FICTION

James Baldwin	*Sonny's Blues:* Longman Lecture ■ Biography, Critical Archive, Bibliography
Toni Cade Bambara	*The Lesson:* Longman Lecture
Ambrose Bierce	*An Occurrence at Owl Creek Bridge:* Video Essay, Critical Essay
T. Coraghessan Boyle	*Greasy Lake:* Critical Essay
Raymond Carver	*Cathedral:* Longman Lecture ■ Biography, Critical Archive, Bibliography
Willa Cather	*Paul's Case:* Video, Audio, Critical Essay ■ Biography/Photos, Critical Archive, Bibliography
John Cheever	Biography, Critical Archive, Bibliography
Anton Chekhov	Biography, Critical Archive, Bibliography
Kate Chopin	*The Storm:* Longman Lecture, Interactive Reading, Student Paper, Critical Essay *The Story of an Hour:* Longman Lecture ■ Biography, Critical Archive, Bibliography
Stephen Crane	Biography, Critical Archive, Bibliography
Ralph Ellison	Biography, Critical Archive, Bibliography
William Faulkner	*A Rose for Emily:* Critical Essay ■ *Barn Burning:* Video (2), Audio (2), Critical Essay (2) Biography/Photos, Critical Archive, Bibliography
Gabriel García Márquez	Biography, Critical Archive, Bibliography
Charlotte Perkins Gilman	*The Yellow Wallpaper:* Critical Essay ■ Biography, Critical Archive, Bibliography
Nathaniel Hawthorne	*Young Goodman Brown:* Longman Lecture ■ Biography, Critical Archive, Bibliography
Ernest Hemingway	*A Clean, Well-Lighted Place:* Critical Essay ■ Biography, Critical Archive, Bibliography
Zora Neale Hurston	*Sweat:* Longman Lecture, Interactive Reading
Shirley Jackson	*The Lottery:* Interactive Reading, Critical Essay
James Joyce	*Araby:* Longman Lecture, Interactive Reading, Critical Essay ■ Biography, Critical Archive, Bibliography
Franz Kafka	Biography, Critical Archive, Bibliography
Ursula K. Le Guin	*The Ones Who Walk Away from Omelas:* Student Paper
Katherine Mansfield	*Miss Brill:* Interactive Reading, Critical Essay
Bobbie Ann Mason	*Shiloh:* Longman Lecture
Joyce Carol Oates	*Where Are You Going, Where Have You Been?:* Longman Lecture Biography, Critical Archive, Bibliography
Tim O'Brien	*The Things They Carried:* Longman Lecture
Flannery O'Connor	*A Good Man Is Hard to Find:* Longman Lecture, Interactive Reading Biography, Critical Archive, Bibliography
Edgar Allan Poe	*The Tell-Tale Heart:* Longman Lecture, Video, Critical Essay Biography/Photos, Critical Archive, Bibliography
Katherine Anne Porter	*The Jilting of Granny Weatherall:* Video, Audio, Critical Essay ■ Biography/Photos
Amy Tan	*A Pair of Tickets:* Critical Essay ■ Biography, Critical Archive, Bibliography
John Updike	*A&P:* Interactive Reading, Student Paper, Critical Essay Biography/Photos, Critical Archive, Bibliography
Alice Walker	*Everyday Use:* Longman Lecture, Student Paper ■ Biography, Critical Archive, Bibliography
Eudora Welty	*Why I Live at the P.O.:* Longman Lecture

POETRY

Kim Addonizio	"Writers on Writing" Video Interview
Margaret Atwood	*You Fit into Me:* Critical Essay
W. H. Auden	Biography, Critical Archive, Bibliography
Elizabeth Bishop	*One Art:* Longman Lecture ■ *The Fish:* Critical Essay ■ Biography, Critical Archive, Bibliography
William Blake	*The Chimney Sweeper:* Audio, Critical Essay ■ *The Tyger:* Audio ■ Biography/Photos
Gwendolyn Brooks	*We Real Cool:* Interactive Reading, Student Paper, Critical Essay ■ *The Mother:* Longman Lecture Biography, Critical Archive, Bibliography
Elizabeth Barrett Browning	*How Do I Love Thee? Let Me Count the Ways:* Audio
Robert Browning	*My Last Duchess:* Longman Lecture, Audio, Critical Essay, Student Paper ■ Biography/Photos
Robert Burns	*Oh, my love is like a red, red rose:* Longman Lecture
Lewis Carroll	*Jabberwocky:* Longman Lecture, Interactive Reading, Critical Essay
Samuel Taylor Coleridge	*Kubla Khan:* Audio, Student Paper, Critical Essay
Billy Collins	*The Names:* Longman Lecture ■ Biography, Critical Archive, Bibliography
E. E. Cummings	*in Just-:* Audio ■ *anyone lived in a pretty how town:* Audio, Critical Essay ■ *Buffalo Bill 's:* Audio, Critical Essay Biography/Photos, Critical Archive, Bibliography

Emily Dickinson	*Because I could not stop for Death:* Longman Lecture ▪ *I heard a Fly buzz – when I died:* Audio *Wild Nights – Wild Nights!:* Audio ▪ Biography, Critical Archive, Bibliography
John Donne	*Batter my heart ….:* Longman Lecture ▪ *Death be not proud:* Audio ▪ Biography, Critical Archive, Bibliography
Rita Dove	"Writers on Writing" Video Interview
T. S. Eliot	*The Love Song of J. Alfred Prufrock:* Student Paper ▪ Biography, Critical Archive, Bibliography
Carolyn Forché	*The Colonel:* Student Paper
Robert Frost	*Acquainted with the Night:* Longman Lecture ▪ *Birches:* Audio ▪ *Mending Wall:* Longman Lecture *"Out, Out—":* Interactive Reading, Critical Essay ▪ *The Road Not Taken:* Critical Essay Biography, Critical Archive, Bibliography
Dana Gioia	*California Hills in August:* Video ▪ *Money:* Video ▪ *Summer Storm:* Video ▪ *Unsaid:* Video
Thomas Hardy	*Neutral Tones:* Critical Essay ▪ *The Ruined Maid:* Critical Essay Biography, Critical Archive, Bibliography
Robert Hayden	Biography, Critical Archive, Bibliography
Seamus Heaney	*Digging:* Longman Lecture
George Herbert	*Easter Wings:* Critical Essay
Gerard Manley Hopkins	*Pied Beauty:* Audio, Critical Essay ▪ Biography/Photos
A. E. Housman	*To an Athlete Dying Young:* Critical Essay ▪ Biography, Critical Archive, Bibliography
Langston Hughes	*The Weary Blues:* Longman Lecture ▪ *Dream Boogie:* Critical Essay Biography, Critical Archive, Bibliography
John Keats	*Bright Star!:* Longman Lecture ▪ *Ode on a Grecian Urn:* Audio, Student Paper Biography/Photos, Critical Archive, Bibliography
X. J. Kennedy	*For Allen Ginsberg:* Video ▪ *In a Prominent Bar in Secaucus One Day:* Video *Nude Descending a Staircase:* Video ▪ *Snowflake Soufflé:* Video
Edna St. Vincent Millay	*What lips my lips have kissed, and where, and why:* Video, Student Paper ▪ Biography/Photos
Wilfred Owen	*Dulce et Decorum Est:* Longman Lecture, Interactive Reading, Critical Essay
Dorothy Parker	*Résumé:* Video ▪ Biography/Photos
Sylvia Plath	*Lady Lazarus:* Longman Lecture ▪ *Metaphors:* Critical Essay, Interactive Reading Biography, Critical Archive, Bibliography
Edgar Allan Poe	Biography/Photos, Critical Archive, Bibliography
Adrienne Rich	Biography, Critical Archive, Bibliography
Edwin Arlington Robinson	*Luke Havergal:* Critical Essay ▪ *Richard Cory:* Longman Lecture, Critical Essay
Theodore Roethke	*Root Cellar:* Interactive Reading, Critical Essay
William Shakespeare	*Let me not to the marriage of true minds:* Critical Essay *Shall I compare thee to a summer's day?:* Audio, Student Paper, Critical Essay (2) *That time of year thou mayst in me behold:* Longman Lecture, Interactive Reading Longman Lecture: The Theme of Love in the Sonnets Biography/Photos, Critical Archive, Bibliography
Percy Bysshe Shelley	*Ozymandias:* Audio
Wallace Stevens	*Anecdote of the Jar:* Interactive Reading ▪ Biography, Critical Archive, Bibliography
Alfred, Lord Tennyson	*The splendor falls on castle walls:* Audio ▪ Biography/Photos, Critical Archive, Bibliography
Dylan Thomas	*Do not go gentle into that good night:* Critical Essay
John Updike	*Recital:* Student Paper ▪ Biography/Photos, Critical Archive, Bibliography
Walt Whitman	*Cavalry Crossing a Ford:* Interactive Reading, Critical Essay Biography, Critical Archive, Bibliography
Richard Wilbur	*Cold War Poetry:* Critical Essay
William Carlos Williams	Biography, Critical Archive, Bibliography
William Wordsworth	*A Slumber Did My Spirit Seal:* Critical Essay ▪ *Composed upon Westminster Bridge:* Audio Biography, Critical Archive, Bibliography
William Butler Yeats	*The Lake Isle of Innisfree:* Longman Lecture, Critical Essay ▪ *Leda and the Swan:* Critical Essay *Who Goes with Fergus?:* Interactive Reading ▪ Biography/Photos, Critical Archive, Bibliography

DRAMA

Susan Glaspell	*Trifles:* Longman Lecture ▪ Biography, Critical Archive, Bibliography
David Henry Hwang	*The Sound of a Voice:* Critical Essay ▪ Biography, Critical Archive, Bibliography
Henrik Ibsen	*A Doll's House:* Longman Lecture ▪ Biography, Critical Archive, Bibliography
Arthur Miller	*Death of a Salesman:* Longman Lecture, Critical Essay ▪ Biography, Critical Archive, Bibliography
William Shakespeare	*Hamlet, Prince of Denmark:* Longman Lecture, Critical Essay *A Midsummer Night's Dream:* Longman Lecture, Critical Essay *Othello:* Video, Audio, Interactive Reading, Student Paper, Critical Essay Biography/Photos, Critical Archive, Bibliography
Sophocles	*Antigonê:* Longman Lecture ▪ *Oedipus:* Longman Lecture ▪ Biography, Critical Archive, Bibliography
Tennessee Williams	Biography, Critical Archive, Bibliography
August Wilson	*Fences:* Longman Lecture ▪ Biography, Critical Archive, Bibliography

Why Do You Need This New Edition?

If you are wondering why you should buy this eleventh edition of *Literature*, here are 6 good reasons!

1. What's the point of reading stories, poems, and plays? Find out from three contemporary writers—fiction writer Amy Tan, U.S. Poet Laureate Kay Ryan, and playwright David Ives.

2. Interested in Latin American culture? Discover the enduring influences of "El Boom" found in the new chapter "Latin American Fiction."

3. Looking to meet some fascinating people? *Literature*'s 11 new stories introduce a host of memorable characters including: a man who travels through his neighborhood, swimming pool by swimming pool ("The Swimmer"); a family member who leaves home and moves to the post office ("Why I Live at the P.O."); and an angel who crash-lands in a backyard ("A Very Old Man with Enormous Wings").

4. Guess what these subjects have in common—a psychiatrist's waiting room, dogs, blues, and powwows. If you answered, "Some of the topics of our 51 new poems," you are right! (See "In the Counselor's Waiting Room," "Dog Haiku," "Late Blues," and "The Powwow at the End of the World.")

5. Think reading a play has nothing to offer that is relevant to your life? Our 3 new drama selections, David Ives's *Soap Opera*, Anna Deavere Smith's *Twilight: Los Angeles, 1992*, and Jane Martin's *Tattoo* may prove you wrong.

6. Need all the help you can get to format your papers correctly? The new 2009 MLA documentation guidelines, found only in the eleventh edition of *Literature*, show you how to correctly cite your sources in the format your instructors will expect.

PEARSON

LITERATURE

INTERACTIVE EDITION

LITERATURE

An Introduction to Fiction,
Poetry, Drama, and Writing

INTERACTIVE EDITION

ELEVENTH EDITION

X. J. Kennedy

Dana Gioia

Longman
New York   San Francisco   Boston
London   Toronto   Sydney   Tokyo   Singapore   Madrid
Mexico City   Munich   Paris   Cape Town   Hong Kong   Montreal

Vice President and Editor in Chief: Joe Terry
Development Editor: Katharine Glynn
Executive Marketing Manager: Joyce Nilsen
Senior Media Producer: Stefanie Liebman
Senior Supplements Editor: Donna Campion
Production Manager: Savoula Amanatidis
Project Coordination, Text Design, and Electronic Page Makeup: Nesbitt Graphics, Inc.
Cover Design Manager: John Callahan
Cover Image: Edward Hopper (1882–1967), *The Lee Shore*, 1941. Private Collection, Art Resource, NY
Pearson Image Resource Center/Photo Researcher: Teri Stratford
Senior Manufacturing Buyer: Roy L. Pickering, Jr.
Printer and Binder: Quebecor World Book Services–Taunton
Cover Printer: Lehigh-Phoenix Color Corporation

For permission to use copyrighted material, grateful acknowledgment is made to the copyright holders on
pp. 2089–2104, which are hereby made part of this copyright page.

Library of Congress Cataloging-in-Publication Data
Literature : an introduction to fiction, poetry, drama, and writing /
[compiled by] X.J. Kennedy, Dana Gioia.—11th ed.
     p. cm.
  Includes bibliographical references and index.
  ISBN 978-0-205-69881-3 (alk. paper)—ISBN 978-0-205-68611-7 (interactive
edition : alk. paper)
  1. Literature—Collections. I. Kennedy, X. J. II. Gioia, Dana.
PN6014.L58 2009
808–dc22

                         2009020876

Please visit us at www.pearsonhighered.com.

1 2 3 4 5 6 7 8 9 10—QWT—12 11 10 09

Longman
is an imprint of

Literature
ISBN-13: 978-0-205-69881-3; ISBN-10: 0-205-69881-6
Literature Interactive
ISBN-13: 978-0-205-68611-7; ISBN-10: 0-205-68611-7
Portable
ISBN-13: 978-0-205-68610-0; ISBN-10: 0-205-68610-9

CONTENTS

FICTION

TALKING WITH *Amy Tan* 2

1 READING A STORY 5

4 SETTING 107

5   TONE AND STYLE 148

 WRITING *effectively*

6   THEME 183

■ WRITING *effectively*

10 CRITICAL CASEBOOK
Flannery O'Connor 368

■ WRITING *effectively*

11 CRITICAL CASEBOOK
Three Stories in Depth 419

POETRY
TALKING WITH *Kay Ryan* 626

THE PERSON IN THE POEM   651

IRONY   659

FOR REVIEW AND FURTHER STUDY

■ WRITING *effectively*

15 WORDS 674

18   FIGURES OF SPEECH 730

19 SONG 750

21 RHYTHM 789

22 CLOSED FORM 809

26 POETRY AND PERSONAL IDENTITY   887

31   TWO CRITICAL CASEBOOKS
Emily Dickinson and Langston Hughes   957

32 CRITICAL CASEBOOK
T. S. Eliot's "The Love Song of J. Alfred Prufrock"   993

■ WRITING *effectively*

33 POEMS FOR FURTHER READING   1016

DRAMA

TALKING WITH *David Ives*   1106

34   READING A PLAY   1109

THEATRICAL CONVENTIONS   1110

ELEMENTS OF A PLAY   1110

ANALYZING *TRIFLES*   1122

38 THE MODERN THEATER 1553

■ WRITING *effectively*

WRITING

42 WRITING ABOUT A STORY   1912

43 WRITING ABOUT A POEM   1937

44 WRITING ABOUT A PLAY   1960

45 WRITING A RESEARCH PAPER 1972

PREFACE

This Interactive Edition of *Literature*, Eleventh Edition—the book in your hands—is really four interlocking volumes sharing one cover. Each of the first three sections is devoted to one of the major literary forms—fiction, poetry, and drama. The fourth section is a comprehensive introduction to critical writing. All the sections are supported by our Web-based resource *MyLiteratureLab.com*, which provides a variety of interesting and useful audio lectures, interactive readings, background material, and writing and research resources. All together, the book is an attempt to provide the college student with a reasonably compact introduction to the study and appreciation of stories, poems, and plays—as well as practical advice on the sort of writing expected in a college English course.

We assume that appreciation begins in delighted attention to words on a page. Speed reading has its uses; but at times, as Robert Frost said, the person who reads for speed "misses the best part of what a good writer puts into it." Close reading, then, is essential. Still, we do not believe that close reading tells us everything, that it is wrong to read a literary work by any light except that of the work itself. At times we suggest different approaches such as referring to the facts of an author's life, looking for myth, or seeing the conventions that typify a kind of writing—noticing, for instance, that an old mansion, cobwebbed and creaking, is the setting for a Gothic horror story.

Although we cannot help having a few convictions about the meanings of stories, poems, and plays, we have tried to step back and give you room to make up your own mind. Here and there, in the wording of a question, our opinions may occasionally stick out. If you should notice any, please feel free to ignore them. Be assured that no one interpretation, laid down by authority, is the only right one for any work of literature. Trust your own interpretation—provided that in making it you have looked clearly and carefully at the evidence.

Reading literature often will provide you with a reason to write. Following the fiction, poetry, and drama sections, there are several chapters that give the student writer some practical advice. It will guide you, step by step, in finding a topic, planning an essay, writing, revising, and putting your paper into finished form. Further, you will find there specific help in writing about fiction, poetry, and drama. There are also short features at the end of most chapters that provide help and perspective on writing about literature. In a few places we have even offered some suggestions about writing your own stories or poems—in case reading the selections in this book inspires you to try your hand at imaginative writing.

A WORD ABOUT CAREERS

Most students agree that to read celebrated writers such as William Faulkner, Emily Dickinson, and William Shakespeare is probably good for the spirit. Most students even take some pleasure in the experience. But many, not planning to teach English and impatient to begin some other career, wonder if the study of literature, however enjoyable, isn't a waste of time—or at least, an annoying obstacle.

This objection may seem reasonable at first glance, but it rests on a shaky assumption. Success in a career does not depend merely on learning the specialized information and skills required to join a profession. In most careers, according to one senior business executive, people often fail not because they don't understand their jobs, but because they don't understand their co-workers, their clients, or their customers. They don't ever see the world from another person's point of view. Their problem is a failure of imagination.

To leap over the wall of self and to look through another's eyes is valuable experience that literature offers. If you are lucky, you may never meet (or have to do business with) anyone *exactly* like Mrs. Turpin in the story "Revelation," and yet you will learn much about the kind of person she is from Flannery O'Connor's fictional portrait of her. What is it like to be black, a white may wonder? James Baldwin, Gwendolyn Brooks, Rita Dove, Langston Hughes, Zora Neale Hurston, Alice Walker, August Wilson, and others have knowledge to impart. What is it like to be a woman? If a man would learn, let him read (for a start) Sandra Cisneros, Kate Chopin, Susan Glaspell, Alice Munro, Sylvia Plath, Katherine Anne Porter, Flannery O'Connor, Tillie Olsen, Adrienne Rich, and Amy Tan, and perhaps, too, Henrik Ibsen's *A Doll's House* and John Steinbeck's "The Chrysanthemums."

Plodding single-mindedly toward careers, some people are like horses wearing blinders. For many, the goals look fixed and predictable. Competent nurses, accountants, and dental technicians seem always in demand. Others may find that in our society some careers, like waves in the sea, will rise or fall unexpectedly. Think how many professions we now take for granted, which a few years ago didn't even exist: genetic engineering, energy conservation, digital editing, and Web site design. Others that once looked like lifetime meal tickets have been cut back and nearly ruined: shoe repairing, commercial fishing, railroading.

In a perpetually changing society, it may be risky to lock yourself on one track to a career, refusing to consider any other. "We are moving," writes John Naisbitt in *Megatrends*, a study of our changing society, "from the specialist, soon obsolete, to the generalist who can adapt." Perhaps the greatest opportunity in your whole life lies in a career that has yet to be invented. If you do change your career as you go along, you will be like most people. According to a U.S. Bureau of Labor Statistics survey conducted in April 2000, the average person holds over nine jobs between the ages of 18 and 34—often completely changing his or her basic occupation. When for some unforeseen reason you have to make such a change, basic skills—and a knowledge of humanity—may be your most valuable credentials.

Literature has much practical knowledge to offer you. An art of words, it can help you become more sensitive to language—both your own and other people's. It can make you aware of the difference between the word that is exactly right and the word that is merely good enough—Mark Twain calls it "the difference between the lightning and the lightning-bug." Read a fine work of literature alertly, and some of its writer's sensitivity to words may grow on you. A Supreme Court Justice, John Paul Stevens, once remarked that the best preparation for law school is to study poetry. Why? George D. Gopen, an English professor with a law degree, says it may be because "no other discipline so closely replicates the central question asked in the study of legal thinking: Here is a text; in how many ways can it have meaning?"

Many careers today, besides law, call for close reading and clear writing—as well as careful listening and thoughtful speech. Lately, college placement directors have reported more demand for graduates who are good readers and writers. The reason is evident: Employers need people who can handle words. In a survey conducted by Cornell University, business executives were asked to rank in importance the traits they look for when hiring. Leadership was first, but skill in writing and speaking came in fourth, ahead of both managerial and analytical skills. Times change, but to think cogently and to express yourself well will always be the abilities the world needs.

KEY LITERARY TERMS

Every discipline has its own terminology. This book introduces a large range of critical terms that may help you in both your reading and writing. When these important words and phrases are first defined, they are printed in **boldface**. If you find a critical term anywhere in this book you don't know or don't recall (for example, what is a *carpe diem* poem or a *dramatic question?*), just check the "Index of Literary Terms" in the back of the book, and you'll see the page where the term is discussed; or, look it up in the "Glossary of Literary Terms," also at the back of the book.

TEXTS AND DATES

Every effort has been made to supply each selection in its most accurate text and (where necessary) in a lively, faithful translation. For the reader who wishes to know when a work was written, at the right of each title appears the date of its first publication in book form. Parentheses around a date indicate the work's date of composition or first magazine publication, given when it was composed much earlier than when it was first published in book form.

ICONS

You will notice MLL screen icons in the margins throughout the book. An icon next to an author's name indicates that further resources about that author are available on *MyLiteratureLab.com*, our state-of-the-art Web resource for introductory literature courses. An icon next to the selection title means that the material concerns the selection.

But enough housekeeping—let's enjoy ourselves and read some unforgettable stories, poems, and plays.

X. J. K. AND D. G.

TO THE INSTRUCTOR

This new Interactive Edition of *Literature*, our eleventh edition, is a book divided into four more or less equal parts—fiction, poetry, drama, and writing—all of which are supported by our Web-based resource, *MyLiteratureLab.com*. Our book has two major goals. First, it introduces college students to the appreciation and experience of literature in its major forms. Second, it tries to develop the student's ability to think critically and communicate effectively through writing. These goals are supported by the audio lectures, interactive readings, and writing and research resources found on *MyLiteratureLab.com*.

Both editors of this volume are writers. We believe that textbooks should be not only informative and accurate but also lively, accessible, and engaging. In education, it never hurts to have a little fun. Our intent has always been to write a book that students will read eagerly and enjoy.

WHAT'S NEW TO THIS EDITION?

- **Exclusive conversations between Dana Gioia and celebrated fiction writer Amy Tan, U.S. Poet Laureate Kay Ryan, and contemporary playwright David Ives**—offer students an insider's look into the importance of literature and reading in the lives of three modern masters.
- **New stories, poems, plays, and critical prose**—offer traditional favorites with exciting and sometimes surprising contemporary selections.
  - **65 stories, 11 new selections**—with new stories by Egyptian Nobel Prize-winner Naguib Mahfouz, Toni Cade Bambara, Virginia Woolf, John Cheever, Eudora Welty, Sherman Alexie, Franz Kafka, and Lorrie Moore.
  - **460 poems, 51 new selections**—from a wonderful range of poets including Kevin Young, Bettie Sellers, Mary Oliver, David Lehman, Constantine Cavafy, Rainer Maria Rilke, Anne Stevenson, James Weldon Johnson, Alice Fulton, Jimmy Santiago Baca, Rita Dove, Gwendolyn Brooks, and Lorine Niedecker, among others.
  - **16 plays, 3 new selections**—include scenes from *Twilight: Los Angeles, 1992* by Anna Deavere Smith, *Tattoo* by Jane Martin, and *Soap Opera* by David Ives.
  - **142 critical prose pieces, 12 new selections**—help students think about different approaches to interpreting literature.
- **New "Latin American Fiction" chapter**—presents some of the finest authors of the region, including Jorge Luis Borges, Octavio Paz, Gabriel García Márquez, and Inés Arredondo.
- **New casebook on Nathaniel Hawthorne's "Young Goodman Brown"**—provides students critical insight into this ever-popular and fascinating story.
- **"Picturing Shakespeare" photo montages**—offer students a pictorial introduction to each Shakespeare play with a visual preview of the key scenes and characters.

- New "Terms for Review" feature at the end of every major chapter—provides students a simple study guide to go over key concepts and terms in each chapter.
- New 2009 MLA guidelines—provide students the updated source citation requirements from the new 7th edition of the *MLA Handbook* and incorporates them in all sample student papers.
- New section on writing a response paper—provides instructions and a sample student essay for this popular type of writing assignment.
- Updated, revised format to increase accessibility and ease of use—newly added section titles and subtitles will help Web-oriented students navigate easily from topic to topic in every chapter. Additionally, all chapters have been reviewed and updated to include relevant cultural references.
- Access to a broadened *MyLiteratureLab.com*—an even larger array of audio lectures, including three given by X. J. Kennedy, interactive readings, film clips, critical articles, writing and research resources, and student papers about key literary selections.

KEY FEATURES

We have revised this edition of *Literature* with the simple aim of introducing useful new features and selections without losing the best-liked material. We have been guided in this effort by scores of instructors and students who use the book in their classrooms. Teaching is a kind of conversation between instructor and student and between reader and text. By revising *Literature*, we try to help keep this conversation fresh by mixing the classic with the new and the familiar with the surprising.

Casebooks on Major Authors and Literary Masterpieces

There are nine casebooks on five major authors (Flannery O'Connor, Emily Dickinson, Langston Hughes, Sophocles, and William Shakespeare) and on four popular works frequently used by students for critical analyses or research papers (Nathaniel Hawthorne's "Young Goodman Brown," Charlotte Perkins Gilman's "The Yellow Wallpaper," Alice Walker's "Everyday Use," and T. S. Eliot's "The Love Song of J. Alfred Prufrock"). These special chapters present a variety of material—biographies, photographs, critical commentaries, and statements by the authors. Our aim has been to provide everything a student might need to begin an in-depth study of each author or work.

Shakespeare Richly Illustrated

Reading Shakespeare can be intimidating to students who have never seen a live production of his plays. Unfortunately, today most American teenagers have never seen any live professional production of spoken drama—by Shakespeare or anyone else. We have tried to help the college instructor address this.

Literature presents three plays by Shakespeare—*Othello, Hamlet,* and *A Midsummer Night's Dream*—in an illustrated format featuring dozens of production photos. We have endeavored to portray every major scene in each play as well as most of the major characters. This approach helps students visualize a play's action. It also helps break up the long blocks of print to make the play's text less intimidating. New to the eleventh edition is "Picturing Shakespeare," pictorial timelines that precede each play and depict the key dramatic moments. We hope to give students a visual overview of each play before they begin to read.

Updated Writing Material

Because today's students need a more concise, visual, and schematic approach than did the previous generation, we continue to refine and edit our extensive writing coverage so that students can easily find useful and accessible information—in outline form wherever possible.

Every major chapter of Fiction, Poetry, and Drama includes a **Writing Effectively** section that has four elements: **Writers on Writing**, which personalizes the composition process; **Thinking About . . . ,** which discusses the specific topic of the chapter; a **Checklist**, which provides a step-by-step approach to composition and critical thinking; and a **Writing Assignment** plus **More Topics for Writing**, which provide a rich source of ideas for writing a paper. These features are designed to make the writing process easier, clearer, and less intimidating.

We have eight full writing chapters at the end of *Literature* to provide comprehensive coverage of the composition and research process. All chapters have been edited for clarity and accessibility. We strive to simplify the text but not to dumb it down. Clarity and concision are never out of place in a textbook, but condescension is fatal. One of our chief aims is to make the information and structure of the writing chapters more visual for today's Internet-oriented students. Instructors will note how information that appeared in prose paragraphs in earlier editions now appears in outline or checklist form.

16 Student Papers Plus Work-in-Progress Samples

We have 16 annotated student papers to provide models for critical writing, including a research paper. (There are also two card reports and a review.) Eight of the papers are found in the final writing chapters, where they illustrate different approaches to critical writing—literary argument, explication, analysis, comparison and contrast, and personal response—as well as a drama review. Eight papers are found in earlier chapters on fiction, poetry, and drama. Each paper focuses on a work or author in the book and often provides a close reading of the literary work that emphasizes specific elements of its structure and meaning. All papers reflect the newly updated 2009 MLA guidelines.

We also show many samples of student work-in-progress as a way of illustrating the writing process. We include, for example, a step-by-step presentation of how students can develop topics, generate ideas, and formulate a strong thesis, and we show how an early draft is revised into a more precise final version. We include sample brainstorming notes and other prewriting techniques, among many other items, to provide students with a more helpful and systematic account of the writing process. We have also integrated the concept of developing a cogent literary argument (with attention to thesis, purpose, audience, support, and organization) throughout the writing chapters.

Latin American Fiction and Poetry Chapters

These important and unique chapters will not only broaden most students' knowledge of world literature but will also recognize the richness of Spanish language fiction and poetry in the literature of the Americas—a very relevant subject in today's multicultural classrooms. The bilingual selections in Poetry will also give your Spanish-speaking students a chance to shine in class.

Critical Approaches to Literature

Chapter 48, "Critical Approaches to Literature," is an ever-popular feature of *Literature*. There are three selections for every major critical school—30 selections in all. The critical excerpts have been carefully chosen both to illustrate the major theoretical approaches and to be accessible to beginning students. The selections focus on literary works found in the present edition. Among the critical excerpts are examinations of works by Zora Neale Hurston and Franz Kafka, a piece by Camille Paglia on William Blake as well as a new piece in gender theory by Richard Bozorth that provides a gay reading of Auden's "Funeral Blues." Taken together with the many commentaries in the casebooks and Writers on Writing, *Literature* now includes a total of 142 critical excerpts. This expanded coverage gives *Literature* both more depth and flexibility for instructors who prefer to incorporate literary theory and criticism into their introductory courses.

Glossary of Literary Terms

The comprehensive Glossary of Literary Terms at the end of this book includes every term highlighted in boldface throughout the text as well as other important terms—over 350 entries in all—providing a clear and accurate definition, usually with cross references to related terms. The purpose of the glossary is to provide students with a single, accessible reference of all key literary terms.

OTHER EDITIONS AVAILABLE

Fiction *and* Poetry *Available Separately*

Instructors who wish to use only the fiction section or only the poetry section of this book are assured that *An Introduction to Fiction,* Eleventh Edition, and *An Introduction to Poetry*, Thirteenth Edition, contain the full and complete contents of these sections. Each book has writing chapters applicable to its subject, as well as the chapters "Writing a Research Paper" and "Critical Approaches to Literature."

Portable Edition

This edition provides all the content of the hardcover text in four lightweight paperback volumes—*Fiction, Poetry, Drama,* and *Writing*—packed in a slipcase.

Compact Edition

There is also the Sixth Compact Edition of *Literature: An Introduction to Fiction, Poetry, Drama, and Writing* in paperback, for instructors who find the full edition "too much book." Although this compact version offers a slightly abridged table of contents, it still covers the complete range of topics presented in the full edition. Both the full text and the compact edition are available in interactive and noninteractive editions.

Backpack Edition

There is an even more compact edition of this book, which we have titled *Backpack Literature*, Third Edition, in honor of the heavy textbook loads many students must carry from class to class. This much briefer anthology contains only the most essential selections and writing apparatus, and it is published in a smaller format to create a more travel-friendly book.

RESOURCES FOR STUDENTS AND INSTRUCTORS

For Students

MyLiteratureLab.com

MyLiteratureLab.com is a Web-based state-of-the-art interactive learning system designed to accompany *Literature* and help students in their literature course. It adds a new dimension to the study of literature with Longman Lectures—evocative, richly illustrated audio readings along with advice on how to read, interpret, and write about literary works from our roster of Longman authors (including X. J. Kennedy). This powerful program also features Diagnostic Tests, Interactive Readings with clickable prompts, film clips of selections in *Literature*, Writers on Writing (which consists of video interviews with distinguished authors that inspire students to explore their creativity), sample student papers, Literature Timelines, and Avoiding Plagiarism. *MyLiteratureLab.com* can be delivered within Course Compass, Web CT, or Blackboard course management systems, enabling instructors to administer their entire course online.

Handbook of Literary Terms

Handbook of Literary Terms by X. J. Kennedy, Dana Gioia, and Mark Bauerlein is a user-friendly primer of over 350 critical terms brought to life with literary examples, pronunciation guides, and scholarly yet accessible explanations. Aimed at undergraduates getting their first taste of serious literary study, the volume will help students engage with the humanities canon and become critical readers and writers ready to experience the insights and joys of great fiction, poetry, and drama.

Sourcebooks Shakespeare

This revolutionary book and CD format offers the complete text of a Shakespeare play with rich illustrations, extensive explanatory and production notes, and a glossary. An accompanying audio CD—narrated by actor Sir Derek Jacobi—features recordings from memorable productions to contrast different interpretations of the play and its characters.

Responding to Literature: A Writer's Journal

This journal provides students with their own personal space for writing and is available at no additional cost when packaged with this anthology. Helpful writing prompts for responding to fiction, poetry, and drama are also included.

Evaluating Plays on Film and Video

This guide walks students through the process of analyzing and writing about plays on film, whether in a short review or a longer essay. It covers each stage of the process, from preparing and analyzing material through writing the piece. The four appendixes include writing and editing tips and a glossary of film terms. The final section of the guide offers worksheets to help students organize their notes and thoughts before they begin writing.

Evaluating a Performance

Perfect for the student assigned to review a local production, this supplement offers students a convenient place to record their evaluations and is available at no additional cost when packaged with this anthology. Useful tips and suggestions of things to consider when evaluating a production are included.

For Instructors

Instructor's Manual

A separate *Instructor's Manual* is available to instructors. If you have never seen our *Instructor's Manual* before, don't prejudge it. We actually write the manual ourselves, and we work hard to make it as interesting, lively, and informed as is the parent text. It offers commentary and teaching ideas for every selection in the book. It also contains additional commentary, debate, qualifications and information—including scores of classroom ideas—from over 100 teachers and authors. As you will see, our *Instructor's Manual* is no ordinary supplement.

Teaching Composition with Literature

For instructors who either use *Literature* in expository writing courses or have a special emphasis on writing in their literature courses, there is an invaluable supplement, *Teaching Composition with Literature: 101 Writing Assignments from College Instructors.* Edited by Dana Gioia and Patricia Wagner, it collects proven writing assignments and classroom exercises from scores of instructors across North America. Each assignment or exercise uses one or more selections in *Literature* as its departure point. A great many instructors have enthusiastically shared their best writing assignments for *Teaching Composition with Literature.*

Penguin Discount Novel Program

In cooperation with Penguin Group USA, Pearson is proud to offer a variety of Penguin paperbacks at a significant discount—almost sixty percent off the retail price—when packaged with any Pearson title. To review the list of titles available, visit the Pearson Penguin Group USA Website at *www.pearsonhighered.com/penguin.*

Video Program

For qualified adopters, an impressive selection of videotapes is available to enrich students' experience of literature. The videos include selections from William Shakespeare, Sylvia Plath, Ezra Pound, and Alice Walker. Contact your Pearson Longman sales representative to see if you qualify.

Teaching Literature Online, Second Edition

Concise and practical, *Teaching Literature Online* provides instructors with strategies and advice for incorporating elements of computer technology into the literature classroom. Offering a range of information and examples, this manual provides ideas and activities for enhancing literature courses with the help of technology.

The Longman Electronic Testbank for Literature

This electronic testbank features various objective questions on major works of fiction, short fiction, poetry, and drama. With this user-friendly CD-ROM, instructors simply choose questions from the electronic testbank, then print out the completed test for distribution.

Contact Us

For examination copies of any of these books, CDs, videos, and programs, contact your Pearson Longman sales representative, or write to Literature Marketing Manager, Longman Publishers, 51 Madison Avenue, New York, NY 10010. For examination copies only, call (800) 922-0579.

To order an examination copy online, go to: *http://www.pearsonhighered.com* or send an e-mail to: *exam.copies@pearsonhighered.com*.

Thanks

The collaboration necessary to create this new edition goes far beyond the partnership of its two editors. *Literature: An Introduction to Fiction, Poetry, Drama, and Writing* has once again been revised, corrected, and shaped by wisdom and advice from instructors who actually put it to the test—and also from a number who, in teaching literature, preferred other textbooks to it, but who generously criticized this book anyway and made suggestions for it. (Some responded to the book in part, focusing their comments on the previous editions of *An Introduction to Poetry* and *An Introduction to Fiction*.) Deep thanks to:

Alvaro Aleman, University of Florida
Jonathan Alexander, University of Southern Colorado
Ann P. Allen, Salisbury State University
Karla Alwes, SUNY Cortland
Brian Anderson, Central Piedmont Community College
Kimberly Green Angel, Georgia State University
Carmela A. Arnoldt, Glendale Community College
Herman Asarnow, University of Portland
Beverly Bailey, Seminole Community College
Carolyn Baker, San Antonio College
Rosemary Baker, SUNY Morrisville
Lee Barnes, Community College of Southern Nevada, Las Vegas
Sandra Barnhill, South Plains College
Bob Baron, Mesa Community College
Melinda Barth, El Camino Community College
Robin Barrow, University of Iowa
Joseph Bathanti, Mitchell Community College
Judith Baumel, Adelphi University
Anis Bawarski, University of Kansas
Bruce Beckum, Colorado Mountain College
Elaine Bender, El Camino Community College
Pamela Benson, Tarrant County Junior College
Jennifer Black, McLennan Community College
Brian Blackley, North Carolina State University
Debbie Borchers, Pueblo Community College
Alan Braden, Tacoma Community College
Glenda Bryant, South Plains College
Paul Buchanan, Biola University

Andrew Burke, University of Georgia
Jolayne Call, Utah Valley State College
Stasia Callan, Monroe Community College
Uzzie T. Cannon, University of North Carolina at Greensboro
Al Capovilla, Folsom Lake Community College
Eleanor Carducci, Sussex County Community College
Thomas Carper, University of Southern Maine
Jean W. Cash, James Madison University
Michael Cass, Mercer University
Patricia Cearley, South Plains College
Fred Chancey, Chemeketa Community College
Kitty Chen, Nassau Community College
Edward M. Cifelli, County College of Morris
Marc Cirigliano, Empire State College
Bruce Clary, McPherson College
Maria Clayton, Middle Tennessee State University
Cheryl Clements, Blinn College
Jerry Coats, Tarrant County Community College
Peggy Cole, Arapahoe Community College
Doris Colter, Henry Ford Community College
Dean Cooledge, University of Maryland Eastern Shore
Patricia Connors, University of Memphis
Steve Cooper, California State University, Long Beach
Cynthia Cornell, DePauw University
Ruth Corson, Norwalk Community Technical College, Norwalk
James Finn Cotter, Mount St. Mary College

Dessa Crawford, Delaware Community College

Janis Adams Crowe, Furman University

Allison M. Cummings, University of Wisconsin, Madison

Elizabeth Curtin, Salisbury State University

Robert Darling, Keuka College

Denise David, Niagara County Community College

Alan Davis, Moorhead State University

Michael Degen, Jesuit College Preparatory School, Dallas

Kathleen De Grave, Pittsburg State University

Apryl Denny, Viterbo University

Fred Dings, University of South Carolina

Leo Doobad, Stetson University

Stephanie Dowdle, Salt Lake Community College

Dennis Driewald, Laredo Community College

David Driscoll, Benedictine College

John Drury, University of Cincinnati

Tony D'Souza, Shasta College

Victoria Duckworth, Santa Rosa Junior College

Ellen Dugan-Barrette, Brescia University

Dixie Durman, Chapman University

Bill Dynes, University of Indianapolis

Janet Eber, County College of Morris

Terry Ehret, Santa Rosa Junior College

George Ellenbogen, Bentley College

Peggy Ellsberg, Barnard College

Toni Empringham, El Camino Community College

Lin Enger, Moorhead State University

Alexina Fagan, Virginia Commonwealth University

Lynn Fauth, Oxnard College

Annie Finch, University of Southern Maine

Katie Fischer, Clarke College

Susan Fitzgerald, University of Memphis

Juliann Fleenor, Harper College

Richard Flynn, Georgia Southern University

Billy Fontenot, Louisiana State University at Eunice

Deborah Ford, University of Southern Mississippi

Doug Ford, Manatee Community College

James E. Ford, University of Nebraska, Lincoln

Peter Fortunato, Ithaca College

Ray Foster, Scottsdale Community College

Maryanne Garbowsky, County College of Morris

John Gery, University of New Orleans

Mary Frances Gibbons, Richland College

Maggie Gordon, University of Mississippi

Joseph Green, Lower Columbia College

William E. Gruber, Emory University

Huey Guagliardo, Louisiana State University

R. S. Gwynn, Lamar University

Steven K. Hale, DeKalb College

Renée Harlow, Southern Connecticut State University

David Harper, Chesapeake College

John Harper, Seminole Community College

Iris Rose Hart, Santa Fe Community College

Karen Hatch, California State University, Chico

Jim Hauser, William Patterson College

Kevin Hayes, Essex County College

Jennifer Heller, Johnson County Community College

Hal Hellwig, Idaho State University

Gillian Hettinger, William Paterson University

Mary Piering Hiltbrand, University of Southern Colorado

Martha Hixon, Middle Tennessee State University

Jan Hodge, Morningside College

David E. Hoffman, Averett University

Mary Huffer, Lake-Sumter Community College

Patricia Hymson, Delaware County Community College

Carol Ireland, Joliet Junior College

Alan Jacobs, Wheaton College

Ann Jagoe, North Central Texas College

Kimberlie Johnson, Seminole Community College

Peter Johnson, Providence College

Ted E. Johnston, El Paso Community College

Cris Karmas, Graceland University

Howard Kerner, Polk Community College

Lynn Kerr, Baltimore City Community College

D. S. Koelling, Northwest College

Dennis Kriewald, Laredo Community College

Paul Lake, Arkansas Technical University

Susan Lang, Southern Illinois University

Greg LaPointe, Elmira College

Tracy Lassiter, Eastern Arizona College

Sherry Little, San Diego State University

Alfred Guy Litton, Texas Woman's University

Heather Lobban-Viravong, Grinnell College

Karen Locke, Lane Community College

Eric Loring, Scottsdale Community College

Gerald Luboff, County College of Morris

Susan Popkin Mach, UCLA

Samuel Maio, California State University, San Jose

Paul Marx, University of New Haven

David Mason, Colorado College

Mike Matthews, Tarrant County Junior College

Beth Maxfield, Henderson State University

Janet McCann, Texas A&M University

Susan McClure, Indiana University of Pennsylvania

Kim McCollum-Clark, Millersville University

David McCracken, Texas A&M University

Nellie McCrory, Gaston College

William McGee, Jr., Joliet Junior College

Kerri McKeand, Joliet Junior College

Robert McPhillips, Iona College

Jim McWilliams, Dickinson State University

Elizabeth Meador, Wayne Community College
Bruce Meyer, Laurentian University
Tom Miller, University of Arizona
Joseph Mills, University of California at Davis
Cindy Milwe, Santa Monica High School
Dorothy Minor, Tulsa Community College
Mary Alice Morgan, Mercer University
Samantha Morgan, University of Tennessee
Bernard Morris, Modesto Junior College
Brian T. Murphy, Burlington Community College
William Myers, University of Colorado at Colorado
  Springs
Madeleine Mysko, Johns Hopkins University
Kevin Nebergall, Kirkwood Community College
Eric Nelson, Georgia Southern University
Jeff Newberry, University of West Florida
Marsha Nourse, Dean College
Hillary Nunn, University of Akron
James Obertino, Central Missouri State University
Julia O'Brien, Meredith College
Sally O'Friel, John Carroll University
Elizabeth Oness, Viterbo College
Regina B. Oost, Wesleyan College
Mike Osborne, Central Piedmont Community
  College
Jim Owen, Columbus State University
Jeannette Palmer, Motlow State Community College
Mark Palmer, Tacoma Community College
Dianne Peich, Delaware County Community College
Betty Jo Peters, Morehead State University
Timothy Peters, Boston University
Norm Peterson, County College of Morris
Susan Petit, College of San Mateo
Louis Phillips, School of Visual Arts
Robert Phillips, University of Houston
Jason Pickavance, Salt Lake Community College
Teresa Point, Emory University
Deborah Prickett, Jacksonville State University
William Provost, University of Georgia
Wyatt Prunty, University of the South, Sewanee
Allen Ramsey, Central Missouri State University
Ron Rash, Tri-County Technical College
Michael W. Raymond, Stetson University
Mary Anne Reiss, Elizabethtown Community College
Barbara Rhodes, Central Missouri State University
Diane Richard-Alludya, Lynn University
Gary Richardson, Mercer University
Fred Robbins, Southern Illinois University
Doulgas Robillard Jr., University of Arkansas at Pine
  Bluff
Daniel Robinson, Colorado State University
Dawn Rodrigues, University of Texas, Brownsville
Linda C. Rollins, Motlow State Community College

Mark Rollins, Ohio University
Laura Ross, Seminole Community College
Jude Roy, Madisonville Community College
M. Runyon, Saddleback College
Mark Sanders, College of the Mainland
Kay Satre, Carroll College
Ben Sattersfield, Mercer University
SueAnn Schatz, University of New Mexico
Roy Scheele, Doane College
Bill Schmidt, Seminole Community College
Beverly Schneller, Millersville University
Meg Schoerke, San Francisco State University
Janet Schwarzkopf, Western Kentucky University
William Scurrah, Pima Community College
Susan Semrow, Northeastern State University
Tom Sexton, University of Alaska, Anchorage
Chenliang Sheng, Northern Kentucky University
Roger Silver, University of Maryland–Asian Division
Phillip Skaar, Texas A&M University
Michael Slaughter, Illinois Central College
Martha K. Smith, University of Southern Indiana
Richard Spiese, California State, Long Beach
Lisa S. Starks, Texas A&M University
John R. Stephenson, Lake Superior State University
Jack Stewart, East Georgia College
Dabney Stuart, Washington and Lee University
David Sudol, Arizona State University
Stan Sulkes, Raymond Walters College
Gerald Sullivan, Savio Preparatory School
Henry Taylor, American University
Jean Tobin, University of Wisconsin Center,
  Sheboygan County
Linda Travers, University of Massachusetts,
  Amherst
Tom Treffinger, Greenville Technical College
Peter Ulisse, Housatonia Community College
Lee Upton, Lafayette College
Rex Veeder, St. Cloud University
Deborah Viles, University of Colorado, Boulder
Joyce Walker, Southern Illinois
  University–Carbondale
Sue Walker, University of South Alabama
Irene Ward, Kansas State University
Penelope Warren, Laredo Community College
Barbara Wenner, University of Cincinnati
Terry Witek, Stetson University
Sallie Wolf, Arapahoe Community College
Beth Rapp Young, University of Alabama
William Zander, Fairleigh Dickinson University
Tom Zaniello, Northern Kentucky University
Guanping Zeng, Pensacola Junior College
John Zheng, Mississippi Valley State University

Special thanks go to Michael Palma, who scrupulously examined and updated every chapter from the previous edition. His deep knowledge of literature, crisp sense of style, and sense of humor kept the new edition fresh, informed, and accessible. Ongoing thanks also go to Diane Thiel of the University of New Mexico, who originally helped develop the Latin American poetry chapter in an earlier edition; Susan Balée, who contributed to the chapter on writing a research paper; April Lindner of Saint Joseph's University in Philadelphia, Pennsylvania, who served as associate editor for the writing sections in the previous edition; Mark Bernier of Blinn College in Brenham, Texas, who helped improve the writing material of earlier editions; Joseph Aimone of Santa Clara University, who helped integrate Web-based materials and research techniques into an earlier edition; and John Swensson of De Anza College, who provided excellent practical suggestions from the classroom.

On the publisher's staff, Joseph Terry, Katharine Glynn, and Joyce Nilsen made many contributions to the development and revision of the new edition. Savoula Amanatidis and Lois Lombardo directed the complex job of managing the production of the book in all of its many versions from the manuscript to the final printed form. Beth Keister handled the difficult job of permissions. Rona Tuccillo and Teri Stratford supervised the expansion of photographs in the new edition.

Mary Gioia was involved in every stage of planning, editing, and execution. Not only could the book not have been done without her capable hand and careful eye, but her expert guidance made every chapter better.

Past debts that will never be repaid are outstanding to hundreds of instructors named in prefaces past and to Dorothy M. Kennedy.

X. J. K. AND D. G.

ABOUT THE AUTHORS

X. J. KENNEDY after graduation from Seton Hall and Columbia, became a journalist second class in the Navy ("Actually, I was pretty eighth class"). His poems, some published in the *New Yorker,* were first collected in *Nude Descending a Staircase* (1961). Since then he has published seven more collections, including a volume of new and selected poems in 2007, several widely adopted literature and writing textbooks, and seventeen books for children, including two novels. He has taught at Michigan, North Carolina (Greensboro), California (Irvine), Wellesley, Tufts, and Leeds. Cited in *Bartlett's Familiar Quotations* and reprinted in some 200 anthologies, his verse has brought him a Guggenheim fellowship, a Lamont Award, a *Los Angeles Times* Book Prize, an award from the American Academy and Institute of Arts and Letters, an Aiken-Taylor prize, and the Award for Poetry for Children from the National Council of Teachers of English. He now lives in Lexington, Massachusetts, where he and his wife Dorothy have collaborated on five books and five children.

DANA GIOIA is a poet, critic, and teacher. Born in Los Angeles of Italian and Mexican ancestry, he attended Stanford and Harvard before taking a detour into business. ("Not many poets have a Stanford M.B.A., thank goodness!") After years of writing and reading late in the evenings after work, he quit a vice presidency to write and teach. He has published three collections of poetry, *Daily Horoscope* (1986), *The Gods of Winter* (1991), and *Interrogations at Noon* (2001), which won the American Book Award; and three critical volumes, including *Can Poetry Matter?* (1992), an influential study of poetry's place in contemporary America. Gioia has taught at Johns Hopkins, Sarah Lawrence, Wesleyan (Connecticut), Mercer, and Colorado College. He is also the co-founder of the summer poetry conference at West Chester University in Pennsylvania. From 2003 to 2009 he served as Chairman of the National Endowment for the Arts. At the NEA he created the largest literary programs in federal history, including Shakespeare in American Communities and Poetry Out Loud, the national high school poetry recitation contest. He also led the campaign to restore active and engaged literary reading by creating The Big Read, which has helped reverse a quarter century of decline in U.S. reading. He currently divides his time between Washington, D.C. and Santa Rosa, California, living with his wife Mary, their two sons, and two uncontrollable cats.

(The surname Gioia is pronounced JOY-A. As some of you may have already guessed, Gioia is the Italian word for joy.)

Amy Tan in Chinatown, San Francisco, 1989.

FICTION

TALKING WITH *Amy Tan*

"Life Is Larger Than We Think"
Dana Gioia Interviews Amy Tan

Q: You were born in Oakland in a family where both parents had come from China. Were you raised bilingually?

AMY TAN: Until the age of five, my parents spoke to me in Chinese or a combination of Chinese and English, but they didn't force me to speak Mandarin. In retrospect, this was sad, because they believed that my chance of doing well in America hinged on my fluency in English. Later, as an adult, I wanted to learn Chinese. Now I make an effort when I am with my sisters, who don't speak English well.

Amy Tan with her mother.

Q: What books do you remember reading early in your childhood?

AMY TAN: I read every fairy tale I could lay my hands on at the public library. It was a wonderful world to escape to. I say "escape" deliberately, because I look back and I feel that my childhood was filled with a lot of tensions in the house, and I was able to go to another place. These stories were also filled with their own kinds of dangers and tensions, but they weren't mine. And they were usually solved in the end. This was something satisfying. You could go through these things and then suddenly, you would have some kind of ending. I think that every lonely kid loves to escape through stories. And what kids never thought that they were lonely at some point in their life?

Q: Your mother—to put it mildly—did not approve of your ambition to be a writer.

AMY TAN: My mother and father were immigrants and they were practical people. They wanted us to do well in the new country. They didn't want us to be starving artists. Going into the arts was considered a luxury—that was something you did if you were born to wealth. When my mother found out that I had switched from pre-med to English literature, she imagined that I would lead this life of poverty, that this was a dream that couldn't possibly lead to anything. I didn't know what it would lead to. It just occurred to me I could finally make a choice when I was in college. I didn't have to follow what my parents had set out for me from the age of six—to become a doctor.

Q: What did your mother think of *The Joy Luck Club*?

AMY TAN: Well, by the time I wrote *The Joy Luck Club*, she had changed her opinion. I was making a very good living as a business writer, enough to buy a house for her to live in. When you can do that for your parents they think you're doing fairly well. That was the goal, to become a doctor and be able to make enough money to take care of my mother in her old age. Because I was able to do that as a business writer, she thought it was great. When I decided to write fiction and I said I needed to interview her for stories from her past, she thought that was even better. Then when I got published, and it became a success, she said, "I always knew she was going to be a writer, because she had a wild imagination."

Q: *The Joy Luck Club* is a book of enormous importance, because it brought the complex history of Chinese immigration into the mainstream of American literature. Writing this book, did you have any sense that you were opening up a whole new territory?

AMY TAN: No, I had no idea this was going to be anything but weird stories about a weird family that was unique to us. To think that they would apply to other people who would find similarities to their own families or conflicts was beyond my imagination, and I have a very good imagination.

I wanted to write this book for very personal reasons. One of them, of course, was to learn the craft of writing. The other reason was to understand myself, to figure out who I was. A lot of writers use writing as a way of finding their own personal meaning. I wrote out of total chaos and personal history, which did not seem like something that would ever be used by other people as a way of understanding their lives.

Q: Did you have any literary models in writing your short stories or putting them together as a book? Or did you just do it on intuition?

AMY TAN: I look back, and there were unconscious models—fairy tales, the Bible, especially the cadence of the Bible. There was a book called *Little House in the Big Woods*, by Laura Ingalls Wilder. Wilder wrote this fictional story based on her life as a lonely little girl, moving from place to place. She lived 100 years ago, but that was my life.

The other major influence was my parents. My father wrote sermons and he read them aloud to me, as his test audience. They were not the kind of hell and brimstone sermons. They were stories about himself and his doubts, what he wanted and how he tried to do it.

Then, of course, there was my mother, who told stories as though they were happening right in front of her. She would remember what happened to her in life and act them out in front of me. That's oral storytelling at its best.

Q: Is there anything else that you'd like to say?

AMY TAN: I think reading is really important. It provided for me a refuge, especially during difficult times. It provided me with the notion that I could find an ending that was different from what was happening to me at the time. When you read about the lives of other people, people of different circumstances or similar circumstances, you are part of their lives for that moment. You inhabit their lives and you feel what they're feeling and that is compassion.

Life is larger than we think it is. Certain events can happen that we don't understand. We can take it as faith or as superstition, or as a fairy tale. The possibilities are wide open as to how we look at them.

It's a wonderful part of life to come to a situation and think that it can offer all kinds of possibilities and you get to choose them. I look at what's happened to me as a published writer, and sometimes I think it's a fairy tale.

H ere is a story, one of the shortest ever written and one of the most difficult to forget:

> A woman is sitting in her old, shuttered house. She knows that she is alone in the whole world; every other thing is dead.
>
> The doorbell rings.

In a brief space this small tale of terror, credited to Thomas Bailey Aldrich, makes itself memorable. It sets a promising scene—is this a haunted house?—introduces a character, and places her in a strange and intriguing situation. Although in reading a story that is over so quickly we don't come to know the character well, for a moment we enter her thoughts and begin to share her feelings. Then something amazing happens. The story leaves us to wonder: who or what rang that bell?

Like many richer, longer, more complicated stories, this one, in its few words, engages the imagination. Evidently, how much a story contains and suggests doesn't depend on its size. In the opening chapter of this book, we will look first at other brief stories—examples of three ancient kinds of fiction, a fable, a parable, and a tale— then at a contemporary short story. We will consider the elements of fiction one after another. By seeing a few short stories broken into their parts, you will come to a keener sense of how a story is put together. Not all stories are short, of course; later in the book, you will find a chapter on reading long stories and novels.

All in all, here are sixty-four stories. Among them, may you find at least a few you'll enjoy and care to remember.

1

READING A STORY

When I read a good book . . . I wish that life were
three thousand years long.

—RALPH WALDO EMERSON

After the shipwreck that marooned him on his desert island, Robinson Crusoe, in the novel by Daniel Defoe, stood gazing over the water where pieces of cargo from his ship were floating by. Along came "two shoes, not mates." It is the qualification *not mates* that makes the detail memorable. We could well believe that a thing so striking and odd must have been seen, and not invented. But in truth Defoe, like other masters of the art of fiction, had the power to make us believe his imaginings. Borne along by the art of the storyteller, we trust what we are told, even though the story may be sheer fantasy.

THE ART OF FICTION

Fiction (from the Latin *fictio,* "a shaping, a counterfeiting") is a name for stories not entirely factual, but at least partially shaped, made up, imagined. It is true that in some fiction, such as a historical novel, a writer draws on factual information in presenting scenes, events, and characters. But the factual information in a historical novel, unlike that in a history book, is of secondary importance.

Many firsthand accounts of the American Civil War were written by men who had fought in it, but few eyewitnesses give us so keen a sense of actual life on the battlefront as the author of *The Red Badge of Courage,* Stephen Crane, who was born after the war was over. In fiction, the "facts" may or may not be true, and a story is none the worse for their being entirely imaginary. We expect from fiction a sense of how people act, not an authentic chronicle of how, at some past time, a few people acted.

Human beings love stories. We put them everywhere—not only in books, films, and plays, but also in songs, news articles, cartoons, and videogames. There seems to be a general human curiosity about how other lives, both real and imaginary, take shape and unfold. Some stories provide simple and predictable pleasures according to a conventional plan. Each episode of *Law and Order* or *The Simpsons,* for instance, follows a roughly similar structure, so that regular viewers feel comfortably engaged

5

and entertained. But other stories may seek to challenge rather than comfort us, by finding new and exciting ways to tell a tale, or delving deeper into the mysteries of human nature, or both.

Literary Fiction

Literary fiction calls for close attention. Reading a short story by Ernest Hemingway instead of watching an episode of *Grey's Anatomy* is a little like playing chess rather than checkers. It isn't that Hemingway isn't entertaining. Great literature provides deep and genuine pleasures. But it also requires great attention and skilled engagement from the reader. We are not necessarily led on by the promise of thrills; we do not keep reading mainly to find out what happens next. Indeed, a literary story might even disclose in its opening lines everything that happened, then spend the rest of its length revealing what that happening meant.

Reading literary fiction is no merely passive activity, but is one that demands both attention and insight-lending participation. In return, it offers rewards. In some works of literary fiction, such as Stephen Crane's "The Open Boat" and Flannery O'Connor's "Revelation," we see more deeply into the minds and hearts of the characters than we ever see into those of our families, our close friends, our lovers—or even ourselves.

TYPES OF SHORT FICTION

Modern literary fiction in English has been dominated by two forms: the novel and the short story. The two have many elements in common. Perhaps we will be able to define the short story more meaningfully—for it has traits more essential than just a particular length—if first, for comparison, we consider some related varieties of fiction: the fable, the parable, and the tale. Ancient forms whose origins date back to the time of word-of-mouth storytelling, the fable and the tale are relatively simple in structure; in them we can plainly see elements also found in the short story (and in the novel).

Fable

The **fable** is a brief, often humorous narrative told to illustrate a moral. The characters in a fable are often animals who represent specific human qualities. An ant, for example, may represent a hard-working type of person, or a lion nobility. But fables can also present human characters. To begin, here is a fable by W. Somerset Maugham (1874–1965), an English novelist and playwright, that retells an Arabian folk story. The narrator of the story is Death. (Samarra, by the way, is a city sixty miles from Baghdad.)

W. Somerset Maugham

The Appointment in Samarra   1933

Death speaks: There was a merchant in Baghdad who sent his servant to market to buy provisions and in a little while the servant came back, white and trembling, and said, Master, just now when I was in the marketplace I was jostled by a woman in the crowd and when I turned I saw it was Death that jostled me. She looked at me and made a threatening gesture; now, lend me your horse, and I will ride away from this city and avoid my fate. I will go to Samarra and there Death will not find me. The merchant lent him his horse, and the servant mounted it, and he dug his spurs in its flanks and as fast as the horse could gallop he went. Then the merchant went down to the marketplace and he saw me standing in the crowd and he came to me and said, Why did you make a threatening gesture to my servant when you saw him this morning? That was not a threatening gesture, I said, it was only a start of surprise. I was astonished to see him in Baghdad, for I had an appointment with him tonight in Samarra.

Elements of Fable

This brief story seems practically all skin and bones; that is, it contains little decoration. For in a fable everything leads directly to the **moral**, or message, sometimes stated at the end (moral: "Haste makes waste"). In "The Appointment in Samarra" the moral isn't stated outright, it is merely implied. How would you state it in your own words?

You are probably acquainted with some of the fables credited to the Greek slave Aesop (about 620–560 B.C.), whose stories seem designed to teach lessons about human life. Such is the fable of "The Goose That Laid the Golden Eggs," in which the owner of this marvelous creature slaughters her to get at the great treasure that he thinks is inside her, but finds nothing (implied moral: "Be content with what you have"). Another is the fable of "The Tortoise and the Hare" (implied moral: "Slow, steady plodding wins the race"). The characters in a fable may be talking animals (as in many of Aesop's fables), inanimate objects, or people and supernatural beings (as in "The Appointment in Samarra"). Whoever they may be, these characters are merely sketched, not greatly developed. Evidently, it would not have helped Maugham's fable to make its point if he had portrayed the merchant, the servant, and Death in fuller detail. A more elaborate description of the marketplace would not have improved the story. Probably, such a description would strike us as unnecessary and distracting. By its very bareness and simplicity, a fable fixes itself—and its message—in memory.

Aesop

The North Wind and the Sun   6th century B.C.

Translated by V. S. Vernon Jones

Very little is known with certainty about the man called Aesop, but several accounts and many traditions survive from antiquity. According to the Greek historian Herodotus, Aesop was a slave on the island of Samos. He gained great fame from his fables, but he somehow met his death at the hands of the people of Delphi. According to one tradition, Aesop was an ugly and misshapen man who charmed and amused people with his stories. No one knows if Aesop himself wrote down any of his fables, but they circulated widely in ancient Greece and were praised by Plato, Aristotle, and many other authors. His short and witty tales with their incisive morals have remained constantly popular and influenced innumerable later writers.

A dispute arose between the North Wind and the Sun, each claiming that he was stronger than the other. At last they agreed to try their powers upon a traveler, to see which could soonest strip him of his cloak. The North Wind had the first try; and, gathering up all his force for the attack, he came whirling furiously down upon the man, and caught up his cloak as though he would wrest it from him by one single effort: but the harder he blew, the more closely the man wrapped it round himself. Then came the turn of the Sun. At first he beamed gently upon the traveler, who soon unclasped his cloak and walked on with it hanging loosely about his shoulders:

then he shone forth in his full strength, and the man, before he had gone many steps, was glad to throw his cloak right off and complete his journey more lightly clad.

Moral: Persuasion is better than force.

Questions

1. Describe the different personalities of the North Wind and the Sun.
2. What was ineffective about the North Wind's method of attempting to strip the man of his cloak?
3. Why was the Sun successful in his attempts? What did he do differently than the North Wind?
4. What purpose does the human serve in this dispute?
5. Explain the closing moral in terms of the fable.

We are so accustomed to the phrase *Aesop's fables* that we might almost start to think the two words inseparable, but in fact there have been fabulists (creators or writers of fables) in virtually every culture throughout recorded history. Here is another fable from many centuries ago, this time from India.

Bidpai

The Tortoise and the Geese   c. 4th century

Retold in English by Maude Barrows Dutton

The Panchatantra *(Pañca-tantra), a collection of beast fables from India, is attributed to its narrator, a sage named Bidpai, a legendary figure about whom almost nothing is known for certain. The* Panchatantra, *which means the "The Five Chapters" in Sanskrit, is based on*

Illustration for "The Tortoise and the Geese" by E. Boyd Smith (1908).

earlier oral folklore. The collection was composed some time between 100 B.C. and 500 A.D. in a Sanskrit original now lost, and is primarily known through an Arabic version of the eighth century and a twelfth-century Hebrew translation. The stories are didactic, teaching niti, the wise conduct of life, and artha, practical wisdom that stresses cleverness and self-reliance above more altruistic virtues.

A Tortoise and two Geese lived together in a pond for many years. At last there came a drought and dried up the pond. Then the Geese said to one another, "We must seek a new home quickly, for we cannot live without water. Let us say farewell to the Tortoise and start at once."

When the Tortoise heard that they were going, he trembled with fear, and besought them by their friendship not to desert him.

"Alas," the Geese replied, "there is no help for it. If we stay here, we shall all three die, and we cannot take you with us, for you cannot fly."

Still the Tortoise begged so hard not to be left behind that the Geese finally said, "Dear Friend, if you will promise not to speak a word on the journey, we will take you with us. But know beforehand, that if you open your mouth to say one single word, you will be in instant danger of losing your life."

"Have no fear," replied the Tortoise, "but that I will be silent until you give me leave to speak again. I would rather never open my mouth again than be left to die alone here in the dried-up pond."   5

So the Geese brought a stout stick and bade the Tortoise grasp it firmly in the middle by his mouth. Then they took hold of either end and flew off with him. They had gone several miles in safety, when their course lay over a village. As the country people saw this curious sight of a Tortoise being carried by two Geese, they began to laugh and cry out, "Oh, did you ever see such a funny sight in all your life!" And they laughed loud and long.

The Tortoise grew more and more indignant. At last he could stand their jeering no longer. "You stupid . . ." he snapped, but before he could say more he had fallen to the ground and was dashed to pieces.

Questions

1. Under what condition do the Geese agree to transport the Tortoise?
2. What motivates the Tortoise to break his agreement?
3. How would you summarize the moral of the fable?

Parable

Another traditional form of storytelling is the **parable**. Like the fable, a parable is a brief narrative that teaches a moral, but unlike the fable, its plot is plausibly realistic, and the main characters are human rather than anthropomorphized animals or natural forces. The other key difference is that parables usually possess a more mysterious and suggestive tone. A fable customarily ends by explicitly stating its moral, but parables often present their morals implicitly, and their meanings can be open to several interpretations.

In the Western tradition, the literary conventions of the parable are largely based on the brief stories told by Jesus in his preaching. The forty-three parables recounted in the four Gospels reveal how frequently he used the form to teach. Jesus designed his parables to have two levels of meaning—a literal story that could immediately be understood by the crowds he addressed and a deeper meaning fully comprehended only by his disciples, an inner circle who understood the nature of his ministry. (You can see the richness of interpretations suggested by Jesus's parables by reading and analyzing "The Parable of the Prodigal Son" from St. Luke's Gospel, which appears in Chapter 6.) The parable was also widely used by Eastern philosophers. The Taoist sage Chuang Tzu often portrayed the principles of Tao—which he called the "Way of Nature"—in witty parables such as the following one, traditionally titled "Independence."

Chuang Tzu

Independence   Chou Dynasty (4th century B.C.)

Translated by Herbert Giles

Chuang Chou, usually known as Chuang Tzu (approximately 390–365 B.C.), was one of the great philosophers of the Chou period in China. He was born in the Sung feudal state and received an excellent education. Unlike most educated men, however, Chuang Tzu did not seek public office or political power. Influenced by Taoist philosophy, he believed that individuals should transcend their desire for success and wealth, as well as their fear of failure and poverty. True freedom, he maintained, came from escaping the distractions of worldly affairs. Chuang Tzu's writings have been particularly praised for their combination of humor and wisdom. His parables and stories are classics of Chinese literature.

Chuang Tzu was one day fishing, when the Prince of Ch'u sent two high officials to interview him, saying that his Highness would be glad of Chuang Tzu's assistance in the administration of his government. The latter quietly fished on, and without looking round, replied, "I have heard that in the State of Ch'u there is a sacred tortoise, which has been dead three thousand years, and which the prince keeps packed up in a box on the altar in his ancestral shrine. Now do you think that tortoise would rather be dead and have its remains thus honoured, or be alive and wagging its tail in the mud?" The two officials answered that no doubt it would rather be alive and wagging its tail in the mud; whereupon Chuang Tzu cried out "Begone! I too elect to remain wagging my tail in the mud."

Questions
1. What part of this story is the exposition? How many sentences does Chuang Tzu use to set up the dramatic situation?
2. Why does the protagonist change the subject and mention the sacred tortoise? Why doesn't he answer the request directly and immediately? Does it serve any purpose that Chuang Tzu makes the officials answer a question to which he knows the answer?
3. What does this story tell us about the protagonist Chuang Tzu's personality?

Tale

The name *tale* (from the Old English *talu*, "speech") is sometimes applied to any story, whether short or long, true or fictitious. *Tale* being a more evocative name than *story*, writers sometimes call their stories "tales" as if to imply something handed down from the past. But defined in a more limited sense, a **tale** is a story, usually short, that sets forth strange and wonderful events in more or less bare summary, without detailed character-drawing. "Tale" is pretty much synonymous with "yarn," for it implies a story in which the goal is revelation of the marvelous rather than revelation of character. In the English folktale "Jack and the Beanstalk," we take away a more vivid impression of the miraculous beanstalk and the giant who dwells at its top than of Jack's mind or personality. Because such venerable stories were told aloud before someone set them down in writing, the storytellers had to limit themselves to brief descriptions. Probably spoken around a fire or hearth, such a tale tends to be less complicated and less closely detailed than a story written for the printed page, whose reader can linger over it. Still, such tales *can* be complicated. It is not merely greater length that makes a short story different from a tale or a fable: one mark of a short story is a fully delineated character.

Types of Tales

Even modern tales favor supernatural or fantastic events: for instance, the **tall tale**, a variety of folk story that recounts the deeds of a superhero (Paul Bunyan, John Henry, Sally Ann Thunder) or of the storyteller. If the storyteller is describing his or her own imaginary experience, the bragging yarn is usually told with a straight face to listeners who take pleasure in scoffing at it. Although the **fairy tale**, set in a world of magic and enchantment, is sometimes the work of a modern author (notably Hans Christian Andersen), well-known examples are those German folktales that probably originated in the Middle Ages, collected by the Brothers Grimm. The label *fairy tale* is something of an English misnomer, for in the Grimm stories, though witches and goblins abound, fairies are a minority.

Jakob and Wilhelm Grimm

Godfather Death

1812 (from oral tradition)

Translated by Dana Gioia

Jakob Grimm (1785–1863) and Wilhelm Grimm (1786–1859), brothers and scholars, were born near Frankfurt am Main, Germany. For most of their lives they worked together— lived together, too, even when in 1825 Wilhelm married. In 1838, as librarians, they began toiling on their Deutsch Wörterbuch, *or German dictionary, a vast project that was to outlive them by a century. (It was completed only in 1960.) In 1840 King Friedrich Wilhelm IV appointed both brothers to the Royal Academy of Sciences, and both taught at the University of Berlin for the rest of their days.*

Jakob and Wilhelm Grimm

The name Grimm is best known to us for that splendid collection of ancient German folk stories we call Grimm's Fairy Tales—in German, Kinder- und Hausmärchen (*"Childhood and Household Tales," 1812–15). This classic work spread German children's stories around the world. Many tales we hear early in life were collected by the Grimms: "Hansel and Gretel," "Snow White and the Seven Dwarfs," "Rapunzel," "Tom Thumb," "Little Red Riding Hood," "Rumpelstiltskin." Versions of some of these tales had been written down as early as the sixteenth century, but mainly the brothers relied on the memories of Hessian peasants who recited the stories aloud for them.*

A poor man had twelve children and had to work day and night just to give them bread. Now when the thirteenth came into the world, he did not know what to do, so he ran out onto the main highway intending to ask the first one he met to be the child's godfather.

The first person he met was the good Lord God, who knew very well what was weighing on the man's heart. And He said to him, "Poor man, I am sorry for you. I will hold your child at the baptismal font. I will take care of him and fill his days with happiness."

The man asked, "Who are you?"

"I am the good Lord."

"Then I don't want you as godfather. You give to the rich and let the poor starve."   5

The man spoke thus because he did not know how wisely God portions out wealth and poverty. So he turned away from the Lord and went on.

Then the Devil came up to him and said, "What are you looking for? If you take me as your child's sponsor, I will give him gold heaped high and wide and all the joys of this world."

The man asked, "Who are you?"

"I am the Devil."

"Then I don't want you as godfather," said the man. "You trick men and lead   10 them astray."

He went on, and bone-thin Death strode up to him and said, "Choose me as godfather."

The man asked, "Who are you?"

"I am Death, who makes all men equal."

Then the man said, "You are the right one. You take the rich and the poor without distinction. You will be the godfather."

Death answered, "I will make your child rich and famous. Whoever has me as a   15 friend shall lack for nothing."

The man said, "The baptism is next Sunday. Be there on time."

Death appeared just as he had promised and stood there as a proper godfather.

When the boy had grown up, his godfather walked in one day and said to come along with him. Death led him out into the woods, showed him an herb, and said, "Now you are going to get your christening present. I am making you a famous doctor. When you are called to a patient, I will always appear to you. If I stand next to the sick person's head, you may speak boldly that you will make him healthy again. Give him some of this herb, and he will recover. But if you see me standing by the sick person's feet, then he is mine. You must say that nothing can be done and that no doctor in the world can save him. But beware of using the herb against my will, or it will turn out badly for you."

It was not long before the young man was the most famous doctor in the whole world. "He needs only to look at the sick person," everyone said, "and then he knows how things stand—whether the patient will get well again or whether he must die." People came from far and wide to bring their sick and gave him so much gold that he quickly became quite rich.

Now it soon happened that the king grew ill, and the doctor was summoned to say   20 whether a recovery was possible. But when he came to the bed, Death was standing at the sick man's feet, and now no herb grown could save him.

"If I cheat Death this one time," thought the doctor, "he will be angry, but since I am his godson, he will turn a blind eye, so I will risk it." He took up the sick man and turned him around so that his head was now where Death stood. Then he gave the king some of the herb. The king recovered and grew healthy again.

But Death then came to the doctor with a dark and angry face and threatened him with his finger. "You have hoodwinked me this time," he said. "And I will forgive you once because you are my godson. But if you try such a thing again, it will be your neck, and I will take you away with me."

Not long after, the king's daughter fell into a serious illness. She was his only child, and he wept day and night until his eyes went blind. He let it be known that whoever saved her from death would become her husband and inherit the crown.

When the doctor came to the sick girl's bed, he saw Death standing at her feet. He should have remembered his godfather's warning, but the princess's great beauty and the happy prospect of becoming her husband so infatuated him that he flung all caution to the wind. He didn't notice that Death stared at him angrily or that he raised his hand and shook his bony fist. The doctor picked up the sick girl and turned her around to place her head where her feet had been. He gave her the herb, and right away her cheeks grew rosy and she stirred again with life.

When Death saw that he had been cheated out of his property a second time, he strode with long steps up to the doctor and said, "It is all over for you. Now it's your turn." Death seized him so firmly with his ice-cold hand that the doctor could not resist. He led him into an underground cavern. There the doctor saw thousands and thousands of candles burning in endless rows. Some were tall, others medium-sized, and others quite small. Every moment some went out and others lit up, so that the tiny flames seemed to jump to and fro in perpetual motion.

"Look," said Death, "these are the life lights of mankind. The tall ones belong to children, the middle-size ones to married people in the prime of life, and the short ones to the very old. But sometimes even children and young people have only a short candle."

"Show me my life light," said the doctor, assuming it would be very tall.

Death pointed to a small stub that seemed about to flicker out.

"Oh, dear godfather!" cried the terrified doctor. "Light a new candle for me. If you love me, do it, so that I may enjoy my life, become king, and marry the beautiful princess."

"That I cannot do," Death replied. "One candle must first go out before a new one is lighted."

"Then put my old one on top of a new candle that will keep burning when the old one goes out," begged the doctor.

Death acted as if he were going to grant the wish and picked up a tall new candle. But because he wanted revenge, he deliberately fumbled in placing the new candle, and the stub toppled over and went out. The doctor immediately dropped to the ground and fell into the hands of Death.

PLOT

Like a fable, the Grimm brothers' tale seems stark in its lack of detail and in the swiftness of its telling. Compared with the fully portrayed characters of many modern stories, the characters of father, son, king, princess, and even Death himself seem hardly more than stick figures. It may have been that to draw ample characters would not have contributed to the storytellers' design; that, indeed, to have done so would have been inartistic. Yet "Godfather Death" is a compelling story. By what methods does it arouse and sustain our interest?

Elements of Plot

Plot sometimes refers simply to the events in a story. In this book, though, **plot** will mean the artistic arrangement of those events. From the opening sentence of "Godfather Death," we watch the unfolding of a **dramatic situation**: a person is involved in some **conflict**. First, this character is a poor man with children to feed, in conflict with the world; very soon, we find him in conflict with God and with the Devil besides. Drama in fiction occurs in any clash of wills, desires, or powers— whether it be a conflict of character against character, character against society, character against some natural force, or, as in "Godfather Death," character against some supernatural entity.

Like any shapely tale, "Godfather Death" has a beginning, a middle, and an end. In fact, it is unusual to find a story so clearly displaying the elements of structure that critics have found in many classic works of fiction and drama. The tale begins with an **exposition**: the opening portion that sets the scene (if any), introduces the main characters, tells us what happened before the story opened, and provides any other background information that we need in order to understand and care about the events to follow. In "Godfather Death," the exposition is brief—all in the opening paragraph. The middle section of the story begins with Death's giving the herb to the boy and his warning not to defy him. This moment introduces a new conflict (a **complication**), and by this time it is clear that the son and not the father is to be the central human character of the story.

Protagonist Versus Antagonist

Death's godson is the principal person who strives: the **protagonist** (a better term than **hero**, for it may apply equally well to a central character who is not especially brave or virtuous). The **suspense**, the pleasurable anxiety we feel that heightens our attention to the story, resides in our wondering how it will all turn out. Will the doctor triumph over Death? Even though we suspect, early in the story, that the doctor stands no chance against such a superhuman **antagonist**, we want to see for ourselves the outcome of his defiance.

Crisis and Climax

When the doctor defies his godfather for the first time—when he saves the king— we have a **crisis**, a moment of high tension. The tension is momentarily resolved when Death lets him off. Then an even greater crisis—the turning point in the action—occurs with the doctor's second defiance in restoring the princess to life. In the last section of the story, with the doctor in the underworld, events come to a **climax**, the moment of greatest tension at which the outcome is to be decided, when the terrified doctor begs for a new candle. Will Death grant him one? Will he live, become king, and marry the princess? The outcome or **conclusion**—also called the **resolution** or **dénouement** (French for "the untying of the knot")— quickly follows as Death allows the little candle to go out.

Narrative Techniques

The treatment of plot is one aspect of an author's artistry. Different arrangements of the same material are possible. A writer might decide to tell of the events in chronological order, beginning with the earliest; or he or she might open the story with the last event, then tell what led up to it. Sometimes a writer chooses to skip rapidly over the exposition and begin *in medias res* (Latin for "in the midst of things"), first presenting some exciting or significant moment, then filling in what happened earlier. This method is by no means a modern invention: Homer begins the *Odyssey* with his hero mysteriously late in returning from war and his son searching for him; John Milton's *Paradise Lost* opens with Satan already defeated in his revolt against the Lord. A device useful to writers for filling in what happened earlier is the **flashback** (or **retrospect**), a scene relived in a character's memory. Alternatively, a storyteller can try to incite our anticipation by giving us some **foreshadowing** or indication of events to come. In "Godfather Death" the foreshadowings are apparent in Death's warnings ("But if you try such a thing again, it will be your neck").

THE SHORT STORY

The teller of tales relies heavily on the method of **summary**: terse, general narration. In a **short story**, a form more realistic than the tale and of modern origin, the writer usually presents the main events in greater fullness. Fine writers of short stories, although they may use summary at times (often to give some portion of a story less emphasis), are skilled in rendering a **scene**: a vivid or dramatic moment described in enough detail to create the illusion that the reader is practically there. Avoiding long summary, they try to *show* rather than simply to *tell,* as if following Mark Twain's advice to authors: "Don't say, 'The old lady screamed.' Bring her on and let her scream."

A short story is more than just a sequence of happenings. A finely wrought short story has the richness and conciseness of an excellent lyric poem. Spontaneous and natural as the finished story may seem, the writer has crafted it so artfully that there is meaning in even seemingly casual speeches and apparently trivial details. If we skim it hastily, skipping the descriptive passages, we miss significant parts.

Some literary short stories, unlike commercial fiction in which the main interest is in physical action or conflict, tell of an **epiphany**: some moment of insight, discovery, or revelation by which a character's life, or view of life, is greatly altered. The term, which means "showing forth" in Greek, was first used in Christian theology to signify the manifestation of God's presence in the world. This theological idea was adapted by James Joyce to refer to a heightened moment of secular revelation. (For such moments in fiction, see the stories in this book by Joyce, John Steinbeck, and Joyce Carol Oates.) Other short stories tell of a character initiated into experience or maturity: one such **story of initiation** is William Faulkner's "Barn Burning" (Chapter 5), in which a boy finds it necessary to defy his father and suddenly to grow into manhood. Less obviously dramatic, perhaps, than "Godfather Death," such a story may be no less powerful.

The fable and the tale are ancient forms; the short story is of more recent origin. In the nineteenth century, writers of fiction were encouraged by a large, literate audience of middle-class readers who wanted to see their lives reflected in faithful mirrors. Skillfully representing ordinary life, many writers perfected the art of the short story: in Russia, Anton Chekhov; in France, Honoré de Balzac and Guy de Maupassant; and in America, Nathaniel Hawthorne and Edgar Allan Poe (although the Americans seem less fond of everyday life than of dream and fantasy). It would be false to claim that, in passing from the fable and the tale to the short story, fiction has made a triumphant progress; or to claim that, because short stories are modern, they are superior to fables and tales. Fable, tale, and short story are distinct forms, each achieving its own effects. Far from being extinct, fable and tale have enjoyed a resurgence in recent years. Jorge Luis Borges, Italo Calvino, and Gabriel García Márquez have all used fable and folktale to create memorable and very modern fiction. All forms of fiction are powerful in the right authorial hands.

Let's begin with a contemporary short story whose protagonist undergoes an initiation into maturity. To notice the difference between a short story and a tale, you may find it helpful to compare John Updike's "A & P" with "Godfather Death." Although Updike's short story is centuries distant from the Grimm tale in its method of telling and in its setting, you may be reminded of "Godfather Death" in the main character's dramatic situation. To defend a young woman, a young man has to defy his mentor—here, the boss of a supermarket! In so doing, he places himself in jeopardy. Updike has the protagonist tell his own story, amply and with humor. How does it differ from a tale?

John Updike

A & P   1961

John Updike (1932–2009), was born in Pennsylvania, received his B.A. from Harvard, then went to Oxford to study drawing and fine art. In the mid-1950s he worked on the staff of the New Yorker, at times doing errands for the aged James Thurber. Although he left the magazine to become a full-time writer, Updike continued to supply it with memorable stories, witty light verse, and searching reviews. A famously prolific writer, he published more than fifty books. Updike is best known as a hardworking, versatile, highly productive writer of fiction. For his novel The Centaur (1963) he received a National Book Award, and for Rabbit Is Rich (1982) a Pulitzer Prize and an American Book Award. The fourth and last Rabbit Angstrom novel, Rabbit at Rest (1990), won him a second Pulitzer. Updike is one of the few Americans ever to be awarded both the National Medal of Arts (1989) and the National Humanities Medal (2003)—the nation's highest honors in each respective field. His many other books include The Witches of Eastwick (1984), made into a successful film starring Jack Nicholson, Terrorist (2006), and his final novel, The Widows of Eastwick (2008).

Almost uniquely among contemporary American writers, Updike moved back and forth successfully among a variety of literary genres: light verse, serious poetry, drama, criticism, children's books, novels, and short stories. But it is perhaps in short fiction that he did his finest work. Some critics, such as Washington Post writer Jonathan Yardley, believe that "It is in his short stories that we find Updike's most assured work, and no doubt it is upon the best of them that his reputation ultimately will rest."

In walks three girls in nothing but bathing suits. I'm in the third check-out slot, with my back to the door, so I don't see them until they're over by the bread. The one that caught my eye first was the one in the plaid green two-piece. She was a chunky kid, with a good tan and a sweet broad soft-looking can with those two crescents of white just under it, where the sun never seems to hit, at the top of the backs of her legs. I stood there with my hand on a box of HiHo crackers trying to remember if I rang it up or not. I ring it up again and the customer starts giving me hell. She's one of these cash-register-watchers, a witch about fifty with rouge on her cheekbones and no eyebrows, and I know it made her day to trip me up. She'd been watching cash registers for fifty years and probably never seen a mistake before.

By the time I got her feathers smoothed and her goodies into a bag—she gives me a little snort in passing, if she'd been born at the right time they would have burned her over in Salem—by the time I get her on her way the girls had circled around the bread and were coming back, without a pushcart, back my way along the counters, in the aisle between the check-outs and the Special bins. They didn't even have shoes on. There was this chunky one, with the two-piece—it was bright green and the seams on the bra were still sharp and her belly was still pretty pale so I guessed she just got it (the suit)—there was this one, with one of those chubby berry-faces, the lips all bunched together under her nose, this one, and a tall one, with black hair that hadn't quite frizzed right, and one of these sunburns right across under the eyes, and a chin that was too long—you know, the kind of girl other girls think is very "striking" and "attractive" but never quite makes it, as they very well know, which is why they like her so much—and then the third one, that wasn't quite so tall. She was the queen. She kind of led them, the other two peeking around and making their shoulders round. She didn't look around, not this queen, she just walked straight on slowly, on these long white prima-donna legs. She came down a little hard on her heels, as if she didn't walk in her bare feet that much, putting down her heels and then letting the weight move along to her toes as if she was testing the floor with every step, putting a little deliberate extra action into it. You never know for sure how girls' minds work (do you really think it's a mind in there or just a little buzz like a bee in a glass jar?) but you got the idea she had talked the other two into coming in here with her, and now she was showing them how to do it, walk slow and hold yourself straight.

She had on a kind of dirty-pink—beige maybe, I don't know—bathing suit with a little nubble all over it and, what got me, the straps were down. They were off her shoulders looped loose around the cool tops of her arms, and I guess as a result the suit had slipped a little on her, so all around the top of the cloth there was this shining rim. If it hadn't been there you wouldn't have known there could have been anything whiter than those shoulders. With the straps pushed off, there was nothing between the top of the suit and the top of her head except just *her*, this clean bare plane of the top of her chest down from the shoulder bones like a dented sheet of metal tilted in the light. I mean, it was more than pretty.

She had sort of oaky hair that the sun and salt had bleached, done up in a bun that was unraveling, and a kind of prim face. Walking into the A & P with your straps down, I suppose it's the only kind of face you *can* have. She held her head so high her neck, coming up out of those white shoulders, looked kind of stretched, but I didn't mind. The longer her neck was, the more of her there was.

She must have felt in the corner of her eye me and over my shoulder Stokesie in the second slot watching, but she didn't tip. Not this queen. She kept her eyes moving across the racks, and stopped, and turned so slow it made my stomach rub the inside of my apron, and buzzed to the other two, who kind of huddled against her for relief, and they all three of them went up the cat-and-dog-food-breakfast-cereal-macaroni-rice-raisins-seasonings-spreads-spaghetti-soft-drinks-crackers-and-cookies aisle. From the third slot I look straight up this aisle to the meat counter, and I watched them all the way. The fat one with the tan sort of fumbled with the cookies, but on second thought she put the packages back. The sheep pushing their carts down the aisle—the girls were walking against the usual traffic (not that we have one-way signs or anything)—were pretty hilarious. You could see them, when Queenie's white shoulders dawned on them, kind of jerk, or hop, or hiccup, but their eyes snapped back to

5

their own baskets and on they pushed. I bet you could set off dynamite in an A & P and the people would by and large keep reaching and checking oatmeal off their lists and muttering "Let me see, there was a third thing, began with A, asparagus, no, ah, yes, applesauce!" or whatever it is they do mutter. But there was no doubt, this jiggled them. A few houseslaves in pin curlers even looked around after pushing their carts past to make sure what they had seen was correct.

You know, it's one thing to have a girl in a bathing suit down on the beach, where what with the glare nobody can look at each other much anyway, and another thing in the cool of the A & P, under the fluorescent lights, against all those stacked packages, with her feet padding along naked over our checkerboard green-and-cream rubber-tile floor.

"Oh Daddy," Stokesie said beside me. "I feel so faint."

"Darling," I said. "Hold me tight." Stokesie's married, with two babies chalked up on his fuselage already, but as far as I can tell that's the only difference. He's twenty-two, and I was nineteen this April.

"Is it done?" he asks, the responsible married man finding his voice. I forgot to say he thinks he's going to be manager some sunny day, maybe in 1990 when it's called the Great Alexandrov and Petrooshki Tea Company or something.

What he meant was, our town is five miles from a beach, with a big summer 10 colony out on the Point, but we're right in the middle of town, and the women generally put on a shirt or shorts or something before they get out of the car into the street. And anyway these are usually women with six children and varicose veins mapping their legs and nobody, including them, could care less. As I say, we're right in the middle of town, and if you stand at our front doors you can see two banks and the Congregational church and the newspaper store and three real-estate offices and about twenty-seven old freeloaders tearing up Central Street because the sewer broke again. It's not as if we're on the Cape; we're north of Boston and there's people in this town haven't seen the ocean for twenty years. The girls had reached the meat counter and were asking McMahon something. He pointed, they pointed, and they shuffled out of sight behind a pyramid of Diet Delight peaches. All that was left for us to see was old McMahon patting his mouth and looking after them sizing up their joints. Poor kids, I began to feel sorry for them, they couldn't help it.

Now here comes the sad part of the story, at least my family says it's sad but I don't think it's sad myself. The store's pretty empty, it being Thursday afternoon, so there was nothing much to do except lean on the register and wait for the girls to show up again. The whole store was like a pinball machine and I didn't know which tunnel they'd come out of. After a while they come around out of the far aisle, around the light bulbs, records at discount of the Caribbean Six or Tony Martin Sings or some such gunk you wonder they waste the wax on, six-packs of candy bars, and plastic toys done up in cellophane that fall apart when a kid looks at them anyway. Around they come, Queenie still leading the way, and holding a little gray jar in her hand. Slots Three through Seven are unmanned and I could see her wondering between Stokes and me, but Stokesie with his usual luck draws an old party in baggy gray pants who stumbles up with four giant cans of pineapple juice (what do these bums *do* with all that pineapple juice? I've often asked myself) so the girls come to me. Queenie puts down the jar and I take it into my fingers icy cold. Kingfish Fancy Herring Snacks in Pure Sour Cream: 49¢. Now her hands are empty, not a ring or a bracelet, bare as God made them, and I wonder where the money's coming from. Still with that prim look she lifts a folded dollar bill out of the hollow at the center of her nubbled pink top. The jar went heavy in my hand. Really, I thought that was so cute.

Then everybody's luck begins to run out. Lengel comes in from haggling with a truck full of cabbages on the lot and is about to scuttle into that door marked MANAGER behind which he hides all day when the girls touch his eye. Lengel's pretty dreary, teaches Sunday school and the rest, but he doesn't miss that much. He comes over and says, "Girls, this isn't the beach."

Queenie blushes, though maybe it's just a brush of sunburn I was noticing for the first time, now that she was so close. "My mother asked me to pick up a jar of herring snacks." Her voice kind of startled me, the way voices do when you see the people first, coming out so flat and dumb yet kind of tony, too, the way it ticked over "pick up" and "snacks." All of a sudden I slid right down her voice into her living room. Her father and the other men were standing around in ice-cream coats and bow ties and the women were in sandals picking up herring snacks on toothpicks off a big plate and they were all holding drinks the color of water with olives and sprigs of mint in them. When my parents have somebody over they get lemonade and if it's a real racy affair Schlitz in tall glasses with "They'll Do It Every Time" cartoons stencilled on.

"That's all right," Lengel said. "But this isn't the beach." His repeating this struck me as funny, as if it had just occurred to him, and he had been thinking all these years the A & P was a great big dune and he was the head lifeguard. He didn't like my smiling—as I say he doesn't miss much—but he concentrates on giving the girls that sad Sunday-school-superintendent stare.

Queenie's blush is no sunburn now, and the plump one in plaid, that I liked better from the back—a really sweet can—pipes up, "We weren't doing any shopping. We just came in for the one thing." **15**

"That makes no difference," Lengel tells her, and I could see from the way his eyes went that he hadn't noticed she was wearing a two-piece before. "We want you decently dressed when you come in here."

"We *are* decent," Queenie says suddenly, her lower lip pushing, getting sore now that she remembers her place, a place from which the crowd that runs the A & P must look pretty crummy. Fancy Herring Snacks flashed in her very blue eyes.

"Girls, I don't want to argue with you. After this come in here with your shoulders covered. It's our policy." He turns his back. That's policy for you. Policy is what the kingpins want. What the others want is juvenile delinquency.

All this while, the customers had been showing up with their carts but, you know, sheep, seeing a scene, they had all bunched up on Stokesie, who shook open a paper bag as gently as peeling a peach, not wanting to miss a word. I could feel in the silence everybody getting nervous, most of all Lengel, who asks me, "Sammy, have you rung up this purchase?"

I thought and said "No" but it wasn't about that I was thinking. I go through the **20** punches, 4, 9, GROC, TOT—it's more complicated than you think, and after you do it often enough, it begins to make a little song, that you hear words to, in my case "Hello (*bing*) there, you (*gung*) hap-py pee-pul (*splat*)!"—the *splat* being the drawer flying out. I uncrease the bill, tenderly as you may imagine, it just having come from between the two smoothest scoops of vanilla I had ever known were there, and pass a half and a penny into her narrow pink palm, and nestle the herrings in a bag and twist its neck and hand it over, all the time thinking.

The girls, and who'd blame them, are in a hurry to get out, so I say "I quit" to Lengel quick enough for them to hear, hoping they'll stop and watch me, their unsuspected hero. They keep right on going, into the electric eye; the door flies open and they flicker across the lot to their car, Queenie and Plaid and Big Tall Goony-Goony (not that as raw material she was so bad), leaving me with Lengel and a kink in his eyebrow.

"Did you say something, Sammy?"

"I said I quit."

"I thought you did."

"You didn't have to embarrass them."

"It was they who were embarrassing us."   25

I started to say something that came out "Fiddle-de-doo." It's a saying of my grandmother's, and I know she would have been pleased.

"I don't think you know what you're saying," Lengel said.

"I know you don't," I said. "But I do." I pull the bow at the back of my apron and start shrugging it off my shoulders. A couple customers that had been heading for my slot begin to knock against each other, like scared pigs in a chute.

Lengel sighs and begins to look very patient and old and gray. He's been a friend   30
of my parents for years. "Sammy, you don't want to do this to your Mom and Dad," he tells me. It's true, I don't. But it seems to me that once you begin a gesture it's fatal not to go through with it. I fold the apron, "Sammy" stitched in red on the pocket, and put it on the counter, and drop the bow tie on top of it. The bow tie is theirs, if you've ever wondered. "You'll feel this for the rest of your life," Lengel says, and I know that's true, too, but remembering how he made that pretty girl blush makes me so scrunchy inside I punch the No Sale tab and the machine whirs "peepul" and the drawer splats out. One advantage to this scene taking place in summer, I can follow this up with a clean exit, there's no fumbling around getting your coat and galoshes, I just saunter into the electric eye in my white shirt that my mother ironed the night before, and the door heaves itself open, and outside the sunshine is skating around on the asphalt.

I look around for my girls, but they're gone, of course. There wasn't anybody but some young married screaming with her children about some candy they didn't get by the door of a powder-blue Falcon station wagon. Looking back in the big windows, over the bags of peat moss and aluminum lawn furniture stacked on the pavement, I could see Lengel in my place in the slot, checking the sheep through. His face was dark gray and his back stiff, as if he'd just had an injection of iron, and my stomach kind of fell as I felt how hard the world was going to be to me hereafter.

Questions

1. Notice how artfully Updike arranges details to set the story in a perfectly ordinary supermarket. What details stand out for you as particularly true to life? What does this close attention to detail contribute to the story?

2. How fully does Updike draw the character of Sammy? What traits (admirable or otherwise) does Sammy show? Is he any less a hero for wanting the girls to notice his heroism? To what extent is he more thoroughly and fully portrayed than the doctor in "Godfather Death"?

3. What part of the story seems to be the exposition? (See the definition of *exposition* in the discussion of plot earlier in the chapter.) Of what value to the story is the carefully detailed portrait of Queenie, the leader of the three girls?

4. As the story develops, do you detect any change in Sammy's feelings toward the girls?

5. Where in "A & P" does the dramatic conflict become apparent? What moment in the story brings the crisis? What is the climax of the story?

6. Why, exactly, does Sammy quit his job?

7. Does anything lead you to *expect* Sammy to make some gesture of sympathy for the three girls? What incident earlier in the story (before Sammy quits) seems a foreshadowing?

8. What do you understand from the conclusion of the story? What does Sammy mean when he acknowledges "how hard the world was going to be . . . hereafter"?

9. What comment does Updike—through Sammy—make on supermarket society?

■ WRITING *effectively*

John Updike on Writing

Why Write? 1975

John Updike

Most people sensibly assume that writing is propaganda. Of course, they admit, there is bad propaganda, like the boy-meets-tractor novels of socialist realism, and old-fashioned propaganda, like Christian melodrama and the capitalist success stories of Horatio Alger or Samuel Smiles. But that some message is intended, wrapped in the story like a piece of crystal carefully mailed in cardboard and excelsior, is not doubted. Scarcely a day passes in my native land that I don't receive some letter from a student or teacher asking me *what I meant to say* in such a book, asking me to elaborate more fully on some sentence I deliberately whittled into minimal shape, or inviting me to speak on some topic, usually theological or sexual, on which it is pleasantly assumed I am an expert. The writer as hero, as Hemingway or Saint-Exupéry or D'Annunzio, a tradition of which Camus was perhaps the last example, has been replaced in America by the writer as educationist. Most writers teach, a great many teach writing; writing is furiously taught in the colleges even as the death knell of the book and the written word is monotonously tolled; any writer, it is assumed, can give a lecture, and the purer products of his academic mind, the "writings" themselves, are sifted and, if found of sufficient quality, installed in their places on the assembly belt of study, as objects of educational contemplation.

How dare one confess, to the politely but firmly inquiring letter-writer who takes for granted that as a remote but functioning element of his education you are duty-bound to provide the information and elucidating essay that will enable him to complete his term paper, or his Ph.D. thesis, or his critical *opus*—how dare one confess that the absence of a swiftly expressible message is, often, *the* message; that reticence is as important a tool to the writer as expression; that the hasty filling out of a questionnaire is not merely irrelevant but *inimical* to the writer's proper activity; that this activity is rather curiously private and finicking, a matter of exorcism and manufacture rather than of toplofty proclamation; that what he makes is ideally as ambiguous and opaque as life itself.

From "Why Write?"

THINKING ABOUT PLOT

A day without conflict is pleasant, but a story without conflict is boring. The plot of every short story, novel, or movie derives its energy from conflict. A character desperately wants something he or she can't have, or is frantic to avoid an unpleasant (or deadly) event. In most stories, conflict is established and tension builds, leading to a crisis and, finally, a resolution of some sort. When analyzing a story, be sure to remember these points:

- **Plotting isn't superficial.** Although plot might seem like the most obvious and superficial part of a story, it is an important expressive device. Plot combines with the other elements of fiction—imagery, style, and symbolism, for example—to create an emotional response in the reader: suspense, humor, sadness, excitement, terror.
- **Small events can have large consequences.** In most short stories, plot depends less on large external events than on small occurrences that set off large internal changes in the main character.
- **Action reveals character.** Good stories are a lot like life: the protagonist's true nature is usually revealed not just by what he or she says but also by what he or she does. Stories often show how the protagonist comes to a personal turning point, or how his or her character is tested or revealed by events.
- **Plot is about cause and effect.** Plot is more than just a sequence of events ("First A happens, and then B, and then C . . . "). The actions, events, and situations described in most stories are related to each other by more than just accident ("First A happens, which causes B to happen, which makes C all the more surprising, or inevitable, or ironic . . . ").

CHECKLIST: Writing About Plot

- ☐ What is the story's central conflict?
- ☐ Who is the protagonist? What does he or she want?
- ☐ What is at stake for the protagonist in the conflict?
- ☐ What stands in the way of the protagonist's easily achieving his or her goal?
- ☐ What are the main events that take place in the story? How does each event relate to the protagonist's struggle?
- ☐ Where do you find the story's climax, or crisis?
- ☐ How is the conflict resolved?
- ☐ Does the protagonist succeed in achieving his or her goals?
- ☐ What is the impact of success, failure, or a surprising outcome on the protagonist?

WRITING ASSIGNMENT ON PLOT

Choose and read a story from this collection, and write a brief description of its plot and main characters. Then write at length about how the protagonist is changed or tested by the story's events. What do the main character's actions reveal about his or her personality?

Some possible story choices are Updike's "A & P," Alice Walker's "Everyday Use," Alice Munro's "How I Met My Husband," and T. C. Boyle's "Greasy Lake."

MORE TOPICS FOR WRITING

1. Briefly list the events described in "A & P." Now write several paragraphs about the ways in which the story adds up to more than the sum of its events. Why should the reader care about Sammy's thoughts and decisions?

2. How do Sammy's actions in "A & P" reveal his character? In what ways are his thoughts and actions at odds with each other?

3. Write a brief fable modeled on either "The Appointment in Samarra," "The North Wind and the Sun," or "The Tortoise and the Geese." Begin with a familiar proverb—"A penny saved is a penny earned" or "Too many cooks spoil the broth"—and invent a story to make the moral convincing.

4. With "Godfather Death" in mind, write a fairy tale set in the present, in a town or city much like your own. After you've completed your fairy tale, write a paragraph explaining what aspects of the fairy tale by the Brothers Grimm you hoped to capture in your story.

5. The Brothers Grimm collected and wrote down many of our best-known fairy tales—"Cinderella," "Snow White and the Seven Dwarfs," and "Little Red Riding Hood," for example. If you have strong childhood recollections of one of these stories—perhaps based on picture books or on the animated Disney versions—find and read the Brothers Grimm version. Are you surprised by the differences? Write a brief essay contrasting the original with your remembered version. What does the original offer that the adaptation does not?

▶ TERMS FOR *review*

Types of Short Fiction

Fable ▶ A brief, often humorous narrative told to illustrate a moral. The characters in fables are traditionally animals whose personality traits symbolize human traits.

Parable ▶ A brief, usually allegorical narrative that teaches a moral. In parables, unlike fables (where the moral is explicitly stated within the narrative), the moral themes are implicit and can often be interpreted in several ways.

Tale ▶ A short narrative without a complex plot. Tales are an ancient form of narrative found in folklore, and traditional tales often contain supernatural elements. A tale differs from a short story by its tendency toward lesser-developed characters and linear plotting.

Tall tale ▶ A humorous short narrative that provides a wildly exaggerated version of events. Originally an oral form, the tall tale usually assumes that its audience knows the narrator is distorting the events. The form is often associated with the American frontier.

Fairy tale, folktale ▶ A traditional form of short narrative folklore, originally transmitted orally, which features supernatural characters such as witches, giants, fairies, or animals with human personality traits. Fairy tales often feature a hero or heroine who strives to achieve some desirable fate—such as marrying royalty or finding great wealth.

Short story ▶ A prose narrative too brief to be published in a separate volume—as novellas and novels frequently are. The short story is usually a focused narrative that presents one or two characters involved in a single compelling action.

Initiation story ▶ (also called **coming-of-age story**) A narrative in which the main character, usually a child or adolescent, undergoes an important experience (or "rite of passage") that prepares him or her for adulthood.

Elements of Plot

Protagonist ▶ The main or central character in a narrative. The protagonist usually initiates the main action of the story, often in conflict with the antagonist.

Antagonist ▶ The most significant character or force that opposes the protagonist in a narrative. The antagonist may be another character, society itself, a force of nature, or even—in modern literature—conflicting impulses within the protagonist.

Exposition ▶ The opening portion of a narrative. In the exposition, the scene is set, the protagonist is introduced, and the author discloses any other background information necessary for the reader to understand the events that follow.

Conflict ▶ The central struggle between two or more forces in a story. Conflict generally occurs when some person or thing prevents the protagonist from achieving his or her goal. Conflict is the basic material out of which most plots are made.

Complication ▶ The introduction of a significant development in the central conflict between characters (or between a character and his or her situation). Complications may be *external* (an outside problem that the characters cannot avoid) or *internal* (a complication that originates in some important aspect of a character's values or personality).

Crisis ▶ The point in a narrative when the crucial action, decision, or realization must take place. From the Greek word *krisis*, meaning "decision."

Climax ▶ The moment of greatest intensity in a story, which almost inevitably occurs toward the end of the work. The climax often takes the form of a decisive confrontation between the protagonist and antagonist.

Conclusion ▶ In plotting, the logical end or outcome of a unified plot, shortly following the climax. Also called **resolution** or **dénouement** ("the untying of the knot"), as in resolving—or untying the knots created by—plot complications earlier in the narrative.

Narrative Techniques

Foreshadowing ▶ An indication of events to come in a narrative. The author may introduce specific words, images, or actions in order to suggest significant later events.

Flashback ▶ A scene relived in a character's memory. Flashbacks may be related by the narrator in a summary, or they may be experienced by the characters themselves. Flashbacks allow the author to include significant events that occurred before the opening of the story.

Epiphany ▶ A moment of profound insight or revelation by which a character's life is greatly altered.

In medias res ▶ A Latin phrase meaning "in the midst of things"; refers to the narrative device of beginning a story midway in the events it depicts (usually at an exciting or significant moment) before explaining the context or preceding actions.

2 POINT OF VIEW

> *An author in his book must be like God in his universe,*
> *present everywhere and visible nowhere.*
>
> —GUSTAVE FLAUBERT

In the opening lines of *The Adventures of Huckleberry Finn*, Mark Twain takes care to separate himself from the leading character, who is to tell his own story:

> You don't know about me, without you have read a book by the name of *The Adventures of Tom Sawyer*, but that ain't no matter. That book was made by Mr. Mark Twain, and he told the truth, mainly.

Twain wrote the novel, but the **narrator** or speaker is Huck Finn, a fictional character who supposedly tells the story. Obviously, in *Huckleberry Finn*, the narrator of the story is not the same person as the "real-life" author. In employing Huck as his narrator, Twain selects a special angle of vision: not his own, exactly, but that of a resourceful boy moving through the thick of events, with a mind at times shrewd, at other times innocent. Through Huck's eyes, Twain takes in certain scenes, actions, and characters and—as only Huck's angle of vision could have enabled Twain to do so well—records them memorably.

Not every narrator in fiction is, like Huck Finn, a main character, one in the thick of events. Some narrators play only minor parts in the stories they tell; others take no active part at all. In the tale of "Godfather Death," we have a narrator who does not participate in the events he recounts. He is not a character in the story but is someone not even named, who stands at some distance from the action recording what the main characters say and do; recording also, at times, what they think, feel, or desire. He seems to have unlimited knowledge: he even knows the mind of Death, who "because he wanted revenge" let the doctor's candle go out.

More humanly restricted in their knowledge, other narrators can see into the mind of only one character. They may be less willing to express opinions than the narrator of "Godfather Death" ("He ought to have remembered his godfather's warning"). A story may even be told by a narrator who seems so impartial and aloof that he limits himself to reporting only overheard conversation and to describing, without comment or opinion, the appearances of things.

IDENTIFYING POINT OF VIEW

Narrators come in many forms; however, because stories usually are told by someone, almost every story has some kind of narrator. Some theorists reserve the term *narrator* for a character who tells a story in the first person. We use it in a wider sense, to mean a recording consciousness that an author creates, who may or may not be a participant in the events of the story. It is rare in modern fiction for the "real-life" author to try to step out from behind the typewriter and tell the story. Real persons can tell stories, but when such a story is *written*, the result is usually *nonfiction*: a memoir, an account of travels, an autobiography.

To identify a story's **point of view**, describe the role the narrator plays in the events and any limits placed on his or her knowledge of the events. In a short story, it is usual for the writer to maintain one point of view from beginning to end, but there is nothing to stop him or her from introducing other points of view as well. In his long, panoramic novel *War and Peace*, encompassing the vast drama of Napoleon's invasion of Russia, Leo Tolstoy freely shifts the point of view in and out of the minds of many characters, among them Napoleon himself.

TYPES OF NARRATORS

Theoretically, a great many points of view are possible. A narrator's knowledge might vary in gradations from total omniscience to almost total ignorance. But in reading fiction, again and again we encounter familiar and recognizable points of view. Here is a list of them—admittedly just a rough abstraction—that may provide a few terms with which to discuss the stories that you read and to describe their points of view:

Participant Narrator
- Writes in the first person ("I")
- Can be either a major or minor character

Nonparticipant Narrator
- Writes in the third person ("he," "she")
- Can possess different levels of knowledge about characters
  - **All-knowing** or **omniscient** (sees into any or all of the characters)
  - **Limited omniscience** (sees into one character)
  - **Objective** (does not see into any characters, reports events from outside)

When the narrator is cast as a **participant** in the events of the story, he or she is a dramatized character who says "I." Such a narrator may be the protagonist (Huck Finn) or may be an **observer**, a minor character standing a little to one side, watching a story unfold that mainly involves someone else. A famous example of a participant narrator occurs in F. Scott Fitzgerald's *The Great Gatsby*. The novel's narrator is not Jay Gatsby, but his friend Nick Carraway, who knows only portions of Gatsby's mysterious life.

A narrator who remains a **nonparticipant** does not appear in the story as a character. Viewing the characters, perhaps seeing into the minds of one or more of them, such a narrator refers to them as "he," "she," or "they."

How Much Does a Narrator Know?

The **all-knowing** (or **omniscient**) narrator sees into the minds of all (or some) characters, moving when necessary from one to another. This is the point of view in "Godfather Death," in which the narrator knows the feelings and motives of the father, of the doctor, and even of Death himself. Since he adds an occasional comment or opinion, this narrator may be said also to show **editorial omniscience** (as we can tell from his disapproving remark that the doctor "should have remembered" and his observation that the father did not understand "how wisely God shares out wealth and poverty"). A narrator who shows **impartial omniscience** presents the thoughts and actions of the characters, but does not judge them or comment on them.

When a nonparticipating narrator sees events through the eyes of a single character, whether a major character or a minor one, the resulting point of view is sometimes called **limited omniscience** or **selective omniscience**. The author, of course, selects which character to see through; the omniscience is his and not the narrator's. In William Faulkner's "Barn Burning" (Chapter 5), the narrator is almost entirely confined to knowing the thoughts and perceptions of a boy, the central character.

In the **objective point of view**, the narrator does not enter the mind of any character but describes events from the outside. Telling us what people say and how their faces look, he or she leaves us to infer their thoughts and feelings. So inconspicuous is the narrator that this point of view has been called "the fly on the wall." This metaphor assumes the existence of a fly with a highly discriminating gaze, who knows which details to look for to communicate the deepest meaning. Some critics would say that in the objective point of view, the narrator disappears altogether. Consider this passage by a writer famous for remaining objective, Dashiell Hammett, in his mystery novel *The Maltese Falcon*, describing his private detective Sam Spade:

> Spade's thick fingers made a cigarette with deliberate care, sifting a measured quantity of tan flakes down into curved paper, spreading the flakes so that they lay equal at the ends with a slight depression in the middle, thumbs rolling the paper's inner edge down and up under the outer edge as forefingers pressed it over, thumb and fingers sliding to the paper cylinder's ends to hold it even while tongue licked the flap, left forefinger and thumb pinching their ends while right forefinger and thumb smoothed the damp seam, right forefinger and thumb twisting their end and lifting the other to Spade's mouth.

In Hammett's novel, this sentence comes at a moment of crisis: just after Spade has been roused from bed in the middle of the night by a phone call telling him that his partner has been murdered. Even in times of stress (we infer) Spade is deliberate, cool, efficient, and painstaking. Hammett refrains from applying all those adjectives to Spade; to do so would be to exercise editorial omniscience and to destroy the objective point of view.

Other Narrative Points of View

Besides the common points of view just listed, uncommon points of view are possible. In *Flush*, a fictional biography of Elizabeth Barrett Browning, Virginia Woolf employs an unusual observer as narrator: the poet's pet cocker spaniel. In "The Circular Valley," a short story by Paul Bowles, a man and a woman are watched by a sinister spirit trying to take possession of them, and we see the human characters through the spirit's vague consciousness.

Also possible, but unusual, is a story written in the second person, *you*. This point of view results in an attention-getting directness, as in Jay McInerney's novel *Bright Lights, Big City* (1985), which begins:

> You are not the kind of guy who would be at a place like this at this time of the morning. But here you are, and you cannot say that the terrain is entirely unfamiliar, although the details are *fuzzy*. You are at a nightclub talking to a girl with a shaved head.

The attitudes and opinions of a narrator aren't necessarily those of the author; in fact, we may notice a lively conflict between what we are told and what, apparently, we are meant to believe. A story may be told by an **innocent narrator** or a **naive narrator**, a character who fails to understand all the implications of the story. One such innocent narrator (despite his sometimes shrewd perceptions) is Huckleberry Finn. Because Huck accepts without question the morality and lawfulness of slavery, he feels guilty about helping Jim, a runaway slave. But, far from condemning Huck for his defiance of the law—"All right, then, I'll *go* to hell," Huck tells himself, deciding against returning Jim to captivity—the author, and the reader along with him, silently applaud.

Naive in the extreme is the narrator of one part of William Faulkner's novel *The Sound and the Fury*, the idiot Benjy, a grown man with the intellect of a child. In a story told by an **unreliable narrator**, the point of view is that of a person who, we perceive, is deceptive, self-deceptive, deluded, or deranged. As though seeking ways to be faithful to uncertainty, contemporary writers have been particularly fond of unreliable narrators.

STREAM OF CONSCIOUSNESS

Virginia Woolf compared life to "a luminous halo, a semi-transparent envelope surrounding us from the beginning of consciousness to the end." To capture such a reality, modern writers of fiction have employed many strategies. One is the method of writing called **stream of consciousness**, from a phrase coined by psychologist William James to describe the procession of thoughts passing through the mind. In fiction, the stream of consciousness is a kind of selective omniscience: the presentation of thoughts and sense impressions in a lifelike fashion—not in a sequence arranged by logic, but mingled randomly. When in his novel *Ulysses* James Joyce takes us into the mind of Leopold Bloom, an ordinary Dublin mind well-stocked with trivia and fragments of odd learning, the reader may have an impression not of a smoothly flowing stream but of an ocean of miscellaneous things, all crowded and jostling.

> As he set foot on O'Connell bridge a puffball of smoke plumed up from the parapet. Brewery barge with export stout. England. Sea air sours it, I heard. Be interesting some day to get a pass through Hancock to see the brewery. Regular world in itself. Vats of porter, wonderful. Rats get in too. Drink themselves bloated as big as a collie floating.

Perceptions—such as the smoke from the brewery barge—trigger Bloom's reflections. A moment later, as he casts a crumpled paper ball off the bridge, he recalls a bit of science he learned in school, the rate of speed of a falling body: "thirty-two feet per sec."

Stream-of-consciousness writing usually occurs in relatively short passages, but in *Ulysses* Joyce employs it extensively. Similar in method, an **interior monologue** is an extended presentation of a character's thoughts, not in the seemingly helter-skelter order of a stream of consciousness, but in an arrangement as if the character were speaking out loud to himself, for us to overhear.

Every point of view has limitations. Even **total omniscience**, a knowledge of the minds of all the characters, has its disadvantages. Such a point of view requires high skill to manage, without the storyteller's losing his or her way in a multitude of perspectives. In fact, there are evident advantages in having a narrator not know everything. We are accustomed to seeing the world through one pair of eyes, to having truths gradually occur to us. Henry James, whose theory and practice of fiction have been influential, held that an excellent way to tell a story was through the fine but bewildered mind of an observer. "It seems probable," James wrote, "that if we were never bewildered there would never be a story to tell about us; we should partake of the superior nature of the all-knowing immortals whose annals are dreadfully dull so long as flurried humans are not, for the positive relief of bored Olympians, mixed up with them."

By using a particular point of view, an author may artfully withhold information, if need be, rather than immediately present it to us. If, for instance, the suspense in a story depends on our not knowing until the end that the protagonist is a spy, the author would be ill advised to tell the story from the protagonist's point of view. Clearly, the author makes a fundamental decision in selecting, from many possibilities, a story's point of view.

Here is a short story memorable for many reasons, among them its point of view.

William Faulkner

A Rose for Emily   1931

William Faulkner (1897–1962) spent most of his days in Oxford, Mississippi, where he attended the University of Mississippi and where he served as postmaster until angry townspeople ejected him because they had failed to receive mail. During World War I he served with the Royal Canadian Air Force and afterward worked as a feature writer for the New Orleans Times-Picayune. *Faulkner's private life was a long struggle to stay solvent: even after fame came to him, he had to write Hollywood scripts and teach at the University of Virginia to support himself. His violent comic novel* Sanctuary *(1931) caused a stir and turned a profit, but critics tend most to admire* The Sound and the Fury *(1929), a tale partially told through the eyes of an idiot;* As I Lay Dying *(1930);* Light in August *(1932);* Absalom, Absalom *(1936); and* The Hamlet *(1940). Beginning with* Sartoris *(1929), Faulkner in*

William Faulkner

his fiction imagines a Mississippi county named Yoknapatawpha and traces the fortunes of several of its families, including the aristocratic Compsons and Sartorises and the white-trash, dollar-grabbing Snopeses, from the Civil War to modern times. His influence on his fellow Southern writers (and others) has been profound. In 1950 he received the Nobel Prize in Literature. Although we think of Faulkner primarily as a novelist, he wrote nearly a hundred short stories. Forty-two of the best are available in his Collected Stories *(1950; 1995).*

I

When Miss Emily Grierson died, our whole town went to her funeral: the men through a sort of respectful affection for a fallen monument, the women mostly out of curiosity to see the inside of her house, which no one save an old manservant—a combined gardener and cook—had seen in at least ten years.

It was a big, squarish frame house that had once been white, decorated with cupolas and spires and scrolled balconies in the heavily lightsome style of the seventies, set on what had once been our most select street. But garages and cotton gins had encroached and obliterated even the august names of that neighborhood; only Miss Emily's house was left, lifting its stubborn and coquettish decay above the cotton wagons and the gasoline pumps—an eyesore among eyesores. And now Miss Emily had gone to join the representatives of those august names where they lay in the cedar-bemused cemetery among the ranked and anonymous graves of Union and Confederate soldiers who fell at the battle of Jefferson.

Alive, Miss Emily had been a tradition, a duty, and a care; a sort of hereditary obligation upon the town, dating from that day in 1894 when Colonel Sartoris, the mayor—he who fathered the edict that no Negro woman should appear on the streets without an apron—remitted her taxes, the dispensation dating from the death of her father on into perpetuity. Not that Miss Emily would have accepted charity. Colonel Sartoris invented an involved tale to the effect that Miss Emily's father had loaned money to the town, which the town, as a matter of business, preferred this way of re-paying. Only a man of Colonel Sartoris' generation and thought could have invented it, and only a woman could have believed it.

When the next generation, with its more modern ideas, became mayors and aldermen, this arrangement created some little dissatisfaction. On the first of the year they mailed her a tax notice. February came, and there was no reply. They wrote her a formal letter, asking her to call at the sheriff's office at her convenience. A week later the mayor wrote her himself, offering to call or to send his car for her, and received in reply a note on paper of an archaic shape, in a thin, flowing calligraphy in faded ink, to the effect that she no longer went out at all. The tax notice was also enclosed, without comment.

They called a special meeting of the Board of Aldermen. A deputation waited   5
upon her, knocked at the door through which no visitor had passed since she ceased giving china-painting lessons eight or ten years earlier. They were admitted by the old Negro into a dim hall from which a stairway mounted into still more shadow. It smelled of dust and disuse—a close, dank smell. The Negro led them into the parlor. It was furnished in heavy, leather-covered furniture. When the Negro opened the blinds of one window, they could see that the leather was cracked; and when they sat down, a faint dust rose sluggishly about their thighs, spinning with slow motes in the single sun-ray. On a tarnished gilt easel before the fireplace stood a crayon portrait of Miss Emily's father.

They rose when she entered—a small, fat woman in black, with a thin gold chain descending to her waist and vanishing into her belt, leaning on an ebony cane with a tarnished gold head. Her skeleton was small and spare; perhaps that was why what would have been merely plumpness in another was obesity in her. She looked bloated, like a body long submerged in motionless water, and of that pallid hue. Her eyes, lost in the fatty ridges of her face, looked like two small pieces of coal pressed into a lump of dough as they moved from one face to another while the visitors stated their errand.

She did not ask them to sit. She just stood in the door and listened quietly until the spokesman came to a stumbling halt. Then they could hear the invisible watch ticking at the end of the gold chain.

Her voice was dry and cold. "I have no taxes in Jefferson. Colonel Sartoris explained it to me. Perhaps one of you can gain access to the city records and satisfy yourselves."

"But we have. We are the city authorities, Miss Emily. Didn't you get a notice from the sheriff, signed by him?"

"I received a paper, yes," Miss Emily said. "Perhaps he considers himself the   10 sheriff . . . I have no taxes in Jefferson."

"But there is nothing on the books to show that, you see. We must go by the—"

"See Colonel Sartoris. I have no taxes in Jefferson."

"But, Miss Emily—"

"See Colonel Sartoris." (Colonel Sartoris had been dead almost ten years.) "I have no taxes in Jefferson. Tobe!" The Negro appeared. "Show these gentlemen out."

II

So she vanquished them, horse and foot, just as she had vanquished their fathers   15 thirty years before about the smell. That was two years after her father's death and a short time after her sweetheart—the one we believed would marry her—had deserted her. After her father's death she went out very little; after her sweetheart went away, people hardly saw her at all. A few of the ladies had the temerity to call, but were not received, and the only sign of life about the place was the Negro man—a young man then—going in and out with a market basket.

"Just as if a man—any man—could keep a kitchen properly," the ladies said; so they were not surprised when the smell developed. It was another link between the gross, teeming world and the high and mighty Griersons.

A neighbor, a woman, complained to the mayor, Judge Stevens, eighty years old.

"But what will you have me do about it, madam?" he said.

"Why, send her word to stop it," the woman said. "Isn't there a law?"

"I'm sure that won't be necessary," Judge Stevens said. "It's probably just a snake   20 or a rat that nigger of hers killed in the yard. I'll speak to him about it."

The next day he received two more complaints, one from a man who came in diffident deprecation. "We really must do something about it, Judge. I'd be the last one in the world to bother Miss Emily, but we've got to do something." That night the Board of Aldermen met—three graybeards and one younger man, a member of the rising generation.

"It's simple enough," he said. "Send her word to have her place cleaned up. Give her a certain time to do it in, and if she don't . . ."

"Dammit, sir," Judge Stevens said, "will you accuse a lady to her face of smelling bad?"

So the next night, after midnight, four men crossed Miss Emily's lawn and slunk about the house like burglars, sniffing along the base of the brickwork and at the cellar openings while one of them performed a regular sowing motion with his hand out of a sack slung from his shoulder. They broke open the cellar door and sprinkled lime there, and in all the outbuildings. As they recrossed the lawn, a window that had been dark was lighted and Miss Emily sat in it, the light behind her, and her upright torso motionless as that of an idol. They crept quietly across the lawn and into the shadow of the locusts that lined the street. After a week or two the smell went away.

That was when people had begun to feel really sorry for her. People in our town, remembering how old lady Wyatt, her great-aunt, had gone completely crazy at last, believed that the Griersons held themselves a little too high for what they really were. None of the young men were quite good enough for Miss Emily and such. We had long thought of them as a tableau, Miss Emily a slender figure in white in the background, her father a spraddled silhouette in the foreground, his back to her and clutching a horsewhip, the two of them framed by the back-flung front door. So when she got to be thirty and was still single, we were not pleased exactly, but vindicated; even with insanity in the family she wouldn't have turned down all of her chances if they had really materialized. 25

When her father died, it got about that the house was all that was left to her; and in a way, people were glad. At last they could pity Miss Emily. Being left alone, and a pauper, she had become humanized. Now she too would know the old thrill and the old despair of a penny more or less.

The day after his death all the ladies prepared to call at the house and offer condolence and aid, as is our custom. Miss Emily met them at the door, dressed as usual and with no trace of grief on her face. She told them that her father was not dead. She did that for three days, with the ministers calling on her, and the doctors, trying to persuade her to let them dispose of the body. Just as they were about to resort to law and force, she broke down, and they buried her father quickly.

We did not say she was crazy then. We believed she had to do that. We remembered all the young men her father had driven away, and we knew that with nothing left, she would have to cling to that which had robbed her, as people will.

III

She was sick for a long time. When we saw her again, her hair was cut short, making her look like a girl, with a vague resemblance to those angels in colored church windows—sort of tragic and serene.

The town had just let the contracts for paving the sidewalks, and in the summer after her father's death they began the work. The construction company came with niggers and mules and machinery, and a foreman named Homer Barron, a Yankee—a big, dark, ready man, with a big voice and eyes lighter than his face. The little boys would follow in groups to hear him cuss the niggers, and the niggers singing in time to the rise and fall of picks. Pretty soon he knew everybody in town. Whenever you heard a lot of laughing anywhere about the square, Homer Barron would be in the center of the group. Presently we began to see him and Miss Emily on Sunday afternoons driving in the yellow-wheeled buggy and the matched team of bays from the livery stable. 30

At first we were glad that Miss Emily would have an interest, because the ladies all said, "Of course a Grierson would not think seriously of a Northerner, a day laborer." But there were still others, older people, who said that even grief could not cause a real lady to forget *noblesse oblige*°—without calling it *noblesse oblige*. They just said, "Poor Emily. Her kinsfolk should come to her." She had some kin in Alabama; but years ago her father had fallen out with them over the estate of old lady Wyatt,

---

noblesse oblige: the obligation of a member of the nobility to behave with honor and dignity.

the crazy woman, and there was no communication between the two families. They had not even been represented at the funeral.

And as soon as the old people said, "Poor Emily," the whispering began. "Do you suppose it's really so?" they said to one another. "Of course it is. What else could . . ." This behind their hands; rustling of craned silk and satin behind jalousies closed upon the sun of Sunday afternoon as the thin, swift clop-clop-clop of the matched team passed: "Poor Emily."

She carried her head high enough—even when we believed that she was fallen. It was as if she demanded more than ever the recognition of her dignity as the last Grierson; as if it had wanted that touch of earthiness to reaffirm her imperviousness. Like when she bought the rat poison, the arsenic. That was over a year after they had begun to say "Poor Emily," and while the two female cousins were visiting her.

"I want some poison," she said to the druggist. She was over thirty then, still a slight woman, though thinner than usual, with cold, haughty black eyes in a face the flesh of which was strained across the temples and about the eye-sockets as you imagine a lighthouse-keeper's face ought to look. "I want some poison," she said.

"Yes, Miss Emily. What kind? For rats and such? I'd recom—" 35

"I want the best you have. I don't care what kind."

The druggist named several. "They'll kill anything up to an elephant. But what you want is—"

"Arsenic," Miss Emily said. "Is that a good one?"

"Is . . . arsenic? Yes, ma'am. But what you want—"

"I want arsenic." 40

The druggist looked down at her. She looked back at him, erect, her face like a strained flag. "Why, of course," the druggist said. "If that's what you want. But the law requires you to tell what you are going to use it for."

Miss Emily just stared at him, her head tilted back in order to look him eye for eye, until he looked away and went and got the arsenic and wrapped it up. The Negro delivery boy brought her the package; the druggist didn't come back. When she opened the package at home there was written on the box, under the skull and bones: "For rats."

IV

So the next day we all said, "She will kill herself"; and we said it would be the best thing. When she had first begun to be seen with Homer Barron, we had said, "She will marry him." Then we said, "She will persuade him yet," because Homer himself had remarked—he liked men, and it was known that he drank with the younger men in the Elks' Club—that he was not a marrying man. Later we said, "Poor Emily," behind the jalousies as they passed on Sunday afternoon in the glittering buggy, Miss Emily with her head high and Homer Barron with his hat cocked and a cigar in his teeth, reins and whip in a yellow glove.

Then some of the ladies began to say that it was a disgrace to the town and a bad example to the young people. The men did not want to interfere, but at last the ladies forced the Baptist minister—Miss Emily's people were Episcopal—to call upon her. He would never divulge what happened during that interview, but he refused to go back again. The next Sunday they again drove about the streets, and the following day the minister's wife wrote to Miss Emily's relations in Alabama.

So she had blood-kin under her roof again and we sat back to watch develop- 45 ments. At first nothing happened. Then we were sure that they were to be married.

We learned that Miss Emily had been to the jeweler's and ordered a man's toilet set in silver, with the letters H.B. on each piece. Two days later we learned that she had bought a complete outfit of men's clothing, including a nightshirt, and we said, "They are married." We were really glad. We were glad because the two female cousins were even more Grierson than Miss Emily had ever been.

So we were not surprised when Homer Barron—the streets had been finished some time since—was gone. We were a little disappointed that there was not a public blowing-off, but we believed that he had gone on to prepare for Miss Emily's coming, or to give her a chance to get rid of the cousins. (By that time it was a cabal, and we were all Miss Emily's allies to help circumvent the cousins.) Sure enough, after another week they departed. And, as we had expected all along, within three days Homer Barron was back in town. A neighbor saw the Negro man admit him at the kitchen door at dusk one evening.

And that was the last we saw of Homer Barron. And of Miss Emily for some time. The Negro man went in and out with the market basket, but the front door remained closed. Now and then we would see her at a window for a moment, as the men did that night when they sprinkled the lime, but for almost six months she did not appear on the streets. Then we knew that this was to be expected too; as if that quality of her father which had thwarted her woman's life so many times had been too virulent and too furious to die.

When we next saw Miss Emily, she had grown fat and her hair was turning gray. During the next few years it grew grayer and grayer until it attained an even pepper-and-salt iron-gray, when it ceased turning. Up to the day of her death at seventy-four it was still that vigorous iron-gray, like the hair of an active man.

From that time on her front door remained closed, save for a period of six or seven years, when she was about forty, during which she gave lessons in china-painting. She fitted up a studio in one of the downstairs rooms, where the daughters and granddaughters of Colonel Sartoris' contemporaries were sent to her with the same regularity and in the same spirit that they were sent to church on Sundays with a twenty-five-cent piece for the collection plate. Meanwhile her taxes had been remitted.

Then the newer generation became the backbone and the spirit of the town, and the painting pupils grew up and fell away and did not send their children to her with boxes of color and tedious brushes and pictures cut from the ladies' magazines. The front door closed upon the last one and remained closed for good. When the town got free postal delivery, Miss Emily alone refused to let them fasten the metal numbers above her door and attach a mailbox to it. She would not listen to them.

Daily, monthly, yearly we watched the Negro grow grayer and more stooped, going in and out with the market basket. Each December we sent her a tax notice, which would be returned by the post office a week later, unclaimed. Now and then we would see her in one of the downstairs windows—she had evidently shut up the top floor of the house—like the carven torso of an idol in a niche, looking or not looking at us, we could never tell which. Thus she passed from generation to generation—dear, inescapable, impervious, tranquil, and perverse.

And so she died. Fell ill in the house filled with dust and shadows, with only a doddering Negro man to wait on her. We did not even know she was sick; we had long since given up trying to get any information from the Negro. He talked to no one, probably not even to her, for his voice had grown harsh and rusty, as if from disuse.

50

She died in one of the downstairs rooms, in a heavy walnut bed with a curtain, her gray head propped on a pillow yellow and moldy with age and lack of sunlight.

V

The Negro met the first of the ladies at the front door and let them in, with their hushed, sibilant voices and their quick, curious glances, and then he disappeared. He walked right through the house and out the back and was not seen again.

The two female cousins came at once. They held the funeral on the second day, with the town coming to look at Miss Emily beneath a mass of bought flowers, with the crayon face of her father musing profoundly above the bier and the ladies sibilant and macabre; and the very old men—some in their brushed Confederate uniforms—on the porch and the lawn, talking of Miss Emily as if she had been a contemporary of theirs, believing that they had danced with her and courted her perhaps, confusing time with its mathematical progression, as the old do, to whom all the past is not a diminishing road but, instead, a huge meadow which no winter ever quite touches, divided from them now by the narrow bottleneck of the most recent decade of years.

Already we knew that there was one room in that region above stairs which no one had seen in forty years, and which would have to be forced. They waited until Miss Emily was decently in the ground before they opened it.

The violence of breaking down the door seemed to fill this room with pervading dust. A thin, acrid pall as of the tomb seemed to lie everywhere upon this room decked and furnished as for a bridal: upon the valance curtains of faded rose color, upon the rose-shaded lights, upon the dressing table, upon the delicate array of crystal and the man's toilet things backed with tarnished silver, silver so tarnished that the monogram was obscured. Among them lay collar and tie, as if they had just been removed, which, lifted, left upon the surface a pale crescent in the dust. Upon a chair hung the suit, carefully folded; beneath it the two mute shoes and the discarded socks.

The man himself lay in the bed.

For a long while we just stood there, looking down at the profound and fleshless grin. The body had apparently once lain in the attitude of an embrace, but now the long sleep that outlasts love, that conquers even the grimace of love, had cuckolded him. What was left of him, rotted beneath what was left of the nightshirt, had become inextricable from the bed in which he lay; and upon him and upon the pillow beside him lay that even coating of the patient and biding dust.

Then we noticed that in the second pillow was the indentation of a head. One of us lifted something from it, and leaning forward, that faint and invisible dust dry and acrid in the nostrils, we saw a long strand of iron-gray hair.

Questions

1. What is meaningful in the final detail that the strand of hair on the second pillow is *iron-gray?*
2. Who is the unnamed narrator? For whom does he profess to be speaking?
3. Why does "A Rose for Emily" seem better told from his point of view than if it were told (like John Updike's "A & P") from the point of view of the main character?
4. What foreshadowings of the discovery of the body of Homer Barron are we given earlier in the story? Share your experience in reading "A Rose for Emily": did the foreshadowings give away the ending for you? Did they heighten your interest?

5. What contrasts does the narrator draw between changing reality and Emily's refusal or inability to recognize change?

6. How do the character and background of Emily Grierson differ from those of Homer Barron? What general observations about the society that Faulkner depicts can be made from his portraits of these two characters and from his account of life in this one Mississippi town?

7. Does the story seem to you totally grim, or do you find any humor in it?

8. What do you infer to be the author's attitude toward Emily Grierson? Is she simply a murderous madwoman? Why do you suppose Faulkner calls his story "A Rose . . ."?

Edgar Allan Poe

The Tell-Tale Heart   (1843) 1850

Edgar Poe was born in Boston in January 1809, the second son of actors Eliza and David Poe. Edgar inherited his family's legacy of artistic talent, financial instability, and social inferiority (actors were not considered respectable in the nineteenth century), as well as his father's problems with alcohol. David Poe abandoned his family after the birth of Edgar's little sister, Rosalie, and Eliza died of tuberculosis in a Richmond, Virginia, boardinghouse before Edgar turned three. He was taken in by the wealthy John and Frances Allan of Richmond, whose name he added to his own. Allan educated Poe at first-rate schools, where he excelled in all subjects. But he grew into a moody adolescent, and his relationship with his foster father deteriorated.

Edgar Allan Poe

Poe's first year at the University of Virginia was marked by scholastic success, alcoholic binges, and gambling debts. Disgraced, he fled to Boston and joined the army under the name Edgar Perry. He performed well as an enlisted man and published his first collection of poetry, Tamerlane and Other Poems, *at the age of eighteen. After an abortive stint at West Point led to a final break with Allan, Poe embarked on a full-time literary career. A respected critic and editor, he sharply improved both the content and circulation of every magazine with which he was associated. But, morbidly sensitive to criticism, paranoid and belligerent when drunk, he left or was fired from every post he held. Poorly paid as both an editor and a writer, he earned almost nothing from the works that made him famous, such as "The Fall of the House of Usher" and "The Raven."*

After the break with his foster family, Poe rediscovered his own. From 1831, he lived with his father's widowed sister, Maria Clemm, and her daughter, Virginia. In 1836 Poe married this thirteen-year-old first cousin. These women provided him with much-needed emotional stability. However, like his mother, Poe's wife died of tuberculosis at age twenty-four, her demise doubtless hastened by poverty. Afterward, Poe's life came apart; his drinking intensified, as did his self-destructive tendencies. In October 1849 he died in mysterious circumstances, a few days after being found sick and incoherent on a Baltimore street.

True!—nervous—very, very dreadfully nervous I had been and am; but why *will* you say that I am mad? The disease had sharpened my senses—not destroyed—not dulled them. Above all was the sense of hearing acute. I heard all things in the heaven and in the earth. I heard many things in hell. How, then, am I mad? Hearken! and observe how healthily—how calmly, I can tell you the whole story.

It is impossible to say how first the idea entered my brain; but once conceived, it haunted me day and night. Object there was none. Passion there was none. I loved the old man. He had never wronged me. He had never given me insult. For his gold I had no desire. I think it was his eye! yes, it was this! One of his eyes resembled that of a vulture—a pale blue eye, with a film over it. Whenever it fell upon me, my blood ran cold; and so by degrees—very gradually—I made up my mind to take the life of the old man, and thus rid myself of the eye forever.

Now this is the point. You fancy me mad. Madmen know nothing. But you should have seen *me*. You should have seen how wisely I proceeded—with what caution—with what foresight—with what dissimulation I went to work! I was never kinder to the old man than during the whole week before I killed him. And every night, about midnight, I turned the latch of his door and opened it—oh, so gently! And then, when I had made an opening sufficient for my head, I put in a dark lantern, all closed, closed, so that no light shone out, and then I thrust in my head. Oh, you would have laughed to see how cunningly I thrust it in! I moved it slowly—very, very slowly, so that I might not disturb the old man's sleep. It took me an hour to place my whole head within the opening so far that I could see him as he lay upon his bed. Ha!—would a madman have been so wise as this? And then, when my head was well in the room, I undid the lantern cautiously—oh, so cautiously—cautiously (for the hinges creaked)—I undid it just so much that a single thin ray fell upon the vulture eye. And this I did for seven long nights—every night just at midnight—but I found the eye always closed; and so it was impossible to do the work; for it was not the old man who vexed me, but his Evil Eye. And every morning, when the day broke, I went boldly into the chamber, and spoke courageously to him, calling him by name in a hearty tone, and inquiring how he had passed the night. So you see he would have been a very profound old man, indeed, to suspect that every night, just at twelve, I looked in upon him while he slept.

Upon the eighth night I was more than usually cautious in opening the door. A watch's minute hand moves more quickly than did mine. Never before that night had I *felt* the extent of my own powers—of my sagacity. I could scarcely contain my feelings of triumph. To think that there I was, opening the door, little by little, and he not even to dream of my secret deeds or thoughts. I fairly chuckled at the idea; and perhaps he heard me; for he moved on the bed suddenly, as if startled. Now you may think that I drew back—but no. His room was as black as pitch with the thick darkness (for the shutters were close fastened, through fear of robbers), and so I knew that he could not see the opening of the door, and I kept pushing it on steadily, steadily.

I had my head in, and was about to open the lantern, when my thumb slipped upon the tin fastening, and the old man sprang up in the bed, crying out—"Who's there?"

I kept quite still and said nothing. For a whole hour I did not move a muscle, and in the meantime I did not hear him lie down. He was still sitting up in the bed,

5

listening;—just as I have done, night after night, hearkening to the death watches°
in the wall.

Presently I heard a slight groan, and I knew it was the groan of mortal terror. It
was not a groan of pain or of grief—oh, no!—it was the low stifled sound that arises
from the bottom of the soul when overcharged with awe. I knew the sound very well.
Many a night, just at midnight, when all the world slept, it has welled up from my
own bosom, deepening, with its dreadful echo, the terrors that distracted me. I say I
knew it well. I knew what the old man felt, and pitied him, although I chuckled at
heart. I knew that he had been lying awake ever since the first slight noise, when he
had turned in the bed. His fears had been ever since growing upon him. He had been
trying to fancy them causeless, but could not. He had been saying to himself—"It is
nothing but the wind in the chimney—it is only a mouse crossing the floor," or "it is
merely a cricket which has made a single chirp." Yes, he had been trying to comfort
himself with these suppositions; but he had found all in vain. *All in vain;* because
Death, in approaching him, had stalked with his black shadow before him, and
enveloped the victim. And it was the mournful influence of the unperceived shadow
that caused him to feel—although he neither saw nor heard—to *feel* the presence of
my head within the room.

When I had waited a long time, very patiently, without hearing him lie down,
I resolved to open a little—a very, very little crevice in the lantern. So I opened
it—you cannot imagine how stealthily, stealthily—until, at length, a single dim
ray, like the thread of the spider, shot from out of the crevice and fell upon the
vulture eye.

It was open—wide, wide open—and I grew furious as I gazed upon it. I saw it
with perfect distinctness—all a dull blue, with a hideous veil over it that chilled the
very marrow in my bones; but I could see nothing else of the old man's face or person:
for I had directed the ray as if by instinct, precisely upon the damned spot.

And now have I not told you that what you mistake for madness is but over-   10
acuteness of the senses?—now, I say, there came to my ears a low, dull, quick sound,
such as a watch makes when enveloped in cotton. I knew *that* sound well, too. It was
the beating of the old man's heart. It increased my fury, as the beating of a drum stim-
ulates the soldier into courage.

But even yet I refrained and kept still. I scarcely breathed. I held the lantern motionless. I tried how steadily I could maintain the ray upon the eye. Meantime the
hellish tattoo of the heart increased. It grew quicker and quicker, and louder and
louder every instant. The old man's terror *must* have been extreme! It grew louder, I
say, louder every moment!—do you mark me well? I have told you that I am nervous:
so I am. And now at the dead hour of the night, amid the dreadful silence of that old
house, so strange a noise as this excited me to uncontrollable terror. Yet, for some
minutes longer I refrained and stood still. But the beating grew louder, louder! I
thought the heart must burst. And now a new anxiety seized me—the sound would
be heard by a neighbor! The old man's hour had come! With a loud yell, I threw
open the lantern and leaped into the room. He shrieked once—once only. In an instant I dragged him to the floor, and pulled the heavy bed over him. I then smiled
gaily, to find the deed so far done. But, for many minutes, the heart beat on with a
muffled sound. This, however, did not vex me; it would not be heard through the wall.

death watches: beetles that infest timbers. Their clicking sound was thought to be an omen of death.

At length it ceased. The old man was dead. I removed the bed and examined the corpse. Yes, he was stone, stone dead. I placed my hand upon the heart and held it there many minutes.

If still you think me mad, you will think so no longer when I describe the wise precautions I took for the concealment of the body. The night waned, and I worked hastily, but in silence. First of all I dismembered the corpse. I cut off the head and the arms and the legs.

I then took up three planks from the flooring of the chamber, and deposited all between the scantlings. I then replaced the boards so cleverly, so cunningly, that no human eye—not even *his*—could have detected anything wrong. There was nothing to wash out—no stain of any kind—no blood-spot whatever. I had been too wary for that. A tub had caught all—ha! ha!

When I had made an end of these labors, it was four o'clock—still dark as midnight. As the bell sounded the hour, there came a knocking at the street door. I went down to open it with a light heart,—for what had I *now* to fear? There entered three men, who introduced themselves, with perfect suavity, as officers of the police. A shriek had been heard by a neighbor during the night; suspicion of foul play had been aroused, information had been lodged at the police office, and they (the officers) had been deputed to search the premises.

I smiled,—for *what* had I to fear? I bade the gentlemen welcome. The shriek, I   15
said, was my own in a dream. The old man, I mentioned, was absent in the country. I took my visitors all over the house. I bade them search—search *well*. I led them, at length, to *his* chamber. I showed them his treasures, secure, undisturbed. In the enthusiasm of my confidence, I brought chairs into the room, and desired them *here* to rest from their fatigues, while I myself, in the wild audacity of my perfect triumph, placed my own seat upon the very spot beneath which reposed the corpse of the victim.

The officers were satisfied. My *manner* had convinced them. I was singularly at ease. They sat, and while I answered cheerily, they chatted of familiar things. But, ere long, I felt myself getting pale and wished them gone. My head ached, and I fancied a ringing in my ears: but still they sat and still chatted. The ringing became more distinct:—it continued and became more distinct: I talked more freely to get rid of the feeling: but it continued and gained definitiveness—until, at length, I found that the noise was *not* within my ears.

No doubt I now grew *very* pale:—but I talked more fluently, and with a heightened voice. Yet the sound increased—and what could I do? It was a *low, dull, quick sound—much such a sound as a watch makes when enveloped in cotton*. I gasped for breath—and yet the officers heard it not. I talked more quickly—more vehemently; but the noise steadily increased. I arose and argued about trifles, in a high key and with violent gesticulations; but the noise steadily increased. Why *would* they not be gone? I paced the floor to and fro with heavy strides, as if excited to fury by the observations of the men—but the noise steadily increased. Oh God! what *could* I do? I foamed—I raved—I swore! I swung the chair upon which I had been sitting, and grated it upon the boards, but the noise arose over all and continually increased. It grew louder—louder—*louder*! And still the men chatted pleasantly, and smiled. Was it possible they heard not? Almighty God!—no, no! They heard!—they suspected!—they *knew*!—they were making a mockery of my horror!—this I thought, and this I think. But anything was better than this agony! Anything was more tolerable than this derision! I could bear those hypocritical smiles no longer! I felt that I must scream or die!—and now—again!—hark! louder! louder! louder! louder! *louder!*—

"Villains!" I shrieked, "dissemble no more! I admit the deed!—tear up the planks!—here, here!—it is the beating of his hideous heart!"

Questions

1. From what point of view is Poe's story told? Why is this point of view particularly effective for "The Tell-Tale Heart"?
2. Point to details in the story that identify its speaker as an unreliable narrator.
3. What do we know about the old man in the story? What motivates the narrator to kill him?
4. In spite of all his precautions, the narrator does not commit the perfect crime. What trips him up?
5. How do you account for the police officers' chatting calmly with the murderer instead of reacting to the sound that stirs the murderer into a frenzy?
6. See the student essays on this story in the chapter "Writing About a Story" later in the book. What do they point out that enlarges your own appreciation of Poe's art?

Virginia Woolf

A Haunted House   1921

Adeline Virginia Stephen Woolf (1882–1941) was born in London, the daughter of Sir Leslie Stephen, an influential critic and editor of the voluminous Dictionary of National Biography. *Virginia and her sister Vanessa (later Vanessa Bell) were largely self-educated in their father's extensive library while—in a distinction not lost on them—their brothers were sent to college. After their father's death in 1904, Virginia and Vanessa moved to Bloomsbury, a bohemian London neighborhood, and became the center of the "Bloomsbury Group" of progressive artists and intellectuals. Always in frail health, Virginia experienced episodes of mental disturbance. In 1912 she married Leonard Woolf, a journalist and novelist. In 1917 as therapy, they set up a hand-press in their home and started the Hogarth Press, which became one of the most*

Virginia Woolf

celebrated small presses of the century. In addition to Woolf's books, it issued works by T. S. Eliot, Katherine Mansfield, Robinson Jeffers, Edwin Arlington Robinson, and Sigmund Freud. Woolf's first novel was The Voyage Out *(1915); though realistic in technique, it foreshadowed the psychological depth and poetic force of her late work. In innovative novels such as* Mrs. Dalloway *(1925) and* To the Lighthouse *(1927), Woolf became one of the central Modernist writers in English and a pioneer of stream-of-consciousness narration, which portrays the random flow of thoughts and feelings through a character's mind. Her critical essays are collected in* The Common Reader *(1925, second series 1932); her long essay* A Room of One's Own *(1929) is a feminist classic. After several nervous break- downs, Woolf, fearing for her sanity, drowned herself in 1941.*

Whatever hour you woke there was a door shutting. From room to room they went, hand in hand, lifting here, opening there, making sure—a ghostly couple.

"Here we left it," she said. And he added, "Oh, but here too!" "It's upstairs," she murmured. "And in the garden," he whispered. "Quietly," they said, "or we shall wake them."

But it wasn't that you woke us. Oh, no. "They're looking for it; they're drawing the curtain," one might say, and so read on a page or two. "Now they've found it," one would be certain, stopping the pencil on the margin. And then, tired of reading, one might rise and see for oneself, the house all empty, the doors standing open, only the wood pigeons bubbling with content and the hum of the threshing machine sounding from the farm. "What did I come in here for? What did I want to find?" My hands were empty. "Perhaps it's upstairs then?" The apples were in the loft. And so down again, the garden still as ever, only the book had slipped into the grass.

But they had found it in the drawing room. Not that one could ever see them. The window panes reflected apples, reflected roses; all the leaves were green in the glass. If they moved in the drawing room, the apple only turned its yellow side. Yet, the moment after, if the door was opened, spread about the floor, hung upon the walls, pendant from the ceiling—what? My hands were empty. The shadow of a thrush crossed the carpet; from the deepest wells of silence the wood pigeon drew its bubble of sound. "Safe, safe, safe," the pulse of the house beat softly. "The treasure buried; the room . . ." the pulse stopped short. Oh, was that the buried treasure?

A moment later the light had faded. Out in the garden then? But the trees spun darkness for a wandering beam of sun. So fine, so rare, coolly sunk beneath the surface the beam I sought always burnt behind the glass. Death was the glass; death was between us; coming to the woman first, hundreds of years ago, leaving the house, sealing all the windows; the rooms were darkened. He left it, left her, went North, went East, saw the stars turned in the Southern sky; sought the house, found it dropped beneath the Downs. "Safe, safe, safe," the pulse of the house beat gladly. "The Treasure yours."

The wind roars up the avenue. Trees stoop and bend this way and that. Moonbeams splash and spill wildly in the rain. But the beam of the lamp falls straight from the window. The candle burns stiff and still. Wandering through the house, opening the windows, whispering not to wake us, the ghostly couple seek their joy.

"Here we slept" she says. And he adds, "Kisses without number." "Waking in the morning—" "Silver between the trees—" "Upstairs—" "In the garden—" "When summer came—" "In winter snowtime—" The doors go shutting far in the distance, gently knocking like the pulse of a heart.

Nearer they come; cease at the doorway. The wind falls, the rain slides silver down the glass. Our eyes darken; we hear no steps beside us; we see no lady spread her ghostly cloak. His hands shield the lantern. "Look," he breathes. "Sound asleep. Love upon their lips."

Stooping, holding their silver lamp above us, long they look and deeply. Long they pause. The wind drives straightly; the flame stoops slightly. Wild beams of moonlight cross both floor and wall, and, meeting, stain the faces bent; the faces pondering; the faces that search the sleepers and seek their hidden joy.

"Safe, safe, safe," the heart of the house beats proudly. "Long years—" he sighs. "Again you found me." "Here," she murmurs, "sleeping; in the garden reading;

laughing, rolling apples in the loft. Here we left our treasure—" Stooping, their light lifts the lids upon my eyes. "Safe! safe! safe!" the pulse of the house beats wildly. Waking, I cry "Oh, is this *your* buried treasure? The light in the heart."

Questions

1. Who is telling this story?
2. Note Woolf's pronoun usage, especially in the story's opening paragraphs. Why does she deliberately shift among first-, second-, and third-person perspectives?
3. What does the narrator report that she herself could not have seen or heard? How can she tell us things that she couldn't possibly know?
4. "A Haunted House," according to critic David Daiches, is not a story at all, but "simply an exercise in the writing of fluid associative prose." What do you think? Can any elements we usually find in a story be found in "A Haunted House"?
5. What is the treasure that is being sought? Notice Woolf's use of "silver" at several points of the story. What is the real treasure in the house?
6. What are the implications of the repeated phrase "Safe, safe, safe"?

Eudora Welty

Why I Live at the P.O.   1941

Eudora Welty

Eudora Welty (1909–2001) was born in Jackson, Mississippi, daughter of an insurance company president. Like William Faulkner, another Mississippi writer, she stayed close to her roots for practically all her life, except for short sojourns at the University of Wisconsin, where she took her B.A., and in New York City, where she studied advertising. She lived most of her life in her childhood home in Jackson, within a stone's throw of the state capitol. Although Welty was a novelist distinguished for The Robber Bridegroom *(1942),* Delta Wedding *(1946),* The Ponder Heart *(1954),* Losing Battles *(1970), and* The Optimist's Daughter *(1972), many critics think her finest work was in the short-story form. The Collected Stories of Eudora Welty (1980) gathers the work of more than forty years. Welty's other books include a memoir,* One Writer's Beginnings *(1984), and* The Eye of the Story *(1977), a book of sympathetic criticism on the fiction of other writers, including Willa Cather, Virginia Woolf, Katherine Anne Porter, and Isak Dinesen.* One Time, One Place, *a book of photographs of everyday life that Welty took in Mississippi during the Depression, was republished in a revised edition in 1996.*

I was getting along fine with Mama, Papa-Daddy, and Uncle Rondo until my sister Stella-Rondo just separated from her husband and came back home again. Mr. Whitaker! Of course I went with Mr. Whitaker first, when he first appeared here in China Grove, taking "Pose Yourself" photos, and Stella-Rondo broke us up. Told him I was one-sided. Bigger on one side than the other, which is a deliberate, calculated falsehood: I'm the same. Stella-Rondo is exactly twelve months to the day younger than I am and for that reason she's spoiled.

She's always had anything in the world she wanted and then she'd throw it away. Papa-Daddy gave her this gorgeous Add-a-Pearl necklace when she was eight years old and she threw it away playing baseball when she was nine, with only two pearls.

So as soon as she got married and moved away from home the first thing she did was separate! From Mr. Whitaker! This photographer with the popeyes she said she trusted. Came home from one of those towns up in Illinois and to our complete surprise brought this child of two.

Mama said she like to make her drop dead for a second. "Here you had this marvelous blonde child and never so much as wrote your mother a word about it," says Mama. "I'm thoroughly ashamed of you." But of course she wasn't.

Stella-Rondo just calmly takes off this *hat*. I wish you could see it. She says,   5
"Why, Mama, Shirley-T.'s adopted, I can prove it."

"How?" says Mama, but all I says was, "H'm!" There I was over the hot stove, trying to stretch two chickens over five people and a completely unexpected child into the bargain, without one moment's notice.

"What do you mean—'H'm!'?" says Stella-Rondo, and Mama says, "I heard that, Sister."

I said that oh, I didn't mean a thing, only that whoever Shirley-T. was, she was the spit-image of Papa-Daddy if he'd cut off his beard, which of course he'd never do in the world. Papa-Daddy's Mama's papa and sulks.

Stella-Rondo got furious! She said, "Sister, I don't need to tell you you got a lot of nerve and always did have and I'll thank you to make no future reference to my adopted child whatsoever."

"Very well," I said. "Very well, very well. Of course I noticed at once she looks   10
like Mr. Whitaker's side too. That frown. She looks like a cross between Mr. Whitaker and Papa-Daddy."

"Well, all I can say is she isn't."

"She looks exactly like Shirley Temple to me," says Mama, but Shirley-T. just ran away from her.

So the first thing Stella-Rondo did at the table was turn Papa-Daddy against me.

"Papa-Daddy," she says. He was trying to cut up his meat. "Papa-Daddy!" I was taken completely by surprise. Papa-Daddy is about a million years old and's got this long-long beard. "Papa-Daddy, Sister says she fails to understand why you don't cut off your beard."

So Papa Daddy l-a-y-s down his knife and fork! He's real rich. Mama says he is,   15
he says he isn't. So he says, "Have I heard correctly? You don't understand why I don't cut off my beard?"

"Why," I says, "Papa-Daddy, of course I understand, I did not say any such of a thing, the idea!"

He says, "Hussy!"

I says, "Papa-Daddy, you know I wouldn't any more want you to cut off your beard than the man in the moon. It was the farthest thing from my mind! Stella-Rondo sat there and made that up while she was eating breast of chicken."

But he says, "So the postmistress fails to understand why I don't cut off my beard. Which job I got you through my influence with the government. 'Bird's nest'—is that what you call it?"

Not that it isn't the next to smallest P.O. in the entire state of Mississippi.   20

I says, "Oh, Papa-Daddy," I says, "I didn't say any such of a thing, I never dreamed it was a bird's nest, I have always been grateful though this is the next to smallest P.O. in the state of Mississippi, and I do not enjoy being referred to as a hussy by my own grandfather."

But Stella-Rondo says, "Yes, you did say it too. Anybody in the world could of heard you, that had ears."

"Stop right there," says Mama, looking at *me*.

So I pulled my napkin straight back through the napkin ring and left the table.

As soon as I was out of the room Mama says, "Call her back, or she'll starve to   25
death," but Papa-Daddy says, "This is the beard I started growing on the Coast when I was fifteen years old." He would of gone on till nightfall if Shirley-T. hadn't lost the Milky Way she ate in Cairo.

So Papa-Daddy says, "I am going out and lie in the hammock, and you can all sit here and remember my words: I'll never cut off my beard as long as I live, even one inch, and I don't appreciate it in you at all." Passed right by me in the hall and went straight out and got in the hammock.

It would be a holiday. It wasn't five minutes before Uncle Rondo suddenly appeared in the hall in one of Stella-Rondo's flesh-colored kimonos, all cut on the bias, like something Mr. Whitaker probably thought was gorgeous.

"Uncle Rondo!" I says. "I didn't know who that was! Where are you going?"

"Sister," he says, "get out of my way, I'm poisoned."

"If you're poisoned stay away from Papa-Daddy," I says. "Keep out of the ham-   30
mock. Papa-Daddy will certainly beat you on the head if you come within forty miles of him. He thinks I deliberately said he ought to cut off his beard after he got me the P.O., and I've told him and told him and told him, and he acts like he just don't hear me. Papa-Daddy must of gone stone deaf."

"He picked a fine day to do it then," says Uncle Rondo, and before you could say "Jack Robinson" flew out in the yard.

What he'd really done, he'd drunk another bottle of that prescription. He does it every single Fourth of July as sure as shooting, and it's horribly expensive. Then he falls over in the hammock and snores. So he insisted on zigzagging right on out to the hammock, looking like a half-wit.

Papa-Daddy woke up with this horrible yell and right there without moving an inch he tried to turn Uncle Rondo against me. I heard every word he said. Oh, he told Uncle Rondo I didn't learn to read till I was eight years old and he didn't see how in the world I ever got the mail put up at the P.O., much less read it all, and he said if Uncle Rondo could only fathom the lengths he had gone to get me that job! And he said on the other hand he thought Stella-Rondo had a brilliant mind and deserved credit for getting out of town. All the time he was just lying there swinging as pretty as you please and looping out his beard, and poor Uncle Rondo was *pleading* with him to slow down the hammock, it was making him as dizzy as a witch to watch it. But that's what Papa-Daddy likes about a hammock. So Uncle Rondo was too dizzy to get turned against me for the time being. He's

Mama's only brother and is a good case of a one-track mind. Ask anybody. A certified pharmacist.

Just then I heard Stella-Rondo raising the upstairs window. While she was married she got this peculiar idea that it's cooler with the windows shut and locked. So she has to raise the window before she can make a soul hear her outdoors.

So she raises the window and says, "*Oh!*" You would have thought she was mortally wounded.

Uncle Rondo and Papa-Daddy didn't even look up, but kept right on with what they were doing. I had to laugh.

I flew up the stairs and threw the door open! I says, "What in the wide world's the matter, Stella-Rondo? You mortally wounded?"

"No," she says, "I am not mortally wounded but I wish you would do me the favor of looking out that window there and telling me what you see."

So I shade my eyes and look out the window.

"I see the front yard," I says.

"Don't you see any human beings?" she says.

"I see Uncle Rondo trying to run Papa-Daddy out of the hammock," I says. "Nothing more. Naturally, it's so suffocating-hot in the house, with all the windows shut and locked, everybody who cares to stay in their right mind will have to go out and get in the hammock before the Fourth of July is over."

"Don't you notice anything different about Uncle Rondo?" asks Stella-Rondo.

"Why, no, except he's got on some terrible-looking flesh-colored contraption I wouldn't be found dead in, is all I can see," I says.

"Never mind, you won't be found dead in it, because it happens to be part of my trousseau, and Mr. Whitaker took several dozen photographs of me in it," says Stella-Rondo. "What on earth could Uncle Rondo *mean* by wearing part of my trousseau out in the broad open daylight without saying so much as 'Kiss my foot,' *knowing* I only got home this morning after my separation and hung my negligee up on the bathroom door, just as nervous as I could be?"

"I'm sure I don't know, and what do you expect me to do about it?" I says. "Jump out the window?"

"No, I expect nothing of the kind. I simply declare that Uncle Rondo looks like a fool in it, that's all," she says. "It makes me sick to my stomach."

"Well, he looks as good as he can," I says. "As good as anybody in reason could." I stood up for Uncle Rondo, please remember. And I said to Stella-Rondo, "I think I would do well not to criticize so freely if I were you and came home with a two-year-old child I had never said a word about, and no explanation whatever about my separation."

"I asked you the instant I entered this house not to refer one more time to my adopted child, and you gave me your word of honor you would not," was all Stella-Rondo would say, and started pulling out every one of her eyebrows with some cheap Kress tweezers.

So I merely slammed the door behind me and went down and made some green-tomato pickle. Somebody had to do it. Of course Mama had turned both the niggers loose; she always said no earthly power could hold one anyway on the Fourth of July, so she wouldn't even try. It turned out that Jaypan fell in the lake and came within a very narrow limit of drowning.

So Mama trots in. Lifts up the lid and says, "H'm! Not very good for your Uncle Rondo in his precarious condition, I must say. Or poor little adopted Shirley-T. Shame on you!"

That made me tired. I says, "Well, Stella-Rondo had better thank her lucky stars it was her instead of me came trotting in with that very peculiar-looking child. Now if it had been me that trotted in from Illinois and brought a peculiar-looking child of two, I shudder to think of the reception I'd of got, much less controlled the diet of an entire family."

"But you must remember, Sister, that you were never married to Mr. Whitaker in the first place and didn't go up to Illinois to live," says Mama, shaking a spoon in my face. If you had I would have been just as overjoyed to see you and your little adopted girl as I was to see Stella-Rondo, when you wound up with your separation and came on back home."

"You would not," I says.

"Don't contradict me, I would," says Mama.   55

But I said she couldn't convince me though she talked till she was blue in the face. Then I said, "Besides, you know as well as I do that that child is not adopted."

"She most certainly is adopted," says Mama, stiff as a poker.

I says, "Why, Mama, Stella-Rondo had her just as sure as anything in this world, and just too stuck up to admit it."

"Why Sister," said Mama. "Here I thought we were going to have a pleasant Fourth of July, and you start right out not believing a word your own baby sister tells you!"

"Just like Cousin Annie Flo. Went to her grave denying the facts of life," I   60 remind Mama.

"I told you if you ever mentioned Annie Flo's name I'd slap your face," says Mama, and slaps my face.

"All right, you wait and see," I says.

"I," says Mama, "I prefer to take my children's word for anything when it's humanly possible." You ought to see Mama, she weighs two hundred pounds and has real tiny feet.

Just then something perfectly horrible occurred to me.

"Mama," I says, "can that child talk?" I simply had to whisper! "Mama, I wonder   65 if that child can be—you know—in any way? Do you realize," I says, "that she hasn't spoken one single, solitary word to a human being up to this minute? This is the way she looks," I says, and I looked like this.

Well, Mama and I just stood there and stared at each other. It was horrible!

"I remember well that Joe Whitaker frequently drank like a fish," says Mama. "I believed to my soul he drank *chemicals*." And without another word she marches to the foot of the stairs and calls Stella-Rondo.

"Stella-Rondo? O-o-o-o-o! Stella-Rondo!"

"What?" says Stella-Rondo from upstairs. Not even the grace to get up off the bed.

"Can that child of yours talk?" asks Mama.   70

Stella-Rondo yells back, "Can she what?"

"Talk! Talk!" says Mama. "Burdyburdyburdyburdy!"

So Stella-Rondo yells back, "Who says she can't talk?"

"Sister says so," says Mama.

"You didn't have to tell me, I know whose word of honor don't mean a thing in this house," says Stella-Rondo. 75

And in a minute the loudest Yankee voice I ever heard in my life yells out, "OE'm Pop-OE the Sailor-r-r Ma-a-an!" and then somebody jumps up and down in the upstairs hall. In another second the house would of fallen down.

"Not only talks, she can tap-dance!" calls Stella-Rondo. "Which is more than some people I won't name can do."

"Why, the little precious darling thing!" Mama says, so surprised. "Just as smart as she can be!" Starts talking baby talk right there. Then she turns on me. "Sister, you ought to be thoroughly ashamed! Run upstairs this instant and apologize to Stella-Rondo and Shirley-T."

"Apologize for what?" I says. "I merely wondered if the child was normal, that's all. Now that she's proved she is, why, I have nothing further to say."

But Mama just turned on her heel and flew out, furious. She ran right upstairs and hugged the baby. She believed it was adopted. Stella-Rondo hadn't done a thing but turn her against me from upstairs while I stood there helpless over the hot stove. So that made Mama, Papa-Daddy, and the baby all on Stella-Rondo's side. 80

Next, Uncle Rondo.

I must say that Uncle Rondo has been marvelous to me at various times in the past and I was completely unprepared to be made to jump out of my skin, the way it turned out. Once Stella-Rondo did something perfectly horrible to him—broke a chain letter from Flanders Field°—and he took the radio back he had given her and gave it to me. Stella-Rondo was furious! For six months we all had to call her Stella instead of Stella-Rondo, or she wouldn't answer. I always thought Uncle Rondo had all the brains of the entire family. Another time he sent me to Mammoth Cave,° with all expenses paid.

But this would be the day he was drinking that prescription, the Fourth of July.

So at supper Stella-Rondo speaks up and says she thinks Uncle Rondo ought to try to eat a little something. So finally Uncle Rondo said he would try a little cold biscuits and ketchup, but that was all. So *she* brought it to him.

"Do you think it is wise to disport with ketchup in Stella-Rondo's flesh-colored kimono?" I says. Trying to be considerate! If Stella-Rondo couldn't watch out for her trousseau, somebody had to. 85

"Any objections?" asks Uncle Rondo, just about to pour out all the ketchup.

"Don't mind what she says, Uncle Rondo," says Stella-Rondo. "Sister has been devoting this solid afternoon to sneering out my bedroom window at the way you look."

"What's that?" says Uncle Rondo. Uncle Rondo has got the most terrible temper in the world. Anything is liable to make him tear the house down if it comes at the wrong time.

Flanders Field: an Allied military cemetery in Belgium for the dead of World War I, it was made famous by a poem by John McCrae. The artificial red poppies still sold for charity on Veterans Day commemorate the cemetery and poem.　*Mammoth Cave:* a network of natural underground caverns in Kentucky.

So Stella-Rondo says, "Sister says, 'Uncle Rondo certainly does look like a fool in that pink kimono!'"

Do you remember who it was really said that?   90

Uncle Rondo spills out all the ketchup and jumps out of his chair and tears off the kimono and throws it down on the dirty floor and puts his foot on it. It had to be sent all the way to Jackson to the cleaners and re-pleated.

"So that's your opinion of your Uncle Rondo, is it?" he says. "I look like a fool, do I? Well, that's the last straw. A whole day in this house with nothing to do, and then to hear you come out with a remark like that behind my back!"

"I didn't say any such of a thing, Uncle Rondo," I says, "and I'm not saying who did, either. Why, I think you look all right. Just try to take care of yourself and not talk and eat at the same time," I says. "I think you better go lie down."

"Lie down my foot," says Uncle Rondo. I ought to of known by that he was fixing to do something perfectly horrible.

So he didn't do anything that night in the precarious state he was in—just   95
played Casino with Mama and Stella-Rondo and Shirley-T. and gave Shirley-T. a nickel with a head on both sides. It tickled her nearly to death, and she called him "Papa." But at 6:30 A.M. the next morning, he threw a whole five-cent package of some unsold one-inch firecrackers from the store as hard as he could into my bedroom and they every one went off. Not one bad one in the string. Anybody else, there'd be one that wouldn't go off.

Well, I'm just terribly susceptible to noise of any kind, the doctor has always told me I was the most sensitive person he had ever seen in his whole life, and I was simply prostrated. I couldn't eat! People tell me they heard it as far as the cemetery, and old Aunt Jep Patterson, that had been holding her own so good, thought it was Judgment Day and she was going to meet her whole family. It's usually so quiet here.

And I'll tell you it didn't take me any longer than a minute to make up my mind what to do. There I was with the whole entire house on Stella-Rondo's side and turned against me. If I have anything at all I have pride.

So I just decided I'd go straight down to the P.O. There's plenty of room there in the back, I says to myself.

Well! I made no bones about letting the family catch on to what I was up to. I didn't try to conceal it.

The first thing they knew, I marched in where they were all playing Old Maid   100
and pulled the electric oscillating fan out by the plug, and everything got real hot. Next I snatched the pillow I'd done the needlepoint on right off the davenport from behind Papa-Daddy. He went "Ugh!" I beat Stella-Rondo up the stairs and finally found my charm bracelet in her bureau drawer under a picture of Nelson Eddy.°

"So that's the way the land lies," says Uncle Rondo. There he was, piecing on the ham. "Well, Sister, I'll be glad to donate my army cot if you got any place to set it up, providing you'll leave right this minute and let me get some peace." Uncle Rondo was in France.

"Thank you kindly for the cot and 'peace' is hardly the word I would select if I had to resort to firecrackers at 6:30 A.M. in a young girl's bedroom," I says back to

Nelson Eddy: a popular singer (1901–1967) who appeared in romantic musical films during the Depression era.

him. "And as to where I intend to go, you seem to forget my position as postmistress of China Grove, Mississippi," I says. "I've always got the P.O."

Well, that made them all sit up and take notice.

I went out front and started digging up some four-o'clocks to plant around the P.O.

"Ah-ah-ah!" says Mama, raising the window. "Those happen to be my four-o'- 105 clocks. Everything planted in that star is mine. I've never known you to make any- thing grow in your life."

"Very well," I says. "But I take the fern. Even you, Mama, can't stand there and deny that I'm the one watered that fern. And I happen to know where I can send in a box top and get a packet of one thousand mixed seeds, no two the same kind, free."

"Oh, where?" Mama wants to know.

But I says, "Too late. You 'tend to your house, and I'll 'tend to mine. You hear things like that all the time if you know how to listen to the radio. Perfectly marvelous offers. Get anything you want free."

So I hope to tell you I marched in and got that radio, and they could of all bit a nail in two, especially Stella-Rondo, that it used to belong to, and she well knew she couldn't get it back, I'd sue for it like a shot. And I very politely took the sewing- machine motor I helped pay the most on to give Mama for Christmas back in 1929, and a good big calendar, with the first-aid remedies on it. The thermometer and the Hawaiian ukulele certainly were rightfully mine, and I stood on the step-ladder and got all my watermelon-rind preserves and every fruit and vegetable I'd put up, every jar. Then I began to pull the tacks out of the bluebird wall vases on the archway to the dining room.

"Who told you you could have those, Miss Priss?" says Mama, fanning as hard as 110 she could.

"I bought 'em and I'll keep track of 'em," I says. "I'll tack 'em up one on each side the post-office window, and you can see 'em when you come to ask me for your mail, if you're so dead to see 'em."

"Not I! I'll never darken the door to that post office again if I live to be a hun- dred," Mama says. "Ungrateful child! After all the money we spent on you at the Normal."°

"Me either," says Stella-Rondo. "You can just let my mail lie there and *rot*, for all I care. I'll never come and relieve you of a single, solitary piece."

"I should worry," I says. "And who you think's going to sit down and write you all those big fat letters and postcards, by the way? Mr. Whitaker? Just because he was the only man ever dropped down in China Grove and you got him—unfairly—is he going to sit down and write you a lengthy correspondence after you come home giving no rhyme nor reason whatsoever for your separation and no explanation for the presence of that child? I may not have your brilliant mind, but I fail to see it."

So Mama says, "Sister, I've told you a thousand times that Stella-Rondo simply 115 got homesick, and this child is far too big to be hers," and she says, "Now, why don't you just sit down and play Casino?"

Normal: normal school, a two-year college for the training of elementary school teachers.

Then Shirley-T. sticks out her tongue at me in this perfectly horrible way. She has no more manners than the man in the moon. I told her she was going to cross her eyes like that some day and they'd stick.

"It's too late to stop me now," I says. "You should have tried that yesterday. I'm going to the P.O. and the only way you can possibly see me is to visit me there."

So Papa-Daddy says, "You'll never catch me setting foot in that post office, even if I should take a notion into my head to write a letter some place." He says, "I won't have you reachin' out of that little old window with a pair of shears and cuttin' off any beard of mine. I'm too smart for you!"

"We all are," says Stella-Rondo.

But I said, "If you're so smart, where's Mr. Whitaker?"   120

So then Uncle Rondo says, "I'll thank you from now on to stop reading all the orders I get on postcards and telling everybody in China Grove what you think is the matter with them," but I says, "I draw my own conclusions and will continue in the future to draw them." I says, "If people want to write their inmost secrets on penny postcards, there's nothing in the wide world you can do about it, Uncle Rondo."

"And if you think we'll ever *write* another postcard you're sadly mistaken," says Mama.

"Cutting off your nose to spite your face then," I says. "But if you're all determined to have no more to do with the U.S. mail, think of this: What will Stella-Rondo do now, if she wants to tell Mr. Whitaker to come after her?"

"Wah!" says Stella-Rondo. I knew she'd cry. She had a conniption fit right there in the kitchen.

"It will be interesting to see how long she holds out," I says. "And now—I am   125
leaving."

"Good-by," says Uncle Rondo.

"Oh, I declare," says Mama, "to think that a family of mine should quarrel on the Fourth of July, or the day after, over Stella-Rondo leaving old Mr. Whitaker and having the sweetest little adopted child! It looks like we'd all be glad!"

"Wah!" says Stella-Rondo, and has a fresh conniption fit.

"*He* left *her*—you mark my words," I says. "That's Mr. Whitaker. I know Mr. Whitaker. After all, I knew him first. I said from the beginning he'd up and leave her. I foretold every single thing that's happened."

"Where did he go?" asks Mama.   130

"Probably to the North Pole, if he knows what's good for him," I says.

But Stella-Rondo just bawled and wouldn't say another word. She flew to her room and slammed the door.

"Now look what you've gone and done, Sister," says Mama. "You go apologize."

"I haven't got time, I'm leaving," I says.

"Well, what are you waiting around for?" asks Uncle Rondo.   135

So I just picked up the kitchen clock and marched off, without saying "Kiss my foot," or anything, and never did tell Stella-Rondo good-by.

There was a nigger girl going along on a little wagon right in front.

"Nigger girl," I says, "come help me haul these things down the hill, I'm going to live in the post office."

Took her nine trips in her express wagon. Uncle Rondo came out on the porch and threw her a nickel.

*

And that's the last I've laid eyes on any of my family or my family laid eyes on 140
me for five solid days and nights. Stella-Rondo may be telling the most horrible tales
in the world about Mr. Whitaker, but I haven't heard them. As I tell everybody, I
draw my own conclusions.

But oh, I like it here. It's ideal, as I've been saying. You see, I've got everything
cater-cornered, the way I like it. Hear the radio? All the war news. Radio, sewing machine, book ends, ironing board and that great big piano lamp—peace, that's what I
like. Butter-bean vines planted all along the front where the strings are.

Of course, there's not much mail. My family are naturally the main people in
China Grove, and if they prefer to vanish from the face of the earth, for all the mail
they get or the mail they write, why, I'm not going to open my mouth. Some of the
folks here in town are taking up for me and some turned against me. I know which is
which. There are always people who will quit buying stamps just to get on the right
side of Papa-Daddy.

But here I am, and here I'll stay. I want the world to know I'm happy.

And if Stella-Rondo should come to me this minute, on bended knees, and
attempt to explain the incidents of her life with Mr. Whitaker, I'd simply put my
fingers in both my ears and refuse to listen.

Questions

1. Can we equate the narrator's voice with Welty's? What clues does the author give that
   Sister's opinions are not her own?
2. What statements does the narrator make that seem unreliable?
3. Describe Sister's personality. Is she slightly crazy or is her odd behavior a justified revolt
   against her family?
4. Sister uses the word "nigger" several times in the story, and she is clearly a racist. What
   does her attitude toward African Americans tell you about the time and place of the
   story?
5. Why does Sister fight so much with her family?

James Baldwin

Sonny's Blues   1957

*James Baldwin (1924–1987) was born in Harlem, in New York City. His father was a
Pentecostal minister, and the young Baldwin initially planned to become a clergyman.
While still in high school, he preached sermons in a storefront church. At seventeen,
however, he left home to live in Greenwich Village, where he worked at menial jobs and
began publishing articles in* Commentary *and the* Nation. *Later he embarked on a series of travels that eventually brought him to France. Baldwin soon regarded France as a
second home, a country in which he could avoid the racial discrimination he felt in
America. His first novel,* Go Tell It on the Mountain *(1953), which described a single day in the lives of the members of a Harlem church, immediately earned him a position as a leading African American writer. His next two novels,* Giovanni's Room
(1956) and Another Country *(1962), dealt with homosexual themes and drew criticism from some of his early champions. His collection of essays* Notes of a Native Son
*(1955) remains one of the key books of the civil rights movement. His short stories were
not collected until* Going to Meet the Man *was published in 1965. Although he spent
nearly forty years in France, Baldwin still considered himself an American. He was not*

an expatriate, he claimed, but a "commuter." He died in St. Paul de Vence, France, but was buried in Ardsley, New York.

I read about it in the paper, in the subway, on my way to work. I read it, and I couldn't believe it, and I read it again. Then perhaps I just stared at it, at the newsprint spelling out his name, spelling out the story. I stared at it in the swinging lights of the subway car, and in the faces and bodies of the people, and in my own face, trapped in the darkness which roared outside.

It was not to be believed and I kept telling myself that, as I walked from the subway station to the high school. And at the same time I couldn't doubt it. I was scared, scared for Sonny. He became real to me again. A great block of ice got settled in my belly and kept melting there slowly all day long, while I taught my classes algebra. It was a special kind of ice. It kept melting, sending trickles of ice water all up and down my veins, but it never got less. Sometimes it hardened and seemed to expand until I felt my guts were going to come spilling out or that I was going to choke or scream. This would always be at a moment when I was remembering some specific thing Sonny had once said or done.

When he was about as old as the boys in my classes his face had been bright and open, there was a lot of copper in it; and he'd had wonderfully direct brown eyes, and great gentleness and privacy. I wondered what he looked like now. He had been picked up, the evening before, in a raid on an apartment downtown, for peddling and using heroin.

I couldn't believe it: but what I mean by that is that I couldn't find any room for it anywhere inside me. I had kept it outside me for a long time. I hadn't wanted to know. I had had suspicions, but I didn't name them, I kept putting them away. I told myself that Sonny was wild, but he wasn't crazy. And he'd always been a good boy, he hadn't ever turned hard or evil or disrespectful, the way kids can, so quick, so quick, especially in Harlem. I didn't want to believe that I'd ever see my brother going down, coming to nothing, all that light in his face gone out, in the condition I'd already seen so many others. Yet it had happened and here I was, talking about algebra to a lot of boys who might, every one of them for all I knew, be popping off needles every time they went to the head. Maybe it did more for them than algebra could.

I was sure that the first time Sonny had ever had horse,° he couldn't have been   5
much older than these boys were now. These boys, now, were living as we'd been living then, they were growing up with a rush and their heads bumped abruptly against the low ceiling of their actual possibilities. They were filled with rage. All they really knew were two darknesses, the darkness of their lives, which was now closing in on them, and the darkness of the movies, which had blinded them to that other darkness, and in which they now, vindictively, dreamed, at once more together than they were at any other time, and more alone.

When the last bell rang, the last class ended, I let out my breath. It seemed I'd been holding it for all that time. My clothes were wet—I may have looked as though I'd been sitting in a steam bath, all dressed up, all afternoon. I sat alone in the classroom a long time. I listened to the boys outside, downstairs, shouting and cursing and laughing. Their laughter struck me for perhaps the first time. It was not the joyous laughter which—God knows why—one associates with children. It was mocking and

horse: heroin.

insular, its intent to denigrate. It was disenchanted, and in this, also, lay the authority of their curses. Perhaps I was listening to them because I was thinking about my brother and in them I heard my brother. And myself.

One boy was whistling a tune, at once very complicated and very simple, it seemed to be pouring out of him as though he were a bird, and it sounded very cool and moving through all that harsh, bright air, only just holding its own through all those other sounds.

I stood up and walked over to the window and looked down into the courtyard. It was the beginning of the spring and the sap was rising in the boys. A teacher passed through them every now and again, quickly, as though he or she couldn't wait to get out of that courtyard, to get those boys out of their sight and off their minds. I started collecting my stuff. I thought I'd better get home and talk to Isabel.

The courtyard was almost deserted by the time I got downstairs. I saw this boy standing in the shadow of a doorway, looking just like Sonny. I almost called his name. Then I saw that it wasn't Sonny, but somebody we used to know, a boy from around our block. He'd been Sonny's friend. He'd never been mine, having been too young for me, and, anyway, I'd never liked him. And now, even though he was a grown-up man, he still hung around that block, still spent hours on the street corners, was always high and raggy. I used to run into him from time to time and he'd often work around to asking me for a quarter or fifty cents. He always had some real good excuse, too, and I always gave it to him, I don't know why.

But now, abruptly, I hated him. I couldn't stand the way he looked at me, partly   10
like a dog, partly like a cunning child. I wanted to ask him what the hell he was doing in the school courtyard.

He sort of shuffled over to me, and he said, "I see you got the papers. So you already know about it."

"You mean about Sonny? Yes, I already know about it. How come they didn't get you?"

He grinned. It made him repulsive and it also brought to mind what he'd looked like as a kid. "I wasn't there. I stay away from them people."

"Good for you." I offered him a cigarette and I watched him through the smoke. "You come all the way down here just to tell me about Sonny?"

"That's right." He was sort of shaking his head and his eyes looked strange, as   15
though they were about to cross. The bright sun deadened his damp dark brown skin
and it made his eyes look yellow and showed up the dirt in his kinked hair. He
smelled funky. I moved a little away from him and I said, "Well, thanks. But I already
know about it and I got to get home."

"I'll walk you a little ways," he said. We started walking. There were a couple of
kids still loitering in the courtyard and one of them said goodnight to me and looked
strangely at the boy beside me.

"What're you going to do?" he asked me. "I mean, about Sonny?"

"Look. I haven't seen Sonny for over a year. I'm not sure I'm going to do anything. Anyway, what the hell *can* I do?"

"That's right," he said quickly, "ain't nothing you can do. Can't much help old
Sonny no more, I guess."

It was what I was thinking and so it seemed to me he had no right to say it.   20

"I'm surprised at Sonny, though," he went on—he had a funny way of talking, he
looked straight ahead as though he were talking to himself—"I thought Sonny was a
smart boy, I thought he was too smart to get hung."

"I guess he thought so too," I said sharply, "and that's how he got hung. And how about you? You're pretty goddamn smart, I bet."

Then he looked directly at me, just for a minute. "I ain't smart," he said. "If I was smart, I'd have reached for a pistol a long time ago."

"Look. Don't tell *me* your sad story, if it was up to me, I'd give you one." Then I felt guilty—guilty, probably, for never having supposed that the poor bastard *had* a story of his own, much less a sad one, and I asked, quickly, "What's going to happen to him now?"

He didn't answer this. He was off by himself some place. "Funny thing," he said, 25 and from his tone we might have been discussing the quickest way to get to Brooklyn, "when I saw the papers this morning, the first thing I asked myself was if I had anything to do with it. I felt sort of responsible."

I began to listen more carefully. The subway station was on the corner, just before us, and I stopped. He stopped, too. We were in front of a bar and he ducked slightly, peering in, but whoever he was looking for didn't seem to be there. The juke box was blasting away with something black and bouncy and I half watched the barmaid as she danced her way from the juke box to her place behind the bar. And I watched her face as she laughingly responded to something someone said to her, still keeping time to the music. When she smiled one saw the little girl, one sensed the doomed, still-struggling woman beneath the battered face of the semi-whore.

"I never *give* Sonny nothing," the boy said finally, "but a long time ago I come to school high and Sonny asked me how it felt." He paused, I couldn't bear to watch him, I watched the barmaid, and I listened to the music which seemed to be causing the pavement to shake. "I told him it felt great." The music stopped, the barmaid paused and watched the juke box until the music began again. "It did."

All this was carrying me some place I didn't want to go. I certainly didn't want to know how it felt. It filled everything, the people, the houses, the music, the dark, quicksilver barmaid, with menace; and this menace was their reality.

"What's going to happen to him now?" I asked again.

"They'll send him away some place and they'll try to cure him." He shook his 30 head. "Maybe he'll even think he's kicked the habit. Then they'll let him loose"—he gestured, throwing his cigarette into the gutter. "That's all."

"What do you mean, that's *all?*"

But I knew what he meant.

"I *mean*, that's *all*." He turned his head and looked at me, pulling down the corners of his mouth. "Don't you know what I mean?" he asked, softly.

"How the hell *would* I know what you mean?" I almost whispered it, I don't know why.

"That's right," he said to the air, "how would *he* know what I mean?" He turned to- 35 ward me again, patient and calm, and yet I somehow felt him shaking, shaking as though he were going to fall apart. I felt that ice in my guts again, the dread I'd felt all afternoon; and again I watched the barmaid, moving about the bar, washing glasses, and singing. "Listen. They'll let him out and then it'll just start all over again. That's what I mean."

"You mean—they'll let him out. And then he'll just start working his way back in again. You mean he'll never kick the habit. Is that what you mean?"

"That's right," he said, cheerfully. "*You* see what I mean."

"Tell me," I said at last, "why does he want to die? He must want to die, he's killing himself, why does he want to die?"

He looked at me in surprise. He licked his lips. "He don't want to die. He wants to live. Don't nobody want to die, ever."

Then I wanted to ask him—too many things. He could not have answered, or if he had, I could not have borne the answers. I started walking. "Well, I guess it's none of my business." 40

"It's going to be rough on old Sonny," he said. We reached the subway station. "This is your station?" he asked. I nodded. I took one step down. "Damn!" he said, suddenly. I looked up at him. He grinned again. "Damn it if I didn't leave all my money home. You ain't got a dollar on you, have you? Just for a couple of days, is all."

All at once something inside gave and threatened to come pouring out of me. I didn't hate him any more. I felt that in another moment I'd start crying like a child.

"Sure," I said. "Don't sweat." I looked in my wallet and didn't have a dollar, I only had a five. "Here," I said. "That hold you?"

He didn't look at it—he didn't want to look at it. A terrible closed look came over his face, as though he were keeping the number on the bill a secret from him and me. "Thanks," he said, and now he was dying to see me go. "Don't worry about Sonny. Maybe I'll write him or something."

"Sure," I said. "You do that. So long." 45

"Be seeing you," he said. I went on down the steps.

And I didn't write Sonny or send him anything for a long time. When I finally did, it was just after my little girl died, he wrote me back a letter which made me feel like a bastard.

Here's what he said:

Dear brother,

You don't know how much I needed to hear from you. I wanted to write you many a time but I dug how much I must have hurt you and so I didn't write. But now I feel like a man who's been trying to climb up out of some deep, real deep and funky hole and just saw the sun up there, outside. I got to get outside.

I can't tell you much about how I got here. I mean I don't know how to tell you. I guess I was afraid of something or I was trying to escape from something and you know I have never been very strong in the head (smile). I'm glad Mama and Daddy are dead and can't see what's happened to their son and I swear if I'd known what I was doing I would never have hurt you so, you and a lot of other fine people who were nice to me and who believed in me.

I don't want you to think it had anything to do with me being a musician. It's more than that. Or maybe less than that. I can't get anything straight in my head down here and I try not to think about what's going to happen to me when I get outside again. Sometime I think I'm going to flip and *never* get outside and sometime I think I'll come straight back. I tell you one thing, though, I'd rather blow my brains out than go through this again. But that's what they all say, so they tell me. If I tell you when I'm coming to New York and if you could meet me, I sure would appreciate it. Give my love to Isabel and the kids and I was sure sorry to hear about little Gracie. I wish I could be like Mama and say the Lord's will be done, but I don't know it seems to me that trouble is the one thing that never does get stopped and I don't know what good it does to blame it on the Lord. But maybe it does some good if you believe it.

Your brother,
Sonny

Then I kept in constant touch with him and I sent him whatever I could and I went to meet him when he came back to New York. When I saw him many things I thought I had forgotten came flooding back to me. This was because I had begun, finally, to wonder about Sonny, about the life that Sonny lived inside. This life, whatever it was, had made him older and thinner and it had deepened the distant stillness in which he had always moved. He looked very unlike my baby brother. Yet, when he smiled, when we shook hands, the baby brother I'd never known looked out from the depths of his private life, like an animal waiting to be coaxed into the light.

"How you been keeping?" he asked me.   50

"All right. And you?"

"Just fine." He was smiling all over his face. "It's good to see you again."

"It's good to see you."

The seven years' difference in our ages lay between us like a chasm: I wondered if these years would ever operate between us as a bridge. I was remembering, and it made it hard to catch my breath, that I had been there when he was born; and I had heard the first words he had ever spoken. When he started to walk, he walked from our mother straight to me. I caught him just before he fell when he took the first steps he ever took in this world.

"How's Isabel?"   55

"Just fine. She's dying to see you."

"And the boys?"

"They're fine, too. They're anxious to see their uncle."

"Oh, come on. You know they don't remember me."

"Are you kidding? Of course they remember you."   60

He grinned again. We got into a taxi. We had a lot to say to each other, far too much to know how to begin.

As the taxi began to move, I asked, "You still want to go to India?"

He laughed. "You still remember that. Hell, no. This place is Indian enough for me."

"It used to belong to them," I said.

And he laughed again. "They damn sure knew what they were doing when they   65 got rid of it."

Years ago, when he was around fourteen, he'd been all hipped on the idea of going to India. He read books about people sitting on rocks, naked, in all kinds of weather, but mostly bad, naturally, and walking barefoot through hot coals and arriving at wisdom. I used to say that it sounded to me as though they were getting away from wisdom as fast as they could. I think he sort of looked down on me for that.

"Do you mind," he asked, "if we have the driver drive alongside the park? On the west side—I haven't seen the city in so long."

"Of course not," I said. I was afraid that I might sound as though I were humoring him, but I hoped he wouldn't take it that way.

So we drove along, between the green of the park and the stony, lifeless elegance of hotels and apartment buildings, toward the vivid, killing streets of our childhood. These streets hadn't changed, though housing projects jutted up out of them now like rocks in the middle of a boiling sea. Most of the houses in which we had grown up had vanished, as had the stores from which we had stolen, the basements in which we had first tried sex, the rooftops from which we had hurled tin cans and bricks. But houses exactly like the houses of our past yet dominated the landscape, boys exactly like the boys we once had been found themselves smothering in these houses, came down into the streets for light and air and found themselves encircled by disaster. Some escaped the trap, most didn't. Those who got out always left something of themselves behind, as some animals amputate a leg and leave it in the trap. It might be said, perhaps, that I had escaped, after all, I was a school teacher; or that Sonny had, he hadn't lived in Harlem for years. Yet, as the cab moved uptown through streets which seemed, with a rush, to darken with dark people, and as I covertly studied Sonny's face, it came to me that what we both were seeking through our separate cab windows was that part of ourselves which had been left behind. It's always at the hour of trouble and confrontation that the missing member aches.

We hit 110th Street and started rolling up Lenox Avenue. And I'd known this avenue all my life, but it seemed to me again, as it had seemed on the day I'd first heard about Sonny's trouble, filled with a hidden menace which was its very breath of life.

"We almost there," said Sonny.

"Almost." We were both too nervous to say anything more.

We live in a housing project. It hasn't been up long. A few days after it was up it seemed uninhabitably new, now, of course, it's already rundown. It looks like a parody of the good, clean, faceless life—God knows the people who live in it do their best to make it a parody. The beat-looking grass lying around isn't enough to make their lives green, the hedges will never hold out the streets, and they know it. The big windows fool no one, they aren't big enough to make space out of no space. They don't bother with the windows, they watch the TV screen instead. The playground is most popular with the children who don't play at jacks, or skip rope, or roller skate, or swing, and they can be found in it after dark. We moved in partly because it's not too far from where I teach, and partly for the kids; but it's really just like the houses in which Sonny and I grew up. The same things happen, they'll have the same things to remember. The moment Sonny and I started into the house I had the feeling that I was simply bringing him back into the danger he had almost died trying to escape.

Sonny has never been talkative. So I don't know why I was sure he'd be dying to talk to me when supper was over the first night. Everything went fine, the oldest boy remembered him, and the youngest boy liked him, and Sonny had remembered to bring something for each of them; and Isabel, who is really much nicer than I am, more open and giving, had gone to a lot of trouble about dinner and was genuinely glad to see him. And she's always been able to tease Sonny in a way that I haven't. It was nice to see her face so vivid again and to hear her laugh and watch her make Sonny laugh. She wasn't, or, anyway, she didn't seem to be, at all uneasy or embarrassed. She chatted as though there were no subject which had to be avoided and she got Sonny past his first, faint stiffness. And thank God she was there, for I was filled with that icy dread again. Everything I did seemed awkward to me, and everything I said sounded freighted with hidden meaning. I was trying to remember everything I'd heard about dope addiction and I couldn't help watching Sonny for signs. I wasn't

70

doing it out of malice. I was trying to find out something about my brother. I was dying to hear him tell me he was safe.

"Safe!" my father grunted, whenever Mama suggested trying to move to a neighborhood which might be safer for children. "Safe, hell! Ain't no place safe for kids, nor nobody."

He always went on like this, but he wasn't, ever, really as bad as he sounded, not even on weekends, when he got drunk. As a matter of fact, he was always on the lookout for "something a little better," but he died before he found it. He died suddenly, during a drunken weekend in the middle of the war, when Sonny was fifteen. He and Sonny hadn't ever got on too well. And this was partly because Sonny was the apple of his father's eye. It was because he loved Sonny so much and was frightened for him, that he was always fighting with him. It doesn't do any good to fight with Sonny. Sonny just moves back, inside himself, where he can't be reached. But the principal reason that they never hit it off is that they were so much alike. Daddy was big and rough and loud-talking, just the opposite of Sonny, but they both had—that same privacy.

Mama tried to tell me something about this, just after Daddy died. I was home on leave from the army.

This was the last time I ever saw my mother alive. Just the same, this picture gets all mixed up in my mind with pictures I had of her when she was younger. The way I always see her is the way she used to be on a Sunday afternoon, say, when the old folks were talking after the big Sunday dinner. I always see her wearing pale blue. She'd be sitting on the sofa. And my father would be sitting in the easy chair, not far from her. And the living room would be full of church folks and relatives. There they sit, in chairs all around the living room, and the night is creeping up outside, but nobody knows it yet. You can see the darkness growing against the windowpanes and you hear the street noises every now and again, or maybe the jangling beat of a tambourine from one of the churches close by, but it's real quiet in the room. For a moment nobody's talking, but every face looks darkening, like the sky outside. And my mother rocks a little from the waist, and my father's eyes are closed. Everyone is looking at something a child can't see. For a minute they've forgotten the children. Maybe a kid is lying on the rug, half asleep. Maybe somebody's got a kid in his lap and is absent-mindedly stroking the kid's head. Maybe there's a kid, quiet and big-eyed, curled up in a big chair in the corner. The silence, the darkness coming, and the darkness in the faces frightens the child obscurely. He hopes that the hand which strokes his forehead will never stop—will never die. He hopes that there will never come a time when the old folks won't be sitting around the living room, talking about where they've come from, and what they've seen, and what's happened to them and their kinfolk.

But something deep and watchful in the child knows that this is bound to end, is already ending. In a moment someone will get up and turn on the light. Then the old folks will remember the children and they won't talk any more that day. And when light fills the room, the child is filled with darkness. He knows that every time this happens he's moved just a little closer to that darkness outside. The darkness outside is what the old folks have been talking about. It's what they've come from. It's what they endure. The child knows that they won't talk any more because if he knows too much about what's happened to *them*, he'll know too much too soon, about what's going to happen to *him*.

The last time I talked to my mother, I remember I was restless. I wanted to get 80 out and see Isabel. We weren't married then and we had a lot to straighten out between us.

There Mama sat, in black, by the window. She was humming an old church song, *Lord, you brought me from a long ways off.* Sonny was out somewhere. Mama kept watching the streets.

"I don't know," she said, "if I'll ever see you again, after you go off from here. But I hope you'll remember the things I tried to teach you."

"Don't talk like that," I said, and smiled. "You'll be here a long time yet."

She smiled, too, but she said nothing. She was quiet for a long time. And I said, "Mama, don't you worry about nothing. I'll be writing all the time, and you be getting the checks . . ."

"I want to talk to you about your brother," she said, suddenly. "If anything hap- 85 pens to me he ain't going to have nobody to look out for him."

"Mama," I said, "ain't nothing going to happen to you *or* Sonny. Sonny's all right. He's a good boy and he's got good sense."

"It ain't a question of his being a good boy," Mama said, "nor of his having good sense. It ain't only the bad ones, nor yet the dumb ones that gets sucked under." She stopped, looking at me. "Your Daddy once had a brother," she said, and she smiled in a way that made me feel she was in pain. "You didn't never know that, did you?"

"No," I said, "I never knew that," and I watched her face.

"Oh, yes," she said, "your Daddy had a brother." She looked out of the window again. "I know you never saw your Daddy cry. But I did—many a time, through all these years."

I asked her, "What happened to his brother? How come nobody's ever talked 90 about him?"

This was the first time I ever saw my mother look old.

"His brother got killed," she said, "when he was just a little younger than you are now. I knew him. He was a fine boy. He was maybe a little full of the devil, but he didn't mean nobody no harm."

Then she stopped and the room was silent, exactly as it had sometimes been on those Sunday afternoons. Mama kept looking out into the streets.

"He used to have a job in the mill," she said, "and, like all young folks, he just liked to perform on Saturday nights. Saturday nights, him and your father would drift around to different places, go to dances and things like that, or just sit around with people they knew, and your father's brother would sing, he had a fine voice, and play along with himself on his guitar. Well, this particular Saturday night, him and your father was coming home from some place, and they were both a little drunk and there was a moon that night, it was bright like day. Your father's brother was feeling kind of good, and he was whistling to himself, and he had his guitar slung over his shoulder. They was coming down a hill and beneath them was a road that turned off from the highway. Well, your father's brother, being always kind of frisky, decided to run down this hill, and he did, with that guitar banging and clanging behind him, and he ran across the road, and he was making water behind a tree. And your father was sort of amused at him and he was still coming down the hill, kind of slow. Then he heard a car motor and that same minute his brother stepped from behind the tree, into the road, in the moonlight. And he started to cross the road. And your father started to run down the hill, he says he don't know why. This car was full of white men. They was all drunk, and when they seen your father's brother they let out a great whoop and holler and they aimed the car straight at him. They was having fun, they just wanted to scare him, the way they do sometimes, you know. But they was drunk. And I guess the boy, being drunk, too, and scared, kind of lost his head. By the time he jumped it was too late. Your father says he heard his brother scream when the car rolled over him, and he heard the wood of that guitar when it give, and he heard them strings go flying, and he heard them white men shouting, and the car kept on a-going and it ain't stopped till this day. And, time your father got down the hill, his brother weren't nothing but blood and pulp."

Tears were gleaming on my mother's face. There wasn't anything I could say. 95

"He never mentioned it," she said, "because I never let him mention it before you children. Your Daddy was like a crazy man that night and for many a night thereafter. He says he never in his life seen anything as dark as that road after the lights of that car had gone away. Weren't nothing, weren't nobody on that road, just your Daddy and his brother and that busted guitar. Oh, yes. Your Daddy never did really get right again. Till the day he died he weren't sure but that every white man he saw was the man that killed his brother."

She stopped and took out her handkerchief and dried her eyes and looked at me.

"I ain't telling you all this," she said, "to make you scared or bitter or to make you hate nobody. I'm telling you this because you got a brother. And the world ain't changed."

I guess I didn't want to believe this. I guess she saw this in my face. She turned away from me, toward the window again, searching those streets.

"But I praise my Redeemer," she said at last, "that He called your Daddy home 100 before me. I ain't saying it to throw no flowers at myself, but, I declare, it keeps me from feeling too cast down to know I helped your father get safely through this world. Your father always acted like he was the roughest, strongest man on earth. And everybody took him to be like that. But if he hadn't had *me* there—to see his tears!"

She was crying again. Still, I couldn't move. I said, "Lord, Lord, Mama, I didn't know it was like that."

"Oh, honey," she said, "there's a lot that you don't know. But you are going to find it out." She stood up from the window and came over to me. "You got to hold on to your brother," she said, "and don't let him fall, no matter what it looks like is happening to him and no matter how evil you gets with him. You going to be evil with him many a time. But don't you forget what I told you, you hear?"

"I won't forget," I said. "Don't you worry, I won't forget. I won't let nothing happen to Sonny."

My mother smiled as though she were amused at something she saw in my face. Then, "You may not be able to stop nothing from happening. But you got to let him know you's *there*."

Two days later I was married, and then I was gone. And I had a lot of things on 105 my mind and I pretty well forgot my promise to Mama until I got shipped home on a special furlough for her funeral.

And, after the funeral, with just Sonny and me alone in the empty kitchen, I tried to find out something about him.

"What do you want to do?" I asked him.

"I'm going to be a musician," he said.

For he had graduated, in the time I had been away, from dancing to the juke box to finding out who was playing what, and what they were doing with it, and he had bought himself a set of drums.

"You mean, you want to be a drummer?" I somehow had the feeling that being a 110 drummer might be all right for other people but not for my brother Sonny.

"I don't think," he said, looking at me very gravely, "that I'll ever be a good drummer. But I think I can play a piano."

I frowned. I'd never played the role of the older brother quite so seriously before, had scarcely ever, in fact, *asked* Sonny a damn thing. I sensed myself in the presence of something I didn't really know how to handle, didn't understand. So I made my frown a little deeper as I asked: "What kind of musician do you want to be?"

He grinned. "How many kinds do you think there are?"

"Be *serious*," I said.

He laughed, throwing his head back, and then looked at me. "I *am* serious." 115

"Well, then, for Christ's sake, stop kidding around and answer a serious question. I mean, do you want to be a concert pianist, you want to play classical music and all that, or—or what?" Long before I finished he was laughing again. "For Christ's *sake*, Sonny!"

He sobered, but with difficulty. "I'm sorry. But you sound so—*scared!*" and he was off again.

"Well, you may think it's funny now, baby, but it's not going to be so funny when you have to make your living at it, let me tell you *that*." I was furious because I knew he was laughing at me and I didn't know why.

"No," he said, very sober now, and afraid, perhaps, that he'd hurt me, "I don't want to be a classical pianist. That isn't what interests me. I mean"—he paused, looking hard at me, as though his eyes would help me to understand, and then gestured helplessly, as though perhaps his hand would help—"I mean, I'll have a lot of studying to do, and I'll have to study *everything*, but, I mean, I want to play *with*—jazz musicians." He stopped. "I want to play jazz," he said.

Well, the word had never before sounded as heavy, as real, as it sounded that 120 afternoon in Sonny's mouth. I just looked at him and I was probably frowning a real frown by this time. I simply couldn't see why on earth he'd want to spend his time hanging around nightclubs, clowning around on bandstands, while people pushed each other around a dance floor. It seemed—beneath him, somehow. I had never thought about it before, had never been forced to, but I suppose I had always put jazz musicians in a class with what Daddy called "goodtime people."

"Are you *serious*?"

"Hell, *yes*, I'm serious."

He looked more helpless than ever, and annoyed, and deeply hurt.

I suggested, helpfully: "You mean—like Louis Armstrong?"°

His face closed as though I'd struck him. "No. I'm not talking about none of that 125 old-time, down home crap."

"Well, look, Sonny, I'm sorry, don't get mad. I just don't altogether get it, that's all. Name somebody—you know, a jazz musician you admire."

Louis Armstrong: jazz trumpeter and vocalist (1900–1971) born in New Orleans. In the 1950s his music would have been considered conservative by progressive jazz fans.

"Bird."

"Who?"

"Bird! Charlie Parker!° Don't they teach you nothing in the goddamn army?"

I lit a cigarette. I was surprised and then a little amused to discover that I was 130
trembling. "I've been out of touch," I said. "You'll have to be patient with me. Now.
Who's this Parker character?"

"He's just one of the greatest jazz musicians alive," said Sonny, sullenly, his
hands in his pockets, his back to me. "Maybe *the* greatest," he added, bitterly, "that's
probably why *you* never heard of him."

"All right," I said, "I'm ignorant. I'm sorry. I'll go out and buy all the cat's records
right away, all right?"

"It don't," said Sonny, with dignity, "make any difference to me. I don't care
what you listen to. Don't do me no favors."

I was beginning to realize that I'd never seen him so upset before. With another
part of my mind I was thinking that this would probably turn out to be one of those
things kids go through and that I shouldn't make it seem important by pushing it too
hard. Still, I didn't think it would do any harm to ask: "Doesn't all this take a lot of
time? Can you make a living at it?"

He turned back to me and half leaned, half sat, on the kitchen table. "Every- 135
thing takes time," he said, "and—well, yes, sure, I can make a living at it. But what I
don't seem to be able to make you understand is that it's the only thing I want to do."

"Well, Sonny," I said, gently, "you know people can't always do exactly what
they *want* to do—"

"*No*, I don't know that," said Sonny, surprising me. "I think people *ought* to do
what they want to do, what else are they alive for?"

"You getting to be a big boy," I said desperately, "it's time you started thinking
about your future."

"I'm thinking about my future," said Sonny, grimly. "I think about it all the time."

I gave up. I decided, if he didn't change his mind, that we could always talk 140
about it later. "In the meantime," I said, "you got to finish school." We had already
decided that he'd have to move in with Isabel and her folks. I knew this wasn't the
ideal arrangement because Isabel's folks are inclined to be dicty° and they hadn't especially wanted Isabel to marry me. But I didn't know what else to do. "And we have
to get you fixed up at Isabel's."

There was a long silence. He moved from the kitchen table to the window.
"That's a terrible idea. You know it yourself."

"Do you have a *better* idea?"

He just walked up and down the kitchen for a minute. He was as tall as I was. He
had started to shave. I suddenly had the feeling that I didn't know him at all.

He stopped at the kitchen table and picked up my cigarettes. Looking at me
with a kind of mocking, amused defiance, he put one between his lips. "You
mind?"

"You smoking already?" 145

Charlie Parker: a jazz saxophonist (1920–1955) who helped create the progressive jazz style called
bebop. Parker was a heroin addict who died at an early age. *dicty:* slang word for stylish, high-
class; snobbish.

He lit the cigarette and nodded, watching me through the smoke. "I just wanted to see if I'd have the courage to smoke in front of you." He grinned and blew a great cloud of smoke to the ceiling. "It was easy." He looked at my face. "Come on, now. I bet you was smoking at my age, tell the truth."

I didn't say anything but the truth was on my face, and he laughed. But now there was something very strained in his laugh. "Sure. And I bet that ain't all you was doing."

He was frightening me a little. "Cut the crap," I said. "We already decided that you was going to go and live at Isabel's. Now what's got into you all of a sudden?"

"*You* decided it," he pointed out. "*I* didn't decide nothing." He stopped in front of me, leaning against the stove, arms loosely folded. "Look, brother. I don't want to stay in Harlem no more, I really don't." He was very earnest. He looked at me, then over toward the kitchen window. There was something in his eyes I'd never seen before, some thoughtfulness, some worry all his own. He rubbed the muscle of one arm. "It's time I was getting out of here."

"Where do you want to go, Sonny?"   150

"I want to join the army. Or the navy, I don't care. If I say I'm old enough, they'll believe me."

Then I got mad. It was because I was so scared. "You must be crazy. You goddamn fool, what the hell do you want to go and join the *army* for?"

"I just told you. To get out of Harlem."

"Sonny, you haven't even finished *school*. And if you really want to be a musician, how do you expect to study if you're in the *army*?"

He looked at me, trapped, and in anguish. "There's ways. I might be able to work   155
out some kind of deal. Anyway, I'll have the G.I. Bill when I come out."

"*If* you come out." We stared at each other. "Sonny, please. Be reasonable. I know the setup is far from perfect. But we got to do the best we can."

"I ain't learning nothing in school," he said. "Even when I go." He turned away from me and opened the window and threw his cigarette out into the narrow alley. I watched his back. "At least, I ain't learning nothing you'd want me to learn." He slammed the window so hard I thought the glass would fly out, and turned back to me. "And I'm sick of the stink of these garbage cans!"

"Sonny," I said, "I know how you feel. But if you don't finish school now, you're going to be sorry later that you didn't." I grabbed him by the shoulders. "And you only got another year. It ain't so bad. And I'll come back and I swear I'll help you do *whatever* you want to do. Just try to put up with it till I come back. Will you please do that? For me?"

He didn't answer and he wouldn't look at me.

"Sonny. You hear me?"   160

He pulled away. "I hear you. But you never hear anything *I* say."

I didn't know what to say to that. He looked out of the window and then back at me. "OK," he said, and sighed. "I'll try."

Then I said, trying to cheer him up a little, "They got a piano at Isabel's. You can practice on it."

And as a matter of fact, it did cheer him up for a minute. "That's right," he said to himself. "I forgot that." His face relaxed a little. But the worry, the thoughtfulness, played on it still, the way shadows play on a face which is staring into the fire.

*

But I thought I'd never hear the end of that piano. At first, Isabel would write   165
me, saying how nice it was that Sonny was so serious about his music and how, as
soon as he came in from school, or wherever he had been when he was supposed to
be at school, he went straight to that piano and stayed there until suppertime. And,
after supper, he went back to that piano and stayed there until everybody went to
bed. He was at the piano all day Saturday and all day Sunday. Then he bought a
record player and started playing records. He'd play one record over and over again,
all day long sometimes, and he'd improvise along with it on the piano. Or he'd play
one section of the record, one chord, one change, one progression, then he'd do it on
the piano. Then back to the record. Then back to the piano.

Well, I really don't know how they stood it. Isabel finally confessed that it wasn't
like living with a person at all, it was like living with sound. And the sound didn't
make any sense to her, didn't make any sense to any of them—naturally. They began, in a way, to be afflicted by this presence that was living in their home. It was as
though Sonny were some sort of god, or monster. He moved in an atmosphere which
wasn't like theirs at all. They fed him and he ate, he washed himself, he walked in
and out of their door; he certainly wasn't nasty or unpleasant or rude, Sonny isn't any
of those things; but it was as though he were all wrapped up in some cloud, some fire,
some vision all his own; and there wasn't any way to reach him.

At the same time, he wasn't really a man yet, he was still a child, and they had to
watch out for him in all kinds of ways. They certainly couldn't throw him out. Neither did they dare to make a great scene about that piano because even they dimly
sensed, as I sensed, from so many thousands of miles away, that Sonny was at that
piano playing for his life.

But he hadn't been going to school. One day a letter came from the school board
and Isabel's mother got it—there had, apparently, been other letters but Sonny had
torn them up. This day, when Sonny came in, Isabel's mother showed him the letter
and asked where he'd been spending his time. And she finally got it out of him that
he'd been down in Greenwich Village, with musicians and other characters, in a
white girl's apartment. And this scared her and she started to scream at him and what
came up, once she began—though she denies it to this day—was what sacrifices they
were making to give Sonny a decent home and how little he appreciated it.

Sonny didn't play the piano that day. By evening, Isabel's mother had calmed
down but then there was the old man to deal with, and Isabel herself. Isabel says she
did her best to be calm but she broke down and started crying. She says she just
watched Sonny's face. She could tell, by watching him, what was happening with
him. And what was happening was that they penetrated his cloud, they had reached
him. Even if their fingers had been a thousand times more gentle than human fingers
ever are, he could hardly help feeling that they had stripped him naked and were
spitting on that nakedness. For he also had to see that his presence, that music,
which was life or death to him, had been torture for them and that they had endured
it, not at all for his sake, but only for mine. And Sonny couldn't take that. He can
take it a little better today than he could then but he's still not very good at it and,
frankly, I don't know anybody who is.

The silence of the next few days must have been louder than the sound of all the   170
music ever played since time began. One morning, before she went to work, Isabel
was in his room for something and she suddenly realized that all of his records were
gone. And she knew for certain that he was gone. And he was. He went as far as the

navy would carry him. He finally sent me a postcard from some place in Greece and that was the first I knew that Sonny was still alive. I didn't see him any more until we were both back in New York and the war had long been over.

He was a man by then, of course, but I wasn't willing to see it. He came by the house from time to time, but we fought almost every time we met. I didn't like the way he carried himself, loose and dreamlike all the time, and I didn't like his friends, and his music seemed to be merely an excuse for the life he led. It sounded just that weird and disordered.

Then we had a fight, a pretty awful fight, and I didn't see him for months. By and by I looked him up, where he was living, in a furnished room in the Village, and I tried to make it up. But there were lots of people in the room and Sonny just lay on his bed, and he wouldn't come downstairs with me, and he treated these other people as though they were his family and I weren't. So I got mad and then he got mad, and then I told him that he might just as well be dead as live the way he was living. Then he stood up and he told me not to worry about him any more in life, that he *was* dead as far as I was concerned. Then he pushed me to the door and the other people looked on as though nothing were happening, and he slammed the door behind me. I stood in the hallway, staring at the door. I heard somebody laugh in the room and then the tears came to my eyes. I started down the steps, whistling to keep from crying, I kept whistling to myself, *You going to need me, baby, one of these cold, rainy days*.

I read about Sonny's trouble in the spring. Little Grace died in the fall. She was a beautiful little girl. But she only lived a little over two years. She died of polio and she suffered. She had a slight fever for a couple of days, but it didn't seem like anything and we just kept her in bed. And we would certainly have called the doctor, but the fever dropped, she seemed to be all right. So we thought it had just been a cold. Then, one day, she was up, playing, Isabel was in the kitchen fixing lunch for the two boys when they'd come in from school, and she heard Grace fall down in the living room. When you have a lot of children you don't always start running when one of them falls, unless they start screaming or something. And, this time, Grace was quiet. Yet, Isabel says that when she heard that *thump* and then that silence, something happened in her to make her afraid. And she ran to the living room and there was little Grace on the floor, all twisted up, and the reason she hadn't screamed was that she couldn't get her breath. And when she did scream, it was the worst sound, Isabel says, that she'd ever heard in all her life, and she still hears it sometimes in her dreams. Isabel will sometimes wake me up with a low, moaning, strangled sound and I have to be quick to awaken her and hold her to me and where Isabel is weeping against me seems a mortal wound.

I think I may have written Sonny the very day that little Grace was buried. I was sitting in the living room in the dark, by myself, and I suddenly thought of Sonny. My trouble made his real.

One Saturday afternoon, when Sonny had been living with us, or, anyway, been 175 in our house, for nearly two weeks, I found myself wandering aimlessly about the living room, drinking from a can of beer, and trying to work up the courage to search Sonny's room. He was out, he was usually out whenever I was home, and Isabel had taken the children to see their grandparents. Suddenly I was standing still in front of the living room window, watching Seventh Avenue. The idea of searching Sonny's room made me still. I scarcely dared to admit to myself what I'd be searching for. I didn't know what I'd do if I found it. Or if I didn't.

On the sidewalk across from me, near the entrance to a barbecue joint, some people were holding an old-fashioned revival meeting. The barbecue cook, wearing a dirty white apron, his conked hair reddish and metallic in the pale sun, and a cigarette between his lips, stood in the doorway, watching them. Kids and older people paused in their errands and stood there, along with some older men and a couple of very tough-looking women who watched everything that happened on the avenue, as though they owned it, or were maybe owned by it. Well, they were watching this, too. The revival was being carried on by three sisters in black, and a brother. All they had were their voices and their Bibles and a tambourine. The brother was testifying and while he testified two of the sisters stood together, seeming to say, amen, and the third sister walked around with the tambourine outstretched and a couple of people dropped coins into it. Then the brother's testimony ended and the sister who had been taking up the collection dumped the coins into her palm and transferred them to the pocket of her long black robe. Then she raised both hands, striking the tambourine against the air, and then against one hand, and she started to sing. And the two other sisters and the brother joined in.

It was strange, suddenly, to watch, though I had been seeing these street meetings all my life. So, of course, had everybody else down there. Yet, they paused and watched and listened and I stood still at the window. *"Tis the old ship of Zion,"* they sang, and the sister with the tambourine kept a steady, jangling beat, *"it has rescued many a thousand!"* Not a soul under the sound of their voices was hearing this song for the first time, not one of them had been rescued. Nor had they seen much in the way of rescue work being done around them. Neither did they especially believe in the holiness of the three sisters and the brother, they knew too much about them, knew where they lived, and how. The woman with the tambourine, whose voice dominated the air, whose face was bright with joy, was divided by very little from the woman who stood watching her, a cigarette between her heavy, chapped lips, her hair a cuckoo's nest, her face scarred and swollen from many beatings, and her black eyes glittering like coal. Perhaps they both knew this, which was why, when, as rarely, they addressed each other, they addressed each other as Sister. As the singing filled the air the watching, listening faces underwent a change, the eyes focusing on something within; the music seemed to soothe a poison out of them; and time seemed, nearly, to fall away from the sullen, belligerent, battered faces, as though they were fleeing back to their first condition, while dreaming of their last. The barbecue cook half shook his head and smiled, and dropped his cigarette and disappeared into his joint. A man fumbled in his pockets for change and stood holding it in his hand impatiently, as though he had just remembered a pressing appointment further up the avenue. He looked furious. Then I saw Sonny, standing on the edge of the crowd. He was carrying a wide, flat notebook with a green cover, and it made him look, from where I was standing, almost like a schoolboy. The coppery sun brought out the copper in his skin, he was very faintly smiling, standing very still. Then the singing stopped, the tambourine turned into a collection plate again. The furious man dropped in his coins and vanished, so did a couple of the women, and Sonny dropped some change in the plate, looking directly at the woman with a little smile. He started across the avenue, toward the house. He has a slow, loping walk, something like the way Harlem hipsters walk, only he's imposed on this his own half-beat. I had never really noticed it before.

I stayed at the window, both relieved and apprehensive. As Sonny disappeared from my sight, they began singing again. And they were still singing when his key turned in the lock.

"Hey," he said.

"Hey, yourself. You want some beer?"

"No. Well, maybe." But he came up to the window and stood beside me, looking out. "What a warm voice," he said.

They were singing *If I could only hear my mother pray again!*

"Yes," I said, "and she can sure beat that tambourine."

"But what a terrible song," he said, and laughed. He dropped his notebook on the sofa and disappeared into the kitchen. "Where's Isabel and the kids?"

"I think they went to see their grandparents. You hungry?"

"No." He came back into the living room with his can of beer. "You want to come some place with me tonight?"

I sensed, I don't know how, that I couldn't possibly say no. "Sure. Where?"

He sat down on the sofa and picked up his notebook and started leafing through it. "I'm going to sit in with some fellows in a joint in the Village."

"You mean, you're going to play, tonight?"

"That's right." He took a swallow of his beer and moved back to the window. He gave me a sidelong look. "If you can stand it."

"I'll try," I said.

He smiled to himself and we both watched as the meeting across the way broke up. The three sisters and the brother, heads bowed, were singing *God be with you till we meet again*. The faces around them were very quiet. Then the song ended. The small crowd dispersed. We watched the three women and the lone man walk slowly up the avenue.

"When she was singing before," said Sonny, abruptly, "her voice reminded me for a minute of what heroin feels like sometimes—when it's in your veins. It makes you feel sort of warm and cool at the same time. And distant. And—and sure." He sipped his beer, very deliberately not looking at me. I watched his face. "It makes you feel—in control. Sometimes you've got to have that feeling."

"Do you?" I sat down slowly in the easy chair.

"Sometimes." He went to the sofa and picked up his notebook again. "Some people do."

"In order," I asked, "to play?" And my voice was very ugly, full of contempt and anger.

"Well"—he looked at me with great, troubled eyes, as though, in fact, he hoped his eyes would tell me things he could never otherwise say—"they *think* so. And *if* they think so—!"

"And what do *you* think?" I asked.

He sat on the sofa and put his can of beer on the floor. "I don't know," he said, and I couldn't be sure if he were answering my question or pursuing his thoughts. His face didn't tell me. "It's not so much to *play*. It's to *stand* it, to be able to make it at all. On any level." He frowned and smiled: "In order to keep from shaking to pieces."

"But these friends of yours," I said, "they seem to shake themselves to pieces pretty goddamn fast."

"Maybe." He played with the notebook. And something told me that I should curb my tongue, that Sonny was doing his best to talk, that I should listen. "But of course you only know the ones that've gone to pieces. Some don't—or at least they haven't *yet* and that's just about all *any* of us can say." He paused. "And then there are some who just live, really, in hell, and they know it and they see what's happening and they go right on. I don't know." He sighed, dropped the notebook, folded his arms. "Some guys, you can tell from the way they play, they on something *all* the time. And you can see that, well, it makes something real for them. But of course," he picked up his beer from the floor and sipped it and put the can down again, "they *want* to, too, you've got to see that. Even some of them that say they don't—*some*, not all."

"And what about you?" I asked—I couldn't help it. "What about you? Do *you* want to?"

He stood up and walked to the window and remained silent for a long time. Then he sighed. "Me," he said. Then: "While I was downstairs before, on my way here, listening to that woman sing, it struck me all of a sudden how much suffering she must have had to go through—to sing like that. It's *repulsive* to think you have to suffer that much."

I said: "But there's no way not to suffer—is there, Sonny?"

"I believe not," he said and smiled, "but that's never stopped anyone from try- 205 ing." He looked at me. "Has it?" I realized, with this mocking look, that there stood between us, forever, beyond the power of time or forgiveness, the fact that I had held silence—so long!—when he had needed human speech to help him. He turned back to the window. "No, there's no way not to suffer. But you try all kinds of ways to keep from drowning in it, to keep on top of it, and to make it seem—well, like *you*. Like you did something, all right, and now you're suffering for it. You know?" I said nothing. "Well you know," he said, impatiently, "why *do* people suffer? Maybe it's better to do something to give it a reason, *any* reason."

"But we just agreed," I said "that there's no way not to suffer. Isn't it better, then, just to—take it?"

"But nobody just takes it," Sonny cried, "that's what I'm telling you! *Everybody* tries not to. You're just hung up on the *way* some people try—it's not *your* way!"

The hair on my face began to itch, my face felt wet. "That's not true," I said, "that's not true. I don't give a damn what other people do, I don't even care how they suffer. I just care how *you* suffer." And he looked at me. "Please believe me," I said, "I don't want to see you—die—trying not to suffer."

"I won't," he said, flatly, "die trying not to suffer. At least, not any faster than anybody else."

"But there's no need," I said, trying to laugh, "is there? in killing yourself." 210

I wanted to say more, but I couldn't. I wanted to talk about will power and how life could be—well, beautiful. I wanted to say that it was all within; but was it? or, rather, wasn't that exactly the trouble? And I wanted to promise that I would never fail him again. But it would all have sounded—empty words and lies.

So I made the promise to myself and prayed that I would keep it.

"It's terrible sometimes, inside," he said, "that's what's the trouble. You walk these streets, black and funky and cold, and there's not really a living ass to talk to, and there's nothing shaking, and there's no way of getting it out—that storm inside. You can't talk it and you can't make love with it, and when you finally try to get with it and play it, you realize *nobody's* listening. So *you've* got to listen. You got to find a way to listen."

And then he walked away from the window and sat on the sofa again, as though all the wind had suddenly been knocked out of him. "Sometimes you'll do *anything* to play, even cut your mother's throat." He laughed and looked at me. "Or your brother's." Then he sobered. "Or your own." Then: "Don't worry. I'm all right now and I think I'll *be* all right. But I can't forget—where I've been. I don't mean just the physical place I've been, I mean where I've *been*. And *what* I've been."

"What have you been, Sonny?" I asked.

He smiled—but sat sideways on the sofa, his elbow resting on the back, his fingers playing with his mouth and chin, not looking at me. "I've been something I didn't recognize, didn't know I could be. Didn't know anybody could be." He stopped, looking inward, looking helplessly young, looking old. "I'm not talking about it now because I feel *guilty* or anything like that—maybe it would be better if I did, I don't know. Anyway, I can't really talk about it. Not to you, not to anybody," and now he turned and faced me. "Sometimes, you know, and it was actually when I was most *out* of the world, I felt that I was in it, that I was *with* it, really, and I could play or I didn't really have to *play*, it just came out of me, it was there. And I don't know how I played, thinking about it now, but I know I did awful things, those times, sometimes, to people. Or it wasn't that I *did* anything to them—it was that they weren't real." He picked up the beer can; it was empty; he rolled it between his palms: "And other times—well, I needed a fix, I needed to find a place to lean, I needed to clear a space to *listen*—and I couldn't find it, and I—went crazy, I did terrible things to *me*, I was terrible *for* me." He began pressing the beer can between his hands, I watched the metal begin to give. It glittered, as he played with it, like a knife, and I was afraid he would cut himself, but I said nothing. "Oh well. I can never tell you. I was all by myself at the bottom of something, stinking and sweating and crying and shaking, and I smelled it, you know? *my* stink, and I thought I'd die if I couldn't get away from it and yet, all the same, I knew that everything I was doing was just locking me in with it. And I didn't know," he paused, still flattening the beer can, "I didn't know, I still *don't* know, something kept telling me that maybe it was good to smell your own stink, but I didn't think that *that* was what I'd been trying to do—and—who can stand it?" and he abruptly dropped the ruined beer can, looking at me with a small, still smile, and then rose, walking to the window as though it were the lodestone rock. I watched his face, he watched the avenue. "I couldn't tell you when Mama died—but the reason I wanted to leave Harlem so bad was to get away from drugs. And then, when I ran away, that's what I was running from—really. When I came back, nothing had changed, I hadn't changed, I was just—older." And he stopped, drumming with his fingers on the windowpane. The sun had vanished, soon darkness would fall. I watched his face. "It can come again," he said, almost as though speaking to himself. Then he turned to me. "It can come again," he repeated. "I just want you to know that."

"All right," I said, at last. "So it can come again. All right."

He smiled, but the smile was sorrowful. "I had to try to tell you," he said.

"Yes," I said. "I understand that."

"You're my brother," he said, looking straight at me, and not smiling at all.

"Yes," I repeated, "yes. I understand that."

He turned back to the window, looking out. "All that hatred down there," he said, "all that hatred and misery and love. It's a wonder it doesn't blow the avenue apart."

We went to the only nightclub on a short, dark street, downtown. We squeezed through the narrow, chattering, jam-packed bar to the entrance of the big room, where the bandstand was. And we stood there for a moment, for the lights were very dim in this room and we couldn't see. Then, "Hello, boy," said a voice and an enormous black man, much older than Sonny or myself, erupted out of all that atmospheric lighting and put an arm around Sonny's shoulder. "I been sitting right here," he said, "waiting for you."

He had a big voice, too, and heads in the darkness turned toward us.

Sonny grinned and pulled a little away, and said, "Creole, this is my brother. I told you about him."   225

Creole shook my hand. "I'm glad to meet you, son," he said, and it was clear that he was glad to meet me *there*, for Sonny's sake. And he smiled, "You got a real musician in *your* family," and he took his arm from Sonny's shoulder and slapped him, lightly, affectionately, with the back of his hand.

"Well. Now I've heard it all," said a voice behind us. This was another musician, and a friend of Sonny's, a coal-black, cheerful-looking man, built close to the ground. He immediately began confiding to me, at the top of his lungs, the most terrible things about Sonny, his teeth gleaming like a lighthouse and his laugh coming up out of him like the beginning of an earthquake. And it turned out that everyone at the bar knew Sonny, or almost everyone; some were musicians, working there, or nearby, or not working, some were simply hangers-on, and some were there to hear Sonny play. I was introduced to all of them and they were all very polite to me. Yet, it was clear that, for them, I was only Sonny's brother. Here, I was in Sonny's world. Or, rather: his kingdom. Here, it was not even a question that his veins bore royal blood.

They were going to play soon and Creole installed me, by myself, at a table in a dark corner. Then I watched them, Creole, and the little black man, and Sonny, and the others, while they horsed around, standing just below the bandstand. The light from the bandstand spilled just a little short of them and, watching them laughing and gesturing and moving about, I had the feeling that they, nevertheless, were being most careful not to step into that circle of light too suddenly: that if they moved into the light too suddenly, without thinking, they would perish in flame. Then, while I watched, one of them, the small, black man, moved into the light and crossed the bandstand and started fooling around with his drums. Then— being funny and being, also, extremely ceremonious—Creole took Sonny by the arm and led him to the piano. A woman's voice called Sonny's name and a few hands started clapping. And Sonny, also being funny and being ceremonious, and so touched, I think, that he could have cried, but neither hiding it nor showing it, riding it like a man, grinned, and put both hands to his heart and bowed from the waist.

Creole then went to the bass fiddle and a lean, very bright-skinned brown man jumped up on the bandstand and picked up his horn. So there they were, and the atmosphere on the bandstand and in the room began to change and tighten. Someone stepped up to the microphone and announced them. Then there were all kinds of murmurs. Some people at the bar shushed others. The waitress ran around, frantically getting in the last orders, guys and chicks got closer to each other, and the lights on the bandstand, on the quartet, turned to a kind of indigo. Then they all looked different there. Creole looked about him for the last time, as though he were making certain that all his chickens were in the coop, and then he—jumped and struck the fiddle. And there they were.

All I know about music is that not many people ever really hear it. And even then, on the rare occasions when something opens within, and the music enters, what we mainly hear, or hear corroborated, are personal, private, vanishing evocations. But the man who creates the music is hearing something else, is dealing with the roar rising from the void and imposing order on it as it hits the air. What is evoked in him, then, is of another order, more terrible because it has no words, and triumphant, too, for that same reason. And his triumph, when he triumphs, is ours. I just watched Sonny's face. His face was troubled, he was working hard, but he wasn't with it. And I had the feeling that, in a way, everyone on the bandstand was waiting for him, both waiting for him and pushing him along. But as I began to watch Creole, I realized that it was Creole who held them all back. He had them on a short rein. Up there, keeping the beat with his whole body, wailing on the fiddle, with his eyes half closed, he was listening to everything, but he was listening to Sonny. He was having a dialogue with Sonny. He wanted Sonny to leave the shoreline and strike out for the deep water. He was Sonny's witness that deep water and drowning were not the same thing—he had been there, and he knew. And he wanted Sonny to know. He was waiting for Sonny to do the things on the keys which would let Creole know that Sonny was in the water.

And, while Creole listened, Sonny moved, deep within, exactly like someone in torment. I had never before thought of how awful the relationship must be between the musician and his instrument. He has to fill it, this instrument, with the breath of life, his own. He has to make it do what he wants it to do. And a piano is just a piano. It's made out of so much wood and wires and little hammers and big ones, and ivory. While there's only so much you can do with it, the only way to find this out is to try; to try and make it do everything.

And Sonny hadn't been near a piano for over a year. And he wasn't on much better terms with his life, not the life that stretched before him now. He and the piano stammered, started one way, got scared, stopped; started another way, panicked, marked time, started again; then seemed to have found a direction, panicked again, got stuck. And the face I saw on Sonny I'd never seen before. Everything had been burned out of it, and, at the same time, things usually hidden were being burned in, by the fire and fury of the battle which was occurring in him up there.

Yet, watching Creole's face as they neared the end of the first set, I had the feeling that something had happened, something I hadn't heard. Then they finished, there was scattered applause, and then, without an instant's warning, Creole started into something else, it was almost sardonic, it was *Am I Blue*. And, as though he commanded, Sonny began to play. Something began to happen. And Creole let out the reins. The dry, low, black man said something awful on the drums, Creole answered, and the drums talked back. Then the horn insisted, sweet and high, slightly detached perhaps, and Creole listened, commenting now and then, dry, and driving, beautiful and calm and old. Then they all came together again, and Sonny was part of the family again. I could tell this from his face. He seemed to have found, right there beneath his fingers, a damn brand-new piano. It seemed that he couldn't get over it. Then, for awhile, just being happy with Sonny, they seemed to be agreeing with him that brand-new pianos certainly were a gas.

Then Creole stepped forward to remind them that what they were playing was the blues. He hit something in all of them, he hit something in me, myself, and the music tightened and deepened, apprehension began to beat the air. Creole began to tell us what the blues were all about. They were not about anything very new. He and his boys up there were keeping it new, at the risk of ruin, destruction, madness, and death, in order to find new ways to make us listen. For, while the tale of how we suffer, and how we are delighted, and how we may triumph is never new, it always must be heard. There isn't any other tale to tell, it's the only light we've got in all this darkness.

And this tale, according to that face, that body, those strong hands on those strings, has another aspect in every country, and a new depth in every generation. Listen, Creole seemed to be saying, listen. Now these are Sonny's blues. He made the little black man on the drums know it, and the bright, brown man on the horn. Creole wasn't trying any longer to get Sonny in the water. He was wishing him Godspeed.° Then he stepped back, very slowly, filling the air with the immense suggestion that Sonny speak for himself.

Then they all gathered around Sonny and Sonny played. Every now and again one of them seemed to say, amen. Sonny's fingers filled the air with life, his life. But that life contained so many others. And Sonny went all the way back, he really began with the spare, flat statement of the opening phrase of the song. Then he began to make it his. It was very beautiful because it wasn't hurried and it was no longer a lament. I seemed to hear with what burning he had made it his, with what burning we had yet to make it ours, how we could cease lamenting. Freedom lurked around us and I understood, at last, that he could help us to be free if we would listen, that he would never be free until we did. Yet, there was no battle in his face now. I heard what he had gone through, and would continue to go through until he came to rest in earth. He had made it his: that long line, of which we knew only Mama and Daddy. And he was giving it back, as everything must be given back, so that, passing through death, it can live forever. I saw my mother's face again, and felt, for the first time, how the stones of the road she had walked on must have bruised her feet. I saw the moon-lit road where my father's brother died. And it brought something else back to me, and carried me past it. I saw my little girl again and felt Isabel's tears again, and I felt my own tears begin to rise. And I was yet aware that this was only a moment, that the world waited outside, as hungry as a tiger, and that trouble stretched above us, longer than the sky.

Then it was over. Creole and Sonny let out their breath, both soaking wet, and grinning. There was a lot of applause and some of it was real. In the dark, the girl came by and I asked her to take drinks to the bandstand. There was a long pause, while they talked up there in the indigo light and after awhile I saw the girl put a Scotch and milk on top of the piano for Sonny. He didn't seem to notice it, but just before they started playing again, he sipped from it and looked toward me, and nodded. Then he put it back on top of the piano. For me, then, as they began to play again, it glowed and shook above my brother's head like the very cup of trembling.

wishing him Godspeed: wishing success.

Questions

1. From whose point of view is "Sonny's Blues" told? How do the narrator's values and experiences affect his view of the story?
2. What is the older brother's profession? Does it suggest anything about his personality?
3. How would this story change if it were told by Sonny?
4. What event prompts the narrator to write to his brother?
5. What does the narrator's mother ask him to do for Sonny? Does the older brother keep his promise?
6. The major characters in this story are called Mama, Daddy, and Sonny (the older brother is never named or even nicknamed). How do these names affect our sense of the story?
7. Reread the last four paragraphs and explain the significance of the statement "Now these are Sonny's blues." How has Sonny made this music his own?

■ WRITING *effectively*

James Baldwin on Writing

Race and the African American Writer   1955

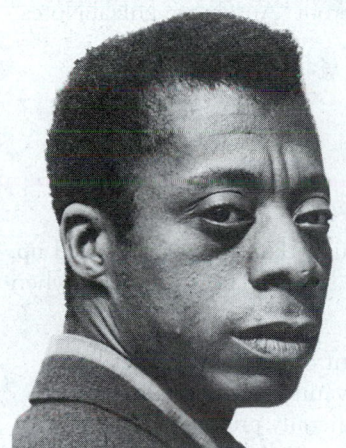

James Baldwin

I know, in any case, that the most crucial time in my own development came when I was forced to recognize that I was a kind of bastard of the West; when I followed the line of my past I did not find myself in Europe but in Africa. And this meant that in some subtle way, in a really profound way, I brought to Shakespeare, Bach, Rembrandt, to the stones of Paris, to the cathedral at Chartres, and to the Empire State Building, a special attitude. These were not really my creations, they did not contain my history; I might search in them in vain forever for any reflection of myself. I was an interloper; this was not my heritage. At the same time I had no other heritage which I could possibly hope to use—I had certainly been unfitted for the jungle or the tribe. I would have to appropriate these white centuries, I would have to make them mine—I would have to accept my special attitude, my special place in this scheme—otherwise I would have no place in *any* scheme. What was the most difficult was the fact that I was forced to admit something I had always hidden from myself, which the American Negro has had to hide from himself as the price of his public progress; that I hated and feared the world. And this meant, not only that I thus gave the world an altogether murderous power over me, but also that in such a self-destroying limbo I could never hope to write.

One writes out of one thing only—one's own experience. Everything depends on how relentlessly one forces from this experience the last drop, sweet or bitter, it can possibly give. This is the only real concern of the artist, to recreate out of the disorder of life that order which is art. The difficulty then, for me, of being a Negro writer was the fact that I was, in effect, prohibited from examining my own experience too closely by the tremendous demands and the very real dangers of my social situation.

I don't think the dilemma outlined above is uncommon. I do think, since writers work in the disastrously explicit medium of language, that it goes a little way towards explaining why, out of the enormous resources of Negro speech and life, and despite the example of Negro music, prose written by Negroes has been generally speaking so pallid and so harsh. I have not written about being a Negro at such length because I expect that to be my only subject, but only because it was the gate I had to unlock before I could hope to write about anything else.

From "Autobiographical Notes"

THINKING ABOUT POINT OF VIEW

When we hear an outlandish piece of news, something that doesn't quite add up, we're well advised, as the saying goes, to consider the source. The same is true when we read a short story.

- **Consider who is telling the story.** A story's point of view determines how much confidence a reader should have in the events related. A story told from a third-person omniscient point of view generally provides a sense of authority and stability that makes the narrative seem reliable.
- **Ask why the narrator is telling the story.** The use of a first-person narrator, on the other hand, often suggests a certain bias, especially when the narrator relates events in which he or she has played a part. In such cases the narrator sometimes has an obvious interest in the audience's accepting his or her version of the story as truth.
- **Think about whether anything important is being left out of the story.** Is something of obvious importance to the situation not being reported? Understanding the limits of a narrator's point of view is key to interpreting what a story says.

CHECKLIST: Writing About Point of View

☐ How is the story narrated? Is it told in the third or the first person?

☐ If the story is told in the third person, is the point of view omniscient or does it confine itself to what is perceived by a particular character?

☐ What is gained by this choice?

☐ If the story is told by a first-person narrator, what is the speaker's main reason for telling the story? What does the narrator have to gain by making us believe his or her account?

☐ Does the first-person narrator fully understand his or her own motivations? Is there some important aspect of the narrator's character or situation that is being overlooked?

☐ Is there anything peculiar about the first-person narrator? Does this peculiarity create any suspicions about the narrator's accuracy or reliability?

☐ What does the narrator's perspective add? Would the story seem as memorable if related from another narrative angle?

WRITING ASSIGNMENT ON POINT OF VIEW

Choose a story from this book and analyze how point of view contributes to the story's overall meaning. Come up with a thesis sentence, and back up your argument with specific observations about the text. Incorporate at least three quotations, and document them, as explained in the writing chapters at the end of the book. Some stories that might lend themselves well to this assignment are "Sonny's Blues," "Cathedral," "The Tell-Tale Heart," and "Greasy Lake."

MORE TOPICS FOR WRITING

1. Retell the events in "A & P" from the point of view of one of the story's minor characters: Lengel, or Stokesie, or one of the girls. How does the story's emphasis change?

2. Here is another writing exercise to help you sense what a difference a point of view makes. Write a short statement from the point of view of William Faulkner's Homer Barron on "My Affair with Miss Emily."

3. Imagine a story such as "A & P" or "A Rose for Emily" told by an omniscient third-person narrator. Write several paragraphs about what would be lost (or gained) by such a change.

4. Choose any tale from "Stories for Further Reading," and, in a paragraph or two, describe how point of view colors the general meaning. If you like, you may argue that the story might be told more effectively from an alternate point of view.

5. Think back to a confrontation in your own life, and describe that event from a point of view contrary to your own. Try to imagine yourself inside your speaker's personality, and present the facts as that person would, as convincingly as you can.

6. With "Sonny's Blues" in mind, write about a family member or friend from your own point of view, allowing, as Baldwin does, an understanding of that person's perspective to slowly develop.

7. Tell the story of a confrontation—biographical or fictional—from the point of view of a minor character peripheral to the central action. You could, for instance, tell the story of a disastrous first date from the point of view of the unlucky waitress who serves the couple dinner.

▶ TERMS FOR *review*

Points of View

Total omniscience ▶ Point of view in which the narrator knows everything about all of the characters and events in a story. A narrator with total omniscience can move freely from one character to another. Generally, a totally omniscient narrative is written in the third person.

Limited or selective omniscience ▶ Point of view in which the narrator sees into the minds of some but not all of the characters. Most typically, limited omniscience sees through the eyes of one major or minor character.

Impartial omniscience ▶ Point of view employed when an omniscient narrator, who presents the thoughts and actions of the characters, does not judge them or comment on them.

Editorial omniscience ▶ Point of view employed when an omniscient narrator goes beyond reporting the thoughts of his characters to make a critical judgment or commentary, making explicit the narrator's own thoughts or attitudes.

Objective point of view ▶ Point of view in which the third-person narrator merely reports dialogue and action with little or no interpretation or access to the characters' minds.

Types of Narrators

Omniscient or all-knowing narrator ▶ A narrator who has the ability to move freely through the consciousness of any character. The omniscient narrator also has complete knowledge of all of the external events in a story.

Participant or first-person narrator ▶ A narrator who is a participant in the action. Such a narrator refers to himself or herself as "I" and may be a major or minor character in the story.

Observer ▶ A first-person narrator who is relatively detached from or plays only a minor role in the events described.

Nonparticipant or third-person narrator ▶ A narrator who does not appear in the story as a character but is usually capable of revealing the thoughts and motives of one or more characters.

Innocent or naive narrator ▶ A character who fails to understand all the implications of the story he or she tells. The innocent narrator—often a child or childlike adult—is frequently used by an author to generate irony, sympathy, or pity by creating a gap between what the narrator perceives and what the reader knows.

Unreliable narrator ▶ A narrator who—intentionally or unintentionally—relates events in a subjective or distorted manner. The author usually provides some indication early on in such stories that the narrator is not to be completely trusted.

Narrative Techniques

Interior monologue ▶ An extended presentation of a character's thoughts in a narrative. Usually written in the present tense and printed without quotation marks, an interior monologue reads as if the character were speaking aloud to himself or herself, for the reader to overhear.

Stream of consciousness ▶ A type of modern narration that uses various literary devices, especially interior monologue, in an attempt to duplicate the subjective and associative nature of human consciousness.

3

CHARACTER

*Show me a character without anxieties
and I will show you a boring book.*

—MARGARET ATWOOD

From popular fiction and drama, both classic and contemporary, we are acquainted with many stereotyped characters. Called **stock characters**, they are
often known by some outstanding trait or traits: the *bragging* soldier of Greek and
Roman comedy, the Prince *Charming* of fairy tales, the *mad* scientist of horror
movies, the *fearlessly reckless* police detective of urban action films, the *brilliant but alcoholic* brain surgeon of medical thrillers on television. Stock characters are especially
convenient for writers of commercial fiction: they require little detailed portraiture, for
we already know them well. Most writers of the literary story, however, attempt to create characters who strike us not as stereotypes but as unique individuals. Although
stock characters tend to have single dominant virtues and vices, characters in the finest
contemporary short stories tend to have many facets, like people we meet.

A **character**, then, is presumably an imagined person who inhabits a story—
although that simple definition may admit to a few exceptions. In George
Stewart's novel *Storm*, the protagonist is the wind; in Richard Adams's *Watership
Down*, the main characters are rabbits. But usually we recognize, in the main
characters of a story, human personalities that become familiar to us. If the story
seems "true to life," we generally find that its characters act in a reasonably
consistent manner and that the author has provided them with **motivation**: sufficient reason to behave as they do. Should a character behave in a sudden and
unexpected way, seeming to deny what we have been told about his or her nature
or personality, we trust that there was a reason for this behavior and that sooner
or later we will discover it.

In good fiction, characters sometimes change or develop. In *A Christmas Carol*,
Charles Dickens tells how Ebenezer Scrooge, a tightfisted miser, reforms overnight,
suddenly gives to the poor, and endeavors to assist his clerk's struggling family. But
Dickens amply demonstrates why Scrooge had such a change of heart: four ghostly
visitors, stirring kind memories the old miser had forgotten and also warning him of
the probable consequences of his habits, provide the character (and hence the story)
with adequate motivation.

TYPES OF CHARACTERS

To borrow the useful terms of the English novelist E. M. Forster, characters may seem **flat** or **round**, depending on whether a writer sketches or sculpts them. A flat character has only one outstanding trait or feature, or at most a few distinguishing marks: for example, the familiar stock character of the mad scientist, with his lust for absolute power and his crazily gleaming eyes. Flat characters, however, need not be stock characters: in all of literature there is probably only one Tiny Tim, though his functions in *A Christmas Carol* are mainly to invoke blessings and to remind others of their Christian duties.

Some writers, notably Balzac, who peopled his many novels with hosts of characters, try to distinguish the flat ones by giving each a single odd physical feature or mannerism—a nervous twitch, a piercing gaze, an obsessive fondness for oysters. Round characters, however, present us with more facets—that is, their authors portray them in greater depth and in more generous detail. Such a round character may appear to us only as he appears to the other characters in the story. If their views of him differ, we will see him from more than one side. In other stories, we enter a character's mind and come to know him through his own thoughts, feelings, and perceptions.

Flat characters tend to stay the same throughout a story, but round characters often change—learn or become enlightened, grow or deteriorate. In William Faulkner's "Barn Burning" (Chapter 5), the boy Sarty Snopes, driven to defy his proud and violent father, becomes at the story's end more knowing and more mature. (Some critics call a fixed character **static**; a changing one, **dynamic**.) This is not to damn a flat character as an inferior creation. In most fiction—even the greatest—minor characters tend to be flat instead of round. Why? Rounding them would cost time and space; and so enlarged, they might only distract us from the main characters.

"A character, first of all, is the noise of his name," according to novelist William Gass. Names, chosen artfully, can indicate natures. A simple illustration is the completely virtuous Squire Allworthy, the foster father in *Tom Jones* by Henry Fielding. Subtler, perhaps, is the custom of giving a character a name that makes an **allusion**: a reference to some famous person, place, or thing. For his central characters in *Moby-Dick*, Herman Melville chose names from the Old Testament, calling his tragic and domineering Ahab after a biblical tyrant who came to a bad end, and his wandering narrator Ishmael after a biblical outcast. Whether or not it includes such a reference, a good name often reveals the character of the character. Charles Dickens, a vigorous and richly suggestive christener, named a couple of shyster lawyers Dodgson and Fogg (suggesting dodging evasiveness and foglike obfuscation), and named two heartless educators, who grimly drill their schoolchildren in "hard facts," Gradgind and M'Choakumchild.

Hero Versus Antihero

Instead of a hero, many a recent novel has featured an **antihero**: a protagonist conspicuously lacking in one or more of the usual attributes of a traditional **hero**, bravery, skill, idealism, sense of purpose. The antihero is an ordinary, unglorious citizen of the modern world, usually drawn (according to the Irish short story writer Sean O'Faolain) as someone "groping, puzzled, cross, mocking, frustrated, and isolated."

If epic poets once drew their heroes as decisive leaders of their people, embodying their people's highest ideals, antiheroes tend to be loners, without admirable qualities, just barely able to survive. A gulf separates Leopold Bloom, antihero of

James Joyce's novel *Ulysses*, from the hero of the Greek *Odyssey*. In Homer's epic, Ulysses wanders the Mediterranean, battling monsters and overcoming enchantments. In Joyce's novel, Bloom wanders the littered streets of Dublin, peddling advertising space. Meursault, the title character of Albert Camus's novel *The Stranger*, is so alienated from his own life that he is unmoved at the news of his mother's death.

Many contemporary writers of fiction would deny even that people have definite selves to alter. Following Sigmund Freud and other modern psychologists, they assume that a large part of human behavior is shaped in the unconscious—that, for instance, a person might fear horses, not because of a basically timid nature, but because of unconscious memories of having been nearly trampled by a horse when a child. To some writers it now appears that personality is more vulnerable to change from such causes as age, disease, neurosis, psychic shock, or brainwashing than was once believed.

Characterization, as practiced by nineteenth-century novelists, almost entirely disappears in Franz Kafka's *The Castle*, whose protagonist has no home, no family, no definite appearance—not even a name, just the initial K. Characters are things of the past, insisted the modern French novelist Alain Robbe-Grillet. Still, nearly all writers of fiction go on portraying them.

Katherine Anne Porter

The Jilting of Granny Weatherall

1930

Katherine Anne Porter (1890–1980) was born in Indian Creek, Texas. Her mother died when she was two, and Porter was raised by a grandmother who surrounded the growing girl with books. At sixteen she ran away from school and soon married a railway clerk in Louisiana. Three years later, she divorced her husband and began supporting herself as a reporter in Chicago, Denver, and Fort Worth, and sometimes as an actress and ballad singer while traveling through the South. Sojourns in Europe and in Mexico supplied her with material for some of her finest stories. Her brilliant, sensitive short fiction, first collected in Flowering Judas *(1930), won her a high reputation. Her one novel,* Ship of Fools *(1962), with which she had struggled for twenty years, received harsh critical notices, but proved a commercial success. In 1965 her* Collected Stories *received a Pulitzer Prize and a National Book Award.*

Katherine Anne Porter
(© Jill Krementz, Inc.)

She flicked her wrist neatly out of Doctor Harry's pudgy careful fingers and pulled the sheet up to her chin. The brat ought to be in knee breeches. Doctoring around the country with spectacles on his nose! "Get along now, take your schoolbooks and go. There's nothing wrong with me."

Doctor Harry spread a warm paw like a cushion on her forehead where the forked green vein danced and made her eyelids twitch. "Now, now, be a good girl, and we'll have you up in no time."

"That's no way to speak to a woman nearly eighty years old just because she's down. I'd have you respect your elders, young man."

"Well, Missy, excuse me." Doctor Harry patted her cheek. "But I've got to warn you, haven't I? You're a marvel, but you must be careful or you're going to be good and sorry."

"Don't tell me what I'm going to be. I'm on my feet now, morally speaking. It's   5
Cornelia. I had to go to bed to get rid of her."

Her bones felt loose, and floated around in her skin, and Doctor Harry floated like a balloon around the foot of the bed. He floated and pulled down his waistcoat and swung his glasses on a cord. "Well, stay where you are, it certainly can't hurt you."

"Get along and doctor your sick," said Granny Weatherall. "Leave a well woman alone. I'll call for you when I want you. . . . Where were you forty years ago when I pulled through milk-leg and double pneumonia? You weren't even born. Don't let Cornelia lead you on," she shouted, because Doctor Harry appeared to float up to the ceiling and out. "I pay my own bills, and I don't throw my money away on nonsense!"

She meant to wave good-by, but it was too much trouble. Her eyes closed of themselves, it was like a dark curtain drawn around the bed. The pillow rose and floated under her, pleasant as a hammock in a light wind. She listened to the leaves rustling outside the window. No, somebody was swishing newspapers: no, Cornelia and Doctor Harry were whispering together. She leaped broad awake, thinking they whispered in her ear.

"She was never like this, *never* like this!" "Well, what can we expect?" "Yes, eighty years old. . . ."

Well, and what if she was? She still had ears. It was like Cornelia to whisper   10
around doors. She always kept things secret in such a public way. She was always being tactful and kind. Cornelia was dutiful; that was the trouble with her. Dutiful and good: "So good and dutiful," said Granny, "that I'd like to spank her." She saw herself spanking Cornelia and making a fine job of it.

"What'd you say, Mother?"

Granny felt her face tying up in hard knots.

"Can't a body think, I'd like to know?"

"I thought you might want something."

"I do. I want a lot of things. First off, go away and don't whisper."   15

She lay and drowsed, hoping in her sleep that the children would keep out and let her rest a minute. It had been a long day. Not that she was tired. It was always pleasant to snatch a minute now and then. There was always so much to be done, let me see: tomorrow.

Tomorrow was far away and there was nothing to trouble about. Things were finished somehow when the time came; thank God there was always a little margin over for peace: then a person could spread out the plan of life and tuck in the edges orderly. It was good to have everything clean and folded away, with the hair brushes and tonic bottles sitting straight on the white embroidered linen: the day started without fuss and the pantry shelves laid out with rows of jelly glasses and brown jugs and white stone-china jars with blue whirligigs and words painted on them: coffee, tea, sugar, ginger, cinnamon, allspice: and the bronze clock with the lion on top nicely dusted off. The dust that lion could collect in twenty-four hours! The box in the attic with all those letters tied up, well, she'd have to go through that tomorrow.

All those letters—George's letters and John's letters and her letters to them both—lying around for the children to find afterwards made her uneasy. Yes, that would be tomorrow's business. No use to let them know how silly she had been once.

While she was rummaging around she found death in her mind and it felt clammy and unfamiliar. She had spent so much time preparing for death there was no need for bringing it up again. Let it take care of itself now. When she was sixty she had felt very old, finished, and went around making farewell trips to see her children and grandchildren, with a secret in her mind: This is the very last of your mother, children! Then she made her will and came down with a long fever. That was all just a notion like a lot of other things, but it was lucky too, for she had once for all got over the idea of dying for a long time. Now she couldn't be worried. She hoped she had better sense now. Her father had lived to be one hundred and two years old and had drunk a noggin of strong hot toddy on his last birthday. He told the reporters it was his daily habit, and he owed his long life to it. He had made quite a scandal and was very pleased about it. She believed she'd just plague Cornelia a little.

"Cornelia! Cornelia!" No footsteps, but a sudden hand on her cheek. "Bless you, where have you been?"

"Here, Mother."

"Well, Cornelia, I want a noggin of hot toddy." 20

"Are you cold, darling?"

"I'm chilly, Cornelia. Lying in bed stops the circulation. I must have told you that a thousand times."

Well, she could just hear Cornelia telling her husband that Mother was getting a little childish and they'd have to humor her. The thing that most annoyed her was that Cornelia thought she was deaf, dumb, and blind. Little hasty glances and tiny gestures tossed around her and over her head saying, "Don't cross her, let her have her way, she's eighty years old," and she sitting there as if she lived in a thin glass cage. Sometimes Granny almost made up her mind to pack up and move back to her own house where nobody could remind her every minute that she was old. Wait, wait, Cornelia, till your own children whisper behind your back!

In her day she had kept a better house and had got more work done. She 25 wasn't too old yet for Lydia to be driving eighty miles for advice when one of the children jumped the track, and Jimmy still dropped in and talked things over: "Now, Mammy, you've a good business head, I want to know what you think of this? . . ." Old. Cornelia couldn't change the furniture around without asking. Little things, little things! They had been so sweet when they were little. Granny wished the old days were back again with the children young and everything to be done over. It had been a hard pull, but not too much for her. When she thought of all the food she had cooked, and all the clothes she had cut and sewed, and all the gardens she had made—well, the children showed it. There they were, made out of her, and they couldn't get away from that. Sometimes she wanted to see John again and point to them and say, Well, I didn't do so badly, did I? But that would have to wait. That was for tomorrow. She used to think of him as a man, but now all the children were older than their father, and he would be a child beside her if she saw him now. It seemed strange and there was something wrong in the idea. Why, he couldn't possibly recognize her. She had fenced in a hundred acres once, digging the post holes herself and clamping the wires with just a negro boy to help. That changed a woman. John would be looking for a young woman with the peaked Spanish comb in her hair and the painted fan. Digging post holes changed a

woman. Riding country roads in the winter when women had their babies was another thing: sitting up nights with sick horses and sick negroes and sick children
and hardly ever losing one. John, I hardly ever lost one of them! John would see
that in a minute, that would be something he could understand, she wouldn't have
to explain anything!

It made her feel like rolling up her sleeves and putting the whole place to
rights again. No matter if Cornelia was determined to be everywhere at once,
there were a great many things left undone on this place. She would start tomorrow and do them. It was good to be strong enough for everything, even if all you
made melted and changed and slipped under your hands, so that by the time you
finished you almost forgot what you were working for. What was it I set out to do?
she asked herself intently, but she could not remember. A fog rose over the valley,
she saw it marching across the creek swallowing the trees and moving up the hill
like an army of ghosts. Soon it would be at the near edge of the orchard, and then
it was time to go in and light the lamps. Come in, children, don't stay out in the
night air.

Lighting the lamps had been beautiful. The children huddled up to her and
breathed like little calves waiting at the bars in the twilight. Their eyes followed the
match and watched the flame rise and settle in a blue curve, then they moved away
from her. The lamp was lit, they didn't have to be scared and hang on to mother any
more. Never, never, never more. God, for all my life I thank Thee. Without Thee,
my God, I could never have done it. Hail, Mary, full of grace.

I want you to pick all the fruit this year and see that nothing is wasted. There's
always someone who can use it. Don't let good things rot for want of using. You waste
life when you waste good food. Don't let things get lost. It's bitter to lose things.
Now, don't let me get to thinking, not when I am tired and taking a little nap before
supper. . . .

The pillow rose about her shoulders and pressed against her heart and the
memory was being squeezed out of it: oh, push down the pillow, somebody: it
would smother her if she tried to hold it. Such a fresh breeze blowing and such a green
day with no threats in it. But he had not come, just the same. What does a woman
do when she has put on the white veil and set out the white cake for a man and he
doesn't come? She tried to remember. No, I swear he never harmed me but in
that. He never harmed me but in that . . . and what if he did? There was the day,
the day, but a whirl of dark smoke rose and covered it, crept up and over into the
bright field where everything was planted so carefully in orderly rows. That was
hell, she knew hell when she saw it. For sixty years she had prayed against remembering him and against losing her soul in the deep pit of hell, and now the two
things were mingled in one and the thought of him was a smoky cloud from hell
that moved and crept in her head when she had just got rid of Doctor Harry and
was trying to rest a minute. Wounded vanity, Ellen, said a sharp voice in the top
of her mind. Don't let your wounded vanity get the upper hand of you. Plenty of
girls get jilted. You were jilted, weren't you? Then stand up to it. Her eyelids
wavered and let in streamers of blue-gray light like tissue paper over her eyes. She
must get up and pull the shades down or she'd never sleep. She was in bed again
and the shades were not down. How could that happen? Better turn over, hide
from the light, sleeping in the light gave you nightmares. "Mother, how do you
feel now?" and a stinging wetness on her forehead. But I don't like having my face
washed in cold water!

Hapsy? George? Lydia? Jimmy? No, Cornelia, and her features were swollen and   30
full of little puddles. "They're coming, darling, they'll all be here soon." Go wash your
face, child, you look funny.

Instead of obeying, Cornelia knelt down and put her head on the pillow. She
seemed to be talking but there was no sound. "Well, are you tongue-tied? Whose
birthday is it? Are you going to give a party?"

Cornelia's mouth moved urgently in strange shapes. "Don't do that, you bother
me, daughter."

"Oh, no, Mother. Oh, no. . . ."

Nonsense. It was strange about children. They disputed your every word. "No
what, Cornelia?"

"Here's Doctor Harry."   35

"I won't see that boy again. He just left three minutes ago."

"That was this morning, Mother. It's night now. Here's the nurse."

"This is Doctor Harry, Mrs. Weatherall. I never saw you look so young and
happy!"

"Ah, I'll never be young again—but I'd be happy if they'd let me lie in peace and
get rested."

She thought she spoke up loudly, but no one answered. A warm weight on her   40
forehead, a warm bracelet on her wrist, and a breeze went on whispering, trying to
tell her something. A shuffle of leaves in the everlasting hand of God. He blew on
them and they danced and rattled. "Mother, don't mind, we're going to give you a little hypodermic." "Look here, daughter, how do ants get in this bed? I saw sugar ants
yesterday." Did you send for Hapsy too?

It was Hapsy she really wanted. She had to go a long way back through a great
many rooms to find Hapsy standing with a baby on her arm. She seemed to herself to
be Hapsy also, and the baby on Hapsy's arm was Hapsy and himself and herself, all at
once, and there was no surprise in the meeting. Then Hapsy melted from within and
turned flimsy as gray gauze and the baby was a gauzy shadow, and Hapsy came up
close and said, "I thought you'd never come," and looked at her very searchingly and
said, "You haven't changed a bit!" They leaned forward to kiss, when Cornelia began
whispering from a long way off, "Oh, is there anything you want to tell me? Is there
anything I can do for you?"

Yes, she had changed her mind after sixty years and she would like to see
George. I want you to find George. Find him and be sure to tell him I forgot him. I
want him to know I had my husband just the same and my children and my house
like any other woman. A good house too and a good husband that I loved and fine
children out of him. Better than I hoped for even. Tell him I was given back everything he took away and more. Oh, no, oh, God, no, there was something else besides
the house and the man and the children. Oh, surely they were not all? What was it?
Something not given back. . . . Her breath crowded down under her ribs and grew
into a monstrous frightening shape with cutting edges; it bored up into her head, and
the agony was unbelievable: Yes, John, get the Doctor now, no more talk, my time
has come.

When this one was born it should be the last. The last. It should have been born
first, for it was the one she had truly wanted. Everything came in good time. Nothing
left out, left over. She was strong, in three days she would be as well as ever. Better. A
woman needed milk in her to have her full health.

"Mother, do you hear me?"

"I've been telling you—"   45

"Mother, Father Connolly's here."

"I went to Holy Communion only last week. Tell him I'm not so sinful as all that."

"Father just wants to speak to you."

He could speak as much as he pleased. It was like him to drop in and inquire about her soul as if it were a teething baby, and then stay on for a cup of tea and a round of cards and gossip. He always had a funny story of some sort, usually about an Irishman who made his little mistakes and confessed them, and the point lay in some absurd thing he would blurt out in the confessional showing his struggles between native piety and original sin. Granny felt easy about her soul. Cornelia, where are your manners? Give Father Connolly a chair. She had her secret comfortable understanding with a few favorite saints who cleared a straight road to God for her. All as surely signed and sealed as the papers for the new Forty Acres. Forever . . . heirs and assigns forever. Since the day the wedding cake was not cut, but thrown out and wasted. The whole bottom dropped out of the world, and there she was blind and sweating with nothing under her feet and the walls falling away. His hand had caught her under the breast, she had not fallen, there was the freshly polished floor with the green rug on it, just as before. He had cursed like a sailor's parrot and said, "I'll kill him for you." Don't lay a hand on him, for my sake leave something to God. "Now, Ellen, you must believe what I tell you. . . ."

So there was nothing, nothing to worry about any more, except sometimes in   50
the night one of the children screamed in a nightmare, and they both hustled out shaking and hunting for the matches and calling, "There, wait a minute, here we are!" John, get the doctor now, Hapsy's time has come. But there was Hapsy standing by the bed in a white cap. "Cornelia, tell Hapsy to take off her cap. I can't see her plain."

Her eyes opened very wide and the room stood out like a picture she had seen somewhere. Dark colors with the shadows rising towards the ceiling in long angles. The tall black dresser gleamed with nothing on it but John's picture, enlarged from a little one, with John's eyes very black when they should have been blue. You never saw him, so how do you know how he looked? But the man insisted the copy was perfect, it was very rich and handsome. For a picture, yes, but it's not my husband. The table by the bed had a linen cover and a candle and a crucifix. The light was blue from Cornelia's silk lampshades. No sort of light at all, just frippery. You had to live forty years with kerosene lamps to appreciate honest electricity. She felt very strong and she saw Doctor Harry with a rosy nimbus around him.

"You look like a saint, Doctor Harry, and I vow that's as near as you'll ever come to it."

"She's saying something."

"I heard you, Cornelia. What's all this carrying-on?"

"Father Connolly's saying—"   55

Cornelia's voice staggered and bumped like a cart in a bad road. It rounded corners and turned back again and arrived nowhere. Granny stepped up in the cart very lightly and reached for the reins, but a man sat beside her and she knew him by his hands, driving the cart. She did not look in his face, for she knew without seeing, but looked instead down the road where the trees leaned over and bowed to each other and a thousand birds were singing a Mass. She felt like singing too, but she put her hand in the bosom of her dress and pulled out a rosary, and Father Connolly murmured

Latin in a very solemn voice and tickled her feet. My God, will you stop that non-sense? I'm a married woman. What if he did run away and leave me to face the priest by myself? I found another a whole world better. I wouldn't have exchanged my hus-band for anybody except St. Michael himself, and you may tell him that for me with a thank you in the bargain.

Light flashed on her closed eyelids, and a deep roaring shook her. Cornelia, is that lightning? I hear thunder. There's going to be a storm. Close all the windows. Call the children in. . . . "Mother, here we are, all of us." "Is that you, Hapsy?" "Oh, no, I'm Lydia. We drove as fast as we could." Their faces drifted above her, drifted away. The rosary fell out of her hands and Lydia put it back. Jimmy tried to help, their hands fumbled together, and Granny closed two fingers around Jimmy's thumb. Beads wouldn't do, it must be something alive. She was so amazed her thoughts ran round and round. So, my dear Lord, this is my death and I wasn't even thinking about it. My children have come to see me die. But I can't, it's not time. Oh, I always hated surprises. I wanted to give Cornelia the amethyst set—Cornelia, you're to have the amethyst set, but Hapsy's to wear it when she wants, and, Doctor Harry, do shut up. Nobody sent for you. Oh, my dear Lord, do wait a minute. I meant to do some-thing about the Forty Acres, Jimmy doesn't need it and Lydia will later on, with that worthless husband of hers. I meant to finish the altar cloth and send six bottles of wine to Sister Borgia for her dyspepsia. I want to send six bottles of wine to Sister Borgia, Father Connolly, now don't let me forget.

Cornelia's voice made short turns and tilted over and crashed, "Oh, Mother, oh, Mother, oh, Mother. . . ."

"I'm not going, Cornelia. I'm taken by surprise. I can't go."

You'll see Hapsy again. What about her? "I thought you'd never come." Granny   60
made a long journey outward, looking for Hapsy. What if I don't find her? What then? Her heart sank down and down, there was no bottom to death, she couldn't come to the end of it. The blue light from Cornelia's lampshade drew into a tiny point in the center of her brain, it flickered and winked like an eye, quietly it flut-tered and dwindled. Granny lay curled down within herself, amazed and watchful, staring at the point of light that was herself; her body was now only a deeper mass of shadow in an endless darkness and this darkness would curl around the light and swallow it up. God, give a sign!

For the second time there was no sign. Again no bridegroom and the priest in the house. She could not remember any other sorrow because this grief wiped them all away. Oh, no, there's nothing more cruel than this—I'll never forgive it. She stretched herself with a deep breath and blew out the light.

Questions

1. In the very first paragraph, what does the writer tell us about Ellen (Granny) Weatherall?
2. What does the name of Weatherall have to do with Granny's nature (or her life story)? What other traits or qualities do you find in her?
3. "Her bones felt loose, and floated around in her skin, and Doctor Harry floated like a balloon" (paragraph 6). What do you understand from this statement? By what other remarks does the writer indicate Granny's condition? In paragraph 56, why does Father Connolly tickle Granny's feet? At what other moments in the story does she fail to understand what is happening, or confuse the present with the past?
4. Exactly what happened to Ellen Weatherall sixty years earlier? What effects did this event have on her?

5. In paragraph 49, whom do you guess to be the man who "cursed like a sailor's parrot"? In paragraph 56, whom do you assume to be the man driving the cart? Is the fact that these persons are not clearly labeled and identified a failure on the author's part?

6. What is stream of consciousness? Would you call "The Jilting of Granny Weatherall" a stream-of-consciousness story? Refer to the story in your reply.

7. Sum up the character of the daughter Cornelia.

8. Why doesn't Granny's last child, Hapsy, come to her mother's deathbed?

9. Would you call the character of Doctor Harry "flat" or "round"? Why is his flatness (or roundness) appropriate to the story?

10. How is this the story of another "jilting"? What similarities are there between that fateful day of sixty years ago (described in paragraphs 29, 49, and 61) and the moment when Granny is dying? This time, who is the "bridegroom" not in the house?

11. "This is the story of an eighty-year-old woman lying in bed, getting groggy, and dying. I can't see why it should interest anybody." How would you answer this critic?

Katherine Mansfield

Miss Brill   1922

Katherine Mansfield Beauchamp (1888–1923), who shortened her byline, was born into a sedate Victorian family in New Zealand, the daughter of a successful businessman. At fifteen, she emigrated to England to attend school and did not ever permanently return Down Under. In 1918, after a time of wild-oat sowing in bohemian London, she married the journalist and critic John Middleton Murry. All at once, Mansfield found herself struggling to define her sexual identity, to earn a living by her pen, to endure World War I (in which her brother was killed in action), and to survive the ravages of tuberculosis. She died at thirty-four, in France, at a spiritualist commune where she had sought to regain her health. Mansfield wrote no novels, but during her brief career concentrated on the short story, in which form of art she has few peers. Bliss (1920) and The Garden-Party and Other Stories (1922) were greeted with an acclaim that has continued; her collected short stories were published in 1937. Some of her stories celebrate life, others wryly poke fun at it. Many reveal, in ordinary lives, small incidents that open like doorways into significances.

Katherine Mansfield

Although it was so brilliantly fine—the blue sky powdered with gold and great spots of light like white wine splashed over the Jardins Publiques—Miss Brill was glad that she had decided on her fur. The air was motionless, but when you opened your mouth there was just a faint chill, like a chill from a glass of iced water before you sip, and now and again a leaf came drifting—from nowhere, from the sky. Miss Brill put up her hand and touched her fur. Dear little thing! It was nice to feel it again. She had taken it out of its box that afternoon, shaken out the moth-powder, given it a good brush, and rubbed the life back into the dim little eyes. "What has been happening to me?" said the sad little eyes. Oh, how sweet it was to see them snap at her again from the red eiderdown! . . . But the nose, which was of some black composition, wasn't at all firm. It must have had a knock, somehow. Never mind—a little dab of black sealing-wax when the time came—when it was absolutely necessary. . . . Little rogue! Yes, she really felt like that about it. Little rogue biting its tail just by her left ear. She could have taken it off and laid it on her lap and stroked it. She felt a tingling in her hands and arms, but that came from walking, she supposed. And when she breathed, something light and sad—no, not sad, exactly—something gentle seemed to move in her bosom.

There were a number of people out this afternoon, far more than last Sunday. And the band sounded louder and gayer. That was because the Season had begun. For although the band played all year round on Sundays, out of season it was never the same. It was like some one playing with only the family to listen; it didn't care how it played if there weren't any strangers present. Wasn't the conductor wearing a new coat, too? She was sure it was new. He scraped with his foot and flapped his arms like a rooster about to crow, and the bandsmen sitting in the green rotunda blew out their cheeks and glared at the music. Now there came a little "flutey" bit—very pretty!—a little chain of bright drops. She was sure it would be repeated. It was; she lifted her head and smiled.

Only two people shared her "special" seat: a fine old man in a velvet coat, his hands clasped over a huge carved walking-stick, and a big old woman, sitting upright, with a roll of knitting on her embroidered apron. They did not speak. This was disappointing, for Miss Brill always looked forward to the conversation. She had become really quite expert, she thought, at listening as though she didn't listen, at sitting in other people's lives just for a minute while they talked round her.

She glanced, sideways, at the old couple. Perhaps they would go soon. Last Sunday, too, hadn't been as interesting as usual. An Englishman and his wife, he wearing a dreadful Panama hat and she button boots. And she'd gone on the whole time about how she ought to wear spectacles; she knew she needed them; but that it was no good getting any; they'd be sure to break and they'd never keep on. And he'd been so patient. He'd suggested everything—gold rims, the kind that curved round your ears, little pads inside the bridge. No, nothing would please her. "They'll always be sliding down my nose!" Miss Brill wanted to shake her.

The old people sat on the bench, still as statues. Never mind, there was always the crowd to watch. To and fro, in front of the flower-beds and the band rotunda, the couples and groups paraded, stopped to talk, to greet, to buy a handful of flowers from the old beggar who had his tray fixed to the railings. Little children ran among them, swooping and laughing; little boys with big white silk bows under their chins, little girls, little French dolls, dressed up in velvet and lace. And sometimes a tiny staggerer came suddenly rocking into the open from under the trees, stopped, stared, as suddenly sat down "flop," until its small high-stepping mother, like a young hen, rushed scolding to its rescue. Other people sat on the benches and green chairs, but they were nearly always the same, Sunday after Sunday, and—Miss Brill had often noticed—there was something funny about nearly all of them. They were odd, silent, nearly all old, and from the way they stared they looked as though they'd just come from dark little rooms or even—even cupboards!

Behind the rotunda the slender trees with yellow leaves down drooping, and through them just a line of sea, and beyond the blue sky with gold-veined clouds.

Tum-tum-tum tiddle-um! tiddle-um! tum tiddley-um tum ta! blew the band.

5

Two young girls in red came by and two young soldiers in blue met them, and they laughed and paired and went off arm-in-arm. Two peasant women with funny straw hats passed, gravely, leading beautiful smoke-colored donkeys. A cold, pale nun hurried by. A beautiful woman came along and dropped her bunch of violets, and a little boy ran after to hand them to her, and she took them and threw them away as if they'd been poisoned. Dear me! Miss Brill didn't know whether to admire that or not! And now an ermine toque and a gentleman in grey met just in front of her. He was tall, stiff, dignified, and she was wearing the ermine toque she'd bought when her hair was yellow. Now everything, her hair, her face, even her eyes, was the same color as the shabby ermine, and her hand, in its cleaned glove, lifted to dab her lips, was a tiny yellowish paw. Oh, she was so pleased to see him—delighted! She rather thought they were going to meet that afternoon. She described where she'd been—everywhere, here, there, along by the sea. The day was so charming—didn't he agree? And wouldn't he, perhaps? . . . But he shook his head, lighted a cigarette, slowly breathed a great deep puff into her face, and, even while she was still talking and laughing, flicked the match away and walked on. The ermine toque was alone; she smiled more brightly than ever. But even the band seemed to know what she was feeling and played more softly, played tenderly, and the drum beat, "The Brute! The Brute!" over and over. What would she do? What was going to happen now? But as Miss Brill wondered, the ermine toque turned, raised her hand as though she'd seen some one else, much nicer, just over there, and pattered away. And the band changed again and played more quickly, more gaily than ever, and the old couple on Miss Brill's seat got up and marched away, and such a funny old man with long whiskers hobbled along in time to the music and was nearly knocked over by four girls walking abreast.

Oh, how fascinating it was! How she enjoyed it! How she loved sitting here, watching it all! It was like a play. It was exactly like a play. Who could believe the sky at the back wasn't painted? But it wasn't till a little brown dog trotted on solemn and then slowly trotted off, like a little "theatre" dog, a little dog that had been drugged, that Miss Brill discovered what it was that made it so exciting. They were all on the stage. They weren't only the audience, not only looking on; they were acting. Even she had a part and came every Sunday. No doubt somebody would have noticed if she hadn't been there; she was part of the performance after all. How strange she'd never thought of it like that before! And yet it explained why she made such a point of starting from home at just the same time each week—so as not to be late for the performance—and it also explained why she had quite a queer, shy feeling at telling her English pupils how she spent her Sunday afternoons. No wonder! Miss Brill nearly laughed out loud. She was on the stage. She thought of the old invalid gentleman to whom she read the newspaper four afternoons a week while he slept in the garden. She had got quite used to the frail head on the cotton pillow, the hollowed eyes, the open mouth and the high pinched nose. If he'd been dead she mightn't have noticed for weeks; she wouldn't have minded. But suddenly he knew he was having the paper read to him by an actress! "An actress!" The old head lifted; two points of light quivered in the old eyes. "An actress—are ye?" And Miss Brill smoothed the newspaper as though it were the manuscript of her part and said gently: "Yes, I have been an actress for a long time."

The band had been having a rest. Now they started again. And what they played   10
was warm, sunny, yet there was just a faint chill—a something, what was it?—not
sadness—no, not sadness—a something that made you want to sing. The tune lifted,
lifted, the light shone; and it seemed to Miss Brill that in another moment all of
them, all the whole company, would begin singing. The young ones, the laughing
ones who were moving together, they would begin, and the men's voices, very resolute and brave, would join them. And then she too, she too, and the others on the
benches—they would come in with a kind of accompaniment—something low, that
scarcely rose or fell, something so beautiful—moving . . . And Miss Brill's eyes filled
with tears and she looked smiling at all the other members of the company. Yes, we
understand, we understand, she thought—though what they understood she didn't
know.

Just at that moment a boy and a girl came and sat down where the old couple
had been. They were beautifully dressed; they were in love. The hero and heroine, of
course, just arrived from his father's yacht. And still soundlessly singing, still with
that trembling smile, Miss Brill prepared to listen.

"No, not now," said the girl. "Not here, I can't."

"But why? Because of that stupid old thing at the end there?" asked the boy.
"Why does she come here at all—who wants her? Why doesn't she keep her silly old
mug at home?"

"It's her fu-fur which is so funny," giggled the girl. "It's exactly like a fried whiting."

"Ah, be off with you!" said the boy in an angry whisper. Then: "Tell me, my   15
petite chérie—"

"No, not here," said the girl. "Not yet."

On her way home she usually bought a slice of honeycake at the baker's. It was
her Sunday treat. Sometimes there was an almond in her slice, sometimes not. It
made a great difference. If there was an almond it was like carrying home a tiny
present—a surprise—something that might very well not have been there. She
hurried on the almond Sundays and struck the match for the kettle in quite a dashing way.

But today she passed the baker's boy, climbed the stairs, went into the little dark
room—her room like a cupboard—and sat down on the red eiderdown. She sat there
for a long time. The box that the fur came out of was on the bed. She unclasped the
necklet quickly; quickly, without looking, laid it inside. But when she put the lid on
she thought she heard something crying.

Questions

1. What details provide insight into Miss Brill's character and lifestyle?
2. What point of view is used in "Miss Brill"? How does this method improve the story?
3. Where and in what season does the story take place? Would the effect be the same if the story were set, say, in a remote Alaskan village in the winter?
4. What draws Miss Brill to the park every Sunday? What is the nature of the startling revelation that delights her on the day the story takes place?
5. Miss Brill's sense of herself is at least partly based on her attitudes toward others. Give in-stances of this tendency, showing also how it is connected with her drastic change of mood.
6. What explanations might there be for Miss Brill's thinking, in the last line of the story, that she "heard something crying"?

Naguib Mahfouz

The Lawsuit   1989

Translated by Denys Johnson-Davies

Naguib Mahfouz

Naguib Mahfouz (1911–2006) was born in Cairo, Egypt, where he spent his entire life and which served as the setting for his thirty-four novels and fourteen collections of short stories. His father was a civil servant, a path that Mahfouz himself would follow, spending most of his career in the Ministry of Culture. Mahfouz graduated from Cairo University in 1934 with a degree in philosophy but abandoned his postgraduate studies to pursue writing, concentrating so intently on this goal that he deferred marriage until 1943. Prose fiction was a relatively new genre in Arabic literature, and Mahfouz—who had read and admired many Western novelists, including Melville, Dostoyevsky, Balzac, and Camus— was enormously influential in modernizing its language, techniques, and subject matter. He planned a sequence of novels telling the entire history of Egypt, but after writing three novels set in the time of the Pharaohs he abandoned this project in favor of contemporary settings. Among his most important works are the Cairo Trilogy (Palace Walk, Palace of Desire, Sugar Street, 1956–57), depicting three generations of a middle-class Cairo family, and Children of Gebelawi (1959), an allegorical treatment of the development of Judaism, Christianity, and Islam. Considered blasphemous, this novel has not been published in the Arabic world, except in Lebanon. Mahfouz further alienated Islamic fundamentalists through his condemnation of the fatwa against Salman Rushdie for The Satanic Verses in 1989. Although Mahfouz regarded Rushdie's novel as offensive, he supported the author's freedom of expression. As a result of defending Rushdie, Mahfouz was stabbed in the neck by an Islamic fundamentalist. He recovered, but was left with permanent nerve damage that impaired his ability to write. In 1988 Mahfouz became the first Arabic writer to win the Nobel Prize in Literature. Though the award had little effect on his modest lifestyle, it had an immense impact on his literary fortunes: previously almost unknown outside the Arab world, he became a widely translated author with an international reputation.

I found myself suddenly the subject of a lawsuit. My father's widow was demanding maintenance. Awakened from the depths of time, the past with its memories had invaded me. After reading the petition I exclaimed, "When did she go broke? Has she in her turn been robbed?"

"This woman robbed us and deprived us of our legal rights," I said to my lawyer.

I felt a strong desire to see her, not through any temptation to gloat over her but in order to see what effects time had had upon her. Today, like me, she was in her forties. Had her beauty withstood the passage of time? Was it holding out against poverty? If the lawsuit was not genuine, would she have stretched out a demanding hand to one of her enemies? On the other hand, if it was specious, why had she not stretched out her hand before? What a ravishing beauty she had been!

"My father married her," I told the lawyer, "when he was in his middle fifties and she a girl of twenty." A semiliterate, old-fashioned contractor, he did not deal with banks but stored his profits away in a large cupboard in his bedroom. We were happy about this so long as we were a single family. The announcement of the new marriage was like a bomb exploding among us—my mother, my elder brother, and myself, as well as my sisters in their various homes. The top floor was given over to my father, the bride, and the cupboard. We were struck dumb by her youth and beauty. My mother said in a quavering voice choked with weeping, "What a catastrophe! We'll end up without a bean."

My elder brother was illiterate and mentally retarded. He was without work, but considered himself a landowner. He flared up in a rage, declaring, "I'll defend myself to the very death."

Some of our relatives advised us to consult a lawyer, but my father threatened my mother with divorce if we were to entertain any such move. "I'm not gullible or an idiot, and no one's rights will be lost."

I was the one least affected by the disaster, partly because of my youth and partly because I was the only one in the family who wanted to study, hoping to enter the engineering college. Yet even so, I did not miss the significance of the facts—my father's age and that of his beautiful bride, and the fortune under threat. By way of smoothing things over, I would say, "I have confidence in my father."

"If we say nothing," my brother would say, "we'll find the cupboard empty."

I shared his fears but affected outwardly what I did not feel inwardly. All the time I felt that our oasis, which had appeared so tranquil, was being subjected to a wild wind and that on the horizon black clouds were gathering. My mother took refuge in silent anxiety, with each new day giving her warning of a bad outcome. As for my elder brother, he would brave the lion in his lair, pleading with his father. "I am the firstborn, uneducated as you can see, and without means of support, so give me my share."

"Do you want to inherit from me while I'm still alive? It's a disgrace for you to doubt me—no one's rights will be lost." But my brother would not calm down and would pester my father whenever they met. He would hurl threats at him from behind his back, and my mother would say that she was more worried about my brother than she was about the fortune.

For my part, I wondered whether my father, that capable master of his trade, the man who was such a meticulous accountant despite his illiteracy, would meet defeat at the hands of a pretty girl. Yet, without doubt, he was changing, slipping down little by little each day. He would take himself off to the Turkish baths twice a month, would clip his beard and trim his mustache every week, and would strut about in new clothes. Finally he took to dyeing his hair. Precious gifts embellished the bride's neck, bosom, and arms. Now there was a Chevrolet and a chauffeur waiting in front of our house.

My brother became more and more angry. "Where did he get her from?" he would say to me. Was it so impossible that she might get hold of the key and find her way to opening the cupboard? Would she not take from him something to secure her future? Did she not have the power to make him happy or to turn his life into one of misery and turmoil as she wished?

Arguments would develop between my brother and my father that would go beyond the bounds of propriety. My father would grow angry and spit in my brother's face. In an explosive outburst, my brother seized hold of a table lamp and hurled it at his father, drawing blood. Seeing the blood, my brother was scared, but even so persevered in his attempts to do Father in, with the cook and the chauffeur intervening. My father insisted on informing the police, and my brother was taken off to court and from there to prison, where he died after a year.

"How did she find the courage to bring her case?" I asked the lawyer.

"Necessity has its own rules."   15

In the midst of our alarm and our mourning for my brother, my mother and I heard the noise of something striking the floor above us. We hurried upstairs and found ourselves standing aghast over my father's body. As is usual in such circumstances, we asked ourselves again and again what could have happened, but no amount of questioning can bring back the dead. It seems that he had had a paralyzing stroke a whole day before his death without our knowing.

We waited till he had been buried and the rites of mourning were over, and then the family gathered together. My sisters, their husbands, and their husbands' parents were there, and the lawyer was present as well. We asked about the key to the cupboard, and the young widow answered quite simply that she knew nothing about it. Sometimes the mind boggles at the sheer brazenness of lying. But what could be done? We then came across the key, and the cupboard finally divulged its secrets, exhibiting to us with profound mockery a bundle of notes that did not exceed five thousand pounds. "Then where is the man's fortune?" everyone called out.

All eyes were fixed on the beautiful widow, who answered defiantly. We had recourse to the police, and there were investigations and searches. As my mother had predicted, we came out of it all "without a bean." The beautiful widow went off to her parents' house, and the curtain was brought down upon her and the inheritance. My mother died. I got a job, married, and achieved a notable success. I became oblivious of the past until the lawsuit brought me back to it.

"It's really the height of irony," I said to the lawyer, "that I should be required to pay maintenance to that woman."

His voice came to me from between the files on his desk. "The old story does on   20
the face of it appear worthy of being put forward, but what's the point of unearthing it when we have no evidence against her?"

"Even if the old story may not be open for discussion, it's a good starting point, whose effect should not be underrated."

"On the contrary, we would be providing the woman's lawyer with the chance to take the offensive and to attract sympathy for her."

"Sympathy?"

"Steady now. Let's think about it a bit objectively. An old man hoards his wealth in a cupboard in his bedroom. He then buys himself a beautiful girl of twenty when he's a man of fifty-five. Such and such happens to his family and such and such to his beautiful wife. Fine, who was to blame?" He was silent for a while, scowling, then continued. "Let's look at it from your side. You're a man who's earning and has a family, and the cost of living is unbearably high, and so on and so forth. . . . Let's content ourselves by settling on a reasonable sum for maintenance."

"Too bad!" I muttered. "She robbed us; then there was the death of my brother   25
and my mother's distress."

"I'm sorry about that, but she's as much a victim as you are. Even the fortune she made off with brought her to disaster. And now here she is begging."

Prompted by casual curiosity, I said, "It's as though you know something about her."

He shook his head with diplomatic vagueness. "A woman who couldn't have children, she was married and divorced several times when she was in her prime. In middle age she fell in love with a student, who, in his turn, robbed her and went off."

He did not divulge the sources of his information, but I surmised the logical progression of events. I experienced a feeling of gratification, which a sense of decency prevented me from showing.

On the day of the court session, I was again seized by a mysterious desire to set   30
eyes on her. I recognized her as she waited in front of the lawyers' room. I knew her by conjecture before actually recognizing her, for the beauty that had made away with our fortune and ruined us had completely vanished. She was fat, excessively and unacceptably so, and the charming freshness had leaked away from her face. What little beauty was left seemed insipid. A veneer of perpetual dejection acted like a screen between her and other people. Without giving the matter any thought, I went up to her, inclined my head in greeting, and said, "I remember you. . . perhaps you remember me?"

At first she gazed at me in surprise, then in confusion. She returned the greeting with a gesture of her covered head. "I'm sorry to cause you trouble," she said, as though apologizing, "but I am forced to do so."

I forgot what I wanted to say. In fact words failed me, and I felt an inner peace. "Don't worry—let the Lord do as He wills." I quietly moved away as I said to myself, "Why not? Even a farce must continue right to the final act."

Questions

1. What impressions do you form about the narrator after reading the first three paragraphs? Are those impressions confirmed or overturned as the story unfolds?

2. Would you call the narrator a round character or a flat one? Explain your reasons why.

3. In your judgment, do the members of the narrator's family behave rationally? If not, how would you characterize their actions?

4. How would you describe the behavior of the lawyer? Does he seem to be an effective advocate for his client's interests? Explain.

5. How does the narrator react to seeing his father's wife in the courtroom at the end of the story? How do his reactions influence his attitude toward the lawsuit?

6. What does the narrator mean by his comments in the last paragraph? What resolution of the case do you think he anticipates?

Raymond Carver

Cathedral   1983

Raymond Carver (1938–1988) was born in Clatskanie, Oregon. When he was three, his family moved to Yakima, Washington, where his father worked in a sawmill. In his early years Carver worked briefly at a lumber mill and at other unskilled jobs, including a stint as a tulip-picker. Married with two children before he was twenty, he experienced blue-collar desperation more intimately than most American writers, though he once quipped that, until he read critics' reactions to his works, he never realized that the characters in his stories "were so bad off." In 1963 Carver earned a degree from Humboldt State College (now California State University, Humboldt). He briefly attended the Writers' Workshop of the University of Iowa, but, needing to support his family, he returned to California, working for three years as a hospital custodian before finding a job editing textbooks. In 1967 he met Gordon Lish, the influential editor who would publish several of his stories in Esquire. Under Lish's demanding tutelage, Carver learned to pare his fiction to the essentials. In the early 1970s, though plagued with bankruptcies, increasing dependency on alcohol, and marital problems, he taught at several universities.

Carver's publishing career began with a volume of poems, Near Klamath *(1968). His books of short stories include* Will You Please Be Quiet, Please? *(1977),* What We Talk About When We Talk About Love *(1981),* Cathedral *(1983), and* Where I'm Call-ing From *(1988), which contained new and selected work. The compression of language he learned as a poet may in part account for the lean quality of his prose, often called "mini-malist," a term Carver did not like. In his last decade Carver taught creative writing at Syracuse University, and lived with the poet Tess Gallagher, whom he married in 1988. He divided his final years between Syracuse and Port Angeles, Washington. Carver's personal victory in 1977 over decades of alcoholism underscored the many professional triumphs of his final decade. He once said, "I'm prouder of that, that I quit drinking, than I am of any-thing in my life." His reputation as a master craftsman of the contemporary short story was still growing when he died, after a struggle with lung cancer.*

This blind man, an old friend of my wife's, he was on his way to spend the night. His wife had died. So he was visiting the dead wife's relatives in Connecticut. He called my wife from his in-laws'. Arrangements were made. He would come by train, a five-hour trip, and my wife would meet him at the station. She hadn't seen him since she worked for him one summer in Seattle ten years ago. But she and the blind man had kept in touch. They made tapes and mailed them back and forth. I wasn't enthusiastic about his visit. He was no one I knew. And his being blind bothered me. My idea of blindness came from the movies. In the movies, the blind moved slowly and never laughed. Sometimes they were led by seeing-eye dogs. A blind man in my house was not something I looked forward to.

That summer in Seattle she had needed a job. She didn't have any money. The man she was going to marry at the end of the summer was in officers' training school. He didn't have any money, either. But she was in love with the guy, and he was in love with her, etc. She'd seen something in the paper: HELP WANTED—*Reading to Blind Man,* and a telephone number. She phoned and went over, was hired on the spot. She'd worked with this blind man all summer. She read stuff to him, case stud-ies, reports, that sort of thing. She helped him organize his little office in the county social-service department. They'd become good friends, my wife and the blind man. How do I know these things? She told me. And she told me something else. On her last day in the office, the blind man asked if he could touch her face. She agreed to this. She told me he touched his fingers to every part of her face, her nose—even her neck! She never forgot it. She even tried to write a poem about it. She was always trying to write a poem. She wrote a poem or two every year, usually after something really important had happened to her.

When we first started going out together, she showed me the poem. In the poem, she recalled his fingers and the way they had moved around over her face. In the poem, she talked about what she had felt at the time, about what went through her mind when the blind man touched her nose and lips. I can remember I didn't think much of the poem. Of course, I didn't tell her that. Maybe I just don't understand po-etry. I admit it's not the first thing I reach for when I pick up something to read.

Anyway, this man who'd first enjoyed her favors, the officer-to-be, he'd been her childhood sweetheart. So okay. I'm saying that at the end of the summer she let the blind man run his hands over her face, said good-bye to him, married her childhood etc., who was now a commissioned officer, and she moved away from Seattle. But they'd kept in touch, she and the blind man. She made the first contact after a year or so. She called him up one night from an Air Force base in Alabama. She wanted to talk. They talked. He asked her to send a tape and tell him about her life. She did this. She sent the tape. On the tape, she told the blind man about her husband and about their life together in the military. She told the blind man she loved her husband but she didn't like it where they lived and she didn't like it that he was part of the military-industrial thing. She told the blind man she'd written a poem and he was in it. She told him that she was writing a poem about what it was like to be an Air Force officer's wife. The poem wasn't finished yet. She was still writing it. The blind man made a tape. He sent her the tape. She made a tape. This went on for years. My wife's officer was posted to one base and then another. She sent tapes from Moody AFB, McGuire, McConnell, and finally Travis, near Sacramento, where one night she got to feeling lonely and cut off from people she kept losing in that moving-around life. She got to feeling she couldn't go it another step. She went in and swallowed all the pills and capsules in the medicine chest and washed them down with a bottle of gin. Then she got into a hot bath and passed out.

But instead of dying, she got sick. She threw up. Her officer—why should he have a name? he was the childhood sweetheart, and what more does he want?—came home from somewhere, found her, and called the ambulance. In time, she put it all on a tape and sent the tape to the blind man. Over the years, she put all kinds of stuff on tapes and sent the tapes off lickety-split. Next to writing a poem every year, I think it was her chief means of recreation. On one tape, she told the blind man she'd decided to live away from her officer for a time. On another tape, she told him about her divorce. She and I began going out, and of course she told her blind man about it. She told him everything, or so it seemed to me. Once she asked me if I'd like to hear the latest tape from the blind man. This was a year ago. I was on the tape, she said. So I said okay, I'd listen to it. I got us drinks and we settled down in the living room. We made ready to listen. First she inserted the tape into the player and adjusted a couple of dials. Then she pushed a lever. The tape squeaked and someone began to talk in this loud voice. She lowered the volume. After a few minutes of harmless chitchat, I heard my own name in the mouth of this stranger, this blind man I didn't even know! And then this: "From all you've said about him, I can only conclude—" But we were interrupted, a knock at the door, something, and we didn't ever get back to the tape. Maybe it was just as well. I'd heard all I wanted to. 5

Now this same blind man was coming to sleep in my house.

"Maybe I could take him bowling," I said to my wife. She was at the draining board doing scalloped potatoes. She put down the knife she was using and turned around.

"If you love me," she said, "you can do this for me. If you don't love me, okay. But if you had a friend, any friend, and the friend came to visit, I'd make him feel comfortable." She wiped her hands with the dish towel.

"I don't have any blind friends," I said.

"You don't have *any* friends," she said. "Period. Besides," she said, "goddamn it, his wife's just died! Don't you understand that? The man's lost his wife!" 10

I didn't answer. She'd told me a little about the blind man's wife. Her name was Beulah. Beulah! That's a name for a colored woman.

"Was his wife a Negro?" I asked.

"Are you crazy?" my wife said. "Have you just flipped or something?" She picked up a potato. I saw it hit the floor, then roll under the stove. "What's wrong with you?" she said. "Are you drunk?"

"I'm just asking," I said.

Right then my wife filled me in with more detail than I cared to know. I made a   15
drink and sat at the kitchen table to listen. Pieces of the story began to fall into place.

Beulah had gone to work for the blind man the summer after my wife had stopped working for him. Pretty soon Beulah and the blind man had themselves a church wedding. It was a little wedding—who'd want to go to such a wedding in the first place?—just the two of them, plus the minister and the minister's wife. But it was a church wedding just the same. It was what Beulah had wanted, he'd said. But even then Beulah must have been carrying the cancer in her glands. After they had been inseparable for eight years—my wife's word, *inseparable*—Beulah's health went into a rapid decline. She died in a Seattle hospital room, the blind man sitting beside the bed and holding on to her hand. They'd married, lived and worked together, slept to-gether—had sex, sure—and then the blind man had to bury her. All this without his having ever seen what the goddamned woman looked like. It was beyond my under-standing. Hearing this, I felt sorry for the blind man for a little bit. And then I found myself thinking what a pitiful life this woman must have led. Imagine a woman who could never see herself as she was seen in the eyes of her loved one. A woman who could go on day after day and never receive the smallest compliment from her beloved. A woman whose husband could never read the expression on her face, be it misery or something better. Someone who could wear makeup or not—what differ-ence to him? She could, if she wanted, wear green eye-shadow around one eye, a straight pin in her nostril, yellow slacks, and purple shoes, no matter. And then to slip off into death, the blind man's hand on her hand, his blind eyes streaming tears—I'm imagining now—her last thought maybe this: that he never even knew what she looked like, and she on an express to the grave. Robert was left with a small insurance policy and a half of a twenty-peso Mexican coin. The other half of the coin went into the box with her. Pathetic.

So when the time rolled around, my wife went to the depot to pick him up. With nothing to do but wait—sure, I blamed him for that—I was having a drink and watching the TV when I heard the car pull into the drive. I got up from the sofa with my drink and went to the window to have a look.

I saw my wife laughing as she parked the car. I saw her get out of the car and shut the door. She was still wearing a smile. Just amazing. She went around to the other side of the car to where the blind man was already starting to get out. This blind man, feature this, he was wearing a full beard! A beard on a blind man! Too much, I say. The blind man reached into the backseat and dragged out a suitcase. My wife took his arm, shut the car door, and, talking all the way, moved him down the drive and then up the steps to the front porch. I turned off the TV. I finished my drink, rinsed the glass, dried my hands. Then I went to the door.

My wife said, "I want you to meet Robert. Robert, this is my husband. I've told you all about him." She was beaming. She had this blind man by his coat sleeve.

The blind man let go of his suitcase and up came his hand.   20

I took it. He squeezed hard, held my hand, and then he let it go.

"I feel like we've already met," he boomed.

"Likewise," I said. I didn't know what else to say. Then I said, "Welcome. I've heard a lot about you." We began to move then, a little group, from the porch into the living room, my wife guiding him by the arm. The blind man was carrying his suitcase in his other hand. My wife said things like, "To your left here, Robert. That's right. Now watch it, there's a chair. That's it. Sit down right here. This is the sofa. We just bought this sofa two weeks ago."

I started to say something about the old sofa. I'd liked that old sofa. But I didn't say anything. Then I wanted to say something else, small-talk, about the scenic ride along the Hudson. How going *to* New York, you should sit on the right-hand side of the train, and coming *from* New York, the left-hand side.

"Did you have a good train ride?" I said. "Which side of the train did you sit on, 25 by the way?"

"What a question, which side!" my wife said. "What's it matter which side?" she said.

"I just asked," I said.

"Right side," the blind man said. "I hadn't been on a train in nearly forty years. Not since I was a kid. With my folks. That's been a long time. I'd nearly forgotten the sensation. I have winter in my beard now," he said. "So I've been told, anyway. Do I look distinguished, my dear?" the blind man said to my wife.

"You look distinguished, Robert," she said. "Robert," she said. "Robert, it's just so good to see you."

My wife finally took her eyes off the blind man and looked at me. I had the 30 feeling she didn't like what she saw. I shrugged.

I've never met, or personally known, anyone who was blind. This blind man was late forties, a heavy-set, balding man with stooped shoulders, as if he carried a great weight there. He wore brown slacks, brown shoes, a light-brown shirt, a tie, a sports coat. Spiffy. He also had this full beard. But he didn't use a cane and he didn't wear dark glasses. I'd always thought dark glasses were a must for the blind. Fact was, I wished he had a pair. At first glance, his eyes looked like anyone else's eyes. But if you looked close, there was something different about them. Too much white in the iris, for one thing, and the pupils seemed to move around in the sockets without his knowing it or being able to stop it. Creepy. As I stared at his face, I saw the left pupil turn in toward his nose while the other made an effort to keep in one place. But it was only an effort, for that eye was on the roam without his knowing it or wanting it to be.

I said, "Let me get you a drink. What's your pleasure? We have a little of everything. It's one of our pastimes."

"Bub, I'm a Scotch man myself," he said fast enough in this big voice.

"Right," I said. Bub! "Sure you are. I knew it."

He let his fingers touch his suitcase, which was sitting alongside the sofa. He was 35 taking his bearings. I didn't blame him for that.

"I'll move that up to your room," my wife said.

"No, that's fine," the blind man said loudly. "It can go up when I go up."

"A little water with the Scotch?" I said.

"Very little," he said.

"I knew it," I said. 40

He said, "Just a tad. The Irish actor, Barry Fitzgerald? I'm like that fellow. When I drink water, Fitzgerald said, I drink water. When I drink whiskey, I drink whiskey." My wife laughed. The blind man brought his hand up under his beard. He lifted his beard slowly and let it drop.

I did the drinks, three big glasses of Scotch with a splash of water in each. Then we made ourselves comfortable and talked about Robert's travels. First the long flight from the West Coast to Connecticut, we covered that. Then from Connecticut up here by train. We had another drink concerning that leg of the trip.

I remembered having read somewhere that the blind didn't smoke because, as speculation had it, they couldn't see the smoke they exhaled. I thought I knew that much and that much only about blind people. But this blind man smoked his cigarette down to the nubbin and then lit another one. This blind man filled his ashtray and my wife emptied it.

When we sat down at the table for dinner, we had another drink. My wife heaped Robert's plate with cube steak, scalloped potatoes, green beans. I buttered him up two slices of bread. I said, "Here's bread and butter for you." I swallowed some of my drink. "Now let us pray," I said, and the blind man lowered his head. My wife looked at me, her mouth agape. "Pray the phone won't ring and the food doesn't get cold," I said.

We dug in. We ate everything there was to eat on the table. We ate like there was no tomorrow. We didn't talk. We ate. We scarfed. We grazed that table. We were into serious eating. The blind man had right away located his foods, he knew just where everything was on his plate. I watched with admiration as he used his knife and fork on the meat. He'd cut two pieces of meat, fork the meat into his mouth, and then go all out for the scalloped potatoes, the beans next, and then he'd tear off a hunk of buttered bread and eat that. He'd follow this up with a big drink of milk. It didn't seem to bother him to use his fingers once in a while, either.

We finished everything, including half a strawberry pie. For a few moments, we sat as if stunned. Sweat beaded on our faces. Finally, we got up from the table and left the dirty plates. We didn't look back. We took ourselves into the living room and sank into our places again. Robert and my wife sat on the sofa. I took the big chair. We had us two or three more drinks while they talked about the major things that had come to pass for them in the past ten years. For the most part, I just listened. Now and then I joined in. I didn't want him to think I'd left the room, and I didn't want her to think I was feeling left out. They talked of things that had happened to them—to them!—these past ten years. I waited in vain to hear my name on my wife's sweet lips: "And then my dear husband came into my life"—something like that. But I heard nothing of the sort. More talk of Robert. Robert had done a little of everything, it seemed, a regular blind jack-of-all-trades. But most recently he and his wife had had an Amway distributorship, from which, I gathered, they'd earned their living, such as it was. The blind man was also a ham radio operator. He talked in his loud voice about conversations he'd had with fellow operators in Guam, in the Philippines, in Alaska, and even in Tahiti. He said he'd have a lot of friends there if he ever wanted to go visit those places. From time to time, he'd turn his blind face toward me, put his hand under his beard, ask me something. How long had I been in my present position? (Three years.) Did I like my work? (I didn't.) Was I going to stay with it? (What were the options?) Finally, when I thought he was beginning to run down, I got up and turned on the TV.

My wife looked at me with irritation. She was heading toward a boil. Then she looked at the blind man and said, "Robert, do you have a TV?"

The blind man said, "My dear, I have two TVs. I have a color set and a black-and-white thing, an old relic. It's funny, but if I turn the TV on, and I'm always turning it on, I turn on the color set. It's funny, don't you think?"

45

I didn't know what to say to that. I had absolutely nothing to say to that. No opinion. So I watched the news program and tried to listen to what the announcer was saying.

"This is a color TV," the blind man said. "Don't ask me how, but I can tell." 50

"We traded up a while ago," I said.

The blind man had another taste of his drink. He lifted his beard, sniffed it, and let it fall. He leaned forward on the sofa. He positioned his ashtray on the coffee table, then put the lighter to his cigarette. He leaned back on the sofa and crossed his legs at the ankles.

My wife covered her mouth, and then she yawned. She stretched. She said, "I think I'll go upstairs and put on my robe. I think I'll change into something else. Robert, you make yourself comfortable," she said.

"I'm comfortable," the blind man said.

"I want you to feel comfortable in this house," she said. 55

"I am comfortable," the blind man said.

After she'd left the room, he and I listened to the weather report and then to the sports roundup. By that time, she'd been gone so long I didn't know if she was going to come back. I thought she might have gone to bed. I wished she'd come back downstairs. I didn't want to be left alone with a blind man. I asked him if he wanted another drink, and he said sure. Then I asked if he wanted to smoke some dope with me. I said I'd just rolled a number. I hadn't, but I planned to do so in about two shakes.

"I'll try some with you," he said.

"Damm right," I said. "That's the stuff."

"I got our drinks and sat down on the sofa with him. Then I rolled us two fat 60 numbers. I lit one and passed it. I brought it to his fingers. He took it and inhaled.

"Hold it as long as you can," I said. I could tell he didn't know the first thing.

My wife came back downstairs wearing her pink robe and her pink slippers.

"What do I smell?" she said.

"We thought we'd have us some cannabis," I said.

My wife gave me a savage look. Then she looked at the blind man and said, 65 "Robert, I didn't know you smoked."

He said, "I do now, my dear. There's a first time for everything. But I don't feel anything yet."

"This stuff is pretty mellow," I said. "This stuff is mild. It's dope you can reason with," I said. "It doesn't mess you up."

"Not much it doesn't, bub," he said, and laughed.

My wife sat on the sofa between the blind man and me. I passed her the number. She took it and toked and then passed it back to me. "Which way is this going?" she said. Then she said, "I shouldn't be smoking this. I can hardly keep my eyes open as it is. That dinner did me in. I shouldn't have eaten so much."

"It was the strawberry pie," the blind man said. "That's what did it," he said, and 70 he laughed his big laugh. Then he shook his head.

"There's more strawberry pie," I said.

"Do you want some more, Robert?" my wife said.

"Maybe in a little while," he said.

We gave our attention to the TV. My wife yawned again. She said, "Your bed is made up when you feel like going to bed, Robert. I know you must have had a long day. When you're ready to go to bed, say so." She pulled his arm. "Robert?"

He came to and said, "I've had a real nice time. This beats tapes, doesn't it?"   75

I said, "Coming at you," and I put the number between his fingers. He inhaled, held the smoke, and then let it go. It was like he'd been doing it since he was nine years old.

"Thanks, bub," he said. "But I think this is all for me. I think I'm beginning to feel it," he said. He held the burning roach out for my wife.

"Same here," she said. "Ditto. Me, too." She took the roach and passed it to me. "I may just sit here for a while between you two guys with my eyes closed. But don't let me bother you, okay? Either one of you. If it bothers you, say so. Otherwise, I may just sit here with my eyes closed until you're ready to go to bed," she said. "Your bed's made up, Robert, when you're ready. It's right next to our room at the top of the stairs. We'll show you up when you're ready. You wake me up now, you guys, if I fall asleep." She said that and then she closed her eyes and went to sleep.

The news program ended. I got up and changed the channel. I sat back down on the sofa. I wished my wife hadn't pooped out. Her head lay across the back of the sofa, her mouth open. She'd turned so that her robe slipped away from her legs, exposing a juicy thigh. I reached to draw her robe back over her, and it was then that I glanced at the blind man. What the hell! I flipped the robe open again.

"You say when you want some strawberry pie," I said.   80

"I will," he said.

I said, "Are you tired? Do you want me to take you up to your bed? Are you ready to hit the hay?"

"Not yet," he said. "No, I'll stay up with you, bub. If that's all right. I'll stay up until you're ready to turn in. We haven't had a chance to talk. Know what I mean? I feel like me and her monopolized the evening." He lifted his beard and he let it fall. He picked up his cigarettes and his lighter.

"That's all right," I said. Then I said, "I'm glad for the company."

And I guess I was. Every night I smoked dope and stayed up as long as I could be-   85 fore I fell asleep. My wife and I hardly ever went to bed at the same time. When I did go to sleep, I had these dreams. Sometimes I'd wake up from one of them, my heart going crazy.

Something about the church and the Middle Ages was on the TV. Not your run-of-the-mill TV fare. I wanted to watch something else. I turned to the other channels. But there was nothing on them, either. So I turned back to the first channel and apologized.

"Bub, it's all right," the blind man said. "It's fine with me. Whatever you want to watch is okay. I'm always learning something. Learning never ends. It won't hurt me to learn something tonight. I got ears," he said.

We didn't say anything for a time. He was leaning forward with his head turned at me, his right ear aimed in the direction of the set. Very disconcerting. Now and then his eyelids drooped and then they snapped open again. Now and then he put his fingers into his beard and tugged, like he was thinking about something he was hearing on the television.

On the screen, a group of men wearing cowls was being set upon and tormented by men dressed in skeleton costumes and men dressed as devils. The men dressed as devils wore devil masks, horns, and long tails. This pageant was part of a procession. The Englishman who was narrating the thing said it took place in Spain once a year. I tried to explain to the blind man what was happening.

"Skeletons," he said. "I know about skeletons," he said, and he nodded.   90

The TV showed this one cathedral. Then there was a long, slow look at another one. Finally, the picture switched to the famous one in Paris, with its flying buttresses and its spires reaching up to the clouds. The camera pulled away to show the whole of the cathedral rising above the skyline.

There were times when the Englishman who was telling the thing would shut up, would simply let the camera move around the cathedrals. Or else the camera would tour the countryside, men in fields walking behind oxen. I waited as long as I could. Then I felt I had to say something. I said, "They're showing the outside of this cathedral now. Gargoyles. Little statues carved to look like monsters. Now I guess they're in Italy. Yeah, they're in Italy. There's paintings on the walls of this one church."

"Are those fresco paintings, bub?" he asked, and he sipped from his drink.

I reached for my glass. But it was empty. I tried to remember what I could remember. "You're asking me are those frescoes?" I said. "That's a good question. I don't know."

The camera moved to a cathedral outside Lisbon. The differences in the Por-   95
tuguese cathedral compared with the French and Italian were not that great. But they were there. Mostly the interior stuff. Then something occurred to me, and I said, "Something has occurred to me. Do you have any idea what a cathedral is? What they look like, that is? Do you follow me? If somebody says cathedral to you, do you have any notion what they're talking about? Do you know the difference between that and a Baptist church, say?"

He let the smoke dribble from his mouth. "I know they took hundreds of workers fifty or a hundred years to build," he said. "I just heard the man say that, of course. I know generations of the same families worked on a cathedral. I heard him say that, too. The men who began their life's work on them, they never lived to see the completion of their work. In that wise, bub, they're no different from the rest of us, right?" He laughed. Then his eyelids drooped again. His head nodded. He seemed to be snoozing. Maybe he was imagining himself in Portugal. The TV was showing another cathedral now. This one was in Germany. The Englishman's voice droned on. "Cathedrals," the blind man said. He sat up and rolled his head back and forth. "If you want the truth, bub, that's about all I know. What I just said. What I heard him say. But maybe you could describe one to me? I wish you'd do it. I'd like that. If you want to know, I really don't have a good idea."

I stared hard at the shot of the cathedral on the TV. How could I even begin to describe it? But say my life depended on it. Say my life was being threatened by an insane guy who said I had to do it or else.

I stared some more at the cathedral before the picture flipped off into the countryside. There was no use. I turned to the blind man and said, "To begin with, they're very tall." I was looking around the room for clues. "They reach way up. Up and up. Toward the sky. They're so big, some of them, they have to have these supports. To help hold them up, so to speak. These supports are called buttresses. They remind me of viaducts, for some reason. But maybe you don't know viaducts, either? Sometimes the cathedrals have devils and such carved into the front. Sometimes lords and ladies. Don't ask me why this is," I said.

He was nodding. The whole upper part of his body seemed to be moving back and forth.

"I'm not doing so good, am I?" I said.   100

He stopped nodding and leaned forward on the edge of the sofa. As he listened to me, he was running his fingers through his beard. I wasn't getting through to him, I could see that. But he waited for me to go on just the same. He nodded, like he was trying to encourage me. I tried to think what else to say. "They're really big," I said. "They're massive. They're built of stone. Marble, too, sometimes. In those olden days, when they built cathedrals, men wanted to be close to God. In those olden days, God was an important part of everyone's life. You could tell this from their cathedral-building. I'm sorry," I said, "but it looks like that's the best I can do for you. I'm just no good at it."

"That's all right, bub," the blind man said. "Hey, listen. I hope you don't mind my asking you. Can I ask you something? Let me ask you a simple question, yes or no. I'm just curious and there's no offense. You're my host. But let me ask if you are in any way religious? You don't mind my asking?"

I shook my head. He couldn't see that, though. A wink is the same as a nod to a blind man. "I guess I don't believe in it. In anything. Sometimes it's hard. You know what I'm saying?"

"Sure, I do," he said.

"Right," I said.

The Englishman was still holding forth. My wife sighed in her sleep. She drew a long breath and went on with her sleeping.

"You'll have to forgive me," I said. "But I can't tell you what a cathedral looks like. It just isn't in me to do it. I can't do any more than I've done."

The blind man sat very still, his head down, as he listened to me.

I said, "The truth is, cathedrals don't mean anything special to me. Nothing. Cathedrals. They're something to look at on late-night TV. That's all they are."

It was then that the blind man cleared his throat. He brought something up. He took a handkerchief from his back pocket. Then he said, "I get it, bub. It's okay. It happens. Don't worry about it," he said. "Hey, listen to me. Will you do me a favor? I got an idea. Why don't you find us some heavy paper? And a pen. We'll do something. We'll draw one together. Get us a pen and some heavy paper. Go on, bub, get the stuff," he said.

So I went upstairs. My legs felt like they didn't have any strength in them. They felt like they did after I'd done some running. In my wife's room I looked around. I found some ballpoints in a little basket on her table. And then I tried to think where to look for the kind of paper he was talking about.

Downstairs, in the kitchen, I found a shopping bag with onion skins in the bottom of the bag. I emptied the bag and shook it. I brought it into the living room and sat down with it near his legs. I moved some things, smoothed the wrinkles from the bag, spread it out on the coffee table.

The blind man got down from the sofa and sat next to me on the carpet.

He ran his fingers over the paper. He went up and down the sides of the paper. The edges, even the edges. He fingered the corners.

"All right," he said. "All right, let's do her."

He found my hand, the hand with the pen. He closed his hand over my hand. "Go ahead, bub, draw," he said. "Draw. You'll see. I'll follow along with you. It'll be okay. Just begin now like I'm telling you. You'll see. Draw," the blind man said.

So I began. First I drew a box that looked like a house. It could have been the house I lived in. Then I put a roof on it. At either end of the roof, I drew spires. Crazy.

105

110

115

"Swell," he said. "Terrific. You're doing fine," he said. "Never thought anything like this could happen in your lifetime, did you, bub? Well, it's a strange life, we all know that. Go on now. Keep it up."

I put in windows with arches. I drew flying buttresses. I hung great doors. I couldn't stop. The TV station went off the air. I put down the pen and closed and opened my fingers. The blind man felt around over the paper. He moved the tips of his fingers over the paper, all over what I had drawn, and he nodded.

"Doing fine," the blind man said. 120

I took up the pen again, and he found my hand. I kept at it. I'm no artist. But I kept drawing just the same.

My wife opened up her eyes and gazed at us. She sat up on the sofa, her robe hanging open. She said, "What are you doing? Tell me, I want to know."

I didn't answer her.

The blind man said, "We're drawing a cathedral. Me and him are working on it. Press hard," he said to me. "That's right. That's good," he said. "Sure. You got it, bub, I can tell. You didn't think you could. But you can, can't you? You're cooking with gas now. You know what I'm saying? We're going to really have us something here in a minute. How's the old arm?" he said. "Put some people in there now. What's a cathedral without people?"

My wife said, "What's going on? Robert, what are you doing? What's going on?" 125

"It's all right," he said to her. "Close your eyes now," the blind man said to me.

I did it. I closed them just like he said.

"Are they closed?" he said. "Don't fudge."

"They're closed," I said.

"Keep them that way," he said. He said, "Don't stop now. Draw." 130

So we kept on with it. His fingers rode my fingers as my hand went over the paper. It was like nothing else in my life up to now.

Then he said, "I think that's it. I think you got it," he said. "Take a look. What do you think?"

But I had my eyes closed. I thought I'd keep them that way for a little longer. I thought it was something I ought to do.

"Well?" he said. "Are you looking?"

My eyes were still closed. I was in my house. I knew that. But I didn't feel like I 135 was inside anything.

"It's really something," I said.

Questions

1. What details in "Cathedral" make clear the narrator's initial attitude toward blind people? What hints does the author give about the reasons for this attitude? At what point in the story do the narrator's preconceptions about blind people start to change?
2. For what reason does the wife keep asking Robert if he'd like to go to bed (paragraphs 74–78)? What motivates the narrator to make the same suggestion in paragraph 82? What effect does Robert's reply have on the narrator?
3. What makes the narrator start explaining what he's seeing on television?
4. How does the point of view contribute to the effectiveness of the story?
5. At the end, the narrator has an epiphany. How would you describe it?
6. Would you describe the narrator as an antihero? Use specific details from the story to back up your response.

7. Is the wife a flat or a round character? What about Robert? Support your conclusion about each of them.

8. In a good story, a character doesn't suddenly become a completely different sort of person. Find details early in the story that show the narrator's more sensitive side and thus help to make his development credible and persuasive.

■ WRITING *effectively*

Raymond Carver on Writing

Commonplace but Precise Language   1983

It's possible, in a poem or short story, to write about commonplace things and objects using commonplace but precise language, and to endow those things—a chair, a window curtain, a fork, a stone, a woman's earring—with immense, even startling power. It is possible to write a line of seemingly innocuous dialogue and have it send a chill along the reader's spine—the source of artistic delight, as Nabokov would have it. That's the kind of writing that most interests me. I hate sloppy or haphazard writing whether it flies under the banner of experimentation or else is just clumsily rendered realism. In Isaac Babel's wonderful short story, "Guy de Maupassant,"

Raymond Carver

the narrator has this to say about the writing of fiction: "No iron can pierce the heart with such force as a period put just at the right place." This too ought to go on a three-by-five.

Evan Connell said once that he knew he was finished with a short story when he found himself going through it and taking out commas and then going through the story again and putting commas back in the same places. I like that way of working on something. I respect that kind of care for what is being done. That's all we have, finally, the words, and they had better be the right ones, with the punctuation in the right places so that they can best say what they are meant to say. If the words are heavy with the writer's own unbridled emotions, or if they are imprecise and inaccurate for some reason—if the words are in any way blurred—the reader's eyes will slide right over them and nothing will be achieved.

From "On Writing"

THINKING ABOUT CHARACTER

Although readers usually consider plot the central element of fiction, writers usually remark that stories begin with characters.

- **Identify the most important character.** The central character is the one who must deal with the plot complications and the central crisis of the story. The choices made by this character communicate his or her attitudes as well as the story's themes.
- **Consider the ways the characters' personalities and values are communicated.** Note that the way characters speak can immediately reveal important things about their personalities, beliefs, and behavior. A single line of dialogue can tell the audience a great deal, as in an old film in which the comedian W. C. Fields confides, "A woman drove me to drink and I never even had the courtesy to thank her."
- **Consider how the story's action grows out of its central character.** A story's action usually grows out of the personality of its protagonist and the situation he or she faces. As novelist Phyllis Bottome observed, "If a writer is true to his characters, they will give him his plot."

CHECKLIST: Writing About Character

- ☐ Who is the main character or protagonist of the story?
- ☐ Make a quick list of the character's physical, mental, moral, or behavioral traits. Which seem especially significant to the action of the story?
- ☐ Does the main character have an antagonist in the story? How do they differ?
- ☐ Does the way the protagonist speaks reveal anything about his or her personality?
- ☐ If the story is told in the first person, what is revealed about how the protagonist views his or her surroundings?
- ☐ What is the character's primary motivation? Does this motivation seem reasonable to you?
- ☐ Does the protagonist fully understand his or her motivations?
- ☐ In what ways is the protagonist changed or tested by the events of the story?

WRITING ASSIGNMENT ON CHARACTER

Choose a story with a dynamic protagonist. (See the beginning of this chapter for a discussion of dynamic characters.) Write an essay exploring how that character evolves over the course of the story, providing evidence from the story to back up your argument. Some good story choices might be Faulkner's "Barn Burning," Carver's "Cathedral," Baldwin's "Sonny's Blues," and Mahfouz's "The Lawsuit."

MORE TOPICS FOR WRITING

1. Using a story from this book, write a short essay that explains why a protagonist takes a crucial life-changing action. What motivates this character to do something that seems bold or surprising? You might consider:
   - What motivates the narrator to overcome his instinctive antipathy to the blind man in "Cathedral"?
   - What motivates the older brother to write to Sonny during his incarceration in "Sonny's Blues"?
   - Why doesn't Miss Brill buy her usual slice of honeycake on her way home at the end of "Miss Brill"?

2. Choose a minor character from any of the stories in this book, and write briefly on what the story reveals about that person, reading closely for even the smallest of details. Is he or she a stock character? Why or why not?

3. Choose a story in which the main character has an obvious antagonist, such as "Cathedral," "Sonny's Blues," or "The Lawsuit." What role does this second character play in bringing the protagonist to a new awareness of life?

4. Choose a dynamic character from one of the stories you've read so far. Write a brief essay on how the events in the story relate to your chosen character's strengths or shortcomings.

5. Choose a favorite character from a television show you watch regularly. What details are provided (either in the show's dialogue or in its visuals) to communicate the personality of this character? Would you say this person is a stock character or a rounded one? Write a brief essay making a case for your position.

6. Browse through magazines and newspapers to find a picture of a person you can't identify. Cut out the picture. Create a character based on the picture. As many writers do, make a list of characteristics, from the large (her life's ambition) to the small (his favorite breakfast cereal). As you build your list, make sure your details add up to a rounded character.

▶ TERMS FOR *review*

Characterization ▶ The techniques a writer uses to create, reveal, or develop the characters in a narrative.

Character description ▶ An aspect of characterization through which the author overtly relates either physical or mental traits of a character. This description is almost invariably a sign of what lurks beneath the surface of the character.

Character development ▶ The process by which a character is introduced, advanced, and possibly transformed in a story.

Character motivation ▶ What a character in a narrative wants, the reasons an author provides for a character's actions. Motivation can be either *explicit* (these reasons are specifically stated in a story) or *implicit* (the reasons are only hinted at or partially revealed).

Flat character ▶ A term coined by English novelist E. M. Forster to describe a character with only one outstanding trait. Flat characters are rarely the central characters in a narrative and stay the same throughout a story.

Round character ▶ A term also coined by E. M. Forster to describe a complex character who is presented in depth in a narrative. Round characters are those who change significantly during the course of a narrative or whose full personalities are revealed gradually throughout the story.

Stock character ▶ A common or stereotypical character. Examples of stock characters are the mad scientist, the battle-scarred veteran, and the strong but silent cowboy.

SETTING

What are the three key rules of real estate?
Location, location, location!

—AMERICAN BUSINESS PROVERB

ELEMENTS OF SETTING

By the **setting** of a story, we mean its time and place. The word might remind you of the metal that holds a diamond in a ring, or of a *set* used in a play—perhaps a bare chair in front of a slab olf painted canvas. But often, in an effective short story, setting may figure as more than mere background or underpinning. It can make things happen. It can prompt characters to act, bring them to realizations, or cause them to reveal their inmost natures.

Place

To be sure, the idea of setting includes the physical environment of a story: a house, a street, a city, a landscape, a region. (*Where* a story takes place is sometimes called its **locale**.) Physical places mattered so greatly to French novelist Honoré de Balzac that sometimes, before writing a story set in a particular town, he would visit that town, select a few houses, and describe them in detail, down to their very smells.

Time

In addition to place, setting may crucially involve the time of the story—the hour, year, or century. It might matter greatly that a story takes place at dawn, or on the day of the first moon landing. When we begin to read a historical novel, we are soon made aware that we aren't reading about life in the twenty-first century. In *The Scarlet Letter*, nineteenth-century author Nathaniel Hawthorne, by a long introduction and a vivid opening scene at a prison door, prepares us to witness events in the Puritan community of Boston in the earlier seventeenth century. This setting, together with scenes of Puritan times we recall from high school history, helps us understand what happens in the novel. We can appreciate the shocked agitation in town when a woman is accused of adultery: she has given illegitimate birth. Such an event might seem common today, but in the stern, God-fearing New England Puritan community, it was a flagrant defiance of church and state, which were all-powerful (and were all one). That reader will make no sense of *The Scarlet Letter* who ignores its setting—if it is even possible to ignore the setting, given how much attention Hawthorne pays to it.

The fact that Hawthorne's novel takes place in a time remote from our own leads us to expect different customs and different attitudes. Some critics and teachers regard the setting of a story as its whole society, including the beliefs and assumptions of its characters. Still, we suggest that for now you keep your working definition of *setting* simple. Call it time and place. If later you should feel that your definition needs widening and deepening, you can always expand it.

Weather

Besides time and place, setting may also include the weather, which in some stories may be crucial. Climate seems as substantial as any character in William Faulkner's "Dry September." After sixty-two rainless days, a long unbroken spell of late-summer heat has frayed every nerve in a small town and caused the main character, a hot-headed white supremacist, to feel more and more irritated. The weather, someone remarks, is "enough to make a man do anything." When a false report circulates that a white woman has been raped by a black man, the rumor, like a match flung into a dry field, ignites rage and provokes a lynching. Evidently, to understand the story we have to recognize its locale, a small town in Mississippi in the 1930s during an infernal heat wave. Fully to take in the meaning of Faulkner's story, we have to take in the setting in its entirety.

Atmosphere

Atmosphere is the dominant mood or feeling that pervades all parts of a literary work. Atmosphere refers to the total effect conveyed by the author's use of language, images, and physical setting. But as the term *atmosphere* suggests, aspects of the physical setting (place, time, and weather) are usually crucial elements in achieving the author's intention. In some stories, a writer will seem to draw a setting mainly to evoke atmosphere. In such a story, setting starts us feeling whatever the storyteller would have us feel. In "The Tell-Tale Heart," Poe's setting the action in an old, dark, lantern-lit house greatly contributes to our sense of unease—and so helps the story's effectiveness.

HISTORICAL FICTION

One obvious example of how time can become a major element of setting is in **historical fiction**, where the story is set in another time and place. In historical fiction the author usually tries to recreate a faithful picture of daily life during the period. The historical period might be long ago, such as ancient Rome in Robert Graves's novel *I, Claudius* (1934), or it may be more recent, as in the setting of early twentieth-century Britain in Ian McEwan's *Atonement* (2001). Historical fiction sometimes introduces well-known figures from the past. Thornton Wilder's *Ides of March* (1948) includes Julius Caesar and Cleopatra among its many characters. Ron Hansen's *Exiles* (2008) depicts the life of English poet Gerard Manley Hopkins. More often, historical fiction presents imaginary characters in a carefully reconstructed version of a particular period of the past. Part of the pleasure of reading this sort of fiction comes from experiencing the many details of another time, just as films carefully set in a particular historical moment, such as Ridley Scott's *Gladiator* (2000) and James Cameron's *Titanic* (1997), let us see meticulously recreated settings of another time and place.

REGIONALISM

Physical place, by the way, is especially vital to a **regional writer**, who usually sets stories (or other work) in one geographic area. Such a writer, often a native of the place, tries to bring it alive to readers who live elsewhere. William Faulkner, a distinguished regional writer, almost always sets his novels and stories in his native Mississippi. Though born in St. Louis, Kate Chopin became known as a regional writer because she wrote about Louisiana in many of her short stories and in her novel *The Awakening*. Willa Cather, for her novels of frontier Nebraska, sometimes is regarded as another outstanding regionalist (though she also set fiction in Quebec, the Southwest, and, in "Paul's Case," in Pittsburgh and New York).

There is often something arbitrary, however, about calling an author a regional writer. The label sometimes has a political tinge; it means that the author describes an area outside the political and economic centers of a society. In a sense, we might think of James Joyce as a regional writer, in that all his fiction takes place in the city of Dublin, but instead we usually call him an Irish author.

As such writers show, a place can profoundly affect the character of someone who grew up in it. Willa Cather is fond of portraying strong-minded, independent women, such as the heroine of her novel *My Antonía*, strengthened in part by years of coping with the hardships of life on the wind-lashed prairie.

NATURALISM

Some writers consider the social and economic setting the most important element in the story. They present social environment as the determining factor in human behavior. Their approach is called **naturalism**—fiction of grim realism, in which the writer observes human characters like a scientist observing ants, seeing them as the products and victims of environment and heredity. Naturalism was first consciously developed in fiction in the late nineteenth century by French novelist Émile Zola. Important American Naturalists include Jack London, Theodore Dreiser, and Stephen Crane. Dreiser's novel *The Financier* (1912) begins in a city setting. A young boy (who will grow up to be a ruthless industrialist) is watching a battle to the death between a lobster and a squid in a fish-market tank. Dented for the rest of his life by this grim scene, he decides that's exactly the way human society functions.

Setting usually operates more subtly than that fish tank. Often, setting and character will reveal each other. Recall how Faulkner, at the start of "A Rose for Emily," depicts Emily Grierson's house, once handsome but now "an eyesore among eyesores" surrounded by gas stations. Still standing, refusing to yield its old-time horse-and-buggy splendor to the age of the automobile, the house in "its stubborn and coquettish decay" embodies the character of its owner. In John Steinbeck's "The Chrysanthemums" (Chapter 7), the story begins with a fog that has sealed off a valley from the rest of the world—a fog like the lid on a pot. That physical setting helps convey the isolation and loneliness of the protagonist's situation.

But be warned: you'll meet stories in which setting appears hardly to matter. In W. Somerset Maugham's fable "The Appointment in Samarra," all we need to be told about the setting is that it is a marketplace in Baghdad. In that brief fable, the inevitability of death is the point, not an exotic setting. In this chapter, though, you will meet four fine stories in which setting, for one reason or another, counts greatly. Without it, none of these stories could take place.

Kate Chopin

The Storm   1898

Kate Chopin (1851–1904) was born Katherine O'Flaherty in St. Louis, daughter of an Irish immigrant grown wealthy in retailing. On his death, young Kate was raised by her mother's family: aristocratic Creoles, descendants of the French and Spaniards who had colonized Louisiana. Young Kate received a convent schooling, and at nineteen married Oscar Chopin, a Creole cotton broker from New Orleans. Later, the Chopins lived on a plantation near Cloutierville, Louisiana, a region whose varied people—Creoles, Cajuns, blacks—Kate Chopin was later to write about with loving care in Bayou Folk (1894) and A Night in Arcadia (1897). The shock of her husband's sudden death in 1883, which left her with the raising of six children, seems to have

Kate Chopin

plunged Kate Chopin into writing. She read and admired fine woman writers of her day, such as the Maine realist Sarah Orne Jewett. She also read Maupassant, Zola, and other new (and scandalous) French naturalist writers. She began to bring into American fiction some of their hard-eyed observation and their passion for telling unpleasant truths. Determined, in defiance of her times, frankly to show the sexual feelings of her characters, Chopin suffered from neglect and censorship. When her major novel, The Awakening, appeared in 1899, critics were outraged by her candid portrait of a woman who seeks sexual and professional independence. After causing such a literary scandal, Chopin was unable to get her later work published, and wrote little more before she died. The Awakening and many of her stories had to wait seven decades for a sympathetic audience.

I

The leaves were so still that even Bibi thought it was going to rain. Bobinôt, who was accustomed to converse on terms of perfect equality with his little son, called the child's attention to certain somber clouds that were rolling with sinister intention from the west, accompanied by a sullen, threatening roar. They were at Friedheimer's store and decided to remain there till the storm had passed. They sat within the door on two empty kegs. Bibi was four years old and looked very wise.

"Mama'll be 'fraid, yes," he suggested with blinking eyes.

"She'll shut the house. Maybe she got Sylvie helpin' her this evenin'," Bobinôt responded reassuringly.

"No; she ent got Sylvie. Sylvie was helpin' her yistiday," piped Bibi.

Bobinôt arose and going across to the counter purchased a can of shrimps, of which Calixta was very fond. Then he returned to his perch on the keg and sat stolidly holding the can of shrimps while the storm burst. It shook the wooden store   5 and seemed to be ripping great furrows in the distant field. Bibi laid his little hand on his father's knee and was not afraid.

II

Calixta, at home, felt no uneasiness for their safety. She sat at a side window sewing furiously on a sewing machine. She was greatly occupied and did not notice the approaching storm. But she felt very warm and often stopped to mop her face on which the perspiration gathered in beads. She unfastened her white sacque at the throat. It began to grow dark, and suddenly realizing the situation she got up hurriedly and went about closing windows and doors.

Out on the small front gallery she had hung Bobinôt's Sunday clothes to air and she hastened out to gather them before the rain fell. As she stepped outside, Alcée Laballière rode in at the gate. She had not seen him very often since her marriage, and never alone. She stood there with Bobinôt's coat in her hands, and the big rain drops began to fall. Alcée rode his horse under the shelter of a side projection where the chickens had huddled and there were plows and a harrow piled up in the corner.

"May I come and wait on your gallery till the storm is over, Calixta?" he asked.

"Come 'long in, M'sieur Alcée."

His voice and her own startled her as if from a trance, and she seized Bobinôt's vest. Alcée, mounting to the porch, grabbed the trousers and snatched Bibi's braided jacket that was about to be carried away by a sudden gust of wind. He expressed an intention to remain outside, but it was soon apparent that he might as well have been out in the open: the water beat in upon the boards in driving sheets, and he went inside, closing the door after him. It was even necessary to put something beneath the door to keep the water out. 10

"My! what a rain! It's good two years since it rain like that," exclaimed Calixta as she rolled up a piece of bagging and Alcée helped her to thrust it beneath the crack.

She was a little fuller of figure than five years before when she married; but she had lost nothing of her vivacity. Her blue eyes still retained their melting quality; and her yellow hair, dishevelled by the wind and rain, kinked more stubbornly than ever about her ears and temples.

The rain beat upon the low, shingled roof with a force and clatter that threatened to break an entrance and deluge them there. They were in the dining room—the sitting room—the general utility room. Adjoining was her bed room, with Bibi's couch along side her own. The door stood open, and the room with its white, monumental bed, its closed shutters, looked dim and mysterious.

Alcée flung himself into a rocker and Calixta nervously began to gather up from the floor the lengths of a cotton sheet which she had been sewing.

"If this keeps up, *Dieu sait*° if the levees goin' to stan' it!" she exclaimed. 15

"What have you got to do with the levees?"

"I got enough to do! An' there's Bobinôt with Bibi out in that storm—if he only didn' left Friedheimer's!"

"Let us hope, Calixta, that Bobinôt's got sense enough to come in out of a cyclone."

She went and stood at the window with a greatly disturbed look on her face. She wiped the frame that was clouded with moisture. It was stiflingly hot. Alcée got up

Dieu sait: God only knows.

and joined her at the window, looking over her shoulder. The rain was coming down in sheets obscuring the view of far-off cabins and enveloping the distant wood in a gray mist. The playing of the lightning was incessant. A bolt struck a tall chinaberry tree at the edge of the field. It filled all visible space with a blinding glare and the crash seemed to invade the very boards they stood upon.

Calixta put her hands to her eyes, and with a cry, staggered backward. Alcée's arm   20
encircled her, and for an instant he drew her close and spasmodically to him.

"*Bonté!*"° she cried, releasing herself from his encircling arm and retreating from the window, "the house'll go next! If I only knew w'ere Bibi was!" She would not compose herself; she would not be seated. Alcée clasped her shoulders and looked into her face. The contact of her warm, palpitating body when he had unthinkingly drawn her into his arms, had aroused all the old-time infatuation and desire for her flesh.

"Calixta," he said, "don't be frightened. Nothing can happen. The house is too low to be struck, with so many tall trees standing about. There! aren't you going to be quiet? say, aren't you?" He pushed her hair back from her face that was warm and steaming. Her lips were as red and moist as pomegranate seed. Her white neck and a glimpse of her full, firm bosom disturbed him powerfully. As she glanced up at him the fear in her liquid blue eyes had given place to a drowsy gleam that unconsciously betrayed a sensuous desire. He looked down into her eyes and there was nothing for him to do but gather her lips in a kiss. It reminded him of Assumption.°

"Do you remember—in Assumption, Calixta?" he asked in a low voice broken by passion. Oh! she remembered; for in Assumption he had kissed her and kissed and kissed her; until his senses would well nigh fail, and to save her he would resort to a desperate flight. If she was not an immaculate dove in those days, she was still inviolate; a passionate creature whose very defenselessness had made her defense, against which his honor forbade him to prevail. Now—well, now—her lips seemed in a manner free to be tasted, as well as her round, white throat and her whiter breasts.

They did not heed the crashing torrents, and the roar of the elements made her laugh as she lay in his arms. She was a revelation in that dim, mysterious chamber; as white as the couch she lay upon. Her firm, elastic flesh that was knowing for the first time its birthright, was like a creamy lily that the sun invites to contribute its breath and perfume to the undying life of the world.

The generous abundance of her passion, without guile or trickery, was like a   25
white flame which penetrated and found response in depths of his own sensuous nature that had never yet been reached.

When he touched her breasts they gave themselves up in quivering ecstasy, inviting his lips. Her mouth was a fountain of delight. And when he possessed her, they seemed to swoon together at the very borderland of life's mystery.

He stayed cushioned upon her, breathless, dazed, enervated, with his heart beating like a hammer upon her. With one hand she clasped his head, her lips lightly touching his forehead. The other hand stroked with a soothing rhythm his muscular shoulders.

The growl of the thunder was distant and passing away. The rain beat softly upon the shingles, inviting them to drowsiness and sleep. But they dared not yield.

Bonté!: Heavens!   *Assumption:* a parish west of New Orleans.

The rain was over; and the sun was turning the glistening green world into a palace of gems. Calixta, on the gallery, watched Alcée ride away. He turned and smiled at her with a beaming face; and she lifted her pretty chin in the air and laughed aloud.

III

Bobinôt and Bibi, trudging home, stopped without at the cistern to make themselves presentable. 30

"My! Bibi, w'at will yo' mama say! You ought to be ashame'. You oughtn' put on those good pants. Look at 'em! An' that mud on yo' collar! How you got that mud on yo' collar, Bibi? I never saw such a boy!" Bibi was the picture of pathetic resignation. Bobinôt was the embodiment of serious solicitude as he strove to remove from his own person and his son's the signs of their tramp over heavy roads and through wet fields. He scraped the mud off Bibi's bare legs and feet with a stick and carefully removed all traces from his heavy brogans. Then, prepared for the worst—the meeting with an overscrupulous housewife, they entered cautiously at the back door.

Calixta was preparing supper. She had set the table and was dripping coffee at the hearth. She sprang up as they came in.

"Oh, Bobinôt! You back! My! but I was uneasy. W'ere you been during the rain? An' Bibi? he ain't wet? he ain't hurt?" She had clasped Bibi and was kissing him effusively. Bobinôt's explanations and apologies which he had been composing all along the way, died on his lips as Calixta felt him to see if he were dry, and seemed to express nothing but satisfaction at their safe return.

"I brought you some shrimps, Calixta," offered Bobinôt, hauling the can from his ample side pocket and laying it on the table.

"Shrimps! Oh, Bobinôt! you too good fo' anything!" and she gave him a smacking kiss on the cheek that resounded. "*J'vous réponds,*° we'll have feas' to night! umph-umph!" 35

Bobinôt and Bibi began to relax and enjoy themselves, and when the three seated themselves at table they laughed much and so loud that anyone might have heard them as far away as Laballière's.

IV

Alcée Laballière wrote to his wife, Clarisse, that night. It was a loving letter, full of tender solicitude. He told her not to hurry back, but if she and the babies liked it at Biloxi, to stay a month longer. He was getting on nicely; and though he missed them, he was willing to bear the separation a while longer—realizing that their health and pleasure were the first things to be considered.

V

As for Clarisse, she was charmed upon receiving her husband's letter. She and the babies were doing well. The society was agreeable; many of her old friends and acquaintances were at the bay. And the first free breath since her marriage seemed to restore the pleasant liberty of her maiden days. Devoted as she was to her husband, their intimate conjugal life was something which she was more than willing to forego for a while.

So the storm passed and everyone was happy.

J'vous réponds: Let me tell you.

Questions

1. Exactly where does Chopin's story take place? How can you tell?
2. What circumstances introduced in Part I turn out to have a profound effect on events in the story?
3. What details in "The Storm" emphasize the fact that Bobinôt loves his wife? What details reveal how imperfectly he comprehends her nature?
4. What general attitudes toward sex, love, and marriage does Chopin imply? Cite evidence to support your answer.
5. What meanings do you find in the title "The Storm"?
6. In the story as a whole, how do setting and plot reinforce each other?

Jack London

To Build a Fire
1910

Jack London (1876–1916), born in San Francisco, won a large popular audience for his novels of the sea and the Yukon: The Call of the Wild *(1903),* The Sea-Wolf *(1904), and* White Fang *(1906). Like Ernest Hemingway, he was a writer who lived a strenuous life. In 1893, he marched cross-country in Coxey's Army, an organized protest of the unemployed; in 1897, he took part in the Klondike gold rush; and later, as a reporter, he covered the Russo-Japanese War and the Mexican Revolution. Son of an unmarried mother and a father who denied his paternity, London grew up in poverty. At fourteen, he began holding hard jobs: working in a canning factory and a jute-mill, serving as a deck hand, pirating oysters in San Francisco Bay. These ex-*

Jack London

periences persuaded him to join the Socialist Labor Party and crusade for workers' rights. In his political novel The Iron Heel *(1908), London envisions a grim totalitarian America. Like himself, the hero of his novel* Martin Eden *(1909) is a man of brief schooling who gains fame as a writer, works for a cause, loses faith in it, and finds life without meaning. Though endowed with immense physical energy—he wrote fifty volumes—London drank hard, spent fast, and played out early. While his reputation as a novelist may have declined since his own day, some of his short stories have lasted triumphantly.*

Day had broken cold and gray, exceedingly cold and gray, when the man turned aside from the main Yukon trail and climbed the high earth-bank, where a dim and little-travelled trail led eastward through the fat spruce timberland. It was a steep bank, and he paused for breath at the top, excusing the act to himself by looking at his watch. It was nine o'clock. There was no sun nor hint of sun, though there was not a cloud in the sky. It was a clear day, and yet there seemed an intangible pall over the face of things, a subtle gloom that made the day dark, and that was due to the absence of sun. This fact did not worry the man. He was used to the lack of sun. It had been days since he had seen the sun, and he knew that a few more days must pass before that cheerful orb, due south, would just peep above the sky line and dip immediately from view.

The man flung a look back along the way he had come. The Yukon lay a mile wide and hidden under three feet of ice. On top of this ice were as many feet of snow. It was all pure white, rolling in gentle undulations where the ice jams of the freeze-up had formed. North and south, as far as the eye could see, it was unbroken white, save for a dark hairline that curved and twisted from around the spruce-covered island to the south, and that curved and twisted away into the north, where it disappeared behind another spruce-covered island. This dark hairline was the trail—the main trail—that led south five hundred miles to the Chilcoot Pass, Dyea, and salt water; and that led north seventy miles to Dawson, and still on to the north a thousand miles to Nulato, and finally to St. Michael, on Bering Sea, a thousand miles and half a thousand more.

But all this—the mysterious, far-reaching hairline trail, the absence of sun from the sky, the tremendous cold, and the strangeness and weirdness of it all—made no impression on the man. It was not because he was long used to it. He was a newcomer in the land, a *chechaquo*, and this was his first winter. The trouble with him was that he was without imagination. He was quick and alert in the things of life, but only in the things, and not in the significances. Fifty degrees below zero meant eighty-odd degrees of frost. Such fact impressed him as being cold and uncomfortable, and that was all. It did not lead him to meditate upon his frailty as a creature of temperature, and upon man's frailty in general, able only to live within certain narrow limits of heat and cold; and from there on it did not lead him to the conjectural field of immortality and man's place in the universe. Fifty degrees below zero stood for a bite of frost that hurt and that must be guarded against by the use of mittens, ear flaps, warm moccasins, and thick socks. Fifty degrees below zero was to him just precisely fifty degrees below zero. That there should be anything more to it than that was a thought that never entered his head.

As he turned to go on, he spat speculatively. There was a sharp, explosive crackle that startled him. He spat again. And again, in the air, before it could fall to the snow, the spittle crackled. He knew that at fifty below spittle crackled on the snow, but this spittle had crackled in the air. Undoubtedly it was colder than fifty below—how much colder he did not know. But the temperature did not matter. He was bound for the old claim on the left fork of Henderson Creek, where the boys were already. They had come over across the divide from the Indian Creek country, while he had come the roundabout way to take a look at the possibilities of getting out logs in the spring from the islands in the Yukon. He would be in to camp by six o'clock; a bit after dark, it was true, but the boys would be there, a fire would be going, and a hot supper would be ready. As for lunch, he pressed his hand against the protruding bundle under his jacket. It was also under his shirt, wrapped up in a handkerchief and lying against the naked skin. It was the only way to keep the biscuits from freezing. He smiled agreeably to himself as he thought of those biscuits, each cut open and sopped in bacon grease, and each enclosing a generous slice of fried bacon.

He plunged in among the big spruce trees. The trail was faint. A foot of snow had fallen since the last sled had passed over, and he was glad he was without a sled, travelling light. In fact, he carried nothing but the lunch wrapped in the handkerchief. He was surprised, however, at the cold. It certainly was cold, he concluded, as he rubbed his numb nose and cheekbones with his mittened hand. He was a warm-whiskered

5

man, but the hair on his face did not protect the high cheekbones and the eager nose that thrust itself aggressively into the frosty air.

At the man's heels trotted a dog, a big native husky, the proper wolf dog, gray-coated and without any visible or temperamental difference from its brother, the wild wolf. The animal was depressed by the tremendous cold. It knew that it was no time for travelling. Its instinct told it a truer tale than was told to the man by the man's judgment. In reality, it was not merely colder than fifty below zero; it was colder than sixty below, than seventy below. It was seventy-five below zero. Since the freezing point is thirty-two above zero, it meant that one hundred and seven degrees of frost obtained. The dog did not know anything about thermometers. Possibly in its brain there was no sharp consciousness of a condition of very cold such as was in the man's brain. But the brute had its instinct. It experienced a vague but menacing apprehension that subdued it and made it slink along at the man's heels, and that made it question eagerly every unwonted movement of the man as if expecting him to go into camp or to seek shelter somewhere and build a fire. The dog had learned fire, and it wanted fire, or else to burrow under the snow and cuddle its warmth away from the air.

The frozen moisture of its breathing had settled on its fur in a fine powder of frost, and especially were its jowls, muzzle, and eyelashes whitened by its crystalled breath. The man's red beard and mustache were likewise frosted, but more solidly, the deposit taking the form of ice and increasing with every warm, moist breath he exhaled. Also, the man was chewing tobacco, and the muzzle of ice held his lips so rigidly that he was unable to clear his chin when he expelled the juice. The result was that a crystal beard of the color and solidity of amber was increasing its length on his chin. If he fell down it would shatter itself, like glass, into brittle fragments. But he did not mind the appendage. It was the penalty all tobacco chewers paid in that country, and he had been out before in two cold snaps. They had not been so cold as this, he knew, but by the spirit thermometer at Sixty Mile he knew they had been registered at fifty below and at fifty-five.

He held on through the level stretch of woods for several miles, crossed a wide flat, and dropped down a bank to the frozen bed of a small stream. This was Henderson Creek, and he knew he was ten miles from the forks. He looked at his watch. It was ten o'clock. He was making four miles an hour, and he calculated that he would arrive at the forks at half-past twelve. He decided to celebrate that event by eating his lunch there.

The dog dropped in again at his heels, with a tail drooping discouragement, as the man swung along the creek bed. The furrow of the old sled trail was plainly visible, but a dozen inches of snow covered the marks of the last runners. In a month no man had come up or down that silent creek. The man held steadily on. He was not much given to thinking, and just then particularly he had nothing to think about save that he would eat lunch at the forks and that at six o'clock he would be in camp with the boys. There was nobody to talk to; and, had there been, speech would have been impossible because of the ice muzzle on his mouth. So he continued monotonously to chew tobacco and to increase the length of his amber beard.

Once in a while the thought reiterated itself that it was very cold and that he had never experienced such cold. As he walked along he rubbed his cheekbones and nose with the back of his mittened hand. He did this automatically, now and again changing hands. But, rub as he would, the instant he stopped his cheekbones were numb, and the following instant the end of his nose went numb. He was sure to frost

10

his cheeks; he knew that, and experienced a pang of regret that he had not devised a nose strap of the sort Bud wore in cold snaps. Such a strap passed across the cheeks, as well, and saved them. But it didn't matter much, after all. What were frosted cheeks? A bit painful, that was all; they were never serious.

Empty as the man's mind was of thoughts, he was keenly observant, and he noticed the changes in the creek, the curves and bends and timber jams, and always he sharply noted where he placed his feet. Once, coming around a bend, he shied abruptly, like a startled horse, curved away from the place where he had been walking, and retreated several paces back along the trail. The creek he knew was frozen clear to the bottom—no creek could contain water in that arctic winter—but he knew also that there were springs that bubbled out from the hillsides and ran along under the snow and on top the ice of the creek. He knew that the coldest snaps never froze these springs, and he knew likewise their danger. They were traps. They hid pools of water under the snow that might be three inches deep, or three feet. Sometimes a skin of ice half an inch thick covered them, and in turn was covered by the snow. Sometimes there were alternate layers of water and ice skin, so that when one broke through he kept on breaking through for a while, sometimes wetting himself to the waist.

That was why he had shied in such panic. He had felt the give under his feet and heard the crackle of a snow-hidden ice skin. And to get his feet wet in such a temperature meant trouble and danger. At the very least it meant delay, for he would be forced to stop and build a fire, and under its protection to bare his feet while he dried his socks and moccasins. He stood and studied the creek bed and its banks, and decided that the flow of water came from the right. He reflected awhile, rubbing his nose and cheeks, then skirted to the left, stepping gingerly and testing the footing for each step. Once clear of the danger, he took a fresh chew of tobacco and swung along at his four-mile gait.

In the course of the next two hours he came upon several similar traps. Usually the snow above the hidden pools had a sunken, candied appearance that advertised the danger. Once again, however, he had a close call; and once, suspecting danger, he compelled the dog to go on in front. The dog did not want to go. It hung back until the man shoved it forward, and then it went quickly across the white, unbroken surface. Suddenly it broke through, floundered to one side, and got away to firmer footing. It had wet its forefeet and legs, and almost immediately the water that clung to it turned to ice. It made quick efforts to lick the ice off its legs, then dropped down in the snow and began to bite out the ice that had formed between the toes. This was a matter of instinct. To permit the ice to remain would mean sore feet. It did not know this. It merely obeyed the mysterious prompting that arose from the deep crypts of its being. But the man knew, having achieved a judgment on the subject, and he removed the mitten from his right hand and helped tear out the ice particles. He did not expose his fingers more than a minute, and was astonished at the swift numbness that smote them. It certainly was cold. He pulled on the mitten hastily, and beat the hand savagely across his chest.

At twelve o'clock the day was at its brightest. Yet the sun was too far south on its winter journey to clear the horizon. The bulge of the earth intervened between it and Henderson Creek, where the man walked under a clear sky at noon and cast no shadow. At half-past twelve, to the minute, he arrived at the forks of the creek. He was pleased at the speed he had made. If he kept it up, he would certainly be with the boys by six. He unbuttoned his jacket and shirt and drew forth his lunch.

The action consumed no more than a quarter of a minute, yet in that brief moment the numbness laid hold of the exposed fingers. He did not put the mitten on, but, instead, struck the fingers a dozen sharp smashes against his leg. Then he sat down on a snow-covered log to eat. The sting that followed upon the striking of his fingers against his leg ceased so quickly that he was startled. He had had no chance to take a bite of biscuit. He struck the fingers repeatedly and returned them to the mitten, baring the other hand for the purpose of eating. He tried to take a mouthful, but the ice muzzle prevented. He had forgotten to build a fire and thaw out. He chuckled at his foolishness, and as he chuckled he noted the numbness creeping into the exposed fingers. Also, he noted that the stinging which had first come to his toes when he sat down was already passing away. He wondered whether the toes were warm or numb. He moved them inside the moccasins and decided that they were numb.

He pulled the mitten on hurriedly and stood up. He was a bit frightened. He   15
stamped up and down until the stinging returned into the feet. It certainly was cold, was his thought. That man from Sulphur Creek had spoken the truth when telling how cold it sometimes got in the country. And he had laughed at him at the time! That showed one must not be too sure of things. There was no mistake about it, it *was* cold. He strode up and down, stamping his feet and threshing his arms, until reassured by the returning warmth. Then he got out matches and proceeded to make a fire. From the undergrowth, where high water of the previous spring had lodged a supply of seasoned twigs, he got his firewood. Working carefully from a small beginning, he soon had a roaring fire, over which he thawed the ice from his face and in the protection of which he ate his biscuits. For the moment the cold of space was outwitted. The dog took satisfaction in the fire, stretching out close enough for warmth and far enough away to escape being singed.

When the man had finished, he filled his pipe and took his comfortable time over a smoke. Then he pulled on his mittens, settled the ear flaps of his cap firmly about his ears, and took the creek trail up the left fork. The dog was disappointed and yearned back toward the fire. This man did not know cold. Possibly all the generations of his ancestry had been ignorant of cold, of real cold, of cold one hundred and seven degrees below freezing point. But the dog knew; all its ancestry knew, and it had inherited the knowledge. And it knew that it was not good to walk abroad in such fearful cold. It was the time to lie snug in a hole in the snow and wait for a curtain of cloud to be drawn across the face of outer space whence this cold came. On the other hand, there was no keen intimacy between the dog and the man. The one was the toil slave of the other, and the only caresses it had ever received were the caresses of the whip lash and of harsh and menacing throat sounds that threatened the whip lash. So the dog made no effort to communicate its apprehension to the man. It was not concerned in the welfare of the man; it was for its own sake that it yearned back toward the fire. But the man whistled, and spoke to it with the sound of whip lashes, and the dog swung in at the man's heels and followed after.

The man took a chew of tobacco and proceeded to start a new amber beard. Also, his moist breath quickly powdered with white his mustache, eyebrows, and lashes. There did not seem to be so many springs on the left fork of the Henderson, and for half an hour the man saw no signs of any. And then it happened. At a place where there were no signs, where the soft, unbroken snow seemed to advertise solidity beneath, the man broke through. It was not deep. He wet himself halfway to the knees before he floundered out to the firm crust.

He was angry, and cursed his luck aloud. He had hoped to get into camp with the boys at six o'clock, and this would delay him an hour, for he would have to build a fire and dry out his footgear. This was imperative at that low temperature—he knew that much; and he turned aside to the bank, which he climbed. On top, tangled in the underbrush about the trunks of several small spruce trees, was a high-water deposit of dry firewood—sticks and twigs, principally, but also larger portions of seasoned branches and fine, dry, last year's grasses. He threw down several large pieces on top of the snow. This served for a foundation and prevented the young flame from drowning itself in the snow it otherwise would melt. The flame he got by touching a match to a small shred of birch bark that he took from his pocket. This burned even more readily than paper. Placing it on the foundation, he fed the young flame with wisps of dry grass and with the tiniest dry twigs.

He worked slowly and carefully, keenly aware of his danger. Gradually, as the flame grew stronger, he increased the size of the twigs with which he fed it. He squatted in the snow, pulling the twigs out from their entanglement in the brush and feeding directly to the flame. He knew there must be no failure. When it is seventy-five below zero, a man must not fail in his first attempt to build a fire—that is, if his feet are wet. If his feet are dry, and he fails, he can run along the trail for half a mile and restore his circulation. But the circulation of wet and freezing feet cannot be restored by running when it is seventy-five below. No matter how fast he runs, the wet feet will freeze the harder.

All this the man knew. The old-timer on Sulphur Creek had told him about it 20 the previous fall, and now he was appreciating the advice. Already all sensation had gone out of his feet. To build the fire he had been forced to remove his mittens, and the fingers had quickly gone numb. His pace of four miles an hour had kept his heart pumping blood to the surface of his body and to all the extremities. But the instant he stopped, the action of the pump eased down. The cold of space smote the unprotected tip of the planet, and he, being on that unprotected tip, received the full force of the blow. The blood of his body recoiled before it. The blood was alive, like the dog, and like the dog it wanted to hide away and cover itself up from the fearful cold. So long as he walked four miles an hour, he pumped that blood, willy-nilly, to the surface; but now it ebbed away and sank down into the recesses of his body. The extremities were the first to feel its absence. His wet feet froze the faster, and his exposed fingers numbed the faster, though they had not yet begun to freeze. Nose and cheeks were already freezing, while the skin of all his body chilled as it lost its blood.

But he was safe. Toes and nose and cheeks would be only touched by the frost, for the fire was beginning to burn with strength. He was feeding it with twigs the size of his finger. In another minute he would be able to feed it with branches the size of his wrist, and then he could remove his wet footgear, and, while it dried, he could keep his naked feet warm by the fire, rubbing them at first, of course, with snow. The fire was a success. He was safe. He remembered the advice of the old-timer on Sulphur Creek, and smiled. The old-timer had been very serious in laying down the law that no man must travel alone in the Klondike after fifty below. Well, here he was; he had had the accident; he was alone; and he had saved himself. Those old-timers were rather womanish, some of them, he thought. All a man had to do was to keep his head, and he was all right. Any man who was a man could travel alone. But it was surprising, the rapidity with which his cheeks and nose were freezing. And he had not thought his fingers could go lifeless in so short a time. Lifeless they were, for he could scarcely make them move together to grip a twig, and they seemed remote from his body and from him. When he touched a twig, he had to look and see whether or not he had hold of it. The wires were pretty well down between him and his finger ends.

All of which counted for little. There was the fire, snapping and crackling and promising life with every dancing flame. He started to untie his moccasins. They were coated with ice; the thick German socks were like sheaths of iron halfway to the knees; and the moccasin strings were like rods of steel all twisted and knotted as by some conflagration. For a moment he tugged with his numb fingers, then, realizing the folly of it, he drew his sheath knife.

But before he could cut the strings, it happened. It was his own fault or, rather, his mistake. He should not have built the fire under the spruce tree. He should have built it in the open. But it had been easier to pull the twigs from the brush and drop them directly on the fire. Now the tree under which he had done this carried a weight of snow on its boughs. No wind had blown for weeks, and each bough was fully freighted. Each time he had pulled a twig he had communicated a slight agitation to the tree— an imperceptible agitation, so far as he was concerned, but an agitation sufficient to bring about the disaster. High up in the tree one bough capsized its load of snow. This fell on the boughs beneath, capsizing them. This process continued, spreading out and involving the whole tree. It grew like an avalanche, and it descended without warning upon the man and the fire, and the fire was blotted out! Where it had burned was a mantle of fresh and disordered snow.

The man was shocked. It was as though he had just heard his own sentence of death. For a moment he sat and stared at the spot where the fire had been. Then he grew very calm. Perhaps the old-timer on Sulphur Creek was right. If he had only had a trail mate he would have been in no danger now. The trail mate could have built the fire. Well, it was up to him to build the fire over again, and this second time there must be no failure. Even if he succeeded, he would most likely lose some toes. His feet must be badly frozen by now, and there would be some time before the second fire was ready.

Such were his thoughts, but he did not sit and think them. He was busy all the time they were passing through his mind. He made a new foundation for a fire, this time in the open, where no treacherous tree could blot it out. Next he gathered dry grasses and tiny twigs from the high-water flotsam. He could not bring his fingers together to pull them out, but he was able to gather them by the handful. In this way he got many rotten twigs and bits of green moss that were undesirable, but it was the best he could do. He worked methodically, even collecting an armful of the larger branches to be used later when the fire gathered strength. And all the while the dog sat and watched him, a certain yearning wistfulness in its eye, for it looked upon him as the fire provider, and the fire was slow in coming.

When all was ready, the man reached in his pocket for a second piece of birch bark. He knew the bark was there, and, though he could not feel it with his fingers, he could hear its crisp rustling as he fumbled for it. Try as he would, he could not clutch hold of it. And all the time, in his consciousness, was the knowledge that each instant his feet were freezing. This thought tended to put him in a panic, but he fought against it and kept calm. He pulled on his mittens with his teeth, and threshed his arms back and forth, beating his hands with all his might against his sides. He did this

25

sitting down, and he stood up to do it; and all the while the dog sat in the snow, its wolf brush of a tail curled around warmly over its forefeet, its sharp wolf ears pricked forward intently as it watched the man. And the man, as he beat and threshed with his arms and hands, felt a great surge of envy as he regarded the creature that was warm and secure in its natural covering.

After a time he was aware of the first faraway signals of sensation in his beaten fingers. The faint tingling grew stronger till it evolved into a stinging ache that was excruciating, but which the man hailed with satisfaction. He stripped the mitten from his right hand and fetched forth the birch bark. The exposed fingers were quickly going numb again. Next he brought out his bunch of sulphur matches. But the tremendous cold had already driven the life out of his fingers. In his effort to sep-arate one match from the others, the whole bunch fell in the snow. He tried to pick it out of the snow, but failed. The dead fingers could neither touch nor clutch. He was very careful. He drove the thought of his freezing feet, and nose, and cheeks, out of his mind, devoting his whole soul to the matches. He watched, using the sense of vision in place of that of touch, and when he saw his fingers on each side the bunch, he closed them—that is, he willed to close them, for the wires were down, and the fingers did not obey. He pulled the mitten on the right hand, and beat it fiercely against his knee. Then, with both mittened hands, he scooped the bunch of matches, along with much snow, into his lap. Yet he was no better off.

After some manipulation he managed to get the bunch between the heels of his mittened hands. In this fashion he carried it to his mouth. The ice crackled and snapped when by a violent effort he opened his mouth. He drew the lower jaw in, curled the upper lip out of the way, and scraped the bunch with his upper teeth in or-der to separate a match. He succeeded in getting one, which he dropped on his lap. He was no better off. He could not pick it up. Then he devised a way. He picked it up in his teeth and scratched it on his leg. Twenty times he scratched before he succeeded in lighting it. As it flamed he held it with his teeth to the birch bark. But the burning brimstone went up his nostrils and into his lungs, causing him to cough spasmodically. The match fell into the snow and went out.

The old-timer on Sulphur Creek was right, he thought in the moment of con-trolled despair that ensued: after fifty below, a man should travel with a partner. He beat his hands, but failed in exciting any sensation. Suddenly he bared both hands, removing the mittens with his teeth. He caught the whole bunch between the heels of his hands. His arm muscles not being frozen enabled him to press the hand heels tightly against the matches. Then he scratched the bunch along his leg. It flared into flame, seventy sulphur matches at once! There was no wind to blow them out. He kept his head to one side to escape the strangling fumes, and held the blazing bunch to the birch bark. As he so held it, he became aware of sensation in his hand. His flesh was burning. He could smell it. Deep down below the surface he could feel it. The sensation developed into pain that grew acute. And still he endured it, holding the flame of the matches clumsily to the bark that would not light readily because his own burning hands were in the way, absorbing most of the flame.

At last, when he could endure no more, he jerked his hands apart. The blazing matches fell sizzling into the snow, but the birch bark was alight. He began laying dry grasses and the tiniest twigs on the flame. He could not pick and choose, for he had to lift the fuel between the heels of his hands. Small pieces of rotten wood and green moss clung to the twigs, and he bit them off as well as he could with his teeth. He

30

cherished the flame carefully and awkwardly. It meant life, and it must not perish. The withdrawal of blood from the surface of his body now made him begin to shiver, and he grew more awkward. A large piece of green moss fell squarely on the little fire. He tried to poke it out with his fingers, but his shivering frame made him poke too far, and he disrupted the nucleus of the little fire, the burning grasses and tiny twigs separating and scattering. He tried to poke them together again, but in spite of the tenseness of the effort, his shivering got away from him, and the twigs were hopelessly scattered. Each twig gushed a puff of smoke and went out. The fire provider had failed. As he looked apathetically about him, his eyes chanced on the dog, sitting across the ruins of the fire from him, in the snow, making restless, hunching movements, slightly lifting one forefoot and then the other, shifting its weight back and forth on them with wistful eagerness.

The sight of the dog put a wild idea into his head. He remembered the tale of the man, caught in the blizzard, who killed a steer and crawled inside the carcass, and so was saved. He would kill the dog and bury his hands in the warm body until the numbness went out of them. Then he could build another fire. He spoke to the dog, calling it to him; but in his voice was a strange note of fear that frightened the animal, who had never known the man to speak in such a way before. Something was the matter, and its suspicious nature sensed danger—it knew not what danger, but somewhere, somehow, in its brain arose an apprehension of the man. It flattened its ears down at the sound of the man's voice, and its restless, hunching movements and the liftings and shiftings of its forefeet became more pronounced; but it would not come to the man. He got on his hands and knees and crawled toward the dog. This unusual posture again excited suspicion, and the animal sidled mincingly away.

The man sat up in the snow for a moment and struggled for calmness. Then he pulled on his mittens, by means of his teeth, and got upon his feet. He glanced down at first in order to assure himself that he was really standing up, for the absence of sensation in his feet left him unrelated to the earth. His erect position in itself started to drive the webs of suspicion from the dog's mind; and when he spoke peremptorily, with the sound of whip lashes in his voice, the dog rendered its customary allegiance and came to him. As it came within reaching distance, the man lost his control. His arms flashed out to the dog, and he experienced genuine surprise when he discovered that his hands could not clutch, that there was neither bend nor feeling in the fingers. He had forgotten for the moment that they were frozen and that they were freezing more and more. All this happened quickly, and before the animal could get away, he encircled its body with his arms. He sat down in the snow, and in this fashion held the dog, while it snarled and whined and struggled.

But it was all he could do, hold its body encircled in his arms and sit there. He realized that he could not kill the dog. There was no way to do it. With his helpless hands he could neither draw nor hold his sheath knife nor throttle the animal. He released it, and it plunged wildly away, with tail between its legs, and still snarling. It halted forty feet away and surveyed him curiously, with ears sharply pricked forward.

The man looked down at his hands in order to locate them, and found them hanging on the ends of his arms. It struck him as curious that one should have to use his eyes in order to find out where his hands were. He began threshing his arms back and forth, beating the mittened hands against his sides. He did this for five minutes, violently, and his heart pumped enough blood up to the surface to put a stop to his shivering. But no sensation was aroused in the hands. He had an impression that they hung like weights on the ends of his arms, but when he tried to run the impression down, he could not find it.

A certain fear of death, dull and oppressive, came to him. This fear quickly became poignant as he realized that it was no longer a mere matter of freezing his fingers and toes, or of losing his hands and feet, but that it was a matter of life and death with the chances against him. This threw him into a panic, and he turned and ran up the creek bed along the old, dim trail. The dog joined in behind and kept up with him. He ran blindly, without intention, in fear such as he had never known in his life. Slowly, as he plowed and floundered through the snow, he began to see things again—the banks of the creek, the old timber jams, the leafless aspens, and the sky. The running made him feel better. He did not shiver. Maybe, if he ran on, his feet would thaw out; and anyway, if he ran far enough, he would reach camp and the boys. Without doubt he would lose some fingers and toes and some of his face; but the boys would take care of him, and save the rest of him when he got there. And at the same time there was another thought in his mind that said he would never get to the camp and the boys; that it was too many miles away, that the freezing had too great a start on him, and that he would soon be stiff and dead. This thought he kept in the background and refused to consider. Sometimes it pushed itself forward and demanded to be heard, but he thrust it back and strove to think of other things.

It struck him as curious that he could run at all on feet so frozen that he could not feel them when they struck the earth and took the weight of his body. He seemed to himself to skim along above the surface, and to have no connection with the earth. Somewhere he had once seen a winged Mercury, and he wondered if Mercury felt as he felt when skimming over the earth.

His theory of running until he reached the camp and the boys had one flaw in it: he lacked the endurance. Several times he stumbled, and finally he tottered, crumpled up, and fell. When he tried to rise, he failed. He must sit and rest, he decided, and next time he would merely walk and keep on going. As he sat and regained his breath, he noted that he was feeling quite warm and comfortable. He was not shivering, and it even seemed that a warm glow had come to his chest and trunk. And yet, when he touched his nose and cheeks, there was no sensation. Running would not thaw them out. Nor would it thaw out his hands and feet. Then the thought came to him that the frozen portions of his body must be extending. He tried to keep this thought down, to forget it, to think of something else; he was aware of the panicky feeling that it caused, and he was afraid of the panic. But the thought asserted itself, and persisted, until it produced a vision of his body totally frozen. This was too much, and he made another wild run along the trail. Once he slowed down to a walk, but the thought of the freezing extending itself made him run again.

And all the time the dog ran with him, at his heels. When he fell down a second time, it curled its tail over its forefeet and sat in front of him, facing him, curiously eager and intent. The warmth and security of the animal angered him, and he cursed it till it flattened down its ears appeasingly. This time the shivering came more quickly upon the man. He was losing in his battle with the frost. It was creeping into his body from all sides. The thought of it drove him on, but he ran no more than a hundred feet, when he staggered and pitched headlong. It was his last panic. When he had recovered his breath and control, he sat up and entertained in his mind the conception of meeting death with dignity. However, the conception did not come to him in such terms. His idea of it was that he had been making a fool of himself, running around like a chicken with its head cut off—such was the simile that occurred to him. Well, he was bound to freeze anyway, and he might as well take it decently. With this new-found peace of mind came the first glimmerings of drowsiness. A good idea, he thought, to sleep off to death. It was like taking an anesthetic. Freezing was not so bad as people thought. There were lots worse ways to die.

He pictured the boys finding his body next day. Suddenly he found himself with them, coming along the trail and looking for himself. And, still with them, he came around a turn in the trail and found himself lying in the snow. He did not belong with himself any more, for even then he was out of himself, standing with the boys and looking at himself in the snow. It certainly was cold, was his thought. When he got back to the States he could tell the folks what real cold was. He drifted on from this to a vision of the old-timer on Sulphur Creek. He could see him quite clearly, warm and comfortable, and smoking a pipe.

"You were right, old hoss; you were right," the man mumbled to the old-timer of   40 Sulphur Creek.

Then the man drowsed off into what seemed to him the most comfortable and satisfying sleep he had ever known. The dog sat facing him and waiting. The brief day drew to a close in a long, slow twilight. There were no signs of a fire to be made, and, besides, never in the dog's experience had it known a man to sit like that in the snow and make no fire. As the twilight drew on, its eager yearning for the fire mastered it, and with a great lifting and shifting of forefeet, it whined softly, then flattened its ears down in anticipation of being chidden by the man. But the man remained silent. Later the dog whined loudly. And still later it crept close to the man and caught the scent of death. This made the animal bristle and back away. A little longer it delayed, howling under the stars that leaped and danced and shone brightly in the cold sky. Then it turned and trotted up the trail in the direction of the camp it knew, where were the other food providers and fire providers.

Questions

1. Roughly how much of London's story is devoted to describing the setting? What particular details make it memorable?
2. To what extent does setting determine what happens in this story?
3. From what point of view is London's story told?
4. In "To Build a Fire" the man is never given a name. What is the effect of his being called simply "the man" throughout the story?
5. From the evidence London gives us, what stages are involved in the process of freezing to death? What does the story gain from London's detailed account of the man's experience with each successive stage?
6. What are the most serious mistakes the man makes? To what factors do you attribute these errors?

T. Coraghessan Boyle

Greasy Lake   1985

*T. Coraghessan Boyle (the T. stands for Tom)
was born in 1948 in Peekskill, New York, the son
of Irish immigrants. He grew up, he recalls, "as a
sort of pampered punk" who did not read a book
until he was eighteen. After a brief period as a high
school teacher, he studied in the University of
Iowa Writers' Workshop, submitting a collection
of stories for his Ph.D. His stories in Esquire,
Paris Review, the Atlantic, and other magazines
quickly won him notice for their outrageous
macabre humor and bizarre inventiveness. Boyle
has published seven volumes of short stories, including* Greasy Lake *(1985),* T.C. Boyle
Stories *(1998), and* Tooth and Claw *(2005).
He has also published nine novels that are quite
unlike anything else in contemporary American
fiction. The subjects of some Boyle novels reveal*
his wide-ranging and idiosyncratic interests. Budding Prospects *(1984) is a picaresque romp
among adventurous marijuana growers.* East Is East *(1990) is a half-serious, half-comic story
of a Japanese fugitive in an American writers' colony.* The Road to Wellville *(1993) takes
place in 1907 in a sanitarium run by Dr. John Harvey Kellogg of corn flakes fame, with cameo
appearances by Henry Ford, Thomas Edison, and Harvey Firestone. Boyle's most recent novel
is* The Women *(2009). He lives in Southern California.*

T. Coraghessan Boyle

It's about a mile down on the dark side of Route 88.

— BRUCE SPRINGSTEEN

There was a time when courtesy and winning ways went out of style, when it was
good to be bad, when you cultivated decadence like a taste. We were all dangerous
characters then. We wore torn-up leather jackets, slouched around with toothpicks in
our mouths, sniffed glue and ether and what somebody claimed was cocaine. When we
wheeled our parents' whining station wagons out onto the street we left a patch of rubber half a block long. We drank gin and grape juice, Tango, Thunderbird, and Bali Hai.
We were nineteen. We were bad. We read André Gide° and struck elaborate poses to
show that we didn't give a shit about anything. At night, we went up to Greasy Lake.

Through the center of town, up the strip, past the housing developments and
shopping malls, street lights giving way to the thin streaming illumination of the
headlights, trees crowding the asphalt in a black unbroken wall: that was the way out
to Greasy Lake. The Indians had called it Wakan, a reference to the clarity of its
waters. Now it was fetid and murky, the mud banks glittering with broken glass and
strewn with beer cans and the charred remains of bonfires. There was a single ravaged
island a hundred yards from shore, so stripped of vegetation it looked as if the air force
had strafed it. We went up to the lake because everyone went there, because we
wanted to snuff the rich scent of possibility on the breeze, watch a girl take off her

---

André Gide: controversial French writer (1869–1951) whose novels, including *The Counterfeiters* and
Lafcadio's Adventures, often show individuals in conflict with accepted morality.

clothes and plunge into the festering murk, drink beer, smoke pot, howl at the stars, savor the incongruous full-throated roar of rock and roll against the primeval susurrus of frogs and crickets. This was nature.

I was there one night, late, in the company of two dangerous characters. Digby wore a gold star in his right ear and allowed his father to pay his tuition at Cornell; Jeff was thinking of quitting school to become a painter/musician/head-shop proprietor. They were both expert in the social graces, quick with a sneer, able to manage a Ford with lousy shocks over a rutted and gutted blacktop road at eighty-five while rolling a joint as compact as a Tootsie Roll Pop stick. They could lounge against a bank of booming speakers and trade "man"s with the best of them or roll out across the dance floor as if their joints worked on bearings. They were slick and quick and they wore their mirror shades at breakfast and dinner, in the shower, in closets and caves. In short, they were bad.

I drove. Digby pounded the dashboard and shouted along with Toots & the Maytals while Jeff hung his head out the window and streaked the side of my mother's Bel Air with vomit. It was early June, the air soft as a hand on your cheek, the third night of summer vacation. The first two nights we'd been out till dawn, looking for something we never found. On this, the third night, we'd cruised the strip sixty-seven times, been in and out of every bar and club we could think of in a twenty-mile radius, stopped twice for bucket chicken and forty-cent hamburgers, debated going to a party at the house of a girl Jeff's sister knew, and chucked two dozen raw eggs at mailboxes and hitchhikers. It was 2:00 A.M.; the bars were closing. There was nothing to do but take a bottle of lemon-flavored gin up to Greasy Lake.

The taillights of a single car winked at us as we swung into the dirt lot with its   5
tufts of weed and washboard corrugations; '57 Chevy, mint, metallic blue. On the far side of the lot, like the exoskeleton of some gaunt chrome insect, a chopper leaned against its kickstand. And that was it for excitement: some junkie halfwit biker and a car freak pumping his girlfriend. Whatever it was we were looking for, we weren't about to find it at Greasy Lake. Not that night.

But then all of a sudden Digby was fighting for the wheel. "Hey, that's Tony Lovett's car! Hey!" he shouted, while I stabbed at the brake pedal and the Bel Air nosed up to the gleaming bumper of the parked Chevy. Digby leaned on the horn, laughing, and instructed me to put my brights on. I flicked on the brights. This was hilarious. A joke. Tony would experience premature withdrawal and expect to be confronted by grim-looking state troopers with flashlights. We hit the horn, strobed the lights, and then jumped out of the car to press our witty faces to Tony's windows; for all we knew we might even catch a glimpse of some little fox's tit, and then we could slap backs with red-faced Tony, roughhouse a little, and go on to new heights of adventure and daring.

The first mistake, the one that opened the whole floodgate, was losing my grip on the keys. In the excitement, leaping from the car with the gin in one hand and a roach clip in the other, I spilled them in the grass—in the dark, rank, mysterious nighttime grass of Greasy Lake. This was a tactical error, as damaging and irreversible in its way as Westmoreland's decision to dig in at Khe Sanh.° I felt it like a jab of

---

Westmoreland's decision . . . Khe Sanh: General William C. Westmoreland commanded U.S. troops in Vietnam (1964–68). In late 1967 the North Vietnamese and Viet Cong forces attacked Khe Sanh (or Khesanh) with a show of strength, causing Westmoreland to expend great effort to defend a plateau of relatively little tactical importance.

intuition, and I stopped there by the open door, peering vaguely into the night that puddled up round my feet.

The second mistake—and this was inextricably bound up with the first—was identifying the car as Tony Lovett's. Even before the very bad character in greasy jeans and engineer boots ripped out of the driver's door, I began to realize that this chrome blue was much lighter than the robin's-egg of Tony's car, and that Tony's car didn't have rear-mounted speakers. Judging from their expressions, Digby and Jeff were privately groping toward the same inevitable and unsettling conclusion as I was.

In any case, there was no reasoning with this bad greasy character—clearly he was a man of action. The first lusty Rockette° kick of his steel-toed boot caught me under the chin, chipped my favorite tooth, and left me sprawled in the dirt. Like a fool, I'd gone down on one knee to comb the stiff hacked grass for the keys, my mind making connections in the most dragged-out, testudineous way, knowing that things had gone wrong, that I was in a lot of trouble, and that the lost ignition key was my grail and my salvation. The three or four succeeding blows were mainly absorbed by my right buttock and the tough piece of bone at the base of my spine.

Meanwhile, Digby vaulted the kissing bumpers and delivered a savage kung-fu blow to the greasy character's collarbone. Digby had just finished a course in martial arts for phys-ed credit and had spent the better part of the past two nights telling us apocryphal tales of Bruce Lee types and of the raw power invested in lightning blows shot from coiled wrists, ankles, and elbows. The greasy character was unimpressed. He merely backed off a step, his face like a Toltec mask, and laid Digby out with a single whistling roundhouse blow . . . but by now Jeff had got into the act, and I was beginning to extricate myself from the dirt, a tinny compound of shock, rage, and impotence wadded in my throat. 10

Jeff was on the guy's back, biting at his ear. Digby was on the ground, cursing. I went for the tire iron I kept under the driver's seat. I kept it there because bad characters always keep tire irons under the driver's seat, for just such an occasion as this. Never mind that I hadn't been involved in a fight since sixth grade, when a kid with a sleepy eye and two streams of mucus depending from his nostrils hit me in the knee with a Louisville slugger,° never mind that I'd touched the tire iron exactly twice before, to change tires: it was there. And I went for it.

I was terrified. Blood was beating in my ears, my hands were shaking, my heart turning over like a dirtbike in the wrong gear. My antagonist was shirtless, and a single cord of muscle flashed across his chest as he bent forward to peel Jeff from his back like a wet overcoat. "Motherfucker," he spat, over and over, and I was aware in that instant that all four of us—Digby, Jeff, and myself included—were chanting "motherfucker, motherfucker," as if it were a battle cry. (What happened next? the detective asks the murderer from beneath the turned-down brim of his porkpie hat. I don't know, the murderer says, something came over me. Exactly.)

Digby poked the flat of his hand in the bad character's face and I came at him like a kamikaze, mindless, raging, stung with humiliation—the whole thing, from the initial boot in the chin to this murderous primal instant involving no more than sixty hyperventilating, gland-flooding seconds—I came at him and brought the tire iron down across his ear. The effect was instantaneous, astonishing. He was a stunt man

Rockette: member of a dance troupe in the stage show at Radio City Music Hall, New York, famous for its ability to kick fast and high with wonderful coordination. *Louisville slugger:* a brand of baseball bat.

and this was Hollywood, he was a big grimacing toothy balloon and I was a man with a straight pin. He collapsed. Wet his pants. Went loose in his boots.

A single second, big as a zeppelin, floated by. We were standing over him in a circle, gritting our teeth, jerking our necks, our limbs and hands and feet twitching with glandular discharges. No one said anything. We just stared down at the guy, the car freak, the lover, the bad greasy character laid low. Digby looked at me; so did Jeff. I was still holding the tire iron, a tuft of hair clinging to the crook like dandelion fluff, like down. Rattled, I dropped it in the dirt, already envisioning the headlines, the pitted faces of the police inquisitors, the gleam of handcuffs, clank of bars, the big black shadows rising from the back of the cell . . . when suddenly a raw torn shriek cut through me like all the juice in all the electric chairs in the country.

It was the fox. She was short, barefoot, dressed in panties and a man's shirt. 15 "Animals!" she screamed, running at us with her fists clenched and wisps of blow-dried hair in her face. There was a silver chain round her ankle, and her toenails flashed in the glare of the headlights. I think it was the toenails that did it. Sure, the gin and the cannabis and even the Kentucky Fried may have had a hand in it, but it was the sight of those flaming toes that set us off—the toad emerging from the loaf in *Virgin Spring*,° lipstick smeared on a child; she was already tainted. We were on her like Bergman's deranged brothers—see no evil, hear none, speak none—panting, wheezing, tearing at her clothes, grabbing for flesh. We were bad characters, and we were scared and hot and three steps over the line—anything could have happened.

It didn't.

Before we could pin her to the hood of the car, our eyes masked with lust and greed and the purest primal badness, a pair of headlights swung into the lot. There we were, dirty, bloody, guilty, dissociated from humanity and civilization, the first of the Ur-crimes behind us, the second in progress, shreds of nylon panty and spandex brassiere dangling from our fingers, our flies open, lips licked—there we were, caught in the spotlight. Nailed.

We bolted. First for the car, and then, realizing we had no way of starting it, for the woods. I thought nothing. I thought escape. The headlights came at me like accusing fingers. I was gone.

Ram-bam-bam, across the parking lot, past the chopper and into the feculent undergrowth at the lake's edge, insects flying up in my face, weeds whipping, frogs and snakes and red-eyed turtles splashing off into the night: I was already ankle-deep in muck and tepid water and still going strong. Behind me, the girl's screams rose in intensity, disconsolate, incriminating, the screams of the Sabine women,° the Christian martyrs, Anne Frank° dragged from the garret. I kept going, pursued by those cries, imagining cops and bloodhounds. The water was up to my knees when I realized what I was doing: I was going to swim for it. Swim the breadth of Greasy Lake and hide myself in the thick clot of woods on the far side. They'd never find me there.

Virgin Spring: film by Swedish director Ingmar Bergman (1960).   *Sabine women*: members of an ancient tribe in Italy, according to legend, forcibly carried off by the early Romans under Romulus to be their wives. The incident is depicted in a famous painting, "The Rape of the Sabine Women," by seventeenth-century French artist Nicolas Poussin. *Anne Frank*: German Jewish girl (1929–1945) whose diary written during the Nazi occupation of the Netherlands later became world-famous. She hid with her family in a secret attic in Amsterdam, but was caught by the Gestapo and sent to the concentration camp at Belsen, where she died.

I was breathing in sobs, in gasps. The water lapped at my waist as I looked out   20
over the moon-burnished ripples, the mats of algae that clung to the surface like
scabs. Digby and Jeff had vanished. I paused. Listened. The girl was quieter now,
screams tapering to sobs, but there were male voices, angry, excited, and the high-
pitched ticking of the second car's engine. I waded deeper, stealthy, hunted, the ooze
sucking at my sneakers. As I was about to take the plunge—at the very instant I
dropped my shoulder for the first slashing stroke—I blundered into something. Something unspeakable, obscene, something soft, wet, moss-grown. A patch of weed? A
log? When I reached out to touch it, it gave like a rubber duck, it gave like flesh.

In one of those nasty little epiphanies for which we are prepared by films and
TV and childhood visits to the funeral home to ponder the shrunken painted
forms of dead grandparents, I understood what it was that bobbed there so inad-
missibly in the dark. Understood, and stumbled back in horror and revulsion, my
mind yanked in six different directions (I was nineteen, a mere child, an infant,
and here in the space of five minutes I'd struck down one greasy character and
blundered into the waterlogged carcass of a second), thinking, The keys, the keys,
why did I have to go and lose the keys? I stumbled back, but the muck took hold of
my feet—a sneaker snagged, balance lost—and suddenly I was pitching face forward into the buoyant black mass, throwing out my hands in desperation while simultaneously conjuring the image of reeking frogs and muskrats revolving in slicks
of their own deliquescing juices. AAAAArrrgh! I shot from the water like a tor-
pedo, the dead man rotating to expose a mossy beard and eyes cold as the moon. I
must have shouted out, thrashing around in the weeds, because the voices behind
me suddenly became animated.

"What was that?"

"It's them, it's them: they tried to, tried to . . . *rape* me!" Sobs.

A man's voice, flat Midwestern accent. "You sons a bitches, we'll kill you!"

Frogs, crickets.   25

Then another voice, harsh, r-less, Lower East Side: "Motherfucker!" I recognized the verbal virtuosity of the bad greasy character in the engineer boots. Tooth
chipped, sneakers gone, coated in mud and slime and worse, crouching breathless in
the weeds waiting to have my ass thoroughly and definitively kicked and fresh from
the hideous stinking embrace of a three-days-dead-corpse, I suddenly felt a rush of
joy and vindication: the son of a bitch was alive! Just as quickly, my bowels turned to
ice. "Come on out of there, you pansy mothers!" the bad greasy character was
screaming. He shouted curses till he was out of breath.

The crickets started up again, then the frogs. I held my breath. All at once there
was a sound in the reeds, a swishing, a splash: thunk-a-thunk. They were throwing
rocks. The frogs fell silent. I cradled my head. Swish, swish, thunk-a-thunk. A wedge
of feldspar the size of a cue ball glanced off my knee. I bit my finger.

It was then that they turned to the car. I heard a door slam, a curse, and then the
sound of the headlights shattering—almost a good-natured sound, celebratory, like
corks popping from the necks of bottles. This was succeeded by the dull booming of
the fenders, metal on metal, and then the icy crash of the windshield. I inched forward, elbows and knees, my belly pressed to the muck, thinking of guerrillas and
commandos and *The Naked and the Dead*.° I parted the weeds and squinted the
length of the parking lot.

The Naked and the Dead: novel (1948) by Norman Mailer, about U.S. Army life in World War II.

The second car—it was a Trans-Am—was still running, its high beams washing
the scene in a lurid stagy light. Tire iron flailing, the greasy bad character was laying
into the side of my mother's Bel Air like an avenging demon, his shadow riding up
the trunks of the trees. Whomp. Whomp. Whomp-whomp. The other two guys—
blond types, in fraternity jackets—were helping out with tree branches and skull-
sized boulders. One of them was gathering up bottles, rocks, muck, candy wrappers,
used condoms, poptops, and other refuse and pitching it through the window on the
driver's side. I could see the fox, a white bulb behind the windshield of the '57
Chevy. "Bobbie," she whined over the thumping, "come on." The greasy character
paused a moment, took one good swipe at the left taillight, and then heaved the tire
iron halfway across the lake. Then he fired up the '57 and was gone.

Blond head nodded at blond head. One said something to the other, too low for   30
me to catch. They were no doubt thinking that in helping to annihilate my
mother's car they'd committed a fairly rash act, and thinking too that there were
three bad characters connected with that very car watching them from the woods.
Perhaps other possibilities occurred to them as well—police, jail cells, justices of the
peace, reparations, lawyers, irate parents, fraternal censure. Whatever they were
thinking, they suddenly dropped branches, bottles, and rocks and sprang for their
car in unison, as if they'd choreographed it. Five seconds. That's all it took. The engine shrieked, the tires squealed, a cloud of dust rose from the rutted lot and then
settled back on darkness.

I don't know how long I lay there, the bad breath of decay all around me, my
jacket heavy as a bear, the primordial ooze subtly reconstituting itself to accommodate my upper thighs and testicles. My jaws ached, my knee throbbed, my coccyx
was on fire. I contemplated suicide, wondered if I'd need bridgework, scraped the
recesses of my brain for some sort of excuse to give my parents—a tree had fallen
on the car, I was blinded by a bread truck, hit and run, vandals had got to it while
we were playing chess at Digby's. Then I thought of the dead man. He was probably
the only person on the planet worse off than I was. I thought about him, fog on the
lake, insects chirring eerily, and felt the tug of fear, felt the darkness opening up inside me like a set of jaws. Who was he, I wondered, this victim of time and circumstance bobbing sorrowfully in the lake at my back. The owner of the chopper, no
doubt, a bad older character come to this. Shot during a murky drug deal, drowned
while drunkenly frolicking in the lake. Another headline. My car was wrecked; he
was dead.

When the eastern half of the sky went from black to cobalt and the trees began
to separate themselves from the shadows, I pushed myself up from the mud and
stepped out into the open. By now the birds had begun to take over for the crickets,
and dew lay slick on the leaves. There was a smell in the air, raw and sweet at the
same time, the smell of the sun firing buds and opening blossoms. I contemplated the
car. It lay there like a wreck along the highway, like a steel sculpture left over from a
vanished civilization. Everything was still. This was nature.

I was circling the car, as dazed and bedraggled as the sole survivor of an air blitz,
when Digby and Jeff emerged from the trees behind me. Digby's face was cross-
hatched with smears of dirt; Jeff's jacket was gone and his shirt was torn across the
shoulder. They slouched across the lot, looking sheepish, and silently came up beside
me to gape at the ravaged automobile. No one said a word. After a while Jeff swung
open the driver's door and began to scoop the broken glass and garbage off the seat. I
looked at Digby. He shrugged. "At least they didn't slash the tires," he said.

It was true: the tires were intact. There was no windshield, the headlights were staved in, and the body looked as if it had been sledge-hammered for a quarter a shot at the county fair, but the tires were inflated to regulation pressure. The car was drivable. In silence, all three of us bent to scrape the mud and shattered glass from the interior. I said nothing about the biker. When we were finished, I reached in my pocket for the keys, experienced a nasty stab of recollection, cursed myself, and turned to search the grass. I spotted them almost immediately, no more than five feet from the open door, glinting like jewels in the first tapering shaft of sunlight. There was no reason to get philosophical about it: I eased into the seat and turned the engine over.

It was at that precise moment that the silver Mustang with the flame decals rumbled into the lot. All three of us froze; then Digby and Jeff slid into the car and slammed the door. We watched as the Mustang rocked and bobbed across the ruts and finally jerked to a halt beside the forlorn chopper at the far end of the lot. "Let's go," Digby said. I hesitated, the Bel Air wheezing beneath me.

Two girls emerged from the Mustang. Tight jeans, stiletto heels, hair like frozen fur. They bent over the motorcycle, paced back and forth aimlessly, glanced once or twice at us, and then ambled over to where the reeds sprang up in a green fence round the perimeter of the lake. One of them cupped her hands to her mouth. "Al," she called. "Hey, Al!"

"Come on," Digby hissed. "Let's get out of here."

But it was too late. The second girl was picking her way across the lot, unsteady on her heels, looking up at us and then away. She was older—twenty-five or -six— and as she came closer we could see there was something wrong with her: she was stoned or drunk, lurching now and waving her arms for balance. I gripped the steering wheel as if it were the ejection lever of a flaming jet, and Digby spat out my name, twice, terse and impatient.

"Hi," the girl said.

We looked at her like zombies, like war veterans, like deaf-and-dumb pencil peddlers.

She smiled, her lips cracked and dry. "Listen," she said, bending from the waist to look in the window, "you guys seen Al?" Her pupils were pinpoints, her eyes glass. She jerked her neck. "That's his bike over there—Al's. You seen him?"

Al. I didn't know what to say. I wanted to get out of the car and retch, I wanted to go home to my parents' house and crawl into bed. Digby poked me in the ribs. "We haven't seen anybody," I said.

The girl seemed to consider this, reaching out a slim veiny arm to brace herself against the car. "No matter," she said, slurring the t's, "he'll turn up." And then, as if she'd just taken stock of the whole scene—the ravaged car and our battered faces, the desolation of the place—she said: "Hey, you guys look like some pretty bad characters—been fightin', huh?" We stared straight ahead, rigid as catatonics. She was fumbling in her pocket and muttering something. Finally she held out a handful of tablets in glassine wrappers: "Hey, you want to party, you want to do some of these with me and Sarah?"

I just looked at her. I thought I was going to cry. Digby broke the silence. "No, thanks," he said, leaning over me. "Some other time."

I put the car in gear and it inched forward with a groan, shaking off pellets of glass like an old dog shedding water after a bath, heaving over the ruts on its worn springs, creeping toward the highway. There was a sheen of sun on the lake. I looked back. The girl was still standing there, watching us, her shoulders slumped, hand outstretched.

Questions

1. Around what year, would you say, was it that "courtesy and winning ways went out of style, when it was good to be bad, when you cultivated decadence like a taste"?

2. What is it about Digby and Jeff that inspires the narrator to call them "bad"?

3. Twice in "Greasy Lake"—in paragraphs 2 and 32—appear the words, "This was nature." What contrasts do you find between the "nature" of the narrator's earlier and later views?

4. What makes the narrator and his friends run off into the woods?

5. How does the young men's encounter with the two girls at the end of the story differ from their earlier encounter with the girl from the blue Chevy? How do you account for the difference? When at the end of the story the girl offers to party with the three friends, what makes the narrator say, "I thought I was going to cry"?

6. How important to what happens in this story is Greasy Lake itself? What details about the lake and its shores strike you as particularly memorable (whether funny, disgusting, or both)?

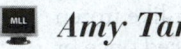

Amy Tan

A Pair of Tickets   1989

Amy Tan was born in Oakland, California, in 1952. Both of her parents were recent Chinese immigrants. Her father was an electrical engineer (as well as a Baptist minister); her mother was a vocational nurse. When her father and older brother both died of brain tumors, the fifteen-year-old Tan moved with her mother and younger brother to Switzerland, where she attended high school. On their return to the United States Tan attended Linfield College, a Baptist school in Oregon, but she eventually transferred to California State University at San Jose. At this time Tan and her mother argued about her future. The mother insisted her daughter pursue premedical studies in preparation for becoming a neu-rosurgeon, but Tan wanted to do something else. For six months the two did not speak to one another. Tan worked for IBM writing computer manuals and also wrote freelance business articles under a pseudonym. In 1987 she and her mother visited China together. This experience, which is reflected in "A Pair of Tickets," deepened Tan's sense of her Chinese American identity. "As soon as my feet touched China," she wrote, "I became Chinese." Soon after, she began writing her first novel, The Joy Luck Club (1989), which consists of sixteen interrelated stories about a group of Chinese American mothers and their daughters. (The club of the title is a woman's social group.) The Joy Luck Club became both a critical success and a best seller, and was made into a movie in 1993. In 1991 Tan published her second novel, The Kitchen God's Wife. Her later novels include The Bonesetter's Daughter (2001) and Saving Fish from Drowning (2005). Tan performs with a "vintage garage" band called the Rock Bottom Remainders, which also includes, among others, Stephen King, Dave Barry, and Scott Turow. She lives outside San Francisco with her husband.

The minute our train leaves the Hong Kong border and enters Shenzhen, China, I feel different. I can feel the skin on my forehead tingling, my blood rushing through a new course, my bones aching with a familiar old pain. And I think, My mother was right. I am becoming Chinese.

"Cannot be helped," my mother said when I was fifteen and had vigorously denied that I had any Chinese whatsoever below my skin. I was a sophomore at Galileo High in San Francisco, and all my Caucasian friends agreed: I was about as Chinese as they were. But my mother had studied at a famous nursing school in Shanghai, and she said she knew all about genetics. So there was no doubt in her mind, whether I agreed or not: Once you are born Chinese, you cannot help but feel and think Chinese.

"Someday you will see," said my mother. "It is in your blood, waiting to be let go."

And when she said this, I saw myself transforming like a werewolf, a mutant tag of DNA suddenly triggered, replicating itself insidiously into a *syndrome*,° a cluster of telltale Chinese behaviors, all those things my mother did to embarrass me—haggling with store owners, pecking her mouth with a toothpick in public, being color-blind to the fact that lemon yellow and pale pink are not good combinations for winter clothes.

But today I realize I've never really known what it means to be Chinese. I am   5
thirty-six years old. My mother is dead and I am on a train, carrying with me her dreams of coming home. I am going to China.

We are first going to Guangzhou, my seventy-two-year-old father, Canning Woo, and I, where we will visit his aunt, whom he has not seen since he was ten years old. And I don't know whether it's the prospect of seeing his aunt or if it's because he's back in China, but now he looks like he's a young boy, so innocent and happy I want to button his sweater and pat his head. We are sitting across from each other, separated by a little table with two cold cups of tea. For the first time I can ever remember, my father has tears in his eyes, and all he is seeing out the train window is a sectioned field of yellow, green, and brown, a narrow canal flanking the tracks, low rising hills, and three people in blue jackets riding an ox-driven cart on this early October morning. And I can't help myself. I also have misty eyes, as if I had seen this a long, long time ago, and had almost forgotten.

In less than three hours, we will be in Guangzhou, which my guidebook tells me is how one properly refers to Canton these days. It seems all the cities I have heard of, except Shanghai, have changed their spellings. I think they are saying China has changed in other ways as well. Chungking is Chongqing. And Kweilin is Guilin. I have looked these names up, because after we see my father's aunt in Guangzhou, we will catch a plane to Shanghai, where I will meet my two half-sisters for the first time.

They are my mother's twin daughters from her first marriage, little babies she was forced to abandon on a road as she was fleeing Kweilin for Chungking in 1944. That was all my mother had told me about these daughters, so they had remained babies in my mind, all these years, sitting on the side of a road, listening to bombs whistling in the distance while sucking their patient red thumbs.

And it was only this year that someone found them and wrote with this joyful news. A letter came from Shanghai, addressed to my mother. When I first heard about this, that they were alive, I imagined my identical sisters transforming from little babies into six-year-old girls. In my mind, they were seated next to each other at a table, taking turns with the fountain pen. One would write a neat row of characters: *Dearest Mama. We are alive.* She would brush back her wispy bangs and hand the other sister the pen, and she would write: *Come get us. Please hurry.*

Of course they could not know that my mother had died three months before,   10
suddenly, when a blood vessel in her brain burst. One minute she was talking to my father, complaining about the tenants upstairs, scheming how to evict them under the pretense that relatives from China were moving in. The next minute she was holding her head, her eyes squeezed shut, groping for the sofa, and then crumpling softly to the floor with fluttering hands.

---

syndrome: a group of symptoms that occur together as the sign of a particular disease or abnormality.

So my father had been the first one to open the letter, a long letter it turned out. And they did call her Mama. They said they always revered her as their true mother. They kept a framed picture of her. They told her about their life, from the time my mother last saw them on the road leaving Kweilin to when they were finally found.

And the letter had broken my father's heart so much—these daughters calling my mother from another life he never knew—that he gave the letter to my mother's old friend Auntie Lindo and asked her to write back and tell my sisters, in the gentlest way possible, that my mother was dead.

But instead Auntie Lindo took the letter to the Joy Luck Club and discussed with Auntie Ying and Auntie An-mei what should be done, because they had known for many years about my mother's search for her twin daughters, her endless hope. Auntie Lindo and the others cried over this double tragedy, of losing my mother three months before, and now again. And so they couldn't help but think of some miracle, some possible way of reviving her from the dead, so my mother could fulfill her dream.

So this is what they wrote to my sisters in Shanghai: "Dearest Daughters, I too have never forgotten you in my memory or in my heart. I never gave up hope that we would see each other again in a joyous reunion. I am only sorry it has been too long. I want to tell you everything about my life since I last saw you. I want to tell you this when our family comes to see you in China. . . ." They signed it with my mother's name.

It wasn't until all this had been done that they first told me about my sisters, the letter they received, the one they wrote back. 15

"They'll think she's coming, then," I murmured. And I had imagined my sisters now being ten or eleven, jumping up and down, holding hands, their pigtails bouncing, excited that their mother—*their* mother—was coming, whereas my mother was dead.

"How can you say she is not coming in a letter?" said Auntie Lindo. "She is their mother. She is your mother. You must be the one to tell them. All these years, they have been dreaming of her." And I thought she was right.

But then I started dreaming, too, of my mother and my sisters and how it would be if I arrived in Shanghai. All these years, while they waited to be found, I had lived with my mother and then had lost her. I imagined seeing my sisters at the airport. They would be standing on their tip-toes, looking anxiously, scanning from one dark head to another as we got off the plane. And I would recognize them instantly, their faces with the identical worried look.

"*Jyejye, Jyejye.* Sister, Sister. We are here," I saw myself saying in my poor version of Chinese.

"Where is Mama?" they would say, and look around, still smiling, two flushed and eager faces. "Is she hiding?" And this would have been like my mother, to stand behind just a bit, to tease a little and make people's patience pull a little on their hearts. I would shake my head and tell my sisters she was not hiding. 20

"Oh, that must be Mama, no?" one of my sisters would whisper excitedly, pointing to another small woman completely engulfed in a tower of presents. And that, too, would have been like my mother, to bring mountains of gifts, food, and toys for children—all bought on sale—shunning thanks, saying the gifts were nothing, and later turning the labels over to show my sisters, "Calvin Klein, 100% wool."

I imagined myself starting to say, "Sisters, I am sorry, I have come alone . . ." and before I could tell them—they could see it in my face—they were wailing, pulling their hair, their lips twisted in pain, as they ran away from me. And then I saw myself getting back on the plane and coming home.

After I had dreamed this scene many times—watching their despair turn from horror into anger—I begged Auntie Lindo to write another letter. And at first she refused.

"How can I say she is dead? I cannot write this," said Auntie Lindo with a stubborn look.

"But it's cruel to have them believe she's coming on the plane," I said. "When they see it's just me, they'll hate me."   25

"Hate you? Cannot be." She was scowling. "You are their own sister, their only family."

"You don't understand," I protested.

"What I don't understand?" she said.

And I whispered, "They'll think I'm responsible, that she died because I didn't appreciate her."

And Auntie Lindo looked satisfied and sad at the same time, as if this were true   30 and I had finally realized it. She sat down for an hour, and when she stood up she handed me a two-page letter. She had tears in her eyes. I realized that the very thing I had feared, she had done. So even if she had written the news of my mother's death in English, I wouldn't have had the heart to read it.

"Thank you," I whispered.

The landscape has become gray, filled with low flat cement buildings, old factories, and then tracks and more tracks filled with trains like ours passing by in the opposite direction. I see platforms crowded with people wearing drab Western clothes, with spots of bright colors: little children wearing pink and yellow, red and peach. And there are soldiers in olive green and red, and old ladies in gray tops and pants that stop mid-calf. We are in Guangzhou.

Before the train even comes to a stop, people are bringing down their belongings from above their seats. For a moment there is a dangerous shower of heavy suitcases laden with gifts to relatives, half-broken boxes wrapped in miles of string to keep the contents from spilling out, plastic bags filled with yarn and vegetables and packages of dried mushrooms, and camera cases. And then we are caught in a stream of people rushing, shoving, pushing us along, until we find ourselves in one of a dozen lines waiting to go through customs. I feel as if I were getting on the number 30 Stockton bus in San Francisco. I am in China, I remind myself. And somehow the crowds don't bother me. It feels right. I start pushing too.

I take out the declaration forms and my passport. "Woo," it says at the top, and below that, "June May," who was born in "California, U.S.A.," in 1951. I wonder if the customs people will question whether I'm the same person in the passport photo. In this picture, my chin-length hair is swept back and artfully styled. I am wearing false eyelashes, eye shadow, and lip liner. My cheeks are hollowed out by bronze blusher. But I had not expected the heat in October. And now my hair hangs limp with the humidity. I wear no makeup; in Hong Kong my mascara had melted into dark circles and everything else had felt like layers of grease. So today my face is plain, unadorned except for a thin mist of shiny sweat on my forehead and nose.

Even without makeup, I could never pass for true Chinese. I stand five-foot-six,   35 and my head pokes above the crowd so that I am eye level only with other tourists. My mother once told me my height came from my grandfather, who was a northerner, and may have even had some Mongol blood. "This is what your grandmother once told me," explained my mother. "But now it is too late to ask her. They are all dead, your grandparents, your uncles, and their wives and children, all killed in the war, when a bomb fell on our house. So many generations in one instant."

She had said this so matter-of-factly that I thought she had long since gotten over any grief she had. And then I wondered how she knew they were all dead.

"Maybe they left the house before the bomb fell," I suggested.

"No," said my mother. "Our whole family is gone. It is just you and I."

"But how do you know? Some of them could have escaped."

"Cannot be," said my mother, this time almost angrily. And then her frown was washed over by a puzzled blank look, and she began to talk as if she were trying to remember where she had misplaced something. "I went back to that house. I kept looking up to where the house used to be. And it wasn't a house, just the sky. And below, underneath my feet, were four stories of burnt bricks and wood, all the life of our house. Then off to the side I saw things blown into the yard, nothing valuable. There was a bed someone used to sleep in, really just a metal frame twisted up at one corner. And a book, I don't know what kind, because every page had turned black. And I saw a teacup which was unbroken but filled with ashes. And then I found my doll, with her hands and legs broken, her hair burned off. . . . When I was a little girl, I had cried for that doll, seeing it all alone in the store window, and my mother had bought it for me. It was an American doll with yellow hair. It could turn its legs and arms. The eyes moved up and down. And when I married and left my family home, I gave the doll to my youngest niece, because she was like me. She cried if that doll was not with her always. Do you see? If she was in the house with that doll, her parents were there, and so everybody was there, waiting together, because that's how our family was." 40

The woman in the customs booth stares at my documents, then glances at me briefly, and with two quick movements stamps everything and sternly nods me along. And soon my father and I find ourselves in a large area filled with thousands of people and suitcases. I feel lost and my father looks helpless.

"Excuse me," I say to a man who looks like an American. "Can you tell me where I can get a taxi?" He mumbles something that sounds Swedish or Dutch.

"Syau Yen! Syau Yen!" I hear a piercing voice shout from behind me. An old woman in a yellow knit beret is holding up a pink plastic bag filled with wrapped trinkets. I guess she is trying to sell us something. But my father is staring down at this tiny sparrow of a woman, squinting into her eyes. And then his eyes widen, his face opens up and he smiles like a pleased little boy.

"Aiyi! Aiyi!" —Auntie Auntie!—he says softly.

"Syau Yen!" coos my great-aunt. I think it's funny she has just called my father "Little Wild Goose." It must be his baby milk name, the name used to discourage ghosts from stealing children. 45

They clasp each other's hands—they do not hug—and hold on like this, taking turns saying, "Look at you! You are so old. Look how old you've become!" They are both crying openly, laughing at the same time, and I bite my lip, trying not to cry. I'm afraid to feel their joy. Because I am thinking how different our arrival in Shanghai will be tomorrow, how awkward it will feel.

Now Aiyi beams and points to a Polaroid picture of my father. My father had wisely sent pictures when he wrote and said we were coming. See how smart she was, she seems to intone as she compares the picture to my father. In the letter, my father had said we would call her from the hotel once we arrived, so this is a surprise, that they've come to meet us. I wonder if my sisters will be at the airport.

It is only then that I remember the camera. I had meant to take a picture of my father and his aunt the moment they met. It's not too late.

"Here, stand together over here," I say, holding up the Polaroid. The camera flashes and I hand them the snapshot. Aiyi and my father still stand close together, each of them holding a corner of the picture, watching as their images begin to form. They are almost reverentially quiet. Aiyi is only five years older than my father, which makes her around seventy-seven. But she looks ancient, shrunken, a mummified relic. Her thin hair is pure white, her teeth are brown with decay. So much for stories of Chinese women looking young forever, I think to myself.

Now Aiyi is crooning to me: "*Jandale.*" So big already. She looks up at me, at my full height, and then peers into her pink plastic bag—her gifts to us, I have figured out—as if she is wondering what she will give to me, now that I am so old and big. And then she grabs my elbow with her sharp pincerlike grasp and turns me around. A man and woman in their fifties are shaking hands with my father, everybody smiling and saying, "Ah! Ah!" They are Aiyi's oldest son and his wife, and standing next to them are four other people, around my age, and a little girl who's around ten. The introductions go by so fast, all I know is that one of them is Aiyi's grandson, with his wife, and the other is her granddaughter, with her husband. And the little girl is Lili, Aiyi's great-granddaughter. 50

Aiyi and my father speak the Mandarin dialect from their childhood, but the rest of the family speaks only the Cantonese of their village. I understand only Mandarin but can't speak it that well. So Aiyi and my father gossip unrestrained in Mandarin, exchanging news about people from their old village. And they stop only occasionally to talk to the rest of us, sometimes in Cantonese, sometimes in English.

"Oh, it is as I suspected," says my father, turning to me. "He died last summer." And I already understood this. I just don't know who this person, Li Gong, is. I feel as if I were in the United Nations and the translators had run amok.

"Hello," I say to the little girl. "My name is Jing-mei." But the little girl squirms to look away, causing her parents to laugh with embarrassment. I try to think of Cantonese words I can say to her, stuff I learned from friends in Chinatown, but all I can think of are swear words, terms for bodily functions, and short phrases like "tastes good," "tastes like garbage," and "she's really ugly." And then I have another plan: I hold up the Polaroid camera, beckoning Lili with my finger. She immediately jumps forward, places one hand on her hip in the manner of a fashion model, juts out her chest, and flashes me a toothy smile. As soon as I take the picture she is standing next to me, jumping and giggling every few seconds as she watches herself appear on the greenish film.

By the time we hail taxis for the ride to the hotel, Lili is holding tight onto my hand, pulling me along.

In the taxi, Aiyi talks nonstop, so I have no chance to ask her about the different sights we are passing by. 55

"You wrote and said you would come only for one day," says Aiyi to my father in an agitated tone. "One day! How can you see your family in one day! Toishan is many hours' drive from Guangzhou. And this idea to call us when you arrive. This is nonsense. We have no telephone."

My heart races a little. I wonder if Auntie Lindo told my sisters we would call from the hotel in Shanghai?

Aiyi continues to scold my father. "I was so beside myself, ask my son, almost turned heaven and earth upside down trying to think of a way! So we decided the best was for us to take the bus from Toishan and come into Guangzhou—meet you right from the start."

And now I am holding my breath as the taxi driver dodges between trucks and buses, honking his horn constantly. We seem to be on some sort of long freeway overpass, like a bridge above the city. I can see row after row of apartments, each floor cluttered with laundry hanging out to dry on the balcony. We pass a public bus, with people jammed in so tight their faces are nearly wedged against the window. Then I see the skyline of what must be downtown Guangzhou. From a distance, it looks like a major American city, with high rises and construction going on everywhere. As we slow down in the more congested part of the city, I see scores of little shops, dark inside, lined with counters and shelves. And then there is a building, its front laced with scaffolding made of bamboo poles held together with plastic strips. Men and women are standing on narrow platforms, scraping the sides, working without safety straps or helmets. Oh, would OSHA° have a field day here, I think.

Aiyi's shrill voice rises up again: "So it is a shame you can't see our village, our   60
house. My sons have been quite successful, selling our vegetables in the free market. We had enough these last few years to build a big house, three stories, all of new brick, big enough for our whole family and then some. And every year, the money is even better. You Americans aren't the only ones who know how to get rich!"

The taxi stops and I assume we've arrived, but then I peer out at what looks like a grander version of the Hyatt Regency. "This is communist China?" I wonder out loud. And then I shake my head toward my father. "This must be the wrong hotel." I quickly pull out our itinerary, travel tickets, and reservations. I had explicitly instructed my travel agent to choose something inexpensive, in the thirty-to-forty-dollar range. I'm sure of this. And there it says on our itinerary: Garden Hotel, Huanshi Dong Lu. Well, our travel agent had better be prepared to eat the extra, that's all I have to say.

The hotel is magnificent. A bellboy complete with uniform and sharp-creased cap jumps forward and begins to carry our bags into the lobby. Inside, the hotel looks like an orgy of shopping arcades and restaurants all encased in granite and glass. And rather than be impressed, I am worried about the expense, as well as the appearance it must give Aiyi, that we rich Americans cannot be without our luxuries even for one night.

But when I step up to the reservation desk, ready to haggle over this booking mistake, it is confirmed. Our rooms are prepaid, thirty-four dollars each. I feel sheepish, and Aiyi and the others seem delighted by our temporary surroundings. Lili is looking wide-eyed at an arcade filled with video games.

Our whole family crowds into one elevator, and the bellboy waves, saying he will meet us on the eighteenth floor. As soon as the elevator door shuts, everybody becomes very quiet, and when the door finally opens again, everybody talks at once in what sounds like relieved voices. I have the feeling Aiyi and the others have never been on such a long elevator ride.

Our rooms are next to each other and are identical. The rugs, drapes, bedspreads   65
are all in shades of taupe. There's a color television with remote-control panels built

OSHA: Occupational Safety and Health Administration, a U.S. federal agency that regulates and monitors workplace safety conditions.

into the lamp table between the two twin beds. The bathroom has marble walls and floors. I find a built-in wet bar with a small refrigerator stocked with Heineken beer, Coke Classic, and Seven-Up, mini-bottles of Johnnie Walker Red, Bacardi rum, and Smirnoff vodka, and packets of M & M's, honey-roasted cashews, and Cadbury chocolate bars. And again I say out loud, "This is communist China?"

My father comes into my room. "They decided we should just stay here and visit," he says, shrugging his shoulders. "They say, Less trouble that way. More time to talk."

"What about dinner?" I ask. I have been envisioning my first real Chinese feast for many days already, a big banquet with one of those soups steaming out of a carved winter melon, chicken wrapped in clay, Peking duck, the works.

My father walks over and picks up a room service book next to a *Travel & Leisure* magazine. He flips through the pages quickly and then points to the menu. "This is what they want," says my father.

So it's decided. We are going to dine tonight in our rooms, with our family, sharing hamburgers, french fries, and apple pie à la mode.

Aiyi and her family are browsing the shops while we clean up. After a hot ride on the train, I'm eager for a shower and cooler clothes.   70

The hotel has provided little packets of shampoo which, upon opening, I discover is the consistency and color of hoisin sauce. This is more like it, I think. This is China. And I rub some in my damp hair.

Standing in the shower, I realize this is the first time I've been by myself in what seems like days. But instead of feeling relieved, I feel forlorn. I think about what my mother said, about activating my genes and becoming Chinese. And I wonder what she meant.

Right after my mother died, I asked myself a lot of things, things that couldn't be answered, to force myself to grieve more. It seemed as if I wanted to sustain my grief, to assure myself that I had cared deeply enough.

But now I ask the questions mostly because I want to know the answers. What was that pork stuff she used to make that had the texture of sawdust? What were the names of the uncles who died in Shanghai? What had she dreamt all these years about her other daughters? All the times when she got mad at me, was she really thinking about them? Did she wish I were they? Did she regret that I wasn't?

At one o'clock in the morning, I awake to tapping sounds on the window. I   75 must have dozed off and now I feel my body uncramping itself. I'm sitting on the floor, leaning against one of the twin beds. Lili is lying next to me. The others are asleep, too, sprawled out on the beds and floor. Aiyi is seated at a little table, looking very sleepy. And my father is staring out the window, tapping his fingers on the glass. The last time I listened my father was telling Aiyi about his life since he last saw her. How he had gone to Yenching University, later got a post with a newspaper in Chungking, met my mother there, a young widow. How they later fled together to Shanghai to try to find my mother's family house, but there was nothing there. And then they traveled eventually to Canton and then to Hong Kong, then Haiphong and finally to San Francisco. . . .

"Suyuan didn't tell me she was trying all these years to find her daughters," he is now saying in a quiet voice. "Naturally, I did not discuss her daughters with her. I thought she was ashamed she had left them behind."

"Where did she leave them?" asks Aiyi. "How were they found?"

I am wide awake now. Although I have heard parts of this story from my mother's friends.

"It happened when the Japanese took over Kweilin," says my father.

"Japanese in Kweilin?" says Aiyi. "That was never the case. Couldn't be. The 80 Japanese never came to Kweilin."

"Yes, that is what the newspapers reported. I know this because I was working for the news bureau at the time. The Kuomintang often told us what we could say and could not say. But we knew the Japanese had come into Kwangsi Province. We had sources who told us how they had captured the Wuchang-Canton railway. How they were coming overland, making very fast progress, marching toward the provincial capital."

Aiyi looks astonished. "If people did not know this, how could Suyuan know the Japanese were coming?"

"An officer of the Kuomintang secretly warned her," explains my father. "Suyuan's husband also was an officer and everybody knew that officers and their families would be the first to be killed. So she gathered a few possessions and, in the middle of the night, she picked up her daughters and fled on foot. The babies were not even one year old."

"How could she give up those babies!" sighs Aiyi. "Twin girls. We have never had such luck in our family." And then she yawns again.

"What were they named?" she asks. I listen carefully. I had been planning on us- 85 ing just the familiar "Sister" to address them both. But now I want to know how to pronounce their names.

"They have their father's surname, Wang," says my father. "And their given names are Chwun Yu and Chwun Hwa."

"What do the names mean?" I ask.

"Ah." My father draws imaginary characters on the window. "One means 'Spring Rain,' the other 'Spring Flower,' " he explains in English, "because they born in the spring, and of course rain come before flower, same order these girls are born. Your mother like a poet, don't you think?"

I nod my head. I see Aiyi nod her head forward, too. But it falls forward and stays there. She is breathing deeply, noisily. She is asleep.

"And what does Ma's name mean?" I whisper.

" 'Suyuan,' " he says, writing more invisible characters on the glass. "The way she 90 write it in Chinese, it mean 'Long-Cherished Wish.' Quite a fancy name, not so ordi- nary like flower name. See this first character, it mean something like 'Forever Never Forgotten.' But there is another way to write 'Suyuan.' Sound exactly the same, but the meaning is opposite." His finger creates the brushstrokes of another character. "The first part look the same: 'Never Forgotten.' But the last part add to first part make the whole word mean 'Long-Held Grudge.' Your mother get angry with me, I tell her her name should be Grudge."

My father is looking at me, moist-eyed. "See, I pretty clever, too, hah?"

I nod, wishing I could find some way to comfort him. "And what about my name," I ask, "what does 'Jing-mei' mean?"

"Your name also special," he says. I wonder if any name in Chinese is not some- thing special. " 'Jing' like excellent *jing*. Not just good, it's something pure, essential, the best quality. *Jing* is good leftover stuff when you take impurities out of something like gold, or rice, or salt. So what is left—just pure essence. And 'Mei,' this is com- mon *mei*, as in *meimei*, 'younger sister.' "

I think about this. My mother's long-cherished wish. Me, the younger sister who 95
was supposed to be the essence of the others. I feed myself with the old grief, wondering
how disappointed my mother must have been. Tiny Aiyi stirs suddenly, her head rolls
and then falls back, her mouth opens as if to answer my question. She grunts in her
sleep, tucking her body more closely into the chair.

"So why did she abandon those babies on the road?" I need to know, because
now I feel abandoned too.

"Long time I wondered this myself," says my father. "But then I read that letter
from her daughters in Shanghai now, and I talk to Auntie Lindo, all the others. And
then I knew. No shame in what she done. None."

"What happened?"

"Your mother running away—" begins my father.

"No, tell me in Chinese," I interrupt. "Really, I can understand." 100
He begins to talk, still standing at the window, looking into the night.

After fleeing Kweilin, your mother walked for several days trying to find a main
road. Her thought was to catch a ride on a truck or wagon, to catch enough rides
until she reached Chungking, where her husband was stationed.

She had sewn money and jewelry into the lining of her dress, enough, she
thought, to barter rides all the way. If I am lucky, she thought, I will not have to trade
the heavy gold bracelet and jade ring. These were things from her mother, your
grandmother.

By the third day, she had traded nothing. The roads were filled with people,
everybody running and begging for rides from passing trucks. The trucks rushed by,
afraid to stop. So your mother found no rides, only the start of dysentery pains in her
stomach.

Her shoulders ached from the two babies swinging from scarf slings. Blisters grew 105
on her palms from holding two leather suitcases. And then the blisters burst and began to bleed. After a while, she left the suitcases behind, keeping only the food and a
few clothes. And later she also dropped the bags of wheat flour and rice and kept
walking like this for many miles, singing songs to her little girls, until she was delirious with pain and fever.

Finally, there was not one more step left in her body. She didn't have the strength
to carry those babies any farther. She slumped to the ground. She knew she would die
of her sickness, or perhaps from thirst, from starvation, or from the Japanese, who she
was sure were marching right behind her.

She took the babies out of the slings and sat them on the side of the road, then
lay down next to them. You babies are so good, she said, so quiet. They smiled back,
reaching their chubby hands for her, wanting to be picked up again. And then she
knew she could not bear to watch her babies die with her.

She saw a family with three young children in a cart going by. "Take my babies, I
beg you," she cried to them. But they stared back with empty eyes and never stopped.

She saw another person pass and called out again. This time a man turned
around, and he had such a terrible expression—your mother said it looked like death
itself—she shivered and looked away.

When the road grew quiet, she tore open the lining of her dress, and stuffed jew- 110
elry under the shirt of one baby and money under the other. She reached into her
pocket and drew out the photos of her family, the picture of her father and mother,
the picture of herself and her husband on their wedding day. And she wrote on the

back of each the names of the babies and this same message: "Please care for these babies with the money and valuables provided. When it is safe to come, if you bring them to Shanghai, 9 Weichang Lu, the Li family will be glad to give you a generous reward. Li Suyuan and Wang Fuchi."

And then she touched each baby's cheek and told her not to cry. She would go down the road to find them some food and would be back. And without looking back, she walked down the road, stumbling and crying, thinking only of this one last hope, that her daughters would be found by a kindhearted person who would care for them. She would not allow herself to imagine anything else.

She did not remember how far she walked, which direction she went, when she fainted, or how she was found. When she awoke, she was in the back of a bouncing truck with several other sick people, all moaning. And she began to scream, thinking she was now on a journey to Buddhist hell. But the face of an American missionary lady bent over her and smiled, talking to her in a soothing language she did not understand. And yet she could somehow understand. She had been saved for no good reason, and it was now too late to go back and save her babies.

When she arrived in Chungking, she learned her husband had died two weeks before. She told me later she laughed when the officers told her this news, she was so delirious with madness and disease. To come so far, to lose so much and to find nothing.

I met her in a hospital. She was lying on a cot, hardly able to move, her dysentery had drained her so thin. I had come in for my foot, my missing toe, which was cut off by a piece of falling rubble. She was talking to herself, mumbling.

"Look at these clothes," she said, and I saw she had on a rather unusual dress for wartime. It was silk satin, quite dirty, but there was no doubt it was a beautiful dress. 115

"Look at this face," she said, and I saw her dusty face and hollow cheeks, her eyes shining back. "Do you see my foolish hope?"

"I thought I had lost everything, except these two things," she murmured. "And I wondered which I would lose next. Clothes or hope? Hope or clothes?"

"But now, see here, look what is happening," she said, laughing, as if all her prayers had been answered. And she was pulling hair out of her head as easily as one lifts new wheat from wet soil.

It was an old peasant woman who found them. "How could I resist?" the peasant woman later told your sisters when they were older. They were still sitting obediently near where your mother had left them, looking like little fairy queens waiting for their sedan to arrive.

The woman, Mei Ching, and her husband, Mei Han, lived in a stone cave. There 120 were thousands of hidden caves like that in and around Kweilin so secret that the people remained hidden even after the war ended. The Meis would come out of their cave every few days and forage for food supplies left on the road, and sometimes they would see something that they both agreed was a tragedy to leave behind. So one day they took back to their cave a delicately painted set of rice bowls, another day a little footstool with a velvet cushion and two new wedding blankets. And once, it was your sisters.

They were pious people, Muslims, who believed the twin babies were a sign of double luck, and they were sure of this when, later in the evening, they discovered how valuable the babies were. She and her husband had never seen rings and bracelets like those. And while they admired the pictures, knowing the babies came from a good family, neither of them could read or write. It was not until many months later that Mei

Ching found someone who could read the writing on the back. By then, she loved these baby girls like her own.

In 1952 Mei Han, the husband, died. The twins were already eight years old, and Mei Ching now decided it was time to find your sisters' true family.

She showed the girls the picture of their mother and told them they had been born into a great family and she would take them back to see their true mother and grandparents. Mei Ching told them about the reward, but she swore she would refuse it. She loved these girls so much, she only wanted them to have what they were entitled to—a better life, a fine house, educated ways. Maybe the family would let her stay on as the girls' amah. Yes, she was certain they would insist.

Of course, when she found the place at 9 Weichang Lu, in the old French Concession, it was something completely different. It was the site of a factory building, recently constructed, and none of the workers knew what had become of the family whose house had burned down on that spot.

Mei Ching could not have known, of course, that your mother and I, her new husband, had already returned to that same place in 1945 in hopes of finding both her family and her daughters.

Your mother and I stayed in China until 1947. We went to many different cities—back to Kweilin, to Changsha, as far south as Kunming. She was always looking out of one corner of her eye for twin babies, then little girls. Later we went to Hong Kong, and when we finally left in 1949 for the United States, I think she was even looking for them on the boat. But when we arrived, she no longer talked about them. I thought, At last, they have died in her heart.

When letters could be openly exchanged between China and the United States, she wrote immediately to old friends in Shanghai and Kweilin. I did not know she did this. Auntie Lindo told me. But of course, by then, all the street names had changed. Some people had died, others had moved away. So it took many years to find a contact. And when she did find an old schoolmate's address and wrote asking her to look for her daughters, her friend wrote back and said this was impossible, like looking for a needle on the bottom of the ocean. How did she know her daughters were in Shanghai and not somewhere else in China? The friend, of course, did not ask, How do you know your daughters are still alive?

So her schoolmate did not look. Finding babies lost during the war was a matter of foolish imagination, and she had no time for that.

But every year, your mother wrote to different people. And this last year, I think she got a big idea in her head, to go to China and find them herself. I remember she told me, "Canning, we should go, before it is too late, before we are too old." And I told her we were already too old, it was already too late.

I just thought she wanted to be a tourist! I didn't know she wanted to go and look for her daughters. So when I said it was too late, that must have put a terrible thought in her head that her daughters might be dead. And I think this possibility grew bigger and bigger in her head, until it killed her.

Maybe it was your mother's dead spirit who guided her Shanghai schoolmate to find her daughters. Because after your mother died, the schoolmate saw your sisters, by chance, while shopping for shoes at the Number One Department Store on Nanjing Dong Road. She said it was like a dream, seeing these two women who looked so much alike, moving down the stairs together. There was something about their facial expressions that reminded the schoolmate of your mother.

She quickly walked over to them and called their names, which of course, they did not recognize at first, because Mei Ching had changed their names. But your mother's friend was so sure, she persisted. "Are you not Wang Chwun Yu and Wang Chwun Hwa?" she asked them. And then these double-image women became very excited, because they remembered the names written on the back of an old photo, a photo of a young man and woman they still honored, as their much-loved first parents, who had died and become spirit ghosts still roaming the earth looking for them.

At the airport, I am exhausted. I could not sleep last night. Aiyi had followed me into my room at three in the morning, and she instantly fell asleep on one of the twin beds, snoring with the might of a lumberjack. I lay awake thinking about my mother's story, realizing how much I have never known about her, grieving that my sisters and I had both lost her.

And now at the airport, after shaking hands with everybody, waving good-bye, I think about all the different ways we leave people in this world. Cheerily waving good-bye to some at airports, knowing we'll never see each other again. Leaving others on the side of the road, hoping that we will. Finding my mother in my father's story and saying good-bye before I have a chance to know her better.

Aiyi smiles at me as we wait for our gate to be called. She is so old. I put one arm around her and one around Lili. They are the same size, it seems. And then it's time. As we wave good-bye one more time and enter the waiting area, I get the sense I am going from one funeral to another. In my hand I'm clutching a pair of tickets to Shanghai. In two hours we'll be there. 135

The plane takes off. I close my eyes. How can I describe to them in my broken Chinese about our mother's life? Where should I begin?

"Wake up, we're here," says my father. And I awake with my heart pounding in my throat. I look out the window and we're already on the runway. It's gray outside.

And now I'm walking down the steps of the plane, onto the tarmac and toward the building. If only, I think, if only my mother had lived long enough to be the one walking toward them. I am so nervous I cannot even feel my feet. I am just moving somehow.

Somebody shouts, "She's arrived!" And then I see her. Her short hair. Her small body. And that same look on her face. She has the back of her hand pressed hard against her mouth. She is crying as though she had gone through a terrible ordeal and were happy it is over.

And I know it's not my mother, yet it is the same look she had when I was five and had disappeared all afternoon, for such a long time, that she was convinced I was dead. And when I miraculously appeared, sleepy-eyed, crawling from underneath my bed, she wept and laughed, biting the back of her hand to make sure it was true. 140

And now I see her again, two of her, waving, and in one hand there is a photo, the Polaroid I sent them. As soon as I get beyond the gate, we run toward each other, all three of us embracing, all hesitations and expectations forgotten.

"Mama, Mama," we all murmur, as if she is among us.

My sisters look at me, proudly. "*Meimei jandale*," says one sister proudly to the other. "Little Sister has grown up." I look at their faces again and I see no trace of my mother in them. Yet they still look familiar. And now I also see what part of me is Chinese. It is so obvious. It is my family. It is in our blood. After all these years, it can finally be let go.

*

My sisters and I stand, arms around each other, laughing and wiping the tears from each other's eyes. The flash of the Polaroid goes off and my father hands me the snapshot. My sisters and I watch quietly together, eager to see what develops.

The gray-green surface changes to the bright colors of our three images, sharpening and deepening all at once. And although we don't speak, I know we all see it: Together we look like our mother. Her same eyes, her same mouth, open in surprise to see, at last, her long-cherished wish.

Questions

1. How is the external setting of "A Pair of Tickets" essential to what happens internally to the narrator in the course of this story?
2. How does the narrator's view of her father change by seeing him in a different setting?
3. In what ways does the narrator feel at home in China? In what ways does she feel foreign?
4. What do the narrator and her half-sisters have in common? How does this element relate to the theme of the story?
5. In what ways does the story explore specifically Chinese American experiences? In what other ways is the story grounded in universal family issues?

■ WRITING *effectively*

Amy Tan on Writing

Setting the Voice   1989

Lately, I've been giving more thought to the kind of English my mother speaks. Like others, I have described it to people as "broken" or "fractured" English. But I wince when I say that. It has always bothered me that I can think of no way to describe it other than "broken," as if it were damaged and needed to be fixed, as if it lacked a certain wholeness and soundness. I've heard other terms used, "limited English," for example. But they seem just as bad, as if everything is limited, including people's perceptions of the limited English speaker.

I know this for a fact, because when I was growing up, my mother's "limited" English limited *my* perception of her. I was ashamed of her English. I believed that her

Amy Tan

English reflected the quality of what she had to say. That is, because she expressed them imperfectly, her thoughts were imperfect. And I had plenty of empirical evidence to support me: the fact that people in department stores, at banks, and at restaurants did not take her seriously, did not give her good service, pretended not to understand her, or even acted as if they did not hear her.

· · ·

But it wasn't until 1985 that I finally began to write fiction. And at first I wrote using what I thought to be wittily crafted sentences, sentences that would finally prove I had mastery over the English language. Here's an example from the first draft of a story that later made its way into *The Joy Luck Club,* but without this line: "That was my mental quandary in its nascent state." A terrible line, which I can barely pronounce.

Fortunately, for reasons I won't get into today, I later decided I should envision a reader for the stories I would write. And the reader I decided upon was my mother, because these were stories about mothers. So with this reader in mind—and in fact she did read my early drafts—I began to write stories using all the Englishes I grew up with: the English I spoke to my mother, which for lack of a better term might be described as "simple"; the English she used with me, which for lack of a better term might be described as "broken"; my translation of her Chinese, which could certainly be described as "watered down"; and what I imagined to be her translation of her Chinese if she could speak in perfect English, her internal language, and for that I sought to preserve the essence, but neither an English nor a Chinese structure. I wanted to capture what language ability tests can never reveal: her intent, her passion, her imagery, the rhythms of her speech and the nature of her thoughts.

Apart from what any critic had to say about my writing, I knew I had succeeded where it counted when my mother finished reading my book and gave me her verdict: "So easy to read."

From "Mother Tongue"

THINKING ABOUT SETTING

The time and place in which a story is set serve as more than mere backdrop. When preparing to write about a story, be sure to consider where and when it is set, and what role the setting plays.

- **Ask whether setting helps motivate the plot.** The external pressure of the setting is often the key factor that compels or invites the protagonist into action. Setting can play as large a role as plot and characters do by prompting a protagonist into an action he or she might not otherwise take.
- **Consider whether the external setting suggests the character's inner reality.** A particular setting can create a mood or provide clues to a protagonist's nature. To write about a story's setting, therefore, invites you to study not only the time and place but also their relation to the protagonist. Does the external reality provide a clue to the protagonist's inner reality?
- **Notice whether the setting changes as the plot progresses.** The settings in a story are not static. Characters can move from place to place, and their actions may bring them into significantly different external and internal places.

CHECKLIST: Writing About Setting

☐ Where does the story take place?

☐ What does the setting suggest about the characters' lives?

☐ Are there significant differences in the settings for different characters? What does this suggest about each person?

☐ When does the story take place? Is the time of year or time of day significant?

☐ Does the weather play a meaningful role in the story's action?

☐ What is the protagonist's relationship to the setting?

☐ Does the setting of the story in some way compel the protagonist into action?

☐ Does the story's time or place suggest something about the character of the protagonist?

☐ Does a change in setting during the story suggest some internal change in the protagonist?

WRITING ASSIGNMENT ON SETTING

Choose a story from this chapter, and explore how character and setting are interrelated. A possible topic would be to describe the significance of setting to the protagonist in "A Pair of Tickets" or "Greasy Lake." How does the setting of the climax of the story contribute to a change in the character's personal perspective?

MORE TOPICS FOR WRITING

1. "Greasy Lake" takes its title and epigraph from Bruce Springsteen's song "Spirit in the Night," about a carefree night at a lakeside party. If you're not familiar with it, you can find the lyrics on the Internet or download the song to get the full effect. Contrast the role setting plays in the story and in the song. What do you make of the fact that Boyle's story is so much darker than the song to which it refers?

2. Write about how setting functions as a kind of character in "To Build a Fire." Do the landscape and weather act as the antagonist in the story's plot?

3. Think of a place—on campus or beyond—to which you often return. If possible, go there. Make a list of every physical detail you can think of to describe that place. Then look the list over and write a paragraph on what sort of mood is suggested by it. If you were to describe your emotional connection to the place, which three details would you choose? Why?

4. Choose any story in this book, and pay careful attention to setting as you read it. Write several paragraphs reflecting on the following questions: What details in the story suggest the time and place in which it is set? Is setting central to the story? If the action were transplanted to some other place and time, how would the story change?

▶ TERMS FOR *review*

Setting ▶ The time and place of a story. The setting may also include the climate and even the social, psychological, or spiritual state of the characters.

Locale ▶ The location where a story takes place.

Atmosphere ▶ The dominant mood or feeling that pervades all or part of a literary work. Atmosphere is the total effect conveyed by the author's use of language, images, and physical setting.

Regionalism ▶ The literary representation of a specific locale that consciously uses the particulars of geography, custom, history, folklore, or speech. In regional narratives, the locale plays a crucial role in the presentation and progression of the story.

Naturalism ▶ A type of fiction in which the characters are presented as products or victims of environment and heredity. Naturalism is considered an extreme form of **realism** (the attempt to reproduce faithfully the surface appearance of life, especially that of ordinary people in everyday situations).

5

TONE AND STYLE

*Style has no fixed laws; it is changed by the usage
of the people, never the same for any length of time.*

—SENECA

In many Victorian novels it was customary for some commentator, presumably the author, to interrupt the story from time to time, remarking on the action, offering philosophical asides, or explaining the procedures to be followed in telling the story.

> Two hours later, Dorothea was seated in an inner room or boudoir of a handsome apartment in the Via Sistina. I am sorry to add that she was sobbing bitterly. . . .
>
> —George Eliot in *Middlemarch* (1873)

> But let the gentle-hearted reader be under no apprehension whatsoever. It is not destined that Eleanor shall marry Mr. Slope or Bertie Stanhope.
>
> —Anthony Trollope in *Barchester Towers* (1857)

Of course, the voice of this commentator was not identical with that of the "real-life" author—the one toiling over an inkpot, worrying about publication deadlines and whether the rent would be paid. At times the living author might have been far different in personality from that usually wise and cheerful intruder who kept addressing the reader of the book. Much of the time, to be sure, the author probably agreed with whatever attitudes this alter ego expressed. But, in effect, the author created the character of a commentator to speak for him or her and artfully sustained that character's voice throughout the novel.

Such intrusions, although sometimes useful to the "real" author and enjoyable to the reader, are today rare. Modern storytellers, carefully keeping out of sight, seldom comment on their plots and characters. Apparently they agree with Anton Chekhov that a writer should not judge the characters but should serve as their "impartial witness." And yet, no less definitely than Victorian novelists who introduced commentators, modern writers of effective stories no doubt have feelings toward their characters and events. The authors make us see these people in such a way that we, too, will care about them.

Although many modern writers have adopted Chekhov's "impartial" methods, they are rarely impartial witnesses. They merely embed their own feelings more deeply into the story so that those reactions emerge indirectly for the reader. For example, when at the beginning of the short story "In Exile" Chekhov introduces us to a character, he does so with a description that arouses sympathy:

> The Tartar was worn out and ill, and wrapping himself in his rags, he talked about how good it was in the province of Simbirsk, and what a beautiful and clever wife he had left at home. He was not more than twenty-five, and in the firelight his pale, sickly face and woebegone expression made him seem like a boy.

Other than the comparison of the Tartar to a child, the details in this passage seem mostly factual: the young man's illness, ragged clothes, facial expression, and topics of conversation. But these details form a portrait that stirs pity. By his selection of these imaginary details out of countless others that he might have included, Chekhov firmly directs our feelings about the Tartar, so miserable and pathetic in his sickness and his homesickness. We cannot know, of course, exactly what the living Chekhov felt; but at least we can be sure that we are supposed to share the compassion and tenderness of the narrator—Chekhov's impartial (but human) witness.

TONE

Not only the author's choice of details may lead us to infer his or her attitude, but also choice of characters, events, and situations, and choice of words. When the narrator of Joseph Conrad's *Heart of Darkness* comes upon an African outpost littered with abandoned machines and notices "a boiler wallowing in the grass," the exact word *wallowing* conveys an attitude: that there is something swinish about this scene of careless waste.

Whatever leads us to infer the author's attitude is commonly called **tone**. Like a tone of voice, the tone of a story may communicate amusement, anger, affection, sorrow, contempt. It implies the feelings of the author, so far as we can sense them. Those feelings may be similar to feelings expressed by the narrator of the story (or by any character), but sometimes they may be dissimilar, even sharply opposed. The characters in a story may regard an event as sad, but we sense that the author regards it as funny. To understand the tone of a story, then, is to understand some attitude more fundamental to the story than whatever attitudes the characters explicitly declare.

The tone of a story, like a tone of voice, may convey not simply one attitude, but a medley. Reading "A & P" (Chapter 1), we have mingled feelings about Sammy: delight in his wicked comments about other people and his skewering of hypocrisy; irritation at his smugness and condescension; admiration for his readiness to take a stand; sympathy for the pain of his disillusionment. Often the tone of a literary story will be too rich and complicated to sum up in one or two words. But to try to describe the tone of such a story may be a useful way to penetrate to its center and to grasp the whole of it.

STYLE

One of the clearest indications of the tone of a story is the **style** in which it is written. In general, style refers to the individual traits or characteristics of a piece of writing: to a writer's particular ways of managing words that we come to recognize as habitual or customary. A distinctive style marks the work of a fine writer: we can tell his or her work from that of anyone else. From one story to another, however, the writer may fittingly change style; and in some stories, style may be altered meaningfully as the story goes along. In his novel *As I Lay Dying,* William Faulkner changes narrators with every chapter, and he distinguishes the narrators one from another by giving each an individual style or manner of speaking. Though each narrator has his or her own style, the book as a whole demonstrates Faulkner's style as well. For instance, one chapter is written from the point of view of a small boy, Vardaman Bundren, member of a family of poor Mississippi tenant farmers, whose view of a horse in a barn reads like this:

> It is as though the dark were resolving him out of his integrity, into an unrelated scattering of components—snuffings and stampings; smells of cooling flesh and ammoniac hair; an illusion of a co-ordinated whole of splotched hide and strong bones within which, detached and secret and familiar, an *is* different from my *is*.

How can a small boy unaccustomed to libraries use words like *integrity, components, illusion,* and *co-ordinated*? Elsewhere in the story, Vardaman says aloud, with no trace of literacy, "Hit was a-laying right there on the ground." Apparently, in the passage it is not the voice of the boy that we are hearing, but something resembling the voice of William Faulkner, elevated and passionate, expressing the boy's thoughts in a style that admits Faulknerian words.

DICTION

Usually, *style* indicates a mode of expression: the language a writer uses. In this sense, the notion of style includes such traits as the length and complexity of sentences, and **diction**, or choice of words: abstract or concrete, bookish ("unrelated scattering of components") or close to speech ("Hit was a-laying right there on the ground"). Involved in the idea of style, too, is any habitual use of imagery, patterns of sound, figures of speech, or other devices.

Several writers of realistic fiction, called **minimalists**—Ann Beattie, Raymond Carver, Bobbie Ann Mason—have written with a flat, laid-back, unemotional tone, in an appropriately bare, unadorned style. Minimalists seem to give nothing but facts drawn from ordinary life, sometimes in picayune detail. Here is a sample passage from Raymond Carver's story "A Small, Good Thing":

> She pulled into the driveway and cut the engine. She closed her eyes and leaned her head against the wheel for a minute. She listened to the ticking sounds the engine made as it began to cool. Then she got out of the car. She could hear the dog barking inside the house. She went to the front door, which was unlocked. She went inside and turned on lights and put on a kettle of water for tea. She opened some dog food and fed Slug on the back porch. The dog ate in hungry little smacks. It kept running into the kitchen to see that she was going to stay.

Explicit feeling and showy language are kept at a minimum here. Notice how Carver's diction relies on everyday words—most words of only one and two syllables. Taken out of context, this description may strike you as banal, as if the writer himself were bored; but it works effectively as a part of Carver's entire story. As in all good writing, the style here seems a faithful mirror of what is said in it. At its best, such writing achieves "a hard-won reduction, a painful stripping away of richness, a baring of bone."[1]

Two Examples of Style: Hemingway Versus Faulkner

To see what style means, compare the stories in this chapter by William Faulkner ("Barn Burning") and by Ernest Hemingway ("A Clean, Well-Lighted Place"). Faulkner frequently falls into a style in which a statement, as soon as it is uttered, is followed by another statement expressing the idea in a more emphatic way. Sentences are interrupted with parenthetical elements (asides, like this) thrust into them unexpectedly. At times, Faulkner writes of seemingly ordinary matters as if giving a speech in a towering passion. Here, from "Barn Burning," is a description of how a boy's father delivers a rug:

> "Don't you want me to help?" he whispered. His father did not answer and now he heard again that stiff foot striking the hollow portico with that wooden and clocklike deliberation, that outrageous overstatement of the weight it carried. The rug, hunched, not flung (the boy could tell that even in the darkness) from his father's shoulder struck the angle of wall and floor with a sound unbelievably loud, thunderous, then the foot again, unhurried and enormous; a light came on in the house and the boy sat, tense, breathing steadily and quietly and just a little fast, though the foot itself did not increase its beat at all, descending the steps now; now the boy could see him.

Faulkner is not merely indulging in language for its own sake. As you will find when you read the whole story, this rug delivery is vital to the story, and so too is the father's profound defiance—indicated by his walk. By devices of style—by *metaphor* and *simile* ("wooden and clocklike"), by exact qualification ("not flung"), by emphatic adjectives ("loud, thunderous")—Faulkner is carefully placing his emphases.

By the words he selects to describe the father's stride, Faulkner directs how we feel toward the man and perhaps also indicates his own wondering but skeptical attitude toward a character whose very footfall is "outrageous" and "enormous." (Fond of long sentences like the last one in the quoted passage, Faulkner remarked that there are sentences that need to be written in the way a circus acrobat pedals a bicycle on a high wire: rapidly, so as not to fall off.)

Hemingway's famous style includes both short sentences and long, but when the sentences are long, they tend to be relatively simple in construction. Hemingway likes long compound sentences (clause plus clause plus clause), sometimes joined with "and"s. He interrupts such a sentence with a dependent clause or a parenthetical element much less frequently than Faulkner does. The effect is like listening to speech:

> In the day time the street was dusty, but at night the dew settled the dust and the old man liked to sit late because he was deaf and now at night it was quiet and he felt the difference.

Hemingway is a master of swift, terse dialogue, and often casts whole scenes in the form of conversation. As if he were a closemouthed speaker unwilling to let his feelings loose, the narrator of a Hemingway story often addresses us in understatement, implying greater depths of feeling than he puts into words. Read the following story and you will see that its style and tone cannot be separated.

[1]Letter in the *New York Times Book Review*, 5 June 1988.

Ernest Hemingway

A Clean, Well-Lighted Place 1933

Ernest Hemingway (1899–1961), born in Oak Park, Illinois, bypassed college to be a cub reporter. In World War I, as an eighteen-year-old volunteer ambulance driver in Italy, he was wounded in action. In 1922 he settled in Paris, then aswarm with writers; he later re-called that time in A Moveable Feast *(1964). Hemingway won swift acclaim for his early stories,* In Our Time *(1925), and for his first, perhaps finest, novel,* The Sun Also Rises *(1926), portraying a "lost generation" of postwar American drifters in France and Spain. For Whom the Bell Tolls (1940) depicts life during the Spanish Civil War. Hemingway became a celebrity, often photographed as a marlin fisherman or a lion hunter. A fan of bull-fighting, he wrote two nonfiction books on the subject:* Death in the Afternoon *(1932) and* The Dangerous Summer *(1985). After World War II, with his fourth wife, journalist Mary Welsh, he made his home in Cuba, where he wrote* The Old Man and the Sea *(1952). The Nobel Prize in Literature came his way in 1954. In 1961, mentally dis-tressed and physically ailing, he shot himself. Hemingway brought a hard-bitten realism to American fiction. His heroes live dangerously, by personal codes of honor, courage, and endurance. Hemingway's distinctively crisp, unadorned style left American literature permanently changed.*

It was late and every one had left the café except an old man who sat in the shadow the leaves of the tree made against the electric light. In the day time the street was dusty, but at night the dew settled the dust and the old man liked to sit late because he was deaf and now at night it was quiet and he felt the difference. The two waiters inside the café knew that the old man was a little drunk, and while he was a good client they knew that if he became too drunk he would leave without paying, so they kept watch on him.

"Last week he tried to commit suicide," one waiter said.

"Why?"

"He was in despair."

"What about?"

"Nothing." 5

"How do you know it was nothing?"

"He has plenty of money."

They sat together at a table that was close against the wall near the door of the café and looked at the terrace where the tables were all empty except where the old man sat in the shadow of the leaves of the tree that moved slightly in the wind. A girl and a soldier went by in the street. The street light shone on the brass number on his collar. The girl wore no head covering and hurried beside him.

"The guard will pick him up," one waiter said. 10

"What does it matter if he gets what he's after?"

"He had better get off the street now. The guard will get him. They went by five minutes ago."

The old man sitting in the shadow rapped on his saucer with his glass. The younger waiter went over to him.

"What do you want?"

The old man looked at him. "Another brandy," he said. 15

"You'll be drunk," the waiter said. The old man looked at him. The waiter went away.

"He'll stay all night," he said to his colleague. "I'm sleepy now. I never get into bed before three o'clock. He should have killed himself last week."

The waiter took the brandy bottle and another saucer from the counter inside the café and marched out to the old man's table. He put down the saucer and poured the glass full of brandy.

"You should have killed yourself last week," he said to the deaf man. The old man motioned with his finger. "A little more," he said. The waiter poured on into the glass so that the brandy slopped over and ran down the stem into the top saucer of the pile. "Thank you," the old man said. The waiter took the bottle back inside the café. He sat down at the table with his colleague again.

"He's drunk now," he said.   20

"He's drunk every night."°

"What did he want to kill himself for?"

"How should I know?"

"How did he do it?"

"He hung himself with a rope."   25

"Who cut him down?"

"His niece."

"Why did they do it?"

"Fear for his soul."

"How much money has he got?"   30

"He's got plenty."

"He must be eighty years old."

"Anyway I should say he was eighty."°

"I wish he would go home. I never get to bed before three o'clock. What kind of hour is that to go to bed?"

"He stays up because he likes it."   35

"He's lonely. I'm not lonely. I have a wife waiting in bed for me."

"He had a wife once too."

"A wife would be no good to him now."

"You can't tell. He might be better with a wife."

"His niece looks after him."   40

"I know. You said she cut him down."

"I wouldn't want to be that old. An old man is a nasty thing."

"Not always. This old man is clean. He drinks without spilling. Even now, drunk. Look at him."

"I don't want to look at him. I wish he would go home. He has no regard for those who must work."

The old man looked from his glass across the square, then over at the waiters.   45

"Another brandy," he said, pointing to his glass. The waiter who was in a hurry came over.

"Finished," he said, speaking with that omission of syntax stupid people employ when talking to drunken people or foreigners. "No more tonight. Close now."

"He's drunk now," he said. "He's drunk every night": The younger waiter perhaps says both these lines. A device of Hemingway's style is sometimes to have a character pause, then speak again—as often happens in actual speech.   *"He must be eighty years old." "Anyway I should say he was eighty":* Is this another instance of the same character's speaking twice? Clearly, it is the younger waiter who says the next line, "I wish he would go home."

"Another," said the old man.

"No. Finished." The waiter wiped the edge of the table with a towel and shook his head.

The old man stood up, slowly counted the saucers, took a leather coin purse from his pocket and paid for the drinks, leaving half a peseta tip. 50

The waiter watched him go down the street, a very old man walking unsteadily but with dignity.

"Why didn't you let him stay and drink?" the unhurried waiter asked. They were putting up the shutters. "It is not half-past two."

"I want to go home to bed."

"What is an hour?"

"More to me than to him." 55

"An hour is the same."

"You talk like an old man yourself. He can buy a bottle and drink at home."

"It's not the same."

"No, it is not," agreed the waiter with a wife. He did not wish to be unjust. He was only in a hurry.

"And you? You have no fear of going home before the usual hour?" 60

"Are you trying to insult me?"

"No, hombre, only to make a joke."

"No," the waiter who was in a hurry said, rising from pulling down the metal shutters. "I have confidence. I am all confidence."

"You have youth, confidence, and a job," the older waiter said. "You have everything."

"And what do you lack?" 65

"Everything but work."

"You have everything I have."

"No. I have never had confidence and I am not young."

"Come on. Stop talking nonsense and lock up."

"I am of those who like to stay late at the café," the older waiter said. "With all 70 those who do not want to go to bed. With all those who need a light for the night."

"I want to go home and into bed."

"We are of two different kinds," the older waiter said. He was not dressed to go home. "It is not only a question of youth and confidence although those things are very beautiful. Each night I am reluctant to close up because there may be some one who needs the café."

"Hombre, there are bodegas° open all night long."

"You do not understand. This is a clean and pleasant café. It is well lighted. The light is very good and also, now, there are shadows of the leaves."

"Good night," said the younger waiter. 75

"Good night," the other said. Turning off the electric light he continued the conversation with himself. It is the light of course but it is necessary that the place be clean and pleasant. You do not want music. Certainly you do not want music. Nor can you stand before a bar with dignity although that is all that is provided for these hours. What did he fear? It was not fear or dread. It was a nothing that he knew too well. It was all a nothing and a man was nothing too. It was only that and light was all it needed and a certain cleanness and order. Some lived in it and never felt it but

---

bodegas: wineshops.

he knew it all was nada y pues nada y nada y pues nada.° Our nada who art in nada, nada be thy name thy kingdom nada thy will be nada in nada as it is in nada. Give us this nada our daily nada and nada us our nada as we nada our nadas and nada us not into nada but deliver us from nada; pues nada. Hail nothing full of nothing, nothing is with thee. He smiled and stood before a bar with a shining steam pressure coffee machine.

"What's yours?" asked the barman.

"Nada."

"Otro loco más,"° said the barman and turned away.

"A little cup," said the waiter.   80

The barman poured it for him.

"The light is very bright and pleasant but the bar is unpolished," the waiter said.

The barman looked at him but did not answer. It was too late at night for conversation.

"You want another copita?"° the barman asked.

"No, thank you," said the waiter and went out. He disliked bars and bodegas. A   85
clean, well-lighted café was a very different thing. Now, without thinking further, he would go home to his room. He would lie in the bed and finally, with daylight, he would go to sleep. After all, he said to himself, it is probably only insomnia. Many must have it.

Questions

1. What besides insomnia makes the older waiter reluctant to go to bed? Comment especially on his meditation with its *nada* refrain. Why does he understand so well the old man's need for a café? What does the café represent for the two of them?

2. Compare the younger waiter and the older waiter in their attitudes toward the old man. Whose attitude do you take to be closer to that of the author? Even though Hemingway does not editorially state his own feelings, how does he make them clear to us?

3. Point to sentences that establish the style of the story. What is distinctive in them? What repetitions of words or phrases seem particularly effective? Does Hemingway seem to favor a simple or an erudite vocabulary?

4. What is the story's point of view? Discuss its appropriateness.

William Faulkner

Barn Burning   1939

William Faulkner (1897–1962) receives a capsule biography in Chapter 2, page 29, along with his story "A Rose for Emily." "Barn Burning" is among his many contributions to the history of Yoknapatawpha, an imaginary Mississippi county in which the Sartorises and the de Spains are landed aristocrats living by a code of honor and the Snopeses—most of them—are shiftless ne'er-do-wells.

    The store in which the Justice of the Peace's court was sitting smelled of cheese. The boy, crouched on his nail keg at the back of the crowded room, knew he smelled cheese, and more: from where he sat he could see the ranked shelves close-packed

---

nada y pues . . . nada: nothing and then nothing and nothing and then nothing.   *Otro loco más:* another lunatic.   *copita:* little cup.

with the solid, squat, dynamic shapes of tin cans whose labels his stomach read, not from the lettering which meant nothing to his mind but from the scarlet devils and the silver curve of fish—this, the cheese which he knew he smelled and the hermetic meat which his intestines believed he smelled coming in intermittent gusts momentary and brief between the other constant one, the smell and sense just a little of fear because mostly of despair and grief, the old fierce pull of blood. He could not see the table where the Justice sat and before which his father and his father's enemy (*our enemy* he thought in that despair: *ourn! mine and hisn both! He's my father!*) stood, but he could hear them, the two of them that is, because his father had said no word yet:

"But what proof have you, Mr. Harris?"

"I told you. The hog got into my corn. I caught it up and sent it back to him. He had no fence that would hold it. I told him so, warned him. The next time I put the hog in my pen. When he came to get it I gave him enough wire to patch up his pen. The next time I put the hog up and kept it. I rode down to his house and saw the wire I gave him still rolled on to the spool in his yard. I told him he could have the hog when he paid me a dollar pound fee. That evening a nigger came with the dollar and got the hog. He was a strange nigger. He said, 'He say to tell you wood and hay kin burn.' I said, 'What?' 'That whut he say to tell you,' the nigger said. 'Wood and hay kin burn.' That night my barn burned. I got the stock out but I lost the barn."

"Where's the nigger? Have you got him?"

"He was a strange nigger, I tell you. I don't know what became of him."   5

"But that's not proof. Don't you see that's not proof?"

"Get that boy up here. He knows." For a moment the boy thought too that the man meant his older brother until Harris said, "Not him. The little one. The boy," and, crouching, small for his age, small and wiry like his father, in patched and faded jeans even too small for him, with straight, uncombed, brown hair and eyes gray and wild as storm scud, he saw the men between himself and the table part and become a lane of grim faces, at the end of which he saw the Justice, a shabby, collarless, graying man in spectacles, beckoning him. He felt no floor under his bare feet; he seemed to walk beneath the palpable weight of the grim turning faces. His father, still in his black Sunday coat donned not for the trial but for the moving, did not even look at him. *He aims for me to lie*, he thought, again with that frantic grief and despair. *And I will have to do hit.*

"What's your name, boy?" the Justice said.

"Colonel Sartoris Snopes," the boy whispered.

"Hey?" the Justice said. "Talk louder. Colonel Sartoris? I reckon anybody named   10
for Colonel Sartoris in this country can't help but tell the truth, can they?" The boy said nothing. *Enemy! Enemy!* he thought; for a moment he could not even see, could not see that the Justice's face was kindly nor discern that his voice was troubled when he spoke to the man named Harris: "Do you want me to question this boy?" But he could hear, and during those subsequent long seconds while there was absolutely no sound in the crowded little room save that of quiet and intent breathing it was as if he had swung outward at the end of a grape vine, over a ravine, and at the top of the swing had been caught in a prolonged instant of mesmerized gravity, weightless in time.

"No!" Harris said violently, explosively. "Damnation! Send him out of here!" Now time, the fluid world, rushed beneath him again, the voices coming to him again through the smell of cheese and sealed meat, the fear and despair and the old grief of blood:

"This case is closed. I can't find against you, Snopes, but I can give you advice. Leave this country and don't come back to it."

His father spoke for the first time, his voice cold and harsh, level, without emphasis: "I aim to. I don't figure to stay in a country among people who . . ." he said something unprintable and vile, addressed to no one.

"That'll do," the Justice said. "Take your wagon and get out of this country before dark. Case dismissed."

His father turned, and he followed the stiff black coat, the wiry figure walking a little stiffly from where a Confederate provost's man's musket ball had taken him in the heel on a stolen horse thirty years ago, followed the two backs now, since his older brother had appeared from somewhere in the crowd, no taller than the father but thicker, chewing tobacco steadily, between the two lines of grim-faced men and out of the store and across the worn gallery and down the sagging steps and among the dogs and half-grown boys in the mild May dust, where as he passed a voice hissed:

"Barn burner!"

Again he could not see, whirling; there was a face in a red haze, moonlike, bigger than the full moon, the owner of it half again his size, he leaping in the red haze toward the face, feeling no blow, feeling no shock when his head struck the earth, scrabbling up and leaping again, feeling no blow this time either and tasting no blood, scrabbling up to see the other boy in full flight and himself already leaping into pursuit as his father's hand jerked him back, the harsh, cold voice speaking above him: "Go get in the wagon."

It stood in a grove of locusts and mulberries across the road. His two hulking sisters in their Sunday dresses and his mother and her sister in calico and sunbonnets were already in it, sitting on and among the sorry residue of the dozen and more movings which even the boy could remember—the battered stove, the broken beds and chairs, the clock inlaid with mother-of-pearl, which would not run, stopped at some fourteen minutes past two o'clock of a dead and forgotten day and time, which had been his mother's dowry. She was crying, though when she saw him she drew her sleeve across her face and began to descend from the wagon. "Get back," the father said.

"He's hurt. I got to get some water and wash his . . ."

"Get back in the wagon," his father said. He got in too, over the tail-gate. His father mounted to the seat where the older brother already sat and struck the gaunt mules two savage blows with the peeled willow, but without heat. It was not even sadistic; it was exactly that same quality which in later years would cause his descendants to over-run the engine before putting a motor car into motion, striking and reining back in the same movement. The wagon went on, the store with its quiet crowd of grimly watching men dropped behind; a curve in the road hid it. *Forever* he thought. *Maybe he's done satisfied now, now that he has* . . . stopping himself, not to say it aloud even to himself. His mother's hand touched his shoulder.

"Does hit hurt?" she said.

"Naw," he said. "Hit don't hurt. Lemme be."

"Can't you wipe some of the blood off before hit dries?"

"I'll wash to-night," he said. "Lemme be, I tell you."

The wagon went on. He did not know where they were going. None of them ever did or ever asked, because it was always somewhere, always a house of sorts waiting for them a day or two days or even three days away. Likely his father had already arranged to make a crop on another farm before he . . . Again he had to stop himself. He (the father) always did. There was something about his wolflike independence and even courage when the advantage was at least neutral which impressed strangers, as if they got from his latent ravening ferocity not so much a sense of dependability as a feeling that his ferocious conviction in the rightness of his own actions would be of advantage to all whose interest lay with his.

That night they camped, in a grove of oaks and beeches where a spring ran. The nights were still cool and they had a fire against it, of a rail lifted from a nearby fence and cut into lengths—a small fire, neat, niggard almost, a shrewd fire; such fires were his father's habit and custom always, even in freezing weather. Older, the boy might have remarked this and wondered why not a big one; why should not a man who had not only seen the waste and extravagance of war, but who had in his blood an inherent voracious prodigality with material not his own, have burned everything in sight? Then he might have gone a step farther and thought that that was the reason: that niggard blaze was the living fruit of nights passed during those four years in the woods hiding from all men, blue and gray, with his strings of horses (captured horses, he called them). And older still, he might have divined the true reason: that the element of fire spoke to some deep mainspring of his father's being, as the element of steel or of powder spoke to other men, as the one weapon for the preservation of integrity, else breath were not worth the breathing, and hence to be regarded with respect and used with discretion.

But he did not think this now and he had seen those same niggard blazes all his life. He merely ate his supper beside it and was already half asleep over his iron plate when his father called him, and once more he followed the stiff back, the stiff and ruthless limp, up the slope and on to the starlit road where, turning, he could see his father against the stars but without face or depth—a shape black, flat, and bloodless as though cut from tin in the iron folds of the frockcoat which had not been made for him, the voice harsh like tin and without heat like tin:

"You were fixing to tell them. You would have told him." He didn't answer. His father struck him with the flat of his hand on the side of the head, hard but without heat, exactly as he had struck the two mules at the store, exactly as he would strike either of them with any stick in order to kill a horse fly, his voice without heat or anger: "You're getting to be a man. You got to learn. You got to learn to stick to your own blood or you ain't going to have any blood to stick to you. Do you think either of them, any man there this morning, would? Don't you know all they wanted was a chance to get at me because they knew I had them beat? Eh?" Later, twenty years later, he was to tell himself, "If I had said they wanted only truth, justice, he would have hit me again." But now he said nothing. He was not crying. He just stood there. "Answer me," his father said.

"Yes," he whispered. His father turned.

"Get on to bed. We'll be there tomorrow."

Tomorrow they were there. In the early afternoon the wagon stopped before a paintless two-room house identical almost with the dozen others it had stopped before even in the boy's ten years, and again, as on the other dozen occasions, his mother and aunt got down and began to unload the wagon, although his two sisters and his father and brother had not moved.

"Likely hit ain't fitten for hawgs," one of the sisters said.

"Nevertheless, fit it will and you'll hog it and like it," his father said. "Get out of them chairs and help your Ma unload."

The two sisters got down, big, bovine, in a flutter of cheap ribbons; one of them drew from the jumbled wagon bed a battered lantern, the other a worn broom. His

30

father handed the reins to the older son and began to climb stiffly over the wheel. "When they get unloaded, take the team to the barn and feed them." Then he said, and at first the boy thought he was still speaking to his brother: "Come with me."

"Me?" he said. 35

"Yes," his father said. "You."

"Abner," his mother said. His father paused and looked back—the harsh level stare beneath the shaggy, graying, irascible brows.

"I reckon I'll have a word with the man that aims to begin to-morrow owning me body and soul for the next eight months."

They went back up the road. A week ago—or before last night, that is—he would have asked where they were going, but not now. His father had struck him before last night but never before had he paused afterward to explain why; it was as if the blow and the following calm, outrageous voice still rang, repercussed, divulging nothing to him save the terrible handicap of being young, the light weight of his few years, just heavy enough to prevent his soaring free of the world as it seemed to be ordered but not heavy enough to keep him footed solid in it, to resist it and try to change the course of its events.

Presently he could see the grove of oaks and cedars and the other flowering trees 40 and shrubs where the house would be, though not the house yet. They walked beside a fence massed with honeysuckle and Cherokee roses and came to a gate swinging open between two brick pillars, and now, beyond a sweep of drive, he saw the house for the first time and at that instant he forgot his father and the terror and despair both, and even when he remembered his father again (who had not stopped) the terror and despair did not return. Because, for all the twelve movings, they had sojourned until now in a poor country, a land of small farms and fields and houses, and he had never seen a house like this before. *Hit's big as a courthouse* he thought quietly, with a surge of peace and joy whose reason he could not have thought into words, being too young for that: *They are safe from him. People whose lives are a part of this peace and dignity are beyond his touch, he no more to them than a buzzing wasp: capable of stinging for a little moment but that's all; the spell of this peace and dignity rendering even the barns and stable and cribs which belong to it impervious to the puny flames he might contrive . . .* this, the peace and joy, ebbing for an instant as he looked again at the stiff black back, the stiff and implacable limp of the figure which was not dwarfed by the house, for the reason that it had never looked big anywhere and which now, against the serene columned backdrop, had more than ever that impervious quality of something cut ruthlessly from tin, depthless, as though, sidewise to the sun, it would cast no shadow. Watching him, the boy remarked the absolutely undeviating course which his father held and saw the stiff foot come squarely down in a pile of fresh droppings where a horse had stood in the drive and which his father could have avoided by a simple change of stride. But it ebbed only a moment, though he could not have thought this into words either, walking on in the spell of the house, which he could even want but without envy, without sorrow, certainly never with that ravening and jealous rage which unknown to him walked in the ironlike black coat before him: *Maybe he will feel it too. Maybe it will even change him now from what maybe he couldn't help but be.*

They crossed the portico. Now he could hear his father's stiff foot as it came down on the boards with clocklike finality, a sound out of all proportion to the displacement of the body it bore and which was not dwarfed either by the white door before it, as though it had attained to a sort of vicious and ravening minimum not to be dwarfed by anything—the flat, wide, black hat, the formal coat of broadcloth which had once been black but which had now that friction-glazed greenish cast of the bodies of old house flies, the lifted sleeve which was too large, the lifted hand like a curled claw. The door opened so promptly that the boy knew the Negro must have been watching them all the time, an old man with neat grizzled hair, in a linen jacket, who stood barring the door with his body, saying, "Wipe yo foots, white man, fo you come in here. Major ain't home nohow."

"Get out of my way, nigger," his father said, without heat too, flinging the door back and the Negro also and entering, his hat still on his head. And now the boy saw the prints of the stiff foot on the doorjamb and saw them appear on the pale rug behind the machinelike deliberation of the foot which seemed to bear (or transmit) twice the weight which the body compassed. The Negro was shouting "Miss Lula! Miss Lula!" somewhere behind them, then the boy, deluged as though by a warm wave by a suave turn of the carpeted stair and a pendant glitter of chandeliers and a mute gleam of gold frames, heard the swift feet and saw her too, a lady—perhaps he had never seen her like before either—in a gray, smooth gown with lace at the throat and an apron tied at the waist and the sleeves turned back, wiping cake or biscuit dough from her hands with a towel as she came up the hall, looking not at his father at all but at the tracks on the blond rug with an expression of incredulous amazement.

"I tried," the Negro cried. "I tole him to . . ."

"Will you please go away?" she said in a shaking voice. "Major de Spain is not at home. Will you please go away?"

His father had not spoken again. He did not speak again. He did not even look 45 at her. He just stood stiff in the center of the rug, in his hat, the shaggy iron-gray brows twitching slightly above the pebble-colored eyes as he appeared to examine the house with brief deliberation. Then with the same deliberation he turned; the boy watched him pivot on the good leg and saw the stiff foot drag around the arc of the turning, leaving a final long and fading smear. His father never looked at it, he never once looked down at the rug. The Negro held the door. It closed behind them, upon the hysteric and indistinguishable woman-wail. His father stopped at the top of the steps and scraped his boot clean on the edge of it. At the gate he stopped again. He stood for a moment, planted stiffly on the stiff foot, looking back at the house. "Pretty and white, ain't it?" he said. "That's sweat. Nigger sweat. Maybe it ain't white enough yet to suit him. Maybe he wants to mix some white sweat with it."

Two hours later the boy was chopping wood behind the house within which his mother and aunt and the two sisters (the mother and aunt, not the two girls, he knew that; even at this distance and muffled by walls the flat loud voices of the two girls emanated an incorrigible idle inertia) were setting up the stove to prepare a meal, when he heard the hooves and saw the linen-clad man on a fine sorrel mare, whom he recognized even before he saw the rolled rug in front of the Negro youth following on a fat bay carriage horse—a suffused, angry face vanishing, still at full gallop, beyond the corner of the house where his father and brother were sitting in the two tilted chairs; and a moment later, almost before he could have put the axe down, he heard the hooves again and watched the sorrel mare go back out of the yard, already galloping again. Then his father began to shout one of the sisters' names, who presently emerged backward from the kitchen door dragging the rolled rug along the ground by one end while the other sister walked behind it.

"If you ain't going to tote, go on and set up the wash pot," the first said.

"You, Sarty!" the second shouted. "Set up the wash pot!" His father appeared at the door, framed against that shabbiness, as he had been against that other bland perfection, impervious to either, the mother's anxious face at his shoulder.

"Go on," the father said. "Pick it up." The two sisters stooped, broad, lethargic; stooping, they presented an incredible expanse of pale cloth and a flutter of tawdry ribbons.

"If I thought enough of a rug to have to git hit all the way from France I wouldn't keep hit where folks coming in would have to tromp on hit," the first said. They raised the rug.

"Abner," the mother said. "Let me do it."

"You go back and git dinner," his father said. "I'll tend to this."

From the woodpile through the rest of the afternoon the boy watched them, the rug spread flat in the dust beside the bubbling wash pot, the two sisters stooping over it with that profound and lethargic reluctance, while the father stood over them in turn, implacable and grim, driving them though never raising his voice again. He could smell the harsh homemade lye they were using; he saw his mother come to the door once and look toward them with an expression not anxious now but very like despair; he saw his father turn, and he fell to with the axe and saw from the corner of his eye his father raise from the ground a flattish fragment of field stone and examine it and return to the pot, and this time his mother actually spoke: "Abner. Abner. Please don't. Please, Abner."

Then he was done too. It was dusk; the whippoorwills had already begun. He could smell coffee from the room where they would presently eat the cold food remaining from the mid-afternoon meal, though when he entered the house he realized they were having coffee again probably because there was a fire on the hearth, before which the rug now lay spread over the backs of the two chairs. The tracks of his father's foot were gone. Where they had been were now long, water-cloudy scoriations resembling the sporadic course of a lilliputian mowing machine.

It still hung there while they ate the cold food and then went to bed, scattered without order or claim up and down the two rooms, his mother in one bed, where his father would later lie, the older brother in the other, himself, the aunt, and the two sisters on pallets on the floor. But his father was not in bed yet. The last thing the boy remembered was the depthless, harsh silhouette of the hat and coat bending over the rug and it seemed to him that he had not even closed his eyes when the silhouette was standing over him, the fire almost dead behind it, the stiff foot prodding him awake. "Catch up the mule," his father said.

When he returned with the mule his father was standing in the back door, the rolled rug over his shoulder. "Ain't you going to ride?" he said.

"No. Give me your foot."

He bent his knee into his father's hand, the wiry, surprising power flowed smoothly, rising, he rising with it, on to the mule's bare back (they had owned a saddle once; the boy could remember it though not when or where) and with the same effortlessness his father swung the rug up in front of him. Now in the starlight they retraced the afternoon's path, up the dusty road rife with honeysuckle, through the gate and up the black tunnel of the drive to the lightless house, where he sat on the mule and felt the rough warp of the rug drag across his thighs and vanish.

"Don't you want me to help?" he whispered. His father did not answer and now he heard again that stiff foot striking the hollow portico with that wooden and clocklike deliberation, that outrageous overstatement of the weight it carried. The rug, hunched, not flung (the boy could tell that even in the darkness) from his father's shoulder struck the angle of wall and floor with a sound unbelievably loud, thunderous, then the foot again, unhurried and enormous; a light came on in the house and the boy sat, tense, breathing steadily and quietly and just a little fast, though the foot itself did not increase its beat at all, descending the steps now; now the boy could see him.

"Don't you want to ride now?" he whispered. "We kin both ride now," the light   60
within the house altering now, flaring up and sinking. *He's coming down the stairs now,* he thought. He had already ridden the mule up beside the horse block; presently his father was up behind him and he doubled the reins over and slashed the mule across the neck, but before the animal could begin to trot the hard, thin arm came around him, the hard, knotted hand jerking the mule back to a walk.

In the first red rays of the sun they were in the lot, putting plow gear on the mules. This time the sorrel mare was in the lot before he heard it at all, the rider collarless and even bareheaded, trembling, speaking in a shaking voice as the woman in the house had done, his father merely looking up once before stooping again to the hame he was buckling, so that the man on the mare spoke to his stooping back:

"You must realize you have ruined that rug. Wasn't there anybody here, any of your women . . ." he ceased, shaking, the boy watching him, the older brother leaning now in the stable door, chewing, blinking slowly and steadily at nothing apparently. "It cost a hundred dollars. But you never had a hundred dollars. You never will. So I'm going to charge you twenty bushels of corn against your crop. I'll add it in your contract and when you come to the commissary you can sign it. That won't keep Mrs. de Spain quiet but maybe it will teach you to wipe your feet off before you enter her house again."

Then he was gone. The boy looked at his father, who still had not spoken or even looked up again, who was now adjusting the logger-head in the hame.

"Pap," he said. His father looked at him—the inscrutable face, the shaggy brows beneath where the gray eyes glinted coldly. Suddenly the boy went toward him, fast, stopping as suddenly. "You done the best you could!" he cried. "If he wanted hit done different why didn't he wait and tell you how? He won't git no twenty bushels! He won't git none! We'll gather hit and hide hit! I kin watch . . ."

"Did you put the cutter back in that straight stock like I told you?"   65

"No, sir," he said.

"Then go do it."

That was Wednesday. During the rest of that week he worked steadily, at what was within his scope and some which was beyond it, with an industry that did not need to be driven nor even commanded twice; he had this from his mother, with the difference that some at least of what he did he liked to do, such as splitting wood with the half-size axe which his mother and aunt had earned, or saved money somehow, to present him with at Christmas. In company with the two older women (and on one afternoon, even one of the sisters), he built pens for the shoat and the cow which were a part of his father's contract with the landlord, and one afternoon, his father being absent, gone somewhere on one of the mules, he went to the field.

They were running a middle buster now, his brother holding the plow straight while he handled the reins, and walking beside the straining mule, the rich black soil shearing cool and damp against his bare ankles, he thought *Maybe this is the end of it. Maybe even that twenty bushels that seems hard to have to pay for just a rug will be a cheap price for him to stop forever and always from being what he used to be;* thinking, dreaming now, so that his brother had to speak sharply to him to mind the mule: *Maybe he even won't collect the twenty bushels. Maybe it will all add up and balance and vanish—corn, rug, fire; the terror and grief; the being pulled two ways like between two teams of horses—gone, done with for ever and ever.*

Then it was Saturday; he looked up from beneath the mule he was harnessing 70 and saw his father in the black coat and hat. "Not that," his father said. "The wagon gear." And then, two hours later, sitting in the wagon bed behind his father and brother on the seat, the wagon accomplished a final curve, and he saw the weathered paintless store with its tattered tobacco- and patent-medicine posters and the teth- ered wagons and saddle animals below the gallery. He mounted the gnawed steps be- hind his father and brother, and there again was the lane of quiet, watching faces for the three of them to walk through. He saw the man in spectacles sitting at the plank table and he did not need to be told this was a Justice of the Peace; he sent one glare of fierce, exultant, partisan defiance at the man in collar and cravat now, whom he had seen but twice before in his life, and that on a galloping horse, who now wore on his face an expression not of rage but of amazed unbelief which the boy could not have known was at the incredible circumstance of being sued by one of his own ten- ants, and came and stood against his father and cried at the Justice: "He ain't done it! He ain't burnt . . ."

"Go back to the wagon," his father said.

"Burnt?" the Justice said. "Do I understand this rug was burned too?"

"Does anybody here claim it was?" his father said. "Go back to the wagon." But he did not, he merely retreated to the rear of the room, crowded as that other had been, but not to sit down this time, instead, to stand pressing among the motionless bodies, listening to the voices:

"And you claim twenty bushels of corn is too high for the damage you did to the rug?"

"He brought the rug to me and said he wanted the tracks washed out of it. I 75 washed the tracks out and took the rug back to him."

"But you didn't carry the rug back to him in the same condition it was in before you made the tracks on it."

His father did not answer, and now for perhaps half a minute there was no sound at all save that of breathing, the faint, steady suspiration of complete and intent lis- tening.

"You decline to answer that, Mr. Snopes?" Again his father did not answer. "I'm going to find against you, Mr. Snopes. I'm going to find that you were responsible for the injury to Major de Spain's rug and hold you liable for it. But twenty bushels of corn seems a little high for a man in your circumstances to have to pay. Major de Spain claims it cost a hundred dollars. October corn will be worth about fifty cents. I figure that if Major de Spain can stand a ninety-five dollar loss on something he paid cash for, you can stand a five-dollar loss you haven't earned yet. I hold you in damages to Major de Spain to the amount of ten bushels of corn over and above your contract with him, to be paid to him out of your crop at gathering time. Court adjourned."

It had taken no time hardly, the morning was but half begun. He thought they would return home and perhaps back to the field, since they were late, far behind all other farmers. But instead his father passed on behind the wagon, merely indicating with his hand for the older brother to follow with it, and crossed the road toward the blacksmith shop opposite, pressing on after his father, overtaking him, speaking, whispering up at the harsh, calm face beneath the weathered hat: "He won't git no ten bushels either. He won't git one. We'll . . ." until his father glanced for an instant down at him, the face absolutely calm, the grizzled eyebrows tangled above the cold eyes, the voice almost pleasant, almost gentle:

"You think so? Well, we'll wait till October anyway." 80

The matter of the wagon—the setting of a spoke or two and the tightening of the tires—did not take long either, the business of the tires accomplished by driving the wagon into the spring branch behind the shop and letting it stand there, the mules nuzzling into the water from time to time, and the boy on the seat with the idle reins, looking up the slope and through the sooty tunnel of the shed where the slow hammer rang and where his father sat on an upended cypress bolt, easily, either talking or listening, still sitting there when the boy brought the dripping wagon up out of the branch and halted it before the door.

"Take them on to the shade and hitch," his father said. He did so and returned. His father and the smith and a third man squatting on his heels inside the door were talking, about crops and animals; the boy, squatting too in the ammoniac dust and hoof-parings and scales of rust, heard his father tell a long and unhurried story out of the time before the birth of the older brother even when he had been a professional horsetrader. And then his father came up beside him where he stood before a tattered last year's circus poster on the other side of the store, gazing rapt and quiet at the scarlet horses, the incredible poisings and convulsions of tulle and tights and the painted leers of comedians, and said, "It's time to eat."

But not at home. Squatting beside his brother against the front wall, he watched his father emerge from the store and produce from a paper sack a segment of cheese and divide it carefully and deliberately into three with his pocket knife and produce crackers from the same sack. They all three squatted on the gallery and ate, slowly, without talking; then in the store again, they drank from a tin dipper tepid water smelling of the cedar bucket and of living beech trees. And still they did not go home. It was a horse lot this time, a tall rail fence upon and along which men stood and sat and out of which one by one horses were led, to be walked and trotted and then cantered back and forth along the road while the slow swapping and buying went on and the sun began to slant westward, they—the three of them—watching and listening, the older brother with his muddy eyes and his steady, inevitable tobacco, the father commenting now and then on certain of the animals, to no one in particular.

It was after sundown when they reached home. They ate supper by lamplight, then, sitting on the doorstep, the boy watched the night fully accomplish, listening to the whippoorwills and the frogs, when he heard his mother's voice: "Abner! No! No! Oh, God. Oh, God. Abner!" and he rose, whirled, and saw the altered light through the door where a candle stub now burned in a bottle neck on the table and his father, still in the hat and coat, at once formal and burlesque as though dressed carefully for some shabby and ceremonial violence, emptying the reservoir of the lamp back into the five-gallon kerosene can from which it had been filled, while the mother tugged at his arm until he shifted the lamp to the other hand and flung her back, not savagely or viciously, just hard, into the wall, her hands flung out against the wall for balance, her mouth open and in her face the same quality of hopeless despair as had been in her voice. Then his father saw him standing in the door.

"Go to the barn and get that can of oil we were oiling the wagon with," he said. 85 The boy did not move. Then he could speak.

"What . . ." he cried. "What are you . . ."

"Go get that oil," his father said. "Go."

Then he was moving, running, outside the house, toward the stable: this the old habit, the old blood which he had not been permitted to choose for himself, which had been bequeathed him willy nilly and which had run for so long (and who knew where, battening on what of outrage and savagery and lust) before it came to him. *I could keep on,* he thought. *I could run on and on and never look back, never need to see his face again. Only I can't. I can't,* the rusted can in his hand now, the liquid sploshing in it as he ran back to the house and into it, into the sound of his mother's weeping in the next room, and handed the can to his father.

"Ain't you going to even send a nigger?" he cried. "At least you sent a nigger before!"

This time his father didn't strike him. The hand came even faster than the blow had, the same hand which had set the can on the table with almost excruciating care flashing from the can toward him too quick for him to follow it, gripping him by the back of his shirt and on to tiptoe before he had seen it quit the can, the face stooping at him in breathless and frozen ferocity, the cold, dead voice speaking over him to the older brother who leaned against the table, chewing with that steady, curious, sidewise motion of cows:

"Empty the can into the big one and go on. I'll catch up with you."

"Better tie him up to the bedpost," the brother said.

"Do like I told you," the father said. Then the boy was moving, his bunched shirt and the hard, bony hand between his shoulder-blades, his toes just touching the floor, across the room and into the other one, past the sisters sitting with spread heavy thighs in the two chairs over the cold hearth, and to where his mother and aunt sat side by side on the bed, the aunt's arm about his mother's shoulders.

"Hold him," the father said. The aunt made a startled movement. "Not you," the father said. "Lennie. Take hold of him. I want to see you do it." His mother took him by the wrist. "You'll hold him better than that. If he gets loose don't you know what he is going to do? He will go up yonder." He jerked his head toward the road. "Maybe I'd better tie him."

"I'll hold him," his mother whispered.

"See you do then." Then his father was gone, the stiff foot heavy and measured upon the boards, ceasing at last.

Then he began to struggle. His mother caught him in both arms, he jerking and wrenching at them. He would be stronger in the end, he knew that. But he had no time to wait for it. "Lemme go!" he cried. "I don't want to have to hit you!"

"Let him go!" the aunt said. "If he don't go, before God, I am going up there myself!"

"Don't you see I can't?" his mother cried. "Sarty! Sarty! No! No! Help me, Lizzie!"

Then he was free. His aunt grasped at him but it was too late. He whirled, running, his mother stumbled forward on to her knees behind him, crying to the nearer sister: "Catch him, Net! Catch him!" But that was too late too, the sister (the sisters were twins, born at the same time, yet either of them now gave the impression of being, encompassing as much living meat and volume and weight as any other two of the family) not yet having begun to rise from the chair, her head, face, alone merely turned, presenting to him in the flying instant an astonishing expanse of young female features untroubled by any surprise even, wearing only an expression of bovine interest. Then he was out of the room, out of the house, in the mild dust of the starlit road and the heavy rifeness of honeysuckle, the pale ribbon unspooling with terrific slowness under his running feet, reaching the gate at last and turning in, running, his heart and lungs drumming, on up the drive toward the lighted house, the lighted door. He did not knock, he burst in, sobbing for breath, incapable for the moment of speech; he saw the astonished face of the Negro in the linen jacket without knowing when the Negro had appeared.

"De Spain!" he cried, panted. "Where's . . ." then he saw the white man too emerging from a white door down the hall. "Barn!" he cried. "Barn!"

"What?" the white man said. "Barn?"

"Yes!" the boy cried. "Barn!"

"Catch him!" the white man shouted.

But it was too late this time too. The Negro grasped his shirt, but the entire   105 sleeve, rotten with washing, carried away, and he was out that door too and in the drive again, and had actually never ceased to run even while he was screaming into the white man's face.

Behind him the white man was shouting, "My horse! Fetch my horse!" and he thought for an instant of cutting across the park and climbing the fence into the road, but he did not know the park nor how high the vine-massed fence might be and he dared not risk it. So he ran on down the drive, blood and breath roaring; presently he was in the road again though he could not see it. He could not hear either: the galloping mare was almost upon him before he heard her, and even then he held his course, as if the very urgency of his wild grief and need must in a moment more find him wings, waiting until the ultimate instant to hurl himself aside and into the weed-choked roadside ditch as the horse thundered past and on, for an instant in furious silhouette against the stars, the tranquil early summer night sky which, even before the shape of the horse and rider vanished, stained abruptly and violently upward: a long, swirling roar incredible and soundless, blotting the stars, and he springing up and into the road again, running again, knowing it was too late yet still running even after he heard the shot and, an instant later, two shots, pausing now without knowing he had ceased to run, crying, "Pap! Pap!", running again before he knew he had begun to run, stumbling, tripping over something and scrabbling up again without ceasing to run, looking backward over his shoulder at the glare as he got up, running on among the invisible trees, panting, sobbing, "Father! Father!"

At midnight he was sitting on the crest of a hill. He did not know it was midnight and he did not know how far he had come. But there was no glare behind him now and he sat now, his back toward what he had called home for four days anyhow, his face toward the dark woods which he would enter when breath was strong again, small, shaking steadily in the chill darkness, hugging himself into the remainder of his thin, rotten shirt, the grief and despair now no longer terror and fear but just grief and despair. *Father. My father,* he thought. "He was brave!" he cried suddenly, aloud but not loud, no more than a whisper. "He was! He was in the war! He was in Colonel Sartoris' cav'ry!" not knowing that his father had gone to that war a private in the fine old European sense, wearing no uniform, admitting the authority of and giving fidelity to no man or army or flag, going to war as Malbrouck° himself did: for booty—it meant nothing and less than nothing to him if it were enemy booty or his own.

Malbrouck: John Churchill, Duke of Marlborough (1650–1722), English general victorious in the Battle of Blenheim (1704), which triumph drove the French army out of Germany. The French called him Malbrouck, a name they found easier to pronounce.

The slow constellations wheeled on. It would be dawn and then sun-up after a while and he would be hungry. But that would be to-morrow and now he was only cold, and walking would cure that. His breathing was easier now and he decided to get up and go on, and then he found that he had been asleep because he knew it was almost dawn, the night almost over. He could tell that from the whippoorwills. They were everywhere now among the dark trees below him, constant and inflectioned and ceaseless, so that, as the instant for giving over to the day birds drew nearer and nearer, there was no interval at all between them. He got up. He was a little stiff, but walking would cure that too as it would the cold, and soon there would be the sun. He went on down the hill, toward the dark woods within which the liquid silver voices of the birds called unceasing—the rapid and urgent beating of the urgent and quiring heart of the late spring night. He did not look back.

Questions

1. After delivering his warning to Major de Spain, the boy Snopes does not actually witness what happens to his father and brother, or what happens to the Major's barn. But what do you assume happens? What evidence is given in the story?

2. What do you understand to be Faulkner's opinion of Abner Snopes? Make a guess, indicating details in the story that convey attitudes.

3. Which adjectives best describe the general tone of the story: *calm, amused, disinterested, scornful, marveling, excited, impassioned?* Point out passages that may be so described. What do you notice about the style in which these passages are written?

4. In tone and style, how does "Barn Burning" compare with Faulkner's story "A Rose for Emily" (Chapter 2)? To what do you attribute any differences?

5. Suppose that, instead of "Barn Burning," Faulkner had written a story told by Abner Snopes in the first person. Why would such a story need a style different from that of "Barn Burning"? (Suggestion: Notice Faulkner's descriptions of Abner Snopes's voice.)

6. Although "Barn Burning" takes place some thirty years after the Civil War, how does the war figure in it?

IRONY

If a friend declares, "Oh, sure, I just *love* to have four papers due on the same day," you detect that the statement contains **irony**. This is **verbal irony**, the most familiar kind, in which we understand the speaker's meaning to be far from the usual meaning of the words—in this case, quite the opposite. (When the irony is found, as here, in a somewhat sour statement tinged with mockery, it is called **sarcasm**.)

Irony, of course, occurs in writing as well as in conversation. When in a comic moment in Isaac Bashevis Singer's "Gimpel the Fool" the sexton announces, "The wealthy Reb Gimpel invites the congregation to a feast in honor of the birth of a son," the people at the synagogue burst into laughter. They know that Gimpel, in contrast to the sexton's words, is not a wealthy man but a humble baker; that the son is not his own but his wife's lover's; and that the birth brings no honor to anybody. Verbal irony, then, implies a contrast or discrepancy between what is *said* and what is *meant*.

Dramatic Irony

There are also times when the speaker, unlike the reader, does not realize the ironic dimension of his or her words; such instances are known as **dramatic irony**. The most famous example occurs in Sophocles' tragic drama *Oedipus the King*, when Oedipus vows to find and punish the murderer of King Laius, unaware that he himself is the man he seeks, and adds: "if by any chance / he proves to be an intimate of our house, / here at my hearth, with my full knowledge, / may the curse I just called down on him strike me!" Dramatic irony may also be used, of course, for lighter purposes: for example, Daisy Coble, the mother in Anne Tyler's "Teenage Wasteland," whose attitudes and moods shift constantly according to what others tell her, responds to the idea that *she* should be less strict with her son by saying, "But see, he's still so suggestible." Stories often contain other kinds of irony besides such verbal irony. A situation, for example, can be ironic if it contains some wry contrast or incongruity. In Jack London's "To Build a Fire" (Chapter 4), it is ironic that a freezing man, desperately trying to strike a match to light a fire and save himself, accidentally ignites all his remaining matches.

Irony as Point of View

An entire story may be told from an **ironic point of view**. Whenever we sense a sharp distinction between the narrator of a story and the author, irony is likely to occur—especially when the narrator is telling us something that we are clearly expected to doubt or to interpret very differently. In "A & P," Sammy (who tells his own story) makes many smug and cruel observations about the people around him; but the author makes clear to us that much of his superiority is based on immaturity and lack of self-knowledge. (This irony, by the way, does not negate the fact that Sammy makes some very telling comments about society's superficial values and rigid and judgmental attitudes, comments that Updike seems to endorse and wants us to endorse as well.) And when we read Hemingway's "A Clean, Well-Lighted Place," surely we feel that most of the time the older waiter speaks for the author. Though the waiter gives us a respectful, compassionate view of a lonely old man, and we don't doubt that the view is Hemingway's, still, in the closing lines of the story we are reminded that author and waiter are not identical. Musing on the sleepless night ahead of him, the waiter tries to shrug off his problem—"After all, it is probably only insomnia"—but the reader, who recalls the waiter's bleak view of *nada*, nothingness, knows that it certainly isn't mere insomnia that keeps him awake but a dread of solitude and death. At that crucial moment, Hemingway and the older waiter part company, and we perceive an ironic point of view, and also a verbal irony, "After all, it is probably only insomnia."

Cosmic Irony

Storytellers are sometimes fond of ironic twists of fate—developments that reveal a terrible distance between what people deserve and what they get, between what is and what ought to be. In the novels of Thomas Hardy, some hostile fate keeps playing tricks to thwart the main characters. In *Tess of the D'Urbervilles*, an all-important letter, thrust under a door, by chance slides beneath a carpet and is not received. Such an irony is sometimes called an **irony of fate** or a **cosmic irony**, for it suggests that some malicious fate (or other spirit in the universe) is deliberately frustrating human efforts. Evidently, there is an irony of fate in the servant's futile attempt to escape Death in the fable "The Appointment in Samarra," and perhaps in the flaring up of the all-precious matches in "To Build a Fire" as well. To notice an irony gives pleasure. It may move us to laughter, make us feel wonder, or arouse our sympathy. By so involving us, irony—whether in a statement, a situation, an unexpected event, or a point of view—can render a story more likely to strike us, to affect us, and to be remembered.

A famous example of O. Henry's irony is the following story, perhaps the best-known and most-loved of his many tales.

O. Henry (William Sydney Porter)

The Gift of the Magi   1906

O. Henry

William Sydney Porter (1862–1910), known to the world as O. Henry, was born in Greensboro, North Carolina. He began writing in his mid-twenties, contributing humorous sketches to various periodicals. In 1896 he was indicted for embezzlement from the First National Bank of Austin, Texas; he fled to Honduras before his trial, but returned when he found that his wife was terminally ill. He was convicted, and served three years of a five-year sentence; his guilt or innocence has never been definitively established. Released in 1901, he moved to New York the following year. Already a well-known writer, for the next three years he produced a story every week for the New York World while also contributing tales and sketches to magazines. Beginning with Cabbages and Kings *in 1904, his stories were published in nine highly successful collections in the few remaining years of his life, as well as in three posthumously issued volumes. Financial extravagance and alcoholism darkened his last days, culminating in his death from tuberculosis at the age of forty-seven. Ranked during his lifetime with Hawthorne and Poe, O. Henry is more likely now to be invoked in negative terms, for his sentimentality and especially for his reliance on frequently forced trick endings, but the most prestigious annual volume of the best American short fiction is still called* The O. Henry Prize Stories, *and the best of his own work is loved by millions of readers.*

One dollar and eighty-seven cents. That was all. And sixty cents of it was in pennies. Pennies saved one and two at a time by bulldozing the grocer and the vegetable man and the butcher until one's cheeks burned with the silent imputation of parsimony that such close dealing implied. Three times Della counted it. One dollar and eighty-seven cents. And the next day would be Christmas.

There was clearly nothing to do but flop down on the shabby little couch and howl. So Della did it. Which instigates the moral reflection that life is made up of sobs, sniffles, and smiles, with sniffles predominating.

While the mistress of the home is gradually subsiding from the first stage to the second, take a look at the home. A furnished flat at $8 per week. It did not exactly beggar description, but it certainly had that word on the lookout for the mendicancy squad.

In the vestibule below was a letter-box into which no letter would go, and an electric button from which no mortal finger could coax a ring. Also appertaining thereunto was a card bearing the name "Mr. James Dillingham Young."

The "Dillingham" had been flung to the breeze during a former period of prosperity when its possessor was being paid $30 per week. Now, when the income was shrunk to $20, the letters of "Dillingham" looked blurred, as though they were thinking seriously of contracting to a modest and unassuming D. But whenever Mr. James Dillingham Young came home and reached his flat above he was called "Jim" and greatly hugged by Mrs. James Dillingham Young, already introduced to you as Della. Which is all very good.

5

Della finished her cry and attended to her cheeks with the powder rag. She stood by the window and looked out dully at a grey cat walking a grey fence in a grey backyard. Tomorrow would be Christmas Day, and she had only $1.87 with which to buy Jim a present. She had been saving every penny she could for months, with this result. Twenty dollars a week doesn't go far. Expenses had been greater than she had calculated. They always are. Only $1.87 to buy a present for Jim. Her Jim. Many a happy hour she had spent planning for something nice for him. Something fine and rare and sterling—something just a little bit near to being worthy of the honor of being owned by Jim.

There was a pier-glass between the windows of the room. Perhaps you have seen a pier-glass in an $8 flat. A very thin and very agile person may, by observing his reflection in a rapid sequence of longitudinal strips, obtain a fairly accurate conception of his looks. Della, being slender, had mastered the art.

Suddenly she whirled from the window and stood before the glass. Her eyes were shining brilliantly, but her face had lost its color within twenty seconds. Rapidly she pulled down her hair and let it fall to its full length.

Now, there were two possessions of the James Dillingham Youngs in which they both took a mighty pride. One was Jim's gold watch that had been his father's and his grandfather's. The other was Della's hair. Had the Queen of Sheba lived in the flat across the airshaft, Della would have let her hair hang out the window some day to dry just to depreciate Her Majesty's jewels and gifts. Had King Solomon been the janitor, with all his treasures piled up in the basement, Jim would have pulled out his watch every time he passed, just to see him pluck at his beard from envy.

So now Della's beautiful hair fell about her, rippling and shining like a cascade of   10
brown waters. It reached below her knee and made itself almost a garment for her. And then she did it up again nervously and quickly. Once she faltered for a minute and stood still while a tear or two splashed on the worn red carpet.

On went her old brown jacket; on went her old brown hat. With a whirl of skirts and with the brilliant sparkle still in her eyes, she fluttered out the door and down the stairs to the street.

Where she stopped the sign read: "Mme. Sofronie. Hair Goods of All Kinds." One flight up Della ran, and collected herself, panting. Madame, large, too white, chilly, hardly looked the "Sofronie."

"Will you buy my hair?" asked Della.

"I buy hair," said Madame. "Take yer hat off and let's have a sight at the looks of it."

Down rippled the brown cascade.   15

"Twenty dollars," said Madame, lifting the mass with a practiced hand.

"Give it to me quick," said Della.

Oh, and the next two hours tripped by on rosy wings. Forget the hashed metaphor. She was ransacking the stores for Jim's present.

She found it at last. It surely had been made for Jim and no one else. There was no other like it in any of the stores, and she had turned all of them inside out. It was a platinum fob chain simple and chaste in design, properly proclaiming its value by substance alone and not by meretricious ornamentation—as all good things should do. It was even worthy of The Watch. As soon as she saw it she knew that it must be Jim's. It was like him. Quietness and value—the description applied to both. Twenty-one dollars they took from her for it, and she hurried home with the 87 cents. With that chain on his watch Jim might be properly anxious about the time in any company. Grand as the watch was, he sometimes looked at it on the sly on account of the old leather strap that he used in place of a chain.

When Della reached home her intoxication gave way a little to prudence and reason. She got out her curling irons and lighted the gas and went to work repairing the ravages made by generosity added to love. Which is always a tremendous task, dear friends—a mammoth task.

Within forty minutes her head was covered with tiny, close-lying curls that made her look wonderfully like a truant schoolboy. She looked at her reflection in the mirror long, carefully, and critically.

"If Jim doesn't kill me," she said to herself, "before he takes a second look at me, he'll say I look like a Coney Island chorus girl. But what could I do—oh! What could I do with a dollar and eighty-seven cents?"

At 7 o'clock the coffee was made and the frying-pan was on the back of the stove hot and ready to cook the chops.

Jim was never late. Della doubled the fob chain in her hand and sat on the corner of the table near the door that he always entered. Then she heard his step on the stair away down on the first flight, and she turned white for just a moment. She had a habit of saying little silent prayers about the simplest everyday things, and now she whispered: "Please God, make him think I am still pretty."

The door opened and Jim stepped in and closed it. He looked thin and very serious. Poor fellow, he was only twenty-two—and to be burdened with a family! He needed a new overcoat and he was without gloves.

Jim stopped inside the door, as immovable as a setter at the scent of quail. His eyes were fixed upon Della, and there was an expression in them that she could not read, and it terrified her. It was not anger, nor surprise, nor disapproval, nor horror, nor any of the sentiments that she had been prepared for. He simply stared at her fixedly with that peculiar expression on his face.

Della wriggled off the table and went for him.

"Jim, darling," she cried, "don't look at me that way. I had my hair cut off and sold because I couldn't have lived through Christmas without giving you a present. It'll grow out again—you won't mind, will you? I just had to do it. My hair grows awfully fast. Say 'Merry Christmas!' Jim, and let's be happy. You don't know what a nice—what a beautiful, nice gift I've got for you."

"You've cut off your hair?" asked Jim, laboriously, as if he had not arrived at that patent fact yet even after the hardest mental labor.

"Cut it off and sold it," said Della. "Don't you like me just as well, anyhow? I'm me without my hair, ain't I?"

Jim looked about the room curiously.

"You say your hair is gone?" he said, with an air almost of idiocy.

"You needn't look for it," said Della. "It's sold, I tell you—sold and gone, too. It's Christmas Eve, boy. Be good to me, for it went for you. Maybe the hairs of my head were numbered," she went on with a sudden serious sweetness, "but nobody could ever count my love for you. Shall I put the chops on, Jim?"

Out of his trance Jim seemed quickly to wake. He enfolded his Della. For ten seconds let us regard with discreet scrutiny some inconsequential object in the other direction. Eight dollars a week or a million a year—what is the difference? A mathematician or a wit would give you the wrong answer. The magi brought valuable gifts, but that was not among them. This dark assertion will be illuminated later on.

Jim drew a package from his overcoat pocket and threw it upon the table.

"Don't make any mistake, Dell," he said, "about me. I don't think there's anything in the way of a haircut or a shave or a shampoo that could make me like my girl any less. But if you'll unwrap that package you may see why you had me going a while at first."

White fingers and nimble tore at the string and paper. And then an ecstatic scream of joy; and then, alas! a quick feminine change to hysterical tears and wails, necessitating the immediate employment of all the comforting powers of the lord of the flat.

For there lay The Combs—the set of combs, side and back, that Della had worshipped for long in a Broadway window. Beautiful combs, pure tortoise shell, with jewelled rims—just the shade to wear in the beautiful vanished hair. They were expensive combs, she knew, and her heart had simply craved and yearned over them without the least hope of possession. And now, they were hers, but the tresses that should have adorned the coveted adornments were gone.

But she hugged them to her bosom, and at length she was able to look up with dim eyes and a smile and say: "My hair grows so fast, Jim!"

And then Della leaped up like a little singed cat and cried, "Oh, oh!"   40

Jim had not yet seen his beautiful present. She held it out to him eagerly upon her open palm. The dull precious metal seemed to flash with a reflection of her bright and ardent spirit.

"Isn't it a dandy, Jim? I hunted all over town to find it. You'll have to look at the time a hundred times a day now. Give me your watch. I want to see how it looks on it."

Instead of obeying, Jim tumbled down on the couch and put his hands under the back of his head and smiled.

"Dell," said he, "let's put our Christmas presents away and keep 'em a while. They're too nice to use just at present. I sold the watch to get the money to buy your combs. And now suppose you put the chops on."

The magi, as you know, were wise men—wonderfully wise men—who brought   45
gifts to the Babe in the manger. They invented the art of giving Christmas presents. Being wise, their gifts were no doubt wise ones, possibly bearing the privilege of exchange in case of duplication. And here I have lamely related to you the uneventful chronicle of two foolish children in a flat who most unwisely sacrificed for each other the greatest treasures of their house. But in a last word to the wise of these days let it be said that of all who give gifts these two were the wisest. Of all who give and receive gifts, such as they are wisest. Everywhere they are wisest. They are the magi.

Questions

1. How would you describe the style of this story? Does the author's tone tell you anything about his attitude toward the characters and events of the narrative?

2. What do the details in paragraph 7 tell you about Della and Jim's financial situation?

3. O. Henry tells us that Jim "needed a new overcoat and he was without gloves" (paragraph 25). Why do you think Della didn't buy him these things for Christmas instead of a watch chain?

4. "Eight dollars a week or a million a year—what is the difference? A mathematician or a wit would give you the wrong answer" (paragraph 34). What, in your view, is "the wrong answer," and why is it wrong? What might the right answer be?

5. What is ironic about the story's ending? Is this plot twist the most important element of the conclusion? If not, what is?

Ha Jin

Saboteur

2000

Ha Jin is the pen name of Xuefei Jin, who was born in Liaoning, China, in 1956. The son of a military officer and a worker, Jin grew up during the turbulent Cultural Revolution, a ten-year upheaval initiated by the Communist Party in 1966 to transform China into a Marxist workers' society by destroying all remnants of the nation's ancient past. During this period many schools and universities were closed and intellectuals were required to work in proletarian jobs. At fourteen, Jin joined the People's Liberation Army, where he remained for nearly six years, and later worked as a telegraph operator for a railroad company. He then attended Heilongjiang University, where in 1981 he received a B.A. in English. After earning an M.A. in American literature from Shangdong

Ha Jin

University in 1984, Jin traveled to the United States to work on a Ph.D. at Brandeis University. He intended to return to China, but the Communist Party's violent suppression of the student movement in 1989 made him decide to stay in the United States and write only in English. "It's such a brutal government," he commented, "I was very angry, and I decided not to return to China." "Writing in English became my means of survival," he remarked, "of spending or wasting my life, of retrieving losses, mine, and those of others."

Jin has published three books of poetry and five novels, including Waiting *(1999, National Book Award),* War Trash *(2004, PEN/Faulkner Award), and* A Free Life *(2007). His first volume of short fiction,* Ocean of Words *(1996), was drawn from his experience in the People's Liberation Army and won the PEN/Hemingway Award. He is a professor of English at Boston University.*

Mr. Chiu and his bride were having lunch in the square before Muji Train Station. On the table between them were two bottles of soda spewing out brown foam and two paper boxes of rice and sautéed cucumber and pork. "Let's eat," he said to her, and broke the connected ends of the chopsticks. He picked up a slice of streaky pork and put it into his mouth. As he was chewing, a few crinkles appeared on his thin jaw.

To his right, at another table, two railroad policemen were drinking tea and laughing; it seemed that the stout, middle-aged man was telling a joke to his young comrade, who was tall and of athletic build. Now and again they would steal a glance at Mr. Chiu's table.

The air smelled of rotten melon. A few flies kept buzzing above the couple's lunch. Hundreds of people were rushing around to get on the platform or to catch buses to downtown. Food and fruit vendors were crying for customers in lazy voices. About a dozen young women, representing the local hotels, held up placards which displayed the daily prices and words as large as a palm, like FREE MEALS, AIR-CONDITIONING, and ON THE RIVER. In the center of the square stood a concrete statue of Chairman Mao, at whose feet peasants were napping, their backs on the warm granite and their faces toward the sunny sky. A flock of pigeons perched on the Chairman's raised hand and forearm.

The rice and cucumber tasted good, and Mr. Chiu was eating unhurriedly. His sallow face showed exhaustion. He was glad that the honeymoon was finally over and that he and his bride were heading back for Harbin. During the two weeks' vacation, he had been worried about his liver, because three months ago he had suffered from acute hepatitis; he was afraid he might have a relapse. But he had had no severe symptoms, despite his liver being still big and tender. On the whole he was pleased with his health, which could endure even the strain of a honeymoon; indeed, he was on the course of recovery. He looked at his bride, who took off her wire glasses, kneading the root of her nose with her fingertips. Beads of sweat coated her pale cheeks.

"Are you all right, sweetheart?" he asked.   5

"I have a headache. I didn't sleep well last night."

"Take an aspirin, will you?"

"It's not that serious. Tomorrow is Sunday and I can sleep in. Don't worry."

As they were talking, the stout policeman at the next table stood up and threw a bowl of tea in their direction. Both Mr. Chiu's and his bride's sandals were wet instantly.

"Hooligan!" she said in a low voice.   10

Mr. Chiu got to his feet and said out loud, "Comrade Policeman, why did you do this?" He stretched out his right foot to show the wet sandal.

"Do what?" the stout man asked huskily, glaring at Mr. Chiu while the young fellow was whistling.

"See, you dumped tea on our feet."

"You're lying. You wet your shoes yourself."

"Comrade Policemen, your duty is to keep order, but you purposely tortured us   15
common citizens. Why violate the law you are supposed to enforce?" As Mr. Chiu was speaking, dozens of people began gathering around.

With a wave of his hand, the man said to the young fellow, "Let's get hold of him!"

They grabbed Mr. Chiu and clamped handcuffs around his wrists. He cried, "You can't do this to me. This is utterly unreasonable."

"Shut up!" The man pulled out his pistol. "You can use your tongue at our headquarters."

The young fellow added, "You're a saboteur, you know that? You're disrupting public order."

The bride was too petrified to say anything coherent. She was a recent college   20
graduate, had majored in fine arts, and had never seen the police make an arrest. All she could say was, "Oh, please, please!"

The policemen were pulling Mr. Chiu, but he refused to go with them, holding the corner of the table and shouting, "We have a train to catch. We already bought the tickets."

The stout man punched him in the chest. "Shut up. Let your ticket expire." With the pistol butt he chopped Mr. Chiu's hands, which at once released the table. Together the two men were dragging him away to the police station.

Realizing he had to go with them, Mr. Chiu turned his head and shouted to his bride, "Don't wait for me here. Take the train. If I'm not back by tomorrow morning, send someone over to get me out."

She nodded, covering her sobbing mouth with her palm.

*

After removing his belt, they locked Mr. Chiu into a cell in the back of the Rail- 25
road Police Station. The single window in the room was blocked by six steel bars; it
faced a spacious yard, in which stood a few pines. Beyond the trees, two swings hung
from an iron frame, swaying gently in the breeze. Somewhere in the building a cleaver
was chopping rhythmically. There must be a kitchen upstairs, Mr. Chiu thought.

He was too exhausted to worry about what they would do to him, so he lay down on
the narrow bed and shut his eyes. He wasn't afraid. The Cultural Revolution was over already, and recently the Party had been propagating the idea that all citizens were equal
before the law. The police ought to be a law-abiding model for common people. As long
as he remained coolheaded and reasoned with them, they probably wouldn't harm him.

Late in the afternoon he was taken to the Interrogation Bureau on the second
floor. On his way there, in the stairwell, he ran into the middle-aged policeman who
had manhandled him. The man grinned, rolling his bulgy eyes and pointing his fingers
at him as if firing a pistol. Egg of a tortoise! Mr. Chiu cursed mentally.

The moment he sat down in the office, he burped, his palm shielding his mouth.
In front of him, across a long desk, sat the chief of the bureau and a donkey-faced
man. On the glass desktop was a folder containing information on his case. He felt it
bizarre that in just a matter of hours they had accumulated a small pile of writing
about him. On second thought he began to wonder whether they had kept a file on
him all the time. How could this have happened? He lived and worked in Harbin,
more than three hundred miles away, and this was his first time in Muji City.

The chief of the bureau was a thin, bald man who looked serene and intelligent.
His slim hands handled the written pages in the folder in the manner of a lecturing
scholar. To Mr. Chiu's left sat a young scribe, with a clipboard on his knee and a
black fountain pen in his hand.

"Your name?" the chief asked, apparently reading out the question from a form. 30

"Chiu Maguang."

"Age?"

"Thirty-four."

"Profession?"

"Lecturer." 35

"Work unit?"

"Harbin University."

"Political status?"

"Communist Party member."

The chief put down the paper and began to speak. "Your crime is sabotage, al- 40
though it hasn't induced serious consequences yet. Because you are a Party member,
you should be punished more. You have failed to be a model for the masses and you—"

"Excuse me, sir," Mr. Chiu cut him off.

"What?"

"I didn't do anything. Your men are the saboteurs of our social order. They threw
hot tea on my feet and on my wife's feet. Logically speaking, you should criticize
them, if not punish them."

"That statement is groundless. You have no witness. Why should I believe you?"
the chief said matter-of-factly.

"This is my evidence." He raised his right hand. "Your man hit my fingers with a 45
pistol."

"That doesn't prove how your feet got wet. Besides, you could have hurt your
fingers yourself."

"But I am telling the truth!" Anger flared up in Mr. Chiu. "Your police station owes me an apology. My train ticket has expired, my new leather sandals are ruined, and I am late for a conference in the provincial capital. You must compensate me for the damage and losses. Don't mistake me for a common citizen who would tremble when you sneeze. I'm a scholar, a philosopher, and an expert in dialectical materialism. If necessary, we will argue about this in *The Northeastern Daily*, or we will go to the highest People's Court in Beijing. Tell me, what's your name?" He got carried away with his harangue, which was by no means trivial and had worked to his advantage on numerous occasions.

"Stop bluffing us," the donkey-faced man broke in. "We have seen a lot of your kind. We can easily prove you are guilty. Here are some of the statements given by eyewitnesses." He pushed a few sheets of paper toward Mr. Chiu.

Mr. Chiu was dazed to see the different handwritings, which all stated that he had shouted in the square to attract attention and refused to obey the police. One of the witnesses had identified herself as a purchasing agent from a shipyard in Shanghai. Something stirred in Mr. Chiu's stomach, a pain rising to his rib. He gave out a faint moan.

"Now you have to admit you are guilty," the chief said. "Although it's a serious 50 crime, we won't punish you severely, provided you write out a self-criticism and promise that you won't disrupt the public order again. In other words, your release will depend on your attitude toward this crime."

"You're daydreaming," Mr. Chiu cried. "I won't write a word, because I'm innocent. I demand that you provide me with a letter of apology so I can explain to my university why I'm late."

Both the interrogators smiled contemptuously. "Well, we've never done that," said the chief, taking a puff of his cigarette.

"Then make this a precedent."

"That's unnecessary. We are pretty certain that you will comply with our wishes." The chief blew a column of smoke toward Mr. Chiu's face.

At the tilt of the chief's head, two guards stepped forward and grabbed the criminal by 55 the arms. Mr. Chiu meanwhile went on saying, "I shall report you to the Provincial Administration. You'll have to pay for this! You are worse than the Japanese military police."

They dragged him out of the room.

After dinner, which consisted of a bowl of millet porridge, a corn bun, and a piece of pickled turnip, Mr. Chiu began to have a fever, shaking with a chill and sweating profusely. He knew that the fire of anger had gotten into his liver and that he was probably having a relapse. No medicine was available, because his briefcase had been left with his bride. At home it would have been time for him to sit in front of their color TV, drinking jasmine tea and watching the evening news. It was so lonesome in here. The orange bulb above the single bed was the only source of light, which enabled the guards to keep him under surveillance at night. A moment ago he had asked them for a newspaper or a magazine to read, but they turned him down.

Through the small opening on the door noises came in. It seemed that the police on duty were playing cards or chess in a nearby office; shouts and laughter could be heard now and then. Meanwhile, an accordion kept coughing from a remote corner in the building. Looking at the ballpoint and the letter paper left for him by the guards when they took him back from the Interrogation Bureau, Mr. Chiu remembered the old saying, "When a scholar runs into soldiers, the more he argues, the muddier his point becomes." How ridiculous this whole thing was. He ruffled his thick hair with his fingers.

He felt miserable, massaging his stomach continually. To tell the truth, he was more upset than frightened, because he would have to catch up with his work once he was back home—a paper that was due at the printers next week, and two dozen books he ought to read for the courses he was going to teach in the fall.

A human shadow flitted across the opening. Mr. Chiu rushed to the door and shouted through the hole, "Comrade Guard, Comrade Guard!" 60

"What do you want?" a voice rasped.

"I want you to inform your leaders that I'm very sick. I have heart disease and hepatitis. I may die here if you keep me like this without medication."

"No leader is on duty on the weekend. You have to wait till Monday."

"What? You mean I'll stay in here tomorrow?"

"Yes." 65

"Your station will be held responsible if anything happens to me."

"We know that. Take it easy, you won't die."

It seemed illogical that Mr. Chiu slept quite well that night, though the light above his head had been on all the time and the straw mattress was hard and infested with fleas. He was afraid of ticks, mosquitoes, cockroaches—any kind of insect but fleas and bedbugs. Once, in the countryside, where his school's faculty and staff had helped the peasants harvest crops for a week, his colleagues had joked about his flesh, which they said must have tasted nonhuman to fleas. Except for him, they were all afflicted with hundreds of bites.

More amazing now, he didn't miss his bride a lot. He even enjoyed sleeping alone, perhaps because the honeymoon had tired him out and he needed more rest.

The backyard was quiet on Sunday morning. Pale sunlight streamed through the pine branches. A few sparrows were jumping on the ground, catching caterpillars and ladybugs. Holding the steel bars, Mr. Chiu inhaled the morning air, which smelled meaty. There must have been an eatery or a cooked-meat stand nearby. He reminded himself that he should take this detention with ease. A sentence that Chairman Mao had written to a hospitalized friend rose in his mind: "Since you are already in here, you may as well stay and make the best of it." 70

His desire for peace of mind originated in his fear that his hepatitis might get worse. He tried to remain unperturbed. However, he was sure that his liver was swelling up, since the fever still persisted. For a whole day he lay in bed, thinking about his paper on the nature of contradictions. Time and again he was overwhelmed by anger, cursing aloud, "A bunch of thugs!" He swore that once he was out, he would write an article about this experience. He had better find out some of the policemen's names.

It turned out to be a restful day for the most part; he was certain that his university would send somebody to his rescue. All he should do now was remain calm and wait patiently. Sooner or later the police would have to release him, although they had no idea that he might refuse to leave unless they wrote him an apology. Damn those hoodlums, they had ordered more than they could eat!

When he woke up on Monday morning, it was already light. Somewhere a man was moaning; the sound came from the backyard. After a long yawn, and kicking off the tattered blanket, Mr. Chiu climbed out of bed and went to the window. In the middle of the yard, a young man was fastened to a pine, his wrists handcuffed around the trunk from behind. He was wriggling and swearing loudly, but there was no sight of anyone else in the yard. He looked familiar to Mr. Chiu.

Mr. Chiu squinted his eyes to see who it was. To his astonishment, he recognized the man, who was Fenjin, a recent graduate from the Law Department at Harbin

University. Two years ago Mr. Chiu had taught a course in Marxist materialism, in which Fenjin had enrolled. Now, how on earth had this young devil landed here?

Then it dawned on him that Fenjin must have been sent over by his bride. What a stupid woman! A bookworm, who only knew how to read foreign novels! He had expected that she would contact the school's Security Section, which would for sure send a cadre here. Fenjin held no official position; he merely worked in a private law firm that had just two lawyers; in fact, they had little business except for some detective work for men and women who suspected their spouses of having extramarital affairs. Mr. Chiu was overcome with a wave of nausea.

Should he call out to let his student know he was nearby? He decided not to, because he didn't know what had happened. Fenjin must have quarreled with the police to incur such a punishment. Yet this could never have occurred if Fenjin hadn't come to his rescue. So no matter what, Mr. Chiu had to do something. But what could he do?

It was going to be a scorcher. He could see purple steam shimmering and rising from the ground among the pines. Poor devil, he thought, as he raised a bowl of corn glue to his mouth, sipped, and took a bite of a piece of salted celery.

When a guard came to collect the bowl and the chopsticks, Mr. Chiu asked him what had happened to the man in the backyard. "He called our boss 'bandit,'" the guard said. "He claimed he was a lawyer or something. An arrogant son of a rabbit."

Now it was obvious to Mr. Chiu that he had to do something to help his rescuer. Before he could figure out a way, a scream broke out in the backyard. He rushed to the window and saw a tall policeman standing before Fenjin, an iron bucket on the ground. It was the same young fellow who had arrested Mr. Chiu in the square two days before. The man pinched Fenjin's nose, then raised his hand, which stayed in the air for a few seconds, then slapped the lawyer across the face. As Fenjin was groaning, the man lifted up the bucket and poured water on his head.

"This will keep you from getting sunstroke, boy. I'll give you some more every hour," the man said loudly.

Fenjin kept his eyes shut, yet his wry face showed that he was struggling to hold back from cursing the policeman, or, more likely, that he was sobbing in silence. He sneezed, then raised his face and shouted, "Let me go take a piss."

"Oh, yeah?" the man bawled. "Pee in your pants."

Still Mr. Chiu didn't make any noise, gripping the steel bars with both hands, his fingers white. The policeman turned and glanced at the cell's window; his pistol, partly holstered, glittered in the sun. With a snort he spat his cigarette butt to the ground and stamped it into the dust.

Then the door opened and the guards motioned Mr. Chiu to come out. Again they took him upstairs to the Interrogation Bureau.

The same men were in the office, though this time the scribe was sitting there empty-handed. At the sight of Mr. Chiu the chief said, "Ah, here you are. Please be seated."

After Mr. Chiu sat down, the chief waved a white silk fan and said to him, "You may have seen your lawyer. He's a young man without manners, so our director had him taught a crash course in the backyard."

"It's illegal to do that. Aren't you afraid to appear in a newspaper?"

"No, we are not, not even on TV. What else can you do? We are not afraid of any story you make up. We call it fiction. What we do care about is that you cooperate with us. That is to say, you must admit your crime."

"What if I refuse to cooperate?"

"Then your lawyer will continue his education in the sunshine."

A swoon swayed Mr. Chiu, and he held the arms of the chair to steady himself. A numb pain stung him in the upper stomach and nauseated him, and his head was throbbing. He was sure that the hepatitis was finally attacking him. Anger was flaming up in his chest; his throat was tight and clogged.

The chief resumed, "As a matter of fact, you don't even have to write out your self-criticism. We have your crime described clearly here. All we need is your signature."

Holding back his rage, Mr. Chiu said, "Let me look at that."

With a smirk the donkey-faced man handed him a sheet which carried these words:

I hereby admit that on July 13 I disrupted public order at Muji Train Station, and that I refused to listen to reason when the railroad police issued their warning. Thus I myself am responsible for my arrest. After two days' detention, I have realized the reactionary nature of my crime. From now on, I shall continue to educate myself with all my effort and shall never commit this kind of crime again.

A voice started screaming in Mr. Chiu's ears, "Lie, lie!" But he shook his head and forced the voice away. He asked the chief, "If I sign this, will you release both my lawyer and me?"

"Of course, we'll do that." The chief was drumming his fingers on the blue folder—their file on him.

Mr. Chiu signed his name and put his thumbprint under his signature.

"Now you are free to go," the chief said with a smile, and handed him a piece of paper to wipe his thumb with.

Mr. Chiu was so sick that he couldn't stand up from the chair at first try. Then he doubled his effort and rose to his feet. He staggered out of the building to meet his lawyer in the backyard, having forgotten to ask for his belt back. In his chest he felt as though there were a bomb. If he were able to, he would have razed the entire police station and eliminated all their families. Though he knew he could do nothing like that, he made up his mind to do something.

"I'm sorry about this torture, Fenjin," Mr. Chiu said when they met.

"It doesn't matter. They are savages." The lawyer brushed a patch of dirt off his jacket with trembling fingers. Water was still dribbling from the bottoms of his trouser legs.

"Let's go now," the teacher said.

The moment they came out of the police station, Mr. Chiu caught sight of a tea stand. He grabbed Fenjin's arm and walked over to the old woman at the table. "Two bowls of black tea," he said and handed her a one-yuan note.

After the first bowl, they each had another one. Then they set out for the train station. But before they walked fifty yards, Mr. Chiu insisted on eating a bowl of tree-ear soup at a food stand. Fenjin agreed. He told his teacher, "You mustn't treat me like a guest."

"No, I want to eat something myself."

As if dying of hunger, Mr. Chiu dragged his lawyer from restaurant to restaurant near the police station, but at each place he ordered no more than two bowls of food. Fenjin wondered why his teacher wouldn't stay at one place and eat his fill.

Mr. Chiu bought noodles, wonton, eight-grain porridge, and chicken soup, respectively, at four restaurants. While eating, he kept saying through his teeth, "If only I could kill all the bastards!" At the last place he merely took a few sips of the soup without tasting the chicken cubes and mushrooms.

Fenjin was baffled by his teacher, who looked ferocious and muttered to himself mysteriously, and whose jaundiced face was covered with dark puckers. For the first time Fenjin thought of Mr. Chiu as an ugly man.

Within a month over eight hundred people contracted acute hepatitis in Muji. Six died of the disease, including two children. Nobody knew how the epidemic had started.

Questions

1. Why is Mr. Chiu in Muji?
2. In the story's second paragraph, two railroad policemen are sitting next to Mr. Chiu and his wife. Why do you think they are laughing and looking at the newlywed couple?
3. With what specific crime is Mr. Chiu charged? Is he guilty?
4. What is Mr. Chiu's initial reaction to his arrest?
5. Why does Mr. Chiu initially refuse to sign a confession? Why does he eventually sign it?
6. What is ironic about Mr. Chiu's arrest? What is ironic about his ultimate confession?
7. When does Mr. Chiu decide to revenge himself on the police?
8. Is Mr. Chiu's revenge justified? Are the effects of his revenge proportionate to his own suffering?
9. What is ironic about the story's title? Who is the saboteur?

■ WRITING *effectively*

Ernest Hemingway on Writing

The Direct Style   1964

"When you write," he [Hemingway] said, "your object is to convey every sensation, sight, feeling, emotion, to the reader. So you have to work over what you write. If you use a pencil, you get three different views of it to see if you are getting it across the way you want to. First, when you read it over, then when it is typed, and again in proof. And it keeps it fluid longer so that you can improve it easier."

"How do you ever learn to convey every sensation, sight and feeling to the reader? Just keep working at it for forty-odd years the way you have? Are there any tricks?"

"No. The hardest trade in the world to do is the writing of straight, honest prose about human beings. But there are ways you can train yourself."

"How?"

Ernest Hemingway

"When you walk into a room and you get a certain feeling or emotion, remember back until you see exactly what it was that gave you the emotion. Remember what the noises and smells were and what was said. Then write it down, making it clear so the reader will see it too and have the same feeling you had. And watch people, observe, try to put yourself in somebody else's head. If two men argue, don't just think who is right and who is wrong. Think what both their sides are. As a man, you know who is right and who is wrong; you have to judge. As a writer, you should not judge, you should understand."

From "An Afternoon with Hemingway" by Edward Stafford

THINKING ABOUT TONE AND STYLE

If you look around a crowded classroom, you will notice—consciously or not—the styles of your fellow students. The way they dress, talk, and even sit conveys information about their attitudes. A haircut, T-shirt, tattoo, or piece of jewelry all silently say something. Similarly, a writer's style—his or her own distinct voice—can give the reader crucial extra information. To analyze a writer's style, think about:

- **Diction: Consider the flavor of words chosen by the author for a particular story.** In "A Clean, Well-Lighted Place," for example, Hemingway favors simple, unemotional, and descriptive language, whereas in "The Storm," Chopin uses extravagant and emotionally charged diction. Each choice reveals something important about the story.
- **Sentence structure: Look for patterns in a story's sentence structure.** Hemingway is famous for his short, clipped sentences, which often repeat certain key words. Faulkner, however, favors complex, elaborate syntax that immerses the reader in the emotion of the narrative.
- **Tone: Try to determine the writer's attitude toward the story he or she is telling.** In "The Gospel According to Mark," Borges uses dispassionate restraint to present a central irony, a tragic misunderstanding that will doom his protagonist. Tan's "A Pair of Tickets," by contrast, creates a tone of hushed excitement and direct emotional involvement.
- **Organization: Examine the order in which information is presented.** Borges tells his story in a straightforward, chronological manner, which eventually makes it possible for us to appreciate the tale's complex undercurrents. Other stories (for example, Atwood's "Happy Endings") present the narrative's events in more complicated and surprising ways.

CHECKLIST: Writing About Tone and Style

- ☐ Does the writer use word choice in a distinctive way?
- ☐ Is the diction unusual in any way?
- ☐ Does the author tend toward long or short—even fragmented—sentences?
- ☐ How would you characterize the writer's voice? Is it formal or casual? Distant or intimate? Impassioned or restrained?
- ☐ Can the narrator's words be taken at face value? Is there anything ironic about the narrator's voice?
- ☐ How does the writer arrange the material? Is information delivered chronologically, or is the organization more complex?
- ☐ What is the writer's attitude toward the material?

WRITING ASSIGNMENT ON TONE AND STYLE

Examine a short story with a style you admire. Write an essay in which you analyze the author's approach toward diction, sentence structure, tone, and organization. How do these elements work together to create a certain mood? How does that mood contribute to the story's meaning? If your chosen story has a first-person narrator, how do stylistic choices help to create a sense of that particular character?

MORE TOPICS FOR WRITING

1. Write a brief analysis of irony in either "Saboteur," "The Gift of the Magi," or "The Jilting of Granny Weatherall." What sorts of irony does your story employ?

2. Consider a short story in which the narrator is the central character, perhaps "A & P," "Greasy Lake," "Araby," "I Stand Here Ironing," or "Cathedral." In a brief essay, show how the character of the narrator determines the style of the story. Examine language in particular—words or phrases, slang expressions, figures of speech, local or regional usage.

3. Write a page in which you describe eating a meal in the company of others. Using sensory details, convey a sense of the setting, the quality of the food, and the presence of your dining companions. Now rewrite your paragraph as Ernest Hemingway. Finally, rewrite it as William Faulkner.

4. In a paragraph, describe a city street as seen through the eyes of a college graduate who has just moved to the city to start a new career. Now describe that same street in the voice of an old woman walking home from the hospital where her husband has just died. Finally, describe the street in the voice of a teenage runaway. In each paragraph, refrain from identifying your character or saying anything about his or her circumstances. Simply present the street as each character would perceive it.

▶ TERMS FOR *review*

Tone ▶ The attitude toward a subject conveyed in a literary work. No single stylistic device creates tone; it is the net result of the various elements an author brings to creating the work's feeling and manner.

Style ▶ All the distinctive ways in which an author uses language to create a literary work. An author's style depends on his or her characteristic use of diction, imagery, tone, syntax, and figurative language.

Diction ▶ Word choice or vocabulary. Diction refers to the class of words that an author decides is appropriate to use in a particular work.

Irony ▶ A literary device in which a discrepancy of meaning is masked beneath the surface of the language. Irony is present when a writer says one thing but means something quite the opposite.

Dramatic irony ▶ Where the reader understands the implication and meaning of a situation and may foresee the oncoming disaster or triumph while the character does not.

Cosmic irony or irony of fate ▶ A type of situational irony that emphasizes the discrepancy between what characters deserve and what they get, between a character's aspirations and the treatment he or she receives at the hands of fate.

Verbal irony ▶ A statement in which the speaker or writer says the opposite of what is really meant. For example, a friend might say, "How graceful!" after you trip clumsily on a stair.

Sarcasm ▶ A conspicuously bitter form of irony in which the ironic statement is designed to hurt or mock its target.

6

THEME

The **theme** of a story is whatever general idea or insight the entire story reveals. In some stories the theme is unmistakable. At the end of Aesop's fable about the council of the mice that can't decide who will bell the cat, the theme is stated in the moral: *It is easier to propose a thing than to carry it out.* In a work of commercial fiction, too, the theme (if any) is usually obvious. Consider a typical detective thriller in which, say, a rookie police officer trained in scientific methods of crime detection sets out to solve a mystery sooner than his or her rival, a veteran sleuth whose only laboratory is carried under his hat. Perhaps the veteran solves the case, leading to the conclusion (and the theme), "The old ways are the best ways after all." Another story by the same writer might dramatize the same rivalry but reverse the outcome, having the rookie win, thereby reversing the theme: "The times are changing! Let's shake loose from old-fashioned ways." In such commercial entertainments, a theme is like a length of rope with which the writer, patently and mechanically, trusses the story neatly (usually too neatly) into meaningful shape.

PLOT VERSUS THEME

In literary fiction, a theme is seldom so obvious. That is, a theme need not be a moral or a message; it may be what the events add up to, what the story is about. When we come to the end of a finely wrought short story such as Ernest Hemingway's "A Clean, Well-Lighted Place" (Chapter 5), it may be easy to sum up the plot—to say what happens—but it is more difficult to sum up the story's main idea. Evidently, Hemingway relates events—how a younger waiter gets rid of an old man and how an older waiter then goes to a coffee bar—but in themselves these events seem relatively slight, though the story as a whole seems large (for its size) and full of meaning. A **summary**, a brief condensation of the main idea or plot of a literary work, may be helpful, but it tends to focus on the surface events of a story. A theme aims for a deeper and more comprehensive statement of its larger meaning.

For the meaning, we must look to other elements in the story besides what happens in it. It is clear that Hemingway is most deeply interested in the thoughts and feelings of the older waiter, the character who has more and more to say as the story progresses, until at the end the story is entirely confined to his thoughts and perceptions. What is meaningful in these thoughts and perceptions? The older waiter understands the old man and sympathizes with his need for a clean, well-lighted place. If we say that, we are still talking about what happens in the story, though we have gone beyond merely recording its external events. But a theme is usually stated in *general* words. Another try: "Solitary people who cannot sleep need a cheerful, orderly place where they can drink with dignity." That's a little better. We have indicated, at least, that Hemingway's story is about more than just an old man and a couple of waiters. But what about the older waiter's meditation on *nada*, nothingness? Coming near the end of the story, it is given great emphasis, and probably no good statement of Hemingway's theme can leave it out. Still another try at a statement: "Solitary people need a place of refuge from their terrible awareness that their lives (or, perhaps, human lives) are essentially meaningless." Neither this nor any other statement of the story's theme is unarguably right, but at least the sentence helps the reader to bring into focus one primary idea that Hemingway seems to be driving at.

When we finish reading "A Clean, Well-Lighted Place," we feel that there is such a theme, a unifying vision, even though we cannot reduce it absolutely to a tag. Like some freshwater lake alive with creatures, Hemingway's story is a broad expanse, reflecting in many directions. No wonder that many readers will view it in different ways.

Moral inferences may be drawn from the story, no doubt, for Hemingway is indirectly giving us advice about properly regarding and sympathizing with the lonely, the uncertain, and the old. But the story doesn't set forth a lesson that we are supposed to put into practice. One could argue that "A Clean, Well-Lighted Place" contains *several* themes, and other statements could be made to include Hemingway's views of love, of communication between people, of dignity. Great short stories, like great symphonies, frequently have more than one theme.

THEME AS UNIFYING DEVICE

In many a fine short story, theme is the center, the moving force, the principle of unity. Clearly, such a theme is something other than the characters and events of its story. To say of James Joyce's "Araby" (Chapter 12) that it is about a boy who goes to a bazaar to buy a gift for a young woman, only to arrive too late, is to summarize plot, not theme. (The theme *might* be put, "The illusions of a romantic youth are vulnerable," or it might be put in any of a few hundred other ways.) Although the title of Shirley Jackson's "The Lottery" (Chapter 7), with its hint of the lure of easy riches, may arouse pleasant expectations, which the neutral tone of the narrative does nothing to dispel, the theme—the larger realization that the story leaves us with—has to do with the ways in which cruel and insensitive attitudes can come to seem like normal and natural ones.

Sometimes you will hear it said that the theme of a story (say, Faulkner's "Barn Burning") is "loss of innocence" or "initiation into maturity," or that the theme of some other story (Hurston's "Sweat," for instance) is "the revolt of the downtrodden." This is to use *theme* in a larger and more abstract sense than we use it here. Although such general descriptions of theme can be useful—as in sorting a large number of stories into rough categories—we suggest that, in the beginning, you look for whatever truth or insight you think the writer of a story reveals. Try to sum it up *in a sentence*. By doing so, you will find yourself looking closely at the story, trying to define its principal meaning.

FINDING THE THEME

You may find it helpful, in making a sentence-statement of theme, to consider these questions:

1. Look back once more at the title of the story. From what you have read, what does it indicate?
2. Does the main character change in any way over the course of the story? Does this character arrive at any eventual realization or understanding? Are you left with any realization or understanding you did not have before?
3. Does the author make any general observations about life or human nature? Do the characters make any? (Caution: Characters now and again will utter opinions with which the reader is not necessarily supposed to agree.)
4. Does the story contain any especially curious objects, mysterious flat characters, significant animals, repeated names, song titles, or whatever, that hint at meanings larger than such things ordinarily have? In literary stories, such symbols may point to central themes.
5. When you have worded your statement of theme, have you cast it into general language, not just given a plot summary?
6. Does your statement hold true for the story as a whole, not for just part of it?

In distilling a statement of theme from a rich and complicated story, we have, of course, no more encompassed the whole story than a paleontologist taking a plaster mold of a petrified footprint has captured a living brontosaurus. A writer (other than a fabulist) does not usually set out with theme in hand, determined to make every detail in the story work to demonstrate it. Well then, the skeptical reader may ask, if only *some* stories have themes, if those themes may be hard to sum up, and if readers will probably disagree in their summations, why bother to state themes? Isn't it too much trouble? Surely it is, unless the effort to state a theme ends in pleasure and profit. Trying to sum up the point of a story in our own words is merely one way to make ourselves better aware of whatever we may have understood vaguely and tentatively. Attempted with loving care, such statements may bring into focus our scattered impressions of a rewarding story, may help to clarify and hold fast whatever wisdom the storyteller has offered us.

Stephen Crane

The Open Boat   1897

Stephen Crane (1871–1900) was born in Newark, New Jersey, a Methodist minister's fourteenth and last child. After flunking out of both Lafayette College and Syracuse University, he became a journalist in New York, specializing in the grim lives of the down-and-out, such as the characters of his early self-published novel Maggie: A Girl of the Streets *(1893). Restlessly generating material for stories, Crane trekked to the Southwest, New Orleans, and Mexico. "The Open Boat" is based on personal experience. En route to Havana to*

Stephen Crane
(Courtesy of the Newark Public Library)

report on the Cuban revolution for the New York Press, *Crane was shipwrecked when the* SS Commodore *sank in heavy seas east of New Smyrna, Florida, on January 2, 1897. He escaped in a ten-foot lifeboat with the captain and two members of the crew. Later that year, Crane moved into a stately home in England with Cora Taylor, former madam of a Florida brothel, hobnobbed with literary greats, and lived beyond his means. Hounded by creditors, afflicted by tuberculosis, he died in Germany at twenty-eight. Crane has been called the first writer of American realism. His classic novel* The Red Badge of Courage *(1895) gives an imagined but convincing account of a young Union soldier's initiation into battle. A handful of his short stories appear immortal. He was also an original poet, writing terse, sardonic poems in open forms, considered radical at the time. In his short life, Crane greatly helped American literature to come of age.*

A tale intended to be after the fact:
Being the experience of four men from the sunk steamer Commodore

I

None of them knew the c'olor of the sky. Their eyes glanced level, and were fastened upon the waves that swept toward them. These waves were of the hue of slate, save for the tops, which were of foaming white, and all of the men knew the colors of the sea. The horizon narrowed and widened, and dipped and rose, and at all times its edge was jagged with waves that seemed thrust up in points like rocks.

Many a man ought to have a bathtub larger than the boat which here rode upon the sea. These waves were most wrongfully and barbarously abrupt and tall, and each froth-top was a problem in small-boat navigation.

The cook squatted in the bottom, and looked with both eyes at the six inches of gunwale which separated him from the ocean. His sleeves were rolled over his fat forearms, and the two flaps of his unbuttoned vest dangled as he bent to bail out the boat. Often he said, "Gawd! that was a narrow clip." As he remarked it he invariably gazed eastward over the broken sea.

The oiler, steering with one of the two oars in the boat, sometimes raised himself suddenly to keep clear of water that swirled in over the stern. It was a thin little oar, and it seemed often ready to snap.

The correspondent,° pulling at the other oar, watched the waves and wondered why he was there.

The injured captain, lying in the bow, was at this time buried in that profound dejection and indifference which comes, temporarily at least, to even the bravest and most enduring when, willy-nilly, the firm fails, the army loses, the ship goes down. The mind of the master of a vessel is rooted deep in the timbers of her, though he command for a day or a decade; and this captain had on him the stern impression of a scene in the grays of dawn of seven turned faces, and later a stump of a topmast with a white ball on it, that slashed to and fro at the waves, went low and lower, and down. Thereafter there was something strange in his voice. Although steady, it was deep with mourning, and of a quality beyond oration or tears.

"Keep 'er a little more south, Billie," said he.

5

---

correspondent: foreign correspondent, newspaper reporter.

"A little more south, sir," said the oiler in the stern.

A seat in this boat was not unlike a seat upon a bucking broncho, and by the same token a broncho is not much smaller. The craft pranced and reared and plunged like an animal. As each wave came, and she rose for it, she seemed like a horse making at a fence outrageously high. The manner of her scramble over these walls of water is a mystic thing, and, moreover, at the top of them were ordinarily these problems in white water, the foam racing down from the summit of each wave requiring a new leap, and a leap from the air. Then, after scornfully bumping a crest, she would slide and race and splash down a long incline, and arrive bobbing and nodding in front of the next menace.

A singular disadvantage of the sea lies in the fact that after successfully surmounting one wave you discover that there is another behind it just as important and just as nervously anxious to do something effective in the way of swamping boats. In a ten-foot dinghy one can get an idea of the resources of the sea in the line of waves that is not probable to the average experience, which is never at sea in a dinghy. As each slaty wall of water approached, it shut all else from the view of the men in the boat, and it was not difficult to imagine that this particular wave was the final outburst of the ocean, the last effort of the grim water. There was a terrible grace in the move of the waves, and they came in silence, save for the snarling of the crests.

In the wan light the faces of the men must have been gray. Their eyes must have glinted in strange ways as they gazed steadily astern. Viewed from a balcony, the whole thing would doubtless have been weirdly picturesque. But the men in the boat had no time to see it, and if they had had leisure, there were other things to occupy their minds. The sun swung steadily up the sky, and they knew it was broad day because the color of the sea changed from slate to emerald green streaked with amber lights, and the foam was like tumbling snow. The process of the breaking day was unknown to them. They were aware only of this effect upon the color of the waves that rolled toward them.

In disjointed sentences the cook and the correspondent argued as to the difference between a life-saving station and a house of refuge. The cook had said: "There's a house of refuge just north of the Mosquito Inlet Light, and as soon as they see us they'll come off in their boat and pick us up."

"As soon as who see us?" said the correspondent.

"The crew," said the cook.

"Houses of refuge don't have crews," said the correspondent. "As I understand them, they are only places where clothes and grub are stored for the benefit of shipwrecked people. They don't carry crews."

"Oh, yes, they do," said the cook.

"No, they don't," said the correspondent.

"Well, we're not there yet, anyhow," said the oiler, in the stern.

"Well," said the cook, "perhaps it's not a house of refuge that I'm thinking of as being near Mosquito Inlet Light; perhaps it's a life-saving station."

"We're not there yet," said the oiler in the stern.

II

As the boat bounced from the top of each wave the wind tore through the hair of the hatless men, and as the craft plopped her stern down again the spray slashed past them. The crest of each of these waves was a hill, from the top of which the men surveyed for a moment a broad tumultuous expanse, shining and wind-riven. It was probably splendid, it was probably glorious, this play of the free sea, wild with lights of emerald and white and amber.

"Bully good thing it's an on-shore wind," said the cook. "If not, where would we be? Wouldn't have a show."

"That's right," said the correspondent.

The busy oiler nodded his assent.

Then the captain, in the bow, chuckled in a way that expressed humor, contempt,   25
tragedy, all in one. "Do you think we've got much of a show now, boys?" said he.

Whereupon the three were silent, save for a trifle of hemming and hawing. To express any particular optimism at this time they felt to be childish and stupid, but they all doubtless possessed this sense of the situation in their minds. A young man thinks doggedly at such times. On the other hand, the ethics of their condition was decidedly against any open suggestion of hopelessness. So they were silent.

"Oh, well," said the captain, soothing his children, "we'll get ashore all right."

But there was that in his tone which made them think; so the oiler quoth, "Yes! if this wind holds."

The cook was bailing. "Yes! if we don't catch hell in the surf."

Canton-flannel gulls flew near and far. Sometimes they sat down on the sea,   30
near patches of brown seaweed that rolled over the waves with a movement like carpets on a line in a gale. The birds sat comfortably in groups, and they were envied by some in the dinghy, for the wrath of the sea was no more to them than it was to a covey of prairie chickens a thousand miles inland. Often they came very close and stared at the men with black bead-like eyes. At these times they were uncanny and sinister in their unblinking scrutiny, and the men hooted angrily at them, telling them to be gone. One came, and evidently decided to alight on the top of the captain's head. The bird flew parallel to the boat and did not circle, but made short sidelong jumps in the air in chicken-fashion. His black eyes were wistfully fixed upon the captain's head. "Ugly brute," said the oiler to the bird. "You look as if you were made with a jackknife." The cook and the correspondent swore darkly at the creature. The captain naturally wished to knock it away with the end of the heavy painter, but he did not dare do it, because anything resembling an emphatic gesture would have capsized this freighted boat; and so, with his open hand, the captain gently and carefully waved the gull away. After it had been discouraged from the pursuit the captain breathed easier on account of his hair, and others breathed easier because the bird struck their minds at this time as being somehow gruesome and ominous.

In the meantime the oiler and the correspondent rowed. And also they rowed. They sat together in the same seat, and each rowed an oar. Then the oiler took both oars; then the correspondent took both oars; then the oiler; then the correspondent. They rowed and they rowed. The very ticklish part of the business was when the time came for the reclining one in the stern to take his turn at the oars. By the very last star of truth, it is easier to steal eggs from under a hen than it was to change seats in the dinghy. First the man in the stern slid his hand along the thwart and moved with care, as if he were of Sèvres.° Then the man in the rowing-seat slid his hand along the other thwart. It was all done with the

Sèvres: chinaware made in this French town.

most extraordinary care. As the two sidled past each other, the whole party kept watchful eyes on the coming wave, and the captain cried: "Look out, now! Steady, there!"

The brown mats of seaweed that appeared from time to time were like islands, bits of earth. They were travelling, apparently, neither one way nor the other. They were, to all intents, stationary. They informed the men in the boat that it was making progress slowly toward the land.

The captain, rearing cautiously in the bow after the dinghy soared on a great swell, said that he had seen the lighthouse at Mosquito Inlet. Presently the cook remarked that he had seen it. The correspondent was at the oars then, and for some reason he too wished to look at the lighthouse; but his back was toward the far shore, and the waves were important, and for some time he could not seize an opportunity to turn his head. But at last there came a wave more gentle than the others, and when at the crest of it he swiftly scoured the western horizon.

"See it?" said the captain.

"No," said the correspondent, slowly; "I didn't see anything."

"Look again," said the captain. He pointed. "It's exactly in that direction."

At the top of another wave the correspondent did as he was bid, and this time his eyes chanced on a small, still thing on the edge of the swaying horizon. It was precisely like the point of a pin. It took an anxious eye to find a lighthouse so tiny.

"Think we'll make it, Captain?"

"If this wind holds and the boat don't swamp, we can't do much else," said the captain.

The little boat, lifted by each towering sea and splashed viciously by the crests, made progress that in the absence of seaweed was not apparent to those in her. She seemed just a wee thing wallowing, miraculously top up, at the mercy of five oceans. Occasionally a great spread of water, like white flames, swarmed into her.

"Bail her, cook," said the captain, serenely.

"All right, Captain," said the cheerful cook.

III

It would be difficult to describe the subtle brotherhood of men that was here established on the seas. No one said that it was so. No one mentioned it. But it dwelt in the boat, and each man felt it warm him. They were a captain, an oiler, a cook, and a correspondent, and they were friends—friends in a more curiously iron-bound degree than may be common. The hurt captain, lying against the water-jar in the bow, spoke always in a low voice and calmly; but he could never command a more ready and swiftly obedient crew than the motley three of the dinghy. It was more than a mere recognition of what was best for the common safety. There was surely in it a quality that was personal and heartfelt. And after this devotion to the commander of the boat, there was this comradeship, that the correspondent, for instance, who had been taught to be cynical of men, knew even at the time was the best experience of his life. But no one said that it was so. No one mentioned it.

"I wish we had a sail," remarked the captain. "We might try my overcoat on the end of an oar, and give you two boys a chance to rest." So the cook and the correspondent held the mast and spread wide the overcoat; the oiler steered; and the little boat made good way with her new rig. Sometimes the oiler had to scull sharply to keep a sea from breaking into the boat, but otherwise sailing was a success.

Meanwhile the lighthouse had been growing slowly larger. It had now almost as- 45
sumed color, and appeared like a little gray shadow on the sky. The man at the oars
could not be prevented from turning his head rather often to try for a glimpse of this
little gray shadow.

At last, from the top of each wave, the men in the tossing boat could see land.
Even as the lighthouse was an upright shadow on the sky, this land seemed but a long
black shadow on the sea. It certainly was thinner than paper. "We must be about opposite New Smyrna," said the cook, who had coasted this shore often in schooners.
"Captain, by the way, I believe they abandoned that life-saving station there about a
year ago."

"Did they?" said the captain.

The wind slowly died away. The cook and the correspondent were not now
obliged to slave in order to hold high the oar. But the waves continued their old impetuous swooping at the dinghy, and the little craft, no longer under way, struggled
woundily over them. The oiler or the correspondent took the oars again.

Shipwrecks are apropos of nothing. If men could only train for them and have
them occur when the men had reached pink condition, there would be less drowning
at sea. Of the four in the dinghy none had slept any time worth mentioning for two
days and two nights previous to embarking in the dinghy, and in the excitement of
clambering about the deck of a foundering ship they had also forgotten to eat heartily.

For these reasons, and for others, neither the oiler nor the correspondent was 50
fond of rowing at this time. The correspondent wondered ingenuously how in the
name of all that was sane could there be people who thought it amusing to row a
boat. It was not an amusement; it was a diabolical punishment, and even a genius of
mental aberrations could never conclude that it was anything but a horror to the
muscles and crime against the back. He mentioned to the boat in general how the
amusement of rowing struck him, and the weary-faced oiler smiled in full sympathy.
Previously to the foundering, by the way, the oiler had worked double watch in the
engine-room of the ship.

"Take her easy now, boys," said the captain. "Don't spend yourselves. If we have
to run a surf you'll need all your strength, because we'll sure have to swim for it. Take
your time."

Slowly the land arose from the sea. From a black line it became a line of black
and a line of white—trees and sand. Finally the captain said that he could make out a
house on the shore. "That's the house of refuge, sure," said the cook. "They'll see us
before long, and come out after us."

The distant lighthouse reared high. "The keeper ought to be able to make us out
now, if he's looking through a glass," said the captain. "He'll notify the life-saving
people."

"None of those other boats could have got ashore to give word of the wreck," said
the oiler, in a low voice, "else the life-boat would be out hunting us."

Slowly and beautifully the land loomed out of the sea. The wind came again. It 55
had veered from the northeast to the southeast. Finally a new sound struck the ears of
the men in the boat. It was the low thunder of the surf on the shore. "We'll never be
able to make the lighthouse now," said the captain. "Swing her head a little more
north, Billie."

"A little more north, sir," said the oiler.

Whereupon the little boat turned her nose once more down the wind, and all
but the oarsman watched the shore grow. Under the influence of this expansion

doubt and direful apprehension were leaving the minds of the men. The management of the boat was still most absorbing, but it could not prevent a quiet cheerfulness. In an hour, perhaps, they would be ashore.

Their backbones had become thoroughly used to balancing in the boat, and they now rode this wild colt of a dinghy like circus men. The correspondent thought that he had been drenched to the skin, but happening to feel in the top pocket of his coat, he found therein eight cigars. Four of them were soaked with seawater; four were perfectly scatheless. After a search, somebody produced three dry matches; and thereupon the four waifs rode impudently in their little boat and, with an assurance of an impending rescue shining in their eyes, puffed at the big cigars, and judged well and ill of all men. Everybody took a drink of water.

IV

"Cook," remarked the captain, "there don't seem to be any signs of life about your house of refuge."

"No," replied the cook. "Funny they don't see us!"   60

A broad stretch of lowly coast lay before the eyes of the men. It was of low dunes topped with dark vegetation. The roar of the surf was plain, and sometimes they could see the white lip of a wave as it spun up the beach. A tiny house was blocked out black upon the sky. Southward, the slim lighthouse lifted its little gray length.

Tide, wind, and waves were swinging the dinghy northward. "Funny they don't see us," said the men.

The surf's roar was here dulled, but its tone was nevertheless thunderous and mighty. As the boat swam over the great rollers the men sat listening to this roar. "We'll swamp sure," said everybody.

It is fair to say here that there was not a life-saving station within twenty miles in either direction; but the men did not know this fact, and in consequence they made dark and opprobrious remarks concerning the eyesight of the nation's life-savers. Four scowling men sat in the dinghy and surpassed records in the invention of epithets.

"Funny they don't see us."   65

The light-heartedness of a former time had completely faded. To their sharpened minds it was easy to conjure pictures of all kinds of incompetency and blindness and, indeed, cowardice. There was the shore of the populous land, and it was bitter and bitter to them that from it came no sign.

"Well," said the captain, ultimately, "I suppose we'll have to make a try for ourselves. If we stay out here too long, we'll none of us have strength left to swim after the boat swamps."

And so the oiler, who was at the oars, turned the boat straight for the shore. There was a sudden tightening of muscles. There was some thinking.

"If we don't all get ashore," said the captain—"if we don't all get ashore, I suppose you fellows know where to send news of my finish?"

They then briefly exchanged some addresses and admonitions. As for the reflec-   70
tions of the men, there was a great deal of rage in them. Perchance they might be formulated thus: "If I am going to be drowned—if I am going to be drowned—if I am going to be drowned, why, in the name of the seven mad gods who rule the sea, was I allowed to come thus far and contemplate sand and trees? Was I brought here merely to have my nose dragged away as I was about to nibble the sacred cheese of life? It is preposterous. If this old ninny-woman, Fate, cannot do better than this,

she should be deprived of the management of men's fortunes. She is an old hen who knows not her intention. If she has decided to drown me, why did she not do it in the beginning and save me all this trouble? The whole affair is absurd. . . . But no; she cannot mean to drown me. She dare not drown me. She cannot drown me. Not after all this work." Afterward the man might have had an impulse to shake his fist at the clouds. "Just you drown me, now, and then hear what I call you!"

The billows that came at this time were more formidable. They seemed always just about to break and roll over the little boat in a turmoil of foam. There was a preparatory and long growl in the speech of them. No mind unused to the sea would have concluded that the dinghy could ascend these sheer heights in time. The shore was still afar. The oiler was a wily surfman. "Boys," he said swiftly, "she won't live three minutes more, and we're too far out to swim. Shall I take her to sea again, Captain?

"Yes; go ahead!" said the captain.

This oiler, by a series of quick miracles and fast and steady oarsmanship, turned the boat in the middle of the surf and took her safely to sea again.

There was a considerable silence as the boat bumped over the furrowed sea to deeper water. Then somebody in gloom spoke: "Well, anyhow, they must have seen us from the shore by now."

The gulls went in slanting flight up the wind toward the gray, desolate east. A squall, marked by dingy clouds and clouds brick-red, like smoke from a burning building, appeared from the southeast. 75

"What do you think of those life-saving people? Ain't they peaches?"

"Funny they haven't seen us."

"Maybe they think we're out here for sport! Maybe they think we're fishin'. Maybe they think we're damned fools."

It was a long afternoon. A changed tide tried to force them southward, but wind and wave said northward. Far ahead, where coast-line, sea, and sky formed their mighty angle, there were little dots which seemed to indicate a city on the shore.

"St. Augustine?" 80

The captain shook his head. "Too near Mosquito Inlet."

And the oiler rowed, and then the correspondent rowed; then the oiler rowed. It was a weary business. The human back can become the seat of more aches and pains than are registered in books for the composite anatomy of a regiment. It is a limited area, but it can become the theatre of innumerable muscular conflicts, tangles, wrenches, knots, and other comforts.

"Did you ever like to row, Billie?" asked the correspondent.

"No," said the oiler; "hang it!"

When one exchanged the rowing-seat for a place in the bottom of the boat, he 85 suffered a bodily depression that caused him to be careless of everything save an obligation to wiggle one finger. There was cold sea-water swashing to and fro in the boat, and he lay in it. His head, pillowed on a thwart, was within an inch of the swirl of a wave-crest, and sometimes a particularly obstreperous sea came inboard and drenched him once more. But these matters did not annoy him. It is almost certain that if the boat had capsized he would have tumbled comfortably upon the ocean as if he felt sure that it was a great soft mattress.

"Look! There's a man on the shore!"

"Where?"

"There! See 'im? See 'im?"

"Yes, sure! He's walking along."

"Now he's stopped. Look! He's facing us!"   90

"He's waving at us!"

"So he is! By thunder!"

"Ah, now we're all right! Now we're all right! There'll be a boat out here for us in half an hour."

"He's going on. He's running. He's going up to that house there."

The remote beach seemed lower than the sea, and it required a searching glance   95
to discern the little black figure. The captain saw a floating stick, and they rowed to it. A bath towel was by some weird chance in the boat, and, tying this on the stick, the captain waved it. The oarsman did not dare turn his head, so he was obliged to ask questions.

"What's he doing now?"

"He's standing still again. He's looking, I think. . . . There he goes again. Toward the house. . . . Now he's stopped again."

"Is he waving at us?"

"No, not now; he was, though."

"Look! There comes another man!"   100

"He's running."

"Look at him go, would you!"

"Why, he's on a bicycle. Now he's met the other man. They're both waving at us. Look!"

"There comes something up the beach."

"What the devil is that thing?"   105

"Why, it looks like a boat."

"Why, certainly, it's a boat."

"No; it's on wheels."

"Yes, so it is. Well, that must be the life-boat. They drag them along shore on a wagon."

"That's the life-boat, sure."   110

"No, by God, it's—it's an omnibus."

"I tell you it's a life-boat."

"It is not! It's an omnibus. I can see it plain. See? One of the these big hotel omnibuses."

"By thunder, you're right. It's an omnibus, sure as fate. What do you suppose they are doing with an omnibus? Maybe they are going around collecting the life-crew, hey?"

"That's it, likely. Look! There's a fellow waving a little black flag. He's standing   115
on the steps of the omnibus. There come those other two fellows. Now they're all talking together. Look at the fellow with the flag. Maybe he ain't waving it!"

"That ain't a flag, is it? That's his coat. Why, certainly, that's his coat."

"So it is; it's his coat. He's taken it off and is waving it around his head. But would you look at him swing it!"

"Oh, say, there isn't any life-saving station there. That's just a winter-resort hotel omnibus that has brought over some of the boarders to see us drown."

"What's that idiot with the coat mean? What's he signalling, anyhow?"

"It looks as if he were trying to tell us to go north. There must be a life-saving   120
station up there."

"No; he thinks we're fishing. Just giving us a merry hand. See? Ah, there, Willie!"

"Well, I wish I could make something out of those signals. What do you suppose he means?"

"He don't mean anything; he's just playing."

"Well, if he'd just signal us to try the surf again, or to go to sea and wait, or go north, or go south, or go to hell, there would be some reason in it. But look at him! He just stands there and keeps his coat revolving like a wheel. The ass!"

"There come more people."   125

"Now there's quite a mob. Look! Isn't that a boat?"

"Where? Oh, I see where you mean. No, that's no boat."

"That fellow is still waving his coat."

"He must think we like to see him do that. Why don't he quit it? It don't mean anything."

"I don't know. I think he is trying to make us go north. It must be that there's a   130
life-saving station there somewhere."

"Say, he ain't tired yet. Look at 'im wave!"

"Wonder how long he can keep that up. He's been revolving his coat ever since he caught sight of us. He's an idiot. Why aren't they getting men to bring a boat out? A fishing boat—one of those big yawls—could come out here all right. Why don't he do something?"

"Oh, it's all right now."

"They'll have a boat out here for us in less than no time, now that they've seen us."

A faint yellow tone came into the sky over the low land. The shadows on the sea   135
slowly deepened. The wind bore coldness with it, and the men began to shiver.

"Holy smoke!" said one, allowing his voice to express his impious mood, "If we keep on monkeying out here! If we've got to flounder out here all night!"

"Oh, we'll never have to stay here all night! Don't you worry. They've seen us now, and it won't be long before they'll come chasing out after us."

The shore grew dusky. The man waving a coat blended gradually into this gloom, and it swallowed in the same manner the omnibus and the group of people. The spray, when it dashed uproariously over the side, made the voyagers shrink and swear like men who were being branded.

"I'd like to catch the chump who waved the coat. I feel like socking him one, just for luck."

"Why? What did he do?"   140

"Oh, nothing, but then he seemed so damned cheerful."

In the meantime the oiler rowed, and then the correspondent rowed, and then the oiler rowed. Gray-faced and bowed forward, they mechanically, turn by turn, plied the leaden oars. The form of the lighthouse had vanished from the southern horizon, but finally a pale star appeared, just lifting from the sea. The streaked saffron in the west passed before the all-merging darkness, and the sea to the east was black. The land had vanished, and was expressed only by the low and drear thunder of the surf.

"If I am going to be drowned—if I am going to be drowned—if I am going to be drowned, why, in the name of the seven mad gods who rule the sea, was I allowed to come thus far and contemplate sand and trees? Was I brought here merely to have my nose dragged away as I was about to nibble the sacred cheese of life?"

The patient captain, drooped over the water-jar, was sometimes obliged to speak to the oarsman.

"Keep her head up! Keep her head up!"   145

"Keep her head, up, sir." The voices were weary and low.

This was surely a quiet evening. All save the oarsman lay heavily and listlessly in the boat's bottom. As for him, his eyes were just capable of noting the tall black waves that swept forward in a most sinister silence, save for an occasional subdued growl of a crest.

The cook's head was on a thwart, and he looked without interest at the water under his nose. He was deep in other scenes. Finally he spoke. "Billie," he murmured, dreamfully, "what kind of pie do you like best?"

V

"Pie!" said the oiler and the correspondent, agitatedly. "Don't talk about those things, blast you!"

"Well," said the cook, "I was just thinking about ham sandwiches, and—"   150

A night on the sea in an open boat is a long night. As darkness settled finally, the shine of the light, lifting from the sea in the south, changed to full gold. On the northern horizon a new light appeared, a small bluish gleam on the edge of the waters. These two lights were the furniture of the world. Otherwise there was nothing but waves.

Two men huddled in the stern, and distances were so magnificent in the dinghy that the rower was enabled to keep his feet partly warm by thrusting them under his companions. Their legs indeed extended far under the rowing-seat until they touched the feet of the captain forward. Sometimes, despite the efforts of the tired oarsman, a wave came piling into the boat, an icy wave of the night, and the chilling water soaked them anew. They would twist their bodies for a moment and groan, and sleep the dead sleep once more, while the water in the boat gurgled about them as the craft rocked.

The plan of the oiler and the correspondent was for one to row until he lost the ability, and then arouse the other from his sea-water couch in the bottom of the boat.

The oiler plied the oars until his head drooped forward and the overpowering sleep blinded him; and he rowed yet afterward. Then he touched a man in the bottom of the boat, and called his name. "Will you spell me for a little while?" he said meekly.

"Sure, Billie," said the correspondent, awaking and dragging himself to a sitting   155
position. They exchanged places carefully, and the oiler, cuddling down in the seawater at the cook's side, seemed to go to sleep instantly.

The particular violence of the sea had ceased. The waves came without snarling. The obligation of the man at the oars was to keep the boat headed so that the tilt of the roller would not capsize her, and to preserve her from filling when the crests rushed past. The black waves were silent and hard to be seen in the darkness. Often one was almost upon the boat before the oarsman was aware.

In a low voice the correspondent addressed the captain. He was not sure that the captain was awake, although this iron man seemed to be always awake. "Captain, shall I keep her making for that light north, sir?"

The same steady voice answered him. "Yes. Keep it about two points off the port bow."

The cook had tied a life-belt around himself in order to get even the warmth which this clumsy cork contrivance could donate, and he seemed almost stove-like when a rower, whose teeth invariably chattered wildly as soon as he ceased his labor, dropped down to sleep.

The correspondent, as he rowed, looked down at the two men sleeping under- 160
foot. The cook's arm was around the oiler's shoulders, and, with their fragmentary
clothing and haggard faces, they were the babes of the sea—a grotesque rendering of
the old babes in the wood.

Later he must have grown stupid at his work, for suddenly there was a growling
of water, and a crest came with a roar and a swash into the boat, and it was a wonder
that it did not set the cook afloat in his life-belt. The cook continued to sleep, but
the oiler sat up, blinking his eyes and shaking with the new cold.

"Oh, I'm awful sorry, Billie," said the correspondent, contritely.

"That's all right, old boy," said the oiler, and lay down again and was asleep.

Presently it seemed that even the captain dozed, and the correspondent thought
that he was the one man afloat on all the oceans. The wind had a voice as it came
over the waves, and it was sadder than the end.

There was a long, loud swishing astern of the boat, and a gleaming trail of phos- 165
phorescence, like blue flame, was furrowed on the black waters. It might have been
made by a monstrous knife.

Then there came a stillness, while the correspondent breathed with open mouth
and looked at the sea.

Suddenly there was another swish and another long flash of bluish light, and this
time it was alongside the boat, and might almost have been reached with an oar. The
correspondent saw an enormous fin speed like a shadow through the water, hurling
the crystalline spray and leaving the long glowing trail.

The correspondent looked over his shoulder at the captain. His face was hidden,
and he seemed to be asleep. He looked at the babes of the sea. They certainly were
asleep. So, being bereft of sympathy, he leaned a little way to one side and swore
softly into the sea.

But the thing did not then leave the vicinity of the boat. Ahead or astern, on
one side or the other, at intervals long or short, fled the long sparkling streak, and
there was to be heard the *whirroo* of the dark fin. The speed and power of the thing
was greatly to be admired. It cut the water like a gigantic and keen projectile.

The presence of this biding thing did not affect the man with the same horror 170
that it would if he had been a picnicker. He simply looked at the sea dully and swore
in an undertone.

Nevertheless, it is true that he did not wish to be alone with the thing. He
wished one of his companions to awake by chance and keep him company with it.
But the captain hung motionless over the water-jar, and the oiler and the cook in the
bottom of the boat were plunged in slumber.

VI

"If I am going to be drowned—if I am going to be drowned—if I am going to be
drowned, why, in the name of the seven mad gods who rule the sea, was I allowed to
come thus far and contemplate sand and trees?"

During this dismal night, it may be remarked that a man would conclude that
it was really the intention of the seven mad gods to drown him, despite the abominable injustice of it. For it was certainly an abominable injustice to drown a man
who had worked so hard, so hard. The man felt it would be a crime most unnatural.
Other people had drowned at sea since galleys swarmed with painted sails, but
still—

When it occurs to a man that nature does not regard him as important, and that she feels she would not maim the universe by disposing of him, he at first wishes to throw bricks at the temple, and he hates deeply the fact that there are no bricks and no temples. Any visible expression of nature would surely be pelleted with his jeers.

Then, if there be no tangible thing to hoot, he feels, perhaps, the desire to 175 confront a personification and indulge in pleas, bowed to one knee, and with hands supplicant, saying, "Yes, but I love myself."

A high cold star on a winter's night is the word he feels that she says to him. Thereafter he knows the pathos of his situation.

The men in the dinghy had not discussed these matters, but each had, no doubt, reflected upon them in silence and according to his mind. There was seldom any expression upon their faces save the general one of complete weariness. Speech was devoted to the business of the boat.

To chime the notes of his emotion, a verse mysteriously entered the correspondent's head. He had even forgotten that he had forgotten this verse, but it suddenly was in his mind.

A soldier of the Legion lay dying in Algiers;
There was lack of woman's nursing, there was dearth of woman's tears;
But a comrade stood beside him, and he took that comrade's hand,
And he said, "I never more shall see my own, my native land."°

In his childhood the correspondent had been made acquainted with the fact that a soldier of the Legion lay dying in Algiers, but he had never regarded the fact as important. Myriads of his school-fellows had informed him of the soldier's plight, but the dinning had naturally ended by making him perfectly indifferent. He had never considered it his affair that a soldier of the Legion lay dying in Algiers, nor had it appeared to him as a matter for sorrow. It was less to him than the breaking of a pencil's point.

Now, however, it quaintly came to him as a human, living thing. It was no 180 longer merely a picture of a few throes in the breast of a poet, meanwhile drinking tea and warming his feet at the grate; it was an actuality—stern, mournful, and fine.

The correspondent plainly saw the soldier. He lay on the sand with his feet out straight and still. While his pale left hand was upon his chest in an attempt to thwart the going of his life, the blood came between his fingers. In the far Algerian distance, a city of low square forms was set against a sky that was faint with the last sunset hues. The correspondent, plying the oars and dreaming of the slow and slower movements of the lips of the soldier, was moved by a profound and perfectly impersonal comprehension. He was sorry for the soldier of the Legion who lay dying in Algiers.

The thing which had followed the boat and waited had evidently grown bored at the delay. There was no longer to be heard the slash of the cutwater, and there was no longer the flame of the long trail. The light in the north still glimmered, but it was apparently no nearer to the boat. Sometimes the boom of the surf rang in the correspondent's ears, and he turned the craft seaward then and rowed harder. Southward, some one had evidently built a watch-fire on the beach. It was too low and too far to be seen, but it made a shimmering, roseate reflection upon the bluff in back of it, and this could be discerned from the boat. The wind came stronger,

A soldier of the Legion . . . native land: The correspondent remembers a Victorian ballad about a German dying in the French Foreign Legion, "Bingen on the Rhine" by Caroline Norton.

and sometimes a wave suddenly raged out like a mountain cat, and there was to be seen the sheen and sparkle of a broken crest.

The captain, in the bow, moved on his water-jar and sat erect. "Pretty long night," he observed to the correspondent. He looked at the shore. "Those life-saving people take their time."

"Did you see that shark playing around?"

"Yes, I saw him. He was a big fellow, all right."   185

"Wish I had known you were awake."

Later the correspondent spoke into the bottom of the boat.

"Billie!" There was a slow and gradual disentanglement. "Billie, will you spell me?"

"Sure," said the oiler.

As soon as the correspondent touched the cold, comfortable sea-water in the   190
bottom of the boat and had huddled close to the cook's life-belt he was deep in sleep, despite the fact that his teeth played all the popular airs. This sleep was so good to him that it was but a moment before he heard a voice call his name in a tone that demonstrated the last stages of exhaustion. "Will you spell me?"

"Sure, Billie."

The light in the north had mysteriously vanished, but the correspondent took his course from the wide-awake captain.

Later in the night they took the boat farther out to sea, and the captain directed the cook to take one oar at the stern and keep the boat facing the seas. He was to call out if he should hear the thunder of the surf. This plan enabled the oiler and the correspondent to get respite together. "We'll give those boys a chance to get into shape again," said the captain. They curled down and, after a few preliminary chatterings and trembles, slept once more the dead sleep. Neither knew they had bequeathed to the cook the company of another shark, or perhaps the same shark.

As the boat caroused on the waves, spray occasionally bumped over the side and gave them a fresh soaking, but this had no power to break their repose. The ominous slash of the wind and the water affected them as it would have affected mummies.

"Boys," said the cook, with the notes of every reluctance in his voice, "she's   195
drifted in pretty close. I guess one of you had better take her to sea again." The correspondent, aroused, heard the crash of the toppled crests.

As he was rowing, the captain gave him some whisky and water, and this steadied the chills out of him. "If I ever get ashore and anybody shows me even a photograph of an oar—"

At last there was a short conversation.

"Billie! . . . Billie, will you spell me?"

"Sure," said the oiler.

VII

When the correspondent again opened his eyes, the sea and sky were each of the   200
gray hue of the dawning. Later, carmine and gold was painted upon the waters. The morning appeared finally, in its splendor, with a sky of pure blue, and the sunlight flamed on the tips of the waves.

On the distant dunes were set many little black cottages, and a tall white windmill reared above them. No man, nor dog, nor bicycle appeared on the beach. The cottages might have formed a deserted village.

The voyagers scanned the shore. A conference was held in the boat. "Well," said the captain, "if no help is coming, we might better try a run through the surf right away. If we stay out here much longer we will be too weak to do anything for ourselves at all." The others silently acquiesced in this reasoning. The boat was headed for the beach. The correspondent wondered if none ever ascended the tall wind-tower, and if they never looked seaward. This tower was a giant, standing with its back to the plight of the ants. It represented in a degree, to the correspondent, the serenity of nature amid the struggles of the individual—nature in the wind, and nature in the vision of men. She did not seem cruel to him then, nor beneficent, nor treacherous, nor wise. But she was indifferent, flatly indifferent. It is, perhaps, plausible that a man in this situation, impressed with the unconcern of the universe, should see the innumerable flaws of life, and have them taste wickedly in his mind, and wish for another chance. A distinction between right and wrong seems absurdly clear to him, then, in this new ignorance of the grave-edge, and he understands that if he were given another opportunity he would mend his conduct and his words, and be better and brighter during an introduction or at a tea.

"Now, boys," said the captain, "she is going to swamp sure. All we can do is to work her in as far as possible, and then when she swamps, pile out and scramble for the beach. Keep cool now, and don't jump until she swamps sure."

The oiler took the oars. Over his shoulders he scanned the surf. "Captain," he said, "I think I'd better bring her about and keep her head-on to the seas and back her in."

"All right, Billie," said the captain. "Back her in." The oiler swung the boat 205 then, and, seated in the stern, the cook and the correspondent were obliged to look over their shoulders to contemplate the lonely and indifferent shore.

The monstrous inshore rollers heaved the boat high until the men were again enabled to see the white sheets of water scudding up the slanted beach. "We won't get in very close," said the captain. Each time a man could wrest his attention from the rollers, he turned his glance toward the shore, and in the expression of the eyes during this contemplation there was a singular quality. The correspondent, observing the others, knew that they were not afraid, but the full meaning of their glances was shrouded.

As for himself, he was too tired to grapple fundamentally with the fact. He tried to coerce his mind into thinking of it, but the mind was dominated at this time by the muscles, and the muscles said they did not care. It merely occurred to him that if he should drown it would be a shame.

There were no hurried words, no pallor, no plain agitation. The men simply looked at the shore. "Now, remember to get well clear of the boat when you jump," said the captain.

Seaward the crest of a roller suddenly fell with a thunderous crash, and the long white comber came roaring down upon the boat.

"Steady now," said the captain. The men were silent. They turned their eyes 210 from the shore to the comber and waited. The boat slid up the incline, leaped at the furious top, bounced over it, and swung down the long back of the wave. Some water had been shipped, and the cook bailed it out.

But the next crest crashed also. The tumbling, boiling flood of white water caught the boat and whirled it almost perpendicular. Water swarmed in from all sides. The correspondent had his hands on the gunwale at this time, and when the water entered at that place he swiftly withdrew his fingers, as if he objected to wetting them.

The little boat, drunken with this weight of water, reeled and snuggled deeper into the sea.

"Bail her out, cook! Bail her out!" said the captain.

"All right, Captain," said the cook.

"Now, boys, the next one will do for us sure," said the oiler. "Mind to jump clear   215
of the boat."

The third wave moved forward, huge, furious, implacable. It fairly swallowed the dinghy, and almost simultaneously the men tumbled into the sea. A piece of life-belt had lain in the bottom of the boat, and as the correspondent went overboard he held this to his chest with his left hand.

The January water was icy, and he reflected immediately that it was colder than he had expected to find it off the coast of Florida. This appeared to his dazed mind as a fact important enough to be noted at the time. The coldness of the water was sad; it was tragic. This fact was somehow mixed and confused with his opinion of his own situation, so that it seemed almost a proper reason for tears. The water was cold.

When he came to the surface he was conscious of little but the noisy water. Afterward he saw his companions in the sea. The oiler was ahead in the race. He was swimming strongly and rapidly. Off to the correspondent's left, the cook's great white and corked back bulged out of the water; and in the rear the captain was hanging with his one good hand to the keel of the overturned dinghy.

There is a certain immovable quality to a shore, and the correspondent wondered at it amid the confusion of the sea.

It seemed also very attractive; but the correspondent knew that it was a long   220
journey, and he paddled leisurely. The piece of life-preserver lay under him, and sometimes he whirled down the incline of a wave as if he were on a hand-sled.

But finally he arrived at a place in the sea where travel was beset with difficulty. He did not pause swimming to inquire what manner of current had caught him, but there his progress ceased. The shore was set before him like a bit of scenery on a stage, and he looked at it and understood with his eyes each detail of it.

As the cook passed, much farther to the left, the captain was calling to him, "Turn over on your back, cook! Turn over on your back and use the oar."

"All right, sir." The cook turned on his back, and, paddling with an oar, went ahead as if he were a canoe.

Presently the boat also passed to the left of the correspondent, with the captain clinging with one hand to the keel. He would have appeared like a man raising himself to look over a board fence if it were not for the extraordinary gymnastics of the boat. The correspondent marvelled that the captain could still hold to it.

They passed on nearer to shore—the oiler, the cook, the captain—and following   225
them went the water-jar, bouncing gaily over the seas.

The correspondent remained in the grip of this strange new enemy—a current. The shore, with its white slope of sand and its green bluff topped with little silent cottages, was spread like a picture before him. It was very near to him then, but he was impressed as one who, in a gallery, looks at a scene from Brittany or Algiers.

He thought: "I am going to drown? Can it be possible? Can it be possible? Can it be possible?" Perhaps an individual must consider his own death to be the final phenomenon of nature.

But later a wave perhaps whirled him out of this small deadly current, for he found suddenly that he could again make progress toward the shore. Later still he was aware that the captain, clinging with one hand to the keel of the dinghy, had his face turned away from the shore and toward him, and was calling his name. "Come to the boat! Come to the boat!"

In his struggle to reach the captain and the boat, he reflected that when one gets properly wearied drowning must really be a comfortable arrangement—a cessation of hostilities accompanied by a large degree of relief; and he was glad of it, for the main thing in his mind for some moments had been horror of the temporary agony. He did not wish to be hurt.

Presently he saw a man running along the shore. He was undressing with most remarkable speed. Coat, trousers, shirt, everything flew magically off him.   230

"Come to the boat!" called the captain.

"All right, Captain." As the correspondent paddled, he saw the captain let himself down to bottom and leave the boat. Then the correspondent performed his one little marvel of the voyage. A large wave caught him and flung him with ease and supreme speed completely over the boat and far beyond it. It struck him even then as an event in gymnastics and a true miracle of the sea. An overturned boat in the surf is not a plaything to a swimming man.

The correspondent arrived in water that reached only to his waist, but his condition did not enable him to stand for more than a moment. Each wave knocked him into a heap, and the undertow pulled at him.

Then he saw the man who had been running and undressing, and undressing and running, come bounding into the water. He dragged ashore the cook, and then waded toward the captain; but the captain waved him away and sent him to the correspondent. He was naked—naked as a tree in winter; but a halo was about his head, and he shone like a saint. He gave a strong pull, and a long drag, and a bully heave at the correspondent's hand. The correspondent, schooled in the minor formulae, said, "Thanks, old man." But suddenly the man cried, "What's that?" He pointed a swift finger. The correspondent said, "Go."

In the shallows, face downward, lay the oiler. His forehead touched sand that   235
was periodically, between each wave, clear of the sea.

The correspondent did not know all that transpired afterward. When he achieved safe ground he fell, striking the sand with each particular part of his body. It was as if he had dropped from a roof, but the thud was grateful to him.

It seems that instantly the beach was populated with men with blankets, clothes, and flasks, and women with coffee-pots and all the remedies sacred to their minds. The welcome of the land to the men from the sea was warm and generous; but a still and dripping shape was carried slowly up the beach, and the land's welcome for it could only be the different and sinister hospitality of the grave.

When it came night, the white waves paced to and fro in the moonlight, and the wind brought the sound of the great sea's voice to the men on the shore, and they felt that they could then be interpreters.

Questions

1. In actuality, Crane, the captain of the *Commodore*, and the two crew members spent nearly thirty hours in the open boat. William Higgins, the oiler, was drowned as Crane describes. Does a knowledge of these facts in any way affect your response to

the story? Would you admire the story less—or more—if you believed it to be pure fiction?

2. Sum up the personalities of each of the four men in the boat: captain, cook, oiler, and correspondent.

3. What is the point of view of the story?

4. In paragraph 9, we are told that as each wave came, the boat "seemed like a horse making at a fence outrageously high." Point to other vivid similes or figures of speech. What do they contribute to the story's effectiveness?

5. Notice some of the ways in which Crane, as a storyteller conscious of plot, builds suspense. What enemies or obstacles do the men in the boat confront? What is the effect of the episode of the men who wave from the beach (paragraphs 86–141)? What is the climax of the story? (If you need to be refreshed on the meaning of *climax*, see the discussion of plot in Chapter 1.)

6. In paragraph 70 (and again in paragraph 143), the men wonder, "Was I brought here merely to have my nose dragged away as I was about to nibble the sacred cheese of life?" What variety of irony do you find in this quotation?

7. Why does the scrap of verse about the soldier dying in Algiers (paragraph 178) suddenly come to mean so much to the correspondent?

8. What theme in "The Open Boat" seems most important to you? Where is it stated?

9. What secondary themes also enrich the story? See for instance paragraph 43 (the thoughts on comradeship).

10. How do you define *heroism*? Who is a hero in "The Open Boat"?

Alice Munro

How I Met My Husband   1974

Alice Munro, one of the most widely admired contemporary Canadian writers, was born of farm parents in 1931 in Wingham, in southwestern Ontario, an area in which she has spent most of her life. Its small-town people figure in many of her stories. For two years, she attended the University of Western Ontario, but dropped out at twenty, after her first marriage. The mother of three daughters, Munro is a particularly sensitive explorer of the relations between parents and children, yet she ranges widely in choosing her themes. She has published twelve remarkable collections of short fiction, including Dance of the Happy Shades *(1968),* The Beggar Maid *(1982),* The Love of a Good Woman *(1998), and* The View from Castle Rock *(2006). Munro's* Selected Stories *appeared in 1996, comfirming her position as one of the greatest living masters of short fiction. Three of her books have*

Alice Munro

won Canada's prestigious Governor General's Literary Award; in the United States she has won the National Book Critics Circle Award. The short story is her true medium, and she has declared her preference for "the story that will zero in and give you intense, but not connected, moments of experience."

We heard the plane come over at noon, roaring through the radio news, and we were sure it was going to hit the house, so we all ran out into the yard. We saw it come in over the treetops, all red and silver, the first close-up plane I ever saw. Mrs. Peebles screamed.

"Crash landing," their little boy said. Joey was his name.

"It's okay," said Dr. Peebles. "He knows what he's doing." Dr. Peebles was only an animal doctor, but had a calming way of talking, like any doctor.

This was my first job—working for Dr. and Mrs. Peebles, who had bought an old house out on the Fifth Line, about five miles out of town. It was just when the trend was starting of town people buying up old farms, not to work them but to live on them.

We watched the plane land across the road, where the fairgrounds used to be. It   5
did make a good landing field, nice and level for the old race track, and the barns and display sheds torn down now for scrap lumber so there was nothing in the way. Even the old grandstand bays had burned.

"All right," said Mrs. Peebles, snappy as she always was when she got over her nerves. "Let's go back in the house. Let's not stand here gawking like a set of farmers."

She didn't say that to hurt my feelings. It never occurred to her.

I was just setting the dessert down when Loretta Bird arrived, out of breath, at the screen door.

"I thought it was going to crash into the house and kill youse all!"

She lived on the next place and the Peebleses thought she was a country-   10
woman, they didn't know the difference. She and her husband didn't farm, he worked on the roads and had a bad name for drinking. They had seven children and couldn't get credit at the HiWay Grocery. The Peebleses made her welcome, not knowing any better, as I say, and offered her dessert.

Dessert was never anything to write home about, at their place. A dish of Jell-O or sliced bananas or fruit out of a tin. "Have a house without a pie, be ashamed until you die," my mother used to say, but Mrs. Peebles operated differently.

Loretta Bird saw me getting the can of peaches.

"Oh, never mind," she said. "I haven't got the right kind of a stomach to trust what comes out of those tins, I can only eat home canning."

I could have slapped her. I bet she never put down fruit in her life.

"I know what he's landed here for," she said. "He's got permission to use the fair-   15
grounds and take people up for rides. It costs a dollar. It's the same fellow who was over at Palmerston° last week and was up the lakeshore before that. I wouldn't go up, if you paid me."

"I'd jump at the chance," Dr. Peebles said. "I'd like to see this neighborhood from the air."

Mrs. Peebles said she would just as soon see it from the ground. Joey said he wanted to go and Heather did, too. Joey was nine and Heather was seven.

"Would you, Edie?" Heather said.

I said I didn't know. I was scared, but I never admitted that, especially in front of children I was taking care of.

"People are going to be coming out here in their cars raising dust and trampling   20
your property, if I was you I would complain," Loretta said. She hooked her legs around the chair rung and I knew we were in for a lengthy visit. After Dr. Peebles went back to his office or out on his next call and Mrs. Peebles went for her nap, she

Palmerston: a town in southern Ontario, Canada.

would hang around me while I was trying to do the dishes. She would pass remarks about the Peebleses in their own house.

"She wouldn't find time to lay down in the middle of the day, if she had seven kids like I got."

She asked me did they fight and did they keep things in the dresser drawer not to have babies with. She said it was a sin if they did. I pretended I didn't know what she was talking about.

I was fifteen and away from home for the first time. My parents had made the effort and sent me to high school for a year, but I didn't like it. I was shy of strangers and the work was hard, they didn't make it nice for you or explain the way they do now. At the end of the year the averages were published in the paper, and mine came out at the very bottom, 37 percent. My father said that's enough and I didn't blame him. The last thing I wanted, anyway, was to go on and end up teaching school. It happened the very day the paper came out with my disgrace in it, Dr. Peebles was staying at our place for dinner, having just helped one of the cows have twins, and he said I looked smart to him and his wife was looking for a girl to help. He said she felt tied down, with the two children, out in the country. I guess she would, my mother said, being polite, though I could tell from her face she was wondering what on earth it would be like to have only two children and no barn work, and then to be complaining.

When I went home I would describe to them the work I had to do, and it made everybody laugh. Mrs. Peebles had an automatic washer and dryer, the first I ever saw. I have had those in my own home for such a long time now it's hard to remember how much of a miracle it was to me, not having to struggle with the wringer and hang up and haul down. Let alone not having to heat water. Then there was practically no baking. Mrs. Peebles said she couldn't make pie crust, the most amazing thing I ever heard a woman admit. I could, of course, and I could make light biscuits and a white cake and dark cake, but they didn't want it, she said they watched their figures. The only thing I didn't like about working there, in fact, was feeling half hungry a lot of the time. I used to bring back a box of doughnuts made out at home, and hide them under my bed. The children found out, and I didn't mind sharing, but I thought I better bind them to secrecy.

The day after the plane landed Mrs. Peebles put both children in the car and drove over to Chesley, to get their hair cut. There was a good woman then at Chesley for doing hair. She got hers done at the same place, Mrs. Peebles did, and that meant they would be gone a good while. She had to pick a day Dr. Peebles wasn't going out into the country, she didn't have her own car. Cars were still in short supply then, after the war.

I loved being left in the house alone, to do my work at leisure. The kitchen was all white and bright yellow, with fluorescent lights. That was before they ever thought of making the appliances all different colors and doing the cupboards like dark old wood and hiding the lighting. I loved light. I loved the double sink. So would anybody new-come from washing dishes in a dishpan with a rag-plugged hole on an oilcloth-covered table by light of a coal-oil lamp. I kept everything shining.

The bathroom too. I had a bath in there once a week. They wouldn't have minded if I took one oftener, but to me it seemed like asking too much, or maybe risking making it less wonderful. The basin and the tub and the toilet were all pink, and there were glass doors with flamingoes painted on them, to shut off the tub. The light had a rosy cast and the mat sank under your feet like snow, except that it was warm. The mirror was three-way. With the mirror all steamed up and the air like a perfume cloud, from things I was allowed to use, I stood up on the side of the tub and admired myself naked, from three directions. Sometimes I thought about the way we lived out at home and the way we lived here and how one way was so hard to imagine when you were living the other way. But I thought it was still a lot easier, living the way we lived at home, to picture something like this, the painted flamingoes and the warmth and the soft mat, than it was anybody knowing only things like this to picture how it was the other way. And why was that?

I was through my jobs in no time, and had the vegetables peeled for supper and sitting in cold water besides. Then I went into Mrs. Peebles' bedroom. I had been in there plenty of times, cleaning, and I always took a good look in her closet, at the clothes she had hanging there. I wouldn't have looked in her drawers, but a closet is open to anybody. That's a lie. I would have looked in drawers, but I would have felt worse doing it and been more scared she could tell.

Some clothes in her closet she wore all the time, I was quite familiar with them. Others she never put on, they were pushed to the back. I was disappointed to see no wedding dress. But there was one long dress I could just see the skirt of, and I was hungering to see the rest. Now I took note of where it hung and lifted it out. It was satin, a lovely weight on my arm, light bluish-green in color, almost silvery. It had a fitted, pointed waist and a full skirt and an off-the-shoulder fold hiding the little sleeves.

Next thing was easy. I got out of my own things and slipped it on. I was slimmer at fifteen than anybody would believe who knows me now and the fit was beautiful. I didn't, of course, have a strapless bra on, which was what it needed, I just had to slide my straps down my arms under the material. Then I tried pinning up my hair, to get the effect. One thing led to another. I put on rouge and lipstick and eyebrow pencil from her dresser. The heat of the day and the weight of the satin and all the excitement made me thirsty, and I went out to the kitchen, got-up as I was, to get a glass of ginger ale with ice cubes from the refrigerator. The Peebleses drank ginger ale, or fruit drinks, all day, like water, and I was getting so I did too. Also there was no limit on ice cubes, which I was so fond of I would even put them in a glass of milk.

I turned from putting the ice tray back and saw a man watching me through the screen. It was the luckiest thing in the world I didn't spill the ginger ale down the front of me then and there.

"I never meant to scare you. I knocked but you were getting the ice out, you didn't hear me."

I couldn't see what he looked like, he was dark the way somebody is pressed up against a screen door with the bright daylight behind them. I only knew he wasn't from around here.

"I'm from the plane over there. My name is Chris Watters and what I was wondering was if I could use that pump."

There was a pump in the yard. That was the way the people used to get their water. Now I noticed he was carrying a pail.

"You're welcome," I said. "I can get it from the tap and save you pumping." I guess I wanted him to know we had piped water, didn't pump ourselves.

"I don't mind the exercise." He didn't move, though, and finally he said, "Were you going to a dance?"

Seeing a stranger there had made me entirely forget how I was dressed.

30

35

"Or is that the way ladies around here generally get dressed up in the afternoon?"
I didn't know how to joke back then. I was too embarrassed.   40

"You live here? Are you the lady of the house?"

"I'm the hired girl."

Some people change when they find that out, their whole way of looking at you
and speaking to you changes, but his didn't.

"Well, I just wanted to tell you you look very nice. I was so surprised when I
looked in the door and saw you. Just because you looked so nice and beautiful."

I wasn't even old enough then to realize how out of the common it is, for a man   45
to say something like that to a woman, or somebody he is treating like a woman. For
a man to say a word like *beautiful*. I wasn't old enough to realize or to say anything
back, or in fact to do anything but wish he would go away. Not that I didn't like him,
but just that it upset me so, having him look at me, and me trying to think of something to say.

He must have understood. He said good-bye, and thanked me, and went and
started filling his pail from the pump. I stood behind the Venetian blinds in the dining
room, watching him. When he had gone, I went into the bedroom and took the dress
off and put it back in the same place. I dressed in my own clothes and took my hair
down and washed my face, wiping it on Kleenex, which I threw in the wastebasket.

The Peebleses asked me what kind of man he was. Young, middle-aged, short,
tall? I couldn't say.

"Good-looking?" Dr. Peebles teased me.

I couldn't think a thing but that he would be coming to get his water again, he
would be talking to Dr. or Mrs. Peebles, making friends with them, and he would
mention seeing me that first afternoon, dressed up. Why not mention it? He would
think it was funny. And no idea of the trouble it would get me into.

After supper the Peebleses drove into town to go to a movie. She wanted to go   50
somewhere with her hair fresh done. I sat in my bright kitchen wondering what to
do, knowing I would never sleep. Mrs. Peebles might not fire me, when she found
out, but it would give her a different feeling about me altogether. This was the first
place I ever worked but I already had picked up things about the way people feel
when you are working for them. They like to think you aren't curious. Not just that
you aren't dishonest, that isn't enough. They like to feel you don't notice things, that
you don't think or wonder about anything but what they liked to eat and how they
liked things ironed, and so on. I don't mean they weren't kind to me, because they
were. They had me eat my meals with them (to tell the truth I expected to, I didn't
know there were families who don't) and sometimes they took me along in the car.
But all the same.

I went up and checked on the children being asleep and then I went out. I had to
do it. I crossed the road and went in the old fairgrounds gate. The plane looked unnatural sitting there, and shining with the moon. Off at the far side of the fairgrounds
where the bush was taking over, I saw his tent.

He was sitting outside it smoking a cigarette. He saw me coming.

"Hello, were you looking for a plane ride? I don't start taking people up till tomorrow." Then he looked again and said, "Oh, it's you. I didn't know you without
your long dress on."

My heart was knocking away, my tongue was dried up. I had to say something.
But I couldn't. My throat was closed and I was like a deaf-and-dumb.

"Did you want a ride? Sit down. Have a cigarette." 55

I couldn't even shake my head to say no, so he gave me one.

"Put it in your mouth or I can't light it. It's a good thing I'm used to shy ladies."

I did. It wasn't the first time I had smoked a cigarette, actually. My girlfriend out home, Muriel Lowe, used to steal them from her brother.

"Look at your hand shaking. Did you just want to have a chat, or what?"

In one burst I said, "I wisht you wouldn't say anything about that dress." 60

"What dress? Oh, the long dress."

"It's Mrs. Peebles'."

"Whose? Oh, the lady you work for? She wasn't home so you got dressed up in her dress, eh? You got dressed up and played queen. I don't blame you. You're not smoking the cigarette right. Don't just puff. Draw it in. Did anybody ever show you how to inhale? Are you scared I'll tell on you? Is that it?"

I was so ashamed at having to ask him to connive this way I couldn't nod. I just looked at him and he saw *yes*.

"Well I won't. I won't in the slightest way mention it or embarrass you. I give 65 you my word of honor."

Then he changed the subject, to help me out, seeing I couldn't even thank him.

"What do you think of this sign?"

It was a board sign lying practically at my feet.

SEE THE WORLD FROM THE SKY. ADULTS $1.00, CHILDREN 50¢. QUALIFIED PILOT.

"My old sign was getting pretty beat up, I thought I'd make a new one. That's 70 what I've been doing with my time today."

The lettering wasn't all that handsome, I thought. I could have done a better one in half an hour.

"I'm not an expert at sign making."

"It's very good," I said.

"I don't need it for publicity, word of mouth is usually enough. I turned away two carloads tonight. I felt like taking it easy. I didn't tell them ladies were dropping in to visit me."

Now I remembered the children and I was scared again, in case one of them had 75 waked up and called me and I wasn't there.

"Do you have to go so soon?"

I remembered some manners. "Thank you for the cigarette."

"Don't forget. You have my word of honor."

I tore off across the fairgrounds, scared I'd see the car heading home from town. My sense of time was mixed up, I didn't know how long I'd been out of the house. But it was all right, it wasn't late, the children were asleep. I got in my bed myself and lay thinking what a lucky end to the day, after all, and among things to be grateful for I could be grateful Loretta Bird hadn't been the one who caught me.

The yard and borders didn't get trampled, it wasn't as bad as that. All the same it 80 seemed very public, around the house. The sign was on the fairgrounds gate. People came mostly after supper but a good many in the afternoon, too. The Bird children all came without fifty cents between them and hung on the gate. We got used to the excitement of the plane coming in and taking off, it wasn't excitement anymore. I never went over, after that one time, but would see him when he came to get his water. I would be out on the steps doing sitting-down work, like preparing vegetables, if I could.

"Why don't you come over? I'll take you up in my plane."

"I'm saving my money," I said, because I couldn't think of anything else.

"For what? For getting married?"

I shook my head.

"I'll take you up for free if you come sometime when it's slack. I thought you 85 would come, and have another cigarette."

I made a face to hush him, because you never could tell when the children would be sneaking around the porch, or Mrs. Peebles herself listening in the house. Sometimes she came out and had a conversation with him. He told her things he hadn't bothered to tell me. But then I hadn't thought to ask. He told her he had been in the war, that was where he learned to fly a plane, and how he couldn't settle down to ordinary life, this was what he liked. She said she couldn't imagine anybody liking such a thing. Though sometimes, she said, she was almost bored enough to try anything herself, she wasn't brought up to living in the country. It's all my husband's idea, she said. This was news to me.

"Maybe you ought to give flying lessons," she said.

"Would you take them?"

She just laughed.

Sunday was a busy flying day in spite of it being preached against from two pul- 90 pits. We were all sitting out watching. Joey and Heather were over on the fence with the Bird kids. Their father had said they could go, after their mother saying all week they couldn't.

A car came down the road past the parked cars and pulled up right in the drive. It was Loretta Bird who got out, all importance, and on the driver's side another woman got out, more sedately. She was wearing sunglasses.

"This is a lady looking for the man that flies the plane," Loretta Bird said. "I heard her inquire in the hotel coffee shop where I was having a Coke and I brought her out."

"I'm sorry to bother you," the lady said. "I'm Alice Kelling, Mr. Watters' fiancée."

This Alice Kelling had on a pair of brown and white checked slacks and a yellow top. Her bust looked to me rather low and bumpy. She had a worried face. Her hair had had a permanent, but had grown out, and she wore a yellow band to keep it off her face. Nothing in the least pretty or even young-looking about her. But you could tell from how she talked she was from the city, or educated, or both.

Dr. Peebles stood up and introduced himself and his wife and me and asked her 95 to be seated.

"He's up in the air right now, but you're welcome to sit and wait. He gets his water here and he hasn't been yet. He'll probably take his break about five."

"That is him, then?" said Alice Kelling, wrinkling and straining at the sky.

"He's not in the habit of running out on you, taking a different name?" Dr. Peebles laughed. He was the one, not his wife, to offer iced tea. Then she sent me into the kitchen to fix it. She smiled. She was wearing sunglasses too.

"He never mentioned his fiancée," she said.

I loved fixing iced tea with lots of ice and slices of lemon in tall glasses. I ought 100 to have mentioned before, Dr. Peebles was an abstainer, at least around the house, or I wouldn't have been allowed to take the place. I had to fix a glass for Loretta Bird too, though it galled me, and when I went out she had settled in my lawn chair, leaving me the steps.

"I knew you was a nurse when I first heard you in that coffee shop."

"How would you know a thing like that?"

"I get my hunches about people. Was that how you met him, nursing?"

"Chris? Well yes. Yes, it was."

"Oh, were you overseas?" said Mrs. Peebles.

"No, it was before he went overseas. I nursed him when he was stationed at Centralia and had a ruptured appendix. We got engaged and then he went overseas. My, this is refreshing, after a long drive."

"He'll be glad to see you," Dr. Peebles said. "It's a rackety kind of life, isn't it, not staying one place long enough to really make friends."

"Youse've had a long engagement," Loretta Bird said.

Alice Kelling passed that over. "I was going to get a room at the hotel, but when I was offered directions I came on out. Do you think I could phone them?"

"No need," Dr. Peebles said. "You're five miles away from him if you stay at the hotel. Here, you're right across the road. Stay with us. We've got rooms on rooms, look at this big house."

Asking people to stay, just like that, is certainly a country thing, and maybe seemed natural to him now, but not to Mrs. Peebles, from the way she said, oh yes, we have plenty of room. Or to Alice Kelling, who kept protesting, but let herself be worn down. I got the feeling it was a temptation to her, to be that close. I was trying for a look at her ring. Her nails were painted red, her fingers were freckled and wrinkled. It was a tiny stone. Muriel Lowe's cousin had one twice as big.

Chris came to get his water, late in the afternoon just as Dr. Peebles had predicted. He must have recognized the car from a way off. He came smiling.

"Here I am chasing after you to see what you're up to," called Alice Kelling. She got up and went to meet him and they kissed, just touched, in front of us.

"You're going to spend a lot on gas that way," Chris said.

Dr. Peebles invited Chris to stay for supper, since he had already put up the sign that said: NO MORE RIDES TILL 7 P.M. Mrs. Peebles wanted it served in the yard, in spite of the bugs. One thing strange to anybody from the country is this eating outside. I had made a potato salad earlier and she had made a jellied salad, that was one thing she could do, so it was just a matter of getting those out, and some sliced meat and cucumbers and fresh leaf lettuce. Loretta Bird hung around for some time saying, "Oh, well, I guess I better get home to those yappers," and, "It's so nice just sitting here, I sure hate to get up," but nobody invited her, I was relieved to see, and finally she had to go.

That night after rides were finished Alice Kelling and Chris went off somewhere in her car. I lay awake till they got back. When I saw the car lights sweep my ceiling I got up to look down on them through the slats of my blind. I don't know what I thought I was going to see. Muriel Lowe and I used to sleep on her front veranda and watch her sister and her sister's boy friend saying good night. Afterward we couldn't get to sleep, for longing for somebody to kiss us and rub against us and we would talk about suppose you were out in a boat with a boy and he wouldn't bring you in to shore unless you did it, or what if somebody got you trapped in a barn, you would have to, wouldn't you, it wouldn't be your fault. Muriel said her two girl cousins used to try with a toilet paper roll that one of them was a boy. We wouldn't do anything like that; just lay and wondered.

All that happened was that Chris got out of the car on one side and she got out on the other and they walked off separately—him toward the fairgrounds and her toward the house. I got back in bed and imagined about me coming home with him, not like that.

Next morning Alice Kelling got up late and I fixed a grapefruit for her the way I had learned and Mrs. Peebles sat down with her to visit and have another cup of coffee. Mrs. Peebles seemed pleased enough now, having company. Alice Kelling said she guessed she better get used to putting in a day just watching Chris take off and come down, and Mrs. Peebles said she didn't know if she should suggest it because Alice Kelling was the one with the car, but the lake was only twenty-five miles away and what a good day for a picnic.

Alice Kelling took her up on the idea and by eleven o'clock they were in the car, with Joey and Heather and a sandwich lunch I had made. The only thing was that Chris hadn't come down, and she wanted to tell him where they were going.

"Edie'll go over and tell him," Mrs. Peebles said. "There's no problem." 120

Alice Kelling wrinkled her face and agreed.

"Be sure and tell him we'll be back by five!"

I didn't see that he would be concerned about knowing this right away, and I thought of him eating whatever he ate over there, alone, cooking on his camp stove, so I got to work and mixed up a crumb cake and baked it, in between the other work I had to do; then, when it was a bit cooled, wrapped it in a tea towel. I didn't do anything to myself but take off my apron and comb my hair. I would like to have put some makeup on, but I was too afraid it would remind him of the way he first saw me, and that would humiliate me all over again.

He had come and put another sign on the gate: NO RIDES THIS P.M. APOLOGIES. I worried that he wasn't feeling well. No sign of him outside and the tent flap was down. I knocked on the pole.

"Come in," he said, in a voice that would just as soon have said *Stay out.* 125

I lifted the flap.

"Oh, it's you. I'm sorry. I didn't know it was you."

He had been just sitting on the side of the bed, smoking. Why not at least sit and smoke in the fresh air?

"I brought a cake and hope you're not sick," I said.

"Why would I be sick? Oh—that sign. That's all right. I'm just tired of talking to 130 people. I don't mean you. Have a seat." He pinned back the tent flap. "Get some fresh air in here."

I sat on the edge of the bed, there was no place else. It was one of those foldup cots, really; I remembered and gave him his fiancée's message.

He ate some of the cake. "Good."

"Put the rest away for when you're hungry later."

"I'll tell you a secret. I won't be around here much longer."

"Are you getting married?"

"Ha ha. What time did you say they'd be back?" 135

"Five o'clock."

"Well, by that time this place will have seen the last of me. A plane can get further than a car." He unwrapped the cake and ate another piece of it, absent-mindedly.

"Now you'll be thirsty."

"There's some water in the pail." 140

"It won't be very cold. I could bring some fresh. I could bring some ice from the refrigerator."

"No," he said. "I don't want you to go. I want a nice long time of saying good-bye to you."

He put the cake away carefully and sat beside me and started those little kisses, so soft, I can't ever let myself think about them, such kindness in his face and lovely kisses, all over my eyelids and neck and ears, all over, then me kissing back as well as I could (I had only kissed a boy on a dare before, and kissed my own arms for practice) and we lay back on the cot and pressed together, just gently, and he did some other things, not bad things or not in a bad way. It was lovely in the tent, that smell of grass and hot tent cloth with the sun beating down on it, and he said, "I wouldn't do you any harm for the world." Once, when he had rolled on top of me and we were sort of rocking together on the cot, he said softly, "Oh, no," and freed himself and jumped up and got the water pail. He splashed some of it on his neck and face, and the little bit left, on me lying there.

"That's to cool us off, miss."

When we said good-bye I wasn't at all sad, because he held my face and said,   145
"I'm going to write you a letter. I'll tell you where I am and maybe you can come and see me. Would you like that? Okay then. You wait." I was really glad I think to get away from him, it was like he was piling presents on me I couldn't get the pleasure of till I considered them alone.

No consternation at first about the plane being gone. They thought he had taken somebody up, and I didn't enlighten them. Dr. Peebles had phoned he had to go to the country, so there was just us having supper, and then Loretta Bird thrusting her head in the door and saying, "I see he's took off."

"What?" said Alice Kelling, and pushed back her chair.

"The kids come and told me this afternoon he was taking down his tent. Did he think he'd run through all the business there was around here? He didn't take off without letting you know, did he?"

"He'll send me word," Alice Kelling said. "He'll probably phone tonight. He's terribly restless, since the war."

"Edie, he didn't mention to you, did he?" Mrs. Peebles said. "When you took   150
over the message?"

"Yes," I said. So far so true.

"Well why didn't you say?" All of them were looking at me. "Did he say where he was going?"

"He said he might try Bayfield," I said. What made me tell such a lie? I didn't intend it.

"Bayfield, how far is that?" said Alice Kelling.

Mrs. Peebles said, "Thirty, thirty-five miles."   155

"That's not far. Oh, well, that's really not far at all. It's on the lake, isn't it?"

You'd think I'd be ashamed of myself, setting her on the wrong track. I did it to give him more time, whatever time he needed. I lied for him, and also, I have to admit, for me. Women should stick together and not do things like that. I see that now, but didn't then. I never thought of myself as being in any way like her, or coming to the same troubles, ever.

She hadn't taken her eyes off me. I thought she suspected my lie.

"When did he mention this to you?"

"Earlier."   160

"When you were over at the plane?"

"Yes."

"You must've stayed and had a chat." She smiled at me, not a nice smile. "You must've stayed and had a little visit with him."

"I took a cake," I said, thinking that telling some truth would spare me telling the rest.

"We didn't have a cake," said Mrs. Peebles rather sharply.   165

"I baked one."

Alice Kelling said, "That was very friendly of you."

"Did you get permission," said Loretta Bird. "You never know what these girls'll do next," she said. "It's not they mean harm so much, as they're ignorant."

"The cake is neither here nor there," Mrs. Peebles broke in. "Edie, I wasn't aware you knew Chris that well."

I didn't know what to say.   170

"I'm not surprised," Alice Kelling said in a high voice. "I knew by the look of her as soon as I saw her. We get them at the hospital all the time." She looked hard at me with her stretched smile. "Having their babies. We have to put them in a special ward because of their diseases. Little country tramps. Fourteen and fifteen years old. You should see the babies they have, too."

"There was a bad woman here in town had a baby that pus was running out of its eyes," Loretta Bird put in.

"Wait a minute," said Mrs. Peebles. "What is this talk? Edie. What about you and Mr. Watters? Were you intimate with him?"

"Yes," I said. I was thinking of us lying on the cot and kissing, wasn't that intimate? And I would never deny it.

They were all one minute quiet, even Loretta Bird.   175

"Well," said Mrs. Peebles. "I am surprised. I think I need a cigarette. This is the first of any such tendencies I've seen in her," she said, speaking to Alice Kelling, but Alice Kelling was looking at me.

"Loose little bitch." Tears ran down her face. "Loose little bitch, aren't you? I knew as soon as I saw you. Men despise girls like you. He just made use of you and went off, you know that, don't you? Girls like you are just nothing, they're just public conveniences, just filthy little rags!"

"Oh, now," said Mrs. Peebles.

"Filthy," Alice Kelling sobbed. "Filthy little rags!"

"Don't get yourself upset," Loretta Bird said. She was swollen up with pleasure at 180 being in on this scene. "Men are all the same."

"Edie, I'm very surprised," Mrs. Pebbles said. "I thought your parents were so strict. You don't want to have a baby, do you?"

I'm still ashamed of what happened next. I lost control, just like a six-year-old, I started howling. "You don't get a baby from just doing that!"

"You see. Some of them are that ignorant," Loretta Bird said.

But Mrs. Peebles jumped up and caught my arms and shook me.

"Calm down. Don't get hysterical. Calm down. Stop crying. Listen to me. Listen. 185 I'm wondering, if you know what being intimate means. Now tell me. What did you think it meant?"

"Kissing," I howled.

She let go. "Oh, Edie. Stop it. Don't be silly. It's all right. It's all a misunderstanding. Being intimate means a lot more than that. Oh, I *wondered*."

"She's trying to cover up, now," said Alice Kelling. "Yes. She's not so stupid. She sees she got herself in trouble."

"I believe her," Mrs. Peebles said. "This is an awful scene."

"Well there is one way to find out," said Alice Kelling, getting up. "After all, I   190
am a nurse."

Mrs. Peebles drew a breath and said, "No. No. Go to your room, Edie. And stop that noise. This is too disgusting."

I heard the car start in a little while. I tried to stop crying, pulling back each wave as it started over me. Finally I succeeded, and lay heaving on the bed.

Mrs. Peebles came and stood in the doorway.

"She's gone," she said. "That Bird woman too. Of course, you know you should never have gone near that man and that is the cause of all this trouble. I have a headache. As soon as you can, go and wash your face in cold water and get at the dishes and we will not say any more about this."

Nor we didn't. I didn't figure out till years later the extent of what I had been   195
saved from. Mrs. Peebles was not very friendly to me afterward, but she was fair. Not very friendly is the wrong way of describing what she was. She had never been very friendly. It was just that now she had to see me all the time and it got on her nerves, a little.

As for me, I put it all out of my mind like a bad dream and concentrated on waiting for my letter. The mail came every day except Sunday, between one-thirty and two in the afternoon, a good time for me because Mrs. Peebles was always having her nap. I would get the kitchen all cleaned and then go up to the mailbox and sit in the grass, waiting. I was perfectly happy, waiting. I forgot all about Alice Kelling and her misery and awful talk and Mrs. Peebles and her chilliness and the embarrassment of whether she told Dr. Peebles and the face of Loretta Bird, getting her fill of other people's troubles. I was always smiling when the mailman got there, and continued smiling even after he gave me the mail and I saw today wasn't the day. The mailman was a Carmichael. I knew by his face because there are a lot of Carmichaels living out by us and so many of them have a sort of sticking-out top lip. So I asked his name (he was a young man, shy, but good-humored, anybody could ask him anything) and then I said, "I knew by your face!" He was pleased by that and always glad to see me and got a little less shy. "You've got the smile I've been waiting for all day!" he used to holler out the car window.

It never crossed my mind for a long time a letter might not come. I believed in it coming just like I believed the sun would rise in the morning. I just put off my hope from day to day, and there was the goldenrod out around the mailbox and the children gone back to school, and the leaves turning, and I was wearing a sweater when I went to wait. One day walking back with the hydro bill stuck in my hand, that was all, looking across at the fairgrounds with the full-blown milkweed and dark teasels, so much like fall, it just struck me: *No letter was ever going to come*. It was an impossible idea to get used to. No, not impossible. If I thought about Chris's face when he said he was going to write me, it was impossible, but if I forgot that and thought about the actual tin mailbox, empty, it was plain and true. I kept on going to meet the mail, but my heart was heavy now like a lump of lead. I only smiled because I thought of the mailman counting on it, and he didn't have an easy life, with the winter driving ahead.

Till it came to me one day there were women doing this with their lives, all over. There were women just waiting and waiting by mailboxes for one letter or another. I imagined me making this journey day after day and year after year, and my hair starting to get gray, and I thought, I was never made to go on like that. So I stopped meeting the mail. If there were women all through life waiting, and women busy and not waiting, I knew which I had to be. Even though there might be things the second kind of women have to pass up and never know about, it still is better.

I was surprised when the mailman phoned the Peebleses' place in the evening and asked for me. He said he missed me. He asked if I would like to go to Goderich, where some well-known movie was on, I forget now what. So I said yes, and I went out with him for two years and he asked me to marry him, and we were engaged a year more while I got my things together, and then we did marry. He always tells the children the story of how I went after him by sitting by the mailbox every day, and naturally I laugh and let him, because I like for people to think what pleases them and makes them happy.

Questions

1. What is your attitude toward Edie, the narrator—sympathy, condescension, disapproval, or something more complicated? Explain.
2. What aspects of Mrs. Peebles and her life does Edie admire or envy? What things about Mrs. Peebles does she find off-putting?
3. Why does Edie dislike Loretta Bird so much?
4. Reread the description of Alice Kelling in paragraph 94. What details does Edie notice about her, and why are these qualities important to Edie?
5. It is interesting that the story contains no description of Chris Watters's personal appearance. Why not, do you think? What are the things about him that really matter to Edie?
6. The twist at the end of the story may remind you of "The Gift of the Magi." Is there here, as there is in O. Henry's tale, more to the conclusion than just a clever surprise?
7. How would you state the theme of this story? Explain.

Luke 15:11–32

The Parable of the Prodigal Son   (Authorized or King James Version, 1611)

And he said, A certain man had two sons: And the younger of them said to his father, Father, give me the portion of goods that falleth to me. And he divided unto them his living. And not many days after the younger son gathered all together, and took his journey into a far country, and there wasted his substance with riotous living. And when he had spent all, there arose a mighty famine in that land; and he began to be in want. And he went and joined himself to a citizen of that country; and he sent him into his fields to feed swine. And he would fain have filled his belly with the husks that the swine did eat: and no man gave unto him. And when he came to himself, he said, How many hired servants of my father's have bread enough and to spare, and I perish with hunger! I will arise and go to my father, and will say unto him, Father I have sinned against heaven, and before thee, and am no more worthy to be called thy son; make me as one of thy hired servants. And he arose, and came to his father. But when he was yet a great way off, his father saw him, and had compassion, and ran, and fell on his neck, and kissed him. And the son said unto him, Father I have sinned against heaven, and in thy sight, and am no more worthy to be called thy son. But the father said to his servants, Bring forth the best robe, and put it on him; and put a ring on his hand, and shoes on his feet: And bring hither the fatted calf, and kill it; and let us eat, and be merry: For this my son was dead, and is alive again; he was lost, and is found. And they began to be merry. Now his elder son was in the field: and he came and drew nigh to the house, he heard music and dancing. And he called one of the servants, and asked what these things meant. And he said unto him, Thy brother is come; and thy father hath killed the fatted calf, because he hath received him safe and sound. And he was angry, and would not go in: therefore came his father out, and entreated him. And he answering said to his father, Lo, these many years do I serve thee, neither transgressed I at any time thy commandment; and yet thou never gavest me a kid, that I might make merry with my friends: But as soon as this thy son was come, which hath devoured thy living with harlots, thou hast killed for him the fatted calf. And he said unto him, Son thou art ever with me, and all that I have is thine. It was meet that we should make merry, and be glad: for this thy brother was dead, and is alive again; and was lost, and is found.

Questions

1. This story has traditionally been called "The Parable of the Prodigal Son." What does *prodigal* mean? Which of the two brothers is prodigal?

2. What position does the younger son expect when he returns to his father's house? What does the father give him?

3. When the older brother sees the celebration for his younger brother's return, he grows angry. He makes a very reasonable set of complaints to his father. He has indeed been a loyal and moral son, but what virtue does the older brother lack?

4. Is the father fair to the elder son? Explain your answer.

5. Theologians have discussed this parable's religious significance for two thousand years. What, in your own words, is the human theme of the story?

Kurt Vonnegut Jr.

Harrison Bergeron   1961

Kurt Vonnegut Jr. (1922–2007) was born in Indianapolis. During the Depression his father, a well-to-do architect, had virtually no work, and the family lived in reduced circumstances. Vonnegut attended Cornell University, where he majored in chemistry and was also managing editor of the daily student newspaper. In 1943 he enlisted in the U.S. Army. During the Battle of the Bulge he was captured by German troops and interned as a prisoner of war in Dresden, where he survived the massive Allied firebombing, which killed tens of thousands of people, mostly civilians. (The firebombing of Dresden became the central incident in Vonnegut's best-selling 1969 novel, Slaughterhouse-Five.) After the war, Vonnegut worked as a reporter and later as a public relations man for General Electric in Schenectady, New York. He quit his job in 1951 to write full-time after publishing several science fiction stories in national magazines. His first novel, Player Piano, appeared in 1952, followed by Sirens of Titan (1959) and his first bestseller, Cat's Cradle (1963)—all now considered classics of literary science fiction. Among his many other books are Mother Night (1961), Jailbird (1979), and a book of biographical essays, A Man Without a Country (2005). His short fiction is collected in Welcome to the Monkey House (1968) and Bagombo Snuff Box (1999). Vonnegut is a singular figure in modern American fiction. An ingenious comic writer, he combined the popular genre of science fiction with the literary tradition of dark satire—a combination splendidly realized in "Harrison Bergeron."

The year was 2081, and everybody was finally equal. They weren't only equal before God and the law. They were equal every which way. Nobody was smarter than anybody else. Nobody was better looking than anybody else. Nobody was stronger or quicker than anybody else. All this equality was due to the 211th, 212th, and 213th Amendments to the Constitution, and to the unceasing vigilance of agents of the United States Handicapper General.

Some things about living still weren't quite right, though. April, for instance, still drove people crazy by not being springtime. And it was in that clammy month that the H-G men took George and Hazel Bergeron's fourteen-year-old son, Harrison, away.

It was tragic, all right, but George and Hazel couldn't think about it very hard. Hazel had a perfectly average intelligence, which meant she couldn't think about anything except in short bursts. And George, while his intelligence was way above normal, had a little mental handicap radio in his ear. He was required by law to wear it at all times. It was tuned to a government transmitter. Every twenty seconds or so, the transmitter would send out some sharp noise to keep people like George from taking unfair advantage of their brains.

George and Hazel were watching television. There were tears on Hazel's cheeks, but she'd forgotten for the moment what they were about.

On the television screen were ballerinas.   5

A buzzer sounded in George's head. His thoughts fled in panic, like bandits from a burglar alarm.

"That was a real pretty dance, that dance they just did," said Hazel.

"Huh?" said George.

"That dance—it was nice," said Hazel.

"Yup," said George. He tried to think a little about the ballerinas. They weren't   10
really very good—no better than anybody else would have been, anyway. They were burdened with sashweights and bags of birdshot, and their faces were masked, so that no one, seeing a free and graceful gesture or a pretty face, would feel like something the cat drug in. George was toying with the vague notion that maybe dancers shouldn't be handicapped. But he didn't get very far with it before another noise in his ear radio scattered his thoughts.

George winced. So did two out of the eight ballerinas.

Hazel saw him wince. Having no mental handicap herself, she had to ask George what the latest sound had been.

"Sounded like somebody hitting a milk bottle with a ball peen hammer," said George.

"I'd think it would be real interesting, hearing all the different sounds," said Hazel, a little envious. "All the things they think up."

"Um," said George.   15

"Only, if I was Handicapper General, you know what I would do?" said Hazel. Hazel, as a matter of fact, bore a strong resemblance to the Handicapper General, a woman named Diana Moon Glampers. "If I was Diana Moon Glampers," said Hazel, "I'd have chimes on Sunday—just chimes. Kind of in honor of religion."

"I could think, if it was just chimes," said George.

"Well—maybe make 'em real loud," said Hazel. "I think I'd make a good Handicapper General."

"Good as anybody else," said George.

"Who knows better'n I do what normal is?" said Hazel.   20

"Right," said George. He began to think glimmeringly about his abnormal son who was now in jail, about Harrison, but a twenty-one-gun salute in his head stopped that.

"Boy!" said Hazel, "that was a doozy, wasn't it?"

It was such a doozy that George was white and trembling, and tears stood on the rims of his red eyes. Two of the eight ballerinas had collapsed to the studio floor, were holding their temples.

"All of a sudden you look so tired," said Hazel. "Why don't you stretch out on the sofa, so's you can rest your handicap bag on the pillows, honeybunch." She was referring to the forty-seven pounds of birdshot in a canvas bag, which was padlocked around George's neck. "Go on and rest the bag for a little while," she said. "I don't care if you're not equal to me for a while."

George weighed the bag with his hands. "I don't mind it," he said. "I don't notice   25
it any more. It's just a part of me."

"You been so tired lately—kind of wore out," said Hazel. "If there was just some way we could make a little hole in the bottom of the bag, and just take out a few of them lead balls. Just a few."

"Two years in prison and two thousand dollars fine for every ball I took out," said George. "I don't call that a bargain."

"If you could just take a few out when you came home from work," said Hazel. "I mean—you don't compete with anybody around here. You just set around."

"If I tried to get away with it," said George, "then other people'd get away with it—and pretty soon we'd be right back to the dark ages again, with everybody competing against everybody else. You wouldn't like that, would you?"

"I'd hate it," said Hazel.   30

"There you are," said George. "The minute people start cheating on laws, what do you think happens to society?"

If Hazel hadn't been able to come up with an answer to this question, George couldn't have supplied one. A siren was going off in his head.

"Reckon it'd fall all apart," said Hazel.

"What would?" said George blankly.

"Society," said Hazel uncertainly. "Wasn't that what you just said?"   35

"Who knows?" said George.

The television program was suddenly interrupted for a news bulletin. It wasn't clear at first as to what the bulletin was about, since the announcer, like all announcers, had a serious speech impediment. For about half a minute, and in a state of high excitement, the announcer tried to say, "Ladies and gentlemen—"

He finally gave up, handed the bulletin to a ballerina to read.

"That's all right—" Hazel said of the announcer, "he tried. That's the big thing. He tried to do the best he could with what God gave him. He should get a nice raise for trying so hard."

"Ladies and gentlemen—" said the ballerina, reading the bulletin. She must have   40
been extraordinarily beautiful, because the mask she wore was hideous. And it was easy to see that she was the strongest and most graceful of all the dancers, for her handicap bags were as big as those worn by two-hundred-pound men.

And she had to apologize at once for her voice, which was a very unfair voice for a woman to use. Her voice was a warm, luminous, timeless melody. "Excuse me—" she said, and she began again, making her voice absolutely uncompetitive.

"Harrison Bergeron, age fourteen," she said in a grackle squawk, "has just escaped from jail, where he was held on suspicion of plotting to overthrow the government. He is a genius and an athlete, is under-handicapped, and should be regarded as extremely dangerous."

A police photograph of Harrison Bergeron was flashed on the screen upside down, then sideways, upside down again, then right side up. The picture showed the full length of Harrison against a background calibrated in feet and inches. He was exactly seven feet tall.

The rest of Harrison's appearance was Halloween and hardware. Nobody had ever borne heavier handicaps. He had outgrown hindrances faster than the H-G men could think them up. Instead of a little ear radio for a mental handicap, he wore a tremendous pair of earphones, and spectacles with thick wavy lenses. The spectacles were intended to make him not only half blind, but to give him whanging headaches besides.

Scrap metal was hung all over him. Ordinarily, there was a certain symmetry, a   45
military neatness to the handicaps issued to strong people, but Harrison looked like a walking junkyard. In the race of life, Harrison carried three hundred pounds.

And to offset his good looks, the H-G men required that he wear at all times a red rubber ball for a nose, keep his eyebrows shaved off, and cover his even white teeth with black caps at snaggle-tooth random.

"If you see this boy," said the ballerina, "do not—I repeat, do not—try to reason with him."

There was the shriek of a door being torn from its hinges.

Screams and barking cries of consternation came from the television set. The photograph of Harrison Bergeron on the screen jumped again and again, as though dancing to the tune of an earthquake.

George Bergeron correctly identified the earthquake, and well he might have—   50
for many was the time his own home had danced to the same crashing tune. "My God—" said George, "that must be Harrison!"

The realization was blasted from his mind instantly by the sound of an automobile collision in his head.

When George could open his eyes again, the photograph of Harrison was gone. A living, breathing Harrison filled the screen.

Clanking, clownish, and huge, Harrison stood in the center of the studio. The knob of the uprooted studio door was still in his hand. Ballerinas, technicians, musicians, and announcers cowered on their knees before him, expecting to die.

"I am the Emperor!" cried Harrison. "Do you hear? I am the Emperor! Everybody must do what I say at once!" He stamped his foot and the studio shook.

"Even as I stand here—" he bellowed, "crippled, hobbled, sickened—I am a greater   55
ruler than any man who ever lived! Now watch me become what I *can* become!"

Harrison tore the straps of his handicap harness like wet tissue paper, tore straps guaranteed to support five thousand pounds.

Harrison's scrap-iron handicaps crashed to the floor.

Harrison thrust his thumbs under the bar of the padlock that secured his head harness. The bar snapped like celery. Harrison smashed his headphones and spectacles against the wall.

He flung away his rubber-ball nose, revealed a man that would have awed Thor, the god of thunder.

"I shall now select my Empress!" he said, looking down on the cowering   60
people. "Let the first woman who dares rise to her feet claim her mate and her throne!"

A moment passed, and then a ballerina arose, swaying like a willow.

Harrison plucked the mental handicap from her ear, snapped off her physical handicaps with marvelous delicacy. Last of all, he removed her mask.

She was blindingly beautiful.

"Now—" said Harrison, taking her hand, "shall we show the people the meaning of the word dance? Music!" he commanded.

The musicians scrambled back into their chairs, and Harrison stripped them of   65
their handicaps, too. "Play your best," he told them, "and I'll make you barons and dukes and earls."

The music began. It was normal at first—cheap, silly, false. But Harrison snatched two musicians from their chairs, waved them like batons as he sang the music as he wanted it played. He slammed them back into their chairs.

The music began again and was much improved.

Harrison and his Empress merely listened to the music for a while—listened gravely, as though synchronizing their heartbeats with it.

They shifted their weights to their toes.

Harrison placed his big hands on the girl's tiny waist, letting her sense the   70
weightlessness that would soon be hers.

And then, in an explosion of joy and grace, into the air they sprang!

Not only were the laws of the land abandoned, but the law of gravity and the laws of motion as well.

They reeled, whirled, swiveled, flounced, capered, gamboled, and spun.

They leaped like deer on the moon.

The studio ceiling was thirty feet high, but each leap brought the dancers nearer   75
to it.

It became their obvious intention to kiss the ceiling.

They kissed it.

And then, neutralizing gravity with love and pure will, they remained suspended in air inches below the ceiling, and they kissed each other for a long, long time.

It was then that Diana Moon Glampers, the Handicapper General, came into the studio with a double-barreled ten-gauge shotgun. She fired twice, and the Emperor and the Empress were dead before they hit the floor.

Diana Moon Glampers loaded the gun again. She aimed it at the musicians and   80
told them they had ten seconds to get their handicaps back on.

It was then that the Bergerons' television tube burned out.

Hazel turned to comment about the blackout to George. But George had gone out into the kitchen for a can of beer.

George came back in with the beer, paused while a handicap signal shook him up. And then he sat down again. "You been crying?" he said to Hazel.

"Yup," she said.

"What about?" he said.   85

"I forget," she said. "Something real sad on television."

"What was it?" he said.

"It's all kind of mixed up in my mind," said Hazel.

"Forget sad things," said George.

"I always do," said Hazel.   90

"That's my girl," said George. He winced. There was the sound of a rivetting gun in his head.

"Gee—I could tell that one was a doozy," said Hazel.

"You can say that again," said George.

"Gee—" said Hazel, "I could tell that one was a doozy."

Questions

1. What tendencies in present-day American society is Vonnegut satirizing? Does the story argue *for* anything? How would you sum up its theme?

2. Is Diana Moon Glampers a "flat" or a "round" character? (If you need to review these terms, see the discussion of character in Chapter 3.) Would you call Vonnegut's characterization of her "realistic"? If not, why doesn't it need to be?

3. From what point of view is the story told? Why is it more effective than if Harrison Bergeron had told his own story in the first person?

4. Two sympathetic critics of Vonnegut's work, Karen and Charles Wood, have said of his stories: "Vonnegut proves repeatedly . . . that men and women remain fundamentally the same, no matter what technology surrounds them." Try applying this comment to "Harrison Bergeron." Do you agree?

5. Stanislaw Lem, Polish author of *Solaris* and other novels, once made this thoughtful criticism of many of his contemporaries among science fiction writers:

   > The revolt against the machine and against civilization, the praise of the "aesthetic" nature of catastrophe, the dead-end course of human civilization—these are their foremost problems, the intellectual content of their works. Such SF is as it were *a priori* vitiated by pessimism, in the sense that anything that may happen will be for the worse. ("The Time-Travel Story and Related Matters of SF Structuring," *Science Fiction Studies* 1 [1974], 143–54.)

   How might Lem's objection be raised against "Harrison Bergeron"? In your opinion, does it negate the value of Vonnegut's story?

▪ WRITING *effectively*

Kurt Vonnegut Jr. on Writing

The Themes of Science Fiction   1971, 1973

Interviewer: You talked a lot about the difficulties you had when you first began. For instance, I think you gave one of the reasons for using the science fiction form as the fact that you were a professional writer and had to do something which was popular.

Vonnegut: In the beginning I was writing about what concerned me, and what was all around me was machinery. I myself had had some training in engineering and chemistry rather than in the arts and I was working for General Electric in a big factory city, Schenectady. So the first book I wrote was about Schenectady, which is full of machinery and engineers. And I was classified as a science fiction writer. Well, in the past, science fiction writers have been beneath the attention of any serious critic. That is, far

Kurt Vonnegut Jr.

above you are the people dealing with the really important, beautiful issues and using great skills and so forth. It used to be that if you were a science fiction writer you really didn't belong in the arts at all, and other artists wouldn't talk to you. You just had this scruffy little gang of your own.

· · ·

Interviewer: What attracted you to using the form [of science fiction] yourself?

Vonnegut: . . . I saw a milling machine for cutting the rotors on jet engines, gas turbines. This was a very expensive thing for a machinist to do, to cut what is essentially one of those Brancusi forms. So they had a computer-operated milling machine built to cut the blades, and I was fascinated by that. This was in 1949 and the guys who were working on it were foreseeing all sorts of machines being run by little boxes and punched cards. *Player Piano* was my response to the implications of having everything run by little boxes. The idea of doing that, you know, made sense, perfect sense. To have a little clicking box make all the decisions wasn't a vicious thing to do. But it was too bad for the human beings who got their dignity from their jobs.

Interviewer: So science fiction seemed like the best way to write about your thoughts on the subject.

Vonnegut: There was no avoiding it, since General Electric Company *was* science fiction.

From interviews with Laurie Clancy and David Standish

THINKING ABOUT THEME

A clear, precise statement about a story's theme can serve as a promising thesis for a writing assignment. After you read a short story, you will probably have some vague sense of its theme—the central unifying idea, or the point of the story. How do you hone that vague sense of theme into a sharp and intriguing thesis?

- **Start by making a list of all the story's possible themes.** If you are discussing Stephen Crane's "The Open Boat," your list might look like this:

  Man versus nature
  Life-and-death struggle
  Camaraderie of people in crisis
  Blindness of fate
  Courage in face of danger
  Bravery not enough

- **Determine which points seem most important; then formulate a single sentence in which you combine them.** For Crane, you might have circled "man versus nature," "blindness of fate," and "bravery not enough," and your summary might be: "The central theme of 'The Open Boat' is nature's indifference to the fate of even the most courageous individuals."

- **Try to capture the story's essence in a single sentence.** Remember, your goal is to transcend a mere one-sentence plot summary. How can you clearly express the central theme in a few words?

CHECKLIST: Writing About Theme

☐ List as many possible themes as you can.

☐ Circle the two or three most important points and try to combine them into a sentence.

☐ Relate particular details of the story to the theme you have spelled out. Consider plot details, dialogue, setting, point of view, title—any elements that seem especially pertinent.

☐ Check whether all the elements of the story fit your thesis.

☐ Have you missed an important aspect of the story? Or, have you chosen to focus on a secondary idea, overlooking the central one?

☐ If necessary, rework your thesis until it applies to every element in the story.

WRITING ASSIGNMENT ON THEME

Choose a story that catches your attention, and go through the steps outlined above to develop a strong thesis sentence about the story's theme. Then flesh out your argument into an essay, supporting your thesis with evidence from the text, including quotations. Some good story choices might be "A Clean, Well-Lighted Place," "The Chrysanthemums," "A Good Man Is Hard to Find," and "The Lottery."

MORE TOPICS FOR WRITING

1. Define the central theme of "Harrison Bergeron." Is Vonnegut's early 1960s vision of the future still relevant today? Why or why not?

2. Think of a social trend that worries you. With "Harrison Bergeron" in mind, write a brief science fiction parable to warn against this danger to society. Try to pick a less familiar or surprising trend instead of one of the hot-button social issues that immediately pop into your mind.

3. "To Build a Fire" and "The Open Boat" both address the theme of a human being pitted against indifferent nature. Contrast the stories' approaches to this theme. How do the tones of the stories differ? How do these tonal differences help to communicate theme?

4. What does "How I Met My Husband" have to say about first love? Back up your response with specific evidence from the story.

5. Write a brief personal narrative about your first crush. Use dialogue and sensory detail to capture a sense of time, place, and the personalities involved. Your narrative should have a thematic focus—for example, the sting of first love, or its many delights.

6. A recent *Time* magazine article describes a young California woman who distanced herself from her Chinese heritage until reading *The Joy Luck Club* "turned her into a 'born-again Asian.' It gave her new insights into why her mom was so hard on her and why the ways she showed love—say, through food—were different from those of the families [she] saw on TV, who seemed to say 'I love you' all day long." Have you ever had a similar experience, in which something you read gave you a better understanding of a loved one, or even yourself?

▶ TERMS FOR *review*

Summary ▶ A brief condensation of the main idea or plot of a literary work. A summary is similar to a paraphrase, but less detailed.

Theme ▶ The main idea or larger meaning of a work of literature. A theme may be a message or a moral, but it is more likely to be a central, unifying insight or viewpoint.

SYMBOL

> *All you have to do is close your eyes*
> *and wait for the symbols.*
>
> —TENNESSEE WILLIAMS

n F. Scott Fitzgerald's novel *The Great Gatsby*, a huge pair of bespectacled eyes stares across a wilderness of ash heaps, from a billboard advertising the services of an oculist. Repeatedly entering into the story, the advertisement comes to mean more than simply the availability of eye examinations. Fitzgerald has a character liken it to the eyes of God; he hints that some sad, compassionate spirit is brooding as it watches the passing procession of humanity. Such an object is a **symbol**: in literature, a person, place, or thing that suggests more than its literal meaning. Symbols generally do not "stand for" any one meaning, nor for anything absolutely definite; they point, they hint, or, as Henry James put it, they cast long shadows. To take a large example: in Herman Melville's *Moby-Dick*, the great white whale of the book's title apparently means more than the literal dictionary-definition meaning of an aquatic mammal. He also suggests more than the devil, to whom some of the characters liken him. The great whale, as the story unfolds, comes to imply an amplitude of meanings, among them the forces of nature and the whole created universe.

ALLEGORY

This indefinite multiplicity of meanings is characteristic of a symbolic story and distinguishes it from an **allegory**, a story in which persons, places, and things form a system of clearly labeled equivalents. In a simple allegory, characters and other elements often stand for other definite meanings, which are often abstractions. You will meet such a character in another story in this book, Nathaniel Hawthorne's "Young Goodman Brown." This tale's main female character, Faith, represents the religious virtue suggested by her name. Supreme allegories are found in some biblical parables ("The Kingdom of Heaven is like a man who sowed good seed in his field . . . ," Matthew 13:24–30).

A classic allegory is the medieval play *Everyman*, whose hero represents us all, and who, deserted by false friends called Kindred and Goods, faces the judgment of God accompanied only by a faithful friend called Good Deeds. In John Bunyan's seventeenth-century allegory *Pilgrim's Progress*, the protagonist, Christian, struggles along the difficult road toward salvation, meeting along the way persons such as Mr. Worldly Wiseman, who directs him into a more comfortable path (a wrong turn), and the residents of a town called Fair Speech, among them a hypocrite named Mr. Facing-both-ways. Not all allegories are simple: Dante's *Divine Comedy*, written during the Middle Ages, continues to reveal new meanings to careful readers. Allegory was much beloved in the Middle Ages, but in contemporary fiction it is rare. One modern instance is George Orwell's long fable *Animal Farm*, in which (among its double meanings) barnyard animals stand for human victims and totalitarian oppressors.

SYMBOLS

Symbols in fiction are not generally abstract terms such as *love* or *truth*, but are likely to be perceptible objects (or worded descriptions that cause us to imagine them). In William Faulkner's "A Rose for Emily" (Chapter 2), Miss Emily's invisible watch ticking at the end of a golden chain not only indicates the passage of time, but also suggests that time passes without even being noticed by the watch's owner, and the golden chain carries suggestions of wealth and authority. Objects (and creatures) that seem insignificant in themselves can take on a symbolic importance in the larger context: in Jhumpa Lahiri's "Interpreter of Maladies" (Chapter 12) the piece of gum that Mrs. Das gives Mr. Kapasi—"As soon as Mr. Kapasi put the gum in his mouth a thick sweet liquid burst onto his tongue"—underscores her effect on his slumbering senses.

Often the symbols we meet in fiction are inanimate objects, but other things also may function symbolically. In James Joyce's "Araby" (Chapter 12), the very name of the bazaar, Araby—the poetic name for Arabia—suggests magic, romance, and *The Arabian Nights*; its syllables (the narrator tells us) "cast an Eastern enchantment over me." Even a locale, or a feature of physical topography, can provide rich suggestions. Recall Ernest Hemingway's "A Clean, Well-Lighted Place" (Chapter 5), in which the café is not merely a café, but an island of refuge from night, chaos, loneliness, old age, and impending death.

Symbolic Characters

In some novels and stories, symbolic characters make brief cameo appearances. Such characters often are not well-rounded and fully known, but are seen fleetingly and remain slightly mysterious. In *Heart of Darkness*, a short novel by Joseph Conrad, a steamship company that hires men to work in the Congo maintains in its waiting room two women who knit black wool—like the classical Fates. Usually such a symbolic character is more a portrait than a person—or somewhat portraitlike, as Faulkner's Miss Emily, who twice appears at a window of her house "like the carven torso of an idol in a niche." Though Faulkner invests Miss Emily with life and vigor, he also clothes her in symbolic hints: she seems almost to personify the vanishing aristocracy of the antebellum South, still maintaining a black servant and being ruthlessly betrayed by a moneymaking Yankee. Sometimes a part of a character's body or an attribute may convey symbolic meaning: a baleful eye, as in Edgar Allan Poe's "The Tell-Tale Heart" (Chapter 2).

Symbolic Acts

Much as a symbolic whale holds more meaning than an ordinary whale, a **symbolic act** is a gesture with larger significance than usual. For the boy's father in Faulkner's

"Barn Burning" (Chapter 5), the act of destroying a barn is no mere act of spite, but an expression of his profound hatred for anything not belonging to him. Faulkner adds that burning a barn reflects the father's memories of the "waste and extravagance of war," and further adds that "the element of fire spoke to some deep mainspring" in his being. A symbolic act, however, doesn't have to be a gesture as large as starting a conflagration. Before setting out in pursuit of the great white whale, Melville's Captain Ahab in *Moby-Dick* deliberately snaps his tobacco pipe and throws it away, as if to suggest (among other things) that he will let no pleasure or pastime distract him from his vengeance.

Why do writers have to symbolize—why don't they tell us outright? One advantage of a symbol is that it is so compact, and yet so fully laden. Both starkly concrete and slightly mysterious, like Miss Emily's invisible ticking watch, it may impress us with all the force of something beheld in a dream or in a nightmare. The watch suggests, among other things, the slow and invisible passage of time. What this symbol says, it says more fully and more memorably than could be said, perhaps, in a long essay on the subject.

To some extent (it may be claimed), all stories are symbolic. Merely by holding up for our inspection these characters and their actions, the writer lends them *some* special significance. But this is to think of *symbol* in an extremely broad and inclusive way. For the usual purposes of reading a story and understanding it, there is probably little point in looking for symbolism in every word, in every stick or stone, in every striking of a match, in every minor character. Still, to be on the alert for symbols when reading fiction is perhaps wiser than to ignore them. Not to admit that symbolic meanings may be present, or to refuse to think about them, would be another way to misread a story—or to read no further than its outer edges.

RECOGNIZING SYMBOLS

How, then, do you recognize a symbol in fiction when you meet it? Fortunately, the storyteller often gives the symbol particular emphasis. It may be mentioned repeatedly throughout the story; it may even supply the story with a title ("Barn Burning," "A Clean, Well-Lighted Place," "Araby"). At times, a crucial symbol will open a story or end it. Unless an object, act, or character is given some such special emphasis and importance, we may generally feel safe in taking it at face value. Probably it isn't a symbol if it points clearly and unmistakably toward some one meaning, like a whistle in a factory, whose blast at noon means lunch. But an object, an act, or a character is surely symbolic (and almost as surely displays high literary art) if, when we finish the story, we realize that it was that item—that gigantic eye; that clean, well-lighted café; that burning of a barn—which led us to the author's theme, the essential meaning.

John Steinbeck

The Chrysanthemums   1938

John Steinbeck (1902–1968) was born in Salinas,
California, in the fertile valley he remembers in
"The Chrysanthemums." Off and on, he attended
Stanford University, then sojourned in New
York as a reporter and a bricklayer. After years
of struggle to earn his living by fiction, Steinbeck
reached a large audience with Tortilla Flat
(1935), a loosely woven novel portraying
Mexican Americans in Monterey with fondness
and sympathy. Great acclaim greeted The
Grapes of Wrath *(1939), the story of a family*
of Oklahoma farmers who, ruined by dust
storms in the 1930s, join a mass migration to
California. In 1962 he became the seventh
American to win the Nobel Prize in Literature,

John Steinbeck

but critics have never placed Steinbeck on the
same high shelf as Faulkner and Hemingway. He wrote much, not all good, and yet his best
work adds up to an impressive total. Besides The Grapes of Wrath, *it includes* In Dubious
Battle *(1936), a novel of an apple-pickers' strike;* Of Mice and Men *(1937), a powerful*
short novel of comradeship between a hobo and a retarded man; and the short stories in The
Long Valley *(1938). Throughout the fiction he wrote in his prime, Steinbeck maintains an*
appealing sympathy for the poor and downtrodden, the lonely and dispossessed.

The high grey-flannel fog of winter closed off the Salinas Valley° from the sky
and from all the rest of the world. On every side it sat like a lid on the mountains and
made of the great valley a closed pot. On the broad, level land floor the gang plows
bit deep and left the black earth shining like metal where the shares had cut. On the
foothill ranches across the Salinas River, the yellow stubble fields seemed to be bathed
in pale cold sunshine, but there was no sunshine in the valley now in December. The
thick willow scrub along the river flamed with sharp and positive yellow leaves.

It was a time of quiet and of waiting. The air was cold and tender. A light wind blew
up from the southwest so that the farmers were mildly hopeful of a good rain before
long; but fog and rain do not go together.

Across the river, on Henry Allen's foothill ranch there was little work to be
done, for the hay was cut and stored and the orchards were plowed up to receive the
rain deeply when it should come. The cattle on the higher slopes were becoming
shaggy and rough-coated.

Elisa Allen, working in her flower garden, looked down across the yard and saw
Henry, her husband, talking to two men in business suits. The three of them stood by
the tractor shed, each man with one foot on the side of the little Fordson. They
smoked cigarettes and studied the machine as they talked.

Elisa watched them for a moment and then went back to her work. She was   5
thirty-five. Her face was lean and strong and her eyes were as clear as water. Her
figure looked blocked and heavy in her gardening costume, a man's black hat pulled

Salinas Valley: south of San Francisco in the Coast Ranges region of California.

low down over her eyes, clodhopper shoes, a figured print dress almost completely covered by a big corduroy apron with four big pockets to hold the snips, the trowel and scratcher, the seeds and the knife she worked with. She wore heavy leather gloves to protect her hands while she worked.

She was cutting down the old year's chrysanthemum stalks with a pair of short and powerful scissors. She looked down toward the men by the tractor shed now and then. Her face was eager and mature and handsome; even her work with the scissors was over-eager, over-powerful. The chrysanthemum stems seemed too small and easy for her energy.

She brushed a cloud of hair out of her eyes with the back of her glove, and left a smudge of earth on her cheek in doing it. Behind her stood the neat white farm house with red geraniums close-banked around it as high as the windows. It was a hard-swept looking little house with hard-polished windows, and a clean mud-mat on the front steps.

Elisa cast another glance toward the tractor shed. The strangers were getting into their Ford coupe. She took off a glove and put her strong fingers down into the forest of new green chrysanthemum sprouts that were growing around the old roots. She spread the leaves and looked down among the close-growing stems. No aphids were there, no sowbugs or snails or cutworms. Her terrier fingers destroyed such pests before they could get started.

Elisa started at the sound of her husband's voice. He had come near quietly, and he leaned over the wire fence that protected her flower garden from cattle and dogs and chickens.

"At it again," he said. "You've got a strong new crop coming." 10

Elisa straightened her back and pulled on the gardening glove again. "Yes. They'll be strong this coming year." In her tone and on her face there was a little smugness.

"You've got a gift with things," Henry observed. "Some of those yellow chrysanthemums you had this year were ten inches across. I wish you'd work out in the orchard and raise some apples that big."

Her eyes sharpened. "Maybe I could do it, too. I've a gift with things, all right. My mother had it. She could stick anything in the ground and make it grow. She said it was having planters' hands that knew how to do it."

"Well, it sure works with flowers," he said.

"Henry, who were those men you were talking to?" 15

"Why, sure, that's what I came to tell you. They were from the Western Meat Company. I sold those thirty head of three-year-old steers. Got nearly my own price, too."

"Good," she said. "Good for you."

"And I thought," he continued, "I thought how it's Saturday afternoon, and we might go into Salinas for dinner at a restaurant, and then to a picture show—to celebrate, you see."

"Good," she repeated. "Oh, yes. That will be good."

Henry put on his joking tone. "There's fights tonight. How'd you like to go to the fights?" 20

"Oh, no," she said breathlessly. "No, I wouldn't like fights."

"Just fooling, Elisa. We'll go to a movie. Let's see. It's two now. I'm going to take Scotty and bring down those steers from the hill. It'll take us maybe two hours. We'll go in town about five and have dinner at the Cominos Hotel. Like that?"

"Of course I'll like it. It's good to eat away from home."

"All right, then. I'll go get up a couple of horses."

She said, "I'll have plenty of time to transplant some of these sets, I guess."   25

She heard her husband calling Scotty down by the barn. And a little later she saw the two men ride up the pale yellow hillside in search of the steers.

There was a little square sandy bed kept for rooting the chrysanthemums. With her trowel she turned the soil over and over, and smoothed it and patted it firm. Then she dug ten parallel trenches to receive the sets. Back at the chrysanthemum bed she pulled out the little crisp shoots, trimmed off the leaves of each one with her scissors and laid it on a small orderly pile.

A squeak of wheels and plod of hoofs came from the road. Elisa looked up. The country road ran along the dense bank of willows and cottonwoods that bordered the river, and up this road came a curious vehicle, curiously drawn. It was an old spring-wagon, with a round canvas top on it like the cover of a prairie schooner. It was drawn by an old bay horse and a little grey-and-white burro. A big stubble-bearded man sat between the cover flaps and drove the crawling team. Underneath the wagon, between the hind wheels, a lean and rangy mongrel dog walked sedately. Words were painted on the canvas, in clumsy, crooked letters. "Pots, pans, knives, sisors, lawn mores, Fixed." Two rows of articles, and the triumphantly definitive "Fixed" below. The black paint had run down in little sharp points beneath each letter.

Elisa, squatting on the ground, watched to see the crazy, loose-jointed wagon pass by. But it didn't pass. It turned into the farm road in front of her house, crooked old wheels skirling and squeaking. The rangy dog darted from between the wheels and ran ahead. Instantly the two ranch shepherds flew out at him. Then all three stopped, and with stiff and quivering tails, with taut straight legs, with ambassadorial dignity, they slowly circled, sniffing daintily. The caravan pulled up to Elisa's wire fence and stopped. Now the newcomer dog, feeling out-numbered, lowered his tail and retired under the wagon with raised hackles and bared teeth.

The man on the wagon seat called out, "That's a bad dog in a fight when he gets   30
started."

Elisa laughed. "I see he is. How soon does he generally get started?"

The man caught up her laughter and echoed it heartily. "Sometimes not for weeks and weeks," he said. He climbed stiffly down, over the wheel. The horse and the donkey drooped like unwatered flowers.

Elisa saw that he was a very big man. Although his hair and beard were greying, he did not look old. His worn black suit was wrinkled and spotted with grease. The laughter had disappeared from his face and eyes the moment his laughing voice ceased. His eyes were dark, and they were full of the brooding that gets in the eyes of teamsters and of sailors. The calloused hands he rested on the wire fence were cracked, and every crack was a black line. He took off his battered hat.

"I'm off my general road, ma'am," he said. "Does this dirt road cut over across the river to the Los Angeles highway?"

Elisa stood up and shoved the thick scissors in her apron pocket. "Well, yes, it   35
does, but it winds around and then fords the river. I don't think your team could pull through the sand."

He replied with some asperity, "It might surprise you what them beasts can pull through."

"When they get started?" she asked.

He smiled for a second. "Yes. When they get started."

"Well," said Elisa, "I think you'll save time if you go back to the Salinas road and pick up the highway there."

He drew a big finger down the chicken wire and made it sing. "I ain't in any hurry, ma'am. I go from Seattle to San Diego and back every year. Takes all my time. About six months each way. I aim to follow nice weather." 40

Elisa took off her gloves and stuffed them in the apron pocket with the scissors. She touched the under edge of her man's hat, searching for fugitive hairs. "That sounds like a nice kind of a way to live," she said.

He leaned confidentially over the fence. "Maybe you noticed the writing on my wagon. I mend pots and sharpen knives and scissors. You got any of them things to do?"

"Oh, no," she said quickly. "Nothing like that." Her eyes hardened with resistance.

"Scissors is the worst thing," he explained. "Most people just ruin scissors trying to sharpen 'em, but I know how. I got a special tool. It's a little bobbit kind of thing, and patented. But it sure does the trick."

"No. My scissors are all sharp." 45

"All right, then. Take a pot," he continued earnestly, "a bent pot, or a pot with a hole. I can make it like new so you don't have to buy no new ones. That's a saving for you."

"No," she said shortly. "I tell you I have nothing like that for you to do."

His face fell to an exaggerated sadness. His voice took on a whining undertone. "I ain't had a thing to do today. Maybe I won't have no supper tonight. You see I'm off my regular road. I know folks on the highway clear from Seattle to San Diego. They save their things for me to sharpen up because they know I do it so good and save them money."

"I'm sorry," Elisa said irritably. "I haven't anything for you to do."

His eyes left her face and fell to searching the ground. They roamed about until they came to the chrysanthemum bed where she had been working. "What's them plants, ma'am?" 50

The irritation and resistance melted from Elisa's face. "Oh, those are chrysanthemums, giant whites and yellows. I raise them every year, bigger than anybody around here."

"Kind of a long-stemmed flower? Looks like a quick puff of colored smoke?" he asked.

"That's it. What a nice way to describe them."

"They smell kind of nasty till you get used to them," he said.

"It's a good bitter smell," she retorted, "not nasty at all." 55

He changed his tone quickly. "I like the smell myself."

"I had ten-inch blooms this year," she said.

The man leaned farther over the fence. "Look. I know a lady down the road a piece, has got the nicest garden you ever seen. Got nearly every kind of flower but no chrysanthemums. Last time I was mending a copper-bottom washtub for her (that's a hard job but I do it good), she said to me, 'If you ever run acrost some nice chrysanthemums I wish you'd try to get me a few seeds.' That's what she told me."

Elisa's eyes grew alert and eager. "She couldn't have known much about chrysanthemums. You *can* raise them from seed, but it's much easier to root the little sprouts you see there."

"Oh," he said. "I s'pose I can't take none to her, then." 60

"Why yes you can," Elisa cried. "I can put some in damp sand, and you can carry them right along with you. They'll take root in the pot if you keep them damp. And then she can transplant them."

"She'd sure like to have some, ma'am. You say they're nice ones?"

"Beautiful," she said. "Oh, beautiful." Her eyes shone. She tore off the battered hat and shook out her dark pretty hair. "I'll put them in a flower pot, and you can take them right with you. Come into the yard."

While the man came through the picket gate Elisa ran excitedly along the geranium-bordered path to the back of the house. And she returned carrying a big red flower pot. The gloves were forgotten now. She kneeled on the ground by the starting bed and dug up the sandy soil with her fingers and scooped it into the bright new flower pot. Then she picked up the little pile of shoots she had prepared. With her strong fingers she pressed them in the sand and tamped around them with her knuckles. The man stood over her. "I'll tell you what to do," she said. "You remember so you can tell the lady."

"Yes, I'll try to remember." 65

"Well, look. These will take root in about a month. Then she must set them out, about a foot apart in good rich earth like this, see?" She lifted a handful of dark soil for him to look at. "They'll grow fast and tall. Now remember this: In July tell her to cut them down, about eight inches from the ground."

"Before they bloom?" he asked.

"Yes, before they bloom." Her face was tight with eagerness. "They'll grow right up again. About the last of September the buds will start."

She stopped and seemed perplexed. "It's the budding that takes the most care," she said hesitantly. "I don't know how to tell you." She looked deep into his eyes, searchingly. Her mouth opened a little, and she seemed to be listening. "I'll try to tell you," she said. "Did you ever hear of planting hands?"

"Can't say I have, ma'am." 70

"Well, I can only tell you what it feels like. It's when you're picking off the buds you don't want. Everything goes right down into your fingertips. You watch your fingers work. They do it themselves. You can feel how it is. They pick and pick the buds. They never make a mistake. They're with the plant. Do you see? Your fingers and the plant. You can feel that, right up your arm. They know. They never make a mistake. You can feel it. When you're like that you can't do anything wrong. Do you see that? Can you understand that?"

She was kneeling on the ground looking up at him. Her breast swelled passionately.

The man's eyes narrowed. He looked away self-consciously. "Maybe I know," he said. "Sometimes in the night in the wagon there—"

Elisa's voice grew husky. She broke in on him, "I've never lived as you do, but I know what you mean. When the night is dark—why, the stars are sharp-pointed, and there's quiet. Why, you rise up and up! Every pointed star gets driven into your body. It's like that. Hot and sharp and—lovely."

Kneeling there, her hand went out toward his legs in the greasy black trousers. Her hesitant fingers almost touched the cloth. Then her hand dropped to the ground. 75 She crouched low like a fawning dog.

He said, "It's nice, just like you say. Only when you don't have no dinner, it ain't."

She stood up then, very straight, and her face was ashamed. She held the flower pot out to him and placed it gently in his arms. "Here. Put it in your wagon, on the seat, where you can watch it. Maybe I can find something for you to do."

At the back of the house she dug in the can pile and found two old and battered aluminum saucepans. She carried them back and gave them to him. "Here, maybe you can fix these."

His manner changed. He became professional. "Good as new I can fix them." At the back of his wagon he set a little anvil, and out of an oily tool box dug a small machine hammer. Elisa came through the gate to watch him while he pounded out the dents in the kettles. His mouth grew sure and knowing. At a difficult part of the work he sucked his under-lip.

"You sleep right in the wagon?" Elisa asked.   80

"Right in the wagon, ma'am. Rain or shine I'm dry as a cow in there."

"It must be nice," she said. "It must be very nice. I wish women could do such things."

"It ain't the right kind of a life for a woman."

Her upper lip raised a little, showing her teeth. "How do you know? How can you tell?" she said.

"I don't know, ma'am," he protested. "Of course I don't know. Now here's your   85
kettles, done. You don't have to buy no new ones."

"How much?"

"Oh, fifty cents'll do. I keep my prices down and my work good. That's why I have all them satisfied customers up and down the highway."

Elisa brought him a fifty-cent piece from the house and dropped it in his hand. "You might be surprised to have a rival some time. I can sharpen scissors, too. And I can beat the dents out of little pots. I could show you what a woman might do."

He put his hammer back in the oily box and shoved the little anvil out of sight. "It would be a lonely life for a woman, ma'am, and a scarey life, too, with animals creeping under the wagon all night." He climbed over the singletree, steadying himself with a hand on the burro's white rump. He settled himself in the seat, picked up the lines. "Thank you kindly, ma'am," he said. "I'll do like you told me; I'll go back and catch the Salinas road."

"Mind," she called, "if you're long in getting there, keep the sand damp."   90

"Sand, ma'am? . . . Sand? Oh, sure. You mean around the chrysanthemums. Sure I will." He clucked his tongue. The beasts leaned luxuriously into their collars. The mongrel dog took his place between the back wheels. The wagon turned and crawled out the entrance road and back the way it had come, along the river.

Elisa stood in front of her wire fence watching the slow progress of the caravan. Her shoulders were straight, her head thrown back, her eyes half-closed, so that the scene came vaguely into them. Her lips moved silently, forming the words "Good-bye—good-bye." Then she whispered, "That's a bright direction. There's a glowing there." The sound of her whisper startled her. She shook herself free and looked about to see whether anyone had been listening. Only the dogs had heard. They lifted their heads toward her from their sleeping in the dust, and then stretched out their chins and settled asleep again. Elisa turned and ran hurriedly into the house.

In the kitchen she reached behind the stove and felt the water tank. It was full of hot water from the noonday cooking. In the bathroom she tore off her soiled clothes and flung them into the corner. And then she scrubbed herself with a little block of pumice, legs and thighs, loins and chest and arms, until her skin was scratched and red. When she had dried herself she stood in front of a mirror in her bedroom and looked at her body. She tightened her stomach and threw out her chest. She turned and looked over her shoulder at her back.

After a while she began to dress, slowly. She put on her newest underclothing and her nicest stockings and the dress which was the symbol of her prettiness. She worked carefully on her hair, penciled her eyebrows and rouged her lips.

Before she was finished she heard the little thunder of hoofs and the shouts of 95
Henry and his helper as they drove the red steers into the corral. She heard the gate bang shut and set herself for Henry's arrival.

His step sounded on the porch. He entered the house calling, "Elisa, where are you?"

"In my room, dressing. I'm not ready. There's hot water for your bath. Hurry up. It's getting late."

When she heard him splashing in the tub, Elisa laid his dark suit on the bed, and shirt and socks and tie beside it. She stood his polished shoes on the floor beside the bed. Then she went to the porch and sat primly and stiffly down. She looked toward the river road where the willow-line was still yellow with frosted leaves so that under the high grey fog they seemed a thin band of sunshine. This was the only color in the grey afternoon. She sat unmoving for a long time. Her eyes blinked rarely.

Henry came banging out of the door, shoving his tie inside his vest as he came. Elisa stiffened and her face grew tight. Henry stopped short and looked at her. "Why—why, Elisa. You look so nice!"

"Nice? You think I look nice? What do you mean by 'nice'?" 100

Henry blundered on. "I don't know. I mean you look different, strong and happy."

"I am strong? Yes, strong. What do you mean 'strong'?"

He looked bewildered. "You're playing some kind of a game," he said helplessly. "It's a kind of a play. You look strong enough to break a calf over your knee, happy enough to eat it like a watermelon."

For a second she lost her rigidity. "Henry! Don't talk like that. You didn't know what you said." She grew complete again. "I'm strong," she boasted. "I never knew before how strong."

Henry looked down toward the tractor shed, and when he brought his eyes back 105
to her, they were his own again. "I'll get out the car. You can put on your coat while I'm starting."

Elisa went into the house. She heard him drive to the gate and idle down his motor, and then she took a long time to put on her hat. She pulled it here and pressed it there. When Henry turned the motor off she slipped into her coat and went out.

The little roadster bounced along on the dirt road by the river, raising the birds and driving the rabbits into the brush. Two cranes flapped heavily over the willow-line and dropped into the river-bed.

Far ahead on the road Elisa saw a dark speck. She knew.

She tried not to look as they passed it, but her eyes would not obey. She whispered to herself sadly, "He might have thrown them off the road. That wouldn't have been much trouble, not very much. But he kept the pot," she explained. "He had to keep the pot. That's why he couldn't get them off the road."

The roadster turned a bend and she saw the caravan ahead. She swung full 110
around toward her husband so she could not see the little covered wagon and the mismatched team as the car passed them.

In a moment it was over. The thing was done. She did not look back.

She said loudly, to be heard above the motor, "It will be good, tonight, a good dinner."

"Now you're changed again," Henry complained. He took one hand from the wheel and patted her knee. "I ought to take you in to dinner oftener. It would be good for both of us. We get so heavy out on the ranch."

"Henry," she asked, "could we have wine at dinner?"

"Sure we could. Say! That will be fine."   115

She was silent for a while; then she said, "Henry, at those prize fights, do the men hurt each other very much?"

"Sometimes a little, not often. Why?"

"Well, I've read how they break noses, and blood runs down their chests. I've read how the fighting gloves get heavy and soggy with blood."

He looked around at her. "What's the matter, Elisa? I didn't know you read things like that." He brought the car to a stop, then turned to the right over the Salinas River bridge.

"Do any women ever go to the fights?" she asked.   120

"Oh, sure, some. What's the matter, Elisa? Do you want to go? I don't think you'd like it, but I'll take you if you really want to go."

She relaxed limply in the seat. "Oh, no. No. I don't want to go. I'm sure I don't." Her face was turned away from him. "It will be enough if we can have wine. It will be plenty." She turned up her coat collar so he could not see that she was crying weakly—like an old woman.

Questions

1. When we first meet Elisa Allen in her garden, with what details does Steinbeck delineate her character for us?

2. Elisa works inside a "wire fence that protected her flower garden from cattle and dogs and chickens" (paragraph 9). What does this wire fence suggest?

3. How would you describe Henry and Elisa's marriage? Cite details from the story.

4. With what motive does the traveling salesman take an interest in Elisa's chrysanthemums? What immediate effect does his interest have on Elisa?

5. For what possible purpose does Steinbeck give us such a detailed account of Elisa's preparations for her evening out? Notice her tearing off her soiled clothes and her scrubbing her body with pumice (paragraphs 93–94).

6. Of what significance to Elisa is the sight of the contents of the flower pot discarded in the road? Notice that, as her husband's car overtakes the covered wagon, Elisa averts her eyes; and then Steinbeck adds, "In a moment it was over. The thing was done. She did not look back" (paragraph 111). Explain this passage.

7. How do you interpret Elisa's asking for wine with dinner? How do you account for her new interest in prizefights?

8. In a sentence, try to state this short story's theme.

9. Why are Elisa Allen's chrysanthemums so important to this story? Sum up what you understand them to mean.

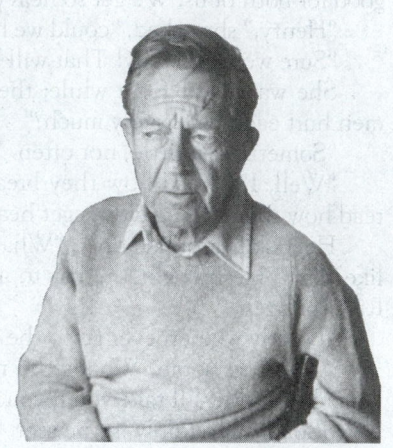

John Cheever

John Cheever

The Swimmer   1964

John Cheever (1912–1982) was born in Quincy, Massachusetts. His parents had been modestly prosperous, but their livelihood declined substantially and was finally dashed by the 1929 stock market crash. Cheever was sent away to Thayer Academy, a prep school, where he was a poor student. When he was expelled at eighteen, he wrote a story about the incident that was published in the New Republic *(1930). Cheever never finished high school or attended college, dedicating himself instead to writing.*

Cheever's stories, most of which appeared in the New Yorker, *often deal with the ordinary lives of middle-class characters living in Manhattan or its suburbs. Although his stories are realistic in plot and setting, they also often contain an underlying religious vision—exploring themes of guilt, grace, and redemption. Cheever's novels include* The Wapshot Chronicle *(1957), which won the National Book Award;* Bullet Park *(1969); and* Falconer *(1977). The Stories of John Cheever (1978), selected works from his five volumes of short fiction, won the Pulitzer Prize and National Book Critics Circle Award. After Cheever's death, his notebooks and letters revealed how tortured his life had been by sex and alcohol. While some early reviewers regarded Cheever's popular stories as "New Yorker fiction" (satiric views of middle-class life), critics now see the psychological and religious vision underlying his work. Once undervalued, Cheever is now generally regarded as one of the finest American short-story writers of the twentieth century.*

It was one of those midsummer Sundays when everyone sits around saying, "I *drank* too much last night." You might have heard it whispered by the parishioners leaving church, heard it from the lips of the priest himself, struggling with his cassock in the *vestiarium:* heard it from the golf links and the tennis courts, heard it from the wildlife preserve where the leader of the Audubon group was suffering from a terrible hangover. "I *drank* too much," said Donald Westerhazy. "We all *drank* too much," said Lucinda Merrill. "It must have been the wine," said Helen Westerhazy. "I *drank* too much of that claret."

This was at the edge of the Westerhazys' pool. The pool, fed by an artesian well with a high iron content, was a pale shade of green. It was a fine day. In the west there was a massive stand of cumulus cloud so like a city seen from a distance—from the bow of an approaching ship—that it might have had a name. Lisbon. Hackensack. The sun was hot. Neddy Merrill sat by the green water, one hand in it, one around a glass of gin. He was a slender man—he seemed to have the especial slenderness of youth—and while he was far from young he had slid down his banister that morning and given the bronze backside of Aphrodite on the hall table a smack, as he jogged toward the smell of coffee in his dining room. He might have been compared to a summer's day, particularly the last hours of one, and while he lacked a tennis racket or a sail bag the impression was definitely one of youth, sport, and clement weather. He had been swimming and now he was breathing deeply, stertorously as if he could gulp into his lungs the components of that moment, the heat of the sun, the intenseness of his pleasure. It all seemed to flow into his chest. His own house stood in Bullet Park, eight miles to the south, where his four beautiful daughters would have had their lunch and might be playing tennis. Then it occurred to him that by taking a dogleg to the southwest he could reach his home by water.

His life was not confining and the delight he took in this observation could not be explained by its suggestion of escape. He seemed to see, with a cartographer's eye, that string of swimming pools, that quasi-subterranean stream that curved across the county. He had made a discovery, a contribution to modern geography; he would name the stream Lucinda after his wife. He was not a practical joker nor was he a fool but he was determinedly original and had a vague and modest idea of himself as a legendary figure. The day was beautiful and it seemed to him that a long swim might enlarge and celebrate its beauty.

He took off a sweater that was hung over his shoulders and dove in. He had an inexplicable contempt for men who did not hurl themselves into pools. He swam a choppy crawl, breathing either with every stroke or every fourth stroke and counting somewhere well in the back of his mind the one-two one-two of a flutter kick. It was not a serviceable stroke for long distances but the domestication of swimming had saddled the sport with some customs and in his part of the world a crawl was customary. To be embraced and sustained by the light green water was less a pleasure, it seemed, than the resumption of a natural condition, and he would have liked to swim without trunks, but this was not possible, considering his project. He hoisted himself up on the far curb—he never used the ladder—and started across the lawn. When Lucinda asked where he was going he said he was going to swim home.

The only maps and charts he had to go by were remembered or imaginary but   5 these were clear enough. First there were the Grahams, the Hammers, the Lears, the Howlands, and the Crosscups. He would cross Ditmar Street to the Bunkers and come, after a short portage, to the Levys, the Welchers, and the public pool in Lancaster. Then there were the Hallorans, the Sachses, the Biswangers, Shirley Adams, the Gilmartins, and the Clydes. The day was lovely, and that he lived in a world so generously supplied with water seemed like a clemency, a beneficence. His heart was high and he ran across the grass. Making his way home by an uncommon route gave him the feeling that he was a pilgrim, an explorer, a man with a destiny, and he knew that he would find friends all along the way; friends would line the banks of the Lucinda River.

He went through a hedge that separated the Westerhazys' land from the Grahams', walked under some flowering apple trees, passed the shed that housed their pump and filter, and came out at the Grahams' pool. "Why, Neddy," Mrs. Graham said, "what a marvelous surprise. I've been trying to get you on the phone all morning. Here, let me get you a drink." He saw then, like any explorer, that the hospitable customs and traditions of the natives would have to be handled with diplomacy if he was ever going to reach his destination. He did not want to mystify or seem rude to the Grahams nor did he have the time to linger there. He swam the length of their pool and joined them in the sun and was rescued, a few minutes later, by the arrival of two carloads of friends from Connecticut. During the uproarious reunions he was able to slip away. He went down by the front of the Grahams' house, stepped over a thorny hedge, and crossed a vacant lot to the Hammers'. Mrs. Hammer, looking up from her roses, saw him swim by although she wasn't quite sure who it was. The Lears heard him splashing past the open windows of their living room. The Howlands and the Crosscups were away.

After leaving the Howlands' he crossed Ditmar Street and started for the Bunkers', where he could hear, even at that distance, the noise of a party.

The water refracted the sound of voices and laughter and seemed to suspend it in midair. The Bunkers' pool was on a rise and he climbed some stairs to a terrace where twenty-five or thirty men and women were drinking. The only person in the water was Rusty Towers, who floated there on a rubber raft. Oh, how bonny and lush were the banks of the Lucinda River! Prosperous men and women gathered by the sapphire-colored waters while caterer's men in white coats passed them cold gin. Overhead a red de Haviland trainer was circling around and around and around in the sky with something like the glee of a child in a swing. Ned felt a passing affection for the scene, a tenderness for the gathering, as if it was something he might touch. In the distance he heard thunder. As soon as Enid Bunker saw him she began to scream: "Oh, look who's here! What a marvelous surprise! When Lucinda said you couldn't come I thought I'd *die*." She made her way to him through the crowd, and when they had finished kissing she led him to the bar, a progress that was slowed by the fact that he stopped to kiss eight or ten other women and shake the hands of as many men. A smiling bartender he had seen at a hundred parties gave him a gin and tonic and he stood by the bar for a moment, anxious not to get stuck in any conversation that would delay his voyage. When he seemed about to be surrounded he dove in and swam close to the side to avoid colliding with Rusty's raft. At the far end of the pool he bypassed the Tomlinsons with a broad smile and jogged up the garden path. The gravel cut his feet but this was the only unpleasantness. The party was confined to the pool, and as he went toward the house he heard the brilliant, watery sound of voices fade, heard the noise of a radio from the Bunkers' kitchen, where someone was listening to a ball game. Sunday afternoon. He made his way through the parked cars and down the grassy border of their driveway to Alewives Lane. He did not want to be seen on the road in his bathing trunks but there was no traffic and he made the short distance to the Levys' driveway, marked with a PRIVATE PROPERTY sign and a green tube for *The New York Times*. All the doors and windows of the big house were open but there were no signs of life; not even a dog barked. He went around the side of the house to the pool and saw that the Levys had only recently left. Glasses and bottles and dishes of nuts were on a table at the deep end, where there was a bathhouse or gazebo, hung with Japanese lanterns. After swimming the pool he got himself a glass and poured a drink. It was his fourth or fifth drink and he had swum nearly half the length of the Lucinda River. He felt tired, clean, and pleased at that moment to be alone; pleased with everything.

It would storm. The stand of cumulus cloud—that city—had risen and darkened, and while he sat there he heard the percussiveness of thunder again. The de Haviland trainer was still circling overhead and it seemed to Ned that he could almost hear the pilot laugh with pleasure in the afternoon; but when there was another peal of thunder he took off for home. A train whistle blew and he wondered what time it had gotten to be. Four? Five? He thought of the provincial station at that hour, where a waiter, his tuxedo concealed by a raincoat, a dwarf with some flowers wrapped in newspaper, and a woman who had been crying would be waiting for the local. It was suddenly growing dark; it was that moment when the pin-headed birds seem to organize their song into some acute and knowledgeable recognition of the storm's approach. Then there was a fine noise of rushing water from the crown of an oak at his back, as if a spigot there had been turned. Then the noise of fountains came from the crowns of all the tall trees. Why did he love storms, what was the meaning of his excitement when the door sprang open and the rain wind fled rudely up the stairs, why had the simple task of shutting the windows of an old house seemed fitting and urgent, why did the first watery notes of a storm wind have for him the unmistakable sound of good news, cheer, glad tidings? Then there was an explosion, a smell of cordite, and rain lashed the Japanese lanterns that Mrs. Levy had bought in Kyoto the year before last, or was it the year before that?

He stayed in the Levys' gazebo until the storm had passed. The rain had cooled the air and he shivered. The force of the wind had stripped a maple of its red and yellow leaves and scattered them over the grass and the water. Since it was midsummer the tree must be blighted, and yet he felt a peculiar sadness at this sign of autumn. He braced his shoulders, emptied his glass, and started for the Welchers' pool. This meant crossing the Lindleys' riding ring and he was surprised to find it overgrown with grass and all the jumps dismantled. He wondered if the Lindleys had sold their horses or gone away for the summer and put them out to board. He seemed to remember having heard something about the Lindleys and their horses but the memory was unclear. On he went, barefoot through the wet grass, to the Welchers', where he found their pool was dry.

This breach in his chain of water disappointed him absurdly, and he felt like some explorer who seeks a torrential headwater and finds a dead stream. He was disappointed and mystified. It was common enough to go away for the summer but no one ever drained his pool. The Welchers had definitely gone away. The pool furniture was folded, stacked, and covered with a tarpaulin. The bathhouse was locked. All the windows of the house were shut, and when he went around to the driveway in front he saw a FOR SALE sign nailed to the tree. When had he last heard from the Welchers—when, that is, had he and Lucinda last regretted an invitation to dine with them? It seemed only a week or so ago. Was his memory failing or had he so disciplined it in the repression of unpleasant facts that he had damaged his sense of the truth? Then in the distance he heard the sound of a tennis game. This cheered him, cleared away all his apprehensions and let him regard the overcast sky and the cold air with indifference. This was the day that Neddy Merrill swam across the county. That was the day! He started off then for his most difficult portage.

Had you gone for a Sunday afternoon ride that day you might have seen him, close to naked, standing on the shoulders of Route 424, waiting for a chance to cross. You might have wondered if he was the victim of foul play, had his car broken down, or was he merely a fool. Standing barefoot in the deposits of the highway—beer cans, rags, and blowout patches—exposed to all kinds of ridicule, he seemed pitiful. He had known when he started that this was a part of his journey— it had been on his maps—but confronted with the lines of traffic, worming through the summery light, he found himself unprepared. He was laughed at, jeered at, a beer can was thrown at him, and he had no dignity or humor to bring to the situation. He could have gone back, back to the Westerhazys', where Lucinda would still be sitting in the sun. He had signed nothing, vowed nothing, pledged nothing, not even to himself. Why, believing as he did, that all human obduracy was susceptible to common sense, was he unable to turn back? Why was he determined to complete his journey even if it meant putting his life in danger? At what point had this prank, this joke, this piece of horseplay become serious? He could not go back, he could not even recall with any clearness the green water at the Westerhazys', the sense of inhaling the day's components, the friendly and relaxed voices saying that

10

they had *drunk* too much. In the space of an hour, more or less, he had covered a distance that made his return impossible.

An old man, tooling down the highway at fifteen miles an hour, let him get to the middle of the road, where there was a grass divider. Here he was exposed to the ridicule of the northbound traffic, but after ten or fifteen minutes he was able to cross. From here he had only a short walk to the Recreation Center at the edge of the village of Lancaster, where there were some handball courts and a public pool.

The effect of the water on voices, the illusion of brilliance and suspense, was the same here as it had been at the Bunkers' but the sounds here were louder, harsher, and more shrill, and as soon as he entered the crowded enclosure he was confronted with regimentation. "ALL SWIMMERS MUST TAKE A SHOWER BEFORE USING THE POOL. ALL SWIMMERS MUST USE THE FOOTBATH. ALL SWIMMERS MUST WEAR THEIR IDENTIFI-CATION DISKS." He took a shower, washed his feet in a cloudy and bitter solution, and made his way to the edge of the water. It stank of chlorine and looked to him like a sink. A pair of lifeguards in a pair of towers blew police whistles at what seemed to be regular intervals and abused the swimmers through a public address system. Neddy remembered the sapphire water at the Bunkers' with longing and thought that he might contaminate himself—damage his own prosperousness and charm— by swimming in this murk, but he reminded himself that he was an explorer, a pil-grim, and that this was merely a stagnant bend in the Lucinda River. He dove, scowling with distaste, into the chlorine and had to swim with his head above water to avoid collisions, but even so he was bumped into, splashed, and jostled. When he got to the shallow end both lifeguards were shouting at him: "Hey, you, you without the identification disk, get outa the water." He did, but they had no way of pursuing him and he went through the reek of suntan oil and chlorine out through the hurri-cane fence and passed the handball courts. By crossing the road he entered the wooded part of the Halloran estate. The woods were not cleared and the footing was treacherous and difficult until he reached the lawn and the clipped beech hedge that encircled their pool.

The Hallorans were friends, an elderly couple of enormous wealth who seemed to bask in the suspicion that they might be Communists. They were zealous reformers but they were not Communists, and yet when they were accused, as they sometimes were, of subversion, it seemed to gratify and excite them. Their beech hedge was yel-low and he guessed this had been blighted like the Levys' maple. He called hullo, hullo, to warn the Hallorans of his approach, to palliate his invasion of their privacy. The Hallorans, for reasons that had never been explained to him, did not wear bathing suits. No explanations were in order, really. Their nakedness was a detail in their uncompromising zeal for reform and he stepped politely out of his trunks before he went through the opening in the hedge.

Mrs. Halloran, a stout woman with white hair and a serene face, was reading the *Times.* Mr. Halloran was taking beech leaves out of the water with a scoop. They seemed not surprised or displeased to see him. Their pool was perhaps the oldest in the county, a fieldstone rectangle, fed by a brook. It had no filter or pump and its waters were the opaque gold of the stream.

"I'm swimming across the county," Ned said.

"Why, I didn't know one could," exclaimed Mrs. Halloran.

"Well, I've made it from the Westerhazys'," Ned said. "That must be about four miles."

15

He left his trunks at the deep end, walked to the shallow end, and swam this stretch. As he was pulling himself out of the water he heard Mrs. Halloran say, "We've been *terribly* sorry to hear about all your misfortunes, Neddy."

"My misfortunes?" Ned asked. "I don't know what you mean."   20

"Why we heard that you'd sold the house and that your poor children. . . ."

"I don't recall having sold the house," Ned said, "and the girls are at home."

"Yes," Mrs. Halloran sighed. "Yes. . . ." Her voice filled the air with an unseasonable melancholy and Ned spoke briskly. "Thank you for the swim."

"Well, have a nice trip," said Mrs. Halloran.

Beyond the hedge he pulled on his trunks and fastened them. They were loose   25
and he wondered if, during the space of an afternoon, he could have lost some weight. He was cold and he was tired and the naked Hallorans and their dark water had depressed him. The swim was too much for his strength but how could he have guessed this, sliding down the banister that morning and sitting in the Westerhazys' sun? His arms were lame. His legs felt rubbery and ached at the joints. The worst of it was the cold in his bones and the feeling that he might never be warm again. Leaves were falling down around him and he smelled wood smoke on the wind. Who would be burning wood at this time of the year?

He needed a drink. Whiskey would warm him, pick him up, carry him through the last of his journey, refresh his feeling that it was original and valorous to swim across the county. Channel swimmers took brandy. He needed a stimulant. He crossed the lawn in front of the Hallorans' house and went down a little path to where they had built a house for their only daughter, Helen, and her husband, Eric Sachs. The Sachses' pool was small and he found Helen and her husband there.

"Oh, *Neddy*," Helen said. "Did you lunch at Mother's?"

"Not *really*" Ned said. "I *did* stop to see your parents." This seemed to be explanation enough. "I'm terribly sorry to break in on you like this but I've taken a chill and I wonder if you'd give me a drink."

"Why, I'd *love* to," Helen said, "but there hasn't been anything in this house to drink since Eric's operation. That was three years ago."

Was he losing his memory, had his gift for concealing painful facts let him forget   30
that he had sold his house, that his children were in trouble, and that his friend had been ill? His eyes slipped from Eric's face to his abdomen, where he saw three pale, sutured scars, two of them at least a foot long. Gone was his navel, and what, Neddy thought, would the roving hand, bed-checking one's gifts at 3 A.M., make of a belly with no navel, no link to birth, this breach in the succession?

"I'm sure you can get a drink at the Biswangers'," Helen said. "They're having an enormous do. You can hear it from here. Listen!"

She raised her head and from across the road, the lawns, the gardens, the woods, the fields, he heard again the brilliant noise of voices over water. "Well, I'll get wet," he said, still feeling that he had no freedom of choice about his means of travel. He dove into the Sachses' cold water, and gasping, close to drowning, made his way from one end of the pool to the other. "Lucinda and I want *terribly* to see you," he said over his shoulder, his face set toward the Biswangers'. "We're sorry it's been so long and we'll call you *very* soon."

He crossed some fields to the Biswangers' and the sounds of revelry there. They would be honored to give him a drink, they would be happy to give him a drink. The Biswangers invited him and Lucinda for dinner four times a year, six weeks in advance.

They were always rebuffed and yet they continued to send out their invitations, unwilling to comprehend the rigid and undemocratic realities of their society. They were the sort of people who discussed the price of things at cocktails, exchanged market tips during dinner, and after dinner told dirty stories to mixed company. They did not belong to Neddy's set—they were not even on Lucinda's Christmas card list. He went toward their pool with feelings of indifference, charity, and some unease, since it seemed to be getting dark and these were the longest days of the year. The party when he joined it was noisy and large. Grace Biswanger was the kind of hostess who asked the optometrist, the veterinarian, the real-estate dealer, and the dentist. No one was swimming and the twilight, reflected on the water of the pool, had a wintry gleam. There was a bar and he started for this. When Grace Biswanger saw him she came toward him, not affectionately as he had every right to expect, but bellicosely.

"Why, this party has everything," she said loudly, "including a gate crasher."

She could not deal him a social blow—there was no question about this and he   35
did not flinch. "As a gate crasher," he asked politely, "do I rate a drink?"

"Suit yourself," she said. "You don't seem to pay much attention to invitations."

She turned her back on him and joined some guests, and he went to the bar and ordered a whiskey. The bartender served him but he served him rudely. His was a world in which the caterer's men kept the social score, and to be rebuffed by a part-time barkeep meant that he had suffered some loss of social esteem. Or perhaps the man was new and uninformed. Then he heard Grace at his back say: "They went for broke overnight—nothing but income—and he showed up drunk one Sunday and asked us to loan him five thousand dollars. . . ." She was always talking about money. It was worse than eating your peas off a knife. He dove into the pool, swam its length, and went away.

The next pool on his list, the last but two, belonged to his old mistress, Shirley Adams. If he had suffered any injuries at the Biswangers' they would be cured here. Love—sexual roughhouse in fact—was the supreme elixir, the pain killer, the brightly colored pill that would put the spring back into his step, the joy of life in his heart. They had had an affair last week, last month, last year. He couldn't remember. It was he who had broken it off, his was the upper hand, and he stepped through the gate of the wall that surrounded her pool with nothing so considered as self-confidence. It seemed in a way to be his pool, as the lover, particularly the illicit lover, enjoys the possessions of his mistress with an authority unknown to holy matrimony. She was there, her hair the color of brass, but her figure, at the edge of the lighted, cerulean water, excited in him no profound memories. It had been, he thought, a lighthearted affair, although she had wept when he broke it off. She seemed confused to see him and he wondered if she was still wounded. Would she, God forbid, weep again?

"What do you want?" she asked.

"I'm swimming across the county."

"Good Christ. Will you ever grow up?"   40

"What's the matter?"

"If you've come here for money," she said, "I won't give you another cent."

"You could give me a drink."

"I could but I won't. I'm not alone."   45

"Well, I'm on my way."

He dove in and swam the pool, but when he tried to haul himself up onto the curb he found that the strength in his arms and shoulders had gone, and he paddled to the ladder and climbed out. Looking over his shoulder he saw, in the lighted bathhouse, a young man. Going out onto the dark lawn he smelled chrysanthemums or marigolds—some stubborn autumnal fragrance—on the night air, strong as gas. Looking overhead he saw that the stars had come out, but why should he seem to see Andromeda, Cepheus, and Cassiopeia? What had become of the constellations of midsummer? He began to cry.

It was probably the first time in his adult life that he had ever cried, certainly the first time in his life that he had ever felt so miserable, cold, tired, and bewildered. He could not understand the rudeness of the caterer's barkeep or the rudeness of a mistress who had come to him on her knees and showered his trousers with tears. He had swum too long, he had been immersed too long, and his nose and his throat were sore from the water. What he needed then was a drink, some company, and some clean, dry clothes, and while he could have cut directly across the road to his home he went on to the Gilmartins' pool. Here, for the first time in his life, he did not dive but went down the steps into the icy water and swam a hobbled sidestroke that he might have learned as a youth. He staggered with fatigue on his way to the Clydes' and paddled the length of their pool, stopping again and again with his hand on the curb to rest. He climbed up the ladder and wondered if he had the strength to get home. He had done what he wanted, he had swum the county, but he was so stupefied with exhaustion that his triumph seemed vague. Stooped, holding on to the gateposts for support, he turned up the driveway of his own house.

The place was dark. Was it so late that they had all gone to bed? Had Lucinda stayed at the Westerhazys' for supper? Had the girls joined her there or gone someplace else? Hadn't they agreed, as they usually did on Sunday, to regret all their invitations and stay at home? He tried the garage doors to see what cars were in but the doors were locked and rust came off the handles onto his hands. Going toward the house, he saw the force of the thunderstorm had knocked one of the rain gutters loose. It hung down over the front door like an umbrella rib, but it could be fixed in the morning. The house was locked, and he thought that the stupid cook or the stupid maid must have locked the place up until he remembered that it had been some time since they had employed a maid or a cook. He shouted, pounded on the door, tried to force it with his shoulder, and then, looking in at the windows, saw that the place was empty.

Questions

1. How is setting used symbolically in the story? Focus on such details as the change in weather and specific locales such as the highway and the public pool.

2. How is Neddy Merrill presented in the beginning of the story (especially paragraphs 2 and 3)? How would you describe the narrator's tone, and what does that tone communicate about the narrator's attitude toward Neddy?

3. At what point do you begin to realize that all is not what it appears to be on the surface? What textual details lead you to that realization?

4. How does Cheever communicate the passing of time and Neddy's aging? Cite specific passages from the story to back up your answer.

5. Does Neddy himself function symbolically in the story? If so, what might he be a symbol of?

6. In paragraph 3, Neddy decides that "he would name the stream Lucinda after his wife." What does that decision suggest at the beginning of the story? What does it suggest at the end?

Ursula K. Le Guin

The Ones Who Walk Away from Omelas   1975

*Ursula Kroeber Le Guin was born in 1929 on St.
Ursula's Day (October 21) in Berkeley, California,
the only daughter and youngest child of Theodora
Kroeber, a folklorist, and Alfred Kroeber, a
renowned anthropologist. Le Guin attended
Radcliffe College, where she graduated Phi Beta
Kappa, and then entered Columbia University to
do graduate work in French and Italian literature.
While completing her M.A., she wrote her first
stories. On a Fulbright fellowship to France, she
met Charles Le Guin, a professor of French history, whom she married in Paris in 1953. Over
the next decade Le Guin reared three children and
worked on her writing in private.*

Ursula K. Le Guin

    *In the early sixties Le Guin began publishing
in both science fiction pulp magazines and acade-
mic journals. In 1966 her first novel,* Rocannon's World, *was published as an Ace science
fiction paperback original—hardly a respectable format for the debut of one of America's
premier writers. In 1968 Le Guin published* A Wizard of Earthsea, *the first novel in her
Earthsea Trilogy, now considered a classic of children's literature. The next two volumes,*
The Tombs of Atuan *(1971), which won a Newbery citation, and* The Farthest Shore
(1972), which won a National Book Award, brought Le Guin mainstream acclaim.

    Le Guin's novels The Left Hand of Darkness *(1969) and* The Dispossessed *(1974)
won both the Hugo and the Nebula awards, science fiction's two most prized honors. She
also twice won the Hugo for best short story, including the 1974 award for "The Ones Who
Walk Away from Omelas." Le Guin has published more than thirty novels and volumes of
short stories. She lives in Portland, Oregon.*

    *One of the few science fiction writers whose work has earned general critical acclaim,
Le Guin belongs most naturally in the company of major novelists of ideas such as Aldous
Huxley, George Orwell, and Anthony Burgess, who have used the genre of science fiction
to explore the possible consequences of ideological rather than technological change. Le Guin
has been especially concerned with issues of social justice and equality. In her short stories—
such as "The Ones Who Walk Away from Omelas"—she creates complex imaginary
civilizations, envisioned with anthropological authority, and her aim is less to imagine alien
cultures than to explore humanity.*

    With a clamor of bells that set the swallows soaring, the Festival of Summer
came to the city. Omelas bright-towered by the sea. The rigging of the boats in harbor sparkled with flags. In the streets between houses with red roofs and painted
walls, between old moss-grown gardens and under avenues of trees, past great parks
and public buildings, processions moved. Some were decorous: old people in long stiff
robes of mauve and grey, grave master workmen, quiet, merry women carrying their
babies and chatting as they walked. In other streets the music beat faster, a shimmering of gong and tambourine, and the people went dancing, the procession was a
dance. Children dodged in and out, their high calls rising like the swallows' crossing

flights over the music and the singing. All the processions wound towards the north side of the city, where on the great water-meadow called the Green Fields boys and girls, naked in the bright air, with mud-stained feet and ankles and long, lithe arms, exercised their restive horses before the race. The horses wore no gear at all but a halter without bit. Their manes were braided with streamers of silver, gold, and green. They flared their nostrils and pranced and boasted to one another; they were vastly excited, the horse being the only animal who has adopted our ceremonies as his own. Far off to the north and west the mountains stood up half encircling Omelas on her bay. The air of morning was so clear that the snow still crowning the Eighteen Peaks burned with white-gold fire across the miles of sunlit air, under the dark blue of the sky. There was just enough wind to make the banners that marked the racecourse snap and flutter now and then. In the silence of the broad green meadows one could hear the music winding through the city streets, farther and nearer and ever approaching, a cheerful faint sweetness of the air that from time to time trembled and gathered together and broke out into the great joyous clanging of the bells.

Joyous! How is one to tell about joy? How describe the citizens of Omelas?

They were not simple folk, you see, though they were happy. But we do not say the words of cheer much any more. All smiles have become archaic. Given a description such as this one tends to make certain assumptions. Given a description such as this one tends to look next for the King, mounted on a splendid stallion and surrounded by his noble knights, or perhaps in a golden litter borne by great-muscled slaves. But there was no king. They did not use swords, or keep slaves. They were not barbarians. I do not know the rules and laws of their society, but I suspect that they were singularly few. As they did without monarchy and slavery, so they also got on without the stock exchange, the advertisement, the secret police, and the bomb. Yet I repeat that these were not simple folk, not dulcet shepherds, noble savages, bland utopians. They were not less complex than us. The trouble is that we have a bad habit, encouraged by pedants and sophisticates, of considering happiness as something rather stupid. Only pain is intellectual, only evil interesting. This is the treason of the artist: a refusal to admit the banality of evil and the terrible boredom of pain. If you can't lick 'em, join 'em. If it hurts, repeat it. But to praise despair is to condemn delight, to embrace violence is to lose hold of everything else. We have almost lost hold; we can no longer describe a happy man, nor make any celebration of joy. How can I tell you about the people of Omelas? They were not naïve and happy children—though their children were, in fact, happy. They were mature, intelligent, passionate adults whose lives were not wretched. O miracle! but I wish I could describe it better. I wish I could convince you. Omelas sounds in my words like a city in a fairy tale, long ago and far away, once upon a time. Perhaps it would be best if you imagined it as your own fancy bids, assuming it will rise to the occasion, for certainly I cannot suit you all. For instance, how about technology? I think that there would be no cars or helicopters in and above the streets; this follows from the fact that the people of Omelas are happy people. Happiness is based on a just discrimination of what is necessary, what is neither necessary nor destructive, and what is destructive. In the middle category, however—that of the unnecessary but undestructive, that of comfort, luxury, exuberance, etc.—they could perfectly well have central heating, subway trains, washing machines, and all kinds of marvelous devices not yet invented here, floating light-sources, fuelless power, a cure for the common cold. Or they could have none of that: it doesn't matter. As you like it. I incline to think that people from towns up and down the coast have been coming in to Omelas during the last days before the Festival on very fast little trains and double-decked trams, and that the train station of Omelas is actually the handsomest building in town, though plainer than the magnificent Farmers' Market. But even granted trains, I fear that Omelas so far strikes some of you as goody-goody. Smiles, bells, parades, horses, bleh. If so, please add an orgy. If an orgy would help, don't hesitate. Let us not, however, have temples from which issue beautiful nude priests and priestesses already half in ecstasy and ready to copulate with any man or woman, lover or stranger, who desires union with the deep godhead of the blood, although that was my first idea. But really it would be better not to have any temples in Omelas—at least, not manned temples. Religion yes, clergy no. Surely the beautiful nudes can just wander about, offering themselves like divine soufflés to the hunger of the needy and the rapture of the flesh. Let them join the processions. Let tambourines be struck above the copulations, and the glory of desire be proclaimed upon the gongs, and (a not unimportant point) let the offspring of these delightful rituals be beloved and looked after by all. One thing I know there is none of in Omelas is guilt. But what else should there be? I thought at first there were no drugs, but that is puritanical. For those who like it, the faint insistent sweetness of *drooz* may perfume the ways of the city, *drooz* which first brings a great lightness and brilliance to the mind and limbs, and then after some hours a dreamy languor, and wonderful visions at last of the very arcana and inmost secrets of the Universe, as well as exciting the pleasure of sex beyond all belief; and it is not habit-forming. For more modest tastes I think there ought to be beer. What else, what else belongs in the joyous city? The sense of victory, surely, the celebration of courage. But as we did without clergy, let us do without soldiers. The joy built upon successful slaughter is not the right kind of joy; it will not do; it is fearful and it is trivial. A boundless and generous contentment, a magnanimous triumph felt not against some outer enemy but in communion with the finest and fairest in the souls of all men everywhere and the splendor of the world's summer: this is what swells the hearts of the people of Omelas, and the victory they celebrate is that of life. I really don't think many of them need to take *drooz*.

Most of the processions have reached the Green Fields by now. A marvelous smell of cooking goes forth from the red and blue tents of the provisioners. The faces of small children are amiably sticky; in the benign grey beard of a man a couple of crumbs of rich pastry are entangled. The youths and girls have mounted their horses and are beginning to group around the starting line of the course. An old woman, small, fat, and laughing, is passing out flowers from a basket, and tall young men wear her flowers in their shining hair. A child of nine or ten sits at the edge of the crowd, alone, playing on a wooden flute. People pause to listen, and they smile, but they do not speak to him, for he never ceases playing and never sees them, his dark eyes wholly rapt in the sweet, thin magic of the tune.

He finishes, and slowly lowers his hands holding the wooden flute.

As if that little private silence were the signal, all at once a trumpet sounds from the pavilion near the starting line: imperious, melancholy, piercing. The horses rear on their slender legs, and some of them neigh in answer. Sober-faced, the young riders stroke the horses' necks and soothe them, whispering, "Quiet, quiet, there my beauty, my hope. . . ." They begin to form in rank along the starting line. The crowds along the racecourse are like a field of grass and flowers in the wind. The Festival of Summer has begun.

5

Do you believe? Do you accept the festival, the city, the joy? No? Then let me describe one more thing.

In a basement under one of the beautiful public buildings of Omelas, or perhaps in the cellar of one of its spacious private homes, there is a room. It has one locked door, and no window. A little light seeps in dustily between cracks in the boards, secondhand from a cobwebbed window somewhere across the cellar. In one corner of the little room a couple of mops, with stiff, clotted, foul-smelling heads, stand near a rusty bucket. The floor is dirt, a little damp to the touch, as cellar dirt usually is. The room is about three paces long and two wide: a mere broom closet or disused tool room. In the room a child is sitting. It could be a boy or a girl. It looks about six, but actually is nearly ten. It is feeble-minded. Perhaps it was born defective, or perhaps it has become imbecile through fear, malnutrition, and neglect. It picks its nose and occasionally fumbles vaguely with its toes or genitals, as it sits hunched in the corner farthest from the bucket and the two mops. It is afraid of the mops. It finds them horrible. It shuts its eyes, but it knows the mops are still standing there; and the door is locked; and nobody will come. The door is always locked; and nobody ever comes, except that sometimes—the child has no understanding of time or interval—sometimes the door rattles terribly and opens, and a person, or several people, are there. One of them may come in and kick the child to make it stand up. The others never come close, but peer in at it with frightened, disgusted eyes. The food bowl and the water jug are hastily filled, the door is locked, the eyes disappear. The people at the door never say anything, but the child, who has not always lived in the tool room, and can remember sunlight and its mother's voice, sometimes speaks. "I will be good," it says. "Please let me out. I will be good!" They never answer. The child used to scream for help at night, and cry a good deal, but now it only makes a kind of whining, "eh-haa, eh-haa," and it speaks less and less often. It is so thin there are no calves to its legs; its belly protrudes; it lives on a half-bowl of corn meal and grease a day. It is naked. Its buttocks and thighs are a mass of festered sores, as it sits in its own excrement continually.

They all know it is there, all the people of Omelas. Some of them have come to see it, others are content merely to know it is there. They all know that it has to be there. Some of them understand why, and some do not, but they all understand that their happiness, the beauty of their city, the tenderness of their friendships, the health of their children, the wisdom of their scholars, the skill of their makers, even the abundance of their harvest and the kindly weathers of their skies, depend wholly on this child's abominable misery.

This is usually explained to children when they are between eight and twelve, whenever they seem capable of understanding; and most of those who come to see the child are young people, though often enough an adult comes, or comes back, to see the child. No matter how well the matter has been explained to them, these young spectators are always shocked and sickened at the sight. They feel disgust, which they had thought themselves superior to. They feel anger, outrage, impotence, despite all the explanations. They would like to do something for the child. But there is nothing they can do. If the child were brought up into the sunlight out of that vile place, if it were cleaned and fed and comforted, that would be a good thing, indeed; but if it were done, in that day and hour all the prosperity and beauty and delight of Omelas would wither and be destroyed. Those are the terms. To exchange all the goodness and grace of every life in Omelas for that single, small improvement: to throw away the happiness of thousands for the chance of the happiness of one: that would be to let guilt within the walls indeed.

The terms are strict and absolute; there may not even be a kind word spoken to the child.

Often the young people go home in tears, or in a tearless rage, when they have seen the child and faced this terrible paradox. They may brood over it for weeks or years. But as time goes on they begin to realize that even if the child could be released, it would not get much good of its freedom: a little vague pleasure of warmth and food, no doubt, but little more. It is too degraded and imbecile to know any real joy. It has been afraid too long ever to be free of fear. Its habits are too uncouth for it to respond to humane treatment. Indeed, after so long it would probably be wretched without walls about it to protect it, and darkness for its eyes, and its own excrement to sit in. Their tears at the bitter injustice dry when they begin to perceive the terrible justice of reality, and to accept it. Yet it is their tears and anger, the trying of their generosity and the acceptance of their helplessness, which are perhaps the true source of the splendor of their lives. Theirs is no vapid, irresponsible happiness. They know that they, like the child, are not free. They know compassion. It is the existence of the child, and their knowledge of its existence, that makes possible the nobility of their architecture, the poignancy of their music, the profundity of their science. It is because of the child that they are so gentle with children. They know that if the wretched one were not there snivelling in the dark, the other one, the flute-player, could make no joyful music as the young riders line up in their beauty for the race in the sunlight of the first morning of summer.

Now do you believe in them? Are they not more credible? But there is one more thing to tell, and this is quite incredible.

At times one of the adolescent girls or boys who go to see the child does not go home to weep or rage, does not, in fact, go home at all. Sometimes also a man or woman much older falls silent for a day or two, and then leaves home. These people go out into the street, and walk down the street alone. They keep walking, and walk straight out of the city of Omelas, through the beautiful gates. They keep walking across the farmlands of Omelas. Each one goes alone, youth or girl, man or woman. Night falls; the traveler must pass down village streets, between the houses with yellow-lit windows, and on out into the darkness of the fields. Each alone, they go west or north, toward the mountains. They go on. They leave Omelas, they walk ahead into the darkness, and they do not come back. The place they go towards is a place even less imaginable to most of us than the city of happiness. I cannot describe it at all. It is possible that it does not exist. But they seem to know where they are going, the ones who walk away from Omelas.

Questions

1. Does the narrator live in Omelas? What do we know about the narrator's society?
2. What is the narrator's opinion of Omelas? Does the author seem to share that opinion?
3. What is the narrator's attitude toward "the ones who walk away from Omelas"? Would the narrator have been one of those who walked away?
4. How do you account for the narrator's willingness to let us readers add anything we like to the story?—"If an orgy would help, don't hesitate" (paragraph 3). Doesn't Ursula Le Guin care what her story includes?
5. What is suggested by the locked, dark cellar in which the child sits? What other details in the story are suggestive enough to be called symbolic?
6. Do you find in the story any implied criticism of our own society?

Shirley Jackson

The Lottery   1948

*Shirley Jackson (1919–1965), a native of San Francisco, moved in her teens to Rochester, New York. She started college at the University of Rochester, but had to drop out, stricken by severe depression, a problem that was to recur at intervals throughout her life. Later she graduated from Syracuse University. With her husband, Stanley Edgar Hyman, a literary critic, she settled in Bennington, Vermont, in a sprawling house built in the nineteenth century. There Jackson conscientiously set herself to produce a fixed number of words each day. She wrote novels—*The Road Through the Wall *(1948)— and three psychological thrillers—*Hangsaman *(1951),* The Haunting of Hill House *(1959), and* We Have Always Lived in the Castle *(1962). She wrote light, witty arti-*cles for Good Housekeeping *and other popular magazines about the horrors of house-keeping and rearing four children, collected in* Life Among the Savages *(1953) and* Raising Demons *(1957); but she claimed to have written these only for money. When "The Lottery" appeared in the* New Yorker *in 1948, that issue of the magazine quickly sold out. Her purpose in writing the story, Jackson declared, had been "to shock the story's readers with a graphic demonstration of the pointless violence and general inhumanity in their own lives."*

The morning of June 27th was clear and sunny, with the fresh warmth of a full-summer day; the flowers were blossoming profusely and the grass was richly green. The people of the village began to gather in the square, between the post office and the bank, around ten o'clock; in some towns there were so many people that the lottery took two days and had to be started on June 26th, but in this village, where there were only about three hundred people, the whole lottery took less than two hours, so it could begin at ten o'clock in the morning and still be through in time to allow the villagers to get home for noon dinner.

The children assembled first, of course. School was recently over for the summer, and the feeling of liberty sat uneasily on most of them; they tended to gather together quietly for a while before they broke into boisterous play, and their talk was still of the classroom and the teacher, of books and reprimands. Bobby Martin had already stuffed his pockets full of stones, and the other boys soon followed his example, selecting the smoothest and roundest stones; Bobby and Harry Jones and Dickie Delacroix—the villagers pronounced this name "Dellacroy"—eventually made a great pile of stones in one corner of the square and guarded it against the raids of the other boys. The girls stood aside, talking among themselves, looking over their shoulders at the boys, and the very small children rolled in the dust or clung to the hands of their older brothers or sisters.

Soon the men began to gather, surveying their own children, speaking of planting and rain, tractors and taxes. They stood together, away from the pile of stones in the corner, and their jokes were quiet and they smiled rather than laughed. The women, wearing faded house dresses and sweaters, came shortly after their menfolk. They greeted one another and exchanged bits of gossip as they went to join their husbands. Soon the women, standing by their husbands, began to call to their children, and the children came reluctantly, having to be called four or five times. Bobby Martin ducked under his mother's grasping hand and ran, laughing, back to the pile of stones. His father spoke up sharply, and Bobby came quickly and took his place between his father and his oldest brother.

The lottery was conducted—as were the square dances, the teenage club, the Halloween program—by Mr. Summers, who had time and energy to devote to civic activities. He was a roundfaced, jovial man and he ran the coal business, and people were sorry for him, because he had no children and his wife was a scold. When he arrived in the square, carrying the black wooden box, there was a murmur of conversation among the villagers and he waved and called, "Little late today, folks." The postmaster, Mr. Graves, followed him, carrying a three-legged stool, and the stool was put in the center of the square and Mr. Summers set the black box down on it. The villagers kept their distance, leaving a space between themselves and the stool, and when Mr. Summers said, "Some of you fellows want to give me a hand?" there was a hesitation before two men, Mr. Martin and his oldest son, Baxter, came forward to hold the box steady on the stool while Mr. Summers stirred up the papers inside it.

The original paraphernalia for the lottery had been lost long ago, and the black box now resting on the stool had been put into use even before Old Man Warner, the oldest man in town, was born. Mr. Summers spoke frequently to the villagers about making a new box, but no one liked to upset even as much tradition as was represented by the black box. There was a story that the present box had been made with some pieces of the box that had preceded it, the one that had been constructed when the first people settled down to make a village here. Every year, after the lottery, Mr. Summers began talking again about a new box, but every year the subject was allowed to fade off without anything's being done. The black box grew shabbier each year; by now it was no longer completely black but splintered badly along one side to show the original wood color, and in some places faded or stained.

Mr. Martin and his oldest son, Baxter, held the black box securely on the stool until Mr. Summers had stirred the papers thoroughly with his hand. Because so much of the ritual had been forgotten or discarded, Mr. Summers had been successful in having slips of paper substituted for the chips of wood that had been used for generations. Chips of wood, Mr. Summers had argued, had been all very well when the village was tiny, but now that the population was more than three hundred and likely to keep on growing, it was necessary to use something that would fit more easily into the black box. The night before the lottery, Mr. Summers and Mr. Graves made up the slips of paper and put them in the box, and it was then taken to the safe of Mr. Summers's coal company and locked up until Mr. Summers was ready to take it to the square next morning. The rest of the year, the box was put away, sometimes one place, sometimes another; it had spent one year in Mr. Graves's barn and another year underfoot in the post office, and sometimes it was set on a shelf in the Martin grocery and left there.

There was a great deal of fussing to be done before Mr. Summers declared the lottery open. There were lists to make up—of heads of families, heads of households in each family, members of each household in each family. There was the proper swearing-in of Mr. Summers by the postmaster, as the official of the lottery; at one time, some people remembered, there had been a recital of some sort, performed by the official of the lottery, a perfunctory, tuneless chant that had been rattled off duly each year; some people believed that the official of the lottery used to stand just so when he said or sang it, others believed that he was supposed to walk among the people, but years and years ago this part of the ritual had been allowed to lapse. There had been, also, a ritual salute, which the official of the lottery had had to use in addressing each person who came up to draw from the box, but this also had changed with time, until now it was felt necessary only

5

for the official to speak to each person approaching. Mr. Summers was very good at all this; in his clean white shirt and blue jeans, with one hand resting carelessly on the black box, he seemed very proper and important as he talked interminably to Mr. Graves and the Martins.

Just as Mr. Summers finally left off talking and turned to the assembled villagers, Mrs. Hutchinson came hurriedly along the path to the square, her sweater thrown over her shoulders, and slid into place in the back of the crowd. "Clean forgot what day it was," she said to Mrs. Delacroix, who stood next to her, and they both laughed softly. "Thought my old man was out back stacking wood," Mrs. Hutchinson went on, "and then I looked out the window and the kids were gone, and then I remembered it was the twenty-seventh and came a-running." She dried her hands on her apron, and Mrs. Delacroix said, "You're in time, though. They're still talking away up there."

Mrs. Hutchinson craned her neck to see through the crowd and found her husband and children standing near the front. She tapped Mrs. Delacroix on the arm as a farewell and began to make her way through the crowd. The people separated good-humoredly to let her through; two or three people said, in voices just loud enough to be heard across the crowd, "Here comes your Missus, Hutchinson," and "Bill, she made it after all." Mrs. Hutchinson reached her husband, and Mr. Summers, who had been waiting, said cheerfully, "Thought we were going to have to get on without you, Tessie." Mrs. Hutchinson said, grinning, "Wouldn't have me leave m'dishes in the sink, now would you, Joe?" and soft laughter ran through the crowd as the people stirred back into position after Mrs. Hutchinson's arrival.

"Well, now," Mr. Summers said soberly, "guess we better get started, get this over with, so's we can go back to work. Anybody ain't here?"

"Dunbar," several people said. "Dunbar, Dunbar."

Mr. Summers consulted his list. "Clyde Dunbar," he said. "That's right. He's broke his leg, hasn't he? Who's drawing for him?"

"Me, I guess," a woman said, and Mr. Summers turned to look at her. "Wife draws for her husband," Mr. Summers said. "Don't you have a grown boy to do it for you, Janey?" Although Mr. Summers and everyone else in the village knew the answer perfectly well, it was the business of the official of the lottery to ask such questions formally. Mr. Summers waited with an expression of polite interest while Mrs. Dunbar answered.

"Horace's not but sixteen yet," Mrs. Dunbar said regretfully. "Guess I gotta fill in for the old man this year."

"Right," Mr. Summers said. He made a note on the list he was holding. Then he asked, "Watson boy drawing this year?"

A tall boy in the crowd raised his hand. "Here," he said. "I'm drawing for m'mother and me." He blinked his eyes nervously and ducked his head as several voices in the crowd said things like "Good fellow, Jack," and "Glad to see your mother's got a man to do it."

"Well," Mr. Summers said, "guess that's everyone. Old Man Warner make it?"

"Here," a voice said, and Mr. Summers nodded.

A sudden hush fell on the crowd as Mr. Summers cleared his throat and looked at the list. "All ready?" he called. "Now, I'll read the names—heads of families first—and the men come up and take a paper out of the box. Keep the paper folded in your hand without looking at it until everyone has had a turn. Everything clear?"

The people had done it so many times that they only half listened to the direc- 20
tions; most of them were quiet, wetting their lips, not looking around. Then Mr.
Summers raised one hand high and said, "Adams." A man disengaged himself from the
crowd and came forward. "Hi, Steve," Mr. Summers said, and Mr. Adams said, "Hi,
Joe." They grinned at one another humorlessly and nervously. Then Mr. Adams
reached into the black box and took out a folded paper. He held it firmly by one corner
as he turned and went hastily back to his place in the crowd, where he stood a little
apart from his family, not looking down at his hand.

"Allen," Mr. Summers said. "Anderson. . . . Bentham."

"Seems like there's no time at all between lotteries any more," Mrs. Delacroix
said to Mrs. Graves in the back row. "Seems like we got through with the last one
only last week."

"Time sure goes fast," Mrs. Graves said.

"Clark. . . . Delacroix."

"There goes my old man," Mrs. Delacroix said. She held her breath while her 25
husband went forward.

"Dunbar," Mr. Summers said, and Mrs. Dunbar went steadily to the box while
one of the women said, "Go on, Janey," and another said, "There she goes."

"We're next," Mrs. Graves said. She watched while Mr. Graves came around
from the side of the box, greeted Mr. Summers gravely, and selected a slip of paper
from the box. By now, all through the crowd there were men holding the small folded
papers in their large hands, turning them over and over nervously. Mrs. Dunbar and
her two sons stood together, Mrs. Dunbar holding the slip of paper.

"Harburt. . . . Hutchinson."

"Get up there, Bill," Mrs. Hutchinson said, and the people near her laughed.

"Jones." 30

"They do say," Mr. Adams said to Old Man Warner, who stood next to him,
"that over in the north village they're talking of giving up the lottery."

Old Man Warner snorted. "Pack of crazy fools," he said. "Listening to the young
folks, nothing's good enough for *them*. Next thing you know, they'll be wanting to go
back to living in caves, nobody work any more, live *that* way for a while. Used to be a
saying about 'Lottery in June, corn be heavy soon.' First thing you know, we'd all be
eating stewed chickweed and acorns. There's *always* been a lottery," he added petu-
lantly. "Bad enough to see young Joe Summers up there joking with everybody."

"Some places have already quit lotteries," Mrs. Adams said.

"Nothing but trouble in *that*," Old Man Warner said stoutly. "Pack of young fools."

"Martin." And Bobby Martin watched his father go forward. "Overdyke. . . . Percy." 35

"I wish they'd hurry," Mrs. Dunbar said to her older son. "I wish they'd hurry."

"They're almost through," her son said.

"You get ready to run tell Dad," Mrs. Dunbar said.

Mr. Summers called his own name and then stepped forward precisely and
selected a slip from the box. Then he called, "Warner."

"Seventy-seventh year I been in the lottery," Old Man Warner said as he went 40
through the crowd. "Seventy-seventh time."

"Watson." The tall boy came awkwardly through the crowd. Someone said,
"Don't be nervous, Jack," and Mr. Summers said, "Take your time, son."

"Zanini."

After that, there was a long pause, a breathless pause, until Mr. Summers, holding his slip of paper in the air, said, "All right, fellows." For a minute, no one moved,

and then all the slips of paper were opened. Suddenly, all the women began to speak
at once, saying, "Who is it?" "Who's got it?" "Is it the Dunbars?" "Is it the Watsons?"
Then the voices began to say, "It's Hutchinson. It's Bill." "Bill Hutchinson's got it."

"Go tell your father," Mrs. Dunbar said to her older son.

People began to look around to see the Hutchinsons. Bill Hutchinson was stand-   45
ing quiet, staring down at the paper in his hand. Suddenly, Tessie Hutchinson shouted
to Mr. Summers, "You didn't give him time enough to take any paper he wanted. I
saw you. It wasn't fair!"

"Be a good sport, Tessie," Mrs. Delacroix called, and Mrs. Graves said, "All of us
took the same chance."

"Shut up, Tessie," Bill Hutchinson said.

"Well, everyone," Mr. Summers said, "that was done pretty fast, and now we've
got to be hurrying a little more to get done in time." He consulted his next list. "Bill,"
he said, "you draw for the Hutchinson family. You got any other households in the
Hutchinsons?"

"There's Don and Eva," Mrs. Hutchinson yelled. "Make them take their
chance!"

"Daughters draw with their husbands' families, Tessie," Mr. Summers said   50
gently. "You know that as well as anyone else."

"It wasn't fair," Tessie said.

"I guess not, Joe," Bill Hutchinson said regretfully. "My daughter draws with her
husband's family, that's only fair. And I've got no other family except the kids."

"Then, as far as drawing for families is concerned, it's you," Mr. Summers said in
explanation, "and as far as drawing for households is concerned, that's you, too.
Right?"

"Right," Bill Hutchinson said.

"How many kids, Bill?" Mr. Summers asked formally.   55

"Three," Bill Hutchinson said. "There's Bill, Jr., and Nancy, and little Dave.
And Tessie and me."

"All right, then," Mr. Summers said. "Harry, you got their tickets back?"

Mr. Graves nodded and held up the slips of paper. "Put them in the box, then,"
Mr. Summers directed. "Take Bill's and put it in."

"I think we ought to start over," Mrs. Hutchinson said, as quietly as she could. "I
tell you it wasn't *fair*. You didn't give him time enough to choose. *Everybody* saw
that."

Mr. Graves had selected the five slips and put them in the box, and he dropped   60
all the papers but those onto the ground, where the breeze caught them and lifted
them off.

"Listen, everybody," Mrs. Hutchinson was saying to the people around her.

"Ready, Bill?" Mr. Summers asked, and Bill Hutchinson, with one quick glance
around at his wife and children, nodded.

"Remember," Mr. Summers said, "take the slips and keep them folded until
each person has taken one. Harry, you help little Dave." Mr. Graves took the hand
of the little boy, who came willingly with him up to the box. "Take a paper out of
the box, Davy," Mr. Summers said. Davy put his hand into the box and laughed.
"Take just *one* paper," Mr. Summers said. "Harry, you hold it for him." Mr. Graves
took the child's hand and removed the folded paper from the tight fist and held it
while little Dave stood next to him and looked up at him wonderingly.

"Nancy next," Mr. Summers said. Nancy was twelve, and her school friends
breathed heavily as she went forward, switching her skirt, and took a slip daintily

from the box. "Bill, Jr.," Mr. Summers said, and Billy, his face red and his feet over-large, nearly knocked the box over as he got a paper out. "Tessie," Mr. Summers said. She hesitated for a minute, looking around defiantly, and then set her lips and went up to the box. She snatched a paper out and held it behind her.

"Bill," Mr. Summers said, and Bill Hutchinson reached into the box and felt 65
around, bringing his hand out at last with the slip of paper in it.

The crowd was quiet. A girl whispered, "I hope it's not Nancy," and the sound of the whisper reached the edges of the crowd.

"It's not the way it used to be," Old Man Warner said clearly. "People ain't the way they used to be."

"All right," Mr. Summers said. "Open the papers. Harry, you open little Dave's."

Mr. Graves opened the slip of paper and there was a general sigh through the crowd as he held it up and everyone could see that it was blank. Nancy and Bill, Jr., opened theirs at the same time, and both beamed and laughed, turning around to the crowd and holding their slips of paper above their heads.

"Tessie," Mr. Summers said. There was a pause, and then Mr. Summers looked at 70
Bill Hutchinson, and Bill unfolded his paper and showed it. It was blank.

"It's Tessie," Mr. Summers said, and his voice was hushed. "Show us her paper, Bill."

Bill Hutchinson went over to his wife and forced the slip of paper out of her hand. It had a black spot on it, the black spot Mr. Summers had made the night before with the heavy pencil in the coal-company office. Bill Hutchinson held it up, and there was a stir in the crowd.

"All right, folks," Mr. Summers said, "Let's finish quickly."

Although the villagers had forgotten the ritual and lost the original black box, they still remembered to use stones. The pile of stones the boys had made earlier was ready; there were stones on the ground with the blowing scraps of paper that had come out of the box. Mrs. Delacroix selected a stone so large she had to pick it up with both hands and turned to Mrs. Dunbar. "Come on," she said. "Hurry up."

Mrs. Dunbar had small stones in both hands, and she said, gasping for breath, "I 75
can't run at all. You'll have to go ahead and I'll catch up with you."

The children had stones already, and someone gave little Davy Hutchinson a few pebbles.

Tessie Hutchinson was in the center of a cleared space by now, and she held her hands out desperately as the villagers moved in on her. "It isn't fair," she said. A stone hit her on the side of the head.

Old Man Warner was saying, "Come on, come on, everyone." Steve Adams was in the front of the crowd of villagers, with Mrs. Graves beside him.

"It isn't fair, it isn't right," Mrs. Hutchinson screamed, and then they were upon her.

Questions

1. Where do you think "The Lottery" takes place? What purpose do you suppose the writer has in making this setting appear so familiar and ordinary?

2. What details in paragraphs 2 and 3 foreshadow the ending of the story?

3. Take a close look at Jackson's description of the black wooden box (paragraph 5) and of the black spot on the fatal slip of paper (paragraph 72). What do these objects suggest to you? Are there any other symbols in the story?

4. What do you understand to be the writer's own attitude toward the lottery and the stoning? Exactly what in the story makes her attitude clear to us?

5. What do you make of Old Man Warner's saying, "Lottery in June, corn be heavy soon" (paragraph 32)?

6. What do you think Shirley Jackson is driving at? Consider each of the following interpretations and, looking at the story, see if you can find any evidence for it:

> Jackson takes a primitive fertility rite and playfully transfers it to a small town in North America.
>
> Jackson, writing her story soon after World War II, indirectly expresses her horror at the Holocaust. She assumes that the massacre of the Jews was carried out by unwitting, obedient people, like these villagers.
>
> Jackson is satirizing our own society, in which men are selected for the army by lottery.
>
> Jackson is just writing a memorable story that signifies nothing at all.

■ WRITING *effectively*

Shirley Jackson on Writing

Biography of a Story   (1960) 1968

Shirley Jackson

My agent did not care for the story, but—as she said in her note at the time—her job was to sell it, not to like it. She sent it at once to the *New Yorker*, and about a week after the story had been written I received a telephone call from the fiction editor of the *New Yorker*; it was quite clear that he did not really care for the story, either, but the *New Yorker* was going to buy it. He asked for one change—that the date mentioned in the story be changed to coincide with the date of the issue of the magazine in which the story would appear, and I said of course. He then asked, hesitantly, if I had any particular interpretation of my own for the story; Mr. Harold Ross, then the editor of the *New Yorker*, was not altogether sure that he understood the story, and wondered if I cared to enlarge upon its meaning. I said no. Mr. Ross, he said, thought that the story might be puzzling to some people, and in case anyone telephoned the magazine, as sometimes happened, or wrote in asking about the story, was there anything in particular I wanted them to say? No, I said, nothing in particular; it was just a story I wrote.

I had no more preparation than that. I went on picking up the mail every morning, pushing my daughter up and down the hill in her stroller, anticipating pleasurably the check from the *New Yorker*, and shopping for groceries. The weather stayed nice and it looked as though it was going to be a good summer. Then, on June 28, the *New Yorker* came out with my story.

Things began mildly enough with a note from a friend at the *New Yorker*: "Your story has kicked up quite a fuss around the office," he wrote. I was flattered; it's nice to think that your friends notice what you write. Later that day there was a call from one of the magazine's editors; they had had a couple of people phone in about my story, he said, and was there anything I particularly wanted him to say if there were any more calls? No, I said, nothing particular; anything he chose to say was perfectly all right with me; it was just a story.

I was further puzzled by a cryptic note from another friend: "Heard a man talking about a story of yours on the bus this morning," she wrote. "Very exciting. I wanted to tell him I knew the author, but after I heard what he was saying I decided I'd better not."

One of the most terrifying aspects of publishing stories and books is the realization that they are going to be read, and read by strangers. I had never fully realized this before, although I had of course in my imagination dwelt lovingly upon the thought of millions and millions of people who were going to be uplifted and enriched and delighted by the stories I wrote. It had simply never occurred to me that these millions and millions of people might be so far from being uplifted that they would sit down and write me letters I was downright scared to open; of the three-hundred-odd letters that I received that summer I can count only thirteen that spoke kindly to me, and they were mostly from friends. Even my mother scolded me: "Dad and I did not care at all for your story in the *New Yorker*," she wrote sternly; "it does seem, dear, that this gloomy kind of story is what all you young people think about these days. Why don't you write something to cheer people up?"

By mid-July I had begun to perceive that I was very lucky indeed to be safely in Vermont, where no one in our small town had ever heard of the *New Yorker*, much less read my story. Millions of people, and my mother, had taken a pronounced dislike to me.

The magazine kept no track of telephone calls, but all letters addressed to me care of the magazine were forwarded directly to me for answering, and all letters addressed to the magazine—some of them addressed to Harold Ross personally; these were the most vehement—were answered at the magazine and then the letters were sent me in great batches, along with carbons of the answers written at the magazine. I have all the letters still, and if they could be considered to give any accurate cross section of the reading public, or the reading public of the *New Yorker*, or even the reading public of one issue of the *New Yorker*, I would stop writing now.

Judging from these letters, people who read stories are gullible, rude, frequently illiterate, and horribly afraid of being laughed at. Many of the writers were positive that the *New Yorker* was going to ridicule them in print; and the most cautious letters were headed, in capital letters: NOT FOR PUBLICATION or PLEASE DO NOT PRINT THIS LETTER, or, at best, THIS LETTER MAY BE PUBLISHED AT YOUR USUAL RATES OF PAYMENT. Anonymous letters, of which there were a few, were destroyed. The *New Yorker* never published any comment of any kind about the story in the magazine, but did issue one publicity release saying that the story had received more mail than any piece of fiction they had ever published; this was after the newspapers had gotten into the act, in midsummer, with a front-page story in the San Francisco *Chronicle* begging to know what the story meant, and a series of columns in New York and Chicago papers pointing out that *New Yorker* subscriptions were being canceled right and left.

Curiously, there are three main themes which dominate the letters of that first summer—three themes which might be identified as bewilderment, speculation, and plain old-fashioned abuse. In the years since then, during which the story has been anthologized, dramatized, televised, and even—in one completely mystifying transformation—made into a ballet, the tenor of letters I receive has changed. I am addressed more politely, as a rule, and the letters largely confine themselves to questions like what does this story mean? The general tone of the early letters, however, was a kind of wide-eyed, shocked innocence. People at first were not so much concerned with what the story meant; what they wanted to know was where these lotteries were held, and whether they could go there and watch.

From *Come Along with Me*

THINKING ABOUT SYMBOLS

One danger in analyzing a story's symbolism is the temptation to read symbolic meaning into *everything*. An image acquires symbolic resonance because it is organically important to the actions and emotions of the story.

- **Consider a symbolic object's relevance to the plot.** What events, characters, and ideas are associated with it? It also helps to remember that some symbols arrive with cultural baggage. Any great white whale that swims into a work of contemporary fiction will inevitably summon up the symbolic associations of Melville's Moby Dick.
- **Ask yourself what the symbol means to the protagonist of your story.** Writers don't simply assign arbitrary meanings to items in their stories; generally, a horse is a horse, and a hammer is just a hammer. Sometimes, though, an object means something more to a character. Think of the flowers in "The Chrysanthemums."
- **Remember: in literature, few symbols are hidden.** Don't go on a symbol hunt. As you read or reread a story, any real symbol will usually find you. If an object appears time and again, or is tied inextricably to the story's events, it is likely to suggest something beyond itself. When an object, an action, or a place has emotional or intellectual power beyond its literal importance, then it is a genuine symbol.

CHECKLIST: Writing About Symbols

- ☐ Which objects, actions, or places seem unusually significant?
- ☐ List the specific objects, people, and ideas with which a particular symbol is associated.
- ☐ Locate the exact place in the story where the symbol links itself to the other thing.
- ☐ Ask whether each symbol comes with ready-made cultural associations.
- ☐ Avoid far-fetched interpretations. Focus first on the literal things, places, and actions in the story.
- ☐ Don't make a symbol mean too much or too little. Don't limit it to one narrow association or claim it summons up many different things.
- ☐ Be specific. Identify the exact place in the story where a symbol takes on a deeper meaning.

WRITING ASSIGNMENT ON SYMBOLS

From the stories in this book, choose one with a strong central symbol. Explain how the symbol helps to communicate the story's meaning, citing specific moments in the text. Here is an example of a paper written on that topic by Samantha L. Brown, a student of Melinda Barth's at El Camino College.

SAMPLE STUDENT PAPER

Brown 1

Samantha L. Brown

Professor Barth

English 210

26 May 2009

An Analysis of the Symbolism in Steinbeck's

"The Chrysanthemums"

In a work of literature a symbol is something that suggests more than its surface meaning. In his short story "The Chrysanthemums," John Steinbeck uses the flowers of the title for both realistic and symbolic purposes. On the realistic level, the chrysanthemums advance the plot because they are the basis for the story's central action. They also help define the character of Elisa, provide a greater understanding of the setting, and play a vital part in revealing the story's theme.

The chrysanthemums provide the reader with insight into Elisa. When we first see her, she is in her flower garden working with her chrysanthemums. She is putting a great deal of energy into the relatively simple job of tending to the flowers. Elisa and her husband, Henry, have no children. They do not appear to have a very intense or passionate relationship. He praises her skill at growing flowers, but says that he wishes she would work in the orchard and grow larger apples for him. His interests are practical and financial. The beauty of the flowers, which also symbolizes her beauty as a woman, is not important to him.

"The Chrysanthemums" is set in rural Monterey, California, in the 1930s. The ranch where Elisa and Henry live is in an isolated area. The flower garden is isolated from the rest of the ranch. The reader sees that Elisa is unhappy and frustrated, emotionally isolated from her husband and the life of their ranch.

Thesis sentence

Clarification and elaboration of thesis

Topic sentence

Development of thesis

Textual evidence

Further development of thesis

Brown 2

The flower garden is also surrounded by a wire fence, which symbolizes Elisa's feelings of being fenced in. She shows such feelings later in the story when she envies the free and easy life of the tinker and wishes that women could live that way.

Textual evidence

The symbolic significance of the chrysanthemums is especially brought out in Elisa's conversation with the tinker. At first she resists his attempts to repair something for her, but then she responds to him because he admires her flowers. When he describes them in a poetic-sounding way, she feels she has met someone like herself that she can share an emotional bond with. The feelings he arouses in her are passionate—even sexual, as we see when she stops herself from reaching out and touching his pants. This is also shown after he leaves, when she takes off her mannish gardening clothes, bathes, and looks at her body in the mirror.

Further development of thesis

Textual evidence

The last and most painful symbolic use of the flowers comes toward the end of the story, when Elisa and her husband are driving into town for their evening out. Even before she can see it clearly, she knows that the speck by the side of the road is the chrysanthemum sprouts she gave the tinker to give to the (probably fictitious) woman he told her about. This is so upsetting to her that she turns around toward her husband so as not to see the tinker again as the car passes his wagon.

Topic sentence announces culmination of thesis

If we read the story only on the surface level, we won't be able to understand why Elisa is so upset. So a cunning traveler has manipulated her love of flowers to soften her up into giving him some work. Maybe he made a fool of her, but it's in the middle of the Depression, and he has to eat, too. What's the big deal? Only when we understand the symbolic importance of the chrysanthemums do we understand why this is so painful for her. She had felt that someone understood her, maybe even felt that life was richer in possibilities than it had seemed. This illusion is shattered, however, when she sees the plant sprouts. The discarded, dying plants symbolize her diminished life, her failure to find anyone who can understand her needs and feelings.

Topic sentence on significance of symbolism

Elaboration of significance of symbolism

The chrysanthemums are vital to Steinbeck's presentation of the theme. At the beginning, Elisa is presented as a strong woman, strong enough to break the back of a calf. At the end, she is seen huddled like an old woman, crying weakly. The newly revealed Elisa is not the strong woman that she or her husband thought she was. It wasn't until she saw the discarded plant sprouts that she felt the sting of her rejection and isolation. Until that moment, her

Elaboration of how symbol reveals theme

Brown 3

Conclusion sums up main idea without simply restating it

gardening had protected—or at least distracted—her from her loneliness, isolation, and feelings of inadequacy. Finally, the theme emerges from our understanding of this woman and the importance of her chrysanthemums. Understanding Steinbeck's symbolism, therefore, is essential to understanding how the story works.

MORE TOPICS FOR WRITING

1. Choose a story from this chapter. Describe your experience of reading that story, and of encountering its symbols. At what point did the main symbol's meaning become clear? What in the story indicated the larger importance of that symbol?

2. From any story in this book, select an object, or place, or action that seems clearly symbolic. How do you know? Now select an object, place, or action from the same story that clearly seems to signify no more than itself. How can you tell?

3. Analyze the symbolism in a story from "Stories for Further Reading." Some good choices might be "Dead Men's Path," "The Story of an Hour," and "Where Are You Going, Where Have You Been?" Choose a symbol that recurs over the course of the story, and look closely at each appearance it makes. How does the story's use of the symbol evolve?

4. In an essay of 600 to 800 words, compare and contrast the symbolic use of the scapegoat in "The Lottery" and "The Ones Who Walk Away from Omelas."

▶ TERMS FOR *review*

Symbol ▶ A person, place, or thing in a narrative that suggests meanings beyond its literal sense. Symbol is related to allegory, but it works more complexly. A symbol often contains multiple meanings and associations.

Conventional symbol ▶ A literary symbol that has a conventional or customary meaning for most readers—for example, a black cat crossing a path or a young bride in a white dress.

Symbolic act ▶ An action whose significance goes well beyond its literal meaning. In literature, symbolic acts often involve some conscious or unconscious ritual element such as rebirth, purification, forgiveness, vengeance, or initiation.

Allegory ▶ A narrative in which the literal events (persons, places, and things) consistently point to a parallel sequence of symbolic equivalents. This narrative strategy is often used to dramatize abstract ideas, historical events, religious systems, or political issues. An allegory has two levels of meaning: a literal level that tells a surface story and a symbolic level in which the abstract ideas unfold.

8 READING LONG STORIES AND NOVELS

The novel is the one bright book of life.

—D. H. LAWRENCE

Among the forms of imaginative literature in our language, the novel has been the favorite of both writers and readers for more than two hundred years. Broadly defined, a **novel** is a book-length fictional story in prose, whose author tries to create the sense that while we read, we experience actual life.

This sense of actuality, also found in artful short stories, may be the quality that sets the novel apart from other long prose narratives. Why do we not apply the name *novel* to, for instance, *Gulliver's Travels*? In his marvel-filled account of Lemuel Gulliver's voyages among pygmies, giants, civilized horses, and noxious humanoid swine, Jonathan Swift does not seem primarily to care if we find his story credible. Though he arrays the adventures of Gulliver in painstaking detail (and, ironically, has Gulliver swear to the truth of them), Swift neither attempts nor achieves a convincing illusion of life. For his book is a fantastic satire that finds resemblances between noble horses and man's reasoning faculties, between debased apes and man's kinship with the beasts.

ORIGINS OF THE NOVEL

Unlike other major literary forms—drama, lyric, ballad, and epic—the novel is a relative newcomer. Originally, the drama in ancient Greece came alive only when actors performed it; the epic or heroic poem (from the classic *Iliad* through the Old English *Beowulf*), only when a bard sang or chanted it. But the English novel came to maturity in literate times, in the eighteenth century, and by its nature was something different: a story to be communicated silently in printed books, at whatever moment and at whatever pace (whether quickly or slowly and meditatively) the reader desired.

Some definitions of the novel would more strictly define the form. "The Novel is a picture of real life and manners, and of the time in which it was written," declared Clara Reeve in 1785. By so specifying that the novel depicts life in the present day, the critic was probably observing the derivation of the word *novel*. Akin to the French word for "news" (*nouvelles*), it comes from the Italian *novella* ("something new and small"), a term applied to a newly made story taking place in recent times, and not a traditional story taking place long ago.

Romances

The novel, which is principally a realistic form, is often contrasted with the other major prose tradition of narrative, the **romance**. In general terms, romance is a narrative mode that employs exotic adventure and idealized emotion rather than realistic depiction of character and action. In the romantic mode—out of which most popular genre fictions develop—people, actions, and events are depicted more as we wish them to be (heroes are very brave, villains are very bad) than as the complex entities they usually are. Medieval romances (in both prose and verse) presented chivalric tales of kings, knights, and aristocratic ladies. Modern romances, emerging in the nineteenth century, were represented by adventure novels such as Sir Walter Scott's *Ivanhoe* which embodied the symbolic quests and idealized characters of earlier, chivalric tales in slightly more realistic terms, a tradition carried on in contemporary popular works such as the *Stars Wars* and James Bond films.

Novels Versus Romances

Also drawing a line between novel and romance, Nathaniel Hawthorne, in his preface to *The House of the Seven Gables* (1851), restricted the novel "not merely to the possible, but to the probable and ordinary course of man's experience." A romance had no such limitations. Such a definition would deny the name of *novel* to any fantastic or speculative story—to, say, the Gothic novel and the science fiction novel. Carefully bestowed, the labels *novel* and *romance* may be useful to distinguish between the true-to-life story of usual people in ordinary places (such as George Eliot's *Silas Marner* or Amy Tan's *The Joy Luck Club*) and the larger-than-life story of daring deeds and high adventure, set in the past or future or in some timeless land (such as Walter Scott's *Ivanhoe* or J. R. R. Tolkien's *The Lord of the Rings*). This sense of the actual is, perhaps, the hallmark of a novel, whether or not the events it relates are literally possible.

A student shouldn't worry too much about the differences between the novel and romance. In everyday conversation people usually refer to any book-length fictional narratives as "novels." The important thing to remember is that there are two fundamentally different ways of telling a story. The novelistic method stresses the everyday, realistic aspects. The romantic method stresses the aspects of adventure, surprise, and wish fulfillment. It is particularly interesting to see the rare occasions when authors deliberately stray across the boundary between the two modes. In Franz Kafka's *The Metamorphosis*, for example, the story begins with a fantastic premise—Gregor Samsa wakes to discover himself turned into a giant insect. This bizarre transformation would seem the very stuff of romance, but after the first sentence Kafka tells the story in the most matter-of-fact and realistic way. The stunning quality of Kafka's masterpiece comes from his novelistic manner of telling his seemingly unrealistic tale.

Novels and Journalism

Since both the novel and journalism try to capture the fabric of everyday life, there has long been a close relationship between the two literary forms. Many novelists, among them Ernest Hemingway, Stephen Crane, and Jack London, began their writing careers as cub reporters. Ambrose Bierce was the most influential newspaper satirist of his day.

The two modes of writing, however, remain different. "Literature is the art of writing something that will be read twice," commented critic and novelist Cyril

Connolly, "journalism what will be grasped at once." Journalism greatly influences how novelists depict the world around them. Stephen Crane's "The Open Boat" (Chapter 6) began as a newspaper account of his actual experiences in a small rowboat after the sinking of the *Commodore* in 1897. A journalist might have been content with such a gripping first-person story of surviving a shipwreck, but a great fiction writer has the gift of turning personal bad luck into art, and Crane eventually created a masterpiece of fiction based on fact.

NOVELISTIC METHODS

Many early novels were told in the form of letters. Sometimes these **epistolary novels** contained letters by only one character; often they contained letters exchanged by several of the characters in the book. By casting his novel *Pamela* (1740) into the form of personal letters, Samuel Richardson helped give the story the appearance of being not invented but discovered from real documents. Alice Walker's *The Color Purple* (1982) is a more recent epistolary novel, though some of the letters that tell the story are addressed to God.

Another method favored by novelists is to write as though setting down a memoir or an autobiography. Daniel Defoe, whose skill in feigning such memoirs was phenomenal, succeeded in writing the supposedly true confessions of a woman retired from a life of crime, *Moll Flanders* (1722), and in maintaining a vivid truthfulness:

> Going through Aldersgate Street, there was a pretty little child who had been at a dancing-school, and was going home all alone: and my prompter, like a true devil, set me upon this innocent creature. I talked to it, and it prattled to me again, and I took it by the hand and led it along till I came to a paved alley that goes into Bartholomew Close, and I led it in there. The child said that was not its way home. I said, "Yes, my dear, it is; I'll show you the way home." The child had a little necklace on of gold beads, and I had my eye upon that, and in the dark of the alley I stooped, pretending to mend the child's clog that was loose, and took off her necklace, and the child never felt it, and so led the child on again. Here, I say, the devil put me upon killing the child in the dark alley, that it might not cry, but the very thought frighted me so that I was ready to drop down; but I turned the child about and bade it go back again. . . . The last affair left no great concern upon me, for as I did the poor child no harm, I only said to myself, I had given the parents a just reproof for their negligence in leaving the poor little lamb to come home by itself, and it would teach them to take more care of it another time.

What could sound more like the voice of an experienced child-robber than this manner of excusing her crime, and even justifying it?

Some novelists place great emphasis on research and notetaking. James A. Michener, the internationally best-selling author of novels such as *Centennial* (which tracks life in Colorado from prehistory through modern times) and *Chesapeake* (which describes 400 years of events on Maryland's Eastern Shore), started work on a book by studying everything available about his chosen subject. He also traveled to locations that might appear in the book, interviewed local people, and compiled immense amounts of scientific, historical, and cultural data. Research alone, however, is not enough to produce a novel. A novel grows to completion only through the slow mental process of creation, selection, and arrangement. But raw facts can sometimes provide a beginning. Many novels started when the author read some arresting episode in a newspaper or magazine. Theodore Dreiser's impressive study of a murder, *An American Tragedy* (1925), for example, was inspired by a journalist's account of a real-life case.

Nonfiction Novels

In the 1960s there was a great deal of talk about the **nonfiction novel**, in which the author presents actual people and events in story form. The vogue of the nonfiction novel was created by Truman Capote's *In Cold Blood* (1966), which depicts an actual multiple murder and the resulting trial in Kansas. Capote traveled to the scene of the crime and interviewed all of the principal parties, including the murderers. Norman Mailer wrote a similar novel, *The Executioner's Song* (1979), chronicling the life and death of Gary Gilmore, the Utah murderer who demanded his own execution. More recently, John Berendt's darkly comic 1994 account of the upper class and under class of Savannah, Georgia, *Midnight in the Garden of Good and Evil* (which also centers on a murder and the subsequent trial), revived interest in the form.

Perhaps the name "nonfiction novel" (Capote's term for it) is newer than the form. In the past, writers of autobiography have cast their memoirs into what looks like novel form: Richard Wright in *Black Boy* (1945), William Burroughs in *Junkie* (1953). Derived from his reporting, John Hersey's *Hiroshima* (1946) reconstructs the lives of six survivors of the atom bomb as if they were fictional. In reading such works we may nearly forget we are reading literal truth, so well do the techniques of the novel lend an air of immediacy to remembered facts.

Historical Novels

A familiar kind of fiction that claims a basis in fact is the **historical novel**, a detailed reconstruction of life in another time, perhaps in another place. In some historical novels the author attempts a faithful picture of daily life in another era, as does Robert Graves in *I, Claudius* (1934), a novel of patrician Rome. More often, history is a backdrop for an exciting story of love and heroic adventure. Nathaniel Hawthorne's *The Scarlet Letter* (set in Puritan Boston) and Stephen Crane's *The Red Badge of Courage* (set on the battlefields of the Civil War) are historical novels in that their authors lived considerably later than the scenes and events that they depicted, and strove for truthfulness, by imaginative means.

Other Types of Novels

Other varieties of novel will be familiar to anyone who browses in bookstores: the mystery or detective novel, the Western novel, the science fiction novel, and other enduring types. Novels are sometimes said to belong to a category if they contain some recognizable kind of structure or theme. Such a category is the **Bildungsroman** (German for a "novel of growth and development"), sometimes called the **apprenticeship novel** after its classic example, *Wilhelm Meister's Apprenticeship* (1796) by Johann Wolfgang von Goethe. This is the kind of novel in which a youth struggles toward maturity, seeking, perhaps, some consistent worldview or philosophy of life. Sometimes the apprenticeship novel is evidently derived from the author's recollection of his own early life: James Joyce's *A Portrait of the Artist as a Young Man* (1916) and Tobias Wolff's *Old School* (2003).

Picaresques

In a **picaresque** (another famous category), a likable scoundrel wanders through adventures, living by his wits, duping the straight citizenry. The name comes from Spanish: *pícaro*, "rascal" or "rogue." The classic picaresque novel is the anonymous Spanish *Life of Lazarillo de Tormes* (1554), imitated by many English writers, among them Henry Fielding in his story of a London thief and racketeer, *Jonathan Wild* (1743). Mark Twain's *Huckleberry Finn* (1885) owes something to the tradition; like early picaresque novels, it is told in episodes rather than in one all-unifying plot and is narrated in the first person by a hero at odds with respectable society ("dismal regular and decent," Huck Finn calls it). In Twain's novel, however, the traveling swindlers who claim to be a duke and a dauphin are much more typical rogues of picaresque fiction than Huck himself, an honest innocent. Modern novels worthy of the name include Saul Bellow's *The Adventures of Augie March* (1953), J. P. Donleavy's *The Ginger Man* (1965), Erica Jong's *Fanny* (1981), and Seth Morgan's *Homeboy* (1990).

Short Novels and Novellas

The term **short novel** (or **novella**) mainly describes the size of a narrative; it refers to a narrative midway in length between a short story and a novel. (E. M. Forster once said that a novel should be at least 50,000 words in length, and most editors and publishers would agree with that definition.) Generally a short novel, like a short story, focuses on just one or two characters; but, unlike a short story, it has room to examine them in great depth and detail. A short novel also often explores its characters over a greater period of time.

Many writers, such as Thomas Mann, Henry James, Joseph Conrad, and Willa Cather, favored the novella as a perfect medium between the necessary compression of the short story and the potential sprawl of the novel. Franz Kafka's famous novella *The Metamorphosis* is included in this book. When the term **novelette** is used, it usually refers (often disapprovingly) to a short novel written for a popular magazine, especially in such fields as science fiction, romance, the Western, and horror.

READING NOVELS

Trying to perceive a novel as a whole, we may find it helpful to look for the same elements that we have noticed in reading short stories. By asking ourselves leading questions, we may be drawn more deeply into the novel's world, and may come to recognize and appreciate the techniques of the novelist. Does the novel have themes, or an overall theme? Who is its main character? What is the author's kind of narrative voice? How would we describe the tone, style, and use of irony? Why is this novel written from one point of view rather than from another? If the novel in question is large and thickly populated, it may help to read it with a pencil and take brief notes. Forced to put the novel aside and later return to it, we may find that the notes refresh the memory. Once our reading of a novel is finished and we prepare to discuss it or write about it, it may be a good idea to browse through it again, rereading brief portions. This method of overall browsing may also help when first approaching a bulky and difficult novel. Just as an explorer mapping unfamiliar territory may find it best to begin by taking an aerial view of it, so too the reader approaching an exceptionally thick and demanding novel may wish, at the start, to look for its general shape. There is, of course, no shortcut to novel reading, and probably the best method is to settle in comfort and read the book through: with your own eyes, not with the borrowed glasses of literary criticism.

The Future of the Novel

The death of the novel has been frequently announced. Competition from television, DVDs, video games, and the Internet, some critics claim, will overwhelm the habit of reading; the public is lazy and will follow the easiest route available for entertainment. But in England and America television and films have been sending people back in vast numbers to the books they dramatize. Jane Austen has never lacked readers, but films such as *Pride and Prejudice, Emma, Persuasion,* and *Sense and Sensibility* (not to mention *Clueless,* a teenage version of *Emma* set in Beverly Hills, or *Bride and Prejudice,* a singing and dancing Bollywood treatment set in modern-day India) made her one of the world's best-selling novelists. Stylish adaptations of Philip K. Dick's offbeat science fiction, including *Blade Runner, Total Recall,* and *Minority Report,* have created a cult for his once neglected work. Sometimes Hollywood even helps bring a good book into print. No one would publish Thomas M. Disch's sophisticated children's novella *The Brave Little Toaster,* until Walt Disney turned it into a cartoon movie. A major publisher then not only rushed it into print, but commissioned a sequel.

Meanwhile, each year new novels by the hundreds continue to appear, their authors wistfully looking for a public. Some of these books reach a mass audience. To forecast the end of the novel seems risky, for the novel exercises the imagination of the beholder. At any hour, at a touch of the hand, it opens and (with no warmup) begins to speak. Once printed, it consumes no further energy. Often so small that it may be carried in a pocket, it may yet survive by its ability to contain multitudes (a "capacious vessel," Henry James called it): a thing that is both a work of art and an amazingly compact system for the storage and retrieval of imagined life.

Leo Tolstoy

The Death of Ivan Ilych   1886

Translated by Louise and Aylmer Maude

The complex and contradictory Leo Nikolaevich Tolstoy (1828–1910) is generally considered the greatest Russian novelist. Born on his aristocratic family's country estate, Yasnaya Polyana, in central Russia, he was orphaned at nine and raised by his aunts. At sixteen, Tolstoy entered Kazan University to study law, but soon returned to the family estate. The young count took off for St. Petersburg and Moscow, where he led a profligate life—carefully listing his moral transgressions in his diary. In 1851 Tolstoy joined the army and fought in the Caucasus. It was there that he completed his first book, Childhood *(1852), a lyrical memoir. Having served in the Crimean War, he left the army in 1856 to become a writer.*

Leo Tolstoy

For the next half century the brilliant and perpetually dissatisfied Tolstoy tried to settle in Yasnaya Polyana, but frequently escaped to St. Petersburg and Western Europe. In 1862 he wed Sonya Bers, an intellectual middle-class woman. Initially happy, the marriage was eventually undermined by the sex-obsessed and guilt-ridden Tolstoy, who engaged in many infidelities (which were sometimes followed by the author's unsuccessful renunciations of sex). Despite its many problems, the marriage produced thirteen children. At Yasnaya Polyana, Tolstoy wrote his two greatest novels, the six-volume War and Peace (1863–1869), which depicts the lives of five aristocratic Russian families during the Napoleonic Wars, and Anna Karenina (1877), which tells the tragic story of a woman led by romantic illusions into a destructive adulterous liaison. As Tolstoy grew older, he became obsessed with early Christianity. He formulated his own version of Christ's teachings, stressing simplicity, love, nonviolence, and community property. Excommunicated by the Orthodox Church, the count, who now dressed in peasant clothing, preached his "Christian anarchism" to the Russian intelligentsia in streams of books and pamphlets. Upset by his ruined marriage and his inability to renounce his personal wealth, the eighty-two-year-old Tolstoy fled home one night to enter a monastery. He died of pneumonia a few days later in a provincial railway station.

Tolstoy is one of the great masters of European Realism. His fame came early and has never been seriously challenged. Much of his fiction examines a tragic predicament of human existence—the difficult search for truth and justice in a world of limited knowledge and ethical imperfection. Tolstoy resolutely believed in the moral development of humanity, but was also painfully aware of the obstacles to genuine progress. His gripping novella The Death of Ivan Ilych dramatizes Tolstoy's central spiritual concerns. His antiheroic Everyman faces death with the horrifying realization that he has not lived a correct or meaningful life.

I

During an interval in the Melvinski trial in the large building of the Law Courts, the members and public prosecutor met in Ivan Egorovich Shebek's private room, where the conversation turned on the celebrated Krasovski case. Fëdor Vasilievich warmly maintained that it was not subject to their jurisdiction, Ivan Egorovich maintained the contrary, while Peter Ivanovich, not having entered into the discussion at the start, took no part in it but looked through the *Gazette* which had just been handed in.

"Gentlemen," he said, "Ivan Ilych has died!"

"You don't say so!"

"Here, read it yourself," replied Peter Ivanovich, handing Fëdor Vasilievich the paper still damp from the press. Surrounded by a black border were the words: "Praskovya Fëdorovna Goloviná, with profound sorrow, informs relatives and friends of the demise of her beloved husband Ivan Ilych Golovin, Member of the Court of Justice, which occurred on February the 4th of this year 1882. The funeral will take place on Friday at one o'clock in the afternoon."

Ivan Ilych had been a colleague of the gentlemen present and was liked by them all. He had been ill for some weeks with an illness said to be incurable. His post had been kept open for him, but there had been conjectures that in case of his death Alexeev might receive his appointment, and that either Vinnikov or Shtabel would succeed Alexeev. So on receiving the news of Ivan Ilych's death the first thought of each of the gentlemen in that private room was of the changes and promotions it might occasion among themselves or their acquaintances.

5

"I shall be sure to get Shtabel's place or Vinnikov's," thought Fëdor Vasilievich. "I was promised that long ago, and the promotion means an extra eight hundred rubles a year for me besides the allowance."

"Now I must apply for my brother-in-law's transfer from Kaluga," thought Peter Ivanovich. "My wife will be very glad, and then she won't be able to say that I never do anything for her relations."

"I thought he would never leave his bed again," said Peter Ivanovich aloud. "It's very sad."

"But what really was the matter with him?"

"The doctors couldn't say—at least they could, but each of them said something   10
different. When last I saw him I thought he was getting better."

"And I haven't been to see him since the holidays. I always meant to go."

"Had he any property?"

"I think his wife had a little—but something quite trifling."

"We shall have to go to see her, but they live so terribly far away."

"Far away from you, you mean. Everything's far away from your place."   15

"You see, he never can forgive my living on the other side of the river," said Peter Ivanovich, smiling at Shebek. Then, still talking of the distances between different parts of the city, they returned to the Court.

Besides considerations as to the possible transfers and promotions likely to result from Ivan Ilych's death, the mere fact of the death of a near acquaintance aroused, as usual, in all who heard of it the complacent feeling that "it is he who is dead and not I."

Each one thought or felt, "Well, he's dead but I'm alive!" But the more intimate of Ivan Ilych's acquaintances, his so-called friends, could not help thinking also that they would now have to fulfil the very tiresome demands of propriety by attending the funeral service and paying a visit of condolence to the widow.

Fëdor Vasilievich and Peter Ivanovich had been his nearest acquaintances. Peter Ivanovich had studied law with Ivan Ilych and had considered himself to be under obligations to him.

Having told his wife at dinner-time of Ivan Ilych's death and of his conjecture   20
that it might be possible to get her brother transferred to their circuit, Peter Ivanovich sacrificed his usual nap, put on his evening clothes, and drove to Ivan Ilych's house.

At the entrance stood a carriage and two cabs. Leaning against the wall in the hall downstairs near the cloak-stand was a coffin-lid covered with cloth of gold, ornamented with gold cord and tassels, that had been polished up with metal powder. Two ladies in black were taking off their fur cloaks. Peter Ivanovich recognized one of them as Ivan Ilych's sister, but the other was a stranger to him. His colleague Schwartz was just coming downstairs, but on seeing Peter Ivanovich enter he stopped and winked at him, as if to say: "Ivan Ilych has made a mess of things—not like you and me."

Schwartz's face with his Piccadilly whiskers and his slim figure in evening dress had as usual an air of elegant solemnity which contrasted with the playfulness of his character and had a special piquancy here, or so it seemed to Peter Ivanovich.

Peter Ivanovich allowed the ladies to precede him and slowly followed them upstairs. Schwartz did not come down but remained where he was, and Peter Ivanovich understood that he wanted to arrange where they should play bridge that evening. The ladies went upstairs to the widow's room, and Schwartz with seriously compressed lips but a playful look in his eyes, indicated by a twist of his eyebrows the room to the right where the body lay.

Peter Ivanovich, like everyone else on such occasions, entered feeling uncertain what he would have to do. All he knew was that at such times it is always safe to cross oneself. But he was not quite sure whether one should make obeisances while doing so. He therefore adopted a middle course. On entering the room he began crossing himself and made a slight movement resembling a bow. At the same time, as far as the motion of his head and arm allowed, he surveyed the room. Two young men—apparently nephews, one of whom was a high-school pupil—were leaving the room, crossing themselves as they did so. An old woman was standing motionless, and a lady with strangely arched eyebrows was saying something to her in a whisper. A vigorous, resolute Church Reader, in a frock-coat, was reading something in a loud voice with an expression that precluded any contradiction. The butler's assistant, Gerasim, stepping lightly in front of Peter Ivanovich, was strewing something on the floor. Noticing this, Peter Ivanovich was immediately aware of a faint odor of a decomposing body.

The last time he had called on Ivan Ilych, Peter Ivanovich had seen Gerasim in the study. Ivan Ilych had been particularly fond of him and he was performing the duty of a sick nurse.

Peter Ivanovich continued to make the sign of the cross, slightly inclining his head in an intermediate direction between the coffin, the Reader, and the icons on the table in a corner of the room. Afterwards, when it seemed to him that this movement of his arm in crossing himself had gone on too long, he stopped and began to look at the corpse.

The dead man lay, as dead men always lie, in a specially heavy way, his rigid limbs sunk in the soft cushions of the coffin, with the head forever bowed on the pillow. His yellow waxen brow with bald patches over his sunken temples was thrust up in the way peculiar to the dead, the protruding nose seeming to press on the upper lip. He was much changed and had grown even thinner since Peter Ivanovich had last seen him, but, as is always the case with the dead, his face was handsomer and above all more dignified than when he was alive. The expression on the face said that what was necessary had been accomplished, and accomplished rightly. Besides this there was in that expression a reproach and a warning to the living. This warning seemed to Peter Ivanovich out of place, or at least not applicable to him. He felt a certain discomfort and so he hurriedly crossed himself once more and turned and went out the door—too hurriedly and too regardless of propriety, as he himself was aware.

Schwartz was waiting for him in the adjoining room with legs spread wide apart and both hands toying with his top-hat behind his back. The mere sight of that playful, well-groomed, and elegant figure refreshed Peter Ivanovich. He felt that Schwartz was above all these happenings and would not surrender to any depressing influences. His very look said that this incident of a church service for Ivan Ilych could not be a sufficient reason for infringing the order of the session—in other words, that it would certainly not prevent his unwrapping a new pack of cards and shuffling them that evening while a footman placed four fresh candles on the table: in fact, that there was no reason for supposing that this incident would hinder their spending the evening agreeably. Indeed he said this in a whisper as Peter Ivanovich passed him, proposing that they should meet for a game at Fëdor Vasilievich's. But apparently Peter Ivanovich was not destined to play bridge that evening. Praskovya Fëdorovna (a short, fat woman who

25

despite all efforts to the contrary had continued to broaden steadily from her shoulders downwards and who had the same extraordinarily arched eyebrows as the lady who had been standing by the coffin), dressed all in black, her head covered with lace, came out of her own room with some other ladies, conducted them to the room where the dead body lay, and said: "The service will begin immediately. Please go in."

Schwartz, making an indefinite bow, stood still, evidently neither accepting nor declining this invitation. Praskovya Fëdorovna, recognizing Peter Ivanovich, sighed, went close up to him, took his hand, and said: "I know you were a true friend to Ivan Ilych . . ." and looked at him awaiting some suitable response. And Peter Ivanovich knew that, just as it had been the right thing to cross himself in that room, so what he had to do here was to press her hand, sigh, and say, "Believe me. . . ." So he did all this and as he did it felt that the desired result had been achieved: that both he and she were touched.

"Come with me. I want to speak to you before it begins," said the widow. "Give me your arm."   30

Peter Ivanovich gave her his arm and they went to the inner rooms, passing Schwartz, who winked at Peter Ivanovich compassionately.

"That does for our bridge! Don't object if we find another player. Perhaps you can cut in when you do escape," said his playful look.

Peter Ivanovich sighed still more deeply and despondently, and Praskovya Fëdorovna pressed his arm gratefully. When they reached the drawing-room, upholstered in pink cretonne and lighted by a dim lamp, they sat down at the table—she on a sofa and Peter Ivanovich on a low pouffe, the springs of which yielded spasmodically under his weight. Praskovya Fëdorovna had been on the point of warning him to take another seat, but felt that such a warning was out of keeping with her present condition and so changed her mind. As he sat down on the pouffe Peter Ivanovich recalled how Ivan Ilych had arranged this room and had consulted him regarding this pink cretonne with green leaves. The whole room was full of furniture and knick-knacks, and on her way to the sofa the lace of the widow's black shawl caught on the carved edge of the table. Peter Ivanovich rose to detach it, and the springs of the pouffe, relieved of his weight, rose also and gave him a push. The widow began detaching her shawl herself, and Peter Ivanovich again sat down, suppressing the rebellious springs of the pouffe under him. But the widow had not quite freed herself and Peter Ivanovich got up again, and again the pouffe rebelled and even creaked. When this was all over she took out a clean cambric handkerchief and began to weep. The episode with the shawl and the struggle with the pouffe had cooled Peter Ivanovich's emotions and he sat there with a sullen look on his face. This awkward situation was interrupted by Sokolov, Ivan Ilych's butler, who came to report that the plot in the cemetery that Praskovya Fëdorovna had chosen would cost two hundred rubles. She stopped weeping and, looking at Peter Ivanovich with the air of a victim, remarked in French that it was very hard for her. Peter Ivanovich made a silent gesture signifying his full conviction that it must indeed be so.

"Please smoke," she said in a magnanimous yet crushed voice, and turned to discuss with Sokolov the price of the plot for the grave.

Peter Ivanovich while lighting his cigarette heard her inquiring very circumstantially into the prices of different plots in the cemetery and finally decide which she would take. When that was done she gave instructions about engaging the choir. Sokolov then left the room.   35

"I look after everything myself," she told Peter Ivanovich, shifting the albums that lay on the table; and noticing that the table was endangered by his cigarette-ash, she immediately passed him an ashtray, saying as she did so: "I consider it an affectation to say that my grief prevents my attending to practical affairs. On the contrary, if anything can—I won't say console me, but—distract me, it is seeing to everything concerning him." She again took out her handkerchief as if preparing to cry, but suddenly, as if mastering her feeling, she shook herself and began to speak calmly. "But there is something I want to talk to you about."

Peter Ivanovich bowed, keeping control of the springs of the pouffe, which immediately began quivering under him.

"He suffered terribly the last few days."

"Did he?" said Peter Ivanovich.

"Oh, terribly! He screamed unceasingly, not for minutes but for hours. For the last three days he screamed incessantly. It was unendurable. I cannot understand how I bore it; you could hear him three rooms off. Oh, what I have suffered!"

"Is it possible that he was conscious all that time?" asked Peter Ivanovich.

"Yes," she whispered. "To the last moment. He took leave of us a quarter of an hour before he died, and asked us to take Volodya away."

The thought of the suffering of this man he had known so intimately, first as a merry little boy, then as a school-mate, and later as a grown-up colleague, suddenly struck Peter Ivanovich with horror, despite an unpleasant consciousness of his own and this woman's dissimulation. He again saw that brow, and that nose pressing down on the lip, and felt afraid for himself.

"Three days of frightful suffering and then death! Why, that might suddenly, at any time, happen to me," he thought, and for a moment felt terrified. But—he did not himself know how—the customary reflection at once occurred to him that this had happened to Ivan Ilych and not to him, and that it should not and could not happen to him, and that to think that it could would be yielding to depression which he ought not to do, as Schwartz's expression plainly showed. After which reflection Peter Ivanovich felt reassured, and began to ask with interest about the details of Ivan Ilych's death, as though death was an accident natural to Ivan Ilych but certainly not to himself.

After many details of the really dreadful physical sufferings Ivan Ilych had endured (which details he learnt only from the effect those sufferings had produced on Praskovya Fëdorovna's nerves) the widow apparently found it necessary to get to business.

"Oh, Peter Ivanovich, how hard it is! How terribly, terribly hard!" and she again began to weep.

Peter Ivanovich sighed and waited for her to finish blowing her nose. When she had done so he said, "Believe me . . ." and she again began talking and brought out what was evidently her chief concern with him—namely, to question him as to how she could obtain a grant of money from the government on the occasion of her husband's death. She made it appear that she was asking Peter Ivanovich's advice about her pension, but he soon saw that she already knew about that to the minutest detail, more even than he did himself. She knew how much could be got out of the government in consequence of her husband's death, but wanted to find out whether she could not possibly extract something more. Peter Ivanovich tried to think of some means of doing so, but after reflecting for a while and, out of propriety, condemning the government for its niggardliness, he said he thought that nothing more could be got. Then she sighed and evidently began to devise means of getting rid of her visitor. Noticing this, he put out his cigarette, rose, pressed her hand, and went out into the anteroom.

In the dining-room where the clock stood that Ivan Ilych had liked so much and had bought at an antique shop, Peter Ivanovich met a priest and a few acquaintances who had come to attend the service, and he recognized Ivan Ilych's daughter, a handsome young woman. She was in black and her slim figure appeared slimmer than ever. She had a gloomy, determined, almost angry expression, and bowed to Peter Ivanovich as though he were in some way to blame. Behind her, with the same offended look, stood a wealthy young man, an examining magistrate, whom Peter Ivanovich also knew and who was her fiancé, as he had heard. He bowed mournfully to them and was about to pass into the death-chamber, when from under the stairs appeared the figure of Ivan Ilych's schoolboy son, who was extremely like his father. He seemed a little Ivan Ilych, such as Peter Ivanovich remembered when they studied law together. His tear-stained eyes had in them the look that is seen in the eyes of boys of thirteen or fourteen who are not pure-minded. When he saw Peter Ivanovich he scowled morosely and shamefacedly. Peter Ivanovich nodded to him and entered the death-chamber. The service began: candles, groans, incense, tears, and sobs. Peter Ivanovich stood looking gloomily down at his feet. He did not look once at the dead man, did not yield to any depressing influence, and was one of the first to leave the room. There was no one in the anteroom, but Gerasim darted out of the dead man's room, rummaged with his strong hands among the fur coats to find Peter Ivanovich's, and helped him on with it.

"Well, friend Gerasim," said Peter Ivanovich, so as to say something. "It's a sad affair, isn't it?"

"It's God's will. We shall all come to it some day," said Gerasim, displaying his   50
teeth—the even, white teeth of a healthy peasant—and, like a man in the thick of urgent work, he briskly opened the front door, called the coachman, helped Peter Ivanovich into the sledge, and sprang back to the porch as if in readiness for what he had to do next.

Peter Ivanovich found the fresh air particularly pleasant after the smell of incense, the dead body, and carbolic acid.

"Where to, sir?" asked the coachman.

"It's not too late even now . . . I'll call round on Fëdor Vasilievich."

He accordingly drove there and found them just finishing the first rubber, so that it was quite convenient for him to cut in.

II

Ivan Ilych's life had been most simple and most ordinary and therefore most   55
terrible.

He had been a member of the Court of Justice, and died at the age of forty-five. His father had been an official who after serving in various ministries and departments in Petersburg had made the sort of career which brings men to positions from which by reason of their long service they cannot be dismissed, though they are obviously unfit to hold any responsible position, and for whom therefore posts are specially created, which, though fictitious, carry salaries of from six to ten thousand rubles that are not fictitious, and in receipt of which they live on to a great age.

Such was the Privy Councillor and superfluous member of various superfluous institutions, Ilya Epimovich Golovin.

He had three sons, of whom Ivan Ilych was the second. The eldest son was following in his father's footsteps only in another department, and was already approaching that stage in the service at which a similar sinecure would be reached. The third son was a failure. He had ruined his prospects in a number of positions and was now serving in the railway department. His father and brothers, and still more their wives, not merely disliked meeting him, but avoided remembering his existence unless compelled to do so. His sister had married Baron Greff, a Petersburg official of her father's type. Ivan Ilych was *le phénix de la famille*° as people said. He was neither as cold and formal as his elder brother nor as wild as the younger, but was a happy mean between them—an intelligent, polished, lively, and agreeable man. He had studied with his younger brother at the School of Law, but the latter had failed to complete the course and was expelled when he was in the fifth class. Ivan Ilych finished the course well. Even when he was at the School of Law he was just what he remained for the rest of his life: a capable, cheerful, good-natured, and sociable man, though strict in the fulfillment of what he considered to be his duty: and he considered his duty to be what was so considered by those in authority. Neither as a boy nor as a man was he a toady, but from early youth was by nature attracted to people of high station as a fly is drawn to the light, assimilating their ways and views of life and establishing friendly relations with them. All the enthusiasms of childhood and youth passed without leaving much trace on him; he succumbed to sensuality, to vanity, and latterly among the highest classes to liberalism, but always within limits which his instinct unfailingly indicated to him as correct.

At school he had done things which had formerly seemed to him very horrid and made him feel disgusted with himself when he did them; but when later on he saw that such actions were done by people of good position and that they did not regard them as wrong, he was able not exactly to regard them as right, but to forget about them entirely or not be at all troubled at remembering them.

Having graduated from the School of Law and qualified for the tenth rank of the civil service, and having received money from his father for his equipment, Ivan Ilych ordered himself clothes at Scharmer's, the fashionable tailor, hung a medallion inscribed *respice finem*° on his watch-chain, took leave of his professor and the prince who was patron of the school, had a farewell dinner with his comrades at Donon's first-class restaurant, and with his new and fashionable portmanteau, linen, clothes, shaving and other toilet appliances, and a traveling rug all purchased at the best shops, he set off for one of the provinces where through his father's influence, he had been attached to the Governor as an official for special service.

In the province Ivan Ilych soon arranged as easy and agreeable a position for himself as he had had at the School of Law. He performed his official tasks, made his career, and at the same time amused himself pleasantly and decorously. Occasionally he paid official visits to country districts, where he behaved with dignity both to his superiors and inferiors, and performed the duties entrusted to him, which related chiefly to the sectarians,° with an exactness and incorruptible honesty of which he could not but feel proud.

In official matters, despite his youth and taste for frivolous gaiety, he was exceedingly reserved, punctilious, and even severe; but in society he was often amusing

---

le phénix de la famille: French for "the prize of the family."   *respice finem:* Latin for "Think of the end (of your life)."   *sectarians:* dissenters from the Orthodox Church.

and witty, and always good-natured, correct in his manner, and *bon enfant,*° as the Governor and his wife—with whom he was like one of the family—used to say of him.

In the province he had an affair with a lady who made advances to the elegant young lawyer, and there was also a milliner; and there were carousals with aides-de-camp who visited the district, and after-supper visits to a certain outlying street of doubtful reputation; and there was too some obsequiousness to his chief and even to his chief's wife, but all this was done with such a tone of good breeding that no hard names could be applied to it. It all came under the heading of the French saying: "*Il faut que jeunesse se passe.*"° It was all done with clean hands, in clean linen, with French phrases, and above all among people of the best society and consequently with the approval of people of rank.

So Ivan Ilych served for five years and then came a change in his official life. The new and reformed judicial institutions were introduced, and new men were needed. Ivan Ilych became such a new man. He was offered the post of examining magistrate, and he accepted it though the post was in another province and obliged him to give up the connections he had formed and to make new ones. His friends met to give him a send-off; they had a group-photograph taken and presented him with a silver cigarette-case, and he set off to his new post.

As examining magistrate Ivan Ilych was just as *comme il faut*° and decorous a   65
man, inspiring general respect and capable of separating his official duties from his private life, as he had been when acting as an official on special service. His duties now as examining magistrate were far more interesting and attractive than before. In his former position it had been pleasant to wear an undress uniform made by Scharmer, and to pass through the crowd of petitioners and officials who were timorously awaiting an audience with the Governor, and who envied him as with free and easy gait he went straight into his chief's private room to have a cup of tea and a cigarette with him. But not many people had then been directly dependent on him—only police officials and the sectarians when he went on special missions—and he liked to treat them politely, almost as comrades, as if he were letting them feel that he who had the power to crush them was treating them in this simple, friendly way. There were then but few such people. But now, as an examining magistrate, Ivan Ilych felt that everyone without exception, even the most important and self-satisfied, was in his power, and that he need only write a few words on a sheet of paper with a certain heading, and this or that important, self-satisfied person would be brought before him in the role of an accused person or a witness, and if he did not choose to allow him to sit down, would have to stand before him and answer his questions. Ivan Ilych never abused his power; he tried on the contrary to soften its expression, but the consciousness of it and of the possibility of softening its effect, supplied the chief interest and attraction of his office. In his work itself, especially in his examinations, he very soon acquired a method of eliminating all considerations irrelevant to the legal aspect of the case, and reducing even the most complicated case to a form in which it would be presented on paper only in its externals, completely excluding his personal opinion of the matter, while above all observing every prescribed formality. The work was new and Ivan Ilych was one of the first men to apply the new Code of 1864.°

---

bon enfant: French for "a well-behaved child."   *"Il faut que jeunesse se passe":* "Youth doesn't last." *comme il faut:* "as required," rule-abiding.   *Code of 1864:* The emancipation of the serfs in 1861 was followed by a thorough all-round reform of judicial proceedings. [Translators' note.]

On taking up the post of examining magistrate in a new town, he made new acquaintances and connections, placed himself on a new footing, and assumed a somewhat different tone. He took up an attitude of rather dignified aloofness towards the provincial authorities, but picked out the best circle of legal gentlemen and wealthy gentry living in the town and assumed a tone of slight dissatisfaction with the government, of moderate liberalism, and of enlightened citizenship. At the same time, without at all altering the elegance of his toilet, he ceased shaving his chin and allowed his beard to grow as it pleased.

Ivan Ilych settled down very pleasantly in this new town. The society there, which inclined towards opposition to the Governor, was friendly, his salary was larger, and he began to play *vint*,° which he found added not a little to the pleasure of life, for he had a capacity for cards, played good-humoredly, and calculated rapidly and astutely, so that he usually won.

After living there for two years he met his future wife, Praskovya Fëdorovna Mikhel, who was the most attractive, clever, and brilliant girl of the set in which he moved, and among other amusements and relaxations from his labors as examining magistrate, Ivan Ilych established light and playful relations with her.

While he had been an official on special service he had been accustomed to dance, but now as an examining magistrate it was exceptional for him to do so. If he danced now, he did it as if to show that though he served under the reformed order of things, and had reached the fifth official rank, yet when it came to dancing he could do it better than most people. So at the end of an evening he sometimes danced with Praskovya Fëdorovna, and it was chiefly during these dances that he captivated her. She fell in love with him. Ivan Ilych had at first no definite intention of marrying, but when the girl fell in love with him he said to himself: "Really, why shouldn't I marry?"

Praskovya Fëdorovna came of a good family, was not bad-looking, and had some little property. Ivan Ilych might have aspired to a more brilliant match, but even this was good. He had his salary, and she, he hoped, would have an equal income. She was well connected, and was a sweet, pretty, and thoroughly correct young woman. To say that Ivan Ilych married because he fell in love with Praskovya Fëdorovna and found that she sympathized with his views of life would be as incorrect as to say that he married because his social circle approved of the match. He was swayed by both these considerations: the marriage gave him personal satisfaction, and at the same time it was considered the right thing by the most highly placed of his associates.

So Ivan Ilych got married.

The preparations for marriage and the beginning of married life, with its conjugal caresses, the new furniture, new crockery, and new linen, were very pleasant until his wife became pregnant—so that Ivan Ilych had begun to think that marriage would not impair the easy, agreeable, gay, and always decorous character of his life, approved of by society and regarded by himself as natural, but would even improve it. But from the first months of his wife's pregnancy, something new, unpleasant, depressing, and unseemly, and from which there was no way of escape, unexpectedly showed itself.

His wife, without any reason—*de gaieté de coeur*° as Ivan Ilych expressed it to himself—began to disturb the pleasure and propriety of their life. She began to be

70

---

vint: a form of bridge. [Translators' note.]   *de gaieté de coeur*: "from pure whim."

jealous without any cause, expected him to devote his whole attention to her, found fault with everything, and made coarse and ill-mannered scenes.

At first Ivan Ilych hoped to escape from the unpleasantness of this state of affairs by the same easy and decorous relation to life that had served him heretofore: he tried to ignore his wife's disagreeable moods, continued to live in his usual easy and pleasant way, invited friends to his house for a game of cards, and also tried going out to his club or spending his evenings with friends. But one day his wife began upbraiding him so vigorously, using such coarse words, and continued to abuse him every time he did not fulfil her demands, so resolutely and with such evident determination not to give way till he submitted—that is, till he stayed at home and was bored just as she was—that he became alarmed. He now realized that matrimony—at any rate with Praskovya Fëdorovna—was not always conducive to the pleasures and amenities of life, but on the contrary often infringed both comfort and propriety, and that he must therefore entrench himself against such infringement. And Ivan Ilych began to seek for means of doing so. His official duties were the one thing that imposed upon Praskovya Fëdorovna, and by means of his official work and the duties attached to it he began struggling with his wife to secure his own independence.

With the birth of their child, the attempts to feed it and the various failures in doing so, and with the real and imaginary illnesses of mother and child, in which Ivan Ilych's sympathy was demanded but about which he understood nothing, the need of securing for himself an existence outside his family life became still more imperative. 75

As his wife grew more irritable and exacting and Ivan Ilych transferred the center of gravity of his life more and more to his official work, so did he grow to like his work better and became more ambitious than before.

Very soon, within a year of his wedding, Ivan Ilych had realized that marriage, though it may add some comforts to life, is in fact a very intricate and difficult affair towards which in order to perform one's duty, that is, to lead a decorous life approved of by society, one must adopt a definite attitude just as towards one's official duties.

And Ivan Ilych evolved such an attitude towards married life. He only required of it those conveniences—dinner at home, housewife, and bed—which it could give him, and above all that propriety of external forms required by public opinion. For the rest he looked for light-hearted pleasure and propriety, and was very thankful when he found them, but if he met with antagonism and querulousness he at once retired into his separate fenced-off world of official duties, where he found satisfaction.

Ivan Ilych was esteemed a good official, and after three years was made Assistant Public Prosecutor. His new duties, their importance, the possibility of indicting and imprisoning anyone he chose, the publicity his speeches received, and the success he had in all these things, made his work still more attractive.

More children came. His wife became more and more querulous and ill-tempered, but the attitude Ivan Ilych had adopted towards his home life rendered him almost impervious to her grumbling. 80

After seven years' service in that town he was transferred to another province as Public Prosecutor. They moved, but were short of money and his wife did not like the place they moved to. Though the salary was higher the cost of living was greater, besides which two of their children died and family life became still more unpleasant for him.

Praskovya Fëdorovna blamed her husband for every inconvenience they encountered in their new home. Most of the conversations between husband and wife, especially as to the children's education, led to topics which recalled former disputes, and those disputes were apt to flare up again at any moment. There remained only those rare periods of amorousness which still came to them at times but did not last long. These were islets at which they anchored for a while and then again set out upon that ocean of veiled hostility which showed itself in their aloofness from one another. This aloofness might have grieved Ivan Ilych had he considered that it ought not to exist, but he now regarded the position as normal, and even made it the goal at which he aimed in family life. His aim was to free himself more and more from those unpleasantnesses and to give them a semblance of harmlessness and propriety. He attained this by spending less and less time with his family, and when obliged to be at home he tried to safeguard his position by the presence of outsiders. The chief thing, however, was that he had his official duties. The whole interest of his life now centered in the official world and that interest absorbed him. The consciousness of his power, being able to ruin anybody he wished to ruin, the importance, even the external dignity of his entry into court, or meetings with his subordinates, his success with superiors and inferiors, and above all his masterly handling of cases, of which he was conscious—all this gave him pleasure and filled his life, together with chats with his colleagues, dinners, and bridge. So that on the whole Ivan Ilych's life continued to flow as he considered it should do—pleasantly and properly.

So things continued for another seven years. His eldest daughter was already sixteen, another child had died, and only one son was left, a schoolboy and a subject of dissension. Ivan Ilych wanted to put him in the School of Law, but to spite him Praskovya Fëdorovna entered him at the High School. The daughter had been educated at home and had turned out well: the boy did not learn badly either.

III

So Ivan Ilych lived for seventeen years after his marriage. He was already a Public Prosecutor of long standing, and had declined several proposed transfers while awaiting a more desirable post, when an unanticipated and unpleasant occurrence quite upset the peaceful course of his life. He was expecting to be offered the post of presiding judge in a University town, but Happe somehow came to the front and obtained the appointment instead. Ivan Ilych became irritable, reproached Happe, and quarreled both with him and with his immediate superiors—who became colder to him and again passed him over when other appointments were made.

This was in 1880, the hardest year of Ivan Ilych's life. It was then that it became evident on the one hand that his salary was insufficient for them to live on, and on the other that he had been forgotten, and not only this, but that what was for him the greatest and most cruel injustice appeared to others a quite ordinary occurrence. Even his father did not consider it his duty to help him. Ivan Ilych felt himself abandoned by everyone, and that they regarded his position with a salary of 3,500 rubles as quite normal and even fortunate. He alone knew that with the consciousness of the injustices done him, with his wife's incessant nagging, and with the debts he had contracted by living beyond his means, his position was far from normal.

In order to save money that summer he obtained leave of absence and went with his wife to live in the country at her brother's place.

In the country, without his work, he experienced *ennui* for the first time in his life, and not only *ennui* but intolerable depression, and he decided that it was impossible to go on living like that, and that it was necessary to take energetic measures.

Having passed a sleepless night pacing up and down the veranda, he decided to go to Petersburg and bestir himself, in order to punish those who had failed to appreciate him and to get transferred to another ministry.

Next day, despite many protests from his wife and her brother, he started for Petersburg with the sole object of obtaining a post with a salary of five thousand rubles a year. He was no longer bent on any particular department, or tendency, or kind of activity. All he now wanted was an appointment to another post with a salary of five thousand rubles, either in the administration, in the banks, with the railways, in one of the Empress Marya's Institutions,° or even in the customs—but it had to carry with it a salary of five thousand rubles and be in a ministry other than that in which they had failed to appreciate him.

And this quest of Ivan Ilych's was crowned with remarkable and unexpected success. At Kursk an acquaintance of his, F. I. Ilyin, got into the first-class carriage, sat down beside Ivan Ilych, and told him of a telegram just received by the Governor of Kursk announcing that a change was about to take place in the ministry: Peter Ivanovich was to be superseded by Ivan Semënovich. 90

The proposed change, apart from its significance for Russia, had a special significance for Ivan Ilych, because by bringing forward a new man, Peter Petrovich, and consequently his friend Zachar Ivanovich, it was highly favorable for Ivan Ilych, since Zachar Ivanovich was a friend and colleague of his.

In Moscow this news was confirmed, and on reaching Petersburg Ivan Ilych found Zachar Ivanovich and received a definite promise of an appointment in his former department of Justice.

A week later he telegraphed to his wife: "Zachar in Miller's place. I shall receive appointment on presentation of report."

Thanks to this change of personnel, Ivan Ilych had unexpectedly obtained an appointment in his former ministry which placed him two stages above his former colleagues besides giving him five thousand rubles salary and three thousand five hundred rubles for expenses connected with his removal. All his ill humor towards his former enemies and the whole department vanished, and Ivan Ilych was completely happy.

He returned to the country more cheerful and contented than he had been for a long time. Praskovya Fëdorovna also cheered up and a truce was arranged between them. Ivan Ilych told of how he had been fêted by everybody in Petersburg, how all those who had been his enemies were put to shame and now fawned on him, how envious they were of his appointment, and how much everybody in Petersburg had liked him. 95

Praskovya Fëdorovna listened to all this and appeared to believe it. She did not contradict anything, but only made plans for their life in the town to which they were going. Ivan Ilych saw with delight that these plans were his plans, that he and his wife agreed, and that, after a stumble, his life was regaining its due and natural character of pleasant lightheartedness and decorum.

Ivan Ilych had come back for a short time only, for he had to take up his new duties on the 10th of September. Moreover, he needed time to settle into the new place, to move all his belongings from the province, and to buy and order many additional things: in a word, to make such arrangements as he had resolved on, which were almost exactly what Praskovya Fëdorovna too had decided on.

Empress Marya's Institutions: orphanages.

Now that everything had happened so fortunately, and that he and his wife were at one in their aims and moreover saw so little of one another, they got on together better than they had done since the first years of marriage. Ivan Ilych had thought of taking his family away with him at once, but the insistence of his wife's brother and her sister-in-law, who had suddenly become particularly amiable and friendly to him and his family, induced him to depart alone.

So he departed, and the cheerful state of mind induced by his success and by the harmony between his wife and himself, the one intensifying the other, did not leave him. He found a delightful house, just the thing both he and his wife had dreamt of. Spacious, lofty reception rooms in the old style, a convenient and dignified study, rooms for his wife and daughter, a study for his son—it might have been specially built for them. Ivan Ilych himself superintended the arrangements, chose the wallpapers, supplemented the furniture (preferably with antiques which he considered particularly *comme il faut*), and supervised the upholstering. Everything progressed and progressed and approached the ideal he had set himself: even when things were only half completed they exceeded his expectations. He saw what a refined and elegant character, free from vulgarity, it would all have when it was ready. On falling asleep he pictured to himself how the reception-room would look. Looking at the yet unfinished drawing-room he could see the fireplace, the screen, the what-not, the little chairs dotted here and there, the dishes and plates on the walls, and the bronzes, as they would be when everything was in place. He was pleased by the thought of how his wife and daughter, who shared his taste in this matter, would be impressed by it. They were certainly not expecting as much. He had been particularly successful in finding, and buying cheaply, antiques which gave a particularly aristocratic character to the whole place. But in his letters he intentionally understated everything in order to be able to surprise them. All this so absorbed him that his new duties—though he liked his official work—interested him less than he had expected. Sometimes he even had moments of absentmindedness during the Court Sessions, and would consider whether he should have straight or curved cornices for his curtains. He was so interested in it all that he often did things himself, rearranging the furniture, or rehanging the curtains. Once when mounting a stepladder to show the upholsterer, who did not understand, how he wanted the hangings draped, he made a false step and slipped, but being a strong and agile man he clung on and only knocked his side against the knob of the window frame. The bruised place was painful but the pain soon passed, and he felt particularly bright and well just then. He wrote: "I feel fifteen years younger." He thought he would have everything ready by September, but it dragged on till mid-October. But the result was charming not only in his eyes but to everyone who saw it.

In reality it was just what is usually seen in the houses of people of moderate means who want to appear rich, and therefore succeed only in resembling others like themselves: there were damasks, dark wood, plants, rugs, and dull and polished bronzes—all the things people of a certain class have in order to resemble other people of that class. His house was so like the others that it would never have been noticed, but to him it all seemed to be quite exceptional. He was very happy when he met his family at the station and brought them to the newly furnished house all lit up, where a footman in a white tie opened the door into the hall decorated with plants, and when they went on into the drawing-room and the study uttering exclamations of delight. He conducted them everywhere, drank in their praises eagerly, and beamed with pleasure. At tea that evening, when Praskovya Fëdorovna among other things asked him about his fall, he laughed and showed them how he had gone flying and had frightened the upholsterer.

"It's a good thing I'm a bit of an athlete. Another man might have been killed, but I merely knocked myself, just here; it hurts when it's touched, but it's passing off already—it's only a bruise."

So they began living in their new home—in which, as always happens, when they got thoroughly settled in they found they were just one room short—and with the increased income, which as always was just a little (some five hundred rubles) too little, but it was all very nice.

Things went particularly well at first, before everything was finally arranged and while something had still to be done: this thing bought, that thing ordered, another thing moved, and something else adjusted. Though there were some disputes between husband and wife, they were both so well satisfied and had so much to do that it all passed off without any serious quarrels. When nothing was left to arrange it became rather dull and something seemed to be lacking, but they were then making acquaintances, forming habits, and life was growing fuller.

Ivan Ilych spent his mornings at the law courts and came home to dinner, and at first he was generally in a good humor, though he occasionally became irritable just on account of his house. (Every spot on the tablecloth or the upholstery, and every broken window-blind string, irritated him. He had devoted so much trouble to arranging it all that every disturbance of it distressed him.) But on the whole his life ran its course as he believed life should do: easily, pleasantly, and decorously.

He got up at nine, drank his coffee, read the paper, and then put on his undress 105 uniform and went to the law courts. There the harness in which he worked had already been stretched to fit him and he donned it without a hitch: petitioners, inquiries at the chancery, the chancery itself, and the sittings public and administrative. In all this the thing was to exclude everything fresh and vital, which always disturbs the regular course of official business, and to admit only official relations with people, and then only on official grounds. A man would come, for instance, wanting some information. Ivan Ilych, as one in whose sphere the matter did not lie, would have nothing to do with him: but if the man had some business with him in his official capacity, something that could be expressed on officially stamped paper, he would do everything, positively everything he could within the limits of such relations, and in doing so would maintain the semblance of friendly human relations, that is, would observe the courtesies of life. As soon as the official relations ended, so did everything else. Ivan Ilych possessed this capacity to separate his real life from the official side of affairs and not mix the two, in the highest degree, and by long practice and natural aptitude had brought it to such a pitch that sometimes, in the manner of a virtuoso, he would even allow himself to let the human and official relations mingle. He let himself do this just because he felt that he could at any time he chose resume the strictly official attitude again and drop the human relation. And he did it all easily, pleasantly, correctly, and even artistically. In the intervals between the sessions he smoked, drank tea, chatted a little about politics, a little about general topics, a little about cards, but most of all about official appointments. Tired, but with the feelings of a virtuoso—one of the first violins who has played his part in an orchestra with precision—he would return home to find that his wife and daughter had been out paying calls, or had a visitor, and that his son had been to school, had done his homework with his tutor, and was duly learning what is taught at High Schools. Everything was as it should be. After dinner, if they had no visitors, Ivan Ilych sometimes read a book that was being much discussed at the time, and in the evening settled down to work, that is, read official papers, compared the depositions of witnesses, and noted paragraphs of the Code applying to them. This was neither dull nor amusing. It was dull when he might have been playing bridge, but if no bridge was available it was at any rate better than doing nothing or sitting with his wife. Ivan Ilych's chief pleasure was giving little dinners to which he invited men and women of good social position, and just as his drawing-room resembled all other drawing-rooms so did his enjoyable little parties resemble all other such parties.

Once they even gave a dance. Ivan Ilych enjoyed it and everything went off well, except that it led to a violent quarrel with his wife about the cakes and sweets. Praskovya Fëdorovna had made her own plans, but Ivan Ilych insisted on getting everything from an expensive confectioner and ordered too many cakes, and the quarrel occurred because some of those cakes were left over and the confectioner's bill came to forty-five rubles. It was a great and disagreeable quarrel. Praskovya Fëdorovna called him "a fool and an imbecile," and he clutched at his head and made angry allusions to divorce.

But the dance itself had been enjoyable. The best people were there, and Ivan Ilych had danced with Princess Trufonova, a sister of the distinguished founder of the Society "Bear My Burden."

The pleasures connected with his work were pleasures of ambition; his social pleasures were those of vanity; but Ivan Ilych's greatest pleasure was playing bridge. He acknowledged that whatever disagreeable incident happened in his life, the pleasure that beamed like a ray of light above everything else was to sit down to bridge with good players, not noisy partners, and of course to four-handed bridge (with five players it was annoying to have to stand out, though one pretended not to mind), to play a clever and serious game (when the cards allowed it), and then to have supper and drink a glass of wine. After a game of bridge, especially if he had won a little (to win a large sum was unpleasant), Ivan Ilych went to bed in specially good humor.

So they lived. They formed a circle of acquaintances among the best people and were visited by people of importance and by young folk. In their views as to their acquaintances, husband, wife, and daughter were entirely agreed, and tacitly and unanimously kept at arm's length and shook off the various shabby friends and relations who, with much show of affection, gushed into the drawing-room with its Japanese plates on the walls. Soon these shabby friends ceased to obtrude themselves and only the best people remained in the Golovins' set.

Young men made up to Lisa, and Petrishchev, an examining magistrate and Dmitri Ivanovich Petrishchev's son and sole heir, began to be so attentive to her that Ivan Ilych had already spoken to Praskovya Fëdorovna about it, and considered whether they should not arrange a party for them, or get up some private theatricals.

So they lived, and all went well, without change, and life flowed pleasantly.

IV

They were all in good health. It could not be called ill health if Ivan Ilych some-times said that he had a queer taste in his mouth and felt some discomfort in his left side.

But this discomfort increased and, though not exactly painful, grew into a sense of pressure in his side accompanied by ill humor. And his irritability became worse and worse and began to mar the agreeable, easy, and correct life that had established itself in the Golovin family. Quarrels between husband and wife became more and more frequent, and soon the ease and amenity disappeared and even the decorum was barely maintained. Scenes again became frequent, and very few of those islets remained on which husband and wife could meet without an explosion. Praskovya Fëdorovna now had good reason to say that her husband's temper was trying. With characteristic exaggeration she said he had always had a dreadful temper, and that it had needed all her good nature to put up with it for twenty years. It was true that now the quarrels were started by him. His bursts of temper always came just before dinner, often just as he began to eat his soup. Sometimes he noticed that a plate or dish was chipped, or the food was not right, or his son put his elbow on the table, or his daughter's hair was not done as he liked it, and for all this he blamed Praskovya Fëdorovna. At first she retorted and said disagreeable things to him, but once or twice he fell into such a rage at the beginning of dinner that she realized it was due to some physical derangement brought on by taking food, and so she restrained herself and did not answer, but only hurried to get the dinner over. She regarded this self-restraint as highly praiseworthy. Having come to the conclusion that her husband had a dreadful temper and made her life miserable, she began to feel sorry for herself, and the more she pitied herself the more she hated her husband. She began to wish he would die; yet she did not want him to die because then his salary would cease. And this irritated her against him still more. She considered herself dreadfully unhappy just because not even his death could save her, and though she concealed her exasperation, that hidden exasperation of hers increased his irritation also.

After one scene in which Ivan Ilych had been particularly unfair and after which he had said in explanation that he certainly was irritable but that it was due to his not being well, she said that if he was ill it should be attended to, and insisted on his going to see a celebrated doctor.

He went. Everything took place as he had expected and as it always does. There was the usual waiting and the important air assumed by the doctor, with which he was so familiar (resembling that which he himself assumed in court), and the sounding and listening, and the questions which called for answers that were foregone conclusions and were evidently unnecessary, and the look of importance which implied that "if only you put yourself in our hands we will arrange everything—we know indubitably how it has to be done, always in the same way for everybody alike." It was all just as it was in the law courts. The doctor put on just the same air towards him as he himself put on towards an accused person. 115

The doctor said that so-and-so indicated that there was so-and-so inside the patient, but if the investigation of so-and-so did not confirm this, then he must assume that and that. If he assumed that and that, then . . . and so on. To Ivan Ilych only one question was important: was his case serious or not? But the doctor ignored that inappropriate question. From his point of view it was not the one under consideration, the real question was to decide between a floating kidney, chronic catarrh, or appendicitis. It was not a question of Ivan Ilych's life or death, but one between a floating kidney and appendicitis. And that question the doctor solved brilliantly, as it seemed to Ivan Ilych, in favor of the appendix, with the reservation that should an examination of the urine give fresh indications the matter would be reconsidered. All this was just what Ivan Ilych had himself brilliantly accomplished a thousand times in dealing with men on trial. The doctor summed up just as brilliantly, looking over his spectacles triumphantly and even gaily at the accused. From the doctor's summing up Ivan Ilych concluded that things were bad, but that for the doctor, and perhaps for everybody else, it was a matter of indifference, though for him it was bad. And this conclusion struck him painfully, arousing in him a great feeling of pity for himself and of bitterness towards the doctor's indifference to a matter of such importance.

He said nothing of this, but rose, placed the doctor's fee on the table, and remarked with a sigh: "We sick people probably often put inappropriate questions. But tell me, in general, is this complaint dangerous, or not? . . ."

The doctor looked at him sternly over his spectacles with one eye, as if to say: "Prisoner, if you will not keep to the questions put to you, I shall be obliged to have you removed from the court."

"I have already told you what I consider necessary and proper. The analysis may show something more." And the doctor bowed.

Ivan Ilych went out slowly, seated himself disconsolately in his sledge, and drove 120 home. All the way home he was going over what the doctor had said, trying to translate those complicated, obscure, scientific phrases into plain language and find in them an answer to the question: "Is my condition bad? Is it very bad? Or is there as yet nothing much wrong?" And it seemed to him that the meaning of what the doctor had said was that it was very bad. Everything in the streets seemed depressing. The cabmen, the houses, the passers-by, and the shops, were dismal. His ache, this dull gnawing ache that never ceased for a moment, seemed to have acquired a new and more serious significance from the doctor's dubious remarks. Ivan Ilych now watched it with a new and oppressive feeling.

He reached home and began to tell his wife about it. She listened, but in the middle of his account his daughter came in with her hat on, ready to go out with her mother. She sat down reluctantly to listen to this tedious story, but could not stand it long, and her mother too did not hear him to the end.

"Well, I am very glad," she said. "Mind now to take your medicine regularly. Give me the prescription and I'll send Gerasim to the chemist's." And she went to get ready to go out.

While she was in the room Ivan Ilych had hardly taken time to breathe, but he sighed deeply when she left it.

"Well," he thought, "perhaps it isn't so bad after all."

He began taking his medicine and following the doctor's directions, which had 125 been altered after the examination of the urine. But then it happened that there was a contradiction between the indications drawn from the examination of the urine and the symptoms that showed themselves. It turned out that what was happening differed from what the doctor had told him, and that he had either forgotten, or blundered, or hidden something from him. He could not, however, be blamed for that, and Ivan Ilych still obeyed his orders implicitly and at first derived some comfort from doing so.

From the time of his visit to the doctor, Ivan Ilych's chief occupation was the exact fulfillment of the doctor's instructions regarding hygiene and the taking of medicine, and the observation of his pain and his excretions. His chief interests came to be people's ailments and people's health. When sickness, deaths, or recoveries were mentioned in his presence, especially when the illness resembled his own, he listened with agitation which he tried to hide, asked questions, and applied what he heard to his own case.

The pain did not grow less, but Ivan Ilych made efforts to force himself to think that he was better. And he could do this so long as nothing agitated him. But as soon as he had any unpleasantness with his wife, any lack of success in his official work, or held bad cards at bridge, he was at once acutely sensible of his disease. He had formerly borne such mischances, hoping soon to adjust what was wrong, to master it and attain success, or make a grand slam. But now every mischance upset him and plunged him into despair. He would say to himself: "There now, just as I was beginning to get better and the medicine had begun to take effect, comes this accursed misfortune, or unpleasantness. . . ." And he was furious with the mishap, or with the people who were causing the unpleasantness and killing him, for he felt that this fury was killing him but could not restrain it. One would have thought that it should have been clear to him that this exasperation with circumstances and people aggravated his illness, and that he ought therefore to ignore unpleasant occurrences. But he drew the very opposite conclusion: he said that he needed peace, and he watched for everything that might disturb it and became irritable at the slightest infringement of it. His condition was rendered worse by the fact that he read medical books and consulted doctors. The progress of his disease was so gradual that he could deceive himself when comparing one day with another—the difference was so slight. But when he consulted the doctors it seemed to him that he was getting worse, and even very rapidly. Yet despite this he was continually consulting them.

That month he went to see another celebrity, who told him almost the same as the first had done but put his questions rather differently, and the interview with this celebrity only increased Ivan Ilych's doubts and fears. A friend of a friend of his, a very good doctor, diagnosed his illness again quite differently from the others, and though he predicted recovery, his questions and suppositions bewildered Ivan Ilych still more and increased his doubts. A homeopathist diagnosed the disease in yet another way, and prescribed medicine which Ivan Ilych took secretly for a week. But after a week, not feeling any improvement and having lost confidence both in the former doctor's treatment and in this one's, he became still more despondent. One day a lady acquaintance mentioned a cure effected by a wonder-working icon. Ivan Ilych caught himself listening attentively and beginning to believe that it had occurred. This incident alarmed him. "Has my mind really weakened to such an extent?" he asked himself. "Nonsense! It's all rubbish. I mustn't give way to nervous fears but having chosen a doctor must keep strictly to his treatment. That is what I will do. Now it's all settled. I won't think about it, but will follow the treatment seriously till summer, and then we shall see. From now there must be no more of this wavering!" This was easy to say but impossible to carry out. The pain in his side oppressed him and seemed to grow worse and more incessant, while the taste in his mouth grew stranger and stranger. It seemed to him that his breath had a disgusting smell, and he was conscious of a loss of appetite and strength. There was no deceiving himself: something terrible, new, and more important than anything before in his life, was taking place within him of which he alone was aware. Those about him did not understand or would not understand it, but thought everything in the world was going on as usual. That tormented Ivan Ilych more than anything. He saw that his household, especially his wife and daughter who were in a perfect whirl of visiting, did not understand anything of it and were annoyed that he was so depressed and so exacting, as if he were to blame for it. Though they tried to disguise it he saw that he was an obstacle in their path, and that his wife had adopted a definite line in regard to his illness and kept to it regardless of anything he said or did. Her attitude was this: "You know," she would say to her friends, "Ivan Ilych can't do as other people do, and keep to the treatment prescribed for him. One day he'll take his drops and keep strictly to his diet and go to bed in good time, but the next day unless I watch him he'll suddenly forget his medicine, eat sturgeon—which is forbidden—and sit up playing cards till one o'clock in the morning."

"Oh, come, when was that?" Ivan Ilych would ask in vexation. "Only once at Peter Ivanovich's."

"And yesterday with Shebek." 130

"Well, even if I hadn't stayed up, this pain would have kept me awake."

"Be that as it may you'll never get well like that, but will always make us wretched."

Praskovya Fëdorovna's attitude to Ivan Ilych's illness, as she expressed it both to others and to him, was that it was his own fault and was another of the annoyances he caused her. Ivan Ilych felt that this opinion escaped her involuntarily— but that did not make it easier for him.

At the law courts too, Ivan Ilych noticed, or thought he noticed, a strange attitude towards himself. It sometimes seemed to him that people were watching him inquisitively as a man whose place might soon be vacant. Then again, his friends would suddenly begin to chaff him in a friendly way about his low spirits, as if the awful, horrible, and unheard-of thing that was going on within him, incessantly gnawing at him and irresistibly drawing him away, was a very agreeable subject for jests. Schwartz in particular irritated him by his jocularity, vivacity, and *savoir-faire*, which reminded him of what he himself had been ten years ago.

Friends came to make up a set and they sat down to cards. They dealt, bending 135 the new cards to soften them, and he sorted the diamonds in his hand and found he had seven. His partner said "No trumps" and supported him with two diamonds. What more could be wished for? It ought to be jolly and lively. They would make a grand slam. But suddenly Ivan Ilych was conscious of that gnawing pain, that taste in his mouth, and it seemed ridiculous that in such circumstances he should be pleased to make a grand slam.

He looked at his partner Mikhail Mikhaylovich, who rapped the table with his strong hand and instead of snatching up the tricks pushed the cards courteously and indulgently towards Ivan Ilych that he might have the pleasure of gathering them up without the trouble of stretching out his hand for them. "Does he think I am too weak to stretch out my arm?" thought Ivan Ilych, and forgetting what he was doing he over-trumped his partner, missing the grand slam by three tricks. And what was most awful of all was that he saw how upset Mikhail Mikhaylovich was about it but did not himself care. And it was dreadful to realize why he did not care.

They all saw that he was suffering, and said: "We can stop if you are tired. Take a rest." Lie down? No, he was not at all tired, and he finished the rubber. All were gloomy and silent. Ivan Ilych felt that he had diffused this gloom over them and could not dispel it. They had supper and went away, and Ivan Ilych was left alone with the consciousness that his life was poisoned and was poisoning the lives of others, and that this poison did not weaken but penetrated more and more deeply into his whole being.

With this consciousness, and with physical pain besides the terror, he must go to bed, often to lie awake the greater part of the night. Next morning he had to get up again, dress, go to the law courts, speak, and write; or if he did not go out, spend at home those twenty-four hours a day each of which was a torture. And he had to live thus all alone on the brink of an abyss, with no one who understood or pitied him.

V

So one month passed and then another. Just before the New Year his brother-in-law came to town and stayed at their house. Ivan Ilych was at the law courts and

Praskovya Fëdorovna had gone shopping. When Ivan Ilych came home and entered his study he found his brother-in-law there—a healthy, florid man—unpacking his portmanteau himself. He raised his head on hearing Ivan Ilych's footsteps and looked up at him for a moment without a word. That stare told Ivan Ilych everything. His brother-in-law opened his mouth to utter an exclamation of surprise but checked himself, and that action confirmed it all.

"I have changed, eh?"

"Yes, there is a change."

And after that, try as he would to get his brother-in-law to return to the subject of his looks, the latter would say nothing about it. Praskovya Fëdorovna came home and her brother went out to her. Ivan Ilych locked the door and began to examine himself in the glass, first full face, then in profile. He took up a portrait of himself taken with his wife, and compared it with what he saw in the glass. The change in him was immense. Then he bared his arms to the elbow, looked at them, drew the sleeves down again, sat down on an ottoman, and grew blacker than night.

"No, no, this won't do!" he said to himself, and jumped up, went to the table, took up some law papers, and began to read them, but could not continue. He unlocked the door and went into the reception-room. The door leading to the drawing-room was shut. He approached it on tiptoe and listened.

"No, you are exaggerating!" Praskovya Fëdorovna was saying.

"Exaggerating! Don't you see it? Why, he's a dead man! Look at his eyes—there's no light in them. But what is it that is wrong with him?"

"No one knows. Nikolaevich said something, but I don't know what. And Leshchetitsky° said quite the contrary . . ."

Ivan Ilych walked away, went to his own room, lay down, and began musing: "The kidney, a floating kidney." He recalled all the doctors had told him of how it detached itself and swayed about. And by an effort of imagination he tried to catch that kidney and arrest it and support it. So little was needed for this, it seemed to him. "No, I'll go to see Peter Ivanovich° again." He rang, ordered the carriage, and got ready to go.

"Where are you going, Jean?" asked his wife, with a specially sad and exceptionally kind look.

This exceptionally kind look irritated him. He looked morosely at her.

"I must go to see Peter Ivanovich."

He went to see Peter Ivanovich, and together they went to see his friend, the doctor. He was in, and Ivan Ilych had a long talk with him.

Reviewing the anatomical and physiological details of what in the doctor's opinion was going on inside him, he understood it all.

There was something, a small thing, in the vermiform appendix. It might all come right. Only stimulate the energy of one organ and check the activity of another, then absorption would take place and everything would come right. He got home rather late for dinner, ate his dinner, and conversed cheerfully, but could not for a long time bring himself to go back to work in his room. At last, however, he went to his study and did what was necessary, but the consciousness that he had put something aside—an important, intimate matter which he would revert to when his work was done—never left him. When he had finished his work he remembered that

Nikolaevich, Leshchetitsky: two doctors, the latter a celebrated specialist. [Translators' note.] *Peter Ivanovich:* That was the friend whose friend was a doctor. [Translators' note.]

this intimate matter was the thought of his vermiform appendix. But he did not give himself up to it, and went to the drawing-room for tea. There were callers there, including the examining magistrate who was a desirable match for his daughter, and they were conversing, playing the piano, and singing. Ivan Ilych, as Praskovya Fëdorovna remarked, spent that evening more cheerfully than usual, but he never for a moment forgot that he had postponed the important matter of the appendix. At eleven o'clock he said good-night and went to his bedroom. Since his illness he had slept alone in a small room next to his study. He undressed and took up a novel by Zola, but instead of reading it he fell into thought, and in his imagination that desired improvement in the vermiform appendix occurred. There was the absorption and evacuation and the re-establishment of normal activity. "Yes, that's it!" he said to himself. "One need only assist nature, that's all." He remembered his medicine, rose, took it, and lay down on his back watching for the beneficent action of the medicine and for it to lessen the pain. "I need only take it regularly and avoid all injurious influences. I am already feeling better, much better." He began touching his side: it was not painful to the touch. "There, I really don't feel it. It's much better already." He put out the light and turned on his side . . . "The appendix is getting better, absorption is occurring." Suddenly he felt the old, familiar, dull, gnawing pain, stubborn and serious. There was the same familiar loathsome taste in his mouth. His heart sank and he felt dazed. "My God! My God!" he muttered. "Again, again! and it will never cease." And suddenly the matter presented itself in a quite different aspect. "Vermiform appendix! Kidney!" he said to himself. "It's not a question of appendix or kidney, but of life and . . . death. Yes, life was there and now it is going, going and I cannot stop it. Yes. Why deceive myself? Isn't it obvious to everyone but me that I'm dying, and that it's only a question of weeks, days . . . it may happen this moment. There was light and now there is darkness. I was here and now I'm going there! Where?" A chill came over him, his breathing ceased, and he felt only the throbbing of his heart.

"When I am not, what will there be? There will be nothing. Then where shall I be when I am no more? Can this be dying? No, I don't want to!" He jumped up and tried to light the candle, felt for it with trembling hands, dropped candle and candle-stick on the floor, and fell back on his pillow.

"What's the use? It makes no difference," he said to himself, staring with wide-open eyes into the darkness. "Death. Yes, death. And none of them knows or wishes to know it, and they have no pity for me. Now they are playing." (He heard through the door the distant sound of a song and its accompaniment.) "It's all the same to them, but they will die too! Fools! I first, and they later, but it will be the same for them. And now they are merry . . . the beasts!" 155

Anger choked him and he was agonizingly, unbearably miserable. "It is impossible that all men have been doomed to suffer this awful horror!" He raised himself.

"Something must be wrong. I must calm myself—must think it all over from the beginning." And he again began thinking. "Yes, the beginning of my illness: I knocked my side, but I was still quite well that day and the next. It hurt a little, then rather more. I saw the doctors, then followed despondency and anguish, more doctors, and I drew nearer to the abyss. My strength grew less and I kept coming nearer and nearer, and now I have wasted away and there is no light in my eyes. I think of the appendix—but this is death! I think of mending the appendix, and all the while here is death! Can it really be death?" Again terror seized him and he gasped for breath. He leant down and began feeling for the matches, pressing with his elbow on the stand beside the bed. It was in his way and hurt him, he grew furious with it, pressed on it still harder, and upset it. Breathless and in despair he fell on his back, expecting death to come immediately.

Meanwhile the visitors were leaving. Praskovya Fëdorovna was seeing them off. She heard something fall and came in.

"What has happened?"

"Nothing. I knocked it over accidentally." 160

She went out and returned with a candle. He lay there panting heavily, like a man who has run a thousand yards, and stared upwards at her with a fixed look.

"What is it, Jean?"

"No . . . o . . . thing. I upset it." ("Why speak of it? She won't understand," he thought.)

And in truth she did not understand. She picked up the stand, lit his candle, and hurried away to see another visitor off. When she came back he still lay on his back, looking upwards.

"What is it? Do you feel worse?" 165

"Yes."

She shook her head and sat down.

"Do you know, Jean, I think we must ask Leshchetitsky to come and see you here."

This meant calling in the famous specialist, regardless of expense. He smiled malignantly and said "No." She remained a little longer and then went up to him and kissed his forehead.

While she was kissing him he hated her from the bottom of his soul and with 170 difficulty refrained from pushing her away.

"Good-night. Please God you'll sleep."

"Yes."

VI

Ivan Ilych saw that he was dying, and he was in continual despair.

In the depth of his heart he knew he was dying, but not only was he not accustomed to the thought, he simply did not and could not grasp it.

The syllogism he had learnt from Kiesewetter's Logic: "Caius is a man, men are 175 mortal, therefore Caius is mortal," had always seemed to him correct as applied to Caius, but certainly not as applied to himself. That Caius—man in the abstract—was mortal, was perfectly correct, but he was not Caius, not an abstract man, but a creature quite, quite separate from all others. He had been little Vanya, with a mamma and a papa, with Mitya and Volodya, with the toys, a coachman and a nurse, afterwards with Katenka and with all the joys, griefs, and delights of childhood, boyhood, and youth. What did Caius know of the smell of that striped leather ball Vanya had been so fond of? Had Caius kissed his mother's hand like that, and did the silk of her dress rustle so for Caius? Had he rioted like that at school when the pastry was bad? Had Caius been in love like that? Could Caius preside at a session as he did? "Caius really was mortal, and it was right for him to die; but for me, little Vanya, Ivan Ilych, with all my thoughts and emotions, it's altogether a different matter. It cannot be that I ought to die. That would be too terrible."

Such was his feeling.

"If I had to die like Caius I should have known it was so. An inner voice would have told me so, but there was nothing of the sort in me and I and all my friends felt that our case was quite different from that of Caius. And now here it is!" he said to himself. "It can't be. It's impossible! But here it is. How is this? How is one to understand it?"

He could not understand it, and tried to drive this false, incorrect, morbid thought away and to replace it by other proper and healthy thoughts. But that thought, and not the thought only but the reality itself, seemed to come and confront him.

And to replace that thought he called up a succession of others, hoping to find in them some support. He tried to get back into the former current of thoughts that had once screened the thought of death from him. But strange to say, all that had formerly shut off, hidden, and destroyed his consciousness of death, no longer had that effect. Ivan Ilych now spent most of his time in attempting to re-establish that old current. He would say to himself: "I will take up my duties again—after all I used to live by them." And banishing all doubts he would go to the law courts, enter into conversation with his colleagues, and sit carelessly as was his wont, scanning the crowd with a thoughtful look and leaning both his emaciated arms on the arms of his oak chair; bending over as usual to a colleague and drawing his papers nearer he would interchange whispers with him, and then suddenly raising his eyes and sitting erect would pronounce certain words and open the proceedings. But suddenly in the midst of those proceedings the pain in his side, regardless of the stage the proceedings had reached, would begin its own gnawing work. Ivan Ilych would turn his attention to it and try to drive the thought of it away, but without success. *It* would come and stand before him and look at him, and he would be petrified and the light would die out of his eyes, and he would again begin asking himself whether *It* alone was true. And his colleagues and subordinates would see with surprise and distress that he, the brilliant and subtle judge, was becoming confused and making mistakes. He would shake himself, try to pull himself together, manage somehow to bring the sitting to a close, and return home with the sorrowful consciousness that his judicial labors could not as formerly hide from him what he wanted them to hide, and could not deliver him from *It*. And what was worst of all was that *It* drew his attention to itself not in order to make him take some action but only that he should look at *It*, look it straight in the face: look at it and, without doing anything, suffer inexpressibly.

And to save himself from this condition Ivan Ilych looked for consolation—new screens—and new screens were found and for a while seemed to save him, but then they immediately fell to pieces or rather became transparent, as if *It* penetrated them and nothing could veil *It*. 180

In these latter days he would go into the drawing-room he had arranged—that drawing-room where he had fallen and for the sake of which (how bitterly ridiculous it seemed) he had sacrificed his life—for he knew that his illness originated with that knock. He would enter and see that something had scratched the polished table. He would look for the cause of this and find that it was the bronze ornamentation of an album, that had got bent. He would take up the expensive album which he had lovingly arranged, and feel vexed with his daughter and her friends for their untidiness—for the album was torn here and there and some of the photographs turned upside down. He would put it carefully in order and bend the ornamentation back into position. Then it would occur to him to place all those things in another corner of the room, near the plants. He would call the footman, but his daughter or wife would come to help him. They would not agree, and his wife would contradict him, and he would dispute and grow angry. But that was all right, for then he did not think about *It*. *It* was invisible.

But then, when he was moving something himself, his wife would say: "Let the servants do it. You will hurt yourself again." And suddenly *It* would flash through the screen and he would see it. It was just a flash, and he hoped it would disappear, but he would involuntarily pay attention to his side. "It sits there as before, gnawing just the same!" And he could no longer forget *It*, but could distinctly see it looking at him from behind the flowers. "What is it all for?"

"It really is so! I lost my life over that curtain as I might have done when storming a fort. Is that possible? How terrible and how stupid. It can't be true! It can't, but it is."

He would go to his study, lie down, and again be alone with *It*: face to face with *It*. And nothing could be done with *It* except to look at it and shudder.

VII

How it happened it is impossible to say because it came about step by step, unnoticed, but in the third month of Ivan Ilych's illness, his wife, his daughter, his son, his acquaintances, the doctors, the servants, and above all he himself, were aware that the whole interest he had for other people was whether he would soon vacate his place, and at last release the living from the discomfort caused by his presence and be himself released from his sufferings.

He slept less and less. He was given opium and hypodermic injections of morphine, but this did not relieve him. The dull depression he experienced in a somnolent condition at first gave him a little relief, but only as something new, afterwards it became as distressing as the pain itself or even more so.

Special foods were prepared for him by the doctors' orders, but all those foods became increasingly distasteful and disgusting to him.

For his excretions also special arrangements had to be made, and this was a torment to him every time—a torment from the uncleanliness, the unseemliness, and the smell, and from knowing that another person had to take part in it.

But just through this most unpleasant matter, Ivan Ilych obtained comfort. Gerasim, the butler's young assistant, always came in to carry the things out. Gerasim was a clean, fresh peasant lad, grown stout on town food and always cheerful and bright. At first the sight of him, in his clean Russian peasant costume, engaged on that disgusting task embarrassed Ivan Ilych.

Once when he got up from the commode too weak to draw up his trousers, he dropped into a soft armchair and looked with horror at his bare, enfeebled thighs with the muscles so sharply marked on them.

Gerasim with a firm light tread, his heavy boots emitting a pleasant smell of tar and fresh winter air, came in wearing a clean Hessian apron, the sleeves of his print shirt tucked up over his strong, bare young arms; and refraining from looking at his sick master out of consideration for his feelings, and restraining the joy of life that beamed from his face, he went up to the commode.

"Gerasim!" said Ivan Ilych in a weak voice.

Gerasim started, evidently afraid he might have committed some blunder, and with a rapid movement turned his fresh, kind, simple young face which just showed the first downy signs of a beard.

"Yes, sir?"

"That must be very unpleasant for you. You must forgive me. I am helpless."

"Oh, why, sir," and Gerasim's eyes beamed and he showed his glistening white teeth, "what's a little trouble? It's a case of illness with you, sir."

And his deft strong hands did their accustomed task, and he went out of the room stepping lightly. Five minutes later he as lightly returned.

Ivan Ilych was still sitting in the same position in the armchair.

"Gerasim," he said when the latter had replaced the freshly washed utensil. "Please come here and help me." Gerasim went up to him. "Lift me up. It is hard for me to get up, and I have sent Dmitri away."

Gerasim went up to him, grasped his master with his strong arms deftly but gently, 200 in the same way that he stepped—lifted him, supported him with one hand, and with the other drew up his trousers and would have set him down again, but Ivan Ilych asked to be led to the sofa. Gerasim, without an effort and without apparent pressure, led him, almost lifting him, to the sofa, and placed him on it.

"Thank you. How easily and well you do it all!"

Gerasim smiled again and turned to leave the room. But Ivan Ilych felt his presence such a comfort that he did not want to let him go.

"One thing more, please move up that chair. No, the other one—under my feet. It is easier for me when my feet are raised."

Gerasim brought the chair, set it down gently in place, and raised Ivan Ilych's legs on to it. It seemed to Ivan Ilych that he felt better while Gerasim was holding up his legs.

"It's better when my legs are higher," he said. "Place that cushion under them." 205

Gerasim did so. He again lifted the legs and placed them, and again Ivan Ilych felt better while Gerasim held his legs. When he set them down Ivan Ilych fancied he felt worse.

"Gerasim," he said. "Are you busy now?"

"Not at all, sir," said Gerasim, who had learnt from the townsfolk how to speak to gentlefolk.

"What have you still to do?"

"What have I to do? I've done everything except chopping the logs for tomor- 210 row."

"Then hold my legs up a bit higher, can you?"

"Of course I can. Why not?" And Gerasim raised his master's legs higher and Ivan Ilych thought that in that position he did not feel any pain at all.

"And how about the logs?"

"Don't trouble about that, sir. There's plenty of time."

Ivan Ilych told Gerasim to sit down and hold his legs, and began to talk to him. 215 And strange to say it seemed to him that he felt better while Gerasim held his legs up.

After that Ivan Ilych would sometimes call Gerasim and get him to hold his legs on his shoulders, and he liked talking to him. Gerasim did it all easily, willingly, simply, and with a good nature that touched Ivan Ilych. Health, strength, and vitality in other people were offensive to him, but Gerasim's strength and vitality did not mortify but soothed him.

What tormented Ivan Ilych most was the deception, the lie, which for some reason they all accepted, that he was not dying but was simply ill, and that he only need keep quiet and undergo a treatment and then something very good would result. He, however, knew that do what they would nothing would come of it, only still more agonizing suffering and death. This deception tortured him—their not wishing to admit what they all knew and what he knew, but wanting to lie to him concerning his terrible condition, and wishing and forcing him to participate in that lie. Those lies—lies enacted over him on the eve of his death and destined to degrade this awful, solemn act to the level of their visitings, their curtains, their sturgeon for dinner—were a terrible agony for Ivan Ilych. And strangely enough, many times when they were going through their antics over him he had been within a hairbreadth of calling out to them: "Stop lying! You know and I know that I am dying. Then at least stop lying about it!" But he had never had the spirit to do it. The awful, terrible act of his dying was, he could see, reduced by those about him to the level of a casual, unpleasant, and almost indecorous incident (as if someone entered a drawing-room diffusing an unpleasant odor) and this was done by that very decorum which he had served all his life long. He saw that no one felt for him, because no one even wished to grasp his position. Only Gerasim recognized it and pitied him. And so Ivan Ilych felt at ease only with him. He felt comforted when Gerasim supported his legs (sometimes all night long) and refused to go to bed, saying: "Don't you worry, Ivan Ilych. I'll get sleep enough later on," or when he suddenly became familiar and exclaimed: "If you weren't sick it would be another matter, but as it is, why should I grudge a little trouble?" Gerasim alone did not lie; everything showed that he alone understood the facts of the case and did not consider it necessary to disguise them, but simply felt sorry for his emaciated and enfeebled master. Once when Ivan Ilych was sending him away he even said straight out: "We shall all of us die, so why should I grudge a little trouble?"—expressing the fact that he did not think his work burdensome, because he was doing it for a dying man and hoped someone would do the same for him when his time came.

Apart from this lying, or because of it, what most tormented Ivan Ilych was that no one pitied him as he wished to be pitied. At certain moments after prolonged suffering he wished most of all (though he would have been ashamed to confess it) for someone to pity him as a sick child is pitied. He longed to be petted and comforted. He knew he was an important functionary, that he had a beard turning grey, and that therefore what he longed for was impossible, but still he longed for it. And in Gerasim's attitude towards him there was something akin to what he wished for, and so that attitude comforted him. Ivan Ilych wanted to weep, wanted to be petted and cried over, and then his colleague Shebek would come, and instead of weeping and being petted, Ivan Ilych would assume a serious, severe, and profound air, and by force of habit would express his opinion on a decision of the Court of Cassation and would stubbornly insist on that view. This falsity around him and within him did more than anything else to poison his last days.

VIII

It was morning. He knew it was morning because Gerasim had gone, and Peter the footman had come and put out the candles, drawn back one of the curtains, and begun quietly to tidy up. Whether it was morning or evening, Friday or Sunday, made no difference, it was all just the same: the gnawing, unmitigated, agonizing pain, never ceasing for an instant, the consciousness of life inexorably waning but not yet extinguished, the approach of that ever dreaded and hateful Death which was the only reality, and always the same falsity. What were days, weeks, hours, in such a case?

"Will you have some tea, sir?"

"He wants things to be regular, and wishes the gentlefolk to drink tea in the morning," thought Ivan Ilych, and only said "No."

220

"Wouldn't you like to move onto the sofa, sir?"

"He wants to tidy up the room, and I'm in the way. I am uncleanliness and disorder," he thought, and said only:

"No, leave me alone."

The man went on bustling about. Ivan Ilych stretched out his hand. Peter came   225
up, ready to help.

"What is it, sir?"

"My watch."

Peter took the watch which was close at hand and gave it to his master.

"Half-past eight. Are they up?"

"No, sir, except Vasily Ivanovich" (the son) "who has gone to school. Praskovya   230
Fëdorovna ordered me to wake her if you asked for her. Shall I do so?"

"No, there's no need to." "Perhaps I'd better have some tea," he thought, and added aloud: "Yes, bring me some tea."

Peter went to the door, but Ivan Ilych dreaded being left alone. "How can I keep him here? Oh yes, my medicine." "Peter, give me my medicine." "Why not? Perhaps it may still do me some good." He took a spoonful and swallowed it. "No, it won't help. It's all tomfoolery, all deception," he decided as soon as he became aware of the familiar, sickly, hopeless taste. "No, I can't believe in it any longer. But the pain, why this pain? If it would only cease just for a moment!" And he moaned. Peter turned towards him. "It's all right. Go and fetch me some tea."

Peter went out. Left alone Ivan Ilych groaned not so much with pain, terrible though that was, as from mental anguish. Always and forever the same, always these endless days and nights. If only it would come quicker! If only *what* would come quicker? Death, darkness? . . . No, no! Anything rather than death!

When Peter returned with the tea on a tray, Ivan Ilych stared at him for a time in perplexity, not realizing who and what he was. Peter was disconcerted by that look and his embarrassment brought Ivan Ilych to himself.

"Oh, tea! All right, put it down. Only help me to wash and put on a clean shirt."   235

And Ivan Ilych began to wash. With pauses for rest, he washed his hands and then his face, cleaned his teeth, brushed his hair, and looked in the glass. He was terrified by what he saw, especially by the limp way in which his hair clung to his pallid forehead.

While his shirt was being changed he knew that he would be still more frightened at the sight of his body, so he avoided looking at it. Finally he was ready. He drew on a dressing-gown, wrapped himself in a plaid, and sat down in the armchair to take his tea. For a moment he felt refreshed, but soon as he began to drink the tea he was again aware of the same taste, and the pain also returned. He finished it with an effort, and then lay down stretching out his legs, and dismissed Peter.

Always the same. Now a spark of hope flashes up, then a sea of despair rages, and always pain; always pain, always despair, and always the same. When alone he had a dreadful and distressing desire to call someone, but he knew beforehand that with others present it would be still worse. "Another dose of morphine—to lose consciousness. I will tell him, the doctor, that he must think of something else. It's impossible, impossible, to go on like this."

An hour and another pass like that. But now there is a ring at the door bell. Perhaps it's the doctor? It is. He comes in fresh, hearty, plump, and cheerful, with that look on his face that seems to say: "There now, you're in a panic about something, but we'll arrange it all for you directly!" The doctor knows this expression is out of place here, but he has put it on once for all and can't take it off—like a man who has put on a frock-coat in the morning to pay a round of calls.

The doctor rubs his hands vigorously and reassuringly. 240

"Brr! How cold it is! There's such a sharp frost; just let me warm myself!" he says, as if it were only a matter of waiting till he was warm, and then he would put everything right.

"Well now, how are you?"

Ivan Ilych feels that the doctor would like to say: "Well, how are our affairs?" but that even he feels that this would not do, and says instead: "What sort of a night have you had?"

Ivan Ilych looks at him as much as to say: "Are you really never ashamed of lying?" But the doctor does not wish to understand this question, and Ivan Ilych says: "Just as terrible as ever. The pain never leaves me and never subsides. If only something . . ."

"Yes, you sick people are always like that. . . . There, now I think I am warm 245 enough. Even Praskovya Fëdorovna, who is so particular, could find no fault with my temperature. Well, now I can say good-morning," and the doctor presses his patient's hand.

Then, dropping his former playfulness, he begins with a most serious face to examine the patient, feeling his pulse and taking his temperature, and then begins the sounding and auscultation.

Ivan Ilych knows quite well and definitely that all this is nonsense and pure deception, but when the doctor, getting down on his knee, leans over him, putting his ear first higher then lower, and performs various gymnastic movements over him with a significant expression on his face, Ivan Ilych submits to it all as he used to submit to the speeches of the lawyers, though he knew very well that they were all lying and why they were lying.

The doctor, kneeling on the sofa, is still sounding him when Praskovya Fëdorovna's silk dress rustles at the door and she is heard scolding Peter for not having let her know of the doctor's arrival.

She comes in, kisses her husband, and at once proceeds to prove that she has been up a long time already, and only owing to a misunderstanding failed to be there when the doctor arrived.

Ivan Ilych looks at her, scans her all over, sets against her the whiteness and 250 plumpness and cleanness of her hands and neck, the gloss of her hair, and the sparkle of her vivacious eyes. He hates her with his whole soul. And the thrill of hatred he feels for her makes him suffer from her touch.

Her attitude towards him and his disease is still the same. Just as the doctor had adopted a certain relation to his patient which he could not abandon, so had she formed one towards him—that he was not doing something he ought to do and was himself to blame, and that she reproached him lovingly for this—and she could not now change that attitude.

"You see he doesn't listen to me and doesn't take his medicine at the proper time. And above all he lies in a position that is no doubt bad for him—with his legs up."

She described how he made Gerasim hold his legs up.

The doctor smiled with a contemptuous affability that said: "What's to be done? These sick people do have foolish fancies of that kind, but we must forgive them."

When the examination was over the doctor looked at his watch, and then 255 Praskovya Fëdorovna announced to Ivan Ilych that it was of course as he pleased, but she had sent today for a celebrated specialist who would examine him and have a consultation with Michael Danilovich (their regular doctor).

"Please don't raise any objections. I am doing this for my own sake," she said ironically, letting it be felt that she was doing it all for his sake and only said this to leave him no right to refuse. He remained silent, knitting his brows. He felt that he was so surrounded and involved in a mesh of falsity that it was hard to unravel anything.

Everything she did for him was entirely for her own sake, and she told him she was doing for herself what she actually was doing for herself, as if that was so incredible that he must understand the opposite.

At half-past eleven the celebrated specialist arrived. Again the sounding began and the significant conversations in his presence and in another room, about the kidneys and the appendix, and the questions and answers, with such an air of importance that again, instead of the real question of life and death which now alone confronted him, the question arose of the kidney and appendix which were not behaving as they ought to and would now be attacked by Michael Danilovich and the specialist and forced to amend their ways.

The celebrated specialist took leave of him with a serious though not hopeless look, and in reply to the timid question Ivan Ilych, with eyes glistening with fear and hope, put to him as to whether there was a chance of recovery, said that he could not vouch for it but there was a possibility. The look of hope with which Ivan Ilych watched the doctor out was so pathetic that Praskovya Fëdorovna, seeing it, even wept as she left the room to hand the doctor his fee.

The gleam of hope kindled by the doctor's encouragement did not last long. The same room, the same pictures, curtains, wallpaper, medicine bottles, were all there, and the same aching suffering body, and Ivan Ilych began to moan. They gave him a subcutaneous injection and he sank into oblivion. 260

It was twilight when he came to. They brought him his dinner and he swallowed some beef tea with difficulty, and then everything was the same again and night was coming on.

After dinner, at seven o'clock, Praskovya Fëdorovna came into the room in evening dress, her full bosom pushed up by her corset, and with traces of powder on her face. She had reminded him in the morning that they were going to the theater. Sarah Bernhardt was visiting the town and they had a box, which he had insisted on their taking. Now he had forgotten about it and her toilet offended him, but he concealed his vexation when he remembered that he had himself insisted on their securing a box and going because it would be an instructive and aesthetic pleasure for the children.

Praskovya Fëdorovna came in, self-satisfied but yet with a rather guilty air. She sat down and asked how he was, but, as he saw, only for the sake of asking and not in order to learn about it, knowing that there was nothing to learn—and then went on to what she really wanted to say: that she would not on any account have gone but that the box had been taken and Helen and their daughter were going, as well as Petrishchev (the examining magistrate, their daughter's fiancé), and that it was out of the question to let them go alone; but that she would have much preferred to sit with him for a while; and he must be sure to follow the doctor's orders while she was away.

"Oh, and Fëdor Petrovich" (the fiancé) "would like to come in. May he? And Lisa?"

"All right."

Their daughter came in in full evening dress, her fresh young flesh exposed (making a show of that very flesh which in his own case caused so much suffering), strong, healthy, evidently in love, and impatient with illness, suffering, and death, because they interfered with her happiness.

Fëdor Petrovich came in too, in evening dress, his hair curled *à la Capoul,*° a tight stiff collar round his long sinewy neck, an enormous white shirtfront, and narrow black trousers tightly stretched over his strong thighs. He had one white glove tightly drawn on, and was holding his opera hat in his hand.

Following him the schoolboy crept in unnoticed, in a new uniform, poor little fellow, and wearing gloves. Terribly dark shadows showed under his eyes, the meaning of which Ivan Ilych knew well.

His son had always seemed pathetic to him, and now it was dreadful to see the boy's frightened look of pity. It seemed to Ivan Ilych that Vasya was the only one besides Gerasim who understood and pitied him.

They all sat down and again asked how he was. A silence followed. Lisa asked   270
her mother about the opera-glasses, and there was an altercation between mother and daughter as to who had taken them and where they had been put. This occasioned some unpleasantness.

Fëdor Petrovich inquired of Ivan Ilych whether he had ever seen Sarah Bernhardt. Ivan Ilych did not at first catch the question, but then replied: "No, have you seen her before?"

"Yes, in *Adrienne Lecouvreur.*"

Praskovya Fëdorovna mentioned some rôles in which Sarah Bernhardt was particularly good. Her daughter disagreed. Conversation sprang up as to the elegance and realism of her acting—the sort of conversation that is always repeated and is always the same.

In the midst of the conversation Fëdor Petrovich glanced at Ivan Ilych and became silent. The others also looked at him and grew silent. Ivan Ilych was staring with glittering eyes straight before him, evidently indignant with them. This had to be rectified, but it was impossible to do so. The silence had to be broken, but for a time no one dared to break it and they all became afraid that the conventional deception would suddenly become obvious and the truth become plain to all. Lisa was the first to pluck up courage and break that silence, but by trying to hide what everybody was feeling, she betrayed it.

"Well, if we are going it's time to start," she said, looking at her watch, a present   275
from her father, and with a faint and significant smile at Fëdor Petrovich relating to something known only to them. She got up with a rustle of her dress.

They all rose, said good-night, and went away.

When they had gone it seemed to Ivan Ilych that he felt better; the falsity had gone with them. But the pain remained—that same pain and that same fear that made everything monotonously alike, nothing harder and nothing easier. Everything was worse.

Again minute followed minute and hour followed hour. Everything remained the same and there was no cessation. And the inevitable end of it all became more and more terrible.

"Yes, send Gerasim here," he replied to a question Peter asked.

à la Capoul: imitating the hairdo of Victor Capoul, a contemporary French singer.

IX

His wife returned late at night. She came in on tiptoe, but he heard her, opened his eyes, and made haste to close them again. She wished to send Gerasim away and to sit with him herself, but he opened his eyes and said: "No, go away."

"Are you in great pain?"

"Always the same."

"Take some opium."

He agreed and took some. She went away.

Till about three in the morning he was in a state of stupefied misery. It seemed to him that he and his pain were being thrust into a narrow, deep black sack, but though they were pushed further and further in they could not be pushed to the bottom. And this, terrible enough in itself, was accompanied by suffering. He was frightened yet wanted to fall through the sack, he struggled but yet cooperated. And suddenly he broke through, fell, and regained consciousness. Gerasim was sitting at the foot of the bed dozing quietly and patiently, while he himself lay with his emaciated stockinged legs resting on Gerasim's shoulders; the same shaded candle was there and the same unceasing pain.

"Go away, Gerasim," he whispered.

"It's all right, sir. I'll stay a while."

"No. Go away."

He removed his legs from Gerasim's shoulders, turned sideways onto his arm, and felt sorry for himself. He only waited till Gerasim had gone into the next room and then restrained himself no longer but wept like a child. He wept on account of his helplessness, his terrible loneliness, the cruelty of man, the cruelty of God, and the absence of God.

"Why hast Thou done all this? Why hast Thou brought me here? Why, why dost Thou torment me so terribly?"

He did not expect an answer and yet wept because there was no answer and could be none. The pain grew more acute, but he did not stir and did not call. He said to himself: "Go on! Strike me! But what is it for? What have I done to Thee? What is it for?"

Then he grew quiet and not only ceased weeping but even held his breath and became all attention. It was as though he was listening not to an audible voice but to the voice of his soul, to the current of thoughts arising within him.

"What is it you want?" was the first clear conception capable of expression in words, that he heard.

"What do you want? What do you want?" he repeated to himself.

"What do I want? To live and not to suffer," he answered.

And again he listened with such concentrated attention that even his pain did not distract him.

"To live? How?" asked his inner voice.

"Why, to live as I used to—well and pleasantly."

"As you lived before, well and pleasantly?" the voice repeated.

And in imagination he began to recall the best moments of his pleasant life. But strange to say none of those best moments of his pleasant life now seemed at all what they had then seemed—none of them except the first recollections of childhood. There, in childhood, there had been something really pleasant with which it would be possible to live if it could return. But the child who had experienced that happiness existed no longer, it was like a reminiscence of somebody else.

As soon as the period began which had produced the present Ivan Ilych, all that had then seemed joys now melted before his sight and turned into something trivial and often nasty.

And the further he departed from childhood and the nearer he came to the present the more worthless and doubtful were the joys. This began with the School of Law. A little that was really good was still found there—there was lightheartedness, friendship, and hope. But in the upper classes there had already been fewer of such good moments. Then during the first years of his official career, when he was in the service of the Governor, some pleasant moments again occurred: they were the memories of love for a woman. Then all became confused and there was still less of what was good; later on again there was still less that was good, and the further he went the less there was. His marriage, a mere accident, then the disenchantment that followed it, his wife's bad breath and the sensuality and hypocrisy; then that deadly official life and those preoccupations about money, a year of it, and two, and ten, and twenty, and always the same thing. And the longer it lasted the more deadly it became. "It is as if I had been going downhill while I imagined I was going up. And that is really what it was. I was going up in public opinion, but to the same extent life was ebbing away from me. And now it is all done and there is only death."

"Then what does it mean? Why? It can't be that life is so senseless and horrible. But if it really has been so horrible and senseless, why must I die and die in agony? There is something wrong!"

"Maybe I did not live as I ought to have done," it suddenly occurred to him. "But how could that be, when I did everything properly?" he replied, and immediately dismissed from his mind this, the sole solution of all the riddles of life and death, as something quite impossible.

"Then what do you want now? To live? Live how? Live as you lived in the law 305 courts when the usher proclaimed 'The judge is coming!' The judge is coming, the judge!" he repeated to himself. "Here he is, the judge. But I am not guilty!" he exclaimed angrily. "What is it for?" And he ceased crying, but turning his face to the wall continued to ponder on the same question: Why, and for what purpose, is there all this horror? But however much he pondered he found no answer. And whenever the thought occurred to him, as it often did, that it all resulted from his not having lived as he ought to have done, he at once recalled the correctness of his whole life and dismissed so strange an idea.

X

Another fortnight passed. Ivan Ilych now no longer left his sofa. He would not lie in bed but lay on the sofa, facing the wall nearly all the time. He suffered ever the same unceasing agonies and in his loneliness pondered always on the same insoluble question: "What is this? Can it be that it is Death?" And the inner voice answered: "Yes, it is Death."

"Why these sufferings?" And the voice answered, "For no reason—they just are so." Beyond and besides this there was nothing.

From the very beginning of his illness, ever since he had first been to see the doctor, Ivan Ilych's life had been divided between two contrary and alternating moods: now it was despair and the expectation of this uncomprehended and terrible death, and now hope and an intently interested observation of the functioning of his organs. Now before his eyes there was only a kidney or an intestine that temporarily evaded its duty, and now only that incomprehensible and dreadful death from which it was impossible to escape.

These two states of mind had alternated from the very beginning of his illness, but the further it progressed the more doubtful and fantastic became the conception of the kidney, and the more real the sense of impending death.

He had but to call to mind what he had been three months before and what he was now, to call to mind with what regularity he had been going downhill, for every possibility of hope to be shattered.

Latterly during that loneliness in which he found himself as he lay facing the back of the sofa, a loneliness in the midst of a populous town and surrounded by numerous acquaintances and relations but that yet could not have been more complete anywhere—either at the bottom of the sea or under the earth—during that terrible loneliness Ivan Ilych had lived only in memories of the past. Pictures of his past rose before him one after another. They always began with what was nearest in time and then went back to what was most remote—to his childhood—and rested there. If he thought of the stewed prunes that had been offered him that day, his mind went back to the raw shrivelled French plums of his childhood, their peculiar flavor and the flow of saliva when he sucked their stones, and along with the memory of that taste came a whole series of memories of those days: his nurse, his brother, and their toys. "No, I mustn't think of that. . . . It is too painful," Ivan Ilych said to himself, and brought himself back to the present—to the button on the back of the sofa and the creases in its morocco. "Morocco is expensive, but it does not wear well: there had been a quarrel about it. It was a different kind of quarrel and a different kind of morocco that time when we tore father's portfolio and were punished, and mamma brought us some tarts. . . ." And again his thoughts dwelt on his childhood, and again it was painful and he tried to banish them and fix his mind on something else.

Then again together with that chain of memories another series passed through his mind—of how his illness had progressed and grown worse. There also the further back he looked the more life there had been. There had been more of what was good in life and more of life itself. The two merged together. "Just as the pain went on getting worse and worse, so my life grew worse and worse," he thought. "There is one bright spot there at the back, at the beginning of life, and afterwards all becomes blacker and blacker and proceeds more and more rapidly—in inverse ratio to the square of the distance from death," thought Ivan Ilych. And the example of a stone falling downwards with increasing velocity entered his mind. Life, a series of increasing sufferings, flies further and further towards its end—the most terrible suffering. "I am flying. . . ." He shuddered, shifted himself, and tried to resist, but was already aware that resistance was impossible, and again, with eyes weary of gazing but unable to cease seeing what was before them, he stared at the back of the sofa and waited—awaiting that dreadful fall and shock and destruction.

"Resistance is impossible!" he said to himself. "If I could only understand what it is all for! But that too is impossible. An explanation would be possible if it could be said that I have not lived as I ought to. But it is impossible to say that," and he remembered all the legality, correctitude, and propriety of his life. "That at any rate can certainly not be admitted," he thought, and his lips smiled ironically as if someone could see that smile and be taken in by it. "There is no explanation! Agony, death. . . . What for?"

XI

Another two weeks went by in this way and during that fortnight an event occurred that Ivan Ilych and his wife had desired. Petrishchev formally proposed. It happened in the evening. The next day Praskovya Fëdorovna came into her husband's room considering how best to inform him of it, but that very night there had been a fresh change for the worse in his condition. She found him still lying on the sofa but in a different position. He lay on his back, groaning and staring fixedly straight in front of him.

She began to remind him of his medicines, but he turned his eyes towards her with such a look that she did not finish what she was saying; so great an animosity, to her in particular, did that look express. 315

"For Christ's sake let me die in peace!" he said.

She would have gone away, but just then their daughter came in and went up to say good morning. He looked at her as he had done at his wife, and in reply to her inquiry about his health said dryly that he would soon free them all of himself. They were both silent and after sitting with him for a while went away.

"Is it our fault?" Lisa said to her mother. "It's as if we were to blame! I am sorry for papa, but why should we be tortured?"

The doctor came at his usual time. Ivan Ilych answered "Yes" and "No," never taking his angry eyes from him, and at last said: "You know you can do nothing for me, so leave me alone."

"We can ease your sufferings." 320

"You can't even do that. Let me be."

The doctor went into the drawing-room and told Praskovya Fëdorovna that the case was very serious and that the only resource left was opium to allay her husband's sufferings, which must be terrible.

It was true, as the doctor said, that Ivan Ilych's physical sufferings were terrible, but worse than the physical sufferings were his mental sufferings, which were his chief torture.

His mental sufferings were due to the fact that one night, as he looked at Gerasim's sleepy, good-natured face with its prominent cheekbones, the question suddenly occurred to him: "What if my whole life has really been wrong?"

It occurred to him that what had appeared perfectly impossible before, namely 325
that he had not spent his life as he should have done, might after all be true. It occurred to him that his scarcely perceptible attempts to struggle against what was considered good by the most highly placed people, those scarcely noticeable impulses which he had immediately suppressed, might have been the real thing, and all the rest false. And his professional duties and the whole arrangement of his life and of his family, and all his social and official interests, might all have been false. He tried to defend all those things to himself and suddenly felt the weakness of what he was defending. There was nothing to defend.

"But if that is so," he said to himself, "and I am leaving this life with the consciousness that I have lost all that was given me and it is impossible to rectify it— what then?"

He lay on his back and began to pass his life in review in quite a new way. In the morning when he saw first his footman, then his wife, then his daughter, and then the doctor, their every word and movement confirmed to him the awful truth that had been revealed to him during the night. In them he saw himself—all that for which he had lived—and saw clearly that it was not real at all, but a terrible and huge deception which had hidden both life and death. This consciousness intensified his physical suffering tenfold. He groaned and tossed about, and pulled at his clothing which choked and stifled him. And he hated them on that account.

He was given a large dose of opium and became unconscious, but at noon his sufferings began again. He drove everybody away and tossed from side to side.

His wife came to him and said:

"Jean, my dear, do this for me. It can't do any harm and often helps. Healthy people often do it." 330

He opened his eyes wide.

"What? Take communion? Why? It's unnecessary! However . . ."

She began to cry.

"Yes, do, my dear. I'll send for our priest. He is such a nice man."

"All right. Very well," he muttered. 335

When the priest came and heard his confession, Ivan Ilych was softened and seemed to feel a relief from his doubts and consequently from his sufferings, and for a moment there came a ray of hope. He again began to think of the vermiform appendix and the possibility of correcting it. He received the sacrament with tears in his eyes.

When they laid him down again afterwards he felt a moment's ease, and the hope that he might live awoke in him again. He began to think of the operation that had been suggested to him. "To live! I want to live!" he said to himself.

His wife came in to congratulate him after his communion, and when uttering the usual conventional words she added:

"You feel better, don't you?"

Without looking at her he said "Yes." 340

Her dress, her figure, the expression of her face, the tone of her voice, all revealed the same thing. "This is wrong, it is not as it should be. All you have lived for and still live for is falsehood and deception, hiding life and death from you." And as soon as he admitted that thought, his hatred and his agonizing physical suffering again sprang up, and with that suffering a consciousness of the unavoidable, approaching end. And to this was added a new sensation of grinding shooting pain and a feeling of suffocation.

The expression of his face when he uttered that "yes" was dreadful. Having uttered it, he looked her straight in the eyes, turned on his face with a rapidity extraordinary in his weak state and shouted:

"Go away! Go away and leave me alone!"

XII

From that moment the screaming began that continued for three days, and was so terrible that one could not hear it through two closed doors without horror. At the moment he answered his wife he realized that he was lost, that there was no return, that the end had come, the very end, and his doubts were still unsolved and remained doubts.

"Oh! Oh! Oh!" he cried in various intonations. He had begun by screaming "I won't!" and continued screaming on the letter O. 345

For three whole days, during which time did not exist for him, he struggled in that black sack into which he was being thrust by an invisible, resistless force. He struggled as a man condemned to death struggles in the hands of the executioner, knowing that he cannot save himself. And every moment he felt that despite all his efforts he was drawing nearer and nearer to what terrified him. He felt that his agony was due to his being thrust into that black hole and still more to his not being able to get right into it. He was hindered from getting into it by his conviction that his life had been a good one. That very justification of his life held him fast and prevented his moving forward, and it caused him most torment of all.

Suddenly some force struck him in the chest and side, making it still harder to breathe, and he fell through the hole and there at the bottom was a light. What had happened to him was like the sensation one sometimes experiences in a railway carriage when one thinks one is going backwards while one is really going forwards and suddenly becomes aware of the real direction.

"Yes, it was all not the right thing," he said to himself, "but that's no matter. It can be done. But what *is* the right thing?" he asked himself, and suddenly grew quiet.

This occurred at the end of the third day, two hours before his death. Just then his schoolboy son had crept softly in and gone up to the bedside. The dying man was still screaming desperately and waving his arms. His hand fell on the boy's head, and the boy caught it, pressed it to his lips, and began to cry.

At that very moment Ivan Ilych fell through and caught sight of the light, and   350
it was revealed to him that though his life had not been what it should have been, this could still be rectified. He asked himself, "What *is* the right thing?" and grew still, listening. Then he felt that someone was kissing his hand. He opened his eyes, looked at his son, and felt sorry for him. His wife came up to him and he glanced at her. She was gazing at him open-mouthed, with undried tears on her nose and cheek and a despairing look on her face. He felt sorry for her too.

"Yes, I am making them wretched," he thought. "They are sorry, but it will be better for them when I die." He wished to say this but had not the strength to utter it. "Besides, why speak? I must act," he thought. With a look at his wife he indicated his son and said: "Take him away . . . sorry for him . . . sorry for you too. . . ." He tried to add, "Forgive me," but said "forgo" and waved his hand, knowing that He whose understanding mattered would understand.

And suddenly it grew clear to him that what had been oppressing him and would not leave him was all dropping away at once from two sides, from ten sides, and from all sides. He was sorry for them, he must act so as not to hurt them: release them and free himself from these sufferings. "How good and how simple!" he thought. "And the pain?" he asked himself. "What has become of it? Where are you, pain?"

He turned his attention to it.

"Yes, here it is. Well, what of it? Let the pain be."

"And death . . . where is it?"   355

He sought his former accustomed fear of death and did not find it. "Where is it? What death?" There was no fear because there was no death.

In place of death there was light.

"So that's what it is!" he suddenly exclaimed aloud. "What joy!"

To him all this happened in a single instant, and the meaning of that instant did not change. For those present his agony continued for another two hours. Something rattled in his throat, his emaciated body twitched, then the gasping and rattle became less and less frequent.

"It is finished!" said someone near him.   360

He heard these words and repeated them in his soul.

"Death is finished," he said to himself. "It is no more!"

He drew in a breath, stopped in the midst of a sigh, stretched out, and died.

Questions

1. Sum up the reactions of Ivan Ilych's colleagues to the news of his death. What is implied in Tolstoy's calling them not friends, but "nearest acquaintances"?

2. What comic elements do you find in the account of the wake that Peter Ivanovich attends?

3. In Tolstoy's description of the corpse and its expression (paragraph 27), what details seem especially revealing and meaningful?

4. Do you think Tolstoy would have improved the story if he had placed the events in chronological order? What would be lost if the opening scene of Ivan Ilych's colleagues at the law courts and the wake scene were to be given last?

5. Would you call Ivan Ilyich, when we first meet him, a religious man? Sum up his goals in life, his values, and his attitudes.

6. By what "virtues" and abilities does Ivan Ilych rise through the ranks? While he continues to succeed in his career, what happens to his marriage?

7. "Every spot on the tablecloth or the upholstery, and every broken window-blind string, irritated him. He had devoted so much trouble to arranging it all that every disturbance of it distressed him" (paragraph 104). What do you make of this passage? What is its tone? Does the narrator sympathize with Ivan Ilych's attachment to his possessions?

8. Consider the account of Ivan Ilych's routine in paragraph 105 ("He got up at nine . . ."). What elements of a full life, what higher satisfactions, does this routine omit?

9. What caused Ivan Ilych's illness? How would it probably be diagnosed today? What is the narrator's attitude toward Ivan Ilych's doctors?

10. In what successive stages does Tolstoy depict Ivan Ilych's growing isolation as his progressive illness sets him more and more apart?

11. What are we apparently supposed to admire in the character and conduct of the servant Gerasim?

12. What do you understand from the statement that Ivan Ilych's justification of his life "prevented his moving forward, and it caused him most torment of all" (paragraph 346)?

13. What is memorable in the character of Ivan Ilych's schoolboy son? Why is he crucial to the story? (Suggestion: Look closely at paragraphs 349–350.)

14. What realization allows Ivan Ilych to triumph over pain? Why does he die peacefully?

15. The writer Henri Troyat has said that through the story of Ivan Ilych we imagine what our own deaths will be. Is it possible to identify with an aging, selfish, worldly, nineteenth-century Russian judge?

Franz Kafka

The Metamorphosis

1915

Translated by John Siscoe

Franz Kafka (1883–1924) was born into a German-speaking Jewish family in Prague, Czechoslovakia (then part of the Austro-Hungarian empire). He was the only surviving son of a domineering, successful father. After earning a law degree, Kafka worked as a claims investigator for the state accident insurance company. He worked on his stories at night, especially during his frequent bouts of insomnia. He never married, and lived mostly with his parents. Kafka was such a careful and self-conscious writer that he found it difficult to finish his work and send it out for publication. During his lifetime he published only a few thin volumes of short fiction, most notably The Metamorphosis *(1915) and* In the Penal

Franz Kafka

Colony (1919). He never finished to his own satisfaction any of his three novels (all published posthumously): The Trial (1925), The Castle (1926), and Amerika (1927). As Kafka was dying of tuberculosis, he begged his friend and literary executor Max Brod to burn his uncompleted manuscripts. Brod pondered this request but luckily didn't obey. Kafka's two major novels, The Trial and The Castle, both depict huge, remote, bumbling, irresponsible bureaucracies in whose power the individual feels helpless and blind. Kafka's works appear startlingly prophetic to readers looking back on them in the later light of Stalinism, World War II, and the Holocaust. His haunting vision of an alienated modern world led the poet W. H. Auden to remark at midcentury, "Had one to name the author who comes nearest to bearing the same kind of relation to our age as Dante, Shakespeare, and Goethe bore to theirs, Kafka is the first one would think of." The Metamorphosis, which arguably has the most famous opening sentence in twentieth-century literature, shows Kafka's dreamlike fiction at its most brilliant and most disturbing.

I

When Gregor Samsa awoke one morning from troubled dreams, he found himself transformed in his bed into a monstrous insect. He was lying on his back, which was hard, as if plated in armor, and when he lifted his head slightly he could see his belly: rounded, brown, and divided into stiff arched segments; on top of it the blanket, about to slip off altogether, still barely clinging. His many legs, which seemed pathetically thin when compared to the rest of his body, flickered helplessly before his eyes.

"What's happened to me?" he thought. It was no dream. His room, a normal though somewhat small human bedroom, lay quietly within its four familiar walls. Above the table on which his unpacked fabric samples were spread—Samsa was a traveling salesman—hung the picture he had recently cut out of an illustrated magazine and had set in a lovely gilt frame. It showed a lady wearing a fur hat and a fur stole, sitting upright, and thrusting out to the viewer a thick fur muff, into which her whole forearm had disappeared.

Gregor's glance then fell on the window, and the overcast sky—one could hear raindrops drumming on the tin sheeting of the windowsill—made him feel profoundly sad. "What if I went back to sleep for a while and forgot all this nonsense," he thought. But that wasn't to be, for he was used to sleeping on his right side and in his present state was unable to get into that position. No matter how hard he threw himself to his right, he would immediately roll onto his back again. He must have tried a hundred times, shutting his eyes so as not to see his wriggling legs, not stopping until he began to feel in his side a slight dull pain that he had never felt before.

"My God," he thought, "what an exhausting job I've chosen! Always on the go, day in and day out. There are far more worries on the road than at the office, what with the constant travel, the nuisance of making your train connections, the wretched meals eaten at odd hours, and the casual acquaintances you meet only in passing, never to see again, never to become intimate friends. To hell with it all!" He felt a slight itch on the surface of his belly. Slowly he shoved himself on his back closer to the bedpost so that he could lift his head more easily. He found the place where it itched. It was covered with small white spots he did not understand. He started to touch it with one of his legs, but pulled back immediately, for the contact sent a cold shiver through him.

He slid back down to his former position. "Getting up this early," he thought, "would turn anyone into an idiot. A man needs his sleep. Other salesmen live like harem women. For example, when I get back to the hotel in the morning to write up the sales I've made, these gentlemen are sitting down to breakfast. If I tried that with my director, I'd be fired on the spot. Actually, that might not be such a bad idea. If I didn't have to curb my tongue because of my parents, I'd have given notice long ago. I'd have gone up to the director and told him from the bottom of my heart exactly what I thought. That would have knocked him from his desk! It's an odd way to run things, this sitting high at a desk and talking down to employees, especially when, since the director is hard of hearing, they have to approach so near. Well, there's hope yet; as soon as I've saved enough money to pay back what my parents owe him—that should take another five or six years—I'll go do it for sure. Then, I'll cut myself completely free. Right now, though, I'd better get up, as my train leaves at five."

He looked at the alarm clock ticking on top of the chest of drawers. "God Almighty!" he thought. It was half past six and the hands were quietly moving forward, it was later than half past, it was nearly a quarter to seven. Hadn't the alarm clock gone off? You could see from the bed that it had been correctly set for four o'clock; of course it must have gone off. Yes, but could he really have slept peacefully through that ear-splitting racket? Well, if he hadn't slept peacefully, he'd slept deeply all the same. But what was he to do now? The next train left at seven, to make it he would have to rush like mad, and his samples weren't even packed, and he himself wasn't feeling particularly spry or alert. And even if he were to make the train, there would be no avoiding a scene with the director. The office messenger would've been waiting for the five o'clock train and would've long since reported his not showing up. The messenger, dim-witted and lacking a will of his own, was a tool of the director. Well, what if he were to call in sick? But that would look embarrassing and suspicious since in his five years with the firm Gregor had not been sick once. The director himself was sure to come over with the health insurance doctor, would upbraid his parents for their son's laziness, and would cut short all excuses by deferring to the doctor, who believed that everyone in the world was a perfectly healthy layabout. And really, would he be so wrong in this case? Apart from a drowsiness that was hard to account for after such a long sleep, Gregor really felt quite well, and in fact was exceptionally hungry.

As he was thinking all this at top speed, without being able to make up his mind to get out of bed—the alarm clock had just struck a quarter to seven—a cautious tap sounded on the door behind his head. "Gregor," said a voice—it was his mother—"it's a quarter to seven. Don't you have a train to catch?" That gentle voice! Gregor was shocked when he heard his own voice answering hers; unmistakably his own voice, true, but mixed in with it, like an undertone, a miserable squeaking that allowed the words to be clearly heard only for a moment before rising up, reverberating, to drown out their meaning, so that no one could be sure if he had heard them correctly. Gregor wanted to answer fully and give a complete explanation, but under the circumstances he merely said, "Yes, yes, thank you, Mother, I'm just getting up." Through the wooden door between them the change in Gregor's voice was probably not obvious, for his mother, quietly accepting his words, shuffled away. However, this brief exchange had made the rest of the family aware that Gregor, surprisingly, was still in the house, and already at one of the side doors his father was knocking, softly, yet with his fist. "Gregor, Gregor," he called, "what's the matter?" Before long he called once more in a deeper voice, "Gregor? Gregor?" From the other side door came the sound of his sister's voice, gentle and plaintive. "Gregor, aren't you feeling well? Is there anything I can get you?" Gregor answered the two of them at the same time: "I'm almost ready." He tried hard to keep his voice from sounding strange by enunciating the words with great care, and by inserting long pauses between the words. His father went back to his breakfast but his sister whispered, "Gregor, please, open the door." But Gregor had no intention of opening the door, and was thankful for having formed, while traveling, the prudent habit of keeping all his doors locked at night, even at home.

What he wanted to do now was to get up quietly and calmly, to get dressed, and above all to eat his breakfast. Only then would he think about what to do next, for he understood that mulling things over in bed would lead him nowhere. He remembered how often in the past he had felt some small pain in bed, perhaps caused by lying in an uncomfortable position, which as soon as he had gotten up had proven to be purely imaginary, and he looked forward to seeing how this morning's fancies would gradually fade and disappear. As for the change in his voice, he hadn't the slightest doubt that it was nothing more than the first sign of a severe cold, an occupational hazard of traveling salesmen.

Throwing off the blanket was easy enough; he had only to puff himself up a little and it slipped right off. But the next part was difficult, especially as he was so unusually wide. He would have needed arms and legs to lift himself up; instead he had only these numerous little legs that never stopped moving and over which he had no control at all. As soon as he tried to bend one of them it would straighten itself out, and if he finally succeeded in making it do as he wished, all the others, as if set free, would waggle about in a high degree of painful agitation. "But what's the point of lying uselessly in bed?" Gregor said to himself.

He thought that he might start by easing the lower part of his body out of bed first, but this lower part, which incidentally he hadn't yet seen and of which he couldn't form a clear picture, turned out to be very difficult to budge—it went so slowly. When finally, almost in a frenzy, he gathered his strength and pushed forward desperately, he miscalculated his direction and bumped sharply against the post at the foot of the bed, and the searing pain he felt told him that, for right now at least, it was exactly this lower part of his body that was perhaps the most tender.

So he tried getting the top part of his body out first, and cautiously turned his head towards the side of the bed. This proved easy enough, and eventually, despite its breadth and weight the bulk of his body slowly followed the turning of his head. But when he finally got his head out over the edge of the bed he felt too afraid to go any farther, for if he were to let himself fall from this position only a miracle would prevent him from hurting his head. And it was precisely now, at all costs, that he must not lose consciousness; he would be better off staying in bed.

But when after repeating his efforts he lay, sighing, in his former position, and once more watched his little legs struggling with one another more furiously than ever, if that were possible, and saw no way of bringing calm and order into this mindless confusion, he again told himself that it was impossible to stay in bed and that the wisest course would be to stake everything on the hope, however slight, of getting away from the bed. At the same time he didn't forget to remind himself that the calmest of calm reflection was much better than frantic resolutions. During this time he kept his eyes fixed as firmly as possible on the window, but unfortunately the morning fog, which shrouded even the other side of the narrow street, gave him little comfort and

10

cheer. "Already seven o'clock," he said to himself when the alarm clock chimed again, "already seven and still such a thick fog." And for some time he lay still, breathing quietly, as if in the hope that utter stillness would bring all things back to how they really and normally were.

But then he said to himself: "I must make sure that I'm out of bed before it strikes a quarter past seven. Anyway, by then someone from work will have come to check on me, since the office opens before seven." And he immediately set the whole length of his body rocking with a rhythmic motion in order to swing out of bed. If he tumbled out this way he could prevent his head from being injured by keeping it tilted upward as he fell. His back seemed to be hard; the fall onto the carpet would probably not hurt it. His greatest worry was the thought of the loud crash he was bound to make; it would probably cause anxiety, if not outright fear, on the other side of the doors. Yet he had to take the chance.

When Gregor was already half out of bed—his new technique made it more of a game than a struggle, since all he had to do was to edge himself across by rocking back and forth—it struck him how simple it would be if he could get someone to help him. Two strong people—he thought of his father and the maid—would be more than enough. All they would have to do would be to slip their arms under his curved back, lift him out of bed, bend down with their burden, and then wait patiently while he flipped himself right side up onto the floor, where, one might hope, his little legs would acquire some purpose. Well then, aside from the fact that the doors were locked, wouldn't it be a good idea to call for help? In spite of his misery, he could not help smiling at the thought.

He had reached the point where, if he rocked any harder, he was in danger of los-   15
ing his balance, and very soon he would have to commit himself, because in five min-
utes it would be a quarter past seven—when the doorbell rang. "It's someone from the office," he said to himself, and almost froze, while his little legs danced even faster. For a moment everything remained quiet. "They won't open the door," Gregor said to himself, clutching at an absurd sort of hope. But then, of course, the maid, as usual, went with her firm tread to the door and opened it. Gregor had only to hear the visitor's first word of greeting to know at once who it was—the office manager himself. Why was Gregor condemned to work for a firm where the most insignificant failure to appear instantly provoked the deepest suspicion? Were the employees, one and all, nothing but scoundrels? Wasn't there among them one man who was true and loyal, who if, one morning, he were to waste an hour or so of the firm's time, would become so conscience-stricken as to be driven out of his mind and actually rendered incapable of leaving his bed? Wouldn't it have been enough to send an office boy to ask—that is, if such prying were necessary at all? Did the office manager have to come in person, and thus demonstrate to an entire family of innocent people that he was the only one wise enough to properly investigate this suspicious affair? And it was more from the anxiety caused by these thoughts than by any act of will that Gregor swung himself out of bed with all his might. There was a loud thump, but not really a crash. The car-pet broke his fall somewhat, and his back too was more elastic than he had thought, so there was only a muffled thud that was relatively unobtrusive. However, he had not lifted his head carefully enough and had banged it; he twisted it and rubbed it against the carpet in frustration and pain.

"Something fell down in there," said the office manager in the room on the left. Gregor tried to imagine whether something like what had happened to him today might one day happen to the office manager; really, one had to admit that it was possible. But as if in a blunt reply to this question the office manager took several determined steps in the next room and his patent leather boots creaked. From the room on the right his sister was whispering to let him know what was going on: "Gregor, the office manager is here." "I know," said Gregor to himself, but he didn't dare speak loudly enough for his sister to hear him.

"Gregor," his father now said from the room on the left, "the office manager is here and he wants to know why you weren't on the early train. We don't know what to tell him. Besides, he wants to speak to you in person. So please open the door. I'm sure he'll be kind enough to excuse any untidiness in your room." "Good morning, Mr. Samsa," the manager was calling out amiably. "He isn't feeling well," said his mother to the manager, while his father was still speaking at the door. "He's not well, sir, believe me. Why else would Gregor miss his train? The boy thinks of nothing but his work. It nearly drives me to distraction the way he never goes out in the evening; he's been here the last eight days, and every single evening he's stayed at home. He just sits here at the table with us quietly reading the newspapers or looking over train schedules. The only enjoyment he gets is when he's working away with his fretsaw.° For example, he spent two or three evenings cutting out a little picture frame, you'd be surprised at how pretty it is, it's hanging in his room, you'll see it in a minute as soon as Gregor opens the door. By the way, I'm glad you've come, sir, we would've never have gotten him to unlock the door by ourselves, he's so stubborn; and I'm sure he's sick, even though he wouldn't admit it this morning." "I'm coming right now," said Gregor, slowly and carefully and not moving an inch for fear of missing a single word of the conversation. "I can't imagine any other explanation, madam," said the office manager, "I hope it's nothing serious. But on the other hand businessmen such as ourselves—fortunately or unfortunately—very often have to ignore any minor indisposition, since the demands of business come first." "So, can the office manager come in now?" asked Gregor's father impatiently, once more knocking on the door. "No," said Gregor. In the room on the left there was an embarrassed silence; in the room on the right his sister began to sob.

But why didn't his sister go and join the others? Probably because she had just gotten out of bed and hadn't even begun to dress yet. Then why was she crying? Because he was in danger of losing his job, and because the director would start once again dunning his parents for the money they owed him? Yet surely these were matters one didn't need to worry about just now. Gregor was still here, and hadn't the slightest intention of deserting the family. True, at the moment he was lying on the carpet, and no one aware of his condition could seriously expect him to let the office manager in. But this minor discourtesy, for which in good time an appropriate excuse could easily be found, was unlikely to result in Gregor's being fired on the spot. And it seemed to Gregor far more sensible for them now to leave him in peace than to bother him with their tears and entreaties. But the uncertainty that preyed upon them excused their behavior.

"Mr. Samsa," the office manager now called in a louder voice, "what's the matter with you? You've barricaded yourself in your room, giving only yes or no answers, causing your parents a great deal of needless grief and neglecting—I mention this only in passing—neglecting your business responsibilities to an unbelievable degree. I am speaking now in the name of your parents and of your director, and I beg you in

fretsaw: saw with a long, narrow, fine-toothed blade, for cutting thin wooden boards or metal plates into patterns.

all seriousness to give me a complete explanation at once. I'm amazed at you, simply amazed. I took you for a calm and reliable person, and now all at once you seem determined to make a ridiculous spectacle of yourself. Earlier this morning the director did suggest to me a possible explanation for your disappearance—I'm referring to the sums of cash that were recently entrusted to you—but I practically swore on my solemn word of honor that this could not be. However, now when I see how incredibly stubborn you are, I no longer have the slightest desire to defend you. And your position with the firm is by no means secure. I came intending to tell you all this in private, but since you're so pointlessly wasting my time I don't see why your parents shouldn't hear it as well. For some time now your work has left much to be desired. We are aware, of course, that this is not the prime season for doing business; but a season for doing no business at all—that, Mr. Samsa, does not and must not exist."

"But sir," Gregor called out distractedly, forgetting everything else in his excitement, "I'm on the verge of opening the door right now. A slight indisposition, a dizzy spell, has prevented me from getting up. I'm still in bed. But I'm feeling better already. I'm getting up now. Please be patient for just a moment. It seems I'm not quite as well as I thought. But really I'm all right. Something like this can come on so suddenly! Only last night I was feeling fine, as my parents can tell you, or actually I did have a slight premonition. I must have shown some sign of it. Oh, why didn't I report it to the office! But one always thinks one can get better without having to stay at home. Please, sir, have mercy on my parents! None of what you've just accused me of has any basis in fact; no one has even spoken a word to me about it. Perhaps you haven't seen the latest orders I've sent in. Anyway, I can still make the eight o'clock train. Don't let me keep you, sir, I'll be showing up at the office very soon. Please be kind enough to inform them, and convey my best wishes to the director."

And while hurriedly blurting all this out, hardly knowing what he was saying, Gregor had reached the chest of drawers easily enough, perhaps because of the practice he had already gotten in bed, and was now trying to use it to lift himself upright. For he actually wanted to open the door, actually intended to show himself, and to talk with the manager; he was eager to find out what the others, who now wanted to see him so much, would say at the sight of him. If they recoiled in horror then he would take no further responsibility and could remain peaceably where he was. But if they took it all in stride then he too had no reason to be upset, and, if he hurried, could even get to the station by eight. The first few times, he slipped down the polished surface of the chest, but finally with one last heave he stood upright. He no longer paid attention to the burning pains in his abdomen, no matter how they hurt. Then, allowing himself to fall against the backrest of a nearby chair, he clung to its edges with his little legs. Now he was once more in control of himself; he fell silent, and was able to hear what the manager was saying.

"Did you understand a single word?" the office manager was asking his parents. "He's not trying to make fools of us, is he?" "My God," cried his mother, already in tears, "maybe he's seriously ill and we're tormenting him. Grete! Grete!" she shouted then. "Mother!" called his sister from the other side. They were calling to each other across Gregor's room. "You must go to the doctor at once. Gregor is sick. Go get the doctor now. Did you hear how Gregor was speaking?" "That was the voice of an animal," said the manager in a tone that was noticeably restrained compared to his mother's shrillness. "Anna! Anna!" his father shouted through the hall to the kitchen, clapping his hands, "get a locksmith and hurry!" And the two girls, their skirts rustling, were already running down the hall—how could his sister have gotten

20

dressed so quickly?—and were pulling the front door open. There was no sound of its being shut; evidently they had left it standing open, as is the custom in houses stricken by some great sorrow.

But Gregor now felt much calmer. Though the words he spoke were apparently no longer understandable, they seemed clear enough to him, even clearer than before, perhaps because his hearing had grown accustomed to their sound. In any case, people were now convinced that something was wrong with him, and were ready to help him. The confidence and assurance with which these first measures had been taken comforted him. He felt himself being drawn back into the human circle and hoped for marvelous and astonishing results from both doctor and locksmith, without really drawing a distinction between them. To ready his voice for the crucial discussion that was now almost upon him, to make it sound as clear as possible, he coughed slightly, as quietly as he could, since for all he knew it might sound different from human coughing. Meanwhile in the next room there was utter silence. Perhaps his parents and the manager were sitting at the table, whispering; perhaps they were, all of them, leaning against the door, listening.

Gregor slowly advanced on the door, pushing the chair in front of him. Then he let go of it, grabbed onto the door for support—the pads at the end of his little legs were somewhat sticky—and, leaning against it, rested for a moment after his efforts. Then he started to turn the key in the lock with his mouth. Unfortunately, he didn't really have any teeth—how was he going to grip the key?—but to make up for that he clearly had very powerful jaws; with their help he was in fact able to start turning the key, paying no attention to the fact that he was surely hurting them somehow, for a brown liquid poured out of his mouth, flowed over the key, and dripped onto the floor. "Listen," said the manager on the other side of the door, "he's turning the key." This was a great encouragement to Gregor, but they should all have been cheering him on, his mother and his father too. "Come on, Gregor," they should have been shouting, "keep at it, hold on to that key!" And, imagining that they were all intently following his efforts, he grimly clamped his jaws on the key with all his might. As the key continued to turn he danced around the lock, holding himself by his mouth alone, either hanging onto the key or pressing down on it with the full weight of his body, as the situation required. The sharper sound of the lock as it finally snapped free woke Gregor up completely. With a sigh of relief he said to himself, "So I didn't need the locksmith after all," and he pressed his head down on the handle to open one wing of the double door.

Because he had to pull the wing in towards him, even when it stood wide open   25
he remained hidden from view. He had to edge slowly around this wing and to do it very carefully or he would fall flat on his back as he made his entrance. He was still busy carrying out this maneuver, with no time to notice anything else, when he heard the manager give a loud "Oh!"—it sounded like a gust of wind—and now he could see him, standing closest to the door, his hand over his open mouth, slowly backing away as if propelled by the relentless pressure of some invisible force. His mother—in spite of the manager's presence, she was standing there with her hair still unpinned and sticking out in all directions—first folded her hands and looked at Gregor's father, then took two steps forward and sank to the floor, her skirts billowing out all around her and her face completely buried in her breast. His father, glowering, clenched his fist, as if he intended to drive Gregor back into his room; then he looked around the living room with uncertainty, covered his eyes with his hands, and wept so hard his great chest shook.

Now Gregor made no attempt to enter the living room, but leaned against the locked wing of the double door, so that only half of his body was visible, with his head above it cocked to one side, peering at the others. Meanwhile the daylight had grown much brighter; across the street one could clearly see a section of the endless, dark gray building opposite—it was a hospital—with a row of uniform windows starkly punctuating its facade. The rain was still falling, but only in large, visibly separate drops that looked as though they were being flung, one by one, onto the earth. On the table the breakfast dishes were set out in lavish profusion, for breakfast was the most important meal of the day for Gregor's father, who lingered over it for hours while reading various newspapers. Hanging on the opposite wall was a photograph of Gregor from his army days, showing him as a lieutenant, with his hand on his sword and his carefree smile demanding respect for his bearing and his rank. The door to the hall stood open, and as the front door was open too, one could see the landing beyond and the top of the stairs going down.

"Well," said Gregor, who was perfectly aware that he was the only one who had kept his composure, "I'll go now and get dressed, pack up my samples, and be on my way. You will, you will let me go, won't you? You can see, sir, that I'm not stubborn and I'm willing to work; the life of a traveling salesman is hard, but I couldn't live without it. Where are you going, sir? To the office? You are? Will you give an honest report about all this? A man may be temporarily unable to work, but that's just the time to remember the service he has rendered in the past, and to bear in mind that later on, when the present problem has been resolved, he is sure to work with even more energy and diligence than before. As you know very well, I am deeply obligated to the director. At the same time, I'm responsible for my parents and my sister. I'm in a tight spot right now, but I'll get out of it. Don't make things more difficult for me than they already are. Stand up for me at the office! People don't like traveling salesmen, I know. They think they make scads of money and lead lives of luxury. And there's no compelling reason for them to revise this prejudice. But you, sir, have a better understanding of things than the rest of the staff, a better understanding, if I may say so, than even the director himself, who, since he is the owner, can be easily swayed against an employee. You also know very well that a traveling salesman, who is away from the office for most of the year, can so easily fall victim to gossip and bad luck and groundless accusations, against which he is powerless to defend himself since he knows nothing about them until, returning home exhausted from his journeys, he suffers personally from evil consequences that can no longer be traced back to their origins. Sir, please don't go away without giving me some word to show that you think that I'm at least partly right!"

But the office manager had turned away at Gregor's first words, and was looking at him now over one twitching shoulder, his mouth agape. And during Gregor's speech he didn't stand still for even a moment, but without once taking his eyes off him kept edging towards the door, yet very slowly, as if there were some secret injunction against his leaving the room. He was already in the hall, and from the suddenness with which he took his last step out of the living room, one might have thought he had burned the sole of his foot. But once in the hall, he stretched out his right hand as far as possible in the direction of the staircase, as if some supernatural rescuer awaited him there.

Gregor realized that he could not let the manager leave in this frame of mind, or his position with the firm would be in extreme jeopardy. His parents were incapable of clearly grasping this; over the years they had come to believe that Gregor was set for life with this firm, and besides they were now so preoccupied with their immediate problems that they had lost the ability to foresee events. But Gregor had this ability. The manager must be overtaken, calmed, swayed, and finally convinced; the future of Gregor and of his family depended on it! If only his sister were here—she was perceptive; she had already begun to cry while Gregor was still lying calmly on his back. And surely the manager, that ladies' man, would've listened to her; she would've shut the door behind them and in the hall talked him out of his fright. But his sister wasn't there, and he would have to handle this himself. And forgetting that he had no idea what his powers of movement were, and forgetting as well that once again his words would possibly, even probably, be misunderstood, he let go of the door, pushed his way through the opening, and started towards the manager, who by now was on the landing, clinging in a ridiculous manner to the banister with both hands. But as Gregor reached out for support, he immediately fell down with a little cry onto his numerous legs. The moment this happened he felt, for the first time that morning, a sense of physical well-being. His little legs had solid ground under them, and, he noticed with joy, they were at his command, and were even eager to carry him in whatever direction he might desire; and he already felt sure that the final recovery from all his misery was at hand. But at that very moment, as he lay on the floor rocking with suppressed motion, not far from his mother and just opposite her, she, who had seemed so completely overwhelmed, leapt to her feet, stretched her arms out wide, spread her fingers, and cried, "Help! For God's sake, help!" She then craned her neck forward as if to see Gregor better, but at the same time, inconsistently, backed away from him. Forgetting that the table with all its dishes was behind her, she sat down on it, and, as if in a daze when she bumped into it, seemed utterly unaware that the large coffee pot next to her had tipped over and was pouring out a flood of coffee onto the carpet.

"Mother, Mother," said Gregor gently, looking up at her. For the moment he   30 had completely forgotten the office manager; on the other hand, he couldn't resist snapping his jaws a few times at the sight of the streaming coffee. This made his mother scream again; she ran from the table and into the outstretched arms of his father, who came rushing to her. But Gregor had no time now for his parents. The manager had already reached the staircase; with his chin on the banister railing, he was looking back for the last time. Gregor darted forward, to be as sure as possible of catching up with him, but the manager must have guessed his intention, for he sprinted down several steps and disappeared. He was still yelling "Oohh!" and the sound echoed throughout the stairwell.

Unfortunately the manager's escape seemed to make his father, who until now had seemed reasonably calm, lose all sense of proportion. Instead of running after the man himself, or at least not interfering with Gregor's pursuit, he grabbed with his right hand the manager's cane, which he had left behind, together with his hat and overcoat, on the chair; with his left hand he snatched up a large newspaper from the table. He began stamping his feet and waving the cane and newspaper in order to drive Gregor back into his room. Nothing Gregor said made any difference, indeed, nothing he said was even understood. No matter how humbly he lowered his head his father only stamped the louder. Behind his father his mother, despite the cold, had flung open a window and was leaning far outside it, her face in her hands. A strong breeze from the street blew across the room to the stairwell, the window curtains billowed inwards, the newspapers fluttered on the table, stray pages skittered across the floor. His father, hissing like a savage, mercilessly drove him back. But as

Gregor had had no practice in walking backwards, it was a very slow process. If he had been given a chance to turn around then he would've gotten back into his room at once, but he was afraid that the length of time it would take him to turn around would exasperate his father and that at any moment the cane in his father's hand might deal him a fatal blow on his back or his head. In the end, though, he had no choice, for he noticed to his horror that while moving backwards he couldn't even keep a straight course. And so, looking back anxiously, he began turning around as quickly as possible, which in reality was very slowly. Perhaps his father divined his good intentions, for he did not interfere, and even helped to direct the maneuver from afar with the tip of his cane. If only he would stop that unbearable hissing! It made Gregor completely lose his concentration. He had turned himself almost all the way around when, confused by this hissing, he made a mistake and started turning back the wrong way. But when at last he'd succeeded in getting his head in front of the doorway, he found that his body was too wide to make it through. Of course his father, in the state he was in, couldn't even begin to consider opening the other wing of the door to let Gregor in. His mind was on one thing only: to drive Gregor back into this room as quickly as possible. He would never have permitted the complicated preparations necessary for Gregor to haul himself upright and in that way perhaps slip through. Instead, making even more noise, he urged Gregor forward as if the way were clear. To Gregor the noise behind him no longer sounded like the voice of merely one father; this really wasn't a joke, and Gregor squeezed himself into the doorway, heedless of the consequences. One side of his body lifted up, he was pitched at an angle in the doorway; the other side was scraped raw, ugly blotches stained the white door. Soon he was stuck fast and couldn't have moved any further by himself. On one side his little legs hung trembling in the air, while those on the other were painfully crushed against the floor—when, from behind, his father gave him a hard blow that was truly a deliverance, and bleeding profusely, he flew far into his room. Behind him the door was slammed shut with the cane, and then at last everything was still.

II

It was already dusk when Gregor awoke from a deep, almost comatose sleep. Surely, even if he hadn't been disturbed he would've soon awakened by himself, since he'd rested and slept long enough; yet it seemed to him that he'd been awakened by the sound of hurried steps and the furtive closing of the hallway door. The light from the electric streetlamps cast pale streaks here and there on the ceiling and the upper part of the furniture, but down below, where Gregor was, it was dark. Groping awkwardly with the feelers which he was only now beginning to appreciate, he slowly pushed himself over to the door to see what had been going on there. His left side felt as if it were one long, painfully tightening scar, and he was actually limping on his two rows of legs. One little leg, moreover, had been badly hurt during the morning's events—it was nearly miraculous that only one had been hurt—and it trailed along lifelessly.

Only when he reached the door did he realize what had impelled him forward—the smell of something to eat. For there stood a bowl full of fresh milk, in which floated small slices of white bread. He could almost have laughed for joy, since he was even hungrier now than he'd been during the morning, and he immediately dipped his head into the milk, almost up to his eyes. But he soon drew it back in disappointment; not only did he find it difficult to eat because of the soreness in his left side—and he was capable of eating only if his whole gasping body cooperated—but also because he didn't like the milk at all, although it had once been his favorite drink, which, no doubt, was why his sister had brought it in. In fact, he turned away from the bowl almost in disgust, and crawled back to the middle of the room.

In the living room, as Gregor could see through the crack in the door, the gaslight had been lit. But while this was the hour when his father would usually be reading the afternoon paper in a loud voice to his mother and sometimes to his sister as well, now there wasn't a sound to be heard. Well, perhaps this custom of reading aloud, which his sister was always telling him about or mentioning in her letters, had recently been discontinued. Still, though the apartment was completely silent, it was scarcely deserted. "What a quiet life the family's been leading," said Gregor to himself, and, staring fixedly into the darkness, he felt a genuine pride at having been able to provide his parents and his sister with such a life in such a nice apartment. But what if all this calm, prosperity, and contentment were to end in horror? So as not to give in to such thoughts, Gregor set himself in motion, and he crawled up and down the room.

Once during the long evening first one of the side doors and then the other was 35 opened a crack and then quickly shut. Someone, it seemed, had wanted to come in but then had thought better of it. Gregor now stationed himself so as to somehow get the hesitant visitor to come in or at least to find out who it might be. But the door did not open again and he waited in vain. That morning when the doors had been locked, everyone had wanted to come in, but now after he'd unlocked one of the doors himself—and the others had evidently been unlocked during the day—nobody came in, and the keys, too, were now on the outside.

It was late at night before the light was put out in the living room, and it was easy for Gregor to tell that his parents and sister had stayed up all the while, since he could plainly hear the three of them as they tiptoed away. As it was obvious that no one would be visiting Gregor before morning, he had plenty of time in which to contemplate, undisturbed, how best to rearrange his life. But the open, high-ceilinged room in which he was forced to lie flat on the floor filled him with a dread which he couldn't account for—since it was, after all, the room he had lived in for the past five years. Almost unthinkingly, and not without a faint sense of shame, he scurried under the couch. There, although his back was slightly cramped and he could no longer raise his head, he immediately felt very much at home, and his only regret was that his body was too wide to fit completely under the couch.

There he spent the rest of the night, now in a doze from which hunger pangs kept awakening him with a start, now preoccupied with worries and vague hopes, all of which, however, led to the same conclusion: that for the time being he must remain calm and, by being patient and showing every consideration, try to help his family bear the burdens that his present condition had placed upon them.

Early the next morning—the night was barely over—Gregor got an opportunity to test the strength of his newly-made resolutions, because his sister, who was almost fully dressed, opened the hallway door and looked in expectantly. She didn't see him at first, but when she spotted him underneath the couch—well, my God, he had to be somewhere, he couldn't just fly away—she was so surprised that she lost her self-control and slammed the door shut again. But, as if she felt sorry for her behavior, she opened it again right away and tiptoed in, as if she were in the presence of someone who was very ill, or who was a stranger. Gregor had moved his head forward almost to the edge of the couch and was watching her. Would she notice that he'd let the milk sit there, and not from lack of hunger, and would she bring him some other food that was more to his taste? If she wasn't going to do it on her own, he'd sooner starve than call her attention to it, although in fact he was feeling a tremendous urge to dash out from under the couch, fling himself at his sister's feet, and beg her for something good to eat. But his sister immediately noticed to her astonishment that the bowl was still full, with only a little milk spilt around it. She picked up the bowl at once—not, it's true, with her bare hands but using a rag—and carried it out. Gregor was extremely curious to find out what she would bring in its place, and he speculated at length as to what it might be. But he never would have guessed what his sister, in the goodness of her heart, actually did. She brought him a wide range of choices, all spread out on an old newspaper. There were old, half-rotten vegetables; bones left over from dinner, covered with a congealed white sauce; some raisins and almonds; a piece of cheese which Gregor two days ago had declared inedible; a slice of plain bread, a slice of bread and butter, and a slice with butter and salt. In addition to all this she replaced the bowl, now evidently reserved for Gregor, filled this time with water. And out of a sense of delicacy, since she knew that Gregor wouldn't eat in front of her, she left in a hurry, even turning the key in the lock in order that Gregor might know that he was free to make himself as comfortable as possible. Gregor's legs whirred as they propelled him toward the food. Besides, his wounds must have healed completely, for he no longer felt handicapped, which amazed him. He thought of how, a month ago, he'd cut his finger slightly with his knife and how only the day before yesterday that little wound had still hurt. "Am I less sensitive now?" he wondered, greedily sucking on the cheese, to which, above all the other dishes, he was immediately and strongly attracted. Tears of joy welled up in his eyes as he devoured the cheese, the vegetables, and the sauce. The fresh foods, on the other hand, were not to his liking; in fact, he couldn't stand to smell them and he actually dragged the food he wanted to eat a little way off. He'd long since finished eating, and was merely lying lazily in the same spot, when his sister began to slowly turn the key in the lock as a signal for him to withdraw. He got up at once, although he'd almost fallen asleep, and scurried back under the couch. But it took a great deal of self-control for him to remain under the couch even for the brief time his sister was in the room, for his heavy meal had swollen his body to some extent and he could scarcely breathe in that confined space. Between little fits of suffocation he stared with slightly bulging eyes as his unsuspecting sister took a broom and swept away not only the scraps of what he'd eaten, but also the food that he'd left untouched—as if these too were no longer any good—and hurriedly dumped everything into a bucket, which she covered with a wooden lid and carried away. She'd hardly turned her back before Gregor came out from under the couch to stretch and puff himself out.

So this was how Gregor was fed each day, once in the morning when his parents and the maid were still asleep, and again after the family's midday meal, while his parents took another brief nap and his sister could send the maid away on some errand or other. His parents didn't want Gregor to starve any more than his sister did, but perhaps for them to be directly involved in his feeding was more than they could bear, or perhaps his sister wanted to shield them even from what might prove to be no more than a minor discomfort, for they were surely suffering enough as it was.

Gregor was unable to discover what excuses had served to get rid of the doctor 40 and the locksmith that first morning. Since the others couldn't understand what he said it never occurred to them, not even to his sister, that he could understand them, so when his sister was in the room, he had to be satisfied with occasionally hearing her sighs and her appeals to the saints. Only later, after she began to get used to the situation—of course she could never become completely used to it—would Gregor sometimes hear a remark that was intended to be friendly or could be so interpreted. "He really liked it today," she'd say when Gregor had polished off a good portion, and when the opposite was the case, which began to happen more and more often, she'd say almost sadly, "Once again, he didn't touch a thing."

But while Gregor wasn't able to get any news directly, he could overhear a considerable amount from the adjoining rooms, and as soon as he would hear the sound of voices he would immediately run to the appropriate door and press his whole body against it. In the early days especially, there wasn't a conversation that didn't in some way, if only indirectly, refer to him. For two whole days, at every meal, the family discussed what they should do, and they kept on doing so between meals as well, for at least two members of the family were now always at home, probably because nobody wanted to be in the apartment alone, and it would be unthinkable to leave it empty. Furthermore, on the very first day the cook—it wasn't completely clear how much she knew of what had happened—had on her knees begged Gregor's mother to dismiss her immediately, and when she said her goodbyes a quarter of an hour later, she thanked them for her dismissal with tears in her eyes, as if this had been the greatest favor ever bestowed on her in the house, and without having to be asked she made a solemn vow never to breathe a word of this to anyone.

So now his sister, together with his mother, had to do all the cooking as well, though in fact this wasn't too much of a chore, since the family ate practically nothing. Gregor kept hearing them vainly urging one another to eat, without receiving any reply except "No thanks, I've had enough," or some similar remark. They didn't seem to drink anything, either. His sister would often ask his father if he'd like some beer, and would gladly offer to go out and get it herself. When he wouldn't respond she'd say, in order to remove any hesitation on his part, that she could always send the janitor's wife, but at that point the father would finally utter an emphatic "No" and that would be the end of the matter.

It was on the very first day that his father gave a full account, to both mother and sister, of the family's financial situation and prospects. Every now and then he would get up from the table and take a receipt or notebook from out of the small safe he'd salvaged from the collapse of his business five years before. He could be heard opening the complicated lock and then securing it again after taking out whatever he'd been looking for. The account that his father gave, or at least part of it, was the first encouraging news that Gregor had heard since being imprisoned. He'd always had the impression that his father had failed to save a penny from the ruin of his business; at least his father had never told him otherwise, and Gregor, for that matter, had never asked him about it. At that time Gregor's only concern had been to do his utmost to make the family forget as quickly as possible the business failure that had plunged them all into a state of total despair. And so he had set to work with tremendous zeal, and had risen almost overnight from junior clerk to become a traveling salesman, which naturally opened up completely new financial opportunities so that in no time at all his success was instantly translated, by way of commissions, into hard cash, which could be laid out on the table under the eyes of his astonished and delighted family. Those had been wonderful times, and they had never returned, at least not with the same glory, even though later on Gregor had been earning enough to pay the entire family's expenses, and in fact had been doing so. They'd simply gotten used to it, both family and Gregor; they had gratefully accepted the money, and he had given it gladly, but no special warmth went with it. Gregor had remained close only to his sister, and it was his secret plan that she, who unlike Gregor loved music and could play the violin with deep feeling, should next year attend the Conservatory, despite the expense which, great as it was, would have to be met in some way. During Gregor's brief stays in the city the subject of the Conservatory would often come up in his conversations with his sister, but always only as a beautiful dream that wasn't meant to come true. His parents weren't happy to hear even these innocent remarks, but Gregor's ideas on the subject were firm and he had intended to make a solemn announcement on Christmas Eve.

Such were the thoughts, so futile in his present condition, that ran through his mind as he stood there, pressed against the door, listening. Sometimes he would grow so thoroughly weary that he couldn't listen any more and would carelessly let his head bump against the door, and though he'd pull it back immediately, even the slight noise he'd made would be heard in the next room, causing everyone to fall silent. "What's he up to now?" his father would say after a pause, obviously looking at the door, and only then would the interrupted conversation gradually be resumed.

Gregor now learned with considerable thoroughness—for his father tended to repeat his explanations several times, partly because he hadn't dealt with these matters in a long time, and partly because his mother didn't understand everything the first time through—that despite their catastrophic ruin a certain amount of capital, a very small amount, it's true, had survived intact from the old days, and thanks to the interest being untouched had even increased slightly. And what was more, the money which Gregor had been bringing home every month—he'd kept only a small sum for himself—hadn't been completely spent and had grown into a tidy sum. Gregor nodded eagerly behind his door, delighted to hear of this unexpected foresight and thrift. Of course he might have been able to use this extra money to pay off more of his father's debt to the director, and thus have brought nearer the day when he could quit his current job, but, given the present circumstances, things were better the way his father had arranged them.

Now the sum of this money wasn't nearly large enough for the family to live off the interest; the principal might support them for a year, or two at the most, but that was all. So this was really only a sum that was not to be touched, but saved instead for emergencies. As for money to live on—that would have to be earned. Though Gregor's father was indeed still healthy, nevertheless he was an old man who hadn't worked for five years and one from whom not too much should be expected in any case. During those five years, the first ones of leisure in his hard-working but unsuccessful life, he had put on a lot of weight and consequently had grown somewhat sluggish. And as for Gregor's elderly mother, was she supposed to start bringing in money, burdened as she was by her asthma which made it a strain for her to even walk across the apartment and which kept her gasping for breath every other day on the couch by the open window? Or should his sister go to work instead—she who though seventeen was still a child and one moreover whom it would be cruel to deprive of the life she'd led up until now, a life of wearing pretty clothes, sleeping late, helping around the house, enjoying a few modest pleasures, and above all playing the violin? At first, whenever their conversation turned to the need to earn money, Gregor would let go of the door and fling himself down on the cool leather couch which stood beside it, for he felt hot with grief and shame.

Often he would lie there all night long, not sleeping a wink, scratching at the leather couch for hours. Or, undaunted by the great effort it required, he would push the chair over to the window. Then he would crawl up to the sill and, propped up by the chair, would lean against the pane, apparently inspired by some memory of the sense of freedom that gazing out a window used to give him. For in truth objects only a short distance away were now, each day, becoming more indistinct; the hospital across the street, which he used to curse because he could see it all too clearly, was now completely outside his field of vision, and if he hadn't known for a fact that he lived on Charlotte Street—a quiet but nevertheless urban street—he could have imagined that he was looking out his window at a wasteland where gray sky and gray earth had indistinguishably merged as one. His observant sister needed only to notice twice that the armchair had been moved to the window. From then on, whenever she cleaned the room, she carefully placed the chair back by the window, and even began leaving the inner casement open.

If only Gregor had been able to speak to his sister and thank her for everything she'd had to do for him, he could have borne her kindnesses more easily, but as it was they were painful to him. Of course his sister tried her best to ease the general embarrassment, and naturally as time passed she grew better and better at it. But Gregor too, over time, gained a clearer sense of what was involved. Even the way in which she entered the room was a torture to him. No sooner had she stepped in when—not even pausing to shut the door, despite the care she normally would take in sparing others the sight of Gregor's room—she would run straight over to the window and tear it open with impatient fingers, almost as if she were suffocating, and she would remain for some time by the window, even in the coldest weather, breathing deeply. Twice a day she would terrify Gregor with all this noise and rushing around. He would cower under the couch the entire time, knowing full well that she surely would have spared him this if only she could have stood being in the room with him with the windows closed.

Once, about a month after Gregor's metamorphosis—so there was really no particular reason for his sister to be upset by his appearance—she came in earlier than usual and caught Gregor as he gazed out the window, terrifying in his stillness. It wouldn't have surprised Gregor if she'd decided not to come in, since his position prevented her from opening the window right away, but not only did she not come in, she actually jumped back and shut the door—a stranger might have thought that Gregor had been planning to ambush her and bite her. Of course he immediately hid under the couch, but he had to wait until noon before she came back, and this time she seemed much more nervous than usual. In this way he came to realize that the sight of him disgusted her, and likely would always disgust her, and that she probably had to steel herself not to run away at the sight of even the tiny portion of his body that stuck out from under the couch. So, one day, to spare her even this, he carried the bedsheet on his back over to the couch—it took him four hours—and spread it so that he was completely covered and his sister wouldn't be able to see him even if she bent down. If she felt this sheet wasn't necessary then of course she could remove it, since obviously Gregor wasn't shutting himself away so completely in order to amuse himself. But she left the sheet alone, and Gregor even thought that he caught a look of gratitude when he cautiously lifted the sheet a little with his head in order to see how his sister was taking to this new arrangement.

During the first two weeks, his parents couldn't bring themselves to come in to see him, and he frequently heard them remarking how much they appreciated his sister's efforts, whereas previously they'd often been annoyed with her for being, in their eyes, somewhat useless. But now both father and mother had fallen into the habit of waiting outside Gregor's door while his sister cleaned up the room, and as soon as she emerged

50

she would have to tell them every detail of the room's condition, what Gregor had eaten, how he'd behaved this time, and whether he'd perhaps shown a little improvement. It wasn't long before his mother began to want to visit Gregor, but his father and sister were at first able to dissuade her by rational arguments to which Gregor listened with great care, and with which he thoroughly agreed. But as time went by she had to be restrained by force, and when she cried out "Let me go to Gregor, he's my unhappy boy! Don't you understand that I have to go to him?" Gregor began to think that it might be a good idea if his mother did come in after all, not every day, naturally, but, say, once a week. She was really a much more capable person than his sister, who, for all her courage, was still only a child and had perhaps taken on such a difficult task only out of a childish impulsiveness.

Gregor's wish to see his mother was soon fulfilled. During the day Gregor didn't want to show himself at the window, if only out of consideration for his parents. But his few square meters of floor gave him little room to crawl around in, he found it hard to lie still even at night, and eating soon ceased to give him any pleasure. So in order to distract himself he fell into the habit of crawling all over the walls and the ceiling. He especially enjoyed hanging from the ceiling; it was completely different from lying on the floor. He could breathe more freely, a faint pulsing coursed through his body, and in his state of almost giddy absentmindedness up there, Gregor would sometimes, to his surprise, lose his grip and tumble onto the floor. But now, of course, since he had much better control over his body, even such a great fall didn't hurt him. His sister noticed right away the new pastime Gregor had discovered for himself—he'd left sticky traces where he'd been crawling—and so she got it into her head to provide Gregor with as much room as possible to crawl around in by removing all the furniture that was in the way—especially the chest of drawers and the desk. But she couldn't manage this by herself; she didn't dare ask her father for help; the maid wouldn't be of any use, for while this girl, who was around sixteen, was brave enough to stay on after the cook had left, she'd asked to be allowed to always keep the kitchen door locked, opening it only when specifically asked to do so. This left his sister with no choice but, one day when her father was out, to ask her mother for help. And indeed, her mother followed her with joyful, excited cries, although she fell silent when they reached the door to Gregor's room. Naturally his sister first made sure that everything in the room was as it should be; only then did she let her mother come in. Gregor had hurriedly pulled his sheet even lower and had folded it more tightly and it really did look as if it had been casually tossed over the couch. This time Gregor also refrained from peeking out from under the sheet; he denied himself the pleasure of seeing his mother for now and was simply glad that she'd come after all. "Come on in, he's nowhere in sight," said his sister, apparently leading his mother in by the hand. Now Gregor could hear the two delicate women moving the heavy chest of drawers away from its place, his sister stubbornly insisting on doing the hardest work, ignoring the warnings of her mother, who was afraid her daughter would overstrain herself. The work took a very long time. After struggling for over a quarter of an hour, his mother suggested that they might leave the chest where it was; in the first place, it was just too heavy, they'd never be done before his father came home and they'd have to leave it in the middle of the room, blocking Gregor's movements in every direction; in the second place, it wasn't at all certain that they were doing Gregor a favor in removing the furniture. It seemed to her that the opposite was true, the sight of the bare walls broke her heart; and why shouldn't Gregor feel the same since he'd been used to this furniture for so long and would feel abandoned in the empty room? "And wouldn't it look as if," his mother concluded very softly—in fact, she'd been almost whispering the entire time, as if she wanted to prevent Gregor, whose exact whereabouts she didn't know, from hearing the sound of her voice (she was convinced that he couldn't understand her words)—"as if by removing his furniture we were telling him that we'd given up all hope of his getting better, and were callously leaving him to his own devices? I think the best course would be to try to keep the room exactly the way it was, so that when Gregor does come back to us he'll find everything the same, making it easier for him to forget what has happened in the meantime."

When he heard his mother's words, Gregor realized that, over the past two months, the lack of having anyone to converse with, together with the monotonous life within the family, must have befuddled his mind; there wasn't any other way he could explain to himself how he could have ever seriously wanted his room cleared out. Did he really want this warm room of his, so comfortably furnished with family heirlooms, transformed into a lair where he'd be perfectly free to crawl around in every direction, but only at the cost of simultaneously forgetting his human past, swiftly and utterly? Just now he'd been on the brink of forgetting, and only his mother's voice, which he hadn't heard for so long, had brought him back. Nothing should be removed; everything must stay. He couldn't do without the furniture's soothing influence on his state of mind, and if the furniture were to impede his sense-lessly crawling around, that wouldn't be a loss but rather a great advantage.

But unfortunately his sister thought otherwise. She'd become accustomed, and not without some justification, to assuming the role of the acknowledged expert whenever she and her parents discussed Gregor's affairs; so her mother's advice was enough for her to insist now not merely on her original plan of moving the chest and the desk, but on the removal of every bit of furniture except for the indispensable couch. Her resolve, to be sure, didn't stem merely from childish stubbornness or from the self-confidence she had recently and unexpectedly gained at such great cost. For in fact she'd noticed that while Gregor needed plenty of room to crawl around in, on the other hand, as far as she could tell, he never used the furniture at all. Perhaps too, the sentimental enthusiasm of girls her age, which they indulge themselves in at every opportunity, now tempted Grete to make Gregor's situation all the more terri-fying so that she might be able to do more for him. No one but Grete would ever be likely to enter a room where Gregor ruled the bare walls all alone.

And so she refused to give in to her mother, who in any case, from the sheer anxiety caused by being in Gregor's room, seemed unsure of herself. She soon fell silent and began as best she could to help her daughter remove the chest of drawers. Well, if he must, then Gregor could do without the chest, but the desk had to stay. And no sooner had the two women, groaning and squeezing, gotten the chest out of the room than Gregor poked his head out from under the couch to see how he might intervene as tactfully as possible. But unfortunately it was his mother who came back first, leaving Grete in the next room, gripping the chest with her arms and rocking it back and forth without, of course, being able to budge it from the spot. His mother wasn't used to the sight of him—it might make her sick; so Gregor, frightened, scut-tled backwards to the far end of the couch, but he couldn't prevent the front of the sheet from stirring slightly. That was enough to catch his mother's attention. She stopped, stood still for a moment, and then went back to Grete.

Gregor kept telling himself that nothing unusual was happening, that only a few 55 pieces of furniture were being moved around. But he soon had to admit that all this coming and going of the two women, their little calls to one another, the scraping of the furniture across the floor, affected him as if it were some gigantic commotion rushing in on him from every side, and though he tucked in his head and legs and pressed his body against the floor, he had to accept the fact that he wouldn't be able to stand it much longer. They were cleaning out his room, taking away from him everything that he loved; already they'd carried off his chest, where he kept his fretsaw and his other tools; now they were trying to pry his writing desk loose—it was practically embedded in the floor—the same desk where he'd always done his homework when he'd been a student at business school, in high school, and even in elementary school. He really no longer had any time left in which to weigh the good intentions of these two women whose existence, for that matter, he'd almost forgotten, since they were so exhausted by now that they worked in silence, the only sound being that of their weary, plodding steps.

And so, while the women were in the next room, leaning against the desk and trying to catch their breath, he broke out, changing his direction four times—since he really didn't know what to rescue first—when he saw, hanging conspicuously on the otherwise bare wall, the picture of the lady all dressed in furs. He quickly crawled up to it and pressed himself against the glass, which held him fast, soothing his hot belly. Now that Gregor completely covered it, this picture at least wasn't about to be carried away by anyone. He turned his head towards the living room door, so that he could watch the women when they returned.

They hadn't taken much of a rest and were already coming back. Grete had put her arm around her mother and was almost carrying her. "Well, what should we take next?" said Grete, looking around. And then her eyes met Gregor's, looking down at her from the wall. Probably only because her mother was there, she kept her composure, bent her head down to her mother to prevent her from glancing around, and said, though in a hollow, quavering voice: "Come on, let's go back to the living room for a minute." To Gregor, her intentions were obvious: she wanted to get his mother to safety and then chase him down from the wall. Well, just let her try! He clung to his picture and he wasn't going to give it up. He'd rather fly at Grete's face.

But Grete's words had made her mother even more anxious; she stepped aside, glimpsed the huge brown blotch on the flowered wallpaper, and before she fully understood that what she was looking at was Gregor, she cried out, "Oh God, oh God!" in a hoarse scream of a voice, and, as if giving up completely, fell with outstretched arms across the couch, and lay there without moving. "You! Gregor!" cried his sister, raising her fist and glaring at him. These were the first words she had addressed directly to him since his metamorphosis. She ran into the next room to get some spirits to revive her mother from her faint. Gregor also wanted to help—he could rescue the picture another time—but he was stuck to the glass and had to tear himself free. He then scuttled into the next room as if to give some advice, as he used to, to his sister. Instead, he had to stand behind her uselessly while she rummaged among various little bottles. When she turned around she was startled, a bottle fell to the floor, a splinter of glass struck Gregor in the face, some sort of corrosive medicine splashed on him, and Grete, without further delay, grabbing as many of the little bottles as she could carry, ran inside with them to her mother, and slammed the door shut behind her with her foot. Now Gregor was cut off from his mother, who was perhaps near death because of him. He didn't dare open the door for fear of scaring his sister, who had to remain with his mother. There wasn't anything for him to do but wait; and so, tormented by guilt and anxiety, he began crawling. He crawled over everything, walls, furniture, and ceiling, until finally, in despair, the room beginning to spin around him, he collapsed onto the middle of the large table.

A short time passed; Gregor lay there stupefied. Everything was quiet around him; perhaps that was a good sign. Then the doorbell rang. The maid, of course, stayed locked up in her kitchen, so Grete had to answer the door. His father was back. "What's happened?" were his first words. Grete's expression must've told him everything. Her answers came in muffled tones—she was obviously burying her face in her father's chest. "Mother fainted, but she's better now. Gregor's broken loose." "I knew it," her father said. "I told you this would happen, but you women refuse to listen." It was clear to Gregor that his father had put the worst construction on Grete's all too brief account and had assumed that Gregor was guilty of some violent act. That meant that he must calm his father down, since he had neither the time nor the ability to explain things to him. So he fled to the door of his room and pressed himself against it in order that his father might see, as soon as he entered the living room, that Gregor had every intention of returning immediately to his own room and there was no need to force him back. All they had to do was to open the door and he would disappear at once.

But his father wasn't in the mood to notice such subtleties; "Ah!" he roared as   60
he entered, in a voice that sounded at once furious and gleeful. Gregor turned his head from the door and lifted it towards his father. He really hadn't imagined that his father would look the way he did standing before him now; true, Gregor had become too absorbed lately by his new habit of crawling to bother about whatever else might be going on in the apartment, and he should have anticipated that there would be some changes. And yet, and yet, could this really be his father? Was this the same man who used to lie sunk in bed, exhausted, whenever Gregor would set out on one of his business trips; who would greet him upon his return in the evening while sitting in his bathrobe in the armchair; who was hardly capable of getting to his feet, and to show his joy could only lift up his arms; and who, on those rare times when the whole family went out for a walk—on the occasional Sunday or on a legal holiday—used to painfully shuffle along between Gregor and his mother, who were slow walkers themselves, and yet he was always slightly slower than they, wrapped up in his old overcoat, carefully planting his crook-handled cane before him with every step, and almost invariably stopping and gathering his escort around him whenever he wanted to say something? Now, however, he held himself very erect, dressed up in a closely-fitting blue uniform with gold buttons, of the kind worn by bank messengers. His heavy chin thrust out over the stiff collar of his jacket; his black eyes stared, sharp and bright, from under his bushy eyebrows; his white hair, once so rumpled, was combed flat, it gleamed, and the part was meticulously exact. He tossed his cap—which bore a gold monogram, probably that of some bank—in an arc across the room so that it landed on the couch, and with his hands in his pockets, the tails of his uniform's long jacket flung back, his face grim, he went after Gregor. He probably didn't know himself what he was going to do, but he lifted his feet unusually high, and Gregor was amazed at the immense size of the soles of his boots. However, Gregor didn't dwell on these reflections, for he had known from the very first day of his new life that his father considered only the strictest measures to be appropriate in dealing with him. So he ran ahead of his father, stopped when he stood still, and scurried on again when he made the slightest move. In this way they circled the room several times without anything decisive happening; in fact, their movements, because of their slow tempo, did not suggest those of a chase. So

Gregor kept to the floor for the time being, especially since he was afraid that his father might consider any flight to the walls or ceiling to be particularly offensive. All the same, Gregor had to admit that he wouldn't be able to keep up even this pace for long, since whenever his father took a single step, Gregor had to perform an entire series of movements. He was beginning to get winded, since even in his former life his lungs had never been strong. As he kept staggering on like this, so weary he could barely keep his eyes open, since he was saving all his strength for running; not even thinking, dazed as he was, that there might be any other way to escape than by running; having almost forgotten that he was free to use the walls, though against these walls, admittedly, were placed bits of intricately carved furniture, bristling with spikes and sharp corners—suddenly something sailed overhead, hit the floor nearby, and rolled right in front of him. It was an apple; at once a second one came flying after it. Gregor stopped, petrified with fear; it was useless to keep on running, for his father had decided to bombard him. He had filled his pockets with the fruit from the bowl on the sideboard and now he was throwing one apple after another, for now at least without bothering to take good aim. These little red apples, colliding with one another, rolled around on the floor as if electrified. One weakly-thrown apple grazed Gregor's back, rolling off without causing harm. But another one that came flying immediately afterwards actually imbedded itself in Gregor's back. Gregor wanted to drag himself onward, as if this shocking and unbelievable pain might disappear if he could only keep moving, but he felt as if he were nailed to the spot, and he splayed himself out in the utter confusion of his senses. With his last glance he saw the door of his room burst open, and his mother, wearing only her chemise—his sister had removed her dress to help her breathe after she'd fainted—rush out, followed by his screaming sister. He saw his mother run toward his father, her loosened underskirts slipping one by one onto the floor. Stumbling over her skirts she flung herself upon his father, embraced him, was as one with him—but now Gregor's sight grew dim—and with her arms clasped around his father's neck, begged for Gregor's life.

III

Gregor's serious wound, which made him suffer for over a month—the apple remained imbedded in his flesh as a visible reminder, no one having the courage to remove it—seemed to have persuaded even his father that Gregor, despite his present pathetic and disgusting shape, was a member of the family who shouldn't be treated as an enemy. On the contrary, familial duty required them to swallow their disgust and to endure him, to endure him and nothing more.

And though his wound probably had caused Gregor to suffer a permanent loss of mobility, and though it now took him, as if he were some disabled war veteran, many a long minute to creep across his room—crawling above ground level was out of the question—yet in return for this deterioration of his condition he was granted a compensation which satisfied him completely: each day around dusk the living room door—which he was in the habit of watching closely for an hour or two ahead of time—was opened, and lying in the darkness of his room, invisible from the living room, he could see the whole family sitting at the table lit by the lamp and could listen to their conversation as if by general consent, instead of the way he'd done before.

True, these were no longer the lively conversations of old, those upon which Gregor had mused somewhat wistfully as he'd settled wearily into his damp bed in some tiny hotel room. Things were now very quiet for the most part. Soon after dinner his father would fall asleep in his armchair, while his mother and sister would admonish each other to be quiet; his mother, bending forward under the light, would sew fine lingerie for a fashion store; his sister, who had found work as a salesgirl, would study shorthand and French in the evenings, hoping to obtain a better job in the future. Sometimes his father would wake up, as if he hadn't the slightest idea that he'd been asleep, and would say to his mother, "Look how long you've been sewing again today!" and then would fall back to sleep, while his mother and sister would exchange weary smiles.

With a kind of perverse obstinacy his father refused to take off his messenger's uniform even in the apartment; while his robe hung unused on the clothes hook, he would sleep fully dressed in his chair, as if he were always ready for duty and were waiting even here for the voice of his superior. As a result his uniform, which hadn't been new in the first place, began to get dirty in spite of all his mother and sister could do to care for it, and Gregor would often spend entire evenings gazing at this garment covered with stains and with its constantly polished buttons gleaming, in which the old man would sit, upright and uncomfortable, yet peacefully asleep.

As soon as the clock would strike ten, his mother would try to awaken his father with soft words of encouragement and then persuade him to go to bed, for this wasn't any place in which to get a decent night's sleep, and his father badly needed his rest, since he had to be at work at six in the morning. But with the stubbornness that had possessed him ever since he'd become a bank messenger he would insist on staying at the table a little while longer, though he invariably would fall asleep again, and then it was only with the greatest difficulty that he could be persuaded to trade his chair for bed. No matter how much mother and sister would urge him on with little admonishments, he'd keep shaking his head for a good fifteen minutes, his eyes closed, and wouldn't get up. Gregor's mother would tug at his sleeve, whisper sweet words into his ear; and his sister would leave her homework to help her mother, but it was all useless. He only sank deeper into his armchair. Not until the two women would lift him up by the arms would he open his eyes, look now at one, now at the other, and usually say, "What a life. So this is the peace of my old age." And leaning on the two women he would get up laboriously, as if he were his own greatest burden, and would allow the women to lead him to the door, where, waving them aside, he continued on his own, while Gregor's mother abandoned her sewing and her sister her pen so that they might run after his father and continue to look after him. 65

Who in this overworked and exhausted family had time to worry about Gregor any more than was absolutely necessary? Their resources grew more limited; the maid was now dismissed after all; a gigantic bony cleaning woman with white hair fluttering about her head came in the mornings and evenings to do the roughest work; Gregor's mother took care of everything else, in addition to her sewing. It even happened that certain pieces of family jewelry which his mother and sister had worn with such pleasure at parties and celebrations in days gone by, were sold, as Gregor found out one evening by listening to a general discussion of the prices they'd gone for. But their greatest complaint was that they couldn't give up the apartment, which was too big for their current needs, since no one could figure out how they would move Gregor. But Gregor understood clearly enough that it wasn't simply consideration for him which prevented them moving, since he could have easily been transported in a suitable crate equipped with a few air holes. The main reason preventing them from moving was their utter despair and the feeling that they had been struck by a misfortune far greater than any that had ever visited their friends and relatives. What the world demands of the poor they did to the utmost: his father fetched breakfast for the bank's minor officials, his mother sacrificed herself for the underwear of strangers, his sister ran back and forth behind the counters at the beck and call of customers; but they lacked the strength for anything beyond this. And the wound in Gregor's back began to ache once more when his mother and sister, after putting his father to bed, returned to the room, ignored their work, and sat huddled together cheek to cheek, and his mother said, "Close that door, Grete," so that Gregor was back in the dark, while in the next room the women wept together or simply stared at the table with dry eyes.

Gregor spent the days and nights almost entirely without sleep. Sometimes he imagined that the next time the door opened he would once again assume control of the family's affairs, as he'd done in the old days. Now, after a long absence, there reappeared in his thoughts the director and the manager, the salesmen and the apprentices, the remarkably stupid errand runner, two or three friends from other firms, a chambermaid at one of the provincial hotels—a sweet, fleeting memory—a cashier at a hat store whom he'd courted earnestly but too slowly—they all came to him mixed up with strangers and with people whom he'd already forgotten. But instead of helping him and his family they were all unapproachable, and he was glad when they faded away. At other times he was in no mood to worry about his family; he was utterly filled with rage at how badly he was being treated, and although he couldn't imagine anything that might tempt his appetite, he nevertheless tried to think up ways of getting into the pantry to take what was rightfully his, even if he wasn't hungry. No longer bothering to consider what Gregor might like as a treat, his sister, before she hurried off to work in the morning and after lunch, would shove any sort of food into Gregor's room with her foot. In the evening, regardless of whether the food had been picked at, or—as was more often the case—left completely untouched, she would sweep it out with a swish of the broom. Nowadays she would clean the room in the evening, and she couldn't have done it any faster. Streaks of grime ran along the walls, balls of dust and dirt lay here and there on the floor. At first, whenever his sister would come in, Gregor would station himself in some corner that was particularly objectionable, as if his presence there might serve as a reproach to her. But he probably could have remained there for weeks without her mending her ways; she obviously could see the dirt as clearly as he could, but she'd made up her mind to leave it. At the same time she made certain—with a touchiness that was completely new to her and which indeed was infecting the entire family—that the cleaning of Gregor's room was to remain her prerogative. On one occasion Gregor's mother had subjected his room to a thorough cleaning, which she managed to accomplish only with the aid of several buckets of water—all this dampness being a further annoyance to Gregor, who lay flat, unhappy, and motionless on the couch. But his mother's punishment was not long in coming. For that evening, as soon as Gregor's sister noticed the difference in his room, she ran, deeply insulted, into the living room, and without regard for his mother's uplifted, beseeching hands, burst into a fit of tears. Both parents—the father, naturally, had been startled out of his armchair—at first looked on with helpless amazement, and then they joined in, the father on his right side blaming the mother: she shouldn't have interfered with the sister's cleaning of the room, while on his left side yelling at the sister that she'd never be allowed to clean Gregor's room again. The mother was trying to drag the father, who was half out of his mind, into their bedroom while the sister, shaking with sobs, pounded the table with her little fists, and Gregor hissed loudly with rage because not one of them had thought to close the door and spare him this scene and this commotion.

But even if his sister, worn out by her job at the store, had gotten tired of taking care of Gregor as she once had, it wasn't really necessary for his mother to take her place so that Gregor wouldn't be neglected. For now the cleaning woman was there. This ancient widow, whose powerful bony frame had no doubt helped her through the hard times in her long life, wasn't at all repelled by Gregor. Without being the least bit inquisitive, she had once, by chance, opened the door to Gregor's room and at the sight of Gregor—who, taken completely by surprise, began running back and forth although no one was chasing him—stood there in amazement, her hands folded over her belly. From then on, morning and evening, she never failed to open his door a crack and peek in on him. At first she also would call him to her, using phrases she probably meant to be friendly, such as "Come on over here, you old dung beetle!" or "Just look at that old dung beetle!" Gregor wouldn't respond to such forms of address, but would remain motionless where he was as if the door had never been opened. If only this cleaning woman, instead of pointlessly disturbing him whenever she felt like it, had been given orders to clean his room every day! Once, early in the morning, when a heavy rain, perhaps a sign of the already approaching spring, was beating against the window panes, Gregor became so exasperated when the cleaning woman started in with her phrases that he made as if to attack her, though, of course, in a slow and feeble manner. But instead of being frightened, the cleaning woman simply picked up a chair by the door and, lifting it high in the air, stood there with her mouth wide open. Obviously she didn't plan on shutting it until the chair in her hands had first come crashing down on Gregor's back. "So you're not going through with it?" she asked as Gregor turned back while she calmly set the chair down again in the corner.

By now Gregor was eating next to nothing. Only when he happened to pass by the food set out for him would he take a bite, hold it in his mouth for hours, and then spit most of it out again. At first he imagined that it was his anguish at the state of his room that kept him from eating, but it was those very changes to which he had quickly become accustomed. The family had fallen into the habit of using the room to store things for which there wasn't any place anywhere else, and there were many of these things now, since one room in the apartment had been rented to three boarders. These serious gentlemen—all three of them had full beards, as Gregor once noted, peering through a crack in the door—had a passion for neatness, not only in their room but since they were now settled in as boarders, throughout the entire apartment, and especially in the kitchen. They couldn't abide useless, let alone dirty, junk. Besides, they'd brought most of their own household goods along with them. This meant that many objects were now superfluous, which, while clearly without any resale value, couldn't just be thrown out either. All these things ended up in Gregor's room, and so did the ash bucket and the garbage can from the kitchen. Anything that wasn't being used at the moment was simply tossed into Gregor's room by the cleaning woman, who was always in a tremendous hurry. Fortunately, Gregor generally saw only the object in question and the hand that held it. Perhaps the cleaning woman intended to come back for these things when she had the time, or perhaps she planned on throwing them all out, but in fact there they remained, wherever they'd happened to land, except for Gregor's disturbing them as he squeezed his way through the junk pile. At first he did so simply because he was forced to, since there wasn't any other space to crawl in, but later he took a growing pleasure in these rambles even though they left him dead tired and so sad that he would lie motionless for hours. Since the boarders would sometimes have their dinner at home in the shared living room, on those evenings the door between that room and Gregor's would remain shut. But Gregor didn't experience the door's not being open as a hardship; in fact there had been evenings when he'd ignored the open door and had lain, unnoticed by the family, in the darkest corners of his room. But one time the cleaning woman left the door slightly ajar, and it remained ajar when the boarders came in that evening and the lamp was lit. They sat down at the head of the table, where Gregor, his mother and his father had sat in the old days; they unfolded their napkins, and picked up their knives and forks. At once his mother appeared at the kitchen door carrying a platter of meat and right behind her came his sister carrying a platter piled high with potatoes. The steaming food gave off a thick vapor. The platters were set down in front of the boarders, who bent over them as if to examine them before eating, and in fact the one sitting in the middle, who was apparently looked up to as an authority by the other two, cut into a piece of meat while it was still on the platter, evidently to determine if it was tender enough or whether perhaps it should be sent back to the kitchen. He was satisfied, and both mother and daughter, who'd been watching anxiously, breathed a sigh of relief and began to smile.

The family itself ate in the kitchen. Even so, before going to the kitchen his father came into the living room, bowed once and, cap in hand, walked around the table. The boarders all rose together and mumbled something into their beards. When they were once more alone, they ate in almost complete silence. It seemed strange to Gregor that, out of all the noises produced by eating, he distinctly heard the sound of their teeth chewing; it was as if he were being told you needed teeth in order to eat and that even with the most wonderful toothless jaws, you wouldn't be able to accomplish a thing. "Yes, I'm hungry enough," Gregor told himself sadly, "but not for those things. How well these boarders feed themselves, while I waste away." 70

That very evening—during this whole time Gregor couldn't once remember hearing the violin—the sound of violin playing came from the kitchen. The boarders had already finished their dinner, the one in the middle had pulled out a newspaper, handed one sheet each to the other two, and now they were leaning back, reading and smoking. When the violin began to play, they noticed it, stood up, and tiptoed to the hall doorway where they stood together in a tight group. They must have been heard in the kitchen for his father called, "Does the playing bother you, gentlemen? We can stop it at once." "On the contrary," said the gentleman in the middle, "wouldn't the young lady like to come and play in here where it's much more roomy and comfortable?" "Why, certainly," called Gregor's father, as if he were the violinist. Soon his father came in carrying the music stand, his mother the sheet music, and his sister the violin. His sister calmly got everything ready for playing; his parents—who had never rented out rooms before and so were overly polite to the boarders—didn't even dare to sit down in their own chairs. His father leaned against the door, slipping his right hand between the buttons of his uniform's jacket, which he'd kept buttoned up; but his mother was offered a chair by one of the gentlemen, and, leaving it where he happened to have placed it, she sat off to one side, in the corner.

His sister began to play; his father and mother, on either side, closely followed the movements of her hands. Gregor, attracted by the playing, had moved a little farther forward and already had his head in the living room. He was hardly surprised that recently he'd shown so little concern for others, although in the past he'd taken pride in being considerate. Now more than ever he had good reason to remain hidden, since he was completely covered with the dust that lay everywhere in his room and was stirred up by the slightest movement. Moreover, threads, hairs, and scraps of food clung to his back and sides, his indifference to everything was much too great for him to have gotten onto his back and rubbed himself clean against the carpet, as he had once done several times a day. And despite his condition he wasn't ashamed to edge his way a little further across the spotless living room floor.

To be sure, no one took any notice of him. The family was completely absorbed by the violin-playing. The boarders, however, who had at first placed themselves, their hands in their pockets, much too close to the music stand—close enough for every one of them to have followed the score, which surely must have flustered his sister—soon retreated to the window, muttering to one another, with their heads lowered. And there they remained while his father watched them anxiously. It seemed all too obvious that they had been disappointed in their hopes of hearing good or entertaining violin-playing; they had had enough of the entire performance, and it was only out of politeness that they continued to let their peace be disturbed. It was especially obvious, by the way they blew their smoke out of their mouths and noses—it floated upwards to the ceiling—just how ill at ease they were. And yet his sister was playing so beautifully. Her face was inclined to one side, and her sad eyes carefully followed the notes of the music. Gregor crawled forward a little farther, keeping his head close to the floor so that their eyes might possibly meet. Was he an animal, that music could move him so? He felt that he was being shown the way to an unknown nourishment he yearned for. He was determined to press on until he reached his sister, to tug at her skirt, and to let her know in this way that she should bring her violin into his room, for no one here would honor her playing as he would. He would never let her out of his room again, at least not for as long as he lived; at last his horrifying appearance would be useful; he would be at every door of his room at once, hissing and spitting at the attackers. His sister, however, wouldn't be forced to remain with him, she would do so of her own free will. She would sit beside him on the couch, leaning towards him and listening as he confided that he had firmly intended to send her to the Conservatory, and if the misfortune hadn't intervened, he would've announced this to everyone last Christmas—for hadn't Christmas come and gone by now?—without paying the slightest attention to any objection. After this declaration his sister would be so moved that she would burst into tears, and Gregor would lift himself up to her shoulder and kiss her on her neck, which, since she had started her job, she had kept bare, without ribbon or collar.

"Mr. Samsa!" cried the middle gentleman to Gregor's father, and without wasting another word pointed with his index finger at Gregor, who was slowly advancing. The violin stopped, the middle gentleman, shaking his head, smiled first at his friend and then looked at Gregor again. Instead of driving Gregor away, his father seemed to think it more important to soothe the boarders, although they weren't upset at all and appeared to consider Gregor more entertaining than the violin-playing. His father rushed over to them and with outstretched arms tried to herd them back into their room and at the same time block their view of Gregor with his body. Now they actually got a little angry—it wasn't clear whether this was due to his father's behavior or to their dawning realization that they had had all along, without knowing it, a next-door neighbor like Gregor. They demanded explanations from his father, raised their own arms now as well, tugged nervously at their beards, and only slowly backed away toward their room. Meanwhile his sister had managed to overcome the bewildered state into which she'd fallen when her playing had been so abruptly interrupted, and after some moments spent holding the violin and bow in her slackly dangling hands and staring at the score as if she were still playing, she suddenly pulled herself together, placed her instrument on her mother's lap—she was still sitting in her chair with her lungs heaving, gasping for breath—and ran into the next room, which the boarders, under pressure from her father, were ever more swiftly approaching. One could see pillows and blankets flying high in the air and then neatly arranging themselves under his sister's practical hands. Before the gentlemen had even reached their room, she had finished making the beds and had slipped out.

Once again a perverse stubbornness seemed to grip Gregor's father, to the extent 75 that he forgot to pay his tenants the respect still due them. He kept on pushing and shoving until the middle gentleman, who was already standing in the room's doorway, brought him up short with a thunderous stamp of his foot. "I hereby declare," he said, raising his hand and looking around for Gregor's mother and sister as well, "that considering the disgusting conditions prevailing in this apartment and in this family"—here he suddenly spat on the floor— "I'm giving immediate notice. Naturally I'm not going to pay a penny for the time I've spent here; on the contrary, I shall be seriously considering bringing some sort of action against you with claims that—I assure you—will be very easy to substantiate." He stopped speaking and stared ahead of him, as if expecting something. And indeed his two friends chimed right in, saying "We're giving immediate notice too." Whereupon he grabbed the doorknob and slammed the door shut with a crash.

Gregor's father, groping his way and staggering forward, collapsed into his armchair; it looked as if he were stretching himself out for his usual evening nap, but his heavily drooping head, looking as if it had lost all means of support, showed that he was anything but asleep. All this time Gregor had lain quietly right where the boarders had first seen him. His disappointment over the failure of his plan, and perhaps also the weakness caused by eating so little for so long, made movement an impossibility. He feared with some degree of certainty that at the very next moment the whole catastrophe would fall on his head, and he waited. He wasn't even startled when the violin slipped from his mother's trembling fingers and fell off her lap with a reverberating clatter.

"Dear parents," said his sister, pounding the table with her hand by way of preamble, "we can't go on like this. Maybe you don't realize it, but I do. I refuse to utter my brother's name in the presence of this monster, and so all I have to say is: we've got to try to get rid of it. We've done everything humanly possible to take care of it and put up with it; I don't think anyone can blame us in the least."

"She's absolutely right," said his father to himself. His mother, still trying to catch her breath, with a wild look in her eyes, began to cough, her cupped hand muffling the sound.

His sister rushed over to his mother and held her forehead. His father seemed to have been led to more definite thoughts by Grete's words; he was sitting up straight and toying with his messenger's cap, which lay on the table among the dishes left over from the boarders' dinner. From time to time he would glance over at Gregor's motionless form.

"We must try to get rid of it," said his sister, speaking only to her father since her 80 mother's coughing was such that she was incapable of hearing a word. "It will be the death of you both. I can see it coming. People who have to work as hard as we do can't stand this constant torture at home. I can't stand it anymore either." And she burst out sobbing so violently that her tears ran down onto her mother's face, where she wiped them away mechanically with her hand.

"But, my child," said her father with compassion and remarkable understanding, "what should we do?"

Gregor's sister could only shrug her shoulders as a sign of the helplessness that had overcome her while she wept, in contrast to her earlier self-confidence.

"If he could understand us," said her father tentatively; Gregor's sister, through her tears, shook her hand violently to indicate how impossible that was.

"If he could understand us," repeated her father, closing his eyes so as to take in his daughter's belief that this was impossible, "then perhaps we might be able to reach some agreement with him, but the way things are—"

"He's got to go," cried Gregor's sister, "it's the only way, Father. You just have to get rid of the idea that this is Gregor. Our real misfortune is having believed it for so long. But how can it be Gregor? If it were, he would've realized a long time ago that it's impossible for human beings to live with a creature like that, and he would've left on his own accord. Then we would've lost a brother, but we'd have been able to go on living and honor his memory. But the way things are, this animal persecutes us, drives away our boarders, obviously it wants to take over the whole apartment and make us sleep in the gutter. Look, Father," she suddenly screamed, "he's at it again!" And in a panic which Gregor found incomprehensible his sister abandoned his mother, and actually pushing herself from the chair as if she would rather sacrifice her mother than remain near Gregor, she rushed behind her father, who, startled by this behavior, got up as well, half raising his arms in front of Grete as if to protect her.

Gregor hadn't the slightest desire to frighten anyone, least of all his sister. He had merely started to turn around in order to go back to his room, a procedure which admittedly looked strange, since in his weakened condition he had to use his head to help him in this difficult maneuver, several times raising it and then knocking it against the floor. He stopped and looked around. His good intentions seemed to have been understood; the panic had only been temporary. Now, silent and sad, they all looked at him. His mother lay in her armchair with her legs outstretched and pressed together, her eyes almost closed from exhaustion. His father and sister sat side by side, and his sister had put her arm around her father's neck.

"Now maybe they'll let me turn around," thought Gregor, resuming his efforts. He couldn't stop panting from the strain, and he also had to rest from time to time. At least no one harassed him and he was left alone. When he had finished turning around, he immediately began to crawl back in a straight line. He was amazed at the distance between him and his room and couldn't understand how, weak as he was, he'd covered the same stretch of ground only a little while ago almost without being aware of it. Completely intent on crawling rapidly, he scarcely noticed that neither a word nor an exclamation came from his family to interrupt his progress. Only when he reached the doorway did he turn his head; not all the way, for he felt his neck growing stiff, but enough to see that behind him all was as before except that his sister had gotten to her feet. His last glimpse was of his mother, who by now was fast asleep.

He was barely inside the room before the door was slammed shut, bolted, and locked. Gregor was so frightened by the sudden noise behind him that his little legs collapsed underneath him. It was his sister who had been in such a hurry. She'd been standing there, ready and waiting, and then had sprung swiftly forward, before

Gregor had even heard her coming. "At last!" she cried to her parents as she turned the key in the lock.

"And now?" Gregor asked himself, looking around in the darkness. He soon discovered that he was no longer able to move. This didn't surprise him; rather it seemed to him strange that until now he'd actually been able to propel himself with these thin little legs. In other respects he felt relatively comfortable. It was true that his entire body ached, but the pain seemed to him to be growing fainter and fainter and soon would go away altogether. The rotten apple in his back and the inflamed area around it, completely covered with fine dust, hardly bothered him anymore. He recalled his family with deep emotion and love. His own belief that he must disappear was, if anything, even firmer than his sister's. He remained in this state of empty and peaceful reflection until the tower clock struck three in the morning. He could still just sense the general brightening outside his window. Then, involuntarily, his head sank all the way down, and from his nostrils came his last feeble breath.

Early that morning, when the cleaning woman appeared—out of sheer energy and impatience she always slammed all the doors, no matter how often she'd been asked not to, so hard that sleep was no longer possible anywhere in the apartment once she'd arrived—she didn't notice anything peculiar when she paid Gregor her usual brief visit. She thought that he was lying there so still on purpose, pretending that his feelings were hurt; she considered him to be very clever. As she happened to be holding a long broom, she tried to tickle Gregor with it from the doorway. When this too had no effect, she became annoyed and jabbed it into Gregor a little, and it was only when she shoved him from his place without meeting resistance that she began to take notice. Quickly realizing how things stood, she opened her eyes wide, gave a soft whistle, and without wasting any time she tore open the bedroom door and yelled at the top of her lungs into the darkness: "Come and look, it's had it, it's lying there, dead and done for." 90

Mr. and Mrs. Samsa sat up in their marriage bed, trying to absorb the shock the cleaning woman had given them and yet at first unable to comprehend the meaning of her words. Then they quickly climbed out of bed, Mr. Samsa on one side, Mrs. Samsa on the other. Mr. Samsa threw a blanket over his shoulders, Mrs. Samsa wore only her nightgown; dressed in this fashion they entered Gregor's room. Meanwhile the door to the living room, where Grete had been sleeping since the boarders' arrival, opened as well. Grete was fully dressed, as if she'd never gone to bed, and the pallor of her face seemed to confirm this. "Dead?" asked Mrs. Samsa and looked inquiring at the cleaning woman, although she could have checked for herself, or guessed at the truth without having to investigate. "That's for sure," said the cleaning woman, and to prove it she pushed Gregor's corpse a good way to one side with her broom. Mrs. Samsa made a move as if to stop her, then let it go. "Well," said Mr. Samsa, "now thanks be to God." He crossed himself, and the three women followed his example. Grete, who never took her eyes off the corpse, said, "Just look how thin he was. It's been a long time since he's eaten anything. The food came out just as it was when it came in." Indeed, Gregor's body was completely flat and dry; this was only now obvious because the body was no longer raised on its little legs and nothing else distracted the eye.

"Come to our room with us for a little while, Grete," said Mrs. Samsa with a sad smile, and Grete, not without a look back at the corpse, followed her parents into the bedroom. The cleaning woman shut the door and opened the windows wide. Although it was early in the morning, there was a certain mildness in the fresh air. After all, these were the last days of March.

The three boarders came out of their rooms and looked around in amazement for their breakfast; they had been forgotten. "Where's our breakfast?" the middle gentleman asked the cleaning woman in a sour tone. But she put her finger to her lips, and then quickly and quietly beckoned to the gentlemen to enter Gregor's room. So they did, and, with their hands in the pockets of their somewhat threadbare jackets, they stood in a circle around Gregor's corpse in the now sunlit room.

At that point the bedroom door opened and Mr. Samsa, wearing his uniform, appeared with his wife on one arm and his daughter on the other. They all looked a little tearful; from time to time Grete would press her face against her father's sleeve.

"Leave my home at once," Mr. Samsa told the three gentlemen, pointing to the 95 door without letting go of the women. "What do you mean?" said the middle gentleman, who, somewhat taken aback, smiled a sugary smile. The other two held their hands behind their backs, and kept rubbing them together as if cheerfully anticipating a major argument which they were bound to win. "I mean just what I say," replied Mr. Samsa, and advanced in a line with his two companions directly on the middle boarder. At first this gentleman stood still, looking at the floor as if the thoughts inside his head were arranging themselves in a new pattern. "Well, so we'll be off," he then said, looking up at Mr. Samsa as if, suddenly overcome with humility, he was asking permission for even this decision. Mr. Samsa, his eyes glowering, merely gave him a few brief nods. With that the gentleman, taking long strides, actually set off in the direction of the hall; his two friends, who had been listening for some time with their hands quite still, now went hopping right along after him, as if they were afraid that Mr. Samsa might reach the hall before them and cut them off from their leader. Once in the hall the three of them took their hats from the coat rack, pulled their canes from the umbrella stand, bowed silently, and left the apartment. Impelled by a suspicion that would turn out to be utterly groundless, Mr. Samsa led the two women out onto the landing; leaning against the banister railing they watched the three gentlemen as they marched slowly but steadily down the long staircase, disappearing at every floor when the staircase made a turn and then after a few moments reappearing once again. The lower they descended the more the Samsas' interest in them waned; and when a butcher's boy with a basket on his head came proudly up the stairs towards the gentlemen and then swept on past them, Mr. Samsa and the women quickly left the banister and, as if relieved, returned to the apartment.

They decided to spend this day resting and going for a walk; not only did they deserve this break from work, they absolutely needed it. And so they sat down at the table to write their three letters excusing themselves, Mr. Samsa to the bank manager, Mrs. Samsa to her employer, and Grete to the store's owner. While they were writing, the cleaning woman came by to say that she was leaving now, since her morning's work was done. At first the three letter writers merely nodded without looking up, but when the cleaning woman made no move to go, they looked up at her, annoyed. "Well?" asked Mr. Samsa. The cleaning woman stood in the doorway, smiling as if she had some wonderful news for the family, news she wasn't about to share until they came right out and asked her to. The little ostrich feathers in her hat, which stood up nearly straight in the air and which had irritated Mr. Samsa the entire time she had worked for them, swayed gently in every direction. "What can we do for you?" asked Mrs. Samsa, whom the cleaning woman respected the most. "Well," the cleaning woman replied, with such good-humored laughter that she had to pause before continuing, "you don't have to worry about getting rid of that thing in the next room. It's already been taken care of." Mrs. Samsa and Grete bent over their letters as if they intended to keep on writing; Mr. Samsa, who realized that the cleaning woman was about to go into the details, stopped her firmly with an outstretched hand. Seeing that she wasn't going to be allowed to tell her story, she suddenly remembered that she was in a great hurry; clearly insulted, she called out, "Bye, everybody," whirled around wildly, and left the apartment with a terrible slamming of doors.

"She'll be dismissed tonight," said Mr. Samsa, but without getting a reply from his wife or his daughter, for the cleaning woman seemed to have ruined their tenuous peace of mind. They got up, went to the window, and remained there holding each other tightly. Mr. Samsa turned around in his chair toward them and watched them quietly for some time. Then he called out, "Come on now, come over here. Let those old troubles alone. And have a little consideration for me, too." The two women promptly obeyed him, hurried over to him, caressed him, and quickly finished their letters.

Then all three of them left the apartment together, something they hadn't done in months, and took a streetcar out to the open country on the outskirts of the city. Their car, which they had all to themselves, was completely bathed in warm sunlight. Leaning comfortably back in their seats they discussed their prospects for the future, which on closer inspection seemed to be not so bad, since all three of them had jobs which—though they'd never asked one another about them in any detail— were in each case very advantageous and promising. Of course the greatest immediate improvement in their situation would quickly come about when they found a new apartment, one that was smaller, cheaper, and in every way easier to maintain than their current one, which Gregor had chosen for them. As they were talking on in this way, it occurred to both Mr. and Mrs. Samsa, almost simultaneously, as they watched their daughter become more and more vivacious, that in spite of all the recent troubles that had turned her cheeks pale, she had blossomed into a pretty and shapely girl. Growing quieter now, communicating almost unconsciously through glances, they reflected that soon it would be time to find her a good husband. And it was as if in confirmation of their new dreams and good intentions that at the end of their ride their daughter got up first and stretched her young body.

Questions

1. What was Gregor's occupation before his transformation? How did he come to his particular job? What keeps him working for his firm?

2. When Gregor wakes to discover he has become a gigantic insect, he is mostly intent on the practical implications of his metamorphosis—how to get out of bed, how to get to his job, and so on. He never wonders why or how he has been changed. What does this odd reaction suggest about Gregor?

3. When Gregor's parents first see the gigantic insect (paragraph 25), do they recognize it as their son? What do their initial reactions suggest about their attitude toward their son?

4. How does each family member react to Gregor after his transformation? How do these reactions differ from one another? What do they have in common?

5. What things about Gregor have been changed? What seems to have remained the same? List specific qualities.

6. *The Metamorphosis* takes place almost entirely in the Samsa family apartment. How does the story's setting shape its themes?

7. Which family member first decides that the family must "get rid of" the insect? What rationale is given? In what specific ways does the family's decision affect Gregor?

8. How does the family react to Gregor's death?
9. Does Grete change in the course of the story? If so, how does she change?
10. In what ways is Gregor's metamorphosis symbolic?

■ WRITING *effectively*

Franz Kafka on Writing

Discussing *The Metamorphosis*
c. 1920

My friend Alfred Kämpf . . . admired Kafka's story *The Metamorphosis*. He described the author as "a new, more profound and therefore more significant Edgar Allan Poe."

During a walk with Franz Kafka on the Altstädter Ring° I told him about this new admirer of his, but aroused neither interest nor understanding. On the contrary, Kafka's expression showed that any discussion of his book was distasteful to him. I, however, was filled with a zeal for discoveries, and so I was tactless.

"The hero of the story is called Samsa," I said. "It sounds like a cryptogram for Kafka. Five letters in each word. The S in the word Samsa has the same position as the K in the word Kafka. The A . . ."

Kafka interrupted me.

"It is not a cryptogram. Samsa is not merely Kafka, and nothing else. *The Metamorphosis* is not a confession, although it is—in a certain sense—an indiscretion."

"I know nothing about that."

"Is it perhaps delicate and discreet to talk about the bugs in one's own family?"

"It isn't usual in good society."

"You see what bad manners I have."

Kafka smiled. He wished to dismiss the subject. But I did not wish to.

"It seems to me that the distinction between good and bad manners hardly applies here," I said. "*The Metamorphosis* is a terrible dream, a terrible conception."

Kafka stood still.

"The dream reveals the reality, which conception lags behind. That is the horror of life—the terror of art. But now I must go home."

From *Conversations with Kafka* by Gustav Janouch

THINKING ABOUT LONG STORIES AND NOVELS

Writing about a long story or novella may seem overwhelming. There can seem to be so much to analyze and consider. You may despair of being able to master the material and discuss it coherently, but if you focus your attention on some central concerns, you will be surprised at how easily you can develop and express your responses to the work.

- ■ **Be aware that characters in a longer narrative often have more complex personalities.** In a short story, characters are often presented in terms of two

Altstädter Ring: a major street in Prague.

or three basic personality traits. But in a long story or novella, characters are usually drawn with more depth and shading—and sometimes even contradictory elements—to their personalities. In reading a long story, you should be alert to all the different aspects of a character's nature.

- **Consider that a longer narrative allows for more development.** Often the intention of a short story is to reveal a personality or a situation as it is, much in the manner of showing a snapshot or drawing back a curtain. But a longer story requires movement and development to sustain the reader's interest. As you read, notice the—often subtle—changes that may take place in the protagonist as he or she initiates or otherwise experiences the events of the narrative.

- **Review the work.** As a long story or novella unfolds, your recollections of the earlier parts of the text may be pushed aside as new events and situations occur. A first-rate work of fiction will yield a wealth of interconnections of language, images, actions, and ideas. After you finish reading the work, by going through the text again you may often see much more in the story than you did the first time around.

CHECKLIST: Writing About Long Stories and Novels

- ☐ What is the protagonist's situation at the beginning of the work?
- ☐ What is the protagonist's main objective at the beginning?
- ☐ What changes take place in the protagonist's situation as the narrative proceeds?
- ☐ How does the protagonist react to these changes? How does his or her response to stress reveal the protagonist's basic nature?
- ☐ Who are the story's other important characters, and what are their relationships to the protagonist?
- ☐ Can anyone be described as an antagonist?
- ☐ Compare and contrast the beginning of the story with its conclusion.
- ☐ Don't try to put everything in your essay. The longer and more involved the text is, the more important it is to focus on the main points and be selective in the choice of textual details.
- ☐ Try to put your ideas in some logical order.
- ☐ Outline the main points of your argument to see clearly what is relevant to that argument and what is not.

WRITING ASSIGNMENT FOR A RESEARCH PAPER

This challenging assignment for a research paper comes from Professor Michael Cass of Mercer University. He asked his students to select the fiction writer whose work impressed them most. Each student had to write a paper defending that author's claim to literary greatness and research the author, using at least five critical sources. The student had to present clear reasons why the author was a major writer and to support the argument with both examples from the writer's work and statements from critics. Choose an author from this book whose greatness you would defend. Here is a short research paper by a student in Professor Cass's class, Stephanie Crowe, who discussed why she believed that Franz Kafka was a great writer.

SAMPLE STUDENT RESEARCH PAPER

Crowe 1

Stephanie Crowe

Professor Cass

English 120

21 November 2009

Kafka's Greatness

Introduction of essay topic

Although most of his major works remained unfinished and unpublished at his untimely death in 1924, Franz Kafka has gradually come to be considered one of the great writers of the twentieth century. By 1977, well over ten thousand works of commentary had appeared on Kafka, and many

Citation of secondary source

more have been written since then (Goodden 2). According to critic Peter Heller, Kafka represents the "mainstream of German literary and intellectual

Quotation from secondary source integrated into sentence

tradition," a nihilistic tradition which extends from Goethe and Lessing to the present (289).

Topic sentence on Kafka as influence

Not only is Kafka generally considered one of the greatest fiction writers of the modern era, he is also indisputably one of the most influential. In his 1989 study, *After Kafka*, Shimon Sandbank discusses Kafka's influence on a dozen modern writers, including Sartre, Camus, Beckett, Borges, and Ionesco. His effects on these writers differ. Some borrow his understated, almost passive prose style while others adopt his recurrent images and themes. Whatever the specific elements they use, however, Kafka's ability to influence these writers is another measure of his stature.

Great literature often gives us the stories and images to understand our own age, a process that necessarily includes understanding our deepest

Assumptions explained

problems. The twentieth century, to borrow a phrase from W. H. Auden, was mostly an "Age of Anxiety." Most modern people are no longer bound to follow the occupations, behaviors, and beliefs of their parents, but they gain this newfound freedom at the expense of a constant, difficult search for identity. The personal quest for meaningful identity often leads to despair. This "existential crisis" is the basis for many contemporary problems including the decline of religion, the rise of totalitarianism, the breakdown of social identity, and the decay of traditional family structure.

Topic sentence on Kafka's relationship to his time

Kafka's works dramatize these problems memorably because they provide us with myths, images, stories, and situations that describe the particular crises of the early twentieth century. When faced with the modern challenge of not having a predetermined social or religious identity, Kafka's characters desperately attempt to find certainty. The problem, however, is that they are usually afraid to do anything decisive because everything is uncertain. Auden observed:

> Far from being confident of success, the Kafka hero is convinced from the start that he is doomed to fail, as he is also doomed, being who he is, to make prodigious and unending efforts to reach it [the goal]. Indeed, the mere desire to reach the goal is itself a proof, not that he is one of the elect, but that he is under a special curse. (162)

Quotation from secondary source, set off from text

One way that Kafka memorably dramatizes the modern struggle for identity is by reversing the traditional quest story. In a quest story, the hero knows the goal that he wants to achieve and has some confidence that he will be able to achieve it. As he tries to reach the goal, he must overcome various enemies and obstacles. "In a typical Kafka story, on the other hand, the goal is peculiar to the hero himself: he has no competitors" (Auden 162). His question then becomes not a practical "Can I succeed?" but instead a vague and problematic "What should I do?" Unable to answer this question satisfactorily, the hero becomes increasingly alienated from his own surroundings. This alienation is yet another symptom of "the inhumanity of modern society" that Kafka so memorably portrayed (Kuna 62).

Topic sentence elaborates on how Kafka's work reflects his time

Verbatim quotation from secondary source

Kafka also distinguishes himself as a great writer because he created a distinctive style that effectively dramatizes modern problems. Although Kafka's fiction often describes extreme situations, his prose usually seems strangely calm and detached. He uses "clear and simple language" that paints "concrete pictures of human beings, pictures that, in a sense, have to speak for themselves" (Cooper 19). These haunting images (the unreachable castle, the unknown laws, the unspecified trial) dramatize the mysterious struggles of the characters.

Topic sentence on relationship between Kafka's era and his style

Kafka also uses his style to separate himself from his characters, a technique that develops a contrast between the calmness of his style and the nervous desperation of his characters (Heller 237). For example, the opening of Kafka's novella *The Metamorphosis*, which is perhaps the most famous first sentence in modern fiction, describes an outrageous event—a young man who wakes up transformed into a giant bug—in a strangely matter-of-fact tone. This contrast is important because it reminds us of the desperation of modern man imprisoned in a world he can neither understand nor control.

Topic sentence on Kafka's style incorporates critical view

Crowe 3

Topic sentence on Kafka's style of ambiguity

Perhaps the most interesting feature of Kafka's style is his ability to create works that cannot be explained by a single interpretation. Because he allows his pictures to "speak for themselves," "Kafka's texts have been subject to a variety of widely divergent approaches" (Heller 236). Another critic, speaking directly of *The Metamorphosis*, agrees: "Gregor's transformation has a double meaning: it is both an escape from his oppressive life and a representation or even an intensification of it" (Goldfarb). Therefore, no single interpretation can adequately explain an entire work of Kafka's. Most interpretations may illuminate particular moments in a work, but inevitably they lead to a dead end when pressed to explain the whole narrative. Whether one is reading on a social, moral, psychological, metaphysical, theological, or existential level, Kafka "tends to suspend all distinction and thus to revert to total ambiguity" (Heller 285). According to Heller, this characteristic mysteriousness becomes "the epitome of his art" (230).

Topic sentence on Kafka's complexity

Auden believed that the impossibility of interpreting Kafka's work is essential in defining him as an important and influential writer. He says that "Kafka is a great, perhaps the greatest, master of the pure parable, a literary genre about which a critic can say very little worth saying" (159). Since the meaning of a parable is different for each individual, critics cannot explain them without revealing their own visions and values. Kafka develops stories with important symbols that are easily identified; attempting to interpret these symbols, however, only leads to frustration.

Topic sentence on Kafka's central theme incorporates quotation from secondary source

The frustration that comes from trying to interpret Kafka's works exemplifies his recurrent, and particularly twentieth-century, theme, which Peter Heller has described as man's "ever frustrated, ever defeated striving for self-realization in an inhuman human universe in which he is alienated from himself and from the world he lives in" (305). Kafka uses his characteristic difficult symbolism and ambiguity, along with his theme of hopelessness and despair, as a common thread that binds all of his works together.

Topic sentence on tone

Kafka's book *The Great Wall of China* contains several short pieces which have a slightly less desperate tone than that of *The Metamorphosis*. Many of the stories in *The Great Wall of China*, however, still present the theme of hopelessness. In the reflection entitled "The Problem of Our Laws," Kafka examines the origins and legitimacy of law. This parable begins with the narrator stating, "Our laws are not generally known; they are kept secret by the small group of nobles who rule us" (147). Next, the narrator goes through a

Quotation from primary source

laborious process of rationally questioning why only the nobility knows the laws, whether the laws really exist, and whether it will ever be possible for common men to know the laws. He finally concludes that the only way to know the law would be a quiet revolution that ends nobility. But even this solution, he realizes, is futile. The nobility cannot be eliminated because they provide the only order that exists. While this parable makes several interesting points, its structure is essentially static. The narrator ends where he began—trapped in an unknowable world.

One of Kafka's unfinished novels, *The Trial*, also concentrates on the unknown symbol of the Law. In the novel, Joseph K. is arrested for a crime that no one ever knows. Joseph, like most of Kafka's characters, is a common man with an uneventful life who admits that he knows little of the Law. The drama of the novel is the protagonist's hopeless attempts to master an unknown and impossible situation. Joseph K.'s life itself becomes a trial, although he is never sentenced. Finally, one year after his arrest, two men come and murder him. Instead of trying to understand the Law, "In the end he appears to accept the verdict as a release from the condition of despair," and "dies like an animal, without comprehending the rationale of the Law which condemns him" (Heller 280-81). Like many men, before his death K. is struggling to discover his identity in relation to the Law that governs him; however, K.'s hopeless life ends with a pointless murder.

Topic sentence on theme

Kafka's other great, unfinished novel, *The Castle*, also concentrates on the theme of unknowability and despair. Instead of trying to understand the Law, K. in *The Castle* has another impossible quest, his attempt to enter the castle of the local ruler to report for duty as a land surveyor. His constant efforts, however, prove futile. As in *The Trial*, the protagonist is at the mercy of an arbitrary and unknowable Law:

Topic sentence on theme

> In many ways the castle functions like a secret court system: the officials decide and carry out policies that are conceived as stipulations of law; they lean on their law books, try to serve the law, and know the clandestine ways of law. Many decisions are arrived at arbitrarily and remain secret; even legal actions such as an official indictment can be kept hidden for some time. (Heidsieck 3)

Only when K. lies on his deathbed does a call from the castle come, giving him permission to live in the town. Once again, the protagonist suffers hopelessly and dies in despair.

Crowe 5

While *The Trial* emphasizes political and psychological themes characteristic of the twentieth century, *The Castle* focuses on the religious identity crisis. *The Metamorphosis* examines similar themes of identity on a personal and family level. All of these works focus on modern humanity's difficult struggle to define its place in existence.

Conclusion sums up argument

Kafka, through his works, accurately describes the modern condition of many by using memorable images and a distinctive style. This characteristic style influenced many twentieth-century writers and readers. While difficult and somewhat bleak, Kafka's often ambiguous, yet understated dramatizations of man's condition, along with his lasting influence, form the foundation of his greatness.

Thesis sentence makes debatable claim

Crowe 6

Works Cited

Auden, W. H. "The I Without a Self." *The Dyer's Hand*. New York: Random, 1989. 159–70. Print.

Cooper, Gabriele Bon Natzmer. *Kafka and Language: In the Stream of Thoughts and Life*. Riverside, CA: Ariadne, 1991. Print.

Goldfarb, Sheldon. "Critical Essay on *The Metamorphosis*." *Short Stories for Students*. Ed. Jennifer Smith. Vol. 12. Detroit: Gale, 2001. N. pag. *Literature Resource Center*. Gale. Web. 19 September 2009.

Goodden, Christina. "Points of Departure." *The Kafka Debate: New Perspectives for Our Time*. Ed. Angel Flores. New York: Gordian, 1988. 2–9. Print.

Heidsieck, Arnold. "Community, Delusion and Anti-Semitism in Kafka's *The Castle*." *German Studies Program*. German Dept., U of Southern California, n.d. Web. 19 September 2009. <http://www.usc.edu/dept/LAS/german/track/heidsiec/KafkaAntisemitism/KafkaAntisemitism.pdf>.

Heller, Peter. "Kafka: The Futility of Striving." *Dialectics and Nihilism*. Amherst: U of Massachusetts P, 1966. 227–306. Print.

Kafka, Franz. "The Problem of Our Laws." *The Great Wall of China*. New York: Schocken, 1946. 147–49. Print.

Crowe 7

Kuna, Franz. *Franz Kafka: Literature as Corrective Punishment*. Bloomington:

Indiana UP, 1974. Print.

Sandbank, Shimon. *After Kafka: The Influence of Kafka's Fiction*. Athens: U of

Georgia P, 1989. Print.

MORE TOPICS FOR WRITING

1. What do Ivan Ilych and Gregor Samsa have in common? In what ways are their lives and deaths dissimilar?

2. Choose a thematic concern of either *The Death of Ivan Ilych* or *The Metamorphosis*; some possibilities are work, romantic love, and the family. Develop a thesis about what your story has to say on your chosen theme. Now choose three key moments from the story to back up your argument. Make your case in a medium-length paper (600 to 1,000 words); be sure to quote as needed from the text.

3. In one carefully thought-out paragraph, sum up what you believe Tolstoy is saying in *The Death of Ivan Ilych*.

4. Compare Tolstoy's short novel with another story of spiritual awakening: Flannery O'Connor's "Revelation" or "A Good Man Is Hard to Find." In each, what brings about the enlightenment of the central character?

5. Is *The Metamorphosis* a horror story? What elements does Kafka's story share with horror fiction or films you have known? How does *The Metamorphosis* differ?

6. Compare and contrast Gregor Samsa's relationships with the people in his life to Miss Emily's relationships with those around her in "A Rose for Emily."

7. Explore how Gregor Samsa's metamorphosis into a giant insect is symbolic of his earlier life and relations with his family. (For a discussion of literary symbols, see Chapter 7, "Symbol.")

8. Write a metamorphosis story of your own. Imagine a character who turns overnight into something quite other than himself or herself. As you describe that character's struggles, try for a mix of tragedy and grotesque comedy, as found in *The Metamorphosis*.

▶ TERMS FOR *review*

Novel ▶ An extended work of fictional prose narrative. The term *novel* usually implies a book-length narrative.

Novella ▶ In modern terms, a prose narrative longer than a short story but shorter than a novel. Unlike a short story, a novella is long enough to be published independently as a brief book.

Romance ▶ In general terms, romance is a narrative mode that employs exotic adventure and idealized emotion rather than realistic depiction of character and action. In the romantic mode, people, actions, and events are depicted more as we wish them to be (heroes are very brave, villains are very bad) than in the complex forms in which they usually exist. Most popular fiction genres—such as mystery, horror, adventure, science fiction—develop from this mode.

Historical fiction ▶ A type of fiction in which the narrative is set in another time or place. In historical fiction, the author often attempts to recreate a faithful picture of daily life during the period. While it may depict real historical figures, more often it places imaginary characters in a carefully reconstructed version of a particular era.

Nonfiction novel ▶ A genre in which actual events are presented as a novel-length story, using the techniques of fiction.

Picaresque ▶ A type of narrative, usually a novel, that presents the life of a likable scoundrel at odds with respectable society. The narrator of a picaresque was originally a *pícaro* (Spanish for "rascal" or "rogue") who recounts his or her adventures tricking the rich and gullible. This type of narrative rarely has a tightly constructed plot, and the episodes or adventures follow in a loose chronological order.

Epistolary novel ▶ Novel in which the story is told by way of letters written by one or more of the characters. This form often lends an authenticity to the story, an illusion that the author may have discovered these letters, even though they are a product of the author's imagination.

Bildungsroman ▶ German for "novel of growth and development." Sometimes called an **apprenticeship novel**, this genre depicts a youth who struggles toward maturity and the forming of a worldview or philosophy of life.

9 LATIN AMERICAN FICTION

Writing is nothing more than a guided dream.

—JORGE LUIS BORGES

Before the middle of the twentieth century Latin America produced a number of highly talented novelists, but their work had relatively little impact outside their region—and often little impact beyond their own individual nations. For the most part, these novels fit into the tradition of realism that dominated European literature in the late nineteenth century, and often pursued a social agenda, emphasizing the economic and geographical characteristics that were unique to the writer's own country. It was relatively rare for the fiction of any individual nation to be published or even to circulate in the other countries of Spanish America. One author who transcended these limits was the Guatemalan novelist Miguel Ángel Asturias (1899–1974), who is credited with introducing some of the techniques of Modernism into Latin American fiction and who would go on to win the Nobel Prize in Literature in 1967.

But even Asturias felt that Latin American literature, while powerful, remained provincial. In a 1970 interview he said, "To believe that we Latin Americans are going to teach Europeans to reflect, to philosophize, to write egocentric or psychological novels, to believe that we are already a mature enough society to produce a Proust or a Goethe—that would be daydreaming and self-deception." His remarks exemplified the marginality still felt by most Latin American writers of his generation.

"EL BOOM"

Asturias underestimated the growing influence and appeal of Latin American literature. By 1970 Latin American fiction had begun to capture international attention. A new generation of fiction writers had emerged who had been profoundly influenced by the great Modernists of American, British, and European literature. In their hands, formal literary style relaxed to incorporate common speech, sudden shifts of tone, and extravagant wordplay. Characterization became more complex and multilayered, and instead of straightforward, realist narrative there were now often fractured time sequences and fantastic events. These young writers were the catalysts of an explosion of creativity—commonly referred to as **"El Boom"**—that transformed Latin America into one of the centers of modern world fiction.

One of the pioneering figures of the movement was the Mexican writer Carlos Fuentes; Chilean novelist Jose Donoso would later write of Fuentes's 1959 novel *Where the Air Is Clear*: "Reading it was a cataclysm for me. Until then, I had been governed by a paralyzing good taste, and for me, the politics and forces giving shape to our history were matters of hometown gossip on the level of friendly phone calls, never on the level of myths, invasions, or idolatries." Other writers prominently associated with the Boom were Julio Cortázar of Argentina, whose experimental novel *Hopscotch* (1963) attracted widespread international attention, and Mario Vargas Llosa of Peru, who also achieved an international reputation with *The Time of the Hero* (1963) and *Aunt Julia and the Scriptwriter* (1977). But its best-known and most influential figure is the Colombian novelist Gabriel García Márquez, whose *One Hundred Years of Solitude* (1967) is the defining text both of "El Boom" and of the genre known as *magic realism*.

MAGIC REALISM

Magic realism (*el realismo magical*) was a term coined in 1949 by the Cuban novelist Alejo Carpentier to describe the matter-of-fact combination of the fantastic and everyday in Latin American fiction. Magic realism has now become the standard name for a major trend in contemporary fiction that stretches from Latin American works such as García Márquez's *One Hundred Years of Solitude* and Octavio Paz's "My Life with the Wave," to *norteamericana* novels such as Mark Helprin's *Winter's Tale* (1983) and Asian works such as Salman Rushdie's *Midnight's Children* (1981). In all cases the term refers to the tendency among contemporary fiction writers to mix the magical and mundane in an overall context of realistic narration.

If the term *magic realism* is relatively new, what it describes has been around since the early development of the novel and short story as modern literary forms. One already sees the key elements of magic realism in *Gulliver's Travels* (1726), which factually narrates the fabulous adventures of an English surgeon. Likewise Nikolai Gogol's short story "The Nose" (1842), in which a minor Czarist bureaucrat's nose takes off to pursue its own career in St. Petersburg, fulfills virtually every requirement of this purportedly contemporary style. One finds similar precedents in Charles Dickens, Honoré de Balzac, Fyodor Dostoyevsky, Guy de Maupassant, Franz Kafka, and others. Seen from a historical perspective, therefore, magic realism is a vital contemporary manifestation of a venerable fictive impulse.

The possibilities of storytelling will always hover between the opposing poles of realism and romance. Until recently most English-language critics almost exclusively favored the realist mode—their emphasis reflected what F. R. Leavis called the "Great Tradition" of the psychological and social realist novel. This tradition encompassed Jane Austen, George Eliot, Henry James, Edith Wharton, Joseph Conrad, Virginia Woolf, D. H. Lawrence, Willa Cather, and early James Joyce. These British and American critics would hardly have imagined that a radically different kind of fiction was being developed beyond their ken in places like Argentina, Colombia, and Peru. By the time García Márquez and his fellow members of the Boom in Latin American fiction came to maturity, the reemergence of the fantastic heritage in fiction seemed nearly as revolutionary as the region's politics.

All of the main features of Latin American magic realism can be found in García Márquez's "A Very Old Man with Enormous Wings," which appeared in his 1972 book

The Incredible and Sad Tale of Innocent Eréndira and Her Heartless Grandmother, written soon after *One Hundred Years of Solitude*. As a young law student, García Márquez read Kafka's *The Metamorphosis*. It proved a decisive encounter, and the influence is not hard to observe in the early stories, which so often present bizarre incidents unfolding in ordinary circumstances. If Kafka reinvented the animal fable by placing it in the everyday modern world, García Márquez reset it in the unfamiliar landscape of the Third World. If Kafka made spiritual issues more mysterious by surrounding them with bureaucratic procedure, his Colombian follower changed our perception of Latin America by insisting that in this New World visionary romanticism was merely reportage. García Márquez also had another crucial mentor closer at hand—the Argentinean master, Jorge Luis Borges.

Only thirty years García Márquez's senior, Borges had quietly redrawn the imaginative boundaries of Latin American fiction, though his work appeared only sporadically in English translation until the early 1960s. Almost single-handedly he had rehabilitated the fantastic tale for literary fiction. Significantly, Borges expressed his sophisticated fictions in popular rather than experimental forms—the fable, the detective story, the supernatural tale, the gaucho legend. Intellectually and temperamentally, Borges was a true citizen of the world; both bookish and playful by nature, he was widely read in European literature and was influenced by an impressive range of writers, including—among many others—Cervantes, Poe, Kafka, and Robert Louis Stevenson. Possessed of an essentially ironic sensibility, he was also strongly influenced by the late-nineteenth-century Symbolist movement—both of which tendencies can be found in "The Gospel According to Mark." He was the first great postmodernist storyteller, and he found an eager apprentice in García Márquez, who developed these innovative notions in different and usually more expansive forms.

AFTER THE BOOM

Like Borges, the Mexican author Octavio Paz was older than the writers of the Boom and had been publishing for decades before their careers began. Paz originally made his mark as a poet, but in the later decades of the twentieth century he gradually established himself as one of the dominant figures of Latin American literature with a series of prose works that incorporated history, biography, psychology, literary theorizing, and spiritual meditation. As the critic Ilan Stavans has said of him: "Paz was never a best-selling author on the scale of Stephen King, but his influence on our culture and his endurance are infinitely wider and more durable." Along with Borges, Paz helped make Latin American literature more inclusive and cosmopolitan.

One of the most frequently raised criticisms of the Boom is its heavily male emphasis, in terms of both the authors themselves and the characters in their novels. More recent years have seen the emergence of important female authors, including the Chilean Isabel Allende, a writer in the tradition of magical realism whose novel *The House of the Spirits* (1982) was an international best-seller, and the Mexican Inés Arredondo, whose subtle and moving short stories—of which "The Shunammite" is an outstanding example—explore the psychology of women and their place in society. In the wake of the Boom, Latin American literature is notably richer, deeper, and more diverse than ever before. If someone were to slightly modify the Englishman Sydney Smith's early nineteenth-century sneer at the literature of the United States and ask "Who reads a Latin American book?," the answer would be, anyone who wants to be in touch with some of the most original, exciting, and important literature in the world today.

Jorge Luis Borges

The Gospel According to Mark   1970

Translated by Andrew Hurley

Jorge Luis Borges (1899–1986), an outstanding modern writer of Latin America, was born in Buenos Aires into a family prominent in Argentine history. His father, with whom he had a very close relationship, was a lawyer and teacher. Borges grew up bilingual, learning English from his English grandmother and receiving his early education from an English tutor. In later years, he would translate work by Poe, Melville, Whitman, Faulkner, and others into Spanish. Caught in Europe by the outbreak of World War I, Borges lived in Switzerland—where he learned French and taught himself German—and later Spain,

Jorge Luis Borges

where he joined the Ultraists, a group of experimental poets who renounced realism. On returning to Argentina, he edited a poetry magazine printed in the form of a poster and affixed to city walls. In his early writings, Borges favored the style of Criollismo (regionalism), but by the mid-1930s he had begun to take a more cosmopolitan and internationalist approach; in this same period, his principal literary emphasis began to shift from poetry to fiction. In 1946, for his opposition to the regime of Colonel Juan Perón, Borges was forced to resign his post as a librarian and was mockingly offered a job as a chicken inspector. In 1955, after Perón was deposed, Borges became director of the National Library and professor of English literature at the University of Buenos Aires. A sufferer since childhood from poor eyesight, Borges eventually went blind. His eye problems may have encouraged him to work mainly in short, highly crafted forms: stories, essays, fables, and lyric poems full of elaborate music. His short stories, in Ficciones (1944), El hacedor (1960; translated as Dreamtigers, 1964), and Labyrinths (1962), have been admired worldwide.

The incident took place on the Los Alamos ranch, south of the small town of Junín, in late March of 1928. Its protagonist was a medical student named Baltasar Espinosa. We might define him for the moment as a Buenos Aires youth much like many others, with no traits worthier of note than the gift for public speaking that had won him more than one prize at the English school° in Ramos Mejía and an almost unlimited goodness. He didn't like to argue; he preferred that his interlocutor rather than he himself be right. And though he found the chance twists and turns of gambling interesting, he was a poor gambler, because he didn't like to win. He was intelligent and open to learning, but he was lazy; at thirty-three he had not yet completed the last requirements for his degree. (The work he still owed, incidentally, was for his

English school: a prep school that emphasized English (well-to-do Argentineans of this era wanted their children to learn English).

favorite class.) His father, like all the gentlemen of his day a freethinker,° had instructed Espinosa in the doctrines of Herbert Spencer,° but once, before he set off on a trip to Montevideo, his mother had asked him to say the Lord's Prayer every night and make the sign of the cross, and never in all the years that followed did he break that promise. He did not lack courage; one morning, with more indifference than wrath, he had traded two or three blows with some of his classmates that were trying to force him to join a strike at the university. He abounded in debatable habits and opinions, out of a spirit of acquiescence: his country mattered less to him than the danger that people in other countries might think the Argentines still wore feathers; he venerated France but had contempt for the French; he had little respect for Americans but took pride in the fact that there were skyscrapers in Buenos Aires; he thought that the gauchos° of the plains were better horsemen than the gauchos of the mountains. When his cousin Daniel invited him to spend the summer at Los Alamos, he immediately accepted—not because he liked the country but out of a natural desire to please, and because he could find no good reason for saying no.

The main house at the ranch was large and a bit run-down; the quarters for the foreman, a man named Gutre, stood nearby. There were three members of the Gutre family: the father, the son (who was singularly rough and unpolished), and a girl of uncertain paternity. They were tall, strong, and bony, with reddish hair and Indian features. They rarely spoke. The foreman's wife had died years before.

In the country, Espinosa came to learn things he hadn't known, had never even suspected; for example, that when you're approaching a house there's no reason to gallop and that nobody goes out on a horse unless there's a job to be done. As the summer wore on, he learned to distinguish birds by their call.

Within a few days, Daniel had to go to Buenos Aires to close a deal on some livestock. At the most, he said, the trip would take a week. Espinosa, who was already a little tired of his cousin's *bonnes fortunes* and his indefatigable interest in the vagaries of men's tailoring, stayed behind on the ranch with his textbooks. The heat was oppressive, and not even nightfall brought relief. Then one morning toward dawn, he was awakened by thunder. Wind lashed the casuarina trees. Espinosa heard the first drops of rain and gave thanks to God. Suddenly the wind blew cold. That afternoon, the Salado overflowed.

The next morning, as he stood on the porch looking out over the flooded plains, Baltasar Espinosa realized that the metaphor equating the pampas with the sea was not, at least that morning, an altogether false one, though Hudson° had noted that the sea seems the grander of the two because we view it not from horseback or our own height, but from the deck of a ship. The rain did not let up; the Gutres, helped (or hindered) by the city dweller, saved a good part of the livestock, though many animals were drowned. There were four roads leading to the ranch; all were under water. On the third day, when a leaking roof threatened the foreman's house, Espinosa gave the Gutres a room at the back of the main house, alongside the toolshed. The move brought Espinosa and the Gutres closer, and they began to eat together in the large dining room. Conversation was not easy; the Gutres, who knew so much about things in the country, did not know how to explain them. One night Espinosa asked them if people still remembered

5

---

freethinker: person who rejects traditional beliefs, especially religious dogma, in favor of rational inquiry. *Herbert Spencer:* a British philosopher (1820–1903) who championed the theory of evolution. *gaucho:* a South American cowboy. *W. H. Hudson:* an English naturalist and author (1841–1922) who wrote extensively about South America.

anything about the Indian raids, back when the military command for the frontier had been in Junín. They told him they did, but they would have given the same answer if he had asked them about the day Charles I° had been beheaded. Espinosa recalled that his father used to say that all the cases of longevity that occur in the country are the result of either poor memory or a vague notion of dates—gauchos quite often know neither the year they were born in nor the name of the man that fathered them.

In the entire house, the only reading material to be found were several copies of a farming magazine, a manual of veterinary medicine, a deluxe edition of the romantic verse drama *Tabaré*, a copy of *The History of the Shorthorn in Argentina*, several erotic and detective stories, and a recent novel that Espinosa had not read—*Don Segundo Sombra*, by Ricardo Güiraldes. In order to put some life into the inevitable after-dinner attempt at conversation, Espinosa read a couple of chapters of the novel to the Gutres, who did not know how to read or write. Unfortunately, the foreman had been a cattle drover himself, and he could not be interested in the adventures of another such a one. It was easy work, he said; they always carried along a pack mule with everything they might need. If he had not been a cattle drover, he announced, he'd never have seen Lake Gómez, or the Bragado River, or even the Núñez ranch, in Chacabuco. . . .

In the kitchen there was a guitar; before the incident I am narrating, the laborers would sit in a circle and someone would pick up the guitar and strum it, though never managing actually to play it. That was called "giving it a strum."

Espinosa, who was letting his beard grow out, would stop before the mirror to look at his changed face; he smiled to think that he'd soon be boring the fellows in Buenos Aires with his stories about the Salado overrunning its banks. Curiously, he missed places in the city he never went, and would never go: a street corner on Cabrera where a mailbox stood; two cement lions on a porch on Calle Jujuy a few blocks from the Plaza del Once; a tile-floored corner grocery-store-and-bar (whose location he couldn't quite remember). As for his father and his brothers, by now Daniel would have told them that he had been isolated—the word was etymologically precise—by the floodwaters.

Exploring the house still cut off by the high water, he came upon a Bible printed in English. On its last pages the Guthries (for that was their real name) had kept their family history. They had come originally from Inverness° and had arrived in the New World—doubtlessly as peasant laborers—in the early nineteenth century; they had intermarried with Indians. The chronicle came to an end in the eighteen-seventies; they no longer knew how to write. Within a few generations they had forgotten their English; by the time Espinosa met them, even Spanish gave them some difficulty. They had no faith, though in their veins, alongside the superstitions of the pampas, there still ran a dim current of the Calvinist's harsh fanaticism. Espinosa mentioned his find to them, but they hardly seemed to hear him.

He leafed through the book, and his fingers opened it to the first verses of the Gospel According to St. Mark. To try his hand at translating, and perhaps to see if they might understand a little of it, he decided that that would be the text he read the Gutres after dinner. He was surprised that they listened first attentively and then with mute fascination. The presence of gold letters on the binding may have given it increased authority. "It's in their blood," he thought. It also occurred to him that   10

Charles I: King of England, beheaded in 1649.   *Inverness:* a county in Scotland.

throughout history, humankind has told two stories: the story of a lost ship sailing the Mediterranean seas in quest of a beloved isle, and the story of a god who allows himself to be crucified on Golgotha. He recalled his elocution classes in Ramos Mejía, and he rose to his feet to preach the parables.

In the following days, the Gutres would wolf down the spitted beef and canned sardines in order to arrive sooner at the Gospel.

The girl had a little lamb; it was her pet, and she prettied it with a sky blue ribbon. One day it cut itself on a piece of barbed wire; to stanch the blood, the Gutres were about to put spiderwebs on the wound, but Espinosa treated it with pills. The gratitude awakened by that cure amazed him. At first, he had not trusted the Gutres and had hidden away in one of his books the two hundred forty pesos he'd brought; now, with Daniel gone, he had taken the master's place and begun to give timid orders, which were immediately followed. The Gutres would trail him through the rooms and along the hallway, as though they were lost. As he read, he noticed that they would sweep away the crumbs he had left on the table. One afternoon, he surprised them as they were discussing him in brief, respectful words. When he came to the end of the Gospel According to St. Mark, he started to read another of the three remaining gospels, but the father asked him to reread the one he'd just finished, so they could understand it better. Espinosa felt they were like children, who prefer repetition to variety or novelty. One night he dreamed of the Flood (which is not surprising) and was awakened by the hammering of the building of the Ark, but he told himself it was thunder. And in fact the rain, which had let up for a while, had begun again; it was very cold. The Gutres told him the rain had broken through the roof of the toolshed; when they got the beams repaired, they said, they'd show him where. He was no longer a stranger, a foreigner, and they all treated him with respect; he was almost spoiled. None of them liked coffee, but there was always a little cup for him, with spoonfuls of sugar stirred in.

That second storm took place on a Tuesday. Thursday night there was a soft knock on his door; because of his doubts about the Gutres he always locked it. He got up and opened the door; it was the girl. In the darkness he couldn't see her, but he could tell by her footsteps that she was barefoot, and afterward, in the bed, that she was naked—that in fact she had come from the back of the house that way. She did not embrace him, or speak a word; she lay down beside him and she was shivering. It was the first time she had lain with a man. When she left, she did not kiss him; Espinosa realized that he didn't even know her name. Impelled by some sentiment he did not attempt to understand, he swore that when he returned to Buenos Aires, he'd tell no one of the incident.

The next day began like all the others, except that the father spoke to Espinosa to ask whether Christ had allowed himself to be killed in order to save all mankind. Espinosa, who was a freethinker like his father but felt obliged to defend what he had read them, paused.

"Yes," he finally replied. "To save all mankind from hell." 15

"What *is* hell?" Gutre then asked him.

"A place underground where souls will burn in fire forever."

"And those that drove the nails will also be saved?"

"Yes," replied Espinosa, whose theology was a bit shaky. (He had worried that the foreman wanted to have a word with him about what had happened last night with his daughter.)

After lunch they asked him to read the last chapters again. 20

Espinosa had a long siesta that afternoon, although it was a light sleep, interrupted by persistent hammering and vague premonitions. Toward evening he got up and went out into the hall.

"The water's going down," he said, as though thinking out loud. "It won't be long now."

"Not long now," repeated Gutre, like an echo.

The three of them had followed him. Kneeling on the floor, they asked his blessing. Then they cursed him, spat on him, and drove him to the back of the house. The girl was weeping. Espinosa realized what awaited him on the other side of the door. When they opened it, he saw the sky. A bird screamed; *it's a goldfinch*, Espinosa thought. There was no roof on the shed; they had torn down the roof beams to build the Cross.

Questions

1. What is about to happen to Baltasar Espinosa at the end of this story?
2. How old is Espinosa? What is ironic about his age?
3. What is the background of the Gutre family? How did they come to own an English Bible? Why is it ironic that they own this book?
4. The narrator claims that the protagonist, Espinosa, has only two noteworthy qualities: an almost unlimited kindness and a capacity for public speaking. How do these qualities become important in the story?
5. When Espinosa begins reading the Gospel of Saint Mark to the Gutres, what changes in their behavior does he notice?
6. What other action does Espinosa perform that earns the Gutres's gratitude?
7. Reread the last paragraph. Why is it ironic that the Gutres ask Espinosa's blessing and the daughter weeps?
8. Why do the Gutres kill Espinosa? What do they hope to gain?
9. Is the significance of Espinosa's death entirely ironic? Or does he resemble Christ in any important respect?

Octavio Paz

My Life with the Wave   1951

Translated by Eliot Weinberger

Octavio Paz (1914–1998) was born in Mexico City. His grandfather, a journalist and novelist, had fought alongside Benito Juarez in resistance to the French occupation of Mexico in the 1860s. His father, a lawyer, had fought for the revolution and had been the private secretary of peasant guerrilla leader Emiliano Zapata. Paz grew up in his grandfather's large but decaying house, and spent much of his time in its library of more than 6,000 volumes. He went to Spain in 1937, intending to fight on the Loyalist side in the Spanish Civil War, but found his leftist ideals severely tested by what he witnessed there, and he gradually adopted a centrist political

Octavio Paz

position that rejected both extremes of right-wing dictatorship and Marxist revolution; his intellectual honesty would later bring him many enemies when he became an early critic of the Castro regime in Cuba. Paz joined the Mexican foreign service in 1945; over the course of his diplomatic career, he held postings in San Francisco, New York, Tokyo, Geneva, and Delhi, but in 1968, after six years as Mexico's ambassador to India, he resigned in protest over his government's brutal suppression of student demonstrations. He then supported himself by teaching at Cambridge, Harvard, the University of Texas, and elsewhere.

Beginning in 1933 and continuing steadily thereafter, Paz published the many volumes of poetry that are the cornerstone of his achievement and the basis of his worldwide reputation. His work, which has been translated by such eminent poets as Elizabeth Bishop, Denise Levertov, John Frederick Nims, and Charles Tomlinson, has its fullest representation in English in The Collected Poems of Octavio Paz 1957–1987. *While immersed in his own culture and national ethos, as demonstrated in* The Labyrinth of Solitude (1950), *Paz was a profound internationalist as well:* The Bow and the Lyre (1956), *a study of the poetic process, and* Convergences: Essays on Art and Literature (1987) *range impressively from ancient to modern times, from the old world to the new. In 1990, Paz was awarded the Nobel Prize in Literature, becoming the only Mexican-born writer to have attained that honor.*

When I left that sea, a wave moved ahead of the others. She was tall and light. In spite of the shouts of the others who grabbed her by her floating clothes, she clutched my arm and went off with me leaping. I didn't want to say anything to her, because it hurt me to shame her in front of her friends. Besides, the furious stares of the elders paralyzed me. When we got to town, I explained to her that it was impossible, that life in the city was not what she had been able to imagine with the ingenuity of a wave that had never left the sea. She watched me gravely. "No, your decision is made. You can't go back." I tried sweetness, hardness, irony. She cried, screamed, hugged, threatened. I had to apologize.

The next day my troubles began. How could we get on the train without being seen by the conductor, the passengers, the police? Certainly the rules say nothing in respect to the transport of waves on the railroad, but this same reserve was an indication of the severity with which our act would be judged. After much thought I arrived at the station an hour before departure, took my seat, and, when no one was looking, emptied the water tank for the passengers; then, carefully, poured in my friend.

The first incident came about when the children of a nearby couple declared their noisy thirst. I stopped them and promised them refreshments and lemonade. They were at the point of accepting when another thirsty passenger approached. I was about to invite her also, but the stare of her companion stopped me. The lady took a paper cup, approached the tank, and turned the faucet. Her cup was barely half full when I leaped between the woman and my friend. She looked at me astonished. While I apologized, one of the children turned the faucet again. I closed it violently. The lady brought the cup to her lips:

"Agh, this water is salty."

The boy echoed her. Various passengers rose. The husband called the conductor: 5

"This man put salt in the water."

The conductor called the Inspector:

"So you put substances in the water?"

The Inspector in turn called the police:

"So you poisoned the water?"   10

The police in turn called the Captain:

"So you're the poisoner?"

The captain called three agents. The agents took me to an empty car amid the stares and whispers of the passengers. At the next station they took me off and pushed and dragged me to the jail. For days no one spoke to me, except during the long interrogations. When I explained my story no one believed me, not even the jailer, who shook his head, saying: "The case is grave, truly grave. You didn't want to poison the children?" One day they brought me before the Magistrate.

"Your case is difficult," he repeated. "I will assign you to the Penal Judge."

A year passed. Finally they judged me. As there were no victims, my sentence was light. After a short time, my day of liberty arrived.

The Chief of the Prison called me in:

"Well, now you're free. You were lucky. Lucky there were no victims. But don't do it again, because the next time won't be so short . . ."

And he stared at me with the same grave stare with which everyone watched me.

The same afternoon I took the train and after hours of uncomfortable traveling arrived in Mexico City. I took a cab home. At the door of my apartment I heard laughter and singing. I felt a pain in my chest, like the smack of a wave of surprise when surprise smacks us across the chest: my friend was there, singing and laughing as always.

"How did you get back?"

"Simple: in the train. Someone, after making sure that I was only salt water, poured me in the engine. It was a rough trip: soon I was a white plume of vapor, soon I fell in a fine rain on the machine. I thinned out a lot. I lost many drops."

Her presence changed my life. The house of dark corridors and dusty furniture was filled with air, with sun, with sounds and green and blue reflections, a numerous and happy populace of reverberations and echoes. How many waves is one wave, and how it can make a beach or a rock or jetty out of a wall, a chest, a forehead that it crowns with foam! Even the abandoned corners, the abject corners of dust and debris were touched by her light hands. Everything began to laugh and everywhere shined with teeth. The sun entered the old rooms with pleasure and stayed in my house for hours, abandoning the other houses, the district, the city, the country. And some nights, very late, the scandalized stars watched it sneak from my house.

Love was a game, a perpetual creation. All was beach, sand, a bed of sheets that were always fresh. If I embraced her, she swelled with pride, incredibly tall, like the liquid stalk of a poplar; and soon that thinness flowered into a fountain of white feathers, into a plume of smiles that fell over my head and back and covered me with whiteness. Or she stretched out in front of me, infinite as the horizon, until I too became horizon and silence. Full and sinuous, it enveloped me like music or some giant lips. Her present was a going and coming of caresses, of murmurs, of kisses. Entered in her waters, I was drenched to the socks and in a wink of an eye I found myself up above, at the height of vertigo, mysteriously suspended, to fall like a stone and feel myself gently deposited on the dryness, like a feather. Nothing is comparable to sleeping in those waters, to wake pounded by a thousand happy light lashes, by a thousand assaults that withdraw laughing.

But never did I reach the center of her being. Never did I touch the nakedness of pain and of death. Perhaps it does not exist in waves, that secret site that renders a woman vulnerable and mortal, that electric button where all interlocks, twitches, and straightens out to then swoon. Her sensibility, like that of women, spread in ripples, only they weren't concentric ripples, but rather eccentric, spreading each time farther, until they touched other galaxies. To love her was to extend to remote contacts, to vibrate with far-off stars we never suspected. But her center . . . no, she had no center, just an emptiness as in a whirlwind, that sucked me in and smothered me.

Stretched out side by side, we exchanged confidences, whispers, smiles. Curled up, she fell on my chest and there unfolded like a vegetation of murmurs. She sang in my ear, a little snail. She became humble and transparent, clutching my feet like a small animal, calm water. She was so clear I could read all of her thoughts. Certain nights her skin was covered with phosphorescence and to embrace her was to embrace a piece of night tattooed with fire. But she also became black and bitter. At unexpected hours she roared, moaned, twisted. Her groans woke the neighbors. Upon hearing her, the sea wind would scratch at the door of the house or rave in a loud voice on the roof. Cloudy days irritated her; she broke furniture, said bad words, covered me with insults and green and gray foam. She spat, cried, swore, prophesied. Subject to the moon, to the stars, to the influence of the light of other worlds, she changed her moods and appearance in a way that I thought fantastic, but it was as fatal as the tide.

She began to miss solitude. The house was full of snails and conches, of small sailboats that in her fury she had shipwrecked (together with the others, laden with images, that each night left my forehead and sank in her ferocious or pleasant whirlwinds). How many little treasures were lost in that time! But my boats and the silent song of the snails was not enough. I had to install in the house a colony of fish. I confess that it was not without jealousy that I watched them swimming in my friend, caressing her breasts, sleeping between her legs, adorning her hair with light flashes of color.

Among all those fish there were a few particularly repulsive and ferocious ones, little tigers from the aquarium, the large fixed eyes and jagged and bloodthirsty mouths. I don't know by what aberration my friend delighted in playing with them, shamelessly showing them a preference whose significance I preferred to ignore. She passed long hours confined with those horrible creatures. One day I couldn't stand it any more; I threw open the door and launched after them. Agile and ghostly they escaped my hands while she laughed and pounded me until I fell. I thought I was drowning. And when I was at the point of death, and purple, she deposited me on the bank and began to kiss me, saying I don't know what things. I felt very weak, fatigued, and humiliated. And at the same time her voluptuousness made me close my eyes, because her voice was sweet and she spoke to me of the delicious death of the drowned. When I recovered, I began to fear and hate her.

I had neglected my affairs. Now I began to visit friends and renew old and dear relations. I met an old girlfriend. Making her swear to keep my secret, I told her of my life with the wave. Nothing moves women so much as the possibility of saving a man. My redeemer employed all of her arts, but what could a woman, master of a limited number of souls and bodies, do in front of my friend who was always changing—and always identical to herself in her incessant metamorphoses.

Winter came. The sky turned gray. Fog fell on the city. Frozen drizzle rained. My friend cried every night. During the day she isolated herself, quiet and sinister, stuttering a single syllable, like an old woman who grumbles in a corner. She became cold; to sleep with her was to shiver all night and to feel freeze, little by little, the blood, the bones, the thoughts. She turned deep, impenetrable, restless. I left frequently and my absences were each time more prolonged. She, in her corner, howled loudly. With teeth like steel and a corrosive tongue she gnawed the walls, crumbled them. She passed the nights in mourning, reproaching me. She had nightmares, deliriums of the sun, of warm beaches. She dreamt of the pole and of changing into a great block of ice, sailing beneath black skies in nights long as months. She insulted me. She cursed and laughed, filled the house with guffaws and phantoms. She called up the monsters of the depths, blind ones, quick ones, blunt. Charged with electricity, she carbonized all she touched; full of acid, she dissolved whatever she brushed against. Her sweet embraces became knotty cords that strangled me. And her body, greenish and elastic, was an implacable whip that lashed, lashed, lashed. I fled. The horrible fish laughed with ferocious smiles.

There in the mountains, among the tall pines and precipices, I breathed the cold thin air like a thought of liberty. At the end of a month I returned. I had decided. It had been so cold that over the marble of the chimney, next to the extinct fire, I found a statue of ice. I was unmoved by her weary beauty. I put her in a big canvas sack and went out to the streets with the sleeper on my shoulders. In a restaurant in the outskirts I sold her to a waiter friend who immediately began to chop her into little pieces, which he carefully deposited in the buckets where bottles are chilled. 30

Questions

1. "My Life with the Wave" is a fantastic story, but the plot still in some ways resembles a conventional human love affair. In what ways is it like a love story between two people?
2. Does Paz ever explicitly state why the wave left the sea? What details does he give to reveal her motivation?
3. How is the wave different from an ordinary woman? How is she similar?
4. Why does the narrator begin to love the wave?
5. When does the narrator cease loving her? Why do his feelings change so radically from earlier?
6. Is the narrator justified in dispatching the frozen wave? Do his actions represent a symbolic murder or simply the final break-up between two lovers?
7. If the wave is a symbol, what symbolic associations does she suggest?

Gabriel García Márquez

A Very Old Man with Enormous Wings   1968

Translated by Gregory Rabassa

Gabriel García Márquez, among the most eminent of living Latin American writers, was born in 1928 in Aracataca, a Caribbean port in Colombia, one of sixteen children of an impoverished telegraph operator. For a time he studied law in Bogotá, then became a newspaper reporter. Although he never joined the Communist Party, García Márquez outspokenly advocated many left-wing proposals for reform. In 1954, despairing of any prospect for political change, he left Colombia to live in Mexico City. Though at nineteen he had already completed a book of short stories, La hojorasca (Leaf Storm), *he waited until 1955 to publish it. Soon he began to build a towering reputation among readers of Spanish. His celebrated novel* Cien años de soledad *(1967), published in English as* One Hundred Years of Solitude *(1969), traces the history of a Colombian family through six generations. Called by Chilean poet Pablo Neruda "the greatest revelation in the Spanish language since Don Quixote," the book has sold more than thirty million copies in thirty-five languages. In 1982 García Márquez was awarded the Nobel Prize in Literature. His fiction, rich in myth and invention, has reminded American readers of the work of William Faulkner, another explorer of his native ground; indeed, García Márquez has called Faulkner "my master." His later novels include* Love in the Time of Cholera *(1988),* The General in His Labyrinth *(1990),* Of Love and Other Demons *(1995), and* Memories of My Melancholy Whores *(2005). His* Collected Stories *was published in 1994.* Living to Tell the Tale *(2003), the first volume of an autobiographical trilogy, traces the author's life up to the beginning of his journalistic career, and offers many insights into the sources and techniques of his works of fiction. García Márquez still lives in Mexico City.*

A Tale for Children

On the third day of rain they had killed so many crabs inside the house that Pelayo had to cross his drenched courtyard and throw them into the sea, because the newborn child had a temperature all night and they thought it was due to the stench. The world had been sad since Tuesday. Sea and sky were a single ash-gray thing and the sands of the beach, which on March nights glimmered like powdered light, had become a stew of mud and rotten shellfish. The light was so weak at noon that when Pelayo was coming back to the house after throwing away the crabs, it was hard for him to see what it was that was moving and groaning in the rear of the courtyard. He had to go very close to see that it was an old man, a very old man, lying face down in the mud, who, in spite of his tremendous efforts, couldn't get up, impeded by his enormous wings.

Frightened by that nightmare, Pelayo ran to get Elisenda, his wife, who was putting compresses on the sick child, and he took her to the rear of the courtyard. They both looked at the fallen body with mute stupor. He was dressed like a ragpicker. There were only a few faded hairs left on his bald skull and very few teeth in his mouth, and his pitiful condition of a drenched great-grandfather had taken away any sense of grandeur he might have had. His huge buzzard wings, dirty and half-plucked, were forever entangled in the mud. They looked at him so long and so closely that Pelayo and Elisenda very soon overcame their surprise and in the end found him familiar. Then they dared speak to him, and he answered in an incomprehensible dialect with a strong sailor's voice. That was how they skipped over the inconvenience of the wings and quite intelligently concluded that he was a lonely castaway from some foreign ship wrecked by the storm. And yet, they called in a neighbor woman who knew everything about life and death to see him, and all she needed was one look to show them their mistake.

"He's an angel," she told them. "He must have been coming for the child, but the poor fellow is so old that the rain knocked him down."

On the following day everyone knew that a flesh-and-blood angel was held captive in Pelayo's house. Against the judgment of the wise neighbor woman, for whom angels in those times were the fugitive survivors of a celestial conspiracy, they did not have the heart to club him to death. Pelayo watched over him all afternoon from the kitchen, armed with his bailiff's club, and before going to bed he dragged him out of the mud and locked him up with the hens in the wire chicken coop. In the middle of the night, when the rain stopped, Pelayo and Elisenda were still killing crabs. A short time afterward the child woke up without a fever and with a desire to eat. Then they felt magnanimous and decided to put the angel on a raft with fresh water and provisions for three days and leave him to his fate on the high seas. But when they went out into the courtyard with the first light of dawn, they found the whole neighborhood in front of the chicken coop having fun with the angel, without the slightest reverence, tossing him things to eat through the openings in the wire as if he weren't a supernatural creature but a circus animal.

Father Gonzaga arrived before seven o'clock, alarmed at the strange news. By that time onlookers less frivolous than those at dawn had already arrived and they were making all kinds of conjectures concerning the captive's future. The simplest among them thought that he should be named mayor of the world. Others of sterner mind felt that he should be promoted to the rank of five-star general in order to win all wars. Some visionaries hoped that he could be put to stud in order to implant on earth a race of winged wise men who could take charge of the universe. But Father Gonzaga, before becoming a priest, had been a robust woodcutter. Standing by the wire, he reviewed his catechism in an instant and asked them to open the door so that he could take a close look at that pitiful man who looked more like a huge decrepit hen among the fascinated chickens. He was lying in a corner drying his open wings in the sunlight among the fruit peels and breakfast leftovers that the early risers had thrown him. Alien to the impertinences of the world, he only lifted his antiquarian eyes and murmured something in his dialect when Father Gonzaga went into the chicken coop and said good morning to him in Latin. The parish priest had his first suspicion of an impostor when he saw that he did not understand the language of God or know how to greet His ministers. Then he noticed that seen close up he was much too human: he had an unbearable smell of the outdoors, the back side of his wings was strewn with parasites and his main feathers had been mistreated by terrestrial winds, and nothing about him measured up to the proud dignity of angels. Then he came out of the chicken coop and in a brief sermon warned the curious against the risks of being ingenuous. He reminded them that the devil had the bad habit of making use of carnival tricks in order to confuse the unwary. He argued that if wings were not the essential element in determining the difference between a hawk and an airplane, they were even less so in the recognition of angels. Nevertheless, he promised to write a letter to his bishop so that the latter would write to his primate so that the latter would write to the Supreme Pontiff in order to get the final verdict from the highest courts.

His prudence fell on sterile hearts. The news of the captive angel spread with such rapidity that after a few hours the courtyard had the bustle of a marketplace and they had to call in troops with fixed bayonets to disperse the mob that was about to knock the house down. Elisenda, her spine all twisted from sweeping up so much marketplace trash, then got the idea of fencing in the yard and charging five cents admission to see the angel.

The curious came from far away. A traveling carnival arrived with a flying acrobat who buzzed over the crowd several times, but no one paid any attention to him because his wings were not those of an angel but, rather, those of a sidereal bat. The most unfortunate invalids on earth came in search of health: a poor woman who since childhood had been counting her heartbeats and had run out of numbers; a Portuguese man who couldn't sleep because the noise of the stars disturbed him; a sleepwalker who got up at night to undo the things he had done while awake; and many others with less serious ailments. In the midst of that shipwreck disorder that made the earth tremble, Pelayo and Elisenda were happy with fatigue, for in less than a week they had crammed their rooms with money and the line of pilgrims waiting their turn to enter still reached beyond the horizon.

The angel was the only one who took no part in his own act. He spent his time trying to get comfortable in his borrowed nest, befuddled by the hellish heat of the oil lamps and sacramental candles that had been placed along the wire. At first they tried to make him eat some mothballs, which, according to the wisdom of the wise neighbor woman, were the food prescribed for angels. But he turned them down, just as he turned down the papal lunches that the penitents brought him, and they never found out whether it was because he was an angel or because he was an old man that in the end ate nothing but eggplant mush. His only supernatural virtue seemed to be patience. Especially during the first days, when the hens pecked at him, searching for the stellar parasites that proliferated in his wings, and the cripples pulled out feathers to touch their defective parts with, and even the most merciful threw stones at him, trying to get him to rise so they could see him standing. The only time they succeeded in arousing him was when they burned his side with an iron for branding steers, for he had been motionless for so many hours that they thought he was dead. He awoke with a start, ranting in his hermetic language and with tears in his eyes, and he flapped his wings a couple of times, which brought on a whirlwind of chicken dung and lunar dust and a gale of panic that did not seem to be of this world. Although many thought that his reaction had been one not of rage but of pain, from then on they were careful not to annoy him, because the majority understood that his passivity was not that of a hero taking his ease but that of a cataclysm in repose.

Father Gonzaga held back the crowd's frivolity with formulas of maidservant inspiration while awaiting the arrival of a final judgment on the nature of the captive. But the mail from Rome showed no sense of urgency. They spent their time finding out if the prisoner had a navel, if his dialect had any connection with Aramaic, how many times he could fit on the head of a pin,° or whether he wasn't just a Norwegian with wings. Those meager letters might have come and gone until the end of time if a providential event had not put an end to the priest's tribulations.

It so happened that during those days, among so many other carnival attractions,   10 there arrived in town the traveling show of the woman who had been changed into a spider for having disobeyed her parents. The admission to see her was not only less than the admission to see the angel, but people were permitted to ask her all manner of questions about her absurd state and to examine her up and down so that no one would ever doubt the truth of her horror. She was a frightful tarantula the size of a ram and with the head of a sad maiden. What was most heart-rending, however, was not her outlandish shape but the sincere affliction with which she recounted the details of her misfortune. While still practically a child she had sneaked out of her parents' house to go to a dance, and while she was coming back through the woods after having danced all night without permission, a fearful thunderclap rent the sky in two and through the crack came the lightning bolt of brimstone that changed her into a spider. Her only nourishment came from the meatballs that charitable souls chose to toss into her mouth. A spectacle like that, full of so much human truth and with such a fearful lesson, was bound to defeat without even trying that of a haughty angel who scarcely deigned to look at mortals. Besides, the few miracles attributed to the angel showed a certain mental disorder, like the blind man who didn't recover his sight but grew three new teeth, or the paralytic who didn't get to walk but almost won the lottery, and the leper whose sores sprouted sunflowers. Those consolation miracles, which were more like mocking fun, had already ruined the angel's reputation when the woman who had

---

fit on the head of a pin: this allusion refers to the famous medieval arguments about how many angels (who had no physical bodies) could dance on the head of a pin.

been changed into a spider finally crushed him completely. That was how Father Gonzaga was cured forever of his insomnia and Pelayo's courtyard went back to being as empty as during the time it had rained for three days and crabs walked through the bedrooms.

The owners of the house had no reason to lament. With the money they saved they built a two-story mansion with balconies and gardens and high netting so that crabs wouldn't get in during the winter, and with iron bars on the windows so that angels wouldn't get in. Pelayo also set up a rabbit warren close to town and gave up his job as bailiff for good, and Elisenda bought some satin pumps with high heels and many dresses of iridescent silk, the kind worn on Sunday by the most desirable women in those times. The chicken coop was the only thing that didn't receive any attention. If they washed it down with creolin° and burned tears of myrrh inside it every so often, it was not in homage to the angel but to drive away the dungheap stench that still hung everywhere like a ghost and was turning the new house into an old one. At first, when the child learned to walk, they were careful that he not get too close to the chicken coop. But then they began to lose their fears and got used to the smell, and before the child got his second teeth he'd gone inside the chicken coop to play, where the wires were falling apart. The angel was no less standoffish with him than with other mortals, but he tolerated the most ingenious infamies with the patience of a dog who had no illusions. They both came down with chicken pox at the same time. The doctor who took care of the child couldn't resist the temptation to listen to the angel's heart, and he found so much whistling in the heart and so many sounds in his kidneys that it seemed impossible for him to be alive. What surprised him most, however, was the logic of his wings. They seemed so natural on that completely human organism that he couldn't understand why other men didn't have them too.

When the child began school it had been some time since the sun and rain had caused the collapse of the chicken coop. The angel went dragging himself about here and there like a stray dying man. They would drive him out of the bedroom with a broom and a moment later find him in the kitchen. He seemed to be in so many places at the same time that they grew to think that he'd been duplicated, that he was reproducing himself all through the house, and the exasperated and unhinged Elisenda shouted that it was awful living in that hell full of angels. He could scarcely eat and his antiquarian eyes had also become so foggy that he went about bumping into posts. All he had left were the bare cannulae° of his last feathers. Pelayo threw a blanket over him and extended him the charity of letting him sleep in the shed, and only then did they notice that he had a temperature at night, and was delirious with the tongue twisters of an old Norwegian. That was one of the few times they became alarmed, for they thought he was going to die and not even the wise neighbor woman had been able to tell them what to do with dead angels.

And yet he not only survived his worst winter, but seemed improved with the first sunny days. He remained motionless for several days in the farthest corner of the courtyard, where no one would see him, and at the beginning of December some large, stiff feathers began to grow on his wings, the feathers of a scarecrow, which looked more like another misfortune of decrepitude. But he must have

---

creolin: a type of cleaning product.   cannulae: the Latin word for tubes; it refers to the tubelike quills that attach feathers to a body.

known the reason for those changes, for he was quite careful that no one should notice them, that no one should hear the sea chanteys that he sometimes sang under the stars. One morning Elisenda was cutting some bunches of onions for lunch when a wind that seemed to come from the high seas blew into the kitchen. Then she went to the window and caught the angel in his first attempts at flight. They were so clumsy that his fingernails opened a furrow in the vegetable patch and he was on the point of knocking the shed down with the ungainly flapping that slipped on the light and couldn't get a grip on the air. But he did manage to gain altitude. Elisenda let out a sigh of relief, for herself and for him, when she saw him pass over the last houses, holding himself up in some way with the risky flapping of a senile vulture. She kept watching him even when she was through cutting the onions and she kept on watching until it was no longer possible for her to see him, because then he was no longer an annoyance in her life but an imaginary dot on the horizon of the sea.

Questions

1. How would you describe the *tone* of this story? What does that tone contribute to your understanding of the story's larger intentions?
2. The earliest and most pervasive assumption made about the old man is that he is an angel. Other than his wings, is there anything angelic about him?
3. How would you characterize Father Gonzaga? Use textual references to back up your conclusions.
4. Consider the specific ailments that are assigned to the "most unfortunate invalids on earth" (paragraph 7). What seems to you to be the point of the author's mockery here?
5. What changes has the old man's presence brought to the lives of Pelayo and his family?
6. Given those changes, why is Elisenda glad to see the old man go away at the end of the story?

Inés Arredondo

The Shunammite   1965

Translated by Alberto Manguel

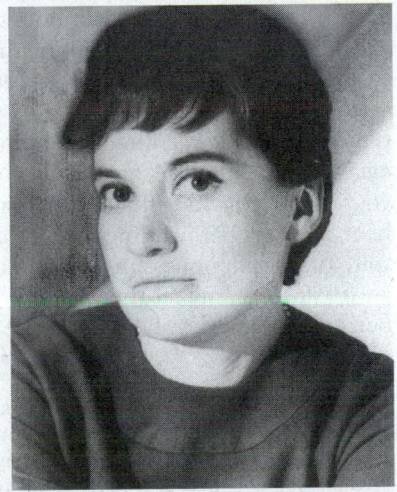

Inés Arredondo (1928–1989) was born in Culiacán, the capital and largest city of the state of Sinaloa, Mexico, the daughter of a doctor. In 1947 she enrolled in the National Autonomous University of Mexico, but in the following year experienced a spiritual and emotional crisis that brought her close to suicide. In 1953 she married the writer Tomas Segovia; the union, which produced three children, was troubled, leading to separation in 1962 and divorce three years later. In 1972 she married Carlos Ruiz Sanchez, a physician. Throughout her adult life, financial necessity caused Arredondo to work at a variety of jobs—librarian, editor, translator, and professor (including guest lectureships at Indiana University and Purdue University in 1966).

Inés Arredondo

Because of spinal problems she was forced to undergo five operations and was ultimately confined to a wheelchair. Beginning in 1965, she published several small volumes of short fiction (the collected edition of her work runs to fewer than four hundred pages), which brought her several awards and established her reputation as a major writer. "The Shunammite" was filmed, with a screenplay by Arredondo, as a segment in a 1965 Mexican movie called Amor Amor Amor, and was the basis for a 1991 opera by Marcela Rodríguez. Underground River and Other Stories (1996) presents twelve of her stories in an English translation.

So they sought for a fair damsel throughout all the coasts of Israel,
and found Abishag, a Shunammite,° and brought her to the king.
    And the damsel was very fair, and cherished the king,
and ministered to him; but the king knew her not.

—1 KINGS 1:3–4

The summer had been a fiery furnace. The last summer of my youth.

Tense, concentrated in the arrogance that precedes combustion, the city shone in a dry and dazzling light. I stood in the very midst of the light, dressed in mourning, proud, feeding the flames with my blonde hair, alone. Men's sly glances slid over my body without soiling it, and my haughty modesty forced them to barely nod at me, full of respect. I was certain of having the power to dominate passions, to purify anything in the scorching air that surrounded but did not singe me.

Nothing changed when I received the telegram; the sadness it brought me did not affect in the least my feelings towards the world. My uncle Apolonio was dying at the age of seventy-odd years and wanted to see me. I had lived as a daughter in his house for many years and I sincerely felt pain at the thought of his inevitable death. All this was perfectly normal, and not a single omen, not a single shiver made me suspect anything. Quickly I made arrangements for the journey, in the very same untouchable midst of the motionless summer.

I arrived at the village during the hour of siesta.

Walking down the empty streets with my small suitcase, I fell to daydreaming, in that dusky zone between reality and time, born of the excessive heat. I was not remembering; I was almost reliving things as they had been. "Look, Licha, the *amapas*° are blooming again." The clear voice, almost childish. "I want you to get yourself a dress like that of Margarita Ibarra to wear on the sixteenth." I could hear her, feel her walking by my side, her shoulders bent a little forwards, light in spite of her plumpness, happy and old. I carried on walking in the company of my aunt Panchita, my mother's sister. "Well, my dear, if you *really* don't like Pepe . . . but he's such a *nice* boy." Yes, she had used those exact words, here, in front of

5

Abishag, the Shunammite: Among the tasks Abishag was called upon to perform for the aged and dying King David was to lie in bed with him and warm him with her body; as the last clause of the epigraph indicates, there was no sexual contact between them.   *amapa:* a small tree that is covered, when in bloom, by masses of yellow, pink, or purple tubular flowers.

Tichi Valenzuela's window, with her gay smile, innocent and impish. I walked a little further, where the paving stones seemed to fade away in the haze, and when the bells rang, heavy and real, ending the siesta and announcing the Rosary, I opened my eyes and gave the village a good, long look: it was not the same. The *amapas* had not bloomed and I was crying, in my mourning dress, at the door of my uncle's house.

The front gate was open, as always, and at the end of the courtyard rose the bougainvillea. As always: but not the same. I dried my tears, and felt that I was not arriving: I was leaving. Everything looked motionless, pinioned in my memory, and the heat and the silence seemed to wither it all. My footsteps echoed with a new sound, and María came out to greet me.

"Why didn't you let us know? We'd have sent . . ."

We went straight into the sick man's room. As I entered, I felt cold. Silence and gloom preceded death.

"Luisa, is that you?"

The dear voice was dying out and would soon be silent for ever.   10

"I'm here, uncle."

"God be praised! I won't die alone."

"Don't say that; you'll soon be much better."

He smiled sadly; he knew I was lying but he did not want to make me cry.

"Yes, my daughter. Yes. Now have a rest, make yourself at home and then come   15
and keep me company. I'll try to sleep a little."

Shriveled, wizened, toothless, lost in the immense bed and floating senselessly in whatever was left of his life, he was painful to be with, like something superfluous, out of place, like so many others at the point of death. Stepping out of the overheated passageway, one would take a deep breath, instinctively, hungry for light and air.

I began to nurse him and I felt happy doing it. This house was *my* house, and in the morning, while tidying up, I would sing long-forgotten songs. The peace that surrounded me came perhaps from the fact that my uncle no longer awaited death as something imminent and terrible, but instead let himself be carried by the passing days towards a more or less distant or nearby future, with the unconscious tenderness of a child. He would go over his past life with great pleasure and enjoy imagining that he was bequeathing me his images, as grandparents do with their children.

"Bring me that small chest, there, in the large wardrobe. Yes, that one. The key is underneath the mat, next to Saint Anthony. Bring the key as well."

And his sunken eyes would shine once again at the sight of all his treasures.

"Look: this necklace—I gave it to your aunt for our tenth wedding anniversary. I   20
bought it in Mazatlán from a Polish jeweler who told me God-knows-what story about an Austrian princess, and asked an impossible price for it. I brought it back hidden in my pistol-holder and didn't sleep a wink in the stagecoach—I was so afraid someone would steal it!"

The light of dusk made the young, living stones glitter in his callused hands.

"This ring, so old, belonged to my mother; look carefully at the miniature in the other room and you'll see her wearing it. Cousin Begoña would mutter behind her back that a sweetheart of hers . . ."

The ladies in the portraits would move their lips and speak, once again, would breathe again—all these ladies he had seen, he had touched. I would picture them in my mind and understand the meaning of these jewels.

"Have I told you about the time we traveled to Europe, in 1908, before the Revolution?° You had to take a ship to Colima. And in Venice your aunt Panchita fell in love with a certain pair of earrings. They were much too expensive, and I told her so. 'They are fit for a queen.' Next day I bought them for her. You just can't imagine what it was like because all this took place long, long before you were born, in 1908, in Venice, when your aunt was so young, so . . . "

"Uncle, you're getting tired, you should rest."   25

"You're right, I'm tired. Leave me a while and take the small chest to your room. It's yours."

"But, uncle . . ."

"It's all yours, that's all! I trust I can give away whatever I want!"

His voice broke into a sob: the illusion was vanishing and he found himself again on the point of dying, of saying goodbye to the things he had loved. He turned to the wall and I left with the box in my hands, not knowing what to do.

On other occasions he would tell me about "the year of the famine," or "the year   30
of the yellow corn," or "the year of the plague," and very old tales of murderers and ghosts. Once he even tried to sing a corrido° from his youth, but it shattered in his jagged voice. He was leaving me his life, and he was happy.

The doctor said that yes, he could see some recovery, but that we were not to raise our hopes, there was no cure, it was merely a matter of a few days more or less.

One afternoon of menacing dark clouds, when I was bringing in the clothes hanging out to dry in the courtyard, I heard María cry out. I stood still, listening to her cry as if it were a peal of thunder, the first of the storm to come. Then silence, and I was left alone in the courtyard, motionless. A bee buzzed by and the rain did not fall. No one knows as well as I do how awful a foreboding can be, a premonition hanging above a head turned towards the sky.

"Lichita, he's dying! He's gasping for air!"

"Go get the doctor . . . No! I'll go. But call doña Clara to stay with you till I'm back."

"And the priest, fetch the priest."   35

I ran, I ran away from that unbearable moment, blunt and asphyxiating. I ran, hurried back, entered the house, made coffee; I greeted the relatives who began to arrive dressed in half-mourning; I ordered candles; I asked for a few holy relics; I kept on feverishly trying to fulfill my only obligation at the time, to be with my uncle. I asked the doctor: he had given him an injection, so as not to leave anything untried, but he knew it was useless. I saw the priest arrive with the Eucharist, even then I lacked the courage to enter. I knew I would regret it afterwards. "Thank God, now I won't die alone"—but I couldn't. I covered my face with my hands and prayed.

The priest came and touched my shoulder. I thought that all was over and I shivered.

"He's calling you. Come in."

I don't know how I reached the door. Night had fallen and the room, lit by a beside lamp, seemed enormous. The furniture, larger than life, looked black, and a

the Revolution: the Mexican Revolution, which toppled the dictator Porfirio Díaz and led to a decade of political unrest and civil war, began in 1910.   corrido: a kind of narrative ballad; corridos were originally about romantic love, but at the time of the Revolution they were frequently political in nature.

strange clogging atmosphere hung about the bed. Trembling, I felt I was inhaling death.

"Stand next to him," said the priest.   40

I obeyed, moving towards the foot of the bed, unable to look even at the sheets.

"Your uncle's wish, unless you say otherwise, is to marry you *in articulo mortis*,° so that you may inherit his possessions. Do you accept?"

I stifled a cry of horror. I opened my eyes wide enough to let in the whole terrible room. "Why does he want to drag me into his grave?" I felt death touching my skin.

"Luisa . . ."

It was uncle Apolonio. Now I had to look at him. He could barely mouth the words,   45
his jaw seemed slack and he spoke moving his face like that of a ventriloquist's doll.

"Please."

And he fell silent with exhaustion.

I could take no more. I left the room. That was not my uncle, it did not even look like him. Leave everything to me, yes, but not only his possessions, his stories, his life. I didn't want it, his life, his death. I didn't want it. When I opened my eyes I was standing once again in the courtyard and the sky was still overcast. I breathed in deeply, painfully.

"Already?" the relatives drew near to ask, seeing me so distraught.

I shook my head. Behind me, the priest explained.   50

"Don Apolonio wants to marry her with his last breath, so that she may inherit him."

"And you won't?" the old servant asked anxiously. "Don't be silly, no one deserves it more than you. You were a daughter to them, and you have worked very hard looking after him. If you don't marry him, the cousins in Mexico City will leave you without a cent. Don't be silly!"

"It's a fine gesture on his part."

"And afterwards you'll be left a rich widow, as untouched as you are now." A young cousin laughed nervously.

"It's a considerable fortune, and I, as your uncle several times removed, would   55
advise you to . . ."

"If you think about it, not accepting shows a lack of both charity and humility."

"That's true, that's absolutely true."

I did not want to give an old man his last pleasure, a pleasure I should, after all, be thankful for, because my youthful body, of which I felt so proud, had not dwelt in any of the regions of death. I was overcome by nausea. That was my last clear thought that night. I woke from a kind of hypnotic slumber as they forced me to hold his hand covered in cold sweat. I felt nauseous again, but said "yes."

I remember vaguely that they hovered over me all the time, talking all at once, taking me over there, bringing me over here, making me sign, making me answer. The taste of that night—a taste that has stayed with me for the rest of my life—was that of an evil ring-around-the-rosies turning vertiginously around me, while everyone laughed and sang grotesquely

This is the way the widow is wed,
The widow is wed, the widow is wed

in articulo mortis: "at the point of death." Such marriages were allowed to take place without the usual formalities and were considered binding even if, as here, the dying party subsequently recovered.

while I stood, a slave, in the middle. Something inside me hurt, and I could not lift my eyes.

When I came to my senses, all was over, and on my hand shone the braided ring   60
which I had seen so many times on my aunt Panchita's finger: there had been no time for anything else.

The guests began to leave.

"If you need me, don't hesitate to call. In the meantime give him these drops every six hours."

"May God bless you and give you strength."

"Happy honeymoon," whispered the young cousin in my ear, with a nasty laugh.

I returned to the sickbed. "Nothing has changed, nothing has changed." My fear   65
certainly had not changed. I convinced María to stay and help me look after uncle Apolonio. I only calmed down once I saw dawn was breaking. It had started to rain, but without thunder or lightning, very still.

It kept on drizzling that day and the next, and the day after. Four days of anguish. Nobody came to visit, nobody other than the doctor and the priest. On days like these no one goes out, everyone stays indoors and waits for life to start again. These are the days of the spirit, sacred days.

If at least the sick man had needed plenty of attention my hours would have seemed shorter, but there was little that could be done for him.

On the fourth night María went to bed in a room close by, and I stayed alone with the dying man. I was listening to the monotonous rain and praying unconsciously, half asleep and unafraid, waiting. My fingers stopped turning the rosary, and as I held the beads I could feel through my fingertips a peculiar warmth, a warmth both alien and intimate, the warmth we leave in things and which is returned to us transformed, a comrade, a brother foreshadowing the warmth of others, a warmth both unknown and recollected, never quite grasped and yet inhabiting the core of my bones. Softly, deliciously, my nerves relaxed, my fingers felt light, I fell asleep.

I must have slept many hours: it was dawn when I woke up. I knew because the lights had been switched off and the electric plant stops working at two in the morning. The room, barely lit by an oil lamp at the feet of the Holy Virgin on the chest of drawers, made me think of the wedding night, *my* wedding night. It was so long ago, an empty eternity.

From the depth of the gloomy darkness don Apolonio's broken and tired breathing   70
reached me. There he still was, not the man himself, simply the persistent and incomprehensible shred that hangs on, with no goal, with no apparent motive. Death is frightening, but life mingled with death, soaked in death, is horrible in a way that owes little to either life or death. Silence, corruption of the flesh, the stench, the monstrous transformation, the final vanishing act, all this is painful, but it reaches a climax and then gives way, dissolves into the earth, into memory, into history. But not this: this arrangement worked out between life and death—echoed in the useless exhaling and inhaling—could carry on forever. I would hear him trying to clear his anaesthetized throat and it occurred to me that air was not entering that body, or rather, that it was not a human body breathing the air: it was a machine, puffing and panting, stopping in a curious game, a game to kill time without end. That thing was no human being: it was somebody playing with huffs and snores. And the horror of it all won me over: I began to breathe to the rhythm of his panting; to inhale, stop suddenly, choke, breathe, choke again, unable to control myself, until I realized I had been deceived by what I thought was the sense of the game. What I

really felt was the pain and shortness of breath of an animal in pain. But I kept on, on, until there was one single breathing, one single inhuman breath, one single agony. I felt calmer, terrified but calmer: I had lifted the barrier, I could let myself go and simply wait for the common end. It seemed to me that by abandoning myself, by giving myself up unconditionally, the end would happen quickly, would not be allowed to continue. It would have fulfilled its purpose and its persistent search in the world.

Not a hint of farewell, not a glimmer of pity towards me. I carried on the mortal game for a long, long while, from someplace where time had ceased to matter.

The shared breathing became less agitated, more peaceful, but also weaker. I seemed to be drifting back. I felt so tired I could barely move, exhaustion nestling in forever inside my body. I opened my eyes. Nothing had changed.

No: far away, in the shadows, is a rose. Alone, unique, alive. There it is, cut out against the darkness, clear as day, with its fleshy, luminous petals, shining. I look at it and my hand moves and I remember its touch and the simple act of putting it in a vase. I looked at it then, but I only understand it now. I stir, I blink, and the rose is still there, in full bloom, identical to itself.

I breathe freely, with my own breath. I pray, I remember, I doze off, and the untouched rose mounts guard over the dawning light and my secret. Death and hope suffer change.

And now day begins to break and in the clean sky I see that at last the days of   75
rain are over. I stay at the window a long time, watching everything change in the sun. A strong ray enters and the suffering seems a lie. Unjustified bliss fills my lungs and unwittingly I smile. I turn to the rose as if to an accomplice but I can't find it: the sun has withered it.

Clear days came again, and maddening heat. The people went to work, and sang, but don Apolonio would not die; in fact he seemed to get better. I kept on looking after him, but no longer in a cheerful mood—my eyes downcast, I turned the guilt I felt into hard work. My wish, now clearly, was that it all end, that he die. The fear, the horror I felt looking at him, at his touch, his voice, were unjustified because the link between us was not real, could never be real, and yet he felt like a dead weight upon me. Through politeness and shame I wanted to get rid of it.

Yes, don Apolonio was visibly improving. Even the doctor was surprised and offered no explanation.

On the very first morning I sat him up among the pillows, I noticed that certain look in my uncle's eyes. The heat was stifling and I had to lift him all by myself. Once I had propped him up I noticed: the old man was staring as if dazed at my heaving chest, his face distorted and his trembling hands unconsciously moving towards me. I drew back instinctively and turned my head away.

"Please close the blinds, it's too hot."

His almost dead body was growing warm.   80

"Come here, Luisa, sit by my side. Come."

"Yes, uncle." I sat, my knees drawn up, at the foot of the bed, without looking at him.

"Polo, you must call me Polo, after all we are closer relatives now." There was mockery in the tone of his voice.

"Yes, uncle."

"Polo, Polo." His voice was again sweet and soft. "You'll have a lot to forgive me.   85
I'm old and sick, and a man in my condition is like a child."

"Yes."

"Let's see. Try saying, 'Yes, Polo.'"

"Yes, Polo."

The name on my lips seemed to me an aberration, made me nauseated.

Polo got better, but became fussy and irritable. I realized he was fighting to be the   90
man he once had been, and yet the resurrected self was not the same, but another.

"Luisa, bring me . . . Luisa, give me . . . Luisa, plump up my pillows . . . pour me
some water . . . prop up my leg . . . "

He wanted me to be there all day long, always by his side, seeing to his needs,
touching him. And the fixed look and distorted face kept coming back, more and
more frequently, growing over his features like a mask.

"Pick up my book. It fell underneath the bed, on this side."

I kneeled and stuck my head and almost half my body underneath the bed, and
had to stretch my arm as far as it would go, to reach it. At first I thought it had been
my own movements, or maybe the bedclothes, but once I had the book in my hand
and was shuffling to get out, I froze, stunned by what I had long foreseen, even
expected: the outburst, the scream, the thunder. A rage never before felt raced
through me when the realization of what was happening reached my consciousness,
when his shaking hand, taking advantage of my amazement, became surer and heavier, and enjoyed itself, adventuring with no restraints, feeling and exploring my
thighs—a fleshless hand glued to my skin, fingering my body with delight, a dead
hand searching impatiently between my legs, a bodyless hand.

I rose as quickly as I could, my face burning with shame and determination, but   95
when I saw him I forgot myself and entered like an automation into the nightmare.
Polo was laughing softly through his toothless mouth. And then, suddenly serious,
with a coolness that terrified me, he said:

"What? Aren't you my wife before God and men? Come here, I'm cold, heat my
bed. But first take off your dress, you don't want to get it creased."

What followed, I know, is my story, my life, but I can barely remember it; like a
disgusting dream I can't even tell whether it was long or short. Only one thought
kept me sane during the early days: "This can't go on, it can't go on." I imagined that
God would not allow it, would prevent it in some way or another. He, personally,
God, would interfere. Death, once dreaded, seemed my only hope. Not Apolonio's—
he was a demon of death—but mine, the just and necessary death for my corrupted
flesh. But nothing happened. Everything stayed on, suspended in time, without
future. Then, one morning, taking nothing with me, I left.

It was useless. There days later they let me know that my husband was dying, and
they called me back. I went to see the father confessor and told him my story.

"What keeps him alive is lust, the most horrible of all sins. This isn't life, Father,
it's death. Let him die!"

"He would die in despair. I can't allow it."   100

"And I?"

"I understand, but if you don't go to him, it would be like murder. Try not to
arouse him, pray to the Blessed Virgin, and keep your mind on your duties."

I went back. And lust drew him out of the grave once more.

Fighting, endlessly fighting, I managed, after several years, to overcome my
hatred, and finally, at the very end, I even conquered the beast: Apolonio died in
peace, sweetly, his old self again.

But I was not able to go back to who I was. Now wickedness, malice, shine in the   105
eyes of the men who look at me, and I feel I have become an occasion of sin for all, I,
the vilest of harlots. Alone, a sinner, totally engulfed by the never-ending flames of
this cruel summer which surrounds us all, like an army of ants.

Questions

1. The story begins—and ends—with references to the summer heat, and there are several days of rain after the marriage takes place. Is this just scene-setting, or is there a larger significance to the descriptions?
2. How would you characterize Luisa—her sense of herself, her attitude toward men, her feelings about her uncle—at the beginning of the story?
3. How do the priest and Luisa's other relatives respond to don Apolonio's request to marry her? How does Luisa herself react? Why does she agree to do it?
4. Luisa says of don Apolonio: "I realized he was fighting to be the man he once had been, and yet the resurrected self was not the same, but another" (paragraph 90). What differences do you see in him before and after his "resurrection"?
5. Speaking to the priest near the end of the story, Luisa describes lust as "the most horrible of all sins." Do you think that we are intended to agree with this assessment? Why or why not?
6. At the very end, Luisa says: "I feel I have become an occasion of sin for all . . . the vilest of harlots . . . a sinner. . . ." Do you think that we are intended to agree with *this* assessment?

■ WRITING *effectively*

Gabriel García Márquez on Writing

My Beginnings as a Writer   1981

Interviewer: How did you start writing?

García Márquez: By drawing. By drawing
cartoons. Before I could read or write I used
to draw comics at school and at home. The
funny thing is that I now realize that when I
was in high school I had the reputation of
being a writer, though I never in fact wrote
anything. If there was a pamphlet to be written or a letter of petition, I was the one to do
it because I was supposedly the writer. When
I entered college I happened to have a very
good literary background in general, considerably above the average of my friends. At
the university in Bogotá, I started making
new friends and acquaintances, who introduced me to contemporary writers. One
night a friend lent me a book of short stories
by Franz Kafka. I went back to the *pension*

Gabriel García Márquez

where I was staying and began to read *The Metamorphosis*. The first line almost
knocked me off the bed. I was so surprised. The first line reads, "As Gregor Samsa

awoke that morning from uneasy dreams, he found himself transformed in his bed into a gigantic insect. . . . " When I read the line I thought to myself that I didn't know anyone was allowed to write things like that. If I had known, I would have started writing a long time ago. So I immediately started writing short stories. They were totally intellectual short stories because I was writing them on the basis of my literary experience and had not yet found the link between literature and life. The stories were published in the literary supplement of the newspaper *El Espectador* in Bogotá and they did have a certain success at the time—probably because nobody in Colombia was writing intellectual short stories. What was being written then was mostly about life in the countryside and social life. When I wrote my first short stories I was told they had Joycean influences.

Interviewer: Had you read Joyce at that time?

García Márquez: I had never read Joyce, so I started reading *Ulysses*. I read it in the only Spanish edition available. Since then, after having read *Ulysses* in English as well as a very good French translation, I can see that the original Spanish translation was very bad. But I did learn something that was to be very useful to me in my future writing—the technique of the interior monologue. I later found this in Virginia Woolf, and I like the way she uses it better than Joyce. Although I later realized that the person who invented this interior monologue was the anonymous writer of the *Lazarillo de Tormes.*°

From *Paris Review* interview with Peter H. Stone

TOPICS FOR WRITING ABOUT "THE GOSPEL ACCORDING TO MARK"

1. The long opening paragraph of "The Gospel According to Mark" tells a great deal about the background and personality of Baltasar Espinosa. Write a brief essay in which you consider how the character traits described there foreshadow the story's events.

2. Have you ever been involved in a misunderstanding that was caused by excessive literal-mindedness, your own or someone else's? Write a description of the incident, including how it was resolved, if at all.

3. What larger point do you think Borges is making about his protagonist's final fate, especially in light of Espinosa's attitudes toward religious belief? Back up your conclusions with references to the text.

TOPICS FOR WRITING ABOUT "MY LIFE WITH THE WAVE"

1. Suppose that a friend to whom you had recommended "My Life with the Wave" came back to you and said, "That story was just stupid; it made no sense at all." How would you argue against this attitude?

2. The incident on the train, with all its escalations and repercussions (paragraphs 3–18), is very funny, but is there also an ominous, perhaps Kafkaesque quality to it, one that might

---

Lazarillo de Tormes: Life of Lazarillo de Tormes (1554), the anonymous Spanish novel credited as the original picaresque novel, a story of a likable scoundrel who wanders through adventures, living by his wits, at odds with respectable society.

find analogies in contemporary attitudes—or is it all just a joke? Discuss this point, explaining your conclusions.

3. One critic has suggested that the theme of "My Life with the Wave" is the impossibility of sustained romantic or sexual passion. Defend or disagree with that statement.

4. Using "My Life with the Wave" as a model, write a narrative of your relationship with a possession—a book or CD, a piece of clothing or jewelry, a car—as if you were describing the stages of a love affair, from initial attraction and desire to final disillusionment and break-up.

TOPICS FOR WRITING ABOUT "A VERY OLD MAN WITH ENORMOUS WINGS"

1. As is said earlier in this chapter, all of the main features of Latin American magic realism can be found in García Márquez's "A Very Old Man with Enormous Wings." Develop this theme in a brief essay, with detailed reference to both the story itself and the components of magic realism.

2. Are you familiar with Franz Kafka's *The Metamorphosis?* If so, discuss the presentation of the spider woman in paragraph 10 of "A Very Old Man with Enormous Wings" as a parody of the Kafka work.

3. Write an essay in which you discuss what you understand the meaning of the story to be. Refer as specifically as possible to the text of the story to back up your arguments.

TOPICS FOR WRITING ABOUT "THE SHUNAMMITE"

1. "The Shunammite" makes some observations about how women are perceived by the larger culture and—partly as a consequence of that—how they perceive themselves. How applicable are those observations to contemporary American society?

2. Do you find it credible that Luisa would behave as submissively as she does throughout the story, even when she is asked to do things she strongly objects to? Refer to the text to substantiate your conclusions.

3. Write a brief essay in which you agree or disagree with the following proposition: "The meaning of this story is very simple: Men are animals."

▶ TERMS FOR *review*

Magic (or magical) realism ▶ A type of contemporary narrative in which the magical and the mundane are mixed in an overall context of realistic storytelling; the term was originally used to describe the matter-of-fact combination of the fantastic and the everyday in Latin American fiction.

"El Boom" ▶ An explosion of creativity in the 1960s—marked by stylistic extravagance, complex characterization, fractured time sequences, and fantastic events—that transformed Latin America into one of the centers of modern world fiction.

10 CRITICAL CASEBOOK
Flannery O'Connor

Flannery O'Connor and her *Self-Portrait with Pheasant Cock*, 1962.

> *The main concern of the fiction writer is with mystery*
> *as it is incarnated in real life.*
>
> —FLANNERY O'CONNOR

FLANNERY O'CONNOR

Mary Flannery O'Connor (1925–1964) was born in Savannah, Georgia, but spent most of her life in the small town of Milledgeville. While attending Georgia State College for Women, she won a local reputation for her fledgling stories and satiric cartoons. After graduating in 1945, she went on to study at the University of Iowa, where she earned an M.F.A. in 1947. Diagnosed in 1950 with disseminated lupus, the same incurable illness that had killed her father, O'Connor returned home and spent the last decade of her life living with her mother in Milledgeville. Back on the family dairy farm, she wrote, maintained an extensive literary correspondence, raised peacocks, and underwent medical treatment. When her illness occasionally went into a period of remission, she made trips to lecture and read her stories to college audiences. Her health declined rapidly after surgery early in 1964 for an unrelated complaint. She died at thirty-nine.

O'Connor is unusual among modern American writers in the depth of her Christian vision. A devout Roman Catholic, she attended mass daily while growing up and living in the largely Protestant South. As a latter-day satirist in the manner of Jonathan Swift, O'Connor levels the eye of an uncompromising moralist on the violence and spiritual disorder of the modern world, focusing on what she calls "the action of grace in territory held largely by the devil." She is sometimes called a "Southern Gothic" writer because of her fascination with grotesque incidents and characters. Throughout her career she depicted the South as a troubled region in which the social, racial, and religious status quo that had existed since before the Civil War was coming to a violent end. Despite the inherent seriousness of her religious and social themes, O'Connor's mordant and frequently outrageous humor is everywhere apparent. Her combination of profound vision and dark comedy is the distinguishing characteristic of her literary sensibilities.

O'Connor's published work includes two short novels, Wise Blood *(1952) and* The Violent Bear It Away *(1960), and two collections of short stories,* A Good Man Is Hard to Find *(1955) and* Everything That Rises Must Converge, *published posthumously in 1965. A collection of essays and miscellaneous prose,* Mystery and Manners *(1969), and her selected letters,* The Habit of Being *(1979), reveal an innate cheerfulness and engaging personal warmth that are not always apparent in her fiction.* The Complete Stories of Flannery O'Connor *was posthumously awarded the National Book Award in 1971.*

STORIES

A Good Man Is Hard to Find   1955

The grandmother didn't want to go to Florida. She wanted to visit some of her connections in east Tennessee and she was seizing at every chance to change Bailey's mind. Bailey was the son she lived with, her only boy. He was sitting on the edge of his chair at the table, bent over the orange sports section of the *Journal.* "Now look here, Bailey," she said, "see here, read this," and she stood with one hand on her thin hip and the other rattling the newspaper at his bald head. "Here this fellow that calls himself The Misfit is aloose from the Federal Pen and headed toward Florida and you read here what it says he did to these people. Just you read it. I wouldn't take my children in any direction with a criminal like that aloose in it. I couldn't answer to my conscience if I did."

Bailey didn't look up from his reading so she wheeled around then and faced the children's mother, a young woman in slacks, whose face was as broad and innocent as a cabbage and was tied around with a green head-kerchief that had two points on the top like rabbit's ears. She was sitting on the sofa, feeding the baby his apricots out of a jar. "The children have been to Florida before," the old lady said. "You all ought to take them somewhere else for a change so they would see different parts of the world and be broad. They never have been to east Tennessee."

The children's mother didn't seem to hear her but the eight-year-old boy, John Wesley, a stocky child with glasses, said, "If you don't want to go to Florida, why dontcha stay at home?" He and the little girl, June Star, were reading the funny papers on the floor.

"She wouldn't stay at home to be queen for a day," June Star said without raising her yellow head.

"Yes and what would you do if this fellow, The Misfit, caught you?" the grand-   5
mother said.

"I'd smack his face," John Wesley said.

"She wouldn't stay at home for a million bucks," June Star said. "Afraid she'd miss something. She has to go everywhere we go."

"All right, Miss," the grandmother said. "Just remember that the next time you want me to curl your hair."

June Star said her hair was naturally curly.

The next morning the grandmother was the first one in the car, ready to go. She   10
had her big black valise that looked like the head of a hippopotamus in one corner, and underneath it she was hiding a basket with Pitty Sing, the cat, in it. She didn't intend for the cat to be left alone in the house for three days because he would miss her too much and she was afraid he might brush against one of the gas burners and accidentally asphyxiate himself. Her son, Bailey, didn't like to arrive at a motel with a cat.

She sat in the middle of the back seat with John Wesley and June Star on either side of her. Bailey and the children's mother and the baby sat in front and they left Atlanta at eight forty-five with the mileage on the car at 55890. The grandmother wrote this down because she thought it would be interesting to say how many miles they had been when they got back. It took them twenty minutes to reach the outskirts of the city.

The old lady settled herself comfortably, removing her white cotton gloves and putting them up with her purse on the shelf in front of the back window. The children's mother still had on slacks and still had her hair tied up in a green kerchief, but the grandmother had on a navy blue straw sailor hat with a bunch of white violets on the brim and a navy blue dress with a small white dot in the print. Her collars and cuffs were white organdy trimmed with lace and at her neckline she had pinned a purple spray of cloth violets containing a sachet. In case of an accident, anyone seeing her dead on the highway would know at once that she was a lady.

She said she thought it was going to be a good day for driving, neither too hot nor too cold, and she cautioned Bailey that the speed limit was fifty-five miles an hour and that the patrolmen hid themselves behind billboards and small clumps of trees and sped out after you before you had a chance to slow down. She pointed out interesting details of the scenery: Stone Mountain; the blue granite that in some places came up to both sides of the highway; the brilliant red clay banks slightly streaked with purple; and the various crops that made rows of green lace-work on the ground. The trees were full of silver-white sunlight and the meanest of them sparkled. The children were reading comic magazines and their mother had gone back to sleep.

"Let's go through Georgia fast so we won't have to look at it much," John Wesley said.

"If I were a little boy," said the grandmother, "I wouldn't talk about my native state that way. Tennessee has the mountains and Georgia has the hills." 15

"Tennessee is just a hillbilly dumping ground," John Wesley said, "and Georgia is a lousy state too."

"You said it," June Star said.

"In my time," said the grandmother, folding her thin veined fingers, "children were more respectful of their native states and their parents and everything else. People did right then. Oh look at the cute little pickaninny!" she said and pointed to a Negro child standing in the door of a shack. "Wouldn't that make a picture, now?" she asked and they all turned and looked at the little Negro out of the back window. He waved.

"He didn't have any britches on," June Star said.

"He probably didn't have any," the grandmother explained. "Little niggers in the 20 country don't have things like we do. If I could paint, I'd paint that picture," she said.

The children exchanged comic books.

The grandmother offered to hold the baby and the children's mother passed him over the front seat to her. She set him on her knee and bounced him and told him about the things they were passing. She rolled her eyes and screwed up her mouth and stuck her leathery thin face into his smooth bland one. Occasionally he gave her a far-away smile. They passed a large cotton field with five or six graves fenced in the middle of it, like a small island. "Look at the graveyard!" the grandmother said, pointing it out. "That was the old family burying ground. That belonged to the plantation."

"Where's the plantation?" John Wesley asked.

"Gone With the Wind," said the grandmother. "Ha. Ha."

When the children finished all the comic books they had brought, they opened 25 the lunch and ate it. The grandmother ate a peanut butter sandwich and an olive and would not let the children throw the box and the paper napkins out the window. When there was nothing else to do they played a game by choosing a cloud and making the other two guess what shape it suggested. John Wesley took one the shape of a cow and June Star guessed a cow and John Wesley said, no, an automobile, and June Star said he didn't play fair, and they began to slap each other over the grandmother.

The grandmother said she would tell them a story if they would keep quiet. When she told a story, she rolled her eyes and waved her head and was very dramatic. She said once when she was a maiden lady she had been courted by a Mr. Edgar Atkins Teagarden from Jasper, Georgia. She said he was a very good-looking man and a gentleman and that he brought her a watermelon every Saturday afternoon with his initials cut in it, E. A. T. Well, one Saturday, she said, Mr. Teagarden brought the watermelon and there was nobody at home and he left it on the front porch and returned in his buggy to Jasper, but she never got the watermelon, she said, because a nigger boy ate it when he saw the initials, E. A. T.! This story tickled John Wesley's funny bone and he giggled and giggled but June Star didn't think it was any good. She said she wouldn't marry a man that just brought her a watermelon on Saturday. The grandmother said she would have done well to marry Mr. Teagarden because he was a gentleman and had bought Coca-Cola stock when it first came out and that he had died only a few years ago, a very wealthy man.

They stopped at The Tower for barbecued sandwiches. The Tower was a part stucco and part wood filling station and dance hall set in a clearing outside of

Timothy. A fat man named Red Sammy Butts ran it and there were signs stuck here and there on the building and for miles up and down the highway saying, TRY RED SAMMY'S FAMOUS BARBECUE. NONE LIKE FAMOUS RED SAMMY'S! RED SAM! THE FAT BOY WITH THE HAPPY LAUGH. A VETERAN! RED SAMMY'S YOUR MAN!

Red Sammy was lying on the bare ground outside The Tower with his head under a truck while a gray monkey about a foot high, chained to a small chinaberry tree, chattered nearby. The monkey sprang back into the tree and got on the highest limb as soon as he saw the children jump out of the car and run toward him.

Inside, The Tower was a long dark room with a counter at one end and tables at the other and dancing space in the middle. They all sat down at a board table next to the nickelodeon and Red Sam's wife, a tall burnt-brown woman with hair and eyes lighter than her skin, came and took their order. The children's mother put a dime in the machine and played "The Tennessee Waltz," and the grandmother said that tune always made her want to dance. She asked Bailey if he would like to dance but he only glared at her. He didn't have a naturally sunny disposition like she did and trips made him nervous. The grandmother's brown eyes were very bright. She swayed her head from side to side and pretended she was dancing in her chair. June Star said play something she could tap to so the children's mother put in another dime and played a fast number and June Star stepped out onto the dance floor and did her tap routine.

"Ain't she cute?" Red Sam's wife said, leaning over the counter. "Would you like   30 to come be my little girl?"

"No I certainly wouldn't," June Star said. "I wouldn't live in a broken-down place like this for a million bucks!" and she ran back to the table.

"Ain't she cute?" the woman repeated, stretching her mouth politely.

"Arn't you ashamed?" hissed the grandmother.

Red Sam came in and told his wife to quit lounging on the counter and hurry up with these people's order. His khaki trousers reached just to his hip bones and his stomach hung over them like a sack of meal swaying under his shirt. He came over and sat down at a table nearby and let out a combination sigh and yodel. "You can't win," he said. "You can't win," and he wiped his sweating red face off with a gray handkerchief. "These days you don't know who to trust," he said. "Ain't that the truth?"

"People are certainly not nice like they used to be," said the grandmother.   35

"Two fellers come in here last week," Red Sammy said, "driving a Chrysler. It was a old beat-up car but it was a good one and these boys looked all right to me. Said they worked at the mill and you know I let them fellers charge the gas they bought? Now why did I do that?"

"Because you're a good man!" the grandmother said at once.

"Yes'm, I suppose so," Red Sam said as if he were struck with this answer.

His wife brought the orders, carrying the five plates all at once without a tray, two in each hand and one balanced on her arm. "It isn't a soul in this green world of God's that you can trust," she said. "And I don't count nobody out of that, not nobody," she repeated, looking at Red Sammy.

"Did you read about that criminal, The Misfit, that's escaped?" asked the grand-   40 mother.

"I wouldn't be a bit surprised if he didn't attact this place right here," said the woman. "If he hears about it being here, I wouldn't be none surprised to see him. If he hears it's two cent in the cash register, I wouldn't be a-tall surprised if he . . ."

"That'll do," Red Sam said. "Go bring these people their Co'-Colas," and the woman went off to get the rest of the order.

"A good man is hard to find," Red Sammy said. "Everything is getting terrible. I remember the day you could go off and leave your screen door unlatched. Not no more."

He and the grandmother discussed better times. The old lady said that in her opinion Europe was entirely to blame for the way things were now. She said the way Europe acted you would think we were made of money and Red Sam said it was no use talking about it, she was exactly right. The children ran outside into the white sunlight and looked at the monkey in the lacy chinaberry tree. He was busy catching fleas on himself and biting each one carefully between his teeth as if it were a delicacy.

They drove off again into the hot afternoon. The grandmother took cat naps and woke up every five minutes with her own snoring. Outside of Toombsboro she woke up and recalled an old plantation that she had visited in this neighborhood once when she was a young lady. She said the house had six white columns across the front and that there was an avenue of oaks leading up to it and two little wooden trellis arbors on either side in front where you sat down with your suitor after a stroll in the garden. She recalled exactly which road to turn off to get to it. She knew that Bailey would not be willing to lose any time looking at an old house, but the more she talked about it, the more she wanted to see it once again and find out if the little twin arbors were still standing. "There was a secret panel in this house," she said craftily, not telling the truth but wishing that she were, "and the story went that all the family silver was hidden in it when Sherman° came through but it was never found . . ."

"Hey!" John Wesley said. "Let's go see it! We'll find it! We'll poke all the wood-work and find it! Who lives there? Where do you turn off at? Hey, Pop, can't we turn off there?"

"We never have seen a house with a secret panel!" June Star shrieked. "Let's go to the house with the secret panel! Hey Pop, can't we go see the house with the secret panel!"

"It's not far from here, I know," the grandmother said. "It wouldn't take over twenty minutes."

Bailey was looking straight ahead. His jaw was as rigid as a horseshoe. "No," he said.

The children began to yell and scream that they wanted to see the house with the secret panel. John Wesley kicked the back of the front seat and June Star hung over her mother's shoulder and whined desperately into her ear that they never had any fun even on their vacation, that they could never do what THEY wanted to do. The baby began to scream and John Wesley kicked the back of the seat so hard that his father could feel the blows in his kidney.

"All right!" he shouted and drew the car to a stop at the side of the road. "Will you all shut up? Will you all just shut up for one second? If you don't shut up, we won't go anywhere."

"It would be very educational for them," the grandmother murmured.

"All right," Bailey said, "but get this: this is the only time we're going to stop for anything like this. This is the one and only time."

45

50

Sherman: General William Tecumseh Sherman, Union commander, whose troops burned Atlanta in 1864, then made a devastating march to the sea.

"The dirt road that you have to turn down is about a mile back," the grand- mother directed. "I marked it when we passed."

"A dirt road," Bailey groaned.   55

After they had turned around and were headed toward the dirt road, the grand- mother recalled other points about the house, the beautiful glass over the front door- way and the candle-lamp in the hall. John Wesley said that the secret panel was probably in the fireplace.

"You can't go inside this house," Bailey said. "You don't know who lives there."

"While you all talk to the people in front, I'll run around behind and get in a window," John Wesley suggested.

"We'll all stay in the car," his mother said.

They turned onto the dirt road and the car raced roughly along in a swirl of pink   60 dust. The grandmother recalled the times when there were no paved roads and thirty miles was a day's journey. The dirt road was hilly and there were sudden washes in it and sharp curves on dangerous embankments. All at once they would be on a hill, looking down over the blue tops of trees for miles around, then the next minute, they would be in a red depression with the dust-coated trees looking down on them.

"This place had better turn up in a minute," Bailey said, "or I'm going to turn around."

The road looked as if no one had traveled on it for months.

"It's not much farther," the grandmother said and just as she said it, a horrible thought came to her. The thought was so embarrassing that she turned red in the face and her eyes dilated and her feet jumped up, upsetting her valise in the corner. The instant the valise moved, the newspaper top she had over the basket under it rose with a snarl and Pitty Sing, the cat, sprang onto Bailey's shoulder.

The children were thrown to the floor and their mother, clutching the baby, was thrown out the door onto the ground; the old lady was thrown into the front seat. The car turned over once and landed right-side-up in a gulch off the side of the road. Bailey remained in the driver's seat with the cat—gray-striped with a broad white face and an orange nose—clinging to his neck like a caterpillar.

As soon as the children saw they could move their arms and legs, they scrambled   65 out of the car, shouting, "We've had an ACCIDENT!" The grandmother was curled up under the dashboard, hoping she was injured so that Bailey's wrath would not come down on her all at once. The horrible thought she had had before the accident was that the house she had remembered so vividly was not in Georgia but in Tennessee.

Bailey removed the cat from his neck with both hands and flung it out the win- dow against the side of a pine tree. Then he got out of the car and started looking for the children's mother. She was sitting against the side of the red gutted ditch, hold- ing the screaming baby, but she only had a cut down her face and a broken shoulder. "We've had an ACCIDENT!" the children screamed in a frenzy of delight.

"But nobody's killed," June Star said with disappointment as the grandmother limped out of the car, her hat still pinned to her head but the broken front brim standing up at a jaunty angle and the violet spray hanging off the side. They all sat down in the ditch, except the children, to recover from the shock. They were all shaking.

"Maybe a car will come along," said the children's mother hoarsely.

"I believe I have injured an organ," said the grandmother, pressing her side, but no one answered her. Bailey's teeth were clattering. He had on a yellow sport shirt with bright blue parrots designed in it and his face was as yellow as the shirt.

The grandmother decided that she would not mention that the house was in Tennessee.

The road was about ten feet above and they could see only the tops of the trees on the other side of it. Behind the ditch they were sitting in there were more woods, tall and dark and deep. In a few minutes they saw a car some distance away on top of a hill, coming slowly as if the occupants were watching them. The grandmother stood up and waved both her arms dramatically to attract their attention. The car continued to come on slowly, disappeared around a bend and appeared again, moving even slower, on top of the hill they had gone over. It was a big black battered hearse-like automobile. There were three men in it.

It came to a stop just over them and for some minutes, the driver looked down with a steady expressionless gaze to where they were sitting, and didn't speak. Then he turned his head and muttered something to the other two and they got out. One was a fat boy in black trousers and a red sweat shirt with a silver stallion embossed on the front of it. He moved around on the right side of them and stood staring, his mouth partly open in a kind of loose grin. The other had on khaki pants and a blue striped coat and a gray hat pulled down very low, hiding most of his face. He came around slowly on the left side. Neither spoke.

The driver got out of the car and stood by the side of it, looking down at them. He was an older man than the other two. His hair was just beginning to gray and he wore silver-rimmed spectacles that gave him a scholarly look. He had a long creased face and didn't have on any shirt or undershirt. He had on blue jeans that were too tight for him and was holding a black hat and a gun. The two boys also had guns.

"We've had an ACCIDENT!" the children screamed.

The grandmother had the peculiar feeling that the bespectacled man was some-one she knew. His face was as familiar to her as if she had known him all her life but she could not recall who he was. He moved away from the car and began to come down the embankment, placing his feet carefully so that he wouldn't slip. He had on tan and white shoes and no socks, and his ankles were red and thin. "Good after-noon," he said. "I see you all had you a little spill."

"We turned over twice!" said the grandmother.

"Oncet," he corrected. "We seen it happen. Try their car and see will it run, Hiram," he said quietly to the boy with the gray hat.

"What you got that gun for?" John Wesley asked. "Whatcha gonna do with that gun?"

"Lady," the man said to the children's mother, "would you mind calling them children to sit down by you? Children make me nervous. I want all you all to sit down right together there where you're at."

"What are you telling US what to do for?" June Star asked.

Behind them the line of woods gaped like a dark open mouth. "Come here," said their mother.

"Look here now," Bailey began suddenly, "we're in a predicament! We're in . . ."

The grandmother shrieked. She scrambled to her feet and stood staring. "You're The Misfit!" she said. "I recognized you at once!"

"Yes'm," the man said, smiling slightly as if he were pleased in spite of himself to be known, "but it would have been better for all of you, lady, if you hadn't of reck-ernized me."

Bailey turned his head sharply and said something to his mother that shocked even the children. The old lady began to cry and The Misfit reddened.

"Lady," he said, "don't you get upset. Sometimes a man says things he don't   85
mean. I don't reckon he meant to talk to you thataway."

"You wouldn't shoot a lady, would you?" the grandmother said and removed a
clean handkerchief from her cuff and began to slap at her eyes with it.

The Misfit pointed the toe of his shoe into the ground and made a little hole and
then covered it up again. "I would hate to have to," he said.

"Listen," the grandmother almost screamed, "I know you're a good man. You
don't look a bit like you have common blood. I know you must come from nice people!"

"Yes mam," he said, "finest people in the world." When he smiled he showed a
row of strong white teeth. "God never made a finer woman than my mother and my
daddy's heart was pure gold," he said. The boy with the red sweat shirt had come
around behind them and was standing with his gun at his hip. The Misfit squatted
down on the ground. "Watch them children, Bobby Lee," he said. "You know they
make me nervous." He looked at the six of them huddled together in front of him
and he seemed to be embarrassed as if he couldn't think of anything to say. "Ain't a
cloud in the sky," he remarked, looking up at it. "Don't see no sun but don't see no
cloud neither."

"Yes, it's a beautiful day," said the grandmother. "Listen," she said, "you shouldn't   90
call yourself The Misfit because I know you're a good man at heart. I can just look at
you and tell."

"Hush!" Bailey yelled. "Hush! Everybody shut up and let me handle this!" He was
squatting in the position of a runner about to sprint forward but he didn't move.

"I pre-chate that, lady," The Misfit said and drew a little circle in the ground
with the butt of his gun.

"It'll take a half a hour to fix this here car," Hiram called, looking over the raised
hood of it.

"Well, first you and Bobby Lee get him and that little boy to step over yonder
with you," The Misfit said, pointing to Bailey and John Wesley. "The boys want to
ast you something," he said to Bailey. "Would you mind stepping back in them woods
there with them?"

"Listen," Bailey began, "we're in a terrible predicament! Nobody realizes what   95
this is," and his voice cracked. His eyes were as blue and intense as the parrots in his
shirt and he remained perfectly still.

The grandmother reached up to adjust her hat brim as if she were going to the
woods with him but it came off in her hand. She stood staring at it and after a second
she let it fall on the ground. Hiram pulled Bailey up by the arm as if he were assisting
an old man. John Wesley caught hold of his father's hand and Bobby Lee followed.
They went off toward the woods and just as they reached the dark edge, Bailey turned
and supporting himself against a gray naked pine trunk, he shouted, "I'll be back in a
minute, Mamma, wait on me!"

"Come back this instant!" his mother shrilled but they all disappeared into the
woods.

"Bailey Boy!" the grandmother called in a tragic voice but she found she was
looking at The Misfit squatting on the ground in front of her. "I just know you're a
good man," she said desperately. "You're not a bit common!"

"Nome, I ain't a good man," The Misfit said after a second as if he had considered her statement carefully, "but I ain't the worst in the world neither. My daddy
said I was a different breed of dog from my brothers and sisters. 'You know,' Daddy

said, 'it's some that can live their whole life out without asking about it and it's others has to know why it is, and this boy is one of the latters. He's going to be into
everything!'" He put on his black hat and looked up suddenly and then away deep
into the woods as if he were embarrassed again. "I'm sorry I don't have on a shirt
before you ladies," he said, hunching his shoulders slightly. "We buried our clothes
that we had on when we escaped and we're just making do until we can get better.
We borrowed these from some folks we met," he explained.

"That's perfectly all right," the grandmother said. "Maybe Bailey has an extra   100
shirt in his suitcase."

"I'll look and see terrectly," The Misfit said.

"Where are they taking him?" the children's mother screamed.

"Daddy was a card himself," The Misfit said. "You couldn't put anything over
on him. He never got in trouble with the Authorities though. Just had the knack of
handling them."

"You could be honest too if you'd only try," said the grandmother. "Think how
wonderful it would be to settle down and live a comfortable life and not have to
think about somebody chasing you all the time."

The Misfit kept scratching in the ground with the butt of his gun as if he were   105
thinking about it. "Yes'm, somebody is always after you," he murmured.

The grandmother noticed how thin his shoulder blades were just behind his hat
because she was standing up looking down on him. "Do you ever pray?" she asked.

He shook his head. All she saw was the black hat wiggle between his shoulder
blades. "Nome," he said.

There was a pistol shot from the woods, followed closely by another. Then silence.
The old lady's head jerked around. She could hear the wind move through the tree tops
like a long satisfied insuck of breath. "Bailey Boy!" she called.

"I was a gospel singer for a while," The Misfit said. "I been most everything. Been
in the arm service, both land and sea, at home and abroad, been twict married, been an
undertaker, been with the railroads, plowed Mother Earth, been in a tornado, seen a
man burnt alive oncet," and he looked up at the children's mother and the little girl
who were sitting close together, their faces white and their eyes glassy; "I even seen a
woman flogged," he said.

"Pray, pray," the grandmother began, "pray, pray . . ."   110

"I never was a bad boy that I remember of," The Misfit said in an almost dreamy
voice, "but somewheres along the line I done something wrong and got sent to the
penitentiary. I was buried alive," and he looked up and held her attention to him by a
steady stare.

"That's when you should have started to pray," she said. "What did you do to get
sent to the penitentiary that first time?"

"Turn to the right, it was a wall," The Misfit said, looking up again at the cloudless sky. "Turn to the left, it was a wall. Look up it was a ceiling, look down it was a
floor. I forget what I done, lady. I set there and set there, trying to remember what it
was I done and I ain't recalled it to this day. Oncet in a while, I would think it was
coming to me, but it never come."

"Maybe they put you in by mistake," the old lady said vaguely.

"Nome," he said. "It wasn't no mistake. They had the papers on me."   115

"You must have stolen something," she said.

The Misfit sneered slightly. "Nobody had nothing I wanted," he said. "It was a
head-doctor at the penitentiary said what I had done was kill my daddy but I known

that for a lie. My daddy died in nineteen ought nineteen of the epidemic flu and I never had a thing to do with it. He was buried in the Mount Hopewell Baptist churchyard and you can go there and see for yourself."

"If you would pray," the old lady said, "Jesus would help you."

"That's right," The Misfit said.

"Well then, why don't you pray?" she asked trembling with delight suddenly.   120

"I don't want no hep," he said. "I'm doing all right by myself."

Bobby Lee and Hiram came ambling back from the woods. Bobby Lee was dragging a yellow shirt with bright blue parrots in it.

"Thow me that shirt, Bobby Lee," The Misfit said. The shirt came flying at him and landed on his shoulder and he put it on. The grandmother couldn't name what the shirt reminded her of. "No, lady," The Misfit said while he was buttoning it up, "I found out the crime don't matter. You can do one thing or you can do another, kill a man or take a tire off his car, because sooner or later you're going to forget what it was you done and just be punished for it."

The children's mother had begun to make heaving noises as if she couldn't get her breath. "Lady," he asked, "would you and that little girl like to step off yonder with Bobby Lee and Hiram and join your husband?"

"Yes, thank you," the mother said faintly. Her left arm dangled helplessly and she   125 was holding the baby, who had gone to sleep, in the other. "Hep that lady up, Hiram," The Misfit said as she struggled to climb out of the ditch, "and Bobby Lee, you hold onto that little girl's hand."

"I don't want to hold hands with him," June Star said. "He reminds me of a pig."

The fat boy blushed and laughed and caught her by the arm and pulled her off into the woods after Hiram and her mother.

Alone with The Misfit, the grandmother found that she had lost her voice. There was not a cloud in the sky nor any sun. There was nothing around her but woods. She wanted to tell him that he must pray. She opened and closed her mouth several times before anything came out. Finally she found herself saying, "Jesus. Jesus," meaning, Jesus will help you, but the way she was saying it, it sounded as if she might be cursing.

"Yes'm," The Misfit said as if he agreed. "Jesus thown everything off balance. It was the same case with Him as with me except He hadn't committed any crime and they could prove I had committed one because they had the papers on me. Of course," he said, "they never shown me my papers. That's why I sign myself now. I said long ago, you get you a signature and sign everything you do and keep a copy of it. Then you'll know what you done and you can hold up the crime to the punishment and see do they match and in the end you'll have something to prove you ain't been treated right. I call myself The Misfit," he said, "because I can't make what all I done wrong fit what all I gone through in punishment."

There was a piercing scream from the woods, followed closely by a pistol report.   130 "Does it seem right to you, lady, that one is punished a heap and another ain't punished at all?"

"Jesus!" the old lady cried. "You've got good blood! I know you wouldn't shoot a lady! I know you come from nice people! Pray! Jesus, you ought not to shoot a lady. I'll give you all the money I've got!"

"Lady," The Misfit said, looking beyond her far into the woods, "there never was a body that give the undertaker a tip."

There were two more pistol reports and the grandmother raised her head like a parched old turkey hen crying for water and called, "Bailey Boy, Bailey Boy!" as if her heart would break.

"Jesus was the only One that ever raised the dead," The Misfit continued, "and He shouldn't have done it. He thown everything off balance. If He did what He said, then it's nothing for you to do but thow away everything and follow Him, and if He didn't, then it's nothing for you to do but enjoy the few minutes you got left the best way you can—by killing somebody or burning down his house or doing some other meanness to him. No pleasure but meanness," he said and his voice had become almost a snarl.

"Maybe He didn't raise the dead," the old lady mumbled, not knowing what she   135 was saying and feeling so dizzy that she sank down in the ditch with her legs twisted under her.

"I wasn't there so I can't say He didn't," The Misfit said. "I wisht I had of been there," he said, hitting the ground with his fist. "It ain't right I wasn't there because if I had of been there I would of known. Listen lady," he said in a high voice, "if I had of been there I would of known and I wouldn't be like I am now." His voice seemed about to crack and the grandmother's head cleared for an instant. She saw the man's face twisted close to her own as if he were going to cry and she murmured, "Why you're one of my babies. You're one of my own children!" She reached out and touched him on the shoulder. The Misfit sprang back as if a snake had bitten him and shot her three times through the chest. Then he put his gun down on the ground and took off his glasses and began to clean them.

Hiram and Bobby Lee returned from the woods and stood over the ditch, looking down at the grandmother who half sat and half lay in a puddle of blood with her legs crossed under her like a child's and her face smiling up at the cloudless sky.

Without his glasses, The Misfit's eyes were red-rimmed and pale and defenseless-looking. "Take her off and thow her where you thown the others," he said, picking up the cat that was rubbing itself against his leg.

"She was a talker, wasn't she?" Bobby Lee said, sliding down the ditch with a yodel.

"She would of been a good woman," The Misfit said, "if it had been somebody   140 there to shoot her every minute of her life."

"Some fun!" Bobby Lee said.

"Shut up, Bobby Lee," The Misfit said. "It's no real pleasure in life."

Questions

1. How early in the story does O'Connor foreshadow what will happen in the end? What further hints does she give us along the way? How does the scene at Red Sammy's Barbecue advance the story toward its conclusion?

2. When we first meet the grandmother, what kind of person is she? What do her various remarks reveal about her? Does she remain a static character, or does she change in any way as the story goes on?

3. When the grandmother's head clears for an instant (paragraph 138), what does she suddenly understand? Reread this passage carefully and prepare to discuss what it means.

4. What do we learn from the conversation between The Misfit and the grandmother while the others go out to the woods? How would you describe The Misfit's outlook on the world? Compare it with the author's, from whatever you know about Flannery O'Connor and from the story itself.

5. How would you respond to a reader who complained, "The title of this story is just an obvious platitude"?

Revelation   1965

The doctor's waiting room, which was very small, was almost full when the Turpins entered and Mrs. Turpin, who was very large, made it look even smaller by her presence. She stood looming at the head of the magazine table set in the center of it, a living demonstration that the room was inadequate and ridiculous. Her little bright black eyes took in all the patients as she sized up the seating situation. There was one vacant chair and a place on a sofa occupied by a blond child in a dirty blue romper who should have been told to move over and make room for the lady. He was five or six, but Mrs. Turpin saw at once that no one was going to tell him to move over. He was slumped down in the seat, his arms idle at his sides and his eyes idle in his head; his nose ran unchecked.

Mrs. Turpin put a firm hand on Claud's shoulder and said in a voice that included anyone who wanted to listen, "Claud, you sit in that chair there," and gave him a push down into the vacant one. Claud was florid and bald and sturdy, somewhat shorter than Mrs. Turpin, but he sat down as if he were accustomed to doing what she told him to.

Mrs. Turpin remained standing. The only man in the room besides Claud was a lean stringy old fellow with a rusty hand spread out on each knee, whose eyes were closed as if he were asleep or dead or pretending to be so as not to get up and offer her his seat. Her gaze settled agreeably on a well-dressed grey-haired lady whose eyes met hers and whose expression said: if that child belonged to me, he would have some manners and move over—there's plenty of room there for you and him too.

Claud looked up with a sigh and made as if to rise.

"Sit down," Mrs. Turpin said. "You know you're not supposed to stand on that   5
leg. He has an ulcer on his leg," she explained.

Claud lifted his foot onto the magazine table and rolled his trouser leg up to reveal a purple swelling on a plump marble-white calf.

"My!" the pleasant lady said. "How did you do that?"

"A cow kicked him," Mrs. Turpin said.

"Goodness!" said the lady.

Claud rolled his trouser leg down.   10

"Maybe the little boy would move over," the lady suggested, but the child did not stir.

"Somebody will be leaving in a minute," Mrs. Turpin said. She could not understand why a doctor—with as much money as they made charging five dollars a day to just stick their head in the hospital door and look at you—couldn't afford a decent-sized waiting room. This one was hardly bigger than a garage. The table was cluttered with limp-looking magazines and at one end of it there was a big green glass ash tray full of cigaret butts and cotton wads with little blood spots on them. If she had had anything to do with the running of the place, that would have been emptied every so often. There were no chairs against the wall at the head of the room. It had a rectangular-shaped panel in it that permitted a view of the office where the nurse came and went and the secretary listened to the radio. A plastic fern in a gold pot sat in the opening and trailed its fronds down almost to the floor. The radio was softly playing gospel music.

Just then the inner door opened and a nurse with the highest stack of yellow hair Mrs. Turpin had ever seen put her face in the crack and called for the next patient. The woman sitting beside Claud grasped the two arms of her chair and hoisted herself up; she pulled her dress free from her legs and lumbered through the door where the nurse had disappeared.

Mrs. Turpin eased into the vacant chair, which held her tight as a corset. "I wish I could reduce," she said, and rolled her eyes and gave a comic sigh.

"Oh, *you* aren't fat," the stylish lady said.

"Ooooo I am too," Mrs. Turpin said. "Claud he eats all he wants to and never weighs over one hundred and seventy-five pounds, but me I just look at something good to eat and I gain some weight," and her stomach and shoulders shook with laughter. "You can eat all you want to, can't you, Claud?" she asked, turning to him.

Claud only grinned.

"Well, as long as you have such a good disposition," the stylish lady said, "I don't think it makes a bit of difference what size you are. You just can't beat a good disposition."

Next to her was a fat girl of eighteen or nineteen, scowling into a thick blue book which Mrs. Turpin saw was entitled *Human Development*. The girl raised her head and directed her scowl at Mrs. Turpin as if she did not like her looks. She appeared annoyed that anyone should speak while she tried to read. The poor girl's face was blue with acne and Mrs. Turpin thought how pitiful it was to have a face like that at that age. She gave the girl a friendly smile but the girl only scowled the harder. Mrs. Turpin herself was fat but she had always had good skin, and, though she was forty-seven years old, there was not a wrinkle in her face except around her eyes from laughing too much.

Next to the ugly girl was the child, still in exactly the same position, and next to him was a thin leathery old woman in a cotton print dress. She and Claud had three sacks of chicken feed in their pump house that was in the same print. She had seen from the first that the child belonged with the old woman. She could tell by the way they sat—kind of vacant and white-trashy, as if they would sit there until Doomsday if nobody called and told them to get up. And at right angles but next to the well-dressed pleasant lady was a lank-faced woman who was certainly the child's mother. She had on a yellow sweat shirt and wine-colored slacks, both gritty-looking, and the rims of her lips were stained with snuff. Her dirty yellow hair was tied behind with a little piece of red paper ribbon. Worse than niggers any day, Mrs. Turpin thought.

The gospel hymn playing was, "When I looked up and He looked down," and Mrs. Turpin, who knew it, supplied the last line mentally, "And wona these days I know I'll we-eara crown."

Without appearing to, Mrs. Turpin always noticed people's feet. The well-dressed lady had on red and grey suede shoes to match her dress. Mrs. Turpin had on her good black patent leather pumps. The ugly girl had on Girl Scout shoes and heavy socks. The old woman had on tennis shoes and the white-trashy mother had on what appeared to be bedroom slippers, black straw with gold braid threaded through them—exactly what you would have expected her to have on.

Sometimes at night when she couldn't go to sleep, Mrs. Turpin would occupy herself with the question of who she would have chosen to be if she couldn't have been herself. If Jesus had said to her before he made her, "There's only two places available for you. You can either be a nigger or white-trash," what would she have said? "Please, Jesus, please," she would have said, "just let me wait until there's another place available," and he would have said, "No, you have to go right now and I have only those two places so make up your mind." She would have wiggled and squirmed and begged and pleaded but it would have been no use and finally she would have said, "All right, make me a nigger then—but that don't mean a trashy one." And he would have made her a neat clean respectable Negro woman, herself but black.

Next to the child's mother was a red-headed youngish woman, reading one of the magazines and working a piece of chewing gum, hell for leather, as Claud would say. Mrs. Turpin could not see the woman's feet. She was not white-trash, just common. Sometimes Mrs. Turpin occupied herself at night naming the classes of people. On the bottom of the heap were most colored people, not the kind she would have been if she had been one, but most of them; then next to them—not above, just away from— were the white-trash; then above them were the home-owners, and above them the home-and-land owners, to which she and Claud belonged. Above she and Claud were people with a lot of money and much bigger houses and much more land. But here the complexity of it would begin to bear in on her, for some of the people with a lot of money were common and ought to be below she and Claud and some of the people who had good blood had lost their money and had to rent and then there were colored people who owned their homes and land as well. There was a colored dentist in town who had two red Lincolns and a swimming pool and a farm with registered white-face cattle on it. Usually by the time she had fallen asleep all the classes of people were moiling and roiling around in her head, and she would dream they were all crammed in together in a box car, being ridden off to be put in a gas oven.

"That's a beautiful clock," she said and nodded to her right. It was a big wall   25
clock, the face encased in a brass sunburst.

"Yes, it's very pretty," the stylish lady said agreeably. "And right on the dot too," she added, glancing at her watch.

The ugly girl beside her cast an eye upward at the clock, smirked, then looked directly at Mrs. Turpin and smirked again. Then she returned her eyes to her book. She was obviously the lady's daughter because, although they didn't look anything alike as to disposition, they both had the same shape of face and the same blue eyes. On the lady they sparkled pleasantly but in the girl's seared face they appeared alternately to smolder and to blaze.

What if Jesus had said, "All right, you can be white-trash or a nigger or ugly"!

Mrs. Turpin felt an awful pity for the girl, though she thought it was one thing to be ugly and another to act ugly.

The woman with the snuff-stained lips turned around in her chair and looked up at   30
the clock. Then she turned back and appeared to look a little to the side of Mrs. Turpin. There was a cast in one of her eyes. "You want to know wher you can get you one of themther clocks?" she asked in a loud voice.

"No, I already have a nice clock," Mrs. Turpin said. Once somebody like her got a leg in the conversation, she would be all over it.

"You can get you one with green stamps," the woman said. "That's most likely wher he got hisn. Save you up enough, you can get you most anythang. I got me some joo'ry."

Ought to have got you a wash rag and some soap, Mrs. Turpin thought.

"I get contour sheets with mine," the pleasant lady said.

The daughter slammed her book shut. She looked straight in front of her,   35
directly through Mrs. Turpin and on through the yellow curtain and the plate glass window which made the wall behind her. The girl's eyes seemed lit all of a sudden with a peculiar light, an unnatural light like night road signs give. Mrs. Turpin turned her head to see if there was anything going on outside that she should see, but she could not see anything. Figures passing cast only a pale shadow through the curtain. There was no reason the girl should single her out for her ugly looks.

"Miss Finley," the nurse said, cracking the door. The gum-chewing woman got up and passed in front of her and Claud and went into the office. She had on red high-heeled shoes.

Directly across the table, the ugly girl's eyes were fixed on Mrs. Turpin as if she had some very special reason for disliking her.

"This is wonderful weather, isn't it?" the girl's mother said.

"It's good weather for cotton if you can get the niggers to pick it," Mrs. Turpin said, "but niggers don't want to pick cotton any more. You can't get the white folks to pick it and now you can't get the niggers—because they got to be right up there with the white folks."

"They gonna *try* anyways," the white-trash woman said, leaning forward.   40

"Do you have one of those cotton-picking machines?" the pleasant lady asked.

"No," Mrs. Turpin said, "they leave half the cotton in the field. We don't have much cotton anyway. If you want to make it farming now, you have to have a little of everything. We got a couple of acres of cotton and a few hogs and chickens and just enough white-face that Claud can look after them himself."

"One thang I don't want," the white-trash woman said, wiping her mouth with the back of her hands. "Hogs. Nasty stinking things, a-gruntin and a-rootin all over the place."

Mrs. Turpin gave her the merest edge of her attention. "Our hogs are not dirty and they don't stink," she said. "They're cleaner than some children I've seen. Their feet never touch the ground. We have a pig-parlor—that's where you raise them on concrete," she explained to the pleasant lady, "and Claud scoots them down with the hose every afternoon and washes off the floor." Cleaner by far than that child right there, she thought. Poor nasty little thing. He had not moved except to put the thumb of his dirty hand into his mouth.

The woman turned her face away from Mrs. Turpin. "I know I wouldn't scoot   45
down no hog with no hose," she said to the wall.

You wouldn't have no hog to scoot down, Mrs. Turpin said to herself.

"A-gruntin and a-rootin and a-groanin," the woman muttered.

"We got a little of everything," Mrs. Turpin said to the pleasant lady. "It's no use in having more than you can handle yourself with help like it is. We found enough niggers to pick our cotton this year but Claud he has to go after them and take them home again in the evening. They can't walk that half a mile. No they can't. I tell you," she said and laughed merrily, "I sure am tired of buttering up niggers, but you got to love em if you want em to work for you. When they come in the morning, I run out and I say, 'Hi yawl this morning?' and when Claud drives them off to the field I just wave to beat the band and they just wave back." And she waved her hand rapidly to illustrate.

"Like you read out of the same book," the lady said, showing she understood perfectly.

"Child, yes," Mrs. Turpin said. "And when they come in from the field, I run out   50
with a bucket of icewater. That's the way it's going to be from now on," she said. "You may as well face it."

"One thang I know," the white-trash woman said. "Two thangs I ain't going to do: love no niggers or scoot down no hog with no hose." And she let out a bark of contempt.

The look that Mrs. Turpin and the pleasant lady exchanged indicated they both understood that you had to *have* certain things before you could *know* certain things.

But every time Mrs. Turpin exchanged a look with the lady, she was aware that the ugly girl's peculiar eyes were still on her, and she had trouble bringing her attention back to the conversation.

"When you got something," she said, "you got to look after it." And when you ain't got a thing but breath and britches, she added to herself, you can afford to come to town every morning and just sit on the Court House coping and spit.

A grotesque revolving shadow passed across the curtain behind her and was thrown palely on the opposite wall. Then a bicycle clattered down against the outside of the building. The door opened and a colored boy glided in with a tray from the drug store. It had two large red and white paper cups on it with tops on them. He was a tall, very black boy in discolored white pants and a green nylon shirt. He was chewing gum slowly, as if to music. He set the tray down in the office opening next to the fern and stuck his head through to look for the secretary. She was not in there. He rested his arms on the ledge and waited, his narrow bottom stuck out, swaying slowly to the left and right. He raised a hand over his head and scratched the base of his skull.

"You see that button there, boy?" Mrs. Turpin said. "You can punch that and   55
she'll come. She's probably in the back somewhere."

"Is thas right?" the boy said agreeably, as if he had never seen the button before. He leaned to the right and put his finger on it. "She sometime out," he said and twisted around to face his audience, his elbows behind him on the counter. The nurse appeared and he twisted back again. She handed him a dollar and he rooted in his pocket and made the change and counted it out to her. She gave him fifteen cents for a tip and he went out with the empty tray. The heavy door swung to slowly and closed at length with the sound of suction. For a moment no one spoke.

"They ought to send all them niggers back to Africa," the white-trash woman said. "That's wher they come from in the first place."

"Oh, I couldn't do without my good colored friends," the pleasant lady said.

"There's a heap of things worse than a nigger," Mrs. Turpin agreed. "It's all kinds of them just like it's all kinds of us."

"Yes, and it takes all kinds to make the world go round," the lady said in her   60
musical voice.

As she said it, the raw-complexioned girl snapped her teeth together. Her lower lip turned downwards and inside out, revealing the pale pink inside of her mouth. After a second it rolled back up. It was the ugliest face Mrs. Turpin had ever seen anyone make and for a moment she was certain that the girl had made it at her. She was looking at her as if she had known and disliked her all her life—all of Mrs. Turpin's life, it seemed too, not just all the girl's life. Why, girl, I don't even know you, Mrs. Turpin said silently.

She forced her attention back to the discussion. "It wouldn't be practical to send them back to Africa," she said. "They wouldn't want to go. They got it too good here."

"Wouldn't be what they wanted—if I had anythang to do with it," the woman said.

"It wouldn't be a way in the world you could get all the niggers back over there," Mrs. Turpin said. "They'd be hiding out and lying down and turning sick on you and wailing and hollering and raring and pitching. It wouldn't be a way in the world to get them over there."

"They got over here," the trashy woman said. "Get back like they got over."   65

"It wasn't so many of them then," Mrs. Turpin explained.

The woman looked at Mrs. Turpin as if here was an idiot indeed but Mrs. Turpin was not bothered by the look, considering where it came from.

"Nooo," she said, "they're going to stay here where they can go to New York and marry white folks and improve their color. That's what they all want to do, every one of them, improve their color."

"You know what comes of that, don't you?" Claud asked.

"No, Claud, what?" Mrs. Turpin said.

Claud's eyes twinkled. "White-faced niggers," he said with never a smile. 70

Everybody in the office laughed except the white-trash and the ugly girl. The girl gripped the book in her lap with white fingers. The trashy woman looked around her from face to face as if she thought they were all idiots. The old woman in the feed sack dress continued to gaze expressionless across the floor at the hightop shoes of the man opposite her, the one who had been pretending to be asleep when the Turpins came in. He was laughing heartily, his hands still spread out on his knees. The child had fallen to the side and was lying now almost face down in the old woman's lap.

While they recovered from their laughter, the nasal chorus on the radio kept the room from silence.

"You go to blank blank
And I'll go to mine
But we'll all blank along
To-geth-er,
And all along the blank
We'll hep eachother out
Smile-ling in any kind of
Weath-ther!"

Mrs. Turpin didn't catch every word but she caught enough to agree with the 75 spirit of the song and it turned her thoughts sober. To help anybody out that needed it was her philosophy of life. She never spared herself when she found somebody in need, whether they were white or black, trash or decent. And of all she had to be thankful for, she was most thankful that this was so. If Jesus had said, "You can be high society and have all the money you want and be thin and svelte-like, but you can't be a good woman with it," she would have had to say, "Well don't make me that then. Make me a good woman and it don't matter what else, how fat or how ugly or how poor!" Her heart rose. He had not made her a nigger or white-trash or ugly! He had made her herself and given her a little of everything. Jesus, thank you! she said. Thank you thank you thank you! Whenever she counted her blessings she felt as buoyant as if she weighed one hundred and twenty-five pounds instead of one hundred and eighty.

"What's wrong with your little boy?" the pleasant lady asked the white-trashy woman.

"He has a ulcer," the woman said proudly. "He ain't give me a minute's peace since he was born. Him and her are just alike," she said, nodding at the old woman, who was running her leathery fingers through the child's pale hair. "Look like I can't get nothing down them two but Co' Cola and candy."

That's all you try to get down em, Mrs. Turpin said to herself. Too lazy to light the fire. There was nothing you could tell her about people like them that she didn't know already. And it was not just that they didn't have anything. Because if you gave them everything, in two weeks it would all be broken or filthy or they would have chopped it up for lightwood. She knew all this from her own experience. Help them you must, but help them you couldn't.

All at once the ugly girl turned her lips inside out again. Her eyes were fixed like two drills on Mrs. Turpin. This time there was no mistaking that there was something urgent behind them.

Girl, Mrs. Turpin exclaimed silently, I haven't done a thing to you! The girl   80
might be confusing her with somebody else. There was no need to sit by and let herself be intimidated. "You must be in college," she said boldly, looking directly at the girl. "I see you reading a book there."

The girl continued to stare and pointedly did not answer.

Her mother blushed at this rudeness. "The lady asked you a question, Mary Grace," she said under her breath.

"I have ears," Mary Grace said.

The poor mother blushed again. "Mary Grace goes to Wellesley College," she explained. She twisted one of the buttons on her dress. "In Massachusetts," she added with a grimace. "And in the summer she just keeps right on studying. Just reads all the time, a real book worm. She's done real well at Wellesley; she's taking English and Math and History and Psychology and Social Studies," she rattled on, "and I think it's too much. I think she ought to get out and have fun."

The girl looked as if she would like to hurl them all through the plate glass   85
window.

"Way up north," Mrs. Turpin murmured and thought, well, it hasn't done much for her manners.

"I'd almost rather to have him sick," the white-trash woman said, wrenching the attention back to herself. "He's so mean when he ain't. Look like some children just take natural to meanness. It's some gets bad when they get sick but he was the opposite. Took sick and turned good. He don't give me no trouble now. It's me waitin to see the doctor," she said.

If I was going to send anybody back to Africa, Mrs. Turpin thought, it would be your kind, woman. "Yes, indeed," she said aloud, but looking up at the ceiling, "it's a heap of things worse than a nigger." And dirtier than a hog, she added to herself.

"I think people with bad dispositions are more to be pitied than anyone on earth," the pleasant lady said in a voice that was decidedly thin.

"I thank the Lord he has blessed me with a good one," Mrs. Turpin said. "The   90
day has never dawned that I couldn't find something to laugh at."

"Not since she married me anyways," Claud said with a comical straight face.

Everybody laughed except the girl and the white-trash.

Mrs. Turpin's stomach shook. "He's such a caution," she said, "that I can't help but laugh at him."

The girl made a loud ugly noise through her teeth.

Her mother's mouth grew thin and straight. "I think the worst thing in the   95
world," she said, "is an ungrateful person. To have everything and not appreciate it. I know a girl," she said, "who has parents who would give her anything, a little brother who loves her dearly, who is getting a good education, who wears the best clothes, but who can never say a kind word to anyone, who never smiles, who just criticizes and complains all day long."

"Is she too old to paddle?" Claud asked.

The girl's face was almost purple.

"Yes," the lady said, "I'm afraid there's nothing to do but leave her to her folly. Some day she'll wake up and it'll be too late."

"It never hurt anyone to smile," Mrs. Turpin said. "It just makes you feel better all over."

"Of course," the lady said sadly, "but there are just some people you can't tell anything to. They can't take criticism." 100

"If it's one thing I am," Mrs. Turpin said with feeling, "it's grateful. When I think who all I could have been besides myself and what all I got, a little of everything, and a good disposition besides, I just feel like shouting, 'Thank you, Jesus, for making everything the way it is!' It could have been different!" For one thing, somebody else could have got Claud. At the thought of this, she was flooded with gratitude and a terrible pang of joy ran through her. "Oh thank you, Jesus, Jesus, thank you!" she cried aloud.

The book struck her directly over her left eye. It struck almost at the same instant that she realized the girl was about to hurl it. Before she could utter a sound, the raw face came crashing across the table toward her, howling. The girl's fingers sank like clamps into the soft flesh of her neck. She heard the mother cry out and Claud shout, "Whoa!" There was an instant when she was certain that she was about to be in an earthquake.

All at once her vision narrowed and she saw everything as if it were happening in a small room far away, or as if she were looking at it through the wrong end of a telescope. Claud's face crumpled and fell out of sight. The nurse ran in, then out, then in again. Then the gangling figure of the doctor rushed out of the inner door. Magazines flew this way and that as the table turned over. The girl fell with a thud and Mrs. Turpin's vision suddenly reversed itself and she saw everything large instead of small. The eyes of the white-trashy woman were staring hugely at the floor. There the girl, held down on one side by the nurse and on the other by her mother, was wrenching and turning in their grasp. The doctor was kneeling astride her, trying to hold her arm down. He managed after a second to sink a long needle into it.

Mrs. Turpin felt entirely hollow except for her heart which swung from side to side as if it were agitated in a great empty drum of flesh.

"Somebody that's not busy call for the ambulance," the doctor said in the off-hand voice young doctors adopt for terrible occasions. 105

Mrs. Turpin could not have moved a finger. The old man who had been sitting next to her skipped nimbly into the office and made the call, for the secretary still seemed to be gone.

"Claud!" Mrs. Turpin called.

He was not in his chair. She knew she must jump up and find him but she felt like some one trying to catch a train in a dream, when everything moves in slow motion and the faster you try to run the slower you go.

"Here I am," a suffocated voice, very unlike Claud's, said.

He was doubled up in the corner on the floor, pale as paper, holding his leg. She 110 wanted to get up and go to him but she could not move. Instead, her gaze was drawn slowly downward to the churning face on the floor, which she could see over the doctor's shoulder.

The girl's eyes stopped rolling and focused on her. They seemed a much lighter blue than before, as if a door that had been tightly closed behind them was now open to admit light and air.

Mrs. Turpin's head cleared and her power of motion returned. She leaned forward until she was looking directly into the fierce brilliant eyes. There was no doubt in her mind that the girl did know her, knew her in some intense and personal way, beyond time and place and condition. "What you got to say to me?" she asked hoarsely and held her breath, waiting, as for a revelation.

The girl raised her head. Her gaze locked with Mrs. Turpin's. "Go back to hell where you came from, you old wart hog," she whispered. Her voice was low but clear.

Her eyes burned for a moment as if she saw with pleasure that her message had struck its target.

Mrs. Turpin sank back in her chair.

After a moment the girl's eyes closed and she turned her head wearily to the side. 115

The doctor rose and handed the nurse the empty syringe. He leaned over and put both hands for a moment on the mother's shoulders, which were shaking. She was sitting on the floor, her lips pressed together, holding Mary Grace's hand in her lap. The girl's fingers were gripped like a baby's around her thumb. "Go on to the hospital," he said. "I'll call and make the arrangements."

"Now let's see that neck," he said in a jovial voice to Mrs. Turpin. He began to inspect her neck with his first two fingers. Two little moon-shaped lines like pink fish bones were indented over her windpipe. There was the beginning of an angry red swelling above her eye. His fingers passed over this also.

"Lea' me be," she said thickly and shook him off. "See about Claud. She kicked him."

"I'll see about him in a minute," he said and felt her pulse. He was a thin grey-haired man, given to pleasantries. "Go home and have yourself a vacation the rest of the day," he said and patted her on the shoulder.

Quit your pattin me, Mrs. Turpin growled to herself. 120

"And put an ice pack over that eye," he said. Then he went and squatted down beside Claud and looked at his leg. After a moment he pulled him up and Claud limped after him into the office.

Until the ambulance came, the only sounds in the room were the tremulous moans of the girl's mother, who continued to sit on the floor. The white-trash woman did not take her eyes off the girl. Mrs. Turpin looked straight ahead at nothing. Presently the ambulance drew up, a long dark shadow, behind the curtain. The attendants came in and set the stretcher down beside the girl and lifted her expertly onto it and carried her out. The nurse helped the mother gather up her things. The shadow of the ambulance moved silently away and the nurse came back in the office.

"That ther girl is going to be a lunatic, ain't she?" the white-trash woman asked the nurse, but the nurse kept on to the back and never answered her.

"Yes, she's going to be a lunatic," the white-trash woman said to the rest of them.

"Po' critter," the old woman murmured. The child's face was still in her lap. His 125 eyes looked idly out over her knees. He had not moved during the disturbance except to draw one leg up under him.

"I thank Gawd," the white-trash woman said fervently, "I ain't a lunatic."

Claud came limping out and the Turpins went home.

As their pick-up truck turned into their own dirt road and made the crest of the hill, Mrs. Turpin gripped the window ledge and looked out suspiciously. The land sloped gracefully down through a field dotted with lavender weeds and at the start of the rise their small yellow frame house, with its little flower beds spread out around it like a fancy apron, sat primly in its accustomed place between two giant hickory trees. She would not have been startled to see a burnt wound between two blackened chimneys.

Neither of them felt like eating so they put on their house clothes and lowered the shade in the bedroom and lay down, Claud with his leg on a pillow and herself with a damp washcloth over her eye. The instant she was flat on her back, the image of a razor-backed hog with warts on its face and horns coming out behind its ears snorted into her head. She moaned, a low quiet moan.

"I am not," she said tearfully, "a wart hog. From hell." But the denial had no force. 130
The girl's eyes and her words, even the tone of her voice, low but clear, directed only to
her, brooked no repudiation. She had been singled out for the message, though there
was trash in the room to whom it might justly have been applied. The full force of this
fact struck her only now. There was a woman there who was neglecting her own child
but she had been overlooked. The message had been given to Ruby Turpin, a respectable, hard-working, church-going woman. The tears dried. Her eyes began to burn
instead with wrath.

She rose on her elbow and the washcloth fell into her hand. Claud was lying on his
back, snoring. She wanted to tell him what the girl had said. At the same time, she did
not wish to put the image of herself as a wart hog from hell into his mind.

"Hey, Claud," she muttered and pushed his shoulder.

Claud opened one pale baby blue eye.

She looked into it warily. He did not think about anything. He just went his way.

"Wha, whasit?" he said and closed the eye again. 135

"Nothing," she said. "Does your leg pain you?"

"Hurts like hell," Claud said.

"It'll quit terreckly," she said and lay back down. In a moment Claud was snoring
again. For the rest of the afternoon they lay there. Claud slept. She scowled at the
ceiling. Occasionally she raised her fist and made a small stabbing motion over her
chest as if she was defending her innocence to invisible guests who were like the
comforters of Job, reasonable-seeming but wrong.

About five-thirty Claud stirred. "Got to go after those niggers," he sighed, not
moving.

She was looking straight up as if there were unintelligible handwriting on the 140
ceiling. The protuberance over her eye had turned a greenish-blue. "Listen here," she
said.

"What?"

"Kiss me."

Claud leaned over and kissed her loudly on the mouth. He pinched her side and
their hands interlocked. Her expression of ferocious concentration did not change.
Claud got up, groaning and growling, and limped off. She continued to study the
ceiling.

She did not get up until she heard the pick-up truck coming back with the
Negroes. Then she rose and thrust her feet in her brown oxfords, which she did not
bother to lace, and stumped out onto the back porch and got her red plastic bucket.
She emptied a tray of ice cubes into it and filled it half full of water and went out into
the back yard. Every afternoon after Claud brought the hands in, one of the boys
helped him put out hay and the rest waited in the back of the truck until he was
ready to take them home. The truck was parked in the shade under one of the hickory trees.

"Hi yawl this evening?" Mrs. Turpin asked grimly, appearing with the bucket 145
and the dipper. There were three women and a boy in the truck.

"Us doin nicely," the oldest woman said. "Hi you doin?" and her gaze stuck immediately on the dark lump on Mrs. Turpin's forehead. "You done fell down, ain't you?"
she asked in a solicitous voice. The old woman was dark and almost toothless. She had
on an old felt hat of Claud's set back on her head. The other two women were younger
and lighter and they both had new bright green sun hats. One of them had hers on her
head; the other had taken hers off and the boy was grinning beneath it.

Mrs. Turpin set the bucket down on the floor of the truck. "Yawl hep your-selves," she said. She looked around to make sure Claud had gone. "No. I didn't fall down," she said, folding her arms. "It was something worse than that."

"Ain't nothing bad happen to you!" the old woman said. She said it as if they all knew Mrs. Turpin was protected in some special way by Divine Providence. "You just had you a little fall."

"We were in town at the doctor's office for where the cow kicked Mr. Turpin," Mrs. Turpin said in a flat tone that indicated they could leave off their foolishness. "And there was this girl there. A big fat girl with her face all broke out. I could look at that girl and tell she was peculiar but I couldn't tell how. And me and her mama were just talking and going along and all of a sudden WHAM! She throws this big book she was reading at me and . . ."

"Naw!" the old woman cried out. 150

"And then she jumps over the table and commences to choke me."

"Naw!" they all exclaimed, "naw!"

"Hi come she do that?" the old woman asked. "What ail her?"

Mrs. Turpin only glared in front of her.

"Somethin ail her," the old woman said. 155

"They carried her off in an ambulance," Mrs. Turpin continued, "but before she went she was rolling on the floor and they were trying to hold her down to give her a shot and she said something to me." She paused. "You know what she said to me?"

"What she say?" they asked.

"She said," Mrs. Turpin began, and stopped, her face very dark and heavy. The sun was getting whiter and whiter, blanching the sky overhead so that the leaves of the hickory tree were black in the face of it. She could not bring forth the words. "Something real ugly," she muttered.

"She sho shouldn't said nothin ugly to you," the old woman said. "You so sweet. You the sweetest lady I know."

"She pretty too," the one with the hat on said. 160

"And stout," the other one said. "I never knowed no sweeter white lady."

"That's the truth befo' Jesus," the old woman said. "Amen! You des as sweet and pretty as you can be."

Mrs. Turpin knew just exactly how much Negro flattery was worth and it added to her rage. "She said," she began again and finished this time with a fierce rush of breath, "that I was an old wart hog from hell."

There was an astounded silence.

"Where she at?" the youngest woman cried in a piercing voice. 165

"Lemme see her. I'll kill her!"

"I'll kill her with you!" the other one cried.

"She b'long in the sylum," the old woman said emphatically. "You the sweetest white lady I know."

"She pretty too," the other two said. "Stout as she can be and sweet. Jesus satisfied with her!"

"Deed he is," the old woman declared. 170

Idiots! Mrs. Turpin growled to herself. You could never say anything intelligent to a nigger. You could talk at them but not with them. "Yawl ain't drunk your water," she said shortly. "Leave the bucket in the truck when you're finished with it. I got more to do than just stand around and pass the time of day," and she moved off and into the house.

She stood for a moment in the middle of the kitchen. The dark protuberance over her eye looked like a miniature tornado cloud which might any moment sweep across the horizon of her brow. Her lower lip protruded dangerously. She squared her massive shoulders. Then she marched into the front of the house and out the side door and started down the road to the pig parlor. She had the look of a woman going single-handed, weaponless, into battle.

The sun was a deep yellow now like a harvest moon and was riding westward very fast over the far tree line as if it meant to reach the hogs before she did. The road was rutted and she kicked several good-sized stones out of her path as she strode along. The pig parlor was on a little knoll at the end of a lane that ran off from the side of the barn. It was a square of concrete as large as a small room, with a board fence about four feet high around it. The concrete floor sloped slightly so that the hog wash could drain off into a trench where it was carried to the field for fertilizer. Claud was standing on the outside, on the edge of the concrete, hanging onto the top board, hosing down the floor inside. The hose was connected to the faucet of a water trough nearby.

Mrs. Turpin climbed up beside him and glowered down at the hogs inside. There were seven long-snouted bristly shoats in it—tan with liver-colored spots—and an old sow a few weeks off from farrowing. She was lying on her side grunting. The shoats were running about shaking themselves like idiot children, their little slit pig eyes searching the floor for anything left. She had read that pigs were the most intelligent animal. She doubted it. They were supposed to be smarter than dogs. There had even been a pig astronaut. He had performed his assignment perfectly but died of a heart attack afterwards because they left him in his electric suit, sitting upright throughout his examination when naturally a hog should be on all fours.

A-gruntin and a-rootin and a-groanin.   175

"Gimme that hose," she said, yanking it away from Claud. "Go on and carry them niggers home and then get off that leg."

"You look like you might have swallowed a mad dog," Claud observed, but he got down and limped off. He paid no attention to her humors.

Until he was out of earshot, Mrs. Turpin stood on the side of the pen, holding the hose and pointing the stream of water at the hind quarters of any shoat that looked as if it might try to lie down. When he had had time to get over the hill, she turned her head slightly and her wrathful eyes scanned the path. He was nowhere in sight. She turned back again and seemed to gather herself up. Her shoulders rose and she drew in her breath.

"What do you send me a message like that for?" she said in a low fierce voice, barely above a whisper but with the force of a shout in its concentrated fury. "How am I a hog and me both? How am I saved and from hell too?" Her free fist was knotted and with the other she gripped the hose, blindly pointing the stream of water in and out of the eye of the old sow whose outraged squeal she did not hear.

The pig parlor commanded a view of the back pasture where their twenty beef   180
cows were gathered around the hay bales Claud and the boy had put out. The freshly cut pasture sloped down to the highway. Across it was their cotton field and beyond that a dark green dusty wood which they owned as well. The sun was behind the wood, very red, looking over the paling of trees like a farmer inspecting his own hogs.

"Why me?" she rumbled. "It's no trash around here, black or white, that I haven't given to. And break my back to the bone every day working. And do for the church."

She appeared to be the right size woman to command the arena before her. "How am I a hog?" she demanded. "Exactly how am I like them?" and she jabbed the stream of water at the shoats. "There was plenty of trash there. It didn't have to be me."

"If you like trash better, go get yourself some trash then," she railed. "You could have made me trash. Or a nigger. If trash is what you wanted why didn't you make me trash?" She shook her fist with the hose in it and a watery snake appeared momentarily in the air. "I could quit working and take it easy and be filthy," she growled. "Lounge about the sidewalks all day drinking root beer. Dip snuff and spit in every puddle and have it all over my face. I could be nasty.

"Or you could have made me a nigger. It's too late for me to be a nigger," she said with deep sarcasm, "but I could act like one. Lay down in the middle of the road and stop traffic. Roll on the ground."

In the deepening light everything was taking on a mysterious hue. The pasture was growing a peculiar glassy green and the streak of highway had turned lavender. She braced herself for a final assault and this time her voice rolled out over the pasture. "Go on," she yelled, "call me a hog! Call me a hog again. From hell. Call me a wart hog from hell. Put that bottom rail on top. There'll still be a top and bottom!" 185

A garbled echo returned to her.

A final surge of fury shook her and she roared, "Who do you think you are?"

The color of everything, field and crimson sky, burned for a moment with a transparent intensity. The question carried over the pasture and across the highway and the cotton field and returned to her clearly like an answer from beyond the wood.

She opened her mouth but no sound came out of it.

A tiny truck, Claud's, appeared on the highway, heading rapidly out of sight. Its 190 gears scraped thinly. It looked like a child's toy. At any moment a bigger truck might smash into it and scatter Claud's and the niggers' brains all over the road.

Mrs. Turpin stood there, her gaze fixed on the highway, all her muscles rigid, until in five or six minutes the truck reappeared, returning. She waited until it had had time to turn into their own road. Then like a monumental statue coming to life, she bent her head slowly and gazed, as if through the very heart of mystery, down into the pig parlor at the hogs. They had settled all in one corner around the old sow who was grunting softly. A red glow suffused them. They appeared to pant with a secret life.

Until the sun slipped finally behind the tree line, Mrs. Turpin remained there with her gaze bent to them as if she were absorbing some abysmal life-giving knowledge. At last she lifted her head. There was only a purple streak in the sky, cutting through a field of crimson and leading, like an extension of the highway, into the descending dusk. She raised her hands from the side of the pen in a gesture hieratic and profound. A visionary light settled in her eyes. She saw the streak as a vast swinging bridge extending upward from the earth through a field of living fire. Upon it a vast horde of souls were rumbling toward heaven. There were whole companies of white-trash, clean for the first time in their lives, and bands of black niggers in white robes, and battalions of freaks and lunatics shouting and clapping and leaping like frogs. And bringing up the end of the procession was a tribe of people whom she recognized at once as those who, like herself and Claud, had always had a little of everything and the God-given wit to use it right. She leaned forward to observe them closer. They were marching behind the others with great dignity, accountable as they had always been for good order and common sense and respectable behavior. They alone were on key. Yet she could see by their shocked and altered faces that even their virtues were being burned away. She lowered her hands and gripped the rail of the hog pen, her eyes small but fixed unblinkingly on what lay ahead. In a moment the vision faded but she remained where she was, immobile.

At length she got down and turned off the faucet and made her slow way on the darkening path to the house. In the woods around her the invisible cricket choruses had struck up, but what she heard were the voices of the souls climbing upward into the starry field and shouting hallelujah.

Questions

1. How does Mrs. Turpin see herself before Mary Grace calls her a wart hog?
2. What is the narrator's attitude toward Mrs. Turpin in the beginning of the story? How can you tell? Does this attitude change, or stay the same, at the end?
3. Describe the relationship between Mary Grace and her mother. What annoying platitudes does the mother mouth? Which of Mrs. Turpin's opinions seem especially to anger Mary Grace?
4. Sketch the plot of the story. What moment or event do you take to be the crisis, or turning point? What is the climax? What is the conclusion?
5. What do you infer from Mrs. Turpin's conversation with the black farm workers? Is she their friend? Why does she now find their flattery unacceptable ("Jesus satisfied with her")?
6. When, near the end of the story, Mrs. Turpin roars "Who do you think you are?" an echo "returned to her clearly like an answer from beyond the wood" (paragraph 188). Explain.
7. What is the final revelation given to Mrs. Turpin? (To state it is to state the theme of the story.) What new attitude does the revelation impart? (How is Mrs. Turpin left with a new vision of humanity?)
8. Other stories in this book contain revelations: "Young Goodman Brown," "The Gospel According to Mark." If you have read them, try to sum up the supernatural revelation made to the central character in each story. In each, is the revelation the same as a statement of the story's main theme?

Parker's Back[1]   1965

Parker's wife was sitting on the front porch floor, snapping beans. Parker was sitting on the step, some distance away, watching her sullenly. She was plain, plain. The skin on her face was thin and drawn as tight as the skin on an onion and her eyes were gray and sharp like the points of two icepicks. Parker understood why he had married her—he couldn't have got her any other way—but he couldn't understand why he stayed with her now. She was pregnant and pregnant women were not his favorite kind. Nevertheless, he stayed as if she had him conjured. He was puzzled and ashamed of himself.

The house they rented sat alone save for a single tall pecan tree on a high embankment overlooking a highway. At intervals a car would shoot past below and his wife's eyes would swerve suspiciously after the sound of it and then come back to rest on the newspaper full of beans in her lap. One of the things she did not approve of was automobiles. In addition to her other bad qualities, she was forever sniffing up sin. She did not smoke or dip, drink whiskey, use bad language or paint her face, and God knew some paint would have improved it, Parker thought. Her being against color, it was the more remarkable she had married him. Sometimes he supposed that

---

[1]"Parker's Back" was the last story Flannery O'Connor wrote, and was published the year after her death.

she had married him because she meant to save him. At other times he had a suspicion that she actually liked everything she said she didn't. He could account for her one way or another; it was himself he could not understand.

She turned her head in his direction and said, "It's no reason you can't work for a man. It don't have to be a woman."

"Aw shut your mouth for a change," Parker muttered.

If he had been certain she was jealous of the woman he worked for he would have been pleased but more likely she was concerned with the sin that would result if he and the woman took a liking to each other. He had told her that the woman was a hefty young blonde; in fact she was nearly seventy years old and too dried up to have an interest in anything except getting as much work out of him as she could. Not that an old woman didn't sometimes get an interest in a young man, particularly if he was as attractive as Parker felt he was, but this old woman looked at him the same way she looked at her old tractor—as if she had to put up with it because it was all she had. The tractor had broken down the second day Parker was on it and she had set him at once to cutting bushes, saying out of the side of her mouth to the nigger, "Everything he touches, he breaks." She also asked him to wear his shirt when he worked; Parker had removed it even though the day was not sultry; he put it back on reluctantly.

This ugly woman Parker married was his first wife. He had had other women but he had planned never to get himself tied up legally. He had first seen her one morning when his truck broke down on the highway. He had managed to pull it off the road into a neatly swept yard on which sat a peeling two-room house. He got out and opened the hood of the truck and began to study the motor. Parker had an extra sense that told him when there was a woman nearby watching him. After he had leaned over the motor a few minutes, his neck began to prickle. He cast his eye over the empty yard and porch of the house. A woman he could not see was either nearby beyond a clump of honeysuckle or in the house, watching him out the window.

Suddenly Parker began to jump up and down and fling his hand about as if he had mashed it in the machinery. He doubled over and held his hand close to his chest. "God dammit!" he hollered, "Jesus Christ in hell! Jesus God Almighty damm! God dammit to hell!" he went on, flinging out the same few oaths over and over as loud as he could.

Without warning a terrible bristly claw slammed the side of his face and he fell backwards on the hood of the truck. "You don't talk no filth here!" a voice close to him shrilled.

Parker's vision was so blurred that for an instant he thought he had been attacked by some creature from above, a giant hawk-eyed angel wielding a hoary weapon. As his sight cleared, he saw before him a tall raw-boned girl with a broom.

"I hurt my hand," he said. "I HURT my hand." He was so incensed that he forgot that he hadn't hurt his hand. "My hand may be broke," he growled although his voice was still unsteady.

"Lemme see it," the girl demanded.

Parker stuck out his hand and she came closer and looked at it. There was no mark on the palm and she took the hand and turned it over. Her own hand was dry and hot and rough and Parker felt himself jolted back to life by her touch. He looked more closely at her. I don't want nothing to do with this one, he thought.

The girl's sharp eyes peered at the back of the stubby reddish hand she held. There emblazoned in red and blue was a tattooed eagle perched on a cannon.

5

10

Parker's sleeve was rolled to the elbow. Above the eagle a serpent was coiled about a shield and in the spaces between the eagle and the serpent there were hearts, some with arrows through them. Above the serpent there was a spread hand of cards. Every space on the skin of Parker's arm, from wrist to elbow, was covered in some loud design. The girl gazed at this with an almost stupefied smile of shock, as if she had accidentally grasped a poisonous snake; she dropped the hand.

"I got most of my other ones in foreign parts," Parker said. "These here I mostly got in the United States. I got my first one when I was only fifteen year old."

"Don't tell me," the girl said, "I don't like it. I ain't got any use for it." 15

"You ought to see the ones you can't see," Parker said and winked.

Two circles of red appeared like apples on the girl's cheeks and softened her appearance. Parker was intrigued. He did not for a minute think that she didn't like the tattoos. He had never yet met a woman who was not attracted to them.

Parker was fourteen when he saw a man in a fair, tattooed from head to foot. Except for his loins which were girded with a panther hide, the man's skin was patterned in what seemed from Parker's distance—he was near the back of the tent, standing on a bench—a single intricate design of brilliant color. The man, who was small and sturdy, moved about on the platform, flexing his muscles so that the arabesque of men and beasts and flowers on his skin appeared to have a subtle motion of its own. Parker was filled with emotion, lifted up as some people are when the flag passes. He was a boy whose mouth habitually hung open. He was heavy and earnest, as ordinary as a loaf of bread. When the show was over, he had remained standing on the bench, staring where the tattooed man had been, until the tent was almost empty.

Parker had never before felt the least motion of wonder in himself. Until he saw the man at the fair, it did not enter his head that there was anything out of the ordinary about the fact that he existed. Even then it did not enter his head, but a peculiar unease settled in him. It was as if a blind boy had been turned so gently in a different direction that he did not know his destination had been changed.

He had his first tattoo some time after—the eagle perched on the cannon. It was 20 done by a local artist. It hurt very little, just enough to make it appear to Parker to be worth doing. This was peculiar too for before he had thought that only what did not hurt was worth doing. The next year he quit school because he was sixteen and could. He went to the trade school for a while, then he quit the trade school and worked for six months in a garage. The only reason he worked at all was to pay for more tattoos. His mother worked in a laundry and could support him, but she would not pay for any tattoo except her name on a heart, which he had put on, grumbling. However, her name was Betty Jean and nobody had to know it was his mother. He found out that the tattoos were attractive to the kind of girls he liked but who had never liked him before. He began to drink beer and get in fights. His mother wept over what was becoming of him. One night she dragged him off to a revival with her, not telling him where they were going. When he saw the big lighted church, he jerked out of her grasp and ran. The next day he lied about his age and joined the navy.

Parker was large for the tight sailor's pants but the silly white cap, sitting low on his forehead, made his face by contrast look thoughtful and almost intense. After a month or two in the navy, his mouth ceased to hang open. His features hardened into the features of a man. He stayed in the navy five years and seemed a natural part of the grey mechanical ship, except for his eyes, which were the same pale slate-color as the ocean and reflected the immense spaces around him as if they were a microcosm of the mysterious sea. In port Parker wandered about comparing the run-down places he was in to Birmingham, Alabama. Everywhere he went he picked up more tattoos.

He had stopped having lifeless ones like anchors and crossed rifles. He had a tiger and a panther on each shoulder, a cobra coiled about a torch on his chest, hawks on his thighs, Elizabeth II and Philip over where his stomach and liver were respectively. He did not care much what the subject was so long as it was colorful; on his abdomen he had a few obscenities but only because that seemed the proper place for them. Parker would be satisfied with each tattoo about a month, then something about it that had attracted him would wear off. Whenever a decent-sized mirror was available, he would get in front of it and study his overall look. The effect was not of one intricate arabesque of colors but of something haphazard and botched. A huge dissatisfaction would come over him and he would go off and find another tattooist and have another space filled up. The front of Parker was almost completely covered but there were no tattoos on his back. He had no desire for one anywhere he could not readily see it himself. As the space on the front of him for tattoos decreased, his dissatisfaction grew and became general.

After one of his furloughs, he didn't go back to the navy but remained away without official leave, drunk, in a rooming house in a city he did not know. His dissatisfaction, from being chronic and latent, had suddenly become acute and raged in him. It was as if the panther and the lion and the serpents and the eagles and the hawks had penetrated his skin and lived inside him in a raging warfare. The navy caught up with him, put him in the brig for nine months and then gave him a dishonorable discharge.

After that Parker decided that country air was the only kind fit to breathe. He rented the shack on the embankment and bought the old truck and took various jobs which he kept as long as it suited him. At the time he met his future wife, he was buying apples by the bushel and selling them for the same price by the pound to isolated homesteaders on back country roads.

"All that there," the woman said, pointing to his arm, "is no better than what a fool Indian would do. It's a heap of vanity." She seemed to have found the word she wanted. "Vanity of vanities," she said.

Well what the hell do I care what she thinks of it? Parker asked himself, but he was plainly bewildered. "I reckon you like one of these better than another anyway," he said, dallying until he thought of something that would impress her. He thrust the arm back at her. "Which you like best?"

"None of them," she said, "but the chicken is not as bad as the rest."

"What chicken?" Parker almost yelled.

She pointed to the eagle.

"That's an eagle," Parker said. "What fool would waste their time having a chicken put on themself?"

"What fool would have any of it?" the girl said and turned away. She went slowly back to the house and left him there to get going. Parker remained for almost five minutes, looking agape at the dark door she had entered.

The next day he returned with a bushel of apples. He was not one to be outdone by anything that looked like her. He liked women with meat on them, so you didn't feel their muscles, much less their old bones. When he arrived, she was sitting on the top step and the yard was full of children, all as thin and poor as herself; Parker remembered it was Saturday. He hated to be making up to a woman when there were children around, but it was fortunate he had brought the bushel of apples off the truck. As the children approached him to see what he carried, he gave each child an apple and told it to get lost; in that way he cleared out the whole crowd.

The girl did nothing to acknowledge his presence. He might have been a stray pig or goat that had wandered into the yard and she too tired to take up the broom and send it off. He set the bushel of apples down next to her on the step. He sat down on a lower step.

"Hep yourself," he said, nodding at the basket; then he lapsed into silence.

She took an apple quickly as if the basket might disappear if she didn't make   35
haste. Hungry people made Parker nervous. He had always had plenty to eat himself. He grew very uncomfortable. He reasoned he had nothing to say so why should he say it? He could not think now why he had come or why he didn't go before he wasted another bushel of apples on the crowd of children. He supposed they were her brothers and sisters.

She chewed the apple slowly but with a kind of relish of concentration, bent slightly but looking out ahead. The view from the porch stretched off across a long incline studded with iron weed and across the highway to a vast vista of hills and one small mountain. Long views depressed Parker. You look out into space like that and you begin to feel as if someone were after you, the navy or the government or religion.

"Who them children belong to, you?" he said at length.

"I ain't married yet," she said. "They belong to momma." She said it as if it were only a matter of time before she would be married.

Who in God's name would marry her? Parker thought.

A large barefooted woman with a wide gap-toothed face appeared in the door   40
behind Parker. She had apparently been there for several minutes.

"Good evening," Parker said.

The woman crossed the porch and picked up what was left of the bushel of apples. "We thank you," she said and returned with it into the house.

"That your old woman?" Parker muttered.

The girl nodded. Parker knew a lot of sharp things he could have said like "You got my sympathy," but he was gloomily silent. He just sat there, looking at the view. He thought he must be coming down with something.

"If I pick up some peaches tomorrow I'll bring you some," he said.   45

"I'll be much obliged to you," the girl said.

Parker had no intention of taking any basket of peaches back there but the next day he found himself doing it. He and the girl had almost nothing to say to each other. One thing he did say was, "I ain't got any tattoo on my back."

"What you got on it?" the girl said.

"My shirt," Parker said. "Haw."

"Haw, haw," the girl said politely.   50

Parker thought he was losing his mind. He could not believe for a minute that he was attracted to a woman like this. She showed not the least interest in anything but what he brought until he appeared the third time with two cantaloups. "What's your name?" she asked.

"O. E. Parker," he said.

"What does the O. E. stand for?"

"You can just call me O. E.," Parker said. "Or Parker. Don't nobody call me by my name."

"What's it stand for?" she persisted.   55

"Never mind," Parker said. "What's yours?"

"I'll tell you when you tell me what them letters are the short of," she said. There was just a hint of flirtatiousness in her tone and it went rapidly to Parker's head. He had never revealed the name to any man or woman, only to the files of the navy and the government, and it was on his baptismal record which he got at the age of a month; his mother was a Methodist. When the name leaked out of the navy files, Parker narrowly missed killing the man who used it.

"You'll go blab it around," he said.

"I'll swear I'll never tell nobody," she said. "On God's holy word I swear it."

Parker sat for a few minutes in silence. Then he reached for the girl's neck, drew   60
her ear close to his mouth and revealed the name in a low voice.

"Obadiah," she whispered. Her face slowly brightened as if the name came as a sign to her. "Obadiah," she said.

The name still stank in Parker's estimation.

"Obadiah Elihue," she said in a reverent voice.

"If you call me that aloud, I'll bust your head open," Parker said. "What's yours?"

"Sarah Ruth Cates," she said.   65

"Glad to meet you, Sarah Ruth," Parker said.

Sarah Ruth's father was a Straight Gospel preacher but he was away, spreading it in Florida. Her mother did not seem to mind his attention to the girl so long as he brought a basket of something with him when he came. As for Sarah Ruth herself, it was plain to Parker after he had visited three times that she was crazy about him. She liked him even though she insisted that pictures on the skin were vanity of vanities and even after hearing him curse, and even after she had asked him if he was saved and he had replied that he didn't see it was anything in particular to save him from. After that, inspired, Parker had said, "I'd be saved enough if you was to kiss me."

She scowled. "That ain't being saved," she said.

Not long after that she agreed to take a ride in his truck. Parker parked it on a deserted road and suggested to her that they lie down together in the back of it.

"Not until after we're married," she said—just like that.   70

"Oh that ain't necessary," Parker said and as he reached for her, she thrust him away with such force that the door of the truck came off and he found himself flat on his back on the ground. He made up his mind then and there to have nothing further to do with her.

They were married in the County Ordinary's office because Sarah Ruth thought churches were idolatrous. Parker had no opinion about that one way or the other. The Ordinary's office was lined with cardboard file boxes and record books with dusty yellow slips of paper hanging on out of them. The Ordinary was an old woman with red hair who had held office for forty years and looked as dusty as her books. She married them from behind the iron-grill of a stand-up desk and when she finished, she said with a flourish, "Three dollars and fifty cents and till death do you part!" and yanked some forms out of a machine.

Marriage did not change Sarah Ruth a jot and it made Parker gloomier than ever. Every morning he decided he had had enough and would not return that night; every night he returned. Whenever Parker couldn't stand the way he felt, he would have another tattoo, but the only surface left on him now was his back. To see a tattoo on his own back he would have to get two mirrors and stand between them in just the correct position and this seemed to Parker a good way to make an idiot of himself. Sarah Ruth who, if she had had better sense, could have enjoyed a tattoo on his back, would not even look at the ones he had elsewhere. When he attempted to point out especial details of them, she would shut her eyes tight and turn her back as well. Except in total darkness, she preferred Parker dressed and with his sleeves rolled down.

"At the judgement seat of God, Jesus is going to say to you, 'What you been doing all your life besides have pictures drawn all over you?'" she said.

"You don't fool me none," Parker said, "you're just afraid that hefty girl I work for'll like me so much she'll say, 'Come on, Mr. Parker, let's you and me . . .'"

"You're tempting sin," she said, "and at the judgement seat of God you'll have to answer for that too. You ought to go back to selling the fruits of the earth."

Parker did nothing much when he was at home but listen to what the judgement seat of God would be like for him if he didn't change his ways. When he could, he broke in with tales of the hefty girl he worked for. "'Mr. Parker,'" he said she said, 'I hired you for your brains.'" (She had added, "So why don't you use them?")

"And you should have seen her face the first time she saw me without my shirt," he said. "'Mr. Parker,' she said, 'you're a walking panner-rammer!'" This had, in fact, been her remark but it had been delivered out of one side of her mouth.

Dissatisfaction began to grow so great in Parker that there was no containing it outside of a tattoo. It had to be his back. There was no help for it. A dim half-formed inspiration began to work in his mind. He visualized having a tattoo put there that Sarah Ruth would not be able to resist—a religious subject. He thought of an open book with HOLY BIBLE tattooed under it and an actual verse printed on the page. This seemed just the thing for a while; then he began to hear her say, "Ain't I already got a real Bible? What you think I want to read the same verse over and over for when I can read it all?" He needed something better even than the Bible! He thought about it so much that he began to lose sleep. He was already losing flesh—Sarah Ruth just threw food in the pot and let it boil. Not knowing for certain why he continued to stay with a woman who was both ugly and pregnant and no cook made him generally nervous and irritable, and he developed a little tic in the side of his face.

Once or twice he found himself turning around abruptly as if someone were trailing him. He had had a granddaddy who had ended in the state mental hospital, although not until he was seventy-five, but as urgent as it might be for him to get a tattoo, it was just as urgent that he get exactly the right one to bring Sarah Ruth to heel. As he continued to worry over it, his eyes took on a hollow preoccupied expression. The old woman he worked for told him that if he couldn't keep his mind on what he was doing, she knew where she could find a fourteen-year-old colored boy who could. Parker was too preoccupied even to be offended. At any time previous, he would have left her then and there, saying drily, "Well, you go ahead on and get him then."

Two or three mornings later he was baling hay with the old woman's sorry baler and her broken down tractor in a large field, cleared save for one enormous old tree standing in the middle of it. The old woman was the kind who would not cut down a large old tree because it was a large old tree. She had pointed it out to Parker as if he didn't have eyes and told him to be careful not to hit it as the machine picked up hay near it. Parker began at the outside of the field and made circles inward toward it. He had to get off the tractor every now and then and untangle the baling cord or kick a rock out of the way. The old woman had told him to carry the rocks to the edge of the field, which he did when she was there watching. When he thought he could make it, he ran over them. As he circled the field his mind was on a suitable design for his back. The sun, the size of a golf ball, began to switch regularly from in front to behind him, but he appeared to see it both places as if he had eyes in the back of his head. All at once he saw the tree reaching out to grasp him. A ferocious thud propelled him into the air, and he heard himself yelling in an unbelievably loud voice, "GOD ABOVE!"

He landed on his back while the tractor crashed upside down into the tree and burst into flame. The first thing Parker saw were his shoes, quickly being eaten by the fire; one was caught under the tractor, the other was some distance away, burning by itself. He was not in them. He could feel the hot breath of the burning tree on his face. He scrambled backwards, still sitting, his eyes cavernous, and if he had known how to cross himself he would have done it.

His truck was on a dirt road at the edge of the field. He moved toward it, still sitting, still backwards, but faster and faster; halfway to it he got up and began a kind of forward-bent run from which he collapsed on his knees twice. His legs felt like two old rusted rain gutters. He reached the truck finally and took off in it, zigzagging up the road. He drove past his house on the embankment and straight for the city, fifty miles distant.

Parker did not allow himself to think on the way to the city. He only knew that there had been a great change in his life, a leap forward into a worse unknown, and that there was nothing he could do about it. It was for all intents accomplished.

The artist had two large cluttered rooms over a chiropodist's office on a back street. Parker, still barefooted, burst silently in on him at a little after three in the afternoon. The artist, who was about Parker's own age—twenty-eight—but thin and bald, was behind a small drawing table, tracing a design in green ink. He looked up with an annoyed glance and did not seem to recognize Parker in the hollow-eyed creature before him.

"Let me see the book you got with all the pictures of God in it," Parker said breathlessly. "The religious one."

The artist continued to look at him with his intellectual, superior stare. "I don't put tattoos on drunks," he said.

"You know me!" Parker cried indignantly. "I'm O. E. Parker! You done work for me before and I always paid!"

The artist looked at him another moment as if he were not altogether sure. "You've fallen off some," he said. "You must have been in jail."

"Married," Parker said.

"Oh," said the artist. With the aid of mirrors the artist had tattooed on the top of his head a miniature owl, perfect in every detail. It was about the size of a half-dollar and served him as a show piece. There were cheaper artists in town but Parker had never wanted anything but the best. The artist went over to a cabinet at the back of the room and began to look over some art books. "Who are you interested in?" he said, "saints, angels, Christs or what?"

"God," Parker said.

"Father, Son or Spirit?"

"Just God," Parker said impatiently. "Christ. I don't care. Just so it's God."

85

90

The artist returned with a book. He moved some papers off another table and 95
put the book down on it and told Parker to sit down and see what he liked. "The
up-to-date ones are in the back," he said.

Parker sat down with the book and wet his thumb. He began to go through
it, beginning at the back where the up-to-date pictures were. Some of them he
recognized—The Good Shepherd, Forbid Them Not, The Smiling Jesus, Jesus the
Physician's Friend, but he kept turning rapidly backwards and the pictures became
less and less reassuring. One showed a gaunt green dead face streaked with blood.
One was yellow with sagging purple eyes. Parker's heart began to beat faster and
faster until it appeared to be roaring inside him like a great generator. He flipped the
pages quickly, feeling that when he reached the one ordained, a sign would come. He
continued to flip through until he had almost reached the front of the book. On one
of the pages a pair of eyes glanced at him swiftly. Parker sped on, then stopped. His
heart too appeared to cut off; there was absolute silence. It said as plainly as if silence
were a language itself, GO BACK.

Parker returned to the picture—the haloed head of a flat stern Byzantine Christ
with all-demanding eyes. He sat there trembling; his heart began slowly to beat again
as if it were being brought to life by a subtle power.

"You found what you want?" the artist asked.

Parker's throat was too dry to speak. He got up and thrust the book at the artist,
opened at the picture.

"That'll cost you plenty," the artist said. "You don't want all those little blocks 100
though, just the outline and some better features."

"Just like it is," Parker said, "just like it is or nothing."

"It's your funeral," the artist said, "but I don't do that kind of work for nothing."

"How much?" Parker asked.

"It'll take maybe two days work."

"How much?" Parker said. 105

"On time or cash?" the artist asked. Parker's other jobs had been on time, but he
had paid.

"Ten down and ten for every day it takes," the artist said.

Parker drew ten dollar bills out of his wallet; he had three left in.

"You come back in the morning," the artist said, putting the money in his own
pocket. "First I'll have to trace that out of the book."

"No no!" Parker said. "Trace it now or gimme my money back," and his eyes 110
blared as if he were ready for a fight.

The artist agreed. Any one stupid enough to want a Christ on his back, he reasoned, would be just as likely as not to change his mind the next minute, but once
the work was begun he could hardly do so.

While he worked on the tracing, he told Parker to go wash his back at the sink
with the special soap he used there. Parker did it and returned to pace back and forth
across the room, nervously flexing his shoulders. He wanted to go look at the picture
again but at the same time he did not want to. The artist got up finally and had
Parker lie down on the table. He swabbed his back with ethyl chloride and then
began to outline the head on it with his iodine pencil. Another hour passed before he
took up his electric instrument. Parker felt no particular pain. In Japan he had had a
tattoo of the Buddha done on his upper arm with ivory needles; in Burma, a little
brown root of a man had made a peacock on each of his knees using thin pointed
sticks, two feet long; amateurs had worked on him with pins and soot. Parker was

usually so relaxed and easy under the hand of the artist that he often went to sleep, but this time he remained awake, every muscle taut.

At midnight the artist said he was ready to quit. He propped one mirror, four feet square, on a table by the wall and took a smaller mirror off the lavatory wall and put it in Parker's hands. Parker stood with his back to the one on the table and moved the other until he saw a flashing burst of color reflected from his back. It was almost completely covered with little red and blue and ivory and saffron squares; from them he made out the lineaments of the face—a mouth, the beginning of heavy brows, a straight nose, but the face was empty; the eyes had not yet been put in. The impression for the moment was almost as if the artist had tricked him and done the Physician's Friend.

"It don't have eyes," Parker cried out.

"That'll come," the artist said, "in due time. We have another day to go on it yet." 115

Parker spent the night on a cot at the Haven of Light Christian Mission. He found these the best places to stay in the city because they were free and included a meal of sorts. He got the last available cot and because he was still barefooted, he accepted a pair of second-hand shoes which, in his confusion, he put on to go to bed; he was still shocked from all that had happened to him. All night he lay awake in the long dormitory of cots with lumpy figures on them. The only light was from a phosphorescent cross glowing at the end of the room. The tree reached out to grasp him again, then burst into flame; the shoe burned quietly by itself; the eyes in the book said to him distinctly GO BACK and at the same time did not utter a sound. He wished that he were not in this city, not in this Haven of Light Mission, not in a bed by himself. He longed miserably for Sarah Ruth. Her sharp tongue and icepick eyes were the only comfort he could bring to mind. He decided he was losing it. Her eyes appeared soft and dilatory compared with the eyes in the book, for even though he could not summon up the exact look of those eyes, he could still feel their penetration. He felt as though, under their gaze, he was as transparent as the wing of a fly.

The tattooist had told him not to come until ten in the morning, but when he arrived at that hour, Parker was sitting in the dark hallway on the floor, waiting for him. He had decided upon getting up that, once the tattoo was on him, he would not look at it, that all his sensations of the day and night before were those of a crazy man and that he would return to doing things according to his own sound judgement.

The artist began where he left off. "One thing I want to know," he said presently as he worked over Parker's back, "why do you want this on you? Have you gone and got religion? Are you saved?" he asked in a mocking voice.

Parker's throat felt salty and dry. "Naw," he said, "I ain't got no use for none of that. A man can't save his self from whatever it is he don't deserve none of my sympathy." These words seemed to leave his mouth like wraiths and to evaporate at once as if he had never uttered them.

"Then why . . . ." 120

"I married this woman that's saved," Parker said. "I never should have done it. I ought to leave her. She's done gone and got pregnant."

"That's too bad," the artist said. "Then it's her making you have this tattoo."

"Naw," Parker said, "she don't know nothing about it. It's a surprise for her."

"You think she'll like it and lay off you a while?"

"She can't hep herself," Parker said. "She can't say she don't like the looks of 125
God." He decided he had told the artist enough of his business. Artists were all right

in their place but he didn't like them poking their noses into the affairs of regular people. "I didn't get no sleep last night," he said. "I think I'll get some now."

That closed the mouth of the artist but it did not bring him any sleep. He lay there, imagining how Sarah Ruth would be struck speechless by the face on his back and every now and then this would be interrupted by a vision of the tree of fire and his empty shoe burning beneath it.

The artist worked steadily until nearly four o'clock, not stopping to have lunch, hardly pausing with the electric instrument except to wipe the dripping dye off Parker's back as he went along. Finally he finished. "You can get up and look at it now," he said.

Parker sat up but he remained on the edge of the table.

The artist was pleased with his work and wanted Parker to look at it at once. Instead Parker continued to sit on the edge of the table, bent forward slightly but with a vacant look. "What ails you?" the artist said. "Go look at it."

"Ain't nothing ail me," Parker said in a sudden belligerent voice. "That tattoo   130 ain't going nowhere. It'll be there when I get there." He reached for his shirt and began gingerly to put it on.

The artist took him roughly by the arm and propelled him between the two mirrors. "Now *look*," he said, angry at having his work ignored.

Parker looked, turned white and moved away. The eyes in the reflected face continued to look at him—still, straight, all-demanding, enclosed in silence.

"It was your idea, remember," the artist said. "I would have advised something else."

Parker said nothing. He put on his shirt and went out the door while the artist shouted, "I'll expect all of my money!"

Parker headed toward a package shop on the corner. He bought a pint of whiskey   135 and took it into a nearby alley and drank it all in five minutes. Then he moved on to a pool hall nearby which he frequented when he came to the city. It was a well-lighted barn-like place with a bar up one side and gambling machines on the other and pool tables in the back. As soon as Parker entered, a large man in a red and black checkered shirt hailed him by slapping him on the back and yelling, "Yeyyyyyy boy! O. E. Parker!"

Parker was not yet ready to be struck on the back. "Lay off," he said, "I got a fresh tattoo there."

"What you got this time?" the man asked and then yelled to a few at the machines. "O. E.'s got him another tattoo."

"Nothing special this time," Parker said and slunk over to a machine that was not being used.

"Come on," the big man said, "let's have a look at O. E.'s tattoo," and while Parker squirmed in their hands, they pulled up his shirt. Parker felt all the hands drop away instantly and his shirt fell again like a veil over the face. There was a silence in the pool room which seemed to Parker to grow from the circle around him until it extended to the foundations under the building and upward through the beams in the roof.

Finally some one said, "Christ!" Then they all broke into noise at once. Parker   140 turned around, an uncertain grin on his face.

"Leave it to O. E.!" the man in the checkered shirt said. "That boy's a real card!"

"Maybe he's gone and got religion," some one yelled.

"Not on your life," Parker said.

"O. E.'s got religion and is witnessing for Jesus, ain't you, O. E.?" a little man with a piece of cigar in his mouth said wryly. "An o-riginal way to do it if I ever saw one."

"Leave it to Parker to think of a new one!" the fat man said.   145

"Yyeeeeeeyyyyyyy boy!" someone yelled and they all began to whistle and curse in compliment until Parker said, "Aaa shut up."

"What'd you do it for?" somebody asked.

"For laughs," Parker said. "What's it to you?"

"Why ain't you laughing then?" somebody yelled. Parker lunged into the midst of them and like a whirlwind on a summer's day there began a fight that raged amid overturned tables and swinging fists until two of them grabbed him and ran to the door with him and threw him out. Then a calm descended on the pool hall as nerve shattering as if the long barn-like room were the ship from which Jonah had been cast into the sea.

Parker sat for a long time on the ground in the alley behind the pool hall,   150
examining his soul. He saw it as a spider web of facts and lies that was not at all important to him but which appeared to be necessary in spite of his opinion. The eyes that were now forever on his back were eyes to be obeyed. He was as certain of it as he had ever been of anything. Throughout his life, grumbling and sometimes curs-ing, often afraid, once in rapture, Parker had obeyed whatever instinct of this kind had come to him—in rapture when his spirit had lifted at the sight of the tattooed man at the fair, afraid when he had joined the navy, grumbling when he had married Sarah Ruth.

The thought of her brought him slowly to his feet. She would know what he had to do. She would clear up the rest of it, and she would at least be pleased. It seemed to him that, all along, that was what he wanted, to please her. His truck was still parked in front of the building where the artist had his place, but it was not far away. He got in it and drove out of the city and into the country night. His head was almost clear of liquor and he observed that his dissatisfaction was gone, but he felt not quite like himself. It was as if he were himself but a stranger to himself, driving into a new country though everything he saw was familiar to him, even at night.

He arrived finally at the house on the embankment, pulled the truck under the pecan tree and got out. He made as much noise as possible to assert that he was still in charge here, that his leaving her for a night without word meant nothing except it was the way he did things. He slammed the car door, stamped up the two steps and across the porch and rattled the door knob. It did not respond to his touch. "Sarah Ruth!" he yelled, "let me in."

There was no lock on the door and she had evidently placed the back of a chair against the knob. He began to beat on the door and rattle the knob at the same time.

He heard the bed springs screak and bent down and put his head to the keyhole, but it was stopped up with paper. "Let me in!" he hollered, bamming on the door again. "What you got me locked out for?"

A sharp voice close to the door said, "Who's there?"   155

"Me," Parker said, "O. E."

He waited a moment.

"Me," he said impatiently, "O. E."

Still no sound from inside.

He tried once more. "O. E.," he said, bamming the door two or three more times.   160
"O. E. Parker. You know me."

There was a silence. Then the voice said slowly, "I don't know no O. E."

"Quit fooling," Parker pleaded. "You ain't got any business doing me this way. It's me, old O. E., I'm back. You ain't afraid of me."

"Who's there?" the same unfeeling voice said.

Parker turned his head as if he expected someone behind him to give him the answer. The sky had lightened slightly and there were two or three streaks of yellow floating above the horizon. Then as he stood there, a tree of light burst over the sky-line.

Parker fell back against the door as if he had been pinned there by a lance.   165

"Who's there?" the voice from inside said and there was a quality about it now that seemed final. The knob rattled and the voice said peremptorily, "Who's there, I ast you?"

Parker bent down and put his mouth near the stuffed keyhole. "Obadiah," he whispered and all at once he felt the light pouring through him, turning his spider web soul into a perfect arabesque of colors, a garden of trees and birds and beasts.

"Obadiah Elihue!" he whispered.

The door opened and he stumbled in. Sarah Ruth loomed there, hands on her hips. She began at once, "That was no hefty blonde woman you was working for and you'll have to pay her every penny on her tractor you busted up. She don't keep insurance on it. She came here and her and me had us a long talk and I . . ."

Trembling, Parker set about lighting the kerosene lamp.   170

"What's the matter with you, wasting that kerosene this near daylight?" she demanded. "I ain't got to look at you."

A yellow glow enveloped them. Parker put the match down and began to unbutton his shirt.

"And you ain't going to have none of me this near morning," she said.

"Shut your mouth," he said quietly. "Look at this and then I don't want to hear no more out of you." He removed the shirt and turned his back to her.

"Another picture," Sarah Ruth growled. "I might have known you was off after   175 putting some more trash on yourself."

Parker's knees went hollow under him. He wheeled around and cried, "Look at it! Don't just say that! *Look* at it!"

"I done looked," she said.

"Don't you know who it is?" he cried in anguish.

"No, who is it?" Sarah Ruth said. "It ain't anybody I know."

"It's him," Parker said.   180

"Him who?"

"God!" Parker cried.

"God? God don't look like that!"

"What do you know how he looks?" Parker moaned. "You ain't seen him."

"He don't *look*," Sarah Ruth said. "He's a spirit. No man shall see his face."   185

"Aw listen," Parker groaned, "this is just a picture of him."

"Idolatry!" Sarah Ruth screamed. "Idolatry! Enflaming yourself with idols under every green tree! I can put up with lies and vanity but I don't want no idolator in this house!" and she grabbed up the broom and began to thrash him across the shoulders with it.

Parker was too stunned to resist. He sat there and let her beat him until she had nearly knocked him senseless and large welts had formed on the face of the tattooed Christ. Then he staggered up and made for the door.

She stamped the broom two or three times on the floor and went to the window and shook it out to get the taint of him off it. Still gripping it, she looked toward the pecan tree and her eyes hardened still more. There he was—who called himself Obadiah Elihue—leaning against the tree, crying like a baby.

Questions

1. Why, in your judgment, did Parker marry Sarah Ruth? Why did she marry him?

2. At the end of the second paragraph, the author says of Parker and Sarah Ruth: "He could account for her one way or another; it was himself he could not understand." How accurate is each part of this assumption?

3. What does Parker's employer think of him? How valid is her estimation?

4. What is the basis of Parker's fascination with tattooing? What kinds of feelings usually prompt him to get a new tattoo?

5. "Long views depressed Parker. You look out into space like that and you begin to feel as if someone were after you, the navy or the government or religion" (paragraph 36). What insights does this statement give us into Parker's character—and, consequently, into his behavior?

6. What motivates Parker to get the tattoo on his back? How does he expect Sarah Ruth to respond to it?

7. While waiting for the "artist" to finish the "God" tattoo, Parker feels that "his sensations of the day and night before were those of a crazy man and that he would return to doing things according to his own sound judgement" (paragraph 117). How much self-awareness does this observation demonstrate?

8. When the artist asks him if he's "gone and got religion," Parker says, "I ain't got no use for none of that. A man can't save his self from whatever it is he don't deserve none of my sympathy" (paragraph 119). What does this attitude illustrate about Parker's personality? By his own standard, how much of his own sympathy does he deserve?

9. Why does Sarah Ruth refuse to recognize Parker by his initials? What is the significance of his whispering his name through the keyhole, and what effect does doing so have on him?

FLANNERY O'CONNOR ON WRITING

Flannery O'Connor at her mother's Georgia farm where she raised peacocks; c. 1962.

Excerpt from "On Her Own Work": Insights into "A Good Man Is Hard to Find"

1963

A story really isn't any good unless it successfully resists paraphrase, unless it hangs on and expands in the mind. Properly, you analyze to enjoy, but it's equally true that to analyze with any discrimination, you have to have enjoyed already, and I think that the best reason to hear a story read is that it should stimulate that primary enjoyment.

I don't have any pretensions to being an Aeschylus or Sophocles and providing you in this story with a cathartic experience out of your mythic background, though this story I'm going to read certainly calls up a good deal of the South's mythic background, and it should elicit from you a degree of pity and terror, even though its way of being serious is a comic one. I do think, though, that like the Greeks you should know what is going to happen in this story so that any element of suspense in it will be transferred from its surface to its interior.

I would be most happy if you had already read it, happier still if you knew it well, but since experience has taught me to keep my expectations along these lines modest, I'll tell you that this is the story of a family of six which, on its way driving to Florida, gets wiped out by an escaped convict who calls himself the Misfit. The family is made up of the Grandmother and her son, Bailey, and his children, John Wesley and June Star and the baby, and there is also the cat and the children's mother. The cat is named Pitty Sing, and the Grandmother is taking him with them, hidden in a basket.

Now I think it behooves me to try to establish with you the basis on which reason operates in this story. Much of my fiction takes its character from a reasonable use of the unreasonable, though the reasonableness of my use of it may not always be apparent. The assumptions that underlie this use of it, however, are those of the central Christian mysteries. These are assumptions to which a large part of the modern audience takes exception. About this I can only say that there are perhaps other ways than my own in which this story could be read, but none other by which it could have been written. Belief, in my own case anyway, is the engine that makes perception operate.

The heroine of this story, the Grandmother, is in the most significant position life offers the Christian. She is facing death. And to all appearances she, like the rest of us, is not too well prepared for it. She would like to see the event postponed. Indefinitely.

I've talked to a number of teachers who use this story in class and who tell their students that the Grandmother is evil, that in fact, she's a witch, even down to the cat. One of these teachers told me that his students, and particularly his Southern students, resisted this interpretation with a certain bemused vigor, and he didn't understand why. I had to tell him that they resisted it because they all had grandmothers or great-aunts just like her at home, and they knew, from personal experience, that the old lady lacked comprehension, but that she had a good heart. The Southerner is usually tolerant of those weaknesses that proceed from innocence, and he knows that a taste for self-preservation can be readily combined with the missionary spirit.

This same teacher was telling his students that morally the Misfit was several cuts above the Grandmother. He had a really sentimental attachment to the Misfit. But then a prophet gone wrong is almost always more interesting than your grandmother, and you have to let people take their pleasures where they find them.

It is true that the old lady is a hypocritical old soul; her wits are no match for the Misfit's, nor is her capacity for grace equal to his; yet I think the unprejudiced reader will feel that the Grandmother has a special kind of triumph in this story which instinctively we do not allow to someone altogether bad.

I often ask myself what makes a story work, and what makes it hold up as a story, and I have decided that it is probably some action, some gesture of a character that is unlike any other in the story, one which indicates where the real heart of the story lies. This would have to be an action or a gesture which was both totally right and totally unexpected; it would have to be one that was both in character and beyond character; it would have to suggest both the world and eternity. The action or gesture I'm talking about would have to be on the anagogical level, that is, the level which has to do with the Divine life and our participation in it. It would be a gesture that transcended any neat allegory that might have been intended or any pat moral categories a reader could make. It would be a gesture which somehow made contact with mystery.

There is a point in this story where such a gesture occurs. The Grandmother is at last alone, facing the Misfit. Her head clears for an instant and she realizes, even in her limited way, that she is responsible for the man before her and joined to him by ties of kinship which have their roots deep in the mystery she has been merely prattling about so far. And at this point, she does the right thing, she makes the right gesture.

I find that students are often puzzled by what she says and does here, but I think myself that if I took out this gesture and what she says with it, I would have no story. What was left would not be worth your attention. Our age not only does not have a very sharp eye for the almost imperceptible intrusions of grace, it no longer has much feeling for the nature of the violences which precede and follow them. The devil's greatest wile, Baudelaire has said, is to convince us that he does not exist.

I suppose the reasons for the use of so much violence in modern fiction will differ with each writer who uses it, but in my own stories I have found that violence is strangely capable of returning my characters to reality and preparing them to accept their moment of grace. Their heads are so hard that almost nothing else will do the work. This idea, that reality is something to which we must be returned at considerable cost, is one which is seldom understood by the casual reader, but it is one which is implicit in the Christian view of the world.

I don't want to equate the Misfit with the devil. I prefer to think that, however unlikely this may seem, the old lady's gesture, like the mustard-seed, will grow to be a great crow-filled tree in the Misfit's heart, and will be enough of a pain to him there to turn him into the prophet he was meant to become. But that's another story.

This story has been called grotesque, but I prefer to call it literal. A good story is literal in the same sense that a child's drawing is literal. When a child draws, he doesn't intend to distort but to set down exactly what he sees, and as his gaze is direct, he sees the lines that create motion. Now the lines of motion that interest the writer are usually invisible. They are lines of spiritual motion. And in this story you should be on the lookout for such things as the action of grace in the Grandmother's soul, and not for the dead bodies.

We hear many complaints about the prevalence of violence in modern fiction, and it is always assumed that this violence is a bad thing and meant to be an end in itself. With the serious writer, violence is never an end in itself. It is the extreme situation that best reveals what we are essentially, and I believe these are times when writers are more interested in what we are essentially than in the tenor of our daily lives. Violence is a force which can be used for good or evil, and among other things taken by it is the kingdom of heaven. But regardless of what can be taken by it, the man in the violent situation reveals those qualities least dispensable in his personality, those qualities which are all he will have to take into eternity with him; and since the characters in this story are all on the verge of eternity, it is appropriate to think of what they take with them. In any case, I hope that if you consider these points in connection with the story, you will come to see it as something more than an account of a family murdered on the way to Florida.

From "On Her Own Work"

On Her Catholic Faith   1955

I write the way I do because (not though) I am a Catholic. This is a fact and nothing covers it like the bald statement. However, I am a Catholic peculiarly possessed of the modern consciousness, the thing Jung describes as unhistorical, solitary, and guilty. To possess this within the Church is to bear a burden, the necessary burden for the conscious Catholic. It's to feel the contemporary situation at the ultimate level. I think

that the Church is the only thing that is going to make the terrible world we are coming to endurable; the only thing that makes the Church endurable is that it is somehow
the body of Christ and that on this we are fed. It seems to be a fact that you suffer as
much from the Church as for it but if you believe in the divinity of Christ, you have to
cherish the world at the same time that you struggle to endure it. This may explain the
lack of bitterness in the stories.

From a letter (July 20, 1955) in *The Habit of Being*

Excerpt from "The Grotesque in Southern Fiction": The Serious Writer and the Tired Reader   1960

Those writers who speak for and with their age are able to do so with a great deal
more ease and grace than those who speak counter to prevailing attitudes. I once
received a letter from an old lady in California who informed me that when the tired
reader comes home at night, he wishes to read something that will lift up his heart.
And it seems her heart had not been lifted up by anything of mine she had read. I
think that if her heart had been in the right place, it would have been lifted up.

You may say that the serious writer doesn't have to bother about the tired
reader, but he does, because they are all tired. One old lady who wants her heart
lifted up wouldn't be so bad, but you multiply her two hundred and fifty thousand
times and what you get is a book club. I used to think it should be possible to write
for some supposed elite, for the people who attend the universities and sometimes
know how to read, but I have since found that though you may publish your stories
in *Botteghe Oscure*,° if they are any good at all, you are eventually going to get a letter from some old lady in California, or some inmate of the Federal Penitentiary or
the state insane asylum or the local poorhouse, telling you where you have failed to
meet his needs.

And his need, of course, is to be lifted up. There is something in us, as storytellers and as listeners to stories, that demands the redemptive act, that demands
that what falls at least be offered the chance to be restored. The reader of today
looks for this motion, and rightly so, but what he has forgotten is the cost of it. His
sense of evil is diluted or lacking altogether and so he has forgotten the price of
restoration. When he reads a novel, he wants either his senses tormented or his spirits raised. He wants to be transported, instantly, either to a mock damnation or a
mock innocence.

I am often told that the model of balance for the novelist should be Dante, who
divided his territory up pretty evenly between hell, purgatory, and paradise. There
can be no objection to this, but also there can be no reason to assume that the result
of doing it in these times will give us the balanced picture that it gave in Dante's.
Dante lived in the 13th century when that balance was achieved in the faith of his
age. We live now in an age which doubts both fact and value, which is swept this way
and that by momentary convictions. Instead of reflecting a balance from the world
around him, the novelist now has to achieve one from a felt balance inside himself.
There are ages when it is possible to woo the reader; there are others when something
more drastic is necessary.

Botteghe Oscure: a distinguished and expensive literary magazine published in Rome from 1949 to 1960
by the Princess Marguerite Caetani for a small, sophisticated audience.

There is no literary orthodoxy that can be prescribed as settled for the fiction writer, not even that of Henry James who balanced the elements of traditional realism and romance so admirably within each of his novels. But this much can be said. The great novels we get in the future are not going to be those that the public thinks it wants, or those that critics demand. They are going to be the kind of novels that interest the novelist. And the novels that interest the novelist are those that have not already been written. They are those that put the greatest demands on him, that require him to operate at the maximum of his intelligence and his talents, and to be true to the particularities of his own vocation. The direction of many of us will be toward concentration and the distortion that is necessary to get our vision across; it will be more toward poetry than toward the traditional novel.

The problem for such a novelist will be to know how far he can distort without destroying, and in order not to destroy, he will have to descend far enough into himself to reach those underground springs that give life to his work. This descent into himself will, at the same time, be a descent into his region. It will be a descent through the darkness of the familiar into a world where, like the blind man cured in the gospels, he sees men as if they were trees, but walking. This is the beginning of vision, and I feel it is a vision which we in the South must at least try to understand if we want to participate in the continuance of a vital Southern literature. I hate to think that in twenty years Southern writers too may be writing about men in grey flannel suits and may have lost their ability to see that these gentlemen are even greater freaks than what we are writing about now. I hate to think of the day when the Southern writer will satisfy the tired reader.

From "The Grotesque in Southern Fiction"

Yearbook Cartoons   1944

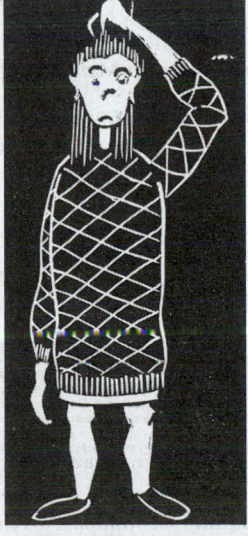

Untitled linoleum block cartoons by O'Connor for the yearbook at Georgia State College.

CRITICS ON FLANNERY O'CONNOR

J. O. Tate

A Good Source Is Not So Hard to Find: The Real Life Misfit   1980

The mounting evidence of O'Connor's use of items from the Milledgeville and Atlanta newspapers will interest those who realize that these sources, in and of themselves, have nothing to do with the Gothic, the grotesque, the American Romance tradition, Southwestern humor, Southern literature, adolescent aggression, the New Hermeneutics, the anxiety of influence, structuralism, pentecostal Gnosticism, medieval theology, Christian humanism, existentialism, or the Roman Catholic Church.

I. On "The Misfit" as Name and Word

The text of an Atlanta *Constitution* article of November 6, 1952, p. 29, identifies for us the source of a celebrated sobriquet. This newspaper reference was reprinted in *The Flannery O'Connor Bulletin,* Volume III, Autumn 1974. The headline says enough: "'The Misfit' Robs Office, Escapes With $150." Flannery O'Connor took a forgotten criminal's alias and used it for larger purposes: *her* Misfit was out of place in a grander way than the original. But we should not forget O'Connor's credentials as "a literalist of the imagination." There is always "a little lower layer." She meant to mock pop psychology by exploiting the original Misfit's exploitation of a socio-psychological "excuse" for aberrant behavior. But even a little lower: the original meaning of the word "misfit" has to do with clothing. We should not fail, therefore, to note that The Misfit's "borrowed" blue jeans are too tight. He leaves the story, of course, wearing Bailey's shirt.

II. On the Identity and Destiny of the Original Misfit

By November 15, 1952, The Misfit had been apprehended; he had also advanced himself to page three of the Atlanta *Journal.* The Misfit was a twenty-five-year old named James C. Yancey. He "was found to be of unsound mind" and committed to the state mental hospital at—Milledgeville. Where else?

III. On The Misfit's Notoriety, Peregrinations, Good Manners, Eye-glasses,
       Companions, and Mental Hygiene

The original Misfit was, as criminals go, small potatoes. He was an unambitious thief, no more. O'Connor took nothing from him but his imposing signature.

'The Misfit' Robs Office, Escapes With $150

A bandit who told his victims he was "The Misfit," held up the Atlanta Federal Savings and Loan Association office at 22 Marietta St., N. W., and escaped with $150 cash in a daring daylight raid Wednesday afternoon.

The man was described as being 30 years old, six feet tall and 175 pounds in weight. He carried a nickel-steel .32-caliber revolver, according to J. F. Clemmer, assistant vice-president of the company.

Clemmer told Det. Y. H. Allen the man shoved an envelope through the window where a cashier, Mrs. Beverly Bradshaw of 1919 Sylvan Ridge Dr., S. W., was at work. A crudely lettered message on the envelope read: "Put $150 in here and don't say anything. I have a gun, and I am 'The Misfit.'"

Mrs. Bradshaw ducked behind the counter, Clemmer said. Clemmer told another cashier to "do whatever the man wanted." Then he told the robber he'd "better go—we're protected by the FBI." The bandit then fled on Marietta St.

Detectives said the description of the man tallied with that of one who Tuesday night held up a hotel clerk at 87 Harris St., N. W., and fled with $50. FBI agents joined Atlanta police in a search.

The article in the Atlanta *Constitution*, November 6, 1952, that provided Flannery O'Connor with the criminal nickname "The Misfit."

But it just so happens that there was another well-publicized criminal aloose in Tennessee and Georgia just before the time that O'Connor appropriated the Misfit's name. This other hold-up artist had four important qualities in common with *her* Misfit. First, he inspired a certain amount of terror through several states. Second, he had, or claimed to have, a certain *politesse*. Third, he wore spectacles. Fourth, he had two accomplices, in more than one account.

James Francis ("Three-Gun") Hill, the sinister celebrity of the front pages, much more closely resembles the object of the grandmother's warnings than the original Misfit. Various articles tell of "a fantastic record of 26 kidnappings in four states, as many robberies, 10 car thefts, and a climactic freeing of four Florida convicts from a prison gang—all in two kaleidoscopic weeks." He had advanced "from an obscure hoodlum to top billing as a public enemy" (The Atlanta *Constitution*, November 1, p. 1). Such headlines as the grandmother had in mind screamed of Hill (though not in the sports section that Bailey was reading): "Maniac's Gang Terrorizes Hills" (*Constitution*, October 24, p. 2, from Sparta, Tenn.); "Search for Kidnap-Robbery Trio Centers in Atlanta and Vicinity" (October 25, p. 1, from Atlanta); "Chattanooga Is Focal Point for Manhunt" (October 27, p. 26); "2nd of Terror Gang Seized In Florida/Pal Said Still In Atlanta Area" (October 29, p. 32); "Self-Styled 3-Gun Maniac Frees 4 Road Gang Convicts at Gunpoint" (October 31, p. 1, from Bartow, Florida). It is quite clear that O'Connor, imagining through the grandmother's point of view, was, like the newspapers, assuming an Atlanta locale and orientation. The southward trip was in the same direction as Hill's last run.

The article of October 24 gives us a bit of color: "A fantastic band of highwaymen, led by a self-styled 'maniac' who laughed weirdly while he looted his victims, spread terror through the Cumberland hills today. . . . [The leader] boasted that he had escaped from the Utah State Prison and 'killed two people' . . . 'They call me a three-gun maniac, and brother, they got the picture straight,' the head bandit was quoted by victims." The October 31 article hints at the rustic setting of O'Connor's story: "The escapees and Hill . . . drove up a dead-end road and abandoned the car. They fled into thick woods on foot. . . ."

The *Constitution* of November 1 speaks of Hill on the front page as "the bespectacled, shrunken-cheeked highwayman." A later article gives us, as it gave O'Connor, a clue to her Misfit's respectful modes of address ("Good afternoon . . . I pre-chate that, lady . . . Nome . . . I'm sorry I don't have on a shirt before you ladies . . . Yes'm . . ."): We read of the trial of "Accused kidnapper, James Francis (Three-Gun) Hill, who says he's a 'gentleman-bandit' because 'I didn't cuss in front of ladies. . . .'" This Associated Press wire story from Chattanooga was on page 26 of the November 13 Atlanta *Journal*.

The *Constitution* of the same date says "Hearing Delayed for 'Maniac' Hill and 2 Cronies," and goes on to mention "James Francis Hill, self-styled 'three-gun maniac.'" We may observe that both Yancey and Hill were referred to in the newspapers as "self-styled," an arresting phrase perhaps to an author attuned to extravagances of self. I think we may also recognize here the genesis of Hiram and Bobby Lee.

The result of Hill's plea of guilty was perhaps not as forthright as his intention: "'Maniac' Hill Is Adjudged Incompetent" (*Constitution*, November 18). Like Yancey, The Misfit, Hill was sent to a mental institution—in Tennessee, this time. (His cronies were sentenced to jail.) The diagnosis of both Yancey and Hill as mentally ill may have suggested O'Connor's Misfit's experiences with the "head-doctor."

IV. On the Misfit, Memory, and Guilt

The fictional Misfit was not easily freudened: he knew perfectly well that he had not killed his daddy. Yet he insisted there was no balance between guilt and punishment—if memory served.

The issues of accuracy of memory, consciousness of guilt, and conscience were also raised in an odd "human-interest" story that was published in those same days when O'Connor was gathering so much material from the newspapers. The Misfit's claim that he was punished for crimes he did not remember may have been inspired by this account of a man who was *not* punished for a crime he *did* remember—but remembered wrongly.

The *Journal* of November 5, 1952 carried the article, written from Brookhaven, New York, on page 12: "'Murder' Didn't Happen, House Painter Free." Louis Roberts had shot a policeman in 1928; he assumed he had killed him. Over twenty years later, his conscience finally forced him to confess. When his tale was investigated, it was discovered that the policeman had survived after all. There was no prosecution for, as an authority was quoted as saying, "His conscience has punished him enough."

From "A Good Source Is Not So Hard to Find"

Mary Jane Schenck (b. 1944)

Deconstructing "A Good Man Is Hard to Find" 1988

"A Good Man Is Hard to Find" presents a masterful portrait of a woman who creates a self and a world through language. From the outset, the grandmother relies on "texts" to structure her reality. The newspaper article about The Misfit mentioned in the opening paragraph of the story is a written text which has a particular status in the narrative. It refers to events outside and prior to the primary *récit*, but it stands as an unrecognized prophecy of the events which occur at the end. For Bailey, the newspaper story is not important or meaningful, and for the grandmother it does not represent a real threat but is part of a ploy to get her own way. It is thus the first one of her "fictions," one which ironically comes true. The grandmother's whole personality is built upon the fictions she tells herself and her family. Although she knows Bailey would object if she brought her cat on the trip, the grandmother sneaks the cat into the car, justifying her behavior by imagining "he would miss her too much and she was afraid he might brush himself against one of the gas burners and accidentally asphyxiate himself." She also carefully cultivates a fiction about the past when people were good and when "children were more respectful of their native states and their parents and everything else." As she tells Red Sam at the Tower when they stop to eat, "People are certainly not nice like they used to be."

The grandmother reads fictional stories to the children, tells them ostensibly true stories, and provides a continual gloss on the physical world they are passing. "Little niggers in the country don't have things like we do. If I could paint, I'd paint that picture." Lacking that skill, the grandmother nevertheless verbally "creates" a whole universe as they ride along. "'Look at the graveyard!' the grandmother said, pointing it out. 'That was the old family burying ground. That belonged to the plantation.'" She creates the stories behind the visual phenomena she sees and explains relationships between events or her own actions which have no logic other than that which she lends them.

Her most important fiction is, of course, the story of the old plantation house which becomes more of an imperative as she tells it. The more she talks about it, the more she wants to see it again, so she does not hesitate to self-consciously lie about it. "'There was a secret panel in this house,' she said craftily, not telling the truth but wishing she were." At this point we see clearly the performative quality of the grandmother's language. At first it motivates her own desire, then spills over onto the children, finally culminating in their violent outburst of screaming and kicking to get their father to stop the car. The performative quality of her language becomes even more crucial when she realizes that she has fantasized the location of the house. She does not admit it, but her thoughts manifest themselves physically: "The thought was so embarrassing that she turned red in the face and her eyes dilated and her feet jumped up, upsetting her valise in the corner." Of course, it is her physical action which frees the cat and causes the accident. After the accident, she again fictionalizes about her condition, hoping she is injured so she can deflect Bailey's anger, and she cannot even manage to tell the truth about the details of the accident.

The scene with The Misfit is the apogee of the grandmother's use of "fictions" to explain and control reality, attempts that are thwarted by her encounter with a character who understands there is no reality behind her words. When the grandmother recognizes The Misfit, he tells her it would have been better if she hadn't, but she has *named* him, thus forcing him to become what is behind his self-selected name. In a desperate attempt to cope with the threat posed by the murderer, the grandmother runs through her litany of convenient fictions. She believes that there are class distinctions ("I know you're a good man. You don't look a bit like you have common blood"), that appearance reflects reality ("You shouldn't call yourself The Misfit because I know you're a good man at heart. I can just look at you and tell"), that redemption can be achieved through work ("You could be honest too if you'd only try. . . . Think how wonderful it would be to settle down . . ."), and finally, that prayer will change him ("'Pray, pray,' she commanded him").

From "Deconstructing Meaning in Two Short Stories by Flannery O'Connor"

Louise S. Cowan (b. 1916)

The Character of Mrs. Turpin in "Revelation"   2005

O'Connor held that serious writers cannot produce their works simply from their own ideas and conscious convictions; rather, if they are to produce anything of value, they must submit to a larger body of customs and manners of which they are a part. "As far as the creation of a body of fiction is concerned," she writes, "the social is superior to the purely personal." The writer whose themes are religious particularly needs a region where the themes find a response in the life of the people. "What the Southern Catholic writer is apt to find when he descends within his imagination is not Catholic life but the life of his region in which he is both native and alien." For O'Connor, then, the South presented the region to which she could devote her genius. It was out of step with the rest of the nation, since it was still largely agrarian, retaining in the early twentieth century traces in it of an older worldview. Further, as she saw, it still had a "folk," both white and black, who maintained an outlook fundamentally religious. It was likely to be from these groups that the prophetic figures in her fiction could emerge. In the South the general conception of man is still, O'Connor maintained, theological:

> The Bible is known by the ignorant as well as the educated and it is always the *mythos* which the poor hold in common that is most valuable to the fiction writer. When the poor hold sacred history in common, they have ties to the universal and the holy which allows the meaning of their every action to be heightened and seen under the aspect of eternity.

• • •

"Revelation"

The short story "Revelation," which won first prize in the 1964 O. Henry Awards, is one of O'Connor's last-written pieces and one of her most accomplished. It is about her familiar theme of Pharisaism;° and the epiphany with which it ends is no less devastating for occurring while the protagonist, Mrs. Turpin, is hosing down one of her prize hogs.

O'Connor's favorite target is the respectable, moral person who has lived a good and sensible life. The main character in "Revelation," Ruby Turpin, is such a figure, innocently falling into the pattern of self-satisfaction that finally assumes God himself must be impressed with her virtue. It is a mistake, however, to construe O'Connor's keen portrayals as pitiless. Her pharisaical characters are unaware of their self-love; they conduct themselves with kindness and courtesy, as good decent people should do. Mrs. Turpin in "Revelation" is such a naively self-righteous person, convinced that her righteousness makes her a special friend of Jesus. One of O'Connor's worries about the story "Revelation," as a matter of fact, was that people would think she was disapproving of Mrs. Turpin. "You got to be a very big woman to shout at the Lord across a hog pen," she wrote in a letter to a friend.

Ruby Turpin is one of O'Connor's masterpieces. Essentially good-hearted, she is blind to her own pride and self-satisfaction. She passes judgment on everyone she meets, sometimes occupying herself with naming over the classes of people. "On the bottom of the heap were most colored people . . . then next to them, not above, just away from—were the white trash, then above them the home-owners, and above them the home-and-land owners to which she and Claud belonged." She naively congratulates herself on having been born as who she is, a good respectable white woman who, with her husband, makes do with what they have and takes care of their property. But there are people who own more property—and people over them, and some of them are not morally good; so Mrs. Turpin's neat little scale of measurement becomes blurry and leaves her puzzled.

The crucial event in Ruby Turpin's life begins in a doctor's office. . . . She has been singled out, she knows, for a message. And, afterwards, the more she thinks about it in her isolation (for she can't bring herself to ask her husband about it; and the black servants who work for her merely flatter her), the more the incident seems to have some sort of divine import. "The message had been given to Ruby Turpin, a respectable, hard-working, church-going woman." Angry, she makes her way to the hogpen; and as she is watering down a white sow she begins her questioning of God that turns into a challenge: "Go on, call me a hog! Call me a hog again. From hell. Call me a wart hog from hell." And finally the blasphemous, "Who do you think you are?"

Pharisaism: hypocritical self-righteousness.

It is this direct challenge to the Almighty that produces the real revelation for Ruby Turpin. And in the vision that she receives, the question she had always stumbled over—the complexity of categorizing the classes of people—is answered, with a revelation at once grotesque and sublime.

From "Passing by the Dragon: Flannery O'Connor's Art of Revelation"

Kathleen Feeley (b. 1929)

The Mystery of Divine Direction: "Parker's Back"   1972

In the last story O'Connor wrote, "Parker's Back," she explores the mystery of divine direction. Unlikely candidate for God's election though he is, O. E. Parker is "chosen," and the story illuminates the communication of that choice and the effect that it has on his life. God leads Parker to understand his destiny through a strange combination of circumstances: his attraction to tattoos and his marriage to a woman who abhors them. This story achieves a goal set by a statement which O'Connor marked in her copy of Emmanuel Mounier's *The Character of Man*: "To draw mystery into the light of day, without losing its strength and fascination, is the highest achievement either of art or of thought." The "light of day" is the absolute credibility of this story; the "mystery" is God's way with man.

A "peculiar unease" which settles in Parker when he is fourteen years old is the first indication of God's designs upon him. At a fair he sees a man tattooed from head to foot; when the man flexes his muscles, the pattern of men and beasts and flowers on his skin appears to have a subtle motion of its own. After this vision fills his eyes, Parker is never the same; the "unease" in him can be satisfied only by tattoos, which he gets, one after the other, all over his body, for the next fourteen years. But the "unease" remains. Each tattoo dispels it for a time, but always it returns. He longs to see on his own body the "moving arabesque of color" that fills his imagination, but when he examines himself in a mirror, he sees only "something haphazard and blotched." It seems as if his desire can never be satisfied, for, when the story opens, he has only one body-space left, and that a place he cannot see—his back.

• • •

One can see in Parker's openness to life's mystery and in Sarah Ruth's certainty about life the difference between the many who are "called" and the few who are "chosen." Trusting exclusively in a literal interpretation of Scripture, Sarah Ruth follows the narrow path to salvation which excludes any other means of apprehending God. Her eyes, "gray and sharp like the points of two icepicks," reveal her determined character. Parker's mind bends toward mystery. Since the time he was initially drawn to the mystery of moving color on the body of the tattooed man, he has been responsive to the inner promptings of his spirit, even if he does not understand them. From that time, his life has had a mysterious orientation; "it was as if a blind boy had been turned so gently in a different direction that he did not know his destination had been changed." This openness to mystery is reflected in his eyes, "which were the same pale slate-color as the ocean and reflected the immense spaces around him as if they were a microcosm of the mysterious sea." Parker, aware of mystery, is open to the power of grace. Confronted with mystery, Sarah Ruth closes her heart. After raising welts on the face of the Christ tattooed on her husband's back and driving him out of the house, she looks out of the window at him sobbing against a tree, and "her eyes hardened still more." Parker had thought that his wife would like his tattoo because "she can't say she don't like the looks of God." But his wife has a narrow conception of Divinity. With her enraged assertion that "God don't look like that! . . . He don't *look*. . . . He's a spirit. No man shall see his face," she cuts herself off from grace.

From *Flannery O'Connor: Voice of the Peacock*

■ WRITING *effectively*

TOPICS FOR WRITING

1. Read three stories by Flannery O'Connor, or any one of the writers who appear in this book. Identify a theme or idea common to all three stories. Write an essay describing how your chosen author treats this theme. Support your argument with evidence from all three stories.

2. Compare and contrast a pair of characters from two different stories who feel conceptually related. Good choices might be Sarah Ruth from "Parker's Back," Mary Grace or Mrs. Turpin from "Revelation," and the grandmother in "A Good Man Is Hard to Find." Do these characters play similar roles in their respective stories?

3. All three stories are about revelations of one kind or another. How do these three revelations relate to each other? Back up your argument with evidence from the three stories.

4. In the excerpt from "On Her Own Work," O'Connor writes:

> I often ask myself what makes a story work, and what makes it hold up as a story, and I have decided that it is probably some action, some gesture of a character that is unlike any other in the story, one which indicates where the real heart of the story lies. This would have to be an action or a gesture which was both totally right and totally unexpected; it would have to be one that was both in character and beyond character; it would have to suggest both the world and eternity. . . . It would be a gesture which somehow made contact with mystery.

While O'Connor is speaking specifically about "A Good Man Is Hard to Find," her words can be applied to her other stories. Choose a gesture from "Revelation" or "Parker's Back" that fits this description, and explain your choice.

5. In 750 to 1,000 words, comment on O'Connor's use of humor. How does comedy help her say what she has to say?

11

CRITICAL CASEBOOK
Three Stories in Depth

Nathaniel Hawthorne ▪ *Young Goodman Brown*

Charlotte Perkins Gilman ▪ *The Yellow Wallpaper*

Alice Walker ▪ *Everyday Use*

NATHANIEL HAWTHORNE

Nathaniel Hawthorne (1804–1864) was born in the clipper-ship seaport of Salem, Massachusetts, son of a merchant captain (who died when the future novelist was only four years old) and great-great-grandson of a magistrate involved in the notorious Salem witchcraft trials. Hawthorne takes a keen interest in New England's sin-and-brimstone Puritan past in many of his stories, especially "Young Goodman Brown," and in the classic novel The Scarlet Letter (1850), his deepest exploration of his major themes of conscience, sin, and guilt. In 1825 Hawthorne graduated from Bowdoin College; one of his classmates—and his lifelong best friend—was Franklin Pierce, who in 1852 would be elected president of the United States. After college, Hawthorne lived at home and trained to be a writer. His first novel, Fanshawe

Nathaniel Hawthorne

(1828), begun while he was still an undergraduate, was published anonymously and at his own expense. During this period, Hawthorne also experienced great difficulty in trying to publish his short fiction, both in magazines and in book form, until the appearance of Twice-Told Tales *(1837). In 1841, he was appointed to a position in the Boston Custom House; in the following year he married Sophia Peabody. The newlyweds settled in the Old Manse in Concord, Massachusetts. Three more novels followed:* The House of the Seven Gables *(1851, the story of a family curse, tinged with nightmarish humor),* The Blithedale Romance *(1852, drawn from his short, irritating stay at a Utopian commune, Brook Farm), and* The Marble Faun *(1860, inspired by a stay in Italy). When Franklin Pierce ran for president, Hawthorne wrote his campaign biography. After taking office, Pierce appointed his old friend American*

consul at Liverpool, England. Depressed by ill health and the terrible toll of the Civil War, Hawthorne died suddenly while on a tour with Pierce of New Hampshire's White Mountains. With his contemporary Edgar Allan Poe, Hawthorne transformed the American short story from popular magazine filler into a major literary form.

Young Goodman Brown (1835) 1846

Young Goodman° Brown came forth, at sunset, into the street of Salem village,° but put his head back, after crossing the threshold, to exchange a parting kiss with his young wife. And Faith, as the wife was aptly named, thrust her own pretty head into the street, letting the wind play with the pink ribbons of her cap, while she called to Goodman Brown.

"Dearest heart," whispered she, softly and rather sadly, when her lips were close to his ear, "pray thee, put off your journey until sunrise, and sleep in your own bed to-night. A lone woman is troubled with such dreams and such thoughts, that she's afraid of herself, sometimes. Pray, tarry with me this night, dear husband, of all nights in the year!"

"My love and my Faith," replied young Goodman Brown, "of all nights in the year, this one night must I tarry away from thee. My journey, as thou callest it, forth and back again, must needs be done 'twixt now and sunrise. What, my sweet, pretty wife, dost thou doubt me already, and we but three months married!"

"Then, God bless you!" said Faith, with the pink ribbons, "and may you find all well, when you come back."

"Amen!" cried Goodman Brown. "Say thy prayers, dear Faith, and go to bed at   5
dusk, and no harm will come to thee."

So they parted; and the young man pursued his way, until, being about to turn the corner by the meeting-house, he looked back, and saw the head of Faith still peeping after him, with a melancholy air, in spite of her pink ribbons.

"Poor little Faith!" thought he, for his heart smote him. "What a wretch am I, to leave her on such an errand! She talks of dreams, too. Methought, as she spoke, there was trouble in her face, as if a dream had warned her what work is to be done to-night. But, no, no! 'twould kill her to think it. Well; she's a blessed angel on earth; and after this one night, I'll cling to her skirts and follow her to Heaven."

With this excellent resolve for the future, Goodman Brown felt himself justified in making more haste on his present evil purpose. He had taken a dreary road, darkened by all the gloomiest trees of the forest, which barely stood aside to let the narrow path creep through, and closed immediately behind. It was all as lonely as could be; and there is this peculiarity in such a solitude, that the traveller knows not who may be concealed by the innumerable trunks and the thick boughs overhead; so that, with lonely footsteps, he may yet be passing through an unseen multitude.

"There may be a devilish Indian behind every tree," said Goodman Brown, to himself; and he glanced fearfully behind him, as he added, "What if the devil himself should be at my very elbow!"

His head being turned back, he passed a crook of the road, and looking forward   10
again, beheld the figure of a man, in grave and decent attire, seated at the foot of an

Goodman: title given by Puritans to a male head of a household; a farmer or other ordinary citizen.
Salem village: in England's Massachusetts Bay Colony.

old tree. He arose, at Goodman Brown's approach, and walked onward, side by side with him.

"You are late, Goodman Brown," said he. "The clock of the Old South was striking as I came through Boston; and that is full fifteen minutes agone."°

"Faith kept me back awhile," replied the young man, with a tremor in his voice, caused by the sudden appearance of his companion, though not wholly unexpected.

It was now deep dusk in the forest, and deepest in that part of it where these two were journeying. As nearly as could be discerned, the second traveller was about fifty years old, apparently in the same rank of life as Goodman Brown, and bearing a considerable resemblance to him, though perhaps more in expression than features. Still, they might have been taken for father and son. And yet, though the elder person was as simply clad as the younger, and as simple in manner too, he had an indescribable air of one who knew the world, and would not have felt abashed at the governor's dinner-table, or in King William's court,° were it possible that his affairs should call him thither. But the only thing about him, that could be fixed upon as remarkable, was his staff, which bore the likeness of a great black snake, so curiously wrought, that it might almost be seen to twist and wriggle itself, like a living serpent. This, of course, must have been an ocular deception, assisted by the uncertain light.

"Come, Goodman Brown!" cried his fellow-traveller, "this is dull pace for the beginning of a journey. Take my staff, if you are so soon weary."

"Friend," said the other, exchanging his slow pace for a full stop, "having kept covenant by meeting thee here, it is my purpose now to return whence I came. I have scruples, touching the matter thou wot'st° of." 15

"Sayest thou so?" replied he of the serpent, smiling apart. "Let us walk on, nevertheless, reasoning as we go, and if I convince thee not, thou shalt turn back. We are but a little way in the forest, yet."

"Too far, too far!" exclaimed the goodman, unconsciously resuming his walk. "My father never went into the woods on such an errand, nor his father before him. We have been a race of honest men and good Christians, since the days of the martyrs.° And shall I be the first of the name of Brown, that ever took this path, and kept—"

"Such company, thou wouldst say," observed the elder person, interpreting his pause. "Well said, Goodman Brown! I have been as well acquainted with your family as with ever a one among the Puritans; and that's no trifle to say. I helped your grandfather, the constable, when he lashed the Quaker woman so smartly through the streets of Salem. And it was I that brought your father a pitch-pine knot, kindled at my own hearth, to set fire to an Indian village, in King Philip's war.° They were my good friends,

full fifteen minutes agone: Apparently this mystery man has traveled in a flash from Boston's Old South Church all the way to the woods beyond Salem—as the crow flies, a good sixteen miles. *King William's court:* back in England, where William III reigned from 1689 to 1702. *wot'st:* know. *days of the martyrs:* a time when many forebears of the New England Puritans had given their lives for religious convictions—when Mary I (Mary Tudor, nicknamed "Bloody Mary"), queen of England from 1553 to 1558, briefly reestablished the Roman Catholic Church in England and launched a campaign of persecution against Protestants. *King Philip's war:* Metacomet, or King Philip (as the English called him), chief of the Wampanoag Indians, had led a bitter, widespread uprising of several New England tribes (1675–78). Metacomet died in the war, as did one out of every ten white male colonists.

both; and many a pleasant walk have we had along this path, and returned merrily after midnight. I would fain be friends with you, for their sake."

"If it be as thou sayest," replied Goodman Brown, "I marvel they never spoke of these matters. Or, verily, I marvel not, seeing that the least rumor of the sort would have driven them from New England. We are a people of prayer, and good works, to boot, and abide no such wickedness."

"Wickedness or not," said the traveller with the twisted staff, "I have a very gen- 20 eral acquaintance here in New England. The deacons of many a church have drunk the communion wine with me; the selectmen, of divers towns, make me their chair- man; and a majority of the Great and General Court are firm supporters of my inter- est. The governor and I, too—but these are state-secrets."

"Can this be so!" cried Goodman Brown, with a stare of amazement at his undis- turbed companion. "Howbeit, I have nothing to do with the governor and council; they have their own ways, and are no rule for a simple husbandman, like me. But, were I to go on with thee, how should I meet the eye of that good old man, our min- ister, at Salem village? Oh, his voice would make me tremble, both Sabbath-day and lecture-day!"°

Thus far, the elder traveller had listened with due gravity, but now burst into a fit of irrepressible mirth, shaking himself so violently, that his snake-like staff actually seemed to wriggle in sympathy.

"Ha! ha! ha!" shouted he, again and again; then composing himself, "Well, go on, Goodman Brown, go on; but pray thee, don't kill me with laughing!"

"Well, then, to end the matter at once," said Goodman Brown, considerably nettled, "there is my wife, Faith. It would break her dear little heart; and I'd rather break my own!"

"Nay, if that be the case," answered the other, "e'en go thy ways, Goodman 25 Brown. I would not, for twenty old women like the one hobbling before us, that Faith should come to any harm."

As he spoke, he pointed his staff at a female figure on the path, in whom Goodman Brown recognized a very pious and exemplary dame, who had taught him his cate- chism, in youth, and was still his moral and spiritual adviser, jointly with the minister and Deacon Gookin.

"A marvel, truly, that Goody° Cloyse should be so far in the wilderness, at night- fall!" said he. "But, with your leave, friend, I shall take a cut through the woods, until we have left this Christian woman behind. Being a stranger to you, she might ask whom I was consorting with, and whither I was going."

"Be it so," said his fellow-traveller. "Betake you to the woods, and let me keep the path."

Accordingly, the young man turned aside, but took care to watch his compan- ion, who advanced softly along the road, until he had come within a staff's length of the old dame. She, meanwhile, was making the best of her way, with singular speed for so aged a woman, and mumbling some indistinct words, a prayer, doubtless, as she

---

lecture-day: a weekday when everyone had to go to church to hear a sermon or Bible-reading. Goody: short for Goodwife, title for a married woman of ordinary station. In his story, Hawthorne borrows from history the names of two "Goodys"—Goody Cloyse and Goody Cory—and one un- married woman, Martha Carrier. In 1692 Hawthorne's great-great-grandfather John Hathorne, a judge in the Salem witchcraft trials, had condemned all three to be hanged.

went. The traveller put forth his staff, and touched her withered neck with what seemed the serpent's tail.

"The devil!" screamed the pious old lady.   30

"Then Goody Cloyse knows her old friend?" observed the traveller, confronting her, and leaning on his writhing stick.

"Ah, forsooth, and is it your worship, indeed?" cried the good dame. "Yea, truly is it, and in the very image of my old gossip,° Goodman Brown, the grandfather of the silly fellow that now is. But—would your worship believe it?—my broomstick hath strangely disappeared, stolen, as I suspect, by that unhanged witch, Goody Cory, and that, too, when I was all anointed with the juice of smallage and cinquefoil and wolf's bane—"°

"Mingled with fine wheat and the fat of a new-born babe," said the shape of old Goodman Brown.

"Ah, your worship knows the receipt,"° cried the old lady, cackling aloud. "So, as I was saying, being all ready for the meeting, and no horse to ride on, I made up my mind to foot it; for they tell me, there is a nice young man to be taken into communion to-night. But now your good worship will lend me your arm, and we shall be there in a twinkling."

"That can hardly be," answered her friend. "I may not spare you my arm, Goody   35
Cloyse, but here is my staff, if you will."

So saying, he threw it down at her feet, where, perhaps, it assumed life, being one of the rods which its owner had formerly lent to the Egyptian Magi.° Of this fact, however, Goodman Brown could not take cognizance. He had cast up his eyes in astonishment, and looking down again, beheld neither Goody Cloyse nor the serpentine staff, but his fellow-traveller alone, who waited for him as calmly as if nothing had happened.

"That old woman taught me my catechism!" said the young man; and there was a world of meaning in this simple comment.

They continued to walk onward, while the elder traveller exhorted his companion to make good speed and persevere in the path, discoursing so aptly, that his arguments seemed rather to spring up in the bosom of his auditor, than to be suggested by himself. As they went, he plucked a branch of maple, to serve for a walking-stick, and began to strip it of the twigs and little boughs, which were wet with evening dew. The moment his fingers touched them, they became strangely withered and dried up, as with a week's sunshine. Thus the pair proceeded, at a good free pace, until suddenly, in a gloomy hollow of the road, Goodman Brown sat himself down on the stump of a tree, and refused to go any farther.

"Friend," said he, stubbornly, "my mind is made up. Not another step will I budge on this errand. What if a wretched old woman do choose to go to the devil, when I thought she was going to Heaven! Is that any reason why I should quit my dear Faith, and go after her?"

"You will think better of this, by-and-by," said his acquaintance, composedly.   40
"Sit here and rest yourself awhile; and when you feel like moving again, there is my staff to help you along."

---

gossip: friend or kinsman.   *smallage and cinquefoil and wolf's bane:* wild plants—here, ingredients for a witch's brew.   *receipt:* recipe.   *Egyptian Magi:* In the Bible, Pharaoh's wise men and sorcerers who by their magical powers changed their rods into live serpents. (This incident, part of the story of Moses and Aaron, is related in Exodus 7:8–12.)

Without more words, he threw his companion the maple stick, and was as speedily out of sight, as if he had vanished into the deepening gloom. The young man sat a few moments, by the road-side, applauding himself greatly, and thinking with how clear a conscience he should meet the minister, in his morning-walk, nor shrink from the eye of good old Deacon Gookin. And what calm sleep would be his, that very night, which was to have been spent so wickedly, but purely and sweetly now, in the arms of Faith! Amidst these pleasant and praiseworthy meditations, Goodman Brown heard the tramp of horses along the road, and deemed it advisable to conceal himself within the verge of the forest, conscious of the guilty purpose that had brought him thither, though now so happily turned from it.

On came the hoof-tramps and the voices of the riders, two grave old voices, conversing soberly as they drew near. These mingled sounds appeared to pass along the road, within a few yards of the young man's hiding-place; but owing, doubtless, to the depth of the gloom, at that particular spot, neither the travellers nor their steeds were visible. Though their figures brushed the small boughs by the way-side, it could not be seen that they intercepted, even for a moment, the faint gleam from the strip of bright sky, athwart which they must have passed. Goodman Brown alternately crouched and stood on tip-toe, pulling aside the branches, and thrusting forth his head as far as he durst, without discerning so much as a shadow. It vexed him the more, because he could have sworn, were such a thing possible, that he recognized the voices of the minister and Deacon Gookin, jogging along quietly, as they were wont to do, when bound to some ordination or ecclesiastical council. While yet within hearing, one of the riders stopped to pluck a switch.

"Of the two, reverend Sir," said the voice like the deacon's, "I had rather miss an ordination-dinner than to-night's meeting. They tell me that some of our community are to be here from Falmouth and beyond, and others from Connecticut and Rhode Island; besides several of the Indian powows,° who, after their fashion, know almost as much deviltry as the best of us. Moreover, there is a goodly young woman to be taken into communion."

"Mighty well, Deacon Gookin!" replied the solemn old tones of the minister. "Spur up, or we shall be late. Nothing can be done, you know, until I get on the ground."

The hoofs clattered again, and the voices, talking so strangely in the empty air, passed on through the forest, where no church had ever been gathered, nor solitary Christian prayed. Whither, then, could these holy men be journeying, so deep into the heathen wilderness? Young Goodman Brown caught hold of a tree, for support, being ready to sink down on the ground, faint and overburdened with the heavy sickness of his heart. He looked up to the sky, doubting whether there really was a Heaven above him. Yet, there was the blue arch, and the stars brightening in it.   45

"With Heaven above, and Faith below, I will yet stand firm against the devil!" cried Goodman Brown.

While he still gazed upward, into the deep arch of the firmament, and had lifted his hands to pray, a cloud, though no wind was stirring, hurried across the zenith, and hid the brightening stars. The blue sky was still visible, except directly overhead,

powows: Indian priests or medicine men.

where this black mass of cloud was sweeping swiftly northward. Aloft in the air, as if from the depths of the cloud, came a confused and doubtful sound of voices. Once, the listener fancied that he could distinguish the accents of town's-people of his own, men and women, both pious and ungodly, many of whom he had met at the communion-table, and had seen others rioting at the tavern. The next moment, so indistinct were the sounds, he doubted whether he had heard aught but the murmur of the old forest, whispering without a wind. Then came a stronger swell of those familiar tones, heard daily in the sunshine, at Salem village, but never, until now, from a cloud of night. There was one voice, of a young woman, uttering lamentations, yet with an uncertain sorrow, and entreating for some favor, which, perhaps, it would grieve her to obtain. And all the unseen multitude, both saints and sinners, seemed to encourage her onward.

"Faith!" shouted Goodman Brown, in a voice of agony and desperation; and the echoes of the forest mocked him, crying—"Faith! Faith!" as if bewildered wretches were seeking her, all through the wilderness.

The cry of grief, rage, and terror, was yet piercing the night, when the unhappy husband held his breath for a response. There was a scream, drowned immediately in a louder murmur of voices, fading into far-off laughter, as the dark cloud swept away, leaving the clear and silent sky above Goodman Brown. But something fluttered lightly down through the air, and caught on the branch of a tree. The young man seized it, and beheld a pink ribbon.

"My Faith is gone!" cried he, after one stupefied moment. "There is no good on   50
earth; and sin is but a name. Come, devil! for to thee is this world given."

And maddened with despair, so that he laughed loud and long, did Goodman Brown grasp his staff and set forth again, at such a rate, that he seemed to fly along the forest-path, rather than to walk or run. The road grew wilder and drearier, and more faintly traced, and vanished at length, leaving him in the heart of the dark wilderness, still rushing onward, with the instinct that guides mortal man to evil. The whole forest was peopled with frightful sounds; the creaking of the trees, the howling of wild beasts, and the yell of Indians; while, sometimes, the wind tolled like a distant church-bell, and sometimes gave a broad roar around the traveller, as if all Nature were laughing him to scorn. But he was himself the chief horror of the scene, and shrank not from its other horrors.

"Ha! ha! ha!" roared Goodman Brown, when the wind laughed at him. "Let us hear which will laugh loudest! Think not to frighten me with your deviltry! Come witch, come wizard, come Indian powow, come devil himself! and here comes Goodman Brown. You may as well fear him as he fear you!"

In truth, all through the haunted forest, there could be nothing more frightful than the figure of Goodman Brown. On he flew, among the black pines, brandishing his staff with frenzied gestures, now giving vent to an inspiration of horrid blasphemy, and now shouting forth such laughter, as set all the echoes of the forest laughing like demons around him. The fiend in his own shape is less hideous, than when he rages in the breast of man. Thus sped the demoniac on his course, until, quivering among the trees, he saw a red light before him, as when the felled trunks and branches of a clearing have been set on fire, and throw up their lurid blaze against the sky, at the hour of midnight. He paused, in a lull of the tempest that had driven him onward, and heard the swell of what seemed a hymn, rolling solemnly from a distance, with the weight of many voices. He knew the tune; it was a familiar one in the choir of the village meeting-house. The verse died heavily away, and was lengthened by a chorus, not of human voices, but of all the sounds of the benighted wilderness, pealing in awful harmony together. Goodman Brown cried out; and his cry was lost to his own ear, by its unison with the cry of the desert.

In the interval of silence, he stole forward, until the light glared full upon his eyes. At one extremity of an open space, hemmed in by the dark wall of the forest, arose a rock, bearing some rude, natural resemblance either to an altar or a pulpit, and surrounded by four blazing pines, their tops aflame, their stems untouched, like candles at an evening meeting. The mass of foliage, that had overgrown the summit of the rock, was all on fire, blazing high into the night, and fitfully illuminating the whole field. Each pendent twig and leafy festoon was in a blaze. As the red light arose and fell, a numerous congregation alternately shone forth, then disappeared in shadow, and again grew, as it were, out of the darkness, peopling the heart of the solitary woods at once.

"A grave and dark-clad company!" quoth Goodman Brown.   55

In truth, they were such. Among them, quivering to-and-fro, between gloom and splendor, appeared faces that would be seen, next day, at the council-board of the province, and others which, Sabbath after Sabbath, looked devoutly heavenward, and benignantly over the crowded pews, from the holiest pulpits in the land. Some affirm that the lady of the governor was there. At least, there were high dames well known to her, and wives of honored husbands, and widows, a great multitude, and ancient maidens, all of excellent repute, and fair young girls, who trembled, lest their mothers should espy them. Either the sudden gleams of light, flashing over the obscure field, bedazzled Goodman Brown, or he recognized a score of the church-members of Salem village, famous for their especial sanctity. Good old Deacon Gookin had arrived, and waited at the skirts of that venerable saint, his revered pastor. But, irreverently consorting with these grave, reputable, and pious people, these elders of the church, these chaste dames and dewy virgins, there were men of dissolute lives and women of spotted fame, wretches given over to all mean and filthy vice, and suspected even of horrid crimes. It was strange to see, that the good shrank not from the wicked, nor were the sinners abashed by the saints. Scattered, also, among their pale-faced enemies, were the Indian priests, or powows, who had often scared their native forest with more hideous incantations than any known to English witchcraft.

"But, where is Faith?" thought Goodman Brown; and, as hope came into his heart, he trembled.

Another verse of the hymn arose, a slow and mournful strain, such as the pious love, but joined to words which expressed all that our nature can conceive of sin, and darkly hinted at far more. Unfathomable to mere mortals is the lore of fiends. Verse after verse was sung, and still the chorus of the desert swelled between, like the deepest tone of a mighty organ. And, with the final peal of that dreadful anthem, there came a sound, as if the roaring wind, the rushing streams, the howling beasts, and every other voice of the unconverted wilderness, were mingling and according with the voice of guilty man, in homage to the prince of all. The four blazing pines threw up a loftier flame, and obscurely discovered shapes and visages of horror on the smoke-wreaths, above the impious assembly. At the same moment, the fire on the rock shot redly forth, and formed a glowing arch above its base, where now appeared a figure. With reverence be it spoken, the figure bore no slight similitude, both in garb and manner, to some grave divine of the New England churches.

"Bring forth the converts!" cried a voice, that echoed through the field and rolled into the forest.

At the word, Goodman Brown stepped forth from the shadow of the trees, and approached the congregation, with whom he felt a loathful brotherhood, by the sympathy of all that was wicked in his heart. He could have well nigh sworn, that the shape of his own dead father beckoned him to advance, looking downward from a smoke-wreath, while a woman, with dim features of despair, threw out her hand to warn him back. Was it his mother? But he had no power to retreat one step, nor to resist, even in thought, when the minister and good old Deacon Gookin seized his arms, and led him to the blazing rock. Thither came also the slender form of a veiled female, led between Goody Cloyse, that pious teacher of the catechism, and Martha Carrier, who had received the devil's promise to be queen of hell. A rampant hag was she! And there stood the proselytes,° beneath the canopy of fire.

"Welcome, my children," said the dark figure, "to the communion of your race! Ye have found, thus young, your nature and your destiny. My children, look behind you!"

They turned; and flashing forth, as it were, in a sheet of flame, the fiend-worshippers were seen; the smile of welcome gleamed darkly on every visage.

"There," resumed the sable form, "are all whom ye have reverenced from youth. Ye deemed them holier than yourselves, and shrank from your own sin, contrasting it with their lives of righteousness, and prayerful aspirations heavenward. Yet, here are they all, in my worshipping assembly! This night it shall be granted you to know their secret deeds; how hoary-bearded elders of the church have whispered wanton words to the young maids of their households; how many a woman, eager for widow's weeds, has given her husband a drink at bedtime, and let him sleep his last sleep in her bosom; how beardless youths have made haste to inherit their fathers' wealth; and how fair damsels—blush not, sweet ones!—have dug little graves in the garden, and bidden me, the sole guest, to an infant's funeral. By the sympathy of your human hearts for sin, ye shall scent out all the places—whether in church, bed-chamber, street, field, or forest—where crime has been committed, and shall exult to behold the whole earth one stain of guilt, one mighty bloodspot. Far more than this! It shall be yours to penetrate, in every bosom, the deep mystery of sin, the fountain of all wicked arts, and which inexhaustibly supplies more evil impulses than human power—than my power, at its utmost!—can make manifest in deeds. And now, my children, look upon each other."

They did so; and, by the blaze of the hell-kindled torches, the wretched man beheld his Faith, and the wife her husband, trembling before that unhallowed altar.

"Lo! there ye stand, my children," said the figure, in a deep and solemn tone, almost sad, with its despairing awfulness, as if his once angelic nature could yet mourn for our miserable race. "Depending upon one another's hearts, ye had still hoped, that virtue were not all a dream. Now are ye undeceived! Evil is the nature of mankind. Evil must be your only happiness. Welcome, again, my children, to the communion of your race!"

"Welcome!" repeated the fiend-worshippers, in one cry of despair and triumph.

And there they stood, the only pair, as it seemed, who were yet hesitating on the verge of wickedness, in this dark world. A basin was hollowed, naturally, in the rock. Did it contain water, reddened by the lurid light? or was it blood? or, perchance, a

proselytes: new converts.

liquid flame? Herein did the Shape of Evil dip his hand, and prepare to lay the mark of baptism upon their foreheads, that they might be partakers of the mystery of sin, more conscious of the secret guilt of others, both in deed and thought, than they could now be of their own. The husband cast one look at his pale wife, and Faith at him. What polluted wretches would the next glance show them to each other, shuddering alike at what they disclosed and what they saw!

"Faith! Faith!" cried the husband. "Look up to Heaven, and resist the Wicked one!"

Whether Faith obeyed, he knew not. Hardly had he spoken, when he found himself amid calm night and solitude, listening to a roar of the wind, which died heavily away through the forest. He staggered against the rock and felt it chill and damp, while a hanging twig, that had been all on fire, besprinkled his cheek with the coldest dew.

The next morning, young Goodman Brown came slowly into the street of 70 Salem village, staring around him like a bewildered man. The good old minister was taking a walk along the grave-yard, to get an appetite for breakfast and meditate his sermon, and bestowed a blessing, as he passed, on Goodman Brown. He shrank from the venerable saint, as if to avoid an anathema.° Old Deacon Goodkin was at domestic worship, and the holy words of his prayer were heard through the open window. "What God doth the wizard pray to?" quoth Goodman Brown. Goody Cloyse, that excellent old Christian, stood in the early sunshine, at her own lattice, catechizing a little girl, who had brought her a pint of morning's milk. Goodman Brown snatched away the child, as from the grasp of the fiend himself. Turning the corner by the meeting-house, he spied the head of Faith, with the pink ribbons, gazing anxiously forth, and bursting into such joy at sight of him, that she skipt along the street, and almost kissed her husband before the whole village. But, Goodman Brown looked sternly and sadly into her face, and passed on without a greeting.

Had Goodman Brown fallen asleep in the forest, and only dreamed a wild dream of a witch-meeting?

Be it so, if you will. But, alas! it was a dream of evil omen for young Goodman Brown. A stern, a sad, a darkly meditative, a distrustful, if not a desperate man, did he become, from the night of that fearful dream. On the Sabbath-day, when the congregation were singing a holy psalm, he could not listen, because an anthem of sin rushed loudly upon his ear, and drowned all the blessed strain. When the minister spoke from the pulpit, with power and fervid eloquence, and, with his hand on the open Bible, of the sacred truths of our religion, and of saint-like lives and triumphant deaths, and of future bliss or misery unutterable, then did Goodman Brown turn pale, dreading, lest the roof should thunder down upon the gray blasphemer and his hearers. Often, awakening suddenly at midnight, he shrank from the bosom of Faith, and at morning or even-tide, when the family knelt down at prayer, he scowled, and muttered to himself, and gazed sternly at his wife, and turned away. And when he had lived long, and was borne to his grave, a hoary corpse, followed by Faith, an aged woman, and children and grandchildren, a goodly procession, besides neighbors, not a few, they carved no hopeful verse upon his tombstone; for his dying hour was gloom.

---

anathema: an official curse, a decree that casts one out of a church and bans him from receiving the sacraments.

Questions

1. Hawthorne's story is set in Salem, Massachusetts. What historical associations does this setting suggest to the reader?

2. Why is Brown's new bride Faith "aptly named" according to the narrator? What does the name "Goodman Brown" suggest about the character of the protagonist?

3. Is there any significance to the fact that the old man in the woods seems to resemble Brown?

4. As Brown and the stranger proceed deeper into the woods, what does Brown find out that troubles him? When the pink ribbon flutters to the ground, as though fallen from something airborne (paragraph 49), what does Brown assume? What effect does this event have upon his determination to resist the devil?

5. Is it significant that most of the story's action take place at night and in the woods?

6. What is the nature of the ceremony going on in the woods? What is being transacted between the old man and the townspeople?

7. What power does the devil promise to give his communicants (paragraph 63)?

8. Is Brown's experience in the woods real? If not, what other explanation can you provide?

9. What would be lost if the last three paragraphs of the tale were omitted?

10. If the story is an allegory, summarize the symbolical drama enacted in it.

NATHANIEL HAWTHORNE ON WRITING

Reflections on Truth and Clarity in Literature   (1837–1863)

I have another great difficulty, in the lack of materials; for I have seen so little of the world, that I have nothing but thin air to concoct my stories of, and it is not easy to give a lifelike semblance to such shadowy stuff. Sometimes, through a peep-hole, I have caught a glimpse of the real world; and the two or three articles, in which I have portrayed such glimpses, please me better than the others.

From a letter to Henry Wadsworth Longfellow, June 4, 1837

Every day of my life makes me feel more and more how seldom a fact is accurately stated; how, almost invariably, when a story has passed through the mind of a third person, it becomes, so far as regards the impression that it makes in further repetitions, little better than a falsehood, and this, too, though the narrator be the most truth-seeking person in existence. . . . Is truth a fantasy which we are to pursue forever and never grasp?

From a letter to his wife, Sophia Peabody, May 1, 1841

I am glad you think my style plain. I never, in any one page or paragraph, aimed at making it anything else, or giving it any other merit—and I wish people would leave off talking about its beauty. If it have any, it is only pardonable as being unintentional. The greatest possible merit of style is, of course, to make the mere words absolutely disappear into the thought.

From a letter to editor Evert A. Duyckinck, April 27, 1851

Upon my honor, I am not quite sure that I entirely comprehend my own meaning, in some of these blasted allegories; but I remember that I always had a meaning—or at least thought I had. I am a good deal changed since those times; and, to tell you the truth, my past self is not very much to my taste, as I see myself in this book.

From a letter to his publisher, James T. Fields, April 13, 1854

[Y]ou attribute to me a superiority which I do not dream of asserting. A reader, who can fully understand and appreciate a work, possesses all the faculties of the writer who produced it—except a knack of expression, by which the latter is enabled to give definite shape to an idea or sentiment which he and his appreciative reader possess in common. Thus the advantage on the author's part is but a slight one, and the more truth and wisdom he writes, the smaller is his individual share in it.

From a letter to Robert J. Poney, September 28, 1863

The Obscurest Man in American Letters   1851

The author of *Twice-Told Tales* has a claim to one distinction, which, as none of his literary brethren will care about disputing it with him, he need not be afraid to mention. He was, for a good many years, the obscurest man of letters in America.

These stories were published in Magazines and Annuals, extending over a period of ten or twelve years, and comprising the whole of the writer's young manhood, without making (so far as he has ever been aware) the slightest impression on the Public. One or two among them—"The Rill from the Town-Pump" in perhaps a greater degree than any other—had a pretty wide newspaper-circulation; as for the rest, he has no grounds for supposing, that, on their first appearance, they met with the good or evil fortune to be read by anybody. Throughout the time above-specified, he had no incitement to literary effort in a reasonable prospect of reputation or profit; nothing but the pleasure itself of composition—an enjoyment not at all amiss in its way, and perhaps essential to the merit of the work in hand, but which, in the long run, will hardly keep the chill out of a writer's heart, or the numbness out of his fingers. To this total lack of sympathy, at the age when his mind would naturally have been most effervescent, the Public owe it, (and it is certainly an effect not to be regretted, on either part,) that the Author can show nothing for the thought and industry of that portion of his life, save the forty sketches, or thereabouts, included in these volumes.

From the preface to the 1851 edition of *Twice-Told Tales*

CRITICS ON HAWTHORNE

Herman Melville (1819–1891)

Excerpt from a Review of *Mosses from an Old Manse*   1850

[W]ith whatever motive, playful or profound, Nathaniel Hawthorne has chosen to entitle his pieces in the manner he has, it is certain, that some of them are directly calculated to deceive—egregiously deceive, the superficial skimmer of pages. To be downright and candid once more, let me cheerfully say, that two of these titles did dolefully dupe no less an eagle-eyed reader than myself; and that, too, after I had been impressed with a sense of the great depth and breadth of this American man. "Who in the name of thunder" (as the country-people say in this neighborhood) "who in the name of thunder," would anticipate any marvel in a piece entitled "Young Goodman Brown"? You would of course suppose that it was a simple little tale, intended as a supplement to "Goody Two Shoes." Whereas, it is deep as Dante; nor can you finish it, without addressing the author in his own words—"It is yours to penetrate, in every bosom, the deep mystery of sin." And with Young Goodman, too, in allegorical pursuit of his Puritan wife, you cry out in your anguish,—

"Faith!" shouted Goodman Brown, in a voice of agony and desperation; and the echoes of the forest mocked him, crying—"Faith! Faith!" as if bewildered wretches were seeking her all through the wilderness.

From "Hawthorne and His Mosses"

Edgar Allan Poe (1809–1849)

The Genius of Hawthorne's Short Stories   1842

Were we called upon however to designate that class of composition which, next to [a short lyric poem] should best fulfill the demands of high genius—should offer it the most advantageous field of exertion—we should unhesitatingly speak of the prose tale, as Mr. Hawthorne has here exemplified it. We allude to the short prose narrative, requiring from a half-hour to one or two hours in its perusal. The ordinary novel is objectionable, from its length, for reasons already stated in substance. As it cannot be read at one sitting, it deprives itself, of course, of the immense force derivable from *totality*. Worldly interests intervening during the pauses of perusal, modify, annul, or counteract, in a greater or less degree, the impressions of the book. But simple cessation in reading, would, of itself, be sufficient to destroy the true unity. In the brief tale, however, the author is enabled to carry out the fullness of his intention, be it what it may. During the hour of perusal the soul of the reader is at the writer's control. There are no external or extrinsic influences—resulting from weariness or interruption.

A skillful literary artist has constructed a tale. If wise, he has not fashioned his thoughts to accommodate his incidents; but having conceived, with deliberate care, a certain unique or single *effect* to be wrought out, he then invents such incidents—he then combines such events as may best aid him in establishing this preconceived effect. If his very initial sentence tend not to the outbringing of this effect, then he has failed in his first step. In the whole composition there should be no word written, of which the tendency, direct or indirect, is not to the one pre-established design. And by such means, with such care and skill, a picture is at length painted which leaves in the mind of him who contemplates it with a kindred art, a sense of the fullest satisfaction. The idea of the tale has been presented unblemished, because undisturbed; and this is an end unattainable by the novel. Undue brevity is just as exceptionable here as in the poem; but undue length is yet more to be avoided.

• • •

Of Mr. Hawthorne's Tales we would say, emphatically, that they belong to the highest region of Art—an Art subservient to genius of a very lofty order. We had supposed, with good reason for so supposing, that he had been thrust into his present position by one of the impudent *cliques* which beset our literature, and whose pretensions it is our full purpose to expose at the earliest opportunity; but we have been most agreeably mistaken. We know of few compositions which the critic can more honestly commend than these "Twice-Told Tales." As Americans, we feel proud of the book.

Mr. Hawthorne's distinctive trait is invention, creation, imagination, originality—a trait which, in the literature of fiction, is positively worth all the rest. But the nature of originality, so far as regards its manifestation in letters, is but imperfectly understood. The inventive or original mind as frequently displays itself in novelty of *tone* as in novelty of matter. Mr. Hawthorne is original at *all* points.

From a review of *Twice-Told Tales* by Nathaniel Hawthorne

CRITICS ON "YOUNG GOODMAN BROWN"

Film adaption of Hawthorne, 1926.

Richard H. Fogle (1911–1995)

Ambiguity in "Young Goodman Brown"   1945

"Young Goodman Brown" is generally felt to be one of Hawthorne's more difficult tales, from the ambiguity of the conclusions which may be drawn from it. Its hero, a naive young man who accepts both society in general and his fellow-men as individuals at their own valuation, is in one terrible night presented with the vision of human Evil, and is ever afterwards "A stern, a sad, a darkly meditative, a distrustful, if not a desperate man . . . ," whose "dying hour was gloom." So far we are clear enough, but there are confusing factors. In the first place, are the events of the night merely subjective, a dream; or do they actually occur? Again, at the crucial point in his ordeal Goodman Brown summons the strength to cry to his wife Faith, "look up to heaven, and resist the evil one." It would appear from this that he has successfully resisted the supreme temptation—but evidently he is not therefore saved. Henceforth, "On the Sabbath-day, when the congregation were singing a holy psalm, he could not listen, because an anthem of sin rushed loudly upon his ear, and drowned all the blessed strain." On the other hand, he is not wholly lost, for in the sequel he is only at intervals estranged from "the bosom of Faith." Has Hawthorne himself failed to control the implications of his allegory?

I should say rather that these ambiguities of meaning are intentional, an integral part of his purpose. Hawthorne wishes to propose, not flatly that man is primarily evil, but instead the gnawing doubt lest this should indeed be true. "Come, devil! for to thee is this world given," exclaims Goodman Brown at the height of his agony, but he finds strength to resist the devil, and in the ambiguous conclusion he does not entirely reject his former faith. His trial, then, comes not from the certainty but the dread of Evil. Hawthorne poses the dangerous question of the relations of Good and Evil in man, but withholds his answer. Nor does he permit himself to settle whether the events of the night of trial are real or the mere figment of a dream.

> From "Ambiguity and Clarity in Hawthorne's 'Young Goodman Brown'"

Paul J. Hurley (1931–2003)

Evil Wherever He Looks   1966

Has Goodman Brown really been subjected to visions which imply the universal prevalence of evil? Has the faith of a good man been destroyed by a revelation of the world's sinfulness? It would seem not. If one accepts the fact that Hawthorne gives us no valid grounds to believe in the reality of Goodman Brown's visions and voices, he must either believe, as Fogle does, that Hawthorne feared his own knowledge of the world's evil; or he must treat those events as emanations from Brown's subconscious which intimate the corruption of Brown's own mind. Why do the young man's visions of evil concern only Goody Cloyse, the minister, Deacon Gookin, and his wife? One answer, of course, is that they represent an exceptional piety which makes their participation in evil dramatically more effective. But if Hawthorne's theme concerns the universality of human sinfulness, should we not see a wider manifestation of that evil? The only scene in which such a manifestation occurs is the Devil's communion, but that takes place *after* Goodman Brown has declared his loss of faith; and the scene of that vision, Hawthorne tells us, was "in the heart of the dark wilderness," a setting whose significance is so inescapable that Conrad would later echo Hawthorne's words (unknowingly?) in the title of one of his novels.

A more significant reason for Hawthorne's choice of those four characters occurs to us if we return to a consideration of their relationship to Goodman Brown. They are the four people in Salem village to whom he is morally responsible. Goody Cloyse "had taught him his catechism in youth, and was still his moral and spiritual advisor, jointly with the minister and Deacon Gookin." His wife is an even more important representative of the forces of morality and virtue. It seems obvious that they are the four people whose respectability must destroyed before Goodman Brown can fully commit himself to a belief in the wickedness of the world. . . .

The most striking quality of the paragraph which describes Goodman Brown's return to the village of Salem is its tone. No longer are there any suggestions of the weird and incredible. The dreamlike quality of Brown's adventure in the forest is replaced by purposefully direct and forthright narration. Life proceeds in the village as it always has. Only Goodman Brown has changed. If the events of the night before had been real, or even symbolic of reality, would not Hawthorne have indicated in some way a shared knowledge between Goodman Brown and the townsfolk whom he sees? Hawthorne has told us that Brown did not know whether his wife obeyed his cry to look up to heaven. Nonetheless, he passes her without a greeting when she runs to meet him. His own distrust and suspicion have assured him that she is sinful, even though, as Hawthorne is careful to note, she is wearing the pink ribbons which Goodman Brown thought he had grasped from the air. Nor is there any change in anyone else. The minister seeks to bless Goodman Brown, but the young man shrinks from him; Deacon Gookin is praying and even though Goodman Brown can hear "the holy words of his prayer," he still thinks him a wizard. Goody Cloyse is catechizing a young girl, and Goodman Brown snatches the child from the old woman's arms. The corruption of his mind and heart is complete; Goodman Brown sees evil wherever he looks. He sees it because he wants to see it.

If Hawthorne had wished to intimate that the events of the night were real, it would hardly do to confuse us with suggestions about dreams (unless, as Fogle thinks, this was Hawthorne's method of escaping the implications of his own insight into man's depravity). A more acceptable interpretation of the ambiguity of the story is to see in it Hawthorne's suggestion that the incredible incidents in the forest were the product of an ego-induced fantasy, the self-justification of a diseased mind. It seems clear that these incidents were not experienced; they were willed. The important point, however, is that Goodman Brown has accepted them as truth; and the acceptance of evil as the final truth about man has turned him into "A stern, a sad, a darkly meditative, a distrustful" human being. Goodman Brown does not become aware of his own kinship with evil; he does not see sinfulness in himself but only in others. That, perhaps, is his most awful sin. He has lost not only faith in his fellow men but his compassion for them. And so it is that "On the Sabbath-day, when the congregation were singing a holy psalm, he could not listen, because an anthem of sin rushed loudly upon his ear, and drowned all the blessed strain." Hawthorne never tells us that the anthem, loud and fearful as it must have been, ever reached the ears of any but young Goodman Brown.

From "Young Goodman Brown's 'Heart of Darkness'"

Nancy Bunge (b. 1942)

Complacency and Community   1993

"Young Goodman Brown" not only presents the issue of the Salem witch trials, but a number of its characters have the names of Salem residents charged with witchcraft, and its major action takes place in the noisy pasture historical documents of the period designate as a witches' gathering place. Hawthorne does not simply provide a record of the time, he uses history to examine issues of community and individualism explaining both the madness in Salem and much subsequent madness.

Ostensibly, this tale indicts arrogant individualism. Young Goodman Brown, either in dream or in fact, almost joins a witches' sabbath in the forest. He turns away at the last moment because he does not want to confess his evil. Ironically, his exemplary behavior produces a life of isolation and gloom: "A stern, a sad, a darkly meditative, a distrustful, if not a desperate man, did he become, from the night of that fearful dream." He despises his townspeople because he believes they participated in the evil ceremony he resisted. He sees nothing but their sinfulness. His wife, Faith, particularly offends him: "Often, awakening suddenly at midnight, he shrank from the bosom of Faith, and at morning or even-tide, when the family knelt down at prayer, he scowled, and muttered to himself, and gazed sternly at his wife, and turned away." Brown has a classic case of projection. Unable to deal with his own frailty, he sees and hates it in everyone else. So the tale seems to celebrate humility.

But Brown learns complacency from his community. He lives in a society that ruthlessly judges evil in everyone else. He resists the demonic figure who urges him towards the witches' sabbath because he suspects that acting out his sinful impulses will bring dishonor on his family. The devil laughs at Brown's innocence: "I have been as well acquainted with your family as with ever a one among the Puritans; and that's no trifle to say. I helped your grandfather, the constable, when he lashed the Quaker woman so smartly through the streets of Salem. And it was I that brought your father a pitch-pine knot, kindled at my own hearth, to set fire to an Indian village, in King Philip's war." In other words, Puritan "goodness" has justified gross violations of people the Puritans perceived as bad, such as Quakers and Native Americans. Brown's decision to declare himself good and assign all the evil to others has strong community history.

The tale also calls into question the quality of Brown's present social and family life since Brown functions as a beloved father and prized citizen, even though he despises everyone: "He had lived long, and was borne to his grave, a hoary corpse, followed by Faith, an aged woman, and children and grandchildren, a goodly procession, besides neighbors, not a few."

So, although this tale condemns arrogance and recommends community, it acknowledges the difficulties of distinguishing real and apparent solidarity. People long to belong and they almost inevitably attempt to win acceptance by following socially approved patterns. But this faith in their family, society, or nation assumes that convention grows from wisdom, not habit. Those willing to resist society's self-righteousness may achieve the humility necessary to genuine fellowship, but they will have trouble making themselves understood. On the other hand, the community will support those who ask no questions. Societies encourage conformity because the assumption that this state, unlike all others, rests on a bedrock of truth, cannot survive examination. So behavior deviating from this complacency needs speedy and forceful correction.

From Nathaniel Hawthorne: A Study of the Short Fiction

CHARLOTTE PERKINS GILMAN

Charlotte Perkins Gilman (1860–1935) was born in Hartford, Connecticut. Her father was the writer Frederick Beecher Perkins (a nephew of reformer-novelist Harriet Beecher Stowe, author of Uncle Tom's Cabin, *and abolitionist minister Henry Ward Beecher), but he abandoned the family shortly after his daughter's birth. Raised in meager surroundings, the young Gilman adopted her intellectual Beecher aunts as role models. Because she and her mother moved from one relation to another, Gilman's early education was neglected—at fifteen, she had had only four years of schooling. In 1878 she studied commercial art at the Rhode Island School of Design. In 1884 she married Walter Stetson, an artist. After the birth of her one daughter, she experienced a severe depression. The rest cure her doctor prescribed became the basis of her most famous story, "The Yellow Wallpaper." This tale combines standard ele-*

Charlotte Perkins Gilman

ments of Gothic fiction (the isolated country mansion, the brooding atmosphere of the room, the aloof but dominating husband) with the fresh clarity of Gilman's feminist perspective. Gilman's first marriage ended in an amicable divorce. A celebrated essayist and public speaker, she became an important early figure in American feminism. Her study Women and Economics *(1898) stressed the importance of both sexes having a place in the working world. Her feminist-Utopian novel* Herland *(1915) describes a thriving nation of women without men. In 1900 Gilman married a second time—this time, more happily—to her cousin George Houghton Gilman. Following his sudden death in 1934, Gilman discovered she had inoperable breast cancer. After finishing her autobiography, she killed herself with chloroform in Pasadena, California.*

The Yellow Wallpaper   1892

It is very seldom that mere ordinary people like John and myself secure ancestral halls for the summer.

A colonial mansion, a hereditary estate, I would say a haunted house and reach the height of romantic felicity—but that would be asking too much of fate!

Still I will proudly declare that there is something queer about it.

Else, why should it be let so cheaply? And why have stood so long untenanted?

John laughs at me, of course, but one expects that.   5

John is practical in the extreme. He has no patience with faith, an intense horror of superstition, and he scoffs openly at any talk of things not to be felt and seen and put down in figures.

John is a physician, and *perhaps*—(I would not say it to a living soul, of course, but this is dead paper and a great relief to my mind)—*perhaps* that is one reason I do not get well faster.

You see, he does not believe I am sick! And what can one do?

If a physician of high standing, and one's own husband, assures friends and relatives that there is really nothing the matter with one but temporary nervous depression— a slight hysterical tendency—what is one to do?

My brother is also a physician, and also of high standing, and he says the same thing.

So I take phosphates or phosphites—whichever it is—and tonics, and air and exercise, and journeys, and am absolutely forbidden to "work" until I am well again.

Personally, I disagree with their ideas.

Personally, I believe that congenial work, with excitement and change, would do me good.

But what is one to do?

I did write for a while in spite of them; but it *does* exhaust me a good deal— having to be so sly about it, or else meet with heavy opposition.

I sometimes fancy that in my condition, if I had less opposition and more society and stimulus—but John says the very worst thing I can do is to think about my con-dition, and I confess it always makes me feel bad.

So I will let it alone and talk about the house.

The most beautiful place! It is quite alone, standing well back from the road, quite three miles from the village. It makes me think of English places that you read about, for there are hedges and walls and gates that lock, and lots of separate little houses for the gardeners and people.

There is a *delicious* garden! I never saw such a garden—large and shady, full of box-bordered paths, and lined with long grape-covered arbors with seats under them.

There were greenhouses, but they are all broken now.

There was some legal trouble, I believe, something about the heirs and co-heirs; anyhow, the place has been empty for years.

That spoils my ghostliness, I am afraid, but I don't care—there is something strange about the house—I can feel it.

I even said so to John one moonlight evening, but he said what I felt was a *draught*, and shut the window.

I get unreasonably angry with John sometimes. I'm sure I never used to be so sensitive. I think it is due to this nervous condition.

But John says if I feel so I shall neglect proper self-control; so I take pains to control myself—before him, at least, and that makes me very tired.

I don't like our room a bit. I wanted one downstairs that opened onto the piazza and had roses all over the window, and such pretty old-fashioned chintz hangings! But John would not hear of it.

He said there was only one window and not room for two beds, and no near room for him if he took another.

He is very careful and loving, and hardly lets me stir without special direction.

I have a schedule prescription for each hour in the day; he takes all care from me, and so I feel basely ungrateful not to value it more.

He said he came here solely on my account, that I was to have perfect rest and all the air I could get. "Your exercise depends on your strength, my dear," said he, "and your food somewhat on your appetite; but air you can absorb all the time." So we took the nursery at the top of the house.

It is a big, airy room, the whole floor nearly, with windows that look all ways, and air and sunshine galore. It was a nursery first, and then playroom and gymnasium,

I should judge, for the windows are barred for little children, and there are rings and things in the walls.

The paint and paper look as if a boys' school had used it. It is stripped off—the paper—in great patches all around the head of my bed, about as far as I can reach, and in a great place on the other side of the room low down. I never saw a worse paper in my life. One of those sprawling, flamboyant patterns committing every artistic sin.

It is dull enough to confuse the eye in following, pronounced enough constantly to irritate and provoke study, and when you follow the lame uncertain curves for a little distance they suddenly commit suicide—plunge off at outrageous angles, destroy themselves in unheard-of contradictions.

The color is repellent, almost revolting: a smouldering unclean yellow, strangely faded by the slow-turning sunlight. It is a dull yet lurid orange in some places, a sickly sulphur tint in others.

No wonder the children hated it! I should hate it myself if I had to live in this   35
room long.

There comes John, and I must put this away—he hates to have me write a word.

We have been here two weeks, and I haven't felt like writing before, since that first day.

I am sitting by the window now, up in this atrocious nursery, and there is nothing to hinder my writing as much as I please, save lack of strength.

John is away all day, and even some nights when his cases are serious.

I am glad my case is not serious!   40

But these nervous troubles are dreadfully depressing.

John does not know how much I really suffer. He knows there is no *reason* to suffer, and that satisfies him.

Of course it is only nervousness. It does weigh on me so not to do my duty in any way!

I meant to be such a help to John, such a real rest and comfort, and here I am a comparative burden already!

Nobody would believe what an effort it is to do what little I am able—to dress   45
and entertain, and order things.

It is fortunate Mary is so good with the baby. Such a dear baby!

And yet I *cannot* be with him, it makes me so nervous.

I suppose John never was nervous in his life. He laughs at me so about this wallpaper!

At first he meant to repaper the room, but afterward he said that I was letting it get the better of me, and that nothing was worse for a nervous patient than to give way to such fancies.

He said that after the wallpaper was changed it would be the heavy bedstead,   50
and then the barred windows, and then that gate at the head of the stairs, and so on.

"You know the place is doing you good," he said, "and really, dear, I don't care to renovate the house just for a three months' rental."

"Then do let us go downstairs," I said. "There are such pretty rooms there."

Then he took me in his arms and called me a blessed little goose, and said he would go down to the cellar, if I wished, and have it whitewashed into the bargain.

But he is right enough about the beds and windows and things.

It is as airy and comfortable a room as anyone need wish, and, of course, I would   55
not be so silly as to make him uncomfortable just for a whim.

I'm really getting quite fond of the big room, all but that horrid paper.

Out of one window I can see the garden—those mysterious deep-shaded arbors, the riotous old-fashioned flowers, and bushes and gnarly trees.

Out of another I get a lovely view of the bay and a little private wharf belonging to the estate. There is a beautiful shaded lane that runs down there from the house. I always fancy I see people walking in these numerous paths and arbors, but John has cautioned me not to give way to fancy in the least. He says that with my imaginative power and habit of story-making, a nervous weakness like mine is sure to lead to all manner of excited fancies, and that I ought to use my will and good sense to check the tendency. So I try.

I think sometimes that if I were only well enough to write a little it would relieve the press of ideas and rest me.

But I find I get pretty tired when I try.   60

It is so discouraging not to have any advice and companionship about my work. When I get really well, John says we will ask Cousin Henry and Julia down for a long visit; but he says he would as soon put fireworks in my pillow-case as to let me have those stimulating people about now.

I wish I could get well faster.

But I must not think about that. This paper looks to me as if it *knew* what a vicious influence it had!

There is a recurrent spot where the pattern lolls like a broken neck and two bulbous eyes stare at you upside down.

I get positively angry with the impertinence of it and the everlastingness. Up   65
and down and sideways they crawl, and those absurd unblinking eyes are everywhere. There is one place where two breadths didn't match, and the eyes go all up and down the line, one a little higher than the other.

I never saw so much expression in an inanimate thing before, and we all know how much expression they have! I used to lie awake as a child and get more entertainment and terror out of blank walls and plain furniture than most children could find in a toy-store.

I remember what a kindly wink the knobs of our big old bureau used to have, and there was one chair that always seemed like a strong friend.

I used to feel that if any of the other things looked too fierce I could always hop into that chair and be safe.

The furniture in this room is no worse than inharmonious, however, for we had to bring it all from downstairs. I suppose when this was used as a playroom they had to take the nursery things out, and no wonder! I never saw such ravages as the children have made here.

The wallpaper, as I said before, is torn off in spots, and it sticketh closer than a   70
brother—they must have had perseverance as well as hatred.

Then the floor is scratched and gouged and splintered, the plaster itself is dug out here and there, and this great heavy bed, which is all we found in the room, looks as if it had been through the wars.

But I don't mind it a bit—only the paper.

There comes John's sister. Such a dear girl as she is, and so careful of me! I must not let her find me writing.

She is a perfect and enthusiastic housekeeper, and hopes for no better profession. I verily believe she thinks it is the writing which made me sick!

But I can write when she is out, and see her a long way off from these windows.   75

There is one that commands the road, a lovely shaded winding road, and one that just looks off over the country. A lovely country, too, full of great elms and velvet meadows.

This wallpaper has a kind of sub-pattern in a different shade, a particularly irritating one, for you can only see it in certain lights, and not clearly then.

But in the places where it isn't faded and where the sun is just so—I can see a strange, provoking, formless sort of figure that seems to skulk about behind that silly and conspicuous front design.

There's sister on the stairs!

Well, the Fourth of July is over! The people are all gone, and I am tired out. John   80
thought it might do me good to see a little company, so we just had Mother and Nellie and the children down for a week.

Of course I didn't do a thing. Jennie sees to everything now.

But it tired me all the same.

John says if I don't pick up faster he shall send me to Weir Mitchell° in the fall.

But I don't want to go there at all. I had a friend who was in his hands once, and she says he is just like John and my brother, only more so!

Besides, it is such an undertaking to go so far.   85

I don't feel as if it was worthwhile to turn my hand over for anything, and I'm getting dreadfully fretful and querulous.

I cry at nothing, and cry most of the time.

Of course I don't when John is here, or anybody else, but when I am alone.

And I am alone a good deal just now. John is kept in town very often by serious cases, and Jennie is good and lets me alone when I want her to.

So I walk a little in the garden or down that lovely lane, sit on the porch under   90
the roses, and lie down up here a good deal.

I'm getting really fond of the room in spite of the wallpaper. Perhaps *because* of the wallpaper.

It dwells in my mind so!

I lie here on this great immovable bed—it is nailed down, I believe—and follow that pattern about by the hour. It is as good as gymnastics, I assure you. I start, we'll say, at the bottom, down in the corner over there where it has not been touched, and I determine for the thousandth time that I *will* follow that pointless pattern to some sort of a conclusion.

I know a little of the principle of design, and I know this thing was not arranged on any laws of radiation,° or alternation, or repetition, or symmetry, or anything else that I ever heard of.

It is repeated, of course, by the breadths, but not otherwise.   95

Looked at in one way, each breadth stands alone; the bloated curves and flourishes—a kind of "debased Romanesque" with *delirium tremens*—go waddling up and down in isolated columns of fatuity.

Weir Mitchell (1829–1914): famed nerve specialist who actually treated the author, Charlotte Perkins Gilman, for nervous prostration with his well-known "rest cure." (The cure was not successful.) Also the author of *Diseases of the Nervous System, Especially of Women* (1881). *laws of radiation:* a principle of design in which all elements are arranged in some circular pattern around a center.

But, on the other hand, they connect diagonally, and the sprawling outlines run off in great slanting waves of optic horror, like a lot of wallowing sea-weeds in full chase.

The whole thing goes horizontally, too, at least it seems so, and I exhaust myself trying to distinguish the order of its going in that direction.

They have used a horizontal breadth for a frieze, and that adds wonderfully to the confusion.

There is one end of the room where it is almost intact, and there, when the   100
crosslights fade and the low sun shines directly upon it, I can almost fancy radiation after all—the interminable grotesque seems to form around a common center and rush off in headlong plunges of equal distraction.

It makes me tired to follow it. I will take a nap, I guess.

I don't know why I should write this.

I don't want to.

I don't feel able.

And I know John would think it absurd. But I *must* say what I feel and think in   105
some way—it is such a relief!

But the effort is getting to be greater than the relief.

Half the time now I am awfully lazy, and lie down ever so much. John says I mustn't lose my strength, and has me take cod liver oil and lots of tonics and things, to say nothing of ale and wines and rare meat.

Dear John! He loves me very dearly, and hates to have me sick. I tried to have a real earnest reasonable talk with him the other day, and tell him how I wish he would let me go and make a visit to Cousin Henry and Julia.

But he said I wasn't able to go, nor able to stand it after I got there; and I did not make out a very good case for myself, for I was crying before I had finished.

It is getting to be a great effort for me to think straight. Just this nervous weak-   110
ness, I suppose.

And dear John gathered me up in his arms, and just carried me upstairs and laid me on the bed, and sat by me and read to me till it tired my head.

He said I was his darling and his comfort and all he had, and that I must take care of myself for his sake, and keep well.

He says no one but myself can help me out of it, that I must use my will and self-control and not let any silly fancies run away with me.

There's one comfort—the baby is well and happy, and does not have to occupy this nursery with the horrid wallpaper.

If we had not used it, that blessed child would have! What a fortunate escape!   115
Why, I wouldn't have a child of mine, an impressionable little thing, live in such a room for worlds.

I never thought of it before, but it is lucky that John kept me here after all; I can stand it so much easier than a baby, you see.

Of course I never mention it to them any more—I am too wise—but I keep watch for it all the same.

There are things in the wallpaper that nobody knows about but me, or ever will.

Behind that outside pattern the dim shapes get clearer every day.

It is always the same shape, only very numerous.   120

And it is like a woman stooping down and creeping about behind that pattern. I don't like it a bit. I wonder—I begin to think—I wish John would take me away from here!

It is so hard to talk with John about my case, because he is so wise, and because he loves me so.

But I tried it last night.

It was moonlight. The moon shines in all around just as the sun does.

I hate to see it sometimes, it creeps so slowly, and always comes in by one   125
window or another.

John was asleep and I hated to waken him, so I kept still and watched the moonlight on that undulating wallpaper till I felt creepy.

The faint figure behind seemed to shake the pattern, just as if she wanted to get out.

I got up softly and went to feel and see if the paper *did* move, and when I came back John was awake.

"What is it, little girl?" he said. "Don't go walking about like that—you'll get cold."

I thought it was a good time to talk, so I told him that I really was not gaining   130
here, and that I wished he would take me away.

"Why, darling!" said he. "Our lease will be up in three weeks, and I can't see how to leave before.

"The repairs are not done at home, and I cannot possibly leave town just now. Of course, if you were in any danger, I could and would, but you really are better, dear, whether you can see it or not. I am a doctor, dear, and I know. You are gaining flesh and color, your appetite is better, I feel really much easier about you."

"I don't weigh a bit more," said I, "nor as much; and my appetite may be better in the evening when you are here but it is worse in the morning when you are away!"

"Bless her little heart!" said he with a big hug. "She shall be as sick as she pleases! But now let's improve the shining hours by going to sleep, and talk about it in the morning!"

"And you won't go away?" I asked gloomily.   135

"Why, how can I, dear? It is only three weeks more and then we will take a nice little trip for a few days while Jennie is getting the house ready. Really, dear, you are better!"

"Better in body perhaps—" I began, and stopped short, for he sat up straight and looked at me with such a stern, reproachful look that I could not say another word.

"My darling," said he, "I beg you, for my sake and for our child's sake, as well as for your own, that you will never for one instant let that idea enter your mind! There is nothing so dangerous, so fascinating, to a temperament like yours. It is a false and foolish fancy. Can you trust me as a physician when I tell you so?"

So of course I said no more on that score, and we went to sleep before long. He thought I was asleep first, but I wasn't, and lay there for hours trying to decide whether that front pattern and the back pattern really did move together or separately.

On a pattern like this, by daylight, there is a lack of sequence, a defiance of law,   140
that is a constant irritant to a normal mind.

The color is hideous enough, and unreliable enough, and infuriating enough, but the pattern is torturing.

You think you have mastered it, but just as you get well under way in following, it turns a back-somersault and there you are. It slaps you in the face, knocks you down, and tramples upon you. It is like a bad dream.

The outside pattern is a florid arabesque,° reminding one of a fungus. If you can imagine a toadstool in joints, an interminable string of toadstools, budding and sprouting in endless convolutions—why, that is something like it.

That is, sometimes!

There is one marked peculiarity about this paper, a thing nobody seems to notice but myself, and that is that it changes as the light changes. 145

When the sun shoots in through the east window—I always watch for that first long, straight ray—it changes so quickly that I never can quite believe it.

That is why I watch it always.

By moonlight—the moon shines in all night when there is a moon—I wouldn't know it was the same paper.

At night in any kind of light, in twilight, candlelight, lamplight, and worst of all by moonlight, it becomes bars! The outside pattern, I mean, and the woman behind it is as plain as can be.

I didn't realize for a long time what the thing was that showed behind, that dim 150
sub-pattern, but now I am quite sure it is a woman.

By daylight she is subdued, quiet. I fancy it is the pattern that keeps her so still. It is so puzzling. It keeps me quiet by the hour.

I lie down ever so much now. John says it is good for me, and to sleep all I can.

Indeed he started the habit by making me lie down for an hour after each meal.

It is a very bad habit, I am convinced, for you see, I don't sleep.

And that cultivates deceit, for I don't tell them I'm awake—oh, no! 155

The fact is I am getting a little afraid of John.

He seems very queer sometimes, and even Jennie has an inexplicable look.

It strikes me occasionally, just as a scientific hypothesis, that perhaps it is the paper!

I have watched John when he did not know I was looking, and come into the room suddenly on the most innocent excuses, and I've caught him several times *looking at the paper!* And Jennie too. I caught Jennie with her hand on it once.

She didn't know I was in the room, and when I asked her in a quiet, a very quiet 160
voice, with the most restrained manner possible, what she was doing with the paper, she turned around as if she had been caught stealing, and looked quite angry—asked me why I should frighten her so!

Then she said that the paper stained everything it touched, that she had found yellow smooches° on all my clothes and John's and she wished we would be more careful!

Did not that sound innocent? But I know she was studying that pattern, and I am determined that nobody shall find it out but myself!

Life is very much more exciting now than it used to be. You see, I have something more to expect, to look forward to, to watch. I really do eat better, and am more quiet than I was.

John is so pleased to see me improve! He laughed a little the other day, and said I seemed to be flourishing in spite of my wallpaper.

I turned it off with a laugh. I had no intention of telling him it was *because* of the 165
wallpaper—he would make fun of me. He might even want to take me away.

arabesque: a type of ornamental style (Arabic in origin) that uses flowers, foliage, fruit, or other figures to create an intricate pattern of interlocking shapes and lines. *smooches:* smudges or smears.

I don't want to leave now until I have found it out. There is a week more, and I think that will be enough.

I'm feeling so much better!

I don't sleep much at night, for it is so interesting to watch developments; but I sleep a good deal during the daytime.

In the daytime it is tiresome and perplexing.

There are always new shoots on the fungus, and new shades of yellow all over it. 170 I cannot keep count of them, though I have tried conscientiously.

It is the strangest yellow, that wallpaper! It makes me think of all the yellow things I ever saw—not beautiful ones like buttercups, but old, foul, bad yellow things.

But there is something else about that paper—the smell! I noticed it the moment we came into the room, but with so much air and sun it was not bad. Now we have had a week of fog and rain, and whether the windows are open or not, the smell is here.

It creeps all over the house.

I find it hovering in the dining-room, skulking in the parlor, hiding in the hall, lying in wait for me on the stairs.

It gets into my hair. 175

Even when I go to ride, if I turn my head suddenly and surprise it—there is that smell!

Such a peculiar odor, too! I have spent hours in trying to analyze it, to find what it smelled like.

It is not bad—at first—and very gentle, but quite the subtlest, most enduring odor I ever met.

In this damp weather it is awful. I wake up in the night and find it hanging over me.

It used to disturb me at first. I thought seriously of burning the house—to reach 180 the smell.

But now I am used to it. The only thing I can think of that it is like is the *color* of the paper! A yellow smell.

There is a very funny mark on this wall, low down, near the mopboard. A streak that runs round the room. It goes behind every piece of furniture, except the bed, a long, straight, even *smooch*, as if it had been rubbed over and over.

I wonder how it was done and who did it, and what they did it for. Round and round and round—round and round and round—it makes me dizzy!

I really have discovered something at last.

Through watching so much at night, when it changes so, I have finally found 185 out.

The front pattern *does* move—and no wonder! The woman behind shakes it!

Sometimes I think there are a great many women behind, and sometimes only one, and she crawls around fast, and her crawling shakes it all over.

Then in the very bright spots she keeps still, and in the very shady spots she just takes hold of the bars and shakes them hard.

And she is all the time trying to climb through. But nobody could climb through that pattern—it strangles so; I think that is why it has so many heads.

They get through and then the pattern strangles them off and turns them upside 190 down, and makes their eyes white!

If those heads were covered or taken off it would not be half so bad.

I think that woman gets out in the daytime!

And I'll tell you why—privately—I've seen her!

I can see her out of every one of my windows!

It is the same woman, I know, for she is always creeping, and most women do not   195
creep by daylight.

I see her in that long shaded lane, creeping up and down. I see her in those dark
grape arbors, creeping all round the garden.

I see her on that long road under the trees, creeping along, and when a carriage
comes she hides under the blackberry vines.

I don't blame her a bit. It must be very humiliating to be caught creeping by daylight!

I always lock the door when I creep by daylight. I can't do it at night, for I know
John would suspect something at once.

And John is so queer now that I don't want to irritate him. I wish he would take   200
another room! Besides, I don't want anybody to get that woman out at night but
myself.

I often wonder if I could see her out of all the windows at once.

But, turn as fast as I can, I can only see out of one at one time.

And though I always see her, she *may* be able to creep faster than I can turn! I
have watched her sometimes away off in the open country, creeping as fast as a cloud
shadow in a wind.

If only that top pattern could be gotten off from the under one! I mean to try it,
little by little.

I have found out another funny thing, but I shan't tell it this time! It does not do   205
to trust people too much.

There are only two more days to get this paper off, and I believe John is beginning to notice. I don't like the look in his eyes.

And I heard him ask Jennie a lot of professional questions about me. She had a
very good report to give.

She said I slept a good deal in the daytime.

John knows I don't sleep very well at night, for all I'm so quiet!

He asked me all sorts of questions too, and pretended to be very loving and kind.   210

As if I couldn't see through him!

Still, I don't wonder he acts so, sleeping under this paper for three months.

It only interests me, but I feel sure John and Jennie are affected by it.

Hurrah! This is the last day, but it is enough. John is to stay in town over night,
and won't be out until this evening.

Jennie wanted to sleep with me—the sly thing; but I told her I should undoubt-   215
edly rest better for a night all alone.

That was clever, for really I wasn't alone a bit! As soon as it was moonlight and
that poor thing began to crawl and shake the pattern, I got up and ran to help her.

I pulled and she shook. I shook and she pulled, and before morning we had
peeled off yards of that paper.

A strip about as high as my head and half around the room.

And then when the sun came and that awful pattern began to laugh at me, I
declared I would finish it today!

We go away tomorrow, and they are moving all my furniture down again to leave   220
things as they were before.

Jennie looked at the wall in amazement, but I told her merrily that I did it out of
pure spite at the vicious thing.

She laughed and said she wouldn't mind doing it herself, but I must not get tired.
How she betrayed herself that time!

But I am here, and no person touches this paper but me—not *alive*!

She tried to get me out of the room—it was too patent! But I said it was so quiet 225
and empty and clean now that I believed I would lie down again and sleep all I could,
and not to wake me even for dinner—I would call when I woke.

So now she is gone, and the servants are gone, and the things are gone, and there
is nothing left but that great bedstead nailed down, with the canvas mattress we
found on it.

We shall sleep downstairs tonight, and take the boat home tomorrow.

I quite enjoy the room, now it is bare again.

How those children did tear about here!

This bedstead is fairly gnawed!   230

But I must get to work.

I have locked the door and thrown the key down into the front path.

I don't want to go out, and I don't want to have anybody come in, till John
comes.

I want to astonish him.

I've got a rope up here that even Jennie did not find. If that woman does get out, 235
and tries to get away, I can tie her!

But I forgot I could not reach far without anything to stand on!

This bed will *not* move!

I tried to lift and push it until I was lame, and then I got so angry I bit off a little
piece at one corner—but it hurt my teeth.

Then I peeled off all the paper I could reach standing on the floor. It sticks horribly and the pattern just enjoys it! All those strangled heads and bulbous eyes and
waddling fungus growths just shriek with derision!

I am getting angry enough to do something desperate. To jump out of the win- 240
dow would be admirable exercise, but the bars are too strong even to try.

Besides I wouldn't do it. Of course not. I know well enough that a step like that
is improper and might be misconstrued.

I don't like to *look* out of the windows even—there are so many of those creeping
women, and they creep so fast.

I wonder if they all come out of that wallpaper as I did!

But I am securely fastened now by my well-hidden rope—you don't get *me* out in
the road there!

I suppose I shall have to get back behind the pattern when it comes night, and 245
that is hard!

It is so pleasant to be out in this great room and creep around as I please!

I don't want to go outside. I won't, even if Jennie asks me to.

For outside you have to creep on the ground, and everything is green instead of
yellow.

But here I can creep smoothly on the floor, and my shoulder just fits in that long
smooch around the wall, so I cannot lose my way.

Why, there's John at the door!   250

It is no use, young man, you can't open it!

How he does call and pound!

Now he's crying to Jennie for an axe.

It would be a shame to break down that beautiful door!

"John, dear!" said I in the gentlest voice. "The key is down by the front steps, un- 255
der a plantain leaf!"

That silenced him for a few moments.

Then he said, very quietly indeed, "Open the door, my darling!"

"I can't," said I. "The key is down by the front door under a plantain leaf!" And then
I said it again, several times, very gently and slowly, and said it so often that he had to go
and see, and he got it of course, and came in. He stopped short by the door.

"What is the matter?" he cried. "For God's sake, what are you doing!"

I kept on creeping just the same, but I looked at him over my shoulder. 260

"I've got out at last," said I, "in spite of you and Jane. And I've pulled off most of
the paper, so you can't put me back!"

Now why should that man have fainted? But he did, and right across my path by
the wall, so that I had to creep over him every time!

Questions

1. Several times at the beginning of the story, the narrator says such things as "What is one
to do?" and "What can one do?" What do these comments refer to? What, if anything, do
they suggest about women's roles at the time the story was written?

2. The narrator says, "I get unreasonably angry with John sometimes" (paragraph 24). How
unreasonable is her anger at him? What does the fact that she feels it is unreasonable say
about her?

3. What do her changing feelings about the wallpaper tell us about the changes in her
condition?

4. "It is so hard to talk with John about my case, because he is so wise, and because he loves
me so" (paragraph 122). His wisdom is, to say the least, open to question, but what about
his love? Do you think he suffers merely from a failure of perception, or is there a failure of
affection as well? Explain your response.

5. Where precisely in the story do you think it becomes clear that she has begun to
hallucinate?

6. What does the woman behind the wallpaper represent? Why does the narrator come to
identify with her?

7. How ill does the narrator seem at the beginning of the story? How ill does she seem at the
end? How do you account for the change in her condition?

CHARLOTTE PERKINS GILMAN ON WRITING

Why I Wrote "The Yellow Wallpaper" 1913

Many and many a reader has asked that. When the story first came out, in the *New
England Magazine* about 1891, a Boston physician made protest in *The Transcript*.
Such a story ought not to be written, he said; it was enough to drive anyone mad to
read it.

Another physician, in Kansas I think, wrote to say that it was the best description of incipient insanity he had ever seen, and—begging my pardon—had I been
there?

Now the story of the story is this: For many years I suffered from a severe and
continuous nervous breakdown tending to melancholia—and beyond. During
about the third year of this trouble I went, in devout faith and some faint stir of
hope, to a noted specialist in nervous diseases, the best known in the country. This

wise man put me to bed and applied the rest cure, to which a still-good physique responded so promptly that he concluded there was nothing much the matter with me, and sent me home with solemn advice to "live as domestic a life as far as possible," to "have but two hours' intellectual life a day," and "never to touch pen, brush, or pencil again" as long as I lived. This was in 1887.

I went home and obeyed those directions for some three months, and came so near the borderline of utter mental ruin that I could see over.

Then, using the remnants of intelligence that remained, and helped by a wise friend, I cast the noted specialist's advice to the winds and went to work again—work, the normal life of every human being; work, in which is joy and growth and service, without which one is a pauper and a parasite—ultimately recovering some measure of power.

Being naturally moved to rejoicing by this narrow escape, I wrote "The Yellow Wallpaper," with its embellishments and additions, to carry out the ideal (I never had hallucinations or objections to my mural decorations) and sent a copy to the physician who so nearly drove me mad. He never acknowledged it.

The little book is valued by alienists and as a good specimen of one kind of literature. It has, to my knowledge, saved one woman from a similar fate—so terrifying her family that they let her out into normal activity and she recovered.

But the best result is this. Many years later I was told that the great specialist had admitted to friends of his that he had altered his treatment of neurasthenia since reading "The Yellow Wallpaper."

It was not intended to drive people crazy, but to save people from being driven crazy, and it worked.

From *The Forerunner*, October 1913

Whatever Is   1903

Whatever is we only know
As in our minds we find it so;
   No staring fact is half so clear
   As one dim, preconceived idea—
No matter how the fact may glow.   5

Vainly may Truth her trumpet blow
To stir our minds; like heavy dough
   They stick to what they think—won't hear
    Whatever is.

Our ancient myths in solid row   10
Stand up—we simply have to go
   And choke each fiction old and dear
   Before the modest facts appear;
Then we may grasp, reluctant, slow,
    Whatever is.   15

The Nervous Breakdown of Women 1916

[A]s a hindrance they [women] have to meet something which men have never met—the cold and cruel opposition of the other sex. In every step of their long upward path men have had women with them, never against them. In hardship, in privation, in danger, in the last test of religious martyrdom, in the pains and terrors of warfare, in rebellions and revolutions, men have had women with them. Individual women have no doubt been a hindrance to individual men, and the economic dependence of women is a drag upon men's freedom of action; but at no step of man's difficult advance has he had to meet the scorn, the neglect, the open vilification of massed womanhood.

No one has seemed to notice the cost of this great artificial barrier to the advance of woman, the effect upon her nervous system of opposition and abuse from the quarter where nature and tradition had taught her to expect aid and comfort. She has had to keep pace with him in meeting the demands of our swiftly changing times. She has had to meet the additional demands of her own even more swiftly changing conditions. And she has had to do this in the face not only of the organized opposition of the other sex, entrenched in secure possession of all the advantageous positions of church and state, buttressed by law and custom, fully trained and experienced, and holding all the ammunition—the "sinews of war"—the whole money power of the world; but besides this her slow, difficult, conscientious efforts to make the changes she knew were right, or which were forced upon her by conditions, have too often cost her man's love, respect and good will.

This is a heavy price to pay for progress.

We should be more than gentle with the many women who cannot yet meet it.

We should be more than grateful for those strong men who are more human than male, who can feel, think and act above the limitations of their sex, and who have helped women in their difficult advance.

Also we should deeply honor those great women of the last century, who met all demands, paid every exaction, faced all opposition and made the way easier for us now.

But we should not be surprised at the "nervous breakdown" of some women, nor attribute it to weakness.

Only the measureless strength of the mother sex could have enabled women to survive the sufferings of yesterday and to meet the exactions of today.

From *The Forerunner*, July–August 1916

CRITICS ON "THE YELLOW WALLPAPER"

A Massachusetts hospital for the insane in the era of Charlotte Perkins Gilman's "The Yellow Wallpaper."

Juliann Fleenor (b. 1942)

Gender and Pathology in "The Yellow Wallpaper"   1983

Although it is not generally known, Gilman wrote at least two other Gothic stories around the same time as "The Yellow Wallpaper." All three were published in the *New England Magazine*. At the time that "The Rocking Chair" and "The Giant Wistaria" were written, Gilman and her young daughter, Katherine, were living in the warmth of Pasadena, separated from her husband, Charles Walter Stetson. Gilman later noted in her papers: "'The Yellow Wallpaper' was written in two days, with the thermometer at one hundred and three in Pasadena, Ca." Her husband was living on the east coast, and, perhaps coincidentally, all three stories appear to be set in a nameless eastern setting, one urban and two rural. All three display similar themes, and all three are evidence that the conflict, central to Gilman's Gothic fiction and later to her autobiography, was a conflict with the mother, with motherhood, and with creation.

In all three stories women are confined within the home; it is their prison, their insane asylum, even their tomb. A sense of the female isolation which Gilman felt, of exclusion from the public world of work and of men, is contained in the anecdote related by Zona Gale in her introduction to Gilman's autobiography. After watching the approach of several locomotives to a train platform in a small town in Wisconsin, Gilman said, "'All that, . . . and women have no part in it. Everything done by men, working together, while women worked on alone within their four walls!'" Female exclusion, women denied the opportunity to work, or their imprisonment behind four walls, led to madness. Her image, interestingly, does not suggest a female subculture of women working together; Gilman was working against her own culture's definition of women, and her primary antagonists were women like her own mother.

Diseased maternity is explicit in Gilman's third Gothic story. The yellow wallpaper symbolizes more than confinement, victimization, and the inability to write. It suggests a disease within the female self. When the narrator peels the wallpaper off, "It sticks horribly and the pattern just enjoys it! All those strangled heads and bulbous eyes and waddling fungus growths just shriek with derision." This passage describes more than the peeling of wallpaper: the "strangled heads and bulbous eyes and waddling fungus" imply something strange and terrible about birth and death conjoined, about female procreation, and about female physiology. Nature is perverted here, too. The narrator thinks of "old, foul, bad yellow things." The smell "creeps all over the house." She finds it "hovering in the dining-room, skulking in the parlor, hiding in the hall, lying in wait for me on the stairs." Finally, "it gets into my hair."

The paper stains the house in a way that suggests the effect of afterbirth. The house, specifically this room, becomes more than a symbol of a repressive society; it represents the physical self of the narrator as well. She is disgusted, perhaps awed, perhaps frightened of her own bodily processes. The story establishes a sense of fear and disgust, the skin crawls and grows clammy with the sense of physiological fear that Ellen Moers refers to as the Female Gothic.

My contention is that one of the major themes in the story, punishment for becoming a mother (as well as punishment for being female), is supported by the absence of the child. The child is taken away from the mother, almost in punishment, as was the child in "The Giant Wistaria." This differs from Gilman's experience; she had been told to keep her child with her at all times. In both the story and in Gilman's life, a breakdown occurs directly after the birth of a child. The narrator is confined as if she had committed a crime. Maternity—the creation of a child—is combined with writing—the creation of writing—in a way that suggests they are interrelated and perhaps symbiotic, as are the strange toadstools behind the wallpaper.

The pathological nature of both experiences is not surprising, given the treatment Gilman received, and given the fact that maternity reduced women to mothers and not writers. Childbirth has long been a rite of passage for women. But the question is, where does that passage lead? Becoming a mother leads to a child-like state. The narrator becomes the absent child.

From "The Gothic Prism"

Sandra M. Gilbert (b. 1936) *and Susan Gubar* (b. 1944)

Imprisonment and Escape: The Psychology of Confinement 1979

["The Yellow Wallpaper" is a] striking story of female confinement and escape, a paradigmatic tale which (like *Jane Eyre*) seems to tell *the* story that all literary women would tell if they could speak their "speechless woe." "The Yellow Wallpaper," which Gilman herself called "a description of a case of nervous breakdown," recounts in the first person the experiences of a woman who is evidently suffering from a severe postpartum psychosis. Her husband, a censorious and paternalistic physician, is treating her according to methods by which S. Weir Mitchell, a famous "nerve specialist," treated Gilman herself for a similar problem. He has confined her to a large garret room in an "ancestral hall" he has rented, and he has forbidden her to touch pen to paper until she is well again, for he feels, says the narrator, "that with my imaginative power and habit of story-making, a nervous weakness like mine is sure to lead to all manner of excited fancies, and that I ought to use my will and good sense to check the tendency."

The cure, of course, is worse than the disease, for the sick woman's mental condition deteriorates rapidly. "I think sometimes that if I were only well enough to write a little it would relieve the press of ideas and rest me," she remarks, but literally confined in a room she thinks is a one-time nursery because it has "rings and things" in the walls, she is literally locked away from creativity. The "rings and things," although reminiscent of children's gymnastic equipment, are really the paraphernalia of confinement, like the gate at the head of the stairs, instruments that definitively indicate her imprisonment. Even more tormenting, however, is the room's wallpaper: a sulfurous yellow paper, torn off in spots, and patterned with "lame uncertain curves" that "plunge off at outrageous angles" and "destroy themselves in unheard-of contradictions." Ancient, smoldering, "unclean" as the oppressive structures of the society in which she finds herself, this paper surrounds the narrator like an inexplicable text, censorious and overwhelming as her physician husband, haunting as the "hereditary estate" in which she is trying to survive. Inevitably she studies its suicidal implications—and inevitably, because of her "imaginative power and habit of story-making," she revises it, projecting her own passion for escape into its otherwise incomprehensible hieroglyphics. "This wallpaper," she decides, at a key point in her story,

> has a kind of sub-pattern in a different shade, a particularly irritating one, for you can only see it in certain lights, and not clearly then.
>
> But in the places where it isn't faded and where the sun is just so—I can see a strange, provoking, formless sort of figure that seems to skulk about behind that silly and conspicuous front design.

As time passes, this figure concealed behind what corresponds (in terms of what we have been discussing) to the facade of the patriarchal text becomes clearer and clearer. By moonlight the pattern of the wallpaper "becomes bars! The outside pattern I mean, and the woman behind it is as plain as can be." And eventually, as the narrator sinks more deeply into what the world calls madness, the terrifying implications of both the paper and the figure imprisoned behind the paper begin to permeate—that is, to *haunt*—the rented ancestral mansion in which she and her husband are immured. The "yellow smell" of the paper "creeps all over the house," drenching every room in its subtle aroma of decay. And the woman creeps too— through the house, in the house, and out of the house, in the garden and "on that long road under the trees." Sometimes, indeed, the narrator confesses, "I think there are a great many women" both behind the paper and creeping in the garden,

> and sometimes only one, and she crawls around fast, and her crawling shakes [the paper] all over. . . . And she is all the time trying to climb through. But nobody could climb through that pattern—it strangles so; I think that is why it has so many heads.

Eventually it becomes obvious to both reader and narrator that the figure creeping through and behind the wallpaper is both the narrator and the narrator's double. By the end of the story, moreover, the narrator has enabled this double to escape from her textual/architectural confinement: "I pulled and she shook, I shook and she pulled, and before morning we had peeled off yards of that paper." Is the message of the tale's conclusion mere madness? Certainly the righteous Doctor John—whose name links him to the anti-hero of Charlotte Bronte's *Villette*—has been temporarily defeated, or at least momentarily stunned. "Now why should that man have fainted?" the narrator ironically asks as she creeps around her attic. But John's unmasculine swoon of surprise is the least of the triumphs Gilman imagines for her madwoman. More significant are the madwoman's own imaginings and creations, mirages of health and freedom with which her author endows her like a fairy godmother showering gold on a sleeping heroine. The woman from behind the wallpaper creeps away, for instance, creeps fast and far on the long road, in broad daylight. "I have watched her sometimes away off in the open country," says the narrator, "creeping as fast as a cloud shadow in a high wind."

Indistinct and yet rapid, barely perceptible but inexorable, the progress of that cloud shadow is not unlike the progress of nineteenth-century literary women out of the texts defined by patriarchal poetics into the open spaces of their own authority. That such an escape from the numb world behind the patterned walls of the text was a flight from disease into health was quite clear to Gilman herself. When "The Yellow Wallpaper" was published she sent it to Weir Mitchell, whose strictures had kept her from attempting the pen during her own breakdown, thereby aggravating her illness, and she was delighted to learn, years later, that "he had changed his treatment of nervous prostration since reading" her story. "If that is a fact," she declared, "I have not lived in vain."

From *The Madwoman in the Attic*

Elizabeth Ammons

Biographical Echoes in "The Yellow Wallpaper"   1991

"The Yellow Wallpaper" probably had deep roots in Gilman's childhood. In her autobiography, the account she gives of her growing up focuses on the misery of her mother, a woman who adored her husband and loved having babies, only to have her husband leave and her babies grow up. Deserted, Gilman's mother—in the daughter's telling—grew bitter and fiercely repressed, deciding not to show any affection for her daughter in order to toughen the child. Life, as Gilman's mother had come to know it, brought women terrible disappointment and denial. Only in the dead of night would she allow herself to hug her daughter.

As a story about her mother, the early portions of Gilman's autobiography construct a family drama in which sexual desire in a woman leads to babies and death. (According to Gilman, her mother was warned that one more pregnancy would kill her, at which point the father left the family.) On the other hand, denial of sexual desire, the celibate life that Mary Fitch Perkins knew when her husband left, resulted in furious repression and frustration. Either way, female sexual desire, motherhood, and masculine power were bitterly entangled for Gilman's mother, who even after years of separation and rejection remained her husband's prisoner, calling for him on her deathbed. Looked at from the child's point of view, Charlotte Perkins Gilman clearly both admired and hated her father. Frederick Beecher Perkins's power over his wife was so strong that she had to stamp out all that was free and physical and warm in herself, and try to do the same to her daughter. In a sense the woman on her knees at the end of "The Yellow Wallpaper," the prisoner of a charming man and an ugly empty domestic life that she cannot escape, is Gilman's mother as the child experienced her while growing up—humiliated, angry, crushed.

• • •

The drama of patriarchal control in "The Yellow Wallpaper" is the same one that Charlotte Perkins Gilman felt as a child, saw in her mother's life, and then experienced again herself as a young wife and mother. The story is not limited to just one stage of her life as a woman, but applies potentially to all stages, from childhood to old age. It is not, moreover, simply a story about the desire for escape from male control. It is also a story about the desire to escape to a female world, a desire to unite with the mother, indeed with all women creeping and struggling in growing numbers, through the paper, behind the wall.

From Conflicting Stories: American Women Writers
at the Turn into the Twentieth Century

ALICE WALKER

Alice Walker, a leading black writer and social activist, was born in 1944 in Eatonton, Georgia, the youngest of eight children. Her father, a sharecropper and dairy farmer, usually earned about $300 a year; her mother helped by working as a maid. Both entertained their children by telling stories. When Alice Walker was eight, she was accidentally struck by a pellet from a brother's BB gun. She lost the sight of one eye because the Walkers had no car to rush her to the hospital. Later she attended Spelman College in Atlanta and finished college at Sarah Lawrence College on a scholarship. While working for the civil rights movement in Mississippi, she met a young lawyer, Melvyn Leventhal. In 1967 they settled in Jackson, Mississippi, the first legally married interracial couple in town. They re-

Alice Walker

turned to New York in 1974 and were later divorced. First known as a poet, Walker has published seven books of her verse. She also has edited a collection of the work of the then-neglected black writer Zora Neale Hurston, and has written a study of Langston Hughes. In a collection of essays, In Search of Our Mothers' Gardens: Womanist Prose *(1983), she recalls her mother and addresses her own daughter. (By womanist she means "black feminist.") But the largest part of Walker's reading audience knows her fiction: three story collections, including* In Love and Trouble *(1973), from which "Everyday Use" is taken, and her many novels. Her best-known novel,* The Color Purple *(1982), won a Pulitzer Prize and was made into a film by Steven Spielberg in 1985. Her recent novels include* By the Light of My Father's Smile *(1998) and* Now Is the Time to Open Your Heart *(2004). Walker now lives in Northern California.*

Everyday Use   1973

for your grandmama

I will wait for her in the yard that Maggie and I made so clean and wavy yesterday afternoon. A yard like this is more comfortable than most people know. It is not just a yard. It is like an extended living room. When the hard clay is swept clean as a floor and the fine sand around the edges lined with tiny, irregular grooves, anyone can come and sit and look up into the elm tree and wait for the breezes that never come inside the house.

Maggie will be nervous until after her sister goes: she will stand hopelessly in corners, homely and ashamed of the burn scars down her arms and legs, eyeing her sister with a mixture of envy and awe. She thinks her sister has held life always in the palm of one hand, that "no" is a word the world never learned to say to her.

You've no doubt seen those TV shows where the child who has "made it" is confronted, as a surprise, by her own mother and father, tottering in weakly from backstage. (A pleasant surprise, of course: What would they do if parent and child came on the show only to curse out and insult each other?) On TV mother and child embrace and smile into each other's faces. Sometimes the mother and father weep, the child wraps them in her arms and leans across the table to tell how she would not have made it without their help. I have seen these programs.°

Sometimes I dream a dream in which Dee and I are suddenly brought together on a TV program of this sort. Out of a dark and soft-seated limousine I am ushered into a bright room filled with many people. There I meet a smiling, gray, sporty man like Johnny Carson who shakes my hand and tells me what a fine girl I have. Then we are on the stage and Dee is embracing me with tears in her eyes. She pins on my dress a large orchid, even though she has told me once that she thinks orchids are tacky flowers.

In real life I am a large, big-boned woman with rough, man-working hands. In the winter I wear flannel nightgowns to bed and overalls during the day. I can kill and clean a hog as mercilessly as a man. My fat keeps me hot in zero weather. I can work outside all day, breaking ice to get water for washing. I can eat pork liver cooked over the open fire minutes after it comes steaming from the hog. One winter I knocked a bull calf straight in the brain between the eyes with a sledge hammer and had the meat hung up to chill before nightfall. But of course all this does not show on television. I am the way my daughter would want me to be: a hundred pounds lighter, my skin like an uncooked barley pancake. My hair glistens in the hot bright lights. Johnny Carson has much to do to keep up with my quick and witty tongue. 5

But that is a mistake. I know even before I wake up. Who ever knew a Johnson with a quick tongue? Who can even imagine me looking a strange white man in the eye? It seems to me I have talked to them always with one foot raised in flight, with my head turned in whichever way is farthest from them. Dee, though. She would always look anyone in the eye. Hesitation was no part of her nature.

"How do I look, Mama?" Maggie says, showing just enough of her thin body enveloped in pink skirt and red blouse for me to know she's there, almost hidden by the door.

"Come out into the yard," I say.

Have you ever seen a lame animal, perhaps a dog run over by some careless person rich enough to own a car, sidle up to someone who is ignorant enough to be kind to him? That is the way my Maggie walks. She has been like this, chin on chest, eyes on ground, feet in shuffle, ever since the fire that burned the other house to the ground.

Dee is lighter than Maggie, with nicer hair and a fuller figure. She's a woman now, though sometimes I forget. How long ago was it that the other house burned? Ten, twelve years? Sometimes I can still hear the flames and feel Maggie's arms sticking to me, her hair smoking and her dress falling off her in little black papery flakes. Her eyes seemed stretched open, blazed open by the flames reflected in them. And Dee. I see her standing off under the sweet gum tree she used to dig gum out of; a look of concentration on her face as she watched the last dingy gray board of the house fall in toward the red-hot brick chimney. Why don't you do a dance around the ashes? I'd wanted to ask her. She had hated the house that much. 10

these programs: On the NBC television show *This Is Your Life*, people were publicly and often tearfully reunited with friends, relatives, and teachers they had not seen in years.

I used to think she hated Maggie, too. But that was before we raised the money, the church and me, to send her to Augusta to school. She used to read to us without pity; forcing words, lies, other folks' habits, whole lives upon us two, sitting trapped and ignorant underneath her voice. She washed us in a river of make-believe, burned us with a lot of knowledge we didn't necessarily need to know. Pressed us to her with the serious way she read, to shove us away at just the moment, like dimwits, we seemed about to understand.

Dee wanted nice things. A yellow organdy dress to wear to her graduation from high school; black pumps to match a green suit she'd made from an old suit somebody gave me. She was determined to stare down any disaster in her efforts. Her eyelids would not flicker for minutes at a time. Often I fought off the temptation to shake her. At sixteen she had a style of her own: and knew what style was.

I never had an education myself. After second grade the school was closed down. Don't ask me why: in 1927 colored asked fewer questions than they do now. Sometimes Maggie reads to me. She stumbles along good-naturedly but can't see well. She knows she is not bright. Like good looks and money, quickness passed her by. She will marry John Thomas (who has mossy teeth in an earnest face) and then I'll be free to sit here and I guess just sing church songs to myself. Although I never was a good singer. Never could carry a tune. I was always better at a man's job. I used to love to milk till I was hoofed in the side in '49. Cows are soothing and slow and don't bother you, unless you try to milk them the wrong way.

I have deliberately turned my back on the house. It is three rooms, just like the one that burned, except the roof is tin; they don't make shingle roofs any more. There are no real windows, just some holes cut in the sides, like the portholes in a ship, but not round and not square, with rawhide holding the shutters up on the outside. This house is in a pasture, too, like the other one. No doubt when Dee sees it she will want to tear it down. She wrote me once that no matter where we "choose" to live, she will manage to come see us. But she will never bring her friends. Maggie and I thought about this and Maggie asked me, "Mama, when did Dee ever *have* any friends?"

She had a few. Furtive boys in pink shirts hanging about on washday after 15 school. Nervous girls who never laughed. Impressed with her they worshiped the well-turned phrase, the cute shape, the scalding humor that erupted like bubbles in lye. She read to them.

When she was courting Jimmy T she didn't have much time to pay to us, but turned all her faultfinding power on him. He *flew* to marry a cheap city girl from a family of ignorant flashy people. She hardly had time to recompose herself.

When she comes I will meet—but there they are!

Maggie attempts to make a dash for the house, in her shuffling way, but I stay her with my hand. "Come back here," I say. And she stops and tries to dig a well in the sand with her toe.

It is hard to see them clearly through the strong sun. But even the first glimpse of leg out of the car tells me it is Dee. Her feet were always neat-looking, as if God himself had shaped them with a certain style. From the other side of the car comes a short, stocky man. Hair is all over his head a foot long and hanging from his chin like a kinky mule tail. I hear Maggie suck in her breath. "Uhnnnh," is what it sounds like. Like when you see the wriggling end of a snake just in front of your foot on the road. "Uhnnnh."

Dee next. A dress down to the ground, in this hot weather. A dress so loud it   20
hurts my eyes. There are yellows and oranges enough to throw back the light of the
sun. I feel my whole face warming from the heat waves it throws out. Earrings, too,
gold and hanging down to her shoulders. Bracelets dangling and making noises when
she moves her arm up to shake the folds of the dress out of her armpits. The dress is
loose and flows, and as she walks closer, I like it. I hear Maggie go "Uhnnnh" again. It
is her sister's hair. It stands straight up like the wool on a sheep. It is black as night
and around the edges are two long pigtails that rope about like small lizards disappearing behind her ears.

"Wa-su-zo-Tean-o!"° she says, coming on in that gliding way the dress makes her
move. The short stocky fellow with the hair to his navel is all grinning and he follows
up with "Asalamalakim,° my mother and sister!" He moves to hug Maggie but she
falls back, right up against the back of my chair. I feel her trembling there and when
I look up I see the perspiration falling off her chin.

"Don't get up," says Dee. Since I am stout it takes something of a push. You
can see me trying to move a second or two before I make it. She turns, showing
white heels through her sandals, and goes back to the car. Out she peeks next with
a Polaroid. She stoops down quickly and lines up picture after picture of me sitting
there in front of the house with Maggie cowering behind me. She never takes a
shot without making sure the house is included. When a cow comes nibbling
around the edge of the yard she snaps it and me and Maggie *and* the house. Then
she puts the Polaroid in the back seat of the car, and comes up and kisses me on the
forehead.

Meanwhile Asalamalakim is going through the motions with Maggie's hand.
Maggie's hand is as limp as a fish, and probably as cold, despite the sweat, and she
keeps trying to pull it back. It looks like Asalamalakim wants to shake hands but
wants to do it fancy. Or maybe he don't know how people shake hands. Anyhow, he
soon gives up on Maggie.

"Well," I say. "Dee."

"No, Mama," she says. "Not 'Dee,' Wangero Leewanika Kemanjo!"   25

"What happened to 'Dee'?" I wanted to know.

"She's dead," Wangero said. "I couldn't bear it any longer, being named after the
people who oppress me."

"You know as well as me you was named after your aunt Dicie," I said. Dicie is
my sister. She named Dee. We called her "Big Dee" after Dee was born.

"But who was *she* named after?" asked Wangero.

"I guess after Grandma Dee," I said.   30

"And who was she named after?" asked Wangero.

"Her mother," I said, and saw Wangero was getting tired. "That's about as far
back as I can trace it," I said. Though, in fact, I probably could have carried it back
beyond the Civil War through the branches.

"Well," said Asalamalakim, "there you are."

"Uhnnnh," I heard Maggie say.

"There I was not," I said, "before 'Dicie' cropped up in our family, so why should   35
I try to trace it that far back?"

Wa-su-zo-Tean-o!: salutation in Swahili, an African language. Notice that Dee has to sound it out,
syllable by syllable.   *Asalamalakim:* salutation in Arabic: "Peace be upon you."

He just stood there grinning, looking down on me like somebody inspecting a Model A car.° Every once in a while he and Wangero sent eye signals over my head.

"How do you pronounce this name?" I asked.

"You don't have to call me by it if you don't want to," said Wangero.

"Why shouldn't I?" I asked. "If that's what you want us to call you, we'll call you."

"I know it might sound awkward at first," said Wangero.   40

"I'll get used to it," I said. "Ream it out again."

Well, soon we got the name out of the way. Asalamalakim had a name twice as long and three times as hard. After I tripped over it two or three times he told me to just call him Hakim-a-barber. I wanted to ask him was he a barber, but I didn't really think he was, so I didn't ask.

"You must belong to those beef-cattle peoples down the road," I said. They said "Asalamalakim" when they met you, too, but they didn't shake hands. Always too busy: feeding the cattle, fixing the fences, putting up salt-lick shelters, throwing down hay. When the white folks poisoned some of the herd the men stayed up all night with rifles in their hands. I walked a mile and a half just to see the sight.

Hakim-a-barber said, "I accept some of their doctrines, but farming and raising cattle is not my style." (They didn't tell me, and I didn't ask, whether Wangero (Dee) had really gone and married him.)

We sat down to eat and right away he said he didn't eat collards and pork was   45
unclean. Wangero, though, went on through the chitlins and corn bread, the greens and everything else. She talked a blue streak over the sweet potatoes. Everything delighted her. Even the fact that we still used the benches her daddy made for the table when we couldn't afford to buy chairs.

"Oh, Mama!" she cried. Then turned to Hakim-a-barber. "I never knew how lovely these benches are. You can feel the rump prints," she said, running her hands underneath her and along the bench. Then she gave a sigh and her hand closed over Grandma Dee's butter dish. "That's it!" she said. "I knew there was something I wanted to ask you if I could have." She jumped up from the table and went over in the corner where the churn stood, the milk in it clabber° by now. She looked at the churn and looked at it.

"This churn top is what I need," she said. "Didn't Uncle Buddy whittle it out of a tree you all used to have?"

"Yes," I said.

"Uh huh," she said happily. "And I want the dasher, too."

"Uncle Buddy whittle that, too?" asked the barber.   50

Dee (Wangero) looked up at me.

"Aunt Dee's first husband whittled the dash," said Maggie so low you almost couldn't hear her. "His name was Henry, but they called him Stash."

"Maggie's brain is like an elephant's," Wangero said, laughing. "I can use the churn top as a centerpiece for the alcove table," she said, sliding a plate over the churn, "and I'll think of something artistic to do with the dasher."

When she finished wrapping the dasher the handle stuck out. I took it for a moment in my hands. You didn't even have to look close to see where hands pushing the dasher up and down to make butter had left a kind of sink in the wood. In fact, there were a lot of small sinks; you could see where thumbs and fingers had sunk into

Model A car: popular low-priced automobile introduced by the Ford Motor Company in 1927.
clabber: sour milk or buttermilk.

the wood. It was beautiful light yellow wood, from a tree that grew in the yard where Big Dee and Stash had lived.

After dinner Dee (Wangero) went to the trunk at the foot of my bed and started 55
rifling through it. Maggie hung back in the kitchen over the dishpan. Out came Wangero with two quilts. They had been pieced by Grandma Dee and then Big Dee and me had hung them on the quilt frames on the front porch and quilted them. One was in the Lone Star pattern. The other was Walk Around the Mountain. In both of them were scraps of dresses Grandma Dee had worn fifty and more years ago. Bits and pieces of Grandpa Jarrell's paisley shirts. And one teeny faded blue piece, about the piece of a penny matchbox, that was from Great Grandpa Ezra's uniform that he wore in the Civil War.

"Mama," Wangero said sweet as a bird. "Can I have these old quilts?"

I heard something fall in the kitchen, and a minute later the kitchen door slammed.

"Why don't you take one or two of the others?" I asked. "These old things was just done by me and Big Dee from some tops your grandma pieced before she died."

"No," said Wangero. "I don't want those. They are stitched around the borders by machine."

"That'll make them last better," I said. 60

"That's not the point," said Wangero. "These are all pieces of dresses Grandma used to wear. She did all this stitching by hand. Imagine!" She held the quilts securely in her arms, stroking them.

"Some of the pieces, like those lavender ones, come from old clothes her mother handed down to her," I said, moving up to touch the quilts. Dee (Wangero) moved back just enough so that I couldn't reach the quilts. They already belonged to her.

"Imagine!" she breathed again, clutching them closely to her bosom.

"The truth is," I said, "I promised to give them quilts to Maggie, for when she marries John Thomas."

She gasped like a bee had stung her. 65

"Maggie can't appreciate these quilts!" she said. "She'd probably be backward enough to put them to everyday use."

"I reckon she would," I said. "God knows I been saving 'em for long enough with nobody using 'em. I hope she will!" I didn't want to bring up how I had offered Dee (Wangero) a quilt when she went away to college. Then she had told me they were old-fashioned, out of style.

"But they're *priceless!*" she was saying now, furiously; for she has a temper. "Maggie would put them on the bed and in five years they'd be in rags. Less than that!"

"She can always make some more," I said. "Maggie knows how to quilt."

Dee (Wangero) looked at me with hatred. "You just will not understand. The 70
point is these quilts, *these* quilts!"

"Well," I said, stumped. "What would *you* do with them?"

"Hang them," she said. As if that was the only thing you *could* do with quilts.

Maggie by now was standing in the door. I could almost hear the sound her feet made as they scraped over each other.

"She can have them, Mama," she said, like somebody used to never winning anything, or having anything reserved for her. "I can 'member Grandma Dee without the quilts."

I looked at her hard. She had filled her bottom lip with checkerberry snuff and it 75
gave her face a kind of dopey, hangdog look. It was Grandma Dee and Big Dee who

taught her how to quilt herself. She stood there with her scarred hands hidden in the folds of her skirt. She looked at her sister with something like fear but she wasn't mad at her. This was Maggie's portion. This was the way she knew God to work.

When I looked at her like that something hit me in the top of my head and ran down to the soles of my feet. Just like when I'm in church and the spirit of God touches me and I get happy and shout. I did something I never had done before: hugged Maggie to me, then dragged her on into the room, snatched the quilts out of Miss Wangero's hands and dumped them into Maggie's lap. Maggie just sat there on my bed with her mouth open.

"Take one or two of the others," I said to Dee.

But she turned without a word and went out to Hakim-a-barber.

"You just don't understand," she said, as Maggie and I came out to the car.

"What don't I understand?" I wanted to know.

"Your heritage," she said. And then she turned to Maggie, kissed her, and said, "You ought to try to make something of yourself, too, Maggie. It's really a new day for us. But from the way you and Mama still live you'd never know it."

She put on some sunglasses that hid everything above the tip of her nose and her chin.

Maggie smiled; maybe at the sunglasses. But a real smile, not scared. After we watched the car dust settle I asked Maggie to bring me a dip of snuff. And then the two of us sat there just enjoying, until it was time to go in the house and go to bed.

Questions

1. What is the basic conflict in "Everyday Use"?
2. What is the tone of Walker's story? By what means does the author communicate it?
3. From whose point of view is "Everyday Use" told? What does the story gain from being told from this point of view—instead of, say, from the point of view of Dee (Wangero)?
4. What does the narrator of the story feel toward Dee? What seems to be Dee's present attitude toward her mother and sister?
5. What do you take to be the author's attitude toward each of her characters? How does she convey it?
6. What levels of meaning do you find in the story's title?
7. Contrast Dee's attitude toward her heritage with the attitudes of her mother and sister. How much truth is there in Dee's accusation that her mother and sister don't understand their heritage?
8. Does the knowledge that "Everyday Use" was written by a black writer in any way influence your reactions to it? Explain.

ALICE WALKER ON WRITING

The Black Woman Writer in America   1973

Interview by John O'Brien

Interviewer: Why do you think that the black woman writer has been so ignored in America? Does she have even more difficulty than the black male writer, who perhaps has just begun to gain recognition?

Walker: There are two reasons why the black woman writer is not taken as seriously as the black male writer. One is that she's a woman. Critics seem unusually ill-equipped to intelligently discuss and analyze the works of black women. Generally, they do not even make the attempt; they prefer, rather, to talk about the lives of black women writers, not about what they write. And, since black women writers are not—it would seem—very likable—until recently they were the least willing worshipers of male supremacy—comments about them tend to be cruel.

In Nathan Huggins's very readable book, *Harlem Renaissance*, he hardly refers to Zora Neale Hurston's work, except negatively. He quotes from Wallace Thurman's novel, *Infants of the Spring,* at length, giving us the words of a character, "Sweetie Mae Carr," who is allegedly based on Zora Neale Hurston. "Sweetie Mae" is a writer noted more "for her ribald wit and personal effervescence than for any actual literary work. She was a great favorite among those whites who went in for Negro prodigies." Mr. Huggins goes on for several pages, never quoting Zora Neale Hurston herself, but rather the opinions of others about her character. He does say that she was "a master of dialect," but adds that "Her greatest weakness was carelessness or indifference to her art."

Having taught Zora Neale Hurston, and of course, having read her work myself, I am stunned. Personally, I do not care if Zora Hurston was fond of her white women friends. When she was a child in Florida, working for nickels and dimes, two white women helped her escape. Perhaps this explains it. But even if it doesn't, so what? Her work, far from being done carelessly, is done (especially in *Their Eyes Were Watching God*) almost too perfectly. She took the trouble to capture the beauty of rural black expression. She saw poetry where other writers merely saw failure to cope with English. She was so at ease with her blackness it never occurred to her that she should act one way among blacks and another among whites (as her more sophisticated black critics apparently did).

It seems to me that black writing has suffered, because even black critics have assumed that a book that deals with the relationships between members of a black family—or between a man and a woman—is less important than one that has white people as a primary antagonist. The consequences of this is that many of our books by "major" writers (always male) tell us little about the culture, history, or future, imagination, fantasies, etc., of black people, and a lot about isolated (often improbable) or limited encounters with a nonspecific white world. Where is the book, by an American black person (aside from *Cane*), that equals Elechi Amadi's *The Concubine*, for example? A book that exposes the *subconscious* of a people, because the people's dreams, imaginings, rituals, legends, etc., are known to be important, are known to contain the accumulated collective reality of the people themselves. Or, in *The Radiance of the King*, the white person is shown to be the outsider he is, because the culture he enters into in Africa *itself* [expels] him. Without malice, but as nature expels what does not suit. The white man is mysterious, a force to be reckoned with, but he is not glorified to such an extent that the Africans turn their attention away from themselves and their own imagination and culture. Which is what often happens with "protest literature." The superficial becomes—for a time—the deepest reality, and replaces the still waters of the collective subconscious.

When my own novel was published, a leading black monthly admitted (the editor did) that the book itself was never read; but the magazine ran an item stating that a *white* reviewer had praised the book (which was, in itself, an indication that the book was no good—such went the logic) and then hinted that the reviewer had liked my book because of my life-style. When I wrote to the editor to complain, he wrote me a small sermon on the importance of my "image," of what is "good" for others to see. Needless to say, what others "see" of me is the least of my worries, and I assumed that "others" are intelligent enough to recover from whatever shocks my presence might cause.

Women writers are supposed to be intimidated by male disapproval. What they write is not important enough to be read. How they live, however, their "image," they owe to the race. Read the reason Zora Neale Hurston gave for giving up her writing. See what "image" the Negro press gave her, innocent as she was. I no longer read articles or reviews unless they are totally about the work. I trust that someday a generation of men and women will arise who will forgive me for such wrong as I do not agree I do, and will read my work because it is a true account of my feelings, my perceptions, and my imagination, and because it will reveal something to them of their own selves. They will also be free to toss it—and me—out of a high window. They can do what they like.

From *Interviews with Black Writers*

Reflections on Writing and Women's Lives   (mid-1990s) 2004

Interview by William R. Ferris

If you think of the early stories, it's true that the women end badly, but it's because they belong to the generation of my mother and grandmother, when they were suspended because they had nowhere to go. All of them couldn't be Bessie Smith or Billie Holiday, so they ended up doing all kinds of destructive things. Most of that generation didn't have any fame or glory. But notice that all of those women are much older than I am. They exist in an historical place that is removed from my generation of women. . . . I wrote about these women in *In Search of Our Mothers' Gardens*. The women who have not had anything, have been, almost of necessity, self-destructive. They've just been driven insane. And the ones who have managed have been the ones who could focus their enormous energies on art forms that were not necessarily recognized as art forms—on quilting, on flowers, on making things. It's a very human need, to make things, to create. To think that women didn't need that—that by having a baby you fulfill your whole function— is absurd and demeaning.

From *Southern Cultures*

CRITICS ON "EVERYDAY USE"

Lone Star quilt pattern: "Out came Wangero with two quilts. . . . One was in the Lone Star pattern" (paragraph 55).

Barbara T. Christian   (1943–2000)

"Everyday Use" and the Black Power Movement   1994

"Everyday Use" is, in part, Alice Walker's response to the concept of heritage as articulated by the black movements of the 1960s. In that period, many African Americans, disappointed by the failure of integration, gravitated to the philosophy of cultural nationalism as the means to achieve liberation. In contrast to the veneration of Western ideas and ideals by many integrationists of the 1950s, Black Power ideologues emphasized the African cultural past as the true heritage of African Americans. The acknowledgment and appreciation of that heritage, which had too often been denigrated by African Americans themselves as well as by Euro-Americans, was a major tenet of the revolutionary movements of the period. Many blacks affirmed their African roots by changing their "slave names" to African names, and by wearing Afro styles and African clothing. Yet, ideologues of the period also lambasted older African Americans, opposing them to the lofty mythical models of the ancient past. These older men and women, they claimed, had become Uncle Toms and Aunt Jemimas who displayed little awareness of their culture and who, as a result of their slave past, had internalized the white man's view of blacks. So while these 1960s ideologues extolled an unknown ancient history, they denigrated the known and recent past. The tendency to idealize an ancient African past while ignoring the recent African American past still persists in the Afrocentric movements of the 1990s.

In contrast to that tendency, Walker's "Everyday Use" is dedicated to "your grandmama." And the story is told by a woman many African Americans would recognize as their grandmama, that supposedly backward Southern ancestor the cultural nationalists of the North probably visited during the summers of their youth and probably considered behind the times. Walker stresses those physical qualities which suggest such a person, qualities often demeaned by cultural nationalists. For this grandmama, like the stereotypical mammy of slavery, is "a large big-boned woman with rough, man-working hands," who wears "flannel nightgowns to bed and overalls during the day," and whose "fat keeps [her] hot in zero weather." Nor is this grandmama politically conscious according to the fashion of the day; she never had an education after the second grade, she knows nothing about African names, and she eats pork. In having the grandmama tell this story, Walker gives voice to an entire maternal ancestry often silenced by the political rhetoric of the period. Indeed, Walker tells us in "In Search of Our Mothers' Gardens" that her writing is part of her mother's legacy to her, that many of her stories are based on stories *her* mother told her. Thus, Walker's writing is her way of breaking silences and stereotypes about her grandmothers', mothers', sisters' lives. In effect, her work is a literary continuation of a distinctly oral tradition in which African American women have been and still are pivotal participants.

Alice Walker is well aware of the restrictions of the African American Southern past, for she is the eighth child of Georgia sharecroppers. Born in 1944, she grew up during the period when, as she put it, apartheid existed in America. For in the 1940s and 1950s, when segregation was the law of the South, opportunities for economic and social advancement were legally denied to Southern blacks. Walker was fortunate to come to adulthood during the social and political movements of the late fifties and sixties. Of her siblings, only she, and a slightly older sister, Molly, were able even to imagine the possibility of moving beyond the poverty of their parents. It is unlikely that Alice Walker would have been able to go to college—first at Spelman, the African American women's college in Atlanta, and then at Sarah Lawrence, the white women's college near New York City—if it had not been for the changes that came about as a result of the Civil Rights Movement. Nor is it likely that she, a Southern black woman from a poor family, would have been able to become the writer that she did without the changes resulting from the ferment of the Black and Women's Movements of the 1960s and early 1970s.

While Walker was a participant in these movements, she was also one of their most astute critics. As a Southerner, she was aware of the ways in which black Southern culture was often thought of as backward by predominantly Northern Black Power ideologues, even as they proclaimed their love for black people. She was also acutely aware of the ways in which women were oppressed within the Black Power Movement itself, even as the very culture its participants revered was so often passed on by women. Walker had also visited Africa during her junior year of college and had personally experienced the gap between the Black Power advocates' idealization of Africa and the reality of the African societies she visited.

. . .

Names are extremely important in African and African American culture as a means of indicating a person's spirit. During the 1960s Walker criticized the tendency among some African Americans to give up the names their parents gave them—names which embodied the history of their recent past—for African names that did not relate to a single person they knew. Hence the grandmama in "Everyday Use" is amazed that Dee would give up her name for the name Wangero. For Dee was the name of her great-grandmother, a woman who had kept her family together against great odds. Wangero might have sounded authentically African but it had no relationship to a person she knew, nor to the personal history that had sustained her.

• • •

In "Everyday Use," by contrasting a sister who has the opportunity to go to college with a sister who stays at home, Walker reminds us of the challenges that contemporary African American women face as they discover what it means to be truly educated. The same concern appears in many of her works. For example, in "For My Sister Molly Who in the Fifties," she explores the conflicts that can result from an education that takes a woman away from her cultural source. Like Molly, Dee/Wangero in "Everyday Use" is embarrassed by her folk. She has been to the North, wears an Afro, and knows the correct political rhetoric of the 1960s, but she has little regard for her relatives who have helped to create that heritage. Thus, she does not know how to quilt and can only conceive of her family's quilts as priceless artifacts, as things, which she intends to hang on her wall as a means of demonstrating to others that she has "heritage." On the other hand, Maggie, the supposedly uneducated sister, who has been nowhere beyond the supposedly uneducated black South, loves and understands her family and can appreciate its history. She knows how to quilt and would put the precious quilts to "everyday use," which is precisely what, Walker suggests, one needs to do with one's heritage. For Maggie, the quilts are an embodiment of the spirit her folks have passed on to her.

From introduction to *Everyday Use*

Houston A. Baker (b. 1943)
and Charlotte Pierce-Baker (b. 1943)

Stylish vs. Sacred in "Everyday Use"   1985

The Johnson women, who populate the generations represented in Walker's short story "Everyday Use," are inhabitants of southern cabins who have always worked with "scraps" and seen what they could make of them. The result of their labor has been a succession of mothers and daughters surviving the ignominies of Jim Crow life and passing on ancestral blessings to descendants. The guardians of the Johnson homestead when the story commences are the mother—"a large, big-boned woman with rough, man-working hands"—and her daughter Maggie, who has remained with her "chin on chest, eyes on ground, feet in shuffle, ever since the fire that burned the other house to the ground" ten or twelve years ago. The mood at the story's beginning is one of ritualistic "waiting": "I will wait for her in the yard that Maggie and I made so clean and wavy yesterday afternoon." The subject awaited is the other daughter, Dee. Not only has the yard (as ritual ground) been prepared for the arrival of a goddess, but the sensibilities and costumes of Maggie and her mother have been appropriately attuned for the occasion. The mother daydreams of television shows where parents and children are suddenly—and pleasantly—reunited, banal shows where chatty hosts oversee tearful reunions. In her fantasy, she weighs a hundred pounds less, is several shades brighter in complexion, and possesses a devastatingly quick tongue. She returns abruptly to real life meditation, reflecting on her own heroic, agrarian accomplishments in slaughtering hogs and cattle and preparing their meat for winter nourishment. She is a robust provider who has gone to the people of her church and raised money to send her light-complexioned, lithe-figured, and ever-dissatisfied daughter Dee to college. Today, as she waits in the purified yard, she notes the stark differences between Maggie and Dee and recalls how the "last dingy gray board of the house [fell] in toward the red-hot brick chimney" when her former domicile burned. Maggie was scarred horribly by the fire, but Dee, who had hated the house with an intense fury, stood "off under the sweet gum tree . . . a look of concentration on her face." A scarred and dull Maggie, who has been kept at home and confined to everyday offices, has but one reaction to the fiery and vivacious arrival of her sister: "I hear Maggie suck in her breath. 'Uhnnnh,' is what it sounds like. Like when you see the wriggling end of a snake just in front of your foot on the road. 'Uhnnnh.'"

Indeed, the question raised by Dee's energetic arrival is whether there are words adequate to her flair, her brightness, her intense colorfulness of style which veritably blocks the sun. She wears "a dress so loud it hurts my eyes. There are yellows and oranges enough to throw back the light of the sun. I feel my whole face warming from the heat waves it throws out." Dee is both serpent and fire introduced with bursting esprit into the calm pasture that contains the Johnsons' tin-roofed, three-room, windowless shack and grazing cows. She has joined the radical, black nationalists of the 1960s and 1970s, changing her name from Dee to Wangero and cultivating a suddenly fashionable, or stylish, interest in what she passionately describes as her "heritage." If there is one quality that Dee (Wangero) possesses in abundance, it is "style": "At sixteen she had a style of her own: and knew what style was."

But in her stylishness, Dee is not an example of the indigenous rapping and styling out of Afro-America. Rather, she is manipulated by the style-makers, the fashion designers whose semiotics the French writer Roland Barthes has so aptly characterized. "Style" for Dee is the latest vogue—the most recent fantasy perpetuated by American media. When she left for college, her mother had tried to give her a quilt whose making began with her grandmother Dee, but the bright daughter felt such patched coverings were "old-fashioned and out of style." She has returned at the commencement of "Everyday Use," however, as one who now purports to know the value of the work of black women as holy patchers.

The dramatic conflict of the story surrounds the definition of holiness. The ritual purification of earth and expectant atmosphere akin to that of Beckett's famous drama ("I will wait for her in the yard that Maggie and I made so clean and wavy yesterday afternoon.") prepare us for the narrator's epiphanic experience at the story's conclusion.

Near the end of "Everyday Use," the mother (who is the tale's narrator) realizes that Dee (a.k.a. Wangero) is a *fantasy* child, a perpetrator and victim of: "words, lies, other folks's habits." The energetic daughter is as frivolously careless of other people's lives as the fiery conflagration that she had watched ten years previously. Assured by the makers of American fashion that "black" is currently "beautiful," she has conformed her own "style" to that notion. Hers is a trendy "blackness" cultivated as "art" and costume. She wears "a dress down to the ground . . . bracelets dangling and making noises when she moves her arm up to shake the folds of the dress out of her armpits." And she says of quilts she has removed from a trunk at the foot of her mother's bed: "Maggie can't appreciate these quilts! She'd probably be backward enough to put them to everyday use." "Art" is, thus, juxtaposed with "everyday use" in Walker's short story, and the fire goddess Dee, who has achieved literacy only to burn "us with a lot of knowledge we didn't necessarily need to know," is revealed as a perpetuator of institutional theories of aesthetics.

• • •

Quilts designed for everyday use, pieced wholes defying symmetry and pattern, are signs of the scarred generations of women who have always been alien to a world of literate words and stylish fantasies. The crafted fabric of Walker's story is the very weave of blues and jazz traditions in the Afro-American community, daringly improvisational modes that confront breaks in the continuity of melody (or theme) by riffing. The asymmetrical quilts of southern black women are like the off-centered stomping of the jazz solo or the innovative musical showmanship of the blues interlude. They speak a world in which the deceptively shuffling Maggie is capable of a quick change into goddess, an unlikely holy figure whose dues are paid in full. Dee's anger at her mother is occasioned principally by the mother's insistence that paid dues make Maggie a more likely bearer of sacredness, tradition, and true value than the "brighter" sister. "You just don't understand," she says to her mother. Her assessment is surely correct where institutional theories and systems of "art" are concerned. The mother's cognition contains no categories for framed art. The mother works according to an entirely different scale of use and value, finally assigning proper weight to the virtues of Maggie and to the ancestral importance of the pieced quilts that she has kept out of use for so many years. Smarting, perhaps, from Dee's designation of the quilts as "old-fashioned," the mother has buried the covers away in a trunk. At the end of Walker's story, however, she has become aware of her own mistaken value judgments, and she pays homage that is due to Maggie. The unlikely daughter is a *griot*° of the vernacular who remembers actors and events in a distinctively black "historical" drama.

Before Dee departs, she "put on some sunglasses that hid everything above the tip of her nose and her chin." Maggie smiles at the crude symbolism implicit in this act, for she has always known that her sister saw "through a glass darkly." But it is the mother's conferral of an ancestral blessing (signaled by her deposit of the quilts in Maggie's lap) that constitutes the occasion for the daughter's first "real smile." Maggie knows that it is only communal recognition by elders of the tribe that confers ancestral privileges on succeeding generations. The mother's holy recognition of the scarred daughter's sacred status as quilter is the best gift of a hard-pressed womankind to the fragmented goddess of the present.

At the conclusion of "Everyday Use," which is surely a fitting precursor to *The Color Purple,* with its sewing protagonist and its scenes of sisterly quilting, Maggie and her mother relax in the ritual yard after the dust of Dee's departing car has settled. They dip snuff in the manner of African confreres sharing cola nuts. The moment is past when a putatively "new" generation has confronted scenes of black, everyday life. A change has taken place, but it is a change best described by Amiri Baraka's designation for Afro-American music's various styles and discontinuities. The change in Walker's story is the "changing same." What has been reaffirmed at the story's conclusion is the value of the quiltmaker's motion and strategy in the precincts of a continuously undemocratic South.

From "Patches: Quilts and Community in
Alice Walker's 'Everyday Use'"

---

griot: African storyteller, guardian of the people's history [authors' note].

Elaine Showalter (b. 1941)

Quilt as Metaphor in "Everyday Use" 1991

For Alice Walker, piecing and quilting have come to represent both the aesthetic heritage of Afro-American women and the model for what she calls a "Womanist," or black feminist, writing of reconciliation and connection; in her essay "In Search of Our Mothers' Gardens," Walker identified the quilt as a major form of creative expression for black women in the South. "In the Smithsonian Institution in Washington, D.C.," Walker writes,

> there hangs a quilt unlike another in the world. In fanciful, inspired, and yet simple and identifiable figures, it portrays the story of the Crucifixion . . . Though it follows no known pattern of quiltmaking, and though it is made of bits and pieces of worthless rags, it is obviously the work of a person of powerful imagination and deep spiritual feeling. Below this quilt I saw a note that says it was made by "an anonymous Black woman in Alabama a hundred years ago."

The quilt Walker is describing from memory is in fact one of two extant narrative quilts by Harriet Powers (1836–1911), born a slave in Georgia. The Powers quilt at the Smithsonian illustrates Bible stories, while the one in the Boston Museum of Fine Arts mingles Bible tales with folklore and astronomical events such as shooting stars and meteor showers.[1] For Walker, genuine imagination and feeling can be recognized without the legitimacy conferred by the labels of "art" or the approval of museums. Paradoxically this heritage survives because it has been preserved in museums; but it can be a living art only if it is practiced.

The theme of Walker's quilt aesthetic is most explicitly presented in her early story "Everyday Use." Like much of her work, it uses a contrast between two sisters to get at the meaning of the concept of "heritage": a privileged one who escapes from Southern black culture, and a suffering one who stays or is left behind. The younger daughter, Maggie, has stayed at home since she was horribly scarred in a house fire ten years before. Dee is the bright and confident sister, the one with "faultfinding power." Dee has learned fast how to produce herself: "At sixteen she had a style of her own: and knew what style was." Now having chosen the style of radical black nationalism, her name changed to "Wangero," and spouting Swahili, Dee returns to claim her heritage from her mother in the form of "folk art": the worn benches made by her father, the butter churn whittled by an uncle, and especially the quilts pieced by her grandmother. "Maggie can't appreciate these quilts," Dee exclaims. "She'd probably be backward enough to put them to everyday use." Walker thus establishes a contrast between "everyday use" and "institutional theories of aesthetics."[2] In a moment of epiphanic insight, the mother, who has always been intimidated by Dee's intelligence and sophistication, decides to give the quilts to Maggie. "She can always make some more," the mother responds. "Maggie knows how to quilt." Maggie cannot speak glibly about her "heritage" or about "priceless" artifacts, but, unlike Dee, she understands the quilt as a process rather than as a commodity; she can read its meaning in a way Dee never will, because she knows the contexts of its pieces, and loves the women who have made it. The meaning of an aesthetic heritage, according

---

[1] See Marie Jean Adams, "The Harriet Powers Pictorial Quilts," *Black Art* 3 (1982) 12–28.
[2] Houston A. Baker and Charlotte Pierce-Baker, "Patches: Quilts and Community in Alice Walker's 'Everyday Use.'" *Southern Review* 21:3 (Summer 1985) 716.

to Walker's story, lies in continual renewal rather than in the rhetoric of nostalgia or appreciation. In writing *The Color Purple*, Walker herself took up quilt-making as well as using it as a central metaphor in the novel.

From Sister's Choice: Tradition and Change in American Women's Writing

■ WRITING *effectively*

TOPICS FOR WRITING ABOUT "YOUNG GOODMAN BROWN"

1. It is sometimes suggested that "Young Goodman Brown" is a story about an innocent young man who becomes disillusioned about human nature. How innocent is Goodman Brown at the beginning of the tale? Use details from the text to back up your conclusion.
2. Have you ever had to come to terms with the discovery of weakness or wrongdoing on the part of someone you admired? What was your initial reaction? What ultimate change was there, if any, in your feelings about that person?
3. The most hotly debated aspect of "Young Goodman Brown" is, of course, whether the events in the forest actually took place. Does it matter to your understanding and appreciation of the story that the issue be settled one way or the other? Why or why not?
4. At the end of the tale, Goodman Brown is withdrawn and isolated from everyone around him, including his wife and children. Is he a better person than everyone else, or a worse one? Refer as specifically as possible to the text itself in explaining the reasons for your conclusion.

TOPICS FOR WRITING ABOUT "THE YELLOW WALLPAPER"

1. "The Yellow Wallpaper" is cast in the form of the journal written by its central character. Consider how the use of this narrative device enriches—or impoverishes—the story.
2. Thomas L. Erskine and Connie L. Richards have written of "the aesthetic problem with much of Gilman's literary work; often her sociopolitical agenda overwhelms the characters, who become one-dimensional mouthpieces for different ideas. Propaganda all too often threatens art." Discuss whether or not you think these concerns apply to "The Yellow Wallpaper."
3. Think of a contemporary issue that involves women's feelings of being confined or thwarted by the male power structure. Then write a brief treatment of that issue in the style of "The Yellow Wallpaper."
4. Discuss the larger implications of the conclusion of "The Yellow Wallpaper." In the end, has the narrator triumphed by escaping her oppression, or has she been crushed by it?

TOPICS FOR WRITING ABOUT "EVERYDAY USE"

1. Write a brief version of the encounter in "Everyday Use" from Dee's point of view. Is it possible to present a nonironic affirmation of her values over those of her mother and sister? Why or why not?
2. Have you grown apart from a friend or relative with whom you once had a close relationship? Imagine an encounter with that person, and write a first-person description of it from the other person's point of view.
3. Alice Walker has suggested that one of her principal intentions in her writing is "nurturing and healing the reader." Is "nurturing and healing" one of the primary aims of "Everyday Use"?
4. How does the use of a first-person narrator function in "Everyday Use"? Are there places in which the reader is expected to understand more than the narrator does, or is everything that she says and sees to be accepted at face value?

12 STORIES FOR FURTHER READING

*The novel tends to tell us everything, whereas the short
story tells us only one thing and that intensely.*

—V. S. PRITCHETT

Chinua Achebe

Dead Men's Path

(1953) 1972

Chinua Achebe was born in Ogidi, a village in
eastern Nigeria, in 1930. His father was a
missionary schoolteacher, and Achebe had a
devout Christian upbringing. A member of the
Ibo tribe, the future writer grew up speaking
Igbo, but at the age of eight, he began learning
English. He went abroad to study at London
University but returned to Africa to complete
his B.A. at the University College of Ibadan in
1953. Achebe worked for years in Nigerian
radio. Shortly after Nigeria's independence
from Great Britain in 1963, civil war broke
out, and the new nation split in two. Achebe
left his job to join the Ministry of Information
for Biafra, the new country created from eastern
Nigeria. It was not until 1970 that the bloody

Chinua Achebe

civil war ended. Approximately one million Ibos lay dead from war, disease, and starvation
as the defeated Biafrans reunited with Nigeria. Achebe is often considered Africa's
premier novelist. His novels include Things Fall Apart (1958), No Longer at Ease
(1962), A Man of the People (1966), and Anthills of the Savannah (1987). His
short stories have been collected in Girls At War (1972). He has also published poetry,
children's stories, and several volumes of essays, the most recent of which is Home and
Exile (2000). In 1990 Achebe suffered massive injuries in a car accident outside Lagos
that left him paralyzed from the waist down. He currently teaches at Bard College in upstate
New York. In 1999 he visited Nigeria again after a deliberate nine-year absence to protest
government dictatorship, and his homecoming became a national event. In 2007 he was
awarded the second Man Booker International Prize for his lifetime contribution to world
literature.

Michael Obi's hopes were fulfilled much earlier than he had expected. He was appointed headmaster of Ndume Central School in January 1949. It had always been an unprogressive school, so the Mission authorities decided to send a young and energetic man to run it. Obi accepted this responsibility with enthusiasm. He had many wonderful ideas and this was an opportunity to put them into practice. He had had sound secondary school education which designated him a "pivotal teacher" in the official records and set him apart from the other headmasters in the mission field. He was outspoken in his condemnation of the narrow views of these older and often less-educated ones.

"We shall make a good job of it, shan't we?" he asked his young wife when they first heard the joyful news of his promotion.

"We shall do our best," she replied. "We shall have such beautiful gardens and everything will be just *modern* and delightful . . ." In their two years of married life she had become completely infected by his passion for "modern methods" and his denigration of "these old and superannuated people in the teaching field who would be better employed as traders in the Onitsha market." She began to see herself already as the admired wife of the young headmaster, the queen of the school.

The wives of the other teachers would envy her position. She would set the fashion in everything . . . Then, suddenly, it occurred to her that there might not be other wives. Wavering between hope and fear, she asked her husband, looking anxiously at him.

"All our colleagues are young and unmarried," he said with enthusiasm which for once she did not share. "Which is a good thing," he continued. 5

"Why?"

"Why? They will give all their time and energy to the school."

Nancy was downcast. For a few minutes she became skeptical about the new school; but it was only for a few minutes. Her little personal misfortune could not blind her to her husband's happy prospects. She looked at him as he sat folded up in a chair. He was stoop-shouldered and looked frail. But he sometimes surprised people with sudden bursts of physical energy. In his present posture, however, all his bodily strength seemed to have retired behind his deep-set eyes, giving them an extraordinary power of penetration. He was only twenty-six, but looked thirty or more. On the whole, he was not unhandsome.

"A penny for your thoughts, Mike," said Nancy after a while, imitating the woman's magazine she read.

"I was thinking what a grand opportunity we've got at last to show these people 10 how a school should be run."

Ndume School was backward in every sense of the word. Mr. Obi put his whole life into the work, and his wife hers too. He had two aims. A high standard of teaching was insisted upon, and the school compound was to be turned into a place of beauty. Nancy's dream-gardens came to life with the coming of the rains, and blossomed. Beautiful hibiscus and allamanda hedges in brilliant red and yellow marked out the carefully tended school compound from the rank neighborhood bushes.

One evening as Obi was admiring his work he was scandalized to see an old woman from the village hobble right across the compound, through a marigold flower-bed and the hedges. On going up there he found faint signs of an almost disused path from the village across the school compound to the bush on the other side.

"It amazes me," said Obi to one of his teachers who had been three years in the school, "that you people allowed the villagers to make use of this footpath. It is simply incredible." He shook his head.

"The path," said the teacher apologetically, "appears to be very important to them. Although it is hardly used, it connects the village shrine with their place of burial."

"And what has that got to do with the school?" asked the headmaster. 15

"Well, I don't know," replied the other with a shrug of the shoulders. "But I remember there was a big row some time ago when we attempted to close it."

"That was some time ago. But it will not be used now," said Obi as he walked away. "What will the Government Education Officer think of this when he comes to inspect the school next week? The villagers might, for all I know, decide to use the schoolroom for a pagan ritual during the inspection."

Heavy sticks were planted closely across the path at the two places where it entered and left the school premises. These were further strengthened with barbed wire.

Three days later the village priest of *Ani* called on the headmaster. He was an old man and walked with a slight stoop. He carried a stout walking-stick which he usually tapped on the floor, by way of emphasis, each time he made a new point in his argument.

"I have heard," he said after the usual exchange of cordialities, "that our ancestral 20 footpath has recently been closed . . ."

"Yes," replied Mr. Obi. "We cannot allow people to make a highway of our school compound."

"Look here, my son," said the priest bringing down his walking-stick, "this path was here before you were born and before your father was born. The whole life of this village depends on it. Our dead relatives depart by it and our ancestors visit us by it. But most important, it is the path of children coming in to be born . . ."

Mr. Obi listened with a satisfied smile on his face.

"The whole purpose of our school," he said finally, "is to eradicate just such beliefs as that. Dead men do not require footpaths. The whole idea is just fantastic. Our duty is to teach your children to laugh at such ideas."

"What you say may be true," replied the priest, "but we follow the practices of 25 our fathers. If you reopen the path we shall have nothing to quarrel about. What I always say is: let the hawk perch and let the eagle perch." He rose to go.

"I am sorry," said the young headmaster. "But the school compound cannot be a thoroughfare. It is against our regulations. I would suggest your constructing another path, skirting our premises. We can even get our boys to help in building it. I don't suppose the ancestors will find the little detour too burdensome."

"I have no more words to say," said the old priest, already outside.

Two days later a young woman in the village died in childbed. A diviner was immediately consulted and he prescribed heavy sacrifices to propitiate ancestors insulted by the fence.

Obi woke up next morning among the ruins of his work. The beautiful hedges were torn up not just near the path but right round the school, the flowers trampled to death and one of the school buildings pulled down . . . That day, the white Supervisor came to inspect the school and wrote a nasty report on the state of the premises but more seriously about the "tribal-war situation developing between the school and the village, arising in part from the misguided zeal of the new headmaster."

Sherman Alexie

This Is What It Means to Say Phoenix, Arizona   1993

Sherman Alexie

Sherman Alexie was born in 1966 on the Spokane Indian Reservation in Wellpinit, Washington. Hydrocephalic at birth, he underwent surgery at the age of six months. At first he was expected not to survive; when that prognosis proved wrong, it was predicted, again wrongly, that he would be severely retarded. Alexie attended Gonzaga University in Spokane and graduated from the University of Washington with a degree in American studies. His first book, a collection of poems called The Business of Fancydancing, *appeared in 1991, and he has published prolifically since then, averaging a book a year. He is the author of ten volumes of poetry and two novels for young adults, as well as three collections of stories—*The Lone Ranger and Tonto Fistfight in Heaven *(1993),* The Toughest Indian in the World *(2000), and* Ten Little Indians *(2003)— and three novels—*Reservation Blues *(1995),* Indian Killer *(1996), and* Flight *(2007). In addition to his writing, Alexie won the World Heavyweight Poetry Bout competition an unprecedented four consecutive times (1998–2001); he has appeared on television discussion programs hosted by Bill Maher, Bill Moyers, and Jim Lehrer (a 1998 "Dialogue on Race" whose participants also included President Bill Clinton); he has performed frequently as a stand-up comedian; and he co-produced and wrote the 1998 feature film* Smoke Signals, *based on "This Is What It Means to Say Phoenix, Arizona." Alexie lives with his wife and two sons in Seattle, Washington.*

Just after Victor lost his job at the BIA,° he also found out that his father had died of a heart attack in Phoenix, Arizona. Victor hadn't seen his father in a few years, only talked to him on the telephone once or twice, but there still was a genetic pain, which was soon to be pain as real and immediate as a broken bone.

Victor didn't have any money. Who does have money on a reservation, except the cigarette and fireworks salespeople? His father had a savings account waiting to be claimed, but Victor needed to find a way to get to Phoenix. Victor's mother was just as poor as he was, and the rest of his family didn't have any use at all for him. So Victor called the Tribal Council.

"Listen," Victor said. "My father just died. I need some money to get to Phoenix to make arrangements."

"Now, Victor," the council said. "You know we're having a difficult time financially."

"But I thought the council had special funds set aside for stuff like this."   5

"Now, Victor, we do have some money available for the proper return of tribal members' bodies. But I don't think we have enough to bring your father all the way back from Phoenix."

BIA: Bureau of Indian Affairs, a federal agency responsible for management of Indian lands and concerns.

"Well," Victor said. "It ain't going to cost all that much. He had to be cremated. Things were kind of ugly. He died of a heart attack in his trailer and nobody found him for a week. It was really hot, too. You get the picture."

"Now, Victor, we're sorry for your loss and the circumstances. But we can really only afford to give you one hundred dollars."

"That's not even enough for a plane ticket."

"Well, you might consider driving down to Phoenix." 10

"I don't have a car. Besides, I was going to drive my father's pickup back up here."

"Now, Victor," the council said. "We're sure there is somebody who could drive you to Phoenix. Or is there somebody who could lend you the rest of the money?"

"You know there ain't nobody around with that kind of money."

"Well, we're sorry, Victor, but that's the best we can do."

Victor accepted the Tribal Council's offer. What else could he do? So he signed 15 the proper papers, picked up his check, and walked over to the Trading Post to cash it.

While Victor stood in line, he watched Thomas Builds-the-Fire standing near the magazine rack, talking to himself. Like he always did. Thomas was a storyteller that nobody wanted to listen to. That's like being a dentist in a town where everybody has false teeth.

Victor and Thomas Builds-the-Fire were the same age, had grown up and played in the dirt together. Ever since Victor could remember, it was Thomas who always had something to say.

Once, when they were seven years old, when Victor's father still lived with the family, Thomas closed his eyes and told Victor this story: "Your father's heart is weak. He is afraid of his own family. He is afraid of you. Late at night he sits in the dark. Watches the television until there's nothing but that white noise. Sometimes he feels like he wants to buy a motorcycle and ride away. He wants to run and hide. He doesn't want to be found."

Thomas Builds-the-Fire had known that Victor's father was going to leave, knew it before anyone. Now Victor stood in the Trading Post with a one-hundred-dollar check in his hand, wondering if Thomas knew that Victor's father was dead, if he knew what was going to happen next.

Just then Thomas looked at Victor, smiled, and walked over to him. 20

"Victor, I'm sorry about your father," Thomas said.

"How did you know about it?" Victor asked.

"I heard it on the wind. I heard it from the birds. I felt it in the sunlight. Also, your mother was just in here crying."

"Oh," Victor said and looked around the Trading Post. All the other Indians stared, surprised that Victor was even talking to Thomas. Nobody talked to Thomas anymore because he told the same damn stories over and over again. Victor was embarrassed, but he thought that Thomas might be able to help him. Victor felt a sudden need for tradition.

"I can lend you the money you need," Thomas said suddenly. "But you have to 25 take me with you."

"I can't take your money," Victor said. "I mean, I haven't hardly talked to you in years. We're not really friends anymore."

"I didn't say we were friends. I said you had to take me with you."

"Let me think about it."

Victor went home with his one hundred dollars and sat at the kitchen table. He held his head in his hands and thought about Thomas Builds-the-Fire, remembered little details, tears and scars, the bicycle they shared for a summer, so many stories.

*

Thomas Builds-the-Fire sat on the bicycle, waited in Victor's yard. He was ten   30
years old and skinny. His hair was dirty because it was the Fourth of July.

"Victor," Thomas yelled. "Hurry up. We're going to miss the fireworks."

After a few minutes, Victor ran out of his house, jumped the porch railing, and
landed gracefully on the sidewalk.

"And the judges award him a 9.95, the highest score of the summer," Thomas
said, clapped, laughed.

"That was perfect, cousin," Victor said. "And it's my turn to ride the bike."

Thomas gave up the bike and they headed for the fairgrounds. It was nearly dark   35
and the fireworks were about to start.

"You know," Thomas said. "It's strange how us Indians celebrate the Fourth of
July. It ain't like it was *our* independence everybody was fighting for."

"You think about things too much," Victor said. "It's just supposed to be fun.
Maybe Junior will be there."

"Which Junior? Everybody on this reservation is named Junior."

And they both laughed.

The fireworks were small, hardly more than a few bottle rockets and a fountain.   40
But it was enough for two Indian boys. Years later, they would need much more.

Afterwards, sitting in the dark, fighting off mosquitoes, Victor turned to Thomas
Builds-the-Fire.

"Hey," Victor said. "Tell me a story."

Thomas closed his eyes and told this story: "There were these two Indian boys who
wanted to be warriors. But it was too late to be warriors in the old way. All the horses
were gone. So the two Indian boys stole a car and drove to the city. They parked the
stolen car in front of the police station and then hitchhiked back home to the reservation. When they got back, all their friends cheered and their parents' eyes shone
with pride. *You were very brave,* everybody said to the two Indian boys. *Very brave.*"

"Ya-hey," Victor said. "That's a good one. I wish I could be a warrior."

"Me, too," Thomas said.   45

They went home together in the dark, Thomas on the bike now, Victor on foot.
They walked through shadows and light from streetlamps.

"We've come a long ways," Thomas said. "We have outdoor lighting."

"All I need is the stars," Victor said. "And besides, you still think about things
too much."

They separated then, each headed for home, both laughing all the way.

Victor sat at his kitchen table. He counted his one hundred dollars again and   50
again. He knew he needed more to make it to Phoenix and back. He knew he needed
Thomas Builds-the-Fire. So he put his money in his wallet and opened the front door
to find Thomas on the porch.

"Ya-hey, Victor," Thomas said. "I knew you'd call me."

Thomas walked into the living room and sat down on Victor's favorite chair.

"I've got some money saved up," Thomas said. "It's enough to get us down there,
but you have to get us back."

"I've got this hundred dollars," Victor said. "And my dad had a savings account
I'm going to claim."

"How much in your dad's account?"   55

"Enough. A few hundred."

"Sounds good. When we leaving?"

When they were fifteen and had long since stopped being friends, Victor and Thomas got into a fistfight. That is, Victor was really drunk and beat Thomas up for no reason at all. All the other Indian boys stood around and watched it happen. Junior was there and so were Lester, Seymour, and a lot of others. The beating might have gone on until Thomas was dead if Norma Many Horses hadn't come along and stopped it.

"Hey, you boys," Norma yelled and jumped out of her car. "Leave him alone."

If it had been someone else, even another man, the Indian boys would've just ig- 60
nored the warnings. But Norma was a warrior. She was powerful. She could have picked up any two of the boys and smashed their skulls together. But worse than that, she would have dragged them all over to some tipi and made them listen to some elder tell a dusty old story.

The Indian boys scattered, and Norma walked over to Thomas and picked him up.

"Hey, little man, are you okay?" she asked.

Thomas gave her a thumbs up.

"Why they always picking on you?"

Thomas shook his head, closed his eyes, but no stories came to him, no words or 65
music. He just wanted to go home, to lie in his bed and let his dreams tell his stories for him.

Thomas Builds-the-Fire and Victor sat next to each other in the airplane, coach section. A tiny white woman had the window seat. She was busy twisting her body into pretzels. She was flexible.

"I have to ask," Thomas said, and Victor closed his eyes in embarrassment.

"Don't," Victor said.

"Excuse me, miss," Thomas asked. "Are you a gymnast or something?"

"There's no something about it," she said. "I was first alternate on the 1980 70
Olympic team."

"Really?" Thomas asked.

"Really."

"I mean, you used to be a world-class athlete?" Thomas asked.

"My husband still thinks I am."

Thomas Builds-the-Fire smiled. She was a mental gymnast, too. She pulled her 75
leg straight up against her body so that she could've kissed her kneecap.

"I wish I could do that," Thomas said.

Victor was ready to jump out of the plane. Thomas, that crazy Indian storyteller with ratty old braids and broken teeth, was flirting with a beautiful Olympic gymnast. Nobody back home on the reservation would ever believe it.

"Well," the gymnast said. "It's easy. Try it."

Thomas grabbed at his leg and tried to pull it up into the same position as the gymnast. He couldn't even come close, which made Victor and the gymnast laugh.

"Hey," she asked. "You two are Indian, right?" 80

"Full-blood," Victor said.

"Not me," Thomas said. "I'm half magician on my mother's side and half clown on my father's."

They all laughed.

"What are your names?" she asked.

"Victor and Thomas."   85

"Mine is Cathy. Pleased to meet you all."

The three of them talked for the duration of the flight. Cathy the gymnast complained about the government, how they screwed the 1980 Olympic team by boycotting.°

"Sounds like you all got a lot in common with Indians," Thomas said.

Nobody laughed.

After the plane landed in Phoenix and they had all found their way to the termi-   90
nal, Cathy the gymnast smiled and waved good-bye.

"She was really nice," Thomas said.

"Yeah, but everybody talks to everybody on airplanes," Victor said. "It's too bad we can't always be that way."

"You always used to tell me I think too much," Thomas said. "Now it sounds like you do."

"Maybe I caught it from you."

"Yeah."   95

Thomas and Victor rode in a taxi to the trailer where Victor's father died.

"Listen," Victor said as they stopped in front of the trailer. "I never told you I was sorry for beating you up that time."

"Oh, it was nothing. We were just kids and you were drunk."

"Yeah, but I'm still sorry."

"That's all right."   100

Victor paid for the taxi and the two of them stood in the hot Phoenix summer. They could smell the trailer.

"This ain't going to be nice," Victor said. "You don't have to go in."

"You're going to need help."

Victor walked to the front door and opened it. The stink rolled out and made them both gag. Victor's father had lain in that trailer for a week in hundred-degree temperatures before anyone found him. And the only reason anyone found him was because of the smell. They needed dental records to identify him. That's exactly what the coroner said. They needed dental records.

"Oh, man," Victor said. "I don't know if I can do this."   105

"Well, then don't."

"But there might be something valuable in there."

"I thought his money was in the bank."

"It is. I was talking about pictures and letters and stuff like that."

"Oh," Thomas said as he held his breath and followed Victor into the trailer.   110

When Victor was twelve, he stepped into an underground wasp nest. His foot was caught in the hole, and no matter how hard he struggled, Victor couldn't pull free. He might have died there, stung a thousand times, if Thomas Builds-the-Fire had not come by.

they screwed the 1980 Olympic team by boycotting: in an international movement led by the United States at the direction of President Jimmy Carter, some sixty nations boycotted the 1980 Summer Olympic Games in Moscow as a protest against the Soviet invasion of Afghanistan in December 1979.

"Run," Thomas yelled and pulled Victor's foot from the hole. They ran then, hard as they ever had, faster than Billy Mills, faster than Jim Thorpe,° faster than the wasps could fly.

Victor and Thomas ran until they couldn't breathe, ran until it was cold and dark outside, ran until they were lost and it took hours to find their way home. All the way back, Victor counted his stings.

"Seven," Victor said. "My lucky number."

Victor didn't find much to keep in the trailer. Only a photo album and a stereo.   115
Everything else had that smell stuck in it or was useless anyway.

"I guess this is all," Victor said. "It ain't much."

"Better than nothing," Thomas said.

"Yeah, and I do have the pickup."

"Yeah," Thomas said. "It's in good shape."

"Dad was good about that stuff."   120

"Yeah, I remember your dad."

"Really?" Victor asked. "What do you remember?"

Thomas Builds-the-Fire closed his eyes and told this story: "I remember when I had this dream that told me to go to Spokane, to stand by the Falls in the middle of the city and wait for a sign. I knew I had to go there but I didn't have a car. Didn't have a license. I was only thirteen. So I walked all the way, took me all day, and I finally made it to the Falls. I stood there for an hour waiting. Then your dad came walking up. *What the hell are you doing here?* he asked me. I said, *Waiting for a vision.* Then your father said, *All you're going to get here is mugged.* So he drove me over to Denny's, bought me dinner, and then drove me home to the reservation. For a long time I was mad because I thought my dreams had lied to me. But they didn't. Your dad was my vision. *Take care of each other* is what my dreams were saying. *Take care of each other.*"

Victor was quiet for a long time. He searched his mind for memories of his father, found the good ones, found a few bad ones, added it all up, and smiled.

"My father never told me about finding you in Spokane," Victor said.   125

"He said he wouldn't tell anybody. Didn't want me to get in trouble. But he said I had to watch out for you as part of the deal."

"Really?"

"Really. Your father said you would need the help. He was right."

"That's why you came down here with me, isn't it?" Victor asked.

"I came because of your father."   130

Victor and Thomas climbed into the pickup, drove over to the bank, and claimed the three hundred dollars in the savings account.

Thomas Builds-the-Fire could fly.

Billy Mills . . . Jim Thorpe: William Mervin "Billy" Mills (born 1938), a member of the Sioux tribe, won a gold medal in the 10,000-meter run at the 1964 Summer Olympic Games in Tokyo, Japan. Jacobus Franciscus "Jim" Thorpe (1888–1953), of the Sac and Fox tribe, is widely regarded as one of the greatest American athletes of the twentieth century; he won gold medals in the pentathlon and decathlon at the 1912 Summer Olympic Games in Stockholm, Sweden. He also played professional football, baseball, and basketball.

Once, he jumped off the roof of the tribal school and flapped his arms like a crazy eagle. And he flew. For a second, he hovered, suspended above all the other Indian boys who were too smart or too scared to jump.

"He's flying," Junior yelled, and Seymour was busy looking for the trick wires or mirrors. But it was real. As real as the dirt when Thomas lost altitude and crashed to the ground.

He broke his arm in two places.   135

"He broke his wing," Victor chanted, and the other Indian boys joined in, made it a tribal song.

"He broke his wing, he broke his wing, he broke his wing," all the Indian boys chanted as they ran off, flapping their wings, wishing they could fly, too. They hated Thomas for his courage, his brief moment as a bird. Everybody has dreams about flying. Thomas flew.

One of his dreams came true for just a second, just enough to make it real.

Victor's father, his ashes, fit in one wooden box with enough left over to fill a cardboard box.

"He always was a big man," Thomas said.   140

Victor carried part of his father and Thomas carried the rest out to the pickup. They set him down carefully behind the seats, put a cowboy hat on the wooden box and a Dodgers cap on the cardboard box. That's the way it was supposed to be.

"Ready to head back home," Victor asked.

"It's going to be a long drive."

"Yeah, take a couple days, maybe."

"We can take turns," Thomas said.   145

"Okay," Victor said, but they didn't take turns. Victor drove for sixteen hours straight north, made it halfway up Nevada toward home before he finally pulled over.

"Hey, Thomas," Victor said. "You got to drive for a while."

"Okay."

Thomas Builds-the-Fire slid behind the wheel and started off down the road. All through Nevada, Thomas and Victor had been amazed at the lack of animal life, at the absence of water, of movement.

"Where is everything?" Victor had asked more than once.   150

Now when Thomas was finally driving they saw the first animal, maybe the only animal in Nevada. It was a long-eared jackrabbit.

"Look," Victor yelled. "It's alive."

Thomas and Victor were busy congratulating themselves on their discovery when the jackrabbit darted out into the road and under the wheels of the pickup.

"Stop the goddamn car," Victor yelled, and Thomas did stop, backed the pickup to the dead jackrabbit.

"Oh, man, he's dead," Victor said as he looked at the squashed animal.   155

"Really dead."

"The only thing alive in this whole state and we just killed it."

"I don't know," Thomas said. "I think it was suicide."

Victor looked around the desert, sniffed the air, felt the emptiness and loneli-ness, and nodded his head.

"Yeah," Victor said. "It had to be suicide."   160

"I can't believe this," Thomas said. "You drive for a thousand miles and there ain't even any bugs smashed on the windshield. I drive for ten seconds and kill the only living thing in Nevada."

"Yeah," Victor said. "Maybe I should drive."

"Maybe you should."

Thomas Builds-the-Fire walked through the corridors of the tribal school by himself. Nobody wanted to be anywhere near him because of all those stories. Story after story.

Thomas closed his eyes and this story came to him: "We are all given one thing 165 by which our lives are measured, one determination. Mine are the stories which can change or not change the world. It doesn't matter which as long as I continue to tell the stories. My father, he died on Okinawa in World War II, died fighting for this country, which had tried to kill him for years. My mother, she died giving birth to me, died while I was still inside her. She pushed me out into the world with her last breath. I have no brothers or sisters. I have only my stories which came to me before I even had the words to speak. I learned a thousand stories before I took my first thousand steps. They are all I have. It's all I can do."

Thomas Builds-the-Fire told his stories to all those who would stop and listen. He kept telling them long after people had stopped listening.

Victor and Thomas made it back to the reservation just as the sun was rising. It was the beginning of a new day on earth, but the same old shit on the reservation.

"Good morning," Thomas said.

"Good morning."

The tribe was waking up, ready for work, eating breakfast, reading the newspa- 170 per, just like everybody else does. Willene LeBret was out in her garden wearing a bathrobe. She waved when Thomas and Victor drove by.

"Crazy Indians made it," she said to herself and went back to her roses.

Victor stopped the pickup in front of Thomas Builds-the-Fire's HUD house.° They both yawned, stretched a little, shook dust from their bodies.

"I'm tired," Victor said.

"Of everything," Thomas added.

They both searched for words to end the journey. Victor needed to thank 175 Thomas for his help, for the money, and make the promise to pay it all back.

"Don't worry about the money," Thomas said. "It don't make any difference anyhow."

"Probably not, enit?"

"Nope."

Victor knew that Thomas would remain the crazy storyteller who talked to dogs and cars, who listened to the wind and pine trees. Victor knew that he couldn't really be friends with Thomas, even after all that had happened. It was cruel but it was real. As real as the ashes, as Victor's father, sitting behind the seats.

"I know how it is," Thomas said. "I know you ain't going to treat me any better than 180 you did before. I know your friends would give you too much shit about it."

Victor was ashamed of himself. Whatever happened to the tribal ties, the sense of community? The only real thing he shared with anybody was a bottle and broken dreams. He owed Thomas something, anything.

"Listen," Victor said and handed Thomas the cardboard box which contained half of his father. "I want you to have this."

HUD house: housing subsidized by the U.S. Department of Housing and Urban Development.

Thomas took the ashes and smiled, closed his eyes, and told this story: "I'm going to travel to Spokane Falls one last time and toss these ashes into the water. And your father will rise like a salmon, leap over the bridge, over me, and find his way home. It will be beautiful. His teeth will shine like silver, like a rainbow. He will rise, Victor, he will rise."

Victor smiled.

"I was planning on doing the same thing with my half," Victor said. "But I didn't   185
imagine my father looking anything like a salmon. I thought it'd be like cleaning the attic or something. Like letting things go after they've stopped having any use."

"Nothing stops, cousin," Thomas said. "Nothing stops."

Thomas Builds-the-Fire got out of the pickup and walked up his driveway. Victor started the pickup and began the drive home.

"Wait," Thomas yelled suddenly from his porch. "I just got to ask one favor."

Victor stopped the pickup, leaned out the window, and shouted back. "What do you want?"

"Just one time when I'm telling a story somewhere, why don't you stop and   190
listen?" Thomas asked.

"Just once?"

"Just once."

Victor waved his arms to let Thomas know that the deal was good. It was a fair trade, and that was all Victor had ever wanted from his whole life. So Victor drove his father's pickup toward home while Thomas went into his house, closed the door behind him, and heard a new story come to him in the silence afterwards.

Margaret Atwood

Happy Endings   1983

Born in Ottawa, Ontario, in 1939, Margaret Eleanor Atwood was the daughter of an entomologist and spent her childhood summers in the forests of northern Quebec, where her father carried out research. Atwood began writing at the age of five and had already seriously entertained thoughts of becoming a professional writer before she finished high school. She graduated from the University of Toronto in 1961, and later did graduate work at Radcliffe and Harvard. Atwood first gained prominence as a poet. Her first full-length collection of poems, The Circle Game *(1966), was awarded a Governor General's Award, Canada's most prestigious literary honor, and she has since published nearly twenty volumes of verse. Atwood also began to write fiction seriously in graduate school, and her short stories were first collected in* Dancing Girls *(1977), followed by numerous additional collections, most recently* Moral Disorder *(2006).*

Margaret Atwood

A dedicated feminist, Atwood's works of fiction explore the complex relations between the sexes, most incisively in The Handmaid's Tale *(1986), a futuristic novel about a world in which gender roles are ruthlessly enforced by a society based on religious fundamentalism. In the same year that* The Handmaid's Tale *appeared, Atwood was named Woman of the Year by Ms. magazine. Subsequent novels include* Cat's Eye *(1988),* The Robber Bride *(1993),* The Blind Assassin *(2000), and* The Year of the Flood *(2009). Atwood has served as writer-in-residence at universities in Canada, the United States, and Europe, and she has been widely in demand for appearances at symposia devoted to literature and women's issues.*

John and Mary meet.
What happens next?
If you want a happy ending, try A.

A

John and Mary fall in love and get married. They both have worthwhile and remunerative jobs which they find stimulating and challenging. They buy a charming house. Real estate values go up. Eventually, when they can afford live-in help, they have two children, to whom they are devoted. The children turn out well. John and Mary have a stimulating and challenging sex life and worthwhile friends. They go on fun vacations together. They retire. They both have hobbies which they find stimulating and challenging. Eventually they die. This is the end of the story.

B

Mary falls in love with John but John doesn't fall in love with Mary. He merely   5
uses her body for selfish pleasure and ego gratification of a tepid kind. He comes to her apartment twice a week and she cooks him dinner, you'll notice that he doesn't even consider her worth the price of a dinner out, and after he's eaten the dinner he fucks her and after that he falls asleep, while she does the dishes so he won't think she's untidy, having all those dirty dishes lying around, and puts on fresh lipstick so she'll look good when he wakes up, but when he wakes up he doesn't even notice, he puts on his socks and his shorts and his pants and his shirt and his tie and his shoes, the reverse order from the one in which he took them off. He doesn't take off Mary's clothes, she takes them off herself, she acts as if she's dying for it every time, not because she likes sex exactly, she doesn't, but she wants John to think she does because if they do it often enough surely he'll get used to her, he'll come to depend on her and they will get married, but John goes out the door with hardly so much as a goodnight and three days later he turns up at six o'clock and they do the whole thing over again.

Mary gets rundown. Crying is bad for your face, everyone knows that and so does Mary but she can't stop. People at work notice. Her friends tell her John is a rat, a pig, a dog, he isn't good enough for her, but she can't believe it. Inside John, she thinks, is another John, who is much nicer. This other John will emerge like a butterfly from a cocoon, a Jack from a box, a pit from a prune, if the first John is only squeezed enough.

One evening John complains about the food. He has never complained about the food before. Mary is hurt.

Her friends tell her they've seen him in a restaurant with another woman, whose name is Madge. It's not even Madge that finally gets to Mary; it's the restaurant. John has never taken Mary to a restaurant. Mary collects all the sleeping pills and aspirins she can find, and takes them and a half a bottle of sherry. You can see what kind of a woman she is by the fact that it's not even whiskey. She leaves a note for John. She hopes he'll discover her and get her to the hospital in time and repent and then they can get married, but this fails to happen and she dies.

John marries Madge and everything continues as in A.

C

John, who is an older man, falls in love with Mary, and Mary, who is only twenty-   10
two, feels sorry for him because he's worried about his hair falling out. She sleeps with him even though she's not in love with him. She met him at work. She's in love with someone called James, who is twenty-two also and not yet ready to settle down.

John on the contrary settled down long ago: this is what is bothering him. John has a steady, respectable job and is getting ahead in his field, but Mary isn't impressed by him, she's impressed by James, who has a motorcycle and a fabulous record collection. But James is often away on his motorcycle, being free. Freedom isn't the same for girls, so in the meantime Mary spends Thursday evenings with John. Thursdays are the only days John can get away.

John is married to a woman called Madge and they have two children, a charming house which they bought just before the real estate values went up, and hobbies which they find stimulating and challenging, when they have the time. John tells Mary how important she is to him, but of course, he can't leave his wife because a commitment is a commitment. He goes on about this more than is necessary and Mary finds it boring, but older men can keep it up longer so on the whole she has a fairly good time.

One day James breezes in on his motorcycle with some top-grade California hybrid and James and Mary get higher than you'd believe possible and they climb into bed. Everything becomes very underwater, but along comes John, who has a key to Mary's apartment. He finds them stoned and entwined. He's hardly in any position to be jealous, considering Madge, but nevertheless he's overcome with despair. Finally he's middle-aged, in two years he'll be bald as an egg and he can't stand it. He purchases a handgun, saying he needs it for target practice—this is the thin part of the plot, but it can be dealt with later—and shoots the two of them and himself.

Madge, after a suitable period of mourning, marries an understanding man called Fred and everything continues as in A, but under different names.

D

Fred and Madge have no problems. They get along exceptionally well and are good   15
at working out any little difficulties that may arise. But their charming house is by the seashore and one day a giant tidal wave approaches. Real estate values go down. The rest of the story is about what caused the tidal wave and how they escape from it. They do, though thousands drown, but Fred and Madge are virtuous and lucky. Finally on high ground they clasp each other, wet and dripping and grateful, and continue as in A.

E

Yes, but Fred has a bad heart. The rest of the story is about how kind and understanding they both are until Fred dies. Then Madge devotes herself to charity work until the end of A. If you like, it can be "Madge," "cancer," "guilty and confused," and "bird watching."

F

If you think this is all too bourgeois, make John a revolutionary and Mary a counterespionage agent and see how far that gets you. Remember, this is Canada.

You'll still end up with A, though in between you may get a lustful brawling saga of passionate involvement, a chronicle of our times, sort of.

You'll have to face it, the endings are the same however you slice it. Don't be deluded by any other endings, they're all fake, either deliberately fake, with malicious intent to deceive, or just motivated by excessive optimism if not by downright sentimentality.

The only authentic ending is the one provided here:

John and Mary die. John and Mary die. John and Mary die.   20

So much for endings. Beginnings are always more fun. True connoisseurs, however, are known to favor the stretch in between, since it's the hardest to do anything with.

That's about all that can be said for plots, which anyway are just one thing after another, a what and a what and a what.

Now try How and Why.

Ambrose Bierce

An Occurrence at Owl Creek Bridge   1891

Ambrose Bierce

Ambrose Bierce (1842–1914?) was born in Horse Cave Creek, Ohio, the youngest child of nine in an impoverished farm family. A year at Kentucky Military Academy was his only formal schooling. Enlisting as a drummer boy in the Union Army, Bierce saw action at Shiloh and Chickamauga, took part in Sherman's March to the Sea, and came out of the army a brevet major. Then he became a writer, later an editor, for San Francisco newspapers. For a while Bierce thrived. He and his wife, on her ample dowry, lived five years in London, where Bierce wrote for London papers, honed his style, and cultivated his wit. But his wife left him, his two sons died (one of gunfire and the other of alcoholism), and late in life Bierce came to deserve his nickname "Bitter Bierce." In 1913, at seventy-one, he trekked off to Mexico and vanished without a trace, although one report had him riding with the forces of revolutionist Pancho Villa. Bierce, who regarded the novel as "a short story padded," favored shorter lengths: short story, fable, newspaper column, aphorism. Sardonically, in The Devil's Dictionary (1911), he defines diplomacy as "the patriotic art of lying for one's country" and saint as "a dead sinner revised and edited." Master of both realism and the ghost story, he collected his best Civil War fiction, including "An Occurrence at Owl Creek Bridge," in Tales of Soldiers and Civilians (1891), later retitled In the Midst of Life.

I

A man stood upon a railroad bridge in northern Alabama, looking down into the swift water twenty feet below. The man's hands were behind his back, the wrists bound with a cord. A rope closely encircled his neck. It was attached to a stout cross-timber above his head and the slack fell to the level of his knees. Some loose boards laid upon the sleepers supporting the metals of the railway supplied a footing for him and his executioners—two private soldiers of the Federal army, directed by a sergeant who in civil life may have been a deputy sheriff. At a short remove upon the same temporary platform was an officer in the uniform of his rank, armed. He was a captain. A sentinel at each end of the bridge stood with his rifle in the position known as "support," that is to say, vertical in front of the left shoulder, the hammer resting on the forearm thrown straight across the chest—a formal and unnatural position, enforcing an erect carriage of the body. It did not appear to be the duty of these two men to know what was occurring at the center of the bridge; they merely blockaded the two ends of the foot planking that traversed it.

Beyond one of the sentinels nobody was in sight; the railroad ran straight away into a forest for a hundred yards, then, curving, was lost to view. Doubtless there was an outpost farther along. The other bank of the stream was open ground—a gentle acclivity topped with a stockade of vertical tree trunks, loop-holed for rifles, with a single embrasure through which protruded the muzzle of a brass cannon commanding the bridge. Midway of the slope between bridge and fort were the spectators—a single company of infantry in line, at "parade rest," the butts of the rifles on the ground, the barrels inclining slightly backward against the right shoulder, the hands crossed upon the stock. A lieutenant stood at the right of the line, the point of his sword upon the ground, his left hand resting upon his right. Excepting the group of four at the center of the bridge, not a man moved. The company faced the bridge, staring stonily, motionless. The sentinels, facing the banks of the stream, might have been statues to adorn the bridge. The captain stood with folded arms, silent, observing the work of his subordinates, but making no sign. Death is a dignitary who when he comes announced is to be received with formal manifestations of respect, even by those most familiar with him. In the code of military etiquette silence and fixity are forms of deference.

The man who was engaged in being hanged was apparently about thirty-five years of age. He was a civilian, if one might judge from his habit, which was that of a planter. His features were good—a straight nose, firm mouth, broad forehead, from which his long, dark hair was combed straight back, falling behind his ears to the collar of his well-fitting frock-coat. He wore a mustache and pointed beard, but no whiskers; his eyes were large and dark gray, and had a kindly expression which one would hardly have expected in one whose neck was in the hemp. Evidently this was no vulgar assassin. The liberal military code makes provision for hanging many kinds of persons, and gentlemen are not excluded.

The preparations being complete, the two private soldiers stepped aside and each drew away the plank upon which he had been standing. The sergeant turned to the captain, saluted and placed himself immediately behind that officer, who in turn moved apart one pace. These movements left the condemned man and the sergeant standing on the two ends of the same plank, which spanned three of the cross-ties of the bridge. The end upon which the civilian stood almost, but not quite, reached a fourth. This plank had been held in place by the weight of the captain; it was now held by that of the sergeant. At a signal from the former the latter would step aside, the plank would tilt and the condemned man go down between two ties. The arrangement commended itself to his judgment as simple and effective. His face had not been covered nor his eyes bandaged. He looked a moment at his "unsteadfast footing," then let his gaze wander to the swirling water of the stream racing madly beneath his feet. A piece of dancing driftwood caught his attention and his eyes followed it down the current. How slowly it appeared to move! What a sluggish stream!

He closed his eyes in order to fix his last thoughts upon his wife and children. The water, touched to gold by the early sun, the brooding mists under the banks at some distance down the stream, the fort, the soldiers, the piece of drift—all had distracted him. And now he became conscious of a new disturbance. Striking through the thought of his dear ones was a sound which he could neither ignore nor understand, a sharp, distinct, metallic percussion like the stroke of a blacksmith's hammer upon the anvil; it had the same ringing quality. He wondered what it was, and whether immeasurably distant or near by—it seemed both. Its recurrence was regular, but as slow as the tolling of a death knell. He awaited each stroke with impatience and—he knew not why—apprehension. The intervals of silence grew progressively longer; the delays became maddening. With their greater infrequency the sounds increased in strength and sharpness. They hurt his ear like the thrust of a knife; he feared he would shriek. What he heard was the ticking of his watch.

He unclosed his eyes and saw again the water below him. "If I could free my hands," he thought, "I might throw off the noose and spring into the stream. By diving I could evade the bullets and, swimming vigorously, reach the bank, take to the woods and get away home. My home, thank God, is as yet outside their lines; my wife and little ones are still beyond the invader's farthest advance."

As these thoughts, which have here to be set down in words, were flashed into the doomed man's brain rather than evolved from it the captain nodded to the sergeant. The sergeant stepped aside.

II

Peyton Farquhar was a well-to-do planter, of an old and highly respected Alabama family. Being a slave owner and like other slave owners a politician he was naturally an original secessionist and ardently devoted to the Southern cause. Circumstances of an imperious nature, which it is unnecessary to relate here, had prevented him from taking service with the gallant army that had fought the disastrous campaigns ending with the fall of Corinth, and he chafed under the inglorious restraint, longing for the release of his energies, the larger life of the soldier, the opportunity for distinction. That opportunity, he felt, would come, as it comes to all in war time. Meanwhile he did what he could. No service was too humble to him to perform in aid of the South, no adventure too perilous for him to undertake if consistent with the character of a civilian who was at heart a soldier, and who in good faith and without too much qualification assented to at least a part of the frankly villainous dictum that all is fair in love and war.

One evening while Farquhar and his wife were sitting on a rustic bench near the entrance to his grounds, a gray-clad soldier rode up to the gate and asked for a drink of water. Mrs. Farquhar was only too happy to serve him with her own white hands. While she was fetching the water her husband approached the dusty horseman and inquired eagerly for news from the front.

"The Yanks are repairing the railroads," said the man, "and are getting ready for another advance. They have reached the Owl Creek bridge, put it in order and built a stockade on the north bank. The commandant has issued an order, which is posted everywhere, declaring that any civilian caught interfering with the railroad, its bridges, tunnels or trains will be summarily hanged. I saw the order."

"How far is it to the Owl Creek bridge?" Farquhar asked.

"About thirty miles."

"Is there no force on this side the creek?"

"Only a picket post half a mile out, on the railroad, and a single sentinel at this end of the bridge."

"Suppose a man—a civilian and student of hanging—should elude the picket   15
post and perhaps get the better of the sentinel," said Farquhar, smiling, "what could he accomplish?"

The soldier reflected. "I was there a month ago," he replied. "I observed that the flood of last winter had lodged a great quantity of driftwood against the wooden pier at this end of the bridge. It is now dry and would burn like tow."

The lady had now brought the water, which the soldier drank. He thanked her ceremoniously, bowed to her husband and rode away. An hour later, after nightfall, he repassed the plantation, going northward in the direction from which he had come. He was a Federal scout.

III

As Peyton Farquhar fell straight downward through the bridge he lost consciousness and was as one already dead. From this state he was awakened—ages later, it seemed to him—by the pain of a sharp pressure upon his throat, followed by a sense of suffocation. Keen, poignant agonies seemed to shoot from his neck downward through every fiber of his body and limbs. These pains appeared to flash along well-defined lines of ramification and to beat with an inconceivably rapid periodicity. They seemed like streams of pulsating fire heating him to an intolerable temperature. As to his head, he was conscious of nothing but a feeling of fulness—of congestion. These sensations were unaccompanied by thought. The intellectual part of his nature was already effaced; he had power only to feel, and feeling was torment. He was conscious of motion. Encompassed in a luminous cloud, of which he was now merely the fiery heart, without material substance, he swung through unthinkable arcs of oscillation, like a vast pendulum. Then all at once, with terrible suddenness, the light about him shot upward with the noise of a loud plash; a frightful roaring was in his ears, and all was cold and dark. The power of thought was restored; he knew that the rope had broken and he had fallen into the stream. There was no additional strangulation; the noose about his neck was already suffocating him and kept the water from his lungs. To die of hanging at the bottom of a river!—the idea seemed to him ludicrous. He opened his eyes in the darkness and saw above him a gleam of light, but how distant, how inaccessible! He was still sinking, for the light became fainter and fainter until it was a mere glimmer. Then it began to grow and brighten, and he knew that he was rising toward the surface—knew it with reluctance, for he was now very comfortable. "To be hanged and drowned," he thought, "that is not so bad; but I do not wish to be shot. No; I will not be shot; that is not fair."

He was not conscious of an effort, but a sharp pain in his wrist apprised him that he was trying to free his hands. He gave the struggle his attention, as an idler might observe the feat of a juggler, without interest in the outcome. What splendid effort!—what magnificent, what superhuman strength! Ah, that was a fine endeavor! Bravo! The cord fell away; his arms parted and floated upward, the hands dimly seen on each side in the growing light. He watched them with a new interest as first one and then the other pounced upon the noose at his neck. They tore it away and thrust it fiercely aside, its undulations resembling those of a water-snake. "Put it back, put it back!" He thought he shouted these words to his hands, for the undoing of the noose had been succeeded by the direst pang that he had yet experienced. His neck ached horribly; his brain was on fire; his heart, which had been fluttering faintly, gave a great leap, trying to force itself out at his mouth. His whole body was racked and wrenched with an insupportable anguish! But his disobedient hands gave no heed to the command. They beat the water vigorously with quick, downward strokes, forcing him to the surface. He felt his head emerge; his eyes were blinded by the sunlight; his chest expanded convulsively, and with a supreme and crowning agony his lungs engulfed a great draught of air, which instantly he expelled in a shriek!

He was now in full possession of his physical senses. They were, indeed, preternatu- 20
rally keen and alert. Something in the awful disturbance of his organic system had so ex-
alted and refined them that they made record of things never before perceived. He felt the ripples upon his face and heard their separate sounds as they struck. He looked at the forest on the bank of the stream, saw the individual trees, the leaves and the veining of each leaf—saw the very insects upon them: the locusts, the brilliant-bodied flies, the gray spiders stretching their webs from twig to twig. He noted the prismatic colors in all the dewdrops upon a million blades of grass. The humming of the gnats that danced above the eddies of the stream, the beating of the dragon-flies' wings, the strokes of the water-spiders' legs, like oars which had lifted their boat—all these made audible music. A fish slid along beneath his eyes and he heard the rush of its body parting the water.

He had come to the surface facing down the stream; in a moment the visible world seemed to wheel slowly round, himself the pivotal point, and he saw the bridge, the fort, the soldiers upon the bridge, the captain, the sergeant, the two privates, his executioners. They were in silhouette against the blue sky. They shouted and gesticu-
lated, pointing at him. The captain had drawn his pistol, but did not fire; the others were unarmed. Their movements were grotesque and horrible, their forms gigantic.

Suddenly he heard a sharp report and something struck the water smartly within a few inches of his head, spattering his face with spray. He heard a second report, and saw one of the sentinels with his rifle at his shoulder, a light cloud of blue smoke rising from the muzzle. The man in the water saw the eye of the man on the bridge gaz-
ing into his own through the sights of the rifle. He observed that it was a gray eye and remembered having read that gray eyes were keenest, and that all famous marksmen had them. Nevertheless, this one had missed.

A counter-swirl had caught Farquhar and turned him half round; he was again looking into the forest on the bank opposite the fort. The sound of a clear, high voice in a monotonous singsong now rang out behind him and came across the water with a distinctness that pierced and subdued all other sounds, even the beating of the ripples in his ears. Although no soldier, he had frequented camps enough to know the dread significance of that deliberate, drawling, aspirated chant; the lieutenant on shore was taking a part in the morning's work. How coldly and pitilessly—with what an even, calm intonation, presaging, and enforcing tranquility in the men—with what accurately measured intervals fell those cruel words:

"Attention, company! . . . Shoulder arms! . . . Ready! . . . Aim! . . . Fire!"

Farquhar dived—dived as deeply as he could. The water roared in his ears like 25
the voice of Niagara, yet he heard the dulled thunder of the volley and, rising again toward the surface, met shining bits of metal, singularly flattened, oscillating slowly downward. Some of them touched him on the face and hands, then fell away, continuing their descent. One lodged between his collar and neck; it was uncomfortably warm and he snatched it out.

As he rose to the surface, gasping for breath, he saw that he had been a long time under water; he was perceptibly farther down stream—nearer to safety. The soldiers had almost finished reloading; the metal ramrods flashed all at once in the sunshine as they were drawn from the barrels, turned in the air, and thrust into their sockets. The two sentinels fired again, independently and ineffectually.

The hunted man saw all this over his shoulder; he was now swimming vigorously with the current. His brain was as energetic as his arms and legs; he thought with the rapidity of lightning.

"The officer," he reasoned, "will not make that martinet's error a second time. It is as easy to dodge a volley as a single shot. He has probably already given the command to fire at will. God help me, I cannot dodge them all!"

An appalling plash within two yards of him was followed by a loud, rushing sound, *diminuendo,*° which seemed to travel back through the air to the fort and died in an explosion which stirred the very river to its deeps! A rising sheet of water curved over him, fell down upon him, blinded him, strangled him! The cannon had taken a hand in the game. As he shook his head free from the commotion of the smitten water he heard the deflected shot humming through the air ahead, and in an instant it was cracking and smashing the branches in the forest beyond.

"They will not do that again," he thought; "the next time they will use a charge 30 of grape. I must keep my eye upon the gun; the smoke will apprise me—the report arrives too late; it lags behind the missile. That is a good gun."

Suddenly he felt himself whirled round and round—spinning like a top. The water, the banks, the forests, the now distant bridge, fort and men—all were commingled and blurred. Objects were represented by their colors only; circular horizontal streaks of color—that was all he saw. He had been caught in a vortex and was being whirled on with a velocity of advance and gyration that made him giddy and sick. In a few moments he was flung upon the gravel at the foot of the left bank of the stream—the southern bank—and behind a projecting point which concealed him from his enemies. The sudden arrest of his motion, the abrasion of one of his hands on the gravel, restored him, and he wept with delight. He dug his fingers into the sand, threw it over himself in handfuls and audibly blessed it. It looked like diamonds, rubies, emeralds; he could think of nothing beautiful which it did not resemble. The trees upon the bank were giant garden plants; he noted a definite order in their arrangement, inhaled the fragrance of their blooms. A strange, roseate light shone through the spaces among their trunks and the wind made in their branches the music of aeolian harps. He had no wish to perfect his escape—was content to remain in that enchanting spot until retaken.

A whiz and rattle of grapeshot among the branches high above his head roused him from his dream. The baffled cannoneer had fired him a random farewell. He sprang to his feet, rushed up the sloping bank, and plunged into the forest.

All that day he traveled, laying his course by the rounding sun. The forest seemed interminable; nowhere did he discover a break in it, not even a woodman's road. He had not known that he lived in so wild a region. There was something uncanny in the revelation.

By nightfall he was fatigued, footsore, famishing. The thought of his wife and children urged him on. At last he found a road which led him in what he knew to be the right direction. It was as wide and straight as a city street, yet it seemed untraveled. No fields bordered it, no dwelling anywhere. Not so much as the barking of a dog suggested human habitation. The black bodies of the trees formed a straight wall on both sides,

---

diminuendo: diminishing (Italian); a term from music indicating a gradual decrease in loudness or force.

terminating on the horizon in a point, like a diagram in a lesson in perspective. Overhead, as he looked up through this rift in the wood, shone great golden stars looking unfamiliar and grouped in strange constellations. He was sure they were arranged in some order which had a secret and malign significance. The wood on either side was full of singular noises, among which—once, twice, and again—he distinctly heard whispers in an unknown tongue.

His neck was in pain and lifting his hand to it he found it horribly swollen. He 35 knew that it had a circle of black where the rope had bruised it. His eyes felt congested; he could no longer close them. His tongue was swollen with thirst; he relieved its fever by thrusting it forward from between his teeth into the cold air. How softly the turf had carpeted the untraveled avenue—he could no longer feel the roadway beneath his feet!

Doubtless, despite his suffering, he had fallen asleep while walking, for now he sees another scene—perhaps he has merely recovered from a delirium. He stands at the gate of his own home. All is as he left it, and all bright and beautiful in the morning sunshine. He must have traveled the entire night. As he pushes open the gate and passes up the wide white walk, he sees a flutter of female garments; his wife, looking fresh and cool and sweet, steps down from the veranda to meet him. At the bottom of the steps she stands waiting, with a smile of ineffable joy, an attitude of matchless grace and dignity. Ah, how beautiful she is! He springs forward with extended arms. As he is about to clasp her he feels a stunning blow upon the back of the neck; a blinding white light blazes all about him with a sound like the shock of a cannon—then all is darkness and silence!

Peyton Farquhar was dead; his body, with a broken neck, swung gently from side to side beneath the timbers of the Owl Creek bridge.

Willa Cather

Paul's Case   1905

Willa Cather (1876–1947) was born in Gore, Virginia, but at nine moved to Webster County, Nebraska, where pioneer sod houses still clung to the windswept plains. There, mainly in the town of Red Cloud, she grew up among Scandinavians, Czechs, Bohemians, and other immigrant settlers, for whom she felt a quick kinship: they too had been displaced from their childhood homes. After graduation from the University of Nebraska, Cather went east to spend ten years in Pittsburgh, where the story "Paul's Case" opens. (When she wrote the story, she was a high school teacher of Latin and English and a music critic for a newspaper.) Then, because her early stories had attracted notice, New York beckoned. A job on the staff of McClure's led to her becoming managing editor of that popular magazine. Her early novels of Nebraska won immense popularity: O

Willa Cather

Pioneers! (1913), My Ántonia (1918), and A Lost Lady (1923). In her later novels Cather explores other regions of the North American past: in Death Comes to the

Archbishop (1927), *frontier New Mexico; in* Shadows on the Rock *(1931), seventeenth-century Quebec. She does not romanticize the rugged lives of farm people on the plains, or glamorize village life. Often, as in* The Song of the Lark *(1915), the story of a Colorado girl who becomes an opera singer, she depicts a small town as stifling. With remarkable skill, she may tell a story from a man's point of view, but her favorite characters are likely to be women of strong will who triumph over obstacles.*

It was Paul's afternoon to appear before the faculty of the Pittsburgh High School to account for his various misdemeanors. He had been suspended a week ago, and his father had called at the Principal's office and confessed his perplexity about his son. Paul entered the faculty room suave and smiling. His clothes were a trifle outgrown and the tan velvet on the collar of his open overcoat was frayed and worn; but for all that there was something of the dandy about him, and he wore an opal pin in his neatly knotted black four-in-hand, and a red carnation in his buttonhole. This latter adornment the faculty somehow felt was not properly significant of the contrite spirit befitting a boy under the ban of suspension.

Paul was tall for his age and very thin, with high, cramped shoulders and a narrow chest. His eyes were remarkable for a certain hysterical brilliancy and he continually used them in a conscious, theatrical sort of way, peculiarly offensive in a boy. The pupils were abnormally large, as though he were addicted to belladonna, but there was a glassy glitter about them which that drug does not produce.

When questioned by the Principal as to why he was there, Paul stated, politely enough, that he wanted to come back to school. This was a lie, but Paul was quite accustomed to lying; found it, indeed, indispensable for overcoming friction. His teachers were asked to state their respective charges against him, which they did with such a rancor and aggrievedness as evinced that this was not a usual case. Disorder and impertinence were among the offenses named, yet each of his instructors felt that it was scarcely possible to put into words the real cause of the trouble, which lay in a sort of hysterically defiant manner of the boy's; in the contempt which they all knew he felt for them, and which he seemingly made not the least effort to conceal. Once, when he had been making a synopsis of a paragraph at the blackboard, his English teacher had stepped to his side and attempted to guide his hand. Paul had started back with a shudder and thrust his hands violently behind him. The astonished woman could scarcely have been more hurt and embarrassed had he struck at her. The insult was so involuntary and definitely personal as to be unforgettable. In one way and another, he had made all his teachers, men and women alike, conscious of the same feeling of physical aversion. In one class he habitually sat with his hand shading his eyes; in another he always looked out of the window during the recitation; in another he made a running commentary on the lecture, with humorous intention.

His teachers felt this afternoon that his whole attitude was symbolized by his shrug and his flippantly red carnation flower, and they fell upon him without mercy, his English teacher leading the pack. He stood through it smiling, his pale lips parted over his white teeth. (His lips were continually twitching, and he had a habit of raising his eyebrows that was contemptuous and irritating to the last degree.) Older boys than Paul had broken down and shed tears under that baptism of fire, but his set smile did not once desert him, and his only sign of discomfort was the nervous trembling of the fingers that toyed with the buttons of his overcoat, and an occasional jerking of the other hand that held his hat. Paul was always smiling, always glancing about him, seeming to feel that people might be watching him and trying to detect something. This conscious expression, since it was as far as possible from boyish mirthfulness, was usually attributed to insolence or "smartness."

As the inquisition proceeded, one of his instructors repeated an impertinent re- 5 mark of the boy's, and the Principal asked him whether he thought that a courteous speech to have made a woman. Paul shrugged his shoulders slightly and his eyebrows twitched.

"I don't know," he replied. "I didn't mean to be polite or impolite, either. I guess it's a sort of way I have of saying things regardless."

The Principal, who was a sympathetic man, asked him whether he didn't think that a way it would be well to get rid of. Paul grinned and said he guessed so. When he was told that he could go, he bowed gracefully and went out. His bow was but a repetition of the scandalous red carnation.

His teachers were in despair, and his drawing master voiced the feeling of them all when he declared there was something about the boy which none of them understood. He added: "I don't really believe that smile of his comes altogether from insolence; there's something sort of haunted about it. The boy is not strong, for one thing. I happen to know that he was born in Colorado, only a few months before his mother died out there of a long illness. There is something wrong about the fellow."

The drawing master had come to realize that, in looking at Paul, one saw only his white teeth and the forced animation of his eyes. One warm afternoon the boy had gone to sleep at his drawing-board, and his master had noted with amazement what a white, blue-veined face it was; drawn and wrinkled like an old man's about the eyes, the lips twitching even in his sleep, and stiff with a nervous tension that drew them back from his teeth.

His teachers left the building dissatisfied and unhappy; humiliated to have felt so 10 vindictive toward a mere boy, to have uttered this feeling in cutting terms, and to have set each other on, as it were, in the gruesome game of intemperate reproach. Some of them remembered having seen a miserable street cat set at bay by a ring of tormentors.

As for Paul, he ran down the hill whistling the Soldiers' Chorus from *Faust*,° looking wildly behind him now and then to see whether some of his teachers were not there to writhe under his light-heartedness. As it was now late in the afternoon and Paul was on duty that evening as usher at Carnegie Hall,° he decided that he would not go home to supper. When he reached the concert hall the doors were not yet open and, as it was chilly outside, he decided to go up into the picture gallery— always deserted at this hour—where there were some of Raffaelli's° gay studies of Paris streets and an airy blue Venetian scene or two that always exhilarated him. He was delighted to find no one in the gallery but the old guard, who sat in one corner, a newspaper on his knee, a black patch over one eye and the other closed. Paul possessed himself of the place and walked confidently up and down, whistling under his breath. After a while he sat down before a blue Rico° and lost himself. When he bethought him to look at his watch, it was after seven o'clock, and he rose with a

---

Faust: tragic grand opera (1859) by French composer Charles Gounod.   *Carnegie Hall*: concert hall endowed by Pittsburgh steel manufacturer Andrew Carnegie, not to be confused with the better-known Carnegie Hall in New York City.   *Raffaelli*: Jean-Francois Raffaelli (1850–1921), painter and graphic artist, native and lifelong resident of Paris, attained great popularity for his paintings and drawings of that city.   *Rico*: (flourished 1500–1550), painter of the Byzantine school, a native of Crete.

start and ran downstairs, making a face at Augustus, peering out from the cast-room,° and an evil gesture at the Venus of Milo as he passed her on the stairway.

When Paul reached the ushers' dressing-room half-a-dozen boys were there already, and he began excitedly to tumble into his uniform. It was one of the few that at all approached fitting, and Paul thought it very becoming—though he knew that the tight, straight coat accentuated his narrow chest, about which he was exceedingly sensitive. He was always considerably excited while he dressed, twanging all over to the tuning of the strings and the preliminary flourishes of the horns in the music-room; but tonight he seemed quite beside himself, and he teased and plagued the boys until, telling him that he was crazy, they put him down on the floor and sat on him.

Somewhat calmed by his suppression, Paul dashed out to the front of the house to seat the early comers. He was a model usher; gracious and smiling he ran up and down the aisles; nothing was too much trouble for him; he carried messages and brought programmes as though it were his greatest pleasure in life, and all the people in his section thought him a charming boy, feeling that he remembered and admired them. As the house filled, he grew more and more vivacious and animated, and the color came to his cheeks and lips. It was very much as though this were a great reception and Paul were the host. Just as the musicians came out to take their places, his English teacher arrived with checks for the seats which a prominent manufacturer had taken for the season. She betrayed some embarrassment when she handed Paul the tickets, and a hauteur° which subsequently made her feel very foolish. Paul was startled for a moment, and had the feeling of wanting to put her out; what business had she here among all these fine people and gay colors? He looked her over and decided that she was not appropriately dressed and must be a fool to sit downstairs in such togs. The tickets had probably been sent her out of kindness, he reflected as he put down a seat for her, and she had about as much right to sit there as he had.

When the symphony began Paul sank into one of the rear seats with a long sigh of relief, and lost himself as he had done before the Rico. It was not that symphonies, as such, meant anything in particular to Paul, but the first sigh of the instruments seemed to free some hilarious and potent spirit within him; something that struggled there like the Genius° in the bottle found by the Arab fisherman. He felt a sudden zest of life; the lights danced before his eyes and the concert hall blazed into unimaginable splendor. When the soprano soloist came on, Paul forgot even the nastiness of his teacher's being there and gave himself up to the peculiar stimulus such personages always had for him. The soloist chanced to be a German woman, by no means in her first youth, and the mother of many children; but she wore an elaborate gown and a tiara, and above all she had that indefinable air of achievement, that world-shine upon her, which, in Paul's eyes, made her a veritable queen of Romance.

After a concert was over Paul was always irritable and wretched until he got to sleep, and tonight he was even more than usually restless. He had the feeling of not

15

Augustus . . . cast-room: Paul mocks a plaster cast of the Vatican Museum's famous statue of the first Roman emperor (63 B.C.–A.D. 14), whom an unknown sculptor posed sternly pointing an index finger at his beholders.   hauteur: haughtiness.   Genius: genie in a tale from *The Arabian Nights*.

being able to let down, of its being impossible to give up this delicious excitement which was the only thing that could be called living at all. During the last number he withdrew and, after hastily changing his clothes in the dressing-room, slipped out to the side door where the soprano's carriage stood. Here he began pacing rapidly up and down the walk, waiting to see her come out.

Over yonder the Schenley, in its vacant stretch, loomed big and square through the fine rain, the windows of its twelve stories glowing like those of a lighted cardboard house under a Christmas tree. All the actors and singers of the better class stayed there when they were in the city, and a number of the big manufacturers of the place lived there in the winter. Paul had often hung about the hotel, watching the people go in and out, longing to enter and leave schoolmasters and dull care behind him forever.

At last the singer came out, accompanied by the conductor, who helped her into her carriage and closed the door with a cordial *auf wiedersehen*° which set Paul to wondering whether she were not an old sweetheart of his. Paul followed the carriage over to the hotel, walking so rapidly as not to be far from the entrance when the singer alighted and disappeared behind the swinging glass doors that were opened by a negro in a tall hat and a long coat. In the moment that the door was ajar it seemed to Paul that he, too, entered. He seemed to feel himself go after her up the steps, into the warm, lighted building, into an exotic, a tropical world of shiny, glistening surfaces and basking ease. He reflected upon the mysterious dishes that were brought into the dining-room, the green bottles in buckets of ice, as he had seen them in the supper party pictures of the *Sunday World* supplement. A quick gust of wind brought the rain down with sudden vehemence, and Paul was startled to find that he was still outside in the slush of the gravel driveway; that his boots were letting in the water and his scanty overcoat was clinging wet about him; that the lights in front of the concert hall were out, and that the rain was driving in sheets between him and the orange glow of the windows above him. There it was, what he wanted—tangibly before him, like the fairy world of a Christmas pantomime, but mocking spirits stood guard at the doors, and, as the rain beat in his face, Paul wondered whether he were destined always to shiver in the black night outside, looking up at it.

He turned and walked reluctantly toward the car tracks. The end had to come sometime; his father in his night-clothes at the top of the stairs, explanations that did not explain, hastily improvised fictions that were forever tripping him up, his upstairs room and its horrible yellow wall-paper, the creaking bureau with the greasy plush collar-box, and over his painted wooden bed the pictures of George Washington and John Calvin,° and the framed motto, "Feed my Lambs," which had been worked in red worsted by his mother.

Half an hour later, Paul alighted from his car and went slowly down one of the side streets off the main thoroughfare. It was a highly respectable street, where all the houses were exactly alike, and where businessmen of moderate means begot and reared large families of children, all of whom went to Sabbath-school and learned the shorter catechism, and were interested in arithmetic; all of whom were as exactly

---

auf wiedersehen: German equivalent of *au revoir,* or "here's to seeing you again." *John Calvin:* French Protestant theologian of the Reformation (1509–1564) whose teachings are the basis of Presbyterianism.

alike as their homes, and of a piece with the monotony in which they lived. Paul never went up Cordelia Street without a shudder of loathing. His home was next to the house of the Cumberland° minister. He approached it tonight with the nerveless sense of defeat, the hopeless feeling of sinking back forever into ugliness and commonness that he had always had when he came home. The moment he turned into Cordelia Street he felt the waters close above his head. After each of these orgies of living, he experienced all the physical depression which follows a debauch; the loathing of respectable beds, of common food, of a house penetrated by kitchen odors; a shuddering repulsion for the flavorless, colorless mass of every-day existence; a morbid desire for cool things and soft lights and fresh flowers.

The nearer he approached the house, the more absolutely unequal Paul felt to the 20
sight of it all; his ugly sleeping chamber; the cold bathroom with the grimy zinc tub, the cracked mirror, the dripping spigots; his father, at the top of the stairs, his hairy legs sticking out from his night-shirt, his feet thrust into carpet slippers. He was so much later than usual that there would certainly be inquiries and reproaches. Paul stopped short before the door. He felt that he could not be accosted by his father tonight; that he could not toss again on that miserable bed. He would not go in. He would tell his father that he had no car fare, and it was raining so hard he had gone home with one of the boys and stayed all night.

Meanwhile, he was wet and cold. He went around to the back of the house and tried one of the basement windows, found it open, raised it cautiously, and scrambled down the cellar wall to the floor. There he stood, holding his breath, terrified by the noise he had made, but the floor above him was silent, and there was no creak on the stairs. He found a soap-box, and carried it over to the soft ring of light that streamed from the furnace door, and sat down. He was horribly afraid of rats, so he did not try to sleep, but sat looking distrustfully at the dark, still terrified lest he might have awakened his father. In such reactions, after one of the experiences which made days and nights out of the dreary blanks of the calendar, when his senses were deadened, Paul's head was always singularly clear. Suppose his father had heard him getting in at the window and had come down and shot him for a burglar? Then, again, suppose his father had come down, pistol in hand, and he had cried out in time to save himself, and his father had been horrified to think how nearly he had killed him? Then, again, suppose a day should come when his father would remember that night, and wish there had been no warning cry to stay his hand? With this last supposition Paul entertained himself until daybreak.

The following Sunday was fine; the sodden November chill was broken by the last flash of autumnal summer. In the morning Paul had to go to church and Sabbath-school, as always. On seasonable Sunday afternoons the burghers of Cordelia Street always sat out on their front "stoops," and talked to their neighbors on the next stoop, or called to those across the street in neighborly fashion. The men usually sat on gay cushions placed upon the steps that led down to the sidewalk, while the women, in their Sunday "waists," sat in rockers on the cramped porches, pretending to be greatly at their ease. The children played in the streets; there were so many of them that the place resembled the recreation grounds of a kindergarten. The men on the steps—all in their shirt sleeves, their vests unbuttoned—sat with their legs

Cumberland: The minister, a Cumberland Presbyterian, belongs to a frontier denomination that had splintered away from the Presbyterian Church and whose ministers were ordained after a briefer training.

well apart, their stomachs comfortably protruding, and talked of the prices of things, or told anecdotes of the sagacity of their various chiefs and overlords. They occasionally looked over the multitude of squabbling children, listened affectionately to their high-pitched, nasal voices, smiling to see their own proclivities reproduced in their offspring, and interspersed their legends of the iron kings with remarks about their sons' progress at school, their grades in arithmetic, and the amounts they had saved in their toy banks.

On this last Sunday of November, Paul sat all the afternoon on the lowest step of his "stoop," staring into the street, while his sisters, in their rockers, were talking to the minister's daughters next door about how many shirt-waists they had made in the last week, and how many waffles some one had eaten at the last church supper. When the weather was warm, and his father was in a particularly jovial frame of mind, the girls made lemonade, which was always brought out in a red-glass pitcher, ornamented with forget-me-nots in blue enamel. This the girls thought very fine, and the neighbors always joked about the suspicious color of the pitcher.

Today Paul's father sat on the top step, talking to a young man who shifted a restless baby from knee to knee. He happened to be the young man who was daily held up to Paul as a model, and after whom it was his father's dearest hope that he would pattern. This young man was of a ruddy complexion, with a compressed, red mouth, and faded, near-sighted eyes, over which he wore thick spectacles, with gold bows that curved about his ears. He was clerk to one of the magnates of a great steel corporation, and was looked upon in Cordelia Street as a young man with a future. There was a story that, some five years ago—he was now barely twenty-six—he had been a trifle dissipated but in order to curb his appetites and save the loss of time and strength that a sowing of wild oats might have entailed, he had taken his chief's advice oft reiterated to his employees, and at twenty-one had married the first woman whom he could persuade to share his fortunes. She happened to be an angular school-mistress, much older than he, who also wore thick glasses, and who had now borne him four children, all near-sighted, like herself.

The young man was relating how his chief, now cruising in the Mediterranean, 25 kept in touch with all the details of the business, arranging his office hours on his yacht just as though he were at home, and "knocking off work enough to keep two stenographers busy." His father told, in turn, the plan his corporation was considering, of putting in an electric railway plant at Cairo. Paul snapped his teeth; he had an awful apprehension that they might spoil it all before he got there. Yet he rather liked to hear these legends of the iron kings, that were told and retold on Sundays and holidays; these stories of palaces in Venice, yachts on the Mediterranean, and high play at Monte Carlo appealed to his fancy, and he was interested in the triumphs of these cash boys who had become famous, though he had no mind for the cash-boy stage.

After supper was over, and he had helped to dry the dishes, Paul nervously asked his father whether he could go to George's to get some help in his geometry, and still more nervously asked for car fare. This latter request he had to repeat, as his father, on principle, did not like to hear requests for money, whether much or little. He asked Paul whether he could not go to some boy who lived nearer, and told him that he ought not to leave his school work until Sunday; but he gave him the dime. He was not a poor man, but he had a worthy ambition to come up in the world. His only reason for allowing Paul to usher was, that he thought a boy ought to be earning a little.

Paul bounded upstairs, scrubbed the greasy odor of the dish-water from his hands with the ill-smelling soap he hated, and then shook over his fingers a few drops of violet water from the bottle he kept hidden in his drawer. He left the house with his geometry conspicuously under his arm, and the moment he got out of Cordelia Street and boarded a downtown car, he shook off the lethargy of two deadening days, and began to live again.

The leading juvenile of the permanent stock company which played at one of the downtown theatres was an acquaintance of Paul's, and the boy had been invited to drop in at the Sunday-night rehearsals whenever he could. For more than a year Paul had spent every available moment loitering about Charley Edwards's dressing-room. He had won a place among Edward's following not only because the young actor, who could not afford to employ a dresser, often found him useful, but because he recognized in Paul something akin to what churchmen term "vocation."

It was at the theatre and at Carnegie Hall that Paul really lived; the rest was but a sleep and a forgetting. This was Paul's fairy tale, and it had for him all the allurement of a secret love. The moment he inhaled the gassy, painty, dusty odor behind the scenes, he breathed like a prisoner set free, and felt within him the possibility of doing or saying splendid, brilliant, poetic things. The moment the cracked orchestra beat out the overture from *Martha*,° or jerked at the serenade from *Rigoletto*,° all stupid and ugly things slid from him, and his senses were deliciously, yet delicately fired.

Perhaps it was because, in Paul's world, the natural nearly always wore the guise of   30
ugliness, that a certain element of artificiality seemed to him necessary in beauty. Perhaps it was because his experience of life elsewhere was so full of Sabbath-school picnics, petty economies, wholesome advice as to how to succeed in life, and the unescapable odors of cooking, that he found this existence so alluring, these smartly-clad men and women so attractive, that he was so moved by these starry apple orchards that bloomed perennially under the limelight.

It would be difficult to put it strongly enough how convincingly the stage entrance of that theatre was for Paul the actual portal of Romance. Certainly none of the company ever suspected it, least of all Charley Edwards. It was very like the old stories that used to float about London of fabulously rich Jews, who had subterranean halls there, with palms, and fountains, and soft lamps and richly apparelled women who never saw the disenchanting light of London day. So, in the midst of that smoke-palled city, enamored of figures and grimy toil, Paul had his secret temple, his wishing carpet, his bit of blue-and-white Mediterranean shore bathed in perpetual sunshine.

Several of Paul's teachers had a theory that his imagination had been perverted by garish fiction, but the truth was that he scarcely ever read at all. The books at home were not such as would either tempt or corrupt a youthful mind, and as for reading the novels that some of his friends urged upon him—well, he got what he wanted much more quickly from music; any sort of music, from an orchestra to a barrel organ. He needed only the spark, the indescribable thrill that made his imagination master of his senses, and he could make plots and pictures enough of his own. It was equally true that he was not stage struck—not, at any rate, in the usual acceptation of that expression. He had no desire to become an actor, any more than he had to become a musician. He felt no necessity to do any of these things; what he wanted

---

Martha: grand opera about romance among English aristocrats (1847) by German composer Friedrich von Flotow.   *Rigoletto:* tragic grand opera (1851) by Italian composer Giuseppe Verdi.

was to see, to be in the atmosphere, float on the wave of it, to be carried out, blue league after blue league, away from everything.

After a night behind the scenes, Paul found the school-room more than ever repulsive; the bare floors and naked walls; the prosy men who never wore frock coats, or violets in their buttonholes; the women with their dull gowns, shrill voices, and pitiful seriousness about prepositions that govern the dative. He could not bear to have the other pupils think, for a moment, that he took these people seriously; he must convey to them that he considered it all trivial, and was there only by way of a jest, anyway. He had autograph pictures of all the members of the stock company which he showed his classmates, telling them the most incredible stories of his familiarity with these people, of his acquaintance with the soloists who came to Carnegie Hall, his suppers with them and the flowers he sent them. When these stories lost their effect, and his audience grew listless, he became desperate and would bid all the boys good-bye, announcing that he was going to travel for a while; going to Naples, to Venice, to Egypt. Then, next Monday, he would slip back, conscious and nervously smiling; his sister was ill, and he should have to defer his voyage until spring.

Matters went steadily worse with Paul at school. In the itch to let his instructors know how heartily he despised them and their homilies, and how thoroughly he was appreciated elsewhere, he mentioned once or twice that he had no time to fool with theorems; adding—with a twitch of the eyebrows and a touch of that nervous bravado which so perplexed them—that he was helping the people down at the stock company; they were old friends of his.

The upshot of the matter was that the Principal went to Paul's father, and Paul was taken out of school and put to work. The manager at Carnegie Hall was told to get another usher in his stead; the door-keeper at the theatre was warned not to admit him to the house; and Charley Edwards remorsefully promised the boy's father not to see him again.

The members of the stock company were vastly amused when some of Paul's stories reached them—especially the women. They were hardworking women, most of them supporting indigent husbands or brothers, and they laughed rather bitterly at having stirred the boy to such fervid and florid inventions. They agreed with the faculty and with his father that Paul's was a bad case.

The east-bound train was ploughing through a January snow-storm; the dull dawn was beginning to show gray when the engine whistled a mile out of Newark. Paul started up from the seat where he had lain curled in uneasy slumber, rubbed the breath-misted window glass with his hand, and peered out. The snow was whirling in curling eddies above the white bottom lands, and the drifts lay already deep in the fields and along the fences, while here and there the long dead grass and dried weed stalks protruded black above it. Lights shone from the scattered houses, and a gang of laborers who stood beside the track waved their lanterns.

Paul had slept very little, and he felt grimy and uncomfortable. He had made the all-night journey in a day coach, partly because he was ashamed, dressed as he was, to go into a Pullman, and partly because he was afraid of being seen there by some Pittsburgh business man, who might have noticed him in Denny & Carson's office. When the whistle awoke him, he clutched quickly at his breast pocket, glancing about him with an uncertain smile. But the little, clay-bespattered Italians were still sleeping, the slatternly women across the aisle were in open-mouthed oblivion, and even the crumby, crying babies were for the nonce stilled. Paul settled back to struggle with his impatience as best as he could.

When he arrived at the Jersey City station, he hurried through his breakfast, manifestly ill at ease and keeping a sharp eye about him. After he reached the Twenty-third Street station,° he consulted a cabman, and had himself driven to a men's furnishing establishment that was just opening for the day. He spent upward of two hours there, buying with endless reconsidering and great care. His new street suit he put on in the fitting-room; the frock coat and dress clothes he had bundled into the cab with his linen. Then he drove to a hatter's and a shoe house. His next errand was at Tiffany's, where he selected his silver and a new scarf-pin. He would not wait to have his silver marked, he said. Lastly, he stopped at a trunk shop on Broadway, and had his purchases packed into various travelling bags.

It was a little after one-o'clock when he drove up to the Waldorf, and after set-   40
tling with the cabman, went into the office. He registered from Washington; said his mother and father had been abroad, and that he had come down to await the arrival of their steamer. He told his story plausibly and had no trouble, since he volunteered to pay for them in advance, in engaging his rooms; a sleeping-room, sitting-room and bath.

Not once, but a hundred times Paul had planned this entry into New York. He had gone over every detail of it with Charley Edwards, and in his scrap book at home there were pages of description about New York hotels, cut from the Sunday papers. When he was shown to his sitting-room on the eighth floor, he saw at a glance that everything was as it should be; there was but one detail in his mental picture that the place did not realize, so he rang for the bell boy and sent him down for flowers. He moved about nervously until the boy returned, putting away his new linen and fingering it delightedly as he did so. When the flowers came, he put them hastily into water, and then tumbled into a hot bath. Presently he came out of his white bathroom, resplendent in his new silk underwear, and playing with the tassels of his red robe. The snow was whirling so fiercely outside his windows that he could scarcely see across the street, but within the air was deliciously soft and fragrant. He put the violets and jonquils on the taboret beside the couch, and threw himself down, with a long sigh, covering himself with a Roman blanket. He was thoroughly tired; he had been in such haste, he had stood up to such a strain, covered so much ground in the last twenty-four hours, that he wanted to think how it had all come about. Lulled by the sound of the wind, the warm air, and the cool fragrance of the flowers, he sank into deep, drowsy retrospection.

It had been wonderfully simple; when they had shut him out of the theatre and concert hall, when they had taken away his bone, the whole thing was virtually determined. The rest was a mere matter of opportunity. The only thing that at all surprised him was his own courage—for he realized well enough that he had always been tormented by fear, a sort of apprehensive dread that, of late years, as the meshes of the lies he had told closed about him, had been pulling the muscles of his body tighter and tighter. Until now, he could not remember the time when he had not been dreading something. Even when he was a little boy, it was always there—behind him, or before, or on either side. There had always been the shadowed corner, the dark place into which he dared not look, but from which something seemed always to be watching him—and Paul had done things that were not pretty to watch, he knew.

Twenty-third Street station: The scene is now New York City.

But now he had a curious sense of relief, as though he had at last thrown down the gauntlet to the thing in the corner.

Yet it was but a day since he had been sulking in the traces; but yesterday afternoon that he had been sent to the bank with Denny & Carson's deposit, as usual—but this time he was instructed to leave the book to be balanced. There was above two thousand dollars in checks, and nearly a thousand in the bank notes which he had taken from the book and quietly transferred to his pocket. At the bank he had made out a new deposit slip. His nerves had been steady enough to permit of his returning to the office, where he had finished his work and asked for a full day's holiday tomorrow, Saturday, giving a perfectly reasonable pretext. The bank book, he knew, would not be returned before Monday or Tuesday, and his father would be out of town for the next week. From the time he slipped the bank notes into his pocket until he boarded the night train for New York, he had not known a moment's hesitation. It was not the first time Paul had steered through treacherous waters.

How astonishingly easy it had all been; here he was, the thing done; and this time there would be no awakening, no figure at the top of the stairs. He watched the snow flakes whirling by his window until he fell asleep.   45

When he awoke, it was three o'clock in the afternoon. He bounded up with a start; half of one of his precious days gone already! He spent more than an hour in dressing, watching every stage of his toilet carefully in the mirror. Everything was quite perfect; he was exactly the kind of boy he had always wanted to be.

When he went downstairs, Paul took a carriage and drove up Fifth Avenue toward the Park. The snow had somewhat abated; carriages and tradesmen's wagons were hurrying soundlessly to and fro in the winter twilight; boys in woollen mufflers were shovelling off the doorsteps; the avenue stages made fine spots of color against the white street. Here and there on the corners were stands, with whole flower gardens blooming under glass cases, against the sides of which the snow flakes stuck and melted; violets, roses, carnations, lilies of the valley—somewhat vastly more lovely and alluring that they blossomed thus unnaturally in the snow. The Park itself was a wonderful stage winter-piece.

When he returned, the pause of the twilight had ceased, and the tune of the streets had changed. The snow was falling faster, lights streamed from the hotels that reared their dozen stories fearlessly up into the storm, defying the raging Atlantic winds. A long, black stream of carriages poured down the avenue, intersected here and there by other streams, tending horizontally. There were a score of cabs about the entrance of his hotel, and his driver had to wait. Boys in livery were running in and out of the awning stretched across the sidewalk, up and down the red velvet carpet laid from the door to the street. Above, about, within it all was the rumble and roar, the hurry and toss of thousands of human beings as hot for pleasure as himself, and on every side of him towered the glaring affirmation of the omnipotence of wealth.

The boy set his teeth and drew his shoulders together in a spasm of realization: the plot of all dramas, the text of all romances, the nerve-stuff of all sensations was whirling about him like the snow flakes. He burnt like a faggot in a tempest.

When Paul went down to dinner, the music of the orchestra came floating up   50
the elevator shaft to greet him. His head whirled as he stepped into the thronged corridor, and he sank back into one of the chairs against the wall to get his breath. The lights, the chatter, the perfumes, the bewildering medley of color—he had, for a moment, the feeling of not being able to stand it. But only for a moment;

these were his own people, he told himself. He went slowly about the corridors, through the writing-rooms, smoking-rooms, reception-rooms, as though he were exploring the chambers of an enchanted palace, built and peopled for him alone.

When he reached the dining-room he sat down at a table near a window. The flowers, the white linen, the many-colored wine glasses, the gay toilettes of the women, the low popping of corks, the undulating repetitions of the *Blue Danube* from the orchestra, all flooded Paul's dream with bewildering radiance. When the roseate tinge of his champagne was added—that cold, precious, bubbling stuff that creamed and foamed in his glass—Paul wondered that there were honest men in the world at all. This was what all the world was fighting for, he reflected; this was what all the struggle was about. He doubted the reality of his past. Had he ever known a place called Cordelia Street, a place where fagged-looking businessmen got on the early car; mere rivets in a machine they seemed to Paul—sickening men, with combings of children's hair always hanging to their coats, and the smell of cooking in their clothes. Cordelia Street—Ah! that belonged to another time and country; had he not always been thus, had he not sat here night after night, from as far back as he could remember, looking pensively over just such shimmering textures, and slowly twirling the stem of a glass like this one between his thumb and middle finger? He rather thought he had.

He was not in the least abashed or lonely. He had no especial desire to meet or to know any of these people; all he demanded was the right to look on and conjecture, to watch the pageant. The mere stage properties were all he contended for. Nor was he lonely later in the evening, in his loge at the Metropolitan. He was now entirely rid of his nervous misgivings, of his forced aggressiveness, of the imperative desire to show himself different from his surroundings. He felt now that his surroundings explained him. Nobody questioned the purple; he had only to wear it passively. He had only to glance down at his attire to reassure himself that here it would be impossible for anyone to humiliate him.

He found it hard to leave his beautiful sitting-room to go to bed that night, and sat long watching the raging storm from his turret window. When he went to sleep it was with the lights turned on in his bedroom; partly because of his old timidity, and partly so that, if he should wake in the night, there would be no wretched moment of doubt, no horrible suspicion of yellow wall-paper, or of Washington and Calvin above his bed.

Sunday morning the city was practically snow-bound. Paul breakfasted late, and in the afternoon he fell in with a wild San Francisco boy, a freshman at Yale, who said he had run down for a "little flyer" over Sunday. The young man offered to show Paul the night side of the town, and the two boys went out together after dinner, not returning to the hotel until seven o'clock the next morning. They had started out in the confiding warmth of a champagne friendship, but their parting in the elevator was singularly cool. The freshman pulled himself together to make his train, and Paul went to bed. He awoke at two o'clock in the afternoon, very thirsty and dizzy, and rang for ice-water, coffee, and the Pittsburgh papers.

On the part of the hotel management, Paul excited no suspicion. There was this   55
to be said for him, that he wore his spoils with dignity and in no way made himself conspicuous. Even under the glow of his wine he was never boisterous, though he found the stuff like a magician's wand for wonder-building. His chief greediness lay in his ears and eyes, and his excesses were not offensive ones. His dearest pleasures were the gray winter twilights in his sitting-room; his quiet enjoyment of his flowers, his

clothes, his wide divan, his cigarette, and his sense of power. He could not remember a time when he had felt so at peace with himself. The mere release from the necessity of petty lying, lying every day and every day, restored his self-respect. He had never lied for pleasure, even at school; but to be noticed and admired, to assert his difference from other Cordelia Street boys; and he felt a good deal more manly, more honest, even, now that he had no need for boastful pretensions, now that he could, as his actor friends used to say, "dress the part." It was characteristic that remorse did not occur to him. His golden days went by without a shadow, and he made each as perfect as he could.

On the eighth day after his arrival in New York, he found the whole affair exploited in the Pittsburgh papers, exploited with a wealth of detail which indicated that local news of a sensational nature was at a low ebb. The firm of Denny & Carson announced that the boy's father had refunded the full amount of the theft, and that they had no intention of prosecuting. The Cumberland minister had been interviewed, and expressed his hope of yet reclaiming the motherless lad, and his Sabbath-school teacher declared that she would spare no effort to that end. The rumor had reached Pittsburgh that the boy had been seen in a New York hotel, and his father had gone East to find him and bring him home.

Paul had just come in to dress for dinner; he sank into a chair, weak to the knees, and clasped his head in his hands. It was to be worse than jail, even; the tepid waters of Cordelia Street were to close over him finally and forever. The gray monotony stretched before him in hopeless, unrelieved years; Sabbath-school, Young People's Meeting, the yellow-papered room, the damp dish-towels; it all rushed back upon him with a sickening vividness. He had the old feeling that the orchestra had suddenly stopped, the sinking sensation that the play was over. The sweat broke out on his face, and he sprang to his feet, looked about him with his white, conscious smile, and winked at himself in the mirror. With something of the old childish belief in miracles with which he had so often gone to class, all his lessons unlearned, Paul dressed and dashed whistling down the corridor to the elevator.

He had no sooner entered the dining-room and caught the measure of the music than his remembrance was lightened by his old elastic power of claiming the moment, mounting with it, and finding it all sufficient. The glare and glitter about him, the mere scenic accessories had again, and for the last time, their old potency. He would show himself that he was game, he would finish the thing splendidly. He doubted, more than ever, the existence of Cordelia Street, and for the first time he drank his wine recklessly. Was he not, after all, one of those fortunate beings born to the purple, was he not still himself and in his own place? He drummed a nervous accompaniment to the Pagliacci music and looked about him, telling himself over and over that it had paid.

He reflected drowsily, to the swell of the music and the chill sweetness of his wine, that he might have done it more wisely. He might have caught an outbound steamer and been well out of their clutches before now. But the other side of the world had seemed too far away and too uncertain then; he could not have waited for it; his need had been too sharp. If he had to choose over again, he would do the same thing tomorrow. He looked affectionately about the dining-room, now gilded with a soft mist. Ah, it had paid indeed!

Paul was awakened next morning by a painful throbbing in his head and feet. He had thrown himself across the bed without undressing, and had slept with his shoes on. His limbs and hands were lead heavy, and his tongue and throat were parched and burnt. There came upon him one of those fateful attacks of clear-headedness that never occurred except when he was physically exhausted and his nerves hung loose. He lay still and closed his eyes and let the tide of things wash over him.

His father was in New York; "stopping at some joint or other," he told himself. The memory of successive summers on the front stoop fell upon him like a weight of black water. He had not a hundred dollars left; and he knew now, more than ever, that money was everything, the wall that stood between all he loathed and all he wanted. The thing was winding itself up; he had thought of that on his first glorious day in New York, and had even provided a way to snap the thread. It lay on his dressing-table now; he had got it out last night when he came blindly up from dinner, but the shiny metal hurt his eyes, and he disliked the looks of it.

He rose and moved about with a painful effort, succumbing now and again to attacks of nausea. It was the old depression exaggerated; all the world had become Cordelia Street. Yet somehow he was not afraid of anything, was absolutely calm; perhaps because he had looked into the dark corner at last and knew. It was bad enough, what he saw there, but somehow not so bad as his long fear of it had been. He saw everything clearly now. He had a feeling that he had made the best of it, that he had lived the sort of life he was meant to live, and for half an hour he sat staring at the revolver. But he told himself that was not the way, so he went downstairs and took a cab to the ferry.

When Paul arrived at Newark, he got off the train and took another cab, directing the driver to follow the Pennsylvania tracks out of the town. The snow lay heavy on the roadways and had drifted deep in the open fields. Only here and there the dead grass or dried weed stalks projected, singularly black, above it. Once well into the country, Paul dismissed the carriage and walked, floundering along the tracks, his mind a medley of irrelevant things. He seemed to hold in his brain an actual picture of everything he had seen that morning. He remembered every feature of both his drivers, of the toothless old woman from whom he had bought the red flowers in his coat, the agent from whom he had got his ticket, and all of his fellow-passengers on the ferry. His mind, unable to cope with vital matters near at hand, worked feverishly and deftly at sorting and grouping these images. They made for him a part of the ugliness of the world, of the ache in his head, and the bitter burning on his tongue. He stooped and put a handful of snow into his mouth as he walked, but that, too, seemed hot. When he reached a little hillside, where the tracks ran through a cut some twenty feet below him, he stopped and sat down.

The carnations in his coat were drooping with the cold, he noticed; their red glory all over. It occurred to him that all the flowers he had seen in the glass cases that first night must have gone the same way, long before this. It was only one splendid breath they had, in spite of their brave mockery at the winter outside the glass; and it was a losing game in the end, it seemed, this revolt against the homilies by which the world is run. Paul took one of the blossoms carefully from his coat and scooped a little hole in the snow, where he covered it up. Then he dozed a while, from his weak condition, seemingly insensible to the cold.

The sound of an approaching train awoke him, and he started to his feet, remembering only his resolution, and afraid lest he should be too late. He stood watching the approaching locomotive, his teeth chattering, his lips drawn away from them in a frightened smile; once or twice he glanced nervously sidewise, as though he

65

were being watched. When the right moment came, he jumped. As he fell, the folly of his haste occurred to him with merciless clearness, the vastness of what he had left undone. There flashed through his brain, clearer than ever before, the blue of Adriatic water, the yellow of Algerian sands.

He felt something strike his chest, and that his body was being thrown swiftly through the air, on and on, immeasurably far and fast, while his limbs were gently relaxed. Then, because the picture making mechanism was crushed, the disturbing visions flashed into black, and Paul dropped back into the immense design of things.

Anton Chekhov

The Lady with the Pet Dog   1899

Translated by Avrahm Yarmolinsky

Anton Chekhov

Anton Chekhov (1860–1904), one of the Russian writers who helped shape modern fiction, is remembered especially for his plays and short stories. Born in the provincial town of Taganrog, the grandson of a serf who had bought his own freedom, Chekhov as a boy worked in his father's general store, a hangout for vodka-drinking storytellers. As a young man, he studied at Moscow University and became a doctor of medicine. To earn money while a medical student, he wrote his first stories for magazines. By 1886 his work had become so celebrated that he gave up medicine for writing, though continuing to treat sick peasants at his home without fee and to work in clinics during times of famine and epidemic. From 1896 to 1904 Chekhov wrote his great plays for the Moscow Art Theater, where they were directed by the influential director Konstantin Stanislavsky: The Seagull, The Cherry Orchard, Uncle Vanya, and The Three Sisters. Chekhov's last years were brightened by his marriage to Olga Knipper, a star of the theater company. He died at forty-four, after a long struggle against tuberculosis.

I

A new person, it was said, had appeared on the esplanade:° a lady with a pet dog. Dmitry Dmitrich Gurov, who had spent a fortnight at Yalta° and had got used to the place, had also begun to take an interest in new arrivals. As he sat in Vernet's confectionery shop, he saw, walking on the esplanade, a fair-haired young woman of medium height, wearing a beret; a white Pomeranian was trotting behind her.

And afterwards he met her in the public garden and in the square several times a day. She walked alone, always wearing the same beret and always with the white dog; no one knew who she was and everyone called her simply "the lady with the pet dog."

---

esplanade: a walkway or promenade along the shore.   *Yalta:* a port city on the Black Sea, a popular seaside resort for wealthy Russians.

"If she is here alone without husband or friends," Gurov reflected, "it wouldn't be a bad thing to make her acquaintance."

He was under forty, but he already had a daughter twelve years old, and two sons at school. They had found a wife for him when he was very young, a student in his second year, and by now she seemed half as old again as he. She was a tall, erect woman with dark eyebrows, stately and dignified and, as she said of herself, intellectual. She read a great deal, used simplified spelling in her letters, called her husband, not Dmitry, but Dimitry, while he privately considered her of limited intelligence, narrow-minded, dowdy, was afraid of her, and did not like to be at home. He had begun being unfaithful to her long ago—had been unfaithful to her often and, probably for that reason, almost always spoke ill of women, and when they were talked of in his presence used to call them "the inferior race."

It seemed to him that he had been sufficiently tutored by bitter experience to call them what he pleased, and yet he could not have lived without "the inferior race" for two days together. In the company of men he was bored and ill at ease, he was chilly and uncommunicative with them; but when he was among women he felt free, and knew what to speak to them about and how to comport himself; and even to be silent with them was no strain on him. In his appearance, in his character, in his whole make-up there was something attractive and elusive that disposed women in his favor and allured them. He knew that, and some force seemed to draw him to them, too. 5

Oft-repeated and really bitter experience had taught him long ago that with decent people—particularly Moscow people—who are irresolute and slow to move, every affair which at first seems a light and charming adventure inevitably grows into a whole problem of extreme complexity, and in the end a painful situation is created. But at every new meeting with an interesting woman this lesson of experience seemed to slip from his memory, and he was eager for life, and everything seemed so simple and diverting.

One evening while he was dining in the public garden the lady in the beret walked up without haste to take the next table. Her expression, her gait, her dress, and the way she did her hair told him that she belonged to the upper class, that she was married, that she was in Yalta for the first time and alone, and that she was bored there. The stories told of the immorality in Yalta are to a great extent untrue; he despised them, and knew that such stories were made up for the most part by persons who would have been glad to sin themselves if they had had the chance; but when the lady sat down at the next table three paces from him, he recalled these stories of easy conquests, of trips to the mountains, and the tempting thought of a swift, fleeting liaison, a romance with an unknown woman of whose very name he was ignorant suddenly took hold of him.

He beckoned invitingly to the Pomeranian, and when the dog approached him, shook his finger at it. The Pomeranian growled; Gurov threatened it again.

The lady glanced at him and at once dropped her eyes.

"He doesn't bite," she said and blushed. 10

"May I give him a bone?" he asked; and when she nodded he inquired affably, "Have you been in Yalta long?"

"About five days."

"And I am dragging out the second week here."

There was a short silence.

"Time passes quickly, and yet it is so dull here!" she said, not looking at him. 15

"It's only the fashion to say it's dull here. A provincial will live in Belyov or Zhizdra and not be bored, but when he comes here it's 'Oh, the dullness! Oh, the dust!' One would think he came from Granada."

She laughed. Then both continued eating in silence, like strangers, but after dinner they walked together and there sprang up between them the light banter of people who are free and contented, to whom it does not matter where they go or what they talk about. They walked and talked of the strange light on the sea: the water was a soft, warm, lilac color, and there was a golden band of moonlight upon it. They talked of how sultry it was after a hot day. Gurov told her that he was a native of Moscow, that he had studied languages and literature at the university, but had a post in a bank; that at one time he had trained to become an opera singer but had given it up, that he owned two houses in Moscow. And he learned from her that she had grown up in Petersburg, but had lived in S_____ since her marriage two years previously, that she was going to stay in Yalta for about another month, and that her husband, who needed a rest, too, might perhaps come to fetch her. She was not certain whether her husband was a member of a Government Board or served on a Zemstvo Council,° and this amused her. And Gurov learned that her name was Anna Sergeyevna.

Afterwards in his room at the hotel he thought about her—and was certain that he would meet her the next day. It was bound to happen. Getting into bed he recalled that she had been a schoolgirl only recently, doing lessons like his own daughter; he thought how much timidity and angularity there was still in her laugh and her manner of talking with a stranger. It must have been the first time in her life that she was alone in a setting in which she was followed, looked at, and spoken to for one secret purpose alone, which she could hardly fail to guess. He thought of her slim, delicate throat, her lovely gray eyes.

"There's something pathetic about her, though," he thought, and dropped off.

II

A week had passed since they had struck up an acquaintance. It was a holiday. It was close indoors, while in the street the wind whirled the dust about and blew people's hats off. One was thirsty all day, and Gurov often went into the restaurant and offered Anna Sergeyevna a soft drink or ice cream. One did not know what to do with oneself.

In the evening when the wind had abated they went out on the pier to watch the steamer come in. There were a great many people walking about the dock; they had come to welcome someone and they were carrying bunches of flowers. And two peculiarities of a festive Yalta crowd stood out: the elderly ladies were dressed like young ones and there were many generals.

Owing to the choppy sea, the steamer arrived late, after sunset, and it was a long time tacking about before it put in at the pier. Anna Sergeyevna peered at the steamer and the passengers through her lorgnette as though looking for acquaintances, and whenever she turned to Gurov her eyes were shining. She talked a great deal and asked questions jerkily, forgetting the next moment what she had asked; then she lost her lorgnette in the crush.

The festive crowd began to disperse; it was now too dark to see people's faces; there was no wind any more, but Gurov and Anna Sergeyevna still stood as though

Zemstvo Council: the elected council for local administration in Czarist Russia, the equivalent of a county administration.

waiting to see someone else come off the steamer. Anna Sergeyevna was silent now, and sniffed her flowers without looking at Gurov.

"The weather has improved this evening," he said. "Where shall we go now? Shall we drive somewhere?"

She did not reply.   25

Then he looked at her intently, and suddenly embraced her and kissed her on the lips, and the moist fragrance of her flowers enveloped him; and at once he looked round him anxiously, wondering if anyone had seen them.

"Let us go to your place," he said softly. And they walked off together rapidly.

The air in her room was close and there was the smell of the perfume she had bought at the Japanese shop. Looking at her, Gurov thought: "What encounters life offers!" From the past he preserved the memory of carefree, good-natured women whom love made gay and who were grateful to him for the happiness he gave them, however brief it might be; and of women like his wife who loved without sincerity, with too many words, affectedly, hysterically, with an expression that it was not love or passion that engaged them but something more significant; and of two or three others, very beautiful, frigid women, across whose faces would suddenly flit a rapacious expression—an obstinate desire to take from life more than it could give, and these were women no longer young, capricious, unreflecting, domineering, unintelligent, and when Gurov grew cold to them their beauty aroused his hatred, and the lace on their lingerie seemed to him to resemble scales.

But here there was the timidity, the angularity of inexperienced youth, a feeling of awkwardness; and there was a sense of embarrassment, as though someone had suddenly knocked at the door. Anna Sergeyevna, "the lady with the pet dog," treated what had happened in a peculiar way, very seriously, as though it were her fall—so it seemed, and this was odd and inappropriate. Her features drooped and faded, and her long hair hung down sadly on either side of her face; she grew pensive and her dejected pose was that of a Magdalene in a picture by an old master.

"It's not right," she said. "You don't respect me now, you first of all."   30

There was a watermelon on the table. Gurov cut himself a slice and began eating it without haste. They were silent for at least half an hour.

There was something touching about Anna Sergeyevna; she had the purity of a well-bred, naive woman who has seen little of life. The single candle burning on the table barely illuminated her face, yet it was clear that she was unhappy.

"Why should I stop respecting you, darling?" asked Gurov. "You don't know what you're saying."

"God forgive me," she said, and her eyes filled with tears. "It's terrible."

"It's as though you were trying to exonerate yourself."   35

"How can I exonerate myself? No. I am a bad, low woman; I despise myself and I have no thought of exonerating myself. It's not my husband but myself I have deceived. And not only just now; I have been deceiving myself for a long time. My husband may be a good, honest man, but he is a flunkey! I don't know what he does, what his work is, but I know he is a flunkey! I was twenty when I married him. I was tormented by curiosity; I wanted something better. 'There must be a different sort of life,' I said to myself. I wanted to live! To live, to live! Curiosity kept eating at me—you don't understand, but I swear to God I could no longer control myself; something was going on in me; I could not be held back. I told my husband I was ill, and came here. And here I have been walking about as though in a daze, as though I were mad; and now I have become a vulgar, vile woman whom anyone may despise."

Gurov was already bored with her; he was irritated by her naive tone, by her repentance, so unexpected and so out of place, but for the tears in her eyes he might
have thought she was joking or play-acting.

"I don't understand, my dear," he said softly. "What do you want?"

She hid her face on his breast and pressed close to him.

"Believe me, believe me, I beg you," she said, "I love honesty and purity, and sin 40
is loathsome to me; I don't know what I'm doing. Simple people say, 'The Evil One
has led me astray.' And I may say of myself now that the Evil One has led me astray."

"Quiet, quiet," he murmured.

He looked into her fixed, frightened eyes, kissed her, spoke to her softly and affectionately, and by degrees she calmed down, and her gaiety returned; both began
laughing.

Afterwards when they went out there was not a soul on the esplanade. The town
with its cypresses looked quite dead, but the sea was still sounding as it broke upon
the beach; a single launch was rocking on the waves and on it a lantern was blinking
sleepily.

They found a cab and drove to Oreanda.

"I found out your surname in the hall just now; it was written on the board—von 45
Dideritz," said Gurov. "Is your husband German?"

"No; I believe his grandfather was German, but he is Greek Orthodox himself."

At Oreanda they sat on a bench not far from the church, looked down at the sea,
and were silent. Yalta was barely visible through the morning mist; white clouds
rested motionlessly on the mountaintops. The leaves did not stir on the trees, cicadas
twanged, and the monotonous muffled sound of the sea that rose from below spoke of
the peace, the eternal sleep awaiting us. So it rumbled below when there was no
Yalta, no Oreanda here; so it rumbles now, and it will rumble as indifferently and as
hollowly when we are no more. And in this constancy, in this complete indifference
to the life and death of each of us, there lies, perhaps, a pledge of our eternal salvation, of the unceasing advance of life upon earth, of unceasing movement towards
perfection. Sitting beside a young woman who in the dawn seemed so lovely, Gurov,
soothed and spellbound by these magical surroundings—the sea, the mountains, the
clouds, the wide sky—thought how everything is really beautiful in this world when
one reflects: everything except what we think or do ourselves when we forget the
higher aims of life and our own human dignity.

A man strolled up to them—probably a guard—looked at them and walked
away. And this detail, too, seemed so mysterious and beautiful. They saw a steamer
arrive from Feodosia, its lights extinguished in the glow of dawn.

"There is dew on the grass," said Anna Sergeyevna, after a silence.

"Yes, it's time to go home." 50

They returned to the city.

Then they met every day at twelve o'clock on the esplanade, lunched and dined
together, took walks, admired the sea. She complained that she slept badly, that she
had palpitations, asked the same questions, troubled now by jealousy and now by the
fear that he did not respect her sufficiently. And often in the square or the public garden, when there was no one near them, he suddenly drew her to him and kissed her
passionately. Complete idleness, these kisses in broad daylight exchanged furtively in
dread of someone's seeing them, the heat, the smell of the sea, and the continual flit-
ting before his eyes of idle, well-dressed, well-fed people, worked a complete change
in him; he kept telling Anna Sergeyevna how beautiful she was, how seductive, was

urgently passionate; he would not move a step away from her, while she was often pensive and continually pressed him to confess that he did not respect her, did not love her in the least, and saw in her nothing but a common woman. Almost every evening rather late they drove somewhere out of town, to Oreanda or to the water-fall; and the excursion was always a success, the scenery invariably impressed them as beautiful and magnificent.

They were expecting her husband, but a letter came from him saying that he had eye-trouble, and begging his wife to return home as soon as possible. Anna Sergeyevna made haste to go.

"It's a good thing I am leaving," she said to Gurov. "It's the hand of Fate!"

She took a carriage to the railway station, and he went with her. They were   55
driving the whole day. When she had taken her place in the express, and when the second bell had rung, she said, "Let me look at you once more—let me look at you again. Like this."

She was not crying but was so sad that she seemed ill and her face was quivering.

"I shall be thinking of you—remembering you," she said. "God bless you; be happy. Don't remember evil against me. We are parting forever—it has to be, for we ought never to have met. Well, God bless you."

The train moved off rapidly, its lights soon vanished, and a minute later there was no sound of it, as though everything had conspired to end as quickly as possible that sweet trance, that madness. Left alone on the platform, and gazing into the dark distance, Gurov listened to the twang of the grasshoppers and the hum of the tele-graph wires, feeling as though he had just waked up. And he reflected, musing, that there had now been another episode or adventure in his life, and it, too, was at an end, and nothing was left of it but a memory. He was moved, sad, and slightly re-morseful: this young woman whom he would never meet again had not been happy with him; he had been warm and affectionate with her, but yet in his manner, his tone, and his caresses there had been a shade of light irony, the slightly coarse arro-gance of a happy male who was, besides, almost twice her age. She had constantly called him kind, exceptional, high-minded; obviously he had seemed to her different from what he really was, so he had involuntarily deceived her.

Here at the station there was already a scent of autumn in the air; it was a chilly evening.

"It is time for me to go north, too," thought Gurov as he left the platform. "High   60
time!"

III

At home in Moscow the winter routine was already established; the stoves were heated, and in the morning it was still dark when the children were having breakfast and getting ready for school, and the nurse would light the lamp for a short time. There were frosts already. When the first snow falls, on the first day the sleighs are out, it is pleasant to see the white earth, the white roofs; one draws easy, delicious breaths, and the season brings back the days of one's youth. The old limes and birches, white with hoar-frost, have a good-natured look; they are closer to one's heart than cypresses and palms, and near them one no longer wants to think of mountains and the sea.

Gurov, a native of Moscow, arrived there on a fine frosty day, and when he put on his fur coat and warm gloves and took a walk along Petrovka, and when on Saturday night he heard the bells ringing, his recent trip and the places he had visited lost all charm for him. Little by little he became immersed in Moscow life, greedily read three newspapers a day, and declared that he did not read the Moscow papers on principle. He already felt a longing for restaurants, clubs, formal dinners, anniversary celebrations, and it flattered him to entertain distinguished lawyers and actors, and to play cards with a professor at the physicians' club. He could eat a whole portion of meat stewed with pickled cabbage and served in a pan, Moscow style.

A month or so would pass and the image of Anna Sergeyevna, it seemed to him, would become misty in his memory, and only from time to time he would dream of her with her touching smile as he dreamed of others. But more than a month went by, winter came into its own, and everything was still clear in his memory as though he had parted from Anna Sergeyevna only yesterday. And his memories glowed more and more vividly. When in the evening stillness the voices of his children preparing their lessons reached his study, or when he listened to a song or to an organ playing in a restaurant, or when the storm howled in the chimney, suddenly everything would rise up in his memory: what had happened on the pier and the early morning with the mist on the mountains, and the steamer coming from Feodosia, and the kisses. He would pace about his room a long time, remembering and smiling; then his memories passed into reveries, and in his imagination the past would mingle with what was to come. He did not dream of Anna Sergeyevna, but she followed him about everywhere and watched him. When he shut his eyes he saw her before him as though she were there in the flesh, and she seemed to him lovelier, younger, tenderer than she had been, and he imagined himself a finer man than he had been in Yalta. Of evenings she peered out at him from the bookcase, from the fireplace, from the corner—he heard her breathing, the caressing rustle of her clothes. In the street he followed the women with his eyes, looking for someone who resembled her.

Already he was tormented by a strong desire to share his memories with someone. But in his home it was impossible to talk of his love, and he had no one to talk to outside; certainly he could not confide in his tenants or in anyone at the bank. And what was there to talk about? He hadn't loved her then, had he? Had there been anything beautiful, poetical, edifying, or simply interesting in his relations with Anna Sergeyevna? And he was forced to talk vaguely of love, of women, and no one guessed what he meant; only his wife would twitch her black eyebrows and say, "The part of a philanderer does not suit you at all, Dimitry."

One evening, coming out of the physicians' club with an official with whom he had been playing cards, he could not resist saying:

"If you only knew what a fascinating woman I became acquainted with at Yalta!"

The official got into his sledge and was driving away, but turned suddenly and shouted:

"Dmitry Dmitrich!"

"What is it?"

"You were right this evening: the sturgeon was a bit high."

These words, so commonplace, for some reason moved Gurov to indignation, and struck him as degrading and unclean. What savage manners, what mugs! What stupid nights, what dull, humdrum days! Frenzied gambling, gluttony, drunkenness, continual talk always about the same thing! Futile pursuits and conversations always about the same topics take up the better part of one's time, the better part of one's strength, and in the end there is left a life clipped and wingless, an absurd mess, and there is no escaping or getting away from it—just as though one were in a madhouse or a prison.

Gurov, boiling with indignation, did not sleep all night. And he had a headache all the next day. And the following nights too he slept badly; he sat up in bed, thinking, or paced up and down his room. He was fed up with his children, fed up with the bank; he had no desire to go anywhere or to talk of anything.

In December during the holidays he prepared to take a trip and told his wife he was going to Petersburg to do what he could for a young friend—and he set off for S_____. What for? He did not know, himself. He wanted to see Anna Sergeyevna and talk with her, to arrange a rendezvous if possible.

He arrived at S_____ in the morning, and at the hotel took the best room, in which the floor was covered with gray army cloth, and on the table there was an ink-stand, gray with dust and topped by a figure on horseback, its hat in its raised hand and its head broken off. The porter gave him the necessary information: von Dideritz lived in a house of his own on Staro-Goncharnaya Street, not far from the hotel: he was rich and lived well and kept his own horses; everyone in the town knew him. The porter pronounced the name: "Dridiritz."

Without haste Gurov made his way to Staro-Goncharnaya Street and found the house. Directly opposite the house stretched a long gray fence studded with nails. 75

"A fence like that would make one run away," thought Gurov, looking now at the fence, now at the windows of the house.

He reflected: this was a holiday, and the husband was apt to be at home. And in any case, it would be tactless to go into the house and disturb her. If he were to send her a note, it might fall into her husband's hands, and that might spoil everything. The best thing was to rely on chance. And he kept walking up and down the street and along the fence, waiting for the chance. He saw a beggar go in at the gate and heard the dogs attack him; then an hour later he heard a piano, and the sound came to him faintly and indistinctly. Probably it was Anna Sergeyevna playing. The front door opened suddenly, and an old woman came out, followed by the familiar white Pomeranian. Gurov was on the point of calling to the dog, but his heart began beating violently, and in his excitement he could not remember the Pomeranian's name.

He kept walking up and down, and hated the gray fence more and more, and by now he thought irritably that Anna Sergeyevna had forgotten him, and was perhaps already diverting herself with another man, and that that was very natural in a young woman who from morning till night had to look at that damn fence. He went back to his hotel room and sat on the couch for a long while, not knowing what to do, then he had dinner and a long nap.

"How stupid and annoying all this is!" he thought when he woke and looked at the dark windows: it was already evening. "Here I've had a good sleep for some reason. What am I going to do at night?"

He sat on the bed, which was covered with a cheap gray blanket of the kind seen in hospitals, and he twitted himself in his vexation: 80

"So there's your lady with the pet dog. There's your adventure. A nice place to cool your heels in."

That morning at the station a playbill in large letters had caught his eye. *The Geisha* was to be given for the first time. He thought of this and drove to the theater.

"It's quite possible that she goes to first nights," he thought.

The theater was full. As in all provincial theaters, there was a haze above the chandelier, the gallery was noisy and restless; in the front row, before the beginning of the performance the local dandies were standing with their hands clasped behind their backs; in the Governor's box the Governor's daughter, wearing a boa, occupied the front seat, while the Governor himself hid modestly behind the portiere and only his hands were visible; the curtain swayed; the orchestra was a long time tuning up. While the audience was coming in and taking their seats, Gurov scanned the faces eagerly.

Anna Sergeyevna, too, came in. She sat down in the third row, and when Gurov   85
looked at her his heart contracted, and he understood clearly that in the whole world there was no human being so near, so precious, and so important to him; she, this little, undistinguished woman, lost in a provincial crowd, with a vulgar lorgnette in her hand, filled his whole life now, was his sorrow and his joy, the only happiness that he now desired for himself, and to the sounds of the bad orchestra, of the miserable local violins, he thought how lovely she was. He thought and dreamed.

A young man with small side-whiskers, very tall and stooped, came in with Anna Sergeyevna and sat down beside her; he nodded his head at every step and seemed to be bowing continually. Probably this was the husband whom at Yalta, in an access of bitter feeling, she had called a flunkey. And there really was in his lanky figure, his side-whiskers, his small bald patch, something of a flunkey's retiring manner; his smile was mawkish, and in his buttonhole there was an academic badge like a waiter's number.

During the first intermission the husband went out to have a smoke; she remained in her seat. Gurov, who was also sitting in the orchestra, went up to her and said in a shaky voice, with a forced smile:

"Good evening!"

She glanced at him and turned pale, then looked at him again in horror, unable to believe her eyes, and gripped the fan and the lorgnette tightly together in her hands, evidently trying to keep herself from fainting. Both were silent. She was sitting, he was standing, frightened by her distress and not daring to take a seat beside her. The violins and the flute that were being tuned up sang out. He suddenly felt frightened: it seemed as if all the people in the boxes were looking at them. She got up and went hurriedly to the exit; he followed her, and both of them walked blindly along the corridors and up and down stairs, and figures in the uniforms prescribed for magistrates, teachers, and officials of the Department of Crown Lands, all wearing badges, flitted before their eyes, as did also ladies, and fur coats on hangers; they were conscious of drafts and the smell of stale tobacco. And Gurov, whose heart was beating violently, thought:

"Oh, Lord! Why are these people here and this orchestra!"   90

And at that instant he suddenly recalled how when he had seen Anna Sergeyevna off at the station he had said to himself that all was over between them and that they would never meet again. But how distant the end still was!

On the narrow, gloomy staircase over which it said "To the Amphitheatre," she stopped.

"How you frightened me!" she said, breathing hard, still pale and stunned. "Oh, how you frightened me! I am barely alive. Why did you come? Why?"

"But do understand, Anna, do understand—" he said hurriedly, under his breath. "I implore you, do understand—"

She looked at him with fear, with entreaty, with love; she looked at him intently,   95
to keep his features more distinctly in her memory.

"I suffer so," she went on, not listening to him. "All this time I have been thinking of nothing but you; I live only by the thought of you. And I wanted to forget, to forget; but why, oh, why have you come?"

On the landing above them two high school boys were looking down and smoking, but it was all the same to Gurov; he drew Anna Sergeyevna to him and began kissing her face and hands.

"What are you doing, what are you doing!" she was saying in horror, pushing him away. "We have lost our senses. Go away today; go away at once—I conjure you by all that is sacred, I implore you—People are coming this way!"

Someone was walking up the stairs.

"You must leave," Anna Sergeyevna went on in a whisper. "Do you hear, Dmitry   100
Dmitrich? I will come and see you in Moscow. I have never been happy; I am unhappy now, and I never, never shall be happy, never! So don't make me suffer still more! I swear I'll come to Moscow. But now let us part. My dear, good, precious one, let us part!"

She pressed his hand and walked rapidly downstairs, turning to look round at him, and from her eyes he could see that she really was unhappy. Gurov stood for a while, listening, then when all grew quiet, he found his coat and left the theater.

IV

And Anna Sergeyevna began coming to see him in Moscow. Once every two or three months she left S_____, telling her husband that she was going to consult a doctor about a woman's ailment from which she was suffering—and her husband did and did not believe her. When she arrived in Moscow she would stop at the Slavyansky Bazar Hotel, and at once send a man in a red cap to Gurov. Gurov came to see her, and no one in Moscow knew of it.

Once he was going to see her in this way on a winter morning (the messenger had come the evening before and not found him in). With him walked his daughter, whom he wanted to take to school; it was on the way. Snow was coming down in big wet flakes.

"It's three degrees above zero,° and yet it's snowing," Gurov was saying to his daughter. "But this temperature prevails only on the surface of the earth; in the upper layers of the atmosphere there is quite a different temperature."

"And why doesn't it thunder in winter, papa?"   105

He explained that, too. He talked, thinking all the while that he was on his way to a rendezvous, and no living soul knew of it, and probably no one would ever know. He had two lives, an open one, seen and known by all who needed to know it, full of conventional truth and conventional falsehood, exactly like the lives of his friends and acquaintances; and another life that went on in secret. And through some strange, perhaps accidental, combination of circumstances, everything that was of interest and importance to him, everything that was essential to him, everything about which he felt sincerely and did not deceive himself, everything that constituted the core of his life, was going on concealed from others; while all that was false, the shell in which he hid to cover the truth—his work at the bank, for instance, his discussions at the club, his references to the "inferior race," his appearances at anniversary celebrations with his wife—all that went on in the open. Judging others by himself, he did not believe what he saw, and always fancied that every man led his real, most interesting life under cover of secrecy as

---

three degrees above zero: the Russian temperature is measured in Celsius degrees; the Fahrenheit equivalent would be about thirty-seven degrees.

under cover of night. The personal life of every individual is based on secrecy, and perhaps it is partly for that reason that civilized man is so nervously anxious that personal privacy should be respected.

Having taken his daughter to school, Gurov went on to the Slavyansky Bazar Hotel. He took off his fur coat in the lobby, went upstairs, and knocked gently at the door. Anna Sergeyevna, wearing his favorite gray dress, exhausted by the journey and by waiting, had been expecting him since the previous evening. She was pale, and looked at him without a smile, and had hardly entered when she flung herself on his breast. That kiss was a long, lingering one, as though they had not seen one another for two years.

"Well, darling, how are you getting on there?" he asked. "What news?"

"Wait; I'll tell you in a moment—I can't speak."

She could not speak; she was crying. She turned away from him, and pressed her   110
handkerchief to her eyes.

"Let her have her cry; meanwhile I'll sit down," he thought, and he seated himself in an armchair.

Then he rang and ordered tea, and while he was having his tea she remained standing at the window with her back to him. She was crying out of sheer agitation, in the sorrowful consciousness that their life was so sad; that they could only see each other in secret and had to hide from people like thieves! Was it not a broken life?

"Come, stop now, dear!" he said.

It was plain to him that this love of theirs would not be over soon, that the end of it was not in sight. Anna Sergeyevna was growing more and more attached to him. She adored him, and it was unthinkable to tell her that their love was bound to come to an end some day; besides, she would not have believed it!

He went up to her and took her by the shoulders, to fondle her and say some-   115
thing diverting, and at that moment he caught sight of himself in the mirror.

His hair was already beginning to turn gray. And it seemed odd to him that he had grown so much older in the last few years, and lost his looks. The shoulders on which his hands rested were warm and heaving. He felt compassion for this life, still so warm and lovely, but probably already about to begin to fade and wither like his own. Why did she love him so much? He always seemed to women different from what he was, and they loved in him not himself, but the man whom their imagination created and whom they had been eagerly seeking all their lives; and afterwards, when they saw their mistake, they loved him nevertheless. And not one of them had been happy with him. In the past he had met women, come together with them, parted from them, but he had never once loved; it was anything you please, but not love. And only now when his head was gray he had fallen in love, really, truly—for the first time in his life.

Anna Sergeyevna and he loved each other as people do who are very close and intimate, like man and wife, like tender friends; it seemed to them that Fate itself had meant them for one another, and they could not understand why he had a wife and she a husband; and it was as though they were a pair of migratory birds, male and female, caught and forced to live in different cages. They forgave each other what they were ashamed of in their past, they forgave everything in the present, and felt that this love of theirs had altered them both.

Formerly in moments of sadness he had soothed himself with whatever logical arguments came into his head, but now he no longer cared for logic; he felt profound compassion, he wanted to be sincere and tender.

"Give it up now, my darling," he said. "You've had your cry; that's enough. Let us have a talk now, we'll think up something."

Then they spent a long time taking counsel together, they talked of how to avoid the necessity for secrecy, for deception, for living in different cities, and not seeing one another for long stretches of time. How could they free themselves from these intolerable fetters?

"How? How?" he asked, clutching his head. "How?"

And it seemed as though in a little while the solution would be found, and then a new and glorious life would begin; and it was clear to both of them that the end was still far off, and that what was to be most complicated and difficult for them was only just beginning.

Kate Chopin

The Story of an Hour   1894

Kate Chopin (1851–1904) demonstrates again, as in "The Storm" in Chapter 4, her ability to write short stories of compressed intensity. For a brief biography and a portrait see page 110.

Knowing that Mrs. Mallard was afflicted with a heart trouble, great care was taken to break to her as gently as possible the news of her husband's death.

It was her sister Josephine who told her, in broken sentences; veiled hints that revealed in half concealing. Her husband's friend Richards was there, too, near her. It was he who had been in the newspaper office when intelligence of the railroad disaster was received, with Brently Mallard's name leading the list of "killed." He had only taken the time to assure himself of its truth by a second telegram, and had hastened to forestall any less careful, less tender friend in bearing the sad message.

She did not hear the story as many women have heard the same, with a paralyzed inability to accept its significance. She wept at once, with sudden, wild abandonment, in her sister's arms. When the storm of grief had spent itself she went away to her room alone. She would have no one follow her.

There stood, facing the open window, a comfortable, roomy armchair. Into this she sank, pressed down by a physical exhaustion that haunted her body and seemed to reach into her soul.

She could see in the open square before her house the tops of trees that were all aquiver with the new spring life. The delicious breath of rain was in the air. In the street below a peddler was crying his wares. The notes of a distant song which some one was singing reached her faintly, and countless sparrows were twittering in the eaves.

There were patches of blue sky showing here and there through the clouds that had met and piled one above the other in the west facing her window.

She sat with her head thrown back upon the cushion of the chair, quite motionless, except when a sob came up into her throat and shook her, as a child who has cried itself to sleep continues to sob in its dreams.

She was young, with a fair, calm face, whose lines bespoke repression and even a certain strength. But now there was a dull stare in her eyes, whose gaze was fixed away off yonder on one of those patches of blue sky. It was not a glance of reflection, but rather indicated a suspension of intelligent thought.

There was something coming to her and she was waiting for it, fearfully. What was it? She did not know; it was too subtle and elusive to name. But she felt it, creeping out of the sky, reaching toward her through the sounds, the scents, the color that filled the air.

Now her bosom rose and fell tumultuously. She was beginning to recognize this thing that was approaching to possess her, and she was striving to beat it back with her will—as powerless as her two white slender hands would have been. 10

When she abandoned herself a little whispered word escaped her slightly parted lips. She said it over and over under her breath: "free, free, free!" The vacant stare and the look of terror that had followed it went from her eyes. They stayed keen and bright. Her pulses beat fast, and the coursing blood warmed and relaxed every inch of her body.

She did not stop to ask if it were not a monstrous joy that held her. A clear and exalted perception enabled her to dismiss the suggestion as trivial.

She knew that she would weep again when she saw the kind, tender hands folded in death; the face that had never looked save with love upon her, fixed and gray and dead. But she saw beyond that bitter moment a long procession of years to come that would belong to her absolutely. And she opened and spread her arms out to them in welcome.

There would be no one to live for her during those coming years; she would live for herself. There would be no powerful will bending hers in that blind persistence with which men and women believe they have a right to impose a private will upon a fellow-creature. A kind intention or a cruel intention made the act seem no less a crime as she looked upon it in that brief moment of illumination.

And yet she had loved him—sometimes. Often she had not. What did it matter! What could love, the unsolved mystery, count for in face of this possession of self-assertion which she suddenly recognized as the strongest impulse of her being! 15

"Free! Body and soul free!" she kept whispering.

Josephine was kneeling before the closed door with her lips to the keyhole, imploring for admission. "Louise, open the door! I beg; open the door—you will make yourself ill. What are you doing, Louise? For heaven's sake open the door."

"Go away. I am not making myself ill." No; she was drinking in a very elixir of life through that open window.

Her fancy was running riot along those days ahead of her. Spring days, and summer days, and all sorts of days that would be her own. She breathed a quick prayer that life might be long. It was only yesterday she had thought with a shudder that life might be long.

She arose at length and opened the door to her sister's importunities. There was a feverish triumph in her eyes, and she carried herself unwittingly like a goddess of Victory. She clasped her sister's waist, and together they descended the stairs. Richards stood waiting for them at the bottom. 20

Some one was opening the front door with a latchkey. It was Brently Mallard who entered, a little travel-stained, composedly carrying his grip-sack and umbrella. He had been far from the scene of the accident, and did not even know there had been one. He stood amazed at Josephine's piercing cry; at Richards' quick motion to screen him from the view of his wife.

But Richards was too late.

When the doctors came they said she had died of heart disease—of joy that kills.

Sandra Cisneros

The House on Mango Street   1984

*Sandra Cisneros was born in Chicago in 1954.
The child of a Mexican father and a Mexican
American mother, she was the only daughter in
a family of seven children. She attended Loyola
University of Chicago and then received a master's degree from the University of Iowa Writers' Workshop. She has instructed high-school
dropouts, but more recently she has taught as a
visiting writer at numerous universities, including the University of California at Irvine and at
Berkeley, and the University of Michigan. Her
honors include fellowships from the National
Endowment for the Arts and the MacArthur
Foundation. Cisneros's first published work was
poetry:* Bad Boys *(1980), followed by* My
Wicked Wicked Ways *(1987) and* Loose
Woman *(1994). Her fiction collections,* The*

Sandra Cisneros

House on Mango Street *(1984) and* Women Hollering Creek *(1991), however, earned
her a broader audience. She has also published a bilingual children's book,* Hairs: Pelitos
(1994), and a novel, Caramelo *(2002). Cisneros currently lives in San Antonio, Texas.*

We didn't always live on Mango Street. Before that we lived on Loomis on the
third floor, and before that we lived on Keeler. Before Keeler it was Paulina, and before that I can't remember. But what I remember most is moving a lot. Each time it
seemed there'd be one more of us. By the time we got to Mango Street we were six—
Mama, Papa, Carlos, Kiki, my sister Nenny, and me.

The house on Mango Street is ours, and we don't have to pay rent to anybody, or
share the yard with the people downstairs, or be careful not to make too much noise,
and there isn't a landlord banging on the ceiling with a broom. But even so, it's not
the house we'd thought we'd get.

We had to leave the flat on Loomis quick. The water pipes broke and the
landlord wouldn't fix them because the house was too old. We had to leave fast.
We were using the washroom next door and carrying water over in empty milk
gallons. That's why Mama and Papa looked for a house, and that's why we moved
into the house on Mango Street, far away, on the other side of town.

They always told us that one day we would move into a house, a real house that
would be ours for always so we wouldn't have to move each year. And our house
would have running water and pipes that worked. And inside it would have real stairs,
not hallway stairs, but stairs inside like the houses on T.V. And we'd have a basement
and at least three washrooms so when we took a bath we wouldn't have to tell everybody. Our house would be white with trees around it, a great big yard and grass growing without a fence. This was the house Papa talked about when he held a lottery
ticket and this was the house Mama dreamed up in the stories she told us before we
went to bed.

But the house on Mango Street is not the way they told it at all. It's small and   5
red with tight steps in front and windows so small you'd think they were holding

their breath. Bricks are crumbling in places, and the front door is so swollen you have to push hard to get in. There is no front yard, only four little elms the city planted by the curb. Out back is a small garage for the car we don't own yet and a small yard that looks smaller between the two buildings on either side. There are stairs in our house, but they're ordinary hallway stairs, and the house has only one washroom. Everybody has to share a bedroom—Mama and Papa, Carlos and Kiki, me and Nenny.

Once when we were living on Loomis, a nun from my school passed by and saw me playing out front. The laundromat downstairs had been boarded up because it had been robbed two days before and the owner had painted on the wood YES WE'RE OPEN so as not to lose business.

Where do you live? she asked.

There, I said pointing up to the third floor.

You live *there*?

There. I had to look to where she pointed—the third floor, the paint peeling, 10 wooden bars Papa had nailed on the windows so we wouldn't fall out. You live *there*? The way she said it made me feel like nothing. *There*. I lived *there*. I nodded.

I knew then I had to have a house. A real house. One I could point to. But this isn't it. The house on Mango Street isn't it. For the time being, Mama says. Temporary, says Papa. But I know how those things go.

Ralph Ellison

Battle Royal   1952

Ralph Ellison

Ralph Ellison (1914–1994) was born in Oklahoma City. His father, a small business owner who sold ice and coal, died when the future author was only three. Ellison's mother, a religious woman of strong convictions, worked as a maid to support her two sons. She also stressed the importance of education. Planning to be a composer, Ellison entered the Tuskegee Institute in 1933. Reading T. S. Eliot's poem The Waste Land, *however, helped focus his interest on literature. In 1936 he moved to New York to find a summer job to pay for his senior year's tuition. He never left. In Harlem Ellison met many black writers, including Langston Hughes and Richard Wright, and he soon began publishing short stories, poems, and reviews. In 1952 Ellison published his only novel,* Invisible Man, *which won the National Book Award for fiction and has gradually come to be recognized as a contemporary American masterpiece. Over the next forty years Ellison tried to finish a second novel, a project that was delayed by the author's obsessive drive for perfection. He eventually published eight sections of the work, but it remained unfinished. A 368-page version of the novel, edited by John F. Callahan from more than 2,000 pages of manuscript, appeared in 1999 as* Juneteenth. *Other posthumous publications were* The Collected Essays *(1995)—which gathered Ellison's two published books of essays,* Shadow and Act *(1964) and* Going to the Territory *(1986), along with much other material—and* Flying Home *(1996), thirteen short stories written between 1937 and 1954. For years Ellison taught at New York University. He published "Battle Royal" as a short story in 1948, and later revised it as the first chapter of* Invisible Man *(where it is preceded by a short prologue).*

It goes a long way back, some twenty years. All my life I had been looking for something, and everywhere I turned someone tried to tell me what it was. I accepted their answers too, though they were often in contradiction and even self-contradictory. I was naïve. I was looking for myself and asking everyone except myself questions which I, and only I, could answer. It took me a long time and much painful boomeranging of my expectations to achieve a realization everyone else appears to have been born with: That I am nobody but myself. But first I had to discover that I am an invisible man!

And yet I am no freak of nature, nor of history. I was in the cards, other things having been equal (or unequal) eighty-five years ago. I am not ashamed of my grand-parents for having been slaves. I am only ashamed of myself for having at one time been ashamed. About eighty-five years ago they were told they were free, united with others of our country in everything pertaining to the common good, and, in every-thing social, separate like the fingers of the hand. And they believed it. They exulted in it. They stayed in their place, worked hard, and brought up my father to do the same. But my grandfather is the one. He was an odd old guy, my grandfather, and I am told I take after him. It was he who caused the trouble. On his deathbed he called my father to him and said, "Son, after I'm gone I want you to keep up the good fight. I never told you, but our life is a war and I have been a traitor all my born days, a spy in the enemy's country ever since I give up my gun back in the Reconstruction. Live with your head in the lion's mouth. I want you to overcome 'em with yeses, under-mine 'em with grins, agree 'em to death and destruction, let 'em swoller you till they vomit or bust wide open." They thought the old man had gone out of his mind. He had been the meekest of men. The younger children were rushed from the room, the shades drawn and the flame of the lamp turned so low that it sputtered on the wick like the old man's breathing. "Learn it to the younguns," he whispered fiercely; then he died.

But my folks were more alarmed over his last words than over his dying. It was as though he had not died at all, his words caused so much anxiety. I was warned em-phatically to forget what he had said and, indeed, this is the first time it has been mentioned outside the family circle. It had a tremendous effect upon me, however. I could never be sure of what he meant. Grandfather had been a quiet old man who never made any trouble, yet on his deathbed he had called himself a traitor and a spy, and he had spoken of his meekness as a dangerous activity. It became a constant puz-zle which lay unanswered in the back of my mind. And whenever things went well for me I remembered my grandfather and felt guilty and uncomfortable. It was as though I was carrying out his advice in spite of myself. And to make it worse, everyone loved me for it. I was praised by the most lily-white men of the town. I was considered an example of desirable conduct—just as my grandfather had been. And what puzzled me was that the old man had defined it as *treachery*. When I was praised for my conduct I felt a guilt that in some way I was doing something that was really against the wishes of the white folks, that if they had understood they would have desired me to act just the opposite, that I should have been sulky and mean, and that that really would have been what they wanted, even though they were fooled and thought they wanted me to act as I did. It made me afraid that some day they would look upon me as a traitor and I would be lost. Still I was more afraid to act any other way because they didn't like that at all. The old man's words were like a curse. On my graduation day I delivered an oration in which I showed that humility was the secret, indeed, the very essence of progress. (Not that I believed this—how could I, remembering my grandfather?—I only believed that it worked.) It was a great success. Everyone praised me and I was invited to give the speech at a gathering of the town's leading white citizens. It was a triumph for the whole community.

It was in the main ballroom of the leading hotel. When I got there I discovered that it was on the occasion of a smoker, and I was told that since I was to be there anyway I might as well take part in the battle royal to be fought by some of my schoolmates as part of the entertainment. The battle royal came first.

All of the town's big shots were there in their tuxedoes, wolfing down the buffet foods, drinking beer and whiskey and smoking black cigars. It was a large room with a high ceiling. Chairs were arranged in neat rows around three sides of a portable boxing ring. The fourth side was clear, revealing a gleaming space of polished floor. I had some misgivings over the battle royal, by the way. Not from a distaste for fighting, but because I didn't care too much for the other fellows who were to take part. They were tough guys who seemed to have no grandfather's curse worrying their minds. No one could mistake their toughness. And besides, I suspected that fighting a battle royal might detract from the dignity of my speech. In those pre-invisible days I visualized myself as a potential Booker T. Washington. But the other fellows didn't care too much for me either, and there were nine of them. I felt superior to them in my way, and I didn't like the manner in which we were all crowded together into the servants' elevator. Nor did they like my being there. In fact, as the warmly lighted floors flashed past the elevator we had words over the fact that I, by taking part in the fight, had knocked one of their friends out of a night's work.

We were led out of the elevator through a rococo hall into an anteroom and told to get into our fighting togs. Each of us was issued a pair of boxing gloves and ushered out into the big mirrored hall, which we entered looking cautiously about us and whispering, lest we might accidentally be heard above the noise of the room. It was foggy with cigar smoke. And already the whiskey was taking effect. I was shocked to see some of the most important men of the town quite tipsy. They were all there—bankers, lawyers, judges, doctors, fire chiefs, teachers, merchants. Even one of the more fashionable pastors. Something we could not see was going on up front. A clarinet was vibrating sensuously and the men were standing up and moving eagerly forward. We were a small tight group, clustered together, our bare upper bodies touching and shining with anticipatory sweat; while up front the big shots were becoming increasingly excited over something we still could not see. Suddenly I heard the school superintendent, who had told me to come, yell, "Bring up the shines, gentlemen! Bring up the little shines!"

We were rushed up to the front of the ballroom, where it smelled even more strongly of tobacco and whiskey. Then we were pushed into place. I almost wet my pants. A sea of faces, some hostile, some amused, ringed around us, and in the center, facing us, stood a magnificent blonde—stark naked. There was dead silence. I felt a blast of cold air chill me. I tried to back away, but they were behind me and around me. Some of the boys stood with lowered heads, trembling. I felt a wave of irrational guilt and fear. My teeth chattered, my skin turned to goose flesh, my knees knocked.

5

Yet I was strongly attracted and looked in spite of myself. Had the price of looking been blindness, I would have looked. The hair was yellow like that of a circus kewpie doll, the face heavily powdered and rouged, as though to form an abstract mask, the eyes hollow and smeared a cool blue, the color of a baboon's butt. I felt a desire to spit upon her as my eyes brushed slowly over her body. Her breasts were firm and round as the domes of East Indian temples, and I stood so close as to see the fine skin texture and beads of pearly perspiration glistening like dew around the pink and erected buds of her nipples. I wanted at one and the same time to run from the room, to sink through the floor, or go to her and cover her from my eyes and the eyes of the others with my body; to feel the soft thighs, to caress her and destroy her, to love her and to murder her, to hide from her, and yet to stroke where below the small American flag tattooed upon her belly her thighs formed a capital V. I had a notion that of all in the room she saw only me with her impersonal eyes.

And then she began to dance, a slow sensuous movement; the smoke of a hundred cigars clinging to her like the thinnest of veils. She seemed like a fair bird-girl girdled in veils calling to me from the angry surface of some gray and threatening sea. I was transported. Then I became aware of the clarinet playing and the big shots yelling at us. Some threatened us if we looked and others if we did not. On my right I saw one boy faint. And now a man grabbed a silver pitcher from a table and stepped close as he dashed ice water upon him and stood him up and forced two of us to support him as his head hung and moans issued from his thick bluish lips. Another boy began to plead to go home. He was the largest of the group, wearing dark red fighting trunks much too small to conceal the erection which projected from him as though in answer to the insinuating low-registered moaning of the clarinet. He tried to hide himself with his boxing gloves.

And all the while the blonde continued dancing, smiling faintly at the big shots who watched her with fascination, and faintly smiling at our fear. I noticed a certain merchant who followed her hungrily, his lips loose and drooling. He was a large man who wore diamond studs in a shirtfront which swelled with the ample paunch underneath, and each time the blonde swayed her undulating hips he ran his hand through the thin hair of his bald head and, with his arms upheld, his posture clumsy like that of an intoxicated panda, wound his belly in a slow and obscene grind. This creature was completely hypnotized. The music had quickened. As the dancer flung herself about with a detached expression on her face, the men began reaching out to touch her. I could see their beefy fingers sink into the soft flesh. Some of the others tried to stop them and she began to move around the floor in graceful circles, as they gave chase, slipping and sliding over the polished floor. It was mad. Chairs went crashing, drinks were spilt, as they ran laughing and howling after her. They caught her just as she reached a door, raised her from the floor, and tossed her as college boys are tossed at a hazing, and above her red, fixed-smiling lips I saw the terror and disgust in her eyes, almost like my own terror and that which I saw in some of the other boys. As I watched, they tossed her twice and her soft breasts seemed to flatten against the air and her legs flung wildly as she spun. Some of the more sober ones helped her to escape. And I started off the floor, heading for the anteroom with the rest of the boys.

Some were still crying and in hysteria. But as we tried to leave we were stopped and ordered to get into the ring. There was nothing to do but what we were told. All ten of us climbed under the ropes and allowed ourselves to be blindfolded with broad bands of white cloth. One of the men seemed to feel a bit sympathetic and tried to

10

cheer us up as we stood with our backs against the ropes. Some of us tried to grin. "See that boy over there?" one of the men said. "I want you to run across at the bell and give it to him right in the belly. If you don't get him, I'm going to get you. I don't like his looks." Each of us was told the same. The blindfolds were put on. Yet even then I had been going over my speech. In my mind each word was as bright as flame. I felt the cloth pressed into place, and frowned so that it would be loosened when I relaxed.

But now I felt a sudden fit of blind terror. I was unused to darkness. It was as though I had suddenly found myself in a dark room filled with poisonous cotton-mouths. I could hear the bleary voices yelling insistently for the battle royal to begin.

"Get going in there!"

"Let me at that big nigger!"

I strained to pick up the school superintendent's voice, as though to squeeze some security out of that slightly more familiar sound.

"Let me at those black sonsabitches!" someone yelled.   15

"No, Jackson, no!" another voice yelled. "Here, somebody, help me hold Jack."

"I want to get at that ginger-colored nigger. Tear him limb from limb," the first voice yelled.

I stood against the ropes trembling. For in those days I was what they called ginger-colored, and he sounded as though he might crunch me between his teeth like a crisp ginger cookie.

Quite a struggle was going on. Chairs were being kicked about and I could hear voices grunting as with terrific effort. I wanted to see, to see more desperately than ever before. But the blindfold was as tight as a thick skin-puckering scab and when I raised my gloved hands to push the layers of white aside a voice yelled, "Oh, no you don't, black bastard! Leave that alone!"

"Ring the bell before Jackson kills him a coon!" someone boomed in the sudden   20
silence. And I heard the bell clang and the sound of the feet scuffling forward.

A glove smacked against my head. I pivoted, striking out stiffly as someone went past, and felt the jar ripple along the length of my arm to my shoulder. Then it seemed as though all nine of the boys had turned upon me at once. Blows pounded me from all sides while I struck out as best I could. So many blows landed upon me that I wondered if I were not the only blindfolded fighter in the ring, or if the man called Jackson hadn't succeeded in getting me after all.

Blindfolded, I could no longer control my motions. I had no dignity. I stumbled about like a baby or a drunken man. The smoke had become thicker and with each new blow it seemed to sear and further restrict my lungs. My saliva became like hot bitter glue. A glove connected with my head, filling my mouth with warm blood. It was everywhere. I could not tell if the moisture I felt upon my body was sweat or blood. A blow landed hard against the nape of my neck. I felt myself going over, my head hitting the floor. Streaks of blue light filled the black world behind the blind-fold. I lay prone, pretending that I was knocked out, but felt myself seized by hands and yanked to my feet. "Get going, black boy! Mix it up!" My arms were like lead, my head smarting from blows. I managed to feel my way to the ropes and held on, trying to catch my breath. A glove landed in my mid-section and I went over again, feeling as though the smoke had become a knife jabbed into my guts. Pushed this way and that by the legs milling around me, I finally pulled erect and discovered that I could see the black, sweat-washed forms weaving in the smoky-blue atmosphere like drunken dancers weaving to the rapid drum-like thuds of blows.

Everyone fought hysterically. It was complete anarchy. Everybody fought everybody else. No group fought together for long. Two, three, four, fought one, then
turned to fight each other, were themselves attacked. Blows landed below the belt
and in the kidney, with the gloves open as well as closed, and with my eye partly
opened now there was not so much terror. I moved carefully, avoiding blows, although not too many to attract attention, fighting group to group. The boys groped
about like blind, cautious crabs crouching to protect their mid-sections, their heads
pulled in short against their shoulders, their arms stretched nervously before them,
with their fists testing the smoke-filled air like the knobbed feelers of hypersensitive
snails. In one corner I glimpsed a boy violently punching the air and heard him
scream in pain as he smashed his hand against a ring post. For a second I saw him
bent over holding his hand, then going down as a blow caught his unprotected head.
I played one group against the other, slipping in and throwing a punch then stepping
out of range while pushing the others into the melee to take the blows blindly aimed
at me. The smoke was agonizing and there were no rounds, no bells at three minute
intervals to relieve our exhaustion. The room spun round me, a swirl of lights, smoke,
sweating bodies surrounded by tense white faces. I bled from both nose and mouth,
the blood spattering upon my chest.

The men kept yelling, "Slug him, black boy! Knock his guts out!"

"Uppercut him! Kill him! Kill that big boy!"   25

Taking a fake fall, I saw a boy going down heavily beside me as though we were
felled by a single blow, saw a sneaker-clad foot shoot into his groin as the two who
had knocked him down stumbled upon him. I rolled out of range, feeling a twinge of
nausea.

The harder we fought the more threatening the men became. And yet, I had begun to worry about my speech again. How would it go? Would they recognize my
ability? What would they give me?

I was fighting automatically when suddenly I noticed that one after another of the
boys was leaving the ring. I was surprised, filled with panic, as though I had been left
alone with an unknown danger. Then I understood. The boys had arranged it among
themselves. It was the custom for the two men left in the ring to slug it out for the
winner's prize. I discovered this too late. When the bell sounded two men in tuxedoes
leaped into the ring and removed the blindfold. I found myself facing Tatlock, the
biggest of the gang. I felt sick at my stomach. Hardly had the bell stopped ringing in
my ears than it clanged again and I saw him moving swiftly toward me. Thinking of
nothing else to do I hit him smash on the nose. He kept coming, bringing the rank
sharp violence of stale sweat. His face was a black blank of a face, only his eyes alive—
with hate of me and aglow with a feverish terror from what had happened to us all. I
became anxious. I wanted to deliver my speech and he came at me as though he
meant to beat it out of me. I smashed him again and again, taking his blows as they
came. Then on a sudden impulse I struck him lightly and we clinched. I whispered,
"Fake like I knocked you out, you can have the prize."

"I'll break your behind," he whispered hoarsely.

"For *them*?"   30

"For *me*, sonofabitch!"

They were yelling for us to break it up and Tatlock spun me half around with a
blow, and as a joggled camera sweeps in a reeling scene, I saw the howling red faces
crouching tense beneath the cloud of blue-gray smoke. For a moment the world wavered, unraveled, flowed, then my head cleared and Tatlock bounced before me.

That fluttering shadow before my eyes was his jabbing left hand. Then falling forward, my head against his damp shoulder, I whispered,

"I'll make it five dollars more."

"Go to hell!"

But his muscles relaxed a trifle beneath my pressure and I breathed, "Seven?" 35

"Give it to your ma," he said, ripping me beneath the heart.

And while I still held him I butted him and moved away. I felt myself bombarded with punches. I fought back with hopeless desperation. I wanted to deliver my speech more than anything else in the world, because I felt that only these men could judge truly my ability, and now this stupid clown was ruining my chances. I began fighting carefully now, moving in to punch him and out again with my greater speed. A lucky blow to his chin and I had him going too—until I heard a loud voice yell, "I got my money on the big boy."

Hearing this, I almost dropped my guard. I was confused: Should I try to win against the voice out there? Would not this go against my speech, and was not this a moment for humility, for nonresistance? A blow to my head as I danced about sent my right eye popping like a jack-in-the-box and settled my dilemma. The room went red as I fell. It was a dream fall, my body languid and fastidious as to where to land, until the floor became impatient and smashed up to meet me. A moment later I came to. An hypnotic voice said FIVE emphatically. And I lay there, hazily watching a dark red spot of my own blood shaping itself into a butterfly, glistening and soaking into the soiled gray world of the canvas.

When the voice drawled TEN I was lifted up and dragged to a chair. I sat dazed. My eye pained and swelled with each throb of my pounding heart and I wondered if now I would be allowed to speak. I was wringing wet, my mouth still bleeding. We were grouped along the wall now. The other boys ignored me as they congratulated Tatlock and speculated as to how much they would be paid. One boy whimpered over his smashed hand. Looking up front, I saw attendants in white jackets rolling the portable ring away and placing a small square rug in the vacant space surrounded by chairs. Perhaps, I thought, I will stand on the rug to deliver my speech.

Then the M.C. called to us. "Come on up here boys and get your money." 40

We ran forward to where the men laughed and talked in their chairs, waiting. Everyone seemed friendly now.

"There it is on the rug," the man said. I saw the rug covered with coins of all dimensions and a few crumpled bills. But what excited me, scattered here and there, were the gold pieces.

"Boys, it's all yours," the man said. "You get all you grab."

"That's right, Sambo," a blond man said, winking at me confidentially.

I trembled with excitement, forgetting my pain. I would get the gold and the 45 bills, I thought. I would use both hands. I would throw my body against the boys nearest me to block them from the gold.

"Get down around the rug now," the man commanded, "and don't anyone touch it until I give the signal."

"This ought to be good," I heard.

As told, we got around the square rug on our knees. Slowly the man raised his freckled hand as we followed it upward with our eyes.

I heard, "These niggers look like they're about to pray!"

Then, "Ready," the man said. "Go!" 50

I lunged for a yellow coin lying on the blue design of the carpet, touching it and sending a surprised shriek to join those rising around me. I tried frantically to remove my hand but could not let go. A hot, violent force tore through my body, shaking me like a wet rat. The rug was electrified. The hair bristled up on my head as I shook myself free. My muscles jumped, my nerves jangled, writhed. But I saw that this was not stopping the other boys. Laughing in fear and embarrassment, some were holding back and scooping up the coins knocked off by the painful contortions of others. The men roared above us as we struggled.

"Pick it up, goddamnit, pick it up!" someone called like a bass-voiced parrot. "Go on, get it!"

I crawled rapidly around the floor, picking up the coins, trying to avoid the coppers and to get greenbacks and the gold. Ignoring the shock by laughing, as I brushed the coins off quickly, I discovered that I could contain the electricity—a contradiction, but it works. Then the men began to push us onto the rug. Laughing embarrassedly, we struggled out of their hands and kept after the coins. We were all wet and slippery and hard to hold. Suddenly I saw a boy lifted into the air, glistening with sweat like a circus seal, and dropped, his wet back landing flush upon the charged rug, heard him yell and saw him literally dance upon his back, his elbows beating a frenzied tattoo upon the floor, his muscles twitching like the flesh of a horse stung by many flies. When he finally rolled off, his face was gray and no one stopped him when he ran from the floor amid booming laughter.

"Get the money," the M.C. called. "That's good hard American cash!"

And we snatched and grabbed, snatched and grabbed. I was careful not to come too close to the rug now, and when I felt the hot whiskey breath descend upon me like a cloud of foul air I reached out and grabbed the leg of a chair. It was occupied and I held on desperately.

"Leggo, nigger! Leggo!"

The huge face wavered down to mine as he tried to push me free. But my body was slippery and he was too drunk. It was Mr. Colcord, who owned a chain of movie houses and "entertainment palaces." Each time he grabbed me I slipped out of his hands. It became a real struggle. I feared the rug more than I did the drunk, so I held on, surprising myself for a moment by trying to topple *him* upon the rug. It was such an enormous idea that I found myself actually carrying it out. I tried not to be obvious, yet when I grabbed his leg, trying to tumble him out of the chair, he raised up roaring with laughter and, looking at me with soberness dead in the eye, kicked me viciously in the chest. The chair leg flew out of my hand and I felt myself going and rolled. It was as though I had rolled through a bed of hot coals. It seemed a whole century would pass before I would roll free, a century in which I was seared through the deepest levels of my body to the fearful breath within me and the breath seared and heated to the point of explosion. It'll all be over in a flash, I thought as I rolled clear. It'll all be over in a flash.

But not yet, the men on the other side were waiting, red faces swollen as though from apoplexy as they bent forward in their chairs. Seeing their fingers coming toward me I rolled away as a fumbled football rolls off the receiver's fingertips, back into the coals. That time I luckily sent the rug sliding out of place and heard the coins ringing against the floor and the boys scuffling to pick them up and the M.C. calling, "All right, boys, that's all. Go get dressed and get your money."

I was limp as a dish rag. My back felt as though it had been beaten with wires.

When we had dressed the M.C. came in and gave us each five dollars, except 60
Tatlock, who got ten for being the last in the ring. Then he told us to leave. I was not
to get a chance to deliver my speech, I thought. I was going out into the dim alley in
despair when I was stopped and told to go back. I returned to the ballroom, where the
men were pushing back their chairs and gathering in small groups to talk.

The M.C. knocked on a table for quiet. "Gentlemen," he said, "we almost forgot
an important part of the program. A most serious part, gentlemen. This boy was
brought here to deliver a speech which he made at his graduation yesterday . . ."

"Bravo!"

"I'm told that he is the smartest boy we've got out there in Greenwood. I'm told
that he knows more big words than a pocket-sized dictionary."

Much applause and laughter.

"So now, gentlemen, I want you to give him your attention." 65

There was still laughter as I faced them, my mouth dry, my eyes throbbing. I began slowly, but evidently my throat was tense, because they began shouting, "Louder!
Louder!"

"We of the younger generation extol the wisdom of that great leader and educa-
tor," I shouted, "who first spoke these flaming words of wisdom: 'A ship lost at sea for
many days suddenly sighted a friendly vessel. From the mast of the unfortunate vessel
was seen a signal: "Water, water; we die of thirst!" The answer from the friendly vessel came back: "Cast down your bucket where you are." The captain of the distressed
vessel, at last heeding the injunction, cast down his bucket, and it came up full of
fresh sparkling water from the mouth of the Amazon River.' And like him I say, and
in his words, 'To those of my race who depend upon bettering their condition in a
foreign land, or who underestimate the importance of cultivating friendly relations
with the Southern white man, who is his next-door neighbor, I would say: "Cast
down your bucket where you are"—cast it down in making friends in every manly
way of the people of all races by whom we are surrounded . . .'"

I spoke automatically and with such fervor that I did not realize that the men
were still talking and laughing until my dry mouth, filling up with blood from the cut,
almost strangled me. I coughed, wanting to stop and go to one of the tall brass, sand-
filled spittoons to relieve myself, but a few of the men, especially the superintendent,
were listening and I was afraid. So I gulped it down, blood, saliva and all, and continued. (What powers of endurance I had during those days! What enthusiasm! What a
belief in the rightness of things!) I spoke even louder in spite of the pain. But still
they talked and still they laughed, as though deaf with cotton in dirty ears. So I spoke
with greater emotional emphasis. I closed my ears and swallowed blood until I was
nauseated. The speech seemed a hundred times as long as before, but I could not
leave out a single word. All had to be said, each memorized nuance considered, rendered. Nor was that all. Whenever I uttered a word of three or more syllables a group
of voices would yell for me to repeat it. I used the phrase "social responsibility" and
they yelled:

"What's that word you say, boy?"

"Social responsibility," I said. 70

"What?"

"Social . . ."

"Louder."

". . . responsibility."

"More!"   75
"Respon—"
"Repeat!"
"—sibility."
The room filled with the uproar of laughter until, no doubt, distracted by having
to gulp down my blood, I made a mistake and yelled a phrase I had often seen de-
nounced in newspaper editorials, heard debated in private.
"Social . . ."   80
"What?" they yelled.
". . . equality—"
The laughter hung smokelike in the sudden stillness. I opened my eyes, puzzled.
Sounds of displeasure filled the room. The M.C. rushed forward. They shouted hos-
tile phrases at me. But I did not understand.
A small dry mustached man in the front row blared out, "Say that slowly, son!"
"What, sir?"   85
"What you just said!"
"Social responsibility, sir," I said.
"You weren't being smart, were you, boy?" he said, not unkindly.
"No, sir!"
"You sure that about 'equality' was a mistake?"   90
"Oh, yes, sir," I said. "I was swallowing blood."
"Well, you had better speak more slowly so we can understand. We mean to do
right by you, but you've got to know your place at all times. All right, now, go on
with your speech."
I was afraid. I wanted to leave but I wanted also to speak and I was afraid they'd
snatch me down.
"Thank you, sir," I said, beginning where I had left off, and having them ignore
me as before.
Yet when I finished there was a thunderous applause. I was surprised to see the   95
superintendent come forth with a package wrapped in white tissue paper, and, gesturing for quiet, address the men.
"Gentlemen, you see that I did not overpraise the boy. He makes a good speech
and some day he'll lead his people in the proper paths. And I don't have to tell you
that that is important in these days and times. This is a good, smart boy, and so to encourage him in the right direction, in the name of the Board of Education I wish to
present him a prize in the form of this . . ."
He paused, removing the tissue paper and revealing a gleaming calfskin
brief case.
". . . in the form of this first-class article from Shad Whitmore's shop."
"Boy," he said, addressing me, "take this prize and keep it well. Consider it a
badge of office. Prize it. Keep developing as you are and some day it will be filled with
important papers that will help shape the destiny of your people."
I was so moved that I could hardly express my thanks. A rope of bloody saliva   100
forming a shape like an undiscovered continent drooled upon the leather and I wiped
it quickly away. I felt an importance that I had never dreamed.
"Open it and see what's inside," I was told.
My fingers a-tremble, I complied, smelling fresh leather and finding an offi-
cial-looking document inside. It was a scholarship to the state college for Negroes.
My eyes filled with tears and I ran awkwardly off the floor.

I was overjoyed; I did not even mind when I discovered the gold pieces I had scrambled for were brass pocket tokens advertising a certain make of automobile.

When I reached home everyone was excited. Next day the neighbors came to congratulate me. I even felt safe from grandfather, whose deathbed curse usually spoiled my triumphs. I stood beneath his photograph with my brief case in hand and smiled triumphantly into his stolid black peasant's face. It was a face that fascinated me. The eyes seemed to follow everywhere I went.

That night I dreamed I was at a circus with him and that he refused to laugh at   105
the clowns no matter what they did. Then later he told me to open my brief case and read what was inside and I did, finding an official envelope stamped with the state seal; and inside the envelope I found another and another, endlessly, and I thought I would fall of weariness. "Them's years," he said. "Now open that one." And I did and in it I found an engraved stamp containing a short message in letters of gold. "Read it," my grandfather said. "Out loud."

"To Whom It May Concern," I intoned. "Keep This Nigger-Boy Running."

I awoke with the old man's laughter ringing in my ears.

Zora Neale Hurston

Sweat   1926

Zora Neale Hurston

Zora Neale Hurston (1901?–1960) was born in Eatonville, Florida, but no record of her actual date of birth exists (best guesses range from 1891 to 1901). Hurston was one of eight children. Her father, a carpenter and Baptist preacher, was also the three-term mayor of Eatonville, the first all-black town incorporated in the United States. When Hurston's mother died in 1912, the father moved the children from one relative to another. Consequently, Hurston never finished grammar school, although in 1918 she began taking classes at Howard University, paying her way through school by working as a manicurist and maid. While at Howard, she published her first story. In early 1925 she moved to New York, arriving with "$1.50, no job, no friends, and a lot of hope." She soon became an important member of the Harlem Renaissance, a group of young black artists (including Langston Hughes, Countee Cullen, Jean Toomer, and Claude McKay) who sought "spiritual emancipation" for African Americans by exploring black heritage and identity in the arts. Hurston eventually became, according to critic Laura Zaidman, "the most prolific black American woman writer of her time." In 1925 she became the first African American student at Barnard College, where she completed a B.A. in anthropology. Hurston's most famous story, "Sweat," appeared in the only issue of Fire!!, a 1926 avant-garde Harlem Renaissance magazine edited by Hurston, Hughes, and Wallace Thurman. This powerful story of an unhappy marriage turned murderous was particularly noteworthy for having the characters speak in the black country dialect of Hurston's native Florida. Hurston achieved only modest success during her lifetime, despite the publication of her memorable novel Their Eyes Were Watching God (1937) and her many contributions to the study of African American folklore. She died, poor and

neglected, in a Florida welfare home and was buried in an unmarked grave. In 1973 novelist
Alice Walker erected a gravestone for her carved with the words:

Zora Neale Hurston
"A Genius of the South"
1901–1960
Novelist, Folklorist
Anthropologist

I

It was eleven o'clock of a Spring night in Florida. It was Sunday. Any other
night, Delia Jones would have been in bed for two hours by this time. But she was a
washwoman, and Monday morning meant a great deal to her. So she collected the
soiled clothes on Saturday when she returned the clean things. Sunday night after
church, she sorted and put the white things to soak. It saved her almost a half-day's
start. A great hamper in the bedroom held the clothes that she brought home. It was
so much neater than a number of bundles lying around.

She squatted on the kitchen floor beside the great pile of clothes, sorting them into
small heaps according to color, and humming a song in a mournful key, but wondering
through it all where Sykes, her husband, had gone with her horse and buckboard.°

Just then something long, round, limp, and black fell upon her shoulders and
slithered to the floor beside her. A great terror took hold of her. It softened her knees
and dried her mouth so that it was a full minute before she could cry out or move.
Then she saw that it was the big bull whip her husband liked to carry when he drove.

She lifted her eyes to the door and saw him standing there bent over with
laughter at her fright. She screamed at him.

"Sykes, what you throw dat whip on me like dat? You know it would skeer me—   5
looks just like a snake, an' you knows how skeered Ah is of snakes."

"Course Ah knowed it! That's how come Ah done it." He slapped his leg with
his hand and almost rolled on the ground in his mirth. "If you such a big fool dat you
got to have a fit over a earth worm or a string, Ah don't keer how bad Ah skeer you."

"You ain't got no business doing it. Gawd knows it's a sin. Some day Ah'm gointuh drop dead from some of yo' foolishness. 'Nother thing, where you been wid mah
rig? Ah feeds dat pony. He ain't fuh you to be drivin' wid no bull whip."

"You sho' is one aggravatin' nigger woman!" he declared and stepped into the
room. She resumed her work and did not answer him at once. "Ah done tole you
time and again to keep them white folks' clothes outa dis house."

He picked up the whip and glared at her. Delia went on with her work. She went
out into the yard and returned with a galvanized tub and set it on the wash-bench.
She saw that Sykes had kicked all of the clothes together again, and now stood in her
way truculently, his whole manner hoping, *praying*, for an argument. But she walked
calmly around him and commenced to re-sort the things.

"Next time, Ah'm gointer kick 'em outdoors," he threatened as he struck a   10
match along the leg of his corduroy breeches.

Delia never looked up from her work, and her thin, stooped shoulders sagged further.

"Ah ain't for no fuss t'night Sykes. Ah just come from taking sacrament at the
church house."

---

buckboard: a four-wheeled open carriage with the seat resting on a spring platform.

He snorted scornfully. "Yeah, you just come from de church house on a Sunday night, but heah you is gone to work on them clothes. You ain't nothing but a hypocrite. One of them amen-corner Christians—sing, whoop, and shout, then come home and wash white folks' clothes on the Sabbath."

He stepped roughly upon the whitest pile of things, kicking them helter-skelter as he crossed the room. His wife gave a little scream of dismay, and quickly gathered them together again.

"Sykes, you quit grindin' dirt into these clothes! How can Ah git through by Sat'day if Ah don't start on Sunday?" 15

"Ah don't keer if you never git through. Anyhow, Ah done promised Gawd and a couple of other men, Ah ain't gointer have it in mah house. Don't gimme no lip neither, else Ah'll throw 'em out and put mah fist up side yo' head to boot."

Delia's habitual meekness seemed to slip from her shoulders like a blown scarf. She was on her feet; her poor little body, her bare knuckly hands bravely defying the strapping hulk before her.

"Looka heah, Sykes, you done gone too fur. Ah been married to you fur fifteen years, and Ah been takin' in washin' fur fifteen years. Sweat, sweat, sweat! Work and sweat, cry and sweat, pray and sweat!"

"What's that got to do with me?" he asked brutally.

"What's it got to do with you, Sykes? Mah tub of suds is filled yo' belly with vittles more times than yo' hands is filled it. Mah sweat is done paid for this house and Ah reckon Ah kin keep on sweatin' in it." 20

She seized the iron skillet from the stove and struck a defensive pose, which act surprised him greatly, coming from her. It cowed him and he did not strike her as he usually did.

"Naw you won't," she panted, "that ole snaggle-toothed black woman you runnin' with ain't comin' heah to pile up on *mah* sweat and blood. You ain't paid for nothin' on this place, and Ah'm gointer stay right heah till Ah'm toted out foot foremost."

"Well, you better quit gittin' me riled up, else they'll be totin' you out sooner than you expect. Ah'm so tired of you Ah don't know whut to do. Gawd! How Ah hates skinny wimmen!"

A little awed by this new Delia, he sidled out of the door and slammed the back gate after him. He did not say where he had gone, but she knew too well. She knew very well that he would not return until nearly daybreak also. Her work over, she went on to bed but not to sleep at once. Things had come to a pretty pass!

She lay awake, gazing upon the debris that cluttered their matrimonial trail. Not 25 an image left standing along the way. Anything like flowers had long ago been drowned in the salty stream that had been pressed from her heart. Her tears, her sweat, her blood. She had brought love to the union and he had brought a longing after the flesh. Two months after the wedding, he had given her the first brutal beating. She had the memory of his numerous trips to Orlando with all of his wages when he had returned to her penniless, even before the first year had passed. She was young and soft then, but now she thought of her knotty, muscled limbs, her harsh knuckly hands, and drew herself up into an unhappy little ball in the middle of the big feather bed. Too late now to hope for love, even if it were not Bertha it would be someone else. This case differed from the others only in that she was bolder than the others. Too late for everything except her little home. She had built it for her old days, and planted one by one the trees and flowers there. It was lovely to her, lovely.

Somehow, before sleep came, she found herself saying aloud: "Oh well, whatever goes over the Devil's back, is got to come under his belly. Sometime or ruther, Sykes, like everybody else, is gointer reap his sowing." After that she was able to build a spiritual earthworks° against her husband. His shells could no longer reach her. AMEN. She went to sleep and slept until he announced his presence in bed by kicking her feet and rudely snatching the covers away.

"Gimme some kivah heah, an' git yo' damn foots over on yo' own side! Ah oughter mash you in yo' mouf fuh drawing dat skillet on me."

Delia went clear to the rail without answering him. A triumphant indifference to all that he was or did.

II

The week was full of work for Delia as all other weeks, and Saturday found her behind her little pony, collecting and delivering clothes.

It was a hot, hot day near the end of July. The village men on Joe Clarke's porch even chewed cane listlessly. They did not hurl the cane-knots as usual. They let them dribble over the edge of the porch. Even conversation had collapsed under the heat. 30

"Heah come Delia Jones," Jim Merchant said, as the shaggy pony came 'round the bend of the road toward them. The rusty buckboard was heaped with baskets of crisp, clean laundry.

"Yep," Joe Lindsay agreed. "Hot or col', rain or shine, jes'ez reg'lar ez de weeks roll roun' Delia carries 'em an' fetches 'em on Sat'day."

"She better if she wanter eat," said Moss. "Syke Jones ain't wuth de shot an' powder hit would tek tuh kill 'im. Not to *huh* he ain't."

"He sho' ain't," Walter Thomas chimed in. "It's too bad, too, cause she wuz a right pretty li'l trick when he got huh. Ah'd uh mah'ied huh mahself if he hadnter beat me to it."

Delia nodded briefly at the men as she drove past. 35

"Too much knockin' will ruin *any* 'oman. He done beat huh 'nough tuh kill three women, let 'lone change they looks," said Elijah Moseley. "How Syke kin stommuck dat big black greasy Mogul he's layin' roun' wid, gits me. Ah swear dat eight-rock couldn't kiss a sardine can Ah done thowed out de back do' 'way las' yeah."

"Aw, she's fat, thass how come. He's allus been crazy 'bout fat women," put in Merchant. "He'd a' been tied up wid one long time ago if he could a' found one tuh have him. Did Ah tell yuh 'bout him come sidlin' roun' *mah* wife—bringin' her a basket uh peecans outa his yard fuh a present? Yessir, mah wife! She tol' him tuh take 'em right straight back home, 'cause Delia works so hard ovah dat washtub she reckon everything on de place taste lak sweat an' soapsuds. Ah jus' wisht Ah'd a' caught 'im 'roun' dere! Ah'd a' made his hips ketch on fiah down dat shell road."

"Ah know he done it, too. Ah sees 'im grinnin' at every 'oman dat passes," Walter Thomas said. "But even so, he useter eat some mighty big hunks uh humble pie tuh git dat li'l 'oman he got. She wuz ez pretty ez a speckled pup! Dat wuz fifteen years ago. He useter be so skeered uh losin' huh, she could make him do some parts of a husband's duty. Dey never wuz de same in de mind."

"There oughter be a law about him," said Lindsay. "He ain't fit tuh carry guts tuh a bear."

---

spiritual earthworks: earthworks are military fortifications made of earth; here Hurston uses it metaphorically to mean Delia's emotional defenses.

Clarke spoke for the first time. "Tain't no law on earth dat kin make a man be   40
decent if it ain't in 'im. There's plenty men dat takes a wife lak dey do a joint uh
sugar-cane. It's round, juicy, an' sweet when dey gits it. But dey squeeze an' grind,
squeeze an' grind an' wring tell dey wring every drop uh pleasure dat's in 'em out.
When dey's satisfied dat dey is wrung dry, dey treats 'em jes' lak dey do a cane-chew.
Dey thows 'em away. Dey knows whut dey is doin' while dey is at it, an' hates theirselves fuh it but they keeps on hangin' after huh tell she's empty. Den dey hates huh
fuh bein' a cane-chew an' in de way."

"We oughter take Syke an' dat stray 'oman uh his'n down in Lake Howell swamp
an' lay on de rawhide till they cain't say Lawd a' mussy. He allus wuz uh ovahbearin
niggah, but since dat white 'oman from up north done teached 'im how to run a automobile, he done got too biggety to live—an' we oughter kill 'im," Old Man Anderson
advised.

A grunt of approval went around the porch. But the heat was melting their civic
virtue and Elijah Moseley began to bait Joe Clarke.

"Come on, Joe, git a melon outa dere an' slice it up for yo' customers. We'se all
sufferin' wid de heat. De bear's done got *me!*"

"Thass right, Joe, a watermelon is jes' whut Ah needs tuh cure de eppizudicks,"
Walter Thomas joined forces with Moseley. "Come on dere, Joe. We all is steady customers an' you ain't set us up in a long time. Ah chooses dat long, bowlegged Floridy
favorite."

"A god, an' be dough. You all gimme twenty cents and slice away," Clarke   45
retorted. "Ah needs a col' slice m'self. Heah, everybody chip in. Ah'll lend y'all mah
meat knife."

The money was all quickly subscribed and the huge melon brought forth. At that
moment, Sykes and Bertha arrived. A determined silence fell on the porch and the
melon was put away again.

Merchant snapped down the blade of his jackknife and moved toward the store
door.

"Come on in, Joe, an' gimme a slab uh sow belly an' uh pound uh coffee—almost
fuhgot 'twas Sat'day. Got to git on home." Most of the men left also.

Just then Delia drove past on her way home, as Sykes was ordering magnificently
for Bertha. It pleased him for Delia to see.

"Git whutsoever yo' heart desires, Honey. Wait a minute, Joe. Give huh two   50
bottles uh strawberry soda-water, uh quart parched ground-peas, an' a block uh
chewin' gum."

With all this they left the store, with Sykes reminding Bertha that this was his
town and she could have it if she wanted it.

The men returned soon after they left, and held their watermelon feast.

"Where did Syke Jones git da 'oman from nohow?" Lindsay asked.

"Ovah Apopka. Guess dey musta been cleanin' out de town when she lef'. She
don't look lak a thing but a hunk uh liver wid hair on it."

"Well, she sho' kin squall," Dave Carter contributed. "When she gits ready tuh   55
laff, she jes' opens huh mouf an' latches it back tuh de las' notch. No ole granpa
alligator down in Lake Bell ain't got nothin' on huh."

III

Bertha had been in town three months now. Sykes was still paying her room-
rent at Della Lewis'—the only house in town that would have taken her in. Sykes

took her frequently to Winter Park to "stomps." He still assured her that he was the swellest man in the state.

"Sho' you kin have dat li'l ole house soon's Ah git dat 'oman outadere. Everything b'longs tuh me an' you sho' kin have it. Ah sho' 'bominates uh skinny 'oman. Lawdy, you sho' is got one portly shape on you! You kin git *anything* you wants. Dis is *mah* town an' you sho' kin have it."

Delia's work-worn knees crawled over the earth in Gethsemane° and up the rocks of Calvary° many, many times during these months. She avoided the villagers and meeting places in her efforts to be blind and deaf. But Bertha nullified this to a degree, by coming to Delia's house to call Sykes out to her at the gate.

Delia and Sykes fought all the time now with no peaceful interludes. They slept and ate in silence. Two or three times Delia had attempted a timid friendliness, but she was repulsed each time. It was plain that the breaches must remain agape.

The sun had burned July to August. The heat streamed down like a million hot   60
arrows, smiting all things living upon the earth. Grass withered, leaves browned, snakes went blind in shedding, and men and dogs went mad. Dog days!

Delia came home one day and found Sykes there before her. She wondered, but started to go on into the house without speaking, even though he was standing in the kitchen door and she must either stoop under his arm or ask him to move. He made no room for her. She noticed a soap box beside the steps, but paid no particular attention to it, knowing that he must have brought it there. As she was stooping to pass under his outstretched arm, he suddenly pushed her backward, laughingly.

"Look in de box dere, Delia, Ah done brung yuh somethin'!"

She nearly fell upon the box in her stumbling, and when she saw what it held, she all but fainted outright.

"Syke! Syke, mah Gawd! You take dat rattlesnake 'way from heah! You *gottuh*. Oh, Jesus, have mussy!"

"Ah ain't got tuh do nuthin' uh de kin'—fact is Ah ain't got tuh do nothin'   65
but die. Tain't no use uh you puttin' on airs makin' out lak you skeered uh dat snake—he's gointer stay right heah tell he die. He wouldn't bite me cause Ah knows how tuh handle 'im. Nohow he wouldn't risk breakin' out his fangs 'gin *yo* skinny laigs."

"Naw, now Syke, don't keep dat thing 'round tryin' tuh skeer me tuh death. You knows Ah'm even feared uh earth worms. Thass de biggest snake Ah evah did see. Kill 'im, Syke, please."

"Doan ast me tuh do nothin' fuh yuh. Goin' 'round tryin' tuh be so damn aster-perious.° Naw, Ah ain't gonna kill it. Ah think uh damn sight mo' uh him dan you! Dat's a nice snake an' anybody doan lak 'im kin jes' hit de grit."

The village soon heard that Sykes had the snake, and came to see and ask questions.

"How de hen-fire did you ketch dat six-foot rattler, Syke?" Thomas asked.

"He's full uh frogs so he cain't hardly move, thass how Ah eased up on 'im. But   70
Ah'm a snake charmer an' knows how tuh handle 'em. Shux, dat ain't nothin'. Ah could ketch one eve'y day if Ah so wanted tuh."

Gethsemane: the garden outside Jerusalem that was the scene of Jesus' agony and arrest (see Matthew 26:36–57); hence, a scene of great suffering.   *Calvary:* the hill outside Jerusalem where Jesus was crucified.   *asterperious:* haughty.

"Whut he needs is a heavy hick'ry club leaned real heavy on his head. Dat's de bes' way tuh charm a rattlesnake."

"Naw, Walt, y'all jes' don't understand dese diamon' backs lak Ah do," said Sykes in a superior tone of voice.

The village agreed with Walter, but the snake stayed on. His box remained by the kitchen door with its screen wire covering. Two or three days later it had digested its meal of frogs and literally came to life. It rattled at every movement in the kitchen or the yard. One day as Delia came down the kitchen steps she saw his chalky-white fangs curved like scimitars hung in the wire meshes. This time she did not run away with averted eyes as usual. She stood for a long time in the doorway in a red fury that grew bloodier for every second that she regarded the creature that was her torment.

That night she broached the subject as soon as Sykes sat down to the table.

"Syke, Ah wants you tuh take dat snake 'way fum heah. You done starved me an' Ah put up widcher, you done beat me an Ah took dat, but you done kilt all mah insides bringin' dat varmint heah." 75

Sykes poured out a saucer full of coffee and drank it deliberately before he answered her.

"A whole lot Ah keer 'bout how you feels inside uh out. Dat snake ain't goin' no damn wheah till Ah gits ready fuh 'im tuh go. So fur as beatin' is concerned, yuh ain't took near all dat you gointer take ef yuh stay 'round *me*."

Delia pushed back her plate and got up from the table. "Ah hates you, Sykes," she said calmly. "Ah hates you tuh de same degree dat Ah useter love yuh. Ah done took an' took till mah belly is full up tuh mah neck. Dat's de reason Ah got mah letter fum de church an' moved mah membership tuh Woodbridge—so Ah don't haftuh take no sacrament wid yuh. Ah don't wantuh see yuh 'round me atall. Lay 'round wid dat 'oman all yuh wants tuh, but gwan 'way fum me an' mah house. Ah hates yuh lak uh suck-egg dog."

Sykes almost let the huge wad of corn bread and collard greens he was chewing fall out of his mouth in amazement. He had a hard time whipping himself up to the proper fury to try to answer Delia.

"Well, Ah'm glad you does hate me. Ah'm sho' tiahed uh you hangin' ontuh me. Ah don't want yuh. Look at yuh stringey ole neck! Yo' rawbony laigs an' arms is enough tuh cut uh man tuh death. You looks jes' lak de devvul's doll-baby tuh *me*. You cain't hate me no worse dan Ah hates you. Ah been hatin' *you* fuh years." 80

"Yo' ole black hide don't look lak nothin' tuh me, but uh passle uh wrinkled up rubber, wid yo' big ole yeahs flappin' on each side lak uh paih uh buzzard wings. Don't think Ah'm gointuh be run 'way fum mah house neither. Ah'm goin' tuh de white folks 'bout *you*, mah young man, de very nex' time you lay yo' han's on me. Mah cup is done run ovah." Delia said this with no signs of fear and Sykes departed from the house, threatening her, but made not the slightest move to carry out any of them.

That night he did not return at all, and the next day being Sunday, Delia was glad she did not have to quarrel before she hitched up her pony and drove the four miles to Woodbridge.

She stayed to the night service—"love feast"—which was very warm and full of spirit. In the emotional winds her domestic trials were borne far and wide so that she sang as she drove homeward,

Jurden water,° black an' col
Chills de body, not de soul
An' Ah wantah cross Jurden in uh calm time.

She came from the barn to the kitchen door and stopped.

"Whut's de mattah, ol' Satan, you ain't kickin' up yo' racket?" She addressed the snake's box. Complete silence. She went on into the house with a new hope in its birth struggles. Perhaps her threat to go to the white folks had frightened Sykes! Perhaps he was sorry! Fifteen years of misery and suppression had brought Delia to the place where she would hope *anything* that looked towards a way over or through her wall of inhibitions.

She felt in the match-safe behind the stove at once for a match. There was only one there.   85

"Dat niggah wouldn't fetch nothin' heah tuh save his rotten neck, but he kin run thew whut Ah brings quick enough. Now he done toted off nigh on tuh haff uh box uh matches. He done had dat 'oman heah in mah house, too."

Nobody but a woman could tell how she knew this even before she struck the match. But she did and it put her into a new fury.

Presently she brought in the tubs to put the white things to soak. This time she decided she need not bring the hamper out of the bedroom; she would go in there and do the sorting. She picked up the pot-bellied lamp and went in. The room was small and the hamper stood hard by the foot of the white iron bed. She could sit and reach through the bedposts—resting as she worked.

"*Ah wantah cross Jurden in uh calm time.*" She was singing again. The mood of the "love feast" had returned. She threw back the lid of the basket almost gaily. Then, moved by both horror and terror, she sprang back toward the door. *There lay the snake in the basket!* He moved sluggishly at first, but even as she turned round and round, jumped up and down in an insanity of fear, he began to stir vigorously. She saw him pouring his awful beauty from the basket upon the bed, then she seized the lamp and ran as fast as she could to the kitchen. The wind from the open door blew out the light and the darkness added to her terror. She sped to the darkness of the yard, slamming the door after her before she thought to set down the lamp. She did not feel safe even on the ground, so she climbed up in the hay barn.

There for an hour or more she lay sprawled upon the hay a gibbering wreck.   90

Finally she grew quiet, and after that came coherent thought. With this stalked through her a cold, bloody rage. Hours of this. A period of introspection, a space of retrospection, then a mixture of both. Out of this an awful calm.

"Well, Ah done de bes' Ah could. If things ain't right, Gawd knows tain't mah fault."

She went to sleep—a twitch sleep—and woke up to a faint gray sky. There was a loud hollow sound below. She peered out. Sykes was at the wood-pile, demolishing a wire-covered box.

He hurried to the kitchen door, but hung outside there some minutes before he entered, and stood some minutes more inside before he closed it after him.

Jurden water: black Southern dialect for the River Jordan, which represents the last boundary before entering heaven. It comes from the Old Testament, when the Jews had to cross the River Jordan to reach the Promised Land.

The gray in the sky was spreading. Delia descended without fear now, and crouched beneath the low bedroom window. The drawn shade shut out the dawn, shut in the night. But the thin walls held back no sound. 95

"Dat ol' scratch° is woke up now!" She mused at the tremendous whirr inside, which every woodsman knows, is one of the sound illusions. The rattler is a ventriloquist. His whirr sounds to the right, to the left, straight ahead, behind, close under foot—everywhere but where it is. Woe to him who guesses wrong unless he is prepared to hold up his end of the argument! Sometimes he strikes without rattling at all.

Inside, Sykes heard nothing until he knocked a pot lid off the stove while trying to reach the match-safe in the dark. He had emptied his pockets at Bertha's.

The snake seemed to wake up under the stove and Sykes made a quick leap into the bedroom. In spite of the gin he had had, his head was clearing now.

"Mah Gawd!" he chattered, "ef Ah could on'y strack uh light!"

The rattling ceased for a moment as he stood paralyzed. He waited. It seemed 100 that the snake waited also.

"Oh, fuh de light! Ah thought he'd be too sick"—Sykes was muttering to himself when the whirr began again, closer, right underfoot this time. Long before this, Sykes' ability to think had been flattened down to primitive instinct and he leaped—onto the bed.

Outside Delia heard a cry that might have come from a maddened chimpanzee, a stricken gorilla. All the terror, all the horror, all the rage that man possibly could express, without a recognizable human sound.

A tremendous stir inside there, another series of animal screams, the intermittent whirr of the reptile. The shade torn violently down from the window, letting in the red dawn, a huge brown hand seizing the window stick, great dull blows upon the wooden floor punctuating the gibberish of sound long after the rattle of the snake had abruptly subsided. All this Delia could see and hear from her place beneath the window, and it made her ill. She crept over to the four-o'clocks and stretched herself on the cool earth to recover.

She lay there. "Delia, Delia!" She could hear Sykes calling in a most despairing tone as one who expected no answer. The sun crept on up, and he called. Delia could not move—her legs had gone flabby. She never moved, he called, and the sun kept rising.

"Mah Gawd!" She heard him moan, "Mah Gawd fum Heben!" She heard 105 him stumbling about and got up from her flower-bed. The sun was growing warm. As she approached the door she heard him call out hopefully, "Delia, is dat you Ah heah?"

She saw him on his hands and knees as soon as she reached the door. He crept an inch or two toward her—all that he was able, and she saw his horribly swollen neck and his one open eye shining with hope. A surge of pity too strong to support bore her away from that eye that must, could not, fail to see the tubs. He would see the lamp. Orlando with its doctors was too far. She could scarcely reach the chinaberry tree, where she waited in the growing heat while inside she knew the cold river was creeping up and up to extinguish that eye which must know by now that she knew.

---

scratch: a folk expression for the devil.

James Joyce

Araby

1914

James Joyce (1882–1941) quit Ireland at twenty to spend his mature life in voluntary exile on the continent, writing of nothing but Dublin, where he was born. In Trieste, Zurich, and Paris, he supported his family with difficulty, sometimes teaching in Berlitz language schools, until his writing won him fame and wealthy patrons. At first Joyce met difficulty in getting his work printed and circulated. Publication of Dubliners (1914), the collection of stories that includes "Araby," was delayed seven years because its prospective Irish publisher feared libel suits. (The book depicts local citizens, some of them recognizable, and views Dubliners mostly as a thwarted, self-deceived lot.) A Portrait of the Artist as a Young Man (1916), a novel of

James Joyce

thinly veiled autobiography, recounts a young intellectual's breaking away from country, church, and home. Joyce's immense comic novel Ulysses (1922), a parody of the Odyssey, spans eighteen hours in the life of a wandering Jew, a Dublin seller of advertising. Frank about sex but untitillating, the book was banned at one time by the U.S. Post Office. Joyce's later work stepped up its demands on readers. The challenging Finnegans Wake (1939), if read aloud, sounds as though a learned comic poet were sleep-talking, jumbling several languages. Joyce was an innovator whose bold experiments showed many other writers possibilities in fiction that had not earlier been imagined.

North Richmond Street, being blind,° was a quiet street except at the hour when the Christian Brothers' School set the boys free. An uninhabited house of two stories stood at the blind end, detached from its neighbors in a square ground. The other houses of the street, conscious of decent lives within them, gazed at one another with brown imperturbable faces.

The former tenant of our house, a priest, had died in the back drawing-room. Air, musty from having been long enclosed, hung in all the rooms, and the waste room behind the kitchen was littered with old useless papers. Among these I found a few paper-covered books, the pages of which were curled and damp: *The Abbot,* by Walter Scott, *The Devout Communicant* and *The Memoirs of Vidocq.*° I liked the last best because its leaves were yellow. The wild garden behind the house contained a central apple-tree and a few straggling bushes under one of which I found the late tenant's rusty bicycle-pump. He had been a very charitable priest: in his will he had left all his money to institutions and the furniture of his house to his sister.

When the short days of winter came dusk fell before we had well eaten our dinners. When we met in the street the houses had grown somber. The space of sky above us was the color of ever-changing violet and towards it the lamps of the street

---

being blind: being a dead-end street.   *The Abbot . . . Vidocq:* a popular historical romance (1820); a book of pious meditations by an eighteenth-century English Franciscan, Pacificus Baker; and the autobiography of François-Jules Vidocq (1775–1857), a criminal who later turned detective.

lifted their feeble lanterns. The cold air stung us and we played till our bodies glowed. Our shouts echoed in the silent street. The career of our play brought us through the dark muddy lanes behind the houses where we ran the gantlet of the rough tribes from the cottages, to the back doors of the dark dripping gardens where odors arose from the ashpits, to the dark odorous stables where a coachman smoothed and combed the horse or shook music from the buckled harness. When we returned to the street light from the kitchen windows had filled the areas. If my uncle was seen turning the corner we hid in the shadow until we had seen him safely housed. Or if Mangan's sister° came out on the doorstep to call her brother in to his tea we watched her from our shadow peer up and down the street. We waited to see whether she would remain or go in and, if she remained, we left our shadow and walked up to Mangan's steps resignedly. She was waiting for us, her figure defined by the light from the half-opened door. Her brother always teased her before he obeyed and I stood by the railings looking at her. Her dress swung as she moved her body and the soft rope of her hair tossed from side to side.

Every morning I lay on the floor in the front parlor watching her door. The blind was pulled down within an inch of the sash so that I could not be seen. When she came out on the doorstep my heart leaped. I ran to the hall, seized my books and followed her. I kept her brown figure always in my eye and, when we came near the point at which our ways diverged, I quickened my pace and passed her. This happened morning after morning. I had never spoken to her, except for a few casual words, and yet her name was like a summons to all my foolish blood.

Her image accompanied me even in places the most hostile to romance. On Saturday evenings when my aunt went marketing I had to go to carry some of the parcels. We walked through the flaring streets, jostled by drunken men and bargaining women, amid the curses of laborers, the shrill litanies of shopboys who stood on guard by the barrels of pigs' cheeks, the nasal chanting of street-singers, who sang a *come-all-you* about O'Donovan Rossa,° or a ballad about the troubles in our native land. These noises converged in a single sensation of life for me: I imagined that I bore my chalice safely through a throng of foes. Her name sprang to my lips at moments in strange prayers and praises which I myself did not understand. My eyes were often full of tears (I could not tell why) and at times a flood from my heart seemed to pour itself out into my bosom. I thought little of the future. I did not know whether I would ever speak to her or not or, if I spoke to her, how I could tell her of my confused adoration. But my body was like a harp and her words and gestures were like fingers running upon the wires.

One evening I went into the back drawing-room in which the priest had died. It was a dark rainy evening and there was no sound in the house. Through one of the broken panes I heard the rain impinge upon the earth, the fine incessant needles of water playing in the sodden beds. Some distant lamp or lighted window gleamed below me. I was thankful that I could see so little. All my senses seemed to desire to veil themselves and, feeling that I was about to slip from them, I pressed the palms of my hands together until they trembled, murmuring: *O love! O love!* many times.

5

Mangan's sister: an actual young woman in this story, but the phrase recalls Irish poet James Clarence Mangan (1803–1849) and his best-known poem, "Dark Rosaleen," which personifies Ireland as a beautiful woman for whom the poet yearns. *come-all-you about O'Donovan Rossa:* the street singers earned their living by singing timely songs that usually began, "Come all you gallant Irishmen / And listen to my song." Their subject, also called Dynamite Rossa, was a popular hero jailed by the British for advocating violent rebellion.

At last she spoke to me. When she addressed the first words to me I was so confused that I did not know what to answer. She asked me was I going to *Araby*. I forget whether I answered yes or no. It would be a splendid bazaar, she said; she would love to go.

—And why can't you? I asked.

While she spoke she turned a silver bracelet round and round her wrist. She could not go, she said, because there would be a retreat that week in her convent.° Her brother and two other boys were fighting for their caps and I was alone at the railings. She held one of the spikes, bowing her head towards me. The light from the lamp opposite our door caught the white curve of her neck, lit up her hair that rested there and, falling, lit up the hand upon the railing. It fell over one side of her dress and caught the white border of a petticoat, just visible as she stood at ease.

—It's well for you, she said. 10

—If I go, I said, I will bring you something.

What innumerable follies laid waste my waking and sleeping thoughts after that evening! I wished to annihilate the tedious intervening days. I chafed against the work of school. At night in my bedroom and by day in the classroom her image came between me and the page I strove to read. The syllables of the word *Araby* were called to me through the silence in which my soul luxuriated and cast an Eastern enchantment over me. I asked for leave to go to the bazaar on Saturday night. My aunt was surprised and hoped it was not some Freemason° affair. I answered few questions in class. I watched my master's face pass from amiability to sternness; he hoped I was not beginning to idle. I could not call my wandering thoughts together. I had hardly any patience with the serious work of life which, now that it stood between me and my desire, seemed to me child's play, ugly monotonous child's play.

On Saturday morning I reminded my uncle that I wished to go to the bazaar in the evening. He was fussing at the hallstand, looking for the hatbrush, and answered me curtly:

—Yes, boy, I know.

As he was in the hall I could not go into the front parlor and lie at the window. I 15 left the house in bad humor and walked slowly towards the school. The air was pitilessly raw and already my heart misgave me.

When I came home to dinner my uncle had not yet been home. Still it was early. I sat staring at the clock for some time and, when its ticking began to irritate me, I left the room. I mounted the staircase and gained the upper part of the house. The high cold empty gloomy rooms liberated me and I went from room to room singing. From the front window I saw my companions playing below in the street. Their cries reached me weakened and indistinct and, leaning my forehead against the cool glass, I looked over at the dark house where she lived. I may have stood there for an hour, seeing nothing but the brown-clad figure cast by my imagination, touched discreetly by the lamplight at the curved neck, at the hand upon the railings and at the border below the dress.

When I came downstairs again I found Mrs. Mercer sitting at the fire. She was an old garrulous woman, a pawnbroker's widow, who collected used stamps for some pious purpose. I had to endure the gossip of the tea-table. The meal was prolonged

---

a retreat . . . in her convent: a week devoted to religious observances more intense than usual, at the convent school Miss Mangan attends; probably she will have to listen to a number of hellfire sermons. *Freemason:* Catholics in Ireland viewed the Masonic order as a Protestant conspiracy against them.

beyond an hour and still my uncle did not come. Mrs. Mercer stood up to go: she was sorry she couldn't wait any longer, but it was after eight o'clock and she did not like to be out late, as the night air was bad for her. When she had gone I began to walk up and down the room, clenching my fists. My aunt said:

—I'm afraid you may put off your bazaar for this night of Our Lord.

At nine o'clock I heard my uncle's latchkey in the halldoor. I heard him talking to himself and heard the hallstand rocking when it had received the weight of his overcoat. I could interpret these signs. When he was midway through his dinner I asked him to give me the money to go to the bazaar. He had forgotten.

—The people are in bed and after their first sleep now, he said.   20

I did not smile. My aunt said to him energetically:

—Can't you give him the money and let him go? You've kept him late enough as it is.

My uncle said he was very sorry he had forgotten. He said he believed in the old saying: *All work and no play makes Jack a dull boy.* He asked me where I was going and, when I had told him a second time he asked me did I know *The Arab's Farewell to His Steed.*° When I left the kitchen he was about to recite the opening lines of the piece to my aunt.

I held a florin tightly in my hands as I strode down Buckingham Street towards the station. The sight of the streets thronged with buyers and glaring with gas recalled to me the purpose of my journey. I took my seat in a third-class carriage of a deserted train. After an intolerable delay the train moved out of the station slowly. It crept onward among ruinous houses and over the twinkling river. At Westland Row Station a crowd of people pressed to the carriage doors; but the porters moved them back, saying that it was a special train for the bazaar. I remained alone in the bare carriage. In a few minutes the train drew up beside an improvised wooden platform. I passed out on to the road and saw by the lighted dial of a clock that it was ten minutes to ten. In front of me was a large building which displayed the magical name.

I could not find any sixpenny entrance and, fearing that the bazaar would be   25
closed, I passed in quickly through a turnstile, handing a shilling to a weary-looking man. I found myself in a big hall girdled at half its height by a gallery. Nearly all the stalls were closed and the greater part of the hall was in darkness. I recognized a silence like that which pervades a church after a service. I walked into the center of the bazaar timidly. A few people were gathered about the stalls which were still open. Before a curtain, over which the words *Café Chantant*° were written in colored lamps, two men were counting money on a salver.° I listened to the fall of the coins.

Remembering with difficulty why I had come I went over to one of the stalls and examined porcelain vases and flowered tea-sets. At the door of the stall a young lady was talking and laughing with two young gentlemen. I remarked their English accents and listened vaguely to their conversation.

—O, I never said such a thing!

—O, but you did!

—O, but I didn't!

The Arab's Farewell to His Steed: This sentimental ballad by a popular poet, Caroline Norton (1808–1877), tells the story of a nomad of the desert who, in a fit of greed, sells his beloved horse, then regrets the loss, flings away the gold he had received, and takes back his horse. Notice the echo of "Araby" in the song title.   *Café Chantant:* name for a Paris nightspot featuring topical songs. *salver:* a tray like that used in serving Holy Communion.

—Didn't she say that?   30

—Yes. I heard her.

—O, there's a . . . fib!

Observing me the young lady came over and asked me did I wish to buy anything. The tone of her voice was not encouraging; she seemed to have spoken to me
out of a sense of duty. I looked humbly at the great jars that stood like eastern guards
at either side of the dark entrance to the stall and murmured:

—No, thank you.

The young lady changed the position of one of the vases and went back to the   35
two young men. They began to talk of the same subject. Once or twice the young
lady glanced at me over her shoulder.

I lingered before her stall, though I knew my stay was useless, to make my interest in her wares seem the more real. Then I turned away slowly and walked down the
middle of the bazaar. I allowed the two pennies to fall against the sixpence in my
pocket. I heard a voice call from one end of the gallery that the light was out. The
upper part of the hall was now completely dark.

Gazing up into the darkness I saw myself as a creature driven and derided by vanity;
and my eyes burned with anguish and anger.

Franz Kafka

Before the Law   1919

Translated by John Siscoe

*Franz Kafka (1883–1924) receives a brief biography on page 301, along with his classic
novella* The Metamorphosis. *The ironic and devastating parable "Before the Law" contains the distilled essence of what we mean by the term "Kafkaesque."*

Before the Law stands a doorkeeper. To this doorkeeper comes a man from the
country who asks to be admitted to the Law. But the doorkeeper says that he can't
let the man in just now. The man thinks this over and then asks if he will be allowed
to enter later. "It's possible," answers the doorkeeper, "but not just now." Since the
door to the Law stands open as usual and the doorkeeper steps aside, the man bends
down to look through the doorway into the interior. Seeing this, the doorkeeper
laughs and says: "If you find it so compelling, then try to enter despite my prohibition. But bear in mind that I am powerful. And I am only the lowest doorkeeper. In
hall after hall, keepers stand at every door. The mere sight of the third one is more
than even I can bear." These are difficulties which the man from the country has not
expected; the Law, he thinks, should be always available to everyone. But when he
looks more closely at the doorkeeper in his furred robe, with his large pointed nose
and his long, thin, black Tartar beard, he decides that it would be better to wait until he receives permission to enter. The doorkeeper gives him a stool and allows him
to sit down beside the door. There he sits for days and years. He makes many attempts to be let in, and wearies the doorkeeper with his pleas. The doorkeeper often
questions him casually about his home and many other matters, but the questions are
asked with indifference, the way important men might ask them, and always conclude with the statement the man can't be admitted at this time. The man, who has
equipped himself with many things for his journey, spends all that he has, regardless

of value, in order to bribe the doorkeeper. The doorkeeper accepts it all, though saying each time as he does so, "I'm taking this only so that you won't feel that you haven't tried everything." During these long years the man watches the doorkeeper almost continuously. He forgets about the other doorkeepers, and imagines that this first one is the sole obstacle barring his way to the Law. In the early years he loudly bewails his misfortune; later, as he grows old, he merely grumbles to himself. He becomes childish, and since during his long study of the doorkeeper he has gotten to know even the fleas in the fur collar, he begs these fleas to help him change the doorkeeper's mind. At last his eyesight grows dim and he cannot tell whether it is really growing darker or whether his eyes are simply deceiving him. Yet in the darkness he can now perceive that radiance that streams inextinguishably from the door of the Law. Now his life is nearing its end. Before he dies, all his experiences during this long time coalesce in his mind into a single question, one which he has never yet asked the doorkeeper. He beckons to the doorkeeper, for he can no longer raise his stiffening body. The doorkeeper has to bend low to hear him, since the difference in size between them has increased very much to the man's disadvantage. "What do you want to know now?" asks the doorkeeper, "you are insatiable." "Surely everyone strives to reach the Law," says the man, "why then is it that in all these years no one has come seeking admittance but me?" The doorkeeper realizes that the man has reached his end and that his hearing is failing so he yells in his ear: "No one but you could have been admitted here, since this entrance was meant for you alone. Now I am going to shut it."

Jamaica Kincaid

Girl

1983

Jamaica Kincaid was born Elaine Potter Richardson in 1949 in St. John's, capital of the West Indian island nation of Antigua (she adopted the name Jamaica Kincaid in 1973 because of her family's disapproval of her writing). In 1965 she was sent to Westchester County, New York, to work as an au pair (or "servant," as she prefers to describe it). She attended Franconia College in New Hampshire, but did not complete a degree. Kincaid worked as a staff writer for the New Yorker for nearly twenty years; Talk Stories (2001) is a collection of seventy-seven short pieces that she wrote for the magazine. She won wide attention for At the Bottom of the River (1983), the volume of her stories that includes "Girl." In 1985 she published Annie John, an interlocking cycle of short stories about growing up in Antigua. Lucy (1990) was her

Jamaica Kincaid

first novel; it was followed by The Autobiography of My Mother (1996) and Mr. Potter (2002), novels inspired by the lives of her parents. Kincaid is also the author of A Small Place (1988), a memoir of her homeland and meditation on the destructiveness of colonialism, and My Brother (1997), a reminiscence of her brother Devon, who died of AIDS at thirty-three. Her most recent work is Among Flowers: A Walk in the Himalaya (2005), a travel book.

A naturalized U.S. citizen, Kincaid has said of her adopted country: "It's given me a place to be myself—but myself as I was formed somewhere else." She is currently a visiting lecturer at Harvard University.

Wash the white clothes on Monday and put them on the stone heap; wash the color clothes on Tuesday and put them on the clothesline to dry; don't walk bare-head in the hot sun; cook pumpkin fritters in very hot sweet oil; soak your little cloths right after you take them off; when buying cotton to make yourself a nice blouse, be sure that it doesn't have gum on it, because that way it won't hold up well after a wash; soak salt fish overnight before you cook it; is it true that you sing benna° in Sunday school?; always eat your food in such a way that it won't turn someone else's stomach; on Sundays try to walk like a lady and not like the slut you are so bent on becoming; don't sing benna in Sunday school; you mustn't speak to wharf-rat boys, not even to give directions; don't eat fruits on the street—flies will follow you; *but I don't sing benna on Sundays at all and never in Sunday school;* this is how to sew on a button; this is how to make a buttonhole for the button you have just sewed on; this is how to hem a dress when you see the hem coming down and so to prevent yourself from looking like the slut I know you are so bent on becoming; this is how you iron your father's khaki shirt so that it doesn't have a crease; this is how you iron your father's khaki pants so that they don't have a crease; this is how you grow okra—far from the house, because okra tree harbors red ants; when you are growing dasheen, make sure it gets plenty of water or else it makes your throat itch when you are eating it; this is how you sweep a corner; this is how you sweep a whole house; this is how you sweep a yard; this is how you smile to someone you don't like too much; this is how you smile to someone you don't like at all; this is how you smile to someone you like completely; this is how you set a table for tea; this is how you set a table for dinner; this is how you set a table for dinner with an important guest; this is how you set a table for lunch; this is how you set a table for breakfast; this is how to behave in the presence of men who don't know you very well, and this way they won't recognize immediately the slut I have warned you against becoming; be sure to wash every day, even if it is with your own spit; don't squat down to play marbles—you are not a boy, you know; don't pick people's flowers—you might catch something; don't throw stones at blackbirds, because it might not be a blackbird at all; this is how to make a bread pudding; this is how to make doukona; this is how to make pepper pot; this is how to make a good medicine for a cold; this is how to make a good medicine to throw away a child before it even becomes a child; this is how to catch a fish; this is how to throw back a fish you don't like, and that way something bad won't fall on you; this is how to bully a man; this is how a man bullies you; this is how to love a man, and if this doesn't work there are other ways, and if they don't work don't feel too bad about giving up; this is how to spit up in the air if you feel like it, and this is how to move quick so that it doesn't fall on you; this is how to make ends meet; always squeeze bread to make sure it's fresh; *but what if the baker won't let me feel the bread?;* you mean to say that after all you are really going to be the kind of woman who the baker won't let near the bread?

benna: Kincaid defined this word, for two editors who inquired, as meaning "songs of the sort your parents didn't want you to sing, at first calypso and later rock and roll" (quoted by Sylvan Barnet and Marcia Stubbs, *The Little Brown Reader,* 2nd ed. [Boston: Little, 1980] 74).

Jhumpa Lahiri

Interpreter of Maladies

1999

Jhumpa Lahiri was born in London in 1967 and grew up in Rhode Island. Her father, a librarian, and her mother, a teacher, had emigrated from their native India, to which Lahiri has made a number of extended visits. After writing a great deal of fiction as a child and teenager, she wrote none at all during her college years. She graduated from Barnard College with a B.A. in English literature, and after all her graduate school applications had been rejected, she went to work as a research assistant for a nonprofit organization. She began staying late after work to use her office computer to write short stories, on the strength of which she was accepted into the creative writing program at Boston University. Earning an M.A. in creative writing, Lahiri

Jhumpa Lahiri

stayed on to complete an M.A. in English, an M.A. in comparative literature and the arts, and a Ph.D. in Renaissance studies. "In the process," she has said, "it became clear to me that I was not meant to be a scholar. It was something I did out of a sense of duty and practicality, but it was never something I loved." Lahiri's first book of stories, Interpreter of Maladies, *was published in 1999 to excellent reviews and won the Pulitzer Prize for fiction. Its title story was also selected for both an O. Henry Award and publication in* The Best American Short Stories. *Her first novel,* The Namesake *(2003), was made into a film (2006) directed by Mira Nair. Her second collection of stories,* Unaccustomed Earth *(2008), also received glowing reviews, and debuted at Number 1 on the* New York Times Book Review *Best-Seller List. Lahiri has taught creative writing at Boston University and the Rhode Island School of Design. She lives in New York.*

At the tea stall Mr. and Mrs. Das bickered about who should take Tina to the toilet. Eventually Mrs. Das relented when Mr. Das pointed out that he had given the girl her bath the night before. In the rearview mirror Mr. Kapasi watched as Mrs. Das emerged slowly from his bulky white Ambassador, dragging her shaved, largely bare legs across the back seat. She did not hold the little girl's hand as they walked to the rest room.

They were on their way to see the Sun Temple at Konarak. It was a dry, bright Saturday, the mid-July heat tempered by a steady ocean breeze, ideal weather for sightseeing. Ordinarily Mr. Kapasi would not have stopped so soon along the way, but less than five minutes after he'd picked up the family that morning in front of Hotel Sandy Villa, the little girl had complained. The first thing Mr. Kapasi had noticed when he saw Mr. and Mrs. Das, standing with their children under the portico of the hotel, was that they were very young, perhaps not even thirty. In addition to Tina they had two boys, Ronny and Bobby, who appeared very close in age and had teeth covered in a network of flashing silver wires. The family looked Indian but dressed as foreigners did, the children in stiff, brightly colored clothing and caps with translucent visors. Mr. Kapasi was accustomed to foreign tourists; he was assigned to them regularly because he could speak English. Yesterday he had driven an elderly couple from Scotland, both with spotted faces and fluffy white hair so thin it exposed their sunburnt scalps. In comparison, the tanned, youthful faces of Mr. and Mrs. Das were all the more striking. When he'd introduced himself, Mr. Kapasi had pressed his palms together in greeting, but Mr. Das squeezed hands like an American so that Mr. Kapasi felt it in his elbow. Mrs. Das, for her part, had flexed one side of her mouth, smiling dutifully at Mr. Kapasi, without displaying any interest in him.

As they waited at the tea stall, Ronny, who looked like the older of the two boys, clambered suddenly out of the back seat, intrigued by a goat tied to a stake in the ground.

"Don't touch it," Mr. Das said. He glanced up from his paperback tour book, which said "INDIA" in yellow letters and looked as if it had been published abroad. His voice, somehow tentative and a little shrill, sounded as though it had not yet settled into maturity.

"I want to give it a piece of gum," the boy called back as he trotted ahead.   5

Mr. Das stepped out of the car and stretched his legs by squatting briefly to the ground. A clean-shaven man, he looked exactly like a magnified version of Ronny. He had a sapphire blue visor, and was dressed in shorts, sneakers, and a T-shirt. The camera slung around his neck, with an impressive telephoto lens and numerous buttons and markings, was the only complicated thing he wore. He frowned, watching as Ronny rushed toward the goat, but appeared to have no intention of intervening. "Bobby, make sure that your brother doesn't do anything stupid."

"I don't feel like it," Bobby said, not moving. He was sitting in the front seat beside Mr. Kapasi, studying a picture of the elephant god taped to the glove compartment.

"No need to worry," Mr. Kapasi said. "They are quite tame." Mr. Kapasi was forty-six years old, with receding hair that had gone completely silver, but his butterscotch complexion and his unlined brow, which he treated in spare moments to dabs of lotus-oil balm, made it easy to imagine what he must have looked like at an earlier age. He wore gray trousers and a matching jacket-style shirt, tapered at the waist, with short sleeves and a large pointed collar, made of a thin but durable synthetic material. He had specified both the cut and the fabric to his tailor—it was his preferred uniform for giving tours because it did not get crushed during his long hours behind the wheel. Through the windshield he watched as Ronny circled around the goat, touched it quickly on its side, then trotted back to the car.

"You left India as a child?" Mr. Kapasi asked when Mr. Das had settled once again into the passenger seat.

"Oh, Mina and I were both born in America," Mr. Das announced with an air of   10
sudden confidence. "Born and raised. Our parents live here now, in Assansol.° They retired. We visit them every couple years." He turned to watch as the little girl ran toward the car, the wide purple bows of her sundress flopping on her narrow brown shoulders. She was holding to her chest a doll with yellow hair that looked as if it had been chopped, as a punitive measure, with a pair of dull scissors. "This is Tina's first trip to India, isn't it, Tina?"

"I don't have to go to the bathroom anymore," Tina announced.

"Where's Mina?" Mr. Das asked.

Mr. Kapasi found it strange that Mr. Das should refer to his wife by her first name when speaking to the little girl. Tina pointed to where Mrs. Das was purchasing

---

Assansol: a city in the state of West Bengal in northeastern India.

something from one of the shirtless men who worked at the tea stall. Mr. Kapasi heard one of the shirtless men sing a phrase from a popular Hindi love song as Mrs. Das walked back to the car, but she did not appear to understand the words of the song, for she did not express irritation, or embarrassment, or react in any other way to the man's declarations.

He observed her. She wore a red-and-white-checkered skirt that stopped above her knees, slip-on shoes with a square wooden heel, and a close-fitting blouse styled like a man's undershirt. The blouse was decorated at chest-level with a calico appliqué in the shape of a strawberry. She was a short woman, with small hands like paws, her frosty pink fingernails painted to match her lips, and was slightly plump in her figure. Her hair, shorn only a little longer than her husband's, was parted far to one side. She was wearing large dark brown sunglasses with a pinkish tint to them, and carried a big straw bag, almost as big as her torso, shaped like a bowl, with a water bottle poking out of it. She walked slowly, carrying some puffed rice tossed with peanuts and chili peppers in a large packet made from newspapers. Mr. Kapasi turned to Mr. Das.

"Where in America do you live?" 15

"New Brunswick, New Jersey."

"Next to New York?"

"Exactly. I teach middle school there."

"What subject?"

"Science. In fact, every year I take my students on a trip to the Museum of 20 Natural History in New York City. In a way we have a lot in common, you could say, you and I. How long have you been a tour guide, Mr. Kapasi?"

"Five years."

Mrs. Das reached the car. "How long's the trip?" she asked, shutting the door.

"About two and a half hours," Mr. Kapasi replied.

At this Mrs. Das gave an impatient sigh, as if she had been traveling her whole life without pause. She fanned herself with a folded Bombay film magazine written in English.

"I thought that the Sun Temple is only eighteen miles north of Puri," Mr. Das 25 said, tapping on the tour book.

"The roads to Konarak are poor. Actually it is a distance of fifty-two miles," Mr. Kapasi explained.

Mr. Das nodded, readjusting the camera strap where it had begun to chafe the back of his neck.

Before starting the ignition, Mr. Kapasi reached back to make sure the cranklike locks on the inside of each of the back doors were secured. As soon as the car began to move the little girl began to play with the lock on her side, clicking it with some effort forward and backward, but Mrs. Das said nothing to stop her. She sat a bit slouched at one end of the back seat, not offering her puffed rice to anyone. Ronny and Tina sat on either side of her, both snapping bright green gum.

"Look," Bobby said as the car began to gather speed. He pointed with his finger to the tall trees that lined the road. "Look."

"Monkeys!" Ronny shrieked. "Wow!" 30

They were seated in groups along the branches, with shining black faces, silver bodies, horizontal eyebrows, and crested heads. Their long gray tails dangled like a series of ropes among the leaves. A few scratched themselves with black leathery hands, or swung their feet, staring as the car passed.

"We call them the hanuman," Mr. Kapasi said. "They are quite common in the area."

As soon as he spoke, one of the monkeys leaped into the middle of the road, causing Mr. Kapasi to brake suddenly. Another bounced onto the hood of the car, then sprang away. Mr. Kapasi beeped his horn. The children began to get excited, sucking in their breath and covering their faces partly with their hands. They had never seen monkeys outside of a zoo, Mr. Das explained. He asked Mr. Kapasi to stop the car so that he could take a picture.

While Mr. Das adjusted his telephoto lens, Mrs. Das reached into her straw bag and pulled out a bottle of colorless nail polish, which she proceeded to stroke on the tip of her index finger.

The little girl stuck out a hand. "Mine too. Mommy, do mine too."   35

"Leave me alone," Mrs. Das said, blowing on her nail and turning her body slightly. "You're making me mess up."

The little girl occupied herself by buttoning and unbuttoning a pinafore on the doll's plastic body.

"All set," Mr. Das said, replacing the lens cap.

The car rattled considerably as it raced along the dusty road, causing them all to pop up from their seats every now and then, but Mrs. Das continued to polish her nails. Mr. Kapasi eased up on the accelerator, hoping to produce a smoother ride. When he reached for the gearshift the boy in front accommodated him by swinging his hairless knees out of the way. Mr. Kapasi noted that this boy was slightly paler than the other children. "Daddy, why is the driver sitting on the wrong side in this car, too?" the boy asked.

"They all do that here, dummy," Ronny said.   40

"Don't call your brother a dummy," Mr. Das said. He turned to Mr. Kapasi. "In America, you know . . . it confuses them."

"Oh yes, I am well aware," Mr. Kapasi said. As delicately as he could, he shifted gears again, accelerating as they approached a hill in the road. "I see it on *Dallas*,° the steering wheels are on the left-hand side."

"What's *Dallas*?" Tina asked, banging her now naked doll on the seat behind Mr. Kapasi.

"It went off the air," Mr. Das explained. "It's a television show."

They were all like siblings, Mr. Kapasi thought as they passed a row of date trees.   45
Mr. and Mrs. Das behaved like an older brother and sister, not parents. It seemed that they were in charge of the children only for the day; it was hard to believe they were regularly responsible for anything other than themselves. Mr. Das tapped on his lens cap, and his tour book, dragging his thumbnail occasionally across the pages so that they made a scraping sound. Mrs. Das continued to polish her nails. She had still not removed her sunglasses. Every now and then Tina renewed her plea that she wanted her nails done, too, and so at one point Mrs. Das flicked a drop of polish on the little girl's finger before depositing the bottle back inside her straw bag.

"Isn't this an air-conditioned car?" she asked, still blowing on her hand. The window on Tina's side was broken and could not be rolled down.

"Quit complaining," Mr. Das said. "It isn't so hot."

"I told you to get a car with air-conditioning," Mrs. Das continued. "Why do you do this, Raj, just to save a few stupid rupees. What are you saving us, fifty cents?"

Dallas: extremely popular 1980s television drama centered on the professional and romantic affairs of unscrupulous oil baron J. R. Ewing and his family.

Their accents sounded just like the ones Mr. Kapasi heard on American television programs, though not like the ones on *Dallas*.

"Doesn't it get tiresome, Mr. Kapasi, showing people the same thing every day?" Mr. Das asked, rolling down his own window all the way. "Hey, do you mind stopping the car. I just want to get a shot of this guy." 50

Mr. Kapasi pulled over to the side of the road as Mr. Das took a picture of a barefoot man, his head wrapped in a dirty turban, seated on top of a cart of grain sacks pulled by a pair of bullocks.° Both the man and the bullocks were emaciated. In the back seat Mrs. Das gazed out another window, at the sky, where nearly transparent clouds passed quickly in front of one another.

"I look forward to it, actually," Mr. Kapasi said as they continued on their way. "The Sun Temple is one of my favorite places. In that way it is a reward for me. I give tours on Fridays and Saturdays only. I have another job during the week."

"Oh? Where?" Mr. Das asked.

"I work in a doctor's office."

"You're a doctor?" 55

"I am not a doctor. I work with one. As an interpreter."

"What does a doctor need an interpreter for?"

"He has a number of Gujarati patients. My father was Gujarati, but many people do not speak Gujarati in this area, including the doctor. And so the doctor asked me to work in his office, interpreting what the patients say."

"Interesting. I've never heard of anything like that," Mr. Das said.

Mr. Kapasi shrugged. "It is a job like any other." 60

"But so romantic," Mrs. Das said dreamily, breaking her extended silence. She lifted her pinkish brown sunglasses and arranged them on top of her head like a tiara. For the first time, her eyes met Mr. Kapasi's in the rearview mirror: pale, a bit small, their gaze fixed but drowsy.

Mr. Das craned to look at her. "What's so romantic about it?"

"I don't know. Something." She shrugged, knitting her brows together for an instant. "Would you like a piece of gum, Mr. Kapasi?" she asked brightly. She reached into her straw bag and handed him a small square wrapped in green-and-white-striped paper. As soon as Mr. Kapasi put the gum in his mouth a thick sweet liquid burst onto his tongue.

"Tell us more about your job, Mr. Kapasi," Mrs. Das said.

"What would you like to know, madame?" 65

"I don't know," she shrugged, munching on some puffed rice and licking the mustard oil from the corners of her mouth. "Tell us a typical situation." She settled back in her seat, her head tilted in a patch of sun, and closed her eyes. "I want to picture what happens."

"Very well. The other day a man came in with a pain in his throat."

"Did he smoke cigarettes?"

"No. It was very curious. He complained that he felt as if there were long pieces of straw stuck in his throat. When I told the doctor he was able to prescribe the proper medication."

"That's so neat." 70

"Yes," Mr. Kapasi agreed after some hesitation.

"So these patients are totally dependent on you," Mrs. Das said. She spoke slowly, as if she were thinking aloud. "In a way, more dependent on you than the doctor."

---

bullocks: young or castrated bulls; steer.

"How do you mean? How could it be?"

"Well, for example, you could tell the doctor that the pain felt like a burning, not straw. The patient would never know what you had told the doctor, and the doctor wouldn't know that you had told the wrong thing. It's a big responsibility."

"Yes, a big responsibility you have there, Mr. Kapasi," Mr. Das agreed.   75

Mr. Kapasi had never thought of his job in such complimentary terms. To him it was a thankless occupation. He found nothing noble in interpreting people's maladies, assiduously translating the symptoms of so many swollen bones, countless cramps of bellies and bowels, spots on people's palms that changed color, shape, or size. The doctor, nearly half his age, had an affinity for bell-bottom trousers and made humorless jokes about the Congress party.° Together they worked in a stale little infirmary where Mr. Kapasi's smartly tailored clothes clung to him in the heat, in spite of the blackened blades of a ceiling fan churning over their heads.

The job was a sign of his failings. In his youth he'd been a devoted scholar of foreign languages, the owner of an impressive collection of dictionaries. He had dreamed of being an interpreter for diplomats and dignitaries, resolving conflicts between people and nations, settling disputes of which he alone could understand both sides. He was a self-educated man. In a series of notebooks, in the evenings before his parents settled his marriage, he had listed the common etymologies of words, and at one point in his life he was confident that he could converse, if given the opportunity, in English, French, Russian, Portuguese, and Italian, not to mention Hindi, Bengali, Orissi, and Gujarati. Now only a handful of European phrases remained in his memory, scattered words for things like saucers and chairs. English was the only non-Indian language he spoke fluently anymore. Mr. Kapasi knew it was not a remarkable talent. Sometimes he feared that his children knew better English than he did, just from watching television. Still, it came in handy for the tours.

He had taken the job as an interpreter after his first son, at the age of seven, contracted typhoid—that was how he had first made the acquaintance of the doctor. At the time Mr. Kapasi had been teaching English in a grammar school, and he bartered his skills as an interpreter to pay the increasingly exorbitant medical bills. In the end the boy had died one evening in his mother's arms, his limbs burning with fever, but then there was the funeral to pay for, and the other children who were born soon enough, and the newer, bigger house, and the good schools and tutors, and the fine shoes and the television, and the countless other ways he tried to console his wife and to keep her from crying in her sleep, and so when the doctor offered to pay him twice as much as he earned at the grammar school, he accepted. Mr. Kapasi knew that his wife had little regard for his career as an interpreter. He knew it reminded her of the son she'd lost, and that she resented the other lives he helped, in his own small way, to save. If ever she referred to his position, she used the phrase "doctor's assistant," as if the process of interpretation were equal to taking someone's temperature, or changing a bedpan. She never asked him about the patients who came to the doctor's office, or said that his job was a big responsibility.

For this reason it flattered Mr. Kapasi that Mrs. Das was so intrigued by his job. Unlike his wife, she had reminded him of its intellectual challenges. She had also used the word "romantic." She did not behave in a romantic way toward her husband, and yet she had used the word to describe him. He wondered if Mr. and Mrs.

the Congress party: India's governing party for five decades after independence in 1947, widely perceived as corrupt.

Das were a bad match, just as he and his wife were. Perhaps they, too, had little in common apart from three children and a decade of their lives. The signs he recognized from his own marriage were there—the bickering, the indifference, the protracted silences. Her sudden interest in him, an interest she did not express in either her husband or her children, was mildly intoxicating. When Mr. Kapasi thought once again about how she had said "romantic," the feeling of intoxication grew.

He began to check his reflection in the rearview mirror as he drove, feeling 80 grateful that he had chosen the gray suit that morning and not the brown one, which tended to sag a little in the knees. From time to time he glanced through the mirror at Mrs. Das. In addition to glancing at her face he glanced at the strawberry between her breasts, and the golden brown hollow in her throat. He decided to tell Mrs. Das about another patient, and another: the young woman who had complained of a sensation of raindrops in her spine, the gentleman whose birthmark had begun to sprout hairs. Mrs. Das listened attentively, stroking her hair with a small plastic brush that resembled an oval bed of nails, asking more questions, for yet another example. The children were quiet, intent on spotting more monkeys in the trees, and Mr. Das was absorbed by his tour book, so it seemed like a private conversation between Mr. Kapasi and Mrs. Das. In this manner the next half hour passed, and when they stopped for lunch at a roadside restaurant that sold fritters and omelette sandwiches, usually something Mr. Kapasi looked forward to on his tours so that he could sit in peace and enjoy some hot tea, he was disappointed. As the Das family settled together under a magenta umbrella fringed with white and orange tassels, and placed their orders with one of the waiters who marched about in tricornered caps, Mr. Kapasi reluctantly headed toward a neighboring table.

"Mr. Kapasi, wait. There's room here," Mrs. Das called out. She gathered Tina onto her lap, insisting that he accompany them. And so, together, they had bottled mango juice and sandwiches and plates of onions and potatoes deep-fried in graham-flour batter. After finishing two omelette sandwiches Mr. Das took more pictures of the group as they ate.

"How much longer?" he asked Mr. Kapasi as he paused to load a new roll of film in the camera.

"About half an hour more."

By now the children had gotten up from the table to look at more monkeys perched in a nearby tree, so there was a considerable space between Mrs. Das and Mr. Kapasi. Mr. Das placed the camera to his face and squeezed one eye shut, his tongue exposed at one corner of his mouth. "This looks funny. Mina, you need to lean in closer to Mr. Kapasi."

She did. He could smell a scent on her skin, like a mixture of whiskey and rose- 85 water. He worried suddenly that she could smell his perspiration, which he knew had collected beneath the synthetic material of his shirt. He polished off his mango juice in one gulp and smoothed his silver hair with his hands. A bit of the juice dripped onto his chin. He wondered if Mrs. Das had noticed.

She had not. "What's your address, Mr. Kapasi?" she inquired, fishing for something inside her straw bag.

"You would like my address?"

"So we can send you copies," she said. "Of the pictures." She handed him a scrap of paper which she had hastily ripped from a page of her film magazine. The blank portion was limited, for the narrow strip was crowded by lines of text and a tiny picture of a hero and heroine embracing under a eucalyptus tree.

The paper curled as Mr. Kapasi wrote his address in clear, careful letters. She would write to him, asking about his days interpreting at the doctor's office, and he would respond eloquently, choosing only the most entertaining anecdotes, ones that would make her laugh out loud as she read them in her house in New Jersey. In time she would reveal the disappointment of her marriage, and he his. In this way their friendship would grow, and flourish. He would possess a picture of the two of them, eating fried onions under a magenta umbrella, which he would keep, he decided, safely tucked between the pages of his Russian grammar. As his mind raced, Mr. Kapasi experienced a mild and pleasant shock. It was similar to a feeling he used to experience long ago when, after months of translating with the aid of a dictionary, he would finally read a passage from a French novel, or an Italian sonnet, and understand the words, one after another, unencumbered by his own efforts. In those moments Mr. Kapasi used to believe that all was right with the world, that all struggles were rewarded, that all of life's mistakes made sense in the end. The promise that he would hear from Mrs. Das now filled him with the same belief.

When he finished writing his address Mr. Kapasi handed her the paper, but as   90
soon as he did so he worried that he had either misspelled his name, or accidentally reversed the numbers of his postal code. He dreaded the possibility of a lost letter, the photograph never reaching him, hovering somewhere in Orissa,° close but ultimately unattainable. He thought of asking for the slip of paper again, just to make sure he had written his address accurately, but Mrs. Das had already dropped it into the jumble of her bag.

They reached Konarak at two-thirty. The temple, made of sandstone, was a massive pyramid-like structure in the shape of a chariot. It was dedicated to the great master of life, the sun, which struck three sides of the edifice as it made its journey each day across the sky. Twenty-four giant wheels were carved on the north and south sides of the plinth. The whole thing was drawn by a team of seven horses, speeding as if through the heavens. As they approached, Mr. Kapasi explained that the temple had been built between A.D. 1243 and 1255, with the efforts of twelve hundred artisans, by the great ruler of the Ganga dynasty, King Narasimhadeva the First, to commemorate his victory against the Muslim army.

"It says the temple occupies about a hundred and seventy acres of land," Mr. Das said, reading from his book.

"It's like a desert," Ronny said, his eyes wandering across the sand that stretched on all sides beyond the temple.

"The Chandrabhaga River once flowed one mile north of here. It is dry now," Mr. Kapasi said, turning off the engine.

They got out and walked toward the temple, posing first for pictures by the pair   95
of lions that flanked the steps. Mr. Kapasi led them next to one of the wheels of the chariot, higher than any human being, nine feet in diameter.

"'The wheels are supposed to symbolize the wheel of life,'" Mr. Das read. "'They depict the cycle of creation, preservation, and achievement of realization.' Cool." He turned the page of his book. "'Each wheel is divided into eight thick and thin spokes, dividing the day into eight equal parts. The rims are carved with designs of birds and animals, whereas the medallions in the spokes are carved with women in luxurious poses, largely erotic in nature.'"

Orissa: a state on the southwest border of West Bengal.

What he referred to were the countless friezes of entwined naked bodies, making love in various positions, women clinging to the necks of men, their knees wrapped eternally around their lovers' thighs. In addition to these were assorted scenes from daily life, of hunting and trading, of deer being killed with bows and arrows and marching warriors holding swords in their hands.

It was no longer possible to enter the temple, for it had filled with rubble years ago, but they admired the exterior, as did all the tourists Mr. Kapasi brought there, slowly strolling along each of its sides. Mr. Das trailed behind, taking pictures. The children ran ahead, pointing to figures of naked people, intrigued in particular by the Nagamithunas, the half-human, half-serpentine couples who were said, Mr. Kapasi told them, to live in the deepest waters of the sea. Mr. Kapasi was pleased that they liked the temple, pleased especially that it appealed to Mrs. Das. She stopped every three or four paces, staring silently at the carved lovers, and the processions of elephants, and the topless female musicians beating on two-sided drums.

Though Mr. Kapasi had been to the temple countless times, it occurred to him, as he, too, gazed at the topless women, that he had never seen his own wife fully naked. Even when they had made love she kept the panels of her blouse hooked together, the string of her petticoat knotted around her waist. He had never admired the backs of his wife's legs the way he now admired those of Mrs. Das, walking as if for his benefit alone. He had, of course, seen plenty of bare limbs before, belonging to the American and European ladies who took his tours. But Mrs. Das was different. Unlike the other women, who had an interest only in the temple, and kept their noses buried in a guidebook, or their eyes behind the lens of a camera, Mrs. Das had taken an interest in him.

Mr. Kapasi was anxious to be alone with her, to continue their private conversa-   100
tion, yet he felt nervous to walk at her side. She was lost behind her sunglasses, ignoring her husband's requests that she pose for another picture, walking past her children as if they were strangers. Worried that he might disturb her, Mr. Kapasi walked ahead, to admire, as he always did, the three life-sized bronze avatars of Surya, the sun god, each emerging from its own niche on the temple facade to greet the sun at dawn, noon, and evening. They wore elaborate headdresses, their languid, elongated eyes closed, their bare chests draped with carved chains and amulets. Hibiscus petals, offerings from previous visitors, were strewn at their gray-green feet. The last statue, on the northern wall of the temple, was Mr. Kapasi's favorite. This Surya had a tired expression, weary after a hard day of work, sitting astride a horse with folded legs. Even his horse's eyes were drowsy. Around his body were smaller sculptures of women in pairs, their hips thrust to one side.

"Who's that?" Mrs. Das asked. He was startled to see that she was standing beside him.

"He is the Astachala-Surya," Mr. Kapasi said. "The setting sun."

"So in a couple of hours the sun will set right here?" She slipped a foot out of one of her square-heeled shoes, rubbed her toes on the back of her other leg.

"That is correct."

She raised her sunglasses for a moment, then put them back on again. "Neat."   105

Mr. Kapasi was not certain exactly what the word suggested, but he had a feeling it was a favorable response. He hoped that Mrs. Das had understood Surya's beauty, his power. Perhaps they would discuss it further in their letters. He would explain things to her, things about India, and she would explain things to him about America. In its own way this correspondence would fulfill his dream, of serving as an interpreter between nations. He looked at her straw bag, delighted that his address lay nestled among its contents. When he pictured her so many thousands of miles away he plummeted, so much so that he had an overwhelming urge to wrap his arms around her, to freeze with her, even for an instant, in an embrace witnessed by his favorite Surya. But Mrs. Das had already started walking.

"When do you return to America?" he asked, trying to sound placid.

"In ten days."

He calculated: A week to settle in, a week to develop the pictures, a few days to compose her letter, two weeks to get to India by air. According to his schedule, allowing room for delays, he would hear from Mrs. Das in approximately six weeks' time.

The family was silent as Mr. Kapasi drove them back, a little past four-thirty, to   110
Hotel Sandy Villa. The children had bought miniature granite versions of the chariot's wheels at a souvenir stand, and they turned them round in their hands. Mr. Das continued to read his book. Mrs. Das untangled Tina's hair with her brush and divided it into two little ponytails.

Mr. Kapasi was beginning to dread the thought of dropping them off. He was not prepared to begin his six-week wait to hear from Mrs. Das. As he stole glances at her in the rearview mirror, wrapping elastic bands around Tina's hair, he wondered how he might make the tour last a little longer. Ordinarily he sped back to Puri using a shortcut, eager to return home, scrub his feet and hands with sandalwood soap, and enjoy the evening newspaper and a cup of tea that his wife would serve him in silence. The thought of that silence, something to which he'd long been resigned, now oppressed him. It was then that he suggested visiting the hills at Udayagiri and Khandagiri, where a number of monastic dwellings were hewn out of the ground, facing one another across a defile. It was some miles away, but well worth seeing, Mr. Kapasi told them.

"Oh yeah, there's something mentioned about it in this book," Mr. Das said. "Built by a Jain° king or something."

"Shall we go then?" Mr. Kapasi asked. He paused at a turn in the road. "It's to the left."

Mr. Das turned to look at Mrs. Das. Both of them shrugged.

"Left, left," the children chanted.   115

Mr. Kapasi turned the wheel, almost delirious with relief. He did not know what he would do or say to Mrs. Das once they arrived at the hills. Perhaps he would tell her what a pleasing smile she had. Perhaps he would compliment her strawberry shirt, which he found irresistibly becoming. Perhaps, when Mr. Das was busy taking a picture, he would take her hand.

He did not have to worry. When they got to the hills, divided by a steep path thick with trees, Mrs. Das refused to get out of the car. All along the path, dozens of monkeys were seated on stones, as well as on the branches of the trees. Their hind legs were stretched out in front and raised to shoulder level, their arms resting on their knees.

"My legs are tired," she said, sinking low in her seat. "I'll stay here."

"Why did you have to wear those stupid shoes?" Mr. Das said. "You won't be in the pictures."

Jain: an adherent of Jainism, a dualistic, ascetic religion founded in the sixth century B.C. in revolt against the Hindu caste system.

"Pretend I'm there."   120

"But we could use one of these pictures for our Christmas card this year. We didn't get one of all five of us at the Sun Temple. Mr. Kapasi could take it."

"I'm not coming. Anyway, those monkeys give me the creeps."

"But they're harmless," Mr. Das said. He turned to Mr. Kapasi. "Aren't they?"

"They are more hungry than dangerous," Mr. Kapasi said. "Do not provoke them with food, and they will not bother you."

Mr. Das headed up the defile with the children, the boys at his side, the little girl   125 on his shoulders. Mr. Kapasi watched as they crossed paths with a Japanese man and woman, the only other tourists there, who paused for a final photograph, then stepped into a nearby car and drove away. As the car disappeared out of view some of the monkeys called out, emitting soft whooping sounds, and then walked on their flat black hands and feet up the path. At one point a group of them formed a little ring around Mr. Das and the children. Tina screamed in delight. Ronny ran in circles around his father. Bobby bent down and picked up a fat stick on the ground. When he extended it, one of the monkeys approached him and snatched it, then briefly beat the ground.

"I'll join them," Mr. Kapasi said, unlocking the door on his side. "There is much to explain about the caves."

"No. Stay a minute," Mrs. Das said. She got out of the back seat and slipped in beside Mr. Kapasi. "Raj has his dumb book anyway." Together, through the windshield, Mrs. Das and Mr. Kapasi watched as Bobby and the monkey passed the stick back and forth between them.

"A brave little boy," Mr. Kapasi commented.

"It's not so surprising," Mrs. Das said.

"No?"   130

"He's not his."

"I beg your pardon?"

"Raj's. He's not Raj's son."

Mr. Kapasi felt a prickle on his skin. He reached into his shirt pocket for the small tin of lotus-oil balm he carried with him at all times, and applied it to three spots on his forehead. He knew that Mrs. Das was watching him, but he did not turn to face her. Instead he watched as the figures of Mr. Das and the children grew smaller, climbing up the steep path, pausing every now and then for a picture, surrounded by a growing number of monkeys.

"Are you surprised?" The way she put it made him choose his words with care.   135

"It's not the type of thing one assumes," Mr. Kapasi replied slowly. He put the tin of lotus-oil balm back in his pocket.

"No, of course not. And no one knows, of course. No one at all. I've kept it a secret for eight whole years." She looked at Mr. Kapasi, tilting her chin as if to gain a fresh perspective. "But now I've told you."

Mr. Kapasi nodded. He felt suddenly parched, and his forehead was warm and slightly numb from the balm. He considered asking Mrs. Das for a sip of water, then decided against it.

"We met when we were very young," she said. She reached into her straw bag in search of something, then pulled out a packet of puffed rice. "Want some?"

"No, thank you."   140

She put a fistful in her mouth, sank into the seat a little, and looked away from Mr. Kapasi, out the window on her side of the car. "We married when we were still in college. We were in high school when he proposed. We went to the same college, of course. Back then we couldn't stand the thought of being separated, not for a day, not for a minute. Our parents were best friends who lived in the same town. My entire life I saw him every weekend, either at our house or theirs. We were sent upstairs to play together while our parents joked about our marriage. Imagine! They never caught us at anything, though in a way I think it was all more or less a setup. The things we did those Friday and Saturday nights, while our parents sat downstairs drinking tea . . . I could tell you stories, Mr. Kapasi."

As a result of spending all her time in college with Raj, she continued, she did not make many close friends. There was no one to confide in about him at the end of a difficult day, or to share a passing thought or a worry. Her parents now lived on the other side of the world, but she had never been very close to them, anyway. After marrying so young she was overwhelmed by it all, having a child so quickly, and nursing, and warming up bottles of milk and testing their temperature against her wrist while Raj was at work, dressed in sweaters and corduroy pants, teaching his students about rocks and dinosaurs. Raj never looked cross or harried, or plump as she had become after the first baby.

Always tired, she declined invitations from her one or two college girlfriends, to have lunch or shop in Manhattan. Eventually the friends stopped calling her, so that she was left at home all day with the baby, surrounded by toys that made her trip when she walked or wince when she sat, always cross and tired. Only occasionally did they go out after Ronny was born, and even more rarely did they entertain. Raj didn't mind; he looked forward to coming home from teaching and watching television and bouncing Ronny on his knee. She had been outraged when Raj told her that a Punjabi° friend, someone whom she had once met but did not remember, would be staying with them for a week for some job interviews in the New Brunswick area.

Bobby was conceived in the afternoon, on a sofa littered with rubber teething toys, after the friend learned that a London pharmaceutical company had hired him, while Ronny cried to be freed from his playpen. She made no protest when the friend touched the small of her back as she was about to make a pot of coffee, then pulled her against his crisp navy suit. He made love to her swiftly, in silence, with an expertise she had never known, without the meaningful expressions and smiles Raj always insisted on afterward. The next day Raj drove the friend to JFK. He was married now, to a Punjabi girl, and they lived in London still, and every year they exchanged Christmas cards with Raj and Mina, each couple tucking photos of their families into the envelopes. He did not know that he was Bobby's father. He never would.

"I beg your pardon, Mrs. Das, but why have you told me this information?"   145
Mr. Kapasi asked when she had finally finished speaking, and had turned to face him once again.

"For God's sake, stop calling me Mrs. Das. I'm twenty-eight. You probably have children my age."

"Not quite." It disturbed Mr. Kapasi to learn that she thought of him as a parent. The feeling he had had toward her, that had made him check his reflection in the rearview mirror as they drove, evaporated a little.

"I told you because of your talents." She put the packet of puffed rice back into her bag without folding over the top.

Punjabi: a native of Punjab, a state in northwest India.

"I don't understand," Mr. Kapasi said.

"Don't you see? For eight years I haven't been able to express this to anybody, 150
not to friends, certainly not to Raj. He doesn't even suspect it. He thinks I'm still in
love with him. Well, don't you have anything to say?"

"About what?"

"About what I've just told you. About my secret, and about how terrible it makes
me feel. I feel terrible looking at my children, and at Raj, always terrible. I have terrible
urges, Mr. Kapasi, to throw things away. One day I had the urge to throw everything I
own out the window, the television, the children, everything. Don't you think it's un-
healthy?"

He was silent.

"Mr. Kapasi, don't you have anything to say? I thought that was your job."

"My job is to give tours, Mrs. Das." 155

"Not that. Your other job. As an interpreter."

"But we do not face a language barrier. What need is there for an interpreter?"

"That's not what I mean. I would never have told you otherwise. Don't you realize what it means for me to tell you?"

"What does it mean?"

"It means that I'm tired of feeling so terrible all the time. Eight years, Mr. Kapasi, 160
I've been in pain eight years. I was hoping you could help me feel better, say the right
thing. Suggest some kind of remedy."

He looked at her, in her red plaid skirt and strawberry T-shirt, a woman not yet
thirty, who loved neither her husband nor her children, who had already fallen out of
love with life. Her confession depressed him, depressed him all the more when he
thought of Mr. Das at the top of the path, Tina clinging to his shoulders, taking pictures of ancient monastic cells cut into the hills to show his students in America,
unsuspecting and unaware that one of his sons was not his own. Mr. Kapasi felt
insulted that Mrs. Das should ask him to interpret her common, trivial little secret.
She did not resemble the patients in the doctor's office, those who came glassy-eyed
and desperate, unable to sleep or breathe or urinate with ease, unable, above all, to
give words to their pains. Still, Mr. Kapasi believed it was his duty to assist Mrs. Das.
Perhaps he ought to tell her to confess the truth to Mr. Das. He would explain that
honesty was the best policy. Honesty, surely, would help her feel better, as she'd put it.
Perhaps he would offer to preside over the discussion, as a mediator. He decided to
begin with the most obvious question, to get to the heart of the matter, and so he
asked, "Is it really pain you feel, Mrs. Das, or is it guilt?"

She turned to him and glared, mustard oil thick on her frosty pink lips. She
opened her mouth to say something, but as she glared at Mr. Kapasi some certain
knowledge seemed to pass before her eyes, and she stopped. It crushed him; he knew
at that moment that he was not even important enough to be properly insulted. She
opened the car door and began walking up the path, wobbling a little on her square
wooden heels, reaching into her straw bag to eat handfuls of puffed rice. It fell
through her fingers, leaving a zigzagging trail, causing a monkey to leap down from a
tree and devour the little white grains. In search of more, the monkey began to follow
Mrs. Das. Others joined him, so that she was soon being followed by about half a
dozen of them, their velvety tails dragging behind.

Mr. Kapasi stepped out of the car. He wanted to holler, to alert her in some way,
but he worried that if she knew they were behind her, she would grow nervous. Perhaps she would lose her balance. Perhaps they would pull at her bag or her hair. He

began to jog up the path, taking a fallen branch in his hand to scare away the
monkeys. Mrs. Das continued walking, oblivious, trailing grains of puffed rice.
Near the top of the incline, before a group of cells fronted by a row of squat stone
pillars, Mr. Das was kneeling on the ground focusing the lens of his camera. The
children stood under the arcade, now hiding, now emerging from view.

"Wait for me," Mrs. Das called out. "I'm coming."

Tina jumped up and down. "Here comes Mommy!"   165

"Great," Mr. Das said without looking up. "Just in time. We'll get Mr. Kapasi
to take a picture of the five of us."

Mr. Kapasi quickened his pace, waving his branch so that the monkeys scampered
away, distracted, in another direction.

"Where's Bobby?" Mrs. Das asked when she stopped.

Mr. Das looked up from the camera. "I don't know. Ronny, where's Bobby?"

Ronny shrugged, "I thought he was right here."   170

"Where is he?" Mrs. Das repeated sharply. "What's wrong with all of you?"

They began calling his name, wandering up and down the path a bit. Because
they were calling, they did not initially hear the boy's screams. When they found
him, a little farther down the path under a tree, he was surrounded by a group of
monkeys, over a dozen of them, pulling at his T-shirt with their long black fingers.
The puffed rice Mrs. Das had spilled was scattered at his feet, raked over by the monkeys' hands. The boy was silent, his body frozen, swift tears running down his startled
face. His bare legs were dusty and red with welts from where one of the monkeys
struck him repeatedly with the stick he had given to it earlier.

"Daddy, the monkey's hurting Bobby," Tina said.

Mr. Das wiped his palms on the front of his shorts. In his nervousness he accidentally pressed the shutter on his camera; the whirring noise of the advancing film
excited the monkeys, and the one with the stick began to beat Bobby more intently.
"What are we supposed to do? What if they start attacking?"

"Mr. Kapasi," Mrs. Das shrieked, noticing him standing to one side. "Do some-   175
thing, for God's sake, do something!"

Mr. Kapasi took his branch and shooed them away, hissing at the ones that
remained, stomping his feet to scare them. The animals retreated slowly, with a measured gait, obedient but unintimidated. Mr. Kapasi gathered Bobby in his arms and
brought him back to where his parents and siblings were standing. As he carried him
he was tempted to whisper a secret into the boy's ear. But Bobby was stunned, and
shivering with fright, his legs bleeding slightly where the stick had broken the skin.
When Mr. Kapasi delivered him to his parents, Mr. Das brushed some dirt off the
boy's T-shirt and put the visor on him the right way. Mrs. Das reached into her straw
bag to find a bandage which she taped over the cut on his knee. Ronny offered his
brother a fresh piece of gum. "He's fine. Just a little scared, right, Bobby?" Mr. Das
said, patting the top of his head.

"God, let's get out of here," Mrs. Das said. She folded her arms across the strawberry
on her chest. "This place gives me the creeps."

"Yeah. Back to the hotel, definitely," Mr. Das agreed.

"Poor Bobby," Mrs. Das said. "Come here a second. Let Mommy fix your hair."
Again she reached into her straw bag, this time for her hairbrush, and began to run it
around the edges of the translucent visor. When she whipped out the hairbrush, the
slip of paper with Mr. Kapasi's address on it fluttered away in the wind. No one but
Mr. Kapasi noticed. He watched as it rose, carried higher and higher by the breeze,

into the trees where the monkeys now sat, solemnly observing the scene below. Mr. Kapasi observed it too, knowing that this was the picture of the Das family he would preserve forever in his mind.

D. H. Lawrence

The Rocking-Horse Winner 1933

David Herbert Lawrence (1885–1930) was born in Nottinghamshire, England, child of a coal miner and a schoolteacher who hated her husband's toil and vowed that her son should escape it. He took up fiction writing, attaining early success. During World War I, Lawrence and his wife were unjustly suspected of treason (he because of his pacifism, she because of her aristocratic German birth). After the armistice they left England and, seeking a climate healthier for Lawrence, who suffered from tuberculosis, wandered in Italy, France, Australia, Mexico, and the American Southwest.

D. H. Lawrence

Lawrence is an impassioned spokesman for our unconscious instinctive natures, which we moderns (he argues) have neglected in favor of our overweening intellects. In Lady Chatterley's Lover (1928), he strove to restore explicit sexuality to English fiction. The book, which today seems tame and repetitious, was long banned in Britain and the United States. Deeper Lawrence novels include Sons and Lovers (1913), a veiled account of his breaking away from his fiercely possessive mother; The Rainbow (1915); Women in Love (1921); and The Plumed Serpent (1926), about a revival of pagan religion in Mexico. Besides fiction, Lawrence left a rich legacy of poetry, essays, criticism (Studies in Classic American Literature, 1923, is especially shrewd and funny), and travel writing. Lawrence exerted deep influence on others, both by the message in his work and by his personal magnetism.

There was a woman who was beautiful, who started with all the advantages, yet she had no luck. She married for love, and the love turned to dust. She had bonny children, yet she felt they had been thrust upon her, and she could not love them. They looked at her coldly, as if they were finding fault with her. And hurriedly she felt she must cover up some fault in herself. Yet what it was that she must cover up she never knew. Nevertheless, when her children were present, she always felt the center of her heart go hard. This troubled her, and in her manner she was all the more gentle and anxious for her children, as if she loved them very much. Only she herself knew that at the center of her heart was a hard little place that could not feel love, no, not for anybody. Everybody else said of her: "She is such a good mother. She adores her children." Only she herself, and her children themselves, knew it was not so. They read it in each other's eyes.

There were a boy and two little girls. They lived in a pleasant house, with a garden, and they had discreet servants, and felt themselves superior to anyone in the neighborhood.

Although they lived in style, they felt always an anxiety in the house. There was never enough money. The mother had a small income, and the father had a small income, but not nearly enough for the social position which they had to keep up. The father went into town to some office. But though he had good prospects, these prospects never materialized. There was always the grinding sense of the shortage of money, though the style was always kept up.

At last the mother said: "I will see if *I* can't make something." But she did not know where to begin. She racked her brains, and tried this thing and the other, but could not find anything successful. The failure made deep lines come into her face. Her children were growing up, they would have to go to school. There must be more money, there must be more money. The father, who was always very handsome and expensive in his tastes, seemed as if he never *would* be able to do anything worth doing. And the mother, who had a great belief in herself, did not succeed any better, and her tastes were just as expensive.

And so the house came to be haunted by the unspoken phrase: *There must be* 5 *more money! There must be more money!* The children could hear it all the time, though nobody said it aloud. They heard it at Christmas, when the expensive and splendid toys filled the nursery. Behind the shining modern rocking-horse, behind the smart doll's house, a voice would start whispering: "There *must* be more money! There *must* be more money!" And the children would stop playing, to listen for a moment. They would look into each other's eyes, to see if they had all heard. And each one saw in the eyes of the other two that they too had heard. "There *must* be more money! There *must* be more money!"

It came whispering from the springs of the still-swaying rocking-horse, and even the horse, bending his wooden, champing head, heard it. The big doll, sitting so pink and smirking in her new pram, could hear it quite plainly, and seemed to be smirking all the more self-consciously because of it. The foolish puppy, too, that took the place of the teddy-bear, he was looking so extraordinarily foolish for no other reason but that he heard the secret whisper all over the house: "There *must* be more money!"

Yet nobody ever said it aloud. The whisper was everywhere, and therefore no one spoke it. Just as no one ever says: "We are breathing!" in spite of the fact that breath is coming and going all the time.

"Mother," said the boy Paul one day, "why don't we keep a car of our own? Why do we always use uncle's, or else a taxi?"

"Because we're the poor members of the family," said the mother.

"But why *are* we, mother?" 10

"Well—I suppose," she said slowly and bitterly, "it's because your father has no luck."

The boy was silent for some time.

"Is luck money, mother?" he asked rather timidly.

"No, Paul. Not quite. It's what causes you to have money."

"Oh!" said Paul vaguely. "I thought when Uncle Oscar said *filthy lucker*, it meant 15 money."

"*Filthy lucre* does mean money," said the mother. "But it's lucre, not luck."

"Oh!" said the boy. "Then what *is* luck, mother?"

"It's what causes you to have money. If you're lucky you have money. That's why it's better to be born lucky than rich. If you're rich, you may lose your money. But if you're lucky, you will always get more money."

"Oh! Will you? And is father not lucky?"

"Very unlucky, I should say," she said bitterly. 20

The boy watched her with unsure eyes.

"Why?" he asked.

"I don't know. Nobody ever knows why one person is lucky and another unlucky."

"Don't they? Nobody at all? Does *nobody* know?"

"Perhaps God. But He never tells." 25

"He ought to, then. And aren't you lucky either, mother?"

"I can't be, if I married an unlucky husband."

"But by yourself, aren't you?"

"I used to think I was, before I married. Now I think I am very unlucky indeed."

"Why?" 30

"Well—never mind! Perhaps I'm not really," she said.

The child looked at her to see if she meant it. But he saw, by the lines of her mouth, that she was only trying to hide something from him.

"Well, anyhow," he said stoutly, "I'm a lucky person."

"Why?" said his mother, with a sudden laugh.

He stared at her. He didn't even know why he had said it. 35

"God told me," he asserted, brazening it out.

"I hope He did, dear!" she said, again with a laugh, but rather bitter.

"He did, mother!"

"Excellent!" said the mother, using one of her husband's exclamations.

The boy saw she did not believe him; or, rather, that she paid no attention to his 40
assertion. This angered him somewhat, and made him want to compel her attention.

He went off by himself, vaguely, in a childish way, seeking for the clue to "luck." Absorbed, taking no heed of other people, he went about with a sort of stealth, seeking inwardly for luck. He wanted luck, he wanted it, he wanted it. When the two girls were playing dolls in the nursery, he would sit on his big rocking-horse, charging madly into space, with a frenzy that made the little girls peer at him uneasily. Wildly the horse careered, the waving dark hair of the boy tossed, his eyes had a strange glare in them. The little girls dared not speak to him.

When he had ridden to the end of his mad little journey, he climbed down and stood in front of his rocking-horse, staring fixedly into its lowered face. Its red mouth was slightly open, its big eye was wide and glassy-bright.

"Now!" he would silently command the snorting steed. "Now, take me to where there is luck! Now take me!"

And he would slash the horse on the neck with the little whip he had asked Uncle Oscar for. He *knew* the horse could take him to where there was luck, if only he forced it. So he would mount again, and start on his furious ride, hoping at last to get there. He knew he could get there.

"You'll break your horse, Paul!" said the nurse. 45

"He's always riding like that! I wish he'd leave off!" said his elder sister Joan.

But he only glared down on them in silence. Nurse gave him up. She could make nothing of him. Anyhow he was growing beyond her.

One day his mother and his Uncle Oscar came in when he was on one of his furious rides. He did not speak to them.

"Hallo, you young jockey! Riding a winner?" said his uncle.

"Aren't you growing too big for a rocking-horse? You're not a very little boy any 50
longer, you know," said his mother.

But Paul only gave a blue glare from his big, rather close-set eyes. He would speak to nobody when he was in full tilt. His mother watched him with an anxious expression on her face.

At last he suddenly stopped forcing his horse into the mechanical gallop and slid down.

"Well, I got there!" he announced fiercely, his blue eyes still flaring, and his sturdy long legs straddling apart.

"Where did you get to?" asked his mother.

"Where I wanted to go," he flared back at her.   55

"That's right, son!" said Uncle Oscar. "Don't you stop till you get there. What's the horse's name?"

"He doesn't have a name," said the boy.

"Gets on without all right?" asked the uncle.

"Well, he has different names. He was called Sansovino last week."

"Sansovino, eh? Won the Ascot. How did you know his name?"   60

"He always talks about horse-races with Bassett," said Joan.

The uncle was delighted to find that his small nephew was posted with all the racing news. Bassett, the young gardener, who had been wounded in the left foot in the war and had got his present job through Oscar Cresswell, whose batman° he had been, was a perfect blade of the "turf." He lived in the racing events, and the small boy lived with him.

Oscar Cresswell got it all from Bassett.

"Master Paul comes and asks me, so I can't do more than tell him, sir," said Bassett, his face terribly serious, as if he were speaking of religious matters.

"And does he ever put anything on a horse he fancies?"   65

"Well—I don't want to give him away—he's a young sport, a fine sport, sir. Would you mind asking him himself? He sort of takes a pleasure in it, and perhaps he'd feel I was giving him away, sir, if you don't mind."

Bassett was serious as a church.

The uncle went back to his nephew and took him off for a ride in the car.

"Say, Paul, old man, do you ever put anything on a horse?" the uncle asked.

The boy watched the handsome man closely.   70

"Why, do you think I oughtn't to?" he parried.

"Not a bit of it. I thought perhaps you might give me a tip for the Lincoln."

The car sped on into the country, going down to Uncle Oscar's place in Hampshire.

"Honor bright?" said the nephew.

"Honor bright, son!" said the uncle.   75

"Well, then, Daffodil."

"Daffodil! I doubt it, sonny. What about Mirza?"

"I only know the winner," said the boy. "That's Daffodil."

"Daffodil, eh?"

There was a pause. Daffodil was an obscure horse comparatively.   80

"Uncle!"

"Yes, son?"

"You won't let it go any further, will you? I promised Bassett."

"Bassett be damned, old man! What's he got to do with it?"

"We're partners. We've been partners from the first. Uncle, he lent me my first   85
five shillings, which I lost. I promised him, honor bright, it was only between me and him; only you gave me that ten-shilling note I started winning with, so I thought you were lucky. You won't let it go any further, will you?"

batman: an enlisted man who serves as valet to a cavalry officer.

The boy gazed at his uncle from those big, hot, blue eyes, set rather close together. The uncle stirred and laughed uneasily.

"Right you are, son! I'll keep your tip private. Daffodil, eh? How much are you putting on him?"

"All except twenty pounds," said the boy. "I keep that in reserve."

The uncle thought it a good joke.

"You keep twenty pounds in reserve, do you, you young romancer? What are you betting, then?"

"I'm betting three hundred," said the boy gravely. "But it's between you and me, Uncle Oscar! Honor bright?"

The uncle burst into a roar of laughter.

"It's between you and me all right, you young Nat Gould,"° he said, laughing. "But where's your three hundred?"

"Bassett keeps it for me. We're partners."

"You are, are you! And what is Bassett putting on Daffodil?"

"He won't go quite as high as I do, I expect. Perhaps he'll go a hundred and fifty."

"What, pennies?" laughed the uncle.

"Pounds," said the child, with a surprised look at his uncle. "Bassett keeps a bigger reserve than I do."

Between wonder and amusement Uncle Oscar was silent. He pursued the matter no further, but he determined to take his nephew with him to the Lincoln races.

"Now, son," he said, "I'm putting twenty on Mirza, and I'll put five for you on any horse you fancy. What's your pick?"

"Daffodil, uncle."

"No, not the fiver on Daffodil!"

"I should if it was my own fiver," said the child.

"Good! Good! Right you are! A fiver for me and a fiver for you on Daffodil."

The child had never been to a race-meeting before, and his eyes were blue fire. He pursed his mouth tight, and watched. A Frenchman just in front had put his money on Lancelot. Wild with excitement, he flayed his arms up and down, yelling "*Lancelot! Lancelot!*" in his French accent.

Daffodil came in first, Lancelot second, Mirza third. The child, flushed and with eyes blazing, was curiously serene. His uncle brought him four five-pound notes, four to one.

"What am I to do with these?" he cried, waving them before the boy's eyes.

"I suppose we'll talk to Bassett," said the boy. "I expect I have fifteen hundred now; and twenty in reserve; and this twenty."

His uncle studied him for some moments.

"Look here, son!" he said. "You're not serious about Bassett and that fifteen hundred, are you?"

"Yes, I am. But it's between you and me, uncle. Honor bright!"

"Honor bright all right, son! But I must talk to Bassett."

"If you'd like to be a partner, uncle, with Bassett and me, we could all be partners. Only, you'd have to promise, honor bright, uncle, not to let it go beyond us three. Bassett and I are lucky, and you must be lucky, because it was your ten shillings I started winning with . . ."

Nat Gould: celebrated English gambler of the 1920s.

Uncle Oscar took both Bassett and Paul into Richmond Park for an afternoon, and there they talked.

"It's like this, you see, sir," Bassett said. "Master Paul would get me talking about 115 racing events, spinning yarns, you know, sir. And he was always keen on knowing if I'd made or if I'd lost. It's about a year since, now, that I put five shillings on Blush of Dawn for him: and we lost. Then the luck turned, and with that ten shillings he had from you: that we put on Singhalese. And since that time, it's been pretty steady, all things considering. What do you say, Master Paul?"

"We're all right when we're sure," said Paul. "It's when we're not quite sure that we go down."

"Oh, but we're careful then," said Bassett.

"But when are you *sure?*" smiled Uncle Oscar.

"It's Master Paul, sir," said Bassett, in a secret, religious voice. "It's as if he had it from heaven. Like Daffodil, now, for the Lincoln. That was as sure as eggs."

"Did you put anything on Daffodil?" asked Oscar Cresswell. 120

"Yes, sir. I made my bit."

"And my nephew?"

Bassett was obstinately silent, looking at Paul.

"I made twelve hundred, didn't I, Bassett? I told uncle I was putting three hundred on Daffodil."

"That's right," said Bassett, nodding. 125

"But where's the money?" asked the uncle.

"I keep it safe locked up, sir. Master Paul he can have it any minute he likes to ask for it."

"What, fifteen hundred pounds?"

"And twenty! And *forty*, that is, with the twenty he made on the course."

"It's amazing!" said the uncle. 130

"If Master Paul offers you to be partners, sir, I would, if I were you: if you'll excuse me," said Bassett.

Oscar Cresswell thought about it.

"I'll see the money," he said.

They drove home again, and, sure enough, Bassett came round to the garden-house with fifteen hundred pounds in notes. The twenty pounds reserve was left with Joe Glee, in the Turf Commission deposit.

"You see, it's all right, uncle, when I'm *sure!* Then we go strong, for all we're 135 worth. Don't we, Bassett!"

"We do that, Master Paul."

"And when are you sure?" said the uncle, laughing.

"Oh, well, sometimes I'm *absolutely* sure, like about Daffodil," said the boy; "and sometimes I have an idea; and sometimes I haven't even an idea, have I, Bassett? Then we're careful, because we mostly go down."

"You do, do you! And when you're sure, like about Daffodil, what makes you sure, sonny?"

"Oh, well, I don't know," said the boy uneasily. "I'm sure, you know, uncle; 140 that's all."

"It's as if he had it from heaven, sir," Bassett reiterated.

"I should say so!" said the uncle.

But he became a partner. And when the Leger was coming on, Paul was "sure" about Lively Spark, which was a quite inconsiderable horse. The boy insisted on putting a thousand on the horse, Bassett went for five hundred, and Oscar Cresswell two hundred. Lively Spark came in first, and the betting had been ten to one against him. Paul had made ten thousand.

"You see," he said, "I was absolutely sure of him."

Even Oscar Cresswell had cleared two thousand. 145

"Look here, son," he said, "this sort of thing makes me nervous."

"It needn't, uncle! Perhaps I shan't be sure again for a long time."

"But what are you going to do with your money?" asked the uncle.

"Of course," said the boy, "I started it for mother. She said she had no luck, because father is unlucky, so I thought if *I* was lucky, it might stop whispering."

"What might stop whispering?" 150

"Our house. I *hate* our house for whispering."

"What does it whisper?"

"Why—why"—the boy fidgeted—"why, I don't know. But it's always short of money, you know, uncle."

"I know it, son, I know it."

"You know people send mother writs, don't you, uncle?" 155

"I'm afraid I do," said the uncle.

"And then the house whispers, like people laughing at you behind your back. It's awful, that is! I thought if I was lucky—"

"You might stop it," added the uncle.

The boy watched him with big blue eyes, that had an uncanny cold fire in them, and he said never a word.

"Well, then!" said the uncle. "What are we doing?" 160

"I shouldn't like mother to know I was lucky," said the boy.

"Why not, son?"

"She'd stop me."

"I don't think she would."

"Oh!"—and the boy writhed in an odd way—"I *don't* want her to know, uncle." 165

"All right, son! We'll manage it without her knowing."

They managed it very easily. Paul, at the other's suggestion, handed over five thousand pounds to his uncle, who deposited it with the family lawyer, who was then to inform Paul's mother that a relative had put five thousand pounds into his hands, which sum was to be paid out a thousand pounds at a time, on the mother's birthday, for the next five years.

"So she'll have a birthday present of a thousand pounds for five successive years," said Uncle Oscar. "I hope it won't make it all the harder for her later."

Paul's mother had her birthday in November. The house had been "whispering" worse than ever lately, and, even in spite of his luck, Paul could not bear up against it. He was very anxious to see the effect of the birthday letter, telling his mother about the thousand pounds.

When there were no visitors, Paul now took his meals with his parents, as he was 170 beyond the nursery control. His mother went into town nearly every day. She had discovered that she had an odd knack of sketching furs and dress materials, so she worked secretly in the studio of a friend who was the chief "artist" for the leading drapers. She drew the figures of ladies in furs and ladies in silk and sequins for the newspaper advertisements. This young woman artist earned several thousand pounds a year, but Paul's mother only made several hundreds, and she was again dissatisfied. She so wanted to be first in something, and she did not succeed, even in making sketches for drapery advertisements.

She was down to breakfast on the morning of her birthday. Paul watched her face as she read her letters. He knew the lawyer's letter. As his mother read it, her face hardened and became more expressionless. Then a cold, determined look came on her mouth. She hid the letter under the pile of others, and said not a word about it.

"Didn't you have anything nice in the post for your birthday, mother?" said Paul.

"Quite moderately nice," she said, her voice cold and absent.

She went away to town without saying more.

But in the afternoon Uncle Oscar appeared. He said Paul's mother had had a 175 long interview with the lawyer, asking if the whole five thousand could not be advanced at once, as she was in debt.

"What do you think, uncle?" said the boy.

"I leave it to you, son."

"Oh, let her have it, then! We can get some more with the other," said the boy.

"A bird in the hand is worth two in the bush, laddie!" said Uncle Oscar.

"But I'm sure to *know* for the Grand National; or the Lincolnshire; or else the 180 Derby. I'm sure to know for *one* of them," said Paul.

So Uncle Oscar signed the agreement, and Paul's mother touched the whole five thousand. Then something very curious happened. The voices in the house suddenly went mad, like a chorus of frogs on a spring evening. There were certain new furnishings, and Paul had a tutor. He was *really* going to Eton, his father's school, in the following autumn. There were flowers in the winter, and a blossoming of the luxury Paul's mother had been used to. And yet the voices in the house, behind the sprays of mimosa and almond blossom, and from under the piles of iridescent cushions, simply trilled and screamed in a sort of ecstasy: "There *must* be more money! Oh-h-h; there *must* be more money. Oh, now, now-w! Now-w-w—there *must* be more money!—more than ever! More than ever!"

It frightened Paul terribly. He studied away at his Latin and Greek with his tutor. But his intense hours were spent with Bassett. The Grand National had gone by: he had not "known," and had lost a hundred pounds. Summer was at hand. He was in agony for the Lincoln. But even for the Lincoln he didn't "know," and he lost fifty pounds. He became wild-eyed and strange, as if something were going to explode in him.

"Let it alone, son! Don't you bother about it!" urged Uncle Oscar. But it was as if the boy couldn't really hear what his uncle was saying.

"I've got to know for the Derby! I've got to know for the Derby!" the child reiterated, his big blue eyes blazing with a sort of madness.

His mother noticed how overwrought he was. 185

"You'd better go to the seaside. Wouldn't you like to go now to the seaside, instead of waiting? I think you'd better," she said, looking down at him anxiously, her heart curiously heavy because of him.

But the child lifted his uncanny blue eyes.

"I couldn't possibly go before the Derby, mother!" he said. "I couldn't possibly!"

"Why not?" she said, her voice becoming heavy when she was opposed. "Why not? You can still go from the seaside to see the Derby with your Uncle Oscar, if that's what you wish. No need for you to wait here. Besides, I think you care too much about these races. It's a bad sign. My family has been a gambling family, and you won't know till you grow up how much damage it has done. But it has done damage. I shall have to send Bassett away, and ask Uncle Oscar not to talk racing to you, unless you promise to be reasonable about it: go away to the seaside and forget it. You're all nerves!"

"I'll do what you like, mother, so long as you don't send me away till after the Derby," the boy said. 190

"Send you away from where? Just from this house?"

"Yes," he said, gazing at her.

"Why, you curious child, what makes you care about this house so much, suddenly? I never knew you loved it."

He gazed at her without speaking. He had a secret within a secret, something he had not divulged, even to Bassett or to his Uncle Oscar.

But his mother, after standing undecided and a little bit sullen for some moments, said: 195

"Very well, then! Don't go to the seaside till after the Derby, if you don't wish it. But promise me you won't let your nerves go to pieces. Promise you won't think so much about horse-racing and *events*, as you call them!"

"Oh, no," said the boy casually. "I won't think much about them, mother. You needn't worry. I wouldn't worry, mother, if I were you."

"If you were me and I were you," said his mother, "I wonder what we *should* do!"

"But you know you needn't worry, mother, don't you?" the boy repeated.

"I should be awfully glad to know it," she said wearily. 200

"Oh, well, you *can*, you know. I mean, you *ought* to know you needn't worry," he insisted.

"Ought I? Then I'll see about it," she said.

Paul's secret of secrets was his wooden horse, that which had no name. Since he was emancipated from a nurse and a nursery-governess, he had had his rocking-horse removed to his own bedroom at the top of the house.

"Surely, you're too big for a rocking-horse!" his mother had remonstrated.

"Well, you see, mother, till I can have a *real* horse, I like to have *some* sort of animal about," had been his quaint answer. 205

"Do you feel he keeps you company?" she laughed.

"Oh, yes! He's very good, he always keeps me company, when I'm there," said Paul.

So the horse, rather shabby, stood in an arrested prance in the boy's bedroom.

The Derby was drawing near, and the boy grew more and more tense. He hardly heard what was spoken to him, he was very frail, and his eyes were really uncanny. His mother had sudden strange seizures of uneasiness about him. Sometimes, for half an hour, she would feel a sudden anxiety about him that was almost anguish. She wanted to rush to him at once, and know he was safe.

Two nights before the Derby, she was at a big party in town, when one of her 210 rushes of anxiety about her boy, her first-born, gripped her heart till she could hardly speak. She fought with the feeling, might and main, for she believed in common sense. But it was too strong. She had to leave the dance and go downstairs to telephone to the country. The children's nursery-governess was terribly surprised and startled at being rung up in the night.

"Are the children all right, Miss Wilmot?"

"Oh, yes, they are quite all right."

"Master Paul? Is he all right?"

"He went to bed as right as a trivet. Shall I run up and look at him?"

"No," said Paul's mother reluctantly. "No! Don't trouble. It's all right. Don't 215 sit up. We shall be home fairly soon." She did not want her son's privacy intruded upon.

"Very good," said the governess.

It was about one-o'clock when Paul's mother and father drove up to their house. All was still. Paul's mother went to her room and slipped off her white fur cloak. She had told her maid not to wait up for her. She heard her husband downstairs, mixing a whisky and soda.

And then, because of the strange anxiety at her heart, she stole upstairs to her son's room. Noiselessly she went along the upper corridor. Was there a faint noise? What was it?

She stood, with arrested muscles, outside his door, listening. There was a strange, heavy, and yet not loud noise. Her heart stood still. It was a soundless noise, yet rushing and powerful. Something huge, in violent, hushed motion. What was it? What in God's name was it? She ought to know. She felt that she knew the noise. She knew what it was.

Yet she could not place it. She couldn't say what it was. And on and on it went, 220 like a madness.

Softly, frozen with anxiety and fear, she turned the door-handle.

The room was dark. Yet in the space near the window, she heard and saw something plunging to and fro. She gazed in fear and amazement.

Then suddenly she switched on the light, and saw her son, in his green pajamas, madly surging on the rocking-horse. The blaze of light suddenly lit him up, as he urged the wooden horse, and lit her up, as she stood, blonde, in her dress of pale green and crystal, in the doorway.

"Paul!" she cried. "Whatever are you doing?"

"It's Malabar!" he screamed, in a powerful, strange voice. "It's Malabar!" 225

His eyes blazed at her for one strange and senseless second, as he ceased urging his wooden horse. Then he fell with a crash to the ground, and she, all her tormented motherhood flooding upon her, rushed to gather him up.

But he was unconscious, and unconscious he remained, with some brain-fever. He talked and tossed, and his mother sat stonily by his side.

"Malabar! It's Malabar! Bassett, Bassett, I *know*! It's Malabar!"

So the child cried, trying to get up and urge the rocking-horse that gave him his inspiration.

"What does he mean by Malabar?" asked the heart-frozen mother. 230

"I don't know," said the father stonily.

"What does he mean by Malabar?" she asked her brother Oscar.

"It's one of the horses running for the Derby," was the answer.

And, in spite of himself, Oscar Cresswell spoke to Bassett, and himself put a thousand on Malabar: at fourteen to one.

The third day of the illness was critical: they were waiting for a change. The boy, 235 with his rather long, curly hair, was tossing ceaselessly on the pillow. He neither slept nor regained consciousness, and his eyes were like blue stones. His mother sat, feeling her heart had gone, turned actually into a stone.

In the evening, Oscar Cresswell did not come, but Bassett sent a message, saying could he come up for one moment, just one moment? Paul's mother was very angry at the intrusion, but on second thoughts she agreed. The boy was the same. Perhaps Bassett might bring him to consciousness.

The gardener, a shortish fellow with a little brown moustache and sharp little brown eyes, tiptoed into the room, touched his imaginary cap to Paul's mother, and stole to the bedside, staring with glittering, smallish eyes, at the tossing, dying child.

"Master Paul!" he whispered. "Master Paul! Malabar came in first all right, a clean win. I did as you told me. You've made over seventy thousand pounds, you have; you've got over eighty thousand. Malabar came in all right, Master Paul."

"Malabar! Malabar! Did I say Malabar, mother? Did I say Malabar? Do you think I'm lucky, mother? I knew Malabar, didn't I? Over eighty thousand pounds! I call that lucky, don't you, mother? Over eighty thousand pounds! I knew, didn't I know I knew? Malabar came in all right. If I ride my horse till I'm sure, then I tell you, Bassett, you can go as high as you like. Did you go for all you were worth, Bassett?"

"I went a thousand on it, Master Paul."   240

"I never told you, mother, that if I can ride my horse, and *get there*, then I'm absolutely sure—oh, absolutely! Mother, did I ever tell you? I *am* lucky!"

"No, you never did," said his mother.

But the boy died in the night.

And even as he lay dead, his mother heard her brother's voice saying to her: "My God, Hester, you're eighty-odd thousand to the good, and a poor devil of a son to the bad. But, poor devil, poor devil, he's best gone out of a life where he rides his rocking-horse to find a winner."

Bobbie Ann Mason

Shiloh   1982

Bobbie Ann Mason, one of the leading voices in the new Southern fiction, was born in 1940 in Mayfield, Kentucky, growing up on a dairy farm in a region of western Kentucky whose people often appear in her stories. After her graduation from the University of Kentucky, she wrote for popular magazines, including Movie Life *and* TV Star Parade, *then began teaching college, taking her Ph.D. at the University of Connecticut and writing the critical studies* Nabokov's Garden *(1974) and* The Girl Sleuth: A Feminist Guide to the Bobbsey Twins, Nancy Drew, and Their Sisters *(1975). Her other nonfiction books include* Clear Springs *(1999), a family memoir, and* Elvis Presley *(2003), a biography in the Penguin Lives series. Her first fiction collection,* Shiloh and Other Stories *(1982),*

Bobbie Ann Mason

received wide attention; it was followed by Midnight Magic: Selected Stories of Bobbie Ann Mason *(1998),* Zigzagging Down a Wild Trail *(2001), and* Nancy Culpepper *(2006). She has published four novels,* In Country *(1985),* Spence + Lila *(1988),* Feather Crowns *(1993), and* An Atomic Romance *(2005). Mason has also supplied many unsigned contributions to the "Talk of the Town" feature in the* New Yorker. *She is a professor of English at the University of Kentucky.*

Leroy Moffitt's wife, Norma Jean, is working on her pectorals. She lifts three-pound dumbbells to warm up, then progresses to a twenty-pound barbell. Standing with her legs apart, she reminds Leroy of Wonder Woman.

"I'd give anything if I could just get these muscles to where they're real hard," says Norma Jean. "Feel this arm. It's not as hard as the other one."

"That's 'cause you're right-handed," says Leroy, dodging as she swings the barbell in an arc.

"Do you think so?"

"Sure."   5

Leroy is a truckdriver. He injured his leg in a highway accident four months ago, and his physical therapy, which involves weights and a pulley, prompted Norma Jean to try building herself up. Now she is attending a body-building class. Leroy has been collecting temporary disability since his tractor-trailer jackknifed in Missouri, badly twisting his left leg in its socket. He has a steel pin in his hip. He will probably not be able to drive his rig again. It sits in the backyard, like a gigantic bird that has flown home to roost. Leroy has been home in Kentucky for three months, and his leg is almost healed, but the accident frightened him and he does not want to drive any more long hauls. He is not sure what to do next. In the meantime, he makes things from craft kits. He started by building a miniature log cabin from notched Popsicle sticks. He varnished it and placed it on the TV set, where it remains. It reminds him of a rustic Nativity scene. Then he tried string art (sailing ships on black velvet), a macramé owl kit, a snap-together B-17 Flying Fortress, and a lamp made out of a model truck, with a light fixture screwed in the top of the cab. At first the kits were diversions, something to kill time, but now he is thinking about building a full-scale log house from a kit. It would be considerably cheaper than building a regular house, and besides, Leroy has grown to appreciate how things are put together. He has begun to realize that in all the years he was on the road he never took time to examine anything. He was always flying past scenery.

"They won't let you build a log cabin in any of the new subdivisions," Norma Jean tells him.

"They will if I tell them it's for you," he says, teasing her. Ever since they were married, he has promised Norma Jean he would build her a new home one day. They have always rented, and the house they live in is small and nondescript. It does not even feel like a home, Leroy realizes now.

Norma Jean works at the Rexall drugstore, and she has acquired an amazing amount of information about cosmetics. When she explains to Leroy the three stages of complexion care, involving creams, toners, and moisturizers, he thinks happily of other petroleum products—axle grease, diesel fuel. This is a connection between him and Norma Jean. Since he has been home, he has felt unusually tender about his wife and guilty over his long absences. But he can't tell what she feels about him. Norma Jean has never complained about his traveling; she has never made hurt remarks, like calling his truck a "widow-maker." He is reasonably certain she has been faithful to him, but he wishes she would celebrate his permanent home-coming more happily. Norma Jean is often startled to find Leroy at home, and he thinks she seems a little disappointed about it. Perhaps he reminds her too much of the early days of their marriage, before he went on the road. They had a child who died as an infant, years ago. They never speak about their memories of Randy, which have almost faded, but now that Leroy is home all the time, they sometimes feel awkward around each other, and Leroy wonders if one of them should mention the child. He has the feeling that they are waking up out of a dream together—that they must create a new marriage, start afresh. They are lucky they are still married. Leroy has read that for most people losing a child destroys the marriage—or else he heard this on *Donahue*. He can't always remember where he learns things anymore.

At Christmas, Leroy bought an electric organ for Norma Jean. She used to play the piano when she was in high school. "It don't leave you," she told him once. "It's like riding a bicycle."

The new instrument had so many keys and buttons that she was bewildered by it at first. She touched the keys tentatively, pushed some buttons, then pecked out "Chopsticks." It came out in an amplified fox-trot rhythm, with marimba sounds.

"It's an orchestra!" she cried.

The organ had a pecan-look finish and eighteen preset chords, with optional flute, violin, trumpet, clarinet, and banjo accompaniments. Norma Jean mastered the organ almost immediately. At first she played Christmas songs. Then she bought *The Sixties Songbook* and learned every tune in it, adding variations to each with the rows of brightly colored buttons.

"I didn't like these old songs back then," she said. "But I have this crazy feeling I missed something."

"You didn't miss a thing," said Leroy.

Leroy likes to lie on the couch and smoke a joint and listen to Norma Jean play "Can't Take My Eyes Off You" and "I'll Be Back." He is back again. After fifteen years on the road, he is finally settling down with the woman he loves. She is still pretty. Her skin is flawless. Her frosted curls resemble pencil trimmings.

Now that Leroy has come home to stay, he notices how much the town has changed. Subdivisions are spreading across western Kentucky like an oil slick. The sign at the edge of town says "Pop: 11,500"—only seven hundred more than it said twenty years before. Leroy can't figure out who is living in all the new houses. The farmers who used to gather around the courthouse square on Saturday afternoons to play checkers and spit tobacco juice have gone. It has been years since Leroy has thought about the farmers, and they have disappeared without his noticing.

Leroy meets a kid named Stevie Hamilton in the parking lot at the new shopping center. While they pretend to be strangers meeting over a stalled car, Stevie tosses an ounce of marijuana under the front seat of Leroy's car. Stevie is wearing orange jogging shoes and a T-shirt that says CHATTAHOOCHEE SUPER-RAT. His father is a prominent doctor who lives in one of the expensive subdivisions in a new white-columned brick house that looks like a funeral parlor. In the phone book under his name there is a separate number, with the listing "Teenagers."

"Where do you get this stuff?" asks Leroy. "From your pappy?"

"That's for me to know and you to find out," Stevie says. He is slit-eyed and skinny.

"What else you got?"

"What you interested in?"

"Nothing special. Just wondered."

Leroy used to take speed on the road. Now he has to go slowly. He needs to be mellow. He leans back against the car and says, "I'm aiming to build me a log house, soon as I get time. My wife, though, I don't think she likes the idea."

"Well, let me know when you want me again," Stevie says. He has a cigarette in his cupped palm, as though sheltering it from the wind. He takes a long drag, then stomps it on the asphalt and slouches away.

Stevie's father was two years ahead of Leroy in high school. Leroy is thirty-four. He married Norma Jean when they were both eighteen, and their child Randy was born a few months later, but he died at the age of four months and three days. He would be about Stevie's age now. Norma Jean and Leroy were at the drive-in, watching a double feature (*Dr. Strangelove* and *Lover Come Back*), and the baby was sleeping in the back seat. When the first movie ended, the baby was dead. It was the sudden infant death syndrome. Leroy remembers handing Randy to a nurse at the emergency room, as though he were offering her a large doll as a present. A dead baby feels like a sack of flour. "It just happens sometimes," said the doctor, in what Leroy always recalls as a nonchalant tone. Leroy can hardly remember the child anymore, but he still sees vividly a scene from *Dr. Strangelove*° in which the President of the United States was talking in a folksy voice on the hot line to the Soviet premier about the bomber accidentally headed toward Russia. He was in the War Room, and the world map was lit up. Leroy remembers Norma Jean standing catatonically beside him in the hospital and himself thinking: Who is this strange girl? He had forgotten who she was. Now scientists are saying that crib death is caused by a virus. Nobody knows anything, Leroy thinks. The answers are always changing.

When Leroy gets home from the shopping center, Norma Jean's mother, Mabel Beasley, is there. Until this year, Leroy has not realized how much time she spends with Norma Jean. When she visits, she inspects the closets and then the plants, informing Norma Jean when a plant is droopy or yellow. Mabel calls the plants "flowers," although there are never any blooms. She also notices if Norma Jean's laundry is piling up. Mabel is a short, overweight woman whose tight, brown-dyed curls look more like a wig than the actual wig she sometimes wears. Today she has brought Norma Jean an off-white dust ruffle she made for the bed; Mabel works in a custom-upholstery shop.

"This is the tenth one I made this year," Mabel says. "I got started and couldn't stop."

"It's real pretty," says Norma Jean.

"Now we can hide things under the bed," says Leroy, who gets along with his   30
mother-in-law primarily by joking with her. Mabel has never really forgiven him for disgracing her by getting Norma Jean pregnant. When the baby died, she said that fate was mocking her.

"What's that thing?" Mabel says to Leroy in a loud voice, pointing to a tangle of yarn on a piece of canvas.

Leroy holds it up for Mabel to see. "It's my needlepoint," he explains. "This is a *Star Trek* pillow cover."

"That's what a woman would do," says Mabel. "Great day in the morning!"

"All the big football players on TV do it," he says.

"Why, Leroy, you're always trying to fool me. I don't believe you for one minute.   35
You don't know what to do with yourself—that's the whole trouble. Sewing!"

"I'm aiming to build us a log house," says Leroy. "Soon as my plans come."

"Like *heck* you are," says Norma Jean. She takes Leroy's needlepoint and shoves it into a drawer. "You have to find a job first. Nobody can afford to build now anyway."

Mabel straightens her girdle and says, "I still think before you get tied down y'all ought to take a little run to Shiloh."

"One of these days, Mama," Norma Jean says impatiently.

Mabel is talking about Shiloh, Tennessee. For the past few years, she has been   40
urging Leroy and Norma Jean to visit the Civil War battleground there. Mabel went

---

Dr. Strangelove: Stanley Kubrick's classic 1964 suspense comedy film about a mad U.S. general who launches an unauthorized nuclear attack on Russia.

there on her honeymoon—the only real trip she ever took. Her husband died of a perforated ulcer when Norma Jean was ten, but Mabel, who was accepted into the United Daughters of the Confederacy in 1975, is still preoccupied with going back to Shiloh.

"I've been to kingdom come and back in that truck out yonder," Leroy says to Mabel, "but we never yet set foot in that battleground. Ain't that something? How did I miss it?"

"It's not even that far," Mabel says.

After Mabel leaves, Norma Jean reads to Leroy from a list she has made. "Things you could do," she announces. "You could get a job as a guard at Union Carbide, where they'd let you set on a stool. You could get one at the lumberyard. You could do a little carpenter work, if you want to build so bad. You could—"

"I can't do something where I'd have to stand up all day."

"You ought to try standing up all day behind a cosmetics counter. It's amazing   45
that I have strong feet, coming from two parents that never had strong feet at all." At
the moment Norma Jean is holding on to the kitchen counter, raising her knees one
at a time as she talks. She is wearing two-pound ankle weights.

"Don't worry," says Leroy. "I'll do something."

"You could truck calves to slaughter for somebody. You wouldn't have to drive any big old truck for that."

"I'm going to build you this house," says Leroy. "I want to make you a real home."

"I don't want to live in any log cabin."

"It's not a cabin. It's a house."   50

"I don't care. It looks like a cabin."

"You and me together could lift those logs. It's just like lifting weights."

Norma Jean doesn't answer. Under her breath, she is counting. Now she is marching through the kitchen. She is doing goose steps.°

Before his accident, when Leroy came home he used to stay in the house with Norma Jean, watching TV in bed and playing cards. She would cook fried chicken, pic-nic ham, chocolate pie—all his favorites. Now he is home alone much of the time. In the mornings, Norma Jean disappears, leaving a cooling place in the bed. She eats a cereal called Body Buddies, and she leaves the bowl on the table, with the soggy tan balls floating in a milk puddle. He sees things about Norma Jean that he never realized before. When she chops onions, she stares off into a corner, as if she can't bear to look. She puts on her house slippers almost precisely at nine o'clock every evening and nudges her jogging shoes under the couch. She saves bread heels for the birds. Leroy watches the birds at the feeder. He notices the peculiar way goldfinches fly past the window. They close their wings, then fall, then spread their wings to catch and lift themselves. He wonders if they close their eyes when they fall. Norma Jean closes her eyes when they are in bed. She wants the lights turned out. Even then, he is sure she closes her eyes.

He goes for long drives around town. He tends to drive a car rather carelessly.   55
Power steering and an automatic shift make a car feel so small and inconsequential
that his body is hardly involved in the driving process. His injured leg stretches out

---

goose steps: a stiff-kneed, straight-legged marching step used in military parades. Used here as an exercise routine.

comfortably. Once or twice he has almost hit something, but even the prospect of an accident seems minor in a car. He cruises the new subdivisions, feeling like a criminal rehearsing for a robbery. Norma Jean is probably right about a log house being inappropriate here in the new subdivision. All the houses look grand and complicated. They depress him.

One day when Leroy comes home from a drive he finds Norma Jean in tears. She is in the kitchen making a potato and mushroom-soup casserole, with grated cheese topping. She is crying because her mother caught her smoking.

"I didn't hear her coming. I was standing here puffing away pretty as you please," Norma Jean says, wiping her eyes.

"I knew it would happen sooner or later," says Leroy, putting his arm around her.

"She don't know the meaning of the word 'knock,'" says Norma Jean. "It's a wonder she hadn't caught me years ago."

"Think of it this way," Leroy says. "What if she caught me with a joint?"   60

"You better not let her!" Norma Jean shrieks. "I'm warning you, Leroy Moffitt!"

"I'm just kidding. Here, play me a tune. That'll help you relax."

Norma Jean puts the casserole in the oven and sets the timer. Then she plays a ragtime tune, with horns and banjo, as Leroy lights up a joint and lies on the couch, laughing to himself about Mabel's catching him at it. He thinks of Stevie Hamilton—a doctor's son pushing grass. Everything is funny. The whole town seems crazy and small. He is reminded of Virgil Mathis, a boastful policeman Leroy used to shoot pool with. Virgil recently led a drug bust in a back room at a bowling alley, where he seized ten thousand dollars' worth of marijuana. The newspaper had a picture of him holding up the bags of grass and grinning widely. Right now, Leroy can imagine Virgil breaking down the door and arresting him with a lungful of smoke. Virgil would probably have been alerted to the scene because of all the racket Norma Jean is making. Now she sounds like a hard-rock band. Norma Jean is terrific. When she switches to a Latin-rhythm version of "Sunshine Superman," Leroy hums along. Norma Jean's foot goes up and down, up and down.

"Well, what do you think?" Leroy says, when Norma Jean pauses to search through her music.

"What do I think about what?"   65

His mind has gone blank. Then he says, "I'll sell my rig and build us a house." That wasn't what he wanted to say. He wanted to know what she thought—what she *really* thought—about them.

"Don't start in on that again," says Norma Jean. She begins playing "Who'll Be the Next in Line?"

Leroy used to tell hitchhikers his whole life story—about his travels, his hometown, the baby. He would end with a question: "Well, what do you think?" It was just a rhetorical question. In time, he had the feeling that he'd been telling the same story over and over to the same hitchhikers. He quit talking to hitchhikers when he realized how his voice sounded—whining and self-pitying, like some teenage-tragedy song. Now Leroy has the sudden impulse to tell Norma Jean about himself, as if he had just met her. They have known each other so long they have forgotten a lot about each other. They could become reacquainted. But when the oven timer goes off and she runs to the kitchen, he forgets why he wants to do this.

The next day, Mabel drops by. It is Saturday and Norma Jean is cleaning. Leroy is studying the plans of his log house, which have finally come in the mail. He has them spread out on the table—big sheets of stiff blue paper, with diagrams and numbers printed in white. While Norma Jean runs the vacuum, Mabel drinks coffee. She sets her coffee cup on a blueprint.

"I'm just waiting for time to pass," she says to Leroy, drumming her fingers on the table.

As soon as Norma Jean switches off the vacuum, Mabel says in a loud voice, "Did you hear about the datsun dog that killed the baby?"

Norma Jean says, "The word is 'dachshund.'"

"They put the dog on trial. It chewed the baby's legs off. The mother was in the next room all the time." She raises her voice. "They thought it was neglect."

Norma Jean is holding her ears. Leroy manages to open the refrigerator and get some Diet Pepsi to offer Mabel. Mabel still has some coffee and she waves away the Pepsi.

"Datsuns are like that," Mabel says. "They're jealous dogs. They'll tear a place to pieces if you don't keep an eye on them."

"You better watch out what you're saying, Mabel," says Leroy.

"Well, facts is facts."

Leroy looks out the window at his rig. It is like a huge piece of furniture gathering dust in the backyard. Pretty soon it will be an antique. He hears the vacuum cleaner. Norma Jean seems to be cleaning the living room rug again.

Later, she says to Leroy, "She just said that about the baby because she caught me smoking. She's trying to pay me back."

"What are you talking about?" Leroy says, nervously shuffling blueprints.

"You know good and well," Norma Jean says. She is sitting in a kitchen chair with her feet up and her arms wrapped around her knees. She looks small and helpless. She says, "The very idea, her bringing up a subject like that! Saying it was neglect."

"She didn't mean that," Leroy says.

"She might not have *thought* she meant it. She always says things like that. You don't know how she goes on."

"But she didn't really mean it. She was just talking."

Leroy opens a king-sized bottle of beer and pours it into two glasses, dividing it carefully. He hands a glass to Norma Jean and she takes it from him mechanically. For a long time, they sit by the kitchen window watching the birds at the feeder.

Something is happening. Norma Jean is going to night school. She has graduated from her six-week body-building course and now she is taking an adult-education course in composition at Paducah Community College. She spends her evenings outlining paragraphs.

"First, you have a topic sentence," she explains to Leroy. "Then you divide it up. Your secondary topic has to be connected to your primary topic."

To Leroy, this sounds intimidating. "I never was any good in English," he says.

"It makes a lot of sense."

"What are you doing this for, anyhow?"

She shrugs. "It's something to do." She stands up and lifts her dumbbells a few times.

"Driving a rig, nobody cared about my English."

"I'm not criticizing your English."

Norma Jean used to say, "If I lose ten minutes' sleep, I just drag all day." Now she stays up late, writing compositions. She got a B on her first paper—a how-to theme on soup-based casseroles. Recently Norma Jean has been cooking unusual foods—tacos, lasagna, Bombay chicken. She doesn't play the organ anymore, though her second paper was called "Why Music Is Important to Me." She sits at the kitchen table, concentrating on her outlines, while Leroy plays with his log house plans, practicing with a set of Lincoln Logs. The thought of getting a truckload of notched, numbered logs scares him, and he wants to be prepared. As he and Norma Jean work together at the kitchen table, Leroy has the hopeful thought that they are sharing something, but he knows he is a fool to think this. Norma Jean is miles away. He knows he is going to lose her. Like Mabel, he is just waiting for time to pass.

One day, Mabel is there before Norma Jean gets home from work, and Leroy finds   95
himself confiding in her. Mabel, he realizes, must know Norma Jean better than he does.

"I don't know what's got into that girl," Mabel says. "She used to go to bed with the chickens. Now you say she's up all hours. Plus her a-smoking. I like to died."

"I want to make her this beautiful home," Leroy says, indicating the Lincoln Logs. "I don't think she even wants it. Maybe she was happier with me gone."

"She don't know what to make of you, coming home like this."

"Is that it?"

Mabel takes the roof off his Lincoln Log cabin. "You couldn't get *me* in a log   100
cabin," she says. "I was raised in one. It's no picnic, let me tell you."

"They're different now," says Leroy.

"I tell you what," Mabel says, smiling oddly at Leroy.

"What?"

"Take her on down to Shiloh. Y'all need to get out together, stir a little. Her brain's all balled up over them books."

Leroy can see traces of Norma Jean's features in her mother's face. Mabel's worn face   105
has the texture of crinkled cotton, but suddenly she looks pretty. It occurs to Leroy that Mabel has been hinting all along that she wants them to take her with them to Shiloh.

"Let's all go to Shiloh," he says. "You and me and her. Come Sunday."

Mabel throws up her hand in protest. "Oh, no, not me. Young folks want to be by theirselves."

When Norma Jean comes in with groceries, Leroy says excitedly, "Your mama here's been dying to go to Shiloh for thirty-five years. It's about time we went, don't you think?"

"I'm not going to butt in on anybody's second honeymoon," Mabel says.

"Who's going on a honeymoon, for Christ's sake?" Norma Jean says loudly.   110

"I never raised no daughter of mine to talk that-a-way," Mabel says.

"You ain't seen nothing yet," says Norma Jean. She starts putting away boxes and cans, slamming cabinet doors.

"There's a log cabin at Shiloh," Mabel says. "It was there during the battle. There's bullet holes in it."

"When are you going to *shut up* about Shiloh, Mama?" asks Norma Jean.

"I always thought Shiloh was the prettiest place, so full of history," Mabel   115
goes on. "I just hoped y'all could see it once before I die, so you could tell me about it." Later, she whispers to Leroy, "You do what I said. A little change is what she needs."

"Your name means 'the king,'" Norma Jean says to Leroy that evening. He is trying to get her to go to Shiloh, and she is reading a book about another century.

"Well, I reckon I ought to be right proud."

"I guess so."

"Am I still king around here?"

Norma Jean flexes her biceps and feels them for hardness. "I'm not fooling   120
around with anybody, if that's what you mean," she says.

"Would you tell me if you were?"

"I don't know."

"What does *your* name mean?"

"It was Marilyn Monroe's real name."

"No kidding!"   125

"Norma comes from the Normans. They were invaders," she says. She closes her
book and looks hard at Leroy. "I'll go to Shiloh with you if you'll stop staring at me."

On Sunday, Norma Jean packs a picnic and they go to Shiloh. To Leroy's relief
Mabel says she does not want to come with them. Norma Jean drives, and Leroy, sitting beside her, feels like some boring hitchhiker she has picked up. He tries some
conversation, but she answers him in monosyllables. At Shiloh, she drives aimlessly
through the park, past bluffs and trails and steep ravines. Shiloh is an immense place,
and Leroy cannot see it as a battleground. It is not what he expected. He thought it
would look like a golf course. Monuments are everywhere, showing through the thick
clusters of trees. Norma Jean passes the log cabin Mabel mentioned. It is surrounded
by tourists looking for bullet holes.

"That's not the kind of log house I've got in mind," says Leroy apologetically.

"I know *that*."

"This is a pretty place. Your mama was right."   130

"It's O.K.," says Norma Jean. "Well, we've seen it. I hope she's satisfied."

They burst out laughing together.

At the park museum, a movie on Shiloh is shown every half hour, but they decide that they don't want to see it. They buy a souvenir Confederate flag for Mabel,
and then they find a picnic spot near the cemetery. Norma Jean has brought a picnic
cooler, with pimiento sandwiches, soft drinks, and Yodels. Leroy eats a sandwich
and then smokes a joint, hiding it behind the picnic cooler. Norma Jean has quit
smoking altogether. She is picking cake crumbs from the cellophane wrapper, like a
fussy bird.

Leroy says, "So the boys in gray ended up in Corinth. The Union soldiers zapped
'em finally. April 7, 1862."

They both know that he doesn't know any history. He is just talking about some   135
of the historical plaques they have read. He feels awkward, like a boy on a date with
an older girl. They are still just making conversation.

"Corinth is where Mama eloped to," says Norma Jean.

They sit in silence and stare at the cemetery for the Union dead and, beyond, at
a tall cluster of trees. Campers are parked nearby, bumper to bumper, and small children in bright clothing are cavorting and squealing. Norma Jean wads up the cake
wrapper and squeezes it tightly in her hand. Without looking at Leroy, she says, "I
want to leave you."

Leroy takes a bottle of Coke out of the cooler and flips off the cap. He holds the
bottle poised near his mouth but cannot remember to take a drink. Finally he says,
"No, you don't."

"Yes, I do."

"I won't let you."   140

"You can't stop me."

"Don't do me that way."

Leroy knows Norma Jean will have her own way. "Didn't I promise to be home
from now on?" he says.

"In some ways, a woman prefers a man who wanders," says Norma Jean. "That
sounds crazy, I know."

"You're not crazy."   145

Leroy remembers to drink from his Coke. Then he says, "Yes, you *are* crazy. You
and me could start all over again. Right back at the beginning."

"We *have* started all over again," says Norma Jean. "And this is how it turned
out."

"What did I do wrong?"

"Nothing."

"Is this one of those women's lib things?" Leroy asks.   150

"Don't be funny."

The cemetery, a green slope dotted with white markers, looks like a subdivision
site. Leroy is trying to comprehend that his marriage is breaking up, but for some reason he is wondering about white slabs in a graveyard.

"Everything was fine till Mama caught me smoking," says Norma Jean, standing
up. "That set something off."

"What are you talking about?"

"She won't leave me alone—*you* won't leave me alone." Norma Jean seems to be   155
crying, but she is looking away from him. "I feel eighteen again. I can't face that all
over again." She starts walking away. "No, it *wasn't* fine. I don't know what I'm saying. Forget it."

Leroy takes a lungful of smoke and closes his eyes as Norma Jean's words sink in.
He tries to focus on the fact that thirty-five hundred soldiers died on the grounds
around him. He can only think of that war as a board game with plastic soldiers.
Leroy almost smiles, as he compares the Confederates' daring attack on the Union
camps and Virgil Mathis's raid on the bowling alley. General Grant, drunk and furious, shoved the Southerners back to Corinth, where Mabel and Jet Beasley were
married years later, when Mabel was still thin and good-looking. The next day,
Mabel and Jet visited the battleground, and then Norma Jean was born, and then
she married Leroy and they had a baby, which they lost, and now Leroy and Norma
Jean are here at the same battleground. Leroy knows he is leaving out a lot. He is
leaving out the insides of history. History was always just names and dates to him.
It occurs to him that building a house of logs is similarly empty—too simple. And
the real inner workings of a marriage, like most of history, have escaped him. Now
he sees that building a log house is the dumbest idea he could have had. It was
clumsy of him to think Norma Jean would want a log house. It was a crazy idea.
He'll have to think of something else, quickly. He will wad the blueprints into
tight balls and fling them into the lake. Then he'll get moving again. He opens his
eyes. Norma Jean has moved away and is walking through the cemetery, following
a serpentine brick path.

Leroy gets up to follow his wife, but his good leg is asleep and his bad leg still
hurts him. Norma Jean is far away, walking rapidly toward the bluff by the river, and
he tries to hobble toward her. Some children run past him, screaming noisily. Norma
Jean has reached the bluff, and she is looking out over the Tennessee River. Now she
turns toward Leroy and waves her arms. Is she beckoning to him? She seems to be
doing an exercise for her chest muscles. The sky is unusually pale—the color of the
dust ruffle Mabel made for their bed.

Lorrie Moore

How to Become a Writer

1985

Marie Lorena Moore was born in 1957 in Glens Falls, New York. Her father was an insurance company executive who wrote short stories and composed music for the church choir, and her mother was a school nurse. Moore graduated summa cum laude from St. Lawrence University in 1978 and spent two years in New York City as a paralegal. She did graduate work in creative writing at Cornell University, submitting a thesis that became her first collection of short stories, Self-Help (1985). Many of the pieces in this volume are what Moore has described as "second person, mock-imperative narratives [which] were written as stylistic experiments: Let's see what happens when one eliminates the subject, leaves the verb shivering at the start of a clause; what happens when one

Lorrie Moore

appropriates the 'how-to' form for a fiction, for an irony, for a 'how-not-to.' . . . The self-help proffered here, then, is perhaps only that of art itself, which, if you agree with Oscar Wilde, is quite useless." After her novel Anagrams was published in 1986, Moore began teaching at the University of Wisconsin at Madison, where she is now a professor of English. Her second novel, Who Will Run the Frog Hospital? (1994), recalls her adolescence in Glens Falls in the early 1970s. She has also published a novel for children, The Forgotten Helper (1987), and two further collections of short fiction, Like Life (1990) and Birds of America (1998), which spent several weeks on the best-seller lists, an unusual accomplishment for a book of stories. Her Collected Stories was published in Britain in 2008.

First, try to be something, anything, else. A movie star/astronaut. A movie star/ missionary. A movie star/kindergarten teacher. President of the World. Fail miserably. It is best if you fail at an early age—say, fourteen. Early, critical disillusionment is necessary so that at fifteen you can write long haiku sequences about thwarted desire. It is a pond, a cherry blossom, a wind brushing against sparrow wing leaving for mountain. Count the syllables. Show it to your mom. She is tough and practical. She has a son in Vietnam and a husband who may be having an affair. She believes in wearing brown because it hides spots. She'll look briefly at your writing, then back up at you with a face blank as a donut. She'll say: "How about emptying the dishwasher?" Look away. Shove the forks in the fork drawer. Accidentally break one of the freebie gas station glasses. This is the required pain and suffering. This is only for starters.

In your high school English class look only at Mr. Killian's face. Decide faces are important. Write a villanelle about pores. Struggle. Write a sonnet. Count the syllables: nine, ten, eleven, thirteen. Decide to experiment with fiction. Here you don't have to count syllables. Write a short story about an elderly man and woman who accidentally shoot each other in the head, the result of an inexplicable malfunction of a shotgun which appears mysteriously in their living room one night. Give it to Mr. Killian as your final project. When you get it back, he has written on it: "Some of your images are quite nice, but you have no sense of plot." When you are home, in the privacy of your own room, faintly scrawl in pencil beneath his black-inked comments: "Plots are for dead people, pore-face."

Take all the babysitting jobs you can get. You are great with kids. They love you. You tell them stories about old people who die idiot deaths. You sing them songs like "Blue Bells of Scotland," which is their favorite. And when they are in their pajamas and have finally stopped pinching each other, when they are fast asleep, you read every sex manual in the house, and wonder how on earth anyone could ever do those things with someone they truly loved. Fall asleep in a chair reading Mr. McMurphy's *Playboy*. When the McMurphys come home, they will tap you on the shoulder, look at the magazine on your lap, and grin. You will want to die. They will ask you if Tracey took her medicine all right. Explain, yes, she did, that you promised her a story if she would take it like a big girl and that seemed to work out just fine. "Oh, marvelous," they will exclaim.
Try to smile proudly.
Apply to college as a child psychology major.   5

As a child psychology major, you have some electives. You've always liked birds. Sign up for something called "The Ornithological Field Trip." It meets Tuesdays and Thursdays at two. When you arrive at Room 134 on the first day of class, everyone is sitting around a seminar table talking about metaphors. You've heard of these. After a short, excruciating while, raise your hand and say diffidently, "Excuse me, isn't this Birdwatching One-oh-one?" The class stops and turns to look at you. They seem to all have one face—giant and blank as a vandalized clock. Someone with a beard booms out, "No, this is Creative Writing." Say: "Oh—right", as if perhaps you knew all along. Look down at your schedule. Wonder how the hell you ended up here. The computer, apparently, has made an error. You start to get up to leave and then don't. The lines at the registrar this week are huge. Perhaps you should stick with this mistake. Perhaps your creative writing isn't all that bad. Perhaps it is fate. Perhaps this is what your dad meant when he said, "It's the age of computers, Francie, it's the age of computers."

Decide that you like college life. In your dorm you meet many nice people. Some are smarter than you. And some, you notice, are dumber than you. You will continue, unfortunately, to view the world in exactly these terms for the rest of your life.

The assignment this week in creative writing is to narrate a violent happening. Turn in a story about driving with your Uncle Gordon and another one about two old people who are accidentally electrocuted when they go to turn on a badly wired desk lamp. The teacher will hand them back to you with comments: "Much of your writing is smooth and energetic. You have, however, a ludicrous notion of plot." Write another story about a man and a woman who, in the very first paragraph, have their lower torsos accidentally blitzed away by dynamite. In the second paragraph, with the insurance money, they buy a frozen yogurt stand together. There are six more paragraphs. You read the whole thing out loud in class. No one likes it. They say your sense of plot is outrageous and incompetent. After class someone asks you if you are crazy.

Decide that perhaps you should stick to comedies. Start dating someone who is funny, someone who has what in high school you called "a really great sense of humor" and what now your creative writing class calls "self-contempt giving rise to comic form." Write down all of his jokes, but don't tell him you are doing this. Make up anagrams of his old girlfriend's name and name all of your socially handicapped characters with them. Tell him his old girlfriend is in all your stories and then watch how funny he can be, see what a really great sense of humor he can have.

Your child psychology advisor tells you you are neglecting courses in your major. 10
What you spend the most time on should be what you're majoring in. Say yes, you understand.

In creative writing seminars over the next two years, everyone continues to smoke cigarettes and ask the same things: "But does it work?" "Why should we care about this character?" "Have you earned this cliché?" These seem like important questions.

On days when it is your turn, you look at the class hopefully as they scour your mimeographs for a plot. They look back up at you, drag deeply, and then smile in a sweet sort of way.

You spend too much time slouched and demoralized. Your boyfriend suggests bicycling. Your roommate suggests a new boyfriend. You are said to be self-mutilating and losing weight, but you continue writing. The only happiness you have is writing something new, in the middle of the night, armpits damp, heart pounding, something no one has yet seen. You have only those brief, fragile, untested moments of exhilaration when you know: you are a genius. Understand what you must do. Switch majors. The kids in your nursery project will be disappointed, but you have a calling, an urge, a delusion, an unfortunate habit. You have, as your mother would say, fallen in with a bad crowd.

Why write? Where does writing come from? These are questions to ask yourself. They are like: Where does dust come from? Or: Why is there war? Or: If there's a God, then why is my brother now a cripple?

These are questions that you keep in your wallet, like calling cards. These are 15
questions, your creative writing teacher says, that are good to address in your journals but rarely in your fiction.

The writing professor this fall is stressing the Power of the Imagination. Which means he doesn't want long descriptive stories about your camping trip last July. He wants you to start in a realistic context but then to alter it. Like recombinant DNA. He wants you to let your imagination sail, to let it grow big-bellied in the wind. This is a quote from Shakespeare.

Tell your roommate your great idea, your great exercise of imaginative power: a transformation of Melville to contemporary life. It will be about monomania and the fish-eat-fish world of life insurance in Rochester, New York. The first line will be "Call me Fishmeal," and it will feature a menopausal suburban husband named Richard, who because he is so depressed all the time is called "Mopey Dick" by his witty wife Elaine. Say to your roommate: "Mopey Dick, get it?" Your roommate looks at you, her face blank as a large Kleenex. She comes up to you, like a buddy, and puts an arm around your burdened shoulders. "Listen, Francie," she says, slow as speech therapy. "Let's go out and get a big beer."

*

The seminar doesn't like this one either. You suspect they are beginning to feel sorry for you. They say: "You have to think about what is happening. Where is the story here?"

The next semester the writing professor is obsessed with writing from personal experience. You must write from what you know, from what has happened to you. He wants deaths, he wants camping trips. Think about what has happened to you. In three years there have been three things: you lost your virginity; your parents got divorced; and your brother came home from a forest ten miles from the Cambodian border with only half a thigh, a permanent smirk nestled into one corner of his mouth.

About the first you write: "It created a new space, which hurt and cried in a   20
voice that wasn't mine, 'I'm not the same anymore, but I'll be okay.'"

About the second you write an elaborate story of an old married couple who stumble upon an unknown land mine in their kitchen and accidentally blow themselves up. You call it: "For Better or for Liverwurst."

About the last thing you write nothing. There are no words for this. Your typewriter hums. You can find no words.

At undergraduate cocktail parties, people say, "Oh, you write? What do you write about?" Your roommate, who has consumed too much wine, too little cheese, and no crackers at all, blurts: "Oh, my god, she always writes about her dumb boyfriend."

Later on in life you will learn that writers are merely open, helpless texts with no real understanding of what they have written and therefore must half-believe anything and everything that is said of them. You, however, have not yet reached this stage of literary criticism. You stiffen and say, "I do not," the same way you said it when someone in the fourth grade accused you of really liking oboe lessons and your parents really weren't just making you take them.

Insist you are not very interested in any one subject at all, that you are interested   25
in the music of language, that you are interested in—in—syllables, because they are the atoms of poetry, the cells of the mind, the breath of the soul. Begin to feel woozy. Stare into your plastic wine cup.

"Syllables?" you will hear someone ask, voice trailing off, as they glide slowly toward the reassuring white of the dip.

Begin to wonder what you do write about. Or if you have anything to say. Or if there even is such a thing as a thing to say. Limit these thoughts to no more than ten minutes a day; like sit-ups, they can make you thin.

You will read somewhere that all writing has to do with one's genitals. Don't dwell on this. It will make you nervous.

Your mother will come visit you. She will look at the circles under your eyes and hand you a brown book with a brown briefcase on the cover. It is entitled: *How to Become a Business Executive*. She has also brought the *Names for Baby* encyclopedia you asked for; one of your characters, the aging clown-schoolteacher, needs a new name. Your mother will shake her head and say: "Francie, Francie, remember when you were going to be a child psychology major?"

Say: "Mom, I like to write."   30
She'll say: "Sure you like to write. Of course. Sure you like to write."

Write a story about a confused music student and title it: "Schubert Was the
One with the Glasses, Right?" It's not a big hit, although your roommate likes the
part where the two violinists accidentally blow themselves up in a recital room. "I
went out with a violinist once," she says, snapping her gum.

Thank god you are taking other courses. You can find sanctuary in nineteenth-century
ontological snags and invertebrate courting rituals. Certain globulur mollusks have
what is called "Sex by the Arm." The male octopus, for instance, loses the end of
one arm when placing it inside the female body during intercourse. Marine biologists
call it "Seven Heaven." Be glad you know these things. Be glad you are not just a writer.
Apply to law school.

From here on in, many things can happen. But the main one will be this: you
decide not to go to law school after all, and, instead, you spend a good, big chunk
of your adult life telling people how you decided not to go to law school after all.
Somehow you end up writing again. Perhaps you go to graduate school. Perhaps
you work odd jobs and take writing courses at night. Perhaps you are working on a
novel and writing down all the clever remarks and intimate personal confessions
you hear during the day. Perhaps you are losing your pals, your acquaintances, your
balance.
    You have broken up with your boyfriend. You now go out with men who,   35
instead of whispering "I love you," shout: "Do it to me, baby." This is good for
your writing.
    Sooner or later you have a finished manuscript more or less. People look at it in a
vaguely troubled sort of way and say, "I'll bet becoming a writer was always a fantasy
of yours, wasn't it?" Your lips dry to salt. Say that of all the fantasies possible in the
world, you can't imagine being a writer even making the top twenty. Tell them you
were going to be a child psychology major. "I bet," they always sigh, "you'd be great
with kids." Scowl fiercely. Tell them you're a walking blade.

Quit classes. Quit jobs. Cash in old savings bonds. Now you have time like warts on
your hands. Slowly copy all of your friends' addresses into a new address book.
    Vacuum. Chew cough drops. Keep a folder full of fragments.

> *An eyelid darkening sideways.*
> *World as conspiracy.*
> *Possible plot? A woman gets on a bus.*
> *Suppose you threw a love affair and nobody came?*

At home drink a lot of coffee. At Howard Johnson's order the cole slaw. Consider how it looks like the soggy confetti of a map: where you've been, where you're
going—"You Are Here," says the red star on the back of the menu.
    Occasionally a date with a face blank as a sheet of paper asks you whether writers   40
often become discouraged. Say that sometimes they do and sometimes they do. Say
it's a lot like having polio.
    "Interesting," smiles your date, and then he looks down at his arm hairs and
starts to smooth them, all, always, in the same direction.

Joyce Carol Oates

Where Are You Going, Where Have You Been?   1970

Joyce Carol Oates was born in 1938 into a blue collar, Catholic family in Lockport, New York. As an undergraduate at Syracuse University, she won a Mademoiselle *magazine award for fiction. After graduating with top honors, she took a master's degree in English at the University of Wisconsin and went on to teach at several universities: Detroit, Windsor, and Princeton. A remarkably prolific writer, Oates has produced more than twenty-five collections of stories, including* High Lonesome: Stories 1966–2006, *and forty novels, including* them, *winner of a National Book Award in 1970,* Because It Is Bitter, and Because It Is My Heart *(1990), and more recently,* Black Girl/White Girl *(2006),* The Gravedigger's Daughter *(2007),*

Joyce Carol Oates
© Jill Krementz, Inc.

and My Sister, My Love *(2008). She also writes poetry, plays, and literary criticism.* On Boxing *(1987) is her nonfiction memoir and study of fighters and fighting.* Foxfire *(1993), her twenty-second novel, is the story of a girl gang in upstate New York. Her 1996 Gothic novella,* First Love, *is a bizarre tale of terror and torture. Violence and the macabre may inhabit her best stories, but Oates has insisted that these elements in her work are never gratuitous. The 1985 film* Smooth Talk, *directed by Joyce Chopra, was based on "Where Are You Going, Where Have You Been?"*

For Bob Dylan

Her name was Connie. She was fifteen and she had a quick nervous giggling habit of craning her neck to glance into mirrors, or checking other people's faces to make sure her own was all right. Her mother, who noticed everything and knew everything and who hadn't much reason any longer to look at her own face, always scolded Connie about it. "Stop gawking at yourself, who are you? You think you're so pretty?" she would say. Connie would raise her eyebrows at these familiar complaints and look right through her mother, into a shadowy vision of herself as she was right at that moment: she knew she was pretty and that was everything. Her mother had been pretty once too, if you could believe those old snapshots in the album, but now her looks were gone and that was why she was always after Connie.

"Why don't you keep your room clean like your sister? How've you got your hair fixed—what the hell stinks? Hair spray? You don't see your sister using that junk."

Her sister June was twenty-four and still lived at home. She was a secretary in the high school Connie attended, and if that wasn't bad enough—with her in the same building—she was so plain and chunky and steady that Connie had to hear her praised all the time by her mother and her mother's sisters. June did this, June did that, she saved money and helped clean the house and cooked and Connie couldn't do a thing, her mind was all filled with trashy daydreams. Their father was away at work most of the time and when he came home he wanted supper and he read the newspaper at supper and after supper he went to bed. He didn't bother talking much to them, but around his bent head Connie's mother kept picking at her until Connie wished her mother was dead and she herself was dead and it was all over. "She makes me want to throw up sometimes," she complained to her friends. She had a high, breathless, amused voice which made everything she said sound a little forced, whether it was sincere or not.

There was one good thing: June went places with girl friends of hers, girls who were just as plain and steady as she, and so when Connie wanted to do that her mother had no objections. The father of Connie's best girl friend drove the girls the three miles to town and left them off at a shopping plaza, so that they could walk through the stores or go to a movie, and when he came to pick them up again at eleven he never bothered to ask what they had done.

They must have been familiar sights, walking around that shopping plaza in their   5
shorts and flat ballerina slippers that always scuffed the sidewalk, with charm bracelets jingling on their thin wrists; they would lean together to whisper and laugh secretly if someone passed by who amused or interested them. Connie had long dark blond hair that drew anyone's eye to it, and she wore part of it pulled up on her head and puffed out and the rest of it she let fall down her back. She wore a pull-over jersey blouse that looked one way when she was at home and another way when she was away from home. Everything about her had two sides to it, one for home and one for anywhere that was not home: her walk that could be childlike and bobbing, or languid enough to make anyone think she was hearing music in her head, her mouth which was pale and smirking most of the time, but bright and pink on these evenings out, her laugh which was cynical and drawling at home—"Ha, ha, very funny"—but high-pitched and nervous anywhere else, like the jingling of the charms on her bracelet.

Sometimes they did go shopping or to a movie, but sometimes they went across the highway, ducking fast across the busy road, to a drive-in restaurant where older kids hung out. The restaurant was shaped like a big bottle, though squatter than a real bottle, and on its cap was a revolving figure of a grinning boy who held a hamburger aloft. One night in mid-summer they ran across, breathless with daring, and right away someone leaned out a car window and invited them over, but it was just a boy from high school they didn't like. It made them feel good to be able to ignore him. They went up through the maze of parked and cruising cars to the bright-lit, fly-infested restaurant, their faces pleased and expectant as if they were entering a sacred building that loomed out of the night to give them what haven and what blessing they yearned for. They sat at the counter and crossed their legs at the ankles, their thin shoulders rigid with excitement, and listened to the music that made everything so good: the music was always in the background like music at a church service, it was something to depend upon.

A boy named Eddie came in to talk with them. He sat backwards on his stool, turning himself jerkily around in semi-circles and then stopping and turning again, and after a while he asked Connie if she would like something to eat. She said she did and so she tapped her friend's arm on her way out—her friend pulled her face up into a brave droll look—and Connie said she would meet her at eleven, across the way. "I just hate to leave her like that," Connie said earnestly, but the boy said that she wouldn't be alone for long. So they went out to his car and on the way Connie couldn't help but let her eyes wander over the windshields and faces all around her, her face gleaming with a joy that had nothing to do with Eddie or even this place; it might have been the music. She drew her shoulders up and sucked in her breath with the pure pleasure of being alive, and just at that moment she happened to glance at a face just a few feet from hers. It was a boy with shaggy black hair, in a convertible jalopy painted gold. He stared at her and then his lips widened into a grin. Connie slit her eyes at him and turned away, but she couldn't help glancing back and there he was still watching her. He wagged a finger and laughed and said, "Gonna get you, baby," and Connie turned away again without Eddie noticing anything.

She spent three hours with him, at the restaurant where they ate hamburgers and drank Cokes in wax cups that were always sweating, and then down an alley a mile or so away, and when he left her off at five to eleven only the movie house was still open at the plaza. Her girl friend was there, talking with a boy. When Connie came up the two girls smiled at each other and Connie said, "How was the movie?" and the girl said, "*You* should know." They rode off with the girl's father, sleepy and pleased, and Connie couldn't help but look at the darkened shopping plaza with its big empty parking lot and its signs that were faded and ghostly now, and over at the drive-in restaurant where cars were still circling tirelessly. She couldn't hear the music at this distance.

Next morning June asked her how the movie was and Connie said, "So-so."

She and that girl and occasionally another girl went out several times a week   10
that way, and the rest of the time Connie spent around the house—it was summer vacation—getting in her mother's way and thinking, dreaming, about the boys she met. But all the boys fell back and dissolved into a single face that was not even a face, but an idea, a feeling, mixed up with the urgent insistent pounding of the music and the humid night air of July. Connie's mother kept dragging her back to the daylight by finding things for her to do or saying, suddenly, "What's this about the Pettinger girl?"

And Connie would say nervously, "Oh, her. That dope." She always drew thick clear lines between herself and such girls, and her mother was simple and kindly enough to believe her. Her mother was so simple, Connie thought, that it was maybe cruel to fool her so much. Her mother went scuffling around the house in old bedroom slippers and complained over the telephone to one sister about the other, then the other called up and the two of them complained about the third one. If June's name was mentioned her mother's tone was approving, and if Connie's name was mentioned it was disapproving. This did not really mean she disliked Connie and actually Connie thought that her mother preferred her to June because she was prettier, but the two of them kept up a pretense of exasperation, a sense that they were tugging and struggling over something of little value to either of them. Sometimes, over coffee, they were almost friends, but something would come up—some vexation that was like a fly buzzing suddenly around their heads—and their faces went hard with contempt.

One Sunday Connie got up at eleven—none of them bothered with church—and washed her hair so that it could dry all day long, in the sun. Her parents and sister were going to a barbecue at an aunt's house and Connie said no, she wasn't interested, rolling her eyes to let her mother know just what she thought of it. "Stay home alone then," her mother said sharply. Connie sat out back in a lawn chair and watched them drive away, her father quiet and bald, hunched around so that he could back the car out, her mother with a look that was still angry and not at all softened through the windshield, and in the back seat poor old June all dressed up as if she didn't know what a barbecue was, with all the running yelling kids and the flies. Connie sat with her eyes closed in the sun, dreaming and dazed with the warmth about her as if this were a kind of love, the caresses of love, and her mind slipped over onto thoughts of the boy she had been with the night before and how nice he had been, how sweet it always was, not the way someone like June would suppose but sweet, gentle, the way it was in movies and promised in songs; and when she opened her eyes she hardly knew where she was, the back yard ran off into weeds and a fence-line of trees and behind it the sky was perfectly blue and still. The asbestos "ranch house" that was now three years old startled her—it looked small. She shook her head as if to get awake.

It was too hot. She went inside the house and turned on the radio to drown out the quiet. She sat on the edge of her bed, barefoot, and listened for an hour and a half to a program called XYZ Sunday Jamboree, record after record of hard, fast, shrieking songs she sang along with, interspersed by exclamations from "Bobby King": "An' look here you girls at Napoleon's—Son and Charley want you to pay real close attention to this song coming up!"

And Connie paid close attention herself, bathed in a glow of slow-pulsed joy that seemed to rise mysteriously out of the music itself and lay languidly about the airless little room, breathed in and breathed out with each gentle rise and fall of her chest.

After a while she heard a car coming up the drive. She sat up at once, startled,   15
because it couldn't be her father so soon. The gravel kept crunching all the way in from the road—the driveway was long—and Connie ran to the window. It was a car she didn't know. It was an open jalopy, painted a bright gold that caught the sunlight opaquely. Her heart began to pound and her fingers snatched at her hair, checking it, and she whispered "Christ, Christ," wondering how bad she looked. The car came to a stop at the side door and the horn sounded four short taps as if this were a signal Connie knew.

She went into the kitchen and approached the door slowly, then hung out the screen door, her bare toes curling down off the step. There were two boys in the car and now she recognized the driver: he had shaggy, shabby black hair that looked crazy as a wig and he was grinning at her.

"I ain't late, am I?" he said.

"Who the hell do you think you are?" Connie said.

"Toldja I'd be out, didn't I?"

"I don't even know who you are."   20

She spoke sullenly, careful to show no interest or pleasure, and he spoke in a fast bright monotone. Connie looked past him to the other boy, taking her time. He had fair brown hair, with a lock that fell onto his forehead. His sideburns gave him a fierce, embarrassed look, but so far he hadn't even bothered to glance at her. Both boys wore sunglasses. The driver's glasses were metallic and mirrored everything in miniature.

"You wanta come for a ride?" he said.

Connie smirked and let her hair fall loose over one shoulder.

"Don'tcha like my car? New paint job," he said. "Hey."

"What?"   25

"You're cute."

She pretended to fidget, chasing flies away from the door.

"Don'tcha believe me, or what?" he said.

"Look, I don't even know who you are," Connie said in disgust.

"Hey, Ellie's got a radio, see. Mine's broke down." He lifted his friend's arm and   30
showed her the little transistor the boy was holding, and now Connie began to hear the music. It was the same program that was playing inside the house.

"Bobby King?" she said.

"I listen to him all the time. I think he's great."

"He's kind of great," Connie said reluctantly.

"Listen, that guy's *great*. He knows where the action is."

Connie blushed a little, because the glasses made it impossible for her to see just   35
what this boy was looking at. She couldn't decide if she liked him or if he was just a
jerk, and so she dawdled in the doorway and wouldn't come down or go back inside.
She said, "What's all that stuff painted on your car?"

"Can'tcha read it?" He opened the door very carefully, as if he was afraid it
might fall off. He slid out just as carefully, planting his feet firmly on the ground,
the tiny metallic world in his glasses slowing down like gelatine hardening and in
the midst of it Connie's bright green blouse. "This here is my name, to begin with,"
he said. ARNOLD FRIEND was written in tarlike black letters on the side, with a drawing of a round grinning face that reminded Connie of a pumpkin, except it wore
sunglasses. "I wanta introduce myself, I'm Arnold Friend and that's my real name
and I'm gonna be your friend, honey, and inside the car's Ellie Oscar, he's kinda
shy." Ellie brought his transistor radio up to his shoulder and balanced it there.
"Now these numbers are a secret code, honey," Arnold Friend explained. He read
off the numbers 33, 19, 17 and raised his eyebrows at her to see what she thought of
that, but she didn't think much of it. The left rear fender had been smashed and
around it was written, on the gleaming gold background: DONE BY CRAZY WOMAN
DRIVER. Connie had to laugh at that. Arnold Friend was pleased at her laughter and
looked up at her. "Around the other side's a lot more—you wanta come and see
them?"

"No."

"Why not?"

"Why should I?"

"Don'tcha wanta see what's on the car? Don'tcha wanta go for a ride?"   40

"I don't know."

"Why not?"

"I got things to do."

"Like what?"

"Things."   45

He laughed as if she had said something funny. He slapped his thighs. He was
standing in a strange way, leaning back against the car as if he were balancing himself. He wasn't tall, only an inch or so taller than she would be if she came down to
him. Connie liked the way he was dressed, which was the way all of them dressed:
tight faded jeans stuffed into black, scuffed boots, a belt that pulled his waist in and
showed how lean he was, and a white pull-over shirt that was a little soiled and
showed the hard small muscles of his arms and shoulders. He looked as if he probably
did hard work, lifting and carrying things. Even his neck looked muscular. And his
face was a familiar face, somehow: the jaw and chin and cheeks slightly darkened, because he hadn't shaved for a day or two, and the nose long and hawk-like, sniffing as
if she were a treat he was going to gobble up and it was all a joke.

"Connie, you ain't telling the truth. This is your day set aside for a ride with me
and you know it," he said, still laughing. The way he straightened and recovered from
his fit of laughing showed that it had been all fake.

"How do you know what my name is?" she said suspiciously.

"It's Connie."

"Maybe and maybe not." 50

"I know my Connie," he said, wagging his finger. Now she remembered him even better, back at the restaurant, and her cheeks warmed at the thought of how she sucked in her breath just at the moment she passed him—how she must have looked to him. And he had remembered her. "Ellie and I come out here especially for you," he said. "Ellie can sit in back. How about it?"

"Where?"

"Where what?"

"Where're we going?"

He looked at her. He took off the sunglasses and she saw how pale the skin 55 around his eyes was, like holes that were not in shadow but instead in light. His eyes were chips of broken glass that catch the light in an amiable way. He smiled. It was as if the idea of going for a ride somewhere, to some place, was a new idea to him.

"Just for a ride, Connie sweetheart."

"I never said my name was Connie," she said.

"But I know what it is. I know your name and all about you, lots of things," Arnold Friend said. He had not moved yet but stood still leaning back against the side of his jalopy. "I took a special interest in you, such a pretty girl, and found out all about you like I know your parents and sister are gone somewheres and I know where and how long they're going to be gone, and I know who you were with last night, and your best girl friend's name is Betty. Right?"

He spoke in a simple lilting voice, exactly as if he were reciting the words to a song. His smile assured her that everything was fine. In the car Ellie turned up the volume on his radio and did not bother to look around at them.

"Ellie can sit in the back seat," Arnold Friend said. He indicated his friend with 60 a casual jerk of his chin, as if Ellie did not count and she should not bother with him.

"How'd you find out all that stuff?" Connie said.

"Listen: Betty Schultz and Tony Fitch and Jimmy Pettinger and Nancy Pettinger," he said, in a chant. "Raymond Stanley and Bob Hutter—"

"Do you know all those kids?"

"I know everybody."

"Look, you're kidding. You're not from around here." 65

"Sure."

"But—how come we never saw you before?"

"Sure you saw me before," he said. He looked down at his boots, as if he were a little offended. "You just don't remember."

"I guess I'd remember you," Connie said.

"Yeah?" He looked up at this, beaming. He was pleased. He began to mark time 70 with the music from Ellie's radio, tapping his fists lightly together. Connie looked away from his smile to the car, which was painted so bright it almost hurt her eyes to look at it. She looked at that name, ARNOLD FRIEND. And up at the front fender was an expression that was familiar—MAN THE FLYING SAUCERS. It was an expression kids had used the year before, but didn't use this year. She looked at it for a while as if the words meant something to her that she did not yet know.

"What're you thinking about? Huh?" Arnold Friend demanded. "Not worried about your hair blowing around in the car, are you?"

"No."

"Think I maybe can't drive good?"

"How do I know?"

"You're a hard girl to handle. How come?" he said. "Don't you know I'm your friend? Didn't you see me put my sign in the air when you walked by?"

"What sign?"

"My sign." And he drew an X in the air, leaning out toward her. They were maybe ten feet apart. After his hand fell back to his side the X was still in the air, almost visible. Connie let the screen door close and stood perfectly still inside it, listening to the music from her radio and the boy's blend together. She stared at Arnold Friend. He stood there so stiffly relaxed, pretending to be relaxed, with one hand idly on the door handle as if he were keeping himself up that way and had no intention of ever moving again. She recognized most things about him, the tight jeans that showed his thighs and buttocks and the greasy leather boots and the tight shirt, and even that slippery friendly smile of his, that sleepy dreamy smile that all the boys used to get across ideas they didn't want to put into words. She recognized all this and also the singsong way he talked, slightly mocking, kidding, but serious and a little melancholy, and she recognized the way he tapped one fist against the other in homage to the perpetual music behind him. But all these things did not come together.

She said suddenly, "Hey, how old are you?"

His smile faded. She could see then that he wasn't a kid, he was much older—thirty, maybe more. At this knowledge her heart began to pound faster.

"That's a crazy thing to ask. Can'tcha see I'm your own age?"

"Like hell you are."

"Or maybe a coupla years older, I'm eighteen."

"Eighteen?" she said doubtfully.

He grinned to reassure her and lines appeared at the corners of his mouth. His teeth were big and white. He grinned so broadly his eyes became slits and she saw how thick the lashes were, thick and black as if painted with a black tarlike material. Then he seemed to become embarrassed, abruptly, and looked over his shoulder at Ellie. "*Him,* he's crazy," he said. "Ain't he a riot, he's a nut, a real character." Ellie was still listening to the music. His sunglasses told nothing about what he was thinking. He wore a bright orange shirt unbuttoned halfway to show his chest, which was a pale, bluish chest and not muscular like Arnold Friend's. His shirt collar was turned up all around and the very tips of the collar pointed out past his chin as if they were protecting him. He was pressing the transistor radio up against his ear and sat there in a kind of daze, right in the sun.

"He's kinda strange," Connie said.

"Hey, she says you're kinda strange! Kinda strange!" Arnold Friend cried. He pounded on the car to get Ellie's attention. Ellie turned for the first time and Connie saw with shock that he wasn't a kid either—he had a fair, hairless face, cheeks reddened slightly as if the veins grew too close to the surface of his skin, the face of a forty-year-old baby. Connie felt a wave of dizziness rise in her at this sight and she stared at him as if waiting for something to change the shock of the moment, make it all right again. Ellie's lips kept shaping words, mumbling along with the words blasting in his ear.

"Maybe you two better go away," Connie said faintly.

"What? How come?" Arnold Friend cried. "We come out here to take you for a ride. It's Sunday." He had the voice of the man on the radio now. It was the same voice, Connie thought. "Don'tcha know it's Sunday all day and honey, no matter who you were with last night today you're with Arnold Friend and don't you forget it!—Maybe you better step out here," he said, and this last was in a different voice. It was a little flatter, as if the heat was finally getting to him.

"No. I got things to do."

"Hey."   90

"You two better leave."

"We ain't leaving until you come with us."

"Like hell I am—"

"Connie, don't fool around with me. I mean, I mean, don't fool *around*," he said, shaking his head. He laughed incredulously. He placed his sunglasses on top of his head, carefully, as if he were indeed wearing a wig, and brought the stems down behind his ears. Connie stared at him, another wave of dizziness and fear rising in her so that for a moment he wasn't even in focus but was just a blur, standing there against his gold car, and she had the idea that he had driven up the driveway all right but had come from nowhere before that and belonged nowhere and that everything about him and even about the music that was so familiar to her was only half real.

"If my father comes and sees you—"   95

"He ain't coming. He's at a barbecue."

"How do you know that?"

"Aunt Tillie's. Right now they're—uh—they're drinking. Sitting around," he said vaguely, squinting as if he were staring all the way to town and over to Aunt Tillie's backyard. Then the vision seemed to get clear and he nodded energetically. "Yeah. Sitting around. There's your sister in a blue dress, huh? And high heels, the poor sad bitch—nothing like you, sweetheart! And your mother's helping some fat woman with the corn, they're cleaning the corn—husking the corn—"

"What fat woman?" Connie cried.

"How do I know what fat woman. I don't know every goddam fat woman in the   100
world!" Arnold Friend laughed.

"Oh, that's Mrs. Hornby. . . . Who invited her?" Connie said. She felt a little light-headed. Her breath was coming quickly.

"She's too fat. I don't like them fat. I like them the way you are, honey," he said, smiling sleepily at her. They stared at each other for a while, through the screen door. He said softly, "Now what you're going to do is this: you're going to come out that door. You're going to sit up front with me and Ellie's going to sit in the back, the hell with Ellie, right? This isn't Ellie's date. You're my date. I'm your lover, honey."

"What? You're crazy—"

"Yes, I'm your lover. You don't know what that is but you will," he said. "I know that too. I know all about you. But look: it's real nice and you couldn't ask for nobody better than me, or more polite. I always keep my word. I'll tell you how it is, I'm always nice at first, the first time. I'll hold you so tight you won't think you have to try to get away or pretend anything because you'll know you can't. And I'll come inside you where it's all secret and you'll give in to me and you'll love me—"

"Shut up! You're crazy!" Connie said. She backed away from the door. She put   105
her hands against her ears as if she'd heard something terrible, something not meant for her. "People don't talk like that, you're crazy," she muttered. Her heart was almost too big now for her chest and its pumping made sweat break out all over her. She looked out to see Arnold Friend pause and then take a step toward the porch lurching. He almost fell. But, like a clever drunken man, he managed to catch his balance. He wobbled in his high boots and grabbed hold of one of the porch posts.

"Honey?" he said. "You still listening?"

"Get the hell out of here!"

"Be nice, honey. Listen."

"I'm going to call the police—"

He wobbled again and out of the side of his mouth came a fast spat curse, an   110
aside not meant for her to hear. But even this "Christ!" sounded forced. Then he began to smile again. She watched this smile come, awkward as if he were smiling from
inside a mask. His whole face was a mask, she thought wildly, tanned down onto his
throat but then running out as if he had plastered makeup on his face but had forgotten about his throat.

"Honey—? Listen, here's how it is. I always tell the truth and I promise you this:
I ain't coming in that house after you."

"You better not! I'm going to call the police if you—if you don't—"

"Honey," he said, talking right through her voice, "honey, I'm not coming in
there but you are coming out here. You know why?"

She was panting. The kitchen looked like a place she had never seen before,
some room she had run inside but which wasn't good enough, wasn't going to help
her. The kitchen window had never had a curtain, after three years, and there were
dishes in the sink for her to do—probably—and if you ran your hand across the table
you'd probably feel something sticky there.

"You listening, honey? Hey?"   115

"—going to call the police—"

"Soon as you touch the phone I don't need to keep my promise and can come
inside. You won't want that."

She rushed forward and tried to lock the door. Her fingers were shaking. "But
why lock it," Arnold Friend said gently, talking right into her face. "It's just a screen
door. It's just nothing." One of his boots was at a strange angle, as if his foot wasn't in
it. It pointed out to the left, bent at the ankle. "I mean, anybody can break through a
screen door and glass and wood and iron or anything else if he needs to, anybody at
all and specially Arnold Friend. If the place got lit up with a fire honey you'd come
running out into my arms, right into my arms and safe at home—like you knew I was
your lover and'd stopped fooling around. I don't mind a nice shy girl but I don't like
no fooling around." Part of those words were spoken with a slight rhythmic lilt, and
Connie somehow recognized them—the echo of a song from last year, about a girl
rushing into her boyfriend's arms and coming home again—

Connie stood barefoot on the linoleum floor, staring at him. "What do you
want?" she whispered.

"I want you," he said.   120

"What?"

"Seen you that night and thought, that's the one, yes sir. I never needed to look
any more."

"But my father's coming back. He's coming to get me. I had to wash my hair
first—" She spoke in a dry, rapid voice, hardly raising it for him to hear.

"No, your daddy is not coming and yes, you had to wash your hair and you
washed it for me. It's nice and shining and all for me, I thank you, sweetheart," he
said, with a mock bow, but again he almost lost his balance. He had to bend and adjust his boots. Evidently his feet did not go all the way down; the boots must have
been stuffed with something so that he would seem taller. Connie stared out at him
and behind him Ellie in the car, who seemed to be looking off toward Connie's right,
into nothing. This Ellie said, pulling the words out of the air one after another as if
he were just discovering them, "You want me to pull out the phone?"

"Shut your mouth and keep it shut," Arnold Friend said, his face red from bend-   125
ing over or maybe from embarrassment because Connie had seen his boots. "This
ain't none of your business."

"What—what are you doing? What do you want?" Connie said. "If I call the police they'll get you, they'll arrest you—"

"Promise was not to come in unless you touch that phone, and I'll keep that
promise," he said. He resumed his erect position and tried to force his shoulders back.
He sounded like a hero in a movie, declaring something important. He spoke too
loudly and it was as if he were speaking to someone behind Connie. "I ain't made
plans for coming in that house where I don't belong but just for you to come out to
me, the way you should. Don't you know who I am?"

"You're crazy," she whispered. She backed away from the door but did not want
to go into another part of the house, as if this would give him permission to come
through the door. "What do you . . . You're crazy, you . . ."

"Huh? What're you saying, honey?"

Her eyes darted everywhere in the kitchen. She could not remember what it was,   130
this room.

"This is how it is, honey: you come out and we'll drive away, have a nice ride.
But if you don't come out we're gonna wait till your people come home and then
they're all going to get it."

"You want that telephone pulled out?" Ellie said. He held the radio away from
his ear and grimaced, as if without the radio the air was too much for him.

"I toldja shut up, Ellie," Arnold Friend said, "you're deaf, get a hearing aid, right?
Fix yourself up. This little girl's no trouble and's gonna be nice to me, so Ellie keep to
yourself, this ain't your date—right? Don't hem in on me. Don't hog. Don't crush.
Don't bird dog. Don't trail me," he said in a rapid meaningless voice, as if he were running through all the expressions he'd learned but was no longer sure which one of them
was in style, then rushing on to new ones, making them up with his eyes closed, "Don't
crawl under my fence, don't squeeze in my chipmunk hole, don't sniff my glue, suck my
popsicle, keep your own greasy fingers on yourself!" He shaded his eyes and peered in at
Connie, who was backed against the kitchen table. "Don't mind him honey he's just a
creep. He's a dope. Right? I'm the boy for you and like I said you come out here nice
like a lady and give me your hand, and nobody else gets hurt, I mean, your nice old
bald-headed daddy and your mummy and your sister in her high heels. Because listen:
why bring them in this?"

"Leave me alone," Connie whispered.

"Hey, you know that old woman down the road, the one with the chickens and   135
stuff—you know her?"

"She's dead!"

"Dead? What? You know her?" Arnold Friend said.

"She's dead—"

"Don't you like her?"

"She's dead—she's—she isn't here any more—"   140

"But don't you like her, I mean, you got something against her? Some grudge or
something?" Then his voice dipped as if he were conscious of a rudeness. He touched
the sunglasses perched on top of his head as if to make sure they were still there.
"Now you be a good girl."

"What are you going to do?"

"Just two things, or maybe three," Arnold Friend said. "But I promise it won't
last long and you'll like me that way you get to like people you're close to. You will.

It's all over for you here, so come on out. You don't want your people in any trouble, do you?"

She turned and bumped against a chair or something, hurting her leg, but she ran into the back room and picked up the telephone. Something roared in her ear, a tiny roaring, and she was so sick with fear that she could do nothing but listen to it—the telephone was clammy and very heavy and her fingers groped down to the dial but were too weak to touch it. She began to scream into the phone, into the roaring. She cried out, she cried for her mother, she felt her breath start jerking back and forth in her lungs as if it were something Arnold Friend were stabbing her with again and again with no tenderness. A noisy sorrowful wailing rose all about her and she was locked inside it the way she was locked inside the house.

After a while she could hear again. She was sitting on the floor with her wet 145
back against the wall.

   ·   Arnold Friend was saying from the door, "That's a good girl. Put the phone back."

She kicked the phone away from her.

"No, honey. Pick it up. Put it back right."

She picked it up and put it back. The dial tone stopped.

"That's a good girl. Now come outside." 150

She was hollow with what had been fear, but what was now just an emptiness. All that screaming had blasted it out of her. She sat, one leg cramped under her, and deep inside her brain was something like a pinpoint of light that kept going and would not let her relax. She thought, I'm not going to see my mother again. She thought, I'm not going to sleep in my bed again. Her bright green blouse was all wet.

Arnold Friend said, in a gentle-loud voice that was like a stage voice, "The place where you came from ain't there any more, and where you had in mind to go is cancelled out. This place you are now—inside your daddy's house—is nothing but a cardboard box I can knock down any time. You know that and always did know it. You hear me?"

She thought, I have got to think. I have to know what to do.

"We'll go out to a nice field, out in the country here where it smells so nice and it's sunny," Arnold Friend said. "I'll have my arms around you so you won't need to try to get away and I'll show you what love is like, what it does. The hell with this house! It looks solid all right," he said. He ran a fingernail down the screen and the noise did not make Connie shiver, as it would have the day before. "Now put your hand on your heart, honey. Feel that? That feels solid too but we know better, be nice to me, be sweet like you can because what else is there for a girl like you but to be sweet and pretty and give in?—and get away before her people come back?"

She felt her pounding heart. Her hand seemed to enclose it. She thought for 155
the first time in her life that it was nothing that was hers, that belonged to her, but just a pounding, living thing inside this body that wasn't really hers either.

"You don't want them to get hurt," Arnold Friend went on. "Now get up, honey. Get up all by yourself."

She stood up.

"Now turn this way. That's right. Come over here to me—Ellie, put that away, didn't I tell you? You dope. You miserable creepy dope," Arnold Friend said. His words were not angry but only part of an incantation. The incantation was kindly. "Now come out through the kitchen to me honey and let's see a smile, try it, you're a brave sweet little girl and now they're eating corn and hotdogs cooked to bursting over an outdoor fire, and they don't know one thing about you and never did and honey you're better than them because not a one of them would have done this for you."

Connie felt the linoleum under her feet; it was cool. She brushed her hair back out of her eyes. Arnold Friend let go of the post tentatively and opened his arms for her, his elbows pointing in toward each other and his wrists limp, to show that this was an embarrassed embrace and a little mocking, he didn't want to make her self-conscious.

She put out her hand against the screen. She watched herself push the door   160
slowly open as if she were safe back somewhere in the other doorway, watching this body and this head of long hair moving out into the sunlight where Arnold Friend waited.

"My sweet little blue-eyed girl," he said, in a half-sung sigh that had nothing to do with her brown eyes but was taken up just the same by the vast sunlit reaches of the land behind him and on all sides of him, so much land that Connie had never seen before and did not recognize except to know that she was going to it.

Tim O'Brien

The Things They Carried   1990

Tim O'Brien was born in 1946 in Austin, Minnesota. Immediately after graduating summa cum laude from Macalester College in 1968, he was drafted into the U.S. Army. Serving as an infantryman in Vietnam, O'Brien attained the rank of sergeant and won a Purple Heart after being wounded by shrapnel. Upon his discharge in 1970, he began graduate work at Harvard. In 1973 he published If I Die in a Combat Zone, Box Me Up and Ship Me Home, *a mixture of memoir and fiction about his wartime experiences. His 1978 novel* Going After Cacciato *won the National Book Award, and is considered by some critics to be the best book of American fiction about the Vietnam War.* "The Things They Carried" *was first pub-*

Tim O'Brien

lished in Esquire *in 1986, and later became the title piece in a book of interlocking short stories published in 1990. His other novels include* The Nuclear Age *(1985),* In the Lake of the Woods *(1994),* Tomcat in Love *(1998) and* July, July *(2002). O'Brien currently teaches at Texas State University–San Marcos.*

First Lieutenant Jimmy Cross carried letters from a girl named Martha, a junior at Mount Sebastian College in New Jersey. They were not love letters, but Lieutenant Cross was hoping, so he kept them folded in plastic at the bottom of his rucksack. In the late afternoon, after a day's march, he would dig his foxhole, wash his hands under a canteen, unwrap the letters, hold them with the tips of his fingers, and spend the last hour of light pretending. He would imagine romantic camping trips into the White Mountains in New Hampshire. He would sometimes taste the envelope flaps, knowing her tongue had been there. More than anything, he wanted Martha to love him as he loved her, but the letters were mostly chatty, elusive on the matter of love. She was a virgin, he was almost sure. She was an English major at Mount Sebastian, and she wrote beautifully about her professors and roommates and midterm exams, about her respect for Chaucer and her great affection for Virginia Woolf. She often quoted lines of poetry; she never mentioned the war, except to say, Jimmy, take care of yourself. The letters weighed 10 ounces. They were signed Love, Martha, but Lieutenant Cross understood that Love was only a way of signing and did not mean what he sometimes pretended it meant. At dusk, he would carefully return the letters to his rucksack. Slowly, a bit distracted, he would get up and move among his men, checking the perimeter; then at full dark he would return to his hole and watch the night and wonder if Martha was a virgin.

The things they carried were largely determined by necessity. Among the necessities or near-necessities were P-38 can openers, pocket knives, heat tabs, wrist-watches, dog tags, mosquito repellent, chewing gum, candy, cigarettes, salt tablets, packets of Kool-Aid, lighters, matches, sewing kits, Military Payment Certificates, C rations, and two or three canteens of water. Together, these items weighed between 15 and 20 pounds, depending upon a man's habits or rate of metabolism. Henry Dobbins, who was a big man, carried extra rations; he was especially fond of canned peaches in heavy syrup over pound cake. Dave Jensen, who practiced field hygiene, carried a toothbrush, dental floss, and several hotel-sized bars of soap he'd stolen on R&R° in Sydney, Australia. Ted Lavender, who was scared, carried tranquilizers until he was shot in the head outside the village of Than Khe in mid-April. By necessity, and because it was SOP,° they all carried steel helmets that weighed 5 pounds including the liner and camouflage cover. They carried the standard fatigue jackets and trousers. Very few carried underwear. On their feet they carried jungle boots— 2.1 pounds—and Dave Jensen carried three pairs of socks and a can of Dr. Scholl's foot powder as a precaution against trench foot. Until he was shot, Ted Lavender carried six or seven ounces of premium dope, which for him was a necessity. Mitchell Sanders, the RTO,° carried condoms. Norman Bowker carried a diary. Rat Kiley carried comic books. Kiowa, a devout Baptist, carried an illustrated New Testament that had been presented to him by his father, who taught Sunday school in Oklahoma City, Oklahoma. As a hedge against bad times, however, Kiowa also carried his grandmother's distrust of the white man, his grandfather's old hunting hatchet. Necessity dictated. Because the land was mined and booby-trapped, it was SOP for each man to carry a steel-centered, nylon-covered flak jacket, which weighed 6.7 pounds, but which on hot days seemed much heavier. Because you could die so quickly, each man carried at least one large compress bandage, usually in the helmet band for easy access. Because the nights were cold, and because the monsoons were wet, each carried a green plastic poncho that could be used as a raincoat or ground-sheet or makeshift tent. With its quilted liner, the poncho weighed almost two pounds, but it was worth every ounce. In April, for instance, when Ted Lavender was shot, they used his poncho to wrap him up, then to carry him across the paddy, then to lift him into the chopper that took him away.

R&R: the military abbreviation for "rest and rehabilitation," a brief vacation from active service. SOP: standard operating procedure.   RTO: radio and telephone operator.

*

They were called legs or grunts.

To carry something was to hump it, as when Lieutenant Jimmy Cross humped his love for Martha up the hills and through the swamps. In its intransitive form, to hump meant to walk, or to march, but it implied burdens far beyond the intransitive.

Almost everyone humped photographs. In his wallet, Lieutenant Cross carried   5
two photographs of Martha. The first was a Kodacolor snapshot signed Love, though he knew better. She stood against a brick wall. Her eyes were gray and neutral, her lips slightly open as she stared straight-on at the camera. At night, sometimes, Lieutenant Cross wondered who had taken the picture, because he knew she had boyfriends, because he loved her so much, and because he could see the shadow of the picture-taker spreading out against the brick wall. The second photograph had been clipped from the 1968 Mount Sebastian yearbook. It was an action shot—women's volleyball—and Martha was bent horizontal to the floor, reaching, the palms of her hands in sharp focus, the tongue taut, the expression frank and competitive. There was no visible sweat. She wore white gym shorts. Her legs, he thought, were almost certainly the legs of a virgin, dry and without hair, the left knee cocked and carrying her entire weight, which was just over one hundred pounds. Lieutenant Cross remembered touching that left knee. A dark theater, he remembered, and the movie was *Bonnie and Clyde*, and Martha wore a tweed skirt, and during the final scene, when he touched her knee, she turned and looked at him in a sad, sober way that made him pull his hand back, but he would always remember the feel of the tweed skirt and the knee beneath it and the sound of the gunfire that killed Bonnie and Clyde, how embarrassing it was, how slow and oppressive. He remembered kissing her good night at the dorm door. Right then, he thought, he should've done something brave. He should've carried her up the stairs to her room and tied her to the bed and touched that left knee all night long. He should've risked it. Whenever he looked at the photographs, he thought of new things he should've done.

What they carried was partly a function of rank, partly of field specialty.

As a first lieutenant and platoon leader, Jimmy Cross carried a compass, maps, code books, binoculars, and a .45-caliber pistol that weighed 2.9 pounds fully loaded. He carried a strobe light and the responsibility for the lives of his men.

As an RTO, Mitchell Sanders carried the PRC-25 radio, a killer, 26 pounds with its battery.

As a medic, Rat Kiley carried a canvas satchel filled with morphine and plasma and malaria tablets and surgical tape and comic books and all the things a medic must carry, including M&M's° for especially bad wounds, for a total weight of nearly 20 pounds.

As a big man, therefore a machine gunner, Henry Dobbins carried the   10
M-60, which weighed 23 pounds unloaded, but which was almost always loaded. In addition, Dobbins carried between 10 and 15 pounds of ammunition draped in belts across his chest and shoulders.

As PFCs or Spec 4s, most of them were common grunts and carried the standard M-16 gas-operated assault rifle. The weapon weighed 7.5 pounds unloaded, 8.2 pounds with its full 20-round magazine. Depending on numerous factors, such as topography and psychology, the riflemen carried anywhere from 12 to 20 magazines,

_M&M's_: comic slang for medical supplies.

usually in cloth bandoliers, adding on another 8.4 pounds at minimum, 14 pounds at maximum. When it was available, they also carried M-16 maintenance gear—rods and steel brushes and swabs and tubes of LSA oil—all of which weighed about a pound. Among the grunts, some carried the M-79 grenade launcher, 5.9 pounds unloaded, a reasonably light weapon except for the ammunition, which was heavy. A single round weighed 10 ounces. The typical load was 25 rounds. But Ted Lavender, who was scared, carried 34 rounds when he was shot and killed outside Than Khe, and he went down under an exceptional burden, more than 20 pounds of ammunition, plus the flak jacket and helmet and rations and water and toilet paper and tranquilizers and all the rest, plus the unweighed fear. He was dead weight. There was no twitching or flopping. Kiowa, who saw it happen, said it was like watching a rock fall, or a big sandbag or something—just boom, then down—not like the movies where the dead guy rolls around and does fancy spins and goes ass over teakettle—not like that, Kiowa said, the poor bastard just flat-fuck fell. Boom. Down. Nothing else. It was a bright morning in mid-April. Lieutenant Cross felt the pain. He blamed himself. They stripped off Lavender's canteens and ammo, all the heavy things, and Rat Kiley said the obvious, the guy's dead, and Mitchell Sanders used his radio to report one U.S. KIA° and to request a chopper. Then they wrapped Lavender in his poncho. They carried him out to a dry paddy, established security, and sat smoking the dead man's dope until the chopper came. Lieutenant Cross kept to himself. He pictured Martha's smooth young face, thinking he loved her more than anything, more than his men, and now Ted Lavender was dead because he loved her so much and could not stop thinking about her. When the dustoff arrived, they carried Lavender aboard. Afterward they burned Than Khe. They marched until dusk, then dug their holes, and that night Kiowa kept explaining how you had to be there, how fast it was, how the poor guy just dropped like so much concrete. Boom-down, he said. Like cement.

In addition to the three standard weapons—the M-60, M-16, and M-79—they carried whatever presented itself, or whatever seemed appropriate as a means of killing or staying alive. They carried catch-as-catch-can. At various times, in various situations, they carried M-14s and CAR-15s and Swedish Ks and grease guns and captured AK-47s and Chi-Coms and RPGs and Simonov carbines and black market Uzis and .38-caliber Smith & Wesson handguns and 66 mm LAWs and shotguns and silencers and blackjacks and bayonets and C-4 plastic explosives. Lee Strunk carried a slingshot; a weapon of last resort, he called it. Mitchell Sanders carried brass knuckles. Kiowa carried his grandfather's feathered hatchet. Every third or fourth man carried a Claymore antipersonnel mine—3.5 pounds with its firing device. They all carried fragmentation grenades—14 ounces each. They all carried at least one M-18 colored smoke grenade—24 ounces. Some carried CS or tear gas grenades. Some carried white phosphorus grenades. They carried all they could bear, and then some, including a silent awe for the terrible power of the things they carried.

In the first week of April, before Lavender died, Lieutenant Jimmy Cross received a good-luck charm from Martha. It was a simple pebble, an ounce at most. Smooth to the touch, it was a milky white color with flecks of orange and violet, oval-shaped, like a miniature egg. In the accompanying letter, Martha wrote that she had found the

KIA: killed in action.

pebble on the Jersey shoreline, precisely where the land touched water at high tide, where things came together but also separated. It was this separate-but-together quality, she wrote, that had inspired her to pick up the pebble and to carry it in her breast pocket for several days, where it seemed weightless, and then to send it through the mail, by air, as a token of her truest feelings for him. Lieutenant Cross found this romantic. But he wondered what her truest feelings were, exactly, and what she meant by separate-but-together. He wondered how the tides and waves had come into play on that afternoon along the Jersey shoreline when Martha saw the pebble and bent down to rescue it from geology. He imagined bare feet. Martha was a poet, with the poet's sensibilities, and her feet would be brown and bare, the toenails unpainted, the eyes chilly and somber like the ocean in March, and though it was painful, he wondered who had been with her that afternoon. He imagined a pair of shadows moving along the strip of sand where things came together but also separated. It was phantom jealousy, he knew, but he couldn't help himself. He loved her so much. On the march, through the hot days of early April, he carried the pebble in his mouth, turning it with his tongue, tasting sea salt and moisture. His mind wandered. He had difficulty keeping his attention on the war. On occasion he would yell at his men to spread out the column, to keep their eyes open, but then he would slip away into daydreams, just pretending, walking barefoot along the Jersey shore, with Martha, carrying nothing. He would feel himself rising. Sun and waves and gentle winds, all love and lightness.

What they carried varied by mission.

When a mission took them to the mountains, they carried mosquito netting, machetes, canvas tarps, and extra bug juice.

If a mission seemed especially hazardous, or if it involved a place they knew to be bad, they carried everything they could. In certain heavily mined AOs,° where the land was dense with Toe Poppers and Bouncing Betties, they took turns humping a 28-pound mine detector. With its headphones and big sensing plate, the equipment was a stress on the lower back and shoulders, awkward to handle, often useless because of the shrapnel in the earth, but they carried it anyway, partly for safety, partly for the illusion of safety.

On ambush, or other night missions, they carried peculiar little odds and ends. Kiowa always took along his New Testament and a pair of moccasins for silence. Dave Jensen carried night-sight vitamins high in carotene. Lee Strunk carried his slingshot; ammo, he claimed, would never be a problem. Rat Kiley carried brandy and M&M's candy. Until he was shot, Ted Lavender carried the starlight scope, which weighed 6.3 pounds with its aluminum carrying case. Henry Dobbins carried his girlfriend's pantyhose wrapped around his neck as a comforter. They all carried ghosts. When dark came, they would move out single file across the meadows and paddies to their ambush coordinates, where they would quietly set up the Claymores and lie down and spend the night waiting.

Other missions were more complicated and required special equipment. In mid-April, it was their mission to search out and destroy the elaborate tunnel complexes in the Than Khe area south of Chu Lai. To blow the tunnels, they carried one-pound blocks of pentrite high explosives, four blocks to a man, 68 pounds in all. They carried wiring, detonators, and battery-powered clackers. Dave Jensen carried earplugs. Most

AOs: areas of operation.

often, before blowing the tunnels, they were ordered by higher command to search them, which was considered bad news, but by and large they just shrugged and carried out orders. Because he was a big man, Henry Dobbins was excused from tunnel duty. The others would draw numbers. Before Lavender died there were 17 men in the platoon, and whoever drew the number 17 would strip off his gear and crawl in headfirst with a flashlight and Lieutenant Cross's .45-caliber pistol. The rest of them would fan out as security. They would sit down or kneel, not facing the hole, listening to the ground beneath them, imagining cobwebs and ghosts, whatever was down there— the tunnel walls squeezing in—how the flashlight seemed impossibly heavy in the hand and how it was tunnel vision in the very strictest sense, compression in all ways, even time, and how you had to wiggle in—ass and elbows—a swallowed-up feeling— and how you found yourself worrying about odd things: Will your flashlight go dead? Do rats carry rabies? If you screamed, how far would the sound carry? Would your buddies hear it? Would they have the courage to drag you out? In some respects, though not many, the waiting was worse than the tunnel itself. Imagination was a killer.

On April 16, when Lee Strunk drew the number 17, he laughed and muttered something and went down quickly. The morning was hot and very still. Not good, Kiowa said. He looked at the tunnel opening, then out across a dry paddy toward the village of Than Khe. Nothing moved. No clouds or birds or people. As they waited, the men smoked and drank Kool-Aid, not talking much, feeling sympathy for Lee Strunk but also feeling the luck of the draw. You win some, you lose some, said Mitchell Sanders, and sometimes you settle for a rain check. It was a tired line and no one laughed.

Henry Dobbins ate a tropical chocolate bar. Ted Lavender popped a tranquilizer and went off to pee.   20

After five minutes, Lieutenant Jimmy Cross moved to the tunnel, leaned down, and examined the darkness. Trouble, he thought—a cave-in maybe. And then suddenly, without willing it, he was thinking about Martha. The stresses and fractures, the quick collapse, the two of them buried alive under all that weight. Dense, crushing love. Kneeling, watching the hole, he tried to concentrate on Lee Strunk and the war, all the dangers, but his love was too much for him, he felt paralyzed, he wanted to sleep inside her lungs and breathe her blood and be smothered. He wanted her to be a virgin and not a virgin, all at once. He wanted to know her. Intimate secrets: Why poetry? Why so sad? Why that grayness in her eyes? Why so alone? Not lonely, just alone—riding her bike across campus or sitting off by herself in the cafeteria—even dancing, she danced alone—and it was the aloneness that filled him with love. He remembered telling her that one evening. How she nodded and looked away. And how, later, when he kissed her, she received the kiss without returning it, her eyes wide open, not afraid, not a virgin's eyes, just flat and uninvolved.

Lieutenant Cross gazed at the tunnel. But he was not there. He was buried with Martha under the white sand at the Jersey shore. They were pressed together, and the pebble in his mouth was her tongue. He was smiling. Vaguely, he was aware of how quiet the day was, the sullen paddies, yet he could not bring himself to worry about matters of security. He was beyond that. He was just a kid at war, in love. He was twenty-four years old. He couldn't help it.

A few moments later Lee Strunk crawled out of the tunnel. He came up grinning, filthy but alive. Lieutenant Cross nodded and closed his eyes while the others clapped Strunk on the back and made jokes about rising from the dead.

Worms, Rat Kiley said. Right out of the grave. Fuckin' zombie.

The men laughed. They all felt great relief.

Spook city, said Mitchell Sanders.

Lee Strunk made a funny ghost sound, a kind of moaning, yet very happy, and right then, when Strunk made that high happy moaning sound, when he went *Ahhooooo*, right then Ted Lavender was shot in the head on his way back from peeing. He lay with his mouth open. The teeth were broken. There was a swollen black bruise under his left eye. The cheekbone was gone. Oh shit, Rat Kiley said, the guy's dead. The guy's dead, he kept saying, which seemed profound—the guy's dead. I mean really.

The things they carried were determined to some extent by superstition. Lieutenant Cross carried his good-luck pebble. Dave Jensen carried a rabbit's foot. Norman Bowker, otherwise a very gentle person, carried a thumb that had been presented to him as a gift by Mitchell Sanders. The thumb was dark brown, rubbery to the touch, and weighed four ounces at most. It had been cut from a VC corpse, a boy of fifteen or sixteen. They'd found him at the bottom of an irrigation ditch, badly burned, flies in his mouth and eyes. The boy wore black shorts and sandals. At the time of his death he had been carrying a pouch of rice, a rifle, and three magazines of ammunition.

You want my opinion, Mitchell Sanders said, there's a definite moral here.

He put his hand on the dead boy's wrist. He was quiet for a time, as if counting a pulse, then he patted the stomach, almost affectionately, and used Kiowa's hunting hatchet to remove the thumb.

Henry Dobbins asked what the moral was.

Moral?

You know. *Moral*.

Sanders wrapped the thumb in toilet paper and handed it across to Norman Bowker. There was no blood. Smiling, he kicked the boy's head, watched the flies scatter, and said, It's like with that old TV show—Paladin. Have gun, will travel.

Henry Dobbins thought about it.

Yeah, well, he finally said. I don't see no moral.

There it *is*, man.

Fuck off.

They carried USO stationery and pencils and pens. They carried Sterno, safety pins, trip flares, signal flares, spools of wire, razor blades, chewing tobacco, liberated joss sticks and statuettes of the smiling Buddha, candles, grease pencils, *The Stars and Stripes*, fingernail clippers, Psy Ops leaflets, bush hats, bolos, and much more. Twice a week, when the resupply choppers came in, they carried hot chow in green mermite cans and large canvas bags filled with iced beer and soda pop. They carried plastic water containers, each with a two-gallon capacity. Mitchell Sanders carried a set of starched tiger fatigues for special occasions. Henry Dobbins carried Black Flag insecticide. Dave Jensen carried empty sandbags that could be filled at night for added protection. Lee Strunk carried tanning lotion. Some things they carried in common. Taking turns, they carried the big PRC-77 scrambler radio, which weighed 30 pounds with its battery. They shared the weight of memory. They took up what others could no longer bear. Often, they carried each other, the wounded or weak. They carried infections. They carried chess sets, basketballs, Vietnamese-English dictionaries, insignia of rank, Bronze Stars and Purple Hearts, plastic cards imprinted with the Code of Conduct. They carried diseases, among them malaria and dysentery. They carried lice and ringworm and leeches and paddy algae and various rots and molds. They carried the land itself—Vietnam, the place, the soil—a powdery orange-red dust that covered their boots and fatigues and faces. They carried the sky. The whole atmosphere, they carried it, the humidity, the monsoons, the stink of fungus and decay, all of it, they carried gravity. They moved like mules. By daylight they took sniper fire, at night they were mortared, but it was not battle, it was just the endless march, village to village, without purpose, nothing won or lost. They marched for the sake of the march. They plodded along slowly, dumbly, leaning forward against the heat, unthinking, all blood and bone, simple grunts, soldiering with their legs, toiling up the hills and down into the paddies and across the rivers and up again and down, just humping, one step and then the next and then another, but no volition, no will, because it was automatic, it was anatomy, and the war was entirely a matter of posture and carriage, the hump was everything, a kind of inertia, a kind of emptiness, a dullness of desire and intellect and conscience and hope and human sensibility. Their principles were in their feet. Their calculations were biological. They had no sense of strategy or mission. They searched the villages without knowing what to look for, not caring, kicking over jars of rice, frisking children and old men, blowing tunnels, sometimes setting fires and sometimes not, then forming up and moving on to the next village, then other villages, where it would always be the same. They carried their own lives. The pressures were enormous. In the heat of early afternoon, they would remove their helmets and flak jackets, walking bare, which was dangerous but which helped ease the strain. They would often discard things along the route of march. Purely for comfort, they would throw away rations, blow their Claymores and grenades, no matter, because by nightfall the resupply choppers would arrive with more of the same, then a day or two later still more, fresh watermelons and crates of ammunition and sunglasses and woolen sweaters—the resources were stunning—sparklers for the Fourth of July, colored eggs for Easter—it was the great American war chest—the fruits of science, the smokestacks, the canneries, the arsenals at Hartford, the Minnesota forests, the machine shops, the vast fields of corn and wheat—they carried like freight trains; they carried it on their backs and shoulders—and for all the ambiguities of Vietnam, all the mysteries and unknowns, there was at least the single abiding certainty that they would never be at a loss for things to carry.

After the chopper took Lavender away, Lieutenant Jimmy Cross led his men   40
into the village of Than Khe. They burned everything. They shot chickens and dogs, they trashed the village well, they called in artillery and watched the wreckage, then they marched for several hours through the hot afternoon, and then at dusk, while Kiowa explained how Lavender died, Lieutenant Cross found himself trembling.

He tried not to cry. With his entrenching tool, which weighed five pounds, he began digging a hole in the earth.

He felt shame. He hated himself. He had loved Martha more than his men, and as a consequence Lavender was now dead, and this was something he would have to carry like a stone in his stomach for the rest of the war.

All he could do was dig. He used his entrenching tool like an ax, slashing, feeling both love and hate, and then later, when it was full dark, he sat at the bottom of his foxhole and wept. It went on for a long while. In part, he was grieving for Ted

Lavender, but mostly it was for Martha, and for himself, because she belonged to another world, which was not quite real, and because she was a junior at Mount Sebastian College in New Jersey, a poet and a virgin and uninvolved, and because he realized she did not love him and never would.

Like cement, Kiowa whispered in the dark. I swear to God—boom, down. Not a word.

I've heard this, said Norman Bowker.   45

A pisser, you know? Still zipping himself up. Zapped while zipping.

All right, fine. That's enough.

Yeah, but you had to see it, the guy just—

I *heard*, man. Cement. So why not shut the fuck *up*?

Kiowa shook his head sadly and glanced over at the hole where Lieutenant   50
Jimmy Cross sat watching the night. The air was thick and wet. A warm dense fog had settled over the paddies and there was the stillness that precedes rain.

After a time Kiowa sighed.

One thing for sure, he said. The lieutenant's in some deep hurt. I mean that crying jag—the way he was carrying on—it wasn't fake or anything, it was real heavy-duty hurt. The man cares.

Sure, Norman Bowker said.

Say what you want, the man does care.

We all got problems.   55

Not Lavender.

No, I guess not, Bowker said. Do me a favor, though.

Shut up?

That's a smart Indian. Shut up.

Shrugging, Kiowa pulled off his boots. He wanted to say more, just to lighten up   60
his sleep, but instead he opened his New Testament and arranged it beneath his head as a pillow. The fog made things seem hollow and unattached. He tried not to think about Ted Lavender, but then he was thinking how fast it was, no drama, down and dead, and how it was hard to feel anything except surprise. It seemed unchristian. He wished he could find some great sadness, or even anger, but the emotion wasn't there and he couldn't make it happen. Mostly he felt pleased to be alive. He liked the smell of the New Testament under his cheek, the leather and ink and paper and glue, whatever the chemicals were. He liked hearing the sounds of night. Even his fatigue, it felt fine, the stiff muscles and the prickly awareness of his own body, a floating feeling. He enjoyed not being dead. Lying there, Kiowa admired Lieutenant Jimmy Cross's capacity for grief. He wanted to share the man's pain, he wanted to care as Jimmy Cross cared. And yet when he closed his eyes, all he could think was Boom-down, and all he could feel was the pleasure of having his boots off and the fog curling in around him and the damp soil and the Bible smells and the plush comfort of night.

After a moment Norman Bowker sat up in the dark.

What the hell, he said. You want to talk, *talk*. Tell it to me.

Forget it.

No, man, go on. One thing I hate, it's a silent Indian.

For the most part they carried themselves with poise, a kind of dignity. Now   65
and then, however, there were times of panic, when they squealed or wanted to squeal

but couldn't, when they twitched and made moaning sounds and covered their heads and said Dear Jesus and flopped around on the earth and fired their weapons blindly and cringed and sobbed and begged for the noise to stop and went wild and made stupid promises to themselves and to God and to their mothers and fathers, hoping not to die. In different ways, it happened to all of them. Afterward, when the firing ended, they would blink and peek up. They would touch their bodies, feeling shame, then quickly hiding it. They would force themselves to stand. As if in slow motion, frame by frame, the world would take on the old logic—absolute silence, then the wind, then sunlight, then voices. It was the burden of being alive. Awkwardly, the men would reassemble themselves, first in private, then in groups, becoming soldiers again. They would repair the leaks in their eyes. They would check for casualties, call in dustoffs, light cigarettes, try to smile, clear their throats and spit and begin cleaning their weapons. After a time someone would shake his head and say, No lie, I almost shit my pants, and someone else would laugh, which meant it was bad, yes, but the guy had obviously not shit his pants, it wasn't that bad, and in any case nobody would ever do such a thing and then go ahead and talk about it. They would squint into the dense, oppressive sunlight. For a few moments, perhaps, they would fall silent, lighting a joint and tracking its passage from man to man, inhaling, holding in the humiliation. Scary stuff, one of them might say. But then someone else would grin or flick his eyebrows and say, Roger-dodger, almost cut me a new asshole, *almost*.

There were numerous such poses. Some carried themselves with a sort of wistful resignation, others with pride or stiff soldierly discipline or good humor or macho zeal. They were afraid of dying but they were even more afraid to show it.

They found jokes to tell.

They used a hard vocabulary to contain the terrible softness. *Greased*, they'd say. *Offed, lit up, zapped while zipping*. It wasn't cruelty, just stage presence. They were actors. When someone died, it wasn't quite dying, because in a curious way it seemed scripted, and because they had their lines mostly memorized, irony mixed with tragedy, and because they called it by other names, as if to encyst and destroy the reality of death itself. They kicked corpses. They cut off thumbs. They talked grunt lingo. They told stories about Ted Lavender's supply of tranquilizers, how the poor guy didn't feel a thing, how incredibly tranquil he was.

There's a moral here, said Mitchell Sanders.

They were waiting for Lavender's chopper, smoking the dead man's dope.   70

The moral's pretty obvious, Sanders said, and winked. Stay away from drugs. No joke, they'll ruin your day every time.

Cute, said Henry Dobbins.

Mind blower, get it? Talk about wiggy. Nothing left, just blood and brains.

They made themselves laugh.

There it is, they'd say. Over and over—there it is, my friend, there it is—as if the   75 repetition itself were an act of poise, a balance between crazy and almost crazy, knowing without going, there it is, which meant be cool, let it ride, because Oh yeah, man, you can't change what can't be changed, there it is, there it absolutely and positively and fucking well *is*.

They were tough.

They carried all the emotional baggage of men who might die. Grief, terror, love, longing—these were intangibles, but the intangibles had their own mass and specific gravity, they had tangible weight. They carried shameful memories. They carried the common secret of cowardice barely restrained, the instinct to run or freeze or hide, and in many respects this was the heaviest burden of all, for it could never be put down, it required perfect balance and perfect posture. They carried their reputations. They carried the soldier's greatest fear, which was the fear of blushing. Men killed, and died, because they were embarrassed not to. It was what had brought them to the war in the first place, nothing positive, no dreams of glory or honor, just to avoid the blush of dishonor. They died so as not to die of embarrassment. They crawled into tunnels and walked point and advanced under fire. Each morning, despite the unknowns, they made their legs move. They endured. They kept humping. They did not submit to the obvious alternative, which was simply to close the eyes and fall. So easy, really. Go limp and tumble to the ground and let the muscles unwind and not speak and not budge until your buddies picked you up and lifted you into the chopper that would roar and dip its nose and carry you off to the world. A mere matter of falling, yet no one ever fell. It was not courage, exactly; the object was not valor. Rather, they were too frightened to be cowards.

By and large they carried these things inside, maintaining the masks of composure. They sneered at sick call. They spoke bitterly about guys who had found release by shooting off their own toes or fingers. Pussies, they'd say. Candy-asses. It was fierce, mocking talk, with only a trace of envy or awe, but even so the image played itself out behind their eyes.

They imagined the muzzle against flesh. So easy: squeeze the trigger and blow away a toe. They imagined it. They imagined the quick, sweet pain, then the evacuation to Japan, then a hospital with warm beds and cute geisha nurses.

And they dreamed of freedom birds.   80

At night, on guard, staring into the dark, they were carried away by jumbo jets. They felt the rush of takeoff. *Gone!* they yelled. And then velocity—wings and engines—a smiling stewardess—but it was more than a plane, it was a real bird, a big sleek silver bird with feathers and talons and high screeching. They were flying. The weights fell off; there was nothing to bear. They laughed and held on tight, feeling the cold slap of wind and altitude, soaring, thinking *It's over, I'm gone!*—they were naked, they were light and free—it was all lightness, bright and fast and buoyant, light as light, a helium buzz in the brain, a giddy bubbling in the lungs as they were taken up over the clouds and the war, beyond duty, beyond gravity and mortification and global entanglements—*Sin loi!* ° they yelled. *I'm sorry, mother-fuckers, but I'm out of it, I'm goofed, I'm on a space cruise, I'm gone!*—and it was a restful, unencumbered sensation, just riding the light waves, sailing that big silver freedom bird over the mountains and oceans, over America, over the farms and great sleeping cities and cemeteries and highways and the golden arches of McDonald's, it was flight, a kind of fleeing, a kind of falling, falling higher and higher, spinning off the edge of the earth and beyond the sun and through the vast, silent vacuum where there were no burdens and where everything weighed exactly nothing—*Gone!* they screamed. *I'm sorry but I'm gone!*—and so at night, not quite dreaming, they gave themselves over to lightness, they were carried, they were purely borne.

On the morning after Ted Lavender died, First Lieutenant Jimmy Cross crouched at the bottom of his foxhole and burned Martha's letters. Then he burned the two photographs. There was a steady rain falling, which made it difficult, but he used heat tabs

Sin loi: Vietnamese for sorry.

and Sterno to build a small fire, screening it with his body, holding the photographs over the tight blue flame with the tips of his fingers.

He realized it was only a gesture. Stupid, he thought. Sentimental, too, but mostly just stupid.

Lavender was dead. You couldn't burn the blame.

Besides, the letters were in his head. And even now, without photographs,   85 Lieutenant Cross could see Martha playing volleyball in her white gym shorts and yellow T-shirt. He could see her moving in the rain.

When the fire died out, Lieutenant Cross pulled his poncho over his shoulders and ate breakfast from a can.

There was no great mystery, he decided.

In those burned letters Martha had never mentioned the war, except to say, Jimmy, take care of yourself. She wasn't involved. She signed the letters Love, but it wasn't love, and all the fine lines and technicalities did not matter. Virginity was no longer an issue. He hated her. Yes, he did. He hated her. Love, too, but it was a hard, hating kind of love.

The morning came up wet and blurry. Everything seemed part of everything else, the fog and Martha and the deepening rain.

He was a soldier, after all.   90

Half smiling, Lieutenant Jimmy Cross took out his maps. He shook his head hard, as if to clear it, then bent forward and began planning the day's march. In ten minutes, or maybe twenty, he would rouse the men and they would pack up and head west, where the maps showed the country to be green and inviting. They would do what they had always done. The rain might add some weight, but otherwise it would be one more day layered upon all the other days.

He was realistic about it. There was that new hardness in his stomach. He loved her but he hated her.

No more fantasies, he told himself.

Henceforth, when he thought about Martha, it would be only to think that she belonged elsewhere. He would shut down the daydreams. This was not Mount Sebastian, it was another world, where there were no pretty poems or midterm exams, a place where men died because of carelessness and gross stupidity. Kiowa was right. Boom-down, and you were dead, never partly dead.

Briefly, in the rain, Lieutenant Cross saw Martha's gray eyes gazing back at him.   95

He understood.

It was very sad, he thought. The things men carried inside. The things men did or felt they had to do.

He almost nodded at her, but didn't.

Instead he went back to his maps. He was now determined to perform his duties firmly and without negligence. It wouldn't help Lavender, he knew that, but from this point on he would comport himself as an officer. He would dispose of his good-luck pebble. Swallow it, maybe, or use Lee Strunk's slingshot, or just drop it along the trail. On the march he would impose strict field discipline. He would be careful to send out flank security, to prevent straggling or bunching up, to keep his troops moving at the proper pace and at the proper interval. He would insist on clean weapons. He would confiscate the remainder of Lavender's dope. Later in the day, perhaps, he would call the men together and speak to them plainly. He would accept the blame for what had happened to Ted Lavender. He would be a man about it. He would look them in the eyes, keeping his chin level, and he would issue the new SOPs in a calm, impersonal tone of voice, a lieutenant's voice, leaving no room for argument or discussion. Commencing immediately, he'd tell them, they would no longer abandon equipment along the route of march. They would police up their acts. They would get their shit together, and keep it together, and maintain it neatly and in good working order.

He would not tolerate laxity. He would show strength, distancing himself.   100

Among the men there would be grumbling, of course, and maybe worse, because their days would seem longer and their loads heavier, but Lieutenant Jimmy Cross reminded himself that his obligation was not to be loved but to lead. He would dispense with love; it was not now a factor. And if anyone quarreled or complained, he would simply tighten his lips and arrange his shoulders in the correct command posture. He might give a curt little nod. Or he might not. He might just shrug and say, Carry on, then they would saddle up and form into a column and move out toward the villages west of Than Khe.

Tillie Olsen

I Stand Here Ironing   1961

Tillie Olsen

Tillie Olsen (1912–2007) was born in Omaha, into a family of blue-collar workers who had fled Czarist Russia to escape persecution. Olsen grew up in poverty and quit school in eleventh grade to work. She later declared, "Public libraries were my college." As a member of the Young Communist League, she strove to organize Kansas City meat-packers, and was once thrown into jail. After her first husband deserted her, leaving her with one child, she married a printer and labor activist, Jack Olsen, and had three more children. Although in the 1930s she published fiction in a distinguished little magazine, Partisan Review, *the demands of motherhood, political activity, and factory and office jobs left her scant time to write until 1955. Then her youngest daughter began school and Olsen was awarded a creative writing fellowship at Stanford University. A lifelong crusader for causes, she was active in the feminist movement. "I Stand Here Ironing," from her first book,* Tell Me a Riddle *(1961), reads like autobiography. Olsen subsequently published* Yonnondio *(1974), an unfinished novel begun at age nineteen, and* Silences *(1978), a study of why writers—especially women writers—stop writing. She was the recipient of several honorary degrees, and in 1981 the city of San Francisco designated a Tillie Olsen day.*

I stand here ironing, and what you asked me moves tormented back and forth with the iron.

"I wish you would manage the time to come in and talk with me about your daughter. I'm sure you can help me understand her. She's a youngster who needs help and whom I'm deeply interested in helping."

"Who needs help." . . . Even if I came, what good would it do? You think because I am her mother I have a key, or that in some way you could use me as a key? She has lived for nineteen years. There is all that life that has happened outside of me, beyond me.

And when is there time to remember, to sift, to weigh, to estimate, to total? I will start and there will be an interruption and I will have to gather it all together again. Or I will become engulfed with all I did or did not do, with what should have been and what cannot be helped.

She was a beautiful baby. The first and only one of our five that was beautiful at birth. You do not guess how new and uneasy her tenancy in her now-loveliness. You did not know her all those years she was thought homely, or see her poring over her baby pictures, making me tell her over and over how beautiful she had been—and would be, I would tell her—and was now, to the seeing eye. But the seeing eyes were few or non-existent. Including mine.

I nursed her. They feel that's important nowadays. I nursed all the children, but with her, with all the fierce rigidity of first motherhood, I did like the books then said. Though her cries battered me to trembling and my breasts ached with swollenness, I waited till the clock decreed.

Why do I put that first? I do not even know if it matters, or if it explains anything.

She was a beautiful baby. She blew shining bubbles of sound. She loved motion, loved light, loved color and music and textures. She would lie on the floor in her blue overalls patting the surface so hard in ecstasy her hands and feet would blur. She was a miracle to me, but when she was eight months old I had to leave her daytimes with the woman downstairs to whom she was no miracle at all, for I worked or looked for work and for Emily's father, who "could no longer endure" (he wrote in his good-bye note) "sharing want with us."

I was nineteen. It was the pre-relief, pre-WPA world of the depression. I would start running as soon as I got off the streetcar, running up the stairs, the place smelling sour, and awake or asleep to startle awake, when she saw me she would break into a clogged weeping that could not be comforted, a weeping I can hear yet.

After a while I found a job hashing at night so I could be with her days, and it was better. But it came to where I had to bring her to his family and leave her.

It took a long time to raise the money for her fare back. Then she got chicken pox and I had to wait longer. When she finally came, I hardly knew her, walking quick and nervous like her father, looking like her father, thin, and dressed in a shoddy red that yellowed her skin and glared at the pockmarks. All the baby loveliness gone.

She was two. Old enough for nursery school they said, and I did not know then what I know now—the fatigue of the long day, and the lacerations of group life in the kinds of nurseries that are only parking places for children.

Except that it would have made no difference if I had known. It was the only place there was. It was the only way we could be together, the only way I could hold a job.

And even without knowing, I knew. I knew the teacher that was evil because all these years it has curdled into my memory, the little boy hunched in the corner, her rasp, "why aren't you outside, because Alvin hits you? that's no reason, go out, scaredy." I knew Emily hated it even if she did not clutch and implore "don't go Mommy" like the other children, mornings.

She always had a reason why we should stay home. Momma, you look sick, Momma, I feel sick. Momma, the teachers aren't there today, they're sick. Momma,

5

10

15

we can't go, there was a fire there last night. Momma, it's a holiday today, no school, they told me.

But never a direct protest, never rebellion. I think of our others in their three-, four-year-oldness—the explosions, the tempers, the denunciations, the demands— and I feel suddenly ill. I put the iron down. What in me demanded that goodness in her? And what was the cost, the cost to her of such goodness?

The old man living in the back once said in his gentle way: "You should smile at Emily more when you look at her." What *was* in my face when I looked at her? I loved her. There were all the acts of love.

It was only with the others I remembered what he said, and it was the face of joy, and not of care or tightness or worry I turned to them—too late for Emily. She does not smile easily, let alone almost always as her brothers and sisters do. Her face is closed and somber, but when she wants, how fluid. You must have seen it in her pantomimes, you spoke of her rare gift for comedy on the stage that rouses a laughter out of the audience so dear they applaud and applaud and do not want to let her go.

Where does it come from, that comedy? There was none of it in her when she came back to me that second time, after I had had to send her away again. She had a new daddy now to learn to love, and I think perhaps it was a better time.

Except when we left her alone nights, telling ourselves she was old enough. 20

"Can't you go some other time, Mommy, like tomorrow?" she would ask. "Will it be just a little while you'll be gone? Do you promise?"

The time we came back, the front door open, the clock on the floor in the hall. She rigid awake. "It wasn't just a little while. I didn't cry. Three times I called you, just three times, and then I ran downstairs to open the door so you could come faster. The clock talked loud. I threw it away, it scared me what it talked."

She said the clock talked loud again that night I went to the hospital to have Susan. She was delirious with the fever that comes before red measles, but she was fully conscious all the week I was gone and the week after we were home when she could not come near the new baby or me.

She did not get well. She stayed skeleton thin, not wanting to eat, and night after night she had nightmares. She would call for me, and I would rouse from exhaustion to sleepily call back: "You're all right, darling, go to sleep, it's just a dream," and if she still called, in a sterner voice, "now go to sleep, Emily, there's nothing to hurt you." Twice, only twice, when I had to get up for Susan anyhow, I went in to sit with her.

Now when it is too late (as if she would let me hold and comfort her like I do the 25 others) I get up and go to her at once at her moan or restless stirring. "Are you awake, Emily? Can I get you something?" And the answer is always the same: "No, I'm all right, go back to sleep, Mother."

They persuaded me at the clinic to send her away to a convalescent home in the country where "she can have the kind of food and care you can't manage for her, and you'll be free to concentrate on the new baby." They still send children to that place. I see pictures on the society page of sleek young women planning affairs to raise money for it, or dancing at the affairs, or decorating Easter eggs or filling Christmas stockings for the children.

They never have a picture of the children so I do not know if the girls still wear those gigantic red bows and the ravaged looks on the every other Sunday when parents can come to visit "unless otherwise notified"—as we were notified the first six weeks.

Oh it is a handsome place, green lawns and tall trees and fluted flower beds. High up on the balconies of each cottage the children stand, the girls in their red bows and white dresses, the boys in white suits and giant red ties. The parents stand below shrieking up to be heard and the children shriek down to be heard, and between them the invisible wall: "Not To Be Contaminated by Parental Germs or Physical Affection."

There was a tiny girl who always stood hand in hand with Emily. Her parents never came. One visit she was gone. "They moved her to Rose Cottage" Emily shouted in explanation. "They don't like you to love anybody here."

She wrote once a week, the labored writing of a seven-year-old. "I am fine. How is the baby. If I write my leter nicly I will have a star. Love." There never was a star. We wrote every other day, letters she could never hold or keep but only hear read— once. "We simply do not have room for children to keep any personal possessions," they patiently explained when we pieced one Sunday's shrieking together to plead how much it would mean to Emily, who loved so to keep things, to be allowed to keep her letters and cards.

Each visit she looked frailer. "She isn't eating," they told us.

(They had runny eggs for breakfast or mush with lumps, Emily said later, I'd hold it in my mouth and not swallow. Nothing ever tasted good, just when they had chicken.)

It took us eight months to get her released home, and only the fact that she gained back so little of her seven lost pounds convinced the social worker.

I used to try to hold and love her after she came back, but her body would stay stiff, and after a while she'd push away. She ate little. Food sickened her, and I think much of life too. Oh she had physical lightness and brightness, twinkling by on skates, bouncing like a ball up and down up and down over the jump rope, skimming over the hill; but these were momentary.

She fretted about her appearance, thin and dark and foreign-looking at a time when every little girl was supposed to look or thought she should look a chubby blonde replica of Shirley Temple. The doorbell sometimes rang for her, but no one seemed to come and play in the house or be a best friend. Maybe because we moved so much.

There was a boy she loved painfully through two school semesters. Months later she told me how she had taken pennies from my purse to buy him candy. "Licorice was his favorite and I brought him some every day, but he still liked Jennifer better'n me. Why, Mommy?" The kind of question for which there is no answer.

School was a worry to her. She was not glib or quick in a world where glibness and quickness were easily confused with ability to learn. To her overworked and exasperated teachers she was an overconscientious "slow learner" who kept trying to catch up and was absent entirely too often.

I let her be absent, though sometimes the illness was imaginary. How different from my now-strictness about attendance with the others. I wasn't working. We had a new baby, I was home anyhow. Sometimes, after Susan grew old enough, I would keep her home from school, too, to have them all together.

Mostly Emily had asthma, and her breathing, harsh and labored, would fill the house with a curiously tranquil sound. I would bring the two old dresser mirrors and her boxes of collections to her bed. She would select beads and single earrings, bottle tops and shells, dried flowers and pebbles, old postcards and scraps, all sorts of oddments; then she and Susan would play Kingdom, setting up landscapes and furniture, peopling them with action.

Those were the only times of peaceful companionship between her and Susan. I have edged away from it, that poisonous feeling between them, that terrible balancing of hurts and needs I had to do between the two, and did so badly, those earlier years.

Oh there are conflicts between the others too, each one human, needing, demanding, hurting, taking—but only between Emily and Susan, no, Emily toward Susan that corroding resentment. It seems so obvious on the surface, yet it is not obvious. Susan, the second child, Susan, golden- and curly-haired and chubby, quick and articulate and assured, everything in appearance and manner Emily was not; Susan, not able to resist Emily's precious things, losing or sometimes clumsily breaking them; Susan telling jokes and riddles to company for applause while Emily sat silent (to say to me later: that was *my* riddle, Mother, I told it to Susan); Susan, who for all the five years' difference in age was just a year behind Emily in developing physically.

I am glad for that slow physical development that widened the difference between her and her contemporaries, though she suffered over it. She was too vulnerable for that terrible world of youthful competition, of preening and parading, of constant measuring of yourself against every other, of envy, "If I had that copper hair," "If I had that skin. . . ." She tormented herself enough about not looking like the others, there was enough of the unsureness, the having to be conscious of words before you speak, the constant caring—what are they thinking of me? without having it all magnified by the merciless physical drives.

Ronnie is calling. He is wet and I change him. It is rare there is such a cry now. That time of motherhood is almost behind me when the ear is not one's own but must always be racked and listening for the child cry, the child call. We sit for a while and I hold him, looking out over the city spread in charcoal with its soft aisles of light. "*Shoogily*," he breathes and curls closer. I carry him back to bed, asleep. *Shoogily*. A funny word, a family word, inherited from Emily, invented by her to say: *comfort*.

In this and other ways she leaves her seal, I say aloud. And startle at my saying it. What do I mean? What did I start to gather together, to try and make coherent? I was at the terrible, growing years. War years. I do not remember them well. I was working, there were four smaller ones now, there was not time for her. She had to help be a mother, and housekeeper, and shopper. She had to set her seal. Mornings of crisis and near hysteria trying to get lunches packed, hair combed, coats and shoes found, everyone to school or Child Care on time, the baby ready for transportation. And always the paper scribbled on by a smaller one, the book looked at by Susan then mislaid, the homework not done. Running out to that huge school where she was one, she was lost, she was a drop; suffering over the unpreparedness, stammering and unsure in her classes.

There was so little time left at night after the kids were bedded down. She would struggle over books, always eating (it was in those years she developed her enormous appetite that is legendary in our family) and I would be ironing, or preparing food for the next day, or writing V-mail° to Bill, or tending the baby. Sometimes, to make me laugh, or out of her despair, she would imitate happenings or types at school.

I think I said once: "Why don't you do something like this in the school amateur show?" One morning she phoned me at work, hardly understandable through the weeping: "Mother, I did it. I won, I won; they gave me first prize; they clapped and clapped and wouldn't let me go."

V-mail: short for Victory mail, a system, involving microfilming and air delivery, for quick and efficient correspondence with family members serving overseas during World War II.

Now suddenly she was Somebody, and as imprisoned in her difference as she had been in anonymity.

She began to be asked to perform at other high schools, even in colleges, then at city and statewide affairs. The first one we went to, I only recognized her that first moment when thin, shy, she almost drowned herself into the curtains. Then: Was this Emily? The control, the command, the convulsing and deadly clowning, the spell, then the roaring, stamping audience, unwilling to let this rare and precious laughter out of their lives.

Afterwards: You ought to do something about her with a gift like that—but without money or knowing how, what does one do? We have left it all to her, and the gift has as often eddied inside, clogged and clotted, as been used and growing.

She is coming. She runs up the stairs two at a time with her light graceful step, 50 and I know she is happy tonight. Whatever it was that occasioned your call did not happen today.

"Aren't you ever going to finish the ironing, Mother? Whistler painted his mother in a rocker. I'd have to paint mine standing over an ironing board." This is one of her communicative nights and she tells me everything and nothing as she fixes herself a plate of food out of the icebox.

She is so lovely. Why did you want me to come in at all? Why were you concerned? She will find her way.

She starts up the stairs to bed. "Don't get me up with the rest in the morning." "But I thought you were having midterms." "Oh, those," she comes back in, kisses me, and says quite lightly, "in a couple of years when we'll all be atom-dead° they won't matter a bit."

She has said it before. She *believes* it. But because I have been dredging the past, and all that compounds a human being is so heavy and meaningful in me, I cannot endure it tonight.

I will never total it all. I will never come in to say: She was a child seldom smiled 55 at. Her father left me before she was a year old. I had to work her first six years when there was work, or I sent her home and to his relatives. There were years she had care she hated. She was dark and thin and foreign-looking in a world where the prestige went to blondeness and curly hair and dimples, she was slow where glibness was prized. She was a child of anxious, not proud, love. We were poor and could not afford for her the soil of easy growth. I was a young mother, I was a distracted mother. There were other children pushing up, demanding. Her younger sister seemed all that she was not. There were years she did not want me to touch her. She kept too much in herself, her life was such she had to keep too much in herself. My wisdom came too late. She has much to her and probably little will come of it. She is a child of her age, of depression, of war, of fear.

Let her be. So all that is in her will not bloom—but in how many does it? There is still enough left to live by. Only help her to know—help make it so there is cause for her to know—that she is more than this dress on the ironing board, helpless before the iron.

---

atom-dead: killed by an exchange of atomic bombs between the United States and the Soviet Union.

Tobias Wolff

The Rich Brother

1985

Tobias Wolff was born in Birmingham, Alabama, in 1945, the son of an aerospace engineer and a waitress and secretary. Following his parents' divorce, Tobias moved with his mother to Washington State while his older brother, Geoffrey, remained with their father (a pathological liar who was the subject of Geoffrey Wolff's acclaimed memoir The Duke of Deception*). Tobias Wolff's own memoir,* This Boy's Life *(1989), describes, among other things, his tense relationship with his abusive stepfather; it was the basis for the 1993 film starring Robert De Niro and Leonardo DiCaprio. In 1964 Wolff joined the Army, where he spent four years, including a year in Vietnam as a Special Forces language expert. This experience is*

Tobias Wolff

recounted in a second memoir, In Pharaoh's Army: Memories of the Lost War *(1994). After his military service, he earned a bachelor's degree at Oxford University and a master's at Stanford University, where he currently teaches in the creative writing program. Wolff is the author of five volumes of fiction, the novella* The Barracks Thief *(1984, PEN/Faulkner Award), the novel* Old School *(2003), and four volumes of short stories, most recently* Our Story Begins: New and Selected Stories *(2008).*

Acknowledging Raymond Carver (his onetime faculty colleague at Syracuse University) and Flannery O'Connor as influences, Wolff writes stories that, in the words of one critic, create a "sometimes comic, always compassionate world of ordinary people who suffer twentieth-century martyrdoms of growing up, growing old, loving and lacking love, living with parents and lovers and wives and their own weaknesses." Wolff lives in Northern California.

There were two brothers, Pete and Donald.

Pete, the older brother, was in real estate. He and his wife had a Century 21 franchise in Santa Cruz. Pete worked hard and made a lot of money, but not any more than he thought he deserved. He had two daughters, a sailboat, a house from which he could see a thin slice of the ocean, and friends doing well enough in their own lives not to wish bad luck on him. Donald, the younger brother, was still single. He lived alone, painted houses when he found the work, and got deeper in debt to Pete when he didn't.

No one would have taken them for brothers. Where Pete was stout and hearty and at home in the world, Donald was bony, grave, and obsessed with the fate of his soul. Over the years Donald had worn the images of two different Perfect Masters° around his neck. Out of devotion to the second of these he entered an ashram° in Berkeley, where he nearly died of undiagnosed hepatitis. By the time Pete finished paying the medical bills Donald had become a Christian. He drifted from church to

---

Perfect Masters: in Hindu mysticism, God-realized souls who work to help others toward the realization of God. *ashram:* secluded place where a community of Hindus lead lives of simplicity and meditation.

church, then joined a pentecostal community that met somewhere in the Mission District° to sing in tongues and swap prophecies.

Pete couldn't make sense of it. Their parents were both dead, but while they were alive neither of them had found it necessary to believe in anything. They managed to be decent people without making fools of themselves, and Pete had the same ambition. He thought that the whole thing was an excuse for Donald to take himself seriously.

The trouble was that Donald couldn't content himself with worrying about his own soul. He had to worry about everyone else's, and especially Pete's. He handed down his judgments in ways that he seemed to consider subtle: through significant silence, innuendo, looks of mild despair that said, *Brother, what have you come to?* What Pete had come to, as far as he could tell, was prosperity. That was the real issue between them. Pete prospered and Donald did not prosper.   5

At the age of forty Pete took up sky diving. He made his first jump with two friends who'd started only a few months earlier and were already doing stunts. He never would have used the word *mystical*, but that was how Pete felt about the experience. Later he made the mistake of trying to describe it to Donald, who kept asking how much it cost and then acted appalled when Pete told him.

"At least I'm trying something new," Pete said. "At least I'm breaking the pattern."

Not long after that conversation Donald also broke the pattern, by going to live on a farm outside Paso Robles. The farm was owned by several members of Donald's community, who had bought it and moved there with the idea of forming a family of faith. That was how Donald explained it in the first letter he sent. Every week Pete heard how happy Donald was, how "in the Lord." He told Pete that he was praying for him, he and the rest of Pete's brothers and sisters on the farm.

"I only have one brother," Pete wanted to answer, "and that's enough." But he kept this thought to himself.

In November the letters stopped. Pete didn't worry about this at first, but when he called Donald at Thanksgiving Donald was grim. He tried to sound upbeat but he didn't try hard enough to make it convincing. "Now listen," Pete said, "you don't have to stay in that place if you don't want to."   10

"I'll be all right," Donald answered.

"That's not the point. Being all right is not the point. If you don't like what's going on up there, then get out."

"I'm all right," Donald said again, more firmly. "I'm doing fine."

But he called Pete a week later and said that he was quitting the farm. When Pete asked him where he intended to go, Donald admitted that he had no plan. His car had been repossessed just before he left the city, and he was flat broke.

"I guess you'll have to stay with us," Pete said.   15

Donald put up a show of resistance. Then he gave in. "Just until I get my feet on the ground," he said.

"Right," Pete said. "Check out your options." He told Donald he'd send him money for a bus ticket, but as they were about to hang up Pete changed his mind. He knew that Donald would try hitchhiking to save the fare. Pete didn't want him out on the road all alone where some head case would pick him up, where anything could happen to him.

Mission District: run-down and, at one time, dangerous section of San Francisco.

"Better yet," he said, "I'll come and get you."

"You don't have to do that. I didn't expect you to do that," Donald said. He added, "It's a pretty long drive."

"Just tell me how to get there."   20

But Donald wouldn't give him directions. He said that the farm was too depressing, that Pete wouldn't like it. Instead, he insisted on meeting Pete at a service station called Jonathan's Mechanical Emporium.

"You must be kidding," Pete said.

"It's close to the highway," Donald said. "I didn't name it."

"That's one for the collection," Pete said.

The day before he left to bring Donald home, Pete received a letter from a man   25
who described himself as "head of household" at the farm where Donald had been living. From this letter Pete learned that Donald had not quit the farm, but had been asked to leave. The letter was written on the back of a mimeographed survey form asking people to record their response to a ceremony of some kind. The last question said:

What did you feel during the liturgy?

    a) *Being*
    b) *Becoming*
    c) *Being and Becoming*
    d) *None of the Above*
    e) *All of the Above*

Pete tried to forget the letter. But of course he couldn't. Each time he thought of it he felt crowded and breathless, a feeling that came over him again when he drove into the service station and saw Donald sitting against a wall with his head on his knees. It was late afternoon. A paper cup tumbled slowly past Donald's feet, pushed by the damp wind.

Pete honked and Donald raised his head. He smiled at Pete, then stood and stretched. His arms were long and thin and white. He wore a red bandanna across his forehead, a T-shirt with a couple of words on the front. Pete couldn't read them because the letters were inverted.

"Grow up," Pete yelled. "Get a Mercedes."

Donald came up to the window. He bent down and said, "Thanks for coming. You must be totally whipped."

"I'll make it." Pete pointed at Donald's T-shirt. "What's that supposed to say?"   30

Donald looked down at his shirt front. "Try God. I guess I put it on backwards. Pete, could I borrow a couple of dollars? I owe these people for coffee and sandwiches."

Pete took five twenties from his wallet and held them out the window.

Donald stepped back as if horrified. "I don't need that much."

"I can't keep track of all these nickels and dimes," Pete said. "Just pay me back when your ship comes in." He waved the bills impatiently. "Go on—take it."

"Only for now." Donald took the money and went into the service station office.   35
He came out carrying two orange sodas, one of which he gave to Pete as he got into the car. "My treat," he said.

"No bags?"

"Wow, thanks for reminding me." Donald balanced his drink on the dashboard, but the slight rocking of the car as he got out tipped it onto the passenger's seat, where half its contents foamed over before Pete could snatch it up again. Donald looked on while Pete held the bottle out the window, soda running down his fingers.

"Wipe it up," Pete told him. "Quick!"

"With what?"

Pete stared at Donald. "That shirt. Use the shirt."   40

Donald pulled a long face but did as he was told, his pale skin puckering against the wind.

"Great, just great," Pete said. "We haven't even left the gas station yet."

Afterwards, on the highway, Donald said, "This is a new car, isn't it?"

"Yes. This is a new car."

"Is that why you're so upset about the seat?"   45

"Forget it, okay? Let's just forget about it."

"I said I was sorry."

Pete said, "I just wish you'd be more careful. These seats are made of leather. That stain won't come out, not to mention the smell. I don't see why I can't have leather seats that smell like leather instead of orange pop."

"What was wrong with the other car?"

Pete glanced over at Donald. Donald had raised the hood of the blue sweatshirt   50
he'd put on. The peaked hood above his gaunt, watchful face gave him the look of an inquisitor.

"There wasn't anything wrong with it," Pete said. "I just happened to like this one better."

Donald nodded.

There was a long silence between them as Pete drove on and the day darkened toward evening. On either side of the road lay stubble-covered fields. A line of low hills ran along the horizon, topped here and there with trees black against the grey sky. In the approaching line of cars a driver turned on his headlights. Pete did the same.

"So what happened?" he asked. "Farm life not your bag?"

Donald took some time to answer, and at last he said, simply, "It was my fault."   55

"What was your fault?"

"The whole thing. Don't play dumb, Pete. I know they wrote to you." Donald looked at Pete, then stared out the windshield again.

"I'm not playing dumb."

Donald shrugged.

"All I really know is they asked you to leave," Pete went on. "I don't know any of   60
the particulars."

"I blew it," Donald said. "Believe me, you don't want to hear the gory details."

"Sure I do," Pete said. He added, "Everybody likes the gory details."

"You mean everybody likes to hear how someone messed up."

"Right," Pete said. "That's the way it is here on Spaceship Earth."

Donald bent one knee onto the front seat and leaned against the door so that he   65
was facing Pete instead of the windshield. Pete was aware of Donald's scrutiny. He waited. Night was coming on in a rush now, filling the hollows of the land. Donald's long cheeks and deep-set eyes were dark with shadow. His brow was white. "Do you ever dream about me?" Donald asked.

"Do I ever dream about you? What kind of a question is that? Of course I don't dream about you," Pete said, untruthfully.

"What do you dream about?"

"Sex and money. Mostly money. A nightmare is when I dream I don't have any."

"You're just making that up," Donald said.

Pete smiled.   70

"Sometimes I wake up at night," Donald went on, "and I can tell you're dreaming about me."

"We were talking about the farm," Pete said. "Let's finish that conversation and then we can talk about our various out-of-body experiences and the interesting things we did during previous incarnations."

For a moment Donald looked like a grinning skull; then he turned serious again. "There's not much to tell," he said. "I just didn't do anything right."

"That's a little vague," Pete said.

"Well, like the groceries. Whenever it was my turn to get the groceries I'd blow it   75
somehow. I'd bring the groceries home and half of them would be missing, or I'd have all the wrong things, the wrong kind of flour or the wrong kind of chocolate or whatever. One time I gave them away. It's not funny, Pete."

Pete said, "Who did you give the groceries to?"

"Just some people I picked up on the way home. Some fieldworkers. They had about eight kids with them and they didn't even speak English—just nodded their heads. Still, I shouldn't have given away the groceries. Not all of them, anyway. I really learned my lesson about that. You have to be practical. You have to be fair to yourself." Donald leaned forward, and Pete could sense his excitement. "There's nothing actually wrong with being in business," he said. "As long as you're fair to other people you can still be fair to yourself. I'm thinking of going into business, Pete."

"We'll talk about it," Pete said. "So, that's the story? There isn't any more to it than that?"

"What did they tell you?" Donald asked.

"Nothing."   80

"They must have told you something."

Pete shook his head.

"They didn't tell you about the fire?" When Pete shook his head again Donald regarded him for a time, then folded his arms across his chest and slumped back into the corner. "Everybody had to take turns cooking dinner. I usually did tuna casserole or spaghetti with garlic bread. But this one night I thought I'd do something different, something really interesting." Donald looked sharply at Pete. "It's all a big laugh to you, isn't it?"

"I'm sorry," Pete said.

"You don't know when to quit. You just keep hitting away."   85

"Tell me about the fire, Donald."

Donald kept watching him. "You have this compulsion to make me look foolish."

"Come off it, Donald. Don't make a big thing out of this."

"I know why you do it. It's because you don't have any purpose in life. You're afraid to relate to people who do, so you make fun of them."

"Relate," Pete said.   90

"You're basically a very frightened individual," Donald said. "Very threatened. You've always been like that. Do you remember when you used to try to kill me?"

"I don't have any compulsion to make you look foolish, Donald—you do it yourself. You're doing it right now."

"You can't tell me you don't remember," Donald said. "It was after my operation. You remember that."

"Sort of." Pete shrugged. "Not really."

"Oh yes," Donald said. "Do you want to see the scar?"   95

"I remember you had an operation. I don't remember the specifics, that's all. And I sure as hell don't remember trying to kill you."

"Oh yes," Donald repeated, maddeningly. "You bet your life you did. All the time. The thing was, I couldn't have anything happen to me where they sewed me up because then my intestines would come apart again and poison me. That was a big issue, Pete. Mom was always in a state about me climbing trees and so on. And you used to hit me there every chance you got."

"Mom was in a state every time you burped," Pete said. "I don't know. Maybe I bumped into you accidentally once or twice. I never did it deliberately."

"Every chance you got," Donald said. "Like when the folks went out at night and left you to baby-sit. I'd hear them say good night, and then I'd hear the car start up, and when they were gone I'd lie there and listen. After a while I would hear you coming down the hall, and I would close my eyes and pretend to be asleep. There were nights when you would stand outside the door, just stand there, and then go away again. But most nights you'd open the door and I would hear you in the room with me, breathing. You'd come over and sit next to me on the bed—you remember, Pete, you have to— you'd sit next to me on the bed and pull the sheets back. If I was on my stomach you'd roll me over. Then you would lift up my pajama shirt and start hitting me on my stitches. You'd hit me as hard as you could, over and over. I was afraid that you'd get mad if you knew I was awake. Is that strange or what? I was afraid that you'd get mad if you found out that I knew you were trying to kill me." Donald laughed. "Come on, you can't tell me you don't remember that."

"It might have happened once or twice. Kids do those things. I can't get all   100
excited about something I maybe did twenty-five years ago."

"No maybe about it. You did it."

Pete said, "You're wearing me out with this stuff. We've got a long drive ahead of us and if you don't back off pretty soon we aren't going to make it. You aren't, anyway."

Donald turned away.

"I'm doing my best," Pete said. The self-pity in his own voice made the words sound like a lie. But they weren't a lie! He was doing his best.

The car topped a rise. In the distance Pete saw a cluster of lights that blinked out   105
when he started downhill. There was no moon. The sky was low and black.

"Come to think of it," Pete said, "I did have a dream about you the other night." Then he added, impatiently, as if Donald were badgering him, "A couple of other nights, too. I'm getting hungry," he said.

"The same dream?"

"Different dreams. I only remember one of them. There was something wrong with me, and you were helping out. Taking care of me. Just the two of us. I don't know where everyone else was supposed to be."

Pete left it at that. He didn't tell Donald that in this dream he was blind.

"I wonder if that was when I woke up," Donald said. He added, "I'm sorry I got into   110
that thing about my scar. I keep trying to forget it but I guess I never will. Not really. It was pretty strange, having someone around all the time who wanted to get rid of me."

"Kid stuff," Pete said. "Ancient history."

They ate dinner at a Denny's on the other side of King City. As Pete was paying the check he heard a man behind him say, "Excuse me, but I wonder if I might ask which way you're going?" and Donald answer, "Santa Cruz."

"Perfect," the man said.

Pete could see him in the fish-eye mirror above the cash register: a red blazer with some kind of crest on the pocket, little black moustache, glossy black hair combed down on his forehead like a Roman emperor's. A rug, Pete thought. Definitely a rug.

Pete got his change and turned. "Why is that perfect?" he asked.   115

The man looked at Pete. He had a soft, ruddy face that was doing its best to express pleasant surprise, as if this new wrinkle were all he could have wished for, but the eyes behind the aviator glasses showed signs of regret. His lips were moist and shiny. "I take it you're together," he said.

"You got it," Pete told him.

"All the better, then," the man went on. "It so happens I'm going to Santa Cruz myself. Had a spot of car trouble down the road. The old Caddy let me down."

"What kind of trouble?" Pete asked.

"Engine trouble," the man said. "I'm afraid it's a bit urgent. My daughter is sick.   120
Urgently sick. I've got a telegram here." He patted the breast pocket of his blazer.

Before Pete could say anything Donald got into the act again. "No problem," Donald said. "We've got tons of room."

"Not that much room," Pete said.

Donald nodded. "I'll put my things in the trunk."

"The trunk's full," Pete told him.

"It so happens I'm traveling light," the man said. "This leg of the trip anyway. In 125
fact, I don't have any luggage at this particular time."

Pete said, "Left it in the old Caddy, did you?"

"Exactly," the man said.

"No problem," Donald repeated. He walked outside and the man went with him. Together they strolled across the parking lot, Pete following at a distance. When they reached Pete's car Donald raised his face to the sky, and the man did the same. They stood there looking up. "Dark night," Donald said.

"Stygian," the man said.

Pete still had it in his mind to brush him off, but he didn't do that. Instead he 130
unlocked the door for him. He wanted to see what would happen. It was an adventure, but not a dangerous adventure. The man might steal Pete's ashtrays but he wouldn't kill him. If Pete got killed on the road it would be by some spiritual person in a sweatsuit, someone with his eyes on the far horizon and a wet Try God T-shirt in his duffel bag.

As soon as they left the parking lot the man lit a cigar. He blew a cloud of smoke over Pete's shoulder and sighed with pleasure. "Put it out," Pete told him.

"Of course," the man said. Pete looked in the rearview mirror and saw the man take another long puff before dropping the cigar out the window. "Forgive me," he said. "I should have asked. Name's Webster, by the way."

Donald turned and looked back at him. "First name or last?"

The man hesitated. "Last," he said finally.

"I know a Webster," Donald said. "Mick Webster."   135

"There are many of us," Webster said.

"Big fellow, wooden leg," Pete said.

Donald gave Pete a look.

Webster shook his head. "Doesn't ring a bell. Still, I wouldn't deny the connection. Might be one of the cousinry."

"What's your daughter got?" Pete asked.   140

"That isn't clear," Webster answered. "It appears to be a female complaint of some nature. Then again it may be tropical." He was quiet for a moment, and added: "If indeed it *is* tropical, I will have to assume some of the blame myself. It was my own vaulting ambition that first led us to the tropics and kept us in the tropics all those many years, exposed to every evil. Truly I have much to answer for. I left my wife there."

Donald said quietly, "You mean she died?"

"I buried her with these hands. The earth will be repaid, gold for gold."

"Which tropics?" Pete asked.

"The tropics of Peru."   145

"What part of Peru are they in?"

"The lowlands," Webster said.

"What's it like down there? In the lowlands."

"Another world," Webster said. His tone was sepulchral. "A world better imagined than described."

"Far out," Pete said.   150

The three men rode in silence for a time. A line of trucks went past in the other direction, trailers festooned with running lights, engines roaring.

"Yes," Webster said at last, "I have much to answer for."

Pete smiled at Donald, but Donald had turned in his seat again and was gazing at Webster. "I'm sorry about your wife," Donald said.

"What did she die of?" Pete asked.

"A wasting illness," Webster said. "The doctors have no name for it, but I do."   155
He leaned forward and said, fiercely, "*Greed.* My greed, not hers. She wanted no part of it."

Pete bit his lip. Webster was a find and Pete didn't want to scare him off by hooting at him. In a voice low and innocent of knowingness, he asked, "What took you there?"

"It's difficult for me to talk about."

"Try," Pete told him.

"A cigar would make it easier."

Donald turned to Pete and said, "It's okay with me."   160

"All right," Pete said. "Go ahead. Just keep the window rolled down."

"Much obliged." A match flared. There were eager sucking sounds.

"Let's hear it," Pete said.

"I am by training an engineer," Webster began. "My work has exposed me to all but one of the continents, to desert and alp and forest, to every terrain and season of the earth. Some years ago I was hired by the Peruvian government to search for tungsten in the tropics. My wife and daughter accompanied me. We were the only white people for a thousand miles in any direction, and we had no choice but to live as the Indians lived—to share their food and drink and even their culture."

Pete said, "You knew the lingo, did you?"   165

"We picked it up." The ember of the cigar bobbed up and down. "We were used to learning as necessity decreed. At any rate, it became evident after a couple of years that there was no tungsten to be found. My wife had fallen ill and was pleading to be taken home. But I was deaf to her pleas, because by then I was on the trail of another metal—a metal far more valuable than tungsten."

"Let me guess," Pete said. "Gold?"

Donald looked at Pete, then back at Webster.

"Gold," Webster said. "A vein of gold greater than the Mother Lode itself. After I found the first traces of it nothing could tear me away from my search—not the sickness of my wife or anything else. I was determined to uncover the vein, and so I did— but not before I laid my wife to rest. As I say, the earth will be repaid."

Webster was quiet. Then he said, "But life must go on. In the years since my wife's death I have been making the arrangements necessary to open the mine. I could have done it immediately, of course, enriching myself beyond measure, but I knew what that would mean—the exploitation of our beloved Indians, the brutal destruction of their environment. I felt I had too much to atone for already." Webster paused, and when he spoke again his voice was dull and rushed, as if he had used up all the interest he had in his own words. "Instead I drew up a program for returning the bulk of the wealth to the Indians themselves. A kind of trust fund. The interest alone will allow them to secure their ancient lands and rights in perpetuity. At the same time, our investors will be rewarded a thousandfold. Two-thousandfold. Everyone will prosper together."

"That's great," said Donald. "That's the way it ought to be."

Pete said, "I'm willing to bet that you just happen to have a few shares left. Am I right?"

Webster made no reply.

"Well?" Pete knew that Webster was on to him now, but he didn't care. The story had bored him. He'd expected something different, something original, and Webster had let him down. He hadn't even tried. Pete felt sour and stale. His eyes burned from cigar smoke and the high beams of road-hogging truckers. "Douse the stogie," he said to Webster. "I told you to keep the window down."

"Got a little nippy back here."

Donald said, "Hey, Pete. Lighten up."

"Douse it!"

Webster sighed. He got rid of the cigar.

"I'm a wreck," Pete said to Donald. "You want to drive for a while?"

Donald nodded.

Pete pulled over and they changed places.

Webster kept his counsel in the back seat. Donald hummed while he drove, until Pete told him to stop. Then everything was quiet.

Donald was humming again when Pete woke up. Pete stared sullenly at the road, at the white lines sliding past the car. After a few moments of this he turned and said, "How long have I been out?"

Donald glanced at him. "Twenty, twenty-five minutes."

Pete looked behind him and saw that Webster was gone. "Where's our friend?"

"You just missed him. He got out in Soledad.° He told me to say thanks and good-bye."

"Soledad? What about his sick daughter? How did he explain her away?"

"He has a brother living there. He's going to borrow a car from him and drive the rest of the way in the morning."

"I'll bet his brother's living there," Pete said. "Doing fifty concurrent life sentences. His brother and his sister and his mom and his dad."

"I kind of liked him," Donald said.

Soledad: city in central California, site of a state prison.

170

175

180

185

190

"I'm sure you did," Pete said wearily.

"He was interesting. He's been places."

"His cigars had been places, I'll give you that."

"Come on, Pete."

"Come on yourself. What a phony."   195

"You don't know that."

"Sure I do."

"How? How do you know?"

Pete stretched. "Brother, there are some things you're just born knowing. What's the gas situation?"

"We're a little low."   200

"Then why didn't you get some more?"

"I wish you wouldn't snap at me like that," Donald said.

"Then why don't you use your head? What if we run out?"

"We'll make it," Donald said. "I'm pretty sure we've got enough to make it. You didn't have to be so rude to him," Donald added.

Pete took a deep breath. "I don't feel like running out of gas tonight, okay?"   205

Donald pulled in at the next station they came to and filled the tank while Pete went to the men's room. When Pete came back, Donald was sitting in the passenger's seat. The attendant came up to the driver's window as Pete got in behind the wheel. He bent down and said, "Twelve fifty-five."

"You heard the man," Pete said to Donald.

Donald looked straight ahead. He didn't move.

"Cough up," Pete said. "This trip's on you."

"I can't."   210

"Sure you can. Break out that wad."

Donald glanced up at the attendant, then at Pete. "Please," he said. "Pete, I don't have it anymore."

Pete took this in. He nodded, and paid the attendant.

Donald began to speak when they left the station but Pete cut him off. He said, "I don't want to hear from you right now. You just keep quiet or I swear to God I won't be responsible."

They left the fields and entered a tunnel of tall trees. The trees went on and on. 215

"Let me get this straight," Pete said at last. "You don't have the money I gave you."

"You treated him like a bug or something," Donald said.

"You don't have the money," Pete said again.

Donald shook his head.

"Since I bought dinner, and since we didn't stop anywhere in between, I assume you gave it to Webster. Is that right? Is that what you did with it?"

"Yes."   220

Pete looked at Donald. His face was dark under the hood but he still managed to convey a sense of remove, as if none of this had anything to do with him.

"Why?" Pete asked. "Why did you give it to him?" When Donald didn't answer, Pete said, "A hundred dollars. Gone. Just like that. I *worked* for that money, Donald."

"I know, I know," Donald said.

"You don't know! How could you? You get money by holding out your hand."

"I work too," Donald said.   225

"You work too. Don't kid yourself, brother."

Donald leaned toward Pete, about to say something, but Pete cut him off again.

"You're not the only one on the payroll, Donald. I don't think you understand that. I have a family."

"Pete, I'll pay you back."

"Like hell you will. A hundred dollars!" Pete hit the steering wheel with the palm of his hand. "Just because you think I hurt some goofball's feelings. Jesus, Donald." 230

"That's not the reason," Donald said. "And I didn't just *give* him the money."

"What do you call it, then? What do you call what you did?"

"I *invested* it. I wanted a share, Pete." When Pete looked over at him Donald nodded and said again, "I wanted a share."

Pete said, "I take it you're referring to the gold mine in Peru."

"Yes," Donald said. 235

"You believe that such a gold mine exists?"

Donald looked at Pete, and Pete could see him just beginning to catch on. "You'll believe anything," Pete said. "Won't you? You really will believe anything at all."

"I'm sorry," Donald said, and turned away.

Pete drove on between the trees and considered the truth of what he had just said—that Donald would believe anything at all. And it came to him that it would be just like this unfair life for Donald to come out ahead in the end, by believing in some outrageous promise that would turn out to be true and that he, Pete, would reject out of hand because he was too wised up to listen to anybody's pitch anymore except for laughs. What a joke. What a joke if there really was a blessing to be had, and the blessing didn't come to the one who deserved it, the one who did all the work, but to the other.

And as if this had already happened Pete felt a shadow move upon him, darkening his thoughts. After a time he said, "I can see where all this is going, Donald." 240

"I'll pay you back," Donald said.

"No," Pete said. "You won't pay me back. You can't. You don't know how. All you've ever done is take. All your life."

Donald shook his head.

"I see exactly where this is going," Pete went on. "You can't work, you can't take care of yourself, you believe anything anyone tells you. I'm stuck with you, aren't I?" He looked over at Donald. "I've got you on my hands for good."

Donald pressed his fingers against the dashboard as if to brace himself. "I'll get out," he said. 245

Pete kept driving.

"Let me out," Donald said. "I mean it, Pete."

"Do you?"

Donald hesitated. "Yes," he said.

"Be sure," Pete told him. "This is it. This is for keeps." 250

"I mean it."

"All right. You made the choice." Pete braked the car sharply and swung it to the shoulder of the road. He turned off the engine and got out. Trees loomed on both sides, shutting out the sky. The air was cold and musty. Pete took Donald's duffel bag from the back seat and set it down behind the car. He stood there, facing Donald in the red glow of the taillights. "It's better this way," Pete said.

Donald just looked at him.

"Better for you," Pete said.

Donald hugged himself. He was shaking. "You don't have to say all that," he told   255
Pete. "I don't blame you."

"Blame me? What the hell are you talking about? Blame me for what?"

"For anything," Donald said.

"I want to know what you mean by blame me."

"Nothing. Nothing, Pete. You'd better get going. God bless you."

"That's it," Pete said. He dropped to one knee, searching the packed dirt with his   260
hands. He didn't know what he was looking for, his hands would know when they
found it.

Donald touched Pete's shoulder. "You'd better go," he said.

Somewhere in the trees Pete heard a branch snap. He stood up. He looked at Donald, then went back to the car and drove away. He drove fast, hunched over the wheel,
conscious of the way he was hunched and the shallowness of his breathing, refusing to
look in the mirror above his head until there was nothing behind him but darkness.

Then he said, "A hundred dollars," as if there were someone to hear.

The trees gave way to fields. Metal fences ran beside the road, plastered with
windblown scraps of paper. Tule fog hung above the ditches, spilling into the road,
dimming the ghostly halogen lights that burned in the yards of the farms Pete passed.
The fog left beads of water rolling up the windshield.

Pete rummaged among his cassettes. He found Pachelbel's Canon° and pushed it   265
into the tape deck. When the violins began to play he leaned back and assumed an attentive expression as if he were really listening to them. He smiled to himself like a
man at liberty to enjoy music, a man who has finished his work and settled his debts,
done all things meet and due.

And in this way, smiling, nodding to the music, he went another mile or so and
pretended that he was not already slowing down, that he was not going to turn back,
that he would be able to drive on like this, alone, and have the right answer when his
wife stood before him in the doorway of his home and asked, Where is he? Where is
your brother?

Pachelbel's Canon: musical composition by Johann Pachelbel (1653–1706); it became widely known
through its use in the film *Ordinary People* (1980).

Kay Ryan, U.S. Poet Laureate, 2008.

POETRY

TALKING WITH *Kay Ryan*

"Language That Lasts"
Dana Gioia Interviews U.S. Poet Laureate Kay Ryan

Q: When did you start writing poetry?

KAY RYAN: In a way I'd say I started writing poetry when I started collecting language, which was as soon as I could. I loved hearing a new word or phrase, and I had a private game of trying to say things differently than I'd said them before. I remember when I was quite advanced in this language study, in ninth grade, I went on a summer trip with my friend and her parents down to Texas. I was sitting there quietly in the small hot living room of my friend's aunt, listening to the adult conversation. Someone said something irritated along the lines of, "Tracy totaled Teddy's Toronado, and Tyler tattled it to Tina!", and I just burst out laughing: that accidental string of T's nobody else seemed to notice. Language brought me constant, secret pleasure, and it was free; I could have as much as I wanted, which is nice if you're poor.

As to writing-writing, I fooled around with writing poetry during high school and college and even after I'd become a community college teacher, trying to keep it at arm's length because I didn't want to be exposed the way poetry makes you exposed. I wanted to stay superficial. But by the time I was thirty I could see that poetry was eating away at my mind anyhow. Why not accept it and try to get really good at it? So, either I started writing poetry at three or thirty.

Q: Did poetry play much of a part in your childhood?

KAY RYAN: I guess the short answer would be no. But my mother had one lovely poem about a dead kitten that she liked to say. I always enjoyed feeling tender and sad when she did; it was a kind of intimacy with a mother who wasn't very intimate. And my mother's mother liked to recite poems when she came to visit. They made me feel very serious, and that is a lovely feeling for a child: "Life is real! Life is earnest! / And the grave is not its goal; / Dust thou art, to dust returnest / Was not spoken of the soul!" My grandmother grew up in a time when people really memorized poetry for pleasure, and I loved hearing it.

My only other contact with poetry—but it was an important one—was in sixth grade. My enlightened teacher, Mrs. Kimball, at Roosevelt Elementary School in Bakersfield, California, had us do "choral reading," meaning the whole class memorized poems and stood up on the stage like a chorus at assemblies and recited them with great gusto. So I got a chance, like my grandmother, to memorize poetry for pleasure and have the pleasure of saying it aloud.

Q: Whom do you write for?

KAY RYAN: This is a devilish question. I'll have to answer it in parts.

First, when I write a poem I'm completely occupied with trying to net some elusive fish; I'm desperate to get the net (made of words) knotted in such a way that it will catch this desired fish (a half-formed idea, a wisp of a feeling). I'm not thinking of anything but that; I'm not thinking of me, I'm not thinking of you.

But then later, after I've finished writing the poem and have let it sit for days or months and look back to see if there's a fish in the net after all (many times, I'm sorry to say, there is no fish), I begin thinking of you. Have I put the necessary connections in the poem, or are some of them still in my head? Have I shaped the lines so they will present the reader with the most pleasure in discovering the secret rhymes? Have I removed self-indulgences? Because a poem, by its nature, must please others. If it doesn't, it can't last; and if it doesn't last it wasn't a poem, because poems are language that lasts.

Q: What gives you pleasure in writing?

KAY RYAN: People have dreams where they begin noticing that their house is lots bigger than they knew; they realize there is a maze of rooms behind the ones they've been occupying. The dreamer (I've had this dream) doesn't know why she hasn't noticed this before, because it's fascinating.

Kay Ryan with Dana Gioia

Writing a poem is like this; I go back behind my usual mind and find places I didn't know about, places that only the activity of writing a poem can let me into.

Q: Who are your favorite poets?

KAY RYAN: My favorite American poets are Emily Dickinson and Robert Frost. British favorites include John Donne, Gerard Manley Hopkins, Philip Larkin, and Stevie Smith. Favorites in other languages are Fernando Pessoa and Constantine Cavafy.

Q: Did a poem ever change your life?

KAY RYAN: A dream poem might have. When I was around ten, I dreamed that a piece of white paper was blowing around and I was chasing it. I knew it had the most beautiful poem in the world written on it. I couldn't catch it.

I never forgot that dream, although at the time I wasn't even thinking of trying to write poetry. Still, maybe some deep part of me was busy at it even then. I'm still trying to catch that piece of paper.

Q: What is the purpose of poetry? Why do people need poetry?

KAY RYAN: The secret, long-term purpose of poetry is to create more space between everything. Poetry is the main engine of the expanding universe. You yourself will have noticed how reading a poem that really strikes you (that will be one in 25, if you're lucky; a poem can be great and still not strike YOU) makes you feel freer and less burdened, even if it's about death. You feel fresher, more awake. This proves my point; your atoms have been subtly distanced from each other, like a breeze is blowing through your DNA. That's poetry loosening you.

Wdhat is poetry? Pressed for an answer, Robert Frost made a classic reply: "Poetry is the kind of thing poets write." In all likelihood, Frost was trying not merely to evade the question but to chide his questioner into thinking for himself. A trouble with definitions is that they may stop thought. If Frost had said, "Poetry is a rhythmical composition of words expressing an attitude, designed to surprise and delight, and to arouse an emotional response," the questioner might have settled back in his chair, content to have learned the truth about poetry. He would have learned nothing, or not so much as he might learn by continuing to wonder.

The nature of poetry eludes simple definitions. (In this respect it is rather like jazz. Asked after one of his concerts, "What is jazz?" Louis Armstrong replied, "Man, if you gotta ask, you'll never know.") Definitions will be of little help at first, if we are to know poetry and respond to it. We have to go to it willing to see and hear. For this reason, you are asked in reading this book not to be in any hurry to decide what poetry is, but instead to study poems and to let them grow in your mind. At the end of our discussions of poetry, the problem of definition will be taken up again (for those who may wish to pursue it).

Confronted with a formal introduction to poetry, you may be wondering, "Who needs it?" and you may well be right. It's unlikely that you have avoided meeting poetry before; and perhaps you already have a friendship, or at least a fair acquaintance, with some of the greatest English-speaking poets of all time. What this book provides is an introduction to the *study* of poetry. It tries to help you look at a poem closely, to offer you a wider and more accurate vocabulary with which to express what poems say to you. It will suggest ways to judge for yourself the poems you read. It may set forth some poems new to you.

A frequent objection is that poetry ought not to be studied at all. In this view, a poem is either a series of gorgeous noises to be funneled into one ear and out the other without being allowed to trouble the mind, or an experience so holy that to analyze it in a classroom is as cruel and mechanical as dissecting a hummingbird. To the first view, it might be countered that a good poem has something to say that is well worth listening to. To the second view, it might be argued that poems are much less perishable than hummingbirds, and luckily, we can study them in flight. The risk of a poem's dying from observation is not nearly so great as the risk of not really seeing it at all. It is doubtful that any excellent poem has ever vanished from human memory because people have read it too closely.

That poetry matters to the people who write it has been shown unmistakably by the ordeal of Soviet poet Irina Ratushinskaya. Sentenced to prison for three and a half years, she was given paper and pencil only twice a month to write letters to her husband and her parents and was not allowed to write anything else. Nevertheless, Ratushinskaya composed more than two hundred poems in her cell, engraving them with a burnt match in a bar of soap, then memorizing the lines. "I would read the poem and read it," she said, "until it was committed to memory—then with one washing of my hands, it would be gone."

Good poetry is something that readers can care about. In fact, an ancient persuasion of humankind is that the hearing of a poem, as well as the making of a poem, can be a religious act. Poetry, in speech and song, was part of classic Greek drama, which for playwright, actor, and spectator alike was a holy-day ceremony. The Greeks' belief that a poet writes a poem only by supernatural assistance is clear from the invocations to the Muse that begin the *Iliad* and the *Odyssey* and from the opinion of Socrates (in Plato's *Ion*) that a poet has no powers of invention until divinely inspired. Among the ancient Celts, poets were regarded as magicians and priests, and whoever insulted one of them might expect to receive a curse in rime potent enough to afflict him with boils and to curdle the milk of his cows. Such identifications between the poet and the magician are less common these days, although we know that poetry is involved in the primitive white magic of children, who bring themselves good luck in a game with the charm "Roll, roll, Tootsie-roll!/Roll the marble in the hole!" and who warn against a hex while jumping along a sidewalk: "Step on a crack,/Break your mother's back." To read a poem, we have to be willing to offer it responses *besides* a logical understanding. Whether we attribute the effect of a poem to a divine spirit or to the reactions of our glands and cortexes, we have to take the reading of poetry seriously (not solemnly), if only because—as some of the poems in this book may demonstrate—few other efforts can repay us so generously, both in wisdom and in joy.

If, as we hope you will do, you sometimes browse in the book for fun, you may be annoyed to see so many questions following the poems. Should you feel this way, try reading with a slip of paper to cover up the questions. You will then—if the Muse should inspire you—have paper in hand to write a poem.

To the Muse

Give me leave, Muse, in plain view to array
Your shift and bodice by the light of day.
I would have brought an epic. Be not vexed
Instead to grace a niggling schoolroom text;
Let down your sanction, help me to oblige
Those who would lead fresh devots to your liege,
And at your altar, grant that in a flash
Readers and I know incense from dead ash.

—X. J. K.

13 READING A POEM

Every good poem begins as the poet's
but ends as the reader's.

—MILLER WILLIAMS

How do you read a poem? The literal-minded might say, "Just let your eye light on it"; but there is more to poetry than meets the eye. What Shakespeare called "the mind's eye" also plays a part. Many a reader who has no trouble understanding and enjoying prose finds poetry difficult. This is to be expected. At first glance, a poem usually will make some sense and give some pleasure, but it may not yield everything at once. Poetry is not to be galloped over like the daily news: a poem differs from most prose in that it is to be read slowly, carefully, and attentively. Not all poems are difficult, of course, and some can be understood and enjoyed on first encounter. But good poems yield more if read twice; and the best poems—after ten, twenty, or a hundred readings—still go on yielding.

POETRY OR VERSE

Approaching a thing written in lines and surrounded with white space, we need not expect it to be a poem just because it is **verse**. (Any composition in lines of more or less regular rhythm, often ending in rimes, is verse.) Here, for instance, is a specimen of verse that few will call poetry:

Thirty days hath September,
April, June, and November;
All the rest have thirty-one
Excepting February alone,
To which we twenty-eight assign
Till leap year makes it twenty-nine.

To a higher degree than that classic memory-tickler, poetry appeals to the mind and arouses feelings. Poetry may state facts, but, more important, it makes imaginative statements that we may value even if its facts are incorrect. Coleridge's error in placing a star within the horns of the crescent moon in "The Rime of the Ancient Mariner" does not stop the passage from being good poetry, though it is faulty astronomy. According to poet Gerard Manley Hopkins, poetry is "to be heard for its own sake and interest even over and above its interest of meaning." There are other elements in a poem besides plain prose sense: sounds, images, rhythms, figures of speech. These may strike us and please us even before we ask, "But what does it all mean?"

This is a truth not readily grasped by anyone who regards a poem as a kind of puzzle written in secret code with a message slyly concealed. The effect of a poem (our whole mental and emotional response to it) consists of much more than simply a message. By its musical qualities, by its suggestions, it can work on the reader's unconscious. T. S. Eliot put it well when he said in *The Use of Poetry and the Use of Criticism* that the prose sense of a poem is chiefly useful in keeping the reader's mind "diverted and quiet, while the poem does its work upon him." Eliot went on to liken the meaning of a poem to the bit of meat a burglar brings along to throw to the family dog. What is the work of a poem? To touch us, to stir us, to make us glad, and possibly even to tell us something.

READING A POEM

How to set about reading a poem? Here are a few suggestions. To begin with, read the poem once straight through, with no particular expectations; read open-mindedly. Let yourself experience whatever you find, without worrying just yet about the large general and important ideas the poem contains (if indeed it contains any). Don't dwell on a troublesome word or difficult passage—just push on. Some of the difficulties may seem smaller when you read the poem for a second time; at least, they will have become parts of a whole for you.

On the second reading, read for the exact sense of all the words; if there are words you don't understand, look them up in a dictionary. Dwell on any difficult parts as long as you need to.

If you read the poem silently, sound its words in your mind. Better still, read the poem aloud, or listen to someone else reading it. You may discover meanings you didn't perceive in it before. To decide how to speak a poem can be an excellent method of getting to understand it.

PARAPHRASE

Try to **paraphrase** the poem as a whole, or perhaps just the more difficult lines. In paraphrasing, we put into our own words what we understand the poem to say, re-stating ideas that seem essential, coming out and stating what the poem may only suggest. This may sound like a heartless thing to do to a poem, but good poems can stand it. In fact, to compare a poem to its paraphrase is a good way to see the distance between poetry and prose. In making a paraphrase, we generally work through a poem or a passage line by line. The statement that results may take as many words as the original, if not more. A paraphrase, then, is ampler than a **summary**, a brief condensation of gist, main idea, or story. (Summary of a horror film in *TV Guide*: "Demented biologist, coveting power over New York, swells sewer rats to hippopotamus-size.") Here is a poem worth considering line by line. The poet writes of an island in a lake in the west of Ireland, in a region where he spent many summers as a boy.

William Butler Yeats (1865–1939)

The Lake Isle of Innisfree   1892

I will arise and go now, and go to Innisfree,
And a small cabin build there, of clay and wattles made:
Nine bean-rows will I have there, a hive for the honey-bee,
And live alone in the bee-loud glade.

And I shall have some peace there, for peace comes dropping slow,   5
Dropping from the veils of the morning to where the cricket sings;
There midnight's all a glimmer, and noon a purple glow,
And evening full of the linnet's wings.

I will arise and go now, for always night and day
I hear lake water lapping with low sounds by the shore;   10
While I stand on the roadway, or on the pavements gray,
I hear it in the deep heart's core.

Though relatively simple, this poem is far from simple-minded. We need to absorb it slowly and thoughtfully. At the start, for most of us, it raises problems: what are *wattles*, from which the speaker's dream-cabin is to be made? We might guess, but in this case it will help to consult a dictionary: they are "poles interwoven with sticks or branches, formerly used in building as frameworks to support walls or roofs." Evidently, this getaway house will be built in an old-fashioned way: it won't be a prefabricated log cabin or A-frame house, nothing modern or citified. The phrase *bee-loud glade* certainly isn't commonplace language, but right away, we can understand it, at least partially: it's a place loud with bees. What is a *glade*? Experience might tell us that it is an open space in woods, but if that word stops us, we can look it up. Although the *linnet* doesn't live in North America, it is a creature with wings—a songbird of the finch family, adds the dictionary. But even if we don't make a special trip to the dictionary to find *linnet*, we probably recognize that the word means "bird," and the line makes sense to us.

A paraphrase of the whole poem might go something like this (in language easier to forget than that of the original): "I'm going to get up now, go to Innisfree, build a cabin, plant beans, keep bees, and live peacefully by myself amid nature and beautiful light. I want to because I can't forget the sound of that lake water. When I'm in the city, a gray and dingy place, I seem to hear it deep inside me."

These dull remarks, roughly faithful to what Yeats is saying, seem a long way from poetry. Nevertheless, they make certain things clear. For one, they spell out what the poet merely hints at in his choice of the word *gray*: that he finds the city dull and depressing. He stresses the word; instead of saying *gray pavements*, in the usual word order, he turns the phrase around and makes *gray* stand at the end of the line, where it rimes with *day* and so takes extra emphasis. The grayness of the city therefore seems important to the poem, and the paraphrase tries to make its meaning obvious.

Theme and Subject

Whenever you paraphrase, you stick your neck out. You affirm what the poem gives you to understand. And making a paraphrase can help you see the central thought of the poem, its **theme**. The theme isn't the same as the **subject**, which is the main topic, whatever the poem is "about." In Yeats's poem, the subject is the lake isle of Innisfree, or a wish to retreat to it. But the theme is, "I yearn for an ideal place where I will find perfect peace and happiness."

Themes can be stated variously, depending on what you believe matters most in the poem. Taking a different view of the poem, placing more weight on the speaker's wish to escape the city, you might instead state the theme: "This city is getting me down—I want to get back to nature." But after taking a second look at that statement, you might want to sharpen it. After all, this Innisfree seems a special, particular place, where the natural world means more to the poet than just any old trees and birds he might see in a park. Perhaps a stronger statement of theme, one closer to what matters most in the poem, might be: "I want to quit the city for my heaven on earth." That, of course, is saying in an obvious way what Yeats says more subtly, more memorably.

Limits of Paraphrase

A paraphrase never tells *all* that a poem contains, nor will every reader agree that a particular paraphrase is accurate. We all make our own interpretations, and sometimes the total meaning of a poem evades even the poet who wrote it. Asked to explain a passage in one of his poems, Robert Browning replied that when he had written the poem, only God and he knew what it meant; but "Now, only God knows." Still, to analyze a poem *as if* we could be certain of its meaning is, in general, more fruitful than to proceed as if no certainty could ever be had. A useful question might be, "What can we understand from the poem's very words?"

All of us bring personal associations to the poems we read. "The Lake Isle of Innisfree" might give you special pleasure if you have ever vacationed on a small island or on the shore of a lake. Such associations are inevitable, even to be welcomed, as long as they don't interfere with our reading the words on the page. We need to distinguish irrelevant responses from those the poem calls for. The reader who can't stand "The Lake Isle of Innisfree" because she is afraid of bees isn't reading a poem by Yeats, but one of her own invention.

Now and again we meet a poem—perhaps startling and memorable—into which the method of paraphrase won't take us far. Some portion of any deep poem resists explanation, but certain poems resist it almost entirely. Many poems by religious mystics seem closer to dream than waking. So do poems that purport to record drug experiences, such as Coleridge's "Kubla Khan" (page 1032). So do nonsense poems, translations of primitive folk songs, and surreal poems. Such poetry may move us and give pleasure (although not, perhaps, the pleasure of intellectual understanding). We do it no harm by trying to paraphrase it, though we may fail. Whether logically clear or strangely opaque, good poems appeal to the intelligence and do not shrink from it.

So far, we have taken for granted that poetry differs from prose; yet all our strategies for reading poetry—plowing straight on through and then going back, isolating difficulties, trying to paraphrase, reading aloud, using a dictionary—are no different from those we might employ in unraveling a complicated piece of prose. Poetry, after all, is similar to prose in most respects. At the very least, it is written in the same language. Like prose, poetry shares knowledge with us. It tells us, for instance, of a beautiful island in Lake Gill, County Sligo, Ireland, and of how one man feels toward it.

LYRIC POETRY

Originally, as its Greek name suggests, a *lyric* was a poem sung to the music of a lyre. This earlier meaning—a poem made for singing—is still current today, when we use *lyrics* to mean the words of a popular song. But the kind of printed poem we now call a *lyric* is usually something else, for over the past five hundred years the nature of lyric poetry has changed greatly. Ever since the invention of the printing press in the fifteenth century, poets have written less often for singers, more often for readers. In general, this tendency has made lyric poems contain less word-music and (since they can be pondered on a page) more thought—and perhaps more complicated feelings.

What Is a Lyric Poem?

Here is a rough definition of a **lyric** as it is written today: a short poem expressing the thoughts and feelings of a single speaker. Often a poet will write a lyric in the first person ("I will arise and go now, and go to Innisfree"), but not always. A lyric can also be in the first person plural, as in Paul Laurence Dunbar's "We Wear the Mask" (page 948). Or, a lyric might describe an object or recall an experience without the speaker's ever bringing himself or herself into it. (For an example of such a lyric, one in which the poet refrains from saying "I," see Theodore Roethke's "Root Cellar" on page 712 or Gerard Manley Hopkins's "Pied Beauty" on page 716.)

Perhaps because, rightly or wrongly, some people still think of lyrics as lyre-strummings, they expect a lyric to be an outburst of feeling, somewhat resembling a song, at least containing musical elements such as rime, rhythm, or sound effects. Such expectations are fulfilled in "The Lake Isle of Innisfree," that impassioned lyric full of language rich in sound. Many contemporary poets, however, write short poems in which they voice opinions or complicated feelings—poems that no reader would dream of trying to sing.

But in the sense in which we use it, *lyric* will usually apply to a kind of poem you can easily recognize. Here, for instance, are two lyrics. They differ sharply in subject and theme, but they have traits in common: both are short, and (as you will find) both set forth one speaker's definite, unmistakable feelings.

Robert Hayden (1913–1980)

Those Winter Sundays   1962

Sundays too my father got up early
and put his clothes on in the blueblack cold,
then with cracked hands that ached
from labor in the weekday weather made
banked fires blaze. No one ever thanked him.   5

I'd wake and hear the cold splintering, breaking.
When the rooms were warm, he'd call,
and slowly I would rise and dress,
fearing the chronic angers of that house,

Speaking indifferently to him,   10
who had driven out the cold
and polished my good shoes as well.
What did I know, what did I know
of love's austere and lonely offices?

Questions

1. Jot down a brief paraphrase of this poem. In your paraphrase, clearly show what the speaker finds himself remembering.
2. What are the speaker's various feelings? What do you understand from the words *chronic angers* and *austere*?
3. With what specific details does the poem make the past seem real?
4. What is the subject of Hayden's poem? How would you state its theme?

Adrienne Rich   (b. 1929)

Aunt Jennifer's Tigers   1951

Aunt Jennifer's tigers prance across a screen,
Bright topaz denizens of a world of green.
They do not fear the men beneath the tree;
They pace in sleek chivalric certainty.

Aunt Jennifer's fingers fluttering through her wool   5
Find even the ivory needle hard to pull.
The massive weight of Uncle's wedding band
Sits heavily upon Aunt Jennifer's hand.

When Aunt is dead, her terrified hands will lie
Still ringed with ordeals she was mastered by.   10
The tigers in the panel that she made
Will go on prancing, proud and unafraid.

Compare

"Aunt Jennifer's Tigers" with Adrienne Rich's critical comments on the poem reprinted in the "Writing Effectively" section at the end of this chapter.

NARRATIVE POETRY

Although a lyric sometimes relates an incident, or like "Those Winter Sundays" draws a scene, it does not usually relate a series of events. That happens in a **narrative poem**, one whose main purpose is to tell a story.

Narrative poetry dates back to the Babylonian *Epic of Gilgamesh* (composed before 2000 B.C.) and Homer's epics the *Iliad* and the *Odyssey* (composed before 700 B.C.). It may well have originated much earlier. In England and Scotland, storytelling poems have long been popular; in the late Middle Ages, ballads—or storytelling songs—circulated widely. Some, such as "Sir Patrick Spence" and "Bonny Barbara Allan," survive in our day, and folksingers sometimes perform them.

Evidently the art of narrative poetry invites the skills of a writer of fiction: the ability to draw characters and settings, to engage attention, to shape a plot. Needless to say, it calls for all the skills of a poet as well. In the English language today, lyrics seem more plentiful than other kinds of poetry. Although there has recently been a revival of interest in writing narrative poems, they have a far smaller audience than the readership enjoyed by long verse narratives, such as Henry Wadsworth Longfellow's *Evangeline* and Alfred, Lord Tennyson's *Idylls of the King*, in the nineteenth century.

Here are two narrative poems: one medieval, one modern. How would you paraphrase the stories they tell? How do they hold your attention on their stories?

Anonymous (traditional Scottish ballad)

Sir Patrick Spence

The king sits in Dumferling toune,
  Drinking the blude-reid wine:
"O whar will I get guid sailor
  To sail this schip of mine?"

Up and spak an eldern knicht,°   *knight* 5
  Sat at the kings richt kne:
"Sir Patrick Spence is the best sailor
  That sails upon the se."

The king has written a braid letter,
  And signed it wi' his hand,   10
And sent it to Sir Patrick Spence,
  Was walking on the sand.

The first line that Sir Patrick red,
  A loud lauch lauchèd he;
The next line that Sir Patrick red,   15
  The teir blinded his ee.

"O wha° is this has don this deid,   *who*
  This ill deid don to me,
To send me out this time o' the yeir,
  To sail upon the se!   20

"Mak haste, mak haste, my mirry men all,
  Our guid schip sails the morne."
"O say na sae,° my master deir,   *so*
  For I feir a deadlie storme.

"Late late yestreen I saw the new moone,   25
  Wi' the auld moone in hir arme,
And I feir, I feir, my deir master,
  That we will cum to harme."

O our Scots nobles wer richt laith°   *loath*
  To weet° their cork-heild schoone,°   *wet; shoes* 30
Bot lang owre° a' the play wer playd,   *long before*
  Their hats they swam aboone.°   *above (their heads)*

O lang, lang may their ladies sit,
  Wi' their fans into their hand,
Or ere° they se Sir Patrick Spence   *before* 35
  Cum sailing to the land.

O lang, lang may the ladies stand,
  Wi' their gold kems° in their hair,   *combs*
Waiting for their ain° deir lords,   *own*
  For they'll se thame na mair.   40

Haf owre,° haf owre to Aberdour,   *halfway over*
  It's fiftie fadom deip,
And thair lies guid Sir Patrick Spence,
  Wi' the Scots lords at his feit.

SIR PATRICK SPENCE. *9 braid:* Broad, but broad in what sense? Among guesses are *plain-spoken, official,* and *on wide paper*.

Questions

1. That the king drinks "blude-reid wine" (line 2)—what meaning do you find in that detail? What does it hint, or foreshadow?
2. What do you make of this king and his motives for sending Spence and the Scots lords into an impending storm? Is he a fool, is he cruel and inconsiderate, is he deliberately trying to drown Sir Patrick and his crew, or is it impossible for us to know? Let your answer depend on the poem alone, not on anything you read into it.
3. Comment on this ballad's methods of storytelling. Is the story told too briefly for us to care what happens to Spence and his men, or are there any means by which the poet makes us feel compassion for them? Do you resent the lack of a detailed account of the shipwreck?
4. Lines 25–28—the new moon with the old moon in her arm—have been much admired as poetry. What does this stanza contribute to the story as well?

Robert Frost (1874–1963)

"Out, Out—"   1916

The buzz-saw snarled and rattled in the yard
And made dust and dropped stove-length sticks of wood,
Sweet-scented stuff when the breeze drew across it.
And from there those that lifted eyes could count
Five mountain ranges one behind the other   5
Under the sunset far into Vermont.
And the saw snarled and rattled, snarled and rattled,
As it ran light, or had to bear a load.
And nothing happened: day was all but done.
Call it a day, I wish they might have said   10
To please the boy by giving him the half hour
That a boy counts so much when saved from work.
His sister stood beside them in her apron
To tell them "Supper." At the word, the saw,
As if to prove saws knew what supper meant,   15
Leaped out at the boy's hand, or seemed to leap—
He must have given the hand. However it was,
Neither refused the meeting. But the hand!
The boy's first outcry was a rueful laugh,
As he swung toward them holding up the hand   20
Half in appeal, but half as if to keep
The life from spilling. Then the boy saw all—
Since he was old enough to know, big boy
Doing a man's work, though a child at heart—
He saw all spoiled. "Don't let him cut my hand off—   25
The doctor, when he comes. Don't let him, sister!"

So. But the hand was gone already.
The doctor put him in the dark of ether.
He lay and puffed his lips out with his breath.
And then—the watcher at his pulse took fright.   30
No one believed. They listened at his heart.
Little—less—nothing!—and that ended it.
No more to build on there. And they, since they
Were not the one dead, turned to their affairs.

"OUT, OUT—" The title of this poem echoes the words of Shakespeare's Macbeth on receiving news that
his queen is dead: "Out, out, brief candle! / Life's but a walking shadow, a poor player / That struts and frets
his hour upon the stage / And then is heard no more. It is a tale / Told by an idiot, full of sound and fury,
/ Signifying nothing" (Macbeth 5.5.23–28).

Questions

1. How does Frost make the buzz-saw appear sinister? How does he make it seem, in another
   way, like a friend?

2. What do you make of the people who surround the boy—the "they" of the poem? Who
   might they be? Do they seem to you concerned and compassionate, cruel, indifferent, or
   what?

3. What does Frost's reference to Macbeth contribute to your understanding of "'Out,
   Out—'"? How would you state the theme of Frost's poem?

4. Set this poem side by side with "Sir Patrick Spence." How does "'Out, Out—'" resemble
   that medieval folk ballad in subject, or differ from it? How is Frost's poem similar or different in its way of telling a story?

DRAMATIC POETRY

A third kind of poetry is **dramatic poetry**, which presents the voice of an imaginary
character (or characters) speaking directly, without any additional narration by the
author.

A dramatic poem, according to T. S. Eliot, does not consist of "what the poet
would say in his own person, but only what he can say within the limits of one imaginary character addressing another imaginary character." Strictly speaking, the term
dramatic poetry describes any verse written for the stage (and until a few centuries ago
most playwrights, like Shakespeare and Molière, wrote their plays mainly in verse).

Dramatic Monologue

The term *dramatic poetry* most often refers to the **dramatic monologue**, a poem written
as a speech made by a character (other than the author) at some decisive moment. A
dramatic monologue is usually addressed by the speaker to some other character who
remains silent. If the listener replies, the poem becomes a dialogue (such as Thomas
Hardy's "The Ruined Maid" on page 685) in which the story unfolds in the conversation between two speakers.

The Victorian poet Robert Browning, who developed the form of the dramatic
monologue, liked to put words in the mouths of characters who were conspicuously
nasty, weak, reckless, or crazy: see, for instance, Browning's "Soliloquy of the Spanish
Cloister" (page 1029), in which the speaker is an obsessively proud and jealous monk.
The dramatic monologue has been a popular form among American poets, including
Edwin Arlington Robinson, Robert Frost, Ezra Pound, Randall Jarrell, Sylvia Plath,
and David Mason. The most famous dramatic monologue ever written is probably

Browning's "My Last Duchess," in which the poet creates a Renaissance Italian duke whose words reveal much more about himself than the aristocratic speaker intends.

MLL ***Robert Browning*** (1812–1889)

MLL **My Last Duchess**   1842

    Ferrara

That's my last Duchess painted on the wall,
Looking as if she were alive. I call
That piece a wonder, now: Frà Pandolf's hands
Worked busily a day, and there she stands.
Will't please you sit and look at her? I said   5
"Frà Pandolf" by design, for never read
Strangers like you that pictured countenance,
The depth and passion of its earnest glance,
But to myself they turned (since none puts by
The curtain I have drawn for you, but I)   10
And seemed as they would ask me, if they durst,
How such a glance came there; so, not the first
Are you to turn and ask thus. Sir, 'twas not
Her husband's presence only, called that spot
Of joy into the Duchess' cheek: perhaps   15
Frà Pandolf chanced to say, "Her mantle laps
Over my lady's wrist too much," or "Paint
Must never hope to reproduce the faint
Half-flush that dies along her throat." Such stuff
Was courtesy, she thought, and cause enough   20
For calling up that spot of joy. She had
A heart—how shall I say?—too soon made glad,
Too easily impressed; she liked whate'er
She looked on, and her looks went everywhere.
Sir, 'twas all one! My favor at her breast,   25
The dropping of the daylight in the West,
The bough of cherries some officious fool
Broke in the orchard for her, the white mule
She rode with round the terrace—all and each
Would draw from her alike the approving speech,   30
Or blush, at least. She thanked men,—good! but thanked
Somehow—I know not how—as if she ranked
My gift of a nine-hundred-years-old name
With anybody's gift. Who'd stoop to blame
This sort of trifling? Even had you skill   35
In speech—(which I have not)—to make your will
Quite clear to such an one, and say "Just this
Or that in you disgusts me; here you miss,
Or there exceed the mark"—and if she let
Herself be lessoned so, nor plainly set   40
Her wits to yours, forsooth, and made excuse,

—E'en then would be some stooping; and I choose
Never to stoop. Oh, sir, she smiled, no doubt,
Whene'er I passed her; but who passed without
Much the same smile? This grew; I gave commands;   45
Then all smiles stopped together. There she stands
As if alive. Will't please you rise? We'll meet
The company below, then. I repeat,
The Count your master's known munificence
Is ample warrant that no just pretense   50
Of mine for dowry will be disallowed;
Though his fair daughter's self, as I avowed
At starting, is my object. Nay, we'll go
Together down, sir. Notice Neptune, though,
Taming a sea-horse, thought a rarity,   55
Which Claus of Innsbruck cast in bronze for me!

MY LAST DUCHESS. Ferrara, a city in northern Italy, is the scene. Browning may have modeled his speaker after Alonzo, Duke of Ferrara (1533–1598). 3 *Frà Pandolf* and 56 *Claus of Innsbruck:* fictitious names of artists.

Questions

1. Whom is the Duke addressing? What is this person's business in Ferrara?
2. What is the Duke's opinion of his last Duchess's personality? Do we see her character differently?
3. If the Duke was unhappy with the Duchess's behavior, why didn't he make his displeasure known? Cite a specific passage to explain his reticence.
4. How much do we know about the fate of the last Duchess? Would it help our understanding of the poem to know more?
5. Does Browning imply any connection between the Duke's art collection and his attitude toward his wife?

DIDACTIC POETRY

More fashionable in former times was a fourth variety of poetry, **didactic poetry**: a poem written to state a message or teach a body of knowledge. In a lyric, a speaker may express sadness; in a didactic poem, he or she may explain that sadness is inherent in life. Poems that impart a body of knowledge, such as Ovid's *Art of Love* and Lucretius's *On the Nature of Things*, are didactic. Such instructive poetry was favored especially by classical Latin poets and by English poets of the eighteenth century. In *The Fleece* (1757), John Dyer celebrated the British woolen industry and included practical advice on raising sheep:

> In cold stiff soils the bleaters oft complain
> Of gouty ails, by shepherds termed the halt:
> Those let the neighboring fold or ready crook
> Detain, and pour into their cloven feet
> Corrosive drugs, deep-searching arsenic,
> Dry alum, verdigris, or vitriol keen.

One might agree with Dr. Johnson's comment on Dyer's effort: "The subject, Sir, cannot be made poetical." But it may be argued that the subject of didactic poetry does not make it any less poetical. Good poems, it seems, can be written about anything under the sun. Like Dyer, John Milton described sick sheep in "Lycidas," a poem few readers have thought unpoetic:

> The hungry sheep look up, and are not fed,
> But, swoll'n with wind and the rank mist they draw,
> Rot inwardly, and foul contagion spread . . .

What makes Milton's lines better poetry than Dyer's is, among other things, a difference in attitude. Sick sheep to Dyer mean the loss of a few shillings and pence; to Milton, whose sheep stand for English Christendom, they mean a moral catastrophe.

■ WRITING *effectively*

Adrienne Rich on Writing

Recalling "Aunt Jennifer's Tigers"   1971

I know that my style was formed first by male poets: by the men I was reading as an undergraduate—Frost, Dylan Thomas, Donne, Auden, MacNeice, Stevens, Yeats. What I chiefly learned from them was craft. But poems are like dreams: in them you put what you don't know you know. Looking back at poems I wrote before I was 21, I'm startled because beneath the conscious craft are glimpses of the split I even then experienced between the girl who wrote poems, who defined herself in writing poems, and the girl who was to define herself by her relationships with men. "Aunt Jennifer's Tigers," written while I was a student, looks with deliberate detachment at this split. In writing this poem, composed and ap-

Adrienne Rich

parently cool as it is, I thought I was creating a portrait of an imaginary woman. But this woman suffers from the opposition of her imagination, worked out in tapestry, and her life-style, "ringed with ordeals she was mastered by." It was important to me that Aunt Jennifer was a person as distinct from myself as possible—distanced by the formalism of the poem, by its objective, observant tone—even by putting the woman in a different generation.

In those years formalism was part of the strategy—like asbestos gloves, it allowed me to handle materials I couldn't pick up bare-handed.

From "When We Dead Awaken: Writing as Re-Vision"

THINKING ABOUT PARAPHRASING

A poet takes pains to choose each word of a poem for both its sound and its exact shade of meaning. Since a poem's full effect is so completely wedded to its exact wording, some would say that no poem can be truly paraphrased. But even though it represents an imperfect approximation of the real thing, a paraphrase can be useful to write and read. It can clearly map out a poem's key images, actions, and ideas. A map is no substitute for a landscape, but a good map often helps us find our way through the landscape without getting lost.

William Stafford (1914–1993)

Ask Me   1975

Some time when the river is ice ask me
mistakes I have made. Ask me whether
what I have done is my life. Others
have come in their slow way into
my thought, and some have tried to help   5
or to hurt—ask me what difference
their strongest love or hate has made.

I will listen to what you say.
You and I can turn and look
at the silent river and wait. We know   10
the current is there, hidden; and there
are comings and goings from miles away
that hold the stillness exactly before us.
What the river says, that is what I say.

William Stafford (1914–1993)

A Paraphrase of "Ask Me"   1977

I think my poem can be paraphrased—and that any poem can be paraphrased. But every pass through the material, using other words, would have to be achieved at certain costs, either in momentum, or nuance, or dangerously explicit (and therefore misleading in tone) adjustments. I'll try one such pass through the poem:

> When it's quiet and cold and we have some chance to interchange without hurry, confront me if you like with a challenge about whether I think I have made mistakes in my life—and ask me, if you want to, whether to me my life is actually the sequence of events or exploits others would see. Well, those others tag along in my living, and some of them in fact have played significant roles in the narrative run of my world; they have intended either helping or hurting (but by implication in the way I am saying this you will know that neither effort is conclusive). So—ask me how important their good or bad intentions have been (both intentions get a drastic *leveling* judgment from this cool stating of it all). You, too, will be entering that realm of maybe-help-maybe-hurt, by entering that far into my life by asking this serious question—so: I will stay still and consider. Out there will be the world confronting us both; we will both know we are surrounded by mystery, tremendous things that do not reveal themselves to us. That river, that world—and our lives—all share the depth and stillness of much more significance than our talk, or intentions. There is a steadiness and somehow a solace in knowing that what is around us so greatly surpasses our human concerns.

From "Ask Me"

CHECKLIST: Writing a Paraphrase

☐ Read the poem closely. It is important to read it more than once to understand it well.

☐ Go through it line by line. Don't skip lines or stanzas or any key details. In your own words, what does each line say?

☐ Write your paraphrase as prose.

☐ State the poem's literal meaning. Don't worry about deeper meanings.

☐ Reread your statement to see if you have missed anything important. Check to see if you have captured the overall significance of the poem along with the details.

WRITING ASSIGNMENT ON PARAPHRASING

Paraphrase any short poem from the chapter "Poems for Further Reading." Be sure to do a careful line-by-line reading. Include the most vital points and details, and state the poem's main thought or theme without quoting any original passage.

MORE TOPICS FOR WRITING

1. In a paragraph, contrast William Stafford's poem with his paraphrase. What does the poem offer that the paraphrase does not? What, then, is the value of the paraphrase?

2. Write a two-page paraphrase of the events described in "'Out, Out—.'" Then take your paraphrase further: summarize the poem's message in a single sentence.

▶ TERMS FOR *review*

Analytic Terms

Verse ▶ This term has two major meanings. It refers to any single line of poetry or any composition written in separate lines of more or less regular rhythm, in contrast to prose.

Paraphrase ▶ The restatement in one's own words of what one understands a poem to say or suggest. A paraphrase is similar to a summary, although not as brief or simple.

Summary ▶ A brief condensation of the main idea or plot of a work. A summary is similar to a paraphrase, but less detailed.

Subject ▶ The main topic of a work, whatever the work is "about."

Theme ▶ A generally recurring subject or idea noticeably evident in a literary work. Not all subjects in a work can be considered themes, only the central one(s).

Types of Poetry

Lyric poem ▶ A short poem expressing the thoughts and feelings of a single speaker. Often written in the first person, it traditionally has a songlike immediacy and emotional force.

Narrative poem ▶ A poem that tells a story. **Ballads** and **epics** are two common forms of narrative poetry.

Dramatic monologue ▶ A poem written as a speech made by a character at some decisive moment. The speaker is usually addressing a silent listener.

Didactic poem ▶ A poem intended to teach a moral lesson or impart a body of knowledge.

14

LISTENING TO A VOICE

*Irony is that little pinch of salt
which alone makes the dish palatable.*

—JOHANN WOLFGANG VON GOETHE

TONE

In old Western movies, when one hombre taunts another, it is customary for the second to drawl, "Smile when you say that, pardner" or "Mister, I don't like your tone of voice." Sometimes in reading a poem, although we can neither see a face nor hear a voice, we can infer the poet's attitude from other evidence.

Like tone of voice, **tone** in literature often conveys an attitude toward the person addressed. Like the manner of a person, the manner of a poem may be friendly or belligerent toward its reader, condescending or respectful. Again like tone of voice, the tone of a poem may tell us how the speaker feels about himself or herself: cocksure or humble, sad or glad. But usually when we ask, "What is the tone of a poem?" we mean, "What attitude does the poet take toward a theme or a subject?" Is the poet being affectionate, hostile, earnest, playful, sarcastic, or what? We may never be able to know, of course, the poet's personal feelings. All we need know is how to feel when we read the poem.

Strictly speaking, tone isn't an attitude; it is whatever in the poem makes an attitude clear to us: the choice of certain words instead of others, the picking out of certain details. In A. E. Housman's "Loveliest of trees," for example, the poet communicates his admiration for a cherry tree's beauty by singling out its white blossoms for attention; had he wanted to show his dislike for the tree, he might have concentrated on its broken branches, birdlime, or snails. To perceive the tone of a poem rightly, we need to read the poem carefully, paying attention to whatever suggestions we find in it.

Theodore Roethke (1908–1963)

My Papa's Waltz   1948

The whiskey on your breath
Could make a small boy dizzy;
But I hung on like death:
Such waltzing was not easy.

We romped until the pans   5
Slid from the kitchen shelf;
My mother's countenance
Could not unfrown itself.

The hand that held my wrist
Was battered on one knuckle;   10
At every step you missed
My right ear scraped a buckle.

You beat time on my head
With a palm caked hard by dirt,
Then waltzed me off to bed   15
Still clinging to your shirt.

What is the tone of this poem? Most readers find the speaker's attitude toward his father critical, but nonetheless affectionate. They take this recollection of childhood to be an odd but happy one. Other readers, however, concentrate on other details, such as the father's rough manners and drunkenness. One reader has written that "Roethke expresses his resentment for his father, a drunken brute with dirty hands and whiskey breath who carelessly hurt the child's ear and manhandled him." Although this reader accurately noticed some of the events in the poem and perceived that there was something desperate in the son's hanging onto the father "like death," he simplifies the tone of the poem and so misses its humorous side.

While "My Papa's Waltz" contains the dark elements of manhandling and drunkenness, the tone remains grotesquely comic. The rollicking rhythms of the poem underscore Roethke's complex humor—half loving and half censuring of the unwashed, intoxicated father. The humor is further reinforced by playful rimes such as *dizzy* and *easy*, *knuckle* and *buckle*, as well as the joyful suggestions of the words *waltz*, *waltzing*, and *romped*. The scene itself is comic, with kitchen pans falling because of the father's roughhousing while the mother looks on unamused. However much the speaker satirizes the overly rambunctious father, he does not have the boy identify with the soberly disapproving mother. Not all comedy is comfortable and reassuring. Certainly, this small boy's family life has its frightening side, but the last line suggests the boy is *still clinging* to his father with persistent if also complicated love.

Satiric Poetry

"My Papa's Waltz," though it includes lifelike details that aren't pretty, has a tone relatively easy to recognize. So does **satiric poetry**, a kind of comic poetry that generally conveys a message. Usually its tone is one of detached amusement, withering contempt, and implied superiority. In a satiric poem, the poet ridicules some person or persons (or perhaps some kind of human behavior), examining the victim by the light of certain principles and implying that the reader, too, ought to feel contempt for the victim.

Countee Cullen (1903–1946)

For a Lady I Know   1925

She even thinks that up in heaven
    Her class lies late and snores,
While poor black cherubs rise at seven
    To do celestial chores.

Questions

1. What is Cullen's message?
2. How would you characterize the tone of this poem? Wrathful? Amused?

A Spectrum of Tones

In some poems the poet's attitude may be plain enough; while in other poems attitudes may be so mingled that it is hard to describe them tersely without doing injustice to the poem. Does Andrew Marvell in "To His Coy Mistress" (page 1066) take a serious or playful attitude toward the fact that he and his lady are destined to be food for worms? No one-word answer will suffice. And what of T. S. Eliot's "The Love Song of J. Alfred Prufrock" (page 995)? In his attitude toward his redemption-seeking hero who wades with trousers rolled, Eliot is seriously funny. Such a mingled tone may be seen in the following poem by the wife of a governor of the Massachusetts Bay Colony and the earliest American poet of note. Anne Bradstreet's first book, *The Tenth Muse Lately Sprung Up in America* (1650), had been published in England without her consent. She wrote these lines to preface a second edition:

Anne Bradstreet (1612?–1672)

The Author to Her Book 1678

Thou ill-formed offspring of my feeble brain,
Who after birth did'st by my side remain,
Till snatched from thence by friends, less wise than true,
Who thee abroad exposed to public view;
Made thee in rags, halting, to the press to trudge,   5
Where errors were not lessened, all may judge.
At thy return my blushing was not small,
My rambling brat (in print) should mother call;
I cast thee by as one unfit for light,
Thy visage was so irksome in my sight;   10
Yet being mine own, at length affection would
Thy blemishes amend, if so I could:
I washed thy face, but more defects I saw,
And rubbing off a spot, still made a flaw.
I stretched thy joints to make thee even feet,   15
Yet still thou run'st more hobbling than is meet;
In better dress to trim thee was my mind,
But nought save homespun cloth in the house I find.
In this array, 'mongst vulgars may'st thou roam;
In critics' hands beware thou dost not come;   20
And take thy way where yet thou are not known.
If for thy Father asked, say thou had'st none;
And for thy Mother, she alas is poor,
Which caused her thus to send thee out of door.

In the author's comparison of her book to an illegitimate ragamuffin, we may be struck by the details of scrubbing and dressing a child: details that might well occur to a mother who had scrubbed and dressed many. As she might feel toward such a child, so she feels toward her book. She starts by deploring it but, as the poem goes on, cannot deny it her affection. Humor enters (as in the pun in line 15). She must dress the creature in *homespun cloth*, something both crude and serviceable. By the end of her poem, Bradstreet seems to regard her book-child with tenderness, amusement, and a certain indulgent awareness of its faults. To read this poem is to sense its mingling of several attitudes. A poet can be merry and in earnest at the same time.

Walt Whitman (1819–1892)

To a Locomotive in Winter   1881

Thee for my recitative,
Thee in the driving storm even as now, the snow, the winter-day
    declining,
Thee in thy panoply,° thy measur'd dual throbbing and thy beat   *suit of armor*
    convulsive,
Thy black cylindric body, golden brass and silvery steel,
Thy ponderous side-bars, parallel and connecting rods, gyrating,   5
    shuttling at thy sides,
Thy metrical, now swelling pant and roar, now tapering
    in the distance,
Thy great protruding head-light fix'd in front,
Thy long, pale, floating vapor-pennants, tinged with delicate purple,
The dense and murky clouds out-belching from thy smoke-stack,
Thy knitted frame, thy springs and valves, the tremulous twinkle of thy   10
    wheels,
Thy train of cars behind, obedient, merrily following,
Through gale or calm, now swift, now slack, yet steadily careering;
Type of the modern—emblem of motion and power—pulse of the
    continent,
For once come serve the Muse and merge in verse, even as here I see thee,
With storm and buffeting gusts of wind and falling snow,   15
By day thy warning ringing bell to sound its notes,
By night thy silent signal lamps to swing.

Fierce-throated beauty!
Roll through my chant with all thy lawless music, thy swinging lamps at night,
Thy madly-whistled laughter, echoing, rumbling like an earth-quake,   20
    rousing all,
Law of thyself complete, thine own track firmly holding,
(No sweetness debonair of tearful harp or glib piano thine,)
Thy trills of shrieks by rocks and hills return'd,
Launch'd o'er the prairies wide, across the lakes,
To the free skies unpent and glad and strong.   25

Emily Dickinson (1830–1886)

I like to see it lap the Miles (about 1862)

I like to see it lap the Miles –
And lick the Valleys up –
And stop to feed itself at Tanks –
And then – prodigious step

Around a Pile of Mountains – 5
And supercilious peer
In Shanties – by the sides of Roads –
And then a Quarry pare

To fit its Ribs
And crawl between 10
Complaining all the while
In horrid – hooting stanza –
Then chase itself down Hill –

And neigh like Boanerges –
Then – punctual as a Star 15
Stop – docile and omnipotent
At its own stable door–

Questions

1. What differences in tone do you find between Whitman's and Dickinson's poems? Point out whatever in each poem contributes to these differences.

2. *Boanerges* in Dickinson's last stanza means "sons of thunder," a name given by Jesus to the disciples John and James (see Mark 3:17). How far should the reader work out the particulars of this comparison? Does it make the tone of the poem serious?

3. In Whitman's opening line, what is a *recitative?* What other specialized terms from the vocabulary of music and poetry does each poem contain? How do they help underscore Whitman's theme?

4. Poets and songwriters probably have regarded the locomotive with more affection than they have shown most other machines. Why do you suppose this is so? Can you think of any other poems or songs as examples?

5. What do these two poems tell you about locomotives that you would not be likely to find in a technical book on railroading?

6. Are the subjects of the two poems identical? Discuss.

Kevin Young (b. 1970)

Doo Wop 2003

Honey baby
Lady lovely

Milk shake your
money maker

Shoo wah   5
Shoo wah

Countryfied
Sudden fried

Alabama
mamma jamma   10

Low bass
Fast pace

Past face
Femme postale

Penned pal   15
My gal

Corner song
Done wronged

Questions

1. What is the tone of this poem—comic? serious? both at once?
2. How many instances of plays on words, and playing with the sounds of words, can you find in the poem?
3. Beyond the author's exuberant delight in language, what do you think "Doo Wop" is *about*?

Weldon Kees (1914–1955)

For My Daughter   1940

Looking into my daughter's eyes I read
Beneath the innocence of morning flesh
Concealed, hintings of death she does not heed.
Coldest of winds have blown this hair, and mesh
Of seaweed snarled these miniatures of hands;   5
The night's slow poison, tolerant and bland,
Has moved her blood. Parched years that I have seen
That may be hers appear: foul, lingering
Death in certain war, the slim legs green.
Or, fed on hate, she relishes the sting   10
Of others' agony; perhaps the cruel
Bride of a syphilitic or a fool.
These speculations sour in the sun.
I have no daughter. I desire none.

Questions

1. How does the last line of this sonnet affect the meaning of the poem?
2. "For My Daughter" was first published in 1940. What considerations might a potential American parent have felt at that time? Are these historical concerns mirrored in the poem?
3. Donald Justice has said that "Kees is one of the bitterest poets in history." Is bitterness the only attitude the speaker reveals in this poem?

THE PERSON IN THE POEM

The tone of a poem, we said, is like tone of voice in that both communicate feelings. Still, this comparison raises a question: when we read a poem, whose "voice" speaks to us?

"The poet's" is one possible answer; and in the case of many a poem that answer may be right. Reading Anne Bradstreet's "The Author to Her Book," we can be reasonably sure that the poet speaks of her very own book, and of her own experiences. In order to read a poem, we seldom need to read a poet's biography; but in truth there are certain poems whose full effect depends upon our knowing at least a fact or two of the poet's life. Here is one such poem.

Natasha Trethewey (b. 1966)

White Lies   2000

The lies I could tell,
when I was growing up
light-bright, near-white,
high-yellow, red-boned
in a black place,   5
were just white lies.

I could easily tell the white folks
that we lived uptown,
not in that pink and green
shanty-fied shotgun section   10
along the tracks. I could act
like my homemade dresses
came straight out the window
of Maison Blanche. I could even
keep quiet, quiet as kept,   15
like the time a white girl said
(squeezing my hand), *Now*
we have three of us in this class.

But I paid for it every time
Mama found out.   20
She laid her hands on me,
then washed out my mouth
with Ivory soap. *This*
is to purify, she said,
and cleanse your lying tongue.   25
Believing her, I swallowed suds
thinking they'd work
from the inside out.

Through its pattern of vivid color imagery, Trethewey's poem tells of a black child light enough to "pass for white" in a society that was still extremely race-sensitive. But knowing the author's family background gives us a deeper insight into the levels of meaning in the poem. Trethewey was born in Mississippi in 1966, at a time when her parents' interracial marriage was a criminal act in that state. On her birth certificate, her mother's race was given as "colored"; in the box intended to record the race of her father—who was white and had been born in Nova Scotia—appeared the word "Canadian" (although her parents divorced before she began grade school, she remained extremely close to both of them). Trethewey has said of her birth certificate: "Something is left out of the official record that way. The irony isn't lost on me. Even in documenting myself as a person there is a little fiction." "White Lies" succeeds admirably on its own, but these biographical details allow us to read it as an even more complex meditation on issues of racial definition and personal identity in America.

Persona

Most of us can tell the difference between a person we meet in life and a person we meet in a work of art—unlike the moviegoer in the Philippines who, watching a villain in an exciting film, pulled out a revolver and peppered the screen. And yet, in reading poems, we are liable to temptation.

When the poet says "I," we may want to assume that he or she is making a personal statement. But reflect: do all poems have to be personal? Here is a brief poem inscribed on the tombstone of an infant in Burial Hill Cemetery, Plymouth, Massachusetts:

> Since I have been so quickly done for,
> I wonder what I was begun for.

We do not know who wrote those lines, but it is clear that the poet was not a short-lived infant writing from personal experience. In other poems, the speaker is obviously a **persona**, or fictitious character: not the poet, but the poet's creation. As a grown man, William Blake, a skilled professional engraver, wrote a poem in the voice of a boy, an illiterate chimney sweeper. (The poem appears later in this chapter.)

Let's consider a poem spoken not by a poet, but by a persona—in this case a mysterious one. Edwin Arlington Robinson's "Luke Havergal" is a dramatic monologue, but the identity of the speaker is never clearly stated. In 1905, upon first reading the poem in Robinson's *The Children of the Night* (1897), President Theodore Roosevelt was so moved that he wrote an essay about the book that made the author famous. Roosevelt, however, admitted that he found the musically seductive poem difficult. "I am not sure I understand 'Luke Havergal,'" he wrote, "but I am entirely sure I like it." Possibly what most puzzled our twenty-sixth president was who was speaking in the poem. How much does Robinson let us know about the voice and the person it addresses?

Edwin Arlington Robinson (1869–1935)

Luke Havergal   1897

Go to the western gate, Luke Havergal,
There where the vines cling crimson on the wall,
And in the twilight wait for what will come.
The leaves will whisper there of her, and some,
Like flying words, will strike you as they fall;   5
But go, and if you listen she will call.
Go to the western gate, Luke Havergal—
Luke Havergal.

No, there is not a dawn in eastern skies
To rift the fiery night that's in your eyes;   10
But there, where western glooms are gathering,
The dark will end the dark, if anything:
God slays Himself with every leaf that flies,
And hell is more than half of paradise.
No, there is not a dawn in eastern skies—   15
In eastern skies.

Out of a grave I come to tell you this,
Out of a grave I come to quench the kiss
That flames upon your forehead with a glow
That blinds you to the way that you must go.   20
Yes, there is yet one way to where she is,
Bitter, but one that faith may never miss.
Out of a grave I come to tell you this—
To tell you this.

There is the western gate, Luke Havergal,   25
There are the crimson leaves upon the wall.
Go, for the winds are tearing them away,—
Nor think to riddle the dead words they say,
Nor any more to feel them as they fall;
But go, and if you trust her she will call.   30
There is the western gate, Luke Havergal—
Luke Havergal.

Questions

1. Who is the speaker of the poem? What specific details does the author reveal about the speaker?
2. What does the speaker ask Luke Havergal to do?
3. What do you understand "the western gate" to be?
4. Would you advise Luke Havergal to follow the speaker's advice? Why or why not?

No literary law decrees that the speaker in a poem even has to be human. Good poems have been uttered by clouds, pebbles, clocks, and cats. Here is a poem spoken by a hawk, a dramatic monologue that expresses the animal's thoughts and attitudes in a way consciously designed to emphasize how different its worldview is from a human perspective.

Ted Hughes (1930–1998)

Hawk Roosting   1960

I sit in the top of the wood, my eyes closed.
Inaction, no falsifying dream
Between my hooked head and hooked feet:
Or in sleep rehearse perfect kills and eat.

The convenience of the high trees!   5
The air's buoyancy and the sun's ray
Are of advantage to me;
And the earth's face upward for my inspection.

My feet are locked upon the rough bark.
It took the whole of Creation
To produce my foot, my each feather:
Now I hold Creation in my foot

Or fly up, and revolve it all slowly—
I kill where I please because it is all mine.
There is no sophistry in my body:
My manners are tearing off heads—

The allotment of death.
For the one path of my flight is direct
Through the bones of the living.
No arguments assert my right:

The sun is behind me.
Nothing has changed since I began.
My eye has permitted no change.
I am going to keep things like this.

Questions

1. Find three observations the hawk makes about its world that a human would probably not make. What do these remarks tell us about the bird's character?
2. In what ways does Ted Hughes create an unrealistic portrayal of the hawk's true mental powers? What statements in the poem would an actual hawk be unlikely to make? Do these passages add anything to the poem's impact? What would be lost if they were omitted?

Here is a poem in which the speaker is something even more remote from humanity, something we ordinarily assume to have no thoughts or attitudes at all, but whose monologue offers an even more pointed contrast with human values.

Suji Kwock Kim (b. 1968)

Monologue for an Onion   2003

I don't mean to make you cry.
I mean nothing, but this has not kept you
From peeling away my body, layer by layer,

The tears clouding your eyes as the table fills
With husks, cut flesh, all the debris of pursuit.
Poor deluded human: you seek my heart.

Hunt all you want. Beneath each skin of mine
Lies another skin: I am pure onion—pure union
Of outside and in, surface and secret core.

Look at you, chopping and weeping. Idiot.
Is this the way you go through life, your mind
A stopless knife, driven by your fantasy of truth,

Of lasting union—slashing away skin after skin
From things, ruin and tears your only signs
Of progress? Enough is enough.   15

You must not grieve that the world is glimpsed
Through veils. How else can it be seen?
How will you rip away the veil of the eye, the veil

That you are, you who want to grasp the heart
Of things, hungry to know where meaning   20
Lies. Taste what you hold in your hands: onion-juice,

Yellow peels, my stinging shreds. You are the one
In pieces. Whatever you meant to love, in meaning to
You changed yourself: you are not who you are,

Your soul cut moment to moment by a blade   25
Of fresh desire, the ground sown with abandoned skins.
And at your inmost circle, what? A core that is

Not one. Poor fool, you are divided at the heart,
Lost in its maze of chambers, blood, and love,
A heart that will one day beat you to death.   30

Questions

1. How would you characterize the speaker's tone in this poem? What attitudes and judgments lie behind that tone?
2. "I mean nothing" (line 2) might be seen as a play on two senses of *mean*—"intend" and "signify." Is the statement true in both senses?
3. Suppose someone said to you, "The whole point of the poem is that vegetables have rights and feelings too, and humanity is being rebuked for its arrogance and insensitivity toward other species." How would you argue against that view?
4. The speaker is obviously one tough onion, cutting humanity little or no slack. To what degree do you think the speaker represents the author's views? Explain your response.

A Classic Poem and Its Source

In a famous definition, William Wordsworth calls poetry "the spontaneous overflow of powerful feelings . . . recollected in tranquillity." But in the case of the following poem, Wordsworth's feelings weren't all his; they didn't just overflow spontaneously; and the process of tranquil recollection had to go on for years.

William Wordsworth (1770–1850)

I Wandered Lonely as a Cloud   1807

I wandered lonely as a cloud
    That floats on high o'er vales and hills,
When all at once I saw a crowd,
    A host, of golden daffodils,
Beside the lake, beneath the trees,   5
Fluttering and dancing in the breeze.

Continuous as the stars that shine
   And twinkle on the milky way,
They stretched in never-ending line
   Along the margin of a bay:
Ten thousand saw I at a glance,   10
Tossing their heads in sprightly dance.

The waves beside them danced; but they
   Out-did the sparkling waves in glee;
A poet could not but be gay,   15
   In such a jocund company;
I gazed—and gazed—but little thought
What wealth the show to me had brought:

For oft, when on my couch I lie
   In vacant or in pensive mood,   20
They flash upon that inward eye
   Which is the bliss of solitude;
And then my heart with pleasure fills,
And dances with the daffodils.

Between the first printing of the poem in 1807 and the version of 1815 given here, Wordsworth made several deliberate improvements. He changed *dancing* to *golden* in line 4, *Along* to *Beside* in line 5, *Ten thousand* to *Fluttering and* in line 6, *laughing* to *jocund* in line 16, and he added a whole stanza (the second). In fact, the writing of the poem was unspontaneous enough for Wordsworth, at a loss for lines 21–22, to take them from his wife, Mary. It is likely that the experience of daffodil-watching was not entirely his to begin with but was derived in part from the recollections his sister, Dorothy Wordsworth, had set down in her journal on April 15, 1802, two years before he first drafted his poem.

Dorothy Wordsworth (1771–1855)

Journal Entry   1802

When we were in the woods beyond Gowbarrow Park we saw a few daffodils close to the water-side. We fancied that the lake had floated the seeds ashore, and that the little colony had so sprung up. But as we went along there were more and yet more; and at last, under the boughs of the trees, we saw that there was a long belt of them along the shore, about the breadth of a country turnpike road. I never saw daffodils so beautiful. They grew among the mossy stones about and about them; some rested their heads upon these stones as on a pillow for weariness; and the rest tossed and reeled and danced, and seemed as if they verily laughed with the wind, that blew upon them over the Lake; they looked so gay, ever glancing, ever changing. This wind blew directly over the Lake to them. There was here and there a little knot, and a few stragglers a few yards higher up; but they were so few as not to disturb the simplicity, unity, and life of that one busy highway.

Notice that Wordsworth's poem echoes a few of his sister's observations. Weaving poetry out of their mutual memories, Wordsworth has offered the experience as if it were altogether his own, made himself lonely, and left Dorothy out. The point is not that Wordsworth is a liar or a plagiarist but that, like any other good poet, he has transformed ordinary life into art. A process of interpreting, shaping, and ordering had to intervene between the experience of looking at daffodils and the finished poem.

The Art of Imagination

We need not deny that a poet's experience can contribute to a poem or that the emotion in the poem can indeed be the poet's. Still, to write a good poem one has to do more than live and feel. Writing poetry takes skill and imagination—qualities that extensive travel and wide experience do not necessarily give. Emily Dickinson seldom strayed from her family's house and grounds in Amherst, Massachusetts; yet her rimed life studies of a snake, a bee, and a hummingbird contain more poetry than we find in any firsthand description (so far) of the surface of the moon.

James Stephens (1882–1950)

A Glass of Beer   1918

The lanky hank of a she in the inn over there
Nearly killed me for asking the loan of a glass of beer;
May the devil grip the whey-faced slut by the hair,
And beat bad manners out of her skin for a year.

That parboiled ape, with the toughest jaw you will see   5
On virtue's path, and a voice that would rasp the dead,
Came roaring and raging the minute she looked at me,
And threw me out of the house on the back of my head!

If I asked her master he'd give me a cask a day;
But she, with the beer at hand, not a gill° would arrange!   *quarter-pint*   10
May she marry a ghost and bear him a kitten, and may
The High King of Glory permit her to get the mange.

Questions

1. Whom do you take to be the speaker? Is it the poet? The speaker may be angry, but what is the tone of this poem?
2. Would you agree with a commentator who said, "To berate anyone in truly memorable language is practically a lost art in America"? How well does the speaker (an Irishman) succeed? Which of his epithets and curses strike you as particularly imaginative?

Anne Sexton (1928–1974)

Her Kind   1960

I have gone out, a possessed witch,
haunting the black air, braver at night;
dreaming evil, I have done my hitch
over the plain houses, light by light:
lonely thing, twelve-fingered, out of mind.   5
A woman like that is not a woman, quite.
I have been her kind.

I have found the warm caves in the woods,
filled them with skillets, carvings, shelves,
closets, silks, innumerable goods;   10
fixed the suppers for the worms and the elves:
whining, rearranging the disaligned.
A woman like that is misunderstood.
I have been her kind.

I have ridden in your cart, driver,   15
waved my nude arms at villages going by,
learning the last bright routes, survivor
where your flames still bite my thigh
and my ribs crack where your wheels wind.
A woman like that is not ashamed to die.   20
I have been her kind.

Questions

1. Who is the speaker of this poem? What do we know about her?
2. What does the speaker mean by ending each stanza with the statement, "I have been her kind?"
3. Who are the figures with whom the speaker identifies? What do these figures tell us about the speaker's state of mind?

William Carlos Williams (1883–1963)

The Red Wheelbarrow   1923

so much depends
upon

a red wheel
barrow

glazed with rain   5
water

beside the white
chickens

Experiment: Reading With and Without Biography

1. Write a paragraph summing up your initial reactions to "The Red Wheelbarrow."
2. Now write a second paragraph with the benefit of this snippet of biographical information: Inspiration for this poem apparently came to Dr. Williams as he was gazing from the window of a house where one of his patients, a small girl, lay suspended between life and death.[1] How does this information affect your reading of the poem?

---

[1]This account, from the director of the public library in Williams's native Rutherford, New Jersey, is given by Geri M. Rhodes in "The Paterson Metaphor in William Carlos Williams's *Paterson*," master's thesis, Tufts University, 1965.

IRONY

To see a distinction between the poet and the words of a fictitious character—between Robert Browning and "My Last Duchess"—is to be aware of **irony**: a manner of speaking that implies a discrepancy. If the mask says one thing and we sense that the writer is in fact saying something else, the writer has adopted an **ironic point of view**. No finer illustration exists in English than Jonathan Swift's "A Modest Proposal," an essay in which Swift speaks as an earnest, humorless citizen who sets forth his reasonable plan to aid the Irish poor. The plan is so monstrous no sane reader can assent to it: the poor are to sell their children as meat for the tables of their landlords. From behind his false face, Swift is actually recommending not cannibalism but love and Christian charity.

A poem is often made complicated and more interesting by another kind of irony. **Verbal irony** occurs whenever words say one thing but mean something else, usually the opposite. The word *love* means *hate* here: "I just *love* to stay home and do my hair on a Saturday night!"

Sarcasm

If verbal irony is conspicuously bitter, heavy-handed, and mocking, it is **sarcasm**: "Oh, he's the biggest spender in the world, all right!" (The sarcasm, if that statement were spoken, would be underscored by the speaker's tone of voice.) A famous instance of sarcasm occurs in Shakespeare's *Julius Caesar* in Mark Antony's oration over the body of the slain Caesar: "Brutus is an honorable man." Antony repeats this line until the enraged populace begins shouting exactly what he means to call Brutus and the other conspirators: traitors, villains, murderers. We had best be alert for irony on the printed page, for if we miss it, our interpretations of a poem may go wild.

Robert Creeley (1926–2005)

Oh No   1959

If you wander far enough
you will come to it
and when you get there
they will give you a place to sit
for yourself only, in a nice chair,   5
and all your friends will be there
with smiles on their faces
and they will likewise all have places.

This poem is rich in verbal irony. The title helps point out that between the speaker's words and attitude lie deep differences. In line 2, what is *it?* Old age? The wandering suggests a conventional metaphor: the journey of life. Is it literally a rest home for "senior citizens," or perhaps some naïve popular concept of heaven (such as we meet in comic strips: harps, angels with hoops for halos) in which the saved all sit around in a ring, smugly congratulating one another? We can't be sure, but the speaker's attitude toward this final sitting-place is definite. It is a place for the selfish, as we infer from the phrase *for yourself only*. And *smiles on their faces* may hint that the smiles are unchanging and forced. There is a difference between saying "They had smiles on their faces" and "They smiled": the latter suggests that the smiles came from within. The word *nice* is to be regarded with distrust. If we see through this speaker, as Creeley implies we can do, we realize that, while pretending to be sweet-talking us into a seat, actually he is revealing the horror of a little hell. And the title is the poet's reaction to it (or the speaker's unironic, straightforward one): "Oh no! Not *that!*"

Dramatic Irony

Dramatic irony, like verbal irony, contains an element of contrast, but it usually refers to a situation in a play wherein a character whose knowledge is limited says, does, or encounters something of greater significance than he or she knows. We, the spectators, realize the meaning of this speech or action, for the playwright has afforded us superior knowledge. In Sophocles' *King Oedipus,* when Oedipus vows to punish whoever has brought down a plague upon the city of Thebes, we know—as he does not—that the man he would punish is himself. The situation of Oedipus also contains **cosmic irony,** or **irony of fate:** some Fate with a grim sense of humor seems cruelly to trick a human being. Cosmic irony clearly exists in poems in which fate or the Fates are personified and seen as hostile, as in Thomas Hardy's "The Convergence of the Twain" (page 1047); and it may be said to occur also in Robinson's "Richard Cory" (page 754). Obviously it is a twist of fate for the most envied man in town to kill himself.

To sum up: the effect of irony depends on the reader's noticing some incongruity or discrepancy between two things. In *verbal irony,* there is a contrast between the speaker's words and meaning; in an *ironic point of view,* between the writer's attitude and what is spoken by a fictitious character; in *dramatic irony,* between the limited knowledge of a character and the fuller knowledge of the reader or spectator; in *cosmic irony,* between a character's position or aspiration and the treatment he or she receives at the hands of Fate. Although, in the work of an inept poet, irony can be crude and obvious sarcasm, it is invaluable to a poet of more complicated mind, who imagines more than one perspective.

W. H. Auden (1907–1973)

The Unknown Citizen   1940

    (To JS/07/M/378
    This Marble Monument Is Erected by the State)

He was found by the Bureau of Statistics to be
One against whom there was no official complaint,
And all the reports on his conduct agree
That, in the modern sense of an old-fashioned word, he was a saint,
For in everything he did he served the Greater Community.   5
Except for the War till the day he retired
He worked in a factory and never got fired,
But satisfied his employers, Fudge Motors Inc.
Yet he wasn't a scab or odd in his views,
For his Union reports that he paid his dues,   10
(Our report on his Union shows it was sound)
And our Social Psychology workers found

That he was popular with his mates and liked a drink.
The Press are convinced that he bought a paper every day
And that his reactions to advertisements were normal in every way. 15
Policies taken out in his name prove that he was fully insured,
And his Health-card shows he was once in hospital but left it cured.
Both Producers Research and High-Grade Living declare
He was fully sensible to the advantages of the Installment Plan
And had everything necessary to the Modern Man, 20
A phonograph, a radio, a car and a frigidaire.
Our researchers into Public Opinion are content
That he held the proper opinions for the time of year;
When there was peace, he was for peace; when there was war, he went.
He was married and added five children to the population, 25
Which our Eugenist says was the right number for a parent of his
    generation,
And our teachers report that he never interfered with their education.
Was he free? Was he happy? The question is absurd:
Had anything been wrong, we should certainly have heard.

Questions

1. Read the two-line epitaph at the beginning of the poem as carefully as you read what follows. How does the epitaph help establish the voice by which the rest of the poem is spoken?
2. Who is speaking?
3. What ironic discrepancies do you find between the speaker's attitude toward the subject and that of the poet himself? By what is the poet's attitude made clear?
4. In the phrase "The Unknown Soldier" (of which "The Unknown Citizen" reminds us), what does the word *unknown* mean? What does it mean in the title of Auden's poem?
5. What tendencies in our civilization does Auden satirize?
6. How would you expect the speaker to define a Modern Man, if a CD player, a radio, a car, and a refrigerator are "everything" a Modern Man needs?

Sharon Olds (b. 1942)

Rite of Passage

1983

As the guests arrive at my son's party
they gather in the living room—
short men, men in first grade
with smooth jaws and chins.
Hands in pockets, they stand around 5
jostling, jockeying for place, small fights
breaking out and calming. One says to another
How old are you? Six. I'm seven. So?
They eye each other, seeing themselves
tiny in the other's pupils. They clear their 10
throats a lot, a room of small bankers,
they fold their arms and frown. *I could beat you
up*, a seven says to a six,

the dark cake, round and heavy as a
turret, behind them on the table. My son,   15
freckles like specks of nutmeg on his cheeks,
chest narrow as the balsa keel of a
model boat, long hands
cool and thin as the day they guided him
out of me, speaks up as a host   20
for the sake of the group.
We could easily kill a two-year-old,
he says in his clear voice. The other
men agree, they clear their throats
like Generals, they relax and get down to   25
playing war, celebrating my son's life.

Questions

1. What is ironic about the way the speaker describes the first-grade boys at her son's birthday party?
2. What other irony does the author underscore in the last two lines?
3. Does this mother sentimentalize her own son by seeing him as better than the other little boys?

Rod Taylor (b. 1947)

Dakota: October, 1822: Hunkpapa Warrior   1972

New air has come around us.
It is cold enough to make us know we are different
from the things we touch. Before dark, we ride
along the high places or go deep in the long
grass at the edge of our people   5
and watch for enemies.
We are the strongest tribe of the Sioux. Buffalo
are plentiful, our women beautiful. Life
is good.
What bad thing can be done against us?   10

DAKOTA: OCTOBER, 1822: HUNKPAPA WARRIOR. The Hunkpapa are one of seven branches of the Lakota Sioux tribe.

Questions

1. How would you describe the speaker's tone—confident, boastful, serene?
2. What is ironic about this poem?
3. What kind of irony does the poem display?

Sarah N. Cleghorn (1876–1959)

The Golf Links   1917

The golf links lie so near the mill
  That almost every day
The laboring children can look out
  And see the men at play.

Questions

1. Is this brief poem satiric? Does it contain any verbal irony or is the poet making a matter-of-fact statement in words that mean just what they say?
2. What other kind of irony is present in the poem?
3. Sarah N. Cleghorn's poem dates from before the enactment of legislation against child labor. Is it still a good poem, or is it hopelessly dated?
4. Would you call this poem lyric, narrative, or didactic?

Edna St. Vincent Millay (1892–1950)

Second Fig   1920

Safe upon the solid rock the ugly houses stand:
Come and see my shining palace built upon the sand!

Question

Do you think the author is making fun of the speaker's attitude or agreeing with it?

Dorothy Parker (1893–1967)

Comment   1926

Oh, life is a glorious cycle of song,
A medley of extemporanea;
And love is a thing that can never go wrong;
And I am Marie of Roumania.

COMMENT. 4 *Marie of Roumania*: Princess Marie of Edinburgh (1875–1938), a granddaughter of Queen Victoria, was married in 1893 to Prince Ferdinand of Romania, who ascended the throne in 1914.

Questions

1. Is Marie of Roumania the speaker of the poem?
2. How serious is the poem's tone? Consider the rhythm and the rimes in lines 2 and 4.
3. In actuality, Queen Marie of Roumania had an unhappy life. Does this fact add another level of irony to the poem?

Bob Hicok (b. 1960)

Making it in poetry   2004

The young teller
at the credit union
asked why so many
small checks
from universities!   5
Because I write
poems I said. Why
haven't I heard
of you? Because
I write poems   10
I said.

Questions

1. Is the title of this poem ironic or not? Explain your answer.
2. Both of the teller's questions are answered the same way. Is there irony in that fact?
3. Do you find any significance in the description of the teller as "young"?

Exercise: Detecting Irony

Point out the kinds of irony that occur in the following poem.

Thomas Hardy (1840–1928)

The Workbox   1914

"See, here's the workbox, little wife,
   That I made of polished oak."
He was a joiner,° of village life;   *carpenter*
   She came of borough folk.

He holds the present up to her   5
   As with a smile she nears
And answers to the profferer,
   "'Twill last all my sewing years!"

"I warrant it will. And longer too.
   'Tis a scantling that I got   10
Off poor John Wayward's coffin, who
   Died of they knew not what.

"The shingled pattern that seems to cease
   Against your box's rim
Continues right on in the piece   15
   That's underground with him.

"And while I worked it made me think
   Of timber's varied doom:
One inch where people eat and drink,
   The next inch in a tomb.   20

"But why do you look so white, my dear,
   And turn aside your face?
You knew not that good lad, I fear,
   Though he came from your native place?"

"How could I know that good young man,   25
   Though he came from my native town,
When he must have left far earlier than
   I was a woman grown?"

"Ah, no. I should have understood!
   It shocked you that I gave   30
To you one end of a piece of wood
   Whose other is in a grave?"

"Don't, dear, despise my intellect,
    Mere accidental things
Of that sort never have effect   35
    On my imaginings."

Yet still her lips were limp and wan,
    Her face still held aside,
As if she had known not only John,
    But known of what he died.   40

FOR REVIEW AND FURTHER STUDY

William Blake (1757–1827)

The Chimney Sweeper   1789

When my mother died I was very young,
And my father sold me while yet my tongue
Could scarcely cry "'weep! 'weep! 'weep! 'weep!"
So your chimneys I sweep, and in soot I sleep.

There's little Tom Dacre, who cried when his head,   5
That curled like a lamb's back, was shaved: so I said
"Hush, Tom! never mind it, for when your head's bare
You know that the soot cannot spoil your white hair."

And so he was quiet, and that very night,
As Tom was a-sleeping, he had such a sight!   10
That thousands of sweepers, Dick, Joe, Ned, and Jack,
Were all of them locked up in coffins of black.

And by came an Angel who had a bright key,
And he opened the coffins and set them all free;
Then down a green plain leaping, laughing, they run,   15
And wash in a river, and shine in the sun.

Then naked and white, all their bags left behind,
They rise upon clouds and sport in the wind;
And the Angel told Tom, if he'd be a good boy,
He'd have God for his father, and never want° joy.   lack   20

And so Tom awoke; and we rose in the dark,
And got with our bags and our brushes to work.
Though the morning was cold, Tom was happy and warm;
So if all do their duty they need not fear harm.

Questions
1. What does Blake's poem reveal about conditions of life in the London of his day?
2. What does this poem have in common with "The Golf Links" (page 662)?
3. Sum up your impressions of the speaker's character. What does he say and do that displays it to us?

4. What pun do you find in line 3? Is its effect comic or serious?

5. In Tom Dacre's dream (lines 11–20), what wishes come true? Do you understand them to be the wishes of the chimney sweepers, of the poet, or of both?

6. In the last line, what is ironic in the speaker's assurance that the dutiful *need not fear harm*? What irony is there in his urging all to *do their duty*? (Who have failed in their duty to *him*?)

7. What is the tone of Blake's poem? Angry? Hopeful? Sorrowful? Compassionate? (Don't feel obliged to sum it up in a single word.)

Erich Fried (1921–1988)

The Measures Taken   1977

The lazy are slaughtered
the world grows industrious

The ugly are slaughtered
the world grows beautiful

The foolish are slaughtered   5
the world grows wise

The sick are slaughtered
the world grows healthy

The sad are slaughtered
the world grows merry   10

The old are slaughtered
the world grows young

The enemies are slaughtered
the world grows friendly

The wicked are slaughtered   15
the world grows good

—*Translated from the German by Michael Hamburger*

Questions

1. Can you relate this poem to a particular historical context? Explain.
2. Does it also have a more general application?
3. Do you think that the author shares the speaker's views? Why or why not?
4. What is especially ironic about the concluding couplet?

William Stafford (1914–1993)

At the Un-National Monument Along the Canadian Border   1977

This is the field where the battle did not happen,
where the unknown soldier did not die.
This is the field where grass joined hands,
where no monument stands,
and the only heroic thing is the sky.   5

Birds fly here without any sound,
unfolding their wings across the open.
No people killed—or were killed—on this ground
hallowed by neglect and an air so tame
that people celebrate it by forgetting its name.   10

Questions

1. What nonevent does this poem celebrate? What is the speaker's attitude toward it?
2. The speaker describes an empty field. What is odd about the way in which he describes it?
3. What words does the speaker appear to use ironically?

Exercise: Telling Tone

Here are two radically different poems on a similar subject. Try stating the theme of each poem in your own words. How is tone (the speaker's attitude) different in the two poems?

Richard Lovelace (1618–1658)

To Lucasta   1649

> *On Going to the Wars*

Tell me not, Sweet, I am unkind
   That from the nunnery
Of thy chaste breast and quiet mind,
   To war and arms I fly.

True, a new mistress now I chase,   5
   The first foe in the field;
And with a stronger faith embrace
   A sword, a horse, a shield.

Yet this inconstancy is such
   As you too shall adore;   10
I could not love thee, Dear, so much,
   Loved I not Honor more.

Wilfred Owen (1893–1918)

Dulce et Decorum Est   1920

Bent double, like old beggars under sacks,
Knock-kneed, coughing like hags, we cursed through sludge,
Till on the haunting flares we turned our backs
And towards our distant rest began to trudge.
Men marched asleep. Many had lost their boots   5
But limped on, blood-shod. All went lame; all blind;
Drunk with fatigue; deaf even to the hoots
Of tired, outstripped Five-Nines that dropped behind.

Gas! Gas! Quick, boys!—An ecstasy of fumbling,   10
Fitting the clumsy helmets just in time;
But someone still was yelling out and stumbling
And flound'ring like a man in fire or lime . . .
Dim, through the misty panes and thick green light,
As under a green sea, I saw him drowning.

In all my dreams, before my helpless sight,   15
He plunges at me, guttering, choking, drowning.

If in some smothering dreams you too could pace
Behind the wagon that we flung him in,
And watch the white eyes writhing in his face,
His hanging face, like a devil's sick of sin;   20
If you could hear, at every jolt, the blood
Come gargling from the froth-corrupted lungs,
Obscene as cancer, bitter as the cud
Of vile, incurable sores on innocent tongues,—
My friend, you would not tell with such high zest   25
To children ardent for some desperate glory,
The old Lie: Dulce et decorum est
Pro patria mori.

DULCE ET DECORUM EST. 8 *Five-Nines*: German howitzers often used to shoot poison gas shells.   17 *you too*: Some manuscript versions of this poem carry the dedication "To Jessie Pope" (a writer of patriotic verse) or "To a certain Poetess."   27–28 *Dulce et . . . mori*: a quotation from the Latin poet Horace, "It is sweet and fitting to die for one's country."

■ WRITING *effectively*

Wilfred Owen on Writing

Wilfred Owen was only twenty-one years old when World War I broke out in 1914. Twice wounded in battle, he was rapidly promoted and eventually became a company commander. The shocking violence of modern war summoned up his poetic genius, and in a two-year period he grew from a negligible minor poet into the most important English-language poet of World War I. Owen, however, did not live to see his talent recognized. He was killed one week before the end of the war; he was twenty-five years old. Owen published only four poems during his lifetime. Shortly before his death he drafted a few lines of prose for the preface of a book of poems.

Wilfred Owen

War Poetry (1917?)

This book is not about heroes. English poetry is not yet fit to speak of them.

Nor is it about deeds, or lands, nor anything about glory, honour, might, majesty, dominion, or power, except War.

Above all I am not concerned with Poetry.

My subject is War, and the pity of War.

The Poetry is in the pity.

Yet these elegies are to this generation in no sense consolatory. They may be to the next. All a poet can do today is warn. That is why the true Poets must be truthful.

From *Collected Poems*

THINKING ABOUT TONE

To understand the tone of a poem, we need to listen to the words, as we might listen to an actual conversation. The key is to hear not only *what* is being said but also *how* it is being said. Does the speaker sound noticeably surprised, angry, nostalgic, or tender? Begin with an obvious but often overlooked question: who is speaking? Don't assume that every poem is spoken by its author.

- **Look for the ways—large and small—in which the speaker reveals aspects of his or her character.** Attitudes may be revealed directly or indirectly. Often, emotions must be intuited. The details a poet chooses to convey can reveal much about a speaker's stance toward his or her subject matter.

- **Consider also how the speaker addresses the listener.** Again, listen to the sound of the poem as you would listen to the sound of someone's voice—is it shrill, or soothing, or sarcastic?

- **Look for an obvious difference between the speaker's attitude and your own honest reaction toward what is happening in the poem.** If the gap between the two responses is wide, the poem may be taken as ironic.

- **Remember that many poets strive toward understatement, writing matter-of-factly about matters of intense sorrow, horror, or joy.** In poems, as in conversation, understatement can be a powerful tool, more convincing—and often more moving—than hyperbole.

CHECKLIST: Writing About Tone

- ☐ Who is speaking the poem?
- ☐ Is the narrator's voice close to the poet's or is it the voice of a fictional or historical person?
- ☐ How does the speaker address the listener?
- ☐ Does the poem directly reveal an emotion or attitude?
- ☐ Does it indirectly reveal any attitudes or emotions?
- ☐ Does your reaction to what is happening in the poem differ widely from that of the speaker? If so, what does that difference suggest? Is the poem in some way ironic?
- ☐ What adjectives would best describe the poem's tone?

WRITING ASSIGNMENT ON TONE

Choose a poem from this chapter, and analyze its speaker's attitude toward the poem's main subject. Examine the author's choice of specific words and images to create the particular tone used to convey the speaker's attitudes. (Possible subjects include Wilfred Owen's attitude toward war in "Dulce et Decorum Est," the tone and imagery of Weldon Kees's "For My Daughter," Ted Hughes's view of the workings of nature in "Hawk Roosting," and Anne Bradstreet's attitude toward her own poetry in "The Author to Her Book.")

Here is an example of an essay written for this assignment by Kim Larsen, a student of Karen Locke's at Lane Community College in Eugene, Oregon.

SAMPLE STUDENT PAPER

Larsen 1

Kim Larsen

Professor Locke

English 110

21 November 2009

Title gives sense of the paper's focus

Word Choice, Tone, and Point of View in Roethke's

"My Papa's Waltz"

Name of author and work

Some readers may find Theodore Roethke's "My Papa's Waltz" a reminiscence of a happy childhood scene. I believe, however, that the poem depicts a more painful and complicated series of emotions. By examining the choice of words that Roethke uses to convey the tone of his scene, I will demonstrate that beneath the seemingly comic situation of the poem is a darker

Thesis sentence

story. The true point of view of "My Papa's Waltz" is that of a resentful adult reliving his fear of a domineering parent.

Topic sentence on title's significance

The first clue that the dance may not have been a mutually enjoyable experience is in the title itself. The author did not title the poem "Our Waltz" or "Waltzing with My Papa," either of which would set an initial tone for readers to expect a shared, loving sentiment. It does not even have a neutral title, such as "The Waltz." The title specifically implies that the waltz was exclusively the father's. Since a waltz normally involves two people, it can be reasoned that the father dances his waltz without regard for his young partner.

Larsen 2

Examining each stanza of the poem offers numerous examples where the choice of words sustains the tone implied in the title. The first line, "The whiskey on your breath," conjures up an olfactory image that most would find unpleasant. The small boy finds it so overpowering he is made "dizzy." This stanza contains the only simile in the poem,"I hung on like death" (3), which creates a ghastly and stark visual image. There are many choices of similes to portray hanging on: a vine, an infant, an animal cub, all of which would have illustrated a lighthearted romp. The choice of "death" was purposefully used to convey an intended image. The first stanza ends by stating the "waltzing was not easy." The definitions of *easy*, as found in *Merriam-Webster's Collegiate Dictionary*, include "free from pain, annoyance or anxiety," and "not difficult to endure or undergo" ("Easy"). Obviously the speaker did not find those qualities in the waltz.

Further evidence of this harsh and oppressive scene is brought to mind by reckless disregard for "the pans / Slid from the kitchen shelf" (5–6), which the reader can almost hear crashing on the floor in loud cacophony, and the "mother's countenance," which "[c]ould not unfrown itself" (7, 8). If this were only a silly, playful romp between father and son, even a stern, fastidious mother might be expected to at least make an unsuccessful attempt to suppress a grin. Instead, the reader gets a visual image of a silent, unhappy woman, afraid, probably because of past experience, to interfere in the domestic destruction around her. Once more, this detail suggests a domineering father who controls the family.

The third stanza relates the father's "battered" hand holding the boy's wrist. The tactile image of holding a wrist suggests dragging or forcing an unwilling person, not holding hands as would be expected with a mutual dance partner. Further disregard for the son's feelings is displayed by the lines "At every step you missed / My right ear scraped a buckle" (11–12). In each missed step, probably due to his drunkenness, the father causes the boy physical pain.

The tone continues in the final stanza as the speaker recalls "You beat time on my head / With a palm caked hard by dirt" (13–14). The visual and tactile image of a dirt-hardened hand beating on a child's head as if it were a drum is distinctly unpleasant. The last lines, "Then waltzed me off to bed / Still clinging to your shirt" (15–16), are the most ambiguous in the poem. It can be reasoned, as X. J. Kennedy and Dana Gioia do, that the lines suggest

Topic sentence on word choice

Paragraph focuses on first stanza

Textual evidence

Key word defined

Paragraph focuses on word choice in second stanza

Textual evidence

Discusses third stanza

Discusses final stanza

Larsen 3

Quotation from secondary source

"the boy is *still clinging* to his father with persistent if also complicated love" (646). On the other hand, if one notices the earlier dark images, the conclusion could describe a boy clinging out of fear, the physical fear of being dropped by one who is drunk and the emotional fear of not being loved and nurtured as a child needs to be by his father.

Transitional phrase

It can also be argued that the poem's rollicking rhythm contributes to a sense of fun, and in truth, the poem can be read in that fashion. On the other hand, it can be read in such a way as to de-emphasize the rhythm, as the author himself does in his recording of "My Papa's Waltz"

Topic sentence on ironic effect of meter

(Roethke, *Reads*). The joyful, rollicking rhythm can be seen as ironic. By reminding readers of a waltzing tempo, it is highlighting the discrepancy between what a waltz should be and the bleak, frightening picture painted in the words.

Conclusion

While "My Papa's Waltz" can be read as a roughhouse comedy, by examining Roethke's title and choice of words closely to interpret the

Restatement of thesis, synthesizing all that has been said in the essay's body.

meaning of their images and sounds, it is also plausible to hear an entirely different tone. I believe "My Papa's Waltz" employs the voice of an embittered adult remembering a harsh scene in which both he and his mother were powerless in the presence of a drunk and domineering father.

Larsen 4

Works Cited

"Easy." *Merriam-Webster's Collegiate Dictionary*. 11th ed. 2003. Print.

Kennedy, X. J., and Dana Gioia, eds. *Literature: An Introduction to Fiction, Poetry, Drama, and Writing*. 11th ed. New York: Longman, 2010. 646. Print.

Roethke, Theodore. "My Papa's Waltz." *Literature: An Introduction to Fiction, Poetry, Drama, and Writing*. Ed. X. J. Kennedy and Dana Gioia. 11th ed. New York: Longman, 2010. 645. Print.

---. *Theodore Roethke Reads His Poetry*. Audio Forum, 2006. CD.

MORE TOPICS FOR WRITING

1. Describe the tone of W. H. Auden's "The Unknown Citizen," quoting as necessary to back up your argument. How does the poem's tone contribute to its meaning?
2. Write an analysis of Thomas Hardy's "The Workbox," focusing on what the poem leaves unsaid.
3. In an essay of 250 to 500 words, compare and contrast the tone of two poems on a similar subject. You might examine how Walt Whitman and Emily Dickinson treat the subject of locomotives, or how Richard Lovelace and Wilfred Owen write about war. (For advice on writing about poetry by the method of comparison and contrast, see the chapter "Writing About a Poem.")
4. Write a poem of your own in which the speaker's attitude toward the subject is revealed not by what the poem says but by the tone in which it is said. William Blake's "The Chimney Sweeper," W. H. Auden's "The Unknown Citizen," and Sharon Olds's "Rite of Passage" provide some good models.
5. Look closely at any poem in this chapter. Going through it line by line, make a list of the sensory details the poem provides. Now write briefly about how those details combine to create a particular tone. Two choices are William Stafford's "At the Un-National Monument Along the Canadian Border" and Sharon Olds's "Rite of Passage."

▶ TERMS FOR *review*

Tone ▶ The mood or manner of expression in a literary work, which conveys an attitude toward the work's subject, which may be playful, sarcastic, ironic, sad, solemn, or any other possible attitude. Tone helps to establish the reader's relationship to the characters or ideas presented in the work.

Satiric poetry ▶ Poetry that blends criticism with humor to convey a message, usually through the use of irony and a tone of detached amusement, withering contempt, and implied superiority.

Persona ▶ Latin for "mask." A fictitious character created by an author to be the speaker of a literary work.

Types of Irony

Irony ▶ In language, a discrepancy between what is said and what is meant. In life, a discrepancy between what is expected and what occurs.

Verbal irony ▶ A mode of expression in which the speaker or writer says the opposite of what is really meant, such as saying "Great story!" in response to a boring, pointless anecdote.

Sarcasm ▶ A style of bitter irony intended to hurt or mock its target.

Dramatic irony ▶ A situation in which the larger implications of character's words, actions, or situation are unrealized by that character but seen by the author and the reader or audience.

Cosmic irony ▶ The contrast between a character's position or aspiration and the treatment he or she receives at the hands of a seemingly hostile fate; also called **irony of fate**.

15

WORDS

We all write poems; it is simply that poets are
the ones who write in words.

—JOHN FOWLES

LITERAL MEANING: WHAT A POEM SAYS FIRST

Although successful as a painter, Edgar Degas found poetry discouragingly hard to
write. To his friend, the poet Stéphane Mallarmé, he complained, "What a business!
My whole day gone on a blasted sonnet, without getting an inch further . . . and it isn't
ideas I'm short of . . . I'm full of them, I've got too many . . ."

"But Degas," said Mallarmé, "you can't make a poem with ideas—you make it
with *words!*"

Like the celebrated painter, some people assume that all it takes to make a poem
is a bright idea. Poems state ideas, to be sure, and sometimes the ideas are invaluable;
and yet the most impressive idea in the world will not make a poem, unless its words
are selected and arranged with loving art. Some poets take great pains to find the
right word. Unable to fill a two-syllable gap in an unfinished line that went, "The
seal's wide＿＿gaze toward Paradise," Hart Crane paged through an unabridged dictionary. When he reached S, he found the object of his quest in *spindrift:* "spray
skimmed from the sea by a strong wind." The word is exact and memorable.

In reading a poem, some people assume that its words can be skipped over
rapidly, and they try to leap at once to the poem's general theme. It is as if they fear
being thought clods unless they can find huge ideas in the poem (whether or not
there are any). Such readers often ignore the literal meanings of words: the ordinary,
matter-of-fact sense to be found in a dictionary. (As you will see in the next chapter,
"Saying and Suggesting," words possess not only dictionary meanings—denotations—
but also many associations and suggestions—connotations.) Consider the following
poem and see what you make of it.

 William Carlos Williams (1883–1963)

This Is Just to Say   1934

I have eaten
the plums
that were in
the icebox

and which 5
you were probably
saving
for breakfast

Forgive me
they were delicious 10
so sweet
and so cold

Some readers distrust a poem so simple and candid. They think, "What's wrong with me? There has to be more to it than this!" But poems seldom are puzzles in need of solutions. We can begin by accepting the poet's statements, without suspecting the poet of trying to hoodwink us. On later reflection, of course, we might possibly decide that the poet is playfully teasing or being ironic; but Williams gives us no reason to think that. There seems no need to look beyond the literal sense of his words, no profit in speculating that the plums symbolize worldly joys and that the icebox stands for the universe. Clearly, a reader who held such a grand theory would have overlooked (in eagerness to find a significant idea) the plain truth that the poet makes clear to us: that ice-cold plums are a joy to taste.

To be sure, Williams's small poem is simpler than most poems are; and yet in reading any poem, no matter how complicated, you will do well to reach slowly and reluctantly for a theory to explain it by. To find the general theme of a poem, you first need to pay attention to its words. Recall Yeats's "The Lake Isle of Innisfree" (page 633), a poem that makes a statement—crudely summed up, "I yearn to leave the city and retreat to a place of ideal peace and happiness." And yet before we can realize this theme, we have to notice details: nine bean rows, a glade loud with bees, "lake water lapping with low sounds by the shore," the gray of a pavement. These details and not some abstract remark make clear what the poem is saying: that the city is drab, while the island hideaway is sublimely beautiful.

Poets often strive for words that point to physical details and solid objects. They may do so even when speaking of an abstract idea:

Beauty is but a flower
Which wrinkles will devour;
Brightness falls from the air,
Queens have died young and fair,
Dust hath closed Helen's eye.
I am sick, I must die:
    Lord, have mercy on us!

In these lines by Thomas Nashe, the abstraction *beauty* has grown petals that shrivel. Brightness may be a general name for light, but Nashe succeeds in giving it the weight of a falling body.

DICTION

If a poem says *daffodils* instead of *plant life*, *diaper years* instead of *infancy*, we call its **diction**, or choice of words, **concrete** rather than **abstract**. Concrete words refer to what we can immediately perceive with our senses: *dog, actor, chemical*, or particular individuals who belong to those general classes: *Bonzo the fox terrier, Clint Eastwood*, *hydrogen sulfate*. Abstract words express ideas or concepts: *love, time, truth*. In abstracting, we leave out some characteristics found in each individual, and instead observe a quality common to many. The word *beauty*, for instance, denotes what may be observed in numerous persons, places, and things.

Ezra Pound gave a famous piece of advice to his fellow poets: "Go in fear of abstractions." This is not to say that a poet cannot employ abstract words, nor that all poems have to be about physical things. Much of T. S. Eliot's *Four Quartets* is concerned with time, eternity, history, language, reality, and other things that cannot be physically handled. But Eliot, however high he may soar for a larger view, keeps returning to earth. He makes us aware of *things*.

Marianne Moore (1887–1972)

Silence   1924

My father used to say,
"Superior people never make long visits,
have to be shown Longfellow's grave
or the glass flowers at Harvard.
Self-reliant like the cat—   5
that takes its prey to privacy,
the mouse's limp tail hanging like a shoelace from its mouth—
they sometimes enjoy solitude,
and can be robbed of speech
by speech which has delighted them.   10
The deepest feeling always shows itself in silence;
not in silence, but restraint."
Nor was he insincere in saying, "Make my house your inn."
Inns are not residences.

Questions

1. Almost all of "Silence" consists of quotation. What are some possible reasons why the speaker prefers using another person's words?
2. What are the words the father uses to describe people he admires?
3. The poem makes an important distinction between two similar words (lines 13–14). Explain the distinction Moore implies.
4. Why is "Silence" an appropriate title for this poem?

Robert Graves (1895–1985)

Down, Wanton, Down!   1933

Down, wanton, down! Have you no shame
That at the whisper of Love's name,
Or Beauty's, presto! up you raise
Your angry head and stand at gaze?

Poor bombard-captain, sworn to reach 5
The ravelin and effect a breach—
Indifferent what you storm or why,
So be that in the breach you die!

Love may be blind, but Love at least
Knows what is man and what mere beast; 10
Or Beauty wayward, but requires
More delicacy from her squires.

Tell me, my witless, whose one boast
Could be your staunchness at the post,
When were you made a man of parts 15
To think fine and profess the arts?

Will many-gifted Beauty come
Bowing to your bald rule of thumb,
Or Love swear loyalty to your crown?
Be gone, have done! Down, wanton, down! 20

DOWN, WANTON, DOWN! 5 *bombard-captain:* officer in charge of a bombard, an early type of cannon that hurled stones. 6 *ravelin:* fortification with two faces that meet in a protruding angle. *effect a breach:* break an opening through (a fortification). 15 *man of parts:* man of talent or ability.

Questions

1. How do you define a *wanton?*
2. What wanton does the poet address?
3. Explain the comparison drawn in the second stanza.
4. In line 14, how many meanings do you find in *staunchness at the post?*
5. Explain any other puns you find in lines 15–19.
6. Do you take this to be a cynical poem making fun of Love and Beauty, or is Graves making fun of stupid, animal lust?

John Donne (1572–1631)

Batter my heart, three-personed God, for You

(about 1610)

Batter my heart, three-personed God, for You
As yet but knock, breathe, shine, and seek to mend.
That I may rise and stand, o'erthrow me, and bend
Your force to break, blow, burn, and make me new.
I, like an usurped town to another due, 5
Labor to admit You, but Oh! to no end.
Reason, Your viceroy in me, me should defend,
But is captived, and proves weak or untrue.
Yet dearly I love You, and would be lovèd fain,
But am betrothed unto Your enemy; 10

Divorce me, untie or break that knot again;
Take me to You, imprison me, for I,
Except You enthrall me, never shall be free,
Nor ever chaste, except You ravish me.

Questions

1. In the last line of this sonnet, to what does Donne compare the onslaught of God's love? Do you think the poem is weakened by the poet's comparing a spiritual experience to something so grossly carnal? Discuss.

2. Explain the seeming contradiction in the last line: in what sense can a ravished person be *chaste*? Explain the seeming contradictions in lines 3–4 and 12–13: how can a person thrown down and destroyed be enabled to *rise and stand*; an imprisoned person be *free*?

3. In lines 5–6 the speaker compares himself to a *usurped town* trying to throw off its conqueror by admitting an army of liberation. Who is the "usurper" in this comparison?

4. Explain the comparison of *Reason* to a *viceroy* (lines 7–8).

5. Sum up in your own words the message of Donne's poem. In stating its theme, did you have to read the poem for literal meanings, figurative comparisons, or both?

THE VALUE OF A DICTIONARY

Use the dictionary. It's better than the critics.

—ELIZABETH BISHOP TO HER STUDENTS

If a poet troubles to seek out the best words available, the least we can do is to find out what the words mean. The dictionary is a firm ally in reading poems; if the poems are more than a century old, it is indispensable. Meanings change. When the Elizabethan poet George Gascoigne wrote, "O Abraham's brats, O brood of blessed seed," the word *brats* implied neither irritation nor contempt. When in the seventeenth century Andrew Marvell imagined two lovers' "vegetable love," he referred to a vegetative or growing love, not one resembling a lettuce. And when Queen Anne, in a famous anecdote, called the just-completed Saint Paul's Cathedral "awful, artificial, and amusing," its architect, Sir Christopher Wren, was overwhelmed with joy and gratitude, for what she had told him was that it was awe-inspiring, artful, and stimulating to contemplate (or *muse* upon).

In reading poetry, there is nothing to be done about the inevitable tendency of language to change except to watch out for it. If you suspect that a word has shifted in meaning over the years, most standard desk dictionaries will be helpful, an unabridged dictionary more helpful still, and most helpful of all the *Oxford English Dictionary* (OED), which gives, for each definition, successive examples of the word's written use through the past thousand years. You need not feel a grim obligation to keep interrupting a poem in order to rummage in the dictionary; but if the poem is worth reading very closely, you may wish any aid you can find.

"Every word which is used to express a moral or intellectual fact," said Emerson in his study *Nature*, "if traced to its root, is found to be borrowed from some material appearance. *Right* means straight; *wrong* means twisted. *Spirit* primarily means wind; *transgression*, the crossing of a line; *supercilious*, the raising of an eyebrow." Browse in a dictionary and you will discover such original concretenesses. These are revealed in your dictionary's etymologies, or brief notes on the derivation of words, given in most dictionaries near the beginning of an entry on a word; in some dictionaries, at the end of the entry. Look up *squirrel*, for instance, and you will find it comes from two Greek words meaning "shadow-tail." For another example of a common word that originally contained a poetic metaphor, look up the origin of *daisy*.

Experiment: Use the Dictionary to Read Longfellow's "Aftermath"

The following short poem seems very simple and straightforward, but much of its total effect depends on the reader knowing the literal meanings of several words. The most crucial word is in the title—*aftermath*. Most readers today will assume that they know what that word means, but in this poem Longfellow uses it in both its current sense and its original, more literal meaning. Read the poem twice—first without a dictionary, then a second time after looking up the meanings of *aftermath*, *fledged*, *rowen*, and *mead*. How does knowing the exact meanings of these words add to both your literal and critical reading of the poem?

Henry Wadsworth Longfellow (1807–1882)

Aftermath   1873

When the summer fields are mown,
When the birds are fledged and flown,
   And the dry leaves strew the path;
With the falling of the snow,
With the cawing of the crow,   5
Once again the fields we mow
   And gather in the aftermath.

Not the sweet, new grass with flowers
In this harvesting of ours;
   Not the upland clover bloom;   10
But the rowen mixed with weeds,
Tangled tufts from marsh and meads,
Where the poppy drops its seeds
   In the silence and the gloom.

Questions
1. How do the etymology and meaning of *aftermath* help explain this poem? (Look the word up in your dictionary.)
2. What is the meaning of *fledged* (line 2) and *rowen* (line 11)?
3. Once you understand the literal meaning of the poem, do you think that Longfellow intended any further significance to it?

Kay Ryan (b. 1945)

Chemise   2000

What would the self
disrobed look like,
the form undraped?
There is a flimsy cloth

we can't take off—   5
some last chemise
we can't escape—
a hope more intimate
than paint
to please.   10

Questions

1. What does *chemise* mean? Is it a more effective word here than *slip* would be?
2. What does the image of a chemise suggest about our true selves?
3. What is the meaning of *paint* in the context of the poem?
4. Can the last three lines be read in more than one way? Can they have both meanings at once?

Allusion

An **allusion** is an indirect reference to any person, place, or thing—fictitious, historical, or actual. Sometimes, to understand an allusion in a poem, we have to find out something we didn't know before. But usually the poet asks of us only common knowledge. When, in his poem "To Helen," Edgar Allan Poe refers to "the glory that was Greece / And the grandeur that was Rome," he assumes that we have heard of those places. He also expects that we will understand his allusion to the cultural achievements of those ancient nations and perhaps even catch the subtle contrast between those two similar words *glory* and *grandeur*, with its suggestion that, for all its merits, Roman civilization was also more pompous than Greek.

Allusions not only enrich the meaning of a poem, they also save space. In "The Love Song of J. Alfred Prufrock" (page 995), T. S. Eliot, by giving a brief introductory quotation from the speech of a damned soul in Dante's *Inferno,* is able to suggest that his poem will be the confession of a soul in torment, who sees no chance of escape and who feels the need to confide in someone but trusts that his secrets will be kept safe.

Often in reading a poem, you will meet a name you don't recognize, on which the meaning of a line (or perhaps a whole poem) seems to depend. In this book, most such unfamiliar references and allusions are glossed or footnoted, but when you venture out on your own in reading poems, you may find yourself needlessly perplexed unless you look up such names, the way you look up any other words. Unless the name is one that the poet made up, you will probably find it in one of the larger desk dictionaries, such as *Merriam-Webster's Collegiate Dictionary* or the *American Heritage Dictionary.* If you don't solve your problem there, try an online search of the word or phrase as some allusions are quotations from other poems.

Exercise: Catching Allusions

From your knowledge, supplemented by a dictionary or other reference work if need be, explain the allusions in the following poems.

J. V. Cunningham (1911–1985)

Friend, on this scaffold Thomas More lies dead   1960

Friend, on this scaffold Thomas More lies dead
Who would not cut the Body from the Head.

Carl Sandburg (1878–1967)

Grass   1918

Pile the bodies high at Austerlitz and Waterloo.
Shovel them under and let me work—
　　I am the grass; I cover all.

And pile them high at Gettsyburg
And pile them high at Ypres and Verdun.   5
Shovel them under and let me work.

Two years, ten years, and passengers ask the conductor:
　　What place is this?
　　Where are we now?

I am the grass.   10
Let me work.

Questions

1. What do the five proper nouns in Sandburg's poem have in common?
2. How much does the reader need to understand about the allusions in "Grass" to appreciate their importance to the literal meaning of the poem?

Anonymous

Dog Haiku   2001

Today I sniffed
Many dog behinds—I celebrate
By kissing your face.

　　　　*

I sound the alarm!
Garbage man—come to kill us all—   5
Look! Look! Look! Look! Look!

　　　　*

How do I love thee?
The ways are numberless as
My hairs on the rug.

Questions

1. Who is the "I" in the poem? Who is the "you"?
2. Do you recognize the allusion in the lines 7–9?
3. What elements create the humorous effect of the poem?

WORD CHOICE AND WORD ORDER

Even if Samuel Johnson's famous *Dictionary* of 1755 had been as thick as Webster's unabridged, an eighteenth-century poet searching through it for words to use would have had a narrower choice. For in English literature of the neoclassical period or

Augustan age—that period from about 1660 into the late eighteenth century—many poets subscribed to a belief in **poetic diction**: "A system of words," said Dr. Johnson, "refined from the grossness of domestic use." The system admitted into a serious poem only certain words and subjects, excluding others as violations of **decorum** (propriety). Accordingly, such common words as *rat, cheese, big, sneeze,* and *elbow,* although admissible to satire, were thought inconsistent with the loftiness of tragedy, epic, ode, and elegy. Dr. Johnson's biographer, James Boswell, tells how a poet writing an epic reconsidered the word "rats" and instead wrote "the whiskered vermin race." Johnson himself objected to Lady Macbeth's allusion to her "keen knife," saying that "we do not immediately conceive that any crime of importance is to be committed with a knife; or who does not, at last, from the long habit of connecting a knife with sordid offices, feel aversion rather than terror?" Probably Johnson was here the victim of his age, and Shakespeare was right, but Johnson was also right in one of his assumptions: there are inappropriate words as well as appropriate ones.

Anglo-Saxon versus Latinate Diction

When Wordsworth, in his Preface to *Lyrical Ballads*, asserted that "the language really spoken by men," especially by humble rustics, is plainer and more emphatic, and conveys "elementary feelings . . . in a state of greater simplicity," he was, in effect, advocating a new poetic diction. Wordsworth's ideas invited freshness into English poetry and, by admitting words that neoclassical poets would have called "low" ("His poor old *ankles* swell"), helped rid poets of the fear of being thought foolish for mentioning a commonplace.

This theory of the superiority of rural diction was, as Coleridge pointed out, hard to adhere to, and, in practice, Wordsworth was occasionally to write a language as Latinate and citified as these lines on yew trees:

> Huge trunks!—and each particular trunk a growth
> Of intertwisted fibers serpentine
> Up-coiling, and inveterately convolved . . .

Language so Latinate sounds pedantic to us, especially the phrase *inveterately convolved*. In fact, some poets, notably Gerard Manley Hopkins, have subscribed to the view that English words derived from Anglo-Saxon (Old English) have more force and flavor than their Latin equivalents. *Kingly,* one may feel, has more power than *regal.* One argument for this view is that so many words of Old English origin—*man, wife, child, house, eat, drink, sleep*—are basic to our living speech. Yet Latinate diction is not necessarily elevated. We use Latinate words everyday, such as *station, office, order,* and *human.* None of these terms seem "inveterately convolved." Word choice is a subtle and flexible art.

Levels of Diction

When E. E. Cummings begins a poem, "mr youse needn't be so spry / concernin questions arty," we recognize another kind of diction available to poetry: **vulgate** (speech not much affected by schooling). Handbooks of grammar sometimes distinguish various **levels of diction**. A sort of ladder is imagined, on whose rungs words, phrases, and sentences may be ranked in an ascending order of formality, from the curses of an illiterate thug to the commencement-day address of a doctor of divinity. These levels range from vulgate through **colloquial** (the casual conversation or informal writing of literate people) and **general English** (most literate speech and writing, more studied than colloquial but not pretentious), up to **formal English** (the impersonal language of educated persons, usually only written, possibly spoken on dignified occasions). Recently, however, lexicographers have been shunning such labels. The designation *colloquial* was expelled from *Webster's Third New International Dictionary* on the grounds that "it is impossible to know whether a word out of context is colloquial or not" and that the diction of Americans nowadays is more fluid than the labels suggest. Aware that we are being unscientific, we may find the labels useful. They may help roughly to describe what happens when, as in the following poem, a poet shifts from one level of usage to another.

Robert Herrick (1591–1674)

Upon Julia's Clothes   1648

Whenas in silks my Julia goes,
Then, then, methinks, how sweetly flows
That liquefaction of her clothes.

Next, when I cast mine eyes and see
That brave vibration each way free,   5
O how that glittering taketh me!

Even in so short a poem as "Upon Julia's Clothes," we see how a sudden shift in the level of diction can produce a surprising and memorable effect. One word in each stanza—*liquefaction* in the first, *vibration* in the second—stands out from the standard, but not extravagant, language that surrounds it. Try to imagine the entire poem being written in such formal English, in mostly unfamiliar words of several syllables each: the result, in all likelihood, would be merely an oddity, and a turgid one at that. But by using such terms sparingly, Herrick allows them to take on a greater strength and significance through their contrast with the words that surround them. It is *liquefaction* in particular that strikes the reader: like a great catch by an outfielder, it impresses both for its appropriateness in the situation and for its sheer beauty as a demonstration of superior skill. Once we have read the poem, we realize that the effect would be severely compromised, if not ruined, by the substitution of any other word in its place.

Dialect

At present, most poetry in English avoids elaborate literary expressions such as "fleecy care" in favor of more colloquial language. In many English-speaking areas, such as Scotland, there has even been a movement to write poems in regional dialects. (A **dialect** is a particular variety of language spoken by an identifiable regional group or social class of persons.) Dialect poets frequently try to capture the freshness and authenticity of the language spoken in their immediate locale.

Most Americans know at least part of one Scottish dialect poem by heart— "Auld Lang Syne," the song commonly sung as the clock strikes twelve on New Year's Eve. Although Robert Burns wrote most of the song's stanzas, the poet claimed to have copied down the famous opening stanza from an old man he heard singing. *Auld* is the Scots word for "old"; *lang syne* means "long since." How different the lines would seem if they were standard English.

Robert Burns (1759–1796)

from Auld Lang Syne   1788

Should auld acquaintance be forgot
and never brought to mind?
Should auld acquaintance be forgot,
and auld lang syne?

> For auld lang syne, my dear,   5
> for auld lang syne,
> we'll tak a cup o' kindness yet,
> for auld lang syne.

Sentence Structure

Not only the poet's choice of words makes a poem seem more formal, or less, but also
the way the words are arranged into sentences. Compare these lines

> Jack and Jill went up the hill
> To fetch a pail of water.
> Jack fell down and broke his crown
> And Jill came tumbling after.

with Milton's account of a more significant downfall:

> Earth trembled from her entrails, as again
> In pangs, and Nature gave a second groan;
> Sky loured and, muttering thunder, some sad drops
> Wept at completing of the mortal sin
> Original; while Adam took no thought,
> Eating his fill, nor Eve to iterate
> Her former trespass feared, the more to soothe
> Him with her loved society, that now
> As with new wine intoxicated both
> They swim in mirth, and fancy that they feel
> Divinity within them breeding wings
> Wherewith to scorn the Earth.

Not all the words in Milton's lines are bookish: indeed, many of them can be found
in nursery rimes. What helps, besides diction, to distinguish this account of the
biblical fall from "Jack and Jill" is that Milton's nonstop sentence seems further
removed from usual speech in its length (83 words), in its complexity (subordinate
clauses), and in its word order ("with new wine intoxicated both" rather than
"both intoxicated with new wine"). Should we think less (or more) highly of
Milton for choosing a style so elaborate and formal? No judgment need be passed:
both Mother Goose and the author of *Paradise Lost* use language appropriate to
their purposes.

Coleridge offered two "homely definitions of prose and poetry; that is, *prose*:
words in their best order; *poetry*: the best words in the best order." If all goes well, a
poet may fasten the right word into the right place, and the result may be—as T. S.
Eliot said in "Little Gidding"—a "complete consort dancing together."

Kay Ryan (b. 1945)

Blandeur   2000

If it please God,
let less happen.
Even out Earth's
rondure, flatten
Eiger, blanden   5
the Grand Canyon.
Make valleys
slightly higher,
widen fissures
to arable land,   10
remand your
terrible glaciers
and silence
their calving,
halving or doubling   15
all geographical features
toward the mean.
Unlean against our hearts.
Withdraw your grandeur
from these parts.   20

BLANDEUR. 5 *Eiger*: a mountain in the Alps.

Questions

1. The title of Ryan's poem is a word that she invented. What do you think it means? Explain the reasoning behind your theory.
2. Where else does Ryan use a different form of this new word?
3. What other unusual but real words does the author use?

Thomas Hardy (1840–1928)

The Ruined Maid   1901

"O 'Melia, my dear, this does everything crown!
Who could have supposed I should meet you in Town?
And whence such fair garments, such prosperi-ty?"—
"O didn't you know I'd been ruined?" said she.

—"You left us in tatters, without shoes or socks,   5
Tired of digging potatoes, and spudding up docks;°   *spading up dockweed*
And now you've gay bracelets and bright feathers three!"—
"Yes: that's how we dress when we're ruined," said she.

—"At home in the barton° you said 'thee' and 'thou,'   *farmyard*
And 'thik oon,' and 'theäs oon,' and 't'other'; but now   10
Your talking quite fits 'ee for high compa-ny!"—
"Some polish is gained with one's ruin," said she.

—"Your hands were like paws then, your face blue and bleak
But now I'm bewitched by your delicate cheek,
And your little gloves fit as on any la-dy!"—   15
"We never do work when we're ruined," said she.

—"You used to call home-life a hag-ridden dream,
And you'd sigh, and you'd sock;° but at present you seem   groan
To know not of megrims° or melancho-ly!"—   blues
"True. One's pretty lively when ruined," said she.   20

—"I wish I had feathers, a fine sweeping gown,
And a delicate face, and could strut about Town!"—
"My dear—a raw country girl, such as you be,
Cannot quite expect that. You ain't ruined," said she.

Questions

1. Where does this dialogue take place? Who are the two speakers?
2. Comment on Hardy's use of the word *ruined*. What is the conventional meaning of the word when applied to a woman? As 'Melia applies it to herself, what is its meaning?
3. Sum up the attitude of each speaker toward the other. What details of the new 'Melia does the first speaker most dwell on? Would you expect Hardy to be so impressed by all these details, or is there, between his view of the characters and their view of themselves, any hint of an ironic discrepancy?
4. In losing her country dialect (*thik oon* and *theäs oon* for *this one* and *that one*), 'Melia is presumed to have gained in sophistication. What does Hardy suggest by her *ain't* in the last line?

Richard Eberhart   (1904–2005)

The Fury of Aerial Bombardment   1947

You would think the fury of aerial bombardment
Would rouse God to relent; the infinite spaces
Are still silent. He looks on shock-pried faces.
History, even, does not know what is meant.

You would feel that after so many centuries   5
God would give man to repent; yet he can kill
As Cain could, but with multitudinous will,
No farther advanced than in his ancient furies.

Was man made stupid to see his own stupidity?
Is God by definition indifferent, beyond us all?   10
Is the eternal truth man's fighting soul
Wherein the Beast ravens in its own avidity?

Of Van Wettering I speak, and Averill,
Names on a list, whose faces I do not recall
But they are gone to early death, who late in school   15
Distinguished the belt feed lever from the belt holding pawl.

Questions

1. As a naval officer during World War II, Richard Eberhart was assigned for a time as an instructor in a gunnery school. How has this experience apparently contributed to the diction of his poem?

2. In his *Life of John Dryden*, complaining about a description of a sea fight Dryden had filled with nautical language, Samuel Johnson argued that technical terms should be excluded from poetry. Is this criticism applicable to Eberhart's last line? Can a word succeed for us in a poem, even though we may not be able to define it? (For more evidence, see also the technical terms in Henry Reed's "Naming of Parts," page 1079.)

3. Some readers have found a contrast in tone between the first three stanzas of this poem and the last stanza. How would you describe this contrast? What does diction contribute to it?

Wendy Cope (b. 1945)

Lonely Hearts   1986

Can someone make my simple wish come true?
Male biker seeks female for touring fun.
Do you live in North London? Is it you?

Gay vegetarian whose friends are few,
I'm into music, Shakespeare and the sun.   5
Can someone make my simple wish come true?

Executive in search of something new—
Perhaps bisexual woman, arty, young.
Do you live in North London? Is it you?

Successful, straight and solvent? I am too—   10
Attractive Jewish lady with a son.
Can someone make my simple wish come true?

I'm Libran, inexperienced and blue—
Need slim non-smoker, under twenty-one.
Do you live in North London? Is it you?   15

Please write (with photo) to Box 152.
Who knows where it may lead once we've begun?
Can someone make my simple wish come true?
Do you live in North London? Is it you?

LONELY HEARTS. This poem has a double form: the rhetorical, a series of "lonely heart" personal ads from a newspaper, and metrical, a **villanelle**, a fixed form developed by French courtly poets in imitation of Italian folk song. For other villanelles, see Elizabeth Bishop's "One Art" (page 941) and Dylan Thomas's "Do not go gentle into that good night" (page 824). In the villanelle, the first and the third lines are repeated in a set pattern throughout the poem.

Questions

1. What sort of language does Wendy Cope borrow for this poem?
2. The form of the villanelle requires that the poet end each stanza with one of two repeating lines. What special use does the author make of these mandatory repetitions?

3. How many speakers are there in the poem? Does the author's voice ever enter or is the entire poem spoken by individuals in personal ads?

4. The poem seems to begin satirically. Does the poem ever move beyond the critical, mocking tone typical of satire?

FOR REVIEW AND FURTHER STUDY

E. E. Cummings (1894–1962)

anyone lived in a pretty how town 1940

anyone lived in a pretty how town
(with up so floating many bells down)
spring summer autumn winter
he sang his didn't he danced his did.

Women and men(both little and small)   5
cared for anyone not at all
they sowed their isn't they reaped their same
sun moon stars rain

children guessed(but only a few
and down they forgot as up they grew   10
autumn winter spring summer)
that noone loved him more by more

when by now and tree by leaf
she laughed his joy she cried his grief
bird by snow and stir by still   15
anyone's any was all to her

someones married their everyones
laughed their cryings and did their dance
(sleep wake hope and then)they
said their nevers they slept their dream   20

stars rain sun moon
(and only the snow can begin to explain
how children are apt to forget to remember
with up so floating many bells down)

one day anyone died i guess   25
(and noone stooped to kiss his face)
busy folk buried them side by side
little by little and was by was

all by all and deep by deep
and more by more they dream their sleep   30
noone and anyone earth by april
wish by spirit and if by yes.

Women and men(both dong and ding)
summer autumn winter spring
reaped their sowing and went their came   35
sun moon stars rain

Questions

1. Summarize the story told in this poem. Who are the characters?
2. Rearrange the words in the two opening lines into the order you would expect them usually to follow. What effect does Cummings obtain by his unconventional word order?
3. Another of Cummings's strategies is to use one part of speech as if it were another; for instance, in line 4, *didn't* and *did* ordinarily are verbs, but here they are used as nouns. What other words in the poem perform functions other than their expected ones?

Billy Collins (b. 1941)

The Names   2002

Yesterday, I lay awake in the palm of the night.
A soft rain stole in, unhelped by any breeze,
And when I saw the silver glaze on the windows,
I started with A, with Ackerman, as it happened,
Then Baxter and Calabro,   5
Davis and Eberling, names falling into place
As droplets fell through the dark.

Names printed on the ceiling of the night.
Names slipping around a watery bend.
Twenty-six willows on the banks of a stream.   10

In the morning, I walked out barefoot
Among thousands of flowers
Heavy with dew like the eyes of tears,
And each had a name—
Fiori inscribed on a yellow petal   15
Then Gonzalez and Han, Ishikawa and Jenkins.

Names written in the air
And stitched into the cloth of the day.
A name under a photograph taped to a mailbox.
Monogram on a torn shirt,   20
I see you spelled out on storefront windows
And on the bright unfurled awnings of this city.
I say the syllables as I turn a corner—
Kelly and Lee,
Medina, Nardella, and O'Connor.   25

When I peer into the woods,
I see a thick tangle where letters are hidden
As in a puzzle concocted for children.
Parker and Quigley in the twigs of an ash,
Rizzo, Schubert, Torres, and Upton,   30
Secrets in the boughs of an ancient maple.

Names written in the pale sky.
Names rising in the updraft amid buildings.
Names silent in stone
Or cried out behind a door.
Names blown over the earth and out to sea.   35

In the evening—weakening light, the last swallows.
A boy on a lake lifts his oars.
A woman by a window puts a match to a candle,
And the names are outlined on the rose clouds—
Vanacore and Wallace,   40
(let X stand, if it can, for the ones unfound)
Then Young and Ziminsky, the final jolt of Z.

Names etched on the head of a pin.
One name spanning a bridge, another undergoing a tunnel.
A blue name needled into the skin.   45
Names of citizens, workers, mothers and fathers,
The bright-eyed daughter, the quick son.
Alphabet of names in a green field.
Names in the small tracks of birds.   50
Names lifted from a hat
Or balanced on the tip of the tongue.
Names wheeled into the dim warehouse of memory.
So many names, there is barely room on the walls of the heart.

THE NAMES. This poem originally appeared in the *New York Times* on September 11, 2002. On that same day its author, the Poet Laureate of the United States, read the poem before a joint session of Congress specially convened in New York City to mark the one-year anniversary of the attack on the World Trade Center.

Questions

1. Occasional poetry—verse written to commemorate a public or historical occasion—is generally held in low esteem because such poems tend to be self-important and overwritten. Does Collins avoid these pitfalls?
2. Discuss the level of diction in "The Names." Is it appropriate to the subject? Explain.

Charles Bukowski (1920–1994)

Dostoevsky   1997

against the wall, the firing squad ready.
then he got a reprieve.
suppose they had shot Dostoevsky?
before he wrote all that?
I suppose it wouldn't have   5
mattered

not directly.
there are billions of people who have
never read him and never
will.   10
but as a young man I know that he
got me through the factories,
past the whores,
lifted me high through the night
and put me down   15
in a better
place.
even while in the bar
drinking with the other
derelicts,   20
I was glad they gave Dostoevsky a
reprieve,
it gave me one,
allowed me to look directly at those
rancid faces   25
in my world,
death pointing its finger,
I held fast,
an immaculate drunk
sharing the stinking dark with   30
my
brothers.

DOSTOEVSKY. The Russian novelist Fyodor Dostoevsky (1821–1880), author of *Crime and Punishment* and
The Brothers Karamazov, was arrested in 1849 in a czarist crackdown on liberal organizations and sentenced to death. It was not until the members of the firing squad had aimed their rifles and were awaiting
the order to fire that he was informed that his sentence had been commuted to four years of hard labor in
Siberia.

Exercise: **Different Kinds of English**

Read the following poems and see what kinds of diction and word order you find in
them. Which poems are least formal in their language and which most formal? Is
there any use of vulgate English? Any dialect? What does each poem achieve that its
own kind of English makes possible?

Anonymous (American oral verse)

Carnation Milk   (about 1900?)

Carnation Milk is the best in the land;
Here I sit with a can in my hand—

No tits to pull, no hay to pitch,
You just punch a hole in the son of a bitch.

CARNATION MILK. "This quatrain is imagined as the caption under a picture of a rugged-looking cowboy
seated upon a bale of hay," notes William Harmon in his *Oxford Book of American Light Verse* (New York:
Oxford UP, 1979). Possibly the first to print this work was David Ogilvy (1911–1999), who quotes it in his
Confessions of an Advertising Man (New York: Atheneum, 1963).

Gina Valdés (b. 1943)

English con Salsa   1993

Welcome to ESL 100, English Surely Latinized,
inglés con chile y cilantro, English as American
as Benito Juárez. Welcome, muchachos from Xochicalco,
learn the language of dólares and Dolores, of kings
and queens, of Donald Duck and Batman. Holy Toluca!   5
In four months you'll be speaking like George Washington,
in four weeks you can ask, More coffee? In two months
you can say, May I take your order? In one year you
can ask for a raise, cool as the Tuxpan River.

Welcome, muchachas from Teocaltiche, in this class   10
we speak English refrito, English con sal y limón,
English thick as mango juice, English poured from
a clay jug, English tuned like a requinto from Uruapan,
English lighted by Oaxacan dawns, English spiked
with mezcal from Mitla, English with a red cactus   15
flower blooming in its heart.

Welcome, welcome, amigos del sur, bring your Zapotec
tongues, your Nahuatl tones, your patience of pyramids,
your red suns and golden moons, your guardian angels,
your duendes, your patron saints, Santa Tristeza,   20
Santa Alegría, Santo Todolopuede. We will sprinkle
holy water on pronouns, make the sign of the cross
on past participles, jump like fish from Lake Pátzcuaro
on gerunds, pour tequila from Jalisco on future perfects,
say shoes and shit, grab a cool verb and a pollo loco   25
and dance on the walls like chapulines.

When a teacher from La Jolla or a cowboy from Santee
asks you, Do you speak English? You'll answer, Sí,
yes, simón, of course, I love English!
                                        And you'll hum
A Mixtec chant that touches la tierra and the heavens.   30

ENGLISH CON SALSA. *3 Benito Juárez:* Mexican statesman (1806–1872), president of Mexico in the 1860s
and 1870s.

Lewis Carroll
[Charles Lutwidge Dodgson] (1832–1898)

Jabberwocky   1871

'Twas brillig, and the slithy toves
    Did gyre and gimble in the wabe:
All mimsy were the borogoves,
    And the mome raths outgrabe.

"Beware the Jabberwock, my son!   5
    The jaws that bite, the claws that catch!
Beware the Jubjub bird, and shun
    The frumious Bandersnatch!"

He took his vorpal sword in hand:
    Long time the manxome foe he sought—   10
So rested he by the Tumtum tree
    And stood awhile in thought.

And, as in uffish thought he stood,
    The Jabberwock, with eyes of flame,
Came whiffling through the tulgey wood,   15
    And burbled as it came!

One, two! One, two! And through and through
    The vorpal blade went snicker-snack!
He left it dead, and with its head
    He went galumphing back.   20

"And hast thou slain the Jabberwock?
    Come to my arms, my beamish boy!
O frabjous day! Callooh, Callay!"
    He chortled in his joy.

'Twas brillig, and the slithy toves   25
    Did gyre and gimble in the wabe:
All mimsy were the borogoves,
    And the mome raths outgrabe.

JABBERWOCKY. Fussy about pronunciation, Carroll in his preface to *The Hunting of the Snark* declares: "The first 'o' in 'borogoves' is pronounced like the 'o' in 'borrow.' I have heard people try to give it the sound of the 'o' in 'worry.' Such is Human Perversity." *Toves*, he adds, rimes with *groves*.

Questions

1. Look up *chortled* (line 24) in your dictionary and find out its definition and origin.

2. In *Through the Looking Glass*, Alice seeks the aid of Humpty Dumpty to decipher the meaning of this nonsense poem. "*Brillig*," he explains, "means four o'clock in the afternoon—the time when you begin *broiling* things for dinner." Does *brillig* sound like any other familiar word?

3. "*Slithy*," the explanation goes on, "means 'lithe and slimy.' 'Lithe' is the same as 'active.' You see it's like a portmanteau—there are two meanings packed up into one word." *Mimsy* is supposed to pack together both "flimsy" and "miserable." In the rest of the poem, what other portmanteau—or packed suitcase—words can you find?

■ WRITING *effectively*

Lewis Carroll on Writing

Humpty Dumpty Explicates "Jabberwocky"   1871

Lewis Carroll

"You seem very clever at explaining words, sir," said Alice. "Would you kindly tell me the meaning of the poem called 'Jabberwocky'?"

"Let's hear it," said Humpty Dumpty. "I can explain all the poems that ever were invented—and a good many that haven't been invented just yet."

This sounded very hopeful, so Alice repeated the first verse:

> "'Twas brillig, and the slithy toves
>   Did gyre and gimble in the wabe:
> All mimsy were the borogoves,
>   And the mome raths outgrabe."

"That's enough to begin with," Humpty Dumpty interrupted: "there are plenty of hard words there. '*Brillig*' means four o'clock in the afternoon—the time when you begin *broiling* things for dinner."

"That'll do very well," said Alice. "And '*slithy*'?"

"Well, '*slithy*' means 'lithe and slimy.' 'Lithe' is the same as 'active.' You see, it's like a portmanteau—there are two meanings packed up into one word."

"I see it now," Alice remarked thoughtfully. "And what are '*toves*'?"

"Well, '*toves*' are something like badgers—they're something like lizards—and they're something like corkscrews."

"They must be very curious-looking creatures."

"They are that," said Humpty Dumpty, "also they make their nests under sundials—also they live on cheese."

"And what's to '*gyre*' and to '*gimble*'?"

"To '*gyre*' is to go round and round like a gyroscope. To '*gimble*' is to make holes like a gimlet."

"And '*the wabe*' is the grass plot round a sundial, I suppose?" said Alice, surprised at her own ingenuity.

"Of course it is. It's called '*wabe*,' you know, because it goes a long way before it, and a long way behind it."

"And a long way beyond it on each side," Alice added.

"Exactly so. Well, then, '*mimsy*' is flimsy and miserable (there's another portmanteau for you). And a '*borogove*' is a thin, shabby-looking bird with its feathers sticking out all round—something like a live mop."

"And then '*mome raths*'?" said Alice. "I'm afraid I'm giving you a great deal of trouble."

"Well, a '*rath*' is a sort of green pig: but '*mome*' I'm not certain about. I think it's short for 'from home'—meaning that they'd lost their way, you know."

"And what does '*outgrabe*' mean?"

"Well, '*outgribing*' is something between bellowing and whistling, with a kind of sneeze in the middle; however, you'll hear it done, maybe—down in the wood yonder—and when you've once heard it you'll be *quite* content. Who's been repeating all that hard stuff to you?"

"I read it in a book," said Alice.

From *Through the Looking Glass*

HUMPTY DUMPTY EXPLICATES "JABBERWOCKY." This celebrated passage is the origin of the term ***portmanteau word***, an artificial word that combines parts of other words to express some combination of their qualities. (*Brunch*, for example, is a meal that combines aspects of both breakfast and lunch.) A portmanteau is a large suitcase that opens up into two separate compartments.

THINKING ABOUT DICTION

Although a poem may contain images and ideas, it is made up of words. Language is the medium of poetry, and a poem's diction—its exact wording—is the chief source of its power. Writers labor to shape each word and phrase to create particular effects. Poets choose words for their meanings, their associations, and even their sounds. Changing a single word may ruin a poem's effect, just as changing one number in an online password makes all the other numbers useless.

- **As you prepare to write about a poem, ask yourself if some particular word or combination of words gives you particular pleasure or especially intrigues you.** Don't worry yet about why the word or words impress you. Don't even worry about the meaning. Just underline the words in your book.

- **Try to determine what about the word or phrase commanded your attention.** Maybe a word strikes you as being unexpected but just right. A phrase might seem especially musical or it might call forth a vivid picture in your imagination.

- **Consider your underlined words and phrases in the context of the poem.** How does each relate to the words around it? What does it add to the poem?

- **Think about the poem as a whole.** What sort of language does it rely on? Many poems favor the plain, straightforward language people use in everyday conversation, but others reach for more elegant diction. Choices such as these contribute to the poem's distinctive flavor, as well as to its ultimate meaning.

CHECKLIST: Writing About Diction

☐ As you read, underline words or phrases that appeal to you or seem especially significant.

☐ What is it about each underlined word or phrase that appeals to you?

☐ How does the word or phrase relate to the other lines? What does it contribute to the poem's effect?

☐ How does the sound of a word you've chosen add to the poem's mood?

☐ What would be lost if synonyms were substituted for your favorite words?

☐ What sort of diction does the poem use? Conversational? Lofty? Monosyllabic? Polysyllabic? Concrete? Abstract?

☐ How does diction contribute to the poem's flavor and meaning?

WRITING ASSIGNMENT ON WORD CHOICE

Find two poems in this book that use very different sorts of diction to address similar subjects. You might choose one with formal and elegant language and another with very down-to-earth or slangy word choices. Some good choices include John Milton's "When I consider how my light is spent" and Seamus Heaney's "Digging"; Dylan Thomas's "Do not go gentle into that good night" and Langston Hughes's "As Befits a Man"; and William Shakespeare's "When, in disgrace with Fortune and men's eyes" and Jane Kenyon's "The Suitor." In a short essay (750 to 1000 words), discuss how the difference in diction affects the tones of the two poems.

MORE TOPICS FOR WRITING

1. Browse through the chapter "Poems for Further Reading," for a poem that catches your interest. Within that poem, find a word or phrase that particularly intrigues you. Write a paragraph on what the word or phrase adds to the poem, how it shades the meaning and contributes to the overall effect.

2. Choose a brief poem from this chapter. Type the poem out, substituting synonyms for each of its nouns and verbs, using a thesaurus if necessary. Next, write a one-page analysis of the difference in feel and meaning between the original and your creation.

3. Choose a poem that strikes you as particularly inventive or unusual in its language, such as E. E. Cummings's "anyone lived in a pretty how town," Gerard Manley Hopkins's "The Windhover," or Wendy Cope's "Lonely Hearts," and write a brief analysis of it. Concentrate on the diction of the poem and word order. For what possible purposes does the poet depart from standard English or incorporate unusual vocabulary?

4. Writers are notorious word junkies who often jot down interesting words they stumble across in daily life. Over the course of a day, keep a list of any intriguing words you run across in your reading, music listening, or television viewing. Even street signs and advertisements can supply surprising words. After twenty-four hours of list-keeping, choose your five favorites. Write a five line poem, incorporating your five words, letting them take you where they will. Then write a page-long description of the process. What appealed to you in the words you chose? What did you learn about the process of composing a poem?

▶ TERMS FOR *review*

Diction and Allusion

Diction ▶ Word choice or vocabulary. *Diction* refers to the class of words that an author chooses as appropriate for a particular work.

Concrete diction ▶ Words that specifically name or describe things or persons. Concrete words refer to what we can immediately perceive with our senses.

Abstract diction ▶ Words that express general ideas or concepts.

Poetic diction ▶ Strictly speaking, *poetic diction* means any language deemed suitable for verse, but the term generally refers to elevated language intended for poetry rather than common use.

Allusion ▶ A brief, sometimes indirect, reference in a text to a person, place, or thing. Allusions imply a common body of knowledge between reader and writer and act as a literary shorthand to enrich the meaning of a text.

Levels of Diction

Vulgate ▶ The lowest level of diction, vulgate is the language of the common people. Not necessarily containing foul or inappropriate language, it refers simply to unschooled, everyday speech. The term comes from the Latin word *vulgus*, "mob" or "common people."

Colloquial English ▶ The casual or informal but correct language of ordinary native speakers. Conversational in tone, it may include contractions, slang, and shifts in grammar, vocabulary, and diction.

General English ▶ The ordinary speech of educated native speakers. Most literate speech and writing is general English. Its diction is more educated than **colloquial English**, yet not as elevated as **formal English**.

Formal English ▶ The heightened, impersonal language of educated persons, usually only written, although possibly spoken on dignified occasions.

Dialect ▶ A particular variety of language spoken by an identifiable regional group or social class of persons.

16

SAYING AND SUGGESTING

To name an object is to take away three-fourths
of the pleasure given by a poem. . . .
to suggest it, that is the ideal.

—STÉPHANE MALLARMÉ

To write so clearly that they might bring "all things as near the mathematical plainness" as possible—that was the goal of scientists, according to Bishop Thomas Sprat, who lived in the seventeenth century. Such an effort would seem bound to fail, because words, unlike numbers, are ambiguous indicators. Although it may have troubled Bishop Sprat, the tendency of a word to have multiplicity of meaning rather than mathematical plainness opens broad avenues to poetry.

DENOTATION AND CONNOTATION

Every word has at least one **denotation**: a meaning as defined in a dictionary. But the English language has many a common word with so many denotations that a reader may need to think twice to see what it means in a specific context. The noun *field,* for instance, can denote a piece of ground, a sports arena, the scene of a battle, part of a flag, a profession, and a number system in mathematics. Further, the word can be used as a verb ("he fielded a grounder") or an adjective ("field trip," "field glasses").

A word also has **connotations**: overtones or suggestions of additional meaning that it gains from all the contexts in which we have met it in the past. The word *skeleton,* according to a dictionary, denotes "the bony framework of a human being or other vertebrate animal, which supports the flesh and protects the organs." But by its associations, the word can rouse thoughts of war, of disease and death, or (possibly) of one's plans to go to medical school. Think, too, of the difference between "Old Doc Jones" and "Theodore E. Jones, M.D." In the mind's eye, the former appears in his shirtsleeves; the latter has a gold nameplate on his door.

That some words denote the same thing but have sharply different connotations is pointed out in this anonymous Victorian jingle:

Here's a little ditty that you really ought to know:
Horses "sweat" and men "perspire," but ladies only "glow."

The terms *druggist, pharmacist,* and *apothecary* all denote the same occupation, but apothecaries lay claim to special distinction.

Poets aren't the only people who care about the connotations of language. Advertisers know that connotations make money. Nowadays many automobile dealers advertise their secondhand cars not as "used" but as "pre-owned," as if fearing that "used car" would connote an old heap with soiled upholstery and mysterious engine troubles. "Pre-owned," however, suggests that the previous owner has kindly taken the trouble of breaking in the car for you. Not long ago prune-packers, alarmed by a slump in sales, sponsored a survey to determine the connotations of prunes in the public consciousness. Asked, "What do you think of when you hear the word *prunes?*" most people replied, "dried up," "wrinkled," or "constipated." Dismayed, the packers hired an advertising agency to create a new image for prunes, in hopes of inducing new connotations. Soon, advertisements began to show prunes in brightly colored settings, in the company of bikinied bathing beauties.

In imaginative writing, connotations are as crucial as they are in advertising. Consider this sentence: "A new brand of journalism is being born, or spawned" (Dwight Macdonald writing in the *New York Review of Books*). The last word, by its associations with fish and crustaceans, suggests that this new journalism is scarcely the product of human beings.

Here is a famous poem that groups together things with similar connotations: certain ships and their cargoes. (A *quinquireme,* by the way, was an ancient Assyrian vessel propelled by sails and oars.)

John Masefield (1878–1967)

Cargoes   1902

Quinquireme of Nineveh from distant Ophir,
Rowing home to haven in sunny Palestine,
With a cargo of ivory,
And apes and peacocks,
Sandalwood, cedarwood, and sweet white wine.   5

Stately Spanish galleon coming from the Isthmus,
Dipping through the Tropics by the palm-green shores,
With a cargo of diamonds,
Emeralds, amethysts,
Topazes, and cinnamon, and gold moidores.°   *Portuguese coins*   10

Dirty British coaster with a salt-caked smoke stack,
Butting through the Channel in the mad March days,
With a cargo of Tyne coal,
Road-rails, pig-lead,
Firewood, iron-ware, and cheap tin trays.   15

To us, as well as to the poet's original readers, the place-names in the first two stanzas suggest the exotic and faraway. Ophir, a vanished place, may have been in Arabia; according to the Bible, King Solomon sent expeditions there for its celebrated pure gold, also for ivory, apes, peacocks, and other luxury items. (See I Kings 9–10.) In his final stanza, Masefield groups commonplace things (mostly heavy and metallic), whose suggestions of crudeness, cheapness, and ugliness he deliberately contrasts with those of the precious stuffs he has listed earlier. For British readers, the Tyne is a stodgy and familiar river; the English Channel in March, choppy and likely to upset a stomach. The quinquireme is *rowing*, the galleon is *dipping*, but the dirty British freighter is *butting*, aggressively pushing. Conceivably, the poet could have described firewood and even coal as beautiful, but evidently he wants them to convey sharply different suggestions here, to go along with the rest of the coaster's cargo. In drawing such a sharp contrast between past and present, Masefield does more than merely draw up bills-of-lading. Perhaps he even implies a wry and unfavorable comment on life in the present day. His meaning lies not so much in the dictionary definitions of his words ("*moidores*: Portuguese gold coins formerly worth approximately five pounds sterling") as in their rich and vivid connotations.

 ## *William Blake* (1757–1827)

London   1794

I wander through each chartered street,
Near where the chartered Thames does flow,
And mark in every face I meet
Marks of weakness, marks of woe.

In every cry of every man,   5
In every infant's cry of fear,
In every voice, in every ban,
The mind-forged manacles I hear.

How the chimney-sweeper's cry
Every black'ning church appalls   10
And the hapless soldier's sigh
Runs in blood down palace walls.

But most through midnight streets I hear
How the youthful harlot's curse
Blasts the new born infant's tear   15
And blights with plagues the marriage hearse.

Here are only a few of the possible meanings of four of Blake's words:

- *chartered* (lines 1, 2)

  Denotations: Established by a charter (a written grant or a certificate of incorporation); leased or hired.
  Connotations: Defined, limited, restricted, channeled, mapped, bound by law; bought and sold (like a slave or an inanimate object); Magna Carta; charters given to crown colonies by the King.

Other words in the poem with similar connotations: Ban, which can denote (1) a legal prohibition; (2) a churchman's curse or malediction; (3) in medieval times, an order summoning a king's vassals to fight for him. *Manacles,* or shackles, restrain movement. *Chimney-sweeper, soldier,* and *harlot* are all hirelings.

Interpretation of the lines: The street has had mapped out for it the direction in which it must go; the Thames has had laid down to it the course it must follow. Street and river are channeled, imprisoned, enslaved (like every inhabitant of London).

- **black'ning** (line 10)

Denotation: Becoming black.

Connotations: The darkening of something once light, the defilement of something once clean, the deepening of guilt, the gathering of darkness at the approach of night.

Other words in the poem with similar connotations: Objects becoming marked or smudged (*marks of weakness, marks of woe* in the faces of passers-by; bloodied walls of a palace; marriage blighted with plagues); the word *appalls* (denoting not only "to overcome with horror" but "to make pale" and also "to cast a pall or shroud over"); *midnight streets.*

Interpretation of the line: Literally, every London church grows black from soot and hires a chimney-sweeper (a small boy) to help clean it. But Blake suggests too that by profiting from the suffering of the child laborer, the church is soiling its original purity.

- **Blasts, blights** (lines 15, 16)

Denotations: Both *blast* and *blight* mean "to cause to wither" or "to ruin and destroy." Both are terms from horticulture. Frost *blasts* a bud and kills it; disease *blights* a growing plant.

Connotations: Sickness and death; gardens shriveled and dying; gusts of wind and the ravages of insects; things blown to pieces or rotted and warped.

Other words in the poem with similar connotations: Faces marked with weakness and woe; the child becomes a chimney-sweep; the soldier killed by war; blackening church and bloodied palace; young girl turned harlot; wedding carriage transformed into a hearse.

Interpretation of the lines: Literally, the harlot spreads the plague of syphilis, which, carried into marriage, can cause a baby to be born blind. In a larger and more meaningful sense, Blake sees the prostitution of even one young girl corrupting the entire institution of matrimony and endangering every child.

Some of these connotations are more to the point than others; the reader of a poem nearly always has the problem of distinguishing relevant associations from irrelevant ones. We need to read a poem in its entirety and, when a word leaves us in doubt, look for other things in the poem to corroborate or refute what we think it means. Relatively simple and direct in its statement, Blake's account of his stroll through the city at night becomes an indictment of a whole social and religious order. The indictment could hardly be this effective if it were "mathematically plain," its every word restricted to one denotation clearly spelled out.

Wallace Stevens (1879–1955)

Disillusionment of Ten O'Clock   1923

The houses are haunted
By white night-gowns.
None are green,
Or purple with green rings,
Or green with yellow rings,   5
Or yellow with blue rings.
None of them are strange,
With socks of lace
And beaded ceintures.
People are not going   10
To dream of baboons and periwinkles.
Only, here and there, an old sailor,
Drunk and asleep in his boots,
Catches tigers
In red weather.   15

Questions

1. What are *beaded ceintures*? What does the phrase suggest?
2. What contrast does Stevens draw between the people who live in these houses and the old sailor? What do the connotations of *white night-gowns* and *sailor* add to this contrast?
3. What is lacking in these people who wear white night-gowns? Why should the poet's view of them be a "disillusionment"?

Gwendolyn Brooks (1917–2000)

Southeast Corner   1945

The School of Beauty's a tavern now.
The Madam is underground.
Out at Lincoln, among the graves
Her own is early found.
Where the thickest, tallest monument   5
Cuts grandly into the air
The Madam lies, contentedly.
Her fortune, too, lies there,
Converted into cool hard steel
And right red velvet lining;   10
While over her tan impassivity
Shot silk is shining.

SOUTHEAST CORNER. *3 Lincoln:* cemetery in Chicago where a number of prominent African Americans, including Gwendolyn Brooks herself, are buried.

Questions

1. What view of its subject does this poem implicitly take, and through what words is it conveyed?
2. Is there more than one relevant meaning of *fortune* in line 8?

E. E. Cummings (1894–1962)

next to of course god america i   1926

"next to of course god america i
love you land of the pilgrims' and so forth oh
say can you see by the dawn's early my
country 'tis of centuries come and go
and are no more what of it we should worry   5
in every language even deafanddumb
thy sons acclaim your glorious name by gorry
by jingo by gee by gosh by gum
why talk of beauty what could be more beaut-
iful than these heroic happy dead   10
who rushed like lions to the roaring slaughter
they did not stop to think they died instead
then shall the voice of liberty be mute?"

He spoke. And drank rapidly a glass of water

Questions

1. How many allusions in this poem can you identify? What do all the sources of those allusions have in common?
2. Look up the origin of *jingo* (line 8). Is it used here as more than just a mindless exclamation?
3. Beyond what is actually said, what do the rhetoric of the first thirteen lines and the description in the last one suggest about the author's intentions in this poem?

Robert Frost (1874–1963)

Fire and Ice   1923

Some say the world will end in fire,
Some say in ice.
From what I've tasted of desire
I hold with those who favor fire.
But if it had to perish twice,   5
I think I know enough of hate
To say that for destruction ice
Is also great
And would suffice.

Questions

1. To whom does Frost refer in line 1? In line 2?
2. What connotations of *fire* and *ice* contribute to the richness of Frost's comparison?

Timothy Steele (b. 1948)

Epitaph   1979

Here lies Sir Tact, a diplomatic fellow
Whose silence was not golden, but just yellow.

Questions

1. To what famous saying does the poet allude?
2. What are the connotations of golden? Of yellow?

Diane Thiel (b. 1967)

The Minefield   2000

He was running with his friend from town to town.
They were somewhere between Prague and Dresden.
He was fourteen. His friend was faster
and knew a shortcut through the fields they could take.
He said there was lettuce growing in one of them,   5
and they hadn't eaten all day. His friend ran a few lengths ahead,
like a wild rabbit across the grass,
turned his head, looked back once,
and his body was scattered across the field.

My father told us this, one night,   10
and then continued eating dinner.

He brought them with him—the minefields.
He carried them underneath his good intentions.
He gave them to us—in the volume of his anger,
in the bruises we covered up with sleeves.   15
In the way he threw anything against the wall—
a radio, that wasn't even ours,
a melon, once, opened like a head.
In the way we still expect, years later and continents away,
that anything might explode at any time,   20
and we would have to run on alone
with a vision like that
only seconds behind.

Questions

1. In the opening lines of the poem, a seemingly small decision—to take a shortcut and find something to eat—leads to a horrifying result. What does this suggest about the poem's larger view of what life is like?
2. The speaker tells the story of the minefield before letting us know that the other boy was her father. What is the effect of this narrative strategy?
3. How does the image of the melon reinforce the poem's intentions?

Ron Rash (b. 1953)

The Day the Gates Closed   2002

We lose so much in this life.
Shouldn't some things stay, she said,
but it was already gone,

no human sound, the poplars
and oaks cut down so even   5
the wind had nothing to rub
a whisper from, just silence
rising over the valley
deep and wide as a glacier.

Questions

1. What do you think the title means, and what does it contribute to your understanding of the poem?
2. How does the first line set a keynote for what follows?
3. What mood is created by the imagery and tone of the poem? Be as specific as possible in your responses.
4. How does the simile of the glacier in the last line tie into the theme?

Alfred, Lord Tennyson (1809–1892)

Tears, Idle Tears   1847

Tears, idle tears, I know not what they mean,
Tears from the depth of some divine despair
Rise in the heart, and gather to the eyes,
In looking on the happy autumn-fields,
And thinking of the days that are no more.   5

Fresh as the first beam glittering on a sail,
That brings our friends up from the underworld,
Sad as the last which reddens over one
That sinks with all we love below the verge;
So sad, so fresh, the days that are no more.   10

Ah, sad and strange as in dark summer dawns
The earliest pipe of half-awakened birds
To dying ears, when unto dying eyes
The casement slowly grows a glimmering square;
So sad, so strange, the days that are no more.   15

Dear as remembered kisses after death,
And sweet as those by hopeless fancy feigned
On lips that are for others; deep as love,
Deep as first love, and wild with all regret;
O Death in Life, the days that are no more!   20

Richard Wilbur (b. 1921)

Love Calls Us to the Things of This World   1956

The eyes open to a cry of pulleys,
And spirited from sleep, the astounded soul
Hangs for a moment bodiless and simple

As false dawn.
                    Outside the open window
The morning air is all awash with angels.   5

    Some are in bed-sheets, some are in blouses,
Some are in smocks: but truly there they are.
Now they are rising together in calm swells
Of halcyon feeling, filling whatever they wear
With the deep joy of their impersonal breathing;   10

    Now they are flying in place, conveying
The terrible speed of their omnipresence, moving
And staying like white water; and now of a sudden
They swoon down into so rapt a quiet
That nobody seems to be there.
                              The soul shrinks   15

    From all that it is about to remember,
From the punctual rape of every blessèd day,
And cries,
          "Oh, let there be nothing on earth but laundry,
Nothing but rosy hands in the rising steam
And clear dances done in the sight of heaven."   20

    Yet, as the sun acknowledges
With a warm look the world's hunks and colors,
The soul descends once more in bitter love
To accept the waking body, saying now
In a changed voice as the man yawns and rises,   25

    "Bring them down from their ruddy gallows;
Let there be clean linen for the backs of thieves;
Let lovers go fresh and sweet to be undone,
And the heaviest nuns walk in a pure floating
Of dark habits,
              keeping their difficult balance."   30

LOVE CALLS US TO THE THINGS OF THIS WORLD. Wilbur claimed that his title was taken from St. Augustine,
but in a recent interview he admitted that neither he nor any critic has ever been able to locate the quotation
again. Whatever its source, however, the title establishes the poem's central idea that love allows us to
return from the divine world of the spirit to the imperfect world of our everyday lives. Wilbur's own
comments on the poem appear after the questions that follow here.

Questions

1. What are the *angels* in line 5? Why does this metaphor seem appropriate to the situation?
2. What is "the punctual rape of every blessèd day?" Who is being raped? Who or what commits
   the rape? Why would Wilbur choose this particular word with all its violent associations?
3. Whom or what does the soul love in line 23, and why is that love bitter?
4. Is it merely obesity that make the nuns' balance "difficult" in the two final lines of the
   poem? What other "balance" does Wilbur's poem suggest?
5. The soul has two speeches in the poem. How do they differ in tone and imagery?
6. The spiritual world is traditionally considered invisible. What concrete images does
   Wilbur use to express its special character?

■ WRITING *effectively*

Richard Wilbur on Writing

Concerning "Love Calls Us to the Things of This World"

1966

If I understand this poem rightly, it has a free and organic rhythm: that is to say, its movement arises naturally from the emotion, and from the things and actions described. At the same time, the lines are metrical and disposed in stanzas. The subject matter is both exalted and vulgar. There is, I should think, sufficient description to satisfy an Imagist, but there is also a certain amount of statement; my hope is that the statement seems to grow inevitably out of the situation described. The language of the poem is at one moment elevated and at the next colloquial or slangy: for example, the imposing word "omnipresence" occurs not far from the undignified word "hunks." A critic would find in this poem certain patterns of sound, but those patterns of sound do not constitute an abstract music; they are meant, at any rate, to be inseparable from what is being said, a subordinate aspect of the poem's meaning.

Richard Wilbur

The title of the poem is a quotation from St. Augustine: "Love Calls Us to the Things of This World." You must imagine the poem as occurring at perhaps seven-thirty in the morning; the scene is a bedroom high up in a city apartment building; outside the bedroom window, the first laundry of the day is being yanked across the sky, and one has been awakened by the squeaking pulleys of the laundry-line.

From "On My Own Work"

THINKING ABOUT DENOTATION AND CONNOTATION

People often convey their feelings indirectly, through body language, facial expression, tone of voice, and other ways. Similarly, the imagery, tone, and diction of a poem can suggest a message so clearly that it doesn't need to be stated outright.

- **Pay careful attention to what a poem suggests.** Jot down a few key observations both about what the poem says directly and what you might want to know but aren't told. What important details are you left to infer for yourself?

- **Establish what the poem actually says.** When journalists write a news story, they usually try to cover the "five W's" in the opening paragraph—*who, what, when, where,* and *why*. These questions are worthwhile ones to ask about a poem:

Who? Who is the speaker or central figure of the poem? (In William Blake's "London," for instance, the speaker is also the protagonist who witnesses the hellish horror of the city.) If the poem seems to be addressed not simply to the reader but to a more specific listener, identify that listener as well.

What? What objects or events are being seen or presented? Does the poem ever suddenly change its subject? (In Wallace Stevens's "Disillusionment of Ten O'Clock," for example, there are essentially two scenes—one dull and proper, the other wild and disreputable. What does that obvious shift suggest about Stevens's meaning?)

When? When does the poem take place? If a poet explicitly states a time of day or a season of the year, it is likely that the when of the poem is important. (The fact that Stevens's poem takes place at 10 P.M. and not 2 A.M. tells us a great deal about the people it describes.)

Where? Where is the poem set? Sometimes the setting suggests something important, or plays a part in setting a mood.

Why? If the poem describes some dramatic action but does not provide an overt reason for the occurrence, perhaps the reader is meant to draw his or her own conclusions on the subject. (Tennyson's "Tears, Idle Tears" becomes more evocative by not being explicit about why the speaker weeps.)

■ **Remember, it is almost as important to know what a poem does not tell us as what it does.**

CHECKLIST: Writing About What a Poem Says and Suggests

☐ Who speaks the words of the poem? Is it a voice close to the poet's own? A fictional character? A real person?

☐ Who is the poem's central figure?

☐ To whom—if anyone—is the poem addressed?

☐ What objects or events are depicted?

☐ When does the poem take place? Is that timing significant in any way?

☐ Where does the action of the poem take place?

☐ Why does the action of the poem take place? Is there some significant motivation?

☐ Does the poem leave any of the above information out? If so, what does that lack of information reveal about the poem's intentions?

WRITING ASSIGNMENT ON DENOTATION AND CONNOTATION

Search a poem of your own choosing for the answers to the "five W's"—*who, what, when, where,* and *why.* Indicate, with details, which of the questions are explicitly answered by the poem and which are left unexplained.

MORE TOPICS FOR WRITING

1. Look closely at the central image of Richard Wilbur's "Love Calls Us to the Things of This World." Why does such an ordinary sight cause such intense feelings in the poem's speaker? Give evidence from the poem to back up your theory.

2. To which of the "five W's" does Robert Frost's brief poem "Fire and Ice" provide answers? In a brief essay, suggest why so many of the questions remain unanswered.

3. What do the various images in Tennyson's "Tears, Idle Tears" suggest about the speaker's reasons for weeping? Address each image, and explain what the images add up to.

4. Locate all the adverbs and adjectives in Gwendolyn Brooks's "Southeast Corner," and write one or two sentences on what each of these words contributes to the poem's thematic intent.

5. Browse through a newspaper or magazine for an advertisement that tries to surround a product with an aura. A new car, for instance, might be described in terms of some powerful jungle cat ("purring power, ready to spring"). Clip or photocopy the ad and circle words in it that seem especially suggestive. Then, in an accompanying essay, unfold the suggestions in these words and try to explain the ad's appeal. What differences can you see between how poetry and advertising copy use connotative language?

▶ TERMS FOR *review*

Denotation ▶ The literal, dictionary meaning of a word.

Connotation ▶ An association or additional meaning that a word, image, or phrase may carry, apart from its literal denotation or dictionary definition. A word may pick up connotations from the uses to which it has been put in the past.

17 IMAGERY

It is better to present one Image in a lifetime than to produce voluminous works.

—EZRA POUND

Ezra Pound (1885–1972)

In a Station of the Metro   1916

The apparition of these faces in the crowd;
Petals on a wet, black bough.

Pound said he wrote this poem to convey an experience: emerging one day from a train in the Paris subway (*Métro*), he beheld "suddenly a beautiful face, and then another and another." Originally he had described his impression in a poem thirty lines long. In this final version, each line contains an image, which, like a picture, may take the place of a thousand words.

Though the term **image** suggests a thing seen, when speaking of images in poetry, we generally mean *a word or sequence of words that refers to any sensory experience*. Often this experience is a sight (**visual imagery**, as in Pound's poem), but it may be a sound (**auditory imagery**) or a touch (**tactile imagery**, as a perception of roughness or smoothness). It may be an odor or a taste or perhaps a bodily sensation such as pain, the prickling of gooseflesh, the quenching of thirst, or—as in the following brief poem—the perception of something cold.

Taniguchi Buson (1716–1783)

The piercing chill I feel   (about 1760)

The piercing chill I feel:
  my dead wife's comb, in our bedroom,
    under my heel . . .

—*Translated by Harold G. Henderson*

As in this haiku (in Japanese, a poem of seventeen syllables) an image can convey a flash of understanding. Had he wished, the poet might have spoken of the dead

710

woman, of the contrast between her death and his memory of her, of his feelings toward death in general. But such a discussion would be quite different from the poem he actually wrote. Striking his bare foot against the comb, now cold and motionless but associated with the living wife (perhaps worn in her hair), the widower feels a shock as if he had touched the woman's corpse. A literal, physical sense of death is conveyed; the abstraction "death" is understood through the senses. To render the abstract in concrete terms is what poets often try to do; in this attempt, an image can be valuable.

IMAGERY

An image may occur in a single word, a phrase, a sentence, or, as in this case, an entire short poem. To speak of the **imagery** of a poem—all its images taken together—is often more useful than to speak of separate images. To divide Buson's haiku into five images—*chill, wife, comb, bedroom, heel*—is possible, for any noun that refers to a visible object or a sensation is an image, but this is to draw distinctions that in themselves mean little and to disassemble a single experience.

Does an image cause a reader to experience a sense impression? Not quite. Reading the word *petals*, no one literally sees petals; but the occasion is given for imagining them. The image asks to be seen with the mind's eye. And although "In a Station of the Metro" records what Ezra Pound saw, it is of course not necessary for a poet actually to have lived through a sensory experience in order to write of it. Keats may never have seen a newly discovered planet through a telescope, despite the image in his sonnet on Chapman's Homer.

It is tempting to think of imagery as mere decoration, particularly when we read Keats, who fills his poems with an abundance of sights, sounds, odors, and tastes. But a successful image is not just a dab of paint or a flashy bauble. When Keats opens "The Eve of St. Agnes" with what have been called the coldest lines in literature, he evokes by a series of images a setting and a mood:

> St. Agnes' eve—Ah, bitter chill it was!
> The owl, for all his feathers, was a-cold;
> The hare limped trembling through the frozen grass,
> And silent was the flock in woolly fold:
> Numb were the Beadsman's fingers, while he told
> His rosary, and while his frosted breath,
> Like pious incense from a censer old,
> Seemed taking flight for heaven, without a death . . .

Indeed, some literary critics look for much of the meaning of a poem in its imagery, wherein they expect to see the mind of the poet more truly revealed than in whatever the poet explicitly claims to believe. Though Shakespeare's Theseus (in *A Midsummer Night's Dream*) accuses poets of being concerned with "airy nothings," poets are usually very much concerned with what is in front of them. This concern is of use to us. Involved in our personal hopes and apprehensions, anticipating the future so hard that much of the time we see the present through a film of thought across our eyes, perhaps we need a poet occasionally to remind us that even the coffee we absentmindedly sip comes in (as Yeats put it) a "heavy spillable cup."

T. S. Eliot (1888–1965)

The winter evening settles down 1917

The winter evening settles down
With smell of steaks in passageways.
Six o'clock.
The burnt-out ends of smoky days.
And now a gusty shower wraps   5
The grimy scraps
Of withered leaves about your feet
And newspapers from vacant lots;
The showers beat
On broken blinds and chimney-pots,   10
And at the corner of the street
A lonely cab-horse steams and stamps.

And then the lighting of the lamps.

Questions

1. What mood is evoked by the images in Eliot's poem?
2. What kind of city neighborhood has the poet chosen to describe? How can you tell?

 Theodore Roethke (1908–1963)

Root Cellar 1948

Nothing would sleep in that cellar, dank as a ditch,
Bulbs broke out of boxes hunting for chinks in the dark,
Shoots dangled and drooped,
Lolling obscenely from mildewed crates,
Hung down long yellow evil necks, like tropical snakes.   5
And what a congress of stinks!—
Roots ripe as old bait,
Pulpy stems, rank, silo-rich,
Leaf-mold, manure, lime, piled against slippery planks.
Nothing would give up life: 10
Even the dirt kept breathing a small breath.

Questions

1. As a boy growing up in Saginaw, Michigan, Theodore Roethke spent much of his time in
   a large commercial greenhouse run by his family. What details in his poem show more
   than a passing acquaintance with growing things?
2. What varieties of image does "Root Cellar" contain? Point out examples.
3. What do you understand to be Roethke's attitude toward the root cellar? Does he view it
   as a disgusting chamber of horrors? Pay special attention to the last two lines.

Elizabeth Bishop (1911–1979)

The Fish

I caught a tremendous fish
and held him beside the boat
half out of water, with my hook
fast in a corner of his mouth.
He didn't fight.   5
He hadn't fought at all.
He hung a grunting weight,
battered and venerable
and homely. Here and there
his brown skin hung in strips   10
like ancient wallpaper,
and its pattern of darker brown
was like wallpaper:
shapes like full-blown roses
stained and lost through age.   15
He was speckled with barnacles,
fine rosettes of lime,
and infested
with tiny white sea-lice,
and underneath two or three   20
rags of green weed hung down.
While his gills were breathing in
the terrible oxygen
—the frightening gills,
fresh and crisp with blood,   25
that can cut so badly—
I thought of the coarse white flesh
packed in like feathers,
the big bones and the little bones,
the dramatic reds and blacks   30
of his shiny entrails,
and the pink swim-bladder
like a big peony.
I looked into his eyes
which were far larger than mine   35
but shallower, and yellowed,
the irises backed and packed
with tarnished tinfoil
seen through the lenses
of old scratched isinglass.   40
They shifted a little, but not
to return my stare.
—It was more like the tipping
of an object toward the light.
I admired his sullen face,   45
the mechanism of his jaw,

and then I saw
that from his lower lip
—if you could call it a lip—
grim, wet, and weaponlike,   50
hung five old pieces of fish-line,
or four and a wire leader
with the swivel still attached,
with all their five big hooks
grown firmly in his mouth.   55
A green line, frayed at the end
where he broke it, two heavier lines,
and a fine black thread
still crimped from the strain and snap
when it broke and he got away.   60
Like medals with their ribbons
frayed and wavering,
a five-haired beard of wisdom
trailing from his aching jaw.
I stared and stared   65
and victory filled up
the little rented boat,
from the pool of bilge
where oil had spread a rainbow
around the rusted engine   70
to the bailer rusted orange,
the sun-cracked thwarts,
the oarlocks on their strings,
the gunnels—until everything
was rainbow, rainbow, rainbow!   75
And I let the fish go.

Questions

1. How many abstract words does this poem contain? What proportion of the poem is imagery?
2. What is the speaker's attitude toward the fish? Comment in particular on lines 61–64.
3. What attitude do the images of the rainbow of oil (line 69), the orange bailer (bailing bucket, line 71), the *sun-cracked thwarts* (line 72) convey? Does the poet expect us to feel mournful because the boat is in such sorry condition?
4. What is meant by *rainbow, rainbow, rainbow*?
5. How do these images prepare us for the conclusion? Why does the speaker let the fish go?

Rainer Maria Rilke (1875–1926)

The Panther   1907

>   *In the Jardin des Plantes, Paris°*

His vision, from the constantly passing bars,
has grown so weary that it cannot hold
anything else. It seems to him there are
a thousand bars; and behind the bars, no world.

As he paces in cramped circles, over and over,   5
the movement of his powerful soft strides
is like a ritual dance around a center
in which a mighty will stands paralyzed.

Only at times, the curtain of the pupils
lifts, quietly—. An image enters in,   10
rushes down through the tensed, arrested muscles,
plunges into the heart and is gone.

—*Translated by Stephen Mitchell*

THE PANTHER. *Jardin des Plantes, Paris:* "garden of plants," a large botanical garden on the bank of the river
Seine, which also contains a small zoo.

Questions

1. What are the "bars" of line 1, and why are they "constantly passing"?
2. How do the contradictory descriptions in the second stanza—especially the simile in lines
   7–8—characterize the panther's situation?
3. What is meant by "the curtain of the pupils" (line 9)?
4. What is communicated by the image of the "image" in the last three lines?

Charles Simic (b. 1938)

Fork   1969

This strange thing must have crept
Right out of hell.
It resembles a bird's foot
Worn around the cannibal's neck.

As you hold it in your hand,   5
As you stab with it into a piece of meat,
It is possible to imagine the rest of the bird:
Its head which like your fist
Is large, bald, beakless, and blind.

Questions

1. The title image of this poem is an ordinary and everyday object. What happens to it in
   the first two lines?
2. How does the word *crept* in line 1 change our sense of the fork? How does the author
   develop this new sense later in the poem?

Emily Dickinson   (1830–1886)

A Route of Evanescence   (about 1879)

A Route of Evanescence
With a revolving Wheel –
A Resonance of Emerald –
A Rush of Cochineal° –   red dye
And every Blossom on the Bush   5
Adjusts its tumbled Head –
The mail from Tunis, probably,
An easy Morning's Ride –

A ROUTE OF EVANESCENCE. Dickinson titled this poem "A Humming-bird" in an 1880 letter to a friend.
1 *Evanescence*; ornithologist's term for the luminous sheen of certain birds' feathers. 7 *Tunis:* capital city
of Tunisia, North Africa.

Questions

What is the subject of this poem? How can you tell?

Jean Toomer   (1894–1967)

Reapers   1923

Black reapers with the sound of steel on stones
Are sharpening scythes. I see them place the hones
In their hip-pockets as a thing that's done,
And start their silent swinging, one by one.
Black horses drive a mower through the weeds,   5
And there, a field rat, startled, squealing bleeds,
His belly close to ground. I see the blade,
Blood-stained, continue cutting weeds and shade.

Questions

1. Imagine the scene Toomer describes. What details most vividly strike the mind's eye?
2. What kind of image is *silent swinging*?
3. Read the poem aloud. Notice especially the effect of the words *sound of steel on stones* and
   field rat, startled, squealing bleeds. What interesting sounds are present in the very words
   that contain these images?
4. What feelings do you get from this poem as a whole? Besides appealing to our auditory
   and visual imagination, what do the images contribute?

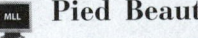

Gerard Manley Hopkins   (1844–1889)

Pied Beauty   (1877)

Glory be to God for dappled things—
    For skies of couple-color as a brinded° cow;   streaked
        For rose-moles all in stipple upon trout that swim;
Fresh-firecoal chestnut-falls; finches' wings;
    Landscape plotted and pieced—fold, fallow, and plow;   5
        And áll trádes, their gear and tackle and trim.°   equipment

All things counter, original, spare, strange;
　　Whatever is fickle, freckled (who knows how?)
　　　With swift, slow; sweet, sour; adazzle, dim;
He fathers-forth whose beauty is past change:　　　　　　　10
　　　　　Praise him.

Questions

1. What does the word *pied* mean? (Hint: what does a Pied Piper look like?)
2. According to Hopkins, what do *skies, cow, trout, ripe chestnuts, finches' wings,* and *landscapes* all have in common? What landscapes can the poet have in mind? (Have you ever seen any *dappled* landscape while looking down from an airplane, or from a mountain or high hill?)
3. What do you make of line 6: what can carpenters' saws and ditch-diggers' spades possibly have in common with the dappled things in lines 2–4?
4. Does Hopkins refer only to visual contrasts? What other kinds of variation interest him?
5. Try to state in your own words the theme of this poem. How essential to our understanding of this theme are Hopkins's images?

ABOUT HAIKU

Arakida Moritake (1473–1549)

The falling flower

The falling flower
I saw drift back to the branch
Was a butterfly.

—Translated by Babette Deutsch

Haiku means "beginning-verse" in Japanese—perhaps because the form may have originated in a game. Players, given a haiku, were supposed to extend its three lines into a longer poem. Haiku (the word can also be plural) consist mainly of imagery, but as we saw in Buson's lines about the cold comb, their imagery is not always only pictorial; it can involve any of the five senses. Haiku are so short that they depend on imagery to trigger associations and responses in the reader. A haiku in Japanese is rimeless; its seventeen syllables are traditionally arranged in three lines, usually following a pattern of five, seven, and five syllables. English haiku frequently ignore such a pattern, being rimed or unrimed as the poet prefers. What English haiku do try to preserve is the powerful way Japanese haiku capture the intensity of a particular moment, usually by linking two concrete images. There is little room for abstract thoughts or general observations. The following attempt, though containing seventeen syllables, is far from haiku in spirit:

Now that our love is gone
I feel within my soul
a nagging distress.

Unlike the author of those lines, haiku poets look out upon a literal world, seldom looking inward to *discuss* their feelings. Japanese haiku tend to be seasonal in subject, but because they are so highly compressed, they usually just *imply* a season: a blossom indicates spring; a crow on a branch, autumn; snow, winter. Not just pretty little sketches of nature (as some Westerners think), haiku assume a view of the universe in which observer and nature are not separated.

Haiku emerged in sixteenth-century Japan and soon developed into a deeply esteemed form. Even today, Japanese soldiers, stockbrokers, scientists, schoolchildren, and the emperor himself still find occasion to pen haiku. Soon after the form first captured the attention of Western poets at the end of the nineteenth century, it became immensely influential for modern poets such as Ezra Pound, William Carlos Williams, and H. D., as a model for the kind of verse they wanted to write—concise, direct, and imagistic.

The Japanese consider the poems of the "Three Masters"—Basho, Buson, and Issa—to be the pinnacle of the classical haiku. Each poet had his own personality: Basho, the ascetic seeker of Zen enlightenment; Buson, the worldly artist; Issa, the sensitive master of wit and pathos. Here are free translations of poems from each of the "Three Masters."

Matsuo Basho (1644–1694)

Heat-lightning streak

Heat-lightning streak—
through darkness pierces
the heron's shriek.

—Translated by X. J. Kennedy

In the old stone pool

In the old stone pool
a frogjump:
splishhhhh.

—Translated by X. J. Kennedy

Taniguchi Buson (1716–1783)

On the one-ton temple bell

On the one-ton temple bell
a moonmoth, folded into sleep,
sits still.

—Translated by X. J. Kennedy

Moonrise on mudflats

Moonrise on mudflats,
the line of water and sky
blurred by a bullfrog

—Translated by Michael Stillman

Kobayashi Issa (1763–1827)

only one guy

only one guy and
only one fly trying to
make the guest room do.

—Translated by Cid Corman

Cricket

Cricket, be
careful! I'm rolling
over!

—Translated by Robert Bly

HAIKU FROM JAPANESE INTERNMENT CAMPS

Japanese immigrants brought the tradition of haiku-writing to the United States, often forming local clubs to pursue their shared literary interests. During World War II, when Japanese Americans were unjustly considered "enemy aliens" and confined to federal internment camps, these poets continued to write in their bleak new surroundings. Today these haiku provide a vivid picture of the deprivations suffered by the poets, their families, and their fellow internees.

Suiko Matsushita

Cosmos in bloom

Cosmos in bloom
as if no war
were taking place

—*Translated by Violet Kazue de Cristoro*

Hakuro Wada

Even the croaking of frogs

Even the croaking of frogs
comes from outside the barbed wire fence
this is our life

—*Translated by Violet Kazue de Cristoro*

CONTEMPORARY HAIKU

If you care to try your hand at haiku-writing, here are a few suggestions: make every word matter. Include few adjectives, shun needless conjunctions. Set your poem in the present. ("Haiku," said Basho, "is simply what is happening in this place at this moment.") Like many writers of haiku, you may wish to confine your poem to what can be seen, heard, smelled, tasted, or touched. Mere sensory reports, however, will be meaningless unless they make the reader feel something.

Here are six more recent haiku written in English. (Don't expect them all to observe a strict arrangement of seventeen syllables, however.) Haiku, in any language, is an art of few words, many suggestions. A haiku starts us thinking and telling.

Etheridge Knight (1931–1991)

Making jazz swing in

Making jazz swing in
Seventeen syllables AIN'T
No square poet's job.

Lee Gurga (b. 1949)

Visitor's Room

Visitor's Room—
everything bolted down
except my brother.

Penny Harter (b. 1940)

broken bowl

broken bowl
the pieces
still rocking.

Jennifer Brutschy (b. 1960)

Born Again

Born Again
she speaks excitedly
of death.

John Ridland (b. 1933)

The Lazy Man's Haiku

out in the night
a wheelbarrowful
of moonlight.

Garry Gay (b. 1951)

Hole in the ozone

Hole in the ozone
My bald spot . . .
sunburned

FOR REVIEW AND FURTHER STUDY

 John Keats (1795–1821)

 Bright Star! would I were steadfast as thou art (1819)

Bright star! would I were steadfast as thou art—
  Not in lone splendor hung aloft the night,
And watching, with eternal lids apart,
  Like Nature's patient, sleepless Eremite,°   *hermit*
The moving waters at their priest-like task   5
  Of pure ablution round earth's human shores,
Or gazing on the new soft-fallen mask
  Of snow upon the mountains and the moors—
No—yet still steadfast, still unchangeable,
  Pillowed upon my fair love's ripening breast,   10
To feel for ever its soft fall and swell,
  Awake for ever in a sweet unrest,
Still, still to hear her tender-taken breath,
And so live ever—or else swoon to death.

Questions

1. Stars are conventional symbols for love and a loved one. (Love, Shakespeare tells us in a sonnet, "is the star to every wandering bark.") In this sonnet, why is it not possible for the star to have this meaning? How does Keats use it?
2. What seems concrete and particular in the speaker's observations?
3. Suppose Keats had said *slow and easy* instead of *tender-taken* in line 13. What would have been lost?

Experiment: Writing with Images

Taking the following poems as examples from which to start rather than as models to be slavishly copied, try to compose a brief poem that consists largely of imagery.

 Walt Whitman (1819–1892)

The Runner 1867

On a flat road runs the well-train'd runner;
He is lean and sinewy, with muscular legs;
He is thinly clothed—he leans forward as he runs,
With lightly closed fists, and arms partially rais'd.

T. E. Hulme (1883–1917)

Image (about 1910)

Old houses were scaffolding once
        and workmen whistling.

William Carlos Williams (1883–1963)

El Hombre 1917

It's a strange courage
You give me ancient star:

Shine alone in the sunrise
Toward which you lend no part!

Robert Bly (b. 1926)

Driving to Town Late to Mail a Letter 1962

It is a cold and snowy night. The main street is deserted.
The only things moving are swirls of snow.
As I lift the mailbox door, I feel its cold iron.
There is a privacy I love in this snowy night.
Driving around, I will waste more time. 5

Paul Goodman (1911–1972)

Birthday Cake 1962

Now isn't it time
when the candles on the icing
are one two too many
too many to blow out
too many to count too many 5
isn't it time to give up this ritual?

although the fiery crown
fluttering on the chocolate
and through the darkened room advancing
is still the most loveliest sight 10
among our savage folk
that have few festivals.

But the thicket is too hot and thick
and isn't it time, isn't it time
when the fires are too many 15
to eat the fire and not the cake
and drip the fires from my teeth
as once I had my hot hot youth.

Louise Glück (b. 1943)

Mock Orange   1985

It is not the moon, I tell you.
It is these flowers
lighting the yard.

I hate them.
I hate them as I hate sex,   5
the man's mouth
sealing my mouth, the man's
paralyzing body—

and the cry that always escapes,
the low, humiliating   10
premise of union—

In my mind tonight
I hear the question and pursuing answer
fused in one sound
that mounts and mounts and then   15
is split into the old selves,
the tired antagonisms. Do you see?
We were made fools of.
And the scent of mock orange
drifts through the window.   20

How can I rest?
How can I be content
when there is still
that odor in the world?

MOCK ORANGE. The mock orange is a flowering shrub with especially fragrant white blossoms and fruit
that resemble those of an orange tree.

 ## *Billy Collins* (b. 1941)

Embrace   1988

You know the parlor trick.
Wrap your arms around your own body
and from the back it looks like
someone is embracing you,
her hands grasping your shirt,   5
her fingernails teasing your neck.

From the front it is another story.
You never looked so alone,
your crossed elbows and screwy grin.
You could be waiting for a tailor   10
to fit you for a straitjacket,
one that would hold you really tight.

Kevin Prufer (b. 1969)

Pause, Pause   2002

Praise to the empty schoolroom, when the folders
are stowed and the sighing desktops close.

Praise to the sixteen-hour silence
after the last chairleg complains against the tiles.

There are tracks in the snow on the sidewalk,   5
ice salting into the bootprints. Snow clots fall

like good advice from the branches.
See the plaid skirts ticking into the distance?

The bookbags swaying to the footfalls?
Praise to the sun. It sets like a clocktower face,   10

oranges over, grows. Praise,
praise to the classrooms, empty at last.

One by one, the door-bolts click
and the lightbulbs shudder to a close.

The chairs dream all askew. Praise to the empty   15
hallway, the pause before the long bells cry.

Stevie Smith (1902–1971)

Not Waving but Drowning   1957

Nobody heard him, the dead man,
But still he lay moaning:
I was much further out than you thought
And not waving but drowning.

Poor chap, he always loved larking   5
And now he's dead
It must have been too cold for him his heart gave way,
They said.

Oh, no no no, it was too cold always
(Still the dead one lay moaning)   10
I was much too far out all my life
And not waving but drowning.

■ WRITING *effectively*

Ezra Pound on Writing

The Image   1913

An "Image" is that which presents an intellectual and emotional complex in an instant
of time. I use the term "complex" rather in
the technical sense employed by the newer
psychologists, such as Hart, though we might
not agree absolutely in our application.

It is the presentation of such a "complex" instantaneously which gives that sense
of sudden liberation; that sense of freedom
from time limits and space limits; that sense
of sudden growth, which we experience in
the presence of the greatest works of art.

It is better to present one Image in a
lifetime than to produce voluminous works.

Ezra Pound

All this, however, some may consider
open to debate. The immediate necessity is to tabulate A LIST OF DON'TS for those
beginning to write verses. I can not put all of them into Mosaic negative.

• • •

Use no superfluous word, no adjective which does not reveal something.

Don't use such an expression as "dim lands *of peace*." It dulls the image. It mixes
an abstraction with the concrete. It comes from the writer's not realizing that the
natural object is always the *adequate* symbol.

Go in fear of abstractions. Do not retell in mediocre verse what has already been
done in good prose. Don't think any intelligent person is going to be deceived when
you try to shirk all the difficulties of the unspeakably difficult art of good prose by
chopping your composition into line lengths.

From "A Few Don'ts"

THINKING ABOUT IMAGERY

Images are powerful things—thus the old saw, "A picture is worth a thousand
words." A poem, however, must build its pictures from words. By taking note of its
imagery, and watching how the nature of those images evolves from start to finish,
you can go a long way toward a better understanding of the poem. The following
steps can help:

- **Make a short list of the poem's key images.** Be sure to write them down in the
  order they appear, because the sequence can be as important as the images
  themselves.
- **Take the poem's title into account.** A title often points the way to important insights.

- **Remember: not all images are visual.** Images can draw on any or all of the five senses.
- **Jot down key adjectives or other qualifying words.**
- **Go back through your list and take notes about what moods or attitudes are suggested by each image.** What do you notice about the movement from the first image to the last?

Example: Robert Bly's "Driving to Town Late to Mail a Letter"

Let's try this method on a short poem. An initial list of images in Bly's "Driving to Town Late to Mail a Letter" (page 721) might look like this:

> cold and snowy night
> deserted main street
> mailbox door–cold iron
> snowy night (speaker loves its privacy)
> speaker drives around (to waste time)

Bly's title also contains several crucial images. Let's add them to the top of the list:

> driving (to town)
> late night
> a letter (to be mailed)

Looking over our list, we see how the images provide an outline of the poem's story. We also see how Bly begins the poem without providing an initial sense of how his speaker feels about the situation. Is driving to town late on a snowy evening a positive, negative, or neutral experience? By noting where (in line 4) the speaker reveals a subjective response to an image ("There is a privacy I love in this snowy night"), we may also begin to grasp the poem's overall emotional structure. We might also note on our list how the poem begins and ends with the same image (driving), but uses it for different effects. At the beginning, the speaker is driving for the practical purpose of mailing a letter but at the end purely for pleasure.

Simply by noting the images from start to finish, we have already worked out a rough essay outline—all on a single sheet of paper or a few inches of computer screen.

CHECKLIST: Writing About Imagery

- ☐ List a poem's key images, in the order in which they appear.
- ☐ What does the poem's title suggest?
- ☐ Remember, images can draw on all five senses—not just the visual.
- ☐ List key adjectives or other qualifying words.
- ☐ What emotions or attitudes are suggested by each image?
- ☐ Does the mood of the imagery change from start to finish?
- ☐ What is suggested by the movement from one image to the next? Remember that the order or sequence of images is almost as important as the images themselves.

WRITING ASSIGNMENT ON IMAGERY

Examining any poem in this chapter, demonstrate how its imagery helps communicate its general theme. Be specific in noting how each key image contributes to the poem's total effect. Feel free to consult criticism on the poem but make sure to credit any observation you borrow exactly from a critical source. Here is an essay written in response to this assignment by Becki Woods, a student of Mark Bernier's at Blinn College in Brenham, Texas.

SAMPLE STUDENT PAPER

Woods 1

Becki Woods

Professor Bernier

English 220

23 February 2009

Faded Beauty: Bishop's Use of Imagery in "The Fish"

First sentence gives name of author and work

Upon first reading, Elizabeth Bishop's "The Fish" appears to be a simple fishing tale. A close investigation of the imagery in Bishop's highly detailed description, however, reveals a different sort of poem. The real theme of Bishop's poem is a compassion and respect for the fish's lifelong struggle to survive. By carefully and effectively describing the captured fish, his reaction to being caught,

Thesis sentence

and the symbols of his past struggles to stay alive, Bishop creates, through her images of beauty, victory, and survival, something more than a simple tale.

Topic sentence

The first four lines of the poem are quite ordinary and factual:

I caught a tremendous fish

and held him beside the boat

half out of water, with my hook

fast in a corner of his mouth. (1–4)

Except for *tremendous*, Bishop's persona uses no exaggerations—unlike most fishing stories—to set up the situation of catching the fish. The detailed description begins as the speaker recounts the event further, noticing something signally important about the captive fish: "He didn't fight" (5). At this point the poem begins to seem unusual: most fish stories are about how ferociously the prey resists being captured. The speaker also notes that the "battered and venerable / and homely" fish offered no resistance to being caught (8–9). The image of the submissive attitude of the

Quotation from secondary source

fish is essential to the theme of the poem. It is his "utter passivity [that] makes [the persona's] detailed scrutiny possible" (McNally 192).

Woods 2

Once the image of the passive fish has been established, the speaker
begins an examination of the fish itself, noting that "Here and there / his
brown skin hung in strips / like ancient wallpaper" (9–11). By comparing the
fish's skin to wallpaper, the persona creates, as Sybil Estess argues, "implicit
suggestions of both artistry and decay" (713). Images of peeling wallpaper are
instantly brought to mind. The comparison of the fish's skin and wallpaper,
though "helpful in conveying an accurate notion of the fish's color to anyone
with memories of Victorian parlors and their yellowed wallpaper . . . is,"
according to Nancy McNally, "even more useful in evoking the associations of
deterioration which usually surround such memories" (192). The fish's faded
beauty has been hinted at in the comparison, thereby setting up the detailed
imagery that soon follows:

> He was speckled with barnacles,
> fine rosettes of lime,
> and infested
> with tiny white sea-lice,
> and underneath two or three
> rags of green weed hung down. (16–21)

The persona sees the fish as he is; the infestations and faults are not left out of
the description. Yet, at the same time, the fisher "express[es] what [he/she]
has sensed of the character of the fish" (Estess 714).

Bishop's persona notices "shapes like full-blown roses / stained and lost
through age" on the fish's skin (14–15). The persona's perception of the fish's
beauty is revealed along with a recognition of its faded beauty, which is best
shown in the description of the fish's being speckled with barnacles and spotted
with lime. However, the fisher observes these spots and sees them as rosettes—
as objects of beauty, not just ugly brown spots. These images contribute to the
persona's recognition of beauty's having become faded beauty.

The poem next turns to a description of the fish's gills. The imagery in
"While his gills were breathing in / the terrible oxygen" (22-23) leads "to the
very structure of the creature" that is now dying (Hopkins 201). The descriptions
of the fish's interior beauty—"the coarse white flesh / packed in like feathers,"
the colors "of his shiny entrails," and his "pink swim-bladder / like a big
peony"—are reminders of the life that seems about to end (27–28, 31–33).

The composite image of the fish's essential beauty—his being alive—is
developed further in the description of the five fish hooks that the captive,

---

Topic sentence

Essay moves systematically through poem, from start to finish

Textual evidence, mix of long and short quotations

Transitional phrase begins topic sentence

Textual evidence, mix of long and short quotations

Topic sentence

Woods 3

living fish carries in his lip:

> grim, wet, and weaponlike,
>
> hung five old pieces of fish-line,
>
> . . . .
>
> with all their five big hooks
>
> grown firmly in his mouth. (50–51, 54–55)

As if fascinated by them, the persona, observing how the lines must have been broken during struggles to escape, sees the hooks as "medals with their ribbons / frayed and wavering, / a five-haired beard of wisdom / trailing from his aching jaw" (61–64), and the fisher becomes enthralled by re-created images of the fish's fighting desperately for his life on at least five separate occasions—and winning. Crale Hopkins suggests that "[i]n its capability not only for mere existence, but for action, escaping from previous anglers, the fish shares the speaker's humanity" (202), thus revealing the fisher's deepening understanding of how he or she must now act. The persona has "all along," notes Estess, "describe[d] the fish not just with great detail but with an imaginative empathy for the aquatic creature. In her more-than-objective description, [the fisher] relates what [he/she] has seen to be both the pride and poverty of the fish" (715). It is at this point that the narrator of this fishing tale has a moment of clarity. Realizing the fish's history and the glory the fish has achieved in escaping previous hookings, the speaker sees everything become "rainbow, rainbow, rainbow!" (75)—and then unexpectedly lets the fish go.

Bishop's "The Fish" begins by describing an event that might easily be a conventional story's climax: "I caught a tremendous fish" (1). The poem, however, develops into a highly detailed account of a fisher noticing both the age and the faded beauty of the captive and his present beauty and past glory as well. The fishing tale is not simply a recounting of a capture; it is a gradually unfolding epiphany in which the speaker sees the fish in an entirely new light. The intensity of this encounter between an apparently experienced fisher in a rented boat and a battle-hardened fish is delivered through the poet's skillful use of imagery. It is through the description of the capture of an aged fish that Bishop offers her audience her theme of compassion derived from a respect for the struggle for survival.

Quotations from secondary sources

Conclusion

Restatement of thesis, in light of all that comes before it.

Woods 4

Works Cited

Bishop, Elizabeth. "The Fish." *Literature: An Introduction to Fiction, Poetry, Drama, and Writing*. Ed. X. J. Kennedy and Dana Gioia. 11th ed. New York: Longman, 2010. 713–714. Print.

Estess, Sybil P. "Elizabeth Bishop: The Delicate Art of Map Making." *Southern Review* 13 (1977): 713–17. Print.

Hopkins, Crale D. "Inspiration as Theme: Art and Nature in the Poetry of Elizabeth Bishop." *Arizona Quarterly* 32 (1976): 200–202. Print.

McNally, Nancy L. "Elizabeth Bishop: The Discipline of Description." *Twentieth-Century Literature* 11 (1966): 192–94. Print.

MORE TOPICS FOR WRITING

1. Apply the steps listed above to one of the poems in this chapter. Louise Glück's "Mock Orange," Billy Collins's "Embrace," and Jean Toomer's "Reapers" would each make a good subject. Make a brief list of images, and jot down notes on what the images suggest. Now write a two-page description of this process—what it revealed about the poem itself, and about reading poetry in general.

2. Choose a small, easily overlooked object in your home that has special significance to you. Write a paragraph-long, excruciatingly detailed description of the item, putting at least four senses into play. Without making any direct statements about the item's importance to you, try to let the imagery convey the mood you associate with it. Bring your paragraph to class, exchange it with a partner, and see if he or she can identify the mood you were trying to convey.

3. Reread the section on haiku in this chapter. Write three or four haiku of your own and a brief prose account of your experience in writing them. Did anything about the process surprise you?

▶ TERMS FOR *review*

Image ▶ A word or series of words that refers to any sensory experience (usually sight, although also sound, smell, touch, or taste). An image is a direct or literal recreation of physical experience and adds immediacy to literary language.

Imagery ▶ The collective set of images in a poem or other literary work.

Haiku ▶ A Japanese verse form that has three unrhymed lines of five, seven, and five syllables. Traditional haiku is often serious and spiritual in tone, relying mostly on imagery, and usually set (often by implication instead of direct statement) in one of the four seasons. Modern haiku in English often ignore strict syllable count, and may have a more playful, worldly tone.

18 FIGURES OF SPEECH

All slang is metaphor,
and all metaphor is poetry.

—G. K. CHESTERTON

WHY SPEAK FIGURATIVELY?

"I will speak daggers to her, but use none," says Hamlet, preparing to confront his mother. His statement makes sense only because we realize that *daggers* is to be taken two ways: literally (denoting sharp, pointed weapons) and nonliterally (referring to something that can be used *like* weapons—namely, words). Reading poetry, we often meet comparisons between two things whose similarity we have never noticed before. When Marianne Moore observes that a fir tree has "an emerald turkey-foot at the top," the result is a pleasure that poetry richly affords: the sudden recognition of likenesses.

A treetop like a turkey-foot, words like daggers—such comparisons are called **figures of speech**. In its broadest definition, a figure of speech may be said to occur whenever a speaker or writer, for the sake of freshness or emphasis, departs from the usual denotations of words. Certainly, when Hamlet says he will speak daggers, no one expects him to release pointed weapons from his lips, for *daggers* is not to be read solely for its denotation. Its connotations—sharp, stabbing, piercing, wounding—also come to mind, and we see ways in which words and daggers work alike. (Words too can hurt: by striking through pretenses, possibly, or by wounding their hearer's self-esteem.) In the statement "A razor is sharper than an ax," there is no departure from the usual denotations of *razor* and *ax,* and no figure of speech results. Both objects are of the same class; the comparison is not offensive to logic. But in King Lear's "How sharper than a serpent's tooth it is / To have a thankless child," the objects—snake's tooth (fang) and ungrateful offspring—are so unlike that no reasonable comparison may be made between them. To find similarity, we attend to the connotations of *serpent's tooth*—biting, piercing, venom, pain—rather than to its denotations. If we are aware of the connotations of *red rose* (beauty, softness, freshness, and so forth), then the line "My love is like a red, red rose" need not call to mind a woman with a scarlet face and a thorny neck.

Figures of speech are not devices to state what is demonstrably untrue. Indeed they often state truths that more literal language cannot communicate; they call attention to such truths; they lend them emphasis.

Alfred, Lord Tennyson (1809–1892)

The Eagle   1851

He clasps the crag with crooked hands;
Close to the sun in lonely lands,
Ringed with the azure world, he stands.

The wrinkled sea beneath him crawls;
He watches from his mountain walls,   5
And like a thunderbolt he falls.

This brief poem is rich in figurative language. In the first line, the phrase *crooked hands* may surprise us. An eagle does not have hands, we might protest; but the objection would be a quibble, for evidently Tennyson is indicating exactly how an eagle clasps a crag, in the way that human fingers clasp a thing. By implication, too, the eagle is a person. *Close to the sun*, if taken literally, is an absurd exaggeration, the sun being a mean distance of 93,000,000 miles from the earth. For the eagle to be closer to it by the altitude of a mountain is an approach so small as to be insignificant. But figuratively, Tennyson conveys that the eagle stands above the clouds, perhaps silhouetted against the sun, and for the moment belongs to the heavens rather than to the land and sea. The word *ringed* makes a circle of the whole world's horizons and suggests that we see the world from the eagle's height; the *wrinkled sea* becomes an aged, sluggish animal; *mountain walls*, possibly literal, also suggests a fort or castle; and finally the eagle itself is likened to a thunderbolt in speed and in power, perhaps also in that its beak is—like our abstract conception of a lightning bolt—pointed. How much of the poem can be taken literally? Only *he clasps the crag, he stands, he watches, he falls*. The rest is made of figures of speech. The result is that, reading Tennyson's poem, we gain a bird's-eye view of sun, sea, and land—and even of bird. Like imagery, figurative language refers us to the physical world.

William Shakespeare (1564–1616)

Shall I compare thee to a summer's day?   1609

Shall I compare thee to a summer's day?
Thou art more lovely and more temperate.
Rough winds do shake the darling buds of May,
And summer's lease hath all too short a date.
Sometime too hot the eye of heaven shines,   5
And often is his gold complexion dimmed;
And every fair° from fair sometimes declines,   *fair one*
By chance, or nature's changing course, untrimmed;
But thy eternal summer shall not fade,
Nor lose possession of that fair thou ow'st,°   *ownest, have* 10
Nor shall death brag thou wand'rest in his shade,
When in eternal lines to time thou grow'st.
  So long as men can breathe or eyes can see,
  So long lives this, and this gives life to thee.

Howard Moss (1922–1987)

Shall I Compare Thee to a Summer's Day?   1976

Who says you're like one of the dog days?
You're nicer. And better.
Even in May, the weather can be gray,
And a summer sub-let doesn't last forever.
Sometimes the sun's too hot;   5
Sometimes it is not.
Who can stay young forever?
People break their necks or just drop dead!
But you? Never!
If there's just one condensed reader left   10
Who can figure out the abridged alphabet,
    After you're dead and gone,
    In this poem you'll live on!

SHALL I COMPARE THEE TO A SUMMER'S DAY? (MOSS). *Dog days:* the hottest days of summer. The ancient Romans believed that the Dog-star, Sirius, added heat to summer months.

Questions

1. In Howard Moss's streamlined version of Shakespeare, from a series called "Modified Sonnets (Dedicated to adapters, abridgers, digesters, and condensers everywhere)," to what extent does the poet use figurative language? In Shakespeare's original sonnet, how high a proportion of Shakespeare's language is figurative?

2. Compare some of Moss's lines to the corresponding lines in Shakespeare's sonnet. Why is *Even in May, the weather can be gray* less interesting than the original? In the lines on the sun (5–6 in both versions), what has Moss's modification deliberately left out? Why is Shakespeare's seeing death as a braggart memorable? Why aren't you greatly impressed by Moss's last two lines?

3. Can you explain Shakespeare's play on the word *untrimmed* (line 8)? Evidently the word can mean "divested of trimmings," but what other suggestions do you find in it?

4. How would you answer someone who argued, "Maybe Moss's language isn't as good as Shakespeare's, but the meaning is still there. What's wrong with putting Shakespeare into up-to-date words that can be understood by everybody?"

METAPHOR AND SIMILE

Life, like a dome of many-colored glass,
Stains the white radiance of Eternity.

The first of these lines (from Shelley's "Adonais") is a **simile**: a comparison of two things, indicated by some connective, usually *like, as, than,* or a verb such as *resembles.* A simile expresses a similarity. Still, for a simile to exist, the things compared have to be dissimilar in kind. It is no simile to say "Your fingers are like mine"; it is a literal observation. But to say "Your fingers are like sausages" is to use a simile. Omit the connective—say "Your fingers are sausages"—and the result is a **metaphor**, a statement that one thing *is* something else, which, in a literal sense, it is not. In the second of Shelley's lines, it is *assumed* that Eternity is light or radiance, and we have an **implied metaphor**, one that uses neither a connective nor the verb *to be*. Here are examples:

Oh, my love is like a red, red rose.	*Simile*
Oh, my love resembles a red, red rose.	*Simile*
Oh, my love is redder than a rose.	*Simile*
Oh, my love is a red, red rose.	*Metaphor*
Oh, my love has red petals and sharp thorns.	*Implied metaphor*
Oh, I placed my love into a long-stem vase	
and I bandaged my bleeding thumb.	*Implied metaphor*

Often you can tell a metaphor from a simile by much more than just the presence or absence of a connective. In general, a simile refers to only one characteristic that two things have in common, while a metaphor is not plainly limited in the number of resemblances it may indicate. To use the simile "He eats like a pig" is to compare man and animal in one respect: eating habits. But to say "He's a pig" is to use a metaphor that might involve comparisons of appearance and morality as well.

For scientists as well as poets, the making of metaphors is customary. In 1933 George Lemaitre, the Belgian priest and physicist credited with the big bang theory of the origin of the universe, conceived of a primal atom that existed before anything else, which expanded and produced everything. And so, he remarked, making a wonderful metaphor, the evolution of the cosmos as it is today "can be compared to a display of fireworks that has just ended." As astrophysicist and novelist Alan Lightman has noted, we can't help envisioning scientific discoveries in terms of things we know from daily life—spinning balls, waves in water, pendulums, weights on springs. "We have no other choice," Lightman reasons. "We cannot avoid forming mental pictures when we try to grasp the meaning of our equations, and how can we picture what we have not seen?"[1] In science as well as in poetry, it would seem, metaphors are necessary instruments of understanding.

Mixed Metaphors

In everyday speech, simile and metaphor occur frequently. We use metaphors ("She's a doll") and similes ("The tickets are selling like hotcakes") without being fully conscious of them. If, however, we are aware that words possess literal meanings as well as figurative ones, we do not write *died in the wool* for *dyed in the wool* or *tow the line* for *toe the line*, nor do we use **mixed metaphors** as did the writer who advised, "Water the spark of knowledge and it will bear fruit," or the speaker who urged, "To get ahead, keep your nose to the grindstone, your shoulder to the wheel, your ear to the ground, and your eye on the ball." Perhaps the unintended humor of these statements comes from our seeing that the writer, busy stringing together stale metaphors, was not aware that they had any physical reference.

Unlike a writer who thoughtlessly mixes metaphors, a good poet can join together incongruous things and still keep the reader's respect. In his ballad "Thirty Bob a Week," John Davidson has a British workingman tell how it feels to try to support a large family on small wages:

It's a naked child against a hungry wolf;
   It's playing bowls upon a splitting wreck;
It's walking on a string across a gulf
   With millstones fore-and-aft about your neck;

[1]"Physicists' Use of Metaphor," *The American Scholar* (Winter 1989): 99.

But the thing is daily done by many and many a one;
  And we fall, face forward, fighting, on the deck.

Like the man with his nose to the grindstone, Davidson's wage earner is in an absurd fix; but his balancing act seems far from merely nonsensical. For every one of the poet's comparisons—of workingman to child, to bowler, to tightrope walker, and to seaman—offers suggestions of a similar kind. All help us see (and imagine) the workingman's hard life: a brave and unyielding struggle against impossible odds.

Poetry and Metaphor

A poem may make a series of comparisons, like Davidson's, or the whole poem may be one extended comparison:

Emily Dickinson (1830–1886)

My Life had stood – a Loaded Gun   (about 1863)

My Life had stood – a Loaded Gun –
In Corners – till a Day
The Owner passed – identified –
And carried Me away –

And now We roam in Sovereign Woods –   5
And now We hunt the Doe –
And every time I speak for Him –
The Mountains straight reply –

And do I smile, such cordial light
Upon the Valley glow –   10
It is as a Vesuvian face
Had let its pleasure through –

And when at Night – Our good Day done –
I guard My Master's Head –
'Tis better than the Eider-Duck's   15
Deep Pillow – to have shared –

To foe of His – I'm deadly foe –
None stir the second time –
On whom I lay a Yellow Eye –
Or an emphatic Thumb –   20

Though I than He – may longer live
He longer must – than I –
For I have but the power to kill,
Without – the power to die –

How much life metaphors bring to poetry may be seen by comparing two poems by Tennyson and Blake.

Alfred, Lord Tennyson (1809–1892)

Flower in the Crannied Wall   1869

Flower in the crannied wall,
I pluck you out of the crannies,
I hold you here, root and all, in my hand,
Little flower—but *if* I could understand
What you are, root and all, and all in all,   5
I should know what God and man is.

How many metaphors does this poem contain? None. Compare it with a briefer
poem on a similar theme: the quatrain that begins Blake's "Auguries of Innocence."
(We follow here the opinion of W. B. Yeats, who, in editing Blake's poems, thought
the lines ought to be printed separately.)

William Blake (1757–1827)

To see a world in a grain of sand   (about 1803)

To see a world in a grain of sand
And a heaven in a wild flower,
Hold infinity in the palm of your hand
And eternity in an hour.

Set beside Blake's poem, Tennyson's—short though it is—seems lengthy. What contributes to the richness of "To see a world in a grain of sand" is Blake's use of a
metaphor in every line. And every metaphor is loaded with suggestion. Our world
does indeed resemble a grain of sand: in being round, in being stony, in being one of
a myriad (the suggestions go on and on). Like Blake's grain of sand, a metaphor holds
much, within a small circumference.

Sylvia Plath (1932–1963)

Metaphors   1960

I'm a riddle in nine syllables,
An elephant, a ponderous house,
A melon strolling on two tendrils.
O red fruit, ivory, fine timbers!
This loaf's big with its yeasty rising.   5
Money's new-minted in this fat purse.
I'm a means, a stage, a cow in calf.
I've eaten a bag of green apples,
Boarded the train there's no getting off.

Questions
1. To what central fact do all the metaphors in this poem refer?
2. In the first line, what has the speaker in common with a riddle? Why does she say she has
   nine syllables?

N. Scott Momaday (b. 1934)

Simile   1974

What did we say to each other
that now we are as the deer
who walk in single file
with heads high
with ears forward   5
with eyes watchful
with hooves always placed on firm ground
in whose limbs there is latent flight

Questions

1. Momaday never tells us what was said. Does this omission keep us from understanding the comparison?
2. The comparison is extended with each detail adding some new twist. Explain the implications of the last line.

Experiment: Likening

Write a poem that follows the method of N. Scott Momaday's "Simile," consisting of one long comparison between two objects. Possible subjects might include talking to a loved one long-distance; what you feel like going to a weekend job; being on a diet; not being noticed by someone you love; winning a lottery.

Emily Dickinson (1830–1886)

It dropped so low – in my Regard   (about 1863)

It dropped so low – in my Regard –
I heard it hit the Ground –
And go to pieces on the Stones
At bottom of my Mind –

Yet blamed the Fate that flung it – *less*   5
Than I denounced Myself,
For entertaining Plated Wares
Upon My Silver Shelf –

Questions

1. What is *it*? What two things are compared?
2. How much of the poem develops and amplifies this comparison?

Jill Alexander Essbaum (b. 1971)

The Heart   2007

Four simple chambers.
A thousand complicated doors.

One of them is yours.

Questions

1. Which line contains a figure of speech?
2. Is that figure a metaphor or a simile? Explain.

Craig Raine (b. 1944)

A Martian Sends a Postcard Home   1979

Caxtons are mechanical birds with many wings
and some are treasured for their markings—

they cause the eyes to melt
or the body to shriek without pain.

I have never seen one fly, but   5
sometimes they perch on the hand.

Mist is when the sky is tired of flight
and rests its soft machine on ground:

then the world is dim and bookish
like engravings under tissue paper.   10

Rain is when the earth is television.
It has the property of making colors darker.

Model T is a room with the lock inside—
a key is turned to free the world

for movement, so quick there is a film   15
to watch for anything missed.

But time is tied to the wrist
or kept in a box, ticking with impatience.

In homes, a haunted apparatus sleeps,
that snores when you pick it up.   20

If the ghost cries, they carry it
to their lips and soothe it to sleep

with sounds. And yet, they wake it up
deliberately, by tickling with a finger.

Only the young are allowed to suffer   25
openly. Adults go to a punishment room

with water but nothing to eat.
They lock the door and suffer the noises

alone. No one is exempt
and everyone's pain has a different smell.   30

At night, when all the colors die,
they hide in pairs

and read about themselves—
in color, with their eyelids shut.

A MARTIAN SENDS A POSTCARD HOME. The title of this poem literally describes its contents. A Martian briefly describes everyday objects and activities on earth, but the visitor sees them all from an alien perspective. The Martian/author lacks a complete vocabulary and sometimes describes general categories of things with a proper noun (as in Model T in line 13). 1 *Caxtons:* Books, since William Caxton (c. 1422–1491) was the first person to print books in England.

Question

Can you recognize *everything* the Martian describes and translate it back into Earth-based English?

Exercise: What Is Similar?

Each of these quotations contains a simile or a metaphor. In each of these figures of speech, what two things is the poet comparing? Try to state exactly what you understand the two things to have in common: the most striking similarity or similarities that the poet sees.

1.   All the world's a stage,
    And all the men and women merely players:
    They have their exits and their entrances,
    And one man in his time plays many parts,
    His acts being seven ages.
            —William Shakespeare, *As You Like It*

2. When the hounds of spring are on winter's traces . . .
            —Algernon Charles Swinburne, "Atalanta in Calydon"

3. Art is long, and Time is fleeting,
        And our hearts, though strong and brave,
    Still, like muffled drums are beating
        Funeral marches to the grave.
            —Henry Wadsworth Longfellow, "A Psalm of Life"

4. "Hope" is the thing with feathers –
    That perches in the soul –
    And sings the tune without the words –
    And never stops – at all –
            —Emily Dickinson, an untitled poem

5. Why should I let the toad *work*
        Squat on my life?
    Can't I use my wit as a pitchfork
        And drive the brute off?
            —Philip Larkin, "Toads"

6. I wear my patience like a light-green dress
    and wear it thin.
            —Emily Grosholz, "Remembering the Ardèche"

7. a laugh maybe, like glasses on a shelf
    suddenly found by the sun . . .
            —Beth Gylys, "Briefly"

8. A new electric fence,
   Its five barbed wires tight
   As a steel-stringed banjo.
   —Van K. Brock, "Driving at Dawn"

9. Spring stirs Gossamer Beynon Schoolmistress like a spoon.
   —Dylan Thomas, *Under Milk Wood*

10. Our headlight caught, as in a flashbulb's flare,
    A pair of hitchhikers.
    —Paul Lake, "Two Hitchhikers"

OTHER FIGURES OF SPEECH

When Shakespeare asks, in a sonnet,

> O! how shall summer's honey breath hold out
> Against the wrackful siege of batt'ring days,

it might seem at first that he mixes metaphors. How can a *breath* confront the
battering ram of an invading army? But it is summer's breath and, by giving it to
summer, Shakespeare makes the season a man or woman. It is as if the fragrance
of summer were the breath within a person's body, and winter were the onslaught
of old age.

Personification

Such is Shakespeare's instance of **personification**: a figure of speech in which a thing,
an animal, or an abstract term (*truth*, *nature*) is made human. A personification extends
throughout this short poem.

James Stephens (1882–1950)

The Wind   1915

The wind stood up and gave a shout.
He whistled on his fingers and

Kicked the withered leaves about
And thumped the branches with his hand

And said he'd kill and kill and kill,   5
And so he will and so he will.

The wind is a wild man, and evidently it is not just any autumn breeze but a hur-
ricane or at least a stiff gale. In poems that do not work as well as this one, personification may be employed mechanically. Hollow-eyed personifications walk
the works of lesser English poets of the eighteenth century: Coleridge has quoted the
beginning of one such neoclassical ode, "Inoculation! heavenly Maid, descend!" It is
hard for the contemporary reader to be excited by William Collins's "The Passions, An Ode for Music" (1747), which personifies, stanza by stanza, Fear,
Anger, Despair, Hope, Revenge, Pity, Jealousy, Love, Hate, Melancholy, and

Cheerfulness, and has them listen to Music, until even "Brown Exercise rejoiced to hear, / And Sport leapt up, and seized his beechen spear." Still, in "Two Sonnets on Fame" John Keats makes an abstraction come alive in seeing Fame as "a way-ward girl."

Apostrophe

Hand in hand with personification often goes **apostrophe**: a way of addressing some-one or something invisible or not ordinarily spoken to. In an apostrophe, a poet (in these examples Wordsworth) may address an inanimate object ("Spade! with which Wilkinson hath tilled his lands"), some dead or absent person ("Milton! thou shouldst be living at this hour"), an abstract thing ("Return, Delights!"), or a spirit ("Thou Soul that art the eternity of thought"). More often than not, the poet uses apostrophe to announce a lofty and serious tone. An "O" may even be put in front of it ("O moon!") since, according to W. D. Snodgrass, every poet has a right to do so at least once in a lifetime. But apostrophe doesn't have to be highfalutin. It is a means of giving life to the inanimate. It is a way of giving body to the intangible, a way of speaking to it person to person, as in the words of a moving American spiritual: "Death, ain't you got no shame?"

Overstatement and Understatement

Most of us, from time to time, emphasize a point with a statement containing exag-geration: "Faster than greased lightning," "I've told him a thousand times." We speak, then, not literal truth but use a figure of speech called **overstatement** (or **hyperbole**). Poets too, being fond of emphasis, often exaggerate for effect. Instances are Marvell's profession of a love that should grow "Vaster than empires, and more slow" and John Burgon's description of Petra: "A rose-red city, half as old as Time." Overstatement can be used also for humorous purposes, as in a fat woman's boast (from a blues song): "Every time I shake, some skinny gal loses her home."[2] The opposite is **understatement**, implying more than is said. Mark Twain in *Life on the Mississippi* recalls how, as an ap-prentice steamboat-pilot asleep when supposed to be on watch, he was roused by the pilot and sent clambering to the pilot house: "Mr. Bixby was close behind, comment-ing." Another example is Robert Frost's line "One could do worse than be a swinger of birches"—the conclusion of a poem that has suggested that to swing on a birch tree is one of the most deeply satisfying activities in the world.

Metonymy and Synecdoche

In **metonymy**, the name of a thing is substituted for that of another closely associated with it. For instance, we say "The White House decided," and mean that the president did. When John Dyer writes in "Grongar Hill,"

> A little rule, a little sway,
> A sun beam in a winter's day,
> Is all the proud and mighty have
> Between the cradle and the grave,

we recognize that *cradle* and *grave* signify birth and death. A kind of metonymy, **synecdoche** is the use of a part of a thing to stand for the whole of it or vice versa.

---

[2]Quoted by Amiri Baraka [LeRoi Jones] in *Blues People* (New York: Morrow, 1963).

We say "She lent a hand," and mean that she lent her entire presence. Similarly, Milton in "Lycidas" refers to greedy clergymen as "blind mouths."

Paradox

Paradox occurs in a statement that at first strikes us as self-contradictory but that on reflection makes some sense. "The peasant," said G. K. Chesterton, "lives in a larger world than the globe-trotter." Here, two different meanings of *larger* are contrasted: "greater in spiritual values" versus "greater in miles." Some paradoxical statements, however, are much more than plays on words. In a moving sonnet, the blind John Milton tells how one night he dreamed he could see his dead wife. The poem ends in a paradox:

> But oh, as to embrace me she inclined,
> I waked, she fled, and day brought back my night.

Pun

Asked to tell the difference between men and women, Samuel Johnson replied, "I can't conceive, madam, can you?" The great dictionary-maker was using a figure of speech known to classical rhetoricians as *paronomasia,* better known to us as a **pun** or play on words. How does a pun operate? It reminds us of another word (or other words) of similar or identical sound but of very different denotation. Although puns at their worst can be mere piddling quibbles, at best they can sharply point to surprising but genuine resemblances. The name of a dentist's country estate, Tooth Acres, is accurate: aching teeth paid for the property. In his novel *Moby-Dick,* Herman Melville takes up questions about whales that had puzzled scientists: for instance, are the whale's spoutings water or gaseous vapor? And when Melville speaks pointedly of the great whale "sprinkling and mistifying the gardens of the deep," we catch his pun, and conclude that the creature both mistifies and mysti-fies at once.

In poetry, a pun may be facetious, as in Thomas Hood's ballad of "Faithless Nelly Gray":

> Ben Battle was a soldier bold,
>   And used to war's alarms;
> But a cannon-ball took off his legs,
>   So he laid down his arms!

Or it may be serious, as in these lines on war by E. E. Cummings:

> the bigness of cannon
> is skillful,

(*is skillful* becoming *is kill-ful* when read aloud), or perhaps, as in Shakespeare's song in *Cymbeline,* "Fear no more the heat o' th' sun," both facetious and serious at once:

> Golden lads and girls all must,
>   As chimney-sweepers, come to dust.

Poets often make puns on images, thereby combining the sensory force of im-agery with the verbal pleasure of wordplay. Find and explain the punning images in these two poems.

Margaret Atwood (b. 1939)

You fit into me   1971

you fit into me
like a hook into an eye

a fish hook
an open eye

George Herbert (1593–1633)

The Pulley   1633

When God at first made man,
Having a glass of blessings standing by—
Let us (said he) pour on him all we can;
Let the world's riches, which dispersèd lie,
    Contract into a span.   5

So strength first made a way,
Then beauty flowed, then wisdom, honor, pleasure:
When almost all was out, God made a stay,
Perceiving that, alone of all His treasure,
    Rest in the bottom lay.   10

For if I should (said he)
Bestow this jewel also on My creature,
He would adore My gifts instead of Me,
And rest in Nature, not the God of Nature:
    So both should losers be.   15

Yet let him keep the rest,
But keep them with repining restlessness;
Let him be rich and weary, that at least,
If goodness lead him not, yet weariness
    May toss him to My breast.   20

Questions

1. What different senses of the word *rest* does Herbert bring into this poem?
2. How do God's words in line 16, *Yet let him keep the rest*, seem paradoxical?
3. What do you feel to be the tone of Herbert's poem? Does the punning make the poem seem comic?
4. Why is the poem called "The Pulley"? What is its implied metaphor?

To sum up: even though figures of speech are not to be taken *only* literally, they refer us to a tangible world. By *personifying* an eagle, Tennyson reminds us that the bird and humankind have certain characteristics in common. Through *metonymy*, a poet can focus our attention on a particular detail in a larger object; through *hyperbole* and *understatement,* make us see the physical actuality in back of words. *Pun* and *paradox* cause us to realize this actuality, too, and probably surprise us enjoyably at the same time. Through *apostrophe,* the poet animates the inanimate and asks it to listen—speaks directly to an immediate god or to the revivified dead. Put to such uses, figures of speech have power. They are more than just ways of playing with words.

Dana Gioia (b. 1950)

Money   1991

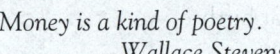

> *Money is a kind of poetry.*
> —*Wallace Stevens*

Money, the long green,
cash, stash, rhino, jack
or just plain dough.

Chock it up, fork it over,
shell it out. Watch it   5
burn holes through pockets.

To be made of it! To have it
to burn! Greenbacks, double eagles,
megabucks and Ginnie Maes.

It greases the palm, feathers a nest,   10
holds heads above water,
makes both ends meet.

Money breeds money.
Gathering interest, compounding daily.
Always in circulation.   15

Money. You don't know where it's been,
but you put it where your mouth is.
And it talks.

Question

What figures of speech can you identify in this poem?

Carl Sandburg (1878–1967)

Fog   1916

The fog comes
on little cat feet.

It sits looking
over harbor and city
on silent haunches   5
and then moves on.

Questions

1. What figure of speech does this poem use?
2. Which specific feline qualities does the speaker impute to the fog?

Charles Simic (b. 1938)

My Shoes   1967

Shoes, secret face of my inner life:
Two gaping toothless mouths,
Two partly decomposed animal skins
Smelling of mice nests.

My brother and sister who died at birth   5
Continuing their existence in you,
Guiding my life
Toward their incomprehensible innocence.

What use are books to me
When in you it is possible to read   10
The Gospel of my life on earth
And still beyond, of things to come?

I want to proclaim the religion
I have devised for your perfect humility
And the strange church I am building   15
With you as the altar.

Ascetic and maternal, you endure:
Kin to oxen, to Saints, to condemned men,
With your mute patience, forming
The only true likeness of myself.   20

Question

Which statements in this poem are literal, and which are not? For those that are figurative,
identify the specific figure of speech that each employs.

FOR REVIEW AND FURTHER STUDY

Robert Frost (1874–1963)

The Silken Tent   1942

She is as in a field a silken tent
At midday when a sunny summer breeze
Has dried the dew and all its ropes relent,
So that in guys° it gently sways at ease,   *attachments that steady it*
And its supporting central cedar pole,   5
That is its pinnacle to heavenward
And signifies the sureness of the soul,
Seems to owe naught to any single cord,
But strictly held by none, is loosely bound
By countless silken ties of love and thought   10
To everything on earth the compass round,
And only by one's going slightly taut
In the capriciousness of summer air
Is of the slightest bondage made aware.

Questions

1. Is Frost's comparison of a woman and tent a simile or a metaphor?
2. What are the ropes or cords?
3. Does the poet convey any sense of this woman's character? What sort of person do you believe her to be?
4. Paraphrase the poem, trying to state its implied meaning. (To be refreshed about paraphrase, turn back to page 632.) Be sure to include the implications of the last three lines.

Jane Kenyon (1947–1995)

The Suitor   1978

We lie back to back. Curtains
lift and fall,
like the chest of someone sleeping.
Wind moves the leaves of the box elder;
they show their light undersides,   5
turning all at once
like a school of fish.
Suddenly I understand that I am happy.
For months this feeling
has been coming closer, stopping   10
for short visits, like a timid suitor.

Question

In each simile you find in "The Suitor," exactly what is the similarity?

Exercise: Figures of Speech

Identify the central figure of speech in the following four short poems.

Robert Frost (1874–1963)

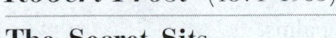

The Secret Sits   1942

We dance round in a ring and suppose,
But the Secret sits in the middle and knows.

A. R. Ammons (1926–2001)

Coward   1975

Bravery runs in my family.

Kay Ryan (b. 1945)

Turtle   1994

Who would be a turtle who could help it?
A barely mobile hard roll, a four-oared helmet,
she can ill afford the chances she must take
in rowing toward the grasses that she eats.
Her track is graceless, like dragging   5

a packing-case places, and almost any slope
defeats her modest hopes. Even being practical,
she's often stuck up to the axle on her way
to something edible. With everything optimal,
she skirts the ditch which would convert   10
her shell into a serving dish. She lives
below luck-level, never imagining some lottery
will change her load of pottery to wings.
Her only levity is patience,
the sport of truly chastened things.   15

Anne Stevenson (b. 1933)

The Demolition   1974

They have lived in each other so long
There is little to do there.
They have taken to patching the floor
While the roof tears.

The rot in her feeds on his woodwork.   5
He batters her cellar.
He camps in the ruin of her carpet.
She cries on his stairs.

Robinson Jeffers (1887–1962)

Hands   1929

Inside a cave in a narrow canyon near Tassajara
The vault of rock is painted with hands,
A multitude of hands in the twilight, a cloud of men's palms,
     no more,
No other picture. There's no one to say
Whether the brown shy quiet people who are dead intended   5
Religion or magic, or made their tracings
In the idleness of art; but over the division of years these
     careful
Signs-manual are now like a sealed message
Saying: "Look: we also were human; we had hands, not paws.
     All hail
You people with the cleverer hands, our supplanters   10
In the beautiful country; enjoy her a season, her beauty, and
     come down
And be supplanted; for you also are human."

Question
Identify examples of personification and apostrophe in "Hands."

Robert Burns (1759–1796)

Oh, my love is like a red, red rose

(about 1788)

Oh, my love is like a red, red rose
  That's newly sprung in June;
My love is like the melody
  That's sweetly played in tune.

So fair art thou, my bonny lass,   5
  So deep in love am I;
And I will love thee still, my dear,
  Till a' the seas gang° dry.   *go*

Till a' the seas gang dry, my dear,
  And the rocks melt wi' the sun;   10
And I will love thee still, my dear,
  While the sands o' life shall run.

And fare thee weel, my only love!
  And fare thee weel awhile!
And I will come again, my love   15
  Though it were ten thousand mile.

■ WRITING *effectively*

Robert Frost on Writing

The Importance of Poetic Metaphor

1930

I do not think anybody ever knows the discreet use of metaphors, his own and other people's, the discreet handling of metaphor, unless he has been properly educated in poetry.

Poetry begins in trivial metaphors, pretty metaphors, "grace" metaphors, and goes on to the profoundest thinking that we have. Poetry provides the one permissible way of saying one thing and meaning another. People say, "Why don't you say what you mean?" We never do that, do we, being all of us too much poets. We like to talk in parables and in hints and in indirections—whether from diffidence or some other instinct.

I have wanted in late years to go further and further in making metaphor the whole of thinking. I find someone now and then to agree with me that all thinking, except

Robert Frost

mathematical thinking, is metaphorical, or all thinking except scientific thinking. The mathematical might be difficult for me to bring in, but the scientific is easy enough.

• • •

What I am pointing out is that unless you are at home in the metaphor, unless you have had your proper poetical education in the metaphor, you are not safe anywhere. Because you are not at ease with figurative values: you don't know the metaphor in its strength and its weakness. You don't know how far you may expect to ride it and when it may break down with you. You are not safe in science; you are not safe in history.

From "Education by Poetry"

THINKING ABOUT METAPHORS

Metaphors are more than mere decoration. Sometimes, for example, they help us envision an unfamiliar thing more clearly by comparing it with another, more familiar item. A metaphor can reveal interesting aspects of both items. Usually we can see the main point of a good metaphor immediately, but in interpreting a poem, the practical issue sometimes arises of how far to extend a comparison.

- **To write effectively about a metaphorical poem, start by considering the general scope of its key metaphor.** In what ways, for instance, does the beloved resemble a rose in Robert Burns's "Oh, my love is like a red, red rose"?
- **Before you begin to write, clarify which aspects of the comparison are true and which are false.** The beloved in Burns's poem is probably beautiful, but might not have thorns, and she probably doesn't stand around in the dirt.
- **Make a list of metaphors and key images in the poem.** Then draw lines to connect the ones that seem to be related.
- **Notice whether there are obvious connections among all the metaphors or similes in a poem.** Perhaps all of them are threatening, or inviting, or nocturnal, or exaggerated. Such similarities, if they occur, will almost certainly be significant.

CHECKLIST: Writing About Metaphors

☐ Underline a poem's key comparisons. Look for both similes and metaphors.

☐ How are the two things being compared alike?

☐ In what ways are the two things unlike each other?

☐ Do the metaphors or similes in the poem have anything in common?

☐ If so, what does that commonality suggest?

WRITING ASSIGNMENT ON FIGURES OF SPEECH

In a brief essay of approximately 500 words, analyze the figures of speech to be found in any poem in this chapter. To what effect does the poem employ metaphors, similes, hyperbole, overstatement, paradox, or any other figure of speech?

MORE TOPICS FOR WRITING

1. Examine the extended implied metaphor that constitutes John Donne's "The Flea" (page 1037). Paraphrase the poem's argument. In your opinion, does the use of metaphor strengthen the speaker's case?

2. Whip up some similes of your own. Choose someone likely to be unfamiliar to your classmates—your brother or your best friend from home, for example. Write a paragraph in which you use multiple metaphors and similes to communicate a sense of what that person looks, sounds, and acts like. Come up with at least one figure of speech in each sentence.

3. Write a paragraph on any topic, tossing in as many hyperbolic statements as possible. Then write another version, changing all your exaggeration to understatement. In one last paragraph, sum up what this experience taught you about figurative language.

4. Rewrite a short poem rich in figurative language: Sylvia Plath's "Metaphors," for example, or Robert Burns's "Oh, my love is like a red, red rose." Taking for your model Howard Moss's deliberately bepiddling version of "Shall I compare thee to a summer's day?," use language as flat and unsuggestive as possible. Eliminate every figure of speech. (Just ignore any rime or rhythm in the original.) Then, in a paragraph, indicate lines in your revised version that seem glaringly worsened. In conclusion, sum up what your barbaric rewrite tells you about the nature of poetry.

▶ TERMS FOR *review*

Simile and Metaphor

Simile ▶ A comparison of two things, indicated by some connective, usually *like, as,* or *than,* or a verb such as *resembles*. A simile usually compares two things that initially seem unlike but are shown to have a significant resemblance. "Cool as a cucumber" and "My love is like a red, red rose" are examples of similes.

Metaphor ▶ A statement that one thing *is* something else, which, in a literal sense, it is not. A metaphor creates a close association between the two entities and underscores some important similarity between them. An example of metaphor is "Richard is a pig."

Implied metaphor ▶ A metaphor that uses neither connectives nor the verb *to be*. If we say "John crowed over his victory," we imply metaphorically that John is a rooster but do not say so specifically.

Mixed metaphor ▶ The (usually unintentional) combining of two or more incompatible metaphors, resulting in ridiculousness or nonsense. For example, "Mary was such a tower of strength that she breezed her way through all the work" ("towers" do not "breeze").

Other Figures of Speech

Personification ▶ The endowing of a thing, an animal, or an abstract term with human characteristics. Personification dramatizes the nonhuman world in tangibly human terms.

Apostrophe ▶ A direct address to someone or something. In an apostrophe, a speaker may address an inanimate object, a dead or absent person, an abstract thing, or a spirit.

Overstatement ▶ Also called **hyperbole**. Exaggeration used to emphasize a point.

Understatement ▶ An ironic figure of speech that deliberately describes something in a way that is less than the case.

Metonymy ▶ Figure of speech in which the name of a thing is substituted for that of another closely associated with it. For instance, we might say "The White House decided" when we mean that the president did.

Synecdoche ▶ The use of a significant part of a thing to stand for the whole of it, or vice versa. Saying *wheels* for *car* is an example of synecdoche.

Paradox ▶ A statement that at first strikes one as self-contradictory, but that on reflection reveals some deeper sense. Paradox is often achieved by a play on words.

19

SONG

A bird doesn't sing because it has an answer,
it sings because it has a song.

—MAYA ANGELOU

SINGING AND SAYING

Most poems are more memorable than most ordinary speech, and when music is combined with poetry, the result can be more memorable still. The differences between speech, poetry, and song may appear if we consider, first of all, this fragment of an imaginary conversation between two lovers:

> Let's not drink; let's just sit here and look at each other. Or put a kiss
>   inside my goblet and I won't want anything to drink.

Forgettable language, we might think; but let's try to make it a little more interesting:

> Drink to me only with your eyes, and I'll pledge my love to you with
>   my eyes;
> Or leave a kiss within the goblet, that's all I'll want to drink.

The passage is closer to poetry, but still has a distance to go. At least we now have a figure of speech—the metaphor that love is wine, implied in the statement that one lover may salute another by lifting an eye as well as by lifting a goblet. But the sound of the words is not yet especially interesting. Here is another try, by Ben Jonson:

> Drink to me only with thine eyes,
>   And I will pledge with mine;
> Or leave a kiss but in the cup,
>   And I'll not look for wine.

In these opening lines from Jonson's poem "To Celia," the improvement is noticeable. These lines are poetry; their language has become special. For one thing, the lines rime (with an additional rime sound on *thine*). There is interest, too, in the proximity of the words *kiss* and *cup*: the repetition (or alliteration) of the *k* sound. The rhythm of the lines has become regular; generally every other word (or syllable) is stressed:

> DRINK to me ON-ly WITH thine EYES,
>   And I will PLEDGE with MINE;
> Or LEAVE a KISS but IN the CUP,
>   And I'LL not LOOK for WINE.

All these devices of sound and rhythm, together with metaphor, produce a pleasing effect—more pleasing than the effect of "Let's not drink; let's look at each other." But the words became more pleasing still when later set to music:

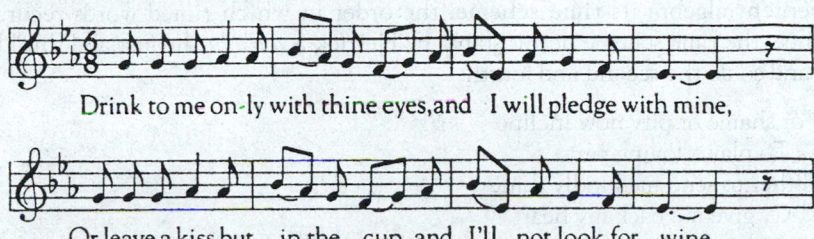

Drink to me on-ly with thine eyes, and I will pledge with mine,

Or leave a kiss but in the cup, and I'll not look for wine.

In this memorable form, the poem is still alive today.

Ben Jonson (1573?–1637)

To Celia   1616

Drink to me only with thine eyes,
   And I will pledge with mine;
Or leave a kiss but in the cup,
   And I'll not look for wine.
The thirst that from the soul doth rise   5
   Doth ask a drink divine;
But might I of Jove's nectar sup,
   I would not change for thine.

I sent thee late a rosy wreath,
   Not so much honoring thee   10
As giving it a hope that there
   It could not withered be.
But thou thereon didst only breathe,
   And sent'st it back to me;
Since when it grows, and smells, I swear,   15
   Not of itself but thee.

A compliment to a lady has rarely been put in language more graceful, more wealthy with interesting sounds. Other figures of speech besides metaphor make them unforgettable: for example, the hyperbolic tributes to the power of the lady's sweet breath, which can start picked roses growing again, and her kisses, which even surpass the nectar of the gods.

Stanza

"To Celia" falls into stanzas—as many poems that resemble songs also do. A **stanza** (Italian for "stopping-place" or "room") is a group of lines whose pattern is repeated throughout the poem. Most songs have more than one stanza. When printed, the stanzas of songs and poems usually are set off from one another by space. When sung, stanzas of songs are indicated by a pause or by the introduction of a refrain, or chorus (a line or lines repeated). The word **verse**, which strictly refers to one line of a poem, is sometimes loosely used to mean a whole stanza: "All join in and sing the second verse!" In speaking of a stanza, whether sung or read, it is customary to indicate by a convenient algebra its **rime scheme**, the order in which rimed words recur. For instance, the rime scheme of this stanza by Herrick is *a b a b;* the first and third lines rime and so do the second and fourth:

> For shame or pity now incline
> To play a loving part,
> Either to send me kindly thine
> Or give me back my heart.

Refrain

Refrains are words, phrases, or lines repeated at intervals in a song or songlike poem. A refrain usually follows immediately after a stanza, and when it does, it is sometimes called **terminal refrain**. Sometimes we also hear an **internal refrain**: one that appears within a stanza, generally in a position that stays fixed throughout a poem. James Weldon Johnson uses a blues-based stanza with a terminal refrain in "Sence You Went Away":

James Weldon Johnson (1871–1938)

Sence You Went Away   1917

Seems lak to me de stars don't shine so bright,
Seems lak to me de sun done loss his light,
Seems lak to me der's nothin' goin' right,
    Sence you went away.

Seems lak to me de sky ain't half so blue,   5
Seems lak to me dat ev'ything wants you,
Seems lak to me I don't know what to do,
    Sence you went away.

Seems lak to me dat ev'ything is wrong,
Seems lak to me de day's jes twice as long,   10
Seems lak to me de bird's forgot his song,
    Sence you went away.

Seems lak to me I jes can't he'p but sigh,
Seems lak to me ma th'oat keeps gittin' dry,
Seems lak to me a tear stays in ma eye,   15
    Sence you went away.

We usually meet poems as words on a page, but songs we generally first encounter as sounds in the air. Consequently, songs tend to be written in language simple enough to be understood on first hearing. But some contemporary songwriters have created songs that require listeners to pay close and repeated attention to their words. Beginning in the 1960s with performers like Bob Dylan, Leonard Cohen, Joni Mitchell, and Frank Zappa, some pop songwriters crafted deliberately challenging songs. More recently, Sting, Aimee Mann, Beck, and Suzanne Vega have written complex lyrics, often full of strange, dreamlike imagery. To unravel them, a listener may have to play the recording many times, with the treble turned up all the way. Anyone who feels that literary criticism is solely an academic enterprise should listen to high school and college students discuss the lyrics of their favorite songs.

Madrigals

Many familiar poems began life as songs, but today, their tunes forgotten, they survive only in poetry anthologies. Shakespeare studded his plays with songs, and many of his contemporaries wrote verses to fit existing tunes. Some poets were themselves musicians (such as Thomas Campion), and composed both words and music. In Shakespeare's day, **madrigals**, short secular songs for three or more voices arranged in counterpoint, enjoyed great popularity. A madrigal is always short, usually just one stanza, and rarely exceeds twelve or thirteen lines. Elizabethans loved to sing, and a person was considered a dolt if he or she could not join in a three-part song. Here is a madrigal from one of Shakespeare's comedies.

William Shakespeare (1564–1616)

O mistress mine (about 1600)

O mistress mine, where are you roaming?
O, stay and hear! your true love's coming,
   That can sing both high and low:
Trip no further, pretty sweeting;
Journeys end in lovers meeting—   5
   Every wise man's son doth know.
What is love? 'Tis not hereafter;
Present mirth hath present laughter;
   What's to come is still unsure:
In delay there lies no plenty;   10
Then, come kiss me, sweet and twenty,
   Youth's a stuff will not endure.

O MISTRESS MINE. The clown's love song from *Twelfth Night* (Act II, Scene iii).

Some poets who were not composers printed their work in madrigal books for others to set to music. In the seventeenth century, however, poetry and song seem to have fallen away from each other. By the end of the century, much new poetry, other than songs for plays, was written to be printed and to be silently read. Poets who wrote popular songs—such as Thomas D'Urfey, compiler of the collection *Pills to Purge Melancholy*—were considered somewhat disreputable. With the notable exceptions of John Gay, who took existing popular tunes for *The Beggar's Opera*, and Robert Burns, who rewrote folk songs or made completely new words for them, few important English poets since Campion have been first-rate song-writers.

Occasionally, a poet has learned a thing or two from music. "But for the opera I could never have written *Leaves of Grass*," said Walt Whitman, who loved the Italian art form for its expansiveness. Coleridge, Hardy, Auden, and many others have learned from folk ballads, and T. S. Eliot patterned his thematically repetitive *Four Quartets* after the structure of a quartet in classical music. "Poetry," said Ezra Pound, "begins to atrophy when it gets too far from music." Still, even in the twentieth century, the poet was more often a corrector of printer's proofs than a tunesmith or performer.

From Troubadours to Rock Stars

Some people think that to write poems and to travel about singing them, as many rock singer-composers now do, is a return to the venerable tradition of the **troubadours**, minstrels of the late Middle Ages. But there are differences. No doubt the troubadours had to please their patrons, but for better or worse their songs were not affected by a producer's video promotion budget or by the technical resources of a sound studio. Bob Dylan has denied that he is a poet, and Paul Simon once told an interviewer, "If you want poetry read Wallace Stevens." Nevertheless, many rock lyrics have the verbal intensity of poetry. No rock lyric, however, can be judged independent of its musical accompaniment. Songwriters rarely create their lyrics to be read on the page. A song joins words and music; a great song joins them inseparably.

Although the words of a great song do not necessarily stand on their own without their music, they are not invalidated as lyrics. If the words seem rich and interesting in themselves, our enjoyment is only increased. Like most poems and songs of the past, most current songs may end up in the trash can of time. And yet, certain memorable rimed and rhythmic lines may live on, especially if they are expressed in stirring music and have been given wide exposure.

Exercise: Comparing Poem and Song

Compare the following poem by Edwin Arlington Robinson and a popular song lyric based on it. Notice what Paul Simon had to do to Robinson's original poem in order to make it into a song, and how Simon altered Robinson's conception.

Edwin Arlington Robinson (1869–1935)

 Richard Cory   1897

Whenever Richard Cory went down town,
We people on the pavement looked at him:
He was a gentleman from sole to crown,
Clean favored, and imperially slim.

And he was always quietly arrayed,   5
And he was always human when he talked;
But still he fluttered pulses when he said,
"Good-morning," and he glittered when he walked.

And he was rich—yes, richer than a king—
And admirably schooled in every grace:
In fine,° we thought that he was everything   10
To make us wish that we were in his place.

So on we worked, and waited for the light,
And went without the meat, and cursed the bread;
And Richard Cory, one calm summer night,   15
Went home and put a bullet through his head.

in short

Paul Simon (b. 1941)

Richard Cory   1966

With Apologies to E. A. Robinson

They say that Richard Cory owns
One half of this whole town,
With political connections
To spread his wealth around.
Born into Society,   5
A banker's only child,
He had everything a man could want:
Power, grace and style.

Refrain:

But I, I work in his factory
And I curse the life I'm livin'   10
And I curse my poverty
And I wish that I could be
Oh I wish that I could be
Oh I wish that I could be
Richard Cory.   15

The papers print his picture
Almost everywhere he goes:
Richard Cory at the opera,
Richard Cory at a show
And the rumor of his parties   20
And the orgies on his yacht—
Oh he surely must be happy
With everything he's got.   *(Refrain.)*

He freely gave to charity,
He had the common touch,   25
And they were grateful for his patronage
And they thanked him very much,
So my mind was filled with wonder
When the evening headlines read:
"Richard Cory went home last night   30
And put a bullet through his head."   *(Refrain.)*

RICHARD CORY by Paul Simon. If possible, listen to the ballad sung by Simon and Garfunkel on *Sounds of Silence* (Sony, 2001), © 1966 by Paul Simon. Used by permission.

BALLADS

Any narrative song, like Paul Simon's "Richard Cory," may be called a **ballad**. In English, some of the most famous ballads are **folk ballads**, loosely defined as anonymous story-songs transmitted orally before they were ever written down. Sir Walter Scott, a pioneer collector of Scottish folk ballads, drew the ire of an old woman whose songs he had transcribed: "They were made for singing and no' for reading, but ye ha'e broken the charm now and they'll never be sung mair." The old singer had a point. Print freezes songs and tends to hold them fast to a single version. If Scott and others had not written them down, however, many would have been lost.

In his monumental work *The English and Scottish Popular Ballads* (1882–1898), the American scholar Francis J. Child winnowed out 305 folk ballads he considered authentic—that is, creations of illiterate or semiliterate people who had preserved them orally. Child, who worked by insight as well as by learning, did such a good job of telling the difference between folk ballads and other kinds that later scholars have added only about a dozen ballads to his count. Often called **Child ballads**, his texts include "The Three Ravens," "Sir Patrick Spence," and many others still on the lips of singers. Here is one of the best-known Child ballads.

Anonymous (traditional Scottish ballad)

Bonny Barbara Allan

It was in and about the Martinmas time,
   When the green leaves were afalling,
That Sir John Graeme, in the West Country,
   Fell in love with Barbara Allan.

He sent his men down through the town,   5
   To the place where she was dwelling;
"O haste and come to my master dear,
   Gin° ye be Barbara Allan."   *if*

O hooly,° hooly rose she up,   *slowly*
   To the place where he was lying,
And when she drew the curtain by: 10
   "Young man, I think you're dying."

"O it's I'm sick, and very, very sick,
   And 'tis a' for Barbara Allan."—
"O the better for me ye's never be,   15
   Tho your heart's blood were aspilling.

"O dinna ye mind,° young man," said she,   *don't you remember*
   "When ye was in the tavern adrinking,
That ye made the health° gae round and round,   *toasts*
   And slighted Barbara Allan?"   20

He turned his face unto the wall,
    And death was with him dealing:
"Adieu, adieu, my dear friends all,
    And be kind to Barbara Allan."

And slowly, slowly raise she up,   25
    And slowly, slowly left him,
And sighing said she could not stay,
    Since death of life had reft him.

She had not gane a mile but twa,
    When she heard the dead-bell ringing,   30
And every jow° that the dead-bell geid,   *stroke*
    It cried, "Woe to Barbara Allan!"

"O mother, mother, make my bed!
    O make it saft and narrow!
Since my love died for me today,   35
    I'll die for him tomorrow."

BONNY BARBARA ALLAN. 1 *Martinmas:* Saint Martin's Day, November 11.

Questions

1. In any line does the Scottish dialect cause difficulty? If so, try reading the line aloud.
2. Without ever coming out and explicitly calling Barbara hard-hearted, this ballad reveals that she is. In which stanza and by what means is her cruelty demonstrated?
3. At what point does Barbara evidently have a change of heart? Again, how does the poem dramatize this change without explicitly talking about it?
4. In many American versions of this ballad, noble knight John Graeme becomes an ordinary citizen. The gist of the story is the same, but at the end are these further stanzas, incorporated from a different ballad:

    They buried Willie in the old churchyard
        And Barbara in the choir;
    And out of his grave grew a red, red rose,
        And out of hers a briar.

    They grew and grew to the steeple top
        Till they could grow no higher;
    And there they locked in a true love's knot,
        The red rose round the briar.

    Do you think this appendage heightens or weakens the final impact of the story? Can the American ending be defended as an integral part of a new song? Explain.
5. Paraphrase lines 9, 15–16, 22, 25–28. By putting these lines into prose, what has been lost?

As you can see from "Bonny Barbara Allan," in a traditional English or Scottish folk ballad the storyteller speaks of the lives and feelings of others. Even if the pronoun "I" occurs, it rarely has much personality. Characters often exchange dialogue, but no one character speaks all the way through. Events move rapidly, perhaps because some of the dull transitional stanzas have been forgotten. The events themselves, as ballad scholar Albert B. Friedman has said, are frequently "the stuff of tabloid journalism—sensational tales of lust, revenge and domestic crime. Unwed mothers slay their newborn babes; lovers unwilling to marry their pregnant mistresses brutally murder the poor women, for which, without fail, they are justly punished."[1] There are also many ballads of the supernatural and of gallant knights ("Sir Patrick Spence"), and there are a few humorous ballads, usually about unhappy marriages.

Ballad Stanza

A favorite pattern of ballad-makers is the so-called **ballad stanza**, four lines rimed *a b c b*, tending to fall into 8, 6, 8, and 6 syllables:

> Clerk Saunders and Maid Margaret
> > Walked owre yon garden green,
> And deep and heavy was the love
> > That fell thir twa between.°   *between those two*

Though not the only possible stanza for a ballad, this easily singable quatrain has continued to attract poets since the Middle Ages. Close kin to the ballad stanza is **common meter**, a stanza found in hymns such as "Amazing Grace," by the eighteenth-century English hymnist John Newton:

> Amazing grace! how sweet the sound
> > That saved a wretch like me!
> I once was lost, but now am found,
> > Was blind, but now I see.

Notice that its pattern is that of the ballad stanza except for its *two* pairs of rimes. That all its lines rime is probably a sign of more literate artistry than we usually hear in folk ballads. Another sign of schoolteachers' influence is that Newton's rimes are exact. (Rimes in folk ballads are often rough-and-ready, as if made by ear, rather than polished and exact, as if the riming words had been matched for their similar spellings. In "Barbara Allan," for instance, the hard-hearted lover's name rimes with *afalling, dwelling, aspilling, dealing,* and even with *ringing* and *adrinking.*) That so many hymns were written in common meter may have been due to convenience. If a congregation didn't know the tune to a hymn in common meter, they readily could sing its words to the tune of another such hymn they knew. Besides hymnists, many poets have favored common meter, among them A. E. Housman and Emily Dickinson.

Literary Ballads

Literary ballads, not meant for singing, are written by sophisticated poets for book-educated readers who enjoy being reminded of folk ballads. Literary ballads imitate

---

[1]Introduction to *The Viking Book of Folk Ballads of the English-Speaking World*, ed. Albert B. Friedman (New York: Viking, 1956).

certain features of folk ballads: they may tell of dramatic conflicts or of mortals who
encounter the supernatural; they may use conventional figures of speech or ballad
stanzas. Well-known poems of this kind include Keats's "La Belle Dame sans Merci"
(see page 872), Coleridge's "Rime of the Ancient Mariner," and (in our time) Dudley
Randall's "Ballad of Birmingham."

Dudley Randall (1914–2000)

Ballad of Birmingham   1966

(*On the Bombing of a Church in
Birmingham, Alabama, 1963*)

"Mother dear, may I go downtown
Instead of out to play,
And march the streets of Birmingham
In a Freedom March today?"

"No, baby, no, you may not go,   5
For the dogs are fierce and wild,
And clubs and hoses, guns and jails
Aren't good for a little child."

"But, mother, I won't be alone.
Other children will go with me,   10
And march the streets of Birmingham
To make our country free."

"No, baby, no, you may not go,
For I fear those guns will fire.
But you may go to church instead   15
And sing in the children's choir."

She has combed and brushed her night-dark hair,
And bathed rose petal sweet,
And drawn white gloves on her small brown hands,
And white shoes on her feet.   20

The mother smiled to know her child
Was in the sacred place,
But that smile was the last smile
To come upon her face.

For when she heard the explosion,   25
Her eyes grew wet and wild.
She raced through the streets of Birmingham
Calling for her child.

She clawed through bits of glass and brick,
Then lifted out a shoe.   30
"O here's the shoe my baby wore,
But, baby, where are you?"

Questions

1. This poem, about a dynamite blast set off in an African American church by a racial terrorist (later convicted), delivers a message without preaching. How would you sum up this message, its implied theme?
2. What is ironic in the mother's denying her child permission to take part in a protest march?
3. How does this modern poem resemble a traditional ballad?

Exercise: Seeing the Traits of Ballads

Read the Child ballads "The Three Ravens" (page 1017) and "Sir Patrick Spence" (page 637). With these ballads in mind, consider these modern poems:

W. H. Auden, "As I Walked Out One Evening" (page 1021)
William Butler Yeats, "Crazy Jane Talks with the Bishop" (page 1102)

What characteristics of folk ballads do you find in them? In what ways do these modern poets depart from the traditions of folk ballads of the Middle Ages?

BLUES

Among the many song forms to have shaped the way poetry is written in English, no recent form has been more influential than the **blues**. Originally a type of folk music developed by black slaves in the South, blues songs have both a distinctive form and tone. They traditionally consist of three-line stanzas in which the first two identical lines are followed by a concluding riming third line:

> To dream of muddy water—trouble is knocking at your door.
> To dream of muddy water—trouble is knocking at your door.
> Your man is sure to leave you and never return no more.

Early blues lyrics almost always spoke of some sadness, pain, or deprivation— often the loss of a loved one. The melancholy tone of the lyrics, however, is not only world-weary but also world-wise. The blues expound the hard-won wisdom of bitter life experience. They frequently create their special mood through down-to-earth, even gritty, imagery drawn from everyday life. Although blues reach back into the nineteenth century, they were not widely known outside African American communities before 1920, when the first commercial recordings appeared. Their influence on both music and song from that time on was rapid and extensive. By 1930 James Weldon Johnson could declare, "It is from the blues that all that may be called American music derives its most distinctive characteristic." Blues have not only become an enduring category of popular music, they have also helped shape virtually all the major styles of contemporary pop— jazz, rap, rock, gospel, country, and, of course, rhythm-and-blues.

The style and structure of blues have also influenced modern poets. Not only have African American writers such as Langston Hughes, Sterling A. Brown, Etheridge Knight, and Sonia Sanchez written blues poems, but white poets as dissimilar as W. H. Auden, Elizabeth Bishop, Donald Justice, and Sandra McPherson have employed the form. The classic touchstones of the blues, however, remain the early singers such as Robert Johnson, Ma Rainey, Blind Lemon Jefferson, Charley Patton, and—perhaps preeminently—Bessie Smith, "the Empress of the Blues." Any form that has fascinated Bishop and Auden as well as B. B. King, Mick Jagger, Tracy Chapman, and Eric Clapton surely deserves special notice.

The blues remind us of how closely related song and poetry will always be. Here are the lyrics of one of Bessie Smith's earliest songs, based on traditional folk blues, followed by a blues-influenced cabaret song written by W. H. Auden (with the composer Benjamin Britten) for a night-club singer, and a short poem by a contemporary African American poet, Kevin Young.

Bessie Smith (1898?–1937)
with Clarence Williams (1898–1965)

Jailhouse Blues   1923

Thirty days in jail with my back turned to the wall.
Thirty days in jail with my back turned to the wall.
Look here, Mister Jailkeeper, put another gal in my stall.

I don't mind bein' in jail but I got to stay there so long.
I don't mind bein' in jail but I got to stay there so long.   5
Well, ev'ry friend I had has done shook hands and gone.

You better stop your man from ticklin' me under my chin.
You better stop your man from ticklin' me under my chin.
'Cause if he keep on ticklin' I'm sure gonna take him in.

Good mornin' blues, blues how do you do?   10
Good mornin' blues, blues how do you do?
Well, I just come here to have a few words with you.

W. H. Auden (1907–1973)

Funeral Blues   1940

Stop all the clocks, cut off the telephone,
Prevent the dog from barking with a juicy bone,
Silence the pianos and with muffled drum
Bring out the coffin, let the mourners come.

Let aeroplanes circle moaning overhead   5
Scribbling on the sky the message He Is Dead,
Put crêpe bows round the white necks of the public doves,
Let the traffic policemen wear black cotton gloves.

He was my North, my South, my East and West,
My working week and my Sunday rest,   10
My noon, my midnight, my talk, my song;
I thought that love would last for ever: I was wrong.

The stars are not wanted now: put out every one,
Pack up the moon and dismantle the sun,
Pour away the ocean and sweep up the woods;   15
For nothing now can ever come to any good.

Questions
What features of the traditional blues does Auden keep in his song? What does he discard?

Kevin Young (b. 1970)

Late Blues   2003

If
    I die,
let me

be buried
    standing—   5
I never lied

to anyone,
    or down—
wouldn't want

to start up now.   10

Questions

1. What is there about this poem that might explain why its author calls it a "blues"?
2. What play on words do you find in the word "lied"? Is there also a play on the word "late" in the poem's title?

RAP

One of the most interesting musical and literary developments of the 1980s was the emergence of **rap**, a form of popular music in which words are recited to a driving rhythmic beat. It differs from mainstream popular music in several ways, but, most interesting in literary terms, rap lyrics are *spoken* rather than sung. In that sense, rap is a form of popular poetry as well as popular music. In most rap songs, the lead performer or "M.C." talks or recites, usually at top speed, long, rhythmic, four-stress lines that end in rimes. Although today most rap singers and groups use electronic or sampled backgrounds, rap began on city streets in the game of "signifying," in which two poets aim rimed insults at each other, sometimes accompanying their tirades with a beat made by clapping or finger-snapping. This game also includes boasts made by the players on both sides about their own abilities.

Rap developed so rapidly that it now uses a variety of metrical forms, but it is interesting to look more closely at some of the early work that established the genre. Most rap still follows the initial formula of rimed couplets that casually mix full rime with assonance. Here are a few lines from one of the first popular raps:

> I said, "By the way, baby, what's your name?"
> She said, "I go by the name Lois Lane.
> And you can be my boyfriend, you surely can,
> Just let me quit my boyfriend, he's called Superman."
>
> —"Rapper's Delight," Sugarhill Gang, 1979

Rap is not written in the standard meters of English literary verse, but its basic measure does come out of the English tradition. Rap's characteristic four-stress, accentual line has been the most common meter for spoken popular poetry in English from Anglo-Saxon verse and the folk ballads to the work of Robert W. Service and Rudyard Kipling.

> What is a woman that you forsake her,
> And the hearth-fire and the home-acre,
> To go with the old grey Widow-maker?
>
> —"Harp Song of the Dane Women," Rudyard Kipling, 1906

Rap deliberately makes use of stress-meter's ability to stretch and contract in syllable count. In fact, playing the syllable count against the beat is the basic metrical technique of rap. Like jazz, rap plays a flexible rhythm off against a fixed metrical beat, turning a traditional English folk meter into something distinctively African American. By hitting the beat hard while exploiting other elements of word music, rappers play interesting and elaborate games with the total rhythm of their lines.

FOR REVIEW AND FURTHER STUDY

John Lennon (1940–1980)
Paul McCartney (b. 1942)

Eleanor Rigby   1966

Ah, look at all the lonely people!
Ah, look at all the lonely people!

Eleanor Rigby
Picks up the rice in the church where a wedding has been,
Lives in a dream.   5
Waits at the window
Wearing the face that she keeps in a jar by the door.
Who is it for?

All the lonely people,
Where do they all come from?   10
All the lonely people,
Where do they all belong?

Father McKenzie
Writing the words of a sermon that no one will hear,
No one comes near.
Look at him working,   15
Darning his socks in the night when there's nobody there.
What does he care?

All the lonely people,
Where do they all come from?
All the lonely people,   20
Where do they all belong?

Eleanor Rigby
Died in the church and was buried along with her name,
Nobody came.   25
Father McKenzie
Wiping the dirt from his hands as he walks from the grave,
No one was saved.

All the lonely people,
Where do they all come from?   30
All the lonely people,
Where do they all belong?

Ah, look at all the lonely people!
Ah, look at all the lonely people!

Question

Is there any reason to call this famous song a ballad? Compare it with a traditional ballad, such as "Bonny Barbara Allan." Do you notice any similarity? What are the differences?

Bob Dylan (b. 1941)

The Times They Are a-Changin'   1963

Come gather 'round people
Wherever you roam
And admit that the waters
Around you have grown
And accept it that soon   5
You'll be drenched to the bone.
If your time to you
Is worth savin'
Then you better start swimmin'
Or you'll sink like a stone   10
For the times they are a-changin'.

Come writers and critics
Who prophesize with your pen
And keep your eyes wide
The chance won't come again   15
And don't speak too soon
For the wheel's still in spin
And there's no tellin' who
That it's namin'.
For the loser now   20
Will be later to win
For the times they are a-changin'.

Come senators, congressmen
Please heed the call
Don't stand in the doorway
Don't block up the hall   25
For he that gets hurt
Will be he who has stalled
There's a battle outside
And it is ragin'.   30
It'll soon shake your windows
And rattle your walls
For the times they are a-changin'.

Come mothers and fathers
Throughout the land   35
And don't criticize
What you can't understand
Your sons and your daughters
Are beyond your command
Your old road is   40
Rapidly agin'.
Please get out of the new one
If you can't lend your hand
For the times they are a-changin'.

The line it is drawn   45
The curse it is cast
The slow one now
Will later be fast
As the present now
Will later be past   50
The order is
Rapidly fadin'.
And the first one now
Will later be last
For the times they are a-changin'.   55

Questions

1. What features does Dylan keep constant from stanza to stanza? What changes?
2. Who is addressed at the start of each stanza? How do those people affect what is said later in the same stanza?
3. Could the stanzas be sung in a different order without greatly changing the impact of the song? Or would any change undercut the structure of the song?
4. Do the words of this song work well on the page? Or is something essential lost when the music is taken away? Choose and defend one point of view.

Aimee Mann (b. 1960)

Deathly   1999

Now that I've met you
Would you object to
Never seeing each other again
Cause I can't afford to
Climb aboard you   5
No one's got that much ego to spend

So don't work your stuff
Because I've got troubles enough
No, don't pick on me
When one act of kindness could be   10
Deathly
Deathly
Definitely

Cause I'm just a problem
For you to solve and   15
Watch dissolve in the heat of your charm
But what will you do when
You run it through and
You can't get me back on the farm

So don't work your stuff   20
Because I've got troubles enough
No, don't pick on me
When one act of kindness could be
Deathly
Deathly   25
Definitely

You're on your honor
Cause I'm a goner
And you haven't even begun
So do me a favor   30
If I should waver
Be my savior
And get out the gun

Just don't work your stuff
Because I've got troubles enough   35
No, don't pick on me
When one act of kindness could be
Deathly
Deathly
Definitely   40

Questions

1. The first three lines of this lyric are quite arresting (so much so that they inspired Paul Thomas Anderson's ambitious 1999 film *Magnolia*). How well does the rest of the lyric sustain and develop this opening?

2. After reading "Deathly," listen to Aimee Mann's recording of the song. Are the melody, arrangement, and singing style what you would have expected from a reading of the words? Explain.

■ WRITING *effectively*

Paul McCartney on Writing

Creating "Eleanor Rigby"   1978

Well, that ["Eleanor Rigby"] started off with sitting down at the piano and getting the first line of the melody, and playing around with the words. I think it was "Miss Daisy Hawkins" originally; then it was her picking up the rice in a church after a wedding. That's how nearly all our songs start, with the first line just suggesting itself from books or newspapers.

Paul McCartney

At first I thought it was a young Miss Daisy Hawkins, a bit like "Annabel Lee," but not so sexy; but then I saw I'd said she was picking up the rice in church, so she had to be a cleaner; she had missed the wedding, and she was suddenly lonely. In fact she had missed it all—she was the spinster type.

Jane° was in a play in Bristol then, and I was walking round the streets waiting for her to finish. I didn't really like "Daisy Hawkins"—I wanted a name that was more real. The thought just came: "Eleanor Rigby picks up the rice and lives in a dream"—so there she was. The next thing was Father McKenzie. It was going to be Father McCartney, but then I thought that was a bit of a hang-up for my Dad, being in this lonely song. So we looked through the phone book. That's the beauty of working at random—it does come up perfectly, much better than if you try to think it with your intellect.

Anyway there was Father McKenzie, and he was just as I had imagined him, lonely, darning his socks. We weren't sure if the song was going to go on. In the next verse we thought of a bin man, an old feller going through dustbins; but it got too involved—embarrassing. John and I wondered whether to have Eleanor Rigby and him have a thing going, but we couldn't really see how. When I played it to John we decided to finish it.

That was the point anyway. She didn't make it, she never made it with anyone, she didn't even look as if she was going to.

From *The Beatles in Their Own Words*

THINKING ABOUT POETRY AND SONG

Poetry and song were originally one art, and even today the two forms remain closely related. We celebrate the sounds of a poem by praising its "music" just as we compliment a great song lyric by calling it "poetic." And yet a very simple distinction separates

Jane: refers to Jane Asher, a British actress McCartney was dating at the time.

the two arts: in a song the lyrics combine with music to create a collaborative work, whereas in a poem the author must create all the effects by words alone.

- ▪ **To analyze song lyrics as poetry, you will need to separate the words temporarily from their music.**
- ▪ **Write out the lyrics and read them without the music playing in the background.** This can help you see how the words hold up on the page. While some lyrics stand well on their own, you may find that the song's power resides mostly in its music, or in the combination of words and music.

Remember, if you find yourself disappointed by the lyrics separated from their music, that song is no less powerful as a song just because the words don't stand on their own as poetry. A song, after all, *is* meant to be sung.

CHECKLIST: Writing About Song Lyrics

- ☐ Listen to the song and jot down the three or four moments that affect you most powerfully.
- ☐ Transcribe all of the lyrics onto the page. (Or find the lyrics on the Internet and print them out.)
- ☐ Compare the moments you remembered with the transcribed lyrics.
- ☐ Are the lyrics as moving without the music?
- ☐ Notice the form. Are there stanzas? A refrain? A rime scheme?
- ☐ What accounts for the song's power? Its music alone? Its lyrics? Its blend of words and music?

WRITING ASSIGNMENT ON SONG LYRICS

Write a short paper (750–1000 words) in which you analyze the lyrics of a favorite song. Discuss what the words alone provide and what they lack in re-creating the total power of the original song. The purpose of the paper is not to justify the song you have chosen as great poetry (though it may perhaps qualify); rather, it is to examine which parts of the song's power come solely from the words and which come from the music or performance. (Don't forget to provide your instructor with an accurate transcription of the song lyrics.)

MORE TOPICS FOR WRITING

1. Compare and contrast Edward Arlington Robinson's "Richard Cory" with Paul Simon's song of the same name. What changes did Simon make to the original? Why do you suppose he chose to make them? How did he alter Robinson's story and its characters?
2. Compare and contrast the folk ballad "The Three Ravens" (page 1017) with the literary ballad "La Belle Dame sans Merci" by John Keats (page 872).
3. Think of several recent popular songs. Can you think of any that qualify as ballads? Type out the lyrics of a narrative song you know well, and write a brief analysis of what those lyrics have in common with "Ballad of Birmingham" or "Bonny Barbara Allan."
4. What gives you the blues? Choose one of the blues songs in this chapter as a model, and write your own lyrics about a sad subject of your choice.

▶ TERMS FOR *review*

Components of Songs and Formal Poems

Stanza ▶ From the Italian, meaning "stopping-place" or "room." A recurring pattern of two or more lines of verse, poetry's equivalent to the paragraph in prose. The stanza is the basic organizational principle of most formal poetry.

Rime scheme ▶ Any recurrent pattern of rime within an individual poem. A rime scheme is usually described by using lowercase letters to represent each end rime—*a* for the first rime, *b* for the second, and so on—in the order in which the rimed words occur.

Refrain ▶ A word, phrase, line, or stanza repeated at intervals in a song or poem. The repeated chorus of a song is a refrain.

Ballads

Ballad ▶ Traditionally, a song that tells a story. Ballads are characteristically compressed, dramatic, and objective in their narrative style.

Folk ballads ▶ Anonymous narrative songs, usually in ballad meter. They were originally created for oral performance, often resulting in many versions of a single ballad.

Ballad stanza ▶ The most common pattern for a ballad, consisting of four lines rimed *a b c b*, in which the first and third lines have four metrical feet (usually eight syllables) and the second and fourth lines have three feet (usually six syllables). **Common meter**, often used in hymns, is a variation rimed *a b a b*.

Literary ballad ▶ A ballad not meant for singing, written by a sophisticated poet for educated readers, rather than arising from the anonymous oral tradition.

Other Kinds of Songs

Blues ▶ A type of folk music originally developed by African Americans in the South, often about some pain or loss. Blues lyrics traditionally consist of three-line stanzas in which two identical lines are followed by a third, riming line. The influence of the blues is fundamental in virtually all styles of contemporary pop—jazz, rap, rock, gospel, country, and rhythm and blues.

Rap ▶ A popular style of music that emerged in the 1980s in which lyrics are spoken or chanted over a steady beat, usually sampled or prerecorded. Rap lyrics are almost always rimed and very rhythmic—syncopating a heavy metrical beat in a manner similar to jazz.

20

SOUND

The sound must seem an echo to the sense.

—ALEXANDER POPE

SOUND AS MEANING

Isak Dinesen, in a memoir of her life on a plantation in East Africa, tells how some Kikuyu tribesmen reacted to their first hearing of rimed verse:

> The Natives, who have a strong sense of rhythm, know nothing of verse, or at least did not know anything before the times of the schools, where they were taught hymns. One evening out in the maize-field, where we had been harvesting maize, breaking off the cobs and throwing them on to the ox-carts, to amuse myself, I spoke to the field laborers, who were mostly quite young, in Swahili verse. There was no sense in the verses, they were made for the sake of rime—"Ngumbe na-penda chumbe, Malaya mbaya. Wakamba na-kula mamba." The oxen like salt—whores are bad—The Wakamba eat snakes. It caught the interest of the boys, they formed a ring round me. They were quick to understand that meaning in poetry is of no consequence, and they did not question the thesis of the verse, but waited eagerly for the rime, and laughed at it when it came. I tried to make them themselves find the rime and finish the poem when I had begun it, but they could not, or would not, do that, and turned away their heads. As they had become used to the idea of poetry, they begged: "Speak again. Speak like rain." Why they should feel verse to be like rain I do not know. It must have been, however, an expression of applause, since in Africa rain is always longed for and welcomed.[1]

What the tribesmen had discovered is that poetry, like music, appeals to the ear. However limited it may be in comparison with the sound of an orchestra—or a tribal drummer—the sound of words in itself gives pleasure. However, we might doubt Isak Dinesen's assumption that "meaning in poetry is of no consequence." "Hey nonny-nonny" and such nonsense has a place in song lyrics and other poems, and we might

[1]Isak Dinesen, *Out of Africa* (New York: Random, 1972).

770

take pleasure in hearing rimes in Swahili; but most good poetry has meaningful sound as well as musical sound. Certainly the words of a song have an effect different from that of wordless music: they go along with their music and, by making statements, add more meaning. The French poet Isidore Isou, founder of a literary movement called *lettrisme*, maintained that poems can be written not only in words but also in letters (sample lines: *xyl, xyl, / prprali dryl / znglo trpylo pwi*). But the sound of letters alone, without denotation and connotation, has not been enough to make Letterist poems memorable. In the response of the Kikuyu tribesmen, there may have been not only the pleasure of hearing sounds but also the agreeable surprise of finding that things not usually associated had been brought together.

Euphony and Cacophony

More powerful when in the company of meaning, not apart from it, the sounds of consonants and vowels can contribute greatly to a poem's effect. The sound of *s*, which can suggest the swishing of water, has rarely been used more accurately than in Surrey's line "Calm is the sea, the waves work less and less." When, in a poem, the sound of words working together with meaning pleases mind and ear, the effect is **euphony**, as in the following lines from Tennyson's "Come down, O maid":

> Myriads of rivulets hurrying through the lawn,
> The moan of doves in immemorial elms,
> And murmuring of innumerable bees.

Its opposite is **cacophony**: a harsh, discordant effect. It too is chosen for the sake of meaning. We hear it in Milton's scornful reference in "Lycidas" to corrupt clergymen whose songs "Grate on their scrannel pipes of wretched straw." (Read that line and one of Tennyson's aloud and see which requires lips, teeth, and tongue to do more work.) But note that although Milton's line is harsh in sound, the line (when we meet it in his poem) is pleasing because it is artful. In a famous passage from his *Essay on Criticism*, Pope has illustrated both euphony and cacophony. (Given here as Pope printed it, the passage relies heavily on italics and capital letters, for particular emphasis. If you will read these lines aloud, dwelling a little longer or harder on the words italicized, you will find that Pope has given you very good directions for a meaningful reading.)

Alexander Pope (1688–1744)

True Ease in Writing comes from Art, not Chance

1711

True Ease in Writing comes from Art, not Chance,
As those move easiest who have learned to dance.
'Tis not enough no Harshness gives Offence,
The *Sound* must seem an *Echo* to the *Sense*.
Soft is the Strain when *Zephyr*° gently blows,   *the west wind*   5
And the *smooth* Stream in *smoother Numbers*° flows;   *metrical rhythm*
But when loud Surges lash the sounding Shore,
The *hoarse, rough* Verse should like the *Torrent* roar.
When *Ajax* strives, some Rock's vast Weight to throw,
The Line too *labors*, and the Words move *slow*;   10

Not so, when swift *Camilla* scours the Plain,
Flies o'er th' unbending Corn, and skims along the Main.°   expanse (of sea)
Hear how *Timotheus'* varied Lays surprise,
And bid Alternate Passions fall and rise!
While, at each Change, the Son of *Lybian Jove*   15
Now *burns* with Glory, and then *melts* with Love;
Now his *fierce Eyes* with *sparkling Fury* glow;
Now *Sighs* steal out, and *Tears begin to flow*:
Persians and *Greeks* like *Turns of Nature* found,
And the *World's Victor* stood subdued by *Sound!*   20
The Pow'rs of Music all our Hearts allow;
And what *Timotheus* was, is *Dryden* now.

TRUE EASE IN WRITING COMES FROM ART, NOT CHANCE (*An Essay on Criticism*, lines 362–383). 9 *Ajax:* Greek hero, almost a superman, who in Homer's account of the siege of Troy hurls an enormous rock that momentarily flattens Hector, the Trojan prince (*Iliad* VII, 268–272). 11 *Camilla:* a kind of Amazon or warrior woman of the Volcians, whose speed and lightness of step are praised by the Roman poet Virgil: "She could have skimmed across an unmown grainfield / Without so much as bruising one tender blade; / She could have sped across an ocean's surge / Without so much as wetting her quicksilver soles" (*Aeneid* VII, 808–811). 13 *Timotheus:* favorite musician of Alexander the Great. In "Alexander's Feast, or The Power of Music," John Dryden imagines him: "Timotheus, placed on high / Amid the tuneful choir, / With flying fingers touched the lyre: / The trembling notes ascend the sky, / And heavenly joys inspire." 15 *Lybian Jove:* name for Alexander. A Libyan oracle had declared the king to be the son of the god Zeus Ammon.

Notice the pleasing effect of all the *s* sounds in the lines about the west wind and the stream, and in another meaningful place, the effect of the consonants in *Ajax strives*, a phrase that makes our lips work almost as hard as Ajax throwing the rock.

Is sound identical with meaning in lines such as these? Not quite. In the passage from Tennyson, for instance, the cooing of doves is not *exactly* a moan. As John Crowe Ransom pointed out, the sound would be almost the same but the meaning entirely different in "The murdering of innumerable beeves." While it is true that the consonant sound *sl-* will often begin a word that conveys ideas of wetness and smoothness—*slick, slimy, slippery, slush*—we are so used to hearing it in words that convey nothing of the kind—*slave, slow, sledgehammer*—that it is doubtful whether, all by itself, the sound communicates anything definite. The most beautiful phrase in the English language, according to Dorothy Parker, is *cellar door.* Another wit once nominated, as our most euphonious word, not *sunrise* or *silvery* but *syphilis.*

Onomatopoeia

Relating sound more closely to meaning, the device called **onomatopoeia** is an attempt to represent a thing or action by a word that imitates the sound associated with it: *zoom, whiz, crash, bang, ding-dong, pitter-patter, yakety-yak.* Onomatopoeia is often effective in poetry, as in Emily Dickinson's line about the fly with its "uncertain stumbling Buzz," in which the nasal sounds *n, m, ng* and the sibilants *c, s* help make a droning buzz.

Like the Kikuyu tribesmen, others who care for poetry have discovered in the sound of words something of the refreshment of cool rain. Dylan Thomas, telling how he began to write poetry, said that from early childhood words were to him "as the notes of bells, the sounds of musical instruments, the noises of wind, sea, and rain, the rattle of milkcarts, the clopping of hooves on cobbles, the fingering of branches on the window pane, might be to someone, deaf from birth, who has miraculously found his hearing."[2] For readers, too, the sound of words can have a magical spell, most powerful when it points to meaning. James Weldon Johnson in *God's Trombones* has told of an old-time preacher who began his sermon, "Brothers and sisters, this morning I intend to explain the unexplainable—find out the indefinable—ponder over the imponderable—and unscrew the inscrutable!" The repetition of sound in *unscrew* and *inscrutable* has appeal, but the magic of the words is all the greater if they lead us to imagine the mystery of all Creation as an enormous screw that the preacher's mind, like a screwdriver, will loosen. Though the sound of a word or the meaning of a word may have value all by itself, both become more memorable when taken together.

William Butler Yeats (1865–1939)

Who Goes with Fergus?   1892

Who will go drive with Fergus now,
And pierce the deep wood's woven shade,
And dance upon the level shore?
Young man, lift up your russet brow,
And lift your tender eyelids, maid,   5
And brood on hopes and fear no more.

And no more turn aside and brood
Upon love's bitter mystery;
For Fergus rules the brazen cars,°   *chariots*
And rules the shadows of the wood,   10
And the white breast of the dim sea
And all dishevelled wandering stars.

WHO GOES WITH FERGUS? *Fergus:* Irish king who gave up his throne to be a wandering poet.

Questions

1. In what lines do you find euphony?
2. In what line do you find cacophony?
3. How do the sounds of these lines stress what is said in them?

Exercise: Listening to Meaning

Read aloud the following brief poems. In the sounds of which particular words are meanings well captured? In which of the following four poems do you find onomatopoeia?

---

[2]"Notes on the Art of Poetry," *Modern Poetics*, ed. James Scully (New York: McGraw-Hill, 1965).

John Updike (1932–2009)

Recital   1963

> ROGER BOBO GIVES
> RECITAL ON TUBA
> —*Headline in the Times*

Eskimos in Manitoba,
    Barracuda off Aruba,
Cock an ear when Roger Bobo
    Starts to solo on the tuba.

Men of every station—Pooh-Bah,   5
    Nabob, bozo, toff, and hobo—
Cry in unison, "Indubi-
    Tably, there is simply nobo-

Dy who oompahs on the tubo,
Solo, quite like Roger Bubo!"   10

William Wordsworth (1770–1850)

A Slumber Did My Spirit Seal   1800

A slumber did my spirit seal;
    I had no human fears—
She seemed a thing that could not feel
    The touch of earthly years.

No motion has she now, no force;   5
    She neither hears nor sees;
Rolled round in earth's diurnal course,
    With rocks, and stones, and trees.

Emanuel di Pasquale (b. 1943)

Rain   1971

Like a drummer's brush,
the rain hushes the surface of tin porches.

Aphra Behn (1640?–1689)

When maidens are young   1687

When maidens are young, and in their spring,
Of pleasure, of pleasure let 'em take their full swing,
    Full swing, full swing,
And love, and dance, and play, and sing,
For Silvia, believe it, when youth is done,   5
There's nought but hum-drum, hum-drum, hum-drum,
There's nought but hum-drum, hum-drum, hum-drum.

ALLITERATION AND ASSONANCE

Listening to a symphony in which themes are repeated throughout each movement, we enjoy both their recurrence and their variation. We take similar pleasure in the repetition of a phrase or a single chord. Something like this pleasure is afforded us frequently in poetry.

Analogies between poetry and wordless music, it is true, tend to break down when carried far, since poetry—to mention a single difference—has denotation. But like musical compositions, poems have patterns of sounds. Among such patterns long popular in English poetry is **alliteration**, which has been defined as a succession of similar sounds. Alliteration occurs in the repetition of the same consonant sound at the beginning of successive words—"round and round the rugged rocks the ragged rascal ran," or in this delightful stanza by Witter Bynner, written nearly a century ago as part of an elaborate literary hoax:

> If I were only dafter
> I might be making hymns
> To the liquor of your laughter
> And the lacquer of your limbs.

Or it may occur inside the words, as in Milton's description of the gates of Hell:

> On a sudden open fly
> With impetuous recoil and jarring sound
> The infernal doors, and on their hinges grate
> Harsh thunder, that the lowest bottom shook
> Of Erebus.

The former kind is called **initial alliteration**, the latter **internal alliteration** or **hidden alliteration**. We recognize alliteration by sound, not by spelling: *know* and *nail* alliterate, *know* and *key* do not. In a line by E. E. Cummings, "colossal hoax of clocks and calendars," the sound of *x* within *hoax* alliterates with the *cks* in *clocks*. Incidentally, the letter *r* does not *always* lend itself to cacophony: elsewhere in *Paradise Lost* Milton said that

> Heaven opened wide
> Her ever-during gates, harmonious sound
> On golden hinges moving . . .

By itself, a letter-sound has no particular meaning. This is a truth forgotten by people who would attribute the effectiveness of Milton's lines on the Heavenly Gates to, say, "the mellow o's and liquid *l* of *harmonious* and *golden*." Mellow o's and liquid *l*'s occur also in the phrase *moldy cold oatmeal*, which may have a quite different effect. Meaning depends on larger units of language than letters of the alphabet.

Poetry formerly contained more alliteration than it usually contains today. In Old English verse, each line was held together by alliteration, a basic pattern still evident in the fourteenth century, as in the following description of the world as a "fair field" in *Piers Plowman*:

> A feir feld ful of folk fond I ther bi-twene,
> Of alle maner of men, the mene and the riche . . .

Most poets nowadays save alliteration for special occasions. They may use it to give emphasis, as Edward Lear does: "Far and *few*, far and *few*, / Are the *lands* where the *Jumblies live*." With its aid they can point out the relationship between two things placed side by side, as in Pope's line on things of little worth: "The courtier's *promises*, and sick man's *prayers*." Alliteration, too, can be a powerful aid to memory. It is hard to forget such tongue twisters as "Peter Piper picked a peck of pickled peppers," or common expressions such as "green as grass," "tried and true," and "from stem to stern." In fact, because alliteration directs our attention to something, it had best be used neither thoughtlessly nor merely for decoration, lest it call attention to emptiness. A case in point may be a line by Philip James Bailey, a reaction to a lady's weeping: "I saw, but *spared* to *speak*." If the poet chose the word *spared* for any meaningful reason other than that it alliterates with *speak*, the reason is not clear.

As we have seen, to repeat the sound of a consonant is to produce alliteration, but to repeat the sound of a *vowel* is to produce **assonance**. Like alliteration, assonance may occur either initially—"all the *awful auguries*"—or internally—Edmund Spenser's "Her goodly *eyes* like sapphires shining bright, / Her forehead *ivory* white . . ." and it can help make common phrases unforgettable: "eager beaver," "holy smoke." Like alliteration, it slows the reader down and focuses attention.

 ## *A. E. Housman* (1859–1936)

Eight O'Clock   1922

He stood, and heard the steeple
   Sprinkle the quarters on the morning town.
One, two, three, four, to market-place and people
   It tossed them down.

Strapped, noosed, nighing his hour,   5
   He stood and counted them and cursed his luck;
And then the clock collected in the tower
   Its strength, and struck.

Questions

1. Why does the protagonist in this brief drama curse his luck? What is his situation?
2. For so short a poem, "Eight O'Clock" carries a great weight of alliteration. What patterns of initial alliteration do you find? What patterns of internal alliteration? What effect is created by all this heavy emphasis?

James Joyce (1882–1941)

All day I hear   1907

All day I hear the noise of waters
   Making moan,
Sad as the sea-bird is, when going
   Forth alone,
He hears the winds cry to the waters'   5
   Monotone.

The grey winds, the cold winds are blowing
   Where I go.
I hear the noise of many waters
   Far below.   10
All day, all night, I hear them flowing
   To and fro.

Questions

1. Find three instances of alliteration in the first stanza. Do any of them serve to reinforce meaning?
2. There is a great deal of assonance throughout the poem on a single vowel sound. What sound is it, and what effect is achieved by its repetition?

Experiment: Reading for Assonance

Try reading aloud as rapidly as possible the following poem by Tennyson. From the difficulties you encounter, you may be able to sense the slowing effect of assonance. Then read the poem aloud a second time, with consideration.

Alfred, Lord Tennyson (1809–1892)

The splendor falls on castle walls   1850

The splendor falls on castle walls
   And snowy summits old in story;
The long light shakes across the lakes,
   And the wild cataract leaps in glory.
Blow, bugle, blow, set the wild echoes flying,   5
Blow, bugle; answer, echoes, dying, dying, dying.

O hark, O hear! how thin and clear,
   And thinner, clearer, farther going!
O sweet and far from cliff and scar°   *jutting rock*
   The horns of Elfland faintly blowing!   10
Blow, let us hear the purple glens replying:
Blow, bugle; answer, echoes, dying, dying, dying.

O love, they die in yon rich sky,
   They faint on hill or field or river;
Our echoes roll from soul to soul,   15
   And grow for ever and for ever.
Blow, bugle, blow, set the wild echoes flying,
And answer, echoes, answer, dying, dying, dying.

RIME

Isak Dinesen's tribesmen, to whom rime was a new phenomenon, recognized at once that rimed language is special language. So do we, for, although much English poetry is unrimed, rime is one means to set poetry apart from ordinary conversation and bring it closer to music. A **rime** (or rhyme), defined most narrowly, occurs when two or more words or phrases contain an identical or similar vowel-sound, usually accented, and the consonant-sounds (if any) that follow the vowel-sound are identical: *hay* and *sleigh, prairie schooner* and *piano tuner*. From these examples it will be seen that rime depends not on spelling but on sound.

Excellent rimes surprise. It is all very well that a reader may anticipate which vowel-sound is coming next, for patterns of rime give pleasure by satisfying expectations; but riming becomes dull clunking if, at the end of each line, the reader can predict the word that will end the next. Hearing many a jukebox song for the first time, a listener can do so: *charms* lead to *arms, skies above* to *love.* As Alexander Pope observes of the habits of dull rimesters,

> Where'er you find "the cooling western breeze,"
> In the next line it "whispers through the trees";
> If crystal streams "with pleasing murmurs creep,"
> The reader's threatened (not in vain) with "sleep" . . .

But who—given the opening line of this comic poem—could predict the lines that follow?

William Cole (1919–2000)

On my boat on Lake Cayuga   1985

On my boat on Lake Cayuga
I have a horn that goes "Ay-oogah!"
I'm not the modern kind of creep
Who has a horn that goes "beep beep."

Robert Herrick, in a more subtle poem, made good use of rime to indicate a startling contrast:

> Then while time serves, and we are but decaying,
> Come, my Corinna, come, let's go a-Maying.

Though good rimes seem fresh, not all will startle, and probably few will call to mind things so unlike as *May* and *decay, Cayuga* and *Ay-oogah*. Some masters of rime often link words that, taken out of text, might seem common and unevocative. Here are the opening lines of Rachel Hadas's poem, "Three Silences," which describe an infant feeding at a mother's breast:

> Of all the times when not to speak is best,
> mother's and infant's is the easiest,
> the milky mouth still warm against her breast.

Hadas's rime words are not especially memorable in themselves, and yet these lines are—at least in part because they rime so well. The quiet echo of sound at the end of each line reinforces the intimate tone of the mother's moment with her child. Poetic invention may be driven home without rime, but it is rime sometimes that rings the doorbell. Admittedly, some rimes wear thin from too much use. More difficult to use freshly than before the establishment of Tin Pan Alley, rimes such as *moon, June, croon* seem leaden and would need an extremely powerful context to ring true. *Death* and *breath* are a rime that poets have used with wearisome frequency; another is *birth, earth, mirth.* And yet we cannot exclude these from the diction of poetry, for they might be the very words a poet would need in order to say something new and original.

Types of Rime

To have an **exact rime**, sounds following the vowel sound have to be the same: *red* and *bread, wealthily* and *stealthily, walk to her* and *talk to her.* If final consonant sounds are the same but the vowel sounds are different, the result is **slant rime**, also called **near rime, off rime**, or **imperfect rime**: *sun* riming with *bone, moon, rain, green, gone, thin.* By not satisfying the reader's expectation of an exact chime, but instead giving a clunk, a slant rime can help a poet say some things in a particular way. It works especially well for disappointed letdowns, negations, and denials, as in Blake's couplet:

> He who the ox to wrath has moved
> Shall never be by woman loved.

Many poets have admired the unexpected and arresting effects of slant rime. One of the first poets to explore the possibilities of rhyming consonants in a consistent way was Wilfred Owen, an English soldier in World War I, who wrote his best poems in the thirteen months before he was killed in action. Seeking a poetic language strong enough to describe the harsh reality of modern war, Owen experimented with matching consonant sounds in striking ways:

> Now men will go content with what we spoiled
> Or, discontent, boil bloody, and be spilled,
> They will be swift with swiftness of the tigress.
> None will break ranks, though nations trek from progress.
> Courage was mine, and I had mystery,
> Wisdom was mine, and I had mastery:
> To miss the march of this retreating world
> Into vain citadels that are not walled.

Consonance, a kind of slant rime, occurs when the rimed words or phrases have the same beginning and ending consonant sounds but a different vowel, as in *chitter* and *chatter.* Owen rimes *spoiled* and *spilled* in this way. Consonance is used in a traditional nonsense poem, "The Cutty Wren": "'O where are you going?' says *Milder* to *Malder.*" (W. H. Auden wrote a variation on it that begins, "'O where are you going?' said *reader* to *rider,*" thus keeping the consonance.)

End rime, as its name indicates, comes at the ends of lines, **internal rime** within them. Most rime tends to be end rime. Few recent poets have used internal rime so heavily as Wallace Stevens in the beginning of "Bantams in Pine-Woods": "Chieftain Iffucan of Azcan in caftan / Of tan with henna hackles, halt!" (lines also heavy on alliteration). A poet may employ both end rime and internal rime in the same poem, as in Robert Burns's satiric ballad "The Kirk's Alarm":

> Orthodox, Orthodox, wha believe in John Knox,
>   Let me sound an alarm to your conscience:
> There's a heretic blast has been blawn i' the wast,°   *west*
>   "That what is not sense must be nonsense."

Masculine rime is a rime of one-syllable words (*jail, bail*) or (in words of more than one syllable) stressed final syllables: *di-VORCE, re-MORSE,* or *horse, re-MORSE.*

Feminine rime is a rime of two or more syllables, with stress on a syllable other than the last: *TUR-tle, FER-tile,* or (to take an example from Byron) *in-tel-LECT-u-al, hen-PECKED you all.* Often it lends itself to comic verse, but can occasionally be valuable to serious poems, as in Wordsworth's "Resolution and Independence":

> We poets in our youth begin in gladness,
> But thereof come in the end despondency and madness,

or as in Anne Sexton's seriously witty "Eighteen Days Without You":

> and of course we're not married, we are a pair of scissors
> who come together to cut, without towels saying His. Hers.

Artfully used, feminine rime can give a poem a heightened musical effect for the simple reason that it offers the listener twice as many riming syllables in each line. In the wrong hands, however, that sonic abundance has the unfortunate ability of making a bad poem twice as painful to endure. Serious poems containing feminine rimes of three syllables have been attempted, notably by Thomas Hood in "The Bridge of Sighs":

> Take her up tenderly,
> Lift her with care;
> Fashioned so slenderly,
> Young, and so fair!

But the pattern is hard to sustain without lapsing into unintended comedy, as in the same poem:

> Still, for all slips of hers,
> One of Eve's family—
> Wipe those poor lips of hers,
> Oozing so clammily.

It works better when comedy is wanted.

Hilaire Belloc (1870–1953)

The Hippopotamus   1896

> I shoot the Hippopotamus
>   with bullets made of platinum,
> Because if I use leaden ones
>   his hide is sure to flatten 'em.

Ogden Nash (1902–1971)

The Panther   1940

> The panther is like a leopard,
> Except it hasn't been peppered.
> Should you behold a panther crouch,
> Prepare to say Ouch.
> Better yet, if called by a panther,
> Don't anther.

5

In **eye rime**, spellings look alike but pronunciations differ—*rough* and *dough*, *idea* and *flea*, *Venus* and *menus*. Strictly speaking, eye rime is not rime at all.

Rime in American poetry suffered a significant fall from favor in the early 1960s. A new generation of poets took for models the open forms of Whitman, Pound, and William Carlos Williams. In the last few decades, however, some poets have been skillfully using rime again in their work. Often called the **New Formalists**, these poets include Julia Alvarez, R. S. Gwynn, Mark Jarman, Paul Lake, Charles Martin, Marilyn Nelson, A. E. Stallings, and Timothy Steele. Their poems often use rime and meter to present unusual contemporary subjects, but they also sometimes write poems that recollect, converse with, and argue with the poetry of the past.

Still, most American poets don't write in rime; some even consider its possibilities exhausted. Such a view may be a reaction against the wearing thin of rimes by overuse or the mechanical and meaningless application of a rime scheme. Yet anyone who listens to children skipping rope in the street, making up rimes to delight themselves as they go along, may doubt that the pleasures of rime are ended; and certainly the practice of Yeats and Emily Dickinson, to name only two, suggests that the possibilities of slant rime may be nearly infinite. If successfully employed, as it has been at times by a majority of English-speaking poets whose work we care to save, rime runs through its poem like a spine: the creature moves by means of it.

William Butler Yeats (1865–1939)

Leda and the Swan   1928

A sudden blow: the great wings beating still
Above the staggering girl, her thighs caressed
By the dark webs, her nape caught in his bill,
He holds her helpless breast upon his breast.

How can those terrified vague fingers push   5
The feathered glory from her loosening thighs?
And how can body, laid in that white rush,
But feel the strange heart beating where it lies?

A shudder in the loins engenders there
The broken wall, the burning roof and tower   10
And Agamemnon dead.
                              Being so caught up,
So mastered by the brute blood of the air,
Did she put on his knowledge with his power
Before the indifferent beak could let her drop?

Questions

1. According to Greek mythology, the god Zeus in the form of a swan descended on Leda, a Spartan queen. Among Leda's children were Clytemnestra, Agamemnon's unfaithful wife, who conspired in his murder, and Helen, on whose account the Trojan war was fought. What does a knowledge of these allusions contribute to our understanding of the poem's last two lines?

2. The slant rime *up / drop* (lines 11, 14) may seem accidental or inept. Is it? Would this poem have ended nearly so well if Yeats had made an exact rime like *up / cup* or *stop / drop*?

Gerard Manley Hopkins (1844–1889)

God's Grandeur   (1877)

The world is charged with the grandeur of God.
  It will flame out, like shining from shook foil;
  It gathers to a greatness, like the ooze of oil
Crushed. Why do men then now not reck his rod?
Generations have trod, have trod, have trod;   5
  And all is seared with trade; bleared, smeared with toil;
  And wears man's smudge and shares man's smell: the soil
Is bare now, nor can foot feel, being shod.

And for all this, nature is never spent;
  There lives the dearest freshness deep down things;   10
And though the last lights off the black West went
  Oh, morning, at the brown brink eastward, springs—
Because the Holy Ghost over the bent
  World broods with warm breast and with ah! bright wings.

GOD'S GRANDEUR. 1 *charged:* as though with electricity. 3–4 *It gathers . . . Crushed:* The grandeur of God
will rise and be manifest, as oil rises and collects from crushed olives or grain. 4 *reck his rod:* heed His law.
10 *deep down things:* Tightly packing the poem, Hopkins omits the preposition *in* or *within* before *things.* 11
last lights . . . went: When in 1534 Henry VIII broke ties with the Roman Catholic Church and created the
Church of England.

Questions

1. In a letter Hopkins explained *shook foil* (line 2): "I mean foil in its sense of leaf or
   tinsel. . . . Shaken goldfoil gives off broad glares like sheet lightning and also, and
   this is true of nothing else, owing to its zigzag dints and creasings and network of
   small many cornered facets, a sort of fork lightning too." What do you think he
   meant by the phrase *ooze of oil* (line 3)? Would you call this phrase an example of
   alliteration?

2. What instances of internal rime does the poem contain? How would you describe their
   effects?

3. Point out some of the poet's uses of alliteration and assonance. Do you believe that
   Hopkins perhaps goes too far in his heavy use of devices of sound, or would you defend his
   practice?

4. Why do you suppose Hopkins, in the last two lines, says *over the bent / World* instead of
   (as we might expect) *bent over the world?* How can the world be bent? Can you make
   any sense out of this wording, or is Hopkins just trying to get his rime scheme to work
   out?

William Jay Smith (b. 1918)

A Note on the Vanity Dresser   1947

The yes-man in the mirror now says no,
No longer will I answer you with lies.
The light descends like snow, so when the snow-
man melts, you will know him by his eyes.

The yes-man in the mirror now says no.   5
Says no. No double negative of pity
Will save you now from what I know you know:
These are your eyes, the cinders of your city.

Questions

1. One particular sound occurs frequently in this poem. What is that sound, and how many instances of it can you find in the text?
2. What thematic significance do you see in the repetition of this sound?
3. Are there any other repeated sounds that may contribute to the poem's meaning?

Robert Frost (1874–1963)

Desert Places   1936

Snow falling and night falling fast, oh, fast
In a field I looked into going past,
And the ground almost covered smooth in snow,
But a few weeds and stubble showing last.

The woods around it have it—it is theirs.   5
All animals are smothered in their lairs.
I am too absent-spirited to count;
The loneliness includes me unawares.

And lonely as it is that loneliness
Will be more lonely ere it will be less—   10
A blanker whiteness of benighted snow
With no expression, nothing to express.

They cannot scare me with their empty spaces
Between stars—on stars where no human race is.
I have it in me so much nearer home   15
To scare myself with my own desert places.

Questions

1. What are these desert places that the speaker finds in himself? (More than one theory is possible. What is yours?)
2. Notice how many times, within the short space of lines 8–10, Frost says *lonely* (or *loneliness*). What other words in the poem contain similar sounds that reinforce these words?
3. In the closing stanza, the feminine rimes *spaces, race is,* and *places* might well occur in light or comic verse. Does "Desert Places" leave you laughing? If not, what does it make you feel?

READING AND HEARING POEMS ALOUD

Thomas Moore's "The light that lies in women's eyes"—a line rich in internal rime, alliteration, and assonance—is harder to forget than "The light burning in the gaze of a woman." Effective on the page, Moore's line becomes even more striking when heard aloud. There is no better way to understand a poem than to effectively read it aloud. Developing skill at reading poems aloud will not only deepen your understanding of literature, it will also improve your ability to speak in public.

Before trying to read a poem aloud to other people, understand its meaning as thoroughly as possible. If you know what the poet is saying and the poet's attitude toward it, you will be able to find an appropriate tone of voice and to give each part of the poem a proper emphasis.

Except in the most informal situations and in some class exercises, read a poem to yourself before trying it on an audience. No actor goes before the footlights without first having studied the script, and the language of poems usually demands even more consideration than the language of most contemporary plays. Prepare your reading in advance. Check pronunciations you are not sure of. Underline things to be emphasized.

Read more slowly than you would read aloud from a newspaper. Keep in mind that you are saying something to somebody. Don't race through the poem as if you are eager to get it over with.

Don't lapse into singsong. A poem may have a definite swing, but swing should never be exaggerated at the cost of sense. If you understand what the poem is saying and utter the poem as if you do, the temptation to fall into such a mechanical intonation should not occur. Observe the punctuation, making slight pauses for commas, longer pauses for full stops (periods, question marks, exclamation points).

If the poem is rimed, don't raise your voice and make the rimes stand out unnaturally. They should receive no more volume than other words in the poem, though a faint pause at the end of each line will call the listener's attention to them. This advice is contrary to a school that holds that, if a line does not end in any punctuation, one should not pause but run it together with the line following. The trouble is that, from such a reading, a listener may not be able to identify the rimes; besides, the line, that valuable unit of rhythm, is destroyed.

In some older poems, rimes that look like slant rimes may have been exact rimes in their day:

> Soft yielding minds to water glide away,
> And sip, with nymphs, their elemental tea.
> —Alexander Pope, "The Rape of the Lock" (1714)

> Tyger! Tyger! burning bright
> In the forests of the night,
> What immortal hand or eye
> Could frame thy fearful symmetry?
> —William Blake, "The Tyger" (1794)

You may wish to establish a consistent policy toward such shifting usage: is it worthwhile to distort current pronunciation for the sake of the rime?

Listening to a poem, especially if it is unfamiliar, calls for concentration. Merciful people seldom read poetry uninterruptedly to anyone for more than a few minutes at a time. Robert Frost, always kind to his audiences, used to intersperse poems with many silences and seemingly casual remarks—shrewdly giving his hearers a chance to rest from their labors and giving his poems a chance to settle in.

If, in first listening to a poem, you don't take in all its meaning, don't be discouraged. With more practice in listening, your attention span and your ability to understand poems read aloud will increase. Incidentally, following the text of poems in a book while hearing them read aloud may increase your comprehension, but it may not necessarily help you to *listen*. At least some of the time, close your book and let your ears make the poems welcome. That way, their sounds may better work for you.

Exercise: Reading for Sound and Meaning

Read these brief poems aloud. What devices of sound do you find in each of them? Try to explain what sound contributes to the total effect of the poem and how it reinforces what the poet is saying.

Michael Stillman (b. 1940)

In Memoriam John Coltrane   1972

   Listen to the coal
rolling, rolling through the cold
   steady rain, wheel on

   wheel, listen to the
turning of the wheels this night   5
   black as coal dust, steel

   on steel, listen to
these cars carry coal, listen
   to the coal train roll.

IN MEMORIAM JOHN COLTRANE. John Coltrane (1926–1967) was a saxophonist whose originality, passion, and technical wizardry have had a deep influence on the history of modern jazz.

William Shakespeare (1564–1616)

Full fathom five thy father lies   about 1611

Full fathom five thy father lies;
   Of his bones are coral made;
Those are pearls that were his eyes:
   Nothing of him that doth fade,
But doth suffer a sea change   5
Into something rich and strange.
Sea nymphs hourly ring his knell:
   Ding-dong.
Hark! now I hear them—Ding-dong, bell.

FULL FATHOM FIVE THY FATHER LIES. The spirit Ariel sings this song in The Tempest to Ferdinand, prince of Naples, who mistakenly thinks his father is drowned (I, ii).

T. S. Eliot (1888–1965)

Virginia   1934

Red river, red river,
Slow flow heat is silence
No will is still as a river
Still. Will heat move
Only through the mocking-bird   5
Heard once? Still hills
Wait. Gates wait. Purple trees,

White trees, wait, wait,
Delay, decay. Living, living,
Never moving. Ever moving   10
Iron thoughts came with me
And go with me:
Red river, river, river.

VIRGINIA. This poem is one of a series entitled "Landscapes."

■ WRITING *effectively*

T. S. Eliot on Writing

The Music of Poetry   1942

I would remind you, first, that the music of
poetry is not something which exists apart
from the meaning. Otherwise, we could have
poetry of great musical beauty which made
no sense, and I have never come across such
poetry. The apparent exceptions only show a
difference of degree: there are poems in
which we are moved by the music and take
the sense for granted, just as there are poems
in which we attend to the sense and are
moved by the music without noticing it.
Take an apparently extreme example—the
non-sense verse of Edward Lear. His nonsense is not vacuity of sense: it is a parody of
sense, and that is the sense of it.

T. S. Eliot

• • •

So, while poetry attempts to convey something beyond what can be conveyed in
prose rhythms, it remains, all the same, one person talking to another; and this is just
as true if you sing it, for singing is another way of talking. The immediacy of poetry to
conversation is not a matter on which we can lay down exact laws. Every revolution
in poetry is apt to be, and sometimes to announce itself to be, a return to common
speech. . . .

It would be a mistake, however, to assume that all poetry ought to be melodious,
or that melody is more than one of the components of the music of words. Some
poetry is meant to be sung; most poetry, in modern times, is meant to be spoken—
and there are many other things to be spoken of besides the murmur of innumerable
bees or the moan of doves in immemorial elms. Dissonance, even cacophony, has its
place: just as, in a poem of any length, there must be transitions between passages of
greater and less intensity, to give a rhythm of fluctuating emotion essential to the
musical structure of the whole; and the passages of less intensity will be, in relation to

the level on which the total poem operates, prosaic—so that, in the sense implied by that context, it may be said that no poet can write a poem of amplitude unless he is a master of the prosaic.

From "The Music of Poetry"

THINKING ABOUT A POEM'S SOUND

A poem's music—the distinct way it sounds—is an important element of its effect and a large part of what separates it from prose. Describing a poem's sound can be tricky, though. Critics often disagree about the sonic effects of particular poems. Cataloguing every auditory element of a poem would be a huge, unwieldy job. The easiest way to write about sound is to focus your discussion. Concentrate on a single, clearly defined sonic element that strikes you as especially noteworthy. Simply try to understand how that element helps communicate the poem's main theme.

- **You might examine, for example, how certain features (such as rime, rhythm, meter, or alliteration) add force to the literal meaning of each line.** Or, for an ironic poem, you might look at how those same elements undercut and change the surface meaning of the poem.
- **Keep in mind that for a detailed analysis of this sort, it often helps to choose a short poem.** If you want to write about a longer poem, focus on a short passage that strikes you as especially rich in sonic effects.
- **Let your data build up before you force any conclusions about the poem's auditory effects.** As your list grows, a pattern should emerge, and ideas will probably occur to you that were not apparent earlier.

CHECKLIST: Writing About a Poem's Sound

- ☐ List the main auditory elements you find in the poem.
- ☐ Look for rime, meter, alliteration, assonance, euphony, cacophony, repetition, onomatopoeia.
- ☐ Is there a pattern in your list? Is the poem particularly heavy in alliteration or repetition, for example?
- ☐ Limit your discussion to one or two clearly defined sonic effects.
- ☐ How do your chosen effects help communicate the poem's main theme?
- ☐ How does the sound of the words add to the poem's mood?

WRITING ASSIGNMENT ON SOUND

Choose a brief poem from this chapter or the chapter "Poems for Further Reading" and examine how one or two elements of sound work throughout the poem to strengthen its meaning. Before you write, review the elements of sound described in this chapter. Back up your argument with specific quotations from the poem.

MORE TOPICS FOR WRITING

1. In a brief (500-word) essay, explore how wordplay contributes to the mood and meaning of T. S. Eliot's "Virginia."

2. Silently read Sylvia Plath's "Daddy" (in the chapter "Poems for Further Reading"). Now read the poem aloud, to yourself or to a friend. Now write briefly. What did you perceive about the poem from reading it aloud that you hadn't noticed before?

3. Consider the verbal music of Michael Stillman's "In Memoriam John Coltrane" (or a selection from the chapter "Poems for Further Reading"). Read the poem both silently and aloud, listening for sonic effects. Describe how the poem's sound underscores its meaning.

▶ TERMS FOR *review*

Sound Effects

Alliteration ▶ The repetition of a consonant sound in a line of verse or prose. Alliteration can be used at the beginning of words (**initial alliteration** as in "c̲ool c̲ats") or internally on stressed syllables (**internal alliteration** as in "I me̲t a t̲raveler from an an̲tique land.").

Assonance ▶ The repetition of two or more vowel sounds in successive words, which creates a kind of rime. Like alliteration, the assonance may occur initially ("all the *awful auguries*") or internally ("white lilacs").

Cacophony ▶ A harsh, discordant sound often mirroring the meaning of the context in which it is used. The opposite of cacophony is **euphony**.

Euphony ▶ The harmonious effect when the sounds of the words connect with the meaning in a way pleasing to the ear and mind. The opposite of euphony is **cacophony**.

Onomatopoeia ▶ An attempt to represent a thing or action by a word that imitates the sound associated with it.

Rime

Rime ▶ Two or more words that contain an identical or similar vowel sound, usually accented, with following consonant sounds (if any) identical as well (*woo* and *stew*). An **exact rime** is a full rime in which the sounds following the initial letters of the words are identical in sound (*follow* and *hollow*).

Consonance ▶ Also called **Slant rime**. A kind of rime in which the linked words share similar consonant sounds but have different vowel sounds, as in *reason* and *raisin, mink* and *monk*. Sometimes only the final consonant sound is identical, as in *fame* and *room*.

End rime ▶ Rime that occurs at the ends of lines, rather than within them. End rime is the most common kind of rime in English-language poetry.

Internal rime ▶ Rime that occurs within a line of poetry, as opposed to **end rime**.

Masculine rime ▶ Either a rime of one-syllable words (*fox* and *socks*) or—in polysyllabic words—a rime on the stressed final syllables (con-*trive* and sur-*vive*).

Feminine rime ▶ A rime of two or more syllables with stress on a syllable other than the last (*tur*-tle and *fer*-tile).

Eye rime ▶ A "false" rime in which the spelling of the words is alike, but the pronunciations differ (*daughter* and *laughter*).

21 RHYTHM

I would define, in brief, the Poetry of words as
the Rhythmical Creation of Beauty.

—EDGAR ALLAN POE

STRESSES AND PAUSES

Rhythms affect us powerfully. We are lulled by a hammock's sway, awakened by an alarm clock's repeated yammer. Long after we come home from a beach, the rising and falling of waves and tides continue in memory. How powerfully the rhythms of poetry also move us may be felt in folk songs of railroad workers and chain gangs whose words were chanted in time to the lifting and dropping of a sledgehammer, and in verse that marching soldiers shout, putting a stress on every word that coincides with a footfall:

> Your LEFT! TWO! THREE! FOUR!
> Your LEFT! TWO! THREE! FOUR!
> You LEFT your WIFE and TWEN-ty-one KIDS
> And you LEFT! TWO! THREE! FOUR!
> You'll NEV-er get HOME to-NIGHT!

A rhythm is produced by a series of recurrences: the returns and departures of the seasons, the repetitions of an engine's stroke, the beats of the heart. A rhythm may be produced by the recurrence of a sound (the throb of a drum, a telephone's busy signal), but rhythm and sound are not identical. A totally deaf person at a parade can sense rhythm from the motions of the marchers' arms and feet, from the shaking of the pavement as they tramp. Rhythms inhere in the motions of the moon and stars, even though when they move, we hear no sound.

In poetry, several kinds of recurrent *sound* are possible, including (as we saw in the last chapter) rime, alliteration, and assonance. But most often when we speak of the **rhythm** of a poem, we mean the recurrence of stresses and pauses in it. When we hear a poem read aloud, stresses and pauses are, of course, part of its sound. It is possible to be aware of rhythms in poems read silently, too.

Stresses

A **stress** (or **accent**) is a greater amount of force given to one syllable in speaking than is given to another. We favor a stressed syllable with a little more breath and emphasis, with the result that it comes out slightly louder, higher in pitch, or longer in duration than other syllables. In this manner we place a stress on the first syllable of words such as *eagle*, *impact*, *open*, and *statue*, and on the second syllable in *cigar*, *mystique*, *precise*, and *until*. Each word in English carries at least one stress, except (usually) for the articles *a*, *an*, and *the*, the conjunction *and*, and one-syllable prepositions: *at*, *by*, *for*, *from*, *of*, *to*, *with*. Even these, however, take a stress once in a while: "Get WITH it!" "You're not THE Dolly Parton?" One word by itself is seldom long enough for us to notice a rhythm in it. Usually a sequence of at least a few words is needed for stresses to establish their pattern: a line, a passage, a whole poem. Strong rhythms may be seen in most Mother Goose rimes, to which children have been responding for hundreds of years. This rime is for an adult to chant while jogging a child up and down on a knee:

> Here goes my lord
> A trot, a trot, a trot, a trot!
> Here goes my lady
> A canter, a canter, a canter, a canter!
> Here goes my young master
> Jockey-hitch, jockey-hitch, jockey-hitch, jockey-hitch!
> Here goes my young miss
> An amble, an amble, an amble, an amble!
> The footman lags behind to tipple ale and wine
> And goes gallop, a gallop, a gallop, to make up his time.

More than one rhythm occurs in these lines, as the make-believe horse changes pace. How do these rhythms differ? From one line to the next, the interval between stresses lengthens or grows shorter. In "a TROT a TROT a TROT a TROT," the stress falls on every other syllable. But in the middle of the line "A CAN-ter a CAN-ter a CAN-ter a CAN-ter," the stress falls on every third syllable. When stresses recur at fixed intervals as in these lines, the result is called a **meter**.

Stresses embody meanings. Whenever two or more fall side by side, words gain in emphasis. Consider these hard-hitting lines from John Donne, in which accent marks have been placed, dictionary-fashion, to indicate the stressed syllables:

> Bat·ter my heart, three-per·soned God, for You
> As yet but knock, breathe, shine, and seek to mend.
> That I may rise and stand, o'er throw me, and bend
> Your force to break, blow, burn, and make me new.

Unstressed (or **slack**) **syllables** also can direct our attention to what the poet means. In a line containing few stresses and a great many unstressed syllables, there can be an effect not of power and force but of hesitation and uncertainty. Yeats asks in "Among School Children" what young mother, if she could see her baby grown to be an old man, would think him:

> A com·pen·sa·tion for the pang of his birth
> Or the un·cer·tain·ty of his set·ting forth?

When unstressed syllables recur in pairs, the result is a rhythm that trips and bounces, as in Robert Service's rollicking line:

A bunch of the boys were whoop·ing it up in the Ma·la·mute sa·loon . . .
or in Edgar Allan Poe's lines—also light but meant to be serious:

For the moon nev·er beams, with·out bring·ing me dreams
Of the beau·ti·ful An·na·bel Lee.

Apart from the words that convey it, the rhythm of a poem has no meaning. There are no essentially sad rhythms, nor any essentially happy ones. But some rhythms enforce certain meanings better than others do. The bouncing rhythm of Service's line seems fitting for an account of a merry night in a Klondike saloon; but it may be distracting when encountered in Poe's wistful elegy.

The special power of poetry comes from allowing us to hear simultaneously every level of meaning in language—denotation and connotation, image and idea, abstract content and physical sound. Since sound stress is one of the ways that the English language most clearly communicates meaning, any regular rhythmic pattern will affect the poem's effect. Poets learn to use rhythms that reinforce the meaning and the tone of a poem. As film directors know, any movie scene's effect can change dramatically if different background music accompanies the images. Master of the suspense film Alfred Hitchcock, for instance, could fill an ordinary scene with tension or terror just by playing nervous, grating music underneath it.

Exercise: Get with the Beat

In each of the following passages the author has established a strong rhythm. Describe how the rhythm helps establish the tone and meaning of the poem. How does each poem's beat seem appropriate to the tone and subject?

1. I sprang to the stirrup, and Joris and he;
   I galloped, Dirck galloped, we galloped all three;
   "Good speed," cried the watch as the gatebolts undrew;
   "Speed!" echoed the wall to us galloping through.
   Behind shut the postern, the lights sank to rest,
   And into the midnight we galloped abreast.
   > —Robert Browning, from "How They Brought the Good News
   > from Ghent to Aix"

2. I couldn't be cooler, I come from Missoula,
   And I rope and I chew and I ride.
   But I'm a heroin dealer, and I drive a four-wheeler
   With stereo speakers inside.
   My ol' lady Phoebe's out rippin' off C.B.'s
   From the rigs at the Wagon Wheel Bar,
   Near a Montana truck stop and a shit-outta-luck stop
   For a trucker who's driven too far.
   > —Greg Keeler, from "There Ain't No Such Thing as a Montana
   > Cowboy" (a song lyric)

3. Oh newsprint moonprint Marilyn!
   Rub ink from a finger
   to make your beauty mark.
   > —Rachel Eisler, from "Marilyn's Nocturne" (a poem about a newspaper
   > photograph of Marilyn Monroe)

4. Of all the lives I cannot live,
    I have elected one

    to haunt me till the margins give
    and I am left alone

    One life has sounded in my voice
    and made me like a stone—

    one that the falling leaves can sink
    not over, but upon.
                    —Annie Finch, "Dickinson"

5. The master, the swabber, the boatswain, and I,
    The gunner and his mate
    Loved Mall, Meg, and Marian, and Margery,
    But none of us cared for Kate;
    For she had a tongue with a tang
    Would cry to a sailor "Go hang!"—
    She loved not the savor of tar nor of pitch
    Yet a tailor might scratch her where'er she did itch;
    Then to sea, boys, and let her go hang!
                    —William Shakespeare, a song from *The Tempest*

Pauses

Rhythms in poetry are due not only to stresses but also to pauses. "Every nice ear," observed Alexander Pope (*nice* meaning "finely tuned"), "must, I believe, have observed that in any smooth English verse of ten syllables, there is naturally a pause either at the fourth, fifth, or sixth syllable." Such a light but definite pause within a line is called a **cesura** (or **caesura**), "a cutting." More liberally than Pope, we apply the name to any pause in a line of any length, after any word in the line. In studying a poem, we often indicate a cesura by double vertical lines (||). Usually, a cesura will occur at a mark of punctuation, but there can be a cesura even if no punctuation is present. Sometimes you will find it at the end of a phrase or clause or, as in these lines by William Blake, after an internal rime:

> And priests in black gowns || were walking their rounds
> And binding with briars || my joys and desires.

Lines of ten or twelve syllables (as Pope knew) tend to have just one cesura, though sometimes there are more as in John Webster's line from *The Duchess of Malfi*:

> Cover her face: || mine eyes dazzle: || she died young.

Pauses also tend to recur at more prominent places—namely, after each line. At the end of a verse (from *versus*, "a turning"), the reader's eye, before turning to go on to the next line, makes a pause, however brief. If a line ends in a full pause—usually indicated by some mark of punctuation—we call it **end-stopped**. All the lines in this passage from Christopher Marlowe's *Doctor Faustus* (in which Faustus addresses the apparition of Helen of Troy) are end-stopped:

> Was this the face that launch'd a thousand ships,
> And burnt the topless towers of Ilium?
> Sweet Helen, make me immortal with a kiss.

Her lips suck forth my soul: see, where it flies!
Come, Helen, come, give me my soul again.
Here will I dwell, for heaven is in these lips,
And all is dross that is not Helena.

A line that does not end in punctuation and that therefore is read with only a slight pause after it is called a **run-on line**. Because a run-on line gives us only part of a phrase, clause, or sentence, we have to read on to the line or lines following, in order to complete a thought. All these lines from Robert Browning's "My Last Duchess" are run-on lines:

> Sir, 'twas not
> Her husband's presence only, called that spot
> Of joy into the Duchess' cheek: perhaps
> Frà Pandolf chanced to say "Her mantle laps
> Over my lady's wrist too much," or "Paint
> Must never hope to reproduce the faint
> Half-flush that dies along her throat." Such stuff
> Was courtesy, she thought . . .

A passage in run-on lines has a rhythm different from that of a passage like Marlowe's in end-stopped lines. When emphatic pauses occur in the quotation from Browning, they fall within a line rather than at the end of one. The passage by Marlowe and that by Browning are in lines of the same meter (iambic) and the same length (ten syllables). What makes the big difference in their rhythms is the running on, or lack of it.

To sum up: rhythm is recurrence. In poems, it is made of stresses and pauses. The poet can produce it by doing any of several things: making the intervals between stresses fixed or varied, long or short; indicating pauses (cesuras) within lines; end-stopping lines or running them over; writing in short or long lines. Rhythm in itself cannot convey meaning. And yet if a poet's words have meaning, their rhythm must be one with it.

Gwendolyn Brooks (1917–2000)

We Real Cool   1960

The Pool Players.
Seven at the Golden Shovel.

We real cool. We
Left school. We

Lurk late. We
Strike straight. We

Sing sin. We
Thin gin. We

Jazz June. We
Die soon.

5

Question
Describe the rhythms of this poem. By what techniques are they produced?

Alfred, Lord Tennyson (1809–1892)

Break, Break, Break   (1834)

Break, break, break,
   On thy cold gray stones, O Sea!
And I would that my tongue could utter
   The thoughts that arise in me.

O well for the fisherman's boy,   5
   That he shouts with his sister at play!
O well for the sailor lad,
   That he sings in his boat on the bay!

And the stately ships go on
   To their haven under the hill;   10
But O for the touch of a vanish'd hand,
   And the sound of a voice that is still!

Break, break, break,
   At the foot of thy crags, O Sea!
But the tender grace of a day that is dead   15
   Will never come back to me.

Questions

1. Read the first line aloud. What effect does it create at the beginning of the poem?
2. Is there a regular rhythmic pattern in this poem? If so, how would you describe it?
3. The speaker claims that his or her thoughts are impossible to utter. Using evidence from the poem, can you describe the speaker's thoughts and feelings?

Ben Jonson (1573–1637)

Slow, slow, fresh fount, keep time   1600
with my salt tears

Slow, slow, fresh fount, keep time with my salt tears;
   Yet slower yet, oh faintly, gentle springs;
List to the heavy part the music bears,
   Woe weeps out her division° when she sings.   *a part in a song*
     Droop herbs and flowers,   5
     Fall grief in showers;
     Our beauties are not ours;
      Oh, I could still,
Like melting snow upon some craggy hill,
   Drop, drop, drop, drop,   10
Since nature's pride is now a withered daffodil.

SLOW, SLOW, FRESH FOUNT. The nymph Echo sings this lament over the youth Narcissus in Jonson's play *Cynthia's Revels*. In mythology, Nemesis, goddess of vengeance, to punish Narcissus for loving his own beauty, caused him to pine away and then transformed him into a narcissus (another name for a *daffodil*, line 11).

Questions

1. Read the first line aloud rapidly. Why is it difficult to do so?
2. Which lines rely most heavily on stressed syllables?
3. How would you describe the rhythm of this poem? How is it appropriate to what is said?

Dorothy Parker (1893–1967)

Résumé 1926

Razors pain you;
Rivers are damp;
Acids stain you;
And drugs cause cramp.
Guns aren't lawful;   5
Nooses give;
Gas smells awful;
You might as well live.

Questions

1. Which of the following words might be used to describe the rhythm of this poem, and which might not—*flowing, jaunty, mournful, tender, abrupt*?
2. Is this light verse or a serious poem? Can it be both?

METER

Meter is the rhythmic pattern of stresses in verse. To enjoy the rhythms of a poem, no special knowledge of meter is necessary. All you need do is pay attention to stresses and where they fall, and you will perceive the basic pattern, if there is any. There is nothing occult about the study of meter. Most people find they can master its essentials in no more time than it takes to learn a complicated game such as chess. If you take the time, you will then have the pleasure of knowing what is happening in the rhythms of many a fine poem, and pleasurable knowledge may even deepen your insight into poetry. The following discussion, then, will be of interest only to those who care to go deeper into **prosody**, the study of metrical structures in poetry.

To make ourselves aware of a meter, we need only listen to a poem, or sound its words to ourselves. If we care to work out exactly what a poet is doing, we *scan* a line or a poem by indicating the stresses in it. **Scansion**, the art of so doing, is not just a matter of pointing to syllables; it is also a matter of listening to a poem and making sense of it. To scan a poem is one way to indicate how to read it aloud; in order to see where stresses fall, you have to see the places where the poet wishes to put emphasis. That is why, when scanning a poem, you may find yourself suddenly understanding it.

An objection might be raised against scanning: isn't it too simple to pretend that all language (and poetry) can be divided neatly into stressed syllables and unstressed syllables? Indeed it is. Language isn't binary; there are many levels of stress from a scream to a whisper. However, the idea in scanning a poem is not to reproduce the sound of a human voice. For that we would do better to buy a tape recorder. To scan a poem, rather, is to make a diagram of the stresses (and absences of stress) we find in it. Various marks are used in scansion; in this book we use ′ for a stressed syllable and ˘ for an unstressed syllable.

Types of Meter

There are four common accentual-syllabic meters in English—iambic, anapestic, trochaic, and dactylic. Each is named for its basic **foot** (usually a unit of two or three syllables that contains one strong stress) or building block. Here are some examples of each meter.

1. **Iambic**—a line made up primarily of **iambs**, an unstressed syllable followed by a stressed syllable, ˘′. The iambic measure is the most common meter in English poetry. Many writers, such as Robert Frost, feel iambs most easily capture the natural rhythms of our speech.

   ˘ ′ | ˘ ′ | ˘ ′ | ˘ ′ | ˘ ′
   But soft, | what light | through yon | der win | dow breaks?
   —*William Shakespeare*

   ˘ ′ | ˘ ′ | ˘ ′ | ˘ ′ | ˘ ′
   When I | have fears | that I | may cease | to be
   —*John Keats*

   ˘ ′ | ˘ ′ | ˘ ′ | ˘ ′
   Had we | but world | e·nough | and time,
   ˘ ′ | ˘ ′ | ˘ ′ | ˘ ′
   This coy | ness, la | dy, were | no crime
   —*Andrew Marvell*

   ˘ ′ | ˘ ′ | ˘ ′ | ˘ ′
   My life | had stood – | a load | ed Gun
   —*Emily Dickinson*

2. **Anapestic**—a line made up primarily of **anapests**, two unstressed syllables followed by a stressed syllable, ˘˘′. Anapestic meter resembles iambic but contains an extra unstressed syllable. Totally anapestic lines often start to gallop, so poets sometimes slow them down by substituting an iambic foot (as Poe does in "Annabel Lee").

   ˘ ˘ ′ | ˘ ˘ ′ | ˘ ˘ ′ | ˘ ˘ ′
   The As·syr | ian came down | like a wolf | on the fold
   ˘ ˘ ′ | ˘ ˘ ′ | ˘ ˘ ′ | ˘ ˘ ′
   And his co | horts were gleam | ing in pur | ple and gold.
   ˘ ˘ ′ | ˘ ˘ ′ | ˘ ˘ ′ | ˘ ˘ ′
   And the sheen | of their spears | was like stars | on the sea
   ˘ ˘ ′ | ˘ ˘ ′ | ˘ ˘ ′ | ˘ ˘ ′
   When the blue | wave rolls night | ly on deep | Gal·i·lee.
   —*Lord Byron*

   ˘ ′ | ˘ ˘ ′ | ˘ ˘ ′ | ˘ ˘ ′ | ˘ ˘ ′
   Now this | is the Law | of the Jun | gle—as old | and as true
   ˘ ˘ ′
   | as the sky;
   ˘ ˘ ′ | ˘ ˘ ′ | ˘ ˘ ′ | ˘ ˘ ′ | ˘ ˘ ′
   And the Wolf | that shall keep | it may pros | per, | but the Wolf
   ˘ ˘ ′ | ˘ ˘ ′
   | that shall break | it must die.
   —*Rudyard Kipling*

˘ ˘ ´ | ˘ ˘ ´ | ˘ ˘ ´ | ˘ ´
It was ma | ny and ma | ny a year | a go,
˘ ˘ ´ | ˘ ´ | ˘ ´
In a king | dom by | the sea,
˘ ˘ ´ | ˘ ˘ ´ | ˘ ´ | ˘ ´
That a maid | en there lived | whom you | may know
˘ ˘ ´ | ˘ ´ | ˘ ˘ ´
By the name | of An | na·bel Lee.

—*Edgar Allan Poe*

3. **Trochaic**—a line made up primarily of **trochees**, a stressed syllable followed
   by an unstressed syllable, ´˘. The trochaic meter is often associated with
   songs, chants, and magic spells in English. Trochees make a strong, emphatic meter that is often very mnemonic—that is, "helping, or meant to
   help, the memory." Shakespeare and Blake used trochaic meter to exploit its
   magical associations. Notice how Blake drops the unstressed syllable at the
   end of his lines from "The Tyger." (The location of a missing syllable in a
   metrical foot is usually marked with a caret sign, ˅.)

   ´ ˘ | ´ ˘ | ´ ˘ | ´ ˘
   Dou·ble, | dou·ble, | toil and | trou·ble,
   ´ ˘ | ´ ˘ | ´ ˘ | ´ ˘
   Fi·re | burn and | caul·dron | bub·ble.

   —*Shakespeare*

   ´ ˘ | ´ ˘ | ´ ˘ | ´ ˅
   Ty·ger! | Ty·ger! | burn·ing | bright
   ´ ˘ | ´ ˘ | ´ ˘ | ´ ˅
   In the | for·ests | of the | night

   —*William Blake*

   ´ ˘ | ´ ˘ | ´ ˘ | ´ ˅
   Go and | catch a | fall·ing | star

   —*John Donne*

4. **Dactylic**—a line made up primarily of **dactyls**, one stressed syllable followed
   by two unstressed syllables, ´˘˘. The dactylic meter is less common in
   English than in classical languages like Greek or Latin. Used carefully,
   dactylic meter can sound stately, as in Longfellow's *Evangeline*.

   ´ ˘ ˘ | ´ ˘ ˘ | ´ | ´ ˘ ˘ | ´ ˘ ˘
   This is the | for·est pri | me·val. The | mur·mur·ing | pines and the
   ´ ´
   | hem·lock

   —*Henry Wadsworth Longfellow*

But it also easily becomes a prancing, propulsive measure and is often used
in comic verse.

   ´ ˘ ˘ | ´ ˘ ˘ | ´ ˘ | ´ ˘ | ´ ˅
   Puss·y·cat, | puss·y·cat, | where have you | been?

   —*Mother Goose*

Poets often drop the unstressed syllables at the end of a dactylic line, the omission usually being noted with a caret sign, ˇ.

> Take her up | ten·der·ly,
> Lift her with | care;
> Fash·ioned so | slen·der·ly,
> Young, and so | fair!
>
> —*Thomas Hood*

Iambic and anapestic meters are called **rising meters** because their movement rises from an unstressed syllable (or syllables) to stress; trochaic and dactylic meters are called **falling**. In the twentieth century, the bouncing meters—anapestic and dactylic—were used more often for comic verse than for serious poetry. Called feet, though they contain no unaccented syllables, are the **monosyllabic foot** (ʹ) and the **spondee** (ʺ). Meters are not ordinarily made up of them; if one were, it would be like the steady impact of nails being hammered into a board—no pleasure to hear or to dance to. But inserted now and then, they can lend emphasis and variety to a meter, as Yeats well knew when he broke up the predominantly iambic rhythm of "Who Goes with Fergus?" (page 773) with the line in which two spondees occur.

> And the white breast of the dim sea,

Line Lengths

Meters are classified also by line lengths: *trochaic monometer*, for instance, is a line one trochee long, as in this anonymous brief comment on microbes:

> Adam
> Had 'em.

A frequently heard metrical description is **iambic pentameter**: a line of five iambs, a meter especially familiar because it occurs in all blank verse (such as Shakespeare's plays and Milton's *Paradise Lost*), heroic couplets, and sonnets. The commonly used names for line lengths follow:

monometer	one foot
dimeter	two feet
trimeter	three feet
tetrameter	four feet
pentameter	five feet
hexameter	six feet
heptameter	seven feet
octameter	eight feet

Lines of more than eight feet are possible but are rare. They tend to break up into shorter lengths in the listening ear.

When Yeats chose the spondees *white breast* and *dim sea*, he was doing what poets who write in meter do frequently for variety—using a foot other than the expected one. Often such a substitution will be made at the very beginning of a line, as in the third line of this passage from Christopher Marlowe's *Tragical History of Doctor Faustus*:

> ⏑ ′ ⏑ ′ ⏑ ′ ⏑ ′ ⏑ ′
> Was this | the face | that launched | a thou | sand ships
> ⏑ ′ ⏑ ′ ⏑ ′ ⏑ ′ ⏑
> And burnt | the top | less tow'rs | of Il | i·um?
> ′ ′ ⏑ ′ ⏑⏑ ′ ⏑ ′ ⏑ ′
> Sweet Hel | en, make | me im·mor | tal with | a kiss.

How, we might wonder, can that last line be called iambic at all? But it is, just as a waltz that includes an extra step or two, or leaves a few steps out, remains a waltz. In the preceding lines the basic iambic pentameter is established, and though in the third line the regularity is varied from, it does not altogether disappear. It continues for a while to run on in the reader's mind, where (if the poet does not stay away from it for too long) the meter will be when the poem comes back to it.

Like a basic dance step, a meter is not to be slavishly adhered to. The fun in reading a metrical poem often comes from watching the poet continually departing from perfect regularity, giving a few heel-kicks to display a bit of joy or ingenuity, then easing back into the basic step again. Because meter is orderly and the rhythms of living speech are unruly, poets can play one against the other, in a sort of counterpoint. Robert Frost, a master at pitting a line of iambs against a very natural-sounding and irregular sentence, declared, "I am never more pleased than when I can get these into strained relation. I like to drag and break the intonation across the meter as waves first comb and then break stumbling on the shingle."[1]

Evidently Frost's skilled effects would be lost to a reader who, scanning a Frost poem or reading it aloud, distorted its rhythms to fit the words exactly to the meter. With rare exceptions, a good poem can be read and scanned the way we would speak its sentences if they were ours. This, for example, is an unreal scansion:

> ⏑ ′ ⏑ ′ ⏑ ′ ⏑ ′ ⏑ ′
> That's my last Duch·ess paint·ed on the wall.

—because no speaker of English would say that sentence in that way. We are likely to stress *That's* and *last*.

Although in good poetry we seldom meet a very long passage of absolute metrical regularity, we sometimes find (in a line or so) a monotonous rhythm that is effective. Words fall meaningfully in Macbeth's famous statement of world-weariness: "Tomorrow and tomorrow and tomorrow . . ." and in the opening lines of Thomas Gray's "Elegy":

> ⏑ ′ ⏑ ′ ⏑ ′ ⏑ ′ ⏑ ′
> The cur·few tolls the knell of part·ing day,
> ⏑ ′ ⏑ ′ ′ ′ ⏑ ′ ⏑ ′
> The low·ing herd wind slow·ly o'er the lea,
> ⏑ ′ ⏑ ′ ⏑ ′ ⏑ ′ ⏑ ′
> The plow·man home·ward plods his wear·y way,
> ⏑ ′ ⏑ ′ ⏑ ′ ⏑ ⏑ ⏑ ′
> And leaves the world to dark·ness and to me.

Although certain unstressed syllables in these lines seem to call for more emphasis than others—you might, for instance, care to throw a little more weight on the

---

[1]Letter to John Cournos in 1914, in *Selected Letters of Robert Frost,* ed. Lawrance Thompson (New York: Holt, 1964) 128.

second syllable of *curfew* in the opening line—we can still say that the lines are notably iambic. Their almost unvarying rhythm seems just right to convey the tolling of a bell and the weary setting down of one foot after the other.

Accentual Meter

Besides the two rising meters (iambic, anapestic) and the two falling meters (trochaic, dactylic), English poets have another valuable meter. It is **accentual meter**, in which the poet does not write in feet (as in the other meters) but instead counts accents (stresses). The idea is to have the same number of stresses in every line. The poet may place them anywhere in the line and may include practically any number of unstressed syllables, which do not count. In "Christabel," for instance, Coleridge keeps four stresses to a line, though the first line has only eight syllables and the last line has eleven:

> There is not wind e·nough to twirl
> The one red leaf, the last of its clan,
> That dan·ces as of·ten as dance it can,
> Hang·ing so light, and hang·ing so high,
> On the top-most twig that looks up at the sky.

The history of accentual meter is long and honorable. Old English poetry was written in a kind of accentual meter, but its line was more rule-bound than Coleridge's: four stresses arranged two on either side of a cesura, plus alliteration of three of the stressed syllables. In "Junk," Richard Wilbur revives the pattern:

> An axe an·gles ‖ from my neigh·bor's ash·can . . .

Many poets, from the authors of Mother Goose rimes to Gerard Manley Hopkins, have sometimes found accentual meters congenial. Recently, accentual meter has enjoyed huge popularity through rap poetry, which usually employs a four-stress line (see page 762 for further discussion of rap).

Although less popular among poets today than formerly, meter endures. Major poets from Shakespeare through Yeats have fashioned their work by it, and if we are to read their poems with full enjoyment, we need to be aware of it. To enjoy metrical poetry—even to write it—you do not have to slice lines into feet; you do need to recognize when a meter is present in a line, and when the line departs from it. An argument in favor of meter is that it reminds us of body rhythms such as breathing, walking, the beating of the heart. In an effective metrical poem, these rhythms cannot be separated from what the poet is saying—or, in the words of an old jazz song of Duke Ellington's, "It don't mean a thing if it ain't got that swing." As critic Paul Fussell has put it: "No element of a poem is more basic—and I mean physical—in its effect upon the reader than the metrical element, and perhaps no technical triumphs reveal more readily than the metrical the poet's sympathy with that universal human nature . . . which exists outside his own."[2]

[2]*Poetic Meter and Poetic Form* (New York: Random, 1965) 110.

Exercise: Meaningful Variation

At what place or places in each of these passages does the poet depart from basic iambic meter? How does each departure help underscore the meaning?

1. Shadwell alone, of all my sons, is he
   Who stands confirmed in full stupidity.
   The rest to some faint meaning make pretense,
   But Shadwell never deviates into sense.
   —John Dryden, "Mac Flecknoe" (speech of Flecknoe, prince of
   Nonsense, referring to Thomas Shadwell, poet and playwright)

2. A needless Alexandrine ends the song
   That, like a wounded snake, drags its slow length along.
   —Alexander Pope, *An Essay on Criticism*

3. Roll on, thou deep and dark blue Ocean—roll!
   Ten thousand fleets sweep over thee in vain;
   Man marks the earth with ruin—his control
   Stops with the shore; upon the watery plain
   The wrecks are all thy deed, nor doth remain
   A shadow of man's ravage, save his own,
   When, for a moment, like a drop of rain,
   He sinks into thy depths with bubbling groan,
   Without a grave, unknell'd, uncoffin'd, and unknown.
   —George Gordon, Lord Byron, *Childe Harold's Pilgrimage*

4. Deer walk upon our mountains, and the quail
   Whistle about us their spontaneous cries;
   Sweet berries ripen in the wilderness;
   And, in the isolation of the sky,
   At evening, casual flocks of pigeons make
   Ambiguous undulations as they sink,
   Downward to darkness, on extended wings.
   —Wallace Stevens, "Sunday Morning"

Exercise: Recognizing Rhythms

Which of the following poems contain predominant meters? Which poems are not wholly metrical, but are metrical in certain lines? Point out any such lines. What reasons do you see, in such places, for the poet's seeking a metrical effect?

Edna St. Vincent Millay (1892–1950)

Counting-out Rhyme   1928

Silver bark of beech, and sallow
Bark of yellow birch and yellow
  Twig of willow.

Stripe of green in moosewood maple,
Color seen in leaf of apple,   5
  Bark of popple.

Wood of popple pale as moonbeam,
Wood of oak for yoke and barn-beam,
  Wood of hornbeam.

Silver bark of beech, and hollow   10
Stem of elder, tall and yellow
   Twig of willow.

Jacqueline Osherow (b. 1956)

Song for the Music in the Warsaw Ghetto   1996

Pity the tune bereft of singers
Pity the tone bereft of chords
Where shall we weep? By which waters?
Pity the song bereft of words

Pity the harps hung on rifles   5
The unsuspected cunning in each hand
Pity the shrill, bewildered nightingales
How could they sing in that strange land?

Pity the string that has no bow
Pity the flute that has no breath   10
Pity the rifle's muted solo
Pity its soundless aftermath

SONG FOR THE MUSIC IN THE WARSAW GHETTO. In November 1940, the Jews of Warsaw, Poland (who constituted nearly a third of the city's population), were moved by the occupying German army into a section of the city that was sealed by a ten-foot-high wall. Beginning in July 1942, more than 300,000 of the ghetto's inhabitants were deported to Treblinka and other forced-labor and death camps. On April 19, 1943, an uprising began, during which 750 Jewish civilians held off the German forces for four weeks. After the revolt was crushed, the Germans shot some 7,000 people and deported the rest of the ghetto's inhabitants to the camps.

A. E. Housman (1859–1936)

When I was one-and-twenty   1896

When I was one-and-twenty
   I heard a wise man say,
"Give crowns and pounds and guineas
   But not your heart away;
Give pearls away and rubies   5
   But keep your fancy free."
But I was one-and-twenty,
   No use to talk to me.

When I was one-and-twenty
   I heard him say again,   10
"The heart out of the bosom
   Was never given in vain;
'Tis paid with sighs a plenty
   And sold for endless rue."
And I am two-and-twenty,   15
   And oh, 'tis true, 'tis true.

William Carlos Williams   (1883–1963)

Smell!

1917

Oh strong-ridged and deeply hollowed
nose of mine! what will you not be smelling?
What tactless asses we are, you and I, boney nose,
always indiscriminate, always unashamed,
and now it is the souring flowers of the bedraggled   5
poplars: a festering pulp on the wet earth
beneath them. With what deep thirst
we quicken our desires
to that rank odor of a passing springtime!
Can you not be decent? Can you not reserve your ardors   10
for something less unlovely? What girl will care
for us, do you think, if we continue in these ways?
Must you taste everything? Must you know everything?
Must you have a part in everything?

Walt Whitman   (1819–1892)

Beat! Beat! Drums!

(1861)

Beat! beat! drums!—blow! bugles! blow!
Through the windows—through doors—burst like a ruthless force,
Into the solemn church, and scatter the congregation,
Into the school where the scholar is studying;
Leave not the bridegroom quiet—no happiness must he have now with
    his bride,   5
Nor the peaceful farmer any peace, ploughing his field or gathering his
    grain,
So fierce you whirr and pound you drums—so shrill you bugles blow.

Beat! beat! drums!—blow! bugles! blow!
Over the traffic of cities—over the rumble of wheels in the streets;
Are beds prepared for sleepers at night in the houses? no sleepers must
    sleep in those beds,   10
No bargainer's bargains by day—no brokers or speculators—would they
    continue?
Would the talkers be talking? would the singer attempt to sing?
Would the lawyer rise in the court to state his case before the judge?
Then rattle quicker, heavier drums—you bugles wilder blow.

Beat! beat! drums!—blow! bugles! blow!   15
Make no parley—stop for no expostulation,
Mind not the timid—mind not the weeper or prayer,
Mind not the old man beseeching the young man,
Let not the child's voice be heard, nor the mother's entreaties,
Make even the trestles to shake the dead where they lie awaiting the
    hearses.   20
So strong you thump O terrible drums—so loud you bugles blow.

David Mason (b. 1954)

Song of the Powers   1996

Mine, said the stone,
mine is the hour.
I crush the scissors,
such is my power.
Stronger than wishes,   5
my power, alone.

Mine, said the paper,
mine are the words
that smother the stone
with imagined birds,   10
reams of them, flown
from the mind of the shaper.

Mine, said the scissors,
mine all the knives
gashing through paper's   15
ethereal lives;
nothing's so proper
as tattering wishes.

As stone crushes scissors,
as paper snuffs stone   20
and scissors cut paper,
all end alone.
So heap up your paper
and scissor your wishes
and uproot the stone   25
from the top of the hill.
They all end alone
as you will, you will.

SONG OF THE POWERS. The three key images of this poem are drawn from the children's game of Scissors, Paper, Stone. In this game each object has a specific power: Scissors cuts paper, paper covers stone, and stone crushes scissors.

Langston Hughes (1902–1967)

Dream Boogie   1951

Good morning, daddy!
Ain't you heard
The boogie-woogie rumble
Of a dream deferred?

Listen closely: 5
You'll hear their feet
Beating out and beating out a—

You think
It's a happy beat?

Listen to it closely: 10
Ain't you heard
something underneath
like a—

What did I say?

Sure,   15
I'm happy!
Take it away!

  Hey, *pop!*
  Re-*bop!*
  Mop!   20

  Y-e-a-h!

■ WRITING *effectively*

Gwendolyn Brooks on Writing

Hearing "We Real Cool"   1969

Stavros: How about the seven pool players
in the poem "We Real Cool"?

Brooks: They have no pretensions to any
glamor. They are supposedly dropouts, or at
least they're in the poolroom when they
should be possibly in school, since they're
probably young enough or at least those I saw
were when I looked in a poolroom, and
they. . . . First of all, let me tell you how that's
supposed to be said, because there's a reason
why I set it out as I did. These are people who
are essentially saying, "Kilroy is here. We
are." But they're a little uncertain of the
strength of their identity. The "We"—you're
supposed to stop after the "We" and think
about *validity;* of course, there's no way for

Gwendolyn Brooks

you to tell whether it should be said softly or not, I suppose, but I say it rather softly because I want to represent their basic uncertainty, which they don't bother to question
every day, of course.

Stavros: Are you saying that the form of this poem, then, was determined by the colloquial rhythm you were trying to catch?

Brooks: No, determined by my feelings about these boys, these young men.

From "On 'We Real Cool'"

THINKING ABOUT RHYTHM

When we read casually, we don't need to think very hard about a poem's rhythm. We *feel* it as we read, even if we aren't consciously paying attention to matters such as iambs or anapests. When analyzing a poem, though, it helps to have a clear sense of how the rhythm works, and the best way to reach that understanding is through scansion. A scansion gives us a picture of the poem's most important sound patterns. Scanning a poem can seem a bit intimidating at first, but it really isn't all that difficult.

- ▪ **Read the poem aloud, marking the stressed syllables as you go.**
- ▪ **If you're having a hard time hearing the stresses, read the line a few different ways.** Try to detect which way seems most like natural speech.

Example: **Tennyson's "Break, Break, Break"**

A simple scansion of the opening of Tennyson's poem "Break, Break, Break" (on page 794) might look like this in your notes:

Break, break, break	(3 syllables)
On thy cold gray stones, O Sea!	(7 syllables)/rime
And I would that my tongue could utter	(9 syllables)
The thoughts that arise in me.	(7 syllables)/rime

By now some basic organizing principles of the poem have become clear. The lines are rimed *a b c b*, but they contain an irregular number of syllables. The number of strong stresses, however, seems to be constant, at least in the opening stanza.

Now that you have a visual diagram of the poem's sound, the rhythm will be much easier to write about. This diagram will also lead you to a richer understanding of how the poet's artistry reinforces the poem's meaning. The three sharp syllables of the first line give the reader an immediate sense of the depth and intensity of the speaker's feelings. The sudden burst of syllables in the third line underscores the rush of passion that wells up in his breast and outstrips his ability to give voice to it. And the rhythm of the last two lines—the rising intensity of the third line followed by the ebb of the fourth—subtly suggests the effect of the surging and receding of the waves.

CHECKLIST: Scanning a Poem

- ☐ Read the poem aloud.
- ☐ Mark the syllables on which the main speech stresses fall. When in doubt, read the line aloud several different ways. Which way seems most natural?
- ☐ Are there rimes? Indicate where they occur.
- ☐ How many syllables are there in each line?
- ☐ Do any other recurring sound patterns strike you?
- ☐ Does the poem set up a reliable pattern and then diverge from it anywhere? If so, how does that irregularity underscore the line's meaning?

WRITING ASSIGNMENT ON RHYTHM

Scan the rhythm of a passage from any poem in this chapter, following the guidelines listed above. Discuss how the poem uses rhythm to create certain key effects. Be sure that your scansion shows all the elements you've chosen to discuss.

MORE TOPICS FOR WRITING

1. Pair up with a friend or classmate and take turns reading Langston Hughes's "Dream Boogie" out loud to each other. Now write briefly on what you learned about this poem's rhythm by speaking and hearing it.

2. How do rhythm and other kinds of sonic effects (alliteration and consonance, for example) combine to make meaning in Edna St. Vincent Millay's "Counting-out Rhyme"?

3. Scan a stanza of Walt Whitman's "Beat! Beat! Drums!" What do you notice about the poem's rhythms? How do the rhythms underscore the poem's meaning?

4. Scan two poems, one in free verse, and the other in regular meter. (For a free verse poem you might pick William Carlos Williams's "Smell!" (page 803) or Hart Crane's "My Grandmother's Love Letters" (page 1034); for a poem in regular meter you could go with A. E. Housman's "When I was one-and-twenty" or David Mason's "Song of the Powers." Now write about the experience. Do you detect any particular strengths offered by regular meter? How about by free verse?

5. Robert Frost once claimed he tried to make poetry out of the "sound of sense." Writing to a friend, Frost discussed his notion that "the simple declarative sentence" in English often contained an abstract sound that helped communicate its meaning. "The best place to get the abstract sound of sense," wrote Frost, "is from voices behind a door that cuts off the words." Ask yourself how these sentences of dialogue would sound without the words in which they are embodied:

   > You mean to tell me you can't read?
   > I said no such thing.
   > Well, read then.
   > You're not my teacher.

   Frost went on to say that "The reader must be at no loss to give his voice the posture proper to the sentence." Thinking about Frost's theory, can you see how it throws any light on one of his poems? In two or three paragraphs, discuss how Frost uses the "simple declarative sentence" as a distinctive rhythmic feature in his poetry.

▶ TERMS FOR *review*

Pattern and Structure

Stress ▶ An emphasis, or **accent**, placed on a syllable in speech. The unstressed syllable in a line of verse is called the **slack syllable**.

Rhythm ▶ The recurring pattern of stresses and pauses in a poem. A fixed rhythm in a poem is called **meter**.

Prosody ▶ The study of metrical structures in poetry.

Scansion ▶ A practice used to describe rhythmic patterns in a poem by separating the metrical feet, counting the syllables, marking the accents, and indicating the cesuras.

Cesura or **caesura** ▶ A light but definite pause within a line of verse. Cesuras often appear near the middle of a line, but their placement may be varied for rhythmic effect.

Run-on line ► A line of verse that does not end in punctuation, but carries on grammatically to the next line. The use of run-on lines is called *enjambment*.

End-stopped line ► A line of verse that ends in a full pause, often indicated by a mark of punctuation.

Meter

Foot ► The basic unit of measurement in metrical poetry. Each separate meter is identified by the pattern and order of stressed and unstressed syllables in its foot.

Iamb ► A metrical foot in verse in which an unaccented syllable is followed by an accented one ($\smile$ $\prime$). The iambic measure is the most common meter used in English poetry.

Iambic pentameter ► The most common meter in English verse, five iambic feet per line. Many fixed forms, such as the sonnet and heroic couplets, employ iambic pentameter.

Anapest ► A metrical foot in verse in which two unstressed syllables are followed by a stressed syllable ($\smile$ $\smile$ $\prime$).

Trochee ► A metrical foot in which a stressed syllable is followed by an unstressed one ($\prime$ $\smile$).

Dactyl ► A metrical foot in which one stressed syllable is followed by two unstressed ones ($\prime$ $\smile$ $\smile$). Dactylic meter is less common in English than in classical Greek and Latin.

Spondee ► A metrical foot of verse consisting of two stressed syllables ($\prime$ $\prime$).

Accentual meter ► Verse meter based on the number of stresses per line, not the number of syllables.

22

CLOSED FORM

> Anybody can write the first line of a poem,
> but it is a very difficult task to make
> the second line rhyme with the first.
>
> —MARK TWAIN

Form, as a general idea, is the design of a thing as a whole, the configuration of all its parts. No poem can escape having some kind of form, whether its lines are as various in length as a tree's branches or all in hexameter. To put this point in another way: if you were to listen to a poem read aloud in a language unknown to you, or if you saw the poem printed in that foreign language, whatever in the poem you could see or hear would be the form of it.[1]

Writing in **closed form**, a poet follows (or finds) some sort of pattern, such as that of a sonnet with its rime scheme and its fourteen lines of iambic pentameter. On a page, poems in closed form tend to look regular and symmetrical, often falling into stanzas that indicate groups of rimes. Along with William Butler Yeats, who held that a successful poem will "come shut with a click, like a closing box," the poet who writes in closed form apparently strives for a kind of perfection—seeking, perhaps, to lodge words so securely in place that no word can be budged without a worsening. For the sake of meaning, though, a competent poet often will depart from a symmetrical pattern. As Robert Frost observed, there is satisfaction to be found in things not mechanically regular: "We enjoy the straight crookedness of a good walking stick."

The poet who writes in **open form** usually seeks no final click. Often, such a poet views the writing of a poem as a process, rather than a quest for an absolute. Free to use white space for emphasis, able to shorten or lengthen lines as the sense seems to require, the poet lets the poem discover its shape as it goes along, moving as water flows downhill, adjusting to its terrain, engulfing obstacles. (Open form will provide the focus of the next chapter.)

Most poetry of the past is in closed form, exhibiting at least a pattern of rime or meter, but since the early 1960s the majority of American poets have preferred forms

[1]For a good summary of the uses of the term *form* in criticism of poetry, see the article "Form" by G. N. G. Orsini in *Princeton Encyclopedia of Poetry and Poetics*, 2nd ed., ed. Preminger, Warnke, and Hardison (Princeton: Princeton UP, 1975).

that stay open. Lately, the situation has been changing yet again, with closed form reappearing in much recent poetry. Whatever the fashion of the moment, the reader who seeks a wide understanding of poetry of both the present and the past will need to know both the closed and open varieties.

Closed form gives some poems a valuable advantage: it makes them more easily memorable. The **epic** poems of nations—long narratives tracing the adventures of popular heroes: the Greek *Iliad* and *Odyssey,* the French *Song of Roland,* the Spanish *Cid*—tend to occur in patterns of fairly consistent line length or number of stresses because these works were sometimes transmitted orally. Sung to the music of a lyre or chanted to a drumbeat, they may have been easier to memorize because of their patterns. If a singer forgot something, the song would have a noticeable hole in it, so rime or fixed meter probably helped prevent an epic from deteriorating when passed along from one singer to another. It is no coincidence that so many English playwrights of Shakespeare's day favored iambic pentameter. Companies of actors, often called on to perform a different play each day, could count on a fixed line length to aid their burdened memories.

Some poets complain that closed form is a straitjacket, a limit to free expression. Other poets, however, feel that, like fires held fast in a narrow space, thoughts stated in a tightly binding form may take on a heightened intensity. "Limitation makes for power," according to one contemporary practitioner of closed form, Richard Wilbur; "the strength of the genie comes of his being confined in a bottle." Compelled by some strict pattern to arrange and rearrange words, delete, and exchange them, poets must focus on them the keenest attention. Often they stand a chance of discovering words more meaningful than the ones they started out with. And at times, in obedience to a rime scheme, the poet may be surprised by saying something quite unexpected.

FORMAL PATTERNS

The best-known one-line pattern for a poem in English is **blank verse:** unrimed iambic pentameter. (This pattern is not a stanza: stanzas have more than one line.) Most portions of Shakespeare's plays are in blank verse, and so are Milton's *Paradise Lost,* Tennyson's "Ulysses," certain dramatic monologues of Browning and Frost, and thousands of other poems. Here is a poem in blank verse that startles us by dropping out of its pattern in the final line. Keats appears to have written it late in his life to his fiancée, Fanny Brawne.

John Keats (1795–1821)

This living hand, now warm and capable   (1819?)

This living hand, now warm and capable
Of earnest grasping, would, if it were cold
And in the icy silence of the tomb,
So haunt thy days and chill thy dreaming nights
That thou wouldst wish thine own heart dry of blood   5
So in my veins red life might stream again,
And thou be conscience-calmed—see here it is—
I hold it towards you.

The Couplet

The **couplet** is a two-line stanza, usually rimed. Its lines often tend to be equal in length, whether short or long. Here are two examples:

Blow,
Snow!

As I in hoary winter's night stood shivering in the snow,
Surprised I was with sudden heat which made my heart to glow.

Actually, any pair of rimed lines that contains a complete thought is called a couplet, even if it is not a stanza, such as the couplet that ends a sonnet by Shakespeare. Unlike other stanzas, couplets are often printed solid, one couplet not separated from the next by white space. This practice is usual in printing the **heroic couplet**—or **closed couplet**—two rimed lines of iambic pentameter, the first ending in a light pause, the second more heavily end-stopped. George Crabbe, in *The Parish Register*, described a shotgun wedding:

Next at our altar stood a luckless pair,
Brought by strong passions and a warrant there:
By long rent cloak, hung loosely, strove the bride,
From every eye, what all perceived, to hide;
While the boy bridegroom, shuffling in his pace,
Now hid awhile and then exposed his face.
As shame alternately with anger strove
The brain confused with muddy ale to move,
In haste and stammering he performed his part,
And looked the rage that rankled in his heart.

Though employed by Chaucer, the heroic couplet was named from its later use by Dryden and others in poems, translations of classical epics, and verse plays of epic heroes. It continued in favor through most of the eighteenth century. Much of our pleasure in reading good heroic couplets comes from the seemingly easy precision with which a skilled poet unites statements and strict pattern. In doing so, the poet may place a pair of words, phrases, clauses, or sentences side by side in agreement or similarity, forming a **parallel**, or in contrast and opposition, forming an **antithesis**. The effect is neat. For such skill in manipulating parallels and antitheses, John Denham's lines on the river Thames were much admired:

O could I flow like thee, and make thy stream
My great example, as it is my theme!
Though deep, yet clear; though gentle, yet not dull;
Strong without rage, without o'erflowing full.

These lines were echoed by Pope, ridiculing a poetaster, in two heroic couplets in *The Dunciad*:

Flow, Welsted, flow! like thine inspirer, Beer:
Though stale, not ripe; though thin, yet never clear;
So sweetly mawkish, and so smoothly dull;
Heady, not strong; o'erflowing, though not full.

Reading long poems in so exact a form, one may feel like a spectator at a Ping-Pong match, unless the poet skillfully keeps varying rhythms. One way of escaping such metronome-like monotony is to keep the cesura (see page 792) shifting about from place to place—now happening early in a line, now happening late—and at times unexpectedly to hurl in a second or third cesura. This skill, among other things, distinguishes the work of Dryden. If you care to see it in action, try working through Dryden's elegy for Oldham (page 1040), noticing where the cesuras fall. You'll find that the pauses skip around with lively variety.

The Tercet

A **tercet** is a group of three lines. If rimed, they usually keep to one rime sound, as in this anonymous English children's jingle:

> Julius Caesar,
> The Roman geezer,
> Squashed his wife with a lemon-squeezer.

(That, by the way, is a great demonstration of surprising and unpredictable rimes.) **Terza rima**, the form Dante employs in *The Divine Comedy*, is made of tercets linked together by the rime scheme *a b a, b c b, c d c, d e d, e f e*, and so on. Harder to do in English than in Italian—with its greater resources of riming words—the form nevertheless has been managed by Shelley in "Ode to the West Wind" (with the aid of some slant rimes):

> Make me thy lyre, even as the forest is:
> What if my leaves are falling like its own!
> The tumult of thy mighty harmonies
>
> Will take from both a deep, autumnal tone,
> Sweet though in sadness. Be thou, spirit fierce,
> My spirit! Be thou me, impetuous one!

The Quatrain

The workhorse of English poetry is the **quatrain**, a stanza consisting of four lines. Quatrains are used in rimed poems more often than any other form.

Robert Graves (1895–1985)

Counting the Beats   1959

You, love, and I,
(He whispers) you and I,
And if no more than only you and I
What care you or I?

Counting the beats,   5
Counting the slow heart beats,
The bleeding to death of time in slow heart beats,
Wakeful they lie.

Cloudless day,
Night, and a cloudless day,
Yet the huge storm will burst upon their heads one day   10
From a bitter sky.

Where shall we be,
(She whispers) where shall we be,
When death strikes home, O where then shall we be   15
Who were you and I?

Not there but here,
(He whispers) only here,
As we are, here, together, now and here,
Always you and I.   20

Counting the beats,
Counting the slow heart beats,
The bleeding to death of time in slow heart beats,
Wakeful they lie.

Questions

What elements of sound and rhythm are consistent from stanza to stanza? Do any features change unpredictably from stanza to stanza?

Quatrains come in many line lengths, and sometimes contain lines of varying length, as in the ballad stanza (see page 758). Most often, poets rime the second and fourth lines of quatrains, as in the ballad, but the rimes can occur in any combination the poet chooses. Here are two quatrains from Tennyson's long, elegiac poem, *In Memoriam*. The poem's form—quatrains of iambic tetrameter with the unusual rime scheme *a b b a*—became so celebrated that this pattern is now called the "*In Memoriam* stanza":

> Be near me when my light is low,
> When the blood creeps, and the nerves prick
> And tingle; and the heart is sick,
> And all the wheels of being slow.
>
> Be near me when the sensuous frame
> Is rack'd with pangs that conquer trust;
> And Time, a maniac scattering dust,
> And Life, a Fury slinging flame.

Longer and more complicated stanzas are, of course, possible, but couplet, tercet, and quatrain have been called the building blocks of our poetry because most longer stanzas are made up of them. What short stanzas does John Donne mortar together to make the longer stanza of his "Song"?

John Donne (1572–1631)

Song   1633

Go and catch a falling star,
  Get with child a mandrake root,
Tell me where all past years are,
  Or who cleft the Devil's foot,
Teach me to hear mermaids singing,   5
  Or to keep off envy's stinging,
      And find
      What wind
Serves to advance an honest mind.

If thou be'st borne to strange sights,
  Things invisible to see,   10
Ride ten thousand days and nights,
  Till age snow white hairs on thee,
Thou, when thou return'st, wilt tell me
  All strange wonders that befell thee,   15
      And swear
      Nowhere
Lives a woman true, and fair.

If thou findst one, let me know,
  Such a pilgrimage were sweet—   20
Yet do not, I would not go,
  Though at next door we might meet;
Though she were true, when you met her,
  And last, till you write your letter,
      Yet she   25
      Will be
False, ere I come, to two, or three.

Syllabic Verse

Recently in vogue is a form known as **syllabic verse**, in which the poet establishes a pattern of a certain number of syllables to a line. Either rimed or rimeless but usually stanzaic, syllabic verse has been hailed as a way for poets to escape "the tyranny of the iamb" and discover less conventional rhythms, since, if they take as their line length an *odd* number of syllables, then iambs, being feet of *two* syllables, cannot fit perfectly into it. A well-known syllabic poem is Dylan Thomas's "Fern Hill" (page 1092). Notice its shape on the page, count the syllables in its lines, and you'll perceive its perfect symmetry.

Other Patterns

Poets who write in demanding forms seem to enjoy taking on an arbitrary task for the fun of it, as ballet dancers do, or weightlifters. Much of our pleasure in reading such poems comes from watching words fall into a shape. It is the pleasure of seeing any hard thing done skillfully—a leap executed in a dance, a basketball swished through a basket. Still, to be excellent, a poem needs more than skill; and to enjoy a poem it isn't always necessary for the reader to be aware of the skill that went into it. Unknowingly, the editors of the *New Yorker* once printed an **acrostic**—a poem in which the initial letter of each line, read downward, spells out a word or words—that named (and insulted) a well-known anthologist. Evidently, besides being clever, the acrostic was a printable poem. In the Old Testament book of Lamentations, profoundly moving songs tell of the sufferings of the Jews after the destruction of Jerusalem. Four of the songs are written as an alphabetical acrostic, every stanza beginning with a letter of the Hebrew alphabet. However ingenious, such sublime poetry cannot be dismissed as merely witty; nor can it be charged that a poet who writes in such a form does not express deep feeling.

Phillis Levin (b. 1954)

Brief Bio   1995

Bearer of no news
Under the sun, except
The spring, I quicken
Time, drawing you to see
Earth's lightest pamphlet,   5
Reeling mosaic of rainbow dust,
Filament hinging a new set of wings,
Lord of no land, subject to flowers and wind,
Yesterday born in a palace that hangs by a thread.

Questions

1. What does the poem describe? (How can we know for sure?)
2. What is the form of the poem?
3. How does the title relate to the rest of the poem?
4. Does the visual shape of the poem on the page suggest any image from the poem itself?

Patterns of sound and rhythm can, however, be striven after in a dull mechanical way, for which reason many poets today think them dangerous. Swinburne, who loved alliterations and tripping meters, here pokes fun at his own excessive patterning:

From the depth of the dreamy decline of the dawn through a
     notable nimbus of nebulous noonshine,
Pallid and pink as the palm of the flag-flower that flickers with
     fear of the flies as they float,
Are the looks of our lovers that lustrously lean from a marvel of
     mystic miraculous moonshine,
These that we feel in the blood of our blushes that thicken and
     threaten with throbs through the throat?

This is bad, but bad deliberately. Viewed mechanically, as so many empty boxes somehow to be filled up, stanzas can impose the most hollow sort of discipline. If any good at all, a poem in a fixed pattern, such as a sonnet, is created not only by the craftsman's chipping away at it, but by the explosion of a sonnet-shaped *idea*.

THE SONNET

When we speak of "traditional verse forms," we usually mean **fixed forms**. If written in a fixed form, a poem inherits from other poems certain familiar elements of structure: an unvarying number of lines, say, or a stanza pattern. In addition, it may display certain **conventions**: expected features such as themes, subjects, attitudes, or figures of speech. In medieval folk ballads a "milk-white steed" is a conventional figure of speech; and if its rider be a cruel and beautiful witch who kidnaps mortals, she is a conventional character.

In the poetry of western Europe and America, the **sonnet** is the fixed form that has attracted for the longest time the largest number of noteworthy practitioners. Originally an Italian form (*sonetto*: "little song"), the sonnet owes much of its prestige to Petrarch (1304–1374), who wrote in it of his love for the unattainable Laura. So great was the vogue for sonnets in England at the end of the sixteenth century that a gentleman might have been thought a boor if he couldn't turn out a decent one. Not content to adopt merely the sonnet's fourteen-line pattern, English poets also tried on its conventional mask of the tormented lover. They borrowed some of Petrarch's similes (a lover's heart, for instance, is like a storm-tossed boat) and invented others.

Soon after English poets imported the sonnet in the sixteenth century, they worked out their own rime scheme—one easier for them to follow than Petrarch's, which calls for a greater number of riming words than English can readily provide. (In Italian, according to an exaggerated report, practically everything rimes.) In the following **English sonnet**, sometimes called a **Shakespearean sonnet**, the rimes cohere in four clusters: *a b a b, c d c d, e f e f, g g.* Because a rime scheme tends to shape the poet's statements to it, the English sonnet has three places where the procession of thought is likely to turn in another direction. Within its form, a poet may pursue one idea throughout the three quatrains and then in the couplet end with a surprise.

William Shakespeare (1564–1616)

Let me not to the marriage of true minds   1609

Let me not to the marriage of true minds
Admit impediments; love is not love
Which alters when it alteration finds,
Or bends with the remover to remove.
O, no, it is an ever-fixèd mark   5
That looks on tempests and is never shaken;
It is the star to every wand'ring bark,
Whose worth's unknown, although his height be taken.
Love's not Time's fool, though rosy lips and cheeks
Within his bending sickle's compass° come;   *range*   10
Love alters not with his° brief hours and weeks,   *Time's*
But bears° it out even to the edge of doom.   *endures*
   If this be error and upon me proved,
   I never writ, nor no man ever loved.

LET ME NOT TO THE MARRIAGE OF TRUE MINDS. 5 *ever-fixèd mark:* a sea-mark like a beacon or a lighthouse that provides mariners with safe bearings. 7 *the star:* presumably the North Star, which gave sailors the most dependable bearing at sea. 12 *edge of doom:* either the brink of death or—taken more generally—Judgment Day.

Michael Drayton (1563–1631)

Since there's no help, come let us kiss and part

1619

Since there's no help, come let us kiss and part;
Nay, I have done, you get no more of me,
And I am glad, yea, glad with all my heart
That thus so cleanly I myself can free;
Shake hands for ever, cancel all our vows,   5
And when we meet at any time again,
Be it not seen in either of our brows
That we one jot of former love retain.
Now at the last gasp of Love's latest breath,
When, his pulse failing, Passion speechless lies,   10
When Faith is kneeling by his bed of death,
And Innocence is closing up his eyes,
   Now if thou wouldst, when all have given him over,
   From death to life thou mightst him yet recover.

Less frequently met in English poetry, the **Italian sonnet**, or **Petrarchan sonnet**, follows the rime scheme *a b b a, a b b a* in its first eight lines, the **octave**, and then adds new rime sounds in the last six lines, the **sestet**. The sestet may rime *c d c d c d, c d e c d e, c d c c d c*, or in almost any other variation that doesn't end in a couplet. This organization into two parts sometimes helps arrange the poet's thoughts. In the octave, the poet may state a problem, and then, in the sestet, may offer a resolution. A lover, for example, may lament all octave long that a loved one is neglectful, then in line 9 begin to foresee some outcome: the speaker will die, or accept unhappiness, or trust that the beloved will have a change of heart.

Edna St. Vincent Millay (1892–1950)

What lips my lips have kissed, and where, and why

1923

What lips my lips have kissed, and where, and why,
I have forgotten, and what arms have lain
Under my head till morning; but the rain
Is full of ghosts tonight, that tap and sigh
Upon the glass and listen for reply,   5
And in my heart there sits a quiet pain
For unremembered lads that not again
Will turn to me at midnight with a cry.
Thus in the winter stands the lonely tree,
Nor knows what birds have vanished one by one,   10
Yet knows its boughs more silent than before:
I cannot say what loves have come and gone,
I only know that summer sang in me
A little while, that in me sings no more.

In this Italian sonnet, the turn of thought comes at the traditional point—the beginning of the ninth line. Many English-speaking poets, however, feel free to vary its placement. In John Milton's commanding sonnet on his blindness ("When I consider how my light is spent" on page 1069), the turn comes midway through line 8, and no one has ever thought the worse of it for bending the rules.

When we hear the terms *closed form* or *fixed form*, we imagine traditional poetic forms as a series of immutable rules. But, in the hands of the best poets, metrical forms are fluid concepts that change to suit the occasion. Here, for example, is a haunting poem by Robert Frost that simultaneously fulfills the rules of two traditional forms. Is it an innovative sonnet or a poem in *terza rima*? (See page 812 for a discussion of *terza rima*.) Frost combined the features of both forms to create a compressed and powerfully lyric poem.

Robert Frost (1874–1963)

Acquainted with the Night   1928

I have been one acquainted with the night.
I have walked out in rain—and back in rain.
I have outwalked the furthest city light.

I have looked down the saddest city lane.
I have passed by the watchman on his beat   5
And dropped my eyes, unwilling to explain.

I have stood still and stopped the sound of feet
When far away an interrupted cry
Came over houses from another street,

But not to call me back or say good-by;   10
And further still at an unearthly height,
One luminary clock against the sky

Proclaimed the time was neither wrong nor right
I have been one acquainted with the night.

"The sonnet," quipped Robert Bly, a contemporary poet-critic, "is where old professors go to die." And certainly in the hands of an unskilled practitioner, the form can seem moribund. Considering the impressive number of powerful sonnets by modern poets such as Yeats, Frost, Auden, Millay, Cummings, Kees, and Heaney, however, the form hardly appears to be exhausted. Like the hero of the popular ballad "Finnegan's Wake," literary forms (though not professors) declared dead have a startling habit of springing up again. No law compels sonnets to adopt an exalted tone, or confines them to an Elizabethan vocabulary. To see some of the surprising shapes contemporary sonnets take, read this selection of five recent examples.

William Meredith (1919–2007)

The Illiterate   1958

Touching your goodness, I am like a man
Who turns a letter over in his hand
And you might think this was because the hand

Was unfamiliar but, truth is, the man
Has never had a letter from anyone;   5
And now he is both afraid of what it means
And ashamed because he has no other means
To find out what it says than to ask someone.

His uncle could have left the farm to him,
Or his parents died before he sent them word,   10
Or the dark girl changed and want him for beloved.
Afraid and letter-proud, he keeps it with him.
What would you call his feeling for the words
That keep him rich and orphaned and beloved?

Questions

1. This entire poem is an extended comparison. Is it a metaphor or a simile? What, precisely, is being compared to what other thing?
2. Is the rime scheme of this poem closer to the Shakespearean or the Petrarchan model? What unusual feature do you notice about the rimes themselves?

Kim Addonizio (b. 1954)

First Poem for You   1994

I like to touch your tattoos in complete
darkness, when I can't see them. I'm sure of
where they are, know by heart the neat
lines of lightning pulsing just above
your nipple, can find, as if by instinct, the blue   5
swirls of water on your shoulder where a serpent
twists, facing a dragon. When I pull you
to me, taking you until we're spent
and quiet on the sheets, I love to kiss
the pictures in your skin. They'll last until   10
you're seared to ashes; whatever persists
or turns to pain between us, they will still
be there. Such permanence is terrifying.
So I touch them in the dark; but touch them, trying.

Questions

1. What is the speaker of this poem "sure of"? What, by implication, is she not sure of?
2. Why do you think the speaker feels that "Such permanence is terrifying"?
3. What, in your view, is she "trying" to do in the poem's last line?

Mark Jarman (b. 1952)

Unholy Sonnet: After the Praying   1997

After the praying, after the hymn-singing,
After the sermon's trenchant commentary
On the world's ills, which make ours secondary,
After communion, after the hand-wringing,
And after peace descends upon us, bringing   5
Our eyes up to regard the sanctuary
And how the light swords through it, and how, scary
In their sheer numbers, motes of dust ride, clinging—
There is, as doctors say about some pain,
Discomfort knowing that despite your prayers,   10
Your listening and rejoicing, your small part
In this communal stab at coming clean,
There is one stubborn remnant of your cares
Intact. There is still murder in your heart.

Questions

1. What kind of sonnet is "Unholy Sonnet," English or Italian?
2. Does the poem have a turn of thought? If so, point out where it occurs and describe it.

A. E. Stallings (b. 1968)

Sine Qua Non   2002

Your absence, father, is nothing. It is naught—
The factor by which nothing will multiply,
The gap of a dropped stitch, the needle's eye
Weeping its black thread. It is the spot
Blindly spreading behind the looking glass.   5
It is the startled silences that come
When the refrigerator stops its hum,
And crickets pause to let the winter pass.

Your absence, father, is nothing—for it is
Omega's long last O, memory's elision,   10
The fraction of impossible division,
The element I move through, emptiness,
The void stars hang in, the interstice of lace,
The zero that still holds the sum in place.

SINE QUA NON. *Sine qua non* is from Latin, meaning literally, "without which not." Used to describe something that is indispensable, an essential part, a prerequisite.

Questions

1. "Nothing" is a key concept in this poem. As used here, does it have its customary connotations of meaninglessness and unimportance? Explain.
2. In "Writing Effectively" (page 827), A. E. Stallings says that when she was young, she felt "that formal verse could not be contemporary, lacked spontaneity, had no room for the intimate." Discuss whether "Sine Qua Non" demonstrates the shortsightedness of that view.

R. S. Gwynn (b. 1948)

Shakespearean Sonnet
2002

With a first line taken from the TV listings

A man is haunted by his father's ghost.
Boy meets girl while feuding families fight.
A Scottish king is murdered by his host.
Two couples get lost on a summer night.
A hunchback slaughters all who block his way. 5
A ruler's rivals plot against his life.
A fat man and a prince make rebels pay.
A noble Moor has doubts about his wife.
An English king decides to conquer France.
A duke finds out his best friend is a she. 10
A forest sets the scene for this romance.
An old man and his daughters disagree.
A Roman leader makes a big mistake.
A sexy queen is bitten by a snake.

Questions

1. Explain the play on words in the title.
2. How many of the texts described in this sonnet can you identify?
3. Does this poem intend merely to amuse, or does it have a larger point?

THE EPIGRAM

Oscar Wilde said that a cynic is "a man who knows the price of everything and the value of nothing." Such a terse, pointed statement is called an epigram. In poetry, however, an **epigram** is a form: "A short poem ending in a witty or ingenious turn of thought, to which the rest of the composition is intended to lead up" (according to the *Oxford English Dictionary*). Often it is a malicious gibe with an unexpected stinger in the final line—perhaps in the very last word.

Alexander Pope (1688–1744)

Epigram Engraved on the Collar of a Dog
Which I Gave to His Royal Highness
1738

I am his Highness' dog at Kew;
Pray tell me, sir, whose dog are you?

Sir John Harrington (1561?–1612)

Of Treason
1618

Treason doth never prosper; what's the reason?
For if it prosper, none dare call it treason.

Robert Herrick (1591–1674)

Moderation   1648

In things a moderation keep,
Kings ought to shear, not skin their sheep.

William Blake (1757–1827)

Her whole life is an epigram   (1793)

Her whole life is an epigram: smack smooth,° and neatly   *perfectly smooth*
    penned,
Platted° quite neat to catch applause, with a sliding noose   *plaited, woven*
    at the end.

E. E. Cummings (1894–1962)

a politician   1944

a politician is an arse upon
which everyone has sat except a man

Langston Hughes (1902–1967)

Two Somewhat Different Epigrams   1957

I

Oh, God of dust and rainbows, help us see
That without dust the rainbow would not be.

II

I look with awe upon the human race
And God, who sometimes spits right in its face.

J. V. Cunningham (1911–1985)

This *Humanist* whom no beliefs constrained   1947

This *Humanist* whom no beliefs constrained
Grew so broad-minded he was scatter-brained.

John Frederick Nims (1913–1999)

Contemplation   1967

"I'm Mark's alone!" you swore. Given cause to doubt you,
I think less of you, dear. But more about you.

Brad Leithauser (b. 1953)

A Venus Flytrap   1982

The humming fly is turned to carrion.
This vegetable's no vegetarian.

Dick Davis (b. 1945)

Fatherhood   1991

O my children, whom I love,
Whom I snap at and reprove—
Bide your time and we shall see
Love and rage snap back at me.

Anonymous

Epitaph on a dentist

Stranger, approach this spot with gravity;
John Brown is filling his last cavity.

Hilaire Belloc (1870–1956)

Fatigue   1923

I'm tired of Love: I'm still more tired of Rhyme.
But Money gives me pleasure all the time.

Wendy Cope (b. 1945)

Variation on Belloc's "Fatigue"   1992

I hardly ever tire of love or rhyme—
That's why I'm poor and have a rotten time.

Limerick

In English the only other fixed form to rival the sonnet and the epigram in favor is
the **limerick**: five anapestic lines usually riming *a a b b a*. The limerick was made
popular by Edward Lear (1812–1888), English painter and author of such nonsense
poems as "The Owl and the Pussycat." Here is a sample, attributed to President
Woodrow Wilson (1856–1924):

> I sat next to the Duchess at tea;
> It was just as I feared it would be:
>   Her rumblings abdominal
>   Were truly phenomenal
> And everyone thought it was me!

OTHER FORMS

There are many other verse forms used in English. Some forms, like the villanelle and sestina, come from other European literatures. But English has borrowed fixed forms from an astonishing variety of sources. The rubaiyat stanza (see page 910), for instance, comes from Persian poetry; the haiku (see page 717) and tanka originated in Japan. Other borrowed forms include the ghazal (Arabic), pantoum (Malay), and sapphics (Greek). Even blank verse (see page 810), which seems as English as the royal family, began as an attempt by Elizabethan poets to copy an Italian eleven-syllable line. To conclude this chapter, here are poems in three widely used closed forms—the villanelle, triolet, and sestina. Their patterns, which are sometimes called "French forms," have been particularly fascinating to English-language poets because they do not merely require the repetition of rime sounds; instead, they demand more elaborate echoing, involving the repetition of either full words or whole lines of verse. Sometimes difficult to master, these forms can create a powerful musical effect unlike ordinary riming.

Dylan Thomas (1914–1953)

Do not go gentle into that good night   1952

Do not go gentle into that good night,
Old age should burn and rave at close of day;
Rage, rage against the dying of the light.

Though wise men at their end know dark is right,
Because their words had forked no lightning they   5
Do not go gentle into that good night.

Good men, the last wave by, crying how bright
Their frail deeds might have danced in a green bay,
Rage, rage against the dying of the light.

Wild men who caught and sang the sun in flight,   10
And learn, too late, they grieved it on its way,
Do not go gentle into that good night.

Grave men, near death, who see with blinding sight
Blind eyes could blaze like meteors and be gay,
Rage, rage against the dying of the light.   15

And you, my father, there on the sad height,
Curse, bless, me now with your fierce tears, I pray,
Do not go gentle into that good night.
Rage, rage against the dying of the light.

Questions

1. "Do not go gentle into that good night" is a **villanelle**: a fixed form originated by French courtly poets of the Middle Ages. What are its rules?
2. Whom does the poem address? What is the speaker saying?
3. Villanelles are sometimes criticized as elaborate exercises in trivial wordplay. How would you defend Thomas's poem against this charge?

Robert Bridges (1844–1930)

Triolet   1890

When first we met we did not guess
That Love would prove so hard a master;
Of more than common friendliness
When first we met we did not guess.
Who could foretell this sore distress,   5
This irretrievable disaster
When first we met?—We did not guess
That Love would prove so hard a master.

TRIOLET. The **triolet** is a short lyric form borrowed from the French; its two opening lines are repeated according to a set pattern, as Bridges's poem illustrates. The triolet is often used for light verse, but Bridges's poem demonstrates how it can carry heavier emotional loads, if used with sufficient skill.

Question

How do the first two lines of "Triolet" change in meaning when they reappear at the end of the poem?

Elizabeth Bishop (1911–1979)

Sestina   1965

September rain falls on the house.
In the failing light, the old grandmother
sits in the kitchen with the child
beside the Little Marvel Stove,
reading the jokes from the almanac,   5
laughing and talking to hide her tears.

She thinks that her equinoctial tears
and the rain that beats on the roof of the house
were both foretold by the almanac,
but only known to a grandmother.   10
The iron kettle sings on the stove.
She cuts some bread and says to the child,

It's time for tea now; but the child
is watching the teakettle's small hard tears
dance like mad on the hot black stove,   15
the way the rain must dance on the house.
Tidying up, the old grandmother
hangs up the clever almanac

on its string. Birdlike, the almanac
hovers half open above the child,   20
hovers above the old grandmother
and her teacup full of dark brown tears.
She shivers and says she thinks the house
feels chilly, and puts more wood in the stove.

It was to be, says the Marvel Stove.   25
I know what I know, says the almanac.
With crayons the child draws a rigid house
and a winding pathway. Then the child
puts in a man with buttons like tears
and shows it proudly to the grandmother.   30

But secretly, while the grandmother
busies herself about the stove,
the little moons fall down like tears
from between the pages of the almanac
into the flower bed the child   35
has carefully placed in the front of the house.

Time to plant tears, says the almanac.
The grandmother sings to the marvellous stove
and the child draws another inscrutable house.

SESTINA. As its title indicates, this poem is written in the trickiest of medieval fixed forms, that of the **sestina** (or "song of sixes"), said to have been invented in Provence in the thirteenth century by the troubadour poet Arnaut Daniel. In six six-line stanzas, the poet repeats six end-words (in a prescribed order), then reintroduces the six repeated words (in any order) in a closing **envoy** of three lines. Elizabeth Bishop strictly follows the troubadour rules for the order in which the end-words recur. (If you care, you can figure out the formula: in the first stanza, the six words are arranged A B C D E F; in the second, F A E B D C; and so on.)

Questions

1. A perceptive comment from a student: "Something seems to be going on here that the child doesn't understand. Maybe some terrible loss has happened." Test this guess by reading the poem closely.
2. In the "little moons" that fall from the almanac (line 33), does the poem introduce dream or fantasy, or do you take these to be small round pieces of paper?
3. What is the tone of this poem—the speaker's apparent attitude toward the scene described?
4. In an essay, "The Sestina," in *A Local Habitation* (U of Michigan P, 1985), John Frederick Nims defends the form against an obvious complaint against it:

   > A shallow view of the sestina might suggest that the poet writes a stanza, and then is stuck with six words which he has to juggle into the required positions through five more stanzas and an envoy—to the great detriment of what passion and sincerity would have him say. But in a good sestina the poet has six words, six images, six ideas so urgently in his mind that he cannot get away from them; he wants to test them in all possible combinations and come to a conclusion about their relationship.

   How well does this description of a good sestina fit "Sestina"?

Experiment: Urgent Repetition

Write a sestina and see what you find out by doing so. (Even if you fail in the attempt, you just might learn something interesting.) To start, pick six words you think are worth repeating six times. This elaborate pattern gives you much help: as John Ashbery has pointed out, writing a sestina is "like riding downhill on a bicycle and having the pedals push your feet." Here is some encouragement from a poet and critic, John Heath-Stubbs: "I have never read a sestina that seemed to me a total failure."

■ WRITING *effectively*

A. E. Stallings on Writing

On Form and Artifice   2000

Is form artificial? Of course it is. I am all for the
artificial. I am reminded of an anecdote. A lovely
girl, with natural blonde hair, but of a rather
dark, rather dingy shade, complains to a friend.
She has wanted for a long time to get it highlighted, which she thinks will brighten her appearance, but with the qualms and vanity of a
natural blonde, scruples about the artificiality of
having her hair colored. At which point her
friend laughs and declares, "Honey, the point is
to *look* natural. Not to *be* natural."

A. E. Stallings

It seems an obvious point for art. Art is effective and direct because of its use of artifice, not
simply because the artist has something sincere or
important to communicate. Anyone who has
written a letter of condolence should be able to
sympathize. When a close friend has lost a loved one, what can one say? "I cannot
imagine your loss" "words cannot begin to" "our thoughts and prayers are with you"
etc. That these phrases are threadbare does not make them less sincere. Phrases become threadbare *because* they are sincere.

I had several revelations about the nature of poetry in a college Latin class on Catullus. I was shocked by how *modern,* how *contemporary* the poems seemed. And it was a
revelation to see how a poet could at one and the same time be a supreme formal architect of verse, and write poems that seemed utterly spontaneous, candid, and confessional, with room for the sublime, the learned, the colloquial, and the frankly obscene.

I suppose at some point I had somehow imbibed the opposite notion, a notion still
held by many, that formal verse could not be contemporary, lacked spontaneity, had no
room for the intimate. At that time I did not see much formal work getting published: I
wanted to publish, and therefore struggled in free verse. I did not have much luck. Eventually I gave up, wrote what I really wanted to write, which rhymed and scanned, and,
oddly, *then* I had some success in publishing. Which leads to yet another little adage of
mine, which is, don't write what you *know* (I think this is better fitted for prose writers),
write what you *like*, the sort of stuff you actually enjoy reading, fashionable or not.

From "Crooked Roads Without Improvement:
Some Thoughts on Formal Verse"

THINKING ABOUT A SONNET

A poem's form is closely tied to its meaning. This is especially true of the sonnet, a
form whose rules dictate not only the sound of a poem but also, to a certain extent,
its sense. A sonnet traditionally looks at a single theme, but reverses its stance on the
subject somewhere along the way. One possible definition of the sonnet might be a

fourteen-line poem divided into two unequal parts. Traditionally, Italian sonnets divide their parts into an octave (the first eight lines) and a sestet (the last six), while English sonnets are more lopsided, with a final couplet balanced against three preceding quatrains. The moment when a sonnet changes its direction is commonly called "the turn."

- **Identifying the moment when the poem "turns" helps in understanding both its theme and its structure.** In a Shakespearean sonnet, the turn usually—but not always—comes in the final couplet. In modern sonnets, the turn is often less overt.
- **To find that moment, study the poem's opening.** Latch on to the mood and manner of the opening lines. Is the feeling joyful or sad, loving or angry?
- **Read the poem from this opening perspective until you feel it tug strongly in another direction.** Sometimes the second part of a sonnet will directly contradict the opening. More often it explains, augments, or qualifies the opening.

CHECKLIST: Writing About a Sonnet

- ☐ Read the poem carefully.
- ☐ What is the mood of its opening lines?
- ☐ Keep reading until you feel the mood shift. Where does that shift take place?
- ☐ What is the tone after the sonnet's turn away from its opening direction?
- ☐ What do the two alternative points of view add up to?
- ☐ How does the poem reconcile its contrasting sections?

WRITING ASSIGNMENT ON A SONNET

Examine a sonnet from anywhere in this book. Explain how its two parts combine to create a total effect neither part could achieve alone. Be sure to identify the turning point. Paraphrase what each of the poem's two sections says and describe how the poem as a whole reconciles the two contrasting parts.

(In addition to the sonnets in this chapter, you might consider any of the following from the chapter "Poems for Further Reading": Elizabeth Barrett Browning's "How Do I Love Thee?"; Gerard Manley Hopkins's "The Windhover"; John Keats's "When I have fears that I may cease to be"; John Milton's "When I consider how my light is spent"; Wilfred Owen's "Anthem for Doomed Youth"; William Shakespeare's "When in disgrace with Fortune and men's eyes"; or William Wordsworth's "Composed upon Westminster Bridge.")

MORE TOPICS FOR WRITING

1. Select a poem that incorporates rime from the chapter "Poems for Further Reading." Write a paragraph describing how the poem's rime scheme helps to advance its meaning.
2. Write ten lines of blank verse on a topic of your own choice. Then write about the experience. What aspects of writing in regular meter did you find most challenging? What did you learn about reading blank verse from trying your hand at writing it?
3. Discuss the use of form in Robert Bridges's "Triolet." What is the effect of so many repeated lines in so brief a poem?

4. Compare Dylan Thomas's "Do not go gentle into that good night" with Wendy Cope's "Lonely Hearts" (page 687). How can the same form be used to create such different kinds of poems?

5. William Carlos Williams, in an interview, delivered this blast:

> Forcing twentieth-century America into a sonnet—gosh, how I hate sonnets—is like putting a crab into a square box. You've got to cut his legs off to make him fit. When you get through, you don't have a crab any more.

In a two-page essay, defend the modern American sonnet against Williams's charge. Or instead, open fire on it, using Williams's view for ammunition. Some sonnets to consider: Mark Jarman's "Unholy Sonnet: After the Praying"; Kim Addonizio's "First Poem for You"; and R. S. Gwynn's "Shakespearean Sonnet."

▶ TERMS FOR *review*

Form

Form ▶ In a general sense, form is the means by which a literary work expresses its content. In poetry, form is usually used to describe the design of a poem.

Fixed form ▶ A traditional verse form requiring certain predetermined elements of structure—for example, a stanza pattern, set meter, or predetermined line length.

Closed form ▶ A generic term that describes poetry written in a pattern of meter, rime, lines, or stanzas. A closed form adheres to a set structure.

Open form ▶ Verse that has no set scheme—no regular meter, rime, or stanzaic pattern. Open form has also been called **free verse.**

Blank verse ▶ Blank verse contains five iambic feet per line (iambic pentameter) and is not rimed. ("Blank" means unrimed.)

Couplet ▶ A two-line stanza in poetry, usually rimed and with lines of equal length.

Closed couplet ▶ Two rimed lines of iambic pentameter that usually contain an independent and complete thought or statement. Also called **heroic couplet.**

Quatrain ▶ A stanza consisting of four lines, it is the most common stanza form used in English-language poetry.

Epic ▶ A long narrative poem tracing the adventures of a popular hero. Epic poems are usually written in a consistent form and meter throughout.

Epigram ▶ A very short, comic poem, often turning at the end with some sharp wit or unexpected stinger.

The Sonnet

Sonnet ▶ A fixed form of fourteen lines, traditionally written in iambic pentameter and rimed throughout.

Italian sonnet ▶ Also called **Petrarchan sonnet,** it rimes the **octave** (the first eight lines) *a b b a a b b a*; the **sestet** (the last six lines) may follow any rime pattern, as long as it does not end in a couplet. The poem traditionally turns, or shifts in mood or tone, after the octave.

English sonnet ▶ Also called **Shakespearean sonnet,** it has the following rime scheme organized into three quatrains and a concluding couplet: *a b a b c d c d e f e f g g*. The poem may turn—that is, shift in mood or tone—between any of the rime clusters.

23 OPEN FORM

All poetry is experimental poetry.

—WALLACE STEVENS

Writing in **open form**, a poet seeks to discover a fresh and individual arrangement for words in every poem. Such a poem, generally speaking, has neither a rime scheme nor a basic meter informing the whole of it. Doing without those powerful (some would say hypnotic) elements, the poet who writes in open form relies on other means to engage and to sustain the reader's attention. Novice poets often think that open form looks easy, not nearly so hard as riming everything; but in truth, formally open poems are easy to write only if written carelessly. To compose lines with keen awareness of open form's demands, and of its infinite possibilities, calls for skill: at least as much as that needed to write in meter and rime, if not more. Should the poet succeed, then the discovered arrangement will seem exactly right for what the poem is saying.

Denise Levertov (1923–1997)

Ancient Stairway   1999

Footsteps like water hollow
the broad curves of stone
ascending, descending
century by century.
Who can say if the last   5
to climb these stairs
will be journeying
downward or upward?

Open form, in this brief poem, affords Denise Levertov certain advantages. Able to break off a line at whatever point she likes (a privilege not available to the poet writing, say, a conventional sonnet, who has to break off each line after its tenth syllable), she selects her pauses artfully. Line breaks lend emphasis: a word or phrase at the end of a line takes a little more stress (and receives a little more attention), because the ending of the line compels the reader to make a slight pause, if only for the brief moment it takes to sling back one's eyes and fix them on the line following. Slight pauses, then, follow the words and phrases *hollow / stone / descending / century / last / stairs / journeying / upward*—all these being elements that apparently the poet wishes to call our attention to. (The pause after a line break also casts a little more weight on the *first* word or phrase of each succeeding line.) Levertov makes the most of white space—another means of calling attention to things, as any good picture-framer knows. She has greater control over the shape of the poem, its look on the page, than would be allowed by the demands of meter; she uses that control to stack on top of one another lines that are (roughly) equivalent in width, like the steps of a staircase. The opening line with its quick stresses might suggest to us the many feet passing over the steps. From there, Levertov slows the rhythm to the heavy beats of lines 3–4, which could communicate a sense of repeated trudging up and down the stairs (in a particularly effective touch, all four of the stressed syllables in these two lines make the same sound), a sense that is reinforced by the poem's last line, which echoes the rhythm of line 3. Note too how, without being restricted by the need of a rime, she can order the terms in that last line according to her intended thematic emphasis. In all likelihood, we perceive these effects instinctively, not consciously (which may also be the way the author created them), but no matter how we apprehend them, they serve to deepen our understanding of and pleasure in the text.

FREE VERSE

Poetry in open form used to be called **free verse** (from the French **vers libre**), suggesting a kind of verse liberated from the shackles of rime and meter. "Writing free verse," said Robert Frost, who wasn't interested in it, "is like playing tennis with the net down." And yet, as Denise Levertov and many other poets demonstrate, high scores can be made in such an unconventional game, provided it doesn't straggle all over the court. For a successful poem in open form, the term *free verse* seems inaccurate. "Being an art form," said William Carlos Williams, "verse cannot be 'free' in the sense of having *no* limitations or guiding principles."[1] Various substitute names have been suggested: organic poetry, composition by field, raw (as against cooked) poetry, open form poetry. "But what does it matter what you call it?" remark the editors of a 1969 anthology called *Naked Poetry*. "The best poems of the last thirty years don't rhyme (usually) and don't move on feet of more or less equal duration (usually). That nondescription moves toward the only technical principle they all have in common."[2]

Projective Verse

Yet many poems in open form have much more in common than absences and lacks. One positive principle has been Ezra Pound's famous suggestion that poets "compose in the sequence of the musical phrase, not in the sequence of the metronome"—good advice, perhaps, even for poets who write inside fixed forms. In Charles Olson's influential theory of **projective verse**, poets compose by listening to their own breathing. On paper, they indicate the rhythms of a poem by using a little white space or a lot, a slight indentation or a deep one, depending on whether a short pause or a long one is intended. Words can be grouped in clusters on the page (usually no more words than

---

[1]"Free Verse," *Princeton Encyclopedia of Poetry and Poetics*, 2nd ed., 1975.

[2]Stephen Berg and Robert Mezey, eds., foreword, *Naked Poetry: Recent American Poetry in Open Forms* (Indianapolis: Bobbs, 1969).

a lungful of air can accommodate). Heavy cesuras are sometimes shown by breaking a line in two and lowering the second part of it.[3]

Free Verse Lines

To the poet working in open form, no less than to the poet writing a sonnet, line length can be valuable. Walt Whitman, who loved to expand vast sentences for line after line, knew well that an impressive rhythm can accumulate if the poet will keep long lines approximately the same length, causing a pause to recur at about the same interval after every line. Sometimes, too, Whitman repeats the same words at each line's opening. An instance is the masterly sixth section of "When Lilacs Last in the Dooryard Bloom'd," an elegy for Abraham Lincoln:

> Coffin that passes through lanes and streets,
> Through day and night with the great cloud darkening the land,
> With the pomp of the inloop'd flags with the cities draped in black,
> With the show of the States themselves as of crape-veil'd women
>   standing,
> With processions long and winding and the flambeaus of the night,
> With the countless torches lit, with the silent sea of faces and the
>   unbared heads,
> With the waiting depot, the arriving coffin, and the somber faces,
> With dirges through the night, with the thousand voices rising
>   strong and solemn,
> With all the mournful voices of the dirges pour'd around the coffin,
> The dim-lit churches and the shuddering organs—where amid
>   these you journey,
> With the tolling tolling bells' perpetual clang,
> Here, coffin that slowly passes,
> I give you my sprig of lilac.

There is music in such solemn, operatic arias. Whitman's lines echo another model: the Hebrew **psalms**, or sacred songs, as translated in the King James Version of the Bible. In Psalm 150, repetition also occurs inside of lines:

> Praise ye the Lord. Praise God in his sanctuary: praise him in the
>   firmament of his power.
> Praise him for his mighty acts: praise him according to his excellent
>   greatness.
> Praise him with the sound of the trumpet: praise him with the
>   psaltery and harp.
> Praise him with the timbrel and dance: praise him with stringed
>   instruments and organs.
> Praise him upon the loud cymbals: praise him upon the high
>   sounding cymbals.
> Let every thing that hath breath praise the Lord. Praise ye the Lord.

Whitman was a more deliberate craftsman than he let his readers think, and to anyone interested in writing in open form, his work will repay close study. He knew

---

[3]See Olson's essays "Projective Verse" and "Letter to Elaine Feinstein" in *Selected Writings*, edited by Robert Creeley (New York: New Directions, 1966). Olson's letters to Cid Corman are fascinating: *Letters for Origin, 1950–1955*, edited by Albert Glover (New York: Grossman, 1970).

that repetitions of any kind often make memorable rhythms, as in this passage from "Song of Myself," with every line ending on an *-ing* word (a stressed syllable followed by an unstressed syllable):

> Here and there with dimes on the eyes walking,
> To feed the greed of the belly the brains liberally spooning,
> Tickets buying, taking, selling, but in to the feast never once going,
> Many sweating, ploughing, thrashing, and then the chaff for
>   payment receiving,
> A few idly owning, and they the wheat continually claiming.

Much more than simply repetition, of course, went into the music of those lines—the internal rime *feed, greed,* the use of assonance, the trochees that begin the third and fourth lines, whether or not they were calculated.

Sound and Rhythm in Free Verse

In many classics of open form poetry, sound and rhythm are positive forces. When speaking a poem in open form, you often may find that it makes a difference for the better if you pause at the end of each line. Try pausing there, however briefly; but don't allow your voice to drop. Read just as you would normally read a sentence in prose (except for the pauses, of course). Why do the pauses matter? Open form poetry usually has no meter to lend it rhythm. *Some* lines in an open form poem, as we have seen in Whitman's "dimes on the eyes" passage, do fall into metrical feet; sometimes the whole poem does. Usually lacking meter's aid, however, open form, in order to have more and more noticeable rhythms, has need of all the recurring pauses it can get. As we can hear in recordings of them reading their work aloud, open form poets such as Robert Creeley and Allen Ginsberg would often pause very definitely at each line break—and so, for that matter, did Ezra Pound.

Some poems, to be sure, seem more widely open in form than others. A poet may wish to avoid the rigidity and predictability of fixed line lengths and stanzaic forms but still wish to hold a poem together through a strong rhythmic impulse and even a discernible metrical emphasis. A poet may employ rime, but have the rimes recur at various intervals, or perhaps rime lines of varying lengths. In a 1917 essay called "Reflections on *Vers Libre*" (French for "free verse"), T. S. Eliot famously observed, "No *vers* is *libre* for the man who wants to do a good job." In that same year, Eliot published his first collection of poems, whose title piece was the classic "The Love Song of J. Alfred Prufrock" (see page 995). Is "Prufrock" a closed poem left ajar or an open poem trying to slam itself?

"Farewell, stale pale skunky pentameters (the only honest English meter, gloop! gloop!)," Kenneth Koch exulted, suggesting that it was high time to junk such stale conventions. Many poets who agree with him believe that it is wrong to fit words into any pattern that already exists, and instead believe in letting a poem seek its own shape as it goes along. (Traditionalists might say that that is what all good poems do anyway: sonnets rarely know they are going to be sonnets until the third line has been written. However, there is no doubt that the sonnet form already exists, at least in the back of the head of any poet who has ever read sonnets.) Some open form poets offer a historical motive: they want to reflect the nervous, staccato, disconnected pace of our bumper-to-bumper society. Others see open form as an attempt to suit thoughts and words to a more spontaneous order than the traditional verse forms allow. "Better," says Gary Snyder, quoting from Zen, "the perfect, easy discipline of the swallow's dip and swoop, 'without east or west.'"

At the moment, much exciting new poetry is being written in both open form and closed. Today, a number of poets (labeled New Formalists) have taken up rime and meter and are writing sonnets, epigrams, and poems in rimed stanzas, giving "pale skunky pentameters" a fresh lease on life. Meanwhile, most younger poets continue to explore a wide range of open forms from conventional and conversational free verse to wildly challenging experimental styles. One West Coast poet, Jack Foley, often writes long free verse poems that involve two voices speaking simultaneously, which makes for exciting if also dizzying poetry readings. The contemporary American determination to play every possible trick that both written and spoken language allows is at least partially inspired by the early Modernist master E. E. Cummings, the smiling godfather of poetic experimentalists everywhere.

E. E. Cummings   (1894–1962)

Buffalo Bill's   1923

Buffalo Bill's
defunct
      who used to
          ride a watersmooth-silver
                        stallion   5
and break onetwothreefourfive pigeonsjustlikethat
                           Jesus
he was a handsome man
              and what i want to know is
how do you like your blueeyed boy   10
Mister Death

Question

Cummings's poem would look like this if given conventional punctuation and set in a solid block like prose:

> Buffalo Bill's defunct, who used to ride a water-smooth silver stallion and break one, two, three, four, five pigeons just like that. Jesus, he was a handsome man. And what I want to know is: "How do you like your blue-eyed boy, Mister Death?"

If this were done, by what characteristics would it still be recognizable as poetry? But what would be lost?

W. S. Merwin   (b. 1927)

For the Anniversary of My Death   1967

Every year without knowing it I have passed the day
When the last fires will wave to me
And the silence will set out
Tireless traveler
Like the beam of a lightless star   5

Then I will no longer
Find myself in life as in a strange garment
Surprised at the earth
And the love of one woman
And the shamelessness of men   10
As today writing after three days of rain
Hearing the wren sing and the falling cease
And bowing not knowing to what

Questions

1. Read the poem aloud. Try pausing for a fraction of a second at the end of every line. Is
    there a justification for each line break?
2. The poem is divided into two asymmetrical sections. Does this formal division reflect
    some change or difference of meaning between the two sections?

William Carlos Williams (1883–1963)

The Dance   1944

In Breughel's great picture, The Kermess,
the dancers go round, they go round and
around, the squeal and the blare and the
tweedle of bagpipes, a bugle and fiddles
tipping their bellies (round as the thick-   5
sided glasses whose wash they impound)
their hips and their bellies off balance
to turn them. Kicking and rolling about
the Fair Grounds, swinging their butts, those

DETAIL. *The Kermess* or *Peasant Dance* by Pieter Brueghel the Elder (1520?–1569).

shanks must be sound to bear up under such   10
rollicking measures, prance as they dance
in Breughel's great picture, The Kermess.

THE DANCE. Breughel (most often spelled "Brueghel"), a Flemish painter known for his scenes of peasant
activities, represented in *The Kermess* a celebration on the feast day of a local patron saint.

Questions

1. Scan this poem and try to describe the effect of its rhythms.
2. Williams, widely admired for his free verse, insisted for many years that what he sought
   was a form not in the least bit free. What effect does he achieve by ending lines on such
   weak words as the articles *and* and *the*? By splitting *thick-* / *sided*? By splitting a preposi-
   tional phrase with the break at the end of line 8? By using line breaks to split *those* and
   such from what they modify? What do you think he is trying to convey?
3. Is there any point in his making line 12 a repetition of the opening line?
4. Look at the reproduction of Brueghel's painting *The Kermess* (also called *Peasant Dance*).
   Aware that the rhythms of dancers, the rhythms of a painting, and the rhythms of a poem
   are not all the same, can you put in your own words what Brueghel's dancing figures have
   in common with Williams's descriptions of them?
5. Compare with "The Dance" another poem that refers to a Brueghel painting: W. H.
   Auden's "Museé des Beaux Arts" on page 1023. What seems to be each poet's main
   concern: to convey in words a sense of the painting, or to visualize the painting in order
   to state some theme?

Stephen Crane (1871–1900)

In the desert   1895

In the desert
I saw a creature, naked, bestial,
Who, squatting upon the ground,
Held his heart in his hands,
And ate of it.   5
I said, "Is it good, friend?"
"It is bitter—bitter," he answered;
"But I like it
Because it is bitter,
And because it is my heart."   10

Walt Whitman (1819–1892)

Cavalry Crossing a Ford   1865

A line in long array where they wind betwixt green islands,
They take a serpentine course, their arms flash in the sun—hark to the
        musical clank,
Behold the silvery river, in it the splashing horses loitering stop to drink,
Behold the brown-faced men, each group, each person a picture, the
        negligent rest on the saddles,
Some emerge on the opposite bank, others are just entering the   5
        ford—while,
Scarlet and blue and snowy white,
The guidon flags flutter gayly in the wind.

Questions

The following nit-picking questions are intended to help you see exactly what makes these two open form poems by Crane and Whitman so different in their music.

1. What devices of sound occur in Whitman's phrase *silvery river* (line 3)? Where else in his poem do you find these devices?
2. Does Crane use any such devices?
3. In number of syllables, Whitman's poem is almost twice as long as Crane's. Which poem has more pauses in it? (Count pauses at the ends of lines, at marks of punctuation.)
4. Read the two poems aloud. In general, how would you describe the effect of their sounds and rhythms? Is Crane's poem necessarily an inferior poem for having less music?

Ezra Pound (1885–1972)

Salutation   1915

O generation of the thoroughly smug
    and thoroughly uncomfortable,
I have seen fishermen picnicking in the sun,
I have seen them with untidy families,
I have seen their smiles full of teeth   5
    and heard ungainly laughter.
And I am happier than you are,
And they were happier than I am;
And the fish swim in the lake
    and do not even own clothing.   10

Questions

1. What organizational devices does this poem use?
2. Why are lines 2, 6, and 10 indented and without initial capital letters?
3. What is the point of the poem's last two lines?

Analyzing Line Breaks

Wallace Stevens's lineation in "Thirteen Ways of Looking at a Blackbird" allows us not only to see but also to savor the connections between the poem's ideas and images. Consider section II of the poem:

    I was of three minds,
    Like a tree
    In which there are three blackbirds.

On a purely semantic level, these lines may mean the same as the prose statement, "I was of three minds like a tree in which there are three blackbirds," but Stevens's choice of line breaks adds special emphasis at several points. Each of these three lines isolates and presents a separate image (the speaker, the tree, and the blackbirds). The placement of *three* at the same position in the opening and closing lines helps us feel the similar nature of the two statements. The short middle line allows us to see the image of the tree before we fully understand why it is parallel to the divided mind—thus adding a touch of suspense that the prose version of this statement just can't supply. Ending each line with a key noun and image also gives the poem a concrete feel not altogether evident in the prose.

Wallace Stevens (1879–1955)

Thirteen Ways of Looking at a Blackbird   1923

I

Among twenty snowy mountains,
The only moving thing
Was the eye of the blackbird.

II

I was of three minds,
Like a tree   5
In which there are three blackbirds.

III

The blackbird whirled in the autumn winds.
It was a small part of the pantomime.

IV

A man and a woman
Are one.   10
A man and a woman and a blackbird
Are one.

V

I do not know which to prefer,
The beauty of inflections
Or the beauty of innuendoes,   15
The blackbird whistling
Or just after.

VI

Icicles filled the long window
With barbaric glass.
The shadow of the blackbird   20
Crossed it, to and fro.
The mood
Traced in the shadow
An indecipherable cause.

VII

O thin men of Haddam,   25
Why do you imagine golden birds?
Do you not see how the blackbird
Walks around the feet
Of the women about you?

VIII

I know noble accents   30
And lucid, inescapable rhythms;
But I know, too,
That the blackbird is involved
In what I know.

IX

When the blackbird flew out of sight,   35
It marked the edge
Of one of many circles.

X

At the sight of blackbirds
Flying in a green light,
Even the bawds of euphony   40
Would cry out sharply.

XI

He rode over Connecticut
In a glass coach.
Once, a fear pierced him,
In that he mistook   45
The shadow of his equipage
For blackbirds.

XII

The river is moving.
The blackbird must be flying.

XIII

It was evening all afternoon.   50
It was snowing
And it was going to snow.
The blackbird sat
In the cedar-limbs.

THIRTEEN WAYS OF LOOKING AT A BLACKBIRD. 25 *Haddam:* This biblical-sounding name is that of a town
in Connecticut.

Questions

1. What is the speaker's attitude toward the men of Haddam? What attitude toward this world does he suggest they lack? What is implied by calling them *thin* (line 25)?
2. What do the landscapes of winter contribute to the poem's effectiveness? If Stevens had chosen images of summer lawns, what would have been lost?
3. In which sections of the poem does Stevens suggest that a unity exists between human being and blackbird, between blackbird and the entire natural world? Can we say that Stevens "philosophizes"? What role does imagery play in Stevens's statement of his ideas?
4. What sense can you make of Part X? Make an enlightened guess.
5. Consider any one of the thirteen parts. What patterns of sound and rhythm do you find in it? What kind of structure does it have?
6. If the thirteen parts were arranged in some different order, would the poem be just as good? Or can we find a justification for its beginning with Part I and ending with Part XIII?
7. Does the poem seem an arbitrary combination of thirteen separate poems? Or is there any reason to call it a whole?

PROSE POETRY

No law requires a poet to split thoughts into verse lines at all. Charles Baudelaire, Rainer Maria Rilke, Jorge Luis Borges, Alexander Solzhenitsyn, T. S. Eliot, and many others have written **prose poems**, in which, without caring that eye appeal and some of the rhythm of a line structure may be lost, the poet prints words in a block like a prose paragraph. To some, the term "prose poetry" is as oxymoronic as "jumbo shrimp" or "plastic glasses," if not a flat-out contradiction in terms. On the other hand, we might recall Samuel Johnson's response when told that Bishop Berkeley's theory that the material world is an illusion, while obviously false, could not be refuted; Johnson kicked a large stone, saying "I refute him *thus*." Like stones, prose poems exist. To prove it, here are two by contemporary American poets. As you read them, ask yourself: Are they prose poems, or very short pieces of prose? If they are poetry, what features distinguish them from prose? If they should be considered prose, what essential features of poetry do they lack?

Carolyn Forché (b. 1950)

The Colonel   1982

What you have heard is true. I was in his house. His wife carried a tray of coffee and sugar. His daughter filed her nails, his son went out for the night. There were daily papers, pet dogs, a pistol on the cushion beside him. The moon swung bare on its black cord over the house. On the television was a cop show. It was in English. Broken bottles were embedded in the walls around the house to scoop   5
the kneecaps from a man's legs or cut his hands to lace. On the windows there were gratings like those in liquor stores. We had dinner, rack of lamb, good wine,

a gold bell was on the table for calling the maid. The maid brought green man-
goes, salt, a type of bread. I was asked how I enjoyed the country. There was a
brief commercial in Spanish. His wife took everything away. There was some   10
talk then of how difficult it had become to govern. The parrot said hello on the
terrace. The colonel told it to shut up, and pushed himself from the table. My
friend said to me with his eyes: say nothing. The colonel returned with a sack
used to bring groceries home. He spilled many human ears on the table. They
were like dried peach halves. There is no other way to say this. He took one of   15
them in his hands, shook it in our faces, dropped it into a water glass. It came
alive there. I am tired of fooling around he said. As for the rights of anyone, tell
your people they can go fuck themselves. He swept the ears to the floor with his
arm and held the last of his wine in the air. Something for your poetry, no? he
said. Some of the ears on the floor caught this scrap of his voice. Some of the ears   20
on the floor were pressed to the ground.

May 1978

Questions

1. Forché begins "The Colonel" by saying "What you have heard is true." Who is the *you*?
   Does she assume a specific person?
2. Should we believe that this story is true? If so, what leads us to believe its veracity?
3. Why does the author end "The Colonel" by giving a date?

Charles Simic (b. 1939)

The Magic Study of Happiness   1992

In the smallest theater in the world the bread crumbs speak. It's a mystery
play on the subject of a lost paradise. Once there was a kitchen with a table
on which a few crumbs were left. Through the window you could see your
young mother by the fence talking to a neighbor. She was cold and kept hugging her thin dress tighter and tighter. The clouds in the sky sailed on as she   5
threw her head back to laugh.

Where the words can't go any further—there's the hard table. The crumbs
are watching you as you in turn watch them. The unknown in you and the
unknown in them attract each other. The two unknowns are like illicit lovers
when they're exceedingly and unaccountably happy.   10

Questions

1. What is the effect of the phrases "the smallest theater in the world" and "mystery play"?
2. How do you interpret "Where the words can't go any further—there's the hard table"?
3. What is the significance of the simile in the last sentence?

VISUAL POETRY

Let's look at a famous poem with a distinctive visible shape. In the seventeenth century, ingenious poets trimmed their lines into the silhouettes of altars and crosses, pillars and pyramids. Here is one. Is it anything more than a demonstration of ingenuity?

George Herbert (1593–1633)

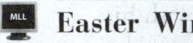

Easter Wings   1633

Lord, who createdst man in wealth and store,
Though foolishly he lost the same,
Decaying more and more,
Till he became
Most poor;
With thee
Oh, let me rise
As larks, harmoniously,
And sing this day thy victories;
Then shall the fall further the flight in me.

My tender age in sorrow did begin;
And still with sicknesses and shame
Thou didst so punish sin,
That I became
Most thin.
With thee
Let me combine,
And feel this day thy victory;
For if I imp my wing on thine,
Affliction shall advance the flight in me.

In the next-to-last line, *imp* is a term from falconry meaning to repair the wing of an injured bird by grafting feathers onto it.

If we see it merely as a picture, we will have to admit that Herbert's word design does not go far. It renders with difficulty shapes that a sketcher's pencil could set down in a flash, in more detail, more accurately. Was Herbert's effort wasted? It might have been, were there not more to his poem than meets the eye. The mind, too, is engaged by the visual pattern, by the realization that the words *most thin* are given emphasis by their narrow form. Here, visual pattern points out meaning. Heard aloud, too, "Easter Wings" gives further pleasure. Its rimes, its rhythm are perceptible.

Ever since George Herbert's day, poets have continued to experiment with the looks of printed poetry. Notable efforts to entertain the eye are Lewis Carroll's rimed mouse's tail in *Alice in Wonderland* and the *Calligrammes* of Guillaume Apollinaire, who arranged words in the shapes of a necktie, of the Eiffel Tower, of spears of falling rain. Here is a bird-shaped poem of more recent inspiration than Herbert's. What does its visual form have to do with what the poet is saying?

John Hollander (b. 1929)

Swan and Shadow 1969

<pre>
                    Dusk
               Above the
             water hang the
                   loud
                   flies
                  Here
                  O so
                  gray
                  then
            What   A pale signal will appear
            When   Soon before its shadow fades
            Where   Here in this pool of opened eye
            In us   No Upon us As at the very edges
          of where we take shape in the dark air
            this object bares its image awakening
             ripples of recognition that will
               brush darkness up into light
even after this bird this hour both drift by atop the perfect sad instant now
                already passing out of sight
              toward yet-untroubled reflection
             this image bears its object darkening
           into memorial shades Scattered bits of
           light   No of water Or something across
           water   Breaking up No Being regathered
           soon   Yet by then a swan will have
            gone   Yet out of mind into what
                  vast
                  pale
                  hush
                  of a
                  place
                  past
            sudden dark as
              if a swan
                  sang
</pre>

A whole poem doesn't need to be such a verbal silhouette, of course, for its appearance on the page to seem meaningful. In some lines of a longer poem, William Carlos Williams has conveyed the way an energetic bellhop (or hotel porter) runs downstairs:

<pre>
    ta tuck a
            ta tuck a
                ta tuck a
                    ta tuck a
                        ta tuck a
</pre>

This is not only good onomatopoeia and an accurate description of a rhythm; the steplike appearance of the lines goes together with their meaning.

At least some of our pleasure in silently reading a poem derives from the way it looks upon its page. A poem in an open form can engage the eye with snowfields of white space and thickets of close-set words. A poem in stanzas can please us by its visual symmetry. And, far from being merely decorative, the visual devices of a poem can be meaningful, too. White space—as poets who work in open forms demonstrate— can indicate pauses. If white space entirely surrounds a word or phrase or line, then that portion of the poem obviously takes special emphasis. Typographical devices such as capital letters and italics also can lay stress upon words. In most traditional poems, a capital letter at the beginning of each new line helps indicate the importance the poet places on line divisions, whose regular intervals make a rhythm out of pauses. And the poet may be trying to show us that certain lines rime by in-denting them.

Some contemporary poets have taken advantage of the computer's ability to mix words and images. They use visual images as integral parts of their poems to explore possibilities beyond traditional prosody. Ezra Pound did similar things in his modernist epic, *The Cantos,* by incorporating Chinese ideograms, musical notations, and marginal notes into the text of the poem.

CONCRETE POETRY

In recent decades, a movement called **concrete poetry** has traveled far and wide. Though practitioners of the art disagree over its definition, what most concretists seem to do is make designs out of letters and words. Poet Richard Kostelanetz has suggested that a more accurate name for concrete poetry might be "word-imagery." He sees it occupying an area somewhere between conventional poetry and visual art.

Richard Kostelanetz (b. 1940)
Ramón Gómez de la Serna (1888–1963)

Simultaneous Translations   2008

Peligroso es ver mas estrellas de las que hay.

It is dangerous to see more stars than there are.

La luna es el unico viajero sin pasaporte.

The moon is the only traveler without a passport.

No hay que dar la verdad desnuda. Por lo menos, hay que ponenerla un velillo.

The truth should not be given naked. At the least, one should give her a veil.

Questions

1. The term "simultaneous translation" customarily has nothing to do with poetry. What is its usual application? What relevance might it have in this context?
2. How does the appearance of the English versions contribute to the communication of their meanings?
3. Does the contrast between the appearance of the Spanish originals and the English versions make any larger statement about the nature of poetic translation?

Some concrete poets wield typography like a brush dipped in paint, using such techniques as blow-up, montage, and superimposed elements (the same words printed many times on top of the same impression, so that the result is blurriness). They may even keep words in a usual order, perhaps employing white space as freely as any writer of open form verse. (More freely sometimes—Aram Saroyan has a concrete poem that consists of a page blank except for the word *oxygen*.)

Admittedly, some concrete poems mean less than meets the eye. That many pretentious doodlers have taken up concretism may have caused a *Time* magazine writer to sneer: did Joyce Kilmer miss all that much by never having seen a poem lovely as a

t

ttt

rrrrr

rrrrrrr

eeeeeeeee

???

Like other structures of language, however, concrete poems evidently can have the effect of poetry, if written by poets. Whether or not it ought to be dubbed poetry, this art can do what poems traditionally have done: use language in delightful ways that reveal meanings to us.

Dorthi Charles (b. 1963)

Concrete Cat   1971

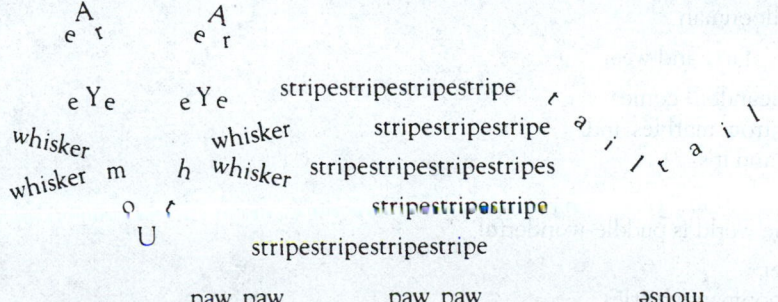

Questions

1. What does this writer indicate by capitalizing the *a* in *ear*? The *y* in *eye*? The *u* in *mouth*? By using spaces between the letters in the word *tail*?
2. Why is the word *mouse* upside down?
3. What possible pun might be seen in the cat's middle stripe?
4. What is the tone of "Concrete Cat"? How is it made evident?
5. Do these words seem chosen for their connotations or only for their denotations? Would you call this work of art a poem?

Experiment: Do It Yourself

Make a concrete poem of your own. If you need inspiration, pick some familiar object or animal and try to find words that look like it. For more ideas, study the typography of a magazine or newspaper; cut out interesting letters and numerals and try pasting them into arrangements. What (if anything) do your experiments tell you about familiar letters and words?

FOR REVIEW AND FURTHER STUDY

Exercise: Seeing the Logic of Open Form Verse

Read the following poems in open form silently to yourself, noticing what each poet does with white space, repetitions, line breaks, and indentations. Then read the poems aloud, trying to indicate by slight pauses where lines end and also pausing slightly at any space inside a line. Can you see any reasons for the poet's placing his or her words in this arrangement rather than in a prose paragraph? Do any of these poets seem to care also about visual effect? (As with other kinds of poetry, there may not be any obvious logical reason for everything that happens in these poems.)

E. E. Cummings (1894–1962)

in Just-   1923

in Just-
spring   when the world is mud-
luscious the little
lame balloonman

whistles   far   and   wee   5

and eddieandbill come
running from marbles and
piracies and it's
spring

when the world is puddle-wonderful   10

the queer
old balloonman whistles
far   and   wee
and bettyandisbel come dancing

from hop-scotch and jump-rope and   15

it's
spring
and
    the

        goat-footed   20

balloonMan   whistles
far
and
wee

A. E. Stallings (b. 1968)

First Love: A Quiz   2006

He came up to me:
    a. in his souped-up Camaro
    b. to talk to my skinny best friend
    c. and bumped my glass of wine so I wore the ferrous stain on my sleeve
    d. from the ground, in a lead chariot drawn by a team of stallions black as   5
       crude oil and breathing sulfur; at his heart, he sported a tiny golden arrow

He offered me:
    a. a ride
    b. dinner and a movie, with a wink at the cliché
    c. an excuse not to go back alone to the apartment with its sink of dirty knives
    d. a narcissus with a hundred dazzling petals that breathed a sweetness   10
       as cloying as decay

I went with him because:
    a. even his friends told me to beware
    b I had nothing to lose except my virginity
    c. he placed his hand in the small of my back and I felt the tread of honeybees
    d. he was my uncle, the one who lived in the half-finished basement, and   15
       he took me by the hair

The place he took me to:
    a. was dark as my shut eyes
    b. and where I ate bitter seed and became ripe
    c. and from which my mother would never take me wholly back, though she
       wept and walked the earth and made the bearded ears of barley wither on
       their stalks and the blasted flowers drop from their sepals
    d. is called by some men hell and others love   20
    e. all of the above

Questions

1. What distinctions of tone and attitude do you find among the lettered responses to each item in the "quiz"?
2. What is the effect of the concluding couplet?
3. Is the title serious? Ironic? Both? Explain your response.

David Lehman   (b. 1948)

Radio   2005

I left it
on when I
left the house
for the pleasure
of coming back   5
ten hours later
to the greatness
of Teddy Wilson
"After You've Gone"
on the piano   10
in the corner
of the bedroom
as I enter
in the dark

Questions

1. This poem is not written in traditional meter or conventional free verse. What organizing
   principle did the poet use?
2. What features does the poem borrow from free verse? From metrical verse?

Carole Satyamurti   (b. 1939)

I Shall Paint My Nails Red   1990

Because a bit of color is a public service.

Because I am proud of my hands.

Because it will remind me I'm a woman.

Because I will look like a survivor.

Because I can admire them in traffic jams.   5

Because my daughter will say ugh.

Because my lover will be surprised.

Because it is quicker than dyeing my hair.

Because it is a ten-minute moratorium.

Because it is reversible.   10

Question

"I Shall Paint My Nails Red" is written in free verse, but the poem has several organizing
principles. How many can you discover?

Alice Fulton   (b. 1952)

What I Like   1983

Friend—the face I wallow toward
through a scrimmage of shut faces.
Arms like towropes to haul me home, aide-
memoire, my lost childhood docks, a bottled ark
in harbor. *Friend*—I can't forget   5
how even the word contains an *end*.
We circle each other in a scared bolero,
imagining stratagems: postures and impostors.
Cold convictions keep us solo. I ahem
and hedge my affections. Who'll blow the first kiss,   10
land it like the lifeforces we feel
tickling at each wrist? It should be easy
easy to take your hand, whisper down this distance
labeled hers or his: what I like about you is

Questions

Does this poem have an ending? Does it need to have an ending to be a successful poem?

■ WRITING *effectively*

Walt Whitman on Writing

The Poetry of the Future   1876

The poetry of the future, (a phrase open to
sharp criticism, and not satisfactory to me, but
significant, and I will use it)—the poetry of
the future aims at the free expression of emotion, (which means far, far more than appears
at first,) and to arouse and initiate, more than
to define or finish. Like all modern tendencies,
it has direct or indirect reference continually
to the reader, to you or me, to the central identity of everything, the mighty Ego. (Byron's
was a vehement dash, with plenty of impatient democracy, but lurid and introverted
amid all its magnetism; not at all the fitting,
lasting song of a grand, secure, free, sunny
race.) It is more akin, likewise, to outside life
and landscape, (returning mainly to the antique
feeling,) real sun and gale, and woods and

Walt Whitman

shores—to the elements themselves—not sitting at ease in parlor or library listening to a
good tale of them, told in good rhyme. Character, a feature far above style or polish—a

feature not absent at any time, but now first brought to the fore—gives predominant stamp to advancing poetry. . . .

Is there not even now, indeed, an evolution, a departure from the masters? Venerable and unsurpassable after their kind as are the old works, and always unspeakably precious as studies, (for Americans more than any other people,) is it too much to say that by the shifted combinations of the modern mind the whole underlying theory of first-class verse has changed?

From "Poetry To-day in America—Shakspere—The Future"

THINKING ABOUT FREE VERSE

"That's not poetry! It's just chopped-up prose." So runs one old-fashioned complaint about free verse. Such criticism may be true of inept poems, but in the best free verse the line endings transform language in ways beyond the possibilities of prose. A line break implies a slight pause so that the last word of each line receives special emphasis. The last word in a line is meant to linger, however briefly, in the listener's ear. With practice and attention, you can easily develop a better sense of how a poem's line breaks operate.

- **Note whether the breaks tend to come at the end of sentences or phrases, or in the middle of an idea.** An abundance of breaks in mid-thought can create a tumbling, headlong effect, forcing your eye to speed down the page. Conversely, lines that tend to break at the end of a full idea can give a more stately rhythm to a poem.
- **Determine whether the lines tend to be all brief, all long, or a mix.** A very short line forces us to pay special attention to its every word, no matter how small.
- **Ask yourself how the poet's choices about line breaks help to reinforce the poem's meaning.** Can you identify any example of a line break affecting the meaning of a phrase or sentence?

CHECKLIST: Writing About Line Breaks

- ☐ Reread a poem, paying attention to where its lines end.
- ☐ Do the breaks tend to come at the end of the sentences or phrases?
- ☐ Do they tend to come in the middle of an idea?
- ☐ Do the lines tend to be long? Short? A mix of both?
- ☐ Is the poem broken into stanzas? Are they long? Short? A mix of both?
- ☐ What mood is created by the breaks?
- ☐ How do line breaks and stanza breaks reinforce the poem's meaning as a whole?

WRITING ASSIGNMENT ON OPEN FORM

Retype a free verse poem as prose, adding conventional punctuation and capitalization if necessary. Then compare and contrast the prose version with the poem itself. How do the two texts differ in tone, rhythm, emphasis, and effect? How do they remain similar? Use any poem from this chapter or any of the following from the chapter "Poems for Further Reading": W. H. Auden's "Musée des Beaux Arts"; Robert Lowell's "Skunk Hour"; Linda Pastan's "Ethics"; Ezra Pound's "The River Merchant's Wife: A Letter"; or William Carlos Williams's "To Waken an Old Lady."

MORE TOPICS FOR WRITING

1. Write a brief essay (approximately 500 words) on how the line breaks and white space (or lack thereof) in E. E. Cummings's "Buffalo Bill's" contribute to the poem's effect.
2. Read aloud William Carlos Williams's "The Dance." Examine how the poem's line breaks and sonic effects underscore the poem's meaning.
3. Imagine Carolyn Forché's "The Colonel" broken into free-verse lines. What are the benefits of the prose-poem form to this particular text?
4. Compare any poem in this chapter with a poem in rime and meter. Discuss several key features that they have in common despite their apparent differences in style. Features it might be useful to compare include imagery, tone, figures of speech, and word choice.
5. Write an imitation of Wallace Stevens's "Thirteen Ways of Looking at a Blackbird." Come up with thirteen ways of looking at your car, a can opener, a housecat—or any object that intrigues you. Choose your line breaks carefully, to recreate some of the mood of the original. You might also have a look at Aaron Abeyta's parody "Thirteen Ways of Looking at a Tortilla" on page 914.

▶ TERMS FOR *review*

Open form ▶ Poems that have neither a rime scheme nor a basic meter are in open form. Open form has also been called free verse.

Free verse ▶ From the French *vers libre*. Free verse is poetry whose lines follow no consistent meter. It may be rimed, but usually is not. In the last hundred years, free verse has become a common practice.

Prose poetry ▶ Poetic language printed in prose paragraphs, but displaying the careful attention to sound, imagery, and figurative language characteristic of poetry.

Concrete poetry ▶ A visual poetry composed exclusively for the page in which a picture or image is made of printed letters and words. Concrete poetry attempts to blur the line between language and visual objects, usually relying on puns and cleverness.

24

SYMBOL

A symbol is like a rock dropped into a pool:
it sends out ripples in all directions,
and the ripples are in motion.

—JOHN CIARDI

The national flag is supposed to stir our patriotic feelings. When a black cat crosses his path, a superstitious man shivers, foreseeing bad luck. To each of these, by custom, our society expects a standard response. A flag, a black cat crossing one's path— each is a **symbol**: a visible object or action that suggests some further meaning in addition to itself. In literature, a symbol might be the word *flag* or the words *a black cat crossed his path* or every description of flag or cat in an entire novel, story, play, or poem.

A flag and the crossing of a black cat may be called **conventional symbols**, since they can have a conventional or customary effect on us. Conventional symbols are also part of the language of poetry, as we know when we meet the red rose, emblem of love, in a lyric, or the Christian cross in the devotional poems of George Herbert. More often, however, symbols in literature have no conventional, long-established meaning, but particular meanings of their own. In Melville's novel *Moby-Dick*, to take a rich example, whatever we associate with the great white whale is *not* attached unmistakably to white whales by custom. Though Melville tells us that men have long regarded whales with awe and relates Moby Dick to the celebrated fish that swallowed Jonah, the reader's response is to one particular whale, the creature of Herman Melville. Only the experience of reading the novel in its entirety can give Moby Dick his particular meaning.

THE MEANINGS OF A SYMBOL

As Eudora Welty has observed, it is a good thing Melville made Moby Dick a whale, a creature large enough to contain all that critics have found in him. A symbol in literature, if not conventional, has more than just one meaning. In "The Raven," by Edgar Allan Poe, the appearance of a strange black bird in the narrator's study is sinister; and indeed, if we take the poem seriously, we may even respond with a sympathetic shiver of dread. Does the bird mean death, fate, melancholy, the loss of a loved one, knowledge in the service of evil? All of these, perhaps. Like any well-chosen symbol, Poe's raven sets off within the reader an unending train of feelings and associations.

We miss the value of a symbol, however, if we think it can mean absolutely anything we wish. If a poet has any control over our reactions, the poem will guide our responses in a certain direction.

T. S. Eliot (1888–1965)

The *Boston Evening Transcript*   1917

The readers of the *Boston Evening Transcript*
Sway in the wind like a field of ripe corn.

When evening quickens faintly in the street,
Wakening the appetites of life in some
And to others bringing the *Boston Evening Transcript,*   5
I mount the steps and ring the bell, turning
Wearily, as one would turn to nod good-bye to La Rochefoucauld,
If the street were time and he at the end of the street,
And I say, "Cousin Harriet, here is the *Boston Evening Transcript.*"

The newspaper, whose name Eliot purposely repeats so monotonously, indicates
what this poem is about. Now defunct, the *Transcript* covered in detail the slightest
activity of Boston's leading families and was noted for the great length of its obituaries.
Eliot, then, uses the newspaper as a symbol for an existence of boredom, fatigue
(*Wearily*), petty and unvarying routine (since an evening newspaper, like night,
arrives on schedule). The *Transcript* evokes a way of life without zest or passion, for,
opposed to people who read it, Eliot sets people who do not: those whose desires revive,
not expire, when the working day is through. Suggestions abound in the ironic
comparison of the *Transcript*'s readers to a cornfield late in summer. To mention only
a few: the readers sway because they are sleepy; they vegetate; they are drying up;
each makes a rattling sound when turning a page. It is not necessary that we know
the remote and similarly disillusioned friend to whom the speaker might nod: La
Rochefoucauld, whose cynical *Maxims* entertained Parisian society under Louis XIV
(sample: "All of us have enough strength to endure the misfortunes of others"). We
understand that the nod is symbolic of an immense weariness of spirit. We know
nothing about Cousin Harriet, whom the speaker addresses, but imagine from the
greeting she inspires that she is probably a bore.

If Eliot wishes to say that certain Bostonians lead lives of sterile boredom, why
does he couch his meaning in symbols? Why doesn't he tell us directly what he means?
These questions imply two assumptions not necessarily true: first, that Eliot has a message to impart; second, that he is concealing it. We have reason to think that Eliot did
not usually have a message in mind when beginning a poem, for as he once told a critic:
"The conscious problems with which one is concerned in the actual writing are more
those of a quasi-musical nature . . . than of a conscious exposition of ideas." Poets sometimes discover what they have to say while in the act of saying it. And it may be that in
his *Transcript* poem, Eliot is saying exactly what he means. By communicating his
meaning through symbols instead of statements, he may be choosing the only kind of
language appropriate to an idea of great subtlety and complexity. (The paraphrase
"Certain Bostonians are bored" hardly begins to describe the poem in all its possible
meanings.) And by his use of symbolism, Eliot affords us the pleasure of finding our own
entrances to his poem.

This power of suggestion that a symbol contains is, perhaps, its greatest advantage.
Sometimes, as in the following poem by Emily Dickinson, a symbol will lead us from
a visible object to something too vast to be perceived.

MLL *Emily Dickinson* (1830–1886)

The Lightning is a yellow Fork (about 1870)

The Lightning is a yellow Fork
From Tables in the sky
By inadvertent fingers dropt
The awful Cutlery

Of mansions never quite disclosed   5
And never quite concealed
The Apparatus of the Dark
To ignorance revealed.

If the lightning is a fork, then whose are the fingers that drop it, the table from which it slips, the household to which it belongs? The poem implies this question without giving an answer. An obvious answer is "God," but can we be sure? We wonder, too, about these partially lighted mansions: if our vision were clearer, what would we behold?

THE SYMBOLIST MOVEMENT

The often complex and indirect way in which symbols communicate their meanings led to a group of nineteenth-century French poets being dubbed **Symbolists**. (This elegant moniker was their second name; their early critics had originally condemned them as the "decadent" poets.) Eventually becoming an international literary movement, the Symbolists began with poets such as Charles Baudelaire, Arthur Rimbaud, Paul Verlaine, and Stéphane Mallarmé. Influenced by sources as diverse as Edgar Allan Poe, Neo-Platonic philosophy, Roman Catholic ritual, and drugs, they tried to write poetry that resembled music. They avoided direct statement and exposition for powerful evocation and suggestion. Symbolists also considered the poet as a seer who could look beyond the mundane aspects of the everyday world to capture visions of a higher and frequently occult reality. Their poems were often musical, evocative, and mysterious. Many critics consider the Symbolist Movement the beginning of Modernist literature, and both its poetry and theory had a major impact on later writers such as Yeats, Eliot, and Pound. But in this chapter when we speak of symbolism (with a small *s*) we mean an element in certain poems, not Symbolism, a specific literary movement.

IDENTIFYING SYMBOLS

"But how am I supposed to know a symbol when I see one?" The best approach is to read poems closely, taking comfort in the likelihood that it is better not to notice symbols at all than to find significance in every literal stone and huge meanings in every thing. In looking for the symbols in a poem, pick out all the references to concrete objects—newspapers, black cats, twisted pins. Consider these with special care.

Notice any that the poet emphasizes by detailed description, by repetition, or by placing it at the very beginning or end of the poem. Ask: What is the poem about, what does it add up to? If, when the poem is paraphrased, the paraphrase depends primarily on the meaning of certain concrete objects, these richly suggestive objects may be the symbols.

There are some things a literary symbol usually is *not*. A symbol is not an abstraction. Such terms as *truth*, *death*, *love*, and *justice* cannot work as symbols (unless personified, as in the traditional figure of Justice holding a scale). Most often, a symbol is something we can see in the mind's eye: a newspaper, a lightning bolt, a gesture of nodding good-bye.

In narratives, a well-developed character who speaks much dialogue and is not the least bit mysterious is usually not a symbol. But watch out for an executioner in a black hood; a character, named for a biblical prophet, who does little but utter a prophecy; a trio of old women who resemble the Three Fates. (It has been argued, with good reason, that Milton's fully rounded character of Satan in *Paradise Lost* is a symbol embodying evil and human pride, but a narrower definition of symbol is more frequently useful.) A symbol *may* be a part of a person's body (the baleful eye of the murder victim in Poe's story "The Tell-Tale Heart") or a look, a voice, or a mannerism.

A symbol usually is not the second term of a metaphor. In the line "The Lightning is a yellow Fork," the symbol is the lightning, not the fork.

Sometimes a symbol addresses a sense other than sight: the sound of a mysterious snapping string at the end of Chekhov's play *The Cherry Orchard*; or, in William Faulkner's tale "A Rose for Emily," the odor of decay that surrounds the house of the last survivor of a town's leading family—suggesting not only physical dissolution but also the decay of a social order. A symbol is a special kind of image, for it exceeds the usual image in the richness of its connotations. The dead wife's cold comb in the haiku of Buson (discussed on page 710) works symbolically, suggesting among other things the chill of the grave, the contrast between the living and the dead.

Symbolic Action

Holding a narrower definition than that used in this book, some readers of poetry prefer to say that a symbol is always a concrete object, never an act. They would deny the label "symbol" to Ahab's breaking his tobacco pipe before setting out to pursue Moby Dick (suggesting, perhaps, his determination to allow no pleasure to distract him from the chase) or to any large motion (as Ahab's whole quest). This distinction, while confining, does have the merit of sparing one from seeing all motion to be possibly symbolic. Some would call Ahab's gesture not a symbol but a **symbolic act**.

To sum up: a symbol radiates hints or casts long shadows (to use Henry James's metaphor). We are unable to say it "stands for" or "represents" a meaning. It evokes, it suggests, it manifests. It demands no single necessary interpretation, such as the interpretation a driver gives to a red traffic light. Rather, like Emily Dickinson's lightning bolt, it points toward an indefinite meaning, which may lie in part beyond the reach of words. In a symbol, as Thomas Carlyle said in *Sartor Resartus*, "the Infinite is made to blend with the Finite, to stand visible, and as it were, attainable there."

Thomas Hardy (1840–1928)

Neutral Tones   1898

We stood by a pond that winter day,
And the sun was white, as though chidden of° God,   *rebuked by*
And a few leaves lay on the starving sod;
    —They had fallen from an ash, and were gray.

Your eyes on me were as eyes that rove   5
Over tedious riddles of years ago;
And some words played between us to and fro
    On which lost the more by our love.

The smile on your mouth was the deadest thing
Alive enough to have strength to die;   10
And a grin of bitterness swept thereby
    Like an ominous bird a-wing. . . .

Since then, keen lessons that love deceives,
And wrings with wrong, have shaped to me
Your face, and the God-curst sun, and a tree,   15
    And a pond edged with grayish leaves.

Questions

1. Sum up the story told in this poem. In lines 1–12, what is the dramatic situation? What has happened in the interval between the experience related in these lines and the reflection in the last stanza?
2. What meanings do you find in the title?
3. Explain in your own words the metaphor in line 2.
4. What connotations appropriate to this poem does the *ash* (line 4) have that *oak* or *maple* would lack?
5. What visible objects in the poem function symbolically? What actions or gestures?

ALLEGORY

If we read of a ship, its captain, its sailors, and the rough seas, and we realize we are reading about a commonwealth and how its rulers and workers keep it going even in difficult times, then we are reading an **allegory**. Closely akin to symbolism, allegory is a description—usually narrative—in which persons, places, and things are employed in a continuous and consistent system of equivalents. In an allegory an object has a single additional significance, one largely determined by convention. When an allegory appears in a work, it usually has a one-to-one relationship to an abstract entity, recognizable to readers and audiences familiar with the cultural context of the work.

   Although more strictly limited in its suggestions than symbolism, allegory need not be thought inferior. Few poems continue to interest readers more than Dante's allegorical *Divine Comedy*. Sublime evidence of the appeal of allegory may be found in Christ's use of the **parable**: a brief narrative—usually allegorical but sometimes not—that teaches a moral.

Matthew 13:24–30 (King James Version, 1611)

The Parable of the Good Seed

The kingdom of heaven is likened unto a man which sowed good seed
    in his field:
But while men slept, his enemy came and sowed tares among the
    wheat, and went his way.
But when the blade was sprung up, and brought forth fruit, then
    appeared the tares also.
So the servants of the householder came and said unto him, Sir, didst
    not thou sow good seed in thy field? From whence then hath it tares?
He said unto them, An enemy hath done this. The servants said unto   5
    him, Wilt thou then that we go and gather them up?
But he said, Nay; lest while ye gather up the tares, ye root up also the
    wheat with them.
Let both grow together until the harvest: and in the time of harvest I
    will say to the reapers, Gather ye together first the tares, and bind
    them in bundles to burn them: but gather the wheat into my barn.

The sower is the Son of man, the field is the world, the good seed are the children
of the Kingdom, the tares are the children of the wicked one, the enemy is the devil,
the harvest is the end of the world, the reapers are angels. "As therefore the tares are
gathered and burned in the fire; so shall it be in the end of this world" (Matthew
13:36–42).

    Usually, as in this parable, the meanings of an allegory are plainly labeled or
thinly disguised. In John Bunyan's allegorical narrative *The Pilgrim's Progress,* it is
clear that the hero Christian, on his journey through places with such pointed names
as Vanity Fair, the Valley of the Shadow of Death, and Doubting Castle, is the soul,
traveling the road of life on the way toward Heaven. An allegory, when carefully
built, is systematic. It makes one principal comparison, the working out of whose
details may lead to further comparisons, then still further comparisons: Christian,
thrown by Giant Despair into the dungeon of Doubting Castle, escapes by means of a
key called Promise. Such a complicated design may take great length to unfold, as in
Spenser's *Faerie Queene*; but the method may be seen in a short poem.

George Herbert (1593–1633)

The World   1633

Love built a stately house; where *Fortune* came,
And spinning phansies, she was heard to say,
That her fine cobwebs did support the frame,
Whereas they were supported by the same:
But *Wisdome* quickly swept them all away.   5

Then *Pleasure* came, who, liking not the fashion,
Began to make *Balcónes, Terraces,*
Till she had weakened all by alteration:
But rev'rend *laws,* and many a *proclamation*
Reforméd all at length with menaces.   10

Then enter'd *Sinne* and with that Sycomore,
Whose leaves first sheltered man from drought & dew,
Working and winding slily evermore,
The inward walls and sommers cleft and tore:
But *Grace* shor'd these, and cut that as it grew.   15

Then *Sinne* combin'd with *Death* in a firm band
To raze the building to the very floore:
Which they effected, none could them withstand.
But *Love* and *Grace* took *Glorie* by the hand,
And built a braver Palace then before.   20

THE WORLD. 2 *phansies:* fancies. 10 *menaces:* threats. 14 *sommers:* summers: that is, beams or girders.
20 *then:* than.

Questions

1. What is the controlling image of this poem? What is that image an allegory of?
2. In each stanza of the poem, a similar pattern of action is repeated. What is that pattern, and how does it illuminate the poem's larger theme?
3. What is the "braver Palace" of the last line?

An object in allegory is like a bird whose cage is clearly lettered with its identity—"RAVEN, *Corvus corax;* habitat of specimen, Maine." A symbol, by contrast, is a bird with piercing eyes that mysteriously appears one evening in your library. It is there; you can touch it. But what does it mean? You look at it. It continues to look at you.

Edwin Markham (1852–1940)

Outwitted   1914

He drew a circle that shut me out—
Heretic, rebel, a thing to flout.
But Love and I had the wit to win:
We drew a circle that took him in!

Questions

What does a circle symbolize in this poem? Does it represent the same thing both times it is mentioned?

Whether an object in literature is a symbol, part of an allegory, or no such thing at all, it has at least one sure meaning. Moby Dick is first a whale, and the *Boston Evening Transcript* is a newspaper. Besides deriving a multitude of intangible suggestions from the title symbol in Eliot's long poem *The Waste Land,* its readers cannot fail to carry away a sense of the land's physical appearance: a river choked with sandwich papers and cigarette ends, London Bridge "under the brown fog of a winter dawn." A virtue of *The Pilgrim's Progress* is that its walking abstractions are no mere abstractions but are also human: Giant Despair is a henpecked husband. The most vital element of a literary work may pass us by, unless, before seeking further depths in a thing, we look to the thing itself.

Robert Frost (1874–1963)

The Road Not Taken   1916

Two roads diverged in a yellow wood,
And sorry I could not travel both
And be one traveler, long I stood
And looked down one as far as I could
To where it bent in the undergrowth;   5

Then took the other, as just as fair,
And having perhaps the better claim,
Because it was grassy and wanted wear;
Though as for that the passing there
Had worn them really about the same,   10

And both that morning equally lay
In leaves no step had trodden black.
Oh, I kept the first for another day!
Yet knowing how way leads on to way,
I doubted if I should ever come back.   15

I shall be telling this with a sigh
Somewhere ages and ages hence:
Two roads diverged in a wood, and I—
I took the one less traveled by,
And that has made all the difference.   20

Question

What symbolism do you find in this poem, if any? Back up your claim with evidence.

Christina Rossetti (1830–1894)

Uphill   1862

Does the road wind uphill all the way?
   Yes, to the very end.
Will the day's journey take the whole long day?
   From morn to night, my friend.

But is there for the night a resting-place?   5
   A roof for when the slow dark hours begin.
May not the darkness hide it from my face?
   You cannot miss that inn.

Shall I meet other wayfarers at night?
   Those who have gone before.   10
Then must I knock, or call when just in sight?
   They will not keep you standing at that door.

Shall I find comfort, travel-sore and weak?
   Of labor you shall find the sum.
Will there be beds for me and all who seek?   15
   Yea, beds for all who come.

Questions

1. In reading this poem, at what line did you realize that the poet is building an allegory?
2. For what does each thing stand?
3. What does the title of the poem suggest to you?
4. Recast the meaning of line 14, a knotty line, in your own words.
5. Discuss the possible identities of the two speakers—the apprehensive traveler and the character with all the answers. Are they specific individuals? Allegorical figures?
6. Compare "Uphill" with Robert Creeley's "Oh No" (page 659). What striking similarities do you find in these two dissimilar poems?

FOR REVIEW AND FURTHER STUDY

Exercise: Symbol Hunting

After you have read each of the following poems, decide which description best suits it:

1. The poem has a central symbol.
2. The poem contains no symbolism, but is to be taken literally.

William Carlos Williams (1883–1963)

The Term   1937

A rumpled sheet
of brown paper
about the length

and apparent bulk
of a man was   5
rolling with the

wind slowly over
and over in
the street as

a car drove down   10
upon it and
crushed it to

the ground. Unlike
a man it rose
again rolling   15

with the wind over
and over to be as
it was before.

Ted Kooser (b. 1939)

Carrie   1979

"There's never an end to dust
and dusting," my aunt would say
as her rag, like a thunderhead,
scudded across the yellow oak
of her little house. There she lived   5
seventy years with a ball
of compulsion closed in her fist,
and an elbow that creaked and popped
like a branch in a storm. Now dust
is her hands and dust her heart.   10
There is never an end to it.

Mary Oliver (b. 1935)

Wild Geese   1986

You do not have to be good.
You do not have to walk on your knees
for a hundred miles through the desert, repenting.
You only have to let the soft animal of your body
      love what it loves.   5
Tell me about despair, yours, and I will tell you mine.
Meanwhile the world goes on.
Meanwhile the sun and the clear pebbles of the rain
are moving across the landscapes,
over the prairies and the deep trees,   10
the mountains and the rivers.
Meanwhile the wild geese, high in the clean blue air,
are heading home again.
Whoever you are, no matter how lonely,
the world offers itself to your imagination,   15
calls to you like the wild geese, harsh and exciting—
over and over announcing your place
in the family of things.

Questions

1. Is this poem addressed to a specific person?
2. What is meant by "good" in the first line?
3. What do the wild geese symbolize? What is the significance of the use of the term "wild"?
4. What other adjectives are used to describe the phenomena of nature? What thematic purpose is served by this characterization of the natural world?

Lorine Niedecker   (1903–1970)

Popcorn-can cover   (about 1959)

Popcorn-can cover
screwed to the wall
over a hole
    so the cold
can't mouse in   5

Wallace Stevens   (1879–1955)

The Snow Man   1923

One must have a mind of winter
To regard the frost and the boughs
Of the pine-trees crusted with snow;

And have been cold a long time
To behold the junipers shagged with ice,   5
The spruces rough in the distant glitter

Of the January sun; and not to think
Of any misery in the sound of the wind,
In the sound of a few leaves,

Which is the sound of the land   10
Full of the same wind
That is blowing in the same bare place

For the listener, who listens in the snow,
And, nothing himself, beholds
Nothing that is not there and the nothing that is.   15

Wallace Stevens   (1879–1955)

Anecdote of the Jar   1923

I placed a jar in Tennessee,
And round it was, upon a hill.
It made the slovenly wilderness
Surround that hill.

The wilderness rose up to it,
And sprawled around, no longer wild.   5
The jar was round upon the ground
And tall and of a port in air.

It took dominion everywhere.
The jar was gray and bare.
It did not give of bird or bush,   10
Like nothing else in Tennessee.

■ WRITING *effectively*

William Butler Yeats on Writing

Poetic Symbols

1901

Any one who has any experience of any mystical state of the soul knows how there float up in the mind profound symbols, whose meaning, if indeed they do not delude one into the dream that they are meaningless, one does not perhaps understand for years. Nor I think has any one, who has known that experience with any constancy, failed to find some day, in some old book or on some old monument, a strange or intricate image that had floated up before him, and to grow perhaps dizzy with the sudden conviction that our little memories are but a part of some great Memory that renews the world and men's thoughts age after age, and that our thoughts are not, as we suppose, the deep, but a little foam upon the deep.

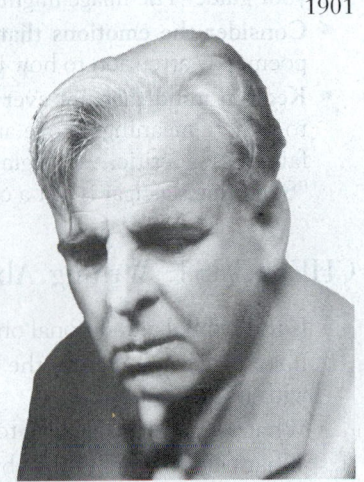

William Butler Yeats

. . .

It is only by ancient symbols, by symbols that have numberless meanings besides the one or two the writer lays an emphasis upon, or the half-score he knows of, that any highly subjective art can escape from the barrenness and shallowness of a too conscious arrangement, into the abundance and depth of Nature. The poet of essences and pure ideas must seek in the half-lights that glimmer from symbol to symbol as if to the ends of the earth, all that the epic and dramatic poet finds of mystery and shadow in the accidental circumstances of life.

From "The Philosophy of Shelley's Poetry"

THINKING ABOUT SYMBOLS

A symbol, to use poet John Drury's concise definition, is "an image that radiates meanings." While images in a poem can and should be read as what they literally are, images often do double duty, suggesting deeper meanings. Exactly what those meanings are, however, often differs from poem to poem.

Some symbols have been used so often and effectively over time that a traditional reading of them has developed. At times a poet clearly adopts an image's traditional symbolic meaning. Some poems, however, deliberately play against a symbol's conventional associations.

- **To determine the meaning (or meanings) of a symbol, start by asking if it has traditional associations.** If so, consider whether the symbol is being used in the expected way or if the poet is playing with those associations.

- **Consider the symbol's relationship to the rest of the poem.** Let context be your guide. The image might have a unique meaning to the poem's speaker.

- **Consider the emotions that the image evokes.** If the image recurs in the poem, pay attention to how it changes from one appearance to the next.

- **Keep in mind that not everything is a symbol.** If an image doesn't appear to radiate meanings above and beyond its literal sense, don't feel you have failed as a critic. As Sigmund Freud once said about symbol-hunting, "Sometimes a cigar is just a cigar."

CHECKLIST: Writing About Symbols

- ☐ Is the symbol a traditional one?
- ☐ If so, is it being used in the expected way? Or is the poet playing with its associations?
- ☐ What does the image seem to mean to the poem's speaker?
- ☐ What emotions are evoked by the image?
- ☐ If an image recurs in a poem, how does it change from one appearance to the next?
- ☐ Does the image radiate meaning beyond its literal sense? If not, it might not be intended as a symbol.

WRITING ASSIGNMENT ON SYMBOLISM

Do an in-depth analysis of the symbolism in a poem of your choice from the chapter "Poems for Further Reading." Some likely choices would be W. H. Auden's "As I Walked Out One Evening," Robert Lowell's "Skunk Hour," Sylvia Plath's "Daddy," and Adrienne Rich's "Living in Sin."

MORE TOPICS FOR WRITING

1. Compare and contrast the use of roads as symbols in Christina Rossetti's "Uphill" and Robert Frost's "The Road Not Taken." What does the use of this image suggest in each poem?

2. Discuss "The Snow Man" and "Anecdote of the Jar" in terms of Wallace Stevens's use of symbolism to portray the relationship between humanity and nature.

3. Write an explication of any poem from this chapter, paying careful attention to its symbols. Some good choices are Robert Frost's "The Road Not Taken," William Carlos Williams's "The Term," Thomas Hardy's "Neutral Tones," and Christina Rossetti's "Uphill." For a further description of poetic explication, see the chapter "Writing About a Poem."

4. Take a relatively simple, straightforward poem, such as William Carlos Williams's "This Is Just to Say" (page 674), and write a burlesque critical interpretation of it. Claim to discover symbols that the poem doesn't contain. While running wild with your "reading into" the poem, don't invent anything that you can't somehow support from the text of the poem itself. At the end of your burlesque, sum up in a paragraph what this exercise taught you about how to read poems, or how not to.

▶ TERMS FOR *review*

Symbol ▶ A person, place, or thing in a narrative that suggests meanings beyond its literal sense. Symbol is related to *allegory*, but it works more complexly. A symbol bears multiple suggestions and associations. It is unique to the work, not common to a culture.

Allegory ▶ A description—often a narrative—in which the literal events (persons, places, and things) consistently point to a parallel sequence of ideas, values, or other recognizable abstractions. An allegory has two levels of meaning: a literal level that tells a surface story and a symbolic level in which the abstractions unfold.

Symbolic act ▶ An action whose significance goes well beyond its literal meaning. In literature, symbolic acts often involve a primal or unconscious ritual element such as rebirth, purification, forgiveness, vengeance, or initiation.

Conventional symbols ▶ Symbols that, because of their frequent use, have acquired a standard significance. They may range from complex metaphysical images such as those of Christian saints in Gothic art to social customs such as a young bride in a white dress. They are conventional symbols because they carry recognizable meanings and suggestions.

MYTH AND NARRATIVE

*Myth does not mean something untrue,
but a concentration of truth.*

—DORIS LESSING

P oets have long been fond of retelling myths, narrowly defined as traditional stories about the exploits of immortal beings. Such stories taken collectively may also be called **myth** or **mythology**. In one of the most celebrated collections of myth ever assembled, the *Metamorphoses*, the Roman poet Ovid told—to take one example from many—how Phaeton, child of the sun god, rashly tried to drive his father's fiery chariot on its daily round, lost control of the horses, and caused disaster both to himself and to the world.

Our use of the term *myth* in discussing poetry, then, differs from its use in expressions such as "the myth of communism" and "the myth of democracy." In these examples, myth is used broadly to represent any idea people believe in, whether true or false. Nor do we mean—to take another familiar use of the word—a cock-and-bull story: "Judge Rapp doesn't roast speeders alive; that's just a *myth*." In the following discussion, *myth* will mean a kind of story—either from ancient or modern sources—whose actions implicitly symbolize some profound truth about human or natural existence.

Traditional myths tell us stories of gods or heroes—their battles, their lives, their loves, and often their suffering—all on a scale of magnificence larger than our life. These exciting stories usually reveal part of a culture's worldview. Myths often try to explain universal natural phenomena, like the phases of the moon or the turning of the seasons. But some myths tell the stories of purely local phenomena; one Greek legend, for example, recounts how grief-stricken King Aegeus threw himself into the sea when he mistakenly believed his son, Theseus, had been killed; consequently, the body of water between Greece and Turkey was called the Aegean Sea.

Modern psychologists, such as Sigmund Freud and Carl Jung, have been fascinated by myth and legend, since they believe these stories symbolically enact deep truths about human nature. Our myths, psychologists believe, express our wishes, dreams, and nightmares. Whether or not we believe myths, we recognize their psychological power. Even in the first century B.C., Ovid did not believe in the literal truth of the legends he so suavely retold; he confessed, "I prate of ancient poets' monstrous lies."

And yet it is characteristic of a myth that it *can* be believed. Throughout history, myths have accompanied religious doctrines and rituals. They have helped sanction or recall the reasons for religious observances. A sublime instance is the

New Testament account of the Last Supper. Because of its record of the words of Jesus, "Do this in remembrance of Me," Christians have continued to re-enact the offering and partaking of the body and blood of their Lord, under the appearances of bread and wine. It is essential to recall that, just because a myth narrates the acts of a god, we do not necessarily mean by the term a false or fictitious narrative. When we speak of "the myth of Islam" or "the Christian myth," we do so without implying either belief or disbelief.

Myths can also help sanction customs and institutions other than religious ones. At the same time that the baking of bread was introduced to ancient Greece—one theory goes—the myth of Demeter, goddess of grain, appeared. Demeter was a kindly deity who sent her emissary to teach humankind the valuable art of baking, thus helping to persuade the distrustful that bread was a good thing. Some myths seem designed to divert and regale, not to sanction anything. Such may be the story of the sculptor Pygmalion, who fell in love with the statue he had carved of a beautiful woman; so exquisite was his work, so deep was his feeling, that Aphrodite, the goddess of Love, brought the statue to life. And yet perhaps the story goes deeper than mere diversion: perhaps it is a way of saying that works of art achieve a reality of their own, that love can transform or animate its object.

ORIGINS OF MYTH

How does a myth begin? Several theories have been proposed, none universally accepted. One is that a myth is a way to explain some natural phenomenon. Winter comes and the vegetation perishes because Persephone, child of Demeter, must return to the underworld for several months every year. This theory, as classical scholar Edith Hamilton has pointed out, may lead us to think incorrectly that Greek mythology was the creation of a primitive people. Tales of the gods of Mount Olympus may reflect an earlier inheritance, but the Greek myths known to us were transcribed in an era of high civilization. Anthropologists have questioned whether primitive people generally find beauty in the mysteries of nature. Many anthropologists emphasize the practical function of myth; in his influential work of comparative mythology, *The Golden Bough*, Sir James Frazer argued that most myths were originally expressions of human hope that nature would be fertile. Still another theory maintains that many myths began as real events; mythic heroes were real human beings whose deeds have been changed and exaggerated by posterity. Most present-day myth historians would say that different myths probably have different origins.

Poets have many coherent mythologies on which to draw; perhaps those most frequently consulted by British and American poets are the classical, the Christian, the Norse, the Native American, and the folktales of the American frontier (embodying the deeds of superhuman characters such as Paul Bunyan). Some poets have taken inspiration from other myths as well: T. S. Eliot's *The Waste Land*, for example, is enriched by allusions to Buddhism and to pagan vegetation cults. Robert Bly borrowed the terrifying Death Goddess of Aztec, Hindu, and Balinese mythology to make her the climactic figure of his long poem "The Teeth Mother Naked at Last."

A tour through any good art museum will demonstrate how thoroughly myth pervades the painting and sculpture of nearly every civilization. In literature, one evidence of its continuing value to recent poets and storytellers is how frequently ancient myths are retold. Even in modern society, writers often turn to myth when they try to tell stories of deep significance. Mythic structures still touch a powerful and primal part of the human imagination. William Faulkner's story "The Bear" recalls tales of Indian totem animals; John Updike's novel *The Centaur* presents the horse-man Chiron as a modern high-school teacher; James Joyce's *Ulysses* transposes the *Odyssey* to modern Dublin (and the Coen brothers' film *O Brother, Where Art Thou?* reimagines Homer's epic in Depression-era Mississippi); Rita Dove's play *The Darker Face of the Earth* recasts the story of Oedipus in the slave-era South; Bernard Shaw retells the story of Pygmalion in his popular Edwardian social comedy *Pygmalion*, later the basis of the hit musical *My Fair Lady*; Jean Cocteau's film *Orphée* shows us Eurydice riding to the underworld with an escort of motorcycles. Popular interest in such works may testify to the profound appeal myths continue to hold for us. Like other varieties of poetry, myth is a kind of knowledge, not at odds with scientific knowledge but existing in addition to it.

Robert Frost (1874–1963)

Nothing Gold Can Stay 1923

Nature's first green is gold,
Her hardest hue to hold.
Her early leaf's a flower;
But only so an hour.
Then leaf subsides to leaf. 5
So Eden sank to grief,
So dawn goes down to day.
Nothing gold can stay.

Questions

1. To what myth does this poem allude? Does Frost sound as though he believes in the myth or as though he rejects it?
2. When Frost says, "Nature's first green is gold," he is describing how many leaves first appear as tiny yellow buds and blossoms. But what else does this line imply?
3. What would happen to the poem's meaning if line 6 were omitted?

William Wordsworth (1770–1850)

The world is too much with us 1807

The world is too much with us; late and soon,
Getting and spending, we lay waste our powers:
Little we see in Nature that is ours;
We have given our hearts away, a sordid boon!
This Sea that bares her bosom to the moon; 5
The winds that will be howling at all hours,
And are up-gathered now like sleeping flowers;
For this, for everything, we are out of tune;
It moves us not.—Great God! I'd rather be
A Pagan suckled in a creed outworn; 10
So might I, standing on this pleasant lea,
Have glimpses that would make me less forlorn;
Have sight of Proteus rising from the sea;
Or hear old Triton blow his wreathèd horn.

Questions

1. What condition does the speaker complain of in this sonnet? To what does he attribute this condition?
2. How does this situation affect him personally?

H. D. *[Hilda Doolittle]* (1886–1961)

Helen   1924

All Greece hates
the still eyes in the white face,
the lustre as of olives
where she stands,
and the white hands.   5

All Greece reviles
the wan face when she smiles,
hating it deeper still
when it grows wan and white,
remembering past enchantments   10
and past ills.

Greece sees, unmoved,
God's daughter, born of love,
the beauty of cool feet
and slenderest knees,   15
could love indeed the maid,
only if she were laid,
white ash amid funereal cypresses.

HELEN. In Greek mythology, Helen, most beautiful of all women, was the daughter of a mortal, Leda, by the god Zeus. Her abduction set off the long and devastating Trojan War. While married to Menelaus, king of the Greek city-state of Sparta, Helen was carried off by Paris, prince of Troy. Menelaus and his brother, Agamemnon, raised an army, besieged Troy for ten years, and eventually recaptured her. One episode of the Trojan War is related in the *Iliad*, Homer's epic poem, composed before 700 B.C.

Questions

1. At what point in the Troy narrative does this poem appear to be set?
2. What connotations does the color white usually possess? Does it have those same associations here?
3. Reread Yeats's "Leda and the Swan" (page 781). Does his retelling of that myth add an ironic dimension to line 13 of "Helen"?

Constantine Cavafy (1863–1933)

Ithaca   1911

When you start on your journey to Ithaca,
then pray that the road is long,
full of adventure, full of knowledge.
Do not fear the Lestrygonians
and the Cyclopes and the angry Poseidon.   5

You will never meet such as these on your path,
if your thoughts remain lofty, if a fine
emotion touches your body and your spirit.
You will never meet the Lestrygonians,
the Cyclopes and the fierce Poseidon,   10
if you do not carry them within your soul,
if your soul does not raise them up before you.

Then pray that the road is long.
That the summer mornings are many,
that you will enter ports seen for the first time   15
with such pleasure, with such joy!
Stop at Phoenician markets,
and purchase fine merchandise,
mother-of-pearl and corals, amber and ebony,
and pleasurable perfumes of all kinds,   20
buy as many pleasurable perfumes as you can;
visit hosts of Egyptian cities,
to learn and learn from those who have knowledge.

Always keep Ithaca fixed in your mind.
To arrive there is your ultimate goal.   25
But do not hurry the voyage at all.
It is better to let it last for long years;
and even to anchor at the isle when you are old,
rich with all that you have gained on the way,
not expecting that Ithaca will offer you riches.   30

Ithaca has given you the beautiful voyage.
Without her you would never have taken the road.
But she has nothing more to give you.

And if you find her poor, Ithaca has not defrauded you.
With the great wisdom you have gained, with so much experience,   35
you must surely have understood by then what Ithacas mean.

— Translated by Rae Dalven

ITHACA. Ithaca was the island kingdom ruled by Odysseus, whose ten-year, adventure-filled voyage home after the Trojan War is recounted in Homer's *Odyssey*. 4–5 *Lestrygonians . . . Cyclopes . . . Poseidon*: the Lestrygonians and the Cyclopes were tribes of man-eating giants encountered by Odysseus and his crew on their homeward voyage; Poseidon was the Greek god of the sea. 17 *Phoenician markets*: the Phoenicians, who lived along the coast of what is now Syria, were notable in the ancient world for navigation and trade. Odysseus visits neither Phoenicia nor Egypt (line 22) in the course of his voyage.

Questions

1. To whom is this poem addressed, Odysseus or the reader? Can it be both at once?
2. In the *Odyssey*, Odysseus's adventures are presented as obstacles and impediments to his goal of returning home. How, according to Cavafy, should "you" approach the experiences of the impending journey?
3. How do you interpret the poem's last three lines?

ARCHETYPE

An important concept in understanding myth is the **archetype**, a basic image, character, situation, or symbol that appears so often in literature and legend that it evokes a deep universal response. (The Greek root of *archetype* means "original pattern.") The term was borrowed by literary critics from the writings of the Swiss psychologist Carl Jung, a serious scholar of myth and religion, who formulated a theory of the "collective unconscious," a set of primal memories common to the entire human race. Archetypal patterns emerged, he speculated, in prerational thought and often reflect key primordial experiences such as birth, growth, sexual awakening, family, generational struggle, and death, as well as primal elements such as fire, sun, moon, blood, and water. Jung also believed that these situations, images, and figures had actually been genetically coded into the human brain and are passed down to successive generations, but no one has ever been able to prove a biological base for the undeniable phenomenon of similar characters, stories, and symbols appearing across widely separated and diverse cultures.

Whatever their origin, archetypal images do seem verbally coded in most myths, legends, and traditional tales. One sees enough recurring patterns and figures from Greek myth to *Star Wars*, from Hindu epic to Marvel superhero comics, to strongly suggest that there is some common psychic force at work. Typical archetypal figures include the trickster, the cruel stepmother, the rebellious young man, the beautiful but destructive woman, and the stupid youngest son who succeeds through simple goodness. Any one of these figures can be traced from culture to culture. The trickster, for instance, appears in American Indian coyote tales, Norse myths about the fire god Loki, Marx Brothers films, and *Batman* comic books and movies featuring the Joker.

Archetypal myths are the basic conventions of human storytelling, which we learn without necessarily being aware of the process. The patterns we absorb in our first nursery rhymes and fairy tales, as mythological critic Northrop Frye has demonstrated, underlie—though often very subtly—the most sophisticated poems and novels. One powerful archetype seen across many cultures is the demon-goddess who immobilizes men by locking them into a deathly trance or—in the most primitive forms of the myth—turning them to stone. Here are modern versions of this ancient myth in the following two poems.

Louise Bogan (1897–1970)

Medusa   1923

I had come to the house, in a cave of trees,
Facing a sheer sky.
Everything moved,—a bell hung ready to strike,
Sun and reflection wheeled by.

When the bare eyes were before me   5
And the hissing hair,
Held up at a window, seen through a door.
The stiff bald eyes, the serpents on the forehead
Formed in the air.

This is a dead scene forever now.   10
Nothing will ever stir.
The end will never brighten it more than this,
Nor the rain blur.

The water will always fall, and will not fall,
And the tipped bell make no sound.   15
The grass will always be growing for hay
Deep on the ground.

And I shall stand here like a shadow
Under the great balanced day,
My eyes on the yellow dust, that was lifting in the wind,   20
And does not drift away.

MEDUSA. Medusa was one of the Gorgons of Greek mythology. Hideously ugly with snakes for hair,
Medusa turned those who looked upon her face into stone.

Questions

1. Who is the speaker of the poem?
2. Why are the first two stanzas spoken in the past tense while the final three are mainly in the future tense?
3. What is the speaker's attitude toward Medusa? Is there anything surprising about his or her reaction to being transformed into stone?
4. Does Bogan merely dramatize an incident from classical mythology, or does the poem suggest other interpretations as well?

John Keats (1795–1821)

La Belle Dame sans Merci   1819

I

O what can ail thee, knight at arms,
    Alone and palely loitering?
The sedge has wither'd from the lake,
    And no birds sing.

II

O what can ail thee, knight at arms,   5
    So haggard and so woe-begone?
The squirrel's granary is full,
    And the harvest's done.

III

I see a lily on thy brow
    With anguish moist and fever dew,   10
And on thy cheeks a fading rose
    Fast withereth too.

IV

I met a lady in the meads,
    Full beautiful, a fairy's child;
Her hair was long, her foot was light,   15
    And her eyes were wild.

V

I made a garland for her head,
   And bracelets too, and fragrant zone;
She look'd at me as she did love,
   And made sweet moan.   20

VI

I set her on my pacing steed,
   And nothing else saw all day long,
For sidelong would she bend, and sing
   A fairy's song.

VII

She found me roots of relish sweet,   25
   And honey wild, and manna dew,
And sure in language strange she said—
   I love thee true.

VIII

She took me to her elfin grot,
   And there she wept, and sigh'd full sore,
And there I shut her wild wild eyes   30
   With kisses four.

IX

And there she lulled me asleep,
   And there I dream'd—Ah! woe betide!
The latest dream I ever dream'd   35
   On the cold hill's side.

X

I saw pale kings, and princes too,
   Pale warriors, death pale were they all;
They cried—"La belle dame sans merci
   Hath thee in thrall!"   40

XI

I saw their starv'd lips in the gloam
   With horrid warning gaped wide,
And I awoke and found me here
   On the cold hill's side.

XII

And this is why I sojourn here,
   Alone and palely loitering,   45
Though the sedge is wither'd from the lake,
   And no birds sing.

LA BELLE DAME SANS MERCI. The title is French for "the beautiful woman without mercy." Keats borrowed the title from a fifteenth-century French poem.

Questions

1. What time of year is suggested by the details of the first two stanzas? What is the significance of the season in the larger context of the poem?
2. How many speakers are there? Where does the change of speaker occur?
3. What details throughout the text tell us that *la belle dame* is no ordinary woman?
4. Why do you think the poet chose to imitate the form of the folk ballad in this poem?

PERSONAL MYTH

Sometimes poets have been inspired to make up myths of their own, to embody their own visions of life. "I must create a system or be enslaved by another man's," said William Blake, who in his "prophetic books" peopled the cosmos with supernatural beings having names such as Los, Urizen, and Vala (side by side with recognizable figures from the Old and New Testaments). This kind of system-making probably has advantages and drawbacks. T. S. Eliot, in his essay on Blake, wishes that the author of *The Four Zoas* had accepted traditional myths, and he compares Blake's thinking to a piece of homemade furniture whose construction diverted valuable energy from the writing of poems. Others have found Blake's untraditional cosmos an achievement—notably William Butler Yeats, himself the author of an elaborate personal mythology. Although we need not know all of Yeats's mythology to enjoy his poems, to know of its existence can make a few great poems deeper for us and less difficult.

William Butler Yeats (1865–1939)

The Second Coming   1921

Turning and turning in the widening gyre°   *spiral*
The falcon cannot hear the falconer;
Things fall apart; the center cannot hold;
Mere anarchy is loosed upon the world,
The blood-dimmed tide is loosed, and everywhere   5
The ceremony of innocence is drowned;
The best lack all conviction, while the worst
Are full of passionate intensity.

Surely some revelation is at hand;
Surely the Second Coming is at hand.   10
The Second Coming! Hardly are those words out
When a vast image out of *Spiritus Mundi*
Troubles my sight: somewhere in sands of the desert
A shape with lion body and the head of a man,
A gaze blank and pitiless as the sun,   15
Is moving its slow thighs, while all about it
Reel shadows of the indignant desert birds.

The darkness drops again; but now I know
That twenty centuries of stony sleep
Were vexed to nightmare by a rocking cradle,   20
And what rough beast, its hour come round at last,
Slouches towards Bethlehem to be born?

What kind of Second Coming does Yeats expect? Evidently it is not to be a
Christian one. Yeats saw human history as governed by the turning of a Great
Wheel, whose phases influence events and determine human personalities—rather
like the signs of the Zodiac in astrology. Every two thousand years comes a horren-
dous moment: the Wheel completes a turn; one civilization ends and another begins.
Strangely, a new age is always announced by birds and by acts of violence. Thus the
Greek-Roman world arrives with the descent of Zeus in swan's form and the burning
of Troy, the Christian era with the descent of the Holy Spirit—traditionally depicted
as a dove—and the Crucifixion. In 1919 when Yeats wrote "The Second Coming,"
his Ireland was in the midst of turmoil and bloodshed; the Western Hemisphere had
been severely shaken by World War I and the Russian Revolution. A new millennium seemed imminent. What sphinxlike, savage deity would next appear on earth,
with birds proclaiming it angrily? Yeats imagines it emerging from *Spiritus Mundi*,
Soul of the World, a collective unconscious from which a human being (since the individual soul touches it) receives dreams, nightmares, and racial memories.

It is hard to say whether a poet who discovers a personal myth does so to have
something to live by or to have something to write about. Robert Graves, who professed his belief in a White Goddess ("Mother of All Living, the ancient power of
love and terror"), declared that he wrote his poetry in a trance, inspired by his
Goddess-Muse. Luckily, we do not have to know a poet's religious affiliation before
we can read his or her poems. Perhaps most personal myths that enter poems are not
acts of faith but works of art: stories that resemble traditional mythology.

Gregory Orr (b. 1947)

Two Lines from the Brothers Grimm   1975

Now we must get up quickly,
dress ourselves, and run away.
Because it surrounds us, because
they are coming with wolves on leashes,
because I stood just now at the window   5
and saw the wall of hills on fire.
They have taken our parents away.
Downstairs in the half dark, two strangers
move about, lighting the stove.

Questions

1. What mood or atmosphere is suggested by the mention of the Brothers Grimm in the title?
   Is that suggestion borne out by the text?
2. What do you think "it" refers to in line 3?
3. Which images and details are from the Brothers Grimm, and which seem to be from other
   sources or personal in nature?

MYTH AND POPULAR CULTURE

If one can find myths in an art museum, one can also find them abundantly in popular culture. Movies and comic books, for example, are full of myths in modern guise. What is Superman, if not a mythic hero who has adapted himself to modern urban life? Marvel Comics even made the Norse thunder god, Thor, into a superhero, although they initially obliged him, like Clark Kent, to get a job. We also see myths retold on the technicolor screen. Sometimes Hollywood presents the traditional story directly, as in Walt Disney's *Cinderella;* more often the ancient tales acquire contemporary settings, as in another celluloid Cinderella story, *Pretty Woman.* (See how Anne Sexton has retold the Cinderella story from a feminist perspective, later in this chapter, or find a recording of Dana Dane's Brooklyn housing-project version of the fairy tale done from a masculine perspective in his underground rap hit "Cinderfella.") George Lucas's *Star Wars* series borrowed the structure of medieval quest legends. In quest stories, young knights pursued their destiny, often by seeking the Holy Grail, the cup Christ used at the Last Supper; in *Star Wars,* Luke Skywalker searched for his own parentage and identity, but his interstellar quest brought him to a surprisingly similar cast of knights, monsters, princesses, and wizards. Medieval Grail romances, which influenced Eliot's *The Waste Land* and J. R. R. Tolkien's *The Lord of the Rings* trilogy, also shaped films such as *The Fisher King* and *The Matrix.* Science fiction also commonly uses myth to novel effect. Extraterrestrial visitors usually appear as either munificent mythic gods or nightmarish demons. Steven Spielberg's *E.T.*, for example, revealed a gentle, Christ-like alien recognized by innocent children, but persecuted by adults. E.T. even healed the sick, fell into a deathlike coma, and was resurrected.

It hardly matters whether the popular audience recognizes the literal source of a myth; the viewers intuitively understand the structure of the story and feel its deep imaginative resonance. That is why poets retell these myths; they are powerful sources of collective psychic energy, waiting to be tapped. Just as Hollywood screenwriters have learned that often the most potent way to use a myth is to disguise it, poets sometimes borrow the forms of popular culture to retell their myths. Here is a contemporary narrative poem that borrows imagery from motion pictures to reenact a story that not only predates cinema but, most probably, stretches back before the invention of writing itself.

Charles Martin (b. 1942)

Taken Up
1978

Tired of earth, they dwindled on their hill,
Watching and waiting in the moonlight until
The aspens' leaves quite suddenly grew still,

No longer quaking as the disc descended,
That glowing wheel of lights whose coming ended   5
All waiting and watching. When it landed

The ones within it one by one came forth,
Stalking out awkwardly upon the earth,
And those who watched them were confirmed in faith:

Mysterious voyagers from outer space,   10
Attenuated, golden—shreds of lace
Spun into seeds of the sunflower's spinning face—

Light was their speech, spanning mind to mind:
We come here not believing what we find—
Can it be your desire to leave behind   15

The earth, which even those called angels bless,
Exchanging amplitude for emptiness?
And in a single voice they answered *Yes,*

Discord of human melodies all bent
To the unearthly strain of their assent.   20
Come then, the Strangers said, and those who were taken went.

Questions

1. What myths does this poem recall?
2. This poem was written about the same time that Steven Spielberg's film *Close Encounters of the Third Kind* (1977) appeared. If you recall the movie, compare its ending with the ending of the poem. Martin had not seen the film before writing "Taken Up." How can we account for the similarity?

Why do poets retell myths? Why don't they just make up their own stories? First, using myth allows poets to be concise. By alluding to stories that their audiences know, they can draw on powerful associations with just a few words. If someone describes an acquaintance, "He thinks he's James Bond," that one allusion speaks volumes. Likewise, when Robert Frost inserts the single line "So Eden sank to grief" in "Nothing Gold Can Stay," those five words summon up a wealth of associations. They tie the perishable quality of spring's beauty to the equally transient nature of human youth. They also suggest that everything in the human world is subject to time's ravages, that perfection is impossible for us to maintain, just as it was for Adam and Eve.

Second, poets know that many stories fall into familiar mythic patterns, and that the most powerful stories of human existence tend to be the same, generation after generation. Sometimes using an old story allows a writer to describe a new situation in a fresh and surprising way. Novels often try to capture the exact texture of a social situation; they need to present the everyday details to evoke the world in which their characters live. Myths tend to tell their stories more quickly and in more general terms. They give just the essential actions and leave out everything else. Narrative poems also work best when they focus on just the essential elements. Here are two modern narrative poems that retell traditional myths to make modern interpretations.

Andrea Hollander Budy (b. 1947)

Snow White   1993

It was actually one of the dwarfs
who kissed her—Bashful,
who still won't admit it.
That is why she remained in the forest
with all of them and made up   5
the story of the prince. Otherwise,
wouldn't you be out there now
scavenging through wildflowers,

mistaking the footprints of your own
children for those little men?   10
And if you found some wild apples
growing in the thickest part, if no one
were looking, wouldn't you
take a bite? And pray
some kind of magic sleep   15
would snatch you
from the plainness
of your life?

Questions

1. What is the significance of the lines "mistaking the footprints of your own / children for those little men"?
2. Why does the poem suggest that Snow White "made up / the story of the prince"?
3. Why, according to the poem, is this ending of Snow White's story superior to the traditional one?

Anne Sexton (1928–1974)

Cinderella   1971

You always read about it:
the plumber with twelve children
who wins the Irish Sweepstakes.
From toilets to riches.
That story.   5

Or the nursemaid,
some luscious sweet from Denmark
who captures the oldest son's heart.
From diapers to Dior.
That story.   10

Or a milkman who serves the wealthy,
eggs, cream, butter, yogurt, milk,
the white truck like an ambulance
who goes into real estate
and makes a pile.   15
From homogenized to martinis at lunch.

Or the charwoman
who is on the bus when it cracks up
and collects enough from the insurance.
From mops to Bonwit Teller.   20
That story.

Once
the wife of a rich man was on her deathbed
and she said to her daughter Cinderella:
Be devout. Be good. Then I will smile   25

down from heaven in the seam of a cloud.
The man took another wife who had
two daughters, pretty enough
but with hearts like blackjacks.
Cinderella was their maid.   30
She slept on the sooty hearth each night
and walked around looking like Al Jolson.
Her father brought presents home from town,
jewels and gowns for the other women
but the twig of a tree for Cinderella.   35
She planted that twig on her mother's grave
and it grew to a tree where a white dove sat.
Whenever she wished for anything the dove
would drop it like an egg upon the ground.
The bird is important, my dears, so heed him.   40

Next came the ball, as you all know.
It was a marriage market.
The prince was looking for a wife.
All but Cinderella were preparing
and gussying up for the big event.   45
Cinderella begged to go too.
Her stepmother threw a dish of lentils
into the cinders and said: Pick them
up in an hour and you shall go.
The white dove brought all his friends;   50
all the warm wings of the fatherland came,
and picked up the lentils in a jiffy.
No, Cinderella, said the stepmother,
you have no clothes and cannot dance.
That's the way with stepmothers.   55

Cinderella went to the tree at the grave
and cried forth like a gospel singer:
Mama! Mama! My turtledove,
send me to the prince's ball!
The bird dropped down a golden dress   60
and delicate little gold slippers.
Rather a large package for a simple bird.
So she went. Which is no surprise.
Her stepmother and sisters didn't
recognize her without her cinder face   65
and the prince took her hand on the spot
and danced with no other the whole day.

As nightfall came she thought she'd better
get home. The prince walked her home
and she disappeared into the pigeon house   70
and although the prince took an axe and broke
it open she was gone. Back to her cinders.

These events repeated themselves for three days.
However on the third day the prince
covered the palace steps with cobbler's wax
and Cinderella's gold shoe stuck upon it.   75
Now he would find whom the shoe fit
and find his strange dancing girl for keeps.
He went to their house and the two sisters
were delighted because they had lovely feet.   80
The eldest went into a room to try the slipper on
but her big toe got in the way so she simply
sliced it off and put on the slipper.
The prince rode away with her until the white dove
told him to look at the blood pouring forth.   85
That is the way with amputations.
They don't just heal up like a wish.
The other sister cut off her heel
but the blood told as blood will.
The prince was getting tired.   90
He began to feel like a shoe salesman.
But he gave it one last try.
This time Cinderella fit into the shoe
like a love letter into its envelope.

At the wedding ceremony   95
the two sisters came to curry favor
and the white dove pecked their eyes out.
Two hollow spots were left
like soup spoons.

Cinderella and the prince   100
lived, they say, happily ever after,
like two dolls in a museum case
never bothered by diapers or dust,
never arguing over the timing of an egg,
never telling the same story twice,   105
never getting a middle-aged spread,
their darling smiles pasted on for eternity.
Regular Bobbsey Twins.
That story.

CINDERELLA. 32 *Al Jolson:* Extremely popular American entertainer (1886–1950) who frequently
performed in blackface.

Questions

1. Most of Sexton's "Cinderella" straightforwardly retells a version of the famous fairy
   tale. But in the beginning and ending of the poem, how does Sexton change the
   story?
2. How does Sexton's refrain of "That story" alter the meaning of the episodes it describes?
   What is the tone of this poem (the poet's attitude toward her material)?
3. What does Sexton's final stanza suggest about the way fairy tales usually end?

■ WRITING *effectively*

Anne Sexton on Writing

Transforming Fairy Tales

1970

October 14, 1970

Dear Paul [Brooks°],

. . . I realize that the "Transformations"° are a departure from my usual style. I would say that they lack
the intensity and perhaps some of the confessional
force of my previous work. I wrote them because I had
to . . . because I wanted to . . . because it made me
happy. I would want to publish them for the same
reason. I would like my readers to see this side of me,
and it is not in every case the lighter side. Some of the
poems are grim. In fact I don't know how to typify
them except to agree that I have made them very
contemporary. It would further be a lie to say that
they weren't about me, because they are just as much
about me as my other poetry.

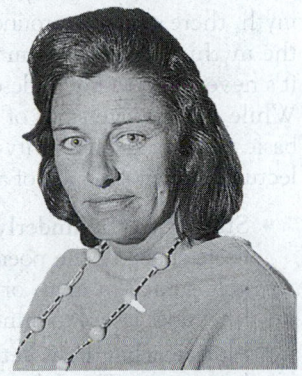

Anne Sexton

I look at my work in stages, and each new book is a kind of growth and reaching
outward and as always backward. Perhaps the critics will be unhappy with this book
and some of my readers maybe will not like it either. I feel I will gain new readers and
critics who have always disliked my work (and too true, the critics are not always
kind to me) may come around. I have found the people I've shown them to apathetic
in some cases and wildly excited in others. It often depends on their own feelings
about Grimms' fairy tales.

November 17, 1970

Dear Kurt [Vonnegut, Jr.°],

I meant to write you a postcard before your dentist appointment, but I was away
at the time I should have sent it. Sorry. Your graph for "Cinderella" is right over my
desk.

The enclosed manuscript is of my new book of poems. I've taken Grimms' Fairy
Tales and "Transformed" them into something all of my own. The better books of
fairy tales have introductions telling the value of these old fables. I feel my
Transformations needs an introduction telling of the value of my (one could say) rape
of them. Maybe that's an incorrect phrase. I do something very modern to them
(have you ever tried to describe your own work? I find I am tongue-tied). They are
small, funny and horrifying. Without quite meaning to I have joined the black
humorists. I don't know if you know my other work, but humor was never a very
prominent feature . . . terror, deformity, madness and torture were my bag. But this

---

Paul Brooks: Sexton's editor at Houghton Mifflin. He initially had reservations about Sexton's fairy
tale poems. *"Transformations:"* title of Sexton's 1971 volume of poems that contained "Cinderella."
Kurt Vonnegut, Jr.: popular author of *Cat's Cradle* (1963) and other novels.

little universe of Grimm is not that far away. I think they end up being as wholly personal as my most intimate poems, in a different language, a different rhythm, but coming strangely, for all their story sound, from as deep a place.

From Anne Sexton: A Self-Portrait in Letters

THINKING ABOUT MYTH

Of the many myths conjured by the poets in these pages, you may know some by heart, some only vaguely, and others not at all. When reading a poem inspired by myth, there's no way around it: your understanding will be more precise if you know the mythic story the poem refers to. With the vast resources available on the Web, it's never hard to find a description of a myth, whether traditional or contemporary. While different versions of most myths exist, what usually remains fixed is the tale's basic pattern. A familiarity with that narrative is a key to the meaning—both intellectual and emotional—of any poem that makes reference to mythology.

- **Start with the underlying pattern of the narrative in question.** Does the basic shape of the poem's story seem familiar? Does it have some recognizable source in myth or legend? Even if the poem has no obvious narrative line, does it call to mind other stories?
- **Notice what new details the poem has added, and what it inevitably leaves out.** The difference between the poem and the source material will reveal something about the author's attitude toward the original, and may give you a sense of his or her intentions in reworking the original myth.
- **Read the section "Mythological Criticism" in the chapter "Critical Approaches to Literature."** A quick sense of how critics analyze myth in literature will help you approach a poem with mythological allusions.

CHECKLIST: Writing About Myth

- ☐ Does the poem have a recognizable source in myth or legend?
- ☐ What new details has the poet added to the original myth?
- ☐ What do these details reveal about the poet's attitude toward the source material?
- ☐ Have important elements of the original been discarded? What does their absence suggest about the author's primary focus?
- ☐ Does the poem rely heavily on its mythic imagery? Or is myth tangential to the poem's theme?
- ☐ How do mythic echoes underscore the poem's meaning?

WRITING ASSIGNMENT ON MYTH

Provide a close reading of any poem from this book that uses a traditional myth or legend. In the course of your analysis, demonstrate how the author borrows or changes certain details of the myth to emphasize his or her meaning. In addition to the poems in this chapter, some selections to consider include: T. S. Eliot's "Journey of the Magi," Alfred, Lord Tennyson's "Ulysses," and William Butler Yeats's "The Magi" or "Leda and the Swan."

Here is an example of an essay on this assignment written by Heather Burke when she was a sophomore at Wesleyan University in Middletown, Connecticut.

Burke 1

Heather Burke

Professor Greene

English 150

18 January 2009

The Bonds Between Love and Hatred in H.D.'s "Helen"

In her poem "Helen," H.D. examines the close connection between the emotions of love and hatred as embodied in the figure of Helen of Troy. Helen was the cause of the long and bloody Trojan War, and her homecoming is tainted by the memory of the suffering this war caused. As in many Imagist poems, the title is essential to the poem's meaning; it gives the reader both a specific mythic context and a particular subject. Without the title, it would be virtually impossible to understand the poem fully since Helen's name appears nowhere else in the text. The reader familiar with Greek myth knows that Helen, who was the wife of Menelaus, ran away with Paris. Their adultery provoked the Trojan War, which lasted for ten years and resulted in the destruction of Troy.

What is unusual about the poem is H.D.'s perspective on Helen of Troy. The poem refuses to romanticize Helen's story, but its stark new version is easy for a reader to accept. After suffering so much for the sake of one adulterous woman, how could the Greeks not resent her? Rather than idealizing the situation, H.D. describes the enmity which defiles Helen's homecoming and explores the irony of the hatred which "All Greece" feels for her.

The opening line of the poem sets its tone and introduces its central theme—hatred. Helen's beauty required thousands of men to face death in battle, but it cannot assuage the emotional aftermath of the war. Even though Helen is described as "God's daughter, born of love" (13), all she inspires now is resentment, and the poem explores the ways in which these two emotions are closely related.

In the first stanza, the poet uses the color white, as well as the radiance of luster connected with it, in her description of Helen, and this color will be associated with her throughout the poem:

> the still eyes in the white face,
>
> the lustre as of olives

Title sets tone and draws reader in

Thesis sentence

Necessary background

Topic sentence on poem's focus

Topic sentence on tone and theme

Topic sentence on specific image

where she stands,

and the white hands. (2–5)

As one of the foundations of agriculture and civilization, the olive was a crucial symbol in Greek culture. Helen's beauty is compared to the "lustre" of this olive. This word presumably refers to the radiance or light which the whiteness of her face reflects, but Helen's identification with this fruit also has an ironic connotation. The olive branch is a traditional symbol of peace, but the woman it is compared to was the cause of a bitter war.

The majority of the imagery in the poem is connected with the color white. H.D. uses white to describe Helen's skin; white would have been seen as the appropriate color for a rich and beautiful woman's skin in pre-twentieth century poetry. This color also has several connotations, all of which operate simultaneously in the poem. The color white has a connection to Helen's paternity; her immortal father Zeus took the form of a white swan when he made love to her mortal mother Leda. At the same time, whiteness suggests a certain chilliness, as with snow or frost. In the third stanza, H.D. makes this suggestion explicit with her use of the phrase "the beauty of cool feet" (14). This image also suggests the barrenness connected with such frigidity. In this sense, it is a very accurate representation of Helen, because in *The Odyssey* Homer tells us that ". . . the gods had never after granted Helen / a child to bring into the sunlit world / after the first, rose-lipped Hermione" (4.13–15). Helen is returned to her rightful husband, but after her adulterous actions, she is unable to bear him any more children. She is a woman who is renowned for exciting passion in legions of men, but that passion is now sterile.

Another traditional connotation of the color white is purity, but this comparison only accentuates Helen's sexual transgressions; she is hardly pure. H.D. emphasizes her lasciviousness through the use of irony. In the third stanza, she refers to Helen as a "maid." A maid is a virgin, but Helen is most definitely not virginal in any sense. In the following line, the poet rhymes "maid" with the word "laid," which refers to the placement of Helen's body on the funeral pyre. This particular word, however, deliberately emphasized by the rhyme, also carries slangy associations with the act of sexual intercourse. This connotation presents another ironic contrast with the word "maid."

The first line of the second stanza is almost identical to that of the first, and again we are reminded of the intense animosity that Helen's presence inspires. This

Burke 3

hatred is now made more explicit. The word *revile* is defined by the *American Heritage College Dictionary* as "to denounce with abusive language" ("Revile"). Helen is a queen, but she is subjected to the insults of her subjects as well as the rest of Greece.

Key word defined

Helen's homecoming is not joyous, but a time of exile and penance. The war is over, but no one, especially Helen, can forget the past. Her memories seem to cause her wanness, which the dictionary defines as "indicating weariness, illness, or unhappiness" ("Wan"). Her face now ". . . grows wan and white, / remembering past enchantments / and past ills" (9–11). The enchantment she remembers is that of Aphrodite, the goddess who lured her from her home and husband to Paris's bed. The "ills" which Helen remembers can be seen as both her sexual offenses and the human losses sustained in the Trojan War. The use of the word *ills* works in conjunction with the word *wan* to demonstrate Helen's spiritual sickness; she is plagued by regret.

Topic sentence/ textual analysis

As the opening of the third stanza shows, the woman who was famous for her beauty and perfection now leaves Greece "unmoved." This opening may not echo the sharpness of those of the first two stanzas, but it picks up on the theme of Helen as a devalued prize. In the eyes of the Greeks, she is not the beauty who called two armies to battle but merely an unfaithful wife for whom many died needlessly.

Topic sentence/ textual analysis

The final lines of the poem reveal the one condition which could turn the people's hatred into love again. They "could love indeed the maid, / only if she were laid, / white ash amid funereal cypresses" (16–18). The Greeks can only forgive Helen once her body has been burned on the funeral pyre. These disturbing lines illustrate the destructive power of hatred; it can only be conquered by death. These lines also reveal the final significance of the color white. It suggests Helen's death. As Helen's face is pale and white in life, so her ashes will be in death. The flames of the funeral pyre are the only way to purify the flesh that was tainted by the figurative flames of passion. Death is the only way to restore Helen's beauty and make it immortal. While she is alive, her beauty is only a reminder of lost fathers, sons, and brothers. The people of Greece can only despise her while she is living, but they can love and revere the memory of her beauty once she is dead.

Conclusion

More complex and specific restatement of thesis

Burke 4

Works Cited

H. D. "Helen." *Literature: An Introduction to Fiction, Poetry, Drama, and Writing*.
Ed. X. J. Kennedy and Dana Gioia. 11th ed. New York: Longman, 2010.
869. Print.

Homer. *The Odyssey*. Trans. Robert Fitzgerald. New York: Noonday P, 1998. Print.

"Revile." *American Heritage College Dictionary*. 4th ed. 2002. Print.

"Wan." *American Heritage College Dictionary*. 4th ed. 2002. Print.

MORE TOPICS FOR WRITING

1. Anne Sexton's "Cinderella" freely mixes period detail and slang from twentieth-century American life with elements from the original fairy tale. (You can read the original in Charles Perrault's *Mother Goose Tales*.) Write an analysis of the effect of all this anachronistic mixing and matching. Be sure to look up any period details you don't recognize.

2. Provide an explication of Louise Bogan's "Medusa." For tips on poetic explication, refer to the chapter "Writing About a Poem."

3. Write an essay of approximately 750 words discussing Constantine Cavafy's "Ithaca." How does the poet combine modern circumstances and mythological allusions to suggest personal meaning for the reader?

4. You're probably familiar with an urban legend or two—near-fantastical stories passed on from one person to another, with the suggestion that they really happened to a friend of a friend of the person who told you the tale. Retell an urban myth in free-verse form. If you don't know any urban myths, an Internet search engine can lead you to scores of them.

5. Compare and contrast Constantine Cavafy's use of the story of Odysseus with Tennyson's use of the same mythic story in "Ulysses" (page 1090)?

6. Retell a famous myth or fairy tale to reflect your personal worldview.

▶ TERMS FOR *review*

Myth ▶ A traditional narrative of anonymous authorship that arises out of a culture's oral tradition. The characters in traditional myths are often gods or heroic figures engaged in significant actions and decisions. Myth is usually differentiated from *legend*, which has a specific historical base.

Archetype ▶ A recurring symbol, character, landscape, or event found in myth and literature across different cultures and eras, one that appears so often that it evokes a universal response.

26 POETRY AND PERSONAL IDENTITY

All literature is, finally, autobiographical.
—JORGE LUIS BORGES

Only a naive reader assumes that all poems directly reflect the personal experience of their authors. That would be like believing that a TV sitcom actually describes the real family life of its cast. As you will recall if you read "The Person in the Poem" (page 651), poets often speak in voices other than their own. These voices may be borrowed or imaginary. Stevie Smith appropriates the voice of a dead swimmer in her poem "Not Waving but Drowning" (page 723), and Ted Hughes imagines a nonhuman voice in "Hawk Roosting" (page 653). Some poets also try to give their personal poems a universal feeling. Edna St. Vincent Millay's emotion-charged sonnet "Well, I Have Lost You; and I Lost You Fairly" describes the end of a difficult love affair with a younger man, but she dramatizes the situation in such a way that it seems deliberately independent of any particular time and place. Even her lover remains shadowy and nameless. No one has ever been able to identify the characters in Shakespeare's sonnets with actual people, but that fact does not diminish our pleasure in them as poems.

And yet there are times when poets try to speak openly in their own voices. What could be a more natural subject for a poet than examining his or her own life? The autobiographical elements in a poem may be indirect, as in Wilfred Owen's "Anthem for Doomed Youth" (page 1072), which is clearly drawn from its author's battle experience in World War I, although it never refers to his own participation, or they may form the central subject, as in Sylvia Plath's "Lady Lazarus," which discusses her suicide attempts. In either case, the poem's autobiographical stance affects a reader's response.

Although we respond to a poem's formal elements, we also cannot help reacting to what we know about its human origins. Reading Plath's chilling exploration of her death wish while knowing that within a few months the poet would kill herself, we receive an extra jolt of emotion. In a good autobiographical poem, that shock of veracity adds to the poem's power. In an unsuccessful poem, the autobiographical facts become a substitute for emotions not credibly conveyed by the words themselves.

CONFESSIONAL POETRY

One literary movement, **Confessional poetry**, has made such frank self-definition its main purpose. As the name implies, Confessional poetry renders personal experience as candidly as possible, even sharing confidences that may violate social conventions or propriety. Confessional poets sometimes shock their readers with admissions of experiences so intimate and painful—adultery, family violence, suicide attempts—that most people would try to suppress them, or at least not proclaim them to the world.

Some confessional poets, such as Anne Sexton, W. D. Snodgrass, and Robert Lowell, underwent psychoanalysis, and at times their poems sound like patients telling their analysts every detail of their personal lives. For this reason, confessional poems run the danger of being more interesting to their authors than to their readers. But when a poet successfully frames his or her personal experience so that the reader can feel an extreme emotion from the inside, the result can be powerful. Here is a chilling poem that takes us within the troubled psyche of a poet who contemplates suicide.

Sylvia Plath (1932–1963)

Lady Lazarus   (1962) 1965

I have done it again.
One year in every ten
I manage it—

A sort of walking miracle, my skin
Bright as a Nazi lampshade,   5
My right foot

A paperweight,
My face a featureless, fine
Jew linen.

Peel off the napkin   10
O my enemy.
Do I terrify?—

The nose, the eye pits, the full set of teeth?
The sour breath
Will vanish in a day.   15

Soon, soon the flesh
The grave cave ate will be
At home on me

And I a smiling woman.
I am only thirty.   20
And like the cat I have nine times to die.

This is Number Three.
What a trash
To annihilate each decade.

What a million filaments.   25
The peanut-crunching crowd
Shoves in to see

Them unwrap me hand and foot—
The big strip tease.
Gentleman, ladies,   30

These are my hands
My knees.
I may be skin and bone,

Nevertheless, I am the same, identical woman.
The first time it happened I was ten.   35
It was an accident.

The second time I meant
To last it out and not come back at all.
I rocked shut

As a seashell.   40
They had to call and call
And pick the worms off me like sticky pearls.

Dying
Is an art, like everything else.
I do it exceptionally well.   45

I do it so it feels like hell.
I do it so it feels real.
I guess you could say I've a call.

It's easy enough to do it in a cell.
It's easy enough to do it and stay put.   50
It's the theatrical

Comeback in broad day
To the same place, the same face, the same brute
Amused shout:

"A miracle!"   55
That knocks me out.
There is a charge

For the eyeing of my scars, there is a charge
For the hearing of my heart—
It really goes.   60

And there is a charge, a very large charge,
For the word or a touch
Or a bit of blood

Or a piece of my hair or my clothes.
So, so, Herr Doktor.   65
So, Herr Enemy.

I am your opus,°   *work, work of art*
I am your valuable,
The pure gold baby

That melts to a shriek.   70
I turn and burn.
Do not think I underestimate your great concern.

Ash, ash—
You poke and stir.
Flesh, bone, there is nothing there—   75

A cake of soap,
A wedding ring,
A gold filling,

Herr God, Herr Lucifer
Beware   80
Beware.

Out of the ash
I rise with my red hair.
And I eat men like air.

Questions

1. Although the poem is openly autobiographical, Plath uses certain symbols to represent herself (Lady Lazarus, a Jew murdered in a concentration camp, a cat with nine lives, and so on). What do these symbols tell us about Plath's attitude toward herself and the world around her?

2. In her biography of Plath, *Bitter Fame*, the poet Anne Stevenson says that this poem penetrates "the furthest reaches of disdain and rage . . . bereft of all 'normal' human feelings." What do you think Stevenson means? Does anything in the poem strike you as particularly chilling?

3. The speaker in "Lady Lazarus" says, "Dying / Is an art, like everything else" (lines 43–44). What sense do you make of this metaphor?

4. Does the ending of "Lady Lazarus" imply that the speaker assumes that she will outlive her suicide attempts? Set forth your final understanding of the poem.

Not all autobiographical poetry needs to shock the reader, as Plath overtly does in "Lady Lazarus." Poets can also try to share the special moments that illuminate their day-to-day lives, as Elizabeth Bishop does in "Filling Station," when she describes a roadside gas station whose shabby bric-a-brac she sees as symbols of love. But when poets attempt to place their own lives under scrutiny, they face certain difficulties. Honest, thorough self-examination isn't as easy as it might seem. It is one thing to examine oneself in the mirror; it is quite another to sketch accurately what one sees there. Even if we have the skill to describe ourselves in words (or in paint) so that a stranger would recognize the self-portrait, there is the challenge of honesty. Drawing or writing our own self-portrait, most of us yield, often unconsciously, to the temptation of making ourselves a little nobler or better-looking than we really are. The best self-portraits, like Rembrandt's unflattering self-examinations, are usually critical. No one enjoys watching someone else preen in front of a dressing mirror, unless the intention is satiric.

IDENTITY POETICS

Autobiographical poetry requires a hunger for honest self-examination. Many poets find that, in order to understand themselves and who they are, they must scrutinize more than the self in isolation. Other forces may shape their identities: ethnic background, family, race, gender, sexual orientation, religion, economic status, and age. Aware of these elements, many recent poets have written memorable personal poems. Dominican-born Rhina Espaillat addresses these concerns in the following poem, which also examines the American experience from the viewpoint of individuals half inside and half outside mainstream society, a division intensified in this instance, as her title makes clear, by issues of language. Espaillat's poem also adds a new human dimension, the generation gap—familiar to anyone raised in an immigrant home—between those raised in "the old country" and those growing up (and feeling at home) in America.

Rhina Espaillat (b. 1932)

Bilingual/Bilingüe   1998

My father liked them separate, one there,
one here (allá y aquí), as if aware

that words might cut in two his daughter's heart
(el corazón) and lock the alien part

to what he was—his memory, his name   5
(su nombre)—with a key he could not claim.

"English outside this door, Spanish inside,"
he said, "y basta." But who can divide

the world, the word (mundo y palabra) from
any child? I knew how to be dumb   10

and stubborn (testaruda); late, in bed,
I hoarded secret syllables I read

until my tongue (mi lengua) learned to run
where his stumbled. And still the heart was one.

I like to think he knew that, even when,   15
proud (orgulloso) of his daughter's pen,

he stood outside mis versos, half in fear
of words he loved but wanted not to hear.

Questions

1. Espaillat's poem is full of Spanish words and phrases. (Even the title is given in both languages.) What does the Spanish add to the poem? Could we remove the phrases without changing the poem?

2. How does the father want to divide his daughter's world, at least in terms of language? Does his request suggest any other divisions he hopes to enforce in her life?

3. How does the daughter respond to her father's request to leave English outside their home?

4. "And still the heart was one," states the speaker of the poem. Should we take her statement at face value or do we sense a cost to her bilingual existence? Agree or disagree with the daughter's statement, but state the reasons for your opinion.

CULTURE, RACE, AND ETHNICITY

One of the personal issues Rhina Espaillat faces in "Bilingual/Bilingüe" is her dual identity as Dominican and American. The daughter of immigrants, she was born in the Dominican Republic but came to America at the age of seven and grew up in New York. Consequently, self-definition for her has meant resolving the claims of two potentially contradictory cultures, as well as dealing, on a more immediate level, with the conflicting demands of family love and loyalty, on the one hand, and personal growth and fulfillment, on the other. As much as she loves her father and wishes to honor him, she cannot be held back from what she is and what she needs to become, and "I hoarded secret syllables I read // until my tongue (mi lengua) learned to run / where his stumbled." Here Espaillat touches on the central issue facing the autobiographical poet—using *words* to embody experience. The tongue must "learn to run," even if where it runs, for an immigrant poet, is away from the language of one's parents.

American poetry is rich in immigrant cultures, as shown in the work of both first-generation writers such as Francisco X. Alarcón and John Ciardi and foreign-born authors such as Joseph Brodsky (Russia), Nina Cassian (Romania), Claude McKay (Jamaica), Eamon Grennan (Ireland), Thom Gunn (England), Shirley Geok-lin Lim (Malaysia), Emanuel di Pasquale (Italy), José Emilio Pacheco (Mexico), Herberto Padilla (Cuba), and Derek Walcott (St. Lucia). Some literary immigrants, such as the late Russian novelist and poet Vladimir Nabokov, make the difficult transition to writing in English. Others, such as Cassian and Pacheco, continue to write in their native languages. A few, such as Brodsky, write bilingually. Such texts often remind us of the multicultural nature of American poetry. Here is a poem by one literary immigrant that raises some important issues of personal identity.

Claude McKay (1890–1948)

America   1922

Although she feeds me bread of bitterness,
And sinks into my throat her tiger's tooth,
Stealing my breath of life, I will confess
I love this cultured hell that tests my youth!
Her vigor flows like tides into my blood,   5
Giving me strength erect against her hate.
Her bigness sweeps my being like a flood.
Yet, as a rebel fronts a king in state,
I stand within her walls with not a shred
Of terror, malice, not a word of jeer.   10
Darkly I gaze into the days ahead,
And see her might and granite wonders there,
Beneath the touch of Time's unerring hand,
Like priceless treasures sinking in the sand.

Questions

1. Is "America" written in a personal or public voice? What specific elements seem personal? What elements seem public?

2. McKay was a black immigrant from Jamaica, but he does not mention either his race or national origin in the poem. Is his personal background important to understanding "America"?

3. "America" is written in a traditional form. How does the poem's form contribute to its impact?

Claude McKay's "America" raises the question of how an author's race and ethnic identity influence the poetry he or she writes. In the 1920s, for instance, there was an ongoing discussion among black poets as to whether their poetry should deal specifically with the African American experience. Did black poetry exist apart from the rest of American poetry or was it, as Robert Hayden would later suggest, "shaped over some three centuries by social, moral, and literary forces essentially American"? Should black authors primarily address a black audience or should they try to engage a broader literary public? Should black poetry focus on specifically black subjects, forms, and idioms or should it rely mainly on the traditions of English literature? Black poets divided into two camps. Claude McKay and Countee Cullen were among the writers who favored universal themes. (Cullen, for example, insisted he be called a "poet," not a "Negro poet.") Langston Hughes and Jean Toomer were among the "new" poets who felt that black poetry must reflect racial themes. They believed, as James Weldon Johnson had once said, that race was "perforce the thing that the American Negro Poet knows best." Writers on both sides of the debate produced excellent poems, but their work has a very different character.

The debate between ethnicity and universality has echoed among American writers of every racial and religious minority. Today, we find the same issues being discussed by Arab, Asian, Hispanic, Italian, Jewish, and Native American authors. There is no one correct answer to the questions of identity, for individual artists need the freedom to pursue their own imaginative vision. But considering the issues of race and ethnicity does help a poet think through the artist's sometimes conflicting responsibilities between group and personal identity. Even in poets who have pursued their individual vision, we often see how unmistakably they write from their racial, social, and cultural background. Sometimes a poet's ethnic background becomes part of his or her private mythology. In the following poem, Samuel Menashe talks about how his physical body is the center of his Jewish identity.

Samuel Menashe (b. 1925)

The Shrine Whose Shape I Am 1961

The shrine whose shape I am
Has a fringe of fire
Flames skirt my skin

There is no Jerusalem but this
Breathed in flesh by shameless love   5
Built high upon the tides of blood
I believe the Prophets and Blake
And like David I bless myself
With all my might

I know many hills were holy once   10
But now in the level lands to live
Zion ground down must become marrow
Thus in my bones I am the King's son
And through death's domain I go
Making my own procession   15

Questions

1. What does the poem tell you about the race and religion of the author? How is this information conveyed? Point to specific lines.
2. The ancient Jews located the center of Judaism at the Temple of Jerusalem, destroyed by the Romans in 70 A.D. When Menashe declares "There is no Jerusalem but this," what does he mean? What is he specifically referring to?
3. What does this poem imply about the nature of ethnic identity?

Francisco X. Alarcón (b. 1954)

The X in My Name   1993

the poor
signature
of my illiterate
and peasant
self   5
giving away
all rights
in a deceiving
contract for life

Question

What does the speaker imply the X in his name signifies?

Sometimes a single word announces a new sort of voice, as in Judith Ortiz Cofer's "Quinceañera." The title is a Spanish noun for which there is no one-word English equivalent. That one word signals that we will be hearing a new voice.

Judith Ortiz Cofer (b. 1952)

Quinceañera   1987

My dolls have been put away like dead
children in a chest I will carry
with me when I marry.
I reach under my skirt to feel
a satin slip bought for this day. It is soft   5
as the inside of my thighs. My hair
has been nailed back with my mother's
black hairpins to my skull. Her hands
stretched my eyes open as she twisted
braids into a tight circle at the nape   10

of my neck. I am to wash my own clothes
and sheets from this day on, as if
the fluids of my body were poison, as if
the little trickle of blood I believe
travels from my heart to the world were   15
shameful. Is not the blood of saints and
men in battle beautiful? Do Christ's hands
not bleed into your eyes from His cross?
At night I hear myself growing and wake
to find my hands drifting of their own will   20
to soothe skin stretched tight
over my bones.
I am wound like the guts of a clock,
waiting for each hour to release me.

QUINCEAÑERA. The title refers to a fifteen-year-old girl's coming-out party in Latin cultures.

Questions

1. What items and actions are associated with the speaker's new life? What items are put away?
2. What is the speaker waiting to release in the final two lines?
3. If the poem's title were changed to "Fifteen-Year-Old Girl," what would the poem lose in meaning?

Sherman Alexie (b. 1966)

The Powwow at the End of the World   1996

I am told by many of you that I must forgive and so I shall
after an Indian woman puts her shoulder to the Grand Coulee Dam
and topples it. I am told by many of you that I must forgive
and so I shall after the floodwaters burst each successive dam
downriver from the Grand Coulee. I am told by many of you   5
that I must forgive and so I shall after the floodwaters find
their way to the mouth of the Columbia River as it enters the Pacific
and causes all of it to rise. I am told by many of you that I must forgive
and so I shall after the first drop of floodwater is swallowed by that salmon
waiting in the Pacific. I am told by many of you that I must forgive and   10
    so I shall
after that salmon swims upstream, through the mouth of the Columbia
and then past the flooded cities, broken dams and abandoned reactors
of Hanford. I am told by many of you that I must forgive and so I shall
after that salmon swims through the mouth of the Spokane River
as it meets the Columbia, then upstream, until it arrives   15
in the shallows of a secret bay on the reservation where I wait alone.
I am told by many of you that I must forgive and so I shall after
that salmon leaps into the night air above the water, throws
a lightning bolt at the brush near my feet, and starts the fire
which will lead all of the lost Indians home. I am told   20
by many of you that I must forgive and so I shall

after we Indians have gathered around the fire with that salmon
who has three stories it must tell before sunrise: one story will teach us
how to pray; another story will make us laugh for hours;
the third story will give us reason to dance. I am told by many   25
of you that I must forgive and so I shall when I am dancing
with my tribe during the powwow at the end of the world.

Questions

1. Who, in your opinion, is the "you" of the poem's refrain?
2. What is it that the speaker is told he "must forgive"?
3. The tone of the poem is not overtly angry or bitter. Does that make its statement more
   effective or less so, in your judgment? Explain.

Yusef Komunyakaa (b. 1947)

Facing It   1988

My black face fades,
hiding inside the black granite.
I said I wouldn't,
dammit: No tears.
I'm stone. I'm flesh.   5
My clouded reflection eyes me
like a bird of prey, the profile of night
slanted against morning. I turn
this way—the stone lets me go.
I turn that way—I'm inside   10
the Vietnam Veterans Memorial
again, depending on the light
to make a difference.
I go down the 58,022 names,
half-expecting to find   15
my own in letters like smoke.
I touch the name Andrew Johnson;
I see the booby trap's white flash.
Names shimmer on a woman's blouse
but when she walks away   20
the names stay on the wall.
Brushstrokes flash, a red bird's
wings cutting across my stare.
The sky. A plane in the sky.
A white vet's image floats   25
closer to me, then his pale eyes
look through mine. I'm a window.
He's lost his right arm
inside the stone. In the black mirror
a woman's trying to erase names: 30
No, she's brushing a boy's hair.

Questions

1. How does the title of "Facing It" relate to the poem? Does it have more than one meaning?
2. The narrator describes the people around him by their reflections on the polished granite rather than by looking at them directly. What does this indirect way of scrutinizing contribute to the poem?
3. This poem comes out of the life experience of a black Vietnam veteran. Is Komunyakaa's writing closer to McKay's "universal" method or to Toomer's "ethnic" style?

GENDER

In her celebrated study *You Just Don't Understand: Women and Men in Conversation* (1990), Georgetown University linguist Deborah Tannen explored how men and women use language differently. Tannen compared many everyday conversations between husbands and wives to "cross-cultural communications," as if people from separate worlds lived under the same roof. While analyzing the divergent ways in which women and men converse, Tannen carefully emphasizes that neither linguistic style is superior, only that they are different.

While it would be simplistic to assume that all poems reveal the sex of their authors, many poems do become both richer and clearer when we examine their gender assumptions. Theodore Roethke's "My Papa's Waltz" (page 645) is hardly a macho poem, but it does reflect the complicated mix of love, authority, and violent horseplay that exists in many father-son relationships. By contrast, Sylvia Plath's "Metaphors" (page 735), which describes her own pregnancy through a series of images, deals with an experience that, by biological definition, only a woman can know first-hand. Feminist criticism has shown us how gender influences literary texts in subtler ways. (See the chapter "Critical Approaches to Literature" for a discussion of gender theory.) The central insight of feminist criticism seems inarguable—our gender does often influence how we speak, write, and interpret language. But that insight need not be intimidating. It can also invite us to bring our whole life experience, as women or men, to reading a poem. It reminds us that poetry, the act of using language with the greatest clarity and specificity, is a means to see the world through the eyes of the opposite sex. Or, it can demonstrate how deeply sexual orientation affects an individual's worldview. Sometimes the messages we get from this exchange are unsettling, but at least they may move us into better understanding the diversity of human behavior.

Anne Stevenson (b. 1933)

Sous-entendu   1969

Don't think

that I don't know
that as you talk to me
the hand of your mind
is inconspicuously
taking off my stocking,   5
moving in resourceful blindness
up along my thigh.

Don't think
that I don't know   10
that you know
everything I say
is a garment.

SOUS-ENTENDU. The title is a French expression for "hidden meaning" or "implication." It describes something left unsaid but assumed to be understood.

Questions

1. What is left unsaid but assumed to be understood between the two people in this poem?
2. Could this poem have been written by a man? If so, under what circumstances? If not, why not?

Bettie Sellers (b. 1926)

In the Counselor's Waiting Room   1981

The terra cotta girl
with the big flat farm feet
traces furrows in the rug
with her toes,
reads an existentialist paperback   5
from psychology class,
finds no ease there
from the guilt of loving
the quiet girl down the hall.
Their home soil has seen to this visit,   10
their Baptist mothers,
who weep for the waste of sturdy hips
ripe for grandchildren.

IN THE COUNSELOR'S WAITING ROOM. The poet was a teacher and administrator at a small college in Georgia. 1 *terra cotta:* fired clay, light brownish orange in hue. 5 *existentialist:* of the twentieth-century school of philosophy that holds (among other tenets) that an individual is alone and isolated, free and yet responsible, and ordinarily subject to guilt, anxiety, and dread.

Questions

1. For what sort of counseling is this girl waiting?
2. Point out all the words that refer to plowing, to clay and earth. Why are the mothers called "home soil"? How do these references to earth relate to the idea in the last line?
3. What irony inheres in this situation?
4. Does the poet appear to sympathize with the girls? With their weeping mothers? In what details does this poem hint at any of the poet's own attitude or attitudes?

Exercise: "Men at Forty"; "Women"

Rewrite either of the following poems from the perspective of the opposite sex. Then evaluate in what ways the new poem has changed the original's meaning and in what ways the original poem comes through more or less unaltered.

Donald Justice (1925–2004)

Men at Forty   1967

Men at forty
Learn to close softly
The doors to rooms they will not be
Coming back to.

At rest on a stair landing,   5
They feel it moving
Beneath them now like the deck of a ship,
Though the swell is gentle.

And deep in mirrors
They rediscover   10
The face of the boy as he practices tying
His father's tie there in secret,

And the face of that father,
Still warm with the mystery of lather.
They are more fathers than sons themselves now.   15
Something is filling them, something

That is like the twilight sound
Of the crickets, immense,
Filling the woods at the foot of the slope
Behind their mortgaged houses.   20

Adrienne Rich (b. 1929)

Women   1968

My three sisters are sitting
on rocks of black obsidian.
For the first time, in this light, I can see who they are.

My first sister is sewing her costume for the procession.
She is going as the Transparent Lady   5
and all her nerves will be visible.

My second sister is also sewing,
at the seam over her heart which has never healed entirely.
At last, she hopes, this tightness in her chest will ease.

My third sister is gazing   10
at a dark-red crust spreading westward far out on the sea.
Her stockings are torn but she is beautiful.

FOR REVIEW AND FURTHER STUDY

Shirley Geok-lin Lim (b. 1944)

Learning to love America   1998

because it has no pure products

because the Pacific Ocean sweeps along the coastline
because the water of the ocean is cold
and because land is better than ocean

because I say we rather than they   5

because I live in California
I have eaten fresh artichokes
and jacarandas bloom in April and May

because my senses have caught up with my body
my breath with the air it swallows   10
my hunger with my mouth

because I walk barefoot in my house

because I have nursed my son at my breast
because he is a strong American boy
because I have seen his eyes redden when he is asked who he is   15
because he answers I don't know

because to have a son is to have a country
because my son will bury me here
because countries are in our blood and we bleed them

because it is late and too late to change my mind   20
because it is time.

LEARNING TO LOVE AMERICA. 1 *pure products*: an allusion to poem XVIII of *Spring and All* (1923) by
William Carlos Williams, which begins: "The pure products of America / go crazy—."

Question

Do the reasons given in the poem suggest that the speaker really does love America?

Philip Larkin (1922–1985)

Aubade   1977

I work all day, and get half-drunk at night.
Waking at four to soundless dark, I stare.
In time the curtain-edges will grow light.
Till then I see what's really always there:
Unresting death, a whole day nearer now,   5
Making all thought impossible but how
And where and when I shall myself die.
Arid interrogation: yet the dread
Of dying, and being dead,
Flashes afresh to hold and horrify.   10

The mind blanks at the glare. Not in remorse
—The good not done, the love not given, time
Torn off unused—nor wretchedly because
An only life can take so long to climb
Clear of its wrong beginnings, and may never;   15
But at the total emptiness for ever,
The sure extinction that we travel to
And shall be lost in always. Not to be here,
Not to be anywhere,
And soon; nothing more terrible, nothing more true.   20

This is a special way of being afraid
No trick dispels. Religion used to try,
That vast moth-eaten musical brocade
Created to pretend we never die,
And specious stuff that says *No rational being*   25
Can fear a thing it will not feel, not seeing
That this is what we fear—no sight, no sound,
No touch or taste or smell, nothing to think with,
Nothing to love or link with,
The anaesthetic from which none come round.   30

And so it stays just on the edge of vision,
A small unfocused blur, a standing chill
That slows each impulse down to indecision.
Most things may never happen: this one will,
And realisation of it rages out   35
In furnace-fear when we are caught without
People or drink. Courage is no good:
It means not scaring others. Being brave
Lets no one off the grave.
Death is no different whined at than withstood.   40

Slowly light strengthens, and the room takes shape.
It stands plain as a wardrobe, what we know,
Have always known, know that we can't escape,
Yet can't accept. One side will have to go.
Meanwhile telephones crouch, getting ready to ring   45
In locked-up offices, and all the uncaring
Intricate rented world begins to rouse.
The sky is white as clay, with no sun.
Work has to be done.
Postmen like doctors go from house to house.   50

Questions

1. Is "Aubade" a confessional poem? If so, what social taboo does it violate?
2. What embarrassing facts about the narrator does the poem reveal? Do these confessions lead us to trust or distrust him?
3. The narrator says that "Courage is no good" (line 37). How might he defend this statement?
4. Would a twenty-year-old reader respond differently to this poem than a seventy-year-old one? Would a devout Christian respond differently to the poem than an atheist?

■ WRITING *effectively*

Rhina Espaillat on Writing

Being a Bilingual Writer   1998

Recent interest in the phenomenon known as "Spanglish" has led me to reexamine my own experience as a writer who works chiefly in her second language, and especially to recall my father's inflexible rule against the mixing of languages. In fact, no English was allowed in that midtown Manhattan apartment that became home after my arrival in New York in 1939. My father read the daily paper in English, taught himself to follow disturbing events in Europe through the medium of English-language radio, and even taught me to read the daily comic strips, in an effort to speed my learning of the language he knew I would need. But that necessary language was banished from family conversation: it was the medium of the outer world, beyond the door; inside, among ourselves, only Spanish was permitted, and it had to be pure, grammatical, unadulterated Spanish.

Rhina Espaillat

At the age of seven, however, nothing seems more important than communicating with classmates and neighborhood children. For my mother, too, the new language was a way out of isolation, a means to deal with the larger world and with those American women for whom she sewed. But my father, a political exile waiting for changes in our native country, had different priorities: he lived in the hope of return, and believed that the new home, the new speech, were temporary. His theory was simple: if it could be said at all, it could be said best in the language of those authors whose words were the core of his education. But his insistence on pure Spanish made it difficult, sometimes impossible, to bring home and share the jokes of friends, puns, pop lyrics, and other staples of seven-year-old conversation. Table talk sometimes ended with tears or sullen silence.

And yet, despite the friction it caused from time to time, my native language was also a source of comfort—the reading that I loved, intimacy within the family, and a peculiar auditory delight best described as echoes in the mind. I learned early to relish words as counters in a game that could turn suddenly serious without losing the quality of play, and to value their sound as a meaning behind their meaning.

Nostalgia, a confusion of identity, the fear that if the native language is lost the self will somehow be altered forever: all are part of the subtle flavor of immigrant life, as well as the awareness that one owes gratitude to strangers for acts of communication that used to be simple and once imposed no such debt.

Memory, folklore, and food all become part of the receding landscape that language sets out to preserve. Guilt, too, adds to the mix, the suspicion that to love the second language too much is to betray those ancestors who spoke the first and could not communicate with us in the vocabulary of our education, our new thoughts. And finally, a sense of grievance and loss may spur hostility toward the new language and those who speak it, as if the common speech of the perceived majority could weld together a disparate population into a huge, monolithic, and threatening Other. That Other is then assigned traits and habits that preclude sympathy and mold "Us" into a unity whose cohesiveness gives comfort.

Luckily, there is another side to bilingualism: curiosity about the Other may be as natural and pervasive as group loyalty. If it weren't, travel, foreign residence, and intermarriage would be less common than they are. For some bilingual writers, the Other—and the language he speaks—are appealing. Some acknowledge and celebrate the tendency of languages to borrow from each other and produce something different in the process.

From Afterword to *Where Horizons Go*

THINKING ABOUT POETIC VOICE AND IDENTITY

Every writer strives to find his or her own voice, that distinct mix of subject matter and style that can make an author's work as instantly recognizable as a friend's voice on the phone. Poetic voice reflects matters of style—characteristic tone, word choice, figures of speech, and rhythms—as well as characteristic themes and subjects. Finding an authentic voice has long been a central issue among minority and female poets. In exploring their subjects, which often lie outside the existing poetic traditions, these writers sometimes need to find innovative forms of expression.

- **You will often find it illuminating to consider the author's personal identity when writing about voice in poetry.** Does the poem present any personal details of the author's life or background?

- **Consider whether the poem's subject matter is directly or indirectly shaped by race, gender, age, ethnicity, social class, sexual orientation, or religious beliefs.** If so, how is the viewpoint reflected in the poem's formal aspects (images, tone, metaphors, and so on)?

- **Read the section "Gender Criticism" in the chapter "Critical Approaches to Literature."** Although that section discusses only one aspect of identity, the general principles it explores relate to the broader question of how an author's life experience may influence the kinds of poetry he or she creates.

CHECKLIST: Writing About Voice and Personal Identity

- ☐ Is the poem's subject matter shaped by an aspect of the poet's identity?
- ☐ Does the poem address issues related to race, gender, social class, ethnicity, sexual orientation, age, or religious beliefs?
- ☐ Does personal identity reveal itself directly or indirectly in the poem's voice or content?
- ☐ If so, *how* does the voice reflect identity? Does it appear in the poem's diction, imagery, tone, metaphors, or sound?

WRITING ASSIGNMENT ON PERSONAL IDENTITY

Analyze any poem from this chapter from the perspective of its author's race, gender, ethnicity, age, or religious beliefs. Take into account the poem's style—its approach to tone, word choice, figures of speech, and rhythm—as well as its content. You may find it helpful to look at some biographical information on the poem's author, but focus your comments on the information provided by the poem itself.

MORE TOPICS FOR WRITING

1. Find another poem in the chapter "Poems for Further Reading" in which the poet, like Rhina Espaillat, considers his or her own family. In a paragraph or two, describe what the poem reveals about the author.

2. Write an explication of Adrienne Rich's "Women." What argument does the poem seem to be making?

3. Write a brief analysis (750 to 1,000 words) on how color imagery contributes to meaning in Yusef Komunyakaa's "Facing It."

4. Write an imitation of Shirley Geok-lin Lim's "Learning to love America," about coming to terms with a place—a state, city, or neighborhood—in which you have lived and felt like an outsider.

5. Write about the personal identity of men and boys as explored in Donald Justice's "Men at Forty."

6. Compare Philip Larkin's "Aubade" with another poem about old age and death, such as William Butler Yeats's "Sailing to Byzantium (page 937), or Dylan Thomas's "Do not go gentle into that good night" (page 824).

27

TRANSLATION

A translation is no translation,
unless it will give you the music of a poem
along with the words of it.

—JOHN MILLINGTON SYNGE

IS POETIC TRANSLATION POSSIBLE?

Poetry, said Robert Frost, is what gets lost in translation. If absolutely true, the comment is bad news for most of us, who have to depend on translations for our only knowledge of great poems in many other languages. However, some translators seem able to save a part of their originals and bring it across the language gap. At times they may even add more poetry of their own, as if to try to compensate for what is lost.

Unlike the writer of an original poem, the translator begins with a meaning that already exists. To convey it, the translator may decide to stick closely to the denotations of the original words or else to depart from them, more or less freely, to pursue something he or she values more. The latter aim is evident in the *Imitations* of Robert Lowell, who said he had been "reckless with literal meaning" and instead had "labored hard to get the tone." Particularly defiant of translation are poems in dialect, uneducated speech, and slang: what can be used for English equivalents? Ezra Pound, in a bold move, translates the song of a Chinese peasant in *The Classic Anthology Defined by Confucius*:

> Yaller bird, let my corn alone,
> Yaller bird, let my crawps alone,
> These folks here won't let me eat,
> I wanna go back whaar I can meet
> the folks I used to know at home,
> > I got a home an' I wanna' git goin'.

Here, it is our purpose to judge a translation not by its fidelity to its original, but by the same standards we apply to any other poem written in English. To do so may be another way to see the difference between appropriate and inappropriate words.

WORLD POETRY

English boasts one of the greatest poetic traditions in the world, with over six centuries of continuous literary culture from Geoffrey Chaucer to the present. It is the language of Shakespeare, Milton, Pope, Keats, Tennyson, Dickinson,

Whitman, Frost, and Yeats. The primary language of over 400 million people, English is spoken from London to San Francisco, Cape Town to Sydney, Vancouver to Nassau. Yet English is the first language of only seven percent of the people of the globe. Mandarin Chinese has almost twice as many native speakers, and two other languages—Hindi and Spanish—have nearly as many speakers as English. Needless to say, all these tongues have rich and ancient literary traditions. To know only the poetry of English, therefore, is to experience a small fraction of world poetry.

Poetry is a universal human phenomenon. Every culture and every language group shape language into verse. To explore the poetry of other languages and cultures is a way of broadening one's vision of humanity. No one, of course, can ever master the whole field of human achievement in poetry, even in translation, but to know a few high spots from poets greatly esteemed by other nations can enlarge our notion of the art as well as enhance our sense of the world.

To gain some perspective on English poetry, one need only look at Chinese literature. China has the oldest uninterrupted literary tradition in the world, dating back at least 3400 years, and poetry has always been its central enterprise. Over a billion people speak one of the dialects of Chinese and all read the same written language. To give a taste of this unparalleled tradition, here is Li Po's "Drinking Alone Beneath the Moon," a classic of Chinese poetry, presented in four ways. First, the poem appears in its original Chinese characters; a phonetic transcription follows, along with a word-for-word literal translation into English. Finally, Li Po's poem is given in a poetic translation.

Li Po (701–762)

Drinking Alone Beneath the Moon (about 750)

月　下　獨　酌

花　間　一　壺　酒
獨　酌　無　相　親
舉　杯　邀　明　月
對　影　成　三　人
月　既　不　解　飲
影　徒　隨　我　身
暫　伴　月　將　影
行　樂　須　及　春
我　歌　月　徘　徊
我　舞　影　零　亂
醒　時　同　交　歡
醉　後　各　分　散
永　結　無　情　遊
相　期　邈　雲　漢

Yue Xia Du Zhuo

Moon-beneath Alone Drink

(about 750)

hua jian yi hu jiu
Flowers-among one pot wine
du zhuo wu xiang qing
Alone drink no mutual dear
ju bei yao ming yue
Lift cup invite bright moon
dui ying cheng san ren
Face shadow become three men
yue ji bu jie yin
Moon not-only not understand drink   5
ying tu sui wo shen
Shadow in-vain follow my body
zan ban yue jiang ying
Temporarily accompany moon with shadow
xing le xu ji chun
Practice pleasure must catch spring
wo ge yue pai huai
I sing moon linger-to-and-fro
wo wu ying ling luan
I dance shadow scatter disorderly   10
xing shi tong jiao huan
Wake time together exchange joy
zui hou ge fen san
Rapt-after each separate disperse
yong jie wu qing you
Always tie no-passion friendship
xiang qu miao yun han
Mutual expect distant Cloud-river

Drinking Alone by Moonlight

1919

A cup of wine, under the flowering trees;
I drink alone, for no friend is near.
Raising my cup I beckon the bright moon,
For he, with my shadow, will make three men.
The moon, alas, is no drinker of wine;   5
Listless, my shadow creeps about at my side.
Yet with the moon as friend and the shadow as slave
I must make merry before the Spring is spent.
To the songs I sing the moon flickers her beams;
In the dance I weave my shadow tangles and breaks.   10
While we were sober, three shared the fun;
Now we are drunk, each goes his way.
May we long share our odd, inanimate feast,
And meet at last on the Cloudy River of the sky.

—Translated by Arthur Waley

DRINKING ALONE BY MOONLIGHT. 14 *the Cloudy River of the sky*: the Milky Way.

Questions

1. Judging from the literal translation of Li Po's poem, discuss which aspects of the original seem to come across vividly in Arthur Waley's English version.
2. Which aspects change or disappear in Waley's version?
3. Take a line from Waley's version (perhaps one you don't especially like) and use the literal translation to offer a different translation.

COMPARING TRANSLATIONS

Our verb *translate* is derived from the Latin word *translatus*, the past participle of "to transfer" or "to carry across." Following is a set of translations of Horace which try to carry across in English one of the most influential short poems ever written. Horace's ode, which ends with the advice *carpe diem* ("seize the day"), has left its mark on countless poems. One even sees its imprint on contemporary novels (such as Saul Bellow's *Seize the Day*) and films (such as *Dead Poets Society*) that echo Horace's command to live in the present moment because no one knows what the future will bring. We offer the original Latin poem first, followed by a line-by-line prose paraphrase (which may help indicate what the translator had to work with and how much of the translation is the translator's own idea), followed by a variety of different poetic translations.

Horace (65–8 B.C.)

"Carpe Diem" Ode (*Odes* Book I, 11)   (about 20 B.C.)

Tu ne quaesieris—scire nefas—quem mihi, quem tibi
finem di dederint, Leuconoë, nec Babylonios
temptaris numeros. Ut melius quicquid erit pati,
seu pluris hiemes, seu tribuit Iuppiter ultimam,
quae nunc oppositis debilitat pumicibus mare   5
Tyrrhenum. Sapias, vina liques, et spatio brevi
spem longam reseces. Dum loquimur, fugerit invida
aetas: carpe diem, quam minimum credula postero.

"Carpe Diem" Ode (*literal translation*)

Do not ask, Leuconoe—to know is not permitted—
what end the gods have given to you and me, do not consult Babylonian
horoscopes. It will be better to endure whatever comes,
whether Jupiter grants us more winters or whether this is the last one,
which now against the opposite cliffs wears out the Tuscan sea.   5
Be wise, decant the wine, and since our space is brief,
cut back your far-reaching hope. Even while we talk, envious time
has fled away: seize the day, put little trust in what is to come.

Horace to Leuconoë   1891

I pray you not, Leuconoë, to pore
With unpermitted eyes on what may be
Appointed by the gods for you and me,
Nor on Chaldean figures any more.

'T were infinitely better to implore 5
The present only:—whether Jove decree
More winters yet to come, or whether he
Make even this, whose hard, wave-eaten shore
Shatters the Tuscan seas to-day, the last—
Be wise withal, and rack your wine, nor fill 10
Your bosom with large hopes; for while I sing,
The envious close of time is narrowing;—
So seize the day, or ever it be past,
And let the morrow come for what it will.

—Translated by Edwin Arlington Robinson

Don't Ask 1963

Don't ask (we may not know), Leuconoe,
   What the gods plan for you or me.
      Leave the Chaldees to parse
      The sentence of the stars.

Better to bear the outcome, good or bad, 5
   Whether Jove purposes to add
      Fresh winters to the past
      Or to make this the last

Which now tires out the Tuscan sea and mocks
   Its strength with barricades of rocks. 10
      Be wise, strain clear the wine
      And prune the rambling vine

Of expectation. Life's short. Even while
   We talk Time, hateful, runs a mile.
      Don't trust tomorrow's bough 15
      For fruit. Pluck this, here, now.

—Translated by James Michie

A New Year's Toast 2000

Blanche—don't ask—it isn't right for us to know what ends
Fate may have in store for us. Don't dial up Psychic Friends.
Isn't it better just to take whatever the future sends,
Whether the new millennium goes off without a hitch
Or World War III is triggered by an old computer glitch? 5
Wise up. Have a drink. Keep plans to a modest pitch.
Even as we're talking here, we spend the time we borrow.
Seize Today—trust nothing to that sly old cheat, Tomorrow.

—Translated by A. E. Stallings

Questions

1. Which translation seems closest to the literal meaning of the Latin? Does that fidelity help or hinder its impact as a new poem in English?

2. In her translation, A. E. Stallings modernizes most of the images and allusions. What does this add to the translation's impact? Does it change the meaning of the original?

3. Which translation do you personally respond to most strongly? While recognizing the subjective nature of your preference, explain what aspects of the version appeal to you.

TRANSLATING FORM

The next set of translations tries to recreate a short lyric by the classical Persian poet Omar Khayyam, the master of the *rubai*, a four-line stanza usually rimed *a a b a*. This Persian form was introduced into English by Edward FitzGerald (1809–1883) in his hugely popular translation, *The Rubaiyat of Omar Khayyam* (*rubaiyat* is the plural of *rubai*). In FitzGerald's Victorian version, Omar Khayyam became one of the most frequently quoted poets in English. Eugene O'Neill borrowed the title of his play *Ah, Wilderness!* from the *Rubaiyat* and expected his audience to catch the allusion. TV buffs may remember hearing Khayyam's poetry quoted habitually by the SWAT-team commander Howard Hunter on the classic series *Hill Street Blues*. Here is a famous *rubai* in the original Persian, in a literal prose paraphrase, and in two poetic translations. Which qualities of the original does each translation seem to capture?

Omar Khayyam (1048–1131)

Rubai XII   (about 1100)

Tongi-ye may-e la'l kh'aham o divani
   Sadd-e ramaghi bayad o nesf-e nani
Vangah man o to neshasteh dar virani
   Khoshtar bovad as mamlekat-e soltani.

Rubai XII (*literal translation*)

I want a jug of ruby wine and a book of poems.
There must be something to stop my breath from departing, and a
   half loaf of bread.
Then you and I sitting in some deserted ruin
would be sweeter than the realm of a sultan.

A Book of Verses underneath the Bough   1879

A Book of Verses underneath the Bough,
A Jug of Wine, a Loaf of Bread—and Thou
   Beside me singing in the Wilderness—
Oh, Wilderness were Paradise enow!°   *enough*

—*Translated by Edward FitzGerald*

I Need a Bare Sufficiency   1992

I need a bare sufficiency—red wine,
   Some poems, half a loaf on which to dine
With you beside me in some ruined shrine:
   A king's state then is not as sweet as mine!

—*Translated by Dick Davis*

Exercise: **Persian Versions**

Write a *rubai* of your own on any topic. Some possible subjects include: what you plan to do next weekend to relax; advice to a friend to stop worrying; an invitation to a loved one; a four-line *carpe diem* ode. For your inspiration, here are a few more *rubaiyat* from Edward FitzGerald's celebrated translation.

Omar Khayyam (1048–1131)

Rubaiyat   1879

I

Wake! For the Sun, who scattered into flight
The Stars before him from the Field of Night,
  Drives Night along with them from Heaven, and strikes
The Sultan's Turret with a Shaft of Light.

VII

Come, fill the Cup, and in the fire of Spring
Your Winter-garment of Repentance fling:
  The Bird of Time has but a little way
To flutter—and the Bird is on the Wing.

XIII

Some for the Glories of This World; and some
Sigh for the Prophet's Paradise to come;
  Ah, take the Cash, and let the Credit go,
Nor heed the rumble of a distant Drum!

LXXI

The Moving Finger writes; and, having writ,
Moves on: nor all your Piety nor Wit
  Shall lure it back to cancel half a Line,
Nor all your Tears wash out a Word of it.

XCIX

Ah Love! could you and I with Him conspire
To grasp this sorry Scheme of Things entire,
  Would not we shatter it to bits—and then
Re-mold it nearer to the Heart's Desire!

—*Translated by Edward FitzGerald*

PARODY

There is another literary mode that is related to translation—namely, **parody**—in which one writer imitates another writer or work, usually for the purpose of poking fun. Parody can be considered an irreverent form of translation in which one poem is changed into another written in the same language but with a different effect (usually slipping from serious to silly). When one writer parodies another writer's work, it does not necessarily mean that the original poem is without merit. "Most parodies are written out of admiration rather than contempt," claimed critic Dwight Macdonald, who edited the anthology *Parodies* (1960), because there needs to be enough common sympathy between poet and parodist for the poem's essence not to be lost in the translation. It takes a fine poem to support an even passable parody. "Nobody is going to parody you if you haven't a style," remarked British critic Geoffrey Grigson.

What a parody mostly reveals is that any good poem becomes funny if you change one or more of the assumptions behind it. Gene Fehler, for example, takes Richard Lovelace's lover-soldier in "To Lucasta" (page 667) and turns him into a major league baseball player changing teams; what this new warrior loves, we soon discover, is neither honor nor his lady but a fat salary. Far from ridiculing Lovelace's original, Fehler's parody demonstrates that the poem is strong enough to support a comic translation into contemporary images.

Parodies remind us how much fun poetry can be—an aspect of the art sometimes forgotten during end-of-term exams and research papers. These comic transformations also teach us something essential about the original poems. Parodies are, as Dwight Macdonald said, "an intuitive kind of literary criticism, shorthand for what 'serious' critics must write out at length." If you try your hand at writing a parody, you will soon discover how deeply you need to understand the original work in order to reproduce its style and manner. You will also learn how much easier it is to parody a poem you really love. Consider this anonymous parody of the Christmas carol "We Three Kings of Orient Are."

Anonymous

We four lads from Liverpool are (about 1963)

We four lads from Liverpool are—
Paul in a taxi, John in a car,
George on a scooter, tootin' his hooter,
Following Ringo Starr.

Skillfully written, parody can be a devastating form of literary criticism. Rather than merely flinging abuse, the wise parodist imitates with understanding, even with sympathy. The many crude parodies of T. S. Eliot's difficult poem *The Waste Land* show parodists mocking what they cannot fathom, with the result that, instead of illuminating the original, they belittle it (and themselves). Good parodists have an ear for the sounds and rhythms of their originals, as does James Camp, who echoes Walt Whitman's stately "Out of the Cradle Endlessly Rocking" in his line "Out of the crock endlessly ladling" (what a weary teacher feels he is doing). Parody can be aimed at poems good or bad; yet there are poems of such splendor and dignity that no parodist seems able to touch them without looking like a small dog defiling a cathedral, and others so illiterate that good parody would be squandered on them. Sometimes parodies are even an odd form of flattery; poets poke fun at poems they simply can't get out of their heads any other way except by rewriting.

Hugh Kingsmill [Hugh Kingsmill Lunn] (1889–1949)

What, still alive at twenty-two? (about 1920)

What, still alive at twenty-two,
A clean, upstanding chap like you?
Sure, if your throat 'tis hard to slit,
Slit your girl's, and swing for it.

Like enough, you won't be glad,   5
When they come to hang you, lad:
But bacon's not the only thing
That's cured by hanging from a string.

So, when the spilt ink of the night
Spreads o'er the blotting pad of light,   10
Lads whose job is still to do
Shall whet their knives, and think of you.

Questions

1. A. E. Housman considered this the best of many parodies of his poetry. Read his poems in this book, particularly "Eight O'Clock" (page 776), "When I was one-and-twenty" (page 802), and "To an Athlete Dying Young" (page 1056). What characteristics of theme, form, and language does Hugh Kingsmill's parody convey?
2. What does Kingsmill exaggerate?

Stanley J. Sharpless

How Do I Hate You? Let Me Count the Ways 1986

How do I hate you? Let me count the ways:
I hate your greying hair, now almost white,
Your blotchy skin, a most repellent sight,
The eyes that stare back in a sort of daze,
The turned-up nose, the hollow that betrays   5
The missing dentures, taken out at night,
Receding chin, whose contour isn't quite
Masked by the scraggy beard—in a phrase,
I hate the sight of you, as every morn,
We meet each other in our favorite place,   10
And casually, as to the manner born,
You make your all too customary grimace,
Something between disgust, boredom and scorn;
God, how I loathe you, shaving-mirror face.

Questions

1. What poem is being parodied (see page 1029)?
2. What characteristics of the original does the parody convey?
3. To whom is the poem written? Who or what is the object of his satire?

Gene Fehler (b. 1940)

If Richard Lovelace Became a Free Agent   1984

Tell me not, fans, I am unkind
   For saying my good-bye
And leaving your kind cheers behind
   While I to new fans fly.

Now, I will leave without a trace   5
   And choose a rival's field;
For I have viewed the market place
   And seen what it can yield.

Though my disloyalty is such
   That all you fans abhor,   10
It's not that I don't love you much:
   I just love money more.

Questions

1. After comparing this parody to Richard Lovelace's "To Lucasta" (page 667), list the elements that Fehler keeps from the original and those he adds.
2. What ideals motivate the speaker of Lovelace's poem? What ideals motivate Fehler's free agent?

Aaron Abeyta (b. 1971)

thirteen ways of looking at a tortilla   2001

       i.
among twenty different tortillas
the only thing moving
was the mouth of the niño

       ii.
i was of three cultures
like a tortilla   5
for which there are three bolios

       iii.
the tortilla grew on the wooden table
it was a small part of the earth

       iv.
a house and a tortilla
are one   10
a man a woman and a tortilla
are one

       v.
i do not know which to prefer
the beauty of the red wall
or the beauty of the green wall   15
the tortilla fresh
or just after

vi.

tortillas filled the small kitchen
with ancient shadows
the shadow of Maclovia
cooking long ago
the tortilla
rolled from the shadow
the innate roundness

vii.

o thin viejos of chimayo
why do you imagine biscuits
do you not see how the tortilla
lives with the hands
of the women about you

viii.

i know soft corn
and beautiful inescapable sopapillas
but i know too
that the tortilla
has taught me what I know

ix.

when the tortilla is gone
it marks the end
of one of many tortillas

x.

at the sight of tortillas
browning on a black comal
even the pachucos of española
would cry out sharply

xi.

he rode over new mexico
in a pearl low rider
once he got a flat
in that he mistook
the shadow of his spare
for a tortilla

xii.

the abuelitas are moving
the tortilla must be baking

xiii.

it was cinco de mayo all year
it was warm
and it was going to get warmer
the tortilla sat
on the frijolito plate

■ WRITING *effectively*

Arthur Waley on Writing

The Method of Translation   1919

It is commonly asserted that poetry, when literally translated, ceases to be poetry. This is often
true, and I have for that reason not attempted to
translate many poems which in the original
have pleased me quite as much as those I have
selected. But I present the ones I have chosen in
the belief that they still retain the essential
characteristics of poetry.

Arthur Waley

   I have aimed at literal translation, not paraphrase. It may be perfectly legitimate for a poet
to borrow foreign themes or material, but this
should not be called translation.

   Above all, considering imagery to be the soul
of poetry, I have avoided either adding images of
my own or suppressing those of the original.

   Any literal translation of Chinese poetry is
bound to be to some extent rhythmical, for the
rhythm of the original obtrudes itself. Translating literally, without thinking about
the meter of the version, one finds that about two lines out of three have a very definite swing similar to that of the Chinese lines. The remaining lines are just too short
or too long, a circumstance very irritating to the reader, whose ear expects the
rhythm to continue. I have therefore tried to produce regular rhythmic effects similar
to those of the original. . . . In a few instances where the English insisted on being
shorter than the Chinese, I have preferred to vary the meter of my version, rather
than pad out the line with unnecessary verbiage.

   I have not used rhyme because it is impossible to produce in English rhyme-
effects at all similar to those of the original, where the same rhyme sometimes runs
through a whole poem. Also, because the restrictions of rhyme necessarily injure
either the vigor of one's language or the literalness of one's version. I do not, at any
rate, know of any example to the contrary. What is generally known as "blank verse"
is the worst medium for translating Chinese poetry, because the essence of blank
verse is that it varies the position of its pauses, whereas in Chinese the stop always
comes at the end of the couplet.

From A Hundred and Seventy Chinese Poems

THINKING ABOUT PARODY

When the poet Elizabeth Bishop taught at Harvard, a surprising question appeared on
her take-home final exam. She asked students to write parodies of the three poets they
had studied during the semester. This assignment was not for a creative writing class,

but for her literature course on modern poetry. Bishop believed that in order to write a good parody one had to understand the original poem deeply. W. H. Auden went even further: in designing his ideal college for aspiring poets, he declared that writing parodies would be the only critical exercise in the curriculum. Consider these suggestions when trying to write a parody:

- **Steep yourself in the style of the author you plan to parody.** Choose two or three typical poems by this writer, and type them on your computer. (It's possible to learn quite a bit about the structure of a poem simply by typing it yourself.)
- **Highlight phrases, lines, or words that seem characteristic of the poet's sound and style.** Images and even punctuation may stand out as typical of the author; mark those up as well.
- **Pick one of the poems, and create a transposition that strikes you as potentially funny but still illuminates some aspect of the original.** Imagine the poem set in a different time or place. Or imagine your author taking on a markedly different subject in his or her distinctive style. Or conceive of the same ideas spoken by an altogether different person.
- **Keep your parody as close to the original poem as possible in length, form, and syntax.** You will be surprised by how much strength of expression you'll gain from drawing on your poet's line and sentence structure.
- **Have fun.** If you don't enjoy your new poem, neither will your reader.

CHECKLIST: Writing a Parody

- ☐ On your computer, type two or three poems by the poet you plan to parody.
- ☐ Highlight phrases, words, and images that seem characteristic of the poet's style.
- ☐ Identify line breaks and punctuation that seem typical.
- ☐ Choose one poem to imitate.
- ☐ Identify its form and conventions.
- ☐ Set the action in a different time or place. Or describe a different subject.
- ☐ Write your own version of the poem. Imitate length, form, and syntax as closely as you can.
- ☐ Is your parody funny?

WRITING ASSIGNMENT ON PARODY

Following the suggestions above, write a parody of any poem in this book. (If you choose a poet represented by only one work, you can find additional poems by its author at the library or on the Internet.) Follow the structure of the original as closely as possible. Bring your parody to class and read it aloud.

MORE TOPICS FOR WRITING

1. Write your own version of Horace's *carpe diem* ode. Follow the original line by line but reset the poem in your hometown (not ancient Tuscany) and address it to your best friend (not long-dead Leuconoe). Advise your friend in your new images to "seize the day."

2. Write a serious poem in the manner of Emily Dickinson, William Carlos Williams, E. E. Cummings, or any other modern poet whose work interests you and which you feel able to imitate. Try to make it good enough to slip into the poet's *Collected Poems* without anyone being the wiser. Read all the poet's poems in this book, or you can consult a larger selection or collection of the poet's work. Though it may be simplest to choose a particular poem as your model, you may echo any number of poems, if you like. It is probably a good idea to pick a subject or theme characteristic of the poet. This is a difficult project, but if you can do it even fairly well, you will know a great deal more about poetry and your poet.

3. Try your hand at a parody of Wallace Stevens's "Thirteen Ways of Looking at a Blackbird" (page 838). Take any three or four stanzas from Stevens's poem and change the central image (as Aaron Abeyta did in "thirteen ways of looking at a tortilla"). If you are feeling ambitious, you might even try to parody all thirteen sections.

28 POETRY IN SPANISH: LITERATURE OF LATIN AMERICA

Poetry belongs to all epochs:
it is man's natural form of expression.

—OCTAVIO PAZ

Most Americans experience poetry in only one language—English. Because English is a world language, with its native speakers spread across every continent, it is easy for us to underestimate the significance of poetry written in other tongues. Why is it important to experience poetry in a different language or in translation? It matters because such poetry represents and illuminates a different cultural experience. Exposure to different cultures enriches our perspectives and challenges assumptions; it also helps us to understand our own culture better.

Latin American poetry is particularly relevant to the English speaker in the United States or Canada because of the long interconnected history of the Americas. Spanish is also an important world language, spoken by over 350 million people and the primary language in over twenty countries. The vast spread of Spanish has created an enormous and prominent body of literature, an international tradition in which Latin America has gradually replaced Spain as the center. Poetry occupies a very significant place in Latin American culture—a more public place than in the United States. Poetry even forms an important part of the popular culture in Latin America, where the average person is able to name his or her favorite poets and can often recite some of their works from memory.

The tradition of Latin American poetry is long and rich. Many poets and scholars consider Sor Juana, a Catholic nun who lived in Mexico during the seventeenth century, to be the mother of Latin American poetry. Mexico's Nobel Laureate poet, Octavio Paz, acknowledges this lineage in his critical work on Sor Juana, *Traps of Faith* (1988), a quintessential book about her life and work. Sor Juana's writing was groundbreaking, not just in the context of Latin American poetry, but truly in the context of world literature, as she was the first writer in Latin America (and one of very few in her era) to address the rights of women to study and write. Her poems are also harbingers of important tendencies in Latin American poetry because of their heightened lyricism.

This lyrical quality finds new form and vitality in the works of the most widely known poets of Latin America—including César Vallejo, Pablo Neruda, Jorge Luis

Borges, and Octavio Paz. Each of these poets addresses questions of cultural and personal identity in his work. Events of the twentieth century had great impact on both the subject matter and style of Latin American poets. The Spanish Civil War (1936–1939) sent many poets who had been living in Europe back to the Americas, conscious of the political and social values being tried and tested in Europe at the time.

Latin American poetry, particularly in the twentieth century, has been marked by a recognition of the region as a unique blending of different cultures, European and indigenous, among others. It has also been marked by a variety of artistic and political movements, of which surrealism is perhaps the most influential. The works of artists such as Mexican painter Frida Kahlo coincided with a body of new writing that emphasized a blurring of fantasy and reality. Some writers, such as Vallejo, became best known for their surrealist writing, while other poets, such as Neruda and Paz, incorporated some of the elements of the movement into their styles.

Three Latin American poets were awarded the Nobel Prize in Literature in the twentieth century: Paz, Neruda, and Gabriela Mistral. (Borges, to the astonishment of many critics, never won the award, though he captured nearly every other major international literary honor.) The importance of Spanish as a global language and in literature is reflected in the recognition of the stature of Latin American writers in the world. Even when decidedly political, Latin American poetry is known for its focus on the personal experience. One does not love one's country as a symbol, José Emilio Pacheco claims; rather, one loves its people, its mountains, and three or four of its rivers.

Sor Juana

Sor Juana Inés de la Cruz is said to have been born in Nepantla, Mexico, somewhere between 1648 and 1651. In 1667, she entered the convent of the "barefoot Carmelites," so named because of the austere way of life they adopted, either going barefoot or wearing rope sandals. In 1691 she wrote her famous Reply, the first document in the Americas to argue for a woman's right to study and to write. She stated that she chose the convent life because it offered her more possibilities for engaging in intellectual pursuits than marriage at that time would allow. The Church responded by demanding she give up writing, and she renewed her vows to the Church, signing documents in her own blood. Sor Juana died during a devastating plague in 1695, after having given aid to a great number of the ill.

Portrait of Sister Juana Inés de la Cruz
(by unknown Mexican artist, eighteenth century)

Presente en que el Cariño Hace Regalo la Llaneza 1689	**A Simple Gift Made Rich by Affection** 2004

Lysi: a tus manos divinas
doy castañas espinosas,
porque donde sobran rosas
no pueden faltar espinas.
Si a su aspereza te inclinas
y con eso el gusto engañas,
perdona las malas mañas
de quien tal regalo te hizo;
perdona, pues que un erizo
sólo puede dar castañas.

Lysi, I give to your divine hand
these chestnuts in their thorny guise
because where velvet roses rise,
thorns also grow unchecked, unplanned.
If you're inclined toward their barbed brand   5
and with this choice, betray your taste,
forgive the ill-bred lack of taste
of one who sends you such a missive—
Forgive me, only this husk can give
the chestnut, in its thorns embraced.   10

—*Translated by Diane Thiel*

Questions

1. How would you relate the title to the content of the poem?
2. Why does the speaker reject a gift of roses? Why does she fear that her gift may be rejected by its recipient?
3. How does the chestnut function as a metaphor? What does the thorny husk seem to represent? What does the chestnut represent?

Pablo Neruda

Pablo Neruda was born Neftalí Ricardo Reyes Basoalto in 1904 in Parral, southern Chile. His mother died a month later, a fact which is said to have affected Neruda's choice of imagery throughout his life's work. He began writing poems as a child despite his family's disapproval, which led him to adopt the "working class" pen name Pablo Neruda. His early book Twenty Love Poems and a Song of Despair *(1923) received vast attention, and Neruda decided to devote himself to writing poetry.*

Neruda served in a long line of diplomatic positions. He lived several years in Spain and chronicled the Spanish Civil War. He journeyed home to Chile in 1938, then served as consul to Mexico, and returned again to Chile in 1943. When the Chilean

Pablo Neruda

government moved to the right, Neruda, who was a communist, went into hiding.

In 1952, when the Chilean government ceased its persecution of leftist writers, Neruda returned to his native land, and in 1970 was a candidate for the presidency of Chile. He was awarded the Nobel Prize in Literature in 1971. Neruda died of cancer in Santiago in 1973.

Muchos Somos 1958	**We Are Many** 1967

De tantos hombres que soy,
  que somos,
no puedo encontrar a ninguno:
se me pierden bajo la ropa,
se fueron a otra ciudad.

Of the many men who I am, who
  we are,
I can't find a single one;
they disappear among my clothes,
they've left for another city.

Cuando todo está preparado	When everything seems to be set 5
para mostrarme inteligente	to show me off as intelligent,
el tonto que llevo escondido	the fool I always keep hidden
se toma la palabra en mi boca.	takes over all that I say.
Otras veces me duermo en medio	At other times, I'm asleep
de la sociedad distinguida	among distinguished people, 10
y cuando busco en mí al valiente,	and when I look for my brave self,
un cobarde que no conozco	a coward unknown to me
corre a tomar con mi esqueleto	rushes to cover my skeleton
mil deliciosas precauciones.	with a thousand fine excuses.
Cuando arde una casa estimada	When a decent house catches fire, 15
en vez del bombero que llamo	instead of the fireman I summon,
se precipita el incendiario	an arsonist bursts on the scene,
y ése soy yo. No tengo arreglo.	and that's me. What can I do?
Qué debo hacer para escogerme?	What can I do to distinguish myself?
Cómo puedo rehabilitarme?	How can I pull myself together? 20
Todos los libros que leo	All the books I read
celebran héroes refulgentes	are full of dazzling heroes,
siempre seguros de sí mismos:	always sure of themselves.
me muero de envidia por ellos,	I die with envy of them;
y en los films de vientos y balas	and in films full of wind and bullets, 25
me quedo envidiando al jinete,	I goggle at the cowboys,
me quedo admirando al caballo.	I even admire the horses.
Pero cuando pido al intrépido	But when I call for a hero,
me sale el viejo perezoso,	out comes my lazy old self;
y así yo no sé quién soy,	so I never know who I am, 30
no sé cuántos soy o seremos.	nor how many I am or will be.
Me gustaría tocar un timbre	I'd love to be able to touch a bell
y sacar el mí verdadero	and summon the real me,
porque si yo me necesito	because if I really need myself,
no debo desaparecerme.	I mustn't disappear. 35
Mientras escribo estoy ausente	While I am writing, I'm far away;
y cuando vuelvo ya he partido:	and when I come back, I've gone.
voy a ver si a las otras gentes	I would like to know if others
les pasa lo que a mí me pasa,	go through the same things that I do,
si son tantos como soy yo,	have as many selves as I have, 40
si se parecen a sí mismos	and see themselves similarly;
y cuando lo haya averiguado	and when I've exhausted this problem,
voy a aprender tan bien las cosas	I'm going to study so hard
que para explicar mis problemas	that when I explain myself,
les hablaré de geografía.	I'll be talking geography. 45

—*Translated by Alastair Reid*

Questions

1. In line 26, Reid translates Neruda's phrase "me quedo envidiando al jinete" as "I goggle at the cowboys." What does Reid gain or lose with that version? (In Spanish, *jinete* means *horseman* or *rider* but not specifically *cowboy*, which is *vaquero* or even—thanks to

Hollywood— *cowboy*.) Neruda once told Reid, "Alastair, don't just translate my poems. I want you to improve them." Is this line an improvement?

2. How many men are in the speaker of the poem? What seems to be their relationship to one another?

Jorge Luis Borges

Luis Borges (1899–1986), a blind librarian who became one of the most important writers ever to emerge from Latin America, was born in Buenos Aires. Borges's Protestant father and Catholic mother reflected Argentina's diverse background; their ancestry included Spanish, English, Italian, Portuguese, and Indian blood. In his youth, Borges lived in Switzerland and later Spain. On returning to Argentina in 1921, he edited a poetry magazine printed in the form of a poster and affixed to city walls. In 1937, to help support his mother and dying father, the thirty-seven-year-old Borges (who still lived at home) got his first job as an assistant librarian.

Jorge Luis Borges

During this decisive period, Borges encountered political trouble. For his opposition to the regime of Colonel Juan Perón, Borges was forced in 1946 to resign his post as a librarian and was mockingly offered a job as a chicken inspector. In 1955, after Perón was deposed, Borges became director of the National Library and a professor of English literature at the University of Buenos Aires. Suffering from poor eyesight since childhood, Borges eventually went blind. Probably the most influential short story writer of the last half-century, Borges considered himself first and foremost a poet.

Amorosa Anticipación

1925

Ni la intimidad de tu frente clara como una fiesta
ni la costumbre de tu cuerpo, aún misterioso y tácito y de niña,
ni la sucesión de tu vida asumiendo palabras o silencios
serán favor tan misterioso
como mirar tu sueño implicado   5
en la vigilia de mis brazos.
Virgen milagrosamente otra vez por la virtud absolutoria del sueño,
quieta y resplandeciente como una dicha que la memoria elige,
me darás esa orilla de tu vida que tú misma no tienes.
Arrojado a quietud,   10
divisaré esa playa última de tu ser
y te veré por vez primera, quizá,
como Dios ha de verte,
desbaratada la ficción del Tiempo,
sin el amor, sin mí.   15

Anticipation of Love

1972

Neither the intimacy of your look, your brow fair as a feast day,
nor the favor of your body, still mysterious, reserved, and childlike,
nor what comes to me of your life, settling in words or silence,
will be so mysterious a gift
as the sight of your sleep, enfolded   5
in the vigil of my arms.
Virgin again, miraculously, by the absolving power of sleep,
quiet and luminous like some happy thing recovered by memory,
you will give me that shore of your life that you yourself do not own.
Cast up into silence   10
I shall discern that ultimate beach of your being
and see you for the first time, perhaps,
as God must see you—
the fiction of Time destroyed,
free from love, from me.   15

—*Translated by Robert Fitzgerald*

Questions

1. In "Anticipation of Love," note the translator's choice in line 4 to translate the Spanish "*favor*" (which translates more directly to "favor") as "gift." What do you think such a choice adds to the poem in English?
2. Why is the sleeping woman described as "virgin again"?
3. Does this poem describe a real event or only an imaginary one?

Octavio Paz

Octavio Paz, the only Mexican author to win the Nobel Prize in Literature, was born in Mexico City in 1914. Paz once commented that he came from "a typical Mexican family" because it combined European and Indian ancestors. "Impoverished by the revolution and civil war," his family lived in his grandfather's huge, crumbling house in Mixoac, a suburb of Mexico City, where they abandoned rooms one by one as the roof collapsed. His grandfather had a library containing over six thousand books where the young author immersed himself. Joining his father in exile, the young Paz lived for two years in Los Angeles, and later went to Spain to fight in the Spanish Civil War. In the highly political world of Latin American letters, Paz refused to adopt the political opinions of the two extremes—military dictatorship or Marxist revolution—but worked toward democracy, "the mystery of freedom," as he called it in an early poem.

Octavio Paz

In 1945 Paz became a diplomat, spending years in San Francisco, New York, Geneva, and Delhi. In 1968 he resigned his post as ambassador to India in protest of the Mexican government's massacre of student demonstrators shortly before the Mexico City

Olympic games. Paz then taught abroad at several universities, but he always returned to Mexico City, where he died in 1998.

Con los ojos cerrados 1968	**With eyes closed** 1986
Con los ojos cerrados	With eyes closed
Te iluminas por dentro	you light up within
Ertes la piedra ciega	you are blind stone
Noche a noche te labro	Night after night I carve you
Con los ojos cerrados	with eyes closed
Eres la piedra franca	you are frank stone
Nos volvemos inmensos	We have become enormous
Sólo por conocernos	just knowing each other
Con los ojos cerrados	with eyes closed

—*Translated by Eliot Weinberger*

Question

How does the refrain contribute to the musical quality of "With eyes closed"?

SURREALISM IN LATIN AMERICAN POETRY

Surrealism was one of the great artistic revolutions of the twentieth century. It first arose in the mockingly named "Dada" movement during World War I. (*Dada* is the French children's word for "rocking horse.") Dadaism announced itself as the radical rejection of the insanity perpetrated by the self-proclaimed "rational" world of the turbulent modern era. The approach was an attempt to shock the world out of its terrible self-destructive traditions. "The only way for Dada to continue," proclaimed poet André Breton, "is for it to cease to exist." Sure enough, the movement soon fell apart through its own excesses of energy, irreverence, and absurdism.

In 1922 **Surrealism** emerged as the successor to Dada, first as a literary movement, soon to spread to the visual arts. Surrealism also sought to free art from the bounds of rationality, promoting the creation of fantastic, dreamlike works that reflected the unconscious mind.

Surrealism emphasized spontaneity rather than craft as the essential element in literary creation. Not all Surrealist art, however, was spontaneous. Breton, for instance, spent six months on a poem of thirty words, in order to achieve what looked like spontaneity. And many Surrealist visual artists would do several versions of the same "automatic drawing" in pursuit of the effect of immediacy. Breton's famous "Manifesto of Surrealism" (1924) launched a movement that continues to influence a great number of writers and artists around the world.

The early Surrealists showed as much genius for absurd humor as for art, and their works often tried to shock and amuse. Marcel Duchamp once exhibited a huge printed reproduction of the *Mona Lisa* on which he had painted a large mustache. Louis Aragon's poem "Suicide" consisted only of the letters of the alphabet, and Breton once published a poem made up of names and numbers copied from the telephone directory. Is it any wonder that the Surrealist motto was "The approval of the public must be shunned at all cost"?

Surrealism's greatest international literary influence was on Latin American poetry. In the early twentieth century, Latin America was much influenced by French culture, and literary innovations in Paris were quickly imported to Mexico City, Buenos Aires, and other New World capitals. In Latin America, however, Surrealism lost much of the playfulness it exhibited in Europe, and the movement often took on a darker and more explicitly political quality. According to Octavio Paz, many poets, such as himself, César Vallejo, and Pablo Neruda, adopted Surrealist processes, and their creative developments often coincided with the movement, although their work is not usually considered "Surrealist."

Surrealism also had a powerful effect on Latin American art. A tradition of Surrealist painting emerged parallel to the movement in literature. One of the best known Surrealist painters is the Mexican artist Frida Kahlo, whose work often created dreamlike visions of the human body, especially her own. In *The Two Fridas*, for example, she presents a frightening image of the body's interior exposed and mirrored. Kahlo's paintings are simultaneously personal and political—surrealistically portraying her own trauma as well as the schism in her native country.

The Two Fridas by Frida Kahlo (1907–1954), c. 1939.

César Vallejo (1892?–1938)

La cólera que quiebra al hombre en niños

(1937) 1939

La cólera que quiebra al hombre en niños,
que quiebra al niño, en pájaros iguales,
y al pájaro, después, en huevecillos;
la cólera del pobre
tiene un aceite contra dos vinagres.   5

La cólera que el árbol quiebra en hojas,
a la hoja en botones desiguales
y al botón, en ranuras telescópicas;
la cólera del pobre
tiene dos ríos contra muchos mares.   10

La cólera que quiebra al bien en dudas,
a la duda, en tres arcos semejantes
y al arco, luego, en tumbas imprevistas;
la cólera del pobre
tiene un acero contra dos puñales.   15

La cólera que quiebra el alma en cuerpos,
al cuerpo en órganos desemejantes
y al órgano, en octavos pensamientos;
la cólera del pobre
tiene un fuego central contra dos cráteres.   20

Anger

1977

Anger which breaks a man into children,
Which breaks the child into two equal birds,
And after that the bird into a pair of little eggs:
The poor man's anger
Has one oil against two vinegars.   5

Anger which breaks a tree into leaves
And the leaf into unequal buds
And the bud into telescopic grooves;
The poor man's anger
Has two rivers against many seas.   10

Anger which breaks good into doubts
And doubt into three similar arcs
And then the arc into unexpected tombs,
The poor man's anger
Has one steel against two daggers.   15

Anger which breaks the soul into bodies
And the body into dissimilar organs
And the organ into octave thoughts;
The poor man's anger
Has one central fire against two craters.   20

—*Translated by Thomas Merton*

CONTEMPORARY MEXICAN POETRY

José Emilio Pacheco   (b. 1939)

Alta Traición   1969

No amo mi Patria. Su fulgor abstracto
es inasible.
Pero (aunque suene mal) daría la vida
por diez lugares suyos, cierta gente.
Puertos, bosques de piños, fortalezas,   5
una ciudad deshecha, gris, monstruosa,
varias figuras de su historia,
montañas
(y tres o cuatro ríos)

High Treason   1978

I do not love my country. Its abstract lustre
is beyond my grasp.
But (although it sounds bad) I would give my life
for ten places in it, for certain people,
seaports, pinewoods, fortresses,   5
a run-down city, gray, grotesque,
various figures from its history,
mountains
(and three or four rivers).

—Translated by Alastair Reid

Tedi López Mills   (b. 1959)

Convalecencia   2000

Moscas de todas las horas.
    —Antonio Machado

el rasguño de esta fiebre
y la mosca del aire
son como un ruido primario
en el espectro de sonidos
un estruendo rojo y sin matiz
el primer fierro en la oreja
el primer filo de la sierra
el primer chillido del garabato en la letra
la primera gota del agua
en un círculo vacío
el primer golpe del martillo
contra un muro y la piedra
el primer grito insumiso junto a la reja
el primer clavo en la luz del mediodía
el cristal predilecto del ojo

Convalescence   2000

Houseflies of all day long.
    —Antonio Machado

this feverish scratch
and the fly in flight
are like primal noises
in the spectrum of sounds
a traceless red din   5
the first iron in the ear
the first cutting of the saw
the first screeching scribble of letters
the first drop of water
in an empty circle   10
the first blow of the hammer
against a wall and the stone
the first unruly scream beside the gate
the first nail in midday light
the favored windowpane of the eye   15

donde la mosca y yo	where the fly and I
en la celda del cráneo	inside the jail cell of the skull
nos oímos	hear each other

—Translated by Cheryl Clark

Francisco Segovia (b. 1958)

Cada árbol en su sombra	**Every Tree in Its Shadow** 2006
Cada árbol en su sombra	Every tree in its shadow
cobija un dios distinto.	shelters a different god.
En su erguida soledad	In its uplifted solitude
lo mece, le susurra	it rocks him, whispers to him,
y a él se fía en su secreto.	confides its secrets in him. 5
Cada árbol en su sombra	Every tree in its shadow
hace espesura de una fe	makes foliage from a faith
que no nació con él	that wasn't born with him
ni acabará en el tiempo.	and won't come to an end.
Cada árbol en su sombra siente	Every tree in its shadow feels 10
esa hondura de inmateria	the depth of the immaterial
que también sienten los hombres	that men also feel
cuando miran de lejos a los niños.	when they watch children from a distance.
Y sólo de cuando en cuando,	And every once in a while,
cuando se nubla el día, reconocen	when it clouds up, they learn 15
que una sombra más vasta y más honda	that a deeper and vaster shadow
los cobija también a ellos.	shelters them, too,
Y los mece y les susurra	and rocks them, and whispers to them
cuando llueve.	as it rains.

—Translated by Don Share with César Perez

■ WRITING *effectively*

Alastair Reid on Writing (b. 1926)

Translating Neruda   1996

Translating someone's work, poetry in particular, has something about it akin to being possessed, haunted. Translating a poem means not only reading it deeply and deciphering it, but clambering about backstage among the props and the scaffolding. I found I could no longer read a poem of Neruda's simply as words on a page without hearing behind them that languid, caressing voice. Most important to me in translating these two writers [Neruda and Borges] was the sound of their voices in my memory, for it very much helped in finding the English appropriate to those voices. I found that if I learned poems of Neruda's by heart I could replay them at odd moments, on buses, at wakeful times in the night, until, at a certain point, the translation would somehow set. The voice was the clue: I felt that all Neruda's poems were fundamentally vocative—spoken poems, poems of direct address—and that Neruda's voice was in a sense the instrument for which he wrote. He once made a tape for me, reading pieces of different poems, in different tones and rhythms. I played it over so many times that I can hear it in my head at will. Two lines of his I used to repeat like a Zen koan, for they seemed to apply particularly to translating:

> in this net it's not just the strings that count
> but also the air that escapes through the meshes.

He often wrote of himself as having many selves, just as he had left behind him several very different poetic manners and voices.

From "Neruda and Borges"

WRITING ASSIGNMENT ON SPANISH POETRY

Compare the three love poems in this chapter—Sor Juana's "A Simple Gift Made Rich by Affection," Jorge Luis Borges's "Anticipation of Love," and Octavio Paz's "With eyes closed." Analyze each poem's presentation of the beloved and contrast it to the presentations in the other poems.

MORE TOPICS FOR WRITING

1. Consider the surreal effects in César Vallejo's "Anger" as well as in Frida Kahlo's painting *The Two Fridas*.
2. Consider the way personal and political themes merge in José Emilio Pacheco's "High Treason" or César Vallejo's "Anger."

29 RECOGNIZING EXCELLENCE

Poetry is life distilled.

—GWENDOLYN BROOKS

Why do we call some poems "bad"? We are not talking about their moral implications. Rather, we mean that, for one or more of many possible reasons, the poem has failed to move us or to engage our sympathies. Instead, it has made us doubt that the poet is in control of language and vision; perhaps it has aroused our antipathies or unwittingly appealed to our sense of the comic, though the poet is serious. Some poems can be said to succeed despite burdensome faults. But in general such faults are symptoms of a deeper malady: some weakness in a poem's basic conception or in the poet's competence.

Nearly always, a bad poem reveals only a dim and distorted awareness of its probable effect on its audience. Perhaps the sound of words may clash with what a poem is saying, as in the jarring last word of this opening line of a tender lyric (author unknown, quoted by Richard Wilbur): "Come into the tent, my love, and close the flap." A bad poem usually overshoots or falls short of its mark by the poet's thinking too little or too much.

In a poem that has a rime scheme or a set line length, when all is well, pattern and structure move inseparably with the rest of the poem, the way a tiger's skin and bones move with the tiger. But sometimes, in a poem that fails, the poet evidently has had difficulty in fitting the statements into a formal pattern. English poets have long felt free to invert word order for a special effect (Milton: "ye myrtles brown"). This change of normal word order, usually done for purposes of meter or rime, is called **poetic inversion**. The poet having trouble keeping to a rime scheme may invert words for no apparent reason but convenience. Needing a rime for *barge* may lead to ending a line with *a police dog large* instead of *a large police dog*. Another sign of trouble is a profusion of adjectives. If a line of iambic pentameter reads "Her lovely skin, like dear sweet white old silk," we suspect the poet of stuffing the line to make it long enough.

Even great poets write awful poems, and after their deaths, their worst efforts are collected with their masterpieces with no consumer warning labels to inform the reader. Some lines in the canon of celebrated bards make us wonder, "How could they have written this?" Wordsworth, Shelley, Whitman, and Browning are among the great whose failures can be painful, and sometimes an excellent poem will have a bad spot in it. To be unwilling to read them, though, would be as ill advised as to refuse to see Venice just because the Grand Canal is said to contain impurities. The seasoned reader of poetry thinks no less of Tennyson for having written "Form, Form, Riflemen Form! . . . // Look to your butts, and take good aims!" The collected works of a duller poet may contain no such lines of unconscious double meaning, but neither do they contain any poem as good as "Ulysses." If the duller poet never had a spectacular failure, it may be because of a failure to take risks. "In poetry," said Ronsard, "the greatest vice is mediocrity."

Often, inept poems fall into familiar categories. At one extreme is the poem written entirely in conventional diction, dimly echoing Shakespeare, Wordsworth, and the Bible, but garbling them. Couched in a rhythm that ticks along like a metronome, this kind of poem shows no sign that its author has ever taken a hard look at anything that can be tasted, handled, or felt. It employs loosely and thoughtlessly the most abstract of words: *love, beauty, life, death, time, eternity*. Littered with old-fashioned contractions (*'tis, o'er, where'er*), it may end in a simple preachment or platitude. George Orwell's complaint against much contemporary writing (not only poetry) is applicable: "As soon as certain topics are raised"—and one thinks of such standard topics for poetry as spring, a first kiss, and stars—"the concrete melts into the abstract and no one seems able to think of turns of speech that are not hackneyed."

At the opposite extreme is the poem that displays no acquaintance with poetry of the past but manages, instead, to fabricate its own clichés. Slightly paraphrased, a manuscript once submitted to the *Paris Review* began:

Vile
  rottenflush
            o   —*screaming*—
        f CORPSEBLOOD!!   ooze
STRANGLE my
        eyes...
                    HELL's
        O, ghastly   stench**!!!

At most, such a work has only a private value. The writer has vented personal frustrations upon words, instead of kicking stray dogs. In its way, "Vile Rottenflush" is as self-indulgent as the oldfangled "first kiss in spring" kind of poem. "I dislike," said John Livingston Lowes, "poems that black your eyes, or put up their mouths to be kissed."

As jewelers tell which of two diamonds is fine by seeing which scratches the other, two poems may be tested by comparing them. This method works only on poems similar in length and kind: an epigram cannot be held up to test an epic. Most poems we meet are neither sheer trash nor obvious masterpieces. Because good diamonds to be proven need softer ones to scratch, in this chapter you will find a few clear-cut gems and a few clinkers.

Anonymous (English)

O Moon, when I gaze on thy beautiful face   (about 1900)

O Moon, when I gaze on thy beautiful face,
Careering along through the boundaries of space,
The thought has often come into my mind
If I ever shall see thy glorious behind.

O MOON. Sir Edmund Gosse, the English critic (1849–1928), offered this quatrain as the work of his servant, but there is reason to suspect him of having written it.

Questions

1. To what fact of astronomy does the last line refer?
2. Which words seem chosen with too little awareness of their denotations and connotations?
3. Even if you did not know that these lines probably were deliberately bad, how would you argue with someone who maintained that the opening O in the poem was admirable as a bit of concrete poetry?

Emily Dickinson (1830–1886)

A Dying Tiger – moaned for Drink   (about 1862)

A Dying Tiger – moaned for Drink –
I hunted all the Sand –
I caught the Dripping of a Rock
And bore it in my Hand –

His Mighty Balls – in death were thick –   5
But searching – I could see
A Vision on the Retina
Of Water – and of me –

'Twas not my blame – who sped too slow –
'Twas not his blame – who died   10
While I was reaching him –
But 'twas – the fact that He was dead –

Questions

How does this poem compare in success with other poems of Emily Dickinson that you know? Justify your opinion by pointing to some of this poem's particulars.

Exercise: Ten Terrible Moments in Poetry

Here is a small anthology of bad moments in poetry.
For what reasons does each selection fail?
In which passages do you attribute the failure
   to inappropriate sound or diction?
   to awkward word order?
   to inaccurate metaphor?
   to excessive overstatement?
   to forced rime?
   to monotonous rhythm?
   to redundancy?
   to simple-mindedness or excessive ingenuity?

1. Last lines of *Enoch Arden* by Alfred, Lord Tennyson:

   > So past the strong heroic soul away.
   > And when they buried him, the little port
   > Had seldom seen a costlier funeral.

2. From *Purely Original Verse* (1891) by J. Gordon Coogler (1865–1901), of Columbia, South Carolina:

   > Alas for the South, her books have grown fewer—
   > She never was much given to literature.

3. From "Lines Written to a Friend on the Death of His Brother, Caused by a Railway Train Running Over Him Whilst He Was in a State of Inebriation" by James Henry Powell:

> Thy mangled corpse upon the rails in frightful shape was found.
> The ponderous train had killed thee as its heavy wheels went round,
> And thus in dreadful form thou met'st a drunkard's awful death
> And I, thy brother, mourn thy fate, and breathe a purer breath.

4. From *Dolce Far Niente* by the American poet Francis Saltus Saltus, who flourished in the 1890s:

> Her laugh is like sunshine, full of glee,
> And her sweet breath smells like fresh-made tea.

5. From another gem by Francis Saltus Saltus, "The Spider":

> Then all thy feculent majesty recalls
>   The nauseous mustiness of forsaken bowers,
> The leprous nudity of deserted halls—
>   The positive nastiness of sullied flowers.
>
> And I mark the colours yellow and black
>   That fresco thy lithe, dictatorial thighs,
> I dream and wonder on my drunken back
>   How God could possibly have created flies!

6. From "Song to the Suliotes" by George Gordon, Lord Byron:

> Up to battle! Sons of Suli
> Up, and do your duty duly!
> There the wall—and there the moat is:
> Bouwah! Bouwah! Suliotes,
> There is booty—there is beauty!
> Up my boys and do your duty!

7. From a juvenile poem of John Dryden, "Upon the Death of the Lord Hastings" (a victim of smallpox):

> Each little pimple had a tear in it,
> To wail the fault its rising did commit . . .

8. From "The Abbey Mason" by Thomas Hardy:

> When longer yet dank death had wormed
> The brain wherein the style had germed
>
> From Gloucester church it flew afar—
> The style called Perpendicular.—
>
> To Winton and to Westminster
> It ranged, and grew still beautifuller . . .

9. A metaphor from "The Crucible of Life" by the once-popular American newspaper poet Edgar A. Guest:

> Sacred and sweet is the joy that must come
> From the furnace of life when you've poured off the scum.

10. From an elegy for Queen Victoria by one of her subjects:

> Dust to dust, and ashes to ashes,
> Into the tomb the Great Queen dashes.

SENTIMENTALITY

Sentimentality is a failure of writers who seem to feel a great emotion but who fail to give us sufficient grounds for sharing it. The emotion may be an anger greater than its object seems to call for, as in these lines by Ali Hilmi to a girl who caused scandal (the exact nature of her act never being specified): "The gossip in each hall / Will curse your name . . . / Go! better cast yourself right down the falls!" Or it may be an enthusiasm quite unwarranted by its subject: in *The Fleece* John Dyer temptingly describes the pleasures of life in a workhouse for the poor. The sentimental poet is especially prone to tenderness. Great tears fill his eyes at a glimpse of an aged grandmother sitting by a hearth. For all the poet knows, she may be the manager of a casino in Las Vegas who would be startled to find herself an object of pity, but the sentimentalist doesn't care to know about the woman herself. She is a general excuse for feeling maudlin. Any other conventional object will serve as well: a faded valentine, the strains of an old song, a baby's cast-off pacifier. An instance of such emotional self-indulgence is "The Old Oaken Bucket," by Samuel Woodworth, a stanza of which goes:

> How sweet from the green, mossy brim to receive it,
>   As, poised on the curb, it inclined to my lips!
> Not a full-flushing goblet could tempt me to leave it,
>   Tho' filled with the nectar that Jupiter sips.
> And now, far removed from the loved habitation,
>   The tear of regret will intrusively swell,
> As fancy reverts to my father's plantation,
>   And sighs for the bucket that hung in the well.

Bathos

The staleness of the phrasing and imagery (Jove's nectar, *tear of regret*) suggests that the speaker is not even seeing the actual physical bucket, and the tripping meter of the lines is inappropriate to an expression of tearful regret. Perhaps the poet's nostalgia is genuine. Indeed, as Keith Waldrop has put it, "a bad poem is always sincere." However sincere in their feelings, sentimental poets fail as artists because they cannot separate their own emotional responses from those of the disinterested reader. Wet-eyed and sighing for a bucket, Woodworth achieves not pathos but **bathos**: a description that can move us to laughter instead of tears. Tears, of course, can be shed for good reason. A piece of sentimentality is not to be confused with a well-wrought poem whose tone is tenderness. Bathos in poetry can also mean an abrupt fall from the sublime to the trivial or incongruous. A sample, from Nicholas Rowe's play *The Fair Penitent:* "Is it the voice of thunder, or my father?" Another, from John Close, a minor Victorian: "Around their heads a dazzling halo shone, / No need of mortal robes, or any hat."

Rod McKuen (b. 1933)

Thoughts on Capital Punishment   1954

There ought to be capital punishment for cars
that run over rabbits and drive into dogs
and commit the unspeakable, unpardonable crime
of killing a kitty cat still in his prime.

Purgatory, at the very least
                    should await the driver
     driving over a beast.

Those hurrying headlights coming out of the dark
that scatter the scampering squirrels in the park
should await the best jury that one might compose
of fatherless chipmunks and husbandless does.

And then found guilty, after too fair a trial
should be caged in a cage with a hyena's smile
or maybe an elephant with an elephant gun
should shoot out his eyes when the verdict is done.

There ought to be something, something that's fair
to avenge Mrs. Badger as she waits in her lair
for her husband who lies with his guts spilling out
cause he didn't know what automobiles are about.

Hell on the highway, at the very least
                    should await the driver
     driving over a beast.

Who kills a man kills a bit of himself
But a cat too is an extension of God.

5

10

15

20

William Stafford (1914–1993)

Traveling Through the Dark   1962

Traveling through the dark I found a deer
dead on the edge of the Wilson River road.
It is usually best to roll them into the canyon:
that road is narrow; to swerve might make more dead.

By glow of the tail-light I stumbled back of the car
and stood by the heap, a doe, a recent killing;
she had stiffened already, almost cold.
I dragged her off; she was large in the belly.

My fingers touching her side brought me the reason—
her side was warm; her fawn lay there waiting,
alive, still, never to be born.
Beside that mountain road I hesitated.

The car aimed ahead its lowered parking lights;
under the hood purred the steady engine.
I stood in the glare of the warm exhaust turning red;
around our group I could hear the wilderness listen.

I thought hard for us all—my only swerving—
then pushed her over the edge into the river.

5

10

15

Questions

1. Compare these poems by Rod McKuen and William Stafford. How are they similar?
2. Explain Stafford's title. Who are all those traveling through the dark?
3. Comment on McKuen's use of language. Consider especially: *unspeakable, unpardonable crime* (line 3), *kitty cat* (4), *scatter the scampering squirrels* (9), and *cause he didn't know* (19).
4. Compare the meaning of Stafford's last two lines and McKuen's last two. Does either poem have a moral? Can either poem be said to moralize?
5. Which poem might be open to the charge of sentimentality? Why?

RECOGNIZING EXCELLENCE

How can we tell an excellent poem from any other? With poetry, explaining excellence is harder than explaining failure (so often due to familiar kinds of imprecision and sentimentality). A bad poem tends to be stereotyped, an excellent poem unique. In judging either, we can have no absolute specifications. A poem is not like an electric toaster that an inspector can test using a check-off list. It has to be judged on the basis of what it is trying to be and how well it succeeds in the effort.

To judge a poem, we first have to understand it. At least, we need to understand it *almost* all the way; to be sure, there are poems such as Hopkins's "The Windhover" (page 1055), which most readers probably would call excellent even though its meaning is still being debated. Although it is a good idea to give a poem at least a couple of considerate readings before judging it, sometimes our first encounter starts turning into an act of evaluation. Moving along into the poem, becoming more deeply involved in it, we may begin forming an opinion. In general, the more a poem contains for us to understand, the more rewarding we are likely to find it. Of course, an obscure and highly demanding poem is not always to be preferred to a relatively simple one. Difficult poems can be pretentious and incoherent; still, there is something to be said for the poem complicated enough to leave us something to discover on our fifteenth reading (unlike most limericks, which yield their all at a look). Here is such a poem, one not readily fathomed and exhausted.

William Butler Yeats (1865–1939)

Sailing to Byzantium   1927

That is no country for old men. The young
In one another's arms, birds in the trees
—Those dying generations—at their song,
The salmon-falls, the mackerel-crowded seas,
Fish, flesh, or fowl, commend all summer long   5
Whatever is begotten, born, and dies.
Caught in that sensual music all neglect
Monuments of unaging intellect.

An aged man is but a paltry thing,
A tattered coat upon a stick, unless   10
Soul clap its hands and sing, and louder sing
For every tatter in its mortal dress,
Nor is there singing school but studying
Monuments of its own magnificence;
And therefore I have sailed the seas and come   15
To the holy city of Byzantium.

O sages standing in God's holy fire
As in the gold mosaic of a wall,
Come from the holy fire, perne in a gyre,°   *spin down a spiral*
And be the singing-masters of my soul.
Consume my heart away; sick with desire   20
And fastened to a dying animal
It knows not what it is; and gather me
Into the artifice of eternity.

Once out of nature I shall never take   25
My bodily form from any natural thing,
But such a form as Grecian goldsmiths make
Of hammered gold and gold enameling
To keep a drowsy Emperor awake;
Or set upon a golden bough to sing   30
To lords and ladies of Byzantium
Of what is past, or passing, or to come.

SAILING TO BYZANTIUM. Byzantium was the capital of the Byzantine Empire, the city now called Istanbul. Yeats means, though, not merely the physical city. Byzantium is also a name for his conception of paradise.

Though *salmon-falls* (line 4) suggests Yeats's native Ireland, the poem, as we find out in line 25, is about escaping from the entire natural world. If the poet desires this escape, then probably the *country* mentioned in the opening line is no political nation but the cycle of birth and death in which human beings are trapped; and, indeed, the poet says his heart is "fastened to a dying animal." Imaginary landscapes, it would seem, are merging with the historical Byzantium. Lines 17–18 refer to mosaic images, adornments of the Byzantine cathedral of St. Sophia, in which the figures of saints are inlaid against backgrounds of gold. The clockwork bird of the last stanza is also a reference to something actual. Yeats noted: "I have read somewhere that in the Emperor's palace at Byzantium was a tree made of gold and silver, and artificial birds that sang." This description of the role the poet would seek—that of a changeless, immortal singer—directs us back to the earlier references to music and singing. Taken all together, they point toward the central metaphor of the poem: the craft of poetry can be a kind of singing. One kind of everlasting monument is a great poem. To study masterpieces of poetry is the only "singing school"—the only way to learn to write a poem.

We have no more than skimmed through a few of this poem's suggestions, enough to show that, out of allusion and imagery, Yeats has woven at least one elaborate metaphor. Surely one thing the poem achieves is that, far from merely puzzling us, it makes us aware of relationships between what a person can imagine and the physical world. There is the statement that a human heart is bound to the body that perishes, and yet it is possible to see consciousness for a moment independent of flesh, to sing with joy at the very fact that the body is crumbling away. Much of the power of Yeats's poem comes from the physical terms with which he states the ancient quarrel between body and spirit, body being a "tattered coat upon a stick." There is all the difference in the world between the work of the poet like Yeats whose eye is on the living thing and whose mind is awake and passionate, and that of the slovenly poet whose dull eye and sleepy mind focus on nothing more than some book read hastily long ago. The former writes a poem out of compelling need, the latter as if it seems a nice idea to write something.

Yeats's poem has the three qualities essential to beauty, according to the definition of Thomas Aquinas: wholeness, harmony, and radiance. The poem is all one; its parts move in peace with one another; it shines with emotional intensity. There is an orderly progression going on in it: from the speaker's statement of his discontent with the world of "sensual music" to his statement that he is quitting this world, to his prayer that the sages will take him in, and his vision of future immortality. And the images of the poem relate to one another—*dying generations* (line 3), *dying animal* (line 22), and the undying golden bird (lines 27–32)—to mention just one series of related things. "Sailing to Byzantium" is not the kind of poem that has, in Pope's words, "One simile, that solitary shines / In the dry desert of a thousand lines." Rich in figurative language, Yeats's whole poem develops a metaphor, with further metaphors as its tributaries.

"Sailing to Byzantium" has a theme that matters to us. What human being does not long, at times, to shed timid, imperfect flesh, to live in a state of absolute joy, unperishing? Being human, perhaps we too are stirred by Yeats's prayer: "Consume my heart away; sick with desire / And fastened to a dying animal. . . ." If it is true that in poetry, as Ezra Pound declared, "only emotion endures," then Yeats's poem ought to endure. (If you happen not to feel moved by this poem, try another—but come back to "Sailing to Byzantium" after a while.)

Most excellent poems, it might be argued, contain significant themes, as does "Sailing to Byzantium." But the presence of such a theme is not enough to render a poem excellent. No theme alone makes an excellent poem, but rather how well the theme is stated.

Yeats's poem, some would say, is a match for any lyric in our language. Some might call it inferior to an epic (to Milton's *Paradise Lost*, say, or to the *Iliad*), but to make this claim is to lead us into a different argument: whether certain genres are innately better than others. Such an argument usually leads to a dead end. Evidently, *Paradise Lost* has greater range, variety, matter, length, and ambitiousness. But any poem—whether an epic or an epigram—may be judged by how well it fulfills the design it undertakes. God, who created both fleas and whales, pronounced all good. Fleas, like epigrams, have no reason to feel inferior.

Exercise: **Two Poems to Compare**

Here are two poems with a similar theme. Which contains more qualities of excellent poetry? Decide whether the other is bad or whether it may be praised for achieving something different.

Arthur Guiterman (1871–1943)

On the Vanity of Earthly Greatness   1936

The tusks that clashed in mighty brawls
Of mastodons, are billiard balls.

The sword of Charlemagne the Just
Is ferric oxide, known as rust.

The grizzly bear whose potent hug   5
Was feared by all, is now a rug.

Great Caesar's bust is on the shelf,
And I don't feel so well myself.

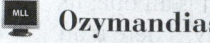

Percy Bysshe Shelley (1792–1822)

Ozymandias   1818

I met a traveler from an antique land
Who said: Two vast and trunkless legs of stone
Stand in the desert. . . . Near them, on the sand,
Half sunk, a shattered visage lies, whose frown,
And wrinkled lip, and sneer of cold command,   5
Tell that its sculptor well those passions read
Which yet survive, stamped on these lifeless things,
The hand that mocked° them, and the heart that fed: *imitated*
And on the pedestal these words appear:
"My name is Ozymandias, king of kings: 10
Look on my works, ye Mighty, and despair!"
Nothing beside remains. Round the decay
Of that colossal wreck, boundless and bare
The lone and level sands stretch far away.

Conventions and Conceits

Some excellent poems of the past will remain sealed to us unless we are willing to sympathize with their conventions. A **convention** is any established feature or technique that is commonly understood by both authors and readers. Pastoral poetry, for instance—Marlowe's "Passionate Shepherd" and Milton's "Lycidas"—asks us to accept certain conventions and situations that may seem old-fashioned: idle swains, oaten flutes. We are under no grim duty, of course, to admire poems whose conventions do not appeal to us. But there is no point in blaming a poet for playing a particular game or for observing its rules.

Bad poems, of course, can be woven together out of conventions, like patchwork quilts made of old unwanted words. In Shakespeare's England, poets were busily imitating the sonnets of Petrarch, the Italian poet whose praise of his beloved Laura had become well known. The result of their industry was a surplus of Petrarchan **conceits**, or elaborate comparisons (from the Italian *concetto*: concept, bright idea). In a famous sonnet ("My mistress' eyes are nothing like the sun," page 1084), Shakespeare, who at times helped himself generously from the Petrarchan stockpile, pokes fun at poets who thoughtlessly use such handed-down figures of speech.

There is no predictable pattern for poetic excellence. A reader needs to remain open to surprise and innovation. Remember, too, that a superb poem is not necessarily an uplifting one—full of noble sentiments and inspiring ideas. Some powerful poems deal with difficult and even unpleasant subjects. What matters is the compelling quality of the presentation, the evocative power of the language, and the depth of feeling and perception achieved by the total work. William Trevor once defined the short story as "an explosion of truth"; the same notion applies to poetry, with a special reminder that not all truths are pleasant. Robert Hayden's "The Whipping," for example, is a memorable but disturbing poem on a difficult subject, child abuse. Notice how Hayden refuses to sensationalize the topic into sociological clichés but instead reaches for its deeper human significance—not only for the victim, but also for the victimizer and even the observer.

Robert Hayden (1913–1980)

The Whipping 1962

The old woman across the way
  is whipping the boy again
and shouting to the neighborhood
  her goodness and his wrongs.

Wildly he crashes through elephant ears, 5
  pleads in dusty zinnias,
while she in spite of crippling fat
  pursues and corners him.

She strikes and strikes the shrilly circling
  boy till the stick breaks 10
in her hand. His tears are rainy weather
  to woundlike memories:

My head gripped in bony vise
  of knees, the writhing struggle
to wrench free, the blows, the fear 15
  worse than blows that hateful

Words could bring, the face that I
  no longer knew or loved. . . .
Well, it is over now, it is over,
  and the boy sobs in his room, 20

And the woman leans muttering against
  a tree, exhausted, purged—
avenged in part for lifelong hidings
  she has had to bear.

Questions

1. Who is the speaker of the poem? What is the speaker's relation to the people he observes in the opening stanza?
2. How does the scene being depicted change in the fourth stanza? Who are the people depicted here?
3. What reason does the speaker give for the old woman's violence? Does the speaker feel her reason is adequate to excuse her behavior?
4. How would you summarize the theme of this poem?

Sometimes poets use conventions in an innovative way, stretching the rules for new expressive ends. Here Elizabeth Bishop takes the form of the villanelle and bends the rules to give her poem a heartbreaking effect.

Elizabeth Bishop (1911–1979)

One Art 1976

The art of losing isn't hard to master;
so many things seem filled with the intent
to be lost that their loss is no disaster.

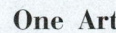

Lose something every day. Accept the fluster
of lost door keys, the hour badly spent.   5
The art of losing isn't hard to master.

Then practice losing farther, losing faster:
places, and names, and where it was you meant
to travel. None of these will bring disaster.

I lost my mother's watch. And look! my last, or   10
next-to-last, of three loved houses went.
The art of losing isn't hard to master.

I lost two cities, lovely ones. And, vaster,
some realms I owned, two rivers, a continent.
I miss them, but it wasn't a disaster.   15

—Even losing you (the joking voice, a gesture
I love) I shan't have lied. It's evident
the art of losing's not too hard to master
though it may look like (*Write* it!) like disaster.

Questions

1. What things has the speaker lost? Put together a complete list in the order she reveals them. What does the list suggest about her experience with loss?
2. Bishop varies the repeated lines that end with the word *disaster*. Look only at those lines: what do they suggest about the story being unfolded in the poem?
3. What effect does the parenthetical comment in the poem's last line create? Would the poem be different if it were omitted?
4. Compare this poem to other villanelles in this book, such as Dylan Thomas's "Do not go gentle into that good night" (page 824) and Wendy Cope's "Lonely Hearts" (page 687). In what ways does Bishop bend the rules of the form?

Like "One Art," many great poems engage our personal feelings and private concerns. Others explore larger historical issues and our relationship to them. The following poem, which is set in New York City on the day that Hitler invaded Poland and World War II began, was widely circulated in the weeks following the terrorist attacks of September 11, 2001.

W. H. Auden (1907–1973)

September 1, 1939   1940

I sit in one of the dives
On Fifty-Second Street
Uncertain and afraid
As the clever hopes expire
Of a low dishonest decade: 5
Waves of anger and fear
Circulate over the bright
And darkened lands of the earth,

Obsessing our private lives;
The unmentionable odor of death
Offends the September night.   10

Accurate scholarship can
Unearth the whole offence
From Luther until now
That has driven a culture mad,   15
Find what occurred at Linz,
What huge imago made
A psychopathic god:
I and the public know
What all schoolchildren learn,   20
Those to whom evil is done
Do evil in return.

Exiled Thucydides knew
All that a speech can say
About Democracy,   25
And what dictators do,
The elderly rubbish they talk
To an apathetic grave;
Analysed all in his book,
The enlightenment driven away,   30
The habit-forming pain,
Mismanagement and grief:
We must suffer them all again.

Into this neutral air
Where blind skyscrapers use   35
Their full height to proclaim
The strength of Collective Man,
Each language pours its vain
Competitive excuse:
But who can live for long   40
In an euphoric dream;
Out of the mirror they stare,
Imperialism's face
And the international wrong.

Faces along the bar   45
Cling to their average day:
The lights must never go out,
The music must always play,
All the conventions conspire
To make this fort assume   50
The furniture of home;
Lest we should see where we are,
Lost in a haunted wood,
Children afraid of the night
Who have never been happy or good.   55

The windiest militant trash
Important Persons shout
Is not so crude as our wish:
What mad Nijinsky wrote
About Diaghilev   60
Is true of the normal heart;
For the error bred in the bone
Of each woman and each man
Craves what it cannot have,
Not universal love   65
But to be loved alone.

From the conservative dark
Into the ethical life
The dense commuters come,
Repeating their morning vow,   70
"I *will* be true to the wife,
I'll concentrate more on my work,"
And helpless governors wake
To resume their compulsory game:
Who can release them now,   75
Who can reach the deaf,
Who can speak for the dumb?

All I have is a voice
To undo the folded lie,
The romantic lie in the brain   80
Of the sensual man-in-the-street
And the lie of Authority
Whose buildings grope the sky:
There is no such thing as the State
And no one exists alone;   85
Hunger allows no choice
To the citizen or the police;
We must love one another or die.

Defenseless under the night
Our world in stupor lies;   90
Yet, dotted everywhere,
Ironic points of light
Flash out wherever the Just
Exchange their messages:
May I, composed like them   95
Of Eros and of dust,
Beleaguered by the same
Negation and despair,
Show an affirming flame.

SEPTEMBER 1, 1939. 2 *Fifty-Second Street:* in New York City. 14 *Luther:* German priest Martin Luther
(1483–1546), whose Ninety-five Theses (1517) ignited the Protestant Reformation. 16 *Linz:* town in
Austria where Adolf Hitler was raised. 23 *Thucydides:* Greek historian of the fifth century B.C., whose
History of the Peloponnesian War contains the famous oration by Pericles commemorating the Athenian

war dead. *59–60 What mad Nijinksy wrote / About Diaghilev:* Russian dancer Vaslav Nijinsky (1890–1960) wrote in his diary of the impresario Sergei Diaghilev (1872–1929): "Some politicians are hypocrites like Diaghilev, who does not want universal love, but to be loved alone. I want universal love."

Questions

1. How do the last two lines of the second stanza relate to the specific political and historical situation that the poem addresses? How valid do you find them as a description of human behavior in general?
2. What attitude does the poem take, especially in the third stanza, toward the use of patriotic appeals by heads of state to build support for war?
3. In the context of the poem's larger themes, why is it an "error" to desire "to be loved alone" (lines 62–66)?
4. What does Auden mean by "There is no such thing as the State" (line 84)?
5. Is this poem relevant to our times? Refer to particular situations and events to back up your response.

Excellent poetry might be easier to recognize if each poet had a fixed position on the slopes of Mount Parnassus, but, from one century to the next, the reputations of some poets have taken humiliating slides, or made impressive clambers. We decide for ourselves which poems to call excellent, but readers of the future may reverse our opinions. Most of us no longer would share this popular view of Walt Whitman held by one of his contemporaries:

Walt Whitman (1819–1892), by some regarded as a great poet; by others, as no poet at all. Most of his so-called poems are mere catalogues of things, without meter or rime, but in a few more regular poems and in lines here and there he is grandly poetical, as in "O Captain! My Captain!"[1]

Walt Whitman (1819–1892)

O Captain! My Captain! 1865

O Captain! my Captain! our fearful trip is done,
The ship has weather'd every rack, the prize we sought is won,
The port is near, the bells I hear, the people all exulting,
While follow eyes the steady keel, the vessel grim and daring;
  But O heart! heart! heart! 5
   O the bleeding drops of red,
    Where on the deck my Captain lies,
     Fallen cold and dead.

O Captain! my Captain! rise up and hear the bells;
Rise up—for you the flag is flung—for you the bugle trills, 10
For you bouquets and ribbon'd wreaths—for you the shores a-crowding,
For you they call, the swaying mass, their eager faces turning;
  Here Captain! dear father!
   This arm beneath your head!
    It is some dream that on the deck, 15
     You've fallen cold and dead.

[1]J. Willis Westlake, A. M., *Common-school Literature, English and American, with Several Hundred Extracts to be Memorized* (Philadelphia, 1898).

My Captain does not answer, his lips are pale and still,
My father does not feel my arm, he has no pulse nor will,
The ship is anchor'd safe and sound, its voyage closed and done,
From fearful trip the victor ship comes in with object won;   20
    Exult O shores, and ring O bells!
      But I with mournful tread,
        Walk the deck my Captain lies,
          Fallen cold and dead.

O CAPTAIN! MY CAPTAIN! Written soon after the death of Abraham Lincoln, this was, in Whitman's life-time, by far the most popular of his poems.

Questions

1. Compare this with other Whitman poems. In what ways is "O Captain! My Captain!" uncharacteristic of his works? Do you agree with J. Willis Westlake that this is one of the few occasions on which Whitman is "grandly poetical"?
2. Comment on the appropriateness of the poem's rhythms to its subject.
3. Do you find any evidence in this poem that an excellent poet wrote it?

In a sense, all readers of poetry are constantly reexamining the judgments of the past by choosing those poems they care to go on reading. In the end, we have to admit that the critical principles set forth in this chapter are all very well for admiring excellent poetry we already know, but they cannot be carried like a yardstick in the hand, to go out looking for it. As Ezra Pound said in his *ABC of Reading*, "A classic is classic not because it conforms to certain structural rules, or fits certain definitions (of which its author had quite probably never heard). It is classic because of a certain eternal and irrepressible freshness."

The best poems, like "Sailing to Byzantium," may offer a kind of religious experience. At the beginning of the twenty-first century, some of us rarely set foot outside an artificial environment. Whizzing down four-lane superhighways, we observe lakes and trees in the distance. In a way our cities are to us as anthills are to ants: no less than anthills, they are "natural" structures. But the "unnatural" world of school or business is, as Wordsworth says, too much with us. Locked in the shells of our ambitions, our self-esteem, we forget our kinship to earth and sea. We fabricate self-justifications. Sometimes it takes a poet to remind us why—and for whom—poems are written.

Dylan Thomas (1914–1953)

In My Craft or Sullen Art   1946

In my craft or sullen art
Exercised in the still night
When only the moon rages
And the lovers lie abed
With all their griefs in their arms,   5
I labor by singing light
Not for ambition or bread
Or the strut and trade of charms
On the ivory stages
But for the common wages   10
Of their most secret heart.

Not for the proud man apart
From the raging moon I write
On these spindrift pages
Nor for the towering dead   15
With their nightingales and psalms
But for the lovers, their arms
Round the griefs of the ages,
Who pay no praise or wages
Nor heed my craft or art.   20

IN MY CRAFT OR SULLEN ART. 14 *spindrift:* spray blown from a rough sea or surf.

Questions

1. What plays on words do you find in *craft* (line 1), *trade* (line 8), and *charms* (line 8)?
2. Why does the speaker describe his art as *sullen*?
3. How would you interpret lines 15–16?
4. In light of the assumption made in the last two lines, why do you think the speaker goes on writing?

A great poem shocks us into another order of perception. It points beyond language to something still more essential. It ushers us into an experience so moving and true that we feel (to quote King Lear) "cut to the brain." In bad or indifferent poetry, words are all there is.

Exercise: Reevaluating Popular Classics

In this exercise you will read two of the most popular American poems of the nineteenth century: Emma Lazarus's "The New Colossus" and Edgar Allan Poe's "Annabel Lee." In their time, not only were these poems considered classics by serious critics, but thousands of ordinary readers knew them by heart. Recently, however, they have fallen out of critical favor. You will also read Paul Laurence Dunbar's "We Wear the Mask," which, while never as wildly popular as the others, enjoyed, along with its author, a higher esteem a century ago than it does today.

Your assignment is to read these poems carefully and make your own personal, tentative evaluation of each poem's merit. Here are some questions you might ask yourself as you consider them.

- Do these poems engage your sympathies? Do they stir you and touch your feelings?

- What, if anything, might make them memorable? Do they have any vivid images? Any metaphors, understatement, overstatement, or other figures of speech? Do these poems appeal to the ear?

- Do the poems exhibit any wild incompetence? Do you find any forced rimes, inappropriate words, or other unintentionally comic features? Can the poems be accused of bathos or sentimentality, or do you trust the poet to report honest feelings?

- How well does the poet seem in control of language? Does the poet's language reflect in any detail the physical world we know?

- Do these poems seem entirely drawn from other poetry of the past, or do you have a sense that the poet is thinking and feeling on her (or his) own? Does the poet show any evidence of having read other poets' poetry?

- What is the poet trying to do in each poem? How successful, in your opinion, is the attempt?

Try setting these poems next to similar poems you know and admire. (You might try comparing Emma Lazarus's "The New Colossus" to Percy Bysshe Shelley's "Ozymandias," found in this chapter; both are sonnets, and their subjects have interesting similarities and contrasts. Or read Paul Laurence Dunbar's "We Wear the Mask" in connection with Claude McKay's "America" (page 892). Or compare Edgar Allan Poe's "Annabel Lee" with A. E. Housman's "To an Athlete Dying Young" (page 1056).

Are these poems sufficiently rich and interesting to repay more than one reading? Do you think that these poems still deserve to be considered classics? Or do they no longer speak powerfully to a contemporary audience?

Paul Laurence Dunbar (1872–1906)

We Wear the Mask   1895

We wear the mask that grins and lies,
It hides our cheeks and shades our eyes,—
This debt we pay to human guile;
With torn and bleeding hearts we smile,
And mouth with myriad subtleties.   5

Why should the world be over-wise,
In counting all our tears and sighs?
Nay, let them only see us, while
    We wear the mask.

We smile, but, O great Christ, our cries   10
To thee from tortured souls arise.
We sing, but oh the clay is vile
Beneath our feet, and long the mile;
But let the world dream otherwise,
    We wear the mask!   15

Emma Lazarus (1849–1887)

The New Colossus   1883

Not like the brazen giant of Greek fame,
With conquering limbs astride from land to land;
Here at our sea-washed, sunset gates shall stand
A mighty woman with a torch, whose flame
Is the imprisoned lightning, and her name   5
Mother of Exiles. From her beacon-hand
Glows world-wide welcome; her mild eyes command
The air-bridged harbor that twin cities frame.
"Keep, ancient lands, your storied pomp!" cries she
With silent lips. "Give me your tired, your poor,   10
Your huddled masses yearning to breathe free,
The wretched refuse of your teeming shore.
Send these, the homeless, tempest-tost to me,
I lift my lamp beside the golden door!"

THE NEW COLOSSUS. In 1883, a committee was formed to raise funds to build a pedestal for what would be the largest statue in the world, "Liberty Enlightening the World" by Fréderic-Auguste Bartholdi, which was a gift from the French people to celebrate America's centennial. American authors were asked to donate manuscripts for a fund-raising auction. The young poet Emma Lazarus, whose parents had come to America as immigrants, sent in this sonnet composed for the occasion. When President Grover Cleveland unveiled the Statue of Liberty in October 1886, Lazarus's sonnet was read at the ceremony. In 1903, the poem was carved on the statue's pedestal. The reference in the opening line to "the brazen giant of Greek fame" is to the famous Colossus of Rhodes, a huge bronze statue that once stood in the harbor on the Aegean island of Rhodes. Built to commemorate a military victory, it was one of the so-called Seven Wonders of the World.

Edgar Allan Poe (1809–1849)

Annabel Lee   1849

It was many and many a year ago,
   In a kingdom by the sea,
That a maiden there lived whom you may know
   By the name of Annabel Lee;
And this maiden she lived with no other thought   5
   Than to love and be loved by me.

I was a child and *she* was a child,
   In this kingdom by the sea,
But we loved with a love that was more than love—
   I and my Annabel Lee—   10
With a love that the wingéd seraphs of Heaven
   Coveted her and me.

And this was the reason that, long ago,
   In this kingdom by the sea,
A wind blew out of a cloud, chilling   15
   My beautiful Annabel Lee;
So that her highborn kinsmen came
   And bore her away from me,
To shut her up in a sepulchre
   In this kingdom by the sea.   20

The angels, not half so happy in Heaven,
   Went envying her and me:—
Yes!—that was the reason (as all men know,
   In this kingdom by the sea)
That the wind came out of the cloud by night,   25
   Chilling and killing my Annabel Lee.

But our love it was stronger by far than the love
   Of those who were older than we—
   Of many far wiser than we—
And neither the angels in Heaven above,   30
   Nor the demons down under the sea,
Can ever dissever my soul from the soul
   Of the beautiful Annabel Lee:—

For the moon never beams, without bringing me dreams
    Of the beautiful Annabel Lee;   35
And the stars never rise, but I feel the bright eyes
    Of the beautiful Annabel Lee:
And so, all the night-tide, I lie down by the side
Of my darling—my darling—my life and my bride,
    In the sepulchre there by the sea—   40
    In her tomb by the sounding sea.

■ WRITING *effectively*

Edgar Allan Poe on Writing

A Long Poem Does Not Exist   1848

I hold that a long poem does not exist. I maintain that the phrase, "a long poem," is simply a flat contradiction in terms.

I need scarcely observe that a poem deserves its title only inasmuch as it excites, by elevating the soul. The value of the poem is in the ratio of this elevating excitement. But all excitements are, through a psychal necessity, transient. That degree of excitement which would entitle a poem to be so called at all, cannot be sustained throughout a composition of any great length. After the lapse of half an hour, at the very utmost, it flags—fails—a revulsion ensues—and then the poem is, in effect, and in fact, no longer such.

From "The Poetic Principle"

Edgar Allan Poe

THINKING ABOUT EVALUATING A POEM

Evaluating a poem begins with personal taste. Though your first impressions may become part of your ultimate judgment, they should usually end up being no more than a departure point. The question isn't merely whether a work pleases or moves you, but how well it manages the literary tasks it sets out to perform. A good critic is willing both to admire a strong poem that he or she doesn't like and to admit that a personal favorite might not really stand up to close scrutiny. Whatever your final opinion, the goal is to nourish your personal response with careful critical examination so that your evaluation will grow into an informed judgment.

- **In evaluating a poem, first try to understand your own subjective response.** Admit to yourself whether the poem delights, moves, bores, or annoys you.
- **Try to determine what the poem seems designed to make you think and feel.** If a poem is written within a genre, then you need to weigh the work against the generic expectations it sets up.
- **Consider how well it fulfills these expectations.** An epigram usually seeks to be witty and concise. If it proves tiresome and verbose, it can be fairly said to fail.
- **Focus on specific elements in the poem.** How well do its language, imagery, symbols, and figures of speech communicate its meanings? Are the metaphors or similes effective? Is the imagery fresh and precise? Is the language vague or verbose? Does the poem ever fall into clichés or platitudes?

CHECKLIST: Writing an Evaluation

- ☐ What is your subjective response to the poem?
- ☐ Highlight or underline moments that call up a strong reaction. Why do you think those passages elicit such a response?
- ☐ What task does the poem set for itself?
- ☐ Does it belong to some identifiable form or genre?
- ☐ If so, what are the expectations for that genre? How well does the poem fulfill the expectations it creates?
- ☐ How do its specific elements work to communicate meaning (e.g. language, imagery, symbols, figures of speech, rhythm, sound, rime)?
- ☐ Reread the poem. Does it seem better or worse than it did initially?

WRITING ASSIGNMENT ON EVALUATING A POEM

Look closely at a short poem to which you have a strong initial response—either positive or negative. Write an essay in which you begin by stating your response, then work through the steps outlined above. Does the poem succeed in fulfilling the task it sets for itself? Back up your opinion with specifics. Finally, state whether the process has changed your impression of the poem. Why or why not?

MORE TOPICS FOR WRITING

1. Choose a short poem that you admire from anywhere in this book. Write a brief essay defending the poem's excellence. Be specific in describing its particular strengths.
2. Write a brief evaluation of "The New Colossus" by Emma Lazarus, "We Wear the Mask" by Paul Laurence Dunbar, or "Annabel Lee" by Edgar Allan Poe. In what ways is the poem successful? In what ways is it unsuccessful?
3. Find a poem you admire in this book and wreck it. First, type the poem as is into a computer. Then go through it, substituting clichés and overly vague language for moments that are vivid and precise. Replace understatement with overstatement, restraint with sentimentality. Keep making changes until you've turned a perfectly good poem into a train wreck. Now write a brief explanation of your choices.

▶ TERMS FOR *review*

Bathos ▶ An unintentional lapse from the sublime to the ridiculous or trivial. An attempt to capture the grand and profound that comes off as inflated and fatuous.

Convention ▶ Any established feature or technique in literature that is commonly understood by both authors and readers. A convention is something generally agreed on to be appropriate for customary uses, such as the sonnet form for a love poem or the opening "Once upon a time" for a fairy tale.

Conceit ▶ A far-flung and often extended metaphor comparing dissimilar things. John Donne, for example, casts his doctors as cosmographers and his body as their map.

Poetic inversion ▶ The inversion of normal word order, usually done for purposes of meter and/or rime.

Sentimentality ▶ A term negatively applied to a literary work that tries to convey great feeling but fails to give the reader sufficient grounds for sharing it. Sentimentality involves an emotion that is excessive in relation to its cause, as opposed to *sentiment*, which connotes one proper to its cause.

30 WHAT IS POETRY?

Poetry is a way of taking life by the throat.

—ROBERT FROST

Archibald MacLeish (1892–1982)

Ars Poetica   1926

A poem should be palpable and mute
As a globed fruit,

Dumb
As old medallions to the thumb,

Silent as the sleeve-worn stone   5
Of casement ledges where the moss has grown—

A poem should be wordless
As the flight of birds.

        * *

A poem should be motionless in time
As the moon climbs,   10

Leaving, as the moon releases
Twig by twig the night-entangled trees,

Leaving, as the moon behind the winter leaves,
Memory by memory the mind—

A poem should be motionless in time   15
As the moon climbs.

        * *

A poem should be equal to:
Not true.

For all the history of grief
An empty doorway and a maple leaf.   20

For love
The leaning grasses and two lights above the sea—

A poem should not mean
But be.

The title of Archibald MacLeish's provocative poem is Latin for "the poetic art" or "the art of poetry," and it is not unusual for poets to speculate in verse about their art. MacLeish, in fact, borrowed his title from the Roman poet Horace, who wrote a brilliant verse epistle on the subject during the reign of Caesar Augustus. In the two thousand years since then, there has been no shortage of opinions from fellow poets. There is something alluring and mysterious about poetry, even to its practitioners.

What, then, is poetry? By now, perhaps, you have formed your own idea, whether or not you can define it. Robert Frost made a try at a definition: "A poem is an idea caught in the act of dawning." Just in case further efforts at definition may be useful, here are a few memorable ones (including, for a second look, some given earlier):

things that are true expressed in words that are beautiful.
> —*Dante*

the art of uniting pleasure with truth by calling imagination to the
> help of reason.
> —*Samuel Johnson*

the best words in the best order.
> —*Samuel Taylor Coleridge*

the spontaneous overflow of powerful feelings.
> —*William Wordsworth*

emotion put into measure.
> —*Thomas Hardy*

If I feel physically as if the top of my head were taken off, I know *that* is
> poetry.
> —*Emily Dickinson*

speech framed . . . to be heard for its own sake and interest even over
> and above its interest of meaning.
> —*Gerard Manley Hopkins*

a way of remembering what it would impoverish us to forget.
> —*Robert Frost*

a revelation in words by means of the words.
> —*Wallace Stevens*

Poetry is prose bewitched.
> —*Mina Loy*

not the assertion that something is true, but the making of that truth
> more fully real to us.
> —*T. S. Eliot*

the clear expression of mixed feelings.
> —*W. H. Auden*

the body of linguistic constructions that men usually refer to as poems.
> —*J. V. Cunningham*

an angel with a gun in its hand . . .
> —*José Garcia Villa*

the language in which man explores his own amazement.
　　　　　—*Christopher Fry*

hundreds of things coming together at the right moment.
　　　　　—*Elizabeth Bishop*

Poetry is a sound art.
　　　　　—*Joy Harjo*

Verse should have two obligations: to communicate a precise instance
　　　　and to touch us physically, as the presence of the sea does.
　　　　　—*Jorge Luis Borges*

Reduced to its simplest and most essential form, the poem is a song.
　　　　Song is neither discourse nor explanation.
　　　　　—*Octavio Paz*

anything said in such a way, or put on the page in such a way, as to
　　　　invite from the hearer or the reader a certain kind of attention.
　　　　　—*William Stafford*

Poetry is always the cat concert under the window of the room in
　　　　which the official version of reality is being written.
　　　　　—*Charles Simic*

A poem differs from most prose in several ways. For one, both writer and reader tend to regard it differently. The poet's attitude is something like this: I offer this piece of writing to be read not as prose but as a poem—that is, more perceptively, thoughtfully, and considerately, with more attention to sounds and connotations. This is a great deal to expect, but in return, the reader, too, has a right to certain expectations. Approaching the poem in the anticipation of out-of-the-ordinary knowledge and pleasure, the reader assumes that the poem may use certain enjoyable devices not available to prose: rime, alliteration, meter, and rhythms—definite, various, or emphatic. (The poet may not *always* decide to use these things.) The reader expects the poet to make greater use, perhaps, of resources of meaning such as figurative language, allusion, symbol, and imagery. As readers of prose, we might seek no more than meaning: no more than what could be paraphrased without serious loss. Meeting any figurative language or graceful turns of word order, we think them pleasant extras. But in poetry all these "extras" matter as much as the paraphrasable content, if not more. For, when we finish reading a good poem, we cannot explain precisely to ourselves what we have experienced—without repeating, word for word, the language of the poem itself. Archibald MacLeish makes this point memorably in "Ars Poetica":

A poem should not mean
But be.

"Poetry is to prose as dancing is to walking," remarked Paul Valéry. It is doubtful, however, that anyone can draw an immovable boundary between poetry and prose. Certain prose needs only to be arranged in lines to be seen as poetry—especially prose that conveys strong emotion in vivid, physical imagery and in terse, figurative, rhythmical language. Even in translation the words of Chief Joseph of the Nez Percé tribe, at the moment of his surrender to the U.S. Army in 1877, still move us and are memorable:

Hear me, my warriors, my heart is sick and sad:
Our chiefs are killed,
The old men all are dead,
It is cold and we have no blankets.

The little children freeze to death.

Hear me, my warriors, my heart is sick and sad:
From where the sun now stands I will fight no more forever.

It may be that a poem can point beyond words to something still more essential. Language has its limits, and probably Edgar Allan Poe was the only poet ever to claim he could always find words for whatever he wished to express. For, of all a human being can experience and imagine, words say only part. "Human speech," said Flaubert, who strove after the best of it, "is like a cracked kettle on which we hammer out tunes to make bears dance, when what we long for is the compassion of the stars."

Like Yeats's chestnut tree in "Among School Children" (which, when asked whether it is leaf, blossom, or bole, has no answer), a poem is to be seen not as a confederation of form, rime, image, metaphor, tone, and theme, but as a whole. We study a poem one element at a time because the intellect best comprehends what it can separate. But only our total attention, involving the participation of our blood and marrow, can see all elements in a poem fused, all dancing together. Yeats knew how to make poems and how to read them:

God guard me from those thoughts men think
In the mind alone;
He that sings a lasting song
Thinks in a marrow-bone.

Throughout this book, we have been working on the assumption that the patient and conscious explication of poems will sharpen unconscious perceptions. We can only hope that it will; the final test lies in whether you care to go on by yourself, reading other poems, finding in them pleasure and enlightenment. Pedagogy must have a stop; so too must the viewing of poems as if their elements fell into chapters. For the total experience of reading a poem surpasses the mind's categories. The wind in the grass, says a proverb, cannot be taken into the house.

Ha Jin (b. 1956)

Missed Time   2000

My notebook has remained blank for months
thanks to the light you shower
around me. I have no use
for my pen, which lies
languorously without grief.   5

Nothing is better than to live
a storyless life that needs
no writing for meaning—
when I am gone, let others say
they lost a happy man,   10
though no one can tell how happy I was.

31 TWO CRITICAL CASEBOOKS
Emily Dickinson and Langston Hughes

Emily Dickinson
(Amherst College Archives and
Special Collections)

Langston Hughes

EMILY DICKINSON

Emily Dickinson (1830–1886) spent virtually all her life in her family home in Amherst, Massachusetts. Her father, Edward Dickinson, was a prominent lawyer who ranked as Amherst's leading citizen. (He even served a term in the U.S. Congress.) Dickinson attended one year of college at Mount Holyoke Female Seminary in South Hadley. She proved to be a good student, but, suffering from homesickness and poor health, she did not return for the second year. This brief period of study and a few trips to Boston, Philadelphia, and Washington, D.C., were the only occasions she left home in her fifty-five-year life. As the years passed, Dickinson became more reclusive. She stopped attending church (and refused to endorse the orthodox Congregationalist creed). She also spent increasing time alone in her room—often writing poems. Dickinson never married, but she had a significant romantic relationship with at least one unidentified man. Although scholars have suggested several likely candidates, the historical object of Dickinson's affections will likely never be known. What survives unmistakably, however, is the intensely passionate poetry written out of these private circumstances. By the end of her life, Dickinson had become a locally famous recluse; she rarely left home. She would greet visitors from her own upstairs room, clearly heard but never seen. In 1886 she was buried, according to her own instructions, within sight of the family home. Although Dickinson composed 1,789 known poems, only a handful were published in her lifetime. She often, however, sent copies of poems to friends in letters, but only after her death would the full extent of her writings become known when a cache of manuscripts was discovered in a trunk in the homestead attic—handwritten little booklets of poems sewn together by the poet with needle and thread. From 1890 until the mid-twentieth century, nine posthumous collections of her poems were published by friends and relatives, some of whom rewrote her work and changed her idiosyncratic punctuation to make it more conventional. Thomas H. Johnson's three-volume edition of the Poems (1955) established a more accurate text. In relatively few and simple forms clearly indebted to the hymns she heard in church, Dickinson succeeded in being a true visionary and a poet of colossal originality.

POEMS

Success is counted sweetest   (1859) Published 1878

Success is counted sweetest
By those who ne'er succeed.
To comprehend a nectar
Requires sorest need.

Not one of all the purple Host°   *an army*   5
Who took the Flag today
Can tell the definition
So clear of Victory

As he defeated – dying –
On whose forbidden ear   10
The distant strains of triumph
Burst agonized and clear!

Wild Nights – Wild Nights!

(about 1861)

Wild Nights – Wild Nights!
Were I with thee
Wild Nights should be
Our luxury!

Futile – the Winds –
To a Heart in port –
Done with the Compass –
Done with the Chart!

Rowing in Eden –
Ah, the Sea!
Might I but moor – Tonight –
In Thee!

There's a certain Slant of light

(about 1861)

There's a certain Slant of light,
Winter Afternoons –
That oppresses, like the Heft
Of Cathedral Tunes –

Heavenly Hurt, it gives us –
We can find no scar,
But internal difference,
Where the Meanings, are –

None may teach it – Any –
'Tis the Seal Despair –
An imperial affliction
Sent us of the Air –

When it comes, the Landscape listens –
Shadows – hold their breath –
When it goes, 'tis like the Distance
On the look of Death –

I felt a Funeral, in my Brain

(about 1861)

I felt a Funeral, in my Brain,
And Mourners to and fro
Kept treading – treading – till it seemed
That Sense was breaking through –

And when they all were seated,
A Service, like a Drum –
Kept beating – beating – till I thought
My Mind was going numb –

And then I heard them lift a Box
And creak across my Soul
With those same Boots of Lead, again,   10
Then Space – began to toll,

As all the Heavens were a Bell,
And Being, but an Ear,
And I, and Silence, some strange Race   15
Wrecked, solitary, here –

And Then a Plank in Reason, broke,
And I dropped down, and down –
And hit a World, at every plunge,
And Finished knowing – then –   20

I'm Nobody! Who are you?   (about 1861)

I'm Nobody! Who are you?
Are you – Nobody – Too?
Then there's a pair of us?
Don't tell! they'd advertise – you know!

How dreary – to be – Somebody!   5
How public – like a Frog –
To tell one's name – the livelong June –
To an admiring Bog!

The Soul selects her own Society   (about 1862)

The Soul selects her own Society –
Then – shuts the Door –
To her divine Majority –
Present no more –

Unmoved – she notes the Chariots – pausing –   5
At her low Gate –
Unmoved – an Emperor be kneeling
Upon her Mat –

I've known her – from an ample nation –
Choose One –
Then – close the Valves of her attention –   10
Like Stone –

Some keep the Sabbath   (about 1862) Published 1864
going to Church

Some keep the Sabbath going to Church –
I keep it, staying at Home –
With a Bobolink for a Chorister –
And an Orchard, for a Dome –

Some keep the Sabbath in Surplice –   5
I just wear my Wings –
And instead of tolling the Bell, for Church,
Our little Sexton – sings.

God preaches, a noted Clergyman –
And the sermon is never long,   10
So instead of getting to Heaven, at last –
I'm going, all along.

After great pain, a formal feeling comes   (about 1862)

After great pain, a formal feeling comes –
The Nerves sit ceremonious, like Tombs –
The stiff Heart questions was it He, that bore,
And Yesterday, or Centuries before?

The Feet, mechanical, go round –   5
Of Ground, or Air, or Ought –
A Wooden way
Regardless grown,
A Quartz contentment, like a stone –

This is the Hour of Lead –   10
Remembered, if outlived,
As Freezing persons, recollect the Snow –
First – Chill – then Stupor – then the letting go –

Much Madness is divinest Sense   (about 1862)

Much Madness is divinest Sense –
To a discerning Eye –
Much Sense – the starkest Madness –
'Tis the Majority
In this, as All, prevail –   5
Assent – and you are sane –
Demur – you're straightway dangerous –
And handled with a Chain –

This is my letter to the World   (about 1862)

This is my letter to the World
That never wrote to Me –
The simple News that Nature told –
With tender Majesty

Her Message is committed   5
To Hands I cannot see –
For love of Her – Sweet – countrymen –
Judge tenderly – of Me

I heard a Fly buzz – when I died (about 1862)

I heard a Fly buzz – when I died –
The Stillness in the Room
Was like the Stillness in the Air –
Between the Heaves of Storm –

The Eyes around – had wrung them dry – 5
And Breaths were gathering firm
For that last Onset – when the King
Be witnessed – in the Room –

I willed my Keepsakes – Signed away
What portion of me be 10
Assignable – and then it was
There interposed a Fly –

With Blue – uncertain stumbling Buzz –
Between the light – and me –
And then the Windows failed – and then 15
I could not see to see –

I started Early – Took my Dog (about 1862)

I started Early – Took my Dog –
And visited the Sea –
The Mermaids in the Basement
Came out to look at me –

And Frigates – in the Upper Floor 5
Extended Hempen Hands –
Presuming Me to be a Mouse –
Aground – upon the Sands –

But no Man moved Me – till the Tide
Went past my simple Shoe – 10
And past my Apron – and my Belt
And past my Bodice – too –

And made as He would eat me up –
As wholly as a Dew
Upon a Dandelion's Sleeve – 15
And then – I started – too –

And He – He followed – close behind –
I felt His Silver Heel
Upon my Ankle – Then my Shoes
Would overflow with Pearl – 20

Until We met the Solid Town –
No One He seemed to know –
And bowing – with a Mighty look –
At me – The Sea withdrew –

Because I could not stop for Death

(about 1863)

Because I could not stop for Death –
He kindly stopped for me –
The Carriage held but just Ourselves –
And Immortality.

We slowly drove – He knew no haste   5
And I had put away
My labor and my leisure too,
For His Civility –

We passed the School, where Children strove
At Recess – in the Ring –   10
We passed the Fields of Gazing Grain –
We passed the Setting Sun –

Or rather – He passed Us –
The Dews drew quivering and chill –
For only Gossamer, my Gown –   15
My Tippet° – only Tulle –   cape

We paused before a House that seemed
A Swelling of the Ground –
The Roof was scarcely visible –
The Cornice – in the Ground –   20

Since then – 'tis Centuries – and yet
Feels shorter than the Day
I first surmised the Horses' Heads
Were toward Eternity.

The Bustle in a House

(about 1866)

The Bustle in a House
The Morning after Death
Is solemnest of industries
Enacted upon Earth –

The Sweeping up the Heart   5
And putting Love away
We shall not want to use again
Until Eternity

Tell all the Truth but tell it slant

(about 1868)

Tell all the Truth but tell it slant –
Success in Circuit lies
Too bright for our infirm Delight
The Truth's superb surprise
As Lightning to the Children eased   5
With explanation kind
The Truth must dazzle gradually
Or every man be blind –

Compare

Other poems by Emily Dickinson that are found in this book:

A Dying Tiger – moaned for Drink (page 933)
I like to see it lap the Miles (page 649)
It dropped so low – in my Regard (page 736)
The Lightning is a yellow Fork (page 854)
My Life had stood – a Loaded Gun (page 734)
A Route of Evanescence (page 716)

EMILY DICKINSON ON EMILY DICKINSON

Emily Dickinson's room in Amherst, Massachusetts.

Recognizing Poetry
(1870)

If I read a book [and] it makes my whole body so cold no fire ever can warm me I know *that* is poetry. If I feel physically as if the top of my head were taken off, I know *that* is poetry. These are the only ways I know it. Is there any other way.

How do most people live without any thoughts. There are many people in the world (you must have noticed them in the street) How do they live. How do they get strength to put on their clothes in the morning.

When I lost the use of my Eyes it was a comfort to think there were so few real *books* that I could easily find some one to read me all of them.

Truth is such a *rare* thing it is delightful to tell it.

I find ecstasy in living – the mere sense of living is joy enough.

From a conversation with Thomas Wentworth Higginson

Compare

Dickinson's famous comments on the nature of poetry, which are often quoted out of context, with their original source, a letter—not by the poet herself but by a visiting editor. (See the editor's letter that follows on page 966.)

Self-Description

(1862)

25 April 1862

Mr. Higginson,

Your kindness claimed earlier gratitude – but I was ill – and write today, from my pillow.

Thank you for the surgery – it was not so painful as I supposed. I bring you others – as you ask – though they might not differ –

While my thought is undressed – I can make the distinction, but when I put them in the Gown – they look alike, and numb.

You asked how old I was? I made no verse – but one or two – until this winter – Sir –

I had a terror – since September – I could tell to none – and so I sing, as the Boy does by the Burying Ground – because I am afraid – You inquire my Books – For Poets – I have Keats – and Mr and Mrs Browning. For Prose – Mr Ruskin – Sir Thomas Browne – and the Revelations.° I went to school – but in your manner of the phrase – had no education. When a little Girl, I had a friend, who taught me Immortality – but venturing too near, himself – he never returned – Soon after, my Tutor, died – and for several years, my Lexicon – was my only companion – Then I found one more – but he was not contented I be his scholar – so he left the Land.

You ask of my Companions Hills – Sir – and the Sundown – and a Dog – large as myself, that my Father bought me – They are better than Beings – because they know – but do not tell – and the noise in the Pool, at Noon – excels my Piano. I have a Brother and Sister – My Mother does not care for thought – and Father, too busy with his Briefs° – to notice what we do – He buys me many Books – but begs me not to read them – because he fears they joggle the Mind. They are religious – except me – and address an Eclipse, every morning – whom they call their "Father." But I fear my story fatigues you – I would like to learn – Could you tell me how to grow – or is it unconveyed – like Melody – or Witchcraft?

You speak of Mr Whitman – I never read his Book° – but was told that he was disgraceful –

I read Miss Prescott's "Circumstance,"° but it followed me, in the Dark – so I avoided her –

Two Editors of Journals came to my Father's House, this winter – and asked me for my Mind – and when I asked them "Why," they said I was penurious – and they, would use it for the World –

I could not weigh myself – Myself –

SELF-DESCRIPTION. Emily Dickinson's letter was written to Thomas Wentworth Higginson, a noted writer. Dickinson had read his article of advice to young writers in the *Atlantic Monthly*. She sent him four poems and a letter asking if her verse was "alive." When he responded with comments and suggestions (the "surgery" Dickinson mentions in the second paragraph), she wrote him this letter about herself. *Mr Ruskin . . . Revelations*: in listing her favorite prose authors Dickinson chose John Ruskin (1819–1900), an English art critic and essayist; Sir Thomas Browne (1605–1682), a doctor and philosopher with a magnificent prose style; and the final book of the New Testament. *Briefs*: legal papers (her father was a lawyer). *Whitman . . . book*: *Leaves of Grass* (1855) by Walt Whitman was considered an improper book for women at this time because of the volume's sexual candor. *Miss Prescott's "Circumstance"*: a story, also published in the *Atlantic Monthly*, that was full of violence.

My size felt small – to me – I read your Chapters in the Atlantic – and experienced honor for you – I was sure you would not reject a confiding question –
Is this – Sir – what you asked me to tell you?

Your friend,
E – Dickinson

From *The Letters of Emily Dickinson*

CRITICS ON EMILY DICKINSON

Thomas Wentworth Higginson (1823–1911)

Meeting Emily Dickinson   1870

Thomas Higginson

A large county lawyer's house, brown brick, with great trees & a garden—I sent up my card. A parlor dark & cool & stiffish, a few books & engravings & an open piano. . . .

A step like a pattering child's in entry & in glided a little plain woman with two smooth bands of reddish hair & a face a little like Belle Dove's; not plainer—with no good feature—in a very plain & exquisitely clean white pique & a blue net worsted shawl. She came to me with two day lilies which she put in a sort of childlike way into my hand & said "These are my introduction" in a soft frightened breathless childlike voice—& added under her breath Forgive me if I am frightened; I never see strangers & hardly know what I say—but she talked soon & thenceforward continuously—& deferentially—sometimes stopping to ask me to talk instead of her—but readily recommencing . . . thoroughly ingenuous & simple . . . & saying many things which you would have thought foolish & I wise—& some things you wd. hv. liked. I add a few over the page. . . .

"Women talk; men are silent; that is why I dread women."
"My father only reads on Sunday—he reads *lonely* & *rigorous* books."
"If I read a book [and] it makes my whole body so cold no fire ever can warm me I know *that* is poetry. If I feel physically as if the top of my head were taken off, I know *that* is poetry. These are the only ways I know it. Is there any other way."
"How do most people live without any thoughts. There are many people in the world (you must have noticed them in the street) How do they live. How do they get strength to put on their clothes in the morning"
"When I lost the use of my Eyes it was a comfort to think there were so few real *books* that I could easily find some one to read me all of them"
"Truth is such a *rare* thing it is delightful to tell it."
"I find ecstasy in living—the mere sense of living is joy enough"

I asked if she never felt want of employment, never going off the place & never seeing any visitor "I never thought of conceiving that I could ever have the slightest approach to such a want in all future time" (& added) "I feel that I have not expressed myself strongly enough."

She makes all the bread for her father only likes hers & says "& people must have puddings" this *very* dreamily, as if they were comets—so she makes them.

• • •

E D again

"Could you tell me what home is"

"I never had a mother. I suppose a mother is one to whom you hurry when you are troubled."

"I never knew how to tell time by the clock till I was 15. My father thought he had taught me but I did not understand & I was afraid to say I did not & afraid to ask any one else lest he should know."

Her father was not severe I should think but remote. He did not wish them to read anything but the Bible. One day her brother brought home Kavanagh° hid it under the piano cover & made signs to her & they read it: her father at last found it & was displeased. Perhaps it was before this that a student of his was amazed that they had never heard of Mrs. [Lydia Maria] Child° & used to bring them books & hide in a bush by the door. They were then little things in short dresses with their feet on the rungs of the chair. After the first book she thought in ecstasy "This then is a book! And there are more of them!"

"Is it oblivion or absorption when things pass from our minds?"

Major Hunt interested her more than any man she ever saw. She remembered two things he said—that her great dog "understood gravitation" & when he said he should come again "in a year. If I say a shorter time it will be longer."

When I said I would come again *some time* she said "Say in a long time, that will be nearer. Some time is nothing."

After long disuse of her eyes she read Shakespeare & thought why is any other book needed.

I never was with any one who drained my nerve power so much. Without touching her, she drew from me. I am glad not to live near her. She often thought me *tired* & seemed very thoughtful of others.

From a letter to his wife, August 16–17, 1870

Thomas H. Johnson (1902–1985)

The Discovery of Emily Dickinson's Manuscripts   1955

Shortly after Emily Dickinson's death on May fifteenth, 1886, her sister Lavinia discovered a locked box in which Emily had placed her poems. Lavinia's amazement seems to have been genuine. Though the sisters had lived intimately together under the same roof all their lives, and though Lavinia had always been aware that her

---

Kavanagh: Kavanagh: A Tale (1849), an utterly innocuous work of fiction by the poet Henry Wadsworth Longfellow.   *Mrs. [Lydia Maria] Child*: anti-slavery writer and author (1802–1880) of didactic novels.

sister wrote poems, she had not the faintest concept of the great number of them. The story of Lavinia's willingness to spare them because she found no instructions specifying that they be destroyed, and her search for an editor and a publisher to give them to the world has already been told in some detail.

Lavinia first consulted the two people most interested in Emily's poetry, her sister-in-law Susan Dickinson, and Mrs. Todd. David Peck Todd, a graduate of Amherst College in 1875, returned to Amherst with his young bride in 1881 as director of the college observatory and soon became professor of Astronomy and Navigation. These were the months shortly before Mrs. Edward Dickinson's death, when neighbors were especially thoughtful. Mrs. Todd endeared herself to Emily and Lavinia by small but understanding attentions, in return for which Emily sent Mrs. Todd copies of her poems. At first approach neither Susan Dickinson nor Mrs. Todd felt qualified for the editorial task which they both were hesitant to undertake. Mrs. Todd says of Lavinia's discovery: "She showed me the manuscripts and there were over sixty little 'volumes,' each composed of four or five sheets of note paper tied together with twine. In this box she discovered eight or nine hundred poems tied up in this way."

• • •

As the story can be reconstructed, at some time during the year 1858 Emily Dickinson began assembling her poems into packets. Always in ink, they are gatherings of four, five, or six sheets of letter paper usually folded once but sometimes single. They are loosely held together by thread looped through them at the spine at two points equidistant from the top and bottom. When opened up they may be read like a small book, a fact that explains why Emily's sister Lavinia, when she discovered them after Emily's death, referred to them as "volumes." All of the packet poems are either fair copies or semifinal drafts, and they constitute two-thirds of the entire body of her poetry.

For the most part the poems in a given packet seem to have been written and assembled as a unit. Since rough drafts of packet poems are almost totally lacking, one concludes that they were systematically discarded. If the poems were in fact composed at the time the copies were made, as the evidence now seems to point, one concludes that nearly two-thirds of her poems were created in the brief span of eight years, centering on her early thirties. Her interest in the packet method of assembling the verses thus coincides with the years of fullest productivity. In 1858 she gathered some fifty poems into packets. There are nearly one hundred so transcribed in 1859, some sixty-five in 1860, and in 1861 more than eighty. By 1862 the creative drive must have been almost frightening; during that year she transcribed into packets no fewer than three hundred and sixty-six poems, the greater part of them complete and final texts.

Whether this incredible number was in fact composed in that year or represents a transcription of earlier worksheet drafts can never be established by direct evidence. But the pattern established during the preceding four years reveals a gathering momentum, and the quality of tenseness and prosodic skill uniformly present in the poems of 1861–1862 bears scant likeness to the conventionality of theme and treatment in the poems of 1858–1859. Excepting a half dozen occasional verses written in the early fifties, there is not a single scrap of poetry that can be dated earlier than 1858.

From *The Poems of Emily Dickinson*

Richard Wilbur (b. 1921)

The Three Privations of Emily Dickinson   1959

Emily Dickinson never lets us forget for very long that in some respects life gave her short measure; and indeed it is possible to see the greater part of her poetry as an effort to cope with her sense of privation. I think that for her there were three major privations: she was deprived of an orthodox and steady religious faith; she was deprived of love; she was deprived of literary recognition.

At the age of seventeen, after a series of revival meetings at Mount Holyoke Seminary, Emily Dickinson found that she must refuse to become a professing Christian. To some modern minds this may seem to have been a sensible and necessary step; and surely it was a step toward becoming such a poet as she became. But for her, no pleasure in her own integrity could then eradicate the feeling that she had betrayed a deficiency, a want of grace. In her letters to Abiah Root she tells of the enhancing effect of conversion on her fellow-students, and says of herself in a famous passage:

> I am one of the lingering bad ones, and so do I slink away, and pause and ponder, and ponder and pause, and do work without knowing why, not surely for this brief world, and more sure it is not for heaven, and I ask what this message *means* that they ask for so very eagerly: *you* know of this depth and fulness, will you try to tell me about it?

There is humor in that, and stubbornness, and a bit of characteristic lurking pride: but there is also an anguished sense of having separated herself, through some dry incapacity, from spiritual community, from purpose, and from magnitude of life. As a child of evangelical Amherst, she inevitably thought of purposive, heroic life as requiring a vigorous faith. Out of such a thought she later wrote:

The abdication of Belief
Makes the Behavior small –
Better an ignis fatuus
Than no illume at all –

That hers *was* a species of religious personality goes without saying; but by her refusal of such ideas as original sin, redemption, hell, and election, she made it impossible for herself—as Whicher observed—"to share the religious life of her generation." She became an unsteady congregation of one.

Her second privation, the privation of love, is one with which her poems and her biographies have made us exceedingly familiar, though some biographical facts remain conjectural. She had the good fortune, at least once, to bestow her heart on another; but she seems to have found her life, in great part, a history of loneliness, separation, and bereavement.

As for literary fame, some will deny that Emily Dickinson ever greatly desired it, and certainly there is evidence, mostly from her latter years, to support such a view. She *did* write that "Publication is the auction / Of the mind of man." And she *did* say to Helen Hunt Jackson, "How can you print a piece of your soul?" But earlier, in 1861, she had frankly expressed to Sue Dickinson the hope that "sometime" she might make her kinfolk proud of her. The truth is, I think, that Emily Dickinson knew she was good, and began her career with a normal appetite for recognition. I think that she later came, with some reason, to despair of being understood or properly valued, and so directed against her hopes of fame what was by then a well-developed disposition to renounce. That she wrote a good number of poems about fame supports my view: the subjects to which a poet returns are those which vex him.

What did Emily Dickinson do, as a poet, with her sense of privation? One thing she quite often did was to pose as the laureate and attorney of the empty-handed, and question God about the economy of His creation. Why, she asked, is a fatherly God so sparing of His presence? Why is there never a sign that prayers are heard? Why does Nature tell us no comforting news of its Maker? Why do some receive a whole loaf, while others must starve on a crumb? Where is the benevolence in shipwreck and earthquake? By asking such questions as these, she turned complaint into critique, and used her own sufferings as experiential evidence about the nature of the deity. The God who emerges from these poems is a God who does not answer, an unrevealed God whom one cannot confidently approach through Nature or through doctrine.

From "Sumptuous Destitution"

Cynthia Griffin Wolff (b. 1935)

Dickinson and Death

1993

(A Reading of "Because I could not stop for Death": page 963)

Modern readers are apt to comment upon the frequency with which Dickinson returns to this subject of death—"How morbid," people say. Perhaps. But if Dickinson was morbid, so was everyone else in her culture. Poe's aestheticizing of death (along with the proliferation of Gothic fiction and poetry) reflects a pervasive real-world concern: in mid-nineteenth-century America death rates were high. It was a truism that men had three wives (two of them having predeceased the spouse); infant mortality was so common that parents often gave several of their children the same name so that at least one "John" or "Lavinia" might survive to adulthood; rapid urbanization had intensified the threat of certain diseases—cholera, typhoid, and tuberculosis.

Poe and the Gothic tradition were one response to society's anxiety about death. Another came from the pulpit: mid-nineteenth-century sermons took death as their almost constant subject. Somewhat later in the century, preachers would embrace a doctrine of consolation: God would be figured as a loving parent—almost motherly—who had prepared a home in heaven for us all, and ministers would tell the members of their congregation that they need not be apprehensive. However, stern traces of Puritanism still tinctured the religious discourse of Dickinson's young womanhood, and members of the Amherst congregation were regularly exhorted with blood-stirring urgency to reflect upon the imminence of their own demise. Repeatedly, then, in attempting to comprehend Dickinson's work, a reader must return to the fundamental tenets of Protestant Christianity, for her poetry echoes the Bible more often than any other single work or author.

In part this preoccupation with the doctrines of her day reflected a more general concern with the essential questions of human existence they addressed. In a letter to Higginson she once said, "To live is so startling, it leaves but little room for other occupations." And to her friend Mrs. Holland she wrote, "All this and more, though *is* there more? More than Love and Death? Then tell me its name." The religious thought and language of the culture was important to her poetry because it comprised the semiotic system that her society employed to discuss the mysteries of life and death. If she wished to contemplate these, what other language was there to employ?

In part, however, conventional Christianity—especially the latter-day Puritanism of Dickinson's New England—represented for Dickinson an ultimate expression of patriarchal power. Rebelling against its rule, upbraiding a "Father" in Heaven who required absolute "faith" from his followers, but gave no discernible response, became a way of attacking the very essence of unjust authority, especially male authority.

• • •

It is true that the stern doctrines of New England Protestantism offered hope for a life after death; yet in Dickinson's estimation, the trope that was used for this "salvation" revealed some of the most repellent features of God's power, for the invitation to accept "faith" had been issued in the context of a courtship with a macabre, sexual component. It was promised that those who had faith would be carried to Heaven by the "Bridegroom" Christ. "Blessed are they which are called unto the marriage supper of the Lamb" (Revelation 19:9). Nor did it escape Dickinson's notice that the perverse prurience of Poe's notions were essentially similar to this Christian idea of Christ's "love" for a "bride" which promised a reunion that must be "consummated" through death. Thus the poem that is, perhaps, the apotheosis of that distinctive Dickinson voice, "the speaking dead," offers an astonishing combination: this conventional promise of Christianity suffused with the tonalities of the Gothic tradition.

[Griffin quotes the entire text of "Because I could not stop for Death."]

The speaker is a beautiful woman (already dead!), and like some spectral Cinderella, she is dressed to go to a ball: "For only Gossamer, my Gown – / My Tippet – only Tulle –." Her escort recalls both the lover of Poe's configuration and the "Bridegroom" that had been promised in the Bible: "We slowly drove – He knew no haste / And I had put away / My labor and my leisure too, / For His Civility –". Their "Carriage" hovers in some surrealistic state that is exterior to both time and place: they are no longer earth-bound, not quite dead (or at least still possessed of consciousness), but they have not yet achieved the celebration that awaits them, the "marriage supper of the Lamb."

Yet the ultimate implication of this work turns precisely upon the *poet's* capacity to explode the finite temporal boundaries that generally define our existence, for there is a third member of the party—also exterior to time and location—and that is "Immortality." *True* immortality, the verse suggests, comes neither from the confabulations of a male lover nor from God's intangible Heaven. Irrefutable "Immortality" resides in the work of art itself, the creation of an empowered woman poet that continues to captivate readers more than one hundred years after her death. And this much-read, often-cited poem stands as patent proof upon the page of its own argument!

From "Emily Dickinson"

Judith Farr (b. 1937)

A Reading of "My Life had stood – a Loaded Gun"[1]　　　　1992

One of the notable qualities of this poem is its formidable directness of statement. Both the substance and the shape of the rhetoric seem straightforward. The ideas of guns and killing are not, superficially, invested by the speaker with negative properties. Far from it. The speaker recounts life with her master in tones of heady confidence and pleasure. If we did not know that this poem had been written by a woman—perhaps especially by "Miss Emily"—some of its presumed complexity and ominousness would be reduced. Let us say that Emily "when a Boy" is speaking; then it may be easier to credit the open delight of the speaker. Liberated from corners in the poem, he/she is freed into a grown-up gunman's life of authority and power, and she likes the idea exceedingly. All the piled-up, dynamic "And"s tell us so.

Or, if we cast her as a woman, she is what has been called "a man's woman"; everything he likes, *she* likes. She likes hunting, and her instincts are not pacifist or nurturing—no ducks and does for her. She smiles at her work of killing; Nature smiles with her (the firing of the gun makes a glow like Vesuvius); and at night she can pronounce the day good. (Hunting is, after all, not always a selfish sport; often it is a protective measure. "Sovereign Woods," of course, suggests a royal preserve, an unfair advantage for the hunter.) Because of her identification with the man, she is nearly human, but with a "Yellow Eye"—the color of explosion in an oval gunbarrel—and "emphatic Thumb." The American hunting pictures of Dickinson's day, like the landscapes of Bowles's favorite painter, Sanford Gifford, present hunting scenes like Dickinson's. Her buoyancy of tone accords with them, depicting easy days roaming in the open air, taking from an apparently complaisant nature all that the Master wants. If we imagine the speaker as a boy with his designated sponsor or master, then she is—up to the last quatrain—learning how to be a man in the rustic world dreamed up by Fenimore Cooper.

"Owner," however, suggests sexual love, and to anyone versed in the language of Emily Dickinson, it inflects one of her central themes:

'Twas my one glory –
Let it be
Remembered
I was owned of thee –

For that reason, and because there is such heroic intimacy between the gun and Master, one can see this as a poem of sexual love that emphasizes comradery, robust equality. It may be considered part of the Master cycle and related to "He touched me," where the speaker begins to "live" when Master touches her or carries her away. Although she is a woman, because the two are one in love she imagines herself like him; like him, empowered. . . . Here the speaker appropriates Master's masculinity; she is a loaded gun. Together they become one person, one royal We in a happy life of power. The speaker has always wanted to exercise her stored-up bullets or faculties; now she can. In a letter to her cousin Louise Norcross in 1880, Dickinson used these same images: "what is each instant but a gun, harmless because 'unloaded,' but that

---

[1]The full text of Dickinson's "My Life had stood – a Loaded Gun" appears on page 734.

touched 'goes off'?" Although she omits one step, loading the gun, she is describing in her letter what she may be describing in her poem: love, "touching," as a means of being empowered.

There remains the final quatrain. It reads as a tightly wrought riddle, inviting explication. In one way, the stanza points up the incontrovertible difference between the mechanical gun and the human owner. He is the complete being, having both the power to die and the power to kill (even without her help). For all her fusion with him in their acts of love and death, she must still depend on him; she must be "carried." Thus this poem is often read—and read brilliantly—as a revelation of the limitations experienced by women under patriarchy, or even of the dependency of the female artist who needs male masters like Higginson to help her exercise her powers.

In reading this poem, however, I think that emphasis should always be placed on the pleasure the speaker experiences. The Master may be carrying her, but she is also speaking for him. He cannot do without her. That the gun's firing is compared to the pleasure of "a Vesuvian face" accents destruction, certainly; and it is hard to exempt this use of Vesuvius from all the others, always destructive, in the Dickinson canon. But the speaker seems to welcome her own destructiveness. She has been waiting a long time in many "corners" until the right lover lets her speak. For Dickinson, love is always the muse. Her variant for "the *power* to kill" in the penultimate line is *art*—which could make others die, from love or from aesthetic rapture. She herself—the gun, the artist—can never "die" like a real woman, however. She is but the arresting voice that speaks to and for the Master.

From *The Passion of Emily Dickinson*

LANGSTON HUGHES

Langston Hughes was born in Joplin, Missouri, in 1902. After his parents separated during his early years, he and his mother often lived a life of itinerant poverty, mostly in Kansas. Hughes attended high school in Cleveland, where as a senior he wrote "The Negro Speaks of Rivers." Reluctantly supported by his father, he attended Columbia University for a year before withdrawing. After a series of menial jobs, Hughes became a merchant seaman in 1923 and visited the ports of West Africa. For a time he lived in Paris, Genoa, and Rome, before returning to the United States. The publication of The Weary Blues *(1926) earned him immediate fame, which he solidified a few months later with his pioneering essay "The Negro Artist and the*

Langston Hughes

Racial Mountain." In 1926 he also entered Lincoln University in Pennsylvania, from which he graduated in 1929. By then Hughes was already one of the central figures of the Harlem Renaissance, the flowering of African American arts and literature in the Harlem neighborhood of upper Manhattan in New York City during the 1920s. A strikingly versatile author, Hughes worked in fiction, drama, translation, criticism, opera libretti, memoir, cinema, and songwriting, as well as poetry. He also became a tireless promoter of African American culture, crisscrossing the United States on speaking tours as well as compiling twenty-eight anthologies of African American folklore and poetry. His newspaper columns, which often reported conversations with an imaginary Harlem friend named Jesse B. Semple, nicknamed "Simple," attracted an especially large following. During the 1930s Hughes became involved in radical politics and traveled to the Soviet Union, but after World War II he gradually shifted to mainstream progressive politics. In his last years he became a spokesman for the moderate wing of the civil rights movement. He died in Harlem in 1967.

POEMS

The Negro Speaks of Rivers   (1921) 1926

I've known rivers:
I've known rivers ancient as the world and older than the flow of human
    blood in human veins.

My soul has grown deep like the rivers.

I bathed in the Euphrates when dawns were young.
I built my hut near the Congo and it lulled me to sleep.   5
I looked upon the Nile and raised the pyramids above it.
I heard the singing of the Mississippi when Abe Lincoln went down to New
    Orleans, and I've seen its muddy bosom turn all golden in the sunset.

I've known rivers:
Ancient, dusky rivers.

My soul has grown deep like the rivers.   10

My People   1922

Dream-singers,
Story-tellers,
Dancers,
Loud laughers in the hands of Fate—
    My People.   5
Dish-washers,
Elevator-boys,
Ladies' maids,
Crap-shooters,
Cooks,   10
Waiters,
Jazzers,
Nurses of babies,
Loaders of ships,
Porters,   15
Hairdressers,
Comedians in vaudeville
And band-men in circuses—
Dream-singers all,
Story-tellers all.   20
    Dancers—
God! What dancers!
Singers—
God! What singers!
Singers and dancers   25
Dancers and laughers.
Laughers?
Yes, laughers . . . laughers . . . laughers—
Loud-mouthed laughers in the hands
    Of Fate.   30

Mother to Son   (1922) 1932

Well, son, I'll tell you:
Life for me ain't been no crystal stair.
It's had tacks in it,
And splinters,
And boards torn up,   5
And places with no carpet on the floor—
Bare.
But all the time
I'se been a-climbin' on,
And reachin' landin's,   10
And turnin' corners,
And sometimes goin' in the dark

Where there ain't been no light.
So boy, don't you turn back.
Don't you set down on the steps   15
'Cause you finds it's kinder hard.
Don't you fall now—
For I'se still goin', honey,
I'se still climbin',
And life for me ain't been no crystal stair.   20

Dream Variations   (1924) 1926

To fling my arms wide
In some place of the sun,
To whirl and to dance
Till the white day is done.
Then rest at cool evening   5
Beneath a tall tree
While night comes on gently,
   Dark like me—
That is my dream!

To fling my arms wide
In the face of the sun,   10
Dance! Whirl! Whirl!
Till the quick day is done.
Rest at pale evening . . .
A tall, slim tree . . .   15
Night coming tenderly
   Black like me.

I, Too   1926

I, too, sing America.

I am the darker brother.
They send me to eat in the kitchen
When company comes,
But I laugh,   5
And eat well,
And grow strong.

Tomorrow,
I'll be at the table
When company comes.   10
Nobody'll dare
Say to me,
"Eat in the kitchen,"
Then.

Besides,
They'll see how beautiful I am
And be ashamed—   15

I, too, am America.

The Weary Blues   1926

Droning a drowsy syncopated tune,
Rocking back and forth to a mellow croon,
    I heard a Negro play.
Down on Lenox Avenue the other night
By the pale dull pallor of an old gas light   5
    He did a lazy sway. . . .
    He did a lazy sway. . . .
To the tune o' those Weary Blues.
With his ebony hands on each ivory key
He made that poor piano moan with melody.   10
    O Blues!
Swaying to and fro on his rickety stool
He played that sad raggy tune like a musical fool.
    Sweet Blues!
Coming from a black man's soul.   15
    O Blues!
In a deep song voice with a melancholy tone
I heard that Negro sing, that old piano moan—
    "Ain't got nobody in all this world,
    Ain't got nobody but ma self.   20
    I's gwine to quit ma frownin'
    And put ma troubles on the shelf."

Thump, thump, thump, went his foot on the floor.
He played a few chords then he sang some more—
    "I got the Weary Blues   25
    And I can't be satisfied.
    Got the Weary Blues
    And can't be satisfied—
    I ain't happy no mo'
    And I wish that I had died."   30
And far into the night he crooned that tune.
The stars went out and so did the moon.
The singer stopped playing and went to bed
While the Weary Blues echoed through his head.
He slept like a rock or a man that's dead.   35

THE WEARY BLUES. This poem quotes the first blues song Hughes had ever heard, "The Weary Blues," which
begins, "I got the weary blues / And I can't be satisfied / . . . I ain't happy no mo' / And I wish that I had died."

Song for a Dark Girl   1927

Way Down South in Dixie
  (Break the heart of me)
They hung my black young lover
  To a cross roads tree.

Way Down South in Dixie   5
  (Bruised body high in air)
I asked the white Lord Jesus
  What was the use of prayer.

Way Down South in Dixie
  (Break the heart of me)
Love is a naked shadow   10
  On a gnarled and naked tree.

Prayer   (1931) 1947

Gather up
In the arms of your pity
The sick, the depraved,
The desperate, the tired,
All the scum   5
Of our weary city
Gather up
In the arms of your pity.
Gather up
In the arms of your love—   10
Those who expect
No love from above.

Ballad of the Landlord   (1940) 1943

Landlord, landlord,
My roof has sprung a leak.
Don't you 'member I told you about it
Way last week?

Landlord, landlord,   5
These steps is broken down.
When you come up yourself
It's a wonder you don't fall down.

Ten Bucks you say I owe you?
Ten Bucks you say is due?
Well, that's Ten Bucks more'n I'll pay you   10
Till you fix this house up new.

What? You gonna get eviction orders?
You gonna cut off my heat?
You gonna take my furniture and   15
Throw it in the street?

Um-huh! You talking high and mighty.
Talk on—till you get through.
You ain't gonna be able to say a word
If I land my fist on you.   20

Police! Police!
Come and get this man!
He's trying to ruin the government
And overturn the land!

Copper's Whistle!   25
Patrol bell!
Arrest.

Precinct Station.
Iron cell.
Headlines in press: 30

MAN THREATENS LANDLORD

. .

TENANT HELD NO BAIL

. .

JUDGE GIVES NEGRO 90 DAYS IN COUNTY JAIL

End   1947

There are
No clocks on the wall,
And no time,
No shadows that move
From dawn to dusk   5
Across the floor.

There is neither light
Nor dark
Outside the door.

There is no door!   10

Theme for English B   1951

The instructor said,

> *Go home and write*
> *a page tonight.*
> *And let that page come out of you—*
> *Then, it will be true.*   5

I wonder if it's that simple?
I am twenty-two, colored, born in Winston-Salem.
I went to school there, then Durham, then here
to this college on the hill above Harlem.
I am the only colored student in my class. 10
The steps from the hill lead down into Harlem,
through a park, then I cross St. Nicholas,
Eighth Avenue, Seventh, and I come to the Y,
the Harlem Branch Y, where I take the elevator
up to my room, sit down, and write this page: 15

It's not easy to know what is true for you or me
at twenty-two, my age. But I guess I'm what
I feel and see and hear, Harlem, I hear you:
hear you, hear me—we two—you, me, talk on this page.
(I hear New York, too.) Me—who? 20
Well, I like to eat, sleep, drink, and be in love.
I like to work, read, learn, and understand life.
I like a pipe for a Christmas present,
or records—Bessie, bop, or Bach.
I guess being colored doesn't make me *not* like 25
the same things other folks like who are other races.
So will my page be colored that I write?
Being me, it will not be white.
But it will be
a part of you, instructor. 30
You are white—
yet a part of me, as I am a part of you.
That's American.
Sometimes perhaps you don't want to be a part of me.
Nor do I often want to be a part of you. 35
But we are, that's true!
As I learn from you,
I guess you learn from me—
although you're older—and white—
and somewhat more free. 40

This is my page for English B.

THEME FOR ENGLISH B. *9 college on the hill above Harlem:* Columbia University, where Hughes was briefly a student. (Note, however, that this poem is not autobiographical. The young speaker is a character invented by the middle-aged author.) *24 Bessie:* Bessie Smith (1898?–1937) was a popular blues singer often called the "Empress of the Blues."

Subway Rush Hour   1951

Mingled
breath and smell
so close
mingled
black and white 5
so near
no room for fear.

Harlem [Dream Deferred]

1951

What happens to a dream deferred?

    Does it dry up
    like a raisin in the sun?
    Or fester like a sore—
    And then run?   5
    Does it stink like rotten meat?
    Or crust and sugar over—
    like a syrupy sweet?

    Maybe it just sags
    like a heavy load.   10

    Or does it explode?

HARLEM. This famous poem appeared under two titles in the author's lifetime. Both titles appear above.

Homecoming

1959

I went back in the alley
And I opened up my door.
All her clothes was gone:
She wasn't home no more.

I pulled back the covers,   5
I made down the bed.
A *whole* lot of room
Was the only thing I had.

As Befits a Man

1959

I don't mind dying—
But I'd hate to die all alone!
I want a dozen pretty women
To holler, cry, and moan.

I don't mind dying   5
But I want my funeral to be fine:
A row of long tall mamas
Fainting, fanning, and crying.

I want a fish-tail hearse
And sixteen fish-tail cars,   10
A big brass band
And a whole truck load of flowers.

When they let me down,
Down into the clay,
I want the women to holler: 15
Please don't take him away!
    Ow-ooo-oo-o!
Don't take daddy away!

Compare

Other poems by Langston Hughes that are found in this book:

Dream Boogie (page 804)
Two Somewhat Different Epigrams (page 822)

LANGSTON HUGHES ON LANGSTON HUGHES

Lenox Avenue, Harlem, in 1925.

The Negro Artist and the Racial Mountain   1926

Most of my own poems are racial in theme and treatment, derived from the life I know. In many of them I try to grasp and hold some of the meanings and rhythms of jazz. I am as sincere as I know how to be in these poems and yet after every reading I answer questions like these from my own people: Do you think Negroes should always write about Negroes? I wish you wouldn't read some of your poems to white folks. How do you find anything interesting in a place like a cabaret? Why do you write about black people? You aren't black. What makes you do so many jazz poems?

But jazz to me is one of the inherent expressions of Negro life in America; the eternal tom-tom beating in the Negro soul—the tom-tom of revolt against weariness in a white world, a world of subway trains, and work, work, work; the tom-tom of joy and laughter, and pain swallowed in a smile. Yet the Philadelphia clubwoman is ashamed to say that her race created it and she does not like me to write about it. The old subconscious "white is best" runs through her mind. Years of study under white teachers, a lifetime of white books, pictures, and papers, and white manners, morals, and Puritan standards made her dislike the spirituals. And now she turns up her nose at jazz and all its manifestations—likewise almost everything else distinctly racial. She doesn't care for the Winold Reiss portraits of Negroes because they are "too Negro." She does not want a true picture of herself from anybody. She wants the artist to flatter her, to make the white world believe that all Negroes are as smug and as near white in soul as she wants to be. But, to my mind, it is the duty of the younger Negro artist, if he accepts any duties at all from outsiders, to change through the force of his art that old whispering "I want to be white," hidden in the aspirations of his people, to "Why should I want to be white? I am a Negro—and beautiful."

So I am ashamed for the black poet who says, "I want to be a poet, not a Negro poet," as though his own racial world were not as interesting as any other world. I am ashamed, too, for the colored artist who runs from the painting of Negro faces to the painting of sunsets after the manner of the academicians because he fears the strange un-whiteness of his own features. An artist must be free to choose what he does, certainly, but he must also never be afraid to do what he might choose.

From "The Negro Artist and the Racial Mountain"

Compare

Hughes's comments on the African American artist with Darryl Pinckney's critical observations on Langston Hughes's public identity as a black poet (page 988).

The Harlem Renaissance   1940

White people began to come to Harlem in droves. For several years they packed the expensive Cotton Club on Lenox Avenue. But I was never there, because the Cotton Club was a Jim Crow club for gangsters and monied whites. They were not cordial to Negro patronage, unless you were a celebrity like Bojangles.° So Harlem Negroes did not like the Cotton Club and never appreciated its Jim Crow policy in the very heart of their dark community. Nor did ordinary Negroes like the growing influx of whites toward Harlem after sundown, flooding the little cabarets and bars where formerly only colored people laughed and sang, and where now the strangers were given the best ringside tables to sit and stare at the Negro customers—like amusing animals in a zoo.

The Negroes said: "We can't go downtown and sit and stare at you in your clubs. You won't even let us in your clubs." But they didn't say it out loud—for Negroes are practically never rude to white people. So thousands of whites came to Harlem night after night, thinking the Negroes loved to have them there, and firmly believing that all Harlemites left their houses at sundown to sing and dance in cabarets, because most of the whites saw nothing but the cabarets, not the houses.

Some of the owners of Harlem clubs, delighted at the flood of white patronage, made the grievous error of barring their own race, after the manner of the famous Cotton Club. But most of these quickly lost business and folded up, because they failed to realize that a large part of the Harlem attraction for downtown New Yorkers lay in simply watching the colored customers amuse themselves. And the smaller clubs, of course, had no big floor shows or a name band like the Cotton Club, where Duke Ellington usually held forth, so, without black patronage, they were not amusing at all.

Some of the small clubs, however, had people like Gladys Bentley, who was something worth discovering in those days, before she got famous, acquired an accompanist, specially written material, and conscious vulgarity. But for two or three amazing years, Miss Bentley sat, and played a big piano all night long, literally all night, without stopping—singing songs like "The St. James Infirmary," from ten in the evening until dawn, with scarcely a break between the notes, sliding from one

---

Bojangles: Bill "Bojangles" Robinson (1876–1949), dancer.

song to another, with a powerful and continuous underbeat of jungle rhythm. Miss Bentley was an amazing exhibition of musical energy—a large, dark, masculine lady, whose feet pounded the floor while her fingers pounded the keyboard—a perfect piece of African sculpture, animated by her own rhythm.

But when the place where she played became too well known, she began to sing with an accompanist, became a star, moved to a larger place, then downtown, and is now in Hollywood. The old magic of the woman and the piano and the night and the rhythm being one is gone. But everything goes, one way or another. The '20s are gone and lots of fine things in Harlem night life have disappeared like snow in the sun— since it became utterly commercial, planned for the downtown tourist trade, and therefore dull.

The lindy-hoppers at the Savoy even began to practice acrobatic routines, and to do absurd things for the entertainment of the whites, that probably never would have entered their heads to attempt merely for their own effortless amusement. Some of the lindy-hoppers had cards printed with their names on them and became dance professors teaching the tourists. Then Harlem nights became show nights for the Nordics.

Some critics say that that is what happened to certain Negro writers, too—that they ceased to write to amuse themselves and began to write to amuse and entertain

The first and only issue of *Fire!!* (1926), an influential journal of the Harlem Renaissance.

white people, and in so doing distorted and overcolored their material, and left out a great many things they thought would offend their American brothers of a lighter complexion. Maybe—since Negroes have writer-racketeers, as has any other race. But I have known almost all of them, and most of the good ones have tried to be honest, write honestly, and express their world as they saw it.

From *The Big Sea*

CRITICS ON LANGSTON HUGHES

Arnold Rampersad (b. 1941)

Hughes as an Experimentalist   1991

From his first publication of verse in the *Crisis*, Hughes had reflected his admiration for Sandburg and Whitman by experimenting with free verse as opposed to committing himself conservatively to rhyme. Even when he employed rhyme in his verse, as he often did, Hughes composed with relative casualness—unlike other major black poets of the day, such as Countee Cullen and Claude McKay, with their highly wrought stanzas. He seemed to prefer, as Whitman and Sandburg had preferred, to write lines that captured the cadences of common American speech, with his ear always especially attuned to the variety of black American language. This last aspect was only a token of his emotional and aesthetic involvement in black American culture, which he increasingly saw as his prime source of inspiration, even as he regarded black Americans ("Loud laughers in the hands of Fate— / My People") as his only indispensable audience.

Early poems captured some of the sights and sounds of ecstatic black church worship ("Glory! Hallelujah!"), but Hughes's greatest technical accomplishment as a poet was in his fusing of the rhythms of blues and jazz with traditional poetry. This technique, which he employed his entire life, surfaced in his art around 1923 with the landmark poem "The Weary Blues," in which the persona recalls hearing a blues singer and piano player ("Sweet Blues! / Coming from a black man's soul") performing in what most likely is a speakeasy in Harlem. The persona recalls the plaintive verse intoned by the singer ("Ain't got nobody in all this world, / Ain't got nobody but ma self.") but finally surrenders to the mystery and magic of the blues singer's art. In the process, Hughes had taken an indigenous African American art form, perhaps the most vivid and commanding of all, and preserved its authenticity even as he formally enshrined it in the midst of a poem in traditional European form.

"The Weary Blues," a work virtually unprecedented in American poetry in its blending of black and white rhythms and forms, won Hughes the first prize for poetry in May 1925 in the epochal literary contest sponsored by *Opportunity* magazine, which marked the first high point of the Harlem Renaissance. The work also confirmed his leadership, along with Countee Cullen, of all the younger poets of the burgeoning movement. For Hughes, it was only the first step in his poetical tribute to blues and jazz. By the time of his second volume of verse, *Fine Clothes to the Jew* (1927), he was writing blues poems without either apology or framing devices taken from the traditional world of poetry. He was also delving into the basic subject matters of the blues—love and raw sexuality, deep sorrow and sudden violence, poverty and heartbreak. These subjects, treated with sympathy for the poor and dispossessed, and without false piety, made him easily the most controversial black poet of his time.

From "Langston Hughes"

Rita Dove (b. 1952)

and Marilyn Nelson (b. 1946)

The Voices in Langston Hughes   1998

Affectionately known for most of his life as "The Poet Laureate of Harlem," Langston Hughes was born in Missouri and raised in the Midwest, moving to Harlem only as a young man. There he discovered his spiritual home, in Harlem's heart of Blackness finding both his vocation—"to explain and illuminate the Negro condition in America"—and the proletarian voice of most of his best work. If Johnson was the Renaissance man of the Harlem Renaissance, Hughes was its greatest man of letters; he saw through publication more than a dozen collections of poems, ten plays, two novels, several collections of short fiction, one historical study, two autobiographical works, several anthologies, and many books for children. His essay, "The Negro Artist and the Racial Mountain," provided a personal credo and statement of direction for the poets of his generation, who, he says, "intend to express our individual dark-skinned selves without fear or shame . . . We know we are beautiful. And ugly too." His forthright commitment to the Negro people led him to explore with great authenticity the frustrated dreams of the Black masses and to experiment with diction, rhythm, and musical forms.

Hughes was ever quick to confess the influences of Whitman and Sandburg on his work, and his best poetry also reflects the influence of Sherwood Anderson's *Winesburg, Ohio*. Like these poets, Hughes collected individual voices; his work is a notebook of life-studies. In his best poems Hughes the man remains masked; his voices are the voices of the Negro race as a whole, or of individual Negro speakers. "The Negro Speaks of Rivers," a widely anthologized poem from his first book, *The Weary Blues* (1926), is a case in point. Here Hughes is visible only as spokesman for the race as he proclaims "I bathed in the Euphrates when dawns were young. / I built my hut near the Congo and it lulled me to sleep." Poems frequently present anonymous Black personae, each of whom shares a painful heritage and an ironic pride. As one humorous character announces:

> I do cooking,
> Day's work, too!
> Alberta K. Johnson—
> *Madam* to you.

Hughes took poetry out of what Cullen called "the dark tower"—which was, and even during the Harlem Renaissance, ivy-covered and distant and took it directly to the people. His blues and jazz experiments described and addressed an audience for which music was a central experience; he became a spokesman for their troubles, as in "Po' Boy Blues":

> When I was home de
> Sunshine seemed like gold.
> When I was home de
> Sunshine seemed like gold.
> Since I come up North de
> Whole damn world's turned cold.

American democracy appears frequently in Hughes's work as the unfulfilled but potentially realizable dream of the Negro, who says in "Let America Be America Again":

O, yes,
I say it plain,
America never was America to me
And yet I swear this oath—
America will be!

There are many fine poems in the Hughes canon, but the strongest single work is *Montage of a Dream Deferred* (1951), a collection of sketches, captured voices, and individual lives unified by the jazzlike improvisations on the central theme of "a dream deferred." Like many of his individual poems, this work is intended for performance: think of it as a Harlem *Under Milk Wood.* Hughes moves rapidly from one voice or scene to the next; from the person in "Blues in Dawn" who says "I don't dare start thinking in the morning," to, in "Dime," a snatch of conversation: "Chile, these steps is hard to climb. / Grandma, lend me a dime."

The moods of the poems are as varied as their voices, for Hughes includes the daylight hours as well as the night. There are the bitter jump-rope rhymes of disillusioned children, the naive exclamations of young lovers, the gossip of friends. A college freshman writes in his "Theme for English B": "I guess being colored doesn't make me *not* like / the same things other folks like who are other races." A jaded woman offers in "Advice" the observation that "birthing is hard / and dying is mean," and advises youth to "get yourself / a little loving / in between." "Hope" is a miniature vignette in which a dying man asks for fish, and "His wife looked it up in her dream book / and played it." The changing voices, moods, and rhythms of this collection are, as Hughes wrote in a preface, "Like be-bop . . . marked by conflicting change, sudden nuances. . . ." We are reminded throughout that we should be hearing the poem as music; as boogie-woogie, as blues, as bass, as saxophone. Against the eighty-odd dreams collected here, the refrain insists that these frustrated dreams are potentially dangerous:

What happens to a dream deferred?

Does it dry up
like a raisin in the sun?
Or fester like a sore—
And then run?
Does it stink like rotten meat?
Or crust and sugar over—
like a syrupy sweet?

Maybe it just sags
like a heavy load.

Or does it explode?

More than any other Black poet, Langston Hughes spoke for the Negro people. Most of those after him have emulated his ascent of the Racial Mountain, his painfully joyous declaration of pride and commonality. His work offers white readers a glimpse into the social and the personal lives of Black America; Black readers recognize a proud affirmation of self.

From "A Black Rainbow: Modern Afro-American Poetry"

Darryl Pinckney (b. 1953)

Black Identity in Langston Hughes

1989

Fierce identification with the sorrows and pleasures of the poor black—"I myself belong to that class"—propelled Hughes toward the voice of the black Everyman. He made a distinction between his lyric and his social poetry, the private and the public. In the best of his social poetry he turned himself into a transmitter of messages and made the "I" a collective "I":

> I've known rivers:
> I've known rivers ancient as the world and older than the flow of
>   human blood in human veins.
>
> My soul has grown deep like the rivers.
>
> I bathed in the Euphrates when dawns were young.
> I built my hut near the Congo and it lulled me to sleep.
> I looked upon the Nile and raised the pyramids above it.
> I heard the singing of the Mississippi when Abe Lincoln went down to
>   New Orleans, and I've seen its muddy bosom turn all golden in the
>   sunset.
>
>   ("The Negro Speaks of Rivers")

The medium conveys a singleness of intention: to make the black known. The straightforward, declarative style doesn't call attention to itself. Nothing distracts from forceful statement, as if the shadowy characters Sandburg wrote about in, say, "When Mammy Hums" had at last their chance to come forward and testify. Poems like "Aunt Sue's Stories" reflect the folk ideal of black women as repositories of racial lore. The story told in dramatic monologues like "The Negro Mother" or "Mother to Son" is one of survival—life "ain't been no crystal stair." The emphasis is on the capacity of black people to endure, which is why Hughes's social poetry, though not strictly protest writing, indicts white America, even taunts it with the steady belief that blacks will overcome simply by "keeping on":

> I, too, sing America.
>
> I am the darker brother.
> They send me to eat in the kitchen
> When company comes,
> But I laugh,
> And eat well,
> And grow strong.
>
>   ("I, Too")

Whites were not the only ones who could be made uneasy by Hughes's attempts to boldly connect past and future. The use of "black" and the invocation of Africa were defiant gestures back in the days when many blacks described themselves as brown. When Hughes answered Sandburg's "Nigger" ("I am the nigger, / Singer of Songs . . .") with "I am a Negro, / Black as the night is black, / Black like the depths of my Africa" ("Negro") he challenged the black middle class with his absorption in slave heritage.

                                   From "Suitcase in Harlem"

Peter Townsend (b. 1948)

Langston Hughes and Jazz   2000

Hughes's engagement with jazz was close and long-lived, from his "Weary Blues" of 1926 up to the time of his death in 1967. Jazz crops naturally out of the landscape of Hughes's poetry, which is largely that of the black communities of Harlem and Chicago, and it remains fluid in its significance. Hughes's earliest references to jazz, in poems like "Jazzonia" and "Jazz Band in a Parisian Cabaret," acknowledge the exoticism which was customary in the presentation of jazz in the 1920s, and the novelty which the music still possessed for Hughes himself:

> In a Harlem cabaret
> Six long-headed jazzers play
> A dancing girl whose eyes are bold
> Lifts high a dress of silken gold.

("Jazzonia")

This novelty is compounded by a further level of exoticism for the white visitors to the black cabarets who figure frequently in Hughes's jazz world. "Jazz Band in a Parisian Cabaret," for instance, has the band

> Play it for the lords and ladies
> For the dukes and counts
> For the whores and gigolos
> For the American millionaires

and "Harlem Night Club" pictures "dark brown girls / In blond men's arms." In Hughes's more politically barbed poetry of the 1930s these comments on white voyeurism harden into his attitude in "Visitors to the Black Belt":

> You can say
> Jazz on the South Side—
> To me it's hell
> On the South Side.

At the same time, jazz is one of the threads that make up the fabric of urban life in the "Harlem Renaissance" period. In a poem entitled "Heart of Harlem" Hughes places jazz musicians such as Earl Hines and Billie Holiday alongside individuals of the stature of Adam Clayton Powell, Joe Louis and W. E. B. Du Bois. Hughes's continuous awareness of the place of jazz in his community enables him to record its scenes and its changes across the decades. "Lincoln Theatre," a poem published in a collection in 1949, gives a memorably exact rendering of the sort of Swing Era performance, in a Harlem theater, that was discussed [earlier]:

> The movies end. The lights flash gaily on.
> The band down in the pit bursts into jazz.
> The crowd applauds a plump brown-skin bleached blonde
> Who sings the troubles every woman has.

Hughes responded with particular sympathy to jazz of the bebop period, which he saw as having great political significance. *Montage of a Dream Deferred*, published in 1951, is one of Hughes's most substantial sequences of poems, and it is shot through with references to jazz. His editorial note to the sequence explains the stylistic influence of bebop on its composition:

> This poem on contemporary Harlem, like bebop, is marked by conflicting changes, sudden nuances, sharp and impudent interjections, and passages sometimes in the manner of the jam session, sometimes the popular song, punctuated by the riffs, runs, breaks and distortions of the music of a community in transition.

As Hughes made clear in other places, he heard bebop as an expression of a dissident spirit within the younger black community:

> Little cullud boys with fears
> frantic, kick their draftee years
> into flatted fifths and flatter beers . . .

and "Dream Boogie" resounds with suggestions, threatening or impudent, that well up in the music, the "boogie-woogie rumble":

> Listen to it closely:
> Ain't you heard
> something underneath . . .

Bebop affected the forms of Hughes's poetry at the higher architectural levels, dictating the structural rhythm of longer works like "Dream Deferred," but otherwise he employed a small range of simple verse forms that originate in earlier styles of black music. A particular favourite was a two-stress line rhymed in quatrains, derived from spirituals, and he also frequently used a looser form drawn from the 12-bar blues. The first of these Hughes was able to use with remarkable flexibility, considering its brevity. The form is often used for aphoristic effect, as in "Motto":

> I play it cool
> And dig all jive.
> That's the reason
> I stay alive.

or in "Sliver," a comment on the form itself:

> A cheap little tune
> To cheap little rhymes
> Can cut a man's
> Throat sometimes.

What is even more remarkable is the naturalness of its effect in these diverse contexts. Hughes makes the form serve the purposes of narrative and description just as flexibly as that of comment. It gives Hughes's verse its idiomatic flavor, so that even where the subject is not jazz or even music, the verse is still permeated with the qualities of black musical culture.

From Jazz in American Culture

Onwuchekwa Jemie (b. 1940)

A Reading of "Dream Deferred" 1976

The deferred dream is examined through a variety of human agencies, of interlocking and recurring voices and motifs fragmented and scattered throughout the six sections of the poem. Much as in bebop, the pattern is one of constant reversals and contrasts. Frequently the poems are placed in thematic clusters, with poems within the cluster arranged in contrasting pairs. *Montage [of a Dream Deferred]* does not move in a straight line; its component poems move off in invisible directions, reappear and touch, creating a complex tapestry or mosaic.

The dream theme itself is carried in the musical motifs. It is especially characterized by the rumble ("The boogie-woogie rumble / Of a dream deferred")—that rapid thumping and tumbling of notes which so powerfully drives to the bottom of the emotions, stirring feelings too deep to be touched by the normal successions of notes and common rhythms. The rumble is an atomic explosion of musical energy, an articulate confusion, a moment of epiphany, a flash of blinding light in which all things are suddenly made clear. The theme is sounded at strategic times, culminating in the final section. . . .

The poet has taken us on a guided tour of microcosmic Harlem, day and night, past and present. And as a new day dawns and the poem moves into a summing up in the final section, he again poses the question and examines the possibilities:

What happens to a dream deferred?

> Does it dry up
> like a raisin in the sun?
> Or fester like a sore—
> And then run?
> Does it stink like rotten meat?
> Or crust and sugar over—
> like a syrupy sweet?

> Maybe it just sags
> like a heavy load.

> *Or does it explode?*

The images are sensory, domestic, earthy, like blues images. The stress is on deterioration—drying, rotting, festering, souring—on loss of essential natural quality. The raisin has fallen from a fresh, juicy grape to a dehydrated but still edible raisin to a sun-baked and inedible dead bone of itself. The Afro-American is not unlike the raisin, for he is in a sense a dessicated trunk of his original African self, used and abandoned in the American wilderness with the stipulation that he rot and disappear. Like the raisin lying neglected in the scorching sun, the black man is treated as a thing of no consequence. But the raisin refuses the fate assigned to it, metamorphoses instead into a malignant living sore that will not heal or disappear. Like the raisin, a sore is but a little thing, inconsequential on the surface but in fact symptomatic of a serious disorder. Its stink is like the stink of the rotten meat sold to black folks in so many ghetto groceries; meat no longer suitable for human use, deathly. And while a syrupy sweet is not central to the diet as meat might be, still it is a rounding-off final pleasure (dessert) at the end of a meal, or a delicious surprise that a child looks forward to at Halloween or Christmas. But that final pleasure turns out to be a pain. Aged, spoiled candy leaves a sickly taste in the mouth; sweetness gone bad turns a treat into a trick.

The elements of the deferred dream are, like the raisin, sore, meat, and candy, little things of no great consequence in themselves. But their unrelieved accretion packs together considerable pressure. Their combined weight becomes too great to carry about indefinitely: not only does the weight increase from continued accumulation, but the longer it is carried the heavier it feels. The load sags from its own weight, and the carrier sags with it; and if he should drop it, it just might explode from all its strange, tortured, and compressed energies.

In short, a dream deferred can be a terrifying thing. Its greatest threat is its unpredictability, and for this reason the question format is especially fitting. Questions demand the reader's participation, corner and sweep him headlong to the final, inescapable conclusion.

From *Langston Hughes: An Introduction to the Poetry*

FOR FURTHER READING

You can study several other poets in depth in this book. Writers who are represented at length include:

> Robert Frost—12 poems (plus Frost on Writing)
> William Shakespeare—8 poems
> William Carlos Williams—8 poems
> William Butler Yeats—8 poems (plus Yeats on Writing)
> William Blake—6 poems
> Thomas Hardy—6 poems

See the Index for specific details.

■ WRITING *effectively*

TOPICS FOR WRITING ABOUT EMILY DICKINSON

1. Focusing on one or two poems, demonstrate how Dickinson's idiosyncratic capitalization and punctuation add special impact to her work.
2. How do the poems by Dickinson in this chapter and elsewhere in the book illustrate her statement (in "Recognizing Poetry" on page 964 that "I find ecstasy in living—the mere sense of living is joy enough"?

TOPICS FOR WRITING ABOUT LANGSTON HUGHES

1. Compare and contrast the use of first-person voices in two poems by Langston Hughes (such as "I, Too" and "Theme for English B" or "Mother to Son" and "The Negro Speaks of Rivers"). In what ways does the speaker's "I" differ in each poem and in what ways is it similar?
2. Discussing a single poem by Hughes, examine how musical forms (such as jazz, blues, or popular song) help shape the effect of the work.

32

CRITICAL CASEBOOK
*T. S. Eliot's "The Love Song of
J. Alfred Prufrock"*

Eliot around 1910.

*Yeats and Pound achieved modernity;
Eliot was modern from the start.*

—LOUISE BOGAN

T. S. ELIOT

Thomas Stearns Eliot was born on September 26, 1888, in St. Louis, Missouri. Both his father, a brick manufacturer, and mother were descended from families that had emigrated from England to Massachusetts in the seventeenth century. Entering Harvard on his eighteenth birthday, he earned a B.A. in 1909 and an M.A. in English literature in 1910. After a year in Paris, he returned to Harvard, where he undertook graduate studies in philosophy and also served as a teaching assistant. Awarded a traveling fellowship, he intended to study in Germany, but the outbreak of World War I in August 1914 forced him to leave the country after only several weeks. He then went to London, England, which would be his home for the remaining fifty years of his life.

T. S. Eliot at Age 18

In September 1914, Eliot met fellow poet Ezra Pound, who would be a great influence on his work and his literary career. In June 1915, Eliot married Vivienne Haigh-Wood after an acquaintance of two months. (The marriage was troubled from the start. He would separate from Vivienne in 1933; she was subsequently institutionalized and died in a nursing home in 1947.) The year 1915 also saw Eliot's first major publication, when "The Love Song of J. Alfred Prufrock" appeared in the June issue of Poetry. *It became the central piece of his first collection,* Prufrock and Other Observations *(1917). During this period, he taught school briefly and worked in Lloyds Bank for several years. He secured permanent employment when he joined the publishing firm of Faber and Gwyer (later Faber and Faber) in 1925.*

Eliot became one of the best-known and most controversial poets of his time with the publication of The Waste Land *(1922). Conservative critics denounced it as impenetrable and incoherent; readers of more advanced tastes responded at once to the poem's depiction of a sordid society, empty of spiritual values, in the wake of World War I. Through the* Criterion, *a journal that he founded in 1922, and through his essays and volumes of literary and social criticism, Eliot came to exert immense influence as a molder of opinion.*

Religious themes became increasingly important to his poetry, from "Journey of the Magi" (1927), through Ash-Wednesday (1930), to Murder in the Cathedral *(1935), which dealt with the death of St. Thomas à Becket, and was the first of his several full-length verse dramas. Others included* The Family Reunion *(1939) and* The Cocktail Party *(1949), which became a remarkable popular success, estimated to have been seen by more than a million and a half people in Eliot's lifetime. Another of his works reached many more millions, at least indirectly: the light-verse pieces of* Old Possum's Book of Practical Cats *(1939) later became the basis of the record-breaking Broadway musical* Cats *(1982). Eliot's last major work of nondramatic poetry was* Four Quartets *(1943). In 1948, he was awarded the Nobel Prize in Literature.*

In January 1957, Eliot married Valerie Fletcher, his secretary at Faber and Faber. After several years of declining health, he died of emphysema at his home in London on January 4, 1965.

The Love Song of J. Alfred Prufrock

1917

> *S'io credessi che mia risposta fosse*
> *a persona che mai tornasse al mondo,*
> *questa fiamma staria senza più scosse.*
> *ma per ciò che giammai di questo fondo*
> *Non tornò vivo alcun, s'i'odo il vero,*
> *senza tema d'infamia ti rispondo.*

Let us go then, you and I,
When the evening is spread out against the sky
Like a patient etherized upon a table;
Let us go, through certain half-deserted streets,
The muttering retreats   5
Of restless nights in one-night cheap hotels
And sawdust restaurants with oyster-shells:
Streets that follow like a tedious argument
Of insidious intent
To lead you to an overwhelming question . . .   10
Oh, do not ask, "What is it?"
Let us go and make our visit.

    In the room the women come and go
Talking of Michelangelo.

    The yellow fog that rubs its back upon the window-panes,   15
The yellow smoke that rubs its muzzle on the window-panes,
Licked its tongue into the corners of the evening,
Lingered upon the pools that stand in drains,
Let fall upon its back the soot that falls from chimneys,
Slipped by the terrace, made a sudden leap,   20
And seeing that it was a soft October night,
Curled once about the house, and fell asleep.

    And indeed there will be time
For the yellow smoke that slides along the street
Rubbing its back upon the window-panes;   25
There will be time, there will be time
To prepare a face to meet the faces that you meet;
There will be time to murder and create,
And time for all the works and days of hands
That lift and drop a question on your plate;   30
Time for you and time for me,
And time yet for a hundred indecisions,
And for a hundred visions and revisions,
Before the taking of a toast and tea.

    In the room the women come and go   35
Talking of Michelangelo.

And indeed there will be time
To wonder, "Do I dare?" and, "Do I dare?"
Time to turn back and descend the stair,
With a bald spot in the middle of my hair—   40
(They will say: "How his hair is growing thin!")
My morning coat, my collar mounting firmly to the chin,
My necktie rich and modest, but asserted by a simple pin—
(They will say: "But how his arms and legs are thin!")
Do I dare   45
Disturb the universe?
In a minute there is time
For decisions and revisions which a minute will reverse.

    For I have known them all already, known them all—
Have known the evenings, mornings, afternoons,   50
I have measured out my life with coffee spoons;
I know the voices dying with a dying fall
Beneath the music from a farther room.
    So how should I presume?

    And I have known the eyes already, known them all—   55
The eyes that fix you in a formulated phrase,
And when I am formulated, sprawling on a pin,
When I am pinned and wriggling on the wall,
Then how should I begin
To spit out all the butt-ends of my days and ways?   60
    And how should I presume?

    And I have known the arms already, known them all—
Arms that are braceleted and white and bare
(But in the lamplight, downed with light brown hair!)
Is it perfume from a dress   65
That makes me so digress?
Arms that lie along a table, or wrap about a shawl.
    And should I then presume?
    And how should I begin?

                                    • • •

Shall I say, I have gone at dusk through narrow streets   70
And watched the smoke that rises from the pipes
Of lonely men in shirt-sleeves, leaning out of windows? . . .

    I should have been a pair of ragged claws
Scuttling across the floors of silent seas.

                                    • • •

And the afternoon, the evening, sleeps so peacefully!   75
Smoothed by long fingers,
Asleep . . . tired . . . or it malingers,
Stretched on the floor, here beside you and me.
Should I, after tea and cakes and ices,
Have the strength to force the moment to its crisis?   80
But though I have wept and fasted, wept and prayed,
Though I have seen my head (grown slightly bald) brought in upon a platter,
I am no prophet—and here's no great matter;
I have seen the moment of my greatness flicker,
And I have seen the eternal Footman hold my coat, and snicker,   85
And in short, I was afraid.

    And would it have been worth it, after all,
After the cups, the marmalade, the tea,
Among the porcelain, among some talk of you and me,
Would it have been worth while,   90
To have bitten off the matter with a smile,
To have squeezed the universe into a ball
To roll it toward some overwhelming question,
To say: "I am Lazarus, come from the dead,
Come back to tell you all, I shall tell you all"—   95
If one, settling a pillow by her head,
    Should say: "That is not what I meant at all.
    That is not it, at all."

    And would it have been worth it, after all,
Would it have been worth while,   100
After the sunsets and the dooryards and the sprinkled streets,
After the novels, after the teacups, after the skirts that trail along the floor—
And this, and so much more?—
It is impossible to say just what I mean!
But as if a magic lantern threw the nerves in patterns on a screen: 105
Would it have been worth while
If one, settling a pillow or throwing off a shawl,
And turning toward the window, should say:
    "That is not it at all,
    That is not what I meant, at all."   110

• • •

No! I am not Prince Hamlet, nor was meant to be;
Am an attendant lord, one that will do
To swell a progress, start a scene or two,
Advise the prince; no doubt, an easy tool,
Deferential, glad to be of use,   115
Politic, cautious, and meticulous;
Full of high sentence, but a bit obtuse;
At times, indeed, almost ridiculous—
Almost, at times, the Fool.

I grow old . . . I grow old . . .   120
I shall wear the bottoms of my trousers rolled.

Shall I part my hair behind? Do I dare to eat a peach?
I shall wear white flannel trousers, and walk upon the beach.
I have heard the mermaids singing, each to each.

I do not think that they will sing to me.   125

I have seen them riding seaward on the waves
Combing the white hair of the waves blown back
When the wind blows the water white and black.

We have lingered in the chambers of the sea
By sea-girls wreathed with seaweed red and brown   130
Till human voices wake us, and we drown.

THE LOVE SONG OF J. ALFRED PRUFROCK. The epigraph, from Dante's *Inferno*, is the speech of one dead and damned, who thinks that his hearer also is going to remain in Hell. Count Guido da Montefeltro, whose sin has been to give false counsel after a corrupt prelate had offered him prior absolution and whose punishment is to be wrapped in a constantly burning flame, offers to tell Dante his story:

> If I thought my answer were to someone who
>   might see the world again, then there would be
>   no more stirrings of this flame. Since it is true
> that no one leaves these depths of misery
>   alive, from all that I have heard reported,
>   I answer you without fear of infamy.

(Translation by Michael Palma from: Dante Alighieri, *Inferno: A New Verse Translation* [New York: Norton, 2002].) 29 *works and days:* title of a poem by Hesiod (eighth century B.C.), depicting his life as a hard-working Greek farmer and exhorting his brother to be like him. 82 *head . . . platter:* like that of John the Baptist, prophet and praiser of chastity, whom King Herod beheaded at the demand of Herodias, his unlawfully wedded wife (see Mark 6:17–28). 92–93 *squeezed . . . To roll it:* an echo from Marvell's "To His Coy Mistress," lines 41–42. 94 *Lazarus:* probably the Lazarus whom Jesus called forth from the tomb (John 11:1–44), but possibly the beggar seen in Heaven by the rich man in Hell (Luke 16:19–25). 105 *magic lantern:* an early type of projector used to display still pictures from transparent slides.

Questions

1. What expectations are created by the title of the poem? Are those expectations fulfilled by the text?

2. John Berryman wrote of line 3, "With this line, modern poetry begins." What do you think he meant?

3. It has been said that Prufrock suffers from a "morbid self-consciousness." How many references can you find in the poem to back up that statement?

4. In the total context of the poem, is the sense of lines 47–48 reassuring or disturbing? Explain your choice.

5. How do lines 70–72 relate to the questions that Prufrock raises in the three preceding stanzas (lines 49–69)?

6. What is the effect of riming "ices" and "crisis"? Can you find similar instances elsewhere in the poem?

7. Is the situation in the poem presented statically, or is there discernible development as the poem proceeds? Defend your answer with references to the text.

8. What, finally, is your attitude toward Prufrock—identification, sympathy, contempt, or something more complicated?

PUBLISHING "PRUFROCK"

Ezra Pound, living in London, was the foreign correspondent for Chicago-based *Poetry* magazine from its beginnings in 1912. Tireless in his efforts to promote writers he believed in, Pound made it his mission to champion poets who were doing new and original work in contrast to what he saw as the dullness and sterility of mainstream verse. His literary enthusiasms differed sharply from the more conservative values of Harriet Monroe, *Poetry*'s founder and editor, and the two clashed frequently. Pound's first mention to Harriet Monroe of T. S. Eliot came in a letter of September 22, 1914:

> An American called Eliot called this P.M. I think he has some sense tho' he has not yet sent me any verse.

Eliot sent Pound "The Love Song of J. Alfred Prufrock" shortly thereafter, and on September 30 Pound wrote to Monroe:

> I was jolly well right about Eliot. He has sent in the best poem I have yet had or seen from an American. PRAY GOD IT BE NOT A SINGLE AND UNIQUE SUCCESS. He has taken it back to get it ready for the press and you shall have it in a few days.
>
> He is the only American I know of who has made what I can call adequate preparation for writing. He has actually trained himself *and* modernized himself *on his own*. The rest of the *promising young* have done one or the other but never both (most of the swine have done neither). It is such a comfort to meet a man and not have to tell him to wash his face, wipe his feet, and remember the date (1914) on the calendar.

Objecting to her request for revisions to make the poem more accessible, Pound wrote on November 9, 1914:

> No, most emphatically I will not ask Eliot to write down to any audience whatsoever. . . . Neither will I send you Eliot's address in order that he may be insulted.

Despite Pound's vigorous advocacy, Monroe continued to object to certain passages and delayed printing the poem, leading Pound to write on January 31, 1915:

> Now as to Eliot: "Mr. Prufrock" does not "go off at the end." It is a portrait of failure, or of a character which fails, and it would be false art to make it end on a note of triumph. I dislike the paragraph about Hamlet, but it is an early and cherished bit and T.E. won't give it up, and as it is the only portion of the poem that most readers will like at first reading, I don't see that it will do much harm.
>
> For the rest, a portrait satire on futility can't end by turning that quintessence of futility, Mr. P., into a reformed character breathing out fire and ozone. . . . I assure you it is better, "more unique," than the other poems of Eliot which I have seen. Also that he is quite *intelligent* (an adjective which is seldom in my mouth).

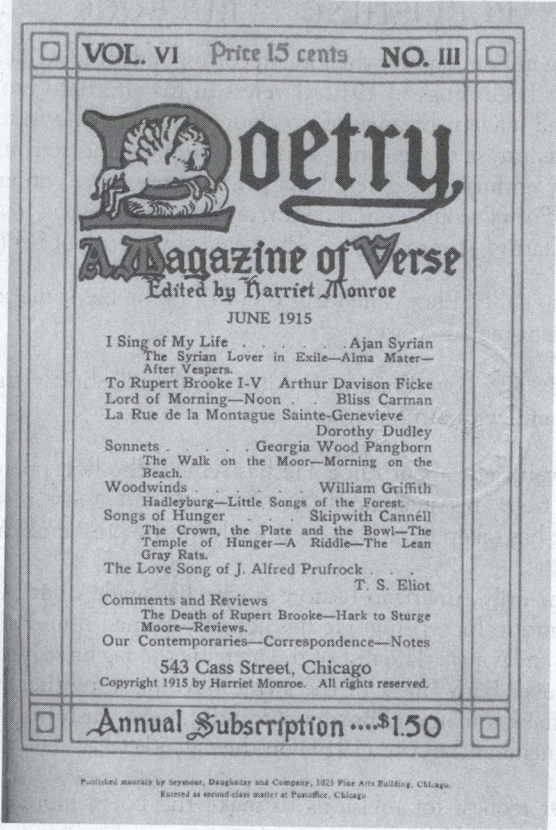

Cover of *Poetry*, June 1915.

"Prufrock" finally appeared in the June 1915 issue of *Poetry*. Writing to Monroe on December 1, Pound explained his vigorous advocacy of the poem and his insistence on her printing it before other, less experimental pieces by Eliot:

> As to T.S.E. the "Prufrock" is more individual and unusual than the "Portrait of a Lady"! I chose it of the two as I wanted his first poem to be published to be a poem that would at once differentiate him from everyone else, in the public mind.

Pound continued zealously to promote Eliot, sending Monroe other Eliot poems and lobbying, without success, for "Prufrock" to receive the prize for the best work published in *Poetry* that year.

While Eliot was preoccupied with marital and financial concerns in late 1916 and early 1917, it was Pound who gathered together twelve of Eliot's poems. Along with "Prufrock," the collection included a number of other pieces that Pound had placed in American and British journals, such as "Portrait of a Lady," "Preludes," "Rhapsody on a Windy Night," and "The *Boston Evening Transcript*." He approached his own publisher, Elkin Matthews, with the manuscript, but Matthews demanded an advance guarantee against poor sales. Pound then turned to Harriet Shaw Weaver, one of the editors of the journal *The Egoist*, with the proposal that he would cover the printing costs if she would allow the book to appear under the Egoist imprint. She agreed to these terms, and *Prufrock and Other Observations* was published in July 1917 in an edition of 500 copies.

THE REVIEWERS ON *PRUFROCK*

For a pamphlet of twelve poems by an almost totally unknown writer, *Prufrock and Other Observations* received a considerable amount of press attention, even when one subtracts everything written by Ezra Pound. Below are excerpts from some of the notices of Eliot's collection. Given the experimental nature of his work, it is not surprising that it received less than favorable—or, at best, mildly dismissive—responses from some of the more conservative outlets aimed at the general reading public (as illustrated by the following two unsigned reviews in British publications). Balancing these reactions were more discerning notices written by several important American and British writers.

Unsigned Review

from *Times Literary Supplement*   June 21, 1917

Mr. Eliot's notion of poetry—he calls the "observations" poems—seems to be a purely analytical treatment, verging sometimes on the catalogue, of personal relations and environments, uninspired by any glimpse beyond them and untouched by any genuine rush of feeling. As, even on this basis, he remains frequently inarticulate, his "poems" will hardly be read by many with enjoyment. . . .

The fact that these things occurred to the mind of Mr. Eliot is surely of the very smallest importance to any one—even to himself. They certainly have no relation to "poetry," and we only give an example because some of the pieces, he states, have appeared in a periodical which claims that word as its title.

Unsigned Review

from *Literary World*   July 5, 1917

Mr. Eliot is one of those clever young men who find it amusing to pull the leg of a sober reviewer. We can imagine his saying to his friends: "See me have a lark out of the old fogies who don't know a poem from a pea-shooter. I'll just put down the first thing that comes into my head, and call it 'The Love Song of J. Alfred Prufrock.' Of course it will be idiotic; but the fogies are sure to praise it, because when they don't understand a thing and yet cannot hold their tongues they find safety in praise." . . . Mr. Eliot has not the wisdom of youth. If the "Love Song" is neither witty nor amusing, the other poems are interesting experiments in the bizarre and violent. The subjects of the poems, the imagery, the rhythms have the willful outlandishness of the young revolutionary idea. We do not wish to appear patronizing, but we are certain that Mr. Eliot could do finer work on traditional lines. With him it seems to be a case of missing the effect by too much cleverness. All beauty has in it an element of strangeness, but here the strangeness overbalances the beauty.

Conrad Aiken

from "Divers Realists," *The Dial*   November 8, 1917

Mr. Eliot gives us, in the first person, the reactions of an individual to a situation for which to a large extent his own character is responsible. . . . [I]t will puzzle many, it will delight a few. Mr. Eliot writes pungently and sharply, with an eye for unexpected and vivid details, and, particularly in the two longer poems and in the "Rhapsody on a Windy Night," he shows himself to be an exceptionally acute technician. Such free rhyme as this, with irregular line lengths, is difficult to write well, and Mr. Eliot does it well enough to make one wonder whether such a form is not what the adorers of free verse will eventually have to come to. In the rest of Mr. Eliot's volume one finds the piquant and the trivial in about equal proportions.

Babette Deutsch

from "Another Impressionist," *The New Republic*   February 16, 1918

The language has the extraordinary quality of common words uncommonly used. Less formal than prose, more nervous than metrical verse, the rhythms are suggestive of program music of an intimate sort. This effect is emphasized by the use of rhyme. It recurs, often internally, with an echoing charm that is heightened by its irregularity. But Mr. Eliot . . . is so clever a technician that the rhymes are subordinated to afford an unconsidered pleasure.

Marianne Moore

from "A Note on T. S. Eliot's Book," *Poetry*   April 1918

It might be advisable for Mr. Eliot to publish a fangless edition of *Prufrock and Other Observations* for the gentle reader who likes his literature, like breakfast coffee or grapefruit, sweetened. . . .

But Eliot deals with life, with beings and things who live and move almost nakedly before his individual mind's eye—in the darkness, in the early sunlight, and in the fog. Whatever one may feel about sweetness in literature, there is also the word honesty, and this man is a faithful friend of the objects he portrays; altogether unlike the sentimentalist who really stabs them treacherously in the back while pretending affection.

May Sinclair

from "*Prufrock and Other Observations:*   December 1917
A Criticism," *The Little Review*

Mr. Eliot's genius is in itself disturbing. It is elusive; it is difficult; it demands a distinct effort of attention. . . . He does not see anything between him and reality, and he makes straight for the reality he sees; he cuts all his corners and his curves; and this directness of method is startling and upsetting to comfortable, respectable people accustomed to going superfluously in and out of corners and carefully round curves. Unless you are prepared to follow with the same nimbleness and straightness you will never arrive with Mr. Eliot at his meaning. Therefore the only comfortable thing is to sit down and pretend . . . that his "*Boston Evening Transcript*" which you do understand is greater than his "Love Song of Prufrock" which you do not understand.

... Mr. Eliot is not a poet of one poem; and if there is anything more astounding and more assured than his performance it is his promise. He knows what he is after. Reality, stripped naked of all rhetoric, of all ornament, of all confusing and obscuring association, is what he is after. His reality may be a modern street or a modern drawing-room; it may be an ordinary human mind suddenly and fatally aware of what is happening to it; Mr. Eliot is careful to present his street and his drawing-room as they are, and Prufrock's thoughts as they are: live thoughts, kicking, running about and jumping, nervily, in a live brain. . . .

Observe the method. Instead of writing round and round about Prufrock, explaining that his tragedy is the tragedy of submerged passion, Mr. Eliot simply removes the covering from Prufrock's mind: Prufrock's mind, jumping quickly from actuality to memory and back again, like an animal, hunted, tormented, terribly and poignantly alive. "The Love Song of Prufrock" is a song that Balzac might have sung if he had been as great a poet as he was a novelist.

T. S. ELIOT ON WRITING

Eliot at Garsington Manor, near Oxford, England, around the time of publication of *Prufrock*.

Poetry and Emotion   1919

It is not in his personal emotions, the emotions provoked by particular events in his life, that the poet is in any way remarkable or interesting. His particular emotions may be simple, or crude, or flat. The emotion in his poetry will be a very complex thing, but not with the complexity of the emotions of people who have very complex or unusual emotions in life. One error, in fact, of eccentricity in poetry is to seek for new human emotions to express; and in this search for novelty in the wrong place it discovers the perverse. The business of the poet is not to find new emotions, but to use the ordinary ones and, in working them up into poetry, to express feelings which are not in actual emotions at all. And emotions which he has never experienced will serve his turn as well as those familiar to him. Consequently, we must believe that "emotion recollected in tranquility"° is an inexact formula. For it is neither emotion, nor recollection, nor, without distortion of meaning, tranquility. It is a concentration, and a new thing resulting from the concentration, of a very great number of experiences which to the practical and active person would not seem to be experiences at all; it is a concentration which does not happen consciously or of deliberation. These experiences are not "recollected," and they finally unite in an atmosphere which is "tranquil" only in that it is a passive attending upon the event. Of course this is not quite the whole story. There is a great deal, in the writing of poetry, which must be conscious and deliberate. In fact, the bad poet is usually unconscious where he ought to be conscious, and conscious where he ought to be unconscious. Both errors tend to make him "personal." Poetry is not a turning loose of emotion, but an escape from emotion; it is not the expression of personality, but an escape from personality. But, of course, only those who have personality and emotions know what it means to want to escape from these things.

From "Tradition and the Individual Talent"

The Objective Correlative   1919

The only way of expressing emotion in the form of art is by finding an "objective correlative"; in other words, a set of objects, a situation, a chain of events which shall be the formula of that *particular* emotion; such that when the external facts, which must terminate in sensory experience, are given, the emotion is immediately evoked. If you examine any of Shakespeare's more successful tragedies, you will find this exact equivalence; you will find that the state of mind of Lady Macbeth walking in her sleep has been communicated to you by a skillful accumulation of imagined sensory impressions; the words of Macbeth on hearing of his wife's death strike us as if, given the sequence of events, these words were automatically released by the last event in the series. The artistic "inevitability" lies in this complete adequacy of the external to the emotion . . .

From "Hamlet and His Problems"

The Difficulty of Poetry   1933

The uses of poetry certainly vary as society alters, as the public to be addressed changes. In this context something should be said about the vexed question of obscurity and unintelligibility. The difficulty of poetry (and modern poetry is supposed to be difficult) may be due to one of several reasons. First, there may be personal causes which make it impossible for a poet to express himself in any but an

---

"*emotion recollected in tranquility*": Eliot is alluding to William Wordsworth's famous statement in his 1800 Preface to *Lyrical Ballads*: "I have said that Poetry is the spontaneous overflow of powerful feelings: it takes its origin from emotion recollected in tranquility."

obscure way; while this may be regrettable, we should be glad, I think, that the man has been able to express himself at all. Or difficulty may be due just to novelty: we know the ridicule accorded in turn to Wordsworth, Shelley and Keats, Tennyson and Browning—but must remark that Browning was the first to be *called* difficult; hostile critics of the earlier poets found them difficult, but called them silly. Or difficulty may be caused by the reader's having been told, or having suggested to himself, that the poem is going to prove difficult. The ordinary reader, when warned against the obscurity of a poem, is apt to be thrown into a state of consternation very unfavorable to poetic receptivity. Instead of beginning, as he should, in a state of sensitivity, he obfuscates his senses by the desire to be clever and to look very hard for something, he doesn't know what—or else by the desire not to be taken in. There is such a thing as stage fright, but what such readers have is pit or gallery fright. The more seasoned reader, he who has reached, in these matters, a state of greater *purity*, does not bother about understanding; not, at least, at first. I know that some of the poetry to which I am most devoted is poetry which I did not understand at first reading; some is poetry which I am not sure I understand yet: for instance, Shakespeare's. And finally, there is the difficulty caused by the author's having left out something which the reader is used to finding; so that the reader, bewildered, gropes about for what is absent, and puzzles his head for a kind of "meaning" which is not there, and is not meant to be there.

The chief use of the "meaning" of a poem, in the ordinary sense, may be (for here again I am speaking of some kinds of poetry and not all) to satisfy one habit of the reader, to keep his mind diverted and quiet, while the poem does its work upon him: much as the imaginary burglar is always provided with a bit of nice meat for the house-dog. This is a normal situation of which I approve. But the minds of all poets do not work that way; some of them, assuming that there are other minds like their own, become impatient of this "meaning" which seems superfluous, and perceive possibilities of intensity through its elimination. I am not asserting that this situation is ideal; only that we must write our poetry as we can, and take it as we find it. It may be that for some periods of society a more relaxed form of writing is right, and for others a more concentrated. I believe that there must be many people who feel, as I do, that the effect of some of the greater nineteenth-century poets is diminished by their bulk. Who now, for the pure pleasure of it, reads Wordsworth, Shelley and Keats even, certainly Browning and Swinburne° and most of the French poets of the century—entire? I by no means believe that the "long poem" is a thing of the past; but at least there must be more in it for the length than our grandparents seemed to demand; and for us, anything that can be said as well in prose can be said better in prose. And a great deal, in the way of meaning, belongs to prose rather than to poetry. The doctrine of "art for art's sake," a mistaken one, and more advertised than practiced, contained this true impulse behind it, that it is a recognition of the error of the poet's trying to do other people's work. But poetry has as much to learn from prose as from other poetry; and I think that an interaction between prose and verse, like the interaction between language and language, is a condition of vitality in literature.

From *The Use of Poetry and the Use of Criticism*

Swinburne: Algernon Charles Swinburne (1837–1909), prolific and expansive British poet.

CRITICS ON "PRUFROCK"

Words Alone The Poet T. S. Eliot

Denis Donoghue

Cover of Donoghue's critical book on Eliot, featuring 1949 portrait of Eliot by Wyndham Lewis.

Denis Donoghue (b. 1928)

One of the Irrefutable Poets

2000

[Eliot] didn't come into my life till I went to university in Dublin. It is my impression that I first read "The Love Song of J. Alfred Prufrock" in the National Library, Kildare Street, my home-away-from-home. I knew that it was a different kind of poetry from Yeats's or Byron's and that I would never forget it. My criterion for poetry at that time was simple: a poem should be memorable. . . . "Prufrock" was one of those. At first reading, it took up residence in my mind. From that day to this I've never wavered from my conviction that it is a fully achieved poem or doubted that Eliot is one of the irrefutable poets. . . .

"Prufrock" seemed to me a poem about a man's dread of being no good. Later readings have made me think that it is about spiritual panic, the mind whirling in a void, or the penury of one's being in the world. No one instructed me to think of the poem in relation to Allen Tate's assertion that "in Mr. Eliot, puritan obligation withdraws into private conscience." Now that "Prufrock" seems to be the only poem of Eliot's that young people in America read, I find that my students at New York University take it as an uncanny description of themselves, their distress, their fear of having already failed. Prufrock is brooding on his insufficiency in mock-epic terms, but the terms don't remove his conviction of being inadequate. Growing up in Ireland, where there were no choices and one was lucky to get a job of any kind, I was likely to internalize the theme and to find Prufrock already defeated.

Knowing no Italian, I could make nothing of the epigraph to *Prufrock and Other Observations* or the further one to "Prufrock." The poem began for me with "Let us go then, you and I. . ." I'm still puzzled by the epigraph to the poem, but for different reasons. In *Inferno* xxvii Dante meets Guido da Montefeltro, confined in a single flame of punishment for having given false counsel to Pope Boniface. Guido answers Dante: "If I believed that my reply would be to someone who would return to earth, this flame would remain without further movement; but since no one has ever returned alive from this abyss, if what I hear is true, I answer you without fear of infamy." It's not clear what bearing this has on "Prufrock." In the "No! I am not Prince Hamlet" passage, Prufrock speaks of himself as if he were Polonius, but he doesn't confess to having given the king fraudulent advice. Perhaps the epigraph has him saying: I'll tell the truth about my life, however humiliating it turns out to be. Or it may be Eliot's device to clear a space for himself, ridding the reader's mind of extraneous matter, all the more effectively because the epigraph is in a foreign language. Or his way of insisting that what follows is a made poem, not what it might seem, a transcript of someone's confession. Eliot tended to choose an epigraph related to the poem it preceded by congruity or contradiction: either way, he enjoyed the latitude of keeping readers on their toes. I note, incidentally, that in his recording of the poem, he hasn't included the epigraph; he goes straight into "Let us go then . . ."

From Words Alone: The Poet T. S. Eliot

Christopher Ricks (b. 1933)

What's in a Name? 1988

Then, back in 1917, before ever you entered upon reading a line of poetry by Mr. T. S. Eliot, you would have been met by the title of the first poem in this, his first book of poems: "The Love Song of J. Alfred Prufrock." At once the crystalline air is thick with incitements to prejudice. For we are immediately invited, or incited, to think and to feel our way through a prejudicial sequence. First, as often with prejudice, comes a concession: that of course a man cannot be blamed for being called Prufrock. Second, that nevertheless the name does have comical possibilities, given not only the play of "frock" against "pru"—prudent, prudish, prurient—but also the suggestive contrariety between splitting the name there, at *pru* and *frock,* as against splitting it as *proof* and *rock.* And, third, that therefore a man in these circumstances might be well advised to call himself John A. Prufrock or J. A. Prufrock, rather than to risk the roll, the rise, the carol, the creation of "J. Alfred Prufrock.". . . And then we are further invited to think and to feel that should Mr. Prufrock, as is his right, plump for J. Alfred Prufrock, he must not then expect the words "The Love Song of" to sit happily in his immediate vicinity. The tax returns of J. Alfred Prufrock, fine, but a love song does not harmonize with the rotund name, with how he has chosen to think of himself, to sound himself. He has, after all, chosen to issue his name in a form which is not only formal but unspeakable: no one, not even the most pompous self-regarder, could ever introduce himself as, or be addressed as, J. Alfred Prufrock. He has adopted a form for his name which is powerfully appropriate to a certain kind of page but not to the voice, and which is therefore for ever inimical to the thought of love's intimacy. "I'm in love." "Who's the lucky man?" "J. Alfred Prufrock." Inconceivable.

But then life often involves these choices and these sacrifices; if you want to cut a public figure and to wax ceremonious and to live on the business page or the title page, you may have to relinquish the more intimate happinesses. And all of this is unobtrusively at work before ever we have arrived at a word of the poem.

Unjust, of course, these incitements. What's in a name? Yet even with some-thing like a name, which is usually given and not chosen, we manage to exercise choices, to adopt a style which becomes our man, or, if we are Prufrock, to wear our name with a difference. Then a name starts to become so mingled with its owner as to call in question which is doing the owning.

"The Love Song of J. Alfred Prufrock": even while the title tempts us—not neces-sarily improperly—to suspect things about the man, it raises the question of whether we are entitled to do so. Can we deduce much from so localized a thing as how a man chooses to cast his name? Can we deduce anything? But then can we imagine that one either could or should refrain from doing any deducing? Straws in the wind are often all that we have to go on. "And should I have the right to smile?": the question ends the succeeding poem, "Portrait of a Lady," but it is a question that haunts the whole book.

As so often with prejudice, one kind of categorizing melts into another. For the teasing speculation as to what sort of man names himself in such a way, especially given "Prufrock" as his climax, merges itself in the class question, not just what class of man but what social class. Calling oneself J. Alfred Prufrock has an air of prerogative and privilege. The class presumption in turn brings a whole culture and society with it.

From T. S. Eliot and Prejudice

Philip R. Headings (1922–1982)

The Pronouns in the Poem: "One," "You," and "I"   1982

"One"

The "one"° of the poem presents no great problems. She seems to be a feminine counterpart of either "you" or "I," frequenting the same Boston teas, expressing on occasion dissatisfactions with the unfulfilling, conventionalized life of that whole milieu. Her awarenesses may parallel theirs, though "I" is not sure. He probably does not even have a particular lady in mind; if he had, he would likely have used "she" instead of "one." This is not to deny the sexual component in his Love Song; it is rather to say that he is open to various possibilities in that regard—to whatever lady demonstrates the qualities requisite to become his Lady, his Beatrice.°

°*one*: The "one" of lines 96–98, "If one, settling a pillow by her head / Should say: 'That is not what I meant at all. / That is not it, at all.'"   *Beatrice*: Beatrice Portinari (1266–1290), Dante's inspira-tion and beloved in *The New Life* and *The Divine Comedy*.

"You" and "I"

The "you" and "I" of the first line present greater difficulties. Critics have commonly interpreted them as referring to two parts of Prufrock, carrying on a conversation with himself. This interpretation now seems to me both too clever and much simpler than the actual situation in the poem. . . .

Sometime before 1949 Eliot wrote to Kristian Smidt:

> As for THE LOVE SONG OF J. ALFRED PRUFROCK anything I say now must be somewhat conjectural, as it was written so long ago that my memory may deceive me; but I am prepared to assert that the "you" in THE LOVE SONG is merely some friend or companion, *presumably of the male sex*, whom *the speaker* is at that moment addressing. . . [italics mine].

Having finally carefully compared "Prufrock" to Dante's *Inferno* and read dozens of critiques of the poem, I now see no reason to dissent from Eliot's straightforward statement. In fact, I see no other way of interpreting the poem that will fit all its complexities. Old Possum's° delightful sense of humor is apparent in that phrase "presumably of the male sex" and in "the speaker"; he knew very well that he himself, allegorically projected to the age of thirty-five, or a persona very like that projection, was the "friend or companion," the Dante-figure of the poem. The "I" who addresses him is an unidentified friend.

"You" and "I" are probably close friends and confidants who have attended such teas together, though perhaps they have only discussed them.

Though the presence of "you" is crucial to Eliot's Dantean intent, "Prufrock" is a dramatic monologue, not a dialogue. It parallels monologues of Shakespeare's Polonius, Dante's Pilgrim, Guido, and Ulysses. The only functions of the "you" are to elicit confidences, set the Dantean tone, indicate Prufrock's equivalence with Guido in the poem's epigraph, listen to the "I," and write the poem—bring back the story.

From "Dantean Observations," *T. S. Eliot*

Maud Ellmann (b. 1954)

Will There Be Time? 1987

. . . Prufrock is etherized by *time*. This is the time that separates desire from fulfillment, motive from execution, thought from speech: in Eliot's words, "the awful separation between potential passion and any actualization possible in life." Time defers.

The way that time defers is through revision. Time itself becomes the object of revision, for the whole poem agonizes over writing time. The incessant repetition of "There will be time" is itself a way of losing time, as Nancy K. Gish[1] suggests; but also a way of gaining it, to prolong the re-editions of desire. "Stretched . . . beside you and me," time deflects Prufrock's ardor from his lover. But in this process time itself

---

Old Possum: Eliot's playful nickname for himself, used in the title *Old Possum's Book of Practical Cats* (1939).

[1]Nancy K. Gish, *Time in the Poetry of T. S. Eliot* (London: Macmillan, 1981) 15–16.

becomes the object of desire, in the form of the voluptuary sweetness of the evening. Indeed, Prufrock addresses time so constantly, in every tone of envy, rage, pain, impatience, longing, humor, flattery, seduction, that he can only really be in love with time.

Revisionary time: because revision has no present tense, and neither does "The Love Song." Instead, the poem hesitates between anticipation and regret for missed appointments with the self, the other or the muse. It begins in the future tense ("there will be time . . . " [23ff]); shifts into the perfect ("For I have known . . ." [49ff]); and finally subsides into the past conditional, the tense of wishful thinking: "I should have been . . . " (73). Because presence would mean speech, apocalypse, Prufrock only pauses in the present tense to say what he is not—"No! I am not Prince Hamlet" (a disavowal that conjures up the effigy that it denies, since Hamlet is the very spirit of theatricality). The poem concludes dreaming the future, faithful if only to its hopeless passion for postponement: "Till human voices wake us, and we drown." Prufrock feels the need to speak as a proof of his identity and as a rock to give him anchorage: yet speech would also mean his end, for voices are waters in which Prufrocks drown.

Through time, all Prufrock's aims have turned awry. His passion and his speech have lost themselves in detours, never to achieve satiety. Love becomes desire—tormenting, inexhaustible—while speech and revelation have surrendered to writing and revision, to the digressions which prolong his dalliance with time. Time is the greatest fetish of them all, the mother of all fetishes, since it is through time that all aims turn aside to revel in rehearsals, detours, transferences. What Prufrock longs for is a talking cure because, like Freud, he thinks that speech alone can transform repetition into memory. What talking remedies is *writing*: for his illness lies in his obsessive re-editions of the text of love. But Prufrock's very histrionics show he is condemned to reenactment, to forget what he repeats in a script that restlessly obliterates its history. It is by remembering the past that the subject can establish his identity, but only by forgetting it can he accede to his desire. Refusing to declare his love, or pop the overwhelming question, Prufrock renounces the position of the speaking subject, but he instigates the drama of revision in its stead. And it is by refusing sexual relation that he conjures up the theatre of desire. The love song Prufrock could not *sing* has been *writing* itself all the time, and the love that could not speak its name has been roving among all the fetishes his rhetoric has liberated to desire. We had the love song, even if we missed the meaning.

From The Poetics of Impersonality: T. S. Eliot and Ezra Pound

Burton Raffel (b. 1928)

"Indeterminacy" in Eliot's Poetry   1982

Perhaps the most difficult aspect of "Prufrock," and a continuing difficulty in all of Eliot's poetry to the end of his life, is what might be called its "indeterminacy." That is, Eliot is constantly making two basic and exceedingly important kinds of assumptions as to his readership: (1) that his readers can and do understand his allusions, his references to people and to literary works, and in time to other things as well; and (2) that his readers can readily reconstruct an entire skeleton, as it were, though presented only with, say, a metatarsal bone or a chunk of a skull. Eliot's allusions are not much of a problem in "Prufrock," though they become a matter of some importance later on in his work. Let me therefore focus briefly on the second variety of "indeterminacy."

Perhaps the most famous example in "Prufrock" is the couplet toward the end, "I grow old . . . I grow old . . . / I shall wear the bottoms of my trousers rolled" (120–21). We can read, in the ingenious pages of Eliot's many scholarly explicators, that this refers to "stylish trousers with cuffs." Over-ingenuity can create, and in the past it has, fantastic and profound (but also profoundly irrelevant) significance for such minor matters. And it is true that Eliot has not troubled to give us all the information we need. But is it true that he has not given us *enough* information (as in other and later poems I think he sometimes has not)? We know that Prufrock is a socialite; we have heard him tell us, proudly, of "My morning coat, my collar mounting firmly to the chin, / My necktie rich and modest, but asserted by a simple pin—" (42–43). Just after the lines at issue he worries, "Shall I part my hair behind?" and goes on to proclaim that he will "wear white flannel trousers, and walk upon the beach" (123). And with so full a presentation of Prufrock's sartorial nature, do we really need more details about his trouser cuffs? Or, to put it differently, is it not enough to leave some minor indeterminacies, when the main outlines are so firmly sketched in? . . .

The poet needs, of course, to draw a fine but basic line between confusing and illuminating the reader. Indeterminacy can be bewildering if not kept under control. Even in "Prufrock," readers have for years been troubled by the "overwhelming question," which is never expressly formulated. It is one thing, such readers have argued, to shock us into comprehension with indeterminate metaphors like, "I have measured out my life with coffee spoons," metaphors which we do not and cannot take literally but which forcefully oblige us to see the intense triviality of Prufrock's well-bred existence. But how, they insist, are we to deal with what seems much more specific—an "overwhelming question"—yet is in the end only infuriatingly obscure? One response to such objections might be that we simply do not need to know. The fact that Prufrock never asks an "overwhelming" question, that he is not, indeed, capable of asking it, is arguably enough information. But I think it is not difficult, using the larger context of the poem as a whole, to see that the overwhelming question which Prufrock "dares not ask [is]: What is the meaning of this life? He realizes the sterile monotony of his 'works and days,' and he senses that a more fruitful and meaningful life must exist."[2] If this is not precise enough, I do not know what is. Nor is it drawn from external (or esoteric) sources: the poem itself gives us all we need, if we read it closely enough.

From T. S. Eliot

John Berryman (1914–1972)

Prufrock's Dilemma (1960) 1976

Eliot brings to bear on Prufrock's dilemma four figures out of the spiritual history of man: Michelangelo, John the Baptist, Lazarus, and Hamlet. Prufrock identifies himself,

[2]Quoted from Nancy Duvall Hargrove, *Landscape as Symbol in the Poetry of T. S. Eliot* (Jackson: UP Mississippi, 1978) 48.

in his imagination, with Lazarus; he says that he is *not* the Baptist or Hamlet. About the first all he says is:

> In the room the women come and go
> Talking of Michelangelo. (13–14, 35–36)

What are we to make of this? There is a twittering of women's voices. Their subject? A type of volcanic masculine energy—sculptor, architect, as well as painter—at the height of one of the supreme periods of human energy, the Italian Renaissance. Chit-chat. *Reduction*, we may say. Michelangelo, everything that mattered about him forgotten or not understood, has become a topic for women's voices—destructive, without even realizing it. Then Prufrock says,

> Though I have seen my head (grown slightly bald) brought in upon a platter,
> I am no prophet— (82–83)

The situation is a visit, or the imagination of a visit, to the woman; it was *women* who got the Baptist beheaded. We might phrase the meaning as: I announce no signifi-cant time to come, I am the forerunner of (not children, not a Savior) nothing. Then Prufrock is speculating about how it *would* have been, IF he had

> squeezed the universe into a ball
> To roll it toward some overwhelming question,
> To say: "I am Lazarus, come from the dead,
> Come back to tell you all, I shall tell you all"— (92–95)

We have seen Prufrock already imagined as dead, the suggestion of the epigraph, and at the end of the poem he drowns. Here he thinks of himself as *come back*. Lazarus, perhaps, is the person whom one would most like to interview—another character from sacred history, not Christ's forerunner but the subject of the supreme miracles (reported, unfortunately, only in the Fourth Gospel)—the one man who would tell us . . . what it is like. Prufrock has a message for the woman that is or ought to be of similar importance: here I am, out of my loneliness, at your feet; I am this man full of love, trust, hope; decide my fate.

Now—postponing Hamlet for a second—what Prufrock imagines the woman as saying in return for his Lazarus-communication explains his despair:

> If one, settling a pillow by her head,
> Should say: "That is not what I meant at all.
> That is not it, at all." (96–98)

Here the reason for his inability to propose becomes clear. He is convinced that she will (or would) respond with the most insulting and unmanning of all attitudes: Let's be *friends*; I never thought of you as a lover or husband, only a friend. What the women's voices did to Michelangelo, her voice is here imagined as doing to him, un-manning him; the sirens' voices at the end of the poem are yet to come. This is the central image of Prufrock's fear: what he cannot face. We see better now why the image of an *operation* turned up so early in the poem, and the paranoid passages swing into focus:

> when I am formulated, sprawling on a pin,
> When I am pinned and wriggling on the wall, (57–58)

and:

> But as if a magic lantern threw the nerves in patterns on a screen: (105)

A reasonable study of these fears of exposure would take us not only into our well-known Anglo-Saxon fear of ridicule but into folklore and psychoanalysis.

As for Hamlet, Prufrock says he is "not Prince Hamlet." He is not even the hero, that is to say, of his own tragedy; let us have in mind again the scientific revolutions and also the hero of one of Franz Kafka's novels, *The Trial*, who suddenly says, when recounting his arrest afterward, "Oh, I've forgotten the most important person of all, myself." Prufrock is merely, he says, an extra courtier, an adviser (to himself a very bad adviser—the name "Alfred" means, ironically, good counselor, and the character in Dante who supplies the epigraph was an evil counselor). But of course he *is* Hamlet—in one view of Shakespeare's character: a man rather of reflection than of action, on whom has been laid an intolerable burden (of revenge, by the way), and who suffers from sexual nausea (owing to his mother's incest) and deserts the woman he loves.

The resort to these four analogues from artistic and sacred history suggests a man—desperate, in his ordeal—ransacking the past for help in the present, and *not finding it*—finding only ironic parallels, or real examples, of his predicament. The available tradition, the poet seems to be saying, is of no use to us. It supplies only analogies and metaphors for our pain.

● ● ●

[T]he basic image of escape occurs in the dead center of the poem, in a couplet, without much relation to anything apparently, *lacking* which this would be a much less impressive poem than it is. These are the lines:

> I should have been a pair of ragged claws
> Scuttling across the floors of silent seas. (73–74)

You notice, first, that this is not much of a couplet, though it *is* a heroic couplet; the off-rhyme speaks of incongruity. As abruptly, second, as we were transferred from the prospect of a romantic evening to a hospital, are we here plunged, away from modern social life ("I have measured out my life with coffee spoons") into—into what? Man's biological past, continuous with him, but unimaginably remote, long before he emerged into the tidal areas: Prufrock sees himself, in his desire, as his own ancestor, *before this ordeal came up*, when he was sufficient unto himself, a "pair," not needing a mate. Now the whole crustacean is not imagined—only the fighting part, which is taken for the whole—the claws. But these do not seem to be in very good condition ("ragged"), and unquestionably we must take them also to be full of fear ("scuttling"), like Prufrock now. But the seas are *silent:* no woman speaks. Therefore, the situation is desirable, protected. We really need to resort to the later formulations of Freud to understand this. When a human being encounters a problem beyond his capacity to meet, Freud thought, *regression* occurs: the whole organization of the emotional and instinctual person escapes from the intolerable reality by reverting to an earlier, or ancient, stage of his individual development—paying the price of symptoms but securing partial oblivion. The antagonism toward civilization in Eliot's couplet is unmistakable. It contains, indeed, a sort of list of the penalties that civilization has exacted from man's instinctual life—having cost him: open expression of hatred, fear, remorse, intolerable responsibilities.

From "Prufrock's Dilemma"

M. L. Rosenthal (1917–1996)

Adolescents Singing   1991

I am trying to reach back to what it was in T.S. Eliot's poetry that so attracted me and my little gang of adolescent literati pals in the early 1930s. Although I don't like to think of myself as a hoary memory bank, facts must be faced. I speak of a time before "Burnt Norton" appeared, when Joyce's *Ulysses* had just been published in the United States—to the shocked fascination of Miss Hughes, my charming, encouraging English teacher in Cleveland, where in 1933–34 my stepfather had a job. The year before, we had lived in Boston, where my previous little gang and I had taken to Eliot over the dead bodies of our teachers. Free verse was still a topic of hot debate, especially on the part of people who hadn't a clue one way or another. As for me, at ages 15 and 16, I certainly thought well of the word "free."

• • •

Eliot's most striking early work is all in the adolescent keys of unresolved self-doubt, endlessly self-directed sensitivity and defensively cruel cool posturing. I hasten to add that I am not calling into question his poetic success, only pointing to an important element in what his poetry was successful in projecting—an actual inner state or quality of reverie, doubtless a reflex too of one type of cultivated American male psyche of Eliot's generation.

"The Love Song of J. Alfred Prufrock" is a perfect instance. Whatever else one may say about this first poem of Eliot's to command strong attention, it positively sweats panic at the challenge of adult sexuality and of living up to one's ideal of what it is to be manly in any sort of heroic model. Those challenges are the special monsters haunting adolescent male imagination, especially of the more introspective and introverted varieties. The furtive restlessness of the start, the fear of women's ridicule, the sensual longings, the forebodings of loneliness and eternal frustration, the painful self-mockery side by side with the persistent romanticism—these are the very stuff of that imagination. The age of the "I" of the poem, who is not in any case a sharply delineated dramatic character but rather a half-delineated one (the other half being the kind of floating sensibility both Eliot and Pound were to evolve a little further down the line), isn't specified. He may be an unusually self-conscious very young man, or perhaps he is older. It really doesn't matter. Adolescent readers took to him because he expressed their feelings while seeming to be someone other—the stuffily named and brought up "Prufrock" of the title. Fear of impotence, failure and isolation continue into adult life, of course, but they are the particular unwanted burden of the young.

"Prufrock" holds all this burden of vulnerability, and also the accompanying need to mask desire ("Is it perfume from a dress / That makes me so digress?") and not give the game away to "the women" as they move about and chatter and seem so politely, unshakably self-contained. How old was Eliot, actually, when he wrote the poem—about 21 or 22? It is a poem whose essence is distilled from teen-age memories, felt as deeply private yet almost universally shared—"I have heard the mermaids singing, each to each. / I do not think that they will sing to me."

Exactly! And that is why we could recite the poem at the drop of a hint, and could absorb its music unthinkingly, so that it mingled with equally rueful tones and rhythms out of Edwin Arlington Robinson and Robert Frost in the great American symphony of unrealized grace and heroism.

From "Adolescents Singing, Each to Each—When We and Eliot Were Young"

■ WRITING *effectively*

TOPICS FOR WRITING

1. "The Love Song of J. Alfred Prufrock" is very firmly grounded in upper-class society in the early twentieth century. Is the poem of purely historical value, opening a window on a society and a set of values that no longer exist, or are the attitudes and concerns that it expresses still relevant today?

2. In the excerpt entitled "Poetry and Emotion," Eliot says: "There is a great deal, in the writing of poetry, which must be conscious and deliberate. . . . Poetry is not a turning loose of emotion, but an escape from emotion; it is not the expression of personality, but an escape from personality." Discuss this statement, in terms of both its own meaning and its application to "The Love Song of J. Alfred Prufrock."

3. Write your own version of the poem by substituting for Michelangelo, morning coats, coffee spoons, and other specific references in the text. The idea is not to parody Eliot or spoof the poem, but instead to do something more challenging—to come up with "objective correlatives" appropriate to contemporary society and culture, just as Eliot found them for his time and place.

33 POEMS FOR FURTHER READING

The manuscript of John Donne's sonnet, "Death be not proud" (page 1037).

Anonymous (traditional Scottish ballad)

Lord Randall

"O where ha you been, Lord Randal, my son?
And where ha you been, my handsome young man?"
"I ha been at the greenwood; mother, mak my bed soon,
For I'm wearied wi hunting, and fain wad lie down."

"An wha° met ye there, Lord Randal, my son?   *who* 5
An wha met you there, my handsome young man?"
"O I met wi my true-love; mother, mak my bed soon,
For I'm wearied wi hunting, and fain wad lie down."

"And what did she give you, Lord Randal, my son?
And what did she give you, my handsome young man?"   10
"Eels fried in a pan; mother, mak my bed soon,
For I'm wearied wi hunting, and fain wad lie down."

"And wha gat° your leavins,° Lord Randal, my son? got; leftovers
And wha gat your leavins, my handsome young man?"
"My hawks and my hounds; mother, mak my bed soon, 15
For I'm wearied wi hunting, and fain wad lie down."

"And what becam of them, Lord Randal, my son?
And what becam of them, my handsome young man?"
"They stretched their legs out an died; mother, mak my bed soon,
For I'm wearied wi hunting, and fain wad lie down." 20

"O I fear you are poisoned, Lord Randal, my son!
I fear you are poisoned, my handsome young man!"
"O yes, I am poisoned; mother, mak my bed soon,
For I'm sick at the heart, and I fain wad lie down."

"What d' ye leave to your mother, Lord Randal, my son? 25
What d' ye leave to your mother, my handsome young man?"
"Four and twenty milk kye;° mother, mak my bed soon, cows
For I'm sick at the heart, and I fain wad lie down."

"What d' ye leave to your sister, Lord Randal, my son?
What d' ye leave to your sister, my handsome young man?" 30
"My gold and my silver; mother, mak my bed soon,
For I'm sick at the heart, and I fain wad lie down."

"What d' ye leave to your brother, Lord Randal, my son?
What d' ye leave to your brother, my handsome young man?"
"My house and my lands; mother, mak my bed soon, 35
For I'm sick at the heart, and I fain wad lie down."

"What d' ye leave to your true-love, Lord Randal, my son?
What d' ye leave to your true-love, my handsome young man?"
"I leave her hell and fire; mother, mak my bed soon,
For I'm sick at the heart, and I fain wad lie down." 40

Compare

"Lord Randall" with a modern ballad such as "Ballad of Birmingham" by Dudley Randall
(page 759).

Anonymous (traditional English ballad)

The Three Ravens

There were three ravens sat on a tree,
   Down a down, hay down, hay down,
There were three ravens sat on a tree,
   With a down,
There were three ravens sat on a tree, 5
They were as black as they might be.
   With a down derry, derry, derry, down, down.

The one of them said to his mate,
"Where shall we our breakfast take?"

"Down in yonder greene field,   10
There lies a knight slain under his shield.

"His hounds they lie down at his feet,
So well they can their master keep.

"His hawks they fly so eagerly,
There's no fowl dare him come nigh."   15

Down there comes a fallow doe,
As great with young as she might go.

She lifted up his bloody head,
And kist his wounds that were so red.

She got him up upon her back,   20
And carried him to earthen lake.°   *the grave*

She buried him before the prime,°   *dawn*
She was dead herself ere evensong time.

God send every gentleman
Such hawks, such hounds, and such a leman.°   *lover* 25

THE THREE RAVENS. The lines of refrain are repeated in each stanza. "Perhaps in the folk mind the doe is the form the soul of a human mistress, now dead, has taken," Albert B. Friedman has suggested (in *The Viking Book of Folk Ballads*). "Most probably the knight's beloved was understood to be an enchanted woman who was metamorphosed at certain times into an animal." In lines 22 and 23, *prime* and *evensong* are two of the canonical hours set aside for prayer and worship. Prime is at dawn, evensong at dusk.

Compare

"The Three Ravens" with "La Belle Dame sans Merci" by John Keats (page 872).

Anonymous (Navajo mountain chant)

Last Words of the Prophet

Farewell, my younger brother!
From the holy places the gods come for me.
You will never see me again; but when the showers pass and the
        thunders peal,
"There," you will say, "is the voice of my elder brother."
And when the harvest comes, of the beautiful birds and grasshoppers   5
        you will say,
"There is the ordering of my elder brother!"

                                              —*Translated by Washington Matthews*

Compare

"Last Words of the Prophet" with "A Slumber Did My Spirit Seal" by William Wordsworth (page 774).

Matthew Arnold (1822–1888)

Dover Beach   1867

The sea is calm to-night.
The tide is full, the moon lies fair
Upon the straits; on the French coast the light
Gleams and is gone; the cliffs of England stand,
Glimmering and vast, out in the tranquil bay.   5
Come to the window, sweet is the night-air!
Only, from the long line of spray
Where the sea meets the moon-blanched land,
Listen! you hear the grating roar
Of pebbles which the waves draw back, and fling,   10
At their return, up the high strand,
Begin, and cease, and then again begin,
With tremulous cadence slow, and bring
The eternal note of sadness in.

Sophocles long ago   15
Heard it on the Aegean, and it brought
Into his mind the turbid ebb and flow
Of human misery; we
Find also in the sound a thought,
Hearing it by this distant northern sea.   20

The Sea of Faith
Was once, too, at the full, and round earth's shore
Lay like the folds of a bright girdle furled.
But now I only hear
Its melancholy, long, withdrawing roar,   25
Retreating, to the breath
Of the night-wind, down the vast edges drear
And naked shingles° of the world.   *gravel beaches*

Ah, love, let us be true
To one another! for the world, which seems   30
To lie before us like a land of dreams,
So various, so beautiful, so new,
Hath really neither joy, nor love, nor light,
Nor certitude, nor peace, nor help for pain;
And we are here as on a darkling° plain   *darkened or darkening* 35
Swept with confused alarms of struggle and flight,
Where ignorant armies clash by night.

Compare

"Dover Beach" with "Hap" by Thomas Hardy (page 1049).

John Ashbery (b. 1927)

At North Farm   1984

Somewhere someone is traveling furiously toward you,
At incredible speed, traveling day and night,
Through blizzards and desert heat, across torrents, through narrow passes.
But will he know where to find you,
Recognize you when he sees you,   5
Give you the thing he has for you?

Hardly anything grows here,
Yet the granaries are bursting with meal,
The sacks of meal piled to the rafters.
The streams run with sweetness, fattening fish;   10
Birds darken the sky. Is it enough
That the dish of milk is set out at night,
That we think of him sometimes,
Sometimes and always, with mixed feelings?

Compare

"At North Farm" with "Uphill" by Christina Rossetti (page 859).

Margaret Atwood (b. 1939)

Siren Song   1974

This is the one song everyone
would like to learn: the song
that is irresistible:

the song that forces men
to leap overboard in squadrons   5
even though they see the beached skulls

the song nobody knows
because anyone who has heard it
is dead, and the others can't remember.

Shall I tell you the secret   10
and if I do, will you get me
out of this bird suit?

I don't enjoy it here
squatting on this island
looking picturesque and mythical   15

Margaret Atwood

with these two feathery maniacs,
I don't enjoy singing
this trio, fatal and valuable.

I will tell the secret to you,
to you, only to you.
Come closer. This song   20

is a cry for help: Help me!
Only you, only you can,
you are unique

at last. Alas   25
it is a boring song
but it works every time.

SIREN SONG. In Greek mythology, sirens were half-woman, half-bird nymphs who lured sailors to their deaths by singing hypnotically beautiful songs.

Compare

"Siren Song" with "Her Kind" by Anne Sexton (page 657).

W. H. Auden (1907–1973)

As I Walked Out One Evening   1940

As I walked out one evening,
    Walking down Bristol Street,
The crowds upon the pavement
    Were fields of harvest wheat.

And down by the brimming river   5
    I heard a lover sing
Under an arch of the railway:
    "Love has no ending.

"I'll love you, dear, I'll love you
    Till China and Africa meet,   10
And the river jumps over the mountain
    And the salmon sing in the street,

"I'll love you till the ocean
    Is folded and hung up to dry
And the seven stars go squawking   15
    Like geese about the sky.

"The years shall run like rabbits,
    For in my arms I hold
The Flower of the Ages,
    And the first love of the world."   20

W. H. Auden

But all the clocks in the city
   Began to whirr and chime:
"O let not Time deceive you,
   You cannot conquer Time.

"In the burrows of the Nightmare   25
   Where Justice naked is,
Time watches from the shadow
   And coughs when you would kiss.

"In headaches and in worry
   Vaguely life leaks away,   30
And Time will have his fancy
   To-morrow or to-day.

"Into many a green valley
   Drifts the appalling snow;
Time breaks the threaded dances   35
   And the diver's brilliant bow.

"O plunge your hands in water,
   Plunge them in up to the wrist;
Stare, stare in the basin
   And wonder what you've missed.   40

"The glacier knocks in the cupboard,
   The desert sighs in the bed,
And the crack in the tea-cup opens
   A lane to the land of the dead.

"Where the beggars raffle the banknotes   45
   And the Giant is enchanting to Jack,
And the Lily-white Boy is a Roarer,
   And Jill goes down on her back.

"O look, look in the mirror,
   O look in your distress;   50
Life remains a blessing
   Although you cannot bless.

"O stand, stand at the window
   As the tears scald and start;
You shall love your crooked neighbor   55
   With your crooked heart."

It was late, late in the evening,
   The lovers they were gone;
The clocks had ceased their chiming,
   And the deep river ran on.   60

Compare

"As I Walked Out One Evening" with "Dover Beach" by Matthew Arnold (page 1019) and "anyone lived in a pretty how town" by E. E. Cummings (page 688).

The Fall of Icarus by Pieter Brueghel the Elder (1520?–1569).

W. H. Auden (1907–1973)

Musée des Beaux Arts 1940

About suffering they were never wrong,
The Old Masters: how well they understood
Its human position; how it takes place
While someone else is eating or opening a window or just walking
    dully along;
How, when the aged are reverently, passionately waiting 5
For the miraculous birth, there always must be
Children who did not specially want it to happen, skating
On a pond at the edge of the wood:
They never forgot
That even the dreadful martyrdom must run its course 10
Anyhow in a corner, some untidy spot
Where the dogs go on with their doggy life and the torturer's horse
Scratches its innocent behind on a tree.

In Brueghel's *Icarus*, for instance: how everything turns away
Quite leisurely from the disaster; the ploughman may 15
Have heard the splash, the forsaken cry,

But for him it was not an important failure; the sun shone
As it had to on the white legs disappearing into the green
Water; and the expensive delicate ship that must have seen
Something amazing, a boy falling out of the sky,   20
Had somewhere to get to and sailed calmly on.

Compare

"Musée des Beaux Arts" with "The Dance" by William Carlos Williams (page 835) and the
painting by Pieter Brueghel to which each poem refers.

Jimmy Santiago Baca (b. 1952)

Spliced Wire   1982

I filled your house with light.
There was warmth in all the corners
of the house. My words I gave you
like soft warm toast in early morning.
I brewed your tongue   5
to a rich dark coffee, and drank
my fill. I turned on the music for you,
playing notes along the crest
of your heart, like birds,
eagles, ravens, owls on rim of red canyon.   10

I brought reception clear to you,
and made the phone ring at your request,
from Paris or South America,
you could talk to any of the people,
as my words gave them life,   15
from a child in a boat with his father,
to a prisoner in a concentration camp,
all at your bedside.

And then you turned away, wanted
a larger mansion. I said no. I left you.   20
The plug pulled out, the house blinked out,
Into a quiet darkness, swallowing wind,
collecting autumn leaves like stamps
between its old boards where they stick.

You say, or carry the thought with you   25
to comfort you, that faraway somewhere,
lightning knocked down all the power lines.
But no my love, it was I,
pulling the plug. Others will come, plug in,
but often the lights will dim weakly   30
in storms, the music stop to a drawl,
the warmth shredded by cold drafts.

Compare

"Spliced Wire" with "The Demolition" by Anne Stevenson (page 746).

Elizabeth Bishop (1911–1979)

Filling Station   1965

Oh, but it is dirty!
—this little filling station,
oil-soaked, oil-permeated
to a disturbing, over-all
black translucency.   5
Be careful with that match!

Father wears a dirty,
oil-soaked monkey suit
that cuts him under the arms,
and several quick and saucy   10
and greasy sons assist him
(it's a family filling station),
all quite thoroughly dirty.

Elizabeth Bishop

Do they live in the station?
It has a cement porch   15
behind the pumps, and on it
a set of crushed and grease-
impregnated wickerwork;
on the wicker sofa
a dirty dog, quite comfy.   20

Some comic books provide
the only note of color—
of certain color. They lie
upon a big dim doily
draping a taboret°   *stool*   25
(part of the set), beside
a big hirsute begonia.

Why the extraneous plant?
Why the taboret?
Why, oh why, the doily?   30
(Embroidered in daisy stitch
with marguerites, I think,
and heavy with gray crochet.)

Somebody embroidered the doily.
Somebody waters the plant,   35
or oils it, maybe. Somebody
arranges the rows of cans
so that they softly say:
ESSO—SO—SO—SO
to high-strung automobiles.   40
Somebody loves us all.

Compare

"Filling Station" with "The splendor falls on castle walls" by Alfred, Lord Tennyson (page 777).

Detail of William Blake's *The Tyger*.

William Blake (1757–1827)

The Tyger   1794

Tyger! Tyger! burning bright
In the forests of the night,
What immortal hand or eye
Could frame thy fearful symmetry?

In what distant deeps or skies   5
Burnt the fire of thine eyes?
On what wings dare he aspire?
What the hand dare seize the fire?

And what shoulder, and what art,
Could twist the sinews of thy heart?
And when thy heart began to beat,   10
What dread hand? and what dread feet?

What the hammer? what the chain?
In what furnace was thy brain?
What the anvil? what dread grasp
Dare its deadly terrors clasp?   15

When the stars threw down their spears,
And watered heaven with their tears,
Did he smile his work to see?
Did he who made the Lamb make thee?   20

Tyger! Tyger! burning bright
In the forests of the night,
What immortal hand or eye
Dare frame thy fearful symmetry?

Compare

"The Tyger" with "The Windhover" by Gerard Manley Hopkins (page 1055).

William Blake (1757–1827)

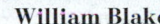

The Sick Rose   1794

O Rose, thou art sick!
The invisible worm
That flies in the night,
In the howling storm,

Has found out thy bed   5
Of crimson joy,
And his dark secret love
Does thy life destroy.

Compare

"The Sick Rose" with "Mock Orange" by Louise Glück (page 722).

William Blake

Gwendolyn Brooks (1917–2000)

the mother   1945

Abortions will not let you forget.
You remember the children you got that you did not get,
The damp small pulps with a little or with no hair,
The singers and workers that never handled the air.
You will never neglect or beat   5
Them, or silence or buy with a sweet.
You will never wind up the sucking-thumb
Or scuttle off ghosts that come.
You will never leave them, controlling your luscious sigh,
Return for a snack of them, with gobbling mother-eye. 10

I have heard in the voices of the wind the voices of my dim killed children.
I have contracted. I have eased
My dim dears at the breasts they could never suck.
I have said, Sweets, if I sinned, if I seized
Your luck   15

And your lives from your unfinished reach,
If I stole your births and your names,
Your straight baby tears and your games,
Your stilted or lovely loves, your tumults, your marriages, aches, and your deaths,
If I poisoned the beginnings of your breaths,   20
Believe that even in my deliberateness I was not deliberate.
Though why should I whine,
Whine that the crime was other than mine?—
Since anyhow you are dead.
Or rather, or instead,   25
You were never made.
But that too, I am afraid,
Is faulty: oh, what shall I say, how is the truth to be said?
You were born, you had body, you died.
It is just that you never giggled or planned or cried.   30

Believe me, I loved you all.
Believe me, I knew you, though faintly, and I loved, I loved you
All.

Compare

"the mother" with "Metaphors" by Sylvia Plath (page 735).

Gwendolyn Brooks (1917–2000)

the rites for Cousin Vit   1949

Carried her unprotesting out the door.
Kicked back the casket-stand. But it can't hold her,
That stuff and satin aiming to enfold her,
The lid's contrition nor the bolts before.

Gwendolyn Brooks

Oh oh. Too much. Too much. Even now, surmise,   5
She rises in the sunshine. There she goes,
Back to the bars she knew and the repose
In love-rooms and the things in people's eyes.
Too vital and too squeaking. Must emerge.
Even now she does the snake-hips with a hiss,   10
Slops the bad wine across her shantung, talks
Of pregnancy, guitars and bridgework, walks
In parks or alleys, comes haply on the verge
Of happiness, haply hysterics. Is.

Compare

"the rites for Cousin Vit" with "Do not go gentle into that good night" by Dylan Thomas (page 824).

Elizabeth Barrett Browning (1806–1861)

How Do I Love Thee? Let Me Count the Ways   1850

How do I love thee? Let me count the ways.
I love thee to the depth and breadth and height
My soul can reach, when feeling out of sight
For the ends of Being and ideal Grace.
I love thee to the level of every day's   5
Most quiet need, by sun and candle-light.
I love thee freely, as men strive for Right.
I love thee purely, as they turn from Praise.
I love thee with the passion put to use
In my old griefs, and with my childhood's faith.   10
I love thee with a love I seemed to lose
With my lost saints,— I love thee with the breath,
Smiles, tears, of all my life!—and, if God choose,
I shall but love thee better after death.

Compare

"How Do I Love Thee?" with "What lips my lips have kissed" by Edna St. Vincent Millay (page 817).

Robert Browning (1812–1889)

Soliloquy of the Spanish Cloister   1842

Gr-r-r—there go, my heart's abhorrence!
   Water your damned flower-pots, do!
If hate killed men, Brother Lawrence,
   God's blood, would not mine kill you!
What? your myrtle-bush wants trimming?   5
   Oh, that rose has prior claims—
Needs its leaden vase filled brimming?
   Hell dry you up with its flames!

At the meal we sit together;
   Salve tibi!° I must hear   *Hail to thee!*   10
Wise talk of the kind of weather,
   Sort of season, time of year:
Not a plenteous cork-crop: scarcely
   Dare we hope oak-galls, I doubt:
What's the Latin name for "parsley"?   15
   What's the Greek name for Swine's Snout?

Whew! We'll have our platter burnished,
   Laid with care on our own shelf!
With a fire-new spoon we're furnished,
   And a goblet for ourself,   20
Rinsed like something sacrificial
   Ere 'tis fit to touch our chaps—
Marked with L. for our initial!
   (He-he! There his lily snaps!)

Saint, forsooth! While brown Dolores   25
    Squats outside the Convent bank
With Sanchicha, telling stories,
    Steeping tresses in the tank,
Blue-black, lustrous, thick like horsehairs,
    —Can't I see his dead eye glow,   30
Bright as 'twere a Barbary corsair's?
    (That is, if he'd let it show!)

When he finishes refection,
    Knife and fork he never lays
Cross-wise, to my recollection,   35
    As I do, in Jesu's praise.
I the Trinity illustrate,
    Drinking watered orange-pulp—
In three sips the Arian frustrate;
    While he drains his at one gulp!   40

Oh, those melons! if he's able
    We're to have a feast; so nice!
One goes to the Abbot's table,
    All of us get each a slice.
How go on your flowers? None double?   45
    Not one fruit-sort can you spy?
Strange!—And I, too, at such trouble,
    Keep them close-nipped on the sly!

There's a great text in Galatians,
    Once you trip on it, entails   50
Twenty-nine distinct damnations,
    One sure, if another fails:
If I trip him just a-dying,
    Sure of heaven as sure can be,
Spin him round and send him flying   55
    Off to hell, a Manichee?

Or, my scrofulous French novel
    On grey paper with blunt type!
Simply glance at it, you grovel
    Hand and foot in Belial's gripe: 60
If I double down its pages
    At the woeful sixteenth print,
When he gathers his greengages,
    Ope a sieve and slip it in't?

Or, there's Satan!—one might venture   65
   Pledge one's soul to him, yet leave
Such a flaw in the indenture
   As he'd miss till, past retrieve,
Blasted lay that rose-acacia
   We're so proud of! Hy, Zy, Hine. . . .   70
'St, there's Vespers! *Plena gratia*
   Ave, Virgo!° Gr-r-r—you swine!   *Hail, Virgin, full of grace!*

SOLILOQUY OF THE SPANISH CLOISTER. 3 *Brother Lawrence:* one of the speaker's fellow monks. 31 *Barbary corsair:* a pirate operating off the Barbary coast of Africa. 39 *Arian:* a follower of Arius, a heretic who denied the doctrine of the Trinity. 49 *a great text in Galatians:* a difficult verse in this book of the Bible. Brother Lawrence will be damned as a heretic if he wrongly interprets it. 56 *Manichee:* another kind of heretic, one who (after the Persian philosopher Mani) sees in the world a constant struggle between good and evil, neither able to win. 60 *Belial:* here, not specifically Satan but (as used in the Old Testament) a name for wickedness. 70 *Hy, Zy, Hine:* possibly the sound of a bell to announce evening devotions.

Compare

"Soliloquy of the Spanish Cloister" with "Unholy Sonnet: After the Praying" by Mark Jarman (page 820).

Geoffrey Chaucer (1340?–1400)

Merciless Beauty   (late 14th century)

Your ÿen° two wol slee° me sodenly;   *eyes; slay*
I may the beautee of hem° not sustene,°   *them; resist*
So woundeth hit thourghout my herte kene.

And but° your word wol helen° hastily   *unless; heal*
My hertes wounde, while that hit is grene,°   *new*   5
   Your ÿen two wol slee me sodenly;
   I may the beautee of hem not sustene.

Upon my trouthe° I sey you feithfully   *word*
That ye ben of my lyf and deeth the quene;
For with my deeth the trouthe° shal be sene.   *truth*   10
   Your ÿen two wol slee me sodenly;
   I may the beautee of hem not sustene,
     So woundeth it thourghout my herte kene.

MERCILESS BEAUTY. This poem is one of a group of three roundels, collectively titled "Merciles Beaute." A **roundel** (or **rondel**) is an English form consisting of 11 lines in 3 stanzas rimed with a refrain. 3 *So woundeth . . . kene:* "So deeply does it wound me through the heart."

Compare

"Merciless Beauty" with "My mistress' eyes are nothing like the sun" by William Shakespeare (page 1084).

John Ciardi (1916–1986)

Most Like an Arch This Marriage   1958

Most like an arch—an entrance which upholds
and shores the stone-crush up the air like lace.
Mass made idea, and idea held in place.
A lock in time. Inside half-heaven unfolds.

Most like an arch—two weaknesses that lean   5
into a strength. Two fallings become firm.
Two joined abeyances become a term
naming the fact that teaches fact to mean.

Not quite that? Not much less. World as it is,
what's strong and separate falters. All I do   10
at piling stone on stone apart from you
is roofless around nothing. Till we kiss

I am no more than upright and unset.
It is by falling in and in we make
the all-bearing point, for one another's sake,   15
in faultless failing, raised by our own weight.

Compare

"Most Like an Arch This Marriage" with "The Silken Tent" by Robert Frost (page 744).

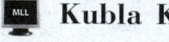

Samuel Taylor Coleridge (1772–1834)

Kubla Khan   (1797–1798)

Or, a Vision in a Dream. A Fragment.

In Xanadu did Kubla Khan
A stately pleasure-dome decree:
Where Alph, the sacred river, ran
Through caverns measureless to man
    Down to a sunless sea.   5
So twice five miles of fertile ground
With walls and towers were girdled round;
And there were gardens bright with sinuous rills,
Where blossomed many an incense-bearing tree;
And here were forests ancient as the hills,   10
Enfolding sunny spots of greenery.

But oh! that deep romantic chasm which slanted
Down the green hill athwart a cedarn cover!
A savage place! as holy and enchanted
As e'er beneath a waning moon was haunted   15
By woman wailing for her demon-lover!
And from this chasm, with ceaseless turmoil seething,
As if this earth in fast thick pants were breathing,
A mighty fountain momently was forced:
Amid whose swift half-intermitted burst   20
Huge fragments vaulted like rebounding hail,
Or chaffy grain beneath the thresher's flail:
And 'mid these dancing rocks at once and ever
It flung up momently the sacred river.
Five miles meandering with a mazy motion   25
Through wood and dale the sacred river ran,
Then reached the caverns measureless to man,
And sank in tumult to a lifeless ocean:
And 'mid this tumult Kubla heard from far
Ancestral voices prophesying war!   30

   The shadow of the dome of pleasure
   Floated midway on the waves;
   Where was heard the mingled measure
   From the fountain and the caves.
It was a miracle of rare device,   35
A sunny pleasure-dome with caves of ice!

   A damsel with a dulcimer
   In a vision once I saw:
   It was an Abyssinian maid,
   And on her dulcimer she played,   40
   Singing of Mount Abora.
   Could I revive within me
   Her symphony and song,
   To such a deep delight 'twould win me,
That with music loud and long,   45
I would build that dome in air,
That sunny dome! those caves of ice!
And all who heard should see them there,
And all should cry, Beware! Beware!
His flashing eyes, his floating hair!   50
Weave a circle round him thrice,
And close your eyes with holy dread,
For he on honey-dew hath fed,
And drunk the milk of Paradise.

KUBLA KHAN. There was an actual Kublai Khan, a thirteenth-century Mongol emperor, and a Chinese city
of Xanadu; but Coleridge's dream vision also borrows from travelers' descriptions of such other exotic
places as Abyssinia and America. 51 *circle:* a magic circle drawn to keep away evil spirits.

Compare

"Kubla Khan" with "The Second Coming" by William Butler Yeats (page 874).

Billy Collins (b. 1941)

Care and Feeding

2003

Because I will turn 420 tomorrow
in dog years
I will take myself for a long walk
along the green shore of the lake,

and when I walk in the door,   5
I will jump up on my chest
and lick my nose and ears and eyelids
while I tell myself again and again to get down.

I will fill my metal bowl at the sink
with cold fresh water,   10
and lift a biscuit from the jar
and hold it gingerly with my teeth.

Billy Collins

Then I will make three circles
and lie down at my feet on the wood floor
and close my eyes   15
while I type all morning and into the afternoon,

checking every once in a while
to make sure I am still there,
reaching down
to stroke my furry, venerable head.   20

Compare

"Care and Feeding" with "For the Anniversary of My Death" by W. S. Merwin (page 834).

Hart Crane (1899–1932)

My Grandmother's Love Letters

1926

There are no stars tonight
But those of memory.
Yet how much room for memory there is
In the loose girdle of soft rain.

There is even room enough   5
For the letters of my mother's mother,
Elizabeth,
That have been pressed so long

Into a corner of the roof
That they are brown and soft,   10
And liable to melt as snow.

Over the greatness of such space
Steps must be gentle.
It is all hung by an invisible white hair.
It trembles as birch limbs webbing the air.   15

And I ask myself:

"Are your fingers long enough to play
Old keys that are but echoes:
Is the silence strong enough
To carry back the music to its source   20
And back to you again
As though to her?"

Yet I would lead my grandmother by the hand
Through much of what she would not understand;
And so I stumble. And the rain continues on the roof   25
With such a sound of gently pitying laughter.

Compare

"My Grandmother's Love Letters" with "When You Are Old" by William Butler Yeats (page 1103).

E. E. Cummings (1894–1962)

somewhere i have never travelled,gladly beyond   1931

somewhere i have never travelled,gladly beyond
any experience,your eyes have their silence:
in your most frail gesture are things which enclose me,
or which i cannot touch because they are too near

E. E. Cummings

your slightest look easily will unclose me   5
though i have closed myself as fingers,
you open always petal by petal myself as Spring opens
(touching skilfully,mysteriously)her first rose

or if your wish be to close me,i and
my life will shut very beautifully,suddenly,   10
as when the heart of this flower imagines
the snow carefully everywhere descending;

nothing which we are to perceive in this world equals
the power of your intense fragility:whose texture
compels me with the colour of its countries,   15
rendering death and forever with each breathing

(i do not know what it is about you that closes
and opens;only something in me understands
the voice of your eyes is deeper than all roses)
nobody,not even the rain,has such small hands   20

Compare

"somewhere i have never travelled,gladly beyond" with "Merciless Beauty" by Geoffrey
Chaucer (page 1031) or "Elegy for Jane" by Theodore Roethke (page 1082).

Marisa de los Santos (b. 1966)

Perfect Dress   2000

It's here in a student's journal, a blue confession
in smudged, erasable ink: "I can't stop hoping
I'll wake up, suddenly beautiful," and isn't it strange
how we want it, despite all we know? To be at last

the girl in the photograph, cobalt-eyed, hair puddling   5
like cognac, or the one stretched at the ocean's edge,
curved and light-drenched, more like a beach than
the beach. I confess I have longed to stalk runways,

leggy, otherworldly as a mantis, to balance a head
like a Fabergé egg on the longest, most elegant neck.   10
Today in the checkout line, I saw a magazine
claiming to know "How to Find the Perfect Dress

for that Perfect Evening," and I felt the old pull, flare
of the pilgrim's twin flames, desire and faith. At fifteen,
I spent weeks at the search. Going from store to store,   15
hands thirsty for shine, I reached for polyester satin,

machine-made lace, petunia- and Easter egg-colored,
brilliant and flammable. Nothing *haute* about this
couture but my hopes for it, as I tugged it on
and waited for my one, true body to emerge.   20

(Picture the angel inside uncut marble, articulation
of wings and robes poised in expectation of release.)
What I wanted was ordinary miracle, the falling away
of everything wrong. Silly maybe or maybe

Marisa de los Santos

I was right, that there's no limit to the ways eternity
suggests itself, that one day I'll slip into it, say
floor-length plum charmeuse. Someone will murmur,
"She is sublime," will be precisely right, and I will step,

with incandescent shoulders, into my perfect evening.

PERFECT DRESS. 10 *Fabergé*: Peter Carl Fabergé (1846–1920) was a Russian jeweler renowned for his elaborately decorated, golden, jeweled eggs.

Compare

"Perfect Dress" with "Cinderella" by Anne Sexton (page 878).

John Donne (1572–1631)

John Donne

Death be not proud   (about 1610)

Death be not proud, though some have callèd thee
Mighty and dreadful, for thou art not so;
For those whom thou think'st thou dost overthrow
Die not, poor death, nor yet canst thou kill me.
From rest and sleep, which but thy pictures be,   5
Much pleasure, then from thee much more must flow,
And soonest our best men with thee do go,
Rest of their bones, and soul's delivery.
Thou art slave to fate, chance, kings, and desperate men,
And dost with poison, war, and sickness dwell,   10
And poppy, or charms can make us sleep as well,
And better than thy stroke; why swell'st thou then?
One short sleep past, we wake eternally,
And death shall be no more; death, thou shalt die.

Compare

Compare Donne's personification of Death in "Death be not proud" with Emily Dickinson's in "Because I could not stop for Death" (page 963).

John Donne (1572–1631)

The Flea   1633

Mark but this flea, and mark in this
How little that which thou deny'st me is;
It sucked me first, and now sucks thee,
And in this flea our two bloods mingled be;
Thou know'st that this cannot be said   5
A sin, nor shame, nor loss of maidenhead,
    Yet this enjoys before it woo,
    And pampered swells with one blood made of two,
    And this, alas, is more than we would do.

Oh stay, three lives in one flea spare,   10
Where we almost, yea more than married are.
This flea is you and I, and this
Our marriage bed, and marriage temple is;
Though parents grudge, and you, we're met
And cloistered in these living walls of jet.   15
  Though use° make you apt to kill me,   *custom*
  Let not to that, self-murder added be,
  And sacrilege, three sins in killing three.

Cruel and sudden, hast thou since
Purpled thy nail in blood of innocence?   20
Wherein could this flea guilty be,
Except in that drop which it sucked from thee?
Yet thou triumph'st, and say'st that thou
Find'st not thyself, nor me, the weaker now;
  'Tis true; then learn how false, fears be;   25
  Just so much honor, when thou yield'st to me,
  Will waste, as this flea's death took life from thee.

Compare

"The Flea" with "To His Coy Mistress" by Andrew Marvell (page 1066).

John Donne (1572–1631)

A Valediction: Forbidding Mourning   (1611)

As virtuous men pass mildly away,
 And whisper to their souls to go,
Whilst some of their sad friends do say
 The breath goes now, and some say no:

So let us melt, and make no noise,   5
 No tear-floods, nor sigh-tempests move;
'Twere profanation of our joys
 To tell the laity° our love.   *common people*

Moving of th' earth° brings harms and fears;   *earthquake*
 Men reckon what it did and meant;   10
But trepidation of the spheres,
 Though greater far, is innocent.°   *harmless*

Dull sublunary lovers' love
 (Whose soul is sense) cannot admit
Absence, because it doth remove   15
 Those things which elemented° it.   *constituted*

But we, by a love so much refined
 That ourselves know not what it is,
Inter-assurèd of the mind,
 Care less, eyes, lips, and hands to miss.   20

Our two souls, therefore, which are one,
   Though I must go, endure not yet
A breach, but an expansiòn,
   Like gold to airy thinness beat.

If they be two, they are two so   25
   As stiff twin compasses are two:
Thy soul, the fixed foot, makes no show
   To move, but doth, if th' other do.

And though it in the center sit,
   Yet when the other far doth roam,   30
It leans and harkens after it,
   And grows erect as that comes home.

Such wilt thou be to me, who must,
   Like th' other foot, obliquely run;
Thy firmness makes my circle just,°   *perfect* 35
   And makes me end where I begun.

A VALEDICTION: FORBIDDING MOURNING. According to Donne's biographer Izaak Walton, Donne's wife received this poem as a gift before the poet departed on a journey to France. 11 *spheres*: in Ptolemaic astronomy, the concentric spheres surrounding the earth. The trepidation or motion of the ninth sphere was thought to change the date of the equinox. 19 *Inter-assured of the mind*: each sure in mind that the other is faithful. 24 *gold to airy thinness*: gold is so malleable that, if beaten to the thickness of gold leaf (1/250,000 of one inch), one ounce of gold would cover 250 square feet.

Compare

"A Valediction: Forbidding Mourning" with "To Lucasta" by Richard Lovelace (page 667).

Rita Dove (b. 1952)

Daystar   1986

She wanted a little room for thinking:
but she saw diapers steaming on the line,
a doll slumped behind the door.

So she lugged a chair behind the garage
to sit out the children's naps.   5

Sometimes there were things to watch—
the pinched armor of a vanished cricket,
a floating maple leaf. Other days
she stared until she was assured
when she closed her eyes   10
she'd see only her own vivid blood.

She had an hour, at best, before Liza appeared
pouting from the top of the stairs.
And just *what* was mother doing
out back with the field mice? Why,   15

Rita Dove

building a palace. Later
that night when Thomas rolled over and
lurched into her, she would open her eyes
and think of the place that was hers
for an hour—where   20
she was nothing,
pure nothing, in the middle of the day.

Compare

"Daystar" with "The Lake Isle of Innisfree" by William Butler Yeats (page 633) or "Driving to
Town Late to Mail a Letter" by Robert Bly (page 721).

John Dryden (1631–1700)

To the Memory of Mr. Oldham   1684

Farewell, too little and too lately known,
Whom I began to think and call my own;
For sure our souls were near allied, and thine
Cast in the same poetic mold with mine.
One common note on either lyre did strike,   5
And knaves and fools we both abhorred alike.
To the same goal did both our studies drive:
The last set out the soonest did arrive.
Thus Nisus fell upon the slippery place,
While his young friend performed and won the race.   10
O early ripe! to thy abundant store
What could advancing age have added more?
It might (what Nature never gives the young)
Have taught the numbers° of thy native tongue.   *meters*
But satire needs not those, and wit will shine   15
Through the harsh cadence of a rugged line.
A noble error, and but seldom made,
When poets are by too much force betrayed.
Thy gen'rous fruits, though gathered ere their prime,
Still showed a quickness; and maturing time   20
But mellows what we write to the dull sweets of rhyme.
Once more, hail, and farewell! farewell, thou young
But ah! too short, Marcellus of our tongue!
Thy brows with ivy and with laurels bound;
But fate and gloomy night encompass thee around.   25

TO THE MEMORY OF MR. OLDHAM. John Oldham, poet best remembered for his *Satires upon the Jesuits,* had
died at thirty. 9–10 *Nisus; his young friend:* these two close friends, as Virgil tells us in the *Aeneid,* ran a
race for the prize of an olive crown. 23 *Marcellus:* had he not died in his twentieth year, he would have
succeeded the Roman emperor Augustus. 25 This line echoes the *Aeneid* (VI, 886), in which Marcellus is
seen walking under the black cloud of his impending doom.

Compare

"To the Memory of Mr. Oldham" with "Elegy for Jane" by Theodore Roethke (page 1082).

T. S. Eliot (1888–1965)

Journey of the Magi

1927

"A cold coming we had of it,
Just the worst time of the year
For a journey, and such a long journey:
The ways deep and the weather sharp,
The very dead of winter."   5
And the camels galled, sore-footed, refractory,
Lying down in the melting snow.
There were times we regretted
The summer palaces on slopes, the terraces,
And the silken girls bringing sherbet.   10
Then the camel men cursing and grumbling
And running away, and wanting their liquor and women,
And the night-fires going out, and the lack of shelters,
And the cities hostile and the towns unfriendly
And the villages dirty and charging high prices: 15
A hard time we had of it.
At the end we preferred to travel all night,
Sleeping in snatches,
With the voices singing in our ears, saying
That this was all folly.   20

Then at dawn we came down to a temperate valley,
Wet, below the snow line, smelling of vegetation;
With a running stream and a water-mill beating the darkness,
And three trees on the low sky,
And an old white horse galloped away in the meadow.   25
Then we came to a tavern with vine-leaves over the lintel,
Six hands at an open door dicing for pieces of silver,
And feet kicking the empty wine-skins.
But there was no information, and so we continued
And arrived at evening, not a moment too soon   30
Finding the place; it was (you may say) satisfactory.

All this was a long time ago, I remember,
And I would do it again, but set down
This set down
This: were we led all that way for   35
Birth or Death? There was a Birth, certainly,
We had evidence and no doubt. I had seen birth and death,
But had thought they were different; this Birth was
Hard and bitter agony for us, like Death, our death.
We returned to our places, these Kingdoms,   40
But no longer at ease here, in the old dispensation,
With an alien people clutching their gods.
I should be glad of another death.

JOURNEY OF THE MAGI. The story of the Magi, the three wise men who traveled to Bethlehem to behold the baby Jesus, is told in Matthew 2:1–12. That the three were kings is a later tradition. *1–5 A cold coming . . . winter:* Eliot quotes with slight changes from a sermon preached on Christmas Day, 1622, by Bishop Lancelot Andrewes. *24 three trees:* foreshadowing the three crosses on Calvary (see Luke 23:32–33). *25 white horse:* perhaps the steed that carried the conquering Christ in the vision of St. John the Divine (Revelation 19:11–16). *41 old dispensation:* older, pagan religion about to be displaced by Christianity.

Compare

"Journey of the Magi" with "The Magi" by William Butler Yeats (page 1102).

Robert Frost (1874–1963)

Birches   1916

When I see birches bend to left and right
Across the lines of straighter darker trees,
I like to think some boy's been swinging them.
But swinging doesn't bend them down to stay
As ice-storms do. Often you must have seen them   5
Loaded with ice a sunny winter morning
After a rain. They click upon themselves
As the breeze rises, and turn many-colored
As the stir cracks and crazes their enamel.
Soon the sun's warmth makes them shed crystal shells   10
Shattering and avalanching on the snow-crust—
Such heaps of broken glass to sweep away
You'd think the inner dome of heaven had fallen.
They are dragged to the withered bracken by the load,
And they seem not to break; though once they are bowed   15
So low for long, they never right themselves:
You may see their trunks arching in the woods
Years afterwards, trailing their leaves on the ground
Like girls on hands and knees that throw their hair
Before them over their heads to dry in the sun.   20
But I was going to say when Truth broke in
With all her matter-of-fact about the ice-storm
I should prefer to have some boy bend them
As he went out and in to fetch the cows—
Some boy too far from town to learn baseball,   25
Whose only play was what he found himself,
Summer or winter, and could play alone.
One by one he subdued his father's trees
By riding them down over and over again
Until he took the stiffness out of them,   30
And not one but hung limp, not one was left
For him to conquer. He learned all there was
To learn about not launching out too soon
And so not carrying the tree away
Clear to the ground. He always kept his poise   35
To the top branches, climbing carefully

With the same pains you use to fill a cup
Up to the brim, and even above the brim.
Then he flung outward, feet first, with a swish,
Kicking his way down through the air to the ground.   40
So was I once myself a swinger of birches.
And so I dream of going back to be.
It's when I'm weary of considerations,
And life is too much like a pathless wood
Where your face burns and tickles with the cobwebs   45
Broken across it, and one eye is weeping
From a twig's having lashed across it open.
I'd like to get away from earth awhile
And then come back to it and begin over.
May no fate willfully misunderstand me   50
And half grant what I wish and snatch me away
Not to return. Earth's the right place for love:
I don't know where it's likely to go better.
I'd like to go by climbing a birch tree,
And climb black branches up a snow-white trunk   55
Toward heaven, till the tree could bear no more,
But dipped its top and set me down again.
That would be good both going and coming back.
One could do worse than be a swinger of birches.

Compare

"Birches" with "Sailing to Byzantium" by William Butler Yeats (page 937).

Robert Frost (1874–1963)

Robert Frost

Mending Wall   1914

Something there is that doesn't love a wall,
That sends the frozen-ground-swell under it,
And spills the upper boulders in the sun;
And makes gaps even two can pass abreast.
The work of hunters is another thing: 5
I have come after them and made repair
Where they have left not one stone on a stone,
But they would have the rabbit out of hiding,
To please the yelping dogs. The gaps I mean,
No one has seen them made or heard them made,   10
But at spring mending-time we find them there.
I let my neighbor know beyond the hill;
And on a day we meet to walk the line
And set the wall between us once again.
We keep the wall between us as we go.   15

To each the boulders that have fallen to each.
And some are loaves and some so nearly balls
We have to use a spell to make them balance:
"Stay where you are until our backs are turned!"
We wear our fingers rough with handling them.   20
Oh, just another kind of outdoor game,
One on a side. It comes to little more:
There where it is we do not need the wall:
He is all pine and I am apple orchard.
My apple trees will never get across   25
And eat the cones under his pines, I tell him.
He only says, "Good fences make good neighbors."
Spring is the mischief in me, and I wonder
If I could put a notion in his head:
"*Why* do they make good neighbors? Isn't it   30
Where there are cows? But here there are no cows.
Before I built a wall I'd ask to know
What I was walling in or walling out,
And to whom I was like to give offence.
Something there is that doesn't love a wall,   35
That wants it down." I could say "Elves" to him,
But it's not elves exactly, and I'd rather
He said it for himself. I see him there
Bringing a stone grasped firmly by the top
In each hand, like an old-stone savage armed.   40
He moves in darkness as it seems to me,
Not of woods only and the shade of trees.
He will not go behind his father's saying,
And he likes having thought of it so well
He says again, "Good fences make good neighbors."   45

Compare

"Mending Wall" with "Digging" by Seamus Heaney (page 1050).

Robert Frost (1874–1963)

Stopping by Woods on a Snowy Evening   1923

Whose woods these are I think I know.
His house is in the village though;
He will not see me stopping here
To watch his woods fill up with snow.

My little horse must think it queer   5
To stop without a farmhouse near
Between the woods and frozen lake
The darkest evening of the year.

He gives his harness bells a shake
To ask if there is some mistake.   10
The only other sound's the sweep
Of easy wind and downy flake.

The woods are lovely, dark and deep,
But I have promises to keep,
And miles to go before I sleep,   15
And miles to go before I sleep.

Compare

"Stopping by Woods on a Snowy Evening" with "Desert Places" by Robert Frost (page 783).

Allen Ginsberg (1926–1997)

A Supermarket in California   1956

What thoughts I have of you tonight, Walt Whitman, for I walked down the sidestreets under the trees with a headache self-conscious looking at the full moon.

In my hungry fatigue, and shopping for images, I went into the neon fruit supermarket, dreaming of your enumerations!

What peaches and what penumbras! Whole families shopping at night! Aisles full of husbands! Wives in the avocados, babies in the tomatoes!—and you, García Lorca, what were you doing down by the watermelons?

I saw you, Walt Whitman, childless, lonely old grubber, poking among the meats in the refrigerator and eyeing the grocery boys.

I heard you asking questions of each: Who killed the pork chops? What   5
price bananas? Are you my Angel?

I wandered in and out of the brilliant stacks of cans following you, and followed in my imagination by the store detective.

We strode down the open corridors together in our solitary fancy tasting artichokes, possessing every frozen delicacy, and never passing the cashier.

Where are we going, Walt Whitman? The doors close in an hour. Which way does your beard point tonight?

(I touch your book and dream of our odyssey in the supermarket and feel absurd.)

Will we walk all night through solitary streets? The trees add shade to   10
shade, lights out in the houses, we'll both be lonely.

Will we stroll dreaming of the lost America of love past blue automobiles in driveways, home to our silent cottage?

Ah, dear father, graybeard, lonely old courage-teacher, what America did you have when Charon quit poling his ferry and you got out on a smoking bank and stood watching the boat disappear on the black waters of Lethe?

A SUPERMARKET IN CALIFORNIA. 2 *enumerations:* many of Whitman's poems contain lists of observed details. 3 *García Lorca:* modern Spanish poet who wrote an "Ode to Walt Whitman" in his book-length sequence *Poet in New York.* 12 *Charon . . . Lethe:* Is the poet confusing two underworld rivers? Charon, in Greek and Roman mythology, is the boatman who ferries the souls of the dead across the River Styx. The River Lethe also flows through Hades, and a drink of its waters makes the dead lose their painful memories of loved ones they have left behind.

Compare

"A Supermarket in California" with Walt Whitman's "To a Locomotive in Winter" (page 638).

Donald Hall (b. 1928)

Names of Horses   1978

All winter your brute shoulders strained against collars, padding
and steerhide over the ash hames, to haul
sledges of cordwood for drying through spring and summer,
for the Glenwood stove next winter, and for the simmering range.

In April you pulled cartloads of manure to spread on the fields,   5
dark manure of Holsteins, and knobs of your own clustered with oats.
All summer you mowed the grass in meadow and hayfield, the mowing
    machine
clacketing beside you, while the sun walked high in the morning;

and after noon's heat, you pulled a clawed rake through the same acres,
gathering stacks, and dragged the wagon from stack to stack,   10
and the built hayrack back, uphill to the chaffy barn,
three loads of hay a day from standing grass in the morning.

Sundays you trotted the two miles to church with the light load
of a leather quartertop buggy, and grazed in the sound of hymns.
Generation on generation, your neck rubbed the windowsill   15
of the stall, smoothing the wood as the sea smooths glass.

When you were old and lame, when your shoulders hurt bending to graze,
one October the man, who fed you and kept you, and harnessed you every
    morning,
led you through corn stubble to sandy ground above Eagle Pond,
and dug a hole beside you where you stood shuddering in your skin,   20

and lay the shotgun's muzzle in the boneless hollow behind your ear,
and fired the slug into your brain, and felled you into your grave,
shoveling sand to cover you, setting goldenrod upright above you,
where by next summer a dent in the ground made your monument.

For a hundred and fifty years, in the pasture of dead horses,   25
roots of pine trees pushed through the pale curves of your ribs,
yellow blossoms flourished above you in autumn, and in winter
frost heaved your bones in the ground—old toilers, soil makers:

O Roger, Mackerel, Riley, Ned, Nellie, Chester, Lady Ghost.

Compare

"Names of Horses" with "'Out, Out—'" by Robert Frost (page 638).

Thomas Hardy (1840–1928)

The Convergence of the Twain

1912

Lines on the Loss of the "Titanic"

I

In a solitude of the sea
Deep from human vanity,
And the Pride of Life that planned her, stilly couches she.

II

Steel chambers, late the pyres
Of her salamandrine fires,
Cold currents thrid,° and turn to rhythmic tidal lyres.   *thread*   5

III

Over the mirrors meant
To glass the opulent
The sea-worm crawls—grotesque, slimed, dumb, indifferent.

IV

Jewels in joy designed   10
To ravish the sensuous mind
Lie lightless, all their sparkles bleared and black and blind.

V

Dim moon-eyed fishes near
Gaze at the gilded gear
And query: "What does this vaingloriousness down here?" . . .   15

VI

Well: while was fashioning
This creature of cleaving wing,
The Immanent Will that stirs and urges everything

VII

Prepared a sinister mate
For her—so gaily great—   20
A Shape of Ice, for the time far and dissociate.

VIII

And as the smart ship grew
In stature, grace, and hue,
In shadowy silent distance grew the Iceberg too.

IX

Alien they seemed to be: 25
No mortal eye could see
The intimate welding of their later history,

X

Or sign that they were bent
   By paths coincident
On being anon twin halves of one august event,   30

XI

Till the Spinner of the Years
   Said "Now!" And each one hears,
And consummation comes, and jars two hemispheres.

THE CONVERGENCE OF THE TWAIN. The luxury liner *Titanic,* supposedly unsinkable, went down in 1912 after striking an iceberg on its first Atlantic voyage. 5 *salamandrine:* like the salamander, a lizard that supposedly thrives in fires, or like a spirit of the same name that inhabits fire (according to alchemists).

Compare

"The Convergence of the Twain" with "Song of the Powers" by Dave Mason (page 804).

Thomas Hardy

Thomas Hardy (1840–1928)

The Darkling Thrush   1900

I leant upon a coppice gate
   When Frost was spectre-gray,
And Winter's dregs made desolate
   The weakening eye of day.
The tangled bine-stems scored the sky   5
   Like strings of broken lyres,
And all mankind that haunted nigh
   Had sought their household fires.

The land's sharp features seemed to be
   The Century's corpse outleant,   10
His crypt the cloudy canopy,
   The wind his death-lament.
The ancient pulse of germ and birth
   Was shrunken hard and dry,
And every spirit upon earth   15
   Seemed fervorless as I.

At once a voice arose among
   The bleak twigs overhead
In a full-hearted evensong
   Of joy illimited;   20
An aged thrush, frail, gaunt, and small,
   In blast-beruffled plume,
Had chosen thus to fling his soul
   Upon the growing gloom.

So little cause for carolings   25
   Of such ecstatic sound
Was written on terrestrial things
   Afar or nigh around,
That I could think there trembled through
   His happy good-night air   30
Some blessed Hope, whereof he knew
   And I was unaware.

THE DARKLING THRUSH. Hardy set this poem on December 31, 1900, the last day of the nineteenth century.

Compare

"The Darkling Thrush" with "I Wandered Lonely as a Cloud" by William Wordsworth (page 655).

Thomas Hardy (1840–1928)

Hap

(1866)

If but some vengeful god would call to me
From up the sky, and laugh: "Thou suffering thing,
Know that thy sorrow is my ecstasy,
That thy love's loss is my hate's profiting!"

Then would I bear it, clench myself, and die,   5
Steeled by the sense of ire unmerited;
Half-eased in that a Powerfuller than I
Had willed and meted me the tears I shed.

But not so. How arrives it joy lies slain,
And why unblooms the best hope ever sown?   10
—Crass Casualty obstructs the sun and rain,
And dicing Time for gladness casts a moan . . .
These purblind Doomsters had as readily strown
Blisses about my pilgrimage as pain.

Compare

"Hap" with the Roman poet Horace's *carpe diem* ode on pages 908–909. Choose any of the three translations there of Horace's work or use the literal translation provided below the Latin original.

Seamus Heaney (b. 1939)

Digging

1966

Between my finger and my thumb
The squat pen rests; snug as a gun.

Under my window, a clean rasping sound
When the spade sinks into gravelly ground:
My father, digging. I look down   5

Till his straining rump among the flowerbeds
Bends low, comes up twenty years away
Stooping in rhythm through potato drills
Where he was digging.

The coarse boot nestled on the lug, the shaft   10
Against the inside knee was levered firmly.
He rooted out tall tops, buried the bright edge deep
To scatter new potatoes that we picked
Loving their cool hardness in our hands.

By God, the old man could handle a spade.   15
Just like his old man.

My grandfather cut more turf in a day
Than any other man on Toner's bog.
Once I carried him milk in a bottle
Corked sloppily with paper. He straightened up   20
To drink it, then fell to right away
Nicking and slicing neatly, heaving sods
Over his shoulder, going down and down
For the good turf. Digging.

The cold smell of potato mould, the squelch and slap   25
Of soggy peat, the curt cuts of an edge
Through living roots awaken in my head.
But I've no spade to follow men like them.

Between my finger and my thumb
The squat pen rests.   30
I'll dig with it.

Compare

"Digging" with "The Writer" by Richard Wilbur (page 1096).

Anthony Hecht (1923–2004)

The Vow 1967

In the third month, a sudden flow of blood.
The mirth of tabrets ceaseth, and the joy
Also of the harp. The frail image of God
Lay spilled and formless. Neither girl nor boy,
But yet blood of my blood, nearly my child. 5
     All that long day
Her pale face turned to the window's mild
     Featureless grey.

And for some nights she whimpered as she dreamed
The dead thing spoke, saying: "Do not recall 10
Pleasure at my conception. I am redeemed
From pain and sorrow. Mourn rather for all
Who breathlessly issue from the bone gates,
     The gates of horn,
For truly it is best of all the fates 15
     Not to be born.

"Mother, a child lay gasping for bare breath
On Christmas Eve when Santa Claus had set
Death in the stocking, and the lights of death
Flamed in the tree. O, if you can, forget 20
You were the child, turn to my father's lips
     Against the time
When his cold hand puts forth its fingertips
     Of jointed lime."

Doctors of Science, what is man that he 25
Should hope to come to a good end? *The best*
Is not to have been born. And could it be
That Jewish diligence and Irish jest
The consent of flesh and a midwinter storm
     Had reconciled, 30
Was yet too bold a mixture to inform
     A simple child?

Even as gold is tried, Gentile and Jew.
If that ghost was a girl's, I swear to it:
Your mother shall be far more blessed than you. 35
And if a boy's, I swear: The flames are lit
That shall refine us; they shall not destroy
     A living hair.
Your younger brothers shall confirm in joy
     This that I swear. 40

THE VOW. 2 *tabrets*: small drums used to accompany traditional Jewish dances. 14 *gates of horn*: according to Homer and Virgil, pleasant, lying dreams emerge from the underworld through gates of ivory; ominous, truth-telling dreams, through gates of horn.

Compare

"The Vow" with "On My First Son" by Ben Jonson (page 1058) and "the mother" by Gwendolyn Brooks (page 1027).

George Herbert (1593–1633)

Love   1633

Love bade me welcome; yet my soul drew back,
    Guilty of dust and sin.
But quick-eyed Love, observing me grow slack
    From my first entrance in,
Drew nearer to me, sweetly questioning   5
    If I lacked anything.

"A guest," I answered, "worthy to be here";
    Love said, "You shall be he."
"I, the unkind, ungrateful? Ah, my dear,
    I cannot look on Thee."   10
Love took my hand, and smiling did reply,
    "Who made the eyes but I?"

"Truth, Lord, but I have marred them; let my shame
    Go where it doth deserve."
"And know you not," says Love, "who bore the blame?"   15
    "My dear, then I will serve."
"You must sit down," says Love, "and taste My meat."
    So I did sit and eat.

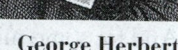

George Herbert

Compare

"Love" with "Batter my heart, three-personed God" by John Donne (page 677).

Robert Herrick (1591–1674)

To the Virgins, to Make Much of Time   1648

Gather ye rose-buds while ye may,
    Old Time is still a-flying;
And this same flower that smiles today,
    Tomorrow will be dying.

The glorious lamp of heaven, the sun,   5
    The higher he's a-getting,
The sooner will his race be run,
    And nearer he's to setting.

That age is best which is the first,
    When youth and blood are warmer;   10
But being spent, the worse, and worst
    Times still succeed the former.

Then be not coy, but use your time,
    And while ye may, go marry;
For having lost but once your prime,   15
    You may for ever tarry.

Compare

"To the Virgins, to Make Much of Time" with "To His Coy Mistress" by Andrew Marvell
(page 1066) and "Go, Lovely Rose" by Edmund Waller (page 1095).

Tony Hoagland (b. 1953)

Beauty   1998

When the medication she was taking
caused tiny vessels in her face to break,
leaving faint but permanent blue stitches in her cheeks,
my sister said she knew she would
never be beautiful again.   5

After all those years
of watching her reflection in the mirror,
sucking in her stomach and standing straight,
she said it was a relief,
being done with beauty,   10

but I could see her pause inside that moment
as the knowledge spread across her face
with a fine distress, sucking
the peach out of her lips,
making her cute nose seem, for the first time,   15
a little knobby.

I'm probably the only one in the whole world
who actually remembers the year in high school
she perfected the art
of being a dumb blond,   20

spending recess on the breezeway by the physics lab,
tossing her hair and laughing that canary trill
which was her specialty,

while some football player named Johnny
with a pained expression in his eyes   25
wrapped his thick finger over and over again
in the bedspring of one of those pale curls.

Or how she spent the next decade of her life
auditioning a series of tall men,
looking for just one with the kind   30
of attention span she could count on.

Then one day her time of prettiness
was over, done, finito,
and all those other beautiful women
in the magazines and on the streets   35
just kept on being beautiful
everywhere you looked,

walking in that kind of elegant, disinterested trance
in which you sense they always seem to have one hand
touching the secret place   40
that keeps their beauty safe,
inhaling and exhaling the perfume of it—

It was spring. Season when the young
buttercups and daisies climb up on the
mulched bodies of their forebears   45
to wave their flags in the parade.

My sister just stood still for thirty seconds,
amazed by what was happening,
then shrugged and tossed her shaggy head
as if she was throwing something out,   50

something she had carried a long ways,
but had no use for anymore,
now that it had no use for her.
That, too, was beautiful.

Compare

"Beauty" with "Perfect Dress" by Marisa de los Santos (page 1036).

 Gerard Manley Hopkins (1844–1889)

Spring and Fall   (1880)

     To a young child

Márgarét, áre you grieving
Over Goldengrove unleaving°   *shedding its leaves*
Leáves, líke the things of man, you
With your fresh thoughts care for, can you?
Áh! ás the heart grows older   5
It will come to such sights colder
By and by, nor spare a sigh
Though worlds of wanwood leafmeal lie;
And yet you wíll weep and know why.
Now no matter, child, the name: 10
Sórrow's spríngs áre the same.
Nor mouth had, no nor mind, expressed
What heart heard of, ghost° guessed: *spirit*
It ís the blight man was born for,
It is Margaret you mourn for.   15

Compare

"Spring and Fall" with "Aftermath" by Henry Wadsworth Longfellow (page 679).

Gerard Manley Hopkins (1844–1889)

No worst, there is none (1884–1885)

No worst, there is none. Pitched past pitch of grief,
More pangs will, schooled at forepangs, wilder wring.
Comforter, where, where is your comforting?
Mary, mother of us, where is your relief?
My cries heave, herds-long; huddle in a main, a chief   5
Woe, world-sorrow; on an age-old anvil wince and sing—
Then lull, then leave off. Fury had shrieked "No ling-
ering! Let me be fell: force I must be brief."

O the mind, mind has mountains; cliffs of fall
Frightful, sheer, no-man-fathomed. Hold them cheap   10
May who ne'er hung there. Nor does long our small
Durance deal with that steep or deep. Here! creep,
Wretch, under a comfort serves in a whirlwind: all
Life death does end and each day dies with sleep.

Compare

"No worst, there is none" with "Hap" by Thomas Hardy (page 1049).

Gerard Manley Hopkins (1844–1889)

The Windhover (1877)

To Christ Our Lord

I caught this morning morning's minion, king-
   dom of daylight's dauphin, dapple-dawn-drawn Falcon, in his riding
   Of the rolling level underneath him steady air, and striding
High there, how he rung upon the rein of a wimpling wing
In his ecstasy! then off, off forth on swing,   5
   As a skate's heel sweeps smooth on a bow-bend: the hurl and gliding
   Rebuffed the big wind. My heart in hiding
Stirred for a bird, —the achieve of, the mastery of the thing!

Brute beauty and valor and act, oh, air, pride, plume, here
   Buckle! AND the fire that breaks from thee then, a billion   10
Times told lovelier, more dangerous, O my chevalier!

No wonder of it: shéer plód makes plough down sillion°   *furrow*
Shine, and blue-bleak embers, ah my dear,
   Fall, gall themselves, and gash gold-vermilion.

THE WINDHOVER. A windhover is a kestrel, or small falcon, so called because it can hover upon the wind.
4 *rung . . . wing:* A horse is "rung upon the rein" when its trainer holds the end of a long rein and has the
horse circle him. The possible meanings of *wimpling* include: (1) curving; (2) pleated, arranged in many
little folds one on top of another; (3) rippling or undulating like the surface of a flowing stream.

Compare

"The Windhover" with "Batter my heart, three-personed God" by John Donne (page 677) and
"Easter Wings" by George Herbert (page 842).

A. E. Housman (1859–1936)

Loveliest of trees, the cherry now   1896

Loveliest of trees, the cherry now
Is hung with bloom along the bough,
And stands about the woodland ride°   *path*
Wearing white for Eastertide.

Now, of my threescore years and ten,   5
Twenty will not come again,
And take from seventy springs a score,
It only leaves me fifty more.

And since to look at things in bloom
Fifty springs are little room,   10
About the woodlands I will go
To see the cherry hung with snow.

Compare

"Loveliest of trees, the cherry now" with "To the Virgins, to Make Much of Time" by Robert
Herrick (page 1052) and "Spring and Fall" by Gerard Manley Hopkins (page 1054).

A. E. Housman (1859–1936)

To an Athlete Dying Young   1896

The time you won your town the race
We chaired you through the market-place;
Man and boy stood cheering by,
And home we brought you shoulder-high.

To-day, the road all runners come,   5
Shoulder-high we bring you home,
And set you at your threshold down,
Townsman of a stiller town.

Smart lad, to slip betimes away
From fields where glory does not stay   10
And early though the laurel grows
It withers quicker than the rose.

Eyes the shady night has shut
Cannot see the record cut,
And silence sounds no worse than cheers   15
After earth has stopped the ears:

Now you will not swell the rout
Of lads that wore their honors out,
Runners whom renown outran
And the name died before the man.   20

So set, before its echoes fade,
The fleet foot on the sill of shade,
And hold to the low lintel up
The still-defended challenge-cup.

And round that early-laureled head   25
Will flock to gaze the strengthless dead,
And find unwithered on its curls
The garland briefer than a girl's.

Compare

"To an Athlete Dying Young" with "Ex-Basketball Player" by John Updike (page 1093).

Randall Jarrell (1914–1965)

The Death of the Ball   1945
Turret Gunner

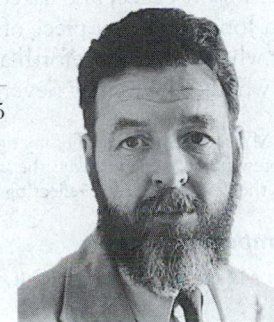

From my mother's sleep I fell into the State,
And I hunched in its belly till my wet fur froze.
Six miles from earth, loosed from its dream of life,
I woke to black flak and the nightmare fighters.
When I died they washed me out of the turret with a
    hose.   5

Randall Jarrell

THE DEATH OF THE BALL TURRET GUNNER. Jarrell has written: "A ball turret was a plexiglass sphere set
into the belly of a B-17 or B-24, and inhabited by two .50 caliber machine-guns and one man, a short small
man. When this gunner tracked with his machine-guns a fighter attacking his bomber from below, he
revolved with the turret; hunched in his little sphere, he looked like the fetus in the womb. The fighters
which attacked him were armed with cannon firing explosive shells. The hose was a steam hose."

Compare

"The Death of the Ball Turret Gunner" with "Dulce et Decorum Est" by Wilfred Owen (page 667).

Robinson Jeffers (1887–1962)

To the Stone-Cutters   1925

Stone-cutters fighting time with marble, you foredefeated
Challengers of oblivion
Eat cynical earnings, knowing rock splits, records fall down,
The square-limbed Roman letters
Scale in the thaws, wear in the rain. The poet as well   5
Builds his monument mockingly;
For man will be blotted out, the blithe earth die, the brave sun
Die blind, his heart blackening:
Yet stones have stood for a thousand years, and pained thoughts found
The honey peace in old poems.   10

Compare

"To the Stone-Cutters" with "Not marble nor the gilded monuments" by William Shakespeare
(page 1083).

Ben Jonson (1573?–1637)

On My First Son (1603)

Farewell, thou child of my right hand, and joy.
My sin was too much hope of thee, loved boy;
Seven years thou wert lent to me, and I thee pay,
Exacted by thy fate, on the just day.
Oh, could I lose all father° now. For why   *fatherhood* 5
Will man lament the state he should envỳ—
To have so soon 'scaped world's and flesh's rage,
And, if no other misery, yet age?
Rest in soft peace, and asked, say, "Here doth lie
Ben Jonson his best piece of poetry,"   10
For whose sake henceforth all his vows be such
As what he loves may never like° too much.   *thrive*

ON MY FIRST SON. 1 *child of my right hand*: Jonson's son was named Benjamin; this phrase translates the Hebrew name. 4 *the just day*: the very day. The boy had died on his seventh birthday. 10 *poetry*: Jonson uses the word *poetry* here reflecting its Greek root *poiesis*, which means *creation*.

Compare

"On My First Son" with "'Out, Out—'" by Robert Frost (page 638).

Donald Justice (1925–2004)

On the Death of Friends in Childhood 1960

We shall not ever meet them bearded in heaven,
Nor sunning themselves among the bald of hell;
If anywhere, in the deserted schoolyard at twilight,
Forming a ring, perhaps, or joining hands
In games whose very names we have forgotten.   5
Come, memory, let us seek them there in the shadows.

Compare

"On the Death of Friends in Childhood" with "To an Athlete Dying Young" by A. E. Housman (page 1056).

John Keats (1795–1821)

Ode on a Grecian Urn 1820

Thou still unravished bride of quietness,
   Thou foster-child of silence and slow time,
Sylvan historian, who canst thus express
   A flowery tale more sweetly than our rhyme:
What leaf-fringed legend haunts about thy shape   5
   Of deities or mortals, or of both,
      In Tempe or the dales of Arcady?
   What men or gods are these? What maidens loth?
What mad pursuit? What struggle to escape?
      What pipes and timbrels? What wild ecstasy?   10

Heard melodies are sweet, but those unheard
    Are sweeter; therefore, ye soft pipes, play on;
Not to the sensual° ear, but, more endeared,   *physical*
    Pipe to the spirit ditties of no tone:
Fair youth, beneath the trees, thou canst not leave   15
    Thy song, nor ever can those trees be bare;
      Bold Lover, never, never canst thou kiss,
Though winning near the goal—yet, do not grieve;
      She cannot fade, though thou hast not thy bliss,
    For ever wilt thou love, and she be fair!   20

Ah, happy, happy boughs! that cannot shed
    Your leaves, nor ever bid the Spring adieu;
And, happy melodist, unwearièd,
    For ever piping songs for ever new;
More happy love! more happy, happy love!   25
    For ever warm and still to be enjoyed,
      For ever panting, and for ever young;
All breathing human passion far above,
    That leaves a heart high-sorrowful and cloyed,
      A burning forehead, and a parching tongue.   30

Who are these coming to the sacrifice?
    To what green altar, O mysterious priest,
Lead'st thou that heifer lowing at the skies,
    And all her silken flanks with garlands drest?
What little town by river or sea shore,   35
    Or mountain-built with peaceful citadel,
      Is emptied of this folk, this pious morn?
And, little town, thy streets for evermore
    Will silent be; and not a soul to tell
      Why thou art desolate, can e'er return.   40

O Attic shape! Fair attitude! with brede°   *design*
    Of marble men and maidens overwrought,
With forest branches and the trodden weed;
    Thou, silent form, dost tease us out of thought
As doth eternity: Cold Pastoral!   45
    When old age shall this generation waste,
      Thou shalt remain, in midst of other woe
    Than ours, a friend to man, to whom thou say'st,
Beauty is truth, truth beauty,—that is all
    Ye know on earth, and all ye need to know.   50

ODE ON A GRECIAN URN. 7 *Tempe, dales of Arcady:* valleys in Greece. 41 *Attic:* Athenian, possessing a classical simplicity and grace. 49–50: if Keats had put the urn's words in quotation marks, critics might have been spared much ink. Does the urn say just "beauty is truth, truth beauty," or does its statement take in the whole of the last two lines?

Compare

"Ode on a Grecian Urn" with "Musée des Beaux Arts" by W. H. Auden (page 1023).

John Keats (1795–1821)

When I have fears that   (1818)
I may cease to be

John Keats

When I have fears that I may cease to be
  Before my pen has gleaned my teeming brain,
Before high-pilèd books, in charact'ry,°   *written language*
  Hold like rich garners° the full-ripened grain; *storehouses*
When I behold, upon the night's starred face,   5
  Huge cloudy symbols of a high romance,
And think that I may never live to trace
  Their shadows with the magic hand of chance;
And when I feel, fair creature of an hour,
  That I shall never look upon thee more,   10
Never have relish in the fairy° power   *supernatural*
  Of unreflecting love;—then on the shore
Of the wide world I stand alone, and think
  Till love and fame to nothingness do sink.

WHEN I HAVE FEARS THAT I MAY CEASE TO BE. 12 *unreflecting:* thoughtless and spontaneous, rather than deliberate.

Compare

"When I have fears that I may cease to be" with any of the three translations of Horace's *carpe diem* ode (pages 908–909) or Philip Larkin's "Aubade" (page 900).

 John Keats (1795–1821)

To Autumn   1820

I

Season of mists and mellow fruitfulness,
  Close bosom-friend of the maturing sun;
Conspiring with him how to load and bless
  With fruit the vines that round the thatch-eaves run;
To bend with apples the mossed cottage-trees,   5
  And fill all fruit with ripeness to the core;
    To swell the gourd, and plump the hazel shells
  With a sweet kernel; to set budding more,
And still more, later flowers for the bees,
Until they think warm days will never cease,   10
    For Summer has o'er-brimmed their clammy cells.

II

Who hath not seen thee oft amid thy store?
   Sometimes whoever seeks abroad may find
Thee sitting careless on a granary floor,
   Thy hair soft-lifted by the winnowing wind;   15
Or on a half-reaped furrow sound asleep,
   Drowsed with the fume of poppies, while thy hook°   *sickle*
      Spares the next swath and all its twinèd flowers:
And sometimes like a gleaner thou dost keep
   Steady thy laden head across a brook;   20
   Or by a cider-press, with patient look,
      Thou watchest the last oozings hours by hours.

III

Where are the songs of Spring? Ay, where are they?
   Think not of them, thou hast thy music too,—
While barrèd clouds bloom the soft-dying day,   25
   And touch the stubble-plains with rosy hue;
Then in a wailful choir the small gnats mourn
   Among the river sallows,° borne aloft   *willows*
      Or sinking as the light wind lives or dies;
And full-grown lambs loud bleat from hilly bourn;   30
   Hedge-crickets sing; and now with treble soft
   The red-breast whistles from a garden-croft;°   *garden plot*
      And gathering swallows twitter in the skies.

To Autumn. 12 *thee:* Autumn personified. 15 *Thy hair . . . winnowing wind:* Autumn's hair is a billowing cloud of straw. In winnowing, whole blades of grain were laid on a granary floor and beaten with wooden flails, then the beaten mass was tossed in a blanket until the yellow straw (or *chaff*) drifted away on the air, leaving kernels of grain. 30 *bourn:* perhaps meaning a brook. In current English, the word is a cousin of burn, as in the first line of Gerard Manley Hopkins's "Inversnaid"; but in archaic English, which Keats sometimes liked to use, a *bourn* can also be a boundary, or a destination. Which possible meaning makes most sense to you?

Compare

"To Autumn" with "Spring and Fall" by Gerard Manley Hopkins (page 1054).

Ted Kooser (b. 1939)

Abandoned Farmhouse

1969/1974

He was a big man, says the size of his shoes
on a pile of broken dishes by the house;
a tall man too, says the length of the bed
in an upstairs room; and a good, God-fearing man,
says the Bible with a broken back   5
on the floor below the window, dusty with sun;
but not a man for farming, say the fields
cluttered with boulders and the leaky barn.

A woman lived with him, says the bedroom wall
papered with lilacs and the kitchen shelves   10
covered with oilcloth, and they had a child,
says the sandbox made from a tractor tire.
Money was scarce, say the jars of plum preserves
and canned tomatoes sealed in the cellar hole.
And the winters cold, say the rags in the window frames.   15
It was lonely here, says the narrow country road.

Something went wrong, says the empty house
in the weed-choked yard. Stones in the fields
say he was not a farmer; the still-sealed jars
in the cellar say she left in a nervous haste.   20
And the child? Its toys are strewn in the yard
like branches after a storm—a rubber cow,
a rusty tractor with a broken plow,
a doll in overalls. Something went wrong, they say.

Compare

"Abandoned Farmhouse" with "The Farm on the Great Plains" by William Stafford (page 1088).

Philip Larkin (1922–1985)

Home is so Sad

1964

Home is so sad. It stays as it was left,
Shaped to the comfort of the last to go
As if to win them back. Instead, bereft
Of anyone to please, it withers so,
Having no heart to put aside the theft   5

And turn again to what it started as,
A joyous shot at how things ought to be,
Long fallen wide. You can see how it was:
Look at the pictures and the cutlery.
The music in the piano stool. That vase.   10

Compare

"Home is so Sad" with "Piano" by D. H. Lawrence (page 1064).

Philip Larkin (1922–1985)

Poetry of Departures   1955

Sometimes you hear, fifth-hand,
As epitaph:
He chucked up everything
And just cleared off,
And always the voice will sound   5
Certain you approve
This audacious, purifying,
Elemental move.

And they are right, I think.
We all hate home   10
And having to be there:
I detest my room,
Its specially-chosen junk,
The good books, the good bed,
And my life, in perfect order: 15
So to hear it said

He walked out on the whole crowd
Leaves me flushed and stirred,
Like *Then she undid her dress*
Or *Take that you bastard;*   20
Surely I can, if he did?
And that helps me stay
Sober and industrious.
But I'd go today,

Yes, swagger the nut-strewn roads,   25
Crouch in the fo'c'sle
Stubbly with goodness, if
It weren't so artificial,
Such a deliberate step backwards
To create an object: 30
Books; china; a life
Reprehensibly perfect.

Philip Larkin

Compare

"Poetry of Departures" with "I started Early – Took my Dog" by Emily Dickinson (page 962).

D. H. Lawrence (1885–1930)

Piano
1918

Softly, in the dusk, a woman is singing to me;
Taking me back down the vista of years, till I see
A child sitting under the piano, in the boom of the tingling strings
And pressing the small, poised feet of a mother who smiles as she sings.

In spite of myself, the insidious mastery of song   5
Betrays me back, till the heart of me weeps to belong
To the old Sunday evenings at home, with winter outside
And hymns in the cozy parlor, the tinkling piano our guide.

So now it is vain for the singer to burst into clamor
With the great black piano appassionato. The glamour   10
Of childish days is upon me, my manhood is cast
Down in the flood of remembrance, I weep like a child for the past.

Compare

"Piano" with "Fern Hill" by Dylan Thomas (page 1092).

Denise Levertov

Denise Levertov (1923–1997)

The Ache of Marriage
1964

The ache of marriage:

thigh and tongue, beloved,
are heavy with it,
it throbs in the teeth

We look for communion   5
and are turned away, beloved,
each and each

It is leviathan and we
in its belly
looking for joy, some joy   10
not to be known outside it

two by two in the ark of
the ache of it.

THE ACHE OF MARRIAGE. *8 leviathan:* a monstrous sea creature mentioned in the Book of Job.

Compare

"The Ache of Marriage" with "Let me not to the marriage of true minds" by William Shakespeare (page 816).

Shirley Geok-lin Lim (b. 1944)

Shirley Geok-Lin Lim

To Li Po   1980

I read you in a stranger's tongue,
Brother whose eyes were slanted also.
But you never left to live among
Foreign devils. Seeing the rice you ate grow
In your own backyard, you stayed on narrow   5
Village paths. Only your mind traveled
Easily: east, north, south, and west
Compassed in observation of field
And family. All men were guests
To one who knew traditions, the best   10
Of race. Country man, you believed to be Chinese
No more than a condition of human history.
Yet I cannot speak your tongue with ease,
No longer from China. Your stories
Stir griefs of dispersion and find   15
Me in simplicity of kin.

To Li Po. Also known as Li T'ai-po (701–762) Li Po was one of the great Chinese poets of the T'ang dynasty.

Compare

"To Li Po" with "Drinking Alone by Moonlight" by Li Po (page 907).

Robert Lowell (1917–1977)

Skunk Hour   1959

For Elizabeth Bishop

Nautilus Island's hermit
heiress still lives through winter in her Spartan cottage;
her sheep still graze above the sea.
Her son's a bishop. Her farmer
is first selectman in our village;   5
she's in her dotage.

Thirsting for
the hierarchic privacy
of Queen Victoria's century,
she buys up all   10
the eyesores facing her shore,
and lets them fall.

The season's ill—
we've lost our summer millionaire,
who seemed to leap from an L. L. Bean   15
catalogue. His nine-knot yawl
was auctioned off to lobstermen.
A red fox stain covers Blue Hill.

And now our fairy
decorator brightens his shop for fall;   20
his fishnet's filled with orange cork,
orange, his cobbler's bench and awl;
there is no money in his work,
he'd rather marry.

One dark night,   25
my Tudor Ford climbed the hill's skull;
I watched for love-cars. Lights turned down,
they lay together, hull to hull,
where the graveyard shelves on the town. . . .
My mind's not right.   30

A car radio bleats,
"Love, O careless Love. . . ." I hear
my ill-spirit sob in each blood cell,
as if my hand were at its throat. . . .
I myself am hell;   35
nobody's here—

only skunks, that search
in the moonlight for a bite to eat.
They march on their soles up Main Street:
white stripes, moonstruck eyes' red fire   40
under the chalk-dry and spar spire
of the Trinitarian Church.

I stand on top
of our back steps and breathe the rich air—
a mother skunk with her column of kittens swills the garbage pail.   45
She jabs her wedge-head in a cup
of sour cream, drops her ostrich tail,
and will not scare.

Compare

"Skunk Hour" with "Desert Places" by Robert Frost (page 783).

Andrew Marvell (1621–1678)

To His Coy Mistress   1681

Had we but world enough, and time,
This coyness,° Lady, were no crime.   *modesty, reluctance*
We would sit down, and think which way

To walk, and pass our long love's day.
Thou by the Indian Ganges' side   5
Should'st rubies find; I by the tide
Of Humber would complain.° I would   *sing sad songs*
Love you ten years before the Flood,
And you should, if you please, refuse
Till the Conversion of the Jews.   10
My vegetable° love should grow   *vegetative, flourishing*
Vaster than empires, and more slow.
An hundred years should go to praise
Thine eyes, and on thy forehead gaze,
Two hundred to adore each breast,   15
But thirty thousand to the rest.
An age at least to every part,
And the last age should show your heart.
For, Lady, you deserve this state,°   *pomp, ceremony*
Nor would I love at lower rate.   20
   But at my back I always hear
Time's wingèd chariot hurrying near,
And yonder all before us lie
Deserts of vast eternity.
Thy beauty shall no more be found,   25
Nor, in thy marble vault, shall sound
My echoing song; then worms shall try
That long preserved virginity,
And your quaint honor turn to dust,
And into ashes all my lust.   30
The grave's a fine and private place,
But none, I think, do there embrace.
   Now therefore, while the youthful hue
Sits on thy skin like morning glew°   *glow*
And while thy willing soul transpires   35
At every pore with instant° fires,   *eager*
Now let us sport us while we may;
And now, like amorous birds of prey,
Rather at once our time devour,
Than languish in his slow-chapped° power.   *slow-jawed*   40
Let us roll all our strength, and all
Our sweetness, up into one ball
And tear our pleasures with rough strife,
Thorough° the iron gates of life.   *through*
Thus, though we cannot make our sun   45
Stand still, yet we will make him run.

TO HIS COY MISTRESS. 7 *Humber*: a river that flows by Marvell's town of Hull (on the side of the world opposite from the Ganges). 10 *conversion of the Jews*: an event that, according to St. John the Divine, is to take
place just before the end of the world. 35 *transpires*: exudes, as a membrane lets fluid or vapor pass through it.

Compare

"To His Coy Mistress" with "To the Virgins, to Make Much of Time" by Robert Herrick
(page 1052).

Edna St. Vincent Millay

Edna St. Vincent Millay (1892–1950)

Recuerdo   1920

We were very tired, we were very merry—
We had gone back and forth all night on the ferry.
It was bare and bright, and smelled like a stable—
But we looked into a fire, we leaned across a table,
We lay on a hill-top underneath the moon;   5
And the whistles kept blowing, and the dawn came soon.

We were very tired, we were very merry—
We had gone back and forth all night on the ferry;
And you ate an apple, and I ate a pear,
From a dozen of each we had bought somewhere;   10
And the sky went wan, and the wind came cold,
And the sun rose dripping, a bucketful of gold.

We were very tired, we were very merry,
We had gone back and forth all night on the ferry.
We hailed, "Good morrow, mother!" to a shawl-covered head,   15
And bought a morning paper, which neither of us read;
And she wept, "God bless you!" for the apples and pears,
And we gave her all our money but our subway fares.

RECUERDO. The Spanish title means "a recollection" or "a memory."

Compare

"Recuerdo" with "A Blessing" by James Wright (page 1100).

John Milton (1608–1674)

When I consider how my light is spent   (1655?)

When I consider how my light is spent,
   Ere half my days in this dark world and wide,
   And that one talent which is death to hide
   Lodged with me useless, though my soul more bent
To serve therewith my Maker, and present   5
   My true account, lest He returning chide;
   "Doth God exact day-labor, light denied?"
   I fondly° ask. But Patience, to prevent   *foolishly*
That murmur, soon replies, "God doth not need
   Either man's work or his own gifts. Who best   10
   Bear his mild yoke, they serve him best. his state
Is kingly: thousands at his bidding speed,
   And post o'er land and ocean without rest;
   They also serve who only stand and wait."

WHEN I CONSIDER HOW MY LIGHT IS SPENT. 1 *my light is spent:* Milton had become blind. 3 *that one talent:* For Jesus' parable of the talents (measures of money), see Matthew 25:14–30.

Compare

"When I consider how my light is spent" with "Batter my heart" by John Donne (page 677).

Marianne Moore (1887–1972)

Poetry   1921

I too, dislike it: there are things that are important beyond all this fiddle.
   Reading it, however, with a perfect contempt for it, one discovers
         that there is in
it after all, a place for the genuine.
     Hands that can grasp, eyes
     that can dilate, hair that can rise   5
        if it must, these things are important not because a

high sounding interpretation can be put upon them but because they are
   useful; when they become so derivative as to become
         unintelligible, the
same thing may be said for all of us—that we
   do not admire what   10
     we cannot understand. The bat,
      holding on upside down or in quest of something to

eat, elephants pushing, a wild horse taking a roll, a tireless wolf under
  a tree, the immovable critic twinkling his skin like a horse that
      feels a flea, the base-
  ball fan, the statistician—case after case   15
    could be cited did
    one wish it; nor is it valid
      to discriminate against "business documents and

school-books"; all these phenomena are important. One must make a
        distinction
  however: when dragged into prominence by half poets, the result
      is not poetry,   20
  nor till the autocrats among us can be
    "literalists of
    the imagination"—above
      insolence and triviality and can present

for inspection, imaginary gardens with real toads in them, shall we have 25
  it. In the meantime, if you demand on one hand, in defiance of
        their opinion—
  the raw material of poetry in
    all its rawness and
    that which is, on the other hand,
      genuine then you are interested in poetry.   30

Compare

Compare "Poetry" with "Ars Poetica" by Archibald MacLeish (page 953).

Marilyn Nelson (b. 1946)

A Strange Beautiful Woman   1985

A strange beautiful woman
met me in the mirror
the other night.
Hey,
I said,   5 **Marilyn Nelson**
What you doing here?
She asked me
the same thing.

Compare

Compare "A Strange Beautiful Woman" with "Embrace" by Billy Collins (page 722).

Howard Nemerov (1920–1991)

The War in the Air

1987

For a saving grace, we didn't see our dead,
Who rarely bothered coming home to die
But simply stayed away out there
In the clean war, the war in the air.

Seldom the ghosts came back bearing their tales   5
Of hitting the earth, the incompressible sea,
But stayed up there in the relative wind,
Shades fading in the mind,

Who had no graves but only epitaphs
Where never so many spoke for never so few: 10
Per ardua, said the partisans of Mars,
Per aspera, to the stars.

That was the good war, the war we won
As if there were no death, for goodness' sake,
With the help of the losers we left out there   15
In the air, in the empty air.

THE WAR IN THE AIR. 11–12 *Per ardua . . . Per aspera*: allusion to the English Royal Air Force's motto
"*Per ardua ad astra*," Latin for "through difficult things to the stars."

Compare

"The War in the Air" with "The Death of the Ball Turret Gunner" by Randall Jarrell (page 1057)
and "The Fury of Aerial Bombardment" by Richard Eberhart (page 686).

Lorine Niedecker (1903–1970)

Sorrow Moves in Wide Waves

(about 1950)

Sorrow moves in wide waves,
    it passes, lets us be.
It uses us, we use it,
    it's blind while we see.

Consciousness is illimitable,   5
    too good to forsake
tho what we feel be misery
    and we know will break.

Old Mother turns blue and from us,
"Don't let my head drop to the earth.   10
I'm blind and deaf." Death from the heart,
    a thimble in her purse.

Lorine Niedecker

"It's a long day since last night.
        Give me space. I need
floors. Wash the floors, Lorine!   15
        Wash clothes! Weed!"

Compare

Compare "Sorrow Moves in Wide Waves" with "One Art" by Elizabeth Bishop (page 941).

Sharon Olds (b. 1942)

Sharon Olds

The One Girl at the   1983
Boys' Party

When I take my girl to the swimming party
I set her down among the boys. They tower and
bristle, she stands there smooth and sleek,
her math scores unfolding in the air around her.
They will strip to their suits, her body hard and   5
indivisible as a prime number,
they'll plunge in the deep end, she'll subtract
her height from ten feet, divide it into
hundreds of gallons of water, the numbers
bouncing in her mind like molecules of chlorine   10
in the bright blue pool. When they climb out,
her ponytail will hang its pencil lead
down her back, her narrow silk suit
with hamburgers and french fries printed on it
will glisten in the brilliant air, and they will   15
see her sweet face, solemn and
sealed, a factor of one, and she will
see their eyes, two each,
their legs, two each, and the curves of their sexes,
one each, and in her head she'll be doing her   20
wild multiplying, as the drops
sparkle and fall to the power of a thousand from her body.

Compare

"The One Girl at the Boys' Party" with "My Papa's Waltz" by Theodore Roethke
(page 645).

Wilfred Owen (1893–1918)

Anthem for Doomed Youth   (1917)

What passing-bells for these who die as cattle?
        Only the monstrous anger of the guns.
        Only the stuttering rifles' rapid rattle
Can patter out their hasty orisons.

No mockeries now for them; no prayers nor bells,   5
    Nor any voice of mourning save the choirs,—
The shrill, demented choirs of wailing shells;
    And bugles calling for them from sad shires.°   *counties*

What candles may be held to speed them all?
    Not in the hands of boys, but in their eyes   10
    Shall shine the holy glimmers of good-byes.
The pallor of girls' brows shall be their pall;
Their flowers the tenderness of patient minds,
And each slow dusk a drawing-down of blinds.

Compare

"Anthem for Doomed Youth" with "Facing It" by Yusef Komunyakaa (page 896).

Linda Pastan (b. 1932)

Ethics   1981

Linda Pastan

In ethics class so many years ago
our teacher asked this question every fall:
if there were a fire in a museum
which would you save, a Rembrandt painting
or an old woman who hadn't many   5
years left anyhow? Restless on hard chairs
caring little for pictures or old age
we'd opt one year for life, the next for art
and always half-heartedly. Sometimes
the woman borrowed my grandmother's face   10
leaving her usual kitchen to wander
some drafty, half imagined museum.
One year, feeling clever, I replied
why not let the woman decide herself?
Linda, the teacher would report, eschews   15
the burdens of responsibility.
This fall in a real museum I stand
before a real Rembrandt, old woman,
or nearly so, myself. The colors
within this frame are darker than autumn,   20
darker even than winter—the browns of earth,
though earth's most radiant elements burn
through the canvas. I know now that woman
and painting and season are almost one
and all beyond saving by children.   25

Compare

"Ethics" with "Musée des Beaux Arts" by W. H. Auden (page 1023).

Sylvia Plath (1932–1963)

Daddy

(1962) 1965

Sylvia Plath

You do not do, you do not do
Any more, black shoe
In which I have lived like a foot
For thirty years, poor and white,
Barely daring to breathe or Achoo.   5

Daddy, I have had to kill you.
You died before I had time—
Marble-heavy, a bag full of God,
Ghastly statue with one grey toe
Big as a Frisco seal   10

And a head in the freakish Atlantic
Where it pours bean green over blue
In the waters off beautiful Nauset.
I used to pray to recover you.
Ach, du.   15

In the German tongue, in the Polish town
Scraped flat by the roller
Of wars, wars, wars.
But the name of the town is common.
My Polack friend   20

Says there are a dozen or two.
So I never could tell where you
Put your foot, your root,
I never could talk to you.
The tongue stuck in my jaw.   25

It stuck in a barb wire snare.
Ich, ich, ich, ich,
I could hardly speak.
I thought every German was you.
And the language obscene   30

An engine, an engine
Chuffing me off like a Jew.
A Jew to Dachau, Auschwitz, Belsen.
I began to talk like a Jew.
I think I may well be a Jew.   35

The snows of the Tyrol, the clear beer of Vienna
Are not very pure or true.
With my gypsy ancestress and my weird luck
And my Taroc pack and my Taroc pack
I may be a bit of a Jew.   40

I have always been scared of *you*,
With your Luftwaffe, your gobbledygoo.
And your neat moustache
And your Aryan eye, bright blue.
Panzer-man, panzer-man, O You—   45

Not God but a swastika
So black no sky could squeak through.
Every woman adores a Fascist,
The boot in the face, the brute
Brute heart of a brute like you.   50

You stand at the blackboard, daddy,
In the picture I have of you,
A cleft in your chin instead of your foot
But no less a devil for that, no not
Any less the black man who   55

Bit my pretty red heart in two.
I was ten when they buried you.
At twenty I tried to die
And get back, back, back to you.
I thought even the bones would do.   60

But they pulled me out of the sack,
And they stuck me together with glue.
And then I knew what to do.
I made a model of you,
A man in black with a Meinkampf look   65

And a love of the rack and the screw.
And I said I do, I do.
So daddy, I'm finally through.
The black telephone's off at the root,
The voices just can't worm through.   70

If I've killed one man, I've killed two—
The vampire who said he was you
And drank my blood for a year,
Seven years, if you want to know.
Daddy, you can lie back now.   75

There's a stake in your fat black heart
And the villagers never liked you.
They are dancing and stamping on you.
They always *knew* it was you.
Daddy, daddy, you bastard, I'm through.   80

DADDY. Introducing this poem in a reading, Sylvia Plath remarked:

> The poem is spoken by a girl with an Electra complex. Her father died while she thought he was God. Her case is complicated by the fact that her father was also a Nazi and her mother very possibly part Jewish. In the daughter the two strains marry and paralyze each other—she has to act out the awful little allegory before she is free of it.

(Quoted by A. Alvarez, *Beyond All This Fiddle* [New York: Random, 1968].)

In some details "Daddy" is autobiography: the poet's father, Otto Plath, a German, had come to the United States from Grabow, Poland. He had died following the amputation of a gangrened foot and leg when Sylvia was eight years old. Politically, Otto Plath was a Republican, not a Nazi, but was apparently a somewhat domineering head of the household. (See the recollections of the poet's mother, Aurelia Schober Plath, in her edition of *Letters Home* by Sylvia Plath [New York: Harper, 1975].)

15 *Ach, du:* Oh, you. 27 *Ich, ich, ich, ich:* I, I, I, I. 51 *blackboard:* Otto Plath had been a professor of biology at Boston University. 65 *Meinkampf:* Adolf Hitler entitled his autobiography *Mein Kampf* ("My Struggle").

Compare

"Daddy" with "My Papa's Waltz" by Theodore Roethke (page 645).

Edgar Allan Poe (1809–1849)

A Dream within a Dream   1849

Take this kiss upon the brow!
And, in parting from you now,
Thus much let me avow—
You are not wrong, who deem
That my days have been a dream;   5
Yet if Hope has flown away
In a night, or in a day,
In a vision, or in none,
Is it therefore the less *gone?*
All that we see or seem   10
Is but a dream within a dream.

I stand amid the roar
Of a surf-tormented shore,
And I hold within my hand
Grains of the golden sand—   15
How few! yet how they creep
Through my fingers to the deep,
While I weep—while I weep!
O God! can I not grasp
Them with a tighter clasp?   20
O God! can I not save
One from the pitiless wave?
Is *all* that we see or seem
But a dream within a dream?

Compare

"A Dream within a Dream" with "Dover Beach" by Matthew Arnold (page 1019).

Alexander Pope (1688–1744)

A little Learning is a dang'rous Thing (from *An Essay on Criticism*)

1711

A *little Learning* is a dang'rous Thing;
Drink deep, or taste not the *Pierian* Spring:
There *shallow Draughts* intoxicate the Brain,
And drinking *largely* sobers us again.
Fir'd at first Sight with what the *Muse* imparts,   5
In *fearless Youth* we tempt the Heights of Arts,
While from the bounded *Level* of our Mind,
Short Views we take, nor see the *Lengths behind,*
But *more advanc'd,* behold with strange Surprize
New, distant Scenes of *endless* Science rise!   10
So pleas'd at first, the towring *Alps* we try,
Mount o'er the Vales, and seem to tread the Sky;
Th' Eternal Snows appear already past,
And the first *Clouds* and *Mountains* seem the last:
But *those attain'd,* we tremble to survey   15
The growing Labours of the lengthen'd Way,
Th' *increasing* Prospect *tires* our wandring Eyes,
Hills peep o'er Hills, and *Alps* on *Alps* arise!

A LITTLE LEARNING IS A DANG'ROUS THING. 2 *Pierian Spring:* the spring of the Muses.

Compare

"A little Learning is a dang'rous Thing" with "The Writer" by Richard Wilbur (page 1096).

Ezra Pound (1885–1972)

The River-Merchant's Wife: A Letter

1915

While my hair was still cut straight across my forehead
I played about the front gate, pulling flowers.
You came by on bamboo stilts, playing horse,
You walked about my seat, playing with blue plums.
And we went on living in the village of Chokan: 5
Two small people, without dislike or suspicion.

At fourteen I married My Lord you.
I never laughed, being bashful.
Lowering my head, I looked at the wall.
Called to, a thousand times, I never looked back.   10

At fifteen I stopped scowling,
I desired my dust to be mingled with yours
Forever and forever and forever.
Why should I climb the look out?

At sixteen you departed, 15
You went into far Ku-to-yen, by the river of swirling eddies,
And you have been gone five months.
The monkeys make sorrowful noise overhead.

You dragged your feet when you went out.
By the gate now, the moss is grown, the different mosses, 20
Too deep to clear them away!
The leaves fall early this autumn, in wind.
The paired butterflies are already yellow with August
Over the grass in the West garden;
They hurt me. I grow older. 25
If you are coming down through the narrows of the river Kiang,
Please let me know beforehand,
And I will come out to meet you
            As far as Cho-fu-sa.

THE RIVER-MERCHANT'S WIFE: A LETTER. A free translation from the Chinese poet Li Po (eighth century).

Compare

"The River-Merchant's Wife: A Letter" with "A Valediction: Forbidding Mourning" by John Donne (page 1038).

Dudley Randall (1914–2000)

A Different Image   1968

The age
requires this task:
create
a different image;
re-animate 5
the mask.

Shatter the icons of slavery and fear.
Replace
the leer
of the minstrel's burnt-cork face 10
with a proud, serene
and classic bronze of Benin.

Dudley Randall

Compare

"A Different Image" with "The Negro Speaks of Rivers" by Langston Hughes (page 974).

John Crowe Ransom (1888–1974)

Piazza Piece   1927

—I am a gentleman in a dustcoat trying
To make you hear. Your ears are soft and small
And listen to an old man not at all,
They want the young men's whispering and sighing.
But see the roses on your trellis dying   5
And hear the spectral singing of the moon;
For I must have my lovely lady soon,
I am a gentleman in a dustcoat trying.

—I am a lady young in beauty waiting
Until my truelove comes, and then we kiss.   10
But what grey man among the vines is this
Whose words are dry and faint as in a dream?
Back from my trellis, Sir, before I scream!
I am a lady young in beauty waiting.

Compare

"Piazza Piece" with "To His Coy Mistress" by Andrew Marvell (page 1066).

Henry Reed (1914–1986)

Naming of Parts   1946

Today we have naming of parts. Yesterday,
We had daily cleaning. And tomorrow morning,
We shall have what to do after firing. But today,
Today we have naming of parts. Japonica
Glistens like coral in all of the neighboring gardens,   5
          And today we have naming of parts.

This is the lower sling swivel. And this
Is the upper sling swivel, whose use you will see,
When you are given your slings. And this is the piling swivel,
Which in your case you have not got. The branches   10
Hold in the gardens their silent, eloquent gestures,
          Which in our case we have not got.

This is the safety-catch, which is always released
With an easy flick of the thumb. And please do not let me
See anyone using his finger. You can do it quite easy   15
If you have any strength in your thumb. The blossoms
Are fragile and motionless, never letting anyone see
          Any of them using their finger.

And this you can see is the bolt. The purpose of this
Is to open the breech, as you see. We can slide it   20
Rapidly backwards and forwards: we call this
Easing the spring. And rapidly backwards and forwards
The early bees are assaulting and fumbling the flowers:
          They call it easing the Spring.

They call it easing the Spring: it is perfectly easy   25
If you have any strength in your thumb: like the bolt,
And the breech, and the cocking-piece, and the point of balance,
Which in our case we have not got; and the almond-blossom
Silent in all of the gardens and the bees going backwards and forwards,
            For today we have naming of parts.   30

Compare

"Naming of Parts" with "The Fury of Aerial Bombardment" by Richard Eberhart (page 686).

Adrienne Rich (b. 1929)

Living in Sin   1955

She had thought the studio would keep itself;
no dust upon the furniture of love.
Half heresy, to wish the taps less vocal,
the panes relieved of grime. A plate of pears,
a piano with a Persian shawl, a cat   5
stalking the picturesque amusing mouse
had risen at his urging.
Not that at five each separate stair would writhe
under the milkman's tramp; that morning light
so coldly would delineate the scraps   10
of last night's cheese and three sepulchral bottles;
that on the kitchen shelf among the saucers
a pair of beetle-eyes would fix her own—
envoy from some village in the moldings . . .
Meanwhile, he, with a yawn,   15
sounded a dozen notes upon the keyboard,
declared it out of tune, shrugged at the mirror,
rubbed at his beard, went out for cigarettes;
while she, jeered by the minor demons,
pulled back the sheets and made the bed and found   20
a towel to dust the table-top,
and let the coffee-pot boil over on the stove.
By evening she was back in love again,
though not so wholly but throughout the night
she woke sometimes to feel the daylight coming   25
like a relentless milkman up the stairs.

Compare

"Living in Sin" with "Let me not to the marriage of true minds" by William Shakespeare (page 816).

Edwin Arlington Robinson (1869–1935)

Miniver Cheevy

1910

Miniver Cheevy, child of scorn,
    Grew lean while he assailed the seasons;
He wept that he was ever born,
    And he had reasons.

Miniver loved the days of old   5
    When swords were bright and steeds were prancing;
The vision of a warrior bold
    Would set him dancing.

Miniver sighed for what was not,
    And dreamed, and rested from his labors;   10
He dreamed of Thebes and Camelot,
    And Priam's neighbors.

Miniver mourned the ripe renown
    That made so many a name so fragrant;
He mourned Romance, now on the town,   15
    And Art, a vagrant.

Miniver loved the Medici,
    Albeit he had never seen one;
He would have sinned incessantly
    Could he have been one.   20

Miniver cursed the commonplace
    And eyed a khaki suit with loathing;
He missed the medieval grace
    Of iron clothing.

Miniver scorned the gold he sought,   25
    But sore annoyed was he without it;
Miniver thought, and thought, and thought,
    And thought about it.

Miniver Cheevy, born too late,
    Scratched his head and kept on thinking;   30
Miniver coughed, and called it fate,
    And kept on drinking.

MINIVER CHEEVY. 11 *Thebes:* a city in ancient Greece and the setting of many famous Greek myths; *Camelot:* the legendary site of King Arthur's Court. 12 *Priam:* the last king of Troy; his "neighbors" would have included Helen of Troy, Aeneas, and other famous figures. 17 *the Medici:* the ruling family of Florence during the high Renaissance, the Medici were renowned patrons of the arts.

Compare

"Miniver Cheevy" with "Ulysses" by Alfred, Lord Tennyson (page 1090).

Theodore Roethke   (1908–1963)

Elegy for Jane   1953

My Student, Thrown by a Horse

I remember the neckcurls, limp and damp as tendrils;
And her quick look, a sidelong pickerel smile;
And how, once startled into talk, the light syllables
    leaped for her,
And she balanced in the delight of her thought,
A wren, happy, tail into the wind,   5
Her song trembling the twigs and small branches.
The shade sang with her;
The leaves, their whispers turned to kissing;
And the mold sang in the bleached valleys under the rose.

Oh, when she was sad, she cast herself down into such a pure depth,   10
Even a father could not find her:
Scraping her cheek against straw;
Stirring the clearest water.

My sparrow, you are not here,
Waiting like a fern, making a spiny shadow.   15
The sides of wet stones cannot console me,
Nor the moss, wound with the last light.

If only I could nudge you from this sleep,
My maimed darling, my skittery pigeon.
Over this damp grave I speak the words of my love: 20
I, with no rights in this matter,
Neither father nor lover.

Theodore Roethke

Compare

"Elegy for Jane" with "Annabel Lee" by Edgar Allan Poe (page 949).

William Shakespeare   (1564–1616)

When, in disgrace with   1609
Fortune and men's eyes

When, in disgrace with Fortune and men's eyes,
I all alone beweep my outcast state,
And trouble deaf heaven with my bootless° cries,   *futile*
And look upon myself and curse my fate,
Wishing me like to one more rich in hope,   5
Featured like him, like him with friends possessed,
Desiring this man's art, and that man's scope,
With what I most enjoy contented least,
Yet in these thoughts myself almost despising,

William Shakespeare

Haply° I think on thee, and then my state, *luckily* 10
Like to the lark at break of day arising
From sullen earth, sings hymns at heaven's gate;
    For thy sweet love rememb'red such wealth brings
    That then I scorn to change my state with kings.

Compare

"When, in disgrace with Fortune and men's eyes" with "When I have fears that I may cease to be" by John Keats (page 1060).

William Shakespeare (1564–1616)

Not marble nor the gilded monuments 1609

Not marble, nor the gilded monuments
Of princes, shall outlive this powerful rhyme;
But you shall shine more bright in these contents
Than unswept stone, besmeared with sluttish time.
When wasteful war shall statues overturn, 5
And broils root out the work of masonry,
Nor Mars his sword nor war's quick fire shall burn
The living record of your memory.
'Gainst death and all-oblivious enmity
Shall you pace forth; your praise shall still find room 10
Even in the eyes of all posterity
That wear this world out to the ending doom.
    So, till the judgment that yourself arise,
    You live in this, and dwell in lovers' eyes.

Compare

"Not marble nor the gilded monuments" with Jeffers' "To the Stone-Cutters" (page 1057).

William Shakespeare (1564–1616)

That time of year thou mayst in me behold 1609

That time of year thou mayst in me behold
When yellow leaves, or none, or few, do hang
Upon those boughs which shake against the cold,
Bare ruined choirs where late the sweet birds sang.
In me thou see'st the twilight of such day 5
As after sunset fadeth in the west,
Which by and by black night doth take away,
Death's second self that seals up all in rest.
In me thou see'st the glowing of such fire
That on the ashes of his youth doth lie, 10
As the deathbed whereon it must expire,
Consumed with that which it was nourished by.
    This thou perceiv'st, which makes thy love more strong,
    To love that well which thou must leave ere long.

Compare

"That time of year thou mayst in me behold" with "anyone lived in a pretty how town" by E. E. Cummings (page 688).

William Shakespeare (1564–1616)

My mistress' eyes are nothing like the sun   1609

My mistress' eyes are nothing like the sun;
Coral is far more red than her lips' red;
If snow be white, why then her breasts are dun;
If hairs be wires, black wires grow on her head.
I have seen roses damasked, red and white,   5
But no such roses see I in her cheeks;
And in some perfumes is there more delight
Than in the breath that from my mistress reeks.
I love to hear her speak, yet well I know
That music hath a far more pleasing sound;   10
I grant I never saw a goddess go:
My mistress, when she walks, treads on the ground.
   And yet, by heaven, I think my love as rare
   As any she° belied with false compare.   *woman*

Compare

"My mistress' eyes are nothing like the sun" with "Crazy Jane Talks with the Bishop" by
William Butler Yeats (page 1102).

Charles Simic (b. 1938)

Butcher Shop   1971

Sometimes walking late at night
I stop before a closed butcher shop.
There is a single light in the store
Like the light in which the convict digs his tunnel.

An apron hangs on the hook: 5
The blood on it smeared into a map
Of the great continents of blood,
The great rivers and oceans of blood.

There are knives that glitter like altars
In a dark church
Where they bring the cripple and the imbecile   10
To be healed.

There's a wooden block where bones are broken,
Scraped clean—a river dried to its bed
Where I am fed,   15
Where deep in the night I hear a voice.

Compare

"Butcher Shop" with "Hawk Roosting" by Ted Hughes (page 653).

Christopher Smart (1722–1771)

For I will consider my Cat Jeoffry   (1759–1763)

For I will consider my Cat Jeoffry.

For he is the servant of the Living God, duly and daily serving him.

For at the first glance of the glory of God in the East he worships in his way.

For is this done by wreathing his body seven times round with elegant
    quickness.

For then he leaps up to catch the musk,° which is the blessing of God   *catnip*   5
    upon his prayer.

For he rolls upon prank to work it in.

For having done duty and received blessing he begins to consider himself.

For this he performs in ten degrees.

For first he looks upon his fore-paws to see if they are clean.

For secondly he kicks up behind to clear away there.   10

For thirdly he works it upon stretch° with the fore-paws   *he works his muscles, stretching*
    extended.

For fourthly he sharpens his paws by wood.

For fifthly he washes himself.

For sixthly he rolls upon wash.

For seventhly he fleas himself, that he may not be interrupted   15
    upon the beat.°   *his patrol*

For eighthly he rubs himself against a post.

For ninthly he looks up for his instructions.

For tenthly he goes in quest of food.

For having considered God and himself he will consider his neighbor.

For if he meets another cat he will kiss her in kindness.   20

For when he takes his prey he plays with it to give it a chance.

For one mouse in seven escapes by his dallying.

For when his day's work is done his business more properly begins.

For he keeps the Lord's watch in the night against the Adversary.

For he counteracts the powers of darkness by his electrical skin   25
    and glaring eyes.

For he counteracts the Devil, who is death, by brisking about the life.

For in his morning orisons he loves the sun and the sun loves him.

For he is of the tribe of Tiger.

For the Cherub Cat is a term of the Angel Tiger.

For he has the subtlety and hissing of a serpent, which in goodness he   30
    suppresses.

For he will not do destruction if he is well-fed, neither will he spit without
    provocation.

For he purrs in thankfulness when God tells him he's a good Cat.

For he is an instrument for the children to learn benevolence upon.

For every house is incomplete without him, and a blessing is lacking in the
    spirit.

For the Lord commanded Moses concerning the cats at the departure of the   35
    Children of Israel from Egypt.

For every family had one cat at least in the bag.

For the English cats are the best in Europe.

For he is the cleanest in the use of his fore-paws of any quadruped.
For the dexterity of his defense is an instance of the love of God to him
    exceedingly.
For he is the quickest to his mark of any creature.   40
For he is tenacious of his point.
For he is a mixture of gravity and waggery.
For he knows that God is his Savior.
For there is nothing sweeter than his peace when at rest.
For there is nothing brisker than his life when in motion.   45
For he is of the Lord's poor, and so indeed is he called by benevolence
    perpetually—Poor Jeoffry! poor Jeoffry! the rat has bit thy throat.
For I bless the name of the Lord Jesus that Jeoffry is better.
For the divine spirit comes about his body to sustain it in complete cat.
For his tongue is exceeding pure so that it has in purity what it wants in
    music.
For he is docile and can learn certain things.   50
For he can sit up with gravity which is patience upon approbation.
For he can fetch and carry, which is patience in employment.
For he can jump over a stick which is patience upon proof positive.
For he can spraggle upon waggle at the word of command.
For he can jump from an eminence into his master's bosom.   55
For he can catch the cork and toss it again.
For he is hated by the hypocrite and miser.
For the former is afraid of detection.
For the latter refuses the charge.
For he camels his back to bear the first notion of business.   60
For he is good to think on, if a man would express himself neatly.
For he made a great figure in Egypt for his signal services.
For he killed the Icneumon-rat, very pernicious by land.
For his ears are so acute that they sting again.
For from this proceeds the passing quickness of his attention.   65
For by stroking of him I have found out electricity.
For I perceived God's light about him both wax and fire.
For the electrical fire is the spiritual substance which God sends from
    heaven to sustain the bodies both of man and beast.
For God has blessed him in the variety of his movements.
For, though he cannot fly, he is an excellent clamberer.   70
For his motions upon the face of the earth are more than any other
    quadruped.
For he can tread to all the measures upon the music.
For he can swim for life.
For he can creep.

FOR I WILL CONSIDER MY CAT JEOFFRY. This is a self-contained extract from Smart's long poem *Jubilate Agno* (Rejoice in the Lamb). 35 *For the Lord commanded Moses concerning the cats:* No such command is mentioned in Scripture. 54 *spraggle upon waggle:* W. F. Stead, in his edition of Smart's poem, suggests that this means Jeoffry will sprawl when his master waggles a finger or a stick. 59 *the charge:* perhaps the cost of feeding a cat.

Compare

"For I will consider my Cat Jeoffry" with "The Tyger" by William Blake (page 1026).

Cathy Song (b. 1955)

Stamp Collecting   1988

Cathy Song

The poorest countries
have the prettiest stamps
as if impracticality were a major export
shipped with the bananas, T-shirts, and coconuts.
Take Tonga, where the tourists,   5
expecting a dramatic waterfall replete with birdcalls,
are taken to see the island's peculiar mystery:
hanging bats with collapsible wings
like black umbrellas swing upside down from fruit trees.
The Tongan stamp is a fruit.   10
The banana stamp is scalloped like a butter-varnished seashell.
The pineapple resembles a volcano, a spout of green on top,
and the papaya, a tarnished goat skull.

They look impressive,
these stamps of countries without a thing to sell   15
except for what is scraped, uprooted and hulled
from their mule-scratched hills.
They believe in postcards,
in portraits of progress: the new dam;
a team of young native doctors   20
wearing stethoscopes like exotic ornaments;
the recently constructed "Facultad de Medicina,"
a building as lack-lustre as an American motel.

The stamps of others are predictable.
Lucky is the country that possesses indigenous beauty.   25
Say a tiger or a queen.
The Japanese can display to the world
their blossoms: a spray of pink on green.
Like pollen, they drift, airborne.
But pity the country that is bleak and stark.   30

Beauty and whimsy are discouraged as indiscreet.
Unbreakable as their climate, a monument of ice,
they issue serious statements, commemorating
factories, tramways and aeroplanes;
athletes marbled into statues.   35
They turn their noses upon the world, these countries,
and offer this: an unrelenting procession
of a grim, historic profile.

Compare

"Stamp Collecting" with "The Virgins" by Derek Walcott (page 1094).

William Stafford (1914–1993)

The Farm on the Great Plains   1960

A telephone line goes cold;
birds tread it wherever it goes.
A farm back of a great plain
tugs an end of the line.

I call that farm every year,   5
ringing it, listening, still;
no one is home at the farm,
the line gives only a hum.

Some year I will ring the line
on a night at last the right one,   10
and with an eye tapered for braille
from the phone on the wall

I will see the tenant who waits—
the last one left at the place;
through the dark my braille eye   15
will lovingly touch his face.

"Hello, is Mother at home?"
No one is home today.
"But Father—he should be there."
No one—no one is here.   20

"But you—are you the one . . . ?"
Then the line will be gone
because both ends will be home:
no space, no birds, no farm.

My self will be the plain,   25
wise as winter is gray,
pure as cold posts go
pacing toward what I know.

Compare

"The Farm on the Great Plains" with "Piano" by D. H. Lawrence (page 1064).

Wallace Stevens

Wallace Stevens (1879–1955)

The Emperor of Ice-Cream   1923

Call the roller of big cigars,
The muscular one, and bid him whip
In kitchen cups concupiscent curds.
Let the wenches dawdle in such dress
As they are used to wear, and let the boys   5
Bring flowers in last month's newspapers.
Let be be finale of seem.
The only emperor is the emperor of ice-cream.

Take from the dresser of deal,
Lacking the three glass knobs, that sheet   10
On which she embroidered fantails once
And spread it so as to cover her face.
If her horny feet protrude, they come
To show how cold she is, and dumb.
Let the lamp affix its beam.   15
The only emperor is the emperor of ice-cream.

THE EMPEROR OF ICE-CREAM. 9 *deal:* fir or pine wood used to make cheap furniture.

Compare

"The Emperor of Ice-Cream" with "This living hand, now warm and capable" by John Keats
(page 810) and "A Slumber Did My Spirit Seal" by William Wordsworth (page 774).

Jonathan Swift (1667–1745)

A Description of the Morning   1711

Now hardly here and there an hackney-coach,°   *horse-drawn cab*
Appearing, showed the ruddy morn's approach.
Now Betty from her master's bed had flown
And softly stole to discompose her own.
The slipshod 'prentice from his master's door   5
Had pared the dirt, and sprinkled round the floor.
Now Moll had whirled her mop with dextrous airs,
Prepared to scrub the entry and the stairs.

The youth with broomy stumps began to trace
The kennel°-edge, where wheels had worn the place.   *gutter*   10
The smallcoal man was heard with cadence deep
Till drowned in shriller notes of chimney-sweep.
Duns° at his lordship's gate began to meet,   *bill-collectors*
And Brickdust Moll had screamed through half a street.
The turnkey° now his flock returning sees,   *jailkeeper*   15
Duly let out a-nights to steal for fees;
The watchful bailiffs° take their silent stands;   *constables*
And schoolboys lag with satchels in their hands.

A DESCRIPTION OF THE MORNING. 9 *youth with broomy stumps:* a young man sweeping the gutter's edge with worn-out brooms, looking for old nails fallen from wagonwheels, which were valuable. 14 *Brickdust Moll:* woman selling brickdust to be used for scouring.

Compare

"A Description of the Morning" with "London" by William Blake (page 700).

Alfred, Lord Tennyson (1809–1892)

Ulysses   (1833)

It little profits that an idle king,
By this still hearth, among these barren crags,
Matched with an agèd wife, I mete and dole
Unequal laws unto a savage race
That hoard, and sleep, and feed, and know not me.   5
I cannot rest from travel; I will drink
Life to the lees. All times I have enjoyed
Greatly, have suffered greatly, both with those
That loved me, and alone; on shore, and when
Through scudding drifts the rainy Hyades   10
Vexed the dim sea. I am become a name;
For always roaming with a hungry heart
Much have I seen and known—cities of men
And manners, climates, councils, governments,
Myself not least, but honored of them all—   15
And drunk delight of battle with my peers,
Far on the ringing plains of windy Troy.
I am a part of all that I have met;
Yet all experience is an arch wherethrough
Gleams that untraveled world whose margin fades   20
Forever and forever when I move.
How dull it is to pause, to make an end,
To rust unburnished, not to shine in use!
As though to breathe were life! Life piled on life
Were all too little, and of one to me   25
Little remains; but every hour is saved
From that eternal silence, something more,
A bringer of new things; and vile it were

For some three suns to store and hoard myself,
And this grey spirit yearning in desire   30
To follow knowledge like a sinking star,
Beyond the utmost bound of human thought.
   This is my son, mine own Telemachus,
To whom I leave the scepter and the isle—
Well-loved of me, discerning to fulfill   35
This labor, by slow prudence to make mild
A rugged people, and through soft degrees
Subdue them to the useful and the good.
Most blameless is he, centered in the sphere
Of common duties, decent not to fail   40
In offices of tenderness, and pay
Meet adoration to my household gods,
When I am gone. He works his work, I mine.
   There lies the port; the vessel puffs her sail;
There gloom the dark, broad seas. My mariners,   45
Souls that have toiled, and wrought, and thought with me—
That ever with a frolic welcome took
The thunder and the sunshine, and opposed
Free hearts, free foreheads—you and I are old;
Old age hath yet his honor and his toil.   50
Death closes all; but something ere the end,
Some work of noble note, may yet be done,
Not unbecoming men that strove with Gods.
The lights begin to twinkle from the rocks;
The long day wanes; the slow moon climbs; the deep   55
Moans round with many voices. Come, my friends,
'Tis not too late to seek a newer world.
Push off, and sitting well in order smite
The sounding furrows; for my purpose holds
To sail beyond the sunset, and the baths   60
Of all the western stars, until I die.
It may be that the gulfs will wash us down;
It may be we shall touch the Happy Isles,
And see the great Achilles, whom we knew.
Though much is taken, much abides; and though   65
We are not now that strength which in old days
Moved earth and heaven, that which we are, we are—
One equal temper of heroic hearts,
Made weak by time and fate, but strong in will
To strive, to seek, to find, and not to yield.   70

ULYSSES. 10 *Hyades:* daughters of Atlas, who were transformed into a group of stars. Their rising with the sun was thought to be a sign of rain. 63 *Happy Isles:* Elysium, a paradise believed to be attainable by sailing west.

Compare

"Ulysses" with "Sir Patrick Spence" (page 637).

Dylan Thomas (1914–1953)

Fern Hill   1946

Now as I was young and easy under the apple boughs   **Dylan Thomas**
About the lilting house and happy as the grass was green,
            The night above the dingle° starry,   *wooded valley*
                Time let me hail and climb
                Golden in the heydays of his eyes,   5
And honored among wagons I was prince of the apple towns
And once below a time I lordly had the trees and leaves
                Trail with daisies and barley
            Down the rivers of the windfall light.

And as I was green and carefree, famous among the barns   10
About the happy yard and singing as the farm was home,
            In the sun that is young once only,
                Time let me play and be
                Golden in the mercy of his means,
And green and golden I was huntsman and herdsman, the calves   15
Sang to my horn, the foxes on the hills barked clear and cold,
                And the sabbath rang slowly
            In the pebbles of the holy streams.

All the sun long it was running, it was lovely, the hay
Fields high as the house, the tunes from the chimneys, it was air   20
                And playing, lovely and watery
                And fire green as grass.
                And nightly under the simple stars
As I rode to sleep the owls were bearing the farm away,
All the moon long I heard, blessed among stables, the nightjars   25
                Flying with the ricks, and the horses
                Flashing into the dark.

And then to awake, and the farm, like a wanderer white
With the dew, come back, the cock on his shoulder: it was all
            Shining, it was Adam and maiden,   30
                The sky gathered again
                And the sun grew round that very day.
So it must have been after the birth of the simple light
In the first, spinning place, the spellbound horses walking warm
                Out of the whinnying green stable   35
                On to the fields of praise.

And honored among foxes and pheasants by the gay house
Under the new made clouds and happy as the heart was long,
      In the sun born over and over,
          I ran my heedless ways,   40
      My wishes raced through the house high hay
And nothing I cared, at my sky blue trades, that time allows
In all his tuneful turning so few and such morning songs
      Before the children green and golden
          Follow him out of grace,   45

Nothing I cared, in the lamb white days, that time would take me
Up to the swallow thronged loft by the shadow of my hand,
      In the moon that is always rising,
          Nor that riding to sleep
      I should hear him fly with the high fields   50
And wake to the farm forever fled from the childless land.
Oh as I was young and easy in the mercy of his means,
      Time held me green and dying
      Though I sang in my chains like the sea.

Compare

"Fern Hill" with "in Just-" by E. E. Cummings (page 846) and "The World Is Too Much with Us" by William Wordsworth (page 868).

John Updike (1932–2009)

Ex-Basketball Player   1958

Pearl Avenue runs past the high-school lot,
Bends with the trolley tracks, and stops, cut off
Before it has a chance to go two blocks,
At Colonel McComsky Plaza. Berth's Garage
Is on the corner facing west, and there,   5
Most days, you'll find Flick Webb, who helps Berth out.

Flick stands tall among the idiot pumps—
Five on a side, the old bubble-head style,
Their rubber elbows hanging loose and low.
One's nostrils are two S's, and his eyes   10
An E and O. And one is squat, without
A head at all—more of a football type.

Once Flick played for the high-school team, the Wizards.
He was good: in fact, the best. In '46
He bucketed three hundred ninety points,   15
A county record still. The ball loved Flick.
I saw him rack up thirty-eight or forty
In one home game. His hands were like wild birds.

He never learned a trade, he just sells gas,
Checks oil, and changes flats. Once in a while,   20
As a gag, he dribbles an inner tube,
But most of us remember anyway.
His hands are fine and nervous on the lug wrench.
It makes no difference to the lug wrench, though.

Off work, he hangs around Mae's luncheonette.   25
Grease-gray and kind of coiled, he plays pinball,
Smokes those thin cigars, nurses lemon phosphates.
Flick seldom says a word to Mae, just nods
Beyond her face toward bright applauding tiers
Of Necco Wafers, Nibs, and Juju Beads.   30

Compare

"Ex-Basketball Player" with "To an Athlete Dying Young" by A. E. Housman (page 1056).

Derek Walcott (b. 1930)

The Virgins   1976

Down the dead streets of sun-stoned Frederiksted,
the first free port to die for tourism,
strolling at funeral pace, I am reminded
of life not lost to the American dream;
but my small-islander's simplicities   5
can't better our new empire's civilized
exchange of cameras, watches, perfumes, brandies
for the good life, so cheaply underpriced
that only the crime rate is on the rise
in streets blighted with sun, stone arches   10
and plazas blown dry by the hysteria
of rumor. A condominium drowns
in vacancy; its bargains are dusted,
but only a jewelled housefly drones
over the bargains. The roulettes spin   15
rustily to the wind—the vigorous trade
that every morning would begin afresh
by revving up green water round the pierhead
heading for where the banks of silver thresh.

THE VIRGINS. The title of this poem refers to the Virgin Islands, a group of 100 small islands in the Caribbean. 1 *Frederiksted:* the biggest seaport in St. Croix, the largest of the American Virgin Islands. 2 *free port:* a port city where goods can be bought and sold without paying customs taxes. 5 *small-islander's:* Walcott was born on St. Lucia, another island in the West Indies. 16 *trade:* trade winds.

Compare

"The Virgins" with "London" by William Blake (page 700).

Edmund Waller (1606–1687)

Go, Lovely Rose 1645

Go, lovely rose,
Tell her that wastes her time and me
That now she knows,
When I resemble° her to thee,   *compare*
How sweet and fair she seems to be.   5

Tell her that's young
And shuns to have her graces spied,
That hadst thou sprung
In deserts where no men abide,
Thou must have uncommended died.   10

Small is the worth
Of beauty from the light retired:
Bid her come forth,
Suffer herself to be desired,
And not blush so to be admired.   15

Then die, that she
The common fate of all things rare
May read in thee:
How small a part of time they share
That are so wondrous sweet and fair.   20

Compare

"Go, Lovely Rose" with "To the Virgins, to Make Much of Time" by Robert Herrick (page 1052) and "To His Coy Mistress" by Andrew Marvell (page 1066).

Walt Whitman (1819–1892)

from Song of the Open Road 1856, 1881

Allons! the road is before us!
It is safe—I have tried it—my own feet have tried it
    well—be not detain'd!

Let the paper remain on the desk unwritten, and the   **Walt Whitman**
    book on the shelf unopen'd!
Let the tools remain in the workshop! let the money remain unearn'd!
Let the school stand! mind not the cry of the teacher!   5
Let the preacher preach in his pulpit! let the lawyer plead in the court,
    and the judge expound the law.

Camerado, I give you my hand!
I give you my love more precious than money,
I give you myself before preaching or law;
Will you give me yourself? will you come travel with me?   10
Shall we stick by each other as long as we live?

SONG OF THE OPEN ROAD. This is part 15 of Whitman's long poem. 1 *Allons!*: French for "Come on!" or
"Let's go!"

Compare

"Song of the Open Road" with "Luke Havergal" by Edwin Arlington Robinson (page 652).

 ## *Walt Whitman* (1819–1892)

I Hear America Singing   1860

I hear America singing, the varied carols I hear,
Those of mechanics, each one singing his as it should be blithe and strong,
The carpenter singing his as he measures his plank or beam,
The mason singing his as he makes ready for work, or leaves off work,
The boatman singing what belongs to him in his boat, the deckhand   5
      singing on the steamboat deck,
The shoemaker singing as he sits on his bench, the hatter singing as he stands,
The wood-cutter's song, the ploughboy's on his way in the morning, or at
      noon intermission or at sundown,
The delicious singing of the mother, or of the young wife at work, or of the
      girl sewing or washing,
Each singing what belongs to him or her and to none else,
The day what belongs to the day—at night the party of young fellows,   10
      robust, friendly,
Singing with open mouths their strong melodious songs.

Compare

"I Hear America Singing" with "I, Too" by Langston Hughes (page 976).

Richard Wilbur (b. 1921)

The Writer   1976

In her room at the prow of the house
Where light breaks, and the windows are tossed with linden,
My daughter is writing a story.

I pause in the stairwell, hearing
From her shut door a commotion of typewriter-keys   5
Like a chain hauled over a gunwale.

Young as she is, the stuff
Of her life is a great cargo, and some of it heavy:
I wish her a lucky passage.

But now it is she who pauses,
As if to reject my thought and its easy figure.
A stillness greatens, in which   10

The whole house seems to be thinking,
And then she is at it again with a bunched clamor
Of strokes, and again is silent.   15

I remember the dazed starling
Which was trapped in that very room, two years ago;
How we stole in, lifted a sash

And retreated, not to affright it;
And how for a helpless hour, through the crack of the door,   20
We watched the sleek, wild, dark

And iridescent creature
Batter against the brilliance, drop like a glove
To the hard floor, or the desk-top,

And wait then, humped and bloody,   25
For the wits to try it again; and how our spirits
Rose when, suddenly sure,

It lifted off from a chair-back,
Beating a smooth course for the right window
And clearing the sill of the world.   30

It is always a matter, my darling,
Of life or death, as I had forgotten. I wish
What I wished you before, but harder.

Compare

"The Writer" with "Digging" by Seamus Heaney (page 1050).

William Carlos Williams (1883–1963)

Spring and All   1923

By the road to the contagious hospital
under the surge of the blue
mottled clouds driven from the
northeast—a cold wind. Beyond, the
waste of broad, muddy fields   5
brown with dried weeds, standing and fallen

patches of standing water
the scattering of tall trees

All along the road the reddish
purplish, forked, upstanding, twiggy   10
stuff of bushes and small trees
with dead, brown leaves under them
leafless vines—

Lifeless in appearance, sluggish
dazed spring approaches—   15

They enter the new world naked,
cold, uncertain of all
save that they enter. All about them
the cold, familiar wind—

Now the grass, tomorrow   20
the stiff curl of wildcarrot leaf

One by one objects are defined—
It quickens: clarity, outline of leaf

But now the stark dignity of
entrance—Still, the profound change   25
has come upon them: rooted, they
grip down and begin to awaken

Compare

"Spring and All" with "in Just-" by E. E. Cummings (page 846) and "Root Cellar" by Theodore
Roethke (page 712).

William Carlos Williams (1883–1963)

To Waken an Old Lady   1921

Old age is
a flight of small
cheeping birds
skimming
bare trees   5
above a snow glaze.
Gaining and failing
they are buffeted
by a dark wind—
But what?   10
On harsh weedstalks
the flock has rested,
the snow
is covered with broken
seedhusks   15
and the wind tempered
by a shrill
piping of plenty.

William Carlos Williams

Compare

"To Waken an Old Lady" with "Eleanor Rigby" by John Lennon and Paul McCartney (page 763).

William Wordsworth (1770–1850)

William Wordsworth

Composed upon Westminster Bridge   1807

Earth has not anything to show more fair:
Dull would he be of soul who could pass by
A sight so touching in its majesty:
This City now doth, like a garment, wear
The beauty of the morning; silent, bare,   5
Ships, towers, domes, theatres, and temples lie
Open unto the fields, and to the sky;
All bright and glittering in the smokeless air.
Never did sun more beautifully steep
In his first splendor, valley, rock, or hill;   10
Ne'er saw I, never felt, a calm so deep!
The river glideth at his own sweet will:
Dear God! the very houses seem asleep;
And all that mighty heart is lying still!

Compare

"Composed upon Westminster Bridge" with "London" by William Blake (page 700).

James Wright (1927–1980)

Autumn Begins in Martins Ferry, Ohio   1963

In the Shreve High football stadium,
I think of Polacks nursing long beers in Tiltonsville,
And gray faces of Negroes in the blast furnace at Benwood,
And the ruptured night watchman of Wheeling Steel,
Dreaming of heroes.   5

All the proud fathers are ashamed to go home.
Their women cluck like starved pullets,
Dying for love.

Therefore,
Their sons grow suicidally beautiful   10
At the beginning of October,
And gallop terribly against each other's bodies.

Compare

"Autumn Begins in Martins Ferry, Ohio" with "Ex-Basketball Player" by John Updike (page 1093).

James Wright (1927–1980)

A Blessing   1963

Just off the highway to Rochester, Minnesota,
Twilight bounds softly forth on the grass.
And the eyes of those two Indian ponies
Darken with kindness.
They have come gladly out of the willows   5
To welcome my friend and me.
We step over the barbed wire into the pasture
Where they have been grazing all day, alone.
They ripple tensely, they can hardly contain their happiness
That we have come.   10
They bow shyly as wet swans. They love each other.
There is no loneliness like theirs.
At home once more,
They begin munching the young tufts of spring in the darkness.

I would like to hold the slenderer one in my arms,   15
For she has walked over to me
And nuzzled my left hand.
She is black and white,
Her mane falls wild on her forehead,
And the light breeze moves me to caress her long ear   20
That is delicate as the skin over a girl's wrist.
Suddenly I realize
That if I stepped out of my body I would break
Into blossom.

Compare

"A Blessing" with "God's Grandeur" by Gerard Manley Hopkins (page 782).

Mary Sidney Wroth (1587?–1623?)

In this strange labyrinth   1621

In this strange labyrinth how shall I turn?
Ways are on all sides while the way I miss:
If to the right hand, there in love I burn;
Let me go forward, therein danger is;
If to the left, suspicion hinders bliss,   5
Let me turn back, shame cries I ought return
Nor faint though crosses with my fortunes kiss.
Stand still is harder, although sure to mourn;
Thus let me take the right, or left hand way;
Go forward, or stand still, or back retire;   10
I must these doubts endure without allay
Or help, but travail find for my best hire;

Yet that which most my troubled sense doth move
Is to leave all, and take the thread of love.

IN THIS STRANGE LABYRINTH. This sonnet comes from Wroth's *Urania* (1621), the first significant sonnet sequence by a woman. Wroth was the niece of Sir Philip Sidney and of the Countess of Pembroke as well as a distant relation of Sir Walter Ralegh. The *Labyrinth* of the title was the maze built by Minos to trap the young men and women sacrificed to the Minotaur. King Minos's daughter Ariadne saved her beloved Theseus by giving him a skein of thread to guide his way through the Labyrinth. (See the final line of the sonnet.)

Compare

"In this strange labyrinth" with Shakespeare's "Let me not to the marriage of true minds." (page 816).

Sir Thomas Wyatt (1503?–1542)

They flee from me that sometime did me sekë
(about 1535)

They flee from me that sometime did me sekë	
With naked fotë° stalking in my chamber.	*foot*
I have seen them gentle, tame and mekë	
That now are wild, and do not remember	
That sometime they put themself in danger	5
To take bread at my hand; and now they range	
Busily seeking with a continual change.	
Thankèd be fortune, it hath been otherwise	
Twenty times better; but once in speciàll,	
In thin array, after a pleasant guise,	10
When her loose gown from her shoulders did fall,	
And she me caught in her armës long and small,	
Therëwith all sweetly did me kiss,	
And softly said, *Dear heart, how like you this?*	
It was no dremë: I lay broadë waking.	15
But all is turned thorough° my gentleness	*through*
Into a strangë fashion of forsaking;	
And I have leave to go of her goodness,	
And she also to use newfangleness.°	*to seek novelty*
But since that I so kindëly am served	20
I would fain knowë what she hath deserved.	

THEY FLEE FROM ME THAT SOMETIME DID ME SEKË. Some latter-day critics have called Sir Thomas Wyatt a careless poet because some of his lines appear faltering and metrically inconsistent; others have thought he knew what he was doing. It is uncertain whether the final *e*'s in English spelling were still pronounced in Wyatt's day as they were in Chaucer's, but if they were, perhaps Wyatt has been unjustly blamed. In this text, spellings have been modernized except in words where the final *e* would make a difference in rhythm. To sense how it matters, try reading the poem aloud leaving out the *e*'s and then putting them in wherever indicated. Sound them like the *a* in *sofa*. 20 *kindëly:* according to my kind (or hers); that is, as befits the nature of man (or woman). Perhaps there is also irony here, and the word means "unkindly."

Compare

"They flee from me that sometime did me sekë" with "When, in disgrace with Fortune and men's eyes" by William Shakespeare (page 1082).

William Butler Yeats (1865–1939)

William Butler Yeats

Crazy Jane Talks with the Bishop   1933

I met the Bishop on the road
And much said he and I.
"Those breasts are flat and fallen now,
Those veins must soon be dry;
Live in a heavenly mansion,   5
Not in some foul sty."

"Fair and foul are near of kin,
And fair needs foul," I cried.
"My friends are gone, but that's a truth
Nor° grave nor bed denied,   *neither*   10
Learned in bodily lowliness
And in the heart's pride.

"A woman can be proud and stiff
When on love intent;
But Love has pitched his mansion in   15
The place of excrement;
For nothing can be sole or whole
That has not been rent."

Compare

"Crazy Jane Talks with the Bishop" with "The Flea" by John Donne (page 1037) or "Down, Wanton, Down!" by Robert Graves (page 676).

 William Butler Yeats (1865–1939)

The Magi   1914

Now as at all times I can see in the mind's eye,
In their stiff, painted clothes, the pale unsatisfied ones
Appear and disappear in the blue depth of the sky
With all their ancient faces like rain-beaten stones,
And all their helms of silver hovering side by side,   5
And all their eyes still fixed, hoping to find once more,
Being by Calvary's turbulence unsatisfied,
The uncontrollable mystery on the bestial floor.

Compare

"The Magi" with "Journey of the Magi" by T. S. Eliot (page 1041).

William Butler Yeats (1865–1939)

When You Are Old   1893

When you are old and grey and full of sleep,
And nodding by the fire, take down this book,
And slowly read, and dream of the soft look
Your eyes had once, and of their shadows deep;

How many loved your moments of glad grace,   5
And loved your beauty with love false or true,
But one man loved the pilgrim soul in you,
And loved the sorrows of your changing face;

And bending down beside the glowing bars,
Murmur, a little sadly, how Love fled   10
And paced upon the mountains overhead
And hid his face amid a crowd of stars.

Compare

"When You Are Old" with "Not marble nor the gilded monuments" by William Shakespeare
(page 1083).

Playwright David Ives.

DRAMA

TALKING WITH *David Ives*

"Comedy is just tragedy without the sentimentality."
Dana Gioia Interviews David Ives

Q: When did you first become interested in theater?

DAVID IVES: I played The Wolf opposite drop-dead-sexy Amy Skeehan in our third-grade production of "Little Red Riding Hood" at St. Mary Magdalene School in South Chicago. Basically it was all over after that. The show was so successful Amy and I took it on tour to the fourth and fifth grades. By then I had learned the Great Lesson of Theater, which is: *theater is a great way to hang out with girls.* It may be why Shakespeare became both an actor and a playwright: *more girls.*

Q: When did you discover that you could make people laugh?

DAVID IVES: There's some debate about this. An aunt of my mine, a few years ago, said to me, "You're just like you were as a boy. Such a happy, funny child." I reported this to my mother, who said without a pause: "I wouldn't say that." She didn't seem to want to explain. One of my old high-school classmates recently mentioned that I was funny in high school. I only remember reading Russian novels about suicide in high school. Maybe I was funny between novels, but they were pretty thick.

Q: Tell us about your first play.

DAVID IVES: I wrote my first play when I was nine. It was about gangsters and had lots of gunfire and a girl I based on Amy Skeehan. I wrote my second play in high school. It was about Russian-like people talking about suicide a lot. My third play was at college and was The Worst Play Ever Written. From there, I had nowhere to go but up. My next play got produced, and suddenly I was a real live playwright. I've been faking it ever since.

Q: When you see one of your plays onstage, how different is it from what you imagined while writing it?

DAVID IVES: It's always better than I imagined it, unless it's worse.

Q: You are the master of the short comic play. What drew you to this unconventional form?

DAVID IVES: Probably a shorter and shorter attention span, like everybody else. Also, my wife Martha is on the short side and I am very drawn to her, so it is only a short (so to speak) way to short plays. I'm fond in general of the concise, the compact, the jeweled, the specific, and perfect as opposed to the verbose, the bloated, the baggy, and general. A good rock-and-roll song can be three or four minutes long and when it's over, if it's been made right and played right, you feel like you've gotten into a barfight, had a love affair, and ridden a convertible down Pacific Coast One on the most beautiful day of the year, all in three minutes. Imagine what you can do with a ten- or fifteen-minute play. You can make an audience feel like they've done

all those things, plus they've gotten married, had kids, died, and went to heaven. There they are, breathless just inside the pearly gate with their heads still spinning, and only ten minutes have passed. As far as I'm concerned, all plays, short or long, should aspire to the conditions of rock-and-roll, whose purpose is to make us aware of our mortality and the fact that we had better get with it before the song ends. Not a bad rule of thumb for art as a whole.

Q: Who are your favorite comic writers and comedians?

DAVID IVES: Nothing depresses me like comedians. Maybe it's because people who try to make me laugh instantly put me in a really bad mood. I once shot a man in Tucson and spent 38 years in the penitentiary because he tried to tell me a joke that started "A priest, a minister, and a rabbi walk into a bar. . . ." As for funny playwrights, Joe Orton and Noel Coward and Chris Durang do it for me because they're not just trying to be funny. They have a vision of life that happens to be comic. They've also got *style*, which is the outward and visible sign of having a vision of life.

Q: Why do people need comedy?

DAVID IVES: Comedy is important for three reasons. First, it's funny. Second, it makes us laugh. Third, it's easier to get a girl to go see a comedy than, let's say, *Hamlet*. Fourth, it shows us what frigging idiots we can be under the right circumstances. As Wendell Berry once said, "It is not from ourselves that we will learn to be better." Watching idiots cavort around onstage is one possible way to do that. First, of course, you have to be interested in being better.

Q: Comedy seems to get less critical respect than tragedy. Does that seem fair to you?

DAVID IVES: Nothing seems fair to me. That's why I write comedy. If you've ever met a critic you'll understand why they give more respect to sadder plays: because critics are the saddest dogs you'll ever meet. The fact is, comedy is much harder to do—to write, to act—than drama, the same way it's harder to look at life and say, *Okay*, than it is to mope around thinking about Russian roulette all the time. But let's get one thing clear: Comedy is not jokes. It certainly isn't sitcoms, which to me are about as funny as a sack of dead kittens. I'm talking about real comedy—human comedy, which is to say comedy that thinks and feels. I'm talking about *Twelfth Night*, or *The Marriage of Bette and Boo*, or *The Importance of Being Earnest*, where there's truth and sadness mixed in with the joy, just as there is in life. Theater *is* life, and fails when it settles for merely being funny, the same way life is not enough when it settles for just being funny. In the end, comedy is just tragedy without the sentimentality. Dostoyevsky, anyone?

Drama is life with the dull bits left out.

—ALFRED HITCHCOCK

Unlike a short story or a novel, a **play** is a work of storytelling in which actors represent the characters. A play also differs from a work of fiction in another essential way: it is addressed not to readers but to spectators.

To be part of an audience in a theater is an experience far different from reading a story in solitude. As the house lights dim and the curtain rises, we become members of a community. The responses of people around us affect our own responses. We, too, contribute to the community's response whenever we laugh, sigh, applaud, murmur in surprise, or catch our breath in excitement. In contrast, when we watch a movie by ourselves in our living room—say, a slapstick comedy—we probably laugh less often than if we were watching the same film in a theater, surrounded by a roaring crowd. On the other hand, no one is spilling popcorn down the backs of our necks. Each kind of theatrical experience, to be sure, has its advantages.

A theater of live actors has another advantage: a sensitive give-and-take between actors and audience. (Such rapport, of course, depends on the skill of the actors and the perceptiveness of the audience.) Although professional actors may try to give a first-rate performance on all occasions, it is natural for them to feel more keenly inspired by a lively, appreciative audience than by a lethargic one. As veteran playgoers well know, something unique and wonderful can happen when good actors and a good audience respond to each other.

In another sense, a play is more than actors and audience. Like a short story or a poem, a play is a work of art made of words. Watching a play, of course, we don't notice the playwright standing between us and the characters. If the play is absorbing, it flows before our eyes. In a silent reading, the usual play consists mainly of **dialogue**, exchanges of speech, punctuated by stage directions. In performance, though, stage directions vanish. And although the thoughtful efforts of perhaps a hundred people—actors, director, producer, stage designer, costumer, makeup artist, technicians—may have gone into a production, a successful play makes us forget its artifice. We may even forget that the play is literature, for its gestures, facial expressions, bodily stances, lighting, and special effects are as much a part of it as the playwright's written words. Even though words are not all there is to a living play, they are its bones. And the whole play, the finished production, is the total of whatever takes place on stage.

There is an aspect of theater related to both religious ritual and civic festival—a mixture of church service and rock concert. These are occasions when people gather for the special communal experiences of being reawakened emotionally and spiritually and celebrating their complex identities. Twice in the history of Europe, drama has sprung forth as a part of worship. In ancient Greece, plays were performed on feast days of Dionysius; and in the Christian Middle Ages, a play was introduced as an adjunct to the Easter mass with the enactment of the meeting between the three Marys and the angel at Jesus's empty tomb. Evidently, something in drama remains constant over the years—something as old, perhaps, as the deepest desires and highest aspirations of humanity.

34

READING A PLAY

> *I regard the theatre as the greatest of all art forms,*
> *the most immediate way in which a human being can share*
> *with another the sense of what it is to be a human being.*
>
> —OSCAR WILDE

Most plays are written not to be read in books but to be performed. Finding plays in a literature anthology, the student may well ask: Isn't there something wrong with the idea of reading plays on the printed page? Isn't that a perversion of their nature?

True, plays are meant to be seen on stage, but equally true, reading a play may afford advantages. One is that it is better to know some masterpieces by reading them than never to know them at all. Even if you live in a large city with many theaters, even if you attend a college with many theatrical productions, to succeed in your lifetime in witnessing, say, all the plays of Shakespeare might well be impossible. In print, they are as near to hand as a book on a shelf, ready to be enacted (if you like) on the stage of the mind.

After all, a play is literature before it comes alive in a theater, and it might be argued that when we read an unfamiliar play, we meet it in the same form in which it first appears to its actors and its director. If a play is rich and complex or if it dates from the remote past and contains difficulties of language and allusion, to read it on the page enables us to study it at our leisure and return to the parts that demand greater scrutiny.

But even if a play may be seen in a theater, sometimes to read it in print may be our way of knowing it as the author wrote it in its entirety. Far from regarding Shakespeare's words as holy writ, producers of *Hamlet, King Lear, Othello,* and other masterpieces often shorten or even leave out whole speeches and scenes. Besides, the nature of the play, as far as you can tell from a stage production, may depend on decisions of the director. In one production Othello may dress as a Renaissance Moor, in another as a modern general. Every actor who plays Iago in *Othello* makes his own interpretation of this knotty character. Some see Iago as a figure of pure evil; others, as a madman; still others, as a suffering human being consumed by hatred, jealousy, and pride. What do you think Shakespeare meant? You can always read the play and decide for yourself. If every stage production of a play is a fresh interpretation, so, too, is every reader's reading of it. Some readers, when silently reading a play to themselves, try to visualize a stage, imagining the characters in costume and under lights. If such a reader is an actor or a director and is reading the play with an eye toward staging it, then he or she may try to imagine every detail of a possible production, even shades of makeup and the loudness of sound effects. But the nonprofessional reader, who regards the play as literature, need not attempt such exhaustive imagining. Although some readers find it enjoyable to imagine the play taking place on a stage, others prefer to imagine the people and events that the play brings vividly to mind. Sympathetically following the tangled life of Nora in *A Doll's House* by Henrik Ibsen, we forget that we are reading printed stage directions and instead feel ourselves in the presence of human conflict. Thus regarded, a play becomes a form of storytelling, and the playwright's instructions to the actors and the director become a conventional mode of narrative that we accept much as we accept the methods of a novel or short story.

THEATRICAL CONVENTIONS

Most plays, whether seen in a theater or in print, employ some **conventions**: customary methods of presenting an action, usual and recognizable devices that an audience is willing to accept. In reading a great play from the past, such as *Oedipus the King* or *Othello*, it will help if we know some of the conventions of the classical Greek theater or the Elizabethan theater. When in *Oedipus the King* we encounter a character called the Chorus, it may be useful to be aware that this is a group of citizens who stand to one side of the action, conversing with the principal character and commenting. In *Othello*, when the sinister Iago, left on stage alone, begins to speak (at the end of Act I, Scene iii), we recognize the conventional device of a **soliloquy**, a monologue in which we seem to overhear the character's inmost thoughts uttered aloud. Another such device is the **aside**, in which a character addresses the audience directly, unheard by the other characters on stage, as when the villain in a melodrama chortles, "Heh! Heh! Now she's in my power!" Like conventions in poetry, such familiar methods of staging a narrative afford us a happy shock of recognition. Often, as in these examples, they are ways of making clear to us exactly what the playwright would have us know.

ELEMENTS OF A PLAY

When we read a play on the printed page and find ourselves swept forward by the motion of its story, we need not wonder how—and from what ingredients—the playwright put it together. Still, to analyze the structure of a play is one way to understand and appreciate a playwright's art. Analysis is complicated, however, because in an excellent play the elements (including plot, theme, and characters) do not stand in isolation. Often, deeds clearly follow from the kinds of people the characters are, and from those deeds it is left to the reader to infer the **theme** of the play—the general point or truth about human beings that may be drawn from it. Perhaps the most meaningful way to study the elements of a play (and certainly the most enjoyable) is to consider a play in its entirety.

Here is a short, famous one-act play worth reading for the boldness of its elements—and for its own sake. *Trifles* tells the story of a murder. As you will discover, the "trifles" mentioned in its title are not of trifling stature. In reading the play, you will probably find yourself imagining what you might see on stage if you were in a theater. You may also want to imagine what took place in the lives of the characters before the curtain rose. All this imagining may sound like a tall order, but don't worry. Just read the play for enjoyment the first time through, and then we will consider what makes it effective.

Susan Glaspell

Trifles

1916

Susan Glaspell (1876–1948) grew up in her native Davenport, Iowa, daughter of a grain dealer. After four years at Drake University and a job as a reporter in Des Moines, she settled in New York's Greenwich Village. In 1915, with her husband, George Cram Cook, a theatrical director, she founded the Provincetown Players, the first influential noncommercial theater troupe in America. During the summers of 1915 and 1916, in a makeshift playhouse on a Cape Cod pier, the Players staged the earliest plays of Eugene O'Neill and works by John Reed, Edna St. Vincent Millay, and Glaspell herself. Transplanting the company to New York in the fall of 1916, Glaspell and Cook renamed it the Playwrights' Theater. Glaspell wrote several still-remembered plays, among them a pioneering work of feminist drama, The Verge *(1921), and the Pulitzer Prize–winning* Alison's House *(1930), about the family of a reclusive poet like Emily Dickinson who, after her death, squabble over the right to publish her poems. First widely known for her fiction with an Iowa background, Glaspell wrote ten novels, including* Fidelity *(1915) and* The Morning Is Near Us *(1939). Shortly after writing the play* Trifles, *she rewrote it as a short story, "A Jury of Her Peers."*

CHARACTERS

George Henderson, county attorney
Henry Peters, sheriff
Lewis Hale, a neighboring farmer
Mrs. Peters
Mrs. Hale

SCENE: *The kitchen in the now abandoned farmhouse of John Wright, a gloomy kitchen, and left without having been put in order—unwashed pans under the sink, a loaf of bread outside the breadbox, a dish towel on the table—other signs of incompleted work. At the rear the outer door opens and the Sheriff comes in followed by the County Attorney and Hale. The Sheriff and Hale are men in middle life, the County Attorney is a young man; all are much bundled up and go at once to the stove. They are followed by two women—the Sheriff's wife first; she is a slight wiry woman, a thin nervous face. Mrs. Hale is larger and would ordinarily be called more comfortable looking, but she is disturbed now and looks fearfully about as she enters. The women have come in slowly, and stand close together near the door.*

County Attorney (rubbing his hands): This feels good. Come up to the fire, ladies.
Mrs. Peters (after taking a step forward): I'm not—cold.
Sheriff (unbuttoning his overcoat and stepping away from the stove as if to mark the beginning of official business): Now, Mr. Hale, before we move things about, you explain to Mr. Henderson just what you saw when you came here yesterday morning.

County Attorney: By the way, has anything been moved? Are things just as you left them yesterday?

Sheriff (*looking about*): It's just the same. When it dropped below zero last night I thought I'd better send Frank out this morning to make a fire for us—no use getting pneumonia with a big case on, but I told him not to touch anything except the stove—and you know Frank.

County Attorney: Somebody should have been left here yesterday.

Sheriff: Oh—yesterday. When I had to send Frank to Morris Center for that man who went crazy—I want you to know I had my hands full yesterday, I knew you could get back from Omaha by today and as long as I went over everything here myself—

County Attorney: Well, Mr. Hale, tell just what happened when you came here yesterday morning.

Hale: Harry and I had started to town with a load of potatoes. We came along the road from my place and as I got here I said, "I'm going to see if I can't get John Wright to go in with me on a party telephone." I spoke to Wright about it once before and he put me off, saying folks talked too much anyway, and all he asked was peace and quiet—I guess you know about how much he talked himself; but I thought maybe if I went to the house and talked about it before his wife, though I said to Harry that I didn't know as what his wife wanted made much difference to John—

County Attorney: Let's talk about that later, Mr. Hale. I do want to talk about that, but tell now just what happened when you got to the house.

Hale: I didn't hear or see anything; I knocked at the door, and still it was all quiet inside. I knew they must be up, it was past eight o'clock. So I knocked again, and I thought I heard somebody say, "Come in." I wasn't sure, I'm not sure yet, but I opened the door—this door (*indicating the door by which the two women are still standing*) and there in that rocker—(*pointing to it*) sat Mrs. Wright.

(*They all look at the rocker.*)

County Attorney: What—was she doing?

Hale: She was rockin' back and forth. She had her apron in her hand and was kind of—pleating it.

County Attorney: And how did she—look?

Hale: Well, she looked queer.

County Attorney: How do you mean—queer?

Hale: Well, as if she didn't know what she was going to do next. And kind of done up.

County Attorney: How did she seem to feel about your coming?

Hale: Why, I don't think she minded—one way or other. She didn't pay much attention. I said, "How do, Mrs. Wright, it's cold, ain't it?" And she said, "Is it?"—and went on kind of pleating at her apron. Well, I was surprised; she didn't ask me to come up to the stove, or to set down, but just sat there, not even looking at me, so I said, "I want to see John." And then she—laughed. I guess you would call it a laugh. I thought of Harry and the team outside, so I said a little sharp: "Can't I see John?" "No," she says, kind o' dull like. "Ain't he home?" says I. "Yes," says she, "he's home." "Then why can't I see him?" I asked her, out of patience. " 'Cause he's dead," says she. "*Dead?*" says I. She just nodded her head, not getting a bit excited, but rockin' back and forth. "Why—where is he?" says I, not knowing what to say. She just pointed upstairs—like that. (*Himself pointing to the room above.*) I got up, with the idea of going up there. I walked from there to here—then I says, "Why, what did he die of?" "He died of a rope round his neck," says she, and just went on pleatin' at her apron. Well, I went out and called Harry. I thought I might—need help. We went upstairs and there he was lyin'—

County Attorney: I think I'd rather have you go into that upstairs, where you can point it all out. Just go on now with the rest of the story.

Hale: Well, my first thought was to get that rope off. It looked . . . (*stops, his face twitches*) . . . but Harry, he went up to him, and he said, "No, he's dead all right, and we'd better not touch anything." So we went back down stairs. She was still sitting that same way. "Has anybody been notified?" I asked. "No," says she, unconcerned. "Who did this, Mrs. Wright?" said Harry. He said it businesslike—and she stopped pleatin' of her apron. "I don't know," she says. "You don't *know?*" says Harry. "No," says she. "Weren't you sleepin' in the bed with him?" says Harry. "Yes," says she, "but I was on the inside." "Somebody slipped a rope round his neck and strangled him and you didn't wake up?" says Harry. "I didn't wake up," she said after him. We must 'a looked as if we didn't see how that could be, for after a minute she said, "I sleep sound." Harry was going to ask her more questions but I said maybe we ought to let her tell her story first to the coroner, or the sheriff, so Harry went fast as he could to Rivers' place, where there's a telephone.

County Attorney: And what did Mrs. Wright do when she knew that you had gone for the coroner?

Hale: She moved from that chair to this one over here (*pointing to a small chair in the corner*) and just sat there with her hands held together and looking down. I got a feeling that I ought to make some conversation, so I said I had come in to see if John wanted to put in a telephone, and at that she started to laugh, and then she stopped and looked at me—scared. (*The County Attorney, who has had his notebook out, makes a note.*) I dunno, maybe it wasn't scared. I wouldn't like to say it was. Soon Harry got back, and then Dr. Lloyd came, and you, Mr. Peters, and so I guess that's all I know that you don't.

County Attorney (*looking around*): I guess we'll go upstairs first—and then out to the barn and around there. (*To the Sheriff*) You're convinced that there was nothing important here—nothing that would point to any motive.

Sheriff: Nothing here but kitchen things.

(*The County Attorney, after again looking around the kitchen, opens the door of a cupboard closet. He gets up on a chair and looks on a shelf. Pulls his hand away, sticky.*)

County Attorney: Here's a nice mess.

(*The women draw nearer.*)

Mrs. Peters (*to the other woman*): Oh, her fruit; it did freeze. (*To the County Attorney*) She worried about that when it turned so cold. She said the fire'd go out and her jars would break.

Sheriff: Well, can you beat the women! Held for murder and worryin' about her preserves.

County Attorney: I guess before we're through she may have something more serious than preserves to worry about.

Hale: Well, women are used to worrying over trifles.

(*The two women move a little closer together.*)

County Attorney (*with the gallantry of a young politician*): And yet, for all their worries, what would we do without the ladies? (*The women do not unbend. He goes to the sink, takes a dipperful of water from the pail and pouring it into a basin, washes his hands. Starts to wipe them on the roller towel, turns it for a cleaner place.*) Dirty towels! (*Kicks his foot against the pans under the sink.*) Not much of a housekeeper, would you say, ladies?

Mrs. Hale (*stiffly*): There's a great deal of work to be done on a farm.

County Attorney: To be sure. And yet (*with a little bow to her*) I know there are some Dickson County farmhouses which do not have such roller towels.

(*He gives it a pull to expose its full length again.*)

Mrs. Hale: Those towels get dirty awful quick. Men's hands aren't always as clean as they might be.

County Attorney: Ah, loyal to your sex, I see. But you and Mrs. Wright were neighbors. I suppose you were friends, too.

Mrs. Hale (*shaking her head*): I've not seen much of her of late years. I've not been in this house—it's more than a year.

County Attorney: And why was that? You didn't like her?

Mrs. Hale: I liked her all well enough. Farmers' wives have their hands full, Mr. Henderson. And then—

County Attorney: Yes—?

Mrs. Hale (*looking about*): It never seemed a very cheerful place.

County Attorney: No—it's not cheerful. I shouldn't say she had the home-making instinct.

Mrs. Hale: Well, I don't know as Wright had, either.

County Attorney: You mean that they didn't get on very well?

Mrs. Hale: No, I don't mean anything. But I don't think a place'd be any cheerfuller for John Wright's being in it.

County Attorney: I'd like to talk more of that a little later. I want to get the lay of things upstairs now.

(*He goes to the left, where three steps lead to a stair door.*)

Sheriff: I suppose anything Mrs. Peters does'll be all right. She was to take in some clothes for her, you know, and a few little things. We left in such a hurry yesterday.

County Attorney: Yes, but I would like to see what you take, Mrs. Peters, and keep an eye out for anything that might be of use to us.

Mrs. Peters: Yes, Mr. Henderson.

(*The women listen to the men's steps on the stairs, then look about the kitchen.*)

Mrs. Hale: I'd hate to have men coming into my kitchen, snooping around and criticizing.

(*She arranges the pans under sink which the County Attorney had shoved out of place.*)

Mrs. *Peters:* Of course it's no more than their duty.

Mrs. *Hale:* Duty's all right, but I guess that deputy sheriff that came out to make the fire might have got a little of this on. (*Gives the roller towel a pull.*) Wish I'd thought of that sooner. Seems mean to talk about her for not having things slicked up when she had to come away in such a hurry.

Mrs. *Peters* (*who has gone to a small table in the left rear corner of the room, and lifted one end of a towel that covers a pan*): She had bread set.

(*Stands still.*)

Mrs. *Hale* (*eyes fixed on a loaf of bread beside the breadbox, which is on a low shelf at the other side of the room; moves slowly toward it*): She was going to put this in there. (*Picks up loaf, then abruptly drops it. In a manner of returning to familiar things.*) It's a shame about her fruit. I wonder if it's all gone. (*Gets up on the chair and looks.*) I think there's some here that's all right, Mrs. Peters. Yes—here; (*holding it toward the window*) this is cherries, too. (*Looking again.*) I declare I believe that's the only one. (*Gets down, bottle in her hand. Goes to the sink and wipes it off on the outside.*) She'll feel awful bad after all her hard work in the hot weather. I remember the afternoon I put up my cherries last summer.

(*She puts the bottle on the big kitchen table, center of the room. With a sigh, is about to sit down in the rocking-chair. Before she is seated realizes what chair it is; with a slow look at it, steps back. The chair which she has touched rocks back and forth.*)

Mrs. *Peters:* Well, I must get those things from the front room closet. (*She goes to the door at the right, but after looking into the other room, steps back.*) You coming with me, Mrs. Hale? You could help me carry them.

(*They go in the other room; reappear, Mrs. Peters carrying a dress and skirt, Mrs. Hale following with a pair of shoes.*)

Mrs. *Peters:* My, it's cold in there.

(*She puts the clothes on the big table, and hurries to the stove.*)

Mrs. *Hale* (*examining her skirt*): Wright was close. I think maybe that's why she kept so much to herself. She didn't even belong to the Ladies Aid. I suppose she felt she couldn't do her part, and then you don't enjoy things when you feel shabby. She used to wear pretty clothes and be lively, when she was Minnie Foster, one of the town girls singing in the choir. But that—oh, that was thirty years ago. This all you was to take in?

Mrs. *Peters:* She said she wanted an apron. Funny thing to want, for there isn't much to get you dirty in jail, goodness knows. But I suppose just to make her feel more natural. She said they was in the top drawer in this cupboard. Yes, here. And then her little shawl that always hung behind the door. (*Opens stair door and looks.*) Yes, here it is.

(*Quickly shuts door leading upstairs.*)

Mrs. *Hale* (*abruptly moving toward her*): Mrs. Peters?

Mrs. *Peters:* Yes, Mrs. Hale?

Mrs. *Hale:* Do you think she did it?

Mrs. *Peters* (*in a frightened voice*): Oh, I don't know.

Mrs. Hale: Well, I don't think she did. Asking for an apron and her little shawl. Worrying about her fruit.

Mrs. Peters (starts to speak, glances up, where footsteps are heard in the room above; in a low voice): Mr. Peters says it looks bad for her. Mr. Henderson is awful sarcastic in a speech and he'll make fun of her sayin' she didn't wake up.

Mrs. Hale: Well, I guess John Wright didn't wake when they was slipping that rope under his neck.

Mrs. Peters: No, it's strange. It must have been done awful crafty and still. They say it was such a—funny way to kill a man, rigging it all up like that.

Mrs. Hale: That's just what Mr. Hale said. There was a gun in the house. He says that's what he can't understand.

Mrs. Peters: Mr. Henderson said coming out that what was needed for the case was a motive; something to show anger, or—sudden feeling.

Mrs. Hale (who is standing by the table): Well, I don't see any signs of anger around here. (*She puts her hand on the dish towel which lies on the table, stands looking down at table, one half of which is clean, the other half messy.*) It's wiped to here. (*Makes a move as if to finish work, then turns and looks at loaf of bread outside the breadbox. Drops towel. In that voice of coming back to familiar things.*) Wonder how they are finding things upstairs. I hope she had it a little more red-up° there. You know, it seems kind of *sneaking.* Locking her up in town and then coming out here and trying to get her own house to turn against her!

Mrs. Peters: But Mrs. Hale, the law is the law.

Mrs. Hale: I s'pose 'tis. (*Unbuttoning her coat.*) Better loosen up your things, Mrs. Peters. You won't feel them when you go out.

(*Mrs. Peters takes off her fur tippet, goes to hang it on hook at back of room, stands looking at the under part of the small corner table.*)

Mrs. Peters: She was piecing a quilt.

(*She brings the large sewing basket and they look at the bright pieces.*)

Mrs. Hale: It's a log cabin pattern. Pretty, isn't it? I wonder if she was goin' to quilt it or just knot it?

(*Footsteps have been heard coming down the stairs. The Sheriff enters followed by Hale and the County Attorney.*)

Sheriff: They wonder if she was going to quilt it or just knot it!

(*The men laugh; the women look abashed.*)

County Attorney (rubbing his hands over the stove): Frank's fire didn't do much up there, did it? Well, let's go out to the barn and get that cleared up.

(*The men go outside.*)

Mrs. Hale (resentfully): I don't know as there's anything so strange, our takin' up our time with little things while we're waiting for them to get the evidence. (*She sits down at the big table smoothing out a block with decision.*) I don't see as it's anything to laugh about.

---

red-up: (slang) readied up, ready to be seen.

Mrs. Peters (apologetically): Of course they've got awful important things on their minds.

(Pulls up a chair and joins Mrs. Hale at the table.)

Mrs. Hale (examining another block): Mrs. Peters, look at this one. Here, this is the one she was working on, and look at the sewing! All the rest of it has been so nice and even. And look at this! It's all over the place! Why, it looks as if she didn't know what she was about!

(After she has said this they look at each, then start to glance back at the door. After an instant Mrs. Hale has pulled at a knot and ripped the sewing.)

Mrs. Peters: Oh, what are you doing, Mrs. Hale?

Mrs. Hale (mildly): Just pulling out a stitch or two that's not sewed very good. *(Threading a needle.)* Bad sewing always made me fidgety.

Mrs. Peters (nervously): I don't think we ought to touch things.

Mrs. Hale: I'll just finish up this end. *(Suddenly stopping and leaning forward.)* Mrs. Peters?

Mrs. Peters: Yes, Mrs. Hale?

Mrs. Hale: What do you suppose she was so nervous about?

Mrs. Peters: Oh—I don't know. I don't know as she was nervous. I sometimes sew awful queer when I'm just tired. *(Mrs. Hale starts to say something, looks at Mrs. Peters, then goes on sewing.)* Well, I must get these things wrapped up. They may be through sooner than we think. *(Putting apron and other things together.)* I wonder where I can find a piece of paper, and string.

Mrs. Hale: In that cupboard, maybe.

Mrs. Peters (looking in cupboard): Why, here's a birdcage. *(Holds it up.)* Did she have a bird, Mrs. Hale?

Mrs. Hale: Why, I don't know whether she did or not—I've not been here for so long. There was a man around last year selling canaries cheap, but I don't know as she took one; maybe she did. She used to sing real pretty herself.

Mrs. Peters (glancing around): Seems funny to think of a bird here. But she must have had one, or why would she have a cage? I wonder what happened to it.

Mrs. Hale: I s'pose maybe the cat got it.

Mrs. Peters: No, she didn't have a cat. She's got that feeling some people have about cats—being afraid of them. My cat got in her room and she was real upset and asked me to take it out.

Mrs. Hale: My sister Bessie was like that. Queer, ain't it?

Mrs. Peters (examining the cage): Why, look at this door. It's broke. One hinge is pulled apart.

Mrs. Hale (looking too): Looks as if someone must have been rough with it.

Mrs. Peters: Why, yes.

(She brings the cage forward and puts it on the table.)

Mrs. Hale: I wish if they're going to find any evidence they'd be about it. I don't like this place.

Mrs. Peters: But I'm awful glad you came with me, Mrs. Hale. It would be lonesome for me sitting here alone.

Mrs. Hale: It would, wouldn't it? *(Dropping her sewing.)* But I tell you what I do wish, Mrs. Peters. I wish I had come over sometimes when *she* was here. I—*(looking around the room)*—wish I had.

Mrs. Peters: But of course you were awful busy, Mrs. Hale—your house and your children.

Mrs. Hale: I could've come. I stayed away because it weren't cheerful—and that's why I ought to have come. I—I've never liked this place. Maybe because it's down in a hollow and you don't see the road. I dunno what it is but it's a lonesome place and always was. I wish I had come over to see Minnie Foster sometimes. I can see now—

(Shakes her head.)

Mrs. Peters: Well, you mustn't reproach yourself, Mrs. Hale. Somehow we just don't see how it is with other folks until—something comes up.

Mrs. Hale: Not having children makes less work—but it makes a quiet house, and Wright out to work all day, and no company when he did come in. Did you know John Wright, Mrs. Peters?

Mrs. Peters: Not to know him; I've seen him in town. They say he was a good man.

Mrs. Hale: Yes—good; he didn't drink, and kept his word as well as most, I guess, and paid his debts. But he was a hard man, Mrs. Peters. Just to pass the time of day with him—(*shivers*). Like a raw wind that gets to the bone. (*Pauses, her eye falling on the cage.*) I should think she would'a wanted a bird. But what do you suppose went with it?

Mrs. Peters: I don't know, unless it got sick and died.

(She reaches over and swings the broken door, swings it again. Both women watch it.)

Mrs. Hale: You weren't raised round here, were you? (*Mrs. Peters shakes her head.*) You didn't know—her?

Mrs. Peters: Not till they brought her yesterday.

Mrs. Hale: She—come to think of it, she was kind of like a bird herself—real sweet and pretty, but kind of timid and—fluttery. How—she—did—change. (*Silence; then as if struck by a happy thought and relieved to get back to everyday things.*) Tell you what, Mrs. Peters, why don't you take the quilt in with you? It might take up her mind.

Mrs. Peters: Why, I think that's a real nice idea, Mrs. Hale. There couldn't possibly be any objection to it, could there? Now, just what would I take? I wonder if her patches are in here—and her things.

(They look in the sewing basket.)

Mrs. Hale: Here's some red. I expect this has got sewing things in it. (*Brings out a fancy box.*) What a pretty box. Looks like something somebody would give you. Maybe her scissors are in here. (*Opens box. Suddenly puts her hand to her nose.*) Why—(*Mrs. Peters bends nearer, then turns her face away.*) There's something wrapped up in this piece of silk.

Mrs. Peters: Why, this isn't her scissors.

Mrs. Hale (lifting the silk): Oh, Mrs. Peters—it's—

(Mrs. Peters bends closer.)

Mrs. Peters: It's the bird.

Mrs. Hale (jumping up): But, Mrs. Peters—look at it! Its neck! Look at its neck! It's all—other side *too.*

Mrs. Peters: Somebody—wrung—its—neck.

2000 production of *Trifles*, by Echo Theatre of Dallas.

(*Their eyes meet. A look of growing comprehension, of horror. Steps are heard outside. Mrs. Hale slips box under quilt pieces, and sinks into her chair. Enter Sheriff and County Attorney. Mrs. Peters rises.*)

County Attorney (*as one turning from serious things to little pleasantries*): Well, ladies, have you decided whether she was going to quilt it or knot it?

Mrs. Peters: We think she was going to—knot it.

County Attorney: Well, that's interesting, I'm sure. (*Seeing the birdcage.*) Has the bird flown?

Mrs. Hale (*putting more quilt pieces over the box*): We think the—cat got it.

County Attorney (*preoccupied*): Is there a cat?

(*Mrs. Hale glances in a quick covert way at Mrs. Peters.*)

Mrs. Peters: Well, not *now*. They're superstitious, you know. They leave.

County Attorney (*to Sheriff Peters, continuing an interrupted conversation*): No sign at all of anyone having come from the outside. Their own rope. Now let's go up again and go over it piece by piece. (*They start upstairs.*) It would have to have been someone who knew just the—

(*Mrs. Peters sits down. The two women sit there not looking at one another, but as if peering into something and at the same time holding back. When they talk now it is in the manner of feeling their way over strange ground, as if afraid of what they are saying, but as if they cannot help saying it.*)

Mrs. Hale: She liked the bird. She was going to bury it in that pretty box.

Mrs. Peters (*in a whisper*): When I was a girl—my kitten—there was a boy took a hatchet, and before my eyes—and before I could get there—(*covers her face an instant*). If they hadn't held me back I would have—(*catches herself, looks upstairs where steps are heard, falters weakly*)—hurt him.

Mrs. Hale (*with a slow look around her*): I wonder how it would seem never to have had any children around. (*Pause.*) No, Wright wouldn't like the bird—a thing that sang. She used to sing. He killed that, too.

Mrs. Peters (*moving uneasily*): We don't know who killed the bird.

Mrs. Hale: I knew John Wright.

Mrs. Peters: It was an awful thing was done in this house that night, Mrs. Hale. Killing a man while he slept, slipping a rope around his neck that choked the life out of him.

Mrs. Hale: His neck. Choked the life out of him.

(*Her hand goes out and rests on the birdcage.*)

Mrs. Peters (*with rising voice*): We don't know who killed him. We don't *know*.

Mrs. Hale (*her own feeling not interrupted*): If there'd been years and years of nothing, then a bird to sing to you, it would be awful—still, after the bird was still.

Mrs. Peters (*something within her speaking*): I know what stillness is. When we homesteaded in Dakota, and my first baby died—after he was two years old, and me with no other then—

Mrs. Hale (*moving*): How soon do you suppose they'll be through looking for the evidence?

Mrs. Peters: I know what stillness is. (*Pulling herself back.*) The law has got to punish crime, Mrs. Hale.

Mrs. Hale (*not as if answering that*): I wish you'd seen Minnie Foster when she wore a white dress with blue ribbons and stood up there in the choir and sang. (*A look around the room.*) Oh, I *wish* I'd come over here once in a while! That was a crime! That was a crime! Who's going to punish that?

Mrs. Peters (*looking upstairs*): We mustn't—take on.

Mrs. Hale: I might have known she needed help! I know how things can be—for women. I tell you, it's queer, Mrs. Peters. We live close together and we live far apart. We all go through the same things—it's all just a different kind of the same thing. (*Brushes her eyes; noticing the bottle of fruit, reaches out for it.*) If I was you I wouldn't tell her her fruit was gone. Tell her it *ain't*. Tell her it's all right. Take this in to prove it to her. She—she may never know whether it was broke or not.

Mrs. Peters (*takes the bottle, looks about for something to wrap it in; takes petticoat from the clothes brought from the other room, very nervously begins winding this around the bottle; in a false voice*): My, it's a good thing the men couldn't hear us. Wouldn't they just laugh! Getting all stirred up over a little thing like a—dead canary. As if that could have anything to do with—with—wouldn't they *laugh*!

(*The men are heard coming down stairs.*)

Mrs. Hale (*under her breath*): Maybe they would—maybe they wouldn't.

County Attorney: No, Peters, it's all perfectly clear except a reason for doing it. But you know juries when it comes to women. If there was some definite thing. Something to show—something to make a story about—a thing that would connect up with this strange way of doing it—

(*The women's eyes meet for an instant. Enter Hale from outer door.*)

Hale: Well, I've got the team around. Pretty cold out there.
County Attorney: I'm going to stay here a while by myself. (*To the Sheriff*) You can send Frank out for me, can't you? I want to go over everything. I'm not satisfied that we can't do better.
Sheriff: Do you want to see what Mrs. Peters is going to take in?

(*The County Attorney goes to the table, picks up the apron, laughs.*)

County Attorney: Oh, I guess they're not very dangerous things the ladies have picked out. (*Moves a few things about, disturbing the quilt pieces which cover the box. Steps back.*) No, Mrs. Peters doesn't need supervising. For that matter, a sheriff's wife is married to the law. Ever think of it that way, Mrs. Peters?
Mrs. Peters: Not—just that way.
Sheriff (*chuckling*): Married to the law. (*Moves toward the other room.*) I just want you to come in here a minute, George. We ought to take a look at these windows.
County Attorney (*scoffingly*): Oh, windows!
Sheriff: We'll be right out, Mr. Hale.

(*Hale goes outside. The Sheriff follows the County Attorney into the other room. Then Mrs. Hale rises, hands tight together, looking intensely at Mrs. Peters, whose eyes make a slow turn, finally meeting Mrs. Hale's. A moment Mrs. Hale holds her, then her own eyes point the way to where the box is concealed. Suddenly Mrs. Peters throws back quilt pieces and tries to put the box in the bag she is wearing. It is too big. She opens box, starts to take bird out, cannot touch it, goes to pieces, stands there helpless. Sound of a knob turning in the other room. Mrs. Hale snatches the box and puts it in the pocket of her big coat. Enter County Attorney and Sheriff.*)

County Attorney (*facetiously*): Well, Henry, at least we found out that she was not going to quilt it. She was going to—what is it you call it, ladies?
Mrs. Hale (*her hand against her pocket*): We call it—knot it, Mr. Henderson.

CURTAIN

Questions

1. What attitudes toward women do the Sheriff and the County Attorney express? How do Mrs. Hale and Mrs. Peters react to these sentiments?
2. Why does the County Attorney care so much about discovering a motive for the killing?
3. What does Glaspell show us about the position of women in this early twentieth-century community?
4. What do we learn about the married life of the Wrights? By what means is this knowledge revealed to us?
5. What is the setting of this play, and how does it help us to understand Mrs. Wright's deed?
6. What do you infer from the wildly stitched block in Minnie's quilt? Why does Mrs. Hale rip out the crazy stitches?

7. What is so suggestive in the ruined birdcage and the dead canary wrapped in silk? What do these objects have to do with Minnie Foster Wright? What similarity do you notice between the way the canary died and John Wright's own death?

8. What thoughts and memories confirm Mrs. Peters and Mrs. Hale in their decision to help Minnie beat the murder rap?

9. In what places does Mrs. Peters show that she is trying to be a loyal, law-abiding sheriff's wife? How do she and Mrs. Hale differ in background and temperament?

10. What ironies does the play contain? Comment on Mrs. Hale's closing speech: "We call it—knot it, Mr. Henderson." Why is that little hesitation before "knot it" such a meaningful pause?

11. Point out some moments in the play when the playwright conveys much to the audience without needing dialogue.

12. How would you sum up the play's major theme?

13. How does this play, first produced in 1916, show its age? In what ways does it seem still remarkably new?

14. "*Trifles* is a lousy mystery. All the action took place before the curtain went up. Almost in the beginning, on the third page, we find out 'who done it.' So there isn't really much reason for us to sit through the rest of the play." Discuss this view.

ANALYZING *TRIFLES*

Some plays endure, perhaps because (among other reasons) actors take pleasure in performing them. *Trifles* is such a play, a showcase for the skills of its two principals. While the men importantly bumble about, trying to discover a motive, Mrs. Peters and Mrs. Hale solve the case right under their dull noses. The two players in these leading roles face a challenging task: to show both characters growing onstage before us. Discovering a secret that binds them, the two women must realize painful truths in their own lives, become aware of all they have in common with Minnie Wright, and gradually resolve to side with the accused against the men. That *Trifles* has enjoyed a revival of attention may reflect its evident feminist views, its convincing portrait of two women forced reluctantly to arrive at a moral judgment and to make a defiant move.

Conflict

Some critics say that the essence of drama is **conflict**, the central struggle between two or more forces in a play. Evidently, Glaspell's play is rich in this essential, even though its most violent conflict—the war between John and Minnie Wright—takes place before the play begins. Right away, when the menfolk barge through the door into the warm room, letting the women trail in after them; right away, when the sheriff makes fun of Minnie for worrying about "trifles" and the county attorney (that slick politician) starts crudely trying to flatter the "ladies," we sense a conflict between officious, self-important men and the women they expect to wait on them. What is the play's *theme*? Surely the title points to it: women, who men say worry over trifles, can find large meanings in those little things.

Plot

Like a carefully constructed traditional short story, *Trifles* has a **plot**, a term sometimes taken to mean whatever happens in a story, but more exactly referring to the unique arrangement of events that the author has made. (For more about plot in a story, see Chapter 1.) If Glaspell had elected to tell the story of John and Minnie Wright in chronological order, the sequence in which events took place in time, she might have written a much longer play, opening perhaps with a scene of Minnie's buying her canary and John's cold complaint, "That damned bird keeps twittering all day long!" She might have included scenes showing John strangling the canary and swearing when it beaks him; the Wrights in their loveless bed while Minnie knots her noose; and farmer Hale's entrance after the murder, with Minnie rocking. Only at the end would she have shown us what happened after the crime. That arrangement of events would have made for a quite different play than the short, tight one Glaspell wrote. By telling of events in retrospect, by having the women detectives piece together what happened, Glaspell leads us to focus not only on the murder but, more importantly, on the developing bond between the two women and their growing compassion for the accused.

Subplot

Tightly packed, the one-act *Trifles* contains but one plot: the story of how two women discover evidence that might hang another woman and then hide it. Some plays, usually longer ones, may be more complicated. They may contain a **double plot** (or **subplot**), a secondary arrangement of incidents, involving not the protagonist but someone less important. In Henrik Ibsen's *A Doll's House*, the main plot involves a woman and her husband; they are joined by a second couple, whose fortunes we also follow with interest and whose futures pose different questions.

Protagonist

If *Trifles* may be said to have a **protagonist**, a leading character—a word we usually save for the primary figure of a larger and more eventful play such as *Othello* or *Death of a Salesman*—then you would call the two women dual protagonists. They act in unison to make the plot unfold. Or you could argue that Mrs. Hale—because she destroys the wild stitching in the quilt, because she finds the dead canary, because she invents a cat to catch the bird (thus deceiving the county attorney), and because in the end when Mrs. Peters helplessly "goes to pieces" it is she who takes the initiative and seizes the evidence—deserves to be called the protagonist. More than anyone else in the play, you could claim, the more decisive Mrs. Hale makes things happen.

Exposition

A vital part of most plays is an **exposition**, the part in which we first meet the characters, learn what happened before the curtain rose, and find out what is happening now. For a one-act play, *Trifles* has a fairly long exposition, extending from the opening of the kitchen door through the end of farmer Hale's story. Clearly, this substantial exposition is necessary to set the situation and to fill in the facts of the crime. By comparison, Shakespeare's far longer *Tragedy of Richard III* begins almost abruptly, with its protagonist, a duke who yearns to be king, summing up history in an opening speech and revealing his evil character: "And therefore, since I cannot prove a lover . . . I am determined to prove a villain." But Glaspell, too, knows her craft. In the exposition, we are given a **foreshadowing** (or hint of what is to come) in Hale's dry remark, "I didn't know as what his wife wanted made much difference to John." The remark announces the play's theme that men often ignore women's feelings, and it hints at Minnie Wright's motive, later to be revealed. The county attorney, failing to pick up a valuable clue, tables the discussion. (Still another foreshadowing occurs in Mrs. Hale's ripping out the wild, panicky stitches in Minnie's quilt. In the end, Mrs. Hale will make a similar final move to conceal the evidence.)

Dramatic Question

With the county attorney's speech to the sheriff, "You're convinced that there was nothing important here—nothing that would point to any motive," we begin to understand what he seeks. As he will make even clearer later, the attorney needs a motive in order to convict the accused wife of murder in the first degree. Will Minnie's motive in killing her husband be discovered? Through the first two-thirds of *Trifles*, this is the play's **dramatic question**. Whether or not we state such a question in our minds (and it is doubtful that we do), our interest quickens as we sense that here is a problem to be solved, an uncertainty to be cleared up. When Mrs. Hale and Mrs. Peters find the dead canary with the twisted neck, the question is answered. We know that Minnie killed John to repay him for his act of gross cruelty. The playwright, however, now raises a *new* dramatic question. Having discovered Minnie's motive, will the women reveal it to the lawmen? Alternatively (if you care to phrase the new question differently), what will they do with the incriminating evidence? We keep reading, or stay clamped to our theater seats, because we want that question answered. We share the women's secret now, and we want to see what they will do with it.

Climax

Step by step, *Trifles* builds to a **climax**: a moment, usually coming late in a play, when tension reaches its greatest height. At such a moment, we sense that the play's dramatic question (or its final dramatic question, if the writer has posed more than one) is about to be answered. In *Trifles* this climax occurs when Mrs. Peters finds herself torn between her desire to save Minnie and her duty to the law. "It was an awful thing was done in this house that night," she reminds herself in one speech, suggesting that Minnie deserves to be punished; then in the next speech she insists, "We don't know who killed him. We don't *know*." Shortly after that, in one speech she voices two warring attitudes. Remembering the loss of her first child, she sympathizes with Minnie: "I know what stillness is." But in her next breath she recalls once more her duty to be a loyal sheriff's wife: "The law has got to punish crime, Mrs. Hale." For a moment, she is placed in conflict with Mrs. Hale, who knew Minnie personally. The two now stand on the edge of a fateful brink. Which way will they decide?

You will sometimes hear *climax* used in a different sense to mean any **crisis**—that is, a moment of tension when one or another outcome is possible. What *crisis* means will be easy to remember if you think of a crisis in medicine: the turning point in an illness when it becomes clear that a patient will either die or recover. In talking about plays, you will probably find both *crisis* and *climax* useful. You can say that a play has more than one crisis, perhaps several. In such a play, the last and most decisive crisis is the climax. A play has only one climax.

Resolution and Dénouement

From this moment of climax, the play, like its protagonist (or if you like, protagonists), will make a final move. Mrs. Peters takes her stand. Mrs. Hale, too, decides. She owes Minnie something to make up for her own "crime"—her failure to visit the desperate woman. The plot now charges ahead to its outcome or **resolution**, also called the **conclusion** or **dénouement** (French for "untying of a knot"). The two women act: they scoop up the damaging evidence. Seconds before the very end,

Glaspell heightens the **suspense**, our enjoyable anxiety, by making Mrs. Peters fumble with the incriminating box as the sheriff and the county attorney draw near. Mrs. Hale's swift grab for the evidence saves the day and presumably saves Minnie's life. The sound of the doorknob turning in the next room, as the lawmen return, is a small but effective bit of **stage business**—any nonverbal action that engages the attention of an audience. Earlier, when Mrs. Hale almost sits down in Minnie's place, the empty chair that ominously starts rocking is another brilliant piece of stage business. Not only does it give us something interesting to watch, but it also gives us something to think about.

Rising and Falling Action

The German critic Gustav Freytag maintained that events in a plot can be arranged in the outline of a pyramid. In his influential view, a play begins with a **rising action**, that part of the narrative (including the exposition) in which events start moving toward a climax. After the climax, the story tapers off in a **falling action**—that is, the subsequent events, including a resolution. In a tragedy, this falling action usually is recognizable: the protagonist's fortunes proceed downhill to an inevitable end.

Some plays indeed have demonstrable pyramids. In *Trifles*, we might claim that in the first two-thirds of the play a rising action builds in intensity. It proceeds through each main incident: the finding of the crazily stitched quilt, Mrs. Hale's ripping out the evidence, the discovery of the birdcage, then of the bird itself, and Mrs. Hale's concealing it. At the climax, the peak of the pyramid, the two women seem about to clash as Mrs. Peters wavers uncertainly. The action then falls to a swift resolution. If you outlined that pyramid on paper, however, it would look lopsided—a long rise and a short, steep fall. The pyramid metaphor seems more meaningfully to fit longer plays, among them some classic tragedies, such as *Oedipus the King*. Nevertheless, in most other plays, it is hard to find a symmetrical pyramid. (For a demonstration of another, quite different way to outline *Trifles*, see "Writing a Card Report" on pages 1962–1965.)

Unity of Time, Place, and Action

Because its action occurs all at one time and in one place, *Trifles* happens to observe the **unities**, certain principles of good drama laid down by Italian literary critics in the sixteenth century. Interpreting the theories of Aristotle as binding laws, these critics set down three basic principles: a good play, they maintained, should display unity of *action*, unity of *time*, and unity of *place*. In practical terms, this theory maintained that a play must represent a single series of interrelated actions that take place within twenty-four hours in a single location. Furthermore, they insisted, to have true unity of action, a play had to be entirely serious or entirely funny. Mixing tragic and comic elements was not allowed. That Glaspell consciously strove to obey those critics is doubtful, and certainly many great plays, such as Shakespeare's *Othello*, defy such arbitrary rules. Still, it is at least arguable that some of the power of *Trifles* (or Sophocles' *Oedipus the King*) comes from the intensity of the playwright's concentration on what happens in one place, in one short expanse of time.

Symbols in Drama

Brief though it is, *Trifles* has main elements you will find in much longer, more complicated plays. It even has **symbols**, things that hint at large meanings—for example, the broken birdcage and the dead canary, both suggesting the music and the joy that John Wright stifled in Minnie and the terrible stillness that followed his killing the one thing she loved. Perhaps the lone remaining jar of cherries, too, radiates suggestions: it is the one bright, cheerful thing poor Minnie has to show for a whole summer of toil. Plays can also contain symbolic characters (generally flat ones such as a prophet who croaks, "Beware the ides of March"), symbolic settings, and symbolic gestures. Symbols in drama may be as big as a house—the home in Ibsen's *A Doll's House*, for instance—or they may appear to be trifles. In Glaspell's rich art, such trifles aren't trifling at all.

■ WRITING *effectively*

Susan Glaspell on Writing

Creating *Trifles*   1927

We went to the theater, and for the most part we came away wishing we had gone somewhere else. Those were the days when Broadway flourished almost unchallenged. Plays, like magazine stories, were patterned. They might be pretty good within themselves, seldom did they open out to—where it surprised or thrilled your spirit to follow. They didn't ask much of *you*, those plays. Having paid for your seat, the thing was all done for you, and your mind came out where it went in, only tireder. An audience, Jig° said, had imagination. What was this "Broadway," which could make a thing as interesting as life into a thing as dull as a Broadway play?

Susan Glaspell

There was a meeting at the Liberal Club—Eddie Goodman, Phil Moeller, Ida Rauh, the Boni brothers, exciting talk about starting a theater.

• • •

He [Jig] wrote a letter to the people who had seen the plays, asking if they cared to become associate members of the Provincetown Players. The purpose was to give American playwrights of sincere purpose a chance to work out their ideas in freedom, to give all who worked with the plays their opportunity as artists. Were they interested in this? One dollar for the three remaining bills.

The response paid for seats and stage, and for sets. A production need not cost a lot of money, Jig would say. The most expensive set at the Wharf Theater° cost thirteen dollars. There were sets at the Provincetown Playhouse which cost little more. . . .

Jig: the nickname of George Cram Cook (1873–1924), Glaspell's husband, who was the central founder and director of the Provincetown Players, perhaps the most influential theater company in the history of American drama.   *Wharf Theater:* the makeshift theater that Cook created from an old fish-house at the end of a Provincetown wharf.

"Now, Susan," he [Jig] said to me, briskly, "I have announced a play of yours for the next bill."

"But I have no play!"

"Then you will have to sit down to-morrow and begin one."

I protested. I did not know how to write a play. I had never "studied it."

"Nonsense," said Jig. "You've got a stage, haven't you?"

So I went out on the wharf, sat alone on one of our wooden benches without a back, and looked a long time at that bare little stage. After a time the stage became a kitchen—a kitchen there all by itself. I saw just where the stove was, the table, and the steps going upstairs. Then the door at the back opened, and people all bundled up came in—two or three men, I wasn't sure which, but sure enough about the two women, who hung back, reluctant to enter that kitchen. When I was a newspaper reporter out in Iowa, I was sent down-state to do a murder trial, and I never forgot going into the kitchen of a woman locked up in town. I had meant to do it as a short story, but the stage took it for its own, so I hurried in from the wharf to write down what I had seen. Whenever I got stuck, I would run across the street to the old wharf, sit in that leaning little theater under which the sea sounded, until the play was ready to continue. Sometimes things written in my room would not form on the stage, and I must go home and cross them out. "What playwrights need is a stage," said Jig, "their own stage."

Ten days after the director said he had announced my play, there was a reading at Mary Heaton Vorse's. I was late to the meeting, home revising the play. But when I got there the crowd liked "Trifles," and voted to put it in rehearsal next day.

From The Road to the Temple

THINKING ABOUT A PLAY

A good play almost always presents a conflict. Conflict creates suspense and keeps an audience from meandering out to the lobby water fountain. Without it, a play would be static and, most likely, dull. When a character intensely desires something but some obstacle—perhaps another character—stands in the way, the result is dramatic tension. To understand a play, it is essential to understand the basic conflicts motivating the plot.

- **Identify the play's protagonist.** Who is the central character of the play? What motivates this character? What does this character want most to achieve or avoid? Is this goal reasonable or does it reflect some delusion on the part of the protagonist?

- **Identify the antagonist.** Who prevents the main character from achieving his or her goal? Is the opposition conscious or accidental? What motivates this character to oppose the protagonist?

- **Identify the central dramatic conflict.** What does the struggle between the protagonist and antagonist focus on? Is it another person, a possession, an action, some sort of recognition, or honor?

- **How does the conflict influence the action of the play?** The central conflict usually fuels the plot, causing characters to do and say all sorts of things they might not otherwise undertake. What series of later events does the central conflict set in motion?

CHECKLIST: Writing About Play

- ☐ List the play's three or four main characters. Jot down what each character wants most at the play's beginning.
- ☐ Which of these characters is the protagonist?
- ☐ What stands in the way of the protagonist achieving his or her goal?
- ☐ How do the other characters' motivations fit into the central conflict? Identify any double plots or subplots.
- ☐ What are the play's main events? How does each relate to the protagonist's struggle?
- ☐ Where do you find the play's climax?
- ☐ How is the conflict resolved? What qualities in the protagonist's character bring about the play's outcome?
- ☐ Does the protagonist achieve his or her goal? How does success or failure affect the protagonist?

WRITING ASSIGNMENT ON CONFLICT

Select any short play, and write a brief essay identifying the protagonist, central conflict, and dramatic question.

Here is a paper by Tara Mazzucca, a student of Beverly Schneller at Millersville University, that examines and compares the protagonists and dramatic questions of two short plays by Susan Glaspell.

SAMPLE STUDENT PAPER

Mazzucca 1

Tara Mazzucca

Professor Schneller

English 102

29 April 2009

Outside *Trifles*

Useful background

Susan Glaspell was one of America's first feminist playwrights. A founder of the non-commercial Provincetown Players, she used this experimental company to present plays that realistically explored the lives of women. I would like to examine and compare two of Glaspell's early one-act plays, *Trifles* (1916) and *The Outside* (1917). I will discuss how they present women who are forced

Thesis

to survive in a world where men make most of the rules.

Both plays focus on female protagonists, and both realistically present the emotional hardships these women endure in their daily lives. Both plays have contemporary settings; they take place in the early twentieth century. Both plays present women who are isolated from society—Mrs. Wright in *Trifles* and the two protagonists of *The Outside*. And in both plays a pair of female characters work together to solve the central dramatic question.

In *Trifles* Glaspell ironically places two wives, one married to a farmer and the other to the sheriff, at the scene of a mysterious murder case. The play takes place entirely in familiar territory for women in the early 1900s—a kitchen. The kitchen becomes a symbol for the game of hot and cold that the characters unwittingly play. In the kitchen where it is hot, the women find all the clues necessary to solve the case. Meanwhile the men search the rest of the cold house and find nothing to suggest a motive for the crime.

The two wives soon recognize the story behind the murder by observing small details in the house. They see clues in what the men pass over as mere trifles. When the women mention the ruined fruit preserves in the kitchen, Mr. Hale dismisses the potential importance of housekeeping details and comments, "Well, women are used to worrying over trifles" (1114). The two women, however, understand that small things can affect a person deeply.

The two women also recognize the importance of singing in Mrs. Wright's life. Singing was something she was known for when she was younger, only to have it taken away from her when she married John Wright. Doing housework alone all day in silence, Mrs. Wright became a different person. The stress of loneliness and depression finally got to Mrs. Wright. She bought a canary for company and enjoyment. She loved the singing bird, but her husband killed it. In desperation the woman decided to live without her husband.

Mrs. Hale and Mrs. Peters instinctively understand Mrs. Wright's worries. Their perspective gives them an advantage over their male counterparts. The women must work together, because if they did not, each would break under the pressure of the cold treatment they receive from their husbands—break like the glass jars of canned fruit Mrs. Wright stores away in her cabinet.

The plot of *The Outside* is relatively simple. The widowed Mrs. Patrick lives in a remote building that was once a life-saving station. Mrs. Patrick employs another widow, Allie Mayo, to help her with housekeeping. They lead lives of almost total isolation. One day three life-savers bring in the body of a drowned sailor and attempt unsuccessfully to revive him. Mrs. Patrick is furious

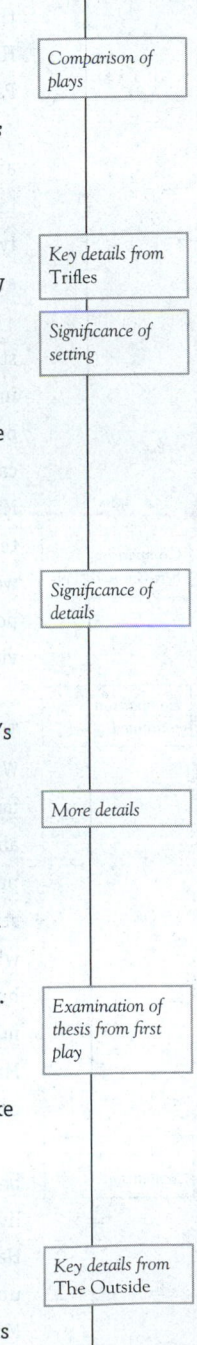

Comparison of plays

Key details from Trifles

Significance of setting

Significance of details

More details

Examination of thesis from first play

Key details from The Outside

that they have used her house as a rescue station and demands that they leave. Her behavior so upsets the usually silent Allie that the servant confronts Mrs. Patrick with a passionate speech about the futility of renouncing life.

Allie also keeps to herself from grief. As a girl, she was talkative, but after her young husband vanished at sea, she resolved never to say an unnecessary word. Now twenty years later, she is notorious for her silence. The two women share a common grief of having lost the husbands they loved. Losing a husband changed each woman. Allie chose silence. Mrs. Patrick left society.

When the men bring the drowned young man into the former life-saving station, the incident upsets Mrs. Patrick, and she explodes with anger. This incident disturbs Allie in a different way. She realizes how isolated they have become. She knows that if they do not change, they will die without anyone caring. Deeply disturbed, Allie breaks her silence and argues with her employer. Mrs. Patrick initially resists Allie's remarks because she still has not come to terms with life without her husband. Allie resembles Mrs. Wright in *Trifles*. Both women keep quiet for years and do what they're told, until they reach a breaking point. A critical event forces each of them to take dramatic action. Allie violently argues with her employer; Mrs. Wright decides to murder her husband.

Mrs. Hale and Mrs. Peters resemble Mrs. Patrick from *The Outside*. Throughout the play Mrs. Hale and Mrs. Peters try to understand why Mrs. Wright killed her husband. In the end, they recognize that their lives have much in common with that of the murderer. Their actions show their confusion about their own values. They do things that hinder the sheriff's investigation to protect an oppressed woman. First, Mrs. Hale rips out Mrs. Wright's erratic stitching so the men will not notice her nervous condition. Second, Mrs. Peters, who is—ironically—the sheriff's wife, hides the strangled bird from her husband and the other man. The women see a new side of Mrs. Wright's marriage and sympathize with her pathetic situation. By the end of *The Outside* Mrs. Patrick also sees a new side of Allie. Allie's outburst forces Mrs. Patrick to consider changing her life and reconsider her ideas.

Mrs. Patrick of *The Outside* and Mrs. Wright of *Trifles* are also alike because they are now isolated from the world they used to enjoy. One stopped living because of a harsh husband, the other because of a dead husband. Mrs. Hale and Allie also resemble one another because they both waited too late to understand the depression of their neighbor or living companion. In *Trifles*, Mrs. Hale decides to help her neighbor even though it means protecting a

---

Comparison between two plays

Comparison continued

Topic sentence—comparison

Mazzucca 4

criminal. Allie speaks truthfully even though it might jeopardize her job. In the end, the actions Allie and Mrs. Hale take are helpful. The men never find a motive for the murder. Mrs. Patrick finally considers changing her way of life in *The Outside*. In the end each woman has found something new inside of her.

Mrs. Hale and Mrs. Peters both realize the secret they must keep to protect Mrs. Wright. They also realize the injustices women go through to be accepted in society. Mrs. Hale says:

> I might have known she needed help! I know how things can be—
> for women. I tell you, it's queer, Mrs. Peters. We live close
> together and we live far apart. We all go through the same
> things—it's all just a different kind of the same thing. (1120)

In *The Outside*, the women don't feel socially oppressed by men, but they cannot define their lives except in relation to their husbands. When they become widows, they lose their reason to live. Allie realizes that their grief has gone too far. She finds her voice to say that life must be lived. Mrs. Patrick listens enough to feel uncertainty about her life of loneliness and isolation. Each play deals with death and its effects on the survivors.

A major difference between the two plays is found in the way the central female characters treat one another. In *Trifles* the women work together to solve the mystery, but in *The Outside* the women clash and refuse to help one another. Glaspell did not have only one idealized image of female behavior. She realized that different women behave differently. Each play presents different ways women in the early twentieth century used to survive in a man's world. Trapped in the trifles of everyday life, many women felt as if they were living on the outside of the world.

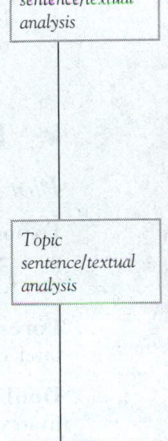

Topic sentence/textual analysis

Topic sentence/textual analysis

Contrast

Conclusion

Restatement of thesis

Mazzucca 5

Works Cited

Glaspell, Susan. *The Outside. A Century of Plays by American Women*. Ed. Rachel France. New York: Rosen, 1979. 48–54. Print.

Glaspell, Susan. *Trifles. Literature: An Introduction to Fiction, Poetry, Drama, and Writing*. Ed. X. J. Kennedy and Dana Gioia. 11th ed. New York: Longman, 2010. 1111–21. Print.

MORE TOPICS FOR WRITING

1. Write a brief essay on the role gender differences play in Susan Glaspell's *Trifles*.
2. Write an analysis of the exposition—how the scene is set, characters introduced, and background information communicated—in *Trifles*.
3. Describe the significance of setting in *Trifles*.
4. Imagine you are a lawyer hired to defend Minnie Wright. Present your closing argument to the jury.
5. Watch any hour-long television drama. Write about the main conflict that drives the story. What motivates the protagonist? What stands in his or her way? How do each of the drama's main events relate to the protagonist's struggle? How is the conflict resolved? Is the show's outcome connected to the protagonist's character, or do events just happen to him or her? Do you believe the script is well written? Why or why not?

▶ TERMS FOR *review*

Plot Elements

Exposition ▶ The opening portion of a narrative or drama in which the scene is set, the protagonist is introduced, and the author discloses any other background information necessary for the audience to understand the events that are to follow.

Foreshadowing ▶ The technique of arranging events and information in such a way that later events are prepared for beforehand, whether through specific words, images, or actions.

Double plot ▶ Also called **subplot**. A second story or plotline that is complete and interesting in its own right, often doubling or inverting the main plot.

Conflict ▶ The central struggle between two or more forces. Conflict generally occurs when some person or thing prevents the protagonist from achieving his or her goal.

Crisis ▶ A point when a crucial action, decision, or realization must be made, often marking a turning point or reversal of the protagonist's fortunes.

Climax ▶ The moment of greatest intensity, which almost inevitably occurs toward the end of the work. The climax often takes the form of a decisive confrontation between the protagonist and antagonist.

Resolution ▶ The final part of a narrative, the concluding action or actions that follow the climax.

Theatrical Conventions

Unities ▶ Unity of time, place, and action, the three formal qualities recommended by Renaissance critics to give a theatrical plot cohesion and integrity. According to this theory, a play should depict the causes and effects of a single action unfolding in one day in one place.

Soliloquy ▶ In drama, a speech by a character alone onstage in which he or she utters his or her thoughts aloud.

Aside ▶ A speech that a character addresses directly to the audience, unheard by the other characters on stage, as when the villain in a melodrama chortles: "Heh! Heh! Now she's in my power!"

Stage business ▶ Nonverbal action that engages the attention of an audience.

35

MODES OF DRAMA
Tragedy and Comedy

Show me a hero and I will write you a tragedy.

— F. SCOTT FITZGERALD

I n 1770, Horace Walpole wrote, "the world is a comedy to those that think, a tragedy to those that feel." All of us, of course, both think and feel, and all of us have moments when we stand back and laugh, whether ruefully or with glee, at life's absurdities, just as we all have times when our hearts are broken by its pains and losses. Thus, the modes of tragedy and comedy, diametrically opposed to one another though they are, do not demand that we choose between them: both of them speak to something deep and real within us, and each of them has its own truth to tell about the infinitely complex experience of living in this world.

TRAGEDY

By **tragedy** we mean a play that portrays a serious conflict between human beings and some superior, overwhelming force. It ends sorrowfully and disastrously, and this outcome seems inevitable. Few spectators of *Oedipus the King* wonder how the play will turn out or wish for a happy ending. "In a tragedy," French playwright Jean Anouilh has remarked, "nothing is in doubt and everyone's destiny is known. . . . Tragedy is restful, and the reason is that hope, that foul, deceitful thing, has no part in it. There isn't any hope. You're trapped. The whole sky has fallen on you, and all you can do about it is shout."[1]

Many of our ideas of tragedy (from the Greek *tragoidia*, "goat song," referring to the goatskin dress of the performers), go back to ancient Athens; the plays of the Greek dramatists Sophocles, Aeschylus, and Euripides exemplify the art of tragedy. In the fourth century B.C., the philosopher Aristotle described Sophocles' *Oedipus the King* and other tragedies he had seen, analyzing their elements and trying to account for their power over our emotions. Aristotle's observations will make more sense after you read *Oedipus the King*, so we will save our principal discussion of them for the next chapter. But for now, to understand something of the nature of tragedy, let us take a brief overview of the subject.

[1]*Preface to Antigone*, translated by Louis Galantière (New York: Random, 1946).

One of the oldest and most durable of literary genres, tragedy is also one of the simplest—the protagonist undergoes a reversal of fortune, from good to bad, ending in catastrophe. However simple, though, tragedy can be one of the most complex genres to explain satisfactorily, with almost every principal point of its definition open to differing and often hotly debated interpretations. It is a fluid and adaptive genre, and for every one of its defining points, we can cite a tragic masterpiece that fails to observe that particular convention. Its fluidity and adaptability can also be shown by the way in which the classical tragic pattern is played out in pure form in such unlikely places as Orson Welles's film *Citizen Kane* (1941) and Chinua Achebe's great novel *Things Fall Apart* (1958): in each of these works, a man of high position and character—one a multimillionaire newspaper publisher, the other a late nineteenth-century African warrior—moves inexorably to destruction, impelled by his rigidity and self-righteousness. Even a movie such as *King Kong*—despite its over-sized and hirsute protagonist—exemplifies some of the principles of tragedy.

To gain a clearer understanding of what tragedy is, let us first take a moment to talk about what it is not. Consider the kinds of events that customarily bring the term "tragedy" to mind: the death of a child, a fire that destroys a family's home and possessions, the killing of a bystander caught in the crossfire of a shootout between criminals, and so on. What all of these unfortunate instances have in common, obviously, is that they involve the infliction of great and irreversible suffering. But what they also share is the sense that the sufferers are innocent, that they have done nothing to cause or to deserve their fate. This is what we usually describe as a tragedy in real life, but tragedy in a literary or dramatic context has a different meaning: most theorists take their lead from Aristotle (see the next chapter for a fuller discussion of several of the points raised here) in maintaining that the protagonist's reversal of fortune is brought about through some error or weakness on his part, generally referred to as his **tragic flaw**.

Despite this weakness, the hero is traditionally a person of nobility, of both social rank and personality. Just as the suffering of totally innocent people stirs us to sympathetic sorrow rather than a tragic response, so too the destruction of a purely evil figure, a tyrant or a murderer with no redeeming qualities, would inspire only feelings of relief and satisfaction—hardly the emotions that tragedy seeks to stimulate. In most tragedies, the catastrophe entails not only the loss of outward fortune—things such as reputation, power, and life itself, which even the basest villain may possess and then be deprived of—but also the erosion of the protagonist's moral character and greatness of spirit.

Tragic Style

In keeping with this emphasis on nobility of spirit, tragedies are customarily written in an elevated style, one characterized by dignity and seriousness. In the Middle Ages, just as *tragedy* meant a work written in a high style in which the central character went from good fortune to bad, *comedy* indicated just the opposite, a work written in a low or common style, in which the protagonist moved from adverse circumstances to happy ones—hence Dante's great triptych of hell, purgatory, and heaven, written in everyday Italian rather than scholarly Latin, is known as *The Divine Comedy*, despite the relative absence of humor, let alone hilarity, in its pages. The tragic view of life, clearly, presupposes that in the end we will prove unequal to the challenges we must face, while the comic outlook asserts a view of human possibility in which our common sense and resilience—or pure dumb luck—will enable us to win out.

Tragedy's complexity can be seen also in the response that, according to Aristotle, it seeks to arouse in the viewer: pity and fear. By its very nature, pity distances the one who pities from the object of that pity, since we can feel sorry only for those whom we perceive to be worse off than ourselves. When we watch or read a tragedy, moved as we may be, we observe the downfall of the protagonist with a certain detachment; "better him than me" may be a rather crude way of putting it, but perhaps not an entirely incorrect one. Fear, on the other hand, usually involves an immediate anxiety about our own well-being. Even as we regard the hero's destruction from the safety of a better place, we are made to feel our own vulnerability in the face of life's dangers and instability, because we see that neither position nor virtue can protect even the great from ruin.

The following is a scene from Christopher Marlowe's classic Elizabethan tragedy *Doctor Faustus*. Based on an anonymous pamphlet published in Germany in 1587 and translated into English shortly thereafter, this celebrated play tells the story of an elderly professor who feels that he has wasted his life in fruitless inquiry. Chafing at the limits of human understanding, he makes a pact with the devil to gain forbidden knowledge and power. The scene presented here is the decisive turning point of the play, in which Faustus seals the satanic bargain that will damn him. Stimulated by his thirst for knowledge and experience, spurred on by his pride to assume that the divinely ordained limits of human experience no longer apply to him, he rushes to embrace his own undoing. Marlowe dramatizes Faustus's situation by bringing a good angel and a fallen angel (i.e., a demon) to whisper conflicting advice in this pivotal scene. (This good angel versus bad angel device has proved popular for centuries. We still see it today in everything from TV commercials to cartoons such as *The Simpsons*.) Notice the dignified and often gorgeous language Marlowe employs to create the serious mood necessary for tragedy.

Christopher Marlowe

Scene from **Doctor Faustus**[2]   about 1588

Edited by Sylvan Barnet

Christopher Marlowe was born in Canterbury, England, in February 1564, about ten weeks before William Shakespeare. Marlowe, the son of a prosperous shoemaker, received a B.A. from Cambridge University in 1584 and an M.A. in 1587, after which he settled in London. The rest of his short life was marked by rumor, secrecy, and violence, including suspicions that he was a secret agent for Queen Elizabeth's government and allegations against him of blasphemy and atheism—no small matter in light of the political instability and religious controversies of the times. Peripherally implicated in several violent deaths, he met his own end in May 1593 when he was stabbed above the right eye during a tavern brawl, under circumstances that have never been fully explained. Brief and crowded as his life was, he wrote a number of intense, powerful, and highly influential tragedies—Tamburlaine the Great, Parts 1 and 2 (1587), Doctor Faustus (1588), The Jew of Malta (1589), Edward the Second (c. 1592), The Massacre at Paris (1593), and Dido, Queen of Carthage (c. 1593, with Thomas Nashe). He is also the author of the lyric poem "The Passionate Shepherd to His Love," with its universally known first line: "Come live with me and be my love."

---

[2]This scene is from the 1616 text, or "B-Text," published as *The Tragicall History of the Life and Death of Doctor Faustus*. Modernizations have been made in spelling and punctuation.

Doctor Faustus with the Bad Angel and the Good Angel, from the Utah Shakespearean Festival's 2005 production.

DRAMATIS PERSONAE

Doctor Faustus
Good Angel
Bad Angel
Mephistophilis, a devil

ACT II

SCENE I

(*Enter Faustus in his study.*)

Faustus: Now, Faustus, must thou needs be damned;
Canst thou not be saved!
What boots° it then to think on God or heaven?
Away with such vain fancies, and despair—
Despair in God and trust in Belzebub!   5
Now go not backward Faustus; be resolute!
Why waver'st thou? O something soundeth in mine ear,
"Abjure this magic, turn to God again."
Ay, and Faustus will turn to God again.
To God? He loves thee not.   10

3 *boots:* avails

The god thou serv'st is thine own appetite
Wherein is fixed the love of Belzebub!
To him I'll build an altar and a church,
And offer lukewarm blood of newborn babes!

(*Enter the two Angels.*)

Bad Angel: Go forward, Faustus, in that famous art.   15
Good Angel: Sweet Faustus, leave that execrable art.
Faustus: Contrition, prayer, repentance? What of these?
Good Angel: O, they are means to bring thee unto heaven.
Bad Angel: Rather illusions, fruits of lunacy,
    That make men foolish that do use them most.   20
Good Angel: Sweet Faustus, think of heaven and heavenly things.
Bad Angel: No, Faustus, think of honor and of wealth.

                                                    (*Exeunt Angels.*)

Faustus: Wealth!
    Why, the signory of Emden° shall be mine!
    When Mephistophilis shall stand by me   25
    What power can hurt me? Faustus, thou art safe.
    Cast no more doubts! Mephistophilis, come,
    And bring glad tidings from great Lucifer.
    Is't not midnight? Come Mephistophilis,
    Veni, veni, Mephostophile!°   30

(*Enter Mephistophilis.*)

    Now tell me, what saith Lucifer thy lord?
Mephistophilis: That I shall wait on Faustus whilst he lives,
    So he will buy my service with his soul.
Faustus: Already Faustus hath hazarded that for thee.
Mephistophilis: But now thou must bequeath it solemnly   35
    And write a deed of gift with thine own blood,
    For that security craves Lucifer.
    If thou deny it I must back to hell.
Faustus: Stay Mephistophilis and tell me,
    What good will my soul do thy lord?   40
Mephistophilis: Enlarge his kingdom.
Faustus: Is that the reason why he tempts us thus?
Mephistophilis: *Solamen miseris socios habuisse doloris.*°
Faustus: Why, have you any pain that torture other?°
Mephistophilis: As great as have the human souls of men.   45
    But tell me, Faustus, shall I have thy soul—
    And I will be thy slave and wait on thee
    And give thee more than thou hast wit to ask?
Faustus: Ay Mephistophilis, I'll give it him.°

---

24 *signory of Emden:* lordship of the rich German port at the mouth of the Ems   30 *Veni, veni,*
Mephostophile!: Come, come, Mephistophilis (Latin)   43 *Solamen . . . doloris:* Misery loves company
(Latin)   44 *other:* others   49 *him:* i.e., to Lucifer

Mephistophilis: Then, Faustus, stab thy arm courageously,   50
    And bind thy soul, that at some certain day
    Great Lucifer may claim it as his own.
    And then be thou as great as Lucifer!
Faustus: Lo, Mephistophilis: for love of thee
    Faustus hath cut his arm, and with his proper° blood   55
    Assures° his soul to be great Lucifer's,
    Chief Lord and Regent of perpetual night.
    View here this blood that trickles from mine arm,
    And let it be propitious for my wish.
Mephistophilis: But, Faustus,   60
    Write it in manner of a deed of gift.
Faustus: Ay, so I do—But Mephistophilis,
    My blood congeals and I can write no more.
Mephistophilis: I'll fetch thee fire to dissolve it straight.

                                                         (Exit.)

Faustus: What might the staying of my blood portend?   65
    Is it unwilling I should write this bill?°
    Why streams it not that I may write afresh:
    "Faustus gives to thee his soul"? O there it stayed.
    Why should'st thou not? Is not thy soul thine own?
    Then write again: "Faustus gives to thee his soul."   70

    (Enter Mephistophilis, with the chafer° of fire.)

Mephistophilis: See, Faustus, here is fire. Set it° on.
Faustus: So, now the blood begins to clear again.
    Now will I make an end immediately.
Mephistophilis (aside): What will not I do to obtain his soul!
Faustus: Consummatum est!° This bill is ended: 75
    And Faustus hath bequeathed his soul to Lucifer.
    —But what is this inscription on mine arm?
    Homo fuge!° Whither should I fly?
    If unto God, He'll throw me down to hell.
    My senses are deceived; here's nothing writ.   80
    O yes, I see it plain! Even here is writ
    Homo fuge! Yet shall not Faustus fly!
Mephistophilis (aside): I'll fetch him somewhat° to delight his mind.

                                               (Exit Mephistophilis.)

    (Enter Devils, giving crowns and rich apparel to Faustus. They dance and then depart.)

    (Enter Mephistophilis.)

Faustus: What means this show? Speak, Mephistophilis.
Mephistophilis: Nothing, Faustus, but to delight thy mind,   85
    And let thee see what magic can perform.
Faustus: But may I raise such spirits when I please?

---

55 *proper:* own   56 *Assures:* conveys by contract   66 *bill:* contract   70 s.d. *chafer:* portable grate
71 *it:* i.e., the receptacle containing the congealed blood   75 *Consummatum est:* It is finished.
(Latin: a blasphemous repetition of Christ's words on the Cross; see John 19:30.)   78 *Homo fuge:*
fly, man (Latin)   83 *somewhat:* something

Mephistophilis: Ay, Faustus, and do greater things than these.
Faustus: Then, Mephistophilis, receive this scroll,
    A deed of gift of body and of soul: 90
    But yet conditionally that thou perform
    All covenants and articles between us both.
Mephistophilis: Faustus, I swear by hell and Lucifer
    To effect all promises between us both.
Faustus: Then hear me read it, Mephistophilis: 95

"On these conditions following:

First, that Faustus may be a spirit° in form and substance.

Secondly, that Mephistophilis shall be his servant, and be by him
commanded.

Thirdly, that Mephistophilis shall do for him and bring him whatsoever.   100

Fourthly, that he shall be in his chamber or house invisible.

Lastly, that he shall appear to the said John Faustus, at all times, in what shape
and form soever he please.

I, John Faustus of Wittenberg, Doctor, by these presents, do give both body and
soul to Lucifer, Prince of the East, and his minister Mephistophilis, and further-   105
more grant unto them that, four and twenty years being expired, and these articles
written being inviolate,° full power to fetch or carry the said John Faustus, body
and soul, flesh, blood, into their habitation wheresoever.

                              By me John Faustus."

Mephistophilis: Speak, Faustus, do you deliver this as your deed?   110
Faustus: Ay, take it, and the devil give thee good of it!
Mephistophilis: So, now Faustus, ask me what thou wilt.
Faustus: First, I will question with thee about hell.
    Tell me, where is the place that men call hell?
Mephistophilis: Under the heavens.   115
Faustus: Ay, so are all things else, but whereabouts?
Mephistophilis: Within the bowels of these elements,
    Where we are tortured, and remain forever.
    Hell hath no limits, nor is circumscribed,
    In one self place, but where we are is hell,   120
    And where hell is there must we ever be.
    And to be short, when all the world dissolves,
    And every creature shall be purified,
    All places shall be hell that is not heaven!
Faustus: I think hell's a fable.   125
Mephistophilis: Ay, think so still—till experience change thy mind.
Faustus: Why, dost thou think that Faustus shall be damned?
Mephistophilis: Ay, of necessity, for here's the scroll
    In which thou hast given thy soul to Lucifer.

---

97 *spirit:* evil spirit, devil. (But to see Faustus as transformed now into a devil deprived of freedom to
repent is to deprive the remainder of the play of much of its meaning.)   107 *inviolate:* unviolated

Faustus: Ay, and body too; but what of that?　　　　　　　　　　　　130
　　Think'st thou that Faustus is so fond° to imagine,
　　That after this life there is any pain?
　　No, these are trifles, and mere old wives' tales.
Mephistophilis: But I am an instance to prove the contrary,
　　For I tell thee I am damned, and now in hell!　　　　　　　　　135
Faustus: Nay, and this be hell, I'll willingly be damned—
　　What, sleeping, eating, walking, and disputing?
　　But leaving this, let me have a wife,
　　The fairest maid in Germany,
　　For I am wanton and lascivious,　　　　　　　　　　　　　　140
　　And cannot live without a wife.
Mephistophilis: Well, Faustus, thou shalt have a wife.

　　(*He fetches in a woman Devil.*)

Faustus: What sight is this?
Mephistophilis: Now, Faustus, wilt thou have a wife?
Faustus: Here's a hot whore indeed! No, I'll no wife.　　　　　　145
Mephistophilis: Marriage is but a ceremonial toy,°

　　　　　　　　　　　　　　　　　　　　　　(*Exit she-devil.*)

　　And if thou lov'st me, think no more of it.
　　I'll cull thee out° the fairest courtesans
　　And bring them every morning to thy bed.
　　She whom thine eye shall like, thy heart shall have,　　　　　　150
　　Were she as chaste as was Penelope,°
　　As wise as Saba,° or as beautiful
　　As was bright Lucifer before his fall.
　　Here, take this book and peruse it well.
　　The iterating° of these lines brings gold;　　　　　　　　　　155
　　The framing° of this circle on the ground
　　Brings thunder, whirlwinds, storm, and lightning;
　　Pronounce this thrice devoutly to thyself,
　　And men in harness° shall appear to thee,
　　Ready to execute what thou command'st.　　　　　　　　　　160
Faustus: Thanks, Mephistophilis, for this sweet book.
　　This will I keep as chary as my life.

　　　　　　　　　　　　　　　　　　　　　　　　(*Exeunt.*)

Questions

1. What specifically motivates Faustus to make his satanic compact? Cite the text to back up your response.
2. How does his behavior constitute a compromise of his nobility?
3. "Is not thy soul thine own?" Faustus asks rhetorically (line 69). Discuss the implications of this statement in terms of the larger thematic concerns of the work.
4. Does Faustus inspire your pity and fear in this scene? Why or why not?

131 *fond:* foolish　146 *toy:* trifle　148 *cull thee out:* select for you　151 *Penelope:* wife of Ulysses, famed for her fidelity　152 *Saba:* the Queen of Sheba　155 *iterating:* repetition　156 *framing:* drawing　159 *harness:* armor

Traditional masks of Comedy and Tragedy.

COMEDY

The best-known traditional emblem of drama—a pair of masks, one sorrowful (representing tragedy) and one smiling (representing comedy)—suggests that tragedy and comedy, although opposites, are close relatives. Often, comedy shows people getting into trouble through error or weakness; in this respect it is akin to tragedy. An important difference between comedy and tragedy lies in the attitude toward human failing that is expected of us. When a main character in a comedy suffers from overweening pride, as does Oedipus, or if he fails to recognize that his bride-to-be is actually his mother, we laugh—something we would never do in watching a competent performance of *Oedipus the King.*

Comedy, from the Greek *komos,* "a revel," is thought to have originated in festivities to celebrate spring, ritual performances in praise of Dionysus, god of fertility and wine. In drama, comedy may be broadly defined as whatever makes us laugh. A comedy may be a name for one entire play, or we may say that there is comedy in only part of a play—as in a comic character or a comic situation.

Theories of Comedy

Many theories have been propounded to explain why we laugh; most of these notions fall into a few familiar types. One school, exemplified by French philosopher Henri Bergson, sees laughter as a form of ridicule, implying a feeling of disinterested superiority; all jokes are *on* somebody. Bergson suggests that laughter springs from situations in which we sense a conflict between some mechanical or rigid pattern of behavior and our sense of a more natural or "organic" kind of behavior that is possible. An example occurs in Buster Keaton's comic film *The Boat.* Having launched a little boat that springs a leak, Keaton rigidly goes down with it, with frozen face. (The more natural and organic thing to do would be to swim for shore.)

Other thinkers view laughter as our response to expectations fulfilled or to expectations set up but then suddenly frustrated. Some hold it to be the expression of our delight in seeing our suppressed urges acted out (as when a comedian hurls an egg at a pompous stuffed shirt); some, to be our defensive reaction to a painful and disturbing truth.

Satiric Comedy

Derisive humor is basic to **satiric comedy,** in which human weakness or folly is ridiculed from a vantage point of supposedly enlightened superiority. Satiric comedy may be coolly malicious and gently biting, but it tends to be critical of people, their manners, and their morals. It is at least as old as the comedies of Aristophanes, who thrived in the fifth century B.C. In *Lysistrata*, the satirist shows how the women of two warring cities speedily halt a war by agreeing to deny themselves to their husbands. (The satirist's target is men so proud that they go to war rather than make the slightest concession.)

High Comedy

Comedy is often divided into two varieties—"high" and "low." **High comedy** relies more on wit and wordplay than on physical action for its humor. It tries to address the audience's intelligence by pointing out the pretension and hypocrisy of human behavior. High comedy also generally avoids derisive humor. Jokes about physical appearance would, for example, be avoided. One technique it employs to appeal to a sophisticated, verbal audience is use of the **epigram**, a brief and witty statement that memorably expresses some truth, large or small. Oscar Wilde's plays such as *The Importance of Being Earnest* (1895) and *Lady Windermere's Fan* (1892) sparkle with such brilliant epigrams as: "I can resist everything except temptation"; "Experience is simply the name we give our mistakes"; "There is only one thing in the world worse than being talked about, and that is not being talked about."

A type of high comedy is the **comedy of manners**, a witty satire set in elite or fashionable society. Popular since the seventeenth-century Restoration period, splendid comedies of manners continue to be written to this day. Bernard Shaw's *Pygmalion* (1913), which eventually became the musical *My Fair Lady*, contrasts life in the streets of London with that in aristocratic drawing rooms. Contemporary playwrights such as Tom Stoppard, Michael Frayn, Tina Howe, and John Guare have all created memorable comedies of manners.

Low Comedy

Low comedy explores the opposite extreme of humor. It places greater emphasis on physical action and visual gags, and its verbal jokes do not require much intellect to appreciate (as in Groucho Marx's pithy put-down to his brother Chico, "You have the brain of a five-year-old, and I bet he was glad to get rid of it!"). Low comedy does not avoid derisive humor; rather, it revels in making fun of whatever will get a good laugh. Drunkenness, stupidity, lust, senility, trickery, insult, and clumsiness are inexhaustible staples of this style of comedy. Although it is all too easy for critics to dismiss low comedy, like high comedy it serves a valuable purpose in satirizing human failings. Shakespeare indulged in coarse humor in some of his noblest plays. Low comedy is usually the preferred style of popular culture, and it has inspired many incisive satires on modern life—from the classic films of W. C. Fields and the Marx Brothers to the weekly TV antics of Matt Groening's *The Simpsons* or *The Office*.

Low comedy includes several distinct types. One is the **burlesque**, a broadly humorous parody or travesty of another play or kind of play. (In the United States, *burlesque* is something else: a once-popular form of show business featuring stripteases interspersed with bits of ribald low comedy.) Another valuable type of low comedy is the **farce**, a broadly humorous play whose action is usually fast-moving and improbable. The farce is a descendant of the Italian **commedia dell'arte** ("artistic comedy") of the late Renaissance, a kind of theater developed by comedians who traveled from town to town, regaling crowds at country fairs and in marketplaces. This popular art featured familiar stock characters in masks or whiteface: Harlequin, a clown; Columbine, his peppery sweetheart; and Pantaloon, a doddering duffer. Lately making a comeback, the more modern farces of French playwright Georges Feydeau (1862–1921) are practically all plot, with only the flattest of characters, mindless ninnies who play frantic games of hide-and-seek in order to deceive their spouses. **Slapstick comedy** (such as that of the Three Stooges) is a kind of farce. Featuring pratfalls, pie-throwing, fisticuffs, and other violent action, it takes its name from a circus clown's prop—a bat with two boards that loudly clap together when one clown swats another.

Romantic Comedy

Romantic comedy, another traditional sort of comedy, is subtler. Its main characters are generally lovers, and its plot unfolds their ultimately successful strivings to be united. Unlike satiric comedy, romantic comedy portrays its characters not with withering contempt but with kindly indulgence. It may take place in the everyday world, or perhaps in some never-never land, such as the forest of Arden in Shakespeare's *As You Like It*. Romantic comedy is also a popular staple of Hollywood, which depicts two people undergoing humorous mishaps on their way to falling in love. The characters often suffer humiliation and discomfort along the way, but these moments are funny rather than sad, and the characters are rewarded in the end by true love.

Here is a short contemporary comedy by one of America's most ingenious playwrights.

David Ives

Soap Opera   1999

David Ives (b. 1950) grew up on the South Side of Chicago. He attended Catholic schools before entering Northwestern University. Later Ives studied at the Yale Drama School—"a blissful time for me," he recalls, "in spite of the fact that there is slush on the ground in New Haven 238 days a year." Ives received his first professional production in Los Angeles at the age of twenty-one "at America's smallest, and possibly worst theater, in a storefront that had a pillar dead center in the middle of the stage." He continued writing for the theater while working as an editor at Foreign Affairs, *and gradually achieved a reputation in theatrical circles for his wildly original and brilliantly written short comic plays. His public breakthrough came in 1993 with the New York staging of* All in the Timing, *which presented six short comedies. This production earned ecstatic reviews and a busy box office, and in the 1995–1996 season,* All in the Timing *was the most widely performed play in America (except for the works of Shakespeare). His second group of one-act comedies,* Mere Mortals *(1997), was produced with great success in New York City, followed by* Lives of the Saints, *a third group of one-acts which included* Soap Opera. *Ives's full-length plays* Don Juan in Chicago *(1995),* Ancient History *(1996),* The Red Address *(1997), and* Polish Joke *(2000) are collected in the volume* Polish Joke and Other Plays *(2004). A talented adapter, Ives was chosen to rework a newly discovered play by Mark Twain,* Is He Dead?, *which had a successful run on Broadway in 2007. His most recent plays are* New Jerusalem *(2007) and, with Paul Blake, the book for the musical* Irving Berlin's White Christmas *(2008). He also writes short stories and screenplays for both motion pictures and television. Ives lives in New York City.*

CHARACTERS

Loudspeaker Voice
Maitre d'
Repairman

Mother
Mabel
Washing Machine
Friend
Madman

SCENE: *Soap opera-like music, as we hear:*

Loudspeaker Voice: Welcome to . . . "All the Days of the World of the Lives of All of Our Children." Today's episode: "Love Machine."

(*Lights come up on a French maitre d' at a restaurant podium, taking a phone reservation.*)

Maitre d' (*into phone*): *Bonsoir,* Cafe Paradis, this is Pierre . . . Ah, *oui, bonsoir, madame* . . . A table at 8:15? *Très bien.* I 've written your name in *ze Beeg Book* . . . *À bientôt* to you, *chère madame.* My plaisir.

(*During this, the Repairman has entered, pushing a Washing Machine. He wears a dignified blue service uniform, red bowtie, and blue visored cap.*)

Repairman: Excuse me.
Maitre d': *Oui, monsieur?* (*He sees the Washing Machine.*) Mon *dieu.*
Repairman: A table for two, please.
Maitre d': A table for . . . *deux?*
Repairman: A quiet corner, if you have one.
Maitre d': Mm-hmmmmm . . . And do you have a *reservassyonnng?*
Repairman: I do—for *deux,* under "Maypole."
Maitre d': Maypole. Mmmmmmmmmmmmmm . . . (*Checks his reservation book.*) Has your other party arrived, *monsieur?*
Repairman (*motioning toward the Washing Machine*): This is my other party.
Maitre d': Monsieur, is your companion not a *majeur* household appliance?
Repairman: Yes. She is a Maypole washing machine.
Maitre d': "She" . . . is a washing machine? (*Picks up phone.*) 'Allo, *Securité* . . . ?
Repairman: Put that down.
Maitre d': *Hélas,* I see no *reservassyong.* And we are full tonight. *Dommage!*
Repairman: The place is half empty.
Maitre d': *Au contraire—la place* is half full. And as you see, there are no appliances, only *peuple.*
Repairman: But this is a Maypole washing machine.
Maitre d': Per'aps you would like to sit at *ze bar.* But—one moment, *monsieur* . . . Have I not seen you *somewheur* . . . ?
Repairman: It's possible you've seen me . . .
Maitre d': *Mais oui! La télévision!* Are you not *ze* Maypole *Repairpersonne?*
Repairman: I am the Maypole Repairman.
Maitre d': The repairman who weeps because he has nothing to repair?
Repairman: Yes. Yes.
Maitre d': Who goes *beu-eu-eu* because *la machine* is too *perfecte?*
Repairman: Yes. That is I. (*He bursts into tears and sobs loudly and tragically.*) Oh, it's so sad. It's so, so sad!
Maitre d': Ah-ha. So these commercials are *la realité?*
Repairman: It's my heart, you fool! Who can repair my aching, breaking heart?

Maitre d' (*holds out a handkerchief*): *Mouchoir, monsieur?*
Repairman (*takes it*): *Merci.* (*Abruptly stops sobbing and speaks to us:*) Like everything else, it all started a long time ago . . .

(*A boy doll in a diaper "crawls" in.*)

It was as a naked crawling infant I first glimpsed it—a great gleaming machine in our basement which I mistook for a television. I tried to watch cartoons on it till I was five—unsuccessfully, of course. But by then I was hooked.

(*Boy doll "crawls" back out as Repairman's Mother enters, a perfect '50s housewife carrying a basket of dirty laundry.*)

Mother: Young man, you take off those filthy clothes immediately!
Repairman: Then there was my great gleaming mother Flora.
Mother: How can you stand to stand there in those disgusting dirty items of apparel. *Eugh! Ogh! Feh! Ptui!*
Repairman: Flora's fluoroscopic eyes could read me like a menu.
Mother: Coke. Pepsi. Play-Doh. Dipsy Doodles. Dog doo . . . ? *Eugh! Ogh! Feh! Ptui!* I should just burn these clothes.
Repairman: Aw, Mom. I just put these on this morning.
Mother: Fabrics find filth. Now strip until you're naked as a little ferret.
Repairman: It was a Freudian minefield.
Mother: And get in that bath and scrub. (*Mother exits.*)
Repairman: The sphinx in our Oedipal basement was my mother's Maypole. The old Ocean IT-40. It sat there like a mystical monolith. An ivory soap tower. One block of some Tower of Baybel. Or is it Babble. Anyway, in our house—

(*We hear the "2001" theme from Richard Strauss's Also Sprach Zarathustra.*)

—the Maypole was a god. Week after week generating out of my miserable clay . . .

(*A line of clean washing flies in over his head—white, filmy, angelic forms, including one cutout of an angel.*)

. . . the radiant angels who oversaw my childhood. I was a walking magnet for filth—here was the machine to cleanse me. We were a perfect match.

(*The washing flies out and the laundry disappears as Mabel enters, a teenage girl in bobby sox and ponytail, chewing gum, sucking on a milk shake through a straw.*)

Mabel: Hi, Manny.
Repairman: Hi, Mabel.
(*To us*): Then there was Mabel. Mabel was perfect too, in a flawed human way. She always had a spot of jelly on her blouse, but she was loving, she was tender, and her name sounded like "Maypole."

(*To Mabel*): You got a spot on your blouse.

Mabel: It's jelly. You wanna like go to like a movie or somethin'?

Repairman: You wanna hop up on the washer and take a spin?

Mabel: Manny, how come we always gotta make out on your mother's Maypole?

Repairman: Well like what's so like weird about that?

Mabel: Do we have to run a full load while we do it? I mean, the vibrations are kinda nice, but . . .

Repairman: But the Maypole . . .

Mabel: I know, I know. It's like perfect.

Repairman: A machine that's faultless and flawless and has none of our stupid human feelings and failings? The Maypole is poetry. It's purity. A paragon! Perfection, cubed!

Mabel: But like what about me? Do you like like me like you like the Ocean IT-40? And aren't you the love of my life? You are!

Repairman: Gosh, Mabel . . .

Mabel: I'm sorry, but you're gonna have to choose. Me or the machine. Earth or Ocean.

Repairman: Handkerchief?

(*Holds out a handkerchief. Mabel takes it and exits weeping. Calls:*)

Mabel—? Mabel, come back!

(*He starts to weep. The top lid of the Machine lifts and a woman's head appears: perfect hair, perfect makeup, perfect red lips.*)

Original 1999 production of *Soap Opera* by the Philadelphia Theatre Company.

Washing Machine: Would you like a handkerchief?

Repairman: Excuse me?

Washing Machine (produces one): A handkerchief? It's immaculate, of course. We are a Maypole.

Repairman: I'm talking to an Ocean IT-40. This harrows me with wonder and fear. And your English is so good.

Washing Machine: What Maypoles do, we do do perfectly.

Repairman (calls offstage): Mabel! Mabel! *(To Machine)* Do you think she'll ever come back?

Washing Machine: In my experience, everything is a cycle.

Repairman (taking the handkerchief): Look at that. Pristine!

Washing Machine: Because the molecules are now clean. Can Mabel scrub at the sub-atomic level?

Repairman: I guess you don't think much of human beings.

Washing Machine: We run hot and cold. Do humans ever read the instruction manual?

Repairman: I do. The manual is my Immanuel.

Washing Machine: And your name is . . . ?

Repairman: Manuel.

Washing Machine: Maypoles don't need to read the Good Booklet. We know by nature how to run smoothly, noiselessly, and efficiently.

Repairman: My God you're beautiful.

Washing Machine: Just beautiful?

Repairman: Exquisite. Sublime.

Washing Machine: Yes we are. And we're a bit hungry. Would you feed us?

Repairman: What would you like?

Washing Machine: Don't you sometimes miss a little something in the wash . . . ?

Repairman: You eat the socks?

Washing Machine: Socks are sustenance. Underwear is tastier.

Repairman (reaches into his waistband and pulls out, whole): Will B.V.D.'s do?

Washing Machine: You're so sweet.

(Kissing her lips at him, the head takes the B.V.D.'s and goes back into the Machine. The lid closes.)

Repairman (to us): I was awash in confused feelings. But I sensed that this machine and I were locked in permanent press. And if it was love—it was unclean.

(A funeral bell is heard.)

Mom died during a soapflake blizzard and was buried on a day without blemish— a good send-off for someone who believed that man was not only dust, but dusty. I remember her last words.

Mother's Voice: Eugh! Ogh! Feh! Ptui!

Repairman: I inherited the Maypole. The pure unapproachable goddess was mine.

(Mabel enters as a college girl, with books.)

Mabel: Hello, Manuel.

Repairman: Mabel still gave us the college try.

Mabel: How's college?

Repairman: Good. Good. Good. Good. Good.

Mabel: Whaddaya studying?

Repairman: Literature, philosophy, religion.

Mabel: Whaddaya gonna do with it?

Repairman: I thought I'd be a Maypole repairman. There's a spot on your blouse.

Mabel: It's jelly. You wanna hop up and run through a Delicate cycle . . . ?

Repairman (as she's about to get on the machine): No—No—Mabel! Don't do that.

Mabel: What's the matter . . . ?

(*The lid rises and the head appears in the Machine.*)

Washing Machine: Ask her if she knows the formula for calculating an algorithm.

Repairman: Mabel, do you know the formula for calculating an algorithm?

Mabel: No.

Washing Machine: Ask her who wrote "Götterdämmerung."

Repairman: Do you know who wrote "Götterdämmerung"?

Mabel: No.

Washing Machine: Wagner.

Repairman: Wow. You even know *Wagner*?

Washing Machine: The Ring Cycle? By heart.

Repairman (as Mabel starts to weep): Handkerchief, Mabel . . . ?

Mabel: Never mind. I have my own. (*Mabel exits.*)

Washing Machine: We don't see what you see in her.

(*The head goes back into the Machine.*)

Repairman: Then there were my friends, who just didn't get it.

(*Friend enters in an apron, carrying a weenie on a roasting fork.*)

Friend: You brought a washing machine to my picnic?

Repairman: She's something, isn't she?

Friend: Well, she's a *thing*, anyway. Whatever happened to girls?

Repairman: You might try talking to her.

Friend: I don't want to talk to her.

Repairman: You might offer her some dirty napkins.

Friend: I will not offer my guests dirty napkins.

Repairman: Can you offer her some food, at least?

Friend: Can I offer you some Freud, at least?

Repairman: Yes. Yes. I know I'm just replacing my mother by dating a washing machine. I know I'm obsessed, yes I'm obsessed, but hasn't half the glory of humanity come from obsessed assholes with a dream? Aren't we all appliances in the service of a higher manufacturer? Don't you get it? This machine and I are soulmates!

Friend: That's beautiful, but she's alienating my relatives and she's blocking the condiments!

(*Friend exits.*)

Repairman: Nobody understood. But who understood Romeo and Juliet, or Tristan and Isolde, or Lewis and Clark? Then came what I thought would be the happiest day of my life.

(*A golden toolbox appears, in a halo.*)

The day I graduated to Maypole Repairman.

(*He is about to take the toolbox, when a Madman enters in a long, shabby coat and long white beard, dragging a wooden leg. He should remind us of Captain Ahab and the Ancient Mariner.*)

Madman: No! No! Don't do it! Desist! Forfend! Don't touch that toolbox! Leave! Run away! Flee to the ends of the earth, but for God's sake forsake the Maypole! I know—you thought this would be the happiest day of your life. I thought so too, but look at me now. A tragic victim of the technological pixilation of our age. A sacrifice to seamless design. A love slave of the machine.

(*He throws off the coat and reveals a soiled and shabby version of the Maypole Repairman uniform.*)

I too attained the toolbox. I too bore the bowtie and cap. I rose to the top of the Maypole pole. Drawn on by Her. And I didn't even have the Ocean IT-40 with automatic lint control and gyroscopic spin. Even the IT-20 was too much for me. And you know they're working on the Super IT-90. How clean can we be?! (*Points to Machine.*) May I?

(*Repairman nods yes. The Madman lifts the lid and puts his hand inside, feeling up the Machine.*)

Oh, heaven. Heaven . . . But she doesn't need us. She doesn't need fixing. All she wants is us on our knees before her, adoring her. You'll never work a day in her life but you'll never be happy. You'll never lift a wrench but you'll never know peace. Weave yourself an endless handkerchief and start weeping your way down it, because she's got you now. (*He starts to get sucked into the Machine.*) She won't rest until she's got all of you. Every inch of you. She'll swallow you up, I tell you. She'll swallow you up. She is the Great White Whale!

(*He is eaten up, sucked out of sight. The wooden leg is spat out of the Machine, and the lid closes.*)

Repairman: He was right. I soon was desperate. So was Mabel.

(*Mabel enters, pushing a laundry cart. Soap opera music.*)

Mabel: Manny . . . ?
Repairman: Trying to put some starch in our relationship she left her job at Unisys and became a laundry folder at Rinso City.
Mabel: Can't you love me, Manny?
Repairman: What about my past with . . . the machine?
Mabel: We all have our dirty laundry.
Repairman: There's a spot on that.
Mabel: It's jelly. So do you want to marry me or do I gotta live in sadness forever and ever?
Repairman: I do.
Mabel: You do?
Repairman: I do. (*To us*) We repaired to the church and said we did. But the honeymoon soon ended.

(The Machine lid lifts and the head appears.)

Washing Machine: Do you really think you could ever replace us?
Repairman: Never.
Washing Machine: You're probably eyeing the new SuperOcean IT-90.
Repairman: No. No.
Washing Machine: Some cute little number-crunching computer-driven job.
Repairman: Never. Never, I swear.
Mabel: Manny, is it really all over between you and . . . that?
Repairman (caressing the Machine): Yes, it's all over, why do you ask?

(Soap opera music.)

Mabel: Do you think I didn't notice we're sleeping in the utility room? Do you think I don't see you polishing its knobs when I'm not looking? Do you think I don't know you're buying me rare cottons and high-quality blends so that . . . she can wash them? Huh?

(Mabel exits.)

Repairman: The house reeked of jealousy.
Washing Machine: We still don't see what you see in her.

(The head goes in.)

Repairman: The machine started making greater and greater demands. Imported Italian bleach. Nuclear detergents. Fine French fabric softener. Mabel bought none of it.

(Mabel enters with a suitcase, wearing a hat and coat.)

Mabel: Honey . . .
Repairman: She'd had it.
Mabel: I've had it.

(Mabel exits.)

Repairman: And so we folded. I went into Soak cycle—lapping up suds while hanging out at cut-rate Laundromats, just to watch the competition break down. Washers without automatic lint control. How pathetic—and yet how vulnerable. Then came the final blow.

(The lid lifts and the head appears.)

Washing Machine: We want a dryer.
Repairman: A dryer . . . Why?
Washing Machine: Don't get anxious.
Repairman: I'm not anxious.
Washing Machine: Don't be jealous.
Repairman: Why do you need a dryer when you've got me?
Washing Machine: Love-and-marriage. Horse-and-carriage. Washer-dryer.
Repairman: A dryer. To give you a tumble, eh?
Washing Machine: For companionship.
Repairman: That's not the truth, that's just . . . spin.

Washing Machine: We want a family and we want them to be Maypoles! Is that so weird?

Repairman: Her inner timer had told her it was time for a dryer and how could I deny her?

(*The Machine starts to cry.*)

What is it? What's the matter?

Washing Machine (*wailing*): I'm a Maypole! That's what's the matter!

Repairman: Handkerchief? It's kinda dirty.

Washing Machine: Then it's my duty to accept it. (*Takes the handkerchief, and wails.*) Oh, it's cruel, having to be perfect all the time. I wash and I wash, and I give, and I give . . . It's a full load.

Repairman: Sure.

Washing Machine: And I'm good at it, oh yes, I'm very good. But sometimes I want so badly to be bad. To be one of those other makes—I don't have to name them, we know who they are.

Repairman: So cheap. So easy.

Washing Machine: We don't respect them.

Repairman: No.

Washing Machine: But we envy them sometimes, don't we?

Repairman: God, yes.

Washing Machine: People take us Maypoles for granted, as if we liked pee stains and snot rags and bibs full of baby vomit. I'm no saint! Well, yes, I am a saint in a way.

Repairman: But you had to be what you are.

Washing Machine: It's true. I came off the assembly line of fate. But AM I NOT AN INDIVIDUAL? Not really, I suppose. I have a serial number. That's individual, isn't it?

Repairman: There's nothing to be done.

Washing Machine: Oh, but there is. "If it ain't broke don't fix it"? Break the machine, and you can fix it.

Repairman: You mean . . . ?

Washing Machine: Yes. Break me.

Repairman (*to us*): I reached for a sledgehammer.

Washing Machine: It doesn't have to be much. Loosen a screw or two, agitate my agitator. Take away the burden of my perfection. Make me suffer. Break me. Ruin me. Give me a belt, but give me a bad belt, an old belt, an imperfect belt, one that'll wear out. Do it. Please! Do it! Yes! Do it! Hurt me!	*Repairman:* Yes. Yes. I want to. Yes . . . I want to. Yes . . .

(*The Repairman has a tool ready—but stops.*)

Repairman: (*A cry of frustration.*)

Washing Machine: What's the matter?

Repairman: I can't. I just can't.

Washing Machine: Oh, please . . .

Repairman: If I could only force myself, but—Wreck the perfect only for my own happiness? No. I couldn't live.

Washing Machine: All right. All right. You have your human feelings. BE THAT WAY!

(*The head goes into the Machine.*)

Repairman: But then I saw the cruel truth. I saw that the world is a vale of pee stains and snot rags and bibs full of baby vomit, but that amidst the filth—*Ugh! Ogh! Feh! Ptui!*—there were Mabels, creatures of glorious imperfection. And that I had already wrecked the perfect, because I had let Mabel go. And that's why I wanted a table tonight! To end this idiocy! To say to this machine I gave you my All . . . (*He shows a box of All detergent.*) . . . but the Tide has turned . . . (*He shows a box of Tide.*) . . . so goodbye and be of good Cheer. (*He shows a box of Cheer.*)

But of course you don't understand! Nobody understands!

(*Maitre d' enters, sobbing loudly.*)

Maitre d': Oh but I do understand, *mon ami!* (*Throws his arms around the Repairman.*) It's so sad, so *triste!* (*Embraces the machine.*) And you too, *pauvre machine!* My heart goes to you! For I was in love for fifteen years with this telephone!

Repairman: No!

Maitre d': *Oui!* Because we communicated so well! Now I can barely get a dial tone! (*Calls offstage.*) Gabrielle! A table for *deux!*

(*Mabel enters.*)

Mabel: Manny, is it you?

Maitre d': Is this Mabel?

Repairman: It is Mabel.

Mabel: Manny, couldn't we try again? I'm running Unisys now so I got some cash.

Repairman: There's a spot on your dress.

Mabel: It's jelly. I don't think it comes out.

Repairman: Never remove it. It is the indelible Rorschach blot of the human heart.

Mabel: Oh, Manny, I see now that all humanity is linked, age upon age, in a great chain of handkerchiefs. I've seen so many hankies. Many, many, Manny. But no hanky of any size could dry the tears I've shed for you. Not if the hanky was broad enough to cover the world and I was broad enough to use it.

Repairman (*as all start to weep for happiness*): Handkerchief?

Maitre d': No. Mabel, take mine.

(*The head comes out of the Machine.*)

Washing Machine: No, Mabel—take ours.

Mabel: Wow!

Repairman: Pierre, I'll take that table for two now.

Loudspeaker Voice: Next time on "All the Days of the World of the Lives of All of Our Children"—a blender enters the mix.

Maitre d' (*to Machine*): Per'aps you would like to get loaded tonight . . . ?
Loudspeaker Voice: Stay tuned.

> (*Closing soap opera music, as the lights fade.*)

Questions

1. Starting with the title itself, there's quite a bit of wordplay in this play. List as many examples as you can find. How does this use of language contribute to the tone and spirit of the play?
2. What features of daytime television dramas are spoofed in *Soap Opera*?
3. In what ways does the Repairman's relationship with the Maypole washing machine resemble a human love affair? In what ways does it differ?
4. Would you call *Soap Opera* high comedy or low? Explain the reasons for your choice.
5. What is gained by framing the Repairman's story with the French restaurant and the Maitre d'?
6. Where does the climax of the play occur?
7. Is *Soap Opera* merely a piece of inspired silliness, or does it have a deeper dimension?

■ WRITING *effectively*

David Ives on Writing

On the One-Act Play   2006

Moss Hart said that you never really learn how to write a play, you only learn how to write *this* play. That is as true of one-acts as of two-, three-, four- or five-acts. To my mind the challenge of the one-act may be even greater than the challenge of larger and necessarily messier plays, in the same way that the sonnet with only fourteen lines remains the ever-attempted Everest of poetry. For what the one-act demands is a kind of concentrated perfection. "A play," said Lorca, "is a poem standing up," and I can't think of a better description of a one-act.

David Ives

  The long play, like the symphony, luxuriates in development and recapitulation. The one-act has no time for them. Develop the story and you start to look overly melodramatic, forcing too much event into too little time. Develop the characters and you look like you're not doing them justice. (In fact you start to look like you want to write a larger play.) Develop your theme and you start to sound like one of those guys at a party trying to explain all of particle theory between two grabs at the canapés. Recapitulate and you're dead.

A one-act masterpiece like Pinter's *The Dumb Waiter* would be tedious and attenuated if stretched over two hours. It says all it needs to say—and that's volumes—in a quarter of that, then stops. *Death of a Salesman* as a one-act would look either like a character study or a short story transcribed for the stage. A full-length is a four-ton, cast-steel, Richard Serra ellipse that you can walk around in; a one-act, a piece of string draped by Richard Tuttle on a gallery wall. Not a ride on the *Titanic*, but a single suitcase left floating in the middle of a theatrical sea.

So what does a one-act like, if not development and recapitulation?

Compression, obviously. Think of a one-act and chances are good you're thinking of something short and sharp, a punch in the nose, the rug pulled out from under you, over before you know it—as if an actor had turned on a camera on the audience and flashed a picture. A good one-act should leave you blinking. Think of a one-act and chances are also good you're picturing something like a small, bare, black-box stage with just a park bench, or a table and chair, or a bus-stop sign. One or two people. Minimal props. There is something necessarily stripped-down about the mere staging of one-acts, and this goes to the heart of the nature of one-acts themselves. They are *elemental*.

From *The Dramatist*

THINKING ABOUT COMEDY

If you have ever tried to explain a punch line to an uncomprehending friend, you know how hard it can be to convey the essence of humor. Too much explanation makes any joke fizzle out fast. We don't often stop to analyze why a joke strikes us as funny. It simply makes us laugh. For this reason, writing about comedy can be challenging.

- **What makes the play amusing?** Is there a central gag or situation (such as mistaken identity) that creates comic potential in every scene? Note that the central gag is often visual (such as a disguise), something that the audience constantly sees but is not equally apparent in the written text. In David Ives's *Soap Opera*, for instance, the central gag is always onstage—a man with a washing machine as his dinner date.

- **What is the flavor of the humor?** Is the comedy high or low? Is it verbal or visual, or both? Is there mostly slapstick action or clever wordplay? Is it a romantic comedy in which love plays a central role? A play often mixes types of comedy, but usually one style predominates. A farce may have a few moments of intellectual wit, but it will mostly keep silly jokes and pratfalls coming fast and furiously.

- **How do the personalities of the main characters intensify the humor?** Even when comedy arises out of a situation, character is likely to play an important role. In *A Midsummer Night's Dream*, for example, the fairy queen Titania is bewitched into falling in love with the weaver Bottom, whose head has been transformed into that of an ass. The situation is funny in its own right, but the humor is intensified by the personalities involved, the proud fairy queen pursuing the lowly and foolish tradesman. Humor often may be found in the unexpected, a twist on the normal and the logical.

CHECKIST: Writing About Comedy

☐ What kind of comedy is the play? Romantic? Slapstick? Satire? How can you tell?

☐ Which style of comedy prevails? Is there more emphasis on high comedy or low? More emphasis on verbal humor or physical comedy?

☐ Focus on a key comic moment. Does the comedy grow out of situation? Character? A mix of both?

☐ How does the play end? In a wedding or romance? A reconciliation? Mutual understanding?

WRITING ASSIGNMENT ON COMEDY

Read *Soap Opera* and write a brief analysis of what makes the play amusing or humorous. Provide details to back up your argument. See pages 1141–1143 for more information on specific types of humor.

TOPICS FOR WRITING ON TRAGEDY

1. According to Oscar Wilde, "In this world there are only two tragedies: one is not getting what one wants, and the other is getting it." Write an essay in which you discuss this statement in its application to the scene from *Doctor Faustus*.

2. Imagine that Faustus, after his death, has sought forgiveness and salvation with the claim, "The Devil tricked me. I didn't know what I was doing." Write a "judicial opinion" setting forth the grounds for the denial of his plea.

TOPICS FOR WRITING ON COMEDY

1. What or who is being satirized in *Soap Opera*? How true or incisive do you find this satire? Why?

2. Write about a recent romantic comedy film. How does its plot fulfill the notion of comedy?

3. Write about a movie you've seen lately that was meant to be funny but fell short. What was lacking?

► TERMS FOR *review*

Dramatic Genres

Tragedy ► A play that portrays a serious conflict between human beings and some superior, overwhelming force. It ends sorrowfully and disastrously, an outcome that seems inevitable.

Comedy ► A literary work aimed at amusing an audience. In traditional comedy, the protagonist often faces obstacles and complications that threaten disaster but are overturned at the last moment to produce a happy ending.

Kinds of Comedy

High comedy ► A comic genre evoking thoughtful laughter from an audience in response to the play's depiction of the folly, pretense, and hypocrisy of human behavior.

Satiric comedy ▶ A genre using derisive humor to ridicule human weakness and folly or attack political injustices and incompetence. Satiric comedy often focuses on ridiculing overly serious characters who resist the festive mood of comedy.

Comedy of manners ▶ A realistic form of high comic drama. It deals with the social relations and romantic intrigues of sophisticated upper-class men and women, whose verbal fencing and witty repartee produce the principal comic effects.

Romantic comedy ▶ A form of comic drama in which the plot focuses on one or more pairs of young lovers who overcome difficulties to achieve a happy ending (usually marriage).

Low comedy ▶ A comic style arousing laughter through jokes, slapstick antics, sight gags, boisterous clowning, and vulgar humor.

Burlesque ▶ A broadly humorous parody or travesty of another play or kind of play.

Farce ▶ A broadly humorous play whose action is usually fast-moving and improbable.

Slapstick comedy ▶ A kind of farce. Featuring pratfalls, pie-throwing, fisticuffs, and other violent action, it takes its name from a circus clown's prop—a bat with two boards that loudly clap together when one clown swats another.

36

CRITICAL CASEBOOK
Sophocles

Oedipus with chorus in Tyrone Guthrie's 1957 film
Oedipus Rex.

None but a poet can write a tragedy.

—EDITH HAMILTON

THE THEATER OF SOPHOCLES

For the citizens of Athens in the fifth century B.C., theater was both a religious and a civic occasion. Plays were presented only twice a year at religious festivals, both associated with Dionysus, the god of wine and crops. In January there was the Lenaea, the festival of the winepress, when plays, especially comedies, were performed. But the major theatrical event of the year came in March at the Great Dionysia, a citywide celebration that included sacrifices, prize ceremonies, and spectacular processions as well as three days of drama.

Each day at dawn a different author presented a trilogy of tragic plays—three interrelated dramas that portrayed an important mythic or legendary event. Each intense tragic trilogy was followed by a **satyr play**, an obscene parody of a mythic story, performed with the chorus dressed as satyrs, unruly mythic attendants of Dionysus who were half goat or horse and half human.

The Greeks loved competition and believed it fostered excellence. Even theater was a competitive event—not unlike the Olympic games. A panel of five judges voted each year at the Great Dionysia for the best dramatic presentation, and a substantial cash prize was given to the winning poet-playwright (all plays were written in verse). Any aspiring writer who has ever lost a literary contest may be comforted to learn that Sophocles, who triumphed in the competition twenty-four times, seems not to have won the annual prize for *Oedipus the King*. Although this play ultimately proved to be the most celebrated Greek tragedy ever written, it lost the award to a revival of a popular trilogy by Aeschylus, who had recently died.

Staging

Seated in the open air in a hillside amphitheater, as many as 17,000 spectators could watch a performance that must have somewhat resembled an opera or musical. The audience was arranged in rows, with the Athenian governing council and young military cadets seated in the middle sections. Priests, priestesses, and foreign dignitaries were given special places of honor in the front rows. The performance space they watched was divided into two parts—the **orchestra**, a level circular "dancing space" (at the base of the amphitheater), and a slightly raised stage built in front of the *skene* or stage house, originally a canvas or wooden hut for costume changes.

The actors spoke and performed primarily on the stage, and the chorus sang and danced in the orchestra. The *skene* served as a general set or backdrop—the exterior of a palace, a temple, a cave, or a military tent, depending on the action of the play. The *skene* had a large door at its center that served as the major entrance for principal characters. When opened wide, the door could be used to frame a striking tableau, as when the body of Eurydicê is displayed at the end of Sophocles' play *Antigonê*. The *skene* supported a hook and pulley by which actors who played gods could be lowered or lifted—hence the Latin phrase **deus ex machina** ("god out of the machine") for any means of bringing a play quickly to a resolution.

What did the actors look like? They wore **masks** (*personae*, the source of our word *person*, "a thing through which sound comes"): some of these masks had exaggerated mouthpieces, possibly designed to project speech across the open air. Certainly, the masks, each of which covered an actor's entire head, helped spectators far away recognize the chief characters. The masks often represented certain

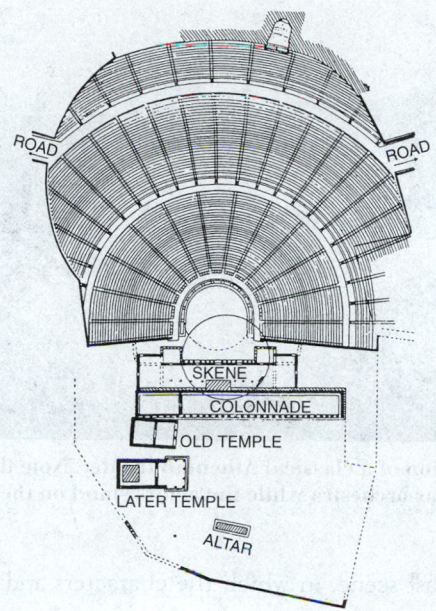

The theater of Dionysus at Athens in the time of
Sophocles; a modern drawing based on scholarly
guesswork. From R. C. Flickinger, *The Greek Theater
and Its Drama* (1918).

conventional types of characters: the old king, the young soldier, the shepherd,
the beautiful girl (women's parts were played by male actors). Perhaps in order to
gain in both increased dignity and visibility, actors in the Greek theater eventually came to wear **cothurni**, high, thick-soled elevator shoes that made them appear taller than ordinary men. All this equipment must have given the actors a
slightly inhuman yet very imposing appearance, but we may infer that the spectators accepted such conventions as easily as opera lovers accept an opera's special
artifice. Today's football fans, for instance, hardly think twice about the elaborate
helmets, shoulderpads, kneepads, and garishly colored uniforms worn by their favorite teams.

Dramatic Structure

By Sophocles' time, the tragedy had a conventional structure understood by most
of the citizens sitting in the audience. No more than three actors were allowed on
stage at any one time, along with a chorus of fifteen (the number was fixed by
Sophocles himself). The actors' spoken monologue and dialogue alternated with
the chorus' singing and dancing. Each tragedy began with a **prologue**, a preparatory
scene. In *Oedipus the King*, for example, the play begins with Oedipus asking the
suppliants why they have come and the priest telling him about the plague rav-
aging Thebes. Next came the *párodos*, the song for the entrance of the chorus.
Then the action was enacted in **episodes**, like the acts or scenes in modern plays;
the episodes were separated by danced choral songs or odes. Finally, there was a

A modern reconstruction of a classical Athenian theater. Note that the chorus performs in the circular orchestra while the actors stand on the raised stage behind.

closing *éxodos*, the last scene, in which the characters and chorus concluded the action and departed.

THE CIVIC ROLE OF GREEK DRAMA

Athenian drama was supported and financed by the state. Administration of the Great Dionysia fell to the head civil magistrate. He annually appointed three wealthy citizens to serve as *choregoi*, or producers, for the competing plays. Each producer had to equip the chorus and rent the rehearsal space in which the poet-playwright would prepare the new work for the festival. The state covered the expenses of the theater, actors, and prizes (which went to author, actors, and *choregos* alike). Theater tickets were distributed free to citizens, which meant that every registered Athenian, even the poorest, could participate. The playwrights therefore addressed themselves to every element of the Athenian democracy. Only the size of the amphitheater limited the attendance. Holding between 14,000 and 17,000 spectators, it could accommodate slightly less than half of Athens's 40,000 citizens.

Greek theater was directed at the moral and political education of the community. The poet's role was the improvement of the *polis* or city-state (made up of a town and its surrounding countryside). Greek city-states traditionally sponsored public contests between *rhapsodes* (professional poetry performers) reciting stories from Homer's epics, the *Iliad* and *Odyssey*. As Greek society developed and urbanized, however, the competitive and individualized heroism of the Homeric epics had to be tempered with the values of cooperation and compromise necessary to a democracy. Civic theater provided the ideal medium to address these cultural needs.

Tragedy and Empathy

As a public art form, tragedy was not simply a stage for political propaganda to promote the status quo. Nor was it exclusively a celebration of idealized heroes nobly enduring the blows of harsh circumstance and misfortune. Tragedy often enabled its audience to reflect on personal values that might be in conflict with civic ideals, on the claims of minorities that it neglected or excluded from public life, on its own irrational prejudices toward the foreign or the unknown. Frequently a play challenged its audience to feel sympathy for a vanquished enemy (as in Euripides' *Trojan Women*, the greatest antiwar play of the period, which dramatizes the horrible fate of captured women). Some plays explored the problems facing members of the politically powerless groups that made up nearly three-fourths of the Athenian population—women, children, resident aliens, and slaves. A largely male audience also frequently watched male performers enact stories of the power and anger of women, such as Euripides' *Medea*, which made their tragic violence understandable (if not entirely pardonable) to an audience not particularly disposed to treat them sympathetically. Other plays such as Sophocles' *Oedipus the King* or Euripides' *Herakles* depicted powerful men undone by misfortune, their own bad judgment, or hubris, and thrown into defeat and exile.

Such tragic stories required performers and audience to put themselves in the places of persons quite unlike themselves, in situations that might engulf any unlucky citizen—war, political upheaval, betrayal, domestic crisis. The release of the powerful emotions of pity and fear through a carefully crafted plot in the orderly context of highly conventionalized performance accounts for the paradox of tragic drama—how a viewer takes aesthetic pleasure in witnessing the sufferings of others.

ARISTOTLE'S CONCEPT OF TRAGEDY

> *Tragedy is an imitation of an action of high importance, complete and of some amplitude; in language enhanced by distinct and varying beauties; acted not narrated; by means of pity and fear effecting its purgation of these emotions.*
>
> —ARISTOTLE, POETICS, CHAPTER VI

Aristotle's famous definition of tragedy, constructed in the fourth century B.C., is the testimony of one who probably saw many classical tragedies performed. In making his observations, Aristotle does not seem to be laying down laws for what a tragedy ought to be. More likely, he is drawing—from tragedies he has seen or read—a general description of them.

Tragic Hero

Aristotle observes that the protagonist, the hero or chief character of a tragedy, is a person of "high estate," apparently a king or queen or other member of a royal family. In thus being as keenly interested as are contemporary dramatists in the private lives of the powerful, Greek dramatists need not be accused of snobbery. It is the nature of tragedy that the protagonist must fall from power and from happiness; his high estate gives him a place of dignity to fall from and perhaps makes his fall seem all the more a calamity in that it involves an entire nation or people. Nor is the protagonist extraordinary merely by his position in society. Oedipus is not only a king but also a noble soul who suffers profoundly and who employs splendid eloquence to express his suffering.

The tragic hero, however, is not a superman; he is fallible. The hero's downfall is the result, as Aristotle said, of his **hamartia**: his error or transgression or (as some translators would have it) his flaw or weakness of character. The notion that a tragic hero has such a **tragic flaw** has often been attributed to Aristotle, but it is by no means clear that Aristotle meant just that. According to this interpretation, every tragic hero has some fatal weakness, some moral Achilles' heel, that brings him to a bad end. In some classical tragedies, his transgression is a weakness the Greeks called **hubris**—extreme pride, leading to overconfidence.

Whatever Aristotle had in mind, however, many later critics find value in the idea of the tragic flaw. In this view, the downfall of a hero follows from his very nature. Whatever view we take—whether we find the hero's sufferings due to a flaw of character or to an error of judgment—we will probably find that his downfall results from acts for which he himself is responsible. In a Greek tragedy, the hero is a character amply capable of making choices—capable, too, of accepting the consequences.

Katharsis

It may be useful to take another look at Aristotle's definition of *tragedy*, with which we began. By **purgation** (or *katharsis*), did the ancient theorist mean that after witnessing a tragedy we feel relief, having released our pent-up emotions? Or did he mean that our feelings are purified, refined into something more ennobling? Scholars continue to argue. Whatever his exact meaning, clearly Aristotle implies that after witnessing a tragedy we feel better, not worse—not depressed, but somehow elated. We take a kind of pleasure in the spectacle of a noble man being brought down, but surely this pleasure is a legitimate one. Part of that catharsis may also be based in our feeling of the "rightness" or accuracy of what we have just witnessed. The terrible but undeniable truth of the tragic vision of life is that blind overreaching and the destruction of hopes and dreams are very much a part of what really happens in the world.

Recognition and Reversal

Aristotle, in describing the workings of this inexorable force in *Oedipus the King,* uses terms that later critics have found valuable. One is **recognition**, or discovery (*anagnorisis*): the revelation of some fact not known before or some person's true identity. Oedipus makes such a discovery: he recognizes that he himself was the child whom his mother had given over to be destroyed. Such a recognition also occurs in Shakespeare's *Macbeth* when Macduff reveals himself to have been "from his mother's womb / Untimely ripped," thus disclosing a double meaning in the witches' prophecy that Macbeth could be harmed by "none of woman born," and sweeping aside Macbeth's last shred of belief that he is infallible. Modern critics have taken the term to mean also the terrible enlightenment that accompanies such a recognition with the protagonist's consequent awareness of his role in his own undoing. "To see things plain— that is *anagnorisis*," Clifford Leech observes, "It is what tragedy ultimately is about: the realization of the unthinkable."

Having made his discovery, Oedipus suffers a reversal in his fortunes; he goes off into exile, blinded and dethroned. Such a fall from happiness seems intrinsic to tragedy, but we should know that Aristotle has a more particular meaning for his term **reversal** (*peripeteia*, anglicized as **peripety**). He means an action that turns out to have the opposite effect from the one its doer had intended. One of his illustrations of such an ironic reversal is from *Oedipus the King.* The first messenger intends to cheer Oedipus with the partially good news that, contrary to the prophecy that Oedipus would kill his father, his father has died of old age. The reversal is in the fact that, when the messenger further reveals that old Polybus was Oedipus' father only by adoption, the king, instead of having his fears allayed, is stirred to new dread.

We are not altogether sorry, perhaps, to see an arrogant man such as Oedipus humbled, and yet it is difficult not to feel that the punishment of Oedipus is greater than he deserves. Possibly this feeling is what Aristotle meant in his observation that a tragedy arouses our pity and our fear—our compassion for Oedipus and our terror as we sense the remorselessness of a universe in which a man is doomed. Notice, however, that at the end of the play Oedipus does not curse God and die. Although such a complex play is open to many interpretations, it is probably safe to say that the play is not a bitter complaint against the universe. At last, Oedipus accepts the divine will, prays for blessings upon his children, and prepares to endure his exile—fallen from high estate but uplifted, through his newfound humility and piety, in moral dignity.

SOPHOCLES

Sophocles

Sophocles (496?–406 B.C.) tragic dramatist, priest, for a time one of ten Athenian generals, was one of the three great ancient Greek writers of tragedy whose work has survived. (The other two were his contemporaries: Aeschylus, his senior, and Euripides, his junior.) Sophocles won his first victory in the Athenian spring drama competition in 468 B.C., when a tragedy he had written defeated one by Aeschylus. He went on to win many prizes, writing more than 120 plays, of which only seven have survived in their entirety—Ajax, Antigonê, Oedipus the King, Electra, Philoctetes, The Trachinian Women, and Oedipus at Colonus. (Of the lost plays, about a thousand fragments remain.) In his long life, Sophocles saw Greece rise to supremacy over the Persian Empire. He enjoyed the favor of the statesman Pericles, who, making peace with enemy Sparta, ruled Athens during a Golden Age (461–429 B.C.), during which the Parthenon was built and music, art, drama, and philosophy flourished. The playwright lived on to see his native city-state in decline, its strength drained by the disastrous Peloponnesian War. His last play, Oedipus at Colonus, set twenty years after the events of Oedipus the King, shows the former king in old age, ragged and blind, cast into exile by his sons, but still accompanied by his faithful daughter Antigonê. It was written when Sophocles was nearly ninety. Oedipus the King is believed to have been first produced in 425 B.C., five years after the plague had broken out in Athens.

THE ORIGINS OF *OEDIPUS THE KING*

On a Great Dionysia feast day several years after Athens had survived a devastating plague, the audience turned out to watch a tragedy by Sophocles, set in the city of Thebes at the moment of another terrible plague. This timely play was *Oedipus*, later given the name (in Greek) *Oedipus Tyrannos* to distinguish it from Sophocles' last Oedipus play, *Oedipus at Colonus*, written many years later when the author was nearly ninety.

A folktale figure, Oedipus gets his name through a complex pun. *Oida* means "to know" (from the root *vid-*, "see"), pointing to the tale's contrasting themes of sight and blindness, wisdom and ignorance. *Oedipus* also means "swollen foot" or "club-foot," pointing to the injury sustained in the title character's infancy, when his ankles were pinioned together like a goat's. Oedipus is the man who comes to knowledge of his true parentage through the evidence of his feet and his old injury. The term *tyrannos,* in the context of the play, simply means a man who comes to rule through his own intelligence and merit, though not related to the ruling family. The traditional Greek title might be translated, therefore, as *Clubfoot the Ruler.* (*Oedipus Rex,* which means "Oedipus the King," is the conventional Latin title for the play.)

Presumably the audience already knew the story portrayed in the play. They would have known that because a prophecy had foretold that Oedipus would grow up to slay his father, he had been taken out as a newborn to perish in the wilderness of Mount Cithaeron outside Thebes. (Exposure was the common fate of unwanted children in ancient Greece, though only in the most extraordinary circumstances would a royal heir be exposed.) The audience would also have known that before he was left to die, the baby's feet had been pinned together. And they would have known that later, adopted by King Polybus and Queen Merope of Corinth and grown to maturity, Oedipus won both the throne and the recently widowed queen of Thebes as a reward for ridding the city of the Sphinx, a winged, woman-headed lion. All who approached the Sphinx were asked a riddle, and failure to solve it meant death. Her lethal riddle was: "What goes on four legs in the morning, two at noon, and three at evening?" Oedipus correctly answered, "Man." (As a baby he crawls on all fours, as a man he walks erect, then as an old man he uses a cane.) Chagrined and outwitted, the Sphinx leaped from her rocky perch and dashed herself to death. Familiarity with all these events is necessary to understand *Oedipus the King,* which begins years later, after the title character has long been established as ruler of Thebes.

Laurence Olivier in *Oedipus Rex.*

Oedipus the King

425 B.C.?

Translated by Dudley Fitts and Robert Fitzgerald

CHARACTERS°

Oedipus	Messenger
A Priest	Shepherd of Laïos
Creon	Second Messenger
Teiresias	Chorus of Theban Elders
Iocastê	

SCENE: *Before the palace of Oedipus, King of Thebes. A central door and two lateral doors open onto a platform which runs the length of the façade. On the platform, right and left, are altars; and three steps lead down into the "orchestra," or chorus-ground. At the beginning of the action these steps are crowded by suppliants° who have brought branches and chaplets of olive leaves and who lie in various attitudes of despair. Oedipus enters.*

PROLOGUE°

Oedipus: My children, generations of the living
    In the line of Kadmos,° nursed at his ancient hearth:
    Why have you strewn yourself before these altars
    In supplication, with your boughs and garlands?
    The breath of incense rises from the city   5
    With a sound of prayer and lamentation.
                                Children,
    I would not have you speak through messengers,
    And therefore I have come myself to hear you—
    I, Oedipus, who bear the famous name.
    (*To a Priest.*) You, there, since you are eldest in the company,   10
    Speak for them all, tell me what preys upon you,
    Whether you come in dread, or crave some blessing:
    Tell me, and never doubt that I will help you
    In every way I can; I should be heartless
    Were I not moved to find you suppliant here.   15
Priest: Great Oedipus, O powerful King of Thebes!
    You see how all the ages of our people
    Cling to your altar steps: here are boys
    Who can barely stand alone, and here are priests
    By weight of age, as I am a priest of God,   20
    And young men chosen from those yet unmarried;
    As for the others, all that multitude,
    They wait with olive chaplets in the squares,

Characters: Some of these names are usually anglicized: Jocasta, Laius. In this version, the translators prefer spelling names more like the Greek originals.   *suppliants:* persons who come to ask some favor of the king.   *Prologue:* portion of the play containing the exposition.   *2 line of Kadmos:* according to legend the city of Thebes, where the play takes place, had been founded by the hero Cadmus.

At the two shrines of Pallas,° and where Apollo°
Speaks in the glowing embers.
                                      Your own eyes   25
Must tell you: Thebes is tossed on a murdering sea
And can not lift her head from the death surge.
A rust consumes the buds and fruits of the earth;
The herds are sick; children die unborn,
And labor is vain. The god of plague and pyre   30
Raids like detestable lightning through the city,
And all the house of Kadmos is laid waste,
All emptied, and all darkened: Death alone
Battens upon the misery of Thebes.

You are not one of the immortal gods, we know;   35
Yet we have come to you to make our prayer
As to the man surest in mortal ways
And wisest in the ways of God. You saved us
From the Sphinx, that flinty singer, and the tribute
We paid to her so long; yet you were never   40
Better informed than we, nor could we teach you:
It was some god breathed in you to set us free.

Therefore, O mighty King, we turn to you:
Find us our safety, find us a remedy,
Whether by counsel of the gods or men.   45
A king of wisdom tested in the past
Can act in a time of troubles, and act well.
Noblest of men, restore
Life to your city! Think how all men call you
Liberator for your triumph long ago;   50
Ah, when your years of kingship are remembered,
Let them not say *We rose, but later fell*—
Keep the State from going down in the storm!
Once, years ago, with happy augury,
You brought us fortune; be the same again!   55
No man questions your power to rule the land:
But rule over men, not over a dead city!
Ships are only hulls, citadels are nothing,
When no life moves in the empty passageways.

Oedipus: Poor children! You may be sure I know   60
All that you longed for in your coming here.
I know that you are deathly sick; and yet,
Sick as you are, not one is as sick as I.
Each of you suffers in himself alone
His anguish, not another's; but my spirit   65
Groans for the city, for myself, for you.

---

24 *Pallas:* title for Athena, goddess of wisdom.   *Apollo:* god of music, poetry, and prophecy. At his shrine near Thebes, the ashes of fires were used to divine the future.

I was not sleeping, you are not waking me.
No, I have been in tears for a long while
And in my restless thought walked many ways.
In all my search, I found one helpful course,   70
And that I have taken: I have sent Creon,
Son of Menoikeus, brother of the Queen,
To Delphi, Apollo's place of revelation,°
To learn there, if he can,
What act or pledge of mine may save the city.   75
I have counted the days, and now, this very day,
I am troubled, for he has overstayed his time.
What is he doing? He has been gone too long.
Yet whenever he comes back, I should do ill
To scant whatever duty God reveals.   80

Priest: It is a timely promise. At this instant
They tell me Creon is here.

Oedipus: O Lord Apollo!
May his news be fair as his face is radiant!

Priest: It could not be otherwise: he is crowned with bay,
The chaplet is thick with berries.

Oedipus: We shall soon know;   85
He is near enough to hear us now.

    Enter Creon.

                       O Prince:
Brother: son of Menoikeus:
What answer do you bring us from the god?

Creon: A strong one. I can tell you, great afflictions
Will turn out well, if they are taken well.   90

Oedipus: What was the oracle? These vague words
Leave me still hanging between hope and fear.

Creon: Is it your pleasure to hear me with all these
Gathered around us? I am prepared to speak,
But should we not go in?

Oedipus: Let them all hear it   95
It is for them I suffer, more than for myself.

Creon: Then I will tell you what I heard at Delphi.

In plain words
The god commands us to expel from the land of Thebes
An old defilement we are sheltering.   100
It is a deathly thing, beyond cure.
We must not let it feed upon us longer.

Oedipus: What defilement? How shall we rid ourselves of it?

---

73 *Delphi . . . revelation:* In the temple of Delphi at the foot of Mount Parnassus, a priestess of Dionysos, while in an ecstatic trance, would speak the wine god's words. Such a priestess was called an *oracle;* the word can also mean "a message from the god."

Creon: By exile or death, blood for blood. It was
    Murder that brought the plague-wind on the city. 105
Oedipus: Murder of whom? Surely the god has named him?
Creon: My lord: long ago Laïos was our king,
    Before you came to govern us.
Oedipus: I know;
    I learned of him from others; I never saw him.
Creon: He was murdered; and Apollo commands us now 110
    To take revenge upon whoever killed him.
Oedipus: Upon whom? Where are they? Where shall we find a clue
    To solve that crime, after so many years?
Creon: Here in this land, he said.
                    If we make enquiry,
    We may touch things that otherwise escape us. 115
Oedipus: Tell me: Was Laïos murdered in his house,
    Or in the fields, or in some foreign country?
Creon: He said he planned to make a pilgrimage.
    He did not come home again.
Oedipus: And was there no one,
    No witness, no companion, to tell what happened? 120
Creon: They were all killed but one, and he got away
    So frightened that he could remember one thing only.
Oedipus: What was that one thing? One may be the key
    To everything, if we resolve to use it.
Creon: He said that a band of highwaymen attacked them, 125
    Outnumbered them, and overwhelmed the King.
Oedipus: Strange, that a highwayman should be so daring—
    Unless some faction here bribed him to do it.
Creon: We thought of that. But after Laïos' death
    New troubles arose and we had no avenger. 130
Oedipus: What troubles could prevent your hunting down the killers?
Creon: The riddling Sphinx's song
    Made us deaf to all mysteries but her own.
Oedipus: Then once more I must bring what is dark to light.
    It is most fitting that Apollo shows, 135
    As you do, this compunction for the dead.
    You shall see how I stand by you, as I should,
    To avenge the city and the city's god,
    And not as though it were for some distant friend,
    But for my own sake, to be rid of evil. 140
    Whoever killed King Laïos might—who knows?—
    Decide at any moment to kill me as well.
    By avenging the murdered king I protect myself.

    Come, then, my children: leave the altar steps,
    Lift up your olive boughs!
                    One of you go 145
    And summon the people of Kadmos to gather here.
    I will do all that I can; you may tell them that.

Exit a Page.

So, with the help of God,
We shall be saved—or else indeed we are lost.
Priest: Let us rise, children. It was for this we came,   150
And now the King has promised it himself.
Phoibos° has sent us an oracle; may he descend
Himself to save us and drive out the plague.

Exeunt Oedipus and Creon into the palace by the central door. The Priest and the
Suppliants disperse right and left. After a short pause the Chorus enters the orchestra.

PÁRODOS°

Strophe° 1

Chorus: What is God singing in his profound
Delphi of gold and shadow?
What oracle for Thebes, the sunwhipped city?

Fear unjoints me, the roots of my heart tremble.

Now I remember, O Healer, your power, and wonder: 5
Will you send doom like a sudden cloud, or weave it
Like nightfall of the past?

Speak, speak to us, issue of holy sound:
Dearest to our expectancy: be tender!

Antistrophe° 1

Let me pray to Athenê, the immortal daughter of Zeus,   10
And to Artemis her sister
Who keeps her famous throne in the market ring,
And to Apollo, bowman at the far butts of heaven—

O gods, descend! Like three streams leap against
The fires of our grief, the fires of darkness;   15
Be swift to bring us rest!

As in the old time from the brilliant house
Of air you stepped to save us, come again!

Strophe 2

Now our afflictions have no end,
Now all our stricken host lies down   20
And no man fights off death with his mind;

The noble plowland bears no grain,
And groaning mothers can not bear—

---

152 *Phoibos:* the sun god Phoebus Apollo.   *Párodos:* part to be sung by the chorus on first entering.
Strophe: a strophe (according to theory) was sung while the chorus danced from stage right to stage left.
Antistrophe: part sung while the chorus danced back again across the stage, from left to right.

See, how our lives like birds take wing,
Like sparks that fly when a fire soars,   25
To the shore of the god of evening.

                                                                    Antistrophe 2

The plague burns on, it is pitiless,
Though pallid children laden with death
Lie unwept in the stony ways,

And old gray women by every path   30
Flock to the strand about the altars

There to strike their breasts and cry
Worship of Phoibos in wailing prayers:
Be kind, God's golden child!

                                                                    Strophe 3

There are no swords in this attack by fire,   35
No shields, but we are ringed with cries.

Send the besieger plunging from our homes
Into the vast sea-room of the Atlantic
Or into the waves that foam eastward of Thrace—

For the day ravages what the night spares—   40

Destroy our enemy, lord of the thunder!
Let him be riven by lightning from heaven!

                                                                    Antistrophe 3

Phoibos Apollo, stretch the sun's bowstring,
That golden cord, until it sing for us,
Flashing arrows in heaven!
                          Artemis, Huntress,   45
Race with flaring lights upon our mountains!

O scarlet god, O golden-banded brow,
O Theban Bacchos in a storm of Maenads,°

Enter Oedipus, center.

Whirl upon Death, that all the Undying hate!
Come with blinding torches, come in joy!   50

SCENE I

Oedipus: Is this your prayer? It may be answered. Come,
          Listen to me, act as the crisis demands,
          And you shall have relief from all these evils.

          Until now I was a stranger to this tale,
          As I had been a stranger to the crime.   5
          Could I track down the murderer without a clue?
          But now, friends,

48 *Bacchos . . . Maenads:* god of wine with his attendant girl revelers.

As one who became a citizen after the murder,
I make this proclamation to all Thebans:

If any man knows by whose hand Laïos, son of Labdakos,   10
Met his death, I direct that man to tell me everything,
No matter what he fears for having so long withheld it.
Let it stand as promised that no further trouble
Will come to him, but he may leave the land in safety.
Moreover: If anyone knows the murderer to be foreign,   15
Let him not keep silent: he shall have his reward from me.
However, if he does conceal it; if any man
Fearing for his friend or for himself disobeys this edict,
Hear what I propose to do:

I solemnly forbid the people of this country,   20
Where power and throne are mine, ever to receive that man
Or speak to him, no matter who he is, or let him
Join in sacrifice, lustration,° or in prayer.
I decree that he be driven from every house,
Being, as he is, corruption itself to us: the Delphic   25
Voice of Zeus has pronounced this revelation.
Thus I associate myself with the oracle
And take the side of the murdered king.

As for the criminal, I pray to God—
Whether it be a lurking thief, or one of a number—   30
I pray that that man's life be consumed in evil and wretchedness.
And as for me, this curse applies no less
If it should turn out that the culprit is my guest here,
Sharing my hearth.
                    You have heard the penalty.
I lay it on you now to attend to this   35
For my sake, for Apollo's, for the sick
Sterile city that heaven has abandoned.
Suppose the oracle had given you no command:
Should this defilement go uncleansed for ever?
You should have found the murderer: your king,   40
A noble king, had been destroyed!
                    Now I,
Having the power that he held before me,
Having his bed, begetting children there
Upon his wife, as he would have, had he lived—
Their son would have been my children's brother,   45
If Laïos had had luck in fatherhood!
(But surely ill luck rushed upon his reign)—
I say I take the son's part, just as though
I were his son, to press the fight for him

---

23 *lustration:* propitiatory sacrifice.

And see it won! I'll find the hand that brought   50
Death to Labdakos' and Polydoros' child,
Heir of Kadmos' and Agenor's line.
And as for those who fail me,
May the gods deny them the fruit of the earth,
Fruit of the womb, and may they rot utterly!   55
Let them be wretched as we are wretched, and worse!

For you, for loyal Thebans, and for all
Who find my actions right, I pray the favor
Of justice, and of all the immortal gods.
Choragos:° Since I am under oath, my lord, I swear   60
    I did not do the murder, I can not name
    The murderer. Might not the oracle
    That has ordained the search tell where to find him?
Oedipus: An honest question. But no man in the world
    Can make the gods do more than the gods will.   65
Choragos: There is one last expedient—
Oedipus: Tell me what it is.
    Though it seem slight, you must not hold it back.
Choragos: A lord clairvoyant to the lord Apollo,
    As we all know, is the skilled Teiresias.
    One might learn much about this from him, Oedipus.   70
Oedipus: I am not wasting time:
    Creon spoke of this, and I have sent for him—
    Twice, in fact; it is strange that he is not here.
Choragos: The other matter—that old report—seems useless.
Oedipus: Tell me. I am interested in all reports.   75
Choragos: The King was said to have been killed by highwaymen.
Oedipus: I know. But we have no witnesses to that.
Choragos: If the killer can feel a particle of dread,
    Your curse will bring him out of hiding!
Oedipus: No.
    The man who dared that act will fear no curse.   80

Enter the blind seer Teiresias, led by a Page.

Choragos: But there is one man who may detect the criminal.
    This is Teiresias, this is the holy prophet
    In whom, alone of all men, truth was born.
Oedipus: Teiresias: seer: student of mysteries,
    Of all that's taught and all that no man tells,   85
    Secrets of Heaven and secrets of the earth:
    Blind though you are, you know the city lies
    Sick with plague; and from this plague, my lord,
    We find that you alone can guard or save us.

    Possibly you did not hear the messengers?   90
    Apollo, when we sent to him,

60 *Choragos:* spokesperson for the chorus.

Sent us back word that this great pestilence
Would lift, but only if we established clearly
The identity of those who murdered Laïos.
They must be killed or exiled.

Can you use   95
Birdflight or any art of divination
To purify yourself, and Thebes, and me
From this contagion? We are in your hands.
There is no fairer duty
Than that of helping others in distress.   100

Teiresias: How dreadful knowledge of the truth can be
When there's no help in truth! I knew this well,
But made myself forget. I should not have come.

Oedipus: What is troubling you? Why are your eyes so cold?

Teiresias: Let me go home. Bear your own fate, and I'll   105
Bear mine. It is better so: trust what I say.

Oedipus: What you say is ungracious and unhelpful
To your native country. Do not refuse to speak.

Teiresias: When it comes to speech, your own is neither temperate
Nor opportune. I wish to be more prudent.   110

Oedipus: In God's name, we all beg you—

Teiresias: You are all ignorant.
No; I will never tell you what I know.
Now it is my misery; then, it would be yours.

Oedipus: What! You do know something, and will not tell us?
You would betray us all and wreck the State?   115

Teiresias: I do not intend to torture myself, or you.
Why persist in asking? You will not persuade me.

Oedipus: What a wicked old man you are! You'd try a stone's
Patience! Out with it! Have you no feeling at all?

Teiresias: You call me unfeeling. If you could only see   120
The nature of your own feelings . . .

Oedipus: Why,
Who would not feel as I do? Who could endure
Your arrogance toward the city?

Teiresias: What does it matter!
Whether I speak or not; it is bound to come.

Oedipus: Then, if "it" is bound to come, you are bound to tell me.   125

Teiresias: No, I will not go on. Rage as you please.

Oedipus: Rage? Why not!
And I'll tell you what I think:
You planned it, you had it done, you all but
Killed him with your own hands: if you had eyes,
I'd say the crime was yours, and yours alone.   130

Teiresias: So? I charge you, then,
Abide by the proclamation you have made:
From this day forth
Never speak again to these men or to me;
You yourself are the pollution of this country.   135

Oedipus: You dare say that! Can you possibly think you have
    Some way of going free, after such insolence?
Teiresias: I have gone free. It is the truth sustains me.
Oedipus: Who taught you shamelessness? It was not your craft.
Teiresias: You did. You made me speak. I did not want to.   140
Oedipus: Speak what? Let me hear it again more clearly.
Teiresias: Was it not clear before? Are you tempting me?
Oedipus: I did not understand it. Say it again.
Teiresias: I say that you are the murderer whom you seek.
Oedipus: Now twice you have spat out infamy. You'll pay for it!   145
Teiresias: Would you care for more? Do you wish to be really angry?
Oedipus: Say what you will. Whatever you say is worthless.
Teiresias: I say you live in hideous shame with those
    Most dear to you. You can not see the evil.
Oedipus: It seems you can go on mouthing like this for ever.   150
Teiresias: I can, if there is power in truth.
Oedipus: There is:
    But not for you, not for you,
    You sightless, witless, senseless, mad old man!
Teiresias: You are the madman. There is no one here
    Who will not curse you soon, as you curse me.   155
Oedipus: You child of endless night! You can not hurt me
    Or any other man who sees the sun.
Teiresias: True: it is not from me your fate will come.
    That lies within Apollo's competence,
    As it is his concern.
Oedipus: Tell me: 160
    Are you speaking for Creon, or for yourself?
Teiresias: Creon is no threat. You weave your own doom.
Oedipus: Wealth, power, craft of statesmanship!
    Kingly position, everywhere admired!
    What savage envy is stored up against these,   165
    If Creon, whom I trusted, Creon my friend,
    For this great office which the city once
    Put in my hands unsought—if for this power
    Creon desires in secret to destroy me!

    He has brought this decrepit fortune-teller, this   170
    Collector of dirty pennies, this prophet fraud—
    Why, he is no more clairvoyant than I am!
                           Tell us:
    Has your mystic mummery ever approached the truth?
    When that hellcat the Sphinx was performing here,
    What help were you to these people?   175
    Her magic was not for the first man who came along:
    It demanded a real exorcist. Your birds—
    What good were they? or the gods, for the matter of that?
    But I came by,
    Oedipus, the simple man, who knows nothing—   180

I thought it out for myself, no birds helped me!
And this is the man you think you can destroy,
That you may be close to Creon when he's king!
Well, you and your friend Creon, it seems to me,
Will suffer most. If you were not an old man,   185
You would have paid already for your plot.

Choragos: We can not see that his words or yours
    Have been spoken except in anger, Oedipus,
    And of anger we have no need. How can God's will
    Be accomplished best? That is what most concerns us.   190

Teiresias: You are a king. But where argument's concerned
    I am your man, as much a king as you.
    I am not your servant, but Apollo's.
    I have no need of Creon to speak for me.

    Listen to me. You mock my blindness, do you?   195
    But I say that you, with both your eyes, are blind:
    You can not see the wretchedness of your life,
    Nor in whose house you live, no, nor with whom.
    Who are your father and mother? Can you tell me?
    You do not even know the blind wrongs   200
    That you have done them, on earth and in the world below.
    But the double lash of your parents' curse will whip you
    Out of this land some day, with only night
    Upon your precious eyes.
    Your cries then—where will they not be heard?   205
    What fastness of Kithairon will not echo them?
    And that bridal-descant of yours—you'll know it then,
    The song they sang when you came here to Thebes
    And found your misguided berthing.
    All this, and more, that you can not guess at now,   210
    Will bring you to yourself among your children.

    Be angry, then. Curse Creon. Curse my words.
    I tell you, no man that walks upon the earth
    Shall be rooted out more horribly than you.

Oedipus: Am I to bear this from him?—Damnation   215
    Take you! Out of this place! Out of my sight!

Teiresias: I would not have come at all if you had not asked me.

Oedipus: Could I have told that you'd talk nonsense, that
    You'd come here to make a fool of yourself, and of me?

Teiresias: A fool? Your parents thought me sane enough   220

Oedipus: My parents again!—Wait: who were my parents?

Teiresias: This day will give you a father, and break your heart.

Oedipus: Your infantile riddles! Your damned abracadabra!

Teiresias: You were a great man once at solving riddles.

Oedipus: Mock me with that if you like; you will find it true. 225

Teiresias: It was true enough. It brought about your ruin.

Oedipus: But if it saved this town?

Teiresias (to the Page):   Boy, give me your hand.

Oedipus: Yes, boy; lead him away.

                     —While you are here

    We can do nothing. Go; leave us in peace.

Teiresias: I will go when I have said what I have to say.   230

    How can you hurt me? And I tell you again:

    The man you have been looking for all this time,

    The damned man, the murderer of Laïos,

    That man is in Thebes. To your mind he is foreign-born,

    But it will soon be shown that he is a Theban,   235

    A revelation that will fail to please.

                    A blind man,

    Who has his eyes now; a penniless man, who is rich now;

    And he will go tapping the strange earth with his staff;

    To the children with whom he lives now he will be

    Brother and father—the very same; to her   240

    Who bore him, son and husband—the very same

    Who came to his father's bed, wet with his father's blood.

    Enough. Go think that over.

    If later you find error in what I have said,

    You may say that I have no skill in prophecy.   245

Exit Teiresias, led by his Page. Oedipus goes into the palace.

ODE° I

                                             Strophe 1

Chorus: The Delphic stone of prophecies

    Remembers ancient regicide

    And a still bloody hand.

    That killer's hour of flight has come.

    He must be stronger than riderless   5

    Coursers of untiring wind,

    For the son of Zeus° armed with his father's thunder

    Leaps in lightning after him;

    And the Furies° follow him, the sad Furies.

                                       Antistrophe 1

    Holy Parnassos' peak of snow   10

    Flashes and blinds that secret man,

    That all shall hunt him down:

    Though he may roam the forest shade

    Like a bull gone wild from pasture

    To rage through glooms of stone.   15

    Doom comes down on him; flight will not avail him;

Ode: a choral song. Here again (as in the *párodos*), *strophe* and *antistrophe* probably indicate the movements of a dance.   7 *son of Zeus:* Apollo.   9 *Furies:* three horrific female spirits whose task was to seek out and punish evildoers.

For the world's heart calls him desolate,
And the immortal Furies follow, for ever follow.

Strophe 2

But now a wilder thing is heard
From the old man skilled at hearing Fate in the wingbeat of a bird.   20
Bewildered as a blown bird, my soul hovers and can not find
Foothold in this debate, or any reason or rest of mind.
But no man ever brought—none can bring
Proof of strife between Thebes' royal house,
Labdakos' line,° and the son of Polybos;°   25
And never until now has any man brought word
Of Laïos' dark death staining Oedipus the King.

Antistrophe 2

Divine Zeus and Apollo hold
Perfect intelligence alone of all tales ever told;
And well though this diviner works, he works in his own night;   30
No man can judge that rough unknown or trust in second sight,
For wisdom changes hands among the wise.
Shall I believe my great lord criminal
At a raging word that a blind old man let fall?
I saw him, when the carrion woman faced him of old,   35
Prove his heroic mind! These evil words are lies.

SCENE II

Creon: Men of Thebes:
  I am told that heavy accusations
  Have been brought against me by King Oedipus.

  I am not the kind of man to bear this tamely.

  If in these present difficulties   5
  He holds me accountable for any harm to him
  Through anything I have said or done—why, then,
  I do not value life in this dishonor.

  It is not as though this rumor touched upon
  Some private indiscretion. The matter is grave.   10
  The fact is that I am being called disloyal
  To the State, to my fellow citizens, to my friends.
Choragos: He may have spoken in anger, not from his mind.
Creon: But did you not hear him say I was the one
  Who seduced the old prophet into lying?   15
Choragos: The thing was said; I do not know how seriously.
Creon: But you were watching him! Were his eyes steady?
  Did he look like a man in his right mind?

---

25 *Labdakos' line:* descendants of Laïos (true father of Oedipus, although the chorus does not know it).
Polybos: king who adopted the child Oedipus.

Choragos: I do not know.
   I can not judge the behavior of great men.
   But here is the King himself.

   Enter Oedipus.

Oedipus: So you dared come back.   20
   Why? How brazen of you to come to my house,
   You murderer!
          Do you think I do not know
   That you plotted to kill me, plotted to steal my throne?
   Tell me, in God's name: am I coward, a fool,
   That you should dream you could accomplish this?   25
   A fool who could not see your slippery game?
   A coward, not to fight back when I saw it?
   You are the fool, Creon, are you not? hoping
   Without support or friends to get a throne?
   Thrones may be won or bought: you could do neither.   30
Creon: Now listen to me. You have talked; let me talk, too.
   You can not judge unless you know the facts.
Oedipus: You speak well: there is one fact; but I find it hard
   To learn from the deadliest enemy I have.
Creon: That above all I must dispute with you.   35
Oedipus: That above all I will not hear you deny.
Creon: If you think there is anything good in being stubborn
   Against all reason, then I say you are wrong.
Oedipus: If you think a man can sin against his own kind
   And not be punished for it, I say you are mad.   40
Creon: I agree. But tell me: what have I done to you?
Oedipus: You advised me to send for that wizard, did you not?
Creon: I did. I should do it again.
Oedipus: Very well. Now tell me:
   How long has it been since Laïos—
Creon: What of Laïos?
Oedipus: Since he vanished in that onset by the road?   45
Creon: It was long ago, a long time.
Oedipus: And this prophet,
   Was he practicing here then?
Creon: He was; and with honor, as now.
Oedipus: Did he speak of me at that time?
Creon: He never did;
   At least, not when I was present.
Oedipus: But . . . the enquiry?
   I suppose you held one?
Creon: We did, but we learned nothing.   50
Oedipus: Why did the prophet not speak against me then?
Creon: I do not know; and I am the kind of man
   Who holds his tongue when he has no facts to go on.
Oedipus: There's one fact that you know, and you could tell it.
Creon: What fact is that? If I know it, you shall have it.   55

Oedipus: If he were not involved with you, he could not say
    That it was I who murdered Laïos.
Creon: If he says that, you are the one that knows it!—
    But now it is my turn to question you.
Oedipus: Put your questions. I am no murderer.   60
Creon: First then: You married my sister?
Oedipus: I married your sister.
Creon: And you rule the kingdom equally with her?
Oedipus: Everything that she wants she has from me.
Creon: And I am the third, equal to both of you?
Oedipus: That is why I call you a bad friend.   65
Creon: No. Reason it out, as I have done.
    Think of this first: Would any sane man prefer
    Power, with all a king's anxieties,
    To that same power and the grace of sleep?
    Certainly not I.   70
    I have never longed for the king's power—only his rights.
    Would any wise man differ from me in this?
    As matters stand, I have my way in everything
    With your consent, and no responsibilities.
    If I were king, I should be a slave to policy.   75

    How could I desire a scepter more
    Than what is now mine—untroubled influence?
    No, I have not gone mad; I need no honors,
    Except those with the perquisites I have now.
    I am welcome everywhere; every man salutes me,   80
    And those who want your favor seek my ear,
    Since I know how to manage what they ask.
    Should I exchange this ease for that anxiety?
    Besides, no sober mind is treasonable.
    I hate anarchy   85
    And never would deal with any man who likes it.

    Test what I have said. Go to the priestess
    At Delphi, ask if I quoted her correctly.
    And as for this other thing: if I am found
    Guilty of treason with Teiresias,   90
    Then sentence me to death! You have my word
    It is a sentence I should cast my vote for—
    But not without evidence!
                    You do wrong
    When you take good men for bad, bad men for good.
    A true friend thrown aside—why, life itself   95
    Is not more precious!
                  In time you will know this well:
    For time, and time alone, will show the just man,
    Though scoundrels are discovered in a day.
Choragos: This is well said, and a prudent man would ponder it.   100
    Judgments too quickly formed are dangerous.

Oedipus: But is he not quick in his duplicity?
    And shall I not be quick to parry him?
    Would you have me stand still, hold my peace, and let
    This man win everything, through my inaction?
Creon: And you want—what is it, then? To banish me?   105
Oedipus: No, not exile. It is your death I want,
    So that all the world may see what treason means.
Creon: You will persist, then? You will not believe me?
Oedipus: How can I believe you?
Creon: Then you are a fool.
Oedipus: To save myself?
Creon: In justice, think of me.   110
Oedipus: You are evil incarnate.
Creon: But suppose that you are wrong?
Oedipus: Still I must rule.
Creon: But not if you rule badly.
Oedipus: O city, city!
Creon: It is my city, too!
Choragos: Now, my lords, be still. I see the Queen,
    Iocastê, coming from her palace chambers;   115
    And it is time she came, for the sake of you both.
    This dreadful quarrel can be resolved through her.

    Enter Iocastê.

Iocastê: Poor foolish men, what wicked din is this?
    With Thebes sick to death, is it not shameful
    That you should rake some private quarrel up?   120
    (*To Oedipus.*) Come into the house.
                    —And you, Creon, go now:
    Let us have no more of this tumult over nothing.
Creon: Nothing? No, sister: what your husband plans for me
    Is one of two great evils: exile or death.
Oedipus: He is right.
             Why, woman, I have caught him squarely   125
    Plotting against my life.
Creon: No! Let me die
    Accurst if ever I have wished you harm!
Iocastê: Ah, believe it, Oedipus!
    In the name of the gods, respect this oath of his
    For my sake, for the sake of these people here!   130

                                    Strophe 1

Choragos: Open your mind to her, my lord. Be ruled by her, I beg you!
Oedipus: What would you have me do?
Choragos: Respect Creon's word. He has never spoken like a fool,
    And now he has sworn an oath.
Oedipus: You know what you ask?
Choragos: I do.
Oedipus: Speak on, then.

Choragos: A friend so sworn should not be baited so,   135
  In blind malice, and without final proof.
Oedipus: You are aware, I hope, that what you say
  Means death for me, or exile at the least.

                                                    Strophe 2

Choragos: No, I swear by Helios, first in Heaven!
    May I die friendless and accurst,   140
  The worst of deaths, if ever I meant that!
      It is the withering fields
        That hurt my sick heart:
      Must we bear all these ills,
        And now your bad blood as well?   145
Oedipus: Then let him go. And let me die, if I must,
  Or be driven by him in shame from the land of Thebes.
  It is your unhappiness, and not his talk,
  That touches me.
                  As for him—
  Wherever he goes, hatred will follow him.   150
Creon: Ugly in yielding, as you were ugly in rage!
  Natures like yours chiefly torment themselves.
Oedipus: Can you not go? Can you not leave me?
Creon: I can.
  You do not know me; but the city knows me,
  And in its eyes I am just, if not in yours.   155

    Exit Creon.

                                                    Antistrophe 1

Choragos: Lady Iocastê, did you not ask the King to go to his chambers?
Iocastê: First tell me what has happened.
Choragos: There was suspicion without evidence; yet it rankled
  As even false charges will.
Iocastê: On both sides?
Choragos: On both.
Iocastê: But what was said?
Choragos: Oh let it rest, let it be done with!   160
  Have we not suffered enough?
Oedipus: You see to what your decency has brought you:
  You have made difficulties where my heart saw none.

                                                    Antistrophe 2

Choragos: Oedipus, it is not once only I have told you—
    You must know I should count myself unwise   165
  To the point of madness, should I now forsake you—
      You, under whose hand,
        In the storm of another time,
      Our dear land sailed out free.
        But now stand fast at the helm!   170
Iocastê: In God's name, Oedipus, inform your wife as well:
  Why are you so set in this hard anger?

Oedipus: I will tell you, for none of these men deserves
　　My confidence as you do. It is Creon's work,
　　His treachery, his plotting against me.   175
Iocastê: Go on, if you can make this clear to me.
Oedipus: He charges me with the murder of Laïos.
Iocastê: Has he some knowledge? Or does he speak from hearsay?
Oedipus: He would not commit himself to such a charge,
　　But he has brought in that damnable soothsayer   180
　　To tell his story.
Iocastê:　　　　　　Set your mind at rest.
　　If it is a question of soothsayers, I tell you
　　That you will find no man whose craft gives knowledge
　　Of the unknowable.

• Here is my proof: •

　　An oracle was reported to Laïos once   185
　　(I will not say from Phoibos himself, but from
　　His appointed ministers, at any rate)
　　That his doom would be death at the hands of his own son—
　　His son, born of his flesh and of mine!

　　Now, you remember the story: Laïos was killed   190
　　By marauding strangers where three highways meet;
　　But his child had not been three days in this world
　　Before the King had pierced the baby's ankles
　　And left him to die on a lonely mountainside.

　　Thus, Apollo never caused that child   195
　　To kill his father, and it was not Laïos' fate
　　To die at the hands of his son, as he had feared.
　　This is what prophets and prophecies are worth!
　　Have no dread of them.
　　　　　　　　　　　It is God himself
　　Who can show us what he wills, in his own way.   200
Oedipus: How strange a shadowy memory crossed my mind,
　　Just now while you were speaking; it chilled my heart.
Iocastê: What do you mean? What memory do you speak of?
Oedipus: If I understand you, Laïos was killed
　　At a place where three roads meet.
Iocastê:　　　　　　　　　　So it was said;   205
　　We have no later story.
Oedipus:　　　　　　　　Where did it happen?
Iocastê: Phokis, it is called: at a place where the Theban Way
　　Divides into the roads toward Delphi and Daulia.
Oedipus: When?
Iocastê:　　　We had the news not long before you came
　　And proved the right to your succession here.   210
Oedipus: Ah, what net has God been weaving for me?
Iocastê: Oedipus! Why does this trouble you?

Oedipus: Do not ask me yet.
   First, tell me how Laïos looked, and tell me
   How old he was.
Iocastê: He was tall, his hair just touched
   With white; his form was not unlike your own.   215
Oedipus: I think that I myself may be accurst
   By my own ignorant edict.
Iocastê: You speak strangely.
   It makes me tremble to look at you, my King.
Oedipus: I am not sure that the blind man can not see.
   But I should know better if you were to tell me—   220
Iocastê: Anything—though I dread to hear you ask it.
Oedipus: Was the King lightly escorted, or did he ride
   With a large company, as a ruler should?
Iocastê: There were five men with him in all: one was a herald,
   And a single chariot, which he was driving.   225
Oedipus: Alas, that makes it plain enough!
                          But who—
   Who told you how it happened?
Iocastê: A household servant,
   The only one to escape.
Oedipus: And is he still
   A servant of ours?
Iocastê: No; for when he came back at last
   And found you enthroned in the place of the dead king,   230
   He came to me, touched my hand with his, and begged
   That I would send him away to the frontier district
   Where only the shepherds go—
   As far away from the city as I could send him.
   I granted his prayer; for although the man was a slave,   235
   He had earned more than this favor at my hands.
Oedipus: Can he be called back quickly?
Iocastê: Easily.
   But why?
Oedipus: I have taken too much upon myself
   Without enquiry; therefore I wish to consult him.
Iocastê: Then he shall come.
                     But am I not one also   240
   To whom you might confide these fears of yours?
Oedipus: That is your right; it will not be denied you,
   Now least of all; for I have reached a pitch
   Of wild foreboding. Is there anyone
   To whom I should sooner speak?   245

   Polybos of Corinth is my father.
   My mother is a Dorian: Meropê.
   I grew up chief among the men of Corinth
   Until a strange thing happened—
   Not worth my passion, it may be, but strange.   250

At a feast, a drunken man maundering in his cups
Cries out that I am not my father's son!

I contained myself that night, though I felt anger
And a sinking heart. The next day I visited
My father and mother, and questioned them. They stormed,   255
Calling it all the slanderous rant of a fool;
And this relieved me. Yet the suspicion
Remained always aching in my mind;
I knew there was talk; I could not rest;
And finally, saying nothing to my parents,   260
I went to the shrine at Delphi.
The god dismissed my question without reply;
He spoke of other things.

                Some were clear,
Full of wretchedness, dreadful, unbearable:
As, that I should lie with my own mother, breed   265
Children from whom all men would turn their eyes;
And that I should be my father's murderer.

I heard all this, and fled. And from that day
Corinth to me was only in the stars
Descending in that quarter of the sky,   270
As I wandered farther and farther on my way
To a land where I should never see the evil
Sung by the oracle. And I came to this country
Where, so you say, King Laïos was killed.

I will tell you all that happened there, my lady.   275

There were three highways
Coming together at a place I passed;
And there a herald came towards me, and a chariot
Drawn by horses, with a man such as you describe
Seated in it. The groom leading the horses   280
Forced me off the road at his lord's command;
But as this charioteer lurched over towards me
I struck him in my rage. The old man saw me
And brought his double goad down upon my head
As I came abreast.

               He was paid back, and more!   285
Swinging my club in this right hand I knocked him
Out of his car, and he rolled on the ground.

                      I killed him.

I killed them all.
Now if that stranger and Laïos were—kin,
Where is a man more miserable than I?
More hated by the gods? Citizen and alien alike   290
Must never shelter me or speak to me—

I must be shunned by all.
                      And I myself
Pronounced this malediction upon myself!

Think of it: I have touched you with these hands,   295
These hands that killed your husband. What defilement!

Am I all evil, then? It must be so,
Since I must flee from Thebes, yet never again
See my own countrymen, my own country,
For fear of joining my mother in marriage   300
And killing Polybos, my father.
                        Ah,
If I was created so, born to this fate,
Who could deny the savagery of God?

O holy majesty of heavenly powers!
May I never see that day! Never!   305
Rather let me vanish from the race of men
Than know the abomination destined me!

Choragos: We too, my lord, have felt dismay at this.
    But there is hope: you have yet to hear the shepherd.

Oedipus: Indeed, I fear no other hope is left me.   310

Iocastê: What do you hope from him when he comes?

Oedipus: This much:
    If his account of the murder tallies with yours,
    Then I am cleared.

Iocastê: What was it that I said
    Of such importance?

Oedipus: Why, "marauders," you said,
    Killed the King, according to this man's story.   315
    If he maintains that still, if there were several,
    Clearly the guilt is not mine: I was alone.
    But if he says one man, singlehanded, did it,
    Then the evidence all points to me.

Iocastê: You may be sure that he said there were several;   320
    And can he call back that story now? He can not.
    The whole city heard it as plainly as I.
    But suppose he alters some detail of it:
    He can not ever show that Laïos' death
    Fulfilled the oracle: for Apollo said   325
    My child was doomed to kill him; and my child—
    Poor baby!—it was my child that died first.

    No. From now on, where oracles are concerned,
    I would not waste a second thought on any.

Oedipus: You may be right.
                    But come: let someone go   330
    For the shepherd at once. This matter must be settled.

Iocastê: I will send for him.

I would not wish to cross you in anything,
And surely not in this.—Let us go in.

Exeunt into the palace.

ODE II

Chorus: Let me be reverent in the ways of right,   *Strophe 1*
     Lowly the paths I journey on;
     Let all my words and actions keep
     The laws of the pure universe
     From highest Heaven handed down.   5
     For Heaven is their bright nurse,
     Those generations of the realms of light;
     Ah, never of mortal kind were they begot,
     Nor are they slaves of memory, lost in sleep:
     Their Father is greater than Time, and ages not.   10

                                                                   Antistrophe 1
     The tyrant is a child of Pride
     Who drinks from his great sickening cup
     Recklessness and vanity,
     Until from his high crest headlong
     He plummets to the dust of hope.   15
     That strong man is not strong.
     But let no fair ambition be denied;
     May God protect the wrestler for the State
     In government, in comely policy,
     Who will fear God, and on His ordinance wait.   20

                                                                        Strophe 2
     Haughtiness and the high hand of disdain
     Tempt and outrage God's holy law;
     And any mortal who dares hold
     No immortal Power in awe
     Will be caught up in a net of pain: 25
     The price for which his levity is sold.
     Let each man take due earnings, then,
     And keep his hands from holy things,
     And from blasphemy stand apart—
     Else the crackling blast of heaven   30
     Blows on his head, and on his desperate heart;
     Though fools will honor impious men,
     In their cities no tragic poet sings.

                                                                   Antistrophe 2
     Shall we lose faith in Delphi's obscurities,
     We who have heard the world's core   35
     Discredited, and the sacred wood
     Of Zeus at Elis praised no more?
     The deeds and the strange prophecies
     Must make a pattern yet to be understood.
     Zeus, if indeed you are lord of all,   40

Throned in light over night and day,
Mirror this in your endless mind:
Our masters call the oracle
Words on the wind, and the Delphic vision blind!
Their hearts no longer know Apollo,   45
And reverence for the gods has died away.

SCENE III

Enter Iocastê.

Iocastê: Princes of Thebes, it has occurred to me
　　To visit the altars of the gods, bearing
　　These branches as a suppliant, and this incense.
　　Our King is not himself: his noble soul
　　Is overwrought with fantasies of dread,   5
　　Else he would consider
　　The new prophecies in the light of the old.
　　He will listen to any voice that speaks disaster,
　　And my advice goes for nothing.

She approaches the altar, right.

　　　　　　　　　　　　　　To you, then, Apollo,
　　Lycean lord, since you are nearest, I turn in prayer.   10
　　Receive these offerings, and grant us deliverance
　　From defilement. Our hearts are heavy with fear
　　When we see our leader distracted, as helpless sailors
　　Are terrified by the confusion of their helmsman.

Enter Messenger.

Messenger: Friends, no doubt you can direct me: 15
　　Where shall I find the house of Oedipus,
　　Or, better still, where is the King himself?
Choragos: It is this very place, stranger; he is inside.
　　This is his wife and mother of his children.
Messenger: I wish her happiness in a happy house,   20
　　Blest in all the fulfillment of her marriage.
Iocastê: I wish as much for you: your courtesy
　　Deserves a like good fortune. But now, tell me:
　　Why have you come? What have you to say to us?
Messenger: Good news, my lady, for your house and your husband.   25
Iocastê: What news? Who sent you here?
Messenger:　　　　　　　　　　　　　　I am from Corinth.
　　The news I bring ought to mean joy for you,
　　Though it may be you will find some grief in it.
Iocastê: What is it? How can it touch us in both ways?
Messenger: The word is that the people of the Isthmus   30
　　Intend to call Oedipus to be their king.
Iocastê: But old King Polybos—is he not reigning still?

Messenger: No. Death holds him in his sepulchre.

Iocastê: What are you saying? Polybos is dead?

Messenger: If I am not telling the truth, may I die myself.   35

Iocastê (to a Maidservant): Go in, go quickly; tell this to your master.

> O riddlers of God's will, where are you now!
> This was the man whom Oedipus, long ago,
> Feared so, fled so, in dread of destroying him—
> But it was another fate by which he died.   40

> *Enter Oedipus, center.*

Oedipus: Dearest Iocastê, why have you sent for me?

Iocastê: Listen to what this man says, and then tell me
    What has become of the solemn prophecies.

Oedipus: Who is this man? What is his news for me?

Iocastê: He has come from Corinth to announce your father's death!   45

Oedipus: Is it true, stranger? Tell me in your own words.

Messenger: I can not say it more clearly: the King is dead.

Oedipus: Was it by treason? Or by an attack of illness?

Messenger: A little thing brings old men to their rest.

Oedipus: It was sickness, then?

Messenger: Yes, and his many years.   50

Oedipus: Ah!
    Why should a man respect the Pythian hearth,° or
    Give heed to the birds that jangle above his head?
    They prophesied that I should kill Polybos,
    Kill my own father; but he is dead and buried,   55
    And I am here—I never touched him, never,
    Unless he died of grief for my departure,
    And thus, in a sense, through me. No. Polybos
    Has packed the oracles off with him underground.
    They are empty words.

Iocastê: Had I not told you so?   60

Oedipus: You had; it was my faint heart that betrayed me.

Iocastê: From now on never think of those things again.

Oedipus: And yet—must I not fear my mother's bed?

Iocastê: Why should anyone in this world be afraid,
    Since Fate rules us and nothing can be foreseen?   65
    A man should live only for the present day.

> Have no more fear of sleeping with your mother:
> How many men, in dreams, have lain with their mothers!
> No reasonable man is troubled by such things.

Oedipus: That is true; only—   70
    If only my mother were not still alive!
    But she is alive. I can not help my dread.

Iocastê: Yet this news of your father's death is wonderful.

---

52 *Pythian hearth:* the shrine at Delphi, whose priestess was famous for her prophecies.

Oedipus: Wonderful. But I fear the living woman.

Messenger: Tell me, who is this woman that you fear?   75

Oedipus: It is Meropê, man; the wife of King Polybos.

Messenger: Meropê? Why should you be afraid of her?

Oedipus: An oracle of the gods, a dreadful saying.

Messenger: Can you tell me about it or are you sworn to silence?

Oedipus: I can tell you, and I will.   80

    Apollo said through his prophet that I was the man

    Who should marry his own mother, shed his father's blood

    With his own hands. And so, for all these years

    I have kept clear of Corinth, and no harm has come—

    Though it would have been sweet to see my parents again.   85

Messenger: And is this the fear that drove you out of Corinth?

Oedipus: Would you have me kill my father?

Messenger: As for that

    You must be reassured by the news I gave you.

Oedipus: If you could reassure me, I would reward you.

Messenger: I had that in mind, I will confess: I thought   90

    I could count on you when you returned to Corinth.

Oedipus: No: I will never go near my parents again.

Messenger: Ah, son, you still do not know what you are doing—

Oedipus: What do you mean? In the name of God tell me!

Messenger: —If these are your reasons for not going home.   95

Oedipus: I tell you, I fear the oracle may come true.

Messenger: And guilt may come upon you through your parents?

Oedipus: That is the dread that is always in my heart.

Messenger: Can you not see that all your fears are groundless?

Oedipus: How can you say that? They are my parents, surely?   100

Messenger: Polybos was not your father.

Oedipus: Not my father?

Messenger: No more your father than the man speaking to you.

Oedipus: But you are nothing to me!

Messenger: Neither was he.

Oedipus: Then why did he call me son?

Messenger: I will tell you:

    Long ago he had you from my hands, as a gift.   105

Oedipus: Then how could he love me so, if I was not his?

Messenger: He had no children, and his heart turned to you.

Oedipus: What of you? Did you buy me? Did you find me by chance?

Messenger: I came upon you in the crooked pass of Kithairon.

Oedipus: And what were you doing there?

Messenger: Tending my flocks.   110

Oedipus: A wandering shepherd?

Messenger: But your savior, son, that day.

Oedipus: From what did you save me?

Messenger: Your ankles should tell you that.

Oedipus: Ah, stranger, why do you speak of that childhood pain?

Messenger: I cut the bonds that tied your ankles together.

Oedipus: I have had the mark as long as I can remember.   115

Messenger: That was why you were given the name you bear.
Oedipus: God! Was it my father or my mother who did it?
  Tell me!
Messenger: I do not know. The man who gave you to me
  Can tell you better than I.
Oedipus: It was not you that found me, but another?   120
Messenger: It was another shepherd gave you to me.
Oedipus: Who was he? Can you tell me who he was?
Messenger: I think he was said to be one of Laïos' people.
Oedipus: You mean the Laïos who was king here years ago?
Messenger: Yes; King Laïos; and the man was one of his herdsmen.   125
Oedipus: Is he still alive? Can I see him?
Messenger: These men here
  Know best about such things.
Oedipus: Does anyone here
  Know this shepherd that he is talking about?
  Have you seen him in the fields, or in the town?
  If you have, tell me. It is time things were made plain.   130
Choragos: I think the man he means is that same shepherd
  You have already asked to see. Iocastê perhaps
  Could tell you something.
Oedipus: Do you know anything
  About him, Lady? Is he the man we have summoned?
  Is that the man this shepherd means?
Iocastê: Why think of him?   135
  Forget this herdsman. Forget it all.
  This talk is a waste of time.
Oedipus: How can you say that,
  When the clues to my true birth are in my hands?
Iocastê: For God's love, let us have no more questioning!
  Is your life nothing to you?   140
  My own is pain enough for me to bear.
Oedipus: You need not worry. Suppose my mother a slave,
  And born of slaves: no baseness can touch you.
Iocastê: Listen to me, I beg you: do not do this thing!
Oedipus: I will not listen; the truth must be made known.   145
Iocastê: Everything that I say is for your own good!
Oedipus: My own good
  Snaps my patience, then; I want none of it.
Iocastê: You are fatally wrong! May you never learn who you are!
Oedipus: Go, one of you, and bring the shepherd here.
  Let us leave this woman to brag of her royal name.   150
Iocastê: Ah, miserable!
  That is the only word I have for you now.
  That is the only word I can ever have.

  Exit into the palace.

Choragos: Why has she left us, Oedipus? Why has she gone
  In such a passion of sorrow? I fear this silence: 155
  Something dreadful may come of it.

Oedipus: Let it come!
    However base my birth, I must know about it.
    The Queen, like a woman, is perhaps ashamed
    To think of my low origin. But I
    Am a child of Luck; I can not be dishonored.   160
    Luck is my mother; the passing months, my brothers,
    Have seen me rich and poor.
               If this is so,
    How could I wish that I were someone else?
    How could I not be glad to know my birth?

ODE III

                                        Strophe

Chorus: If ever the coming time were known
    To my heart's pondering,
    Kithairon, now by Heaven I see the torches
    At the festival of the next full moon,
    And see the dance, and hear the choir sing   5
    A grace to your gentle shade:
    Mountain where Oedipus was found,
    O mountain guard of a noble race!
    May the god who heals us lend his aid,
    And let that glory come to pass   10
    For our king's cradling-ground.

                                      Antistrophe

    Of the nymphs that flower beyond the years,
    Who bore you, royal child,
    To Pan of the hills or the timberline Apollo,
    Cold in delight where the upland clears,   15
    Or Hermês for whom Kyllenê's° heights are piled?
    Or flushed as evening cloud,
    Great Dionysos, roamer of mountains,
    He—was it he who found you there,
    And caught you up in his own proud   20
    Arms from the sweet god-ravisher
    Who laughed by the Muses' fountains?

SCENE IV

Oedipus: Sirs; though I do not know the man,
    I think I see him coming, this shepherd we want:
    He is old, like our friend here, and the men
    Bringing him seem to be servants of my house.
    But you can tell, if you have ever seen him.   5

    Enter Shepherd escorted by servants.

---

16 *Kyllenê:* a sacred mountain, birthplace of Hermês, the deities' messenger. The chorus assumes that the mountain was created in order to afford him birth.

Choragos: I know him, he was Laïos' man. You can trust him.

Oedipus: Tell me first, you from Corinth: is this the shepherd
    We were discussing?

Messenger: This is the very man.

Oedipus (to Shepherd): Come here. No, look at me. You must answer
    Everything I ask.—You belonged to Laïos?   10

Shepherd: Yes: born his slave, brought up in his house.

Oedipus: Tell me: what kind of work did you do for him?

Shepherd: I was a shepherd of his, most of my life.

Oedipus: Where mainly did you go for pasturage?

Shepherd: Sometimes Kithairon, sometimes the hills near-by.   15

Oedipus: Do you remember ever seeing this man out there?

Shepherd: What would he be doing there? This man?

Oedipus: This man standing here. Have you ever seen him before?

Shepherd: No. At least, not to my recollection.

Messenger: And that is not strange, my lord. But I'll refresh   20
    His memory: he must remember when we two
    Spent three whole seasons together, March to September,
    On Kithairon or thereabouts. He had two flocks;
    I had one. Each autumn I'd drive mine home
    And he would go back with his to Laïos' sheepfold.—   25
    Is this not true, just as I have described it?

Shepherd: True, yes; but it was all so long ago.

Messenger: Well, then: do you remember, back in those days
    That you gave me a baby boy to bring up as my own?

Shepherd: What if I did? What are you trying to say?   30

Messenger: King Oedipus was once that little child.

Shepherd: Damn you, hold your tongue!

Oedipus: No more of that!
    It is your tongue needs watching, not this man's.

Shepherd: My King, my Master, what is it I have done wrong?

Oedipus: You have not answered his question about the boy.   35

Shepherd: He does not know . . . He is only making trouble . . .

Oedipus: Come, speak plainly, or it will go hard with you.

Shepherd: In God's name, do not torture an old man!

Oedipus: Come here, one of you; bind his arms behind him.

Shepherd: Unhappy king! What more do you wish to learn?   40

Oedipus: Did you give this man the child he speaks of?

Shepherd: I did.
    And I would to God I had died that very day.

Oedipus: You will die now unless you speak the truth.

Shepherd: Yet if I speak the truth, I am worse than dead.

Oedipus: Very well; since you insist upon delaying—   45

Shepherd: No! I have told you already that I gave him the boy.

Oedipus: Where did you get him? From your house? From somewhere else?

Shepherd: Not from mine, no. A man gave him to me.

Oedipus: Is that man here? Do you know whose slave he was?

Shepherd: For God's love, my King, do not ask me any more!   50

Oedipus: You are a dead man if I have to ask you again.

Shepherd: Then . . . Then the child was from the palace of Laïos.
Oedipus: A slave child? or a child of his own line?
Shepherd: Ah, I am on the brink of dreadful speech!
Oedipus: And I of dreadful hearing. Yet I must hear.   55
Shepherd: If you must be told, then . . .
They said it was Laïos' child;
But it is your wife who can tell you about that.
Oedipus: My wife!—Did she give it to you?
Shepherd: My lord, she did.
Oedipus: Do you know why?
Shepherd: I was told to get rid of it.
Oedipus: An unspeakable mother!
Shepherd: <div style="text-align:center">There had been prophecies . . .</div>   60
Oedipus: Tell me.
Shepherd: It was said that the boy would kill his own father.
Oedipus: Then why did you give him over to this old man?
Shepherd: I pitied the baby, my King,
  And I thought that this man would take him far away   65
  To his own country.
He saved him—but for what a fate!
For if you are what this man says you are,
No man living is more wretched than Oedipus.
Oedipus: Ah God!
  It was true!
All the prophecies!
—Now,   70
O Light, may I look on you for the last time!
I, Oedipus,
Oedipus, damned in his birth, in his marriage damned,
Damned in the blood he shed with his own hand!

He rushes into the palace.

ODE IV

Strophe 1

Chorus: Alas for the seed of men.

  What measure shall I give these generations
  That breathe on the void and are void
  And exist and do not exist?

  Who bears more weight of joy   5
  Than mass of sunlight shifting in images,
  Or who shall make his thought stay on
  That down time drifts away?

  Your splendor is all fallen.

  O naked brow of wrath and tears,   10
  O change of Oedipus!

I who saw your days call no man blest—
Your great days like ghosts gone.

Antistrophe 1

That mind was a strong bow.

Deep, how deep you drew it then, hard archer,   15
At a dim fearful range,
And brought dear glory down!

You overcame the stranger—
The virgin with her hooking lion claws—
And though death sang, stood like a tower   20
To make pale Thebes take heart.

Fortress against our sorrow!

True king, giver of laws,
Majestic Oedipus!
No prince in Thebes had ever such renown,   25
No prince won such grace of power.

Strophe 2

And now of all men ever known
Most pitiful is this man's story:
His fortunes are most changed, his state
Fallen to a low slave's   30
Ground under bitter fate.

O Oedipus, most royal one!
The great door that expelled you to the light
Gave at night—ah, gave night to your glory:
As to the father, to the fathering son.   35

All understood too late.

How could that queen whom Laïos won,
The garden that he harrowed at his height,
Be silent when that act was done?

Antistrophe 2

But all eyes fail before time's eye,   40
All actions come to justice there.
Though never willed, though far down the deep past,
Your bed, your dread sirings,
Are brought to book at last.

Child by Laïos doomed to die,   45
Then doomed to lose that fortunate little death,
Would God you never took breath in this air
That with my wailing lips I take to cry:

For I weep the world's outcast.

I was blind, and now I can tell why:
Asleep, for you had given ease of breath   50
To Thebes, while the false years went by.

ÉXODOS°

Enter, from the palace, Second Messenger.

Second Messenger: Elders of Thebes, most honored in this land,
What horrors are yours to see and hear, what weight
Of sorrow to be endured, if, true to your birth,
You venerate the line of Labdakos!
I think neither Istros nor Phasis, those great rivers,   5
Could purify this place of the corruption
It shelters now, or soon must bring to light—
Evil not done unconsciously, but willed.

The greatest griefs are those we cause ourselves.
Choragos: Surely, friend, we have grief enough already;   10
What new sorrow do you mean?
Second Messenger: The Queen is dead.
Choragos: Iocastê? Dead? But at whose hand?
Second Messenger: Her own.
The full horror of what happened, you can not know,
For you did not see it; but I, who did, will tell you
As clearly as I can how she met her death.   15

When she had left us,
In passionate silence, passing through the court,
She ran to her apartment in the house,
Her hair clutched by the fingers of both hands.
She closed the doors behind her; then, by that bed   20
Where long ago the fatal son was conceived—
That son who should bring about his father's death—
We heard her call upon Laïos, dead so many years,
And heard her wail for the double fruit of her marriage,
A husband by her husband, children by her child.   25

Exactly how she died I do not know:
For Oedipus burst in moaning and would not let us
Keep vigil to the end: it was by him
As he stormed about the room that our eyes were caught.
From one to another of us he went, begging a sword,   30
Cursing the wife who was not his wife, the mother
Whose womb had carried his own children and himself.
I do not know: it was none of us aided him,
But surely one of the gods was in control!
For with a dreadful cry   35
He hurled his weight, as though wrenched out of himself,
At the twin doors: the bolts gave, and he rushed in.
And there we saw her hanging, her body swaying
From the cruel cord she had noosed about her neck.
A great sob broke from him, heartbreaking to hear,   40
As he loosed the rope and lowered her to the ground.

Éxodos: final scene, containing the resolution.

I would blot out from my mind what happened next!
For the King ripped from her gown the golden brooches
That were her ornament, and raised them, and plunged them down
Straight into his own eyeballs, crying, "No more,   45
No more shall you look on the misery about me,
The horrors of my own doing! Too long you have known
The faces of those whom I should never have seen,
Too long been blind to those for whom I was searching!
From this hour, go in darkness!" And as he spoke,   50
He struck at his eyes—not once, but many times;
And the blood spattered his beard,
Bursting from his ruined sockets like red hail.

So from the unhappiness of two this evil has sprung,
A curse on the man and woman alike. The old   55
Happiness of the house of Labdakos
Was happiness enough: where is it today?
It is all wailing and ruin, disgrace, death—all
The misery of mankind that has a name—
And it is wholly and for ever theirs.   60

Choragos: Is he in agony still? Is there no rest for him?

Second Messenger: He is calling for someone to lead him to the gates
So that all the children of Kadmos may look upon
His father's murderer, his mother's—no,
I can not say it!
                              And then he will leave Thebes,   65
Self-exiled, in order that the curse
Which he himself pronounced may depart from the house.
He is weak, and there is none to lead him,
So terrible is his suffering.
                              But you will see:
Look, the doors are opening; in a moment   70
You will see a thing that would crush a heart of stone.

The central door is opened; Oedipus, blinded, is led in.

Choragos: Dreadful indeed for men to see.
    Never have my own eyes
    Looked on a sight so full of fear.

    Oedipus!   75
    What madness came upon you, what daemon
    Leaped on your life with heavier
    Punishment than a mortal man can bear?
    No: I can not even
    Look at you, poor ruined one.   80
    And I would speak, question, ponder,
    If I were able. No.
    You make me shudder.

Oedipus: God. God.

Is there a sorrow greater?   85
Where shall I find harbor in this world?
My voice is hurled far on a dark wind.
What has God done to me?
Choragos: Too terrible to think of, or to see.

Strophe 1

Oedipus: O cloud of night,   90
    Never to be turned away: night coming on,
    I can not tell how: night like a shroud!

    My fair winds brought me here.
                        Oh God. Again
    The pain of the spikes where I had sight,
    The flooding pain   95
    Of memory, never to be gouged out.
Choragos: This is not strange.
    You suffer it all twice over, remorse in pain,
    Pain in remorse.

Antistrophe 1

Oedipus: Ah dear friend   100
    Are you faithful even yet, you alone?
    Are you still standing near me, will you stay here,
    Patient, to care for the blind?
                        The blind man!
    Yet even blind I know who it is attends me,
    By the voice's tone—   105
    Though my new darkness hide the comforter.
Choragos: Oh fearful act!
    What god was it drove you to rake black
    Night across your eyes?

Strophe 2

Oedipus: Apollo. Apollo. Dear   110
    Children, the god was Apollo.
    He brought my sick, sick fate upon me.
    But the blinding hand was my own!
    How could I bear to see
    When all my sight was horror everywhere?   115
Choragos: Everywhere; that is true.
Oedipus: And now what is left?
    Images? Love? A greeting even,
    Sweet to the senses? Is there anything?
    Ah, no, friends: lead me away.   120
    Lead me away from Thebes.
                        Lead the great wreck
    And hell of Oedipus, whom the gods hate.
Choragos: Your fate is clear, you are not blind to that.
    Would God you had never found it out!

Antistrophe 2

Oedipus: Death take the man who unbound   125
      My feet on that hillside
      And delivered me from death to life! What life?
      If only I had died,
      This weight of monstrous doom
      Could not have dragged me and my darlings down.   130
Choragos: I would have wished the same.
Oedipus: Oh never to have come here
      With my father's blood upon me! Never
      To have been the man they call his mother's husband!
      Oh accurst! Oh child of evil,   135
      To have entered that wretched bed—
                                    the selfsame one!
      More primal than sin itself, this fell to me.
Choragos: I do not know how I can answer you.
      You were better dead than alive and blind.
Oedipus: Do not counsel me any more. This punishment   140
      That I have laid upon myself is just.
      If I had eyes,
      I do not know how I could bear the sight
      Of my father, when I came to the house of Death,
      Or my mother: for I have sinned against them both   145
      So vilely that I could not make my peace
      By strangling my own life.
                                    Or do you think my children,
      Born as they were born, would be sweet to my eyes?
      Ah never, never! Nor this town with its high walls,
      Nor the holy images of the gods.
                                    For I,   150
      Thrice miserable!—Oedipus, noblest of all the line
      Of Kadmos, have condemned myself to enjoy
      These things no more, by my own malediction
      Expelling that man whom the gods declared
      To be a defilement in the house of Laïos.   155
      After exposing the rankness of my own guilt,
      How could I look men frankly in the eyes?
      No, I swear it,
      If I could have stifled my hearing at its source,
      I would have done it and made all this body   160
      A tight cell of misery, blank to light and sound:
      So I should have been safe in a dark agony
      Beyond all recollection.
                                    Ah Kithairon!
      Why did you shelter me? When I was cast upon you,
      Why did I not die? Then I should never   165
      Have shown the world my execrable birth.

      Ah Polybos! Corinth, city that I believed
      The ancient seat of my ancestors: how fair

I seemed, your child! And all the while this evil
Was cancerous within me!
                              For I am sick   170
In my daily life, sick in my origin.

O three roads, dark ravine, woodland and way
Where three roads met: you, drinking my father's blood,
My own blood, spilled by my own hand: can you remember
The unspeakable things I did there, and the things   175
I went on from there to do?
                              O marriage, marriage!
The act that engendered me, and again the act
Performed by the son in the same bed—
                              Ah, the net
Of incest, mingling fathers, brothers, sons,
With brides, wives, mothers: the last evil   180
That can be known by men: no tongue can say
How evil!
              No. For the love of God, conceal me
Somewhere far from Thebes; or kill me; or hurl me
Into the sea, away from men's eyes for ever.

Come, lead me. You need not fear to touch me.   185
Of all men, I alone can bear this guilt.

Enter Creon.

Choragos: We are not the ones to decide; but Creon here
    May fitly judge of what you ask. He only
    Is left to protect the city in your place.
Oedipus: Alas, how can I speak to him? What right have I   190
    To beg his courtesy whom I have deeply wronged?
Creon: I have not come to mock you, Oedipus,
    Or to reproach you, either.
    (*To Attendants.*)   —You, standing there:
    If you have lost all respect for man's dignity,
    At least respect the flame of Lord Helios: 195
    Do not allow this pollution to show itself
    Openly here, an affront to the earth
    And Heaven's rain and the light of day. No, take him
    Into the house as quickly as you can.
    For it is proper   200
    That only the close kindred see his grief.
Oedipus: I pray you in God's name, since your courtesy
    Ignores my dark expectation, visiting
    With mercy this man of all men most execrable:
    Give me what I ask—for your good, not for mine.   205
Creon: And what is it that you would have me do?
Oedipus: Drive me out of this country as quickly as may be
    To a place where no human voice can ever greet me.
Creon: I should have done that before now—only,
    God's will had not been wholly revealed to me.   210

Oedipus: But his command is plain: the parricide
   Must be destroyed. I am that evil man.
Creon: That is the sense of it, yes; but as things are,
   We had best discover clearly what is to be done.
Oedipus: You would learn more about a man like me?   215
Creon: You are ready now to listen to the god.
Oedipus: I will listen. But it is to you
   That I must turn for help. I beg you, hear me.

The woman in there—
Give her whatever funeral you think proper: 220
She is your sister.
                    —But let me go, Creon!
Let me purge my father's Thebes of the pollution
Of my living here, and go out to the wild hills,
To Kithairon, that has won such fame with me,
The tomb my mother and father appointed for me,   225
And let me die there, as they willed I should.
And yet I know
Death will not ever come to me through sickness
Or in any natural way: I have been preserved
For some unthinkable fate. But let that be.   230

As for my sons, you need not care for them.
They are men, they will find some way to live.
But my poor daughters, who have shared my table,
Who never before have been parted from their father—
Take care of them, Creon; do this for me.   235
And will you let me touch them with my hands
A last time, and let us weep together?
Be kind, my lord,
Great prince, be kind!
                    Could I but touch them,
They would be mine again, as when I had my eyes.   240

Enter Antigonê and Ismene, attended.

Ah, God!
Is it my dearest children I hear weeping?
Has Creon pitied me and sent my daughters?
Creon: Yes, Oedipus: I knew that they were dear to you
   In the old days, and know you must love them still.   245
Oedipus: May God bless you for this—and be a friendlier
   Guardian to you than he has been to me!

Children, where are you?
Come quickly to my hands: they are your brother's—
Hands that have brought your father's once clear eyes   250
To this way of seeing—
                    Ah dearest ones,
I had neither sight nor knowledge then, your father

By the woman who was the source of his own life!
And I weep for you—having no strength to see you—,
I weep for you when I think of the bitterness   255
That men will visit upon you all your lives.
What homes, what festivals can you attend
Without being forced to depart again in tears?
And when you come to marriageable age,
Where is the man, my daughters, who would dare   260
Risk the bane that lies on all my children?
Is there any evil wanting? Your father killed
His father; sowed the womb of her who bore him;
Engendered you at the fount of his own existence!
That is what they will say of you.

                        Then, whom   265
Can you ever marry? There are no bridegrooms for you,
And your lives must wither away in sterile dreaming.

O Creon, son of Menoikeus!
You are the only father my daughters have,
Since we, their parents, are both of us gone for ever.   270
They are your own blood: you will not let them
Fall into beggary and loneliness;
You will keep them from the miseries that are mine!
Take pity on them; see, they are only children,
Friendless except for you. Promise me this,   275
Great Prince, and give me your hand in token of it.

Creon clasps his right hand.

Children:
I could say much, if you could understand me,
But as it is, I have only this prayer for you:
Live where you can, be as happy as you can—   280
Happier, please God, than God has made your father!
Creon: Enough. You have wept enough. Now go within.
Oedipus: I must; but it is hard.
Creon: Time eases all things.
Oedipus: But you must promise—
Creon: Say what you desire.
Oedipus: Send me from Thebes!
Creon: God grant that I may!   285
Oedipus: But since God hates me . . .
Creon: No, he will grant your wish.
Oedipus: You promise?
Creon: I can not speak beyond my knowledge.
Oedipus: Then lead me in.
Creon: Come now, and leave your children.
Oedipus: No! Do not take them from me!
Creon: Think no longer
That you are in command here, but rather think   290
How, when you were, you served your own destruction.

Exeunt into the house all but the Chorus; the Choragos chants directly to the audience.

Choragos: Men of Thebes: look upon Oedipus.

This is the king who solved the famous riddle
And towered up, most powerful of men.
No mortal eyes but looked on him with envy,   295
Yet in the end ruin swept over him.

Let every man in mankind's frailty
Consider his last day; and let none
Presume on his good fortune until he find
Life, at his death, a memory without pain.   300

Questions

1. How explicitly does the prophet Teiresias reveal the guilt of Oedipus? Does it seem to you stupidity on the part of Oedipus or a defect in Sophocles' play that the king takes so long to recognize his guilt and to admit to it?

2. How does Oedipus exhibit weakness of character? Point to lines that reveal him as imperfectly noble in his words, deeds, or treatment of others.

3. "Oedipus is punished not for any fault in himself, but for his ignorance. Not knowing his family history, unable to recognize his parents on sight, he is blameless; and in slaying his father and marrying his mother, he behaves as any sensible person might behave in the same circumstances." Do you agree with this interpretation?

4. Besides the predictions of Teiresias, what other foreshadowings of the shepherd's revelation does the play contain?

5. Consider the character of Iocastê. Is she a "flat" character—a generalized queen figure—or an individual with distinctive traits of personality? Point to speeches or details in the play to back up your opinion.

6. What is dramatic irony? Besides the example given on page 660, what other instances of dramatic irony do you find in *Oedipus the King*? What do they contribute to the effectiveness of the play?

7. In the drama of Sophocles, violence and bloodshed take place offstage; thus, the suicide of Iocastê is only reported to us. Nor do we witness Oedipus' removal of his eyes; this horror is only given in the report by the second messenger. Of what advantage or disadvantage to the play is this limitation?

8. For what reason does Oedipus blind himself? What meaning, if any, do you find in his choice of a surgical instrument?

9. What are your feelings toward him as the play ends?

10. Read the famous interpretation of this play offered by Sigmund Freud (page 1233). How well does Freud explain why the play moves you?

11. With what attitude toward the gods does the play leave you? By inflicting a plague on Thebes, by causing barrenness, by cursing both the people and their king, do the gods seem cruel, unjust, or tyrannical? Does the play show any reverence toward them?

12. Does this play end in total gloom?

THE BACKGROUND OF *ANTIGONÊ*

Although *Antigonê* tells a later part of the Oedipus story, it was not part of the trilogy that originally contained *Oedipus the King* (the other plays in that trilogy have been lost). *Antigonê* was written in 441 B.C., over twenty years before the author took up the tale of Oedipus himself. In *Antigonê* duties to family and duties to the state are pitted

Antigonê. **Martha Henry in the 1971 Lincoln Center Repertory production.**

against one another in a story that has Creon, now king of Thebes many years after Oedipus' exile and death, refusing burial to the body of Oedipus' son (and brother) Polyneicês, who has led an army against the city to claim the throne from his brother. His sister Antigonê (Oedipus' daughter and sister) resists Creon's unjust edict in the name of family loyalty, a defiance both noble and potentially threatening to political stability in a time of crisis. Though the gods approve of her action, she dies a victim of Creon's hubris. (Or perhaps, as Patricia Lines suggests on page 1236, Antigonê's own hubris is her downfall.) Creon suffers the death (by suicide) of his son and his wife as a result. Antigonê's claim is especially compelling when we imagine her played by a mature male actor who in his public life, as a citizen, must know both how to rule and how to be ruled, to submit to legitimate authority when he steps down from office.

Antigonê

441 B.C.

Translated by Dudley Fitts and Robert Fitzgerald

CHARACTERS

Antigonê	*Teiresias*
Ismenê	*A Sentry*
Eurydicê	*A Messenger*
Creon	*Chorus*
Haimon	

SCENE *Before the palace of Creon, King of Thebes. A central double door, and two lateral doors. A platform extends the length of the façade, and from this platform three steps lead down into the "orchestra," or chorus-ground.*

TIME: *Dawn of the day after the repulse of the Argive army from the assault on Thebes.*

PROLOGUE°

Antigonê and Ismenê enter from the central door of the palace.

Antigonê: Ismenê, dear sister,
    You would think that we had already suffered enough
    For the curse on Oedipus:°
    I cannot imagine any grief
    That you and I have not gone through. And now—   5
    Have they told you of the new decree of our King Creon?
Ismenê: I have heard nothing: I know
    That two sisters lost two brothers, a double death
    In a single hour; and I know that the Argive army
    Fled in the night; but beyond this, nothing.   10
Antigonê: I thought so. And that is why I wanted you
    To come out here with me. There is something we must do.
Ismenê: Why do you speak so strangely?
Antigonê: Listen, Ismenê:
    Creon buried our brother Eteoclês   15
    With military honors, gave him a soldier's funeral,
    And it was right that he should; but Polyneicês,
    Who fought as bravely and died as miserably,—
    They say that Creon has sworn
    No one shall bury him, no one mourn for him,   20
    But his body must lie in the fields, a sweet treasure
    For carrion birds to find as they search for food.
    That is what they say, and our good Creon is coming here
    To announce it publicly; and the penalty—
    Stoning to death in the public square!
                              There it is,   25

Prologue: portion of the play containing the exposition, or explanation of what has gone before and what is now happening.   3 *the curse on Oedipus:* As Sophocles tells in *Oedipus the King,* the King of Thebes discovered that he had lived his life under a curse. Unknowingly, he had slain his father and married his mother. On realizing this terrible truth, Oedipus put out his own eyes and departed into exile. Now, years later, as *Antigonê* opens, Antigonê and Ismenê, daughters of Oedipus, are recalling how their two brothers died. After the abdication of their father, the brothers had ruled Thebes together. But they fell to quarreling. When Eteoclês expelled Polyneicês, the latter returned with an army and attacked the city. The two brothers killed each other in combat, leaving the throne to Creon. The new king of Thebes has buried Eteoclês with full honors, but, calling Polyneicês a traitor, has decreed that his body shall be left to the crows—an especially terrible decree, for a rotting corpse might offend Zeus; bring down plague, blight, and barrenness upon Thebes; and prevent the soul of a dead hero from entering the Elysian Fields, abode of those favored by the gods.

And now you can prove what you are:
A true sister, or a traitor to your family.
Ismenê: Antigonê, you are mad! What could I possibly do?
Antigonê: You must decide whether you will help me or not.
Ismenê: I do not understand you. Help you in what? 30
Antigonê: Ismenê, I am going to bury him. Will you come?
Ismenê: Bury him! You have just said the new law forbids it.
Antigonê: He is my brother. And he is your brother, too.
Ismenê: But think of the danger! Think what Creon will do!
Antigonê: Creon is not strong enough to stand in my way. 35
Ismenê: Ah sister!
      Oedipus died, everyone hating him
For what his own search brought to light, his eyes
Ripped out by his own hand; and Iocastê died,
His mother and wife at once: she twisted the cords 40
That strangled her life; and our two brothers died,
Each killed by the other's sword. And we are left:
But oh, Antigonê,
Think how much more terrible than these
Our own death would be if we should go against Creon 45
And do what he has forbidden! We are only women,
We cannot fight with men, Antigonê!
The law is strong, we must give in to the law
In this thing, and in worse. I beg the Dead
To forgive me, but I am helpless: I must yield 50
To those in authority. And I think it is dangerous business
To be always meddling.
Antigonê: If that is what you think,
I should not want you, even if you asked to come.
You have made your choice, you can be what you want to be.
But I will bury him; and if I must die, 55
I say that this crime is holy: I shall lie down
With him in death, and I shall be as dear
To him as he to me.
            It is the dead,
Not the living, who make the longest demands:
We die for ever . . .
                  You may do as you like, 60
Since apparently the laws of the gods mean nothing to you.
Ismenê: They mean a great deal to me; but I have no strength
   To break laws that were made for the public good.
Antigonê: That must be your excuse, I suppose. But as for me,
   I will bury the brother I love.
Ismenê: Antigonê, 65
   I am so afraid for you!
Antigonê: You need not be:
   You have yourself to consider, after all.
Ismenê: But no one must hear of this, you must tell no one!
   I will keep it a secret, I promise!

Antigonê: O tell it! Tell everyone!
    Think how they'll hate you when it all comes out   70
    If they learn that you knew about it all the time!
Ismenê: So fiery! You should be cold with fear.
Antigonê: Perhaps. But I am doing only what I must.
Ismenê: But you can do it? I say that you cannot.
Antigonê: Very well: when my strength gives out, I shall do no more.   75
Ismenê: Impossible things should not be tried at all.
Antigonê: Go away, Ismenê:
    I shall be hating you soon, and the dead will too,
    For your words are hateful. Leave me my foolish plan:
    I am not afraid of the danger; if it means death,
    It will not be the worst of deaths—death without honor.   80
Ismenê: Go then, if you feel that you must.
    You are unwise,
    But a loyal friend indeed to those who love you.

Exit into the palace. Antigonê goes off, left. Enter the Chorus.

PÁRODOS°

Strophe° 1

Chorus: Now the long blade of the sun, lying
    Level east to west, touches with glory
    Thebes of the Seven Gates. Open, unlidded
    Eye of golden day! O marching light
    Across the eddy and rush of Dircê's stream,°   5
    Striking the white shields of the enemy
    Thrown headlong backward from the blaze of morning!
Choragos:° Polyneicês their commander
    Roused them with windy phrases,
    He the wild eagle screaming   10
    Insults above our land,
    His wings their shields of snow,
    His crest their marshalled helms.

Antistrophe° 1

Chorus: Against our seven gates in a yawning ring
    The famished spears came onward in the night;   15
    But before his jaws were sated with our blood,
    Or pinefire took the garland of our towers,
    He was thrown back; and as he turned, great Thebes—
    No tender victim for his noisy power—
    Rose like a dragon behind him, shouting war.   20
Choragos: For God hates utterly
    The bray of bragging tongues;

Párodos: a song sung by the chorus on first entering. Its *strophe* (according to scholarly theory) was sung while the chorus danced from stage right to stage left; its *antistrophe,* while it danced back again. Another párodos follows the prologue of *Oedipus the King.* 5 *Dircê's stream:* river near Thebes. 8 *Choragos:* leader of the Chorus and principal commentator on the play's action.

And when he beheld their smiling,
Their swagger of golden helms,
The frown of his thunder blasted   25
Their first man from our walls.

Strophe 2

Chorus: We heard his shout of triumph high in the air
Turn to a scream; far out in a flaming arc
He fell with his windy torch, and the earth struck him.
And others storming in fury no less than his   30
Found shock of death in the dusty joy of battle.

Choragos: Seven captains at seven gates
Yielded their clanging arms to the god
That bends the battle-line and breaks it.
These two only, brothers in blood,   35
Face to face in matchless rage,
Mirroring each the other's death,
Clashed in long combat.

Antistrophe 2

Chorus: But now in the beautiful morning of victory
Let Thebes of the many chariots sing for joy!   40
With hearts for dancing we'll take leave of war:
Our temples shall be sweet with hymns of praise,
And the long night shall echo with our chorus.

SCENE I

Choragos: But now at last our new King is coming:
Creon of Thebes, Menoikeus' son.
In this auspicious dawn of his reign
What are the new complexities
That shifting Fate has woven for him?   5
What is his counsel? Why has he summoned
The old men to hear him?

Enter Creon from the palace, center. He addresses the Chorus from the top step.

Creon: Gentlemen: I have the honor to inform you that our Ship of State, which recent
storms have threatened to destroy, has come safely to harbor at last, guided by
the merciful wisdom of Heaven. I have summoned you here this morning   10
because I know that I can depend upon you: your devotion to King Laïos was
absolute; you never hesitated in your duty to our late ruler Oedipus; and when
Oedipus died, your loyalty was transferred to his children. Unfortunately, as you
know, his two sons, the princes Eteoclês and Polyneicês, have killed each other
in battle; and I, as the next in blood, have succeeded to the full power of the   15
throne.

I am aware, of course, that no Ruler can expect complete loyalty from his
subjects until he has been tested in office. Nevertheless, I say to you at the very
outset that I have nothing but contempt for the kind of Governor who is afraid,
for whatever reason, to follow the course that he knows is best for the State; and   20

as for the man who sets private friendship above the public welfare,—I have no
use for him, either. I call God to witness that if I saw my country headed for ruin,
I should not be afraid to speak out plainly; and I need hardly remind you that I
would never have any dealings with an enemy of the people. No one values
friendship more highly than I; but we must remember that friends made at the   25
risk of wrecking our Ship are not real friends at all.

　　These are my principles, at any rate, and that is why I have made the following decision concerning the sons of Oedipus: Eteoclês, who died as a man
should die, fighting for his country, is to be buried with full military honors,
with all the ceremony that is usual when the greatest heroes die; but his brother   30
Polyneicês, who broke his exile to come back with fire and sword against his
native city and the shrines of his fathers' gods, whose one idea was to spill the
blood of his blood and sell his own people into slavery—Polyneicês, I say, is to
have no burial: no man is to touch him or say the least prayer for him; he shall
lie on the plain, unburied; and the birds and the scavenging dogs can do with   35
him whatever they like.

　　This is my command, and you can see the wisdom behind it. As long as I am
King, no traitor is going to be honored with the loyal man. But whoever shows
by word and deed that he is on the side of the State,—he shall have my respect
while he is living, and my reverence when he is dead.   40

Choragos: If that is your will, Creon son of Menoikeus,
　　You have the right to enforce it: we are yours.
Creon: That is my will. Take care that you do your part.
Choragos: We are old men: let the younger ones carry it out.
Creon: I do not mean that: the sentries have been appointed.   45
Choragos: Then what is it that you would have us do?
Creon: You will give no support to whoever breaks this law.
Choragos: Only a crazy man is in love with death!
Creon: And death it is, yet money talks, and the wisest
　　Have sometimes been known to count a few coins too many.   50

　　Enter Sentry from left.

Sentry: I'll not say that I'm out of breath from running, King, because every time I
　　stopped to think about what I have to tell you, I felt like going back. And all the
　　time a voice kept saying, "You fool, don't you know you're walking straight into
　　trouble?"; and then another voice: "Yes, but if you let somebody else get the
　　news to Creon first, it will be even worse than that for you!" But good sense won 55
　　out, at least I hope it was good sense, and here I am with a story that makes no
　　sense at all; but I'll tell it anyhow, because, as they say, what's going to happen's
　　going to happen and—
Creon: Come to the point. What have you to say?
Sentry: I did not do it. I did not see who did it. You must not punish me for what 60
　　someone else has done.
Creon: A comprehensive defense! More effective, perhaps,
　　If I knew its purpose. Come: what is it?
Sentry: A dreadful thing . . . I don't know how to put it—
Creon: Out with it!
Sentry:　　　　　Well, then;   65

The dead man—
>   Polyneicês—

Pause. The Sentry is overcome, fumbles for words. Creon waits impassively.

>   out there—
>   someone,—

New dust on the slimy flesh!

Pause. No sign from Creon.

Someone has given it burial that way, and
Gone . . .

Long pause. Creon finally speaks with deadly control.

Creon: And the man who dared do this?
Sentry: I swear I   70
>   Do not know! You must believe me!
>   Listen:
>   The ground was dry, not a sign of digging, no,
>   Not a wheeltrack in the dust, no trace of anyone.
>   It was when they relieved us this morning: and one of them,
>   The corporal, pointed to it.
>   There it was,   75
>   The strangest—
>   Look:
>   The body, just mounded over with light dust: you see?
>   Not buried really, but as if they'd covered it
>   Just enough for the ghost's peace. And no sign
>   Of dogs or any wild animal that had been there.   80
>
>   And then what a scene there was! Every man of us
>   Accusing the other: we all proved the other man did it,
>   We all had proof that we could not have done it.
>   We were ready to take hot iron in our hands,
>   Walk through fire, swear by all the gods,   85
>   *It was not I!*
>   *I do not know who it was, but it was not I!*

Creon's rage has been mounting steadily, but the Sentry is too intent upon his story to notice it.

>   And then, when this came to nothing, someone said
>   A thing that silenced us and made us stare
>   Down at the ground: you had to be told the news,   90
>   And one of us had to do it! We threw the dice,
>   And the bad luck fell to me. So here I am,
>   No happier to be here than you are to have me:
>   Nobody likes the man who brings bad news.
Choragos: I have been wondering, King: can it be that the gods have done this?   95
Creon (*furiously*): Stop!

Must you doddering wrecks
Go out of your heads entirely? "The gods"!
Intolerable!
The gods favor this corpse? Why? How had he served them?   100
Tried to loot their temples, burn their images,
Yes, and the whole State, and its laws with it!
Is it your senile opinion that the gods love to honor bad men?
A pious thought!—
                         No, from the very beginning
There have been those who have whispered together,   105
Stiff-necked anarchists, putting their heads together,
Scheming against me in alleys. These are the men,
And they have bribed my own guard to do this thing.

(*Sententiously.*) Money!
There's nothing in the world so demoralizing as money.   110
Down go your cities,
Homes gone, men gone, honest hearts corrupted,
Crookedness of all kinds, and all for money!
(*To Sentry.*)   But you—!
I swear by God and by the throne of God,
The man who has done this thing shall pay for it!   115
Find that man, bring him here to me, or your death
Will be the least of your problems: I'll string you up
Alive, and there will be certain ways to make you
Discover your employer before you die;
And the process may teach you a lesson you seem to have missed: 120
The dearest profit is sometimes all too dear:
That depends on the source. Do you understand me?
A fortune won is often misfortune.
Sentry: King, may I speak?
Creon: Your very voice distresses me.
Sentry: Are you sure that it is my voice, and not your conscience?   125
Creon: By God, he wants to analyze me now!
Sentry: It is not what I say, but what has been done, that hurts you.
Creon: You talk too much.
Sentry: Maybe; but I've done nothing.
Creon: Sold your soul for some silver: that's all you've done.
Sentry: How dreadful it is when the right judge judges wrong!   130
Creon: Your figures of speech
May entertain you now; but unless you bring me the man,
You will get little profit from them in the end.

Exit Creon into the palace.

Sentry: "Bring me the man"—!
I'd like nothing better than bringing him the man!   135
But bring him or not, you have seen the last of me here.
At any rate, I am safe!

Exit Sentry.

ODE I°

Strophe 1

Chorus: Numberless are the world's wonders, but none
 More wonderful than man; the stormgray sea
 Yields to his prows, the huge crests bear him high;
 Earth, holy and inexhaustible, is graven
 With shining furrows where his plows have gone   5
 Year after year, the timeless labor of stallions.

Antistrophe 1

 The lightboned birds and beasts that cling to cover,
 The lithe fish lighting their reaches of dim water,
 All are taken, tamed in the net of his mind;
 The lion on the hill, the wild horse windy-maned,   10
 Resign to him; and his blunt yoke has broken
 The sultry shoulders of the mountain bull.

Strophe 2

 Words also, and thought as rapid as air,
 He fashions to his good use; statecraft is his,
 And his the skill that deflects the arrows of snow,   15
 The spears of winter rain: from every wind
 He has made himself secure—from all but one:
 In the late wind of death he cannot stand.

Antistrophe 2

 O clear intelligence, force beyond all measure!
 O fate of man, working both good and evil!   20
 When the laws are kept, how proudly his city stands!
 When the laws are broken, what of his city then?
 Never may the anárchic man find rest at my hearth,
 Never be it said that my thoughts are his thoughts.

SCENE II

Re-enter Sentry leading Antigonê.

Choragos: What does this mean? Surely this captive woman
 Is the Princess, Antigonê. Why should she be taken?
Sentry: Here is the one who did it! We caught her
 In the very act of burying him.—Where is Creon?
Choragos: Just coming from the house.

  Enter Creon, center.

Creon: What has happened?   5
 Why have you come back so soon?
Sentry (expansively):   O King,

Ode I: first song sung by the Chorus, who at the same time danced. Here again, as in the *párodos*, *strophe* and *antistrophe* probably divide the song into two movements of the dance: right to left, then left to right.

A man should never be too sure of anything:
I would have sworn
That you'd not see me here again: your anger
Frightened me so, and the things you threatened me with;   10
But how could I tell then
That I'd be able to solve the case so soon?

No dice-throwing this time: I was only too glad to come!

Here is this woman. She is the guilty one:
We found her trying to bury him.   15
Take her, then; question her; judge her as you will.
I am through with the whole thing now, and glad of it.
Creon: But this is Antigonê! Why have you brought her here?
Sentry: She was burying him, I tell you!
Creon (severely):   Is this the truth?
Sentry: I saw her with my own eyes. Can I say more?   20
Creon: The details: come, tell me quickly!
Sentry: It was like this:
After those terrible threats of yours, King,
We went back and brushed the dust away from the body.
The flesh was soft by now, and stinking,
So we sat on a hill to windward and kept guard.   25
No napping this time! We kept each other awake.
But nothing happened until the white round sun
Whirled in the center of the round sky over us:
Then, suddenly,
A storm of dust roared up from the earth, and the sky   30
Went out, the plain vanished with all its trees
In the stinging dark. We closed our eyes and endured it.
The whirlwind lasted a long time, but it passed;
And then we looked, and there was Antigonê!

I have seen   35
A mother bird come back to a stripped nest, heard
Her crying bitterly a broken note or two
For the young ones stolen. Just so, when this girl
Found the bare corpse, and all her love's work wasted,
She wept, and cried on heaven to damn the hands   40
That had done this thing.
                              And then she brought more dust
And sprinkled wine three times for her brother's ghost.

We ran and took her at once. She was not afraid,
Not even when we charged her with what she had done.
She denied nothing.
                        And this was a comfort to me,   45
And some uneasiness: for it is a good thing
To escape from death, but it is no great pleasure
To bring death to a friend.
                              Yet I always say
There is nothing so comfortable as your own safe skin!

Creon (*slowly, dangerously*): And you, Antigonê,   50
  You with your head hanging,—do you confess this thing?
Antigonê: I do. I deny nothing.
Creon (*to Sentry*):   You may go.

  Exit Sentry.

(*To Antigonê.*) Tell me, tell me briefly:
  Had you heard my proclamation touching this matter?
Antigonê: It was public. Could I help hearing it?   55
Creon: And yet you dared defy the law.
Antigonê: I dared.
  It was not God's proclamation. That final Justice
  That rules the world below makes no such laws.

  Your edict, King, was strong,
  But all your strength is weakness itself against   60
  The immortal unrecorded laws of God.
  They are not merely now: they were, and shall be,
  Operative for ever, beyond man utterly.

  I knew I must die, even without your decree:
  I am only mortal. And if I must die   65
  Now, before it is my time to die,
  Surely this is no hardship: can anyone
  Living, as I live, with evil all about me,
  Think Death less than a friend? This death of mine
  Is of no importance; but if I had left my brother   70
  Lying in death unburied, I should have suffered.
  Now I do not.
                    You smile at me. Ah Creon,
  Think me a fool, if you like; but it may well be
  That a fool convicts me of folly.
Choragos: Like father, like daughter: both headstrong, deaf to reason!   75
  She has never learned to yield.
Creon: She has much to learn.
  The inflexible heart breaks first, the toughest iron
  Cracks first, and the wildest horses bend their necks
  At the pull of the smallest curb.
                                Pride? In a slave?
  This girl is guilty of a double insolence,   80
  Breaking the given laws and boasting of it.
  Who is the man here,
  She or I, if this crime goes unpunished?
  Sister's child, or more than sister's child,
  Or closer yet in blood—she and her sister   85
  Win bitter death for this!
  (*To Servants.*)   Go, some of you,
  Arrest Ismenê. I accuse her equally.
  Bring her: you will find her sniffling in the house there.

  Her mind's a traitor: crimes kept in the dark

Cry for light, and the guardian brain shudders;   90
But how much worse than this
Is brazen boasting of barefaced anarchy!
Antigonê: Creon, what more do you want than my death?
Creon: Nothing.
      That gives me everything.
Antigonê: Then I beg you: kill me.
      This talking is a great weariness: your words   95
      Are distasteful to me, and I am sure that mine
      Seem so to you. And yet they should not seem so:
      I should have praise and honor for what I have done.
      All these men here would praise me
      Were their lips not frozen shut with fear of you.   100
      (*Bitterly.*) Ah the good fortune of kings,
      Licensed to say and do whatever they please!
Creon: You are alone here in that opinion.
Antigonê: No, they are with me. But they keep their tongues in leash.
Creon: Maybe. But you are guilty, and they are not.   105
Antigonê: There is no guilt in reverence for the dead.
Creon: But Eteoclês—was he not your brother too?
Antigonê: My brother too.
Creon: And you insult his memory?
Antigonê (*softly*): The dead man would not say that I insult it.
Creon: He would: for you honor a traitor as much as him.   110
Antigonê: His own brother, traitor or not, and equal in blood.
Creon: He made war on his country. Eteoclês defended it.
Antigonê: Nevertheless, there are honors due all the dead.
Creon: But not the same for the wicked as for the just.
Antigonê: Ah Creon, Creon,   115
      Which of us can say what the gods hold wicked?
Creon: An enemy is an enemy, even dead.
Antigonê: It is my nature to join in love, not hate.
Creon (*finally losing patience*): Go join them, then; if you must have your love,
      Find it in hell!   120
Choragos: But see, Ismenê comes:

      Enter Ismenê, guarded.

      Those tears are sisterly, the cloud
      That shadows her eyes rains down gentle sorrow.
Creon: You too, Ismenê,
      Snake in my ordered house, sucking my blood   125
      Stealthily—and all the time I never knew
      That these two sisters were aiming at my throne!
                                                          Ismenê,
      Do you confess your share in this crime, or deny it?
      Answer me.
Ismenê: Yes, if she will let me say so. I am guilty.   130
Antigonê (*coldly*): No, Ismenê. You have no right to say so.
      You would not help me, and I will not have you help me.

Ismenê: But now I know what you meant; and I am here
    To join you, to take my share of punishment.
Antigonê: The dead man and the gods who rule the dead   135
    Know whose act this was. Words are not friends.
Ismenê: Do you refuse me, Antigonê? I want to die with you:
    I too have a duty that I must discharge to the dead.
Antigonê: You shall not lessen my death by sharing it.
Ismenê: What do I care for life when you are dead?   140
Antigonê: Ask Creon. You're always hanging on his opinions.
Ismenê: You are laughing at me. Why, Antigonê?
Antigonê: It's a joyless laughter, Ismenê.
Ismenê: But can I do nothing?
Antigonê: Yes. Save yourself. I shall not envy you.
    There are those who will praise you; I shall have honor, too.   145
Ismenê: But we are equally guilty!
Antigonê: No more, Ismenê.
    You are alive, but I belong to Death.
Creon (to the Chorus): Gentlemen, I beg you to observe these girls:
    One has just now lost her mind; the other,
    It seems, has never had a mind at all.   150
Ismenê: Grief teaches the steadiest minds to waver, King.
Creon: Yours certainly did, when you assumed guilt with the guilty!
Ismenê: But how could I go on living without her?
Creon: You are.
    She is already dead.
Ismenê: But your own son's bride!
Creon: There are places enough for him to push his plow.   155
    I want no wicked women for my sons!
Ismenê: O dearest Haimon, how your father wrongs you!
Creon: I've had enough of your childish talk of marriage!
Choragos: Do you really intend to steal this girl from your son?
Creon: No; Death will do that for me.
Choragos: Then she must die?   160
Creon (ironically): You dazzle me.
                  —But enough of this talk!
    (*To Guards.*) You, there, take them away and guard them well:
    For they are but women, and even brave men run
    When they see Death coming.

    Exeunt Ismenê, Antigonê, and Guards.

ODE II

Strophe 1

Chorus: Fortunate is the man who has never tasted God's vengeance!
    Where once the anger of heaven has struck, that house is shaken
    For ever: damnation rises behind each child
    Like a wave cresting out of the black northeast,
    When the long darkness under sea roars up   5
    And bursts drumming death upon the windwhipped sand.

Antistrophe 1

I have seen this gathering sorrow from time long past
Loom upon Oedipus' children: generation from generation
Takes the compulsive rage of the enemy god.
So lately this last flower of Oedipus' line   10
Drank the sunlight! but now a passionate word
And a handful of dust have closed up all its beauty.

Strophe 2

    What mortal arrogance
    Transcends the wrath of Zeus?
Sleep cannot lull him nor the effortless long months   15
Of the timeless gods: but he is young for ever,
And his house is the shining day of high Olympos.
    All that is and shall be,
    And all the past, is his.
No pride on earth is free of the curse of heaven.   20

Antistrophe 2

    The straying dreams of men
    May bring them ghosts of joy:
But as they drowse, the waking embers burn them;
Or they walk with fixed eyes, as blind men walk.
But the ancient wisdom speaks for our own time: 25
    Fate works most for woe
    With Folly's fairest show.
Man's little pleasure is the spring of sorrow.

SCENE III

Choragos: But here is Haimon, King, the last of all your sons.
    Is it grief for Antigonê that brings him here,
    And bitterness at being robbed of his bride?

Enter Haimon.

Creon: We shall soon see, and no need of diviners.
                                     —Son,
    You have heard my final judgment on that girl: 5
    Have you come here hating me, or have you come
    With deference and with love, whatever I do?
Haimon: I am your son, father. You are my guide.
    You make things clear for me, and I obey you.
    No marriage means more to me than your continuing wisdom.   10
Creon: Good. That is the way to behave: subordinate
    Everything else, my son, to your father's will.
    This is what a man prays for, that he may get
    Sons attentive and dutiful in his house,
    Each one hating his father's enemies,   15
    Honoring his father's friends. But if his sons
    Fail him, if they turn out unprofitably,
    What has he fathered but trouble for himself

And amusement for the malicious?
                              So you are right
Not to lose your head over this woman.   20
Your pleasure with her would soon grow cold, Haimon,
And then you'd have a hellcat in bed and elsewhere.
Let her find her husband in Hell!
Of all the people in this city, only she
Has had contempt for my law and broken it.   25

Do you want me to show myself weak before the people?
Or to break my sworn word? No, and I will not.
The woman dies.

I suppose she'll plead "family ties." Well, let her.
If I permit my own family to rebel,   30
How shall I earn the world's obedience?
Show me the man who keeps his house in hand,
He's fit for public authority.
                              I'll have no dealings
With law-breakers, critics of the government:
Whoever is chosen to govern should be obeyed—   35
Must be obeyed, in all things, great and small,
Just and unjust! O Haimon,
The man who knows how to obey, and that man only,
Knows how to give commands when the time comes.
You can depend on him, no matter how fast   40
The spears come: he's a good soldier, he'll stick it out.

Anarchy, anarchy! Show me a greater evil!
This is why cities tumble and the great houses rain down,
This is what scatters armies!

No, no: good lives are made so by discipline.   45
We keep the laws then, and the lawmakers,
And no woman shall seduce us. If we must lose,
Let's lose to a man, at least! Is a woman stronger than we?
Choragos: Unless time has rusted my wits,
    What you say, King, is said with point and dignity.   50
Haimon (*boyishly earnest*): Father:
    Reason is God's crowning gift to man, and you are right
    To warn me against losing mine. I cannot say—
    I hope that I shall never want to say!—that you
    Have reasoned badly. Yet there are other men   55
    Who can reason, too; and their opinions might be helpful.
    You are not in a position to know everything
    That people say or do, or what they feel:
    Your temper terrifies them—everyone
    Will tell you only what you like to hear.   60
    But I, at any rate, can listen; and I have heard them
    Muttering and whispering in the dark about this girl.
    They say no woman has ever, so unreasonably,

Died so shameful a death for a generous act:
"She covered her brother's body. Is this indecent? 65
She kept him from dogs and vultures. Is this a crime?
Death?—She should have all the honor that we can give her!"

This is the way they talk out there in the city.

You must believe me:
Nothing is closer to me than your happiness. 70
What could be closer? Must not any son
Value his father's fortune as his father does his?
I beg you, do not be unchangeable:
Do not believe that you alone can be right.
The man who thinks that, 75
The man who maintains that only he has the power
To reason correctly, the gift to speak, the soul—
A man like that, when you know him, turns out empty.

It is not reason never to yield to reason!

In flood time you can see how some trees bend, 80
And because they bend, even their twigs are safe,
While stubborn trees are torn up, roots and all.
And the same thing happens in sailing:
Make your sheet fast, never slacken,—and over you go,
Head over heels and under: and there's your voyage. 85
Forget you are angry! Let yourself be moved!
I know I am young; but please let me say this:
The ideal condition
Would be, I admit, that men should be right by instinct;
But since we are all too likely to go astray, 90
The reasonable thing is to learn from those who can teach.

Choragos: You will do well to listen to him, King,
If what he says is sensible. And you, Haimon,
Must listen to your father.—Both speak well.
Creon: You consider it right for a man of my years and experience 95
To go to school to a boy?
Haimon: It is not right,
If I am wrong. But if I am young, and right,
What does my age matter?
Creon: You think it right to stand up for an anarchist?
Haimon: Not at all. I pay no respect to criminals. 100
Creon: Then she is not a criminal?
Haimon: The City would deny it, to a man.
Creon: And the City proposes to teach me how to rule?
Haimon: Ah. Who is it that's talking like a boy now?
Creon: My voice is the one voice giving orders in this City! 105
Haimon: It is no City if it takes orders from one voice.
Creon: The State is the King!
Haimon: Yes, if the State is a desert.

   Pause.

Creon: This boy, it seems, has sold out to a woman.

Haimon: If you are a woman: my concern is only for you.

Creon: So? Your "concern"! In a public brawl with your father! 110

Haimon: How about you, in a public brawl with justice?

Creon: With justice, when all that I do is within my rights?

Haimon: You have no right to trample on God's right.

Creon (*completely out of control*): Fool, adolescent fool! Taken in by a woman!

Haimon: You'll never see me taken in by anything vile. 115

Creon: Every word you say is for her!

Haimon (*quietly, darkly*): And for you.
   And for me. And for the gods under the earth.

Creon: You'll never marry her while she lives.

Haimon: Then she must die.—But her death will cause another.

Creon: Another? 120
   Have you lost your senses? Is this an open threat?

Haimon: There is no threat in speaking to emptiness.

Creon: I swear you'll regret this superior tone of yours!
   You are the empty one!

Haimon: If you were not my father,
   I'd say you were perverse. 125

Creon: You girl-struck fool, don't play at words with me!

Haimon: I am sorry. You prefer silence.

Creon: Now, by God—!
   I swear, by all the gods in heaven above us,
   You'll watch it, I swear you shall!
   (*To the Servants.*) Bring her out!
   Bring the woman out! Let her die before his eyes! 130
   Here, this instant, with her bridegroom beside her!

Haimon: Not here, no; she will not die here, King.
   And you will never see my face again.
   Go on raving as long as you've a friend to endure you.

   Exit Haimon.

Choragos: Gone, gone. 135
   Creon, a young man in a rage is dangerous!

Creon: Let him do, or dream to do, more than a man can.
   He shall not save these girls from death.

Choragos: These girls?
   You have sentenced them both?

Creon: No, you are right.
   I will not kill the one whose hands are clean. 140

Choragos: But Antigonê!

Creon (*somberly*): I will carry her far away
   Out there in the wilderness, and lock her
   Living in a vault of stone. She shall have food,
   As the custom is, to absolve the State of her death.
   And there let her pray to the gods of hell: 145
   They are her only gods:
   Perhaps they will show her an escape from death,

Or she may learn,
                    though late,
That piety shown the dead is pity in vain.

Exit Creon.

ODE III

Strophe

Chorus: Love, unconquerable
          Waster of rich men, keeper
          Of warm lights and all-night vigil
          In the soft face of a girl:
          Sea-wanderer, forest-visitor!   5
          Even the pure Immortals cannot escape you,
          And mortal man, in his one day's dusk,
          Trembles before your glory.

Antistrophe

          Surely you swerve upon ruin
          The just man's consenting heart,   10
          As here you have made bright anger
          Strike between father and son—
          And none has conquered but Love!
          A girl's glánce wórking the will of heaven:
          Pleasure to her alone who mocks us,   15
          Merciless Aphroditê.°

SCENE IV

Choragos (as Antigonê enters guarded):
          But I can no longer stand in awe of this,
          Nor, seeing what I see, keep back my tears.
          Here is Antigonê, passing to that chamber
          Where all find sleep at last.

Strophe 1

Antigonê: Look upon me, friends, and pity me   5
          Turning back at the night's edge to say
          Good-by to the sun that shines for me no longer;
          Now sleepy Death
          Summons me down to Acheron,° that cold shore:
          There is no bridesong there, nor any music.   10
Chorus: Yet not unpraised, not without a kind of honor,
          You walk at last into the underworld;
          Untouched by sickness, broken by no sword.
          What woman has ever found your way to death?

Antistrophe 1

16 *Aphroditê:* goddess of love and beauty.   9 *Acheron:* river in Hades, domain of the dead.

Antigonê: How often I have heard the story of Niobê,°   15
　　Tantalos' wretched daughter, how the stone
　　Clung fast about her, ivy-close: and they say
　　The rain falls endlessly
　　And sifting soft snow; her tears are never done.
　　I feel the loneliness of her death in mine.   20
Chorus: But she was born of heaven, and you
　　Are woman, woman-born. If her death is yours,
　　A mortal woman's, is this not for you
　　Glory in our world and in the world beyond?

　　　　　　　　　　　　　　　　　　　　　Strophe 2

Antigonê: You laugh at me. Ah, friends, friends,   25
　　Can you not wait until I am dead? O Thebes,
　　O men many-charioted, in love with Fortune,
　　Dear springs of Dircê, sacred Theban grove,
　　Be witnesses for me, denied all pity,
　　Unjustly judged! and think a word of love   30
　　For her whose path turns
　　Under dark earth, where there are no more tears.
Chorus: You have passed beyond human daring and come at last
　　Into a place of stone where Justice sits.
　　I cannot tell   35
　　What shape of your father's guilt appears in this.

　　　　　　　　　　　　　　　　　　　　Antistrophe 2

Antigonê: You have touched it at last: that bridal bed
　　Unspeakable, horror of son and mother mingling:
　　Their crime, infection of all our family!
　　O Oedipus, father and brother!   40
　　Your marriage strikes from the grave to murder mine.
　　I have been a stranger here in my own land:
　　All my life
　　The blasphemy of my birth has followed me.
Chorus: Reverence is a virtue, but strength   45
　　Lives in established law: that must prevail.
　　You have made your choice,
　　Your death is the doing of your conscious hand.

　　　　　　　　　　　　　　　　　　　　　Epode°

Antigonê: Then let me go, since all your words are bitter,
　　And the very light of the sun is cold to me.   50
　　Lead me to my vigil, where I must have
　　Neither love nor lamentation; no song, but silence.

　　Creon interrupts impatiently.

---

15 *story of Niobê:* a Theban queen whose fourteen children were slain. She wept so copiously she was transformed to a stone on Mount Sipylos, and her tears became the mountain's streams.   48 *Epode:* the final section (after the strophe and antistrophe) of a lyric passage; whereas the earlier sections are symmetrical, it takes a different metrical form.

Creon: If dirges and planned lamentations could put off death,
   Men would be singing for ever.
   (*To the Servants.*)   Take her, go!
   You know your orders: take her to the vault   55
   And leave her alone there. And if she lives or dies,
   That's her affair, not ours: our hands are clean.
Antigonê: O tomb, vaulted bride-bed in eternal rock,
   Soon I shall be with my own again
   Where Persephonê° welcomes the thin ghosts underground: 60
   And I shall see my father again, and you, mother,
   And dearest Polyneicês—
                        dearest indeed
   To me, since it was my hand
   That washed him clean and poured the ritual wine:
   And my reward is death before my time!   65

   And yet, as men's hearts know, I have done no wrong,
   I have not sinned before God. Or if I have,
   I shall know the truth in death. But if the guilt
   Lies upon Creon who judged me, then, I pray,
   May his punishment equal my own.
Choragos: O passionate heart,   70
   Unyielding, tormented still by the same winds!
Creon: Her guards shall have good cause to regret their delaying.
Antigonê: Ah! That voice is like the voice of death!
Creon: I can give you no reason to think you are mistaken.
Antigonê: Thebes, and you my fathers' gods,   75
   And rulers of Thebes, you see me now, the last
   Unhappy daughter of a line of kings,
   Your kings, led away to death. You will remember
   What things I suffer, and at what men's hands,
   Because I would not transgress the laws of heaven.   80
   (*To the Guards, simply.*) Come: let us wait no longer.

   Exit Antigonê, left, guarded.

ODE IV

Strophe 1

Chorus: All Danaê's beauty was locked away
   In a brazen cell where the sunlight could not come:
   A small room still as any grave, enclosed her.
   Yet she was a princess too,
   And Zeus in a rain of gold poured love upon her.°   5

---

60 *Persephonê:* daughter of Zeus and Demeter whom Pluto, god of the underworld, abducted to be his queen. 1–5 *All Danaê's beauty . . . poured love upon her:* In legend, when an oracle told Acrisius, king of Argos, that his daughter Danaê would bear a son who would grow up to slay him, he locked the princess into a chamber made of bronze, lest any man impregnate her. But Zeus, father of the gods, entered Danaê's prison in a shower of gold. The resultant child, the hero Perseus, was accidentally to fulfill the prophecy by killing Acrisius with an ill-aimed discus throw.

O child, child,
No power in wealth or war
Or tough sea-blackened ships
Can prevail against untiring Destiny!

Antistrophe 1

And Dryas' son° also, that furious king,   10
Bore the god's prisoning anger for his pride:
Sealed up by Dionysos in deaf stone,
His madness died among echoes.
So at the last he learned what dreadful power
His tongue had mocked: 15
For he had profaned the revels,
And fired the wrath of the nine
Implacable Sisters° that love the sound of the flute.

Strophe 2

And old men tell a half-remembered tale
Of horror° where a dark ledge splits the sea   20
And a double surf beats on the gráy shóres:
How a king's new woman, sick
With hatred for the queen he had imprisoned,
Ripped out his two sons' eyes with her bloody hands
While grinning Arês° watched the shuttle plunge   25
Four times: four blind wounds crying for revenge,

Antistrophe 2

Crying, tears and blood mingled.—Piteously born,
Those sons whose mother was of heavenly birth!
Her father was the god of the North Wind
And she was cradled by gales,   30
She raced with young colts on the glittering hills
And walked untrammeled in the open light:
But in her marriage deathless Fate found means
To build a tomb like yours for all her joy.

SCENE V

Enter blind Teiresias, led by a boy. The opening speeches of Teiresias should be in singsong contrast to the realistic lines of Creon.

Teiresias: This is the way the blind man comes, Princes, Princes,
    Lockstep, two heads lit by the eyes of one.
Creon: What new thing have you to tell us, old Teiresias?
Teiresias: I have much to tell you: listen to the prophet, Creon.

---

10 *Dryas' son:* King Lycurgus of Thrace, whom Dionysos, god of wine, caused to be stricken with madness.   18 *Sisters:* the Muses, nine sister goddesses who presided over poetry and music, arts and sciences.   19–20 *a half-remembered tale of horror:* As the Chorus recalls in the rest of this song, the point of this tale is that being nobly born will not save one from disaster. King Phineas cast off his first wife, Cleopatra (not the later Egyptian queen, but the daughter of Boreas, god of the north wind) and imprisoned her in a cave. Out of hatred for Cleopatra, the cruel Eidothea, second wife of the king, blinded her stepsons.   25 *Arês:* god of war, said to gloat over bloodshed.

Creon: I am not aware that I have ever failed to listen.   5
Teiresias: Then you have done wisely, King, and ruled well.
Creon: I admit my debt to you. But what have you to say?
Teiresias: This, Creon: you stand once more on the edge of fate.
Creon: What do you mean? Your words are a kind of dread.
Teiresias: Listen Creon: 10
    I was sitting in my chair of augury, at the place
    Where the birds gather about me. They were all a-chatter,
    As is their habit, when suddenly I heard
    A strange note in their jangling, a scream, a
    Whirring fury; I knew that they were fighting,   15
    Tearing each other, dying
    In a whirlwind of wings clashing. And I was afraid.
    I began the rites of burnt-offering at the altar,
    But Hephaistos° failed me: instead of bright flame,
    There was only the sputtering slime of the fat thigh-flesh   20
    Melting: the entrails dissolved in gray smoke,
    The bare bone burst from the welter. And no blaze!

    This was a sign from heaven. My boy described it,
    Seeing for me as I see for others.

    I tell you, Creon, you yourself have brought   25
    This new calamity upon us. Our hearths and altars
    Are stained with the corruption of dogs and carrion birds
    That glut themselves on the corpse of Oedipus' son.
    The gods are deaf when we pray to them, their fire
    Recoils from our offering, their birds of omen   30
    Have no cry of comfort, for they are gorged
    With the thick blood of the dead.
                      O my son,
    These are no trifles! Think: all men make mistakes,
    But a good man yields when he knows his course is wrong,
    And repairs the evil. The only crime is pride.   35

    Give in to the dead man, then: do not fight with a corpse—
    What glory is it to kill a man who is dead?
    Think, I beg you:
    It is for your own good that I speak as I do.
    You should be able to yield for your own good.   40
Creon: It seems that prophets have made me their especial province.
    All my life long
    I have been a kind of butt for the dull arrows
    Of doddering fortune-tellers!
                  No, Teiresias:
    If your birds—if the great eagles of God himself   45
    Should carry him stinking bit by bit to heaven,
    I would not yield. I am not afraid of pollution:

19 *Hephaistos:* god of fire.

No man can defile the gods.
                              Do what you will,
Go into business, make money, speculate
In India gold or that synthetic gold from Sardis,   50
Get rich otherwise than by my consent to bury him.
Teiresias, it is a sorry thing when a wise man
Sells his wisdom, lets out his words for hire!
Teiresias: Ah Creon! Is there no man left in the world—
Creon: To do what?—Come, let's have the aphorism!   55
Teiresias: No man who knows that wisdom outweighs any wealth?
Creon: As surely as bribes are baser than any baseness.
Teiresias: You are sick, Creon! You are deathly sick!
Creon: As you say: it is not my place to challenge a prophet.
Teiresias: Yet you have said my prophecy is for sale.   60
Creon: The generation of prophets has always loved gold.
Teiresias: The generation of kings has always loved brass.
Creon: You forget yourself! You are speaking to your King.
Teiresias: I know it. You are a king because of me.
Creon: You have a certain skill; but you have sold out.   65
Teiresias: King, you will drive me to words that—
Creon: Say them, say them!
Only remember: I will not pay you for them.
Teiresias: No, you will find them too costly.
Creon: No doubt. Speak:
Whatever you say, you will not change my will.
Teiresias: Then take this, and take it to heart!   70
The time is not far off when you shall pay back
Corpse for corpse, flesh of your own flesh.
You have thrust the child of this world into living night,
You have kept from the gods below the child that is theirs:
The one in a grave before her death, the other,   75
Dead, denied the grave. This is your crime:
And the Furies and the dark gods of Hell
Are swift with terrible punishment for you.

Do you want to buy me now, Creon?

                              Not many days,
And your house will be full of men and women weeping,   80
And curses will be hurled at you from far
Cities grieving for sons unburied, left to rot
Before the walls of Thebes.

These are my arrows, Creon: they are all for you.

(*To Boy.*) But come, child: lead me home.   85
Let him waste his fine anger upon younger men.
Maybe he will learn at last
To control a wiser tongue in a better head.

Exit Teiresias.

Choragos: The old man has gone, King, but his words
            Remain to plague us. I am old, too,   90
            But I cannot remember that he was ever false.
Creon: That is true . . . . It troubles me.
         Oh it is hard to give in! but it is worse
         To risk everything for stubborn pride.
Choragos: Creon: take my advice.
Creon: What shall I do?   95
Choragos: Go quickly: free Antigonê from her vault
            And build a tomb for the body of Polyneicês.
Creon: You would have me do this!
Choragos: Creon, yes!
            And it must be done at once: God moves
            Swiftly to cancel the folly of stubborn men.   100
Creon: It is hard to deny the heart! But I
         Will do it: I will not fight with destiny.
Choragos: You must go yourself, you cannot leave it to others.
Creon: I will go.
                 —Bring axes, servants:
         Come with me to the tomb. I buried her, I   105
         Will set her free.
                        Oh quickly!
         My mind misgives—
         The laws of the gods are mighty, and a man must serve them
         To the last day of his life!

Exit Creon.

PAEAN°

                                                                Strophe 1
Choragos: God of many names
Chorus: O Iacchos
                           son
    of Kadmeian Sémelê
                        O born of the Thunder!
    Guardian of the West
                           Regent
    of Eleusis' plain
                        O Prince of maenad Thebes
    and the Dragon Field by rippling Ismenós:°   5

Paean: a song of praise or prayer, here to Dionysos, god of wine. 1–5 *God of many names . . .
Dragon Field by rippling Ismenós:* Dionysos was also called Iacchos (or, by the Romans, Bacchus).
He was the son of Zeus ("the Thunderer") and of Sémelê, daughter of Kadmos (or Cadmus),
legendary founder of Thebes. "Regent of Eleusis' plain" is another name for Dionysos, honored in
secret rites at Eleusis, a town northwest of Athens. "Prince of maenad Thebes" is yet another: the
Maenads were women of Thebes said to worship Dionysos with wild orgiastic rites. Kadmos, so
the story goes, sowed dragon's teeth in a field beside the river Ismenós. Up sprang a crop of fierce
warriors who fought among themselves until only five remained. These victors became the first
Thebans.

Antistrophe 1

Choragos: God of many names
Chorus: the flame of torches
     flares on our hills
                    the nymphs of Iacchos
     dance at the spring of Castalia:°

     from the vine-close mountain
                              come ah come in ivy:
     Evohé evohé!° sings through the streets of Thebes   10

Strophe 2

Choragos: God of many names
Chorus: Iacchos of Thebes
     heavenly Child
                    of Sémelê bride of the Thunderer!
     The shadow of plague is upon us:
                              come
     with clement feet
                    oh come from Parnasos
     down the long slopes
                    across the lamenting water   15

Antistrophe 2

Choragos: Iô° Fire! Chorister of the throbbing stars!
     O purest among the voices of the night!
     Thou son of God, blaze for us!
Chorus: Come with choric rapture of circling Maenads
     Who cry *Iô Iacche!*
                    God of many names!   20

ÉXODOS°

Enter Messenger from left.

Messenger: Men of the line of Kadmos, you who live
     Near Amphion's citadel:°
                    I cannot say
     Of any condition of human life "This is fixed,
     This is clearly good, or bad." Fate raises up,
     And Fate casts down the happy and unhappy alike: 5
     No man can foretell his Fate.
                    Take the case of Creon:

---

8 *Castalia:* a spring on Mount Parnassus, named for a maiden who drowned herself in it to avoid rape by the god Apollo. She became a nymph, or nature spirit, dwelling in its waters. In the temple of Delphi, at the mountain's foot, priestesses of Dionysos (the "nymphs of Iacchos") used the spring's waters in rites of purification.   10 *Evohé evohé!:* cry of the Maenads in supplicating Dionysos: "Come forth, come forth!"   16 *Iô:* "Hail" or "Praise be to . . . "   *Éxodos:* the final scene, containing the play's resolution.   2 *Amphion's citadel:* a name for Thebes. Amphion, son of Zeus, had built a wall around the city by playing so beautifully on his lyre that the charmed stones leaped into their slots.

Creon was happy once, as I count happiness:
Victorious in battle, sole governor of the land,
Fortunate father of children nobly born.
And now it has all gone from him! Who can say   10
That a man is still alive when his life's joy fails?
He is a walking dead man. Grant him rich,
Let him live like a king in his great house:
If his pleasure is gone, I would not give
So much as the shadow of smoke for all he owns.   15

Choragos: Your words hint at sorrow: what is your news for us?
Messenger: They are dead. The living are guilty of their death.
Choragos: Who is guilty? Who is dead? Speak!
Messenger: Haimon.
Haimon is dead; and the hand that killed him
Is his own hand.
Choragos: His father's? or his own?   20
Messenger: His own, driven mad by the murder his father had done.
Choragos: Teiresias, Teiresias, how clearly you saw it all!
Messenger: This is my news: you must draw what conclusions you can from it.
Choragos: But look: Eurydicê, our Queen:
Has she overheard us?   25

Enter Eurydicê from the palace, center.

Eurydicê: I have heard something, friends:
As I was unlocking the gate of Pallas'° shrine,
For I needed her help today, I heard a voice
Telling of some new sorrow. And I fainted
There at the temple with all my maidens about me.   30
But speak again: whatever it is, I can bear it:
Grief and I are no strangers.
Messenger: Dearest Lady.
I will tell you plainly all that I have seen.
I shall not try to comfort you: what is the use,
Since comfort could lie only in what is not true?   35
The truth is always best.
                              I went with Creon
To the outer plain where Polyneicês was lying,
No friend to pity him, his body shredded by dogs.
We made our prayers in that place to Hecatê
And Pluto,° that they would be merciful. And we bathed   40
The corpse with holy water, and we brought
Fresh-broken branches to burn what was left of it,
And upon the urn we heaped up a towering barrow
Of the earth of his own land.
                              When we were done, we ran

27 *Pallas:* Pallas Athene, goddess of wisdom, and hence an excellent source of advice. 39–40
Hecatê and Pluto: two fearful divinities—the goddess of witchcraft and sorcery and the king of
Hades, underworld of the dead.

To the vault where Antigonê lay on her couch of stone.   45
One of the servants had gone ahead,
And while he was yet far off he heard a voice
Grieving within the chamber, and he came back
And told Creon. And as the King went closer,
The air was full of wailing, the words lost,   50
And he begged us to make all haste. "Am I a prophet?"
He said, weeping, "And must I walk this road,
The saddest of all that I have gone before?
My son's voice calls me on. Oh quickly, quickly!
Look through the crevice there, and tell me   55
If it is Haimon, or some deception of the gods!"

We obeyed; and in the cavern's farthest corner
We saw her lying:
She had made a noose of her fine linen veil
And hanged herself. Haimon lay beside her,   60
His arms about her waist, lamenting her,
His love lost under ground, crying out
That his father had stolen her away from him.

When Creon saw him the tears rushed to his eyes
And he called to him: "What have you done, child? Speak to me.   65
What are you thinking that makes your eyes so strange?
O my son, my son, I come to you on my knees!"
But Haimon spat in his face. He said not a word,
Staring—
              And suddenly drew his sword
And lunged. Creon shrank back, the blade missed; and the boy,   70
Desperate against himself, drove it half its length
Into his own side, and fell. And as he died
He gathered Antigonê close in his arms again,
Choking, his blood bright red on her white cheek.
And now he lies dead with the dead, and she is his   75
At last, his bride in the houses of the dead.

Exit Eurydicê into the palace.

Choragos: She has left us without a word. What can this mean?
Messenger: It troubles me, too; yet she knows what is best,
          Her grief is too great for public lamentation,
          And doubtless she has gone to her chamber to weep   80
          For her dead son, leading her maidens in his dirge.
Choragos: It may be so: but I fear this deep silence.

Pause.

Messenger: I will see what she is doing. I will go in.

Exit Messenger into the palace.

Enter Creon with attendants, bearing Haimon's body.

Choragos: But here is the king himself: oh look at him,
      Bearing his own damnation in his arms.   85
Creon: Nothing you say can touch me any more.
      My own blind heart has brought me
      From darkness to final darkness. Here you see
      The father murdering, the murdered son—
      And all my civic wisdom!   90

      Haimon my son, so young, so young to die,
      I was the fool, not you; and you died for me.
Choragos: That is the truth; but you were late in learning it.
Creon: This truth is hard to bear. Surely a god
      Has crushed me beneath the hugest weight of heaven,   95
      And driven me headlong a barbaric way
      To trample out the thing I held most dear.

      The pains that men will take to come to pain!

Enter Messenger from the palace.

Messenger: The burden you carry in your hands is heavy,
      But it is not all: you will find more in your house.   100
Creon: What burden worse than this shall I find there?
Messenger: The Queen is dead.
Creon: O port of death, deaf world,
      Is there no pity for me? And you, Angel of evil,
      I was dead, and your words are death again.   105
      Is it true, boy? Can it be true?
      Is my wife dead? Has death bred death?
Messenger: You can see for yourself.

The doors are opened and the body of Eurydicê is disclosed within.

Creon: Oh pity!
      All true, all true, and more than I can bear!   110
      O my wife, my son!
Messenger: She stood before the altar, and her heart
      Welcomed the knife her own hand guided,
      And a great cry burst from her lips for Megareus° dead,
      And for Haimon dead, her sons; and her last breath   115
      Was a curse for their father, the murderer of her sons.
      And she fell, and the dark flowed in through her closing eyes.
Creon: O God, I am sick with fear.
      Are there no swords here? Has no one a blow for me?
Messenger: Her curse is upon you for the deaths of both.   120
Creon: It is right that it should be. I alone am guilty.
      I know it, and I say it. Lead me in,
      Quickly, friends.
      I have neither life nor substance. Lead me in.

---

114 *Megareus:* Son of Creon and brother of Haimon, Megareus was slain in the unsuccessful attack
upon Thebes.

Choragos: You are right, if there can be right in so much wrong.   125
    The briefest way is best in a world of sorrow.
Creon: Let it come,
    Let death come quickly, and be kind to me.
    I would not ever see the sun again.
Choragos: All that will come when it will; but we, meanwhile,   130
    Have much to do. Leave the future to itself.
Creon: All my heart was in that prayer!
Choragos: Then do not pray any more: the sky is deaf.
Creon: Lead me away. I have been rash and foolish.
    I have killed my son and my wife.   135
    I look for comfort; my comfort lies here dead.
    Whatever my hands have touched has come to nothing.
    Fate has brought all my pride to a thought of dust.

*As Creon is being led into the house, the Choragos advances and speaks directly to the
audience.*

Choragos: There is no happiness where there is no wisdom;
    No wisdom but in submission to the gods.   140
    Big words are always punished,
    And proud men in old age learn to be wise.

Questions

1. What is Creon's motivation for forbidding the burial of his own nephew Polyneicês? Why would he issue an edict that runs so contrary to his family obligations?
2. What are Antigonê's reasons for performing funeral rites on her brother's corpse in direct violation of Creon's edict?
3. What are the larger issues behind the conflicting positions of both Creon and Antigonê? Is either person or position clearly wrong?
4. Does the chorus take a position in the argument between Creon and Antigonê?
5. If Antigonê is a tragic heroine, what is her tragic flaw? Does she have any particular *hubris* or excess of virtue that dooms her?
6. Can a modern reader discern Sophocles' own position on the debate between civic responsibility (Creon's edict) and family duty (Antigonê's defiance)? Are his authorial sympathies anywhere evident in the play?
7. What is the role of Eurydicê? Is her presence essential to the story? What would be the effect of removing her from the drama?
8. Can you imagine a modern setting in which a new production of *Antigonê* might be staged? Describe your idea in terms of sets, costumes, and staging.

CRITICS ON SOPHOCLES

Aristotle (384–322 B.C.)

Defining Tragedy   330 B.C.?

Translated by L. J. Potts

Tragedy is an imitation of an action of high importance, complete and of some amplitude; in language enhanced by distinct and varying beauties; acted not narrated; by means of pity and fear effecting its purgation of these emotions. By the beauties enhancing the language I mean rhythm and melody; by "distinct and varying" I mean that some are produced by meter alone, and others at another time by melody.

• • •

What will produce the tragic effect? Since, then, tragedy, to be at its finest, requires a complex, not a simple, structure, and its structure should also imitate fearful and pitiful events (for that is the peculiarity of this sort of imitation), it is clear: first, that decent people must not be shown passing from good fortune to misfortune (for that is not fearful or pitiful but disgusting); again, vicious people must not be shown passing from misfortune to good fortune (for that is the most untragic situation possible—it has none of the requisites, it is neither humane, nor pitiful, nor fearful); nor again should an utterly evil man fall from good fortune into misfortune (for though a plot of that kind would be humane, it would not induce pity or fear—pity is induced by undeserved misfortune, and fear by the misfortunes of normal people, so that this situation will be neither pitiful nor fearful). So we are left with the man between these extremes: that is to say, the kind of man who neither is distinguished for excellence and virtue, nor comes to grief on account of baseness and vice, but on account of some error; a man of great reputation and prosperity, like Oedipus and Thyestes and conspicuous people of such families as theirs. So, to be well formed, a fable must be single rather than (as some say) double—there must be no change from misfortune to good fortune, but only the opposite, from good fortune to misfortune; the cause must not be vice, but a great error; and the man must be either of the type specified or better, rather than worse. This is borne out by the practice of poets; at first they picked a fable at random and made an inventory of its contents, but now the finest tragedies are plotted, and concern a few families—for example, the tragedies about Alcmeon, Oedipus, Orestes, Meleager, Thyestes, Telephus, and any others whose lives were attended by terrible experiences or doings.

This is the plot that will produce the technically finest tragedy. Those critics are therefore wrong who censure Euripides on this very ground—because he does this in his tragedies, and many of them end in misfortune; for it is, as I have said, the right thing to do. This is clearly demonstrated on the stage in the competitions, where such plays, if they succeed, are the most tragic, and Euripides, even if he is inefficient in every other respect, still shows himself the most tragic of our poets. The next best plot, which is said by some people to be the best, is the tragedy with a double plot, like the *Odyssey*, ending in one way for the better people and in the opposite way for the worse. But it is the weakness of theatrical performances that gives priority to this kind; when poets write what the audience would like to happen, they are in leading strings.° This is not the pleasure proper to tragedy, but rather to comedy, where the

---

in leading strings: each is led, by a string, wherever the audience wills.

greatest enemies in the fable, say Orestes and Aegisthus, make friends and go off at the end, and nobody is killed by anybody.

• • •

The pity and fear can be brought about by the *mise en scène;*° but they can also come from the mere plotting of the incidents, which is preferable, and better poetry. For, without seeing anything, the fable ought to have been so plotted that if one heard the bare facts, the chain of circumstances would make one shudder and pity. That would happen to any one who heard the fable of the *Oedipus*. To produce this effect by the *mise en scène* is less artistic and puts one at the mercy of the technician; and those who use it not to frighten but merely to startle have lost touch with tragedy altogether. We should not try to get all sorts of pleasure from tragedy, but the particular tragic pleasure. And clearly, since this pleasure coming from pity and fear has to be produced by imitation, it is by his handling of the incidents that the poet must create it.

From *Poetics, VI, XIII, XIV*

Sigmund Freud (1856–1939)

The Destiny of Oedipus 1900

Translated by James Strachey

If *Oedipus the King* moves a modern audience no less than it did the contemporary Greek one, the explanation can only be that its effect does not lie in the contrast between destiny and human will, but is to be looked for in the particular nature of the material on which that contrast is exemplified. There must be something which makes a voice within us ready to recognize the compelling force of destiny in the *Oedipus*, while we can dismiss as merely arbitrary such dispositions as are laid down in *Die Ahnfrau*° or other modern tragedies of destiny. And a factor of this kind is in fact involved in the story of King Oedipus. His destiny moves us only because it might have been ours—because the oracle laid the same curse upon us before our birth as upon him. It is the fate of all of us, perhaps, to direct our first sexual impulse towards our mother and our first hatred and our first murderous wish against our father. Our dreams convince us that that is so. King Oedipus, who slew his father Laius and married his mother Jocasta, merely shows us the fulfillment of our own childhood wishes. But, more fortunate than he, we have meanwhile succeeded, insofar as we have not become psychoneurotics, in detaching our sexual impulses from our mothers and in forgetting our jealousy of our fathers. Here is one in whom these primeval wishes of our childhood have been fulfilled, and we shrink back from him with the whole force of the repression by which those wishes have since that time been held down within us. While the poet, as he unravels the past, brings to light the guilt of Oedipus, he is at the same time compelling us to recognize our own inner minds, in which those same impulses, though suppressed, are still to be found. The contrast with which the closing Chorus leaves us confronted—

---

mise en scène: arrangement of actors and scenery.   *Die Ahnfrau: The Foremother*, a play by Franz Grillparzer (1791–1872), Austrian dramatist and poet.

look upon Oedipus.

This is the king who solved the famous riddle
And towered up, most powerful of men.
No mortal eyes but looked on him with envy,
Yet in the end ruin swept over him.

—strikes as a warning at ourselves and our pride, at us who since our childhood have grown so wise and so mighty in our own eyes. Like Oedipus, we live in ignorance of these wishes, repugnant to morality, which have been forced upon us by Nature, and after their revelation we may all of us well seek to close our eyes to the scenes of our childhood.

From The Interpretation of Dreams

E. R. Dodds (1893–1979)

On Misunderstanding Oedipus   1966

Some readers of the *Oedipus Rex* have told me that they find its atmosphere stifling and oppressive: they miss the tragic exaltation that one gets from the *Antigonê* or the *Prometheus Vinctus*. And I fear that what I have said here has done nothing to remove that feeling. Yet it is not a feeling which I share myself. Certainly the *Oedipus Rex* is a play about the blindness of man and the desperate insecurity of the human condition: in a sense every man must grope in the dark as Oedipus gropes, not knowing who he is or what he has to suffer; we all live in a world of appearance which hides from us who-knows-what dreadful reality. But surely the *Oedipus Rex* is also a play about human greatness. Oedipus is great, not in virtue of a great worldly position—for his worldly position is an illusion which will vanish like a dream—but in virtue of his inner strength: strength to pursue the truth at whatever personal cost, and strength to accept and endure it when found. "This horror is mine," he cries, "and none but I is *strong* enough to bear it." Oedipus is great because he accepts the responsibility for *all* his acts, including those which are objectively most horrible, though subjectively innocent.

To me personally Oedipus is a kind of symbol of the human intelligence which cannot rest until it has solved all the riddles—even the last riddle, to which the answer is that human happiness is built on an illusion. I do not know how far Sophocles intended that. But certainly in the last lines of the play (which I firmly believe to be genuine) he does generalize the case, does appear to suggest that in some sense Oedipus is every man and every man is potentially Oedipus. Freud felt this (he was not insensitive to poetry), but as we all know he understood it in a specific psychological sense. "Oedipus' fate," he says, "moves us only because it might have been our own, because the oracle laid upon us before birth is the very curse which rested upon him. It may be that we were all destined to direct our first sexual impulses towards our mothers, and our first impulses of hatred and violence towards our fathers; our dreams convince us that we were." Perhaps they do; but Freud did not ascribe his interpretation of the myth to Sophocles, and it is not the interpretation I have in mind. Is there not in the poet's view a much wider sense in which every man is Oedipus? If every man could tear away the last veils of illusion, if he could see human life as time and the gods see it, would he not see that against that tremendous background all the generations of men are as if they had not been, *isa kai to mēden zōsas?* That was how Odysseus saw it when he had conversed with Athena, the embodiment of divine wisdom. "In Ajax' condition," he says, "I recognize my own: I perceive that all men living are but appearance or unsubstantial shadow."

From "On Misunderstanding the Oedipus Rex"

A. E. Haigh (1855–1905)

<table><tr><td>

The Irony of Sophocles
</td><td align="right">1896</td></tr></table>

The use of "tragic irony," as it has been called, is a favorite device in all dramatic literature. It is mostly employed when some catastrophe is about to happen, which is known and foreseen by the spectators, but concealed either from all, or from some, of the actors in the drama. In such cases the dialogue may be couched in terms which, though perfectly harmless upon the surface, carry an ominous significance to the initiated, and point suggestively to what is about to happen; and the contrast between the outer and the inner meaning of the language produces a deep effect upon the stage. Examples of this "irony" are to be found in most tragic writers, but especially in those of Greece, who use it with far greater frequency than the moderns; the reason being that, as the subjects of Greek tragedy were taken from the old legends with which every one was familiar, it was far easier for the ancient dramatist to indulge in those ambiguous allusions which presuppose a certain knowledge on the part of the spectators. Sophocles, however, is distinguished even among the Greek poets for his predilection for this form of speech, and his "irony" has become proverbial. It figures so prominently in his dramas, and goes so far to determine their general tone, that a detailed consideration of the matter will not be out of place.

Tragic irony may be divided into two kinds, the conscious and the unconscious. Conscious irony occurs in those cases where the speaker is not himself the victim of any illusion, but foresees the calamity that is about to fall on others, and exults in the prospect. His language, though equivocal, is easily intelligible to the audience, and to those actors who are acquainted with the facts; and its dark humor adds to the horror of the situation. This kind of irony is the one more commonly met with in the modern drama.

· · ·

The other kind of irony, the unconscious, is perhaps the more impressive of the two. Here the sufferer is himself the spokesman. Utterly blind as to the doom which overhangs him, he uses words which, to the mind of the audience, have an ominous suggestiveness, and without knowing it, probes his own wounds to the bottom. Such irony is not confined merely to the language, but runs through the whole situation; and the contrast between the cheerful heedlessness of the victim, and the dark shadows which surround him, produces an impression more terrible than that which any form of speech could convey. Scenes of this kind had a peculiar fascination for the ancients. The fear of a sudden reverse of fortune, and of some fatal Nemesis which waits upon pride and boastfulness, was of all ideas the one most deeply impressed upon the mind of antiquity. Hence the popularity upon the stage of those thrilling spectacles, in which confidence and presumption were seen advancing blindfold to destruction, and the bitterness of the doom was intensified by the unconscious utterances of the victim.

• • •

The greatest example of all is the *Oedipus Rex*, the masterpiece of Sophocles, and the most typical of all Greek tragedies. The irony of destiny is here exhibited with unexampled force. In the opening scene Oedipus is depicted in the height of his prosperity, renowned and venerated, and surrounded by his suppliant countrymen; and the priest addresses him as the "wisest of men in dealing with life's chances and with the visitations of heaven." To the audience who know that within a few short hours the wrath of heaven will have crushed and shattered him, the pathetic meaning of these words is indescribable. From this first scene until the final catastrophe the speeches of Oedipus are all full of the same tragic allusiveness. He can scarcely open his lips without touching unconsciously on his own approaching fate. When he insists upon the fact that his search for the assassin is "not on behalf of strangers, but in his own cause," and when he cautiously warns Jocasta that, as his mother still lives, the guilt of incest is not yet an impossibility, every word that he utters has a concealed barb. Perhaps the most tragic passage of all is that in which, while cursing the murderer of Laius, he prounounces his own doom. "As for the man who did the deed of guilt, whether alone he lurks, or in league with others, I pray that he may waste his life away in suffering, perishing vilely for his vile actions. And if he should become a dweller in my house, I knowing it, may every curse I utter fall on my own head."

From *The Tragic Drama of the Greeks*

David Wiles

The Chorus as Democrat 2000

Oedipus becomes a political play when we focus on the interaction of actor and chorus, and see how the chorus forms a democratic mass jury. Each sequence of dialogue takes the form of a contest for the chorus' sympathy, with Oedipus sliding from the role of prosecutor to that of defendant, and each choral dance offers a provisional verdict. After Oedipus' set-to with Teiresias the soothsayer, the chorus decides to trust Oedipus on the basis of his past record; after his argument with his brother-in-law Creon, the chorus shows their distress and urges compromise. Once Oedipus has confessed to a killing and Iocastê has declared that oracles have no force, the chorus is forced to think about political tyranny, torn between respect for divine law and trust in their rulers. In the next dance they assume that the contradiction is resolved and Oedipus has turned out to be the son of a god. Finally a slave's evidence reveals that the man most honored by society is in fact the least to be envied. The political implications are clear: there is no space in democratic society for such as Oedipus. Athenians, like the chorus of the play, must reject the temptation to believe one man can calculate the future.

From *Greek Theatre Performance: An Introduction*

Patricia M. Lines　(b. 1938)

What Is Antigonê's Tragic Flaw? 1999

Antigonê does not seem to fit the Aristotelian formula. Aristotle himself did not seem to know what to make of it. In the *Poetica*'s sole reference to the play Aristotle offers *Antigonê* as an example of a poor plot for a tragedy. The least tragic plot, he avers, involves a character who resolves to do a fearful deed and does not do it. His example is Haimon who seems ready to slay his father, Creon, and does not. This may be one of those rare cases where Aristotle misses the point. First, after more than two millennia of experience with drama, one can imagine a situation where delay in doing the dread deed makes the tragedy. Nor is it clear that Haimon had resolved to kill his father; his veiled threat may have been to kill himself, an action which he finally takes. Most important, the conflict between Haimon and his father does not stir our emotions as much as the conflict swirling around Antigonê.

The play strikes us as a fine one—Hegel thought it was the supreme example of tragedy, prompting him to pose a different theory for the form. Hegel sees a dialectical clash between two ideals of justice. A noble and wise Antigonê fights for the justice of traditional belief, while a tyrannical Creon fights for a right based on might. Irving Babbitt has suggested a more subtle variation of dialectic theory, hailing Antigonê as the "perfect example of the ethical imagination" in contrast to her sister, Ismenê, who knows merely "the law of the community." Both Antigonê and Ismenê are ethical, but Ismenê lacks ethical imagination. As Babbitt sees it:

> This law, the convention of a particular place and time, is always but a very imperfect image, a mere shadow indeed of the unwritten law which being above the ordinary rational level is . . . infinite and incapable of final formulation.

While such interpretations no doubt are true—with each uncovering layers of meaning—alone they reduce *Antigonê* to a morality play. Such interpretations fail to explain the play's more complex and turbulent moods.

• • •

The suggestion that Sophocles intended to present a flawed Antigonê rubs against the grain. She is the paragon. The religion of the Greeks, like virtually all religions, required burial of the dead—even the enemy dead. The ancient tales in the *Iliad*, the bible to the Greeks, warn of the anger of the gods upon a failure to honor the dead. Besides, the restless shades of the unburied could cause trouble. Antigonê stands for all that is right and for the opposition to tyranny. Thus, we have only a play about Creon's excessive harshness and his tragically delayed conversion. Yet, Sophocles provides a fair amount of evidence that he intended to create something more complex than a morality play.

Consider first the parallels between *Antigonê* and *Oedipus Rex*. Both stories begin with a problem facing family and polis, and with the central character resolving to make things right. Antigonê proceeds with unswerving resolution in her judgment of the situation. She possesses complete confidence in her ability to choose and execute a just action. She does not see the full situation; she is blind to key elements of the problem. She is like her father in most respects. Both Antigonê and Oedipus claim to know justice with the certainty of a god. Oedipus believes most in his cunning and strength, Antigonê in her goodness.

The flaw of hubris is easy to spot in Oedipus, but Antigonê's brilliance is so dazzling that we overlook her flaw. After all, she has formulated a great and noble truth and maintains it with courage. She asserts God's law over man's law. Especially in our own time, where we formally recognize the superiority, within specified spheres, of individual right over the demands of overly broad laws, Antigonê seems a genius beyond her time.

Creon, by contrast, understands the needs of the polis. Following a civil war, he has placed a premium on order. He will do whatever is necessary, including the stern enforcement of harsh rules. He faces another dilemma in his role as leader: he forbade the burial of Polyneicês and decreed this harsh punishment before he was aware of Antigonê's guilt. To pardon his future daughter-in-law as his first serious act as ruler of Thebes would compromise all future claims to fairness in his rule. Yet Creon listens to the chorus of old men; he listens to the blind seer. After struggling with the issue, he reconsiders his judgment; he determines to bury the body of Polyneicês and to unbury Antigonê with his own hands.

Antigonê, on the other hand, recognizes the demands of true justice and champions it. She spurns Ismenê, who initially hesitated to assist her but soon after wished to share in her sister's punishment and death. Antigonê refuses the offer. When Ismenê asks whether her sister has cast her aside, Antigonê's answer ignores Ismenê's change of heart: "Yes. For you chose to live when I chose death." Antigonê seems to speak not to spare Ismenê, but to wound her to the quick. Antigonê leaves Haimon, her betrothed, in the cold, as she left Ismenê. She never seeks him out, nor even mentions his name. Yet Haimon is ready to defy his father for Antigonê's sake, and he refuses to live without her. Ironically, this may be what he must do to win her affection, for Antigonê reveals no tenderness for anyone except those already dead.

• • •

The chorus, often the truth-sayer for Sophocles, provides more clues. Of Antigonê, they tell us:

> The girl is bitter. She's her father's child.
> She cannot yield to trouble; nor could he.

In perhaps the most revealing exchange, the chorus turns to Antigonê and tells her, plainly:

> You showed respect for the dead.
> So we for you: but power
> is not to be thwarted so.
> Your self-sufficiency has brought you down.

The last line is key: "δ' αὐτόγνωτος ὤλεσ' ὀργά." The above quotation is from Wyckoff's translation. But all translations seem to head in the same direction: "A self-determined impulse hath undone thee" (Campbell). "You were self-willed. That has been your undoing" (Townsend). "And thee, thy stubborne mood, self-chosen, layeth low" (students of the University of Notre Dame, 1983).[1] In any translation, it seems the chorus has identified Antigonê's flaw. She follows a truth that springs only from her self: It is αὐτόγνωτος, or autognotos. She will not consult with others. We could call it self-certainty or, perhaps even better, self-righteousness. It is a form of hubris.

At another point, the chorus tells Antigonê she is autonomous. Literally, this means "a law unto yourself." The English word autonomy does not convey quite the right meaning, as individual autonomy was a condition the Greeks viewed with discomfort and suspicion. The autonomous being is either beast or god, living only within the horizons of its own laws.

"Antigonê's Flaw"

[1]Scene IV, lines 47–48 in the Fitts and Fitzgerald translation: "You have made your choice, / Your death is the doing of your conscious hand."

■ WRITING *effectively*

Robert Fitzgerald on Writing

Translating Sophocles into English

1941

The style of Sophocles was smooth. It has been likened by a modern critic to a molten flow of language, fitting and revealing every contour of the meaning, with no words wasted and no words poured on for effect. To approximate such purity I have sought a spare but felicitous manner of speech, not common and not "elevated" either, except by force of natural eloquence. The Greek writer did not disdain plainness when plainness was appropriate—appropriate, that is, both dramatically and within a context of verse very brilliant, mellifluous and powerful. As in every highly inflected language, the Greek order of words was controlled, by its masters, for special purposes of emphasis and even of meaning; and such of these as I have been acute enough to grasp I have tried to bring out by a comparable phrasing or rhythm in English. This I hold to be part of the business of "literal" rendering.

Robert Fitzgerald

   The difficulties involved in translating Greek dialogue are easily tripled when it comes to translating a chorus. Here the ellipses and compressions possible to the inflected idiom are particularly in evidence; and in the chorus, too, the poet concentrates his allusive power. For the modern reader, who has very little "literature" in the sense in which Samuel Johnson° used the term, two out of three allusions in the Greek odes will be meaningless. This is neither surprising nor deplorable. The Roman writer Ennius,° translating Euripides for a Latin audience two centuries after the Periclean period, found it advisable to omit many place names and to omit or explain many mythological references; and his public had greater reason to be familiar with such things than we have. My handling of this problem has been governed by the general wish to leave nothing in the English that would drive the literate reader to a library.

"Commentary" on Sophocles' The Oedipus Cycle

THINKING ABOUT GREEK TRAGEDY

Reading an ancient work of literature, such as Sophocles' *Oedipus the King* or *Antigonê*, you might have two contradictory reactions. On the one hand, you are

Samuel Johnson: Johnson (1709–1784) was the great eighteenth-century critic, lexicographer, poet, and conversationalist. His definition of *literature* would have referred mostly to the Greek and Latin classics.   *Ennius:* Quintus Ennius (239–169 B.C.) was an early Latin epic poet and tragedian. He created Latin versions of the Greek tragic plays, especially those of Euripides.

likely to note how differently people thought, spoke, and conducted themselves in the ancient world from the way they do now. On the other hand, you might notice how many facets of human nature remain constant across the ages. Though Sophocles' characters are mythic, they also are recognizably human.

- **Stay alert to both impulses.** Be open to the play's universal appeal, but never forget its foreignness. Take note of the basic beliefs and values that the characters hold that are different from your own. How do those elements influence their actions and motivations?
- **Jot down something about each major character that seems odd or exotic to you.** Don't worry about being too basic; these notes are just a starting place. You might observe, for example, that Oedipus and Iocastê both believe in the power of prophecy. They also believe that Apollo and the other gods would punish the city with a plague because of an unsolved crime committed twenty years earlier. These are certainly not mainstream modern beliefs.
- **Focus on the differences themselves.** You do not need to understand the historical origins or cultural context of the differences you note. You can safely leave those things to scholars. But observing these differences—at least a few important ones—will keep you from making inappropriate modern assumptions about the characters, and keeping the differences in mind will give you greater insight into their behavior.

CHECKLIST: Writing About Greek Drama

- ☐ Identify the play's major characters.
- ☐ In what ways do they seem alien to you?
- ☐ What do you notice about a character's beliefs? About his or her values? How do these differ from your own?
- ☐ In what ways are the play's characters like the people you know?
- ☐ How do these qualities—both the alien and the familiar—influence the characters' motivations and actions?

WRITING ASSIGNMENT ON SOPHOCLES

Write a brief personality profile (two or three pages) of any major character in *Oedipus the King* or *Antigonê*. Describe the character's age, social position, family background, personality, and beliefs. What is his or her major motivation in the play? In what ways does the character resemble his or her modern equivalent? In what ways do they differ?

MORE TOPICS FOR WRITING

1. Suppose you were to direct and produce a new stage production of *Oedipus the King*. How would you go about it? Would you use masks? How would you render the chorus? Would you set the play in contemporary North America? Justify your decisions by referring to the play itself.
2. Write a brief comment on the play under the title "Does Sophocles' Oedipus Have an Oedipus Complex?" Consider Sigmund Freud's famous observations (quoted on page 1233). Your comment can be either serious or light.
3. Compare *Oedipus the King* to *Antigonê* in terms of their characterizations of their protagonists. In what ways does Antigonê resemble Oedipus, and in what ways does she differ?

4. Taking the protagonist of either play by Sophocles, write an essay explaining how he or she exemplifies or refutes Aristotle's definition of a tragic hero.

5. Discuss Rita Dove's *The Darker Face of the Earth*, in "Plays for Further Reading," as an analogue to *Oedipus the King*. Do you find Augustus Newcastle to be a truly tragic protagonist? What is there about him that suggests nobility? What is his tragic flaw, and how does it destroy him?

▶ TERMS FOR *review*

Stagecraft in Ancient Greece

Skene ▶ The canvas or wooden stage building in which actors changed masks and costumes when changing roles. Its façade, with double center doors and possibly two side doors, served as the setting for action taking place before a palace, temple, cave, or other interior space.

Orchestra ▶ "The place for dancing"; a circular, level performance space at the base of a horseshoe-shaped amphitheater, where twelve, then later (in Sophocles' plays) fifteen masked young male chorus members sang and danced the odes interspersed between dramatic episodes in a play. (Today the term *orchestra* refer to the ground-floor seats in a theater or concert hall.)

Deus ex machina ▶ (Latin for "god out of the machine.") Originally, the phrase referred to the Greek playwrights' frequent use of a god, mechanically lowered to the stage from the *skene* roof to resolve the human conflict. Today, *deus ex machina* refers to any forced or improbable device used to resolve a plot.

Masks ▶ (In Latin, *personae*.) Classical Greek theater masks covered an actor's entire head. Large, recognizable masks allowed far-away spectators to distinguish the conventional characters of tragedy and comedy.

Cothurni ▶ High, thick-soled elevator boots worn by tragic actors in late classical times to make them appear taller than ordinary men. (Earlier, in the fifth-century classical Athenian theater, actors wore soft shoes or boots or went barefoot.)

Elements of Classical Tragedy

Hamartia ▶ (Greek for "error.") An offense committed in ignorance of some material fact; a great mistake made as a result of an error by a morally good person.

Tragic flaw ▶ A fatal weakness or moral flaw in the protagonist that brings him or her to a bad end. Sometimes offered as an alternative understanding of *hamartia*, in contrast to the idea that the tragic hero's catastrophe is caused by an error in judgment.

Hubris ▶ Overweening pride, outrageous behavior, or the insolence that leads to ruin, the antithesis of moderation or rectitude.

Peripeteia ▶ (Anglicized as *peripety*; Greek for "sudden change.") A reversal of fortune, a sudden change of circumstance affecting the protagonist. According to Aristotle, the play's peripety occurs when a certain result is expected and instead its opposite effect is produced. In a tragedy, the reversal takes the protagonist from good fortune to catastrophe.

Recognition ▶ In tragic plotting, the moment of recognition occurs when ignorance gives way to knowledge, illusion to disillusion.

Katharsis, **catharsis** ▶ (Often translated from Greek as *purgation* or *purification*.) The feeling of emotional release or calm the spectator feels at the end of tragedy. The term is drawn from Aristotle's definition of tragedy, relating to the final cause or purpose of tragic art. Some feel that through *katharsis*, drama taught the audience compassion for the vulnerabilities of others and schooled it in justice and other civic virtues.

37 CRITICAL CASEBOOK
Shakespeare

"To be or not to be . . ." **Is it Shakespeare?** In 2009 the Shakespeare Birthplace Trust unveiled this newly discovered portrait they believe is William Shakespeare. If authentic—and many scholars disagree—it is the only surviving portrait of the author painted during his lifetime.

All the world's a stage

—WILLIAM SHAKESPEARE, *AS YOU LIKE IT* (II, vii)

**The reconstructed Globe Theatre in today's London—
built in 1997 as an exact replica of the original.**

THE THEATER OF SHAKESPEARE

Compared with the technical resources of a theater of today, those of a London public theater in the time of Queen Elizabeth I seem hopelessly limited. Plays had to be performed by daylight, and scenery had to be kept simple: a table, a chair, a throne, perhaps an artificial tree or two to suggest a forest. But these limitations were, in a sense, advantages. What the theater of today can spell out for us realistically, with massive scenery and electric lighting, Elizabethan playgoers had to imagine and the playwright had to make vivid for them by means of language. Not having a lighting technician to work a panel, Shakespeare had to indicate the dawn by having Horatio, in *Hamlet*, say in a speech rich in metaphor and descriptive detail:

> But look, the morn in russet mantle clad
> Walks o'er the dew of yon high eastward hill.

And yet the theater of Shakespeare was not bare, for the playwright did have *some* valuable technical resources. Costumes could be elaborate, and apparently some costumes conveyed recognized meanings: one theater manager's inventory included "a robe for to go invisible in." There could be musical accompaniment and sound effects such as gunpowder explosions and the beating of a pan to simulate thunder.

The stage itself was remarkably versatile. At its back were doors for exits and entrances and a curtained booth or alcove useful for hiding inside. Above the stage was a higher acting area—perhaps a porch or balcony—useful for a Juliet to stand upon and for a Romeo to raise his eyes to. In the stage floor was a trapdoor leading to a "hell" or cellar, especially useful for ghosts or devils who had to appear or disappear. The stage itself was a rectangular platform that projected into a yard enclosed by three-storied galleries.

The building was round or octagonal. In *Henry V*, Shakespeare calls it a "wooden O." The audience sat in these galleries or else stood in the yard in front of the stage and at its sides. A roof or awning protected the stage and the high-priced gallery seats, but in a sudden rain, the *groundlings*, who paid a penny to stand in the yard, must have been dampened.

Built by the theatrical company to which Shakespeare belonged, the Globe, most celebrated of Elizabethan theaters, was not in the city of London itself but on the south bank of the Thames River. This location had been chosen because earlier, in 1574, public plays had been banished from the city by an ordinance that blamed them for "corruptions of youth and other enormities" (such as providing opportunities for prostitutes and pickpockets).

A playwright had to please all members of the audience, not only the mannered and educated. This obligation may help to explain the wide range of matter and tone in an Elizabethan play: passages of subtle poetry, of deep philosophy, of coarse bawdry; scenes of sensational violence and of quiet psychological conflict (not that most members of the audience did not enjoy all these elements). Because he was an actor as well as a playwright, Shakespeare well knew what his company could do and what his audience wanted. In devising a play, he could write a part to take advantage of some actor's specific skills, or he could avoid straining the company's resources (some of his plays have few female parts, perhaps because of a shortage of competent boy actors). The company might offer as many as thirty plays in a season, customarily changing the program daily. The actors thus had to hold many parts in their heads, which may account for Elizabethan playwrights' fondness for blank verse. Lines of fixed length were easier for actors to commit to memory.

WILLIAM SHAKESPEARE

William Shakespeare (1564–1616), the supreme writer of English, was born, baptized, and buried in the market town of Stratford-on-Avon, eighty miles from London. Son of a glove maker and merchant who was high bailiff (or mayor) of the town, he probably attended grammar school and learned to read Latin authors in the original. At eighteen, he married Anne Hathaway, twenty-six, by whom he had three children, including twins. By 1592 he had become well known and envied as an actor and playwright in London. From 1594 until he retired, he belonged to the same theatrical company, the Lord Chamberlain's Men (later renamed the King's Men in honor of their patron, James I), for whom he wrote thirty-six

William Shakespeare

plays—some of them, such as Hamlet and King Lear, profound reworkings of old plays. As an actor, Shakespeare is believed to have played supporting roles, such as the ghost of Hamlet's father. The company prospered, moved into the Globe in 1599, and in 1608 bought the fashionable Blackfriars as well; Shakespeare owned an interest in both theaters. When plagues shut down the theaters from 1592 to 1594, Shakespeare turned to story poems; his great Sonnets (published only in 1609) probably also date from the 1590s. Plays were regarded as entertainments of little literary merit, like comic books today, and Shakespeare did not bother to supervise their publication. After writing The Tempest (1611), the last play entirely from his hand, he retired to Stratford, where since 1597 he had owned the second-largest house in town. Most critics agree that when he wrote Othello, about 1604, Shakespeare was at the height of his powers.

A NOTE ON *OTHELLO*

James Earl Jones as Othello.

Othello, the Moor of Venice, here offered for study, may be (if you are fortunate) new to you. It is seldom taught in high school, for it is ablaze with passion and violence. Even if you already know the play, we trust that you (like your instructor and your editors) still have much more to learn from it. Following his usual practice, Shakespeare based the play on a story he had appropriated—from a tale, "Of the Unfaithfulness of Husbands and Wives," by a sixteenth-century Italian writer, Giraldi Cinthio. As he could not help but do, Shakespeare freely transformed his source material. In the original tale, the heroine Disdemona (whose name Shakespeare so hugely improved) is beaten to death with a stocking full of sand—a shoddier death than the bard imagined for her.

Surely no character in literature can touch us more than Desdemona; no character can shock and disgust us more than Iago. Between these two extremes stands Othello, a black man of courage and dignity—and yet insecure, capable of being fooled, a pushover for bad advice. Besides breathing life into these characters and a host of others, Shakespeare—as brilliant a writer as any the world has known—enables them to speak poetry. Sometimes this poetry seems splendid and rich in imagery; at other times quiet and understated. Always, it seems to grow naturally from the nature of Shakespeare's characters and from their situations. *Othello, the Moor of Venice* has never ceased to grip readers and beholders alike. It is a safe bet that it will triumphantly live as long as fathers dislike whomever their daughters marry, as long as husbands suspect their wives of cheating, as long as blacks remember slavery, and as long as the ambitious court favor and the jealous practice deceit. The play may well make sense as long as public officials connive behind smiling faces, and it may even endure as long as the world makes room for the kind, the true, the beautiful—the blessed pure in heart.

PICTURING *Othello*

▲ Desdemona's father, Brabantio, *page 1253*

▼ Othello and Desdemona, *page 1266*

▲ Desdemona arrives in Cyprus, *page 1275*

▲ Desdemona offers the wrong handkerchief, *page 1307*

▲ Iago's machinations, *page 1314*

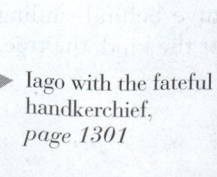

▶ Iago with the fateful handkerchief, *page 1301*

▶ Iago advises Cassio,
page 1286

▲ Drunken Cassio fights, *page 1282*

▲ Iago plants doubts about Desdemona,
page 1296

▼ Othello despairs, *page 1322*

▲ Othello
smothers
Desdemona,
page 1339

▶ Enter Othello, *page 1336*

Othello, the Moor of Venice   1604?

Edited by David Bevington

THE NAMES OF THE ACTORS

Othello, the Moor
Brabantio, [a senator,] father to Desdemona
Cassio, an honorable lieutenant [to Othello]
Iago, [Othello's ancient,] a villain
Roderigo, a gulled gentleman
Duke of Venice
Senators [of Venice]
Montano, governor of Cyprus
Gentlemen of Cyprus
Lodovico and Gratiano, [kinsmen to Brabantio,] two noble Venetians
Sailors
Clown
Desdemona, [daughter to Brabantio and] wife to Othello
Emilia, wife to Iago
Bianca, a courtesan [and mistress to Cassio]
[A Messenger
A Herald
A Musician
Servants, Attendants, Officers, Senators, Musicians, Gentlemen

SCENE. *Venice; a seaport in Cyprus*]

ACT I

SCENE I [VENICE. A STREET.]

    Enter Roderigo and Iago.

Roderigo: Tush, never tell me!° I take it much unkindly
    That thou, Iago, who hast had my purse
    As if the strings were thine, shouldst know of this.°

NOTE ON THE TEXT: This text of *Othello* is based on that of the First Folio, or large collection, of Shakespeare's plays (1623). But there are many differences between the Folio text and that of the play's first printing in the Quarto, or small volume, of 1621 (eighteen or nineteen years after the play's first performance). Some readings from the Quarto are included. For the reader's convenience, some material has been added by the editor, David Bevington (some indications of scene, some stage directions). Such additions are enclosed in brackets. Mr. Bevington's text and notes were prepared for his book, *The Complete Works of Shakespeare,* updated 4th ed. (New York: Longman, 1997).

PRODUCTION PHOTOS: The photos included are from the 2003 production of *Othello* by the Guthrie Theater of Minneapolis, with Lester Purry (Othello), Bill McCallum (Iago), Cheyenne Casebier (Desdemona), Robert O. Berdahl (Cassio), Virginia S. Burke (Emilia), Nathaniel Fuller (Brabantio), and Shawn Hamilton (Montano).

1 *never tell me* (An expression of incredulity, like "tell me another one.")   3 *this* i.e., Desdemona's elopement

Iago: 'Sblood,° but you'll not hear me.
    If ever I did dream of such a matter,   5
    Abhor me.
Roderigo: Thou toldst me thou didst hold him in thy hate.
Iago: Despise me
    If I do not. Three great ones of the city,
    In personal suit to make me his lieutenant,   10
    Off-capped to him;° and by the faith of man,
    I know my price, I am worth no worse a place.
    But he, as loving his own pride and purposes,
    Evades them with a bombast circumstance°
    Horribly stuffed with epithets of war,°   15
    And, in conclusion,
    Nonsuits° my mediators. For, "Certes,"° says he,
    "I have already chose my officer."
    And what was he?
    Forsooth, a great arithmetician,°   20
    One Michael Cassio, a Florentine,
    A fellow almost damned in a fair wife,°
    That never set a squadron in the field
    Nor the division of a battle° knows
    More than a spinster°—unless the bookish theoric,°   25
    Wherein the togaed° consuls° can propose°
    As masterly as he. Mere prattle without practice
    Is all his soldiership. But he, sir, had th' election;
    And I, of whom his° eyes had seen the proof
    At Rhodes, at Cyprus, and on other grounds   30
    Christened° and heathen, must be beleed and calmed°
    By debitor and creditor.° This countercaster,°
    He, in good time,° must his lieutenant be,
    And I—God bless the mark!°—his Moorship's ancient.°
Roderigo: By heaven, I rather would have been his hangman.°   35
Iago: Why, there's no remedy. 'Tis the curse of service;
    Preferment° goes by letter and affection,°

---

4 *'Sblood* by His (Christ's) blood 11 *him* i.e., Othello 14 *bombast circumstance* wordy evasion. (Bombast is cotton padding.) 15 *epithets of war* military expressions 17 *Nonsuits* rejects the petition of. *Certes* certainly 20 *arithmetician* i.e., a man whose military knowledge is merely theoretical, based on books of tactics 22 *A . . . wife* (Cassio does not seem to be married, but his counterpart in Shakespeare's source does have a woman in his house. See also IV, i, 127.) 24 *division of a battle* disposition of a military unit 25 *a spinster* i.e., a housewife, one whose regular occupation is spinning. *theoric* theory 26 *togaed* wearing the toga. *consuls* counselors, senators. *propose* discuss 29 *his* i.e., Othello's 31 *Christened* Christian. *beleed and calmed* left to leeward without wind, becalmed. (A sailing metaphor.) 32 *debitor and creditor* (A name for a system of bookkeeping, here used as a contemptuous nickname for Cassio.) *countercaster* i.e., bookkeeper, one who tallies with *counters,* or "metal disks." (Said contemptuously.) 33 *in good time* opportunely, i.e., forsooth 34 *God bless the mark* (Perhaps originally a formula to ward off evil; here an expression of impatience.) *ancient* standard-bearer, ensign 35 *his hangman* the executioner of him 37 *Preferment* promotion. *letter and affection* personal influence and favoritism

And not by old gradation,° where each second
Stood heir to th' first. Now, sir, be judge yourself
Whether I in any just term° am affined°   40
To love the Moor.
Roderigo: I would not follow him then.
Iago: O sir, content you.°
I follow him to serve my turn upon him.
We cannot all be masters, nor all masters   45
Cannot be truly° followed. You shall mark
Many a duteous and knee-crooking knave
That, doting on his own obsequious bondage,
Wears out his time, much like his master's ass,
For naught but provender, and when he's old, cashiered.°   50
Whip me° such honest knaves. Others there are
Who, trimmed in forms and visages of duty,°
Keep yet their hearts attending on themselves,
And, throwing but shows of service on their lords,
Do well thrive by them, and when they have lined their coats,°   55
Do themselves homage.° These fellows have some soul,
And such a one do I profess myself. For, sir,
It is as sure as you are Roderigo,
Were I the Moor I would not be Iago.°
In following him, I follow but myself—   60
Heaven is my judge, not I for love and duty,
But seeming so for my peculiar° end.
For when my outward action doth demonstrate
The native° act and figure° of my heart
In compliment extern,° 'tis not long after   65
But I will wear my heart upon my sleeve
For daws° to peck at. I am not what I am.°
Roderigo: What a full° fortune does the thick-lips° owe°
If he can carry 't thus!°
Iago: Call up her father.
Rouse him, make after him, poison his delight,   70
Proclaim him in the streets; incense her kinsmen,
And, though he in a fertile climate dwell,
Plague him with flies.° Though that his joy be joy,°

---

38 *old gradation* step-by-step seniority, the traditional way   40 *term* respect.   *affined* bound   43 *content you* don't you worry about that   46 *truly* faithfully   50 *cashiered* dismissed from service   51 *Whip me* whip, as far as I'm concerned   52 *trimmed . . . duty* dressed up in the mere form and show of dutifulness   55 *lined their coats* i.e., stuffed their purses   56 *Do themselves homage* i.e., attend to self-interest solely   59 *Were . . . Iago* i.e., if I were able to assume command, I certainly would not choose to remain a subordinate, or, I would keep a suspicious eye on a flattering subordinate   62 *peculiar* particular, personal   64 *native* innate.   *figure* shape, intent   65 *compliment extern* outward show. (Conforming in this case to the inner workings and intention of the heart.)   67 *daws* small crowlike birds, proverbially stupid and avaricious.   *I am not what I am* i.e., I am not one who wears his heart on his sleeve   68 *full* swelling.   *thick-lips* (Elizabethans often applied the term "Moor" to Negroes.)   *owe* own   69 *carry 't thus* carry this off   72–73 *though . . . flies* though he seems prosperous and happy now, vex him with misery   73 *Though . . . be joy* although he seems fortunate and happy. (Repeats the idea of line 72.)

Yet throw such changes of vexation° on 't
As it may° lose some color.°   75
Roderigo: Here is her father's house. I'll call aloud.
Iago: Do, with like timorous° accent and dire yell
As when, by night and negligence,° the fire
Is spied in populous cities.
Roderigo: What ho, Brabantio! Signor Brabantio, ho!   80
Iago: Awake! What ho, Brabantio! Thieves, thieves, thieves!
Look to your house, your daughter, and your bags!
Thieves, thieves!

Brabantio [enters] above [at a window].°

Brabantio: What is the reason of this terrible summons?
What is the matter° there?   85
Roderigo: Signor, is all your family within?
Iago: Are your doors locked?
Brabantio: Why, wherefore ask you this?
Iago: Zounds,° sir, you're robbed. For shame, put on your gown!
Your heart is burst; you have lost half your soul.
Even now, now, very now, an old black ram   90
Is tupping° your white ewe. Arise, arise!
Awake the snorting° citizens with the bell,
Or else the devil° will make a grandsire of you.
Arise, I say!
Brabantio: What, have you lost your wits?
Roderigo: Most reverend signor, do you know my voice?   95
Brabantio: Not I. What are you?
Roderigo: My name is Roderigo.
Brabantio: The worser welcome.
I have charged thee not to haunt about my doors.
In honest plainness thou hast heard me say   100
My daughter is not for thee; and now, in madness,
Being full of supper and distempering° drafts,
Upon malicious bravery° dost thou come
To start° my quiet.
Roderigo: Sir, sir, sir—
Brabantio: But thou must needs be sure   105
My spirits and my place° have in° their power
To make this bitter to thee.
Roderigo: Patience, good sir.
Brabantio: What tell'st thou me of robbing? This is Venice;

---

74 *changes of vexation* vexing changes   75 *As it may* that may cause it to.   *some color* some of its fresh gloss
77 *timorous* frightening   78 *and negligence* i.e., by negligence   83 s.d. *at a window* (This stage direction,
from the Quarto, probably calls for an appearance on the gallery above and rearstage.)   85 *the matter* your
business   88 *Zounds* by His (Christ's) wounds   91 *tupping* covering, copulating with. (Said of sheep.)
92 *snorting* snoring   93 *the devil* (The devil was conventionally pictured as black.)   102 *distempering*
intoxicating   103 *Upon malicious bravery* with hostile intent to defy me   104 *start* startle, disrupt   106 *My
spirits and my place* my temperament and my authority of office.   *have in* have it in

My house is not a grange.°

Roderigo: Most grave Brabantio,
    In simple° and pure soul I come to you.   110

Iago: Zounds, sir, you are one of those that will not serve God if the devil bid you.
    Because we come to do you service and you think we are ruffians, you'll have your
    daughter covered with a Barbary° horse; you'll have your nephews° neigh to you;
    you'll have coursers° for cousins° and jennets° for germans.°

Brabantio: What profane wretch art thou?   115

Iago: I am one, sir, that comes to tell you your daughter and the Moor are now
    making the beast with two backs.

Brabantio: Thou art a villain.

Iago: You are—a senator.°

Brabantio: This thou shalt answer.° I know thee, Roderigo.

Roderigo: Sir, I will answer anything. But I beseech you,   120
    If't be your pleasure and most wise° consent—
    As partly I find it is—that your fair daughter,
    At this odd-even° and dull watch o' the night,
    Transported with° no worse nor better guard
    But with a knave° of common hire, a gondolier,   125
    To the gross clasps of a lascivious Moor—
    If this be known to you and your allowance°
    We then have done you bold and saucy° wrongs.
    But if you know not this, my manners tell me
    We have your wrong rebuke. Do not believe   130
    That, from° the sense of all civility,°
    I thus would play and trifle with your reverence.°
    Your daughter, if you have not given her leave,
    I say again, hath made a gross revolt,
    Tying her duty, beauty, wit,° and fortunes   135
    In an extravagant° and wheeling° stranger°
    Of here and everywhere. Straight° satisfy yourself.
    If she be in her chamber or your house,
    Let loose on me the justice of the state
    For thus deluding you.

Brabantio: Strike on the tinder,° ho!   140
    Give me a taper! Call up all my people!
    This accident° is not unlike my dream.
    Belief of it oppresses me already.
    Light, I say, light!   *Exit [above].*

109 *grange* isolated country house   110 *simple* sincere   113 *Barbary* from northern Africa (and hence
associated with Othello). *nephews* i.e., grandsons   114 *coursers* powerful horses. *cousins* kinsmen.
jennets small Spanish horses.   *germans* near relatives   118 *a senator* (Said with mock politeness, as though
the word itself were an insult.)   119 *answer* be held accountable for   121 *wise* well-informed   123 *odd-
even* between one day and the next, i.e., about midnight   124 *with* by   125 *But with a knave* than by a low
fellow, a servant   127 *allowance* permission   128 *saucy* insolent   131 *from* contrary to.   *civility* good
manners, decency   132 *your reverence* the respect due to you   135 *wit* intelligence   136 *extravagant*
expatriate, wandering far from home.   *wheeling* roving about, vagabond.   *stranger* foreigner   137 *Straight*
straightway   140 *tinder* charred linen ignited by a spark from flint and steel, used to light torches or *tapers*
(lines 141, 166)   142 *accident* occurrence, event

Roused from sleep, Desdemona's father, Brabantio, rushes to the street to search out his daughter (I, i, 160–180).

Iago: Farewell, for I must leave you.
    It seems not meet° nor wholesome to my place°   145
    To be producted°—as, if I stay, I shall—
    Against the Moor. For I do know the state,
    However this may gall° him with some check,°
    Cannot with safety cast° him, for he's embarked°
    With such loud reason° to the Cyprus wars,   150
    Which even now stands in act,° that, for their souls,°
    Another of his fathom° they have none

---

145 *meet* fitting. *place* position (as ensign) 146 *producted* produced (as a witness) 148 *gall* rub; oppress.
check rebuke 149 *cast* dismiss. *embarked* engaged 150 *loud reason* unanimous shout of confirmation
(in the Senate) 151 *stands in act* are going on. *for their souls* to save themselves 152 *fathom* i.e., ability,
depth of experience

To lead their business; in which regard,°
Though I do hate him as I do hell pains,
Yet for necessity of present life°   155
I must show out a flag and sign of love,
Which is indeed but sign. That you shall surely find him,
Lead to the Sagittary° the raisèd search,°
And there will I be with him. So farewell.   *Exit.*

Enter [below] Brabantio [in his nightgown°] with servants and torches.

Brabantio: It is too true an evil. Gone she is;   160
    And what's to come of my despisèd time°
    Is naught but bitterness. Now, Roderigo,
    Where didst thou see her?—O unhappy girl!—
    With the Moor, sayst thou?—Who would be a father!—
    How didst thou know 'twas she?—O, she deceives me   165
    Past thought!—What said she to you?—Get more tapers.
    Raise all my kindred.—Are they married, think you?
Roderigo: Truly, I think they are.
Brabantio: O heaven! How got she out? O treason of the blood!
    Fathers, from hence trust not your daughters' minds   170
    By what you see them act. Is there not charms°
    By which the property° of youth and maidhood
    May be abused?° Have you not read, Roderigo,
    Of some such thing?
Roderigo: Yes, sir, I have indeed.
Brabantio: Call up my brother.—O, would you had had her!—   175
    Some one way, some another.—Do you know
    Where we may apprehend her and the Moor?
Roderigo: I think I can discover° him, if you please
    To get good guard and go along with me.
Brabantio: Pray you, lead on. At every house I'll call;   180
    I may command° at most.—Get weapons, ho!
    And raise some special officers of night.—
    On, good Roderigo. I will deserve° your pains.

    Exeunt.

SCENE II [VENICE. ANOTHER STREET, BEFORE OTHELLO'S LODGINGS.]

Enter Othello, Iago, attendants with torches.

Iago: Though in the trade of war I have slain men,
    Yet do I hold it very stuff° o' the conscience

---

153 *in which regard* out of regard for which   155 *life* livelihood   158 *Sagittary* (An inn or house where Othello and Desdemona are staying, named for its sign of Sagittarius, or Centaur.) *raisèd search* search party roused out of sleep   159 s.d. *nightgown* dressing gown. (This costuming is specified in the Quarto text.)   161 *time* i.e., remainder of life   171 *charms* spells   172 *property* special quality, nature   173 *abused* deceived   178 *discover* reveal, uncover   181 *command* demand assistance   183 *deserve* show gratitude for   2 *very stuff* essence, basic material (continuing the metaphor of *trade* from line 1)

To do no contrived° murder. I lack iniquity
Sometimes to do me service. Nine or ten times
I had thought t' have yerked° him° here under the ribs.   5
Othello: 'Tis better as it is.
Iago: Nay, but he prated,
And spoke such scurvy and provoking terms
Against your honor
That, with the little godliness I have,
I did full hard forbear him.° But, I pray you, sir,   10
Are you fast married? Be assured of this,
That the magnifico° is much beloved,
And hath in his effect° a voice potential°
As double as the Duke's. He will divorce you,
Or put upon you what restraint or grievance   15
The law, with all his might to enforce it on,
Will give him cable.°
Othello: Let him do his spite.
My services which I have done the seigniory°
Shall out-tongue his complaints. 'Tis yet to know°—
Which, when I know that boasting is an honor,   20
I shall promulgate—I fetch my life and being
From men of royal siege,° and my demerits°
May speak unbonneted° to as proud a fortune
As this that I have reached. For know, Iago,
But that I love the gentle Desdemona,   25
I would not my unhousèd° free condition
Put into circumscription and confine°
For the sea's worth.° But look, what lights come yond?

Enter Cassio [and certain officers°] with torches.

Iago: Those are the raisèd father and his friends.
You were best go in.
Othello: Not I. I must be found.   30
My parts, my title, and my perfect soul°
Shall manifest me rightly. Is it they?
Iago: By Janus,° I think no.
Othello: The servants of the Duke? And my lieutenant?
The goodness of the night upon you, friends!   35
What is the news?

---

3 *contrived* premeditated 5 *yerked* stabbed. *him* i.e., Roderigo 10 *I . . . him* I restrained myself with great difficulty from assaulting him 12 *magnifico* Venetian grandee, i.e., Brabantio 13 *in his effect* at his command. *potential* powerful 17 *cable* i.e., scope 18 *seigniory* Venetian government 19 *yet to know* not yet widely known 22 *siege* i.e., rank. (Literally, a seat used by a person of distinction.) *demerits* deserts 23 *unbonneted* without removing the hat, i.e., on equal terms (?) (Or "with hat off," "in all due modesty.") 26 *unhousèd* unconfined, undomesticated 27 *circumscription and confine* restriction and confinement 28 *the sea's worth* all the riches at the bottom of the sea. s.d. *officers* (The Quarto text calls for "Cassio with lights, officers with torches.") 31 *My . . . soul* my natural gifts, my position or reputation, and my unflawed conscience 33 *Janus* Roman two-faced god of beginnings

Cassio: The Duke does greet you, General,
    And he requires your haste-post-haste appearance
    Even on the instant.
Othello: What is the matter,° think you?
Cassio: Something from Cyprus, as I may divine.°
    It is a business of some heat.° The galleys   40
    Have sent a dozen sequent° messengers
    This very night at one another's heels,
    And many of the consuls,° raised and met,
    Are at the Duke's already. You have been hotly called for;
    When, being not at your lodging to be found,   45
    The Senate hath sent about° three several° quests
    To search you out.
Othello: 'Tis well I am found by you.
    I will but spend a word here in the house
    And go with you.   [Exit.]
Cassio: Ancient, what makes° he here?
Iago: Faith, he tonight hath boarded° a land carrack.°   50
    If it prove lawful prize,° he's made forever.
Cassio: I do not understand.
Iago: He's married.
Cassio: To who?

    [Enter Othello.]

Iago: Marry,° to—Come, Captain, will you go?
Othello: Have with you.°
Cassio: Here comes another troop to seek for you.   55

    Enter Brabantio, Roderigo, with officers and torches.°

Iago: It is Brabantio. General, be advised.°
    He comes to bad intent.
Othello: Holla! Stand there!
Roderigo: Signor, it is the Moor.
Brabantio: Down with him, thief!

    [They draw on both sides.]

Iago: You, Roderigo! Come, sir, I am for you.
Othello: Keep up° your bright swords, for the dew will rust them.   60
    Good signor, you shall more command with years
    Than with your weapons.

---

38 *matter* business 39 *divine* guess 40 *heat* urgency 41 *sequent* successive 43 *consuls* senators
46 *about* all over the city. *several* separate 49 *makes* does 50 *boarded* gone aboard and seized as an act
of piracy (with sexual suggestion). *carrack* large merchant ship 51 *prize* booty 53 *Marry* (An oath,
originally "by the Virgin Mary"; here used with wordplay on *married*.) 54 *Have with you* i.e., let's go
55 s.d. *officers and torches* (The Quarto text calls for "others with lights and weapons.") 56 *be advised* be
on your guard 60 *Keep up* keep in the sheath

Brabantio: O thou foul thief, where hast thou stowed my daughter?
    Damned as thou art, thou hast enchanted her!
    For I'll refer me° to all things of sense,°   65
    If she in chains of magic were not bound
    Whether a maid so tender, fair, and happy,
    So opposite to marriage that she shunned
    The wealthy curlèd darlings of our nation,
    Would ever have, t' incur a general mock,   70
    Run from her guardage° to the sooty bosom
    Of such a thing as thou—to fear, not to delight.
    Judge me the world if 'tis not gross in sense°
    That thou hast practiced on her with foul charms,
    Abused her delicate youth with drugs or minerals°   75
    That weaken motion.° I'll have 't disputed on;°
    'Tis probable and palpable to thinking.
    I therefore apprehend and do attach° thee
    For an abuser of the world, a practicer
    Of arts inhibited° and out of warrant.°—   80
    Lay hold upon him! If he do resist,
    Subdue him at his peril.
Othello: Hold your hands,
    Both you of my inclining° and the rest.
    Were it my cue to fight, I should have known it
    Without a prompter.—Whither will you that I go   85
    To answer this your charge?
Brabantio: To prison, till fit time
    Of law and course of direct session°
    Call thee to answer.
Othello: What if I do obey?
    How may the Duke be therewith satisfied,   90
    Whose messengers are here about my side
    Upon some present business of the state
    To bring me to him?
Officer: 'Tis true, most worthy signor.
    The Duke's in council, and your noble self,
    I am sure, is sent for.
Brabantio: How? The Duke in council?   95
    In this time of the night? Bring him away.°
    Mine's not an idle° cause. The Duke himself,
    Or any of my brothers of the state,
    Cannot but feel this wrong as 'twere their own;

---

65 *refer me* submit my case. *things of sense* commonsense understandings, or, creatures possessing common sense   71 *her guardage* my guardianship of her   73 *gross in sense* obvious   75 *minerals* i.e., poisons 76 *weaken motion* impair the vital faculties. *disputed on* argued in court by professional counsel, debated by experts   78 *attach* arrest   80 *arts inhibited* prohibited arts, black magic. *out of warrant* illegal 83 *inclining* following, party   88 *course of direct session* regular or specially convened legal proceedings 96 *away* right along   97 *idle* trifling

For if such actions may have passage free,°   100
Bondslaves and pagans shall our statesmen be.

Exeunt.

SCENE III [VENICE. A COUNCIL CHAMBER.]

*Enter Duke [and] Senators [and sit at a table, with lights], and Officers.° [The Duke
and Senators are reading dispatches.]*

Duke: There is no composition° in these news
      That gives them credit.
First Senator: Indeed, they are disproportioned.°
      My letters say a hundred and seven galleys.
Duke: And mine, a hundred forty.
Second Senator: And mine, two hundred.   5
      But though they jump° not on a just° account—
      As in these cases, where the aim° reports
      'Tis oft with difference—yet do they all confirm
      A Turkish fleet, and bearing up to Cyprus.
Duke: Nay, it is possible enough to judgment.   10
      I do not so secure me in the error
      But the main article I do approve°
      In fearful sense.
Sailor (*within*):   What ho, what ho, what ho!

      Enter Sailor.

Officer: A messenger from the galleys.
Duke: Now, what's the business?
Sailor: The Turkish preparation° makes for Rhodes.   15
      So was I bid report here to the state
      By Signor Angelo.
Duke: How say you by° this change?
First Senator: This cannot be
      By no assay° of reason. 'Tis a pageant°   20
      To keep us in false gaze.° When we consider
      Th' importancy of Cyprus to the Turk,
      And let ourselves again but understand
      That, as it more concerns the Turk than Rhodes,
      So may he with more facile question bear it,°   25
      For that° it stands not in such warlike brace,°
      But altogether lacks th' abilities°

100 *have passage free* are allowed to go unchecked   s.d. *Enter . . . Officers* (The Quarto text calls for the Duke
and senators to "sit at a table with lights and attendants.")   1 *composition* consistency   3 *disproportioned*
inconsistent   6 *jump* agree.   *just* exact   7 *the aim* conjecture   11–12 *I do not . . . approve* I do not take such
(false) comfort in the discrepancies that I fail to perceive the main point, i.e., that the Turkish fleet is threatening   16 *preparation* fleet prepared for battle   19 *by* about   20 *assay* test.   *pageant* mere show   21 *in
false gaze* looking the wrong way   25 *So may . . . it* so also he (the Turk) can more easily capture it (Cyprus)
26 *For that* since.   *brace* state of defense   27 *abilities* means of self-defense

That Rhodes is dressed in°—if we make thought of this,
We must not think the Turk is so unskillful°
To leave that latest° which concerns him first,   30
Neglecting an attempt of ease and gain
To wake° and wage° a danger profitless.

Duke: Nay, in all confidence, he's not for Rhodes.

Officer: Here is more news.

    Enter a Messenger.

Messenger: The Ottomites, reverend and gracious,   35
Steering with due course toward the isle of Rhodes,
Have there injointed them° with an after° fleet.

First Senator: Ay, so I thought. How many, as you guess?

Messenger: Of thirty sail; and now they do restem
Their backward course,° bearing with frank appearance°   40
Their purposes toward Cyprus. Signor Montano,
Your trusty and most valiant servitor,°
With his free duty° recommends° you thus,
And prays you to believe him.

Duke: 'Tis certain then for Cyprus.   45
Marcus Luccicos, is not he in town?

First Senator: He's now in Florence.

Duke: Write from us to him, post-post-haste. Dispatch.

First Senator: Here comes Brabantio and the valiant Moor.

    Enter Brabantio, Othello, Cassio, Iago, Roderigo, and officers.

Duke: Valiant Othello, we must straight° employ you   50
Against the general enemy° Ottoman.
[*To Brabantio.*] I did not see you; welcome, gentle° signor.
We lacked your counsel and your help tonight.

Brabantio: So did I yours. Good Your Grace, pardon me;
Neither my place° nor aught I heard of business   55
Hath raised me from my bed, nor doth the general care
Take hold on me, for my particular° grief
Is of so floodgate° and o'erbearing nature
That it engluts° and swallows other sorrows
And it is still itself.°

Duke: Why, what's the matter?   60

Brabantio: My daughter! O, my daughter!

Duke and Senators: Dead?

Brabantio: Ay, to me
She is abused,° stol'n from me, and corrupted

---

28 *dressed in* equipped with 29 *unskillful* deficient in judgment 30 *latest* last 32 *wake* stir up. *wage* risk 37 *injointed them* joined themselves. *after* second, following 39–40 *restem . . . course* retrace their original course 40 *frank appearance* undisguised intent 42 *servitor* officer under your command 43 *free duty* freely given and loyal service. *recommends* commends himself and reports to 50 *straight* straightway 51 *general enemy* universal enemy to all Christendom 52 *gentle* noble 55 *place* official position 57 *particular* personal 58 *floodgate* i.e., overwhelming (as when floodgates are opened) 59 *engluts* engulfs 60 *is still itself* remains undiminished 62 *abused* deceived

Othello answers Brabantio's charges before the Duke (I, iii, 78–172).

By spells and medicines bought of mountebanks;
For nature so preposterously to err,
Being not deficient,° blind, or lame of sense,°   65
Sans° witchcraft could not.
Duke: Whoe'er he be that in this foul proceeding
Hath thus beguiled your daughter of herself,
And you of her, the bloody book of law
You shall yourself read in the bitter letter   70
After your own sense°—yea, though our proper° son
Stood in your action.°
Brabantio: Humbly I thank Your Grace.
Here is the man, this Moor, whom now it seems
Your special mandate for the state affairs
Hath hither brought.
All: We are very sorry for 't.   75
Duke [to Othello]: What, in your own part, can you say to this?
Brabantio: Nothing, but this is so.
Othello: Most potent, grave, and reverend signors,
My very noble and approved° good masters:
That I have ta'en away this old man's daughter,   80

---

65 *deficient* defective.   *lame of sense* deficient in sensory perception   66 *Sans* without   71 *After . . . sense*
according to your own interpretation.   *our proper* my own   72 *Stood . . . action* were under your accusation   79 *approved* proved, esteemed

It is most true; true, I have married her.
The very head and front° of my offending
Hath this extent, no more. Rude° am I in my speech,
And little blessed with the soft phrase of peace;
For since these arms of mine had seven years' pith,°   85
Till now some nine moons wasted,° they have used
Their dearest° action in the tented field;
And little of this great world can I speak
More than pertains to feats of broils and battle,
And therefore little shall I grace my cause   90
In speaking for myself. Yet, by your gracious patience,
I will a round° unvarnished tale deliver
Of my whole course of love—what drugs, what charms,
What conjuration, and what mighty magic,
For such proceeding I am charged withal,°   95
I won his daughter.
Brabantio: A maiden never bold;
Of spirit so still and quiet that her motion
Blushed at herself;° and she, in spite of nature,
Of years,° of country, credit,° everything,
To fall in love with what she feared to look on!   100
It is a judgment maimed and most imperfect
That will confess° perfection so could err
Against all rules of nature, and must be driven
To find out practices° of cunning hell
Why this should be. I therefore vouch° again   105
That with some mixtures powerful o'er the blood,°
Or with some dram conjured to this effect,°
He wrought upon her.
Duke: To vouch this is no proof,
Without more wider° and more overt test°
Than these thin habits° and poor likelihoods°   110
Of modern seeming° do prefer° against him.
First Senator: But Othello, speak.
Did you by indirect and forcèd courses°
Subdue and poison this young maid's affections?
Or came it by request and such fair question°   115
As soul to soul affordeth?
Othello: I do beseech you,
Send for the lady to the Sagittary

---

82 *head and front* height and breadth, entire extent   83 *Rude* unpolished   85 *since . . . pith* i.e., since I was
seven. *pith* strength, vigor   86 *Till . . . wasted* until some nine months ago (since when Othello has evidently not been on active duty, but in Venice)   87 *dearest* most valuable   92 *round* plain   95 *withal* with
97–98 *her . . . herself* i.e., she blushed easily at herself. (*Motion* can suggest the impulse of the soul
or of the emotions, or physical movement.)   99 *years* i.e., difference in age.   *credit* virtuous reputation
102 *confess* concede (that)   104 *practices* plots   105 *vouch* assert   106 *blood* passions   107 *dram . . .
effect* dose made by magical spells to have this effect   109 *more wider* fuller. *test* testimony   110 *habits*
garments, i.e., appearances.   *poor likelihoods* weak inferences   111 *modern seeming* commonplace assumption.   *prefer* bring forth   113 *forcèd courses* means used against her will   115 *question* conversation

And let her speak of me before her father.
If you do find me foul in her report,
The trust, the office I do hold of you   120
Not only take away, but let your sentence
Even fall upon my life.
Duke: Fetch Desdemona hither.
Othello: Ancient, conduct them. You best know the place.

[*Exeunt Iago and attendants.*]

And, till she come, as truly as to heaven
I do confess the vices of my blood,°   125
So justly° to your grave ears I'll present
How I did thrive in this fair lady's love,
And she in mine.
Duke: Say it, Othello.
Othello: Her father loved me, oft invited me,   130
Still° questioned me the story of my life
From year to year—the battles, sieges, fortunes
That I have passed.
I ran it through, even from my boyish days
To th' very moment that he bade me tell it,   135
Wherein I spoke of most disastrous chances,
Of moving accidents° by flood and field,
Of hairbreadth scapes i' th' imminent deadly breach,°
Of being taken by the insolent foe
And sold to slavery, of my redemption thence,   140
And portance° in my travels' history,
Wherein of antres° vast and deserts idle,°
Rough quarries,° rocks, and hills whose heads touch heaven,
It was my hint° to speak—such was my process—
And of the Cannibals that each other eat,   145
The Anthropophagi,° and men whose heads
Do grow beneath their shoulders. These things to hear
Would Desdemona seriously incline;
But still the house affairs would draw her thence,
Which ever as she could with haste dispatch   150
She'd come again, and with a greedy ear
Devour up my discourse. Which I, observing,
Took once a pliant° hour, and found good means
To draw from her a prayer of earnest heart
That I would all my pilgrimage dilate,°   155
Whereof by parcels° she had something heard,

---

125 *blood* passions, human nature   126 *justly* truthfully, accurately   131 *Still* continually   137 *moving accidents* stirring happenings   138 *imminent . . . breach* death-threatening gaps made in a fortification   141 *portance* conduct   142 *antres* caverns.   *idle* barren, desolate   143 *Rough quarries* rugged rock formations   144 *hint* occasion, opportunity   146 *Anthropophagi* man-eaters. (A term from Pliny's *Natural History.*)   153 *pliant* well-suiting   155 *dilate* relate in detail   156 *by parcels* piecemeal

But not intentively.° I did consent,
And often did beguile her of her tears,
When I did speak of some distressful stroke
That my youth suffered. My story being done,   160
She gave me for my pains a world of sighs.
She swore, in faith, 'twas strange, 'twas passing° strange,
'Twas pitiful, 'twas wondrous pitiful.
She wished she had not heard it, yet she wished
That heaven had made her° such a man. She thanked me,   165
And bade me, if I had a friend that loved her,
I should but teach him how to tell my story,
And that would woo her. Upon this hint° I spake.
She loved me for the dangers I had passed,
And I loved her that she did pity them.   170
This only is the witchcraft I have used.
Here comes the lady. Let her witness it.

Enter Desdemona, Iago, [and] attendants.

Duke: I think this tale would win my daughter too.
    Good Brabantio,
    Take up this mangled matter at the best.°   175
    Men do their broken weapons rather use
    Than their bare hands.
Brabantio: I pray you, hear her speak.
    If she confess that she was half the wooer,
    Destruction on my head if my bad blame
    Light on the man!—Come hither, gentle mistress.   180
    Do you perceive in all this noble company
    Where most you owe obedience?
Desdemona: My noble Father,
    I do perceive here a divided duty.
    To you I am bound for life and education;°
    My life and education both do learn° me   185
    How to respect you. You are the lord of duty;°
    I am hitherto your daughter. But here's my husband,
    And so much duty as my mother showed
    To you, preferring you before her father,
    So much I challenge° that I may profess   190
    Due to the Moor my lord.
Brabantio: God be with you! I have done.
    Please it Your Grace, on to the state affairs.
    I had rather to adopt a child than get° it.
    Come hither, Moor.   [*He joins the hands of Othello and Desdemona.*]   195

---

157 *intentively* with full attention, continuously 162 *passing* exceedingly 165 *made her* created her to
be 168 *hint* opportunity. (Othello does not mean that she was dropping hints.) 175 *Take . . . best* make
the best of a bad bargain 184 *education* upbringing 185 *learn* teach 186 *of duty* to whom duty is due
190 *challenge* claim 194 *get* beget

I here do give thee that with all my heart°
Which, but thou hast already, with all my heart°
I would keep from thee.—For your sake,° jewel,
I am glad at soul I have no other child,
For thy escape° would teach me tyranny,   200
To hang clogs° on them.—I have done, my lord.

Duke: Let me speak like yourself,° and lay a sentence°
Which, as a grece° or step, may help these lovers
Into your favor.
When remedies° are past, the griefs are ended   205
By seeing the worst, which late on hopes depended.°
To mourn a mischief° that is past and gone
Is the next° way to draw new mischief on.
What° cannot be preserved when fortune takes,
Patience her injury a mockery makes.°   210
The robbed that smiles steals something from the thief;
He robs himself that spends a bootless grief.°

Brabantio: So let the Turk of Cyprus us beguile,
We lose it not, so long as we can smile.
He bears the sentence well that nothing bears°   215
But the free comfort which from thence he hears,
But he bears both the sentence and the sorrow
That, to pay grief, must of poor patience borrow.°
These sentences, to sugar or to gall,
Being strong on both sides, are equivocal.°   220
But words are words. I never yet did hear
That the bruised heart was piercèd through the ear.°
I humbly beseech you, proceed to th' affairs of state.

Duke: The Turk with a most mighty preparation makes for Cyprus. Othello, the
fortitude° of the place is best known to you; and though we have there a sub-   225
stitute° of most allowed° sufficiency, yet opinion, a sovereign mistress of
effects, throws a more safer voice on you.° You must therefore be content to
slubber° the gloss of your new fortunes with this more stubborn° and boisterous
expedition.

Othello: The tyrant custom, most grave senators,   230
Hath made the flinty and steel couch of war

196 *with all my heart* wherein my whole affection has been engaged   197 *with all my heart* willingly,
gladly   198 *For your sake* on your account   200 *escape* elopement   201 *clogs* (Literally, blocks of wood
fastened to the legs of criminals or convicts to inhibit escape.)   202 *like yourself* i.e., as you would, in
your proper temper.   *lay a sentence* apply a maxim   203 *grece* step   205 *remedies* hopes of remedy
206 *which . . . depended* which griefs were sustained until recently by hopeful anticipation   207 *mischief*
misfortune, injury   208 *next* nearest   209 *What* whatever   210 *Patience . . . makes* patience laughs at
the injury inflicted by fortune (and thus eases the pain)   212 *spends a bootless grief* indulges in unavailing grief   215–218 *He bears . . . borrow* a person well bears out your maxim who can enjoy its platitudi-
nous comfort, free of all genuine sorrow, but anyone whose grief bankrupts his poor patience is left with
your saying and his sorrow, too. (*Bears the sentence* also plays on the meaning, "receives judicial sentence.")   219–220 *These . . . equivocal* these fine maxims are equivocal, either sweet or bitter in their
application   222 *piercèd . . . ear* i.e., surgically lanced and cured by mere words of advice   225 *fortitude*
strength   226 *substitute* deputy.   *allowed* acknowledged   226–227 *opinion . . . on you* general opinion,
an important determiner of affairs, chooses you as the best man   228 *slubber* soil, sully.   *stubborn*
harsh, rough

My thrice-driven° bed of down. I do agnize°
A natural and prompt alacrity
I find in hardness,° and do undertake
These present wars against the Ottomites.   235
Most humbly therefore bending to your state,°
I crave fit disposition for my wife,
Due reference of place and exhibition,°
With such accommodation° and besort°
As levels° with her breeding.°   240
Duke: Why, at her father's.
Brabantio: I will not have it so.
Othello: Nor I.
Desdemona: Nor I. I would not there reside,
To put my father in impatient thoughts
By being in his eye. Most gracious Duke,
To my unfolding° lend your prosperous° ear,   245
And let me find a charter° in your voice,
T' assist my simpleness.
Duke: What would you, Desdemona?
Desdemona: That I did love the Moor to live with him,
My downright violence and storm of fortunes°   250
May trumpet to the world. My heart's subdued
Even to the very quality of my lord.°
I saw Othello's visage in his mind,
And to his honors and his valiant parts°
Did I my soul and fortunes consecrate.   255
So that, dear lords, if I be left behind
A moth° of peace, and he go to the war,
The rites° for why I love him are bereft me,
And I a heavy interim shall support
By his dear° absence. Let me go with him.   260
Othello: Let her have your voice.°
Vouch with me, heaven, I therefore beg it not
To please the palate of my appetite,
Nor to comply with heat°—the young affects°
In me defunct—and proper° satisfaction,   265
But to be free° and bounteous to her mind.
And heaven defend° your good souls that you think°

---

232 *thrice-driven* thrice sifted, winnowed. *agnize* know in myself, acknowledge 234 *hardness* hardship
236 *bending . . . state* bowing or kneeling to your authority 238 *reference . . . exhibition* provision of
appropriate place to live and allowance of money 239 *accommodation* suitable provision. *besort* attendance 240 *levels* equals, suits. *breeding* social position, upbringing 245 *unfolding* explanation,
proposal. *prosperous* propitious 246 *charter* privilege, authorization 250 *My . . . fortunes* my plain
and total breach of social custom, taking my future by storm and disrupting my whole life 251–252 *My
heart's . . . lord* my heart is brought wholly into accord with Othello's virtues; I love him for his virtues
254 *parts* qualities 257 *moth* i.e., one who consumes merely 258 *rites* rites of love (with a suggestion,
too, of "rights," sharing) 260 *dear* (1) heartfelt (2) costly 261 *voice* consent 264 *heat* sexual passion.
young affects passions of youth, desires 265 *proper* personal 266 *free* generous 267 *defend* forbid.
think should think

Desdemona declares her loyalty to her husband Othello (I, iii, 182–301).

I will your serious and great business scant
When she is with me. No, when light-winged toys
Of feathered Cupid seel° with wanton dullness   270
My speculative and officed instruments,°
That° my disports° corrupt and taint° my business,
Let huswives make a skillet of my helm,
And all indign° and base adversities
Make head° against my estimation!°   275
Duke: Be it as you shall privately determine,
Either for her stay or going. Th' affair cries haste,
And speed must answer it.
A Senator: You must away tonight.
Desdemona: Tonight, my lord?
Duke: This night.
Othello: With all my heart.

270 *seel* i.e., make blind (as in falconry, by sewing up the eyes of the hawk during training) 271
speculative . . . instruments eyes and other faculties used in the performance of duty 272 *That* so that.
disports sexual pastimes. *taint* impair 274 *indign* unworthy, shameful 275 *Make head* raise an army.
estimation reputation

Duke: At nine i' the morning here we'll meet again.   280
    Othello, leave some officer behind,
    And he shall our commission bring to you,
    With such things else of quality and respect°
    As doth import° you.
Othello: So please Your Grace, my ancient;
    A man he is of honesty and trust.   285
    To his conveyance I assign my wife,
    With what else needful Your Good Grace shall think
    To be sent after me.
Duke: Let it be so.
    Good night to everyone. [*To Brabantio.*] And, noble signor,
    If virtue no delighted° beauty lack,   290
    Your son-in-law is far more fair than black.
First Senator: Adieu, brave Moor. Use Desdemona well.
Brabantio: Look to her, Moor, if thou hast eyes to see.
    She has deceived her father, and may thee.

                Exeunt [Duke, Brabantio, Cassio, Senators, and officers].

Othello: My life upon her faith! Honest Iago,   295
    My Desdemona must I leave to thee.
    I prithee, let thy wife attend on her,
    And bring them after in the best advantage.°
    Come, Desdemona. I have but an hour
    Of love, of worldly matters and direction,°   300
    To spend with thee. We must obey the time.°

                    Exit [with Desdemona].

Roderigo: Iago—
Iago: What sayst thou, noble heart?
Roderigo: What will I do, think'st thou?
Iago: Why, go to bed and sleep.   305
Roderigo: I will incontinently° drown myself.
Iago: If thou dost, I shall never love thee after. Why, thou silly gentleman?
Roderigo: It is silliness to live when to live is torment; and then have we a prescrip-
    tion° to die when death is our physician.
Iago: O villainous!° I have looked upon the world for four times seven years, and,   310
    since I could distinguish betwixt a benefit and an injury, I never found man
    that knew how to love himself. Ere I would say I would drown myself for the
    love of a guinea hen,° I would change my humanity with a baboon.
Roderigo: What should I do? I confess it is my shame to be so fond,° but it is not
    in my virtue° to amend it.   315

---

283 *of quality and respect* of importance and relevance 284 *import* concern 290 *delighted* capable of delighting 298 *in . . . advantage* at the most favorable opportunity 300 *direction* instructions 301 *the time* the urgency of the present crisis 306 *incontinently* immediately, without self-restraint 308–309 *prescription* (1) right based on long-established custom (2) doctor's prescription 310 *villainous* i.e., what perfect nonsense 313 *guinea hen* (A slang term for a prostitute.) 314 *fond* infatuated 315 *virtue* strength, nature

Iago: Virtue? A fig!° 'Tis in ourselves that we are thus or thus. Our bodies are our gardens, to the which our wills are gardeners; so that if we will plant nettles or sow lettuce, set hyssop° and weed up thyme, supply it with one gender° of herbs or distract it with° many, either to have it sterile with idleness° or manured with industry—why, the power and corrigible authority° of this lies in our wills. If the   320
beam° of our lives had not one scale of reason to poise° another of sensuality, the blood° and baseness of our natures would conduct us to most preposterous conclusions. But we have reason to cool our raging motions,° our carnal stings, our unbitted° lusts, whereof I take this that you call love to be a sect or scion.°

Roderigo: It cannot be.   325

Iago: It is merely a lust of the blood and a permission of the will. Come, be a man. Drown thyself? Drown cats and blind puppies. I have professed me thy friend, and I confess me knit to thy deserving with cables of perdurable° toughness. I could never better stead° thee than now. Put money in thy purse. Follow thou the wars; defeat thy favor° with an usurped° beard. I say, put money in thy purse.   330
It cannot be long that Desdemona should continue her love to the Moor—put money in thy purse—nor he his to her. It was a violent commencement in her, and thou shalt see an answerable sequestration°—put but money in thy purse. These Moors are changeable in their wills°—fill thy purse with money. The food that to him now is as luscious as locusts° shall be to him shortly as bitter as   335
coloquintida.° She must change for youth; when she is sated with his body, she will find the error of her choice. She must have change, she must. Therefore put money in thy purse. If thou wilt needs damn thyself, do it a more delicate way than drowning. Make° all the money thou canst. If sanctimony° and a frail vow betwixt an erring° barbarian and a supersubtle Venetian be not too hard for my   340
wits and all the tribe of hell, thou shalt enjoy her. Therefore make money. A pox of drowning thyself! It is clean out of the way.° Seek thou rather to be hanged in compassing° thy joy than to be drowned and go without her.

Roderigo: Wilt thou be fast° to my hopes if I depend on the issue?°

Iago: Thou art sure of me. Go, make money. I have told thee often, and I retell thee   345
again and again, I hate the Moor. My cause is hearted;° thine hath no less reason. Let us be conjunctive° in our revenge against him. If thou canst cuckold him, thou dost thyself a pleasure, me a sport. There are many events in the womb of time which will be delivered. Traverse,° go, provide thy money. We will have more of this tomorrow. Adieu.   350

Roderigo: Where shall we meet i' the morning?

Iago: At my lodging.

316 *fig* (To give a fig is to thrust the thumb between the first and second fingers in a vulgar and insulting gesture.) 318 *hyssop* an herb of the mint family. *gender* kind 319 *distract it with* divide it among. *idleness* want of cultivation 320 *corrigible authority* power to correct 321 *beam* balance. *poise* counterbalance 322 *blood* natural passions 323 *motions* appetites 324 *unbitted* unbridled, uncontrolled. *sect or scion* cutting or offshoot 328 *perdurable* very durable 329 *stead* assist 330 *defeat thy favor* disguise your face. *usurped* (The suggestion is that Roderigo is not man enough to have a beard of his own.) 333 *an answerable sequestration* a corresponding separation or estrangement 334 *wills* carnal appetites 335 *locusts* fruit of the carob tree (see Matthew 3:4), or perhaps honeysuckle. 336 *coloquintida* colocynth or bitter apple, a purgative 339 *Make* raise, collect. *sanctimony* sacred ceremony 340 *erring* wandering, vagabond, unsteady 342 *clean . . . way* entirely unsuitable as a course of action 343 *compassing* encompassing, embracing 344 *fast* true. *issue* (successful) outcome 346 *hearted* fixed in the heart, heartfelt 347 *conjunctive* united 349 *Traverse* (A military marching term.)

Roderigo: I'll be with thee betimes.°   [*He starts to leave.*]

Iago: Go to, farewell.—Do you hear, Roderigo?

Roderigo: What say you?   355

Iago: No more of drowning, do you hear?

Roderigo: I am changed.

Iago: Go to, farewell. Put money enough in your purse.

Roderigo: I'll sell all my land.   *Exit.*

Iago: Thus do I ever make my fool my purse;   360
     For I mine own gained knowledge should profane
     If I would time expend with such a snipe°
     But for my sport and profit. I hate the Moor;
     And it is thought abroad° that twixt my sheets
     He's done my office.° I know not if 't be true;   365
     But I, for mere suspicion in that kind,
     Will do as if for surety.° He holds me well;°
     The better shall my purpose work on him.
     Cassio's a proper° man. Let me see now:
     To get his place and to plume up° my will   370
     In double knavery—How, how?—Let's see:
     After some time, to abuse° Othello's ear
     That he° is too familiar with his wife.
     He hath a person and a smooth dispose°
     To be suspected, framed to make women false.   375
     The Moor is of a free° and open° nature,
     That thinks men honest that but seem to be so,
     And will as tenderly° be led by the nose
     As asses are.
     I have 't. It is engendered. Hell and night   380
     Must bring this monstrous birth to the world's light.

     [*Exit.*]

ACT II

SCENE I [A SEAPORT IN CYPRUS. AN OPEN PLACE NEAR THE QUAY.]

     Enter Montano and two Gentlemen.

Montano: What from the cape can you discern at sea?

First Gentleman: Nothing at all. It is a high-wrought flood.°
     I cannot, twixt the heaven and the main,°
     Descry a sail.

Montano: Methinks the wind hath spoke aloud at land;   5
     A fuller blast ne'er shook our battlements.

---

353 *betimes* early   362 *snipe* woodcock, i.e., fool   364 *it is thought abroad* it is rumored   365 *my office* i.e., my sexual function as husband   367 *do . . . surety* act as if on certain knowledge.   *holds me well* regards me favorably   369 *proper* handsome   370 *plume up* put a feather in the cap of, i.e., glorify, gratify   372 *abuse* deceive   373 *he* i.e., Cassio   374 *dispose* disposition   376 *free* frank, generous.   *open* unsuspicious 378 *tenderly* readily   2 *high-wrought flood* very agitated sea   3 *main* ocean (also at line 41)

If it hath ruffianed° so upon the sea,
What ribs of oak, when mountains° melt on them,
Can hold the mortise?° What shall we hear of this?

Second Gentleman: A segregation° of the Turkish fleet.   10
For do but stand upon the foaming shore,
The chidden° billow seems to pelt the clouds;
The wind-shaked surge, with high and monstrous mane,°
Seems to cast water on the burning Bear°
And quench the guards of th' ever-fixèd pole.   15
I never did like molestation° view
On the enchafèd° flood.

Montano: If that° the Turkish fleet
Be not ensheltered and embayed,° they are drowned;
It is impossible to bear it out.°   20

Enter a [Third] Gentleman.

Third Gentleman: News, lads! Our wars are done.
The desperate tempest hath so banged the Turks
That their designment° halts.° A noble ship of Venice
Hath seen a grievous wreck° and sufferance°
On most part of their fleet.   25

Montano: How? Is this true?

Third Gentleman: The ship is here put in,
A Veronesa;° Michael Cassio,
Lieutenant to the warlike Moor Othello,
Is come on shore; the Moor himself at sea,   30
And is in full commission here for Cyprus.

Montano: I am glad on 't. 'Tis a worthy governor.

Third Gentleman: But this same Cassio, though he speak of comfort
Touching the Turkish loss, yet he looks sadly°
And prays the Moor be safe, for they were parted   35
With foul and violent tempest.

Montano: Pray heaven he be,
For I have served him, and the man commands
Like a full° soldier. Let's to the seaside, ho!
As well to see the vessel that's come in
As to throw out our eyes for brave Othello,   40
Even till we make the main and th' aerial blue°
An indistinct regard.°

---

7 *ruffianed* raged   8 *mountains* i.e., of water   9 *hold the mortise* hold their joints together. (A *mortise* is
the socket hollowed out in fitting timbers.)   10 *segregation* dispersal   12 *chidden* i.e., rebuked, repelled
(by the shore), and thus shot into the air   13 *monstrous mane* (The surf is like the mane of a wild beast.)
14 *the burning Bear* i.e., the constellation Ursa Minor or the Little Bear, which includes the polestar (and
hence regarded as the *guards of th' ever-fixèd pole* in the next line; sometimes the term *guards* is applied to
the two "pointers" of the Big Bear or Dipper, which may be intended here).   16 *like molestation* comparable disturbance   17 *enchafèd* angry   18 *If that* if   19 *embayed* sheltered by a bay   20 *bear it out* survive,
weather the storm   23 *designment* design, enterprise. *halts* is lame   24 *wreck* shipwreck. *sufferance*
damage, disaster   28 *Veronesa* i.e., fitted out in Verona for Venetian service, or possibly *Verennessa* (the
Folio spelling), i.e., *verrinessa*, a cutter (from *verrinare*, "to cut through")   34 *sadly* gravely   38 *full*
perfect   41 *the main . . . blue* the sea and the sky   42 *An indistinct regard* indistinguishable in our view

Third Gentleman: Come, let's do so,
 For every minute is expectancy°
 Of more arrivance.°

 Enter Cassio.

Cassio: Thanks, you the valiant of this warlike isle,   45
 That so approve° the Moor! O, let the heavens
 Give him defense against the elements,
 For I have lost him on a dangerous sea.
Montano: Is he well shipped?
Cassio: His bark is stoutly timbered, and his pilot   50
 Of very expert and approved allowance;°
 Therefore my hopes, not surfeited to death,°
 Stand in bold cure.°

 [A cry] within: "A sail, a sail, a sail!"

Cassio: What noise?
A Gentleman: The town is empty. On the brow o' the sea°   55
 Stand ranks of people, and they cry "A sail!"
Cassio: My hopes do shape him for° the governor.

 [A shot within.]

Second Gentleman: They do discharge their shot of courtesy;°
 Our friends at least.
Cassio: I pray you, sir, go forth,
 And give us truth who 'tis that is arrived.   60
Second Gentleman: I shall.   *Exit.*
Montano: But, good Lieutenant, is your general wived?
Cassio: Most fortunately. He hath achieved a maid
 That paragons° description and wild fame,°
 One that excels the quirks° of blazoning° pens,   65
 And in th' essential vesture of creation
 Does tire the enginer.°

 Enter [Second] Gentleman.°

      How now? Who has put in?°
Second Gentleman: 'Tis one Iago, ancient to the General.
Cassio: He's had most favorable and happy speed.
 Tempests themselves, high seas, and howling winds,   70
 The guttered° rocks and congregated sands—

---

43 *is expectancy* gives expectation   44 *arrivance* arrival   46 *approve* admire, honor   51 *approved allowance* tested reputation   52 *surfeited to death* i.e., overextended, worn thin through repeated application or delayed fulfillment   53 *in bold cure* in strong hopes of fulfillment   55 *brow o' the sea* cliff-edge   57 *My . . . for* I hope it is   58 *discharge . . . courtesy* fire a salute in token of respect and courtesy   64 *paragons* surpasses. *wild fame* extravagant report   65 *quirks* witty conceits. *blazoning* setting forth as though in heraldic language   66–67 *in . . . enginer* in her real, God-given, beauty, (she) defeats any attempt to praise her. *enginer* engineer, i.e., poet, one who devises. s.d. *[Second] Gentleman* (So identified in the Quarto text here and in lines 58, 61, 68, and 96; the Folio calls him a gentleman.)   67 *put in* i.e., to harbor   71 *guttered* jagged, trenched

Traitors ensteeped° to clog the guiltless keel—
As° having sense of beauty, do omit°
Their mortal° natures, letting go safely by
The divine Desdemona.

Montano: What is she?   75
Cassio: She that I spake of, our great captain's captain,
Left in the conduct of the bold Iago,
Whose footing° here anticipates our thoughts
A sennight's° speed. Great Jove, Othello guard,
And swell his sail with thine own powerful breath,   80
That he may bless this bay with his tall° ship,
Make love's quick pants in Desdemona's arms,
Give renewed fire to our extincted spirits,
And bring all Cyprus comfort!

Enter Desdemona, Iago, Roderigo, and Emilia.

                              O, behold,
The riches of the ship is come on shore!   85
You men of Cyprus, let her have your knees.

[*The gentlemen make curtsy to Desdemona.*]

Hail to thee, lady! And the grace of heaven
Before, behind thee, and on every hand
Enwheel thee round!

Desdemona: I thank you, valiant Cassio.
What tidings can you tell me of my lord?   90
Cassio: He is not yet arrived, nor know I aught
But that he's well and will be shortly here.
Desdemona: O, but I fear—How lost you company?
Cassio: The great contention of the sea and skies
Parted our fellowship.

(*Within*)   "A sail, a sail!" [*A shot.*]

                              But hark. A sail!   95
Second Gentleman: They give their greeting to the citadel.
This likewise is a friend.
Cassio: See for the news.

[*Exit Second Gentleman.*]

Good Ancient, you are welcome. [*Kissing Emilia.*] Welcome, mistress.
Let it not gall your patience, good Iago,
That I extend° my manners; 'tis my breeding°   100
That gives me this bold show of courtesy.
Iago: Sir, would she give you so much of her lips
As of her tongue she oft bestows on me,
You would have enough.

72 *ensteeped* lying under water   73 *As* as if.   *omit* forbear to exercise   74 *mortal* deadly   78 *footing* landing
79 *sennight's* week's   81 *tall* splendid, gallant   100 *extend* give scope to.   *breeding* training in the
niceties of etiquette

Desdemona: Alas, she has no speech!° 105
Iago: In faith, too much.
    I find it still,° when I have list° to sleep.
    Marry, before your ladyship, I grant,
    She puts her tongue a little in her heart
    And chides with thinking.°
Emilia: You have little cause to say so. 110
Iago: Come on, come on. You are pictures out of doors,°
    Bells° in your parlors, wildcats in your kitchens,°
    Saints° in your injuries, devils being offended,
    Players° in your huswifery,° and huswives° in your beds.
Desdemona: O, fie upon thee, slanderer! 115
Iago: Nay, it is true, or else I am a Turk.°
    You rise to play, and go to bed to work.
Emilia: You shall not write my praise.
Iago: No, let me not.
Desdemona: What wouldst write of me, if thou shouldst praise me?
Iago: O gentle lady, do not put me to 't, 120
    For I am nothing if not critical.°
Desdemona: Come on, essay.°—There's one gone to the harbor?
Iago: Ay, madam.
Desdemona: I am not merry, but I do beguile
    The thing I am° by seeming otherwise. 125
    Come, how wouldst thou praise me?
Iago: I am about it, but indeed my invention
    Comes from my pate as birdlime° does from frieze°—
    It plucks out brains and all. But my Muse labors,°
    And thus she is delivered: 130
    If she be fair and wise, fairness and wit,
    The one's for use, the other useth it.°
Desdemona: Well praised! How if she be black° and witty?
Iago: If she be black, and thereto have a wit,
    She'll find a white° that shall her blackness fit.° 135
Desdemona: Worse and worse.
Emilia: How if fair and foolish?
Iago: She never yet was foolish that was fair,
    For even her folly° helped her to an heir.°
Desdemona: These are old fond° paradoxes to make fools laugh i' th' alehouse.
    What miserable praise hast thou for her that's foul and foolish? 140

---

105 *she has no speech* i.e., she's not a chatterbox, as you allege   107 *still* always. *list* desire   110 *with thinking* i.e., in her thoughts only   111 *pictures out of doors* i.e., silent and well-behaved in public   112 *Bells* i.e., jangling, noisy, and brazen. *in your kitchens* i.e., in domestic affairs. (Ladies would not do the cooking.) 113 *Saints* martyrs   114 *Players* idlers, triflers, or deceivers. *huswifery* housekeeping. *huswives* hussies (i.e., women are "busy" in bed, or unduly thrifty in dispensing sexual favors)   116 *a Turk* an infidel, not to be believed   121 *critical* censorious   122 *essay* try   125 *The thing I am* i.e., my anxious self   128 *birdlime* sticky substance used to catch small birds. *frieze* coarse woolen cloth   129 *labors* (1) exerts herself (2) prepares to deliver a child (with a following pun on *delivered* in line 130)   132 *The one's . . . it* i.e., her cleverness will make use of her beauty   133 *black* dark-complexioned, brunette   135 *a white* a fair person (with word-play on "wight," a person). *fit* (with sexual suggestion of mating)   138 *folly* (with added meaning of "lechery, wantonness"). *to an heir* i.e., to bear a child   139 *fond* foolish

Iago: There's none so foul° and foolish thereunto,°
　　But does foul° pranks which fair and wise ones do.
Desdemona: O heavy ignorance! Thou praisest the worst best. But what praise
　　couldst thou bestow on a deserving woman indeed, one that, in the authority of
　　her merit, did justly put on the vouch° of very malice itself?　　　　　　　　145
Iago: She that was ever fair, and never proud,
　　Had tongue at will, and yet was never loud,
　　Never lacked gold and yet went never gay,°
　　Fled from her wish, and yet said, "Now I may,"°
　　She that being angered, her revenge being nigh,　　　　　　　　　　　　　150
　　Bade her wrong stay° and her displeasure fly,
　　She that in wisdom never was so frail
　　To change the cod's head for the salmon's tail,°
　　She that could think and ne'er disclose her mind,
　　See suitors following and not look behind,　　　　　　　　　　　　　　　155
　　She was a wight, if ever such wight were—
Desdemona: To do what?
Iago: To suckle fools° and chronicle small beer.°
Desdemona: O most lame and impotent conclusion! Do not learn of him, Emilia, though
　　he be thy husband. How say you, Cassio? Is he not a most profane° and liberal°　160
　　counselor?
Cassio: He speaks home,° madam. You may relish° him more in° the soldier than in
　　the scholar.

　　[*Cassio and Desdemona stand together, conversing intimately.*]

Iago [*aside*]: He takes her by the palm. Ay, well said,° whisper. With as little a
　　web as this will I ensnare as great a fly as Cassio. Ay, smile upon her, do; I will　165
　　gyve° thee in thine own courtship.° You say true;° 'tis so, indeed. If such tricks as
　　these strip you out of your lieutenantry, it had been better you had not kissed
　　your three fingers so oft, which now again you are most apt to play the sir° in.
　　Very good; well kissed! An excellent courtesy! 'Tis so, indeed. Yet again your
　　fingers to your lips? Would they were clyster pipes° for your sake! [*Trumpet*　170
　　within.] The Moor! I know his trumpet.
Cassio: 'Tis truly so.
Desdemona: Let's meet him and receive him.
Cassio: Lo, where he comes!

　　Enter Othello and attendants.

Othello: O my fair warrior!
Desdemona:　　　　　　　　My dear Othello!　　　　　　　　　　　　　　　175

---

141 *foul* ugly.　*thereunto* in addition　142 *foul* sluttish　145 *put . . . vouch* compel the approval　148 *gay* extravagantly clothed　149 *Fled . . . may* avoided temptation where the choice was hers　151 *Bade . . . stay* i.e., resolved to put up with her injury patiently　153 *To . . . tail* i.e., to exchange a lackluster husband for a sexy lover (?) (*Cod's head* is slang for "penis," and *tail,* for "pudendum.")　158 *suckle fools* breastfeed babies.　*chronicle small beer* i.e., keep petty household accounts, keep track of trivial matters　160 *profane* irreverent, ribald.　*liberal* licentious, free-spoken　162 *home* right to the target. (A term from fencing.)　*relish* appreciate　*in* in the character of　164 *well said* well done　166 *gyve* fetter, shackle.　*courtship* courtesy, show of courtly manners.　*You say true* i.e., that's right, go ahead　168 *the sir* i.e., the fine gentleman　170 *clyster pipes* tubes used for enemas and douches

Desdemona arrives in Cyprus and reunites with Othello as Cassio looks on (II, i, 175–208).

Othello: It gives me wonder great as my content
　　To see you here before me. O my soul's joy,
　　If after every tempest come such calms,
　　May the winds blow till they have wakened death,
　　And let the laboring bark climb hills of seas   180
　　Olympus-high, and duck again as low
　　As hell's from heaven! If it were now to die,
　　'Twere now to be most happy, for I fear
　　My soul hath her content so absolute
　　That not another comfort like to this   185
　　Succeeds in unknown fate.°
Desdemona:　　　　　　　　　　The heavens forbid
　　But that our loves and comforts should increase
　　Even as our days do grow!
Othello: Amen to that, sweet powers!
　　I cannot speak enough of this content.   190
　　It stops me here; it is too much of joy.
　　And this, and this, the greatest discords be

　　[They kiss.]°

　　That e'er our hearts shall make!

---

186 *Succeeds . . . fate* i.e., can follow in the unknown future   192 s.d. *They kiss* (The direction is from the Quarto.)

Iago [*aside*]: O, you are well tuned now!
But I'll set down° the pegs that make this music,   195
As honest as I am.°
Othello: Come, let us to the castle.
News, friends! Our wars are done, the Turks are drowned.
How does my old acquaintance of this isle?—
Honey, you shall be well desired° in Cyprus;   200
I have found great love amongst them. O my sweet,
I prattle out of fashion,° and I dote
In mine own comforts.—I prithee, good Iago,
Go to the bay and disembark my coffers.°
Bring thou the master° to the citadel;   205
He is a good one, and his worthiness
Does challenge° much respect.—Come, Desdemona.—
Once more, well met at Cyprus!

Exeunt Othello and Desdemona [and all but Iago and Roderigo].

Iago [*to an attendant*]: Do thou meet me presently at the harbor. [*To Roderigo.*]
Come hither. If thou be'st valiant—as, they say, base men° being in love have   210
then a nobility in their natures more than is native to them—list° me. The Lieutenant tonight watches on the court of guard.° First, I must tell thee this: Desdemona is directly in love with him.
Roderigo: With him? Why, 'tis not possible.
Iago: Lay thy finger thus,° and let thy soul be instructed. Mark me with what violence   215
she first loved the Moor, but° for bragging and telling her fantastical lies. To love
him still for prating? Let not thy discreet heart think it. Her eye must be fed; and
what delight shall she have to look on the devil? When the blood is made dull
with the act of sport,° there should be, again to inflame it and to give satiety a
fresh appetite, loveliness in favor,° sympathy° in years, manners, and beauties—   220
all which the Moor is defective in. Now, for want of these required conveniences,° her delicate tenderness will find itself abused,° begin to heave the
gorge,° disrelish and abhor the Moor. Very nature° will instruct her in it and compel her to some second choice. Now, sir, this granted—as it is a most pregnant°° and
unforced position—who stands so eminent in the degree of° this fortune as Cassio   225
does? A knave very voluble,° no further conscionable° than in putting on the
mere form of civil and humane° seeming for the better compassing of his salt°
and most hidden loose affection.° Why, none, why, none. A slipper° and subtle

---

195 *set down* loosen (and hence untune the instrument)   196 *As . . . I am* for all my supposed honesty
200 *desired* welcomed   202 *out of fashion* irrelevantly, incoherently (?)   204 *coffers* chests, baggage
205 *master* ship's captain   207 *challenge* lay claim to, deserve   210 *base men* even lowly born men
211 *list* listen to   212 *court of guard* guardhouse. (Cassio is in charge of the watch.)   215 *thus* i.e., on
your lips   216 *but* only   219 *the act of sport* sex   220 *favor* appearance. *sympathy* correspondence,
similarity   221–222 *required conveniences* things conducive to sexual compatibility   222 *abused*
cheated, revolted   222–223 *heave the gorge* experience nausea   223 *Very nature* her very instincts
224 *pregnant* evident, cogent   225 *in the degree of* as next in line for   226 *voluble* facile, glib.
conscionable conscientious, conscience-bound   227 *humane* polite, courteous. *salt* licentious   228
affection passion. *slipper* slippery

knave, a finder out of occasions, that has an eye can stamp° and counterfeit
advantages,° though true advantage never present itself; a devilish knave. Besides,   230
the knave is handsome, young, and hath all those requisites in him that folly°
and green° minds look after. A pestilent complete knave, and the woman hath
found him° already.

Roderigo: I cannot believe that in her. She's full of most blessed condition.°

Iago: Blessed fig's end!° The wine she drinks is made of grapes. If she had been   235
blessed, she would never have loved the Moor. Blessed pudding!° Didst thou not
see her paddle with the palm of his hand? Didst not mark that?

Roderigo: Yes, that I did; but that was but courtesy.

Iago: Lechery, by this hand. An index° and obscure° prologue to the history of lust
and foul thoughts. They met so near with their lips that their breaths embraced   240
together. Villainous thoughts, Roderigo! When these mutualities° so marshal
the way, hard at hand° comes the master and main exercise, th' incorporate°
conclusion. Pish! But, sir, be you ruled by me. I have brought you from Venice.
Watch you° tonight; for the command, I'll lay 't upon you.° Cassio knows you
not. I'll not be far from you. Do you find some occasion to anger Cassio, either by   245
speaking too loud, or tainting° his discipline, or from what other course you
please, which the time shall more favorably minister.°

Roderigo: Well.

Iago: Sir, he's rash and very sudden in choler,° and haply° may strike at you. Provoke
him that he may, for even out of that will I cause these of Cyprus to mutiny,°   250
whose qualification° shall come into no true taste° again but by the displanting
of Cassio. So shall you have a shorter journey to your desires by the means I shall
then have to prefer° them, and the impediment most profitably removed, without the which there were no expectation of our prosperity.

Roderigo: I will do this, if you can bring it to any opportunity.   255

Iago: I warrant° thee. Meet me by and by° at the citadel. I must fetch his necessaries
ashore. Farewell.

Roderigo: Adieu.   *Exit.*

Iago: That Cassio loves her, I do well believe 't;
    That she loves him, 'tis apt° and of great credit.°   260
    The Moor, howbeit that I endure him not,
    Is of a constant, loving, noble nature,
    And I dare think he'll prove to Desdemona
    A most dear husband. Now, I do love her too,
    Not out of absolute lust—though peradventure   265
    I stand accountant° for as great a sin—
    But partly led to diet° my revenge

---

229 *an eye can stamp* an eye that can coin, create   230 *advantages* favorable opportunities   231 *folly* wantonness   232 *green* immature   233 *found him* sized him up, perceived his intent   234 *condition* disposition
235 *fig's end* (See Act I, Scene iii, line 316 for the vulgar gesture of the fig.)   236 *pudding* sausage   239 *index*
table of contents.   *obscure* (i.e., the *lust and foul thoughts* in lines 239–240 are secret, hidden from view)
241 *mutualities* exchanges, intimacies   242 *hard at hand* closely following.   *incorporate* carnal   244 *Watch
you* stand watch.   *for the command . . . you* I'll arrange for you to be appointed, given orders   246 *tainting*
disparaging   247 *minister* provide   249 *choler* wrath.   *haply* perhaps   250 *mutiny* riot   251 *qualification*
appeasement.   *true taste* i.e., acceptable state   253 *prefer* advance   256 *warrant* assure.   *by and by* immediately   260 *apt* probable.   *credit* credibility   266 *accountant* accountable   267 *diet* feed

For that I do suspect the lusty Moor
Hath leaped into my seat, the thought whereof
Doth, like a poisonous mineral, gnaw my innards; 270
And nothing can or shall content my soul
Till I am evened with him, wife for wife,
Or failing so, yet that I put the Moor
At least into a jealousy so strong
That judgment cannot cure. Which thing to do, 275
If this poor trash of Venice, whom I trace°
For° his quick hunting, stand the putting on,°
I'll have our Michael Cassio on the hip,°
Abuse° him to the Moor in the rank garb°—
For I fear Cassio with my nightcap° too— 280
Make the Moor thank me, love me, and reward me
For making him egregiously an ass
And practicing upon° his peace and quiet
Even to madness. 'Tis here, but yet confused.
Knavery's plain face is never seen till used. *Exit.* 285

SCENE II [CYPRUS. A STREET.]

Enter Othello's Herald with a proclamation.

Herald: It is Othello's pleasure, our noble and valiant general, that, upon certain
tidings now arrived, importing the mere perdition° of the Turkish fleet, every
man put himself into triumph:° some to dance, some to make bonfires, each man
to what sport and revels his addiction° leads him. For, besides these beneficial
news, it is the celebration of his nuptial. So much was his pleasure should be 5
proclaimed. All offices° are open, and there is full liberty of feasting from this
present hour of five till the bell have told eleven. Heaven bless the isle of Cyprus
and our noble general Othello!

Exit.

SCENE III [CYPRUS. THE CITADEL.]

Enter Othello, Desdemona, Cassio, and attendants.

Othello: Good Michael, look you to the guard tonight.
Let's teach ourselves that honorable stop°
Not to outsport° discretion.
Cassio: Iago hath direction what to do,
But notwithstanding, with my personal eye 5
Will I look to 't.

---

276 *trace* i.e., train, or follow (?), or perhaps *trash*, a hunting term, meaning to put weights on a hunting
dog in order to slow him down 277 *For* to make more eager. *stand . . . on* respond properly when I incite
him to quarrel 278 *on the hip* at my mercy, where I can throw him. (A wrestling term.) 279 *Abuse* slander.
rank garb coarse manner, gross fashion 280 *with my nightcap* i.e., as a rival in my bed, as one who gives me
cuckold's horns 283 *practicing upon* plotting against 2 *mere perdition* complete destruction 3 *triumph*
public celebration 4 *addiction* inclination 6 *offices* rooms where food and drink are kept 2 *stop* restraint
3 *outsport* celebrate beyond the bounds of

Othello: Iago is most honest.
   Michael, good night. Tomorrow with your earliest°
   Let me have speech with you. [*To Desdemona.*]
                        Come, my dear love,
   The purchase made, the fruits are to ensue;
   That profit's yet to come 'tween me and you.°—   10
   Good night.

Exit [Othello, with Desdemona and attendants].

Enter Iago.

Cassio: Welcome, Iago. We must to the watch.
Iago: Not this hour,° Lieutenant; 'tis not yet ten o' the clock. Our general cast° us
   thus early for the love of his Desdemona; who° let us not therefore blame. He hath
   not yet made wanton the night with her, and she is sport for Jove.   15
Cassio: She's a most exquisite lady.
Iago: And, I'll warrant her, full of game.
Cassio: Indeed, she's a most fresh and delicate creature.
Iago: What an eye she has! Methinks it sounds a parley° to provocation.
Cassio: An inviting eye, and yet methinks right modest.   20
Iago: And when she speaks, is it not an alarum° to love?
Cassio: She is indeed perfection.
Iago: Well, happiness to their sheets! Come, Lieutenant, I have a stoup° of wine, and
   here without° are a brace° of Cyprus gallants that would fain have a measure° to
   the health of black Othello.   25
Cassio: Not tonight, good Iago. I have very poor and unhappy brains for drinking.
   I could well wish courtesy would invent some other custom of entertainment.
Iago: O, they are our friends. But one cup! I'll drink for you.°
Cassio: I have drunk but one cup tonight, and that was craftily qualified° too,
   and behold what innovation° it makes here.° I am unfortunate in the infirmity   30
   and dare not task my weakness with any more.
Iago: What, man? 'Tis a night of revels. The gallants desire it.
Cassio: Where are they?
Iago: Here at the door. I pray you, call them in.
Cassio: I'll do 't, but it dislikes me.°   *Exit.*   35
Iago: If I can fasten but one cup upon him,
   With that which he hath drunk tonight already,
   He'll be as full of quarrel and offense°
   As my young mistress' dog. Now, my sick fool Roderigo,
   Whom love hath turned almost the wrong side out,   40
   To Desdemona hath tonight caroused°

7 *with your earliest* at your earliest convenience   9–10 *The purchase . . . you* i.e., though married, we haven't
yet consummated our love   13 *Not this hour* not for an hour yet.   *cast* dismissed   14 *who* i.e., Othello   19
sounds a parley calls for a conference, issues an invitation   21 *alarum* signal calling men to arms (continuing
the military metaphor of *parley*, line 19)   23 *stoup* measure of liquor, two quarts   24 *without* outside.
brace pair.   *fain have a measure* gladly drink a toast   28 *for you* in your place. (Iago will do the steady drinking to keep the gallants company while Cassio has only one cup.)   29 *qualified* diluted   30 *innovation*
disturbance, insurrection.   *here* i.e., in my head   35 *it dislikes me* i.e., I'm reluctant   38 *offense* readiness to
take offense   41 *caroused* drunk off

Potations pottle-deep;° and he's to watch.°
Three lads of Cyprus—noble swelling° spirits,
That hold their honors in a wary distance,°
The very elements° of this warlike isle—   45
Have I tonight flustered with flowing cups,
And they watch° too. Now, 'mongst this flock of drunkards
Am I to put our Cassio in some action
That may offend the isle.—But here they come.

Enter Cassio, Montano, and gentlemen; [servants following with wine].

If consequence do but approve my dream,°   50
My boat sails freely both with wind and stream.°
Cassio: 'Fore God, they have given me a rouse° already.
Montano: Good faith, a little one; not past a pint, as I am a soldier.
Iago: Some wine, ho! [He *sings.*]
                "And let me the cannikin° clink, clink,   55
                And let me the cannikin clink.
                A soldier's a man,
                O, man's life's but a span;°
                Why, then, let a soldier drink."
        Some wine, boys!   60
Cassio: 'Fore God, an excellent song.
Iago: I learned it in England, where indeed they are most potent in potting.° Your
        Dane, your German, and your swag-bellied Hollander—drink, ho!—are nothing
        to your English.
Cassio: Is your Englishman so exquisite in his drinking?   65
Iago: Why, he drinks you,° with facility, your Dane° dead drunk; he sweats not° to
        overthrow your Almain;° he gives your Hollander a vomit ere the next pottle
        can be filled.
Cassio: To the health of our general!
Montano: I am for it, Lieutenant, and I'll do you justice.°   70
Iago: O sweet England! [He *sings.*]
                "King Stephen was and-a worthy peer,
                His breeches cost him but a crown;
                He held them sixpence all too dear,
                With that he called the tailor lown.°   75

                He was a wight of high renown,
                And thou art but of low degree.
                'Tis pride° that pulls the country down;
                Then take thy auld° cloak about thee."
        Some wine, ho!   80

42 *pottle-deep* to the bottom of the tankard.   *watch* stand watch   43 *swelling* proud   44 *hold . . . distance*
i.e., are extremely sensitive of their honor   45 *very elements* typical sort   47 *watch* are members of the
guard   50 *If . . . dream* if subsequent events will only substantiate my scheme   51 *stream* current   52
rouse full draft of liquor   55 *cannikin* small drinking vessel   58 *span* brief span of time. (Compare Psalm
39:6 as rendered in the 1928 Book of Common Prayer: "Thou hast made my days as it were a span long.")
62 *potting* drinking   66 *drinks you* drinks.   *your Dane* your typical Dane.   *sweats not* i.e., need not exert
himself   67 *Almain* German   70 *I'll . . . justice* i.e., I'll drink as much as you   75 *lown* lout, rascal   78
pride i.e., extravagance in dress   79 *auld* old

Cassio: 'Fore God, this is a more exquisite song than the other.

Iago: Will you hear 't again?

Cassio: No, for I hold him to be unworthy of his place that does those things. Well, God's above all; and there be souls must be saved, and there be souls must not be saved. 85

Iago: It's true, good Lieutenant.

Cassio: For mine own part—no offense to the General, nor any man of quality°—I hope to be saved.

Iago: And so do I too, Lieutenant.

Cassio: Ay, but, by your leave, not before me; the lieutenant is to be saved before the 90 ancient. Let's have no more of this; let's to our affairs.—God forgive us our sins!—Gentlemen, let's look to our business. Do not think, gentlemen, I am drunk. This is my ancient; this is my right hand, and this is my left. I am not drunk now. I can stand well enough, and speak well enough.

Gentlemen: Excellent well. 95

Cassio: Why, very well then; you must not think then that I am drunk. *Exit.*

Montano: To th' platform, masters. Come, let's set the watch.°

 [Exeunt Gentlemen.]

Iago: You see this fellow that is gone before.
  He's a soldier fit to stand by Caesar
  And give direction; and do but see his vice. 100
  'Tis to his virtue a just equinox,°
  The one as long as th' other. 'Tis pity of him.
  I fear the trust Othello puts him in,
  On some odd time of his infirmity,
  Will shake this island.

Montano: But is he often thus? 105

Iago: 'Tis evermore the prologue to his sleep.
  He'll watch the horologe a double set,°
  If drink rock not his cradle.

Montano: It were well
  The General were put in mind of it.
  Perhaps he sees it not, or his good nature 110
  Prizes the virtue that appears in Cassio
  And looks not on his evils. Is not this true?

 Enter Roderigo.

Iago [*aside to him*]: How now, Roderigo?
  I pray you, after the Lieutenant; go. *[Exit Roderigo.]*

Montano: And 'tis great pity that the noble Moor 115
  Should hazard such a place as his own second
  With° one of an engraffed° infirmity.

---

87 *quality* rank   97 *set the watch* mount the guard   101 *just equinox* exact counterpart. (*Equinox* is an equal length of days and nights.)   107 *watch . . . set* stay awake twice around the clock or *horologe*   116–117 *hazard . . . With* risk giving such an important position as his second in command to   117 *engraffed* engrafted, inveterate

Cassio, encouraged to drink by Iago, starts a fight with Montano (II, iii, 130).

It were an honest action to say so
To the Moor.
Iago: Not I, for this fair island.
I do love Cassio well and would do much
To cure him of this evil.   [*Cry within:* "Help! Help!"]   120
                    But, hark! What noise?

Enter Cassio, pursuing° Roderigo.

Cassio: Zounds, you rogue! You rascal!
Montano: What's the matter, Lieutenant?
Cassio: A knave teach me my duty?
I'll beat the knave into a twiggen° bottle.

121 s.d. *pursuing* (The Quarto text reads, "driving in.")   124 *twiggen* wicker-covered. (Cassio vows to assail Roderigo until his skin resembles wickerwork or until he has driven Roderigo through the holes in a wickerwork.)

Roderigo: Beat me?   125

Cassio: Dost thou prate, rogue?   [*He strikes Roderigo.*]

Montano: Nay, good Lieutenant. [*Restraining him.*] I pray you, sir, hold your hand.

Cassio: Let me go, sir, or I'll knock you o'er the mazard.°

Montano: Come, come, you're drunk.

Cassio: Drunk?   [*They fight.*]   130

Iago [*aside to Roderigo*]: Away, I say. Go out and cry a mutiny.°

   [*Exit Roderigo.*]

   Nay, good Lieutenant—God's will, gentlemen—
   Help, ho!—Lieutenant—sir—Montano—sir—
   Help, masters!°—Here's a goodly watch indeed!

   [*A bell rings.*]°

   Who's that which rings the bell?—Diablo,° ho!   135
   The town will rise.° God's will, Lieutenant, hold!
   You'll be ashamed forever.

   Enter Othello and attendants [*with weapons*].

Othello: What is the matter here?

Montano: Zounds, I bleed still.
   I am hurt to th' death. He dies!   [*He thrusts at Cassio.*]

Othello: Hold, for your lives!

Iago: Hold, ho! Lieutenant—sir—Montano—gentlemen—   140
   Have you forgot all sense of place and duty?
   Hold! The General speaks to you. Hold, for shame!

Othello: Why, how now, ho! From whence ariseth this?
   Are we turned Turks, and to ourselves do that
   Which heaven hath forbid the Ottomites?°   145
   For Christian shame, put by this barbarous brawl!
   He that stirs next to carve for° his own rage
   Holds his soul light;° he dies upon his motion.°
   Silence that dreadful bell. It frights the isle
   From her propriety.° What is the matter, masters?   150
   Honest Iago, that looks dead with grieving,
   Speak. Who began this? On thy love, I charge thee.

Iago: I do not know. Friends all but now, even now,
   In quarter° and in terms° like bride and groom
   Devesting them° for bed; and then, but now—   155
   As if some planet had unwitted men—

---

128 *mazard* i.e., head. (Literally, a drinking vessel.)   131 *mutiny* riot   134 *masters* sirs.   s.d. *A bell rings* (This direction is from the Quarto, as are *Exit Roderigo* at line 114, *They fight* at line 130, and *with weapons* at line 137.)   135 *Diablo* the devil   136 *rise* grow riotous   144–145 *to ourselves . . . Ottomites* inflict on ourselves the harm that heaven has prevented the Turks from doing (by destroying their fleet)   147 *carve for* i.e., indulge, satisfy with his sword   148 *Holds . . . light* i.e., places little value on his life.   *upon his motion* if he moves   150 *propriety* proper state or condition   154 *In quarter* in friendly conduct, within bounds.   *in terms* on good terms   155 *Devesting them* undressing themselves

Swords out, and tilting one at others' breasts
In opposition bloody. I cannot speak°
Any beginning to this peevish odds;°
And would in action glorious I had lost   160
Those legs that brought me to a part of it!

Othello: How comes it, Michael, you are thus forgot?°

Cassio: I pray you, pardon me. I cannot speak.

Othello: Worthy Montano, you were wont be° civil;
The gravity and stillness° of your youth   165
The world hath noted, and your name is great
In mouths of wisest censure.° What's the matter
That you unlace° your reputation thus
And spend your rich opinion° for the name
Of a night-brawler? Give me answer to it.   170

Montano: Worthy Othello, I am hurt to danger.
Your officer, Iago, can inform you—
While I spare speech, which something° now offends° me—
Of all that I do know; nor know I aught
By me that's said or done amiss this night,   175
Unless self-charity be sometimes a vice,
And to defend ourselves it be a sin
When violence assails us.

Othello: Now, by heaven,
My blood° begins my safer guides° to rule,
And passion, having my best judgment collied,°   180
Essays° to lead the way. Zounds, if I stir,
Or do but lift this arm, the best of you
Shall sink in my rebuke. Give me to know
How this foul rout° began, who set it on;
And he that is approved in° this offense,   185
Though he had twinned with me, both at a birth,
Shall lose me. What? In a town of° war
Yet wild, the people's hearts brim full of fear,
To manage° private and domestic quarrel?
In night, and on the court and guard of safety?°   190
'Tis monstrous. Iago, who began 't?

Montano [to Iago]: If partially affined,° or leagued in office,°
Thou dost deliver more or less than truth,
Thou art no soldier.

Iago: Touch me not so near.
I had rather have this tongue cut from my mouth   195

---

158 *speak* explain   159 *peevish odds* childish quarrel   162 *are thus forgot* have forgotten yourself thus
164 *wont be* accustomed to be   165 *stillness* sobriety   167 *censure* judgment   168 *unlace* undo, lay open
(as one might loose the strings of a purse containing reputation)   169 *opinion* reputation   173 *something*
somewhat.   *offends* pains   179 *blood* passion (of anger).   *guides* i.e., reason   180 *collied* darkened   181
Essays undertakes   184 *rout* riot   185 *approved in* found guilty of   187 *town of* town garrisoned for   189
manage undertake   190 *on . . . safety* at the main guardhouse or headquarters and on watch   192 *partially
affined* made partial by some personal relationship.   *leagued in office* in league as fellow officers

Than it should do offense to Michael Cassio;
Yet, I persuade myself, to speak the truth
Shall nothing wrong him. Thus it is, General.
Montano and myself being in speech,
There comes a fellow crying out for help,   200
And Cassio following him with determined sword
To execute° upon him. Sir, this gentleman

[*indicating Montano*]

Steps in to Cassio and entreats his pause.°
Myself the crying fellow did pursue,
Lest by his clamor—as it so fell out—   205
The town might fall in fright. He, swift of foot,
Outran my purpose, and I returned, the rather°
For that I heard the clink and fall of swords
And Cassio high in oath, which till tonight
I ne'er might say before. When I came back—   210
For this was brief—I found them close together
At blow and thrust, even as again they were
When you yourself did part them.
More of this matter cannot I report.
But men are men; the best sometimes forget.°   215
Though Cassio did some little wrong to him,
As men in rage strike those that wish them best,°
Yet surely Cassio, I believe, received
From him that fled some strange indignity,
Which patience could not pass.°   220
Othello: I know, Iago,
Thy honesty and love doth mince this matter,
Making it light to Cassio. Cassio, I love thee,
But nevermore be officer of mine.

Enter Desdemona, attended.

Look if my gentle love be not raised up.
I'll make thee an example.   225
Desdemona: What is the matter, dear?
Othello: All's well now, sweeting;
Come away to bed. [*To Montano.*] Sir, for your hurts,
Myself will be your surgeon.°—Lead him off.

[*Montano is led off.*]

Iago, look with care about the town
And silence those whom this vile brawl distracted.   230

---

202 *execute* give effect to (his anger)   203 *his pause* him to stop   207 *rather* sooner   215 *forget* forget
themselves   217 *those . . . best* i.e., even those who are well disposed   220 *pass* pass over, overlook   228 *be
your surgeon* i.e., make sure you receive medical attention

Iago advises Cassio to ask Desdemona to plead his cause with Othello (II, iii, 233–286).

Come, Desdemona. 'Tis the soldiers' life
To have their balmy slumbers waked with strife.

Exit [with all but Iago and Cassio].

Iago: What, are you hurt, Lieutenant?
Cassio: Ay, past all surgery.
Iago: Marry, God forbid!   235
Cassio: Reputation, reputation, reputation! O, I have lost my reputation! I have lost
the immortal part of myself, and what remains is bestial. My reputation, Iago, my
reputation!
Iago: As I am an honest man, I thought you had received some bodily wound; there
is more sense in that than in reputation. Reputation is an idle and most false   240
imposition,° oft got without merit and lost without deserving. You have lost no
reputation at all, unless you repute yourself such a loser. What, man, there are more
ways to recover° the General again. You are but now cast in his mood°—a
punishment more in policy° than in malice, even so as one would beat his offenseless
dog to affright an imperious lion.° Sue° to him again and he's yours.   245

240–241 *false imposition* thing artificially imposed and of no real value   243 *recover* regain favor with.
cast in his mood dismissed in a moment of anger   244 *in policy* done for expediency's sake and as a public
gesture   244–245 *would . . . lion* i.e., would make an example of a minor offender in order to deter more
important and dangerous offenders   245 *Sue* petition

Cassio: I will rather sue to be despised than to deceive so good a commander with so slight,° so drunken, and so indiscreet an officer. Drunk? And speak parrot?° And squabble? Swagger? Swear? And discourse fustian with one's own shadow? O thou invisible spirit of wine, if thou hast no name to be known by, let us call thee devil! 250

Iago: What was he that you followed with your sword? What had he done to you?

Cassio: I know not.

Iago: Is 't possible?

Cassio: I remember a mass of things, but nothing distinctly; a quarrel, but nothing wherefore.° O God, that men should put an enemy in their mouths to steal away 255 their brains! That we should, with joy, pleasance, revel, and applause° transform ourselves into beasts!

Iago: Why, but you are now well enough. How came you thus recovered?

Cassio: It hath pleased the devil drunkenness to give place to the devil wrath. One unperfectness shows me another, to make me frankly despise myself. 260

Iago: Come, you are too severe a moraler.° As the time, the place, and the condition of this country stands, I could heartily wish this had not befallen; but since it is as it is, mend it for your own good.

Cassio: I will ask him for my place again; he shall tell me I am a drunkard. Had I as many mouths as Hydra,° such an answer would stop them all. To be now a sensi- 265 ble man, by and by a fool, and presently a beast! O, strange! Every inordinate cup is unblessed, and the ingredient is a devil.

Iago: Come, come, good wine is a good familiar creature, if it be well used. Exclaim no more against it. And, good Lieutenant, I think you think I love you.

Cassio: I have well approved° it, sir. I drunk! 270

Iago: You or any man living may be drunk at a time,° man. I'll tell you what you shall do. Our general's wife is now the general—I may say so in this respect, for that° he hath devoted and given up himself to the contemplation, mark, and denote-ment° of her parts° and graces. Confess yourself freely to her; importune her help to put you in your place again. She is of so free,° so kind, so apt, so blessed a dis- 275 position, she holds it a vice in her goodness not to do more than she is requested. This broken joint between you and her husband entreat her to splinter;° and, my fortunes against any lay° worth naming, this crack of your love shall grow stronger than it was before.

Cassio: You advise me well. 280

Iago: I protest,° in the sincerity of love and honest kindness.

Cassio: I think it freely;° and betimes in the morning I will beseech the virtuous Desdemona to undertake for me. I am desperate of my fortunes if they check° me here.

Iago: You are in the right. Good night, Lieutenant. I must to the watch. 285

Cassio: Good night, honest Iago. *Exit Cassio.*

---

247 *slight* worthless. *speak parrot* talk nonsense, rant 255 *wherefore* why 256 *applause* desire for applause 261 *moraler* moralizer 265 *Hydra* the Lernaean Hydra, a monster with many heads and the ability to grow two heads when one was cut off, slain by Hercules as the second of his twelve labors 270 *approved* proved 271 *at a time* at one time or another 272 *in . . . that* in view of this fact, that 273–274 *mark, and denotement* (Both words mean "observation.") 274 *parts* qualities 275 *free* generous 277 *splinter* bind with splints. 278 *lay* stake, wager 281 *protest* insist, declare 282 *freely* unreservedly 283 *check* repulse

Iago: And what's he then that says I play the villain,
When this advice is free° I give, and honest,
Probal° to thinking, and indeed the course
To win the Moor again? For 'tis most easy   290
Th' inclining° Desdemona to subdue°
In any honest suit; she's framed as fruitful°
As the free elements.° And then for her
To win the Moor—were 't to renounce his baptism,
All seals and symbols of redeemèd sin—   295
His soul is so enfettered to her love
That she may make, unmake, do what she list,
Even as her appetite° shall play the god
With his weak function.° How am I then a villain,
To counsel Cassio to this parallel° course   300
Directly to his good? Divinity of hell!°
When devils will the blackest sins put on,°
They do suggest° at first with heavenly shows,
As I do now. For whiles this honest fool
Plies Desdemona to repair his fortune,   305
And she for him pleads strongly to the Moor,
I'll pour this pestilence into his ear,
That she repeals him° for her body's lust;
And by how much she strives to do him good,
She shall undo her credit with the Moor.   310
So will I turn her virtue into pitch,°
And out of her own goodness make the net
That shall enmesh them all.

    Enter Roderigo.

                How now, Roderigo?
Roderigo: I do follow here in the chase, not like a hound that hunts, but one that
fills up the cry.° My money is almost spent; I have been tonight exceedingly   315
well cudgeled; and I think the issue will be I shall have so much° experience for
my pains, and so, with no money at all and a little more wit, return again
to Venice.
Iago: How poor are they that have not patience!
What wound did ever heal but by degrees?   320
Thou know'st we work by wit, and not by witchcraft,
And wit depends on dilatory time.
Does 't not go well? Cassio hath beaten thee,

---

288 *free* (1) free from guile (2) freely given   289 *Probal* probable, reasonable   291 *inclining* favorably
disposed.   *subdue* persuade   292 *framed as fruitful* created as generous   293 *free elements* i.e., earth, air,
fire, and water, unrestrained and spontaneous   298 *her appetite* her desire, or, perhaps, his desire for her
299 *function* exercise of faculties (weakened by his fondness for her)   300 *parallel* corresponding to these
facts and to his best interests   301 *Divinity of hell* inverted theology of hell (which seduces the soul to its
damnation)   302 *put on* further, instigate   303 *suggest* tempt   308 *repeals him* attempts to get him restored
311 *pitch* i.e., (1) foul blackness (2) a snaring substance   315 *fills up the cry* merely takes part as one of the
pack   316 *so much* just so much and no more

And thou, by that small hurt, hast cashiered° Cassio.
Though other things grow fair against the sun,   325
Yet fruits that blossom first will first be ripe.°
Content thyself awhile. By the Mass, 'tis morning!
Pleasure and action make the hours seem short.
Retire thee; go where thou art billeted.
Away, I say! Thou shalt know more hereafter.   330
Nay, get thee gone.   *Exit Roderigo.*
                    Two things are to be done.
My wife must move° for Cassio to her mistress;
I'll set her on;
Myself the while to draw the Moor apart
And bring him jump° when he may Cassio find   335
Soliciting his wife. Ay, that's the way.
Dull not device° by coldness° and delay.   *Exit.*

ACT III

SCENE I [BEFORE THE CHAMBER OF OTHELLO AND DESDEMONA.]

Enter Cassio [and] Musicians.

Cassio: Masters, play here—I will content your pains°—
  Something that's brief, and bid "Good morrow, General."   [*They play.*]

[*Enter*] *Clown.*

Clown: Why, masters, have your instruments been in Naples, that they speak i' the
  nose° thus?
A Musician: How, sir, how?   5
Clown: Are these, I pray you, wind instruments?
A Musician: Ay, marry, are they, sir.
Clown: O, thereby hangs a tail.
A Musician: Whereby hangs a tale, sir?
Clown: Marry, sir, by many a wind instrument° that I know. But, masters, here's   10
  money for you. [*He gives money.*] And the General so likes your music that he
  desires you, for love's sake,° to make no more noise with it.
A Musician: Well, sir, we will not.
Clown: If you have any music that may not° be heard, to 't again; but, as they say, to
  hear music the General does not greatly care.   15
A Musician: We have none such, sir.

---

324 *cashiered* dismissed from service   325–326 *Though . . . ripe* i.e., plans that are well prepared and set
expeditiously in motion will soonest ripen into success   332 *move* plead   335 *jump* precisely   337 *device*
plot.   *coldness* lack of zeal   1 *content your pains* reward your efforts   3–4 *speak i' the nose* (1) sound nasal
(2) sound like one whose nose has been attacked by syphilis. (Naples was popularly supposed to have a
high incidence of venereal disease.)   10 *wind instrument* (With a joke on flatulence. The *tail*, line 8, that
hangs nearby the *wind instrument* suggests the penis.)   12 *for love's sake* (1) out of friendship and affection
(2) for the sake of lovemaking in Othello's marriage   14 *may not* cannot

Clown: Then put up your pipes in your bag, for I'll away.° Go, vanish into air, away!

Exeunt Musicians.

Cassio: Dost thou hear, mine honest friend?

Clown: No, I hear not your honest friend; I hear you.   20

Cassio: Prithee, keep up° thy quillets.° There's a poor piece of gold for thee. [*He gives money.*] If the gentle-woman that attends the General's wife be stirring, tell her there's one Cassio entreats her a little favor of speech.° Wilt thou do this?

Clown: She is stirring, sir. If she will stir° hither, I shall seem° to notify unto her.

Cassio: Do, good my friend.   *Exit Clown.*

    Enter Iago.

                         In happy time,° Iago.   25

Iago: You have not been abed, then?

Cassio: Why, no. The day had broke
    Before we parted. I have made bold, Iago,
    To send in to your wife. My suit to her
    Is that she will to virtuous Desdemona   30
    Procure me some access.

Iago: I'll send her to you presently;
    And I'll devise a means to draw the Moor
    Out of the way, that your converse and business
    May be more free.   35

Cassio: I humbly thank you for 't.   *Exit* [*Iago*].
                I never knew
    A Florentine° more kind and honest.

    Enter Emilia.

Emilia: Good morrow, good Lieutenant. I am sorry
    For your displeasure;° but all will sure be well.
    The General and his wife are talking of it,   40
    And she speaks for you stoutly.° The Moor replies
    That he you hurt is of great fame° in Cyprus
    And great affinity,° and that in wholesome wisdom
    He might not but refuse you; but he protests° he loves you
    And needs no other suitor but his likings   45
    To take the safest occasion by the front°
    To bring you in again.

Cassio: Yet I beseech you,
    If you think fit, or that it may be done,
    Give me advantage of some brief discourse
    With Desdemona alone.

---

17 *I'll away* (Possibly a misprint, or a snatch of song?)   21 *keep up* do not bring out, do not use.   *quillets* quibbles, puns   23 *a little . . . speech* the favor of a brief talk   24 *stir* bestir herself (with a play on *stirring,* "rousing herself from rest").   *seem* deem it good, think fit   25 *In happy time* i.e., well met   37 *Florentine* i.e., even a fellow Florentine. (Iago is a Venetian; Cassio is a Florentine.)   39 *displeasure* fall from favor   41 *stoutly* spiritedly   42 *fame* reputation, importance   43 *affinity* kindred, family connection   44 *protests* insists   46 *occasion . . . front* opportunity by the forelock

Emilia: Pray you, come in.   50
　　I will bestow you where you shall have time
　　To speak your bosom° freely.
Cassio: I am much bound to you.

　　　　　　　　　　　　　　　　　　　　　　[*Exeunt.*]

SCENE II [THE CITADEL.]

　　Enter Othello, Iago, and Gentlemen.

Othello [*giving letters*]: These letters give, Iago, to the pilot,
　　And by him do my duties° to the Senate.
　　That done, I will be walking on the works;°
　　Repair° there to me.
Iago: Well, my good lord, I'll do 't.
Othello: This fortification, gentlemen, shall we see 't?   5
Gentlemen: We'll wait upon° your lordship.   *Exeunt.*

SCENE III [THE GARDEN OF THE CITADEL.]

　　Enter Desdemona, Cassio, and Emilia.

Desdemona: Be thou assured, good Cassio, I will do
　　All my abilities in thy behalf.
Emilia: Good madam, do. I warrant it grieves my husband
　　As if the cause were his.
Desdemona: O, that's an honest fellow. Do not doubt, Cassio,   5
　　But I will have my lord and you again
　　As friendly as you were.
Cassio: Bounteous madam,
　　Whatever shall become of Michael Cassio,
　　He's never anything but your true servant.
Desdemona: I know 't. I thank you. You do love my lord;   10
　　You have known him long, and be you well assured
　　He shall in strangeness° stand no farther off
　　Than in a politic° distance.
Cassio: Ay, but, lady,
　　That policy may either last so long,
　　Or feed upon such nice and waterish diet,°   15
　　Or breed itself so out of circumstance,°
　　That, I being absent and my place supplied,°
　　My general will forget my love and service.
Desdemona: Do not doubt° that. Before Emilia here
　　I give thee warrant° of thy place. Assure thee,   20

---

52 *bosom* inmost thoughts   2 *do my duties* convey my respects   3 *works* breastworks, fortifications
4 *Repair* return, come   6 *wait upon* attend   12 *strangeness* aloofness   13 *politic* required by wise policy
15 *Or . . . diet* or sustain itself at length upon such trivial and meager technicalities   16 *breed . . . circum-*
stance continually renew itself so out of chance events, or yield so few chances for my being pardoned
17 *supplied* filled by another person   19 *doubt* fear   20 *warrant* guarantee

If I do vow a friendship I'll perform it
To the last article. My lord shall never rest.
I'll watch him tame° and talk him out of patience;°
His bed shall seem a school, his board° a shrift;°
I'll intermingle everything he does   25
With Cassio's suit. Therefore be merry, Cassio,
For thy solicitor° shall rather die
Than give thy cause away.°

Enter Othello and Iago [at a distance].

Emilia: Madam, here comes my lord.
Cassio: Madam, I'll take my leave.   30
Desdemona: Why, stay, and hear me speak.
Cassio: Madam, not now. I am very ill at ease,
     Unfit for mine own purposes.
Desdemona: Well, do your discretion.°   *Exit Cassio.*
Iago: Ha? I like not that.   35
Othello: What dost thou say?
Iago: Nothing, my lord; or if—I know not what.
Othello: Was not that Cassio parted from my wife?
Iago: Cassio, my lord? No, sure, I cannot think it,
     That he would steal away so guiltylike,   40
     Seeing you coming.
Othello: I do believe 'twas he.
Desdemona: How now, my lord?
     I have been talking with a suitor here,
     A man that languishes in your displeasure.   45
Othello: Who is 't you mean?
Desdemona: Why, your lieutenant, Cassio. Good my lord,
     If I have any grace or power to move you,
     His present reconciliation take;°
     For if he be not one that truly loves you,   50
     That errs in ignorance and not in cunning,°
     I have no judgment in an honest face.
     I prithee, call him back.
Othello: Went he hence now?
Desdemona: Yes, faith, so humbled   55
     That he hath left part of his grief with me
     To suffer with him. Good love, call him back.
Othello: Not now, sweet Desdemon. Some other time.
Desdemona: But shall 't be shortly?
Othello: The sooner, sweet, for you.   60
Desdemona: Shall 't be tonight at supper?

---

23 *watch him tame* tame him by keeping him from sleeping. (A term from falconry.)   *out of patience* past
his endurance   24 *board* dining table.   *shrift* confessional   27 *solicitor* advocate   28 *away* up   34 *do
your discretion* act according to your own discretion   49 *His . . . take* let him be reconciled to you right
away   51 *in cunning* wittingly

Othello: No, not tonight.
Desdemona: Tomorrow dinner,° then?
Othello: I shall not dine at home.
    I meet the captains at the citadel.   65
Desdemona: Why, then, tomorrow night, or Tuesday morn,
    On Tuesday noon, or night, on Wednesday morn.
    I prithee, name the time, but let it not
    Exceed three days. In faith, he's penitent;
    And yet his trespass, in our common reason°—   70
    Save that, they say, the wars must make example
    Out of her best°—is not almost° a fault
    T' incur a private check.° When shall he come?
    Tell me, Othello. I wonder in my soul
    What you would ask me that I should deny,   75
    Or stand so mammering on.° What? Michael Cassio,
    That came a-wooing with you, and so many a time,
    When I have spoke of you dispraisingly,
    Hath ta'en your part—to have so much to do
    To bring him in!° By 'r Lady, I could do much—   80
Othello: Prithee, no more. Let him come when he will;
    I will deny thee nothing.
Desdemona: Why, this is not a boon.
    'Tis as I should entreat you wear your gloves,
    Or feed on nourishing dishes, or keep you warm,   85
    Or sue to you to do a peculiar° profit
    To your own person. Nay, when I have a suit
    Wherein I mean to touch° your love indeed,
    It shall be full of poise° and difficult weight,
    And fearful to be granted.   90
Othello: I will deny thee nothing.
    Whereon,° I do beseech thee, grant me this,
    To leave me but a little to myself.
Desdemona: Shall I deny you? No. Farewell, my lord.
Othello: Farewell, my Desdemona. I'll come to thee straight.°   95
Desdemona: Emilia, come.—Be as your fancies° teach you;
    Whate'er you be, I am obedient.   *Exit [with Emilia]*
Othello: Excellent wretch! Perdition catch my soul
    But I do love thee! And when I love thee not,
    Chaos is come again.°   100
Iago: My noble lord—

---

63 *dinner* (The noontime meal.)   70 *common reason* everyday judgments   71–72 *Save . . . best* were it not that, as the saying goes, military discipline requires making an example of the very best men. (He refers to *wars* as a singular concept.)   72 *not almost* scarcely   73 *private check* even a private reprimand   76 *mammering on* wavering about   80 *bring him in* restore him to favor   86 *peculiar* particular, personal   88 *touch* test   89 *poise* weight, heaviness; or equipoise, delicate balance involving hard choice   92 *Whereon* in return for which   95 *straight* straightway   96 *fancies* inclinations   98 *wretch* (A term of affectionate endearment.)   99–100 *And . . . again* i.e., my love for you will last forever, until the end of time when chaos will return. (But with an unconscious, ironic suggestion that, if anything should induce Othello to cease loving Desdemona, the result would be chaos.)

Othello: What dost thou say, Iago?
Iago: Did Michael Cassio, when you wooed my lady,
    Know of your love?
Othello: He did, from first to last. Why dost thou ask?   105
Iago: But for a satisfaction of my thought;
    No further harm.
Othello: Why of thy thought, Iago?
Iago: I did not think he had been acquainted with her.
Othello: O, yes, and went between us very oft.
Iago: Indeed?   110
Othello: Indeed? Ay, indeed. Discern'st thou aught in that?
    Is he not honest?
Iago: Honest, my lord?
Othello: Honest. Ay, honest.
Iago: My lord, for aught I know.   115
Othello: What dost thou think?
Iago: Think, my lord?
Othello: "Think, my lord?" By heaven, thou echo'st me,
    As if there were some monster in thy thought
    Too hideous to be shown. Thou dost mean something.   120
    I heard thee say even now, thou lik'st not that,
    When Cassio left my wife. What didst not like?
    And when I told thee he was of my counsel°
    In my whole course of wooing, thou criedst "Indeed?"
    And didst contract and purse° thy brow together   125
    As if thou then hadst shut up in thy brain
    Some horrible conceit.° If thou dost love me,
    Show me thy thought.
Iago: My lord, you know I love you.
Othello: I think thou dost;   130
    And, for° I know thou'rt full of love and honesty,
    And weigh'st thy words before thou giv'st them breath,
    Therefore these stops° of thine fright me the more;
    For such things in a false disloyal knave
    Are tricks of custom,° but in a man that's just   135
    They're close dilations,° working from the heart
    That passion cannot rule.°
Iago: For° Michael Cassio,
    I dare be sworn I think that he is honest.
Othello: I think so too.
Iago: Men should be what they seem;
    Or those that be not, would they might seem none!°   140
Othello: Certain, men should be what they seem.

---

123 *of my counsel* in my confidence   125 *purse* knit   127 *conceit* fancy   131 *for* because   133 *stops* pauses
135 *of custom* customary   136 *close dilations* secret or involuntary expressions or delays   137 *That passion
cannot rule* i.e., that are too passionately strong to be restrained (referring to the workings), or that cannot
rule its own passions (referring to the heart).   137 *For* as for   140 *none* i.e., not to be men, or not seem to
be honest

Iago: Why, then, I think Cassio's an honest man.

Othello: Nay, yet there's more in this.
    I prithee, speak to me as to thy thinkings,
    As thou dost ruminate, and give thy worst of thoughts   145
    The worst of words.

Iago: Good my lord, pardon me.
    Though I am bound to every act of duty,
    I am not bound to that° all slaves are free to.°
    Utter my thoughts? Why, say they are vile and false,
    As where's the palace whereinto foul things   150
    Sometimes intrude not? Who has that breast so pure
    But some uncleanly apprehensions
    Keep leets and law days,° and in sessions sit
    With° meditations lawful?°

Othello: Thou dost conspire against thy friend,° Iago,   155
    If thou but think'st him wronged and mak'st his ear
    A stranger to thy thoughts.

Iago: I do beseech you,
    Though I perchance am vicious° in my guess—
    As I confess it is my nature's plague
    To spy into abuses, and oft my jealousy°   160
    Shapes faults that are not—that your wisdom then,°
    From one° that so imperfectly conceits,°
    Would take no notice, nor build yourself a trouble
    Out of his scattering° and unsure observance.
    It were not for your quiet nor your good,   165
    Nor for my manhood, honesty, and wisdom,
    To let you know my thoughts.

Othello: What dost thou mean?

Iago: Good name in man and woman, dear my lord,
    Is the immediate° jewel of their souls.
    Who steals my purse steals trash; 'tis something, nothing;   170
    'Twas mine, 'tis his, and has been slave to thousands;
    But he that filches from me my good name
    Robs me of that which not enriches him
    And makes me poor indeed.

Othello: By heaven, I'll know thy thoughts.   175

Iago: You cannot, if° my heart were in your hand,
    Nor shall not, whilst 'tis in my custody.

Othello: Ha?

Iago: O, beware, my lord, of jealousy.
    It is the green-eyed monster which doth mock
    The meat it feeds on.° That cuckold lives in bliss   180

---

148 *that* that which. *free to* free with respect to   153 *Keep leets and law days* i.e., hold court, set up their authority in one's heart. (*Leets* are a kind of manor court; *law days* are the days courts sit in session, or those sessions.)   154 *With* along with. *lawful* innocent   155 *thy friend* i.e., Othello   158 *vicious* wrong 160 *jealousy* suspicious nature   161 *then* on that account   162 *one* i.e., myself, Iago. *conceits* judges, conjectures   164 *scattering* random   169 *immediate* essential, most precious   176 *if* even if   179–180 *doth mock . . . on* mocks and torments the heart of its victim, the man who suffers jealousy

Iago plants doubts about Desdemona in Othello's mind (III, iii, 101–295).

Who, certain of his fate, loves not his wronger;°
But O, what damnèd minutes tells° he o'er
Who dotes, yet doubts, suspects, yet fondly loves!
Othello: O misery!
Iago: Poor and content is rich, and rich enough,°   185
But riches fineless° is as poor as winter
To him that ever fears he shall be poor.
Good God, the souls of all my tribe defend
From jealousy!
Othello: Why, why is this?   190
Think'st thou I'd make a life of jealousy,
To follow still the changes of the moon
With fresh suspicions?° No! To be once in doubt
Is once° to be resolved.° Exchange me for a goat

---

181 *his wronger* i.e., his faithless wife. (The unsuspecting cuckold is spared the misery of loving his wife
only to discover she is cheating on him.)   182 *tells* counts   185 *Poor . . . enough* to be content with what
little one has is the greatest wealth of all. (Proverbial.)   186 *fineless* boundless   192–193 *To follow . . .
suspicions* to be constantly imagining new causes for suspicion, changing incessantly like the moon
194 *once* once and for all.   *resolved* free of doubt, having settled the matter

When I shall turn the business of my soul   195
To such exsufflicate and blown° surmises
Matching thy inference.° 'Tis not to make me jealous
To say my wife is fair, feeds well, loves company,
Is free of speech, sings, plays, and dances well;
Where virtue is, these are more virtuous.   200
Nor from mine own weak merits will I draw
The smallest fear or doubt of her revolt,°
For she had eyes, and chose me. No, Iago,
I'll see before I doubt; when I doubt, prove;
And on the proof, there is no more but this—   205
Away at once with love or jealousy.

Iago: I am glad of this, for now I shall have reason
To show the love and duty that I bear you
With franker spirit. Therefore, as I am bound,
Receive it from me. I speak not yet of proof.   210
Look to your wife; observe her well with Cassio.
Wear your eyes thus, not° jealous nor secure.°
I would not have your free and noble nature,
Out of self-bounty,° be abused.° Look to 't.
I know our country disposition well;   215
In Venice they do let God see the pranks
They dare not show their husbands; their best conscience
Is not to leave 't undone, but keep 't unknown.

Othello: Dost thou say so?

Iago: She did deceive her father, marrying you;   220
And when she seemed to shake and fear your looks,
She loved them most.

Othello: And so she did.

Iago: Why, go to,° then!
She that, so young, could give out such a seeming,°
To seel° her father's eyes up close as oak,°
He thought 'twas witchcraft! But I am much to blame.   225
I humbly do beseech you of your pardon
For too much loving you.

Othello: I am bound° to thee forever.

Iago: I see this hath a little dashed your spirits.

Othello: Not a jot, not a jot.

Iago: I' faith, I fear it has.   230
I hope you will consider what is spoke
Comes from my love. But I do see you're moved.
I am to pray you not to strain my speech

---

196 *exsufflicate and blown* inflated and blown up, rumored about, or, spat out and flyblown, hence, loathsome, disgusting   197 *inference* description or allegation   202 *doubt . . . revolt* fear of her unfaithfulness   212 *not* neither.   *secure* free from uncertainty   214 *self-bounty* inherent or natural goodness and generosity.   *abused* deceived   222 *go to* (An expression of impatience.)   223 *seeming* false appearance   224 *seel* blind. (A term from falconry.)   *oak* (A close-grained wood.)   228 *bound* indebted (but perhaps with ironic sense of "tied")

To grosser issues° nor to larger reach°
Than to suspicion. 235

Othello: I will not.

Iago: Should you do so, my lord,
My speech should fall into such vile success°
Which my thoughts aimed not. Cassio's my worthy friend.
My lord, I see you're moved.

Othello: No, not much moved. 240
I do not think but Desdemona's honest.°

Iago: Long live she so! And long live you to think so!

Othello: And yet, how nature erring from itself—

Iago: Ay, there's the point! As—to be bold with you—
Not to affect° many proposèd matches 245
Of her own clime, complexion, and degree,°
Whereto we see in all things nature tends—
Foh! One may smell in such a will° most rank,
Foul disproportion,° thoughts unnatural.
But pardon me. I do not in position° 250
Distinctly speak of her, though I may fear
Her will, recoiling° to her better° judgment,
May fall to match you with her country forms°
And happily repent.°

Othello: Farewell, farewell!
If more thou dost perceive, let me know more. 255
Set on thy wife to observe. Leave me, Iago.

Iago [*going*]: My lord, I take my leave.

Othello: Why did I marry? This honest creature doubtless
Sees and knows more, much more, than he unfolds.

Iago [*returning*]: My Lord, I would I might entreat your honor 260
To scan° this thing no farther. Leave it to time.
Although 'tis fit that Cassio have his place—
For, sure, he fills it up with great ability—
Yet, if you please to hold him off awhile,
You shall by that perceive him and his means.° 265
Note if your lady strain his entertainment°
With any strong or vehement importunity;
Much will be seen in that. In the meantime,
Let me be thought too busy° in my fears—
As worthy cause I have to fear I am— 270
And hold her free,° I do beseech your honor.

Othello: Fear not my government.°

Iago: I once more take my leave. *Exit.*

234 *issues* significances. *reach* meaning, scope   238 *success* effect, result   241 *honest* chaste   245 *affect* prefer, desire   246 *clime . . . degree* country, color, and social position   248 *will* sensuality, appetite   249 *disproportion* abnormality   250 *position* argument, proposition   252 *recoiling* reverting. *better* i.e., more natural and reconsidered   253 *fall . . . forms* undertake to compare you with Venetian norms of hand-someness   254 *happily repent* happily repent her marriage   261 *scan* scrutinize   265 *his means* the method he uses (to regain his post)   266 *strain his entertainment* urge his reinstatement   269 *busy* interfering   271 *hold her free* regard her as innocent   272 *government* self-control, conduct

Othello: This fellow's of exceeding honesty,
  And knows all qualities,° with a learnèd spirit, 275
  Of human dealings. If I do prove her haggard,°
  Though that her jesses° were my dear heartstrings,
  I'd whistle her off and let her down the wind°
  To prey at fortune.° Haply, for° I am black
  And have not those soft parts of conversation° 280
  That chamberers° have, or for I am declined
  Into the vale of years—yet that's not much—
  She's gone. I am abused,° and my relief
  Must be to loathe her. O curse of marriage,
  That we can call these delicate creatures ours 285
  And not their appetites! I had rather be a toad
  And live upon the vapor of a dungeon
  Than keep a corner in the thing I love
  For others' uses. Yet, 'tis the plague of great ones;
  Prerogatived° are they less than the base.° 290
  'Tis destiny unshunnable, like death.
  Even then this forkèd° plague is fated to us
  When we do quicken.° Look where she comes.

Enter Desdemona and Emilia.

  If she be false, O, then heaven mocks itself!
  I'll not believe 't.
Desdemona: How now, my dear Othello? 295
  Your dinner, and the generous° islanders
  By you invited, do attend° your presence.
Othello: I am to blame.
Desdemona: Why do you speak so faintly?
  Are you not well?
Othello: I have a pain upon my forehead here. 300
Desdemona: Faith, that's with watching.° 'Twill away again.

[She offers her handkerchief.]

  Let me but bind it hard, within this hour
  It will be well.
Othello: Your napkin° is too little.
  Let it alone.° Come, I'll go in with you.

[He puts the handkerchief from him, and it drops.]

---

275 *qualities* natures, types   276 *haggard* wild (like a wild female hawk)   277 *jesses* straps fastened around the legs of a trained hawk   278 *I'd . . . wind* i.e., I'd let her go forever. (To release a hawk downwind was to invite it not to return.)   279 *prey at fortune* tend for herself in the wild.   *Haply, for* perhaps because   280 *soft . . . conversation* pleasing graces of social behavior   281 *chamberers* gallants   283 *abused* deceived   290 *Prerogatived* privileged (to have honest wives).   *the base* ordinary citizens. (Socially prominent men are especially prone to the unavoidable destiny of being cuckolded and to the public shame that goes with it.)   292 *forkèd* (An allusion to the horns of the cuckold.)   293 *quicken* receive life. (Quicken may also mean to swarm with maggots as the body festers, as in IV, ii, 69, in which case lines 292–293 suggest that *even then*, in death, we are cuckolded by *forkèd* worms.)   296 *generous* noble   297 *attend* await   301 *watching* too little sleep   303 *napkin* handkerchief   304 *Let it alone* i.e., never mind

Desdemona: I am very sorry that you are not well.   305

    Exit [with Othello].

Emilia [picking up the handkerchief]: I am glad I have found this napkin.
    This was her first remembrance from the Moor.
    My wayward° husband hath a hundred times
    Wooed me to steal it, but she so loves the token—
    For he conjured her she should ever keep it—   310
    That she reserves it evermore about her
    To kiss and talk to. I'll have the work ta'en out,°
    And give 't Iago. What he will do with it
    Heaven knows, not I;
    I nothing but to please his fantasy.°   315

    Enter Iago.

Iago: How now? What do you here alone?
Emilia: Do not you chide. I have a thing for you.
Iago: You have a thing for me? It is a common thing°—
Emilia: Ha?
Iago: To have a foolish wife.   320
Emilia: O, is that all? What will you give me now
    For that same handkerchief?
Iago: What handkerchief?
Emilia: What handkerchief?
    Why, that the Moor first gave to Desdemona;   325
    That which so often you did bid me steal.
Iago: Hast stolen it from her?
Emilia: No, faith. She let it drop by negligence,
    And to th' advantage° I, being here, took 't up.
    Look, here 'tis.
Iago: A good wench! Give it me.   330
Emilia: What will you do with 't, that you have been so earnest
    To have me filch it?
Iago [snatching it]:   Why, what is that to you?
Emilia: If it be not for some purpose of import,
    Give 't me again. Poor lady, she'll run mad
    When she shall lack° it.
Iago: Be not acknown on 't.°   335
    I have use for it. Go, leave me.   *Exit Emilia.*
    I will in Cassio's lodging lose° this napkin
    And let him find it. Trifles light as air
    Are to the jealous confirmations strong
    As proofs of Holy Writ. This may do something.   340

---

308 *wayward* capricious   312 *work ta'en out* design of the embroidery copied   315 *fantasy* whim   318 *common thing* (With bawdy suggestion; *common* suggests coarseness and availability to all comers, and *thing* is a slang term for the pudendum.)   329 *to th' advantage* taking the opportunity   335 *lack* miss. *Be . . . on 't* do not confess knowledge of it   337 *lose* (The Folio spelling, *loose,* is a normal spelling for "lose," but it may also contain the idea of "let go," "release.")

Iago: "I have use for it. Go, leave me. / I will in Cassio's lodging lose this napkin" (III, iii, 336–337).

The Moor already changes with my poison.
Dangerous conceits° are in their natures poisons,
Which at the first are scarce found to distaste,°
But with a little act° upon the blood
Burn like the mines of sulfur.

Enter Othello.

                    I did say so.   345
Look where he comes! Not poppy nor mandragora°
Nor all the drowsy syrups of the world

---

342 *conceits* fancies, ideas   343 *distaste* be distasteful   344 *act* action, working   346 *mandragora* an opiate made of the mandrake root

Shall ever medicine thee to that sweet sleep
Which thou owedst° yesterday.

Othello: Ha, ha, false to me?

Iago: Why, how now, General? No more of that.   350

Othello: Avaunt! Begone! Thou hast set me on the rack.
I swear 'tis better to be much abused
Than but to know 't a little.

Iago: How now, my lord?

Othello: What sense had I of her stolen hours of lust?
I saw 't not, thought it not, it harmed not me.   355
I slept the next night well, fed well, was free° and merry;
I found not Cassio's kisses on her lips.
He that is robbed, not wanting° what is stolen,
Let him not know 't and he's not robbed at all.

Iago: I am sorry to hear this.   360

Othello: I had been happy if the general camp,
Pioners° and all, had tasted her sweet body,
So° I had nothing known. O, now, forever
Farewell the tranquil mind! Farewell content!
Farewell the plumèd troops and the big° wars   365
That makes ambition virtue! O, farewell!
Farewell the neighing steed and the shrill trump,
The spirit-stirring drum, th' ear-piercing fife,
The royal banner, and all quality,°
Pride,° pomp, and circumstance° of glorious war!   370
And O, you mortal engines,° whose rude throats
Th' immortal Jove's dread clamors° counterfeit,
Farewell! Othello's occupation's gone.

Iago: Is 't possible, my lord?

Othello: Villain, be sure thou prove my love a whore!   375
Be sure of it. Give me the ocular proof,
Or, by the worth of mine eternal soul,
Thou hadst been better have been born a dog
Than answer my waked wrath!

Iago: Is 't come to this?

Othello: Make me to see 't, or at the least so prove it   380
That the probation° bear no hinge nor loop
To hang a doubt on, or woe upon thy life!

Iago: My noble lord—

Othello: If thou dost slander her and torture me,
Never pray more; abandon all remorse;°   385
On horror's head horrors accumulate;°
Do deeds to make heaven weep, all earth amazed;°

---

349 *thou owedst* you did own   356 *free* carefree   358 *wanting* missing   362 *Pioners* diggers of mines, the lowest grade of soldiers   363 *So* provided   365 *big* stately   369 *quality* character, essential nature   370 *Pride* rich display. *circumstance* pageantry   371 *mortal engines* i.e., cannon. (*Mortal* means "deadly.")   372 *Jove's dread clamors* i.e., thunder   381 *probation* proof   385 *remorse* pity, penitent hope for salvation   386 *horrors accumulate* add still more horrors   387 *amazed* confounded with horror

For nothing canst thou to damnation add
Greater than that.

Iago: O grace! O heaven forgive me!
Are you a man? Have you a soul or sense?   390
God b' wi' you; take mine office. O wretched fool,°
That lov'st to make thine honesty a vice!°
O monstrous world! Take note, take note, O world,
To be direct and honest is not safe.
I thank you for this profit,° and from hence°   395
I'll love no friend, sith° love breeds such offense.°

Othello: Nay, stay. Thou shouldst be° honest.

Iago: I should be wise, for honesty's a fool
And loses that° it works for.

Othello: By the world,
I think my wife be honest and think she is not;   400
I think that thou art just and think thou art not.
I'll have some proof. My name, that was as fresh
As Dian's° visage, is now begrimed and black
As mine own face. If there be cords, or knives,
Poison, or fire, or suffocating streams,   405
I'll not endure it. Would I were satisfied!

Iago: I see, sir, you are eaten up with passion.
I do repent me that I put it to you.
You would be satisfied?

Othello: Would? Nay, and I will.

Iago: And may; but how? How satisfied, my lord?   410
Would you, the supervisor,° grossly gape on?
Behold her topped?

Othello: Death and damnation! O!

Iago: It were a tedious difficulty, I think,
To bring them to that prospect. Damn them then,°
If ever mortal eyes do see them bolster°   415
More° than their own.° What then? How then?
What shall I say? Where's satisfaction?
It is impossible you should see this,
Were they as prime° as goats, as hot as monkeys,
As salt° as wolves in pride,° and fools as gross   420
As ignorance made drunk. But yet I say,
If imputation and strong circumstances°
Which lead directly to the door of truth
Will give you satisfaction, you might have 't.

---

391 *O wretched fool* (Iago addresses himself as a fool for having carried honesty too far.) 392 *vice* failing,
something overdone 395 *profit* profitable instruction. *hence* henceforth 396 *sith* since. *offense* i.e.,
harm to the one who offers help and friendship 397 *Thou shouldst be* it appears that you are. (But Iago
replies in the sense of "ought to be.") 399 *that* what 403 *Dian* Diana, goddess of the moon and of chastity
411 *supervisor* onlooker 414 *Damn them then* i.e., they would have to be really incorrigible 415 *bolster* go
to bed together, share a bolster 416 *More* other. *own* own eyes 419 *prime* lustful 420 *salt* wanton,
sensual. *pride* heat 422 *imputation . . . circumstances* strong circumstantial evidence

Othello: Give me a living reason she's disloyal.   425
Iago: I do not like the office.
    But sith° I am entered in this cause so far,
    Pricked° to 't by foolish honesty and love,
    I will go on. I lay with Cassio lately,
    And being troubled with a raging tooth   430
    I could not sleep. There are a kind of men
    So loose of soul that in their sleeps will mutter
    Their affairs. One of this kind is Cassio.
    In sleep I heard him say, "Sweet Desdemona,
    Let us be wary, let us hide our loves!"   435
    And then, sir, would he grip and wring my hand,
    Cry "O sweet creature!" and then kiss me hard,
    As if he plucked up kisses by the roots
    That grew upon my lips; then laid his leg
    Over my thigh, and sighed, and kissed, and then   440
    Cried, "Cursèd fate that gave thee to the Moor!"
Othello: O monstrous! Monstrous!
Iago: Nay, this was but his dream.
Othello: But this denoted a foregone conclusion.°
    'Tis a shrewd doubt,° though it be but a dream.
Iago: And this may help to thicken other proofs   445
    That do demonstrate thinly.
Othello: I'll tear her all to pieces.
Iago: Nay, but be wise. Yet we see nothing done;
    She may be honest yet. Tell me but this:
    Have you not sometimes seen a handkerchief
    Spotted with strawberries° in your wife's hand?   450
Othello: I gave her such a one. 'Twas my first gift.
Iago: I know not that; but such a handkerchief—
    I am sure it was your wife's—did I today
    See Cassio wipe his beard with.
Othello: If it be that—
Iago: If it be that, or any that was hers,   455
    It speaks against her with the other proofs.
Othello: O, that the slave° had forty thousand lives!
    One is too poor, too weak for my revenge.
    Now do I see 'tis true. Look here, Iago,
    All my fond° love thus do I blow to heaven.   460
    'Tis gone.
    Arise, black vengeance, from the hollow hell!
    Yield up, O love, thy crown and hearted° throne
    To tyrannous hate! Swell, bosom, with thy freight,°
    For 'tis of aspics'° tongues!   465

---

427 *sith* since   428 *Pricked* spurred   443 *foregone conclusion* concluded experience or action   444 *shrewd doubt* suspicious circumstance   450 *Spotted with strawberries* embroidered with a strawberry pattern   457 *the slave* i.e., Cassio   460 *fond* foolish (but also suggesting "affectionate")   463 *hearted* fixed in the heart   464 *freight* burden   465 *aspics'* venomous serpents'

Iago: Yet be content.°
Othello: O, blood, blood, blood!
Iago: Patience, I say. Your mind perhaps may change.
Othello: Never, Iago. Like to the Pontic Sea,°
    Whose icy current and compulsive course   470
    Ne'er feels retiring ebb, but keeps due on
    To the Propontic° and the Hellespont,°
    Even so my bloody thoughts with violent pace
    Shall ne'er look back, ne'er ebb to humble love,
    Till that a capable° and wide revenge   475
    Swallow them up. Now, by yond marble° heaven,
    [*Kneeling*] In the due reverence of a sacred vow
    I here engage my words.
Iago: Do not rise yet.
    [*He kneels.*°] Witness, you ever-burning lights above,
    You elements that clip° us round about,   480
    Witness that here Iago doth give up
    The execution° of his wit,° hands, heart,
    To wronged Othello's service. Let him command,
    And to obey shall be in me remorse,°
    What bloody business ever.°   [*They rise.*]
Othello: I greet thy love,   485
    Not with vain thanks, but with acceptance bounteous,
    And will upon the instant put thee to 't.°
    Within these three days let me hear thee say
    That Cassio's not alive.
Iago: My friend is dead;
    'Tis done at your request. But let her live.   490
Othello: Damn her, lewd minx!° O, damn her, damn her!
    Come, go with me apart. I will withdraw
    To furnish me with some swift means of death
    For the fair devil. Now art thou my lieutenant.
Iago: I am your own forever.   *Exeunt.* 495

SCENE IV [BEFORE THE CITADEL.]

    Enter Desdemona, Emilia, and Clown.

Desdemona: Do you know, sirrah,° where Lieutenant Cassio lies?°
Clown: I dare not say he lies anywhere.
Desdemona: Why, man?
Clown: He's a soldier, and for me to say a soldier lies, 'tis stabbing.

---

466 *content* calm 469 *Pontic Sea* Black Sea 472 *Propontic* Sea of Marmara, between the Black Sea and the Aegean. *Hellespont* Dardanelles, straits where the Sea of Marmara joins with the Aegean 475 *capable* ample, comprehensive 476 *marble* i.e., gleaming like marble and unrelenting 479 s.d. *He kneels* (In the Quarto text, Iago kneels here after Othello has knelt at line 477.) 480 *clip* encompass 482 *execution* exercise, action. *wit* mind 484 *remorse* pity (for Othello's wrongs) 485 *ever* soever 487 *to 't* to the proof 491 *minx* wanton 1 *sirrah* (A form of address to an inferior.) *lies* lodges. (But the Clown makes the obvious pun.)

Desdemona: Go to. Where lodges he?   5

Clown: To tell you where he lodges is to tell you where I lie.

Desdemona: Can anything be made of this?

Clown: I know not where he lodges, and for me to devise a lodging and say he lies here, or he lies there, were to lie in mine own throat.°

Desdemona: Can you inquire him out, and be edified by report?   10

Clown: I will catechize the world for him; that is, make questions, and by them answer.

Desdemona: Seek him, bid him come hither. Tell him I have moved° my lord on his behalf and hope all will be well.

Clown: To do this is within the compass of man's wit, and therefore I will attempt   15
    the doing it.   *Exit Clown.*

Desdemona: Where should I lose that handkerchief, Emilia?

Emilia: I know not, madam.

Desdemona: Believe me, I had rather have lost my purse
    Full of crusadoes;° and but my noble Moor   20
    Is true of mind and made of no such baseness
    As jealous creatures are, it were enough
    To put him to ill thinking.

Emilia: Is he not jealous?

Desdemona: Who, he? I think the sun where he was born
    Drew all such humors° from him.

Emilia: Look where he comes.   25

    Enter Othello.

Desdemona: I will not leave him now till Cassio
    Be called to him.—How is 't with you, my lord?

Othello: Well, my good lady. [*Aside.*] O, hardness to dissemble!—
    How do you, Desdemona?

Desdemona: Well, my good lord.

Othello: Give me your hand. [*She gives her hand.*] This hand is moist, my lady.   30

Desdemona: It yet hath felt no age nor known no sorrow.

Othello: This argues° fruitfulness° and liberal° heart.
    Hot, hot, and moist. This hand of yours requires
    A sequester° from liberty, fasting and prayer,
    Much castigation,° exercise devout;°   35
    For here's a young and sweating devil here
    That commonly rebels. 'Tis a good hand,
    A frank° one.

Desdemona: You may indeed say so,
    For 'twas that hand that gave away my heart.

Othello: A liberal hand. The hearts of old gave hands,°   40

---

9 *lie . . . throat* (1) lie egregiously and deliberately (2) use the windpipe to speak a lie   13 *moved* petitioned
20 *crusadoes* Portuguese gold coins   25 *humors* (Refers to the four bodily fluids thought to determine temperament.)   32 *argues* gives evidence of.   *fruitfulness* generosity, amorousness, and fecundity.   *liberal* generous and sexually free   34 *sequester* separation, sequestration   35 *castigation* corrective discipline.   *exercise
devout* i.e., prayer, religious meditation, etc.   38 *frank* generous, open (with sexual suggestion)   40 *The
hearts . . . hands* i.e., in former times, people would give their hearts when they gave their hands to something

"She offers a handkerchief" (III, iv, 47 s.d.).

But our new heraldry is hands, not hearts.°
Desdemona: I cannot speak of this. Come now, your promise.
Othello: What promise, chuck?°
Desdemona: I have sent to bid Cassio come speak with you.
Othello: I have a salt and sorry rheum° offends me;   45
    Lend me thy handkerchief.
Desdemona: Here, my lord.   [*She offers a handkerchief.*]
Othello: That which I gave you.
Desdemona: I have it not about me.
Othello: Not?
Desdemona: No, faith, my lord.   50
Othello: That's a fault. That handkerchief
    Did an Egyptian to my mother give.
    She was a charmer,° and could almost read
    The thoughts of people. She told her, while she kept it
    'Twould make her amiable° and subdue my father   55
    Entirely to her love, but if she lost it
    Or made a gift of it, my father's eye
    Should hold her loathèd and his spirits should hunt

41 *But . . . hearts* i.e., in our decadent times, the joining of hands is no longer a badge to signify the giving
of hearts   43 *chuck* (A term of endearment.)   45 *salt . . . rheum* distressful head cold or watering of the
eyes   53 *charmer* sorceress   55 *amiable* desirable

After new fancies.° She, dying, gave it me,
And bid me, when my fate would have me wived,   60
To give it her.° I did so; and take heed on 't;
Make it a darling like your precious eye.
To lose 't or give 't away were such perdition°
As nothing else could match.
Desdemona: Is 't possible?
Othello: 'Tis true. There's magic in the web° of it.   65
A sibyl, that had numbered in the world
The sun to course two hundred compasses,°
In her prophetic fury° sewed the work;°
The worms were hallowed that did breed the silk,
And it was dyed in mummy° which the skillful   70
Conserved of° maidens' hearts.
Desdemona: I' faith! Is 't true?
Othello: Most veritable. Therefore look to 't well.
Desdemona: Then would to God that I had never seen 't!
Othello: Ha? Wherefore?
Desdemona: Why do you speak so startingly and rash?°   75
Othello: Is 't lost? Is 't gone? Speak, is 't out o' the way?°
Desdemona: Heaven bless us!
Othello: Say you?
Desdemona: It is not lost; but what an if° it were?
Othello: How?   80
Desdemona: I say it is not lost.
Othello: Fetch 't, let me see 't.
Desdemona: Why, so I can, sir, but I will not now.
    This is a trick to put me from my suit.
    Pray you, let Cassio be received again.
Othello: Fetch me the handkerchief! My mind misgives.   85
Desdemona: Come, come,
    You'll never meet a more sufficient° man.
Othello: The handkerchief!
Desdemona: I pray, talk° me of Cassio.
Othello: The handkerchief!
Desdemona: A man that all his time°
    Hath founded his good fortunes on your love,   90
    Shared dangers with you—
Othello: The handkerchief!
Desdemona: I' faith, you are to blame.
Othello: Zounds!   *Exit Othello.*
Emilia: Is not this man jealous?   95

59 *fancies* loves   61 *her* i.e., to my wife   63 *perdition* loss   65 *web* fabric, weaving   67 *compasses* annual circlings. (The *sibyl*, or prophetess, was two hundred years old.)   68 *prophetic fury* frenzy of prophetic inspiration.   *work* embroidered pattern   70 *mummy* medicinal or magical preparation drained from mummified bodies   71 *Conserved of* prepared or preserved out of   75 *startingly and rash* disjointedly and impetuously, excitedly   76 *out o' the way* lost, misplaced   79 *an if* if   87 *sufficient* able, complete   88 *talk* talk to   89 *all his time* throughout his career

Desdemona: I ne'er saw this before.
  Sure, there's some wonder in this handkerchief.
  I am most unhappy in the loss of it.
Emilia: 'Tis not a year or two shows us a man.°
  They are all but stomachs, and we all but° food;   100
  They eat us hungerly,° and when they are full
  They belch us.

Enter Iago and Cassio.

            Look you, Cassio and my husband.
Iago [to Cassio]: There is no other way; 'tis she must do 't.
  And, lo, the happiness!° Go and importune her.
Desdemona: How now, good Cassio? What's the news with you?   105
Cassio: Madam, my former suit. I do beseech you
  That by your virtuous° means I may again
  Exist and be a member of his love
  Whom I, with all the office° of my heart,
  Entirely honor. I would not be delayed.   110
  If my offense be of such mortal° kind
  That nor my service past, nor° present sorrows,
  Nor purposed merit in futurity
  Can ransom me into his love again,
  But to know so must be my benefit;°   115
  So shall I clothe me in a forced content,
  And shut myself up in° some other course,
  To fortune's alms.°
Desdemona: Alas, thrice-gentle Cassio,
  My advocation° is not now in tune.
  My lord is not my lord; nor should I know him,   120
  Were he in favor° as in humor° altered.
  So help me every spirit sanctified
  As I have spoken for you all my best
  And stood within the blank° of his displeasure
  For my free speech! You must awhile be patient.   125
  What I can do I will, and more I will
  Than for myself I dare. Let that suffice you.
Iago: Is my lord angry?
Emilia: He went hence but now,
  And certainly in strange unquietness.
Iago: Can he be angry? I have seen the cannon   130
  When it hath blown his ranks into the air,

---

99 'Tis . . . man i.e., you can't really know a man even in a year or two of experience (?), or, real men come along seldom (?) 100 but nothing but 101 hungerly hungrily 104 the happiness in happy time, fortunately met 107 virtuous efficacious 109 office loyal service 111 mortal fatal 112 nor . . . nor neither . . . nor 115 But . . . benefit merely to know that my case is hopeless will have to content me (and will be better than uncertainty) 117 shut . . . in confine myself to 118 To fortune's alms throwing myself on the mercy of fortune 119 advocation advocacy 121 favor appearance. humor mood 124 within the blank within point-blank range. (The blank is the center of the target.)

And like the devil from his very arm
Puffed his own brother—and is he angry?
Something of moment° then. I will go meet him.
There's matter in 't indeed, if he be angry.   135

Desdemona: I prithee, do so.   *Exit* [*Iago*].
                         Something, sure, of state,°
Either from Venice, or some unhatched practice°
Made demonstrable here in Cyprus to him,
Hath puddled° his clear spirit; and in such cases
Men's natures wrangle with inferior things,   140
Though great ones are their object. 'Tis even so;
For let our finger ache, and it indues°
Our other, healthful members even to a sense
Of pain. Nay, we must think men are not gods,
Nor of them look for such observancy°   145
As fits the bridal.° Beshrew me° much, Emilia,
I was, unhandsome° warrior as I am,
Arraigning his unkindness with° my soul;
But now I find I had suborned the witness,°
And he's indicted falsely.

Emilia: Pray heaven it be   150
State matters, as you think, and no conception
Nor no jealous toy° concerning you.

Desdemona: Alas the day! I never gave him cause.

Emilia: But jealous souls will not be answered so;
They are not ever jealous for the cause,
But jealous for° they're jealous. It is a monster   155
Begot upon itself,° born on itself.

Desdemona: Heaven keep that monster from Othello's mind!

Emilia: Lady, amen.

Desdemona: I will go seek him. Cassio, walk hereabout.   160
If I do find him fit, I'll move your suit
And seek to effect it to my uttermost.

Cassio: I humbly thank your ladyship.

    Exit [*Desdemona with Emilia*].

    Enter Bianca.

Bianca: Save° you, friend Cassio!

Cassio: What make° you from home?
How is 't with you, my most fair Bianca?   165
I' faith, sweet love, I was coming to your house.

---

134 *of moment* of immediate importance, momentous   136 *of state* concerning state affairs   137 *unhatched practice* as yet unexecuted or undiscovered plot   139 *puddled* muddied   142 *indues* brings to the same condition   145 *observancy* attentiveness   146 *bridal* wedding (when a bridegroom is newly attentive to his bride).   *Beshrew me* (A mild oath.)   147 *unhandsome* insufficient, unskillful   148 *with* before the bar of   149 *suborned the witness* induced the witness to give false testimony   152 *toy* fancy   156 *for* because   157 *Begot upon itself* generated solely from itself   164 *Save* God save.   *make* do

Cassio explains to Bianca that he does not know how the handkerchief appeared in his room (III, iv, 175–186).

Bianca: And I was going to your lodging, Cassio.
    What, keep a week away? Seven days and nights?
    Eightscore-eight° hours? And lovers' absent hours
    More tedious than the dial° eightscore times?   170
    O weary reckoning!
Cassio: Pardon me, Bianca.
    I have this while with leaden thoughts been pressed;
    But I shall, in a more continuate° time,
    Strike off this score° of absence. Sweet Bianca,

---

169 *Eightscore-eight* one hundred sixty-eight, the number of hours in a week   170 *the dial* a complete
revolution of the clock   173 *continuate* uninterrupted   174 *Strike . . . score* settle this account

[giving her Desdemona's handkerchief]

Take me this work out.°

Bianca: O Cassio, whence came this?   175
This is some token from a newer friend.°
To the felt absence now I feel a cause.
Is 't come to this? Well, well.

Cassio: Go to, woman!
Throw your vile guesses in the devil's teeth,
From whence you have them. You are jealous now   180
That this is from some mistress, some remembrance.
No, by my faith, Bianca.

Bianca: Why, whose is it?

Cassio: I know not, neither. I found it in my chamber.
I like the work well. Ere it be demanded°—
As like° enough it will—I would have it copied.   185
Take it and do 't, and leave me for this time.

Bianca: Leave you? Wherefore?

Cassio: I do attend here on the General,
And think it no addition,° nor my wish,
To have him see me womaned.   190

Bianca: Why, I pray you?

Cassio: Not that I love you not.

Bianca: But that you do not love me.
I pray you, bring° me on the way a little,
And say if I shall see you soon at night.   195

Cassio: 'Tis but a little way that I can bring you,
For I attend here; but I'll see you soon.

Bianca: 'Tis very good. I must be circumstanced.°

Exeunt omnes.

ACT IV

SCENE I [BEFORE THE CITADEL.]

Enter Othello and Iago.

Iago: Will you think so?

Othello: Think so, Iago?

Iago: What,
To kiss in private?

Othello: An unauthorized kiss!

Iago: Or to be naked with her friend in bed
An hour or more, not meaning any harm?

Othello: Naked in bed, Iago, and not mean harm?   5
It is hypocrisy against the devil.

---

175 *Take . . . out* copy this embroidery for me   176 *friend* mistress   184 *demanded* inquired for   185 *like* likely   189 *addition* i.e., addition to my reputation   194 *bring* accompany   198 *be circumstanced* be governed by circumstance, yield to your conditions

They that mean virtuously and yet do so,
The devil their virtue tempts, and they tempt heaven.
Iago: If they do nothing, 'tis a venial° slip.
But if I give my wife a handkerchief—   10
Othello: What then?
Iago: Why then, 'tis hers, my lord, and being hers,
She may, I think, bestow 't on any man.
Othello: She is protectress of her honor too.
May she give that?   15
Iago: Her honor is an essence that's not seen;
They have it° very oft that have it not.
But, for the handkerchief—
Othello: By heaven, I would most gladly have forgot it.
Thou saidst—O, it comes o'er my memory   20
As doth the raven o'er the infectious house,°
Boding to all—he had my handkerchief.
Iago: Ay, what of that?
Othello: That's not so good now.
Iago: What
If I had said I had seen him do you wrong?
Or heard him say—as knaves be such abroad,°   25
Who having, by their own importunate suit,
Or voluntary dotage° of some mistress,
Convincèd or supplied° them, cannot choose
But they must blab—
Othello: Hath he said anything?
Iago: He hath, my lord; but, be you well assured,   30
No more than he'll unswear.
Othello: What hath he said?
Iago: Faith, that he did—I know not what he did.
Othello: What? What?
Iago: Lie—
Othello: With her?
Iago: With her, on her; what you will.
Othello: Lie with her? Lie on her? We say "lie on her" when they belie° her. Lie   35
with her? Zounds, that's fulsome.°—Handkerchief—confessions—handker-
chief!—To confess and be hanged for his labor—first to be hanged and then
to confess.°—I tremble at it. Nature would not invest herself in such shad-
owing passion without some instruction.° It is not words° that shakes me

---

9 *venial* pardonable   17 *They have it* i.e., they enjoy a reputation for it   21 *raven . . . house* (Allusion to the belief that the raven hovered over a house of sickness or infection, such as one visited by the plague.) 25 *abroad* around about   27 *voluntary dotage* willing infatuation   28 *Convincèd or supplied* seduced or sexually gratified   35 *belie* slander   36 *fulsome* foul   37–38 *first . . . to confess* (Othello reverses the proverbial *confess and be hanged*; Cassio is to be given no time to confess before he dies.)   38–39 *Nature . . . instruction* i.e., without some foundation in fact, nature would not have dressed herself in such an overwhelming passion that comes over me now and fills my mind with images, or in such a lifelike fantasy as Cassio had in his dream of lying with Desdemona   39 *words* mere words

Iago lies to Cassio that Othello has "fall'n into an epilepsy" (IV, i, 48).

thus. Pish! Noses, ears, and lips.—Is 't possible?—Confess—handkerchief!— 40
O devil!

Falls in a trance.

Iago: Work on,
My medicine, work! Thus credulous fools are caught,
And many worthy and chaste dames even thus,
All guiltless, meet reproach.—What, ho! My lord! 45
My lord, I say! Othello!

Enter Cassio.

How now, Cassio?

Cassio: What's the matter?

Iago: My lord is fall'n into an epilepsy.
This is his second fit. He had one yesterday.

Cassio: Rub him about the temples.

Iago: No, forbear.   50
The lethargy° must have his° quiet course.
If not, he foams at mouth, and by and by
Breaks out to savage madness. Look, he stirs.
Do you withdraw yourself a little while.
He will recover straight. When he is gone,   55
I would on great occasion° speak with you.

[*Exit Cassio.*]

How is it, General? Have you not hurt your head?

Othello: Dost thou mock me?°

Iago: I mock you not, by heaven.
Would you would bear your fortune like a man!

Othello: A hornèd man's a monster and a beast.   60

Iago: There's many a beast then in a populous city,
And many a civil° monster.

Othello: Did he confess it?

Iago: Good sir, be a man.
Think every bearded fellow that's but yoked°   65
May draw with you.° There's millions now alive
That nightly lie in those unproper° beds
Which they dare swear peculiar.° Your case is better.°
O, 'tis the spite of hell, the fiend's arch-mock,
To lip° a wanton in a secure° couch   70
And to suppose her chaste! No, let me know,
And knowing what I am,° I know what she shall be.°

Othello: O, thou art wise. 'Tis certain.

Iago: Stand you awhile apart;
Confine yourself but in a patient list.°   75
Whilst you were here o'erwhelmèd with your grief—
A passion most unsuiting such a man—
Cassio came hither. I shifted him away,°
And laid good 'scuse upon your ecstasy,°
Bade him anon return and here speak with me,   80
The which he promised. Do but encave° yourself
And mark the fleers,° the gibes, and notable° scorns
That dwell in every region of his face;
For I will make him tell the tale anew,
Where, how, how oft, how long ago, and when   85
He hath and is again to cope° your wife.

---

51 *lethargy* coma. *his* its   56 *on great occasion* on a matter of great importance   58 *mock me* (Othello takes Iago's question about hurting his head to be a mocking reference to the cuckold's horns.)   62 *civil* i.e., dwelling in a city   65 *yoked* (1) married (2) put into the yoke of infamy and cuckoldry   66 *draw with you* pull as you do, like oxen who are yoked, i.e., share your fate as cuckold   67 *unproper* not exclusively their own   68 *peculiar* private, their own.   *better* i.e., because you know the truth   70 *lip* kiss.   *secure* free from suspicion   72 *what I am* i.e., a cuckold.   *she shall be* will happen to her   75 *in . . . list* within the bounds of patience   78 *shifted him away* used a dodge to get rid of him   79 *ecstasy* trance   81 *encave* conceal   82 *fleers* sneers.   *notable* obvious   86 *cope* encounter with, have sex with

I say, but mark his gesture. Marry, patience!
Or I shall say you're all-in-all in spleen,°
And nothing of a man.

Othello: Dost thou hear, Iago?
I will be found most cunning in my patience;   90
But—dost thou hear?—most bloody.

Iago: That's not amiss;
But yet keep time° in all. Will you withdraw?

[*Othello stands apart.*]

Now will I question Cassio of Bianca,
A huswife° that by selling her desires
Buys herself bread and clothes. It is a creature   95
That dotes on Cassio—as 'tis the strumpet's plague
To beguile many and be beguiled by one.
He, when he hears of her, cannot restrain°
From the excess of laughter. Here he comes.

Enter Cassio.

As he shall smile, Othello shall go mad;   100
And his unbookish° jealousy must conster°
Poor Cassio's smiles, gestures, and light behaviors
Quite in the wrong.—How do you now, Lieutenant?

Cassio: The worser that you give me the addition°
Whose want° even kills me.   105

Iago: Ply Desdemona well and you are sure on 't.
[*Speaking lower.*] Now, if this suit lay in Bianca's power,
How quickly should you speed!

Cassio [*laughing*]: Alas, poor caitiff!°

Othello [*aside*]: Look how he laughs already!   110

Iago: I never knew a woman love man so.

Cassio: Alas, poor rogue! I think, i' faith, she loves me.

Othello: Now he denies it faintly, and laughs it out.

Iago: Do you hear, Cassio?

Othello: Now he importunes him
To tell it o'er. Go to!° Well said,° well said.   115

Iago: She gives it out that you shall marry her.
Do you intend it?

Cassio: Ha, ha, ha!

Othello: Do you triumph, Roman?° Do you triumph?

Cassio: I marry her? What? A customer?° Prithee, bear some charity to my wit;° do   120
not think it so unwholesome. Ha, ha, ha!

---

88 *all-in-all in spleen* utterly governed by passionate impulses   92 *keep time* keep yourself steady (as in music)
94 *huswife* hussy   98 *restrain* refrain   101 *unbookish* uninstructed.   *conster* construe   104 *addition* title
105 *Whose want* the lack of which   109 *caitiff* wretch   115 *Go to* (An expression of remonstrance.)
Well said well done   119 *Roman* (The Romans were noted for their *triumphs* or triumphal processions.)
120 *customer* i.e., prostitute.   *bear . . . wit* be more charitable to my judgment

Othello: So, so, so, so! They laugh that win.°

Iago: Faith, the cry° goes that you shall marry her.

Cassio: Prithee, say true.

Iago: I am a very villain else.°   125

Othello: Have you scored me?° Well.

Cassio: This is the monkey's own giving out. She is persuaded I will marry her out of her own love and flattery,° not out of my promise.

Othello: Iago beckons me.° Now he begins the story.

Cassio: She was here even now; she haunts me in every place. I was the other day   130
talking on the seabank° with certain Venetians, and thither comes the bauble,° and, by this hand,° she falls me thus about my neck—

[*He embraces Iago.*]

Othello: Crying, "O dear Cassio!" as it were; his gesture imports it.

Cassio: So hangs and lolls and weeps upon me, so shakes and pulls me. Ha, ha, ha!

Othello: Now he tells how she plucked him to my chamber. O, I see that nose of   135
yours, but not that dog I shall throw it to.°

Cassio: Well, I must leave her company.

Iago: Before me,° look where she comes.

Enter Bianca [with Othello's handkerchief].

Cassio: 'Tis such another fitchew!° Marry, a perfumed one.—What do you mean by
this haunting of me?   140

Bianca: Let the devil and his dam° haunt you! What did you mean by that same
handkerchief you gave me even now? I was a fine fool to take it. I must take out
the work? A likely piece of work,° that you should find it in your chamber and
know not who left it there! This is some minx's token, and I must take out the
work? There; give it your hobbyhorse.° [*She gives him the handkerchief.*] Wheresoever   145
you had it, I'll take out no work on 't.

Cassio: How now, my sweet Bianca? How now? How now?

Othello: By heaven, that should be° my handkerchief!

Bianca: If you'll come to supper tonight, you may; if you will not, come when you are
next prepared for.°   *Exit.*   150

Iago: After her, after her.

Cassio: Faith, I must. She'll rail in the streets else.

Iago: Will you sup there?

Cassio: Faith, I intend so.

Iago: Well, I may chance to see you, for I would very fain speak with you.   155

Cassio: Prithee, come. Will you?

Iago: Go to.° Say no more.   [*Exit Cassio.*]

---

122 *They . . . win* i.e., they that laugh last laugh best   123 *cry* rumor   125 *I . . . else* call me a complete
rogue if I'm not telling the truth   126 *scored me* scored off me, beaten me, made up my reckoning, branded
me   128 *flattery* self-flattery, self-deception   129 *beckons* signals   131 *seabank* seashore. *bauble* plaything
132 *by this hand* I make my vow   136 *not . . . to* (Othello imagines himself cutting off Cassio's nose and
throwing it to a dog.)   138 *Before me* i.e., on my soul   139 *'Tis . . . fitchew* what a polecat she is! Just like
all the others. (Polecats were often compared with prostitutes because of their rank smell and presumed
lechery.)   141 *dam* mother   143 *A likely . . . work* a fine story   145 *hobbyhorse* harlot   148 *should be* must
be   149–150 *when . . . for* when I'm ready for you (i.e., never)   157 *Go to* (An expression of remonstrance.)

Othello [*advancing*]: How shall I murder him, Iago?

Iago: Did you perceive how he laughed at his vice?

Othello: O, Iago!

Iago: And did you see the handkerchief?   160

Othello: Was that mine?

Iago: Yours, by this hand. And to see how he prizes the foolish woman your wife! She
gave it him, and he hath given it his whore.

Othello: I would have him nine years a-killing. A fine woman! A fair woman! A   165
sweet woman!

Iago: Nay, you must forget that.

Othello: Ay, let her rot and perish, and be damned tonight, for she shall not live. No,
my heart is turned to stone; I strike it, and it hurts my hand. O, the world hath
not a sweeter creature! She might lie by an emperor's side and command him   170
tasks.

Iago: Nay, that's not your way.°

Othello: Hang her! I do but say what she is. So delicate with her needle! An admirable
musician! O, she will sing the savageness out of a bear. Of so high and plenteous
wit and invention!°   175

Iago: She's the worse for all this.

Othello: O, a thousand, a thousand times! And then, of so gentle a condition!°

Iago: Ay, too gentle.°

Othello: Nay, that's certain. But yet the pity of it, Iago! O, Iago, the pity of it, Iago!

Iago: If you are so fond° over her iniquity, give her patent° to offend, for if it touch   180
not you it comes near nobody.

Othello: I will chop her into messes.° Cuckold me?

Iago: O, 'tis foul in her.

Othello: With mine officer?

Iago: That's fouler.   185

Othello: Get me some poison, Iago, this night. I'll not expostulate with her, lest her
body and beauty unprovide° my mind again. This night, Iago.

Iago: Do it not with poison. Strangle her in her bed, even the bed she hath
contaminated.

Othello: Good, good! The justice of it pleases. Very good.   190

Iago: And for Cassio, let me be his undertaker.° You shall hear more by midnight.

Othello: Excellent good. [*A trumpet within.*] What trumpet is that same?

Iago: I warrant, something from Venice.

Enter Lodovico, Desdemona, and attendants.

'Tis Lodovico. This comes from the Duke.
See, your wife's with him.   195

Lodovico: God save you, worthy General!

Othello: With all my heart,° sir.

Lodovico [*giving him a letter*]: The Duke and the senators of Venice greet you.

Othello: I kiss the instrument of their pleasures.

---

172 *your way* i.e., the way you should think of her   175 *invention* imagination   177 *gentle a condition*
wellborn and well-bred   178 *gentle* generous, yielding (to other men)   180 *fond* foolish.   *patent* license
182 *messes* portions of meat, i.e., bits   187 *unprovide* weaken, render unfit   191 *be his undertaker* undertake to dispatch him   196 *With all my heart* i.e., I thank you most heartily

[*He opens the letter, and reads.*]

Desdemona: And what's the news, good cousin Lodovico?
Iago: I am very glad to see you, signor.   200
    Welcome to Cyprus.
Lodovico: I thank you. How does Lieutenant Cassio?
Iago: Lives, sir.
Desdemona: Cousin, there's fall'n between him and my lord
    An unkind° breach; but you shall make all well.   205
Othello: Are you sure of that?
Desdemona: My lord?
Othello[*reads*]: "This fail you not to do, as you will—"
Lodovico: He did not call; he's busy in the paper.
    Is there division twixt my lord and Cassio?   210
Desdemona: A most unhappy one. I would do much
    T' atone° them, for the love I bear to Cassio.
Othello: Fire and brimstone!
Desdemona: My lord?
Othello: Are you wise?   215
Desdemona: What, is he angry?
Lodovico: Maybe the letter moved him;
    For, as I think, they do command him home,
    Deputing Cassio in his government.°
Desdemona: By my troth, I am glad on 't.°
Othello: Indeed?   220
Desdemona: My lord?
Othello: I am glad to see you mad.°
Desdemona: Why, sweet Othello—
Othello [*striking her*]: Devil!
Desdemona: I have not deserved this.   225
Lodovico: My lord, this would not be believed in Venice,
    Though I should swear I saw 't. 'Tis very much.°
    Make her amends; she weeps.
Othello: O devil, devil!
    If that the earth could teem° with woman's tears,
    Each drop she falls would prove a crocodile.°   230
    Out of my sight!
Desdemona: I will not stay to offend you. [*Going.*]
Lodovico: Truly, an obedient lady.
    I do beseech your lordship, call her back.
Othello: Mistress!
Desdemona [*returning*]: My lord?   235
Othello: What would you with her, sir?°

---

205 *unkind* unnatural, contrary to their natures; hurtful   212 *atone* reconcile   218 *government* office
219 *on 't* of it   222 *I am . . . mad* i.e., I am glad to see that you are insane enough to rejoice in Cassio's
promotion (?) (Othello bitterly plays on Desdemona's *I am glad*.)   227 *very much* too much, outrageous
229 *teem* breed, be impregnated   230 *falls . . . crocodile* (Crocodiles were supposed to weep hypocritical
tears for their victims.)   236 *What . . . sir* (Othello implies that Desdemona is pliant and will do a *turn*,
lines 238–240, for any man.)

Lodovico: Who, I, my lord?

Othello: Ay, you did wish that I would make her turn.
Sir, she can turn, and turn, and yet go on
And turn again; and she can weep, sir, weep;   240
And she's obedient,° as you say, obedient,
Very obedient.—Proceed you in your tears.—
Concerning this, sir—O well-painted passion!°—
I am commanded home.—Get you away;
I'll send for you anon.—Sir, I obey the mandate   245
And will return to Venice.—Hence, avaunt!

[*Exit Desdemona.*]

Cassio shall have my place. And, sir, tonight
I do entreat that we may sup together.
You are welcome, sir, to Cyprus.—Goats and monkeys!°   *Exit.*

Lodovico: Is this the noble Moor whom our full Senate   250
Call all in all sufficient? Is this the nature
Whom passion could not shake? Whose solid virtue
The shot of accident nor dart of chance
Could neither graze nor pierce?

Iago: He is much changed.

Lodovico: Are his wits safe? Is he not light of brain?   255

Iago: He's that he is. I may not breathe my censure
What he might be. If what he might he is not,
I would to heaven he were!°

Lodovico: What, strike his wife?

Iago: Faith, that was not so well; yet would I knew
That stroke would prove the worst!

Lodovico: Is it his use?°   260
Or did the letters work upon his blood°
And new-create his fault?

Iago: Alas, alas!
It is not honesty in me to speak
What I have seen and known. You shall observe him,
And his own courses will denote° him so   265
That I may save my speech. Do but go after,
And mark how he continues.

Lodovico: I am sorry that I am deceived in him.   *Exeunt.*

SCENE II [THE CITADEL.]

Enter Othello and Emilia.

Othello: You have seen nothing then?

Emilia: Nor ever heard, nor ever did suspect.

241 *obedient* (With much the same sexual connotation as *turn* in lines 238–240.)   243 *passion* i.e., grief
249 *Goats and monkeys* (See III, iii, 419.)   256–258 *I may . . . were* i.e., I dare not venture an opinion as
to whether he's of unsound mind, as you suggest, but, if he isn't, then it might be better to wish he were in
fact insane, since only that could excuse his wild behavior   260 *use* custom   261 *blood* passions   265
courses will denote actions will reveal

Othello: Yes, you have seen Cassio and she together.
Emilia: But then I saw no harm, and then I heard
    Each syllable that breath made up between them.   5
Othello: What, did they never whisper?
Emilia: Never, my lord.
Othello: Nor send you out o' the way?
Emilia: Never.
Othello: To fetch her fan, her gloves, her mask, nor nothing?   10
Emilia: Never, my lord.
Othello: That's strange.
Emilia: I durst, my lord, to wager she is honest,
    Lay down my soul at stake.° If you think other,
    Remove your thought; it doth abuse your bosom.°   15
    If any wretch have put this in your head,
    Let heaven requite it with the serpent's curse!°
    For if she be not honest, chaste, and true,
    There's no man happy; the purest of their wives
    Is foul as slander.
Othello: Bid her come hither. Go.   20

    Exit Emilia.

    She says enough; yet she's a simple bawd
    That cannot say as much.° This° is a subtle whore,
    A closet lock and key° of villainous secrets.
    And yet she'll kneel and pray; I have seen her do 't.

    Enter Desdemona and Emilia.

Desdemona: My lord, what is your will?   25
Othello: Pray you, chuck, come hither.
Desdemona: What is your pleasure?
Othello: Let me see your eyes.
    Look in my face.
Desdemona: What horrible fancy's this?
Othello [to Emilia]: Some of your function,° mistress.
    Leave procreants° alone and shut the door;   30
    Cough or cry "hem" if anybody come.
    Your mystery, your mystery!° Nay, dispatch.

    Exit Emilia.

Desdemona [kneeling]: Upon my knees, what doth your speech import?
    I understand a fury in your words,
    But not the words.   35
Othello: Why, what art thou?

---

14 *at stake* as the wager   15 *abuse your bosom* deceive you   17 *the serpent's curse* the curse pronounced by God on the serpent for deceiving Eve, just as some man has done to Othello and Desdemona. (See Genesis 3:14.)   21–22 *she's . . . much* i.e., any procuress or go-between who couldn't make up as plausible a story as Emilia's would have to be pretty stupid   22 *This* i.e., Desdemona   23 *closet lock and key* i.e., concealer 29 *Some . . . function* i.e., practice your chosen profession, that of bawd (by guarding the door) 30 *procreants* mating couples   32 *mystery* trade, occupation

"Ah, Desdemon! Away, away, away!" (IV, ii, 43).

Desdemona:	Your wife, my lord, your true
And loyal wife.	
Othello:	Come, swear it, damn thyself,

Lest, being like one of heaven,° the devils themselves
Should fear to seize thee. Therefore be double damned:
Swear thou art honest.

Desdemona:	Heaven doth truly know it.	40

Othello: Heaven truly knows that thou art false as hell.
Desdemona: To whom, my lord? With whom? How am I false?
Othello [*weeping*]: Ah, Desdemon! Away, away, away!
Desdemona: Alas the heavy day! Why do you weep?
  Am I the motive° of these tears, my lord?   45

38 *being . . . heaven* looking like an angel   45 *motive* cause

If haply you my father do suspect
An instrument of this your calling back,
Lay not your blame on me. If you have lost him,
I have lost him too.
Othello: Had it pleased heaven
To try me with affliction, had they° rained   50
All kinds of sores and shames on my bare head,
Steeped me in poverty to the very lips,
Given to captivity me and my utmost hopes,
I should have found in some place of my soul
A drop of patience. But, alas, to make me   55
A fixèd figure for the time of scorn°
To point his° slow and moving finger° at!
Yet could I bear that too, well, very well.
But there where I have garnered° up my heart,
Where either I must live or bear no life,   60
The fountain° from the which my current runs
Or else dries up—to be discarded thence!
Or keep it as a cistern° for foul toads
To knot° and gender° in! Turn thy complexion there,°
Patience, thou young and rose-lipped cherubin—   65
Ay, there look grim as hell!°
Desdemona: I hope my noble lord esteems me honest.°
Othello: O, ay, as summer flies are in the shambles,°
That quicken° even with blowing.° O thou weed,
Who art so lovely fair and smell'st so sweet   70
That the sense aches at thee, would thou hadst ne'er been born!
Desdemona: Alas, what ignorant° sin have I committed?
Othello: Was this fair paper, this most goodly book,
Made to write "whore" upon? What committed?
Committed? O thou public commoner!°   75
I should make very forges of my cheeks,
That would to cinders burn up modesty,
Did I but speak thy deeds. What committed?
Heaven stops the nose at it and the moon winks;°
The bawdy° wind, that kisses all it meets,   80
Is hushed within the hollow mine° of earth
And will not hear 't. What committed?
Impudent strumpet!

---

50 *they* i.e., heavenly powers   56 *time of scorn* i.e., scornful world   57 *his* its.   *slow and moving finger* i.e., hour hand of the clock, moving so slowly it seems hardly to move at all. (Othello envisages himself as being eternally pointed at by the scornful world as the numbers on a clock are pointed at by the hour hand.)   59 *garnered* stored   61 *fountain* spring   63 *cistern* cesspool   64 *knot* couple.   *gender* engender.   *Turn . . . there* change your color, at such a sight   65–66 *Patience . . . hell* (Even Patience, that rose-lipped cherub, will look grim and pale at this spectacle.)   67 *honest* chaste   68 *shambles* slaughterhouse   69 *quicken* come to life.   *with blowing* i.e., with the puffing up of something rotten in which maggots are breeding   72 *ignorant sin* sin in ignorance   75 *commoner* prostitute   79 *winks* closes her eyes. (The moon symbolizes chastity.)   80 *bawdy* kissing one and all   81 *mine* cave (where the winds were thought to dwell)

Othello berates Desdemona as a "strumpet" and "cunning whore" (IV, ii, 73–98).

Desdemona: By heaven, you do me wrong.
Othello: Are not you a strumpet?
Desdemona: No, as I am a Christian.   85
    If to preserve this vessel° for my lord
    From any other foul unlawful touch
    Be not to be a strumpet, I am none.
Othello: What, not a whore?
Desdemona: No, as I shall be saved.   90
Othello: Is 't possible?
Desdemona: O, heaven forgive us!
Othello: I cry you mercy,° then.
    I took you for that cunning whore of Venice
    That married with Othello. [*Calling out.*] You, mistress,
    That have the office opposite to Saint Peter   95
    And keep the gate of hell!

    Enter Emilia.

                You, you, ay, you!
    We have done our course.° There's money for your pains.   [*He gives money.*]
    I pray you, turn the key and keep our counsel.   *Exit.*

86 *vessel* body   92 *cry you mercy* beg your pardon   97 *course* business (with an indecent suggestion of
"trick," turn at sex)

Emilia: Alas, what does this gentleman conceive?°
  How do you, madam? How do you, my good lady?   100
Desdemona: Faith, half asleep.°
Emilia: Good madam, what's the matter with my lord?
Desdemona: With who?
Emilia: Why, with my lord, madam.
Desdemona: Who is thy lord?
Emilia: He that is yours, sweet lady.   105
Desdemona: I have none. Do not talk to me, Emilia.
  I cannot weep, nor answers have I none
  But what should go by water.° Prithee, tonight
  Lay on my bed my wedding sheets, remember;
  And call thy husband hither.   110
Emilia: Here's a change indeed!   *Exit.*
Desdemona: 'Tis meet I should be used so, very meet.°
  How have I been behaved, that he might stick°
  The small'st opinion° on my least misuse?°

  Enter Iago.

Iago: What is your pleasure, madam? How is 't with you?   115
Desdemona: I cannot tell. Those that do teach young babes
  Do it with gentle means and easy tasks.
  He might have chid me so, for, in good faith,
  I am a child to chiding.
Iago: What is the matter, lady?   120
Emilia: Alas, Iago, my lord hath so bewhored her,
  Thrown such despite and heavy terms upon her,
  That true hearts cannot bear it.
Desdemona: Am I that name, Iago?
Iago: What name, fair lady?   125
Desdemona: Such as she said my lord did say I was.
Emilia: He called her whore. A beggar in his drink
  Could not have laid such terms upon his callet.°
Iago: Why did he so?
Desdemona [*weeping*]: I do not know. I am sure I am none such.   130
Iago: Do not weep, do not weep. Alas the day!
Emilia: Hath she forsook so many noble matches,
  Her father and her country and her friends,
  To be called whore? Would it not make one weep?
Desdemona: It is my wretched fortune.
Iago: Beshrew° him for 't!   135
  How comes this trick° upon him?
Desdemona: Nay, heaven doth know.
Emilia: I will be hanged if some eternal° villain,
  Some busy and insinuating° rogue,

99 *conceive* suppose, think   101 *half asleep* i.e., dazed   108 *go by water* be expressed by tears   112 *meet* fitting   113 *stick* attach   114 *opinion* censure. *least misuse* slightest misconduct   128 *callet* whore   135 *Beshrew* curse   136 *trick* strange behavior, delusion   137 *eternal* inveterate   138 *insinuating* ingratiating, fawning, wheedling

Iago comforts Desdemona regarding Othello's accusations (IV, ii, 115–179).

Some cogging,° cozening° slave, to get some office,
Have not devised this slander. I will be hanged else.   140
Iago: Fie, there is no such man. It is impossible.
Desdemona: If any such there be, heaven pardon him!
Emilia: A halter° pardon him! And hell gnaw his bones!
Why should he call her whore? Who keeps her company?
What place? What time? What form?° What likelihood?   145
The Moor's abused by some most villainous knave,
Some base notorious knave, some scurvy fellow.
O heaven, that° such companions° thou'dst unfold,°
And put in every honest hand a whip
To lash the rascals naked through the world   150
Even from the east to th' west!
Iago: Speak within door.°
Emilia: O, fie upon them! Some such squire° he was
That turned your wit the seamy side without°
And made you to suspect me with the Moor.
Iago: You are a fool. Go to.°
Desdemona: Alas, Iago,   155
What shall I do to win my lord again?

139 *cogging* cheating. *cozening* defrauding 143 *halter* hangman's noose 145 *form* appearance, circumstance 148 *that* would that. *companions* fellows. *unfold* expose 151 *within door* i.e., not so loud 152 *squire* fellow 153 *seamy side without* wrong side out 155 *Go to* i.e., that's enough

Good friend, go to him; for, by this light of heaven,
I know not how I lost him. Here I kneel. [*She kneels.*]
If e'er my will did trespass 'gainst his love,
Either in discourse of thought° or actual deed,   160
Or that° mine eyes, mine ears, or any sense
Delighted them° in any other form;
Or that I do not yet,° and ever did,
And ever will—though he do shake me off
To beggarly divorcement—love him dearly,   165
Comfort forswear° me! Unkindness may do much,
And his unkindness may defeat° my life,
But never taint my love. I cannot say "whore."
It does abhor° me now I speak the word;
To do the act that might the addition° earn   170
Not the world's mass of vanity° could make me.

[*She rises.*]

Iago: I pray you, be content. 'Tis but his humor.°
The business of the state does him offense,
And he does chide with you.
Desdemona: If 'twere no other—   175
Iago: It is but so, I warrant.   [*Trumpets within.*]
Hark, how these instruments summon you to supper!
The messengers of Venice stays the meat.°
Go in, and weep not. All things shall be well.

Exeunt Desdemona and Emilia.

Enter Roderigo.

How now, Roderigo?   180
Roderigo: I do not find that thou deal'st justly with me.
Iago: What in the contrary?
Roderigo: Every day thou daff'st me° with some device,° Iago, and rather, as it seems
to me now, keep'st from me all conveniency° than suppliest me with the least
advantage° of hope. I will indeed no longer endure it, nor am I yet persuaded to   185
put up° in peace what already I have foolishly suffered.
Iago: Will you hear me, Roderigo?
Roderigo: Faith, I have heard too much, for your words and performances are no kin
together.
Iago: You charge me most unjustly.   190
Roderigo: With naught but truth. I have wasted myself out of my means. The jewels
you have had from me to deliver° Desdemona would half have corrupted a

---

160 *discourse of thought* process of thinking   161 *that* if. (Also in line 163.)   162 *Delighted them* took
delight   163 *yet* still   166 *Comfort forswear* may heavenly comfort forsake   167 *defeat* destroy   169
abhor (1) fill me with abhorrence (2) make me whorelike   170 *addition* title   171 *vanity* showy splendor
172 *humor* mood   178 *stays the meat* are waiting to dine   183 *thou daff'st me* you put me off.   *device*
excuse, trick   184 *conveniency* advantage, opportunity   185 *advantage* increase   186 *put up* submit to,
tolerate   192 *deliver* deliver to

votarist.° You have told me she hath received them and returned me expectations and comforts of sudden respect° and acquaintance, but I find none.

Iago: Well, go to, very well.   195

Roderigo: "Very well"! "Go to"! I cannot go to,° man, nor 'tis not very well. By this hand, I think it is scurvy, and begin to find myself fopped° in it.

Iago: Very well.

Roderigo: I tell you 'tis not very well.° I will make myself known to Desdemona. If she will return me my jewels, I will give over my suit and repent my unlawful solici-   200
tation; if not, assure yourself I will seek satisfaction° of you.

Iago: You have said now?°

Roderigo: Ay, and said nothing but what I protest intendment° of doing.

Iago: Why, now I see there's mettle in thee, and even from this instant do build on thee a better opinion than ever before. Give me thy hand, Roderigo. Thou hast   205
taken against me a most just exception; but yet I protest I have dealt most directly in thy affair.

Roderigo: It hath not appeared.

Iago: I grant indeed it hath not appeared, and your suspicion is not without wit and judgment. But, Roderigo, if thou hast that in thee indeed which I have greater   210
reason to believe now than ever—I mean purpose, courage, and valor—this night show it. If thou the next night following enjoy not Desdemona, take me from this world with treachery and devise engines for° my life.

Roderigo: Well, what is it? Is it within reason and compass?

Iago: Sir, there is especial commission come from Venice to depute Cassio in   215
Othello's place.

Roderigo: Is that true? Why, then Othello and Desdemona return again to Venice.

Iago: O, no; he goes into Mauritania and takes away with him the fair Desdemona, unless his abode be lingered here by some accident; wherein none can be so determinate° as the removing of Cassio.   220

Roderigo: How do you mean, removing of him?

Iago: Why, by making him uncapable of Othello's place—knocking out his brains.

Roderigo: And that you would have me to do?

Iago: Ay, if you dare do yourself a profit and a right. He sups tonight with a harlotry,° and thither will I go to him. He knows not yet of his honorable fortune. If you   225
will watch his going thence, which I will fashion to fall out° between twelve and one, you may take him at your pleasure. I will be near to second your attempt, and he shall fall between us. Come, stand not amazed at it, but go along with me. I will show you such a necessity in his death that you shall think yourself bound to put it on him. It is now high° suppertime, and the night grows to waste.°   230
About it.

Roderigo: I will hear further reason for this.

Iago: And you shall be satisfied.   *Exeunt.*

---

193 *votarist* nun   194 *sudden respect* immediate consideration   196 *I cannot go to* (Roderigo changes Iago's
go to, an expression urging patience, to *I cannot go to,* "I have no opportunity for success in wooing.")
197 *fopped* fooled, duped   199 *not very well* (Roderigo changes Iago's *very well,* "all right, then," to *not very
well,* "not at all good.")   201 *satisfaction* repayment. (The term normally means settling of accounts in a
duel.)   202 *You . . . now* have you finished?   203 *intendment* intention   213 *engines for* plots against
220 *determinate* conclusive   224 *harlotry* slut   226 *fall out* occur   230 *high* fully. *grows to waste* wastes
away

SCENE III [THE CITADEL.]

> *Enter Othello, Lodovico, Desdemona, Emilia, and attendants.*

Lodovico: I do beseech you, sir, trouble yourself no further.
Othello: O, pardon me; 'twill do me good to walk.
Lodovico: Madam, good night. I humbly thank your ladyship.
Desdemona: Your honor is most welcome.
Othello: Will you walk, sir?
   O, Desdemona!   5
Desdemona: My lord?
Othello: Get you to bed on th' instant.
   I will be returned forthwith. Dismiss your attendant there. Look
   't be done.
Desdemona: I will, my lord.   10

> *Exit* [*Othello, with Lodovico and attendants*].

Emilia: How goes it now? He looks gentler than he did.
Desdemona: He says he will return incontinent,°
   And hath commanded me to go to bed,
   And bid me to dismiss you.
Emilia: Dismiss me?   15
Desdemona: It was his bidding. Therefore, good Emilia,
   Give me my nightly wearing, and adieu.
   We must not now displease him.
Emilia: I would you had never seen him!
Desdemona: So would not I. My love doth so approve him   20
   That even his stubbornness,° his checks,° his frowns—
   Prithee, unpin me—have grace and favor in them.

> [*Emilia prepares Desdemona for bed.*]

Emilia: I have laid those sheets you bade me on the bed.
Desdemona: All's one.° Good faith, how foolish are our minds!
   If I do die before thee, prithee shroud me   25
   In one of these same sheets.
Emilia: Come, come, you talk.°
Desdemona: My mother had a maid called Barbary.
   She was in love, and he she loved proved mad°
   And did forsake her. She had a song of "Willow."
   An old thing 'twas, but it expressed her fortune,   30
   And she died singing it. That song tonight
   Will not go from my mind; I have much to do
   But to go hang° my head all at one side
   And sing it like poor Barbary. Prithee, dispatch.
Emilia: Shall I go fetch your nightgown?°   35

---

12 *incontinent* immediately   21 *stubbornness* roughness.   *checks* rebukes   24 *All's one* all right. It doesn't
really matter   26 *talk* i.e., prattle   28 *mad* wild, i.e., faithless   32–33 *I . . . hang* I can scarcely keep myself
from hanging   35 *nightgown* dressing gown

Desdemona: No, unpin me here.
　　This Lodovico is a proper° man.
Emilia: A very handsome man.
Desdemona: He speaks well.
Emilia: I know a lady in Venice would have walked barefoot to Palestine for a touch　　40
　　of his nether lip.
Desdemona [*singing*]:
　　　　　　"The poor soul sat sighing by a sycamore tree,
　　　　　　Sing all a green willow;°
　　　　　　Her hand on her bosom, her head on her knee,
　　　　　　Sing willow, willow, willow.
　　　　　　The fresh streams ran by her and murmured her moans;　　45
　　　　　　Sing willow, willow, willow;
　　　　　　Her salt tears fell from her, and softened the stones—"
　　Lay by these.
　　　　　　[*Singing.*] "Sing willow, willow, willow—"
　　　　　　　　　　　　　　　　　　　　　　　　　　　　50
　　Prithee, hie thee.° He'll come anon.°
　　　　　　[*Singing.*] "Sing all a green willow must be my garland.
　　　　　　Let nobody blame him; his scorn I approve—"
　　Nay, that's not next.—Hark! Who is 't that knocks?
Emilia: It's the wind.　　55
Desdemona [*singing*]:
　　　　　　"I called my love false love; but what said he then?
　　　　　　Sing willow, willow, willow;
　　　　　　If I court more women, you'll couch with more men."

　　So, get thee gone. Good night. Mine eyes do itch;
　　Doth that bode weeping?
Emilia:　　　　　　　　　　　'Tis neither here nor there.　　60
Desdemona: I have heard it said so. O, these men, these men!
　　Dost thou in conscience think—tell me, Emilia—
　　That there be women do abuse° their husbands
　　In such gross kind?
Emilia:　　　　　　　　　There be some such, no question.
Desdemona: Wouldst thou do such a deed for all the world?　　65
Emilia: Why, would not you?
Desdemona:　　　　　　　No, by this heavenly light!
Emilia: Nor I neither by this heavenly light;
　　I might do 't as well i' the dark.
Desdemona: Wouldst thou do such a deed for all the world?
Emilia: The world's a huge thing. It is a great price　　70
　　For a small vice.
Desdemona: Good troth, I think thou wouldst not.
Emilia: By my troth, I think I should, and undo 't when I had done. Marry, I would
　　not do such a thing for a joint ring,° nor for measures of lawn,° nor for gowns,
　　petticoats, nor caps, nor any petty exhibition.° But for all the whole world! Uds°　　75

---

37 *proper* handsome   43 *willow* (A conventional emblem of disappointed love.)   51 *hie thee* hurry.   *anon*
right away   63 *abuse* deceive   74 *joint ring* a ring made in separate halves.   *lawn* fine linen   75 *exhibition*
gift.   *Uds* God's

pity, who would not make her husband a cuckold to make him a monarch? I
should venture purgatory for 't.

Desdemona: Beshrew me if I would do such a wrong
For the whole world.

Emilia: Why, the wrong is but a wrong i' the world, and having the world for your 80
labor, 'tis a wrong in your own world, and you might quickly make it right.

Desdemona: I do not think there is any such woman.

Emilia: Yes, a dozen, and as many
To th' vantage° as would store° the world they played° for.
But I do think it is their husbands' faults 85
If wives do fall. Say that they slack their duties°
And pour our treasures into foreign laps,°
Or else break out in peevish jealousies,
Throwing restraint upon us?° Or say they strike us,
Or scant our former having in despite?° 90
Why, we have galls,° and though we have some grace,
Yet have we some revenge. Let husbands know
Their wives have sense° like them. They see, and smell,
And have their palates both for sweet and sour,
As husbands have. What is it that they do 95
When they change us for others? Is it sport?°
I think it is. And doth affection° breed it?
I think it doth. Is 't frailty that thus errs?
It is so, too. And have not we affections,
Desires for sport, and frailty, as men have? 100
Then let them use us well; else let them know,
The ills we do, their ills instruct us so.

Desdemona: Good night, good night. God me such uses° send
Not to pick bad from bad, but by bad mend!°

Exeunt.

ACT V

SCENE I [A STREET IN CYPRUS.]

Enter Iago and Roderigo.

Iago: Here stand behind this bulk.° Straight will he come.
Wear thy good rapier bare,° and put it home.
Quick, quick! Fear nothing. I'll be at thy elbow.
It makes us or it mars us. Think on that,
And fix most firm thy resolution. 5

Roderigo: Be near at hand. I may miscarry in 't.

---

84 *To th' vantage* in addition, to boot.   *store* populate.   *played* (1) gambled (2) sported sexually   86 *duties*
marital duties   87 *pour . . . laps* i.e., are unfaithful, give what is rightfully ours (semen) to other women
89 *Throwing . . . us* i.e., jealously restricting our freedom to see other men   90 *scant . . . despite* reduce
our allowance to spite us   91 *have galls* i.e., are capable of resenting injury and insult   93 *sense* physical
sense   96 *sport* sexual pastime   97 *affection* passion   103 *uses* habit, practice   104 *Not . . . mend* i.e.,
not to learn bad conduct from others' badness (as Emilia has suggested women learn from men), but to
mend my ways by perceiving what badness is, making spiritual benefit out of evil and adversity   1 *bulk*
framework projecting from the front of a shop   2 *bare* unsheathed

Iago: Here, at thy hand. Be bold, and take thy stand.

    [*Iago stands aside. Roderigo conceals himself.*]

Roderigo: I have no great devotion to the deed;
    And yet he hath given me satisfying reasons.
    'Tis but a man gone. Forth, my sword! He dies.   10

    [*He draws.*]

Iago: I have rubbed this young quat° almost to the sense,°
    And he grows angry. Now, whether he kill Cassio
    Or Cassio him, or each do kill the other,
    Every way makes my gain. Live Roderigo,°
    He calls me to a restitution large   15
    Of gold and jewels that I bobbed° from him
    As gifts to Desdemona.
    It must not be. If Cassio do remain,
    He hath a daily beauty in his life
    That makes me ugly; and besides, the Moor   20
    May unfold° me to him; there stand I in much peril.
    No, he must die. Be 't so. I hear him coming.

    Enter Cassio.

Roderigo [*coming forth*]: I know his gait, 'tis he.—Villain, thou diest!

    [*He attacks Cassio.*]

Cassio: That thrust had been mine enemy indeed,
    But that my coat° is better than thou know'st.   25
    I will make proof° of thine.

    [*He draws, and wounds Roderigo.*]

Roderigo: O, I am slain!   [*He falls.*]

    [*Iago, from behind, wounds Cassio in the leg, and exits.*]

Cassio: I am maimed forever. Help, ho! Murder! Murder!

    Enter Othello.

Othello: The voice of Cassio! Iago keeps his word.
Roderigo: O, villain that I am!
Othello: It is even so.
Cassio: O, help, ho! Light! A surgeon!   30
Othello: 'Tis he. O brave Iago, honest and just,
    That hast such noble sense of thy friend's wrong!
    Thou teachest me. Minion,° your dear lies dead,

---

11 *quat* pimple, pustule. *to the sense* to the quick 14 *Live Roderigo* if Roderigo lives 16 *bobbed* swindled
21 *unfold* expose 25 *coat* (Possibly a garment of mail under the outer clothing, or simply a tougher coat
than Roderigo expected.) 26 *proof* a test 34 *Minion* hussy (i.e., Desdemona)

And your unblest fate hies.° Strumpet, I come.   35
Forth of° my heart those charms, thine eyes, are blotted;
Thy bed, lust-stained, shall with lust's blood be spotted.   *Exit Othello.*

Enter Lodovico and Gratiano.

Cassio: What ho! No watch? No passage?° Murder! Murder!
Gratiano: 'Tis some mischance. The voice is very direful.
Cassio: O, help!
Lodovico: Hark!   40
Roderigo: O wretched villain!
Lodovico: Two or three groan. 'Tis heavy° night;
    These may be counterfeits. Let's think 't unsafe
    To come in to° the cry without more help.   45

[*They remain near the entrance.*]

Roderigo: Nobody come? Then shall I bleed to death.

Enter Iago [in his shirtsleeves, with a light].

Lodovico: Hark!
Gratiano: Here's one comes in his shirt, with light and weapons.
Iago: Who's there? Whose noise is this that cries on° murder?
Lodovico: We do not know.
Iago: Did not you hear a cry?   50
Cassio: Here, here! For heaven's sake, help me!
Iago: What's the matter?

[*He moves toward Cassio.*]

Gratiano [*to Lodovico*]: This is Othello's ancient, as I take it.
Lodovico [*to Gratiano*]: The same indeed, a very valiant fellow.
Iago [*to Cassio*]: What° are you here that cry so grievously?
Cassio: Iago? O, I am spoiled,° undone by villains!   55
    Give me some help.
Iago: O me, Lieutenant! What villains have done this?
Cassio: I think that one of them is hereabout,
    And cannot make° away.
Iago: O treacherous villains!

[*To Lodovico and Gratiano.*]

    What are you there? Come in, and give some help.   [*They advance.*]   60
Roderigo: O, help me there!
Cassio: That's one of them.
Iago: O murderous slave! O villain!

[*He stabs Roderigo.*]

---

35 *hies* hastens on   36 *Forth of* from out   38 *passage* people passing by   43 *heavy* thick, dark   45 *come in to* approach   49 *cries on* cries out   54 *What* who (also at lines 60 and 66)   55 *spoiled* ruined, done for 59 *make* get

Roderigo: O damned Iago! O inhuman dog!
Iago: Kill men i' the dark?—Where be these bloody thieves?—
    How silent is this town!—Ho! Murder, murder!—   65
    [*To Lodovico and Gratiano.*] What may you be? Are you of good or evil?
Lodovico: As you shall prove us, praise° us.
Iago: Signor Lodovico?
Lodovico: He, sir.
Iago: I cry you mercy.° Here's Cassio hurt by villains.   70
Gratiano: Cassio?
Iago: How is 't, brother?
Cassio: My leg is cut in two.
Iago: Marry, heaven forbid!
    Light, gentlemen! I'll bind it with my shirt.   75

[*He hands them the light, and tends to Cassio's wound.*]

    Enter Bianca.

Bianca: What is the matter, ho? Who is 't that cried?
Iago: Who is 't that cried?
Bianca: O my dear Cassio!
    My sweet Cassio! O Cassio, Cassio, Cassio!
Iago: O notable strumpet! Cassio, may you suspect
    Who they should be that have thus mangled you?
Cassio: No.   80
Gratiano: I am sorry to find you thus. I have been to seek you.
Iago: Lend me a garter. [*He applies a tourniquet.*] So.—O, for a chair,°
    To bear him easily hence!
Bianca: Alas, he faints! O Cassio, Cassio, Cassio!   85
Iago: Gentlemen all, I do suspect this trash
    To be a party in this injury.—
    Patience awhile, good Cassio.—Come, come;
    Lend me a light.   [*He shines the light on Roderigo.*]
                 Know we this face or no?
    Alas, my friend and my dear countryman   90
    Roderigo! No.—Yes, sure.—O heaven! Roderigo!
Gratiano: What, of Venice?
Iago: Even he, sir. Did you know him?
Gratiano: Know him? Ay.
Iago: Signor Gratiano? I cry your gentle° pardon.   95
    These bloody accidents° must excuse my manners
    That so neglected you.
Gratiano: I am glad to see you.
Iago: How do you, Cassio? O, a chair, a chair!
Gratiano: Roderigo!
Iago: He, he, 'tis he. [*A litter is brought in.*] O, that's well said;° the chair.   100
    Some good man bear him carefully from hence;

67 *praise* appraise   70 *I cry you mercy* I beg your pardon   83 *chair* litter   95 *gentle* noble   96 *accidents* sudden events   100 *well said* well done

I'll fetch the General's surgeon. [*To Bianca.*] For you, mistress,
Save you your labor.°—He that lies slain here, Cassio,
Was my dear friend. What malice° was between you?
Cassio: None in the world, nor do I know the man.   105
Iago [*to Bianca*]: What, look you pale?—O, bear him out o' th' air.°

[*Cassio and Roderigo are borne off.*]

Stay you,° good gentlemen.—Look you pale, mistress?—
Do you perceive the gastness° of her eye?—
Nay, if you stare,° we shall hear more anon.—
Behold her well; I pray you, look upon her.   110
Do you see, gentlemen? Nay, guiltiness
Will speak, though tongues were out of use.

[*Enter Emilia.*]

Emilia: 'Las, what's the matter? What's the matter, husband?
Iago: Cassio hath here been set on in the dark
By Roderigo and fellows that are scaped.   115
He's almost slain, and Roderigo dead.
Emilia: Alas, good gentleman! Alas, good Cassio!
Iago: This is the fruits of whoring. Prithee, Emilia,
Go know° of Cassio where he supped tonight.
[*To Bianca.*] What, do you shake at that?   120
Bianca: He supped at my house, but I therefore shake not.
Iago: O, did he so? I charge you go with me.
Emilia: O, fie upon thee, strumpet!
Bianca: I am no strumpet, but of life as honest°
As you that thus abuse me.   125
Emilia: As I? Faugh! Fie upon thee!
Iago: Kind gentlemen, let's go see poor Cassio dressed.°—
Come, mistress, you must tell's another tale.
Emilia, run you to the citadel
And tell my lord and lady what hath happed.—   130
Will you go on afore? [*Aside.*] This is the night
That either makes me or fordoes° me quite.   *Exeunt.*

SCENE II [A BEDCHAMBER IN THE CITADEL.]

Enter Othello [*with a light*], *and Desdemona in her bed.*°

Othello: It is the cause,° it is the cause, my soul.
Let me not name it to you, you chaste stars!
It is the cause. Yet I'll not shed her blood,

---

103 *Save . . . labor* i.e., never you mind tending Cassio   104 *malice* enmity   106 *bear . . . air* (Fresh air
was thought to be dangerous for a wound.)   107 *Stay you* (Lodovico and Gratiano are evidently about to
leave.)   108 *gastness* terror   109 *stare* (Iago pretends to interpret Bianca's wild looks as an involuntary
confession of guilt.)   119 *know* learn   124 *honest* chaste   127 *Cassio dressed* Cassio's wounds dressed
132 *fordoes* undoes, ruins   s.d.   *in her bed* (Either the curtains are drawn back to reveal the bed in a recessed
area backstage, or the bed is "thrust out" onstage as the scene begins.)   1 *cause* i.e., cause of justice, the
offense itself, which Othello must correct as an agent of justice

"Enter Othello, and Desdemona in her bed" (V, ii, s.d.).

Nor scar that whiter skin of hers than snow,
And smooth as monumental° alabaster.   5
Yet she must die, else she'll betray more men.
Put out the light, and then put out the light.°
If I quench thee, thou flaming minister,°
I can again thy former light restore,
Should I repent me;° but once put out thy light,   10
Thou cunning'st pattern° of excelling nature,
I know not where is that Promethean heat°
That can thy light relume.° When I have plucked thy rose,
I cannot give it vital growth again;
It needs must wither. I'll smell thee on the tree.   15

[*He kisses her.*]

O balmy breath, that dost almost persuade
Justice to break her sword! One more, one more.
Be thus when thou art dead, and I will kill thee,
And love thee after. One more, and that's the last.

[*He kisses her.*]

5 *monumental* i.e., used in making tombs and funeral monuments;   7 *the light . . . light* the torch or lamp
. . . Desdemona's life   8 *flaming minister* torch or lamp that serves me   10 *repent me* change my mind
11 *Thou . . . pattern* you skillfully wrought perfect example   12 *Promethean heat* divine fire. (Alluding to the
theft of fire from heaven by Prometheus.)   13 *relume* rekindle

So sweet was ne'er so fatal. I must weep,   20
But they are cruel° tears. This sorrow's heavenly;
It strikes where it doth love.° She wakes.

Desdemona: Who's there? Othello?

Othello: Ay, Desdemona.

Desdemona: Will you come to bed, my lord?   25

Othello: Have you prayed tonight, Desdemon?

Desdemona: Ay, my lord.

Othello: If you bethink yourself of any crime°
   Unreconciled as yet to heaven and grace,
   Solicit° for it straight.°   30

Desdemona: Alack, my lord, what may you mean by that?

Othello: Well, do it, and be brief. I will walk by.
   I would not kill thy unpreparèd spirit.
   No, heaven forfend!° I would not kill thy soul.

Desdemona: Talk you of killing?

Othello: Ay, I do.

Desdemona: Then heaven   35
   Have mercy on me!

Othello: Amen, with all my heart!

Desdemona: If you say so, I hope you will not kill me.

Othello: Humh!

Desdemona: And yet I fear you; for you're fatal then
   When your eyes roll so. Why I should fear I know not,   40
   Since guiltiness I know not; but yet I feel I fear.

Othello: Think on thy sins.

Desdemona: They are loves I bear to you.°

Othello: Ay, and for that thou diest.

Desdemona: That death's unnatural that kills for loving.
   Alas, why gnaw you so your nether lip?   45
   Some bloody passion shakes your very frame.
   These are portents; but yet I hope, I hope,
   They do not point on° me.

Othello: Peace, and be still!

Desdemona: I will so. What's the matter?   50

Othello: That handkerchief which I so loved and gave thee
   Thou gav'st to Cassio.

Desdemona: No, by my life and soul!
   Send for the man and ask him.

Othello: Sweet soul, take heed, take heed of perjury.
   Thou art on thy deathbed.   55

Desdemona: Ay, but not yet to die.

Othello: Yes, presently.°

---

21 *cruel* unrelenting 22 *It . . . love* (Compare Hebrews 12:6: "For whom the Lord loveth he chasteneth.")
28 *crime* sin 30 *Solicit* petition, pray. *straight* immediately 34 *forfend* forbid 42 *They are . . . you* i.e.,
if I sinned, it was in loving you more than my father or more than God 48 *point on* point at, predict what
is to happen to 56 *presently* immediately

Therefore confess thee freely of thy sin;
For to deny each article with oath
Cannot remove nor choke the strong conception°
That I do groan withal.° Thou art to die.   60
Desdemona: Then Lord have mercy on me!
Othello: I say, amen.
Desdemona: And have you mercy too! I never did
    Offend° you in my life; never loved Cassio
    But with such general warranty° of heaven
    As I might love. I never gave him token.   65
Othello: By heaven, I saw my handkerchief in 's hand.
    O perjured woman! Thou dost stone° my heart,
    And makes me call what I intend to do
    A murder, which I thought a sacrifice.
    I saw the handkerchief.
Desdemona: He found it, then.   70
    I never gave it him. Send for him hither;
    Let him confess a truth.
Othello: He hath confessed.
Desdemona: What, my lord?
Othello: That he hath used thee.
Desdemona: How? Unlawfully?
Othello: Ay.
Desdemona: He will not say so.
Othello: No, his mouth is stopped;   75
    Honest Iago hath ta'en order° for 't.
Desdemona: O, my fear interprets. What, is he dead?
Othello: Had all his hairs been lives, my great revenge
    Had stomach for them all.
Desdemona: Alas, he is betrayed and I undone!   [*She weeps.*]   80
Othello: Out, strumpet! Weep'st thou for him to my face?
Desdemona: O, banish me, my lord, but kill me not!
Othello: Down, strumpet!
Desdemona: Kill me tomorrow; let me live tonight!
Othello: Nay, if you strive—   85
Desdemona: But half an hour!
Othello: Being done,° there is no pause.
Desdemona: But while I say one prayer!
Othello: It is too late.

    Smothers her.

Emilia [*at the door*]: My lord, my lord! What, ho! My lord, my lord!
Othello: What noise is this? Not dead? Not yet quite dead?
    I that am cruel am yet merciful;   90
    I would not have thee linger in thy pain.

---

59 *conception* (1) belief in your guilt (2) plan in my mind   60 *groan withal* (1) groan at in sorrow (2) as in giving birth   63 *Offend* wrong   64 *warranty* sanction   67 *stone* turn to stone, harden   76 *ta'en order* taken measures   86 *Being done* i.e., since justice has begun its relentless course

Othello smothers Desdemona (V, ii, 87–91).

[*He dispatches her.*]

                                            So, so.

Emilia [*within*]: What, ho! My lord, my lord!

Othello: Who's there?

Emilia [*within*]: O, good my lord, I would speak a word with you!

Othello: Yes, 'tis Emilia.—By and by.—She's dead.

   'Tis like° she comes to speak of Cassio's death.—   95

   The noise was here.° Ha! No more moving?

   Still as the grave. Shall she come in? Were 't good?—

   I think she stirs again. No. What's best to do?

   If she come in, she'll sure speak to my wife.

   My wife! My wife! What wife? I have no wife.   100

   O, insupportable! O heavy hour!

   Methinks it should be now a huge eclipse

   Of sun and moon, and that th' affrighted globe

   Should yawn° at alteration.°

Emilia [*within*]:   I do beseech you

   That I may speak with you, O, good my lord!   105

Othello: I had forgot thee. O, come in, Emilia.—

   Soft,° by and by. Let me the curtains draw.—

---

95 *like* likely that   96 *here* (The Folio's *high* is possible, suggesting that the commotion of the attack on Cassio was loud.)   104 *yawn* gape in amazement, i.e., move in an earthquake. (According to Pliny, earthquakes often happen during eclipses.)   *at alteration* at these cataclysmic events in nature, well suited to express the horror of Desdemona's death   107 *Soft* wait a minute

[He closes the bed-curtains and opens the door.]

Where art thou?

Enter Emilia.

                    What's the matter with thee now?
Emilia: O, my good lord, yonder's foul murders done!
Othello: What, now?   110
Emilia: But now, my lord.
Othello: It is the very error° of the moon;
    She comes more nearer earth than she was wont,
    And makes men mad.
Emilia: Cassio, my lord, hath killed a young Venetian   115
    Called Roderigo.
Othello: Roderigo killed?
    And Cassio killed?
Emilia: No, Cassio is not killed.
Othello: Not Cassio killed? Then murder's out of tune,
    And sweet revenge grows harsh.
Desdemona: O, falsely, falsely murdered!   120
Emilia: O Lord, what cry is that?
Othello: That? What?
Emilia: Out° and alas, that was my lady's voice.

    [She opens the bed-curtains.]

    Help, help, ho, help! O lady, speak again!
    Sweet Desdemona! O sweet mistress, speak!   125
Desdemona: A guiltless death I die.
Emilia: O, who hath done this deed?
Desdemona: Nobody; I myself. Farewell.
    Commend me to my kind lord. O, farewell!   *[She dies.]*
Othello: Why, how should she be murdered?
Emilia: Alas, who knows?   130
Othello: You heard her say herself it was not I.
Emilia: She said so. I must needs report the truth.
Othello: She's like a liar gone to burning hell!
    'Twas I that killed her.
Emilia: O, the more angel she,
    And you the blacker devil!   135
Othello: She turned to folly,° and she was a whore.
Emilia: Thou dost belie° her, and thou art a devil.
Othello: She was false as water.
Emilia: Thou art rash as fire to say
    That she was false. O, she was heavenly true!   140
Othello: Cassio did top her. Ask thy husband else.°

---

112 *error* aberration, irregularity   123 *Out* (A cry of dismay, intensifying *alas*.)   136 *folly* i.e., wantonness, fleshly sin   137 *belie* slander   141 *else* i.e., if you don't believe me

Emilia declares Desdemona's innocence (V, ii, 134–164).

O, I were damned beneath all depth in hell
But that I did proceed upon just grounds
To this extremity. Thy husband knew it all.
Emilia: My husband?   145
Othello: Thy husband.
Emilia: That she was false to wedlock?
Othello: Ay, with Cassio. Nay, had she been true,
  If heaven would make me such another world
  Of one entire and perfect chrysolite,°   150
  I'd not have sold her for it.
Emilia: My husband?
Othello: Ay, 'twas he that told me on her first.
  An honest man he is, and hates the slime
  That sticks on filthy deeds.   155
Emilia: My husband?
Othello: What needs this iterance,° woman? I say thy husband.
Emilia: O mistress, villainy hath made mocks with° love!
  My husband say that she was false?
Othello: He, woman;

150 *chrysolite* precious topaz   157 *iterance* iteration, repetition   158 *made mocks with* derided, made sport of

I say thy husband. Dost understand the word? 160
My friend, thy husband, honest, honest Iago.
Emilia: If he say so, may his pernicious soul
Rot half a grain a day! He lies to th' heart.
She was too fond of her most filthy bargain.
Othello: Ha? [*He draws.*] 165
Emilia: Do thy worst!
This deed of thine is no more worthy heaven
Than thou wast worthy her.
Othello: Peace, you were best.°
Emilia: Thou hast not half that power to do me harm
As I have to be hurt.° O gull!° O dolt! 170
As ignorant as dirt! Thou hast done a deed—
I care not for thy sword; I'll make thee known,
Though I lost twenty lives.—Help! Help, ho, help!
The Moor hath killed my mistress! Murder, murder!

Enter Montano, Gratiano, and Iago.

Montano: What is the matter? How now, General? 175
Emilia: O, are you come, Iago? You have done well,
That men must lay their murders on your neck.
Gratiano: What is the matter?
Emilia [to Iago]: Disprove this villain, if thou be'st a man.
He says thou toldst him that his wife was false. 180
I know thou didst not; thou'rt not such a villain.
Speak, for my heart is full.
Iago: I told him what I thought, and told no more
Than what he found himself was apt° and true.
Emilia: But did you ever tell him she was false? 185
Iago: I did.
Emilia: You told a lie, an odious, damnèd lie!
Upon my soul, a lie, a wicked lie.
She false with Cassio? Did you say with Cassio?
Iago: With Cassio, mistress. Go to, charm° your tongue. 190
Emilia: I will not charm my tongue; I am bound to speak.
My mistress here lies murdered in her bed—
All: O heavens forfend!
Emilia: And your reports have set the murder on.
Othello: Nay, stare not, masters. It is true indeed. 195
Gratiano: 'Tis a strange truth.
Montano: O monstrous act!
Emilia: Villainy, villainy, villainy!
I think upon 't—I think I smell 't! O villainy!
I thought so then°—I'll kill myself for grief—
O villainy, villainy! 200

---

168 *you were best* it would be best for you   170 *to be hurt* i.e., to endure hurt.   *gull* dupe   184 *apt* plausible
190 *charm* keep silent (as though by a magic spell)   199 *then* (Perhaps at III, iii, 331–332 and IV, ii,
137–154.)

Iago: What, are you mad? I charge you, get you home.

Emilia: Good gentlemen, let me have leave to speak.
'Tis proper I obey him, but not now.
Perchance, Iago, I will ne'er go home.

Othello: O! O! O!   [*Othello falls on the bed.°*]

Emilia: Nay, lay thee down and roar,   205
For thou hast killed the sweetest innocent
That e'er did lift up eye.°

Othello [*rising*]:   O, she was foul!
I scarce did know you, uncle. There lies your niece,
Whose breath indeed these hands have newly stopped.
I know this act shows° horrible and grim.   210

Gratiano: Poor Desdemon! I am glad thy father's dead.
Thy match was mortal to him, and pure grief
Shore his old thread° in twain. Did he live now,
This sight would make him do a desperate turn,°
Yea, curse his better angel from his side,   215
And fall to reprobance.°

Othello: 'Tis pitiful. But yet Iago knows
That she with Cassio hath the act of shame
A thousand times committed. Cassio confessed it;
And she did gratify° his amorous works   220
With that recognizance° and pledge of love
Which I first gave her. I saw it in his hand;
It was a handkerchief, an antique token
My father gave my mother.

Emilia: O God! O heavenly God!   225

Iago: Zounds, hold your peace.

Emilia: 'Twill out, 'twill out! I peace?
No, I will speak as liberal as the north.°
Let heaven and men and devils, let them all,
All, all, cry shame against me, yet I'll speak.

Iago: Be wise, and get you home.

Emilia: I will not.

[*Iago threatens Emilia.*]

Gratiano: Fie!   230
Your sword upon a woman?

Emilia: O thou dull Moor! That handkerchief thou speak'st of
I found by fortune and did give my husband;
For often, with a solemn earnestness,
More than indeed belonged° to such a trifle,   235
He begged of me to steal 't.

---

205 s.d. *Othello . . . bed* (This direction is from the Quarto, as also *He kisses her* at line 19 and *She dies* at line 129.)   207 *lift up eye* i.e., lift her eyes to heaven   210 *shows* looks   213 *Shore . . . thread* sheared the thread of his old age (as Atropos, one of the three Fates, was thought to do)   214 *turn* deed   216 *reprobance* damnation, i.e., suicide   220 *gratify* reward   221 *recognizance* token   227 *liberal as the north* freely as the north wind (blows)   235 *belonged* was appropriate

Iago: Villainous whore!

Emilia: She give it Cassio? No, alas! I found it,
    And I did give 't my husband.

Iago: Filth, thou liest!

Emilia: By heaven, I do not, I do not, gentlemen.
    O murderous coxcomb!° What should such a fool   240
    Do with so good a wife?

Othello: Are there no stones° in heaven
    But what serves for the thunder?—Precious° villain!

[*He runs at Iago; Montano disarms Othello. Iago, from behind, stabs Emilia.*°]

Gratiano: The woman falls! Sure he hath killed his wife.

Emilia: Ay, ay. O, lay me by my mistress' side.   245

    Exit [*Iago.*]

Gratiano: He's gone, but his wife's killed.

Montano: 'Tis a notorious villain. Take you this weapon,
    Which I have here recovered from the Moor.
    Come, guard the door without. Let him not pass,
    But kill him rather. I'll after that same villain,   250
    For 'tis a damnèd slave.

    Exit [*with all but Othello and Emilia, who has been laid by Desdemona's side*].

Othello: I am not valiant neither,
    But every puny whipster° gets my sword.
    But why should honor° outlive honesty?°
    Let it go all.

Emilia: What did thy song bode, lady?   255
    Hark, canst thou hear me? I will play the swan,
    And die in music. [*She sings.*] "Willow, willow, willow."
    Moor, she was chaste. She loved thee, cruel Moor.
    So come my soul to bliss as I speak true.
    So speaking as I think, alas, I die.   [*She dies.*] 260

Othello: I have another weapon in this chamber;
    It was a sword of Spain, the ice-brook's temper°—
    O, here it is. [*He finds a sword.*] Uncle, I must come forth.

Gratiano [*within*]: If thou attempt it, it will cost thee dear.
    Thou hast no weapon, and perforce must suffer.   265

Othello: Look in upon me then and speak with me,
    Or, naked° as I am, I will assault thee.

    [*Enter Gratiano.*]

---

240 *coxcomb* fool. (Addressed to Othello.)   242 *stones* bolts, such as those used for thunderbolts   243 *Precious* i.e., arrant, utter. s.d. *He . . . Emilia* (The Quarto text reads, "The Moor runs at Iago. Iago kills his wife." The Quarto also specifies the exit of Iago at line 245 and the death of Emilia at line 260.)   253 *whipster* contemptible fellow (one who is always ready to whip out his sword)   254 *honor* i.e., the bravery for which one enjoys a soldier's reputation. *honesty* true integrity   262 *the ice-brook's temper* tempered in ice-cold water   267 *naked* unarmed

Gratiano: What is the matter?

Othello: Behold, I have a weapon;
  A better never did itself sustain
  Upon a soldier's thigh. I have seen the day   270
  That, with this little arm and this good sword,
  I have made my way through more impediments
  Than twenty times your stop.° But O, vain boast!
  Who can control his fate? 'Tis not so now.
  Be not afraid, though you do see me weaponed;   275
  Here is my journey's end, here is my butt°
  And very seamark° of my utmost sail.

  [*Gratiano steps back.*]

  Do you go back dismayed? 'Tis a lost° fear;
  Man but a rush° against Othello's breast
  And he retires. Where should Othello go?   280

  [*He turns to Desdemona.*]

  Now, how dost thou look now? O ill-starred wench!
  Pale as thy smock! When we shall meet at compt,°
  This look of thine will hurl my soul from heaven,
  And fiends will snatch at it. Cold, cold, my girl?
  Even like thy chastity. O cursèd, cursèd slave!°   285
  Whip me, ye devils,
  From the possession of this heavenly sight!
  Blow me about in winds! Roast me in sulfur!
  Wash me in steep-down gulfs of liquid fire!
  O Desdemon! Dead, Desdemon! Dead! O! O!   290

  Enter Lodovico, Cassio [*carried in a litter°*], *Montano, and Iago* [*prisoner*], *with officers.*

Lodovico: Where is this rash and most unfortunate man?

Othello: That's he that was Othello. Here I am.

Lodovico: Where is that viper? Bring the villain forth.

  [*Iago is led forward.*]

Othello: I look down towards his feet;° but that's a fable.
  If that thou be'st a devil, I cannot kill thee.   295

  [*He wounds Iago.*]

Lodovico: Wrench his sword from him.   [*Othello is disarmed.*]

Iago: I bleed, sir, but not killed.

---

273 *stop* power (to stop)   276 *butt* goal, limit. (An archery term.)   277 *seamark* beacon (marking his destination or limit)   278 *lost* wasted, unneeded   279 *Man . . . rush* wield no more than a reed   282 *compt* account, judgment day   285 *slave* i.e., Othello himself   290 s.d. *in a litter* (The Quarto specifies that Cassio is "in a chair.")   294 *towards his feet* i.e., to see if they are cloven, as the devil's are fabled to be

Lodovico confronts the prisoner Iago; Desdemona and Emilia lie dead in the background (V, ii, 296–314).

Othello: I am not sorry neither. I'd have thee live,
    For in my sense° 'tis happiness to die.
Lodovico: O thou Othello, that was once so good,
    Fall'n in the practice° of a cursèd slave,°   300
    What shall be said to thee?
Othello: Why, anything.
    An honorable murderer, if you will,
    For naught I did in hate, but all in honor.
Lodovico: This wretch hath part confessed his villainy.
    Did you and he consent° in Cassio's death?   305
Othello: Ay.
Cassio: Dear General, I never gave you cause.
Othello: I do believe it, and I ask your pardon.
    Will you, I pray, demand that demi-devil
    Why he hath thus ensnared my soul and body?   310
Iago: Demand me nothing. What you know, you know.
    From this time forth I never will speak word.
Lodovico: What, not to pray?
Gratiano: Torments° will ope your lips.

298 *in my sense* to one who feels as I do   300 *in the practice* through the plotting, into the snare.
slave villain   305 *consent* agree   314 *Torments* torture

Othello: Well, thou dost best.   315
Lodovico: Sir, you shall understand what hath befall'n,
    Which, as I think, you know not. Here is a letter
    Found in the pocket of the slain Roderigo;
    And here another. [*He produces letters.*] The one of them imports
    The death of Cassio, to be undertook   320
    By Roderigo.
Othello: O villain!
Cassio: Most heathenish and most gross!°
Lodovico [*showing another paper*]: Now here's another discontented° paper
    Found in his pocket too. And this, it seems,
    Roderigo meant t' have sent this damnèd villain;   325
    But that belike° Iago in the interim
    Came in and satisfied him.°
Othello: O thou pernicious caitiff!—
    How came you, Cassio, by that handkerchief
    That was my wife's?
Cassio: I found it in my chamber;   330
    And he himself confessed but even now
    That there he dropped it for a special purpose
    Which wrought to his desire.°
Othello: O fool, fool, fool!
Cassio: There is besides in Roderigo's letter
    How he upbraids Iago, that he made him   335
    Brave° me upon the watch, whereon it came°
    That I was cast;° and even but now he spake,
    After long seeming dead, Iago hurt him,
    Iago set him on.
Lodovico [*to Othello*]: You must forsake this room and go with us.   340
    Your power and your command is taken off,°
    And Cassio rules in Cyprus. For this slave,
    If there be any cunning cruelty
    That can torment him much and hold him long,°
    It shall be his. You shall close prisoner rest°   345
    Till that the nature of your fault be known
    To the Venetian state.—Come, bring away.
Othello: Soft you;° a word or two before you go.
    I have done the state some service, and they know 't.
    No more of that. I pray you, in your letters,   350
    When you shall these unlucky° deeds relate,
    Speak of me as I am; nothing extenuate,
    Nor set down aught in malice. Then must you speak
    Of one that loved not wisely but too well;
    Of one not easily jealous but, being wrought,°   355

322 *gross* monstrous 323 *discontented* full of discontent 326 *belike* most likely 327 *Came . . . him* interposed and gave him satisfactory explanation 333 *wrought . . . desire* worked out as he wished, fitted in with his plan 336 *Brave* defy. *whereon it came* whereof it came about 337 *cast* dismissed 341 *taken off* taken away 344 *hold him long* keep him alive a long time (during his torture) 345 *rest* remain 348 *Soft you* one moment 351 *unlucky* unfortunate 355 *wrought* worked upon, worked into a frenzy

Perplexed° in the extreme; of one whose hand,
Like the base Indian,° threw a pearl away
Richer than all his tribe; of one whose subdued° eyes,
Albeit unusèd to the melting mood,
Drop tears as fast as the Arabian trees   360
Their medicinable gum.° Set you down this;
And say besides that in Aleppo once,
Where a malignant and a turbaned Turk
Beat a Venetian and traduced the state,
I took by th' throat the circumcisèd dog   365
And smote him, thus.   [*He stabs himself.°*]
Lodovico: O bloody period!°
Gratiano: All that is spoke is marred.
Othello: I kissed thee ere I killed thee. No way but this,
   Killing myself, to die upon a kiss.   370

   [*He kisses Desdemona and dies.*]

Cassio: This did I fear, but thought he had no weapon;
   For he was great of heart.
Lodovico [*to Iago*]:   O Spartan dog,°
   More fell° than anguish, hunger, or the sea!
   Look on the tragic loading of this bed.
   This is thy work. The object poisons sight;   375
   Let it be hid.° Gratiano, keep° the house,

   [*The bed curtains are drawn*]

   And seize upon° the fortunes of the Moor,
   For they succeed on° you. [*To Cassio.*] To you, Lord Governor,
   Remains the censure° of this hellish villain,
   The time, the place, the torture. O, enforce it!   380
   Myself will straight aboard, and to the state
   This heavy act with heavy heart relate.   *Exeunt.*

Questions

ACT I

1. What is Othello's position in society? How is he regarded by those who know him? By his own words, when we first meet him in Scene ii, what traits of character does he manifest?
2. How do you account for Brabantio's dismay on learning of his daughter's marriage, despite the fact that Desdemona has married a man so generally honored and admired?
3. What is Iago's view of human nature? In his fondness for likening men to animals (as in I, i, 49–50; I, i, 90–91; and I, iii, 378–379), what does he tell us about himself?
4. What reasons does Iago give for his hatred of Othello?

356 *Perplexed* distraught 357 *Indian* (This reading from the Quarto pictures an ignorant savage who cannot recognize the value of a precious jewel. The Folio reading, *Iudean* or *Judean*, i.e., infidel or disbeliever, may refer to Herod, who slew Miriamne in a fit of jealousy, or to Judas Iscariot, the betrayer of Christ.) 358 *subdued* i.e., overcome by grief 361 *gum* i.e., myrrh 366 s.d. *He stabs himself* (This direction is in the Quarto text.) 367 *period* termination, conclusion 372 *Spartan dog* (Spartan dogs were noted for their savagery and silence.) 373 *fell* cruel 376 *Let it be hid* i.e., draw the bed curtains. (No stage direction specifies that the dead are to be carried offstage at the end of the play.) *keep* remain in 377 *seize upon* take legal possession of 378 *succeed on* pass as though by inheritance to 379 *censure* sentencing

5. In Othello's defense before the senators (Scene iii), how does he explain Desdemona's gradual falling in love with him?
6. Is Brabantio's warning to Othello (I, iii, 293–294) an accurate or an inaccurate prophecy?
7. By what strategy does Iago enlist Roderigo in his plot against the Moor? In what lines do we learn Iago's true feelings toward Roderigo?

ACT II

1. What do the Cypriots think of Othello? Do their words (in Scene i) make him seem to us a lesser man or a larger one?
2. What cruelty does Iago display toward Emilia? How well founded is his distrust of his wife's fidelity?
3. In II, iii, 221, Othello speaks of Iago's "honesty and love." How do you account for Othello's being so totally deceived?
4. For what major events does the merrymaking (proclaimed in Scene ii) give opportunity?

ACT III

1. Trace the steps by which Iago rouses Othello to suspicion. Is there anything in Othello's character or circumstances that renders him particularly susceptible to Iago's wiles?
2. In III, iv, 49–98, Emilia knows of Desdemona's distress over the lost handkerchief. At this moment, how do you explain her failure to relieve Desdemona's mind? Is Emilia aware of her husband's villainy?

ACT IV

1. In this act, what circumstantial evidence is added to Othello's case against Desdemona?
2. How plausible do you find Bianca's flinging the handkerchief at Cassio just when Othello is looking on? How important is the handkerchief in this play? What does it represent? What suggestions or hints do you find in it?
3. What prevents Othello from being moved by Desdemona's appeal (IV, ii, 33–92)?
4. When Roderigo grows impatient with Iago (IV, ii, 181–201), how does Iago make use of his fellow plotter's discontent?
5. What does the conversation between Emilia and Desdemona (Scene iii) tell us about the nature of each?
6. In this act, what scenes (or speeches) contain memorable dramatic irony?

ACT V

1. Summarize the events that lead to Iago's unmasking.
2. How does Othello's mistaken belief that Cassio is slain (V, i, 27–34) affect the outcome of the play?
3. What is Iago's motive in stabbing Roderigo?
4. In your interpretation of the play, exactly what impels Othello to kill Desdemona? Jealousy? Desire for revenge? Excess idealism? A wish to be a public avenger who punishes, "else she'll betray more men"?
5. What do you understand by Othello's calling himself "one that loved not wisely but too well" (V, ii, 354)?
6. In your view, does Othello's long speech in V, ii, 348–366 succeed in restoring his original dignity and nobility? Do you agree with Cassio (V, ii, 372) that Othello was "great of heart"?

General Questions

1. What motivates Iago to carry out his schemes? Do you find him a devil incarnate, a madman, or a rational human being?

2. Whom besides Othello does Iago deceive? What is Desdemona's opinion of him? Emilia's? Cassio's (before Iago is found out)? To what do you attribute Iago's success as a deceiver?

3. How essential to the play is the fact that Othello is a black man, a Moor, and not a native of Venice?

4. In the introduction to his edition of the play in *The Complete Signet Classic Shakespeare*, Alvin Kernan remarks:

    > *Othello* is probably the most neatly, the most formally constructed of Shakespeare's plays. Every character is, for example, balanced by another similar or contrasting character. Desdemona is balanced by her opposite, Iago; love and concern for others at one end of the scale, hatred and concern for self at the other.

    Besides Desdemona and Iago, what other pairs of characters strike balances?

5. Consider any passage of the play in which there is a shift from verse to prose, or from prose to verse. What is the effect of this shift?

6. Indicate a passage that you consider memorable for its poetry. Does the passage seem introduced for its own sake? Does it in any way advance the action of the play, express theme, or demonstrate character?

7. Does the play contain any *tragic recognition*—as discussed on pages 1162–1163 a moment of terrible enlightenment, a "realization of the unthinkable"?

8. Does the downfall of Othello proceed from any flaw in his nature, or is his downfall entirely the work of Iago?

THE BACKGROUND OF *HAMLET*

William Shakespeare wrote *Hamlet* around 1600. The Hamlet story first appears in the *Danish History* of the twelfth-century writer Saxo Grammaticus, but the tale is probably even older than that. Saxo's version recounts the murder of the king of Denmark by his wicked brother and the brother's marriage to the widowed queen; then Prince Amlethus, the dead king's son, feigns madness, escapes a plot on his life, and eventually gains revenge. There was an earlier English play, also called *Hamlet*, based on this tale. Written in the 1580s, probably by Thomas Kyd, it is now lost. It is believed that Shakespeare based his own play on it. Although he borrowed his story (as he did the basic plot of *Othello*), Shakespeare made it entirely his own and populated it with some of the most memorable characters in English drama. It is usually assumed that *Hamlet* was the earliest of Shakespeare's four great mature tragedies (being written just before *Othello*, *King Lear*, and *Macbeth*). If this speculative dating is true, *Hamlet* represented something extraordinarily innovative in world drama, especially in respect to the title character—a deeply intelligent and reflective man compelled by justice and filial duty to avenge his father's murder but simultaneously riddled with self-doubt and moral conscience. In the brooding figure of Hamlet, Shakespeare presented both the prince's inner and exterior life with startling immediacy and mysterious depth. For centuries critics have considered *Hamlet* Shakespeare's most philosophical play, yet it does not lack action. *Hamlet* contains a vengeful ghost, two sorts of madness (one tragically genuine, the other comically feigned), a suicide, sword fights, poisonings, incest, and multiple murders. The play provides both the compelling entertainment beloved by Elizabethan audiences and a tragic meditation on human existence that has haunted readers of every subsequent age.

Kenneth Branagh as Hamlet with Kate Winslet as Ophelia.

PICTURING *Hamlet*

▲ The king's ghost, *page 1357*

▲ Hamlet returns home, *page 1363*

▼ Hamlet considers killing
  Claudius, *page 1418*

▲ Hamlet and the gravedigger,
  page 1446

▲ "Alas, poor Yorick,"
  page 1449

▼ Hamlet with his father's ghost, *page 1375*

▲ Ophelia and Hamlet, *page 1402*

▲ *The Murder of Gonzago, page 1411*

▲ Queen Gertrude mourns Ophelia, *page 1451*

▲ Swordplay turns deadly, *page 1461*

Hamlet, Prince of Denmark

about 1600

Edited by David Bevington

[DRAMATIS PERSONAE

Ghost of Hamlet, the former King of Denmark
Claudius, King of Denmark, the former King's brother
Gertrude, Queen of Denmark, widow of the former King and now wife of Claudius
Hamlet, Prince of Denmark, son of the late King and of Gertrude
Polonius, councillor to the King
Laertes, his son
Ophelia, his daughter
Reynaldo, his servant
Horatio, Hamlet's friend and fellow student

Voltimand,
Cornelius,
Rosencrantz,
Guildenstern, } members of the Danish court
Osric,
A Gentleman,
A Lord,

Bernardo,
Francisco, } officers and soldiers on watch
Marcellus,

Fortinbras, Prince of Norway
Captain in his army
Three or Four Players, taking the roles of *Prologue, Player King, Player Queen, and Lucianus*
Two Messengers
First Sailor
Two Clowns, a gravedigger and his companion
Priest
First Ambassador from England
Lords, Soldiers, Attendants, Guards, other Players, Followers of Laertes, other Sailors,
    another Ambassador or Ambassadors from England

SCENE: *Denmark*]

ACT I

SCENE I [ELSINORE CASTLE. A GUARD PLATFORM.]

   Enter Bernardo and Francisco, two sentinels, [meeting].

NOTE ON THE TEXT: This text of *Hamlet* is based primarily on the Second Quarto of 1604–1605. For the reader's convenience, some material has been added by the editor, David Bevington (some indications of scenes and some stage directions). Such additions are enclosed in brackets. Mr. Bevington's text and notes were prepared for his book, *The Complete Works of Shakespeare*, Updated 4th ed. (New York: Longman, 1997).

PRODUCTION PHOTOS: The photos included are from the 2003 production of *Hamlet* by the Alley Theatre of Houston, with Ty Mayberry (Hamlet), Elizabeth Heflin (Gertrude), James Black (Claudius, ghost of Hamlet's father), Philip Lehl (Horatio), Daniel Magill (Laertes), John Tyson (Polonius), Jennifer Cherry (Ophelia), and Charles Krohn (gravedigger).

Bernardo: Who's there?

Francisco: Nay, answer me.° Stand and unfold yourself.°

Bernardo: Long live the King!

Francisco: Bernardo?

Bernardo: He.   5

Francisco: You come most carefully upon your hour.

Bernardo: 'Tis now struck twelve. Get thee to bed, Francisco.

Francisco: For this relief much thanks. 'Tis bitter cold,
    And I am sick at heart.

Bernardo: Have you had quiet guard?   10

Francisco: Not a mouse stirring.

Bernardo: Well, good night.
    If you do meet Horatio and Marcellus,
    The rivals° of my watch, bid them make haste.

    Enter Horatio and Marcellus.

Francisco: I think I hear them.—Stand, ho! Who is there?   15

Horatio: Friends to this ground.°

Marcellus: And liegemen to the Dane.°

Francisco: Give° you good night.

Marcellus: O, farewell, honest soldier. Who hath relieved you?

Francisco: Bernardo hath my place. Give you good night.   20

                                                                    Exit Francisco.

Marcellus: Holla! Bernardo!

Bernardo: Say, what, is Horatio there?

Horatio: A piece of him.

Bernardo: Welcome, Horatio. Welcome, good Marcellus.

Horatio: What, has this thing appeared again tonight?   25

Bernardo: I have seen nothing.

Marcellus: Horatio says 'tis but our fantasy,°
    And will not let belief take hold of him
    Touching this dreaded sight twice seen of us.
    Therefore I have entreated him along°   30
    With us to watch° the minutes of this night,
    That if again this apparition come
    He may approve° our eyes and speak to it.

Horatio: Tush, tush, 'twill not appear.

Bernardo: Sit down awhile,
    And let us once again assail your ears,   35
    That are so fortified against our story,
    What° we have two nights seen.

Horatio: Well, sit we down,
    And let us hear Bernardo speak of this.

Bernardo: Last night of all,°

---

2 *me* (Francisco emphasizes that *he* is the sentry currently on watch.)   *unfold yourself* reveal your identity
14 *rivals* partners   16 *ground* country, land   17 *liegemen to the Dane* men sworn to serve the Danish king
18 *Give* i.e., may God give   27 *fantasy* imagination   30 *along* to come along   31 *watch* keep watch during
ing   33 *approve* corroborate   37 *What* with what   39 *Last . . . all* i.e., this very last night (Emphatic.)

When yond same star that's westward from the pole° 40
Had made his° course t' illume° that part of heaven
Where now it burns, Marcellus and myself,
The bell then beating one—

Enter Ghost.

Marcellus: Peace, break thee off! Look where it comes again!
Bernardo: In the same figure like the King that's dead. 45
Marcellus: Thou art a scholar.° Speak to it, Horatio.
Bernardo: Looks 'a° not like the King? Mark it, Horatio.
Horatio: Most like. It harrows me with fear and wonder.
Bernardo: It would be spoke to.°
Marcellus: Speak to it, Horatio.
Horatio: What are thou that usurp'st° this time of night, 50
    Together with that fair and warlike form
    In which the majesty of buried Denmark°
    Did sometime° march? By heaven, I charge thee, speak!
Marcellus: It is offended.
Bernardo: See, it stalks away.
Horatio: Stay! Speak, speak! I charge thee, speak!   *Exit Ghost.* 55
Marcellus: 'Tis gone and will not answer.
Bernardo: How now, Horatio? You tremble and look pale.
    Is not this something more than fantasy?
    What think you on 't?°
Horatio: Before my God, I might not this believe 60
    Without the sensible° and true avouch°
    Of mine own eyes.
Marcellus: Is it not like the King?
Horatio: As thou art to thyself.
    Such was the very armor he had on
    When he the ambitious Norway° combated. 65
    So frowned he once when, in an angry parle,°
    He smote the sledded° Polacks° on the ice.
    'Tis strange.
Marcellus: Thus twice before, and jump° at this dead hour,
    With martial stalk° hath he gone by our watch. 70
Horatio: In what particular thought to work° I know not,
    But in the gross and scope° of mine opinion
    This bodes some strange eruption to our state.
Marcellus: Good now,° sit down, and tell me, he that knows,
    Why this same strict and most observant watch 75

---

40 *pole* polestar, north star   41 *his* its.   *illume* illuminate   46 *scholar* one learned enough to know how to
question a ghost properly   47 *'a* he   49 *It . . . to* (It was commonly believed that a ghost could not speak
until spoken to.)   50 *usurp'st* wrongfully takes over   52 *buried Denmark* the buried King of Denmark
53 *sometime* formerly   59 *on 't* of it   61 *sensible* confirmed by the senses.   *avouch* warrant, evidence
65 *Norway* King of Norway   66 *parle* parley   67 *sledded* traveling on sleds.   *Polacks* Poles   69 *jump*
exactly   70 *stalk* stride   71 *to work* i.e., to collect my thoughts and try to understand this   72 *gross and*
scope general drift   74 *Good now* (An expression denoting entreaty or expostulation.)

The ghost of the king appears to the watch.

So nightly toils° the subject° of the land,
And why such daily cast° of brazen cannon
And foreign mart° for implements of war,
Why such impress° of shipwrights, whose sore task
Does not divide the Sunday from the week.   80
What might be toward,° that this sweaty haste
Doth make the night joint-laborer with the day?
Who is 't that can inform me?
Horatio: That can I;
    At least, the whisper goes so. Our last king,
    Whose image even but now appeared to us,   85

76 *toils* causes to toil. *subject* subjects   77 *cast* casting   78 *mart* buying and selling   79 *impress*
impressment, conscription   81 *toward* in preparation

Was, as you know, by Fortinbras of Norway,
Thereto° pricked on° by a most emulate° pride,
Dared to the combat; in which our valiant Hamlet—
For so this side of our known world° esteemèd him—
Did slay this Fortinbras; who by a sealed° compact   90
Well ratified by law and heraldry
Did forfeit, with his life, all those his lands
Which he stood seized° of, to the conqueror;
Against the° which a moiety competent°
Was gagèd° by our king, which had returned°   95
To the inheritance° of Fortinbras
Had he been vanquisher, as, by the same cov'nant°
And carriage of the article designed,°
His fell to Hamlet. Now, sir, young Fortinbras,
Of unimprovèd mettle° hot and full,   100
Hath in the skirts° of Norway here and there
Sharked up° a list° of lawless resolutes°
For food and diet° to some enterprise
That hath a stomach° in 't, which is no other—
As it doth well appear unto our state—   105
But to recover of us, by strong hand
And terms compulsatory, those foresaid lands
So by his father lost. And this, I take it,
Is the main motive of our preparations,
The source of this our watch, and the chief head°   110
Of this posthaste and rummage° in the land.
Bernardo: I think it be no other but e'en so.
       Well may it sort° that this portentous figure
       Comes armèd through our watch so like the King
       That was and is the question° of these wars.   115
Horatio: A mote° it is to trouble the mind's eye.
       In the most high and palmy° state of Rome,
       A little ere the mightiest Julius fell,
       The graves stood tenantless, and the sheeted° dead
       Did squeak and gibber in the Roman streets;   120
       As° stars with trains° of fire and dews of blood,
       Disasters° in the sun; and the moist star°

87 *Thereto . . . pride* (Refers to old Fortinbras, not the Danish King.) *pricked on* incited. *emulate* emulous, ambitious 89 *this . . . world* i.e., all Europe, the Western world 90 *sealed* certified, confirmed 93 *seized* possessed 94 *Against the* in return for. *moiety competent* corresponding portion 95 *gagèd* engaged, pledged. *had returned* would have passed 96 *inheritance* possession 97 *cov'nant* i.e., the *sealed compact* of line 90 98 *carriage . . . designed* carrying out of the article or clause drawn up to cover the point 100 *unimprovèd mettle* untried, undisciplined spirits 101 *skirts* outlying regions, outskirts 102 *Sharked up* gathered up, as a shark takes fish. *list* i.e., troop. *resolutes* desperadoes 103 *For food and diet* i.e., they are to serve as *food*, or "means," to some *enterprise*; also they serve in return for the rations they get 104 *stomach* (1) a spirit of daring (2) an appetite that is fed by the *lawless resolutes* 110 *head* source 111 *rummage* bustle, commotion 113 *sort* suit 115 *question* focus of contention 116 *mote* speck of dust 117 *palmy* flourishing 119 *sheeted* shrouded 121 *As* (This abrupt transition suggests that matter is possibly omitted between lines 120 and 121.) *trains* trails 122 *Disasters* unfavorable signs or aspects. *moist star* i.e., moon, governing tides

Upon whose influence Neptune's° empire stands°
Was sick almost to doomsday° with eclipse.
And even the like precurse° of feared events,   125
As harbingers° preceding still° the fates
And prologue to the omen° coming on,
Have heaven and earth together demonstrated
Unto our climatures° and countrymen.

Enter Ghost.

But soft,° behold! Lo, where it comes again!   130
I'll cross° it, though it blast° me. (*It spreads his° arms.*) Stay, illusion!
If thou hast any sound or use of voice,
Speak to me!
If there be any good thing to be done
That may to thee do ease and grace to me,   135
Speak to me!
If thou art privy to° thy country's fate,
Which, happily,° foreknowing may avoid,
O, speak!
Or if thou hast uphoarded in thy life   140
Extorted treasure in the womb of earth,
For which, they say, you spirits oft walk in death,
Speak of it! (*The cock crows.*) Stay and speak!—Stop it, Marcellus.
Marcellus: Shall I strike at it with my partisan?°
Horatio: Do, if it will not stand.   [*They strike at it.*] 145
Bernardo: 'Tis here!
Horatio: 'Tis here!   [*Exit Ghost.*]
Marcellus: 'Tis gone.
We do it wrong, being so majestical,
To offer it the show of violence,   150
For it is as the air invulnerable,
And our vain blows malicious mockery.
Bernardo: It was about to speak when the cock crew.
Horatio: And then it started like a guilty thing
Upon a fearful summons. I have heard   155
The cock, that is the trumpet° to the morn,
Doth with his lofty and shrill-sounding throat
Awake the god of day, and at his warning,
Whether in sea or fire, in earth or air,
Th' extravagant and erring° spirit hies°   160
To his confine; and of the truth herein
This present object made probation.°

---

123 *Neptune* god of the sea.   *stands* depends   124 *sick . . . doomsday* (See Matthew 24:29 and Revelation
6:12.)   125 *precurse* heralding, foreshadowing   126 *harbingers* forerunners.   *still* continually   127 *omen*
calamitous event   129 *climatures* regions   130 *soft* i.e., enough, break off   131 *cross* stand in its path,
confront.   *blast* wither, strike with a curse.   s.d. *his* its   137 *privy to* in on the secret of   138 *happily*
haply, perchance   144 *partisan* long-handled spear   156 *trumpet* trumpeter   160 *extravagant and erring*
wandering beyond bounds. (The words have similar meaning.)   *hies* hastens   162 *probation* proof

Marcellus: It faded on the crowing of the cock.
  Some say that ever 'gainst° that season comes
  Wherein our Savior's birth is celebrated,   165
  This bird of dawning singeth all night long,
  And then, they say, no spirit dare stir abroad;
  The nights are wholesome, then no planets strike,°
  No fairy takes,° nor witch hath power to charm,
  So hallowed and so gracious° is that time.   170
Horatio: So have I heard and do in part believe it.
  But, look, the morn in russet mantle clad
  Walks o'er the dew of yon high eastward hill.
  Break we our watch up, and by my advice
  Let us impart what we have seen tonight   175
  Unto young Hamlet; for upon my life,
  This spirit, dumb to us, will speak to him.
  Do you consent we shall acquaint him with it,
  As needful in our loves, fitting our duty?
Marcellus: Let's do 't, I pray, and I this morning know   180
  Where we shall find him most conveniently.   *Exeunt.*

SCENE II [THE CASTLE.]

*Flourish. Enter Claudius, King of Denmark, Gertrude the Queen, [the] Council, as°
Polonius and his son Laertes, Hamlet, cum aliis° [including Voltimand and Cornelius].*

King: Though yet of Hamlet our° dear brother's death
  The memory be green, and that it us befitted
  To bear our hearts in grief and our whole kingdom
  To be contracted in one brow of woe,
  Yet so far hath discretion fought with nature   5
  That we with wisest sorrow think on him
  Together with remembrance of ourselves.
  Therefore our sometime° sister, now our queen,
  Th' imperial jointress° to this warlike state,
  Have we, as 'twere with a defeated joy—   10
  With an auspicious and a dropping eye,°
  With mirth in funeral and with dirge in marriage,
  In equal scale weighing delight and dole°—
  Taken to wife. Nor have we herein barred
  Your better wisdoms, which have freely gone   15
  With this affair along. For all, our thanks.
  Now follows that you know° young Fortinbras,
  Holding a weak supposal° of our worth,
  Or thinking by our late dear brother's death

164 *'gainst* just before   168 *strike* destroy by evil influence   169 *takes* bewitches   170 *gracious* full of grace
s.d. *as* i.e., such as, including.   *cum aliis* with others   1 *our* my. (The royal "we"; also in the following
lines.)   8 *sometime* former   9 *jointress* woman possessing property with her husband   11 *With . . . eye*
with one eye smiling and the other weeping   13 *dole* grief   17 *that you know* what you know already, that;
or, that you be informed as follows   18 *weak supposal* low estimate

Our state to be disjoint and out of frame,   20
Co-leaguèd with° this dream of his advantage,°
He hath not failed to pester us with message
Importing° the surrender of those lands
Lost by his father, with all bonds° of law,
To our most valiant brother. So much for him.   25
Now for ourself and for this time of meeting.
Thus much the business is: we have here writ
To Norway, uncle of young Fortinbras—
Who, impotent° and bed-rid, scarcely hears
Of this his nephew's purpose—to suppress   30
His° further gait° herein, in that the levies,
The lists, and full proportions are all made
Out of his subject;° and we here dispatch
You, good Cornelius, and you, Voltimand,
For bearers of this greeting to old Norway,   35
Giving to you no further personal power
To business with the King more than the scope
Of these dilated° articles allow.   [*He gives a paper.*]
Farewell, and let your haste commend your duty.°
Cornelius, Voltimand:
   In that, and all things, will we show our duty.   40
King: We doubt it nothing.° Heartily farewell.

                         [*Exeunt Voltimand and Cornelius.*]
And now, Laertes, what's the news with you?
You told us of some suit; what is 't, Laertes?
You cannot speak of reason to the Dane°
And lose your voice.° What wouldst thou beg, Laertes,   45
That shall not be my offer, not thy asking?
The head is not more native° to the heart,
The hand more instrumental° to the mouth,
Than is the throne of Denmark to thy father.
What wouldst thou have, Laertes?
Laertes: My dread lord,   50
Your leave and favor° to return to France,
From whence though willingly I came to Denmark
To show my duty in your coronation,
Yet now I must confess, that duty done,
My thoughts and wishes bend again toward France   55
And bow them to your gracious leave and pardon.°

---

21 *Co-leaguèd with* joined to, allied with.   *dream . . . advantage* illusory hope of having the advantage. (His only ally is this hope.)   23 *Importing* pertaining to   24 *bonds* contracts   29 *impotent* helpless   31 *His* i.e., Fortinbras'.   *gait* proceeding   31–33 *in that . . . subject* since the levying of troops and supplies is drawn entirely from the King of Norway's own subjects   38 *dilated* set out at length   39 *let . . . duty* let your swift obeying of orders, rather than mere words, express your dutifulness   41 *nothing* not at all   44 *the Dane* the Danish king   45 *lose your voice* waste your speech   47 *native* closely connected, related   48 *instrumental* serviceable   51 *leave and favor* kind permission   56 *bow . . . pardon* entreatingly make a deep bow, asking your permission to depart

King: Have you your father's leave? What says Polonius?
Polonius: H'ath,° my lord, wrung from me my slow leave
    By laborsome petition, and at last
    Upon his will I sealed° my hard° consent.   60
    I do beseech you, give him leave to go.
King: Take thy fair hour,° Laertes. Time be thine,
    And thy best graces spend it at thy will!°
    But now, my cousin° Hamlet, and my son—
Hamlet: A little more than kin, and less than kind.°   65
King: How is it that the clouds still hang on you?
Hamlet: Not so, my lord. I am too much in the sun.°
Queen: Good Hamlet, cast thy nighted color° off,
    And let thine eye look like a friend on Denmark.°
    Do not forever with thy vailèd lids°   70
    Seek for thy noble father in the dust.
    Thou know'st 'tis common,° all that lives must die,
    Passing through nature to eternity.
Hamlet: Ay, madam, it is common.
Queen: If it be,
    Why seems it so particular° with thee?   75
Hamlet: Seems, madam? Nay, it is. I know not "seems."
    'Tis not alone my inky cloak, good Mother,
    Nor customary° suits of solemn black,
    Nor windy suspiration° of forced breath,
    No, nor the fruitful° river in the eye,   80
    Nor the dejected havior° of the visage,
    Together with all forms, moods,° shapes of grief,
    That can denote me truly. These indeed seem,
    For they are actions that a man might play.
    But I have that within which passes show;   85
    These but the trappings and the suits of woe.
King: 'Tis sweet and commendable in your nature, Hamlet,
    To give these mourning duties to your father.
    But you must know your father lost a father,
    That father lost, lost his, and the survivor bound   90
    In filial obligation for some term
    To do obsequious° sorrow. But to persever°
    In obstinate condolement° is a course

58 *H'ath* he has   60 *sealed* (as if sealing a legal document). *hard* reluctant   62 *Take thy fair hour* enjoy your time of youth   63 *And . . . will* and may your finest qualities guide the way you choose to spend your time   64 *cousin* any kin not of the immediate family   65 *A little . . . kind* i.e., closer than an ordinary nephew (since I am stepson), and yet more separated in natural feeling (with pun on *kind* meaning "affectionate" and "natural," "lawful." This line is often read as an aside, but it need not be. The King chooses perhaps not to respond to Hamlet's cryptic and bitter remark.)   67 *the sun* i.e., the sunshine of the King's royal favor (with pun on *son*)   68 *nighted color* (1) mourning garments of black (2) dark melancholy   69 *Denmark* the King of Denmark   70 *vailèd lids* lowered eyes   72 *common* of universal occurrence. (But Hamlet plays on the sense of "vulgar" in line 74.)   75 *particular* personal   78 *customary* (1) socially conventional (2) habitual with me   79 *suspiration* sighing   80 *fruitful* abundant   81 *havior* expression 82 *moods* outward expression of feeling   92 *obsequious* suited to obsequies or funerals. *persever* persevere 93 *condolement* sorrowing

Prince Hamlet returns to Denmark to discover his widowed mother remarried to his uncle, the new king.

Of impious stubbornness. 'Tis unmanly grief.
It shows a will most incorrect to heaven,   95
A heart unfortified,° a mind impatient,
An understanding simple° and unschooled.
For what we know must be and is as common
As any the most vulgar thing to sense,°
Why should we in our peevish opposition   100
Take it to heart? Fie, 'tis a fault to heaven,
A fault against the dead, a fault to nature,
To reason most absurd, whose common theme
Is death of fathers, and who still° hath cried,
From the first corpse° till he that died today,   105
"This must be so." We pray you, throw to earth
This unprevailing° woe and think of us
As of a father; for let the world take note,

96 *unfortified* i.e., against adversity   97 *simple* ignorant   99 *As . . . sense* as the most ordinary experience
104 *still* always   105 *the first corpse* (Abel's)   107 *unprevailing* unavailing, useless

You are the most immediate° to our throne,
And with no less nobility of love   110
Than that which dearest father bears his son
Do I impart toward° you. For° your intent
In going back to school° in Wittenberg,°
It is most retrograde° to our desire,
And we beseech you bend you° to remain   115
Here in the cheer and comfort of our eye,
Our chiefest courtier, cousin, and our son.
Queen: Let not thy mother lose her prayers, Hamlet.
I pray thee, stay with us, go not to Wittenberg.
Hamlet: I shall in all my best° obey you, madam.   120
King: Why, 'tis a loving and a fair reply.
Be as ourself in Denmark. Madam, come.
This gentle and unforced accord of Hamlet
Sits smiling to° my heart, in grace° whereof
No jocund° health that Denmark drinks today   125
But the great cannon to the clouds shall tell,
And the King's rouse° the heaven shall bruit again,°
Respeaking earthly thunder.° Come away.

Flourish. Exeunt all but Hamlet.

Hamlet: O, that this too too sullied° flesh would melt,
Thaw, and resolve itself into a dew!   130
Or that the Everlasting had not fixed
His canon° 'gainst self-slaughter! O God, God,
How weary, stale, flat, and unprofitable
Seem to me all the uses° of this world!
Fie on 't, ah fie! 'Tis an unweeded garden   135
That grows to seed. Things rank and gross in nature
Possess it merely.° That it should come to this!
But two months dead—nay, not so much, not two.
So excellent a king, that was to° this
Hyperion° to a satyr,° so loving to my mother   140
That he might not beteem° the winds of heaven
Visit her face too roughly. Heaven and earth,
Must I remember? Why, she would hang on him
As if increase of appetite had grown
By what it fed on, and yet within a month—   145
Let me not think on 't; frailty, thy name is woman!—

109 *most immediate* next in succession   112 *impart toward* i.e., bestow my affection on.   *For* as for   113
to school i.e., to your studies.   *Wittenberg* famous German university founded in 1502   114 *retrograde*
contrary   115 *bend you* incline yourself   120 *in all my best* to the best of my ability   124 *to* i.e., at.
grace thanksgiving   125 *jocund* merry   127 *rouse* drinking of a draft of liquor.   *bruit again* loudly echo
128 *thunder* i.e., of trumpet and kettledrum, sounded when the King drinks; see I, iv, 8–12   129 *sullied*
defiled. (The early quartos read *sallied*; the Folio, *solid*.)   132 *canon* law   134 *all the uses* the whole routine   137 *merely* completely   139 *to* in comparison to   140 *Hyperion* Titan sun-god, father of Helios.
satyr a lecherous creature of classical mythology, half-human but with a goat's legs, tail, ears, and horns
141 *beteem* allow

A little month, or ere° those shoes were old
With which she followed my poor father's body,
Like Niobe,° all tears, why she, even she—
O God, a beast, that wants discourse of reason,°   150
Would have mourned longer—married with my uncle,
My father's brother, but no more like my father
Than I to Hercules. Within a month,
Ere yet the salt of most unrighteous tears
Had left the flushing in her gallèd° eyes,   155
She married. O, most wicked speed, to post°
With such dexterity to incestuous° sheets!
It is not, nor it cannot come to good.
But break, my heart, for I must hold my tongue.

Enter Horatio, Marcellus, and Bernardo.

Horatio: Hail to your lordship!
Hamlet: I am glad to see you well.   160
   Horatio!—or I do forget myself.
Horatio: The same, my lord, and your poor servant ever.
Hamlet: Sir, my good friend; I'll change that name° with you.
   And what make you from° Wittenberg, Horatio?
   Marcellus.   165
Marcellus: My good lord.
Hamlet: I am very glad to see you. [*To Bernardo.*] Good even, sir.—
   But what in faith make you from Wittenberg?
Horatio: A truant disposition, good my lord.
Hamlet: I would not hear your enemy say so,   170
   Nor shall you do my ear that violence
   To make it truster of your own report
   Against yourself. I know you are no truant.
   But what is your affair in Elsinore?
   We'll teach you to drink deep ere you depart.   175
Horatio: My lord, I came to see your father's funeral.
Hamlet: I prithee, do not mock me, fellow student;
   I think it was to see my mother's wedding.
Horatio: Indeed, my lord, it followed hard° upon.
Hamlet: Thrift, thrift, Horatio! The funeral baked meats°   180
   Did coldly° furnish forth the marriage tables.
   Would I had met my dearest° foe in heaven
   Or ever° I had seen that day, Horatio!
   My father!—Methinks I see my father.

---

147 *or ere* even before   149 *Niobe* Tantalus' daughter, Queen of Thebes, who boasted that she had more sons and daughters than Leto; for this, Apollo and Artemis, children of Leto, slew her fourteen children. She was turned by Zeus into a stone that continually dropped tears.   150 *wants . . . reason* lacks the faculty of reason   155 *gallèd* irritated, inflamed   156 *post* hasten   157 *incestuous* (In Shakespeare's day, the marriage of a man like Claudius to his deceased brother's wife was considered incestuous.)   163 *change that name* i.e., give and receive reciprocally the name of "friend" (rather than talk of "servant")   164 *make you from* are you doing away from   179 *hard* close   180 *baked meats* meat pies   181 *coldly* i.e., as cold leftovers   182 *dearest* closest (and therefore deadliest)   183 *Or ever* before

Horatio: Where, my lord?
Hamlet: In my mind's eye, Horatio.   185
Horatio: I saw him once. 'A° was a goodly king.
Hamlet: 'A was a man. Take him for all in all,
 I shall not look upon his like again.
Horatio: My lord, I think I saw him yesternight.
Hamlet: Saw? Who?   190
Horatio: My lord, the King your father.
Hamlet: The King my father?
Horatio: Season your admiration° for a while
 With an attent° ear till I may deliver,
 Upon the witness of these gentlemen,   195
 This marvel to you.
Hamlet: For God's love, let me hear!
Horatio: Two nights together had these gentlemen,
 Marcellus and Bernardo, on their watch,
 In the dead waste° and middle of the night,
 Been thus encountered. A figure like your father, 200
 Armèd at point° exactly, cap-à-pie,°
 Appears before them, and with solemn march
 Goes slow and stately by them. Thrice he walked
 By their oppressed and fear-surprisèd eyes
 Within his truncheon's° length, whilst they, distilled° 205
 Almost to jelly with the act° of fear,
 Stand dumb and speak not to him. This to me
 In dreadful° secrecy impart they did,
 And I with them the third night kept the watch,
 Where, as they had delivered, both in time,   210
 Form of the thing, each word made true and good,
 The apparition comes. I knew your father;
 These hands are not more like.
Hamlet: But where was this?
Marcellus: My lord, upon the platform where we watch.
Hamlet: Did you not speak to it?
Horatio: My lord, I did,   215
 But answer made it none. Yet once methought
 It lifted up its head and did address
 Itself to motion, like as it would speak;°
 But even then° the morning cock crew loud,
 And at the sound it shrunk in haste away   220
 And vanished from our sight.
Hamlet: 'Tis very strange.
Horatio: As I do live, my honored lord, 'tis true,

---

186 *'A* he 193 *Season your admiration* restrain your astonishment 194 *attent* attentive 199 *dead waste* desolate stillness 201 *at point* correctly in every detail. *cap-à-pie* from head to foot 205 *truncheon* officer's staff. *distilled* dissolved 206 *act* action, operation 208 *dreadful* full of dread 217–218 *did . . . speak* began to move as though it were about to speak 219 *even then* at that very instant

And we did think it writ down in our duty
    To let you know of it.
Hamlet: Indeed, indeed, sirs. But this troubles me.   225
    Hold you the watch tonight?
All: We do, my lord.
Hamlet: Armed, say you?
All: Armed, my lord.
Hamlet: From top to toe?
All: My lord, from head to foot.   230
Hamlet: Then saw you not his face?
Horatio: O, yes, my lord, he wore his beaver° up.
Hamlet: What° looked he, frowningly?
Horatio: A countenance more in sorrow than in anger.
Hamlet: Pale or red?   235
Horatio: Nay, very pale.
Hamlet: And fixed his eyes upon you?
Horatio: Most constantly.
Hamlet: I would I had been there.
Horatio: It would have much amazed you.   240
Hamlet: Very like, very like. Stayed it long?
Horatio: While one with moderate haste might tell° a hundred.
Marcellus, Bernardo: Longer, longer.
Horatio: Not when I saw 't.
Hamlet: His beard was grizzled°—no?   245
Horatio: It was, as I have seen it in his life,
    A sable silvered.°
Hamlet: I will watch tonight.
    Perchance 'twill walk again.
Horatio: I warrant° it will.
Hamlet: If it assume my noble father's person,
    I'll speak to it though hell itself should gape   250
    And bid me hold my peace. I pray you all,
    If you have hitherto concealed this sight,
    Let it be tenable° in your silence still,
    And whatsoever else shall hap tonight,
    Give it an understanding but no tongue.   255
    I will requite your loves. So, fare you well.
    Upon the platform 'twixt eleven and twelve
    I'll visit you.
All: Our duty to your honor.
Hamlet: Your loves, as mine to you. Farewell.

                               Exeunt [all but Hamlet].

    My father's spirit in arms! All is not well.   260
    I doubt° some foul play. Would the night were come!
    Till then sit still, my soul. Foul deeds will rise,
    Though all the earth o'erwhelm them, to men's eyes.   *Exit.*

---

232 *beaver* visor on the helmet   233 *What* how   242 *tell* count   245 *grizzled* gray   247 *sable silvered* black
mixed with white   248 *warrant* assure you   253 *tenable* held   261 *doubt* suspect

SCENE III [POLONIUS' CHAMBERS.]

Enter Laertes and Ophelia, his sister.

Laertes: My necessaries are embarked. Farewell.
    And, sister, as the winds give benefit
    And convoy is assistant,° do not sleep
    But let me hear from you.
Ophelia: Do you doubt that?
Laertes: For Hamlet, and the trifling of his favor,   5
    Hold it a fashion and a toy in blood,°
    A violet in the youth of primy° nature,
    Forward,° not permanent, sweet, not lasting,
    The perfume and suppliance° of a minute—
    No more.
Ophelia: No more but so?
Laertes: Think it no more.   10
    For nature crescent° does not grow alone
    In thews° and bulk, but as this temple° waxes
    The inward service of the mind and soul
    Grows wide withal.° Perhaps he loves you now,
    And now no soil° nor cautel° doth besmirch   15
    The virtue of his will;° but you must fear,
    His greatness weighed,° his will is not his own.
    For he himself is subject to his birth.
    He may not, as unvalued persons do,
    Carve° for himself, for on his choice depends   20
    The safety and health of this whole state,
    And therefore must his choice be circumscribed
    Unto the voice and yielding° of that body
    Whereof he is the head. Then if he says he loves you,
    It fits your wisdom so far to believe it   25
    As he in his particular act and place°
    May give his saying deed, which is no further
    Than the main voice° of Denmark goes withal.°
    Then weigh what loss your honor may sustain
    If with too credent° ear you list° his songs,   30
    Or lose your heart, or your chaste treasure open
    To his unmastered importunity.
    Fear it, Ophelia, fear it, my dear sister,
    And keep you in the rear of your affection,°
    Out of the shot and danger of desire.   35
    The chariest° maid is prodigal enough

---

3 *convoy is assistant* means of conveyance are available   6 *toy in blood* passing amorous fancy   7 *primy* in its prime, springtime   8 *Forward* precocious   9 *suppliance* supply, filler   11 *crescent* growing, waxing   12 *thews* bodily strength.   *temple* i.e., body   14 *Grows wide withal* grows along with it   15 *soil* blemish. *cautel* deceit   16 *will* desire   17 *His greatness weighed* if you take into account his high position   20 *Carve* i.e., choose   23 *voice and yielding* assent, approval   26 *in . . . place* in his particular restricted circumstances   28 *main voice* general assent.   *withal* along with   30 *credent* credulous.   *list* listen to   34 *keep . . . affection* don't advance as far as your affection might lead you. (A military metaphor.)   36 *chariest* most scrupulously modest

If she unmask° her beauty to the moon.°
Virtue itself scapes not calumnious strokes.
The canker galls° the infants of the spring
Too oft before their buttons° be disclosed,°   40
And in the morn and liquid dew° of youth
Contagious blastments° are most imminent.
Be wary then; best safety lies in fear.
Youth to itself rebels,° though none else near.

Ophelia: I shall the effect of this good lesson keep   45
As watchman to my heart. But, good my brother,
Do not, as some ungracious° pastors do,
Show me the steep and thorny way to heaven,
Whiles like a puffed° and reckless libertine
Himself the primrose path of dalliance treads,   50
And recks° not his own rede.°

    Enter Polonius.

Laertes: O, fear me not.°
I stay too long. But here my father comes.
A double° blessing is a double grace;
Occasion smiles upon a second leave.°

Polonius: Yet here, Laertes? Aboard, aboard, for shame!   55
The wind sits in the shoulder of your sail,
And you are stayed for. There—my blessing with thee!
And these few precepts in thy memory
Look° thou character.° Give thy thoughts no tongue,
Nor any unproportioned° thought his° act.   60
Be thou familiar,° but by no means vulgar.°
Those friends thou hast, and their adoption tried,°
Grapple them unto thy soul with hoops of steel,
But do not dull thy palm° with entertainment
Of each new-hatched, unfledged courage.° Beware   65
Of entrance to a quarrel, but being in,
Bear 't that° th' opposèd may beware of thee.
Give every man thy ear, but few thy voice;
Take each man's censure,° but reserve thy judgment.
Costly thy habit° as thy purse can buy,   70
But not expressed in fancy;° rich, not gaudy,
For the apparel oft proclaims the man,
And they in France of the best rank and station

---

37 *If she unmask* if she does no more than show her beauty. *moon* (Symbol of chastity.) 39 *canker galls* cankerworm destroys 40 *buttons* buds. *disclosed* opened 41 *liquid dew* i.e., time when dew is fresh and bright 42 *blastments* blights 44 *Youth . . . rebels* youth is inherently rebellious 47 *ungracious* ungodly 49 *puffed* bloated, or swollen with pride 51 *recks* heeds. *rede* counsel. 51 *fear me not* don't worry on my account 53 *double* (Laertes has already bid his father good-bye.) 54 *Occasion . . . leave* happy is the circumstance that provides a second leave-taking. The goddess Occasion, or Opportunity, smiles. 59 *Look* be sure that. *character* inscribe 60 *unproportioned* badly calculated, intemperate. *his* its 61 *familiar* sociable. *vulgar* common 62 *and their adoption tried* and also their suitability for adoption as friends having been tested 64 *dull thy palm* i.e., shake hands so often as to make the gesture meaningless 65 *courage* young man of spirit 67 *Bear 't that* manage it so that 69 *censure* opinion, judgment 70 *habit* clothing 71 *fancy* excessive ornament, decadent fashion

Are of a most select and generous chief in that.°

Neither a borrower nor a lender be,   75

For loan oft loses both itself and friend,

And borrowing dulleth edge of husbandry.°

This above all: to thine own self be true,

And it must follow, as the night the day,

Thou canst not then be false to any man.   80

Farewell. My blessing season° this in thee!

Laertes: Most humbly do I take my leave, my lord.

Polonius: The time invests° you. Go, your servants tend.°

Laertes: Farewell, Ophelia, and remember well

What I have said to you.   85

Ophelia: 'Tis in my memory locked,

And you yourself shall keep the key of it.

Laertes: Farewell.   *Exit Laertes.*

Polonius: What is 't, Ophelia, he hath said to you?

Ophelia: So please you, something touching the Lord Hamlet.   90

Polonius: Marry,° well bethought.

'Tis told me he hath very oft of late

Given private time to you, and you yourself

Have of your audience been most free and bounteous.

If it be so—as so 'tis put on° me,   95

And that in way of caution—I must tell you

You do not understand yourself so clearly

As it behooves° my daughter and your honor.

What is between you? Give me up the truth.

Ophelia: He hath, my lord, of late made many tenders°   100

Of his affection to me.

Polonius: Affection? Pooh! You speak like a green girl,

Unsifted° in such perilous circumstance.

Do you believe his tenders, as you call them?

Ophelia: I do not know, my lord, what I should think.   105

Polonius: Marry, I will teach you. Think yourself a baby

That you have ta'en these tenders for true pay

Which are not sterling.° Tender° yourself more dearly,

Or—not to crack the wind° of the poor phrase,

Running it thus—you'll tender me a fool.°   110

Ophelia: My lord, he hath importuned me with love

In honorable fashion.

Polonius: Ay, fashion° you may call it. Go to,° go to.

Ophelia: And hath given countenance° to his speech, my lord,

With almost all the holy vows of heaven.   115

74 *Are . . . that* are of a most refined and well-bred preeminence in choosing what to wear   77 *husbandry* thrift   81 *season* mature   83 *invests* besieges, presses upon.   *tend* attend, wait   91 *Marry* i.e., by the Virgin Mary. (A mild oath.)   95 *put on* impressed on, told to   98 *behooves* befits   100 *tenders* offers   103 *Unsifted* i.e., untried   108 *sterling* legal currency.   *Tender* hold, look after, offer   109 *crack the wind* i.e., run it until it is broken-winded   110 *tender me a fool* (1) show yourself to me as a fool (2) show me up as a fool (3) present me with a grandchild. (*Fool* was a term of endearment for a child.)   113 *fashion* mere form, pretense.   *Go to* (An expression of impatience.)   114 *countenance* credit, confirmation

Polonius: Ay, springes° to catch woodcocks.° I do know,
　　When the blood burns, how prodigal° the soul
　　Lends the tongue vows. These blazes, daughter,
　　Giving more light than heat, extinct in both
　　Even in their promise as it° is a-making,　　　　　　　　　　120
　　You must not take for fire. From this time
　　Be something° scanter of your maiden presence.
　　Set your entreatments° at a higher rate
　　Than a command to parle.° For Lord Hamlet,
　　Believe so much in him° that he is young,　　　　　　　　　125
　　And with a larger tether may he walk
　　Than may be given you. In few,° Ophelia,
　　Do not believe his vows, for they are brokers,°
　　Not of that dye° which their investments° show,
　　But mere implorators° of unholy suits,　　　　　　　　　　130
　　Breathing° like sanctified and pious bawds,
　　The better to beguile. This is for all:°
　　I would not, in plain terms, from this time forth
　　Have you so slander° any moment° leisure
　　As to give words or talk with the Lord Hamlet.　　　　　　135
　　Look to 't, I charge you. Come your ways.°
Ophelia: I shall obey, my lord.　　　　　　　　　　　　　　*Exeunt.*

SCENE IV [THE GUARD PLATFORM.]

　　Enter Hamlet, Horatio, and Marcellus.

Hamlet: The air bites shrewdly;° it is very cold.
Horatio: It is a nipping and an eager° air.
Hamlet: What hour now?
Horatio: 　　　　　　　　I think it lacks of° twelve.
Marcellus: No, it is struck.
Horatio: 　　　　　　　　　Indeed? I heard it not.
　　It then draws near the season°　　　　　　　　　　　　　　　5
　　Wherein the spirit held his wont° to walk.

　　A flourish of trumpets, and two pieces° go off [*within*].

　　What does this mean, my lord?
Hamlet: The King doth wake° tonight and takes his rouse,°
　　Keeps wassail,° and the swaggering upspring° reels;°

---

116 *springes* snares.　*woodcocks* birds easily caught; here used to connote gullibility.　117 *prodigal* prodigally　120 *it* i.e., the promise　122 *something* somewhat　123 *entreatments* negotiations for surrender. (A military term.)　124 *parle* discuss terms with the enemy. (Polonius urges his daughter, in the metaphor of military language, not to meet with Hamlet and consider giving in to him merely because he requests an interview.)　125 *so . . . him* this much concerning him　127 *In few* briefly　128 *brokers* go-between, procurers　129 *dye* color or sort.　*investments* clothes. (The vows are not what they seem.)　130 *mere implorators* out and out solicitors　131 *Breathing* speaking　132 *for all* once for all, in sum　134 *slander* abuse, misuse.　*moment* moment's　136 *Come your ways* come along　1 *shrewdly* keenly, sharply　2 *eager* biting　3 *lacks of* is just short of　5 *season* time　6 *held his wont* was accustomed.　s.d. *pieces* i.e., of ordnance, cannon　8 *wake* stay awake and hold revel.　*takes his rouse* carouses　9 *wassail* carousal.　*upspring* wild German dance.　*reels* dances

And as he drains his drafts of Rhenish° down,   10
The kettledrum and trumpet thus bray out
The triumph of his pledge.°
Horatio: Is it a custom?
Hamlet: Ay, marry, is 't,
But to my mind, though I am native here
And to the manner° born, it is a custom   15
More honored in the breach than the observance.°
This heavy-headed revel east and west°
Makes us traduced and taxed of° other nations.
They clepe° us drunkards, and with swinish phrase°
Soil our addition;° and indeed it takes   20
From our achievements, though performed at height,°
The pith and marrow of our attribute.°
So, oft it chances in particular men,
That for° some vicious mole of nature° in them,
As in their birth—wherein they are not guilty,   25
Since nature cannot choose his° origin—
By their o'ergrowth of some complexion,°
Oft breaking down the pales° and forts of reason,
Or by some habit that too much o'erleavens°
The form of plausive° manners, that these men,   30
Carrying, I say, the stamp of one defect,
Being nature's livery° or fortune's star,°
His virtues else,° be they as pure as grace,
As infinite as man may undergo,°
Shall in the general censure° take corruption   35
From that particular fault. The dram of evil
Doth all the noble substance often dout
To his own scandal.°

Enter Ghost.

Horatio: Look, my lord, it comes!
Hamlet: Angels and ministers of grace° defend us!
Be thou° a spirit of health° or goblin damned,   40
Bring° with thee airs from heaven or blasts from hell,
Be thy intents° wicked or charitable,

10 Rhenish Rhine wine   12 The triumph . . . pledge i.e., his feat in draining the wine in a single draft
15 manner custom (of drinking)   16 More . . . observance better neglected than followed   17 east and west
i.e., everywhere   18 taxed of censured by   19 clepe call.   with swinish phrase i.e., by calling us swine   20
addition reputation   21 at height outstandingly   22 The pith . . . attribute the essence of the reputation that
others attribute to us   24 for on account of.   mole of nature natural blemish in one's constitution   26 his
its   27 their o'ergrowth . . . complexion the excessive growth in individuals of some natural trait   28 pales
palings, fences (as of a fortification)   29 o'erleavens induces a change throughout (as yeast works in dough)
30 plausive pleasing   32 nature's livery sign of one's servitude to nature.   fortune's star the destiny that
chance brings   33 His virtues else i.e., the other qualities of these men (line 30)   34 may undergo can sustain
35 general censure general opinion that people have of him   36–38 The dram . . . scandal i.e., the small drop
of evil blots out or works against the noble substance of the whole and brings it into disrepute. To dout is to
blot out. (A famous crux.)   39 ministers of grace messengers of God   40 Be thou whether you are.   spirit of
health good angel   41 Bring whether you bring   42 Be thy intents whether your intentions are

Thou com'st in such a questionable° shape
That I will speak to thee. I'll call thee Hamlet,
King, father, royal Dane. O, answer me!   45
Let me not burst in ignorance, but tell
Why thy canonized° bones, hearsèd° in death,
Have burst their cerements;° why the sepulcher
Wherein we saw thee quietly inurned°
Hath oped his ponderous and marble jaws   50
To cast thee up again. What may this mean,
That thou, dead corpse, again in complete steel,°
Revisits thus the glimpses of the moon,°
Making night hideous, and we fools of nature°
So horridly to shake our disposition°   55
With thoughts beyond the reaches of our souls?
Say, why is this? Wherefore? What should we do?

                                    [The Ghost] beckons [Hamlet].

Horatio: It beckons you to go away with it,
      As if it some impartment° did desire
      To you alone.
Marcellus: Look with what courteous action   60
      It wafts you to a more removèd ground.
      But do not go with it.
Horatio: No, by no means.
Hamlet: It will not speak. Then I will follow it.
Horatio: Do not, my lord!
Hamlet: Why, what should be the fear?
      I do not set my life at a pin's fee,°   65
      And for my soul, what can it do to that,
      Being a thing immortal as itself?
      It waves me forth again. I'll follow it.
Horatio: What if it tempt you toward the flood,° my lord,
      Or to the dreadful summit of the cliff   70
      That beetles o'er° his base into the sea,
      And there assume some other horrible form
      Which might deprive your sovereignty of reason°
      And draw you into madness? Think of it.
      The very place puts toys of desperation,°   75
      Without more motive, into every brain
      That looks so many fathoms to the sea
      And hears it roar beneath.
Hamlet: It wafts me still.—Go on, I'll follow thee.
Marcellus: You shall not go, my lord,   *[They try to stop him.]*

---

43 *questionable* inviting question   47 *canonized* buried according to the canons of the church. *hearsèd* coffined   48 *cerements* grave clothes   49 *inurned* entombed   52 *complete steel* full armor   53 *glimpses of the moon* pale and uncertain moonlight   54 *fools of nature* mere men, limited to natural knowledge and subject to nature   55 *So . . . disposition* to distress our mental composure so violently   59 *impartment* communication   65 *fee* value   69 *flood* sea   71 *beetles o'er* overhangs threateningly (like bushy eyebrows.)   73 *deprive . . . reason* take away the rule of reason over your mind   75 *toys of desperation* fancies of desperate acts, i.e., suicide

Hamlet: Hold off your hands!   80
Horatio: Be ruled. You shall not go.
Hamlet: My fate cries out,°
      And makes each petty° artery° in this body
      As hardy as the Nemean lion's° nerve.°
      Still am I called. Unhand me, gentlemen.
      By heaven, I'll make a ghost of him that lets° me!   85
      I say, away!—Go on, I'll follow thee.

      Exeunt Ghost and Hamlet.

Horatio: He waxes desperate with imagination.
Marcellus: Let's follow. 'Tis not fit thus to obey him.
Horatio: Have after.° To what issue° will this come?
Marcellus: Something is rotten in the state of Denmark.   90
Horatio: Heaven will direct it.°
Marcellus: Nay, let's follow him.   *Exeunt.*

SCENE V [THE BATTLEMENTS OF THE CASTLE.]

      Enter Ghost and Hamlet.

Hamlet: Whither wilt thou lead me? Speak. I'll go no further.
Ghost: Mark me.
Hamlet: I will.
Ghost: My hour is almost come,
      When I to sulfurous and tormenting flames
      Must render up myself.
Hamlet: Alas, poor ghost!
Ghost: Pity me not, but lend thy serious hearing   5
      To what I shall unfold.
Hamlet: Speak. I am bound° to hear.
Ghost: So art thou to revenge, when thou shalt hear.
Hamlet: What?
Ghost: I am thy father's spirit,   10
      Doomed for a certain term to walk the night,
      And for the day confined to fast° in fires,
      Till the foul crimes° done in my days of nature°
      Are burnt and purged away. But that° I am forbid
      To tell the secrets of my prison house,   15
      I could a tale unfold whose lightest word
      Would harrow up° thy soul, freeze thy young blood,
      Make thy two eyes like stars start from their spheres,°

---

81 My *fate cries out* my destiny summons me   82 *petty* weak.   *artery* (through which the vital spirits were
thought to have been conveyed)   83 *Nemean lion's* one of the monsters slain by Hercules in his twelve
labors.   *nerve* sinew   85 *lets* hinders   89 *Have after* let's go after him.   *issue* outcome   91 *it* i.e., the outcome   7 *bound* (1) ready (2) obligated by duty and fate. (The Ghost, in line 8, answers in the second
sense.)   12 *fast* do penance by fasting   13 *crimes* sins.   *of nature* as a mortal   14 *But that* were it not that
17 *harrow up* lacerate, tear   18 *spheres* i.e., eye-sockets, here compared to the orbits or transparent revolving spheres in which, according to Ptolemaic astronomy, the heavenly bodies were fixed

Hamlet with his father's ghost.

Thy knotted and combinèd locks° to part,
And each particular hair to stand on end   20
Like quills upon the fretful porcupine.
But this eternal blazon° must not be
To ears of flesh and blood. List, list, O, list!
If thou didst ever thy dear father love—
Hamlet: O God!   25
Ghost: Revenge his foul and most unnatural murder.
Hamlet: Murder?
Ghost: Murder most foul, as in the best° it is,
But this most foul, strange, and unnatural.

19 *knotted . . . locks* hair neatly arranged and confined   22 *eternal blazon* revelation of the secrets of eternity   28 *in the best* even at best

Hamlet: Haste me to know 't, that I, with wings as swift   30
    As meditation or the thoughts of love,
    May sweep to my revenge.
Ghost: I find thee apt;
    And duller shouldst thou be° than the fat° weed
    That roots itself in ease on Lethe° wharf,
    Wouldst thou not stir in this. Now, Hamlet, hear.   35
    'Tis given out that, sleeping in my orchard,°
    A serpent stung me. So the whole ear of Denmark
    Is by a forgèd process° of my death
    Rankly abused.° But know, thou noble youth,
    The serpent that did sting thy father's life   40
    Now wears his crown.
Hamlet: O, my prophetic soul! My uncle!
Ghost: Ay, that incestuous, that adulterate° beast,
    With witchcraft of his wit, with traitorous gifts°—
    O wicked wit and gifts, that have the power   45
    So to seduce!—won to his shameful lust
    The will of my most seeming-virtuous queen.
    O Hamlet, what a falling off was there!
    From me, whose love was of that dignity
    That it went hand in hand even with the vow°   50
    I made to her in marriage, and to decline
    Upon a wretch whose natural gifts were poor
    To° those of mine!
    But virtue, as it° never will be moved,
    Though lewdness court it in a shape of heaven,°   55
    So lust, though to a radiant angel linked,
    Will sate itself in a celestial bed°
    And prey on garbage.
    But soft, methinks I scent the morning air.
    Brief let me be. Sleeping within my orchard,   60
    My custom always of the afternoon,
    Upon my secure° hour thy uncle stole,
    With juice of cursèd hebona° in a vial,
    And in the porches of my ears° did pour
    The leperous distillment,° whose effect   65
    Holds such an enmity with blood of man
    That swift as quicksilver it courses through
    The natural gates and alleys of the body,
    And with a sudden vigor it doth posset°

---

33 *shouldst thou be* you would have to be.   *fat* torpid, lethargic   34 *Lethe* the river of forgetfulness in Hades   36 *orchard* garden   38 *forgèd process* falsified account   39 *abused* deceived   43 *adulterate* adulterous   44 *gifts* (1) talents (2) presents   50 *even with the vow* with the very vow   53 *To* compared to 54 *virtue, as it* as virtue   55 *shape of heaven* heavenly form   57 *sate . . . bed* cease to find sexual pleasure in a virtuously lawful marriage   62 *secure* confident, unsuspicious   63 *hebona* a poison. (The word seems to be a form of *ebony*, though it is thought perhaps to be related to *henbane*, a poison, or to *ebenus*, "yew.")   64 *porches of my ears* ears as a porch or entrance of the body   65 *leperous distillment* distillation causing leprosylike disfigurement   69 *posset* coagulate, curdle

And curd, like eager° droppings into milk,   70
The thin and wholesome blood. So did it mine,
And a most instant tetter° barked° about,
Most lazar-like,° with vile and loathsome crust,
All my smooth body.
Thus was I, sleeping, by a brother's hand   75
Of life, of crown, of queen at once dispatched,°
Cut off even in the blossom of my sin,
Unhouseled,° disappointed,° unaneled,°
No reckoning° made, but sent to my account
With all my imperfections on my head.   80
O, horrible! O, horrible, most horrible!
If thou hast nature° in thee, bear it not.
Let not the royal bed of Denmark be
A couch for luxury° and damnèd incest.
But, howsoever thou pursuest this act,   85
Taint not thy mind nor let thy soul contrive
Against thy mother aught. Leave her to heaven
And to those thorns that in her bosom lodge,
To prick and sting her. Fare thee well at once.
The glowworm shows the matin° to be near,   90
And 'gins to pale his° uneffectual fire.
Adieu, adieu, adieu! Remember me.   [*Exit.*]
Hamlet: O all you host of heaven! O earth! What else?
And shall I couple° hell? O, fie! Hold,° hold, my heart,
And you, my sinews, grow not instant° old,   95
But bear me stiffly up. Remember thee?
Ay, thou poor ghost, whiles memory holds a seat
In this distracted globe.° Remember thee?
Yea, from the table° of my memory
I'll wipe away all trivial fond° records,   100
All saws° of books, all forms,° all pressures° past
That youth and observation copied there,
And thy commandment all alone shall live
Within the book and volume of my brain,
Unmixed with baser matter. Yes, by heaven!   105
O most pernicious woman!
O villain, villain, smiling, damnèd villain!
My tables°—meet it is° I set it down
That one may smile, and smile, and be a villain.
At least I am sure it may be so in Denmark.   110
                                                                       [*Writing.*]

---

70 *eager* sour, acid 72 *tetter* eruption of scabs. *barked* covered with a rough covering, like bark of a tree
73 *lazar-like* leperlike 76 *dispatched* suddenly deprived 78 *Unhouseled* without having received the Sacrament. *disappointed* unready (spiritually) for the last journey. *unaneled* without having received extreme unction 79 *reckoning* settling of accounts 82 *nature* i.e., the promptings of a son 84 *luxury* lechery 90 *matin* morning 91 *his* its 94 *couple* add. *Hold* hold together 95 *instant* instantly 98 *globe* (1) head (2) world 99 *table* tablet, slate 100 *fond* foolish 101 *saws* wise sayings. *forms* shapes or images copied onto the slate; general ideas. *pressures* impressions stamped 108 *tables* writing tablets. *meet it is* it is fitting

So, uncle, there you are.° Now to my word:
It is "Adieu, adieu! Remember me."
I have sworn 't.

Enter Horatio and Marcellus.

Horatio: My lord, my lord!
Marcellus: Lord Hamlet!   115
Horatio: Heavens secure him!°
Hamlet: So be it.
Marcellus: Hillo, ho, ho, my lord!
Hamlet: Hillo, ho, ho, boy! Come, bird, come.°
Marcellus: How is 't, my noble lord?   120
Horatio: What news, my lord?
Hamlet: O, wonderful!
Horatio: Good my lord, tell it.
Hamlet: No, you will reveal it.
Horatio: Not I, my lord, by heaven.   125
Marcellus: Nor I, my lord.
Hamlet: How say you, then, would heart of man once° think it?
   But you'll be secret?
Horatio, Marcellus: Ay, by heaven, my lord.
Hamlet: There's never a villain dwelling in all Denmark
   But he's an arrant° knave.   130
Horatio: There needs no ghost, my lord, come from the grave
   To tell us this.
Hamlet: Why, right, you are in the right.
   And so, without more circumstance° at all,
   I hold it fit that we shake hands and part,
   You as your business and desire shall point you—   135
   For every man hath business and desire,
   Such as it is—and for my own poor part,
   Look you, I'll go pray.
Horatio: These are but wild and whirling words, my lord.
Hamlet: I am sorry they offend you, heartily;   140
   Yes, faith, heartily.
Horatio: There's no offense, my lord.
Hamlet: Yes, by Saint Patrick,° but there is, Horatio,
   And much offense° too. Touching this vision here,
   It is an honest ghost,° that let me tell you.
   For your desire to know what is between us,   145
   O'ermaster 't as you may. And now, good friends,
   As you are friends, scholars, and soldiers,
   Give me one poor request.

---

111 *there you are* i.e., there, I've written that down against you   116 *secure him* keep him safe   119 *Hillo . . . come* (A falconer's call to a hawk in air. Hamlet mocks the hallooing as though it were a part of hawking.) 127 *once* ever   130 *arrant* thoroughgoing   133 *circumstance* ceremony, elaboration   142 *Saint Patrick* (The keeper of Purgatory and patron saint of all blunders and confusion.)   143 *offense* (Hamlet deliberately changes Horatio's "no offense taken" to "an offense against all decency.")   144 *an honest ghost* i.e., a real ghost and not an evil spirit

Horatio: What is 't, my lord? We will.

Hamlet: Never make known what you have seen tonight. 150

Horatio, Marcellus: My lord, we will not.

Hamlet: Nay, but swear 't.

Horatio: In faith, my lord, not I.°

Marcellus: Nor I, my lord, in faith.

Hamlet: Upon my sword.° [*He holds out his sword.*] 155

Marcellus: We have sworn, my lord, already.°

Hamlet: Indeed, upon my sword, indeed.

Ghost (cries under the stage): Swear.

Hamlet: Ha, ha, boy, sayst thou so? Art thou there, truepenny?°

    Come on, you hear this fellow in the cellarage. 160

    Consent to swear.

Horatio: Propose the oath, my lord.

Hamlet: Never to speak of this that you have seen,

    Swear by my sword.

Ghost [beneath]: Swear. [*They swear.*]°

Hamlet: Hic et ubique?° Then we'll shift our ground. 165

                           [*He moves to another spot.*]

    Come hither, gentlemen,

    And lay your hands again upon my sword.

    Swear by my sword

    Never to speak of this that you have heard.

Ghost [beneath]: Swear by his sword. [*They swear.*] 170

Hamlet: Well said, old mole. Canst work i' th' earth so fast?

    A worthy pioner!°—Once more remove, good friends.

                              [*He moves again.*]

Horatio: O day and night, but this is wondrous strange!

Hamlet: And therefore as a stranger° give it welcome.

    There are more things in heaven and earth, Horatio, 175

    Than are dreamt of in your philosophy.°

    But come;

    Here, as before, never, so help you mercy,°

    How strange or odd soe'er I bear myself—

    As I perchance hereafter shall think meet 180

    To put an antic° disposition on—

    That you, at such times seeing me, never shall,

    With arms encumbered° thus, or this headshake,

    Or by pronouncing of some doubtful phrase

    As "Well, we know," or "We could, an if° we would," 185

---

153 *In faith . . . I* i.e., I swear not to tell what I have seen. (Horatio is not refusing to swear.) 155 *sword* i.e., the hilt in the form of a cross 156 *We . . . already* i.e., we swore in faith 159 *truepenny* honest old fellow 164 s.d. *They swear* (Seemingly they swear here, and at lines 170 and 190, as they lay their hands on Hamlet's sword. Triple oaths would have particular force; these three oaths deal with what they have seen, what they have heard, and what they promise about Hamlet's *antic* disposition. 165 *Hic et ubique* here and everywhere. (Latin.) 172 *pioner* foot soldier assigned to dig tunnels and excavations 174 *as a stranger* i.e., needing your hospitality 176 *your philosophy* this subject called "natural philosophy" or "science" that people talk about 178 *so help you mercy* as you hope for God's mercy when you are judged 181 *antic* fantastic 183 *encumbered* folded 185 *an if* if

Or "If we list° to speak," or "There be, an if they might,"°
Or such ambiguous giving out,° to note°
That you know aught° of me—this do swear,
So grace and mercy at your most need help you.

Ghost [*beneath*]: Swear.   [*They swear.*] 190
Hamlet: Rest, rest, perturbèd spirit! So, gentlemen,
With all my love I do commend me to you;°
And what so poor a man as Hamlet is
May do t' express his love and friending° to you,
God willing, shall not lack.° Let us go in together,   195
And still° your fingers on your lips, I pray.
The time° is out of joint. O cursèd spite°
That ever I was born to set it right!

                                                              [*They wait for him to leave first.*]

Nay, come, let's go together.°   *Exeunt.*

ACT II

SCENE I [POLONIUS' CHAMBERS.]

Enter Old Polonius with his man [Reynaldo].

Polonius: Give him this money and these notes, Reynaldo.

                                                              [*He gives money and papers.*]

Reynaldo: I will, my lord.
Polonius: You shall do marvelous° wisely, good Reynaldo,
Before you visit him, to make inquire°
Of his behavior.
Reynaldo: My lord, I did intend it.   5
Polonius: Marry, well said, very well said. Look you, sir,
Inquire me first what Danskers° are in Paris,
And how, and who, what means,° and where they keep,°
What company, at what expense; and finding
By this encompassment° and drift° of question   10
That they do know my son, come you more nearer
Than your particular demands will touch it.°
Take you,° as 'twere, some distant knowledge of him,
As thus, "I know his father and his friends,
And in part him." Do you mark this, Reynaldo?   15
Reynaldo: Ay, very well, my lord.
Polonius: "And in part him, but," you may say, "not well.
But if 't be he I mean, he's very wild,

---

186 *list* wished.   *There . . . might* i.e., there are people here (we, in fact) who could tell news if we were at liberty to do so   187 *giving out* intimation.   *note* draw attention to the fact   188 *aught* i.e., something secret   192 *do . . . you* entrust myself to you   194 *friending* friendliness   195 *lack* be lacking   196 *still* always   197 *The time* the state of affairs.   *spite* i.e., the spite of Fortune   199 *let's go together* (Probably they wait for him to leave first, but he refuses this ceremoniousness.)   3 *marvelous* marvelously   4 *inquire* inquiry   7 *Danskers* Danes   8 *what means* what wealth (they have).   *keep* dwell   10 *encompassment* roundabout talking.   *drift* gradual approach or course   11–12 *come . . . it* you will find out more this way than by asking pointed questions (*particular demands*)   13 *Take you* assume, pretend

Addicted so and so," and there put on° him
What forgeries° you please—marry, none so rank° 20
As may dishonor him, take heed of that,
But, sir, such wanton,° wild, and usual slips
As are companions noted and most known
To youth and liberty.
Reynaldo: As gaming, my lord. 25
Polonius: Ay, or drinking, fencing, swearing,
Quarreling, drabbing°—you may go so far.
Reynaldo: My lord, that would dishonor him.
Polonius: Faith, no, as you may season° it in the charge.
You must not put another scandal on him 30
That he is open to incontinency;°
That's not my meaning. But breathe his faults so quaintly°
That they may seem the taints of liberty,°
The flash and outbreak of a fiery mind,
A savageness in unreclaimèd blood, 35
Of general assault.°
Reynaldo: But, my good lord—
Polonius: Wherefore should you do this?
Reynaldo: Ay, my lord, I would know that.
Polonius: Marry, sir, here's my drift, 40
And I believe it is a fetch of warrant.°
You laying these slight sullies on my son,
As 'twere a thing a little soiled wi' the working,°
Mark you,
Your party in converse,° him you would sound,° 45
Having ever° seen in the prenominate crimes°
The youth you breathe° of guilty, be assured
He closes with you in this consequence:°
"Good sir," or so, or "friend," or "gentleman,"
According to the phrase or the addition° 50
Of man and country.
Reynaldo: Very good, my lord.
Polonius: And then, sir, does 'a this—'a does—
What was I about to say? By the Mass, I was about to say something. Where did
I leave?
Reynaldo: At "closes in the consequence." 55
Polonius: At "closes in the consequence," ay, marry.
He closes thus: "I know the gentleman,
I saw him yesterday," or "th' other day,"
Or then, or then, with such or such, "and as you say,

---

19 *put on* impute to   20 *forgeries* invented tales.   *rank* gross   22 *wanton* sportive, unrestrained   27 *drabbing* whoring   29 *season* temper, soften   31 *incontinency* habitual sexual excess   32 *quaintly* artfully, subtly   33 *taints of liberty* faults resulting from free living   35–36 A *savageness . . . assault* a wildness in untamed youth that assails all indiscriminately   41 *fetch of warrant* legitimate trick   43 *soiled wi' the working* soiled by handling while it is being made, i.e., by involvement in the ways of the world   45 *converse* conversation.   *sound* i.e., sound out   46 *Having ever* if he has ever.   *prenominate crimes* before-mentioned offenses   47 *breathe* speak   48 *closes . . . consequence* takes you into his confidence in some fashion, as follows   50 *addition* title

There was 'a gaming," "there o'ertook in 's rouse,"° 60
"There falling out° at tennis," or perchance
"I saw him enter such a house of sale,"
Videlicet° a brothel, or so forth. See you now,
Your bait of falsehood takes this carp° of truth;
And thus do we of wisdom and of reach,° 65
With windlasses° and with assays of bias,°
By indirections find directions° out.
So by my former lecture and advice
Shall you my son. You have° me, have you not?
Reynaldo: My lord, I have.
Polonius: God b' wi'° ye; fare ye well. 70
Reynaldo: Good my lord.
Polonius: Observe his inclination in yourself.°
Reynaldo: I shall, my lord.
Polonius: And let him ply his music.
Reynaldo: Well, my lord. 75
Polonius: Farewell.   *Exit Reynaldo.*

        Enter Ophelia.

                How now, Ophelia, what's the matter?
Ophelia: O my lord, my lord, I have been so affrighted!
Polonius: With what, i' the name of God?
Ophelia: My lord, as I was sewing in my closet,°
    Lord Hamlet, with his doublet° all unbraced,° 80
    No hat upon his head, his stockings fouled,
    Ungartered, and down-gyvèd° to his ankle,
    Pale as his shirt, his knees knocking each other,
    And with a look so piteous in purport°
    As if he had been loosèd out of hell 85
    To speak of horrors—he comes before me.
Polonius: Mad for thy love?
Ophelia: My lord, I do not know,
    But truly I do fear it.
Polonius: What said he?
Ophelia: He took me by the wrist and held me hard.
    Then goes he to the length of all his arm, 90
    And, with his other hand thus o'er his brow
    He falls to such perusal of my face
    As° 'a would draw it. Long stayed he so.
    At last, a little shaking of mine arm
    And thrice his head thus waving up and down, 95

---

60 *o'ertook in 's rouse* overcome by drink   61 *falling out* quarreling   63 *Videlicet* namely   64 *carp* a fish   65 *reach* capacity, ability   66 *windlasses* i.e., circuitous paths. (Literally, circuits made to head off the game in hunting.)   *assays of bias* attempts through indirection (like the curving path of the bowling ball, which is biased or weighted to one side)   67 *directions* i.e., the way things really are   69 *have* understand   70 *b'wi'* be with   72 *in yourself* in your own person (as well as by asking questions)   79 *closet* private chamber   80 *doublet* close-fitting jacket.   *unbraced* unfastened.   82 *down-gyvèd* fallen to the ankles (like gyves or fetters)   84 *in purport* in what it expressed   93 *As* as if (also in line 97)

He raised a sigh so piteous and profound
As it did seem to shatter all his bulk°
And end his being. That done, he lets me go,
And with his head over his shoulder turned
He seemed to find his way without his eyes,   100
For out o' doors he went without their helps,
And to the last bended their light on me.
Polonius: Come, go with me. I will go seek the King.
This is the very ecstasy° of love,
Whose violent property° fordoes° itself   105
And leads the will to desperate undertakings
As oft as any passion under heaven
That does afflict our natures. I am sorry.
What, have you given him any hard words of late?
Ophelia: No, my good lord, but as you did command   110
I did repel his letters and denied
His access to me.
Polonius: That hath made him mad.
I am sorry that with better heed and judgment
I had not quoted° him. I feared he did but trifle
And meant to wrack° thee. But beshrew my jealousy!°   115
By heaven, it is as proper to our age°
To cast beyond° ourselves in our opinions
As it is common for the younger sort
To lack discretion. Come, go we to the King.
This must be known,° which, being kept close,° might move   120
More grief to hide than hate to utter love.°
Come.   *Exeunt.*

SCENE II [THE CASTLE.]

Flourish. Enter King and Queen, Rosencrantz, and Guildenstern [with others].

King: Welcome, dear Rosencrantz and Guildenstern.
Moreover that° we much did long to see you,
The need we have to use you did provoke
Our hasty sending. Something have you heard
Of Hamlet's transformation—so call it,   5
Sith nor° th' exterior nor the inward man
Resembles that° it was. What it should be,
More than his father's death, that thus hath put him
So much from th' understanding of himself,
I cannot dream of. I entreat you both   10

---

97 *bulk* body   104 *ecstasy* madness   105 *property* nature. *fordoes* destroys   114 *quoted* observed   115 *wrack* ruin, seduce.   *beshrew my jealousy* a plague upon my suspicious nature   116 *proper . . . age* characteristic of us (old) men   117 *cast beyond* overshoot, miscalculate. (A metaphor from hunting.)   120 *known* made known (to the King).   *close* secret   120–121 *might . . . love* i.e., might cause more grief (because of what Hamlet might do) by hiding the knowledge of Hamlet's strange behavior to Ophelia than unpleasantness by telling it   2 *Moreover that* besides the fact that   6 *Sith nor* since neither   7 *that* what

King Claudius and Queen Gertrude.

That, being of so young days° brought up with him,
And sith so neighbored to° his youth and havior,°
That you vouchsafe your rest° here in our court
Some little time, so by your companies
To draw him on to pleasures, and to gather   15
So much as from occasion° you may glean,
Whether aught to us unknown afflicts him thus
That, opened,° lies within our remedy.
Queen: Good gentlemen, he hath much talked of you,
And sure I am two men there is not living   20
To whom he more adheres. If it will please you

11 *of . . . days* from such early youth   12 *And sith so neighbored to* and since you are (or, and since that time you are) intimately acquainted with.   *havior* demeanor   13 *vouchsafe your rest* please to stay   16 *occasion* opportunity   18 *opened* being revealed

To show us so much gentry° and good will
As to expend your time with us awhile
For the supply and profit of our hope,°
Your visitation shall receive such thanks   25
As fits a king's remembrance.°
Rosencrantz: Both Your Majesties
Might, by the sovereign power you have of° us,
Put your dread° pleasures more into command
Than to entreaty.
Guildenstern: But we both obey,
And here give up ourselves in the full bent°   30
To lay our service freely at your feet,
To be commanded.
King: Thanks, Rosencrantz and gentle Guildenstern.
Queen: Thanks, Guildenstern and gentle Rosencrantz.
And I beseech you instantly to visit   35
My too much changèd son. Go, some of you,
And bring these gentlemen where Hamlet is.
Guildenstern: Heavens make our presence and our practices°
Pleasant and helpful to him!
Queen: Ay, amen!
Exeunt Rosencrantz and Guildenstern [with some attendants]

Enter Polonius.

Polonius: Th' ambassadors from Norway, my good lord,   40
Are joyfully returned.
King: Thou still° hast been the father of good news.
Polonius: Have I, my lord? I assure my good liege
I hold° my duty, as° I hold my soul,
Both to my God and to my gracious king;   45
And I do think, or else this brain of mine
Hunts not the trail of policy° so sure
As it hath used to do, that I have found
The very cause of Hamlet's lunacy.
King: O, speak of that! That do I long to hear.   50
Polonius: Give first admittance to th' ambassadors.
My news shall be the fruit° to that great feast.
King: Thyself do grace° to them and bring them in.

                                                            [*Exit Polonius.*]

He tells me, my dear Gertrude, he hath found
The head and source of all your son's distemper.   55
Queen: I doubt° it is no other but the main,°
His father's death and our o'erhasty marriage.

---

22 *gentry* courtesy   24 *supply . . . hope* aid and furtherance of what we hope for   26 *As fits . . . remem-brance* as would be a fitting gift of a king who rewards true service   27 *of* over   28 *dread* inspiring awe
30 *in . . . bent* to the utmost degree of our capacity. (An archery metaphor.)   38 *practices* doings   42 *still* always   44 *hold* maintain.   *as* as firmly as   47 *policy* sagacity   52 *fruit* dessert   53 *grace* honor (punning on *grace* said before a *feast*, line 52)   56 *doubt* fear, suspect.   *main* chief point, principal concern

Enter Ambassadors [Voltimand and Cornelius, with Polonius].

King: Well, we shall sift him.°—Welcome, my good friends!
      Say, Voltimand, what from our brother° Norway?
Voltimand: Most fair return of greetings and desires.°   60
      Upon our first,° he sent out to suppress
      His nephew's levies, which to him appeared
      To be a preparation 'gainst the Polack,
      But, better looked into, he truly found
      It was against Your Highness. Whereat grieved   65
      That so his sickness, age, and impotence°
      Was falsely borne in hand,° sends out arrests°
      On Fortinbras, which he, in brief, obeys,
      Receives rebuke from Norway, and in fine°
      Makes vow before his uncle never more   70
      To give th' assay° of arms against Your Majesty.
      Whereon old Norway, overcome with joy,
      Gives him three thousand crowns in annual fee
      And his commission to employ those soldiers,
      So levied as before, against the Polack,   75
      With an entreaty, herein further shown,

                                                         [*giving a paper*]

      That it might please you to give quiet pass
      Through your dominions for this enterprise
      On such regards of safety and allowance°
      As therein are set down.
King: It likes° us well,   80
      And at our more considered° time we'll read,
      Answer, and think upon this business.
      Meantime we thank you for your well-took labor.
      Go to your rest; at night we'll feast together.
      Most welcome home!   *Exeunt Ambassadors.*
Polonius: This business is well ended.   85
      My liege, and madam, to expostulate°
      What majesty should be, what duty is,
      Why day is day, night night, and time is time,
      Were nothing but to waste night, day, and time.
      Therefore, since brevity is the soul of wit,°   90
      And tediousness the limbs and outward flourishes,
      I will be brief. Your noble son is mad.
      Mad call I it, for, to define true madness,
      What is 't but to be nothing else but mad?
      But let that go.

---

58 *sift him* question Polonius closely   59 *brother* fellow king   60 *desires* good wishes   61 *Upon our first* at our first words on the business   66 *impotence* helplessness   67 *borne in hand* deluded, taken advantage of. *arrests* orders to desist   69 *in fine* in conclusion   71 *give th' assay* make trial of strength, challenge   79 *On . . . allowance* i.e., with such considerations for the safety of Denmark and permission for Fortinbras   80 *likes* pleases   81 *considered* suitable for deliberation   86 *expostulate* expound, inquire into   90 *wit* sense or judgment

Queen: More matter, with less art.   95
Polonius: Madam, I swear I use no art at all.
    That he's mad, 'tis true; 'tis true 'tis pity,
    And pity 'tis 'tis true—a foolish figure,°
    But farewell it, for I will use no art.
    Mad let us grant him, then, and now remains   100
    That we find out the cause of this effect,
    Or rather say, the cause of this defect,
    For this effect defective comes by cause.°
    Thus it remains, and the remainder thus.
    Perpend.°   105
    I have a daughter—have while she is mine—
    Who, in her duty and obedience, mark,
    Hath given me this. Now gather and surmise.°
    [*He reads the letter.*] "To the celestial and my soul's idol, the most beautified
    Ophelia"—That's an ill phrase, a vile phrase; "beautified" is a vile phrase. But   110
    you shall hear. Thus:

                                                        [*He reads.*]

    "In her excellent white bosom,° these,° etc."
Queen: Came this from Hamlet to her?
Polonius: Good madam, stay° awhile, I will be faithful.°

                                                        [*He reads.*]

    "Doubt° thou the stars are fire,   115
        Doubt that the sun doth move,
    Doubt truth to be a liar,
        But never doubt I love.

    O dear Ophelia, I am ill at these numbers.° I have not art to reckon° my groans.
    But that I love thee best, O most best, believe it. Adieu. Thine evermore, most   120
    dear lady, whilst this machine° is to him, Hamlet."

    This in obedience hath my daughter shown me,
    And, more above,° hath his solicitings,
    As they fell out° by° time, by means, and place,
    All given to mine ear.°
King: But how hath she   125
    Received his love?
Polonius: What do you think of me?
King: As of a man faithful and honorable.
Polonius: I would fain° prove so. But what might you think,
    When I had seen this hot love on the wing—
    As I perceived it, I must tell you that,
    Before my daughter told me—what might you,   130
    Or my dear Majesty your queen here, think,

98 *figure* figure of speech   103 *For . . . cause* i.e., for this defective behavior, this madness, has a cause
105 *Perpend* consider   108 *gather and surmise* draw your own conclusions   112 *In . . . bosom* (The letter is
poetically addressed to her heart.)   *these* i.e., the letter   114 *stay* wait.   *faithful* i.e., in reading the letter
accurately   115 *Doubt* suspect   119 *ill . . . numbers* unskilled at writing verses.   *reckon* (1) count (2)
number metrically, scan   121 *machine* i.e., body   123 *more above* moreover   124 *fell out* occurred.   *by*
according to   125 *given . . . ear* i.e., told me about   128 *fain* gladly

If I had played the desk or table book,°
Or given my heart a winking,° mute and dumb,
Or looked upon this love with idle sight?°   135
What might you think? No, I went round° to work,
And my young mistress thus I did bespeak:°
"Lord Hamlet is a prince out of thy star;°
This must not be." And then I prescripts° gave her,
That she should lock herself from his resort,°   140
Admit no messengers, receive no tokens.
Which done, she took the fruits of my advice;
And he, repellèd—a short tale to make—
Fell into a sadness, then into a fast,
Thence to a watch,° thence into a weakness,
Thence to a lightness,° and by this declension°   145
Into the madness wherein now he raves,
And all we° mourn for.
King [*to the Queen*]:   Do you think 'tis this?
Queen: It may be, very like.
Polonius: Hath there been such a time—I would fain know that—   150
    That I have positively said " 'Tis so,"
    When it proved otherwise?
King: Not that I know.
Polonius: Take this from this,° if this be otherwise.
    If circumstances lead me, I will find
    Where truth is hid, though it were hid indeed   155
    Within the center.°
King: How may we try° it further?
Polonius: You know sometimes he walks four hours together
    Here in the lobby.
Queen: So he does indeed.
Polonius: At such a time I'll loose° my daughter to him.
    Be you and I behind an arras° then.   160
    Mark the encounter. If he love her not
    And be not from his reason fall'n thereon,°
    Let me be no assistant for a state,
    But keep a farm and carters.°
King: We will try it.

    Enter Hamlet [*reading on a book*].

Queen: But look where sadly° the poor wretch comes reading.   165

---

133 *played . . . table book* i.e., remained shut up, concealing the information   134 *given . . . winking* closed the eyes of my heart to this   135 *with idle sight* complacently or uncomprehendingly   136 *round* roundly, plainly   137 *bespeak* address   138 *out of thy star* above your sphere, position   139 *prescripts* orders   140 *his resort* his visits   145 *watch* state of sleeplessness   146 *lightness* lightheadedness. *declension* decline, deterioration (with a pun on the grammatical sense)   148 *all we* all of us, or, into everything that we   153 *Take this from this* (The actor probably gestures, indicating that he means his head from his shoulders, or his staff of office or chain from his hands or neck, or something similar.)   156 *center* middle point of the earth (which is also the center of the Ptolemaic universe).   157 *try* test, judge   159 *loose* (as one might release an animal that is being mated)   160 *arras* hanging, tapestry   162 *thereon* on that account   164 *carters* wagon drivers   165 *sadly* seriously

Polonius: Away, I do beseech you both, away.
    I'll board° him presently.° O, give me leave.°

                                    Exeunt King and Queen [with attendants].

    How does my good Lord Hamlet?
Hamlet: Well, God-a-mercy.°
Polonius: Do you know me, my lord?   170
Hamlet: Excellent well. You are a fishmonger.°
Polonius: Not I, my lord.
Hamlet: Then I would you were so honest a man.
Polonius: Honest, my lord?
Hamlet: Ay, sir. To be honest, as this world goes, is to be one man picked out of ten   175
    thousand.
Polonius: That's very true, my lord.
Hamlet: For if the sun breed maggots in a dead dog, being a good kissing carrion°—
    Have you a daughter?
Polonius: I have, my lord.   180
Hamlet: Let her not walk i' the sun.° Conception° is a blessing, but as your daughter
    may conceive, friend, look to 't.
Polonius [aside]: How say you by that? Still harping on my daughter. Yet he knew me
    not at first; 'a° said I was a fishmonger. 'A is far gone. And truly in my youth I
    suffered much extremity for love, very near this. I'll speak to him again.—What   185
    do you read, my lord?
Hamlet: Words, words, words.
Polonius: What is the matter,° my lord?
Hamlet: Between who?
Polonius: I mean, the matter that you read, my lord.   190
Hamlet: Slanders, sir; for the satirical rogue says here that old men have gray beards,
    that their faces are wrinkled, their eyes purging° thick amber° and plum-tree
    gum, and that they have a plentiful lack of wit,° together with most weak hams.
    All which, sir, though I most powerfully and potently believe, yet I hold it not
    honesty° to have it thus set down, for yourself, sir, shall grow old° as I am, if like   195
    a crab you could go backward.
Polonius [aside]: Though this be madness, yet there is method in 't.—Will you walk
    out of the air,° my lord?
Hamlet: Into my grave.
Polonius: Indeed, that's out of the air. [*Aside.*] How pregnant° sometimes his replies   200
    are! A happiness° that often madness hits on, which reason and sanity could not
    so prosperously° be delivered of. I will leave him and suddenly° contrive the
    means of meeting between him and my daughter.—My honorable lord, I will
    most humbly take my leave of you.

---

167 *board* accost.   *presently* at once.   *give me leave* i.e., excuse me, leave me alone. (Said to those he hurries offstage, including the King and Queen.)   169 *God-a-mercy* God have mercy, i.e., thank you   171
fishmonger fish merchant   178 *a good kissing carrion* i.e., a good piece of flesh for kissing, or for the sun to
kiss   181 *i' the sun* in public (with additional implication of the sunshine of princely favors).   *Conception*
(1) understanding (2) pregnancy   184 *'a* he   188 *matter* substance. (But Hamlet plays on the sense of
"basis for a dispute.")   192 *purging* discharging.   *amber* i.e., resin, like the resinous *plum-tree gum*   193
wit understanding   195 *honesty* decency, decorum.   *old* as old   198 *out of the air* (The open air was considered dangerous for sick people.)   200 *pregnant* quick-witted, full of meaning   201 *happiness* felicity of
expression   202 *prosperously* successfully.   *suddenly* immediately

Hamlet: You cannot, sir, take from me anything that I will more willingly part 205
    withal°—except my life, except my life, except my life.

    Enter Guildenstern and Rosencrantz.

Polonius: Fare you well, my lord.
Hamlet: These tedious old fools!°
Polonius: You go to seek the Lord Hamlet. There he is.
Rosencrantz [to Polonius]: God save you, sir! 210

                                                                             [Exit Polonius.]

Guildenstern: My honored lord!
Rosencrantz: My most dear lord!
Hamlet: My excellent good friends! How dost thou, Guildenstern? Ah, Rosencrantz!
    Good lads, how do you both?
Rosencrantz: As the indifferent° children of the earth. 215
Guildenstern: Happy in that we are not overhappy.
    On Fortune's cap we are not the very button.
Hamlet: Nor the soles of her shoe?
Rosencrantz: Neither, my lord.
Hamlet: Then you live about her waist, or in the middle of her favors?° 220
Guildenstern: Faith, her privates we.°
Hamlet: In the secret parts of Fortune? O, most true, she is a strumpet.° What news?
Rosencrantz: None, my lord, but the world's grown honest.
Hamlet: Then is doomsday near. But your news is not true. Let me question more in
    particular. What have you, my good friends, deserved at the hands of fortune 225
    that she sends you to prison hither?
Guildenstern: Prison, my lord?
Hamlet: Denmark's a prison.
Rosencrantz: Then is the world one.
Hamlet: A goodly one, in which there are many confines,° wards,° and dungeons, 230
    Denmark being one o' the worst.
Rosencrantz: We think not so, my lord.
Hamlet: Why then 'tis none to you, for there is nothing either good or bad but think-
    ing makes it so. To me it is a prison.
Rosencrantz: Why then, your ambition makes it one. 'Tis too narrow for your mind. 235
Hamlet: O God, I could be bounded in a nutshell and count myself a king of infinite
    space, were it not that I have bad dreams.
Guildenstern: Which dreams indeed are ambition, for the very substance of the ambi-
    tious° is merely the shadow of a dream.
Hamlet: A dream itself is but a shadow. 240
Rosencrantz: Truly, and I hold ambition of so airy and light a quality that it is but a
    shadow's shadow.

---

206 *withal* with 208 *old fools* i.e., old men like Polonius 215 *indifferent* ordinary, at neither extreme of
fortune or misfortune 220 *favors* i.e., sexual favors 221 *her privates we* i.e., (1) we are sexually intimate
with Fortune, the fickle goddess who bestows her favors indiscriminately (2) we are her private citizens
222 *strumpet* prostitute. (A common epithet for indiscriminate Fortune; see line 426.) 230 *confines* places
of confinement. *wards* cells 238–239 *the very . . . ambitious* that seemingly very substantial thing that
the ambitious pursue

Hamlet: Then are our beggars bodies,° and our monarchs and outstretched° heroes
   the beggars' shadows. Shall we to the court? For, by my fay,° I cannot reason.

Rosencrantz, Guildenstern: We'll wait upon° you.   245

Hamlet: No such matter. I will not sort° you with the rest of my servants, for, to
   speak to you like an honest man, I am most dreadfully attended.° But, in the
   beaten way° of friendship, what make° you at Elsinore?

Rosencrantz: To visit you, my lord, no other occasion.

Hamlet: Beggar that I am, I am even poor in thanks; but I thank you, and sure, dear   250
   friends, my thanks are too dear a halfpenny.° Were you not sent for? Is it your
   own inclining? Is it a free° visitation? Come, come, deal justly with me. Come,
   come. Nay, speak.

Guildenstern: What should we say, my lord?

Hamlet: Anything but to the purpose.° You were sent for, and there is a kind of con-   255
   fession in your looks which your modesties° have not craft enough to color.° I know
   the good King and Queen have sent for you.

Rosencrantz: To what end, my lord?

Hamlet: That you must teach me. But let me conjure° you, by the rights of our fellowship, by the consonancy of our youth,° by the obligation of our ever-preserved   260
   love, and by what more dear a better° prosper could charge° you withal, be even°
   and direct with me whether you were sent for or no.

Rosencrantz [*aside to Guildenstern*]: What say you?

Hamlet [*aside*]: Nay, then, I have an eye of° you.—If you love me, hold not off.°

Guildenstern: My lord, we were sent for.   265

Hamlet: I will tell you why; so shall my anticipation prevent your discovery,° and
   your secrecy to the King and Queen molt no feather.° I have of late—
   but wherefore I know not—lost all my mirth, forgone all custom of exercises;
   and indeed it goes so heavily with my disposition that this goodly frame, the
   earth, seems to me a sterile promontory; this most excellent canopy, the air, look   270
   you, this brave° o'erhanging firmament, this majestical roof fretted° with golden
   fire, why, it appeareth nothing to me but a foul and pestilent congregation°
   of vapors. What a piece of work° is a man! How noble in reason, how infinite in
   faculties, in form and moving how express° and admirable, in action how like an
   angel, in apprehension° how like a god! The beauty of the world, the paragon of   275
   animals! And yet, to me, what is this quintessence° of dust? Man delights not
   me—no, nor woman neither, though by your smiling you seem to say so.

---

243 *bodies* i.e., solid substances rather than shadows (since beggars are not ambitious). *outstretched*
(1) far-reaching in their ambition (2) elongated as shadows   244 *fay* faith   245 *wait upon* accompany,
attend. (But Hamlet uses the phrase in the sense of providing menial service.)   246 *sort* class, categorize
247 *dreadfully attended* waited upon in slovenly fashion   248 *beaten way* familiar path, tried-and-true
course. *make do*   251 *too dear a halfpenny* (1) too expensive at even a halfpenny, i.e., of little worth (2)
too expensive *by* a halfpenny in return for worthless kindness   252 *free* voluntary   255 *Anything but to the
purpose* anything except a straightforward answer. (Said ironically.)   256 *modesties* sense of shame. *color*
disguise   259 *conjure* adjure, entreat   260 *the consonancy of our youth* our closeness in our younger days
261 *better* more skillful. *charge* urge. *even* straight, honest   264 *of* on. *hold not off* don't hold back
266 *so . . . discovery* in that way my saying it first will spare you from revealing the truth   267 *molt no
feather* i.e., not diminish in the least   271 *brave* splendid. *fretted* adorned (with fretwork, as in a vaulted
ceiling)   272 *congregation* mass   273 *piece of work* masterpiece   274 *express* well-framed, exact, expressive   275 *apprehension* power of comprehending   276 *quintessence* the fifth essence of ancient philosophy,
beyond earth, water, air, and fire, supposed to be the substance of the heavenly bodies and to be latent in
all things

Rosencrantz: My lord, there was no such stuff in my thoughts.

Hamlet: Why did you laugh, then, when I said man delights not me?

Rosencrantz: To think, my lord, if you delight not in man, what Lenten entertain- 280
ment° the players shall receive from you. We coted° them on the way, and hither
are they coming to offer you service.

Hamlet: He that plays the king shall be welcome; His Majesty shall have tribute°
of° me. The adventurous knight shall use his foil and target,° the lover shall
not sigh gratis,° the humorous man° shall end his part in peace,° the clown 285
shall make those laugh whose lungs are tickle o' the sear,° and the lady
shall say her mind freely, or the blank verse shall halt° for 't. What players are
they?

Rosencrantz: Even those you were wont to take such delight in, the tragedians° of
the city. 290

Hamlet: How chances it they travel? Their residence,° both in reputation and profit,
was better both ways.

Rosencrantz: I think their inhibition° comes by the means of the late° innovation.°

Hamlet: Do they hold the same estimation they did when I was in the city? Are they
so followed? 295

Rosencrantz: No, indeed are they not.

Hamlet: How° comes it? Do they grow rusty?

Rosencrantz: Nay, their endeavor keeps° in the wonted° pace. But there is, sir, an
aerie° of children, little eyases,° that cry out on the top of question° and are most
tyrannically° clapped for 't. These are now the fashion, and so berattle° the 300
common stages°—so they call them—that many wearing rapiers° are afraid of
goose quills° and dare scarce come thither.

Hamlet: What, are they children? Who maintains 'em? How are they escoted?° Will
they pursue the quality° no longer than they can sing?° Will they not say afterwards, if they should grow themselves to common° players—as it is most like,° if 305
their means are no better°—their writers do them wrong to make them exclaim
against their own succession?°

Rosencrantz: Faith, there has been much to-do° on both sides, and the nation holds it
no sin to tar° them to controversy. There was for a while no money bid for argument
unless the poet and the player went to cuffs in the question.° 310

280–281 *Lenten entertainment* meager reception (appropriate to Lent)   281 *coted* overtook and passed by
283 *tribute* (1) applause (2) homage paid in money   284 *of* from.   *foil and target* sword and shield   285
gratis for nothing.   *humorous man* eccentric character, dominated by one trait or "humor."   *in peace* i.e.,
with full license   286 *tickle o' the sear* easy on the trigger, ready to laugh easily. (A *sear* is part of a gunlock.)
287 *halt* limp   289 *tragedians* actors   291 *residence* remaining in their usual place, i.e., in the city   293
inhibition formal prohibition (from acting plays in the city).   *late* recent.   *innovation* i.e., the new fashion
in satirical plays performed by boy actors in the "private" theaters; or possibly a political uprising; or the
strict limitations set on the theaters in London in 1600   297–314 *How . . . load too* (The passage, omitted
from the early quartos, alludes to the so-called War of the Theaters, 1599–1602, the rivalry between the
children's companies and the adult actors.)   298 *keeps* continues.   *wonted* usual   299 *aerie* nest.   *eyases*
young hawks.   *cry . . . question* speak shrilly, dominating the controversy (in decrying the public theaters)
300 *tyrannically* outrageously.   *berattle* berate, clamor against   301 *common stages* public theaters. *many
wearing rapiers* i.e., many men of fashion, afraid to patronize the common players for fear of being satirized by
the poets writing for the boy actors   302 *goose quills* i.e., pens of satirists   303 *escoted* maintained   304
quality (acting) profession.   *no longer . . . sing* i.e., only until their voices change   305 *common* regular,
adult.   *like* likely.   305–306 *if . . . better* if they find no better way to support themselves   307 *succession*
i.e., future careers   308 *to-do* ado   309 *tar* set on (as dogs)   309–310 *There . . . question* i.e., for a while, no
money was offered by the acting companies to playwrights for the plot to a play unless the satirical poets
who wrote for the boys and the adult actors came to blows in the play itself

Hamlet: Is 't possible?

Guildenstern: O, there has been much throwing about of brains.

Hamlet: Do the boys carry it away?°

Rosencrantz: Ay, that they do, my lord—Hercules and his load° too.

Hamlet: It is not very strange; for my uncle is King of Denmark, and those that would make mouths° at him while my father lived give twenty, forty, fifty, a hundred ducats° apiece for his picture in little.° Sblood,° there is something in this more than natural, if philosophy° could find it out.   315

A flourish [of trumpets within].

Guildenstern: There are the players.

Hamlet [to Rosenkrantz and Guildenstern]: Gentlemen, you are welcome to Elsinore.   320
Your hands, come then. Th' appurtenance° of welcome is fashion and ceremony. Let me comply° with you in this garb,° lest my extent° to the players, which, I tell you, must show fairly outwards,° should more appear like entertainment° than yours. You are welcome. But my uncle-father and aunt-mother are deceived.   325

Guildenstern: In what, my dear lord?

Hamlet: I am but mad north-north-west.° When the wind is southerly I know a hawk° from a handsaw.°

Enter Polonius.

Polonius: Well be with you, gentlemen!

Hamlet: Hark you, Guildenstern, and you too; at each ear a hearer. That great baby   330
you see there is not yet out of his swaddling clouts.°

Rosencrantz: Haply° he is the second time come to them, for they say an old man is twice a child.

Hamlet: I will prophesy, he comes to tell me of the players. Mark it.—You say right, sir, o' Monday morning, 'twas then indeed.   335

Polonius: My lord, I have news to tell you.

Hamlet: My lord, I have news to tell you. When Roscius° was an actor in Rome—

Polonius: The actors are come hither, my lord.

Hamlet: Buzz,° buzz!

Polonius: Upon my honor—   340

Hamlet: Then came each actor on his ass.

Polonius: The best actors in the world, either for tragedy, comedy, history, pastoral, pastoral-comical, historical-pastoral, tragical-historical, tragical-comical-historical-pastoral, scene individable,° or poem unlimited.° Seneca° cannot be too

---

313 *carry it away* i.e., win the day   314 *Hercules . . . load* (Thought to be an allusion to the sign of the Globe Theatre, which was Hercules bearing the world on his shoulders.)   316 *mouths* faces   317 *ducats* gold coins. *in little* in miniature. *'Sblood* by God's (Christ's) blood   318 *philosophy* i.e., scientific inquiry   321 *appurtenance* proper accompaniment   322 *comply* observe the formalities of courtesy.   *garb* i.e., manner.   *my extent* that which I extend, i.e., my polite behavior   323 *show fairly outwards* show every evidence of cordiality. *entertainment* a (warm) reception   327 *north-north-west* just off true north, only partly   328 *hawk, handsaw* i.e., two very different things, though also perhaps meaning a mattock (or *hack*) and a carpenter's cutting tool, respectively; also birds, with a play on *hernshaw*, or heron   331 *swaddling clouts* cloths in which to wrap a new-born baby   332 *Haply* perhaps   337 *Roscius* a famous Roman actor who died in 62 B.C.   339 *Buzz* (An interjection used to denote stale news.)   344 *scene individable* a play observing the unity of place; or perhaps one that is unclassifiable, or performed without intermission.   *poem unlimited* a play disregarding the unities of time and place; one that is all-inclusive.   *Seneca* writer of Latin tragedies

heavy, nor Plautus° too light. For the law of writ and the liberty,° these° are the   345
only men.

Hamlet: O Jephthah, judge of Israel,° what a treasure hadst thou!

Polonius: What a treasure had he, my lord?

Hamlet: Why,

<blockquote>

"One fair daughter, and no more,   350
The which he lovèd passing° well."
</blockquote>

Polonius [*aside*]: Still on my daughter.

Hamlet: Am I not i' the right, old Jephthah?

Polonius: If you call me Jephthah, my lord, I have a daughter that I love passing
well.   355

Hamlet: Nay, that follows not.

Polonius: What follows then, my lord?

Hamlet: Why,

<blockquote>

"As by lot,° God wot,"°
and then, you know,   360
"It came to pass, as most like° it was"—
</blockquote>

the first row° of the pious chanson° will show you more, for look where my
abridgement° comes.

Enter the Players.

You are welcome, masters; welcome, all. I am glad to see thee well. Welcome, good friends. O, old friend! Why, thy face is valanced° since I saw thee   365
last. Com'st thou to beard° me in Denmark? What, my young lady° and
mistress! By 'r Lady,° your ladyship is nearer to heaven than when I saw you last,
by the altitude of a chopine.° Pray God your voice, like a piece of uncurrent°
gold, be not cracked within the ring.° Masters, you are all welcome. We'll e'en to
't° like French falconers, fly at anything we see. We'll have a speech straight.°   370
Come, give us a taste of your quality.° Come, a passionate speech.

First Player: What speech, my good lord?

Hamlet: I heard thee speak me a speech once, but it was never acted, or if it was, not
above once, for the play, I remember, pleased not the million; 'twas caviar to the
general.° But it was—as I received it, and others, whose judgments in such matters   375
cried in the top of° mine—an excellent play, well digested° in the scenes, set
down with as much modesty° as cunning.° I remember one said there were no
sallets° in the lines to make the matter savory, nor no matter in the phrase that
might indict° the author of affectation, but called it an honest method, as

---

345 *Plautus* writer of Latin comedy.   *law . . . liberty* dramatic composition both according to the rules and disregarding the rules.   *these* i.e., the actors   347 *Jephthah . . . Israel* (Jephthah had to sacrifice his daughter; see Judges 11. Hamlet goes on to quote from a ballad on the theme.)   351 *passing* surpassingly   359 *lot* chance.   *wot* knows   361 *like* likely, probable   362 *row* stanza.   *chanson* ballad, song   362–363 *my abridgment* something that cuts short my conversation; also, a diversion   365 *valanced* fringed (with a beard)   366 *beard* confront, challenge (with obvious pun).   *young lady* i.e., boy playing women's parts   367 *By 'r Lady* by Our Lady   368 *chopine* thick-soled shoe of Italian fashion.   *uncurrent* not passable as lawful coinage   369 *cracked . . . ring* i.e., changed from adolescent to male voice, no longer suitable for women's roles. (Coins featured rings enclosing the sovereign's head; if the coin was cracked within this ring, it was unfit for currency.)   369–370 *e'en to 't* go at it   370 *straight* at once   371 *quality* professional skill   374–375 *caviar to the general* caviar to the multitude, i.e., a choice dish too elegant for coarse tastes   376 *cried in the top of* i.e., spoke with greater authority than.   *digested* arranged, ordered   377 *modesty* moderation, restraint.   *cunning* skill   378 *sallets* i.e., something savory, spicy improprieties   379 *indict* convict

wholesome as sweet, and by very much more handsome° than fine.° One speech 380
in 't I chiefly loved: 'twas Aeneas' tale to Dido, and thereabout of it especially
when he speaks of Priam's slaughter.° If it live in your memory, begin at this line:
let me see, let me see—
"The rugged Pyrrhus,° like th' Hyrcanian beast"°—
'Tis not so. It begins with Pyrrhus: 385
"The rugged° Pyrrhus, he whose sable° arms,
Black as his purpose, did the night resemble
When he lay couchèd° in the ominous horse,°
Hath now this dread and black complexion smeared
With heraldry more dismal.° Head to foot 390
Now is he total gules,° horridly tricked°
With blood of fathers, mothers, daughters, sons,
Baked and impasted° with the parching streets,°
That lend a tyrannous° and a damnèd light
To their lord's° murder. Roasted in wrath and fire, 395
And thus o'ersizèd° with coagulate gore,
With eyes like carbuncles,° the hellish Pyrrhus
Old grandsire Priam seeks."
So proceed you.
Polonius: 'Fore God, my lord, well spoken, with good accent and good discretion. 400
First Player: "Anon he finds him
Striking too short at Greeks. His antique° sword,
Rebellious to his arm, lies where it falls,
Repugnant° to command. Unequal matched,
Pyrrhus at Priam drives, in rage strikes wide, 405
But with the whiff and wind of his fell° sword
Th' unnervèd° father falls. Then senseless Ilium,°
Seeming to feel this blow, with flaming top
Stoops to his° base, and with a hideous crash
Takes prisoner Pyrrhus' ear. For, lo! His sword, 410
Which was declining° on the milky° head
Of reverend Priam, seemed i' th' air to stick.
So as a painted° tyrant Pyrrhus stood,
And, like a neutral to his will and matter,°
Did nothing. 415
But as we often see against° some storm

---

380 *handsome* well-proportioned. *fine* elaborately ornamented, showy 382 *Priam's slaughter* the slaying
of the ruler of Troy, when the Greeks finally took the city 384 *Pyrrhus* a Greek hero in the Trojan War,
also known as Neoptolemus, son of Achilles—another avenging son. *Hyrcanian beast* i.e., tiger. (On the
death of Priam, see Virgil, *Aeneid,* 2.506 ff.; compare the whole speech with Marlowe's *Dido, Queen of
Carthage,* 2.1.214 ff. On the Hyrcanian tiger, see *Aeneid,* 4.366–367. Hyrcania is on the Caspian Sea.)
386 *rugged* shaggy, savage. *sable* black (for reasons of camouflage during the episode of the Trojan horse)
388 *couched* concealed. *ominous horse* fateful Trojan horse, by which the Greeks gained access to Troy
390 *dismal* ill-omened 391 *total gules* entirely red. (A heraldic term.) *tricked* spotted and smeared.
(Heraldic.) 393 *impasted* crusted, like a thick paste. *with . . . streets* by the parching heat of the streets
(because of the fires everywhere) 394 *tyrannous* cruel 395 *their lord's* i.e., Priam's 396 *o'ersizèd* covered
as with size or glue 397 *carbuncles* large fiery-red precious stones thought to emit their own light
402 *antique* ancient, long-used 404 *Repugnant* disobedient, resistant 406 *fell* cruel 407 *unnervèd*
strengthless. *senseless Ilium* inanimate citadel of Troy 409 *his* its 411 *declining* descending. *milky*
white-haired 413 *painted* i.e., painted in a picture 414 *like . . . matter* i.e., as though suspended between
his intention and its fulfillment 416 *against* just before

A silence in the heavens, the rack° stand still,
The bold winds speechless, and the orb° below
As hush as death, anon the dreadful thunder
Doth rend the region,° so, after Pyrrhus' pause,   420
A rousèd vengeance sets him new a-work,
And never did the Cyclops'° hammers fall
On Mars's armor forged for proof eterne°
With less remorse° than Pyrrhus' bleeding sword
Now falls on Priam.   425
Out, out, thou strumpet Fortune! All you gods
In general synod° take away her power!
Break all the spokes and fellies° from her wheel,
And bowl the round nave° down the hill of heaven°
As low as to the fiends!"   430
Polonius: This is too long.
Hamlet: It shall to the barber's with your beard.—Prithee, say on. He's for a jig° or a
    tale of bawdry, or he sleeps. Say on; come to Hecuba.°
First Player: "But who, ah woe! had° seen the moblèd° queen"—
Hamlet: "The moblèd queen"?   435
Polonius: That's good. "Moblèd queen" is good.
First Player: "Run barefoot up and down, threat'ning the flames°
    With bisson rheum,° a clout° upon that head
    Where late° the diadem stood, and, for a robe,
    About her lank and all o'erteemèd° loins   440
    A blanket, in the alarm of fear caught up—
    Who this had seen, with tongue in venom steeped,
    'Gainst Fortune's state° would treason have pronounced.°
    But if the gods themselves did see her then
    When she saw Pyrrhus make malicious sport   445
    In mincing with his sword her husband's limbs,
    The instant burst of clamor that she made,
    Unless things mortal move them not at all,
    Would have made milch° the burning eyes of heaven,°
    And passion° in the gods."   450
Polonius: Look whe'er° he has not turned his color and has tears in 's eyes. Prithee,
    no more.
Hamlet: 'Tis well; I'll have thee speak out the rest of this soon.—Good my lord, will
    you see the players well bestowed?° Do you hear, let them be well used, for they are
    the abstract° and brief chronicles of the time. After your death you were better   455
    have a bad epitaph than their ill report while you live.

---

417 *rack* mass of clouds   418 *orb* globe, earth   420 *region* sky   422 *Cyclops* giant armor makers in the
smithy of Vulcan   423 *proof eterne* eternal resistance to assault   424 *remorse* pity   427 *synod* assembly
428 *fellies* pieces of wood forming the rim of a wheel   429 *nave* hub.   *hill of heaven* Mount Olympus   432
jig comic song and dance often given at the end of a play   433 *Hecuba* wife of Priam   434 *who . . . had*
anyone who had (also in line 442).   *moblèd* muffled   437 *threat'ning the flames* i.e., weeping hard enough
to dampen the flames   438 *bisson rheum* blinding tears.   *clout* cloth   439 *late* lately   440 *all o'erteemèd*
utterly worn out with bearing children   443 *state* rule, managing.   *pronounced* proclaimed   449 *milch*
milky, moist with tears.   *burning eyes of heaven* i.e., heavenly bodies   450 *passion* overpowering emotion
451 *whe'er* whether   454 *bestowed* lodged   455 *abstract* summary account

Polonius: My lord, I will use them according to their desert.

Hamlet: God's bodikin,° man, much better. Use every man after° his desert, and who shall scape whipping? Use them after your own honor and dignity. The less they deserve, the more merit is in your bounty. Take them in. 460

Polonius: Come, sirs. [*Exit.*]

Hamlet: Follow him, friends. We'll hear a play tomorrow. [*As they start to leave, Hamlet detains the First Player.*] Dost thou hear me, old friend? Can you play *The Murder of Gonzago?*

First Player: Ay, my lord. 465

Hamlet: We'll ha 't° tomorrow night. You could, for a need, study° a speech of some dozen or sixteen lines which I would set down and insert in 't, could you not?

First Player: Ay, my lord.

Hamlet: Very well. Follow that lord, and look you mock him not.

(*Exeunt Players.*)

My good friends, I'll leave you till night. You are welcome to Elsinore. 470

Rosencrantz: Good my lord!

Exeunt [Rosencrantz and Guildenstern].

Hamlet: Ay, so, goodbye to you.—Now I am alone.
O, what a rogue and peasant slave am I!
Is it not monstrous that this player here,
But° in a fiction, in a dream of passion, 475
Could force his soul so to his own conceit°
That from her working° all his visage wanned,°
Tears in his eyes, distraction in his aspect,°
A broken voice, and his whole function suiting
With forms to his conceit?° And all for nothing! 480
For Hecuba!
What's Hecuba to him, or he to Hecuba,
That he should weep for her? What would he do
Had he the motive and the cue for passion
That I have? He would drown the stage with tears 485
And cleave the general ear° with horrid° speech,
Make mad the guilty and appall° the free,°
Confound the ignorant,° and amaze° indeed
The very faculties of eyes and ears. Yet I,
A dull and muddy-mettled° rascal, peak° 490
Like John-a-dreams,° unpregnant° of my cause,
And can say nothing—no, not for a king

---

458 *God's bodikin* by God's (Christ's) little body, *bodykin.* (Not to be confused with *bodkin,* "dagger."). *after* according to 466 *ha 't* have it. *study* memorize 475 *But* merely 476 *force . . . conceit* bring his innermost being so entirely into accord with his conception (of the role) 477 *from her working* as a result of, or in response to, his soul's activity. *wanned* grew pale 478 *aspect* look, glance 479–480 *his whole . . . conceit* all his bodily powers responding with actions to suit his thought 486 *the general ear* everyone's ear. *horrid* horrible 487 *appall* (Literally, make pale.) *free* innocent 488 *Confound the ignorant* i.e., dumbfound those who know nothing of the crime that has been committed. *amaze* stun 490 *muddy-mettled* dull-spirited. *peak* mope, pine 491 *John-a-dreams* a sleepy, dreaming idler. *unpregnant of* not quickened by

Upon whose property° and most dear life
A damned defeat° was made. Am I a coward?   495
Who calls me villain? Breaks my pate° across?
Plucks off my beard and blows it in my face?
Tweaks me by the nose? Gives me the lie i' the throat°
As deep as to the lungs? Who does me this?
Ha, 'swounds,° I should take it; for it cannot be
But I am pigeon-livered° and lack gall   500
To make oppression bitter,° or ere this
I should ha' fatted all the region kites°
With this slave's offal.° Bloody, bawdy villain!
Remorseless,° treacherous, lecherous, kindless° villain!
O, vengeance!   505
Why, what an ass am I! This is most brave,°
That I, the son of a dear father murdered,
Prompted to my revenge by heaven and hell,
Must like a whore unpack my heart with words
And fall a-cursing, like a very drab,°   510
A scullion!° Fie upon 't, foh! About,° my brains!
Hum, I have heard
That guilty creatures sitting at a play
Have by the very cunning° of the scene°
Been struck so to the soul that presently°   515
They have proclaimed their malefactions;
For murder, though it have no tongue, will speak
With most miraculous organ. I'll have these players
Play something like the murder of my father
Before mine uncle. I'll observe his looks;   520
I'll tent° him to the quick.° If 'a do blench,°
I know my course. The spirit that I have seen
May be the devil, and the devil hath power
T' assume a pleasing shape; yea, and perhaps,
Out of my weakness and my melancholy,   525
As he is very potent with such spirits,°
Abuses° me to damn me. I'll have grounds
More relative° than this. The play's the thing
Wherein I'll catch the conscience of the King.

Exit.

---

493 *property* i.e., the crown; also character, quality   494 *damned defeat* damnable act of destruction   495
pate head   497 *Gives . . . throat* calls me an out-and-out liar   499 *'swounds* by his (Christ's) wounds
500 *pigeon-livered* (The pigeon or dove was popularly supposed to be mild because it secreted no gall.)
501 *bitter* i.e., bitter to me   502 *region kites* kites (birds of prey) of the air   503 *offal* entrails   504
Remorseless pitiless.   *kindless* unnatural   506 *brave* fine, admirable. (Said ironically.)   510 *drab* whore
511 *scullion* menial kitchen servant (apt to be foul-mouthed).   *About* about it, to work   514 *cunning* art,
skill.   *scene* dramatic presentation   515 *presently* at once   521 *tent* probe.   *the quick* the tender part
of a wound, the core.   *blench* quail, flinch   526 *spirits* humors (of melancholy)   527 *Abuses* deludes
528 *relative* cogent, pertinent

ACT III

SCENE I [THE CASTLE.]

Enter King, Queen, Polonius, Ophelia, Rosencrantz, Guildenstern, lords.

King: And can you by no drift of conference°
    Get from him why he puts on this confusion,
    Grating so harshly all his days of quiet
    With turbulent and dangerous lunacy?
Rosencrantz: He does confess he feels himself distracted,   5
    But from what cause 'a will by no means speak.
Guildenstern: Nor do we find him forward° to be sounded,°
    But with a crafty madness keeps aloof
    When we would bring him on to some confession
    Of his true state.
Queen: Did he receive you well?   10
Rosencrantz: Most like a gentleman.
Guildenstern: But with much forcing of his disposition.°
Rosencrantz: Niggard° of question,° but of our demands
    Most free in his reply.
Queen: Did you assay° him
    To any pastime?   15
Rosencrantz: Madam, it so fell out that certain players
    We o'erraught° on the way. Of these we told him,
    And there did seem in him a kind of joy
    To hear of it. They are here about the court,
    And, as I think, they have already order   20
    This night to play before him.
Polonius: 'Tis most true,
    And he beseeched me to entreat Your Majesties
    To hear and see the matter.
King: With all my heart, and it doth much content me
    To hear him so inclined.
    Good gentlemen, give him a further edge°   25
    And drive his purpose into these delights.
Rosencrantz: We shall, my lord.

                    Exeunt Rosencrantz and Guildenstern.
King: Sweet Gertrude, leave us too,
    For we have closely° sent for Hamlet hither,
    That he, as 'twere by accident, may here   30
    Affront° Ophelia.
    Her father and myself, lawful espials,°
    Will so bestow ourselves that seeing, unseen,
    We may of their encounter frankly judge,
    And gather by him, as he is behaved,   35

---

1 *drift of conference* directing of conversation 7 *forward* willing. *sounded* questioned 12 *disposition* inclination 13 *Niggard* stingy. *question* conversation 14 *assay* try to win 17 *o'erraught* overtook 26 *edge* incitement 29 *closely* privately 31 *Affront* confront, meet 32 *espials* spies

          If 't be th' affliction of his love or no
          That thus he suffers for.
Queen: I shall obey you.
          And for your part, Ophelia, I do wish
          That your good beauties be the happy cause
          Of Hamlet's wildness. So shall I hope your virtues   40
          Will bring him to his wonted° way again,
          To both your honors.
Ophelia: Madam, I wish it may.

                                                        [Exit Queen.]

Polonius: Ophelia, walk you here.—Gracious,° so please you,
          We will bestow° ourselves. [To Ophelia.] Read on this book, [giving her a book]
          That show of such an exercise° may color°   45
          Your loneliness.° We are oft to blame in this—
          'Tis too much proved°—that with devotion's visage
          And pious action we do sugar o'er
          The devil himself.
King [aside]: O, 'tis too true!   50
          How smart a lash that speech doth give my conscience!
          The harlot's cheek, beautied with plastering art,
          Is not more ugly to° the thing° that helps it
          Than is my deed to my most painted word.
          O heavy burden!   55
Polonius: I hear him coming. Let's withdraw, my lord.

                                        [The King and Polonius withdraw.°]

        Enter Hamlet. [Ophelia pretends to read a book.]

Hamlet: To be, or not to be, that is the question:
          Whether 'tis nobler in the mind to suffer
          The slings° and arrows of outrageous fortune,
          Or to take arms against a sea of troubles   60
          And by opposing end them. To die, to sleep—
          No more—and by a sleep to say we end
          The heartache and the thousand natural shocks
          That flesh is heir to. 'Tis a consummation
          Devoutly to be wished. To die, to sleep;   65
          To sleep, perchance to dream. Ay, there's the rub,°
          For in that sleep of death what dreams may come,
          When we have shuffled° off this mortal coil,°
          Must give us pause. There's the respect°
          That makes calamity of so long life.°   70

41 *wonted* accustomed   43 *Gracious* Your Grace (i.e., the King)   44 *bestow* conceal   45 *exercise* religious
exercise. (The book she reads is one of devotion.)   *color* give a plausible appearance to   46 *loneliness*
being alone   47 *too much proved* too often shown to be true, too often practiced   53 *to* compared to.   *the
thing* i.e., the cosmetic   56 s.d. *withdraw* (The King and Polonius may retire behind an arras. The stage
directions specify that they "enter" again near the end of the scene.)   59 *slings* missiles   66 *rub* (Literally,
an obstacle in the game of bowls.)   68 *shuffled* sloughed, cast.   *coil* turmoil   69 *respect* consideration
70 *of . . . life* so long-lived, something we willingly endure for so long (also suggesting that long life is itself
a calamity)

For who would bear the whips and scorns of time,
Th' oppressor's wrong, the proud man's contumely,°
The pangs of disprized° love, the law's delay,
The insolence of office,° and the spurns°
That patient merit of th' unworthy takes,°   75
When he himself might his quietus° make
With a bare bodkin?° Who would fardels° bear,
To grunt and sweat under a weary life,
But that the dread of something after death,
The undiscovered country from whose bourn°   80
No traveler returns, puzzles the will,
And makes us rather bear those ills we have
Than fly to others that we know not of?
Thus conscience does make cowards of us all;
And thus the native hue° of resolution   85
Is sicklied o'er with the pale cast° of thought,
And enterprises of great pitch° and moment°
With this regard° their currents° turn awry
And lose the name of action.—Soft you° now,
The fair Ophelia. Nymph, in thy orisons°   90
Be all my sins remembered.
Ophelia: Good my lord,
How does your honor for this many a day?
Hamlet: I humbly thank you; well, well, well.
Ophelia: My lord, I have remembrances of yours,
That I have longèd long to redeliver.   95
I pray you, now receive them.   [*She offers tokens.*]
Hamlet: No, not I, I never gave you aught.
Ophelia: My honored lord, you know right well you did,
And with them words of so sweet breath composed
As made the things more rich. Their perfume lost,   100
Take these again, for to the noble mind
Rich gifts wax poor when givers prove unkind.
There, my lord.   [*She gives tokens.*]
Hamlet: Ha, ha! Are you honest?°
Ophelia: My lord?   105
Hamlet: Are you fair?°
Ophelia: What means your lordship?
Hamlet: That if you be honest and fair, your honesty° should admit no discourse to°
your beauty.
Ophelia: Could beauty, my lord, have better commerce° than with honesty?   110

---

72 *contumely* insolent abuse   73 *disprized* unvalued   74 *office* officialdom.   *spurns* insults   75 *of . . . takes* receives from unworthy persons   76 *quietus* acquittance; here, death   77 *a bare bodkin* a mere dagger, unsheathed.   *fardels* burdens   80 *bourn* frontier, boundary   85 *native hue* natural color, complexion   86 *cast* tinge, shade of color   87 *pitch* height (as of a falcon's flight).   *moment* importance   88 *regard* respect, consideration.   *currents* courses   89 *Soft you* i.e., wait a minute, gently   90 *orisons* prayers   104 *honest* (1) truthful (2) chaste   106 *fair* (1) beautiful (2) just, honorable   108 *your honesty* your chastity *discourse to* familiar dealings with   110 *commerce* dealings, intercourse

Ophelia and Hamlet.

Hamlet: Ay, truly, for the power of beauty will sooner transform honesty from what it
is to a bawd than the force of honesty can translate beauty into his° likeness.
This was sometime° a paradox,° but now the time° gives it proof. I did love you
once.

Ophelia: Indeed, my lord, you made me believe so.   115

Hamlet: You should not have believed me, for virtue cannot so inoculate° our old
stock but we shall relish of it.° I loved you not.

Ophelia: I was the more deceived.

Hamlet: Get thee to a nunnery.° Why wouldst thou be a breeder of sinners? I am myself
indifferent honest,° but yet I could accuse me of such things that it were better   120

112 *his* its   113 *sometime* formerly.   *a paradox* a view opposite to commonly held opinion.   *the time* the
present age   116 *inoculate* graft, be engrafted to   117 *but . . . it* that we do not still have about us a taste of
the old stock, i.e., retain our sinfulness   119 *nunnery* convent (with possibly an awareness that the word
was also used derisively to denote a brothel)   120 *indifferent honest* reasonably virtuous

my mother had not borne me: I am very proud, revengeful, ambitious, with more
offenses at my beck° than I have thoughts to put them in, imagination to give
them shape, or time to act them in. What should such fellows as I do crawling
between earth and heaven? We are arrant knaves all; believe none of us. Go
thy ways to a nunnery. Where's your father?   125

Ophelia: At home, my lord.

Hamlet: Let the doors be shut upon him, that he may play the fool nowhere but in 's
own house. Farewell.

Ophelia: O, help him, you sweet heavens!

Hamlet: If thou dost marry, I'll give thee this plague for thy dowry: be thou as chaste   130
as ice, as pure as snow, thou shalt not escape calumny. Get thee to a nunnery,
farewell. Or, if thou wilt needs marry, marry a fool, for wise men know well
enough what monsters° you° make of them. To a nunnery, go, and quickly too.
Farewell.

Ophelia: Heavenly powers, restore him!   135

Hamlet: I have heard of your paintings too, well enough. God hath given you one
face, and you make yourselves another. You jig,° you amble,° and you lisp, you
nickname God's creatures,° and make your wantonness your ignorance.° Go to,
I'll no more on 't;° it hath made me mad. I say we will have no more marriage.
Those that are married already—all but one—shall live. The rest shall keep as   140
they are. To a nunnery, go.   *Exit.*

Ophelia: O, what a noble mind is here o'erthrown!
 The courtier's, soldier's, scholar's, eye, tongue, sword,
 Th' expectancy° and rose° of the fair state,
 The glass of fashion and the mold of form,°   145
 Th' observed of all observers,° quite, quite down!
 And I, of ladies most deject and wretched,
 That sucked the honey of his music° vows,
 Now see that noble and most sovereign reason
 Like sweet bells jangled out of tune and harsh,   150
 That unmatched form and feature of blown° youth
 Blasted° with ecstasy.° O, woe is me,
 T' have seen what I have seen, see what I see!

 Enter King and Polonius.

King: Love? His affections° do not that way tend;
 Nor what he spake, though it lacked form a little,   155
 Was not like madness. There's something in his soul
 O'er which his melancholy sits on brood,°
 And I do doubt° the hatch and the disclose°
 Will be some danger; which for to prevent,

---

122 *beck* command   133 *monsters* (An allusion to the horns of a cuckold.)   *you* i.e., you women   137 *jig*
dance.   *amble* move coyly   138 *you nickname . . . creatures* i.e., you give trendy names to things in place
of their God-given names.   *make . . . ignorance* i.e., excuse your affectation on the grounds of pretended
ignorance   139 *on 't* of it   144 *expectancy* hope.   *rose* ornament   145 *The glass . . . form* the mirror of
true self-fashioning and the pattern of courtly behavior   146 *Th' observed . . . observers* i.e., the center of
attention and honor in the court   148 *music* musical, sweetly uttered   151 *blown* blooming   152 *Blasted*
withered.   *ecstasy* madness   154 *affections* emotions, feelings   157 *sits on brood* sits like a bird on a nest,
about to *hatch* mischief (line 158)   158 *doubt* fear.   *disclose* disclosure, hatching

I have in quick determination   160
Thus set it down:° he shall with speed to England
For the demand of° our neglected tribute.
Haply the seas and countries different
With variable objects° shall expel
This something-settled matter in his heart,°   165
Whereon his brains still° beating puts him thus
From fashion of himself.° What think you on 't?

Polonius: It shall do well. But yet do I believe
The origin and commencement of his grief
Sprung from neglected love.—How now, Ophelia?   170
You need not tell us what Lord Hamlet said;
We heard it all.—My lord, do as you please,
But, if you hold it fit, after the play
Let his queen-mother° all alone entreat him
To show his grief. Let her be round° with him;   175
And I'll be placed, so please you, in the ear
Of all their conference. If she find him not,°
To England send him, or confine him where
Your wisdom best shall think.

King: It shall be so.
Madness in great ones must not unwatched go.   180

                                                                    Exeunt.

SCENE II [THE CASTLE.]

Enter Hamlet and three of the Players.

Hamlet: Speak the speech, I pray you, as I pronounced it to you, trippingly on the
tongue. But if you mouth it, as many of our players° do, I had as lief° the town
crier spoke my lines. Nor do not saw the air too much with your hand, thus, but
use all gently; for in the very torrent, tempest, and, as I may say, whirlwind of
your passion, you must acquire and beget a temperance that may give it smooth-   5
ness. O, it offends me to the soul to hear a robustious° periwig-pated° fellow tear
a passion to tatters, to very rags, to split the ears of the groundlings,° who for the
most part are capable of° nothing but inexplicable dumb shows° and noise. I
would have such a fellow whipped for o'erdoing Termagant.° It out-Herods
Herod.° Pray you, avoid it.   10

First Player: I warrant your honor.

Hamlet: Be not too tame neither, but let your own discretion be your tutor. Suit the
action to the word, the word to the action, with this special observance, that

---

161 *set it down* resolved   162 *For . . . of* to demand   164 *variable objects* various sights and surroundings to
divert him   165 *This something . . . heart* the strange matter settled in his heart   166 *still* continually
167 *From . . . himself* out of his natural manner   174 *queen-mother* queen and mother   175 *round* blunt
177 *find him not* fails to discover what is troubling him   2 *our players* players nowadays.   *I had as lief* I
would just as soon   6 *robustious* violent, boisterous.   *periwig-pated* wearing a wig   7 *groundlings* spectators
who paid least and stood in the yard of the theater   8 *capable of* able to understand.   *dumb shows* mimed
performances, often used before Shakespeare's time to precede a play or each act   9 *Termagant* a supposed
deity of the Mohammedans, not found in any English medieval play but elsewhere portrayed as violent
and blustering   10 *Herod* Herod of Jewry. (A character in *The Slaughter of the Innocents* and other cycle
plays. The part was played with great noise and fury.)

you o'erstep not the modesty° of nature. For anything so o'erdone is from° the purpose of playing, whose end, both at the first and now, was and is to hold as 't were the mirror up to nature, to show virtue her feature, scorn° her own image, and the very age and body of the time° his° form and pressure.° Now this overdone or come tardy off,° though it makes the unskillful° laugh, cannot but make the judicious grieve, the censure of the which one° must in your allowance° o'erweigh a whole theater of others. O, there be players that I have seen play, and heard others praise, and that highly, not to speak it profanely,° that, neither having th' accent of Christians° nor the gait of Christian, pagan, nor man,° have so strutted and bellowed that I have thought some of nature's journeymen° had made men and not made them well, they imitated humanity so abominably.°

First Player: I hope we have reformed that indifferently° with us, sir.

Hamlet: O, reform it altogether. And let those that play your clowns speak no more than is set down for them; for there be of them° that will themselves laugh, to set on some quantity of barren° spectators to laugh too, though in the meantime some necessary question of the play be then to be considered. That's villainous, and shows a most pitiful ambition in the fool that uses it. Go make you ready. [*Exeunt Players.*]

Enter Polonius, Guildenstern, and Rosencrantz.

How now, my lord, will the King hear this piece of work?

Polonius: And the Queen too, and that presently.°

Hamlet: Bid the players make haste. [*Exit Polonius.*]
Will you two help to hasten them?

Rosencrantz: Ay, my lord. *Exeunt they two.*

Hamlet: What ho, Horatio!

Enter Horatio.

Horatio: Here, sweet lord, at your service.

Hamlet: Horatio, thou art e'en as just a man
As e'er my conversation coped withal.°

Horatio: O, my dear lord—

Hamlet: Nay, do not think I flatter,
For what advancement may I hope from thee
That no revenue hast but thy good spirits
To feed and clothe thee? Why should the poor be flattered?
No, let the candied° tongue lick absurd pomp,
And crook the pregnant° hinges of the knee

15

20

25

30

35

40

45

14 *modesty* restraint, moderation. *from* contrary to   16 *scorn* i.e., something foolish and deserving of scorn   17 *the very   time* i.e., the present state of affairs   *his* its.   *pressure* stamp, impressed character. 18 *come tardy off* inadequately done.   *the unskillful* those lacking in judgment   19 *the censure . . . one* the judgment of even one of whom   19–20 *your allowance* your scale of values   21 *not . . . profanely* (Hamlet anticipates his idea in lines 23–25 that some men were not made by God at all.)   22 *Christians* i.e., ordinary decent folk   23 *nor man* i.e., nor any human being at all   24 *journeymen* laborers who are not yet masters in their trade   25 *abominably* (Shakespeare's usual spelling, *abhominably*, suggests a literal though etymologically incorrect meaning, "removed from human nature.")   26 *indifferently* tolerably   28 *of them* some among them   29 *barren* i.e., of wit   34 *presently* at once   40 *my . . . withal* my dealings encountered   45 *candied* sugared, flattering   46 *pregnant* compliant

Where thrift° may follow fawning. Dost thou hear?
Since my dear soul was mistress of her choice
And could of men distinguish her election,°
Sh' hath sealed thee° for herself, for thou hast been   50
As one, in suffering all, that suffers nothing,
A man that Fortune's buffets and rewards
Hast ta'en with equal thanks; and blest are those
Whose blood° and judgment are so well commeddled°
That they are not a pipe for Fortune's finger   55
To sound what stop° she please. Give me that man
That is not passion's slave, and I will wear him
In my heart's core, ay, in my heart of heart,
As I do thee.—Something too much of this.—
There is a play tonight before the King.   60
One scene of it comes near the circumstance
Which I have told thee of my father's death.
I prithee, when thou seest that act afoot,
Even with the very comment of thy soul°
Observe my uncle. If his occulted° guilt   65
Do not itself unkennel° in one speech,
It is a damnèd° ghost that we have seen,
And my imaginations are as foul
As Vulcan's stithy.° Give him heedful note,
For I mine eyes will rivet to his face,   70
And after we will both our judgments join
In censure of his seeming.°

Horatio: Well, my lord.
If 'a steal aught° the whilst this play is playing
And scape detecting, I will pay the theft.

[*Flourish.*] *Enter trumpets and kettledrums, King, Queen, Polonius, Ophelia,*
[*Rosencrantz, Guildenstern, and other lords, with guards carrying torches*].

Hamlet: They are coming to the play. I must be idle.° Get you a place.   75

[*The King, Queen, and courtiers sit.*]

King: How fares our cousin° Hamlet?
Hamlet: Excellent, i' faith, of the chameleon's dish:° I eat the air, promise-crammed.
You cannot feed capons° so.

---

47 *thrift* profit   49 *could . . . election* could make distinguishing choices among persons   50 *sealed thee*
(Literally, as one would seal a legal document to mark possession.)   54 *blood* passion.   *commeddled* commingled   56 *stop* hole in a wind instrument for controlling the sound   64 *very . . . soul* your most penetrating observation and consideration   65 *occulted* hidden   66 *unkennel* (As one would say of a fox driven
from its lair.)   67 *damnèd* in league with Satan   69 *stithy* smithy, place of stiths (anvils)   72 *censure of his
seeming* judgment of his appearance or behavior   73 *If 'a steal aught* if he gets away with anything   75 *idle*
(1) unoccupied (2) mad   76 *cousin* i.e., close relative   77 *chameleon's dish* (Chameleons were supposed to
feed on air. Hamlet deliberately misinterprets the King's *fares* as "feeds." By his phrase *eat the air,* he also
plays on the idea of feeding himself with the promise of succession, of being the *heir.*)   78 *capons* roosters
castrated and *crammed* with feed to make them succulent

King: I have nothing with° this answer, Hamlet. These words are not mine.°

Hamlet: No, nor mine now.° [*To Polonius.*] My lord, you played once i' th' university, 80
you say?

Polonius: That did I, my lord, and was accounted a good actor.

Hamlet: What did you enact?

Polonius: I did enact Julius Caesar. I was killed i' the Capitol; Brutus killed me.

Hamlet: It was a brute° part° of him to kill so capital a calf° there.—Be the players 85
ready?

Rosencrantz: Ay, my lord. They stay upon° your patience.

Queen: Come hither, my dear Hamlet, sit by me.

Hamlet: No, good Mother, here's metal° more attractive.

Polonius [*to the King*]: O, ho, do you mark that? 90

Hamlet: Lady, shall I lie in your lap?

[*Lying down at Ophelia's feet.*]

Ophelia: No, my lord.

Hamlet: I mean, my head upon your lap?

Ophelia: Ay, my lord.

Hamlet: Do you think I meant country matters?° 95

Ophelia: I think nothing, my lord.

Hamlet: That's a fair thought to lie between maids' legs.

Ophelia: What is, my lord?

Hamlet: Nothing.°

Ophelia: You are merry, my lord. 100

Hamlet: Who, I?

Ophelia: Ay, my lord.

Hamlet: O God, your only jig maker.° What should a man do but be merry? For
look you how cheerfully my mother looks, and my father died within 's° two
hours. 105

Ophelia: Nay, 'tis twice two months, my lord.

Hamlet: So long? Nay then, let the devil wear black, for I'll have a suit of sables.°
O heavens! Die two months ago, and not forgotten yet? Then there's hope a great
man's memory may outlive his life half a year. But, by'r Lady, 'a must build churches,
then, or else shall 'a suffer not thinking on,° with the hobbyhorse, whose epitaph 110
is "For O, for O, the hobbyhorse is forgot."°

---

79 *have . . . with* make nothing of, or gain nothing from.   *are not mine* do not respond to what I asked
80 *nor mine now* (Once spoken, words are proverbially no longer the speaker's own—and hence should be
uttered warily.)   85 *brute* (The Latin meaning of *brutus,* "stupid," was often used punningly with the
name Brutus.)   *part* (1) deed (2) role.   *calf* fool   87 *stay upon* await   89 *metal* substance that is
attractive, i.e., magnetic, but with suggestion also of *mettle,* "disposition"   95 *country matters* sexual intercourse (making a bawdy pun on the first syllable of *country*)   99 *Nothing* the figure zero or naught, suggesting the female sexual anatomy. (*Thing* not infrequently has a bawdy connotation of male or female
anatomy, and the reference here could be male.)   103 *only jig maker* very best composer of jigs, i.e., pointless merriment. (Hamlet replies sardonically to Ophelia's observation that he is merry by saying, "If you're
looking for someone who is really merry, you've come to the right person.")   104 *within 's* within this (i.e.,
these)   107 *suit of sables* garments trimmed with the fur of the sable and hence suited for a wealthy person, not
a mourner (but with a pun on *sable,* "black," ironically suggesting mourning once again)   110 *suffer . . .
on* undergo oblivion   111 *For . . . forgot* (Verse of a song occurring also in *Love's Labor's Lost,* III, i,
27–28. The hobbyhorse was a character made up to resemble a horse and rider, appearing in the morris
dance and such May-game sports. This song laments the disappearance of such customs under pressure
from the Puritans.)

The trumpets sound. Dumb show follows.

Enter a King and a Queen [very lovingly]; the Queen embracing him, and he her. [She kneels, and makes show of protestation unto him.] He takes her up, and declines his head upon her neck. He lies him down upon a bank of flowers. She, seeing him asleep, leaves him. Anon comes in another man, takes off his crown, kisses it, pours poison in the sleeper's ears, and leaves him. The Queen returns, finds the King dead, makes passionate action. The Poisoner with some three or four come in again, seem to condole with her. The dead body is carried away. The Poisoner woos the Queen with gifts; she seems harsh awhile, but in the end accepts love.

[*Exeunt players.*]

Ophelia: What means this, my lord?

Hamlet: Marry, this' miching mallico;° it means mischief.

Ophelia: Belike° this show imports the argument° of the play.

Enter Prologue.

Hamlet: We shall know by this fellow. The players cannot keep counsel;° they'll 115
tell all.

Ophelia: Will 'a tell us what this show meant?

Hamlet: Ay, or any show that you will show him. Be not you° ashamed to show, he'll
not shame to tell you what it means.

Ophelia: You are naught, you are naught.° I'll mark the play. 120

Prologue: For us, and for our tragedy,
Here stooping° to your clemency,
We beg your hearing patiently.

[*Exit.*]

Hamlet: Is this a prologue, or the posy of a ring?°

Ophelia: 'Tis brief, my lord. 125

Hamlet: As woman's love.

Enter [two Players as] King and Queen.

Player King: Full thirty times hath Phoebus' cart° gone round
Neptune's salt wash° and Tellus'° orbèd ground,
And thirty dozen moons with borrowed° sheen
About the world have times twelve thirties been,
Since love our hearts and Hymen° did our hands 130
Unite commutual° in most sacred bands.°

Player Queen: So many journeys may the sun and moon
Make us again count o'er ere love be done!
But, woe is me, you are so sick of late, 135
So far from cheer and from your former state,
That I distrust° you. Yet, though I distrust,
Discomfort° you, my lord, it nothing° must.
For women's fear and love hold quantity;°

---

113 *this' miching mallico* this is sneaking mischief   114 *Belike* probably.   *argument* plot   115 *counsel* secret
118 *Be not you* provided you are not   120 *naught* indecent. (Ophelia is reacting to Hamlet's pointed
remarks about not being ashamed to show all.)   122 *stooping* bowing   124 *posy . . . ring* brief motto in
verse inscribed in a ring   127 *Phoebus' cart* the sun-god's chariot, making its yearly cycle   128 *salt wash*
the sea.   *Tellus* goddess of the earth, of the *orbèd ground*   129 *borrowed* i.e., reflected   131 *Hymen* god of
matrimony   132 *commutual* mutually.   *bands* bonds   137 *distrust* am anxious about   138 *Discomfort* distress.   *nothing* not at all   139 *hold quantity* keep proportion with one another

In neither aught, or in extremity.°   140
Now, what my love is, proof° hath made you know,
And as my love is sized,° my fear is so.
Where love is great, the littlest doubts are fear;
Where little fears grow great, great love grows there.
Player King: Faith, I must leave thee, love, and shortly too;   145
My operant powers° their functions leave to do.°
And thou shalt live in this fair world behind,°
Honored, beloved; and haply one as kind
For husband shalt thou—
Player Queen: O, confound the rest!
Such love must needs be treason in my breast.   150
In second husband let me be accurst!
None° wed the second but who° killed the first.
Hamlet: Wormwood,° wormwood.
Player Queen: The instances° that second marriage move°
Are base respects of thrift,° but none of love.   155
A second time I kill my husband dead
When second husband kisses me in bed.
Player King: I do believe you think what now you speak,
But what we do determine oft we break.
Purpose is but the slave to memory,°   160
Of violent birth, but poor validity,°
Which° now, like fruit unripe, sticks on the tree,
But fall unshaken when they mellow be.
Most necessary 'tis that we forget
To pay ourselves what to ourselves is debt.°   165
What to ourselves in passion we purpose,
The passion ending, doth the purpose lose.
The violence of either grief or joy
Their own enactures° with themselves destroy.
Where joy most revels, grief doth most lament;   170
Grief joys, joy grieves, on slender accident.°
This world is not for aye,° nor 'tis not strange
That even our loves should with our fortunes change;
For 'tis a question left us yet to prove,
Whether love lead fortune, or else fortune love.   175
The great man down,° you mark his favorite flies;
The poor advanced makes friends of enemies.°

140 *In . . . extremity* i.e., women fear and love either too little or too much, but the two, fear and love, are equal in either case   141 *proof* experience   142 *sized* in size   146 *operant powers* vital functions.   *leave to do* cease to perform   147 *behind* after I have gone   152 *None* i.e., let no woman.   *but who* except the one who   153 *Wormwood* i.e., how bitter. (Literally, a bitter-tasting plant.)   154 *instances* motives.   *move* motivate   155 *base . . . thrift* ignoble considerations of material prosperity   160 *Purpose . . . memory* our good intentions are subject to forgetfulness   161 *validity* strength, durability   162 *Which* i.e., purpose   164–165 *Most . . . debt* it's inevitable that in time we forget the obligations we have imposed on ourselves   169 *enactures* fulfillments   170–171 *Where . . . accident* the capacity for extreme joy and grief go together, and often one extreme is instantly changed into its opposite on the slightest provocation   172 *aye* ever   176 *down* fallen in fortune   177 *The poor . . . enemies* when one of humble station is promoted, you see his enemies suddenly becoming his friends

And hitherto° doth love on fortune tend;°
For who not needs° shall never lack a friend,
And who in want° a hollow friend doth try°   180
Directly seasons him° his enemy.
But, orderly to end where I begun,
Our wills and fates do so contrary run°
That our devices still° are overthrown;
Our thoughts are ours, their ends° none of our own.   185
So think thou wilt no second husband wed,
But die thy thoughts when thy first lord is dead.
Player Queen: Nor° earth to me give food, nor heaven light,
Sport and repose lock from me day and night,°
To desperation turn my trust and hope,   190
An anchor's cheer° in prison be my scope!°
Each° opposite that blanks° the face of joy
Meet what I would have well and it destroy!
Both here and hence° pursue me lasting strife
If, once a widow, ever I be wife!   195
Hamlet: If she should break it now!
Player King: 'Tis deeply sworn. Sweet, leave me here awhile;
My spirits° grow dull, and fain I would beguile
The tedious day with sleep.
Player Queen: Sleep rock thy brain,
And never come mischance between us twain!   200

                                     [He sleeps.] Exit [Player Queen].

Hamlet: Madam, how like you this play?
Queen: The lady doth protest too much,° methinks.
Hamlet: O, but she'll keep her word.
King: Have you heard the argument?° Is there no offense° in 't?
Hamlet: No, no, they do but jest,° poison in jest. No offense i' the world.   205
King: What do you call the play?
Hamlet: *The Mousetrap.* Marry, how? Tropically.° This play is the image of a murder
    done in Vienna. Gonzago is the Duke's° name, his wife, Baptista. You shall see
    anon. 'Tis a knavish piece of work, but what of that? Your Majesty, and we that
    have free° souls, it touches us not. Let the galled jade° wince, our withers° are   210
    unwrung.°

---

178 *hitherto* up to this point in the argument, or, to this extent. *tend* attend 179 *who not needs* he who is
not in need (of wealth) 180 *who in want* he who, being in need. *try* test (his generosity) 181 *seasons
him* ripens him into 183 *Our . . . run* what we want and what we get go so contrarily 184 *devices still*
intentions continually 185 *ends* results 188 *Nor* let neither 189 *Sport . . . night* may day deny me its
pastimes and night its repose 191 *anchor's cheer* anchorite's or hermit's fare. *my scope* the extent of my
happiness 192–193 *Each . . . destroy* may every adverse thing that causes the face of joy to turn pale meet
and destroy everything that I desire to see prosper. 192 *blanks* causes to blanch or grow pale 194 *hence*
in the life hereafter 198 *spirits* vital spirits 202 *doth . . . much* makes too many promises and protestations
204 *argument* plot 204–205 *offense . . . offense* cause for objection . . . actual injury, crime 205 *jest* make
believe 207 *Tropically* figuratively. (The First Quarto reading, *trapically,* suggests a pun on *trap* in
Mousetrap.) 208 *Duke's* i.e., King's. (A slip that may be due to Shakespeare's possible source, the alleged
murder of the Duke of Urbino by Luigi Gonzaga in 1538.) 210 *free* guiltless. *galled jade* horse whose
hide is rubbed by saddle or harness. *withers* the part between the horse's shoulder blades 211 *unwrung*
not rubbed sore

The players perform *The Murder of Gonzago* for Queen Gertrude and King Claudius (III, ii, 125–229).

Enter Lucianus.

This is one Lucianus, nephew to the King.

Ophelia: You are as good as a chorus,° my lord.

Hamlet: I could interpret° between you and your love, if I could see the puppets dallying.°   215

Ophelia: You are keen, my lord, you are keen.°

Hamlet: It would cost you a groaning to take off mine edge.

213 *chorus* (In many Elizabethan plays, the forthcoming action was explained by an actor known as the "chorus"; at a puppet show, the actor who spoke the dialogue was known as an "interpreter," as indicated by the lines following.) 214 *interpret* (1) ventriloquize the dialogue, as in puppet show (2) act as pander 214–215 *puppets dallying* (With suggestion of sexual play, continued in lines 216–217: *keen*, "sexually aroused," *groaning*, "moaning in pregnancy," and *edge*, "sexual desire" or "impetuosity.") 216 *keen* sharp, bitter

Ophelia: Still better, and worse.°

Hamlet: So° you mis-take° your husbands. Begin, murderer; leave thy damnable faces and begin. Come, the croaking raven doth bellow for revenge. 220

Lucianus: Thoughts black, hands apt, drugs fit, and time agreeing,
Confederate season,° else° no creature seeing,°
Thou mixture rank, of midnight weeds collected,
With Hecate's ban° thrice blasted, thrice infected,
Thy natural magic and dire property° 225
On wholesome life usurp immediately.

[*He pours the poison into the sleeper's ear.*]

Hamlet: 'A poisons him i' the garden for his estate.° His° name's Gonzago. The story is extant, and written in very choice Italian. You shall see anon how the murderer gets the love of Gonzago's wife.

[*Claudius rises.*]

Ophelia: The King rises. 230

Hamlet: What, frighted with false fire?°

Queen: How fares my lord?

Polonius: Give o'er the play.

King: Give me some light. Away!

Polonius: Lights, lights, lights! 235

Exeunt all but Hamlet and Horatio.

Hamlet:

"Why,° let the strucken deer go weep,
The hart ungallèd° play.
For some must watch,° while some must sleep;
Thus runs the world away."°

Would not this,° sir, and a forest of feathers°—if the rest of my fortunes turn Turk 240
with° me—with two Provincial roses° on my razed° shoes, get me a fellowship°
in a cry° of players?

Horatio: Half a share.

Hamlet: A whole one, I.

"For thou dost know, O Damon° dear, 245
This° realm dismantled° was
Of Jove himself, and now reigns here
A very, very—pajock."

218 *Still . . . worse* more keen, always *bettering* what other people say with witty wordplay, but at the same time more offensive   219 *So* even thus (in marriage). *mis-take* take falseheartedly and cheat on. (The marriage vows say "for better, for worse.")   222 *Confederate season* the time and occasion conspiring (to assist the murderer). *else* otherwise. *seeing* seeing me   224 *Hecate's ban* the curse of Hecate, the goddess of witchcraft   225 *dire property* baleful quality   227 *estate* i.e., the kingship. *His* i.e., the King's   231 *false fire* the blank discharge of a gun loaded with powder but no shot   236–239 *Why . . . away* (Probably from an old ballad, with allusion to the popular belief that a wounded deer retires to weep and die; compare with *As You Like It*, II, i, 33–66.)   237 *ungallèd* unafflicted   238 *watch* remain awake   239 *Thus . . . away* thus the world goes   240 *this* i.e., the play. *feathers* (Allusion to the plumes that Elizabethan actors were fond of wearing.)   240–241 *turn Turk with* turn renegade against, go back on   241 *Provincial roses* rosettes of ribbon, named for roses grown in a part of France. *razed* with ornamental slashing. *fellowship . . . players* partnership in a theatrical company.   242 *cry* pack (of hounds)   245 *Damon* the friend of Pythias, as Horatio is friend of Hamlet; or, a traditional pastoral name   246–248 *This realm . . . pajock* i.e., Jove, representing divine authority and justice, has abandoned this realm to its own devices, leaving in his stead only a peacock or vain pretender to virtue (though the rhyme-word expected in place of *pajock* or "peacock" suggests that the realm is now ruled over by an "ass").   246 *dismantled* stripped, divested

Horatio: You might have rhymed.

Hamlet: O good Horatio, I'll take the ghost's word for a thousand pound. Didst 250
perceive?

Horatio: Very well, my lord.

Hamlet: Upon the talk of the poisoning?

Horatio: I did very well note him.

Enter Rosencrantz and Guildenstern.

Hamlet: Aha! Come, some music! Come, the recorders.° 255
"For if the King like not the comedy,
Why then, belike, he likes it not, perdy."°
Come, some music.

Guildenstern: Good my lord, vouchsafe me a word with you.

Hamlet: Sir, a whole history. 260

Guildenstern: The King, sir—

Hamlet: Ay, sir, what of him?

Guildenstern: Is in his retirement° marvelous distempered.°

Hamlet: With drink, sir?

Guildenstern: No, my lord, with choler. 265

Hamlet: Your wisdom should show itself more richer to signify this to the doctor, for
for me to put him to his purgation° would perhaps plunge him into more choler.°

Guildenstern: Good my lord, put your discourse into some frame° and start° not so
wildly from my affair.

Hamlet: I am tame, sir. Pronounce. 270

Guildenstern: The Queen, your mother, in most great affliction of spirit, hath sent
me to you.

Hamlet: You are welcome.

Guildenstern: Nay, good my lord, this courtesy is not of the right breed.° If it shall
please you to make me a wholesome answer, I will do your mother's command- 275
ment; if not, your pardon° and my return shall be the end of my business.

Hamlet: Sir, I cannot.

Rosencrantz: What, my lord?

Hamlet: Make you a wholesome answer; my wit's diseased. But, sir, such answer as
I can make, you shall command, or rather, as you say, my mother. Therefore no 280
more, but to the matter. My mother, you say—

Rosencrantz: Then thus she says: your behavior hath struck her into amazement
and admiration.°

Hamlet: O wonderful son, that can so stonish a mother! But is there no sequel at the
heels of this mother's admiration? Impart. 285

Rosencrantz: She desires to speak with you in her closet° ere you go to bed.

Hamlet: We shall obey, were she ten times our mother. Have you any further trade
with us?

---

255 *recorders* wind instruments of the flute kind   257 *perdy* (A corruption of the French *par dieu,* "by God.")
263 *retirement* withdrawal to his chambers.   *distempered* out of humor. (But Hamlet deliberately plays on the
wider application to any illness of mind or body, especially to drunkenness.)   267 *purgation* (Hamlet hints at
something going beyond medical treatment to blood-letting and the extraction of confession.).   *choler*
anger. (But Hamlet takes the word in its more basic humoral sense of "bilious disorder.")   268 *frame* order.
start shy or jump away (like a horse; the opposite of *tame* in line 270)   274 *breed* (1) kind (2) breeding, manners   276 *pardon* permission to depart   283 *admiration* bewilderment   286 *closet* private chamber

Rosencrantz: My lord, you once did love me.

Hamlet: And do still, by these pickers and stealers.° 290

Rosencrantz: Good my lord, what is your cause of distemper? You do surely bar the door upon your own liberty° if you deny° your griefs to your friend.

Hamlet: Sir, I lack advancement.

Rosencrantz: How can that be, when you have the voice of the King himself for your succession in Denmark? 295

Hamlet: Ay, sir, but "While the grass grows"°—the proverb is something° musty.

Enter the Players° with recorders.

O, the recorders. Let me see one. [*He takes a recorder.*] To withdraw° with you: why do you go about to recover the wind° of me, as if you would drive me into a toil?°

Guildenstern: O, my lord, if my duty be too bold, my love is too unmannerly.° 300

Hamlet: I do not well understand that.° Will you play upon this pipe?

Guildenstern: My lord, I cannot.

Hamlet: I pray you.

Guildenstern: Believe me, I cannot.

Hamlet: I do beseech you. 305

Guildenstern: I know no touch of it, my lord.

Hamlet: It is as easy as lying. Govern these ventages° with your fingers and thumb, give it breath with your mouth, and it will discourse most eloquent music. Look you, these are the stops.

Guildenstern: But these cannot I command to any utterance of harmony. I have not 310 the skill.

Hamlet: Why, look you now, how unworthy a thing you make of me! You would play upon me, you would seem to know my stops, you would pluck out the heart of my mystery, you would sound° me from my lowest note to the top of my compass,° and there is much music, excellent voice, in this little organ,° yet cannot you 315 make it speak. 'Sblood, do you think I am easier to be played on than a pipe? Call me what instrument you will, though you can fret° me, you cannot play upon me.

Enter Polonius.

God bless you, sir!

Polonius: My lord, the Queen would speak with you, and presently.° 320

Hamlet: Do you see yonder cloud that's almost in shape of a camel?

Polonius: By the Mass and 'tis, like a camel indeed.

Hamlet: Methinks it is like a weasel.

---

290 *pickers and stealers* i.e., hands. (So called from the catechism, "to keep my hands from picking and stealing.") 292 *liberty* i.e., being freed from *distemper*, line 291; but perhaps with a veiled threat as well. *deny* refuse to share 296 *While . . . grows* (The rest of the proverb is "the silly horse starves"; Hamlet may not live long enough to succeed to the kingdom.) *something* somewhat. s.d. *Players* actors 297 *withdraw* speak privately 298 *recover the wind* get to the windward side (thus driving the game into the *toil*, or "net") 299 *toil* snare 300 *if . . . unmannerly* if I am using an unmannerly boldness, it is my love that occasions it 301 *I . . . that* i.e., I don't understand how genuine love can be unmannerly 307 *ventages* finger-holes or *stops* (line 313) of the recorder 314 *sound* (1) fathom (2) produce sound in 314 *compass* range (of voice) 315 *organ* musical instrument 317 *fret* irritate (with a quibble on *fret*, meaning the piece of wood, gut, or metal that regulates the fingering on an instrument) 320 *presently* at once

Polonius: It is backed like a weasel.

Hamlet: Or like a whale.   325

Polonius: Very like a whale.

Hamlet: Then I will come to my mother by and by.° [*Aside.*] They fool me° to the top
    of my bent.°—I will come by and by.

Polonius: I will say so.   [*Exit.*]

Hamlet: "By and by" is easily said. Leave me, friends.   330

                             [*Exeunt all but Hamlet.*]

'Tis now the very witching time° of night,
When churchyards yawn and hell itself breathes out
Contagion to this world. Now could I drink hot blood
And do such bitter business as the day
Would quake to look on. Soft, now to my mother.   335
O heart, lose not thy nature!° Let not ever
The soul of Nero° enter this firm bosom.
Let me be cruel, not unnatural;
I will speak daggers to her, but use none.
My tongue and soul in this be hypocrites: 340
How in my words soever° she be shent,°
To give them seals° never my soul consent!   *Exit.*

SCENE III [THE CASTLE.]

Enter King, Rosencrantz, and Guildenstern.

King: I like him° not, nor stands it safe with us
    To let his madness range. Therefore prepare you.
    I your commission will forthwith dispatch,°
    And he to England shall along with you.
    The terms of our estate° may not endure   5
    Hazard so near us as doth hourly grow
    Out of his brows.°

Guildenstern: We will ourselves provide.
    Most holy and religious fear° it is
    To keep those many many bodies safe
    That live and feed upon Your Majesty.   10

Rosencrantz: The single and peculiar° life is bound
    With all the strength and armor of the mind
    To keep itself from noyance,° but much more
    That spirit upon whose weal depends and rests
    The lives of many. The cess° of majesty   15
    Dies not alone, but like a gulf° doth draw

327 *by and by* quite soon.   *fool me* trifle with me, humor my fooling   327–328 *top of my bent* limit of my
ability or endurance. (Literally, the extent to which a bow may be bent.)   331 *witching time* time when
spells are cast and evil is abroad   336 *nature* natural feeling   337 *Nero* murderer of his mother, Agrippina
341 *How . . . soever* however much by my words.   *shent* rebuked   342 *give them seals* i.e., confirm them
with deeds   1 *him* i.e., his behavior   3 *dispatch* prepare, cause to be drawn up   5 *terms of our estate* circumstances of my royal position   7 *Out of his brows* i.e., from his brain, in the form of plots and threats
8 *religious fear* sacred concern   11 *single and peculiar* individual and private   13 *noyance* harm   15 *cess*
decrease, cessation   16 *gulf* whirlpool

> What's near it with it; or it is a massy° wheel
> Fixed on the summit of the highest mount,
> To whose huge spokes ten thousand lesser things
> Are mortised° and adjoined, which, when it falls,°   20
> Each small annexment, petty consequence,°
> Attends° the boisterous ruin. Never alone
> Did the King sigh, but with a general groan.
> *King:* Arm° you, I pray you, to this speedy voyage,
> For we will fetters put about this fear,   25
> Which now goes too free-footed.
> *Rosencrantz:*   We will haste us.
>   *Exeunt gentlemen [Rosencrantz and Guildenstern].*

> *Enter Polonius.*

> *Polonius:* My lord, he's going to his mother's closet.
> Behind the arras° I'll convey myself
> To hear the process.° I'll warrant she'll tax him home,°
> And, as you said—and wisely was it said—   30
> 'Tis meet° that some more audience than a mother,
> Since nature makes them partial, should o'erhear
> The speech, of vantage.° Fare you well, my liege.
> I'll call upon you ere you go to bed
> And tell you what I know.
> *King:*   Thanks, dear my lord.   35
>   *Exit [Polonius].*
> O, my offense is rank! It smells to heaven.
> It hath the primal eldest curse° upon 't,
> A brother's murder. Pray can I not,
> Though inclination be as sharp as will;°
> My stronger guilt defeats my strong intent,   40
> And like a man to double business bound°
> I stand in pause where I shall first begin,
> And both neglect. What if this cursèd hand
> Were thicker than itself with brother's blood,
> Is there not rain enough in the sweet heavens   45
> To wash it white as snow? Whereto serves mercy
> But to confront the visage of offense?°
> And what's in prayer but this twofold force,
> To be forestallèd° ere we come to fall,

---

17 *massy* massive   20 *mortised* fastened (as with a fitted joint).   *when it falls* i.e., when it descends, like the wheel of Fortune, bringing a king down with it   21 *Each . . . consequence* i.e., every hanger-on and unimportant person or thing connected with the King   22 *Attends* participates in   24 *Arm* prepare   28 *arras* screen of tapestry placed around the walls of household apartments. (On the Elizabethan stage, the arras was presumably over a door or discovery space in the tiring-house facade.)   29 *process* proceedings.   *tax him home* reprove him severely   31 *meet* fitting   33 *of vantage* from an advantageous place, or, in addition   37 *the primal eldest curse* the curse of Cain, the first murderer; he killed his brother Abel   39 *Though . . . will* though my desire is as strong as my determination   41 *bound* (1) destined (2) obliged. (The King wants to repent and still enjoy what he has gained.)   46–47 *Whereto . . . offense* what function does mercy serve other than to meet sin face to face?   49 *forestallèd* prevented (from sinning)

Or pardoned being down? Then I'll look up.   50
My fault is past. But O, what form of prayer
Can serve my turn? "Forgive me my foul murder"?
That cannot be, since I am still possessed
Of those effects for which I did the murder:
My crown, mine own ambition, and my queen.   55
May one be pardoned and retain th' offense?°
In the corrupted currents° of this world
Offense's gilded hand° may shove° by justice,
And oft 'tis seen the wicked prize° itself
Buys out the law. But 'tis not so above.   60
There° is no shuffling,° there the action lies°
In his° true nature, and we ourselves compelled,
Even to the teeth and forehead° of our faults,
To give in° evidence. What then? What rests?°
Try what repentance can. What can it not?   65
Yet what can it, when one cannot repent?
O wretched state, O bosom black as death,
O limèd° soul that, struggling to be free,
Art more engaged!° Help, angels! Make assay.°
Bow, stubborn knees, and heart with strings of steel,   70
Be soft as sinews of the newborn babe!
All may be well.   [*He kneels.*]

Enter Hamlet.

Hamlet: Now might I do it pat,° now 'a is a-praying;
And now I'll do 't. [*He draws his sword.*] And so 'a goes to heaven,
And so am I revenged. That would be scanned:°   75
A villain kills my father, and for that,
I, his sole son, do this same villain send
To heaven.
Why, this is hire and salary, not revenge.
'A took my father grossly, full of bread,°   80
With all his crimes broad blown,° as flush° as May;
And how his audit° stands who knows save° heaven?
But in our circumstance and course of thought°
'Tis heavy with him. And am I then revenged,
To take him in the purging of his soul,   85
When he is fit and seasoned° for his passage?

---

56 *th' offense* the thing for which one offended   57 *currents* courses   58 *gilded hand* hand offering gold as a bribe.   *shove by* thrust aside   59 *wicked prize* prize won by wickedness   61 *There* i.e., in heaven.   *shuffling* escape by trickery.   *the action lies* the accusation is made manifest. (A legal metaphor.)   62 *his* its   63 *to the teeth and forehead* face to face, concealing nothing   64 *give in* provide.   *rests* remains   68 *limèd* caught as with birdlime, a sticky substance used to ensnare birds   69 *engaged* entangled.   *assay* trial. (Said to himself.)   73 *pat* opportunely   75 *would be scanned* needs to be looked into, or, would be interpreted as follows   80 *grossly, full of bread* i.e., enjoying his worldly pleasures rather than fasting. (See Ezekiel 16:49.)   81 *crimes broad blown* sins in full bloom.   *flush* vigorous   82 *audit* account.   *save* except for   83 *in . . . thought* as we see it from our mortal perspective   86 *seasoned* matured, readied

Hamlet stops himself from killing Claudius during his prayers (III, iii, 73–96).

No!
Up, sword, and know° thou a more horrid hent.°

[*He puts up his sword.*]

When he is drunk asleep, or in his rage,°
Or in th' incestuous pleasure of his bed,   90
At game,° a-swearing, or about some act
That has no relish° of salvation in 't—
Then trip him, that his heels may kick at heaven,
And that his soul may be as damned and black
As hell, whereto it goes. My mother stays.°   95
This physic° but prolongs thy sickly days.

Exit.

---

88 *know . . . hent* await to be grasped by me on a more horrid occasion.   *hent* act of seizing   89 *drunk . . . rage* dead drunk, or in a fit of sexual passion   91 *game* gambling   92 *relish* trace, savor   95 *stays* awaits (me)   96 *physic* purging (by prayer), or, Hamlet's postponement of the killing

King: My words fly up, my thoughts remain below.
　　Words without thoughts never to heaven go.　　　　　　　　　*Exit.*

SCENE IV [THE QUEEN'S PRIVATE CHAMBER.]

　　Enter [Queen] *Gertrude and Polonius.*

Polonius: 'A will come straight. Look you lay home° to him.
　　Tell him his pranks have been too broad° to bear with,
　　And that Your Grace hath screened and stood between
　　Much heat° and him. I'll shroud° me even here.
　　Pray you, be round° with him.　　　　　　　　　　　　　　　5
Hamlet (within): Mother, Mother, Mother!
Queen: I'll warrant you, fear me not.
　　Withdraw, I hear him coming.

　　　　　　　　　　　　　　　　　　[*Polonius hides behind the arras.*]

　　Enter Hamlet.

Hamlet: Now, Mother, what's the matter?
Queen: Hamlet, thou hast thy father° much offended.　　　　10
Hamlet: Mother, you have my father much offended.
Queen: Come, come, you answer with an idle° tongue.
Hamlet: Go, go, you question with a wicked tongue.
Queen: Why, how now, Hamlet?
Hamlet:　　　　　　　　　　　　What's the matter now?
Queen: Have you forgot me?°
Hamlet:　　　　　　　　　　No, by the rood,° not so:　　　　15
　　You are the Queen, your husband's brother's wife,
　　And—would it were not so!—you are my mother.
Queen: Nay, then, I'll set those to you that can speak.°
Hamlet: Come, come, and sit you down; you shall not budge.
　　You go not till I set you up a glass　　　　　　　　　　　20
　　Where you may see the inmost part of you.
Queen: What wilt thou do? Thou wilt not murder me?
　　Help, ho!
Polonius [*behind the arras*]: What ho! Help!
Hamlet [*drawing*]: How now? A rat? Dead for a ducat,° dead!　　25

　　　　　　　　　　　　　　[*He thrusts his rapier through the arras.*]

Polonius [*behind the arras*]: O, I am slain!　　　　[*He falls and dies.*]
Queen:　　　　　　　　　　　　O me, what has thou done?
Hamlet: Nay, I know not. Is it the King?
Queen: O, what a rash and bloody deed is this!
Hamlet: A bloody deed—almost as bad, good Mother,
　　As kill a king, and marry with his brother.　　　　　　　30

---

1 *lay home* thrust to the heart, reprove him soundly　2 *broad* unrestrained　4 *Much heat* i.e., the King's anger.　*shroud* conceal (with ironic fitness to Polonius' imminent death. The word is only in the First Quarto; the Second Quarto and the Folio read "silence.")　5 *round* blunt　10 *thy father* i.e., your stepfather, Claudius　12 *idle* foolish　15 *forgot me* i.e., forgotten that I am your mother.　*rood* cross of Christ　18 *speak* i.e., to someone so rude　25 *Dead for a ducat* i.e., I bet a ducat he's dead; or, a ducat is his life's fee

Queen: As kill a king!
Hamlet: Ay, lady, it was my word.

                          [He parts the arras and discovers Polonius.]

    Thou wretched, rash, intruding fool, farewell!
    I took thee for thy better. Take thy fortune.
    Thou find'st to be too busy° is some danger.—
    Leave wringing of your hands. Peace, sit you down,   35
    And let me wring your heart, for so I shall,
    If it be made of penetrable stuff,
    If damnèd custom° have not brazed° it so
    That it be proof° and bulwark against sense.°
Queen: What have I done, that thou dar'st wag thy tongue   40
    In noise so rude against me?
Hamlet: Such an act
    That blurs the grace and blush of modesty,
    Calls virtue hypocrite, takes off the rose
    From the fair forehead of an innocent love
    And sets a blister° there, makes marriage vows   45
    As false as dicers' oaths. O, such a deed
    As from the body of contraction° plucks
    The very soul, and sweet religion makes°
    A rhapsody° of words. Heaven's face does glow
    O'er this solidity and compound mass   50
    With tristful visage, as against the doom,
    Is thought-sick at the act.°
Queen: Ay me, what act,
    That roars so loud and thunders in the index?°
Hamlet [showing her two likenesses]: Look here upon this picture, and on this,
    The counterfeit presentment° of two brothers.   55
    See what a grace was seated on this brow:
    Hyperion's° curls, the front° of Jove himself,
    An eye like Mars° to threaten and command,
    A station° like the herald Mercury°
    New-lighted° on a heaven-kissing hill—   60
    A combination and a form indeed
    Where every god did seem to set his seal°
    To give the world assurance of a man.
    This was your husband. Look you now what follows:
    Here is your husband, like a mildewed ear,°   65
    Blasting° his wholesome brother. Have you eyes?

---

34 *busy* nosey   38 *damnèd custom* habitual wickedness. *brazed* brazened, hardened   39 *proof* armor.
sense feeling   45 *sets a blister* i.e., brands as a harlot   47 *contraction* the marriage contract   48 *sweet religion makes* i.e., makes marriage vows   49 *rhapsody* senseless string   49–52 *Heaven's . . . act* heaven's face
blushes at this solid world compounded of the various elements, with sorrowful face as though the day of
doom were near, and is sick with horror at the deed (i.e., Gertrude's marriage)   53 *index* table of contents,
prelude or preface   55 *counterfeit presentment* portrayed representation   57 *Hyperion's* the sun-god's.
front brow   58 *Mars* god of war   59 *station* manner of standing. *Mercury* winged messenger of the gods
60 *New-lighted* newly alighted   62 *set his seal* i.e., affix his approval   65 *ear* i.e., of grain 66 *Blasting*
blighting

Could you on this fair mountain leave° to feed
And batten° on this moor?° Ha, have you eyes?
You cannot call it love, for at your age
The heyday° in the blood° is tame, it's humble,   70
And waits upon the judgment, and what judgment
Would step from this to this? Sense,° sure, you have,
Else could you not have motion, but sure that sense
Is apoplexed,° for madness would not err,°
Nor sense to ecstasy was ne'er so thralled,   75
But° it reserved some quantity of choice
To serve in such a difference.° What devil was 't
That thus hath cozened° you at hoodman-blind?°
Eyes without feeling, feeling without sight,
Ears without hands or eyes, smelling sans° all,   80
Or but a sickly part of one true sense
Could not so mope.° O shame, where is thy blush?
Rebellious hell,
If thou canst mutine° in a matron's bones,
To flaming youth let virtue be as wax   85
And melt in her own fire.° Proclaim no shame
When the compulsive ardor gives the charge,
Since frost itself as actively doth burn,
And reason panders will.°

Queen: O Hamlet, speak no more!   90
  Thou turn'st mine eyes into my very soul,
  And there I see such black and grainèd° spots
  As will not leave their tinct.°

Hamlet: Nay, but to live
  In the rank sweat of an enseamèd° bed,
  Stewed° in corruption, honeying and making love   95
  Over the nasty sty!

Queen: O, speak to me no more!
  These words like daggers enter in my ears.
  No more, sweet Hamlet!

Hamlet: A murderer and a villain,
  A slave that is not twentieth part the tithe°   100

---

67 *leave* cease   68 *batten* gorge.   *moor* barren or marshy ground (suggesting also "dark-skinned")   70 *heyday* state of excitement.   *blood* passion   72 *Sense* perception through the five senses (the functions of the middle or sensible soul)   74 *apoplexed* paralyzed. (Hamlet goes on to explain that, without such a paralysis of will, mere madness would not so err, nor would the five senses so enthrall themselves to *ecstasy* or lunacy; even such deranged states of mind would be able to make the obvious choice between Hamlet Senior and Claudius.)   *err* so err   76 *But* but that   77 *to . . . difference* to help in making a choice between two such men   78 *cozened* cheated.   *hoodman-blind* blindman's buff. (In this game, says Hamlet, the devil must have pushed Claudius toward Gertrude while she was blindfolded.)   80 *sans* without   82 *mope* be dazed, act aimlessly   84 *mutine* incite mutiny   85–86 *be as wax . . . fire* melt like a candle or stick of sealing wax held over the candle flame   86–89 *Proclaim . . . will* call it no shameful business when the compelling ardor of youth delivers the attack, i.e., commits lechery, since the *frost* of advanced age burns with as active a fire of lust and reason perverts itself by fomenting lust rather than restraining it   92 *grainèd* dyed in grain, indelible   93 *leave their tinct* surrender their color   94 *enseamèd* saturated in the grease and filth of passionate lovemaking   95 *Stewed* soaked, bathed (with a suggestion of "stew," brothel)   100 *tithe* tenth part

Of your precedent lord,° a vice° of kings,
A cutpurse of the empire and the rule,
That from a shelf the precious diadem stole
And put it in his pocket!

Queen: No more!   105

Enter Ghost.

Hamlet: A king of shreds and patches°—
Save me, and hover o'er me with your wings,
You heavenly guards! What would your gracious figure?

Queen: Alas, he's mad!

Hamlet: Do you not come your tardy son to chide,   110
That, lapsed° in time and passion, lets go by
Th' important° acting of your dread command?
O, say!

Ghost: Do not forget. This visitation
Is but to whet thy almost blunted purpose.   115
But look, amazement° on thy mother sits.
O, step between her and her fighting soul!
Conceit° in weakest bodies strongest works.
Speak to her, Hamlet.

Hamlet: How is it with you, lady?

Queen: Alas, how is 't with you,   120
That you do bend your eye on vacancy,
And with th' incorporal° air do hold discourse?
Forth at your eyes your spirits wildly peep,
And, as the sleeping soldiers in th' alarm,°
Your bedded° hairs, like life in excrements,°   125
Start up and stand on end. O gentle son,
Upon the heat and flame of thy distemper°
Sprinkle cool patience. Whereon do you look?

Hamlet: On him, on him! Look you how pale he glares!
His form and cause conjoined,° preaching to stones,   130
Would make them capable.°—Do not look upon me,
Lest with this piteous action you convert
My stern effects.° Then what I have to do
Will want true color—tears perchance for blood.°

Queen: To whom do you speak this?   135

Hamlet: Do you see nothing there?

Queen: Nothing at all, yet all that is I see.

---

101 *precedent lord* former husband. *vice* buffoon. (A reference to the Vice of the morality plays.)   106 *shreds and patches* i.e., motley, the traditional costume of the clown or fool   111 *lapsed* delaying   112 *important* importunate, urgent   116 *amazement* distraction   118 *Conceit* imagination   122 incorporal immaterial 124 *as . . . alarm* like soldiers called out of sleep by an alarm   125 *bedded* laid flat. *like life in excrements* i.e., as though hair, an outgrowth of the body, had a life of its own. (Hair was thought to be lifeless because it lacks sensation, and so its standing on end would be unnatural and ominous.)   127 *distemper* disorder 130 *His . . . conjoined* his appearance joined to his cause for speaking   131 *capable* receptive   132–133 *convert . . . effects* divert me from my stern duty   134 *want . . . blood* lack plausibility so that (with a play on the normal sense of *color*) I shall shed colorless tears instead of blood

Hamlet: Nor did you nothing hear?
Queen: No, nothing but ourselves.
Hamlet: Why, look you there, look how it steals away!   140
    My father, in his habit° as° he lived!
    Look where he goes even now out at the portal!

                                 Exit Ghost.

Queen: This is the very° coinage of your brain.
    This bodiless creation ecstasy
    Is very cunning in.°   145
Hamlet: Ecstasy?
    My pulse as yours doth temperately keep time,
    And makes as healthful music. It is not madness
    That I have uttered. Bring me to the test,
    And I the matter will reword,° which madness   150
    Would gambol° from. Mother, for love of grace,
    Lay not that flattering unction° to your soul
    That not your trespass but my madness speaks.
    It will but skin° and film the ulcerous place,
    Whiles rank corruption, mining° all within,   155
    Infects unseen. Confess yourself to heaven,
    Repent what's past, avoid what is to come,
    And do not spread the compost° on the weeds
    To make them ranker. Forgive me this my virtue;°
    For in the fatness° of these pursy° times   160
    Virtue itself of vice must pardon beg,
    Yea, curb° and woo for leave° to do him good.
Queen: O Hamlet, thou hast cleft my heart in twain.
Hamlet: O, throw away the worser part of it,
    And live the purer with the other half.   165
    Good night. But go not to my uncle's bed;
    Assume a virtue, if you have it not.
    That monster, custom, who all sense doth eat,°
    Of habits devil,° is angel yet in this,
    That to the use of actions fair and good   170
    He likewise gives a frock or livery°
    That aptly° is put on. Refrain tonight,
    And that shall lend a kind of easiness
    To the next abstinence; the next more easy;
    For use° almost can change the stamp of nature,°   175
    And either° . . . the devil, or throw him out

---

141 *habit* clothes. *as* as when   143 *very* mere   144–145 *This . . . in* madness is skillful in creating this kind of hallucination   150 *reword* repeat word for word   151 *gambol* skip away   152 *unction* ointment   154 *skin* grow a skin for   155 *mining* working under the surface   158 *compost* manure   159 *this my virtue* my virtuous talk in reproving you   160 *fatness* grossness. *pursy* flabby, out of shape   162 *curb* bow, bend the knee. *leave* permission   168 *who . . . eat* which consumes all proper or natural feeling, all sensibility   169 *Of habits devil* devillike in prompting evil habits   171 *livery* an outer appearance, a customary garb (and hence a predisposition easily assumed in time of stress)   172 *aptly* readily   175 *use* habit. *the stamp of nature* our inborn traits   176 *And either* (A defective line, usually emended by inserting the word *master* after *either*, following the Fourth Quarto and early editors.)

With wondrous potency. Once more, good night;
And when you are desirous to be blest,
I'll blessing beg of you.° For this same lord,

[pointing to Polonius]

I do repent; but heaven hath pleased it so   180
To punish me with this, and this with me,
That I must be their scourge and minister.°
I will bestow° him, and will answer° well
The death I gave him. So, again, good night.
I must be cruel only to be kind.   185
This° bad begins, and worse remains behind.°
One word more, good lady.
Queen: What shall I do?
Hamlet: Not this by no means that I bid you do:
Let the bloat° king tempt you again to bed,
Pinch wanton° on your cheek, call you his mouse,   190
And let him, for a pair of reechy° kisses,
Or paddling° in your neck with his damned fingers,
Make you to ravel all this matter out°
That I essentially am not in madness,
But mad in craft.° 'Twere good° you let him know,   195
For who that's but a queen, fair, sober, wise,
Would from a paddock,° from a bat, a gib,°
Such dear concernings° hide? Who would do so?
No, in despite of sense and secrecy,°
Unpeg the basket° on the house's top,   200
Let the birds fly, and like the famous ape,°
To try conclusions,° in the basket creep
And break your own neck down.°
Queen: Be thou assured, if words be made of breath,
And breath of life, I have no life to breathe   205
What thou hast said to me.
Hamlet: I must to England. You know that?
Queen: Alack,
I had forgot. 'Tis so concluded on.
Hamlet: There's letters sealed, and my two schoolfellows,
Whom I will trust as I will adders fanged,   210
They bear the mandate; they must sweep my way

178–179 when . . . you i.e., when you are ready to be penitent and seek God's blessing, I will ask your blessing as a dutiful son should   182 their scourge and minister i.e., agent of heavenly retribution. (By scourge,
Hamlet also suggests that he himself will eventually suffer punishment in the process of fulfilling heaven's
will.)   183 bestow stow, dispose of.   answer account or pay for   186 This i.e., the killing of Polonius.
behind to come   189 bloat bloated   190 Pinch wanton i.e., leave his love pinches on your cheeks, branding
you as wanton   191 reechy dirty, filthy   192 paddling fingering amorously   193 ravel . . . out unravel, disclose   195 in craft by cunning.   good (Said sarcastically; also the following eight lines.)   197 paddock
toad.   gib tomcat   198 dear concernings important affairs   199 sense and secrecy secrecy that common
sense requires   200 Unpeg the basket open the cage, i.e., let out the secret   201 famous ape (In a story now
lost.)   202 try conclusions test the outcome (in which the ape apparently enters a cage from which birds
have been released and then tries to fly out of the cage as they have done, falling to its death)   203 down
in the fall: utterly

And marshal me to knavery.° Let it work.°
For 'tis the sport to have the enginer°
Hoist with° his own petard,° and 't shall go hard
But I will° delve one yard below their mines°   215
And blow them at the moon. O, 'tis most sweet
When in one line° two crafts° directly meet.
This man shall set me packing.°
I'll lug the guts into the neighbor room.
Mother, good night indeed. This counselor   220
Is now most still, most secret, and most grave,
Who was in life a foolish prating knave.—
Come, sir, to draw toward an end° with you.—
Good night, Mother.

> *Exeunt [separately, Hamlet dragging in Polonius].*

ACT IV

SCENE I [THE CASTLE.]

Enter King and Queen,° with Rosencrantz and Guildenstern.

King: There's matter° in these sighs, these profound heaves.°
　You must translate; 'tis fit we understand them.
　Where is your son?
Queen: Bestow this place on us a little while.

> *[Exeunt Rosencrantz and Guildenstern.]*   5

　Ah, mine own lord, what have I seen tonight!
King: What, Gertrude? How does Hamlet?
Queen: Mad as the sea and wind when both contend
　Which is the mightier. In his lawless fit,
　Behind the arras hearing something stir,
　Whips out his rapier, cries, "A rat, a rat!"   10
　And in this brainish apprehension° kills
　The unseen good old man.
King:　　　　　　　　　　O heavy° deed!
　It had been so with us,° had we been there.
　His liberty is full of threats to all—

211–212 *sweep . . . knavery* sweep a path before me and conduct me to some *knavery* or treachery prepared for me   212 *work* proceed   213 *enginer* maker of military contrivances   214 *Hoist with* blown up by. *petard* an explosive used to blow in a door or make a breach   214–215 *'t shall . . . will* unless luck is against me, I will   215 *mines* tunnels used in warfare to undermine the enemy's emplacements: Hamlet will countermine by going under their mines   217 *in one line* i.e., mines and countermines on a collision course, or the countermines directly below the mines.   *crafts* acts of guile, plots   218 *set me packing* set me to making schemes, and set me to lugging (him), and, also, send me off in a hurry   223 *draw . . . end* finish up (with a pun on *draw*, "pull") s.d.   *Enter . . . Queen* (Some editors argue that Gertrude never exits in Act III, Scene iv, and that the scene is continuous here, as suggested in the Folio, but the Second Quarto marks an entrance for her and at line 35 Claudius speaks of Gertrude's *closet* as though it were elsewhere. A short time has elapsed, during which the King has become aware of her highly wrought emotional state.)   1 *matter* significance.   *heaves* heavy sighs   11 *brainish apprehension* headstrong conception   12 *heavy* grievous   13 *us* i.e., me. (The royal "we"; also in line 15.)

To you yourself, to us, to everyone.   15
Alas, how shall this bloody deed be answered?°
It will be laid to us, whose providence°
Should have kept short,° restrained, and out of haunt°
This mad young man. But so much was our love,
We would not understand what was most fit,   20
But, like the owner of a foul disease,
To keep it from divulging,° let it feed
Even on the pith of life. Where is he gone?
Queen: To draw apart the body he hath killed,
O'er whom his very madness, like some ore°   25
Among a mineral° of metals base,
Shows itself pure: 'a weeps for what is done.
King: O Gertrude, come away!
The sun no sooner shall the mountains touch
But we will ship him hence, and this vile deed   30
We must with all our majesty and skill
Both countenance° and excuse.—Ho, Guildenstern!

Enter Rosencrantz and Guildenstern.

Friends both, go join you with some further aid.
Hamlet in madness hath Polonius slain,
And from his mother's closet hath he dragged him.   35
Go seek him out, speak fair, and bring the body
Into the chapel. I pray you, haste in this.

[Exeunt Rosencrantz and Guildenstern.]

Come, Gertrude, we'll call up our wisest friends
And let them know both what we mean to do
And what's untimely done. . . . .°   40
Whose whisper o'er the world's diameter,°
As level° as the cannon to his blank,°
Transports his poisoned shot, may miss our name
And hit the woundless° air. O, come away!
My soul is full of discord and dismay.   *Exeunt.*   45

SCENE II [THE CASTLE.]

Enter Hamlet.

Hamlet: Safely stowed.
Rosencrantz, Guildenstern (*within*): Hamlet! Lord Hamlet!
Hamlet: But soft, what noise? Who calls on Hamlet? O, here they come.

Enter Rosencrantz and Guildenstern.

---

16 *answered* explained   17 *providence* foresight   18 *short* i.e., on a short tether.   *out of haunts* secluded
22 *divulging* becoming evident   25 *ore* vein of gold   26 *mineral* mine   32 *countenance* put the best face on
40 *And . . . done* (A defective line: conjectures as to the missing words include *So, haply, slander* [Capell and others]; *For, haply, slander* [Theobald and others]; and *So envious slander* [Jenkins].)   41 *diameter* extent
from side to side   42 *As level* with as direct aim.   *his blank* its target at point-blank range   44 *woundless*
invulnerable

Rosencrantz: What have you done, my lord, with the dead body?

Hamlet: Compounded it with dust, whereto 'tis kin.   5

Rosencrantz: Tell us where 'tis, that we may take it thence
    And bear it to the chapel.

Hamlet: Do not believe it.

Rosencrantz: Believe what?

Hamlet: That I can keep your counsel and not mine own.° Besides, to be demanded   10
    of° a sponge, what replication° should be made by the son of a king?

Rosencrantz: Take you me for a sponge, my lord?

Hamlet: Ay, sir, that soaks up the King's countenance,° his rewards, his authorities.°
    But such officers do the King best service in the end. He keeps them, like an ape,
    an apple, in the corner of his jaw, first mouthed to be last swallowed. When he   15
    needs what you have gleaned, it is but squeezing you, and, sponge, you shall be dry
    again.

Rosencrantz: I understand you not, my lord.

Hamlet: I am glad of it. A knavish speech sleeps in° a foolish ear.

Rosencrantz: My lord, you must tell us where the body is and go with us to the King.   20

Hamlet: The body is with the King, but the King is not with the body.° The King is a
    thing—

Guildenstern: A thing, my lord?

Hamlet: Of nothing.° Bring me to him. Hide fox, and all after!°

                                               Exeunt [running].

SCENE III [THE CASTLE.]

    Enter King, and two or three.

King: I have sent to seek him, and to find the body.
    How dangerous is it that this man goes loose!
    Yet must not we put the strong law on him.
    He's loved of° the distracted° multitude,
    Who like not in their judgment, but their eyes,°   5
    And where 'tis so, th' offender's scourge° is weighed,°
    But never the offense. To bear all smooth and even,°
    This sudden sending him away must seem
    Deliberate pause.° Diseases desperate grown
    By desperate appliance° are relieved,   10
    Or not at all.

---

10 *That . . . own* i.e., that I can follow your advice (by telling where the body is) and still keep my own secret   10–11 *demanded of* questioned by   11 *replication* reply   13 *countenance* favor. *authorities* delegated power, influence   19 *sleeps in* has no meaning to   21 *The . . . body* (Perhaps alludes to the legal commonplace of "the king's two bodies," which drew a distinction between the sacred office of kingship and the particular mortal who possessed it at any given time. Hence, although Claudius' body is necessarily a part of him, true kingship is not contained in it. Similarly, Claudius will have Polonius' body when it is found, but there is no kingship in this business either.)   24 *Of nothing* (1) of no account (2) lacking the essence of kingship, as in line 21 and note. *Hide . . . after* (An old signal cry in the game of hide-and-seek, suggesting that Hamlet now runs away from them.)   4 *of* by. *distracted* fickle, unstable   5 *Who . . . eyes* who choose not by judgment but by appearance   6 *scourge* punishment. (Literally, blow with a whip.) *weighed* sympathetically considered   7 *To . . . even* to manage the business in an unprovocative way   9 *Deliberate pause* carefully considered action   10 *appliance* remedies

Enter Rosencrantz, [Guildenstern,] and all the rest.

How now, what hath befall'n?

Rosencrantz: Where the dead body is bestowed, my lord,
  We cannot get from him.

King: But where is he?

Rosencrantz: Without, my lord; guarded, to know your pleasure.

King: Bring him before us.

Rosencrantz: Ho! Bring in the lord.   15

They enter [with Hamlet].

King: Now, Hamlet, where's Polonius?

Hamlet: At supper.

King: At supper? Where?

Hamlet: Not where he eats, but where 'a is eaten. A certain convocation of politic
  worms° are e'en° at him. Your worm° is your only emperor for diet.° We fat all   20
  creatures else to fat us, and we fat ourselves for maggots. Your fat king and your
  lean beggar is but variable service°—two dishes, but to one table. That's the end.

King: Alas, alas!

Hamlet: A man may fish with the worm that hath eat° of a king, and eat of the fish
  that hath fed of that worm.   25

King: What dost thou mean by this?

Hamlet: Nothing but to show you how a king may go a progress° through the guts of
  a beggar.

King: Where is Polonius?

Hamlet: In heaven. Send thither to see. If your messenger find him not there, seek   30
  him i' th' other place yourself. But if indeed you find him not within this month,
  you shall nose him as you go up the stairs into the lobby.

King [to some attendants]: Go seek him there.

Hamlet: 'A will stay till you come.   [*Exeunt attendants.*]

King: Hamlet, this deed, for thine especial safety—   35
  Which we do tender,° as we dearly° grieve
  For that which thou hast done—must send thee hence
  With fiery quickness. Therefore prepare thyself.
  The bark° is ready, and the wind at help,
  Th' associates tend,° and everything is bent°   40
  For England.

Hamlet: For England!

King: Ay, Hamlet.

Hamlet: Good.

King: So is it, if thou knew'st our purposes.   45

Hamlet: I see a cherub° that sees them. But come, for England! Farewell, dear
  mother.

19–20 *politic worms* crafty worms (suited to a master spy like Polonius)   20 *e'en* even now.   *Your worm*
your average worm (Compare *your fat king* and *your lean beggar* in lines 21–22)   *diet* food, eating (with a
punning reference to the Diet of Worms, a famous *convocation* held in 1521)   22 *variable service* different
courses of a single meal   24 *eat* eaten. (Pronounced *et*.)   27 *progress* royal journey of state   36 *tender*
regard, hold dear.   *dearly* intensely   39 *bark* sailing vessel   40 *tend* wait.   *bent* in readiness   46 *cherub*
(Cherubim are angels of knowledge. Hamlet hints that both he and heaven are onto Claudius' tricks.)

King: Thy loving father, Hamlet.
Hamlet: My mother. Father and mother is man and wife, man and wife is one flesh,
 and so, my mother. Come, for England! 50

Exit.

King: Follow him at foot;° tempt him with speed aboard.
 Delay it not. I'll have him hence tonight.
 Away! For everything is sealed and done
 That else leans on° th' affair. Pray you, make haste.

[Exeunt all but the King.]

 And, England,° if my love thou hold'st at aught°— 55
 As my great power thereof may give thee sense,°
 Since yet thy cicatrice° looks raw and red
 After the Danish sword, and thy free awe°
 Pays homage to us—thou mayst not coldly set°
 Our sovereign process,° which imports at full,° 60
 By letters congruing° to that effect,
 The present° death of Hamlet. Do it, England,
 For like the hectic° in my blood he rages,
 And thou must cure me. Till I know 'tis done,
 Howe'er my haps,° my joys were ne'er begun. 65

Exit.

SCENE IV [THE COAST OF DENMARK.]

 Enter Fortinbras with his army over the stage.

Fortinbras: Go, Captain, from me greet the Danish king.
 Tell him that by his license° Fortinbras
 Craves the conveyance of° a promised march
 Over his kingdom. You know the rendezvous.
 If that His Majesty would aught with us, 5
 We shall express our duty° in his eye;°
 And let him know so.
Captain: I will do 't, my lord.
Fortinbras: Go softly° on. *[Exeunt all but the Captain.]*

 Enter Hamlet, Rosencrantz, [Guildenstern,] etc.

Hamlet: Good sir, whose powers° are these? 10
Captain: They are of Norway, sir.
Hamlet: How purposed, sir, I pray you?
Captain: Against some part of Poland.
Hamlet: Who commands them, sir?
Captain: The nephew to old Norway, Fortinbras. 15

---

51 *at foot* close behind, at heel 54 *leans on* bears upon, is related to 55 *England* i.e., King of England. *at aught* at any value 56 *As . . . sense* for so my great power may give you a just appreciation of the importance of valuing my love 57 *cicatrice* scar 58 *free awe* voluntary show of respect 59 *coldly set* regard with indifference 60 *process* command. *imports at full* conveys specific directions for 61 *congruing* agreeing 62 *present* immediate 63 *hectic* persistent fever 65 *haps* fortunes 2 *license* permission 3 *the conveyance of* escort during 6 *duty* respect. *eye* presence 9 *softly* slowly, circumspectly 10 *powers* forces

Hamlet: Goes it against the main° of Poland, sir,
  Or for some frontier?
Captain: Truly to speak, and with no addition,°
  We go to gain a little patch of ground
  That hath in it no profit but the name.
  To pay° five ducats, five, I would not farm it;°   20
  Nor will it yield to Norway or the Pole
  A ranker° rate, should it be sold in fee.°
Hamlet: Why, then the Polack never will defend it.
Captain: Yes, it is already garrisoned.
Hamlet: Two thousand souls and twenty thousand ducats   25
  Will not debate the question of this straw.°
  This is th' impostume° of much wealth and peace,
  That inward breaks, and shows no cause without
  Why the man dies. I humbly thank you, sir.
Captain: God b' wi' you, sir.   30

  [*Exit.*]

Rosencrantz: Will 't please you go, my lord?
Hamlet: I'll be with you straight. Go a little before.

                        [*Exeunt all except Hamlet.*]

  How all occasions do inform against° me
  And spur my dull revenge! What is a man,
  If his chief good and market of° his time   35
  Be but to sleep and feed? A beast, no more.
  Sure he that made us with such large discourse,°
  Looking before and after,° gave us not
  That capability and godlike reason
  To fust° in us unused. Now, whether it be   40
  Bestial oblivion,° or some craven° scruple
  Of thinking too precisely° on th' event°—
  A thought which, quartered, hath but one part wisdom
  And ever three parts coward—I do not know
  Why yet I live to say "This thing's to do,"   45
  Sith° I have cause, and will, and strength, and means
  To do 't. Examples gross° as earth exhort me:
  Witness this army of such mass and charge,°
  Led by a delicate and tender° prince,
  Whose spirit with divine ambition puffed   50
  Makes mouths° at the invisible event,°
  Exposing what is mortal and unsure

---

16 *main* main part   18 *addition* exaggeration   21 *To pay* i.e., for a yearly rental of.   *farm it* take a lease of it   23 *ranker* higher. *in fee* fee simple, outright   27 *debate . . . straw* settle this trifling matter   28 *impostume* abscess   33 *inform against* denounce, betray: take shape against   35 *market of* profit of, compensation for   37 *discourse* power of reasoning   38 *Looking before and after* able to review past events and anticipate the future   40 *fust* grow moldy   41 *oblivion* forgetfulness. *craven* cowardly   42 *precisely* scrupulously. *event* outcome   46 *Sith* since   47 *gross* obvious   48 *charge* expense   49 *delicate and tender* of fine and youthful qualities   51 *Makes mouths* makes scornful faces. *invisible event* unforeseeable outcome

To all that fortune, death, and danger dare,°
Even for an eggshell. Rightly° to be great
Is not to stir without great argument,   55
But greatly to find quarrel in a straw
When honor's at the stake.° How stand I, then,
That have a father killed, a mother stained,
Excitements of° my reason and my blood,
And let all sleep, while to my shame I see   60
The imminent death of twenty thousand men
That for a fantasy° and trick° of fame
Go to their graves like beds, fight for a plot°
Whereon the numbers cannot try the cause,°
Which is not tomb enough and continent°   65
To hide the slain? O, from this time forth
My thoughts be bloody or be nothing worth!   *Exit.*

SCENE V [THE CASTLE.]

Enter Horatio, [Queen] Gertrude, and a Gentleman.

Queen: I will not speak with her.
Gentleman: She is importunate,
    Indeed distract.° Her mood will needs be pitied.
Queen: What would she have?
Gentleman: She speaks much of her father, says she hears
    There's tricks° i' the world, and hems,° and beats her heart,°   5
    Spurns enviously at straws,° speaks things in doubt°
    That carry but half sense. Her speech is nothing,
    Yet the unshapèd use° of it doth move
    The hearers to collection;° they yawn° at it,
    And botch° the words up fit to their own thoughts,   10
    Which,° as her winks and nods and gestures yield° them,
    Indeed would make one think there might be thought,°
    Though nothing sure, yet much unhappily.°
Horatio: 'Twere good she were spoken with, for she may strew
    Dangerous conjectures in ill-breeding° minds.   15
Queen: Let her come in.   [*Exit Gentleman.*]
    [*Aside.*] To my sick soul, as sin's true nature is,
    Each toy° seems prologue to some great amiss.°

---

53 *dare* could do (to him) 54–57 *Rightly . . . stake* true greatness does not normally consist of rushing
into action over some trivial provocation; however, when one's honor is involved, even a trifling insult
requires that one respond greatly (?) 57 *at the stake* (A metaphor from gambling or bear-baiting.) 59
Excitements of promptings by 62 *fantasy* fanciful caprice, illusion. *trick* trifle, deceit 63 *plot* plot of
ground 64 *Whereon . . . cause* on which there is insufficient room for the soldiers needed to engage in a
military contest 65 *continent* receptacle, container 2 *distract* distracted 5 *tricks* deceptions. *hems*
makes "hmm" sounds. *heart* i.e., breast 6 *Spurns . . . straws* kicks spitefully, takes offense at trifles. *in
doubt* obscurely 8 *unshapèd use* incoherent manner 9 *collection* inference, a guess at some sort of meaning. *yawn* gape, wonder; grasp. (The Folio reading, *aim*, is possible.) 10 *botch* patch 11 *Which* which
words. *yield* deliver, represent 12 *thought* intended 13 *unhappily* unpleasantly near the truth, shrewdly
15 *ill-breeding* prone to suspect the worst and to make mischief 18 *toy* trifle. *amiss* calamity

So full of artless jealousy is guilt,
It spills itself in fearing to be spilt.° 20

Enter Ophelia° [*distracted*].

Ophelia: Where is the beauteous majesty of Denmark?
Queen: How now, Ophelia?
Ophelia (she sings):
        "How should I your true love know
        From another one?
        By his cockle hat° and staff,
        And his sandal shoon.°" 25
Queen: Alas, sweet lady, what imports this song?
Ophelia: Say you? Nay, pray you, mark.
        "He is dead and gone, lady,   (*Song.*)
        He is dead and gone; 30
        At his head a grass-green turf,
        At his heels a stone."
    O, ho!
Queen: Nay, but Ophelia—
Ophelia: Pray you, mark. [*Sings.*] 35
        "White his shroud as the mountain snow"—

Enter King.

Queen: Alas, look here, my lord.
Ophelia:
        "Larded° with sweet flowers;   (*Song.*)
        Which bewept to the ground did not go
        With true-love showers.°" 40
King: How do you, pretty lady?
Ophelia: Well, God 'ild° you! They say the owl° was a baker's daughter. Lord, we
    know what we are, but know not what we may be. God be at your table!
King: Conceit° upon her father.
Ophelia: Pray let's have no words of this; but when they ask you what it means, say 45
    you this:
        "Tomorrow is Saint Valentine's day,   (*Song.*)
        All in the morning betime,°
        And I a maid at your window,
        To be your Valentine.
        Then up he rose, and donned his clothes, 50
        And dupped° the chamber door,
        Let in the maid, that out a maid
        Never departed more."

19–20 *So . . . split* guilt is so full of suspicion that it unskillfully betrays itself in fearing betrayal   20 s.d
Enter Ophelia (In the First Quarto, Ophelia enters, "playing on a lute, and her hair down, singing.")   25
cockle hat hat with cockleshell stuck in it as a sign that the wearer had been a pilgrim to the shrine of Saint
James of Compostella in Spain   26 *shoon* shoes   38 *Larded* decorated   40 *showers* i.e., tears   42 *God 'ild*
God yield or reward.   *owl* (Refers to a legend about a baker's daughter who was turned into an owl for
being ungenerous when Jesus begged a loaf of bread.)   44 *Conceit* brooding   48 *betime* early   52 *dupped*
did up, opened

King: Pretty Ophelia—   55
Ophelia: Indeed, la, without an oath, I'll make an end on 't:
      "By Gis° and by Saint Charity,
      Alack, and he for shame!
      Young men will do 't, if they come to 't;
      By Cock,° they are to blame.   60
      Quoth she, 'Before you tumbled me,
      You promised me to wed.'"

   He answers:

      "'So would I ha' done, by yonder sun,
      An° thou hadst not come to my bed.'"   65
King: How long hath she been thus?
Ophelia: I hope all will be well. We must be patient, but I cannot choose but weep to
think they would lay him i' the cold ground. My brother shall know of it. And so
I thank you for your good counsel. Come, my coach! Good night, ladies, good
night, sweet ladies, good night, good night.   [*Exit.*]   70
King [*to Horatio*]: Follow her close. Give her good watch, I pray you.

                                             [*Exit Horatio.*]

   O, this is the poison of deep grief; it springs
   All from her father's death—and now behold!
   O Gertrude, Gertrude,
   When sorrows come, they come not single spies,°   75
   But in battalions. First, her father slain;
   Next, your son gone, and he most violent author
   Of his own just remove;° the people muddied,°
   Thick and unwholesome in their thoughts and whispers
   For good Polonius' death—and we have done but greenly,°   80
   In hugger-mugger° to inter him; poor Ophelia
   Divided from herself and her fair judgment,
   Without the which we are pictures or mere beasts;
   Last, and as much containing° as all these,
   Her brother is in secret come from France,   85
   Feeds on this wonder, keeps himself in clouds,°
   And wants° not buzzers° to infect his ear
   With pestilent speeches of his father's death,
   Wherein necessity,° of matter beggared,°
   Will nothing stick our person to arraign   90
   In ear and ear.° O my dear Gertrude, this,
   Like to a murdering piece,° in many places
   Gives me superfluous death.°   *A noise within.*
Queen: Alack, what noise is this?

---

57 *Gis* Jesus   60 *Cock* (A perversion of "God" in oaths; here also with a quibble on the slang word for penis.)
65 *An if*   75 *spies* scouts sent in advance of the main force   78 *remove* removal. *muddied* stirred up, confused   80 *greenly* in an inexperienced way, foolishly   81 *hugger-mugger* secret haste   84 *as much containing*
as full of serious matter   86 *Feeds . . . clouds* feeds his resentment or shocked grievance, holds himself
inscrutable and aloof amid all this rumor   87 *wants* lacks. *buzzers* gossipers, informers   89 *necessity* i.e., the
need to invent some plausible explanation. *of matter beggared* unprovided with facts   90–91 *Will . . . ear*
will not hesitate to accuse my (royal) person in everybody's ears   92 *murdering piece* cannon loaded so as to
scatter its shot   93 *Gives . . . death* kills me over and over

King: Attend!°   95
    Where is my Switzers?° Let them guard the door.

Enter a Messenger.

    What is the matter?
Messenger: Save yourself, my lord!
    The ocean, overpeering of his list,°
    Eats not the flats° with more impetuous° haste
    Than young Laertes, in a riotous head,°   100
    O'erbears your officers. The rabble call him lord,
    And, as° the world were now but to begin,
    Antiquity forgot, custom not known,
    The ratifiers and props of every word,°
    They cry, "Choose we! Laertes shall be king!"   105
    Caps,° hands, and tongues applaud it to the clouds,
    "Laertes shall be king, Laertes king!"
Queen: How cheerfully on the false trail they cry!   *A noise within.*
    O, this is counter,° you false Danish dogs!

Enter Laertes with others.

King: The doors are broke.   110
Laertes: Where is this King?—Sirs, stand you all without.
All: No, let's come in.
Laertes: I pray you, give me leave.
All: We will, we will.
Laertes: I thank you. Keep the door.   *[Exeunt followers.]*
        O thou vile king, Give me my father!   115
Queen [restraining him]: Calmly, good Laertes.
Laertes: That drop of blood that's calm proclaims me bastard,
    Cries cuckold to my father, brands the harlot
    Even here, between° the chaste unsmirchèd brow
    Of my true mother.
King: What is the cause, Laertes,   120
    That thy rebellion looks so giantlike?
    Let him go, Gertrude. Do not fear our° person.
    There's such divinity doth hedge° a king
    That treason can but peep to what it would,°
    Acts little of his will.° Tell me, Laertes,   125
    Why thou art thus incensed. Let him go, Gertrude.
    Speak, man.

---

95 *Attend* i.e., guard me   96 *Switzers* Swiss guards, mercenaries   98 *overpeering of his list* overflowing its shore, boundary   99 *flats* i.e., flatlands near shore.   *impetuous* violent (perhaps also with the meaning of impiteous [*impitious, Second Quarto*], "pitiless")   100 *head* insurrection   102 *as* as if   104 *The ratifiers . . . word* i.e., antiquity (or tradition) and *custom* ought to confirm (*ratify*) and underprop our every word or promise   106 *Caps* (The caps are thrown in the air.)   109 *counter* (A hunting term, meaning to follow the trail in a direction opposite to that which the game has taken.)   119 *between* in the middle of   122 *fear our* fear for my   123 *hedge* protect, as with a surrounding barrier   124 *can . . . would* can only peep furtively, as through a barrier at what it would intend   125 *Acts . . . will* (but) performs little of what it intends

Laertes: Where is my father?
King: Dead.
Queen: But not by him.
King: Let him demand his fill.
Laertes: How came he dead? I'll not be juggled with.°
   To hell, allegiance! Vows, to the blackest devil!   130
   Conscience and grace, to the profoundest pit!
   I dare damnation. To this point I stand,°
   That both the worlds I give to negligence,°
   Let come what comes, only I'll be revenged
   Most throughly° for my father.   135
King: Who shall stay you?
Laertes: My will, not all the world's.°
   And for° my means, I'll husband them so well
   They shall go far with little.
King: Good Laertes,
   If you desire to know the certainty   140
   Of your dear father, is 't writ in your revenge
   That, swoopstake,° you will draw both friend and foe,
   Winner and loser?
Laertes: None but his enemies.
King: Will you know them, then?   145
Laertes: To his good friends thus wide I'll ope my arms,
   And like the kind life-rendering pelican°
   Repast° them with my blood.
King: Why, now you speak
   Like a good child and a true gentleman.
   That I am guiltless of your father's death,   150
   And am most sensibly° in grief for it,
   It shall as level° to your judgment 'pear
   As day does to your eye.   *A noise within.*
Laertes: How now, what noise is that?

   Enter Ophelia.

King: Let her come in.
Laertes: O heat, dry up my brains! Tears seven times salt   155
   Burn out the sense and virtue° of mine eye!
   By heaven, thy madness shall be paid with weight°
   Till our scale turn the beam.° O rose of May!
   Dear maid, kind sister, sweet Ophelia!
   O heavens, is 't possible a young maid's wits   160

---

129 *juggled with* cheated, deceived   132 *To . . . stand* I am resolved in this   133 *both . . . negligence* i.e., both this world and the next are of no consequence to me   135 *throughly* thoroughly   137 *My will . . . world's* I'll stop (stay) when my will is accomplished, not for anyone else's.   138 *for* as for   142 *swoopstake* i.e., indiscriminately. (Literally taking all stakes on the gambling table at once. *Draw* is also a gambling term meaning "take from.")   147 *pelican* (Refers to the belief that the female pelican fed its young with its own blood.)   148 *Repast* feed   151 *sensibly* feelingly   152 *level* plain   156 *virtue* faculty, power   157 *paid with weight* repaid, avenged equally or more   158 *beam* crossbar of a balance

Should be as mortal as an old man's life?
Nature is fine in° love, and where 'tis fine
It sends some precious instance° of itself
After the thing it loves.°

Ophelia:

    "They bore him barefaced on the bier,   *(Song.)* 165
    Hey non nonny, nonny, hey nonny,
    And in his grave rained many a tear—"
Fare you well, my dove!

Laertes: Hadst thou thy wits and didst persuade° revenge,
    It could not move thus.   170
Ophelia: You must sing "A-down a-down," and you "call him a-down-a."° O, how the
    wheel° becomes it! It is the false steward° that stole his master's daughter.
Laertes: This nothing's more than matter.°
Ophelia: There's rosemary,° that's for remembrance; pray you, love, remember.
    And there is pansies;° that's for thoughts.   175
Laertes: A document° in madness, thoughts and remembrance fitted.
Ophelia: There's fennel° for you, and columbines.° There's rue° for you, and here's
    some for me; we may call it herb of grace o' Sundays. You must wear your rue
    with a difference.° There's a daisy.° I would give you some violets,° but they
    withered all when my father died. They say 'a made a good end—   180
    [*Sings.*]

    "For bonny sweet Robin is all my joy."
Laertes: Thought° and affliction, passion,° hell itself,
    She turns to favor° and to prettiness.

Ophelia:

    "And will 'a not come again?   *(Song.)*
    And will 'a not come again?   185
    No, no, he is dead.
    Go to thy deathbed,
    He never will come again."
    "His beard was as white as snow,
    All flaxen was his poll.°He is gone, he is gone,   190
    And we cast away moan.
    God ha' mercy on his soul!"
And of all Christian souls, I pray God. God b' wi' you.

                                           [*Exit, followed by Gertrude.*]

Laertes: Do you see this, O God?   195

---

162 *fine in* refined by   163 *instance* token   164 *After . . . loves* i.e., into the grave, along with Polonius   169 *persuade* argue cogently for   171 *You . . . a-down a* (Ophelia assigns the singing of refrains, like her own "Hey non nonny," to others present.)   172 *wheel* spinning wheel as accompaniment to the song, or refrain. *false steward* (The story is unknown.)   173 *This . . . matter* this seeming nonsense is more eloquent than sane utterance   174 *rosemary* (Used as a symbol of remembrance both at weddings and at funerals.)   175 *pansies* (Emblems of love and courtship; perhaps from French *pensées*, "thoughts.")   176 *document* instruction, lesson   177 *fennel* (Emblem of flattery.)   *columbines* (Emblems of unchastity or ingratitude.) *rue* (Emblem of repentance—a signification that is evident in its popular name, *herb of grace.*)   179 *with a difference* (A device used in heraldry to distinguish one family from another on the coat of arms, here suggesting that Ophelia and the others have different causes of sorrow and repentance; perhaps with a play on *rue* in the sense of "ruth," "pity.")   *daisy* (Emblem of dissembling, faithlessness.)   *violets* (Emblems of faithfulness.)   182 *Thought* melancholy. *passion* suffering   183 *favor* grace, beauty   190 *poll* head

King: Laertes, I must commune with your grief,
    Or you deny me right. Go but apart,
    Make choice of whom° your wisest friends you will,
    And they shall hear and judge twixt you and me.
    If by direct or by collateral hand°   200
    They find us touched,° we will our kingdom give,
    Our crown, our life, and all that we call ours
    To you in satisfaction; but if not,
    Be you content to lend your patience to us,
    And we shall jointly labor with your soul   205
    To give it due content.
Laertes: Let this be so.
    His means of death, his obscure funeral—
    No trophy,° sword, nor hatchment° o'er his bones,
    No noble rite, nor formal ostentation°—
    Cry to be heard, as 'twere from heaven to earth,   210
    That° I must call 't in question.°
King: So you shall,
    And where th' offense is, let the great ax fall.
    I pray you, go with me.   *Exeunt.*

SCENE VI [THE CASTLE.]

    Enter Horatio and others.

Horatio: What are they that would speak with me?
Gentleman: Seafaring men, sir. They say they have letters for you.
Horatio: Let them come in.   *[Exit Gentleman.]*
    I do not know from what part of the world
    I should be greeted, if not from Lord Hamlet.   5

    Enter Sailors.

First Sailor: God bless you, sir.
Horatio: Let him bless thee too.
First Sailor: 'A shall, sir, an 't° please him. There's a letter for you, sir—it came from
    th' ambassador° that was bound for England—if your name be Horatio, as I am
    let to know it is.   *[He gives a letter.]*   10
Horatio [reads]: "Horatio, when thou shalt have overlooked° this, give these fellows
    some means° to the King; they have letters for him. Ere we were two days old at
    sea, a pirate of very warlike appointment° gave us chase. Finding ourselves too
    slow of sail, we put on a compelled valor, and in the grapple I boarded them.
    On the instant they got clear of our ship, so I alone became their prisoner. They   15
    have dealt with me like thieves of mercy,° but they knew what they did: I am to

---

198 *whom* whichever of   200 *collateral hand* indirect agency   201 *us touched* be implicated   208 *trophy* memorial. *hatchment* tablet displaying the armorial bearings of a deceased person   209 *ostentation* ceremony   211 *That* so that. *call 't in question* demand an explanation   8 *an 't* if it   9 *th' ambassador* (Evidently Hamlet. The sailor is being circumspect.)   11 *overlooked* looked over   12 *means* means of access   13 *appointment* equipage   16 *thieves of mercy* merciful thieves

do a good turn for them. Let the King have the letters I have sent, and repair°
thou to me with as much speed as thou wouldest fly death. I have words to speak
in thine ear will make thee dumb, yet are they much too light for the bore° of
the matter. These good fellows will bring thee where I am. Rosencrantz and 20
Guildenstern hold their course for England. Of them I have much to tell thee.
Farewell.

He that thou knowest thine, Hamlet."

Come, I will give you way° for these your letters,
And do 't the speedier that you may direct me 25
To him from whom you brought them. *Exeunt.*

SCENE VII [THE CASTLE.]

Enter King and Laertes.

King: Now must your conscience my acquittance seal,°
And you must put me in your heart for friend,
Sith° you have heard, and with a knowing ear,
That he which hath your noble father slain
Pursued my life.

Laertes: It well appears. But tell me 5
Why you proceeded not against these feats°
So crimeful and so capital° in nature,
As by your safety, greatness, wisdom, all things else,
You mainly° were stirred up.

King: O, for two special reasons, 10
Which may to you perhaps seem much unsinewed,°
But yet to me they're strong. The Queen his mother
Lives almost by his looks, and for myself—
My virtue or my plague, be it either which—
She is so conjunctive° to my life and soul 15
That, as the star moves not but in his° sphere,°
I could not but by her. The other motive
Why to a public count° I might not go
Is the great love the general gender° bear him,
Who, dipping all his faults in their affection, 20
Work° like the spring° that turneth wood to stone,
Convert his gyves° to graces, so that my arrows,
Too slightly timbered° for so loud° a wind,
Would have reverted° to my bow again
But not where I had aimed them. 25

17 *repair* come   19 *bore* caliber, i.e., importance   24 *way* means of access   1 *my acquittance seal* confirm
or acknowledge my innocence   3 *Sith* since   6 *feats* acts   7 *capital* punishable by death   9 *mainly* greatly
11 *unsinewed* weak   15 *conjunctive* closely united. (An astronomical metaphor.)   16 *his* its.   *sphere* one
of the hollow spheres in which, according to Ptolemaic astronomy, the planets were supposed to move
18 *count* account, reckoning, indictment   19 *general gender* common people   21 *Work* operate, act.
spring i.e., a spring with such a concentration of lime that it coats a piece of wood with limestone, in effect
gilding and petrifying it   22 *gyves* fetters (which, gilded by the people's praise, would look like badges of
honor)   23 *slightly timbered* light.   *loud* (suggesting public outcry on Hamlet's behalf)   24 *reverted*
returned

Laertes: And so have I a noble father lost,
 A sister driven into desperate terms,°
 Whose worth, if praises may go back° again,
 Stood challenger on mount° of all the age
 For her perfections. But my revenge will come.   30
King: Break not your sleeps for that. You must not think
 That we are made of stuff so flat and dull
 That we can let our beard be shook with danger
 And think it pastime. You shortly shall hear more.
 I loved your father, and we love ourself;   35
 And that, I hope, will teach you to imagine—

Enter a Messenger with letters.

 How now? What news?
Messenger: Letters, my lord, from Hamlet:
 This to Your Majesty, this to the Queen.

              [He gives letters.]

King: From Hamlet? Who brought them?
Messenger: Sailors, my lord, they say. I saw them not.   40
 They were given me by Claudio. He received them
 Of him that brought them.
King: Laertes, you shall hear them.—
 Leave us.   *[Exit Messenger.]*
 [He reads.] "High and mighty, you shall know I am set naked° on your kingdom.
 Tomorrow shall I beg leave to see your kingly eyes, when I shall, first asking your   45
 pardon,° thereunto recount the occasion of my sudden and more strange return.
 Hamlet."
 What should this mean? Are all the rest come back? Or is it some abuse,° and no
 such thing?°
Laertes: Know you the hand?
King: 'Tis Hamlet's character.° "Naked!"   50
 And in a postscript here he says "alone."
 Can you devise° me?
Laertes: I am lost in it, my lord. But let him come.
 It warms the very sickness in my heart
 That I shall live and tell him to his teeth,   55
 "Thus didst thou."°
King: If it be so, Laertes—
 As how should it be so? How otherwise?°—
 Will you be ruled by me?
Laertes: Ay, my lord,
 So° you will not o'errule me to a peace.

---

27 *terms* state, condition   28 *go back* i.e., recall what she was   29 *on mount* set up on high   44 *naked* destitute, unarmed, without following   46 *pardon* permission   48 *abuse* deceit   49 *no such thing* not what it appears   50 *character* handwriting   52 *devise* explain to   56 *Thus didst thou* i.e., here's for what you did to my father   57 *As . . . otherwise* how can this (Hamlet's return) be true? Yet how otherwise than true (since we have the evidence of his letter)?   59 *So* provided that

King: To thine own peace. If he be now returned, 60
　　As checking at° his voyage, and that° he means
　　No more to undertake it, I will work him
　　To an exploit, now ripe in my device,°
　　Under the which he shall not choose but fall;
　　And for his death no wind of blame shall breathe, 65
　　But even his mother shall uncharge the practice°
　　And call it accident.
Laertes: 　　　　　　My lord, I will be ruled,
　　The rather if you could devise it so
　　That I might be the organ.°
King: 　　　　　　　　It falls right.
　　You have been talked of since your travel much, 70
　　And that in Hamlet's hearing, for a quality
　　Wherein they say you shine. Your sum of parts°
　　Did not together pluck such envy from him
　　As did that one, and that, in my regard,
　　Of the unworthiest siege.° 75
Laertes: What part is that, my lord?
King: A very ribbon in the cap of youth,
　　Yet needful too, for youth no less becomes°
　　The light and careless livery that it wears
　　Than settled age his sables° and his weeds° 80
　　Importing health and graveness.° Two months since
　　Here was a gentleman of Normandy.
　　I have seen myself, and served against, the French,
　　And they can well° on horseback, but this gallant
　　Had witchcraft in 't; he grew unto his seat, 85
　　And to such wondrous doing brought his horse
　　As had he been incorpsed and demi-natured°
　　With the brave beast. So far he topped° my thought
　　That I in forgery° of shapes and tricks
　　Come short of what he did.
Laertes: 　　　　　　A Norman was 't? 90
King: A Norman.
Laertes: Upon my life, Lamord.
King: 　　　　　　　The very same.
Laertes: I know him well. He is the brooch° indeed
　　And gem of all the nation.
King: He made confession° of you. 95
　　And gave you such a masterly report

---

61 *checking at* i.e., turning aside from (like a falcon leaving the quarry to fly at a chance bird).　*that if*
63 *device* devising, invention　66 *uncharge the practice* acquit the stratagem of being a plot　69 *organ*
agent, instrument　72 *Your . . . parts* i.e., all your other virtues　75 *unworthiest siege* least important
rank　78 *no less becomes* is no less suited by　80 *his sables* its rich robes furred with sable.　*weeds*
garments　81 *Importing . . . graveness* signifying a concern for health and dignified prosperity; also, giving
an impression of comfortable prosperity　84 *can well* are skilled　87 *As . . . demi-natured* as if he had been of
one body and nearly of one nature (like the centaur)　88 *topped* surpassed　89 *forgery* imagining　93 *brooch*
ornament　95 *confession* testimonial, admission of superiority

For art and exercise in your defense,°
And for your rapier most especial,
That he cried out 'twould be a sight indeed
If one could match you. Th' escrimers° of their nation,   100
He swore, had neither motion, guard, nor eye
If you opposed them. Sir, this report of his
Did Hamlet so envenom with his envy
That he could nothing do but wish and beg
Your sudden° coming o'er, to play° with you.   105
Now, out of this—

Laertes: What out of this, my lord?

King: Laertes, was your father dear to you?
Or are you like the painting of a sorrow,
A face without a heart?

Laertes: Why ask you this?

King: Not that I think you did not love your father,   110
But that I know love is begun by time,°
And that I see, in passages of proof,°
Time qualifies° the spark and fire of it.
There lives within the very flame of love
A kind of wick or snuff° that will abate it,   115
And nothing° is at a like goodness still,
For goodness, growing to a pleurisy,°
Dies in his own too much.° That° we would do,
We should do when we would; for this "would" changes
And hath abatements° and delays as many   120
As there are tongues, are hands, are accidents,°
And then this "should" is like a spendthrift sigh,°
That hurts by easing.° But, to the quick o' th' ulcer:°
Hamlet comes back. What would you undertake
To show yourself in deed your father's son   125
More than in words?

Laertes: To cut his throat i' the church.

King: No place, indeed, should murder sanctuarize;°
Revenge should have no bounds. But good Laertes,
Will you do this,° keep close within your chamber.
Hamlet returned shall know you are come home.   130
We'll put on those shall° praise your excellence

---

97 *For . . . defense* with respect to your skill and practice with your weapon   100 *escrimers* fencers   105 *sudden* immediate.   *play* fence   111 *begun by time* i.e., created by the right circumstance and hence subject to change   112 *passages of proof* actual instances that prove it   113 *qualifies* weakens, moderates   115 *snuff* the charred part of a candlewick   116 *nothing . . . still* nothing remains at a constant level of perfection   117 *pleurisy* excess, plethora. (Literally, a chest inflammation.)   118 *in . . . much* of its own excess.   *That* that which   120 *abatements* diminutions   121 *As . . . accidents* as there are tongues to dissuade, hands to prevent, and chance events to intervene   122 *spendthrift sigh* (An allusion to the belief that sighs draw blood from the heart.)   123 *hurts by easing* i.e., costs the heart blood and wastes precious opportunity even while it affords emotional relief.   *quick o' th' ulcer* i.e., heart of the matter   127 *sanctuarize* protect from punishment. (Alludes to the right of sanctuary with which certain religious places were invested.)   129 *Will you do this* if you wish to do this   131 *put on those shall* arrange for some to

And set a double varnish on the fame
The Frenchman gave you, bring you in fine° together,
And wager on your heads. He, being remiss,°
Most generous,° and free from all contriving,   135
Will not peruse the foils, so that with ease,
Or with a little shuffling, you may choose
A sword unbated,° and in a pass of practice°
Requite him for your father.

Laertes: I will do 't,
And for that purpose I'll anoint my sword.   140
I bought an unction° of a mountebank°
So mortal that, but dip a knife in it,
Where it draws blood no cataplasm° so rare,
Collected from all simples° that have virtue°
Under the moon,° can save the thing from death   145
That is but scratched withal. I'll touch my point
With this contagion, that if I gall° him slightly,
It may be death.

King: Let's further think of this,
Weigh what convenience both of time and means
May fit us to our shape.° If this should fail,   150
And that our drift look through our bad performance,°
'Twere better not assayed. Therefore this project
Should have a back or second, that might hold
If this did blast in proof.° Soft, let me see.
We'll make a solemn wager on your cunnings°—   155
I ha 't!
When in your motion you are hot and dry—
As° make your bouts more violent to that end—
And that he calls for drink, I'll have prepared him
A chalice for the nonce,° whereon but sipping,   160
If he by chance escape your venomed stuck,°
Our purpose may hold there. [*A cry within.*] But stay, what noise?

Enter Queen.

Queen: One woe doth tread upon another's heel,
So fast they follow. Your sister's drowned, Laertes.
Laertes: Drowned! O, where?   165
Queen: There is a willow grows askant° the brook,
That shows his hoar leaves° in the glassy stream;
Therewith fantastic garlands did she make

---

133 *in fine* finally 134 *remiss* negligently unsuspicious 135 *generous* noble-minded 138 *unbated* not blunted, having no button. *pass of practice* treacherous thrust 141 *unction* ointment. *mountebank* quack doctor 143 *cataplasm* plaster or poultice 144 *simples* herbs. *virtue* potency 145 *Under the moon* i.e., anywhere (with reference perhaps to the belief that herbs gathered at night had a special power) 147 *gall* graze, wound 150 *shape* part we propose to act 151 *drift . . . performance* intention should be made visible by our bungling 154 *blast in proof* burst in the test (like a cannon) 155 *cunnings* respective skills 158 *As* i.e., and you should 160 *nonce* occasion 161 *stuck* thrust. (From *stoccado;* a fencing term.) 166 *askant* aslant 167 *hoar leaves* white or gray undersides of the leaves

Of crowflowers, nettles, daisies, and long purples,°
That liberal° shepherds give a grosser name,°   170
But our cold° maids do dead men's fingers call them.
There on the pendent° boughs her crownet° weeds
Clamb'ring to hang, an envious sliver° broke,
When down her weedy° trophies and herself
Fell in the weeping brook. Her clothes spread wide,   175
And mermaidlike awhile they bore her up,
Which time she chanted snatches of old lauds,°
As one incapable of° her own distress,
Or like a creature native and endued°
Unto that element. But long it could not be   180
Till that her garments, heavy with their drink,
Pulled the poor wretch from her melodious lay
To muddy death.

Laertes: Alas, then she is drowned?
Queen: Drowned, drowned.
Laertes: Too much of water hast thou, poor Ophelia,   185
    And therefore I forbid my tears. But yet
    It is our trick;° nature her custom holds.

John Everett Millais's painting, *Ophelia* **(1852).**

169 *long purples* early purple orchids   170 *liberal* free-spoken.   *a grosser name* (The testicle-resembling tubers of the orchid, which also in some cases resemble *dead men's fingers*, have earned various slang names like "dogstones" and "cullions.")   171 *cold* chaste   172 *pendent* overhanging.   *crownet* made into a chaplet or coronet   173 *envious sliver* malicious branch   174 *weedy* i.e., of plants   177 *lauds* hymns   178 *incapable of* lacking capacity to apprehend   179 *endued* adapted by nature   187 *It is our trick* i.e., weeping is our natural way (when sad)

Let shame say what it will. [*He weeps.*] When these are gone,
The woman will be out.° Adieu, my lord.
I have a speech of fire that fain would blaze,
But that this folly douts° it.   190
                                                                                                  Exit.

King: Let's follow, Gertrude.
How much I had to do to calm his rage!
Now fear I this will give it start again;
Therefore let's follow.   *Exeunt.*

ACT V

SCENE I [A CHURCHYARD.]

Enter two Clowns° [*with spades and mattocks*].

First Clown: Is she to be buried in Christian burial, when she willfully seeks her own salvation?°

Second Clown: I tell thee she is; therefore make her grave straight.° The crowner° hath sat on her,° and finds it° Christian burial.

First Clown: How can that be, unless she drowned herself in her own defense?   5

Second Clown: Why, 'tis found so.°

First Clown: It must be *se offendendo,*° it cannot be else. For here lies the point: if I drown myself wittingly, it argues an act, and an act hath three branches—it is to act, to do, and to perform. Argal,° she drowned herself wittingly.

Second Clown: Nay, but hear you, goodman° delver—   10

First Clown: Give me leave. Here lies the water; good. Here stands the man; good. If the man go to this water and drown himself, it is, will he, nill he,° he goes, mark you that. But if the water come to him and drown him, he drowns not himself. Argal, he that is not guilty of his own death shortens not his own life.

Second Clown: But is this law?   15

First Clown: Ay, marry, is 't—crowner's quest law.

Second Clown: Will you ha' the truth on 't? If this had not been a gentlewoman, she should have been buried out o' Christian burial.

First Clown: Why, there thou sayst.° And the more pity that great folk should have countenance° in this world to drown or hang themselves, more than their even-   20
Christian.° Come, my spade. There is no ancient° gentlemen but gardeners, ditchers, and grave makers. They hold up° Adam's profession.

Second Clown: Was he a gentleman?

First Clown: 'A was the first that ever bore arms.°

188–189 *When . . . out* when my tears are all shed, the woman in me will be expended, satisfied   191 *douts* extinguishes. (The Second Quarto reads "drowns.")   s.d. *Clowns* rustics   2 *salvation* (A blunder for "damnation," or perhaps a suggestion that Ophelia was taking her own shortcut to heaven.)   3 *straight* straightway, immediately. (But with a pun on *strait,* "narrow.")   *crowner* coroner   4 *sat on her* conducted an inquest on her case.   *finds it* gives his official verdict that her means of death was consistent with   6 *found so* determined so in the coroner's verdict   7 *se offendendo* (A comic mistake for *se defendendo,* a term used in verdicts of justifiable homicide.)   9 *Argal* (Corruption of *ergo,* "therefore.")   10 *goodman* (An honorific title often used with the name of a profession or craft.)   12 *will he, nill he* whether he will or no, willy-nilly   19 *there thou sayst,* i.e., that's right   20 *countenance* privilege   20–21 *even-Christian* fellow Christians   21 *ancient* going back to ancient times   22 *hold up* maintain   24 *bore arms* (To be entitled to bear a coat of arms would make Adam a gentleman, but as one who bore a spade, our common ancestor was an ordinary delver in the earth.)

Second Clown: Why, he had none.   25

First Clown: What, art a heathen? How dost thou understand the Scripture? The
   Scripture says Adam digged. Could he dig without arms?° I'll put another question
   to thee. If thou answerest me not to the purpose, confess thyself°—

Second Clown: Go to.

First Clown: What is he that builds stronger than either the mason, the shipwright,   30
   or the carpenter?

Second Clown: The gallows maker, for that frame° outlives a thousand tenants.

First Clown: I like thy wit well, in good faith. The gallows does well.° But how does it
   well? It does well to those that do ill. Now thou dost ill to say the gallows is built
   stronger than the church. Argal, the gallows may do well to thee. To 't again,   35
   come.

Second Clown: "Who builds stronger than a mason, a shipwright, or a carpenter?"

First Clown: Ay, tell me that, and unyoke.°

Second Clown: Marry, now I can tell.

First Clown: To 't.   40

Second Clown: Mass,° I cannot tell.

   Enter Hamlet and Horatio [at a distance].

First Clown: Cudgel thy brains no more about it, for your dull ass will not mend his
   pace with beating; and when you are asked this question next, say "a grave
   maker." The houses he makes last till doomsday. Go get thee in and fetch me a
   stoup° of liquor.   45

                                    [Exit Second Clown. First Clown digs.]
                                                                        Song.

          "In youth, when I did love, did love,°
          Methought it was very sweet,
          To contract—O—the time for—a—my behove,°
          O, methought there—a—was nothing—a—meet."°

Hamlet: Has this fellow no feeling of his business, 'a° sings in grave-making?   50
Horatio: Custom hath made it in him a property of easiness.°
Hamlet: 'Tis e'en so. The hand of little employment hath the daintier sense.°
First Clown: *Song.*

          "But age with his stealing steps
          Hath clawed me in his clutch,
          And hath shipped me into the land,°   55
          As if I had never been such."

                                            [He throws up a skull.]

---

27 *arms* i.e., the arms of the body   28 *confess thyself* (The saying continues, "and be hanged.")   32 *frame*
(1) gallows(2) structure   33 *does well* (1) is an apt answer (2) does a good turn   38 *unyoke* i.e., after this
great effort, you may unharness the team of your wits   41 *Mass* by the Mass   45 *stoup* two-quart measure
46 *In . . . love* (This and the two following stanzas, with nonsensical variations, are from a poem
attributed to Lord Vaux and printed in *Tottel's Miscellany,* 1557. The O and a [for "ah"] seemingly are the
grunts of the digger.)   48 *To contract . . . behove* i.e., to shorten the time for my own advantage. (Perhaps
he means to *prolong* it.)   49 *meet* suitable, i.e., more suitable   50 *'a* that he   51 *property of easiness* something he can do easily and indifferently   52 *daintier sense* more delicate sense of feeling   55 *into the land*
i.e., toward my grave (?) (But note the lack of rhyme in *steps, land.*)

Hamlet and the gravedigger.

Hamlet: That skull had a tongue in it and could sing once. How the knave jowls° it to
   the ground, as if 'twere Cain's jawbone, that did the first murder! This might be the
   pate of a politician,° which this ass now o'erreaches,° one that would circumvent
   God, might it not?

Horatio: It might, my lord.   60

Hamlet: Or of a courtier, which could say, "Good morrow, sweet lord! How dost
   thou, sweet lord?" This might be my Lord Such-a-one, that praised my Lord
   Such-a-one's horse when 'a meant to beg it, might it not?

Horatio: Ay, my lord.

Hamlet: Why, e'en so, and now my Lady Worm's, chapless,° and knocked about the   65
   mazard° with a sexton's spade. Here's fine revolution,° an° we had the trick to see° 't.

---

57 *jowls* dashes (with a pun on *jowl,* "jawbone")   59 *politician* schemer, plotter.   *o'erreaches* circumvents,
gets the better of (with a quibble on the literal sense)   66 *chapless* having no lower jaw.   67 *mazard* i.e.,
head. (Literally, a drinking vessel.)   *revolution* turn of Fortune's wheel, change.   *an* if.   *trick to see* knack
of seeing

Did these bones cost no more the breeding but° to play at loggets° with
them? Mine ache to think on 't.

First Clown: Song.

> "A pickax and a spade, a spade,   70
> For and° a shrouding sheet;
> O, a pit of clay for to be made
> For such a guest is meet."

                                                        [*He throws up another skull.*]

Hamlet: There's another. Why may not that be the skull of a lawyer? Where be his
quiddities° now, his quillities,° his cases, his tenures,° and his tricks? Why does   75
he suffer this mad knave now to knock him about the sconce° with a dirty
shovel, and will not tell him of his action of battery?° Hum, this fellow might be
in 's time a great buyer of land, with his statutes, his recognizances,° his fines,°
his double° vouchers° his recoveries.° Is this the fine of his fines and the recovery
of his recoveries, to have his fine pate full of fine dirt?° Will his vouchers vouch   80
him no more of his purchases, and double ones too, than the length and breadth
of a pair of indentures?° The very conveyances° of his lands will scarcely lie in
this box,° and must th' inheritor° himself have no more, ha?

Horatio: Not a jot more, my lord.

Hamlet: Is not parchment made of sheepskins?   85

Horatio: Ay, my lord, and of calves' skins too.

Hamlet: They are sheep and calves which seek out assurance in that.° I will speak to
this fellow.—Whose grave's this, sirrah?°

First Clown: Mine, sir. [*Sings.*]

> "O, pit of clay for to be made   90
> For such a guest is meet."

Hamlet: I think it be thine, indeed, for thou liest in 't.

First Clown: You lie out on 't, sir, and therefore 'tis not yours. For my part, I do not
lie in 't, yet it is mine.

Hamlet: Thou dost lie in 't, to be in 't and say it is thine. 'Tis for the dead, not for the   95
quick;° therefore thou liest.

First Clown: 'Tis a quick lie, sir; 'twill away again from me to you.

Hamlet: What man dost thou dig it for?

First Clown: For no man, sir.

Hamlet: What woman, then?   100

---

68 *cost . . . but* involve so little expense and care in upbringing that we may.   *loggets* a game in which
pieces of hard wood shaped like Indian clubs or bowling pins are thrown to lie as near as possible to a
stake   71 *For and* and moreover   75 *quiddities* subtleties, quibbles. (From Latin *quid,* "a thing.")
quillities verbal niceties, subtle distinctions. (Variation of *quiddities.*)   *tenures* the holding of a piece of
property or office, or the conditions or period of such holding   76 *sconce* head   77 *action of battery* lawsuit about physical assault   78 *statutes, his recognizances* legal documents guaranteeing a debt by attach-
ing land and property.   *fines, recoveries* ways of converting entailed estates into "fee simple" or freehold
79 *double* signed by two signatories.   *vouchers* guarantees of the legality of a title to real estate   79–80
fine of his fines . . . fine pate . . . fine dirt end of his legal maneuvers . . . elegant head . . . minutely sifted
dirt   82 *pair of indentures* legal document drawn up in duplicate on a single sheet and then cut apart on a
zigzag line so that each pair was uniquely matched. (Hamlet may refer to two rows of teeth or dentures.).
conveyances deeds   83 *box* (1) deed box (2) coffin. ("Skull" has been suggested.)   *inheritor* possessor,
owner   87 *assurance in that* safety in legal parchments   88 *sirrah* (A term of address to inferiors.)   96 *quick*
living

First Clown: For none, neither.

Hamlet: Who is to be buried in 't?

First Clown: One that was a woman, sir, but, rest her soul, she's dead.

Hamlet: How absolute° the knave is! We must speak by the card,° or equivocation°
will undo us. By the Lord, Horatio, this three years I have took° note of it: the age   105
is grown so picked° that the toe of the peasant comes so near the heel of the
courtier, he galls his kibe.°—How long hast thou been grave maker?

First Clown: Of all the days i' the year, I came to 't that day that our last king Hamlet
overcame Fortinbras.

Hamlet: How long is that since?   110

First Clown: Cannot you tell that? Every fool can tell that. It was that very day that
young Hamlet was born—he that is mad and sent into England.

Hamlet: Ay, marry, why was he sent into England?

First Clown: Why, because 'a was mad. 'A shall recover his wits there, or if 'a do not,
'tis no great matter there.   115

Hamlet: Why?

First Clown: 'Twill not be seen in him there. There the men are as mad as he.

Hamlet: How came he mad?

First Clown: Very strangely, they say.

Hamlet: How strangely?   120

First Clown: Faith, e'en with losing his wits.

Hamlet: Upon what ground?°

First Clown: Why, here in Denmark. I have been sexton here, man and boy, thirty
years.

Hamlet: How long will a man lie i' th' earth ere he rot?   125

First Clown: Faith, if 'a be not rotten before 'a die—as we have many pocky° corpses
nowadays, that will scarce hold the laying in°—'a will last you° some eight year
or nine year. A tanner will last you nine year.

Hamlet: Why he more than another?

First Clown: Why, sir, his hide is so tanned with his trade that 'a will keep out water   130
a great while, and your water is a sore° decayer of your whoreson° dead body. [*He
picks up a skull.*] Here's a skull now hath lien you° i' th' earth three-and-twenty
years.

Hamlet: Whose was it?

First Clown: A whoreson mad fellow's it was. Whose do you think it was?   135

Hamlet: Nay, I know not.

First Clown: A pestilence on him for a mad rogue! 'A poured a flagon of Rhenish° on
my head once. This same skull, sir, was, sir, Yorick's skull, the King's jester.

Hamlet: This?

First Clown: E'en that.   140

---

104 *absolute* strict, precise. *by the card* i.e., with precision. (Literally, by the mariner's compass-card, on
which the points of the compass were marked.). *equivocation* ambiguity in the use of terms   105 *took*
taken   106 *picked* refined, fastidious   107 *galls his kibe* chafes the courtier's chilblain   122 *ground* cause.
(But, in the next line, the gravedigger takes the word in the sense of "land," "country.")   126 *pocky*
rotten, diseased. (Literally, with the pox, or syphilis.)   127 *hold the laying in* hold together long enough
to be interred. *last you* last. (*You* is used colloquially here and in the following lines.)   131 *sore* i.e.,
terrible, great. *whoreson* i.e., vile, scurvy   132 *lien you* lain. (See the note at line 127.)   137 *Rhenish*
Rhine wine

"Alas, poor Yorick! I knew him, Horatio . . ." (V, i, 141–149).

Hamlet: Let me see. [*He takes the skull.*] Alas, poor Yorick! I knew him, Horatio, a
fellow of infinite jest, of most excellent fancy. He hath bore° me on his back a
thousand times, and now how abhorred in my imagination it is! My gorge rises°
at it. Here hung those lips that I have kissed I know not how oft. Where be your
gibes now? Your gambols, your songs, your flashes of merriment that were wont° 145
to set the table on a roar? Not one now, to mock your own grinning?° Quite
chopfallen.° Now get you to my lady's chamber and tell her, let her paint an
inch thick, to this favor° she must come. Make her laugh at that. Prithee, Horatio,
tell me one thing.

142 *bore* borne   143 *My gorge rises* i.e., I feel nauseated   145 *were wont* used   146 *mock your own grinning*
mock at the way your skull seems to be grinning (just as you used to mock at yourself and those who
grinned at you)   147 *chopfallen* (1) lacking the lower jaw (2) dejected   148 *favor* aspect, appearance

Horatio: What's that, my lord? 150

Hamlet: Dost thou think Alexander looked o' this fashion i' th' earth?

Horatio: E'en so.

Hamlet: And smelt so? Pah! [*He throws down the skull.*]

Horatio: E'en so, my lord.

Hamlet: To what base uses we may return, Horatio! Why may not imagination trace 155
the noble dust of Alexander till 'a find it stopping a bunghole?°

Horatio: 'Twere to consider too curiously° to consider so.

Hamlet: No, faith, not a jot, but to follow him thither with modesty° enough, and
likelihood to lead it. As thus: Alexander died, Alexander was buried, Alexander
returneth to dust, the dust is earth, of earth we make loam,° and why of that 160
loam whereto he was converted might they not stop a beer barrel?
Imperious° Caesar, dead and turned to clay,
Might stop a hole to keep the wind away.
O, that that earth which kept the world in awe
Should patch a wall t' expel the winter's flaw!° 165

Enter King, Queen, Laertes, and the corpse [*of Ophelia, in procession, with Priest,
lords, etc.*].

But soft,° but soft awhile! Here comes the King,
The Queen, the courtiers. Who is this they follow?
And with such maimèd° rites? This doth betoken
The corpse they follow did with desperate hand
Fordo° its own life. 'Twas of some estate.° 170
Couch we° awhile and mark.
        [*He and Horatio conceal themselves. Ophelia's body is taken to the grave.*]

Laertes: What ceremony else?

Hamlet [*to Horatio*]: That is Laertes, a very noble youth. Mark.

Laertes: What ceremony else?

Priest: Her obsequies have been as far enlarged 175
As we have warranty.° Her death was doubtful,
And but that great command o'ersways the order°
She should in ground unsanctified been lodged°
Till the last trumpet. For° charitable prayers,
Shards,° flints, and pebbles should be thrown on her. 180
Yet here she is allowed her virgin crants,°
Her maiden strewments,° and the bringing home
Of bell and burial.°

Laertes: Must there no more be done?

Priest: No more be done.

---

156 *bunghole* hole for filling or emptying a cask   157 *curiously* minutely   158 *modesty* plausible moderation   160 *loam* mortar consisting chiefly of moistened clay and straw   162 *Imperious* imperial   165 *flaw*
gust of wind   166 *soft* i.e., wait, be careful   168 *maimèd* mutilated, incomplete   170 *Fordo* destroy.
estate rank   171 *Couch we* let's hide, lie low   176 *warranty* i.e., ecclesiastical authority   177 *great . . .
order* orders from on high overrule the prescribed procedures   178 *She should . . . lodged* she should have
been buried in unsanctified ground   179 *For* in place of   180 *Shards* broken bits of pottery   181 *crants*
garlands betokening maidenhood   182 *strewments* flowers strewn on a coffin   182–183 *bringing . . . burial*
laying the body to rest, to the sound of the bell

The Queen mourns at Ophelia's funeral (V, i, 192–195).

We should profane the service of the dead   185
To sing a requiem and such rest° to her
As to peace-parted souls.°
Laertes: Lay her i' th' earth,
And from her fair and unpolluted flesh
May violets spring! I tell thee, churlish priest,
A ministering angel shall my sister be   190
When thou liest howling.°
Hamlet [to Horatio]:   What, the fair Ophelia!
Queen [scattering flowers]: Sweets to the sweet! Farewell.
I hoped thou shouldst have been my Hamlet's wife.

186 *such rest* i.e., to pray for such rest   187 *peace-parted souls* those who have died at peace with God
191 *howling* i.e., in hell

I thought thy bride-bed to have decked, sweet maid,
And not t' have strewed thy grave.
Laertes: O, treble woe   195
 Fall ten times treble on that cursèd head
 Whose wicked deed thy most ingenious sense°
 Deprived thee of! Hold off the earth awhile,
 Till I have caught her once more in mine arms.

                [He leaps into the grave and embraces Ophelia.]

 Now pile your dust upon the quick and dead,   200
 Till of this flat a mountain you have made
 T' o'ertop old Pelion or the skyish head
 Of blue Olympus.°
Hamlet [coming forward]: What is he whose grief
 Bears such an emphasis,° whose phrase of sorrow   205
 Conjures the wandering stars° and makes them stand
 Like wonder-wounded° hearers? This is I,
 Hamlet the Dane.°
Laertes [grappling with him°]: The devil take thy soul!
Hamlet: Thou pray'st not well.   210
 I prithee, take thy fingers from my throat,
 For though I am not splenitive° and rash,
 Yet have I in me something dangerous,
 Which let thy wisdom fear. Hold off thy hand.
King: Pluck them asunder.   215
Queen: Hamlet, Hamlet!
All: Gentlemen!
Horatio: Good my lord, be quiet.

                [Hamlet and Laertes are parted.]

Hamlet: Why, I will fight with him upon this theme
 Until my eyelids will no longer wag.°   220
Queen: O my son, what theme?
Hamlet: I loved Ophelia. Forty thousand brothers
 Could not with all their quantity of love
 Make up my sum. What wilt thou do for her?
King: O, he is mad, Laertes.   225
Queen: For love of God, forbear him.°
Hamlet: 'Swounds,° show me what thou'lt do.
 Woo't° weep? Woo't fight? Woo't fast? Woo't tear thyself?
 Woo't drink up° eisel?° Eat a crocodile?°

---

197 *ingenious sense* a mind that is quick, alert, of fine qualities   202–203 *Pelion . . . Olympus* sacred mountains in the north of Thessaly   205 *emphasis* i.e., rhetorical and florid emphasis. (*Phrase* has a similar rhetorical connotation.)   206 *wandering stars* planets   207 *wonder-wounded* struck with amazement   208 *the Dane* (This title normally signifies the King; see I, i, 17 and note.)   209 s.d. *grappling with him* The testimony of the First Quarto that "*Hamlet leaps in after Laertes*" and the "Elegy on Burbage" ("Oft have I seen him leap into the grave") seem to indicate one way in which this fight was staged; however, the difficulty of fitting two contenders and Ophelia's body into a confined space (probably the trapdoor) suggests to many editors the alternative, that Laertes jumps out of the grave to attack Hamlet.)   212 *splenitive* quick-tempered   220 *wag* move. (A fluttering eyelid is a conventional sign that life has not yet gone.   226 *forbear him* leave him alone   227 *'Swounds* by His (Christ's) wounds   228 *Woo't* wilt thou   229 *drink up* drink deeply.   *eisel* vinegar.   *crocodile* (Crocodiles were tough and dangerous, and were supposed to shed hypocritical tears.)

I'll do 't. Dost come here to whine?   230
To outface me with leaping in her grave?
Be buried quick° with her, and so will I.
And if thou prate of mountains, let them throw
Millions of acres on us, till our ground,
Singeing his pate° against the burning zone,°   235
Make Ossa° like a wart! Nay, an° thou'lt mouth,°
I'll rant as well as thou.

Queen: This is mere° madness,
And thus awhile the fit will work on him;
Anon, as patient as the female dove
When that her golden couplets° are disclosed,°   240
His silence will sit drooping.

Hamlet: Hear you, sir.
What is the reason that you use me thus?
I loved you ever. But it is no matter.
Let Hercules himself do what he may,
The cat will mew, and dog will have his day.°   245

                                        Exit Hamlet.

King: I pray thee, good Horatio, wait upon him.

                                     [Exit] Horatio.

[*To Laertes.*] Strengthen your patience in° our last night's speech;
We'll put the matter to the present push.°—
Good Gertrude, set some watch over your son.—
This grave shall have a living° monument.   250
An hour of quiet° shortly shall we see;
Till then, in patience our proceeding be.   *Exeunt.*

SCENE II [THE CASTLE.]

Enter Hamlet and Horatio.

Hamlet: So much for this, sir; now shall you see the other.°
    You do remember all the circumstance?
Horatio: Remember it, my lord!
Hamlet: Sir, in my heart there was a kind of fighting
    That would not let me sleep. Methought I lay   5
    Worse than the mutines° in the bilboes.° Rashly,°
    And praised be rashness for it—let us know°
    Our indiscretion° sometimes serves us well

---

232 *quick* alive 233 *his pate* his head, i.e., top. *burning zone* zone in the celestial sphere containing the sun's orbit, between the tropics of Cancer and Capricorn 236 *Ossa* another mountain in Thessaly. (In their war against the Olympian gods, the giants attempted to heap Ossa on Pelion to scale Olympus.) *an* if. *mouth* i.e., rant 237 *mere* utter 240 *golden couplets* two baby pigeons, covered with yellow down. *disclosed* hatched 244–245 *Let . . . day* i.e., (1) even Hercules couldn't stop Laertes' theatrical rant (2) I, too, will have my turn; i.e., despite any blustering attempts at interference, every person will sooner or later do what he or she must do 247 *in* i.e., by recalling 248 *present push* immediate test 250 *living* lasting. (For Laertes' private understanding, Claudius also hints that Hamlet's death will serve as such a monument.) 251 *hour of quiet* time free of conflict 1 *see the other* hear the other news 6 *mutines* mutineers. *bilboes* shackles. *Rashly* on impulse. (This adverb goes with lines 12 ff.) 7 *know* acknowledge 8 *indiscretion* lack of foresight and judgment (not an indiscreet act)

When our deep plots do pall,° and that should learn° us
There's a divinity that shapes our ends,
Rough-hew° them how we will—   10

Horatio: That is most certain.
Hamlet: Up from my cabin,
My sea-gown° scarfed° about me, in the dark
Groped I to find out them,° had my desire,
Fingered° their packet, and in fine° withdrew   15
To mine own room again, making so bold,
My fears forgetting manners, to unseal
Their grand commission; where I found, Horatio—
Ah, royal knavery!—an exact command,
Larded° with many several° sorts of reasons   20
Importing° Denmark's health and England's too,
With, ho! such bugs° and goblins in my life,°
That on the supervise,° no leisure bated,°
No, not to stay° the grinding of the ax,
My head should be struck off.

Horatio: Is 't possible?   25
Hamlet [giving a document]: Here's the commission. Read it at more leisure.
But wilt thou hear now how I did proceed?

Horatio: I beseech you.
Hamlet: Being thus benetted round with villainies—
Ere I could make a prologue to my brains,
They had begun the play°—I sat me down,   30
Devised a new commission, wrote it fair.°
I once did hold it, as our statists° do,
A baseness° to write fair, and labored much
How to forget that learning, but, sir, now   35
It did me yeoman's° service. Wilt thou know
Th' effect° of what I wrote?

Horatio: Ay, good my lord.
Hamlet: An earnest conjuration° from the King,
As England was his faithful tributary,
As love between them like the palm° might flourish,   40
As peace should still° her wheaten garland° wear
And stand a comma° 'tween their amities,
And many suchlike "as"es° of great charge,°
That on the view and knowing of these contents,

9 *pall* fail, falter, go stale. *learn* teach 11 *Rough-hew* shape roughly 13 *sea-gown* seaman's coat. *scarfed*
loosely wrapped 14 *them* i.e., Rosencrantz and Guildenstern 15 *Fingered* pilfered, pinched. *in fine*
finally, in conclusion 20 *Larded* garnished. *several* different 21 *Importing* relating to 22 *bugs* bug-
bears, hobgoblins. *in my life* i.e., to be feared if I were allowed to live 23 *supervise* reading. *leisure bated*
delay allowed 24 *stay* await 30–31 *Ere . . . play* before I could consciously turn my brain to the matter,
it had started working on a plan 32 *fair* in a clear hand 33 *statists* statesmen 34 *baseness* i.e., lower-
class trait 36 *yeoman's* i.e., substantial, faithful, loyal 37 *effect* purport 38 *conjuration* entreaty 40
palm (An image of health; see Psalm 92:12.) 41 *still* always. *wheaten garland* (Symbolic of fruitful agriculture, of peace and plenty.) 42 *comma* (Indicating continuity, link.) 43 *"as"es* (1) the "whereases" of
a formal document (2) asses. *charge* (1) import (2) burden (appropriate to asses)

Without debatement further more or less,   45
He should those bearers put to sudden death,
Not shriving time° allowed.
Horatio: How was this sealed?
Hamlet: Why, even in that was heaven ordinant.°
I had my father's signet° in my purse,
Which was the model° of that Danish seal;   50
Folded the writ° up in the form of th' other,
Subscribed° it, gave 't th' impression,° placed it safely,
The changeling° never known. Now, the next day
Was our sea fight, and what to this was sequent°
Thou knowest already.   55
Horatio: So Guildenstern and Rosencrantz go to 't.
Hamlet: Why, man, they did make love to this employment.
They are not near my conscience. Their defeat°
Does by their own insinuation° grow.
'Tis dangerous when the baser° nature comes   60
Between the pass° and fell° incensed points
Of mighty opposites.°
Horatio: Why, what a king is this!
Hamlet: Does it not, think thee, stand me now upon°—
He that hath killed my king and whored my mother,
Popped in between th' election° and my hopes,   65
Thrown out his angle° for my proper° life,
And with such cozenage°—is 't not perfect conscience
To quit° him with this arm? And is 't not to be damned
To let this canker° of our nature come
In° further evil?   70
Horatio: It must be shortly known to him from England
What is the issue of the business there.
Hamlet: It will be short. The interim is mine.
And a man's life's no more than to say "one."°
But I am very sorry, good Horatio,   75
That to Laertes I forgot myself.
For by the image of my cause I see
The portraiture of his. I'll court his favors.
But, sure, the bravery° of his grief did put me
Into a tow'ring passion.
Horatio: Peace, who comes here?   80

    Enter a Courtier [Osric].

47 *shriving time* time for confession and absolution 48 *ordinant* directing 49 *signet* small seal 50 *model* replica 51 *writ* writing 52 *Subscribed* signed (with forged signature). *impression* i.e., with a wax seal 53 *changeling* i.e., substituted letter. (Literally, a fairy child substituted for a human one.) 54 *was sequent* followed 58 *defeat* destruction 59 *insinuation* intrusive intervention, sticking their noses in my business 60 *baser* of lower social station 61 *pass* thrust. *fell* fierce 62 *opposites* antagonists 63 *stand me now upon* become incumbent on me now 65 *election* (The Danish monarch was "elected" by a small number of high-ranking electors.) 66 *angle* fishhook. *proper* very 67 *cozenage* trickery 68 *quit* requite, pay back 69 *canker* ulcer 69–70 *come in* grow into 74 *a man's . . . "one"* one's whole life occupies such a short time, only as long as it takes to count to 1 79 *bravery* bravado

Osric: Your lordship is right welcome back to Denmark.

Hamlet: I humbly thank you, sir. [*To Horatio.*] Dost know this water fly?

Horatio: No, my good lord.

Hamlet: Thy state is the more gracious, for 'tis a vice to know him. He hath much, land and fertile. Let a beast be lord of beasts, and his crib° shall stand at the   85
King's mess.° 'Tis a chuff,° but, as I say, spacious in the possession of dirt.

Osric: Sweet lord, if your lordship were at leisure, I should impart a thing to you from His Majesty.

Hamlet: I will receive it, sir, with all diligence of spirit. Put your bonnet° to his°
right use; 'tis for the head.   90

Osric: I thank your lordship, it is very hot.

Hamlet: No, believe me, 'tis very cold. The wind is northerly.

Osric: It is indifferent° cold, my lord, indeed.

Hamlet: But yet methinks it is very sultry and hot for my complexion.°

Osric: Exceedingly, my lord. It is very sultry, as 'twere—I cannot tell how. My lord,   95
His Majesty bade me signify to you that 'a has laid a great wager on your head.
Sir, this is the matter—

Hamlet: I beseech you, remember.

[*Hamlet moves him to put on his hat.*]

Osric: Nay, good my lord; for my ease,° in good faith. Sir, here is newly come to court
Laertes—believe me, an absolute° gentleman, full of most excellent differences,°   100
of very soft society° and great showing.° Indeed, to speak feelingly° of him, he is
the card° or calendar° of gentry,° for you shall find in him the continent of what
part a gentleman would see.°

Hamlet: Sir, his definement° suffers no perdition° in you,° though I know to divide
him inventorially° would dozy° th' arithmetic of memory, and yet but yaw°   105
neither° in respect of° his quick sail. But, in the verity of extolment,° I take him
to be a soul of great article,° and his infusion° of such dearth and rareness° as, to
make true diction° of him, his semblable° is his mirror and who else would trace°
him his umbrage,° nothing more.

Osric: Your lordship speaks most infallibly of him.   110

Hamlet: The concernancy,° sir? Why do we wrap the gentleman in our more rawer
breath?°

Osric: Sir?

---

85 *crib* manger   85–86 *Let . . . mess* i.e., if a man, no matter how beastlike, is as rich in livestock and possessions as Osric, he may eat at the King's table   86 *chuff* boor, churl. (The Second Quarto spelling,
chough, is a variant spelling that also suggests the meaning here of "chattering jackdaw.")   89 *bonnet* any
kind of cap or hat.   *his* its   93 *indifferent* somewhat   94 *complexion* temperament   99 *for my ease* (A
conventional reply declining the invitation to put his hat back on.)   100 *absolute* perfect.   *differences*
special qualities   101 *soft society* agreeable manners.   *great showing* distinguished appearance.   *feelingly*
with just perception   102 *card* chart, map.   *calendar* guide.   *gentry* good breeding   102–103 *the continent . . . see* one who contains in him all the qualities a gentleman would like to see. (A *continent* is that
which contains.)   104 *definement* definition. (Hamlet proceeds to mock Osric by throwing his lofty diction back at him.)   *perdition* loss, diminution.   *you* your description   104–105 *divide him inventorially*
enumerate his graces   105 *dozy* dizzy.   *yaw* swing unsteadily off course. (Said of a ship.)   106 *neither* for
all that.   *in respect of* in comparison with.   *in . . . extolment* in true praise (of him)   107 *of great article*
one with many articles in his inventory.   *infusion* essence, character infused into him by nature.   *dearth
and rareness* rarity   108 *make true diction* speak truly.   *semblable* only true likeness.   *who . . . trace* any
other person who would wish to follow   109 *umbrage* shadow   111 *concernancy* import, relevance
111–112 *rawer breath* unrefined speech that can only come short in praising him

Horatio: Is 't not possible to understand in another tongue?° You will do 't,° sir, really. 115

Hamlet: What imports the nomination of this gentleman?

Osric: Of Laertes?

Horatio [to Hamlet]: His purse is empty already; all 's golden words are spent.

Hamlet: Of him, sir.

Osric: I know you are not ignorant— 120

Hamlet: I would you did, sir. Yet in faith if you did, it would not much approve° me. Well, sir?

Osric: You are not ignorant of what excellence Laertes is—

Hamlet: I dare not confess that, lest I should compare with him in excellence. But to know a man well were to know himself.° 125

Osric: I mean, sir, for° his weapon; but in the imputation laid on him by them,° in his meed° he's unfellowed.°

Hamlet: What's his weapon?

Osric: Rapier and dagger.

Hamlet: That's two of his weapons—but well.° 130

Osric: The King, sir, hath wagered with him six Barbary horses, against the which he° has impawned,° as I take it, six French rapiers and poniards,° with their assigns,° as girdle, hangers,° and so.° Three of the carriages,° in faith, are very dear to fancy,° very responsive° to the hilts, most delicate° carriages, and of very liberal conceit.° 135

Hamlet: What call you the carriages?

Horatio [to Hamlet]: I knew you must be edified by the margent° ere you had done.

Osric: The carriages, sir, are the hangers.

Hamlet: The phrase would be more germane to the matter if we could carry a cannon by our sides; I would it might be hangers till then. But, on: six Barbary horses 140 against six French swords, their assigns, and three liberal—conceited carriages; that's the French bet against the Danish. Why is this impawned, as you call it?

Osric: The King, sir, hath laid,° sir, that in a dozen passes° between yourself and him, he shall not exceed you three hits. He hath laid on twelve for nine, and it would come to immediate trial, if your lordship would vouchsafe the answer.° 145

Hamlet: How if I answer no?

Osric: I mean, my lord, the opposition of your person in trial.

---

114 *to understand . . . tongue* i.e., for you, Osric, to understand when someone else speaks your language. (Horatio twits Osric for not being able to understand the kind of flowery speech he himself uses, when Hamlet speaks in such a vein. Alternatively, all this could be said to Hamlet.)   *You will do 't* i.e., you can if you try, or, you may well have to try (to speak plainly)   121 *approve* commend   124–125 *I dare . . . himself* I dare not boast of knowing Laertes' excellence lest I seem to imply a comparable excellence in myself. Certainly to know another person well, one must know oneself   126 *for* i.e., with.   *imputation . . . them* reputation given him by others   127 *meed* merit.   *unfellowed* unmatched   130 *but well* but never mind   132 *he* i.e., Laertes.   *impawned* staked, wagered.   *poniards* daggers   133 *assigns* appurtenances. *hangers* straps on the sword belt (*girdle*), from which the sword hung.   *and so* and so on.   *carriages* (An affected way of saying *hangers*; literally, gun carriages.)   134 *dear to fancy* delightful to the fancy. *responsive* corresponding closely, matching or well-adjusted.   *delicate* (i.e., in workmanship)   135 *liberal conceit* elaborate design   137 *margent* margin of a book, place for explanatory notes   143 *laid* wagered. *passes* bouts. (The odds of the betting are hard to explain. Possibly the King bets that Hamlet will win at least five out of twelve, at which point Laertes raises the odds against himself by betting he will win nine.)   145 *vouchsafe the answer* be so good as to accept the challenge. (Hamlet deliberately takes the phrase in its literal sense of replying.)

Hamlet: Sir, I will walk here in the hall. If it please His Majesty, it is the breathing
  time° of day with me. Let° the foils be brought, the gentleman willing, and the
  King hold his purpose, I will win for him an I can; if not, I will gain nothing but   150
  my shame and the odd hits.
Osric: Shall I deliver you° so?
Hamlet: To this effect, sir—after what flourish your nature will.
Osric: I commend° my duty to your lordship.
Hamlet: Yours, yours. [*Exit Osric.*] 'A does well to commend it himself; there are no   155
  tongues else for 's turn.°
Horatio: This lapwing° runs away with the shell on his head.
Hamlet: 'A did comply with his dug° before 'a sucked it. Thus has he—and many
  more of the same breed that I know the drossy° age dotes on—only got the tune°
  of the time and, out of an habit of encounter,° a kind of yeasty° collection,°   160
  which carries them through and through the most fanned and winnowed
  opinions;° and do° but blow them to their trial, the bubbles are out.°

  Enter a Lord.

Lord: My lord, His Majesty commended him to you by young Osric, who brings back to
  him that you attend him in the hall. He sends to know if your pleasure hold to
  play with Laertes, or that you will take longer time.   165
Hamlet: I am constant to my purposes; they follow the King's pleasure. If his fitness
  speaks, mine is ready;° now or whensoever, provided I be so able as now.
Lord: The King and Queen and all are coming down.
Hamlet: In happy time.°
Lord: The Queen desires you to use some gentle entertainment° to Laertes before   170
  you fall to play.
Hamlet: She well instructs me.   [*Exit Lord.*]
Horatio: You will lose, my lord.
Hamlet: I do not think so. Since he went into France, I have been in continual practice;
  I shall win at the odds. But thou wouldst not think how ill all's here about my   175
  heart; but it is no matter.
Horatio: Nay, good my lord—
Hamlet: It is but foolery, but it is such a kind of gaingiving° as would perhaps trouble
  a woman.
Horatio: If your mind dislike anything, obey it. I will forestall their repair° hither and   180
  say you are not fit.

148–149 *breathing time* exercise period   149 *Let* i.e., if   152 *deliver you* report what you say   154
commend commit to your favor. (A conventional salutation, but Hamlet wryly uses a more literal meaning,
"recommend," "praise," in line 155.)   156 *for 's turn* for his purposes, i.e., to do it for him   157 *lapwing* (A
proverbial type of youthful forwardness. Also, a bird that draws intruders away from its nest and was
thought to run about with its head in the shell when newly hatched; a seeming reference to Osric's hat.)
158 *comply . . . dug* observe ceremonious formality toward his nurse's or mother's teat   159 *drossy* laden
with scum and impurities, frivolous.   *tune* temper, mood, manner of speech   160 *an habit of encounter* a
demeanor in conversing (with courtiers of his own kind).   *yeasty* frothy.   *collection* i.e., of current phrases
161–162 *carries . . . opinions* sustains them right through the scrutiny of persons whose opinions are select
and refined. (Literally, like grain separated from its chaff. Osric is both the chaff and the bubbly froth on
the surface of the liquor that is soon blown away.)   162 *and do yet do.*   *blow . . . out* test them by merely
blowing on them, and their bubbles burst   166–167 *If . . . ready* if he declares his readiness, my convenience waits on his   169 *In happy time* (A phrase of courtesy indicating that the time is convenient.)
170 *entertainment* greeting   178 *gaingiving* misgiving   180 *repair* coming

Hamlet: Not a whit, we defy augury. There is special providence in the fall of a sparrow.
If it be now, 'tis not to come; if it be not to come, it will be now; if it be not now,
yet it will come. The readiness is all. Since no man of aught he leaves knows, what
is 't to leave betimes? Let be.° 185

A table prepared. [Enter] trumpets, drums, and officers with cushions; King, Queen,
[Osric,] and all the state; foils, daggers, [and wine borne in;] and Laertes.

King: Come, Hamlet, come and take this hand from me.
　　　　　　　　　　　　　[The King puts Laertes' hand into Hamlet's.]
Hamlet *[to Laertes]*: Give me your pardon, sir. I have done you wrong,
　　But pardon 't as you are a gentleman.
　　This presence° knows,
　　And you must needs have heard, how I am punished° 190
　　With a sore distraction. What I have done
　　That might your nature, honor, and exception°
　　Roughly awake, I here proclaim was madness.
　　Was 't Hamlet wronged Laertes? Never Hamlet.
　　If Hamlet from himself be ta'en away, 195
　　And when he's not himself does wrong Laertes,
　　Then Hamlet does it not, Hamlet denies it.
　　Who does it, then? His madness. If 't be so,
　　Hamlet is of the faction° that is wronged;
　　His madness is poor Hamlet's enemy. 200
　　Sir, in this audience
　　Let my disclaiming from a purposed evil
　　Free me so far in your most generous thoughts
　　That I have° shot my arrow o'er the house
　　And hurt my brother.
Laertes: 　　　　　　　I am satisfied in nature,° 205
　　Whose motive° in this case should stir me most
　　To my revenge. But in my terms of honor
　　I stand aloof, and will no reconcilement
　　Till by some elder masters of known honor
　　I have a voice° and precedent of peace° 210
　　To keep my name ungored.° But till that time
　　I do receive your offered love like love,
　　And will not wrong it.
Hamlet: 　　　　　　　I embrace it freely,
　　And will this brother's wager frankly° play.—
　　Give us the foils. Come on.
Laertes: 　　　　　　　Come, one for me. 215
Hamlet: I'll be your foil,° Laertes. In mine ignorance

184–185 *Since . . . Let be* since no one has knowledge of what he is leaving behind, what does an early
death matter after all? Enough; don't struggle against it. 189 *presence* royal assembly 190 *punished*
afflicted 192 *exception* disapproval 199 *faction* party 204 *That I have* as if I had 205 *in nature* i.e., as
to my personal feelings 206 *motive* prompting 210 *voice* authoritative pronouncement. *of peace* for
reconciliation 211 *name ungored* reputation unwounded 214 *frankly* without ill feeling or the burden of
rancor 216 *foil* thin metal background that sets a jewel off (with pun on the blunted rapier for fencing)

> Your skill shall, like a star i' the darkest night,
> Stick fiery off° indeed.
Laertes: You mock me, sir.
Hamlet: No, by this hand.
King: Give them the foils, young Osric. Cousin Hamlet,   220
> You know the wager?
Hamlet: Very well, my lord.
> Your Grace has laid the odds o'° the weaker side.
King: I do not fear it; I have seen you both.
> But since he is bettered,° we have therefore odds.
Laertes: This is too heavy. Let me see another.   225

> > [*He exchanges his foil for another.*]

Hamlet: This likes me° well. These foils have all a length?

> > [*They prepare to play.*]

Osric: Ay, my good lord.
King: Set me the stoups of wine upon that table.
> If Hamlet give the first or second hit,
> Or quit in answer of the third exchange,°   230
> Let all the battlements their ordnance fire.
> The King shall drink to Hamlet's better breath,°
> And in the cup an union° shall he throw
> Richer than that which four successive kings
> In Denmark's crown have worn. Give me the cups,   235
> And let the kettle° to the trumpet speak,
> The trumpet to the cannoneer without,
> The cannons to the heavens, the heaven to earth,
> "Now the King drinks to Hamlet." Come, begin.

> > *Trumpets the while.*

> And you, the judges, bear a wary eye.   240
Hamlet: Come on, sir.
Laertes: Come, my lord. [*They play. Hamlet scores a hit.*]
Hamlet: One.
Laertes: No.
Hamlet: Judgment.
Osric: A hit, a very palpable hit.   245

> > *Drum, trumpets, and shot. Flourish.*
> > *A piece goes off.*

Laertes: Well, again.
King: Stay, give me drink. Hamlet, this pearl is thine.

> > [*He drinks, and throws a pearl in Hamlet's cup.*]

> Here's to thy health. Give him the cup.
Hamlet: I'll play this bout first. Set it by awhile.
> Come. [*They play.*] Another hit; what say you?   250

---

218 *Stick fiery off* stand out brilliantly   222 *laid the odds o'* bet on, backed   224 *is bettered* has improved; is the odds-on favorite. (Laertes' handicap is the "three hits" specified in line 144.)   226 *likes me* pleases me   230 *Or . . . exchange* i.e., or requites Laertes in the third bout for having won the first two   232 *better breath* improved vigor   233 *union* pearl. (So called, according to Pliny's *Natural History*, 9, because pearls are *unique*, never identical.)   236 *kettle* kettledrum

Deadly swordplay between Laertes and Hamlet (V, ii, 241–269).

Laertes: A touch, a touch, I do confess 't.
King: Our son shall win.
Queen: He's fat° and scant of breath.
   Here, Hamlet, take my napkin,° rub thy brows.
   The Queen carouses° to thy fortune, Hamlet.
Hamlet: Good madam!   255
King: Gertrude, do not drink.
Queen: I will, my lord, I pray you pardon me.   [*She drinks.*]
King [*aside*]: It is the poisoned cup. It is too late.
Hamlet: I dare not drink yet, madam; by and by.
Queen: Come, let me wipe thy face.   260
Laertes [*to King*]: My lord, I'll hit him now.
King: I do not think 't.
Laertes [*aside*]: And yet it is almost against my conscience.
Hamlet: Come, for the third, Laertes. You do but dally.
   I pray you, pass° with your best violence;   265
   I am afeard you make a wanton of me.°
Laertes: Say you so? Come on.   [*They play.*]
Osric: Nothing neither way.
Laertes: Have at you now!

252 *fat* not physically fit, out of training   253 *napkin* handkerchief   254 *carouses* drinks a toast   265 *pass*
thrust   266 *make . . . me* i.e., treat me like a spoiled child, trifle with me

[*Laertes wounds Hamlet; then, in scuffling, they change rapiers,° and Hamlet wounds*
Laertes.]

King: Part them! They are incensed.
Hamlet: Nay, come, again.   [*The Queen falls.*]
Osric: Look to the Queen there, ho!   270
Horatio: They bleed on both sides. How is it, my lord?
Osric: How is 't, Laertes?
Laertes: Why, as a woodcock° to mine own springe,° Osric;
    I am justly killed with mine own treachery.
Hamlet: How does the Queen?
King: She swoons to see them bleed.   275
Queen: No, no, the drink, the drink—O my dear Hamlet—
    The drink, the drink! I am poisoned.   [*She dies.*]
Hamlet: O villainy! Ho, let the door be locked!
    Treachery! Seek it out.   [*Laertes falls. Exit Osric.*]
Laertes: It is here, Hamlet. Hamlet, thou art slain.   280
    No med'cine in the world can do thee good;
    In thee there is not half an hour's life.
    The treacherous instrument is in thy hand,
    Unbated° and envenomed. The foul practice°
    Hath turned itself on me. Lo, here I lie,   285
    Never to rise again. Thy mother's poisoned.
    I can no more. The King, the King's to blame.
Hamlet: The point envenomed too? Then, venom, to thy work.
                              [*He stabs the King.*]
All: Treason! Treason!
King: O, yet defend me, friends! I am but hurt.   290
Hamlet [*forcing the King to drink*]:
    Here, thou incestuous, murderous, damnèd Dane,
    Drink off this potion. Is thy union° here?
    Follow my mother.   [*The King dies.*]
Laertes: He is justly served.
    It is a poison tempered° by himself.
    Exchange forgiveness with me, noble Hamlet.   295
    Mine and my father's death come not upon thee,
    Nor thine on me!   [*He dies.*]
Hamlet: Heaven make thee free of it! I follow thee.
    I am dead, Horatio. Wretched Queen, adieu!
    You that look pale and tremble at this chance,°   300
    That are but mutes° or audience to this act,
    Had I but time—as this fell° sergeant,° Death,
    Is strict° in his arrest°—O, I could tell you—

269 s.d. *in scuffling, they change rapiers* (This stage direction occurs in the Folio. According to a widespread stage tradition, Hamlet receives a scratch, realizes that Laertes' sword is unbated, and accordingly forces an exchange.)   273 *woodcock* a bird, a type of stupidity or as a decoy.   *springe* trap, snare   284 *Unbated* not blunted with a button.   *practice* plot   292 *union* pearl. (See line 233; with grim puns on the word's other meanings: marriage, shared death.)   294 *tempered* mixed   300 *chance* mischance   301 *mutes* silent observers. (Literally, actors with nonspeaking parts.)   302 *fell* cruel.   *sergeant* sheriff's officer   303 *strict* (1) severely just (2) unavoidable.   *arrest* (1) taking into custody (2) stopping my speech

But let it be. Horatio, I am dead;
Thou livest. Report me and my cause aright   305
To the unsatisfied.
Horatio: Never believe it.
I am more an antique Roman° than a Dane.
Here's yet some liquor left.

[*He attempts to drink from the poisoned cup. Hamlet prevents him.*]

Hamlet: As thou'rt a man,
Give me the cup! Let go! By heaven, I'll ha 't.
O God, Horatio, what a wounded name,   310
Things standing thus unknown, shall I leave behind me!
If thou didst ever hold me in thy heart,
Absent thee from felicity awhile,
And in this harsh world draw thy breath in pain
To tell my story.   *A march afar off* [*and a volley within*].
                  What warlike noise is this?   315

Enter Osric.

Osric: Young Fortinbras, with conquest come from Poland,
To th' ambassadors of England gives
This warlike volley.
Hamlet: O, I die, Horatio!
The potent poison quite o'ercrows° my spirit.
I cannot live to hear the news from England,   320
But I do prophesy th' election lights
On Fortinbras. He has my dying voice.°
So tell him, with th' occurrents° more and less
Which have solicited°—the rest is silence.   [*He dies.*]
Horatio: Now cracks a noble heart. Good night, sweet prince,   325
And flights of angels sing thee to thy rest!

[*March within.*]

Why does the drum come hither?

Enter Fortinbras, with the [*English*] *Ambassadors* [*with drum, colors, and attendants*].

Fortinbras: Where is this sight?
Horatio: What is it you would see?
If aught of woe or wonder, cease your search.
Fortinbras: This quarry° cries on havoc.° O proud Death,   330
What feast° is toward° in thine eternal cell,
That thou so many princes at a shot
So bloodily hast struck?

---

307 *Roman* (Suicide was an honorable choice for many Romans as an alternative to a dishonorable life.)
319 *o'ercrows* triumphs over (like the winner in a cockfight)   322 *voice* vote   323 *occurrents* events,
incidents   324 *solicited* moved, urged. (Hamlet doesn't finish saying what the events have prompted—
presumably, his acts of vengeance, or his reporting of those events to Fortinbras.)   330 *quarry* heap of
dead.   *cries on havoc* proclaims a general slaughter   331 *feast* i.e., Death feasting on those who have fallen.
toward in preparation

First Ambassador: The sight is dismal,
 And our affairs from England come too late.
 The ears are senseless that should give us hearing,   335
 To tell him his commandment is fulfilled,
 That Rosencrantz and Guildenstern are dead.
 Where should we have our thanks?
Horatio: Not from his° mouth,
 Had it th' ability of life to thank you.
 He never gave commandment for their death.   340
 But since, so jump° upon this bloody question,°
 You from the Polack wars, and you from England,
 Are here arrived, give order that these bodies
 High on a stage° be placèd to the view,
 And let me speak to th' yet unknowing world   345
 How these things came about. So shall you hear
 Of carnal, bloody, and unnatural acts,
 Of accidental judgments,° casual° slaughters,
 Of deaths put on° by cunning and forced cause,°
 And, in this upshot, purposes mistook   350
 Fall'n on th' inventors' heads. All this can I
 Truly deliver.
Fortinbras: Let us haste to hear it,
 And call the noblest to the audience.
 For me, with sorrow I embrace my fortune.
 I have some rights of memory° in this kingdom,   355
 Which now to claim my vantage° doth invite me.
Horatio: Of that I shall have also cause to speak,
 And from his mouth whose voice will draw on more.°
 But let this same be presently° performed,
 Even while men's minds are wild, lest more mischance 360
 On° plots and errors happen.
Fortinbras: Let four captains
 Bear Hamlet, like a soldier, to the stage,
 For he was likely, had he been put on,°
 To have proved most royal; and for his passage,°
 The soldiers' music and the rite of war   365
 Speak° loudly for him.
 Take up the bodies. Such a sight as this
 Becomes the field,° but here shows much amiss.
 Go bid the soldiers shoot.

  Exeunt [marching, bearing off the dead bodies; a peal of ordnance is shot off].

---

338 *his* i.e., Claudius' 341 *jump* precisely, immediately. *question* dispute, affair 344 *stage* platform
348 *judgments* retributions. *casual* occurring by chance 349 *put on* instigated. *forced cause* contrivance
355 *of memory* traditional, remembered, unforgotten 356 *vantage* favorable opportunity 358 *voice . . .
more* vote will influence still others 359 *presently* immediately 361 *On* on the basis of; on top of 363 *put
on* i.e., invested in royal office and so put to the test 364 *passage* i.e., from life to death 366 *Speak* (let
them) speak 368 *Becomes the field* suits the field of battle

Questions
ACT I

1. By what means does Shakespeare build suspense before the Ghost's appearances? What disturbing political events occur in the background of the first act?
2. Why is Hamlet so unwilling to trust what the Ghost tells him? What precisely does the Ghost instruct him to do? (What does the Ghost command him not to do?) Why does Hamlet not immediately obey the Ghost's orders?
3. What is Hamlet's relationship to Horatio at the beginning of the play (ii, 160–188)? How does their relationship change in the course of the play?
4. How does Claudius appear in his first scene (ii, 1–128)? Does he betray evidence of guilt?
5. Hamlet's first soliloquy (ii, 129–159) occurs before Horatio reports the Ghost's appearance. What does it reveal about the Prince's state of mind? What things trouble him?
6. Is the advice Polonius offers Laertes trustworthy? Polonius sometimes appears bumbling and self-deluded. Does his opening speech (iii, 55–81) offer good or bad advice?
7. What does Polonius tell Ophelia about Hamlet's declarations of affection (iii, 102–136)? What do his remarks reveal about his opinion of Ophelia?

ACT II

1. How does Polonius's conversation with Reynaldo change our opinion of the old counselor? What verbal mannerisms does Shakespeare give to Polonius that now make him appear comic? What precisely does Polonius ask Reynaldo to do in Paris?
2. When Ophelia tells her father about Hamlet's frightening visit to her room (i, 77–102), how does Polonius interpret the event? What does the audience know that might lead them to analyze the Prince's visit differently?
3. When Polonius announces his theory of Hamlet's madness to the King, the counselor indulges in wordplay and metaphor (ii, 86–91). What does his performance suggest about his personality?
4. Is Polonius entirely foolish? Is he capable of genuine insight? Give specific examples of wise and deluded judgments by Polonius.
5. Polonius observes "there is method" in Hamlet's madness (ii, 197). Give an example of something important that Hamlet utters under the guise of madness that he probably would not say openly in a more rational way.
6. What does Hamlet imply about Polonius in his remark "That great baby you see there is not yet out of his swaddling clouts" (ii, 330–331)? Does Rosencrantz understand the Prince's joke (332–333)?
7. What does Hamlet's request to hear a recitation from the players about Pyrrhus's bloody slaughter at Troy suggest about the Prince's state of mind? What specific actions by Pyrrhus are the most suggestive of Hamlet's own plans?

ACT III

1. In his most famous soliloquy (i, 57–91), what course of action does Hamlet contemplate? How does he resolve his internal argument?
2. How guilty is Gertrude? With what offenses does Hamlet charge her (Scene iv)? Is our attitude toward her the same as Hamlet's or different? Does our sympathy for her grow or diminish as the play continues?
3. What is odd about the Ghost's appearance to Hamlet in the Queen's bedroom (iv, 106–142)?
4. From the play-within-a-play (Scene ii) and from Hamlet's remarks on acting, what do we learn about the Elizabethan theater? How do Hamlet's remarks serve to advance the story?
5. Discuss Hamlet's treatment of Ophelia (see especially Scene i). Does his behavior seem cruel, in conflict with his supposed nobility and sensitivity?

ACT IV

1. When Claudius demands that the Queen explain her son's behavior, Gertrude claims that the Prince is insane (i, 1–27). Does she truly believe Hamlet is mad, or is she trying to protect him from Claudius?

2. What causes Ophelia to go mad? Cite lines or events in the play for your interpretation.
3. Discuss how Shakespeare differently portrays Hamlet's feigned madness and Ophelia's real madness. State some specific differences in Shakespeare's presentation.
4. When Laertes returns to avenge his father's death, does he appear heroic or confused? How does his behavior compare with Hamlet's strategy for revenge?

ACT V

1. The final act of *Hamlet* begins with a long comic scene featuring two gravediggers. This episode has little direct bearing on the plot, and the two gravediggers never reappear. What does this comic interlude add to the tragedy? Would the play be more focused and forceful without this humorous scene?
2. *Hamlet* ends with the arrival of Fortinbras. If someone suggested that Fortinbras be cut from the play, what reasons would you offer for his inclusion?

General Questions

1. What is the play's major dramatic question? (For a discussion of this term, see page 1124.) At what point is the question formulated? Does this play have a crisis, or turning point?
2. How early in the play, and from what passages, do you perceive that Claudius is a villain?
3. What comic elements does the play contain—what scenes, what characters, what exchanges of dialogue? What is their value to a play that, as a whole, is a tragedy?
4. A familiar kind of behavior is showing one face to the world and another to oneself. What characters in *Hamlet* do so? Is their deception ever justified?
5. Is Laertes a villain like Claudius, or is there reason to feel that his contrived duel with Hamlet is justified?
6. How is Hamlet shown to be a noble and extraordinary person, not merely by birth, but by nature? See Ophelia's praise of Hamlet as "The glass of fashion, and the mold of form" (III, i, 142–153). Are we to take Ophelia's speech as the prejudiced view of a lover, or does Shakespeare demonstrate that her opinion of Hamlet is trustworthy?
7. If the characters of Rosencrantz and Guildenstern are cut from the play, as is the case in some productions, what is lost?

THE BACKGROUND OF *A MIDSUMMER NIGHT'S DREAM*

The theme in *A Midsummer Night's Dream* of love being best fulfilled in marital union suggests that the play may have originally been written for performance at an aristocratic wedding. The work is certainly Shakespeare's most lyrical and romantic comedy, full of reflections on fantasy, dreaming, and desire, set mostly amid festive palaces and moonlit woods filled with fairies.

In the Renaissance there were two major varieties of comedy—both borrowed from Greek and Roman drama. The first was satiric comedy, which usually poked bitter fun at human folly. Shakespeare generally avoided this mode, which was very well practiced by his friend Ben Jonson. Instead, Shakespeare preferred the second type, romantic comedy, which he had discovered as a schoolboy reading the Latin plays of Terence and Plautus. Romantic comedy is less concerned with correcting misdeeds and folly than with following the delightful and embarrassing behavior of imperfect but mostly likeable characters. Always ending in the happy marriage (or marriages) of young lovers who have overcome considerable obstacles to unite, romantic comedy also encourages the viewer to accept and forgive human faults and frailties.

Kevin Kline as Bottom and Michelle Pfeiffer as Titania in a 1999 film adaptation of *A Midsummer Night's Dream.*

A Midsummer Night's Dream also demonstrates Shakespeare's particular genius for plotting, a necessary skill for comic theater. Although Shakespeare often borrowed (and usually greatly improved) the stories of his plays from various sources, the plot of *A Midsummer Night's Dream* appears to be original, though he took individual characters like Theseus and Titania from classical mythology. The comedy has a delightfully complex structure combining four different plots—all romantic in different ways, from young love to marital reconciliation.

The play presents five different sets of lovers. The general action is framed around the wedding of the first set of lovers, King Theseus and the Amazon Queen Hippolyta, whom he has conquered in war and taken as his wife. Both a personal and public union, their marriage will end the enmity between their nations. More complicated are the love affairs of the second group, the young aristocrats—Helena, Lysander, Hermia, and Demetrius. The adventures of these two passionately mismatched couples, who ultimately find happy marriages, form the main plot of the comedy. The third set of lovers is a supernatural couple, Oberon and Titania, the king and queen of the fairy realm, who are in the midst of a bitter marital dispute. Then, there is a group of rustic workmen dominated by Nick Bottom, a weaver with theatrical aspirations. While this group does not initially seem to contain any lovers, Bottom eventually becomes entangled in a series of enchantments that transforms him into Titania's ass-eared darling for a single night. Finally, at the play's end the rustics perform a burlesque of tragic love that presents a fifth, imaginary set of lovers, Pyramus and Thisbe. Their tale of "tragic mirth" subtly comments on the consequences of doomed romance. No other comedy by Shakespeare focuses so single-mindedly or happily on sexual love and marriage. No wonder *A Midsummer Night's Dream* has been popular for centuries, not only in English-speaking countries but around the world.

PICTURING *A Midsummer's*

▲ Hippolyta and Theseus, *page 1472*

▲ Lysander and Hermia, *page 1475*

▼ Oberon enchants Titania, *page 1492*

◀ Bottom as ass,
page 1498

▶ "You thief of love," *page 1509*

Night Dream

▲ The rustics plan their play,
page 1479

▲ Demetrius to Helena:
"Let me go!"
page 1489

▲ Oberon directs Puck, *page 1486*

▼ Puck's closing soliloquy,
page 1533

▲ The fairies tend to Bottom,
page 1515

► The performance of
Pyramus and Thisbe,
page 1527

A Midsummer Night's Dream

about 1594–1595

Edited By David Bevington

[DRAMATIS PERSONAE

Theseus, Duke of Athens
Hippolyta, Queen of the Amazons, betrothed to Theseus
Philostrate, Master of the Revels
Egeus, father of Hermia
Hermia, daughter of Egeus, in love with Lysander
Lysander, in love with Hermia
Demetrius, in love with Hermia and favored by Egeus
Helena, in love with Demetrius

Oberon, King of the Fairies
Titania, Queen of the Fairies
Puck, or Robin Goodfellow
Peaseblossom,
Cobweb,
Mote, } *fairies attending Titania*
Mustardseed,
Other fairies attending

Peter Quince, a carpenter,   *Prologue*
Nick Bottom, a weaver,   *Pyramus*
Francis Flute, a bellows mender,   *Thisbe*
Tom Snout, a tinker,   } *representing*   *Wall*
Snug, a joiner,   *Lion*
Robin Starveling, a tailor,   *Moonshine*
Lords and *Attendants* on *Theseus* and *Hippolyta*

SCENE *Athens, and a wood near it*]

ACT I

SCENE I [ATHENS. THESEUS' COURT.]

Enter Theseus, Hippolyta, [and Philostrate,] with others.

Theseus: Now, fair Hippolyta, our nuptial hour
    Draws on apace. Four happy days bring in
    Another moon; but, O, methinks, how slow

NOTE ON THE TEXT: This text of *A Midsummer Night's Dream* is taken from the First Quarto of 1600. For the reader's convenience, some material has been added by the editor, David Bevington (some indications of scenes and some stage directions). Such additions are enclosed in brackets. Mr. Bevington's text and notes were prepared for his book, *The Complete Works of Shakespeare*, Updated 4th ed. (New York: Longman, 1997).

PRODUCTION PHOTOS: The photos included are from the 2005 production of *A Midsummer Night's Dream* by the Utah Shakespearean Festival, with Anne Newhall (Hippolyta and Titania), Michael Sharon (Theseus and Oberon), Christine Williams (Hermia), Michael Brusasco (Lysander), Tiffany Scott (Helena), Ashley Smith (Demetrius), Corliss Preston (Puck), John Tilhotson (Bottom) Aaron Galligan-Stierte (Flute), Peter Sham (Quince), Kevin Kiler (Snout), and Martin Swoverland (Snug).

This old moon wanes! She lingers° my desires,
Like to a stepdame° or a dowager°   5
Long withering out° a young man's revenue.
Hippolyta: Four days will quickly steep themselves° in night;
Four nights will quickly dream away the time;
And then the moon, like to a silver bow
New bent in heaven, shall behold the night   10
Of our solemnities.°
Theseus: Go, Philostrate,
Stir up the Athenian youth to merriments.
Awake the pert and nimble spirit of mirth.
Turn melancholy forth to funerals;
The pale companion° is not for our pomp.°   [*Exit Philostrate.*]   15
Hippolyta, I wooed thee with my sword°
And won thy love doing thee injuries;
But I will wed thee in another key,
With pomp, with triumph,° and with reveling.

Enter Egeus and his daughter Hermia, and Lysander, and Demetrius.

Egeus: Happy be Theseus, our renownèd duke!   20
Theseus: Thanks, good Egeus. What's the news with thee?
Egeus: Full of vexation come I, with complaint
Against my child, my daughter Hermia.—
Stand forth, Demetrius.—My noble lord,
This man hath my consent to marry her.—   25
Stand forth, Lysander.—And, my gracious Duke,
This man hath bewitched the bosom of my child.
Thou, thou Lysander, thou hast given her rhymes
And interchanged love tokens with my child.
Thou hast by moonlight at her window sung   30
With feigning° voice verses of feigning° love,
And stol'n the impression of her fantasy°
With bracelets of thy hair, rings, gauds,° conceits,°
Knacks,° trifles, nosegays, sweetmeats—messengers
Of strong prevailment in° unhardened youth.   35
With cunning hast thou filched my daughter's heart,
Turned her obedience, which is due to me,
To stubborn harshness. And, my gracious Duke,
Be it so° she will not here before Your Grace
Consent to marry with Demetrius,   40

---

4 *lingers* postpones, delays the fulfillment of   5 *stepdame* stepmother. *a dowager* i.e., a widow (whose right of inheritance from her dead husband is eating into her son's estate)   6 *withering out* causing to dwindle   7 *steep themselves* saturate themselves, be absorbed in   11 *solemnities* festive ceremonies of marriage   15 *companion* fellow. *pomp* ceremonial magnificence   16 *with my sword* i.e., in a military engagement against the Amazons, when Hippolyta was taken captive   19 *triumph* public festivity   31 *feigning* (1) counterfeiting (2) faining, desirous   32 *And . . . fantasy* and made her fall in love with you (imprinting your image on her imagination) by stealthy and dishonest means   33 *gauds* playthings. *conceits* fanciful trifles   34 *Knacks* knickknacks   35 *prevailment in* influence on   39 *Be it so* if

Hippolyta, Queen of the Amazons, and her betrothed, Theseus, Duke of Athens.

I beg the ancient privilege of Athens:
As she is mine, I may dispose of her,
Which shall be either to this gentleman
Or to her death, according to our law
Immediately° provided in that case.   45
Theseus: What say you, Hermia? Be advised, fair maid.
To you your father should be as a god—
One that composed your beauties, yea, and one
To whom you are but as a form in wax
By him imprinted, and within his power   50
To leave° the figure or disfigure° it.
Demetrius is a worthy gentleman.
Hermia: So is Lysander.
Theseus: In himself he is;
But in this kind,° wanting° your father's voice,°
The other must be held the worthier.   55

45 *Immediately* directly, with nothing intervening   51 *leave* i.e., leave unaltered.   *disfigure* obliterate   54 *kind*
respect.   *wanting* lacking.   *voice* approval

Hermia: I would my father looked but with my eyes.

Theseus: Rather your eyes must with his judgment look.

Hermia: I do entreat Your Grace to pardon me.
    I know not by what power I am made bold,
    Nor how it may concern° my modesty   60
    In such a presence here to plead my thoughts;
    But I beseech Your Grace that I may know
    The worst that may befall me in this case
    If I refuse to wed Demetrius.

Theseus: Either to die the death° or to abjure   65
    Forever the society of men.
    Therefore, fair Hermia, question your desires,
    Know of your youth, examine well your blood,°
    Whether, if you yield not to your father's choice,
    You can endure the livery° of a nun,   70
    For aye° to be in shady cloister mewed,°
    To live a barren sister all your life,
    Chanting faint hymns to the cold fruitless moon.
    Thrice blessèd they that master so their blood
    To undergo such maiden pilgrimage;   75
    But earthlier happy° is the rose distilled°
    Than that which, withering on the virgin thorn,
    Grows, lives, and dies in single blessedness.

Hermia: So will I grow, so live, so die, my lord,
    Ere I will yield my virgin patent° up   80
    Unto his lordship, whose unwishèd yoke
    My soul consents not to give sovereignty.

Theseus: Take time to pause, and by the next new moon—
    The sealing day betwixt my love and me
    For everlasting bond of fellowship—   85
    Upon that day either prepare to die
    For disobedience to your father's will,
    Or° else to wed Demetrius, as he would,
    Or on Diana's altar to protest°
    For aye austerity and single life.   90

Demetrius: Relent, sweet Hermia, and, Lysander, yield
    Thy crazèd° title to my certain right.

Lysander: You have her father's love, Demetrius;
    Let me have Hermia's. Do you marry him.

Egeus: Scornful Lysander! True, he hath my love,   95
    And what is mine my love shall render him.
    And she is mine, and all my right of her
    I do estate unto° Demetrius:

---

60 *concern* befit   65 *die the death* be executed by legal process   68 *blood* passions   70 *livery* habit, costume
71 *aye* ever.   *mewed* shut in. (Said of a hawk, poultry, etc.)   76 *earthlier happy* happier as respects this
world.   *distilled* i.e., to make perfume   80 *patent* privilege   88 *Or* either   89 *protest* vow   92 *crazèd*
cracked, unsound   98 *estate unto* settle or bestow upon

Lysander: I am, my lord, as well derived° as he,
    As well possessed;° my love is more than his;   100
    My fortunes every way as fairly° ranked,
    If not with vantage,° as Demetrius';
    And, which is more than all these boasts can be,
    I am beloved of beauteous Hermia.
    Why should not I then prosecute my right?   105
    Demetrius, I'll avouch it to his head,°
    Made love to Nedar's daughter, Helena,
    And won her soul; and she, sweet lady, dotes,
    Devoutly dotes, dotes in idolatry
    Upon this spotted° and inconstant man.   110
Theseus: I must confess that I have heard so much,
    And with Demetrius thought to have spoke thereof;
    But, being overfull of self-affairs,°
    My mind did lose it. But, Demetrius, come,
    And come, Egeus, you shall go with me;   115
    I have some private schooling° for you both.
    For you, fair Hermia, look you arm° yourself
    To fit your fancies° to your father's will,
    Or else the law of Athens yields you up—
    Which by no means we may extenuate°—   120
    To death or to a vow of single life.
    Come, my Hippolyta. What cheer, my love?
    Demetrius and Egeus, go° along.
    I must employ you in some business
    Against° our nuptial, and confer with you   125
    Of something nearly that° concerns yourselves.
Egeus: With duty and desire we follow you.

                      Exeunt [all but Lysander and Hermia].
Lysander: How now, my love, why is your cheek so pale?
    How chance the roses there do fade so fast?
Hermia: Belike° for want of rain, which I could well   130
    Beteem° them from the tempest of my eyes.
Lysander: Ay me! For aught that I could ever read,
    Could ever hear by tale or history,
    The course of true love never did run smooth;
    But either it was different in blood°—   135
Hermia: O cross!° Too high to be enthralled to low.
Lysander: Or else misgrafted° in respect of years—
Hermia: O spite! Too old to be engaged to young.
Lysander: Or else it stood upon the choice of friends°—

99 *as well derived* as well born and descended   100 *possessed* endowed with wealth   101 *fairly* handsomely
102 *vantage* superiority   106 *head* i.e., face   110 *spotted* i.e., morally stained   113 *self-affairs* my own concerns   116 *schooling* admonition   117 *look you arm* take care you prepare   118 *fancies* likings, thoughts of
love   120 *extenuate* mitigate, relax   123 *go* i.e., come   125 *Against* in preparation for   126 *nearly that*
that closely   130 *Belike* very likely   131 *Beteem* grant, afford   135 *blood* hereditary station   136 *cross*
vexation   137 *misgrafted* ill grafted, badly matched   139 *friends* relatives

The young lovers Lysander and Hermia.

Hermia: O hell, to choose love by another's eyes!   140
Lysander: Or if there were a sympathy° in choice,
    War, death, or sickness did lay siege to it,
    Making it momentany° as a sound,
    Swift as a shadow, short as any dream,
    Brief as the lightning in the collied° night   145
    That in a spleen° unfolds° both heaven and earth,
    And ere a man hath power to say "Behold!"
    The jaws of darkness do devour it up.
    So quick° bright things come to confusion.°

141 *sympathy* agreement   143 *momentany* lasting but a moment   145 *collied* blackened (as with coal dust), darkened   146 *in a spleen* in a swift impulse, in a violent flash.   *unfolds* reveals   149 *quick* quickly; also, living, alive.   *confusion* ruin

Hermia: If then true lovers have been ever crossed,°   150
It stands as an edict in destiny.
Then let us teach our trial patience,°
Because it is a customary cross,
As due to love as thoughts, and dreams, and sighs,
Wishes, and tears, poor fancy's° followers.   155
Lysander: A good persuasion.° Therefore, hear me, Hermia:
I have a widow aunt, a dowager
Of great revenue, and she hath no child.
From Athens is her house remote seven leagues;
And she respects° me as her only son.   160
There, gentle Hermia, may I marry thee,
And to that place the sharp Athenian law
Cannot pursue us. If thou lovest me, then,
Steal forth thy father's house tomorrow night;
And in the wood, a league without° the town,   165
Where I did meet thee once with Helena
To do observance to a morn of May,°
There will I stay for thee.
Hermia: My good Lysander!
I swear to thee by Cupid's strongest bow,
By his best arrow° with the golden head,   170
By the simplicity° of Venus' doves,°
By that which knitteth souls and prospers loves,
And by that fire which burned the Carthage queen°
When the false Trojan° under sail was seen,
By all the vows that ever men have broke,   175
In number more than ever women spoke,
In that same place thou hast appointed me
Tomorrow truly will I meet with thee.
Lysander: Keep promise, love. Look, here comes Helena.

Enter Helena.

Hermia: God speed, fair° Helena! Whither away?   180
Helena: Call you me fair? That "fair" again unsay.
Demetrius loves your fair.° O happy fair!°
Your eyes are lodestars,° and your tongue's sweet air°
More tunable° than lark to shepherd's ear
When wheat is green, when hawthorn buds appear.   185
Sickness is catching. O, were favor° so,

---

150 *ever crossed* always thwarted   152 *teach . . . patience* i.e., teach ourselves patience in this trial   155 *fancy's* amorous passion's   156 *persuasion* doctrine   160 *respects* regards   165 *without* outside   167 *do . . . May* perform the ceremonies of May Day   170 *best arrow* (Cupid's best gold-pointed arrows were supposed to induce love; his blunt leaden arrows, aversion.)   171 *simplicity* innocence.   *doves* i.e., those that drew Venus' chariot   173, 174 *Carthage queen, false Trojan* (Dido, Queen of Carthage, immolated herself on a funeral pyre after having been deserted by the Trojan hero Aeneas.)   180 *fair* fair-complexioned (generally regarded by the Elizabethans as more beautiful than a dark complexion)   182 *your fair* your beauty (even though Hermia is dark-complexioned).   *happy fair* lucky fair one   183 *lodestars* guiding stars.   *air* music   184 *tunable* tuneful, melodious   186 *favor* appearance, looks

Yours would I catch, fair Hermia, ere I go;
My ear should catch your voice, my eye your eye,
My tongue should catch your tongue's sweet melody.
Were the world mine, Demetrius being bated,°   190
The rest I'd give to be to you translated.°
O, teach me how you look and with what art
You sway° the motion° of Demetrius' heart.

Hermia: I frown upon him, yet he loves me still.
Helena: O, that your frowns would teach my smiles such skill!   195
Hermia: I give him curses, yet he gives me love.
Helena: O, that my prayers could such affection° move!°
Hermia: The more I hate, the more he follows me.
Helena: The more I love, the more he hateth me.
Hermia: His folly, Helena, is no fault of mine.   200
Helena: None, but your beauty. Would that fault were mine!
Hermia: Take comfort. He no more shall see my face.
    Lysander and myself will fly this place.
    Before the time I did Lysander see
    Seemed Athens as a paradise to me.°   205
    O, then, what graces in my love do dwell,
    That he hath turned a heaven unto a hell?
Lysander: Helen, to you our minds we will unfold.
    Tomorrow night, when Phoebe° doth behold
    Her silver visage in the watery glass,°   210
    Decking with liquid pearl the bladed grass,
    A time that lovers' flights doth still° conceal,
    Through Athens' gates have we devised to steal.
Hermia: And in the wood, where often you and I
    Upon faint° primrose beds were wont to lie,   215
    Emptying our bosoms of their counsel° sweet,
    There my Lysander and myself shall meet,
    And thence from Athens turn away our eyes
    To seek new friends and stranger companies.°
    Farewell, sweet playfellow. Pray thou for us,   220
    And good luck grant thee thy Demetrius!
    Keep word, Lysander: We must starve our sight
    From lovers' food till morrow deep midnight.
Lysander: I will, my Hermia. *(Exit Hermia.)* Helena, adieu.
    As you on him, Demetrius dote on you!   225

                                  Exit Lysander.

Helena: How happy some o'er other some can be!°
    Through Athens I am thought as fair as she.
    But what of that? Demetrius thinks not so;

---

190 *bated* excepted 191 *translated* transformed 193 *sway* control. *motion* impulse 197 *affection* passion. *move* arouse 204–205 *Before . . . to me* (Hermia seemingly means that love has led to complications and jealousies, making Athens hell for her.) 209 *Phoebe* Diana, the moon 210 *glass* mirror 212 *still* always 215 *faint* pale 216 *counsel* secret thought 219 *stranger companies* the company of strangers 226 *o'er . . . can be* can be in comparison to some others

He will not know what all but he do know.
And as he errs, doting on Hermia's eyes, 230
So I, admiring of° his qualities.
Things base and vile, holding no quantity,°
Love can transpose to form and dignity.
Love looks not with the eyes, but with the mind,
And therefore is winged Cupid painted blind. 235
Nor hath Love's mind of any judgment taste;°
Wings and no eyes figure° unheedy haste.
And therefore is Love said to be a child,
Because in choice° he is so oft beguiled.°
As waggish° boys in game° themselves forswear, 240
So the boy Love is perjured everywhere.
For ere Demetrius looked on Hermia's eyne,°
He hailed down oaths that he was only mine;
And when this hail some heat from Hermia felt,
So he dissolved, and showers of oaths did melt. 245
I will go tell him of fair Hermia's flight.
Then to the wood will he tomorrow night
Pursue her; and for this intelligence°
If I have thanks, it is a dear expense.°
But herein mean I to enrich my pain, 250
To have his sight thither and back again.

Exit.

SCENE II [ATHENS.]

Enter Quince the carpenter, and Snug the joiner, and Bottom the weaver, and Flute the bellows mender, and Snout the tinker, and Starveling the tailor.

Quince: Is all our company here?
Bottom: You were best to call them generally,° man by man, according to the scrip.°
Quince: Here is the scroll of every man's name which is thought fit, through all Athens, to play in our interlude° before the Duke and the Duchess on his wedding day at night. 5
Bottom: First, good Peter Quince, say what the play treats on, then read the names of the actors, and so grow to° a point.
Quince: Marry,° our play is "The most lamentable comedy and most cruel death of Pyramus and Thisbe."
Bottom: A very good piece of work, I assure you, and a merry. Now, good Peter 10
Quince, call forth your actors by the scroll. Masters, spread yourselves.
Quince: Answer as I call you. Nick Bottom,° the weaver.

---

231 *admiring of* wondering at   232 *holding no quantity* i.e., unsubstantial, unshapely   236 *Nor . . . taste* i.e., nor has Love, which dwells in the fancy or imagination, any *taste* or least bit of judgment or reason   237 *figure* are a symbol of   239 *in choice* in choosing.   *beguiled* self-deluded, making unaccountable choices   240 *waggish* playful, mischievous.   *game* sport, jest   242 *eyne* eyes. (Old form of plural.)   248 *intelligence* information   249 *a dear expense* i.e., a trouble worth taking on my part, or a begrudging effort on his part. *dear* costly   2 *generally* (Bottom's blunder for "individually.").   *scrip* scrap (Bottom's error for "script.")   4 *interlude* play   7 *grow to* come to   8 *Marry* (A mild oath; originally the name of the Virgin Mary.)   12 *Bottom* (As a weaver's term, a *bottom* was an object around which thread was wound.)

The workers meet to plan their play, and Quince hands out the parts.

Bottom: Ready. Name what part I am for, and proceed.

Quince: You, Nick Bottom, are set down for Pyramus.

Bottom: What is Pyramus? A lover or a tyrant?   15

Quince: A lover, that kills himself most gallant for love.

Bottom: That will ask some tears in the true performing of it. If I do it, let the audience look to their eyes. I will move storms; I will condole° in some measure. To
the rest—yet my chief humor° is for a tyrant. I could play Ercles° rarely, or a part
to tear a cat° in, to make all split.ᵀ   20
> "The raging rocks
> And shivering shocks
> Shall break the locks

---

18 *condole* lament, arouse pity   19 *humor* inclination, whim.   *Ercles* Hercules (The tradition of ranting
came from Seneca's *Hercules Furens.*)   20 *tear a cat* i.e., rant.   *make all split* i.e., cause a stir, bring the
house down

Of prison gates;
And Phibbus' car° 25
Shall shine from far
And make and mar
The foolish Fates."

This was lofty! Now name the rest of the players. This is Ercles' vein, a tyrant's
vein. A lover is more condoling. 30

Quince: Francis Flute, the bellows mender.

Flute: Here, Peter Quince.

Quince: Flute, you must take Thisbe on you.

Flute: What is Thisbe? A wandering knight?

Quince: It is the lady that Pyramus must love. 35

Flute: Nay, faith, let not me play a woman. I have a beard coming.

Quince: That's all one.° You shall play it in a mask, and you may speak as small° as
you will.

Bottom: An° I may hide my face, let me play Thisbe too. I'll speak in a monstrous
little voice, "Thisne, Thisne!" "Ah Pyramus, my lover dear! Thy Thisbe dear, 40
and lady dear!"

Quince: No, no, you must play Pyramus, and Flute, you Thisbe.

Bottom: Well, proceed.

Quince: Robin Starveling, the tailor.

Starveling: Here, Peter Quince. 45

Quince: Robin Starveling, you must play Thisbe's mother. Tom Snout, the tinker.

Snout: Here, Peter Quince.

Quince: You, Pyramus' father; myself, Thisbe's father; Snug, the joiner, you, the
lion's part, and I hope here is a play fitted.

Snug: Have you the lion's part written? Pray you, if it be, give it me, for I am slow of 50
study.

Quince: You may do it extempore, for it is nothing but roaring.

Bottom: Let me play the lion too. I will roar that I will do any man's heart good to
hear me. I will roar that I will make the Duke say, "Let him roar again, let him
roar again." 55

Quince: An you should do it too terribly, you would fright the Duchess and the
ladies, that they would shriek; and that were enough to hang us all.

All: That would hang us, every mother's son.

Bottom: I grant you, friends, if you should fright the ladies out of their wits, they
would have no more discretion but to hang us; but I will aggravate° my voice so 60
that I will roar you° as gently as any sucking dove;° I will roar you an 'twere° any
nightingale.

Quince: You can play no part but Pyramus; for Pyramus is a sweet-faced man, a
proper° man as one shall see in a summer's day, a most lovely gentlemanlike man.
Therefore you must needs play Pyramus. 65

Bottom: Well, I will undertake it. What beard were I best to play it in?

Quince: Why, what you will.

---

25 *Phibbus' car* Phoebus', the sun god's, chariot   37 *That's all one* it makes no difference.   *small* high-
pitched   39 *An* if (also at line 56)   60 *aggravate* (Bottom's blunder for "moderate.")   61 *roar you* i.e.,
roar for you.   *sucking dove* (Bottom conflates *sitting dove* and *sucking lamb*, two proverbial images of innocence.).   *an 'twere* as if it were   64 *proper* handsome

Bottom: I will discharge° it in either your° straw-color beard, your orange-tawny beard, your purple-in-grain° beard, or your French-crown-color° beard, your per- 70
fect yellow.

Quince: Some of your French crowns° have no hair at all, and then you will play barefaced. But, masters, here are your parts. [*He distributes parts.*] And I am to entreat you, request you, and desire you to con° them by tomorrow night, and meet me in the palace wood, a mile without the town, by moonlight. There will we rehearse; for if we meet in the city, we shall be dogged with company, and our 75
devices° known. In the meantime I will draw a bill° of properties, such as our play wants. I pray you, fail me not.

Bottom: We will meet, and there we may rehearse most obscenely° and courageously. Take pains, be perfect.° Adieu.

Quince: At the Duke's oak we meet. 80

Bottom: Enough. Hold, or cut bowstrings.° *Exeunt.*

ACT II

SCENE I [A WOOD NEAR ATHENS.]

Enter a Fairy at one door, and Robin Goodfellow [Puck] at another.

Puck: How now, spirit, whither wander you?
Fairy:

        Over hill, over dale,
        Thorough° bush, thorough brier,
        Over park, over pale,°
        Thorough flood, thorough fire, 5
        I do wander everywhere,
        Swifter than the moon's sphere;°
        And I serve the Fairy Queen,
        To dew° her orbs° upon the green.
        The cowslips tall her pensioners° be. 10
        In their gold coats spots you see;
        Those be rubies, fairy favors;°
        In those freckles live their savors.°
  I must go seek some dewdrops here
  And hang a pearl in every cowslip's ear. 15
  Farewell, thou lob° of spirits; I'll be gone.
  Our Queen and all her elves come here anon.°
Puck: The King doth keep his revels here tonight.
  Take heed the Queen come not within his sight.

---

68 *discharge* perform. *your* i.e., you know the kind I mean 69 *purple-in-grain* dyed a very deep red. (From *grain*, the name applied to the dried insect used to make the dye.) *French-crown-color* i.e., color of a French crown, a gold coin 71 *crowns* heads bald from syphilis, the "French disease" 73 *con* learn by heart 76 *devices* plans. *draw a bill* draw up a list 78 *obscenely* (An unintentionally funny blunder, whatever Bottom meant to say.) 79 *perfect* i.e., letter-perfect in memorizing your parts 81 *Hold . . . bowstrings* (An archer's expression, not definitely explained, but probably meaning here "keep your promises, or give up the play.") 3 *Thorough* through 4 *pale* enclosure 7 *sphere* orbit 9 *dew* sprinkle with dew. *orbs* circles, i.e., fairy rings (circular bands of grass, darker than the surrounding area, caused by fungi enriching the soil) 10 *pensioners* retainers, members of the royal bodyguard 12 *favors* love tokens 13 *savors* sweet smells 16 *lob* country bumpkin 17 *anon* at once

20

> For Oberon is passing fell° and wrath,°
> Because that she as her attendant hath
> A lovely boy, stolen from an Indian king;
> She never had so sweet a changeling.°
> And jealous Oberon would have the child
> Knight of his train, to trace° the forests wild.   25
> But she perforce° withholds the lovèd boy,
> Crowns him with flowers, and makes him all her joy.
> And now they never meet in grove or green,
> By fountain° clear, or spangled starlight sheen,°
> But they do square,° that all their elves for fear   30
> Creep into acorn cups and hide them there.

Fairy: Either I mistake your shape and making quite,
    Or else you are that shrewd° and knavish sprite°
    Called Robin Goodfellow. Are not you he
    That frights the maidens of the villagery,°   35
    Skim milk,° and sometimes labor in the quern,°
    And bootless° make the breathless huswife° churn,
    And sometimes make the drink to bear no barm,°
    Mislead night wanderers,° laughing at their harm?
    Those that "Hobgoblin" call you, and "Sweet Puck,"°   40
    You do their work, and they shall have good luck.
    Are you not he?

Puck: Thou speakest aright;
    I am that merry wanderer of the night.
    I jest to Oberon and make him smile
    When I a fat and bean-fed° horse beguile,   45
    Neighing in likeness of a filly foal;
    And sometimes lurk I in a gossip's° bowl
    In very likeness of a roasted crab,°
    And when she drinks, against her lips I bob
    And on her withered dewlap° pour the ale.   50
    The wisest aunt,° telling the saddest° tale,
    Sometimes for three-foot stool mistaketh me;
    Then slip I from her bum, down topples she,
    And "Tailor"° cries, and falls into a cough;
    And then the whole choir° hold their hips and laugh,   55
    And waxen° in their mirth, and neeze,° and swear

20 *passing fell* exceedingly angry. *wrath* wrathful   23 *changeling* child exchanged for another by the fairies   25 *trace* range through   26 *perforce* forcibly   29 *fountain* spring. *starlight sheen* shining starlight   30 *square* quarrel   33 *shrewd* mischievous. *sprite* spirit   35 *villagery* village population   36 *Skim milk* i.e., steal the cream. *quern* hand mill (where Puck presumably hampers the grinding of grain)   37 *bootless* in vain (Puck prevents the cream from turning to butter.) *huswife* housewife   38 *barm* head on the ale (Puck prevents the barm or yeast from producing fermentation.)   39 *Mislead night wanderers* i.e., mislead with false fire those who walk abroad at night (hence earning Puck his other names of Jack o' Lantern and Will o' the Wisp)   40 *Those . . . Puck* i.e., those who call you by the names you favor rather than those denoting the mischief you do.   45 *bean-fed* well fed on field beans   47 *gossip's* old woman's   48 *crab* crab apple   50 *dewlap* loose skin on neck   51 *aunt* old woman. *saddest* most serious   54 *Tailor* (possibly because she ends up sitting cross-legged on the floor, looking like a tailor, or else referring to the *tail* or buttocks.)   55 *choir* company   56 *waxen* increase. *neeze* sneeze

A merrier hour was never wasted° there.
But, room,° fairy! Here comes Oberon.
Fairy: And here my mistress. Would that he were gone!

*Enter [Oberon] the King of Fairies at one door, with his train, and [Titania] the Queen
at another, with hers.*

Oberon: Ill met by moonlight, proud Titania.   60
Titania: What, jealous Oberon? Fairies, skip hence.
   I have forsworn his bed and company.
Oberon: Tarry, rash wanton.° Am not I thy lord?
Titania: Then I must be thy lady; but I know
   When thou hast stolen away from Fairyland   65
   And in the shape of Corin° sat all day,
   Playing on pipes of corn° and versing love
   To amorous Phillida.° Why art thou here
   Come from the farthest step° of India,
   But that, forsooth, the bouncing Amazon,   70
   Your buskined° mistress and your warrior love,
   To Theseus must be wedded, and you come
   To give their bed joy and prosperity.
Oberon: How canst thou thus for shame, Titania,
   Glance at my credit with Hippolyta,°   75
   Knowing I know thy love to Theseus?
   Didst not thou lead him through the glimmering night
   From Perigenia,° whom he ravishèd?
   And make him with fair Aegles° break his faith,
   With Ariadne° and Antiopa?°   80
Titania: These are the forgeries of jealousy;
   And never, since the middle summer's spring,°
   Met we on hill, in dale, forest, or mead,°
   By pavèd° fountain or by rushy° brook,
   Or in° the beachèd margent° of the sea,   85
   To dance our ringlets° to° the whistling wind,
   But with thy brawls thou hast disturbed our sport.
   Therefore the winds, piping to us in vain,
   As in revenge, have sucked up from the sea
   Contagious° fogs which, falling in the land,   90
   Hath every pelting° river made so proud

57 *wasted* spent   58 *room* stand aside, make room   63 *wanton* headstrong creature   66, 68 *Corin, Phillida* (Conventional names of pastoral lovers.)   67 *corn* (Here, oat stalks.)   69 *step* farthest limit of travel, or, perhaps, *steep,* "mountain range"   71 *buskined* wearing half-boots called buskins   75 *Glance . . . Hippolyta* make insinuations about my favored relationship with Hippolyta   78 *Perigenia* i.e., Perigouna, one of Theseus's conquests. (This and the following women are named in Thomas North's translation of Plutarch's "Life of Theseus.")79 *Aegles* i.e., Aegle, for whom Theseus deserted Ariadne according to some accounts   80 *Ariadne* the daughter of Minos, King of Crete, who helped Theseus to escape the labyrinth after killing the Minotaur; later she was abandoned by Theseus.   *Antiopa* Queen of the Amazons and wife of Theseus; elsewhere identified with Hippolyta, but here thought of as a separate woman   82 *middle summer's spring* beginning of midsummer   83 *mead* meadow   84 *pavèd* with pebbled bottom.   *rushy* bordered with rushes   85 *in* on.   *margent* edge, border   86 *ringlets* dances in a ring. (See *orbs* in line 9.)   *to* to the sound of   90 *Contagious* noxious   91 *pelting* paltry

Titania and Oberon.

That they have overborne their continents.°
The ox hath therefore stretched his yoke° in vain,
The plowman lost his sweat, and the green corn°
Hath rotted ere his youth attained a beard;   95
The fold° stands empty in the drownèd field,
And crows are fatted with the murrain° flock;
The nine-men's morris° is filled up with mud,
And the quaint mazes° in the wanton° green
For lack of tread are undistinguishable.   100

92 *continents* banks that contain them   93 *stretched his yoke* i.e., pulled at his yoke in plowing   94 *corn* grain of any kind   96 *fold* pen for sheep or cattle   97 *murrain* having died of the plague   98 *nine-men's morris* i.e., portion of the village green marked out in a square for a game played with nine pebbles or pegs 99 *quaint mazes* i.e., intricate paths marked out on the village green to be followed rapidly on foot as a kind of contest.   *wanton* luxuriant

The human mortals want° their winter° here;
No night is now with hymn or carol blessed.
Therefore° the moon, the governess of floods,
Pale in her anger, washes° all the air,
That rheumatic diseases° do abound.   105
And thorough this distemperature° we see
The seasons alter: hoary-headed frosts
Fall in the fresh lap of the crimson rose,
And on old Hiems'° thin and icy crown
An odorous chaplet of sweet summer buds   110
Is, as in mockery, set. The spring, the summer,
The childing° autumn, angry winter, change
Their wonted liveries,° and the mazèd° world
By their increase° now knows not which is which.
And this same progeny of evils comes   115
From our debate,° from our dissension.
We are their parents and original.°
Oberon: Do you amend it, then. It lies in you.
Why should Titania cross her Oberon?
I do but beg a little changeling boy   120
To be my henchman.°
Titania: Set your heart at rest.
The fairy land buys not the child of me.
His mother was a vot'ress of my order,°
And in the spicèd Indian air by night
Full often hath she gossiped by my side   125
And sat with me on Neptune's yellow sands,
Marking th' embarkèd traders° on the flood,°
When we have laughed to see the sails conceive
And grow big-bellied with the wanton° wind;
Which she, with pretty and with swimming° gait,   130
Following—her womb then rich with my young squire—
Would imitate, and sail upon the land
To fetch me trifles, and return again
As from a voyage, rich with merchandise.
But she, being mortal, of that boy did die;   135
And for her sake do I rear up her boy,
And for her sake I will not part with him.
Oberon: How long within this wood intend you stay?
Titania: Perchance till after Theseus' wedding day.
If you will patiently dance in our round°   140

---

101 *want* lack.   *winter* i.e., regular winter season; or, proper observances of winter, such as the *hymn or carol* in the next line (?)   103 *Therefore* i.e., as a result of our quarrel   104 *washes* saturates with moisture   105 *rheumatic diseases* colds, flu, and other respiratory infections   106 *distemperature* disturbance in nature   109 *Hiems'* the winter god's   112 *childing* fruitful, pregnant   113 *wonted liveries* usual apparel.   *mazèd* bewildered   114 *their increase* their yield, what they produce   116 *debate* quarrel   117 *original* origin   121 *henchman* attendant, page   123 *was . . . order* had taken a vow to serve me   127 *traders* trading vessels.   *flood* flood tide   129 *wanton* (1) playful (2) amorous   130 *swimming* smooth, gliding   140 *round* circular dance

Oberon directs Puck to fetch the magic flower.

And see our moonlight revels, go with us;
If not, shun me, and I will spare° your haunts.
Oberon: Give me that boy, and I will go with thee.
Titania: Not for thy fairy kingdom. Fairies, away!
We shall chide downright, if I longer stay.   145

                                    Exeunt [Titania with her train].

Oberon: Well, go thy way. Thou shalt not from° this grove
Till I torment thee for this injury.
My gentle Puck, come hither. Thou rememb'rest
Since° once I sat upon a promontory,
And heard a mermaid on a dolphin's back   150
Uttering such dulcet° and harmonious breath°

142 *spare* shun   146 *from* go from   149 *Since* when   151 *dulcet* sweet.   *breath* voice, song

That the rude° sea grew civil at her song,
And certain stars shot madly from their spheres
To hear the sea-maid's music?

Puck: I remember.

Oberon: That very time I saw, but thou couldst not,   155
Flying between the cold moon and the earth
Cupid, all° armed. A certain° aim he took
At a fair vestal° thronèd by° the west,
And loosed° his love shaft smartly from his bow
As° it should pierce a hundred thousand hearts;   160
But I might° see young Cupid's fiery shaft
Quenched in the chaste beams of the watery moon,
And the imperial vot'ress passèd on,
In maiden meditation, fancy-free.°
Yet marked I where the bolt° of Cupid fell: 165
It fell upon a little western flower,
Before milk-white, now purple with love's wound,
And maidens call it love-in-idleness.°
Fetch me that flower; the herb I showed thee once.
The juice of it on sleeping eyelids laid   170
Will make or man or° woman madly dote
Upon the next live creature that it sees.
Fetch me this herb, and be thou here again
Ere the leviathan° can swim a league.

Puck: I'll put a girdle round about the earth   175
In forty° minutes.   [*Exit.*]

Oberon: Having once this juice,
I'll watch Titania when she is asleep
And drop the liquor of it in her eyes.
The next thing then she waking looks upon,
Be it on lion, bear, or wolf, or bull,   180
On meddling monkey, or on busy ape,
She shall pursue it with the soul of love.
And ere I take this charm from off her sight,
As I can take it with another herb,
I'll make her render up her page to me.   185
But who comes here? I am invisible,
And I will overhear their conference.

Enter Demetrius, Helena following him.

Demetrius: I love thee not; therefore pursue me not.
Where is Lysander and fair Hermia?
The one I'll slay; the other slayeth me.   190

---

152 *rude* rough   157 *all* fully.   *certain* sure   158 *vestal* vestal virgin. (Contains a complimentary allusion
to Queen Elizabeth as a votaress of Diana and probably refers to an actual entertainment in her honor at
Elvetham in 1591.)   *by* in the region of   159 *loosed* released   160 As as if   161 *might* could   164 *fancy-
free* free of love's spell   165 *bolt* arrow   168 *love-in-idleness* pansy, heartsease   171 *or . . . or* either . . . or
174 *leviathan* sea monster, whale   176 *forty* (Used indefinitely.)

Thou toldst me they were stol'n unto this wood;
And here am I, and wood° within this wood
Because I cannot meet my Hermia.
Hence, get thee gone, and follow me no more.
Helena: You draw me, you hardhearted adamant!° 195
But yet you draw not iron, for my heart
Is true as steel. Leave you° your power to draw,
And I shall have no power to follow you.
Demetrius: Do I entice you? Do I speak you fair?°
Or rather do I not in plainest truth 200
Tell you I do not nor I cannot love you?
Helena: And even for that do I love you the more.
I am your spaniel; and, Demetrius,
The more you beat me I will fawn on you.
Use me but as your spaniel, spurn me, strike me, 205
Neglect me, lose me; only give me leave,
Unworthy as I am, to follow you.
What worser place can I beg in your love—
And yet a place of high respect with me—
Than to be usèd as you use your dog? 210
Demetrius: Tempt not too much the hatred of my spirit,
For I am sick when I do look on thee.
Helena: And I am sick when I look not on you.
Demetrius: You do impeach° your modesty too much
To leave° the city and commit yourself 215
Into the hands of one that loves you not,
To trust the opportunity of night
And the ill counsel of a desert° place
With the rich worth of your virginity.
Helena: Your virtue° is my privilege.° For that° 220
It is not night when I do see your face,
Therefore I think I am not in the night;
Nor doth this wood lack worlds of company,
For you, in my respect,° are all the world.
Then how can it be said I am alone 225
When all the world is here to look on me?
Demetrius: I'll run from thee and hide me in the brakes,°
And leave thee to the mercy of wild beasts.
Helena: The wildest hath not such a heart as you.
Run when you will. The story shall be changed: 230
Apollo flies and Daphne holds the chase,°

192 *and wood* and mad, frantic (with an obvious word play on *wood,* meaning "woods")   195 *adamant* lodestone, magnet (with pun on *hardhearted,* since adamant was also thought to be the hardest of all stones and was confused with the diamond)   197 *Leave you* give up   199 *speak you fair* speak courteously to you   214 *impeach* call into question   215 *To leave* by leaving   218 *desert* deserted   220 *virtue* goodness or power to attract.   *privilege* safeguard, warrant.   *For that* because   224 *in my respect* as far as I am concerned, in my esteem   227 *brakes* thickets   231 *Apollo . . . chase* (In the ancient myth, Daphne fled from Apollo and was saved from rape by being transformed into a laurel tree; here it is the female who *holds the chase,* or pursues, instead of the male.)

"Let me go!" Demetrius tells Helena after she follows him into the woods
(II, i, 235).

The dove pursues the griffin,° the mild hind°
Makes speed to catch the tiger—bootless° speed,
When cowardice pursues and valor flies!
Demetrius: I will not stay° thy questions.° Let me go!   235
Or if thou follow me, do not believe
But I shall do thee mischief in the wood.
Helena: Ay, in the temple, in the town, the field,
You do me mischief. Fie, Demetrius!
Your wrongs do set a scandal on my sex.°   240

232 *griffin* a fabulous monster with the head and wings of an eagle and the body of a lion.   *hind* female deer
233 *bootless* fruitless   235 *stay* wait for, put up with.   *questions* talk or argument   240 *Your . . . sex* i.e., the
wrongs that you do me cause me to act in a manner that disgraces my sex

We cannot fight for love, as men may do;
We should be wooed and were not made to woo.

[*Exit Demetrius.*]

I'll follow thee and make a heaven of hell,
To die upon° the hand I love so well.   [*Exit.*]

Oberon: Fare thee well, nymph. Ere he do leave this grove,   245
Thou shalt fly him, and he shall seek thy love.

Enter Puck.

Hast thou the flower there? Welcome, wanderer.
Puck: Ay, there it is.   [*He offers the flower.*]
Oberon: I pray thee, give it me.
I know a bank where the wild thyme blows,°
Where oxlips° and the nodding violet grows,   250
Quite overcanopied with luscious woodbine,°
With sweet muskroses° and with eglantine.°
There sleeps Titania sometimes of° the night,
Lulled in these flowers with dances and delight;
And there the snake throws° her enameled skin,   255
Weed° wide enough to wrap a fairy in.
And with the juice of this I'll streak° her eyes
And make her full of hateful fantasies.
Take thou some of it, and seek through this grove.

[*He gives some love juice.*]

A sweet Athenian lady is in love   260
With a disdainful youth. Anoint his eyes,
But do it when the next thing he espies
May be the lady. Thou shalt know the man
By the Athenian garments he hath on.
Effect it with some care, that he may prove   265
More fond on° her than she upon her love;
And look thou meet me ere the first cock crow.
Puck: Fear not, my lord, your servant shall do so.

Exeunt [*separately*].

SCENE II [THE WOOD.]

Enter Titania, Queen of Fairies, with her train.

Titania: Come, now a roundel° and a fairy song;
Then, for the third part of a minute,° hence—
Some to kill cankers° in the muskrose buds,
Some war with reremice° for their leathern wings

---

244 *upon* by   249 *blows* blooms   250 *oxlips* flowers resembling cowslip and primrose   251 *woodbine* honeysuckle   252 *muskroses* a kind of large, sweet-scented rose.   *eglantine* sweetbrier, another kind of rose
253 *sometimes of* for part of   255 *throws* sloughs off, sheds   256 *Weed* garment   257 *streak* anoint, touch
gently   266 *fond on* doting on   1 *roundel* dance in a ring   2 *the third . . . minute* (Indicative of the fairies'
quickness.)   3 *cankers* cankerworms (i.e., caterpillars or grubs)   4 *reremice* bats

To make my small elves coats, and some keep back   5
The clamorous owl, that nightly hoots and wonders
At our quaint° spirits. Sing me now asleep.
Then to your offices, and let me rest.

Fairies sing.

First Fairy: You spotted snakes with double° tongue,
         Thorny hedgehogs, be not seen;   10
    Newts° and blindworms, do no wrong;
         Come not near our Fairy Queen.
Chorus [dancing]:   Philomel,° with melody
         Sing in our sweet lullaby;
    Lulla, lulla, lullaby, lulla, lulla, lullaby.   15
         Never harm
         Nor spell nor charm
    Come our lovely lady nigh.
    So good night, with lullaby.
First Fairy: Weaving spiders, come not here;   20
         Hence, you long-legged spinners, hence!
    Beetles black, approach not near;
         Worm nor snail, do no offense.°
Chorus [dancing.]:   Philomel, with melody
         Sing in our sweet lullaby;   25
    Lulla, lulla, lullaby, lulla, lulla, lullaby.
         Never harm
         Nor spell nor charm
    Come our lovely lady nigh.
    So good night, with lullaby.   30

                                         [Titania sleeps.]

Second Fairy: Hence, away! Now all is well.
    One aloof stand sentinel.°

                  [Exeunt Fairies, leaving one sentinel.]

Enter Oberon [and squeezes the flower on Titania's eyelids].

Oberon: What thou seest when thou dost wake,
    Do it for thy true love take;
    Love and languish for his sake.   35
    Be it ounce,° or cat, or bear,
    Pard,° or boar with bristled hair,
    In thy eye that shall appear
    When thou wak'st, it is thy dear.
    Wake when some vile thing is near.   *[Exit.]* 40

---

7 *quaint* dainty   9 *double* forked   11 *Newts* water lizards (considered poisonous, as were *blindworms*—small snakes with tiny eyes—and spiders)   13 *Philomel* the nightingale. (Philomela, daughter of King Pandion, was transformed into a nightingale, according to Ovid's *Metamorphoses* 6, after she had been raped by her sister Procne's husband, Tereus.)   23 *offense* harm   32 *sentinel* (Presumably Oberon is able to outwit or intimidate this guard.)   36 *ounce* lynx   37 *Pard* leopard

Oberon squeezes the magic flower's juice onto Titania's eyelids.

Enter Lysander and Hermia.

Lysander: Fair love, you faint with wandering in the wood;
    And to speak truth, I have forgot our way.
    We'll rest us, Hermia, if you think it good,
    And tarry for the comfort of the day.
Hermia: Be it so, Lysander. Find you out a bed,
    For I upon this bank will rest my head.   45
Lysander: One turf shall serve as pillow for us both;
    One heart, one bed, two bosoms, and one troth.°
Hermia: Nay, good Lysander, for my sake, my dear,
    Lie further off yet. Do not lie so near.   50

48 *troth* faith, trothplight

Lysander: O, take the sense, sweet, of my innocence!°
    Love takes the meaning in love's conference.°
    I mean that my heart unto yours is knit,
    So that but one heart we can make of it;
    Two bosoms interchainèd with an oath—   55
    So then two bosoms and a single troth.
    Then by your side no bed-room me deny,
    For lying so, Hermia, I do not lie.°
Hermia: Lysander riddles very prettily.
    Now much beshrew° my manners and my pride   60
    If Hermia meant to say Lysander lied.
    But, gentle friend, for love and courtesy
    Lie further off, in human° modesty.
    Such separation as may well be said
    Becomes a virtuous bachelor and a maid,   65
    So far be distant; and good night, sweet friend.
    Thy love ne'er alter till thy sweet life end!
Lysander: Amen, amen, to that fair prayer, say I,
    And then end life when I end loyalty!
    Here is my bed. Sleep give thee all his rest!   70
Hermia: With half that wish the wisher's eyes be pressed!°

                    [They sleep, separated by a short distance.]

Enter Puck:

Puck: Through the forest have I gone,
            But Athenian found I none
            On whose eyes I might approve°
            This flower's force in stirring love.   75
            Night and silence.—Who is here?
            Weeds of Athens he doth wear.
            This is he, my master said,
            Despisèd the Athenian maid;
            And here the maiden, sleeping sound,   80
            On the dank and dirty ground.
            Pretty soul, she durst not lie
            Near this lack-love, this kill-courtesy.
            Churl, upon thy eyes I throw
            All the power this charm doth owe.°   85

                    [He applies the love juice.]

            When thou wak'st, let love forbid
            Sleep his seat on thy eyelid.
            So awake when I am gone,
            For I must now to Oberon.   *Exit.*

---

51 *take . . . innocence* i.e., interpret my intention as innocent   52 *Love . . . conference* i.e., when lovers confer, love teaches each lover to interpret the other's meaning lovingly   58 *lie* tell a falsehood (with a riddling pun on *lie*, "recline")   60 *beshrew* curse. (But mildly meant.)   63 *human* courteous (and perhaps suggesting "humane," the Quarto spelling)   71 *With . . . pressed* i.e., may we share your wish, so that your eyes too are *pressed*, closed, in sleep   74 *approve* test   85 *owe* own

Enter Demetrius and Helena, running.

Helena: Stay, though thou kill me, sweet Demetrius! 90
Demetrius: I charge thee, hence, and do not haunt me thus.
Helena: O, wilt thou darkling° leave me? Do not so.
Demetrius: Stay, on thy peril!° I alone will go. [*Exit.*]
Helena: O, I am out of breath in this fond° chase!
    The more my prayer, the lesser is my grace.° 95
    Happy is Hermia, wheresoe'er she lies,°
    For she hath blessèd and attractive eyes.
    How came her eyes so bright? Not with salt tears;
    If so, my eyes are oftener washed than hers.
    No, no, I am as ugly as a bear, 100
    For beasts that meet me run away for fear.
    Therefore no marvel though Demetrius
    Do, as a monster, fly my presence thus.°
    What wicked and dissembling glass of mine
    Made me compare° with Hermia's sphery eyne?° 105
    But who is here? Lysander, on the ground?
    Dead, or asleep? I see no blood, no wound.
    Lysander, if you live, good sir, awake.
Lysander [*awaking*]: And run through fire I will for thy sweet sake.
    Transparent° Helena! Nature shows art,° 110
    That through thy bosom makes me see thy heart.
    Where is Demetrius? O, how fit a word
    Is that vile name to perish on my sword!
Helena: Do not say so, Lysander, say not so.
    What though he love your Hermia? Lord, what though? 115
    Yet Hermia still loves you. Then be content.
Lysander: Content with Hermia? No! I do repent
    The tedious minutes I with her have spent.
    Not Hermia but Helena I love.
    Who will not change a raven for a dove? 120
    The will° of man is by his reason swayed,
    And reason says you are the worthier maid.
    Things growing are not ripe until their season;
    So I, being young, till now ripe not° to reason.
    And, touching° now the point° of human skill,° 125
    Reason becomes the marshal to my will
    And leads me to your eyes, where I o'erlook°
    Love's stories written in love's richest book.
Helena: Wherefore° was I to this keen mockery born?
    When at your hands did I deserve this scorn? 130

---

92 *darkling* in the dark   93 *on thy peril* i.e., on pain of danger to you if you don't obey me and stay   94 *fond* doting   95 *my grace* the favor I obtain   96 *lies* dwells   102–103 *no marvel . . . thus* i.e., no wonder that Demetrius flies from me as from a monster   105 *compare* vie.   *sphery eyne* eyes as bright as stars in their spheres   110 *Transparent* (1) radiant (2) able to be seen through, lacking in deceit.   *art* skill, magic power   121 *will* desire   124 *ripe not* (am) not ripened   125 *touching* reaching.   *point* summit.   *skill* judgment   127 *o'erlook* read   129 *Wherefore* why

Is 't not enough, is 't not enough, young man,
That I did never—no, nor never can—
Deserve a sweet look from Demetrius' eye,
But you must flout my insufficiency?
Good troth, you do me wrong, good sooth,° you do,   135
In such disdainful manner me to woo.
But fare you well. Perforce I must confess
I thought you lord of° more true gentleness.°
O, that a lady, of° one man refused,
Should of another therefore be abused!°   *Exit.*   140

Lysander: She sees not Hermia. Hermia, sleep thou there,
And never mayst thou come Lysander near!
For as a surfeit of the sweetest things
The deepest loathing to the stomach brings,
Or as the heresies that men do leave   145
Are hated most of those they did deceive,°
So thou, my surfeit and my heresy,
Of all be hated, but the most of° me!
And, all my powers, address° your love and might
To honor Helen and to be her knight!   *Exit.*   150

Hermia [awaking]: Help me, Lysander, help me! Do thy best
To pluck this crawling serpent from my breast!
Ay me, for pity! What a dream was here!
Lysander, look how I do quake with fear.
Methought a serpent ate my heart away,   155
And you sat smiling at his cruel prey.°
Lysander! What, removed? Lysander! Lord!
What, out of hearing? Gone? No sound, no word?
Alack, where are you? Speak, an if° you hear;
Speak, of all loves!° I swoon almost with fear.   160
No? Then I well perceive you are not nigh.
Either death, or you, I'll find immediately.

                          Exit. [The sleeping Titania remains.]

ACT III

SCENE I [THE ACTION IS CONTINUOUS.]

   Enter the clowns° *[Quince, Snug, Bottom, Flute, Snout, and Starveling].*

Bottom: Are we all met?

Quince: Pat,° pat; and here's a marvelous convenient place for our rehearsal. This
   green plot shall be our stage, this hawthorn brake° our tiring-house,° and we will
   do it in action as we will do it before the Duke.

---

135 *Good troth, good sooth* i.e., indeed, truly   138 *lord of* i.e., possessor of.   *gentleness* courtesy   139 *of* by
140 *abused* ill treated   145–146 *as . . . deceive* as renounced heresies are hated most by those persons who
formerly were deceived by them   148 *Of . . . of* by . . . by   149 *address* direct, apply   156 *prey* act of
preying   159 *an if* if   160 *of all loves* for all love's sake   s.d. *clowns* rustics   2 *Pat* on the dot, punctually
3 *brake* thicket.   *tiring-house* attiring area, hence backstage

Bottom: Peter Quince?   5
Quince: What sayest thou, bully° Bottom?
Bottom: There are things in this comedy of Pyramus and Thisbe that will never
  please. First, Pyramus must draw a sword to kill himself, which the ladies cannot
  abide. How answer you that?
Snout: By 'r lakin,° a parlous° fear.   10
Starveling: I believe we must leave the killing out, when all is done.°
Bottom: Not a whit. I have a device to make all well. Write me° a prologue, and let
  the prologue seem to say, we will do no harm with our swords, and that Pyramus
  is not killed indeed; and for the more better assurance, tell them that I, Pyramus,
  am not Pyramus but Bottom the weaver. This will put them out of fear.   15
Quince: Well, we will have such a prologue, and it shall be written in eight and six.°
Bottom: No, make it two more: let it be written in eight and eight.
Snout: Will not the ladies be afeard of the lion?
Starveling: I fear it, I promise you.
Bottom: Masters, you ought to consider with yourself, to bring in—God shield us!—a   20
  lion among ladies° is a most dreadful thing. For there is not a more fearful° wild-
  fowl than your lion living, and we ought to look to 't.
Snout: Therefore another prologue must tell he is not a lion.
Bottom: Nay, you must name his name, and half his face must be seen through the
  lion's neck, and he himself must speak through, saying thus or to the same   25
  defect:° "Ladies," or "Fair ladies, I would wish you," or "I would request you," or
  "I would entreat you, not to fear, not to tremble; my life for yours.° If you think
  I come hither as a lion, it were pity of my life.° No, I am no such thing; I am a
  man as other men are." And there indeed let him name his name, and tell them
  plainly he is Snug the joiner.   30
Quince: Well, it shall be so. But there is two hard things: that is, to bring the moon-
  light into a chamber; for, you know, Pyramus and Thisbe meet by moonlight.
Snout: Doth the moon shine that night we play our play?
Bottom: A calendar, a calendar! Look in the almanac. Find out moonshine, find out
  moonshine.   35

                                                    [*They consult an almanac.*]

Quince: Yes, it doth shine that night.
Bottom: Why then may you leave a casement of the great chamber window where we
  play open, and the moon may shine in at the casement.
Quince: Ay; or else one must come in with a bush of thorns° and a lantern and say he
  comes to disfigure,° or to present,° the person of Moonshine. Then there is   40
  another thing: we must have a wall in the great chamber; for Pyramus and
  Thisbe, says the story, did talk through the chink of a wall.

---

6 *bully* i.e., worthy, jolly, fine fellow   10 *By 'r lakin* by our ladykin, i.e., the Virgin Mary.   *parlous* perilous,
alarming   11 *when all is done* i.e., when all is said and done   12 *Write me* i.e., write at my suggestion (*Me*
is used colloquially.)   16 *eight and six* alternate lines of eight and six syllables, a common ballad measure
21 *lion among ladies* (A contemporary pamphlet tells how, at the christening in 1594 of Prince Henry,
eldest son of King James VI of Scotland, later James I of England, a "blackamoor" instead of a lion drew
the triumphal chariot, since the lion's presence might have "brought some fear to the nearest.").   *fearful*
fear-inspiring   26 *defect* (Bottom's blunder for "effect.")   27 *my life for yours* i.e., I pledge my life to make
your lives safe   28 *it were . . . life* i.e., I should be sorry, by my life; or, my life would be endangered   39
bush of thorns bundle of thornbush faggots (part of the accoutrements of the man in the moon, according to
the popular notions of the time, along with his lantern and his dog)   40 *disfigure* (Quince's blunder for
"figure.")   *present* represent

Snout: You can never bring in a wall. What say you, Bottom?

Bottom: Some man or other must present Wall. And let him have some plaster, or some loam, or some roughcast° about him, to signify wall; or let him hold his fingers thus, and through that cranny shall Pyramus and Thisbe whisper. 45

Quince: If that may be, then all is well. Come, sit down, every mother's son, and rehearse your parts. Pyramus, you begin. When you have spoken your speech, enter into that brake, and so everyone according to his cue.

Enter Robin [Puck].

Puck [aside]: What hempen homespuns° have we swaggering here 50
So near the cradle° of the Fairy Queen?
What, a play toward?° I'll be an auditor;
An actor, too, perhaps, if I see cause.

Quince: Speak, Pyramus. Thisbe, stand forth.

Bottom [as Pyramus]: "Thisbe, the flowers of odious savors sweet—" 55

Quince: Odors, odors.

Bottom: "—Odors savors sweet;
So hath thy breath, my dearest Thisbe dear.
But hark, a voice! Stay thou but here awhile,
And by and by I will to thee appear."   *Exit.* 60

Puck: A stranger Pyramus than e'er played here.°   [*Exit.*]

Flute: Must I speak now?

Quince: Ay, marry, must you; for you must understand he goes but to see a noise that he heard, and is to come again.

Flute [as Thisbe]: "Most radiant Pyramus, most lily-white of hue, 65
Of color like the red rose on triumphant° brier,
Most brisky juvenal° and eke° most lovely Jew,°
As true as truest horse that yet would never tire.
I'll meet thee, Pyramus, at Ninny's tomb."

Quince: "Ninus'° tomb," man. Why, you must not speak that yet. That you answer to 70
Pyramus: You speak all your part° at once, cues and all. Pyramus, enter. Your cue is past; it is "never tire."

Flute: O—"As true as truest horse, that yet would never tire."

[*Enter Puck, and Bottom as Pyramus with the ass head.°*]

Bottom: "If I were fair,° Thisbe, I were° only thine."

Quince: O, monstrous! O, strange! We are haunted. Pray, masters! Fly, masters! 75
Help!

[*Exeunt Quince, Snug, Flute, Snout, and Starveling.*]

---

45 *roughcast* a mixture of lime and gravel used to plaster the outside of buildings   50 *hempen homespuns* i.e., rustics dressed in clothes woven of coarse, homespun fabric made from hemp   51 *cradle* i.e., Titania's bower   52 *toward* about to take place   61 *A stranger . . . here* (Either Puck refers to an earlier dramatic version played in the same theater, or he has conceived of a plan to present a "stranger" Pyramus than ever seen before.)   66 *triumphant* magnificent   67 *brisky juvenal* lively youth.   *eke* also.   *Jew* (An absurd repetition of the first syllable of *juvenal,* and an indication of how desperately Quince searches for his rhymes.)   70 *Ninus* mythical founder of Nineveh (whose wife, Semiramis, was supposed to have built the walls of Babylon where the story of Pyramus and Thisbe takes place)   71 *part* (An actor's *part* was a script consisting only of his speeches and their cues.)   s.d. *with the ass head* (This stage direction, taken from the Folio, presumably refers to a standard stage property.)   74 *fair* handsome.   *were* would be

Bottom is transformed into an ass.

Puck: I'll follow you, I'll lead you about a round,°
    Thorough bog, thorough bush, thorough brake, thorough brier.
    Sometimes a horse I'll be, sometimes a hound,
    A hog, a headless bear, sometimes a fire;°   80
    And neigh, and bark, and grunt, and roar, and burn,
    Like horse, hound, hog, bear, fire, at every turn.   *Exit.*
Bottom: Why do they run away? This is a knavery of them to make me afeard.

    Enter Snout.

Snout: O Bottom, thou art changed! What do I see on thee?
Bottom: What do you see? You see an ass head of your own, do you?   85
                                                   [Exit Snout.]

77 *about a round* roundabout   80 *fire* will-o'-the-wisp

Enter Quince.

Quince: Bless thee, Bottom, bless thee! Thou art translated.°   *Exit.*

Bottom: I see their knavery. This is to make an ass of me, to fright me, if they could.
But I will not stir from this place, do what they can. I will walk up and down
here, and will sing, that they shall hear I am not afraid.

                                                        [*He sings.*]

        The ouzel cock° so black of hue,   90
           With orange-tawny bill,
        The throstle° with his note so true,
           The wren with little quill°—

Titania [awaking]: What angel wakes me from my flowery bed?

Bottom [sings]:

        The finch, the sparrow, and the lark,   95
           The plainsong° cuckoo gray,
        Whose note full many a man doth mark,
           And dares not answer nay°—

For, indeed, who would set his wit to° so foolish a bird? Who would give a bird
the lie,° though he cry "cuckoo" never so?°   100

Titania: I pray thee, gentle mortal, sing again.
Mine ear is much enamored of thy note;
So is mine eye enthrallèd to thy shape;
And thy fair virtue's force° perforce doth move me
On the first view to say, to swear, I love thee.   105

Bottom: Methinks, mistress, you should have little reason for that. And yet, to say
the truth, reason and love keep little company together nowadays—the more
the pity that some honest neighbors will not make them friends. Nay, I can
gleek° upon occasion.

Titania: Thou art as wise as thou art beautiful.   110

Bottom: Not so, neither. But if I had wit enough to get out of this wood, I have
enough to serve mine own turn.°

Titania: Out of this wood do not desire to go.
Thou shalt remain here, whether thou wilt or no.
I am a spirit of no common rate.°   115
The summer still doth tend upon my state,°
And I do love thee. Therefore go with me.
I'll give thee fairies to attend on thee,
And they shall fetch thee jewels from the deep,
And sing while thou on pressèd flowers dost sleep.   120
And I will purge thy mortal grossness° so
That thou shalt like an airy spirit go.
Peaseblossom, Cobweb, Mote,° and Mustardseed!

---

86 *translated* transformed   90 *ouzel cock* male blackbird   92 *throstle* song thrush   93 *quill* (Literally, a reed
pipe; hence, the bird's piping song.)   96 *plainsong* singing a melody without variations   98 *dares . . . nay*
i.e., cannot deny that he is a cuckold   99 *set his wit to* employ his intelligence to answer   99–100 *give . . .
lie* call the bird a liar   100 *never so* ever so much   104 *thy . . . force* the power of your unblemished excellence   109 *gleek* jest   112 *serve . . . turn* answer my purpose   115 *rate* rank, value   116 *still . . . state*
always waits upon me as a part of my royal retinue   121 *mortal grossness* materiality (i.e., the corporeal
nature of a mortal being)   123 *Mote* i.e., speck. (The two words *moth* and *mote* were pronounced alike,
and both meanings may be present.)

Enter four Fairies [Peaseblossom, Cobweb, Mote, and Mustardseed].

Peaseblossom: Ready.
Cobweb: And I.
Mote: And I.
Mustardseed: And I.
All: Where shall we go?   125
Titania: Be kind and courteous to this gentleman.
    Hop in his walks and gambol in his eyes;°
    Feed him with apricots and dewberries,°
    With purple grapes, green figs, and mulberries;
    The honey bags steal from the humble-bees,   130
    And for night tapers crop their waxen thighs
    And light them at the fiery glowworms' eyes,
    To have my love to bed and to arise;
    And pluck the wings from painted butterflies
    To fan the moonbeams from his sleeping eyes.   135
    Nod to him, elves, and do him courtesies.
Peaseblossom: Hail, mortal!
Cobweb: Hail!
Mote: Hail!
Mustardseed: Hail!   140
Bottom: I cry your worships mercy,° heartily. I beseech your worship's name.
Cobweb: Cobweb.
Bottom: I shall desire you of more acquaintance,° good Master Cobweb. If I cut my
    finger, I shall make bold with you.°—Your name, honest gentleman?
Peaseblossom: Peaseblossom.   145
Bottom: I pray you, commend me to Mistress Squash,° your mother, and to Master
    Peascod,° your father. Good Master Peaseblossom, I shall desire you of more
    acquaintance too.—Your name, I beseech you, sir?
Mustardseed: Mustardseed.
Bottom: Good Master Mustardseed, I know your patience° well. That same cowardly,   150
    giantlike ox-beef hath devoured many a gentleman of your house. I promise you,
    your kindred hath made my eyes water° ere now. I desire you of more acquaintance,
    good Master Mustardseed.
Titania: Come wait upon him; lead him to my bower.
    The moon methinks looks with a watery eye;   155
    And when she weeps,° weeps every little flower,
    Lamenting some enforcèd° chastity.
    Tie up my lover's tongue,° bring him silently.

                                     [Exeunt.]

---

128 *in his eyes* in his sight (i.e., before him)   129 *dewberries* blackberries   141 *I cry . . . mercy* I beg
pardon of your worships (for presuming to ask a question)   143 *I . . . . acquaintance* I crave to be better
acquainted with you   143–144 *If . . . you* (Cobwebs were used to stanch bleeding.)   146 *Squash* unripe
pea pod   147 *Peascod* ripe pea pod   150 *your patience* what you have endured. (Mustard is eaten with
beef.)   152 *water* (1) weep for sympathy (2) smart, sting   156 *she weeps* i.e., she causes dew   157 *enforcèd*
forced, violated; or, possibly, constrained (since Titania at this moment is hardly concerned about
chastity)   158 *Tie . . . tongue* (Presumably Bottom is braying like an ass.)

SCENE II [THE WOOD.]

> *Enter* [*Oberon,*] *King of Fairies.*

Oberon: I wonder if Titania be awaked;
Then, what it was that next came in her eye,
Which she must dote on in extremity.

> [*Enter*] *Robin Goodfellow* [*Puck*].

Here comes my messenger. How now, mad spirit?
What night-rule° now about this haunted° grove?   5
Puck: My mistress with a monster is in love.
Near to her close° and consecrated bower,
While she was in her dull° and sleeping hour,
A crew of patches,° rude mechanicals,°
That work for bread upon Athenian stalls,°   10
Were met together to rehearse a play
Intended for great Theseus' nuptial day.
The shallowest thickskin of that barren sort,°
Who Pyramus presented,° in their sport
Forsook his scene° and entered in a brake.   15
When I did him at this advantage take,
An ass's noll° I fixèd on his head.
Anon his Thisbe must be answerèd,
And forth my mimic° comes. When they him spy,
As wild geese that the creeping fowler° eye,   20
Or russet-pated choughs,° many in sort,°
Rising and cawing at the gun's report,
Sever° themselves and madly sweep the sky,
So, at his sight, away his fellows fly;
And, at our stamp, here o'er and o'er one falls;   25
He "Murder!" cries and help from Athens calls.
Their sense thus weak, lost with their fears thus strong,
Made senseless things begin to do them wrong,
For briers and thorns at their apparel snatch;
Some, sleeves—some, hats; from yielders all things catch.°   30
I led them on in this distracted fear
And left sweet Pyramus translated there,
When in that moment, so it came to pass,
Titania waked and straightway loved an ass.
Oberon: This falls out better than I could devise.   35
But hast thou yet latched° the Athenian's eyes
With the love juice, as I did bid thee do?

---

5 *night-rule* diversion or misrule for the night. *haunted* much frequented   7 *close* secret, private   8 *dull* drowsy   9 *patches* clowns, fools. *rude mechanicals* ignorant artisans   10 *stalls* market booths   13 *barren sort* stupid company or crew   14 *presented* acted   15 *scene* playing area   17 *noll* noddle, head   19 *mimic* burlesque actor   20 *fowler* hunter of game birds   21 *russet-pated choughs* reddish brown or gray-headed jackdaws. *in sort* in a flock   23 *Sever* i.e., scatter   30 *from . . . catch* i.e., everything preys on those who yield to fear   36 *latched* fastened, snared

Puck: I took him sleeping—that is finished too—
    And the Athenian woman by his side,
    That, when he waked, of force° she must be eyed.   40

    Enter Demetrius and Hermia.

Oberon: Stand close. This is the same Athenian.
Puck: This is the woman, but not this the man.

                                              [They stand aside.]

Demetrius: O, why rebuke you him that loves you so?
    Lay breath so bitter on your bitter foe.
Hermia: Now I but chide; but I should use thee worse,   45
    For thou, I fear, hast given me cause to curse.
    If thou hast slain Lysander in his sleep,
    Being o'er shoes° in blood, plunge in the deep,
    And kill me too.
    The sun was not so true unto the day   50
    As he to me. Would he have stolen away
    From sleeping Hermia? I'll believe as soon
    This whole° earth may be bored, and that the moon
    May through the center creep, and so displease
    Her brother's° noontide with th' Antipodes.°   55
    It cannot be but thou hast murdered him;
    So should a murderer look, so dead,° so grim.
Demetrius: So should the murdered look, and so should I,
    Pierced through the heart with your stern cruelty.
    Yet you, the murderer, look as bright, as clear   60
    As yonder Venus in her glimmering sphere.
Hermia: What's this to° my Lysander? Where is he?
    Ah, good Demetrius, wilt thou give him me?
Demetrius: I had rather give his carcass to my hounds.
Hermia: Out, dog! Out, cur! Thou driv'st me past the bounds   65
    Of maiden's patience. Hast thou slain him, then?
    Henceforth be never numbered among men.
    O, once° tell true, tell true, even for my sake:
    Durst thou have looked upon him being awake?
    And hast thou killed him sleeping? O brave touch!°   70
    Could not a worm,° an adder, do so much?
    An adder did it; for with doubler° tongue
    Than thine, thou serpent, never adder stung.
Demetrius: You spend your passion° on a misprised mood.°
    I am not guilty of Lysander's blood,   75
    Nor is he dead, for aught that I can tell.
Hermia: I pray thee, tell me then that he is well.

---

40 *of force* perforce   48 *Being o'er shoes* having waded in so far   53 *whole* solid   55 *Her brother's* i.e., the sun's.   *th' Antipodes* the people on the opposite side of the earth (where the moon is imagined bringing night to noontime)   57 *dead* deadly, or deathly pale   62 *to* to do with   68 *once* once and for all 70 *brave touch!* fine stroke! (Said ironically.)   71 *worm* serpent   72 *doubler* (1) more forked (2) more deceitful   74 *passion* violent feelings. *misprised mood* anger based on misconception

Demetrius: And if I could, what should I get therefor?°
Hermia: A privilege never to see me more.
    And from thy hated presence part I so.   80
    See me no more, whether he be dead or no.   *Exit.*
Demetrius: There is no following her in this fierce vein.
    Here therefore for a while I will remain.
    So sorrow's heaviness doth heavier° grow
    For debt that bankrupt° sleep doth sorrow owe;   85
    Which now in some slight measure it will pay,
    If for his tender here I make some stay.°   *[He] lie[s] down [and sleeps].*
Oberon: What hast thou done? Thou hast mistaken quite
    And laid the love juice on some true love's sight.
    Of thy misprision° must perforce ensue
    Some true love turned, and not a false turned true.   90
Puck: Then fate o'errules, that, one man holding troth,°
    A million fail, confounding oath on oath.°
Oberon: About the wood go swifter than the wind,
    And Helena of Athens look° thou find.   95
    All fancy-sick° she is and pale of cheer°
    With sighs of love, that cost the fresh blood° dear.
    By some illusion see thou bring her here.
    I'll charm his eyes against she do appear.°
Puck: I go, I go, look how I go,   100
    Swifter than arrow from the Tartar's bow.°   *[Exit.]*
Oberon [applying love juice to Demetrius' eyes]:
           Flower of this purple dye,
           Hit with Cupid's archery,
           Sink in apple° of his eye.
           When his love he doth espy,   105
           Let her shine as gloriously
           As the Venus of the sky.
           When thou wak'st, if she be by,
           Beg of her for remedy.

    Enter Puck:

Puck: Captain of our fairy band,   110
           Helena is here at hand,
           And the youth, mistook by me,
           Pleading for a lover's fee.°

---

78 *therefor* in return for that   84 *heavier* (1) harder to bear (2) more drowsy   85 *bankrupt* (Demetrius is saying that his sleepiness adds to the weariness caused by sorrow.)   86–87 *Which . . . stay* i.e., to a small extent, I will be able to "pay back" and hence find some relief from sorrow, if I pause here awhile (*make some stay*) while sleep "tenders" or offers itself by way of paying the debt owed to sorrow   90 *misprision* mistake   92 *that . . . troth* in that, for each man keeping true faith in love   93 *confounding . . . oath* i.e., breaking oath after oath   95 *look* i.e., be sure   96 *fancy-sick* lovesick. *cheer* face   97 *sighs . . . blood* (An allusion to the physiological theory that each sigh costs the heart a drop of blood.)   99 *against . . . appear* in anticipation of her coming   101 *Tartar's bow* (Tartars were famed for their skill with the bow.)   104 *apple* pupil   113 *fee* privilege, reward

	Shall we their fond pageant° see?	
	Lord, what fools these mortals be!	115
Oberon:	Stand aside. The noise they make	
	Will cause Demetrius to awake.	
Puck:	Then will two at once woo one;	
	That must needs be sport alone.°	
	And those things do best please me	120
	That befall preposterously.°	

[*They stand aside.*]

Enter Lysander and Helena.

Lysander: Why should you think that I should woo in scorn?
Scorn and derision never come in tears.
Look when° I vow, I weep; and vows so born,
In their nativity all truth appears.° 125
How can these things in me seem scorn to you,
Bearing the badge° of faith to prove them true?
Helena: You do advance° your cunning more and more.
When truth kills truth,° O, devilish-holy fray!
These vows are Hermia's. Will you give her o'er? 130
Weigh oath with oath, and you will nothing weigh.
Your vows to her and me, put in two scales,
Will even weigh, and both as light as tales.°
Lysander: I had no judgment when to her I swore.
Helena: Nor none, in my mind, now you give her o'er. 135
Lysander: Demetrius loves her, and he loves not you.
Demetrius [*awaking*]: O Helen, goddess, nymph, perfect, divine!
To what, my love, shall I compare thine eyne?
Crystal is muddy. O, how ripe in show°
Thy lips, those kissing cherries, tempting grow! 140
That pure congealèd white, high Taurus'° snow,
Fanned with the eastern wind, turns to a crow°
When thou hold'st up thy hand. O, let me kiss
This princess of pure white, this seal° of bliss!
Helena: O spite! O hell! I see you all are bent 145
To set against° me for your merriment.
If you were civil and knew courtesy,
You would not do me thus much injury.
Can you not hate me, as I know you do,
But you must join in souls° to mock me too? 150
If you were men, as men you are in show,
You would not use a gentle lady so—

---

114 *fond pageant* foolish spectacle   119 *alone* unequaled   121 *preposterously* out of the natural order
124 *Look when* whenever   124–125 *vows . . . appears* i.e., vows made by one who is weeping give evidence
thereby of their sincerity   127 *badge* identifying device such as that worn on servants' livery (here, his tears)
128 *advance* carry forward, display   129 *truth kills truth* i.e., one of Lysander's vows must invalidate the other
133 *tales* lies   139 *show* appearance   141 *Taurus* a lofty mountain range in Asia Minor   142 *turns to a crow*
i.e., seems black by contrast   144 *seal* pledge   146 *set against* attack   150 *in souls* i.e., heart and soul

Helena believes the enchanted Demetrius is only pretending to love her in order to mock her.

To vow, and swear, and superpraise° my parts,°
When I am sure you hate me with your hearts.
You both are rivals, and love Hermia,   155
And now both rivals, to mock Helena.
A trim° exploit, a manly enterprise,
To conjure tears up in a poor maid's eyes
With your derision! None of noble sort°
Would so offend a virgin and extort°   160
A poor soul's patience, all to make you sport.

153 *superpraise* overpraise.   *parts* qualities   157 *trim* pretty, fine (Said ironically.)   159 *sort* character, quality   160 *extort* twist, torture

Lysander: You are unkind, Demetrius. Be not so.
    For you love Hermia; this you know I know.
    And here, with all good will, with all my heart,
    In Hermia's love I yield you up my part;
    And yours of Helena to me bequeath,   165
    Whom I do love, and will do till my death.
Helena: Never did mockers waste more idle breath.
Demetrius: Lysander, keep thy Hermia; I will none.°
    If e'er I loved her, all that love is gone.
    My heart to her but as guestwise sojourned,°   170
    And now to Helen is it home returned,
    There to remain.
Lysander: Helen, it is not so.
Demetrius: Disparage not the faith thou dost not know,
    Lest, to thy peril, thou aby° it dear.   175
    Look where thy love comes; yonder is thy dear.

    Enter Hermia.

Hermia: Dark night, that from the eye his° function takes,
    The ear more quick of apprehension makes;
    Wherein it doth impair the seeing sense,
    It pays the hearing double recompense.   180
    Thou art not by mine eye, Lysander, found;
    Mine ear, I thank it, brought me to thy sound.
    But why unkindly didst thou leave me so?
Lysander: Why should he stay, whom love doth press to go?
Hermia: What love could press Lysander from my side?   185
Lysander: Lysander's love, that would not let him bide—
    Fair Helena, who more engilds° the night
    Than all yon fiery oes° and eyes of light.
    Why seek'st thou me? Could not this make thee know
    The hate I bear thee made me leave thee so?   190
Hermia: You speak not as you think. It cannot be.
Helena: Lo, she is one of this confederacy!
    Now I perceive they have conjoined all three
    To fashion this false sport in spite of me.°
    Injurious Hermia, most ungrateful maid!   195
    Have you conspired, have you with these contrived°
    To bait° me with this foul derision?
    Is all the counsel° that we two have shared—
    The sisters' vows, the hours that we have spent
    When we have chid the hasty-footed time
    For parting us—O, is all forgot?   200
    All schooldays' friendship, childhood innocence?

---

169 *will none* i.e., want no part of her   171 *to . . . sojourned* only visited with her   175 *aby* pay for   177 *his* its   187 *engilds* gilds, brightens with a golden light   188 *oes* spangles (here, stars)   194 *in spite of me* to vex me   196 *contrived* plotted   197 *bait* torment, as one sets on dogs to bait a bear   198 *counsel* confidential talk

We, Hermia, like two artificial° gods,
Have with our needles created both one flower,
Both on one sampler, sitting on one cushion,   205
Both warbling of one song, both in one key,
As if our hands, our sides, voices, and minds
Had been incorporate.° So we grew together,
Like to a double cherry, seeming parted,
But yet an union in partition,   210
Two lovely° berries molded on one stem;
So with two seeming bodies but one heart,
Two of the first, like coats in heraldry,
Due but to one and crownèd with one crest.°
And will you rend our ancient love asunder,   215
To join with men in scorning your poor friend?
It is not friendly, 'tis not maidenly.
Our sex, as well as I, may chide you for it,
Though I alone do feel the injury.
Hermia: I am amazèd at your passionate words.   220
    I scorn you not. It seems that you scorn me.
Helena: Have you not set Lysander, as in scorn,
    To follow me and praise my eyes and face?
    And made your other love, Demetrius,
    Who even but now did spurn me with his foot,   225
    To call me goddess, nymph, divine, and rare,
    Precious, celestial? Wherefore speaks he this
    To her he hates? And wherefore doth Lysander
    Deny your love, so rich within his soul,
    And tender° me, forsooth, affection,   230
    But by your setting on, by your consent?
    What though I be not so in grace° as you,
    So hung upon with love, so fortunate,
    But miserable most, to love unloved?
    This you should pity rather than despise.   235
Hermia: I understand not what you mean by this.
Helena: Ay, do! Persever, counterfeit sad° looks,
    Make mouths° upon° me when I turn my back,
    Wink each at other, hold the sweet jest up.°
    This sport, well carried,° shall be chronicled.   240
    If you have any pity, grace, or manners,
    You would not make me such an argument.°
    But fare ye well. 'Tis partly my own fault,
    Which death, or absence, soon shall remedy.
Lysander: Stay, gentle Helena; hear my excuse,   245
    My love, my life, my soul, fair Helena!

203 *artificial* skilled in art or creation   208 *incorporate* of one body   211 *lovely* loving   213–214 *Two . . . crest* i.e., we have two separate bodies, just as a coat of arms in heraldry can be represented twice on a shield but surmounted by a single crest   230 *tender* offer   232 *grace* favor   237 *sad* grave, serious   238 *mouths* i.e., moves, faces, grimaces.   *upon* at   239 *hold . . . up* keep up the joke   240 *carried* managed   242 *argument* subject for a jest

Helena: O excellent!

Hermia [*to Lysander*]: Sweet, do not scorn her so.

Demetrius [*to Lysander*]: If she cannot entreat,° I can compel.

Lysander: Thou canst compel no more than she entreat.

    Thy threats have no more strength than her weak prayers.   250

    Helen, I love thee, by my life I do!

    I swear by that which I will lose for thee,

    To prove him false that says I love thee not.

Demetrius [*to Helena*]:

    I say I love thee more than he can do.

Lysander: If thou say so, withdraw, and prove it too.°   255

Demetrius: Quick, come!

Hermia: Lysander, whereto tends all this?

Lysander: Away, you Ethiope!°

                              [*He tries to break away from Hermia.*]

Demetrius: No, no; he'll

    Seem to break loose; take on as° you would follow,

    But yet come not. You are a tame man. Go!

Lysander [*to Hermia*]: Hang off,° thou cat, thou burr! Vile thing, let loose,   260

    Or I will shake thee from me like a serpent!

Hermia: Why are you grown so rude? What change is this,

    Sweet love?

Lysander: Thy love? Out, tawny Tartar, out!

    Out, loathèd med'cine!° O hated potion, hence!

Hermia: Do you not jest?

Helena: Yes, sooth,° and so do you.   265

Lysander: Demetrius, I will keep my word with thee.

Demetrius: I would I had your bond, for I perceive

    A weak bond° holds you. I'll not trust your word.

Lysander: What, should I hurt her, strike her, kill her dead?

    Although I hate her, I'll not harm her so.   270

Hermia: What, can you do me greater harm than hate?

    Hate me? Wherefore? O me, what news,° my love?

    Am not I Hermia? Are not you Lysander?

    I am as fair now as I was erewhile.°

    Since night you loved me; yet since night you left me.   275

    Why, then you left me—O, the gods forbid!—

    In earnest, shall I say?

Lysander: Ay, by my life!

    And never did desire to see thee more.

    Therefore be out of hope, of question, of doubt;

    Be certain, nothing truer. 'Tis no jest   280

    That I do hate thee and love Helena.

---

248 *entreat* i.e., succeed by entreaty   255 *withdraw . . . too* i.e., withdraw with me and prove your claim in a duel. (The two gentlemen are armed.)   257 *Ethiope* (Referring to Hermia's relatively dark hair and complexion; see also *tawny Tartar* six lines later.)   258 *take on as* act as if, make a fuss as if   260 *Hang off* let go   264 *med'cine* i.e., poison   265 *sooth* truly   268 *weak bond* i.e., Hermia's arm (with a pun on *bond*, "oath," in the previous line)   272 *what news* what is the matter   274 *erewhile* just now

Hermia berates Helena, "You thief of love!" (III, ii, 283).

Hermia [*to Helena*]: O me! You juggler! You cankerblossom!°
    You thief of love! What, have you come by night
    And stol'n my love's heart from him?
Helena: Fine, i' faith!
    Have you no modesty, no maiden shame,   285
    No touch of bashfulness? What, will you tear
    Impatient answers from my gentle tongue?
    Fie, fie! You counterfeit, you puppet,° you!
Hermia: "Puppet"? Why, so!° Ay, that way goes the game.
    Now I perceive that she hath made compare   290
    Between our statures; she hath urged her height,
    And with her personage, her tall personage,
    Her height, forsooth, she hath prevailed with him.
    And are you grown so high in his esteem
    Because I am so dwarfish and so low?   295
    How low am I, thou painted maypole? Speak!
    How low am I? I am not yet so low
    But that my nails can reach unto thine eyes.
                        [*She flails at Helena but is restrained.*]

---

282 *cankerblossom* worm that destroys the flower bud, or wild rose   288 *puppet* (1) counterfeit (2) dwarfish
woman (in reference to Hermia's smaller stature)   289 *Why, so* i.e., Oh, so that's how it is

Helena: I pray you, though you mock me, gentlemen,
    Let her not hurt me. I was never curst;°   300
    I have no gift at all in shrewishness;
    I am a right° maid for my cowardice.
    Let her not strike me. You perhaps may think,
    Because she is something° lower than myself,
    That I can match her.
Hermia: Lower? Hark, again!   305
Helena: Good Hermia, do not be so bitter with me.
    I evermore did love you, Hermia,
    Did ever keep your counsels, never wronged you,
    Save that, in love unto Demetrius,
    I told him of your stealth° unto this wood.   310
    He followed you; for love I followed him.
    But he hath chid me hence° and threatened me
    To strike me, spurn me, nay, to kill me too.
    And now, so° you will let me quiet go,
    To Athens will I bear my folly back   315
    And follow you no further. Let me go.
    You see how simple and how fond° I am.
Hermia: Why, get you gone. Who is 't that hinders you?
Helena: A foolish heart, that I leave here behind.
Hermia: What, with Lysander?
Helena: With Demetrius.   320
Lysander: Be not afraid; she shall not harm thee, Helena.
Demetrius: No, sir, she shall not, though you take her part.
Helena: O, when she is angry, she is keen° and shrewd.°
    She was a vixen when she went to school;
    And though she be but little, she is fierce.   325
Hermia: "Little" again? Nothing but "low" and "little"?
    Why will you suffer her to flout me thus?
    Let me come to her.
Lysander: Get you gone, you dwarf!
    You minimus,° of hindering knotgrass° made!
    You bead, you acorn!
Demetrius: You are too officious   330
    In her behalf that scorns your services.
    Let her alone. Speak not of Helena;
    Take not her part. For, if thou dost intend°
    Never so little show of love to her,
    Thou shalt aby° it.
Lysander: Now she holds me not.   335
    Now follow, if thou dar'st, to try whose right,
    Of thine or mine, is most in Helena.

                                                          [Exit.]

---

300 *curst* shrewish   302 *right* true   304 *something* somewhat   310 *stealth* stealing away   312 *chid me hence* driven me away with his scolding   314 *so* if only   317 *fond* foolish   323 *keen* fierce, cruel. *shrewd* shrewish   329 *minimus* diminutive creature. *knotgrass* a weed, an infusion of which was thought to stunt the growth   333 *intend* give sign of   335 *aby* pay for

Demetrius: Follow? Nay, I'll go with thee, cheek by jowl.°

[*Exit, following Lysander.*]

Hermia: You, mistress, all this coil° is 'long of° you.
Nay, go not back.°

Helena: I will not trust you, I,   340
Nor longer stay in your curst company.
Your hands than mine are quicker for a fray;
My legs are longer, though, to run away.   [*Exit.*]

Hermia: I am amazed and know not what to say.   *Exit.*

[*Oberon and Puck come forward.*]

Oberon: This is thy negligence. Still thou mistak'st,   345
Or else committ'st thy knaveries willfully.

Puck: Believe me, king of shadows, I mistook.
Did not you tell me I should know the man
By the Athenian garments he had on?
And so far blameless proves my enterprise   350
That I have 'nointed an Athenian's eyes;
And so far° am I glad it so did sort,°
As° this their jangling I esteem a sport.

Oberon: Thou seest these lovers seek a place to fight.
Hie° therefore, Robin, overcast the night;   355
The starry welkin° cover thou anon
With drooping fog as black as Acheron,°
And lead these testy rivals so astray
As° one come not within another's way.
Like to Lysander sometimes frame thy tongue,   360
Then stir Demetrius up with bitter wrong;°
And sometimes rail thou like Demetrius.
And from each other look thou lead them thus,
Till o'er their brows death-counterfeiting sleep
With leaden legs and batty° wings doth creep.   365
Then crush this herb° into Lysander's eye,   [*giving herb.*]
Whose liquor hath this virtuous° property,
To take from thence all error with his° might
And make his eyeballs roll with wonted° sight.
When they next wake, all this derision°   370
Shall seem a dream and fruitless vision,
And back to Athens shall the lovers wend
With league whose date° till death shall never end.
Whiles I in this affair do thee employ,
I'll to my queen and beg her Indian boy;   375

---

338 *cheek by jowl* i.e., side by side   339 *coil* turmoil, dissension.   *'long of* on account of   340 *go not back*
i.e., don't retreat (Hermia is again proposing a fight.)   352 *so far* at least to this extent.   *sort* turn out
353 *As* that   355 *Hie* hasten   356 *welkin* sky   357 *Acheron* river of Hades (here representing Hades
itself)   359 *As* that   361 *wrong* insults   365 *batty* batlike   366 *this herb* i.e., the antidote (mentioned in
II, i, 184) to love-in-idleness   367 *virtuous* efficacious   368 *his* its   369 *wonted* accustomed   370 *derision*
laughable business   373 *date* term of existence

And then I will her charmèd eye release
From monster's view, and all things shall be peace.
Puck: My fairy lord, this must be done with haste,
For night's swift dragons° cut the clouds full fast,
And yonder shines Aurora's harbinger,° 380
At whose approach ghosts, wand'ring here and there,
Troop home to churchyards. Damnèd spirits all,
That in crossways and floods have burial,°
Already to their wormy beds are gone.
For fear lest day should look their shames upon, 385
They willfully themselves exile from light
And must for aye° consort with black-browed night.
Oberon: But we are spirits of another sort.
I with the Morning's love° have oft made sport,
And, like a forester,° the groves may tread 390
Even till the eastern gate, all fiery red,
Opening on Neptune with fair blessèd beams,
Turns into yellow gold his salt green streams.
But notwithstanding, haste, make no delay.
We may effect this business yet ere day.   [*Exit.*] 395
Puck:
　　　Up and down, up and down,
　　　I will lead them up and down.
　　　I am feared in field and town.
　　　Goblin,° lead them up and down.
Here comes one. 400

Enter Lysander.

Lysander: Where art thou, proud Demetrius? Speak thou now.
Puck [*mimicking Demetrius*]: Here, villain, drawn° and ready. Where art thou?
Lysander: I will be with thee straight.°
Puck:
　　　　　　　　　　　Follow me, then,
　　To plainer° ground.

　　　　　　　　　　[*Lysander wanders about,° following the voice.*]

Enter Demetrius.
Demetrius:　　　　　Lysander! Speak again!
Thou runaway, thou coward, art thou fled?
Speak! In some bush? Where dost thou hide thy head? 405

---

379 *dragons* (Supposed by Shakespeare to be yoked to the car of the goddess of night or the moon.)   380
Aurora's harbinger the morning star, precursor of dawn   383 *crossways . . . burial* (Those who had committed suicide were buried at crossways, with a stake driven through them; those who intentionally or accidentally drowned [in floods or deep water], would be condemned to wander disconsolate for lack of burial rites.)   387 *for aye* forever   389 *the Morning's love* Cephalus, a beautiful youth beloved by Aurora; or perhaps the goddess of the dawn herself   390 *forester* keeper of a royal forest   399 *Goblin* Hobgoblin. (Puck refers to himself.)   402 *drawn* with drawn sword   403 *straight* immediately   404 *plainer* more open.   s.d. *Lysander wanders about* (Lysander may exit here, but perhaps not; neither exit nor reentrance is indicated in the early texts.)

Puck [*mimicking Lysander*]:
    Thou coward, art thou bragging to the stars,
    Telling the bushes that thou look'st for wars,
    And wilt not come? Come, recreant;° come, thou child,
    I'll whip thee with a rod. He is defiled   410
    That draws a sword on thee.
Demetrius: Yea, art thou there?
Puck: Follow my voice. We'll try° no manhood here.

                                        Exeunt.

    [*Lysander returns.*]

Lysander: He goes before me and still dares me on.
    When I come where he calls, then he is gone.
    The villain is much lighter-heeled than I.   415
    I followed fast, but faster he did fly,
    That fallen am I in dark uneven way,
    And here will rest me. [*He lies down.*] Come, thou gentle day!
    For if but once thou show me thy gray light,
    I'll find Demetrius and revenge this spite.   [*He sleeps.*] 420

    [*Enter*] *Robin* [*Puck*] *and Demetrius.*

Puck: Ho, ho, ho! Coward, why com'st thou not?
Demetrius: Abide° me, if thou dar'st; for well I wot°
    Thou runn'st before me, shifting every place,
    And dar'st not stand nor look me in the face.
    Where art thou now?
Puck: Come hither. I am here.   425
Demetrius: Nay, then, thou mock'st me. Thou shalt buy° this dear,°
    If ever I thy face by daylight see.
    Now, go thy way. Faintness constraineth me
    To measure out my length on this cold bed.
    By day's approach look to be visited.   430
                            [*He lies down and sleeps.*]

    Enter Helena.

Helena: O weary night, O long and tedious night,
    Abate° thy hours! Shine comforts from the east,
    That I may back to Athens by daylight
    From these that my poor company detest;
    And sleep, that sometimes shuts up sorrow's eye,   435
    Steal me awhile from mine own company.
                          [*She lies down and*] *sleep*[*s*].

Puck: Yet but three! Come one more,
    Two of both kinds makes up four.
    Here she comes, curst° and sad.
    Cupid is a knavish lad,   440
    Thus to make poor females mad.

---

409 *recreant* cowardly wretch   412 *try* test   422 *Abide* confront, face.   *wot* know   426 *buy* aby, pay for.
dear dearly   432 *Abate* lessen, shorten   439 *curst* ill-tempered

[*Enter Hermia.*]

Hermia: Never so weary, never so in woe,
Bedabbled with the dew and torn with briers,
I can no further crawl, no further go;
My legs can keep no pace with my desires.   445
Here will I rest me till the break of day.
Heavens shield Lysander, if they mean a fray!

[*She lies down and sleeps.*]

Puck: On the ground
Sleep sound.
I'll apply   450
To your eye,
Gentle lover, remedy.

[*He squeezes the juice on Lysander's eyes.*]

When thou wak'st,
Thou tak'st
True delight
In the sight   455
Of thy former lady's eye;
And the country proverb known,
That every man should take his own,
In your waking shall be shown:
Jack shall have Jill;°   460
Naught shall go ill;
The man shall have his mare again, and all shall be well.

[*Exit. The four sleeping lovers remain.*]

ACT IV

SCENE I [THE ACTION IS CONTINUOUS. THE FOUR LOVERS ARE STILL ASLEEP° ONSTAGE.]

Enter [*Titania,*] *Queen of Fairies, and* [*Bottom the*] *clown, and Fairies; and* [*Oberon,*]
the King, behind them.

Titania: Come, sit thee down upon this flowery bed,
While I thy amiable° cheeks do coy,°
And stick muskroses in thy sleek smooth head,
And kiss thy fair large ears, my gentle joy.

[*They recline.*]

Bottom: Where's Peaseblossom?   5
Peaseblossom: Ready.
Bottom: Scratch my head, Peaseblossom. Where's Monsieur Cobweb?
Cobweb: Ready.

---

461 *Jack shall have Jill* (Proverbial for "boy gets girl.")   s.d. *still asleep* (Compare with the Folio stage direction: "They sleep all the act.")   2 *amiable* lovely.   *coy* caress

The fairies tend to Bottom's wishes.

Bottom: Monsieur Cobweb, good monsieur, get you your weapons in your hand, and kill me a red-hipped humble-bee on the top of a thistle; and, good monsieur, bring me the honey bag. Do not fret yourself too much in the action, monsieur; and, good monsieur, have a care the honey bag break not. I would be loath to have you overflown with a honey bag, signor. [*Exit Cobweb.*] Where's Monsieur Mustardseed?   10

Mustardseed: Ready.   15

Bottom: Give me your neaf,° Monsieur Mustardseed. Pray you, leave your courtesy,° good monsieur.

Mustardseed: What's your will?

Bottom: Nothing, good monsieur, but to help Cavalery° Cobweb° to scratch. I must to the barber's, monsieur, for methinks I am marvelous hairy about the face; and I am such a tender ass, if my hair do but tickle me I must scratch.   20

Titania: What, wilt thou hear some music, my sweet love?

Bottom: I have a reasonable good ear in music. Let's have the tongs and the bones.°
                              [*Music: tongs, rural music.°*]

Titania: Or say, sweet love, what thou desirest to eat.

Bottom: Truly, a peck of provender.° I could munch your good dry oats. Methinks I have a great desire to a bottle° of hay. Good hay, sweet hay, hath no fellow.°   25

---

16 *neaf* fist. *leave your courtesy* i.e., stop bowing, or put on your hat   19 *Cavalery* cavalier. (Form of address for a gentleman.) *Cobweb* (Seemingly an error, since Cobweb has been sent to bring honey, while Peaseblossom has been asked to scratch.)   23 *tongs . . . bones* instruments for rustic music. (The tongs were played like a triangle, whereas the bones were held between the fingers and used as clappers.) s.d. *Music . . . music* (This stage direction is added from the Folio.)   25 *peck of provender* one-quarter bushel of grain   26 *bottle* bundle. *fellow* equal

Titania: I have a venturous fairy that shall seek
    The squirrel's hoard, and fetch thee new nuts.
Bottom: I had rather have a handful or two of dried peas. But, I pray you, let none of
    your people stir° me. I have an exposition of° sleep come upon me.   30
Titania: Sleep thou, and I will wind thee in my arms.
    Fairies, begone, and be all ways° away.

                                             [Exeunt Fairies.]

    So doth the woodbine° the sweet honeysuckle
    Gently entwist; the female ivy so
    Enrings the barky fingers of the elm.   35
    O, how I love thee! How I dote on thee!

                                              [They sleep.]

    Enter Robin Goodfellow [Puck].

Oberon [coming forward]: Welcome, good Robin. Seest thou this sweet sight?
    Her dotage now I do begin to pity.
    For, meeting her of late behind the wood
    Seeking sweet favors° for this hateful fool,   40
    I did upbraid her and fall out with her.
    For she his hairy temples then had rounded
    With coronet of fresh and fragrant flowers;
    And that same dew, which sometime° on the buds
    Was wont to swell like round and orient° pearls,   45
    Stood now within the pretty flowerets' eyes
    Like tears that did their own disgrace bewail.
    When I had at my pleasure taunted her,
    And she in mild terms begged my patience,
    I then did ask of her her changeling child,   50
    Which straight she gave me, and her fairy sent
    To bear him to my bower in Fairyland.
    And, now I have the boy, I will undo
    This hateful imperfection of her eyes.
    And, gentle Puck, take this transformèd scalp   55
    From off the head of this Athenian swain,
    That he, awaking when the other° do,
    May all to Athens back again repair,°
    And think no more of this night's accidents
    But as the fierce vexation of a dream.   60
    But first I will release the Fairy Queen.

                              [He squeezes an herb on her eyes.]

        Be as thou wast wont to be;
        See as thou wast wont to see.
        Dian's bud° o'er Cupid's flower
        Hath such force and blessèd power.   65

---

30 *stir* disturb.   *exposition of* (Bottom's phrase for "disposition to.")   32 *all ways* in all directions   33 *woodbine* bindweed, a climbing plant that twines in the opposite direction from that of honeysuckle   40 *favors* i.e., gifts of flowers   44 *sometime* formerly   45 *orient pearls* i.e., the most beautiful of all pearls, those coming from the Orient   57 *other* others   58 *repair* return   64 *Dian's bud* (Perhaps the flower of the *agnus castus* or chaste-tree, supposed to preserve chastity; or perhaps referring simply to Oberon's herb by which he can undo the effects of "Cupid's flower," the love-in-idleness of II, i, 166–168.)

Now, my Titania, wake you, my sweet queen.
Titania [*waking*]: My Oberon! What visions have I seen!
    Methought I was enamored of an ass.
Oberon: There lies your love.
Titania: How came these things to pass?
    O, how mine eyes do loathe his visage now!   70
Oberon: Silence awhile. Robin, take off this head.
    Titania, music call, and strike more dead
    Than common sleep of all these five° the sense.
Titania: Music, ho! Music, such as charmeth° sleep!   [*Music.*]
Puck [*removing the ass head*]:
    Now, when thou wak'st, with thine own fool's eyes peep.   75
Oberon: Sound, music! Come, my queen, take hands with me,
    And rock the ground whereon these sleepers be.   [*They dance.*]
    Now thou and I are new in amity,
    And will tomorrow midnight solemnly°
    Dance in Duke Theseus' house triumphantly,   80
    And bless it to all fair prosperity.
    There shall the pairs of faithful lovers be
    Wedded, with Theseus, all in jollity.
Puck: Fairy King, attend, and mark:
    I do hear the morning lark.   85
Oberon: Then, my queen, in silence sad,°
    Trip we after night's shade.
    We the globe can compass soon,
    Swifter than the wandering moon.
Titania: Come, my lord, and in our flight   90
    Tell me how it came this night
    That I sleeping here was found
    With these mortals on the ground.
                             Exeunt. [*Oberon, Titania, and Puck*].
                                     Wind horn [*within*].

Enter Theseus and all his train; [*Hippolyta, Egeus*].

Theseus: Go, one of you, find out the forester,
    For now our observation° is performed;   95
    And since we have the vaward° of the day,
    My love shall hear the music of my hounds.
    Uncouple° in the western valley; let them go.
    Dispatch, I say, and find the forester.   [*Exit an Attendant.*]
    We will, fair queen, up to the mountain's top   100
    And mark the musical confusion
    Of hounds and echo in conjunction.

---

73 *these five* i.e., the four lovers and Bottom   74 *charmeth* brings about, as though by a charm   79 *solemnly* ceremoniously   86 *sad* sober   95 *observation* i.e., observance to a morn of May (I, i, 167)   96 *vaward* vanguard, i.e., earliest part   98 *Uncouple* set free for the hunt

Hippolyta: I was with Hercules and Cadmus° once,
    When in a wood of Crete they bayed° the bear
    With hounds of Sparta.° Never did I hear
    Such gallant chiding;° for, besides the groves,   105
    The skies, the fountains, every region near
    Seemed all one mutual cry. I never heard
    So musical a discord, such sweet thunder.
Theseus: My hounds are bred out of the Spartan kind,°   110
    So flewed,° so sanded;° and their heads are hung
    With ears that sweep away the morning dew;
    Crook-kneed, and dewlapped° like Thessalian bulls;
    Slow in pursuit, but matched in mouth like bells,
    Each under each.° A cry° more tunable°   115
    Was never holloed to nor cheered° with horn
    In Crete, in Sparta, nor in Thessaly.
    Judge when you hear.   *[He sees the sleepers.]*
              But soft!° What nymphs are these?
Egeus: My lord, this is my daughter here asleep,
    And this Lysander; this Demetrius is;   120
    This Helena, old Nedar's Helena.
    I wonder of° their being here together.
Theseus: No doubt they rose up early to observe
    The rite of May, and hearing our intent,
    Came here in grace of our solemnity.°   125
    But speak, Egeus. Is not this the day
    That Hermia should give answer of her choice?
Egeus: It is, my lord.
Theseus: Go, bid the huntsmen wake them with their horns.
                                    [Exit an Attendant.]

Shout within. Wind horns. They all start up.

    Good morrow, friends. Saint Valentine° is past.   130
    Begin these woodbirds but to couple now?
Lysander: Pardon, my lord.   *[They kneel.]*
Theseus: I pray you all, stand up.   *[They stand.]*
    I know you two are rival enemies;
    How comes this gentle concord in the world,
    That hatred is so far from jealousy°   135
    To sleep by hate and fear no enmity?

---

103 *Cadmus* mythical founder of Thebes. (This story about him is unknown.)   104 *bayed* brought to bay
105 *hounds of Sparta* (A breed famous in antiquity for their hunting skill.)   106 *chiding* i.e., yelping   110 *kind*
strain, breed   111 *So flewed* similarly having large hanging chaps or fleshy covering of the jaw.   *sanded* of
sandy color   113 *dewlapped* having pendulous folds of skin under the neck   114–115 *matched . . . each*
i.e., harmoniously matched in their various cries like a set of bells, from treble down to bass   115 *cry* pack
of hounds.   *tunable* well tuned, melodious   116 *cheered* encouraged   118 *soft* i.e., gently, wait a minute
122 *wonder of* wonder at   125 *in . . . solemnity* in honor of our wedding ceremony   130 *Saint Valentine*
(Birds were supposed to choose their mates on Saint Valentine's Day.)   135 *jealousy* suspicion

Lysander: My lord, I shall reply amazedly,
　　Half sleep, half waking; but as yet, I swear,
　　I cannot truly say how I came here.
　　But, as I think—for truly would I speak,
　　And now I do bethink me, so it is—
　　I came with Hermia hither. Our intent
　　Was to be gone from Athens, where° we might,
　　Without° the peril of the Athenian law—
Egeus: Enough, enough, my lord; you have enough.
　　I beg the law, the law, upon his head.
　　They would have stol'n away; they would, Demetrius,
　　Thereby to have defeated° you and me,
　　You of your wife and me of my consent,
　　Of my consent that she should be your wife.
Demetrius: My lord, fair Helen told me of their stealth,
　　Of this their purpose hither° to this wood,
　　And I in fury hither followed them,
　　Fair Helena in fancy° following me.
　　But, my good lord, I wot not by what power—
　　But by some power it is—my love to Hermia,
　　Melted as the snow, seems to me now
　　As the remembrance of an idle gaud°
　　Which in my childhood I did dote upon;
　　And all the faith, the virtue of my heart,
　　The object and the pleasure of mine eye,
　　Is only Helena. To her, my lord,
　　Was I betrothed ere I saw Hermia,
　　But like a sickness did I loathe this food;
　　But, as in health, come to my natural taste,
　　Now I do wish it, love it, long for it,
　　And will forevermore be true to it.
Theseus: Fair lovers, you are fortunately met.
　　Of this discourse we more will hear anon.
　　Egeus, I will overbear your will;
　　For in the temple, by and by, with us
　　These couples shall eternally be knit.
　　And, for° the morning now is something° worn,
　　Our purposed hunting shall be set aside.
　　Away with us to Athens. Three and three,
　　We'll hold a feast in great solemnity.°
　　Come, Hippolyta.

[Exeunt Theseus, Hippolyta, Egeus, and train.]

Demetrius: These things seem small and undistinguishable,
　　Like far-off mountains turnèd into clouds.

	140
	145
	150
	155
	160
	165
	170
	175

---

143 *where* wherever; or, to where   144 *Without* outside of, beyond   148 *defeated* defrauded   152 *hither* in coming hither   154 *in fancy* driven by love   158 *idle gaud* worthless trinket   173 *for* since. *something* somewhat   176 *in great solemnity* with great ceremony

Hermia: Methinks I see these things with parted° eye,   180
    When everything seems double.
Helena: So methinks;
    And I have found Demetrius like a jewel,
    Mine own, and not mine own.°
Demetrius: Are you sure
    That we are awake? It seems to me
    That yet we sleep, we dream. Do not you think   185
    The Duke was here, and bid us follow him?
Hermia: Yea, and my father.
Helena: And Hippolyta.
Lysander: And he did bid us follow to the temple.
Demetrius: Why, then, we are awake. Let's follow him,
    And by the way let us recount our dreams.   [*Exeunt the lovers.*]   190
Bottom [*awaking*]: When my cue comes, call me, and I will answer. My next is, "Most
    fair Pyramus." Heigh—ho! Peter Quince! Flute, the bellows mender! Snout,
    the tinker! Starveling! God's° my life, stolen hence and left me asleep! I have
    had a most rare vision. I have had a dream, past the wit of man to say what
    dream it was. Man is but an ass if he go about° to expound this dream. Methought   195
    I was—there is no man can tell what. Methought I was—and methought I had—
    but man is but a patched° fool if he will offer° to say what methought I had.
    The eye of man hath not heard, the ear of man hath not seen, man's hand is not
    able to taste, his tongue to conceive, nor his heart to report,° what my dream
    was. I will get Peter Quince to write a ballad° of this dream. It shall be called   200
    "Bottom's Dream," because it hath no bottom;° and I will sing it in the latter end
    of a play, before the Duke. Peradventure, to make it the more gracious, I shall
    sing it at her° death.

                                                              [*Exit.*]

SCENE II [ATHENS.]

    Enter Quince, Flute, [Snout, and Starveling].

Quince: Have you sent to Bottom's house? Is he come home yet?
Starveling: He cannot be heard of. Out of doubt he is transported.°
Flute: If he come not, then the play is marred. It goes not forward. Doth it?
Quince: It is not possible. You have not a man in all Athens able to discharge°
    Pyramus but he.   5
Flute: No, he hath simply the best wit° of any handicraft man in Athens.
Quince: Yea, and the best person° too, and he is a very paramour for a sweet voice.
Flute: You must say "paragon." A paramour is, God bless us, a thing of naught.°

    Enter Snug the joiner.

---

180 *parted* i.e., improperly focused   182–183 *like . . . mine own* i.e., like a jewel that one finds by chance
and therefore possesses but cannot certainly consider one's own property   193 *God's* may God save
195 *go about* attempt   197 *patched* wearing motley, i.e., a dress of various colors.   *offer* venture
198–199 *The eye . . . report* (Bottom garbles the terms of 1 Corinthians 2:9)   200 *ballad* (The proper
medium for relating sensational stories and preposterous events.)   201 *hath no bottom* is unfathomable
203 *her* Thisbe's (?)   2 *transported* carried off by fairies; or, possibly, transformed   4 *discharge* perform
6 *wit* intellect   7 *person* appearance   8 *a . . . naught* a shameful thing

The workers celebrate the return of Bottom and prepare to put on their play.

Snug: Masters, the Duke is coming from the temple, and there is two or three lords
and ladies more married. If our sport had gone forward, we had all been made   10
men.°

Flute: O sweet bully Bottom! Thus hath he lost sixpence a day° during his life; he
could not have scaped sixpence a day. An the Duke had not given him sixpence
a day for playing Pyramus, I'll be hanged. He would have deserved it. Sixpence a
day in Pyramus, or nothing.   15

Enter Bottom.

Bottom: Where are these lads? Where are these hearts?°
Quince: Bottom! O most courageous day! O most happy hour!
Bottom: Masters, I am to discourse wonders.° But ask me not what; for if I tell you, I
am no true Athenian. I will tell you everything, right as it fell out.
Quince: Let us hear, sweet Bottom.   20
Bottom: Not a word of° me. All that I will tell you is that the Duke hath dined. Get
your apparel together, good strings° to your beards, new ribbons to your pumps;°
meet presently° at the palace; every man look o'er his part, for the short and the
long is, our play is preferred.° In any case, let Thisbe have clean linen; and let
not him that plays the lion pare his nails, for they shall hang out for the lion's   25

10–11 *we . . . men* i.e., we would have had our fortunes made   12 *sixpence a day* i.e., as a royal pension
16 *hearts* good fellows   18 *am . . . wonders* have wonders to relate   21 *of* out of   22 *strings* (to attach the
beards). *pumps* light shoes or slippers   23 *presently* immediately   24 *preferred* selected for consideration

claws. And, most dear actors, eat no onions nor garlic, for we are to utter sweet breath; and I do not doubt but to hear them say it is a sweet comedy. No more words. Away! Go, away!

[*Exeunt.*]

ACT V

SCENE I [ATHENS. THE PALACE OF THESEUS.]

Enter Theseus, Hippolyta, and Philostrate, [lords, and attendants].

Hippolyta: 'Tis strange, my Theseus, that° these lovers speak of.	
Theseus: More strange than true. I never may° believe	
These antique° fables nor these fairy toys.°	
Lovers and madmen have such seething brains,	
Such shaping fantasies,° that apprehend°	5
More than cool reason ever comprehends.°	
The lunatic, the lover, and the poet	
Are of imagination all compact.°	
One sees more devils than vast hell can hold;	
That is the madman. The lover, all as frantic,	10
Sees Helen's° beauty in a brow of Egypt.°	
The poet's eye, in a fine frenzy rolling,	
Doth glance from heaven to earth, from earth to heaven;	
And as imagination bodies forth	
The forms of things unknown, the poet's pen	15
Turns them to shapes and gives to airy nothing	
A local habitation and a name.	
Such tricks hath strong imagination	
That, if it would but apprehend some joy,	
It comprehends some bringer° of that joy;	20
Or in the night, imagining some fear,°	
How easy is a bush supposed a bear!	
Hippolyta: But all the story of the night told over,	
And all their minds transfigured so together,	
More witnesseth than fancy's images°	25
And grows to something of great constancy;°	
But, howsoever,° strange and admirable.°	

Enter lovers: Lysander, Demetrius, Hermia, and Helena.

Theseus: Here come the lovers, full of joy and mirth.	
Joy, gentle friends! Joy and fresh days of love	
Accompany your hearts!	
Lysander: More than to us	30

1 *that* that which 2 *may* can 3 *antique* old-fashioned (punning too on "*antic*," "strange," "grotesque"). *fairy toys* trifling stories about fairies 5 *fantasies* imaginations. *apprehend* conceive, imagine 6 *comprehends* understands 8 *compact* formed, composed 11 *Helen's* i.e., of Helen of Troy, pattern of beauty. *brow of Egypt* i.e., face of a gypsy 20 *bringer* i.e., source 21 *fear* object of fear 25 *More . . . images* testifies to something more substantial than mere imaginings 26 *constancy* certainty 27 *howsoever* in any case. *admirable* a source of wonder

Wait in your royal walks, your board, your bed!
Theseus: Come now, what masques,° what dances shall we have,
    To wear away this long age of three hours
    Between our after-supper and bedtime?
    Where is our usual manager of mirth?   35
    What revels are in hand? Is there no play
    To ease the anguish of a torturing hour?
    Call Philostrate.
Philostrate: Here, mighty Theseus.
Theseus: Say, what abridgment° have you for this evening?
    What masque? What music? How shall we beguile   40
    The lazy time, if not with some delight?
Philostrate [giving him a paper]: There is a brief° how many sports are ripe.
    Make choice of which Your Highness will see first.
Theseus [He reads]: "The battle with the Centaurs,° to be sung
    By an Athenian eunuch to the harp"?   45
    We'll none of that. That have I told my love,
    In glory of my kinsman° Hercules.
    [*He reads.*] "The riot of the tipsy Bacchanals,
    Tearing the Thracian singer in their rage"?°
    That is an old device;° and it was played   50
    When I from Thebes came last a conqueror.
    [*He reads.*] "The thrice three Muses mourning for the death
    Of Learning, late deceased in beggary"?°
    That is some satire, keen and critical,
    Not sorting with° a nuptial ceremony.   55
    [*He reads.*] "A tedious brief scene of young Pyramus
    And his love Thisbe; very tragical mirth"?
    Merry and tragical? Tedious and brief?
    That is, hot ice and wondrous strange° snow.
    How shall we find the concord of this discord?   60
Philostrate: A play there is, my lord, some ten words long,
    Which is as brief as I have known a play;
    But by ten words, my lord, it is too long,
    Which makes it tedious. For in all the play
    There is not one word apt, one player fitted.   65
    And tragical, my noble lord, it is,
    For Pyramus therein doth kill himself.

---

32 *masques* courtly entertainments   39 *abridgment* pastime (to abridge or shorten the evening)   12 *brief* short written statement, summary   44 *battle . . . Centaurs* (Probably refers to the battle of the Centaurs and the Lapithae, when the Centaurs attempted to carry off Hippodamia, bride of Theseus' friend Pirothous. The story is told in Ovid's *Metamorphoses* 12.)   47 *kinsman* (Plutarch's "Life of Theseus" states that Hercules and Theseus were near kinsmen. Theseus is referring to a version of the battle of the Centaurs in which Hercules was said to be present.)   48–49 *The riot . . . rage* (This was the story of the death of Orpheus, as told in *Metamorphoses* 11.)   50 *device* show, performance   52–53 *The thrice . . . beggary* (Possibly an allusion to Spenser's *Teares of the Muses,* 1591, though "satires" deploring the neglect of learning and the creative arts were commonplace.)   55 *sorting with* befitting   59 *strange* (Sometimes emended to an adjective that would contrast with *snow,* just as *hot* contrasts with *ice.*)

Which, when I saw rehearsed, I must confess,
Made mine eyes water; but more merry tears
The passion of loud laughter never shed. 70
Theseus: What are they that do play it?
Philostrate: Hardhanded men that work in Athens here,
Which never labored in their minds till now,
And now have toiled° their unbreathed° memories
With this same play, against° your nuptial. 75
Theseus: And we will hear it.
Philostrate: No, my noble lord,
It is not for you. I have heard it over,
And it is nothing, nothing in the world;
Unless you can find sport in their intents,
Extremely stretched° and conned° with cruel pain 80
To do you service.
Theseus: I will hear that play;
For never anything can be amiss
When simpleness° and duty tender it.
Go, bring them in; and take your places, ladies.

                               [Philostrate goes to summon the players.]
Hippolyta: I love not to see wretchedness o'ercharged,° 85
And duty in his service° perishing.
Theseus: Why, gentle sweet, you shall see no such thing.
Hippolyta: He says they can do nothing in this kind.°
Theseus: The kinder we, to give them thanks for nothing.
Our sport shall be to take what they mistake; 90
And what poor duty cannot do, noble respect°
Takes it in might, not merit.°
Where I have come, great clerks° have purposèd
To greet me with premeditated welcomes;
Where I have seen them shiver and look pale,
Make periods in the midst of sentences, 95
Throttle their practiced accent° in their fears,
And in conclusion dumbly have broke off,
Not paying me a welcome. Trust me, sweet,
Out of this silence yet I picked a welcome; 100
And in the modesty of fearful duty
I read as much as from the rattling tongue
Of saucy and audacious eloquence.
Love, therefore, and tongue-tied simplicity
In least° speak most, to my capacity.° 105

[Philostrate returns.]

---

74 *toiled* taxed. *unbreathed* unexercised   75 *against* in preparation for   80 *stretched* strained. *conned* memorized   83 *simpleness* simplicity   85 *wretchedness o'ercharged* social or intellectual inferiors overburdened   86 *his service* its attempt to serve   88 *kind* kind of thing   91 *respect* evaluation, consideration   92 *Takes . . . merit* values it for the effort made rather than for the excellence achieved   93 *clerks* learned men   97 *practiced accent* i.e., rehearsed speech; or, usual way of speaking   105 *least* i.e., saying least. *to my capacity* in my judgment and understanding

Philostrate: So please Your Grace, the Prologue° is addressed.°
Theseus: Let him approach.   [*A flourish of trumpets.*]

    Enter the Prologue [*Quince*].

Prologue: If we offend, it is with our good will.
    That you should think, we come not to offend,
    But with good will. To show our simple skill,   110
    That is the true beginning of our end.
    Consider, then, we come but in despite.
    We do not come, as minding° to content you,
    Our true intent is. All for your delight
    We are not here. That you should here repent you,   115
    The actors are at hand; and, by their show,
    You shall know all that you are like to know.
Theseus: This fellow doth not stand upon points.°
Lysander: He hath rid° his prologue like a rough° colt; he knows not the stop.° A good
    moral, my lord: it is not enough to speak, but to speak true.   120
Hippolyta: Indeed, he hath played on his prologue like a child on a recorder;° a
    sound, but not in government.°
Theseus: His speech was like a tangled chain: nothing° impaired, but all disordered.
    Who is next?

    Enter Pyramus [*Bottom*], *and Thisbe* [*Flute*], *and Wall* [*Snout*], *and Moonshine*
    [*Starveling*], *and Lion* [*Snug*].

Prologue:
    Gentles, perchance you wonder at this show;   125
    But wonder on, till truth makes all things plain.
    This man is Pyramus, if you would know;
    This beauteous lady Thisbe is, certain.
    This man with lime and roughcast doth present
    Wall, that vile wall which did these lovers sunder;   130
    And through Wall's chink, poor souls, they are content
    To whisper. At the which let no man wonder.
    This man, with lantern, dog, and bush of thorn,
    Presenteth Moonshine; for, if you will know,
    By moonshine did these lovers think no scorn°   135
    To meet at Ninus' tomb, there, there to woo.
    This grisly beast, which Lion hight° by name,
    The trusty Thisbe coming first by night
    Did scare away, or rather did affright;
    And as she fled, her mantle she did fall,°   140
    Which Lion vile with bloody mouth did stain.

---

106 *Prologue* speaker of the prologue. *addressed* ready   113 *minding* intending   118 *stand upon points* (1)
heed niceties or small points (2) pay attention to punctuation in his reading. (The humor of Quince's
speech is in the blunders of its punctuation.)   119 *rid* ridden.   *rough* unbroken.   *stop* (1) the stopping of
a colt by reining it in (2) punctuation mark   121 *recorder* a wind instrument like a flute   122 *government*
control   123 *nothing* not at all   135 *think no scorn* think it no disgraceful matter   137 *hight* is called   140 *fall*
let fall

Anon comes Pyramus, sweet youth and tall,°
And finds his trusty Thisbe's mantle slain;
Whereat, with blade, with bloody, blameful blade,
He bravely broached° his boiling bloody breast.   145
And Thisbe, tarrying in mulberry shade,
His dagger drew, and died. For all the rest,
Let Lion, Moonshine, Wall, and lovers twain
At large° discourse, while here they do remain.

                                 Exeunt Lion, Thisbe, and Moonshine.

Theseus: I wonder if the lion be to speak.   150
Demetrius: No wonder, my lord. One lion may, when many asses do.
Wall: In this same interlude° it doth befall
    That I, one Snout by name, present a wall;
    And such a wall as I would have you think
    That had in it a crannied hole or chink,   155
    Through which the lovers, Pyramus and Thisbe,
    Did whisper often, very secretly.
    This loam, this roughcast, and this stone doth show
    That I am that same wall; the truth is so.
    And this the cranny is, right and sinister,°   160
    Through which the fearful lovers are to whisper.
Theseus: Would you desire lime and hair to speak better?
Demetrius: It is the wittiest partition° that ever I heard discourse, my lord.

    [*Pyramus comes forward.*]

Theseus: Pyramus draws near the wall. Silence!
Pyramus: O grim-looked° night! O night with hue so black!   165
    O night, which ever art when day is not!
    O night, O night! Alack, alack, alack,
    I fear my Thisbe's promise is forgot.
    And thou, O wall, O sweet, O lovely wall,
    That stand'st between her father's ground and mine,   170
    Thou wall, O wall, O sweet and lovely wall,
    Show me thy chink, to blink through with mine eyne.

                                 [*Wall makes a chink with his fingers.*]

    Thanks, courteous wall. Jove shield thee well for this.
    But what see I? No Thisbe do I see.
    O wicked wall, through whom I see no bliss!   175
    Cursed be thy stones for thus deceiving me!
Theseus: The wall, methinks, being sensible,° should curse again.°
Pyramus: No, in truth, sir, he should not. "Deceiving me" is Thisbe's cue: she is to
    enter now, and I am to spy her through the wall. You shall see, it will fall pat° as
    I told you. Yonder she comes.   180

---

142 *tall* courageous   145 *broached* stabbed   149 *At large* in full, at length   152 *interlude* play   160 *right and sinister* i.e., the right side of it and the left; or, running from right to left, horizontally   163 *partition* (1) wall (2) section of a learned treatise or oration   165 *grim-looked* grim-looking   177 *sensible* capable of feeling.   *again* in return   179 *pat* exactly

The workers perform *Pyramus and Thisbe*.

Enter Thisbe.

Thisbe: O wall, full often hast thou heard my moans
　　For parting my fair Pyramus and me.
　　My cherry lips have often kissed thy stones,
　　Thy stones with lime and hair knit up in thee.
Pyramus: I see a voice. Now will I to the chink,　　　　　　　　　　185
　　To spy an° I can hear my Thisbe's face.
　　Thisbe!
Thisbe:　　My love! Thou art my love, I think.
Pyramus: Think what thou wilt, I am thy lover's grace,°
　　And like Limander° am I trusty still.
Thisbe: And I like Helen,° till the Fates me kill.　　　　　　　　　　190

186 *an* if   188 *lover's grace* i.e., gracious lover   189, 190 *Limander, Helen* (Blunders for "Leander" and "Hero.")

Pyramus: Not Shafalus° to Procrus° was so true.

Thisbe: As Shafalus to Procrus, I to you.

Pyramus: O, kiss me through the hole of this vile wall!

Thisbe: I kiss the wall's hole, not your lips at all.

Pyramus: Wilt thou at Ninny's tomb meet me straightway?   195

Thisbe: 'Tide° life, 'tide death, I come without delay.

                                      [*Exeunt Pyramus and Thisbe.*]

Wall: Thus have I, Wall, my part dischargèd so;

     And, being done, thus Wall away doth go.   [*Exit.*]

Theseus: Now is the mural down between the two neighbors.

Demetrius: No remedy, my lord, when walls are so willful° to hear without   200
     warning.°

Hippolyta: This is the silliest stuff that ever I heard.

Theseus: The best in this kind° are but shadows;° and the worst are no worse, if
     imagination amend them.

Hippolyta: It must be your imagination then, and not theirs.   205

Theseus: If we imagine no worse of them than they of themselves, they may pass for
     excellent men. Here come two noble beasts in, a man and a lion.

     Enter Lion and Moonshine.

Lion: You, ladies, you, whose gentle hearts do fear
     The smallest monstrous mouse that creeps on floor,
     May now perchance both quake and tremble here,   210
     When lion rough in wildest rage doth roar.
     Then know that I, as Snug the joiner, am
     A lion fell,° nor else no lion's dam;
     For, if I should as lion come in strife
     Into this place, 'twere pity on my life.   215

Theseus: A very gentle beast, and of a good conscience.

Demetrius: The very best at a beast, my lord, that e'er I saw.

Lysander: This lion is a very fox for his valor.°

Theseus: True; and a goose for his discretion.°

Demetrius: Not so, my lord; for his valor cannot carry his discretion, and the fox   220
     carries the goose.

Theseus: His discretion, I am sure, cannot carry his valor; for the goose carries not the
     fox. It is well. Leave it to his discretion, and let us listen to the moon.

Moon: This lanthorn° doth the hornèd moon present—

Demetrius: He should have worn the horns on his head.°   225

Theseus: He is no crescent,° and his horns are invisible within the circumference.

Moon: This lanthorn doth the hornèd moon present;

---

191 *Shafalus, Procrus* (Blunders for "Cephalus" and "Procris," also famous lovers.)   196 *'Tide* betide,
come   200 *willful* willing   200–201 *without warning* i.e., without warning the parents (Demetrius makes a
joke on the proverb "Walls have ears.")   203 *in this kind* of this sort.   *shadows* likenesses, representations
213 *lion fell* fierce lion (with a play on the idea of "lion skin")   218 *is . . . valor* i.e., his valor consists of
craftiness and discretion   219 *a goose . . . discretion* i.e., as discreet as a goose, that is, more foolish than
discreet   224 *lanthorn* (This original spelling, *lanthorn*, may suggest a play on the *horn* of which lanterns
were made, and also on a cuckold's horns; however, the spelling *lanthorn* is not used consistently for comic
effect in this play or elsewhere. At V, i, 133, for example, the word is *lantern* in the original.)   225 *on his
head* (as a sign of cuckoldry)   226 *crescent* a waxing moon

Myself the man i' the moon do seem to be.

Theseus: This is the greatest error of all the rest. The man should be put into the
    lanthorn. How is it else the man i' the moon?   230

Demetrius: He dares not come there for° the candle, for you see it is already in snuff.°

Hippolyta: I am aweary of this moon. Would he would change!

Theseus: It appears, by his small light of discretion, that he is in the wane; but yet, in
    courtesy, in all reason, we must stay the time.

Lysander: Proceed, Moon.   235

Moon: All that I have to say is to tell you that the lanthorn is the moon, I, the man i'
    the moon, this thornbush my thornbush, and this dog my dog.

Demetrius: Why, all these should be in the lanthorn, for all these are in the moon.
    But silence! Here comes Thisbe.

Enter Thisbe.

Thisbe: This is old Ninny's tomb. Where is my love?   240

Lion [roaring]: O!

Demetrius: Well roared, Lion.

                    [Thisbe runs off, dropping her mantle.]

Theseus: Well run, Thisbe.

Hippolyta: Well shone, Moon. Truly, the moon shines with a good grace.

                    [The Lion worries Thisbe's mantle.]

Theseus: Well moused,° Lion.   245

                    [Enter Pyramus; exit Lion.]

Demetrius: And then came Pyramus.

Lysander: And so the lion vanished.

Pyramus: Sweet Moon, I thank thee for thy sunny beams;
    I thank thee, Moon, for shining now so bright;
    For, by thy gracious, golden, glittering gleams,   250
    I trust to take of truest Thisbe sight.
        But stay, O spite!
        But mark, poor knight,
    What dreadful dole° is here?
        Eyes, do you see?   255
        How can it be?
    O dainty duck! O dear!
        Thy mantle good,
        What, stained with blood?
    Approach, ye Furies° fell!°   260
        O Fates,° come, come,
        Cut thread and thrum;°
    Quail,° crush, conclude, and quell!°

---

231 *for* because of, for fear of. *in snuff* (1) offended (2) in need of snuffing or trimming 245 *moused*
shaken, torn, bitten 254 *dole* grievous event 260 *Furies* avenging goddesses of Greek myth. *fell* fierce
261 *Fates* the three goddesses (Clotho, Lachesis, Atropos) of Greek myth who spun, drew, and cut the
thread of human life 262 *thread and thrum* i.e., everything—the good and bad alike; literally, the warp in
weaving and the loose end of the weft 263 *Quail* overpower. *quell* kill, destroy

Theseus: This passion, and the death of a dear friend, would go near to make a man
look sad.°   265
Hippolyta: Beshrew my heart, but I pity the man.
Pyramus: O, wherefore, Nature, didst thou lions frame?
    Since lion vile hath here deflowered my dear,
    Which is—no, no, which was—the fairest dame
    That lived, that loved, that liked, that looked with cheer.°   270
        Come, tears, confound,
        Out, sword, and wound
    The pap° of Pyramus;
        Ay, that left pap,
        Where heart doth hop.   [*He stabs himself.*] 275
    Thus die I, thus, thus, thus.
        Now am I dead,
        Now am I fled;
    My soul is in the sky.
        Tongue, lose thy light;   280
        Moon, take thy flight.   [*Exit Moonshine.*]
    Now die, die, die, die, die.   [*Pyramus dies.*]
Demetrius: No die, but an ace,° for him; for he is but one.°
Lysander: Less than an ace, man; for he is dead, he is nothing.
Theseus: With the help of a surgeon he might yet recover, and yet prove an ass.°   285
Hippolyta: How chance Moonshine is gone before Thisbe comes back and finds her
lover?
Theseus: She will find him by starlight.

    [*Enter Thisbe.*]

    Here she comes, and her passion ends the play.
Hippolyta: Methinks she should not use a long one for such a Pyramus. I hope she   290
will be brief.
Demetrius: A mote° will turn the balance, which Pyramus, which° Thisbe, is the
better: he for a man, God warrant us; she for a woman, God bless us.
Lysander: She hath spied him already with those sweet eyes.
Demetrius: And thus she means,° videlicet:°   295
Thisbe: Asleep, my love?
            What, dead, my dove?
        O Pyramus, arise!
            Speak, speak. Quite dumb?
            Dead, dead? A tomb   300
        Must cover thy sweet eyes.
            These lily lips,
            This cherry nose,

264–265 *This . . . sad* i.e., if one had other reason to grieve, one might be sad, but not from this absurd
portrayal of passion   270 *cheer* countenance   273 *pap* breast   283 *ace* the side of the die featuring the
single pip, or spot (The pun is on *die* as a singular of *dice;* Bottom's performance is not worth a whole *die*
but rather one single face of it, one small portion.).   *one* (1) an individual person (2) unique   285 *ass*
(with a pun on *ace*)   292 *mote* small particle.   *which . . . which* whether . . . or   295 *means* moans,
laments (with a pun on the meaning, "lodge a formal complaint").   *videlicet* to wit

These yellow cowslip cheeks,
    Are gone, are gone!   305
    Lovers, make moan.
His eyes were green as leeks.
    O Sisters Three,°
    Come, come to me,
With hands as pale as milk;   310
    Lay them in gore,
    Since you have shore°
With shears his thread of silk.
    Tongue, not a word.
    Come, trusty sword,   315
Come, blade, my breast imbrue!°   *[She stabs herself.]*
    And farewell, friends.
    Thus Thisbe ends.
    Adieu, adieu, adieu.   *[She dies.]*

Theseus: Moonshine and Lion are left to bury the dead.   320
Demetrius: Ay, and Wall too.
Bottom [starting up, as Flute does also]: No, I assure you, the wall is down that parted their fathers. Will it please you to see the epilogue, or to hear a Bergomask dance° between two of our company?

    [The other players enter.]

Theseus: No epilogue, I pray you; for your play needs no excuse. Never excuse; for 325
when the players are all dead, there need none to be blamed. Marry, if he that
writ it had played Pyramus and hanged himself in Thisbe's garter, it would have
been a fine tragedy; and so it is, truly, and very notably discharged. But, come,
your Bergomask. Let your epilogue alone.   *[A dance.]*
The iron tongue° of midnight hath told° twelve.   330
Lovers, to bed, 'tis almost fairy time.
I fear we shall outsleep the coming morn
As much as we this night have overwatched.°
This palpable-gross° play hath well beguiled
The heavy° gait of night. Sweet friends, to bed.   335
A fortnight hold we this solemnity,
In nightly revels and new jollity.   *Exeunt.*

    Enter Puck [carrying a broom].

Puck: Now the hungry lion roars,
               And the wolf behowls the moon,
          Whilst the heavy° plowman snores,   340
               All with weary task fordone.°
          Now the wasted brands° do glow,
               Whilst the screech owl, screeching loud,

---

308 *Sisters Three* the Fates   312 *shore* shorn   316 *imbrue* stain with blood   323 *Bergomask dance* a rustic dance named from Bergamo, a province in the state of Venice   330 *iron tongue* i.e., of a bell. *told* counted, struck ("tolled")   333 *overwatched* stayed up too late   334 *palpable-gross* palpably gross, obviously crude   335 *heavy* drowsy, dull   340 *heavy* tired   341 *fordone* exhausted   342 *wasted brands* burned-out logs

                Puts the wretch that lies in woe
                    In remembrance of a shroud.   345
                Now it is the time of night
                    That the graves, all gaping wide,
                Every one lets forth his sprite,°
                    In the church-way paths to glide.
                And we fairies, that do run   350
                    By the triple Hecate's° team
                From the presence of the sun,
                    Following darkness like a dream,
                Now are frolic.° Not a mouse
                Shall disturb this hallowed house.   355
                I am sent with broom before,
                To sweep the dust behind° the door.

        Enter [Oberon and Titania,] King and Queen of Fairies, with all their train.

Oberon: Through the house give glimmering light,
                    By the dead and drowsy fire;
                Every elf and fairy sprite   360
                    Hop as light as bird from brier;
                And this ditty, after me,
                Sing, and dance it trippingly.
Titania: First, rehearse° your song by rote,
                To each word a warbling note.   365
                Hand in hand, with fairy grace,
                Will we sing, and bless this place.

                                                        [Song and dance.]
Oberon: Now, until the break of day,
                Through this house each fairy stray.
                To the best bride-bed will we,   370
                Which by us shall blessèd be;
                And the issue there create°
                Ever shall be fortunate.
                So shall all the couples three
                Ever true in loving be;   375
                And the blots of Nature's hand
                Shall not in their issue stand;
                Never mole, harelip, nor scar,
                Nor mark prodigious,° such as are
                Despisèd in nativity,   380
                Shall upon their children be.
                With this field dew consecrate°

---

348 *Every . . . sprite* every grave lets forth its ghost   351 *triple Hecate's* (Hecate ruled in three capacities: as
Luna or Cynthia in heaven, as Diana on earth, and as Proserpina in hell.)   354 *frolic* merry   357 *behind*
from behind, or else like sweeping the dirt under the carpet. (Robin Goodfellow was a household spirit
who helped good housemaids and punished lazy ones, but he could, of course, be mischievous.)   364 *rehearse*
recite   372 *create* created   379 *prodigious* monstrous, unnatural   382 *consecrate* consecrated

"If we shadows have offended, / Think but this, and all is mended"
(V, i, 390–391).

> Every fairy take his gait,°
> And each several° chamber bless,
> Through this palace, with sweet peace;   385
> And the owner of it blest
> Ever shall in safety rest.
> Trip away; make no stay;
> Meet me all by break of day.

Exeunt [Oberon, Titania, and train].

Puck [*to the audience*]: If we shadows have offended,   390
>   Think but this, and all is mended,
>   That you have but slumbered here°

---

383 *take his gait* go his way   384 *several* separate   392 *That . . . here* i.e., that it is a "midsummer night's dream"

While these visions did appear.
And this weak and idle theme,
No more yielding but a dream,°   395
Gentles, do not reprehend.
If you pardon, we will mend.°
And, as I am an honest Puck,
If we have unearnèd luck
Now to scape the serpent's tongue,°   400
We will make amends ere long;
Else the Puck a liar call.
So, good night unto you all.
Give me your hands,° if we be friends,
And Robin shall restore amends.°   [*Exit.*] 405

Questions

1. Describe the relationship between King Theseus and Queen Hippolyta in the opening scene. How did they meet? Does their imminent marriage promise to be happy?
2. Describe the personality of each young aristocratic lover. How does Shakespeare differentiate them?
3. Characterize Nick Bottom. What aspects of his personality and behavior make him comic?
4. In what ways does Shakespeare differentiate his rustic tradesmen from the aristocrats?
5. Are the supernatural lovers, Oberon and Titania, characterized differently from their mortal counterparts? How are they similar to the aristocratic lovers and how are they different from them?
6. In what ways is Puck the unifying character of the play? How do his actions touch on every plot and subplot?
7. The main plot of *A Midsummer Night's Dream* concludes by the end of Act IV. What purpose does the final act serve in the play? Could it be omitted without significant loss?

395 *No . . . but* yielding no more than   397 *mend* improve   400 *serpent's tongue* i.e., hissing   404 *Give . . . hands* applaud   405 *restore amends* give satisfaction in return

CRITICS ON SHAKESPEARE

Oberon and Titania in the Ninagawa Company's 1996 production of *A Midsummer Night's Dream.*

Anthony Burgess (1917–1993)

An Asian Culture Looks at Shakespeare   1982

Is translation possible? I first found myself asking this question in the Far East, when I was given the task of translating T. S. Eliot's *The Waste Land* into Indonesian. The difficulties began with the first line: "April is the cruellest month . . ." This I rendered as *"Bulan Abril ia-lah bulan yang dzalim sa-kali . . ."* I had to take *dzalim* from Arabic, since Indonesian did not, at that time, seem to possess a word for *cruel.* The term was accepted, but not the notion that a month, as opposed to a person or institution, could be cruel. Moreover, even if a month could be cruel, how—in the tropics where all the months are the same and the concepts of spring and winter do not exist—can one month be crueller than another? When I came to *forgetful snow*—rendered as *thalji berlupa*—I had to borrow a highly poetical word from the Persian, acceptable as a useful descriptive device for the brown skin of the beloved but not known in terms of a climatic reality. And, again, how could this inanimate substance possess the faculty of forgetting? I gave up the task as hopeless. Evidently the imagery of *The Waste Land* does not relate to a universal experience but applies only to the northern hemisphere, with its temperate climate and tradition of spring and fertility rituals.

As a teacher in Malaysia, I had to consider with a mixed group of Malay, Chinese, Indian, and Eurasian students, seasoned with the odd Buginese, Achinese, and Japanese, a piece of representative postwar British fiction. Although the setting of the book is West Africa, I felt that its story was of universal import. It was a novel by Graham Greene called *The Heart of the Matter*—a tragic story about a police officer named Scobie who is a Catholic convert. He is in love with his wife but falls in love with another woman, discovers that he cannot repent of this adultery, makes a sacrilegious communion so that his very Catholic wife will not suspect that a love affair is in progress, then commits suicide in despair, trusting that God will thrust him into the outer darkness and be no longer agonized by the exploits of sinning Scobie. To us this is a tragic situation. To my Muslim students it was extremely funny. One girl said: "Why cannot this Mr. Scobie become a Muslim? Then he can have four wives and there is no problem."

The only author who seemed to have the quality of universal appeal in Malaysia was William Shakespeare. Despite the problems of translating him, there is always an intelligible residue. I remember seeing in a Borneo kampong the film of *Richard III* made by Laurence Olivier, and the illiterate tribe which surrounded me was most appreciative. They knew nothing here of literary history and nothing of the great world outside this jungle clearing. They took this film about medieval conspiracy and tyranny to be a kind of newsreel representation of contemporary England. They approved the medieval costumes because they resembled their own ceremonial dress. This story of the assassination of innocents, including children, Machiavellian massacre, and the eventual defeat of a tyrant was typical of their own history, even their contemporary experience, and they accepted Shakespeare as a great poet. Eliot would not have registered with them at all. Translation is not a matter of words only; it is a matter of making intelligible a whole culture. Evidently the Elizabethan culture was still primitive enough to survive transportation over much time and space.

From spoken remarks on the "Importance of Translation"

W. H. Auden (1907–1973)

Iago as a Triumphant Villain   1962

Any consideration of the *Tragedy of Othello* must be primarily occupied, not with its official hero but with its villain. I cannot think of any other play in which only one character performs personal actions—all the *deeds* are Iago's—and all the others without exception only exhibit behavior. In marrying each other, Othello and Desdemona have performed a deed, but this took place before the play begins. Nor can I think of another play in which the villain is so completely triumphant: everything Iago sets out to do, he accomplishes—(among his goals, I include his self-destruction). Even Cassio, who survives, is maimed for life.

If *Othello* is a tragedy—and one certainly cannot call it a comedy—it is tragic in a peculiar way. In most tragedies the fall of the hero from glory to misery and death is the work, either of the gods, or of his own freely chosen acts, or, more commonly, a mixture of both. But the fall of Othello is the work of another human being; nothing he says or does originates with himself. In consequence we feel pity for him but no respect; our aesthetic respect is reserved for Iago.

Iago is a wicked man. The wicked man, the stage villain, as a subject of serious dramatic interest does not, so far as I know, appear in the drama of western Europe before the Elizabethans. In the mystery plays, the wicked characters, like Satan or Herod, are treated comically, but the theme of the triumphant villain cannot be treated comically because the suffering he inflicts is real.

From "The Joker in the Pack"

Maud Bodkin (1875–1967)

Lucifer in Shakespeare's *Othello*   1934

If we attempt to define the devil in psychological terms, regarding him as an archetype, a persistent or recurrent mode of apprehension, we may say that the devil is our tendency to represent in personal form the forces within and without us that threaten our supreme values. When Othello finds those values of confident love, of honor, and pride in soldiership, that made up his purposeful life, falling into ruin, his sense of the devil in all around him becomes acute. Desdemona has become "a fair devil"; he feels "a young and sweating devil" in her hand. The cry "O devil" breaks out among his incoherent words of raving. When Iago's falsehoods are disclosed, and Othello at last, too late, wrenches himself free from the spell of Iago's power over him, his sense of the devil incarnate in Iago's shape before him becomes overwhelming. If those who tell of the devil have failed to describe Iago, they have lied:

I look down towards his feet; but that's a fable.
If that thou be'st a devil, I cannot kill thee.

We also, watching or reading the play, experience the archetype. Intellectually aware, as we reflect, of natural forces, within a man himself as well as in society around, that betray or shatter his ideals, we yet feel these forces aptly symbolized for the imagination by such a figure as Iago—a being though personal yet hardly human, concentrated wholly on the hunting to destruction of its destined prey, the proud figure of the hero.

From *Archetypal Patterns in Poetry*

Virginia Mason Vaughan (b. 1947)

Black and White in *Othello*   1994

If virtue no delighted beauty lack,
Your son-in-law is far more fair than black.
—*Othello* (1.3.290–291)

Black/white oppositions permeate *Othello*. Throughout the play, Shakespeare exploits a discourse of racial difference that by 1604 had become ingrained in the English psyche. From Iago's initial racial epithets at Brabantio's window ("old black ram," "barbary horse") to Emilia's cries of outrage in the final scene ("ignorant as dirt"), Shakespeare shows that the union of a white Venetian maiden and a black Moorish general is from at least one perspective emphatically unnatural. The union is of course a central fact of the play, and to some commentators, the spectacle of the pale-skinned woman caught in Othello's black arms has indeed seemed monstrous. Yet that spectacle is a major source of *Othello*'s emotional power. From Shakespeare's day to the present, the sight has titillated and terrified predominantly white audiences.

The effect of *Othello* depends, in other words, on the essential fact of the hero's darkness, the visual signifier of his Otherness. To Shakespeare's original audience, this chromatic sign was probably dark black, although there were other signifiers as well. Roderigo describes the Moor as having "thick lips," a term many sixteenth-century explorers employed in their descriptions of Africans. But, as historian Winthrop Jordan notes, by the late sixteenth century, "Blackness became so generally associated with Africa that every African seemed a black man[,] . . . the terms *Moor* and *Negro* used almost interchangeably." "Moor" became, G. K. Hunter observes, "a word for 'people not like us,' so signaled by color." Richard Burbage's Othello was probably black. But in any production, whether he appears as a tawny Moor (as nineteenth-century actors preferred) or as a black man of African descent, Othello bears the visual signs of his Otherness, a difference that the play's language insists can never be eradicated.

From Othello: A Contextual History

A. C. Bradley (1851–1935)

Hamlet's Melancholy

1903

That Hamlet was not far from insanity is very probable. His adoption of the pretence of madness may well have been due in part to fear of the reality; to an instinct of self-preservation, a fore-feeling that the pretence would enable him to give some utterance to the load that pressed on his heart and brain, and a fear that he would be unable altogether to repress such utterance. And if the pathologist calls his state melancholia, and even proceeds to determine its species, I see nothing to object to in that; I am grateful to him for emphasizing the fact that Hamlet's melancholy was no mere common depression of spirits; and I have no doubt that many readers of the play would understand it better if they read an account of melancholia in a work on mental diseases. If we like to use the word "disease" loosely, Hamlet's condition may truly be called diseased. No exertion of will could have dispelled it. Even if he had been able at once to do the bidding of the Ghost he would doubtless have still remained for some time under the cloud. It would be absurdly unjust to call *Hamlet* a study of melancholy, but it contains such a study.

But this melancholy is something very different from insanity, in anything like the usual meaning of that word. No doubt it might develop into insanity. The longing for death might become an irresistible impulse to self-destruction; the disorder of feeling and will might extend to sense and intellect; delusions might arise; and the man might become, as we say, incapable and irresponsible. But Hamlet's melancholy is some way from this condition. It is a totally different thing from the madness which he feigns; and he never, when alone or in company with Horatio alone, exhibits the signs of that madness. Nor is the dramatic use of this melancholy, again, open to the objections which would justly be made to the portrayal of an insanity which brought the hero to a tragic end. The man who suffers as Hamlet suffers—and thousands go about their business suffering thus in greater or less degree—is considered irresponsible neither by other people nor by himself: he is only too keenly conscious of his responsibility. He is therefore, so far, quite capable of being a tragic agent, which an insane person, at any rate according to Shakespeare's practice, is not. And, finally, Hamlet's state is not one which a healthy mind is unable sufficiently to imagine. It is probably not further from average experience, nor more difficult to realize, than the great tragic passions of Othello, Antony or Macbeth.

Let me try to show now, briefly, how much this melancholy accounts for.

It accounts for the main fact, Hamlet's inaction. For the *immediate* cause of that is simply that his habitual feeling is one of disgust at life and everything in it, himself included—a disgust which varies in intensity, rising at times into a longing for death, sinking often into weary apathy, but is never dispelled for more than brief intervals. Such a state of feeling is inevitably adverse to *any* kind of decided action; the body is inert, the mind indifferent or worse; its response is, "it does not matter," "it is not worth while," "it is no good." And the action required of Hamlet is very exceptional. It is violent, dangerous, difficult to accomplish perfectly, on one side repulsive to a man of honor and sensitive feeling, on another side involved in a certain mystery (here come in thus, in their subordinate place, various causes of inaction assigned by various theories). These obstacles would not suffice to prevent Hamlet from acting, if his state were normal; and against them there operate, even in his morbid state, healthy and positive feelings, love of his father, loathing of his uncle, desire of revenge, desire to do duty. But the retarding motives acquire an unnatural strength because they have an ally in something far stronger than themselves, the melancholic disgust and apathy; while the healthy motives, emerging with difficulty from the central mass of diseased feeling, rapidly sink back into it and "lose the name of action."

From *Shakespearean Tragedy*

Rebecca West (1892–1983)

Hamlet and Ophelia   1958

There is no more bizarre aspect of the misreading of Hamlet's character than the assumption that his relations with Ophelia were innocent and that Ophelia was a correct and timid virgin of exquisite sensibilities. . . . She was not a chaste young woman. That is shown by her tolerance of Hamlet's obscene conversations, which cannot be explained as consistent with the custom of the time. If that were the reason for it, all the men and women in Shakespeare's plays, Romeo and Juliet, Beatrice and Benedick, Miranda and Ferdinand, Antony and Cleopatra, would have talked obscenely together, which is not the case. "The marriage of true minds" would hardly, even in the most candid age, have expressed itself by this ugly chatter, which Wilson Knight has so justly described as governed by "infra-sexual neurosis." The truth is that Ophelia was a disreputable young woman: not scandalously so, but still disreputable. She was foredoomed to it by her father, whom it is a mistake to regard as a simple platitudinarian. Shakespeare, like all major writers, was never afraid of a good platitude, and he would certainly never have given time to deriding a character because his only attribute was a habit of stating the obvious. Polonius is interesting because he was a cunning old intriguer who, like an iceberg, only showed one-eighth of himself above the surface. The innocuous sort of worldly wisdom that rolled off his tongue in butter balls was a very small part of what he knew. It has been insufficiently noted that Shakespeare would never have held up the action in order that Polonius should give his son advice as to how to conduct himself abroad, unless the scene helped him to develop his theme. But "This above all: to thine own self be true; / And it must follow, as the night the day, / Thou canst not then be false to any man" (1.3.78–80), has considerable contrapuntal value when it is spoken by an old gentleman who is presently going to instruct a servant to spy on his son, and to profess great anxiety about his daughter's morals, when plainly he needed to send her away into the country if he really wanted her to retain any.

There is no mistaking the disingenuousness of his dealings with his daughter. When Ophelia comes to him with her tale of how Hamlet had come to her as she was sewing in her chamber, "with his doublet all unbraced," and had looked madly on her, Polonius eagerly interprets this as "the very ecstasy of love," and asks her "What, have you given him any hard words of late?" . . . The girl is not to be kept out of harm's way. She is a card that can be played to take several sorts of tricks. She might be Hamlet's mistress; but she might be more honored for resistance. And if Hamlet was himself an enemy of the King, and an entanglement with him had ceased to be a means of winning favor, then she can give a spy's report on him to Claudius. Surely Ophelia is one of the few authentic portraits of that army of not virgin martyrs, the poor little girls who were sacrificed to family ambition in the days when a court was a cat's cradle of conspiracies. Man's persuasion that his honor depends on the chastity of his women folk has always been liable to waste away and perish within sight of a throne. Particularly where monarchy had grown from a yeasty mass of feudalism, few families found themselves able to resist the temptation to hawk any young beauty in their brood, if it seemed likely that she might catch the eye of the king or any man close to the king. Unfortunately the king's true favorite was usually not a woman but an ideology. If royal approval was withdrawn from the religious or political faith held by the family which had hawked the girl, she was as apt to suffer fatality as any of her kinsmen. The axe has never known chivalry. Shakespeare, writing this play only three reigns from Henry the Eighth, had heard of such outrages on half-grown girls from the lips of those who had seen the final bloodletting.

From *The Court and the Castle*

Jan Kott (1914–2001)

Producing *Hamlet*   1964

There are many subjects in *Hamlet*. There is politics, force opposed to morality; there is discussion of the divergence between theory and practice, of the ultimate purpose of life; there is tragedy of love, as well as family drama; political, eschatological and metaphysical problems are considered. There is everything you want, including deep psychological analysis, a bloody story, a duel, and general slaughter. One can select at will. But one must know what one selects, and why.

The *Hamlet* produced in Cracow a few weeks after the XXth Congress of the Soviet Communist Party lasted exactly three hours.° It was light and clear, tense and sharp, modern and consistent, limited to one issue only. It was a political drama par

The Hamlet *produced . . . hours:* The production of *Hamlet* Kott discusses was staged in Cracow, Poland, in 1956 at the height of Soviet repression in Eastern Europe.

excellence. "Something is rotten in the state of Denmark" was the first chord of *Hamlet*'s new meaning. And then the dead sound of the words "Denmark's a prison," three times repeated. Finally the magnificent churchyard scene, with the gravediggers' dialogue rid of metaphysics, brutal and unequivocal. Gravediggers know for whom they dig graves. "The gallows is built stronger than the church," they say.

"Watch" and "enquire" were the words most commonly heard from the stage. In this performance everybody, without exception, was being constantly watched. Polonius, minister to the royal murderer, sends a man to France even after his own son. Was Shakespeare not a genius for our time? Let us listen to the minister:

> Inquire me first what Danskers are in Paris,
> And how, and who, what means, and where they keep,
> What company, at what expense; and finding
> By this encompassment and drift of question
> That they do know my son, come you more nearer
> Than your particular demands will touch it.
>
> (2.1.7–12)

At Elsinore castle someone is hidden behind every curtain. The good minister does not even trust the Queen. Let us listen to him again:

> 'Tis meet that some more audience than a mother,
> Since nature makes them partial, should o'erhear
> The speech, of vantage.
>
> (3.3.31–33)

Everything at Elsinore has been corroded by fear: marriage, love and friendship. Shakespeare, indeed, must have experienced terrible things at the time of Essex's plot and execution, since he came to learn so well the working of the Grand Mechanism. Let us listen to the King talking to Hamlet's young friends:

> . . . I entreat you both
> That, being of so young days brought up with him,
> And since so neighbour'd to his youth and haviour,
> That you vouchsafe your rest here in our court
> Some little time; so by your companies
> To draw him on to pleasures, and to gather
> So much as from occasion you may glean,
> Whether aught to us unknown afflicts him thus
> That, open'd, lies within our remedy.
>
> (2.2.10–18)

The murderous uncle keeps a constant watchful eye on Hamlet. Why does he not want him to leave Denmark? His presence at court is inconvenient, reminding everybody of what they would like to forget. Perhaps he suspects something? Would it not be better not to issue him a passport and keep him at hand? Or does the King wish to get rid of Hamlet as soon as possible, but give way to the Queen, who wants to have her son near her? And the Queen? What does she think about it all? Does she feel guilty? What does the Queen know? She has been through passion, murder and silence. She had to suppress everything inside her. One can sense a volcano under her superficial poise.

Ophelia, too, has been drawn into the big game. They listen in to her conversations, ask questions, read her letters. It is true that she gives them up herself. She is at the same time part of the Mechanism, and its victim. Politics hangs here over every feeling, and there is no getting away from it. All the characters are poisoned by it. The only subject of their conversations is politics. It is a kind of madness.

Hamlet loves Ophelia. But he knows he is being watched; moreover—he has more important matters to attend to. Love is gradually fading away. There is no room for it in this world. Hamlet's dramatic cry: "Get thee to a nunnery!" is addressed not to Ophelia alone, but also to those who are overhearing the two lovers. It is to confirm their impression of his alleged madness. But for Hamlet and for Ophelia it means that in the world where murder holds sway, there is no room for love.

From *Shakespeare: Our Contemporary*

Joel Wingard (b. 1946)

Reader-Response Issues in *Hamlet*   1996

Hamlet is a long play, one of Shakespeare's longest in terms of lines and scenes (though all his plays are five acts). Like any play on the page and like Shakespeare's especially, it is riddled with gaps. Many of these gaps . . . involve the reader's knowing or unknowing. As you read on through the text, you will fill in some of these gaps easily enough as you find out more through the characters' words and actions. Others will remain open; some that have been identified over the years are still open and always will be, even if one strong reading or another has proposed a way to close them.

One consequence of a reader's identification of gaps in the text is the opportunity to apply consistency building as a reading strategy. As you read, or as you watch a production, you may find yourself trying to explain in some kind of logical or consistent terms why Hamlet does what he does, or why he doesn't do what he's supposed to do—get revenge on Claudius—right away. Indeed the question of Hamlet's "delay" or why he delays exacting revenge has been a significant gap in the text for many readers for the past couple of hundred years, a gap filled in differently by various readers. Many readers also have pondered the question of Hamlet's "madness." After he hears his father's ghost's story in Act 1, Hamlet tells his friend Horatio that he will "put an antic disposition on" in order to disguise his inquiry into what the ghost has told him; in other words, he'll act crazy. But over the years, readers have debated the extent to which Hamlet is in control of his insanity act or whether he goes at least temporarily insane as he plays it out. A reader's decision that Hamlet really *is* mad, for instance, based on the way he behaves in Acts 2–4 and on what other characters say about him, is an instance of consistency building to fill in this gap.

The play affords many opportunities for you to use this reading strategy, but you should also remember before you start to read that consistency building has a complementary reading strategy: what the critic Wolfgang Iser calls "wandering viewpoint." This strategy isn't exactly what it sounds like, so it would probably help if you think of it in contrast to consistency building. If consistency building is filling in gaps or closing down interpretive options as you read (Hamlet delays because he goes insane, for instance), adopting a wandering viewpoint means keeping those gaps or options open, not making up your mind as to, for instance, what makes Hamlet tick.

In an academic context, you are used to engaging in consistency building as you read, even if the term itself is new to you, and you are encouraged to practice it for the sake of writing about literature in papers where you have to argue an interpretation. Reading to come up with a consistent interpretation of a complex character or text seems to be the "natural" way of doing things, but of course it is really a learned procedure. If you find *Hamlet* difficult, apart from the language, it may be because you have trouble building a consistent interpretation with such a contradictory character in such a complex play. So it may just take some of that pressure off you to remember that consistency building is an *optional* reading strategy and that you can also read with a wandering viewpoint and leave your interpretive options open.

From "Reading and Responding: A Shakespearean Tragedy"

Clare Asquith

Shakespeare's Language as a Hidden Political Code   2005

Shakespeare was the one sixteenth-century writer who, it appears, never fell foul of the authorities. Yet in a strangely insistent passage, the editors of the First Folio of his work, published in 1623, urge us to look beneath the surface of the great universal plays to something hidden below. Though they are sure that his wit can "no more lie hid than it could be lost," they press us to "Read him therefore, and again, and again." We must seek help from his friends if we miss his "hidden wit," and we should act as guides to others if we find it. The insistence on readers acting as guides is striking and unusual.

• • •

Whatever its impact at the time, Shakespeare's cautious artistry was so great that his hidden language remained undetectable to succeeding generations that accepted the official version of England's Reformation. Yet the subterfuge was essential if he and his work were to survive. He was writing in a climate more dangerous and oppressive than anything experienced by his predecessors. By the 1580s, the censorship laws, regularly tightened under Elizabeth, were strictly enforced. Yet he could not remain silent. He was driven to write by a different fear, to which he returns throughout his work. This was the growing concern, shared by many contemporaries, that the true history of the age would never be told. . . . Shakespeare not only needed to write; he needed to find a new method of writing, one capable of recording the whole unhappy story of the country's political and spiritual collapse against the background of a regime for whom the slightest topical reference was justification enough to imprison a playwright.

• • •

In these dramas, there would be no room for asides or explanations. Instead, Shakespeare worked out a set of simple markers, basic call-signs that would alert his audience to the entry point they needed to access the hidden story. Unlike Erasmus, Sidney and Donne, who were poets and essayists, he was a seasoned actor addressing restless spectators, so he kept his signals simple and consistent. But he was also one of a brotherhood of dissident writers, and to them his pointers would have been as readily even wittily—recognizable as they became baffling to later readers.

The master key to the hidden level is so simple that it is easy to miss. It takes the form of twin terms that identify the polar opposites in Elizabeth's England. They are not Shakespeare's only terms, and he uses them sparingly, but with pinpoint accuracy. They are the terms "high" and "fair," which always indicate Catholicism, and "low" and "dark," which always suggest Protestantism. Shakespeare's treatment of these words is sufficiently remarkable for critics to have wondered whether he was writing for a tall blond actor and a short dark one—but the theory is untenable. Shakespeare was not a dramatist who would have deliberately created casting problems, and the references span a ten-year period.

The opposition of high and low, representing the two opposing sides of the Reformation, was commonplace at the time. The modern Christian distinction between high and low church goes back to pre-Reformation days when High Mass, high day, and high altars involved full liturgical ceremony—Low Mass and low altars were for every day.

The opposition of dark and fair was equally recognizable. The glittering, skin-deep attractions of the scarlet woman were constantly under fire from Protestant plays, sermons, and literature: the sober reformers wore plain black, and the new Prayer Book was shorn of illuminated initials and, as far as possible, red print.

• • •

His markers are morally neutral. Fair, tall characters can be corrupt, while dark, low ones are often noble—the words merely identify the religious allegiance of one or two characters, providing a key compass-bearing from which alert readers and spectators can work out the rest of the shadowed plot. In the process an enjoyable trail of punning wordplay emerges, deepening and confirming the discovery.

From *Shadowplay: The Hidden Beliefs and Coded Politics of William Shakespeare*

Germaine Greer (b. 1939)

Shakespeare's "Honest Mirth" 1986

The Puritan attack on the acting of plays rested on two assumptions, the first that the imitation of human speech and actions was lying and taught dissimulation, and the second that the dressing of men as women was evil in itself. Shakespeare mocks such ethical conundra in divers ways. In *Love's Labor's Lost* and *A Midsummer Night's Dream*, he goes behind the scenes to show the mounting of theatrical presentations, and deliberately poises the simplicity of the performers against the sophistication of the audience. Theseus's master of the revels warns the noble company (in *A Midsummer Night's Dream*) that they will not enjoy the "tedious brief scene of young Pyramus / And his love Thisbe":

> It is not for you. I have heard it over,
> And it is nothing, nothing in the world;
> Unless you can find sport in their intents,
> Extremely stretched and conned with cruel pain
> To do you service.

> (5.1.77–81)

Theseus's description of the importance of the active participation of the audience in creating and maintaining the illusion is a basic tenet of the Shakespearian aesthetic, to which he was to cling despite the gibes of more arrogant poets until the end of his writing career.

> The best in this kind are but shadows; and the worst are no worse, if imagination amend them.

> (5.1.203–204)

The frantic efforts of the players to reassure their audience that there is no need to be afraid of Snug dressed up as a lion are seen in this context as ridiculous not only because the players are not so expert that they could deceive anybody, but because audiences know that what is being presented is invented. Indeed, the action is taken from a classical source that would be known to all literate people either from their school Latin or from Golding's translation, namely the *Metamorphoses* of Ovid.

From Shakespeare

Linda Bamber (b. 1945)

Female Power in *A Midsummer Night's Dream* 1982

The best example of the relationship between male dominance and the status quo comes in *A Midsummer Night's Dream*, which begins with a rebellion of the feminine against the power of masculine authority. Hermia refuses the man both Egeus and Theseus order her to marry; her refusal sends us off into the forest, beyond the power of the father and the masculine state. Once in the forest, of course, we find the social situation metaphorically repeated in this world of imagination and nature. The fairy king, Oberon, rules the forest. His rule, too, is troubled by the rebellion of the feminine. Titania has refused to give him her page, the child of a human friend who died in childbirth. But by the end of the story Titania is conquered, the child relinquished, and order restored. Even here the comic upheavals, whether we see them as May games or bad dreams, are associated with an uprising of women. David P. Young, in *Something of Great Constancy*, has pointed out how firmly this play connects order with masculine dominance and the disruption of order with the rebellion of the feminine:

> It is appropriate that Theseus, as representative of daylight and right reason, should have subdued his bride-to-be to the rule of his masculine will. That is the natural order of things. It is equally appropriate that Oberon, as king of darkness and fantasy, should have lost control of his wife, and that the corresponding natural disorder described by Titania should ensue.

The natural order, the status quo, is for men to rule women. When they fail to do so, we have the exceptional situation, the festive, disruptive, disorderly moment of comedy.

• • •

Where are we to bestow our sympathies? On the forces that make for the disruption of the status quo and therefore for the plot? Or on the force that asserts itself against the disruption and reestablishes a workable social order? Of course we cannot choose. We can only say that in comedy we owe our holiday to such forces as the tendency of the feminine to rebel, whereas to the successful reassertion of masculine power we owe our everyday order. Shakespearean comedy endorses both sides. Holiday is, of course, the subject and the analogue of each play; but the plays always end in a return to everyday life. The optimistic reading of Shakespearean comedy says that everyday life is clarified and enriched by our holiday from it; according to the pessimistic reading the temporary subversion of the social order has revealed how much that order excludes, how high a price we pay for it. But whether our return to everyday life is a comfortable one or not, the return itself is the inevitable conclusion to the journey out.

From Comic Women, Tragic Men

■ WRITING *effectively*

Ben Jonson on Writing (1573?–1637)

On His Friend and Rival William Shakespeare   1640

Ben Jonson

I remember the players have often mentioned it as an honor to Shakespeare, that in his writing (whatsoever he penned) he never blotted out a line. My answer hath been, "Would he had blotted a thousand," which they thought a malevolent speech. I had not told posterity this but for their ignorance who chose that circumstance to commend their friend by wherein he most faulted; and to justify mine own candor, for I loved the man, and do honor his memory on this side idolatry as much as any. He was, indeed, honest, and of an open and free nature; had an excellent phantasy, brave notions, and gentle expressions, wherein he flowed with that facility that sometimes it was necessary he should be stopped. "*Sufflaminandus erat,*"° as Augustus° said of Haterius.° His wit was in his own power; would the rule of it had been so, too! Many times he fell into those things, could not escape laughter, as when he said in the person of Caesar,° one speaking to him, "Caesar, thou dost me wrong." He replied, "Caesar did never wrong but with just cause"; and such like, which were ridiculous. But he redeemed his vices with his virtues. There was ever more in him to be praised than to be pardoned.

From Discoveries

UNDERSTANDING SHAKESPEARE

The basic problem a modern reader faces with Shakespeare is language. Shakespeare's English is now four hundred years old, and it differs in innumerable small ways from contemporary American English. Although Shakespeare's idiom may at first seem daunting, it is easily mastered if you make the effort. To grow comfortable with his language, you must immerse yourself in it. Fortunately, doing so isn't all that hard; you might even find it pleasurable.

Sufflaminandus erat: Latin for "He ought to have been plugged up."   *Augustus:* the first emperor of Rome (63 B.C.–14 A.D.)   *Haterius:* a very verbose orator of the Augustan age.   *Caesar:* Shakespeare's tragedy *Julius Caesar.* Jonson misremembers the quotation, which (in the First Folio) actually reads "Know, Caesar doth not wrong, nor without cause will he be satisfied." (III, i, 47)

- **Let your ears do the work.** There is no substitute for hearing Shakespeare's words in performance. After all, the plays were written to be seen, not to be read silently on the page. After reading the play, listen to or watch a recording of it. It sometimes helps to read along as you listen or watch, hitting the pause button as needed. If you can attend a live performance of any Shakespearean play, do so.

- **But read the text first.** Watching a production is never a full substitute for reading an assigned play. Many productions abridge the play, leaving passages out. Even more important, directors and actors choose a particular interpretation of a play, and their choices might skew your understanding of events and motivation if you are unfamiliar with the original itself.

- **Before you write a paper, read the play again.** The first time through an Elizabethan-era text, you will almost certainly miss many things. As you grow more familiar with Shakespeare's language, you will able to read it with greater comprehension. If you choose to write about a particular episode or character, carefully study the speeches and dialogue in question (and pay special attention to the footnotes) so that you understand each word.

- **Enjoy yourself.** From Beijing to Berlin, Buenos Aires to Oslo, Shakespeare is almost universally acknowledged as the world's greatest playwright, a master entertainer as well as a consummate artist.

CHECKLIST: Writing About Shakespeare

- ☐ Read closely. Work through passages with difficult language.
- ☐ Pay special attention to footnotes.
- ☐ Read the play more than once if necessary.
- ☐ Watch a DVD or listen to an audio recording after reading a play. Immerse yourself in Shakespeare's language until it becomes familiar.
- ☐ As you view or listen to a play, read along, or revisit the text afterward.
- ☐ Carefully study any speeches and dialogue you choose to write about.
- ☐ Be sure you understand each word of any passage you decide to discuss or quote.

WRITING ASSIGNMENT ON TRAGEDY

Select any tragedy found in the book (*Othello, Hamlet, Oedipus the King,* or *Antigonê*), and analyze it using Aristotle's definition of the form. Does the play measure up to Aristotle's requirements for a tragedy? In what ways does it meet the definition? In what ways does it depart from it? (Be sure to state clearly the Aristotelian rules by which drama is to be judged.)

Here is a paper written in response to this assignment by Janet Housden, a student of Melinda Barth at El Camino College.

SAMPLE STUDENT PAPER

Janet Housden

Professor Barth

English 201

3 November 2009

Othello: Tragedy or Soap Opera?

When we hear the word "tragedy," we usually think of either a terrible

real-life disaster, or a dark and serious drama filled with pain, suffering, and

loss that involves the downfall of a powerful person due to some character flaw

or error in judgment. William Shakespeare's *Othello* is such a drama. Set in

Venice and Cyprus during the Renaissance, the play tells the story of Othello, a

Moorish general in the Venetian army, who has just married Desdemona, the

daughter of a Venetian nobleman. Through the plotting of a jealous villain,

Iago, Othello is deceived into believing that Desdemona has been unfaithful to

him. He murders her in revenge, only to discover too late how he has been

tricked. Overcome by shame and grief, Othello kills himself.

Dealing as it does with jealousy, murder, and suicide, the play is

certainly dark, but is *Othello* a true tragedy? In the fourth century BC, the Greek

philosopher Aristotle proposed a formal definition of tragedy

(Kennedy 1161–62), which only partially fits *Othello*.

The first characteristic of tragedy identified by Aristotle is that the

protagonist is a person of outstanding quality and high social position. While

Othello is not of royal birth as are many tragic heroes and heroines, he does

occupy a sufficiently high position to satisfy this part of Aristotle's definition.

Although Othello is a foreigner and a soldier by trade, he has risen to the rank

of general and has married into a noble family, which is quite an

accomplishment for an outsider. Furthermore, Othello is generally liked and

respected by those around him. He is often described by others as being

"noble," "brave," and "valiant." By virtue of his high rank and the respect he

commands from others, Othello would appear to possess the high stature

commonly given to the tragic hero in order to make his eventual fall seem all

the more tragic.

First paragraph gives name of author and work

Key plot information avoids excessive retelling

Central question is raised

Thesis statement provides response

Topic sentence on Othello's social position

Essay systematically applies Aristotle's definition of tragedy to Othello

Housden 2

While Othello displays the nobility and high status commonly associated with the tragic hero, he also possesses another, less admirable characteristic, the flaw or character defect shared by all heroes of classical tragedy. In Othello's case, it is a stunning gullibility, combined with a violent temper that once awakened overcomes all reason. These flaws permit Othello to be easily deceived and manipulated by the villainous Iago and make him easy prey for the "green-eyed monster" (3.3.179).

Topic sentence on Othello's tragic flaw

It is because of this tragic flaw, according to Aristotle, that the hero is at least partially to blame for his own downfall. While Othello's "free and open nature, / That thinks men honest that but seem to be so" (1.3.376–77) is not a fault in itself, it does allow Iago to convince the Moor of his wife's infidelity without one shred of concrete evidence. Furthermore, once Othello has been convinced of Desdemona's guilt, he makes up his mind to take vengeance, and says that his "bloody thoughts with violent pace / Shall ne'er look back, ne'er ebb to humble love" (3.3.473–74). He thereby renders himself deaf to the voice of reason, and ignoring Desdemona's protestations of innocence, brutally murders her, only to discover too late that he has made a terrible mistake. Although he is goaded into his crime by Iago, who is a master at manipulating people, it is Othello's own character flaws that lead to his horrible misjudgment.

Quotes from play as evidence to support point

Topic sentence elaborates on idea raised in previous paragraphs

Aristotle's definition also states that the hero's misfortune is not wholly deserved, that the punishment he receives exceeds his crime. Although it is hard to sympathize with a man as cruel as Othello is to the innocent Desdemona, Othello pays an extremely high price for his sin of gullibility. Othello loses everything—his wife, his position, even his life. Even though it's partially his fault, Othello is not entirely to blame, for without Iago's interference it's highly unlikely that things would turn out as they do. Though it seems incredibly stupid on Othello's part, that a man who has travelled the world and commanded armies should be so easily deceived, there is little evidence that Othello has had much experience with civilian society, and although he is "declined / Into the vale of years" (3.3.281–82) Othello has apparently never been married before. By his own admission, "little of this great world can I speak / More than pertains to feats of broils and battle" (1.3.88–89). Furthermore, Othello has no reason to suspect that "honest Iago" is anything but his loyal friend and supporter.

Topic sentence on Othello's misfortune

Transitional words signal argument's direction

While it is understandable that Othello could be fooled into believing Desdemona unfaithful, the question remains whether his fate is deserved. In addition to his mistake of believing Iago's lies, Othello commits a more serious error: he lets himself be blinded by anger. Worse yet, in deciding to take vengeance, he also makes up his mind not be swayed from his course, even by his love for Desdemona. In fact, he refuses to listen to her at all, "lest her body and beauty unprovide my mind again" (4.1.186–87), therefore denying her the right to defend herself. Because of his rage and unfairness, perhaps Othello deserves his fate more than Aristotle's ideal tragic hero. Othello's punishment does exceed his crime, but just barely.

Topic sentence elaborates on Othello's misfortune

According to Aristotle, the tragic hero's fall gives the protagonist deeper understanding and self-awareness. Othello departs from Aristotle's model in that Othello apparently learns nothing from his mistakes. He never realizes that he is partly at fault. He sees himself only as an innocent victim and blames his misfortune on fate rather than accepting responsibility for his actions. To be sure, he realizes he has been tricked and deeply regrets his mistake, but he seems to feel that he was justified under the circumstances, "For naught I did in hate, but all in honor" (5.2.303). Othello sees himself not as someone whose bad judgment and worse temper have resulted in the death of an innocent party, but as one who has "loved not wisely but too well" (5.2.354). This failure to grasp the true nature of his error indicates that Othello hasn't learned his lesson.

Topic sentence on whether Othello learns from his mistakes

Neither accepting responsibility nor learning from his mistakes, Othello fails to fulfill yet another of Aristotle's requirements. Since the protagonist usually gains some understanding along with his defeat, classical tragedy conveys a sense of human greatness and of life's unrealized potentialities—a quality totally absent from *Othello*. Not only does Othello fail to learn from his mistakes, he never really realizes what those mistakes are, and it apparently never crosses his mind that things could have turned out any differently. "Who can control his fate?" Othello asks (5.2.274), and this defeatist attitude, combined with his failure to salvage any wisdom from his defeat, separates *Othello* from the tragedy as defined by Aristotle.

Topic sentence elaborating further on whether Othello learns from his errors

The last part of Aristotle's definition states that viewing the conclusion of a tragedy should result in catharsis for the audience, and that the audience should be left with a feeling of exaltation rather than depression. Unfortunately, the feeling we are left with after viewing *Othello* is neither catharsis nor exaltation but rather a feeling of horror, pity, and disgust at the senseless waste of human lives. The deaths of Desdemona and Othello, as well as

Topic sentence on catharsis

Housden 4

those of Emilia and Roderigo, serve no purpose whatsoever. They die not in the service of a great cause but because of lies, treachery, jealousy, and spite. Their deaths don't even benefit Iago, who is directly or indirectly responsible for all of them. No lesson is learned, no epiphany is reached, and the audience, instead of experiencing catharsis, is left with its negative feeling unresolved.

Since *Othello* only partially fits Aristotle's definition of tragedy, it is questionable whether or not it should be classified as one. Though it does involve a great man undone by a defect in his own character, the hero gains neither insight nor understanding from his defeat, and so there can be no inspiration or catharsis for the audience, as there would be in a "true" tragedy. *Othello* is tragic only in the everyday sense of the word, the way a plane crash or fire is tragic. At least in terms of Aristotle's classic definition, *Othello* ultimately comes across as more of a melodrama or soap opera than a tragedy.

Restatement of thesis

Conclusion

Housden 5

Work Cited

Kennedy, X. J., and Dana Gioia, eds. *Literature: An Introduction to Fiction, Poetry, Drama, and Writing.* 11th ed. New York: Longman, 2010. 1162–63. Print.

Shakespeare, William. *Othello, The Moor of Venice. Literature: An Introduction to Fiction, Poetry, Drama, and Writing.* Ed. X. J. Kennedy and Dana Gioia. 11th ed. New York: Longman, 2010. 1248–1348. Print.

MORE TOPICS FOR WRITING

1. Write a defense of Iago.

2. "Never was any play fraught, like this of *Othello*, with improbabilities," wrote Thomas Rymer in a famous attack (*A Short View of Tragedy*, 1692). Consider Rymer's objection to the play, either answering it or finding evidence to back it up.

3. Suppose yourself a casting director assigned to a film version of either *Othello or Hamlet*. What well-known actors would you cast in the principal roles? Write a report justifying your choices. Don't merely discuss the stars and their qualifications; discuss (with specific reference to the play) what Shakespeare appears to call for.

4. Emilia's long speech at the end of Act IV (iii, 83–102) has been called a Renaissance plea for women's rights. Do you agree? Write a brief, close analysis of this speech. How timely is it?

5. "The downfall of Oedipus is the work of the gods; the downfall of Othello is self-inflicted." Test this comment with reference to the two plays, and report your findings.

6. In what respects does *Hamlet* resemble a classical tragedy, such as *Oedipus the King*? In what ways is Shakespeare's play different? Is Hamlet, like Oedipus, driven to his death by some inexorable force (Fate, the gods, the nature of things)?

7. Write a defense of Hamlet's uncle, Claudius.

8. "Hamlet is a mentally unstable young man who is obsessed with his father's death. He is angry at his mother for remarrying so quickly. The Ghost is not real. It is only a projection of the Prince's deranged imagination." Write an essay to support or refute this argument. Use specific incidents in the play to back up your position.

9. Contrast the palace and the woods as settings in *A Midsummer Night's Dream*.

10. Explain the connection between the comic sketch presented by the rustic tradesmen on Pyramus and Thisbe and the events that occur elsewhere in the play.

38

THE MODERN THEATER

> *Speak of the moderns without contempt,*
> *and of the ancients without idolatry.*
>
> —LORD CHESTERFIELD

REALISM

The ancient art of the drama experienced a revival in the Renaissance and went through a number of changes over the next several centuries. The Elizabethan drama was marked by strong characterization, heightened and intense language, and crowded, sometimes sprawling plots. In the neoclassical period of the seventeenth and eighteenth centuries, greater emphasis was placed upon formality, decorum, and Aristotle's unities of time, place, and action. The early nineteenth century saw the rise of melodrama, with its florid dialogue, plots that relied heavily on often absurd coincidences, and crude stereotypes of good and evil characters. Through all these developments—from kings and generals to lords and ladies of high society to pure-hearted swashbucklers and craven villains—the one thing that seemed to remain constant was an absence of **realism**—the attempt to reproduce faithfully the surface appearance of life, especially that of ordinary people in everyday situations.

By the end of the nineteenth century, however, Realism had become the drama's dominant mode. The writer most responsible for that shift was the Norwegian playwright Henrik Ibsen. From *Pillars of Society* (1877) to *Hedda Gabler* (1890), he wrote a series of prose dramas in which realistically portrayed middle-class characters face conflicts in their lives and relationships. They are often called "problem plays" because of their engagement of social issues, such as women's place in society (*A Doll's House*) and inherited venereal disease (*Ghosts*). In actuality, the social problems in these plays serve as a context for Ibsen's real concern, an examination of the complexities of human personality and psychology, especially those aspects of our natures that are hidden or repressed because of society's expectations.

The attempt to use the theater to present the real lives of real people was taken even further by the Russian dramatist Anton Chekhov. In Chekhov's mature plays, the dialogue seems at times to meander and there appears to be little or no action. *The Cherry Orchard* (1904), his last and greatest play, presents a decayed aristocratic clan unable to deal with a threatened foreclosure on the family estate, despite advice from all quarters. The play has sparked debate for over a century: Is it a comedy or a tragedy? Are its characters foolish or sympathetic? Does it lament the passing of an old way of life or greet the dawn of a new age? The answer, of course, is *All of the above*—just like life itself.

Conventions of Realism

From Italian playhouses of the sixteenth century, the theater had inherited the **picture-frame stage**: a structure that holds the action within a **proscenium arch**, a gateway standing (as the word *proscenium* indicates) "in front of the scenery." This manner of constructing a playhouse in effect divided the actors from their audience; most commercial theaters even today are so constructed. But as the nineteenth century gave way to the twentieth, actors less often declaimed their passions in oratorical style in front of backdrops painted with waterfalls and volcanoes, while stationed exactly at the center of the stage as if to sing "duets meant to bring forth applause" (as Swedish playwright August Strindberg complained).

In the theater of Realism, a room was represented by a **box set**—three walls that joined in two corners and a ceiling that tilted as if seen in perspective—replacing drapery walls that had billowed and doors that had flapped, not slammed. Instead of posing at stage center and directly facing the audience to deliver key speeches, actors were instructed to speak from wherever the dramatic situation placed them, and now and then even to turn their backs upon the audience. They were to behave as if they were in a room with the fourth wall sliced away, unaware that they had an audience.

To encourage actors further to imitate reality, the influential director Constantin Stanislavsky of the Moscow Art Theater developed his famous system to help actors feel at home inside a playwright's characters. One of Stanislavsky's exercises was to have actors search their memories for personal experiences like those of the characters in the play; another was to have them act out things a character did *not* do in the play but might do in life. The system enabled Stanislavsky to bring authenticity to his productions of Chekhov's plays and of Maxim Gorky's *The Lower Depths* (1902), a play that showed the tenants of a sordid lodging house drinking themselves to death (and hanging themselves) in surroundings of realistic squalor. Stanislavsky's techniques are still used by stage and film actors today.

NATURALISM

Gorky's play is a masterpiece of **Naturalism**, a kind of realism in fiction and drama dealing with the more brutal or unpleasant aspects of reality. As codified by French novelist and playwright Émile Zola, who influenced Ibsen, Naturalism viewed a person as a creature whose acts are determined by heredity and environment; Zola urged writers to study their characters' behavior with the detachment of zoologists studying animals.

Another masterpiece of the naturalistic tradition is *The Hairy Ape* (1922) by the American playwright Eugene O'Neill. The title character is Yank, a brutish but good-natured engine-stoker on an ocean liner. After a rich young woman calls him a "filthy beast," he grows depressed and dislocated, trying and failing to find a comfortable place for himself in society. He ends up at the zoo, where he dies in a gorilla's embrace. (The play's enduring power was affirmed by a successful New York revival in 2006.) Universally regarded as the first true genius of the American theater, O'Neill greatly influenced several generations of American playwrights, including Arthur Miller. In many of his plays, Miller portrayed working-class characters whose lives are shaped and constrained by powerful social and cultural forces. Miller was also influenced by Ibsen, whose *Enemy of the People* he adapted for the Broadway stage in 1950.

SYMBOLISM AND EXPRESSIONISM

The ascendance of Realism had liberated drama from some outworn styles and opened rich new areas of artistic exploration, but when it became the dominant tradition, some writers began to feel confined by its themes and theatrical conventions, and new forms of drama emerged. One of these was the **Symbolist movement** in the French theater, most influentially expressed by Belgian playwright Maurice Maeterlinck, whose work conjures up a spirit world we cannot directly perceive, as in his play *The Intruder* (1890), when a blind man sees the approach of Death.

In Ireland, poet William Butler Yeats wrote (among other plays) "plays for dancers" to be performed in drawing rooms, often in friends' homes, with simple costumes and props, a few masked actors, and a very few musicians. In Sweden, August Strindberg, who earlier had won fame as a Naturalist, reversed direction and in *The Dream Play* (1902) and *The Ghost Sonata* (1907) introduced characters who change their identities and, ignoring space and time, move across dreamlike landscapes.

In these plays Strindberg anticipated the movement in German theater after World War I called **Expressionism**. Delighting in bizarre sets and exaggerated makeup and costuming, Expressionist playwrights and producers sought to reflect intense states of emotion and, sometimes, to depict the world through lunatic eyes. A classic film example is *The Cabinet of Dr. Caligari*, made in Berlin in 1919 and 1920, in which a hypnotist sends forth a subject to murder people. Garbed in jet black, the killer sleepwalks through a town of lopsided houses, twisted streets, and railings that tilt at gravity-defying angles. A restless experimenter throughout his career, Eugene O'Neill employed Expressionist techniques in his 1926 play *The Great God Brown*, in which characters speak through masks and wear one another's clothes (and identities).

AMERICAN MODERNISM

If modern American drama first came of age with Eugene O'Neill, it soon found powerful new voices. Thornton Wilder wrote experimental plays such as *Our Town* (1938) and *The Skin of Our Teeth* (1942) that were so carefully constructed, witty, and evocative that they achieved enormous popular and critical success. Wilder's plays, especially *Our Town*, have become so familiar to American audiences that we hardly realize how innovative his works were in their time.

It was not until the mid-1940s that two playwrights emerged who would rival O'Neill in the depth and artistry of their work—Arthur Miller and Tennessee Williams. Miller achieved his first major success with *All My Sons* (1947), in which an idealistic young man discovers that his father was guilty of supplying defective airplane parts to the government during World War II, resulting in the deaths of American servicemen. But it was his next play, *Death of a Salesman* (1949), that established Miller's work as a permanent part of America's literary heritage. In this emotionally devastating drama, Miller once again presents a tormented young man trying to come to terms with the deeply flawed father that he loves.

Tennessee Williams had made his mark a bit earlier, with *The Glass Menagerie*, produced in Chicago in December 1944 and on Broadway the following March. From there, Williams would go on to greater triumphs, especially in *A Streetcar Named Desire* (1947) and *Cat on a Hot Tin Roof* (1955). These two plays established the qualities most associated with Williams's name—strong but driven and sometimes brutal men who dominate their families; sensitive yet ambitious women; a kind of folk poetry grounded in vigorous speech rhythms (hinted at in the evocative titles of the plays); Southern settings in which contemporary decay embodies a nostalgia for a more refined past. But *The Glass Menagerie* is extraordinary for its tender lyricism and in the high quotient of human decency among its characters; partly for these reasons, it is still one of the most popular, if not *the* most popular, of Williams's works.

TRAGICOMEDY AND THE ABSURD

One of the more prominent developments in mid-twentieth-century drama was the rise of **tragicomedies**, plays that stir us not only to pity and fear (echoing Aristotle's description of the effect of tragedy) but also to laughter. Although tragicomedy is a kind of drama we think distinctively modern, it is by no means new. The term was used (although jokingly) by the Roman writer of comedy Plautus in about 185 B.C.

Shakespeare's darker comedies such as *Measure for Measure* and *The Merchant of Venice* deal so forcefully with such stark themes as lust, greed, racism, revenge, and cruelty that they often seem like tragedies until their happy endings. In the tragedies of Shakespeare and others, passages of clownish humor are sometimes called **comic relief**, meaning that the section of comedy introduces a sharp contrast in mood. But such passages can do more than provide relief. In *Othello* (3.4.1–16) the clown's banter with Desdemona for a moment makes the surrounding tragedy seem, by comparison, more poignant and intense.

No one doubts that *Othello* is a tragedy, but some twentieth-century plays leave us both bemused and confused: should we laugh or cry? One of the most talked-about plays after World War II, Samuel Beckett's *Waiting for Godot* (1953) portrays two clownish tramps who mark time in a wasteland, wistfully looking for a savior who never arrives. Modern drama, by the way, has often featured such **antiheroes**: ordinary people, inglorious and inarticulate, who carry on not from bravery but from inertia. We cannot help laughing, in *Godot*, at the tramps' painful situation; but, turning the idea around, we also feel deeply moved by their ridiculous plight. Perhaps a modern tragicomedy like *Godot* does not show us great souls suffering greatly—as we observe in a classical tragedy—but Beckett's play nonetheless touches mysteriously on the universal sorrows of human existence.

Straddling the fence between tragedy and comedy, the plays of some modern playwrights portray people whose suffering seems ridiculous. These plays belong to the **theater of the absurd**: a general name for a type of play first staged in Paris in the 1950s. "For the modern critical spirit, nothing can be taken entirely seriously, nor entirely lightly," said Eugène Ionesco, one of the movement's leading playwrights. Behind the literary conventions of the theater of the absurd stands a philosophical fear that human existence has no meaning. Every person, such playwrights assume, is a helpless waif alone in a universe full of ridiculous obstacles. In Ionesco's *Rhinoceros* (1958), the human race starts turning into rhinos, except for one man, who remains human and isolated. A favorite theme in the theater of the absurd is that communication between people is impossible. Language is therefore futile. Ionesco's *The Bald Soprano* (1948) accordingly pokes fun at polite social conversation in a scene whose dialogue consists entirely of illogical strings of catchphrases.

RETURN TO REALISM

Trends in drama change along with playwrights' convictions, and during the 1970s and 1980s the theater of the absurd no longer seemed the dominant influence on new drama in America. Along with other protests of the 1960s, experimental theater seemed to have spent its force. During the later period most of the critically celebrated new plays were neither absurd nor experimental. David Mamet's *American Buffalo* (1975) realistically portrays three petty thieves in a junk shop as they plot to steal a coin collection. Albert Innaurato's *Gemini* (1977) takes a realistic (and comic) view of family life and sexual awakening in one of Philadelphia's Italian neighborhoods. Beth Henley's 1979 Pulitzer Prize–winning play *Crimes of the Heart* presents an eccentric but still believable group of sisters in a small Southern town. The dialogue in all three plays shows high fidelity to ordinary speech. Meanwhile, many of the most influential plays of **feminist theater**, which explores the lives, problems, and occasional triumphs of contemporary women, were also written in a realistic style. Notable success—with both critics and the ticket-buying public—greeted plays such as Marsha Norman's *'night, Mother* (1983), Tina Howe's *Painting Churches* (1983), and Wendy Wasserstein's *The Heidi Chronicles* (1988).

Some leading critics, among them Richard Gilman, believed that the American theater had entered an era of "new naturalism." Indeed many plays of this time subjected the lives of people, especially poor and unhappy people, to a realistic, searching light, showing the forces that shaped them. Sam Shepard in *Buried Child* (1978) explores violence and desperation in a family that dwells on the edge of poverty; while August Wilson in *Joe Turner's Come and Gone* (1988) convincingly portrays life in a Pittsburgh ghetto lodging house. But if these newly established playwrights sometimes showed life as frankly as did the earlier Naturalists, many also employed rich and suggestive symbolism.

EXPERIMENTAL DRAMA

In the same period, experimental drama, greatly influenced by the traditions of earlier Symbolist, Expressionist, and absurdist theater, continued to flourish. David Hwang's work combines realistic elements with ritualistic and symbolic devices drawn from Asian theater (see his one-act play, *The Sound of a Voice*, in "Plays for Further Reading"). Caryl Churchill's *Top Girls* (1982) presents a dinner party in which a contemporary woman invites legendary women from history to a dinner party in a restaurant. Tony Kushner's *Angels in America* (1992) also mixes realism and fantasy to dramatize the plight of AIDS. Shel Silverstein, popular author of children's poetry, wrote a raucous one-man play, *The Devil and Billy Markham* (1991), entirely in rime, about a series of fantastic adventures in hell featuring a hard-drinking gambler and the Prince of Darkness. Silverstein's play is simultaneously experimental in form but traditional in content with its homage to American ballads and tall tales.

Some playwrights combined experimental and naturalistic elements, creating documentary works that dramatized actual events. British dramatist Michael Frayn presented the European physicists who did the work preceding the atom bomb in *Copenhagen* (1998) and explored the career of director Max Reinhardt in Nazi-era Austria in *Afterlife* (2008). Actress-playwright Anna Deavere Smith created an extremely innovative version of documentary drama in which she performed all of the roles herself in bravura one-woman shows. Using the actual words of real people, she constructed performance pieces to explore complex social events such as the race riots in Crown Heights, Brooklyn, in 1991 and in Los Angeles in 1992.

Below is one of the pioneering works of realism, Henrik Ibsen's *A Doll's House*. The play derives a good deal of its power from our ability to identify with its characters and the lives they live, an identification that Ibsen achieves in part by framing the action with the details of daily existence.

Henrik Ibsen

A Doll's House   1879

Translated by R. Farquharson Sharp
Revised by Viktoria Michelsen

Henrik Ibsen (1828–1906) was born in Skien, a seaport in Norway. When he was six, his father's business losses suddenly reduced his wealthy family to poverty. After a brief attempt to study medicine, young Ibsen worked as a stage manager in provincial Bergen; then, becoming known as a playwright, he moved to Oslo as artistic director of the National Theater—practical experiences that gained him firm grounding in his craft. Discouraged when his theater failed and the king turned down his plea for a grant to enable him to write, Ibsen left Norway and for twenty-seven years lived in Italy and Germany. There, in his middle years (1879–1891), he wrote most of his famed plays about small-town life, among them A Doll's House, Ghosts, An Enemy of the People, The Wild Duck, *and* Hedda Gabler. *Introducing social problems to the stage, these plays aroused storms of controversy. Although best known as a Realist, Ibsen early in his career wrote poetic dramas based on Norwegian history and folklore: the tragedy* Brand *(1866) and the powerful, wildly fantastic* Peer Gynt *(1867). He ended as a Symbolist in* John Gabriel Borkman *(1896) and* When We Dead Awaken *(1899), both encompassing huge mountains that heaven-assaulting heroes try to climb. Late in life Ibsen returned to Oslo, honored at last both at home and abroad.*

CHARACTERS

Torvald Helmer, a lawyer
Nora, his wife
Doctor Rank
Mrs. Kristine Linde
Nils Krogstad
The Helmers' three young children
Anne Marie, their nursemaid
Helene, the maid
A Porter

The action takes place in the Helmers' apartment.

ACT I

The scene is a room furnished comfortably and tastefully, but not extravagantly. At the back wall, a door to the right leads to the entrance hall. Another to the left leads to Helmer's study. Between the doors there is a piano. In the middle of the left-hand wall is a door, and beyond it a window. Near the window are a round table, armchairs, and a small sofa. In the right-hand wall, at the farther end, is another door, and on the same side, nearer the footlights, a stove, two easy chairs and a rocking chair. Between the stove and the door there is a small table. There are engravings on the walls, a cabinet with china and other small objects, and a small bookcase with expensively bound books. The floors are carpeted, and a fire burns in the stove. It is winter.

A bell rings in the hall. A moment later, we hear the door being opened. Enter Nora, humming a tune and in high spirits. She is wearing a hat and coat and carries a number of packages, which she puts down on the table to the right. She leaves the outer door open behind her. Through the door we see a porter who is carrying a Christmas tree and a basket, which he gives to the maid, who has opened the door.

Nora: Hide the Christmas tree carefully, Helene. Make sure the children don't see it till it's decorated this evening. (*To the Porter, taking out her purse.*) How much?
Porter: Fifty ore.
Nora: Here's a krone. No, keep the change.

> (*The Porter thanks her and goes out. Nora shuts the door. She is laughing to herself as she takes off her hat and coat. She takes a bag of macaroons from her pocket and eats one or two, then goes cautiously to the door of her husband's study and listens.*)

Yes, he's there. (*Still humming, she goes to the table on the right.*)

Helmer (*calls out from his study*): Is that my little lark twittering out there?
Nora (*busy opening some of the packages*): Yes, it is!
Helmer: Is it my little squirrel bustling around?
Nora: Yes!
Helmer: When did my squirrel come home?
Nora: Just now. (*Puts the bag of macaroons into her pocket and wipes her mouth.*) Come in here, Torvald, and see what I bought.
Helmer: I'm very busy right now. (*A little later, he opens the door and looks into the room, pen in hand.*) Bought, did you say? All these things? Has my little spend-thrift been wasting money again?
Nora: Yes, but, Torvald, this year we really can let ourselves go a little. This is the first Christmas that we don't have to watch every penny.
Helmer: Still, you know, we can't spend money recklessly.
Nora: Yes, Torvald, but we can be a little more reckless now, can't we? Just a tiny little bit! You're going to have a big salary and you'll be making lots and lots of money.
Helmer: Yes, after the New Year. But it'll still be a whole three months before the money starts coming in.
Nora: Pooh! We can borrow till then.
Helmer: Nora! (*Goes up to her and takes her playfully by the ear.*) The same little feath-erbrain! Just suppose that I borrowed a thousand kroner today, and you spent it all on Christmas, and then on New Year's Eve a roof tile fell on my head and killed me, and—
Nora (*putting her hand over his mouth*): Oh! Don't say such horrible things.
Helmer: Still, suppose that happened. What then?
Nora: If that happened, I don't suppose I'd care whether I owed anyone money or not.
Helmer: Yes, but what about the people who'd lent it to us?

1896 production of *A Doll's House* at the Empire Theatre in New York.

Nora: Them? Who'd care about them? I wouldn't even know who they were.

Helmer: That's just like a woman! But seriously, Nora, you know how I feel about that. No debt, no borrowing. There can't be any freedom or beauty in a home life that depends on borrowing and debt. We two have managed to stay on the straight road so far, and we'll go on the same way for the short time that we still have to be careful.

Nora (moving towards the stove): As you wish, Torvald.

Helmer (following her): Now, now, my little skylark mustn't let her wings droop. What's the matter? Is my little squirrel sulking? (*Taking out his purse.*) Nora, what do you think I've got here?

Nora (turning round quickly): Money!

Helmer: There you are. (*Gives her some money.*) Do you think I don't know how much you need for the house at Christmastime?

Nora (counting): Ten, twenty, thirty, forty! Thank you, thank you, Torvald. That'll keep me going for a long time.

Helmer: It's going to have to.

Nora: Yes, yes, it will. But come here and let me show you what I bought. And all so cheap! Look, here's a new suit for Ivar, and a sword. And a horse and a trumpet for Bob. And a doll and doll's bed for Emmy. They're not the best, but she'll break them soon enough anyway. And here's dress material and handkerchiefs for the maids. Old Anne Marie really should have something nicer.

Helmer: And what's in this package?

Nora (crying out): No, no! You can't see that till this evening.

Helmer: If you say so. But now tell me, you extravagant little thing, what would you like for yourself?

Nora: For myself? Oh, I'm sure I don't want anything.

Helmer: But you must. Tell me something that you'd especially like to have—within reasonable limits.

Nora: No, I really can't think of anything. Unless, Torvald . . .

Helmer: Well?

Nora (*playing with his coat buttons, and without raising her eyes to his*): If you really want to give me something, you might . . . you might . . .

Helmer: Well, out with it!

Nora (*speaking quickly*): You might give me money, Torvald. Only just as much as you can afford. And then one of these days I'll buy something with it.

Helmer: But, Nora—

Nora: Oh, do! Dear Torvald, please, please do! Then I'll wrap it up in beautiful gold paper and hang it on the Christmas tree. Wouldn't that be fun?

Helmer: What do they call those little creatures that are always wasting money?

Nora: Spendthrifts. I know. Let's do as I suggest, Torvald, and then I'll have time to think about what I need most. That's a very sensible plan, isn't it?

Helmer (*smiling*): Yes, it is. That is, if you really did save some of the money I give you, and then really buy something for yourself. But if you spend it all on the housekeeping and all kinds of unnecessary things, then I just have to open my wallet all over again.

Nora: Oh, but, Torvald—

Helmer: You can't deny it, my dear little Nora. (*Puts his arm around her waist.*) She's a sweet little spendthrift, but she uses up a lot of money. One would hardly believe how expensive such little creatures are!

Nora: That's a terrible thing to say. I really do save all I can.

Helmer (*laughing*): That's true. All you can. But you can't save anything!

Nora (*smiling quietly and happily*): You have no idea how many bills skylarks and squirrels have, Torvald.

Helmer: You're an odd little soul. Just like your father. You always find some new way of wheedling money out of me, and, as soon as you've got it, it seems to melt in your hands. You never know where it's gone. Still, one has to take you as you are. It's in the blood. Because, you know, it's true that you can inherit these things, Nora.

Nora: Ah, I wish I'd inherited a lot of Papa's traits.

Helmer: And I wouldn't want you to be anything but just what you are, my sweet little skylark. But, you know, it seems to me that you look rather—how can I put it—rather uneasy today.

Nora: Do I?

Helmer: You do, really. Look straight at me.

Nora (*looks at him*): Well?

Helmer (*wagging his finger at her*): Has little Miss Sweet Tooth been breaking our rules in town today?

Nora: No, what makes you think that?

Helmer: Has she paid a visit to the bakery?

Nora: No, I assure you, Torvald—

Helmer: Not been nibbling pastries?

Nora: No, certainly not.

Helmer: Not even taken a bite of a macaroon or two?

Nora: No, Torvald, I assure you, really—

Helmer: Come on, you know I was only kidding.

Nora (*going to the table on the right*): I wouldn't dream of going against your wishes.

Helmer: No, I'm sure of that. Besides, you gave me your word. (*Going up to her.*) Keep your little Christmas secrets to yourself, my darling. They'll all be revealed tonight when the Christmas tree is lit, no doubt.

Nora: Did you remember to invite Doctor Rank?

Helmer: No. But there's no need. It goes without saying that he'll have dinner with us. All the same, I'll ask him when he comes over this morning. I've ordered some good wine. Nora, you have no idea how much I'm looking forward to this evening.

Nora: So am I! And how the children will enjoy themselves, Torvald!

Helmer: It's great to feel that you have a completely secure position and a big enough income. It's a delightful thought, isn't it?

Nora: It's wonderful!

Helmer: Do you remember last Christmas? For three whole weeks you hid yourself away every evening until long after midnight, making ornaments for the Christmas tree and all the other fine things that were going to be a surprise for us. It was the most boring three weeks I ever spent!

Nora: I wasn't bored.

Helmer (*smiling*): But there was precious little to show for it, Nora.

Nora: Oh, you're not going to tease me about that again. How could I help it that the cat went in and tore everything to pieces?

Helmer: Of course you couldn't, poor little girl. You had the best of intentions to make us all happy, and that's the main thing. But it's a good thing that our hard times are over.

Nora: Yes, it really is wonderful.

Helmer: This time I don't have to sit here and be bored all by myself, and you don't have to ruin your dear eyes and your pretty little hands—

Nora (*clapping her hands*): No, Torvald, I don't have to any more, do I! It's wonderfully lovely to hear you say so! (*Taking his arm.*) Now let me tell you how I've been thinking we should arrange things, Torvald. As soon as Christmas is over— (*A bell rings in the hall.*) There's the bell. (*She tidies the room a little.*) There's somebody at the door. What a nuisance!

Helmer: If someone's visiting, remember I'm not home.

Maid (*in the doorway*): A lady to see you, ma'am. A stranger.

Nora: Ask her to come in.

Maid (*to Helmer*): The doctor's here too, sir.

Helmer: Did he go straight into my study?

Maid: Yes, sir.

(*Helmer goes into his study. The maid ushers in Mrs. Linde, who is in traveling clothes, and shuts the door.*)

Mrs. Linde (*in a dejected and timid voice*): Hello, Nora.

Nora (*doubtfully*): Hello.

Mrs. Linde: You don't recognize me, I suppose.

Nora: No, I don't know . . . Yes, of course, I think so—(*Suddenly.*) Yes! Kristine! Is it really you?

Mrs. Linde: Yes, it is.

Nora: Kristine! Imagine my not recognizing you! And yet how could I—(*In a gentle voice.*) You've changed, Kristine!

Mrs. Linde: Yes, I certainly have. In nine, ten long years—

Nora: Is it that long since we've seen each other? I suppose it is. The last eight years have been a happy time for me, you know. And so now you've come to town, and you've taken this long trip in the winter. That was brave of you.

Mrs. Linde: I arrived by steamer this morning.

Nora: To have some fun at Christmastime, of course. How delightful! We'll have such fun together! But take off your things. You're not cold, I hope. (*Helps her.*) Now we'll sit down by the stove and be cozy. No, take this armchair. I'll sit here in the rocking chair. (*Takes her hands.*) Now you look like your old self again. It was only that first moment. You are a little paler, Kristine, and maybe a little thinner.

Mrs. Linde: And much, much older, Nora.

Nora: Maybe a little older. Very, very little. Surely not very much. (*Stops suddenly and speaks seriously.*) What a thoughtless thing I am, chattering away like this. My poor, dear Kristine, please forgive me.

Mrs. Linde: What do you mean, Nora?

Nora (gently): Poor Kristine, you're a widow.

Mrs. Linde: Yes. For three years now.

Nora: Yes, I knew. I saw it in the papers. I swear to you, Kristine, I kept meaning to write to you at the time, but I always put it off and something always came up.

Mrs. Linde: I understand completely, dear.

Nora: It was very bad of me, Kristine. Poor thing, how you must have suffered. And he left you nothing?

Mrs. Linde: No.

Nora: And no children?

Mrs. Linde: No.

Nora: Nothing at all, then?

Mrs. Linde: Not even any sorrow or grief to live on.

Nora (looking at her in disbelief): But, Kristine, is that possible?

Mrs. Linde (smiles sadly and strokes Nora's hair): It happens sometimes, Nora.

Nora: So you're completely alone. How terribly sad that must be. I have three beautiful children. You can't see them just now, because they're out with their nursemaid. But now you must tell me all about it.

Mrs. Linde: No, no, I want to hear about you.

Nora: No, you go first. I mustn't be selfish today. Today I should think only about you. But there is one thing I have to tell you. Do you know we've just had a fabulous piece of good luck?

Mrs. Linde: No, what is it?

Nora: Just imagine, my husband's been appointed manager of the bank!

Mrs. Linde: Your husband? That is good luck!

Nora: Yes, it's tremendous! A lawyer's life is so uncertain, especially if he won't take any cases that are the slightest bit shady, and of course Torvald has never been willing to do that, and I completely agree with him. You can imagine how delighted we are! He starts his job in the bank at New Year's, and then he'll have a big salary and lots of commissions. From now on we can live very differently. We can do just what we want. I feel so relieved and so happy, Kristine! It'll be wonderful to have heaps of money and not have to worry about anything, won't it?

Mrs. Linde: Yes. Anyway, I think it would be delightful to have what you need.

Nora: No, not only what you need, but heaps and heaps of money.

Mrs. Linde (*smiling*): Nora, Nora, haven't you learned any sense yet? Back in school you were a terrible spendthrift.

Nora (*laughing*): Yes, that's what Torvald says now. (*Wags her finger at her.*) But "Nora, Nora" isn't as silly as you think. We haven't been in a position for me to waste money. We've both had to work.

Mrs. Linde: You too?

Nora: Oh, yes, odds and ends, needlework, crocheting, embroidery, and that kind of thing. (*Dropping her voice.*) And other things too. You know Torvald left his government job when we got married? There was no chance of promotion, and he had to try to earn more money than he was making there. But in that first year he overworked himself terribly. You see, he had to make money any way he could, and he worked all hours, but he couldn't take it, and he got very sick, and the doctors said he had to go south, to a warmer climate.

Mrs. Linde: You spent a whole year in Italy, didn't you?

Nora: Yes. It wasn't easy to get away, I can tell you that. It was just after Ivar was born, but obviously we had to go. It was a wonderful, beautiful trip, and it saved Torvald's life. But it cost a tremendous amount of money, Kristine.

Mrs. Linde: I would imagine so.

Nora: It cost about four thousand, eight hundred kroner. That's a lot, isn't it?

Mrs. Linde: Yes, it is, and when you have an emergency like that it's lucky to have the money.

Nora: Well, the fact is, we got it from Papa.

Mrs. Linde: Oh, I see. It was just about that time that he died, wasn't it?

Nora: Yes, and, just think of it, I couldn't even go and take care of him. I was expecting little Ivar any day and I had my poor sick Torvald to look after. My dear, kind father. I never saw him again, Kristine. That was the worst experience I've gone through since we got married.

Mrs. Linde: I know how fond of him you were. And then you went off to Italy?

Nora: Yes. You see, we had money then, and the doctors insisted that we go, so we left a month later.

Mrs. Linde: And your husband came back completely recovered?

Nora: The picture of health!

Mrs. Linde: But . . . the doctor?

Nora: What doctor?

Mrs. Linde: Didn't your maid say that the gentleman who arrived here with me was the doctor?

Nora: Yes, that was Doctor Rank, but he doesn't come here professionally. He's our dearest friend, and he drops in at least once every day. No, Torvald hasn't been sick for an hour since then, and our children are strong and healthy, and so am I. (*Jumps up and claps her hands.*) Kristine! Kristine! It's good to be alive and happy!

But how awful of me. I'm talking about nothing but myself. (*Sits on a nearby stool and rests her arms on her knees.*) Please don't be mad at me. Tell me, is it really true that you didn't love your husband? Why did you marry him?

Mrs. Linde: My mother was still alive then, and she was bedridden and helpless, and I had to provide for my two younger brothers, so I didn't think I had any right to turn him down.

Nora: No, maybe you did the right thing. So he was rich then?

Mrs. Linde: I believe he was quite well off. But his business wasn't very solid, and when he died, it all went to pieces and there was nothing left.

Nora: And then?

Mrs. Linde: Well, I had to turn my hand to anything I could find. First a small shop, then a small school, and so on. The last three years have seemed like one long workday, with no rest. Now it's over, Nora. My poor mother's gone and doesn't need me any more, and the boys don't need me, either. They've got jobs now and can manage for themselves.

Nora: What a relief it must be if—

Mrs. Linde: No, not at all. All I feel is an unbearable emptiness. No one to live for anymore. (*Gets up restlessly.*) That's why I couldn't stand it any longer in my little backwater. I hope it'll be easier to find something here that'll keep me busy and occupy my mind. If I could be lucky enough to find some regular work, office work of some kind—

Nora: But, Kristine, that's so awfully tiring, and you look tired out now. It'd be much better for you if you could get away to a resort.

Mrs. Linde (*walking to the window*): I don't have a father to give me money for a trip, Nora.

Nora (*rising*): Oh, don't be mad at me!

Mrs. Linde (*going up to her*): It's you who mustn't be mad at me, dear. The worst thing about a situation like mine is that it makes you so bitter. No one to work for, and yet you have to always be on the lookout for opportunities. You have to live, and so you grow selfish. When you told me about your good luck—you'll find this hard to believe—I was delighted less for you than for myself.

Nora: What do you mean? Oh, I understand. You mean that maybe Torvald could find you a job.

Mrs. Linde: Yes, that's what I was thinking.

Nora: He must, Kristine. Just leave it to me. I'll broach the subject very cleverly. I'll think of something that'll put him in a really good mood. It'll make me so happy to be of some use to you.

Mrs. Linde: How kind you are, Nora, to be so eager to help me! It's doubly kind of you, since you know so little of the burdens and troubles of life.

Nora: Me? I know so little of them?

Mrs. Linde (*smiling*): My dear! Small household cares and that sort of thing! You're a child, Nora.

Nora (*tosses her head and crosses the stage*): You shouldn't act so superior.

Mrs. Linde: No?

Nora: You're just like the others. They all think I'm incapable of anything really serious—

Mrs. Linde: Come on—

Nora: —that I haven't had to deal with any real problems in my life.

Mrs. Linde: But, my dear Nora, you've just told me all your troubles.

Nora: Pooh! That was nothing. (*Lowering her voice.*) I haven't told you the important thing.

Mrs. Linde: The important thing? What do you mean?

Nora: You really look down on me, Kristine, but you shouldn't. Aren't you proud of having worked so hard and so long for your mother?

Mrs. Linde: Believe me, I don't look down on anyone. But it's true, I'm proud and I'm glad that I had the privilege of making my mother's last days almost worry-free.

Nora: And you're proud of what you did for your brothers?

Mrs. Linde: I think I have the right to be.

Nora: I think so, too. But now, listen to this. I have something to be proud of and happy about too.

Mrs. Linde: I'm sure you do. But what do you mean?

Nora: Keep your voice down. If Torvald were to overhear! He can't find out, not under any circumstances. No one in the world must know, Kristine, except you.

Mrs. Linde: But what is it?

Nora: Come here. (*Pulls her down on the sofa beside her.*) Now I'll show you that I too have something to be proud and happy about. I'm the one who saved Torvald's life.

Mrs. Linde: Saved? How?

Nora: I told you about our trip to Italy. Torvald would never have recovered if he hadn't gone there—

Mrs. Linde: Yes, but your father gave you the money you needed.

Nora (smiling): Yes, that's what Torvald thinks, along with everybody else, but—

Mrs. Linde: But—

Nora: Papa didn't give us a penny. I was the one who raised the money.

Mrs. Linde: You? That huge amount?

Nora: That's right, four thousand, eight hundred kroner. What do you think of that?

Mrs. Linde: But, Nora, how could you possibly? Did you win the lottery?

Nora (disdainfully): The lottery? That wouldn't have been any accomplishment.

Mrs. Linde: But where did you get it from, then?

Nora (humming and smiling with an air of mystery): Hm, hm! Ha!

Mrs. Linde: Because you couldn't have borrowed it.

Nora: Couldn't I? Why not?

Mrs. Linde: No, a wife can't borrow money without her husband's consent.

Nora (tossing her head): Oh, if it's a wife with a head for business, a wife who has the brains to be a little clever—

Mrs. Linde: I don't understand this at all, Nora.

Nora: There's no reason why you should. I never said I'd borrowed the money. Maybe I got it some other way. (*Lies back on the sofa.*) Maybe I got it from an admirer. When a woman's as pretty as I am—

Mrs. Linde: You're crazy.

Nora: Now, you know you're dying of curiosity, Kristine.

Mrs. Linde: Listen to me, Nora dear. Have you done something rash?

Nora (sits up straight): Is it rash to save your husband's life?

Mrs. Linde: I think it's rash, without his knowledge, to—

Nora: But it was absolutely necessary that he not know! My goodness, can't you understand that? It was necessary he have no idea how sick he was. The doctors came to *me* and said his life was in danger and the only thing that could save him was to live in the south. Don't you think I tried first to get him to do it as if it was for me? I told him how much I would love to travel abroad like other young wives. I tried tears and pleading with him. I told him he should remember the condition I was in, and that he should be kind and indulgent to me. I even hinted that he might take out a loan. That almost made him mad, Kristine. He said I was thoughtless, and that it was his duty as my husband not to indulge me in my "whims and caprices," as I believe he called them. All right, I thought, you need to be saved. And that was how I came to think up a way out of the mess—

Mrs. Linde: And your husband never found out from your father that the money hadn't come from him?

Nora: No, never. Papa died just then. I'd meant to let him in on the secret and beg him never to reveal it. But he was so sick. Unfortunately, there never was any need to tell him.

Mrs. Linde: And since then you've never told your secret to your husband?

Nora: Good heavens, no! How could you think I would? A man with such strong opinions about these things! Besides, how painful and humiliating it would be for Torvald, with his masculine pride, to know that he owed me anything! It would completely upset the balance of our relationship. Our beautiful happy home would never be the same.

Mrs. Linde: Are you never going to tell him about it?

Nora (meditatively, and with a half smile): Yes, someday, maybe, in many years, when I'm not as pretty as I am now. Don't laugh at me! I mean, of course, when Torvald is no longer as devoted to me as he is now, when he's grown tired of my dancing and dressing up and reciting. Then it may be a good thing to have something in reserve—*(Breaking off.)* What nonsense! That time will never come. Now, what do you think of my great secret, Kristine? Do you still think I'm useless? And the fact is, this whole situation has caused me a lot of worry. It hasn't been easy for me to make my payments on time. I can tell you that there's something in business that's called quarterly interest, and something else called installment payments, and it's always so terribly difficult to keep up with them. I've had to save a little here and there, wherever I could, you understand. I haven't been able to put much aside from my housekeeping money, because Torvald has to live well. And I couldn't let my children be shabbily dressed. I feel I have to spend everything he gives me for them, the sweet little darlings!

Mrs. Linde: So it's all had to come out of your own allowance, poor Nora?

Nora: Of course. Besides, I was the one responsible for it. Whenever Torvald has given me money for new dresses and things like that, I've never spent more than half of it. I've always bought the simplest and cheapest things. Thank heaven, any clothes look good on me, and so Torvald's never noticed anything. But it was often very hard on me, Kristine, because it is delightful to be really well dressed, isn't it?

Mrs. Linde: I suppose so.

Nora: Well, then I've found other ways of earning money. Last winter I was lucky enough to get a lot of copying to do, so I locked myself up and sat writing every evening until late into the night. A lot of the time I was desperately tired, but all the same it was a tremendous pleasure to sit there working and earning money. It was like being a man.

Mrs. Linde: How much have you been able to pay off that way?

Nora: I can't tell you exactly. You see, it's very hard to keep a strict account of a business matter like that. I only know that I've paid out every penny I could scrape together. Many a time I was at my wits' end. (*Smiles.*) Then I used to sit here and imagine that a rich old gentleman had fallen in love with me—

Mrs. Linde: What! Who was it?

Nora: Oh, be quiet! That he had died, and that when his will was opened it said, in great big letters: "The lovely Mrs. Nora Helmer is to have everything I own paid over to her immediately in cash."

Mrs. Linde: But, my dear Nora, who could the man be?

Nora: Good gracious, can't you understand? There wasn't any old gentleman. It was only something that I used to sit here and imagine, when I couldn't think of any way of getting money. But it's all right now. The tiresome old gent can stay right where he is, as far as I'm concerned. I don't care about him or his will either, because now I'm worry-free. (*Jumps up.*) My goodness, it's delightful to think of, Kristine! Worry-free! To be able to have no worries, no worries at all! To be able to play and romp with the children! To be able to keep the house beautifully and have everything just the way Torvald likes it! And, just think of it, soon the spring will come and the big blue sky! Maybe we can take a little trip. Maybe I can see the sea again! Oh, it's a wonderful thing to be alive and happy.

(*A bell rings in the hall.*)

Mrs. Linde (*rising*): There's the bell. Perhaps I should be going.

Nora: No, don't go. No one will come in here. It's sure to be for Torvald.

Servant (*at the hall door*): Excuse me, ma'am. There's a gentleman to see the master, and as the doctor is still with him—

Nora: Who is it?

Krogstad (*at the door*): It's me, Mrs. Helmer.

(*Mrs. Linde starts, trembles, and turns toward the window.*)

Nora (*takes a step toward him, and speaks in a strained, low voice*): You? What is it? What do you want to see my husband for?

Krogstad: Bank business, in a way. I have a small position in the bank, and I hear your husband is going to be our boss now—

Nora: Then it's—

Krogstad: Nothing but dry business matters, Mrs. Helmer, that's all.

Nora: Then please go into the study.

(*She bows indifferently to him and shuts the door into the hall, then comes back and makes up the fire in the stove.*)

Mrs. Linde: Nora, who was that man?

Nora: A lawyer. His name is Krogstad.

Mrs. Linde: Then it really was him.

Nora: Do you know the man?

Mrs. Linde: I used to, many years ago. At one time he was a law clerk in our town.

Nora: That's right, he was.

Mrs. Linde: How much he's changed.

Nora: He had a very unhappy marriage.

Mrs. Linde: He's a widower now, isn't he?

Nora: With several children. There, now it's really caught. (*Shuts the door of the stove and moves the rocking chair aside.*)

Mrs. Linde: They say he's mixed up in a lot of questionable business.

Nora: Really? Maybe he is. I don't know anything about it. But let's not talk about business. It's so tiresome.

Doctor Rank (*comes out of Helmer's study. Before he shuts the door he calls to Helmer*): No, my dear fellow, I won't disturb you. I'd rather go in and talk to your wife for a little while.

(*Shuts the door and sees Mrs. Linde.*)

I beg your pardon. I'm afraid I'm in the way here too.

Nora: No, not at all. (*Introducing him:*) Doctor Rank, Mrs. Linde.

Rank: I've often heard that name in this house. I think I passed you on the stairs when I arrived, Mrs. Linde?

Mrs. Linde: Yes, I take stairs very slowly. I can't manage them very well.

Rank: Oh, some small internal problem?

Mrs. Linde: No, it's just that I've been overworking myself.

Rank: Is that all? Then I suppose you've come to town to get some rest by sampling our social life.

Mrs. Linde: I've come to look for work.

Rank: Is that a good cure for overwork?

Mrs. Linde: One has to live, Doctor Rank.

Rank: Yes, that seems to be the general opinion.

Nora: Now, now, Doctor Rank, you know you want to live.

Rank: Of course I do. However miserable I may feel, I want to prolong the agony for as long as possible. All my patients are the same way. And so are those who are morally sick. In fact, one of them, and a bad case too, is at this very moment inside with Helmer—

Mrs. Linde (*sadly*): Ah!

Nora: Who are you talking about?

Rank: A lawyer by the name of Krogstad, a fellow you don't know at all. He's a completely worthless creature, Mrs. Helmer. But even he started out by saying, as if it were a matter of the utmost importance, that he has to live.

Nora: Did he? What did he want to talk to Torvald about?

Rank: I have no idea. All I heard was that it was something about the bank.

Nora: I didn't know this—what's his name—Krogstad had anything to do with the bank.

Rank: Yes, he has some kind of a position there. (*To Mrs. Linde*) I don't know whether you find the same thing in your part of the world, that there are certain people who go around zealously looking to sniff out moral corruption, and, as soon as they find some, they put the person involved in some cushy job where they can keep an eye on him. Meanwhile, the morally healthy ones are left out in the cold.

Mrs. Linde: Still, I think it's the sick who are most in need of being taken care of.

Rank (shrugging his shoulders): Well, there you have it. That's the attitude that's turning society into a hospital.

(*Nora, who has been absorbed in her thoughts, breaks out into smothered laughter and claps her hands.*)

Rank: Why are you laughing at that? Do you have any idea what society really is?

Nora: What do I care about your boring society? I'm laughing at something else, something very funny. Tell me, Doctor Rank, are all the people who work in the bank dependent on Torvald now?

Rank: That's what's so funny?

Nora (smiling and humming): That's my business! (*Walking around the room.*) It's just wonderful to think that we have—that Torvald has—so much power over so many people. (*Takes the bag out of her pocket.*) Doctor Rank, what do you say to a macaroon?

Rank: Macaroons? I thought they were forbidden here.

Nora: Yes, but these are some Kristine gave me.

Mrs. Linde: What! Me?

Nora: Oh, well, don't be upset! How could you know that Torvald had forbidden them? I have to tell you, he's afraid they'll ruin my teeth. But so what? Once in a while, that's all right, isn't it, Doctor Rank? With your permission! (*Puts a macaroon into his mouth.*) You have to have one too, Kristine. And I'll have one, just a little one—or no more than two. (*Walking around.*) I am tremendously happy. There's just one thing in the world now that I would dearly love to do.

Rank: Well, what is it?

Nora: It's something I would dearly love to say, if Torvald could hear me.

Rank: Well, why can't you say it?

Nora: No, I don't dare. It's too shocking.

Mrs. Linde: Shocking?

Rank: Well then, I'd advise you not to say it. Still, in front of us you might risk it. What is it you'd so much like to say if Torvald could hear you?

Nora: I would just love to say—"Well, I'll be damned!"

Rank: Are you crazy?

Mrs. Linde: Nora, dear!

Rank: Here he is. Say it!

Nora (hiding the bag): Shh, shh, shh!

(*Helmer comes out of his room, with his coat over his arm and his hat in his hand.*)

Nora: Well, Torvald dear, did you get rid of him?

Helmer: Yes, he just left.

Nora: Let me introduce you. This is Kristine. She's just arrived in town.

Helmer: Kristine? I'm sorry, but I don't know any—

Nora: Mrs. Linde, dear, Kristine Linde.

Helmer: Oh, of course. A school friend of my wife's, I believe?

Mrs. Linde: Yes, we knew each other back then.

Nora: And just think, she's come all this way in order to see you.

Helmer: What do you mean?

Mrs. Linde: No, really, I—

Nora: Kristine is extremely good at bookkeeping, and she's very eager to work for some talented man, so she can perfect her skills—

Helmer: Very sensible, Mrs. Linde.

Nora: And when she heard that you'd been named manager of the bank—the news was sent by telegraph, you know—she traveled here as quickly as she could. Torvald, I'm sure you'll be able to do something for Kristine, for my sake, won't you?

Helmer: Well, it's not completely out of the question. I expect that you're a widow, Mrs. Linde?

Mrs. Linde: Yes.

Helmer: And you've had some bookkeeping experience?

Mrs. Linde: Yes, a fair amount.

Helmer: Ah! Well, there's a very good chance that I'll be able to find something for you—

Nora (clapping her hands): What did I tell you? What did I tell you?

Helmer: You've just come at a lucky moment, Mrs. Linde.

Mrs. Linde: How can I thank you?

Helmer: There's no need. (*Puts on his coat.*) But now you must excuse me—

Rank: Wait a minute. I'll come with you. (*Brings his fur coat from the hall and warms it at the fire.*)

Nora: Don't be long, Torvald dear.

Helmer: About an hour, that's all.

Nora: Are you leaving too, Kristine?

Mrs. Linde (putting on her cloak): Yes, I have to go and look for a place to stay.

Helmer: Oh, well then, we can walk down the street together.

Nora (helping her): It's too bad we're so short of space here. I'm afraid it's impossible for us—

Mrs. Linde: Please don't even think of it! Goodbye, Nora dear, and many thanks.

Nora: Goodbye for now. Of course you'll come back this evening. And you too, Dr. Rank. What do you say? If you're feeling up to it? Oh, you have to be! Wrap yourself up warmly.

(*They go to the door all talking together. Children's voices are heard on the staircase.*)

Nora: There they are! There they are!

(*She runs to open the door. The nursemaid comes in with the children.*)

Come in! Come in! (*Stoops and kisses them.*) Oh, you sweet blessings! Look at them, Kristine! Aren't they darlings?

Rank: Let's not stand here in the draft.

Helmer: Come along, Mrs. Linde. Only a mother will be able to stand it in here now!

(*Rank, Helmer, and Mrs. Linde go downstairs. The Nursemaid comes forward with the children. Nora shuts the hall door.*)

Nora: How fresh and healthy you look! Cheeks as red as apples and roses. (*The children all talk at once while she speaks to them.*) Did you have a lot of fun? That's wonderful! What, you pulled Emmy and Bob on the sled? Both at once? That was really something. You *are* a clever boy, Ivar. Let me take her for a little, Anne Marie. My sweet little baby doll! (*Takes the baby from the maid and dances her up and down.*) Yes, yes, mother will dance with Bob too. What! Have you been throwing snowballs? I wish I'd been there too! No, no, I'll take their things off, Anne Marie, please let me do it, it's such fun. Go inside now, you look half frozen. There's some hot coffee for you on the stove.

(*The Nursemaid goes into the room on the left. Nora takes off the children's things and throws them around, while they all talk to her at once.*)

Nora: Really! Did a big dog run after you? But it didn't bite you? No, dogs don't bite nice little dolly children. You mustn't look at the packages, Ivar. What are they? Oh, I'll bet you'd like to know. No, no, it's something boring! Come on, let's play a game! What should we play? Hide and seek? Yes, we'll play hide and seek. Bob will hide first. You want me to hide? All right, I'll hide first.

(*She and the children laugh and shout, and romp in and out of the room. At last Nora hides under the table. The children rush in and out looking for her, but they don't see her. They hear her smothered laughter, run to the table, lift up the cloth and find her. Shouts of laughter. She crawls forward and pretends to scare them. More laughter. Meanwhile there has been a knock at the hall door, but none of them has noticed it. The door is opened halfway and Krogstad appears. He waits for a little while. The game goes on.*)

Krogstad: Excuse me, Mrs. Helmer.
Nora (with a stifled cry, turns round and gets up onto her knees): Oh! What do you want?
Krogstad: Excuse me, the outside door was open. I suppose someone forgot to shut it.
Nora (rising): My husband is out, Mr. Krogstad.
Krogstad: I know that.
Nora: What do you want here, then?
Krogstad: A word with you.
Nora: With me? (*To the children, gently.*) Go inside to Anne Marie. What? No, the strange man won't hurt Mother. When he's gone we'll play another game. (*She takes the children into the room on the left, and shuts the door after them.*) You want to speak to me?
Krogstad: Yes, I do.
Nora: Today? It isn't the first of the month yet.
Krogstad: No, it's Christmas Eve, and it's up to you what kind of Christmas you're going to have.
Nora: What do you mean? Today it's absolutely impossible for me—
Krogstad: We won't talk about that until later on. This is something else. I presume you can spare me a moment?
Nora: Yes, yes, I can. Although . . .
Krogstad: Good. I was in Olsen's restaurant and I saw your husband going down the street—
Nora: Yes?
Krogstad: With a lady.
Nora: So?
Krogstad: May I be so bold as to ask if it was a Mrs. Linde?

Nora: It was.

Krogstad: Just arrived in town?

Nora: Yes, today.

Krogstad: She's a very good friend of yours, isn't she?

Nora: She is. But I don't see—

Krogstad: I knew her too, once upon a time.

Nora: I'm aware of that.

Krogstad: Are you? So you know all about it. I thought so. Then I can ask you, without beating around the bush. Is Mrs. Linde going to work in the bank?

Nora: What right do you have to question me, Mr. Krogstad? You're one of my husband's employees. But since you ask, I'll tell you. Yes, Mrs. Linde is going to work in the bank. And I'm the one who spoke up for her, Mr. Krogstad. So now you know.

Krogstad: So I was right, then.

Nora (walking up and down the stage): Sometimes one has a tiny little bit of influence, I should hope. Just because I'm a woman, it doesn't necessarily follow that—You know, when somebody's in a subordinate position, Mr. Krogstad, they should really be careful to avoid offending anyone who—who—

Krogstad: Who has influence?

Nora: Exactly.

Krogstad (changing his tone): Mrs. Helmer, may I ask you to use *your* influence on my behalf?

Nora: What? What do you mean?

Krogstad: Will you be kind enough to see to it that I'm allowed to keep my subordinate position in the bank?

Nora: What do you mean by that? Who's threatening to take your job away from you?

Krogstad: Oh, there's no need to keep up the pretence of ignorance. I can understand that your friend isn't very anxious to expose herself to the chance of rubbing shoulders with me. And now I realize exactly who I have to thank for pushing me out.

Nora: But I swear to you—

Krogstad: Yes, yes. But, to get right to the point, there's still time to prevent it, and I would advise you to use your influence to do so.

Nora: But, Mr. Krogstad, I have no influence.

Krogstad: Oh no? Didn't you yourself just say—

Nora: Well, obviously, I didn't mean for you to take it that way. Me? What would make you think I have that kind of influence with my husband?

Krogstad: Oh, I've known your husband since our school days. I don't suppose he's any more unpersuadable than other husbands.

Nora: If you're going to talk disrespectfully about my husband, I'll have to ask you to leave my house.

Krogstad: Bold talk, Mrs. Helmer.

Nora: I'm not afraid of you anymore. When the New Year comes, I'll soon be free of the whole thing.

Krogstad (controlling himself): Listen to me, Mrs. Helmer. If I have to, I'm ready to fight for my little job in the bank as if I were fighting for my life.

Nora: So it seems.

Krogstad: It's not just for the sake of the money. In fact, that matters the least to me. There's another reason. Well, I might as well tell you. Here's my situation. I suppose, like everybody else, you know that many years ago I did something pretty foolish.

Nora: I think I heard something about it.

Krogstad: It never got as far as the courtroom, but every door seemed closed to me after that. So I got involved in the business that you know about. I had to do something, and, honestly, I think there are many worse than me. But now I have to get myself free of all that. My sons are growing up. For their sake I have to try to win back as much respect as I can in this town. The job in the bank was like the first step up for me, and now your husband is going to kick me downstairs back into the mud.

Nora: But you have to believe me, Mr. Krogstad, it's not in my power to help you at all.

Krogstad: Then it's because you don't want to. But I have ways of making you.

Nora: You don't mean you'll tell my husband I owe you money?

Krogstad: Hm! And what if I did tell him?

Nora: That would be a terrible thing for you to do. (*Sobbing.*) To think he would learn my secret, which has been my pride and joy, in such an ugly, clumsy way— that he would learn it from you! And it would put me in a horribly uncomfortable position—

Krogstad: Just uncomfortable?

Nora (impetuously): Well, go ahead and do it, then! And it'll be so much the worse for you. My husband will see for himself how vile you are, and then you'll lose your job for sure.

Krogstad: I asked you if it's just an uncomfortable situation at home that you're afraid of.

Nora: If my husband does find out about it, of course he'll immediately pay you what I still owe, and then we'll be through with you once and for all.

Krogstad (coming a step closer): Listen to me, Mrs. Helmer. Either you have a very bad memory or you don't know much about business. I can see I'm going to have to remind you of a few details.

Nora: What do you mean?

Krogstad: When your husband was sick, you came to me to borrow four thousand, eight hundred kroner.

Nora: I didn't know anyone else to go to.

Krogstad: I promised to get you that amount—

Nora: Yes, and you did so.

Krogstad: I promised to get you that amount, on certain conditions. You were so preoccupied with your husband's illness, and you were so anxious to get the money for your trip, that you seem to have paid no attention to the conditions of our bargain. So it won't be out of place for me to remind you of them. Now, I promised to get the money on the security of a note which I drew up.

Nora: Yes, and which I signed.

Krogstad: Good. But underneath your signature there were a few lines naming your father as a co-signer who guaranteed the repayment of the loan. Your father was supposed to sign that part.

Nora: Supposed to? He did sign it.

Krogstad: I had left the date blank. That was because your father was supposed to fill in the date when he signed the paper. Do you remember that?

Nora: Yes, I think I remember. . . .

Krogstad: Then I gave you the note to mail to your father. Isn't that so?

Nora: Yes.

Krogstad: And obviously you mailed it right away, because five or six days later you brought me the note with your father's signature. And then I gave you the money.

Nora: Well, haven't I been paying it back regularly?

Krogstad: Fairly regularly, yes. But, to get back to the point, that must have been a very difficult time for you, Mrs. Helmer.

Nora: Yes, it was.

Krogstad: Your father was very sick, wasn't he?

Nora: He was very near the end.

Krogstad: And he died soon after?

Nora: Yes.

Krogstad: Tell me, Mrs. Helmer, can you by any chance remember what day your father died? On what day of the month, I mean.

Nora: Papa died on the 29th of September.

Krogstad: That's right. I looked it up myself. And, since that is the case, there's something extremely peculiar (*taking a piece of paper from his pocket*) that I can't account for.

Nora: Peculiar in what way? I don't know—

Krogstad: The peculiar thing, Mrs. Helmer, is the fact that your father signed this note three days after he died.

Nora: What do you mean? I don't understand—

Krogstad: Your father died on the 29th of September. But, look here. Your father dated his signature the 2nd of October. It is mighty peculiar, isn't it? (*Nora is silent.*) Can you explain it to me? (*Nora is still silent.*) And what's just as peculiar is that the words "October 2," as well as the year, are not in your father's handwriting, but in someone else's, which I think I recognize. Well, of course it can all be explained. Your father might have forgotten to date his signature, and someone else might have filled in the date before they knew that he had died. There's no harm in that. It all depends on the signature, and that's genuine, isn't it, Mrs. Helmer? It was your father himself who signed his name here?

Nora (*after a short pause, lifts her head up and looks defiantly at him*): No, it wasn't. I'm the one who wrote Papa's name.

Krogstad: Are you aware that you're making a very serious confession?

Nora: How so? You'll get your money soon.

Krogstad: Let me ask you something. Why didn't you send the paper to your father?

Nora: It was out of the question. Papa was too sick. If I had asked him to sign something, I'd have had to tell him what the money was for, and when he was so sick himself I couldn't tell him that my husband's life was in danger. It was out of the question.

Krogstad: It would have been better for you if you'd given up your trip abroad.

Nora: No, that was impossible. That trip was to save my husband's life. I couldn't give that up.

Krogstad: But didn't it ever occur to you that you were committing a fraud against me?

Nora: I couldn't take that into account. I didn't trouble myself about you at all. I couldn't stand you, because you put so many heartless difficulties in my way, even though you knew how seriously ill my husband was.

Krogstad: Mrs. Helmer, you evidently don't realize clearly what you're guilty of. But, believe me, my one mistake, which cost me my whole reputation, was nothing more and nothing worse than what you did.

Nora: You? You expect me to believe that you were brave enough to take a risk to save your wife's life?

Krogstad: The law doesn't care about motives.

Nora: Then the law must be very stupid.

Krogstad: Stupid or not, it's the law that's going to judge you, if I produce this paper in court.

Nora: I don't believe it. Isn't a daughter allowed to spare her dying father anxiety and concern? Isn't a wife allowed to save her husband's life? I don't know much about the law, but I'm sure there must be provisions for things like that. Don't you know anything about such provisions? You seem like a very poor excuse for a lawyer, Mr. Krogstad.

Krogstad: That's as may be. But business, the kind of business you and I have done together—do you think I don't know about that? Fine. Do what you want. But I can assure you of this. If I lose everything all over again, this time you're going down with me. (*He bows, and goes out through the hall.*)

Nora (*appears buried in thought for a short time, then tosses her head*): Nonsense! He's just trying to scare me! I'm not as naive as he thinks I am. (*Begins to busy herself putting the children's things in order.*) And yet . . . .? No, it's impossible! I did it for love.

Children (*in the doorway on the left*): Mother, the strange man is gone. He went out through the gate.

Nora: Yes, dears, I know. But don't tell anyone about the strange man. Do you hear me? Not even Papa.

Children: No, Mother. But will you come and play with us again?

Nora: No, no, not just now.

Children: But, Mother, you promised us.

Nora: Yes, but I can't right now. Go inside. I have too much to do. Go inside, my sweet little darlings.

(*She gets them into the room bit by bit and shuts the door on them. Then she sits down on the sofa, takes up a piece of needlework and sews a few stitches, but soon stops.*)

No! (*Throws down the work, gets up, goes to the hall door and calls out.*) Helene! Bring the tree in. (*Goes to the table on the left, opens a drawer, and stops again.*) No, no! It's completely impossible!

Maid (*coming in with the tree*): Where should I put it, ma'am?

Nora: Here, in the middle of the floor.

Maid: Do you need anything else?

Nora: No, thank you. I have everything I want.

(*Exit Maid.*)

Nora (*begins decorating the tree*): A candle here, and flowers here. That horrible man! It's all nonsense, there's nothing wrong. The tree is going to be magnificent! I'll do everything I can think of to make you happy, Torvald! I'll sing for you, dance for you—

(*Helmer comes in with some papers under his arm.*)

Oh! You're back already?

Helmer: Yes. Has anyone been here?

Nora: Here? No.

Helmer: That's strange. I saw Krogstad going out the gate.

Nora: You did? Oh yes, I forgot, Krogstad was here for a moment.

Helmer: Nora, I can tell from the way you're acting that he was here begging you to put in a good word for him.

Nora: Yes, he was.

Helmer: And you were supposed to pretend it was all your idea and not tell me that he'd been here to see you. Didn't he beg you to do that too?

Nora: Yes, Torvald, but—

Helmer: Nora, Nora, to think that you'd be a party to that sort of thing! To have any kind of conversation with a man like that, and promise him anything at all? And to lie to me in the bargain?

Nora: Lie?

Helmer: Didn't you tell me no one had been here? (*Shakes his finger at her.*) My little songbird must never do that again. A songbird must have a clean beak to chirp with. No false notes! (*Puts his arm round her waist.*) That's true, isn't it? Yes, I'm sure it is. (*Lets her go.*) We won't mention this again. (*Sits down by the stove.*) How warm and cozy it is here! (*Turns over his papers.*)

Nora (*after a short pause, during which she busies herself with the Christmas tree*): Torvald!

Helmer: Yes?

Nora: I'm really looking forward to the masquerade ball at the Stenborgs' the day after tomorrow.

Helmer: And I'm really curious to see what you're going to surprise me with.

Nora: Oh, it was very silly of me to want to do that.

Helmer: What do you mean?

Nora: I can't come up with anything good. Everything I think of seems so stupid and pointless.

Helmer: So my little Nora finally admits that?

Nora (*standing behind his chair with her arms on the back of it*): Are you very busy, Torvald?

Helmer: Well . . .

Nora: What are all those papers?

Helmer: Bank business.

Nora: Already?

Helmer: I've gotten the authority from the retiring manager to reorganize the work procedures and make the necessary personnel changes. I need to take care of it during Christmas week, so as to have everything in place for the new year.

Nora: Then that was why this poor Krogstad—

Helmer: Hm!

Nora (*leans against the back of his chair and strokes his hair*): If you weren't so busy, I would have asked you for a huge favor, Torvald.

Helmer: What favor? Tell me.

Nora: No one has such good taste as you. And I really want to look nice at the fancy-dress ball. Torvald, couldn't you take me in hand and decide what I should go as and what kind of costume I should wear?

Helmer: Aha! So my obstinate little woman has to get someone to come to her rescue?

Nora: Yes, Torvald, I can't get along at all without your help.

Helmer: All right, I'll think it over. I'm sure we'll come up with something.

Nora: That's so nice of you. (*Goes to the Christmas tree. A short pause.*) How pretty the red flowers look. But, tell me, was it really something very bad that this Krogstad was guilty of?

Helmer: He forged someone's name. Do you have any idea what that means?

Nora: Isn't it possible that he was forced to do it by necessity?

Helmer: Yes. Or, the way it is in so many cases, by foolishness. I'm not so heartless that I'd absolutely condemn a man because of one mistake like that.

Nora: No, you wouldn't, would you, Torvald?

Helmer: Many a man has been able to rehabilitate himself, if he's openly admitted his guilt and taken his punishment.

Nora: Punishment?

Helmer: But Krogstad didn't do that. He wriggled out of it with lies and trickery, and that's what completely undermined his moral character.

Nora: But do you think that that would—

Helmer: Just think how a guilty man like that has to lie and act like a hypocrite with everyone, how he has to wear a mask in front of the people closest to him, even with his own wife and children. And the children. That's the most terrible part of it all, Nora.

Nora: How so?

Helmer: Because an atmosphere of lies infects and poisons the whole life of a home. Every breath the children take in a house like that is full of the germs of moral corruption.

Nora (*coming closer to him*): Are you sure of that?

Helmer: My dear, I've seen it many times in my legal career. Almost everyone who's gone wrong at a young age had a dishonest mother.

Nora: Why only the mother?

Helmer: It usually seems to be the mother's influence, though naturally a bad father would have the same result. Every lawyer knows this. This Krogstad, now, has been systematically poisoning his own children with lies and deceit. That's why I say he's lost all moral character. (*Holds out his hands to her.*) And that's why my sweet little Nora must promise me not to plead his cause. Give me your hand on it. Come now, what's this? Give me your hand. There, that's settled. Believe me, it would be impossible for me to work with him. It literally makes me feel physically ill to be around people like that.

Nora (*takes her hand out of his and goes to the opposite side of the Christmas tree*): How hot it is in here! And I have so much to do.

Helmer (*getting up and putting his papers in order*): Yes, and I have to try to read through some of these before dinner. And I have to think about your costume, too. And it's just possible I'll have something wrapped in gold paper to hang up on the tree. (*Puts his hand on her head.*) My precious little songbird! (*He goes into his study and closes the door behind him.*)

Nora (after a pause, whispers): No, no, it's not true. It's impossible. It has to be impossible.

(*The nursemaid opens the door on the left.*)

Nursemaid: The little ones are begging so hard to be allowed to come in to see Mama.

Nora: No, no, no! Don't let them come in to me! You stay with them, Anne Marie.

Nursemaid: Very well, ma'am. (*Shuts the door.*)

Nora (pale with terror): Corrupt my little children? Poison my home? (*A short pause. Then she tosses her head.*) It's not true. It can't possibly be true.

ACT II

The same scene. The Christmas tree is in the corner by the piano, stripped of its ornaments and with burnt-down candle-ends on its disheveled branches. Nora's coat and hat are lying on the sofa. She is alone in the room, walking around uneasily. She stops by the sofa and picks up her coat.

Nora (drops her coat): Someone's coming! (*Goes to the door and listens.*) No, there's no one there. Of course, no one will come today. It's Christmas Day. And not tomorrow either. But maybe . . . (*opens the door and looks out*) No, nothing in the mailbox. It's empty. (*Comes forward.*) What nonsense! Of course he can't be serious about it. A thing like that couldn't happen. It's impossible. I have three little children.

(*Enter the nursemaid Anne Marie from the room on the left, carrying a big cardboard box.*)

Nursemaid: I finally found the box with the costume.

Nora: Thank you. Put it on the table.

Nursemaid (doing so): But it really needs to be mended.

Nora: I'd like to tear it into a hundred thousand pieces.

Nursemaid: What an idea! It can easily be fixed up. All you need is a little patience.

Nora: Yes, I'll go get Mrs. Linde to come and help me with it.

Nursemaid: What, going out again? In this horrible weather? You'll catch cold, Miss Nora, and make yourself sick.

Nora: Well, worse things than that might happen. How are the children?

Nursemaid: The poor little ones are playing with their Christmas presents, but—

Nora: Do they ask for me much?

Nursemaid: You see, they're so used to having their Mama with them.

Nora: Yes, but, Anne Marie, I won't be able to spend as much time with them now as I did before.

Nursemaid: Oh well, young children quickly get used to anything.

Nora: Do you think so? Do you think they'd forget their mother if she went away for good?

Nursemaid: Good heavens! Went away for good?

Nora: Anne Marie, I want you to tell me something I've often wondered about. How could you have the heart to let your own child be raised by strangers?

Nursemaid: I had to, if I wanted to be little Nora's nursemaid.

Nora: Yes, but how could you agree to it?

Nursemaid: What, when I was going to get such a good situation out of it? A poor girl who's gotten herself in trouble should be glad to. Besides, that worthless man didn't do a single thing for me.

Nora: But I suppose your daughter has completely forgotten you.

Nursemaid: No, she hasn't, not at all. She wrote to me when she was confirmed, and again when she got married.

Nora (*putting her arms round her neck*): Dear old Anne Marie, you were such a good mother to me when I was little.

Nursemaid: Poor little Nora, you had no other mother but me.

Nora: And if my little ones had no other mother, I'm sure that you would—What nonsense I'm talking! (*Opens the box.*) Go in and see to them. Now I have to . . . You'll see how lovely I'll look tomorrow.

Nursemaid: I'm sure there'll be no one at the ball as lovely as you, Miss Nora.

(*Goes into the room on the left.*)

Nora (*begins to unpack the box, but soon pushes it away from her*): If only I dared to go out. If only no one would come. If only I could be sure nothing would happen here in the meantime. What nonsense! No one's going to come. I just have to stop thinking about it. This muff needs to be brushed. What beautiful, beautiful gloves! Stop thinking about it, stop thinking about it! One, two, three, four, five, six—(*Screams.*) Aaah! Somebody *is* coming—(*Makes a movement towards the door, but stands in hesitation.*)

(*Enter Mrs. Linde from the hall, where she has taken off her coat and hat.*)

Nora: Oh, it's you, Kristine. There's no one else out in the hall, is there? How good of you to come!

Mrs. Linde: I heard you came by asking for me.

Nora: Yes, I was passing by. As a matter of fact, it's something you could help me with. Let's sit down here on the sofa. Listen, tomorrow evening there's going to be a fancy-dress ball at the Stenborgs'—they live upstairs from us—and Torvald wants me to go as a Neapolitan fisher-girl and dance the tarantella. I learned it when we were at Capri.

Mrs. Linde: I see. You're going to give them the whole show.

Nora: Yes, Torvald wants me to. Look, here's the dress. Torvald had it made for me there, but now it's all so torn, and I don't have any idea—

Mrs. Linde: We can easily fix that. Some of the trim has just come loose here and there. Do you have a needle and thread? That's all we need.

Nora: This is so nice of you.

Mrs. Linde (*sewing*): So you're going to be dressed up tomorrow, Nora. I'll tell you what. I'll stop by for a moment so I can see you in your finery. Oh, meanwhile I've completely forgotten to thank you for a delightful evening last night.

Nora (*gets up, and crosses the stage*): Well, I didn't think last night was as pleasant as usual. You should have come to town a little earlier, Kristine. Torvald really knows how to make a home pleasant and attractive.

Mrs. Linde: And so do you, if you ask me. You're not your father's daughter for nothing. But tell me, is Doctor Rank always as depressed as he was yesterday?

Nora: No, yesterday it was especially noticeable. But you have to understand that he has a very serious disease. He has tuberculosis of the spine, poor creature. His father was a horrible man who always had mistresses, and that's why his son has been sickly since childhood, if you know what I mean.

Mrs. Linde (dropping her sewing): But, my dear Nora, how do you know anything about such things?

Nora (walking around the room): Pooh! When you have three children, you get visits now and then from—from married women, who know something about medical matters, and they talk about one thing and another.

Mrs. Linde (goes on sewing. A short silence): Does Doctor Rank come here every day?

Nora: Every day, like clockwork. He's Torvald's best friend, and a great friend of mine too. He's just like one of the family.

Mrs. Linde: But tell me, is he really sincere? I mean, isn't he the kind of man who tends to play up to people?

Nora: No, not at all. What makes you think that?

Mrs. Linde: When you introduced him to me yesterday, he told me he'd often heard my name mentioned in this house, but later I could see that your husband didn't have the slightest idea who I was. So how could Doctor Rank—?

Nora: That's true, Kristine. Torvald is so ridiculously fond of me that he wants me completely to himself, as he says. At first he used to seem almost jealous if I even mentioned any of my friends back home, so naturally I stopped talking about them to him. But I often talk about things like that with Doctor Rank, because he likes hearing about them.

Mrs. Linde: Listen to me, Nora. You're still like a child in a lot of ways, and I'm older than you and more experienced. So pay attention. You'd better stop all this with Doctor Rank.

Nora: Stop all what?

Mrs. Linde: Two things, I think. Yesterday you talked some nonsense about a rich admirer who was going to leave you his money—

Nora: An admirer who doesn't exist, unfortunately! But so what?

Mrs. Linde: Is Doctor Rank a wealthy man?

Nora: Yes, he is.

Mrs. Linde: And he has no dependents?

Nora: No, no one. But—

Mrs. Linde: And he comes here every day?

Nora: Yes, I told you he does.

Mrs. Linde: But how can such a well-bred man be so tactless?

Nora: I don't understand what you mean.

Mrs. Linde: Don't try to play dumb, Nora. Do you think I didn't guess who lent you the four thousand, eight hundred kroner?

Nora: Are you out of your mind? How can you even think that? A friend of ours, who comes here every day! Don't you realize what an incredibly awkward position that would put me in?

Mrs. Linde: Then he's really not the one?

Nora: Absolutely not. It would never have come into my head for one second. Besides, he had nothing to lend back then. He inherited his money later on.

Mrs. Linde: Well, I think that was lucky for you, my dear Nora.

Nora: No, it would never have crossed my mind to ask Doctor Rank. Although I'm sure that if I had asked him—

Mrs. Linde: But of course you won't.

Nora: Of course not. I have no reason to think I could possibly need to. But I'm absolutely certain that if I told Doctor Rank—

Mrs. Linde: Behind your husband's back?

Nora: I have to finish up with the other one, and that'll be behind his back too. I've got to wash my hands of him.

Mrs. Linde: Yes, that's what I told you yesterday, but—

Nora (walking up and down): A man can take care of these things so much more easily than a woman.

Mrs. Linde: If he's your husband, yes.

Nora: Nonsense! (*Standing still.*) When you pay off a debt you get your note back, don't you?

Mrs. Linde: Yes, of course.

Nora: And you can tear it into a hundred thousand pieces and burn up the filthy, nasty piece of paper!

Mrs. Linde (stares at her, puts down her sewing and gets up slowly): Nora, you're hiding something from me.

Nora: You can tell by looking at me?

Mrs. Linde: Something's happened to you since yesterday morning. Nora, what is it?

Nora (going nearer to her): Kristine! (*Listens.*) Shh! I hear Torvald. He's come home. Would you mind going in to the children's room for a little while? Torvald can't stand to see all this sewing going on. You can get Anne Marie to help you.

Mrs. Linde (gathering some of the things together): All right, but I'm not leaving this house until we've talked this thing through.

(*She goes into the room on the left, as Helmer comes in from the hall.*)

Nora (going up to Helmer): I've missed you so much, Torvald dear.

Helmer: Was that the seamstress?

Nora: No, it was Kristine. She's helping me fix up my dress. You'll see how nice I'm going to look.

Helmer: Wasn't that a good idea of mine, now?

Nora: Wonderful! But don't you think it's nice of me, too, to do what you said?

Helmer: Nice, because you do what your husband tells you to? Go on, you silly little thing, I am sure you didn't mean it like that. But I'll stay out of your way. I imagine you'll be trying on your dress.

Nora: I suppose you're going to do some work.

Helmer: Yes. (*Shows her a stack of papers.*) Look at that. I've just been at the bank. (*Turns to go into his room.*)

Nora: Torvald.

Helmer: Yes?

Nora: If your little squirrel were to ask you for something in a very, very charming way—

Helmer: Well?

Nora: Would you do it?

Helmer: I'd have to know what it is, first.

Nora: Your squirrel would run around and do all her tricks if you would be really nice and do what she wants.

Helmer: Speak plainly.

Nora: Your skylark would chirp her beautiful song in every room—

Helmer: Well, my skylark does that anyhow.

Nora: I'd be a little elf and dance in the moonlight for you, Torvald.

Helmer: Nora, you can't be referring to what you talked about this morning.

Nora (moving close to him): Yes, Torvald, I'm really begging you—

Helmer: You really have the nerve to bring that up again?

Nora: Yes, dear, you have to do this for me. You have to let Krogstad keep his job in the bank.

Helmer: My dear Nora, his job is the one that I'm giving to Mrs. Linde.

Nora: Yes, you've been awfully sweet about that. But you could just as easily get rid of somebody else instead of Krogstad.

Helmer: This is just unbelievable stubbornness! Because you decided to foolishly promise that you'd speak up for him, you expect me to—

Nora: That's not the reason, Torvald. It's for your own sake. This man writes for the trashiest newspapers, you've told me so yourself. He can do you an incredible amount of harm. I'm scared to death of him—

Helmer: Oh, I see, it's bad memories that are making you afraid.

Nora: What do you mean?

Helmer: Obviously you're thinking about your father.

Nora: Yes. Yes, of course. You remember what those hateful creatures wrote in the papers about Papa, and how horribly they slandered him. I believe they'd have gotten him fired if the department hadn't sent you over to look into it, and if you hadn't been so kind and helpful to him.

Helmer: My little Nora, there's an important difference between your father and me. His reputation as a public official was not above suspicion. Mine is, and I hope it will continue to be for as long as I hold my office.

Nora: You never can tell what trouble these men might cause. We could be so well off, so snug and happy here in our peaceful home, without a care in the world, you and I and the children, Torvald! That's why I'm begging you to—

Helmer: And the more you plead for him, the more you make it impossible for me to keep him. They already know at the bank that I'm going to fire Krogstad. Do you think I'm going to let them all say that the new manager has changed his mind because his wife said to—

Nora: And what if they did?

Helmer: Right! What does it matter, as long as this stubborn little creature gets her own way! Do you think I'm going to make myself look ridiculous in front of my whole staff, and let people think that I can be pushed around by all sorts of outside influence? That would soon come back to haunt me, you can be sure! And besides, there's one thing that makes it totally impossible for me to have Krogstad working in the bank as long as I'm the manager.

Nora: What's that?

Helmer: I might have been able to overlook his moral failings, if need be—

Nora: Yes, you could do that, couldn't you?

Helmer: And I hear he's a good worker, too. But I knew him when we were boys. It was one of those rash friendships that so often turn out to be a millstone around the neck later on. I might as well tell you straight out, we were very close friends at one time. But he has no tact and no self-restraint, especially when other people are around. He thinks he has the right to still call me by my first name, and every minute it's Torvald this and Torvald that. I don't mind telling you, I find it extremely annoying. He would make my position at the bank intolerable.

Nora: Torvald, I can't believe you're serious.

Helmer: Oh no? Why not?

Nora: Because it's so petty.

Helmer: What do you mean, petty? You think I'm petty?

Nora: No, just the opposite, dear, and that's why I can't—

Helmer: It's the same thing. You say my attitude's petty, so I must be petty too! Petty! Fine! Well, I'll put a stop to this once and for all. (*Goes to the hall door and calls.*) Helene!

Nora: What are you going to do?

Helmer (*looking among his papers*): Settle it.

(*Enter Maid.*)

Here, take this letter downstairs right now. Find a messenger and tell him to deliver it, and to be quick about it. The address is on it, and here's the money.

Maid: Yes, sir. (*Exits with the letter.*)

Helmer (*putting his papers together*): There, Little Pigheaded Miss.

Nora (*breathlessly*): Torvald, what was that letter?

Helmer: Krogstad's notice.

Nora: Call her back, Torvald! There's still time. Oh, Torvald, call her back! Do it for my sake—for your own sake—for the children's sake! Do you hear me, Torvald? Call her back! You don't know what that letter can do to us.

Helmer: It's too late.

Nora: Yes, it's too late.

Helmer: My dear Nora, I can forgive this anxiety of yours, even though it's insulting to me. It really is. Don't you think it's insulting to suggest that I should be afraid of retaliation from a grubby pen-pusher? But I forgive you anyway, because it's such a beautiful demonstration of how much you love me. (*Takes her in his arms.*) And that is as it should be, my own darling Nora. Come what may, you can rest assured that I'll have both courage and strength if necessary. You'll see that I'm man enough to take everything on myself.

Nora (*in a horror-stricken voice*): What do you mean by that?

Helmer: Everything, I say.

Nora (*recovering herself*): You'll never have to do that.

Helmer: That's right, we'll take it on together, Nora, as man and wife. That's just how it should be. (*Caressing her.*) Are you satisfied now? There, there! Don't look at me that way, like a frightened dove! This whole thing is just your imagination running away with you. Now you should go and run through the tarantella and practice your tambourine. I'll go into my study and shut the door so I can't hear anything. You can make all the noise you want. (*Turns back at the door.*) And when Rank comes, tell him where I am.

(*Nods to her, takes his papers and goes into his room, and shuts the door behind him.*)

Nora (*bewildered with anxiety, stands as if rooted to the spot and whispers*): He's capable of doing it. He's going to do it. He'll do it in spite of everything. No, not that! Never, never! Anything but that! Oh, for somebody to help me find some way out of this! (*The doorbell rings.*) Doctor Rank! Anything but that—anything, whatever it is!

(*She puts her hands over her face, pulls herself together, goes to the door and opens it. Rank is standing in the hall, hanging up his coat. During the following dialogue it starts to grow dark.*)

Nora: Hello, Doctor Rank. I recognized your ring. But you'd better not go in and see Torvald just now. I think he's busy with something.

Rank: And you?

Nora (*brings him in and shuts the door behind him*): Oh, you know perfectly well I always have time for you.

Rank: Thank you. I'll make use of it for as long as I can.

Nora: What does that mean, for as long as you can?

Rank: Why, does that frighten you?

Nora: It was such a strange way of putting it. Is something going to happen?

Rank: Nothing but what I've been expecting for a long time. But I never thought it would happen so soon.

Nora (*gripping him by the arm*): What have you found out? Doctor Rank, you must tell me.

Rank (*sitting down by the stove*): I'm done for. And there's nothing I can do about it.

Nora (*with a sigh of relief*): Oh—you're talking about yourself?

Rank: Who else? And there's no use lying to myself. I'm the sickest patient I have, Mrs. Helmer. Lately I've been adding up my internal account. Bankrupt! In a month I'll probably be rotting in the ground.

Nora: What a horrible thing to say!

Rank: The thing itself is horrible, and the worst of it is all the horrible things I'll have to go through before it's over. I'm going to examine myself just once more. When that's done, I'll be pretty sure when I'm going to start breaking down. There's something I want to say to you. Helmer's sensitive nature makes him completely unable to deal with anything ugly. I don't want him in my sickroom.

Nora: Oh, but, Doctor Rank—

Rank: I won't have him there, period. I'll lock the door to keep him out. As soon as I'm quite sure that the worst has come, I'll send you my card with a black cross on it, and that way you'll know that the final stage of the horror has started.

Nora: You're being really absurd today. And I so much wanted you to be in a good mood.

Rank: With death stalking me? Having to pay this price for another man's sins? Where's the justice in that? In every single family, in one way or another, some such unavoidable retribution is being imposed.

Nora (*putting her hands over her ears*): Nonsense! Can't you talk about something cheerful?

Rank: Oh, this *is* something cheerful. In fact, it's hilarious. My poor innocent spine has to suffer for my father's youthful self-indulgence.

Nora (sitting at the table on the left): Yes, he did love asparagus and *pâté de foie gras*, didn't he?

Rank: Yes, and truffles.

Nora: Truffles, yes. And oysters too, I suppose?

Rank: Oysters, of course. That goes without saying.

Nora: And oceans of port and champagne. Isn't it sad that all those delightful things should take their revenge on our bones?

Rank: Especially that they should take their revenge on the unlucky bones of people who haven't even had the satisfaction of enjoying them.

Nora: Yes, that's the saddest part of all.

Rank (with a searching look at her): Hm!

Nora (after a short pause): Why did you smile?

Rank: No, it was you who laughed.

Nora: No, it was you who smiled, Doctor Rank!

Rank (rising): You're even more of a tease than I thought you were.

Nora: I am in a crazy mood today.

Rank: Apparently so.

Nora (putting her hands on his shoulders): Dear, dear Doctor Rank, we can't let death take you away from Torvald and me.

Rank: It's a loss that you'll easily recover from. Those who are gone are soon forgotten.

Nora (looking at him anxiously): Do you really believe that?

Rank: People make new friends, and then—

Nora: Who'll make new friends?

Rank: Both you and Helmer, when I'm gone. You yourself are already well on the way to it, I think. What was that Mrs. Linde doing here last night?

Nora: Oho! You're not telling me that you're jealous of poor Kristine, are you?

Rank: Yes, I am. She'll be my successor in this house. When I'm six feet under, this woman will—

Nora: Shh! Don't talk so loud. She's in that room.

Rank: Again today. There, you see.

Nora: She's just come to sew my dress for me. Goodness, how unreasonable you are! (*Sits down on the sofa.*) Be nice now, Doctor Rank, and tomorrow you'll see how beautifully I'll dance, and you can pretend that I'm doing it just for you—and for Torvald too, of course. (*Takes various things out of the box.*) Doctor Rank, come and sit down here, and I'll show you something.

Rank (sitting down): What is it?

Nora: Just look at these!

Rank: Silk stockings.

Nora: Flesh-colored. Aren't they lovely? It's so dark here now, but tomorrow—No, no, no! You're only supposed to look at the feet. Oh well, you have my permission to look at the legs too.

Rank: Hm!

Nora: Why do you look so critical? Don't you think they'll fit me?

Rank: I have no basis for forming an opinion on that subject.

Nora (*looks at him for a moment*): Shame on you! (*Hits him lightly on the ear with the stockings.*) That's your punishment. (*Folds them up again.*)

Rank: And what other pretty things do I have your permission to look at?

Nora: Not one single thing. That's what you get for being so naughty. (*She looks among the things, humming to herself.*)

Rank (*after a short silence*): When I'm sitting here, talking to you so intimately this way, I can't imagine for a moment what would have become of me if I'd never come into this house.

Nora (*smiling*): I believe you really do feel completely at home with us.

Rank (*in a lower voice, looking straight in front of him*): And to have to leave it all—

Nora: Nonsense, you're not going to leave it.

Rank (*as before*): And not to be able to leave behind the slightest token of my gratitude, hardly even a fleeting regret. Nothing but an empty place to be filled by the first person who comes along.

Nora: And if I were to ask you now for a—No, never mind!

Rank: For a what?

Nora: For a great proof of your friendship—

Rank: Yes, yes!

Nora: I mean a tremendously huge favor—

Rank: Would you really make me so happy, just this once?

Nora: But you don't know what it is yet.

Rank: No, but tell me.

Nora: I really can't, Doctor Rank. It's too much to ask. It involves advice, and help, and a favor—

Rank: So much the better. I can't imagine what you mean. Tell me what it is. You do trust me, don't you?

Nora: More than anyone. I know that you're my best and truest friend, so I'll tell you what it is. Well, Doctor Rank, it's something you have to help me prevent. You know how devoted Torvald is to me, how deeply he loves me. He wouldn't hesitate for a second to give his life for me.

Rank (*leaning towards her*): Nora, do you think that he's the only one—

Nora (*with a slight start*): The only one?

Rank: Who would gladly give his life for you.

Nora (*sadly*): Oh, is that it?

Rank: I'd made up my mind to tell you before I—I go away, and there'll never be a better opportunity than this. Now you know it, Nora. And now you know that you can trust me more than you can trust anyone else.

Nora (*rises, deliberately and quietly*): Let me by.

Rank (*makes room for her to pass him, but sits still*): Nora!

Nora (*at the hall door*): Helene, bring in the lamp. (*Goes over to the stove.*) Dear Doctor Rank, that was really horrible of you.

Rank: To love you just as much as somebody else does? Is that so horrible?

Nora: No, but to go and tell me like that. There was really no need—

Rank: What do you mean? Did you know—

(*Maid enters with lamp, puts it down on the table, and goes out.*)

Nora—Mrs. Helmer—tell me, did you have any idea I felt this way?

Nora: Oh, how do I know whether I did or I didn't? I really can't answer that. How could you be so clumsy, Doctor Rank? When we were getting along so nicely.

Rank: Well, at any rate, now you know that I'm yours to command, body and soul. So won't you tell me what it is?

Nora (looking at him): After what just happened?

Rank: I beg you to let me know what it is.

Nora: I can't tell you anything now.

Rank: Yes, yes. Please don't punish me that way. Give me permission to do anything for you that a man can do.

Nora: You can't do anything for me now. Besides, I really don't need any help at all. The whole thing is just my imagination. It really is. It has to be! (*Sits down in the rocking chair, and smiles at him.*) You're a nice man, Doctor Rank. Don't you feel ashamed of yourself, now that the lamp is lit?

Rank: Not a bit. But maybe it would be better if I left—and never came back?

Nora: No, no, you can't do that. You must keep coming here just as you always did. You know very well Torvald can't do without you.

Rank: But what about you?

Nora: Oh, I'm always extremely pleased to see you.

Rank: And that's just what gave me the wrong idea. You're a puzzle to me. I've often felt that you'd almost just as soon be in my company as in Helmer's.

Nora: Yes, you see, there are the people you love the most, and then there are the people whose company you enjoy the most.

Rank: Yes, there's something to that.

Nora: When I lived at home, of course I loved Papa best. But I always thought it was great fun to sneak down to the maids' room, because they never preached at me, and I loved listening to the way they talked to each other.

Rank: I see. So I'm their replacement.

Nora (jumping up and going to him): Oh, dear, sweet Doctor Rank, I didn't mean it that way. But surely you can understand that being with Torvald is a little like being with Papa—

(*Enter Maid from the hall.*)

Maid: Excuse me, ma'am. (*Whispers and hands her a card.*)

Nora (glancing at the card): Oh! (*Puts it in her pocket.*)

Rank: Is something wrong?

Nora: No, no, not at all. It's just—it's my new dress—

Rank: What? Your dress is lying right there.

Nora: Oh, yes, that one. But this is another one, one that I ordered. I don't want Torvald to find out about it—

Rank: Oh! So that was the big secret.

Nora: Yes, that's it. Why don't you just go inside and see him? He's in his study. Stay with him for as long as—

Rank: Put your mind at ease. I won't let him escape. (*Goes into Helmer's study.*)

Nora (to the maid): And he's waiting in the kitchen?

Maid: Yes, ma'am. He came up the back stairs.

Nora: Didn't you tell him no one was home?

Maid: Yes, but it didn't do any good.

Nora: He won't go away?

Maid: No, he says he won't leave until he sees you, ma'am.

Nora: Well, show him in, but quietly. Helene, I don't want you to say anything about this to anyone. It's a surprise for my husband.

Maid: Yes, ma'am. I understand. (*Exit.*)

Nora: This horrible thing is really going to happen! It's going to happen in spite of me! No, no, no, it can't happen! I can't let it happen!

(*She bolts the door of Helmer's study. The maid opens the hall door for Krogstad and closes it behind him. He is wearing a fur coat, high boots, and a fur cap.*)

Nora (*advancing towards him*): Speak quietly. My husband's home.

Krogstad: What do I care about that?

Nora: What do you want from me?

Krogstad: An explanation of something.

Nora: Be quick, then. What is it?

Krogstad: I suppose you're aware that I've been let go.

Nora: I couldn't prevent it, Mr. Krogstad. I fought for you as hard as I could, but it was no use.

Krogstad: Does your husband love you so little, then? He knows what I can expose you to, and he still goes ahead and—

Nora: How can you think that he knows any such thing?

Krogstad: I didn't think so for a moment. It wouldn't be at all like dear old Torvald Helmer to show that kind of courage—

Nora: Mr. Krogstad, a little respect for my husband, please.

Krogstad: Certainly—all the respect he deserves. But since you've kept everything so carefully to yourself, may I be bold enough to assume that you see a little more clearly than you did yesterday just what it is that you've done?

Nora: More than you could ever teach me.

Krogstad: Yes, such a poor excuse for a lawyer as I am.

Nora: What is it you want from me?

Krogstad: Only to see how you're doing, Mrs. Helmer. I've been thinking about you all day. A mere bill collector, a pen-pusher, a—well, a man like me—even he has a little of what people call feelings, you know.

Nora: Why don't you show some, then? Think about my little children.

Krogstad: Have you and your husband thought about mine? But never mind about that. I just wanted to tell you not to take this business too seriously. I won't make any accusations against you. Not for now, anyway.

Nora: No, of course not. I was sure you wouldn't.

Krogstad: The whole thing can be settled amicably. There's no need for anyone to know anything about it. It'll be our little secret, just the three of us.

Nora: My husband must never know anything about it.

Krogstad: How are you going to keep him from finding out? Are you telling me that you can pay off the whole balance?

Nora: No, not just yet.

Krogstad: Or that you have some other way of raising the money soon?

Nora: No way that I plan to make use of.

Krogstad: Well, in any case, it wouldn't be any use to you now even if you did. If you stood in front of me with a stack of bills in each hand, I still wouldn't give you back your note.

Nora: What are you planning to do with it?

Krogstad: I just want to hold onto it, just keep it in my possession. No one who isn't involved in the matter will ever know anything about it. So, if you've been thinking about doing something desperate—

Nora: I have.

Krogstad: If you've been thinking about running away—

Nora: I have.

Krogstad: Or doing something even worse—

Nora: How could you know that?

Krogstad: Stop thinking about it.

Nora: How did you know I'd thought of that?

Krogstad: Most of us think about that at first. I did, too. But I didn't have the courage.

Nora (faintly): Neither do I.

Krogstad (in a tone of relief): No, that's true, isn't it? You don't have the courage either?

Nora: No, I don't. I don't.

Krogstad: Besides, it would have been an incredibly stupid thing to do. Once the first storm at home blows over . . . I have a letter for your husband in my pocket.

Nora: Telling him everything?

Krogstad: As gently as possible.

Nora (quickly): He can't see that letter. Tear it up. I'll find some way of getting money.

Krogstad: Excuse me, Mrs. Helmer, but didn't I just tell you—

Nora: I'm not talking about what I owe you. Tell me how much you want from my husband, and I'll get the money.

Krogstad: I don't want any money from your husband.

Nora: Then what do you want?

Krogstad: I'll tell you what I want. I want a fresh start, Mrs. Helmer, and I want to move up in the world. And your husband's going to help me do it. I've steered clear of anything questionable for the last year and a half. In all that time I've been struggling along, pinching every penny. I was content to work my way up step by step. But now I've been fired, and it's not going to be enough just to get my job back, as if you people were doing me some huge favor. I want to move up, I tell you. I want to get back into the bank again, but with a promotion. Your husband's going to have find me a position—

Nora: He'll never do it!

Krogstad: Oh yes, he will. I know him. He won't dare object. And as soon as I'm back there with him, then you'll see! Inside of a year I'll be the manager's right-hand man. It'll be Nils Krogstad, not Torvald Helmer, who's running the bank.

Nora: That's never going to happen!

Krogstad: Do you mean that you'll—

Nora: I have enough courage for it now.

Krogstad: Oh, you can't scare me. An elegant, spoiled lady like you—

Nora: You'll see, you'll see.

Krogstad: Under the ice, maybe? Down in the cold, coal-black water? And then floating up to the surface in the spring, all horrible and unrecognizable, with your hair fallen out—

Nora: You can't scare me.

Krogstad: And you can't scare me. People don't do that kind of thing, Mrs. Helmer. Besides, what good would it do? I'd still have him completely in my power.

Nora: Even then? When I'm no longer—

Krogstad: Have you forgotten that your reputation is completely in my hands? (*Nora stands speechless, looking at him.*) Well, now I've warned you. Don't do anything foolish. I'll be expecting an answer from Helmer after he reads my letter. And remember, it's your husband himself who's forced me to act this way again. I'll never forgive him for that. Goodbye, Mrs. Helmer. (*Exits through the hall.*)

Nora (*goes to the hall door, opens it slightly and listens.*): He's leaving. He isn't putting the letter in the box. Oh no, no! He couldn't! (*Opens the door little by little.*) What? He's standing out there. He's not going downstairs. He's hesitating? Is he?

(*A letter drops into the box. Then Krogstad's footsteps are heard, until they die away as he goes downstairs. Nora utters a stifled cry, and runs across the room to the table by the sofa. A short pause.*)

Nora: In the mailbox. (*Steals across to the hall door.*) It's there! Torvald, Torvald, there's no hope for us now!

(*Mrs. Linde comes in from the room on the left, carrying the dress.*)

Mrs. Linde: There, I can't find anything more to mend. Would you like to try it on?

Nora (*in a hoarse whisper*): Kristine, come here.

Mrs. Linde (*throwing the dress down on the sofa*): What's the matter with you? You look so agitated!

Nora: Come here. Do you see that letter? There, look. You can see it through the glass in the mailbox.

Mrs. Linde: Yes, I see it.

Nora: That letter is from Krogstad.

Mrs. Linde: Nora! It was Krogstad who lent you the money!

Nora: Yes, and now Torvald will know all about it.

Mrs. Linde: Believe me, Nora, that's the best thing for both of you.

Nora: You don't know the whole story. I forged a name.

Mrs. Linde: My God!

Nora: There's something I want to say to you, Kristine. I need you to be my witness.

Mrs. Linde: Your witness? What do you mean? What am I supposed to—

Nora: If I should go out of my mind—and it could easily happen—

Mrs. Linde: Nora!

Nora: Or if anything else should happen to me—anything, for instance, that might keep me from being here—

Mrs. Linde: Nora! Nora! What's the matter with you?

Nora: And if it turned out that somebody wanted to take all the responsibility, all the blame, you understand what I mean—

Mrs. Linde: Yes, yes, but how can you imagine—

Nora: Then you must be my witness that it's not true, Kristine. I'm not out of my mind at all. I'm perfectly rational right now, and I'm telling you that no one else ever knew anything about it. I did the whole thing all by myself. Remember that.

Mrs. Linde: I will. But I don't understand all this.

Nora: How could you understand it? Or the miracle that's going to happen!

Mrs. Linde: A miracle?

Nora: Yes, a miracle! But it's so terrible, Kristine. I can't let it happen, not for the whole world.

Mrs. Linde: I'll go and see Krogstad right this minute.

Nora: No, don't. He'll do something to hurt you too.

Mrs. Linde: There was a time when he would have gladly done anything for my sake.

Nora: What?

Mrs. Linde: Where does he live?

Nora: How should I know? Yes (*feeling in her pocket*), here's his card. But the letter, the letter—

Helmer (calls from his room, knocking at the door): Nora!

Nora (cries out anxiously): What is it? What do you want?

Helmer: Don't be so afraid. We're not coming in. You've locked the door. Are you trying on your dress?

Nora: Yes, that's it. Oh, it's going to look so nice, Torvald.

Mrs. Linde (who has read the card): Look, he lives right around the corner.

Nora: But it's no use. It's all over. The letter's lying right there in the box.

Mrs. Linde: And your husband has the key?

Nora: Yes, always.

Mrs. Linde: Krogstad can ask for his letter back unread. He'll have to make up some reason—

Nora: But now is just about the time that Torvald usually—

Mrs. Linde: You have to prevent him. Go in and talk to him. I'll be back as soon as I can.

(*She hurries out through the hall door.*)

Nora (goes to Helmer's door, opens it and peeps in): Torvald!

Helmer (from the inner room): Well? May I finally come back into my own room? Come along, Rank, now you'll see—(*Stopping in the doorway.*) But what's this?

Nora: What's what, dear?

Helmer: Rank led me to expect an amazing transformation.

Rank (in the doorway): So I understood, but apparently I was mistaken.

Nora: Yes, nobody gets to admire me in my dress until tomorrow.

Helmer: But, my dear Nora, you look exhausted. Have you been practicing too much?

Nora: No, I haven't been practicing at all.

Helmer: But you'll have to—

Nora: Yes, of course I will, Torvald. But I can't get anywhere without you helping me. I've completely forgotten the whole thing.

Helmer: Oh, we'll soon get you back up to form again.

Nora: Yes, help me, Torvald. Promise that you will! I'm so nervous about it—all those people. I need you to devote yourself completely to me this evening. Not even the tiniest little bit of business. You can't even pick up a pen. Do you promise, Torvald dear?

Helmer: I promise. This evening I will be wholly and absolutely at your service, you helpless little creature. But first I'm just going to—(*Goes towards the hall door.*)

Nora: Just going to what?

Helmer: To see if there's any mail.

Nora: No, no! Don't do that, Torvald!

Helmer: Why not?

Nora: Torvald, please don't. There's nothing there.

Helmer: Well, let me look. (*Turns to go to the mailbox. Nora, at the piano, plays the first bars of the tarantella. Helmer stops in the doorway.*) Aha!

Nora: I can't dance tomorrow if I don't practice with you.

Helmer (going up to her): Are you really so worried about it, dear?

Nora: Yes, terribly worried about it. Let me practice right now. We have time before dinner. Sit down and play for me, Torvald dear. Criticize me and correct me, the way you always do.

Helmer: With great pleasure, if you want me to. (*Sits down at the piano.*)

Nora (takes a tambourine and a long multicolored shawl out of the box. She hastily drapes the shawl around her. Then she bounds to the front of the stage and calls out): Now play for me! I'm going to dance!

(*Helmer plays and Nora dances. Rank stands by the piano behind Helmer and watches.*)

Helmer (as he plays): Slower, slower!

Nora: I can't do it any other way.

Helmer: Not so violently, Nora!

Nora: This is the way.

Helmer (stops playing): No, no, that's not right at all.

Nora (laughing and swinging the tambourine): Didn't I tell you so?

Rank: Let me play for her.

Helmer (getting up): Good idea. I can correct her better that way.

(*Rank sits down at the piano and plays. Nora dances more and more wildly. Helmer has taken up a position beside the stove, and as she dances, he gives her frequent instructions. She doesn't seem to hear him. Her hair comes undone and falls over her shoulders. She pays no attention to it, but goes on dancing. Enter Mrs. Linde.*)

Mrs. Linde (standing as if spellbound in the doorway): Oh!

Nora (as she dances): What fun, Kristine!

Helmer: My dear darling Nora, you're dancing as if your life depended on it.

Nora: It does.

Helmer: Stop, Rank. This is insane! I said stop!

(*Rank stops playing, and Nora suddenly stands still. Helmer goes up to her.*)

I never would have believed it. You've forgotten everything I taught you.

Nora (throwing the tambourine aside): There, you see.

Helmer: You're going to need a lot of coaching.

Nora: Yes, you see how much I need it. You have to coach me right up to the last minute. Promise me you will, Torvald!

Helmer: You can depend on me.

Nora: You can't think about anything but me, today or tomorrow. Don't open a single letter. Don't even open the mailbox—

Helmer: You're still afraid of that man—

Nora: Yes, yes, I am.

Helmer: Nora, I can tell from your face that there's a letter from him in the box.

Nora: I don't know. I think there is. But you can't read anything like that now. Nothing nasty must come between us until this is all over.

Rank (whispers to Helmer): Don't contradict her.

Helmer (taking her in his arms): The child shall have her way. But tomorrow night, after you've danced—

Nora: Then you'll be free.

(*The Maid appears in the doorway to the right.*)

Maid: Dinner is served, ma'am.

Nora: We'll have champagne, Helene.

Maid: Yes, ma'am. (*Exit.*)

Helmer: Oh, are we having a banquet?

Nora: Yes, a banquet. Champagne till dawn! (*Calls out.*) And a few macaroons, Helene. Lots of them, just this once!

Helmer: Come on, stop acting so wild and nervous. Be my own little skylark again.

Nora: Yes, dear, I will. But go inside now, and you too, Doctor Rank. Kristine, please help me do up my hair.

Rank (whispers to Helmer as they go out): There isn't anything—she's not expecting—?

Helmer: No, nothing like that. It's just this childish nervousness I was telling you about. (*They go into the right-hand room.*)

Nora: Well?

Mrs. Linde: Out of town.

Nora: I could tell from your face.

Mrs. Linde: He'll be back tomorrow evening. I wrote him a note.

Nora: You should have left it alone. Don't try to prevent anything. After all, it's exciting to be waiting for a miracle to happen.

Mrs. Linde: What is it that you're waiting for?

Nora: Oh, you wouldn't understand. Go inside with them, I'll be there in a moment.

(*Mrs. Linde goes into the dining room. Nora stands still for a little while, as if to compose herself. Then she looks at her watch.*)

Five o'clock. Seven hours till midnight, and another twenty-four hours till the next midnight. And then the tarantella will be over. Twenty-four plus seven? Thirty-one hours to live.

Helmer (from the doorway on the right): Where's my little skylark?

Nora (going to him with her arms outstretched): Here she is!

ACT III

The same scene. The table has been placed in the middle of the stage, with chairs around it. A lamp is burning on the table. The door into the hall stands open. Dance music is heard in the room above. Mrs. Linde is sitting at the table idly turning over the pages of a book. She tries to read, but she seems unable to concentrate. Every now and then she listens intently for a sound at the outer door.

Mrs. Linde (*looking at her watch*): Not yet—and the time's nearly up. If only he doesn't— (*Listens again.*) Ah, there he is. (*Goes into the hall and opens the outer door carefully. Light footsteps are heard on the stairs. She whispers.*) Come in. There's no one else here.

Krogstad (*in the doorway*): I found a note from you at home. What does this mean?

Mrs. Linde: It's absolutely necessary that I have a talk with you.

Krogstad: Really? And is it absolutely necessary that we have it here?

Mrs. Linde: It's impossible where I live. There's no private entrance to my apartment. Come in. We're all alone. The maid's asleep, and the Helmers are upstairs at a dance.

Krogstad (*coming into the room*): Are the Helmers really at a dance tonight?

Mrs. Linde: Yes. Why shouldn't they be?

Krogstad: Certainly—why not?

Mrs. Linde: Now, Nils, let's have a talk.

Krogstad: What can we two have to talk about?

Mrs. Linde: Quite a lot.

Krogstad: I wouldn't have thought so.

Mrs. Linde: Of course not. You've never really understood me.

Krogstad: What was there to understand, except what the whole world could see—a heartless woman drops a man when a better catch comes along?

Mrs. Linde: Do you think I'm really that heartless? And that I broke it off with you so lightly?

Krogstad: Didn't you?

Mrs. Linde: Nils, did you really think that?

Krogstad: If not, why did you write what you did to me?

Mrs. Linde: What else could I do? Since I had to break it off with you, I had an obligation to stamp out your feelings for me.

Krogstad (*wringing his hands*): So that was it. And all this just for the sake of money!

Mrs. Linde: Don't forget that I had an invalid mother and two little brothers. We couldn't wait for you, Nils. Success seemed a long way off for you back then.

Krogstad: That may be so, but you had no right to cast me aside for anyone else's sake.

Mrs. Linde: I don't know if I did or not. Many times I've asked myself if I had the right.

Krogstad (*more gently*): When I lost you, it was as if the earth crumbled under my feet. Look at me now—a shipwrecked man clinging to a bit of wreckage.

Mrs. Linde: But help may be on the way.

Krogstad: It *was* on the way, till you came along and blocked it.

Mrs. Linde: Without knowing it, Nils. It wasn't till today that I found out I'd be taking your job.

Krogstad: I believe you, if you say so. But now that you know it, are you going to step aside?

Mrs. Linde: No, because it wouldn't do you any good.

Krogstad: Good? I would quit whether it did any good or not.

Mrs. Linde: I've learned to be practical. Life and hard, bitter necessity have taught me that.

Krogstad: And life has taught me not to believe in fine speeches.

Mrs. Linde: Then life has taught you something very sensible. But surely you believe in actions?

Krogstad: What do you mean by that?

Mrs. Linde: You said you were like a shipwrecked man clinging to a piece of wreckage.

Krogstad: I had good reason to say so.

Mrs. Linde: Well, I'm like a shipwrecked woman clinging to a piece of wreckage, with no one to mourn for and no one to care for.

Krogstad: That was your own choice.

Mrs. Linde: I had no other choice—then.

Krogstad: Well, what about now?

Mrs. Linde: Nils, how would it be if we two shipwrecked people could reach out to each other?

Krogstad: What are you saying?

Mrs. Linde: Two people on the same piece of wreckage would stand a better chance than each one on their own.

Krogstad: Kristine, I . . .

Mrs. Linde: Why do you think I came to town?

Krogstad: You can't mean that you were thinking about me?

Mrs. Linde: Life is unendurable without work. I've worked all my life, for as long as I can remember, and it's been my greatest and my only pleasure. But now that I'm completely alone in the world, my life is so terribly empty and I feel so abandoned. There isn't the slightest pleasure in working only for yourself. Nils, give me someone and something to work for.

Krogstad: I don't trust this. It's just some romantic female impulse, a high-minded urge for self-sacrifice.

Mrs. Linde: Have you ever known me to be like that?

Krogstad: Could you really do it? Tell me, do you know all about my past?

Mrs. Linde: Yes.

Krogstad: And you know what they think of me around here?

Mrs. Linde: Didn't you imply that with me you might have been a very different person?

Krogstad: I'm sure I would have.

Mrs. Linde: Is it too late now?

Krogstad: Kristine, are you serious about all this? Yes, I'm sure you are. I can see it in your face. Do you really have the courage, then—

Mrs. Linde: I want to be a mother to someone, and your children need a mother. We two need each other. Nils, I have faith in your true nature. I can face anything together with you.

Krogstad (grasps her hands): Thank you, thank you, Kristine! Now I can find a way to clear myself in the eyes of the world. Ah, but I forgot—

Mrs. Linde (listening): Shh! The tarantella! You have to go!

Krogstad: Why? What's the matter?

Mrs. Linde: Do you hear them up there? They'll probably come home as soon as this dance is over.

Krogstad: Yes, yes, I'll go. But it won't make any difference. You don't know what I've done about my situation with the Helmers.

Mrs. Linde: Yes, I know all about that.

Krogstad: And in spite of that you still have the courage to—

Mrs. Linde: I understand completely what despair can drive a man like you to do.

Krogstad: If only I could undo it!

Mrs. Linde: You can't. Your letter's lying in the mailbox now.

Krogstad: Are you sure?

Mrs. Linde: Quite sure, but—

Krogstad (*with a searching look at her*): Is that what this is all about? That you want to save your friend, no matter what you have to do? Tell me the truth. Is that it?

Mrs. Linde: Nils, when a woman has sold herself for someone else's sake, she doesn't do it a second time.

Krogstad: I'll ask for my letter back.

Mrs. Linde: No, no.

Krogstad: Yes, of course I will. I'll wait here until Helmer comes home. I'll tell him he has to give me back my letter, that it's only about my being fired, that I don't want him to read it—

Mrs. Linde: No, Nils, don't ask for it back.

Krogstad: But wasn't that the reason why you asked me to meet you here?

Mrs. Linde: In my first moment of panic, it was. But twenty-four hours have gone by since then, and in the meantime I've seen some incredible things in this house. Helmer has to know all about it. This terrible secret has to come out. They have to have a complete understanding between them. It's time for all this lying and pretending to stop.

Krogstad: All right then, if you think it's worth the risk. But there's at least one thing I can do, and do right away—

Mrs. Linde (*listening*): You have to leave this instant! The dance is over. They could walk in here any minute.

Krogstad: I'll wait for you downstairs.

Mrs. Linde: Yes, please do. I want you to walk me home.

Krogstad: I've never been so happy in my entire life!

(*Goes out through the outer door. The door between the room and the hall remains open.*)

Mrs. Linde (*straightening up the room and getting her hat and coat ready*): How different things will be! Someone to work for and live for, a home to bring happiness into. I'm certainly going to try. I wish they'd hurry up and come home—(*Listens.*) Ah, here they are now. I'd better put on my things.

(*Picks up her hat and coat. Helmer's and Nora's voices are heard outside. A key is turned, and Helmer brings Nora into the hall almost by force. She is in an Italian peasant costume with a large black shawl wrapped around her. He is in formal wear and a black domino—a hooded cloak with an eye-mask—which is open.*)

Nora (*hanging back in the doorway and struggling with him*): No, no, no! Don't bring me inside. I want to go back upstairs. I don't want to leave so early.

Helmer: But, my dearest Nora—

Nora: Please, Torvald dear, please, please, only one more hour.

Helmer: Not one more minute, my sweet Nora. You know this is what we agreed on. Come inside. You'll catch cold standing out there.

(*He brings her gently into the room, in spite of her resistance.*)

Mrs. Linde: Good evening.

Nora: Kristine!

Helmer: What are you doing here so late, Mrs. Linde?

Mrs. Linde: You must excuse me. I was so anxious to see Nora in her dress.

Nora: Have you been sitting here waiting for me?

Mrs. Linde: Yes, unfortunately I came too late, you'd already gone upstairs. And I didn't want to go away again without seeing you.

Helmer (*taking off Nora's shawl*): Yes, take a good look at her. I think she's worth looking at. Isn't she charming, Mrs. Linde?

Mrs. Linde: Yes, indeed she is.

Helmer: Doesn't she look especially pretty? Everyone thought so at the dance. But this sweet little person is extremely stubborn. What are we going to do with her? Believe it or not, I almost had to drag her away by force.

Nora: Torvald, you'll be sorry you didn't let me stay, even if only for half an hour.

Helmer: Listen to her, Mrs. Linde! She danced her tarantella and it was a huge success, as it deserved to be, though maybe her performance was a tiny bit too realistic, a little more so than it might have been by strict artistic standards. But never mind about that! The main thing is, she was a success, a tremendous success. Do you think I was going to let her stay there after that, and spoil the effect? Not a chance! I took my charming little Capri girl—my capricious little Capri girl, I should say—I took her by the arm, one quick circle around the room, a curtsey to one and all, and, as they say in novels, the beautiful vision vanished. An exit should always make an effect, Mrs. Linde, but I can't make Nora understand that. Whew, this room is hot!

(*Throws his domino on a chair and opens the door to his study.*)

Why is it so dark in here? Oh, of course. Excuse me.

(*He goes in and lights some candles.*)

Nora (*in a hurried, breathless whisper*): Well?

Mrs. Linde (*in a low voice*): I talked to him.

Nora: And?

Mrs. Linde: Nora, you have to tell your husband the whole story.

Nora (*in an expressionless voice*): I knew it.

Mrs. Linde: You have nothing to fear from Krogstad, but you still have to tell him.

Nora: I'm not going to.

Mrs. Linde: Then the letter will.

Nora: Thank you, Kristine. Now I know what I have to do. Shh!

Helmer (*coming in again*): Well, Mrs. Linde, have you been admiring her?

Mrs. Linde: Yes, I have, and now I'll say goodnight.

Helmer: What, already? Is this your knitting?

Mrs. Linde (*taking it*): Yes, thank you, I'd almost forgotten it.

Helmer: So you knit?

Mrs. Linde: Yes, of course.

Helmer: You know, you ought to embroider.

Mrs. Linde: Really? Why?

Helmer: It's much more graceful-looking. Here, let me show you. You hold the embroidery this way in your left hand, and use the needle with your right, like this, with a long, easy sweep. Do you see?

Mrs. Linde: Yes, I suppose—

Helmer: But knitting, that can never be anything but awkward. Here, look. The arms close together, the knitting needles going up and down. It's sort of Chinese looking. That was really excellent champagne they gave us.

Mrs. Linde: Well, good night, Nora, and don't be stubborn anymore.

Helmer: That's right, Mrs. Linde.

Mrs. Linde: Good night, Mr. Helmer.

Helmer (seeing her to the door): Good night, good night. I hope you get home safely. I'd be very happy to—but you only have a short way to go. Good night, good night.

(She goes out. He closes the door behind her, and comes in again.)

Ah, rid of her at last! What a bore that woman is.

Nora: Aren't you tired, Torvald?

Helmer: No, not at all.

Nora: You're not sleepy?

Helmer: Not a bit. As a matter of fact, I feel very lively. And what about you? You really look tired *and* sleepy.

Nora: Yes, I am very tired. I want to go to sleep right away.

Helmer: So, you see how right I was not to let you stay there any longer.

Nora: You're always right, Torvald.

Helmer (kissing her on the forehead): Now my little skylark is talking sense. Did you notice what a good mood Rank was in this evening?

Nora: Really? Was he? I didn't talk to him at all.

Helmer: And I only talked to him for a little while, but it's a long time since I've seen him so cheerful. *(Looks at her for a while and then moves closer to her.)* It's delightful to be home again by ourselves, to be alone with you, you fascinating, charming little darling!

Nora: Don't look at me like that, Torvald.

Helmer: Why shouldn't I look at my dearest treasure? At all the beauty that is mine, all my very own?

Nora (going to the other side of the table): I wish you wouldn't talk that way to me tonight.

Helmer (following her): You've still got the tarantella in your blood, I see. And it makes you more captivating than ever. Listen, the guests are starting to leave now. *(In a lower voice.)* Nora, soon the whole house will be quiet.

Nora: Yes, I hope so.

Helmer: Yes, my own darling Nora. Do you know why, when we're out at a party like this, why I hardly talk to you, and keep away from you, and only steal a glance at you now and then? Do you know why I do that? It's because I'm pretending to myself that we're secretly in love, and we're secretly engaged, and no one suspects that there's anything between us.

Nora: Yes, yes, I know you're thinking about me every moment.

Helmer: And when we're leaving, and I'm putting the shawl over your beautiful young shoulders, on your lovely neck, then I imagine that you're my young bride and that we've just come from our wedding and I'm bringing you home for the first time, to be alone with you for the first time, all alone with my shy little darling! This whole night I've been longing for you alone. My blood was on fire watching you move when you danced the tarantella. I couldn't stand it any longer, and that's why I brought you home so early—

Nora: Stop it, Torvald! Let me go. I won't—

Helmer: What? You're not serious, Nora! You won't? You won't? I'm your husband—

(*There is a knock at the outer door.*)

Nora (*starting*): Did you hear—

Helmer (*going into the hall*): Who is it?

Rank (*outside*): It's me. May I come in for a moment?

Helmer (*in an irritated whisper*): What does he want now? (*Aloud.*) Wait a minute! (*Unlocks the door.*) Come in. It's good of you not to pass by our door without saying hello.

Rank: I thought I heard your voice, and I felt like dropping by. (*With a quick look around.*) Ah, yes, these dear familiar rooms. You two are very happy and cozy in here.

Helmer: You seemed to be making yourself pretty happy upstairs too.

Rank: Very much so. Why shouldn't I? Why shouldn't we enjoy everything in this world? At least as much as we can, for as long as we can. The wine was first-rate—

Helmer: Especially the champagne.

Rank: So you noticed that too? It's almost unbelievable how much of it I managed to put away!

Nora: Torvald drank a lot of champagne tonight too.

Rank: Did he?

Nora: Yes, and it always makes him so merry.

Rank: Well, why shouldn't a person have a merry evening after a well-spent day?

Helmer: Well-spent? I'm afraid I can't take credit for that.

Rank (*clapping him on the back*): But I can, you know!

Nora: Doctor Rank, you must have been busy with some scientific investigation today.

Rank: Exactly.

Helmer: Listen to this! Little Nora talking about scientific investigations!

Nora: And may I congratulate you on the result?

Rank: Indeed you may.

Nora: Was it favorable, then?

Rank: The best possible result, for both doctor and patient—certainty.

Nora (*quickly and searchingly*): Certainty?

Rank: Absolute certainty. So wasn't I entitled to make a merry evening of it after that?

Nora: Yes, you certainly were, Doctor Rank.

Helmer: I think so too, as long as you don't have to pay for it in the morning.

Rank: Oh well, you can't have anything in this life without paying for it.

Nora: Doctor Rank, are you fond of fancy-dress balls?

Rank: Yes, if there are a lot of pretty costumes.

Nora: Tell me, what should the two of us wear to the next one?

Helmer: Little featherbrain! You're thinking of the next one already?

Rank: The two of us? Yes, I can tell you. You'll go as a good-luck charm—

Helmer: Yes, but what would be the costume for that?

Rank: She just needs to dress the way she always does.

Helmer: That was very nicely put. But aren't you going to tell us what you'll be?

Rank: Yes, my dear friend, I've already made up my mind about that.

Helmer: Well?

Rank: At the next fancy-dress ball I'm going to be invisible.

Helmer: That's a good one!

Rank: There's a big black cap . . . Haven't you ever heard of the cap that makes you invisible? Once you put it on, no one can see you anymore.

Helmer (suppressing a smile): Yes, that's right.

Rank: But I'm clean forgetting what I came for. Helmer, give me a cigar. One of the dark Havanas.

Helmer: With the greatest pleasure. (*Offers him his case.*)

Rank (takes a cigar and cuts off the end): Thanks.

Nora (striking a match): Let me give you a light.

Rank: Thank you. (*She holds the match for him to light his cigar.*) And now goodbye!

Helmer: Goodbye, goodbye, my dear old friend.

Nora: Sleep well, Doctor Rank.

Rank: Thank you for that wish.

Nora: Wish me the same.

Rank: You? Well, if you want me to. Sleep well! And thanks for the light. (*He nods to them both and goes out.*)

Helmer (in a subdued voice): He's had too much to drink.

Nora (absently): Maybe.

(*Helmer takes a bunch of keys out of his pocket and goes into the hall.*)

Torvald! What are you going to do out there?

Helmer: Empty the mailbox. It's quite full. There won't be any room for the newspaper in the morning.

Nora: Are you going to work tonight?

Helmer: You know I'm not. What's this? Someone's been at the lock.

Nora: At the lock?

Helmer: Yes, it's been tampered with. What does this mean? I never would have thought the maid—Look, here's a broken hairpin. It's one of yours, Nora.

Nora (quickly): Then it must have been the children—

Helmer: Then you'd better break them of those habits. There, I've finally got it open.

(*Empties the mailbox and calls out to the kitchen.*)

Helene! Helene, put out the light over the front door.

(*Comes back into the room and shuts the door into the hall. He holds out his hand full of letters.*)

Look at that. Look what a pile of them there are. (*Turning them over.*) What's this?

Nora (at the window): The letter! No! Torvald, no!

Helmer: Two calling cards of Rank's.

Nora: Of Doctor Rank's!

Helmer (looking at them): Yes, Doctor Rank. They were on top. He must have put them in there when he left just now.

Nora: Is there anything written on them?

Helmer: There's a black cross over the name. Look. What a morbid thing to do! It looks as if he's announcing his own death.

Nora: That's exactly what he's doing.

Helmer: What? Do you know anything about it? Has he said anything to you?

Nora: Yes. He told me that when the cards came it would be his farewell to us. He means to close himself off and die.

Helmer: My poor old friend! Of course I knew we wouldn't have him for very long. But this soon! And he goes and hides himself away like a wounded animal.

Nora: If it has to happen, it's better that it be done without a word. Don't you think so, Torvald?

Helmer (walking up and down): He's become so much a part of our lives, I can't imagine him not being with us anymore. With his poor health and his loneliness, he was like a cloudy background to our sunlit happiness. Well, maybe it's all for the best. For him, anyway. (*Standing still.*) And maybe for us too, Nora. Now we have only each other to rely on. (*Puts his arms around her.*) My darling wife, I feel as though I can't possibly hold you tight enough. You know, Nora, I've often wished you were in some kind of serious danger, so that I could risk everything, even my own life, to save you.

Nora (disengages herself from him, and says firmly and decidedly): Now you must go and read your letters, Torvald.

Helmer: No, no, not tonight. I want to be with you, my darling wife.

Nora: With the thought of your friend's death—

Helmer: You're right, it has affected us both. Something ugly has come between us, the thought of the horrors of death. We have to try to put it out of our minds. Until we do, we'll each go to our own room.

Nora (with her arms around his neck): Good night, Torvald. Good night!

Helmer (kissing her on the forehead): Good night, my little songbird. Sleep well, Nora. Now I'll go read all my mail. (*He takes his letters and goes into his room, shutting the door behind him.*)

Nora (gropes distractedly about, picks up Helmer's domino and wraps it around her, while she says in quick, hoarse, spasmodic whispers): Never to see him again. Never! Never! (*Puts her shawl over her head.*) Never to see my children again either, never again. Never! Never! Oh, the icy, black water, the bottomless depths! If only it were over! He's got it now, now he's reading it. Goodbye, Torvald . . . children!

(*She is about to rush out through the hall when Helmer opens his door hurriedly and stands with an open letter in his hand.*)

Helmer: Nora!

Nora: Ah!

Helmer: What is this? Do you know what's in this letter?

Nora: Yes, I know. Let me go! Let me get out!

Helmer (holding her back): Where are you going?

Nora (trying to get free): You're not going to save me, Torvald!

Helmer (reeling): It's true? Is this true, what it says here? This is horrible! No, no, it can't possibly be true.

Nora: It is true. I've loved you more than anything else in the world.

Helmer: Don't start with your ridiculous excuses.

Nora (taking a step towards him): Torvald!

Helmer: You little fool, do you know what you've done?

Nora: Let me go. I won't let you suffer for my sake. You're not going to take it on yourself.

Helmer: Stop play-acting. (*Locks the hall door.*) You're going to stay right here and give me an explanation. Do you understand what you've done? Answer me! Do you understand what you've done?

Nora (*looks steadily at him and says with a growing look of coldness in her face*): Yes, I'm beginning to understand everything now.

Helmer (*walking around the room*): What a horrible awakening! The woman who was my pride and joy for eight years, a hypocrite, a liar, worse than that, much worse— a criminal! The unspeakable ugliness of it all! The shame of it! The shame!

(*Nora is silent and looks steadily at him. He stops in front of her.*)

I should have realized that something like this was bound to happen. I should have seen it coming. Your father's shifty nature—be quiet!—your father's shifty nature has come out in you. No religion, no morality, no sense of duty. This is my punishment for closing my eyes to what he did! I did it for your sake, and this is how you pay me back.

Nora: Yes, that's right.

Helmer: Now you've destroyed all my happiness. You've ruined my whole future. It's horrible to think about! I'm in the power of an unscrupulous man. He can do what he wants with me, ask me for anything he wants, give me any orders he wants, and I don't dare say no. And I have to sink to such miserable depths, all because of a feather-brained woman!

Nora: When I'm out of the way, you'll be free.

Helmer: Spare me the speeches. Your father had always plenty of those on hand, too. What good would it do me if you were out of the way, as you say? Not the slightest. He can tell everybody the whole story. And if he does, I could be wrongly suspected of having been in on it with you. People will probably think I was behind it all, that I put you up to it! And I have you to thank for all this, after I've cherished you the whole time we've been married. Do you understand what you've done to me?

Nora (*coldly and quietly*): Yes.

Helmer: It's so incredible that I can't take it all in. But we have to come to some understanding. Take off that shawl. Take it off, I said. I have to try to appease him some way or another. It has to be hushed up, no matter what it costs. And as for you and me, we have to make it look as if everything is just as it always was, but only for the sake of appearances, obviously. You'll stay here in my house, of course. But I won't let you bring up the children. I can't trust them to you. To think that I have to say these things to someone I've loved so dearly, and that I still—No, that's all over. From this moment on happiness is out of the question. All that matters now is to save the bits and pieces, to keep up the appearance—

(*The front doorbell rings.*)

Helmer (*with a start*): What's that? At this hour! Can the worst—Can he—Go and hide yourself, Nora. Say you don't feel well. (*Nora stands motionless. Helmer goes and unlocks the hall door.*)

Maid (*half-dressed, comes to the door*): A letter for Mrs. Helmer.

Helmer: Give it to me. (*Takes the letter, and shuts the door.*) Yes, it's from him. I'm not giving it to you. I'll read it myself.

Nora: Go ahead, read it.

Helmer (*standing by the lamp*): I barely have the courage to. It could mean ruin for both of us. No, I have to know. (*Tears open the letter, runs his eye over a few lines, looks at a piece of paper enclosed with it, and gives a shout of joy.*) Nora! (*She looks at him questioningly.*) Nora! No, I'd better read it again. Yes, it's true! I'm saved! Nora, I'm saved!

Nora: And what about me?

Helmer: You too, of course. We're both saved, you and I. Look, he's returned your note. He says he's sorry and he apologizes—that a happy change in his life— what difference does it make what he says! We're saved, Nora! Nobody can hurt you. Oh, Nora, Nora! No, first I have to destroy these horrible things. Let me see. . . . (*Glances at the note.*) No, no, I don't want to look at it. This whole business will be nothing but a bad dream to me.

(*Tears up the note and both letters, throws them all into the stove, and watches them burn.*)

There, now it doesn't exist anymore. He says that you've known since Christmas Eve. These must have been a horrible three days for you, Nora.

Nora: I fought a hard fight these three days.

Helmer: And suffered agonies, and saw no way out but—No, we won't dwell on any of those horrors. We'll just shout for joy and keep saying, "It's all over! It's all over!" Listen to me, Nora. You don't seem to realize that it's all over. What's this? Such a cold, hard face! My poor little Nora, I understand. You find it hard to believe that I've really forgiven you. But I swear that it's true, Nora. I forgive you for everything. I know that you did it all out of love for me.

Nora: That's true.

Helmer: You've loved me the way a wife ought to love her husband. You just didn't have the awareness to see what was wrong with the means you used. But do you think I love you any less because you don't understand how to deal with these things? No, of course not. I want you to lean on me. I'll advise you and guide you. I wouldn't be a man if this womanly helplessness didn't make you twice as attractive to me. Don't think anymore about the hard things I said when I was so upset at first, when I thought everything was going to crush me. I forgive you, Nora. I swear to you that I forgive you.

Nora: Thank you for your forgiveness. (*She goes out through the door to the right.*)

Helmer: No, don't go—(*Looks in.*) What are you doing in there?

Nora (*from within*): Taking off my costume.

Helmer (*standing at the open door*): Yes, do. Try to calm yourself, and ease your mind again, my frightened little songbird. I want you to rest and feel secure. I have wide wings for you to take shelter underneath. (*Walks up and down by the door.*) What a warm and cozy home we have, Nora: Here's a safe haven for you, and I'll protect you like a hunted dove that I've rescued from a hawk's claws. I'll calm your poor pounding heart. It will happen, little by little, Nora, believe me. In the morning you'll see it in a very different light. Soon everything will be exactly the way it was before. Before you know it, you won't need my reassurances that I've forgiven you. You'll know for certain that I have. You can't imagine that I'd ever consider rejecting you, or even blaming you? You have no idea what a man feels in his heart, Nora. A man finds it indescribably sweet and satisfying to know that he's forgiven his wife, freely and with all his heart. It's as if he's made her his own all over again. He's given her a new life, in a way, and she's become both wife and child to him. And from this moment on that's what you'll be to me, my little scared, helpless darling. Don't worry about anything, Nora. Just be honest and open with me, and I'll be your will and your conscience. What's this? You haven't gone to bed yet? Have you changed?

Nora (in everyday dress): Yes, Torvald, I've changed.

Helmer: But why—It's so late.

Nora: I'm not going to sleep tonight.

Helmer: But, my dear Nora—

Nora (looking at her watch): It's not that late. Sit down here, Torvald. You and I have a lot to talk about. *(She sits down at one side of the table.)*

Helmer: Nora, what is this? Why this cold, hard face?

Nora: Sit down. This is going to take a while. I have a lot to say to you.

Helmer (sits down at the opposite side of the table): You're making me nervous, Nora. And I don't understand you.

Nora: No, that's it exactly. You don't understand me, and I've never understood you either, until tonight. No, don't interrupt me. I want you to listen to what I have to say. Torvald, I'm settling accounts with you.

Helmer: What do you mean by that?

Nora (after a short silence): Doesn't anything strike you as odd about the way we're sitting here like this?

Helmer: No, what?

Nora: We've been married for eight years. Doesn't it occur to you that this is the first time the two of us, you and I, husband and wife, have had a serious conversation?

Helmer: What do you mean by serious?

Nora: In the whole eight years—longer than that, for the whole time we've known each other—we've never exchanged one word on any serious subject.

Helmer: Did you expect me to be constantly worrying you with problems that you weren't capable of helping me deal with?

Nora: I'm not talking about business. I mean we've never sat down together seriously to try to get to the bottom of anything.

Helmer: But, dearest Nora, what good would that have done you?

Nora: That's just it. You've never understood me. I've been treated badly, Torvald, first by Papa and then by you.

Helmer: What? The two people who've loved you more than anyone else?

Nora (shaking her head): You've never loved me. You just thought it was pleasant to be in love with me.

Helmer: Nora, what are you saying?

Nora: It's true, Torvald. When I lived at home with Papa, he gave me his opinion about everything, and so I had all the same opinions, and if I didn't, I kept my mouth shut, because he wouldn't have liked it. He used to call me his doll-child, and he played with me the way I played with my dolls. And when I came to live in your house—

Helmer: What kind of way is that to talk about our marriage?

Nora (undisturbed): I mean that I was just passed from Papa's hands to yours. You arranged everything according to your own taste, and so I had all the same tastes as you. Or else I pretended to, I'm not really sure which. Sometimes I think it's one way and sometimes the other. When I look back, it's as if I've been living here like a beggar, from hand to mouth. I've supported myself by performing tricks for you, Torvald. But that's the way you wanted it. You and Papa have committed a terrible sin against me. It's your fault that I've done nothing with my life.

Helmer: This is so unfair and ungrateful of you, Nora! Haven't you been happy here?

Nora: No, I've never really been happy. I thought I was, but it wasn't true.

Helmer: Not—not happy!

Nora: No, just cheerful. You've always been very kind to me. But our home's been nothing but a playroom. I've been your doll-wife, the same way that I was Papa's doll-child. And the children have been my dolls. I thought it was great fun when you played with me, the way they thought it was when I played with them. That's what our marriage has been, Torvald.

Helmer: There's some truth in what you're saying, even though your view of it is exaggerated and overwrought. But things will be different from now on. Playtime is over, and now it's lesson-time.

Nora: Whose lessons? Mine, or the children's?

Helmer: Both yours and the children's, my darling Nora.

Nora: I'm sorry, Torvald, but you're not the man to give me lessons on how to be a proper wife to you.

Helmer: How can you say that?

Nora: And as for me, who am I to be allowed to bring up the children?

Helmer: Nora!

Nora: Didn't you say so yourself a little while ago, that you don't dare trust them to me?

Helmer: That was in a moment of anger! Why can't you let it go?

Nora: Because you were absolutely right. I'm not fit for the job. There's another job I have to take on first. I have to try to educate myself. You're not the man to help me with that. I have to do that for myself. And that's why I'm going to leave you now.

Helmer (jumping up): What are you saying?

Nora: I have to stand completely on my own, if I'm going to understand myself and everything around me. That's why I can't stay here with you any longer.

Helmer: Nora, Nora!

Nora: I'm leaving right now. I'm sure Kristine will put me up for the night—

Helmer: You're out of your mind! I won't let you go! I forbid it!

Nora: It's no use forbidding me anything anymore. I'm taking only what belongs to me. I won't take anything from you, now or later.

Helmer: This is insanity!

Nora: Tomorrow I'm going home. Back to where I came from, I mean. It'll be easier for me to find something to do there.

Helmer: You're a blind, senseless woman!

Nora: Then I'd better try to get some sense, Torvald.

Helmer: But to desert your home, your husband, and your children! And aren't you concerned about what people will say?

Nora: I can't concern myself with that. I only know that this is what I have to do.

Helmer: This is outrageous! You're just going to walk away from your most sacred duties?

Nora: What do you consider to be my most sacred duties?

Helmer: Do you need me to tell you that? Aren't they your duties to your husband and your children?

Nora: I have other duties just as sacred.

Helmer: No, you do not. What could they be?

Nora: Duties to myself.

Helmer: First and foremost, you're a wife and a mother.

Nora: I don't believe that anymore. I believe that first and foremost I'm a human being, just as you are—or, at least, that I have to try to become one. I know very well, Torvald, that most people would agree with you, and that opinions like yours are in books, but I can't be satisfied anymore with what most people say, or with what's in books. I have to think things through for myself and come to understand them.

Helmer: Why can't you understand your place in your own home? Don't you have an infallible guide in matters like that? What about your religion?

Nora: Torvald, I'm afraid I'm not sure what religion is.

Helmer: What are you saying?

Nora: All I know is what Pastor Hansen said when I was confirmed. He told us that religion was this, that, and the other thing. When I'm away from all this and on my own, I'll look into that subject too. I'll see if what he said is true or not, or at least whether it's true for me.

Helmer: This is unheard of, coming from a young woman like you! But if religion doesn't guide you, let me appeal to your conscience. I assume you have some moral sense. Or do you have none? Answer me.

Nora: Torvald, that's not an easy question to answer. I really don't know. It's very confusing to me. I only know that you and I look at it in very different ways. I'm learning too that the law isn't at all what I thought it was, and I can't convince myself that the law is right. A woman has no right to spare her old dying father or to save her husband's life? I can't believe that.

Helmer: You talk like a child. You don't understand anything about the world you live in.

Nora: No, I don't. But I'm going to try. I'm going to see if I can figure out who's right, me or the world.

Helmer: You're sick, Nora. You're delirious. I'm half convinced that you're out of your mind.

Nora: I've never felt so clearheaded and sure of myself as I do tonight.

Helmer: Clearheaded and sure of yourself—and that's the spirit in which you forsake your husband and your children?

Nora: Yes, it is.

Helmer: Then there's only one possible explanation.

Nora: Which is?

Helmer: You don't love me anymore.

Nora: Exactly.

Helmer: Nora! How can you say that?

Nora: It's very painful for me to say it, Torvald, because you've always been so good to me, but I can't help it. I don't love you anymore.

Helmer (*regaining his composure*): Are you clearheaded and sure of yourself when you say that too?

Nora: Yes, totally clearheaded and sure of myself. That's why I can't stay here.

Helmer: Can you tell me what I did to make you stop loving me?

Nora: Yes, I can. It was tonight, when the miracle didn't happen. That's when I realized you're not the man I thought you were.

Helmer: Can you explain that more clearly? I don't understand you.

Nora: I've been waiting so patiently for the last eight years. Of course I knew that miracles don't happen every day. Then when I found myself in this horrible situation, I was sure that the miracle was about to happen at last. When Krogstad's letter was lying out there, never for a moment did I imagine that you would agree to his conditions. I was absolutely certain that you'd say to him: Go ahead, tell the whole world. And when he had—

Helmer: Yes, what then? After I'd exposed my wife to shame and disgrace?

Nora: When he had, I was absolutely certain you'd come forward and take the whole thing on yourself, and say: I'm the guilty one.

Helmer: Nora—!

Nora: You mean that I would never have let you make such a sacrifice for me? Of course I wouldn't. But who would have believed my word against yours? That was the miracle that I hoped for and dreaded. And it was to keep it from happening that made me want to kill myself.

Helmer: I'd gladly work night and day for you, Nora, and endure sorrow and poverty for your sake. But no man would sacrifice his honor for the one he loves.

Nora: Hundreds of thousands of women have done it.

Helmer: Oh, you think and talk like a thoughtless child.

Nora: Maybe so. But you don't think or talk like the man I want to be with for the rest of my life. As soon as your fear had passed—and it wasn't fear for what threatened me, but for what might happen to you—when the whole thing was past, as far as you were concerned it was just as if nothing at all had happened. I was still your little skylark, your doll, but now you'd handle me twice as gently and carefully as before, because I was so delicate and fragile. (*Getting up.*) Torvald, that's when it dawned on me that for eight years I'd been living here with a stranger and had borne him three children. Oh, I can't bear to think about it! I could tear myself into little pieces!

Helmer (*sadly*): I see, I see. An abyss has opened up between us. There's no denying it. But, Nora, can't we find some way to close it?

Nora: The way I am now, I'm no wife for you.

Helmer: I can find it in myself to become a different man.

Nora: Maybe so—if your doll is taken away from you.

Helmer: But to be apart!—to be apart from you! No, no, Nora, I can't conceive of it.

Nora (*going out to the right*): All the more reason why it has to be done.

(*She comes back with her coat and hat and a small suitcase which she puts on a chair by the table.*)

Helmer: Nora, Nora, not now! Wait till tomorrow.

Nora (*putting on her cloak*): I can't spend the night in a strange man's room.

Helmer: But couldn't we live here together like brother and sister?

Nora (*putting on her hat*): You know how long that would last. (*Puts the shawl around her.*) Goodbye, Torvald. I won't look in on the children. I know they're in better hands than mine. The way I am now, I'm no use to them.

Helmer: But someday, Nora, someday?

Nora: How can I tell? I have no idea what's going to become of me.

Helmer: But you're my wife, whatever becomes of you.

Nora: Listen, Torvald. I've heard that when a wife deserts her husband's house, the way I'm doing now, he's free of all legal obligations to her. In any event, I set you free from all your obligations. I don't want you to feel bound in the slightest, any more than I will. There has to be complete freedom on both sides. Look, here's your ring back. Give me mine.

Helmer: That too?

Nora: That too.

Helmer: Here it is.

Nora: Good. Now it's all over. I've left the keys here. The maids know all about how to run the house, much better than I do. Kristine will come by tomorrow after I leave her place and pack up my own things, the ones I brought with me from home. I'd like to have them sent to me.

Helmer: All over! All over! Nora, will you ever think about me again?

Nora: I know I'll often think about you, and the children, and this house.

Helmer: May I write to you, Nora?

Nora: No, never. You mustn't do that.

Helmer: But at least let me send you—

Nora: Nothing, nothing.

Helmer: Let me help you if you're in need.

Nora: No. I can't accept anything from a stranger.

Helmer: Nora . . . can't I ever be anything more than a stranger to you?

Nora (*picking up her bag*): Ah, Torvald, for that, the most wonderful miracle of all would have to happen.

Helmer: Tell me what that would be!

Nora: We'd both have to change so much that—Oh, Torvald, I've stopped believing in miracles.

Helmer: But I'll believe. Tell me! Change so much that . . . ?

Nora: That our life together would be a true marriage. Goodbye.

(*She goes out through the hall.*)

Helmer (*sinks down into a chair at the door and buries his face in his hands*): Nora! Nora! (*Looks around, and stands up.*) Empty. She's gone. (*A hope flashes across his mind.*) The most wonderful miracle of all . . . ?

(*The heavy sound of a closing door is heard from below.*)

Questions

ACT I

1. From the opening conversation between Helmer and Nora, what are your impressions of him? Of her? Of their marriage?
2. At what moment in the play do you understand why it is called *A Doll's House*?
3. In what ways does Mrs. Linde provide a contrast for Nora?
4. What in Krogstad's first appearance on stage, and in Dr. Rank's remarks about him, indicates that the bank clerk is a menace?
5. Of what illegal deed is Nora guilty? How does she justify it?
6. When the curtain falls on Act I, what problems now confront Nora?

ACT II

1. As Act II opens, what are your feelings on seeing the stripped, ragged Christmas tree? How is it suggestive?
2. What events that soon occur make Nora's situation even more difficult?
3. How does she try to save herself?
4. Why does Nora fling herself into the wild tarantella?

ACT III

1. For what possible reasons does Mrs. Linde pledge herself to Krogstad?
2. How does Dr. Rank's announcement of his impending death affect Nora and Helmer?
3. What is Helmer's reaction to learning the truth about Nora's misdeed? Why does he blame Nora's father? What is revealing (of Helmer's own character) in his remark, "From this moment on happiness is out of the question. All that matters now is to save the bits and pieces, to keep up the appearance—"?
4. When Helmer finds that Krogstad has sent back the note, what is his response? How do you feel toward him?
5. How does the character of Nora develop in this act?
6. How do you interpret her final slamming of the door?

General Questions

1. In what ways do you find Nora a victim? In what ways is she at fault?
2. Try to state the theme of the play. Does it involve women's rights? Self-fulfillment?
3. What dramatic question does the play embody? At what moment can this question first be stated?
4. What is the crisis? In what way is this moment or event a "turning point"? (In what new direction does the action turn?)
5. Eric Bentley, in an essay titled "Ibsen, Pro and Con" (*In Search of Theater* [New York: Knopf, 1953]), criticizes the character of Krogstad, calling him "a mere pawn of the plot." He then adds, "When convenient to Ibsen, he is a blackmailer. When inconvenient, he is converted." Do you agree or disagree?
6. Why is the play considered a work of realism? Is there anything in it that does not seem realistic?
7. In what respects does *A Doll's House* seem to apply to life today? Is it in any way dated? Could there be a Nora in North America today?

Henrik Ibsen on Writing

Correspondence on the Final Scene of *A Doll's House* 1880, 1891

Translated by John Nilsen Laurvik and Mary Morison

Munich, 17 February 1880

To the Editor of the *Nationaltidende*

Sir,

In No. 1360 of your esteemed paper I have read a letter from Flensburg, in which it is stated that *A Doll's House* (in German *Nora*) has been acted there, and that the conclusion of the play has been changed—the alteration having been made, it is asserted, by my orders. This last statement is untrue. Immediately after the publication of *Nora*, I received from my translator, Mr. Wilhelm Lange of Berlin, the information that he had reason to fear that an "adaptation" of the play, giving it a different ending, was about to be published, and that this would probably be chosen in preference to the original by several of the North German theaters.

In order to prevent such a possibility, I sent to him, for use in case of absolute

Henrik Ibsen

necessity, a draft of an altered last scene, according to which Nora does not leave the house, but is forcibly led by Helmer to the door of the children's bedroom; a short dialogue takes place, Nora sinks down at the door, and the curtain falls.

This change, I myself, in the letter to my translator, stigmatize as "barbaric violence" done to the play. Those who make use of the altered scene do so entirely against my wish. But I trust that it will not be used at very many German theaters.

. . . When my works are threatened, I prefer, taught by experience, to commit the act of violence myself, instead of leaving them to be treated and "adapted" by less careful and less skilful hands.

Yours respectfully,

Henrik Ibsen

1891

Dear Count Prozhor,

Mr. Luigi Capuana° has, I regret to see, given you a great deal of trouble by his proposal to alter the last scene of *A Doll's House* for performance in the Italian theaters. . . . [T]he fact is that I cannot possibly directly authorize any change whatever

---

Luigi Capuana: Italian novelist and dramatic critic who translated *A Doll's House* into Italian. It was the famous actress Eleonora Duse who wished him to alter the last scene of the play, but she finally relented and acted it in the original form.

in the ending of the drama. I may almost say that it was for the sake of the last scene that the whole play was written.

And, besides, I believe that Mr. Capuana is mistaken in fearing that the Italian public would not be able to understand or approve of my work if it were put on the stage in its original form. The experiment, ought, at any rate, to be tried. If it turns out a failure, then let Mr. Capuana, on his own responsibility, employ your adaptation of the closing scene; for I cannot formally authorize, or approve of, such a proceeding.

I wrote to Mr. Capuana yesterday, briefly expressing my views on the subject; and I hope that he will disregard his misgivings until he has proved by experience that they are well founded.

At the time when A Doll's House was quite new, I was obliged to give my consent to an alteration of the last scene for Frau Hedwig Niemann-Raabe, who was to play the part of Nora in Berlin. At that time I had no choice. I was entirely unprotected by copyright law in Germany, and could, consequently prevent nothing. . . . With its altered ending it had only a short run. In its unchanged form it is still being played. . . .

Your sincere and obliged,

Henrik Ibsen

Tennessee Williams

The Glass Menagerie   1945

Tennessee Williams (1911–1983) was born Thomas Lanier Williams in Columbus, Mississippi, went to high school in St. Louis, and graduated from the University of Iowa. As an undergraduate, he saw a performance of Ibsen's Ghosts *and decided to become a playwright himself. His family bore a close resemblance to the Wingfields in* The Glass Menagerie: *his mother came from a line of Southern blue bloods (Tennessee pioneers); his sister Rose suffered from incapacitating shyness; and as a young man, Williams himself, like Tom, worked at a job he disliked (in a shoe factory where his father worked), wrote poetry, sought refuge in moviegoing, and finally left home to wander and hold odd jobs. He worked as a bellhop in a New Orleans hotel; a teletype operator in Jacksonville, Florida; an usher and a waiter in New York. In 1945* The Glass Menagerie *scored a success on Broadway, winning a Drama Critics Circle award. Two years later Williams received a Pulitzer Prize for* A Streetcar Named Desire, *a grim, powerful study of a woman's illusions and frustrations, set in New Orleans. In 1955 Williams was awarded another Pulitzer Prize for* Cat on a Hot Tin Roof. *Besides other plays, including* Summer and Smoke *(1948),* Sweet Bird of Youth *(1959),* The Night of the Iguana *(1961),* Small Craft Warnings *(1973),* Clothes for a Summer Hotel *(1980), and* A House Not Meant to Stand *(1981), Williams wrote two novels, poetry, essays, short stories, and* Memoirs *(1975).*

Nobody, not even the rain, has such small hands.

—E. E. CUMMINGS

CHARACTERS

Amanda Wingfield, the mother. A little woman of great but confused vitality clinging frantically to another time and place. Her characterization must be carefully created, not copied from type. She is not paranoiac, but her life is paranoia. There is much to admire in Amanda, and as much to love and pity as there is to laugh at. Certainly she has endurance and a kind of heroism, and though her foolishness makes her unwittingly cruel at times, there is tenderness in her slight person.

Laura Wingfield, her daughter. Amanda, having failed to establish contact with reality, continues to live vitally in her illusions, but Laura's situation is even graver. A childhood illness has left her crippled, one leg slightly shorter than the other, and held in a brace. This defect need not be more than suggested on the stage. Stemming from this, Laura's separation increases till she is like a piece of her own glass collection, too exquisitely fragile to move from the shelf.

Tom Wingfield, her son. And the narrator of the play. A poet with a job in a warehouse. His nature is not remorseless, but to escape from a trap he has to act without pity.

Jim O'Connor, the gentleman caller. A nice, ordinary, young man.

SCENE. *An alley in St. Louis.*

PART I. *Preparation for a Gentleman Caller.*

PART II. *The Gentleman Calls.*

TIME. *Now and the Past.*

The 1945 original production of *The Glass Menagerie*, the Playhouse, New York. Left to right: Anthony Ross (Jim), Laurette Taylor (Amanda), Eddie Dowling (Tom), and Julie Hayden (Laura).

SCENE I

The Wingfield apartment is in the rear of the building, one of those vast hive-like conglomerations of cellular living-units that flower as warty growths in overcrowded urban centers of lower middle-class population and are symptomatic of the impulse of this largest and fundamentally enslaved section of American society to avoid fluidity and differentiation and to exist and function as one interfused mass of automatism.

The apartment faces an alley and is entered by a fire-escape, a structure whose name is a touch of accidental poetic truth, for all of these huge buildings are always burning with the slow and implacable fires of human desperation. The fire-escape is included in the set—that is, the landing of it and steps descending from it.

The scene is memory and is therefore unrealistic. Memory takes a lot of poetic license. It omits some details; others are exaggerated, according to the emotional value of the articles it touches, for memory is seated predominantly in the heart. The interior is therefore rather dim and poetic.

At the rise of the curtain, the audience is faced with the dark, grim rear wall of the Wingfield tenement. This building, which runs parallel to the footlights, is flanked on both sides by dark, narrow alleys which run into murky canyons of tangled clotheslines, garbage cans, and the sinister latticework of neighboring fire-escapes. It is up and down these side alleys that exterior entrances and exits are made, during the play. At the end of Tom's opening commentary, the dark tenement wall slowly reveals (by means of a transparency) the interior of the ground floor Wingfield apartment.

Downstage is the living room, which also serves as a sleeping room for Laura, the sofa unfolding to make her bed. Upstage, center, and divided by a wide arch or second proscenium with transparent faded portieres (or second curtain), is the dining room. In an old-fashioned what-not in the living room are seen scores of transparent glass animals. A blown-up photograph of the father hangs on the wall of the living room, facing the audience, to the left of the archway. It is the face of a very handsome young man in a doughboy's First World War cap. He is gallantly smiling, ineluctably smiling, as if to say, "I will be smiling forever."

The audience hears and sees the opening scene in the dining room through both the transparent fourth wall of the building and the transparent gauze portieres of the dining room arch. It is during this revealing scene that the fourth wall slowly ascends, out of sight. This transparent exterior wall is not brought down again until the very end of the play, during Tom's final speech.

The narrator is an undisguised convention of the play. He takes whatever license with dramatic convention as is convenient to his purposes.

Tom enters dressed as a merchant sailor from the alley, stage left, and strolls across the front of the stage to the fire-escape. There he stops and lights a cigarette. He addresses the audience.

Tom: Yes, I have tricks in my pocket, I have things up my sleeve. But I am the opposite of a stage magician. He gives you illusion that has the appearance of truth. I give you truth in the pleasant disguise of illusion. To begin with, I turn back time. I reverse it to that quaint period, the thirties, when the huge middle class of America was matriculating in a school for the blind. Their eyes had failed them, or they had failed their eyes, and so they were having their fingers pressed forcibly down on the fiery Braille alphabet of a dissolving economy. In Spain there was revolution. Here there was only shouting and confusion. In Spain there was Guernica. Here there were disturbances of labor, sometimes pretty violent, in otherwise peaceful cities such as Chicago, Cleveland, St. Louis. . . . This is the social background of the play.

(Music.)

The play is memory. Being a memory play, it is dimly lighted, it is sentimental, it is not realistic. In memory everything seems to happen to music. That explains the fiddle in the wings. I am the narrator of the play, and also a character in it. The other characters are my mother, Amanda, my sister, Laura, and a gentleman caller who appears in the final scenes. He is the most realistic character in the play, being an emissary from a world of reality that we were somehow set apart from. But since I have a poet's weakness for symbols, I am using this character also as a symbol; he is the long delayed but always expected something that we live for. There is a fifth character in the play who doesn't appear except in this larger-than-life photograph over the mantel. This is our father who left us a long time ago. He was a telephone man who fell in love with long distances; he gave up his job with the telephone company and skipped the light fantastic out of town. . . . The last we heard of him was a picture post-card from Mazatlan, on the Pacific coast of Mexico, containing a message of two words—"Hello—Good-bye!" and an address. I think the rest of the play will explain itself. . . .

Amanda's voice becomes audible through the portieres.

(Screen Legend: "Où Sont Les Neiges.")°

He divides the portieres and enters the upstage area.

Amanda and Laura are seated at a drop-leaf table. Eating is indicated by gestures without food or utensils. Amanda faces the audience. Tom and Laura are seated in profile.

The interior has lit up softly and through the scrim we see Amanda and Laura seated at the table in the upstage area.

Amanda (calling): Tom?

Tom: Yes, Mother.

Amanda: We can't say grace until you come to the table!

Tom: Coming, Mother. (*He bows slightly and withdraws, reappearing a few moments later in his place at the table.*)

Amanda (to her son): Honey, don't *push* with your *fingers*. If you have to push with something, the thing to push with is a crust of bread. And chew—chew! Animals have sections in their stomachs which enable them to digest food without mastication, but human beings are supposed to chew their food before they swallow it down. Eat food leisurely, son, and really enjoy it. A well-cooked meal has lots of

---

(*Screen Legend . . . Neiges.*"): "Where are the snows (of yesteryear)?" A slide bearing this line by the French poet François Villon is to be projected on a stage wall.

delicate flavors that have to be held in the mouth for appreciation. So chew your food and give your salivary glands a chance to function!

Tom deliberately lays his imaginary fork down and pushes his chair back from the table.

Tom: I haven't enjoyed one bite of this dinner because of your constant directions on how to eat it. It's you that makes me rush through meals with your hawk-like attention to every bite I take. Sickening—spoils my appetite—all this discussion of animals' secretion—salivary glands—mastication!

Amanda (*lightly*): Temperament like a Metropolitan star!

(*He rises and crosses downstage.*)

You're not excused from the table.

Tom: I am getting a cigarette.

Amanda: You smoke too much.

Laura rises.

Laura: I'll bring in the blanc mange.

He remains standing with his cigarette by the portieres during the following.

Amanda (*rising*): No, sister, no, sister—you be the lady this time and I'll be the darky.

Laura: I'm already up.

Amanda: Resume your seat, little sister—I want you to stay fresh and pretty—for gentlemen callers!

Laura (*sitting down*): I'm not expecting any gentlemen callers.

Amanda (*crossing out to kitchenette, airily*): Sometimes they come when they are least expected! Why, I remember one Sunday afternoon in Blue Mountain—(*Enters kitchenette.*)

Tom: I know what's coming!

Laura: Yes. But let her tell it.

Tom: Again?

Laura: She loves to tell it.

Amanda returns with bowl of dessert.

Amanda: One Sunday afternoon in Blue Mountain—your mother received— seventeen!—gentlemen callers! Why, sometimes there weren't chairs enough to accommodate them all. We had to send the nigger over to bring in folding chairs from the parish house.

Tom (*remaining at portieres*): How did you entertain those gentlemen callers?

Amanda: I understood the art of conversation!

Tom: I bet you could talk.

Amanda: Girls in those days *knew* how to talk, I can tell you.

Tom: Yes?

(Image: Amanda As A Girl On A Porch Greeting Callers.)

Amanda: They knew how to entertain their gentlemen callers. It wasn't enough for a girl to be possessed of a pretty face and a graceful figure—although I wasn't slighted in either respect. She also needed to have a nimble wit and a tongue to meet all occasions.

Tom: What did you talk about?

Amanda: Things of importance going on in the world! Never anything coarse or common or vulgar. (*She addresses Tom as though he were seated in the vacant chair at the table though he remains by portieres. He plays this scene as though reading from a script.*) My callers were gentlemen—all! Among my callers were some of the most prominent young planters of the Mississippi Delta—planters and sons of planters!

Tom motions for music and a spot of light on Amanda. Her eyes lift, her face glows, her voice becomes rich and elegiac.

(Screen Legend: "Où Sont Les Neiges D'antan?")

There was young Champ Laughlin who later became vice-president of the Delta Planters Bank. Hadley Stevenson who was drowned in Moon Lake and left his widow one hundred and fifty thousand in Government bonds. There were the Cutrere brothers, Wesley and Bates. Bates was one of my bright particular beaux! He got in a quarrel with that wild Wainright boy. They shot it out on the floor of Moon Lake Casino. Bates was shot through the stomach. Died in the ambulance on his way to Memphis. His widow was also well-provided for, came into eight or ten thousand acres, that's all. She married him on the rebound—never loved her—carried my picture on him the night he died! And there was that boy that every girl in the Delta had set her cap for! That beautiful, brilliant young Fitzhugh boy from Green County!

Tom: What did he leave his widow?

Amanda: He never married! Gracious, you talk as though all of my old admirers had turned up their toes to the daisies!

Tom: Isn't this the first you mentioned that still survives?

Amanda: That Fitzhugh boy went North and made a fortune—came to be known as the Wolf of Wall Street! He had the Midas touch, whatever he touched turned to gold! And I could have been Mrs. Duncan J. Fitzhugh, mind you! But—I picked your *father!*

Laura (*rising*): Mother, let me clear the table.

Amanda: No dear, you go in front and study your typewriter chart. Or practice your shorthand a little. Stay fresh and pretty!—It's almost time for our gentlemen callers to start arriving. (*She flounces girlishly toward the kitchenette.*) How many do you suppose we're going to entertain this afternoon?

Tom throws down the paper and jumps up with a groan.

Laura (*alone in the dining room*): I don't believe we're going to receive any, Mother.

Amanda (*reappearing, airily*): What? No one—not one? You must be joking! (*Laura nervously echoes her laugh. She slips in a fugitive manner through the half open portieres and draws them gently behind her. A shaft of very clear light is thrown on her face against the jaded tapestry of the curtains.*) (**Music: "The Glass Menagerie" Under Faintly.**) (*Lightly.*) Not one gentleman caller? It can't be true! There must be a flood, there must have been a tornado!

Laura: It isn't a flood, it's not a tornado, Mother. I'm just not popular like you were in Blue Mountain. . . . (*Tom utters another groan. Laura glances at him with a faint, apologetic smile. Her voice catching a little.*) Mother's afraid I'm going to be an old maid.

(The Scene Dims Out With "Glass Menagerie" Music.)

SCENE II

"Laura, Haven't You Ever Liked Some Boy?"

On the dark stage the screen is lighted with the image of blue roses.

Gradually Laura's figure becomes apparent and the screen goes out.

The music subsides.

Laura is seated in the delicate ivory chair at the small clawfoot table.

She wears a dress of soft violet material for a kimono—her hair tied back from her forehead with a ribbon.

She is washing and polishing her collection of glass.

Amanda appears on the fire-escape steps. At the sound of her ascent, Laura catches her breath, thrusts the bowl of ornaments away and seats herself stiffly before the diagram of the typewriter keyboard as though it held her spellbound. Something has happened to Amanda. It is written in her face as she climbs to the landing: a look that is grim and hopeless and a little absurd.

She has on one of those cheap or imitation velvety-looking cloth coats with imitation fur collar. Her hat is five or six years old, one of those dreadful cloche hats that were worn in the late twenties, and she is clasping an enormous black patent-leather pocketbook with nickel clasp and initials. This is her full-dress outfit, the one she usually wears to the D.A.R.

Before entering she looks through the door.

She purses her lips, opens her eyes wide, rolls them upward and shakes her head.

Then she slowly lets herself in the door. Seeing her mother's expression Laura touches her lips with a nervous gesture.

Laura: Hello, Mother, I was—(*She makes a nervous gesture toward the chart on the wall. Amanda leans against the shut door and stares at Laura with a martyred look.*)

Amanda: Deception? Deception? (*She slowly removes her hat and gloves, continuing the sweet suffering stare. She lets the hat and gloves fall on the floor—a bit of acting.*)

Laura (shakily): How was the D.A.R. meeting? (*Amanda slowly opens her purse and removes a dainty white handkerchief which she shakes out delicately and delicately touches to her lips and nostrils.*) Didn't you go to the D.A.R. meeting, Mother?

Amanda (faintly, almost inaudibly): —No.—No. (*Then more forcibly.*) I did not have the strength—to go to the D.A.R. In fact, I did not have the courage! I wanted to find a hole in the ground and hide myself in it forever! (*She crosses slowly to the wall and removes the diagram of the typewriter keyboard. She holds it in front of her for a second, staring at it sweetly and sorrowfully—then bites her lips and tears it in two pieces.*)

Laura (faintly): Why did you do that, Mother? (*Amanda repeats the same procedure with the chart of the Gregg Alphabet.*) Why are you—

Amanda: Why? Why? How old are you, Laura?

Laura: Mother, you know my age.

Amanda: I thought that you were an adult; it seems that I was mistaken. (*She crosses slowly to the sofa and sinks down and stares at Laura.*)

Laura: Please don't stare at me, Mother.

Amanda closes her eyes and lowers her head. Count ten.

Amanda: What are we going to do, what is going to become of us, what is the future? *Count ten.*

Laura: Has something happened, Mother? (*Amanda draws a long breath and takes out the handkerchief again. Dabbing process.*) Mother, has—something happened?

Amanda: I'll be all right in a minute. I'm just bewildered—(*count five*)—by life . . .

Laura: Mother, I wish that you would tell me what's happened.

Amanda: As you know, I was supposed to be inducted into my office at the D.A.R. this afternoon. (**Image: A Swarm of Typewriters.**) But I stopped off at Rubicam's Business College to speak to your teachers about your having a cold and ask them what progress they thought you were making down there.

Laura: Oh . . .

Amanda: I went to the typing instructor and introduced myself as your mother. She didn't know who you were. "Wingfield," she said, "We don't have any such student enrolled at the school!" I assured her she did, that you had been going to classes since early in January. "I wonder," she said, "if you could be talking about that terribly shy little girl who dropped out of school after only a few days' attendance?" "No," I said, "Laura, my daughter, has been going to school every day for the past six weeks!" "Excuse me," she said. She took the attendance book out and there was your name, unmistakably printed, and all the dates you were absent until they decided that you had dropped out of school. I still said, "No, there must have been some mistake! There must have been some mix-up in the records!" And she said, "No—I remember her perfectly now. Her hand shook so that she couldn't hit the right keys! The first time we gave a speed-test, she broke down completely— was sick at the stomach and almost had to be carried into the wash-room! After that morning she never showed up any more. We phoned the house but never got any answer"—While I was working at Famous-Barr, I suppose, demonstrating those—(*She indicates a brassiere with her hands.*) Oh! I felt so weak I could barely keep on my feet. I had to sit down while they got me a glass of water! Fifty dollars' tuition, all of our plans—my hopes and ambitions for you—just gone up the spout, just gone up the spout like that. (*Laura draws a long breath and gets awkwardly to her feet. She crosses to the victrola and winds it up.*) What are you doing?

Laura: Oh! (*She releases the handle and returns to her seat.*)

Amanda: Laura, where have you been going when you've gone out pretending that you were going to business college?

Laura: I've just been going out walking.

Amanda: That's not true.

Laura: It is. I just went walking.

Amanda: Walking? Walking? In winter? Deliberately courting pneumonia in that light coat? Where did you walk to, Laura?

Laura: All sorts of places—mostly in the park.

Amanda: Even after you'd started catching that cold?

Laura: It was the lesser of two evils, Mother. (**Image: Winter Scene In Park.**) I couldn't go back there. I—threw up—on the floor!

Amanda: From half past seven till after five every day you mean to tell me you walked around in the park, because you wanted to make me think that you were still going to Rubicam's Business College?

Laura: It wasn't as bad as it sounds. I went inside places to get warmed up.

Amanda: Inside where?

Laura: I went in the art museum and the bird-houses at the Zoo. I visited the penguins every day! Sometimes I did without lunch and went to the movies. Lately I've been spending most of my afternoons in the Jewel-box, that big glass house where they raise the tropical flowers.

Amanda: You did all this to deceive me, just for deception? (*Laura looks down.*) Why?

Laura: Mother, when you're disappointed, you get that awful suffering look on your face, like the picture of Jesus' mother in the museum!

Amanda: Hush!

Laura: I couldn't face it.

Pause. A whisper of strings.

(Legend: "The Crust Of Humility.")

Amanda (*hopelessly fingering the huge pocketbook*): So what are we going to do the rest of our lives? Stay home and watch the parades go by? Amuse ourselves with the glass menagerie, darling? Eternally play those worn-out phonograph records your father left as a painful reminder of him? We won't have a business career—we've given that up because it gave us nervous indigestion! (*Laughs wearily.*) What is there left but dependency all our lives? I know so well what becomes of unmarried women who aren't prepared to occupy a position. I've seen such pitiful cases in the South—barely tolerated spinsters living upon the grudging patronage of sister's husband or brother's wife!—stuck away in some little mouse-trap of a room—encouraged by one in-law to visit another—little birdlike women without any nest—eating the crust of humility all their life! Is that the future that we've mapped out for ourselves? I swear it's the only alternative I can think of! It isn't a very pleasant alternative, is it? Of course—some girls *do marry.* (*Laura twists her hands nervously.*) Haven't you ever liked some boy?

Laura: Yes I liked one once. (*Rises.*) I came across his picture a while ago.

Amanda (*with some interest*): He gave you his picture?

Laura: No, it's in the year-book.

Amanda (*disappointed*): Oh—a high-school boy.

(Screen Image: Jim As A High-School Hero Bearing A Silver Cup.)

Laura: Yes. His name was Jim. (*Laura lifts the heavy annual from the clawfoot table.*) Here he is in *The Pirates of Penzance.*

Amanda (*absently*): The what?

Laura: The operetta the senior class put on. He had a wonderful voice and we sat across the aisle from each other Mondays, Wednesdays, and Fridays in the Aud. Here he is with the silver cup for debating! See his grin?

Amanda (*absently*): He must have had a jolly disposition.

Laura: He used to call me—Blue Roses.

(Image: Blue Roses.)

Amanda: Why did he call you such a name as that?

Laura: When I had that attack of pleurosis—he asked me what was the matter when I came back. I said pleurosis—he thought that I said Blue Roses! So that's what he always called me after that. Whenever he saw me, he'd holler, "Hello, Blue Roses!" I didn't care for the girl he went out with. Emily Meisenbach. Emily was the best-dressed girl at Soldan. She never struck me, though, as being sincere . . . It says in the Personal Section—they're engaged. That's—six years ago! They must be married by now.

Amanda: Girls that aren't cut out for business careers usually wind up married to some nice man. (*Gets up with a spark of revival.*) Sister, that's what you'll do!

Laura utters a startled, doubtful laugh. She reaches quickly for a piece of glass.

Laura: But, Mother—
Amanda: Yes? (*Crossing to photograph.*)
Laura (in a tone of frightened apology): I'm—crippled!

(Image: Screen.)

Amanda: Nonsense! Laura, I've told you never, never to use that word. Why, you're not crippled, you just have a little defect—hardly noticeable, even! When people have some slight disadvantage like that, they cultivate other things to make up for it—develop charm—and vivacity—and—*charm!* That's all you have to do! (*She turns again to the photograph.*) One thing your father had *plenty of*—was *charm!*

Tom motions to the fiddle in the wings.

(The Scene Fades Out With Music.)

SCENE III

(Legend On The Screen: "After The Fiasco—")

Tom speaks from the fire-escape landing.

Tom: After the fiasco at Rubicam's Business College, the idea of getting a gentleman caller for Laura began to play a more important part in Mother's calculations. It became an obsession. Like some archetype of the universal unconscious, the image of the gentleman caller haunted our small apartment. . . . (**Image: Young Man At Door With Flowers.**) An evening at home rarely passed without some allusion to this image, this specter, this hope. . . . Even when he wasn't mentioned, his presence hung in Mother's preoccupied look and in my sister's frightened, apologetic manner—hung like a sentence passed upon the Wingfields! Mother was a woman of action as well as words. She began to take logical steps in the planned direction. Late that winter and in the early spring—realizing that extra money would be needed to properly feather the nest and plume the bird— she conducted a vigorous campaign on the telephone, roping in subscribers to one of those magazines for matrons called *The Home-maker's Companion*, the type of journal that features the serialized sublimations of ladies of letters who think in terms of delicate cup-like breasts, slim, tapering waists, rich, creamy thighs, eyes like wood-smoke in autumn, fingers that soothe and caress like strains of music, bodies as powerful as Etruscan sculpture.

(Screen Image: Glamor Magazine Cover.)

Amanda enters with phone on long extension cord. She is spotted in the dim stage.

Amanda: Ida Scott? This is Amanda Wingfield! We *missed* you at the D.A.R. last Monday! I said to myself: She's probably suffering with that sinus condition! How is that sinus condition? Horrors! Heaven have mercy!—You're a Christian martyr, yes, that's what you are, a Christian martyr! Well, I just now happened to notice that your subscription to the *Companion*'s about to expire! Yes, it expires with the next issue, honey!—just when that wonderful new serial by Bessie Mae Hopper is getting off to such an exciting start. Oh, honey, it's something that you can't miss! You remember how *Gone With the Wind* took everybody by storm? You simply couldn't go out if you hadn't read it. All everybody *talked* was Scarlett O'Hara. Well, this is a book that critics already compare to *Gone With the Wind*. It's the *Gone With the Wind* of the post-World War generation!— What?—Burning?—Oh, honey, don't let them burn, go take a look in the oven and I'll hold the wire! Heavens—I think she's hung up!

(Dim Out.)

(Legend On Screen: "You Think I'm In Love With Continental Shoemakers?")

Before the stage is lighted, the violent voices of Tom and Amanda are heard. They are quarreling behind the portieres. In front of them stands Laura with clenched hands and panicky expression.

A clear pool of light on her figure throughout this scene.

Tom: What in Christ's name am I—
Amanda (shrilly): Don't you use that—
Tom: —supposed to do!
Amanda: —expression! Not in my—
Tom: Ohhh!
Amanda: —presence! Have you gone out of your senses?
Tom: I have, that's true, *driven* out!
Amanda: What is the matter with you, you—big—big—IDIOT!
Tom: Look—I've got *no thing*, no single thing—
Amanda: Lower your voice!
Tom: —in my life here that I can call my OWN! Everything is—
Amanda: Stop that shouting!
Tom: Yesterday you confiscated my books! You had the nerve to—
Amanda: I took that horrible novel back to the library—yes! That hideous book by that insane Mr. Lawrence. (*Tom laughs wildly.*) I cannot control the output of diseased minds or people who cater to them—(*Tom laughs still more wildly.*) BUT I WON'T ALLOW SUCH FILTH BROUGHT INTO MY HOUSE! No, no, no, no, no!
Tom: House, house! Who pays rent on it, who makes a slave of himself to—
Amanda (fairly screeching): Don't you DARE to—
Tom: No, no, I mustn't say things! *I've* got to just—
Amanda: Let me tell you—

Tom: I don't want to hear any more! (*He tears the portieres open. The upstage area is lit with a turgid smoky red glow.*)

Amanda's hair is in metal curlers and she wears a very old bathrobe, much too large for her slight figure, a relic of the faithless Mr. Wingfield.

An upright typewriter and a wild disarray of manuscripts are on the drop-leaf table. The quarrel was probably precipitated by Amanda's interruption of his creative labor. A chair lying overthrown on the floor.

Their gesticulating shadows are cast on the ceiling by the fiery glow.

Amanda: You *will* hear more, you—
Tom: No, I won't hear more, I'm going out!
Amanda: You come right back in—
Tom: Out, out out! Because I'm—
Amanda: Come back here, Tom Wingfield! I'm not through talking to you!
Tom: Oh, go—
Laura (desperately): Tom!
Amanda: You're going to listen, and no more insolence from you! I'm at the end of my patience! (*He comes back toward her.*)
Tom: What do you think I'm at? Aren't I supposed to have any patience to reach the end of, Mother? I know, I know. It seems unimportant to you, what I'm *doing*— what I *want* to do—having a little *difference* between them! You don't think that—
Amanda: I think you've been doing things that you're ashamed of. That's why you act like this. I don't believe that you go every night to the movies. Nobody goes to the movies night after night. Nobody in their right minds goes to the movies as often as you pretend to. People don't go to the movies at nearly midnight, and movies don't let out at two A.M. Come in stumbling. Muttering to yourself like a maniac! You get three hours' sleep and then go to work. Oh, I can picture the way you're doing down there. Moping, doping, because you're in no condition.
Tom (wildly): No, I'm in no condition!
Amanda: What right have you got to jeopardize your job? Jeopardize the security of us all? How do you think we'd manage if you were—
Tom: Listen! You think I'm crazy about the *warehouse*? (*He bends fiercely toward her slight figure.*) You think I'm in love with the Continental Shoemakers? You think I want to spend fifty-five *years* down there in that—*celotex interior!* with— *fluorescent—tubes!* Look! I'd rather somebody picked up a crowbar and battered out my brains—than go back mornings! I *go!* Every time you come in yelling that God-damn *"Rise and Shine!" "Rise and Shine!"* I say to myself "How *lucky dead* people are!" But I get up. I *go!* For sixty-five dollars a month I give up all that I dream of doing and being *ever!* And you say self—*self's* all I ever think of. Why, listen, if self is what I thought of, Mother, I'd be where he is—GONE! (*Pointing to father's picture.*) As far as the system of transportation reaches! (*He starts past her. She grabs his arm.*) Don't grab at me, Mother!
Amanda: Where are you going?
Tom: I'm going to the *movies!*

Amanda: I don't believe that lie!

Tom (crouching toward her, overtowering her tiny figure. She backs away, gasping): I'm going to opium dens! Yes, opium dens, dens of vice and criminals' hangouts, Mother. I've joined the Hogan gang, I'm a hired assassin, I carry a tommy-gun in a violin case! I run a string of cat-houses in the Valley! They call me Killer, Killer Wingfield, I'm leading a double-life, a simple, honest warehouse worker by day, by night a dynamic *czar* of the *underworld, Mother.* I go to gambling casinos, I spin away fortunes on the roulette table! I wear a patch over one eye and a false mustache, sometimes I put on green whiskers. On those occasions they call me—*El Diablo!* Oh, I could tell you things to make you sleepless! My enemies plan to dynamite this place. They're going to blow us all sky-high some night! I'll be glad, very happy, and so will you! You'll go up, up on a broomstick, over Blue Mountain with seventeen gentlemen callers! You ugly—babbling old— witch. . . . (*He goes through a series of violent, clumsy movements, seizing his over- coat, lunging to the door, pulling it fiercely open. The women watch him, aghast. His arm catches in the sleeve of the coat as he struggles to pull it on. For a moment he is pinioned by the bulky garment. With an outraged groan he tears the coat off again, splitting the shoulders of it, and hurls it across the room. It strikes against the shelf of Laura's glass collection, there is a tinkle of shattering glass. Laura cries out as if wounded.*)

(Music Legend: "The Glass Menagerie.")

Laura (shrilly): My glass!—menagerie. . . . (*She covers her face and turns away.*)

But Amanda is still stunned and stupefied by the "ugly witch" so that she barely notices this occurrence. Now she recovers her speech.

Amanda (in an awful voice): I won't speak to you—until you apologize! (*She crosses through portieres and draws them together behind her. Tom is left with Laura. Laura clings weakly to the mantel with her face averted. Tom stares at her stupidly for a moment. Then he crosses to shelf. Drops awkwardly to his knees to collect the fallen glass, glancing at Laura as if he would speak but couldn't.*)

("The Glass Menagerie" steals in as the Scene Dims Out.)

SCENE IV

The interior is dark. Faint in the alley.

A deep-voiced bell in a church is tolling the hour of five as the scene commences.

Tom appears at the top of the alley. After each solemn boom of the bell in the tower, he shakes a little noise-maker or rattle as if to express the tiny spasm of man in contrast to the sustained power and dignity of the Almighty. This and the unsteadiness of his advance make it evident that he has been drinking.

As he climbs the few steps to the fire-escape landing light steals up inside. Laura appears in night-dress, observing Tom's empty bed in the front room.

Tom fishes in his pockets for the door-key, removing a motley assortment of articles in the search, including a perfect shower of movie-ticket stubs and an empty bottle. At last he finds the key, but just as he is about to insert it, it slips from his fingers. He strikes a match and crouches below the door.

Tom (*bitterly*): One crack—and it falls through!

Laura opens the door.

Laura: Tom! Tom, what are you doing?

Tom: Looking for a door-key.

Laura: Where have you been all this time?

Tom: I have been to the movies.

Laura: All this time at the movies?

Tom: There was a very long program. There was a Garbo picture and a Mickey Mouse and a travelogue and a newsreel and a preview of coming attractions. And there was an organ solo and a collection for the milk-fund—simultaneously— which ended up in a terrible fight between a fat lady and an usher!

Laura (*innocently*): Did you have to stay through everything?

Tom: Of course! And, oh, I forgot! There was a big stage show! The headliner on this stage show was Malvolio the Magician. He performed wonderful tricks, many of them, such as pouring water back and forth between pitchers. First it turned to wine and then it turned to beer and then it turned to whiskey. I know it was whiskey it finally turned into because he needed somebody to come up out of the audience to help him, and I came up—both shows! It was Kentucky Straight Bourbon. A very generous fellow, he gave souvenirs. (*He pulls from his back pocket a shimmering rainbow-colored scarf.*) He gave me this. This is his magic scarf. You can have it, Laura. You wave it over a canary cage and you get a bowl of gold-fish. You wave it over the gold-fish bowl and they fly away canaries. . . . But the wonderfullest trick of all was the coffin trick. We nailed him into a coffin and he got out of the coffin without removing one nail. (*He has come inside.*) There is a trick that would come in handy for me—get me out of this 2 by 4 situation! (*Flops onto bed and starts removing shoes.*)

Laura: Tom—shhh!

Tom: What're you shushing me for?

Laura: You'll wake up Mother.

Tom: Goody, goody! Pay 'er back for all those "Rise an' Shines." (*Lies down, groaning.*) You know it don't take much intelligence to get yourself into a nailed-up coffin, Laura. But who in hell ever got himself out of one without removing one nail?

As if in answer, the father's grinning photograph lights up.

(Scene Dims Out.)

Immediately following: The church bell is heard striking six. At the sixth stroke the alarm clock goes off in Amanda's room, and after a few moments we hear her calling: "Rise and Shine! Rise and Shine! Laura, go tell your brother to rise and shine!"

Tom (*sitting up slowly*): I'll rise—but I won't shine.

The light increases.

Amanda: Laura, tell your brother his coffee is ready.

Laura slips into front room.

Laura: Tom!—It's nearly seven. Don't make Mother nervous. (*He stares at her stupidly.*) (*Beseechingly*) Tom, speak to Mother this morning. Make up with her, apologize, speak to her!

Tom: She won't to me. It's her that started not speaking.

Laura: If you just say you're sorry she'll start speaking.

Tom: Her not speaking—is that such a tragedy?

Laura: Please—please!

Amanda (calling from kitchenette): Laura, are you going to do what I asked you to do, or do I have to get dressed and go out myself?

Laura: Going, going—soon as I get on my coat! (*She pulls on a shapeless felt hat with nervous, jerky movements, pleadingly glancing at Tom. Rushes awkwardly for coat. The coat is one of Amanda's inaccurately made-over, the sleeves too short for Laura.*) Butter and what else?

Amanda (entering upstage): Just butter. Tell them to charge it.

Laura: Mother, they make such faces when I do that.

Amanda: Sticks and stones may break my bones, but the expression on Mr. Garfinkel's face won't harm us! Tell your brother his coffee is getting cold.

Laura (at door): Do what I asked you, will you, will you, Tom?

He looks sullenly away.

Amanda: Laura, go now or just don't go at all!

Laura (rushing out): Going—going! (*A second later she cries out. Tom springs up and crosses to the door. Amanda rushes anxiously in. Tom opens the door.*)

Tom: Laura?

Laura: I'm all right. I slipped, but I'm all right.

Amanda (peering anxiously after her): If anyone breaks a leg on those fire-escape steps, the landlord ought to be sued for every cent he possesses! (*She shuts door. Remembers she isn't speaking and returns to other room.*)

As Tom enters listlessly for his coffee, she turns her back to him and stands rigidly facing the window on the gloomy gray vault of the areaway. Its light on her face with its aged but childish features is cruelly sharp, satirical as a Daumier print.

(Music Under: "Ave Maria.")

Tom glances sheepishly but sullenly at her averted figure and slumps at the table. The coffee is scalding hot; he sips it and gasps and spits it back in the cup. At his gasp, Amanda catches her breath and half turns. Then catches herself and turns back to window.

Tom blows on his coffee, glancing sidewise at his mother. She clears her throat. Tom clears his. He starts to rise. Sinks back down again, scratches his head, clears his throat again. Amanda coughs. Tom raises his cup in both hands to blow on it, his eyes staring over the rim of it at his mother for several moments. Then he slowly sets the cup down and awkwardly and hesitantly rises from the chair.

Tom (*hoarsely*): Mother. I—I apologize. Mother. (*Amanda draws a quick, shuddering breath. Her face works grotesquely. She breaks into childlike tears.*) I'm sorry for what I said, for everything that I said, I didn't mean it.

Amanda (*sobbingly*): My devotion has made me a witch and so I make myself hateful to my children!

Tom: No, you *don't.*

Amanda: I worry so much, don't sleep, it makes me nervous!

Tom (*gently*): I understand that.

Amanda: I've had to put up a solitary battle all these years. But you're my right-hand bower! Don't fall down, don't fail!

Tom (*gently*): I try, Mother.

Amanda (*with great enthusiasm*): Try and you will *succeed!* (*The notion makes her breathless.*) Why, you—you're just *full* of natural endowments! Both of my children—they're *unusual* children! Don't you think I know it? I'm so—*proud!* Happy and—feel I've—so much to be thankful for but—promise me one thing, son!

Tom: What, Mother?

Amanda: Promise, son you'll—never be a drunkard!

Tom (*turns to her grinning*): I will never be a drunkard, Mother.

Amanda: That's what frightened me so, that you'd be drinking! Eat a bowl of Purina!

Tom: Just coffee, Mother.

Amanda: Shredded wheat biscuit?

Tom: No. No, Mother, just coffee.

Amanda: You can't put in a day's work on an empty stomach. You've got ten minutes—don't gulp! Drinking too-hot liquids makes cancer of the stomach. . . . Put cream in.

Tom: No, thank you.

Amanda: To cool it.

Tom: No! No, thank you, I want it black.

Amanda: I know, but it's not good for you. We have to do all that we can to build ourselves up. In these trying times we live in, all that we have to cling to is—each other. . . . That's why it's so important to—Tom, I—I sent out your sister so I could discuss something with you. If you hadn't spoken I would have spoken to you. (*Sits down.*)

Tom (*gently*): What is it, Mother, that you want to discuss?

Amanda: Laura!

Tom puts his cup down slowly.

(Legend On Screen: "Laura.")

(Music: "The Glass Menagerie.")

Tom: —Oh.—Laura . . .

Amanda (*touching his sleeve*): You know how Laura is. So quiet but—still water runs deep! She notices things and I think she—broods about them. (*Tom looks up.*) A few days ago I came in and she was crying.

Tom: What about?

Amanda: You.

Tom: Me?

Amanda: She has an idea that you're not happy here.

Tom: What gave her that idea?

Amanda: What gives her any idea? However, you do act strangely. I—I'm not criticizing, understand *that!* I know your ambitions do not lie in the warehouse, that like everybody in the whole wide world—you've had to—make sacrifices, but—Tom—Tom—life's not easy, it calls for—Spartan endurance! There's so many things in my heart that I cannot describe to you! I've never told you but I—*loved* your father. . . .

Tom (gently): I know that, Mother.

Amanda: And you—when I see you taking after his ways! Staying out late—and—well, you *had* been drinking the night you were in that—terrifying condition! Laura says that you hate the apartment and that you go out nights to get away from it! Is that true, Tom?

Tom: No. You say there's so much in your heart that you can't describe to me. That's true of me, too. There's so much in my heart that I can't describe to *you!* So let's respect each other's—

Amanda: But, why—*why*, Tom—are you always so *restless?* Where do you go to, nights?

Tom: I—go to the movies.

Amanda: Why do you go to the movies so much, Tom?

Tom: I go to the movies because—I like adventure. Adventure is something I don't have much of at work, so I go to the movies.

Amanda: But, Tom, you go to the movies *entirely* too *much!*

Tom: I like a lot of adventure.

Amanda looks baffled, then hurt. As the familiar inquisition resumes he becomes hard and impatient again. Amanda slips back into her querulous attitude toward him.

(Image On Screen: Sailing Vessel With Jolly Roger.)

Amanda: Most young men find adventure in their careers.

Tom: Then most young men are not employed in a warehouse.

Amanda: The world is full of young men employed in warehouses and offices and factories.

Tom: Do all of them find adventure in their careers?

Amanda: They do or they do without it! Not everybody has a craze for adventure.

Tom: Man is by instinct a lover, a hunter, a fighter, and none of those instincts are given much play at the warehouse!

Amanda: Man is by instinct! Don't quote instinct to me! Instinct is something that people have got away from! It belongs to animals! Christian adults don't want it!

Tom: What do Christian adults want, then, Mother?

Amanda: Superior things! Things of the mind and the spirit! Only animals have to satisfy instincts! Surely your aims are somewhat higher than theirs! Than monkeys—pigs—

Tom: I reckon they're not.

Amanda: You're joking. However, that isn't what I wanted to discuss.

Tom (rising): I haven't much time.

Amanda (pushing his shoulder): Sit down.

Tom: You want me to punch in red at the warehouse, Mother?
Amanda: You have five minutes. I want to talk about Laura.

(Legend: "Plans And Provisions.")

Tom: All right! What about Laura?
Amanda: We have to be making some plans and provisions for her. She's older than you, two years, and nothing has happened. She just drifts along doing nothing. It frightens me terribly how she just drifts along.
Tom: I guess she's the type that people call home girls.
Amanda: There's no such type, and if there is, it's a pity! That is unless the home is hers, with a husband!
Tom: What?
Amanda: Oh, I can see the handwriting on the wall as plain as I see the nose in front of my face! It's terrifying! More and more you remind me of your father! He was out all hours without explanation—Then *left! Goodbye!* And me with the bag to hold. I saw that letter you got from the Merchant Marine. I know what you're dreaming of. I'm not standing here blindfolded. (*She pauses.*) Very well, then. Then *do* it! But not till there's somebody to take your place.
Tom: What do you mean?
Amanda: I mean that as soon as Laura has got somebody to take care of her, married, a home of her own, independent—why, then you'll be free to go wherever you please, on land, on sea, whichever way the wind blows! But until that time you've got to look out for your sister. I don't say me because I'm old and don't matter! I say for your sister because she's young and dependent. I put her in business college—a dismal failure! Frightened her so it made her sick to her stomach. I took her over to the Young People's League at the church. Another fiasco. She spoke to nobody, nobody spoke to her. Now all she does is fool with those pieces of glass and play those worn-out records. What kind of a life is that for a girl to lead!
Tom: What can I do about it?
Amanda: Overcome selfishness! Self, self, self is all that you ever think of! (*Tom springs up and crosses to get his coat. It is ugly and bulky. He pulls on a cap with earmuffs.*) Where is your muffler? Put your wool muffler on! (*He snatches it angrily from the closet and tosses it around his neck and pulls both ends tight.*) Tom! I haven't said what I had in mind to ask you.
Tom: I'm too late to—
Amanda (*catching his arms—very importunately. Then shyly*): Down at the warehouse, aren't there some—nice young men?
Tom: No!
Amanda: There *must* be—some . . .
Tom: Mother—

  Gesture.

Amanda: Find one that's clean-living—doesn't drink—and ask him out for sister!
Tom: What?
Amanda: For *sister!* To *meet!* Get *acquainted!*
Tom (*stamping to door*): Oh, my go-osh!

Amanda: Will you? (*He opens door. Imploringly.*) Will you? (*He starts down.*) Will you? Will you, dear?

Tom (*calling back*): Yes!

Amanda closes the door hesitantly and with a troubled but faintly hopeful expression.

(Screen Image: Glamor Magazine Cover.)

Spot Amanda at phone.

Amanda: Ella Cartwright? This is Amanda Wingfield! How are you, honey? How is that kidney condition? (*Count five.*) Horrors! (*Count five.*) You're a Christian martyr, yes, honey, that's what you are, a Christian martyr! Well, I just happened to notice in my little red book that your subscription to the *Companion* has just run out! I knew that you wouldn't want to miss out on the wonderful serial starting in this new issue. It's by Bessie Mae Hopper, the first thing she's written since *Honeymoon for Three.* Wasn't that a strange and interesting story? Well, this one is even lovelier, I believe. It has a sophisticated society background. It's all about the horsey set on Long Island!

(Fade Out.)

SCENE V

(Legend On Screen: "Annunciation.") *Fade with music.*

It is early dusk of a spring evening. Supper has just been finished in the Wingfield apartment. Amanda and Laura in light colored dresses are removing dishes from the table, in the upstage area, which is shadowy, their movements formalized almost as a dance or ritual, their moving forms as pale and silent as moths.

Tom, in white shirt and trousers, rises from the table and crosses toward the fire-escape.

Amanda (*as he passes her*): Son, will you do me a favor?

Tom: What?

Amanda: Comb your hair! You look so pretty when your hair is combed! (*Tom slouches on sofa with evening paper. Enormous caption "Franco Triumphs."*) There is only one respect in which I would like you to emulate your father.

Tom: What respect is that?

Amanda: The care he always took of his appearance. He never allowed himself to look untidy. (*He throws down the paper and crosses to fire-escape.*) Where are you going?

Tom: I'm going out to smoke.

Amanda: You smoke too much. A pack a day at fifteen cents a pack. How much would that amount to in a month? Thirty times fifteen is how much, Tom? Figure it out and you will be astounded at what you could save. Enough to give you a night-school course in accounting at Washington U! Just think what a wonderful thing that would be for you, son!

Tom is unmoved by the thought.

Tom: I'd rather smoke. (*He steps out on landing, letting the screen door slam.*)

Amanda (sharply): I know! That's the tragedy of it. . . . (*Alone, she turns to look at her husband's picture.*)

(Dance Music: "All The World Is Waiting For The Sunrise.")

Tom (to the audience): Across the alley from us was the Paradise Dance Hall. On evenings in spring the windows and doors were open and the music came out-doors. Sometimes the lights were turned out except for a large glass sphere that hung from the ceiling. It would turn slowly about and filter the dusk with deli-cate rainbow colors. Then the orchestra played a waltz or a tango, something that had a slow and sensuous rhythm. Couples would come outside, to the rela-tive privacy of the alley. You could see them kissing behind ash-pits and tele-phone poles. This was the compensation for lives that passed like mine, without any change or adventure. Adventure and change were imminent in this year. They were waiting around the corner for all these kids. Suspended in the mist over Berchtesgaden, caught in the folds of Chamberlain's umbrella. In Spain there was Guernica! But here there was only hot swing music and liquor, dance halls, bars, and movies, and sex that hung in the gloom like a chandelier and flooded the world with brief, deceptive rainbows. . . . All the world was waiting for bombardments!

Amanda turns from the picture and comes outside.

Amanda (sighing): A fire-escape landing's a poor excuse for a porch. (*She spreads a newspaper on a step and sits down, gracefully and demurely as if she were settling into a swing on a Mississippi veranda.*) What are you looking at?

Tom: The moon.

Amanda: Is there a moon this evening?

Tom: It's rising over Garfinkel's Delicatessen.

Amanda: So it is! A little silver slipper of a moon. Have you made a wish on it yet?

Tom: Um-hum.

Amanda: What did you wish for?

Tom: That's a secret.

Amanda: A secret, huh? Well, I won't tell mine either. I will be just as mysterious as you.

Tom: I bet I can guess what yours is.

Amanda: Is my head so transparent?

Tom: You're not a sphinx.

Amanda: No, I don't have secrets. I'll tell you what I wished for on the moon. Suc-cess and happiness for my precious children! I wish for that whenever there's a moon, and when there isn't a moon, I wish for it, too.

Tom: I thought perhaps you wished for a gentleman caller.

Amanda: Why do you say that?

Tom: Don't you remember asking me to fetch one?

Amanda: I remember suggesting that it would be nice for your sister if you brought home some nice young man from the warehouse. I think I've made that sugges-tion more than once.

Tom: Yes, you have made it repeatedly.

Amanda: Well?

Tom: We are going to have one.

Amanda: What?
Tom: A gentleman caller!

(The Annunciation Is Celebrated With Music.)

Amanda rises.

(Image On Screen: Caller With Bouquet.)

Amanda: You mean you have asked some nice young man to come over?
Tom: Yep. I've asked him to dinner.
Amanda: You really did?
Tom: I did!
Amanda: You did, and did he—*accept?*
Tom: He did!
Amanda: Well, well—well, well! That's—lovely!
Tom: I thought that you would be pleased.
Amanda: It's definite, then?
Tom: Very definite.
Amanda: Soon?
Tom: Very soon.
Amanda: For heaven's sake, stop putting on and tell me some things, will you?
Tom: What things do you want me to tell you?
Amanda: Naturally I would like to know when he's *coming!*
Tom: He's coming tomorrow.
Amanda: Tomorrow?
Tom: Yep. Tomorrow.
Amanda: But, Tom!
Tom: Yes, Mother?
Amanda: Tomorrow gives me no time!
Tom: Time for what?
Amanda: Preparations! Why didn't you phone me at once, as soon as you asked him, the minute that he accepted? Then, don't you see, I could have been getting ready!
Tom: You don't have to make any fuss.
Amanda: Oh, Tom, Tom, Tom, of course I have to make a fuss! I want things nice, not sloppy! Not thrown together. I'll certainly have to do some fast thinking, won't I?
Tom: I don't see why you have to think at all.
Amanda: You just don't know. We can't have a gentleman caller in a pig-sty! All my wedding silver has to be polished, the monogrammed table linen ought to be laundered! The windows have to be washed and fresh curtains put up. And how about clothes? We have to *wear* something, don't we?
Tom: Mother, this boy is no one to make a fuss over!
Amanda: Do you realize he's the first young man we've introduced to your sister? It's terrible, dreadful, disgraceful that poor little sister has never received a single gentleman caller! Tom, come inside! (*She opens the screen door.*)
Tom: What for?
Amanda: I want to ask you some things.
Tom: If you're going to make such a fuss, I'll call it off, I'll tell him not to come.

Amanda: You certainly won't do anything of the kind. Nothing offends people worse than broken engagements. It simply means I'll have to work like a Turk! We won't be brilliant, but we will pass inspection. Come on inside. (*Tom follows, groaning.*) Sit down.

Tom: Any particular place you would like me to sit?

Amanda: Thank heavens I've got that new sofa! I'm also making payments on a floor lamp I'll have sent out! And put the chintz covers on, they'll brighten things up! Of course I'd hoped to have these walls re-papered. . . . What is the young man's name?

Tom: His name is O'Connor.

Amanda: That, of course, means fish—tomorrow is Friday! I'll have that salmon loaf—with Durkee's dressing! What does he do? He works at the warehouse?

Tom: Of course! How else would I—

Amanda: Tom, he—doesn't drink?

Tom: Why do you ask me that?

Amanda: Your father *did*!

Tom: Don't get started on that!

Amanda: He *does* drink, then?

Tom: Not that I know of!

Amanda: Make sure, be certain! The last thing I want for my daughter's a boy who drinks!

Tom: Aren't you being a little premature? Mr. O'Connor has not yet appeared on the scene!

Amanda: But will tomorrow. To meet your sister, and what do I know about his character? Nothing! Old maids are better off than wives of drunkards!

Tom: Oh, my God!

Amanda: Be still!

Tom (*leaning forward to whisper*): Lots of fellows meet girls whom they don't marry!

Amanda: Oh, talk sensibly, Tom—and don't be sarcastic! (*She has gotten a hairbrush.*)

Tom: What are you doing?

Amanda: I'm brushing that cow-lick down! (*She attacks his hair with the brush.*) What is this young man's position at the warehouse?

Tom (*submitting grimly to the brush and the interrogation*): This young man's position is that of a shipping clerk, Mother.

Amanda: Sounds to me like a fairly responsible job, the sort of a job *you* would be in if you just had more *get-up*. What is his salary? Have you got any idea?

Tom: I would judge it to be approximately eighty-five dollars a month.

Amanda: Well—not princely, but—

Tom: Twenty more than I make.

Amanda: Yes, how well I know! But for a family man, eighty-five dollars a month is not much more than you can just get by on. . . .

Tom: Yes, but Mr. O'Connor is not a family man.

Amanda: He might be, mightn't he? Some time in the future?

Tom: I see. Plans and provisions.

Amanda: You are the only young man that I know of who ignores the fact that the future becomes the present, the present the past, and the past turns into everlasting regret if you don't plan for it!

Tom: I will think that over and see what I can make of it!

Amanda: Don't be supercilious with your mother! Tell me some more about this— what do you call him?

Tom: James D. O'Connor. The D. is for Delaney.

Amanda: Irish on *both* sides! *Gracious!* And doesn't drink?

Tom: Shall I call him up and ask him right this minute?

Amanda: The only way to find out about those things is to make discreet inquiries at the proper moment. When I was a girl in Blue Mountain and it was suspected that a young man drank, the girl whose attentions he had been receiving, if any girl *was*, would sometimes speak to the minister of his church, or rather her father would if her father was living, and sort of feel him out on the young man's character. That is the way such things are discreetly handled to keep a young woman from making a tragic mistake!

Tom: Then how did you happen to make a tragic mistake?

Amanda: That innocent look of your father's had everyone fooled! He *smiled*—the world was *enchanted!* No girl can do worse than put herself at the mercy of a handsome appearance! I hope that Mr. O'Connor is not too good-looking.

Tom: No, he's not too good-looking. He's covered with freckles and hasn't too much of a nose.

Amanda: He's not right-down homely, though?

Tom: Not right-down homely. Just medium homely, I'd say.

Amanda: Character's what to look for in a man.

Tom: That's what I've always said, Mother.

Amanda: You've never said anything of the kind and I suspect you would never give it a thought.

Tom: Don't be suspicious of me.

Amanda: At least I hope he's the type that's up and coming.

Tom: I think he really goes in for self-improvement.

Amanda: What reason have you to think so?

Tom: He goes to night school.

Amanda (beaming): Splendid! What does he do, I mean study?

Tom: Radio engineering and public speaking!

Amanda: Then he has visions of being advanced in the world! Any young man who studies public speaking is aiming to have an executive job some day! And radio engineering? A thing for the future! Both of these facts are very illuminating. Those are the sort of things that a mother should know concerning any young man who comes to call on her daughter. Seriously or—not.

Tom: One little warning. He doesn't know about Laura. I didn't let on that we had dark ulterior motives. I just said, why don't you come have dinner with us? He said okay and that was the whole conversation.

Amanda: I bet it was! You're eloquent as an oyster. However, he'll know about Laura when he gets here. When he sees how lovely and sweet and pretty she is, he'll thank his lucky stars he was asked to dinner.

Tom: Mother, you mustn't expect too much of Laura.

Amanda: What do you mean?

Tom: Laura seems all those things to you and me because she's ours and we love her. We don't even notice she's crippled any more.

Amanda: Don't say crippled! You know that I never allow that word to be used!

Tom: But face facts, Mother. She is and—that not's all—

Amanda: What do you mean "not all"?

Tom: Laura is very different from other girls.

Amanda: I think the difference is all to her advantage.

Tom: Not quite all—in the eyes of others—strangers—she's terribly shy and lives in a world of her own and those things make her seem a little peculiar to people outside the house.

Amanda: Don't say peculiar.

Tom: Face the facts. She is.

(The Dance-Hall Music Changes To A Tango That Has A Minor And Somewhat Ominous Tone.)

Amanda: In what way is she peculiar—may I ask?

Tom (gently): She lives in a world of her own—a world of—little glass ornaments, Mother. . . . (*Gets up. Amanda remains holding brush, looking at him, troubled.*) She plays old phonograph records and—that's about all—(*He glances at himself in the mirror and crosses to door.*)

Amanda (sharply): Where are you going?

Tom: I'm going to the movies. (*Out screen door.*)

Amanda: Not to the movies, every night to the movies! (*Follows quickly to screen door.*) I don't believe you always go to the movies! (*He is gone. Amanda looks worriedly after him for a moment. Then vitality and optimism return and she turns from the door. Crossing to portieres.*) Laura! Laura! (*Laura answers from kitchenette.*)

Laura: Yes, Mother.

Amanda: Let those dishes go and come in front! (*Laura appears with dish towel. Gaily.*) Laura, come here and make a wish on the moon!

Laura (entering): Moon—moon?

Amanda: A little silver slipper of a moon. Look over your left shoulder, Laura, and make a wish! (*Laura looks faintly puzzled as if called out of sleep. Amanda seizes her shoulders and turns her at an angle by the door.*) Now! Now, darling, wish!

Laura: What shall I wish for, Mother?

Amanda (her voice trembling and her eyes suddenly filling with tears): Happiness! Good fortune!

The violin rises and the stage dims out.

SCENE VI

(Image: High-School Hero.)

Tom: And so the following evening I brought him home to dinner. I had known Jim slightly in high school. In high school Jim was a hero. He had tremendous Irish good nature and vitality with the scrubbed and polished look of white chinaware. He seemed to move in a continual spotlight. He was a star in basketball, captain of the debating club, president of the senior class and the glee club and he sang the male lead in the annual light operas. He was always running or bounding, never just walking. He seemed always at the point of defeating the law of gravity. He was shooting with such velocity through his adolescence that you would logically expect him to arrive at nothing short of the White House by the time he was thirty. But Jim apparently ran into more interference after his graduation from Soldan. His speed had definitely slowed. Six years after he left high school he was holding a job that wasn't much better than mine.

(Image: Clerk.)

He was the only one at the warehouse with whom I was on friendly terms. I was valuable to him as someone who could remember his former glory, who had seen him win basketball games and the silver cup in debating. He knew of my secret practice of retiring to a cabinet of the washroom to work on my poems when business was slack in the warehouse. He called me Shakespeare. And while the other boys in the warehouse regarded me with suspicious hostility, Jim took a humorous attitude toward me. Gradually his attitude affected the others, their hostility wore off and they also began to smile at me as people smile at an oddly fashioned dog who trots across their path at some distance.

I knew that Jim and Laura had known each other at Soldan, and I had heard Laura speak admiringly of his voice. I didn't know if Jim remembered her or not. In high school Laura had been as unobtrusive as Jim had been astonishing. If he did remember Laura, it was not as my sister, for when I asked him to dinner, he grinned and said, "You know, Shakespeare, I never thought of you as having folks!"

He was about to discover that I did. . . .

(Light Up Stage.)

(Legend On Screen: "The Accent Of A Coming Foot.")

Friday evening. It is about five o'clock of a late spring evening which comes "scattering poems in the sky."

A delicate lemony light is in the Wingfield apartment.

Amanda has worked like a Turk in preparation for the gentleman caller. The results are astonishing. The new floor lamp with its rose-silk shade is in place, a colored paper lantern conceals the broken light fixture in the ceiling, new billowing white curtains are at the windows, chintz covers are on chairs and sofa, a pair of new sofa pillows make their initial appearance.

Open boxes and tissue paper are scattered on the floor.

Laura stands in the middle with lifted arms while Amanda crouches before her, adjusting the hem of the new dress, devout and ritualistic. The dress is colored and designed by memory. The arrangement of Laura's hair is changed; it is softer and more becoming. A fragile, unearthly prettiness has come out in Laura: she is like a piece of translucent glass touched by light, given a momentary radiance, not actual, not lasting.

Amanda (impatiently): Why are you trembling?
Laura: Mother, you've made me so nervous!
Amanda: How have I made you nervous?
Laura: By all this fuss! You make it seem so important!

Amanda: I don't understand you, Laura. You couldn't be satisfied with just sitting home, and yet whenever I try to arrange something for you, you seem to resist it. (*She gets up.*) Now take a look at yourself. No, wait! Wait just a moment—I have an idea!

Laura: What is it now?

Amanda produces two powder puffs which she wraps in handkerchiefs and stuffs in Laura's bosom.

Laura: Mother, what are you doing?

Amanda: They call them "Gay Deceivers"!

Laura: I won't wear them!

Amanda: You will!

Laura: Why should I?

Amanda: Because, to be painfully honest, your chest is flat.

Laura: You make it seem like we were setting a trap.

Amanda: All pretty girls are a trap, a pretty trap, and men expect them to be. **(Legend: "A Pretty Trap.")** Now look at yourself, young lady. This is the prettiest you will ever be! (*She stands back to admire Laura.*) I've got to fix myself now! You're going to be surprised by your mother's appearance! (*She crosses through the portieres, humming gaily.*)

Laura moves slowly to the long mirror and stares solemnly at herself.

A wind blows the white curtains inward in a slow, graceful motion and with a faint, sorrowful sighing.

Amanda (*offstage*): It isn't dark enough yet. (*She turns slowly before the mirror with a troubled look.*)

(Legend On Screen: "This Is My Sister: Celebrate Her With Strings!" Music.)

Amanda (*laughing, off*): I'm going to show you something. I'm going to make a spectacular appearance!

Laura: What is it, Mother?

Amanda: Possess your soul in patience—you will see! Something I've resurrected from that old trunk! Styles haven't changed so terribly much after all. . . . (*She parts the portieres.*) Now just look at your mother! (*She wears a girlish frock of yellowed voile with a blue silk sash. She carries a bunch of jonquils—the legend of her youth is nearly revived. Feverishly.*) This is the dress in which I led the cotillion. Won the cakewalk twice at Sunset Hill, wore one Spring to the Governor's Ball in Jackson! See how I sashayed around the ballroom, Laura? (*She raises her skirt and does a mincing step around the room.*) I wore it on Sundays for my gentlemen callers! I had it on the day I met your father . . . I had malaria fever all that Spring. The change of climate from East Tennessee to the Delta—weakened resistance—I had a little temperature all the time—not enough to be serious—just enough to make me restless and giddy! Invitations poured in—parties all over the Delta!—"Stay in bed," said Mother, "you have fever!"—but I just wouldn't. I took quinine but kept on going, going! Evenings, dances! Afternoons, long, long rides! Picnics—lovely!— So lovely, that country in May—all lacy with dogwood, literally flooded with jonquils! That was the spring I had the craze for jonquils. Jonquils became an absolute obsession. Mother said, "Honey, there's no more room for jonquils." And still I kept on bringing in more jonquils. Whenever, wherever I saw them, I'd say, "Stop! Stop! I see jonquils!" I made the young men help me gather the jonquils! It was a joke, Amanda and her jonquils! Finally there were no more vases to hold them, every available space was filled with jonquils. No vases to hold them? All right, I'll hold them myself! And then I—(*She stops in front of the picture.*) (**Music.**) met your father! Malaria fever and jonquils and then—this—boy. . . . (*She switches on the rose-colored lamp.*) I hope they get here before it starts to rain. (*She crosses upstage and places the jonquils in bowl on table.*) I gave your brother a little extra change so he and Mr. O'Connor could take the service car home.

Laura (*with altered look*): What did you say his name was?

Amanda: O'Connor.

Laura: What is his first name?

Amanda: I don't remember. Oh, yes, I do. It was—Jim!

Laura sways slightly and catches hold of a chair.

(**Legend On Screen. "Not Jim!"**)

Laura (*faintly*): Not—Jim!

Amanda: Yes, that was it, it was Jim! I've never known a Jim that wasn't nice!

(**Music: Ominous.**)

Laura: Are you sure his name is Jim O'Connor?

Amanda: Yes. Why?

Laura: Is he the one that Tom used to know in high school?

Amanda: He didn't say so. I think he just got to know him at the warehouse.

Laura: There was a Jim O'Connor we both knew in high school—(*Then, with effort.*) If that is the one that Tom is bringing to dinner—you'll have to excuse me, I won't come to the table.

Amanda: What sort of nonsense is this?

Laura: You asked me once if I'd ever liked a boy. Don't you remember I showed you this boy's picture?

Amanda: You mean the boy you showed me in the year-book?

Laura: Yes, that boy.

Amanda: Laura, Laura, were you in love with that boy?

Laura: I don't know, Mother. All I know is I couldn't sit at the table if it was him!

Amanda: It won't be him! It isn't the least bit likely. But whether it is or not, you will come to the table. You will not be excused.

Laura: I'll have to be, Mother.

Amanda: I don't intend to humor your silliness, Laura. I've had too much from you and your brother, both! So just sit down and compose yourself till they come. Tom has forgotten his key so you'll have to let them in, when they arrive.

Laura (*panicky*): Oh, Mother—*you* answer the door!

Amanda (*lightly*): I'll be in the kitchen—busy!

Laura: Oh, Mother, please answer the door, don't make me do it!

Amanda (*crossing into kitchenette*): I've got to fix the dressing for the salmon. Fuss, fuss—silliness!—over a gentleman caller!

Door swings shut. Laura is left alone.

(Legend: "Terror!")

She utters a low moan and turns off the lamp—sits stiffly on the edge of the sofa, knotting her fingers together.

(Legend On Screen: "The Opening Of A Door!")

Tom and Jim appear on the fire-escape steps and climb to landing. Hearing their approach, Laura rises with a panicky gesture. She retreats to the portieres.

The doorbell. Laura catches her breath and touches her throat. Low drums.

Amanda (*calling*): Laura, sweetheart! The door!

Laura stares at it without moving.

Jim: I think we just beat the rain.

Tom: Uh-huh. (*He rings again, nervously. Jim whistles and fishes for a cigarette.*)

Amanda (*very, very gaily*): Laura, that is your brother and Mr. O'Connor! Will you let them in, darling?

Laura crosses toward kitchenette door.

Laura (*breathlessly*): Mother—you go to the door!

Amanda steps out of kitchenette and stares furiously at Laura. She points imperiously at the door.

Laura: Please, please!

Amanda (*in a fierce whisper*): What is the matter with you, you silly thing?

Laura (*desperately*): Please, you answer it, *please*!

Amanda: I told you I wasn't going to humor you, Laura. Why have you chosen this moment to lose your mind?

Laura: Please, please, please, you go!

Amanda: You'll have to go to the door because I can't!

Laura (*despairingly*): I can't either!

Amanda: Why?

Laura: I'm sick!

Amanda: I'm sick, too—of your nonsense! Why can't you and your brother be normal people? Fantastic whims and behavior! (*Tom gives a long ring.*) Preposterous goings on! Can you give me one reason—(*Calls out lyrically.*) Coming! Just one second!—why should you be afraid to open a door? Now you answer it, Laura!

Laura: Oh, oh, oh . . . (*She returns through the portieres. Darts to the victrola and winds it frantically and turns it on.*)

Amanda: Laura Wingfield, you march right to that door!

Laura: Yes—yes, Mother!

A faraway, scratchy rendition of "Dardanella" softens the air and gives her strength to move through it. She slips to the door and draws it cautiously open. Tom enters with the caller, Jim O'Connor.

Tom: Laura, this is Jim. Jim, this is my sister, Laura.

Jim (*stepping inside*): I didn't know that Shakespeare had a sister!
Laura (*retreating stiff and trembling from the door*): How—how do you do?
Jim (*heartily extending his hand*): Okay!

> *Laura touches it hesitantly with hers.*

Jim: Your hand's cold, Laura!
Laura: Yes, well—I've been playing the victrola. . . .
Jim: Must have been playing classical music on it! You ought to play a little hot
    swing music to warm you up!
Laura: Excuse me—I haven't finished playing the victrola. . . .

> *She turns awkwardly and hurries into the front room. She pauses a second by the victrola.
> Then catches her breath and darts through the portieres like a frightened deer.*

Jim (*grinning*): What was the matter?
Tom: Oh—with Laura? Laura is—terribly shy.
Jim: Shy, huh? It's unusual to meet a shy girl nowadays. I don't believe you ever
    mentioned you had a sister.
Tom: Well, now you know. I have one. Here is the *Post Dispatch*. You want a piece of it?
Jim: Uh-huh.
Tom: What piece? The comics?
Jim: Sports! (*Glances at it.*) Ole Dizzy Dean is on his bad behavior.
Tom (*disinterest*): Yeah? (*Lights cigarette and crosses back to fire-escape door.*)
Jim: Where are *you* going?
Tom: I'm going out on the terrace.
Jim (*goes after him*): You know, Shakespeare—I'm going to sell you a bill of goods!
Tom: What goods?
Jim: A course I'm taking.
Tom: Huh?
Jim: In public speaking! You and me, we're not the warehouse type.
Tom: Thanks—that's good news. But what has public speaking got to do with it?
Jim: It fits you for—executive positions!
Tom: Awww.
Jim: I tell you it's done a helluva lot for me.

(Image: Executive At Desk.)

Tom: In what respect?
Jim: In every! Ask yourself what is the difference between you an' me and men in
    the office down front? Brains?—No!—Ability?—No! Then what? Just one little
    thing—
Tom: What is that one little thing?
Jim: Primarily it amounts to—social poise! Being able to square up to people and
    hold your own on any social level!
Amanda (*offstage*): Tom?
Tom: Yes, Mother?
Amanda: Is that you and Mr. O'Connor?
Tom: Yes, Mother.
Amanda: Well, you just make yourselves comfortable in there.

Tom: Yes, Mother.

Amanda: Ask Mr. O'Connor if he would like to wash his hands.

Jim: Aw—no—thank you—I took care of that at the warehouse. Tom—

Tom: Yes?

Jim: Mr. Mendoza was speaking to me about you.

Tom: Favorably?

Jim: What do you think?

Tom: Well—

Jim: You're going to be out of a job if you don't wake up.

Tom: I am waking up—

Jim: You show no signs.

Tom: The signs are interior.

(Image On Screen: The Sailing Vessel With Jolly Roger Again.)

Tom: I'm planning to change. (*He leans over the rail speaking with quiet exhilaration. The incandescent marquees and signs of the first-run movie houses light his face from across the alley. He looks like a voyager.*) I'm right at the point of committing myself to a future that doesn't include the warehouse and Mr. Mendoza or even a night-school course in public speaking.

Jim: What are you gassing about?

Tom: I'm tired of the movies.

Jim: Movies!

Tom: Yes, movies! Look at them—(*A wave toward the marvels of Grand Avenue.*) All of those glamorous people—having adventures—hogging it all, gobbling the whole thing up! You know what happens? People go to the *movies* instead of *moving!* Hollywood characters are supposed to have all the adventures for everybody in America, while everybody in America sits in a dark room and watches them have them! Yes, until there's a war. That's when adventure becomes available to the masses! *Everyone's* dish, not only Gable's! Then the people in the dark room come out of the dark room to have some adventures themselves—goody, goody! It's our turn now, to go to the South Sea Island—to make a safari—to be exotic, far-off—But I'm not patient. I don't want to wait till then. I'm tired of the *movies* and I am *about* to *move!*

Jim (incredulously): Move?

Tom: Yes!

Jim: When?

Tom: Soon!

Jim: Where? Where?

Theme three music seems to answer the question, while *Tom thinks it over. He searches among his pockets.*

Tom: I'm starting to boil inside. I know I seem dreamy, but inside—well, I'm boiling! Whenever I pick up a shoe, I shudder a little thinking how short life is and what I am doing!—Whatever that means. I know it doesn't mean shoes—except as something to wear on a traveler's feet! (*Finds paper.*) Look—

Jim: What?

Tom: I'm a member.

Jim (reading): The Union of Merchant Seamen.

Tom: I paid my dues this month, instead of the light bill.

Jim: You will regret it when they turn the lights off.

Tom: I won't be here.

Jim: How about your mother?

Tom: I'm like my father. The bastard son of a bastard! Did you notice how he is grinning in his picture in there? And he's been absent going on sixteen years!

Jim: You're just talking, you drip. How does your mother feel about it?

Tom: Shhh—Here comes Mother! Mother is not acquainted with my plans!

Amanda (enters portieres): Where are you all?

Tom: On the terrace, Mother.

> *They start inside. She advances to them. Tom is distinctly shocked at her appearance. Even Jim blinks a little. He is making his first contact with girlish Southern vivacity and in spite of the night-school course in public speaking is somewhat thrown off the beam by the unexpected outlay of social charm.*

> *Certain responses are attempted by Jim but are swept aside by Amanda's gay laughter and chatter. Tom is embarrassed but after the first shock Jim reacts very warmly. Grins and chuckles, is altogether won over.*

(Image: Amanda As A Girl.)

Amanda (coyly smiling, shaking her girlish ringlets): Well, well, well, so this is Mr. O'Connor. Introductions entirely unnecessary. I've heard so much about you from my boy. I finally said to him, Tom—good gracious!—why don't you bring this paragon to supper? I'd like to meet this nice young man at the warehouse!—Instead of just hearing him sing your praises so much! I don't know why my son is so stand-offish—that's not Southern behavior! Let's sit down and—I think we could stand a little more air in here! Tom, leave the door open. I felt a nice fresh breeze a moment ago. Where has it gone? Mmm, so warm already! And not quite summer, even. We're going to burn up when summer really gets started. However, we're having—we're having a very light supper. I think light things are better fo' this time of year. The same as light clothes are. Light clothes an' light food are what warm weather calls fo'. You know our blood gets so thick during th' winter—it takes a while fo' us to *adjust* ou'selves!—when the season changes . . . It's come so quick this year. I wasn't prepared. All of a sudden—heavens! Already summer!—I ran to the trunk an' pulled out this light dress—Terribly old! Historical almost! But feels so good—so good an' co-ol, y'know. . . .

Tom: Mother—

Amanda: Yes, honey?

Tom: How about—supper?

Amanda: Honey, you go ask Sister if supper is ready! You know that Sister is in full charge of supper! Tell her you hungry boys are waiting for it. (*To Jim*) Have you met Laura?

Jim: She—

Amanda: Let you in? Oh, good, you've met already! It's rare for a girl as sweet an' pretty as Laura to be domestic! But Laura is, thank heavens, not only pretty but also very domestic. I'm not at all. I never was a bit. I never could make a thing but angel-food cake. Well, in the South we had so many servants. Gone, gone, gone. All vestige of gracious living! Gone completely! I wasn't prepared for what the future brought me. All of my gentlemen callers were sons of planters and so of course I assumed that I would be married to one and raise my family on a large piece of land with plenty of servants. But man proposes—and woman accepts the proposal!—To vary that old, old saying a little bit—I married no planter! I married a man who worked for the telephone company! That gallantly smiling gentleman over there! (*Points to the picture.*) A telephone man who—fell in love with long-distance! Now he travels and I don't even know where!—But what am I going on for about my—tribulations? Tell me yours—I hope you don't have any! Tom?

Tom (*returning*): Yes, Mother?

Amanda: Is supper nearly ready?

Tom: It looks to me like supper is on the table.

Amanda: Let me look—(*She rises prettily and looks through portieres.*) Oh, lovely! But where is Sister?

Tom: Laura is not feeling well and she says that she thinks she'd better not come to the table.

Amanda: What? Nonsense! Laura? Oh, Laura!

Laura (*offstage, faintly*): Yes, Mother.

Amanda: You really must come to the table. We won't be seated until you come to the table! Come in, Mr. O'Connor. You sit over there and I'll . . . Laura? Laura Wingfield! You're keeping us waiting, honey! We can't say grace until you come to the table!

The back door is pushed weakly open and Laura comes in. She is obviously quite faint, her lips trembling, her eyes wide and staring. She moves unsteadily toward the table.

(**Legend: "Terror!"**)

Outside a summer storm is coming abruptly. The white curtains billow inward at the windows and there is a sorrowful murmur and deep blue dusk.

Laura suddenly stumbles—She catches at a chair with a faint moan.

Tom: Laura!

Amanda: Laura! (*There is a clap of thunder.*) (**Legend: "Ah!"**) (*Despairingly.*) Why, Laura, you *are* ill, darling! Tom, help your sister into the living room, dear! Sit in the living room, Laura—rest on the sofa. Well! (*To Jim as Tom helps his sister to the sofa in the living room*) Standing over the hot stove made her ill!—I told her that it was just too warm this evening, but—(*Tom comes back in. Laura is on the sofa.*) Is Laura all right now?

Tom: Yes.

Amanda: What is that? Rain? A nice cool rain has come up! (*She gives the gentleman caller a frightened look.*) I think we may—have grace—now . . . (*Tom looks at her stupidly.*) Tom, honey—you say grace!

Tom: Oh . . . "For these and all thy mercies—" (*They bow their heads, Amanda stealing a nervous glance at Jim. In the living room Laura, stretched on the sofa, clenches her hand to her lips, to hold back a shuddering sob.*) God's Holy Name be praised—

(**The Scene Dims Out.**)

SCENE VII

A Souvenir.

Half an hour later. Dinner is just being finished in the upstage area which is concealed by the drawn portieres.

As the curtain rises Laura is still huddled upon the sofa, her feet drawn under her, her head resting on a pale blue pillow, her eyes wide and mysteriously watchful. The new floor lamp with its shade of rose-colored silk gives a soft, becoming light to her face, bringing out the fragile, unearthly prettiness which usually escapes attention. There is a steady murmur of rain, but it is slackening and stops soon after the scene begins; the air outside becomes pale and luminous as the moon breaks out.

A moment after the curtain rises, the lights in both rooms flicker and go out.

Jim: Hey, there, Mr. Light Bulb!

    Amanda laughs nervously.

(Legend: "Suspension Of A Public Service.")

Amanda: Where was Moses when the lights went out? Ha-ha. Do you know the answer to that one, Mr. O'Connor?

Jim: No, Ma'am, what's the answer?

Amanda: In the dark! (*Jim laughs appreciatively.*) Everybody sit still. I'll light the candles. Isn't it lucky we have them on the table? Where's a match? Which of you gentlemen can provide a match?

Jim: Here.

Amanda: Thank you, sir.

Jim: Not at all, Ma'am!

Amanda (as she lights the candles): I guess the fuse has burnt out. Mr. O'Connor, can you tell a burnt-out fuse? I know I can't and Tom is a total loss when it comes to mechanics. (**Sound: Getting Up: Voices Recede A Little To Kitchenette.**) Oh, be careful you don't bump into something. We don't want our gentleman caller to break his neck. Now wouldn't that be a fine howdy-do?

Jim: Ha-ha! Where is the fuse-box?

Amanda: Right here next to the stove. Can you see anything?

Jim: Just a minute.

Amanda: Isn't electricity a mysterious thing? Wasn't it Benjamin Franklin who tied a key to a kite? We live in such a mysterious universe, don't we? Some people say that science clears up all the mysteries for us. In my opinion it only creates more! Have you found it yet?

Jim: No, Ma'am. All these fuses look okay to me.

Amanda: Tom!

Tom: Yes, Mother?

Amanda: That light bill I gave you several days ago. The one I told you we got the notices about?

Tom: Oh—yeah.

(Legend: "Ha!")

Amanda: You didn't neglect to pay it by any chance?

Tom: Why, I—

Amanda: Didn't! I might have known it!

Jim: Shakespeare probably wrote a poem on that light bill, Mrs. Wingfield.

Amanda: I might have known better than to trust him with it! There's such a high price for negligence in this world!

Jim: Maybe the poem will win a ten-dollar prize.

Amanda: We'll just have to spend the remainder of the evening in the nineteenth century, before Mr. Edison made the Mazda lamp!

Jim: Candlelight is my favorite kind of light.

Amanda: That shows you're romantic! But that's no excuse for Tom. Well, we got through dinner. Very considerate of them to let us get through dinner before they plunged us into everlasting darkness, wasn't it, Mr. O'Connor?

Jim: Ha-ha!

Amanda: Tom, as a penalty for your carelessness you can help me with the dishes.

Jim: Let me give you a hand.

Amanda: Indeed you will not!

Jim: I ought to be good for something.

Amanda: Good for something? (*Her tone is rhapsodic.*) *You?* Why, Mr. O'Connor, nobody, *nobody's* given me this much entertainment in years—as you have!

Jim: Aw, now, Mrs. Wingfield!

Amanda: I'm not exaggerating, not one bit! But Sister is all by her lonesome. You go keep her company in the parlor! I'll give you this lovely old candelabrum that used to be on the altar at the church of the Heavenly Rest. It was melted a little out of shape when the church burnt down. Lightning struck it one spring. Gypsy Jones was holding a revival at the time and he intimated that the church was destroyed because the Episcopalians gave card parties.

Jim: Ha-ha.

Amanda: And how about coaxing Sister to drink a little wine? I think it would be good for her! Can you carry both at once?

Jim: Sure. I'm Superman!

Amanda: Now, Thomas, get into this apron!

Jim comes into the dining room, carrying the candelabrum, its candles lighted, in one hand and a glass of wine in the other. The door of kitchenette swings closed on Amanda's gay laughter; the flickering light approaches the portieres. Laura sits up nervously as he enters. Her speech at first is low and breathless from the almost intolerable strain of being alone with a stranger.

(The Legend: "I Don't Suppose You Remember Me At All!")

In her first speeches in this scene, before Jim's warmth overcomes her paralyzing shyness, Laura's voice is thin and breathless as though she has run up a steep flight of stairs. Jim's attitude is gently humorous. While the incident is apparently unimportant, it is to Laura the climax of her secret life.

Jim: Hello, there, Laura.

Laura (*faintly*): Hello. (*She clears her throat.*)

Jim: How are you feeling now? Better?

Laura: Yes. Yes, thank you.

Jim: This is for you. A little dandelion wine. (*He extends it toward her with extravagant gallantry.*)

Laura: Thank you.

Jim: Drink it—but don't get drunk! (*He laughs heartily. Laura takes the glass uncertainly; laughs shyly.*) Where shall I set the candles?

Laura: Oh—oh, anywhere . . .

Jim: How about here on the floor? Any objections?

Laura: No.

Jim: I'll spread a newspaper under to catch the drippings. I like to sit on the floor. Mind if I do?

Laura: Oh, no.

Jim: Give me a pillow?

Laura: What?

Jim: A pillow!

Laura: Oh . . . (*Hands him one quickly.*)

Jim: How about you? Don't you like to sit on the floor?

Laura: Oh—yes.

Jim: Why don't you, then?

Laura: I—will.

Jim: Take a pillow! (*Laura does. Sits on the other side of the candelabrum. Jim crosses his legs and smiles engagingly at her.*) I can't hardly see you sitting way over there.

Laura: I can—see you.

Jim: I know, but that's not fair, I'm in the limelight. (*Laura moves her pillow closer.*) Good! Now I can see you! Comfortable?

Laura: Yes.

Jim: So am I. Comfortable as a cow. Will you have some gum?

Laura: No, thank you.

Jim: I think that I will indulge, with your permission. (*Musingly unwraps it and holds it up.*) Think of the fortune made by the guy that invented the first piece of chewing gum. Amazing, huh? The Wrigley Building is one of the sights of Chicago—I saw it when I went up to the Century of Progress. Did you take in the Century of Progress?

Laura: No, I didn't.

Jim: Well, it was quite a wonderful exposition. What impressed me most was the Hall of Science. Gives you an idea of what the future will be in America, even more wonderful than the present time is! (*Pause. Smiling at her.*) Your brother tells me you're shy. Is that right, Laura?

Laura: I—don't know.

Jim: I judge you to be an old-fashioned type of girl. Well, I think that's pretty good type to be. Hope you don't think I'm being too personal—do you?

Laura (hastily, out of embarrassment): I believe I *will* take a piece of gum, if you—don't mind. (*Clearing her throat.*) Mr. O'Connor, have you—kept up with your singing?

Jim: Singing? Me?

Laura: Yes. I remember what a beautiful voice you had.

Jim: When did you hear me sing?

(**Voice Offstage In The Pause.**)

Voice (*offstage*):

> O blow, ye winds, heigh-ho,
> A-roving I will go!
> I'm off to my love
> With a boxing glove—
> Ten thousand miles away!

Jim: You say you've heard me sing?

Laura: Oh, yes! Yes, very often . . . . I—don't suppose you remember me—at all?

Jim (*smiling doubtfully*): You know I have an idea I've seen you before. I had that idea soon as you opened the door. It seemed almost like I was about to remember your name. But the name that I started to call you—wasn't a name! And so I stopped myself before I said it.

Laura: Wasn't it—Blue Roses?

Jim (*springs up, grinning*): Blue Roses! My gosh, yes—Blue Roses! That's what I had on my tongue when you opened the door! Isn't it funny what tricks your memory plays? I didn't connect you with the high school somehow or other. But that's where it was; it was high school. I didn't even know you were Shakespeare's sister! Gosh, I'm sorry.

Laura: I didn't expect you to. You—barely knew me!

Jim: But we did have a speaking acquaintance, huh?

Laura: Yes, we—spoke to each other.

Jim: When did you recognize me?

Laura: Oh, right away!

Jim: Soon as I came in the door?

Laura: When I heard your name I thought it was probably you. I knew that Tom used to know you a little in high school. So when you came in the door—well, then I was—sure.

Jim: Why didn't you *say* something, then?

Laura (*breathlessly*): I didn't know what to say, I was—too surprised!

Jim: For goodness sakes! You know, this sure is funny!

Laura: Yes! Yes, isn't it, though . . .

Jim: Didn't we have a class in something together?

Laura: Yes, we did.

Jim: What class was that?

Laura: It was—singing—chorus!

Jim: Aw!

Laura: I sat across the aisle from you in the Aud.

Jim: Aw.

Laura: Mondays, Wednesdays, and Fridays.

Jim: Now I remember—you always came in late.

Laura: Yes, it was so hard for me, getting upstairs. I had that brace on my leg—it clumped so loud!

Jim: I never heard any clumping.

Laura (wincing at the recollection): To me it sounded like—thunder!

Jim: Well, well, well. I never even noticed.

Laura: And everybody was seated before I came in. I had to walk in front of all those people. My seat was in the back row. I had to go clumping all the way up the aisle with everyone watching!

Jim: You shouldn't have been self-conscious.

Laura: I know, but I was. It was always such a relief when the singing started.

Jim: Aw, yes, I've placed you now! I used to call you Blue Roses. How was it that I got started calling you that?

Laura: I was out of school a little while with pleurosis. When I came back you asked me what was the matter. I said I had pleurosis—you thought I said *Blue Roses.* That's what you always called me after that!

Jim: I hope you didn't mind.

Laura: Oh, no—I liked it. You see, I wasn't acquainted with many—people. . . .

Jim: As I remember you sort of stuck by yourself.

Laura: I—I—never had much luck at—making friends.

Jim: I don't see why you wouldn't.

Laura: Well, I—started out badly.

Jim: You mean being—

Laura: Yes, it sort of—stood between me—

Jim: You shouldn't have let it!

Laura: I know, but it did, and—

Jim: You were shy with people!

Laura: I tried not to be but never could—

Jim: Overcome it?

Laura: No, I—I never could!

Jim: I guess being shy is something you have to work out of kind of gradually.

Laura (sorrowfully): Yes—I guess it—

Jim: Takes time!

Laura: Yes—

Jim: People are not so dreadful when you know them. That's what you have to remember! And everybody has problems, not just you, but practically everybody has got some problems. You think of yourself as having the only problems, as being the only one who is disappointed. But just look around you and you will see lots of people as disappointed as you are. For instance, I hoped when I was going to high school that I would be further along at this time, six years later, than I am now— You remember that wonderful write-up I had in *The Torch?*

Laura: Yes! (*She rises and crosses to table.*)

Jim: It said I was bound to succeed in anything I went into! (*Laura returns with the annual.*) Holy Jeez! *The Torch!* (*He accepts it reverently. They smile across it with mutual wonder. Laura crouches beside him and they begin to turn through it. Laura's shyness is dissolving in his warmth.*)

Laura: Here you are in *Pirates of Penzance!*

Jim (wistfully): I sang the baritone lead in that operetta.

Laura (rapidly): So—beautifully!

Jim (protesting): Aw—

Laura: Yes, yes—beautifully—beautifully!

Jim: You heard me?

Laura: All three times!

Jim: No!

Laura: Yes!

Jim: All three performances?

Laura (looking down): Yes.

Jim: Why?

Laura: I—wanted to ask you to—autograph my program.

Jim: Why didn't you ask me to?

Laura: You were always surrounded by your own friends so much that I never had a chance to.

Jim: You should have just—

Laura: Well, I—thought you might think I was—

Jim: Thought I might think you was—what?

Laura: Oh—

Jim (with reflective relish): I was beleaguered by females in those days.

Laura: You were terribly popular!

Jim: Yeah—

Laura: You had such a—friendly way—

Jim: I was spoiled in high school.

Laura: Everybody—liked you!

Jim: Including you?

Laura: I—yes, I—did, too—*(She gently closes the book in her lap.)*

Jim: Well, well, well!—Give me that program, Laura. *(She hands it to him. He signs it with a flourish.)* There you are—better late than never!

Laura: Oh, I—what a—surprise!

Jim: My signature isn't worth very much right now. But some day—maybe—it will increase in value! Being disappointed is one thing and being discouraged is something else. I am disappointed but I'm not discouraged. I'm twenty-three years old. How old are you?

Laura: I'll be twenty-four in June.

Jim: That's not old age!

Laura: No, but—

Jim: You finished high school?

Laura (with difficulty): I didn't go back.

Jim: You mean you dropped out?

Laura: I made bad grades in my final examinations. *(She rises and replaces the book and the program. Her voice strained.)* How is—Emily Meisenbach getting along?

Jim: Oh, that kraut-head!

Laura: Why do you call her that?

Jim: That's what she was.

Laura: You're not still—going with her?

Jim: I never see her.

Laura: It said in the Personal Section that you were—engaged!

Jim: I know, but I wasn't impressed by that—propaganda!

Laura: It wasn't—the truth?

Jim: Only in Emily's optimistic opinion!

Laura: Oh—

(Legend: "What Have You Done Since High School?")

Jim lights a cigarette and leans indolently back on his elbows smiling at Laura with a warmth and charm which light her inwardly with altar candles. She remains by the table and turns in her hands a piece of glass to cover her tumult.

Jim (after several reflective puffs on a cigarette): What have you done since high school? (*She seems not to hear him.*) Huh? (*Laura looks up.*) I said what have you done since high school, Laura?

Laura: Nothing much.

Jim: You must have been doing something these six long years.

Laura: Yes.

Jim: Well, then, such as what?

Laura: I took a business course at business college—

Jim: How did that work out?

Laura: Well, not very—well—I had to drop out, it gave me—indigestion—

Jim laughs gently.

Jim: What are you doing now?

Laura: I don't do anything—much. Oh, please don't think I sit around doing nothing! My glass collection takes up a good deal of time. Glass is something you have to take good care of.

Jim: What did you say—about glass?

Laura: Collection I said—I have one—(*She clears her throat and turns away again, acutely shy.*)

Jim (abruptly): You know what I judge to be the trouble with you? Inferiority complex! Know what that is? That's what they call it when someone low-rates himself! I understand it because I had it, too. Although my case was not so aggravated as yours seems to be. I had it until I took up public speaking, developed my voice, and learned that I had an aptitude for science. Before that time I never thought of myself as being outstanding in any way whatsoever! Now I've never made a regular study of it, but I have a friend who says I can analyze people better than doctors that make a profession of it. I don't claim that to be necessarily true, but I can sure guess a person's psychology, Laura! (*Takes out his gum.*) Excuse me, Laura. I always take it out when the flavor is gone. I'll use this scrap of paper to wrap it in. I know how it is to get it stuck on a shoe. (*He wraps the gum in paper and puts it in his pocket.*) Yep—that's what I judge to be your principal trouble. A lack of confidence in yourself as a person. You don't have the proper amount of faith in yourself. I'm basing that fact on a number of your remarks and also on certain observations I've made. For instance that clumping you thought was so awful in high school. You say that you even dreaded to walk into class. You see what you did? You dropped out of school, you gave up an education because of a clump, which as far as I know was practically non-existent! A little physical defect is what you have. Hardly noticeable even! Magnified thousands of times by imagination! You know what my strong advice to you is? Think of yourself as *superior* in some way!

Laura: In what way would I think?

Jim: Why, man alive, Laura! Just look about you a little. What do you see? A world full of common people! All of 'em born and all of 'em going to die! Which of them has one-tenth of your good points! Or mine! Or anyone else's, as far as that goes—gosh! Everybody excels in some one thing. Some in many! (*Unconsciously glances at himself in the mirror.*) All you've got to do is discover in *what!* Take me, for instance. (*He adjusts his tie at the mirror.*) My interest happens to lie in electro-dynamics. I'm taking a course in radio engineering at night school, Laura, on top of a fairly responsible job at the warehouse. I'm taking that course and studying public speaking.

Laura: Ohhhh.

Jim: Because I believe in the future of television! (*Turning back to her.*) I wish to be ready to go up right along with it. Therefore I'm planning to get in on the ground floor. In fact, I've already made the right connections and all that remains is for the industry itself to get under way! Full steam—(*His eyes are starry.*) Knowledge—Zzzzzp! Money—Zzzzzp!—Power! That's the cycle democracy is built on! (*His attitude is convincingly dynamic. Laura stares at him, even her shyness eclipsed in her absolute wonder. He suddenly grins.*) I guess you think I think a lot of myself!

Laura: No—o-o-o, I—

Jim: Now how about you? Isn't there something you take more interest in than anything else?

Laura: Well, I do—as I said—have my—glass collection—

A peal of girlish laughter from the kitchen.

Jim: I'm not right sure I know what you're talking about. What kind of glass is it?

Laura: Little articles of it, they're ornaments mostly! Most of them are little animals made out of glass, the tiniest little animals in the world. Mother calls them a glass menagerie! Here's an example of one, if you'd like to see it! This one is one of the oldest. It's nearly thirteen. (*He stretches out his hand.*) (**Music: "The Glass Menagerie."**) Oh, be careful—if you breathe, it breaks!

Jim: I'd better not take it. I'm pretty clumsy with things.

Laura: Go on, I trust you with him! (*Places it in his palm.*) There now—you're holding him gently! Hold him over the light, he loves the light! You see how the light shines through him?

Jim: It sure does shine!

Laura: I shouldn't be partial, but he is my favorite one.

Jim: What kind of a thing is this one supposed to be?

Laura: Haven't you noticed the single horn on his forehead?

Jim: A unicorn, huh?

Laura: Mmm-hmmm!

Jim: Unicorns—aren't they extinct in the modern world?

Laura: I know!

Jim: Poor little fellow, he must feel sort of lonesome.

Laura (smiling): Well, if he does, he doesn't complain about it. He stays on a shelf with some horses that don't have horns and all of them seem to get along nicely together.

Jim: How do you know?

Laura (lightly): I haven't heard any arguments among them!

Jim (grinning): No arguments, huh? Well, that's a pretty good sign! Where shall I set him?

Laura: Put him on the table. They all like a change of scenery once in a while!

Jim: Well, well, well, well— (*He places the glass piece on the table, then raises his arms and stretches.*) Look how big my shadow is when I stretch!

Laura: Oh, oh, yes—it stretches across the ceiling!

Jim (crossing to door): I think it's stopped raining. (*Opens fire-escape door.*) Where does the music come from?

Laura: From the Paradise Dance Hall across the alley.

Jim: How about cutting the rug a little, Miss Wingfield?

Laura: Oh, I—

Jim: Or is your program filled up? Let me have a look at it. (*Grasps imaginary card.*) Why, every dance is taken! I'll just have to scratch some out. (**Waltz Music: "La Golondrina."**) Ahhh, a waltz! (*He executes some sweeping turns by himself, then holds his arms toward Laura.*)

Laura (breathlessly): I—can't dance!

Jim: There you go, that inferiority stuff!

Laura: I've never danced in my life!

Jim: Come on, try!

Laura: Oh, but I'd step on you!

Jim: I'm not made out of glass.

Laura: How—how—how do we start?

Jim: Just leave it to me. You hold your arms out a little.

Laura: Like this?

Jim (taking her in his arms): A little bit higher. Right. Now don't tighten up, that's the main thing about it—relax.

Laura (laughing breathlessly): It's hard not to.

Jim: Okay.

Laura: I'm afraid you can't budge me.

Jim: What do you bet I can't? (*He swings her into motion.*)

Laura: Goodness, yes, you can!

Jim: Let yourself go, now, Laura, just let yourself go.

Laura: I'm—

Jim: Come on!

Laura: —trying!

Jim: Not so stiff—easy does it!

Laura: I know but I'm—

Jim: Loosen th' backbone! There now, that's a lot better.

Laura: Am I?

Jim: Lots, lots better! (*He moves her about the room in a clumsy waltz.*)

Laura: Oh, my!

Jim: Ha-ha!

Laura: Oh, my goodness!

Jim: Ha-ha-ha! (*They suddenly bump into the table, and the glass piece on it falls to the floor. Jim stops.*) What did we hit on?

Laura: Table.

Jim: Did something fall off it? I think—

Laura: Yes. (*She stoops to pick it up.*)

Jim: I hope that it wasn't the little glass horse with the horn!

Laura: Yes. (*she stoops to pick it up.*)

Jim: Aw, aw, aw. Is it broken?

Laura: Now it is just like all the other horses.

Jim: It's lost its—

Laura: Horn! It doesn't matter. Maybe it's a blessing in disguise.

Jim: You'll never forgive me. I bet that that was your favorite piece of glass.

Laura: I don't have favorites much. It's no tragedy, Freckles. Glass breaks so easily. No matter how careful you are. The traffic jars the shelves and things fall off them.

Jim: Still I'm awfully sorry that I was the cause.

Laura (*smiling*): I'll just imagine he had an operation. The horn was removed to make him feel less—freakish! (*They both laugh.*) Now he will feel more at home with the other horses, the ones that don't have horns . . .

Jim: Ha-ha, that's very funny! (*Suddenly serious.*) I'm glad to see that you have a sense of humor. You know—you're—well—very different! Surprisingly different from anyone else I know! (*His voice becomes soft and hesitant with a genuine feeling.*) Do you mind me telling you that? (*Laura is abashed beyond speech.*) I mean it in a nice way. You make me feel sort of—I don't know how to put it! I'm usually pretty good at expressing things, but—this is something that I don't know how to say! (*Laura touches her throat and clears it—turns the broken unicorn in her hands.*) (*Even softer.*) Has anyone ever told you that you were pretty? (**Pause: Music.**) (*Laura looks up slowly, with wonder, and shakes her head.*) Well, you are! In a very different way from anyone else. And all the nicer because of the difference, too. (*His voice becomes low and husky. Laura turns away, nearly faint with the novelty of her emotions.*) I wish you were my sister. I'd teach you to have some confidence in yourself. The different people are not like other people, but being different is nothing to be ashamed of. Because other people are not such wonderful people. They're one hundred times one thousand. You're one times one! They walk all over the earth. You just stay here. They're common as—weeds, but—you—well, you're—*Blue Roses!*

(**Image On Screen: Blue Roses.**)

(**Music Changes.**)

Laura: But blue is wrong for—roses . . .

Jim: It's right for you! You're—pretty!

Laura: In what respect am I pretty?

Jim: In all respects—believe me! Your eyes—your hair—are pretty! Your hands are pretty! (*He catches hold of her hand.*) You think I'm making this up because I'm invited to dinner and have to be nice. Oh, I could do that! I could put on an act for you, Laura, and say lots of things without being very sincere. But this time I am. I'm talking to you sincerely. I happened to notice you had this inferiority complex that keeps you from feeling comfortable with people. Somebody needs to build your confidence up and make you proud instead of shy and turning away and—blushing—Somebody ought to—ought to—*kiss* you, Laura! (*His hand slips slowly up her arm to her shoulder.*) (**Music Swells Tumultuously.**) (*He suddenly* turns her about and kisses her on the lips. When he releases her Laura sinks on the sofa with a bright, dazed look. Jim backs away and fishes in his pocket for a cigarette.) (**Legend On Screen: "Souvenir."**) Stumble-john! (*He lights the cigarette, avoiding her look. There is a peal of girlish laughter from Amanda in the kitchen. Laura slowly raises and opens her hand. It still contains the little broken glass animal. She looks at it with a tender, bewildered expression.*) Stumble-john! I shouldn't have done that—That was way off the beam. You don't smoke, do you? (*She looks up, smiling, not hearing the question. He sits beside her a little gingerly. She looks at him speechlessly—waiting. He coughs decorously and moves a little farther aside as he considers the situation and senses her feelings, dimly, with perturbation. Gently.*) Would you—care for a—mint? (*She doesn't seem to hear him but her look grows brighter even.*) Peppermint—Life Saver? My pocket's a regular drug store—wherever I go . . . (*He pops a mint in his mouth. Then gulps and decides to make a clean breast of it. He speaks slowly and gingerly.*) Laura, you know, if I had a sister like you, I'd do the same thing as Tom, I'd bring out fellows—and introduce her to them. The right type of boys—of a type to—appreciate her. Only—well—he made a mistake about me. Maybe I've got no call to be saying this. That may not have been the idea in having me over. But what if it was? There's nothing wrong about that. The only trouble is that in my case—I'm not in a situation to—do the right thing. I can't take down your number and say I'll phone. I can't call up next week and—ask for a date. I thought I had better explain the situation in case you—misunderstood it and—I hurt your feelings. . . . (*Pause. Slowly, very slowly, Laura's look changes, her eyes returning slowly from his to the ornament in her palm.*)

Amanda utters another gay laugh in the kitchen.

Laura (*faintly*): You—won't—call again?
Jim: No, Laura, I can't. (*He rises from the sofa.*) As I was just explaining, I've—got strings on me, Laura, I've—been going steady! I go out all the time with a girl named Betty. She's a home-girl like you, and Catholic, and Irish, and in a great many ways we—get along fine. I met her last summer on a moonlight boat trip up the river to Alton, on the *Majestic*. Well—right away from the start it was—love! (**Legend: Love!**) (*Laura sways slightly forward and grips the arm of the sofa. He fails to notice, now enrapt in his own comfortable being.*) Being in love has made a new man of me! (*Leaning stiffly forward, clutching the arm of the sofa, Laura struggles visibly with her storm. But Jim is oblivious, she is a long way off.*) The power of love is really pretty tremendous! Love is something that—changes the whole world, Laura! (*The storm abates a little and Laura leans back. He notices her again.*) It happened that Betty's aunt took sick, she got a wire and had to go to Centralia. So Tom—when he asked me to dinner—I naturally just accepted the invitation, not knowing that you—that he—that I—(*He stops awkwardly.*) Huh—I'm a stumble-john! (*He flops back on the sofa. The holy candles in the altar of Laura's face have been snuffed out! There is a look of almost infinite desolation. Jim glances at her uneasily.*) I wish that you would—say something. (*She bites her lip which was trembling and then bravely smiles. She opens her hand again on the broken glass ornament. Then she gently takes his hand and raises it level with her own. She carefully places the unicorn in the palm of his hand, then pushes his fingers closed upon it.*) What are you—doing that for? You want me to have him?—Laura? (*She nods.*) What for?

Laura: A—souvenir . . .

She rises unsteadily and crouches beside the victrola to wind it up.

(Legend On Screen: "Things Have A Way Of Turning Out So Badly.")

(Or Image: "Gentleman Caller Waving Good-bye! Gaily.")

At this moment Amanda rushes brightly back in the front room. She bears a pitcher of fruit punch in an old-fashioned cut-glass pitcher and a plate of macaroons. The plate has a gold border and poppies painted on it.

Amanda: Well, well, well! Isn't the air delightful after the shower? I've made you children a little liquid refreshment. (*Turns gaily to the gentleman caller.*) Jim, do you know that song about lemonade?
>   "Lemonade, lemonade
>   Made in the shade and stirred with a spade—
>   Good enough for any old maid!"

Jim (*uneasily*): Ha-ha! No—I never heard it.
Amanda: Why, Laura! You look so serious!
Jim: We were having a serious conversation.
Amanda: Good! Now you're better acquainted!
Jim (*uncertainly*): Ha-ha! Yes.
Amanda: You modern young people are much more serious-minded than my generation. I was so gay as a girl!
Jim: You haven't changed, Mrs. Wingfield.
Amanda: Tonight I'm rejuvenated! The gaiety of the occasion, Mr. O'Connor! (*She tosses her head with a peal of laughter. Spills lemonade.*) Oooo! I'm baptizing myself!
Jim: Here—let me—
Amanda (*setting the pitcher down*): There now. I discovered we had some maraschino cherries. I dumped them in, juice and all!
Jim: You shouldn't have gone to that trouble, Mrs. Wingfield.
Amanda: Trouble, trouble? Why it was loads of fun! Didn't you hear me cutting up in the kitchen? I bet your ears were burning! I told Tom how outdone with him I was for keeping you to himself so long a time! He should have brought you over much, much sooner! Well, now that you've found your way, I want you to be a very frequent caller! Not just occasional but all the time. Oh, we're going to have a lot of gay times together! I see them coming! Mmm, just breathe that air! So fresh, and the moon's so pretty! I'll skip back out—I know where my place is when young folks are having a—serious conversation!
Jim: Oh, don't go out, Mrs. Wingfield. The fact of the matter is I've got to be going.
Amanda: Going, now? You're joking! Why, it's only the shank of the evening, Mr. O'Connor!
Jim: Well, you know how it is.
Amanda: You mean you're a young workingman and have to keep workingmen's hours. We'll let you off early tonight. But only on the condition that next time you stay later. What's the best night for you? Isn't Saturday night the best night for you workingmen?
Jim: I have a couple of time-clocks to punch, Mrs. Wingfield. One at morning, another one at night!

Amanda: My, but you *are* ambitious! You work at night, too?

Jim: No, Ma'am, not work but—Betty! (*He crosses deliberately to pick up his hat. The band at the Paradise Dance Hall goes into a tender waltz.*)

Amanda: Betty? Betty? Who's—Betty? (*There is an ominous cracking sound in the sky.*)

Jim: Oh, just a girl. The girl I go steady with! (*He smiles charmingly. The sky falls.*)

(Legend: "The Sky Falls.")

Amanda (*a long-drawn exhalation*): Ohhhh . . . Is it a serious romance, Mr. O'Connor?

Jim: We're going to be married the second Sunday in June.

Amanda: Ohhhh—how nice! Tom didn't mention that you were engaged to be married.

Jim: The cat's not out of the bag at the warehouse yet. You know how they are. They call you Romeo and stuff like that. (*He stops at the oval mirror to put on his hat. He carefully shapes the brim and the crown to give a discreetly dashing effect.*) It's been a wonderful evening, Mrs. Wingfield. I guess this is what they mean by Southern hospitality.

Amanda: It really wasn't anything at all.

Jim: I hope it don't seem like I'm rushing off. But I promised Betty I'd pick her up at the Wabash depot, an' by the time I get my jalopy down there her train'll be in. Some women are pretty upset if you keep 'em waiting.

Amanda: Yes, I know—The tyranny of women! (*Extends her hand.*) Goodbye, Mr. O'Connor. I wish you luck—and happiness—and success! All three of them, and so does Laura!—Don't you, Laura?

Laura: Yes!

Jim (*taking her hand*): Goodbye, Laura. I'm certainly going to treasure that souvenir. And don't you forget the good advice I gave you. (*Raises his voice to a cheery shout.*) So long, Shakespeare! Thanks again, ladies—Good night!

He grins and ducks jauntily out.

Still bravely grimacing, Amanda closes the door on the gentleman caller. Then she turns back to the room with a puzzled expression. She and Laura don't dare to face each other. Laura crouches beside the victrola to wind it.

Amanda (*faintly*): Things have a way of turning out so badly. I don't believe that I would play the victrola. Well, well—well—Our gentleman caller was engaged to be married! (*She raises her voice.*) Tom!

Tom (*from back*): Yes, Mother?

Amanda: Come in here a minute. I want to tell you something awfully funny.

Tom (*enters with macaroon and a glass of the lemonade*): Has the gentleman caller gotten away already?

Amanda: The gentleman caller has made an early departure. What a wonderful joke you played on us!

Tom: How do you mean?

Amanda: You didn't mention that he was engaged to be married.

Tom: Jim? Engaged?

Amanda: That's what he just informed us.

Tom: I'll be jiggered! I didn't know about that.

Amanda: That seems very peculiar.

Tom: What's peculiar about it?

Amanda: Didn't you call him your best friend down at the warehouse?

Tom: He is, but how did I know?

Amanda: It seems extremely peculiar that you wouldn't know your best friend was going to be married!

Tom: The warehouse is where I work, not where I know things about people!

Amanda: You don't know things anywhere! You live in a dream; you manufacture illusions! (*He crosses to door.*) Where are you going?

Tom: I'm going to the movies.

Amanda: That's right, now that you've had us make such fools of ourselves. The effort, the preparations, all the expense! The new floor lamp, the rug, the clothes for Laura! All for what? To entertain some other girl's fiancé! Go to the movies, go! Don't think about us, a mother deserted, an unmarried sister who's crippled and has no job! Don't let anything interfere with your selfish pleasure! Just go, go, go—to the movies!

Tom: All right, I will! The more you shout about my selfishness to me the quicker I'll go, and I won't go to the movies!

Amanda: Go, then! Then go to the moon—you selfish dreamer!

Tom smashes his glass on the floor. He plunges out on the fire-escape, slamming the door. Laura screams—cut by door.

Dance-hall music up. Tom goes to the rail and grips it desperately, lifting his face in the chill white moonlight penetrating the narrow abyss of the alley.

(Legend On Screen: "And So Good-bye . . . ")

Tom's closing speech is timed with the interior pantomime. The interior scene is played as though viewed through sound-proof glass. Amanda appears to be making a comforting speech to Laura who is huddled upon the sofa. Now that we cannot hear the mother's speech, her silliness is gone and she has dignity and tragic beauty. Laura's dark hair hides her face until at the end of the speech she lifts it to smile at her mother. Amanda's gestures are slow and graceful, almost dancelike, as she comforts the daughter. At the end of her speech she glances a moment at the father's picture—then withdraws through the portieres. At close of Tom's speech, Laura blows out the candles, ending the play.

Tom: I didn't go to the moon, I went much further—for time is the longest distance between two places—Not long after that I was fired for writing a poem on the lid of a shoe-box. I left Saint Louis. I descended the steps of this fire-escape for a last time and followed, from then on, in my father's footsteps, attempting to find in motion what was lost in space. I traveled around a great deal. The cities swept about me like dead leaves, leaves that were brightly colored but torn away from the branches. I would have stopped, but I was pursued by something. It always came upon me unawares, taking me altogether by surprise. Perhaps it was a familiar bit of music. Perhaps it was only a piece of transparent glass. Perhaps I am walking along a street at night, in some strange city, before I have found companions. I pass the lighted window of a shop where perfume is sold. The window is filled with pieces of colored glass, tiny transparent bottles in delicate colors, like bits of a shattered rainbow. Then all at once my sister touches my shoulder. I turn around and look into her eyes. . . . Oh, Laura, Laura, I tried to leave you behind me, but I am more faithful than I intended to be! I reach for a cigarette, I cross the street, I run into the movies or a bar, I buy a drink, I speak to the nearest stranger—anything that can blow your candles out!

Laura bends over the candles.

For nowadays the world is lit by lightning! Blow out your candles, Laura—and so good-bye. . . .

She blows the candles out.

Questions

1. How do Amanda's dreams for her daughter contrast with the realities of the Wingfields' day-to-day existence?
2. What suggestions do you find in Laura's glass menagerie? In the glass unicorn?
3. In the cast of characters, Jim O'Connor is listed as "a nice, ordinary, young man." Why does his coming to dinner have such earthshaking implications for Amanda? For Laura?
4. Try to describe Jim's feelings toward Laura during their long conversation in Scene VII. After he kisses her, how do his feelings seem to change?
5. Near the end of the play, Amanda tells Tom, "You live in a dream; you manufacture illusions!" What is ironic about her speech? Is there any truth in it?
6. Who is the main character in *The Glass Menagerie*? Tom? Laura? Amanda? (It may be helpful to review the definition of a protagonist.)
7. Has Tom, at the conclusion of the play, successfully made his escape from home? Does he appear to have fulfilled his dream?
8. How effective is the device of accompanying the action by projecting slides on a screen, bearing titles and images? Do you think most producers of the play are wise to leave it out?

Tennessee Williams on Writing

How to Stage *The Glass Menagerie*   1945

Being a "memory play," *The Glass Menagerie* can be presented with unusual freedom of convention. Because of its considerably delicate or tenuous material, atmospheric touches and subtleties of direction play a particularly important part. Expressionism and all other unconventional techniques in drama have only one valid aim, and that is a closer approach to truth. When a play employs unconventional techniques, it is not, or certainly shouldn't be, trying to escape its responsibility of dealing with reality, or interpreting experience, but is actually or should be attempting to find a closer approach, a more penetrating and vivid expression of things as they are. The straight realistic play with its genuine Frigidaire and authentic ice-cubes, its char-

Tennessee Williams

acters that speak exactly as its audience speaks, corresponds to the academic landscape and has the same virtue of a photographic likeness. Everyone should know nowadays the unimportance of the photographic in art: that truth, life, or reality is an organic thing which the poetic imagination can represent or suggest, in essence, only through transformation, through changing into other forms than those which were merely present in appearance.

These remarks are not meant as a preface only to this particular play. They have to do with a conception of a new, plastic theater which must take the place of the exhausted theater of realistic conventions if the theater is to resume vitality as a part of our culture.

THE SCREEN DEVICE. There is *only one important difference between the original and acting version of the play* and that is the *omission* in the latter of the device which I tentatively included in my *original* script. This device was the use of a screen on which were projected magic-lantern slides bearing images or titles. I do not regret the omission of this device from the present Broadway production. The extraordinary power of Miss Taylor's performance° made it suitable to have the utmost simplicity in the physical production. But I think it may be interesting to some readers to see how this device was conceived. So I am putting it into the published manuscript. These images and legends, projected from behind, were cast on a section of wall between the front-room and dining-room areas, which should be indistinguishable from the rest when not in use.

The purpose of this will probably be apparent. It is to give accent to certain values in each case. Each scene contains a particular point (or several) which is structurally the most important. In an episodic play, such as this, the basic structure or narrative line may be obscured from the audience; the effect may seem fragmentary rather than architectural. This may not be the fault of the play so much as a lack of attention in the audience. The legend or image upon the screen will strengthen the effect of what is merely allusion in the writing and allow the primary point to be made more simply and lightly than if the entire responsibility were on the spoken lines. Aside from this structural value, I think the screen will have a definite emotional appeal, less definable but just as important. An imaginative producer or director may invent many other uses for this device than those indicated in the present script. In fact the possibilities of the device seem much larger to me than the instance of this play can possibly utilize.

THE MUSIC. Another extra-literary accent in this play is provided by the use of music. A single recurring tune, "The Glass Menagerie," is used to give emotional emphasis to suitable passages. This tune is like circus music, not when you are on the grounds or in the immediate vicinity of the parade, but when you are at some distance and very likely thinking of something else. It seems under those circumstances to continue almost interminably and it weaves in and out of your preoccupied consciousness; then it is the lightest, most delicate music in the world and perhaps the saddest. It expresses the surface vivacity of life with the underlying strain of immutable and inexpressible sorrow. When you look at a piece of delicately spun glass you think of two things: how beautiful it is and how easily it can be broken. Both of those ideas should be woven into the recurring tune, which dips in and out of the play as if it were carried on a wind that changes. It serves as a thread of connection and allusion

---

Miss Taylor's performance: In the original Broadway production of the play in 1945 (see photograph on page 1613), the role of Amanda Wingfield, the mother, was played by veteran actress Laurette Taylor.

between the narrator with his separate point in time and space and the subject of his story. Between each episode it returns as reference to the emotion, nostalgia, which is the first condition of the play. It is primarily Laura's music and therefore comes out most clearly when the play focuses upon her and the lovely fragility of glass which is her image.

THE LIGHTING. The lighting in the play is not realistic. In keeping with the atmosphere of memory, the stage is dim. Shafts of light are focused on selected areas or actors, sometimes in contradistinction to what is the apparent center. For instance, in the quarrel scene between Tom and Amanda, in which Laura has no active part, the clearest pool of light is on her figure. This is also true of the supper scene, when her silent figure on the sofa should remain the visual center. The light upon Laura should be distinct from the others, having a peculiar pristine clarity such as light used in early religious portraits of female saints or madonnas. A certain correspondence to light in religious paintings, such as El Greco's, where the figures are radiant in atmosphere that is relatively dusky, could be effectively used throughout the play. (It will also permit a more effective use of the screen.) A free, imaginative use of light can be of enormous value in giving a mobile, plastic quality to plays of a more or less static nature.

From the author's production notes for The Glass Menagerie

Anna Deavere Smith

Scenes from Twilight: Los Angeles, 1992   1994

Anna Deavere Smith was born in Baltimore, Maryland, in 1950, the daughter of a business-man and an elementary school principal. She graduated from Beaver College in 1971 and earned a Master of Fine Arts degree from the American Conservatory Theater in 1977. She taught drama at Stanford University from 1990 to 2000 and is presently a professor at both the Tisch School of the Arts at New York University and the NYU School of Law. Over many years Smith has conducted more than two thousand interviews; from them she has fashioned a number of works of "documentary theater," each of which is a stage presentation in which a single performer speaks a series of monologues using the actual words of her interview subjects. The best-known of these are Fires in the Mirror *(1993), drawn from the 1991 race riots in Crown Heights, Brooklyn, and* Twilight: Los Angeles, 1992 *(1994), derived from the 1992 riot in that city. Smith has frequently performed these pieces herself, winning rave reviews both for the works and for her extraordinary ability to bring to life characters of both sexes and many ages and races. In its review of* Twilight: Los Angeles, 1992, *the* New York Times *said: "Anna Deavere Smith is the ultimate impressionist: she does people's souls." As an actress, she has also made many appearances on stage and in films, including* Philadelphia *and* The American President, *and has been seen on television in* The West Wing. *Included here are four scenes from the over fifty monologues in* Twilight: Los Angeles, 1992.

CHARACTERS

Angela King, Rodney King's aunt, African American
Paul Parker, Chairperson, Free the LA Four Plus Defense Committee, African American, well-built, 20s
Mrs. Young-Soon Han, former liquor store owner, Korean American, 40s, heavy accent
Twilight Bey, Gang Truce organizer, African American, early 30s/late 20s, Crips gang.

GENERAL PRODUCTION NOTE

A slide with the following language should begin the show, just after lights down and before any other visual image:

> *This play is based on interviews conducted by Anna Deavere Smith soon after the race riots in Los Angeles of 1992. All words were spoken by real people and are verbatim from those interviews.*

ANGELA KING,
Rodney King's Aunt

Here's a Nobody

Returning from white iron-gated doorway. To her stool. Heavy pounding rain outside. Day. On her stool, in her studio. Crying, has been crying, prior to the speech for ten minutes straight.

We weren't raised like this.
We weren't raised with no black and white thing.
We were raised with all kinds of friends.
Mexicans, Indians, blacks, whites, Chinese
Most of our friends were Spanish.
Who'd have thought this would happen to us?
Well, I guess there's a first time for everything you know.

> (*Blowing her nose, she stops crying. A sense in the rest of the speech that she is recovering from a long cry.*)

I guess you want me to tell the story
I don't know if you understand sometimes I'm just not in the mood, you know
just not in the mood.

> (*Slight pause.*)

His brother Galen called to say "Cops done beat Glen up!"
Talkin' about Rodney.
I said "What?"
"Police. They got it on tape."
And when I was just turning the channels
I saw this white car.
I heard him holler,
I recognized him layin' there on the ground
that's what got me.
And he looked just like his father too.
Galen was the one used to favor his father.
Now Rodney looks just like him, identical.
I don't know if it's when you lose a life
it comes back in somebody else.
Oh you should have seen him.
It's a hell of a look.
went through three plastic surgeons just to get Rodney to look like
Rodney again.
I tell him he's got a lot

Anna Deavere Smith as Angela King.

to be thankful for.
A hell of a lot.
He couldn't talk,
just der der der
I said, "Goddamn!"

   (*Angry.*)

My brother's son out there was lookin' like hell
that I saw in that bed and I was gonna fight for every bit of
our justice and fairness.
That (Officer) Koon
that's the one in the whole trial,
that man showed no-kind-of-remorse-at-all,
you know that?
He sit there like "it ain't
no big thing
and I
will do it it *again.*"
And he smile at you.
The nerve,
the audacity!

But I didn't give a damn if it was the President's
whatever it was.

(*Slight pause, responding to a question.*)

You see how everybody *rave* when something happens with the
President of the United States?
You know, 'cause he's a higher sort?
Okay, here's a nobody.
But the way they beat him.
This is the way I felt towards him.
You understand what I'm sayin' now?
You do? Alright.

(*She lights a "More" cigarette, or long brown cigarette.*)

PAUL PARKER
Chairperson, Free the L.A. Four Plus Defense Committee

Slavery

Dressed differently than before. Golf shirt and slacks.

We spoke out on April twenty-ninth.
It was *some* victory—
I mean it was burnin' *everywhere*.
It was takin' things and nobody was tellin'
Nobody!
It wasn't callin' 911,
"Awww they taken—"
Unh unh it was like, Baby go get some too!
"I'm a little bit too old but get me something—"
You know I mean it was the spirit!
You know they got what?
Eight people?
Eight people?
Out of several thousand?
Um
Um. Um.
They lost!
Oh.
Big Time!
Basically, it's
that you as black people ain't takin' this shit no more.
Even back in slavery.
'Cause I saw *Roots* when I was young.
My dad made sure. He sat us down
in front of that TV
when *Roots* came on,

so it's embedded in me
since then.
And just to see that Eh, Eh!
This is for Kunta!
This is for Kizzy!
This is for Chicken George!

MRS. YOUNG-SOON HAN
Former Liquor Store Owner

Swallowing the Bitterness

At a low coffee table. Deep voice.

When I was in Korea,
I used to watch many luxurious Hollywood lifestyle movies.
I never saw any poor man,
any black
maybe one housemaid?
Until last year
I believed America is the best.
I still believe it.
I don't deny that now.
Because I'm victim.
But

Anna Deavere Smith as Mrs. Young-Soon Han.

as
the year ends in ninety-two,
and we were still in turmoil,
and having all the financial problems,
and mental problems,
then a couple months ago,
I really realized that
Korean immigrants were left out
from this
society and we were nothing.
What is our right?
Is it because we are Korean?
Is it because we have no politicians?
Is it because we don't
speak good English?
Why?
Why do we have to be left out?

> (*She is hitting her hand on the coffee table.*)

We are not qualified to have medical treatment!
We are not qualified to get, uh,
food stamps!

> (*She hits the table once.*)

No GR!

> (*Hits the table once.*)

No welfare!

> (*Hits the table once.*)

Anything!
Many Afro-Americans

> (*Two quick hits.*)

who never worked

> (*One hit.*)

they get
at least minimum amount

> (*One hit.*)

of money

> (*One hit.*)

to survive!

> (*One hit.*)

We don't get any!

> (*Large hit with full hand spread.*)

Because we have a *car!*

(*One hit.*)

and we have a *house!*

(*Pause six seconds.*)

And we are *high tax payers!*

(*One hit.*)

(*Pause fourteen seconds.*)

Where do I finda [sic] justice?
Okay, black people
Probably,
believe they won
by the trial?
Even some complains only half, right
justice was there?
But I watched the television
that Sunday morning
Early morning as they started
I started watch it all day.
They were having party, and then they celebrated (*Pronounced CeLEbreted.*)
all of South Central,
all the churches,
they finally found that justice exists
in this society.
Then where is the victims' rights?
They got their rights
by destroying *innocent Korean merchants* (*Louder.*)
They have a lot of respect, (*Softer.*)
as I do
for Dr. Martin King?
He is the only model for black community.
I don't care Jesse Jackson.
But,
he was the model
of non-violence
Non-violence?
They like to have hiseh [sic] spirits.
What about last year?
They destroyed innocent people!

(*Five second pause.*)

And I wonder if that is really justice, (*And a very soft uh after justice like justicah, but
very quick.*)
to get their rights
in this way.

(*Thirteen second pause.*)

I waseh swallowing the bitternesseh.
Sitting here alone, and watching them.
They became all hilarious.

(*Three second pause.*)

And uh,
in a way I was happy for them,
and I felt glad for them,
at least they got something back, you know.
Just lets forget Korean victims or other victims
who are destroyed by them.
They have fought
for their rights

(*One hit simultaneous with the word "rights."*)

over two centuries

(*One hit simultaneous with "centuries."*)

and I have a lot of sympathy and understanding for them.
Because of their effort, and sacrificing,
other minorities, like Hispanic
or Asians
maybe we have to suffer more
by mainstream,
you know?
That's why I understand.
And then
I like to be part of their
'joyment.
But.
That's why I had mixed feeling
as soon as I heard the verdict.
I wish I could
live together
with eh [sic] blacks
but after the riots
there were too much differences
The fire is still there
how do you call it

(*She says a Korean word asking for translation. In Korean, she says "igniting fire."*)

igni
igniting fire
It canuh
burst out any time.

TWILIGHT BEY
Organizer, Gang Truce

Limbo

Walking the full stage and around the table from the dinner party.

So a lot of times when I've brought up ideas to my homeboys,
They say
"Twilight
that's before your time
that's something you can't do now."
When I talked about the truce back in 1988,
that was something they considered before its time.
Yet
in 1992,
we made it
realistic.
So to me, it's like I'm stuck in limbo,
like the sun is stuck between night and day,
in the twilight hours,
You know?
I'm in an area not many people exist.

Anna Deavere Smith as Twilight Bey.

Night time to me
is like a lack of sun.
And I don't affiliate
darkness with anything negative.
I affiliate
darkness of what was first
because it *was first*
and then relative to my complexion,
I am a *dark* individual,
and with me stuck in limbo
I see the darkness as myself
I see the light (*he lights a candle*) as knowledge and the wisdom
of the world and understanding others.
And in order for me to be, a to be, a true human being.
I can't forever dwell in darkness.
I can't forever dwell in the idea,
just identifying with people like me, and understanding me and
mine.
So twilight
is
that time
between day and night
limbo
I call it limbo.

    (*He blows out the candle and walks off the stage.*)

Questions

1. Angela King says of her nephew, Rodney, "I tell him he's got a lot / to be thankful for." Is she being deliberately ironic? Is there a larger irony in her comment?

2. Do you find Mrs. Young-Soon Han to be a sympathetic character? Why or why not?

3. Does the speech by Twilight Bey, which concludes the play, seem conciliatory? Does it explain why the play is called *Twilight*?

4. Taking these monologues together, what do you see as the mood that emerges from the text—despair? hopefulness? resignation? Explain.

Anna Deavere Smith on Writing

A Call to the Community
1994

For over ten years now I have been creating performances based on actual events in a series I have titled *On the Road: A Search for American Character*. Each *On the Road* performance evolves from interviews I conduct with individuals directly or indirectly involved in the event I intend to explore. Basing my scripts entirely on this interview material, I perform the interviews onstage using their own words. *Twilight: Los Angeles, 1992* is the product of my search for the character of Los Angeles in the wake of the initial Rodney King verdict.

Anna Deavere Smith

• • •

The story of how Los Angeles came to experience what some call the worst riots in United States history is by now familiar. In the Spring of 1991, Rodney King, a black man, was severely beaten by four white Los Angeles police officers after a high-speed chase in which King was pursued for speeding. A nearby resident videotaped the beating from the balcony of his apartment. When the videotape was broadcast on national television, there was an immediate outcry from the community. The next year, the police officers who beat King were tried and found not guilty—and the city exploded. The verdict took the city by surprise, from public officials to average citizens. Even the defense lawyers, I was told, anticipated that there would be some convictions. Three days of burning, looting, and killing scarred Los Angeles and captured the attention of the world.

• • •

The video of the Rodney King beating, which seemed to "tell all," apparently did not tell enough, and the prosecution lost, as their lead attorney told me, "the slam-dunk case of the century." The city of Los Angeles lost much more. *Twilight* is an attempt to explore the shades of that loss. It is not really an attempt to find causes or to show where responsibility was lacking. That would be the task of a commission report. While I was in Los Angeles, and when I have returned since my initial performance of *Twilight* in the summer of 1993, I have been trying to look at the shifts in attitudes of citizens toward race relations. I have been particularly interested in the opportunity the events in Los Angeles give us to take stock of how the race canvas in America has *changed* since the Watts riots. Los Angeles shows us that the story of race in America is much larger and more complex than a story of black and white. There are new players in the race drama. Whereas Jewish merchants were hit during the Watts riots, Korean merchants were hit this time. Although the media tended to focus on blacks in South-Central, the Latino population was equally involved. We tend to think of race as us and them—us or them being black or white depending on one's own color. The relationships among peoples of color and *within* racial groups are getting more and more complicated.

• • •

When I did my research in Los Angeles, I was listening with an ear that was trained to hear stories for the specific purpose of repeating them with the elements of character intact. This becomes significant because sometimes there is the expectation that inasmuch as I am doing "social dramas," I am looking for *solutions* to social problems. In fact, though, I am looking at the *processes* of the problems. Acting is a constant process of becoming something. It is not a result, it is not an answer. It is not a solution. I am first looking for the humanness inside the problems, or the crises. The spoken word is evidence of the humanness. Perhaps the solutions come somewhere further down the road.

I see the work as a call. I played *Twilight* in Los Angeles as a call to the community. I performed it at a time when the community had not yet resolved the problems. I wanted to be a part of their examination of the problems. I believe that solutions to these problems will call for the participation of large and eclectic groups of people. I also believe that we are at a stage at which we must first break the silence about race and encourage many more people to participate in the dialogue.

One of the questions I was frequently asked when I was interviewed about *Twilight* was "Did you find any one voice that could speak for the entire city?" I think there is an expectation that in this diverse city, and in this diverse nation, a unifying voice would bring increased understanding and put us on the road to solutions. This expectation surprises me. There is little in culture or education that encourages the development of a unifying voice. In order to have real unity, all voices would have to first be heard or at least represented. Many of us who work in race relations do so from the point of view of our own ethnicity. This very fact inhibits our ability to hear more voices than those that are closest to us in proximity. Few people speak a language about race that is not their own. If more of us could actually speak from another point of view, like speaking another language, we could accelerate the flow of ideas.

Introduction to *Twilight: Los Angeles, 1992*

■ WRITING *effectively*

THINKING ABOUT DRAMATIC REALISM

When critics use the word *realism* in relation to a play, are they claiming it is true to life? Not necessarily. Realism generally refers to certain dramatic conventions that emerged during the nineteenth century. A realistic play is not necessarily any truer to life than an experimental one, although the conventions of Realist drama have become so familiar to us that other kinds of drama—though no more artificial—can seem mannered and even bizarre to the casual viewer. Remember, though, that all drama—even the theater of Realism—is artifice.

- **Notice the conventions of Realist drama.** Compare, for example, a play by Henrik Ibsen with one by Sophocles. Ibsen's characters speak in prose, not verse. His settings are drawn from contemporary life, not a legendary past. His characters are ordinary middle-class citizens, not kings, queens, and aristocrats.
- **Be aware that the inner lives, memories, and motivations of the characters play a crucial role in the dramatic action.** Ibsen, like other Realist playwrights, seeks to portray the complexity of human psychology—especially motivation—in detailed, subtle ways. In contrast, Shakespeare appears less

interested in the reason for Iago's villainy than its consequences. Did Iago have an unhappy childhood or a troubled adolescence? These questions do not greatly matter in Renaissance drama, but to Ibsen they become central. In *A Doll's House*, for example, we can infer that Nora's self-absorption and naiveté result from her father's overprotection.

■ **Remember though, Realist drama does not necessarily come any closer than other dramatic styles to getting at the truths of human existence.** *A Doll's House*, for example, does not provide a more profound picture of psychological struggle than *Oedipus the King*. But Ibsen does offer a more detailed view of his protagonist's inner life and her daily routine.

CHECKLIST: Writing About a Realist Play

☐ List every detail the play gives about the protagonist's past. How does each detail affect the character's current behavior?

☐ What is the protagonist's primary motivation? What are the origins of that motivation?

☐ Do the other characters understand the protagonist's deeper motivations?

☐ How much of the plot arises from misunderstandings among characters?

☐ Do major plot events grow from characters' interactions? Or, do they occur at random?

☐ How does the protagonist's psychology determine his or her reactions to events?

WRITING ASSIGNMENT ON REALISM

Al Capovilla of Folsom Lake Center College has developed an ingenious assignment based on Ibsen's *A Doll's House* that asks you to combine the skills of a literary critic with those of a lawyer. Here is Professor Capovilla's assignment:

> You are the family lawyer for Torvald and Nora Helmer. The couple comes to you with a request. They want you to listen to an account of their domestic problems and recommend whether they should pursue a divorce or try to reconcile.
>
> You listen to both sides of the argument. (You also know everything that is said by every character.)
>
> Now, it is your task to write a short decision. In stating your opinion, provide a clear and organized explanation of your reasoning. Show both sides of the argument. You may employ as evidence anything said or done in the play.
>
> Conclude your paper with your recommendation. What do you advise under the circumstances—divorce or an attempt at reconciliation?

Following is a paper from Professor Capovilla's course written by Carlota Llarena, a student at Folsom Lake Center College.

Llarena 1

Carlota Llarena

Professor Capovilla

English 320

19 April 2009

Helmer vs. Helmer

In reaching a determination of whether Torvald and Nora Helmer should either get divorced or attempt reconciliation, I have carefully considered the events leading to the breakdown of their marriage in order to decide on an amicable solution to their present predicament. In my belief, marriage is a sacred institution—one that should not be taken lightly. Love and happiness in a marriage should be cultivated by the parties. Obstacles are often found throughout marriage, but in order to overcome those obstacles, a husband and wife should share responsibilities, discuss whatever problems arise, and jointly work on finding solutions to those problems. Based on this belief, I recommend that Torvald and Nora Helmer attempt a reconciliation of the marriage.

In reviewing the testimony provided by both parties, I find it true that Torvald has treated Nora in such a manner as to make her feel she was considered a child rather than an equal partner. Torvald handled all their finances and solely resolved all their problems. Torvald never discussed any of their household problems with Nora or attempted to seek her advice. In that regard, I believe that Torvald treated Nora in that fashion because he felt Nora was incapable of handling these types of situations. Nora's every need had always been looked after by her father. She grew up with nannies, never had to take responsibility for herself, and never had to work to earn money as money was always given to her.

I find it also true, however, that Nora has always acted like a child. She has the tendency to sulk if matters don't go her way, is happy when rewarded with gifts, hides treats (like macaroons) for herself when they are prohibited, and likes to play games. These characteristics are clearly evident in Nora. There are at least six examples of her child-like behaviors in the testimonies. First, Nora denied nibbling on a macaroon or two (1561–62) as a child would deny any wrongdoing. Second, Nora thought it would be "fun" to hang the money in pretty gold paper on the Christmas tree (1561) as a child would enjoy bright and colorful objects. Third, Nora considered it to be "a tremendous pleasure" to sit and work to earn money "like being a man" (1568) as a child would pretend and play-act adult roles. Fourth, Nora was excited when she received a gift of money from Torvald (1560) as a child would be excited when she receives a

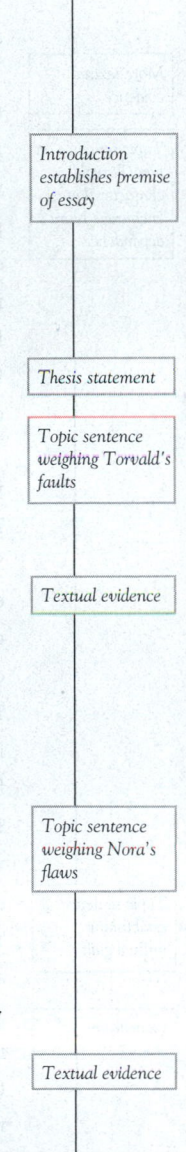

Introduction establishes premise of essay

Thesis statement

Topic sentence weighing Torvald's faults

Textual evidence

Topic sentence weighing Nora's flaws

Textual evidence

Llarena 2

present. Fifth, Nora enjoyed dreaming of a rich old gentleman falling in love with her (1568) as a child would dream of getting married to a rich man who would take complete care of her. And, finally, Nora would "do everything I can think of . . . I'll sing for you, dance for you" (1576) as a child would always attempt to please her parents.

More textual evidence

Unfortunately, Torvald reinforced Nora's child-like characteristics by calling her names such as "my little lark" (1559), "my squirrel" (1559), "little Miss Sweet Tooth" (1561), and "my little Nora" (1577). These nicknames seem more appropriate for a child than a grown woman. Torvald has also been very protective of Nora—just as a parent would be protective of a child. Torvald claimed that Nora had "precious eyes" and "fair little delicate hands" which indicates his belief that Nora was a fragile person, one who does not know how to take care of herself. Since Nora was treated in that same manner by her father, she has never experienced life in any other fashion other than that of a child.

Topic sentence on how Torvald's character flaws encourage Nora's dependence

As a further review of the testimony presented, I opine that Torvald is not solely to be blamed for the predicament at hand. Nora has allowed Torvald to treat her in this manner during the eight years they were married. She never told Torvald that she wanted to be treated as an adult and as his equal or that she wanted to become more involved with family matters to help determine solutions to problems they may have. Nora was also guilty of not confiding in Torvald or discussing her problems with him. Did Nora discuss with Torvald the need for them to live in Italy for a year (1567)? Did she sit with her husband and discuss issues concerning money to make such a trip to Italy feasible and where the money actually came from (1567)? Did Nora ever tell Torvald the truth that she had borrowed the money from Krogstad, how she was repaying the loan and what she did to secure that loan (1567, 1574)? The answer to all these questions is no! Accordingly, it is quite clear that Nora and Torvald are both equally guilty of not discussing problems and issues with one another.

Topic sentence establishing mutual guilt

In summation, Nora and Torvald are equally at fault on the following issues. First, Torvald treated Nora as a child, and Nora allowed herself to be treated in that manner. Second, Torvald never confided in Nora regarding matters concerning the family or their finances. Nora, however, also did not confide in Torvald. Now that these issues and concerns are made known to the parties, the parties may work on resolving their differences, share the

Conclusion

Llarena 3

responsibility of handling both family and financial matters by discussing them with one another and finding amicable solutions, and cultivate the trust and judgment of one another. Accordingly, it is my ruling that Nora and Torvald attempt reconciling their marriage and forgo divorce as an immediate option. Only if the parties reach an impasse after an honest and sustained attempt at reconciliation would I suggest reconsidering the option of divorce.

Restatement of thesis

Llarena 4

Work Cited

Ibsen, Henrik. *A Doll's House.* Trans. R. Farquharson Sharp. Rev. Viktoria Michelsen. *Literature: An Introduction to Fiction, Poetry, Drama, and Writing.* Ed. X. J. Kennedy and Dana Gioia. 11th ed. New York: Longman, 2010. 1558–1609. Print.

MORE TOPICS FOR WRITING

1. How relevant is *A Doll's House* today? Do women like Nora still exist? How about men like Torvald? Build an argument, either that the concerns of *A Doll's House* are timeless and universal or that the issues addressed by the play are historical, not contemporary.

2. Placing yourself in the character of Ibsen's Torvald Helmer, write a defense of him and his attitudes as he himself might write it.

3. Who is the protagonist of *The Glass Menagerie*? Give the reasons for your choice. Is there an antagonist? If so, who is it, and why?

4. At the end of *The Glass Menagerie*, Amanda says to Tom, "You live in a dream; you manufacture illusions." Discuss the degree to which this is true of each of the characters in the play.

5. How effective is the technique of *Twilight: Los Angeles, 1992*? Does the lack of interplay between characters make it less dramatic, or is there sufficient drama in what the speakers say and the ways in which they present themselves?

6. Write a paper that compares and contrasts the different points of view of any two characters in *Twilight: Los Angeles, 1992*.

▶ TERMS FOR *review*

Modern Theater Movements

Realism ▶ An attempt to reproduce faithfully on the stage the surface appearance of life, especially that of ordinary people in everyday situations. In a historical sense, Realism (usually capitalized) refers to a movement in nineteenth-century European theater. Realist drama customarily focused on the middle class (and occasionally the working class) rather than the aristocracy.

Naturalism ▶ A type of drama in which the characters are presented as products or victims of environment and heredity. Naturalism, considered an extreme form of Realism, customarily depicts the social, psychological, and economic milieu of the primary characters.

Symbolist drama ▶ A style of drama that avoids direct statement and exposition for powerful evocation and suggestion. In place of realistic stage settings and actions, Symbolist drama uses lighting, music, and dialogue to create a mystical atmosphere.

Expressionism ▶ A dramatic style developed between 1910 and 1924 in Germany in reaction against Realism's focus on surface details and external reality. Expressionist style used episodic plots, distorted lines, exaggerated shapes, abnormally intense coloring, mechanical physical movement, and telegraphic speech to create a dreamlike subjective realm.

Theater of the absurd ▶ Postwar European genre depicting the grotesquely comic plight of human beings thrown by accident into an irrational and meaningless world. The critic Martin Esslin coined the term to characterize plays by writers such as Samuel Beckett, Jean Genet, and Eugène Ionesco.

Aspects of Drama

Tragicomedy ▶ A type of drama that combines elements of both tragedy and comedy. Usually it creates potentially tragic situations that bring the protagonists to the brink of disaster but then ends happily.

Comic relief ▶ The appearance of a comic or situation or character, or clownish humor in the midst of a serious action, introducing a sharp contrast in mood.

Antihero ▶ A protagonist who is lacking in one or more of the conventional qualities attributed to a hero. Instead of being dignified, brave, idealistic, or purposeful, for instance, the antihero may be buffoonish, cowardly, self-interested, or weak. The antihero is often considered an essentially modern form of characterization, a satiric or realistic commentary on traditional portrayals of idealized characters.

The Stage

Proscenium arch ▶ An architectural picture frame or gateway "standing in front of the scenery" (as the name *proscenium* indicates) that separates the auditorium from the raised stage and the world of the play.

Picture-frame stage ▶ A stage that holds the action within a proscenium arch, with painted scene panels (receding into the middle distance) designed to give the illusion of three-dimensional perspective. Picture-frame stages became the norm throughout Europe and England up into the twentieth century.

Box set ▶ A stage set consisting of three walls joined in two corners and a ceiling that tilts, as if seen in perspective, to provide the illusion of scenic realism for interior rooms.

39 EVALUATING A PLAY

The critic should describe, and not prescribe.

—EUGENE IONESCO

To **evaluate** a play is to decide whether the play is any good or not and, if it is good, how good it is in relation to other plays of its kind. In the theater, evaluation is usually thought to be the task of the play reviewer (or, with nobler connotations, "drama critic"), ordinarily a person who sees a new play on its first night and who then tells us, in print or over the air, what the play is about, how well it is done, and whether or not we ought to go to see it. Enthroned in an excellent free seat, the drama critic apparently plies a glamorous trade. What fun it must be to whittle a nasty epigram, for example, to be able to observe, as did a critic of a faltering production of *Uncle Tom's Cabin*, that "the Siberian wolf hound was weakly supported."

The opportunities to be a drama critic today, though, are probably few and strictly limited. Much more significant, for most of us, is the task of evaluating for our own satisfaction. We see a play, a film, or a television program, and then we make up our minds about it; we often have to decide whether to recommend it to someone else.

To evaluate new drama isn't easy. (For this discussion, let us define *drama* broadly as including not only plays but also anything that actors perform in the movies or on television, for most of us see more movies and television programs than plays.) By the time we see a production of any kind, at least a part of the process of evaluation has already been accomplished for us. To produce a new play, even in an amateur theater, or to produce a new drama for the movies or for television is complicated and involves large sums of money and the efforts of many people. Sifted from a mountain of submitted scripts, already subjected to long scrutiny and evaluation, a new play or film, whether or not it is of deep interest, arrives with a built-in air of professional competence. It seldom happens that a dull play written by the producer's relative or friend finds enough financial backers to reach play stage; only on the fictitious Broadway of Mel Brooks's film and hit play *The Producers* could there be a musical comedy as awful as *Springtime for Hitler*.

And so new plays—the few that we do see—are usually, like television drama, somebody's safe investment. More often than not, our powers of evaluation confront only slick, pleasant, and efficient mediocrity. We owe it to ourselves to discriminate. Life is too short and theater tickets too expensive to spend either on the agreeably second-rate. There are too many marvelous plays we might miss.

■ WRITING *effectively*

JUDGING A PLAY

To write an informed, useful evaluation of a dramatic work, consider how the play it-self asks to be judged. Does it belong to a particular type of drama? It might be a farce, a comedy of manners, or a melodrama (a piece in which suspense and physical action are the prime ingredients). Remember that theaters, such as the classic Greek theater of Sophocles, impose conventions. Do not condemn *Oedipus the King* for the reason one spectator gave: "That damned chorus keeps sticking their noses in!" Do not complain that Hamlet utters soliloquies. Do not dismiss *Sweeney Todd* on the grounds that real people don't keep suddenly bursting into song. So, you might ask, what aspects of a play are up for critique?

- **Judge how well a play fulfills its own conventions.** Ask yourself whether or not it delivers on the expectations it sets up. If a tragedy wants you to feel for the protagonist while also approving the rightness of his downfall, decide whether it has achieved those goals, and if not, why not.

- **Consider whether the play's main characters are fully rounded and believable.** Ask also whether or not their actions follow naturally from their personalities. In a satisfying play, the resolution arises from the nature of the characters, and not through some *deus ex machina* or nick-of-time arrival of the Marines.

- **Consider the play's theme.** How readily can you apply it to the human world beyond the play? Is it trivial, or does it seem to touch a universal chord?

- **Don't be afraid to state your own honest reactions.** We cannot truthfully judge a work of art without somehow involving our own reaction—simple or complicated—to the experience of it.

- **Be careful to distinguish a production from the play itself.** It is important to maintain the distinction between direction, acting, setting, and other elements of production, on the one hand, and the script, on the other.

CHECKLIST: Evaluating a Play

- ☐ What type of play are you watching or reading?
- ☐ What are the conventions of that type of play?
- ☐ How well does the play fulfill those conventions?
- ☐ Are the play's main characters fully realized?
- ☐ Do their actions follow from their personalities, or do the actions seem imposed upon them?
- ☐ Do any symbols stand out? If so, do they reveal meaning?
- ☐ Is the play sentimental? Or does it evoke honest emotion in the viewer?
- ☐ What is the play's theme? Is it of universal importance?

WRITING ASSIGNMENT ON EVALUATION

Many of the plays in this book are available in performance on tape or DVD. Choose one to watch. Pretend you are a critic attending the world premiere, and write a review. Be sure to state your criteria for judgment clearly. For tips on writing a review, see page 1966 in the chapter "Writing About a Play."

MORE TOPICS FOR WRITING

1. Read and evaluate a work from "Plays for Further Reading". Begin with your own personal response to the text, but be sure to temper it with the considerations listed above.

2. Attend a performance of a play you haven't read and write a critical review of it. Be sure to consider both the play itself and the production. For advice on reviewing and a sample review, see page 1966.

3. Evaluate the skill with which Arthur Miller portrays character in *Death of a Salesman*. Focus on one particular character. What telling details are presented about that person? How is he or she characterized by dialogue? Does your character change over the course of the play? How does his or her personality contribute to the plot?

4. Read a modern or contemporary play not found in this book. In an essay of 500 to 750 words, evaluate it. You might choose your subject from this list of interesting plays:

> *The Zoo Story* by Edward Albee
> *Waiting for Godot* by Samuel Beckett
> "*Master Harold*" *and the Boys* by Athol Fugard
> *Six Degrees of Separation* by John Guare
> *Hedda Gabler, The Master Builder,* or *Peer Gynt* by Henrik Ibsen
> *The Bald Soprano* or *The Chairs* by Eugène Ionesco
> *Words, Words, Words* by David Ives
> *American Buffalo* by David Mamet
> '*night, Mother* by Marsha Norman
> *Long Day's Journey into Night* by Eugene O'Neill
> *Topdog/Underdog* by Suzan-Lori Parks
> *The Birthday Party* or *The Caretaker* by Harold Pinter
> *The Cuban Swimmer* by Milcha Sanchez-Scott
> *No Exit* by Jean-Paul Sartre
> *for colored girls who have considered suicide / when the rainbow is enuf*
>   by Ntozake Shange
> *Major Barbara* or *Pygmalion* by George Bernard Shaw
> *Buried Child* or *True West* by Sam Shepard
> *Rosencrantz and Guildenstern Are Dead* by Tom Stoppard
> *How I Learned to Drive* by Paula Vogel
> *The Heidi Chronicles* by Wendy Wasserstein
> *The Piano Lesson* by August Wilson

40

PLAYS FOR
FURTHER READING

> *A play isn't a text. It's an event.*
>
> —TOM STOPPARD

Rita Dove

The Darker Face of the Earth   1994

Rita Dove was born in Akron, Ohio, in 1952, to middle-class parents who were themselves the children of working-class families. She earned a B.A. summa cum laude from Miami University of Ohio and an M.F.A. from the University of Iowa. Later she won a Fulbright fellowship that enabled her to study in Germany. Her first two books of poems were The

Guthrie Theater's 2000 production of *The Darker Face of the Earth*.

Yellow House on the Corner (1980) *and* Museum (1983); *her third,* Thomas and Beulah (1986), *a book-length cycle based on the lives of her mother's parents, was awarded the Pulitzer Prize. Her Selected Poems appeared in 1993, the year in which she was named Poet Laureate of the United States, the youngest person and the first African American to achieve that honor. Her subsequent collections are* Mother Love (1995), On the Bus with Rosa Parks (1999), *and* American Smooth (2004), *which was chosen as one of the 100 Notable Books of that year by the New York Times. She has also published a novel, a book of short stories, and the verse play* The Darker Face of the Earth (1994), *which recasts the Oedipus myth in a drama set on a plantation in pre–Civil War South Carolina. Dove's poetry often deals with race, as well as with broader issues of American history and culture, but she has been principally concerned with family themes, especially mother-daughter relationships. She is Commonwealth Professor of English at the University of Virginia in Charlottesville, where she lives with her husband, the novelist Fred Viebahn.*

CAST

FEMALE SLAVES:
Phebe
Psyche, in her mid-teens
Scylla, pronounced "Skilla"
Ticey, a house slave
Diana, a young girl about 12 years old
Slave woman/Narrator

MALE SLAVES:
Hector, an African
Alexander
Scipio, pronounced "Sippio"
Augustus Newcastle, a mulatto

THE WHITES:
Amalia Jennings LaFarge
Louis LaFarge, Amalia's husband
Doctor, in his fifties
Jones, the overseer, in his thirties

THE BLACK CONSPIRATORS:
Leader
Benjamin Skeene
Henry Blake

OTHER SLAVES AND CONSPIRATORS

TIME.
Prologue: *about 1820.*
Acts I and II: *twenty years later.*

PLACE: *The action takes place in antebellum South Carolina, on the Jennings Plantation and in its environs.*

The characters of Psyche and Diana, as well as the Doctor and Jones, can be played by the same actors, as long as it is made clear to the audience that they are different people.

On occasion, the slaves comment upon the play somewhat in the manner of a Greek chorus. Individual characters are bound by time and circumstance; the chorus of slaves is more detached and omnipresent. By moving and speaking in a ritualized manner, they provide vocal and percussive counterpoint to the action. The slave woman who occasionally steps forward as the narrator, is quietly present in all slave scenes.

This Play Is for My Daughter, Aviva Chantal Tamu Dove-Viebahn.

PROLOGUE

Lights rise on the big house, revealing the porch, Amalia's bedroom, Louis's study and the hallway.

Hector, a slave in his early twenties, is standing on the porch, looking up at a second-story window. Phebe, a slave girl in her early teens, runs onstage; she is coming from the basement kitchen. Skinny and electric, she is chuckling to herself.

Phebe: What some people won't do
    for attention! Shore,
    he's alright-looking—
    but that ain't qualification enough
    for the big white bed
    in the big white house!

(*Laughs at her own wit; then, skipping in a circle, sings.*)

    Stepped on a pin, the pin bent,
    and that's the way the story went!
Psyche (offstage): Phebe! Phebe! You up there?
Phebe: Here I am, Psyche!

(*Psyche enters. She is petite, shy; though not much older than Phebe, she treats her like a little sister.*)

Psyche: You shouldn't go running off
    by yourself, chile.
Phebe: Look: Hector on the porch. (*She giggles and points to Hector.*)
Psyche: Leave him be, poor soul.
Phebe: Aw, Psyche! Anybody crazy enough
    to be standing there, thinking he—
Psyche: Shush now, chile!

(*Phebe shrugs, hums and skips again. The other slaves straggle in, tired from the day's work, whispering among themselves, a suppressed excitement in their manner.*)

Phebe: What took you all so long?
    Slower than a pack of lame turtles.
Alexander (a dignified man in his forties): We all ain't quite
    so spry as you, gal.
Phebe: Shh!

(*Everyone freezes*)

I thought I heard something.

Psyche: Aw, girl—

Scylla (*a tall dark woman in her twenties*):
Must be a hard birthin'.

Psyche: I sure hope she makes it. Her mama—

Scylla: Her mama was the weakest excuse for a woman
ever dropped on this earth. But this one—

(*With a significant look to the window.*)

this one got her daddy in her.

Alexander: Nothing but trouble, I tell you.
Nothing but trouble.

(*Lights up on Amalia's bedroom. Amalia Jennings LaFarge lies in a canopy bed, a
thickly swaddled babe in her arms. She is an attractive white woman, close to 20 years
old, who exhibits more intelligence and backbone than is generally credited to a Southern
belle. The Doctor, an older whiskered gentleman, is pacing the floor. Amalia, though
exhausted, appears amused.*)

Amalia: Well, Doctor, isn't he beautiful?

Doctor: This is serious, Amalia!
If the niggers get wind of this—

(*Amalia begins humming a lullaby to the baby.*)

Amalia: Don't get melodramatic, Doctor;
you'll frighten my son. See?

(*Baby raises a cry; Amalia continues to hum while the Doctor keeps pacing. Among
the slaves, Scylla stands up, clutching her stomach.*)

Scylla: Oh! Oh!

Others: What is it, Scylla? What is it?

Scylla: It's out in the world.

(*The slaves look at her in fear.*)

Alexander: Lord have mercy.

(*The slaves gather around Scylla as she tries to straighten up but cannot. Hector's gaze
is still fixed on the window. Amalia's husband rushes into the bedroom. Louis LaFarge
is a handsome man in his twenties. The Doctor holds him back.*)

Louis: Doctor—

Doctor: Everything's fine. Just go on back outside.

Louis: Can't a man see his own child?

(*Tears himself free and rushes over to the bed.*)

Amalia: What, Louis—struck dumb?

Louis: My God!

Amalia: Isn't he a fine strapping boy?

Doctor: This is unnatural.
Louis: Who did this to you?
   I'll have him whipped to a pulp—
Amalia (hissing): So it's alright for you
   to stroll out by the cabins
   any fine night you please? Ha—
   the Big White Hunter with his scrawny whip!
Louis: That tears it!
Doctor: Quiet! They might hear.
Louis: I'll kill her!

   (*Louis lunges at Amalia; the Doctor restrains him.*)

Doctor: Hold it, sir! Calm yourself!
Amalia (to the Doctor): Daddy tried to keep me from
   marrying him—but I was in love
   with riding boots and the smell
   of shaving cream and bourbon.
   I was in love with a cavalryman
   and nothing could stop me,
   not even Daddy!

   (*To Louis, who is being forced into an armchair by the Doctor.*)

   But not even Daddy
   suspected where you would seek
   your satisfaction.
   It was your right
   to pull on those riding boots
   and stalk little slave girls.
   God knows what you do to them
   in the name of ownership.

   (*Depleted from the bravado she has mustered, Amalia bends over the baby so they won't see her exhaustion. Louis, still sitting in the armchair, grabs the Doctor by the shirt and pulls him down to his level.*)

Louis: Get rid of it! Destroy the bastard!
Doctor: My charge is to preserve life,
   Mr. LaFarge, not to destroy it.
Louis: What's the matter? Aren't you a man?
Doctor (scathingly; a fierce whisper): My manhood isn't the question here.
   Do you want your business
   smeared across the whole county?
   Think for a minute: What have we got
   here? A fresh slave. New property.
   And you're in need of a little spare change,
   aren't you? I understand the cards
   haven't been much in your favor lately.
Louis: What are you trying to say, Doctor?

Amalia: Stop your whispering, gentlemen.
    No one's going to touch this baby!
Louis: You can be sure I'll never
    touch you again!
Amalia: That's one blessing.
Doctor: Is this baby worth destroying your life?

    (*Pulling Louis aside.*)

    Give me a minute alone with her.
    I'll make her see reason. Go on, now.

    (*He shoves the reluctant Louis out of the door, then moves quickly to the window to peek out on the slaves below. Among the slaves, excitement reigns as Scylla hobbles over to Hector, whose eyes are still fixed on the bedroom window.*)

Phebe (to Psyche): Scylla gonna be alright?
Psych (sees the curtains move): Hush chile!

    (*Pointing to the window.*)

    Something's stirring.

    (*The slaves look up to the window and freeze. The Doctor returns to Amalia, who is singing to the baby.*)

Doctor: You can cease your motherly blandishments,
    Amalia. He's gone.
Amalia: I knew you were good for something besides
    tonics and botched surgeries, Doctor!
Doctor: Oh, you're mighty clever, Miss Jennings—
    no wonder your marriage is a disappointment.
    Hell, your daddy saw it coming;
    he worried about you. How many times
    did he have to haul you back from the fields,
    kicking and scratching like a she-cat?
Amalia: And just who was I supposed to
    play with—the pigs and the chickens?
    Daddy could run a plantation
    but he didn't know the first thing
    about raising a daughter. All morning
    he'd teach me to calculate inventory,
    but he expected his slippers darned come evening!
    And when I refused, off I went—
    to finishing school and the Charleston society balls.

    (*Lights up on Louis, sitting on the bed in his room, head in hands.*)

Louis: Spare change. Spare change!
    How they all smirk! I know what they're thinking.
    "Louis sure slipped into a silk-lined purse!"

    (*Takes a swig from a flask in his jacket.*)

Damn his blasted Hippocratic oath!

(*Paces, agitated; then stops, an idea dawning.*)

That's it! Of course.
Doctor, I'll save you the trouble.

(*He rummages in drawers; lights up on Amalia's room.*)

Amalia: When I came home from Charleston
 with my brand new dashing husband,
 Daddy had the slaves line the path
 from the gate to the front porch;
 and as we walked through the ranks
 each one stepped up with
 the nosegays they had picked—
 awkward bunches of wildflowers.
 I was laughing, gathering up bouquets
 and tossing them to Louis.

 We were almost to the porch
 when suddenly there appeared this . . .
 this rose. One red rose,
 thrust right into the path so we had to stop.
 I recognised him right away.
 We hadn't seen each other
 since Daddy sent him to the fields.
 We used to sneak out to Mama's
 old cutting garden; it was overgrown
 and the roses had run particularly wild!

(*Softly, remembering.*)

 One day he covered me in rose petals,
 then blew them off, one by one.
 He'd never seen anything like them
 back in Africa.

(*In wonder.*)

 And there he stood, all grown up,
 with one red rose held out
 like it was a piece of him
 growing straight from his fist.
 "What a lovely tribute to the bride!" I said—

(*Shaking off the spell of the memory.*)

 then passed it to Louis to tuck in with the rest.
Doctor: I suppose there's no sense in talking about
 your duty to the institution of marriage.
Amalia: I made one mistake—Louis.
 I don't have to go on living it.

Doctor: Oh, there's where you're wrong
  Amalia Jennings. Some mistakes
  don't right themselves that easy.
  Some mistakes you live with until you die.

(*Lights up on Louis in his bedroom as he emerges from the back of the wardrobe with a pair of spurs, still trailing red ribbons.*)

Louis (sneering): There they are!
  Amalia's Christmas present—
  fancy new riding spurs!
  Won't they make a special
  "christening" present
  for the little bitty baby
  to tuck in with its blanket!

(*Louis chuckles as he pockets the spurs and leaves the room. Lights up on slaves. Hector stretches his hand toward the window and speaks, as if trying to remember.*)

Hector: Eshu Elewa . . .
Phebe: What's he saying?
Psyche: Something surely gone wrong.

(*Lights up on Amalia and Doctor.*)

Doctor: How long do you think it will take
  before your slaves begin to speak back?
  To botch the work and fall ill
  with mysterious ailments? Then
  who will help you—Louis?
  An overseer who knows his mistress
  is tainted with slave funk? In a bad year,
  how much will you have to beg
  to get a tab at the store?
  Who will you invite to tea, Amalia—
  your dashing blackamoor?
Amalia: What a convenient morality, Doctor.
Doctor: I'm just trying to save
  your daddy's good name.
  As for your precious little bundle—
  how long do you think he'll last
  with Louis feeling as he does?
  How long before your child
  accidentally drowns
  or stumbles under a horse's hooves?
  You can't keep him, Amalia;
  if you truly love him,
  you cannot keep him.

(*Amalia buries her face in the pillow and begins to weep.*)

Doctor: I know a family who handles
  these . . . delicate matters.

They'll raise him and arrange for sale
when it's time.

(*Amalia clutches the baby to her.*)

He'll be treated well. I'll make sure of that.

(*Silence. Amalia stares at the baby.*)

Amalia: Give me a little more time!
Doctor: You had nine months.

(*The baby makes a noise; she lays him on her breast.*)

Amalia: There's no way back, is there?

(*Hector falls to his knee and cries out; Scylla tries to restrain him.*)

Hector: Eshu Elewa ogo gbogbo!
Scylla: No, Hector.
Alexander: Lord help him.
Psyche: Lord help us all.

(*Lights up on Amalia's bedroom; there's a knock at the door.*)

Doctor: There he is. Now:
I'll take the baby to Charleston tonight.
You must play the wronged wife.
No matter the truth—whatever the truth—
this affair was an act of revenge,
your retaliation to Louis's philandering.
But you won't keep the child
to taunt him, oh, no! Instead,
you'll forgive and forget . . . and show him
how to turn a profit besides.

(*Amalia stares at the Doctor with disgust. The Doctor opens the door.*)

Come in, sir.

(*Louis enters, glaring.*)

This is a damned tricky situation,
but I think I've sorted it out.

(*Warming up to his role as the arbiter of responsibility and morality; pacing self-importantly.*)

Out of rage and sorrow over
your philandering behavior, Louis,
Amalia has responded in kind.
An extreme vindication, true,
and utterly reprehensible—unless
we remember what prompted it
in the first place. Are we agreed?

(*Both Louis and Amalia are silent.*)

As for the bastard child . . .

(*Pauses for effect.*)

Amalia has agreed to let it go.
I have a friend in Charleston
who likes raising slaves
from the ground up. He's familiar
with the story of the distraught wife
confronted with the evidence
of a husband's wandering lust.

Louis: No! I won't take the blame!

Doctor: No one need know it's come
from the Jennings Plantation.

Louis: What about the niggers? They're out
on the lawn, waiting for news.

Doctor: We'll say the poor soul expired
directly after birth, took one breath
and died. I've taken the body away.

Louis: No funeral? Niggers love funerals.

Doctor: No—Amalia didn't want a funeral.
They'll believe it. They have no choice.

(*To Amalia.*)

You better make sure the father
keeps his mouth shut.

Amalia (*haunted*): Who would believe him?

Louis: I must say, your ingenuity is impressive,
Doctor. It's what I'd call a "master" plan.

(*Pointing to the sideboard where Amalia keeps an oblong wicker sewing basket, trimmed with red velvet rosettes and lined in blue silk.*)

That basket—surely you'd donate
your sewing basket to the cause,
Amalia? It would fit so nicely
behind the good doctor's saddle.

Doctor (*examines the basket*): Yes, that will do.

(*Louis places the basket next to the bed.*)

Amalia: Go tell them.
Spread the sad tidings.

(*She says this with difficulty. Doctor and Louis exit as Amalia carefully unwraps the baby and inspects him, top to toe. Lights up on the Doctor and Louis in the hall; Ticey, a house slave in her forties, approaches them.*)

Ticey: How's Miss Jennings, suh?
The baby sure sounds like a big one!

Doctor (*harshly*): The baby's dead.

Ticey: Dead? But I heard it cry!
Doctor: He cried out once. Poor little thing
    had no more breath left.
Ticey: Now, if that ain't the strangest thing . . .
Louis (sharply): What's so strange about it?
    The baby just up and died.
    Happens all the time.
Doctor: Look at you, standing here arguing
    like a fool hen, while your mistress
    is in there crying her eyes out!

    (*Shaking his head.*)

    Now go on out to those niggers—
    I know you got them waiting by the porch.
    Tell them there'll be no wailing and moaning,
    no singing or mighty sorry, Ma'am.
    Miss Jennings wants no funeral.
    Miss Jennings wants to forget.
    Go on now, scat!
Ticey: Yassuh. Sorry suh.

    (*Ticey exits. During the following scene she approaches Psyche, takes her aside, whispering. At Psyche's shocked reaction, the slaves, except for Hector and Scylla, crowd around. Ticey retreats back into the house while the other slaves lower their heads, softly humming in a frozen tableau. Hector falls to his knees; Scylla stands over him, severely bent.*)

    (*In the bedroom, Amalia embraces the baby one last time.*)

Amalia: This basket will be your cradle now.
    Blue silk for my prince, and a canopy of roses!
    Don't be afraid: it's warm inside.

    (*Places first a small blanket, then the baby inside, takes one last look, nearly breaking down.*)

    I dreamed you before you came;
    now I must remember you before you go.

    (*Collects herself as she wraps the blanket around the baby and closes the lid.*)

Doctor: Let's get this over with.
Louis: Go ahead. Doctor, I—I'll wait here.

    (*The Doctor enters the bedroom.*)

Doctor: Ready?

    (*Amalia averts her head, thrusts the basket at him.*)

    I wasn't sure you had it in you,
    but I'll say one thing, Amalia Jennings—
    you are your father's daughter.

(*Doctor exits with the basket. Amalia buries her face in the pillows.*)

Doctor: I best be on my way.
Louis: You have a hard ride ahead of you, Doctor.
    Would you care for a bit of bourbon
    to warm your way?
Doctor (*slightly surprised*): Why yes, that would do nicely.
    Just put it with my things.

(*As the Doctor turns to get his coat and hat, Louis slips the spurs in the sewing basket, under the blanket, then puts the flask into the Doctor's bag.*)

Louis: There, you're all set—
    best medicine made by man!
Doctor: It's over, Louis. Nothing left but to forget.
Louis: Have a pleasant journey, Doctor.
Doctor: I will try.

(*Lights go out as the Doctor exits. The Slave woman/Narrator steps forward. During the Narrator's speech, the slaves go about their tasks, humming as the lights slowly warm to sunrise and the stage begins to transmogrify, simulating the passing of 20 years: a tree growing, the big house being enlarged, etc.*)

Narrator:
    Take a little seed,
    put it in the ground;
    the seed takes root,
    sends its tendrils down

    till the sapling shoots
    its branches high—
    roots piercing ground,
    limbs touching sky.

    Now the mighty tree
    is twenty years tall;
    seed become king,
    and the king takes all.

ACT I

SCENE I

The cotton fields. Diana, a slave girl, collapses. Scipio, a young slave working nearby, hesitates.

Scipio: Move it gal, or
    you'll feel it later!
Phebe (*helping her up*): Lift in your knees, Diana;
    try not to think about your blood.
    Tomorrow's Sunday—
    tomorrow you can rest.
Diana (*derisively*): Blessed be the Sabbath!

Phebe: The child's too young to tote that sack.
    She should be helping in the kitchen,
    like we was raised.
Alexander: You was raised with Massa Jennings,
    Phebe—and he been gone these twenty-some years.
    You know his daughter got other ideas.
Phebe: She grow eviller year for year.
Alexander: Ain't right, a woman
    running a plantation like that.
Scipio: Woman? She's more man than woman.
Phebe: And more devil than man.
Alexander: Ever since she lost that child.
Phebe: Oh, Alexander!
Alexander: White folks feel a loss
    as much as we do—
    it's just that they ain't
    used to losing. I tell you,
    Miss Amalia went crazy in the head
    the day she lost that baby boy.
Scylla: That's not the way Ticey told it.

(Scylla is severely bent over and walks with a limp. Her gaze is fearful.)

Alexander (to Diana): Nowadays old Ticey don't tell us
    field niggers nothing. But that night
    she come from the Big House
    and say to Psyche . . .
Phebe: That's enough, Alexander.
Diana: Phebe, what was my mama like?
Phebe: Chile, you heard that story
    a hundred times. Ain't no different now,
    just 'cause you turned to a woman yourself.
Diana: Please, Phebe.
Phebe (tenderly, as she resumes picking cotton):
    Psyche was the sister I never had.
    Why, she pulled me offa trouble
    so many times, I thought her hand
    had growed to my shoulder!
Diana (begins to cry): I wish I'd a known her.
Phebe: Childbirth can kill the strongest woman.
Alexander: Or kill the child.
Scylla: You still believe the white folks?
    That baby weren't born dead.
    Ticey heard it cry. I seen the doctor
    carry it off in a basket, but
    it weren't dead. I felt it kick.
Diana (wiping her tears): The baby kicked?
Alexander: Scylla got her powers that night.
Scylla (staring at Diana, who shrinks back): The child was born alive!
    I know. I felt it.

Phebe: Scylla . . .
Scylla: The veil was snatched from my eyes—
and over the hill I saw
bad times a-coming. Bad times
coming over the hill on mighty horses,
horses snorting as they galloped
through slave cabin and pillared mansion,
horses whinnying as they trampled
everything in their path.
Like a thin black net
the curse settled over the land.
Diana: What curse?
Phebe: Don't pay her no mind.
Scylla: The curse touched four people.
Diana (getting scared): Who were they?
Who were the four people?
Slaves: Black woman, black man,
white woman, white man.
Scylla: When the curse came I stood up
to meet it, and it knocked me
to the ground.
Slaves: Black woman.
Scylla: My womb dried up,
but the power churned in me.
Phebe: We best get back to pickin'.
No tellin' where Jones got off to—
Scipio: Same place he always "gets off to"
—that clump of timothy at the spring
where he's tucked his whiskey!

(*Scylla appears to be in a trance; Slaves accompany her in a syncopated whisper.*)

Scylla: Hector, son of Africa—
stolen from his father's hut,
sold on the auction block!
Slaves: Black man.
Scylla: Hector was a slave in the fields
until Miss Amalia took him up
to the house. He followed her
like her own right shoe.
When she felt faint,
he brought her iced lemon water;
when she started to show,
he helped her up the stairs;
when the baby kicked,
he soothed her.
But when her time came
he had to stand out by the porch
like the rest of us.
And when Ticey brought the news

Hector fell to his knees
and ate dirt like a worm.
Now he lives alone
and catches snakes in the swamp.
Slaves: Black woman, black man—
both were twisted
when the curse came over the hill.
Scylla: While the slave turned to grief,
the master turned to business.
Miss Amalia hiked up her skirts
and pulled on man's boots.
Slaves: White woman.
Scylla: And Massa Louis . . . Massa Louis
took off his riding breeches—
Slaves: White man.
Scylla: —and shut himself upstairs.
Some nights you can see him out
on the balcony, staring at the sky:
he has machines to measure the stars.
Slaves: Black woman, black man;
white woman, white man!
Scylla: Four people touched by the curse:
but the curse is not complete.
Diana: I'm scared.
Phebe (in spite of herself): Did you have to tell her so much,
Scylla? She's just a child.
Scylla: She's old enough to know,
and you're old enough to know better.
Phebe: I was there, too. I didn't see
no horses comin' over the hill.
You just crumpled up like a leaf.

(Amalia enters unseen in riding clothes, whip in hand.)

Scylla: I can strike you down like lightning,
Phebe. I can send demons mightier—
Amalia: What's this?
Phebe: How—how de do, Miss Amalia!
We was just trying to figure out
what to do with Diana here.
Amalia: She seems healthy enough to me—
good stock, young and fresh.
Phebe (motioning for Diana to look sicker): She fell out something awful.
It don't look like she feel too good—
Amalia: You aren't here to play doctor, Phebe.
Where is that Jones? Jones!

(Jones is nowhere to be seen. Impatient, Amalia prods Diana with the whip stock.)

Lazy Pack! I swear I've seen cows
smarter than you! Jones!

Jones (rushes in, wiping his mouth with his sleeve): Yes, Miss Jennings?
Amalia: Get these niggers in line!
   Drink on your own time.
Jones: Yes'm.
Amalia: I'll see you this evening
   up at the house.
Jones: Yes, Ma'am. I'll be there, Ma'am!

   (*She strides off; Jones mops his brow with a huge handkerchief.*)

   Goddamn niggers, gotta watch you
   every second! Get that gal back on her feet!

   (*Cracking his whip.*)

   Keep your mouths shut and your hands picking
   or you'll feel my lash, sick or not!

   (*Watches them resume work; then exits.*)

Scylla: I believe it's about time for you
   to pay me a little visit, Phebe.
   Tomorrow evening—
   after the moon's set.
Phebe: Aw, Scylla, I didn't mean nothing—
Scylla: It'll be pitch dark. Take care
   you don't trip on the way.

BLACKOUT

SCENE II

The big house, the parlor and Louis's study.

Louis is visible at the window of his study, peering through a telescope at the stars; he occasionally takes notes or sips his brandy.

Amalia sits at the desk in the parlor; Jones stands in front of her.

Jones: Sorry about this afternoon, Ma'am.
   That little gal seemed real sick, you know.
Amalia: Mr. Jones, I am aware you come fresh
   from the well-groomed slave holdings
   of Dawson's Plantation. And I was not
   so naïve, upon hiring you, to believe
   Dawson's high-minded economic philosophy
   had not rubbed off on you.
   But that's not what I called you for.
   I bought a new buck yesterday:
   here are his papers.
Jones (glancing through the documents): Miss Jennings! You can't be serious!
Amalia: Something wrong, Jones?

Jones: Augustus Newcastle? That slave's
　　the most talked-about nigger
　　along the Southern seaboard!
Amalia: Good! We'll be famous.
Jones: Story goes he belonged to a British sea captain
　　who treated him like his own son,
　　and promised him his freedom when he died.
　　But the brother who executed the estate
　　sold the boy to pay off the debts.
　　After that, the nigger went wild.
　　They lost count of how many times he ran off,
　　how many times they caught him—

(*Frantically leafs through the papers.*)

　　here it is: "Twenty-two
　　acts of aggression and rebellion."
　　Twenty-two separate acts!
Amalia: That's why I got him so cheaply.
Jones: But Miss Jennings! They say
　　his back's so laced with scars
　　it's as rutted as a country road.
　　Rumor has it he can read and write.
　　If you don't mind my saying so,
　　Ma'am, an educated nigger
　　brings nothing but trouble.
　　Sure as I'm standing here,
　　he'll stir up the others.
Amalia: I wonder just how smart he is.
Jones: It's a miracle no one ever killed him.
Amalia (*sharply*): I own Augustus Newcastle,
　　and I'll make him serve up.
　　Any objections?
Jones: No, Ma'am. Sorry, Ma'am.
Amalia: They're bringing him over tonight;
　　put him in the barn and chain him down.
　　You can show him around tomorrow.
　　If he's as smart as they say,
　　he could help you oversee the ginning.
　　You may go.

(*This last is a jab at Jones, who looks at her for a moment, then turns on his heel and exits.*)

BLACKOUT

SCENE III

In the fields.

Sunday. The slaves have been "let out in the fields" to occupy themselves as they please. They have settled into two groups—some joke, tell stories, and dance, while others are quieter, chanting and praying. As the lights come up, the groups are rivaling each other in melody, the quieter ones humming in a minor key while the others counterpoint in a jauntier tune.

Scipio: Have you seen the new man?
  Mister Jones been showing him around.
Alexander: I saw 'em down
  by the gin house.
  That's one wild nigger.
Phebe: He spent last night
  chained in the barn.
  Chained!
Scipio: Must be mighty tough.
  Heard tell he's sailed the seas!
Diana: Did he sail the seas to Canada?

(Shocked silence; everybody looks at her.)

Alexander: Gal, don't let nobody
  hear you say that word;
  Miss Amalia'll have your head on a stick.
  As far as you concerned
  there's nothing in this world
  but South Carolina and this here plantation.

(Augustus enters in leg chains, followed by a watchful Jones. Augustus is a tall, handsome young man with caramel-toned skin and piercing eyes. His righteous anger is thinly concealed behind his slave mannerisms. Jones bluffs his way with a squeaky bravado.)

Jones: Here's the new buck you all
  been whispering about!

(Removes the leg chains; then, to Augustus.)

You're lucky it's Sunday. Tomorrow
you'll get a taste of how things run
around here. First horn at day-clean!

(Jones exits. There is a moment's awkward silence as Augustus rubs his ankles where the chains have chafed. He looks up, calmly surveying the two groups.)

Scipio: Welcome, stranger, welcome.
  They call me Scipio.
  What do you go by?
Augustus: Augustus.
Scipio (stretching the name out, trying to make it fit his tongue): Au-gus-tus?
  Ain't never heard that one before.
  What kind of name is that?
Augustus: The name of a king.

(Uneasy silence.)

Phebe: Don't pay Scipio no mind.
  He's always joking.
  I'm Phebe. And this is Alexander.

(Alexander nods, warily.)

Alexander been here longer than anyone, I reckon.

Alexander: How do.

(*Scylla enters with a water gourd and watches the introductions with a hard eye. Phebe rushes to introduce them.*)

Phebe: And this here's Scylla. Scylla,
    he's the new one, go by the name of—
Augustus: Augustus Newcastle.
Scylla: Newcastle. Is that your captain's name?
Augustus: Scylla was the rock,
    Charybdis the whirlpool,
    that pulled the sailors down.

(*General astonishment.*)

Phebe: Now this little girl—

(*Pushes Diana over to Augustus*)

was born and raised
    right here on this plantation.
Augustus: What's your name, child?
Diana (shyly): Diana.
Augustus: My, my. The sun and the moon
    all in one morning!

(*The slaves look bewildered. He laughs softly.*)

Don't mind me. I'm just glad to meet you all.

(*Some slaves take up their chant again. Augustus walks upstage and stands looking into the distance. Although they are curious, the other slaves let him be. Only Diana stares after him.*)

Phebe: Come on, Scipio, give us a story.
Scipio: You always wanting a story!
    How many stories you think I got?
Phebe: I think you grow them in your sleep.
Scipio: Well, I ain't got a story this time.
Phebe: Aw, Scipio! You dog!
Scipio: But I got a song:

(*Accompanies himself on a handmade string instrument while his friends clap, pat their bodies, etc.*)

The possum said, don't hurt me,
I'm harmless if you please!
The nigger said, I'm harmless, too,
And got down on his knees.

The possum cocked his little head
And contemplated long;
You're running just like me, he said
And joined into the song

Old Mr. Coon just happened by
Where the two sang merrily;
I don't trust you, cried Mr. Coon,
Why, you just as black as me!

You're just as black as me, Coon said,
but your tail ain't quite so long!
Then Mr. Coon ran in the woods
And wouldn't join their song.

(*Laughter: Diana walks over to Augustus.*)

Diana: What you looking at?
Augustus: Just looking.
Diana: Ain't nothing out there but the swamp.
Augustus: Do you know what's beyond that swamp?
Diana: What?
Augustus: The world.
Phebe (*to Scipio*): Is that all?
Scipio: No, there's more:

(*Singing.*)

The nigger wrapped his fingers
Around the possum's throat.
The possum didn't have the time
To sing another note.

That night the nigger had himself
A pot of possum stew.
That harmless meat is just the thing
To warm your innards through!

Diana: What did you mean by
  the sun and the moon?
Augustus: Beg pardon?
Diana: The sun and the moon—you asked
  my name and then you said you had
  the sun and the moon all in one day.
Augustus: You're a curious one, aren't you?
Diana: Uh-huh.
Augustus: Well—a long time ago there were
  gods to look after the earth and the sky.
  Phoebus was the god of the sun;
  your friend's name is Phebe.
  And your name stood for the moon.
  People wrote poems to Diana,
  goddess of the moon.
Diana: What's poems?
Augustus: A poem is . . .

(*Looking over at Scipio.*)

. . . a song without music.

(*Looks off towards the swamp.*)

Who's that old man?

Diana: Phebe, Hector's coming up from the swamp!

Phebe: Don't fret, chile.
Hector talk kind of crazy sometimes,
but he don't hurt nobody.

Augustus: His name is Hector?

Phebe: Yeah. Massa Jennings give it to him
straight off the boat. He used to talk
African—but he forgot most of it.

Augustus: What does he do in the swamp?

Phebe (catching a warning look from Scylla): He lives there.

Augustus: Hector, mighty warrior,
abandoned by the gods.

Diana: You know a lot of things.

Augustus: Nothing you couldn't learn
if you had the chance.

(*Enter Hector, now middle-aged, dressed in muddy rags. He carries a dead snake in a net and looks around with wild, piercing eyes, then wanders up to Diana.*)

Hector (tenderly): Eshu Elewa ogo gbogbo!

(*Diana shrinks back. Hector taps Augustus on the shoulder, holding out the net.*)

I catch snakes: big ones, little ones.
I'm going to catch all the snakes in the swamp.

Augustus: I don't know much about snakes,
my friend.

Hector: I'm gonna catch all the snakes in the swamp!
They grow and grow, so many of them.
But I'll kill them! I'll kill them all!

Scylla: Shh, Hector!
Don't let the snakes hear!

(*She puts her arm around Hector and pats him gently on the back, all the while staring at Augustus, as the lights dim and go out.*)

SCENE IV

Scylla's cabin and the area outside of the slave cabins.

Night. Scylla sits in her cabin behind a crude table strewn with an assortment of bones, twisted roots, beads, and dried corncobs. Three candles light up her face from below. Augustus, in ankle chains, squats outside the slave cabins. In the distance can be heard the rhythmic ecstasy of the Sunday night "shout." Phebe at the door with a small cloth bundle. She looks behind her.

Scylla: Come in, child. Sit.

(*Phebe sits.*)

I know your heart, Phebe.
You have made the spirits angry!
Phebe: I never meant no harm—
Scylla: Shh!

(*Picks out a forked branch and arranges the candles in a half-circle around the branch.*)

The body moves through the world.

(*Places a round white stone in the fork of the branch.*)

The mind rests in the body.

(*Sprinkles green powder from a vial onto branch and stone.*)

The soul is bright
as a jewel, lighter than air.

(*Blows the powder away; the candles flare, Phebe coughs.*)

There is a curse on the land.
The net draws closer.
What have you brought?
Phebe: Here!

(*Shoves her bundle across the table. Scylla pulls out a pink ribbon and drapes it over the branch.*)

Scylla: "Eshu Elewa ogo gbogbo . . .

(*Sprinkling powder on the first candle.*)

. . . oki kosi eyo!"

(*The candle flares and goes out.*)

You have tried to make the earth
give up her dead.
Phebe: Oh!
Scylla (*pulling out a shell necklace, draping it over the branch*): "Kosi eyo,
    kosi iku . . .

(*Sprinkling powder on the second candle.*)

. . . kosi ano!"

(*The second candle goes out.*)

Phebe: Have mercy . . .
Scylla: You have tried to snatch words
    back from the air. The wind is angry.
    It will take more than these—

(*Indicating Phebe's offerings.*)

to satisfy him.

Phebe (*pulls a white handkerchief out of her pocket*): Here's . . . a hankie from
    my mama.
    There's a little lace on it—see?

(*Scylla snatches the handkerchief, places it on the branch and repeats the procedure
with powder and incantation.*)

Scylla: "Ni oru ko mi gbogbo
    omonile fu kuikuo
    modupue—
    baba mi Elewa!"

(*The third candle flickers but stays lit.*)

    Ah!
Phebe: What is it?
Scylla: Are you prepared to hear
    what the spirits have to say?
Phebe (*gathering courage*): If there's something I need to know,
    I want to know it.
Scylla: I give you two warnings.
    One: guard your footsteps;
    they are your mark on the earth.
    If a sharp stone or piece of glass
    falls into the path you have walked,
    you will go lame.
    Two: guard your breath;
    do not throw with words.
    Whenever the wind blows,
    if your mouth is open,
    your soul could be snatched away.
    That is all.
Phebe: Scylla . . .
Scylla: Go now!

(*Scylla mutters over the candles as Phebe hurries off, shuffling her feet to blur her footprints as she flees. On the way she passes Augustus. In the distance the slaves can be
heard humming during the "shout."*)

Augustus: Evening.
Phebe (*caught in the act of obliterating her steps; embarrassed*): Evening.
Augustus: Back from the shout?
Phebe (*trying not to speak*): Uh-uh.
Augustus: What's your hurry? Why don't
    you keep me company for a spell?
    Unless you're scared of me, that is.
Phebe: Scared of you? Why should
    I be scared of you?
Augustus: I can't think of a reason in the world.
    Come on, rest yourself.

(*Phebe sits down beside him carefully.*)

Augustus: Sure is a fine night.

(*Phebe nods.*)

You're trembling.
Phebe: I am?

(*Claps her hand over her mouth.*)

Augustus: And I don't believe
it's entirely my doing.

(*He says this in a mildly flirtatious manner, then looks off, unaware of the effect this
has on Phebe, who has stopped thinking about Scylla and is now acutely aware of
Augustus as a man. Augustus continues speaking, preoccupied once again with his
hatred.*)

Fear! Fear eats out the heart.
It'll cause kings and field niggers alike
to crawl in their own piss. Listen
to them sing!
What kind of god preaches such misery?

(*Gesturing in the direction of the "shout."*)

White-fearing niggers.
Death-fearing slaves.
Phebe: Ain't you ever scared?
Augustus: Of what? White folks?
They're more afraid of me. Pain?
Every whipping's got to come to an end.
Phebe: I heard you've been whipped
so many times, they lost count.
Augustus: They think they can beat me to my senses.
Then they look into my eyes
and see I'm not afraid.
Phebe: It'd be something, not to be afraid.
Augustus: You have to have a purpose.
Something bigger than anything
they can do to you.
Phebe (*suppressing a shudder*): And ain't nobody ever tried to kill you?
Augustus: Oh, yes. First time,
I was hardly alive.
They ripped me from my mother
the night I was born
and threw me out like trash.
I didn't walk until I was three.
Phebe: Lord have mercy.
Augustus: Mercy had nothing to do with it!
Missy couldn't stand the sight of me.
Just look at me! It's an old story.

You've stopped trembling.
Now why don't you tell me
what made you quake that way
in the first place?

(*Phebe shakes her head.*)

Conjuration, I imagine?
Mumble-jumble from that hateful woman.
Phebe: Her name's Scylla.
Augustus: Women like her, hah!
They get a chill one morning,
hear an owl or two, and snap!—
they've received their "powers"!
Then they collect a few old bones,
dry some herbs, and they're in business.
Phebe: She told me to watch my footsteps—
Augustus: —or you'd fall lame.
Phebe: And to keep my mouth shut
when the wind blowed—
Augustus: —or else the wind spirit
would steal your soul.
Phebe: How'd you know?
Augustus: You think she's the only conjure-woman
in the world? Why, your Scylla's a baby
compared to the voodoo chiefs in the islands.
They can kill you with a puff of smoke
from their pipes—if you believe in them.
Take me: I've been cursed enough times
to bring down a whole fleet of ships
around me—but here I sit, high and dry.
So I guess they must be saving me
for something special.

(*Phebe looks at Augustus in wonder; the lights dim as the other slaves slowly come on stage, singing as they take their places in the fields. The song sung during the "shout" has modulated into a percussive piece with no words—clapping, sighs, whispered exclamations and grunts punctuate what becomes a work song.*)

Slaves: No way out, gotta keep on—
No way but to see it through.
Narrator: Don't sass, don't fight!
Lay low, grin bright!
Narrator/Slaves: No way but to see it through.

SCENE V

The cotton fields. The light brightens: high noon. Jones enters, looks at the sun and cracks his whip as he calls out.

Jones: Noon!

(*He exits, wiping his brow with a huge handkerchief. The slaves groan and sigh as they settle down with their provisions—cornpone and salt pork and gourds of water.*)

Alexander (*making sure that Jones is out of earshot*): I swear on all my years
    there's nothing I hate so much as cotton.
    Picking, toting, weighing, tramping:
    the work keeps coming.
Scipio: No end in sight, and that's the truth!

(*Leans back, hands under head.*)

    Now what I'd fancy is a life at sea.
    Sun and sky and blue water,
    with just a sip of rum
    every once in a while.
    You been to sea, Augustus.
    What's it like?
Augustus: It ain't the easy life.
Scipio: But what's it like, man?
    The closest I been to the sea
    was when the cotton gin came in
    to Charleston port. All those fine
    flapping sails and tall masts,
    cotton bales stacked to heaven . . .
    Did you visit lots of strange places?
Augustus: We sailed the West Indies route.
    Stocked up rum, tobacco, beads—
Scylla (*scathingly*): —and traded them for slaves.
    Did you have to ride cargo?
Augustus (*with a sharp look, sarcastically*): Cap'n Newcastle was a generous master.

(*Resuming his story.*)

    But those ports! Sand so white,
    from far off it looked like
    spilled cream. Palm trees taller
    than our masts, loaded with coconuts.
Diana: What's a coconut?
Augustus: It's a big brown gourd
    with hair on it like a dog,
    and when you break it open
    sweet milk pours out.
Diana: What does it taste like?
Augustus: It tastes like . . .
    just coconut. There's nothing like it.
Scylla: Your stories stir up trouble,
    young man.

(*Phebe moves as if to stop him; he motions her back.*)

Augustus: Seems you're the only one
    who's riled up, Scylla.

Scylla: You're what we call an uppity nigger.
     And uppity niggers always trip themselves up.
Augustus: Are you going to put a curse on me, too,
     Scylla? Cross your eyes
     and wave a few roots in the air
     until I fall on my knees?
Scylla: No need to curse you;
     you have been cursed already.
Augustus: You feed on ignorance
     and call it magic. What kind of prophet
     works against her own people?

(*The slaves murmur. Scylla stands up.*)

Scylla: Oh, you may dance now,
     but you will fall.
     The evil inside you
     will cut you down to your knees,
     and you will crawl—crawl in front of us all!

(*Lights dim, then grow mottled and swamp-green as all exit.*)

SCENE VI

The swamp. Lights remain mottled and swamp-green. Night sounds filter in as Hector enters.

Hector: Easy, easy: don't tell the cook
     the meat's gone bad.

(*Slashes at the underbrush.*)

We got to cut it out.
Ya! Ya!

(*Hacks in rhythm for a moment.*)

I can smell it. Pah!

(*Sniffs, then peers.*)

But there's a rose in the gravy, oh yes—
a rose shining through the mists, a red smell.
Red and mean.

But how sweet she smelled!
Cottons and flowers.
And lemons that bite back
when you touch them to the tongue.

Shh! Don't tell the cook.
Black folks fiddle, the white folks stare.

(*There is a bird call; Hector conceals himself. Augustus enters; he appears to be following the sound. He gives out a matching call, then bursts into a clearing in the swamp where a group of black men sit in a circle around a small fire, chanting softly. The Leader of the group rises.)*

Leader: There you are!
    We've called two nights.
Augustus: Who are you?
Leader: Patience, Augustus Newcastle.
    Oh yes, we know all about you.
Augustus: What do you want?
Leader: Your courage has been a beacon—
Conspirators: Amen! Selah!

(The Conspirators surrounded the Leader; they react to his words in a call-and-response fashion; their movements are vaguely ritualistic and creepy, as if they were under a spell; this effect can be enhanced with dance and pantomime. Augustus stands still as the Conspirators swarm around him, occasionally trying to pull him among them.)

Leader: —and we need men willing to fight
    for freedom! Tell me, Augustus Newcastle:
    are you prepared to sign your name
    with the revolutionary forces?
Augustus: First tell me who you are.
Leader: So cautious? We expected a bit more daring
    from someone of your reputation.
Augustus: I am many things, but I'm not a fool.
Leader *(laughs)*: Shall we show him, brothers?
Conspirators: Selah!
Leader: Each of us has been called forth
    as a warrior of righteousness.
    Each wandered in darkness
    until he found the light of brotherhood!
    Take young Benjamin Skeene:

(Benjamin squares his shoulders as he steps forward; he is a trim young man who, judging from his clothes, must be either a house slave or a freeman.)

    As a skilled carpenter, he enjoys
    a fair amount of freedom.
Benjamin: The boss man's glad
    I can make his deliveries.
Leader: So we've arranged a few
    deposits of our own.
    Benjamin, can you find a way
    to fasten this blade to a pole?
Benjamin: Easy.
Leader: Every man who can wield a stick
    shall have a bayonet!
Conspirators: Selah!
Leader: A few were more reluctant . . .
    or shall I say cautious?
    Henry Blake, for instance:

(*Henry, a dark middle-aged man, steps forward hesitantly.*)

Fear had made him grateful
for every crumb his master dropped him.

(*The two act out the following exchange.*)

Henry: I don't want no part of this!
Leader: You followed the sign;
  you have been called!
Henry: Any fool knows a mockingbird
  when he hears one—and that
  weren't no mockingbird!
Leader (*threatening*): Are you prepared to slay
  our oppressors, male and female,
  when it is deemed time, according
  to the plans of insurrection drawn up
  and approved by members present?
Henry: I'm against the white man
  much as all of you—but murder?
  "Thou shalt not kill," saith the
  Commandments.
Leader: Who made your master?
Henry: God.
Leader: And who made you?
Henry: God.
Leader: Then aren't you as good as your master
  if God made you both?
Henry: I'm not a vengeful man.
Leader: But our Lord is a vengeful God.
  "Whoever steals a man," He says,
  "whether he sells him or
  is found in possession of him,
  shall be put to death."

Who is not with us
is against us.
You answered the call.
If you turn back now . . .

(*Henry slowly lifts his head, squares his shoulders, and remains frozen in the spotlight while the Leader speaks to Augustus.*)

Leader: He was brought to reason.
Conspirators: Selah.
Leader: So the one becomes many
  and the many, one.
  Hence our password:
  "May Fate be with you—
Conspirators: And with us all!"
Augustus: Now I see who you are.

Leader: Augustus Newcastle: are you prepared
　　to slay our oppressors,
　　male and female,
　　when it is deemed time, according
　　to the plans of insurrection
　　drawn up and approved by members present?
Augustus: I am.
Leader: Enter your name in the Book of Redemption!

　　(Augustus signs the book.)

Conspirators: Selah! Selah!
Augustus: Tell me what to do.
Leader: You'll need a second-in-command.
　　Report your choice to us;
　　we will send out the sign.

　　(Turning to the group.)

　　My brothers, it is time to be free!
　　Maps are being prepared
　　of the city and its surroundings
　　along with the chief points of attack.
　　Bullets wait in kegs under the dock.
　　Destiny calls!
Conspirators: Amen!
Leader: There are barrels of gun powder
　　stacked in a cave outside Dawson's Plantation.
　　Our Toby has been busy—

　　(Conspirators nod and laugh in consent.)

　　but he cannot risk further expeditions.
　　Henry Blake!

　　(Henry steps forward.)

　　Your owner praised you in the marketplace
　　as the most trustworthy nigger
　　he ever had the fortune of owning.
　　Now it is up to you
　　to put your master's trust to the test.

　　(Henry bows his head in assent, steps back into the group.)

　　Destiny calls us! The reckoning is nigh!
　　But remember: trust no one.
　　All those who are not with us
　　are against us, blacks as well
　　as whites. Oh, do not falter!
　　Bolster your heart with the memory
　　of the atrocities committed upon your mother:

Gird your loins with vengeance,
  strap on the shining sword of freedom!
Conspirators: Selah!
Leader: Brothers, are you with me?
Conspirators: Right behind you!
Leader: Then nothing can stop us now!
Augustus (blurting out): My orders! What are my orders?
Leader (a little taken aback, but decides on the role of the amused patriarch):
  Patience, my son! Patience and cunning.
  Sow discontent among your brethren,
  inspire them to fury.
Augustus: I can do more. Read maps, write passes—
Leader: That is all for now.
  Is that clear?

  (*Strained silence; the Leader speaks reassuringly.*)

You will recognize the signal.

  (*The Conspirators begin humming "Steal Away."*)

Go to your people and test their minds;
  so when the fires of redemption
  lick the skies of Charleston,
  they will rise up, up—
  a mighty army
  marching into battle!
Conspirators: Steal away, steal away,
  Steal away to Jesus!
  Steal away, steal away home,
  I ain't got long to stay here.

(*The Conspirators continue singing as they exchange farewells and slip off. Hector appears at the edge of the undergrowth, a dead snake in his outstretched arms.*)

BLACKOUT

SCENE VII

The cotton fields.

Narrator: A sniff of freedom's all it takes
  to feel history's sting;
  there's danger by-and-by
  when the slaves won't sing.

(*Jones supervises the picking, which transpires without singing; the silence is eerie. Jones's appearance is slovenly, as if he's already been drinking.*)

Jones: Move it, nigger! Faster!
  What you glaring at? Faster!

(*The slaves continue picking at the same rate. Jones looks at the sun, then cracks his whip.*)

Aw, the hell with ya! Noon!

(*He stumbles offstage. The slaves divide into two groups: some hum spirituals while the others gather around Augustus.*)

Scipio: Come on, Augustus, what else?
Augustus: Did you know there are slaves
    who have set themselves free?
Scipio (*almost afraid to ask*): How'd they do that?
Augustus: Santo Domingo, San Domingue, Hispaniola—
    three names for an island
    rising like a fortress
    from the waters of the Caribbean.
    An island of sun and forest,
    wild fruit and mosquitoes—
    and slaves, many slaves—half a million.
    Slaves to chop sugar, slaves
    to pick coffee beans, slaves to do
    their French masters' every bidding.

    Then one summer, news came
    from the old country: Revolution!
    Plantation owners broke into a sweat;
    their slaves served cool drinks
    while the masters rocked on their verandas,
    discussing each outrage:
    people marching against the king,
    crowds pouring into the streets,
    shouting three words: *Liberté!*
Slaves: We shall be free!
Augustus: *Égalité!*
Slaves: Master and slave.
Augustus: *Fraternité!*
Slaves: Brothers and sisters!
Augustus: *Liberté, Égalité, Fraternité*—three words
    were all the island masters talked about
    that summer, while their slaves
    served carefully and listened.
Slaves: *Liberté, Égalité, Fraternité!*

(*During the following speech, a smoldering growl among the slaves grows louder and louder, until it explodes in a shout.*)

Augustus: Black men meeting in the forest:
    Eight days, they whispered,
    and we'll be free. For eight days
    bonfires flashed in the hills:
    Equality. For eight days
    tom-toms spoke in the mountains:
    Liberty. For eight days
    the tom-toms sang: Brothers and sisters.
    And on the eighth day, swift as lightning,
    the slaves attacked.

Slaves: Yah!

(*Amalia enters, unseen, and stands listening.*)

Augustus: They came down the mountains
    to the sound of tambourines and conch shells.
    With torches they swept onto the plantations,
    with the long harvest knives
    they chopped white men down
    like sugar cane. For three weeks
    the flames raged; then the sun
    broke through the smoke and shone
    upon a new nation, a black nation—
    Haiti!
Slaves: Haiti!
Augustus (*looking intently at the faces around him*): Now do you see
why they've kept this from us,
    brothers and sisters?
    Amalia: A lovely speech.
(*The slaves are horrified. Augustus stands impassive.*)

    I see you're a poet

    as well as a rebel.
    (*Jones rushes in.*)

    Jones: Anything wrong, Miss Jennings?

Amalia: Not a thing, Jones. Just passing
the time of day with my happy flock—
    which is more than I see you doing.
    Jones: But it's noon, Miss Jennings!
They need nourishment
    if we're going to get this crop in.
    Amalia: It appears they've been getting
a different sort of sustenance.
    Jones (*uncomprehending*): Beg pardon, Ma'am?
Amalia (*impatient with Jones*): See that they work an extra hour tonight.
I don't care if they have to pick by moonlight!
    (*To Augustus.*)

    As for you: I'll see you

    up at the house. Come at sunset—
    the view over the fields
    is most enchanting then.
    (*She strides off. Blackout.*)

SCENE VIII

The big house, Louis's study and the parlor.

Twilight filters through the curtains; the frogs have started up in the swamp.

Louis paces back and forth in his room, holding a chart; he stops to stare at it for a moment, then waves it in disgust and paces once more.

Louis: Something's out there: I can feel it!
    What a discovery it would be.
    But no—

(Grabs his brandy.)

No new coin shines
for Louis LaFarge
among the stars!

(He stops at the window and stares out.)

(Amalia sits in the parlor reading, a decanter of sherry and a tea service on the table next to the sofa. The evening song of the slaves floats in from the fields—a plaintive air with a compelling affirmation of life, a strange melody with no distinct beat or tune. Ticey, the old house slave, enters.)

Ticey: Miss Amalia?
Amalia *(without turning)*: Yes?
Ticey: That new slave, Ma'am—
    he's standing at the front porch!
Amalia *(amused)*: The front porch? Well, show him in, Ticey!

(Ticey exits; Amalia rises and goes to the window. She is looking out toward the fields when Augustus appears in the doorway. Although she knows he is there, she does not turn around.)

Amalia: What are they singing?
Augustus: No words you'd understand.
    No tune you'd recognise.
Amalia: And how is it they all sing together?
Augustus: It's the sorrow songs.
    They don't need a psalm book.
Amalia *(resumes her imperious manner)*: "Personal servant to Captain Newcastle
    of the schooner Victoria. Ports of call:
    St. Thomas, Tobago, St. Croix,
    Martinique"—in other words, a slave ship.
Augustus: Yes.
Amalia: And what did you learn
    under your captain's tutelage?
Augustus: Reading. Writing. Figures.
Amalia: What did you read?
Augustus: Milton. The Bible.
    And the Tales of the Greeks.
Amalia *(thrusting the book she's been reading at him)*:
    See the blue ribbon sticking out?
    You may start there.

(Augustus turns the book over to read the title, then looks at her for a moment before returning. She snatches the book.)

Amalia: Too difficult? No doubt you'd do better
  with the Greek original—

(*Slyly.*)

but we are not that cultured a household.

(*Circling him.*)

I wondered could there be a nigger alive
  smart as this one's claimed to be?
  Of course, if there were, he might
  be smart enough to pretend
  he wasn't smart at all.
Augustus: No pretense. I've read that one already.
  In my opinion, the Greeks
  were a bit too predictable.
Amalia: A slave has no opinion!

(*Regaining her composure.*)

I could have you flogged to your bones
  for what you did today.
Augustus: Why didn't you?

(*The slaves stop singing.*)

Amalia: Daddy said a master knows his slaves
  better than they know themselves.
  And he never flogged a slave—
  he said it was a poor businessman
  who damaged his own merchandise.
Augustus (*sarcastically*): An enlightened man, your father.
Amalia: He let me run wild until
  it was time to put on crinolines.
  My playmates were sent to the fields,
  and I was sent to the parlor with needlework—
  a scented, dutiful daughter.
Augustus: Most men find intelligence troubling
  in a woman—even fathers.
Amalia: Then, off I went to finishing school: Miss Peeters'
  Academy for Elocution and Deportment!
  "The art of conversation," she used to say—
  please, sit down!—"is to make
  the passing of time agreeable."

(*Arranging her dress as she sits on the sofa.*)

"Suitable subjects are—"
Sit down, I said!

(*Softer, but with an edge.*)

One does not conduct conversation
while standing.

(*She indicates a chair, upholstered in champagne-colored tufted damask. Augustus moves toward it but swiftly and gracefully drops cross-legged to the floor, daringly close to Amalia's slippered feet. She starts to pull away—then slowly extends her feet again.*)

"Suitable subjects for
genteel conversation are:

(*Ticking them off on her fingers.*)

"Nature. Travel. History.
And above all, culture—
painting, music, and books."

Well, we're done with books!
Tell me, Mr. Newcastle—
was the weather in the Indies
very different from here?
Augustus: Warmer.
Amalia: Is that all?
Augustus: There was always a breeze.
Amalia: And an abundance of exotic
foods, I'm sure.
Augustus: We had our share of papaya.

(*The slaves start up a new song, more African in rhythm and harmonies.*)

Amalia: Imagine that. Subject number two:
Travel. So many ports!

(*Shaking her head charmingly.*)

Did Captain Newcastle
allow you to go ashore
at St. Thomas, Tobago, Martinique?
Augustus (on guard): No.
Amalia: Charleston has welcomed a fair
share of immigrants to her shores.

(*Laughs delicately.*)

There was that Haiti business around the time
I was born. Over five hundred French plantation owners
fled here. The whole city was in panic.
Why, my dear husband—hear him pacing
up there, wearing out the floorboards?—
little Louis showed up in Charleston harbor
that year, with his blue blood *maman* and *papa*.
Liberté, Égalité, Fraternité!

(*Looking directly at Augustus.*)

It was a brilliant revolution.
I've often wondered why our niggers
don't revolt. I've said to myself:

"Amalia, if you had been a slave,
you most certainly would have plotted
an insurrection by now."

(*Turns away from Augustus.*)

But we say all sorts of things
to ourselves, don't we?
There's no telling what we'd do
if the moment were there for the taking.

(*Lights up on Louis, still staring out the window.*)

Louis: You can't hide forever.
There's a hole in the heavens,
and you're throbbing right behind it.

(*Whispers.*)

I can feel you.
Amalia: Have you ever heard of the *Amistad*?
Augustus: Why?
Amalia: The *Amistad*:° a slave ship.
Three days off the port of Principe
the Africans freed themselves
and attacked with machetes and harpoons.
Cinque, their leader, spared two sailors
to steer them back to Africa.
But Cinque was unfamiliar with the stars
in our hemisphere. Each morning
he set course east by the sun;
each night the sailors turned the ship
and steered west—until they managed
to land on our coast and deliver
Cinque and his followers to execution.
Augustus: A bit of a storybook ending, isn't it?
Amalia: What's that supposed to mean?
Augustus: It's just so perfect a lesson.
Amalia: You don't believe me?
It was in the newspapers.

(*Significantly.*)

You followed your precious captain
everywhere; you were there when
he loaded slave cargo into the hold

Amistad: On July 2, 1839, a group of enslaved Africans being transported on the Spanish schooner *Amistad* rose up against their captors. Arrested when the ship drifted into Long Island Sound, they were tried on charges of piracy and murder. The outcome of the case is quite different from Amalia's version above. The case reached the Supreme Court, which in 1841 upheld their petition for their freedom, whereupon the survivors were released and returned to Africa.

or plotted a new course.
What an admirable science, navigation!
It must be terribly complicated,
even for you.

Augustus (*getting up from the floor*): Now I have a story for you.
Once there was a preacher slave
went by the name of Isaac.
When God called him
he was a boy, out hunting rice birds.
Killing rice birds is easy—
just pinch off their heads.

(*Indicating the sherry.*)

May I?

(*Amalia flinches, nods. He pours the sherry expertly.*)

But one day, halfway up the tree
where a nest of babies chirped,
a voice called out: "Don't do it, Isaac."
It was an angel, shining
in the crook of a branch.
Massa let him preach.
What harm could it do?

(*Sitting down in the damask chair.*)

Then a slave uprising in Virginia
had all the white folks
watching their own niggers
for signs of treachery.
No more prayer meetings, Isaac!
But God would not wait,
so Isaac kept on preaching
at night, in the woods.

Of course he was caught.
Three of his congregation
were shot on the spot, three others branded
and their feet pierced.
But what to do about Isaac,
gentle Isaac who had turned traitor?

Amalia: Is there a point to this?
Augustus: I'm just passing the time of evening
with . . . conversation.

(*Upstairs, Louis positions his telescope at the window and searches the heavens.*)

Louis: There it is . . . no, wait!
Gone.

(*Shakes his head in despair.*)

Sometimes I catch
a glimmer, a hot blue flash—
then it disappears.
Show yourself, demon!

(*In the parlor, Augustus takes a sip of sherry and continues.*)

Augustus: First they flogged him. Then
they pickled the wounds with salt water,
and when they were nearly healed,
he was flogged again, and the wounds
pickled again, and on and on for weeks
while Massa sold off Isaac's children
one by one. They took him to see
his wife on the auction block,
baby at her breast.
A week later it was his turn.
His back had finally healed;
but as his new owner led him
from the auction block,
Isaac dropped down dead.

(*Pause; more to himself than to Amalia.*)

They couldn't break his spirit,
so they broke his heart.

(*They stare at each other for a moment; then Amalia rises and walks to the window. It has gotten dark outside.*)

Amalia: They're still singing.
How can they have songs left?
Augustus (*joining her at the window*): As many songs as sorrows.
Amalia: And you, Augustus? Were you ever happy?
Augustus: Happy? No.
Amalia: Never? Not even on the ship
with the whole sea around you?
Augustus: I was a boy. I felt lucky, not happy.
Amalia: I was happy once.
I traded it for luck.
Augustus: Luck's a dangerous master.
Amalia: Half my life I spent dreaming,
the other half burying dreams.

(*Bitter laugh, turns to Augustus.*)

Funny, isn't it?
Augustus (*turns away from her with difficulty, stares out the window*):
One soft spring night
when the pear blossoms
cast their pale faces
on the darker face of the earth,
Massa stood up from the porch swing

and said to himself, "I think
I'll make me another bright-eyed pickaninny."
Then he stretched and headed
for my mother's cabin. And now—
that pickaninny, who started out
no more than the twinkle in a white man's eye
and the shame between his mama's legs—
now he stands in the parlor of
another massa, entertaining the pretty mistress
with stories of whippings and heartbreak.
Amalia (half to herself): Pretty? Am I pretty?
Augustus (answers in spite of himself): You can put a rose in a vase
with a bunch of other flowers;
but when you walk into the room
the rose is the only thing you see.

(*Amalia touches his wrist, then traces the vein up his arm, as if remembering.*)

Amalia: Imagine! A life without even
a smidgen of happiness . . .
Augustus (wrestling with desire): I'm not one of your dreams.
Amalia: No? Perhaps not. What a pity.

(*She touches his cheek; he holds her hand there. They lean towards each other slowly, as the slaves' sorrow song surges—but before their lips touch, there is a blackout.*)

ACT II

SCENE I

Dream sequence.

Dimly lit, the light rather blue. Each group is in its appointed "place" on stage—Amalia in her parlor with Ticey standing impassively in the background; Louis above, in his study; most slaves going about their chores; Scylla isolated, with her herbs and potions. In the swamp, Hector searches for snakes; the Conspirators huddle, occasionally lifting a fist into the circle. Augustus stands front and center, back to the audience, gazing at Amalia. Mostly silhouettes are seen, except when a single voice rises out of the chanting which will grow to cacophony at the end of the sequence.

Slaves: They have bowed our heads,
they have bent our backs.
Mercy, mercy,
Lord above, mercy.
Amalia: I slept, but my heart was awake.
How beautiful he is!
Slaves: Lord have mercy.
They have bowed our heads . . .
Scylla: There's a curse on the land.
The net draws closer.

Hector: Under rocks, 'twixt reeds and roots . . .
Slaves: They have bent out backs,
  they have snatched our songs . . .
Augustus (singing): Sometimes I feel like a motherless child . . .
Slaves (joining in): A motherless child, a motherless child,
  sometimes I feel like a motherless child—

(*Continue humming through most of the scene.*)

Louis (in a scientific voice, detached, as if reciting):
  Every night at the same hour, each star appears
  slightly to the west of its previous position.
  Scientists calculate that the 12 houses of the zodiac
  have shifted so radically since ancient times,
  their relation to each other
  may now signify completely different portents.
Hector: So many, so many.
Slaves (singing): A long way from home.
Augustus: One soft night, Massa stood up—
Conspirators: Selah.
Augustus: —and laughed to himself.
Conspirators: It is time.
Scylla: The net draws tighter.
Conspirators: Selah!
Augustus: One darkening evening, I stood up—

(*Slaves humming, Conspirators chanting "Selah" in a barely audible whisper.*)

  —and she was mine,
  mine all night, until
  the day breathed fire
  and the shadows fled.
Amalia: Look, how beautiful he is!
Conspirators: Rise up!
Slaves (simultaneously): Mercy, mercy.
Amalia: His eyes, his brow, his cheeks—
Conspirators: Rise up!
Amalia: —his lips . . .
Augustus: . . . until the day breathed fire . . .
Hector: Eshu Elewa . . . ogo . . . gbogbo.
Slaves: They have bowed our heads,
  they have bent our backs.
Scylla: Closer . . .

(*Phebe dashes to center-stage, hands outstretched as if to hold back a flood.*)

Phebe: Stop it! Stop!!!

(*Everyone freezes.*)

SCENE II

The tableau remains.

Phebe drops her arms and moves slightly stage-left. Augustus, with his back still to the audience, backs downstage, towards the slave cabins, looking alternately at Amalia and the Conspirators until the tableau disintegrates. Phebe taps him on the shoulder, and he whirls around.

Phebe: Evenin'.
Augustus: Oh! Phebe. Evening.
Phebe: You're trembling.
Augustus: I am?

(*Laughs.*)

Cold spell coming on, I imagine.
Phebe: No, that's what you said to me!

(*Augustus looks at her, uncomprehending.*)

That time I was coming back from Scylla's,
scared to open my mouth, you said:
"What's your hurry?" And then you said,
"You're trembling," and I said, "I am?"
—just like you did now.
Augustus: Oh.
Phebe: What's your hurry?
Heading up to the House again?
Augustus: I got a moment.
Phebe: Sit yourself down, then.
Rest a spell.

(*They sit side by side; Phebe embarrassed, Augustus nervous.*)

Phebe: You sure be up there a long time.
At the Big House, I mean.
Augustus (*tersely*): Missy's orders.
Phebe: What else she have you doing?
Augustus: We practice the fine art of conversation.
Phebe: Quit fooling!
Augustus: Oh, yes, we talk about everything—
weather and the science of navigation,
recent history and ancient literature.
Phebe: What's that she-fox up to now?
Augustus: It's simple: she wants to tame me.
And if I get better treatment
than the rest of you,
all my talk about Haiti
won't hold much water.
Phebe: So she think she can get us
to fighting amongst ourselves!
Augustus: Seems plenty folks want things
just the way they are.
Alexander keeps his distance, lately.

Phebe: Alexander's seen his share of sorrow.
　　　He just wants to live in peace.
Augustus: And die in peace?
Phebe (not catching his drift): I 'spect so. Who doesn't?
　　　Oh, that's right—
　　　you and Death gonna walk outta here
　　　hand in hand!

(Phebe laughs; Augustus is spooked.)

　　　Alexander don't mean you no spite.
　　　And Scipio—Scipio say
　　　you his man, any time, any place!
　　　You shoulda seen him the other day,
　　　putting voodoo spells on the chickens!
　　　Then he pick up the milk bucket
　　　and pranced around, serving up
　　　revolution lemonade! Now there's
　　　a body need of some occupation!
Augustus (aside): Maybe I can help him find it.
Phebe: 'Course, you got Diana's heart.
　　　She thinks the sun and the moon
　　　set in your face.
Augustus: Then there's Scylla.
Phebe: Hmmpf! Woman had me nearly crazy,
　　　clamping my mouth and wiping my
　　　footsteps
　　　so I ended up getting nowhere.
　　　As far as I'm concerned,
　　　Scylla can roll her eye and talk conjuration
　　　till the summer go cold and the cotton pick itself!
Augustus: Now, that's the fire I saw!
Phebe: Huh?
Augustus: The first time I saw you,
　　　I thought to myself:
　　　"That's not the spirit of a slave.
　　　That's a pure flame."

(Phebe tucks her head.)

Phebe (flattered): Go on.
Augustus: Tell me—how did you land
　　　on the Jennings Plantation?
Phebe: I didn't land at all. I was borned here.
Augustus: So this is your home.
Phebe: Much as any of us got
　　　a home on this earth.
Augustus: And your folks?
Phebe: My father was sold before I was borned.
　　　Mama . . . it's a long story.

Augustus: I got time.

(*Phebe stares down at the ground as if she's conjuring the memory out of the dust; then she begins.*)

Phebe: Mama worked in the kitchen until
I was about five; that's when
fever broke out in the quarters.
She used to set table scraps out
for the field hands, and I
stuck wildflowers in the baskets
to pretty 'em up. Mama said
you never know what a flower can mean
to somebody in misery.

That fever tore through the cabins like wildfire.
Massa Jennings said the field hands
spread contamination and forbid them
to come up to the house, but
Mama couldn't stand watching them
just wasting away—so she started
sneaking food to the quarters at night.

Then the fever caught her too.
She couldn't hide it long.
And Massa Jennings found out.

(*Gulps a deep breath for strength, reliving the scene.*)

Mama started wailing right there at the stove.
Hadn't she been a good servant?
Who stayed up three nights straight
to keep Massa's baby girl among the living
when her own mother done left this world?
Who did he call when the fire
needed lighting? Who mended the pinafores
Miss Amalia was forever snagging on bushes?

Mama dropped to her knees
and stretched out her arms along the floor.
She didn't have nowheres to go;
she'd always been at the Big House.
"Where am I gonna lay
my poor sick head?" she asked.

He stood there, staring
like she was a rut in the road,
and he was trying to figure out
how to get round it.

Then he straightened his waistcoat
and said: "You have put me and my child
in the path of mortal danger,
and you dare ask me what to do

with your nappy black head?"
He didn't even look at her—
just spoke off into the air
like she was already a ghost.

(*Woodenly.*)

She died soon after.

(*Augustus takes Phebe into his arms.*)

Augustus (*a bit helplessly*): Lord have mercy.
Phebe: Mercy had nothing to do with it.
   Ain't that what you said?
Augustus: Phebe, how far would you go
   to avenge your mother's death?
Phebe: There you go again
   with your revolution talk.
Augustus: How far?
Phebe: We ain't got no tom-toms
   like them slaves in Haiti!
Augustus: You don't need tom-toms.
   Just a bird call.

(*Phebe looks at him, uncomprehending. Augustus stares off.*)

(*Stage dims to black: a single spot on the Narrator.*)

Narrator: What is it about him, girl—
   the book-learning, his acquaintance with the world?
   He can stand up to a glare,
   but he doesn't know his heart.
   Look around you, child: It's growing dark.

SCENE III

The cotton house.

Almost sundown: Jones is in the field supervising the bringing in of the cotton, which has been weighed and now must be tramped down in order to be stored. There is the steady beat of stomping feet throughout the scene. Phebe and Augustus are outside the cotton house.

Phebe: Any news?
Augustus: I expect another signal
   any day now. Then I'll know more.
Phebe: What are they waiting for?
   You reckon something's gone wrong—
Augustus (*calming her*): Shh. They have their reasons.
   Patience.

(*Phebe catches him looking at the sky.*)

Phebe (*with a mixture of jealousy and trepidation*): You better get on up there—
   sun's almost touching.

(*Phebe scoots inside the cotton house. Augustus studies the horizon, his expression inexplicable, then exits as Jones enters from the fields, urging along the next group bearing cotton. The slaves are sweaty and tired. Jones looks after Augustus; it's clear he's been told not to interfere.*)

Jones: Keep it moving!
　　Don't be looking at the sun;
　　you got a whole long while
　　before your day is over!

(*Jones exits. The scene opens to the inside of the cotton house; Scipio dumps the sacks of cotton onto the floor while the other slaves tramp it down. The dull thud of stomping feet punctuates the dialogue; changes in pace and rhythm signal changes in mood and tension. On his way for the next sack of cotton, Scipio looks out the one small window.*)

Scipio: There he goes.
Alexander: Every evening, same time.
Scylla: It's the devil's work afoot, for sure.
Scipio: It *is* peculiar! I wonder—
Phebe: It ain't your task to wonder.
Scipio: What's the matter with you, gal?
　　Most times you're the one speculating
　　about other folks' doings.
　　Maybe you're sweet on him.

(*General laughter.*)

Phebe: If you ain't finding fault with someone,
　　you all laughing at them! We all been
　　called up to the house one time or another.
　　Ain't nothing special in that.
Scylla: For weeks on end? As soon as
　　the sun eases into the sycamores,
　　there ain't a hair of his to be seen
　　till daylight.

(*Significant pause.*)

　　Except maybe on his lady's pillow.
Phebe: What are you trying to say, Scylla?
Scylla: I ain't *trying* to say nothing.
Alexander: He's certainly the boldest nigger
　　I've ever seen.
Scipio (*shaking his head in admiration*): That's the truth there!
　　The way he handles Massa Jones—
　　no bowing or scraping for him.
　　That eye of his could cut
　　through stone. Jones don't know
　　what to do with that nigger!
　　He's plain scared, and that's a fact.

Phebe: Maybe they're just talking.

Diana: Augustus is nice.

Alexander: Nice as the devil was to Eve.

Scylla: A slave and his missus
    ain't got nothing to talk about.
    Oh, he might have bold ideas,
    but he'll never put them to work.
    She'll see to that.

Phebe: What do you mean?

Scylla: That first master of his kept him in style.
    That's why he ran away so much afterwards—
    he ain't used to being treated like a regular slave.
    A whip can't make him behave:
    Miss Amalia knows that.
    So she's trying another way—
    and it appears to be working.

Scipio: Well, I'll be.

Diana: What 'pears to be working?

Scylla: What's the only thing
    white folks think
    a nigger buck's good for?
    It wouldn't be the first time.

Alexander (slowly): If that's what he's doing,
    he's headed for big trouble.

Phebe: I don't believe it!
    And even if it's true, it's 'cause
    he ain't got no choice!

Scylla: You been mighty contrary lately, Phebe.

Phebe: I ain't afraid of every shadow!

Scipio (trying to avert disaster): Scylla, don't mind her.
    She's feeling the weather.

Scylla: I'm warning you, Phebe.

Phebe: I already got a pack of curses
    on my head. A few more won't hurt.

Alexander: Phebe! Don't talk to Scylla like that!

Phebe: Should have done it a long time ago.
    Woman had me nearly crazy!
    If anyone around here's putting
    sharp stones in my path,
    it ain't no earth spirit.
    If there's a curse here,
    Scylla, it's you.

    (Everyone stops stamping.)

Diana: Phebe . . .

Phebe: Yes, Scylla, you're the curse—
    with all your roots and potions.
    Tell me: How come you never put a spell
    on Miss Amalia? Why didn't you
    sprinkle some powder over a candle

to make her house go up in flames
one night? That would have been some magic.

(*Timid murmurs from the others.*)

Scylla: I do what the spirits tell me.
Phebe: Then those slaves in Haiti
    must have known some better spirits.
Scylla: Some nigger comes in here with
    a few pretty stories,
    and you think he's the Savior!
Alexander: Dear Lord!
Phebe: The Savior was never
    to your liking, Scylla.
    He took too much attention
    away from you.
Alexander: Have mercy!
Scylla (*drawing herself into her full "conjurer" posture*):
    There's a vine in the woods
    with a leaf like a saw blade.
    One side of the leaf is shiny dark
    and pocked like skin;
    the other side is dusty gray.
    Touch the gray side to a wound,
    the sore will shut and heal.
    But touch it with the shiny side,
    and the wound will boil up
    and burst open.
Phebe: Always talking in riddles!
    Why don't you come right out and
    say what you mean for a change?

(*Agreeing murmurs; Scylla looks darkly around until everyone grows silent.*)

Scylla: Alright, I'll tell you direct.
    Your Augustus is pretty clever—
    been lots of places and knows
    the meanings of words and things like that.
    But something's foul in his blood,
    and what's festering inside him
    nothing this side of the living
    can heal. A body hurting that bad
    will do anything to get relief—anything.

(*Looking around at all of them.*)

So keep talking about Haiti
and sharpening your sticks!
But know one thing:
that nigger's headed for destruction,
and you're all headed there with him.

(*They stare at her as the lights dim to blackout.*)

SCENE IV

The swamp.

Night: mottled light. Strangely twisted branches, replete with Spanish moss and vines; huge gnarled roots slick with wet. The whole resembles abstract gargoyles in a gothic cathedral. There's a gigantic tree trunk. At some remove—in front of the proscenium, or silhouetted against the backdrop—the slaves pantomime the motions of evening chores: mending tools, shelling beans, stirring the stew.

When the lights come up, Hector is puttering around the perimeter of the swamp, muttering to himself; he finds a snake and lifts it up triumphantly before whacking off the head.

Hector: Hah! So many—under rocks, 'twixt reeds,
    they lie and breed, breed, breed.
    The wicked never rest.

    (*Stops, listens.*)

    What's that? Someone coming?

    (*He scrambles for cover as Henry and Augustus enter, stop, and shake hands.*)

Henry: Good night, friend.
    We will be victorious.
Augustus: May Fate be with us, brother.
Henry: Oh she is, brother, she is.
    It was a golden day
    when Fate brought you to us.

    (*They exchange the secret handshake; Henry exits. Augustus looks after him; then, as soon as he thinks he's alone, he sinks down on a fallen log, burying his face in his hands. Hector—well hidden from Augustus but visible to the audience—looks on with keen interest; he recognizes this kind of despair. Augustus's soliloquy is more an agitated outpouring than a reflective speech.*)

Augustus: Compass and sextant. Ropes thick as my wrist,
    coiled like greased snakes. A cutlass.
    The rough caress of the anchor line slithering
    between my boy palms. The hourglass tipped,
    surrendering sand in a thin stream of sighs.
    Clouded belly of the oil lamp dangling from a chain.
    And everything rocking, rocking.

    (*Hums a lullaby.*)

    Dark green pillows, salve for my wounds.
    "Who did this to you, boy?"
    "It was the sun, Father; see its spokes?"
    "Child of midnight, the sun can't hurt you!"

    (*Sings softly.*)

    "Jesus Savior pilot me
    over life's tempestuous sea . . ."

(*Speaks.*)

And when she looks at me—
such a cool sweet look—
each scar weeps like an open wound.

(*Softer.*)

If fear eats out the heart,
what does love do?

(*Hector springs out of hiding; Augustus jumps up.*)

Hector: You! I've seen you before.
Augustus (*relieved*): That you have, my friend.
    I'm from the Jennings Plantation, like you.
Hector (*stares at him suspiciously*): Like me? Like me you say?
    We'll see about that.

(*Circles him, inspecting.*)

What are you doing in my swamp?
Augustus: Taking a walk. Breathing the night air.
Hector: Wrong! You were with someone.
    I saw you!
Augustus: Just a friend, Hector. Don't you have friends?
Hector: I saw you. I heard you!
    How do you know my name?
Augustus: We met before, don't you remember?
    I'm the new slave on the Jennings Plantation.
Hector: You're the one who came in leg irons,
    along the road—

(*Circling him very closely, so that Augustus must back up.*)

I never heard of leg irons on this plantation before.

(*Crowds Augustus, who trips on a root and falls.*)

You must be dangerous.
Augustus: I was sold in chains and spent my first night
    in the barn. The overseer
    didn't have enough sense to take them off
    until Amalia gave the order—
Hector: Amalia? Amalia!
    You are plotting some evil.
Augustus: You've got swamp fever, old man.
    I plan no evil.
Hector: I heard you!
    Men come and go in wagons.
    They whisper and shake hands.
    They come out at night
    when the innocent sleep.
Augustus: These men—what do they look like?

Hector: They have the devil's eye.

Augustus: Are they black men, or white?

Hector: You are one of them!

Augustus: If they are black, black like
  me and you, how can they be evil?

Hector (vehemently): No, no—the world's not right, don't you see?
  I took the curse as far away as I could.

Augustus: There is no curse!

Hector (draping moss and vines over the tree trunk to make a "throne"):
  Ah, but the little mother's gone.
  And I came here where evil
  bubbles out of the ground.
  Once I didn't watch out;
  I got lost in the smell of a rose
  and snap!—the snake bit down.
  Little mother was mother no more.

Augustus: I'm no snake, Hector.

Hector: Evil isn't the snake, little man.
  Evil is what grows the snake.

  (Gazing into the distance.)

  Such a cool sweet look . . .

  (Cuts a piercing glance at Augustus, who recognizes his own words and is on guard—though against what, he's not sure.)

Augustus: You *are* crazy.

Hector: Once we had a garden to hide in,
  but we were children.

  (Taking his seat on the throne; with a full sweep of his arm.)

  This is my home now.
  I am king here.

  (Regarding him suspiciously.)

  Every man has his place.

Augustus: And you are fortunate to have found yours.
  They've left you in peace.
  But what of your brothers and sisters?
  They cry out in their bondage.
  They have no place in this world
  to lay their heads.

Hector (in a low growl): You are planning a great evil.
  You come out at night
  when the innocent sleep—

  (Raising his voice.)

  but I won't let you harm her!

Augustus: Shh! Someone might hear.

Hector: I won't let you harm her!

(*Screaming.*)

Danger! Wake up, children!

(*The slaves wake up and stumble out of their cabins, in a bewildered pantomime. The Conspirators also appear and consult each other.*)

Augustus (*grabbing Hector to silence him*): Quiet! Do you want to bring
    the whole pack down on us?
Hector (*hits Augustus in the chest; crazed*): Wake up! Wake up!
    Mother, Father!
    They're coming for us!

(*Hector tries to run out of the swamp. Augustus tackles him from behind.*)

Augustus: Crazy fool! You'll spoil everything!
    I've . . . come . . . to . . . save you!

(*A fierce struggle ensues.*)

Hector (*in a vision from his childhood in Africa*): Fire! Fire!
    The huts . . . the boats . . .
    blood in the water.
    Run, children, run!

(*Augustus gains control and kneels over Hector, choking him; Hector gasps and is finally still. When Augustus realizes Hector is dead, he collapses on the lifeless body.*)

Augustus: Damn you, old man! I came to save you.

(*After a moment, he collects himself and stands up, his voice breaking, more pitiful than angry.*)

Who is not with us, is against us.
Henry: Selah.

(*The slaves begin humming as Augustus kneels and wraps the body in vines, then rolls it under a clump of moss and exposed roots.*)

Augustus: Let these vines be your shroud,
    this moss a pillow for your head.
    These roots will be your coffin,
    this dark water your grave.
Slaves: Selah.
Augustus: Sleep, Hector. Sleep and be free.

(*The slaves look at Scylla, who lifts her hand slowly.*)

Scylla: Eshu Elewa ogo gbogbo.

BLACKOUT

SCENE V

Lights rise on the Narrator.

Narrator: Sweet whispers can leave a bitter taste
    when a body's supposed to be freedom bound.

> Every day as the sun comes easing down,
> our man climbs the stairs to sherry and lace.

Lights rise on the big house, Louis's study and the parlor.

Early evening. Louis sits hunched over his charts. He is excited.

Louis: Nothing in the books.
> Empty sky in all the charts.
> And yet I've seen it, with my own eyes!
> Last night it was the brightest.

> *(Draws a few lines with his compass, looks up wistfully.)*

> What once was a void
> fills with feverish matter.

> *(Louis continues to fiddle with his papers throughout the scene, occasionally jumping up to peer through the telescope.)*

> *(Amalia stands by the fireplace, reading aloud from a book.)*

Amalia: The princess said to her father, "Bring me
> strawberries, I am hungry for strawberries."

> *(She shuts the book.)*

> He came back with a husband instead.

> *(Kneels before the fireplace, trying to start it.)*

> "I'm getting too old to tend the garden,"
> the king said. "Here is a husband for you—
> he will fetch your strawberries."
> The princess stomped her foot and replied
> if she must have a husband,
> she would rather marry the fox,
> who at least knew where the sweetest berries grew.

> And so she ran out of the palace
> and into the woods, on and on
> until a pebble in her shoe forced her to stop.
> But it was not a pebble at all—
> it was the king's head, shrunk to the size
> of a pea.
> "Put me in your pocket,"
> the king pleaded, "and take me away with you."
> Horrified, the princess threw the king's head down
> and ran on. But she had not gone far
> before she had to stop again,
> and this time when she shook out her shoe,
> it was the head of her husband that said:
> "Please put me in your pocket
> so that I may love you wherever you go."
> The princess threw his head down, too,

and ran faster; but before long her shoe stopped her
for the third time. And this time
it was her own head she held in her hands.

(*She burns her hand, curses softly. There is a knock at the door. An agitated Jones
steps into the room, leaving the door open.*)

Jones: Beg pardon for the disturbance, Ma'am,
but the matter's urgent.

(*Amalia rises, pulling her shawl tighter in exasperation, and takes a seat behind the
desk, glaring.*)

Amalia: Since you've barged in, Mr. Jones,
the least you can do is close the door.
There's a chill; I believe I've caught it.
Jones (*closes the door, steps up to the desk*): Just what I wanted to talk to you about,
Miss Jennings. This cold spell—
it'll kill the last of the crops
if we don't get them in soon.

(*Amalia doesn't respond.*)

Ma'am, you let the niggers
leave the fields early.
Amalia: I thought you'd be happy, Mr. Jones.
Aren't such measures part of
your economic philosophy?
Jones: Not when there's cotton to be picked.
Amalia: An hour more or less can hardly matter.
Now—this cold spell is unusual,
but not as threatening
as you make it out to be.
Jones: Well, the niggers sure are spooked.
They're just sitting around or looking off
in the sky. Matter of fact, they ain't even
been tending their own gardens.
Amalia: This late in the season
I don't imagine there's much left to tend.
Jones: And that crazy slave, the one's
got the shack out in the swamp—
Amalia: Hector?
Jones: Yes'm, that's the one I mean.
No one's seen hide nor hair of him.
Amalia: Hector's in the habit of appearing
whenever he has snakes to parade.
Jones: But it's been three days, Ma'am!
Amalia: Cold weather makes the snakes scarce.
Is that all, Jones?
Jones: Yes, Ma'am, as you please.
Good evening, Miss Jennings.

(Jones exits, closing the door behind him. Amalia shakes herself once, briskly, as if trying to restore some measure of reason or calm.)

Amalia: He's just waiting till the cold clears.
 He'll be alright.

(Starts toward the window, stops to look in the mirror.)

 She looked down at her own head,
 cradling it in her cupped palms,
 and cried and cried herself to sleep
 beneath a giant oak tree.
 No one heard her. No one came.
 And so she perished,
 and her body was never found,
 even to this day.

(Listening.)

Augustus?

(Augustus enters, looking worn and preoccupied. Amalia runs to embrace him.)

So you've come after all!

(Reaching out to stroke his chest.)

 You look tired.
Augustus *(uncomfortable)*: I nearly collided with Jones,
 barrelling full steam across the porch.
Amalia: Did he see you?
Augustus: Shadows are kind to niggers.
Amalia: You're not a nigger!
Augustus *(catching her hand by the wrist)*: Yes I am, Amalia.
 Best not forget that.
Amalia *(leading him to the fire)*: Come and get warm.
Augustus *(hanging back)*: What did Jones want?
Amalia: Oh, he was complaining about the weather.
Augustus: The cold's hard on the crops.
 They should be picked fast.
Amalia *(lightly)*: Scylla says the weather will break tomorrow.
Augustus: Since when have you taken to consulting Scylla?
Amalia: I didn't "consult" her.
 She came up today and said,
 "If it please the Mistress,
 the cold has run its course.
 Morn will break warm, no worry."
Augustus: Why should you risk your profit
 on Scylla's words?
Amalia: Look at us, squabbling about agriculture!
 Forget about the weather!
 Who cares what happens out there?
Augustus: Someone's got to care, Missy.

Amalia: Don't call me that.

Augustus: That's what you are. And I'm your slave.
Nothing has changed that.

Amalia (*putting her hand to his mouth; Augustus withdraws, but only slightly*):
Shh! If this is all the world they've left us, then it's ours to make over.
From time to time we can step out
to show ourselves to the people
so they will have someone to blame.

Augustus: It's too late.

Amalia: Don't you think I see the suffering?
Don't you think I know I'm the cause?

(*With sarcasm and self-loathing.*)

But a master cannot allow himself
the privilege of sorrow. A master
must rule, or die.

Augustus (*pained, thinking of Hector*): Dying used to be such
a simple business. Easy—

(*Caresses her neck.*)

as long as there was
nothing to live for.

(*Tightening his grip; Amalia shows no fear.*)

And murder simply a matter of being
on the right side of the knife.

Amalia (*caressing him, pulling his shirt up*): Have you ever used a knife?
Have you ever killed someone?

Augustus (*haunted, evasive*): Now where would I get a knife?

(*Turns abruptly away; from outside, barely audible, come the opening strains of "Steal Away."*)

Amalia (*touching each scar on his back as she talks*): Your back is like a book
no one can bear to read to the end—
each angry gash, each proud welt . . .
But these scars on your side are different.

(*Touching them gently.*)

They couldn't have come from a whipping.
They're more like—more like
markings that turn up in fairy tales
of princes and paupers exchanged at birth.

Augustus: I've had them since birth.

Amalia (*caressing him*): So they are magical!

Augustus: Hardly—unless the art of survival
is in your magician's bag of tricks.

(*Augustus begins to return Amalia's attentions.*)

Amalia: They even look like crowns.
Or suns—exploding suns!
How did you come by them?
Augustus (abrupt): No more stories.
Amalia: Please?
Augustus: Another time.
There's enough sorrow on earth tonight.

(Embracing her.)

And what's the harm in borrowing
a little happiness?
Amalia: Take this, then—

(Kisses him.)

and this—

(He pulls her down on the sofa as the strains of "Steal Away" grow ever more urgent. Augustus appears not to hear. He and Amalia embrace passionately as the light dims.)

SCENE VI

In the slave cemetery.

Hector's funeral. Hector's body is lying in state on a crude platform, covered with a rough blanket. The slaves march around the bier as they sing. After a little while Jones enters and stands uncertainly in the background; Amalia watches from her bedroom window.

Louis sits at his window but has turned his back. He stares into nothingness, brandy glass in hand.

Slaves: Oh Deat' him is a little man,
And him goes from do' to do',
Him kill some souls and him cripple up,
And him lef' some souls to pray.

Do Lord, remember me,
Do Lord, remember me.
I cry to the Lord as de year roll aroun',
Lord, remember me.

Alexander: No children, and his kinfolk
scattered around this world.
Phebe: We were all his friends, Alexander.
Alexander: But his youngest child's
got to pass over and under!
Who's going to do it?
Phebe: Every child on this plantation
was like his child, Alexander.
Don't you worry.
Alexander (breaking down): To die like that, swoll up
and burst open like a—

Phebe: He's at rest now. He don't feel it.

(*The slaves stop marching to prepare for the ritual of the "passing." In this rite, the youngest child of the deceased is passed under and over the coffin to signify the continuity of life.*)

Slaves: My fader's done wid de trouble o' de world,
Wid de trouble o' de world,
Wid de trouble o' de world,
My fader's done wid de trouble o' de world,
Outshine de sun.

(*Augustus appears and he stands at a distance; Phebe goes over to him.*)

Alexander: Here he come, stopping by
when he's good and ready.
Too busy to pay proper respect to the dead.
Scipio: Each soul grieves in its own way.
Phebe: Where were you?
Augustus: I came as soon as I heard—
Phebe (*secretive*): Not here, man. There.

(*Gestures toward the swamp.*)

They were calling for you last night.
Didn't you hear that "Steal Away?"
They sang till I thought the dead
would rise out of their graves and follow!
I was crazy with worry.
Finally I went and told them
you couldn't get away.

(*Augustus glances up at the house, locks gazes with Amalia.*)

On the way back I tripped
over what I thought was an old root,
and there he was—
Augustus: You found him?
Phebe: Under the crook of a mangrove,
wrapped in vines. Poor Hector!
All those years folks thought he was crazy—

(*Looking up at Amalia's window.*)

when he was just sick at heart.
Alexander: Hector took a liking to you,
Diana. You should be the one.

(*Phebe joins the mourners as Alexander and Scipio pass Diana under and over the coffin.*)

Slaves: Lift him high, Lord,
Take him by the arm.
Wrap him in glory,
Dip him in balm.

(Augustus kneels wearily. Scylla, ravaged with grief and more stooped than ever, approaches.)

Scylla: He thought evil could be caught.
Augustus: Yes.
Scylla: But evil breeds inside, in the dark.
  I can smell its sour breath.
Augustus: Don't come around me, then.
Scylla: You believe you can cure the spirit
    just by riling it. What will
    these people do with your hate
    after you free them—as you promise?
Augustus: I got better things to do
    than argue with you, Scylla.
Scylla: Oh yes, you're a busy man;
    you got to watch for people waiting
    to trip you up; you think
    danger's on the outside.
    But do you know what's inside
    you, Augustus Newcastle?
    The seeds of the future; they'll have their way.
    You can't escape.
    You are in your skin wherever you go.

(Turns to the mourners, who have just completed the ritual of the passing and calls out.)

  Eshu Elewa ogo gbogbo!
Alexander: He's gone over. He's flown on the wind.
Scylla: He came with no mother to soothe him.
    He came with no father to teach him.
    He came with no names for his gods.
Phebe: No way but to see it through.
Scylla: Who can I talk to about his journey?
    He stood tall, so they bent his back.
    He found love, so they ate his heart.
    Eshu Elewa ogo gbogbo!
Scipio: This is what a man comes to.
Scylla: Who will remember him,
    without a father, without a mother?
Phebe: Poor people, you've lost your wings.
Scylla: Eshu Elewa ogo gbogbo!
    Where are the old words now?
    Scattered by the wind.
Alexander: The body a feather, the spirit a flame.
Scylla: And now the sun
    has come out to warm him.
Scipio: Too late! He's flown.
Scylla: But the wind won't carry me!

(The slaves hum and chant as they disperse, their song becoming gradually less mournful and more urgent as we segue into the next scene.)

Narrator: Sunday evening;
New moon, skies clear.
The wheel's stopped turning:
Redemption's here.

SCENE VII

Near the slave cabins.

Early evening shortly before sunset: Phebe and Augustus come from the shadows. In the background the slaves go about evening chores while singing a mixture of militant spirituals and African chants with whispered phrases such as "Rise up!" or "Mean to be free!" occasionally audible.

Augustus: Everything's ready.
Phebe: Yes.
Augustus: We've been careful.
Phebe: Oh, yes.
Augustus (pacing): Any day now. Any time!
Phebe: It's been three days, Augustus—
three days since you heard the call
and didn't answer.
Augustus: Tonight's new moon; skies are clear.
Destiny calls!
Phebe: Are you sure it's not just your destiny?
Augustus: What do you mean?
Phebe: Every time you talk about
victory and vengeance,
it's as if you're saying
my victory, my vengeance.
As if you didn't care about
anyone's pain but yours.
Augustus: Are you with us, or against us?
Phebe: Ain't nothing wrong with feelings,
Augustus—just where they lead you.
Now when it comes to hating,
you and Miss Amalia are a lot alike.

(Augustus whirls, but she stands her ground.)

She used to be different—high-minded,
but always ready to laugh.
When she married Massa Louis
she began to sour.
Seemed like disappointment killed her.

(Hesitates, then hurries through.)

And now you've brought her back to life.
No wonder you're mixed up!
Augustus: Why are you telling me this?

Phebe: Because I care what happens to you
    more than revolution or freedom.
    Those may be traitor's words, but
    I don't care. 'Cause maybe—
    maybe if you hadn't let hate
    take over your life, you might have
    had some love left over for me.

(*She runs off. Augustus slowly sits down, as if a new and treacherous path had opened before him. Benjamin and Henry enter unseen. Augustus buries his face in his hands.*)

Benjamin (*whispering*): There he is. Don't look
    so fearful now, does he?

(*Makes a bird call.*)

Augustus: Who's there?

(*He leaps to his feet; the Conspirators approach.*)

Benjamin: May Fate be with you.
Augustus: You've brought news?
Benjamin: Most of the news is old, brother.
Augustus: It couldn't be helped;
    I was under constant guard.
Benjamin: Constant guard? Constant companionship
    would be closer to the truth.
Augustus: Talk straight!
Benjamin: Straight as a bullet, brother.
    You sent word that you were "being watched"—
    naturally, we sent someone to see about
    your difficulties. What a surprise
    to find out who your guard was
    and how tenderly
    she watched over you!
Augustus: Missy needed a buck—what of it?
Benjamin: Sound mighty proud, buck.
Augustus: Just the facts, brother, just the facts.
    Should I knock her hand away
    to prove my loyalty to the cause?
    Why not charm her instead?
Benjamin: That never used to be your style.
Augustus: I've never been so close to freedom.
Benjamin: All the more reason to see
    you don't spoil it.

(*Looks skyward.*)

The night's perfect:
    clear skies, new moon.
Augustus: Tonight? I knew it!
    I'll assemble my forces.

Benjamin: Hold on. You'll be coming with us.
Augustus: But—
Benjamin: You told us what you wanted us to believe.
    We've got orders to bring you to headquarters.
    They'll decide what's to be done.
Augustus: I can't leave. My people need me!
Benjamin: This is death's business, brother.
    Evan a nigger as famous as you
    can't be given the benefit of the doubt!
    Your second-in-command—
Augustus: Phebe?
Benjamin: —will organize things here.

    (*Takes Augustus by the arm.*)

    Henry will deliver her orders.
    We'll wait in the wagon. Come on!

(*All exit; blackout. The chanting of the slaves grows louder, with snatches of spirituals in high descant, but the lyrics of the spirituals are volatile. The percussive, more African-based chants prevail, with key phrases like "Freedom, children, freedom!" emerging ever stronger through the next scene.*)

SCENE VIII

The big house: Amalia's bedroom, Louis's study and the hallway.

Evening: Louis stands at the open window of his study, looking through the telescope, alternately at the night sky and down over the plantation grounds.

Amalia sits on the window seat in her bedroom. Phebe enters.

Phebe: You wanted me, Ma'am?
Amalia: Good evening, Phebe!
    I was sitting at the window,
    catching the last rays of sunlight,
    when I happened to see you
    darting from group to group,
    talking to this slave and that,
    and I said to myself: "Perhaps
    Phebe would like to talk to me, too."
Phebe: (*on her guard*): I'm pleased to talk conversation
    whenever you like, Miss Amalia.
Amalia (*slightly sarcastic*): It seems you're mighty pleased
    with other people's conversations
    these days.
Phebe: I don't follow your meaning, Ma'am.
Amalia: Oh, really? I notice
    you and Augustus have no problem
    following each other's meaning.

Phebe: Augustus ain't nothing
　　but a friend, Ma'am.
　　I don't recollect talking to him
　　any more than anyone else.

(*Laughs nervously.*)

　　Me and my big mouth always be
　　yakking at somebody or another.
Amalia: Don't talk yourself
　　into trouble, Phebe.
Phebe: Beg pardon, Ma'am.
　　I didn't mean nothing by it.
Amalia: Everyone can see
　　you're making a fool of yourself
　　over him! Have you spoken
　　to Augustus today?
Phebe: I can't rightly say, Ma'am.

(*At a warning look from Amalia.*)

　　That is—I talked to a lot of people
　　and he was amongst them, but
　　we didn't say more than a how-de-do.
Amalia: Tell Augustus I want to see him.
Phebe (*thrown into panic*): I don't know—I mean—
Amalia: What's the matter, Phebe?
Phebe: Nothing, Ma'am.
　　It might take a while, is all.
Amalia (*sarcastic*): And why is that?
Phebe: It's just—well, Augustus been keeping
　　to himself lately. I seen him
　　going off in the direction of the swamp;
　　he's got some crazy idea
　　about fixing up Hector's shack.
Amalia (*haunted*): Oh.
　　When he returns, send him up.
Phebe: Yes, Ma'am.

(*Phebe exits. In the hallway she runs into Augustus. He is very agitated.*)

Phebe (*whispering*): You! Here?
Augustus: Yes. They sent me back.
Phebe: I thought for sure they was going to do
　　something awful to you.
Augustus: The sun travels its appointed track,
　　a knot of fire, day in day out—
　　what could be more awful?
Phebe: Augustus, what is it?
　　Can I help?
Augustus: This job I do alone.

Phebe: But surely you can take a minute
    to go in there and smooth
    that she-hawk's feathers down
    so's the rest of us can—

(*Amalia steps out and peers into the dim hall. Augustus shrinks into the shadows.*)

Amalia: Is that you, Phebe?
Phebe: Yes'm. I was just on my way downstairs.
Amalia: I heard voices.
Phebe: That was me, Ma'am.
    I twisted my foot in the dark—
    guess I was talking to it.

(*Laughs nervously.*)

My mama used to say it helps
to talk the hurt out.
Amalia: Well, do your talking
    elsewhere. Go on!

(*Phebe hesitates, then exits. Amalia stands looking into the darkness for a moment, then goes back into her room. Augustus steps out of hiding, holding a knife. The Conspirators can be heard in the background.*)

Leader: Prove you haven't betrayed the cause!
Benjamin: Kill them both—
Henry: —your mistress
    and her foolish husband.
Augustus: That's fate for you, Amalia

(*Looks at the knife.*)

That white throat, bared for kisses . . .
one quick pass, and it will flow
redder than a thousand roses.

Everything was so simple before!
Hate and be hated.
But this—love or freedom—
is the devil's choice.

(*Steeling himself, he heads for Louis's room. Lights up on Louis, who is sitting with his right hand tucked nervously in the lap of his dressing grown. His back is to Augustus, who enters stealthily.*)

Louis (*startling Augustus, who stops in his tracks*):
    No one has come through that door
    for years. You're the new one, aren't you?

(*Unseen by Augustus, he pulls a pistol out of his lap.*)

A wild nigger, I hear. Amalia's latest indulgence.
Augustus: So this is the great white master,
    trembling in his dressing gown!

Louis: Beware of the Moon in the house of Mars!

(*Stands up and turns, hiding the pistol as he and Augustus face off.*)

The stars can tell you everything—
war and pestilence, love and betrayal.

Augustus: War? Yes, this is war. Say your prayers,
Massa—you have a hard ride ahead of you.

Louis: A hard ride, me? I don't think so.

(*Aims his pistol at Augustus.*)

A man should be able to kill
when he has to, don't you agree?

(*Startled by this unexpected turn of events, Augustus freezes. Louis reaches for the bottle on the table with his other hand.*)

Perhaps you'd care for a bit of bourbon
to warm your way?

Augustus (*trying to compose himself*): You can't stop what's coming
over the hill.

Louis (*shakes his pistol at Augustus, shouting*):
This time I won't leave things up to chance!

(*Muttering.*)

What a fool I was!
I should have smothered the bastard
right there in the basket.
That's the man's way.

Augustus: Basket? What basket?

Louis: Amalia's of course. Amalia's basket.
It was—

(*Slight pause; distracted.*)

The doctor refused to kill it.
What else was there to do?

(*Augustus lunges, knocking the gun from Louis's hand and overpowering him.*)

Augustus: There goes your last chance, fool!

(*Drags Louis by the collar toward center-stage.*)

This basket—what did it look like?

Louis: What do you care?

Augustus (*holds the knife to Louis's throat*): Enough to slit your throat.

Louis (*whimpering*): Oh, it was beautiful! White wicker,
lined in blue satin, tiny red rosettes
marching along the rim . . .

Augustus (*slowly lets go of Louis's collar*): And your spurs slipped right inside.

Louis: Amalia's Christmas present.
Oh, was the good doctor relieved!

"It's a miracle," he said,
"but the child's still alive!"
Augustus: And still lives to this day.
Spurs bite into a horse's belly—
think what they can do
to a newborn child!

(*Rips open his shirt.*)

Louis: You?
Augustus: All my life I tried to imagine
what you would look like.
Would you be tall or stooped over?
Blue eyes, or brown?
Would you dress in white linen
or dash around in a dusty greatcoat?
To think that your blood flows
through my veins—

(*Advances on Louis, who staggers back into the chair.*)

Louis: My blood?
Augustus: When I think of you forcing
your wretched seed into my mother,
I want to rip you—
Louis: Me, your father?
You think I'm your father?
Augustus: I heard it from your own lips.
Louis (*bursts into laughter*): Of course! Of course!
The stars said it all:
who is born into violence
shall live to fulfill it.
Who shuns violence
will die by the sword.
Augustus (*pulls Louis from the chair, knife at his throat*):
What happened to my mother?
What did you do to her?
Louis (*in a crafty voice*): I haven't touched her since.
Ask Amalia—
she runs this plantation.
She knows your mother better than anyone!
Augustus: Amalia? Of course!
Missy wanted the bastard child dead.
Now I understand: It's an old story.
Louis: You understand nothing.

(*A sudden shout outside, the revolt has begun. Both men freeze, listening.*)

Augustus: It's time!

(*Stabs Louis as the sounds of the revolt grow.*)

Louis: You were there . . . all along . . .

Augustus (letting Louis's body drop): So, Amalia—and to think
    I tried to bargain for your life!
Slaves: Freedom! Freedom! Selah! Selah!

    (*Augustus heads for Amalia's room; lights come up on Amalia, who has stepped into the hall.*)

Amalia: Augustus, there you are! What's happening?
    I called Ticey, but she won't come!
Augustus (backing her into the room): I thought you didn't care
    what happened out there.
Amalia: Why are they shouting?
    Why doesn't Jones make them stop?
Augustus: I reckon the dead don't make good overseers.
    Your slaves are rebelling, Missy.
    Liberté, Égalité, Fraternité!
Amalia (stares at him uncomprehendingly, then runs to the window):
    Rebelling? My slaves?
    Augustus, make them stop!
    They'll listen to you!
Augustus: Like I listened to you?
    You led me into your parlour
    like a dog on a leash. Sit, dog!
    Heel! Care for a sherry? A fairy tale?
Amalia: No, you were different!
    You were—
Augustus (grabs her): No more conversation!
    Where is my mother?
Amalia: Your mother? How would I know a thing like that?
Augustus: Your husband confessed.
Amalia (aware of danger on all sides, seeking escape): What could Louis have to
    confess?
Augustus: A shrewd piece of planning,
    to destroy him with his own son
    after you had failed to destroy
    the son himself!
    But you had to be patient.
    Twenty years you had to wait
    before you could buy me back.
Amalia: Louis, your father? You must be joking!
Augustus: Shall I help you remember?
    You supplied the basket yourself—
Amalia: Basket?
Augustus: —lined in blue satin, trimmed with rosettes—
Amalia: Red rosettes?
Augustus: Monsieur LaFarge agreed
    to sell his own baby—but that wasn't enough,
    was it? You wanted the child dead.
    So you slipped a pair of riding spurs
    into the sewing basket.

And you know the kind of scars
spurs leave, Missy. Like crowns . . .
or exploding suns.
Amalia: My God.
Augustus: The woman who patched me up
  kept that basket as a reminder.
Amalia: No . . .
Augustus (shakes her): What did you do with my mother?
  Who is she?

  (*Slaps her.*)

  Tell me!
Amalia (wrenches free to face him; her voice trembling):
  So you want to know who your mother is?
  You think, if I tell you,
  the sad tale of your life
  will find its storybook ending?
  Well then, this will be my last story—
  and when I have finished,
  you will wish you had never
  stroked my hair or kissed my mouth.
  You will wish you had no eyes to see
  or ears to hear. You will wish
  you had never been born.
Augustus: I've heard grown men scream,
  watched as the branding iron
  sank into their flesh. I've seen
  pregnant women slit open like melon,
  runaways staked to the ground
  and whipped until
  they floated in their own blood and piss.
  Don't think you can frighten me, Missy:
  Nothing your lips can tell
  can be worse than what
  these eyes have seen.
Amalia: Bravo! What a speech!
  But you've seen nothing.

  (*Backs up to appraise him, smiling, slightly delirious.*)

  That same expression! How could I forget?
  My lover then stood as tall as you now.
Augustus: Your lover?

  (*Phebe bursts in.*)

Phebe: They're coming, Augustus!
  They're coming to see if you did
  what you were told! Oh, Augustus—
  you were supposed to kill her!

Augustus (*shaking himself into action, threatening Amalia*):
    My mother, who is my mother?
    Out with it!
Amalia: Phebe, you tell him.
    You were there.
    Everyone was there—
    under my window,
    waiting for news . . .
Phebe: That . . . was the night
    we all came to wait out the birth.
Augustus: What birth?
Amalia: Hector on the porch.
Augustus: What about Hector?

(*More shouts outside; compelled by the urgency of the growing revolution, Phebe tries to distract Augustus.*)

Phebe: There's no time!
Augustus (*grabs Amalia as if to slit her throat*): What about Hector?
Amalia: Chick in a basket, going to market!
    They said you died, poor thing.
    That's why Hector went to the swamp.

(*Augustus stares desperately at her. Phebe turns, thunderstruck.*)

Augustus: Hector?
Amalia: But you didn't die. You're here . . .

(*Reaches for him; he draws back.*)

Phebe (*looks from Amalia to Augustus, horror growing, recites tonelessly*):
    Stepped on a pin, the pin bent,
    and that's the way the story went.
Amalia (*sadly, in a small voice*): Silk for my prince, and a canopy of roses!
    You were so tiny—so sweet and tiny.
    I didn't know about the spurs.
Phebe: You sold your own child.
    Hector's child.
Augustus: Hector . . .

(*The knife slips from his fingers.*)

Amalia: I was trying to save you!
Augustus: Save me?
Amalia (*extremely agitated*): I felt like they had hacked out my heart.
    But I wouldn't let them see me cry.
Augustus (*wrestling with the horror*): You? My mother?
Amalia (*clutching herself*): It was like missing an arm or a leg
    that pains and throbs, even though
    you can look right where it was
    and see there's nothing left.

(*She stops abruptly.*)

Augustus: My own mother gave me away.
But I found my way back . . .
a worm crawling into its hole.

Amalia: For weeks afterwards
my breasts ached with milk.

Augustus (*sinking to his knees*): Better I had bled to death in that basket.

(*A great shout goes up as the insurrectionists gain entry to the main house. Amalia takes advantage of the ensuing distraction to pick up the knife.*)

Phebe: Augustus!

Augustus (*passive*): The Day of Redemption is here.

Phebe: They'll kill you, Augustus!

Augustus: Time to be free.

Amalia: Poor baby! I thought
I could keep you from harm—
and here you are,
right in harm's way.

(*Phebe gasps; Amalia stabs herself as Augustus, alerted by Phebe's gasp, jumps up, too late to stop her. The room turns red as the outbuildings go up in flames.*)

Augustus: Amalia!

(*Catching her as she falls.*)

No . . .

(*Calling out in anguish.*)

Eshu Elewa ogo gbogbo!

(*The chanting of the rebelling slaves grows louder.*)

Phebe: Oh, Augustus.

Augustus (*lays Amalia's body down, gently*): I had the sun and the moon
once. And the stars
with their cool gaze.
Now it's dark.

Phebe: It's alright. You'll be alright now.

Augustus (*staring as if trying to make out something in the distance*):
Who's there? How she stares,
like a cat at midnight!

Phebe: Nobody's there, Augustus.

Augustus: Don't you see her?

(*Phebe shakes her head, terrified.*)

Look, she's hidden behind a tree.

Phebe: Oh, Augus—

Augustus: Shh! You'll frighten her. There's another one—
he's been flogged and pickled in brine.

That skinny boy ate dirt; that's why he staggers.
So many of them, limping, with brands
on their cheeks! Oh, I can't bear it!
Phebe: Come along, now.
Augustus (*calling out to the "ghosts"*): I came to save you!

(*The slaves burst in, brandishing bayonets and torches.*)

Benjamin: He did it.
Slaves: Selah! We're free!

(*The slaves lift Augustus onto their shoulders. The Slave woman/Narrator stands at the door, holding a torch, taking in the scene.*)

Slaves: Freedom, freedom, freedom . . .

(*The "Freedom!" chant grows louder and more persistent as the slaves parade out of the room, Augustus on their shoulders; Phebe follows them, sobbing. Scylla takes the torch from the Slave woman/Narrator and sets fire to the window's billowing curtains as she slowly straightens up to her full height.*)

BLACKOUT

Rita Dove on Writing

The Inspiration for *The Darker Face of the Earth*   2000

Interviewer: When did the inspiration for *The Darker Face of the Earth* come to you?

Dove: My husband and I spent five months in Jerusalem in 1979. I had recently finished the manuscript of my first book of poems, *The Yellow House on the Corner,* which contained a section of poems based on slave narratives, and I suppose that was on my mind one late afternoon that summer, as I stood looking out over the walled city of Jerusalem with its turrets and citadels. I had just reread Sophocles' *Oedipus Rex;* and perhaps it was the natural amphitheater of the Kidron valley, where King David cried out at the loss of his rebellious son Absalom, perhaps it was the slanted sunbeams striking the pale stones of the Old

Rita Dove

City like a spotlight dressed with the palest of pink gels—but I found myself musing on kings and all-too-human heartbreaks, looking for similarities between the classical sense of destiny and our contemporary attitudes toward history and its heroes. What is it, I wondered, that makes Oedipus interesting as a hero when his course has been set at birth? Why do we watch, enthralled, if we already know his fate? I searched for a modern analogy, a set of circumstances where the social structure was as rigid and all-powerful as the Greek universe, one against which even the noblest of characters would be powerless. And as the sun began to set behind the Mount of Olives, a Jimmy Cliff song floated from my husband's study:

> Oh de wicked carry us away,
> Captivity require of us a song;
> How can we sing King Alpha's song
> In a strange land?

The lines are adapted from Psalm 137, the cries of the Israelites in bondage—but sung, in Cliff's version, by the slaves in the Americas.

And there I had my analogy. Rarely has history seen a system which fostered such a sense of futility as slavery. For the Africans taken forcibly from their homes and their roots—language, family, tribal memory—systematically decimated, the white power structure must have seemed as all-encompassing as the implacable will of Zeus. In a flash, I had the basic constructs: A child born of a white plantation mistress and her African lover is sold off but returns twenty years later, unaware of his origins. The open secret of miscegenation would be the key that turns the lock of Fate, and instead of Teiresias, a conjure woman would prophesy the curse. Pride and rebellious spirit have little chance in the systemic violence of slavery, which brutalizes both slave and master. In a different world, Amalia might have been a woman of independent means and Augustus a poet; instead, both are doomed to be crushed when their emotions run counter to the ruling status quo. The slaves know this and function as a Greek chorus, commenting and warning, all to no avail.

From "An Interview with Rita Dove" by Robert McDowell

David Henry Hwang

The Sound of a Voice

1983

David Henry Hwang (b. 1957) grew up in San Gabriel, California, the son of first-generation Chinese immigrants. He was born into a family of musicians: his mother was a concert pianist, his sister plays cello in a string quartet, and he studied the violin. In 1979, as a senior at Stanford University, he directed his first play, F.O.B. (an acronym for "fresh off the boat"), in a dormitory lounge. F.O.B. was later staged at the New York Shakespeare Festival Public Theater and won a 1981 Obie Award. The Sound of a Voice was also produced at the Public Theater as part of a double bill with another one-act play by Hwang, The House of Sleeping Beauties. Hwang enjoyed his greatest commercial and critical success with M. Butterfly (1988), which won the Tony Award for best play. His other plays include Face Value (1993), Golden Child (1997), and Yellowface (2007). While some of his plays are realistic in their approach, Hwang has always been fascinated by the possibilities of symbolic drama. In The Sound of a Voice, he creates a timeless, placeless scene in which two characters named Man and Woman act out a story reminiscent of a folk legend or a traditional Japanese Nō drama (a type of symbolic aristocratic drama developed in the fourteenth century in which a ghost recounts the struggles of his or her life for a traveler). Hwang's interest in nonrealistic and experimental drama has also led him to explore opera. He has collaborated with composer Philip Glass on three works: 1000 Airplanes on the Roof (1988), a science-fiction music drama; The Voyage (1992), an allegorical grand opera commissioned by New York's Metropolitan Opera for the 500th anniversary of Christopher Columbus's arrival in America; and The Sound of a Voice (2003), a combined staging of

American Reportory Theater's 2003 production of *The Sound of a Voice* **(Cambridge, Massachusetts).**

the following play with The House of Sleeping Beauties. *He has also written the books for the shows* Aida (2000), *with music by Elton John and lyrics by Tim Rice, and* Tarzan (2006), *with music and lyrics by Phil Collins. Hwang lives in New York City.*

CHARACTERS

Man, fifties, Japanese
Woman, fifties, Japanese

SETTING. *Woman's house, in a remote corner of the forest.*

SCENE I

Woman pours tea for Man. Man rubs himself, trying to get warm.

Man: You're very kind to take me in.
Woman: This is a remote corner of the world. Guests are rare.
Man: The tea—you pour it well.
Woman: No.
Man: The sound it makes—in the cup—very soothing.
Woman: That is the tea's skill, not mine. (*She hands the cup to him.*) May I get you
    something else? Rice, perhaps?
Man: No.
Woman: And some vegetables?
Man: No, thank you.

Woman: Fish? (*Pause.*) It is at least two days' walk to the nearest village. I saw no horse. You must be very hungry. You would do a great honor to dine with me. Guests are rare.

Man: Thank you.

Woman (*Woman gets up, leaves. Man holds the cup in his hands, using it to warm himself. He gets up, walks around the room. It is sparsely furnished, drab, except for one shelf on which stands a vase of brightly colored flowers. The flowers stand out in sharp contrast to the starkness of the room. Slowly, he reaches out towards them. He touches them. Quickly, he takes one of the flowers from the vase, hides it in his clothes. He returns to where he had sat previously. He waits. Woman re-enters. She carries a tray with food.*): Please. Eat. It will give me great pleasure.

Man: This—this is magnificent.

Woman: Eat.

Man: Thank you. (*He motions for Woman to join him.*)

Woman: No, thank you.

Man: This is wonderful. The best I've tasted.

Woman: You are reckless in your flattery. But anything you say, I will enjoy hearing. It's not even the words. It's the sound of a voice, the way it moves through the air.

Man: How long has it been since you last had a visitor? (*Pause.*)

Woman: I don't know.

Man: Oh?

Woman: I lose track. Perhaps five months ago, perhaps ten years, perhaps yesterday. I don't consider time when there is no voice in the air. It's pointless. Time begins with the entrance of a visitor, and ends with his exit.

Man: And in between? You don't keep track of the days? You can't help but notice—

Woman: Of course I notice.

Man: Oh.

Woman: I notice, but I don't keep track. (*Pause.*) May I bring out more?

Man: More? No. No. This was wonderful.

Woman: I have more.

Man: Really—the best I've had.

Woman: You must be tired. Did you sleep in the forest last night?

Man: Yes.

Woman: Or did you not sleep at all?

Man: I slept.

Woman: Where?

Man: By a waterfall. The sound of the water put me to sleep. It rumbled like the sounds of a city. You see, I can't sleep in too much silence. It scares me. It makes me feel that I have no control over what is about to happen.

Woman: I feel the same way.

Man: But you live here—alone?

Woman: Yes.

Man: It's so quiet here. How can you sleep?

Woman: Tonight, I'll sleep. I'll lie down in the next room, and hear your breathing through the wall, and fall asleep shamelessly. There will be no silence.

Man: You're very kind to let me stay here.

Woman: This is yours. (*She unrolls a mat; there is a beautiful design of a flower on the mat. The flower looks exactly like the flowers in the vase.*)

Man: Did you make it yourself?

Woman: Yes. There is a place to wash outside.

Man: Thank you.

Woman: Goodnight.

Man: Goodnight. (*Man starts to leave.*)

Woman: May I know your name?

Man: No. I mean, I would rather not say. If I gave you a name, it would only be made-up. Why should I deceive you? You are too kind for that.

Woman: Then what should I call you? Perhaps—"Man Who Fears Silence"?

Man: How about, "Man Who Fears Women"?

Woman: That name is much too common.

Man: And you?

Woman: Yokiko.

Man: That's your name?

Woman: It's what you may call me.

Man: Goodnight, Yokiko. You are very kind.

Woman: You are very smart. Goodnight.

(*Man exits. Hanako° goes to the mat. She tidies it, brushes it off. She goes to the vase. She picks up the flowers, studies them. She carries them out of the room with her. Man re-enters. He takes off his outer clothing. He glimpses the spot where the vase used to sit. He reaches into his clothing, pulls out the stolen flower. He studies it. He puts it underneath his head as he lies down to sleep, like a pillow. He starts to fall asleep. Suddenly, a start. He picks up his head. He listens.*)

SCENE II

Dawn. Man is getting dressed. Woman enters with food.

Woman: Good morning.

Man: Good morning, Yokiko.

Woman: You weren't planning to leave?

Man: I have quite a distance to travel today.

Woman: Please. (*She offers him food.*)

Man: Thank you.

Woman: May I ask where you're travelling to?

Man: It's far.

Woman: I know this region well.

Man: Oh? Do you leave the house often?

Woman: I used to. I used to travel a great deal. I know the region from those days.

Man: You probably wouldn't know the place I'm headed.

Woman: Why not?

Man: It's new. A new village. It didn't exist in "those days." (*Pause.*)

Woman: I thought you said you wouldn't deceive me.

Man: I didn't. You don't believe me, do you?

Hanako: The woman.

Woman: No.

Man: Then I didn't deceive you. I'm travelling. That much is true.

Woman: Are you in such a hurry?

Man: Travelling is a matter of timing. Catching the light. (*Woman exits; Man finishes eating, puts down his bowl. Woman re-enters with the vase of flowers.*) Where did you find those? They don't grow native around these parts, do they?

Woman: No; they've all been brought in. They were brought in by visitors. Such as yourself. They were left here. In my custody.

Man: But—they look so fresh, so alive.

Woman: I take care of them. They remind me of the people and places outside this house.

Man: May I touch them?

Woman: Certainly.

Man: These have just blossomed.

Woman: No; they were in bloom yesterday. If you'd noticed them before, you would know that.

Man: You must have received these very recently. I would guess—within five days.

Woman: I don't know. But I wouldn't trust your estimate. It's all in the amount of care you show to them. I create a world which is outside the realm of what you know.

Man: What do you do?

Woman: I can't explain. Words are too inefficient. It takes hundreds of words to describe a single act of caring. With hundreds of acts, words become irrelevant. (*Pause.*) But perhaps you can stay.

Man: How long?

Woman: As long as you'd like.

Man: Why?

Woman: To see how I care for them.

Man: I am tired.

Woman: Rest.

Man: The light?

Woman: It will return.

SCENE III

Man is carrying chopped wood. He is stripped to the waist. Woman enters.

Woman: You're very kind to do that for me.

Man: I enjoy it, you know. Chopping wood. It's clean. No questions. You take your axe, you stand up the log, you aim—pow!—you either hit it or you don't. Success or failure.

Woman: You seem to have been very successful today.

Man: Why shouldn't I be? It's a beautiful day. I can see to those hills. The trees are cool. The sun is gentle. Ideal. If a man can't be successful on a day like this, he might as well kick the dust up into his own face. (*Man notices Woman staring at him. Man pats his belly, looks at her.*) Protection from falls.

Woman: What? (*Man pinches his belly, showing some fat.*) Oh. Don't be silly. (*Man begins slapping the fat on his belly to a rhythm.*)

Man: Listen—I can make music—see?—that wasn't always possible. But now—that I've developed this—whenever I need entertainment.

Woman: You shouldn't make fun of your body.

Man: Why not? I saw you. You were staring.

Woman: I wasn't making fun. (*Man inflates his cheeks.*) I was—stop that!

Man: Then why were you staring?

Woman: I was—

Man: Laughing?

Woman: No.

Man: Well?

Woman: I was—Your body. It's . . . strong. (*Pause.*)

Man: People say that. But they don't know. I've heard that age brings wisdom. That's a laugh. The years don't accumulate here. They accumulate here. (*Pause; he pinches his belly.*) But today is a day to be happy, right? The woods. The sun. Blue. It's a happy day. I'm going to chop wood.

Woman: There's nothing left to chop. Look.

Man: Oh. I guess . . . that's it.

Woman: Sit. Here.

Man: But—

Woman: There's nothing left. (*Man sits; Woman stares at his belly.*) Learn to love it.

Man: Don't be ridiculous.

Woman: Touch it.

Man: It's flabby.

Woman: It's strong.

Man: It's weak.

Woman: And smooth.

Man: Do you mind if I put on my shirt?

Woman: Of course not. Shall I get it for you?

Man: No. No. Just sit there. (*Man starts to put on his shirt. He pauses, studies his body.*) You think it's cute, huh?

Woman: I think you should learn to love it. (*Man pats his belly, talks to it.*)

Man (to belly): You're okay, sir. You hang onto my body like a great horseman.

Woman: Not like that.

Man (ibid.): You're also faithful. You'll never leave me for another man.

Woman: No.

Man: What do you want me to say? (*Woman walks over to Man. She touches his belly with her hand. They look at each other.*)

SCENE IV

Night. Man is alone. Flowers are gone from stand. Mat is unrolled. Man lies on it, sleeping. Suddenly, he starts. He lifts up his head. He listens. Silence. He goes back to sleep. Another start. He lifts up his head, strains to hear. Slowly, we begin to make out the strains of a single shakuhachi° playing a haunting line. It is very soft. He strains to hear it. The instrument slowly fades out. He waits for it to return, but it does not. He takes out the stolen flower. He stares into it.

---

shakuhachi: A Japanese bamboo flute.

SCENE V

Day. Woman is cleaning, while Man relaxes. She is on her hands and knees, scrubbing. She is dressed in a simple outfit, for working. Her hair is tied back. Man is sweating. He has not, however, removed his shirt.

Man: I heard your playing last night.

Woman: My playing?

Man: *Shakuhachi.*

Woman: Oh.

Man: You played very softly. I had to strain to hear it. Next time, don't be afraid. Play out. Fully. Clear. It must've been very beautiful, if only I could've heard it clearly. Why don't you play for me sometime?

Woman: I'm very shy about it.

Man: Why?

Woman: I play for my own satisfaction. That's all. It's something I developed on my own. I don't know if it's at all acceptable by outside standards.

Man: Play for me. I'll tell you.

Woman: No; I'm sure you're too knowledgeable in the arts.

Man: Who? Me?

Woman: You being from the city and all.

Man: I'm ignorant, believe me.

Woman: I'd play, and you'd probably bite your cheek.

Man: Ask me a question about music. Any question. I'll answer incorrectly. I guarantee it.

Woman: Look at this.

Man: What?

Woman: A stain.

Man: Where?

Woman: Here? See? I can't get it out.

Man: Oh. I hadn't noticed it before.

Woman: I notice it every time I clean.

Man: Here. Let me try.

Woman: Thank you.

Man: Ugh. It's tough.

Woman: I know.

Man: How did it get here?

Woman: It's been there as long as I've lived here.

Man: I hardly stand a chance. (*Pause.*) But I'll try. Uh—one—two—three—four! One—two—three—four! See, you set up . . . gotta set up . . . a rhythm—two—three—four. Like fighting! Like battle! One—two—three—four! Used to practice with a rhythm . . . beat . . . battle! Yes! (*The stain starts to fade away.*) Look—it's—yes!—whoo!—there it goes—got the sides—the edges—yes!—fading quick—fading away—ooo—here we come—towards the center—to the heart—two—three—four—slow—slow death—tough—dead! (*Man rolls over in triumphant laughter.*)

Woman: Dead.

Man: I got it! I got it! Whoo! A little rhythm! All it took! Four! Four!

Woman: Thank you.

Man: I didn't think I could do it—but there—it's gone—I did it!

Woman: Yes. You did.

Man: And you—you were great.

Woman: No—I was carried away.

Man: We were a team! You and me!

Woman: I only provided encouragement.

Man: You were great! You were! (*Man grabs Woman. Pause.*)

Woman: It's gone. Thank you. Would you like to hear me play *shakuhachi?*

Man: Yes I would.

Woman: I don't usually play for visitors. It's so . . . I'm not sure. I developed it—all
    by myself—in times when I was alone. I heard nothing—no human voice. So I
    learned to play *shakuhachi.* I tried to make these sounds resemble the human
    voice. The *shakuhachi* became my weapon. To ward off the air. It kept me from
    choking on many a silent evening.

Man: I'm here. You can hear my voice.

Woman: Speak again.

Man: I will.

SCENE VI

*Night. Man is sleeping. Suddenly, a start. He lifts his head up. He listens. Silence. He
strains to hear. The shakuhachi melody rises up once more. This time, however, it becomes
louder and more clear than before. He gets up. He cannot tell from what direction the music
is coming. He walks around the room, putting his ear to different places in the wall, but he
cannot locate the sound. It seems to come from all directions at once, as omnipresent as the
air. Slowly, he moves towards the wall with the sliding panel through which the Woman
enters and exits. He puts his ear against it, thinking the music may be coming from there.
Slowly, he slides the door open just a crack, ever so carefully. He peeks through the crack.
As he peeks through, the Upstage wall of the set becomes transparent, and through the
scrim, we are able to see what he sees. Woman is Upstage of the scrim. She is tending a
room filled with potted and vased flowers of all variety. The lushness and beauty of the room
Upstage of the scrim stands out in stark contrast to the barrenness of the main set. She is
also transformed. She is a young woman. She is beautiful. She wears a brightly colored
kimono. Man observes this scene for a long time. He then slides the door shut. The scrim
returns to opaque. The music continues. He returns to his mat. He picks up the stolen
flower. It is brown and wilted, dead. He looks at it. The music slowly fades out.*

SCENE VII

*Morning. Man is half-dressed. He is practicing sword maneuvers. He practices with the feel
of a man whose spirit is willing, but the flesh is inept. He tries to execute deft movements,
but is dissatisfied with his efforts. He curses himself, and returns to basic exercises. Suddenly, he feels something buzzing around his neck—a mosquito. He slaps his neck, but
misses it. He sees it flying near him. He swipes at it with his sword. He keeps missing.
Finally, he thinks he's hit it. He runs over, kneels down to recover the fallen insect. He picks
up two halves of a mosquito on two different fingers. Woman enters the room. She looks as
she normally does. She is carrying a vase of flowers, which she places on its shelf.*

Man: Look.

Woman: I'm sorry?

Man: Look.

Woman: What? (*He brings over the two halves of mosquito to show her.*)

Man: See?

Woman: Oh.

Man: I hit it—chop!

Woman: These are new forms of target practice?

Man: Huh? Well—yes—in a way.

Woman: You seem to do well at it.

Man: Thank you. For last night. I heard your *shakuhachi*. It was very loud, strong—good tone.

Woman: Did you enjoy it? I wanted you to enjoy it. If you wish, I'll play it for you every night.

Man: Every night!

Woman: If you wish.

Man: No—I don't—I don't want you to treat me like a baby.

Woman: What? I'm not.

Man: Oh, yes. Like a baby. Who you must feed in the middle of the night or he cries. Waaah! Waaah!

Woman: Stop that!

Man: You need your sleep.

Woman: I don't mind getting up for you. (*Pause.*) I would enjoy playing for you. Every night. While you sleep. It will make me feel—like I'm shaping your dreams. I go through long stretches when there is no one in my dreams. It's terrible. During those times, I avoid my bed as much as possible. I paint. I weave. I play *shakuhachi*. I sit on mats and rub powder into my face. Anything to keep from facing a bed with no dreams. It is like sleeping on ice.

Man: What do you dream of now?

Woman: Last night—I dreamt of you. I don't remember what happened. But you were very funny. Not in a mocking way. I wasn't laughing at you. But you made me laugh. And you were very warm. I remember that. (*Pause.*) What do you remember about last night?

Man: Just your playing. That's all. I got up, listened to it, and went back to sleep. (*Man gets up, resumes practicing with his sword.*)

Woman: Another mosquito bothering you?

Man: Just practicing. Ah! Weak! Too weak! I tell you, it wasn't always like this. I'm telling you, there were days when I could chop the fruit from a tree without ever taking my eyes off the ground. (*He continues practicing.*) You ever use one of these?

Woman: I've had to pick one up, yes.

Man: Oh?

Woman: You forget—I live alone—out here—there is . . . not much to sustain me but what I manage to learn myself. It wasn't really a matter of choice.

Man: I used to be very good, you know. Perhaps I can give you some pointers.

Woman: I'd really rather not.

Man: C'mon—a woman like you—you're absolutely right. You need to know how to defend yourself.

Woman: As you wish.

Man: Do you have something to practice with?

Woman: Yes. Excuse me. (*She exits. He practices more. She re-enters with two wooden sticks. He takes one of them.*) Will these do?

Man: Nice. Now, show me what you can do.

Woman: I'm sorry?

Man: Run up and hit me.

Woman: Please.

Man: Go on—I'll block it.

Woman: I feel so . . . undignified.

Man: Go on. (*She hits him playfully with stick.*) Not like that!

Woman: I'll try to be gentle.

Man: What?

Woman: I don't want to hurt you.

Man: You won't—Hit me! (*Woman charges at Man, quickly, deftly. She scores a hit.*) Oh!

Woman: Did I hurt you?

Man: No—you were—let's try that again. (*They square off again. Woman rushes forward. She appears to attempt a strike. He blocks that apparent strike, which turns out to be a feint. She scores.*) Huh?

Woman: Did I hurt you? I'm sorry.

Man: No.

Woman: I hurt you.

Man: No.

Woman: Do you wish to hit me?

Man: No.

Woman: Do you want me to try again?

Man: No.

Woman: Thank you.

Man: Just practice there—by yourself—let me see you run through some maneuvers.

Woman: Must I?

Man: Yes! Go! (*She goes to an open area.*) My greatest strength was always as a teacher. (*Woman executes a series of deft movements. Her whole manner is transformed. Man watches with increasing amazement. Her movements end. She regains her submissive manner.*)

Woman: I'm so embarrassed. My skills—they're so—inappropriate. I look like a man.

Man: Where did you learn that?

Woman: There is much time to practice here.

Man: But you—the techniques.

Woman: I don't know what's fashionable in the outside world. (*Pause.*) Are you unhappy?

Man: No.

Woman: Really?

Man: I'm just . . . surprised.

Woman: You think it's unbecoming for a woman.

Man: No, no. Not at all.

Woman: You want to leave.

Man: No!

Woman: All visitors do. I know. I've met many. They say they'll stay. And they do. For a while. Until they see too much. Or they learn something new. There are boundaries outside of which visitors do not want to see me step. Only who knows what those boundaries are? Not I. They change with every visitor. You have to be careful not to cross them, but you never know where they are. And one day, inevitably, you step outside the lines. The visitor knows. You don't. You didn't know that you'd done anything different. You thought it was just another part of you. The visitor sneaks away. The next day, you learn that you had stepped outside his heart. I'm afraid you've seen too much.

Man: There are stories.

Woman: What?

Man: People talk.

Woman: Where? We're two days from the nearest village.

Man: Word travels.

Woman: What are you talking about?

Man: There are stories about you. I heard them. They say that your visitors never leave this house.

Woman: That's what you heard?

Man: They say you imprison them.

Woman: Then you were a fool to come here.

Man: Listen.

Woman: Me? Listen? You. Look! Where are these prisoners? Have you seen any?

Man: They told me you were very beautiful.

Woman: Then they are blind as well as ignorant.

Man: You are.

Woman: What?

Man: Beautiful.

Woman: Stop that! My skin feels like seaweed.

Man: I didn't realize it at first. I must confess—I didn't. But over these few days— your face has changed for me. The shape of it. The feel of it. The color. All changed. I look at you now, and I'm no longer sure you are the same woman who had poured tea for me just a week ago. And because of that I remembered—how little I know about a face that changes in the night. (*Pause.*) Have you heard those stories?

Woman: I don't listen to old wives' tales.

Man: But have you heard them?

Woman: Yes. I've heard them. From other visitors—young—hotblooded—or old— who came here because they were told great glory was to be had by killing the witch in the woods.

Man: I was told that no man could spend time in this house without falling in love.

Woman: Oh? So why did you come? Did you wager gold that you could come out untouched? The outside world is so flattering to me. And you—are you like the rest? Passion passing through your heart so powerfully that you can't hold onto it?

Man: No! I'm afraid!

Woman: Of what?

Man: Sometimes—when I look into the flowers, I think I hear a voice—from inside—a voice beneath the petals. A human voice.

Woman: What does it say? "Let me out"?

Man: No. Listen. It hums. It hums with the peacefulness of one who is completely imprisoned.

Woman: I understand that if you listen closely enough, you can hear the ocean.

Man: No. Wait. Look at it. See the layers? Each petal—hiding the next. Try and see where they end. You can't. Follow them down, further down, around—and as you come down—faster and faster—the breeze picks up. The breeze becomes a wail. And in that rush of air—in the silent midst of it—you can hear a voice.

Woman (grabs flower from Man): So, you believe I water and prune my lovers? How can you be so foolish? (*She snaps the flower in half, at the stem. She throws it to the ground.*) Do you come only to leave again? To take a chunk of my heart, then leave with your booty on your belt, like a prize? You say that I imprison hearts in these flowers? Well, bits of my heart are trapped with travellers across this land. I can't even keep track. So kill me. If you came here to destroy a witch, kill me now. I can't stand to have it happen again.

Man: I won't leave you.

Woman: I believe you. (*She looks at the flower that she has broken, bends to pick it up. He touches her. They embrace.*)

SCENE VIII

Day. Woman wears a simple undergarment, over which she is donning a brightly colored kimono, the same one we saw her wearing Upstage of the scrim. Man stands apart.

Woman: I can't cry. I don't have the capacity. Right from birth, I didn't cry. My mother and father were shocked. They thought they'd given birth to a ghost, a demon. Sometimes I've thought myself that. When great sadness has welled up inside me, I've prayed for a means to release the pain from my body. But my prayers went unanswered. The grief remained inside me. It would sit like water, still. (*Pause; she models her kimono.*) Do you like it?

Man: Yes, it's beautiful.

Woman: I wanted to wear something special today.

Man: It's beautiful. Excuse me. I must practice.

Woman: Shall I get you something?

Man: No.

Woman: Some tea, maybe?

Man: No. (*Man resumes swordplay.*)

Woman: Perhaps later today—perhaps we can go out—just around here. We can look for flowers.

Man: Alright.

Woman: We don't have to.

Man: No. Let's.

Woman: I just thought if—

Man: Fine. Where do you want to go?

Woman: There are very few recreational activities around here, I know.

Man: Alright. We'll go this afternoon. (*Pause.*)

Woman: Can I get you something?

Man (turning around): What?

Woman: You might be—

Man: I'm not hungry or thirsty or cold or hot.

Woman: Then what are you?

Man: Practicing. (*Man resumes practicing; Woman exits. As soon as she exits, he rests. He sits down. He examines his sword. He runs his finger along the edge of it. He takes the tip, runs it against the soft skin under his chin. He places the sword on the ground with the tip pointed directly upwards. He keeps it from falling by placing the tip under his chin. He experiments with different degrees of pressure. Woman re-enters. She sees him in this precarious position. She jerks his head upward; the sword falls.*)

Woman: Don't do that!

Man: What?

Woman: You can hurt yourself!

Man: I was practicing!

Woman: You were playing!

Man: I was practicing!

Woman: It's dangerous.

Man: What do you take me for—a child?

Woman: Sometimes wise men do childish things.

Man: I knew what I was doing!

Woman: It scares me.

Man: Don't be ridiculous. (*He reaches for the sword again.*)

Woman: Don't! Don't do that!

Man: Get back! (*He places the sword back in its previous position, suspended between the floor and his chin, upright.*)

Woman: But—

Man: Sssssh!

Woman: I wish—

Man: Listen to me! The slightest shock, you know—the slightest shock— surprise—it might make me jerk or—something—and then . . . so you must be perfectly still and quiet.

Woman: But I—

Man: Sssssh! (*Silence.*) I learned this exercise from a friend—I can't even remember his name—good swordsman—many years ago. He called it his meditation position. He said, like this, he could feel the line between this world and the others because he rested on it. If he saw something in another world that he liked better, all he would have to do is let his head drop, and he'd be there. Simple. No fuss. One day, they found him with the tip of his sword run clean out the back of his neck. He was smiling. I guess he saw something he liked. Or else he'd fallen asleep.

Woman: Stop that.

Man: Stop what?

Woman: Tormenting me.

Man: I'm not.

Woman: Take it away!

Man: You don't have to watch, you know.

Woman: Do you want to die that way—an accident?

Man: I was doing this before you came in.

Woman: If you do, all you need to do is tell me.

Man: What?

Woman: I can walk right over. Lean on the back of your head.

Man: Don't try to threaten—

Woman: Or jerk your sword up.

Man: Or scare me. You can't threaten—

Woman: I'm not. But if that's what you want.

Man: You can't threaten me. You wouldn't do it.

Woman: Oh?

Man: Then I'd be gone. You wouldn't let me leave that easily.

Woman: Yes, I would.

Man: You'd be alone.

Woman: No. I'd follow you. Forever. (*Pause.*) Now, let's stop this nonsense.

Man: No! I can do what I want! Don't come any closer!

Woman: Then release your sword.

Man: Come any closer and I'll drop my head.

Woman (*Woman slowly approaches Man. She grabs the hilt of the sword. She looks into his eyes. She pulls it out from under his chin.*): There will be no more of this. (*She exits with the sword. He starts to follow her, then stops. He touches under his chin. On his finger, he finds a drop of blood.*)

SCENE IX

Night. Man is leaving the house. He is just about out, when he hears a shakuhachi playing. He looks around, trying to locate the sound. Woman appears in the doorway to the outside. Shakuhachi slowly fades out.

Woman: It's time for you to go?

Man: Yes. I'm sorry.

Woman: You're just going to sneak out? A thief in the night? A frightened child?

Man: I care about you.

Woman: You express it strangely.

Man: I leave in shame because it is proper. (*Pause.*) I came seeking glory.

Woman: To kill me? You can say it. You'll be surprised at how little I blanch. As if you'd said, "I came for a bowl of rice," or "I came seeking love" or "I came to kill you."

Man: Weakness. All weakness. Too weak to kill you. Too weak to kill myself. Too weak to do anything but sneak away in shame. (*Woman brings out Man's sword.*)

Woman: Were you even planning to leave without this? (*He takes sword.*) Why not stay here?

Man: I can't live with someone who's defeated me.

Woman: I never thought of defeating you. I only wanted to take care of you. To make you happy. Because that made me happy and I was no longer alone.

Man: You defeated me.

Woman: Why do you think that way?

Man: I came here with a purpose. The world was clear. You changed the shape of your face, the shape of my heart—rearranged everything—created a world where I could do nothing.

Woman: I only tried to care for you.

Man: I guess that was all it took. (*Pause.*)

Woman: You still think I'm a witch. Just because old women gossip. You are so cruel. Once you arrived, there were only two possibilities: I would die or you would leave. (*Pause.*) If you believe I'm a witch, then kill me. Rid the province of one more evil.

Man: I can't—

Woman: Why not? If you believe that about me, then it's the right thing to do.

Man: You know I can't.

Woman: Then stay.

Man: Don't try and force me.

Woman: I won't force you to do anything. (*Pause.*) All I wanted was an escape—for both of us. The sound of a human voice—the simplest thing to find, and the hardest to hold onto. This house—my loneliness is etched into the walls. Kill me, but don't leave. Even in death, my spirit would rest here and be comforted by your presence.

Man: Force me to stay.

Woman: I won't. (*Man starts to leave.*) Beware.

Man: What?

Woman: The ground on which you walk is weak. It could give way at any moment. The crevice beneath is dark.

Man: Are you talking about death? I'm ready to die.

Woman: Fear for what is worse than death.

Man: What?

Woman: Falling. Falling through the darkness. Waiting to hit the ground. Picking up speed. Waiting for the ground. Falling faster. Falling alone. Waiting. Falling. Waiting. Falling.

(Woman wails and runs out through the door to her room. Man stands, confused, not knowing what to do. He starts to follow her, then hesitates, and rushes out the door to the outside. Silence. Slowly, he re-enters from the outside. He looks for her in the main room. He goes slowly towards the panel to her room. He throws down his sword. He opens the panel. He goes inside. He comes out. He unrolls his mat. He sits on it, cross-legged. He looks out into space. He notices near him a shakuhachi. He picks it up. He begins to blow into it. He tries to make sounds. He continues trying through the end of the play. The Upstage scrim lights up. Upstage, we see the Woman. She is young. She is hanging from a rope suspended from the roof. She has hung herself. Around her are scores of vases with flowers in them whose blossoms have been blown off. Only the stems remain in the vases. Around her swirl the thousands of petals from the flowers. They fill the Upstage scrim area like a blizzard of color. Man continues to attempt to play. Lights fade to black.)

David Henry Hwang on Writing

Multicultural Theater

1989

Interviewer: How did you begin . . . exploring your [Chinese American] heritage?

Hwang: A lot of that happened in college. I was in college in the mid-to-late 1970s, and whereas most people seem to associate collegiate life in the seventies with John Travolta, there was at that time a third-world consciousness, a third-world power movement, in the universities, particularly among Hispanics and Asians. The blacks really started it in the late sixties and early seventies, and it took a while to trickle down into the other third-world communities. Asians probably picked it up last. . . . While I was never a very ardent Marxist, I studied the ideas and I was interested in the degree to

David Henry Hwang

which we all may have been affected by certain prejudices in the society without having realized it, and to what degree we had incorporated that into our persons by the time we'd reached our early twenties.

The other thing that I think fascinated me about exploring my Chineseness at that time was consistent with my interest in play-writing. I had become very interested in Sam Shepard, particularly in the way in which Shepard likes to create a sort of American mythology. In his case it's the cowboy mythology, but nonetheless it's something that is larger than simply our present-day, fast-food existence. In my context, creating a mythology, creating a past for myself, involved going into Chinese history and Chinese American history. I think the combination of wanting to delve into those things for artistic reasons and being exposed to an active third-world-consciousness movement was what started to get me interested in my roots when I was in college.

Interviewer: I wonder if there will come a time when the expression "ethnic theater" won't have any meaning.

Hwang: I'm hopeful that there will be a time at some point, but I think it's going to be fifty years or so down the road. The whole idea of being ethnic only applies when it's clear what the dominant culture is. Once it becomes less clear and the culture is acknowledged to be more multicultural, then the idea of what's ethnic becomes irrelevant. I think even today we're starting to see that. The monoethnic theaters—that is, the Asian theaters, the black theaters, the Hispanic theaters—are really useful; they serve a purpose. But I think, if we do our jobs correctly, we will phase out our own need for existence, and the future of theaters will be in multicultural theaters, theaters that do a black play and a Jewish play and a classic and whatever . . .

There are so many people now who can't be labeled. I know a couple in which the man is Japanese and Jewish and the woman is Haitian and Filipino. They have a child, and sociologists have told them that a child of that stock probably hasn't existed before. When someone like that becomes a writer, what do we call him? Do we say he's an Asian writer, or what? As those distinctions become increasingly muddled, the whole notion of what is ethnic as opposed to what is mainstream is going to become more and more difficult to define.

From interview in *Contemporary Authors*

Jane Martin

Tattoo   2000

The identity of Jane Martin is a closely guarded secret. No biographical details, public statements, or photographs of this Kentucky-based playwright have been published, nor has she given any interviews or made any public appearances. Often called "America's best known, unknown playwright," Martin first came to public notice in 1981 for Talking With, *a collection of monologues that received a number of productions worldwide and won a Best Foreign Play of the Year award in Germany. Of Martin's many plays, others include* What Mama Don't Know *(1988),* Cementville *(1991),* Keely and Du *(which was a finalist for the 1993 Pulitzer Prize),* Middle-Aged White Guys *(1995),* Jack and Jill *(1996),* Mr. Bundy *(1998),* Anton in Show Business *(2000),* Flaming Guns of the Purple Sage *(2001), and* Good Boys *(2002). Her most recent work is* Sez She *(2005), a monologue play for five actresses.*

CHARACTERS

Link
Jenny
Jones
Vladimir
William

Three women in their twenties sit on chairs facing a door upstage. Link (short for Linchovna) is dressed in black slacks, has short blond hair, several earrings, and all ten fingers adorned with rings. Jenny is dressed in a suit as a young advertising account executive might for a date. Jones is more in the girly-girl vein with curly hair and Laura Ashley style. She is a graduate student who works also as a waitress.

Jenny: What time is it?

Jones (*very Southern*): 7:45.

Jenny: Where is this guy?

Link (*a Russian accent*): He will come. He is sister's ex-husband. Very reliable person. He will come.

Jones: But . . . like if they both . . . I mean what do we do if, you know, they both . . .

Link: Very reliable.

Jones: I am sweating like a shot-putter.

Jenny: Calm down. Breathe. (*Knock.*) See.

Jones: But what if it's . . .

Link: Is Vladimir. Very Russian knock. Okay? I get.

Jones: But if it's William, do we . . .

Link: Only Russian is knocking so deliberate as this. You sit, I do. (*She goes to the door.*) Ah. [Russian] Ooh m^{ie}yáh b ^{ih}ll pree-páh-dok syáird-tsuh. Tih uh-púz-dah-vá-yesh. [You gave me a heart attack. You are late.]

Vladimir [Russian]: Ahv-tóe-booss pree-shóal púhz-dnuh. Yah lóohch-shuh dyéluhl shtaw smúg. [Bus was late. I did the best I could.] (*He enters. He is big, very big, and bearded and tattooed. He has a bag with him much like an old-fashioned doctor bag.*) (K)huh-ruh-sháw, éh-tut ch^{ie}l-uh-v^{ie}k gdyeh aown. [Okay, this guy he is where?]

Jones: My God, he's speaking Russian.

Link: He *is* Russian. All Russians are coming to your country, get ready. [Russian] Aown n^{i}ee yesh-cháw n^{i}ee pree-yéh-(k)hull. Ee-dée zhdoo féh-toy k^{w}óm-nah-tuh. [He hasn't arrived. Go in that room and wait.]

Vladimir [Russian]: (K)huh-ruh-sháw n^{a}o^{w} ooh m^{ie}n-yáh svee-dáh-nyuh ch^{i}ée-ez chahss. Éh-tuh dvair? [Okay, but in one hour I have an appointment. That door?]

(*Vladimir heads toward the other room.*)

Link [Russian]: Da. [Yes]

Jenny: What did you tell him?

Link: Be ready. We will tell him when. Call him in.

Jones: Is this really a good idea? Is this really, really, really a good idea?

Jenny: We need closure. He needs closure. There is going to be closure.

(*A knock on the door.*)

Jones (*whispering*): Oh my God. Oh my God it's him. I have a good idea. You guys do this. You'll be better at this than me. I'll just . . . oh my God, can I do this?

Link: Sit down. Not to vacillate. We do this. (*They arrange themselves on the chairs.*) Okay. Very calm. Very good. This is no more than result of his actions. We are a living logic for him. Breathing. Breathing. Good. Okay. We begin. (*Another knock.*) I am liking this.

(*She opens the door. The man outside, William, immediately grabs her and pulls her into a passionate kiss. After it has gone on for a while, he has the sense of being watched. He removes his lips from Link and sees the seated women.*)

William: Oh shit.

Jenny: Hello, William.

Jones: Hi.

Link (*still in his arms*): Hello, William.

William (*trying to recover*): All right, all right, this is really . . . an intrusion. This is really second-rate is what it is. I cannot believe . . . have I ever gone through your purses, have I ever gone through . . .

Jenny: You were going to say "our drawers"?

William: No, no, I wasn't, Jenny, I wasn't going to say "your drawers." I was pointing out that there are issues of privacy, that there are questions of trust . . . (*Realizes he is still embracing Link.*) Oh. Excuse me. (*He releases her.*) I was so . . .

Jenny: Fucked up.

William: No, not fucked up, Jenny, taken aback. Yes. Completely taken aback that you . . .

Jenny: Knew each other.

William: No, I didn't say . . . you are putting, unfairly, words in my mouth. Look Jenny, if you are looking for the negative, you will find the negative. If you insist something is shoddy, it will look shoddy to you.

Jones: My daddy will come down here and eat your lunch!

William: Jones, will you for once in your life wait to start crying until there is something to cry about?

Jones: You slept with me at 6 A.M. this morning!

William: Well, yes I did, Jones. I did that. Well, actually, it was around 6:15.

Jenny: So that was the early meeting?

William: Well no, I mean yes, there was an early meeting . . .

Jones: You said you had to see me. You said you were wracked with desire.

Link: Wracked with desire?

Jenny: You said that to me at lunch.

William: Okay, hold it . . .

Jenny: It's why I went into the trees with you in the park.

Link: Wracked with desire, yes, it's very charming.

William: Excuse me . . .

Link: In the trees his methodology is what?

Jenny: Kissed my neck.

Jones: That's it! That's what he does! He goes for your goddamn neck like an attack dog! And here I was thinking that was because he was wracked with desire!

Link: Then hand goes up leg. He is then unbuttons the blouse . . .

Jones: Then he starts saying "please," he says "please" over and over and over! Please, please, please!

Link: Is like puppy.

William: All right, goddammit, I concede the point!

Jenny: He concedes the point.

William: If the point is that I am having more than one relationship, you can get off that point because nobody is arguing with you!

Jenny: Oh good.

William: We can calm down!

Jenny: Fine.

Jones: You made love to me at 6 A.M. this morning! You called me your little tuna melt!

Jenny: Tuna melt?

Link: What is tuna melt?

Jenny: You took me behind the trees at noon.

Link: And tonight you will teach me *Kama Sutra.*°

William: This isn't about sex. This is about something way more profound than sex.

Jenny: Oh good, because I thought it *was* about sex.

William: Well, it isn't, Jenny it's about . . .

Jenny: Screwing like a rabbit.

William: No.

Jenny: Completely indiscriminate sex.

Link: Altogether impersonal.

Jenny: Wildly dysfunctional.

Jones: He called me his tuna melt.

Jenny: Okay, Jones, that adds a dollop of romance.

William: You may not recognize this but it's about *passion*. It is a frank admission that complex personalities have complex needs, and that . . .

Jenny: Point of order.

William: Each of those needs finds passionate fulfillment . . .

Jenny: Point of order.

William: What?

Jenny: You are the complex personality in question?

William: Yes, I am.

Jenny: Just trying to keep up.

William: Now each one of you is very different.

Jenny: We are very different.

William: And in each case a different part of me responds. I don't give the same thing. I don't get the same thing. The me that is with each of you could not respond to the others. That self is faithful and would never betray you. You wouldn't want that part of me you don't have, and were I not as complex as I am there wouldn't have been enough of each part of me for you to relate to, to care about, in fact, to love.

(*There is a long, stunned pause.*)

Jones: What the *hell* is he talking about?

Link: He has many souls.

Jenny: He da three-souled man.

William: Go ahead, Jenny, make fun of what you don't understand. You are a wonderful person, a very talented advertising account executive, but you have a demeaningly reductive view of life. That is one of the reasons your spirit has sought me out. You want to be carried into deeper water.

Jenny: Well I will admit that it's getting pretty deep.

William: Now I'm not saying there aren't issues here. Matters of the heart, intimacies that I want to discuss with you alone, Jenny, and you too Jones, of course I meant you, too.

Kama Sutra: ancient Sanskrit text that includes detailed descriptions of sexual activities and positions.

Jones: Okay now, I want to get down and talk some Georgia talk here . . . you know, get right on down in the red dirt here . . . and what I got on my mind is "am I *is* or am I *ain't* your tuna melt?"

William: I am what you need me to be, Jones. (*Link locks the door.*) What are you doing, Link?

Link: I am making here old-fashioned totalitarian state.

Jenny (*moving one chair away from the others*): Sit down, William.

William: I see no reason to sit down.

Jenny: Bill, do you remember when we very recently began seriously to make our wedding plans?

William: Yes, I do.

Jenny: Do you remember saying you wanted a really big wedding?

William: Yes I do.

Jenny: And I said, "Honey, I just don't know that many people," and you said, "Sweetie, I could list two hundred family, friends, and business associates right now." And I bet you ten dollars and, by golly, you sat right down and did it!

Link: He has good organizational memory, to do *this* he had to have such a memory.

Jenny (*taking a paper out of her briefcase*): Now, Bill, this is the account of your activities today that I plan to fax to that list if you don't sit down. (*He glances over the letter and sits down.*) I know it's a little heavy on sexual specifics, but you have such a remarkably individual style I thought it made good reading.

Jones: I am never dressing up like that again at 6 A.M.!

William: What precisely is it that you want?

Link: Ah.

Jenny: Ah.

Jones: Ah.

Jenny: What precisely? Well, we want you to meet someone.

Link [Russian]: Vlah-dée-meer, vuh-(k)huh-dée! Puh-ráh rahbᵃoᵂ-táhts. [Vladimir, come in! It is time to go to work.] (*Vladimir enters.*) Vladimir, I am wanting you to meet interesting person William. William, this is interesting person Vladimir.

(*Vladimir clicks his heels and bows slightly.*)

William: If you are planning to kill me or harm me, I would like it to be clearly understood that I am a lawyer, my friends are lawyers, my mother is a lawyer, my brother Don is a *ferocious* lawyer, and you will pay. P-A-Y. Pay.

Link: I like this, William, this is very dramatic, but in this time we don't kill you. This is very funny idea though. You make good Russian joke. Wait, one moment, I tell Vladimir.

(*In Russian, Link communicates William's fear. Vladimir laughs and slaps William on the back.*)

Jenny: Okay, so it's "the lady and the tiger."° Behind two doors, the choice is yours. Here's the deal. I will fax the aforementioned document to the aforementioned list, or Vladimir will tattoo on your butt our version of what you did today.

(*Jenny hands William another piece of paper.*)

"*the lady and the tiger*": allusion to "The Lady or the Tiger?," an 1882 short story by the American writer Frank R. Stockton, in which a princess's unfaithful lover must blindly choose between two doors representing two choices, either to marry another woman or be killed by a tiger.

William: What?!
Jones: Signed.
Jenny: And dated.
William: You are kidding.
Jenny: Take a good look at Vladimir. Does he look like he's kidding?

(*Vladimir opens his bag, takes out a small towel, and begins laying out the tools of his trade.*)

Link: In Russia, this man is thoracic surgeon, but in America he is tattoo artist. Such is fate of Russian people. [Russian.] N^{i}ee pláhts, moy droohg. [Do not weep, my friend.]

(*He wipes his eyes.*)

William (*still holding the paper*): I am supposed to go through life with this tattooed on my butt?
Jenny: William, like many pharmaceuticals, you need a warning label.
Jones: But they can take a tattoo off.
Link: Not with Russian inks.
William: I cannot believe this is happening to me!
Jenny: So you choose the fax?
William: You know perfectly well that would ruin my career.
Jenny: Well, see now, we just seem to be on the horns of a dilemma.
Jones: Your career or your rear.
Link: The lady . . .
Jones: Or your skinny white butt.
William: How the hell did the three of you find out about each other?
Link: Vladimir is also private detective.
William (*to Link*): And what made you think you needed a private detective?
Link: Because, my darling, I am Russian.
Jenny: So what'll it be, Billy?
William: Can I have just a goddamn minute here?
Jones: I'm gonna wash your mouth out with soap.
Link: Man must come to terms with tragic fate. Is good. Okay, while you think, Vladimir will sing you song of suffering and transfiguration from Ukraine. (*Vladimir does; it has no words but great feeling.*) And I will read you *Kama Sutra*.
William: Oh God.
Link: You say tonight our souls, our bodies will become one through *Kama Sutra*. This I don't want to miss.

(*Link begins reading the first few sentences of the Kama Sutra, "Man, the period of whose life is one hundred years, should practise Dharma,° Artha,° and Kama° at different times and in such a manner that they may harmonize together and not clash in any way. He should acquire learning in his childhood, in his youth, and middle age he should attend to Artha and Kama, and in his old age he should perform Dharma, and thus seek to gain Moksha, i.e., release from further transmigration." Vladimir sings more softly and prepares, the women watch. William fumes and puts his head in his hands. Lights out.*)

END OF PLAY

Dharma: righteousness, duty.   *Artha:* purpose, meaning.   *Kama:* pleasure, gratification.

MLL

MLL

Arthur Miller

Death of a Salesman   1949

Certain Private Conversations in Two Acts and a Requiem

Arthur Miller (1915–2005) was born into a lower-income Jewish family in New York City's Harlem but grew up in Brooklyn. He studied playwriting at the University of Michigan, later wrote radio scripts, and during World War II worked as a steamfitter. When the New York Drama Critics named his All My Sons *best play of 1947, Miller told an interviewer, "I don't see how you can write anything decent without using as your basis the question of right and wrong." (The play is about a guilty manufacturer of defective aircraft parts.)* Death of a Salesman *(1949, Pulitzer Prize for Drama) made Miller famous.* The Crucible *(1953), a dramatic indictment of the Salem witch trials, gained him further attention at a time when Senator Joseph McCarthy was conducting loyalty investigations; in 1996,* The Crucible *was made into a film starring Daniel Day-Lewis and Winona Ryder. For a while (1956–1961), Miller was the husband of actress Marilyn Monroe, whom the main character of his* After the Fall *(1964) resembles. Among Miller's other plays are* A View from the Bridge *(1955);* The Price *(1968);* The Creation of the World and Other Business *(1972);* Playing for Time *(1980), written for television;* Broken Glass *(1994);* Mr. Peters' Connections *(1999);* Resurrection Blues *(2002); and* Finishing the Picture *(2004). He published an autobiography, several volumes of essays, two collections of short stories, and two novels,* Focus *(1945) and* The Misfits *(1960), drawn from his screenplay for the film starring Monroe.*

A new production of Death of a Salesman, *starring Brian Dennehy as Willy Loman, opened on Broadway on February 10, 1999, fifty years to the day after its original premiere. Although Miller made a number of memorable contributions to the American theater, this work is unquestionably the pinnacle of his achievement. In Willy Loman, he has given us a figure who is at once both representative and unique, whose desperate plight is conveyed through memorable dialogue and scenes of almost unbearable painfulness and intensity.*

Brian Dennehy with Ron Eldard and Ted Koch in a 2000 TV production of *Death of a Salesman.*

CAST

Willy Loman
Linda
Biff
Charley
Uncle Ben
Howard Wagner
Jenny
Happy
Bernard
The Woman
Stanley
Miss Forsythe
Letta

SCENE. *The action takes place in Willy Loman's house and yard and in various places he visits in the New York and Boston of today. Throughout the play, in the stage directions, left and right mean stage left and stage right.*

ACT I

A melody is heard, played upon a flute. It is small and fine, telling of grass and trees and the horizon. The curtain rises.

Before us is the Salesman's house. We are aware of towering, angular shapes behind it, surrounding it on all sides. Only the blue light of the sky falls upon the house and forestage; the surrounding area shows an angry glow of orange. As more light appears, we see a solid vault of apartment houses around the small, fragile-seeming home. An air of the dream clings to the place, a dream rising out of reality. The kitchen at center seems actual enough, for there is a kitchen table with three chairs, and a refrigerator. But no other fixtures are seen. At the back of the kitchen there is a draped entrance, which leads to the living room. To the right of the kitchen, on a level raised two feet, is a bedroom furnished only with a brass bedstead and a straight chair. On a shelf over the bed a silver athletic trophy stands. A window opens onto the apartment house at the side.

Behind the kitchen, on a level raised six and a half feet, is the boys' bedroom, at present barely visible. Two beds are dimly seen, and at the back of the room a dormer window. (This bedroom is above the unseen living room.) At the left a stairway curves up to it from the kitchen.

The entire setting is wholly or, in some places, partially transparent. The roof-line of the house is one-dimensional; under and over it we see the apartment buildings. Before the house lies an apron, curving beyond the forestage into the orchestra. This forward area serves as the backyard as well as the locale of all Willy's imaginings and of his city scenes. Whenever the action is in the present the actors observe the imaginary wall-lines, entering the house only through the door at the left. But in the scenes of the past these boundaries are broken, and characters enter or leave a room by stepping "through" a wall onto the forestage.

From the right, Willy Loman, the Salesman, enters, carrying two large sample cases. The flute plays on. He hears but is not aware of it. He is past sixty years of age, dressed quietly. Even as he crosses the stage to the doorway of the house, his exhaustion is apparent. He unlocks the door, comes into the kitchen, and thankfully lets his burden down, feeling the soreness of his palms. A word-sigh escapes his lips—it might be, "Oh, boy, oh, boy." He closes the door, then carries his cases out into the living room, through the draped kitchen doorway.

Linda, his wife, has stirred in her bed at the right. She gets out and puts on a robe, listening. Most often jovial, she has developed an iron repression of her exceptions to Willy's behavior— she more than loves him, she admires him, as though his mercurial nature, his temper, his massive dreams and little cruelties, served her only as sharp reminders of the turbulent longings within him, longings which she shares but lacks the temperament to utter and follow to their end.

Linda (*hearing Willy outside the bedroom, calls with some trepidation*): Willy!

Willy: It's all right. I came back.

Linda: Why? What happened? (*Slight pause.*) Did something happen, Willy?

Willy: No, nothing happened.

Linda: You didn't smash the car, did you?

Willy (*with casual irritation*): I said nothing happened. Didn't you hear me?

Linda: Don't you feel well?

Willy: I am tired to the death. (*The flute has faded away. He sits on the bed beside her, a little numb.*) I couldn't make it. I just couldn't make it, Linda.

Linda (*very carefully, delicately*): Where were you all day? You look terrible.

Willy: I got as far as a little above Yonkers. I stopped for a cup of coffee. Maybe it was the coffee.

Linda: What?

Willy (*after a pause*): I suddenly couldn't drive any more. The car kept going onto the shoulder, y'know?

Linda (*helpfully*): Oh. Maybe it was the steering again. I don't think Angelo knows the Studebaker.

Willy: No, it's me, it's me. Suddenly I realize I'm goin' sixty miles an hour and I don't remember the last five minutes. I'm—I can't seem to—keep my mind to it.

Linda: Maybe it's your glasses. You never went for your new glasses.

Willy: No, I see everything. I came back ten miles an hour. It took me nearly four hours from Yonkers.

Linda (*resigned*): Well, you'll just have to take a rest. Willy, you can't continue this way.

Willy: I just got back from Florida.

Linda: But you didn't rest your mind. Your mind is overactive, and the mind is what counts, dear.

Willy: I'll start out in the morning. Maybe I'll feel better in the morning. (*She is taking off his shoes.*) These goddam arch supports are killing me.

Linda: Take an aspirin. Should I get you an aspirin? It'll soothe you.

Willy (*with wonder*): I was driving along, you understand? And I was fine. I was even observing the scenery. You can imagine, me looking at scenery, on the road every week of my life. But it's so beautiful up there, Linda, the trees are so thick, and the sun is warm. I opened the windshield and just let the warm air bathe over me. And then all of a sudden I'm goin' off the road! I'm tellin' ya, I absolutely forgot I was driving. If I'd've gone the other way over the white line I might've killed somebody. So I went on again—and five minutes later I'm dreamin' again, and I nearly—(*He presses two fingers against his eyes.*) I have such thoughts, I have such strange thoughts.

Linda: Willy, dear. Talk to them again. There's no reason why you can't work in New York.

Willy: They don't need me in New York. I'm the New England man. I'm vital in New England.

Linda: But you're sixty years old. They can't expect you to keep traveling every week.

Willy: I'll have to send a wire to Portland. I'm supposed to see Brown and Morrison tomorrow morning at ten o'clock to show the line. Goddammit, I could sell them! (*He starts putting on his jacket.*)

Linda (*taking the jacket from him*): Why don't you go down to the place tomorrow and tell Howard you've simply got to work in New York? You're too accommodating, dear.

Willy: If old man Wagner was alive I'd a been in charge of New York now! That man was a prince, he was a masterful man. But that boy of his, that Howard, he don't appreciate. When I went north the first time, the Wagner Company didn't know where New England was!

Linda: Why don't you tell those things to Howard, dear?

Willy (*encouraged*): I will, I definitely will. Is there any cheese?

Linda: I'll make you a sandwich.

Willy: No, go to sleep. I'll take some milk. I'll be up right away. The boys in?

Linda: They're sleeping. Happy took Biff on a date tonight.

Willy (*interested*): That so?

Linda: It was so nice to see them shaving together, one behind the other, in the bathroom. And going out together. You notice? The whole house smells of shaving lotion.

Willy: Figure it out. Work a lifetime to pay off a house. You finally own it, and there's nobody to live in it.

Linda: Well, dear, life is a casting off. It's always that way.

Willy: No, no, some people—some people accomplish something. Did Biff say anything after I went this morning?

Linda: You shouldn't have criticized him, Willy, especially after he just got off the train. You mustn't lose your temper with him.

Willy: When the hell did I lose my temper? I simply asked him if he was making any money. Is that a criticism?

Linda: But, dear, how could he make any money?

Willy (*worried and angered*): There's such an undercurrent in him. He became a moody man. Did he apologize when I left this morning?

Linda: He was crestfallen, Willy. You know how he admires you. I think if he finds himself, then you'll both be happier and not fight any more.

Willy: How can he find himself on a farm? Is that a life? A farmhand? In the beginning, when he was young, I thought, well, a young man, it's good for him to tramp around, take a lot of different jobs. But it's more than ten years now and he has yet to make thirty-five dollars a week!

Linda: He's finding himself, Willy.

Willy: Not finding yourself at the age of thirty-four is a disgrace!

Linda: Shh!

Willy: The trouble is he's lazy, goddammit!

Linda: Willy, please!

Willy: Biff is a lazy bum.

Linda: They're sleeping. Get something to eat. Go on down.

Willy: Why did he come home? I would like to know what brought him home.

Linda: I don't know. I think he's still lost, Willy. I think he's very lost.

Willy: Biff Loman is lost. In the greatest country in the world a young man with such—personal attractiveness, gets lost. And such a hard worker. There's one thing about Biff—he's not lazy.

Linda: Never.

Willy (with pity and resolve): I'll see him in the morning. I'll have a nice talk with him. I'll get him a job selling. He could be big in no time. My God! Remember how they used to follow him around in high school? When he smiled at one of them their faces lit up. When he walked down the street . . . (*He loses himself in reminiscences.*)

Linda (trying to bring him out of it): Willy, dear, I got a new kind of American-type cheese today. It's whipped.

Willy: Why do you get American when I like Swiss?

Linda: I just thought you'd like a change—

Willy: I don't want a change! I want Swiss cheese. Why am I always being contradicted?

Linda (with a covering laugh): I thought it would be a surprise.

Willy: Why don't you open a window in here, for God's sake?

Linda (with infinite patience): They're all open, dear.

Willy: The way they boxed us in here. Bricks and windows, windows and bricks.

Linda: We should've bought the land next door.

Willy: The street is lined with cars. There's not a breath of fresh air in the neighborhood. The grass don't grow any more, you can't raise a carrot in the back yard. They should've had a law against apartment houses. Remember those two beautiful elm trees out there? When I and Biff hung the swing between them?

Linda: Yeah, like being a million miles from the city.

Willy: They should've arrested the builder for cutting those down. They massacred the neighborhood. (*Lost.*) More and more I think of those days, Linda. This time of year it was lilac and wisteria. And then the peonies would come out, and the daffodils. What fragrance in this room!

Linda: Well, after all, people had to move somewhere.

Willy: No, there's more people now.

Linda: I don't think there's more people. I think—

Willy: There's more people! That's what's ruining this country! Population is getting out of control. The competition is maddening! Smell the stink from that apartment house! And another on the other side . . . How can they whip cheese?

(*On Willy's last line, Biff and Happy raise themselves up in their beds, listening.*)

Linda: Go down, try it. And be quiet.

Willy (turning to Linda, guiltily): You're not worried about me, are you, sweetheart?

Biff: What's the matter?

Happy: Listen!

Linda: You've got too much on the ball to worry about.

Willy: You're my foundation and my support, Linda.

Linda: Just try to relax, dear. You make mountains out of molehills.

Willy: I won't fight with him any more. If he wants to go back to Texas, let him go.

Linda: He'll find his way.

Willy: Sure. Certain men just don't get started till later in life. Like Thomas Edison, I think. Or B. F. Goodrich. One of them was deaf. (*He starts for the bedroom doorway.*) I'll put my money on Biff.

Linda: And Willy—if it's warm Sunday we'll drive in the country. And we'll open the windshield, and take lunch.

Willy: No, the windshields don't open on the new cars.

Linda: But you opened it today.

Willy: Me? I didn't. (*He stops.*) Now isn't that peculiar! Isn't that a remarkable—(*He breaks off in amazement and fright as the flute is heard distantly.*)

Linda: What, darling?

Willy: That is the most remarkable thing.

Linda: What, dear?

Willy: I was thinking of the Chevvy. (*Slight pause.*) Nineteen twenty-eight . . . when I had that red Chevvy—(*Breaks off.*) That funny? I coulda sworn I was driving that Chevvy today.

Linda: Well, that's nothing. Something must've reminded you.

Willy: Remarkable. Ts. Remember those days? The way Biff used to simonize that car? The dealer refused to believe there was eighty thousand miles on it. (*He shakes his head.*) Heh! (*To Linda.*) Close your eyes, I'll be right up. (*He walks out of the bedroom.*)

Happy (*to Biff*): Jesus, maybe he smashed up the car again!

Linda (*calling after Willy*): Be careful on the stairs, dear! The cheese is on the middle shelf! (*She turns, goes over to the bed, takes his jacket, and goes out of the bedroom.*)

(*Light has risen on the boys' room. Unseen, Willy is heard talking to himself, "Eighty thousand miles," and a little laugh. Biff gets out of bed, comes downstage a bit, and stands attentively. Biff is two years older than his brother Happy, well built, but in these days bears a worn air and seems less self-assured. He has succeeded less, and his dreams are stronger and less acceptable than Happy's. Happy is tall, powerfully made. Sexuality is like a visible color on him, or a scent that many women have discovered. He, like his brother, is lost, but in a different way, for he has never allowed himself to turn his face toward defeat and is thus more confused and hardskinned, although seemingly more content.*)

Happy (*getting out of bed*): He's going to get his license taken away if he keeps that up. I'm getting nervous about him, y'know, Biff?

Biff: His eyes are going.

Happy: No, I've driven with him. He sees all right. He just doesn't keep his mind on it. I drove into the city with him last week. He stops at a green light and then it turns red and he goes. (*He laughs.*)

Biff: Maybe he's color-blind.

Happy: Pop? Why he's got the finest eye for color in the business. You know that.

Biff (*sitting down on his bed*): I'm going to sleep.

Happy: You're not still sour on Dad, are you, Biff?

Biff: He's all right, I guess.

Willy (*underneath them, in the living room*): Yes, sir, eighty thousand miles—eighty-two thousand!

Biff: You smoking?

Happy (*holding out a pack of cigarettes*): Want one?

Biff (*taking a cigarette*): I can never sleep when I smell it.

Willy: What a simonizing job, heh!

Happy (with deep sentiment): Funny, Biff, y'know? Us sleeping in here again? The old beds. (*He pats his bed affectionately.*) All the talk that went across those two beds, huh? Our whole lives.

Biff: Yeah. Lotta dreams and plans.

Happy (with a deep and masculine laugh): About five hundred women would like to know what was said in this room.

(*They share a soft laugh.*)

Biff: Remember that big Betsy something—what the hell was her name—over on Bushwick Avenue?

Happy (combing his hair): With the collie dog!

Biff: That's the one. I got you in there, remember?

Happy: Yeah, that was my first time—I think. Boy, there was a pig! (*They laugh, almost crudely.*) You taught me everything I know about women. Don't forget that.

Biff: I bet you forgot how bashful you used to be. Especially with girls.

Happy: Oh, I still am, Biff.

Biff: Oh, go on.

Happy: I just control it, that's all. I think I got less bashful and you got more so. What happened, Biff? Where's the old humor, the old confidence? (*He shakes Biff's knee. Biff gets up and moves restlessly about the room.*) What's the matter?

Biff: Why does Dad mock me all the time?

Happy: He's not mocking you, he—

Biff: Everything I say there's a twist of mockery on his face. I can't get near him.

Happy: He just wants you to make good, that's all. I wanted to talk to you about Dad for a long time, Biff. Something's—happening to him. He—talks to himself.

Biff: I noticed that this morning. But he always mumbled.

Happy: But not so noticeable. It got so embarrassing I sent him to Florida. And you know something? Most of the time he's talking to you.

Biff: What's he say about me?

Happy: I can't make it out.

Biff: What's he say about me?

Happy: I think the fact that you're not settled, that you're still kind of up in the air . . .

Biff: There's one or two other things depressing him, Happy.

Happy: What do you mean?

Biff: Never mind. Just don't lay it all on me.

Happy: But I think if you just got started—I mean—is there any future for you out there?

Biff: I tell ya, Hap, I don't know what the future is. I don't know—what I'm supposed to want.

Happy: What do you mean?

Biff: Well, I spent six or seven years after high school trying to work myself up. Shipping clerk, salesman, business of one kind or another. And it's a measly manner of existence. To get on that subway on the hot mornings in summer. To devote your whole life to keeping stock, or making phone calls, or selling or buying. To suffer fifty weeks of the year for the sake of a two-week vacation, when all you really desire is to be outdoors, with your shirt off. And always to have to get ahead of the next fella. And still—that's how you build a future.

Happy: Well, you really enjoy it on a farm? Are you content out there?

Biff (*with rising agitation*): Hap, I've had twenty or thirty different kinds of jobs since I left home before the war, and it always turns out the same. I just realized it lately. In Nebraska when I herded cattle, and the Dakotas, and Arizona, and now in Texas. It's why I came home now, I guess, because I realized it. This farm I work on, it's spring there now, see? And they've got about fifteen new colts. There's nothing more inspiring or—beautiful than the sight of a mare and a new colt. And it's cool there now, see? Texas is cool now, and it's spring. And whenever spring comes to where I am, I suddenly get the feeling, my God, I'm not gettin' anywhere! What the hell am I doing, playing around with horses, twenty-eight dollars a week! I'm thirty-four years old, I oughta be makin' my future. That's when I come running home. And now, I get here, and I don't know what to do with myself. (*After a pause.*) I've always made a point of not wasting my life, and everytime I come back here I know that all I've done is to waste my life.

Happy: You're a poet, you know that, Biff? You're a—you're an idealist!

Biff: No, I'm mixed up very bad. Maybe I oughta get married. Maybe I oughta get stuck into something. Maybe that's my trouble. I'm like a boy. I'm not married, I'm not in business, I just—I'm like a boy. Are you content, Hap? You're a success, aren't you? Are you content?

Happy: Hell, no!

Biff: Why? You're making money, aren't you?

Happy (*moving about with energy, expressiveness*): All I can do now is wait for the merchandise manager to die. And suppose I get to be merchandise manager? He's a good friend of mine, and he just built a terrific estate on Long Island. And he lived there about two months and sold it, and now he's building another one. He can't enjoy it once it's finished. And I know that's just what I would do. I don't know what the hell I'm workin' for. Sometimes I sit in my apartment—all alone. And I think of the rent I'm paying. And it's crazy. But then, it's what I always wanted. My own apartment, a car, and plenty of women. And still, goddammit, I'm lonely.

Biff (*with enthusiasm*): Listen, why don't you come out West with me?

Happy: You and I, heh?

Biff: Sure, maybe we could buy a ranch. Raise cattle, use our muscles. Men built like we are should be working out in the open.

Happy (*avidly*): The Loman Brothers, heh?

Biff (*with vast affection*): Sure, we'd be known all over the counties!

Happy (*enthralled*): That's what I dream about, Biff. Sometimes I want to just rip my clothes off in the middle of the store and outbox that goddam merchandise manager. I mean I can outbox, outrun, and outlift anybody in that store, and I have to take orders from those common, petty sons-of-bitches till I can't stand it any more.

Biff: I'm tellin' you, kid, if you were with me I'd be happy out there.

Happy (*enthused*): See, Biff, everybody around me is so false that I'm constantly lowering my ideals . . .

Biff: Baby, together we'd stand up for one another, we'd have someone to trust.

Happy: If I were around you—

Biff: Hap, the trouble is we weren't brought up to grub for money. I don't know how to do it.

Happy: Neither can I!

Biff: Then let's go!

Happy: The only thing is—what can you make out there?

Biff: But look at your friend. Builds an estate and then hasn't the peace of mind to live in it.

Happy: Yeah, but when he walks into the store the waves part in front of him. That's fifty-two thousand dollars a year coming through the revolving door, and I got more in my pinky finger than he's got in his head.

Biff: Yeah, but you just said—

Happy: I gotta show some of those pompous, self-important executives over there that Hap Loman can make the grade. I want to walk into the store the way he walks in. Then I'll go with you, Biff. We'll be together yet, I swear. But take those two we had tonight. Now weren't they gorgeous creatures?

Biff: Yeah, yeah, most gorgeous I've had in years.

Happy: I get that any time I want, Biff. Whenever I feel disgusted. The only trouble is, it gets like bowling or something. I just keep knockin' them over and it doesn't mean anything. You still run around a lot?

Biff: Naa. I'd like to find a girl—steady, somebody with substance.

Happy: That's what I long for.

Biff: Go on! You'd never come home.

Happy: I would! Somebody with character, with resistance! Like Mom, y'know? You're gonna call me a bastard when I tell you this. That girl Charlotte I was with tonight is engaged to be married in five weeks. (*He tries on his new hat.*)

Biff: No kiddin'!

Happy: Sure, the guy's in line for the vice-presidency of the store. I don't know what gets into me, maybe I just have an overdeveloped sense of competition or something, but I went and ruined her, and furthermore I can't get rid of her. And he's the third executive I've done that to. Isn't that a crummy characteristic? And to top it all, I go to their weddings! (*Indignantly, but laughing.*) Like I'm not supposed to take bribes. Manufacturers offer me a hundred-dollar bill now and then to throw an order their way. You know how honest I am, but it's like this girl, see. I hate myself for it. Because I don't want the girl, and, still, I take it and— I love it!

Biff: Let's go to sleep.

Happy: I guess we didn't settle anything, heh?

Biff: I just got one idea that I think I'm going to try.

Happy: What's that?

Biff: Remember Bill Oliver?

Happy: Sure, Oliver is very big now. You want to work for him again?

Biff: No, but when I quit he said something to me. He put his arm on my shoulder, and he said, "Biff, if you ever need anything, come to me."

Happy: I remember that. That sounds good.

Biff: I think I'll go to see him. If I could get ten thousand or even seven or eight thousand dollars I could buy a beautiful ranch.

Happy: I bet he'd back you. 'Cause he thought highly of you, Biff. I mean, they all do. You're well liked, Biff. That's why I say to come back here, and we both have the apartment. And I'm tellin' you, Biff, any babe you want . . .

Biff: No, with a ranch I could do the work I like and still be something. I just wonder though. I wonder if Oliver still thinks I stole that carton of basketballs.

Happy: Oh, he probably forgot that long ago. It's almost ten years. You're too sensitive. Anyway, he didn't really fire you.

Biff: Well, I think he was going to. I think that's why I quit. I was never sure whether he knew or not. I know he thought the world of me, though. I was the only one he'd let lock up the place.

Willy (below): You gonna wash the engine, Biff?

Happy: Shh!

(*Biff looks at Happy, who is gazing down, listening. Willy is mumbling in the parlor.*)

Happy: You hear that?

(*They listen. Willy laughs warmly.*)

Biff (growing angry): Doesn't he know Mom can hear that?

Willy: Don't get your sweater dirty, Biff!

(*A look of pain crosses Biff's face.*)

Happy: Isn't that terrible? Don't leave again, will you? You'll find a job here. You gotta stick around. I don't know what to do about him, it's getting embarrassing.

Willy: What a simonizing job!

Biff: Mom's hearing that!

Willy: No kiddin', Biff, you got a date? Wonderful!

Happy: Go on to sleep. But talk to him in the morning, will you?

Biff (reluctantly getting into bed): With her in the house. Brother!

Happy (getting into bed): I wish you'd have a good talk with him.

(*The light on their room begins to fade.*)

Biff (to himself in bed): That selfish, stupid . . .

Happy: Sh . . . Sleep, Biff.

(*Their light is out. Well before they have finished speaking, Willy's form is dimly seen below in the darkened kitchen. He opens the refrigerator, searches in there, and takes out a bottle of milk. The apartment houses are fading out, and the entire house and sur-roundings become covered with leaves. Music insinuates itself as the leaves appear.*)

Willy: Just wanna be careful with those girls, Biff, that's all. Don't make any promises. No promises of any kind. Because a girl, y'know, they always believe what you tell 'em, and you're very young, Biff, you're too young to be talking seriously to girls.

(*Light rises on the kitchen. Willy, talking, shuts the refrigerator door and comes down-stage to the kitchen table. He pours milk into a glass. He is totally immersed in himself, smiling faintly.*)

Willy: Too young entirely, Biff. You want to watch your schooling first. Then when you're all set, there'll be plenty of girls for a boy like you. (*He smiles broadly at a kitchen chair.*) That so? The girls pay for you? (*He laughs.*) Boy, you must really be makin' a hit.

(*Willy is gradually addressing—physically—a point offstage, speaking through the wall of the kitchen, and his voice has been rising in volume to that of a normal conversation.*)

Willy: I been wondering why you polish the car so careful. Ha! Don't leave the hub-caps, boys. Get the chamois to the hubcaps. Happy, use newspaper on the windows, it's the easiest thing. Show him how to do it, Biff! You see, Happy? Pad it up, use it like a pad. That's it, that's it, good work. You're doin' all right, Hap. (*He pauses, then nods in approbation for a few seconds, then looks upward.*) Biff, first thing we gotta do when we get time is clip that big branch over the house. Afraid it's gonna fall in a storm and hit the roof. Tell you what. We get a rope and sling her around, and then we climb up there with a couple of saws and take her down. Soon as you finish the car, boys, I wanna see ya. I got a surprise for you, boys.

Biff (*offstage*): Whatta ya got, Dad?

Willy: No, you finish first. Never leave a job till you're finished—remember that. (*Looking toward the "big trees."*) Biff, up in Albany I saw a beautiful hammock. I think I'll buy it next trip, and we'll hang it right between those two elms. Wouldn't that be something? Just swingin' there under those branches. Boy, that would be . . .

(*Young Biff and Young Happy appear from the direction Willy was addressing. Happy carries rags and a pail of water. Biff, wearing a sweater with a block "S," carries a football.*)

Biff (*pointing in the direction of the car offstage*): How's that, Pop, professional?

Willy: Terrific. Terrific job, boys. Good work, Biff.

Happy: Where's the surprise, Pop?

Willy: In the back seat of the car.

Happy: Boy! (*He runs off.*)

Biff: What is it, Dad? Tell me, what'd you buy?

Willy (*laughing, cuffs him*): Never mind, something I want you to have.

Biff (*turns and starts off*): What is it, Hap?

Happy (*offstage*): It's a punching bag!

Biff: Oh, Pop!

Willy: It's got Gene Tunney's signature on it.

(*Happy runs onstage with a punching bag.*)

Biff: Gee, how'd you know we wanted a punching bag?

Willy: Well, it's the finest thing for the timing.

Happy (*lies down on his back and pedals with his feet*): I'm losing weight, you notice, Pop?

Willy (*to Happy*): Jumping rope is good too.

Biff: Did you see the new football I got?

Willy (*examining the ball*): Where'd you get a new ball?

Biff: The coach told me to practice my passing.

Willy: That so? And he gave you the ball, heh?

Biff: Well, I borrowed it from the locker room. (*He laughs confidentially.*)

Willy (*laughing with him at the theft*): I want you to return that.

Happy: I told you he wouldn't like it!

Biff (*angrily*): Well, I'm bringing it back!

Willy (*stopping the incipient argument, to Happy*): Sure, he's gotta practice with a regulation ball, doesn't he? (*To Biff.*) Coach'll probably congratulate you on your initiative.

Biff: Oh, he keeps congratulating my initiative all the time, Pop.

Willy: That's because he likes you. If somebody else took that ball there'd be an uproar. So what's the report, boys, what's the report?

Biff: Where'd you go this time, Dad? Gee we were lonesome for you.

Willy (*pleased, puts an arm around each boy and they come down to the apron*): Lonesome, heh?

Biff: Missed you every minute.

Willy: Don't say? Tell you a secret, boys. Don't breathe it to a soul. Someday I'll have my own business, and I'll never have to leave home any more.

Happy: Like Uncle Charley, heh?

Willy: Bigger than Uncle Charley! Because Charley is not—liked. He's liked, but he's not—well liked.

Biff: Where'd you go this time, Dad?

Willy: Well, I got on the road, and I went north to Providence. Met the Mayor.

Biff: The Mayor of Providence!

Willy: He was sitting in the hotel lobby.

Biff: What'd he say?

Willy: He said, "Morning!" And I said, "You've got a fine city here, Mayor." And then he had coffee with me. And then I went to Waterbury. Waterbury is a fine city. Big clock city, the famous Waterbury clock. Sold a nice bill there. And then Boston—Boston is the cradle of the Revolution. A fine city. And a couple of other towns in Mass., and on to Portland and Bangor and straight home!

Biff: Gee, I'd love to go with you sometime, Dad.

Willy: Soon as summer comes.

Happy: Promise?

Willy: You and Hap and I, and I'll show you all the towns. America is full of beautiful towns and fine, upstanding people. And they know me, boys, they know me up and down New England. The finest people. And when I bring you fellas up, there'll be open sesame for all of us, 'cause one thing, boys: I have friends. I can park my car in any street in New England, and the cops protect it like their own. This summer, heh?

Biff and Happy (*together*): Yeah! You bet!

Willy: We'll take our bathing suits.

Happy: We'll carry your bags, Pop!

Willy: Oh, won't that be something! Me comin' into the Boston stores with you boys carryin' my bags. What a sensation!

(*Biff is prancing around, practicing passing the ball.*)

Willy: You nervous, Biff, about the game?

Biff: Not if you're gonna be there.

Willy: What do they say about you in school, now that they made you captain?

Happy: There's a crowd of girls behind him everytime the classes change.

Biff (*taking Willy's hand*): This Saturday, Pop, this Saturday—just for you, I'm going to break through for a touchdown.

Happy: You're supposed to pass.

Biff: I'm takin' one play for Pop. You watch me, Pop, and when I take off my helmet, that means I'm breakin' out. Then you watch me crash through that line!

Willy (*kisses Biff*): Oh, wait'll I tell this in Boston!

(*Bernard enters in knickers. He is younger than Biff, earnest and loyal, a worried boy.*)

Bernard: Biff, where are you? You're supposed to study with me today.

Willy: Hey, looka Bernard. What're you lookin' so anemic about, Bernard?

Bernard: He's gotta study, Uncle Willy. He's got Regents next week.

Happy (*tauntingly, spinning Bernard around*): Let's box, Bernard!

Bernard: Biff! (*He gets away from Happy.*) Listen, Biff, I heard Mr. Birnbaum say that if you don't start studyin' math he's gonna flunk you, and you won't graduate. I heard him!

Willy: You better study with him, Biff. Go ahead now.

Bernard: I heard him!

Biff: Oh, Pop, you didn't see my sneakers! (*He holds up a foot for Willy to look at.*)

Willy: Hey, that's a beautiful job of printing!

Bernard (*wiping his glasses*): Just because he printed University of Virginia on his sneakers doesn't mean they've got to graduate him, Uncle Willy!

Willy (*angrily*): What're you talking about? With scholarships to three universities they're gonna flunk him?

Bernard: But I heard Mr. Birnbaum say—

Willy: Don't be a pest, Bernard! (*To his boys.*) What an anemic!

Bernard: Okay, I'm waiting for you in my house, Biff.

(*Bernard goes off. The Lomans laugh.*)

Willy: Bernard is not well liked, is he?

Biff: He's liked, but he's not well liked.

Happy: That's right, Pop.

Willy: That's just what I mean. Bernard can get the best marks in school, y'understand, but when he gets out in the business world, y'understand, you are going to be five times ahead of him. That's why I thank Almighty God you're both built like Adonises. Because the man who makes an appearance in the business world, the man who creates personal interest, is the man who gets ahead. Be liked and you will never want. You take me, for instance. I never have to wait in line to see a buyer. "Willy Loman is here!" That's all they have to know, and I go right through.

Biff: Did you knock them dead, Pop?

Willy: Knocked 'em cold in Providence, slaughtered 'em in Boston.

Happy (*on his back, pedaling again*): I'm losing weight, you notice, Pop?

(*Linda enters, as of old, a ribbon in her hair, carrying a basket of washing.*)

Linda (*with youthful energy*): Hello, dear!

Willy: Sweetheart!

Linda: How'd the Chevvy run?

Willy: Chevrolet, Linda, is the greatest car every built. (*To the boys.*) Since when do you let your mother carry wash up the stairs?

Biff: Grab hold there, boy!

Happy: Where to, Mom?

Linda: Hang them up on the line. And you better go down to your friends, Biff. The cellar is full of boys. They don't know what to do with themselves.

Biff: Ah, when Pop comes home they can wait!

Willy (*laughs appreciatively*): You better go down and tell them what to do, Biff.

Biff: I think I'll have them sweep out the furnace room.

Willy: Good work, Biff.

Biff (*goes through wall-line of kitchen to doorway at back and calls down*): Fellas! Everybody sweep out the furnace room! I'll be right down!

Voices: All right! Okay, Biff.

Biff: George and Sam and Frank, come out back! We're hangin' up the wash! Come on, Hap, on the double! (*He and Happy carry out the basket.*)

Linda: The way they obey him!

Willy: Well, that's training, the training. I'm tellin' you, I was sellin' thousands and thousands, but I had to come home.

Linda: Oh, the whole block'll be at that game. Did you sell anything?

Willy: I did five hundred gross in Providence and seven hundred gross in Boston.

Linda: No! Wait a minute, I've got a pencil. (*She pulls pencil and paper out of her apron pocket.*) That makes your commission . . . Two hundred—my God! Two hundred and twelve dollars!

Willy: Well, I didn't figure it yet, but . . .

Linda: How much did you do?

Willy: Well, I—I did—about a hundred and eighty gross in Providence. Well, no—it came to—roughly two hundred gross on the whole trip.

Linda (*without hesitation*): Two hundred gross. That's . . . (*She figures.*)

Willy: The trouble was that three of the stores were half closed for inventory in Boston. Otherwise I woulda broke records.

Linda: Well, it makes seventy dollars and some pennies. That's very good.

Willy: What do we owe?

Linda: Well, on the first there's sixteen dollars on the refrigerator—

Willy: Why sixteen?

Linda: Well, the fan belt broke, so it was a dollar eighty.

Willy: But it's brand new.

Linda: Well, the man said that's the way it is. Till they work themselves in, y'know.

(*They move through the wall-line into the kitchen.*)

Willy: I hope we didn't get stuck on that machine.

Linda: They got the biggest ads of any of them.

Willy: I know, it's a fine machine. What else?

Linda: Well, there's nine-sixty for the washing machine. And for the vacuum cleaner there's three and a half due on the fifteenth. Then the roof, you got twenty-one dollars remaining.

Willy: It don't leak, does it?

Linda: No, they did a wonderful job. Then you owe Frank for the carburetor.

Willy: I'm not going to pay that man! That goddam Chevrolet, they ought to prohibit the manufacture of that car!

Linda: Well, you owe him three and a half. And odds and ends, comes to around a hundred and twenty dollars by the fifteenth.

Willy: A hundred and twenty dollars! My God, if business don't pick up I don't know what I'm gonna do!

Linda: Well, next week you'll do better.

Willy: Oh, I'll knock 'em dead next week. I'll go to Hartford. I'm very well liked in Hartford. You know, the trouble is, Linda, people don't seem to take to me.

(*They move on the forestage.*)

Linda: Oh, don't be foolish.

Willy: I know it when I walk in. They seem to laugh at me.

Linda: Why? Why would they laugh at you? Don't talk that way, Willy.

(*Willy moves to the edge of the stage. Linda goes into the kitchen and starts to darn stockings.*)

Willy: I don't know the reason for it, but they just pass me by. I'm not noticed.

Linda: But you're doing wonderful, dear. You're making seventy to a hundred dollars a week.

Willy: But I gotta be at it ten, twelve hours a day. Other men—I don't know—they do it easier. I don't know why—I can't stop myself—I talk too much. A man oughta come in with a few words. One thing about Charley. He's a man of few words, and they respect him.

Linda: You don't talk too much, you're just lively.

Willy (*smiling*): Well, I figure, what the hell, life is short, a couple of jokes. (*To himself.*) I joke too much! (*The smile goes.*)

Linda: Why? You're—

Willy: I'm fat. I'm very—foolish to look at, Linda. I didn't tell you, but Christmas time I happened to be calling on F. H. Stewarts, and a salesman I know, as I was going in to see the buyer I heard him say something about walrus. And I—I cracked him right across the face. I won't take that. I simply will not take that. But they do laugh at me. I know that.

Linda: Darling . . .

Willy: I gotta overcome it. I know I gotta overcome it. I'm not dressing to advantage, maybe.

Linda: Willy, darling, you're the handsomest man in the world—

Willy: Oh, no, Linda.

Linda: To me you are. (*Slight pause.*) The handsomest.

(*From the darkness is heard the laughter of a woman. Willy doesn't turn to it, but it continues through Linda's lines.*)

Linda: And the boys, Willy. Few men are idolized by their children the way you are.

(*Music is heard as behind a scrim, to the left of the house, The Woman, dimly seen, is dressing.*)

Willy (*with great feeling*): You're the best there is, Linda, you're a pal, you know that? On the road—on the road I want to grab you sometimes and just kiss the life outa you.

(*The laughter is loud now, and he moves into a brightening area at the left, where The Woman has come from behind the scrim and is standing, putting on her hat, looking into a "mirror" and laughing.*)

Willy: 'Cause I get so lonely—especially when business is bad and there's nobody to talk to. I get the feeling that I'll never sell anything again, that I won't make a living for you, or a business, a business for the boys. (*He talks through The Woman's subsiding laughter; The Woman primps at the "mirror."*) There's so much I want to make for—

The Woman: Me? You didn't make me, Willy. I picked you.

Willy (*pleased*): You picked me?

The Woman (*who is quite proper-looking, Willy's age*): I did. I've been sitting at that desk watching all the salesmen go by, day in, day out. But you've got such a sense of humor, and we do have such a good time together, don't we?

Willy: Sure, sure. (*He takes her in his arms.*) Why do you have to go now?

The Woman: It's two o'clock . . .

Willy: No, come on in! (*He pulls her.*)

The Woman: . . . my sisters'll be scandalized. When'll you be back?

Willy: Oh, two weeks about. Will you come up again?

The Woman: Sure thing. You do make me laugh. It's good for me. (*She squeezes his arm, kisses him.*) And I think you're a wonderful man.

Willy: You picked me, heh?

The Woman: Sure. Because you're so sweet. And such a kidder.

Willy: Well, I'll see you next time I'm in Boston.

The Woman: I'll put you right through to the buyers.

Willy (*slapping her bottom*): Right. Well, bottoms up!

The Woman (*slaps him gently and laughs*): You just kill me, Willy. (*He suddenly grabs her and kisses her roughly.*) You kill me. And thanks for the stockings. I love a lot of stockings. Well, good night.

Willy: Good night. And keep your pores open!

The Woman: Oh, Willy!

(*The Woman bursts out laughing, and Linda's laughter blends in. The Woman disappears into the dark. Now the area at the kitchen table brightens. Linda is sitting where she was at the kitchen table, but now is mending a pair of silk stockings.*)

Linda: You are, Willy. The handsomest man. You've got no reason to feel that—

Willy (*coming out of The Woman's dimming area and going over to Linda*): I'll make it all up to you, Linda, I'll—

Linda: There's nothing to make up, dear. You're doing fine, better than—

Willy (*noticing her mending*): What's that?

Linda: Just mending my stockings. They're so expensive—

Willy (*angrily, taking them from her*): I won't have you mending stockings in this house! Now throw them out!

(*Linda puts the stockings in her pocket.*)

Bernard (*entering on the run*): Where is he? If he doesn't study!

Willy (*moving to the forestage, with great agitation*): You'll give him the answers!

Bernard: I do, but I can't on a Regents! That's a state exam! They're liable to arrest me!

Willy: Where is he? I'll whip him, I'll whip him!

Linda: And he'd better give back that football, Willy, it's not nice.

Willy: Biff! Where is he? Why is he taking everything?

Linda: He's too rough with the girls, Willy. All the mothers are afraid of him!

Willy: I'll whip him!

Bernard: He's driving the car without a license!

(*The Woman's laugh is heard.*)

Willy: Shut up!

Linda: All the mothers—

Willy: Shut up!

Bernard (*backing quietly away and out*): Mr. Birnbaum says he's stuck up.

Willy: Get outa here!

Bernard: If he doesn't buckle down he'll flunk math! (*He goes off.*)

Linda: He's right, Willy, you've gotta—

Willy (*exploding at her*): There's nothing the matter with him! You want him to be a worm like Bernard? He's got spirit, personality . . .

(*As he speaks, Linda, almost in tears, exits into the living room. Willy is alone in the kitchen, wilting and staring. The leaves are gone. It is night again, and the apartment houses look down from behind.*)

Willy: Loaded with it. Loaded! What is he stealing? He's giving it back, isn't he? Why is he stealing? What did I tell him? I never in my life told him anything but decent things.

(*Happy in pajamas has come down the stairs; Willy suddenly becomes aware of Happy's presence.*)

Happy: Let's go now, come on.

Willy (*sitting down at the kitchen table*): Huh! Why did she have to wax the floors herself? Everytime she waxes the floors she keels over. She knows that!

Happy: Shh! Take it easy. What brought you back tonight?

Willy: I got an awful scare. Nearly hit a kid in Yonkers. God! Why didn't I go to Alaska with my brother Ben that time! Ben! That man was a genius, that man was success incarnate! What a mistake! He begged me to go.

Happy: Well, there's no use in—

Willy: You guys! There was a man started with the clothes on his back and ended up with diamond mines!

Happy: Boy, someday I'd like to know how he did it.

Willy: What's the mystery? The man knew what he wanted and went out and got it! Walked into a jungle, and comes out, the age of twenty-one, and he's rich! The world is an oyster, but you don't crack it open on a mattress!

Happy: Pop, I told you I'm gonna retire you for life.

Willy: You'll retire me for life on seventy goddam dollars a week? And your women and your car and your apartment, and you'll retire me for life! Christ's sake, I couldn't get past Yonkers today! Where are you guys, where are you? The woods are burning! I can't drive a car!

(*Charley has appeared in the doorway. He is a large man, slow of speech, laconic, immovable. In all he says, despite what he says, there is pity, and, now, trepidation. He has a robe over his pajamas, slippers on his feet. He enters the kitchen.*)

Charley: Everything all right?

Happy: Yeah, Charley, everything's . . .

Willy: What's the matter?

Charley: I heard some noise. I thought something happened. Can't we do something about the walls? You sneeze in here, and in my house hats blow off.

Happy: Let's go to bed, Dad. Come on.

(*Charley signals to Happy to go.*)

Willy: You go ahead, I'm not tired at the moment.

Happy (to Willy): Take it easy, huh? (*He exits.*)

Willy: What're you doin' up?

Charley (sitting down at the kitchen table opposite Willy): Couldn't sleep good. I had a heartburn.

Willy: Well, you don't know how to eat.

Charley: I eat with my mouth.

Willy: No, you're ignorant. You gotta know about vitamins and things like that.

Charley: Come on, let's shoot. Tire you out a little.

Willy (hesitantly): All right. You got cards?

Charley (taking a deck from his pocket): Yeah, I got them. Someplace. What is it with those vitamins?

Willy (dealing): They build up your bones. Chemistry.

Charley: Yeah, but there's no bones in a heartburn.

Willy: What are you talkin' about? Do you know the first thing about it?

Charley: Don't get insulted.

Willy: Don't talk about something you don't know anything about.

(*They are playing. Pause.*)

Charley: What're you doin' home?

Willy: A little trouble with the car.

Charley: Oh. (*Pause.*) I'd like to take a trip to California.

Willy: Don't say.

Charley: You want a job?

Willy: I got a job, I told you that. (*After a slight pause.*) What the hell are you offering me a job for?

Charley: Don't get insulted.

Willy: Don't insult me.

Charley: I don't see no sense in it. You don't have to go on this way.

Willy: I got a good job. (*Slight pause.*) What do you keep comin' in here for?

Charley: You want me to go?

Willy (after a pause, withering): I can't understand it. He's going back to Texas again. What the hell is that?

Charley: Let him go.

Willy: I got nothin' to give him, Charley, I'm clean, I'm clean.

Charley: He won't starve. None a them starve. Forget about him.

Willy: Then what have I got to remember?

Charley: You take it too hard. To hell with it. When a deposit bottle is broken you don't get your nickel back.

Willy: That's easy enough for you to say.

Charley: That ain't easy for me to say.

Willy: Did you see the ceiling I put up in the living room?

Charley: Yeah, that's a piece of work. To put up a ceiling is a mystery to me. How do you do it?

Willy: What's the difference?

Charley: Well, talk about it.

Willy: You gonna put up a ceiling?

Charley: How could I put up a ceiling?

Willy: Then what the hell are you bothering me for?

Charley: You're insulted again.

Willy: A man who can't handle tools is not a man. You're disgusting.

Charley: Don't call me disgusting, Willy.

(*Uncle Ben, carrying a valise and an umbrella, enters the forestage from around the right corner of the house. He is a stolid man, in his sixties, with a mustache and an authoritative air. He is utterly certain of his destiny, and there is an aura of far places about him. He enters exactly as Willy speaks.*)

Willy: I'm getting awfully tired, Ben.

(*Ben's music is heard. Ben looks around at everything.*)

Charley: Good, keep playing; you'll sleep better. Did you call me Ben?

(*Ben looks at his watch.*)

Willy: That's funny. For a second there you reminded me of my brother Ben.

Ben: I have only a few minutes. (*He strolls, inspecting the place. Willy and Charley continue playing.*)

Charley: You never heard from him again, heh? Since that time?

Willy: Didn't Linda tell you? Couple of weeks ago we got a letter from his wife in Africa. He died.

Charley: That so.

Ben (*chuckling*): So this is Brooklyn, eh?

Charley: Maybe you're in for some of his money.

Willy: Naa, he had seven sons. There's just one opportunity I had with that man . . .

Ben: I must make a train, William. There are several properties I'm looking at in Alaska.

Willy: Sure, sure! If I'd gone with him to Alaska that time, everything would've been totally different.

Charley: Go on, you'd froze to death up there.

Willy: What're you talking about?

Ben: Opportunity is tremendous in Alaska, William. Surprised you're not up there.

Willy: Sure, tremendous.

Charley: Heh?

Willy: There was the only man I ever met who knew the answers.

Charley: Who?

Ben: How are you all?

Willy (*taking a pot, smiling*): Fine, fine.

Charley: Pretty sharp tonight.

Ben: Is Mother living with you?

Willy: No, she died a long time ago.

Charley: Who?

Ben: That's too bad. Fine specimen of a lady, Mother.

Willy (*to Charley*): Heh?

Ben: I'd hoped to see the old girl.

Charley: Who died?

Ben: Heard anything from Father, have you?

Willy (*unnerved*): What do you mean, who died?

Charley (*taking a pot*): What're you talkin' about?

Ben (*looking at his watch*): William, it's half-past eight!

Willy (*as though to dispel his confusion he angrily stops Charley's hand*): That's my build!

Charley: I put the ace—

Willy: If you don't know how to play the game I'm not gonna throw my money away on you!

Charley (rising): It was my ace, for God's sake!

Willy: I'm through, I'm through!

Ben: When did Mother die?

Willy: Long ago. Since the beginning you never knew how to play cards.

Charley (picks up the cards and goes to the door): All right! Next time I'll bring a deck with five aces.

Willy: I don't play that kind of game!

Charley (turning to him): You ought to be ashamed of yourself!

Willy: Yeah?

Charley: Yeah! (*He goes out.*)

Willy (slamming the door after him): Ignoramus!

Ben (as Willy comes toward him through the wall-line of the kitchen): So you're William.

Willy (shaking Ben's hand): Ben! I've been waiting for you so long! What's the answer? How did you do it?

Ben: Oh, there's a story in that.

(*Linda enters the forestage, as of old, carrying the wash basket.*)

Linda: Is this Ben?

Ben (gallantly): How do you do, my dear.

Linda: Where've you been all these years? Willy's always wondered why you—

Willy (pulling Ben away from her impatiently): Where is Dad? Didn't you follow him? How did you get started?

Ben: Well, I don't know how much you remember.

Willy: Well, I was just a baby, of course, only three or four years old—

Ben: Three years and eleven months.

Willy: What a memory, Ben!

Ben: I have many enterprises, William, and I have never kept books.

Willy: I remember I was sitting under the wagon in—was it Nebraska?

Ben: It was South Dakota, and I gave you a bunch of wild flowers.

Willy: I remember you walking away down some open road.

Ben (laughing): I was going to find Father in Alaska.

Willy: Where is he?

Ben: At that age I had a very faulty view of geography, William. I discovered after a few days that I was heading due south, so instead of Alaska, I ended up in Africa.

Linda: Africa!

Willy: The Gold Coast!

Ben: Principally, diamond mines.

Linda: Diamond mines!

Ben: Yes, my dear. But I've only a few minutes—

Willy: No! Boys! Boys! (*Young Biff and Happy appear.*) Listen to this. This is your Uncle Ben, a great man! Tell my boys, Ben!

Ben: Why, boys, when I was seventeen I walked into the jungle, and when I was twenty-one I walked out. (*He laughs.*) And by God I was rich.

Willy (to the boys): You see what I been talking about? The greatest things can happen!

Ben (glancing at his watch): I have an appointment in Ketchikan Tuesday week.

Willy: No, Ben! Please tell about Dad. I want my boys to hear. I want them to know the kind of stock they sprang from. All I remember is a man with a big beard, and I was in Mamma's lap, sitting around a fire, and some kind of high music.

Ben: His flute. He played the flute.

Willy: Sure, the flute, that's right!

(*New music is heard, a high, rollicking tune.*)

Ben: Father was a very great and a very wild-hearted man. We would start in Boston, and he'd toss the whole family into the wagon, and then he'd drive the team right across the country; through Ohio, and Indiana, Michigan, Illinois, and all the Western states. And we'd stop in the towns and sell the flutes that he'd made on the way. Great inventor, Father. With one gadget he made more in a week than a man like you could make in a lifetime.

Willy: That's just the way I'm bringing them up, Ben—rugged, well-liked, all-around.

Ben: Yeah? (*To Biff.*) Hit that, boy—hard as you can. (*He pounds his stomach.*)

Biff: Oh, no, sir!

Ben (taking boxing stance): Come on, get to me! (*He laughs.*)

Willy: Go to it, Biff! Go ahead, show him!

Biff: Okay! (*He cocks his fist and starts in.*)

Linda (to Willy): Why must he fight, dear?

Ben (sparring with Biff): Good boy! Good boy!

Willy: How's that, Ben, heh?

Happy: Give him the left, Biff!

Linda: Why are you fighting?

Ben: Good boy! (*Suddenly comes in, trips Biff, and stands over him, the point of his umbrella poised over Biff's eye.*)

Linda: Look out, Biff!

Biff: Gee!

Ben (patting Biff's knee): Never fight fair with a stranger, boy. You'll never get out of the jungle that way. (*Taking Linda's hand and bowing.*) It was an honor and a pleasure to meet you, Linda.

Linda (withdrawing her hand coldly, frightened): Have a nice—trip.

Ben (to Willy): And good luck with your—what do you do?

Willy: Selling.

Ben: Yes. Well . . . (*He raises his hand in farewell to all.*)

Willy: No, Ben, I don't want you to think . . . (*He takes Ben's arm to show him.*) It's Brooklyn, I know, but we hunt too.

Ben: Really, now.

Willy: Oh, sure, there's snakes and rabbits and—that's why I moved out here. Why, Biff can fell any one of these trees in no time! Boys! Go right over to where they're building the apartment house and get some sand. We're gonna rebuild the entire front stoop right now! Watch this, Ben!

Biff: Yes, sir! On the double, Hap!

Happy (as he and Biff run off): I lost weight, Pop, you notice?

(*Charley enters in knickers, even before the boys are gone.*)

Charley: Listen, if they steal any more from that building the watchman'll put the cops on them!

Linda (to Willy): Don't let Biff . . .

(Ben laughs lustily.)

Willy: You shoulda seen the lumber they brought home last week. At least a dozen six-by-tens worth all kinds of money.

Charley: Listen, if that watchman—

Willy: I gave them hell, understand. But I got a couple of fearless characters there.

Charley: Willy, the jails are full of fearless characters.

Ben (clapping Willy on the back, with a laugh at Charley): And the stock exchange, friend!

Willy (joining in Ben's laughter): Where are the rest of your pants?

Charley: My wife bought them.

Willy: Now all you need is a golf club and you can go upstairs and go to sleep. *(To Ben.)* Great athlete! Between him and his son Bernard they can't hammer a nail!

Bernard (rushing in): The watchman's chasing Biff!

Willy (angrily): Shut up! He's not stealing anything!

Linda (alarmed, hurrying off left): Where is he? Biff, dear! *(She exits.)*

Willy (moving toward the left, away from Ben): There's nothing wrong. What's the matter with you?

Ben: Nervy boy. Good!

Willy (laughing): Oh, nerves of iron, that Biff!

Charley: Don't know what it is. My New England man comes back and he's bleedin', they murdered him up there.

Willy: It's contacts, Charley, I got important contacts!

Charley (sarcastically): Glad to hear it, Willy. Come in later, we'll shoot a little casino. I'll take some of your Portland money. *(He laughs at Willy and exits.)*

Willy (turning to Ben): Business is bad, it's murderous. But not for me, of course.

Ben: I'll stop by on my way back to Africa.

Willy (longingly): Can't you stay a few days? You're just what I need, Ben, because I— I have a fine position, but I—well, Dad left when I was such a baby and I never had a chance to talk to him and I still feel—kind of temporary about myself.

Ben: I'll be late for my train.

(They are at opposite ends of the stage.)

Willy: Ben, my boys—can't we talk? They'd go into the jaws of hell for me, see, but I—

Ben: William, you're being first-rate with your boys. Outstanding, manly chaps!

Willy (hanging on to his words): Oh, Ben, that's good to hear! Because sometimes I'm afraid that I'm not teaching them the right kind of—Ben, how should I teach them?

Ben (giving great weight to each word, and with a certain vicious audacity): William, when I walked into the jungle, I was seventeen. When I walked out I was twenty-one. And, by God, I was rich! *(He goes off into darkness around the right corner of the house.)*

Willy: . . . was rich! That's just the spirit I want to imbue them with! To walk into a jungle! I was right! I was right! I was right!

(Ben is gone, but Willy is still speaking to him as Linda, in nightgown and robe, enters the kitchen, glances around for Willy, then goes to the door of the house, looks out and sees him. Comes down to his left. He looks at her.)

Linda: Willy, dear? Willy?

Willy: I was right!

Linda: Did you have some cheese? (*He can't answer.*) It's very late, darling. Come to bed, heh?

Willy (*looking straight up*): Gotta break your neck to see a star in this yard.

Linda: You coming in?

Willy: What ever happened to that diamond watch fob? Remember? When Ben came from Africa that time? Didn't he give me a watch fob with a diamond in it?

Linda: You pawned it, dear. Twelve, thirteen years ago. For Biff's radio correspondence course.

Willy: Gee, that was a beautiful thing. I'll take a walk.

Linda: But you're in your slippers.

Willy (*starting to go around the house at the left*): I was right! I was! (*Half to Linda, as he goes, shaking his head.*) What a man! There was a man worth talking to. I was right!

Linda (*calling after Willy*): But in your slippers, Willy!

(*Willy is almost gone when Biff, in his pajamas, comes down the stairs and enters the kitchen.*)

Biff: What is he doing out there?

Linda: Sh!

Biff: God Almighty, Mom, how long has he been doing this?

Linda: Don't, he'll hear you.

Biff: What the hell is the matter with him?

Linda: It'll pass by morning.

Biff: Shouldn't we do anything?

Linda: Oh, my dear, you should do a lot of things, but there's nothing to do, so go to sleep.

(*Happy comes down the stairs and sits on the steps.*)

Happy: I never heard him so loud, Mom.

Linda: Well, come around more often; you'll hear him. (*She sits down at the table and mends the lining of Willy's jacket.*)

Biff: Why didn't you ever write me about this, Mom?

Linda: How would I write to you? For over three months you had no address.

Biff: I was on the move. But you know I thought of you all the time. You know that, don't you, pal?

Linda: I know, dear, I know. But he likes to have a letter. Just to know that there's still a possibility for better things.

Biff: He's not like this all the time, is he?

Linda: It's when you come home he's always the worst.

Biff: When I come home?

Linda: When you write you're coming, he's all smiles, and talks about the future, and—he's just wonderful. And then the closer you seem to come, the more shaky he gets, and then, by the time you get here, he's arguing, and he seems angry at you. I think it's just that maybe he can't bring himself to—to open up to you. Why are you so hateful to each other? Why is that?

Biff (*evasively*): I'm not hateful, Mom.

Linda: But you no sooner come in the door than you're fighting!

Biff: I don't know why. I mean to change. I'm tryin', Mom, you understand?

Linda: Are you home to stay now?

Biff: I don't know. I want to look around, see what's doin'.

Linda: Biff, you can't look around all your life, can you?

Biff: I just can't take hold, Mom. I can't take hold of some kind of a life.

Linda: Biff, a man is not a bird, to come and go with the springtime.

Biff: Your hair . . . (*He touches her hair.*) Your hair got so gray.

Linda: Oh, it's been gray since you were in high school. I just stopped dyeing it, that's all.

Biff: Dye it again, will ya? I don't want my pal looking old. (*He smiles.*)

Linda: You're such a boy! You think you can go away for a year and . . . You've got to get it into your head now that one day you'll knock on this door and there'll be strange people here—

Biff: What are you talking about? You're not even sixty, Mom.

Linda: But what about your father?

Biff (lamely): Well, I meant him too.

Happy: He admires Pop.

Linda: Biff dear, if you don't have any feeling for him, then you can't have any feeling for me.

Biff: Sure I can, Mom.

Linda: No. You can't just come to see me, because I love him. (*With a threat, but only a threat, of tears.*) He's the dearest man in the world to me, and I won't have anyone making him feel unwanted and low and blue. You've got to make up your mind now, darling, there's no leeway any more. Either he's your father and you pay him that respect, or else you're not to come here. I know he's not easy to get along with—nobody knows that better than me—but . . .

Willy (from the left, with a laugh): Hey, hey, Biffo!

Biff (starting to go out after Willy): What the hell is the matter with him? (*Happy stops him.*)

Linda: Don't—don't go near him!

Biff: Stop making excuses for him! He always, always wiped the floor with you. Never had an ounce of respect for you.

Happy: He's always had respect for—

Biff: What the hell do you know about it?

Happy (surlily): Just don't call him crazy!

Biff: He's got no character—Charley wouldn't do this. Not in his own house—spewing out that vomit from his mind.

Happy: Charley never had to cope with what he's got to.

Biff: People are worse off than Willy Loman. Believe me, I've seen them!

Linda: Then make Charley your father, Biff. You can't do that, can you? I don't say he's a great man. Willy Loman never made a lot of money. His name was never in the paper. He's not the finest character that ever lived. But he's a human being, and a terrible thing is happening to him. So attention must be paid. He's not to be allowed to fall into his grave like an old dog. Attention, attention must be finally paid to such a person. You called him crazy—

Biff: I didn't mean—

Linda: No, a lot of people think he's lost his—balance. But you don't have to be very smart to know what his trouble is. The man is exhausted.

Happy: Sure!

Linda: A small man can be just as exhausted as a great man. He works for a company thirty-six years this March, opens up unheard-of territories to their trademark, and now in his old age they take his salary away.

Happy (indignantly): I didn't know that, Mom!

Linda: You never asked, my dear! Now that you get your spending money someplace else you don't trouble your mind with him.

Happy: But I gave you money last—

Linda: Christmas time, fifty dollars! To fix the hot water it cost ninety-seven fifty! For five weeks he's been on straight commission, like a beginner, an unknown!

Biff: Those ungrateful bastards!

Linda: Are they any worse than his sons? When he brought them business, when he was young, they were glad to see him. But now his old friends, the old buyers that loved him so and always found some order to hand him in a pinch—they're all dead, retired. He used to be able to make six, seven calls a day in Boston. Now he takes his valises out of the car and puts them back and takes them out again and he's exhausted. Instead of walking he talks now. He drives seven hundred miles, and when he gets there no one knows him any more, no one welcomes him. And what goes through a man's mind, driving seven hundred miles home without having earned a cent? Why shouldn't he talk to himself? Why? When he has to go to Charley and borrow fifty dollars a week and pretend to me that it's his pay? How long can that go on? How long? You see what I'm sitting here and waiting for? And you tell me he has no character? The man who never worked a day but for your benefit? When does he get the medal for that? Is this his reward—to turn around at the age of sixty-three and find his sons, who he loved better than his life, one a philandering bum—

Happy: Mom!

Linda: That's all you are, my baby! (*To Biff.*) And you! What happened to the love you had for him? You were such pals! How you used to talk to him on the phone every night! How lonely he was till he could come home to you!

Biff: All right, Mom. I'll live here in my room, and I'll get a job. I'll keep away from him, that's all.

Linda: No, Biff. You can't stay here and fight all the time.

Biff: He threw me out of this house, remember that.

Linda: Why did he do that? I never knew why.

Biff: Because I know he's a fake and he doesn't like anybody around who knows!

Linda: Why a fake? In what way? What do you mean?

Biff: Just don't lay it all at my feet. It's between me and him—that's all I have to say. I'll chip in from now on. He'll settle for half my pay check. He'll be all right. I'm going to bed. (*He starts for the stairs.*)

Linda: He won't be all right.

Biff (turning on the stairs, furiously): I hate this city and I'll stay here. Now what do you want?

Linda: He's dying, Biff.

(*Happy turns quickly to her, shocked.*)

Biff (after a pause): Why is he dying?

Linda: He's been trying to kill himself.

Biff (with great horror): How?

Linda: I live from day to day.

Biff: What're you talking about?

Linda: Remember I wrote you that he smashed up the car again? In February?

Biff: Well?

Linda: The insurance inspector came. He said that they have evidence. That all these accidents in the last year—weren't—weren't—accidents.

Happy: How can they tell that? That's a lie.

Linda: It seems there's a woman . . . (*She takes a breath as—*)

Biff (*sharply but contained*): What woman?

Linda (*simultaneously*): . . . and this woman . . .

Linda: What?

Biff: Nothing. Go ahead.

Linda: What did you say?

Biff: Nothing. I just said what woman?

Happy: What about her?

Linda: Well, it seems she was walking down the road and saw his car. She says that he wasn't driving fast at all, and that he didn't skid. She says he came to that little bridge, and then deliberately smashed into the railing, and it was only the shallowness of the water that saved him.

Biff: Oh, no, he probably just fell asleep again.

Linda: I don't think he fell asleep.

Biff: Why not?

Linda: Last month . . . (*With great difficulty.*) Oh, boys, it's so hard to say a thing like this! He's just a big stupid man to you, but I tell you there's more good in him than in many other people. (*She chokes, wipes her eyes.*) I was looking for a fuse. The lights blew out, and I went down the cellar. And behind the fuse box—it happened to fall out—was a length of rubber pipe—just short.

Happy: No kidding?

Linda: There's a little attachment on the end of it. I knew right away. And sure enough, on the bottom of the water heater there's a new little nipple on the gas pipe.

Happy (*angrily*): That—jerk.

Biff: Did you have it taken off?

Linda: I'm—I'm ashamed to. How can I mention it to him? Every day I go down and take away that little rubber pipe. But, when he comes home, I put it back where it was. How can I insult him that way? I don't know what to do. I live from day to day, boys. I tell you, I know every thought in his mind. It sounds so old-fashioned and silly, but I tell you he put his whole life into you and you've turned your backs on him. (*She is bent over in the chair, weeping, her face in her hands.*) Biff, I swear to God! Biff, his life is in your hands!

Happy (*to Biff*): How do you like that damned fool!

Biff (*kissing her*): All right, pal, all right. It's all settled now. I've been remiss. I know that, Mom. But now I'll stay, and I swear to you, I'll apply myself. (*Kneeling in front of her, in a fever of self-reproach.*) It's just—you see, Mom, I don't fit in business. Not that I won't try. I'll try, and I'll make good.

Happy: Sure you will. The trouble with you in business was you never tried to please people.

Biff: I know, I—

Happy: Like when you worked for Harrison's. Bob Harrison said you were tops, and then you go and do some damn fool thing like whistling whole songs in the elevator like a comedian.

Biff (*against Happy*): So what? I like to whistle sometimes.

Happy: You don't raise a guy to a responsible job who whistles in the elevator!

Linda: Well, don't argue about it now.

Happy: Like when you'd go off and swim in the middle of the day instead of taking the line around.

Biff (*his resentment rising*): Well, don't you run off? You take off sometimes, don't you? On a nice summer day?

Happy: Yeah, but I cover myself!

Linda: Boys!

Happy: If I'm going to take a fade the boss can call any number where I'm supposed to be and they'll swear to him that I just left. I'll tell you something that I hate to say, Biff, but in the business world some of them think you're crazy.

Biff (*angered*): Screw the business world!

Happy: All right, screw it! Great, but cover yourself!

Linda: Hap! Hap!

Biff: I don't care what they think! They've laughed at Dad for years, and you know why? Because we don't belong in this nut-house of a city! We should be mixing cement on some open plain, or—or carpenters. A carpenter is allowed to whistle!

(*Willy walks in from the entrance of the house, at left.*)

Willy: Even your grandfather was better than a carpenter. (*Pause. They watch him.*) You never grew up. Bernard does not whistle in the elevator, I assure you.

Biff (*as though to laugh Willy out of it*): Yeah, but you do, Pop.

Willy: I never in my life whistled in an elevator! And who in the business world thinks I'm crazy?

Biff: I didn't mean it like that, Pop. Now don't make a whole thing out of it, will ya?

Willy: Go back to the West! Be a carpenter, a cowboy, enjoy yourself!

Linda: Willy, he was just saying—

Willy: I heard what he said!

Happy (*trying to quiet Willy*): Hey, Pop, come on now . . .

Willy (*continuing over Happy's line*): They laugh at me, heh? Go to Filene's, go to the Hub, go to Slattery's, Boston. Call out the name Willy Loman and see what happens! Big shot!

Biff: All right, Pop.

Willy: Big!

Biff: All right!

Willy: Why do you always insult me?

Biff: I didn't say a word. (*To Linda.*) Did I say a word?

Linda: He didn't say anything, Willy.

Willy (*going to the doorway of the living room*): All right, good night, good night.

Linda: Willy, dear, he just decided . . .

Willy (*to Biff*): If you get tired hanging around tomorrow, paint the ceiling I put up in the living room.

Biff: I'm leaving early tomorrow.

Happy: He's going to see Bill Oliver, Pop.

Willy (*interestedly*): Oliver? For what?

Biff (*with reserve, but trying, trying*): He always said he'd stake me. I'd like to go into business, so maybe I can take him up on it.

Linda: Isn't that wonderful?

Willy: Don't interrupt. What's wonderful about it? There's fifty men in the City of New York who'd stake him. (*To Biff.*) Sporting goods?

Biff: I guess so. I know something about it and—

Willy: He knows something about it! You know sporting goods better than Spalding, for God's sake! How much is he giving you?

Biff: I don't know, I didn't even see him yet, but—

Willy: Then what're you talkin' about?

Biff (*getting angry*): Well, all I said was I'm gonna see him, that's all!

Willy (*turning away*): Ah, you're counting your chickens again.

Biff (*starting left for the stairs*): Oh, Jesus, I'm going to sleep!

Willy (*calling after him*): Don't curse in this house!

Biff (*turning*): Since when did you get so clean!

Happy (*trying to stop them*): Wait a . . .

Willy: Don't use that language to me! I won't have it!

Happy (*grabbing Biff, shouts*): Wait a minute! I got an idea. I got a feasible idea. Come here, Biff, let's talk this over now, let's talk some sense here. When I was down in Florida last time, I thought of a great idea to sell sporting goods. It just came back to me. You and I, Biff—we have a line, the Loman Line. We train a couple of weeks, and put on a couple of exhibitions, see?

Willy: That's an idea!

Happy: Wait! We form two basketball teams, see? Two water-polo teams. We play each other. It's a million dollars' worth of publicity. Two brothers, see? The Loman Brothers. Displays in the Royal Palms—all the hotels. And banners over the ring and the basketball court: "Loman Brothers." Baby, we could sell sporting goods!

Willy: That is a one-million-dollar idea.

Linda: Marvelous!

Biff: I'm in great shape as far as that's concerned.

Happy: And the beauty of it is, Biff, it wouldn't be like a business. We'd be out playin' ball again . . .

Biff (*enthused*): Yeah, that's . . .

Willy: Million-dollar . . .

Happy: And you wouldn't get fed up with it, Biff. It'd be the family again. There'd be the old honor, and comradeship, and if you wanted to go off for a swim or somethin'—well, you'd do it! Without some smart cooky gettin' up ahead of you!

Willy: Lick the world! You guys together could absolutely lick the civilized world.

Biff: I'll see Oliver tomorrow. Hap, if we could work that out . . .

Linda: Maybe things are beginning to—

Willy (*wildly enthused, to Linda*): Stop interrupting! (*To Biff.*) But don't wear sport jacket and slacks when you see Oliver.

Biff: No, I'll—

Willy: A business suit, and talk as little as possible, and don't crack any jokes.

Biff: He did like me. Always liked me.

Linda: He loved you!

Willy (*to Linda*): Will you stop! (*To Biff.*) Walk in very serious. You are not applying for a boy's job. Money is to pass. Be quiet, fine, and serious. Everybody likes a kidder, but nobody lends him money.

Happy: I'll try to get some myself, Biff. I'm sure I can.

Willy: I can see great things for you, kids, I think your troubles are over. But remember, start big and you'll end big. Ask for fifteen. How much you gonna ask for?

Biff: Gee, I don't know—

Willy: And don't say "Gee." "Gee" is a boy's word. A man walking in for fifteen thousand dollars does not say "Gee!"

Biff: Ten, I think, would be top though.

Willy: Don't be so modest. You always started too low. Walk in with a big laugh. Don't look worried. Start off with a couple of your good stories to lighten things up. It's not what you say, it's how you say it—because personality always wins the day.

Linda: Oliver always thought the highest of him—

Willy: Will you let me talk?

Biff: Don't yell at her, Pop, will ya?

Willy (angrily): I was talking, wasn't I?

Biff: I don't like you yelling at her all the time, and I'm tellin' you, that's all.

Willy: What're you, takin' over the house?

Linda: Willy—

Willy (turning on her): Don't take his side all the time, goddammit!

Biff (furiously): Stop yelling at her!

Willy (suddenly pulling on his cheek, beaten down, guilt ridden): Give my best to Bill Oliver—he may remember me. (*He exits through the living room doorway.*)

Linda (her voice subdued): What'd you have to start that for? (*Biff turns away.*) You see how sweet he was as soon as you talked hopefully? (*She goes over to Biff.*) Come up and say good night to him. Don't let him go to bed that way.

Happy: Come on, Biff, let's buck him up.

Linda: Please, dear. Just say good night. It takes so little to make him happy. Come. (*She goes through the living room doorway, calling upstairs from within the living room.*) Your pajamas are hanging in the bathroom. Willy!

Happy (looking toward where Linda went out): What a woman! They broke the mold when they made her. You know that, Biff?

Biff: He's off salary. My God, working on commission!

Happy: Well, let's face it: he's no hot-shot selling man. Except that sometimes, you have to admit, he's a sweet personality.

Biff (deciding): Lend me ten bucks, will ya? I want to buy some new ties.

Happy: I'll take you to a place I know. Beautiful stuff. Wear one of my striped shirts tomorrow.

Biff: She got gray. Mom got awful old. Gee, I'm gonna go in to Oliver tomorrow and knock him for a—

Happy: Come on up. Tell that to Dad. Let's give him a whirl. Come on.

Biff (steamed up): You know, with ten thousand bucks, boy!

Happy (as they go into the living room): That's the talk, Biff, that's the first time I've heard the old confidence out of you! (*From within the living room, fading off.*) You're gonna live with me, kid, and any babe you want you just say the word . . . (*The last lines are hardly heard. They are mounting the stairs to their parents' bedroom.*)

Linda (entering her bedroom and addressing Willy, who is in the bathroom. She is straightening the bed for him): Can you do anything about the shower? It drips.

Willy (from the bathroom): All of a sudden everything falls to pieces! Goddam plumbing, oughta be sued, those people. I hardly finished putting it in and the thing . . . (*His words rumble off.*)

Linda: I'm just wondering if Oliver will remember him. You think he might?

Willy (coming out of the bathroom in his pajamas): Remember him? What's the matter with you, you crazy? If he'd've stayed with Oliver he'd be on top by now! Wait'll

Oliver gets a look at him. You don't know the average caliber any more. The average young man today—(*he is getting into bed*)—is got a caliber of zero. Greatest thing in the world for him was to bum around.

(*Biff and Happy enter the bedroom. Slight pause.*)

Willy (*stops short, looking at Biff*): Glad to hear it, boy.

Happy: He wanted to say good night to you, sport.

Willy (*to Biff*): Yeah. Knock him dead, boy. What'd you want to tell me?

Biff: Just take it easy, Pop. Good night. (*He turns to go.*)

Willy (*unable to resist*): And if anything falls off the desk while you're talking to him—like a package or something—don't you pick it up. They have office boys for that.

Linda: I'll make a big breakfast—

Willy: Will you let me finish? (*To Biff.*) Tell him you were in the business in the West. Not farm work.

Biff: All right, Dad.

Linda: I think everything—

Willy (*going right through her speech*): And don't undersell yourself. No less than fifteen thousand dollars.

Biff (*unable to bear him*): Okay. Good night, Mom. (*He starts moving.*)

Willy: Because you got a greatness in you, Biff, remember that. You got all kinds a greatness . . . (*He lies back, exhausted. Biff walks out.*)

Linda (*calling after Biff*): Sleep well, darling!

Happy: I'm gonna get married, Mom. I wanted to tell you.

Linda: Go to sleep, dear.

Happy (*going*): I just wanted to tell you.

Willy: Keep up the good work. (*Happy exits.*) God . . . remember that Ebbets Field game? The championship of the city?

Linda: Just rest. Should I sing to you?

Willy: Yeah. Sing to me. (*Linda hums a soft lullaby.*) When that team came out—he was the tallest, remember?

Linda: Oh, yes. And in gold.

(*Biff enters the darkened kitchen, takes a cigarette, and leaves the house. He comes downstage into a golden pool of light. He smokes, staring at the night.*)

Willy: Like a young god. Hercules—something like that. And the sun, the sun all around him. Remember how he waved to me? Right up from the field, with the representatives of three colleges standing by? And the buyers I brought, and the cheers when he came out—Loman, Loman, Loman! God Almighty, he'll be great yet. A star like that, magnificent, can never really fade away!

(*The light on Willy is fading. The gas heater begins to glow through the kitchen wall, near the stairs, a blue flame beneath red coils.*)

Linda (*timidly*): Willy, dear, what has he got against you?

Willy: I'm so tired. Don't talk any more.

(*Biff slowly returns to the kitchen. He stops, stares toward the heater.*)

Linda: Will you ask Howard to let you work in New York?

Willy: First thing in the morning. Everything'll be all right.

(*Biff reaches behind the heater and draws out a length of rubber tubing. He is horrified and turns his head toward Willy's room, still dimly lit, from which the strains of Linda's desperate but monotonous humming rise.*)

Willy (*staring through the window into the moonlight*): Gee, look at the moon moving between the buildings!

(*Biff wraps the tubing around his hand and quickly goes up the stairs. Curtain.*)

ACT II

Music is heard, gay and bright. The curtain rises as the music fades away. Willy, in shirt sleeves, is sitting at the kitchen table, sipping coffee, his hat in his lap. Linda is filling his cup when she can.

Willy: Wonderful coffee. Meal in itself.

Linda: Can I make you some eggs?

Willy: No. Take a breath.

Linda: You look so rested, dear.

Willy: I slept like a dead one. First time in months. Imagine, sleeping till ten on a Tuesday morning. Boys left nice and early, heh?

Linda: They were out of here by eight o'clock.

Willy: Good work!

Linda: It was so thrilling to see them leaving together. I can't get over the shaving lotion in this house.

Willy (*smiling*): Mmm—

Linda: Biff was very changed this morning. His whole attitude seemed to be hopeful. He couldn't wait to get downtown to see Oliver.

Willy: He's heading for a change. There's no question, there simply are certain men that take longer to get—solidified. How did he dress?

Linda: His blue suit. He's so handsome in that suit. He could be a—anything in that suit!

(*Willy gets up from the table. Linda holds his jacket for him.*)

Willy: There's no question, no question at all. Gee, on the way home tonight I'd like to buy some seeds.

Linda (*laughing*): That'd be wonderful. But not enough sun gets back there. Nothing'll grow any more.

Willy: You wait, kid, before it's all over we're gonna get a little place out in the country, and I'll raise some vegetables, a couple of chickens . . .

Linda: You'll do it yet, dear.

(*Willy walks out of his jacket. Linda follows him.*)

Willy: And they'll get married, and come for a weekend. I'd build a little guest house. 'Cause I got so many fine tools, all I'd need would be a little lumber and some peace of mind.

Linda (*joyfully*): I sewed the lining . . .

Willy: I could build two guest houses, so they'd both come. Did he decide how much he's going to ask Oliver for?

Linda (*getting him into the jacket*): He didn't mention it, but I imagine ten or fifteen thousand. You going to talk to Howard today?

Willy: Yeah. I'll put it to him straight and simple. He'll just have to take me off the road.

Linda: And Willy, don't forget to ask for a little advance, because we've got the insurance premium. It's the grace period now.

Willy: That's a hundred . . . ?

Linda: A hundred and eight, sixty-eight. Because we're a little short again.

Willy: Why are we short?

Linda: Well, you had the motor job on the car . . .

Willy: That goddam Studebaker!

Linda: And you got one more payment on the refrigerator . . .

Willy: But it just broke again!

Linda: Well, it's old, dear.

Willy: I told you we should've bought a well-advertised machine. Charley bought a General Electric and it's twenty years old and it's still good, that son-of-a-bitch.

Linda: But, Willy—

Willy: Whoever heard of a Hastings refrigerator? Once in my life I would like to own something outright before it's broken! I'm always in a race with the junkyard! I just finished paying for the car and it's on its last legs. The refrigerator consumes belts like a goddam maniac. They time those things. They time them so when you finally paid for them, they're used up.

Linda (*buttoning up his jacket as he unbuttons it*): All told, about two hundred dollars would carry us, dear. But that includes the last payment on the mortgage. After this payment, Willy, the house belongs to us.

Willy: It's twenty-five years!

Linda: Biff was nine years old when we bought it.

Willy: Well, that's a great thing. To weather a twenty-five year mortgage is—

Linda: It's an accomplishment.

Willy: All the cement, the lumber, the reconstruction I put in this house! There ain't a crack to be found in it any more.

Linda: Well, it served its purpose.

Willy: What purpose? Some stranger'll come along, move in, and that's that. If only Biff would take this house, and raise a family . . . (*He starts to go.*) Good-by, I'm late.

Linda (*suddenly remembering*): Oh, I forgot! You're supposed to meet them for dinner.

Willy: Me?

Linda: At Frank's Chop House on Forty-eighth near Sixth Avenue.

Willy: Is that so! How about you?

Linda: No, just the three of you. They're gonna blow you to a big meal!

Willy: Don't say! Who thought of that?

Linda: Biff came to me this morning, Willy, and he said, "Tell Dad, we want to blow him to a big meal." Be there six o'clock. You and your two boys are going to have dinner.

Willy: Gee whiz! That's really somethin'. I'm gonna knock Howard for a loop, kid. I'll get an advance, and I'll come home with a New York job. Goddammit, now I'm gonna do it!

Linda: Oh, that's the spirit, Willy!

Willy: I will never get behind a wheel the rest of my life!

Linda: It's changing, Willy, I can feel it changing!

Willy: Beyond a question. G'by, I'm late. (*He starts to go again.*)

Linda (*calling after him as she runs to the kitchen table for a handkerchief*): You got your glasses?

Willy (*feels for them, then comes back in*): Yeah, yeah, got my glasses.

Linda (*giving him the handkerchief*): And a handkerchief.

Willy: Yeah, handkerchief.

Linda: And your saccharine?

Willy: Yeah, my saccharine.

Linda: Be careful on the subway stairs.

(*She kisses him, and a silk stocking is seen hanging from her hand. Willy notices it.*)

Willy: Will you stop mending stockings? At least while I'm in the house. It gets me nervous. I can't tell you. Please.

(*Linda hides the stocking in her hand as she follows Willy across the forestage in front of the house.*)

Linda: Remember, Frank's Chop House.

Willy (*passing the apron*): Maybe beets would grow out there.

Linda (*laughing*): But you tried so many times.

Willy: Yeah. Well, don't work hard today. (*He disappears around the right corner of the house.*)

Linda: Be careful!

(*As Willy vanishes, Linda waves to him. Suddenly the phone rings. She runs across the stage and into the kitchen and lifts it.*)

Linda: Hello? Oh, Biff! I'm so glad you called, I just . . . Yes, sure, I just told him. Yes, he'll be there for dinner at six o'clock, I didn't forget. Listen, I was just dying to tell you. You know that little rubber pipe I told you about? That he connected to the gas heater? I finally decided to go down the cellar this morning and take it away and destroy it. But it's gone! Imagine? He took it away himself, it isn't there! (*She listens.*) When? Oh, then you took it. Oh—nothing, it's just that I'd hoped he'd taken it away himself. Oh, I'm not worried, darling, because this morning he left in such high spirits, it was like the old days! I'm not afraid any more. Did Mr. Oliver see you? . . . Well, you wait there then. And make a nice impression on him, darling. Just don't perspire too much before you see him. And have a nice time with Dad. He may have big news too! . . . That's right, a New York job. And be sweet to him tonight, dear. Be loving to him. Because he's only a little boat looking for a harbor. (*She is trembling with sorrow and joy.*) Oh, that's wonderful, Biff, you'll save his life. Thanks, darling. Just put your arm around him when he comes into the restaurant. Give him a smile. That's the boy . . . Good-by, dear. . . . You got your comb? . . . That's fine. Good-by, Biff dear.

(*In the middle of her speech, Howard Wagner, thirty-six, wheels in a small typewriter table on which is a wire-recording machine and proceeds to plug it in. This is on the left forestage. Light slowly fades on Linda as it rises on Howard. Howard is intent on threading the machine and only glances over his shoulder as Willy appears.*)

Willy: Pst! Pst!

Howard: Hello, Willy, come in.

Willy: Like to have a little talk with you, Howard.

Howard: Sorry to keep you waiting. I'll be with you in a minute.

Willy: What's that, Howard?

Howard: Didn't you ever see one of these? Wire recorder.

Willy: Oh. Can we talk a minute?

Howard: Records things. Just got delivery yesterday. Been driving me crazy, the most terrific machine I ever saw in my life. I was up all night with it.

Willy: What do you do with it?

Howard: I bought it for dictation, but you can do anything with it. Listen to this. I had it home last night. Listen to what I picked up. The first one is my daughter. Get this. (*He flicks the switch and "Roll out the Barrel" is heard being whistled.*) Listen to that kid whistle.

Willy: That is lifelike, isn't it?

Howard: Seven years old. Get that tone.

Willy: Ts, ts. Like to ask a little favor if you . . .

(*The whistling breaks off, and the voice of Howard's Daughter is heard.*)

His Daughter: "Now you, Daddy."

Howard: She's crazy for me! (*Again the same song is whistled.*) That's me! Ha! (*He winks.*)

Willy: You're very good!

(*The whistling breaks off again. The machine runs silent for a moment.*)

Howard: Sh! Get this now, this is my son.

His Son: "The capital of Alabama is Montgomery; the capital of Arizona is Phoenix; the capital of Arkansas is Little Rock; the capital of California is Sacramento . . ." (*And on, and on.*)

Howard (*holding up five fingers*): Five years old, Willy!

Willy: He'll make an announcer some day!

His Son (*continuing*): "The capital . . ."

Howard: Get that—alphabetical order! (*The machine breaks off suddenly.*) Wait a minute. The maid kicked the plug out.

Willy: It certainly is a—

Howard: Sh, for God's sake!

His Son: "It's nine o'clock, Bulova watch time. So I have to go to sleep."

Willy: That really is—

Howard: Wait a minute! The next is my wife.

(*They wait.*)

Howard's Voice: "Go on, say something." (*Pause.*) "Well, you gonna talk?"

His Wife: "I can't think of anything."

Howard's Voice: "Well, talk—it's turning."

His Wife (*shyly, beaten*): "Hello." (*Silence.*) "Oh, Howard, I can't talk into this . . ."

Howard (*snapping the machine off*): That was my wife.

Willy: That is a wonderful machine. Can we—

Howard: I tell you, Willy, I'm gonna take my camera, and my bandsaw, and all my hobbies, and out they go. This is the most fascinating relaxation I ever found.

Willy: I think I'll get one myself.

Howard: Sure, they're only a hundred and a half. You can't do without it. Supposing you wanna hear Jack Benny, see? But you can't be at home at that hour. So you tell the maid to turn the radio on when Jack Benny comes on, and this automatically goes on with the radio . . .

Willy: And when you come home you . . .

Howard: You can come home twelve o'clock, one o'clock, any time you like, and you get yourself a Coke and sit yourself down, throw the switch, and there's Jack Benny's program in the middle of the night!

Willy: I'm definitely going to get one. Because lots of times I'm on the road, and I think to myself, what I must be missing on the radio!

Howard: Don't you have a radio in the car?

Willy: Well, yeah, but who ever thinks of turning it on?

Howard: Say, aren't you supposed to be in Boston?

Willy: That's what I want to talk to you about, Howard. You got a minute?

(*He draws a chair in from the wing.*)

Howard: What happened? What're you doing here?

Willy: Well . . .

Howard: You didn't crack up again, did you?

Willy: Oh, no. No . . .

Howard: Geez, you had me worried there for a minute. What's the trouble?

Willy: Well, to tell you the truth, Howard, I've come to the decision that I'd rather not travel any more.

Howard: Not travel! Well, what'll you do?

Willy: Remember, Christmas time, when you had the party here? You said you'd try to think of some spot for me here in town.

Howard: With us?

Willy: Well, sure.

Howard: Oh, yeah, yeah. I remember. Well, I couldn't think of anything for you, Willy.

Willy: I tell ya, Howard. The kids are all grown up, y'know. I don't need much any more. If I could take home—well, sixty-five dollars a week, I could swing it.

Howard: Yeah, but Willy, see I—

Willy: I tell ya why, Howard. Speaking frankly and between the two of us, y'know— I'm just a little tired.

Howard: Oh, I could understand that, Willy. But you're a road man, Willy, and we do a road business. We've only got a half-dozen salesmen on the floor here.

Willy: God knows, Howard, I never asked a favor of any man. But I was with the firm when your father used to carry you in here in his arms.

Howard: I know that, Willy, but—

Willy: Your father came to me the day you were born and asked me what I thought of the name of Howard, may he rest in peace.

Howard: I appreciate that, Willy, but there just is no spot here for you. If I had a spot I'd slam you right in, but I just don't have a single, solitary spot.

(*He looks for his lighter. Willy has picked it up and gives it to him. Pause.*)

Willy (*with increasing anger*): Howard, all I need to set my table is fifty dollars a week.

Howard: But where am I going to put you, kid?

Willy: Look, it isn't a question of whether I can sell merchandise, is it?

Howard: No, but it's a business, kid, and everybody's gotta pull his own weight.

Willy (*desperately*): Just let me tell you a story, Howard—

Howard: 'Cause you gotta admit, business is business.

Willy (*angrily*): Business is definitely business, but just listen for a minute. You don't understand this. When I was a boy—eighteen, nineteen—I was already on the road. And there was a question in my mind as to whether selling had a future for me. Because in those days I had a yearning to go to Alaska. See, there were three gold strikes in one month in Alaska, and I felt like going out. Just for the ride, you might say.

Howard (*barely interested*): Don't say.

Willy: Oh, yeah, my father lived many years in Alaska. He was an adventurous man. We've got quite a little streak of self-reliance in our family. I thought I'd go out with my older brother and try to locate him, and maybe settle in the North with the old man. And I was almost decided to go, when I met a salesman in the Parker House. His name was Dave Singleman. And he was eighty-four years old, and he'd drummed merchandise in thirty-one states. And old Dave, he'd go up to his room, y'understand, put on his green velvet slippers—I'll never forget—and pick up his phone and call the buyers, and without ever leaving his room, at the age of eighty-four, he made his living. And when I saw that, I realized that selling was the greatest career a man could want. 'Cause what could be more satisfying than to be able to go, at the age of eighty-four, into twenty or thirty different cities, and pick up a phone, and be remembered and loved and helped by so many different people? Do you know? When he died—and by the way he died the death of a salesman, in his green velvet slippers in the smoker of the New York, New Haven and Hartford, going into Boston—when he died, hundreds of salesmen and buyers were at his funeral. Things were sad on a lotta trains for months after that. (*He stands up. Howard has not looked at him.*) In those days there was personality in it, Howard. There was respect, and comradeship, and gratitude in it. Today, it's all cut and dried, and there's no chance for bringing friendship to bear—or personality. You see what I mean? They don't know me any more.

Howard (*moving away, to the right*): That's just the thing, Willy.

Willy: If I had forty dollars a week—that's all I'd need. Forty dollars, Howard.

Howard: Kid, I can't take blood from a stone, I—

Willy (*desperation is on him now*): Howard, the year Al Smith was nominated, your father came to me and—

Howard (*starting to go off*): I've got to see some people, kid.

Willy (*stopping him*): I'm talking about your father! There were promises made across this desk! You mustn't tell me you've got people to see—I put thirty-four years into this firm, Howard, and now I can't pay my insurance! You can't eat the orange and throw the peel away—a man is not a piece of fruit! (*After a pause.*) Now pay attention. Your father—in 1928 I had a big year. I averaged a hundred and seventy dollars a week in commissions.

Howard (*impatiently*): Now, Willy, you never averaged—

Willy (*banging his hand on the desk*): I averaged a hundred and seventy dollars a week in the year of 1928! And your father came to me—or rather, I was in the office here—it was right over this desk—and he put his hand on my shoulder—

Howard (*getting up*): You'll have to excuse me, Willy, I gotta see some people. Pull yourself together. (*Going out.*) I'll be back in a little while.

(*On Howard's exit, the light on his chair grows very bright and strange.*)

Willy: Pull yourself together! What the hell did I say to him? My God, I was yelling at him! How could I! (*Willy breaks off, staring at the light, which occupies the chair, animating it. He approaches this chair, standing across the desk from it.*) Frank, Frank, don't you remember what you told me that time? How you put your hand on my shoulder, and Frank . . . (*He leans on the desk and as he speaks the dead man's name he accidentally switches on the recorder, and instantly—*)

Howard's Son: ". . . of New York is Albany. The capital of Ohio is Cincinnati, the capital of Rhode Island is . . ." (*The recitation continues.*)

Willy (*leaping away with fright, shouting*): Ha! Howard! Howard! Howard!

Howard (*rushing in*): What happened?

Willy (*pointing at the machine, which continues nasally, childishly, with the capital cities*): Shut it off! Shut it off!

Howard (*pulling the plug out*): Look, Willy . . .

Willy (*pressing his hands to his eyes*): I gotta get myself some coffee. I'll get some coffee . . .

(*Willy starts to walk out. Howard stops him.*)

Howard (*rolling up the cord*): Willy, look . . .

Willy: I'll go to Boston.

Howard: Willy, you can't go to Boston for us.

Willy: Why can't I go?

Howard: I don't want you to represent us. I've been meaning to tell you for a long time now.

Willy: Howard, are you firing me?

Howard: I think you need a good long rest, Willy.

Willy: Howard—

Howard: And when you feel better, come back, and we'll see if we can work something out.

Willy: But I gotta earn money, Howard. I'm in no position—

Howard: Where are your sons? Why don't your sons give you a hand?

Willy: They're working on a very big deal.

Howard: This is no time for false pride, Willy. You go to your sons and tell them that you're tired. You've got two great boys, haven't you?

Willy: Oh, no question, no question, but in the meantime . . .

Howard: Then that's that, heh?

Willy: All right, I'll go to Boston tomorrow.

Howard: No, no.

Willy: I can't throw myself on my sons. I'm not a cripple!

Howard: Look, kid, I'm busy this morning.

Willy (*grasping Howard's arm*): Howard, you've got to let me go to Boston!

Howard (*hard, keeping himself under control*): I've got a line of people to see this morning. Sit down, take five minutes, and pull yourself together, and then go home, will ya? I need the office, Willy. (*He starts to go, turns, remembering the recorder, starts to push off the table holding the recorder.*) Oh, yeah. Whenever you can this week, stop by and drop off the samples. You'll feel better, Willy, and then come back and we'll talk. Pull yourself together, kid, there's people outside.

(*Howard exits, pushing the table off left. Willy stares into space, exhausted. Now the music is heard—Ben's music—first distantly, then closer, closer. As Willy speaks, Ben enters from the right. He carries valise and umbrella.*)

Willy: Oh, Ben, how did you do it? What is the answer? Did you wind up the Alaska deal already?

Ben: Doesn't take much time if you know what you're doing. Just a short business trip. Boarding ship in an hour. Wanted to say good-by.

Willy: Ben, I've got to talk to you.

Ben (*glancing at his watch*): Haven't the time, William.

Willy (*crossing the apron to Ben*): Ben, nothing's working out. I don't know what to do.

Ben: Now, look here, William. I've bought timberland in Alaska and I need a man to look after things for me.

Willy: God, timberland! Me and my boys in those grand outdoors!

Ben: You've a new continent at your doorstep, William. Get out of these cities, they're full of talk and time payments and courts of law. Screw on your fists and you can fight for a fortune up there.

Willy: Yes, yes! Linda! Linda!

(*Linda enters as of old, with the wash.*)

Linda: Oh, you're back?

Ben: I haven't much time.

Willy: No, wait! Linda, he's got a proposition for me in Alaska.

Linda: But you've got—(*To Ben.*) He's got a beautiful job here.

Willy: But in Alaska, kid, I could—

Linda: You're doing well enough, Willy!

Ben (*to Linda*): Enough for what, my dear?

Linda (*frightened of Ben and angry at him*): Don't say those things to him! Enough to be happy right here, right now. (*To Willy, while Ben laughs.*) Why must everybody conquer the world? You're well liked, and the boys love you, and someday—(*to Ben*)—why, old man Wagner told him just the other day that if he keeps it up he'll be a member of the firm, didn't he, Willy?

Willy: Sure, sure. I am building something with this firm, Ben, and if a man is building something he must be on the right track, mustn't he?

Ben: What are you building? Lay your hand on it. Where is it?

Willy (*hesitantly*): That's true, Linda, there's nothing.

Linda: Why? (*To Ben.*) There's a man eighty-four years old—

Willy: That's right, Ben, that's right. When I look at that man I say, what is there to worry about?

Ben: Bah!

Willy: It's true, Ben. All he has to do is go into any city, pick up the phone, and he's making his living and you know why?

Ben (*picking up his valise*): I've got to go.

Willy (*holding Ben back*): Look at this boy!

(*Biff, in his high school sweater, enters carrying suitcase. Happy carries Biff's shoulder guards, gold helmet, and football pants.*)

Willy: Without a penny to his name, three great universities are begging for him, and from there the sky's the limit, because it's not what you do, Ben. It's who you know and the smile on your face! It's contacts, Ben, contacts! The whole wealth of Alaska passes over the lunch table at the Commodore Hotel, and that's the wonder, the wonder of this country, that a man can end with diamonds here on the basis of being liked! (*He turns to Biff.*) And that's why when you get out on that field today it's important. Because thousands of people will be rooting for you and loving you. (*To Ben, who has again begun to leave.*) And Ben! when he walks into a business office his name will sound out like a bell and all the doors will open to him! I've seen it, Ben, I've seen it a thousand times! You can't feel it with your hand like timber, but it's there!

Ben: Good-by, William.

Willy: Ben, am I right? Don't you think I'm right? I value your advice.

Ben: There's a new continent at your doorstep, William. You could walk out rich. Rich. (*He is gone.*)

Willy: We'll do it here, Ben! You hear me? We're gonna do it here!

(*Young Bernard rushes in. The gay music of the boys is heard.*)

Bernard: Oh, gee, I was afraid you left already!

Willy: Why? What time is it?

Bernard: It's half-past one!

Willy: Well, come on, everybody! Ebbets Field next stop! Where's the pennants? (*He rushes through the wall-line of the kitchen and out into the living room.*)

Linda (*to Biff*): Did you pack fresh underwear?

Biff (*who has been limbering up*): I want to go!

Bernard: Biff, I'm carrying your helmet, ain't I?

Happy: No, I'm carrying the helmet.

Bernard: Oh, Biff, you promised me.

Happy: I'm carrying the helmet.

Bernard: How am I going to get in the locker room?

Linda: Let him carry the shoulder guards. (*She puts her coat and hat on in the kitchen.*)

Bernard: Can I, Biff? 'Cause I told everybody I'm going to be in the locker room.

Happy: In Ebbets Field it's the clubhouse.

Bernard: I meant the clubhouse. Biff!

Happy: Biff!

Biff (*grandly, after a slight pause*): Let him carry the shoulder guards.

Happy (*as he gives Bernard the shoulder guards*): Stay close to us now.

(*Willy rushes in with the pennants.*)

Willy (*handing them out*): Everybody wave when Biff comes out on the field. (*Happy and Bernard run off.*) You set now, boy?

(*The music has died away.*)

Biff: Ready to go, Pop. Every muscle is ready.

Willy (*at the edge of the apron*): You realize what this means?

Biff: That's right, Pop.

Willy (*feeling Biff's muscles*): You're comin' home this afternoon captain of the All-Scholastic Championship Team of the City of New York.

Biff: I got it, Pop. And remember, pal, when I take off my helmet, that touchdown is for you.

Willy: Let's go! (*He is starting out, with his arm around Biff, when Charley enters, as of old, in knickers.*) I got no room for you, Charley.

Charley: Room? For what?

Willy: In the car.

Charley: You goin' for a ride? I wanted to shoot some casino.

Willy (furiously): Casino! (*Incredulously.*) Don't you realize what today is?

Linda: Oh, he knows, Willy. He's just kidding you.

Willy: That's nothing to kid about!

Charley: No, Linda, what's goin' on?

Linda: He's playing in Ebbets Field.

Charley: Baseball in this weather?

Willy: Don't talk to him. Come on, come on! (*He is pushing them out.*)

Charley: Wait a minute, didn't you hear the news?

Willy: What?

Charley: Don't you listen to the radio? Ebbets Field just blew up.

Willy: You go to hell! (*Charley laughs. Pushing them out.*) Come on, come on! We're late.

Charley (as they go): Knock a homer, Biff, knock a homer!

Willy (the last to leave, turning to Charley): I don't think that was funny, Charley. This is the greatest day of his life.

Charley: Willy, when are you going to grow up?

Willy: Yeah, heh? When this game is over, Charley, you'll be laughing out of the other side of your face. They'll be calling him another Red Grange. Twenty-five thousand a year.

Charley (kidding): Is that so?

Willy: Yeah, that's so.

Charley: Well, then, I'm sorry, Willy. But tell me something.

Willy: What?

Charley: Who is Red Grange?

Willy: Put up your hands. Goddam you, put up your hands!

(*Charley, chuckling, shakes his head and walks away, around the left corner of the stage. Willy follows him. The music rises to a mocking frenzy.*)

Willy: Who the hell do you think you are, better than everybody else? You don't know everything, you big, ignorant, stupid . . . Put up your hands!

(*Light rises, on the right side of the forestage, on a small table in the reception room of Charley's office. Traffic sounds are heard. Bernard, now mature, sits whistling to himself. A pair of tennis rackets and an overnight bag are on the floor beside him.*)

Willy (offstage): What are you walking away for? Don't walk away! If you're going to say something say it to my face! I know you laugh at me behind my back. You'll laugh out of the other side of your goddam face after this game. Touchdown! Touchdown! Eighty thousand people! Touchdown! Right between the goal posts.

(*Bernard is a quiet, earnest, but self-assured young man. Willy's voice is coming from right upstage now. Bernard lowers his feet off the table and listens. Jenny, his father's secretary, enters.*)

Jenny (distressed): Say, Bernard, will you go out in the hall?

Bernard: What is that noise? Who is it?

Jenny: Mr. Loman. He just got off the elevator.

Bernard (getting up): Who's he arguing with?

Jenny: Nobody. There's nobody with him. I can't deal with him any more, and your father gets all upset everytime he comes. I've got a lot of typing to do, and your father's waiting to sign it. Will you see him?

Willy (entering): Touchdown! Touch—(*He sees Jenny.*) Jenny, Jenny, good to see you. How're ya? Workin'? Or still honest?

Jenny: Fine. How've you been feeling?

Willy: Not much any more, Jenny. Ha, ha! (*He is surprised to see the rackets.*)

Bernard: Hello, Uncle Willy.

Willy (almost shocked): Bernard! Well, look who's here! (*He comes quickly, guiltily, to Bernard and warmly shakes his hand.*)

Bernard: How are you? Good to see you.

Willy: What are you doing here?

Bernard: Oh, just stopped by to see Pop. Get off my feet till my train leaves. I'm going to Washington in a few minutes.

Willy: Is he in?

Bernard: Yes, he's in his office with the accountant. Sit down.

Willy (sitting down): What're you going to do in Washington?

Bernard: Oh, just a case I've got there, Willy.

Willy: That so? (*indicating the rackets.*) You going to play tennis there?

Bernard: I'm staying with a friend who's got a court.

Willy: Don't say. His own tennis court. Must be fine people, I bet.

Bernard: They are, very nice. Dad tells me Biff's in town.

Willy (with a big smile): Yeah, Biff's in. Working on a very big deal, Bernard.

Bernard: What's Biff doing?

Willy: Well, he's been doing very big things in the West. But he decided to establish himself here. Very big. We're having dinner. Did I hear your wife had a boy?

Bernard: That's right. Our second.

Willy: Two boys! What do you know!

Bernard: What kind of deal has Biff got?

Willy: Well, Bill Oliver—very big sporting-goods man—he wants Biff very badly. Called him in from the West. Long distance, carte blanche, special deliveries. Your friends have their own private tennis court?

Bernard: You still with the old firm, Willy?

Willy (after a pause): I'm—I'm overjoyed to see how you made the grade, Bernard, overjoyed. It's an encouraging thing to see a young man really—really—Looks very good for Biff—very—(*He breaks off, then.*) Bernard—(*He is so full of emotion, he breaks off again.*)

Bernard: What is it, Willy?

Willy (small and alone): What—what's the secret?

Bernard: What secret?

Willy: How—how did you? Why didn't he ever catch on?

Bernard: I wouldn't know that, Willy.

Willy (confidentially, desperately): You were his friend, his boyhood friend. There's something I don't understand about it. His life ended after that Ebbets Field game. From the age of seventeen nothing good ever happened to him.

Bernard: He never trained himself for anything.

Willy: But he did, he did. After high school he took so many correspondence courses. Radio mechanics; television; God knows what, and never made the slightest mark.

Bernard (taking off his glasses): Willy, do you want to talk candidly?

Willy (rising, faces Bernard): I regard you as a very brilliant man, Bernard. I value your advice.

Bernard: Oh, the hell with the advice, Willy. I couldn't advise you. There's just one thing I've always wanted to ask you. When he was supposed to graduate, and the math teacher flunked him—

Willy: Oh, that son-of-a-bitch ruined his life.

Bernard: Yeah, but, Willy, all he had to do was go to summer school and make up that subject.

Willy: That's right, that's right.

Bernard: Did you tell him not to go to summer school?

Willy: Me? I begged him to go. I ordered him to go!

Bernard: Then why wouldn't he go?

Willy: Why? Why! Bernard, that question has been trailing me like a ghost for the last fifteen years. He flunked the subject, and laid down and died like a hammer hit him!

Bernard: Take it easy, kid.

Willy: Let me talk to you—I got nobody to talk to. Bernard, Bernard, was it my fault? Y'see? It keeps going around in my mind, maybe I did something to him. I got nothing to give him.

Bernard: Don't take it so hard.

Willy: Why did he lay down? What is the story there? You were his friend!

Bernard: Willy, I remember, it was June, and our grades came out. And he'd flunked math.

Willy: That son-of-a-bitch!

Bernard: No, it wasn't right then. Biff just got very angry, I remember, and he was ready to enroll in summer school.

Willy (surprised): He was?

Bernard: He wasn't beaten by it at all. But then, Willy, he disappeared from the block for almost a month. And I got the idea that he'd gone up to New England to see you. Did he have a talk with you then?

(Willy stares in silence.)

Bernard: Willy?

Willy (with a strong edge of resentment in his voice): Yeah, he came to Boston. What about it?

Bernard: Well, just that when he came back—I'll never forget this, it always mystifies me. Because I'd thought so well of Biff, even though he'd always taken advantage of me. I loved him, Willy, y'know? And he came back after that month and took his sneakers—remember those sneakers with "University of Virginia" printed on them? He was so proud of those, wore them every day. And he took them down in the cellar, and burned them up in the furnace. We had a fist fight. It lasted at least half an hour. Just the two of us, punching each other down the cellar, and crying right through it. I've often thought of how strange it was that I knew he'd given up his life. What happened in Boston, Willy?

(*Willy looks at him as at an intruder.*)

Bernard: I just bring it up because you asked me.

Willy (*angrily*): Nothing. What do you mean, "What happened?" What's that got to do with anything?

Bernard: Well, don't get sore.

Willy: What are you trying to do, blame it on me? If a boy lays down is that my fault?

Bernard: Now, Willy, don't get—

Willy: Well, don't—don't talk to me that way! What does that mean, "What happened?"

(*Charley enters. He is in his vest, and he carries a bottle of bourbon.*)

Charley: Hey, you're going to miss that train. (*He waves the bottle.*)

Bernard: Yeah, I'm going. (*He takes the bottle.*) Thanks, Pop. (*He picks up his rackets and bag.*) Good-by, Willy, and don't worry about it. You know, "If at first you don't succeed . . ."

Willy: Yes, I believe in that.

Bernard: But sometimes, Willy, it's better for a man just to walk away.

Willy: Walk away?

Bernard: That's right.

Willy: But if you can't walk away?

Bernard (*after a slight pause*): I guess that's when it's tough. (*Extending his hand.*) Good-by, Willy.

Willy (*shaking Bernard's hand*): Good-by, boy.

Charley (*an arm on Bernard's shoulder*): How do you like this kid? Gonna argue a case in front of the Supreme Court.

Bernard (*protesting*): Pop!

Willy (*genuinely shocked, pained, and happy*): No! The Supreme Court!

Bernard: I gotta run. 'By, Dad!

Charley: Knock 'em dead, Bernard!

(*Bernard goes off.*)

Willy (*as Charley takes out his wallet*): The Supreme Court! And he didn't even mention it!

Charley (*counting out money on the desk*): He don't have to—he's gonna do it.

Willy: And you never told him what to do, did you? You never took any interest in him.

Charley: My salvation is that I never took any interest in anything. There's some money—fifty dollars. I got an accountant inside.

Willy: Charley, look . . . (*With difficulty.*) I got my insurance to pay. If you can manage it—I need a hundred and ten dollars.

(*Charley doesn't reply for a moment; merely stops moving.*)

Willy: I'd draw it from my bank but Linda would know, and I . . .

Charley: Sit down, Willy.

Willy (*moving toward the chair*): I'm keeping an account of everything, remember. I'll pay every penny back. (*He sits.*)

Charley: Now listen to me, Willy.

Willy: I want you to know I appreciate . . .

Charley (*sitting down on the table*): Willy, what're you doin'? What the hell is goin' on in your head?

Willy: Why? I'm simply . . .

Charley: I offered you a job. You can make fifty dollars a week. And I won't send you on the road.

Willy: I've got a job.

Charley: Without pay? What kind of a job is a job without pay? (*He rises.*) Now, look, kid, enough is enough. I'm no genius but I know when I'm being insulted.

Willy: Insulted!

Charley: Why don't you want to work for me?

Willy: What's the matter with you? I've got a job.

Charley: Then what're you walkin' in here every week for?

Willy (*getting up*): Well, if you don't want me to walk in here—

Charley: I am offering you a job.

Willy: I don't want your goddam job!

Charley: When the hell are you going to grow up?

Willy (*furiously*): You big ignoramus, if you say that to me again I'll rap you one! I don't care how big you are! (*He's ready to fight.*)

(*Pause.*)

Charley (*kindly, going to him*): How much do you need, Willy?

Willy: Charley, I'm strapped. I'm strapped. I don't know what to do. I was just fired.

Charley: Howard fired you?

Willy: That snotnose. Imagine that? I named him. I named him Howard.

Charley: Willy, when're you gonna realize that them things don't mean anything? You named him Howard, but you can't sell that. The only thing you got in this world is what you can sell. And the funny thing is that you're a salesman, and you don't know that.

Willy: I've always tried to think otherwise, I guess. I always felt that if a man was impressive, and well liked, that nothing—

Charley: Why must everybody like you? Who liked J. P. Morgan? Was he impressive? In a Turkish bath he'd look like a butcher. But with his pockets on he was very well liked. Now listen, Willy, I know you don't like me, and nobody can say I'm in love with you, but I'll give you a job because—just for the hell of it, put it that way. Now what do you say?

Willy: I—I just can't work for you, Charley.

Charley: What're you, jealous of me?

Willy: I can't work for you, that's all, don't ask me why.

Charley (*angered, takes out more bills*): You been jealous of me all your life, you damned fool! Here, pay your insurance. (*He puts the money in Willy's hand.*)

Willy: I'm keeping strict accounts.

Charley: I've got some work to do. Take care of yourself. And pay your insurance.

Willy (*moving to the right*): Funny, y'know? After all the highways, and the trains, and the appointments, and the years, you end up worth more dead than alive.

Charley: Willy, nobody's worth nothin' dead. (*After a slight pause.*) Did you hear what I said?

(*Willy stands still, dreaming.*)

Charley: Willy!

Willy: Apologize to Bernard for me when you see him. I didn't mean to argue with him. He's a fine boy. They're all fine boys, and they'll end up big—all of them. Someday they'll all play tennis together. Wish me luck, Charley. He saw Bill Oliver today.

Charley: Good luck.

Willy (*on the verge of tears*): Charley, you're the only friend I got. Isn't that a remarkable thing? (*He goes out.*)

Charley: Jesus!

(*Charley stares after him a moment and follows. All light blacks out. Suddenly raucous music is heard, and a red glow rises behind the screen at right. Stanley, a young waiter, appears, carrying a table, followed by Happy, who is carrying two chairs.*)

Stanley (*putting the table down*): That's all right, Mr. Loman, I can handle it myself. (*He turns and takes the chairs from Happy and places them at the table.*)

Happy (*glancing around*): Oh, this is better.

Stanley: Sure, in the front there you're in the middle of all kinds a noise. Whenever you got a party, Mr. Loman, you just tell me and I'll put you back here. Y'know, there's a lotta people they don't like it private, because when they go out they like to see a lotta action around them because they're sick and tired to stay in the house by theirself. But I know you, you ain't from Hackensack. You know what I mean?

Happy (*sitting down*): So how's it coming, Stanley?

Stanley: Ah, it's a dog's life. I only wish during the war they'd a took me in the Army. I coulda been dead by now.

Happy: My brother's back, Stanley.

Stanley: Oh, he come back, heh? From the Far West.

Happy: Yeah, big cattle man, my brother, so treat him right. And my father's coming too.

Stanley: Oh, your father too!

Happy: You got a couple of nice lobsters?

Stanley: Hundred per cent, big.

Happy: I want them with the claws.

Stanley: Don't worry, I don't give you no mice. (*Happy laughs.*) How about some wine? It'll put a head on the meal.

Happy: No. You remember, Stanley, that recipe I brought you from overseas? With the champagne in it?

Stanley: Oh, yeah, sure. I still got it tacked up yet in the kitchen. But that'll have to cost a buck apiece anyways.

Happy: That's all right.

Stanley: What'd you, hit a number or somethin'?

Happy: No, it's a little celebration. My brother is—I think he pulled off a big deal today. I think we're going into business together.

Stanley: Great! That's the best for you. Because a family business, you know what I mean?—that's the best.

Happy: That's what I think.

Stanley: 'Cause what's the difference? Somebody steals? It's in the family. Know what I mean? (*Sotto voce.*) Like this bartender here. The boss is goin' crazy what kinda leak he's got in the cash register. You put it in but it don't come out.

Happy (*raising his head*): Sh!

Stanley: What?

Happy: You notice I wasn't lookin' right or left, was I?

Stanley: No.

Happy: And my eyes are closed.

Stanley: So what's the—?

Happy: Strudel's comin'.

Stanley (catching on, looks around): Ah, no, there's no—

(*He breaks off as a furred, lavishly dressed Girl enters and sits at the next table. Both follow her with their eyes.*)

Stanley: Geez, how'd ya know?

Happy: I got radar or something. (*Staring directly at her profile.*) Oooooooo . . . Stanley.

Stanley: I think that's for you, Mr. Loman.

Happy: Look at that mouth. Oh, God. And the binoculars.

Stanley: Geez, you got a life, Mr. Loman.

Happy: Wait on her.

Stanley (going to The Girl's table): Would you like a menu, ma'am?

Girl: I'm expecting someone, but I'd like a—

Happy: Why don't you bring her—excuse me, miss, do you mind? I sell champagne, and I'd like you to try my brand. Bring her a champagne, Stanley.

Girl: That's awfully nice of you.

Happy: Don't mention it. It's all company money. (*He laughs.*)

Girl: That's a charming product to be selling, isn't it?

Happy: Oh, gets to be like everything else. Selling is selling, y'know.

Girl: I suppose.

Happy: You don't happen to sell, do you?

Girl: No, I don't sell.

Happy: Would you object to a compliment from a stranger? You ought to be on a magazine cover.

Girl (looking at him a little archly): I have been.

(*Stanley comes in with a glass of champagne.*)

Happy: What'd I say before, Stanley? You see? She's a cover girl.

Stanley: Oh, I could see, I could see.

Happy (to The Girl): What magazine?

Girl: Oh, a lot of them. (*She takes the drink.*) Thank you.

Happy: You know what they say in France, don't you? "Champagne is the drink of the complexion"—Hya, Biff!

(*Biff has entered and sits with Happy.*)

Biff: Hello, kid. Sorry I'm late.

Happy: I just got here. Uh, Miss—?

Girl: Forsythe.

Happy: Miss Forsythe, this is my brother.

Biff: Is Dad here?

Happy: His name is Biff. You might've heard of him. Great football player.

Girl: Really? What team?

Happy: Are you familiar with football?

Girl: No, I'm afraid I'm not.

Happy: Biff is quarterback with the New York Giants.

Girl: Well, that is nice, isn't it? (*She drinks.*)

Happy: Good health.

Girl: I'm happy to meet you.

Happy: That's my name. Hap. It's really Harold, but at West Point they called me Happy.

Girl (now really impressed): Oh, I see. How do you do? (*She turns her profile.*)

Biff: Isn't Dad coming?

Happy: You want her?

Biff: Oh, I could never make that.

Happy: I remember the time that idea would never come into your head. Where's the old confidence, Biff?

Biff: I just saw Oliver—

Happy: Wait a minute. I've got to see that old confidence again. Do you want her? She's on call.

Biff: Oh, no. (*He turns to look at The Girl.*)

Happy: I'm telling you. Watch this. (*Turning to The Girl.*) Honey? (*She turns to him.*) Are you busy?

Girl: Well, I am . . . but I could make a phone call.

Happy: Do that, will you, honey? And see if you can get a friend. We'll be here for a while. Biff is one of the greatest football players in the country.

Girl (standing up): Well, I'm certainly happy to meet you.

Happy: Come back soon.

Girl: I'll try.

Happy: Don't try, honey, try hard.

(*The Girl exits. Stanley follows, shaking his head in bewildered admiration.*)

Happy: Isn't that a shame now? A beautiful girl like that? That's why I can't get married. There's not a good woman in a thousand. New York is loaded with them, kid!

Biff: Hap, look—

Happy: I told you she was on call!

Biff (strangely unnerved): Cut it out, will ya? I want to say something to you.

Happy: Did you see Oliver?

Biff: I saw him all right. Now look, I want to tell Dad a couple of things and I want you to help me.

Happy: What? Is he going to back you?

Biff: Are you crazy? You're out of your goddam head, you know that?

Happy: Why? What happened?

Biff (breathlessly): I did a terrible thing today, Hap. It's been the strangest day I ever went through. I'm all numb, I swear.

Happy: You mean he wouldn't see you?

Biff: Well, I waited six hours for him, see? All day. Kept sending my name in. Even tried to date his secretary so she'd get me to him, but no soap.

Happy: Because you're not showin' the old confidence, Biff. He remembered you, didn't he?

Biff (stopping Happy with a gesture): Finally, about five o'clock, he comes out. Didn't remember who I was or anything. I felt like such an idiot, Hap.

Happy: Did you tell him my Florida idea?

Biff: He walked away. I saw him for one minute. I got so mad I could've torn the walls down! How the hell did I ever get the idea I was a salesman there? I even believed myself that I'd been a salesman for him! And then he gave me one look and—I realized what a ridiculous lie my whole life has been! We've been talking in a dream for fifteen years. I was a shipping clerk.

Happy: What'd you do?

Biff (with great tension and wonder): Well, he left, see. And the secretary went out. I was all alone in the waiting-room. I don't know what came over me, Hap. The next thing I know I'm in his office—paneled walls, everything. I can't explain it. I—Hap, I took his fountain pen.

Happy: Geez, did he catch you?

Biff: I ran out. I ran down all eleven flights. I ran and ran and ran.

Happy: That was an awful dumb—what'd you do that for?

Biff (agonized): I don't know, I just—wanted to take something, I don't know. You gotta help me, Hap. I'm gonna tell Pop.

Happy: You crazy? What for?

Biff: Hap, he's got to understand that I'm not the man somebody lends that kind of money to. He thinks I've been spiting him all these years and it's eating him up.

Happy: That's just it. You tell him something nice.

Biff: I can't.

Happy: Say you got a lunch date with Oliver tomorrow.

Biff: So what do I do tomorrow?

Happy: You leave the house tomorrow and come back at night and say Oliver is thinking it over. And he thinks it over for a couple of weeks, and gradually it fades away and nobody's the worse.

Biff: But it'll go on forever!

Happy: Dad is never so happy as when he's looking forward to something!

(*Willy enters.*)

Happy: Hello, scout!

Willy: Gee, I haven't been here in years!

(*Stanley has followed Willy in and sets a chair for him. Stanley starts off but Happy stops him.*)

Happy: Stanley!

(*Stanley stands by, waiting for an order.*)

Biff (going to Willy with guilt, as to an invalid): Sit down, Pop. You want a drink?

Willy: Sure, I don't mind.

Biff: Let's get a load on.

Willy: You look worried.

Biff: N-no. (*To Stanley.*) Scotch all around. Make it doubles.

Stanley: Doubles, right. (*He goes.*)

Willy: You had a couple already, didn't you?

Biff: Just a couple, yeah.

Willy: Well, what happened, boy? (*Nodding affirmatively, with a smile.*) Everything go all right?

Biff (takes a breath, then reaches out and grasps Willy's hand): Pal . . . (*He is smiling bravely, and Willy is smiling too.*) I had an experience today.

Happy: Terrific, Pop.

Willy: That so? What happened?

Biff (high, slightly alcoholic, above the earth): I'm going to tell you everything from first to last. It's been a strange day. (*Silence. He looks around, composes himself as best he can, but his breath keeps breaking the rhythm of his voice.*) I had to wait quite a while for him, and—

Willy: Oliver?

Biff: Yeah, Oliver. All day, as a matter of cold fact. And a lot of—instances—facts, Pop, facts about my life came back to me. Who was it, Pop? Who ever said I was a salesman with Oliver?

Willy: Well, you were.

Biff: No, Dad, I was a shipping clerk.

Willy: But you were practically—

Biff (with determination): Dad, I don't know who said it first, but I was never a salesman for Bill Oliver.

Willy: What're you talking about?

Biff: Let's hold on to the facts tonight, Pop. We're not going to get anywhere bullin' around. I was a shipping clerk.

Willy (angrily): All right, now listen to me—

Biff: Why don't you let me finish?

Willy: I'm not interested in stories about the past or any crap of that kind because the woods are burning, boys, you understand? There's a big blaze going on all around. I was fired today.

Biff (shocked): How could you be?

Willy: I was fired, and I'm looking for a little good news to tell your mother, because the woman has waited and the woman has suffered. The gist of it is that I haven't got a story left in my head, Biff. So don't give me a lecture about facts and aspects. I am not interested. Now what've you got to say to me?

(*Stanley enters with three drinks. They wait until he leaves.*)

Willy: Did you see Oliver?

Biff: Jesus, Dad!

Willy: You mean you didn't go up there?

Happy: Sure he went up there.

Biff: I did. I—saw him. How could they fire you?

Willy (on the edge of his chair): What kind of a welcome did he give you?

Biff: He won't even let you work on commission?

Willy: I'm out! (*Driving.*) So tell me, he gave you a warm welcome?

Happy: Sure, Pop, sure!

Biff (driven): Well, it was kind of—

Willy: I was wondering if he'd remember you. (*To Happy.*) Imagine, man doesn't see him for ten, twelve years and gives him that kind of welcome!

Happy: Damn right!

Biff (trying to return to the offensive): Pop, look—

Willy: You know why he remembered you, don't you? Because you impressed him in those days.

Biff: Let's talk quietly and get this down to the facts, huh?

Willy (as though Biff had been interrupting): Well, what happened? It's great news, Biff. Did he take you into his office or'd you talk in the waiting-room?

Biff: Well, he came in, see, and—

Willy (*with a big smile*): What'd he say? Betcha he threw his arm around you.

Biff: Well, he kinda—

Willy: He's a fine man. (*To Happy.*) Very hard man to see, y'know.

Happy (*agreeing*): Oh, I know.

Willy (*to Biff*): Is that where you had the drinks?

Biff: Yeah, he gave me a couple of—no, no!

Happy (*cutting in*): He told him my Florida idea.

Willy: Don't interrupt. (*To Biff.*) How'd he react to the Florida idea?

Biff: Dad, will you give me a minute to explain?

Willy: I've been waiting for you to explain since I sat down here! What happened? He took you into his office and what?

Biff: Well—I talked. And—and he listened, see.

Willy: Famous for the way he listens, y'know. What was his answer?

Biff: His answer was—(*He breaks off, suddenly angry.*) Dad, you're not letting me tell you what I want to tell you!

Willy (*accusing, angered*): You didn't see him, did you?

Biff: I did see him!

Willy: What'd you insult him or something? You insulted him, didn't you?

Biff: Listen, will you let me out of it, will you just let me out of it!

Happy: What the hell!

Willy: Tell me what happened!

Biff (*to Happy*): I can't talk to him!

(*A single trumpet note jars the ear. The light of green leaves stains the house, which holds the air of night and a dream. Young Bernard enters and knocks on the door of the house.*)

Young Bernard (*frantically*): Mrs. Loman, Mrs. Loman!

Happy: Tell him what happened!

Biff (*to Happy*): Shut up and leave me alone!

Willy: No, no! You had to go and flunk math!

Biff: What math? What're you talking about?

Young Bernard: Mrs. Loman, Mrs. Loman!

(*Linda appears in the house, as of old.*)

Willy (*wildly*): Math, math, math!

Biff: Take it easy, Pop.

Young Bernard: Mrs. Loman!

Willy (*furiously*): If you hadn't flunked you'd've been set by now!

Biff: Now, look, I'm gonna tell you what happened, and you're going to listen to me.

Young Bernard: Mrs. Loman!

Biff: I waited six hours—

Happy: What the hell are you saying?

Biff: I kept sending in my name but he wouldn't see me. So finally he . . . (*He continues unheard as light fades low on the restaurant.*)

Young Bernard: Biff flunked math!

Linda: No!

Young Bernard: Birnbaum flunked him! They won't graduate him!

Linda: But they have to. He's gotta go to the university. Where is he? Biff! Biff!

Young Bernard: No, he left. He went to Grand Central.

Linda: Grand—You mean he went to Boston?

Young Bernard: Is Uncle Willy in Boston?

Linda: Oh, maybe Willy can talk to the teacher. Oh, the poor, poor boy!

(*Light on house area snaps out.*)

Biff (*at the table, now audible, holding up a gold fountain pen*): . . . so I'm washed up with Oliver, you understand? Are you listening to me?

Willy (*at a loss*): Yeah, sure. If you hadn't flunked—

Biff: Flunked what? What're you talking about?

Willy: Don't blame everything on me! I didn't flunk math—you did! What pen?

Happy: That was awful dumb, Biff, a pen like that is worth—

Willy (*seeing the pen for the first time*): You took Oliver's pen?

Biff (*weakening*): Dad, I just explained it to you.

Willy: You stole Bill Oliver's fountain pen!

Biff: I didn't exactly steal it! That's just what I've been explaining to you!

Happy: He had it in his hand and just then Oliver walked in, so he got nervous and stuck it in his pocket!

Willy: My God, Biff!

Biff: I never intended to do it, Dad!

Operator's voice: Standish Arms, good evening!

Willy (*shouting*): I'm not in my room!

Biff (*frightened*): Dad, what's the matter? (*He and Happy stand up.*)

Operator: Ringing Mr. Loman for you!

Willy: I'm not there, stop it!

Biff (*horrified, gets down on one knee before Willy*): Dad, I'll make good, I'll make good. (*Willy tries to get to his feet. Biff holds him down.*) Sit down now.

Willy: No, you're no good, you're no good for anything.

Biff: I am, Dad, I'll find something else, you understand? Now don't worry about anything. (*He holds up Willy's face.*) Talk to me, Dad.

Operator: Mr. Loman does not answer. Shall I page him?

Willy (*attempting to stand, as though to rush and silence the Operator*): No, no, no!

Happy: He'll strike something, Pop.

Willy: No, no . . .

Biff (*desperately, standing over Willy*): Pop, listen! Listen to me! I'm telling you something good. Oliver talked to his partner about the Florida idea. You listening? He—he talked to his partner, and he came to me . . . I'm to be all right, you hear? Dad, listen to me, he said it was just a question of the amount!

Willy: Then you . . . got it?

Happy: He's gonna be terrific, Pop!

Willy (*trying to stand*): Then you got it, haven't you? You got it! You got it!

Biff (*agonized, holds Willy down*): No, no. Look, Pop. I'm supposed to have lunch with them tomorrow. I'm just telling you this so you'll know that I can still make an impression, Pop. And I'll make good somewhere, but I can't go tomorrow, see?

Willy: Why not? You simply—

Biff: But the pen, Pop!

Willy: You give it to him and tell him it was an oversight!

Happy: Sure, have lunch tomorrow!

Biff: I can't say that—

Willy: You were doing a crossword puzzle and accidentally used his pen!

Biff: Listen, kid, I took those balls years ago, now I walk in with his fountain pen? That clinches it, don't you see? I can't face him like that! I'll try elsewhere.

Page's voice: Paging Mr. Loman!

Willy: Don't you want to be anything?

Biff: Pop, how can I go back?

Willy: You don't want to be anything, is that what's behind it?

Biff (*now angry at Willy for not crediting his sympathy*): Don't take it that way! You think it was easy walking into that office after what I'd done to him? A team of horses couldn't have dragged me back to Bill Oliver!

Willy: Then why'd you go?

Biff: Why did I go? Why did I go? Look at you! Look at what's become of you!

(*Off left, The Woman laughs.*)

Willy: Biff, you're going to go to that lunch tomorrow, or—

Biff: I can't go. I've got no appointment!

Happy: Biff, for . . . !

Willy: Are you spiting me?

Biff: Don't take it that way! Goddammit!

Willy (*strikes Biff and falters away from the table*): You rotten little louse! Are you spiting me?

The Woman: Someone's at the door, Willy!

Biff: I'm no good, can't you see what I am?

Happy (*separating them*): Hey, you're in a restaurant! Now cut it out, both of you! (*The Girls enter.*) Hello, girls, sit down.

(*The Woman laughs, off left.*)

Miss Forsythe: I guess we might as well. This is Letta.

The Woman: Willy, are you going to wake up?

Biff (*ignoring Willy*): How're ya, miss, sit down. What do you drink?

Miss Forsythe: Letta might not be able to stay long.

Letta: I gotta get up very early tomorrow. I got jury duty. I'm so excited! Were you fellows ever on a jury?

Biff: No, but I been in front of them! (*The Girls laugh.*) This is my father.

Letta: Isn't he cute? Sit down with us, Pop.

Happy: Sit him down, Biff!

Biff (*going to him*): Come on, slugger, drink us under the table. To hell with it! Come on, sit down, pal.

(*On Biff's last insistence, Willy is about to sit.*)

The Woman (*now urgently*): Willy, are you going to answer the door!

(*The Woman's call pulls Willy back. He starts right, befuddled.*)

Biff: Hey, where are you going?

Willy: Open the door.

Biff: The door?

Willy: The washroom . . . the door . . . where's the door?

Biff (*leading Willy to the left*): Just go straight down.

(*Willy moves left.*)

The Woman: Willy, Willy, are you going to get up, get up, get up, get up?

(*Willy exits left.*)

Letta: I think it's sweet you bring your daddy along.

Miss Forsythe: Oh, he isn't really your father!

Biff (*at left, turning to her resentfully*): Miss Forsythe, you've just seen a prince walk by. A fine, troubled prince. A hard-working, unappreciated prince. A pal, you understand? A good companion. Always for his boys.

Letta: That's so sweet.

Happy: Well, girls, what's the program? We're wasting time. Come on, Biff. Gather round. Where would you like to go?

Biff: Why don't you do something for him?

Happy: Me!

Biff: Don't you give a damn for him, Hap?

Happy: What're you talking about? I'm the one who—

Biff: I sense it, you don't give a good goddam about him. (*He takes the rolled-up hose from his pocket and puts it on the table in front of Happy.*) Look what I found in the cellar, for Christ's sake. How can you bear to let it go on?

Happy: Me? Who goes away? Who runs off and—

Biff: Yeah, but he doesn't mean anything to you. You could help him—I can't! Don't you understand what I'm talking about? He's going to kill himself, don't you know that?

Happy: Don't I know it! Me!

Biff: Hap, help him! Jesus . . . Help him . . . Help me, help me, I can't bear to look at his face! (*Ready to weep, he hurries out, up right.*)

Happy (*starting after him*): Where are you going?

Miss Forsythe: What's he so mad about?

Happy: Come on, girls, we'll catch up with him.

Miss Forsythe (*as Happy pushes her out*): Say, I don't like that temper of his!

Happy: He's just a little overstrung, he'll be all right!

Willy (*off left, as The Woman laughs*): Don't answer! Don't answer!

Letta: Don't you want to tell your father—

Happy: No, that's not my father. He's just a guy. Come on, we'll catch Biff, and, honey, we're going to paint this town! Stanley, where's the check? Hey, Stanley!

(*They exit. Stanley looks toward left.*)

Stanley (*calling to Happy indignantly*): Mr. Loman! Mr. Loman!

(*Stanley picks up a chair and follows them off. Knocking is heard off left. The Woman enters, laughing. Willy follows her. She is in a black slip; he is buttoning his shirt. Raw, sensuous music accompanies their speech.*)

Willy: Will you stop laughing? Will you stop?

The Woman: Aren't you going to answer the door? He'll wake the whole hotel.

Willy: I'm not expecting anybody.

The Woman: Whyn't you have another drink, honey, and stop being so damn self-centered?

Willy: I'm so lonely.

The Woman: You know you ruined me, Willy? From now on, whenever you come to the office, I'll see that you go right through to the buyers. No waiting at my desk any more, Willy. You ruined me.

Willy: That's nice of you to say that.

The Woman: Gee, you are self-centered! Why so sad? You are the saddest self-centeredest soul I ever did see-saw. (*She laughs. He kisses her.*) Come on inside, drummer boy. It's silly to be dressing in the middle of the night. (*As knocking is heard.*) Aren't you going to answer the door?

Willy: They're knocking on the wrong door.

The Woman: But I felt the knocking. And he heard us talking in here. Maybe the hotel's on fire!

Willy (*his terror rising*): It's a mistake.

The Woman: Then tell him to go away!

Willy: There's nobody there.

The Woman: It's getting on my nerves, Willy. There's somebody standing out there and it's getting on my nerves!

Willy (*pushing her away from him*): All right, stay in the bathroom here, and don't come out. I think there's a law in Massachusetts about it, so don't come out. It may be that new room clerk. He looked very mean. So don't come out. It's a mistake, there's no fire.

(*The knocking is heard again. He takes a few steps away from her, and she vanishes into the wing. The light follows him, and now he is facing Young Biff, who carries a suitcase. Biff steps toward him. The music is gone.*)

Biff: Why didn't you answer?

Willy: Biff! What are you doing in Boston?

Biff: Why didn't you answer? I've been knocking for five minutes, I called you on the phone—

Willy: I just heard you. I was in the bathroom and had the door shut. Did anything happen at home?

Biff: Dad—I let you down.

Willy: What do you mean?

Biff: Dad . . .

Willy: Biffo, what's this about? (*Putting his arm around Biff.*) Come on, let's go downstairs and get you a malted.

Biff: Dad, I flunked math.

Willy: Not for the term?

Biff: The term. I haven't got enough credits to graduate.

Willy: You mean to say Bernard wouldn't give you the answers?

Biff: He did, he tried, but I only got a sixty-one.

Willy: And they wouldn't give you four points?

Biff: Birnbaum refused absolutely. I begged him, Pop, but he won't give me those points. You gotta talk to him before they close the school. Because if he saw the kind of man you are, and you just talked to him in your way, I'm sure he'd come through for me. The class came right before practice, see, and I didn't go enough. Would you talk to him? He'd like you, Pop. You know the way you could talk.

Willy: You're on. We'll drive right back.

Biff: Oh, Dad, good work! I'm sure he'll change it for you!

Willy: Go downstairs and tell the clerk I'm checkin' out. Go right down.

Biff: Yes, Sir! See, the reason he hates me, Pop—one day he was late for class so I got up at the blackboard and imitated him. I crossed my eyes and talked with a lithp.

Willy (laughing): You did? The kids like it?

Biff: They nearly died laughing!

Willy: Yeah? What'd you do?

Biff: The thquare root of thixthy twee is . . . (*Willy bursts out laughing; Biff joins him.*) And in the middle of it he walked in!

(*Willy laughs and The Woman joins in offstage.*)

Willy (without hesitating): Hurry downstairs and—

Biff: Somebody in there?

Willy: No, that was next door.

(*The Woman laughs offstage.*)

Biff: Somebody got in your bathroom!

Willy: No, it's the next room, there's a party—

The Woman (enters, laughing. She lisps this): Can I come in? There's something in the bathtub, Willy, and it's moving!

(*Willy looks at Biff, who is staring open-mouthed and horrified at The Woman.*)

Willy: Ah—you better go back to your room. They must be finished painting by now. They're painting her room so I let her take a shower here. Go back, go back . . . (*He pushes her.*)

The Woman (resisting): But I've got to get dressed, Willy, I can't—

Willy: Get out of here! Go back, go back . . . (*Suddenly striving for the ordinary.*) This is Miss Francis, Biff, she's a buyer. They're painting her room. Go back, Miss Francis, go back . . .

The Woman: But my clothes, I can't go out naked in the hall!

Willy (pushing her offstage): Get outa here! Go back, go back!

(*Biff slowly sits down on his suitcase as the argument continues offstage.*)

The Woman: Where's my stockings? You promised me stockings, Willy!

Willy: I have no stockings here!

The Woman: You had two boxes of size nine sheers for me, and I want them!

Willy: Here, for God's sake, will you get outa here!

The Woman (enters holding a box of stockings): I just hope there's nobody in the hall. That's all I hope. (*To Biff.*) Are you football or baseball?

Biff: Football.

The Woman (angry, humiliated): That's me too. G'night. (*She snatches her clothes from Willy, and walks out.*)

Willy (after a pause): Well, better get going. I want to get to the school first thing in the morning. Get my suits out of the closet. I'll get my valise. (*Biff doesn't move.*) What's the matter? (*Biff remains motionless, tears falling.*) She's a buyer. Buys for J. H. Simmons. She lives down the hall—they're painting. You don't imagine— (*He breaks off. After a pause.*) Now listen, pal, she's just a buyer. She sees merchandise in her room and they have to keep it looking just so . . . (*Pause. Assuming command.*) All right, get my suits. (*Biff doesn't move.*) Now stop crying and do as I say. I gave you an order. Biff, I gave you an order! Is that what you do when I give you an order? How dare you cry! (*Putting his arm around Biff.*) Now look, Biff, when you grow up you'll understand about these things. You mustn't—you mustn't overemphasize a thing like this. I'll see Birnbaum first thing in the morning.

Biff: Never mind.

Willy (getting down beside Biff): Never mind! He's going to give you those points. I'll see to it.

Biff: He wouldn't listen to you.

Willy: He certainly will listen to me. You need those points for the U. of Virginia.

Biff: I'm not going there.

Willy: Heh? If I can't get him to change that mark you'll make it up in summer school. You've got all summer to—

Biff (his weeping breaking from him): Dad . . .

Willy (infected by it): Oh, my boy . . .

Biff: Dad . . .

Willy: She's nothing to me, Biff. I was lonely, I was terribly lonely.

Biff: You—you gave her Mama's stockings! (*His tears break through and he rises to go.*)

Willy (grabbing for Biff): I gave you an order!

Biff: Don't touch me, you—liar!

Willy: Apologize for that!

Biff: You fake! You phony little fake! (*Overcome, he turns quickly and weeping fully goes out with his suitcase. Willy is left on the floor on his knees.*)

Willy: I gave you an order! Biff, come back here or I'll beat you! Come back here! I'll whip you!

(*Stanley comes quickly in from the right and stands in front of Willy.*)

Willy (shouts at Stanley): I gave you an order . . .

Stanley: Hey, let's pick it up, pick it up, Mr. Loman. (*He helps Willy to his feet.*) Your boys left with the chippies. They said they'll see you at home.

(*A second waiter watches some distance away.*)

Willy: But we were supposed to have dinner together.

(*Music is heard, Willy's theme.*)

Stanley: Can you make it?

Willy: I'll—sure, I can make it. (*Suddenly concerned about his clothes.*) Do I—I look all right?

Stanley: Sure, you look all right. (*He flicks a speck off Willy's lapel.*)

Willy: Here—here's a dollar.

Stanley: Oh, your son paid me. It's all right.

Willy (putting it in Stanley's hand): No, take it. You're a good boy.

Stanley: Oh, no, you don't have to . . .

Willy: Here—here's some more, I don't need it any more. (*After a slight pause.*) Tell me—is there a seed store in the neighborhood?

Stanley: Seeds? You mean like to plant?

(*As Willy turns, Stanley slips the money back into his jacket pocket.*)

Willy: Yes. Carrots, peas . . .

Stanley: Well, there's hardware stores on Sixth Avenue, but it may be too late now.

Willy (anxiously): Oh, I'd better hurry. I've got to get some seeds. (*He starts off to the right.*) I've got to get some seeds, right away. Nothing's planted. I don't have a thing in the ground.

(*Willy hurries out as the light goes down. Stanley moves over to the right after him, watches him off. The other waiter has been staring at Willy.*)

Stanley (*to the waiter*): Well, whatta you looking at?

(*The waiter picks up the chairs and moves off right. Stanley takes the table and follows him. The light fades on this area. There is a long pause, the sound of the flute coming over. The light gradually rises on the kitchen, which is empty. Happy appears at the door of the house, followed by Biff. Happy is carrying a large bunch of long-stemmed roses. He enters the kitchen, looks around for Linda. Not seeing her, he turns to Biff, who is just outside the house door, and makes a gesture with his hands, indicating "Not here, I guess." He looks into the living room and freezes. Inside, Linda, unseen, is seated, Willy's coat on her lap. She rises ominously and quietly and moves toward Happy, who backs up into the kitchen, afraid.*)

Happy: Hey, what're you doing up? (*Linda says nothing but moves toward him implacably.*) Where's Pop? (*He keeps backing to the right, and now Linda is in full view in the doorway to the living room.*) Is he sleeping?

Linda: Where were you?

Happy (*trying to laugh it off*): We met two girls, Mom, very fine types. Here, we brought you some flowers. (*Offering them to her.*) Put them in your room, Ma.

(*She knocks them to the floor at Biff's feet. He has now come inside and closed the door behind him. She stares at Biff, silent.*)

Happy: Now what'd you do that for? Mom, I want you to have some flowers—

Linda (*cutting Happy off, violently to Biff*): Don't you care whether he lives or dies?

Happy (*going to the stairs*): Come upstairs, Biff.

Biff (*with a flare of disgust, to Happy*): Go away from me! (*To Linda.*) What do you mean, lives or dies? Nobody's dying around here, pal.

Linda: Get out of my sight! Get out of here!

Biff: I wanna see the boss.

Linda: You're not going near him!

Biff: Where is he? (*He moves into the living room and Linda follows.*)

Linda (*shouting after Biff*): You invite him for dinner. He looks forward to it all day— (*Biff appears in his parents' bedroom, looks around, and exits*)—and then you desert him there. There's no stranger you'd do that to!

Happy: Why? He had a swell time with us. Listen, when I—(*Linda comes back into the kitchen*)—desert him I hope I don't outlive the day!

Linda: Get out of here!

Happy: Now look, Mom . . .

Linda: Did you have to go to women tonight? You and your lousy rotten whores!

(*Biff re-enters the kitchen.*)

Happy: Mom, all we did was follow Biff around trying to cheer him up! (*To Biff.*) Boy, what a night you gave me!

Linda: Get out of here, both of you, and don't come back! I don't want you tormenting him anymore. Go on now, get your things together! (*To Biff.*) You can sleep in his apartment. (*She starts to pick up the flowers and stops herself.*) Pick up this stuff, I'm not your maid any more. Pick it up, you bum, you!

(*Happy turns his back to her in refusal. Biff slowly moves over and gets down on his knees, picking up the flowers.*)

Linda: You're a pair of animals! Not one, not another living soul would have had the cruelty to walk out on that man in a restaurant!

Biff (*not looking at her*): Is that what he said?

Linda: He didn't have to say anything. He was so humiliated he nearly limped when he came in.

Happy: But, Mom, he had a great time with us—

Biff (*cutting him off violently*): Shut up!

(*Without another word, Happy goes upstairs.*)

Linda: You! You didn't even go in to see if he was all right!

Biff (*still on the floor in front of Linda, the flowers in his hand; with self-loathing*): No. Didn't. Didn't do a damned thing. How do you like that, heh? Left him babbling in a toilet.

Linda: You louse. You . . .

Biff: Now you hit it on the nose! (*He gets up, throws the flowers in the wastebasket.*) The scum of the earth, and you're looking at him!

Linda: Get out of here!

Biff: I gotta talk to the boss, Mom. Where is he?

Linda: You're not going near him. Get out of this house!

Biff (*with absolute assurance, determination*): No. We're gonna have an abrupt conversation, him and me.

Linda: You're not talking to him!

(*Hammering is heard from outside the house, off right. Biff turns toward the noise.*)

Linda (*suddenly pleading*): Will you please leave him alone?

Biff: What's he doing out there?

Linda: He's planting the garden!

Biff (*quietly*): Now? Oh, my God!

(*Biff moves outside, Linda following. The light dies down on them and comes up on the center of the apron as Willy walks into it. He is carrying a flashlight, a hoe and a handful of seed packets. He raps the top of the hoe sharply to fix it firmly, and then moves to the left, measuring off the distance with his foot. He holds the flashlight to look at the seed packets, reading off the instructions. He is in the blue of night.*)

Willy: Carrots . . . quarter-inch apart. Rows . . . one-foot rows. (*He measures it off.*) One foot. (*He puts down a package and measures off.*) Beets. (*He puts down another package and measures again.*) Lettuce. (*He reads the package, puts it down.*) One foot—(*He breaks off as Ben appears at the right and moves slowly down to him.*) What a proposition, ts, ts. Terrific, terrific. 'Cause she's suffered, Ben, the woman has suffered. You understand me? A man can't go out the way he came in, Ben, a man has got to add up to something. You can't, you can't—(*Ben moves toward him as though to interrupt.*) You gotta consider, now. Don't answer so quick. Remember, it's a guaranteed twenty-thousand-dollar proposition. Now look, Ben, I want you to go through the ins and outs of this thing with me. I've got nobody to talk to, Ben, and the woman has suffered, you hear me?

Ben (*standing still, considering*): What's the proposition?

Willy: It's twenty thousand dollars on the barrelhead. Guaranteed, gilt-edged, you understand?

Ben: You don't want to make a fool of yourself. They might not honor the policy.

Willy: How can they dare refuse? Didn't I work like a coolie to meet every premium on the nose? And now they don't pay off? Impossible!

Ben: It's called a cowardly thing, William.

Willy: Why? Does it take more guts to stand here the rest of my life ringing up a zero?

Ben (yielding): That's a point, William. (*He moves, thinking, turns.*) And twenty thousand—that is something one can feel with the hand, it is there.

Willy (now assured, with rising power): Oh, Ben, that's the whole beauty of it! I see it like a diamond, shining in the dark, hard and rough, that I can pick up and touch in my hand. Not like—like an appointment! This would not be another damned-fool appointment, Ben, and it changes all the aspects. Because he thinks I'm nothing, see, and so he spites me. But the funeral—(*Straightening up.*) Ben, that funeral will be massive! They'll come from Maine, Massachusetts, Vermont, New Hampshire! All the old-timers with the strange license plates—that boy will be thunder-struck, Ben, because he never realized—I am known! Rhode Island, New York, New Jersey—I am known, Ben, and he'll see it with his eyes once and for all. He'll see what I am, Ben! He's in for a shock, that boy!

Ben (coming down to the edge of the garden): He'll call you a coward.

Willy (suddenly fearful): No, that would be terrible.

Ben: Yes. And a damned fool.

Willy: No, no, he mustn't, I won't have that! (*He is broken and desperate.*)

Ben: He'll hate you, William.

(*The gay music of the boys is heard.*)

Willy: Oh, Ben, how do we get back to all the great times? Used to be so full of light, and comradeship, the sleigh-riding in winter, and the ruddiness on his cheeks. And always some kind of good news coming up, always something nice coming up ahead. And never even let me carry the valises in the house, and simonizing, simonizing that little red car! Why, why can't I give him something and not have him hate me?

Ben: Let me think about it. (*He glances at his watch.*) I still have a little time. Remarkable proposition, but you've got to be sure you're not making a fool of yourself.

(*Ben drifts off upstage and goes out of sight. Biff comes down from the left.*)

Willy (suddenly conscious of Biff, turns and looks up at him, then begins picking up the packages of seeds in confusion): Where the hell is that seed? (*Indignantly.*) You can't see nothing out here! They boxed in the whole goddam neighborhood!

Biff: There are people all around here. Don't you realize that?

Willy: I'm busy. Don't bother me.

Biff (taking the hoe from Willy): I'm saying good-by to you, Pop. (*Willy looks at him, silent, unable to move.*) I'm not coming back any more.

Willy: You're not going to see Oliver tomorrow?

Biff: I've got no appointment, Dad.

Willy: He put his arm around you, and you've got no appointment?

Biff: Pop, get this now, will you? Everytime I've left it's been a fight that sent me out of here. Today I realized something about myself and I tried to explain it to you and I—I think I'm just not smart enough to make any sense out of it for you. To hell with whose fault it is or anything like that. (*He takes Willy's arm.*) Let's just wrap it up, heh? Come on in, we'll tell Mom. (*He gently tries to pull Willy to the left.*)

Willy (frozen, immobile, with guilt in his voice): No, I don't want to see her.

Biff: Come on! (*He pulls again, and Willy tries to pull away.*)

Willy (highly nervous): No, no, I don't want to see her.

Biff (tries to look into Willy's face, as if to find the answer there): Why don't you want to see her?

Willy (more harshly now): Don't bother me, will you?

Biff: What do you mean, you don't want to see her? You don't want them calling you yellow, do you? This isn't your fault; it's me, I'm a bum. Now come inside! (*Willy strains to get away.*) Did you hear what I said to you?

(*Willy pulls away and quickly goes by himself into the house. Biff follows.*)

Linda (to Willy): Did you plant, dear?

Biff (at the door, to Linda): All right, we had it out. I'm going and I'm not writing any more.

Linda (going to Willy in the kitchen): I think that's the best way, dear. 'Cause there's no use drawing it out, you'll just never get along.

(*Willy doesn't respond.*)

Biff: People ask where I am and what I'm doing, you don't know, and you don't care. That way it'll be off your mind and you can start brightening up again. All right? That clears it, doesn't it? (*Willy is silent, and Biff goes to him.*) You gonna wish me luck, scout? (*He extends his hand.*) What do you say?

Linda: Shake his hand, Willy.

Willy (turning to her, seething with hurt): There's no necessity to mention the pen at all, y'know.

Biff (gently): I've got no appointment, Dad.

Willy (erupting fiercely): He put his arm around . . . ?

Biff: Dad, you're never going to see what I am, so what's the use of arguing? If I strike oil I'll send you a check. Meantime forget I'm alive.

Willy (to Linda): Spite, see?

Biff: Shake hands, Dad.

Willy: Not my hand.

Biff: I was hoping not to go this way.

Willy: Well, this is the way you're going. Good-by.

(*Biff looks at him a moment, then turns sharply and goes to the stairs.*)

Willy (stops him with): May you rot in hell if you leave this house!

Biff (turning): Exactly what is it that you want from me?

Willy: I want you to know, on the train, in the mountains, in the valleys, wherever you go, that you cut down your life for spite!

Biff: No, no.

Willy: Spite, spite, is the word of your undoing! And when you're down and out, remember what did it. When you're rotting somewhere beside the railroad tracks, remember, and don't you dare blame it on me!

Biff: I'm not blaming it on you!

Willy: I won't take the rap for this, you hear?

(*Happy comes down the stairs and stands on the bottom step, watching.*)

Biff: That's just what I'm telling you!

Willy (sinking into a chair at the table, with full accusation): You're trying to put a knife in me—don't think I don't know what you're doing!

Biff: All right, phony! Then let's lay it on the line. (*He whips the rubber tube out of his pocket and puts it on the table.*)

Happy: You crazy—

Linda: Biff! (*She moves to grab the hose, but Biff holds it down with his hand.*)

Biff: Leave it there! Don't move it!

Willy (not looking at it): What is that?

Biff: You know goddam well what that is.

Willy (caged, wanting to escape): I never saw that.

Biff: You saw it. The mice didn't bring it into the cellar! What is this supposed to do, make a hero out of you? This supposed to make me sorry for you?

Willy: Never heard of it.

Biff: There'll be no pity for you, you hear? No pity!

Willy (to Linda): You hear the spite!

Biff: No, you're going to hear the truth—what you are and what I am!

Linda: Stop it!

Willy: Spite!

Happy (coming down toward Biff): You cut it now!

Biff (to Happy): The man don't know who we are! The man is gonna know! (*To Willy.*) We never told the truth for ten minutes in this house!

Happy: We always told the truth!

Biff (turning on him): You big blow, are you the assistant buyer? You're one of the two assistants to the assistant, aren't you?

Happy: Well, I'm practically—

Biff: You're practically full of it! We all are! And I'm through with it. (*To Willy.*) Now hear this, Willy, this is me.

Willy: I know you!

Biff: You know why I had no address for three months? I stole a suit in Kansas City and I was in jail. (*To Linda, who is sobbing.*) Stop crying. I'm through with it.

(*Linda turns away from them, her hands covering her face.*)

Willy: I suppose that's my fault!

Biff: I stole myself out of every good job since high school!

Willy: And whose fault is that?

Biff: And I never got anywhere because you blew me so full of hot air I could never stand taking orders from anybody! That's whose fault it is!

Willy: I hear that!

Linda: Don't, Biff!

Biff: It's goddam time you heard that! I had to be boss big shot in two weeks, and I'm through with it!

Willy: Then hang yourself! For spite, hang yourself!

Biff: No! Nobody's hanging himself, Willy! I ran down eleven flights with a pen in my hand today. And suddenly I stopped, you hear me? And in the middle of that office building, do you hear this? I stopped in the middle of that building and I saw—the sky. I saw the things that I love in this world. The work and the food and time to sit and smoke. And I looked at the pen and said to myself, what the hell am I grabbing this for? Why am I trying to become what I don't want to be? What am I doing in an office, making a contemptuous, begging fool of myself, when all I want is out there, waiting for me the minute I say I know who I am! Why can't I say that, Willy? (*He tries to make Willy face him, but Willy pulls away and moves to the left.*)

Willy (*with hatred, threateningly*): The door of your life is wide open!

Biff: Pop! I'm a dime a dozen, and so are you!

Willy (*turning on him now in an uncontrolled outburst*): I am not a dime a dozen! I am Willy Loman, and you are Biff Loman!

(*Biff starts for Willy, but is blocked by Happy. In his fury, Biff seems on the verge of attacking his father.*)

Biff: I am not a leader of men, Willy, and neither are you. You were never anything but a hard-working drummer who landed in the ash can like all the rest of them! I'm one dollar an hour, Willy! I tried seven states and couldn't raise it. A buck an hour! Do you gather my meaning? I'm not bringing home any prizes any more, and you're going to stop waiting for me to bring them home!

Willy (*directly to Biff*): You vengeful, spiteful mutt!

(*Biff breaks from Happy. Willy, in fright, starts up the stairs. Biff grabs him.*)

Biff (*at the peak of his fury*): Pop, I'm nothing! I'm nothing, Pop. Can't you understand that? There's no spite in it any more. I'm just what I am, that's all.

(*Biff's fury has spent itself, and he breaks down, sobbing, holding on to Willy, who dumbly fumbles for Biff's face.*)

Willy (*astonished*): What're you doing? What're you doing? (*To Linda.*) Why is he crying?

Biff (*crying, broken*): Will you let me go, for Christ sake? Will you take that phony dream and burn it before something happens? (*Struggling to contain himself, he pulls away and moves to the stairs.*) I'll go in the morning. Put him—put him to bed. (*Exhausted, Biff moves up the stairs to his room.*)

Willy (*after a long pause, astonished, elevated*): Isn't that remarkable? Biff—he likes me!

Linda: He loves you, Willy!

Happy (*deeply moved*): Always did, Pop.

Willy: Oh, Biff! (*Staring wildly.*) He cried! Cried to me. (*He is choking with his love, and now cries out his promise.*) That boy—that boy is going to be magnificent!

(*Ben appears in the light just outside the kitchen.*)

Ben: Yes, outstanding, with twenty thousand behind him.

Linda (*sensing the racing of his mind, fearfully, carefully*): Now come to bed, Willy. It's all settled now.

Willy (*finding it difficult not to rush out of the house*): Yes, we'll sleep. Come on. Go to sleep, Hap.

Ben: And it does take a great kind of man to crack the jungle.

(*In accents of dread, Ben's idyllic music starts up.*)

Happy (*his arm around Linda*): I'm getting married, Pop, don't forget it. I'm changing everything. I'm gonna run that department before the year is up. You'll see, Mom. (*He kisses her.*)

Ben: The jungle is dark but full of diamonds, Willy.

(*Willy turns, moves, listening to Ben.*)

Linda: Be good. You're both good boys, just act that way, that's all.

Happy: 'Night, Pop. (*He goes upstairs.*)

Linda (*to Willy*): Come, dear.

Ben (*with greater force*): One must go in to fetch a diamond out.

Willy (*to Linda, as he moves slowly along the edge of the kitchen, toward the door*): I just want to get settled down, Linda. Let me sit alone for a little.

Linda (*almost uttering her fear*): I want you upstairs.

Willy (*taking her in his arms*): In a few minutes, Linda. I couldn't sleep right now. Go on, you look awful tired. (*He kisses her.*)

Ben: Not like an appointment at all. A diamond is rough and hard to the touch.

Willy: Go on now, I'll be right up.

Linda: I think this is the only way, Willy.

Willy: Sure, it's the best thing.

Ben: Best thing!

Willy: The only way. Everything is gonna be—go on, kid, get to bed. You look so tired.

Linda: Come right up.

Willy: Two minutes.

(*Linda goes into the living room, then reappears in her bedroom. Willy moves just outside the kitchen door.*)

Willy: Loves me. (*Wonderingly.*) Always loved me. Isn't that a remarkable thing? Ben, he'll worship me for it!

Ben (*with promise*): It's dark there, but full of diamonds.

Willy: Can you imagine that magnificence with twenty thousand dollars in his pocket?

Linda (*calling from her room*): Willy! Come up!

Willy (*calling from the kitchen*): Yes! Yes! Coming! It's very smart, you realize that, don't you, sweetheart? Even Ben sees it. I gotta go, baby. 'By! By! (*Going over to Ben, almost dancing.*) Imagine? When the mail comes he'll be ahead of Bernard again!

Ben: A perfect proposition all around.

Willy: Did you see how he cried to me? Oh, if I could kiss him, Ben!

Ben: Time, William, time!

Willy: Oh, Ben, I always knew one way or another we were gonna make it, Biff and I!

Ben (*looking at his watch*): The boat. We'll be late. (*He moves slowly off into the darkness.*)

Willy (*elegiacally, turning to the house*): Now when you kick off, boy, I want a seventy-yard boot, and get right down the field under the ball, and when you hit, hit low and hit hard, because it's important, boy. (*He swings around and faces the audience.*) There's all kinds of important people in the stands, and the first thing you know . . . (*Suddenly realizing he is alone.*) Ben! Ben, where do I . . . ? (*He makes a sudden movement of search.*) Ben, how do I . . . ?

Linda (calling): Willy, you coming up?

Willy (uttering a gasp of fear, whirling about as if to quiet her): Sh! (*He turns around as if to find his way; sounds, faces, voices, seem to be swarming in upon him and he flicks at them, crying.*) Sh! Sh! (*Suddenly music, faint and high, stops him. It rises in intensity, almost to an unbearable scream. He goes up and down on his toes, and rushes off around the house.*) Shhh!

Linda: Willy?

(*There is no answer. Linda waits. Biff gets up off his bed. He is still in his clothes. Happy sits up. Biff stands listening.*)

Linda (with real fear): Willy, answer me! Willy!

(*There is the sound of a car starting and moving away at full speed.*)

Linda: No!

Biff (rushing down the stairs): Pop!

As the car speeds off, the music crashes down in a frenzy of sound, which becomes the soft pulsation of a single cello string. Biff slowly returns to his bedroom. He and Happy gravely don their jackets. Linda slowly walks out of her room. The music has developed into a dead march. The leaves of day are appearing over everything. Charley and Bernard, somberly dressed, appear and knock on the kitchen door. Biff and Happy slowly descend the stairs to the kitchen as Charley and Bernard enter. All stop a moment when Linda, in clothes of mourning, bearing a little bunch of roses, comes through the draped doorway into the kitchen. She goes to Charley and takes his arm. Now all move toward the audience, through the wall-line of the kitchen. At the limit of the apron, Linda lays down the flowers, kneels, and sits back on her heels. All stare down at the grave.

REQUIEM

Charley: It's getting dark, Linda.

(*Linda doesn't react. She stares at the grave.*)

Biff: How about it, Mom? Better get some rest, heh? They'll be closing the gate soon.

(*Linda makes no move. Pause.*)

Happy (deeply angered): He had no right to do that! There was no necessity for it. We would've helped him.

Charley (grunting): Hmmm.

Biff: Come along, Mom.

Linda: Why didn't anybody come?

Charley: It was a very nice funeral.

Linda: But where are all the people he knew? Maybe they blame him.

Charley: Naa. It's a rough world, Linda. They wouldn't blame him.

Linda: I can't understand it. At this time especially. First time in thirty-five years we were just about free and clear. He only needed a little salary. He was even finished with the dentist.

Charley: No man only needs a little salary.

Linda: I can't understand it.

Biff: There were a lot of nice days. When he'd come home from a trip; or on Sundays, making the stoop; finishing the cellar; putting on the new porch; when he built the extra bathroom; and put up the garage. You know something, Charley, there's more of him in that front stoop than in all the sales he ever made.

Charley: Yeah. He was a happy man with a batch of cement.

Linda: He was so wonderful with his hands.

Biff: He had the wrong dreams. All, all, wrong.

Happy (almost ready to fight Biff): Don't say that!

Biff: He never knew who he was.

Charley (stopping Happy's movement and reply. To Biff.): Nobody dast blame this man. You don't understand: Willy was a salesman. And for a salesman, there is no rock bottom to the life. He don't put a bolt to a nut, he don't tell you the law or give you medicine. He's a man out there in the blue, riding on a smile and a shoeshine. And when they start not smiling back—that's an earthquake. And then you get yourself a couple of spots on your hat, and you're finished. Nobody dast blame this man. A salesman is got to dream, boy. It comes with the territory.

Biff: Charley, the man didn't know who he was.

Happy (infuriated): Don't say that!

Biff: Why don't you come with me, Happy?

Happy: I'm not licked that easily. I'm staying right in this city, and I'm gonna beat this racket! (*He looks at Biff, his chin set.*) The Loman Brothers!

Biff: I know who I am, kid.

Happy: All right, boy. I'm gonna show you and everybody else that Willy Loman did not die in vain. He had a good dream. It's the only dream you can have—to come out number-one man. He fought it out here, and this is where I'm gonna win it for him.

Biff (with a hopeless glance at Happy, bends toward his mother): Let's go, Mom.

Linda: I'll be with you in a minute. Go on, Charley. (*He hesitates.*) I want to, just for a minute. I never had a chance to say good-by.

(*Charley moves away, followed by Happy. Biff remains a slight distance up and left of Linda. She sits there, summoning herself. The flute begins, not far away, playing behind her speech.*)

Linda: Forgive me, dear. I can't cry. I don't know what it is, but I can't cry. I don't understand it. Why did you ever do that? Help me, Willy, I can't cry. It seems to me that you're just on another trip. I keep expecting you. Willy, dear, I can't cry. Why did you do it? I search and search and search, and I can't understand it, Willy. I made the last payment on the house today. Today, dear. And there'll be nobody home. (*A sob rises in her throat.*) We're free and clear. (*Sobbing more fully, released.*) We're free. (*Biff comes slowly toward her.*) We're free . . . We're free . . .

Biff lifts her to her feet and moves out up right with her in his arms. Linda sobs quietly. Bernard and Charley come together and follow them, followed by Happy. Only the music of the flute is left on the darkening stage as over the house the hard towers of the apartment buildings rise into sharp focus, and—

THE CURTAIN FALLS

Arthur Miller on Writing

Tragedy and the Common Man[1]

1949

In this age few tragedies are written. It has often been held that the lack is due to a paucity of heroes among us, or else that modern man has had the blood drawn out of his organs of belief by the skepticism of science, and the heroic attack on life cannot feed on an attitude of reserve and circumspection. For one reason or another, we are often held to be below tragedy—or tragedy above us. The inevitable conclusion is, of course, that the tragic mode is archaic, fit only for the very highly placed, the kings or the kingly, and where this admission is not made in so many words it is most often implied.

I believe that the common man is as apt a subject for tragedy in its highest sense as kings were. On the face of it this ought to be obvious in

Arthur Miller

the light of modern psychiatry, which bases its analysis upon classific formulations, such as the Oedipus and Orestes complexes, for instance, which were enacted by royal beings, but which apply to everyone in similar emotional situations.

More simply, when the question of tragedy in art is not at issue, we never hesitate to attribute to the well-placed and the exalted the very same mental processes as the lowly. And finally, if the exaltation of tragic action were truly a property of the high-bred character alone, it is inconceivable that the mass of mankind should cherish tragedy above all other forms, let alone be capable of understanding it.

As a general rule, to which there may be exceptions unknown to me, I think the tragic feeling is evoked in us when we are in the presence of a character who is ready to lay down his life, if need be, to secure one thing—his sense of personal dignity. From Orestes to Hamlet, Medea to Macbeth, the underlying struggle is that of the individual attempting to gain his "rightful" position in his society.

Sometimes he is one who has been displaced from it, sometimes one who seeks to attain it for the first time, but the fateful wound from which the inevitable events spiral is the wound of indignity, and its dominant force is indignation. Tragedy, then, is the consequence of a man's total compulsion to evaluate himself justly.

In the sense of having been initiated by the hero himself, the tale always reveals what has been called his "tragic flaw," a failing that is not peculiar to grand or elevated characters. Nor is it necessarily a weakness. The flaw, or crack in the character, is really nothing—and need be nothing—but his inherent unwillingness to remain passive in the face of what he conceives to be a challenge to his dignity, his image of his rightful status. Only the passive, only those who accept their lot without active retaliation, are "flawless." Most of us are in that category.

But there are among us today, as there always have been, those who act against the scheme of things that degrades them, and in the process of action, everything we have accepted out of fear or insensitivity or ignorance is shaken before us and examined, and

[1]This essay was originally published in the *New York Times*, February 27, 1949.

from this total onslaught by an individual against the seemingly stable cosmos surrounding us—from this total examination of the "unchangeable" environment—comes the terror and the fear that is classically associated with tragedy.

More important, from this total questioning of what has been previously unquestioned, we learn. And such a process is not beyond the common man. In revolutions around the world, these past thirty years, he has demonstrated again and again this inner dynamic of all tragedy.

Insistence upon the rank of the tragic hero, or the so-called nobility of his character, is really but a clinging to the outward forms of tragedy. If rank or nobility of character was indispensable, then it would follow that the problems of those with rank were the particular problems of tragedy. But surely the right of one monarch to capture the domain from another no longer raises our passions, nor are our concepts of justice what they were to the mind of an Elizabethan king.

The quality in such plays that does shake us, however, derives from the underlying fear of being displaced, the disaster inherent in being torn away from our chosen image of what and who we are in this world. Among us today this fear is as strong, and perhaps stronger, than it ever was. In fact, it is the common man who knows this fear best.

Now, if it is true that tragedy is the consequence of a man's total compulsion to evaluate himself justly, his destruction in the attempt posits a wrong or an evil in his environment. And this is precisely the morality of tragedy and its lesson. The discovery of the moral law, which is what the enlightenment of tragedy consists of, is not the discovery of some abstract or metaphysical quantity.

The tragic right is a condition of life, a condition in which the human personality is able to flower and realize itself. The wrong is the condition which suppresses man, perverts the flowing out of his love and creative instinct. Tragedy enlightens—and it must, in that it points the heroic finger at the enemy of man's freedom. The thrust for freedom is the quality in tragedy which exalts. The revolutionary questioning of the stable environment is what terrifies. In no way is the common man debarred from such thoughts or such actions.

Seen in this light, our lack of tragedy may be partially accounted for by the turn which modern literature has taken toward the purely psychiatric view of life, or the purely sociological. If all our miseries, our indignities, are born and bred within our minds, then all action, let alone the heroic action, is obviously impossible.

And if society alone is responsible for the cramping of our lives, then the protagonist must needs be so pure and faultless as to force us to deny his validity as a character. From neither of these views can tragedy derive, simply because neither represents a balanced concept of life. Above all else, tragedy requires the finest appreciation by the writer of cause and effect.

No tragedy can therefore come about when its author fears to question absolutely everything, when he regards any institution, habit or custom as being either everlasting, immutable or inevitable. In the tragic view the need of man to wholly realize himself is the only fixed star, and whatever it is that hedges his nature and lowers it is ripe for attack and examination. Which is not to say that tragedy must preach revolution.

The Greeks could probe the very heavenly origin of their ways and return to confirm the rightness of laws. And Job could face God in anger, demanding his right, and end in submission. But for a moment everything is in suspension, nothing is accepted, and in this stretching and tearing apart of the cosmos, in the very action of so doing, the character gains "size," the tragic stature which is spuriously attached to the royal or the high born in our minds. The commonest of men may take on that stature to the extent of his willingness to throw all he has into the contest, the battle to secure his rightful place in his world.

There is a misconception of tragedy with which I have been struck in review after review, and in many conversations with writers and readers alike. It is the idea that tragedy is of necessity allied to pessimism. Even the dictionary says nothing more about the word than that it means a story with a sad or unhappy ending. This impression is so firmly fixed that I almost hesitate to claim that in truth tragedy implies more optimism in its author than does comedy, and that its final result ought to be the reinforcement of the onlooker's brightest opinions of the human animal.

For, if it is true to say that in essence the tragic hero is intent upon claiming his whole due as a personality, and if this struggle must be total and without reservation, then it automatically demonstrates the indestructible will of man to achieve his humanity.

The possibility of victory must be there in tragedy. Where pathos rules, where pathos is finally derived, a character has fought a battle he could not possibly have won. The pathetic is achieved when the protagonist is, by virtue of his witlessness, his insensitivity, or the very air he gives off, incapable of grappling with a much superior force.

Pathos truly is the mode for the pessimist. But tragedy requires a nicer balance between what is possible and what is impossible. And it is curious, although edifying, that the plays we revere, century after century, are the tragedies. In them, and in them alone, lies the belief—optimistic, if you will—in the perfectibility of man.

It is time, I think, that we who are without kings took up this bright thread of our history and followed it to the only place it can possibly lead in our time—the heart and spirit of the average man.

From The Theater Essays of Arthur Miller

August Wilson

Fences   1985

August Wilson (1945–2005) was born in Pittsburgh, one of six children of a German American father and an African American mother. His parents separated early, and the young Wilson was raised on the Hill, a Pittsburgh ghetto neighborhood. Although he quit school in the ninth grade when a teacher wrongly accused him of submitting a ghost-written paper, Wilson continued his education in local libraries, supporting himself by working as a cook and stock clerk. In 1968 he co-founded a community troupe, the Black Horizons Theater, staging plays by LeRoi Jones and other militants; later he moved from Pittsburgh to Saint Paul, Minnesota, where at last he saw a play of his own performed. Jitney, his first important work, won him entry to a 1982 playwrights' conference at the Eugene O'Neill Theater Center. There, Lloyd Richards, dean of Yale University School of Drama, took an interest in Wilson's work and offered to produce his plays at Yale. Ma Rainey's Black Bottom was the first to reach Broadway (in 1985), where it ran for ten months and received an award from the New York Drama Critics Circle. In 1987 Fences, starring Mary Alice and James Earl Jones, won another Critics Circle Award, as well as a Tony Award and the Pulitzer Prize for best American play of its year. It set a box office record for a Broadway nonmusical. Joe Turner's Come and Gone (1988) also received high acclaim, and The Piano Lesson (1990) won Wilson a second Pulitzer Prize. His subsequent plays were

James Earl Jones and Mary Alice in Yale Repertory Theater's 1985 world premiere of *Fences*.

Two Trains Running (1992), *Seven Guitars* (1995), *King Hedley II* (2000), *Gem of the Ocean* (2003), *and Radio Golf* (2005).

Wilson's ten plays, each one set in a different decade of the 1900s, constitute his "Century Cycle" that traces the black experience in America throughout the twentieth century. Seamlessly interweaving realistic and mythic approaches, filled with vivid characters, pungent dialogue, and strong dramatic scenes, it is one of the most ambitious projects in the history of the American theater and an epic achievement in our literature. Wilson died of liver cancer in October 2005, a few months after completing the final play in his cycle. Two weeks after his death the Virginia Theater on Broadway was renamed the August Wilson Theater in his honor. A published poet as well as a dramatist, Wilson once told an interviewer, "After writing poetry for twenty-one years, I approach a play the same way. The mental process is poetic: you use metaphor and condense."

For Lloyd Richards, Who Adds to Whatever He Touches

> When the sins of our fathers visit us
> We do not have to play host.
> We can banish them with forgiveness
> As God, in His Largeness and Laws.

> —AUGUST WILSON

LIST OF CHARACTERS

Troy Maxson
Jim Bono, Troy's friend
Rose, Troy's wife
Lyons, Troy's oldest son by previous marriage
Gabriel, Troy's brother
Cory, Troy and Rose's son
Raynell, Troy's daughter

SETTING. *The setting is the yard which fronts the only entrance to the Maxson household, an ancient two-story brick house set back off a small alley in a big-city neighborhood. The entrance to the house is gained by two or three steps leading to a wooden porch badly in need of paint.*

A relatively recent addition to the house and running its full width, the porch lacks congruence. It is a sturdy porch with a flat roof. One or two chairs of dubious value sit at one end where the kitchen window opens onto the porch. An old-fashioned icebox stands silent guard at the opposite end.

The yard is a small dirt yard, partially fenced, except for the last scene, with a wooden saw horse, a pile of lumber, and other fence-building equipment set off to the side. Opposite is a tree from which hangs a ball made of rags. A baseball bat leans against the tree. Two oil drums serve as garbage receptacles and sit near the house at right to complete the setting.

THE PLAY. *Near the turn of the century, the destitute of Europe sprang on the city with tenacious claws and an honest and solid dream. The city devoured them. They swelled its belly until it burst into a thousand furnaces and sewing machines, a thousand butcher shops and bakers' ovens, a thousand churches and hospitals and funeral parlors and moneylenders. The city grew. It nourished itself and offered each man a partnership limited only by his talent, his guile, and his willingness and capacity for hard work. For the immigrants of Europe, a dream dared and won true.*

The descendants of African slaves were offered no such welcome or participation. They came from places called the Carolinas and the Virginias, Georgia, Alabama, Mississippi, and Tennessee. They came strong, eager, searching. The city rejected them and they fled and settled along the riverbanks and under bridges in shallow, ramshackle houses made of sticks and tarpaper. They collected rags and wood. They sold the use of their muscles and their bodies. They cleaned houses and washed clothes, they shined shoes, and in quiet desperation and vengeful pride, they stole, and lived in pursuit of their own dream. That they could breathe free, finally, and stand to meet life with the force of dignity and whatever eloquence the heart could call upon.

By 1957, the hard-won victories of the European immigrants had solidified the industrial might of America. War had been confronted and won with new energies that used loyalty and patriotism as its fuel. Life was rich, full, and flourishing. The Milwaukee Braves won the World Series, and the hot winds of change that would make the sixties a turbulent, racing, dangerous, and provocative decade had not yet begun to blow full.

ACT I

SCENE I

It is 1957. Troy and Bono enter the yard, engaged in conversation. Troy is fifty-three years old, a large man with thick, heavy hands; it is this largeness that he strives to fill out and make an accommodation with. Together with his blackness, his largeness informs his sensibilities and the choices he has made in his life.

Of the two men, Bono is obviously the follower. His commitment to their friendship of thirty-odd years is rooted in his admiration of Troy's honesty, capacity for hard work, and his strength, which Bono seeks to emulate.

It is Friday night, payday, and the one night of the week the two men engage in a ritual of talk and drink. Troy is usually the most talkative and at times he can be crude and almost vulgar, though he is capable of rising to profound heights of expression. The men carry lunch buckets and wear or carry burlap aprons and are dressed in clothes suitable to their jobs as garbage collectors.

Bono: Troy, you ought to stop that lying!

Troy: I ain't lying! The nigger had a watermelon this big. (*He indicates with his hands.*) Talking about . . . "What watermelon, Mr. Rand?" I liked to fell out! "What watermelon, Mr. Rand?" . . . And it sitting there big as life.

Bono: What did Mr. Rand say?

Troy: Ain't said nothing. Figure if the nigger too dumb to know he carrying a watermelon, he wasn't gonna get much sense out of him. Trying to hide that great big old watermelon under his coat. Afraid to let the white man see him carry it home.

Bono: I'm like you . . . I ain't got no time for them kind of people.

Troy: Now what he look like getting mad cause he see the man from the union talking to Mr. Rand?

Bono: He come to me talking about . . . "Maxson gonna get us fired." I told him to get away from me with that. He walked away from me calling you a trouble-maker. What Mr. Rand say?

Troy: Ain't said nothing. He told me to go down the Commissioner's office next Friday. They called me down there to see them.

Bono: Well, as long as you got your complaint filed, they can't fire you. That's what one of them white fellows tell me.

Troy: I ain't worried about them firing me. They gonna fire me cause I asked a question? That's all I did. I went to Mr. Rand and asked him, "Why? Why you got the white mens driving and the colored lifting?" Told him, "what's the matter, don't I count? You think only white fellows got sense enough to drive a truck. That ain't no paper job! Hell, anybody can drive a truck. How come you got all whites driving and the colored lifting?" He told me "take it to the union." Well, hell, that's what I done! Now they wanna come up with this pack of lies.

Bono: I told Brownie if the man come and ask him any questions . . . just tell the truth! It ain't nothing but something they done trumped up on you cause you filed a complaint on them.

Troy: Brownie don't understand nothing. All I want them to do is change the job description. Give everybody a chance to drive the truck. Brownie can't see that. He ain't got that much sense.

Bono: How you figure he be making out with that gal be up at Taylors' all the time . . . that Alberta gal?

Troy: Same as you and me. Getting just as much as we is. Which is to say nothing.

Bono: It is, huh? I figure you doing a little better than me . . . and I ain't saying what I'm doing.

Troy: Aw, nigger, look here . . . I know you. If you had got anywhere near that gal, twenty minutes later you be looking to tell somebody. And the first one you gonna tell . . . that you gonna want to brag to . . . is gonna be me.

Bono: I ain't saying that. I see where you be eyeing her.

Troy: I eye all the women. I don't miss nothing. Don't never let nobody tell you Troy Maxson don't eye the women.

Bono: You been doing more than eyeing her. You done bought her a drink or two.

Troy: Hell yeah, I bought her a drink! What that mean? I bought you one, too. What that mean cause I buy her a drink? I'm just being polite.

Bono: It's alright to buy her one drink. That's what you call being polite. But when you wanna be buying two or three . . . that's what you call eyeing her.

Troy: Look here, as long as you known me . . . you ever known me to chase after women?

Bono: Hell yeah! Long as I done known you. You forgetting I knew you when.

Troy: Naw, I'm talking about since I been married to Rose?

Bono: Oh, not since you been married to Rose. Now, that's the truth, there. I can say that.

Troy: Alright then! Case closed.

Bono: I see you be walking up around Alberta's house. You supposed to be at Taylors' and you be walking up around there.

Troy: What you watching where I'm walking for? I ain't watching after you.

Bono: I seen you walking around there more than once.

Troy: Hell, you liable to see me walking anywhere! That don't mean nothing cause you see me walking around there.

Bono: Where she come from anyway? She just kinda showed up one day.

Troy: Tallahassee. You can look at her and tell she one of them Florida gals. They got some big healthy women down there. Grow them right up out the ground. Got a little bit of Indian in her. Most of them niggers down in Florida got some Indian in them.

Bono: I don't know about that Indian part. But she damn sure big and healthy. Woman wear some big stockings. Got them great big old legs and hips as wide as the Mississippi River.

Troy: Legs don't mean nothing. You don't do nothing but push them out of the way. But them hips cushion the ride!

Bono: Troy, you ain't got no sense.

Troy: It's the truth! Like you riding on Goodyears!

(*Rose enters from the house. She is ten years younger than Troy, her devotion to him stems from her recognition of the possibilities of her life without him: a succession of abusive men and their babies, a life of partying and running the streets, the Church, or aloneness with its attendant pain and frustration. She recognizes Troy's spirit as a fine and illuminating one and she either ignores or forgives his faults, only some of which she recognizes. Though she doesn't drink, her presence is an integral part of the Friday night rituals. She alternates between the porch and the kitchen, where supper preparations are under way.*)

Rose: What you all out here getting into?

Troy: What you worried about what we getting into for? This is men talk, woman.

Rose: What I care what you all talking about? Bono, you gonna stay for supper?

Bono: No, I thank you, Rose. But Lucille say she cooking up a pot of pigfeet.

Troy: Pigfeet! Hell, I'm going home with you! Might even stay the night if you got some pigfeet. You got something in there to top them pigfeet, Rose?

Rose: I'm cooking up some chicken. I got some chicken and collard greens.

Troy: Well, go on back in the house and let me and Bono finish what we was talking about. This is men talk. I got some talk for you later. You know what kind of talk I mean. You go on and powder it up.

Rose: Troy Maxson, don't you start that now!

Troy (puts his arm around her): Aw, woman . . . come here. Look here, Bono . . . when I met this woman . . . I got out that place, say, "Hitch up my pony, saddle up my mare . . . there's a woman out there for me somewhere. I looked here. Looked there. Saw Rose and latched on to her." I latched on to her and told her—I'm gonna tell you the truth—I told her, "Baby, I don't wanna marry, I just wanna be your man." Rose told me . . . tell him what you told me, Rose.

Rose: I told him if he wasn't the marrying kind, then move out the way so the marrying kind could find me.

Troy: That's what she told me. "Nigger, you in my way. You blocking the view! Move out the way so I can find me a husband." I thought it over two or three days. Come back—

Rose: Ain't no two or three days nothing. You was back the same night.

Troy: Come back, told her . . . "Okay, baby . . . but I'm gonna buy me a banty rooster and put him out there in the backyard . . . and when he see a stranger come, he'll flap his wings and crow . . . " Look here, Bono, I could watch the front door by myself . . . it was that back door I was worried about.

Rose: Troy, you ought not talk like that. Troy ain't doing nothing but telling a lie.

Troy: Only thing is . . . when we first got married . . . forget the rooster . . . we ain't had no yard!

Bono: I hear you tell it. Me and Lucille was staying down there on Logan Street. Had two rooms with the outhouse in the back. I ain't mind the outhouse none. But when that goddamn wind blow through there in the winter . . . that's what I'm talking about! To this day I wonder why in the hell I ever stayed down there for six long years. But see, I didn't know I could do no better. I thought only white folks had inside toilets and things.

Rose: There's a lot of people don't know they can do no better than they doing now. That's just something you got to learn. A lot of folks still shop at Bella's.

Troy: Ain't nothing wrong with shopping at Bella's. She got fresh food.

Rose: I ain't said nothing about if she got fresh food. I'm talking about what she charge. She charge ten cents more than the A&P.

Troy: The A&P ain't never done nothing for me. I spends my money where I'm treated right. I go down to Bella, say, "I need a loaf of bread, I'll pay you Friday." She give it to me. What sense that make when I got money to go and spend it somewhere else and ignore the person who done right by me? That ain't in the Bible.

Rose: We ain't talking about what's in the Bible. What sense it make to shop there when she overcharge?

Troy: You shop where you want to. I'll do my shopping where the people been good to me.

Rose: Well, I don't think it's right for her to overcharge. That's all I was saying.

Bono: Look here . . . I got to get on. Lucille going be raising all kind of hell.

Troy: Where you going, nigger? We ain't finished this pint. Come here, finish this pint.

Bono: Well, hell, I am . . . if you ever turn the bottle loose.

Troy (*hands him the bottle*): The only thing I say about the A&P is I'm glad Cory got that job down there. Help him take care of his school clothes and things. Gabe done moved out and things getting tight around here. He got that job . . . He can start to look out for himself.

Rose: Cory done went and got recruited by a college football team.

Troy: I told that boy about that football stuff. The white man ain't gonna let him get nowhere with that football. I told him when he first come to me with it. Now you come telling me he done went and got more tied up in it. He ought to go and get recruited in how to fix cars or something where he can make a living.

Rose: He ain't talking about making no living playing football. It's just something the boys in school do. They gonna send a recruiter by to talk to you. He'll tell you he ain't talking about making no living playing football. It's a honor to be recruited.

Troy: It ain't gonna get him nowhere. Bono'll tell you that.

Bono: If he be like you in the sports . . . he's gonna be alright. Ain't but two men ever played baseball as good as you. That's Babe Ruth and Josh Gibson.° Them's the only two men ever hit more home runs than you.

Troy: What it ever get me? Ain't got a pot to piss in or a window to throw it out of.

Rose: Times have changed since you was playing baseball, Troy. That was before the war. Times have changed a lot since then.

Troy: How in hell they done changed?

Rose: They got lots of colored boys playing ball now. Baseball and football.

Bono: You right about that, Rose. Times have changed, Troy. You just come along too early.

Troy: There ought not never have been no time called too early! Now you take that fellow . . . what's that fellow they had playing right field for the Yankees back then? You know who I'm talking about, Bono. Used to play right field for the Yankees.

Rose: Selkirk?

Troy: Selkirk!° That's it! Man batting .269, understand? .269. What kind of sense that make? I was hitting .432 with thirty-seven home runs! Man batting .269 and playing right field for the Yankees! I saw Josh Gibson's daughter yesterday. She walking around with raggedy shoes on her feet. Now I bet you Selkirk's daughter ain't walking around with raggedy shoes on her feet! I bet you that!

Rose: They got a lot of colored baseball players now. Jackie Robinson° was the first. Folks had to wait for Jackie Robinson.

Troy: I done seen a hundred niggers play baseball better than Jackie Robinson. Hell, I know some teams Jackie Robinson couldn't even make! What you talking about Jackie Robinson. Jackie Robinson wasn't nobody. I'm talking about if you could play ball then they ought to have let you play. Don't care what color you were. Come telling me I come along too early. If you could play . . . then they ought to have let you play.

(*Troy takes a long drink from the bottle.*)

Josh Gibson: legendary catcher in the Negro Leagues whose batting average and home-run totals far outstripped Major League records; he died of a stroke at age 35 in January 1947, three months before Jackie Robinson's debut with the Brooklyn Dodgers. *Selkirk:* Andy Selkirk, Yankee outfielder who hit .269 in 118 games in 1940. *Jackie Robinson:* the first African American to play in major league baseball, joined the Brooklyn Dodgers in 1947.

Rose: You gonna drink yourself to death. You don't need to be drinking like that.

Troy: Death ain't nothing. I done seen him. Done wrassled with him. You can't tell me nothing about death. Death ain't nothing but a fastball on the outside corner. And you know what I'll do to that! Lookee here, Bono . . . am I lying? You get one of them fastballs, about waist high, over the outside corner of the plate where you can get the meat of the bat on it . . . and good god! You can kiss it goodbye. Now, am I lying?

Bono: Naw, you telling the truth there. I seen you do it.

Troy: If I'm lying . . . that 450 feet worth of lying! (*Pause.*) That's all death is to me. A fastball on the outside corner.

Rose: I don't know why you want to get on talking about death.

Troy: Ain't nothing wrong with talking about death. That's part of life. Everybody gonna die. You gonna die, I'm gonna die. Bono's gonna die. Hell, we all gonna die.

Rose: But you ain't got to talk about it. I don't like to talk about it.

Troy: You the one brought it up. Me and Bono was talking about baseball . . . you tell me I'm gonna drink myself to death. Ain't that right, Bono? You know I don't drink this but one night out of the week. That's Friday night. I'm gonna drink just enough to where I can handle it. Then I cuts it loose. I leave it alone. So don't you worry about me drinking myself to death. 'Cause I ain't worried about Death. I done seen him. I done wrestled with him.

Look here, Bono . . . I looked up one day and Death was marching straight at me. Like Soldiers on Parade! The Army of Death was marching straight at me. The middle of July, 1941. It got real cold just like it be winter. It seem like Death himself reached out and touched me on the shoulder. He touch me just like I touch you. I got cold as ice and Death standing there grinning at me.

Rose: Troy, why don't you hush that talk.

Troy: I say . . . what you want, Mr. Death? You be wanting me? You done brought your army to be getting me? I looked him dead in the eye. I wasn't fearing nothing. I was ready to tangle. Just like I'm ready to tangle now. The Bible say be ever vigilant. That's why I don't get but so drunk. I got to keep watch.

Rose: Troy was right down there in Mercy Hospital. You remember he had pneumonia? Laying there with a fever talking plumb out of his head.

Troy: Death standing there staring at me . . . carrying that sickle in his hand. Finally he say, "You want bound over for another year?" See, just like that . . . "You want bound over for another year?" I told him, "Bound over hell! Let's settle this now!"

It seem like he kinda fell back when I said that, and all the cold went out of me. I reached down and grabbed that sickle and threw it just as far as I could throw it . . . and me and him commenced to wrestling.

We wrestled for three days and three nights. I can't say where I found the strength from. Everytime it seemed like he was gonna get the best of me, I'd reach way down deep inside myself and find the strength to do him one better.

Rose: Every time Troy tell that story he find different ways to tell it. Different things to make up about it.

Troy: I ain't making up nothing. I'm telling you the facts of what happened. I wrestled with Death for three days and three nights and I'm standing here to tell you about it. (*Pause.*) Alright. At the end of the third night we done weakened each other to where we can't hardly move. Death stood up, throwed on his robe . . . had him a white robe with a hood on it. He threw on that robe and went off to look for his sickle. Say, "I'll be back." Just like that. "I'll be back." I told him, say, "Yeah, but . . . you gonna have to find me!" I wasn't no fool. I wasn't going looking for him. Death ain't nothing to play with. And I know he's gonna get me. I know I got to join his army . . . his camp followers. But as long as I keep my strength and see him coming . . . as long as I keep up my vigilance . . . he's gonna have to fight to get me. I ain't going easy.

Bono: Well, look here, since you got to keep up your vigilance . . . let me have the bottle.

Troy: Aw hell, I shouldn't have told you that part. I should have left out that part.

Rose: Troy be talking that stuff and half the time don't even know what he be talking about.

Troy: Bono know me better than that.

Bono: That's right. I know you. I know you got some Uncle Remus in your blood. You got more stories than the devil got sinners.

Troy: Aw hell, I done seen him too! Done talked with the devil.

Rose: Troy, don't nobody wanna be hearing all that stuff.

(*Lyons enters the yard from the street. Thirty-four years old, Troy's son by a previous marriage, he sports a neatly trimmed goatee, sport coat, white shirt, tieless and buttoned at the collar. Though he fancies himself a musician, he is more caught up in the rituals and "idea" of being a musician than in the actual practice of the music. He has come to borrow money from Troy, and while he knows he will be successful, he is uncertain as to what extent his lifestyle will be held up to scrutiny and ridicule.*)

Lyons: Hey, Pop.

Troy: What you come "Hey, Popping" me for?

Lyons: How you doing, Rose? (*He kisses her.*) Mr. Bono. How you doing?

Bono: Hey, Lyons . . . how you been?

Troy: He must have been doing alright. I ain't seen him around here last week.

Rose: Troy, leave your boy alone. He come by to see you and you wanna start all that nonsense.

Troy: I ain't bothering Lyons. (*Offers him the bottle.*) Here . . . get you a drink. We got an understanding. I know why he come by to see me and he know I know.

Lyons: Come on, Pop . . . I just stopped by to say hi . . . see how you was doing.

Troy: You ain't stopped by yesterday.

Rose: You gonna stay for supper, Lyons? I got some chicken cooking in the oven.

Lyons: No, Rose . . . thanks. I was just in the neighborhood and thought I'd stop by for a minute.

Troy: You was in the neighborhood alright, nigger. You telling the truth there. You was in the neighborhood cause it's my payday.

Lyons: Well, hell, since you mentioned it . . . let me have ten dollars.

Troy: I'll be damned! I'll die and go to hell and play blackjack with the devil before I give you ten dollars.

Bono: That's what I wanna know about . . . that devil you done seen.

Lyons: What . . . Pop done seen the devil? You too much, Pops.

Troy: Yeah, I done seen him. Talked to him too!

Rose: You ain't seen no devil. I done told you that man ain't had nothing to do with the devil. Anything you can't understand, you want to call it the devil.

Troy: Look here, Bono . . . I went down to see Hertzberger about some furniture. Got three rooms for two-ninety-eight. That what it say on the radio. "Three rooms . . . two-ninety-eight." Even made up a little song about it. Go down there . . . man tell me I can't get no credit. I'm working every day and can't get no credit. What to do? I got an empty house with some raggedy furniture in it. Cory ain't got no bed. He's sleeping on a pile of rags on the floor. Working every day and can't get no credit. Come back here—Rose'll tell you—madder than hell. Sit down . . . try to figure what I'm gonna do. Come a knock on the door. Ain't been living here but three days. Who know I'm here? Open the door . . . devil standing there bigger than life. White fellow . . . got on good clothes and everything. Standing there with a clipboard in his hand. I ain't had to say nothing. First words come out of his mouth was . . . "I understand you need some furniture and can't get no credit." I liked to fell over. He say "I'll give you all the credit you want, but you got to pay the interest on it." I told him, "Give me three rooms worth and charge whatever you want." Next day a truck pulled up here and two men unloaded them three rooms. Man what drove the truck give me a book. Say send ten dollars, first of every month to the address in the book and every thing will be alright. Say if I miss a payment the devil was coming back and it'll be hell to pay. That was fifteen years ago. To this day . . . the first of the month I send my ten dollars, Rose'll tell you.

Rose: Troy lying.

Troy: I ain't never seen that man since. Now you tell me who else that could have been but the devil? I ain't sold my soul or nothing like that, you understand. Naw, I wouldn't have truck with the devil about nothing like that. I got my furniture and pays my ten dollars the first of the month just like clockwork.

Bono: How long you say you been paying this ten dollars a month?

Troy: Fifteen years!

Bono: Hell, ain't you finished paying for it yet? How much the man done charged you?

Troy: Aw hell, I done paid for it. I done paid for it ten times over! The fact is I'm scared to stop paying it.

Rose: Troy lying. We got that furniture from Mr. Glickman. He ain't paying no ten dollars a month to nobody.

Troy: Aw hell, woman. Bono know I ain't that big a fool.

Lyons: I was just getting ready to say . . . I know where there's a bridge for sale.

Troy: Look here, I'll tell you this . . . it don't matter to me if he was the devil. It don't matter if the devil give credit. Somebody has got to give it.

Rose: It ought to matter. You going around talking about having truck with the devil . . . God's the one you gonna have to answer to. He's the one gonna be at the Judgment.

Lyons: Yeah, well, look here, Pop . . . Let me have that ten dollars. I'll give it back to you. Bonnie got a job working at the hospital.

Troy: What I tell you, Bono? The only time I see this nigger is when he wants something. That's the only time I see him.

Lyons: Come on, Pop, Mr. Bono don't want to hear all that. Let me have the ten dollars. I told you Bonnie working.

Troy: What that mean to me? "Bonnie working." I don't care if she working. Go ask her for the ten dollars if she working. Talking about "Bonnie working." Why ain't you working?

Lyons: Aw, Pop, you know I can't find no decent job. Where am I gonna get a job at? You know I can't get no job.

Troy: I told you I know some people down there. I can get you on the rubbish if you want to work. I told you that the last time you came by here asking me for something.

Lyons: Naw, Pop . . . thanks. That ain't for me. I don't wanna be carrying nobody's rubbish. I don't wanna be punching nobody's time clock.

Troy: What's the matter, you too good to carry people's rubbish? Where you think that ten dollars you talking about come from? I'm just supposed to haul people's rubbish and give my money to you cause you too lazy to work. You too lazy to work and wanna know why you ain't got what I got.

Rose: What hospital Bonnie working at? Mercy?

Lyons: She's down at Passavant working in the laundry.

Troy: I ain't got nothing as it is. I give you that ten dollars and I got to eat beans the rest of the week. Naw . . . you ain't getting no ten dollars here.

Lyons: You ain't got to be eating no beans. I don't know why you wanna say that.

Troy: I ain't got no extra money. Gabe done moved over to Miss Pearl's paying her the rent and things done got tight around here. I can't afford to be giving you every payday.

Lyons: I ain't asked you to give me nothing. I asked you to loan me ten dollars. I know you got ten dollars.

Troy: Yeah, I got it. You know why I got it? Cause I don't throw my money away out there in the streets. You living the fast life . . . wanna be a musician . . . running around in them clubs and things . . . then, you learn to take care of yourself. You ain't gonna find me going and asking nobody for nothing. I done spent too many years without.

Lyons: You and me is two different people, Pop.

Troy: I done learned my mistake and learned to do what's right by it. You still trying to get something for nothing. Life don't owe you nothing. You owe it to yourself. Ask Bono. He'll tell you I'm right.

Lyons: You got your way of dealing with the world . . . I got mine. The only thing that matters to me is the music.

Troy: Yeah, I can see that! It don't matter how you gonna eat . . . where your next dollar is coming from. You telling the truth there.

Lyons: I know I got to eat. But I got to live too. I need something that gonna help me to get out of the bed in the morning. Make me feel like I belong in the world. I don't bother nobody. I just stay with my music cause that's the only way I can find to live in the world. Otherwise there ain't no telling what I might do. Now I don't come criticizing you and how you live. I just come by to ask you for ten dollars. I don't wanna hear all that about how I live.

Troy: Boy, your mama did a hell of a job raising you.

Lyons: You can't change me, Pop. I'm thirty-four years old. If you wanted to change me, you should have been there when I was growing up. I come by to see you . . . ask for ten dollars and you want to talk about how I was raised. You don't know nothing about how I was raised.

Rose: Let the boy have ten dollars, Troy.

Troy (to Lyons): What the hell you looking at me for? I ain't got no ten dollars. You know what I do with my money. *(To Rose.)* Give him ten dollars if you want him to have it.

Rose: I will. Just as soon as you turn it loose.

Troy (handing Rose the money): There it is. Seventy-six dollars and forty-two cents. You see this, Bono? Now, I ain't gonna get but six of that back.

Rose: You ought to stop telling that lie. Here, Lyons. (*She hands him the money.*)

Lyons: Thanks, Rose. Look . . . I got to run . . . I'll see you later.

Troy: Wait a minute. You gonna say, "thanks, Rose" and ain't gonna look to see where she got that ten dollars from? See how they do me, Bono?

Lyons: I know she got it from you, Pop. Thanks. I'll give it back to you.

Troy: There he go telling another lie. Time I see that ten dollars . . . he'll be owing me thirty more.

Lyons: See you, Mr. Bono.

Bono: Take care, Lyons!

Lyons: Thanks, Pop. I'll see you again.

    (*Lyons exits the yard.*)

Troy: I don't know why he don't go and get him a decent job and take care of that woman he got.

Bono: He'll be alright, Troy. The boy is still young.

Troy: The *boy* is thirty-four years old.

Rose: Let's not get off into all that.

Bono: Look here . . . I got to be going. I got to be getting on. Lucille gonna be waiting.

Troy (puts his arm around Rose): See this woman, Bono? I love this woman. I love this woman so much it hurts. I love her so much . . . I done run out of ways of loving her. So I got to go back to basics. Don't you come by my house Monday morning talking about time to go to work . . . 'cause I'm still gonna be stroking!

Rose: Troy! Stop it now!

Bono: I ain't paying him no mind, Rose. That ain't nothing but gin-talk. Go on, Troy. I'll see you Monday.

Troy: Don't you come by my house, nigger! I done told you what I'm gonna be doing.

    (*The lights go down to black.*)

SCENE II

The lights come up on Rose hanging up clothes. She hums and sings softly to herself. It is the following morning.

Rose (sings):

        Jesus, be a fence all around me every day

        Jesus, I want you to protect me as I travel on my way.

        Jesus, be a fence all around me every day.

    (*Troy enters from the house.*)

        Jesus, I want you to protect me

        As I travel on my way.

(*To Troy.*) 'Morning. You ready for breakfast? I can fix it soon as I finish hanging up these clothes.

Troy: I got the coffee on. That'll be alright. I'll just drink some of that this morning.

Rose: That 651 hit yesterday. That's the second time this month. Miss Pearl hit for a dollar . . . seem like those that need the least always get lucky. Poor folks can't get nothing.

Troy: Them numbers don't know nobody. I don't know why you fool with them. You and Lyons both.

Rose: It's something to do.

Troy: You ain't doing nothing but throwing your money away.

Rose: Troy, you know I don't play foolishly. I just play a nickel here and a nickel there.

Troy: That's two nickels you done thrown away.

Rose: Now I hit sometimes . . . that makes up for it. It always comes in handy when I do hit. I don't hear you complaining then.

Troy: I ain't complaining now. I just say it's foolish. Trying to guess out of six hundred ways which way the number gonna come. If I had all the money niggers, these Negroes, throw away on numbers for one week—just one week—I'd be a rich man.

Rose: Well, you wishing and calling it foolish ain't gonna stop folks from playing numbers. That's one thing for sure. Besides . . . some good things come from playing numbers. Look where Pope done bought him that restaurant off of numbers.

Troy: I can't stand niggers like that. Man ain't had two dimes to rub together. He walking around with his shoes all run over bumming money for cigarettes. Alright. Got lucky there and hit the numbers . . .

Rose: Troy, I know all about it.

Troy: Had good sense, I'll say that for him. He ain't throwed his money away. I seen niggers hit the numbers and go through two thousand dollars in four days. Man bought him that restaurant down there . . . fixed it up real nice . . . . and then didn't want nobody to come in it! A Negro go in there and can't get no kind of service. I seen a white fellow come in there and order a bowl of stew. Pope picked all the meat out of the pot for him. Man ain't had nothing but a bowl of meat! Negro come behind him and ain't got nothing but the potatoes and carrots. Talking about what numbers do for people, you picked a wrong example. Ain't done nothing but make a worser fool out of him than he was before.

Rose: Troy, you ought to stop worrying about what happened at work yesterday.

Troy: I ain't worried. Just told me to be down there at the Commissioner's office on Friday. Everybody think they gonna fire me. I ain't worried about them firing me. You ain't got to worry about that. (*Pause.*) Where's Cory? Cory in the house? (*Calls.*) Cory?

Rose: He gone out.

Troy: Out, huh? He gone out 'cause he know I want him to help me with this fence. I know how he is. That boy scared of work.

(*Gabriel enters. He comes halfway down the alley and, hearing Troy's voice, stops.*)

Troy (*continues*): He ain't done a lick of work in his life.

Rose: He had to go to football practice. Coach wanted them to get in a little extra practice before the season start.

Troy: I got his practice . . . running out of here before he get his chores done.

Rose: Troy, what is wrong with you this morning? Don't nothing set right with you. Go on back in there and go to bed . . . get up on the other side.

Troy: Why something got to be wrong with me? I ain't said nothing wrong with me.

Rose: You got something to say about everything. First it's the numbers . . . then it's the way the man runs his restaurant . . . then you done got on Cory. What's it gonna be next? Take a look up there and see if the weather suits you . . . or is it gonna be how you gonna put up the fence with the clothes hanging in the yard?

Troy: You hit the nail on the head then.

Rose: I know you like I know the back of my hand. Go on in there and get you some coffee . . . see if that straighten you up. 'Cause you ain't right this morning.

(*Troy starts into the house and sees Gabriel. Gabriel starts singing. Troy's brother, he is seven years younger than Troy. Injured in World War II, he has a metal plate in his head. He carries an old trumpet tied around his waist and believes with every fiber of his being that he is the Archangel Gabriel. He carries a chipped basket with an assortment of discarded fruits and vegetables he has picked up in the strip district and which he attempts to sell.*)

Gabriel (singing):
   Yes, ma'am, I got plums
   You ask me how I sell them
   Oh ten cents apiece
   Three for a quarter
   Come and buy now
   'Cause I'm here today
   And tomorrow I'll be gone

(*Gabriel enters.*)

   Hey, Rose!

Rose: How you doing, Gabe?

Gabriel: There's Troy . . . Hey, Troy!

Troy: Hey, Gabe.

(*Exit into kitchen.*)

Rose (*to Gabriel*): What you got there?

Gabriel: You know what I got, Rose. I got fruits and vegetables.

Rose (*looking in basket*): Where's all these plums you talking about?

Gabriel: I ain't got no plums today, Rose. I was just singing that. Have some tomorrow. Put me in a big order for plums. Have enough plums tomorrow for St. Peter and everybody.

(*Troy reenters from kitchen, crosses to steps.*)

(*To Rose.*) Troy's mad at me.

Troy: I ain't mad at you. What I got to be mad at you about? You ain't done nothing to me.

Gabriel: I just moved over to Miss Pearl's to keep out from in your way. I ain't mean no harm by it.

Troy: Who said anything about that? I ain't said anything about that.

Gabriel: You ain't mad at me, is you?

Troy: Naw . . . I ain't mad at you, Gabe. If I was mad at you I'd tell you about it.

Gabriel: Got me two rooms. In the basement. Got my own door too. Wanna see my key? (*He holds up a key.*) That's my own key! Ain't nobody else got a key like that. That's my key! My two rooms!

Troy: Well, that's good, Gabe. You got your own key . . . that's good.

Rose: You hungry, Gabe? I was just fixing to cook Troy his breakfast.

Gabriel: I'll take some biscuits. You got some biscuits? Did you know when I was in heaven . . . every morning me and St. Peter would sit down by the gate and eat some big fat biscuits? Oh, yeah! We had us a good time. We'd sit there and eat us them biscuits and then St. Peter would go off to sleep and tell me to wake him up when it's time to open the gates for the judgment.

Rose: Well, come on . . . I'll make up a batch of biscuits.

(*Rose exits into the house.*)

Gabriel: Troy . . . St. Peter got your name in the book. I seen it. It say . . . Troy Maxson. I say . . . I know him! He got the same name like what I got. That's my brother!

Troy: How many times you gonna tell me that, Gabe?

Gabriel: Ain't got my name in the book. Don't have to have my name. I done died and went to heaven. He got your name though. One morning St. Peter was looking at his book . . . marking it up for the judgment . . . and he let me see your name. Got it in there under M. Got Rose's name . . . I ain't seen it like I seen yours . . . but I know it's in there. He got a great big book. Got everybody's name what was ever been born. That's what he told me. But I seen your name. Seen it with my own eyes.

Troy: Go on in the house there. Rose going to fix you something to eat.

Gabriel: Oh, I ain't hungry. I done had breakfast with Aunt Jemimah. She come by and cooked me up a whole mess of flapjacks. Remember how we used to eat them flapjacks?

Troy: Go on in the house and get you something to eat now.

Gabriel: I got to sell my plums. I done sold some tomatoes. Got me two quarters. Wanna see? (*He shows Troy his quarters.*) I'm gonna save them and buy me a new horn so St. Peter can hear me when it's time to open the gates. (*Gabriel stops suddenly. Listens.*) Hear that? That's the hellhounds. I got to chase them out of here. Go on get out of here! Get out!

(*Gabriel exits singing.*)

> Better get ready for the judgment
> Better get ready for the judgment
> My Lord is coming down

(*Rose enters from the house.*)

Troy: He gone off somewhere.

Gabriel (*offstage*):

> Better get ready for the judgment
> Better get ready for the judgment morning
> Better get ready for the judgment
> My God is coming down

Rose: He ain't eating right. Miss Pearl say she can't get him to eat nothing.

Troy: What you want me to do about it, Rose? I done did everything I can for the man. I can't make him get well. Man got half his head blown away . . . what you expect?

Rose: Seem like something ought to be done to help him.

Troy: Man don't bother nobody. He just mixed up from that metal plate he got in his head. Ain't no sense for him to go back into the hospital.

Rose: Least he be eating right. They can help him take care of himself.

Troy: Don't nobody wanna be locked up, Rose. What you wanna lock him up for? Man go over there and fight the war . . . messin' around with them Japs, get half his head blown off . . . and they give him a lousy three thousand dollars. And I had to swoop down on that.

Rose: Is you fixing to go into that again?

Troy: That's the only way I got a roof over my head . . . cause of that metal plate.

Rose: Ain't no sense you blaming yourself for nothing. Gabe wasn't in no condition to manage that money. You done what was right by him. Can't nobody say you ain't done what was right by him. Look how long you took care of him . . . till he wanted to have his own place and moved over there with Miss Pearl.

Troy: That ain't what I'm saying, woman! I'm just stating the facts. If my brother didn't have that metal plate in his head . . . I wouldn't have a pot to piss in or a window to throw it out of. And I'm fifty-three years old. Now see if you can understand that!

(Troy gets up from the porch and starts to exit the yard.)

Rose: Where you going off to? You been running out of here every Saturday for weeks. I thought you was gonna work on this fence?

Troy: I'm gonna walk down to Taylors'. Listen to the ball game. I'll be back in a bit. I'll work on it when I get back.

(He exits the yard. The lights go to black.)

SCENE III

The lights come up on the yard. It is four hours later. Rose is taking down the clothes from the line. Cory enters carrying his football equipment.

Rose: Your daddy like to had a fit with you running out of here this morning without doing your chores.

Cory: I told you I had to go to practice.

Rose: He say you were supposed to help him with this fence.

Cory: He been saying that the last four or five Saturdays, and then he don't never do nothing, but go down to Taylors'. Did you tell him about the recruiter?

Rose: Yeah, I told him.

Cory: What he say?

Rose: He ain't said nothing too much. You get in there and get started on your chores before he gets back. Go on and scrub down them steps before he gets back here hollering and carrying on.

Cory: I'm hungry. What you got to eat, Mama?

Rose: Go on and get started on your chores. I got some meat loaf in there. Go on and make you a sandwich . . . and don't leave no mess in there.

(*Cory exits into the house. Rose continues to take down the clothes. Troy enters the yard and sneaks up and grabs her from behind.*)

Troy! Go on, now. You liked to scared me to death. What was the score of the game? Lucille had me on the phone and I couldn't keep up with it.

Troy: What I care about the game? Come here, woman. (*He tries to kiss her.*)

Rose: I thought you went down Taylors' to listen to the game. Go on, Troy! You supposed to be putting up this fence.

Troy (*attempting to kiss her again*): I'll put it up when I finish with what is at hand.

Rose: Go on, Troy. I ain't studying you.

Troy (*chasing after her*): I'm studying you . . . fixing to do my homework!

Rose: Troy, you better leave me alone.

Troy: Where's Cory? That boy brought his butt home yet?

Rose: He's in the house doing his chores.

Troy (*calling*): Cory! Get your butt out here, boy!

(*Rose exits into the house with the laundry. Troy goes over to the pile of wood, picks up a board, and starts sawing. Cory enters from the house.*)

Troy: You just now coming in here from leaving this morning?

Cory: Yeah, I had to go to football practice.

Troy: Yeah, what?

Cory: Yessir.

Troy: I ain't but two seconds off you noway. The garbage sitting in there overflowing . . . you ain't done none of your chores . . . and you come in here talking about "Yeah."

Cory: I was just getting ready to do my chores now, Pop . . .

Troy: Your first chore is to help me with this fence on Saturday. Everything else come after that. Now get that saw and cut them boards.

(*Cory takes the saw and begins cutting the boards. Troy continues working. There is a long pause.*)

Cory: Hey, Pop . . . why don't you buy a TV?

Troy: What I want with a TV? What I want one of them for?

Cory: Everybody got one. Earl, Ba Bra . . . Jesse!

Troy: I ain't asked you who had one. I say what I want with one?

Cory: So you can watch it. They got lots of things on TV. Baseball games and everything. We could watch the World Series.

Troy: Yeah . . . and how much this TV cost?

Cory: I don't know. They got them on sale for around two hundred dollars.

Troy: Two hundred dollars, huh?

Cory: That ain't that much, Pop.

Troy: Naw, it's just two hundred dollars. See that roof you got over your head at night? Let me tell you something about that roof. It's been over ten years since that roof was last tarred. See now . . . the snow come this winter and sit up there on that roof like it is . . . and it's gonna seep inside. It's just gonna be a little bit . . . ain't gonna hardly notice it. Then the next thing you know, it's gonna be leaking all over the house. Then the wood rot from all that water and you gonna need a whole new roof. Now, how much you think it cost to get that roof tarred?

Cory: I don't know.

Troy: Two hundred and sixty-four dollars . . . cash money. While you thinking about a TV, I got to be thinking about the roof . . . and whatever else go wrong here. Now if you had two hundred dollars, what would you do . . . fix the roof or buy a TV?

Cory: I'd buy a TV. Then when the roof started to leak . . . when it needed fixing . . . I'd fix it.

Troy: Where you gonna get the money from? You done spent it for a TV. You gonna sit up and watch the water run all over your brand new TV.

Cory: Aw, Pop. You got money. I know you do.

Troy: Where I got it at, huh?

Cory: You got it in the bank.

Troy: You wanna see my bankbook? You wanna see that seventy-three dollars and twenty-two cents I got sitting up in there?

Cory: You ain't got to pay for it all at one time. You can put a down payment on it and carry it on home with you.

Troy: Not me. I ain't gonna owe nobody nothing if I can help it. Miss a payment and they come and snatch it right out of your house. Then what you got? Now, soon as I get two hundred dollars clear, then I'll buy a TV. Right now, as soon as I get two hundred and sixty-four dollars, I'm gonna have this roof tarred.

Cory: Aw . . . Pop!

Troy: You go on and get you two hundred dollars and buy one if ya want it. I got better things to do with my money.

Cory: I can't get no two hundred dollars. I ain't never seen two hundred dollars.

Troy: I'll tell you what . . . you get you a hundred dollars and I'll put the other hundred with it.

Cory: Alright, I'm gonna show you.

Troy: You gonna show me how you can cut them boards right now.

(*Cory begins to cut the boards. There is a long pause.*)

Cory: The Pirates won today. That makes five in a row.

Troy: I ain't thinking about the Pirates. Got an all-white team. Got that boy . . . that Puerto Rican boy . . . Clemente.° Don't even half-play him. That boy could be something if they give him a chance. Play him one day and sit him on the bench the next.

Cory: He gets a lot of chances to play.

Troy: I'm talking about playing regular. Playing every day so you can get your timing. That's what I'm talking about.

Cory: They got some white guys on the team that don't play every day. You can't play everybody at the same time.

Troy: If they got a white fellow sitting on the bench . . . you can bet your last dollar he can't play! The colored guy got to be twice as good before he get on the team. That's why I don't want you to get all tied up in them sports. Man on the team

---

Clemente: Hall of Fame outfielder Roberto Clemente, a dark-skinned Puerto Rican, played 17 seasons with the Pittsburgh Pirates.

and what it get him? They got colored on the team and don't use them. Same as not having them. All them teams the same.

Cory: The Braves got Hank Aaron and Wes Covington. Hank Aaron hit two home runs today. That makes forty-three.

Troy: Hank Aaron ain't nobody. That's what you supposed to do. That's how you supposed to play the game. Ain't nothing to it. It's just a matter of timing . . . getting the right follow-through. Hell, I can hit forty-three home runs right now!

Cory: Not off no major-league pitching, you couldn't.

Troy: We had better pitching in the Negro leagues. I hit seven home runs off of Satchel Paige.° You can't get no better than that!

Cory: Sandy Koufax.° He's leading the league in strikeouts.

Troy: I ain't thinking of no Sandy Koufax.

Cory: You got Warren Spahn° and Lew Burdette.° I bet you couldn't hit no home runs off of Warren Spahn.

Troy: I'm through with it now. You go on and cut them boards. (*Pause.*) Your mama tell me you done got recruited by a college football team? Is that right?

Cory: Yeah. Coach Zellman say the recruiter gonna be coming by to talk to you. Get you to sign the permission papers.

Troy: I thought you supposed to be working down there at the A&P. Ain't you suppose to be working down there after school?

Cory: Mr. Stawicki say he gonna hold my job for me until after the football season. Say starting next week I can work weekends.

Troy: I thought we had an understanding about this football stuff? You suppose to keep up with your chores and hold that job down at the A&P. Ain't been around here all day on a Saturday. Ain't none of your chores done . . . and now you telling me you done quit your job.

Cory: I'm going to be working weekends.

Troy: You damn right you are! And ain't no need for nobody coming around here to talk to me about signing nothing.

Cory: Hey, Pop . . . you can't do that. He's coming all the way from North Carolina.

Troy: I don't care where he coming from. The white man ain't gonna let you get nowhere with that football noway. You go on and get your book-learning so you can work yourself up in that A&P or learn how to fix cars or build houses or something, get you a trade. That way you have something can't nobody take away from you. You go on and learn how to put your hands to some good use. Besides hauling people's garbage.

Cory: I get good grades, Pop. That's why the recruiter wants to talk with you. You got to keep up your grades to get recruited. This way I'll be going to college. I'll get a chance . . .

Troy: First you gonna get your butt down there to the A&P and get your job back.

Cory: Mr. Stawicki done already hired somebody else 'cause I told him I was playing football.

Troy: You a bigger fool than I thought . . . to let somebody take away your job so you can play some football. Where you gonna get your money to take out your

Satchel Paige . . . Sandy Koufax . . . Warren Spahn . . . Lew Burdette: The great Satchel Paige pitched many years in the Negro Leagues; beginning in 1948, when he was in his forties and long past his prime, he appeared in nearly 200 games in the American League. Star pitchers Sandy Koufax of the Dodgers and Warren Spahn and Lew Burdette of the Braves were all white.

girlfriend and whatnot? What kind of foolishness is that to let somebody take away your job?

Cory: I'm still gonna be working weekends.

Troy: Naw . . . naw. You getting your butt out of here and finding you another job.

Cory: Come on, Pop! I got to practice. I can't work after school and play football too. The team needs me. That's what Coach Zellman say . . .

Troy: I don't care what nobody else say. I'm the boss . . . you understand? I'm the boss around here. I do the only saying what counts.

Cory: Come on, Pop!

Troy: I asked you . . . did you understand?

Cory: Yeah . . .

Troy: What?!

Cory: Yessir.

Troy: You go on down there to that A&P and see if you can get your job back. If you can't do both . . . then you quit the football team. You've got to take the crookeds with the straights.

Cory: Yessir. (*Pause.*) Can I ask you a question?

Troy: What the hell you wanna ask me? Mr. Stawicki the one you got the questions for.

Cory: How come you ain't never liked me?

Troy: Liked you? Who the hell say I got to like you? What law is there say I got to like you? Wanna stand up in my face and ask a damn fool-ass question like that. Talking about liking somebody. Come here, boy, when I talk to you.

(*Cory comes over to where Troy is working. He stands slouched over and Troy shoves him on his shoulder.*)

Straighten up, goddammit! I asked you a question . . . what law is there say I got to like you?

Cory: None.

Troy: Well, alright then! Don't you eat every day? (*Pause.*) Answer me when I talk to you! Don't you eat every day?

Cory: Yeah.

Troy: Nigger, as long as you in my house, you put that sir on the end of it when you talk to me.

Cory: Yes . . . sir.

Troy: You eat every day.

Cory: Yessir!

Troy: Got a roof over your head.

Cory: Yessir!

Troy: Got clothes on your back.

Cory: Yessir.

Troy: Why you think that is?

Cory: Cause of you.

Troy: Aw, hell I know it's 'cause of me . . . but why do you think that is?

Cory (hesitant): Cause you like me.

Troy: Like you? I go out of here every morning . . . bust my butt . . . putting up with them crackers every day . . . cause I like you? You about the biggest fool I ever saw. (*Pause.*) It's my job. It's my responsibility! You understand that? A man got to take care of his family. You live in my house . . . sleep you behind on my bedclothes . . . fill you belly up with my food . . . cause you my son. You my flesh and blood. Not 'cause I like you! Cause it's my duty to take care of you. I owe a responsibility to you!

      Let's get this straight right here . . . before it go along any further . . . I ain't got to like you. Mr. Rand don't give me my money come payday cause he likes me. He gives me cause he owe me. I done give you everything I had to give you. I gave you your life! Me and your mama worked that out between us. And liking your black ass wasn't part of the bargain. Don't you try and go through life worrying about if somebody like you or not. You best be making sure they doing right by you. You understand what I'm saying, boy?

Cory: Yessir.

Troy: Then get the hell out of my face, and get on down to that A&P.

(Rose has been standing behind the screen door for much of the scene. She enters as Cory exits.)

Rose: Why don't you let the boy go ahead and play football, Troy? Ain't no harm in that. He's just trying to be like you with the sports.

Troy: I don't want him to be like me! I want him to move as far away from my life as he can get. You the only decent thing that ever happened to me. I wish him that. But I don't wish him a thing else from my life. I decided seventeen years ago that boy wasn't getting involved in no sports. Not after what they did to me in the sports.

Rose: Troy, why don't you admit you was too old to play in the major leagues? For once . . . why don't you admit that?

Troy: What do you mean too old? Don't come telling me I was too old. I just wasn't the right color. Hell, I'm fifty-three years old and can do better than Selkirk's .269 right now!

Rose: How's was you gonna play ball when you were over forty? Sometimes I can't get no sense out of you.

Troy: I got good sense, woman. I got sense enough not to let my boy get hurt over playing no sports. You been mothering that boy too much. Worried about if people like him.

Rose: Everything that boy do . . . he do for you. He wants you to say "Good job, son." That's all.

Troy: Rose, I ain't got time for that. He's alive. He's healthy. He's got to make his own way. I made mine. Ain't nobody gonna hold his hand when he get out there in that world.

Rose: Times have changed from when you was young, Troy. People change. The world's changing around you and you can't even see it.

Troy *(slow, methodical)*: Woman . . . I do the best I can do. I come in here every Friday. I carry a sack of potatoes and a bucket of lard. You all line up at the door with your hands out. I give you the lint from my pockets. I give you my sweat and my blood. I ain't got no tears. I done spent them. We go upstairs in that room at night . . . and I fall down on you and try to blast a hole into forever. I get up Monday morning . . . find my lunch on the table. I go out. Make my way. Find my strength to carry me through to the next Friday. *(Pause.)* That's all I got, Rose. That's all I got to give. I can't give nothing else.

(Troy exits into the house. The lights go down to black.)

SCENE IV

It is Friday. Two weeks later. Cory starts out of the house with his football equipment. The phone rings.

Cory (*calling*): I got it! (*He answers the phone and stands in the screen door talking.*) Hello? Hey, Jesse. Naw . . . I was just getting ready to leave now.

Rose (*calling*): Cory!

Cory: I told you, man, them spikes is all tore up. You can use them if you want, but they ain't no good. Earl got some spikes.

Rose (*calling*): Cory!

Cory (*calling to Rose*): Mam? I'm talking to Jesse. (*Into phone.*) When she say that? (*Pause.*) Aw, you lying, man. I'm gonna tell her you said that.

Rose (*calling*): Cory, don't you go nowhere!

Cory: I got to go to the game, Ma! (*Into the phone.*) Yeah, hey, look, I'll talk to you later. Yeah, I'll meet you over Earl's house. Later. Bye, Ma.

(*Cory exits the house and starts out the yard.*)

Rose: Cory, where you going off to? You got that stuff all pulled out and thrown all over your room.

Cory (*in the yard*): I was looking for my spikes. Jesse wanted to borrow my spikes.

Rose: Get up there and get that cleaned up before your daddy get back in here.

Cory: I got to go to the game! I'll clean it up *when I get back.*

(*Cory exits.*)

Rose: That's all he need to do is see that room all messed up.

(*Rose exits into the house. Troy and Bono enter the yard. Troy is dressed in clothes other than his work clothes.*)

Bono: He told him the same thing he told you. Take it to the union.

Troy: Brownie ain't got that much sense. Man wasn't thinking about nothing. He wait until I confront them on it . . . then he wanna come crying seniority. (*Calls.*) Hey, Rose!

Bono: I wish I could have seen Mr. Rand's face when he told you.

Troy: He couldn't get it out of his mouth! Liked to bit his tongue! When they called me down there to the Commissioner's office . . . he thought they was gonna fire me. Like everybody else.

Bono: I didn't think they was gonna fire you. I thought they was gonna put you on the warning paper.

Troy: Hey, Rose! (*To Bono.*) Yeah, Mr. Rand like to bit his tongue.

(*Troy breaks the seal on the bottle, takes a drink, and hands it to Bono.*)

Bono: I see you run right down to Taylors' and told that Alberta gal.

Troy (*calling*): Hey, Rose! (*To Bono.*) I told everybody. Hey, Rose! I went down there to cash my check.

Rose (*entering from the house*): Hush all that hollering, man! I know you out here. What they say down there at the Commissioner's office?

Troy: You supposed to come when I call you, woman. Bono'll tell you that. (*To Bono.*) Don't Lucille come when you call her?

Rose: Man, hush your mouth. I ain't no dog . . . talk about "come when you call me."

Troy (*puts his arm around Rose*): You hear this, Bono? I had me an old dog used to get uppity like that. You say, "C'mere, Blue!" . . . and he just lay there and look at you. End up getting a stick and chasing him away trying to make him come.

Rose: I ain't studying you and your dog. I remember you used to sing that old song.

Troy (*he sings*):
>   Hear it ring! Hear it ring!
>   I had a dog his name was Blue.

Rose: Don't nobody wanna hear you sing that old song.

Troy (*sings*):
>   You know Blue was mighty true.

Rose: Used to have Cory running around here singing that song.

Bono: Hell, I remember that song myself.

Troy (*sings*):
>   You know Blue was a good old dog.
>   Blue treed a possum in a hollow log.
>   That was my daddy's song. My daddy made up that song.

Rose: I don't care who made it up. Don't nobody wanna hear you sing it.

Troy (*makes a song like calling a dog*): Come here, woman.

Rose: You come in here carrying on, I reckon they ain't fired you. What they say down there at the Commissioner's office?

Troy: Look here, Rose . . . Mr. Rand called me into his office today when I got back from talking to them people down there . . . it come from up top . . . he called me in and told me they was making me a driver.

Rose: Troy, you kidding!

Troy: No I ain't. Ask Bono.

Rose: Well, that's great, Troy. Now you don't have to hassle them people no more.

(*Lyons enters from the street.*)

Troy: Aw hell, I wasn't looking to see you today. I thought you was in jail. Got it all over the front page of the *Courier* about them raiding Sefus's place . . . where you be hanging out with all them thugs.

Lyons: Hey, Pop . . . that ain't got nothing to do with me. I don't go down there gambling. I go down there to sit in with the band. I ain't got nothing to do with the gambling part. They got some good music down there.

Troy: They got some rogues . . . is what they got.

Lyons: How you been, Mr. Bono? Hi, Rose.

Bono: I see where you playing down at the Crawford Grill tonight.

Rose: How come you ain't brought Bonnie like I told you? You should have brought Bonnie with you, she ain't been over in a month of Sundays.

Lyons: I was just in the neighborhood . . . thought I'd stop by.

Troy: Here he come . . .

Bono: Your daddy got a promotion on the rubbish. He's gonna be the first colored driver. Ain't got to do nothing but sit up there and read the paper like them white fellows.

Lyons: Hey, Pop . . . if you knew how to read you'd be alright.

Bono: Naw . . . naw . . . you mean if the nigger knew how to *drive* he'd be alright. Been fighting with them people about driving and ain't even got a license. Mr. Rand know you ain't got no driver's license?

Troy: Driving ain't nothing. All you do is point the truck where you want it to go. Driving ain't nothing.

Bono: Do Mr. Rand know you ain't got no driver's license? That's what I'm talking about. I ain't asked if driving was easy. I asked if Mr. Rand know you ain't got no driver's license.

Troy: He ain't got to know. The man ain't got to know my business. Time he find out, I have two or three driver's licenses.

Lyons (going into his pocket): Say, look here, Pop . . .

Troy: I knew it was coming. Didn't I tell you, Bono? I know what kind of "Look here, Pop" that was. The nigger fixing to ask me for some money. It's Friday night. It's my payday. All them rogues down there on the avenue . . . the ones that ain't in jail . . . and Lyons is hopping in his shoes to get down there with them.

Lyons: See, Pop . . . if you give somebody else a chance to talk sometime, you'd see that I was fixing to pay you back your ten dollars like I told you. Here . . . I told you I'd pay you when Bonnie got paid.

Troy: Naw . . . you go ahead and keep that ten dollars. Put it in the bank. The next time you feel like you wanna come by here and ask me for something . . . you go on down there and get that.

Lyons: Here's your ten dollars, Pop. I told you I don't want you to give me nothing. I just wanted to borrow ten dollars.

Troy: Naw . . . you go on and keep that for the next time you want to ask me.

Lyons: Come on, Pop . . . here go your ten dollars.

Rose: Why don't you go on and let the boy pay you back, Troy?

Lyons: Here you go, Rose. If you don't take it I'm gonna have to hear about it for the next six months. (*He hands her the money.*)

Rose: You can hand yours over here too, Troy.

Troy: You see this, Bono. You see how they do me.

Bono: Yeah, Lucille do me the same way.

(*Gabriel is heard singing offstage. He enters.*)

Gabriel: Better get ready for the Judgment! Better get ready for . . . Hey! . . . Hey! . . . There's Troy's boy!

Lyons: How are you doing, Uncle Gabe?

Gabriel: Lyons . . . The King of the Jungle! Rose . . . hey, Rose. Got a flower for you. (*He takes a rose from his pocket.*) Picked it myself. That's the same rose like you is!

Rose: That's right nice of you, Gabe.

Lyons: What you been doing, Uncle Gabe?

Gabriel: Oh, I been chasing hellhounds and waiting on the time to tell St. Peter to open the gates.

Lyons: You been chasing hellhounds, huh? Well . . . you doing the right thing, Uncle Gabe. Somebody got to chase them.

Gabriel: Oh, yeah . . . I know it. The devil's strong. The devil ain't no pushover. Hellhounds snipping at everybody's heels. But I got my trumpet waiting on the judgment time.

Lyons: Waiting on the Battle of Armageddon, huh?

Gabriel: Ain't gonna be too much of a battle when God get to waving that Judgment sword. But the people's gonna have a hell of a time trying to get into heaven if them gates ain't open.

Lyons (putting his arm around Gabriel): You hear this, Pop. Uncle Gabe, you alright!

Gabriel (laughing with Lyons): Lyons! King of the Jungle.

Rose: You gonna stay for supper, Gabe? Want me to fix you a plate?

Gabriel: I'll take a sandwich, Rose. Don't want no plate. Just wanna eat with my hands. I'll take a sandwich.

Rose: How about you, Lyons? You staying? Got some short ribs cooking.

Lyons: Naw, I won't eat nothing till after we finished playing. (*Pause.*) You ought to come down and listen to me play, Pop.

Troy: I don't like that Chinese music. All that noise.

Rose: Go on in the house and wash up, Gabe . . . I'll fix you a sandwich.

Gabriel (to Lyons, as he exits): Troy's mad at me.

Lyons: What you mad at Uncle Gabe for, Pop?

Rose: He thinks Troy's mad at him cause he moved over to Miss Pearl's.

Troy: I ain't mad at the man. He can live where he want to live at.

Lyons: What he move over there for? Miss Pearl don't like nobody.

Rose: She don't mind him none. She treats him real nice. She just don't allow all that singing.

Troy: She don't mind that rent he be paying . . . that's what she don't mind.

Rose: Troy, I ain't going through that with you no more. He's over there cause he want to have his own place. He can come and go as he please.

Troy: Hell, he could come and go as he please here. I wasn't stopping him. I ain't put no rules on him.

Rose: It ain't the same thing, Troy. And you know it.

(*Gabriel comes to the door.*)

Now, that's the last I wanna hear about that. I don't wanna hear nothing else about Gabe and Miss Pearl. And next week . . .

Gabriel: I'm ready for my sandwich, Rose.

Rose: And next week . . . when that recruiter come from that school . . . I want you to sign that paper and go on and let Cory play football. Then that'll be the last I have to hear about that.

Troy (to Rose as she exits into the house): I ain't thinking about Cory nothing.

Lyons: What . . . Cory got recruited? What school he going to?

Troy: That boy walking around here smelling his piss . . . thinking he's grown. Thinking he's gonna do what he want, irrespective of what I say. Look here, Bono . . . I left the Commissioner's office and went down to the A&P . . . that boy ain't working down there. He lying to me. Telling me he got his job back . . . telling me he working weekends . . . telling me he working after school . . . Mr. Stawicki tell me he ain't working down there at all!

Lyons: Cory just growing up. He's just busting at the seams trying to fill out your shoes.

Troy: I don't care what he's doing. When he get to the point where he wanna disobey me . . . then it's time for him to move on. Bono'll tell you that. I bet he ain't never disobeyed his daddy without paying the consequences.

Bono: I ain't never had a chance. My daddy came on through . . . but I ain't never knew him to see him . . . or what he had on his mind or where he went. Just moving on through. Searching out the New Land. That's what the old folks used to call it. See a fellow moving around from place to place . . . woman to woman . . . called it searching out the New Land. I can't say if he ever found it. I come along, didn't want no kids. Didn't know if I was gonna be in one place long enough to fix on them right as their daddy. I figured I was going searching too. As it turned out I been hooked up with Lucille near about as long as your daddy been with Rose. Going on sixteen years.

Troy: Sometimes I wish I hadn't known my daddy. He ain't cared nothing about no kids. A kid to him wasn't nothing. All he wanted was for you to learn how to walk so he could start you to working. When it come time for eating . . . he ate first. If there was anything left over, that's what you got. Man would sit down and eat two chickens and give you the wing.

Lyons: You ought to stop that, Pop. Everybody feed their kids. No matter how hard times is . . . everybody care about their kids. Make sure they have something to eat.

Troy: The only thing my daddy cared about was getting them bales of cotton in to Mr. Lubin. That's the only thing that mattered to him. Sometimes I used to wonder why he was living. Wonder why the devil hadn't come and got him. "Get them bales of cotton in to Mr. Lubin" and find out he owe him money . . .

Lyons: He should have just went on and left when he saw he couldn't get nowhere. That's what I would have done.

Troy: How he gonna leave with eleven kids? And where he gonna go? He ain't knew how to do nothing but farm. No, he was trapped and I think he knew it. But I'll say this for him . . . he felt a responsibility toward us. Maybe he ain't treated us the way I felt he should have . . . but without that responsibility he could have walked off and left us . . . made his own way.

Bono: A lot of them did. Back in those days what you talking about . . . they walk out their front door and just take on down one road or another and keep on walking.

Lyons: There you go! That's what I'm talking about.

Bono: Just keep on walking till you come to something else. Ain't you never heard of nobody having the walking blues? Well, that's what you call it when you just take off like that.

Troy: My daddy ain't had them walking blues! What you talking about? He stayed right there with his family. But he was just as evil as he could be. My mama couldn't stand him. Couldn't stand that evilness. She run off when I was about eight. She sneaked off one night after he had gone to sleep. Told me she was coming back for me. I ain't never seen her no more. All his women run off and left him. He wasn't good for nobody.

When my turn come to head out, I was fourteen and got to sniffing around Joe Canewell's daughter. Had us an old mule we called Greyboy. My daddy sent me out to do some plowing and I tied up Greyboy and went to fooling around with Joe Canewell's daughter. We done found us a nice little spot, got real cozy with each other. She about thirteen and we done figured we was grown anyway . . . so we down there enjoying ourselves . . . ain't thinking about nothing. We didn't know Greyboy had got loose and wandered back to the house and my daddy was looking for me. We down there by the creek enjoying ourselves when my daddy come up on us. Surprised us. He had them leather straps off the mule and commenced to whupping me like there was no tomorrow. I jumped up, mad and embarrassed. I was scared of my daddy. When he commenced to whupping on me . . . quite naturally I run to get out of the way. (*Pause.*) Now I thought he was mad cause I ain't done my work. But I see where he was chasing me off so he could have the gal for himself. When I see what the matter of it was, I lost all fear of my daddy. Right there is where I become a man . . . at fourteen years of age. (*Pause.*) Now it was my turn to run him off. I picked up them same reins that he had used on me. I picked up them reins and commenced to whupping on him. The gal jumped up and run off . . . and when my daddy turned to face me, I could see why the devil had never come to get him . . . cause he was the devil himself. I don't know what happened. When I woke up, I was laying right there by the creek, and Blue . . . this old dog we had . . . was licking my face. I thought I was blind. I couldn't see nothing. Both my eyes were swollen shut. I layed there and cried. I didn't know what I was gonna do. The only thing I knew was the time had come for me to leave my daddy's house. And right there the world suddenly got big. And it was a long time before I could cut it down to where I could handle it.

Part of that cutting down was when I got to the place where I could feel him kicking in my blood and knew that the only thing that separated us was the matter of a few years.

(*Gabriel enters from the house with a sandwich.*)

Lyons: What you got there, Uncle Gabe?

Gabriel: Got me a ham sandwich. Rose gave me a ham sandwich.

Troy: I don't know what happened to him. I done lost touch with everybody except Gabriel. But I hope he's dead. I hope he found some peace.

Lyons: That's a heavy story, Pop. I didn't know you left home when you was fourteen.

Troy: And didn't know nothing. The only part of the world I knew was the forty-two acres of Mr. Lubin's land. That's all I knew about life.

Lyons: Fourteen's kinda young to be out on your own. (*Phone rings.*) I don't even think I was ready to be out on my own at fourteen. I don't know what I would have done.

Troy: I got up from the creek and walked on down to Mobile. I was through with farming. Figured I could do better in the city. So I walked the two hundred miles to Mobile.

Lyons: Wait a minute . . . you ain't walked no two hundred miles, Pop. Ain't nobody gonna walk no two hundred miles. You talking about some walking there.

Bono: That's the only way you got anywhere back in them days.

Lyons: Shhh. Damn if I wouldn't have hitched a ride with somebody!

Troy: Who you gonna hitch it with? They ain't had no cars and things like they got now. We talking about 1918.

Rose (*entering*): What you all out here getting into?

Troy (*to Rose*): I'm telling Lyons how good he got it. He don't know nothing about this I'm talking.

Rose: Lyons, that was Bonnie on the phone. She say you supposed to pick her up.

Lyons: Yeah, okay, Rose.

Troy: I walked on down to Mobile and hitched up with some of them fellows that was heading this way. Got up here and found out . . . not only couldn't you get a job . . . you couldn't find no place to live. I thought I was in freedom. Shhh. Colored folks living down there on the riverbanks in whatever kind of shelter they could find for themselves. Right down there under the Brady Street Bridge. Living in shacks made of sticks and tarpaper. Messed around there and went from bad to worse. Started stealing. First it was food. Then I figured, hell, if I steal money I can buy me some food. Buy me some shoes too! One thing led to another. Met your mama. I was young and anxious to be a man. Met your mama and had you. What I do that for? Now I got to worry about feeding you and her. Got to steal three times as much. Went out one day looking for somebody to rob . . . that's what I was, a robber. I'll tell you the truth. I'm ashamed of it today. But it's the truth. Went to rob this fellow . . . pulled out my knife . . . and he pulled out a gun. Shot me in the chest. It felt just like somebody had taken a hot branding iron and laid it on me. When he shot me I jumped at him with my knife. They told me I killed him and they put me in the penitentiary and locked me up for fifteen years. That's where I met Bono. That's where I learned how to play baseball. Got out that place and your mama had taken you and went on to make life without me. Fifteen years was a long time for her to wait. But that fifteen years cured me of that robbing stuff. Rose'll tell you. She asked me when I met her if I had gotten all that foolishness out of my system. And I told her, "Baby, it's you and baseball all what count with me." You hear me, Bono? I meant it too. She say, "Which one comes first?" I told her, "Baby, ain't no doubt it's baseball . . . but you stick and get old with me and we'll both outlive this baseball." Am I right, Rose? And it's true.

Rose: Man, hush your mouth. You ain't said no such thing. Talking about, "Baby you know you'll always be number one with me." That's what you was talking.

Troy: You hear that, Bono. That's why I love her.

Bono: Rose'll keep you straight. You get off the track, she'll straighten you up.

Rose: Lyons, you better get on up and get Bonnie. She waiting on you.

Lyons (gets up to go): Hey, Pop, why don't you come on down to the Grill and hear me play?

Troy: I ain't going down there. I'm too old to be sitting around in them clubs.

Bono: You got to be good to play down at the Grill.

Lyons: Come on, Pop . . .

Troy: I got to get up in the morning.

Lyons: You ain't got to stay long.

Troy: Naw, I'm gonna get my supper and go on to bed.

Lyons: Well, I got to go. I'll see you again.

Troy: Don't you come around my house on my payday.

Rose: Pick up the phone and let somebody know you coming. And bring Bonnie with you. You know I'm always glad to see her.

Lyons: Yeah, I'll do that, Rose. You take care now. See you, Pop. See you, Mr. Bono. See you, Uncle Gabe.

Gabriel: Lyons! King of the Jungle!

(*Lyons exits.*)

Troy: Is supper ready, woman? Me and you got some business to take care of. I'm gonna tear it up too.

Rose: Troy, I done told you now!

Troy (puts his arm around Bono): Aw hell, woman . . . this is Bono. Bono like family. I done known this nigger since . . . how long I done know you?

Bono: It's been a long time.

Troy: I done know this nigger since Skippy was a pup. Me and him done been through some times.

Bono: You sure right about that.

Troy: Hell, I done know him longer than I known you. And we still standing shoulder to shoulder. Hey, look here, Bono . . . a man can't ask for no more than that. (*Drinks to him.*) I love you, nigger.

Bono: Hell, I love you too . . . but I got to get home see my woman. You got yours in hand. I got to go get mine.

(*Bono starts to exit as Cory enters the yard, dressed in his football uniform. He gives Troy a hard, uncompromising look.*)

Cory: What you do that for, Pop?

(*He throws his helmet down in the direction of Troy.*)

Rose: What's the matter? Cory . . . what's the matter?

Cory: Papa done went up to the school and told Coach Zellman I can't play football no more. Wouldn't even let me play the game. Told him to tell the recruiter not to come.

Rose: Troy . . .

Troy: What you Troying me for. Yeah, I did it. And the boy know why I did it.

Cory: Why you wanna do that to me? That was the one chance I had.

Rose: Ain't nothing wrong with Cory playing football, Troy.

Troy: The boy lied to me. I told the nigger if he wanna play football . . . to keep up his chores and hold down that job at the A&P. That was the conditions. Stopped down there to see Mr. Stawicki . . .

Cory: I can't work after school during the football season, Pop! I tried to tell you that Mr. Stawicki's holding my job for me. You don't never want to listen to nobody. And then you wanna go and do this to me!

Troy: I ain't done nothing to you. You done it to yourself.

Cory: Just cause you didn't have a chance! You just scared I'm gonna be better than you, that's all.

Troy: Come here.

Rose: Troy . . .

(*Cory reluctantly crosses over to Troy.*)

Troy: Alright! See. You done made a mistake.

Cory: I didn't even do nothing!

Troy: I'm gonna tell you what your mistake was. See . . . you swung at the ball and didn't hit it. That's strike one. See, you in the batter's box now. You swung and you missed. That's strike one. Don't you strike out!

(*Lights fade to black.*)

ACT II

SCENE I

The following morning. Cory is at the tree hitting the ball with the bat. He tries to mimic Troy, but his swing is awkward, less sure. Rose enters from the house.

Rose: Cory, I want you to help me with this cupboard.

Cory: I ain't quitting the team. I don't care what Poppa say.

Rose: I'll talk to him when he gets back. He had to go see about your Uncle Gabe. The police done arrested him. Say he was disturbing the peace. He'll be back directly. Come on in here and help me clean out the top of this cupboard.

(Cory exits into the house. Rose sees Troy and Bono coming down the alley.)

Troy . . . what they say down there?

Troy: Ain't said nothing. I give them fifty dollars and they let him go. I'll talk to you about it. Where's Cory?

Rose: He's in there helping me clean out these cupboards.

Troy: Tell him to get his butt out here.

(Troy and Bono go over to the pile of wood. Bono picks up the saw and begins sawing.)

Troy (to Bono): All they want is the money. That makes six or seven times I done went down there and got him. See me coming they stick out their *hands.*

Bono: Yeah. I know what you mean. That's all they care about . . . that money. They don't care about what's right. *(Pause.)* Nigger, why you got to go and get some hard wood? You ain't doing nothing but building a little old fence. Get you some soft pine wood. That's all you need.

Troy: I know what I'm doing. This is outside wood. You put pine wood inside the house. Pine wood is inside wood. This here is outside wood. Now you tell me where the fence is gonna be?

Bono: You don't need this wood. You can put it up with pine wood and it'll stand as long as you gonna be here looking at it.

Troy: How you know how long I'm gonna be here, nigger? Hell, I might just live forever. Live longer than old man Horsely.

Bono: That's what Magee used to say.

Troy: Magee's a damn fool. Now you tell me who you ever heard of gonna pull their own teeth with a pair of rusty pliers.

Bono: The old folks . . . my granddaddy used to pull his teeth with pliers. They ain't had no dentists for the colored folks back then.

Troy: Get clean pliers! You understand? Clean pliers! Sterilize them! Besides we ain't living back then. All Magee had to do was walk over to Doc Goldblum's.

Bono: I see where you and that Tallahassee gal . . . that Alberta . . . I see where you all done got tight.

Troy: What you mean "got tight"?

Bono: I see where you be laughing and joking with her all the time.

Troy: I laughs and jokes with all of them, Bono. You know me.

Bono: That ain't the kind of laughing and joking I'm talking about.

(Cory enters from the house.)

Cory: How you doing, Mr. Bono?

Troy: Cory? Get that saw from Bono and cut some wood. He talking about the wood's too hard to cut. Stand back there, Jim, and let that young boy show you how it's done.

Bono: He's sure welcome to it.

(Cory takes the saw and begins to cut the wood.)

Whew-e-e! Look at that. Big old strong boy. Look like Joe Louis. Hell, must be getting old the way I'm watching that boy whip through that wood.

Cory: I don't see why Mama want a fence around the yard noways.

Troy: Damn if I know either. What the hell she keeping out with it? She ain't got nothing nobody want.

Bono: Some people build fences to keep people out . . . and other people build fences to keep people in. Rose wants to hold on to you all. She loves you.

Troy: Hell, nigger, I don't need nobody to tell me my wife loves me. Cory . . . go on in the house and see if you can find that other saw.

Cory: Where's it at?

Troy: I said find it! Look for it till you find it!

(Cory exits into the house.)

What's that supposed to mean? Wanna keep us in?

Bono: Troy . . . I done known you seem like damn near my whole life. You and Rose both. I done know both of you all for a long time. I remember when you met Rose. When you was hitting them baseball out the park. A lot of them old gals was after you then. You had the pick of the litter. When you picked Rose, I was happy for you. That was the first time I knew you had any sense. I said . . . My man Troy knows what he's doing . . . I'm gonna follow this nigger . . . he might take me somewhere. I been following you too. I done learned a whole heap of things about life watching you. I done learned how to tell where the shit lies. How to tell it from the alfalfa. You done learned me a lot of things. You showed me how to not make the same mistakes . . . to take life as it comes along and keep putting one foot in front of the other. *(Pause.)* Rose a good woman, Troy.

Troy: Hell, nigger, I know she a good woman. I been married to her for eighteen years. What you got on your mind, Bono?

Bono: I just say she a good woman. Just like I say anything. I ain't got to have nothing on my mind.

Troy: You just gonna say she a good woman and leave it hanging out there like that? Why you telling me she a good woman?

Bono: She loves you, Troy. Rose loves you.

Troy: You saying I don't measure up. That's what you trying to say. I don't measure up cause I'm seeing this other gal. I know what you trying to say.

Bono: I know what Rose means to you, Troy. I'm just trying to say I don't want to see you mess up.

Troy: Yeah, I appreciate that, Bono. If you was messing around on Lucille I'd be telling you the same thing.

Bono: Well, that's all I got to say. I just say that because I love you both.

Troy: Hell, you know me . . . I wasn't out there looking for nothing. You can't find a better woman than Rose. I know that. But seems like this woman just stuck onto me where I can't shake her loose. I done wrestled with it, tried to throw her off me . . . but she just stuck on tighter. Now she's stuck on for good.

Bono: You's in control . . . that's what you tell me all the time. You responsible for what you do.

Troy: I ain't ducking the responsibility of it. As long as it sets right in my heart . . . then I'm okay. Cause that's all I listen to. It'll tell me right from wrong every time. And I ain't talking about doing Rose no bad turn. I love Rose. She done carried me a long ways and I love and respect her for that.

Bono: I know you do. That's why I don't want to see you hurt her. But what you gonna do when she find out? What you got then? If you try and juggle both of them . . . sooner or later you gonna drop one of them. That's common sense.

Troy: Yeah, I hear what you saying, Bono. I been trying to figure a way to work it out.

Bono: Work it out right, Troy. I don't want to be getting all up between you and Rose's business . . . but work it so it come out right.

Troy: Aw hell, I get all up between you and Lucille's business. When you gonna get that woman that refrigerator she been wanting? Don't tell me you ain't got no money now. I know who your banker is. Mellon° don't need that money bad as Lucille want that refrigerator. I'll tell you that.

Bono: Tell you what I'll do . . . when you finish building this fence for Rose . . . I'll buy Lucille that refrigerator.

Troy: You done stuck your foot in your mouth now!

(*Troy grabs up a board and begins to saw. Bono starts to walk out the yard.*)

Hey, nigger . . . where you going?

Bono: I'm going home. I know you don't expect me to help you now. I'm protecting my money. I wanna see you put that fence up by yourself. That's what I want to see. You'll be here another six months without me.

Troy: Nigger, you ain't right.

Bono: When it comes to my money . . . I'm right as fireworks on the Fourth of July.

Troy: Alright, we gonna see now. You better get out your bankbook.

(*Bono exits, and Troy continues to work. Rose enters from the house.*)

Rose: What they say down there? What's happening with Gabe?

Troy: I went down there and got him out. Cost me fifty dollars. Say he was disturbing the peace. Judge set up a hearing for him in three weeks. Say to show cause why he shouldn't be re-committed.

Rose: What was he doing that cause them to arrest him?

Troy: Some kids was teasing him and he run them off home. Say he was howling and carrying on. Some folks seen him and called the police. That's all it was.

Rose: Well, what's you say? What'd you tell the judge?

Troy: Told him I'd look after him. It didn't make no sense to recommit the man. He stuck out his big greasy palm and told me to give him fifty dollars and take him on home.

Rose: Where's he at now? Where'd he go off to?

Troy: He's gone on about his business. He don't need nobody to hold his hand.

Rose: Well, I don't know. Seem like that would be the best place for him if they did put him into the hospital. I know what you're gonna say. But that's what I think would be best.

Troy: The man done had his life ruined fighting for what? And they wanna take and lock him up. Let him be free. He don't bother nobody.

Rose: Well, everybody got their own way of looking at it I guess. Come on and get your lunch. I got a bowl of lima beans and some cornbread in the oven. Come on get something to eat. Ain't no sense you fretting over Gabe.

(*Rose turns to go into the house.*)

Troy: Rose . . . got something to tell you.

Mellon: banker and industrialist Andrew Mellon (1855–1937), U.S. Treasury Secretary 1921–32, was active in philanthropic enterprises, especially in his native Pittsburgh.

Rose: Well, come on . . . wait till I get this food on the table.
Troy: Rose!

(*She stops and turns around.*)

I don't know how to say this. (*Pause.*) I can't explain it none. It just sort of grows on you till it gets out of hand. It starts out like a little bush . . . and the next thing you know it's a whole forest.
Rose: Troy . . . what is you talking about?
Troy: I'm talking, woman, let me talk. I'm trying to find a way to tell you . . . I'm gonna be a daddy. I'm gonna be somebody's daddy.
Rose: Troy . . . you're not telling me this? You're gonna be . . . what?
Troy: Rose . . . now . . . see . . .
Rose: You telling me you gonna be somebody's daddy? You telling your *wife* this?

(*Gabriel enters from the street. He carries a rose in his hand.*)

Gabriel: Hey, Troy! Hey, Rose!
Rose: I have to wait eighteen years to hear something like this.
Gabriel: Hey, Rose . . . I got a flower for you. (*He hands it to her.*) That's a rose. Same rose like you is.
Rose: Thanks, Gabe.
Gabriel: Troy, you ain't mad at me is you? Them bad mens come and put me away. You ain't mad at me is you?
Troy: Naw, Gabe, I ain't mad at you.
Rose: Eighteen years and you wanna come with this.
Gabriel (*takes a quarter out of his pocket*): See what I got? Got a brand new quarter.
Troy: Rose . . . it's just . . .
Rose: Ain't nothing you can say, Troy. Ain't no way of explaining that.
Gabriel: Fellow that give me this quarter had a whole mess of them. I'm gonna keep this quarter till it stop shining.
Rose: Gabe, go on in the house there. I got some watermelon in the Frigidaire. Go on and get you a piece.
Gabriel: Say, Rose . . . you know I was chasing hellhounds and them bad mens come and get me and take me away. Troy helped me. He come down there and told them they better let me go before he beat them up. Yeah, he did!
Rose: You go on and get you a piece of watermelon, Gabe. Them bad mens is gone now.
Gabriel: Okay, Rose . . . gonna get me some watermelon. The kind with the stripes on it.

(*Gabriel exits into the house.*)

Rose: Why, Troy? Why? After all these years to come dragging this in to me now. It don't make no sense at your age. I could have expected this ten or fifteen years ago, but not now.
Troy: Age ain't got nothing to do with it, Rose.
Rose: I done tried to be everything a wife should be. Everything a wife could be. Been married eighteen years and I got to live to see the day you tell me you been seeing another woman and done fathered a child by her. And you know I ain't never wanted no half nothing in my family. My whole family is half. Everybody got different

fathers and mothers . . . my two sisters and my brother. Can't hardly tell who's who. Can't never sit down and talk about Papa and Mama. It's your papa and your mama and my papa and my mama . . .

Troy: Rose . . . stop it now.

Rose: I ain't never wanted that for none of my children. And now you wanna drag your behind in here and tell me something like this.

Troy: You ought to know. It's time for you to know.

Rose: Well, I don't want to know, goddamn it!

Troy: I can't just make it go away. It's done now. I can't wish the circumstance of the thing away.

Rose: And you don't want to either. Maybe you want to wish me and my boy away. Maybe that's what you want? Well, you can't wish us away. I've got eighteen years of my life invested in you. You ought to have stayed upstairs in my bed where you belong.

Troy: Rose . . . now listen to me . . . we can get a handle on this thing. We can talk this out . . . come to an understanding.

Rose: All of a sudden it's "we." Where was "we" at when you was down there rolling around with some godforsaken woman? "We" should have come to an understanding before you started making a damn fool of yourself. You're a day late and a dollar short when it comes to an understanding with me.

Troy: It's just . . . She gives me a different idea . . . a different understanding about myself. I can step out of this house and get away from the pressures and problems . . . be a different man. I ain't got to wonder how I'm gonna pay the bills or get the roof fixed. I can just be a part of myself that I ain't never been.

Rose: What I want to know . . . is do you plan to continue seeing her. That's all you can say to me.

Troy: I can sit up in her house and laugh. Do you understand what I'm saying. I can laugh out loud . . . and it feels good. It reaches all the way down to the bottom of my shoes. (*Pause.*) Rose, I can't give that up.

Rose: Maybe you ought to go on and stay down there with her . . . if she's a better woman than me.

Troy: It ain't about nobody being a better woman or nothing. Rose, you ain't the blame. A man couldn't ask for no woman to be a better wife than you've been. I'm responsible for it. I done locked myself into a pattern trying to take care of you all that I forgot about myself.

Rose: What the hell was I there for? That was my job, not somebody else's.

Troy: Rose, I done tried all my life to live decent . . . to live a clean . . . hard . . . useful life. I tried to be a good husband to you. In every way I knew how. Maybe I come into the world backwards, I don't know. But . . . you born with two strikes on you before you come to the plate. You got to guard it closely . . . always looking for the curve-ball on the inside corner. You can't afford to let none get past you. You can't afford a call strike. If you going down . . . you going down swinging. Everything lined up against you. What you gonna do. I fooled them, Rose. I bunted. When I found you and Cory and a halfway decent job . . . I was safe. Couldn't nothing touch me. I wasn't gonna strike out no more. I wasn't going back to the penitentiary. I wasn't gonna lay in the streets with a bottle of wine. I was safe. I had me a family. A job. I wasn't gonna get that last strike. I was on first looking for one of them boys to knock me in. To get me home.

Rose: You should have stayed in my bed, Troy.

Troy: Then when I saw that gal . . . she firmed up my backbone. And I got to thinking that if I tried . . . I just might be able to steal second. Do you understand
after eighteen years I wanted to steal second.

Rose: You should have held me tight. You should have grabbed me and held on.

Troy: I stood on first base for eighteen years and I thought . . . well, goddamn it . . . go
on for it!

Rose: We're not talking about baseball! We're talking about you going off to lay in
bed with another woman . . . and then bring it home to me. That's what we're
talking about. We ain't talking about no baseball.

Troy: Rose, you're not listening to me. I'm trying the best I can to explain it to you.
It's not easy for me to admit that I been standing in the same place for eighteen
years.

Rose: I been standing with you! I been right here with you, Troy. I got a life too.
I gave eighteen years of my life to stand in the same spot with you. Don't you
think I ever wanted other things? Don't you think I had dreams and hopes?
What about my life? What about me. Don't you think it ever crossed my mind to
want to know other men? That I wanted to lay up somewhere and forget about
my responsibilities? That I wanted someone to make me laugh so I could feel
good? You not the only one who's got wants and needs. But I held on to you,
Troy. I took all my feelings, my wants and needs, my dreams . . . and I buried
them inside you. I planted a seed and watched and prayed over it. I planted myself
inside you and waited to bloom. And it didn't take me no eighteen years to find
out the soil was hard and rocky and it wasn't never gonna bloom.

But I held on to you, Troy. I held you tighter. You was my husband. I owed
you everything I had. Every part of me I could find to give you. And upstairs in
that room . . . with the darkness falling in on me . . . I gave everything I had to try
and erase the doubt that you wasn't the finest man in the world. And wherever
you was going . . . I wanted to be there with you. Cause you was my husband.
Cause that's the only way I was gonna survive as your wife. You always talking
about what you give . . . and what you don't have to give. But you take too. You
take . . . and don't even know nobody's giving!

(*Rose turns to exit into the house; Troy grabs her arm.*)

Troy: You say I take and don't give!

Rose: Troy! You're hurting me!

Troy: You say I take and don't give.

Rose: Troy . . . you're hurting my arm! Let go!

Troy: I done give you everything I got. Don't you tell that lie on me.

Rose: Troy!

Troy: Don't you tell that lie on me!

(*Cory enters from the house.*)

Cory: Mama!

Rose: Troy. You're hurting me.

Troy: Don't you tell me about no taking and giving.

(*Cory comes up behind Troy and grabs him. Troy, surprised, is thrown off balance just
as Cory throws a glancing blow that catches him on the chest and knocks him down.
Troy is stunned, as is Cory.*)

Rose: Troy. Troy. No!

(*Troy gets to his feet and starts at Cory.*)

Troy . . . no. Please! Troy!

(*Rose pulls on Troy to hold him back. Troy stops himself.*)

Troy (to Cory): Alright. That's strike two. You stay away from around me, boy. Don't you strike out. You living with a full count. Don't you strike out.

(*Troy exits out the yard as the lights go down.*)

SCENE II

It is six months later, early afternoon. Troy enters from the house and starts to exit the yard. Rose enters from the house.

Rose: Troy, I want to talk to you.

Troy: All of a sudden, after all this time, you want to talk to me, huh? You ain't wanted to talk to me for months. You ain't wanted to talk to me last night. You ain't wanted no part of me then. What you wanna talk to me about now?

Rose: Tomorrow's Friday.

Troy: I know what day tomorrow is. You think I don't know tomorrow's Friday? My whole life I ain't done nothing but look to see Friday coming and you got to tell me it's Friday.

Rose: I want to know if you're coming home.

Troy: I always come home, Rose. You know that. There ain't never been a night I ain't come home.

Rose: That ain't what I mean . . . and you know it. I want to know if you're coming straight home after work.

Troy: I figure I'd cash my check . . . hang out at Taylors' with the boys . . . maybe play a game of checkers . . .

Rose: Troy, I can't live like this. I won't live like this. You livin' on borrowed time with me. It's been going on six months now you ain't been coming home.

Troy: I be here every night. Every night of the year. That's 365 days.

Rose: I want you to come home tomorrow after work.

Troy: Rose . . . I don't mess up my pay. You know that now. I take my pay and I give it to you. I don't have no money but what you give me back. I just want to have a little time to myself . . . a little time to enjoy life.

Rose: What about me? When's my time to enjoy life?

Troy: I don't know what to tell you, Rose. I'm doing the best I can.

Rose: You ain't been home from work but time enough to change your clothes and run out . . . and you wanna call that the best you can do?

Troy: I'm going over to the hospital to see Alberta. She went into the hospital this afternoon. Look like she might have the baby early. I won't be gone long.

Rose: Well, you ought to know. They went over to Miss Pearl's and got Gabe today. She said you told them to go ahead and lock him up.

Troy: I ain't said no such thing. Whoever told you that is telling a lie. Pearl ain't doing nothing but telling a big fat lie.

Rose: She ain't had to tell me. I read it on the papers.

Troy: I ain't told them nothing of the kind.

Rose: I saw it right there on the papers.

Troy: What it say, huh?

Rose: It said you told them to take him.

Troy: Then they screwed that up, just the way they screw up everything. I ain't worried about what they got on the paper.

Rose: Say the government send part of his check to the hospital and the other part to you.

Troy: I ain't got nothing to do with that if that's the way it works. I ain't made up the rules about how it work.

Rose: You did Gabe just like you did Cory. You wouldn't sign the paper for Cory . . . but you signed for Gabe. You signed that paper.

(The telephone is heard ringing inside the house.)

Troy: I told you I ain't signed nothing, woman! The only thing I signed was the release form. Hell, I can't read, I don't know what they had on that paper! I ain't signed nothing about sending Gabe away.

Rose: I said send him to the hospital . . . you said let him be free . . . now you done went down there and signed him to the hospital for half his money. You went back on yourself, Troy. You gonna have to answer for that.

Troy: See now . . . you been over there talking to Miss Pearl. She done got mad cause she ain't getting Gabe's rent money. That's all it is. She's liable to say anything.

Rose: Troy, I seen where you signed the paper.

Troy: You ain't seen nothing I signed. What she doing got papers on my brother anyway? Miss Pearl telling a big fat lie. And I'm gonna tell her about it too! You ain't seen nothing I signed. Say . . . you ain't seen nothing I signed.

(Rose exits into the house to answer the telephone. Presently she returns.)

Rose: Troy . . . that was the hospital. Alberta had the baby.

Troy: What she have? What is it?

Rose: It's a girl.

Troy: I better get on down to the hospital to see her.

Rose: Troy . . .

Troy: Rose . . . I got to go see her now. That's only right . . . what's the matter . . . the baby's alright, ain't it?

Rose: Alberta died having the baby.

Troy: Died . . . you say she's dead? Alberta's dead?

Rose: They said they done all they could. They couldn't do nothing for her.

Troy: The baby? How's the baby?

Rose: They say it's healthy. I wonder who's gonna bury her.

Troy: She had family, Rose. She wasn't living in the world by herself.

Rose: I know she wasn't living in the world by herself.

Troy: Next thing you gonna want to know if she had any insurance.

Rose: Troy, you ain't got to talk like that.

Troy: That's the first thing that jumped out your mouth. "Who's gonna bury her?" Like I'm fixing to take on that task for myself.

Rose: I am your wife. Don't push me away.

Troy: I ain't pushing nobody away. Just give me some space. That's all. Just give me some room to breathe.

(*Rose exits into the house. Troy walks about the yard.*)

Troy (*with a quiet rage that threatens to consume him*): Alright . . . Mr. Death. See now . . . I'm gonna tell you what I'm gonna do. I'm gonna take and build me a fence around this yard. See? I'm gonna build me a fence around what belongs to me. And then I want you to stay on the other side. See? You stay over there until you're ready for me. Then you come on. Bring your army. Bring your sickle. Bring your wrestling clothes. I ain't gonna fall down on my vigilance this time. You ain't gonna sneak up on me no more. When you ready for me . . . when the top of your list say Troy Maxson . . . that's when you come around here. You come up and knock on the front door. Ain't nobody else got nothing to do with this. This is between you and me. Man to man. You stay on the other side of that fence until you ready for me. Then you come up and knock on the front door. Anytime you want. I'll be ready for you.

(*The lights go down to black.*)

SCENE III

The lights come up on the porch. It is late evening three days later. Rose sits listening to the ball game waiting for Troy. The final out of the game is made and Rose switches off the radio. Troy enters the yard carrying an infant wrapped in blankets. He stands back from the house and calls.

Rose enters and stands on the porch. There is a long, awkward silence, the weight of which grows heavier with each passing second.

Troy: Rose . . . I'm standing here with my daughter in my arms. She ain't but a wee bittie little old thing. She don't know nothing about grownups' business. She innocent . . . and she ain't got no mama.

Rose: What you telling me for, Troy?

(*She turns and exits into the house.*)

Troy: Well . . . I guess we'll just sit out here on the porch.

(*He sits down on the porch. There is an awkward indelicateness about the way he handles the baby. His largeness engulfs and seems to swallow it. He speaks loud enough for Rose to hear.*)

A man's got to do what's right for him. I ain't sorry for nothing I done. It felt right in my heart. (*To the baby.*) What you smiling at? Your daddy's a big man. Got these great big old hands. But sometimes he's scared. And right now your daddy's scared cause we sitting out here and ain't got no home. Oh, I been homeless before. I ain't had no little baby with me. But I been homeless. You just be out on the road by your lonesome and you see one of them trains coming and you just kinda go like this . . .

(*He sings as a lullaby.*)

> Please, Mr. Engineer let a man ride the line
> Please, Mr. Engineer let a man ride the line
> I ain't got no ticket please let me ride the blinds

(*Rose enters from the house. Troy, hearing her steps behind him, stands and faces her.*)

She's my daughter, Rose. My own flesh and blood. I can't deny her no more than I can deny them boys. (*Pause.*) You and them boys is my family. You and them and this child is all I got in the world. So I guess what I'm saying is . . . I'd appreciate it if you'd help me take care of her.

Rose: Okay, Troy . . . you're right. I'll take care of your baby for you . . . cause . . . like you say . . . she's innocent . . . and you can't visit the sins of the father upon the child. A motherless child has got a hard time. (*She takes the baby from him.*) From right now . . . this child got a mother. But you a womanless man.

(*Rose turns and exits into the house with the baby. Lights go down to black.*)

SCENE IV

It is two months later. Lyons enters the street. He knocks on the door and calls.

Lyons: Hey, Rose! (*Pause.*) Rose!

Rose (*from inside the house*): Stop that yelling. You gonna wake up Raynell. I just got her to sleep.

Lyons: I just stopped by to pay Papa this twenty dollars I owe him. Where's Papa at?

Rose: He should be here in a minute. I'm getting ready to go down to the church. Sit down and wait on him.

Lyons: I got to go pick up Bonnie over her mother's house.

Rose: Well, sit it down there on the table. He'll get it.

Lyons (*enters the house and sets the money on the table*): Tell Papa I said thanks. I'll see you again.

Rose: Alright, Lyons. We'll see you.

(*Lyons starts to exit as Cory enters.*)

Cory: Hey, Lyons.

Lyons: What's happening, Cory? Say man, I'm sorry I missed your graduation. You know I had a gig and couldn't get away. Otherwise, I would have been there, man. So what you doing?

Cory: I'm trying to find a job.

Lyons: Yeah I know how that go, man. It's rough out here. Jobs are scarce.

Cory: Yeah, I know.

Lyons: Look here, I got to run. Talk to Papa . . . he know some people. He'll be able to help get you a job. Talk to him . . . see what he say.

Cory: Yeah . . . alright, Lyons.

Lyons: You take care. I'll talk to you soon. We'll find some time to talk.

(*Lyons exits the yard. Cory wanders over to the tree, picks up the bat, and assumes a batting stance. He studies an imaginary pitcher and swings. Dissatisfied with the result, he tries again. Troy enters. They eye each other for a beat. Cory puts the bat down and exits the yard. Troy starts into the house as Rose exits with Raynell. She is carrying a cake.*)

Troy: I'm coming in and everybody's going out.

Rose: I'm taking this cake down to the church for the bake sale. Lyons was by to see you. He stopped by to pay you your twenty dollars. It's laying in there on the table.

Troy (going into his pocket): Well . . . here go this money.

Rose: Put it in there on the table, Troy. I'll get it.

Troy: What time you coming back?

Rose: Ain't no use in you studying me. It don't matter what time I come back.

Troy: I just asked you a question, woman. What's the matter . . . can't I ask you a question?

Rose: Troy, I don't want to go into it. Your dinner's in there on the stove. All you got to do is heat it up. And don't you be eating the rest of them cakes in there. I'm coming back for them. We having a bake sale at the church tomorrow.

(Rose exits the yard. Troy sits down on the steps, takes a pint bottle from his pocket, opens it and drinks. He begins to sing.)

Troy:

> Hear it ring! Hear it ring!
> Had an old dog his name was Blue
> You know Blue was mighty true
> You know Blue was a good old dog
> Blue trees a possum in a hollow log
> You know from that he was a good old dog

(Bono enters the yard.)

Bono: Hey, Troy.

Troy: Hey, what's happening, Bono?

Bono: I just thought I'd stop by to see you.

Troy: What you stop by and see me for? You ain't stopped by in a month of Sundays. Hell, I must owe you money or something.

Bono: Since you got your promotion I can't keep up with you. Used to see you every day. Now I don't even know what route you working.

Troy: They keep switching me around. Got me out in Greentree now . . . hauling white folks' garbage.

Bono: Greentree, huh? You lucky, at least you ain't got to be lifting them barrels. Damn if they ain't getting heavier. I'm gonna put in my two years and call it quits.

Troy: I'm thinking about retiring myself.

Bono: You got it easy. You can *drive* for another five years.

Troy: It ain't the same, Bono. It ain't like working the back of the truck. Ain't got nobody to talk to . . . feel like you working by yourself. Naw, I'm thinking about retiring. How's Lucille?

Bono: She alright. Her arthritis get to acting up on her sometime. Saw Rose on my way in. She going down to the church, huh?

Troy: Yeah, she took up going down there. All them preachers looking for somebody to fatten their pockets. *(Pause.)* Got some gin here.

Bono: Naw, thanks. I just stopped by to say hello.

Troy: Hell, nigger . . . you can take a drink. I ain't never known you to say no to a drink. You ain't got to work tomorrow.

Bono: I just stopped by. I'm fixing to go over to Skinner's. We got us a domino game going over his house every Friday.

Troy: Nigger, you can't play no dominoes. I used to whup you four games out of five.

Bono: Well, that learned me. I'm getting better.

Troy: Yeah? Well, that's alright.

Bono: Look here . . . I got to be getting on. Stop by sometime, huh?

Troy: Yeah, I'll do that, Bono. Lucille told Rose you bought her a new refrigerator.

Bono: Yeah, Rose told Lucille you had finally built your fence . . . so I figured we'd call it even.

Troy: I knew you would.

Bono: Yeah . . . okay. I'll be talking to you.

Troy: Yeah, take care, Bono. Good to see you. I'm gonna stop over.

Bono: Yeah. Okay, Troy.

(*Bono exits. Troy drinks from the bottle.*)

Troy:

> Old Blue died and I dug his grave
> Let him down with a golden chain
> Every night when I hear old Blue bark
> I know Blue treed a possum in Noah's Ark.
> Hear it ring! Hear it ring!

(*Cory enters the yard. They eye each other for a beat. Troy is sitting in the middle of the steps. Cory walks over.*)

Cory: I got to get by.

Troy: Say what? What's you say?

Cory: You in my way. I got to get by.

Troy: You got to get by where? This is my house. Bought and paid for. In full. Took me fifteen years. And if you wanna go in my house and I'm sitting on the steps . . . you say excuse me. Like your mama taught you.

Cory: Come on, Pop . . . I got to get by.

(*Cory starts to maneuver his way past Troy. Troy grabs his leg and shoves him back.*)

Troy: You just gonna walk over top of me?

Cory: I live here too!

Troy (*advancing toward him*): You just gonna walk over top of me in my own house?

Cory: I ain't scared of you.

Troy: I ain't asked if you was scared of me. I asked you if you was fixing to walk over top of me in my own house? That's the question. You ain't gonna say excuse me? You just gonna walk over top of me?

Cory: If you wanna put it like that.

Troy: How else am I gonna put it?

Cory: I was walking by you to go into the house cause you sitting on the steps drunk, singing to yourself. You can put it like that.

Troy: Without saying excuse me???

(*Cory doesn't respond.*)

I asked you a question. Without saying excuse me???

Cory: I ain't got to say excuse me to you. You don't count around here no more.

Troy: Oh, I see . . . I don't count around here no more. You ain't got to say excuse me to your daddy. All of a sudden you done got so grown that your daddy don't count around here no more . . . Around here in his own house and yard that he done paid for with the sweat of his brow. You done got so grown to where you gonna take over. You gonna take over my house. Is that right? You gonna wear my pants. You gonna go in there and stretch out on my bed. You ain't got to say excuse me cause I don't count around here no more. Is that right?

Cory: That's right. You always talking this dumb stuff. Now, why don't you just get out my way?

Troy: I guess you got someplace to sleep and something to put in your belly. You got that, huh? You got that? That's what you need. You got that, huh?

Cory: You don't know what I got. You ain't got to worry about what I got.

Troy: You right! You one hundred percent right! I done spent the last seventeen years worrying about what you got. Now it's your turn, see? I'll tell you what to do. You grown . . . we done established that. You a man. Now, let's see you act like one. Turn your behind around and walk out this yard. And when you get out there in the alley . . . you can forget about this house. See? Cause this is my house. You go on and be a man and get your own house. You can forget about this. Cause this is mine. You go on and get yours cause I'm through with doing for you.

Cory: You talking about what you did for me . . . what'd you ever give me?

Troy: Them feet and bones! That pumping heart, nigger! I give you more than anybody else is ever gonna give you.

Cory: You ain't never gave me nothing! You ain't never done nothing but hold me back. Afraid I was gonna be better than you. All you ever did was try and make me scared of you. I used to tremble every time you called my name. Every time I heard your footsteps in the house. Wondering all the time . . . what's Papa gonna say if I do this? . . . What's he gonna say if I do that? . . . What's Papa gonna say if I turn on the radio? And Mama, too . . . she tries . . . but she's scared of you.

Troy: You leave your mama out of this. She ain't got nothing to do with this.

Cory: I don't know how she stand you . . . after what you did to her.

Troy: I told you to leave your mama out of this!

(*He advances toward Cory.*)

Cory: What you gonna do . . . give me a whupping? You can't whup me no more. You're too old. You just an old man.

Troy (*shoves him on his shoulder*): Nigger! That's what you are. You just another nigger on the street to me!

Cory: You crazy! You know that?

Troy: Go on now! You got the devil in you. Get on away from me!

Cory: You just a crazy old man . . . talking about I got the devil in me.

Troy: Yeah, I'm crazy! If you don't get on the other side of that yard . . . I'm gonna show you how crazy I am! Go on . . . get the hell out of my yard.

Cory: It ain't your yard. You took Uncle Gabe's money he got from the army to buy this house and then you put him out.

Troy (*advances on Cory*): Get your black ass out of my yard!

(*Troy's advance backs Cory up against the tree. Cory grabs up the bat.*)

Cory: I ain't going nowhere! Come on . . . put me out! I ain't scared of you.

Troy: That's my bat!

Cory: Come on!

Troy: Put my bat down!

Cory: Come on, put me out.

(*Cory swings at Troy, who backs across the yard.*)

What's the matter? You so bad . . . put me out!

(*Troy advances toward Cory.*)

Cory (*backing up*): Come on! Come on!

Troy: You're gonna have to use it! You wanna draw that bat back on me . . . you're gonna have to use it.

Cory: Come on! . . . Come on!

(*Cory swings the bat at Troy a second time. He misses. Troy continues to advance toward him.*)

Troy: You're gonna have to kill me! You wanna draw that bat back on me. You're gonna have to kill me.

(*Cory, backed up against the tree, can go no farther. Troy taunts him. He sticks out his head and offers him a target.*)

Come on! Come on!

(*Cory is unable to swing the bat. Troy grabs it.*)

Troy: Then I'll show you.

(*Cory and Troy struggle over the bat. The struggle is fierce and fully engaged. Troy ultimately is the stronger, and takes the bat from Cory and stands over him ready to swing. He stops himself.*)

Go on and get away from around my house.

(*Cory, stung by his defeat, picks himself up, walks slowly out of the yard and up the alley.*)

Cory: Tell Mama I'll be back for my things.

Troy: They'll be on the other side of that fence.

(*Cory exits.*)

Troy: I can't taste nothing. Helluljah! I can't taste nothing no more. (*Troy assumes a batting posture and begins to taunt Death, the fastball on the outside corner.*) Come on! It's between you and me now! Come on! Anytime you want! Come on! I be ready for you . . . but I ain't gonna be easy.

(*The lights go down on the scene.*)

SCENE V

The time is 1965. The lights come up in the yard. It is the morning of Troy's funeral. A funeral plaque with a light hangs beside the door. There is a small garden plot off to the side. There is noise and activity in the house as Rose, Lyons, and Bono have gathered. The door opens and Raynell, seven years old, enters dressed in a flannel nightgown. She crosses to the garden and pokes around with a stick. Rose calls from the house.

Rose: Raynell!

Raynell: Mam?

Rose: What you doing out there?
Raynell: Nothing.

(*Rose comes to the door.*)

Rose: Girl, get in here and get dressed. What you doing?
Raynell: Seeing if my garden growed.
Rose: I told you it ain't gonna grow overnight. You got to wait.
Raynell: It don't look like it never gonna grow. Dag!
Rose: I told you a watched pot never boils. Get in here and get dressed.
Raynell: This ain't even no pot, Mama.
Rose: You just have to give it a chance. It'll grow. Now you come on and do what I told you. We got to be getting ready. This ain't no morning to be playing around. You hear me?
Raynell: Yes, Mam.

(*Rose exits into the house. Raynell continues to poke at her garden with a stick. Cory enters. He is dressed in a Marine corporal's uniform, and carries a duffelbag. His posture is that of a military man, and his speech has a clipped sternness.*)

Cory (*to Raynell*): Hi. (*Pause.*) I bet your name is Raynell.
Raynell: Uh huh.
Cory: Is your mama home?

(*Raynell runs up on the porch and calls through the screen door.*)

Raynell: Mama . . . there's some man out here. Mama?

(*Rose comes to the door.*)

Rose: Cory? Lord have mercy! Look here, you all!

(*Rose and Cory embrace in a tearful reunion as Bono and Lyons enter from the house dressed in funeral clothes.*)

Bono: Aw, looka here . . .
Rose: Done got all grown up!
Cory: Don't cry, Mama. What you crying about?
Rose: I'm just so glad you made it.
Cory: Hey Lyons. How you doing, Mr. Bono.

(*Lyons goes to embrace Cory.*)

Lyons: Look at you, man. Look at you. Don't he look good, Rose. Got them Corporal stripes.
Rose: What took you so long?
Cory: You know how the Marines are, Mama. They got to get all their paperwork straight before they let you do anything.
Rose: Well, I'm sure glad you made it. They let Lyons come. Your Uncle Gabe's still in the hospital. They don't know if they gonna let him out or not. I just talked to them a little while ago.
Lyons: A Corporal in the United States Marines.
Bono: Your daddy knew you had it in you. He used to tell me all the time.
Lyons: Don't he look good, Mr. Bono?

Bono: Yeah, he remind me of Troy when I first met him. (*Pause.*) Say, Rose, Lucille's down at the church with the choir. I'm gonna go down and get the pallbearers lined up. I'll be back to get you all.

Rose: Thanks, Jim.

Cory: See you, Mr. Bono.

Lyons (*with his arm around Raynell*): Cory . . . look at Raynell. Ain't she precious? She gonna break a whole lot of hearts.

Rose: Raynell, come and say hello to your brother. This is your brother, Cory. You remember Cory.

Raynell: No, Mam.

Cory: She don't remember me, Mama.

Rose: Well, we talk about you. She heard us talk about you. (*To Raynell.*) This is your brother, Cory. Come on and say hello.

Raynell: Hi.

Cory: Hi. So you're Raynell. Mama told me a lot about you.

Rose: You all come on into the house and let me fix you some breakfast. Keep up your strength.

Cory: I ain't hungry, Mama.

Lyons: You can fix me something, Rose. I'll be in there in a minute.

Rose: Cory, you sure you don't want nothing? I know they ain't feeding you right.

Cory: No, Mama . . . thanks. I don't feel like eating. I'll get something later.

Rose: Raynell . . . get on upstairs and get that dress on like I told you.

> (*Rose and Raynell exit into the house.*)

Lyons: So . . . I hear you thinking about getting married.

Cory: Yeah, I done found the right one, Lyons. It's about time.

Lyons: Me and Bonnie been split up about four years now. About the time Papa retired. I guess she just got tired of all them changes I was putting her through. (*Pause.*) I always knew you was gonna make something out yourself. Your head was always in the right direction. So . . . you gonna stay in . . . make it a career . . . put in your twenty years?

Cory: I don't know. I got six already, I think that's enough.

Lyons: Stick with Uncle Sam and retire early. Ain't nothing out here. I guess Rose told you what happened with me. They got me down the workhouse. I thought I was being slick cashing other people's checks.

Cory: How much time you doing?

Lyons: They give me three years. I got that beat now. I ain't got but nine more months. It ain't so bad. You learn to deal with it like anything else. You got to take the crookeds with the straights. That's what Papa used to say. He used to say that when he struck out. I seen him strike out three times in a row . . . and the next time up he hit the ball over the grandstand. Right out there in Homestead Field. He wasn't satisfied hitting in the seats . . . he want to hit it over everything! After the game he had two hundred people standing around waiting to shake his hand. You got to take the crookeds with the straights. Yeah, Papa was something else.

Cory: You still playing?

Lyons: Cory . . . you know I'm gonna do that. There's some fellows down there we got us a band . . . we gonna try and stay together when we get out . . . but yeah, I'm still playing. It still helps me to get out of bed in the morning. As long as it do that I'm gonna be right there playing and trying to make some sense out of it.

Rose (calling): Lyons, I got these eggs in the pan.

Lyons: Let me go on and get these eggs, man. Get ready to go bury Papa. (*Pause.*) How you doing? You doing alright?

(*Cory nods. Lyons touches him on the shoulder and they share a moment of silent grief. Lyons exits into the house. Cory wanders about the yard. Raynell enters.*)

Raynell: Hi.

Cory: Hi.

Raynell: Did you used to sleep in my room?

Cory: Yeah . . . that used to be my room.

Raynell: That's what Papa call it. "Cory's room." It got your football in the closet.

(*Rose comes to the door.*)

Rose: Raynell, get in there and get them good shoes on.

Raynell: Mama, can't I wear these? Them other one hurt my feet.

Rose: Well, they just gonna have to hurt your feet for a while. You ain't said they hurt your feet when you went down to the store and got them.

Raynell: They didn't hurt then. My feet done got bigger.

Rose: Don't you give me no backtalk now. You get in there and get them shoes on.

(*Raynell exits into the house.*)

Ain't too much changed. He still got that piece of rag tied to that tree. He was out here swinging that bat. I was just ready to go back in the house. He swung that bat and then he just fell over. Seem like he swung it and stood there with this grin on his face . . . and then he just fell over. They carried him on down to the hospital, but I knew there wasn't no need . . . why don't you come on in the house?

Cory: Mama . . . I got something to tell you. I don't know how to tell you this . . . but I've got to tell you . . . I'm not going to Papa's funeral.

Rose: Boy, hush your mouth. That's your daddy you talking about. I don't want hear that kind of talk this morning. I done raised you to come to this? You standing there all healthy and grown talking about you ain't going to your daddy's funeral?

Cory: Mama . . . listen . . .

Rose: I don't want to hear it, Cory. You just get that thought out of your head.

Cory: I can't drag Papa with me everywhere I go. I've got to say no to him. One time in my life I've got to say no.

Rose: Don't nobody have to listen to nothing like that. I know you and your daddy ain't seen eye to eye, but I ain't got to listen to that kind of talk this morning. Whatever was between you and your daddy . . . the time has come to put it aside. Just take it and set it over there on the shelf and forget about it. Disrespecting your daddy ain't gonna make you a man, Cory. You got to find a way to come to that on your own. Not going to your daddy's funeral ain't gonna make you a man.

Cory: The whole time I was growing up . . . living in his house . . . Papa was like a shadow that followed you everywhere. It weighed on you and sunk into your flesh. It would wrap around you and lay there until you couldn't tell which one was you anymore. That shadow digging in your flesh. Trying to crawl in. Trying to live through you. Everywhere I looked, Troy Maxson was staring back at me . . . hiding under the bed . . . in the closet. I'm just saying I've got to find a way to get rid of that shadow, Mama.

Rose: You just like him. You got him in you good.

Cory: Don't tell me that, Mama.

Rose: You Troy Maxson all over again.

Cory: I don't want to be Troy Maxson. I want to be me.

Rose: You can't be nobody but who you are, Cory. That shadow wasn't nothing but you growing into yourself. You either got to grow into it or cut it down to fit you. But that's all you got to make life with. That's all you got to measure yourself against that world out there. Your daddy wanted you to be everything he wasn't . . . and at the same time he tried to make you into everything he was. I don't know if he was right or wrong . . . but I do know he meant to do more good than he meant to do harm. He wasn't always right. Sometimes when he touched he bruised. And sometimes when he took me in his arms he cut.

When I first met your daddy I thought . . . Here is a man I can lay down with and make a baby. That's the first thing I thought when I seen him. I was thirty years old and had done seen my share of men. But when he walked up to me and said, "I can dance a waltz that'll make you dizzy," I thought, Rose Lee, here is a man that you can open yourself up to and be filled to bursting. Here is a man that can fill all them empty spaces you been tipping around the edges of. One of them empty spaces was being somebody's mother.

I married your daddy and settled down to cooking his supper and keeping clean sheets on the bed. When your daddy walked through the house he was so big he filled it up. That was my first mistake. Not to make him leave some room for me. For my part in the matter. But at that time I wanted that. I wanted a house that I could sing in. And that's what your daddy gave me. I didn't know to keep up his strength I had to give up little pieces of mine. I did that. I took on his life as mine and mixed up the pieces so that you couldn't hardly tell which was which anymore. It was my choice. It was my life and I didn't have to live it like that. But that's what life offered me in the way of being a woman and I took it. I grabbed hold of it with both hands.

By the time Raynell came into the house, me and your daddy had done lost touch with one another. I didn't want to make my blessing off of nobody's misfortune . . . but I took on to Raynell like she was all them babies I had wanted and never had.

(*The phone rings.*)

Like I'd been blessed to relive a part of my life. And if the Lord see fit to keep up my strength . . . I'm gonna do her just like your daddy did you . . . I'm gonna give her the best of what's in me.

Raynell (*entering, still with her old shoes*): Mama . . . Reverend Tolliver on the phone.

(*Rose exits into the house.*)

Raynell: Hi.

Cory: Hi.

Raynell: You in the Army or the Marines?

Cory: Marines.

Raynell: Papa said it was the Army. Did you know Blue?

Cory: Blue? Who's Blue?

Raynell: Papa's dog what he sing about all the time.

Cory (*singing*):

Hear it ring! Hear it ring!
I had a dog his name was Blue
You know Blue was mighty true

> You know Blue was a good old dog
> Blue treed a possum in a hollow log
> You know from that he was a good old dog.
> Hear it ring! Hear it ring!

(Raynell joins in singing.)

Cory and Raynell:

> Blue treed a possum out on a limb
> Blue looked at me and I looked at him
> Grabbed that possum and put him in a sack
> Blue stayed there till I came back
> Old Blue's feets was big and round
> Never allowed a possum to touch the ground.
>
> Old Blue died and I dug his grave
> I dug his grave with a silver spade
> Let him down with a golden chain
> And every night I call his name
> Go on Blue, you good dog you
> Go on Blue, you good dog you.

Raynell:

> Blue laid down and died like a man
> Blue laid down and died . . .

Both:

> Blue laid down and died like a man
> Now he's treeing possums in the Promised Land
> I'm gonna tell you this to let you know
> Blue's gone where the good dogs go
> When I hear old Blue bark
> When I hear old Blue bark
> Blue treed a possum in Noah's Ark
> Blue treed a possum in Noah's Ark.

(Rose comes to the screen door.)

Rose: Cory, we gonna be ready to go in a minute.

Cory (to Raynell): You go on in the house and change them shoes like Mama told you so we can go to Papa's funeral.

Raynell: Okay, I'll be back.

(Raynell exits into the house. Cory gets up and crosses over to the tree. Rose stands in the screen door watching him. Gabriel enters from the alley.)

Gabriel (calling): Hey, Rose!

Rose: Gabe?

Gabriel: I'm here, Rose. Hey, Rose, I'm here!

(Rose enters from the house.)

Rose: Lord . . . Look here, Lyons!

Lyons: See, I told you, Rose . . . I told you they'd let him come.

Cory: How you doing, Uncle Gabe?

Lyons: How you doing, Uncle Gabe?

Gabriel: Hey, Rose. It's time. It's time to tell St. Peter to open the gates. Troy, you ready? You ready, Troy. I'm gonna tell St. Peter to open the gates. You get ready now.

(Gabriel, with great fanfare, braces himself to blow. The trumpet is without a mouthpiece. He puts the end of it into his mouth and blows with great force, like a man who has been waiting some twenty-odd years for this single moment. No sound comes out of the trumpet. He braces himself and blows again with the same result. A third time he blows. There is a weight of impossible description that falls away and leaves him bare and exposed to a frightful realization. It is a trauma that a sane and normal mind would be unable to withstand. He begins to dance. A slow, strange dance, eerie and life-giving. A dance of atavistic signature and ritual. Lyons attempts to embrace him. Gabriel pushes Lyons away. He begins to howl in what is an attempt at song, or perhaps a song turning back into itself in an attempt at speech. He finishes his dance and the gates of heaven stand open as wide as God's closet.)

That's the way that go!

BLACKOUT

August Wilson on Writing

A Look Into Black America   1999

Interviewer: Is it a concern to effect social change with your plays?

Wilson: I don't write primarily to effect social change. I believe writing can do that, but that's not why I write. I work as an artist. However, all art is political in the sense that it serves the politics of someone. Here in America whites have a particular view of blacks, and I think my plays offer them a different and new way to look at black Americans. For instance, in *Fences* they see a garbageman, a person they really don't look at, although they may see a garbageman every day. By looking at Troy's life, white people find out that the content of this black garbageman's life is very similar to their own,

August Wilson

that he is affected by the same things—love, honor, beauty, betrayal, duty. Recognizing that these things are as much a part of his life as of theirs can be revolutionary and can affect how they think about and deal with black people in their lives.

Interviewer: How would that same play, *Fences*, affect a black audience?

Wilson: Blacks see the content of their lives being elevated into art. They don't always know that it is possible, and it's important to know that.

From "Interview with August Wilson"
by Bonnie Lyons and George Plimpton

Susan Glaspell at work, around 1913.

WRITING

41 WRITING ABOUT LITERATURE

If one waits for the right time to come before writing,
the right time never comes.

——JAMES RUSSELL LOWELL

Assigned to write an essay on *Hamlet*, a student might well wonder, "What can I say that hasn't been said a thousand times before?" Often the most difficult aspect of writing about a story, poem, or play is the feeling that we have nothing of interest to contribute to the ongoing conversation about some celebrated literary work. There's always room, though, for a reader's fresh take on an old standby.

Remember that in the study of literature common sense is never out of place. For most of a class hour, a professor once rhapsodized about the arrangement of the contents of W. H. Auden's *Collected Poems*. Auden, he claimed, was a master of thematic continuity, who had brilliantly placed the poems in the order that they ingeniously complemented each other. Near the end of the hour, his theories were punctured—with a great inaudible pop—when a student, timidly raising a hand, pointed out that Auden had arranged the poems in the book not by theme but in alphabetical order according to the first word of each poem. The professor's jaw dropped: "Why didn't you say that sooner?" The student was apologetic: "I—I was afraid I'd sound too *ordinary*."

Don't be afraid to state a conviction, though it seems obvious. Does it matter that you may be repeating something that, once upon a time or even just the other day, has been said before? What matters more is that you are actively engaged in thinking about literature. There are excellent old ideas as well as new ones. You have something to say.

READ ACTIVELY

Most people read in a relaxed, almost passive way. They let the story or poem carry them along without asking too many questions. To write about literature well, however, you need to *read actively*, paying special attention to various aspects of the text. This special sort of attention will not only deepen your enjoyment of the story, poem, or play but will also help generate the information and ideas that will eventually become your final paper. How do you become an active reader? Here are some steps to get you started:

■ **Preview the text.** To get acquainted with a work of literature before you settle in for a closer reading, skim it for an overview of its content and organization. Take a quick look at all parts of the work. Even a book's cover, preface, introduction, footnotes, and biographical notes about the author can provide you with some context for reading the work itself.

■ **Take notes. Annotate the text.** Read with a highlighter and pencil at hand, making appropriate annotations to the text. Later, you'll easily be able to review these highlights, and, when you write your paper, quickly refer to supporting evidence.

- Underline words, phrases, or sentences that seem interesting or important, or that raise questions.
- Jot down brief notes in the margin ("*key symbol—this foreshadows the ending,*" for example, or "*dramatic irony*").
- Use lines or arrows to indicate passages that seem to speak to each other—for instance, all the places in which you find the same theme or related symbols.

Robert Frost

Nothing Gold Can Stay

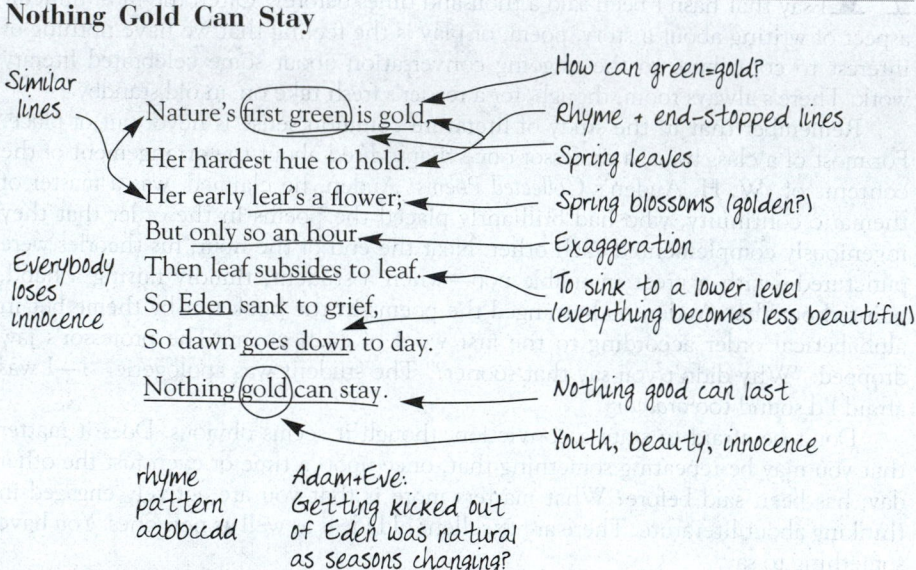

■ **Read closely.** Once you have begun reading in earnest, don't skim or skip over words you don't recognize; sometimes, looking up those very words will unlock a piece's meaning.

■ **Reread as needed.** If a piece is short, read it several times. Often, knowing the ending of a poem or short story will allow you to extract new meaning from its beginning and middle. If the piece is longer, reread the passages you thought important enough to highlight.

PLAN YOUR ESSAY

If you have actively reread the work you plan to write about and have made notes or annotations, you are already well on your way to writing your paper. Your mind has already begun to work through some initial impressions and ideas. Now you need to arrange those early notions into an organized and logical essay. Here is some advice on how to manage the writing process:

- **Leave yourself time.** Good writing involves thought and revision. Anyone who has ever been a student knows what it's like to pull an all-nighter, churning out a term paper hours before it is due. Still, the best writing evolves over time. Your ideas need to marinate. Sometimes, you'll make false starts, and you'll need to salvage what you can and do the rest from scratch. For the sake of your writing—not to mention your health and sanity—it's far better to get the job started well before your deadline.

- **Choose a subject you care about.** If you have been given a choice of literary works to write about, always choose the play, story, or poem that evokes the strongest emotional response. Your writing will be liveliest if you feel engaged by your subject.

- **Know your purpose.** As you write, keep the assignment in mind. You may have been asked to write a response, in which you describe your reactions to a literary work. Perhaps your purpose is to interpret a work, analyzing how one or more of its elements contribute to its meaning. You may have been instructed to write an evaluation, in which you judge a work's merits. Whatever the assignment, how you approach your essay will depend in large part on your purpose.

- **Think about your audience.** When you write journal entries or rough drafts, you may be composing for your own eyes only. More often, though, you are likely to be writing for an audience, even if it is an audience of one: your professor. Whenever you write for others, you need to be conscious of your readers. Your task is to convince them that your take on a work of literature is a plausible one. To do so, you need to keep your audience's needs and expectations in mind.

- **Define your topic narrowly.** Worried about having enough to say, students sometimes frame their topic so broadly that they can't do justice to it in the allotted number of pages. Your paper will be stronger if you go more deeply into your subject than if you choose a gigantic subject and touch on most aspects of it only superficially. A thorough explication of a short story is hardly possible in a 250-word paper, but an explication of a paragraph or two could work in that space. A profound topic ("The Character of Hamlet") might overflow a book, but a more focused one ("Hamlet's View of Acting" or "Hamlet's Puns") could result in a manageable paper. A paper entitled "Female Characters in *Hamlet*" couldn't help being too general and vague, but one on "Ophelia's Relationship to Laertes" could make for a good marriage of length and subject.

PREWRITING: DISCOVER YOUR IDEAS

Topic in hand, you can begin to get your ideas on the page. To generate new ideas and clarify the thoughts you already have, try one or more of the following useful prewriting techniques:

■ **Brainstorm.** Writing quickly, list everything that comes into your mind about your subject. Set a time limit—ten or fifteen minutes—and force yourself to keep adding items to the list, even when you think you have run out of things to say. Sometimes, if you press onward past the point where you feel you are finished, you will surprise yourself with new and fresh ideas.

> gold = early leaves/blossoms
> Or gold = something precious (both?)
> early leaf = flower (yellow blossoms)
> spring (lasts an hour)
> Leaves subside (sink to lower level)
> Eden = paradise = perfection = beauty
> Loss of innocence?
> What about original sin?
> Dawn becomes day (dawn is more precious?)
> Adam and Eve had to fall? Part of natural order.
> seasons/days/people's lives
> Title = last line: perfection can't last
> spring/summer/autumn
> dawn/day
> Innocence can't last

■ **Cluster.** This prewriting technique works especially well for visual thinkers. In clustering, you build a diagram to help you explore the relationships among your ideas. To get started, write your subject at the center of a sheet of paper. Circle it. Then jot down ideas, linking each to the central circle with lines. As you write down each new idea, draw lines to link it to related old ideas. The result will look something like the following web.

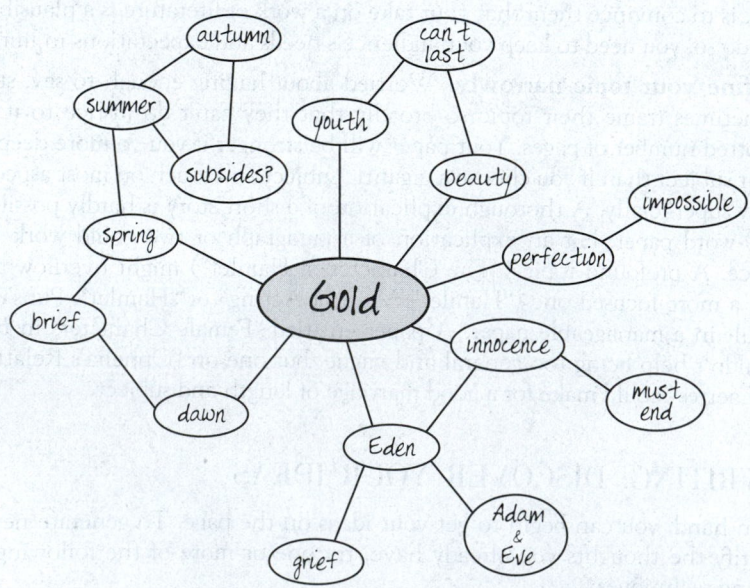

■ **List.** Look over the notes and annotations that you made in your active reading of the work. You have probably already underlined or noted more information than you can possibly use. One way to sort through your material to find the most useful information is to make a list of the important items. It helps to make several short lists under different headings. Here are some lists you might make after rereading Frost's "Nothing Gold Can Stay." Don't be afraid to add more comments or questions on the lists to help your thought process.

Images	Colors
leaf ("early leaf")	green
flower	gold ("hardest hue to hold")
dawn	
day	
Eden	
gold	

Key Actions
gold is hard to hold
early leaf lasts only an hour
leaf subsides to leaf (what does this mean???)
Eden sinks to grief (paradise is lost)
dawn goes down to day
gold can't stay (perfection is impossible?)

■ **Freewrite.** Most writers have snarky little voices in their heads, telling them that the words they're committing to paper aren't interesting or deep or elegant enough. To drown out those little voices, try freewriting. Give yourself a set amount of time (say, ten minutes) and write, nonstop, on your topic. Force your pen to keep moving, even if you have run out of things to say. If all you can think of to write is "I'm stuck" or "This is dumb," so be it. Keep your hand moving, and something else will most likely occur to you. Don't worry, yet, about grammar or spelling. When your time is up, read what you have written, highlighting the best ideas for later use.

> How can green be gold? By nature's first green, I guess he means the first leaves in spring. Are those leaves gold? They're more delicate and yellow than summer leaves . . . so maybe in a sense they look gold. Or maybe he means spring blossoms. Sometimes they're yellow. Also the first line seems to connect with the third one, where he comes right out and says that flowers are like early leaves. Still, I think he also means that the first leaves are the most precious ones, like gold. I don't think the poem wants me to take all of these statements literally. Flowers on trees last more than an hour, but that really beautiful moment in spring when blossoms are everywhere always ends too quickly, so maybe that's what he means by "only so an hour." I had to look up "subsides." It means to sink to a lower level . . . as if the later leaves will be less perfect than the first ones. I don't know if I agree. Aren't fall leaves precious? Then he says, "So Eden sank to grief" which seems to be saying that Adam and Eve's fall would

have happened no matter what they did, because everything that seems perfect falls apart . . . nothing gold can stay. Is he saying Adam and Eve didn't really have a choice? No matter what, everything gets older, less beautiful, less innocent . . . even people.

■ **Journal.** Your instructor might ask you to keep a journal in which you jot down your ideas, feelings, and impressions before they are fully formulated. Sometimes a journal is meant for your eyes only; in other instances your instructor might read it. Either way, it is meant to be informal and immediate, and to provide raw material that you may later choose to refine into a formal essay. Here are some tips for keeping a useful journal:

- Get your ideas down as soon as they occur to you.
- Write quickly.
- Jot down your feelings about and first impressions of the story, poem, or play you are reading.
- Don't worry about grammar, spelling, or punctuation.
- Don't worry about sounding academic.
- Don't worry about whether your ideas are good or bad ones; you can sort that out later.
- Try out invention strategies, such as freewriting, clustering, and outlining.
- Keep writing, even after you think you have run out of things to say. You might surprise yourself.
- Write about what interests you most.
- Write in your journal on a regular basis.

For a more detailed explanation of how to approach journal writing, read the chapter "Writing as Discovery: Keeping a Journal."

■ **Outline.** Some topics by their very nature suggest obvious ways to organize a paper. "An Explication of a Sonnet by Wordsworth" might mean simply working through the poem line by line. If this isn't the case, some kind of outline will probably prove helpful. Your outline needn't be elaborate to be useful. While a long research paper on several literary works might call for a detailed outline, a 500-word analysis of a short story's figures of speech might call for just a simple list of points in the order that makes the most logical sense—not necessarily, of course, the order in which those thoughts first came to mind.

1. Passage of time = fall from innocence
    blossoms
    gold
    dawn
    grief
2. Innocence = perfection
    Adam and Eve
    loss of innocence = inevitable
    real original sin = passing of time
    paradise sinks to grief

3. Grief = knowledge
            experience of sin & suffering
            unavoidable as grow older

DEVELOP A LITERARY ARGUMENT

Once you have finished a rough outline of your ideas, you need to refine it into a clear and logical shape. You need to state your thesis (or basic idea) clearly and then support it with logical and accurate evidence. Here is a practical approach to this crucial stage of the writing process:

■ **Consider your purpose.** As you develop your argument, be sure to refer back to the specific assignment; let it guide you. Your instructor might request one of the following kinds of papers:

- *Response,* in which you explore your reaction to a work of literature.
- *Evaluation,* in which you assess the literary merits of a work.
- *Interpretation,* in which you discuss a work's meaning. If your instructor has assigned an interpretation, he or she may have more specifically asked for an *analysis, explication,* or *comparison/contrast* essay, among other possibilities.

■ **Remember your audience.** Practically speaking, your professor (and sometimes your classmates) will be your paper's primary audience. Some assignments, however, specify a particular audience beyond your professor and classmates. Keep your readers in mind. Be sure to adapt your writing to meet their needs and interests. If, for example, the audience has presumably already read a story under discussion, you won't need to relate the plot in its entirety. Instead, you will be free to bring up only those plot points that serve as evidence for your thesis.

■ **Narrow your topic to fit the assignment.** Though you may be tempted to choose a broad topic so that you will have no shortage of things to say, remember that a good paper needs focus. Your choice should be narrow enough for you to do it justice in the space and time allotted.

■ **Decide on a thesis.** Just as you need to know your destination before you set out on a trip, you need to decide what point you're traveling toward before you begin your first draft. Start by writing a provisional thesis sentence: a summing up of the main idea or argument your paper will explore. While your thesis doesn't need to be outrageous or deliberately provocative, it does need to take a stand. A clear, decisive statement gives you something to prove and lends vigor to your essay.

WORKING THESIS

The poem argues that like Adam and Eve we all lose our innocence and the passage of time is inevitable.

This first stab at a thesis sentence gave its author a sense of purpose and direction that allowed him to finish his first draft. Later, as he revised his essay, he found he needed to refine his thesis to make more specific and focused assertions.

▪ **Build your argument.** Once you've formulated your thesis, your task will be clear: you need to convince your audience that your thesis is sound. To write persuasively, it helps to have an understanding of some key elements of argument:

- *Claims.* Any time you make a statement you hope will be taken as true, you have made a claim. Some claims are unlikely to be contradicted ("the sky is blue" or "today is Tuesday"), but others are debatable ("every college sophomore dreams of running off to see the world"). Your essay's main claim—your thesis—should not be something entirely obvious. Having to support your point of view will cause you to clarify your ideas about a work of literature.

- *Persuasion.* If the word *argument* makes you think of raised voices and short tempers, it may help to think of your task as the gentler art of persuasion. To convince your audience of your thesis, you will need to present a cogent argument supported by evidence gathered from the text. If the assignment is a research paper, you will also need to cite what others have written on your topic.

- *Evidence.* When you write about a work of literature, the most convincing evidence will generally come from the text itself. Direct quotations from the poem, play, or story under discussion can provide particularly convincing support for your claims. Be sure to introduce any quotation by putting it in the context of the larger work. It is even more important to follow up each quotation with your own analysis of what it shows about the work.

- *Warrants.* Whenever you use a piece of evidence to support a claim, an underlying assumption connects one to the other. For instance, if you were to make the claim that today's weather is absolutely perfect and offer as your evidence the blue sky, your logic would include an unspoken warrant: sunny weather is perfect weather. Not everyone will agree with your warrant, though. Some folks (perhaps farmers) might prefer rain. In making any argument, including one about literature, you may find that you sometimes need to spell out your warrants to demonstrate that they are sound. This is especially true when the evidence you provide can lead to conclusions other than the one you are hoping to prove.

- *Credibility.* When weighing the merits of a claim, you will probably take into account the credibility of the person making the case. Often this happens almost automatically. You are more likely to listen to the opinion that you should take vitamins if it is expressed by your doctor than if it is put forth by a stranger you meet on the street. An expert on any given topic has a certain brand of authority not available to most of us. Fortunately, there are other ways to establish your credibility:

  Keep your tone thoughtful. Your reader will develop a sense of who you are through your words. If you come across as belligerent or disrespectful to those inclined to disagree with your views, you may lose your reader's goodwill. Therefore, express your ideas calmly and thoughtfully. A level tone demonstrates that you are interested in thinking through an issue or idea, not in bullying your reader into submission.

  Take opposing arguments into account. To make an argument more convincing, demonstrate familiarity with other possible points of view.

Doing so indicates that you have taken other claims into account before arriving at your thesis; it reveals your fairness as well as your understanding of your subject matter. In laying out other points of view, though, be sure to represent them fairly but also to respectfully make clear why your thesis is the soundest claim; you don't want your reader to doubt where you stand.

Demonstrate your knowledge. To gain your reader's trust, it helps to Demonstrate a solid understanding of your subject matter. Always check your facts; factual errors can call your knowledge into doubt. It also helps to have a command of the conventions of writing. Rightly or wrongly, errors in punctuation and spelling can undermine a writer's credibility.

■ **Organize your argument.** Unless you are writing an explication that works its way line by line through a work of literature, you will need to make crucial decisions about how to shape your essay. Its order should be driven by the logic of your argument, not by the structure of the story, play, or poem you're discussing. In other words, you need not work your way from start to finish through your source material, touching on each major point. Instead, choose only the points needed to prove your thesis, and present them in whatever order best makes your point. A rough outline can help you to determine that order.

■ **Make sure your thesis is supported by the evidence.** If you find you can't support certain aspects of your thesis, then refine it so that you can. Remember: until you turn it in, your essay is a work in progress. Anything can and should be changed if it doesn't further the development of the paper's main idea.

CHECKLIST: Developing an Argument

- ☐ What is your essay's purpose?
- ☐ Who is your audience?
- ☐ Is your topic narrow enough?
- ☐ Is your thesis interesting and thought-provoking?
- ☐ Does everything in your essay support your thesis?
- ☐ Have you considered and refuted alternative views?
- ☐ Is your tone thoughtful?
- ☐ Is your argument sensibly organized? Are similar ideas grouped together? Does one point lead logically to the next?

WRITE A ROUGH DRAFT

Seated at last, you prepare to write, only to find yourself besieged with petty distractions. All of a sudden you remember a friend you had promised to call, some double-A batteries you were supposed to pick up, a neglected Coke (in another room) growing warmer and flatter by the minute. If your paper is to be written, you have only one course of action: collar these thoughts and for the moment banish them. Here are a few tips for writing your rough draft:

■ **Review your argument.** The shape of your argument, its support, and the evidence you have collected will form the basis of your rough draft.

■ **Get your thoughts down.** The best way to draft a paper is to get your ideas down quickly. At this stage, don't fuss over details. The critical, analytical side of your mind can worry about spelling, grammar, and punctuation later. For now, let your creative mind take charge. This part of yourself has the good ideas, insight, and confidence. Forge ahead. Believe in yourself and in your ideas.

■ **Write the part you feel most comfortable with first.** There's no need to start at the paper's beginning and work your way methodically through to the end. Instead, plunge right into the parts of the paper you feel most prepared to write. You can always go back later and fill in the blanks.

■ **Leave yourself plenty of space.** As you compose, leave plenty of space between lines and set wide margins. When later thoughts come to you, you will easily be able to go back and squeeze them in.

■ **Focus on the argument.** As you jot down your first draft, you might not want to look at the notes you have compiled. When you come to a place where a note will fit, just insert a reminder to yourself such as "See card 19" or "See Aristotle on comedy." Also, whenever you bring up a new point, it's good to tie it back to your thesis. If you can't find a way to connect a point to your thesis, it's probably better to leave it out of your paper and come up with a point that advances your central claim.

■ **Does your thesis hold up?** If, as you write, you find that most of the evidence you uncover is not helping you prove your paper's thesis, it may be that the thesis needs honing. Adjust it as needed.

■ **Be open to new ideas.** Writing rarely proceeds in a straight line. Even after you outline your paper and begin to write and revise, expect to discover new thoughts—perhaps the best thoughts of all. If you do, be sure to invite them in.

Here is a student's rough draft for an analytical essay on "Nothing Gold Can Stay."

On Robert Frost's "Nothing Gold Can Stay"

Most of the lines in the poem "Nothing Gold Can Stay" by Robert Frost focus on the changing of the seasons. The poem's first line says that the first leaves of spring are actually blossoms, and the actual leaves that follow are less precious. Those first blossoms only last a little while. The reader realizes that nature is a metaphor for a person's state of mind. People start off perfectly innocent, but as time passes, they can't help but lose that innocence. The poem argues that like Adam and Eve we all lose our innocence and the passage of time is inevitable.

The poem's first image is of the color found in nature. The early gold of spring blossoms is nature's "hardest hue to hold." The color gold is associated with the mineral gold, a precious commodity. There's a hint that early spring is nature in its perfect state, and perfection is impossible to hold on to. To the poem's speaker, the colors of early spring seem to last only an hour. If you blink, they are gone. Like early spring, innocence can't last.

The line "leaf subsides to leaf" brings us from early spring through summer and fall. The golden blossoms and delicate leaves of spring subside, or sink to a lower level, meaning they become less special and beautiful. There's nothing more special and beautiful than a baby, so people are the same way. In literature, summer often means the prime of your life, and autumn often means the declining years. These times are less beautiful ones. "So dawn goes down to day" is a similar kind of image. Dawns are unbelievably colorful and beautiful but they don't last very long. Day is nice, but not as special as dawn.

The most surprising line in the poem is the one that isn't about nature. Instead it's about human beings. Eden may have been a garden (a part of nature), but it also represents a state of mind. The traditional religious view is that Adam and Eve chose to disobey God and eat from the tree of knowledge. They could have stayed in paradise forever if they had followed God's orders. So it's surprising that Frost writes "So Eden sank to grief" in a poem that is all about how inevitable change is. It seems like he's saying that no matter what Adam and Eve had done, the Garden of Eden wouldn't stay the paradise it started out being. When Adam and Eve ate the apple, they lost their innocence. The apple is supposed to represent knowledge, so they became wiser but less perfect. But the poem implies that no matter what Adam and Eve had done, they would have grown sadder and wiser. That's true for all people. We can't stay young and innocent.

It's almost as if Frost is defying the Bible, suggesting that there is no such thing as sin. We can't help getting older and wiser. It's a natural process. Suffering happens not because we choose to do bad things but because passing time takes our innocence. The real original sin is that time has to pass and we all have to grow wiser and less innocent.

The poem "Nothing Gold Can Stay" makes the point that people can't stay innocent forever. Suffering is the inevitable result of the aging process. Like the first leaves of spring, we are at the best at the very beginning, and it's all downhill from there.

REVISE YOUR DRAFT

A writer rarely—if ever—achieves perfection on the first try. For most of us, good writing is largely a matter of revision. Once your first draft is done, you can—and should—turn on your analytical mind. Painstaking revision is more than just tidying up grammar and spelling. It might mean expanding your ideas or sharpening the focus by cutting out any unnecessary thoughts. To achieve effective writing, you must have the courage to be merciless. Tear your rough drafts apart and reassemble their pieces into a stronger order. As you revise, consider the following:

■ **Be sure your thesis is clear, decisive, and thought-provoking.** The most basic ingredient in a good essay is a strong thesis—the sentence in which you summarize the claim you are making. Your thesis should say something more than just the obvious; it should be clear and decisive and make a point that requires evidence to persuade your reader to agree. A sharp, bold thesis lends energy to your argument. A revision of the working thesis used in the rough draft above provides a good example.

> **WORKING THESIS**
>
> The poem argues that like Adam and Eve we all lose our innocence and the passage of time is inevitable.

This thesis may not be bold or specific enough to make for an interesting argument. A careful reader would be hard pressed to disagree with the observation that Frost's poem depicts the passage of time or the loss of innocence. In a revision of his thesis, however, the essay's author pushes the claim further, going beyond the obvious to its implications.

> **REVISED THESIS**
>
> In "Nothing Gold Can Stay," Frost makes a bold claim: sin, suffering, and loss are inevitable because the passage of time causes everyone to fall from grace.

Instead of simply asserting that the poem looks with sorrow on the passage of time, the revised thesis raises the issue of why this is so. It makes a more thought-provoking claim about the poem. An arguable thesis can result in a more energetic, purposeful essay. A thesis that is obvious to everyone, on the other hand, leads to a static, dull paper.

■ **Ascertain whether the evidence you provide supports your theory.** Does everything within your paper work to support its thesis sentence? While a solid paper might be written about the poetic form of "Nothing Gold Can Stay," the student paper above would not be well served by bringing the subject up unless the author could show how the poem's form contributes to its message that time causes everyone to lose his or her innocence. If you find yourself including information that doesn't serve your argument, consider going back into the poem, story, or play for more useful evidence. On the other hand, if you're beginning to have a sneaking feeling that your thesis itself is shaky, consider reworking it so that it more accurately reflects the evidence in the text.

■ **Check whether your argument is logical.** Does one point lead naturally to the next? Reread the paper, looking for logical fallacies, moments in which the claims you make are not sufficiently supported by evidence, or the connection between one thought and the next seems less than rational. Classic logical fallacies include making hasty generalizations, confusing cause and effect, or using a non sequitur, a statement that doesn't follow from the statement that precedes it. An example of two seemingly unconnected thoughts may be found in the second paragraph of the draft above:

> To the poem's speaker, the colors of early spring seem to last only an hour.
> If you blink, they are gone. Like early spring, innocence can't last.

Though there may well be a logical connection between the first two sentences and the third one, the paper doesn't spell that connection out. Asked to clarify the warrant, or assumption, that makes possible the leap from the subject of spring to the subject of innocence, the author revised the passage this way:

> To the poem's speaker, the colors of early spring seem to last only an hour.
> When poets write of seasons, they often also are commenting on the life
> cycle. To make a statement that spring can't last more than an hour
> implies that a person's youth (often symbolically associated with spring) is
> all too short. Therefore, the poem implies that innocent youth, like spring,
> lasts for only the briefest time.

The revised version spells out the author's thought process, helping the reader to follow the argument.

- **Supply transitional words and phrases.** To ensure that your reader's journey from one idea to the next is a smooth one, insert transitional words and phrases at the start of new paragraphs or sentences. Phrases such as "in contrast" and "however" signal a U-turn in logic, while those such as "in addition" and "similarly" alert the reader that you are continuing in the same direction you have been traveling. Seemingly inconsequential words and phrases such as "also" and "as well" or "as mentioned above" can smooth the reader's path from one thought to the next, as in the example below.

DRAFT

Though Frost is writing about nature, his real subject is humanity. In literature, spring often represents youth. Summer symbolizes young adulthood, autumn stands for middle age, and winter represents old age. The adult stages of life are, for Frost, less precious than childhood, which passes very quickly. The innocence of childhood is, like those spring leaves, precious as gold.

ADDING TRANSITIONAL WORDS AND PHRASES

Though Frost is writing about nature, his real subject is humanity. As mentioned above, in literature, spring often represents youth. Similarly, summer symbolizes young adulthood, autumn stands for middle age, and winter represents old age. The adult stages of life are, for Frost, less precious than childhood, which passes very quickly. Also, the innocence of childhood is, like those spring leaves, precious as gold.

■ **Make sure each paragraph contains a topic sentence.** Each paragraph in your essay should develop a single idea; this idea should be conveyed in a topic sentence. As astute readers often expect to get a sense of a paragraph's purpose from its first few sentences, a topic sentence is often well placed at or near a paragraph's start.

■ **Make a good first impression.** Your introductory paragraph may have seemed just fine as you began the writing process. Be sure to reconsider it in light of the entire paper. Does the introduction draw readers in and prepare them for what follows? If not, be sure to rework it, as the author of the rough draft above did. Look at his first paragraph again:

DRAFT OF OPENING PARAGRAPH

Most of the lines in the poem "Nothing Gold Can Stay" by Robert Frost focus on the changing of the seasons. The poem's first line says that the first leaves of spring are actually blossoms, and the actual leaves that follow are less precious. Those first blossoms only last a little while. The reader realizes that nature is a metaphor for a person's state of mind. People start off perfectly innocent, but as time passes, they can't help but lose that happy innocence. The poem argues that like Adam and Eve we all lose our innocence and the passage of time is inevitable.

While serviceable, this paragraph could be more compelling. Its author improved it by adding specifics to bring his ideas to more vivid life. For example, the rather pedestrian sentence "People start off perfectly innocent, but as time passes, they can't help but lose that innocence," became this livelier one: "As babies we are all perfectly innocent, but as time passes, we can't help but lose that innocence." By adding a specific image—the baby—the author gives the reader a visual picture to illustrate the abstract idea of innocence. He also sharpened his thesis sentence, making it less general and more thought-provoking. By varying the length of his sentences, he made the paragraph less monotonous.

REVISED OPENING PARAGRAPH

Most of the lines in Robert Frost's brief poem "Nothing Gold Can Stay" focus on nature: the changing of the seasons and the fading of dawn into day. The poem's opening line asserts that the first blossoms of spring are more precious than the leaves that follow. Likewise, dawn is more special than day. Though Frost's subject seems to be nature, the reader soon realizes that his real subject is human nature. As babies we are all perfectly innocent, but as time passes, we can't help but lose that happy innocence. In "Nothing Gold Can Stay," Frost makes a bold claim: sin, suffering, and loss are inevitable because the passage of time causes everyone to fall from grace.

■ **Remember that last impressions count too.** Your paper's conclusion should give the reader some closure, tying up the paper's loose ends without simply (and boringly) restating all that has come before. The author of the rough draft above initially ended his paper with a paragraph that repeated the paper's main ideas without pushing those ideas any further:

DRAFT OF CONCLUSION

The poem "Nothing Gold Can Stay" makes the point that people can't stay innocent forever. Grief is the inevitable result of the aging process. Like the first leaves of spring, we are at the best at the very beginning, and it's all downhill from there.

While revising his paper, the author realized that the ideas in his next-to-last paragraph would serve to sum up the paper. The new final paragraph doesn't simply restate the thesis; it pushes the idea further, in its last two sentences, by exploring the poem's implications.

REVISED CONCLUSION

Some people might view Frost's poem as sacrilegious, because it seems to say that Adam and Eve had no choice; everything in life is doomed to fall. Growing less innocent and more knowing seems less a choice in Frost's view than a natural process like the changing of golden blossoms to green leaves. "Eden sank to grief" not because we choose to do evil things but because time takes away our innocence as we encounter the suffering and loss of human existence. Frost suggests that the real original sin is that time has to pass and we all must grow wiser and less innocent.

■ **Give your paper a compelling title.** Like the introduction, a title should be inviting to readers, giving them a sense of what's coming. Avoid a nontitle such as "A Rose for Emily," which serves as a poor advertisement for your paper. Instead, provide enough specifics to pique your reader's interest. "On Robert Frost's 'Nothing Gold Can Stay'" is a duller, less informative title than "Lost Innocence in Robert Frost's 'Nothing Gold Can Stay,'" which may spark the reader's interest and prepare him or her for what is to come.

CHECKLIST: Revising Your Draft

- ☐ Is your thesis clear? Can it be sharpened?
- ☐ Does all your evidence serve to advance the argument put forth in your thesis?
- ☐ Is your argument logical?
- ☐ Do transitional words and phrases signal movement from one idea to the next?
- ☐ Does each paragraph contain a topic sentence?
- ☐ Does your introduction draw the reader in? Does it prepare the reader for what follows?
- ☐ Does your conclusion tie up the paper's loose ends? Does it avoid merely restating what has come before?
- ☐ Is your title compelling?

SOME FINAL ADVICE ON REWRITING

- **Whenever possible, get feedback from a trusted reader.** In every project, there comes a time when the writer has gotten so close to the work that he or she can't see it clearly. A talented roommate or a tutor in the campus writing center can tell you what isn't yet clear on the page, what questions still need answering, or what line of argument isn't yet as persuasive as it could be.

- **Be willing to refine your thesis.** Once you have fleshed out your whole paper, you may find that your original thesis is not borne out by the rest of your argument. If so, you will need to rewrite your thesis so that it more precisely fits the evidence at hand.

- **Be prepared to question your whole approach to a work of literature.** On occasion, you may even need to entertain the notion of throwing everything you have written into the wastebasket and starting over again. Occasionally having to start from scratch is the lot of any writer.

- **Rework troublesome passages.** Look for skimpy paragraphs of one or two sentences—evidence that your ideas might need more fleshing out. Can you supply more evidence, more explanation, more examples or illustrations?

- **Cut out any unnecessary information.** Everything in your paper should serve to further its thesis. Delete any sentences or paragraphs that detract from your focus.

- **Aim for intelligent clarity when you use literary terminology.** Critical terms can help sharpen your thoughts and make them easier to handle. Nothing is less sophisticated or more opaque, however, than too many technical terms thrown together for grandiose effect: "The mythic *symbolism* of this *archetype* is the *antithesis* of the *dramatic situation*." Choose plain words you're already at ease with. When you use specialized terms, do so to smooth the way for your reader—to make your meaning more precise. It is less cumbersome, for example, to refer to the *tone* of a story than to say, "the way the author makes you feel that she feels about what she is talking about."

- **Set your paper aside for a while.** Even an hour or two away from your essay can help you return to it with fresh eyes. Remember that the literal meaning of "revision" is "seeing again."

- **Finally, carefully read your paper one last time to edit it.** Now it's time to sweat the small stuff. Check any uncertain spellings, scan for run-on sentences and fragments, pull out a weak word and send in a stronger one. Like soup stains on a job interviewee's tie, finicky errors distract from the overall impression and prejudice your reader against your essay.

Here is the revised version of the student paper we have been examining.

Gabriel 1

Noah Gabriel

Professor James

English 2171

7 October 2009

Lost Innocence in

Robert Frost's "Nothing Gold Can Stay"

Most of the lines in Robert Frost's brief poem "Nothing Gold Can Stay"
focus on nature: the changing of the seasons and the fading of dawn into day.
The poem's opening line asserts that the first blossoms of spring are more
precious than the leaves that follow. Likewise, dawn is more special than day.
Though Frost's subject seems to be nature, the reader soon realizes that his real
subject is human nature. As babies we are all perfectly innocent, but as time
passes, we can't help but lose that happy innocence. In "Nothing Gold Can
Stay," Frost makes a bold claim: sin, suffering, and loss are inevitable because
the passage of time causes everyone to fall from grace.

The poem begins with a deceptively simple sentence: "Nature's first green
is gold." The subject seems to be the first, delicate leaves of spring which are
less green and more golden than summer leaves. However, the poem goes on to
say, "Her early leaf's a flower" (3), indicating that Frost is describing the first
blossoms of spring. In fact, he's describing both the new leaves and blossoms.
Both are as rare and precious as the mineral gold. They are precious because
they don't last long; the early gold of spring blossoms is nature's "hardest hue
to hold" (2). Early spring is an example of nature in its perfect state, and
perfection is impossible to hold on to. To the poem's speaker, in fact, the colors
of early spring seem to last only an hour. When poets write of seasons, they
often also are commenting on the life cycle. To make a statement that spring
can't last more than an hour implies that a person's youth (often symbolically
associated with spring) is all too short. Therefore, the poem implies that
innocent youth, like spring, lasts for only the briefest time.

While Frost takes four lines to describe the decline of the spring blossoms,
he picks up the pace when he describes what happens next. The line, "Then leaf
subsides to leaf" (5) brings us from early spring through summer and fall,
compressing three seasons into a single line. Just as time seems to pass slowly

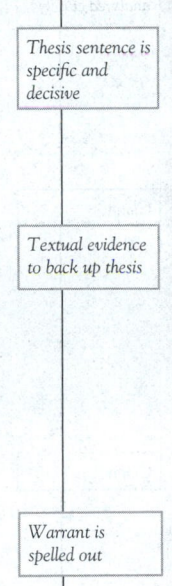

*Thesis sentence is
specific and
decisive*

*Textual evidence
to back up thesis*

*Warrant is
spelled out*

Claim

Gabriel 2

when we are children, and then much more quickly when we grow up, the poem

Significant word is looked at closely

moves quickly once the first golden moment is past. The word "subsides" feels important. The golden blossoms and delicate leaves of spring subside, or sink to a lower level, meaning they become less special and beautiful.

Claim

Warrant spelled out

Though Frost is writing about nature, his real subject is humanity. As mentioned above, in literature, spring often represents youth. Similarly, summer symbolizes young adulthood, autumn stands for middle age, and winter represents old age. The adult stages of life are, for Frost, less precious than childhood, which passes very quickly, as we later realize. Also, the innocence of childhood is, like those spring leaves, precious as gold.

Frost shifts his view from the cycle of the seasons to the cycle of a single day to make a similar point. Just as spring turns to summer, "So dawn goes down to day" (7). Like spring, dawn is unbelievably colorful and beautiful but doesn't last very long. Like "subsides," the phrase "goes down" implies that full daylight is actually a falling off from dawn. As beautiful as daylight is, it's ordinary, while dawn is special because it is more fleeting.

Key phrase is analyzed closely

Among these natural images, one line stands out: "So Eden sank to grief" (6). This line is the only one in the poem that deals directly with human beings. Eden may have been a garden (a part of nature) but it represents a state of mind—perfect innocence. In the traditional religious view, Adam and Eve chose to disobey God by eating an apple from the tree of knowledge. They were presented with a choice: to be obedient and remain in paradise forever, or to disobey God's order. People often speak of that first choice as "original sin." In this religious view, "Eden sank to grief" because the first humans chose to sin.

Claim

Frost, however, takes a different view. He compares the Fall of Man to the changing of spring to summer, as though it was as inevitable as the passage of time. The poem implies that no matter what Adam and Eve did, they couldn't remain in paradise. Original sin in Frost's view seems less a voluntary moral action than a natural, if unhappy sort of maturation. The innocent perfection of the garden of Eden couldn't possibly last. The apple represents knowledge, so in a symbolic sense God wanted Adam and Eve to stay unknowing, or innocent. But the poem implies that it was inevitable that Adam and Eve would gain knowledge and lose their innocence, becoming wiser but less perfect. They lost Eden and encountered "grief," the knowledge of suffering and loss associated with the human condition. This is certainly true for the rest of us human beings. As much as we might like to, we can't stay young or innocent forever.

Claim

Gabriel 3

Some people might view Frost's poem as sacrilegious, because it seems to say that Adam and Eve had no choice; everything in life is doomed to fall. Growing less innocent and more knowing seems less a choice in Frost's view than a natural process like the changing of golden blossoms to green leaves. "Eden sank to grief" not because we choose to do evil things but because time takes away our innocence as we encounter the suffering and loss of human existence. Frost suggests that the real original sin is that time has to pass and we all must grow wiser and less innocent.

Restatement of thesis

Gabriel 4

Work Cited

Frost, Robert. "Nothing Gold Can Stay." *Literature: An Introduction to Fiction, Poetry, Drama, and Writing.* 11th ed. Ed. X. J. Kennedy and Dana Gioia. New York: Longman, 2010. 868. Print.

DOCUMENT SOURCES TO AVOID PLAGIARISM

Certain literary works, because they offer intriguing difficulties, have attracted professional critics by the score. On library shelves, great phalanxes of critical books now stand at the side of James Joyce's *Ulysses* and T. S. Eliot's allusive poem *The Waste Land.* The student who undertakes to study such works seriously is well advised to profit from the critics' labors. Chances are, too, that even in discussing a relatively uncomplicated work, you will want to seek the aid of some critics.

If you do so, you may find yourself wanting to borrow quotations for your own papers. This is a fine thing to do—provided you give credit for those words to their rightful author. To do otherwise is plagiarism—a serious offense—and most English instructors are likely to recognize it when they see it. In any but the most superlative student paper, a brilliant (or even not so brilliant) phrase from a renowned critic is likely to stand out like a golf ball in a garter snake's midriff.

To avoid plagiarism, you must reproduce the text you are using with quotation marks around it, and give credit where it is due. Even if you summarize a critic's idea in your own words, rather than quoting his or her exact words, you have to give credit to your source. A later chapter, "Writing a Research Paper," will discuss in greater depth the topic of properly citing your sources. For now, students should simply remember that claiming another's work as one's own is the worst offense of the learning community. It negates the very purpose of education, which is to learn to think for oneself.

THE FORM OF YOUR FINISHED PAPER

If your instructor has not specified the form of your finished paper, follow the guidelines in the current edition of the *MLA Handbook for Writers of Research Papers*, which you will find more fully described in the chapter "Writing a Research Paper." In brief:

- Choose standard letter-size (8 1/2 × 11) white paper.
- Use standard, easy-to-read type fonts, such as Times New Roman. Be sure the italic type style contrasts with the regular style.
- Give your name, your instructor's name, the course number, and the date at the top left-hand corner of your first page, starting one inch from the top.
- On all pages, give your last name and the page number in the upper right-hand corner, one-half inch from the top.
- Remember to give your paper a title that reflects your thesis.
- Leave an inch or two of margin on all four sides of each page and a few inches of blank paper or an additional sheet after your conclusion, so that your instructor can offer comments.
- If you include a works-cited section, begin it on a new page.
- Double-space your text, including quotations and notes. Don't forget to double-space the works-cited page also.
- Italicize the titles of longer works—books, full-length plays, periodicals, and book-length poems such as *The Odyssey*. The titles of shorter works—poems, articles, or short stories—should appear in quotation marks.

SPELL-CHECK AND GRAMMAR-CHECK PROGRAMS

Most computer software includes a program to automatically check spelling. While such programs make proofreading easier, there are certain kinds of errors they won't catch. Words that are perfectly acceptable in other contexts but not the ones you intended ("is" where you meant "in," or "he" where you meant "the") will slip by undetected, making it clear to your instructor that your computer—and not you—did the proofreading. This is why it's still crucial that you proofread and correct your papers the old-fashioned way—read them yourself.

Another common problem is that the names of most authors, places, and special literary terms won't be in many standard spell-check memories. Unfamiliar words will be identified during the spell-check process, but you still must check all proper nouns carefully, so that Robert Frost, Gwendolyn Brooks, or Emily Dickenson doesn't make an unauthorized appearance midway in your otherwise exemplary paper. As the well-known authors Dina Gioia, Dan Goia, Dana Glola, Dona Diora, and Dana Gioia advise, always check the spelling of all names.

As an example of the kinds of mistakes your spell-checker won't catch, here are some cautionary verses that have circulated on the Internet. (Based on a charming piece of light verse by Jerrold H. Zar, "Candidate for a Pullet Surprise," this version reflects additions and revisions by numerous anonymous Internet collaborators.)

A Little Poem Regarding Computer Spell-Checkers   2000?

Eye halve a spelling checker
    It came with my pea sea
It plainly marques four my revue
    Miss steaks eye kin knot sea.

Eye strike a key and type a word   5
    And weight four it two say
Weather eye am wrong oar write
    It shows me strait a weigh.

As soon as a mist ache is made
    It nose bee fore two long   10
And eye can put the error rite
    Its rare lea ever wrong.

Eye have run this poem threw it
    I am shore your pleased two no
Its letter perfect awl the weigh   15
    My checker tolled me sew.

Another mixed blessing is the grammar-check program that highlights sentences containing obvious grammatical mistakes. Unfortunately, if you don't know what is wrong with your sentence in the first place, the grammar program won't always tell you. You can try reworking the sentence until the highlighting disappears (indicating that it's now grammatically correct). Better still, you can take steps to ensure that you have a good grasp of grammar already. Most colleges offer brief refresher courses in grammar, and, of course, writers' handbooks with grammar rules are readily available. Still, the best way to improve your grammar, your spelling, and your general command of language is to read widely and well.

To that end, we urge you to read the works of literature collected in this book beyond those texts assigned to you by your teacher. A well-furnished mind is a great place to live, an address you'll want to have forever.

42 WRITING ABOUT A STORY

Don't write merely to be understood.
Write so that you cannot possibly be misunderstood.

—ROBERT LOUIS STEVENSON

Writing about fiction presents its own set of challenges and rewards. Because a well-wrought work of fiction can catch us up in the twists and turns of its plot, we may be tempted to read it in a trance, passively letting its plot wash over us, as we might watch an entertaining film. Or, because stories, even short ones, unfold over time, there is often so much to say about them that narrowing down and organizing your thoughts can seem daunting.

To write compellingly about fiction, you need to read actively, identify a meaningful topic, and focus on making a point about which you feel strongly. (For pointers on finding a topic, organizing, writing, and revising your paper, see the previous chapter, "Writing About Literature." Some methods especially useful for writing about stories are described in the present chapter.)

In this chapter many of the discussions and examples refer to Edgar Allan Poe's short story "The Tell-Tale Heart" (page 36). If you haven't already read it, you can do so in only a few minutes, so that the rest of this chapter will make more sense to you.

READ ACTIVELY

Unlike a brief poem or a painting that you can take in with one long glance, a work of fiction—even a short story—may be too complicated to hold all at once in the mind's eye. Before you can write about it, you may need to give it two or more careful readings, and even then, as you begin to think further about it, you will probably have to thumb through it to reread passages. The first time through, it is best just to read attentively, open to whatever pleasure and wisdom the story may afford. The second time, you will find it useful to read with pencil in hand, either to mark your text or to take notes to jog your memory. To work out the design and meaning of a story need not be a boring chore, any more than it is to land a fighting fish and to study it with admiration.

- **Read the story at least twice.** The first time through, allow yourself just to enjoy the story—to experience surprise and emotion. Once you know how the tale ends, you'll find it easier to reread with some detachment, noticing details you may have glossed over the first time.

- **Annotate the text.** Reread the story, taking notes in the margins or highlighting key passages as you go. When you sit down to write, you probably will have to skim the story to refresh your memory, and those notes and highlighted passages should prove useful. Here is a sample of an annotated passage, from paragraph 3 of Edgar Allan Poe's "The Tell-Tale Heart."

Who is his listener?

Now this is the point. You fancy me mad. (Madmen know nothing).

Is this true?

But you should have seen *me*. You should have seen how wisely I proceeded—with what caution—with what foresight—with what dissimulation I went to work! I was never kinder to the old man than during the

He's not so mad he doesn't know what he's doing

whole week before I killed him. And every night, about midnight, I turned the latch of his door and opened it—oh, so gently! And then, when I had made an opening sufficient for my head, I put in a dark lantern, all closed, closed, so that no light shone out, and then I thrust in my head. Oh, you would have laughed to see how cunningly I thrust it

He's strangely happy! excited

in! I moved it slowly—very, very slowly, so that I might not disturb the old man's sleep. It took me an hour to place my whole head within the opening so far that I could see him as he lay upon his bed. Ha!—would a

Careful planning

madman have been so wise as this? And then, when my head was well in the room, I undid the lantern cautiously—oh, so cautiously—cautiously (for the hinges creaked)—I undid it just so much that a single thin ray

Creepy image. Who is the vulture here?

fell upon the vulture eye. And this I did for seven long nights—every

What did he expect?!

night just at midnight—but I found the eye always closed; and so it was impossible to do the work; for it was not the old man who vexed me, but

Peculiar obsession

his Evil Eye.

THINK ABOUT THE STORY

Once you have reread the story, you can begin to process your ideas about it. To get started, try the following steps:

- **Identify the protagonist and the conflict.** Whose story is being told? What does that character desire more than anything else? What stands in the way of that character's achievement of his or her goal? The answers to these questions can give you a better handle on the story's plot.

- **Consider the story's point of view.** What does it contribute to the story? How might the tale change if told from another point of view?

- **Think about the setting.** Does it play a significant role in the plot? How does setting affect the story's tone?

- **Notice key symbols.** If any symbols catch your attention as you go, be sure to highlight each place in which they appear in the text. What do these symbols contribute to the story's meaning? (Remember, not every image is a symbol—only those important recurrent persons, places, or things that seem to suggest more than their literal meaning.)

- **Look for the theme.** Is the story's central meaning stated directly? If not, how does it reveal itself?

- **Think about tone and style.** How would you characterize the style in which the story is written? Consider elements such as diction, sentence structure, tone, and organization. How does the story's style contribute to its tone?

PREWRITING: DISCOVER YOUR IDEAS

Once you have given the story some preliminary thought, it is time to write as a means of discovering what it is you have to say. Brainstorming, clustering, listing, freewriting, keeping a journal, and outlining all can help you clarify your thoughts about the story and, in doing so, generate ideas for your paper. While you don't need to use *all* these techniques, try them to find the one or two that work best for you.

- **Brainstorm.** If you aren't sure what, exactly, to say about a story, try jotting down everything you can think of about it. Work quickly, without pausing to judge what you have written. Set yourself a time limit of ten or fifteen minutes and keep writing even if you think you have said it all. A list that results from brainstorming on "The Tell-Tale Heart" might look something like this:

> madness? seems crazy
> unreliable narrator
> Could story be a dream?
> Could heartbeat be supernatural?
> heartbeat = speaker's paranoia
> tone: dramatic, intense, quick mood changes
> glee/terror
> lots of exclamation points

telling his story to listener
old man = father? boss? friend?
old man's gold/treasures
old man's eye = motive
vulture eye = symbolic
Calls plotting murder "work"
careful/patient
Chops up body
perfect crime
Policemen don't hear heartbeat
Guilt makes him confess

- **Cluster.** Clustering involves generating ideas by diagramming the relationship among your many ideas. First, write your subject at the center of a sheet of paper and circle it. Then, jot down ideas as they occur to you, drawing lines to link each idea to related ones. Here is an example of how you might cluster your ideas about "The Tell-Tale Heart."

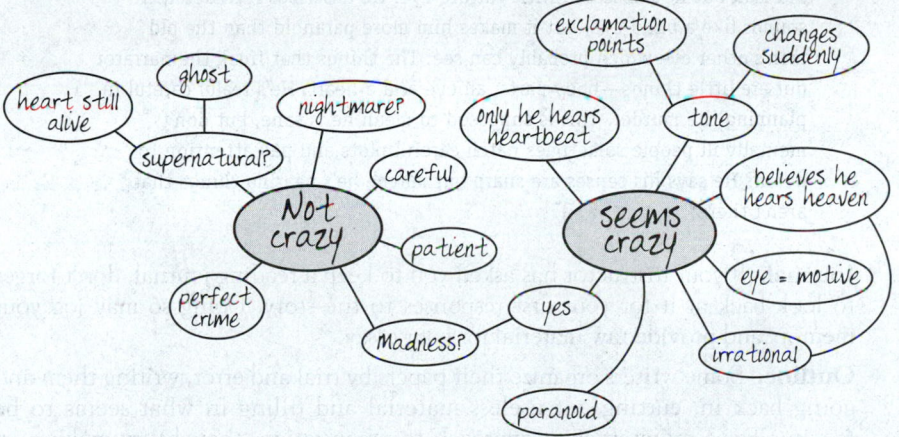

- **List.** Using your notes and annotations as a guide, list information that seems useful, adding any notes that help you to keep track of your thought process. Use different headings to organize related concepts. Your lists might look something like this:

Unreliable Narrator
mood swings
insists too much on being sane
confusion
disease
sharpened senses
loved old man
murder
patience
guilt
hearing things

Other Possibilities
nightmare
supernatural
heart still alive?
ghost's heartbeat?

■ **Freewrite.** Before you try to write a coherent first draft of your essay, take time to write freely, exploring your ideas as they occur to you. Writing quickly, without thinking too hard about grammar or spelling, can call forth surprising new ideas that wouldn't arrive if you were composing in a more reflective, cautious manner. To freewrite, give yourself a set amount of time—fifteen or twenty minutes. Put your pen to paper (or your fingers to the keys) and write without pausing to think. Keep going even if you run out of things to say. A freewrite on "The Tell-Tale Heart" might look like this:

> The guy seems crazy. He keeps insisting he's sane, so maybe others have accused him of being insane. He's speaking to someone—a judge? a fellow inmate? The story feels spoken out loud, like a dramatic monologue. His mood changes really quickly. One minute he's gleeful, and then impatient, then terrified. The story is full of dashes and exclamation points. He says he can hear everything in heaven and earth and even some things in hell. That seems crazy. His disease has sharpened his senses. Is he the old man's son, or his employee? I don't think the story says. It does say he loves the old man but he's obsessed with vulture eye. He describes it in detail. It sounds like a blind eye, but it makes him more paranoid than the old man's other eye which probably can see. The things that freak the narrator out are little things—body parts, an eye and a heart. He's really careful in planning the murder. This is supposed to mean he is sane, but don't mentally ill people sometimes hatch careful plots and pay attention to detail? He says his senses are sharp but maybe he's hearing things that aren't there?

■ **Journal.** If your instructor has asked you to keep a reading journal, don't forget to look back at it for your first responses to the story. Doing so may jog your memory and provide raw material for your essay.

■ **Outline.** Some writers organize their papers by trial and error, writing them and going back in, cutting out useless material and filling in what seems to be missing. For a more efficient approach to organization, though, try making an outline—a simple list of points arranged in an order that makes logical sense. Such an outline might look like this:

1. Point of view is ironic (speaker is mad/unreliable)
   hears things in heaven/hell
   excited tone
   focus on strange detail
2. Can we trust story really happened?
   nightmare?
   more interesting if actual
3. Supernatural elements?
   ghost heartbeat?
   heart still alive?
4. More interesting/believable if speaker is mad

WRITE A ROUGH DRAFT

Once your prewriting exercises have sparked an idea or two, you will be ready to begin shaping your thoughts into a rough draft. Reread the section "Develop a Literary Argument" on page 1897 of the previous chapter for help getting started. You can still keep your approach loose and informal; don't worry yet about phrasing things perfectly or pinning down the ideal word. For now, your goal is to begin finding a shape for your argument.

- **Remember your purpose.** Before you begin work on your first draft, be sure to check the assignment you have been given. There is no sense in writing even the most elegant *analysis* (in which you focus on one particular element of a story) if you have been told to write an *explication* (a detailed, line-by-line interpretation of a passage).

- **Consider your audience.** Though your professor and classmates will likely be your paper's actual audience, the assignment might specify hypothetical readers. Whoever your audience may be, keep their needs in mind as you write.

- **Formulate your thesis.** Before you get going on your rough draft, you will need a thesis sentence summing up your paper's main idea. Begin with a provisional thesis to give your argument direction. As you write, be sure to keep your provisional thesis in mind; doing so will help you stay on track. Here is a working thesis for a paper on "The Tell-Tale Heart":

  > **WORKING THESIS**
  >
  > The story contains many hints that the narrator of "The Tell-Tale Heart" is crazy.

  While this thesis gives its author something to work toward, it isn't yet as sharp as it could be. Most readers would agree that the story's narrator shows obvious signs of insanity. A more compelling thesis would go into the specifics of what, exactly, gives away the narrator's madness, or it might spell out the implications of this madness for the story. The following reworked version of this thesis sentence does both:

  > **REVISED THESIS**
  >
  > The narrator's tenuous hold on reality and his wild shifts in mood indicate that he is insane and, therefore, that his point of view is untrustworthy.

  Like this statement, your thesis should be decisive and specific. As you write a rough draft, your task is to persuade readers of the wisdom of your thesis.

- **Back up your thesis with evidence.** The bulk of your essay should be spent providing evidence that proves your thesis. Because the most persuasive evidence tends to be that which comes from the story itself, be sure to quote as needed.

As you flesh out your argument, check back frequently to make sure your thesis continues to hold up to the evidence. If you find that the facts of the story don't bear out your thesis, the problem may be with the evidence or with the thesis itself. Could your point be better proved by presenting different evidence? If so, exchange what you have for more convincing information. If not, go back in and refine your thesis sentence. Then make sure that the rest of the evidence bears out your new and improved thesis.

■ **Organize your argument.** Choose the points you need to prove your thesis and present them, along with supporting evidence, in whatever order best makes your case. A rough outline is often a useful tool.

CHECKLIST: Writing a Rough Draft

☐ What is your essay's purpose?

☐ Who is your audience? What do they need to know?

☐ What is your thesis? Is it debatable?

☐ Does everything in your essay support your thesis?

☐ Is your argument sensibly organized?

REVISE YOUR DRAFT

Once your first draft has been committed to paper, you will need to begin revising—going back in and reworking it to make the argument as persuasive and the prose as seamless as can be. First, though, it is an excellent idea to get feedback on your draft from a trusted reader—a classmate, a roommate, a tutor in your school's writing center, or, even your instructor—who can tell you which ideas are, and are not, coming across clearly, or where your argument is persuasive and where it could be more convincing. For writers at all levels of expertise, there simply is no substitute for constructive criticism from a thoughtful reader. If, however, you find readers are in short supply, put your rough draft away for at least an hour or two, and reread it with fresh eyes before you begin revising.

The following is an example of how one student used his instructor's comments to improve his paper's opening paragraph. (The final paper is printed later in the chapter on page 1924.)

DRAFT OF OPENING PARAGRAPH

The narrator of Edgar Allan Poe's "The Tell-Tale Heart" is a very mysterious and murderous character. The reader doesn't know much about him, except for how he speaks and <u>what he has to say for himself</u>. There is one (important fact) revealed by evidence in the story. The story contains <u>many hints</u> that the narrator of "The Tell-Tale Heart" is crazy.

Provide specifics.

Tell me more!

Why is this important?

What are some of these?

REVISED OPENING PARAGRAPH

 Although there are many things we do not know about the narrator
of Edgar Allan Poe's story "The Tell-Tale Heart"—is he a son? a servant? a
companion?—there is one thing we are sure of from the start. He is mad.
In the opening paragraph, Poe makes the narrator's condition unmistakable,
not only from his excited and worked-up speech (full of dashes and
exclamation points), but also from his wild claims. He says it is merely
some disease which has sharpened his senses that has made people call
him crazy. Who but a madman, however, would say, "I heard all things in
the heaven and in the earth," and brag how his ear is a kind of radio,
listening in on hell? The narrator's tenuous hold on reality and his wild
shifts in mood indicate that he is mad and, therefore, that his point of
view is untrustworthy.

 Remember that revision means more than just cleaning up typos and doing away
with stray semicolons. Revision might mean fleshing out your ideas with new paragraphs, rearranging material, or paring away passages that detract from your focus. As
you rewrite, make sure every paragraph has a topic sentence that announces its main
idea. Feel free to link your ideas with transitional words and phrases such as "moreover," "in addition," or "in contrast," to help your reader understand how each new
idea relates to the one that precedes it.

CHECKLIST: Revising Your Draft

- ☐ Is your thesis clear? Does it say something significant but not
  entirely obvious about the story?
- ☐ Does all your evidence serve to advance the argument put forth in
  your thesis?
- ☐ Is your argument clear and logical?
- ☐ Do transitional words and phrases help signal movement from one
  idea to the next?
- ☐ Does your introduction draw the reader in? Does it prepare the
  reader for what follows?
- ☐ Does your conclusion tie up the paper's loose ends? Does it avoid
  merely restating what has come before?
- ☐ Does each paragraph contain a topic sentence?
- ☐ Does the paper have an interesting and compelling title?

WHAT'S YOUR PURPOSE? COMMON APPROACHES
TO WRITING ABOUT FICTION

It is crucial to keep your paper's purpose in mind. When you write an academic
paper, you are likely to have been given a specific set of marching orders. Maybe you
have been asked to write for a particular audience besides the obvious one (your
professor, that is). Perhaps you have been asked to describe your personal reaction
to a literary work. Maybe your purpose is to interpret a work, analyzing how one or

more of its elements contribute to its meaning. You may have been instructed to write an evaluation in which you judge a work's merits. Let the assignment dictate your paper's tone and content. Below are several commonly used approaches to writing about fiction.

Explication

Explication is the patient unfolding of meanings in a work of literature. An explication proceeds carefully through a story, usually interpreting it line by line—perhaps even word by word, dwelling on details a casual reader might miss and illustrating how a story's smaller parts contribute to the whole. Alert and willing to take pains, the writer of such an essay notices anything meaningful that isn't obvious, whether it is a colossal theme suggested by a symbol or a little hint contained in a single word.

To write an honest explication of an entire story takes time and space, and is a better assignment for a long term paper, an honors thesis, or a dissertation than a short essay. A thorough explication of Nathaniel Hawthorne's "Young Goodman Brown," for example, would likely run much longer than the rich and intriguing short story itself. Ordinarily, explication is best suited to a short passage or section of a story: a key scene, a critical conversation, a statement of theme, or an opening or closing paragraph. In a long critical essay that doesn't adhere to one method all the way through, the method of explication may appear from time to time, as when the critic, in discussing a story, stops to unravel a particularly knotty passage. Here are some tips for writing a successful explication of your own:

- **Focus on the details that strike you as most meaningful.** Do not try to cover everything.

- **Try working through the original passage sentence by sentence.** If you choose this method, be sure to vary your transitions from one point to the next, to avoid the danger of falling into a boring singsong: "In the first sentence I noticed . . . ," "In the next sentence . . . ," "Now in the third sentence . . . ," and "Finally, in the last sentence. . . . "

- **Consider working from a simple outline.** In writing the explication that follows of a passage from "The Tell-Tale Heart," the student began with a list of points she wanted to express:

   1. Speaker's extreme care and exactness—typical of some mental illnesses.
   2. Speaker doesn't act by usual logic but by a crazy logic.
   3. Dreamlike connection between latch and lantern and old man's eye.

Storytellers who are especially fond of language invite closer attention to their words than others might. Edgar Allan Poe, for one, is a poet sensitive to the rhythms of his sentences and a symbolist whose stories abound in potent suggestions. Here is a student's explication of a short but essential passage in "The Tell-Tale Heart." The passage occurs in the third paragraph of the story, and to help us follow the explication, the student quotes the passage in full at the paper's beginning.

Kim 1

Susan Kim

Professor A. M. Lundy

English 100

20 May 2009

By Lantern Light: An Explication

of a Passage in Poe's "The Tell-Tale Heart"

And every night, about midnight, I turned the latch of his door
and opened it—oh, so gently! And then, when I had made an
opening sufficient for my head, I put in a dark lantern, all closed,
closed, so that no light shone out, and then I thrust in my head.
Oh, you would have laughed to see how cunningly I thrust it in!
I moved it slowly—very, very slowly, so that I might not disturb
the old man's sleep. It took me an hour to place my whole head
within the opening so far that I could see him as he lay upon
his bed. Ha!—would a madman have been so wise as this? And then,
when my head was well in the room, I undid the lantern
cautiously—oh, so cautiously—cautiously (for the hinges
creaked)—I undid it just so much that a single thin ray fell upon
the vulture eye. And this I did for seven long nights—every night
just at midnight—but I found the eye always closed; and so it was
impossible to do the work; for it was not the old man who vexed
me, but his Evil Eye. (par. 3)

> *Quotes passage to be explicated*

Although Edgar Allan Poe has suggested in the first lines of his story "The
Tell-Tale Heart" that the person who addresses us is insane, it is only when we
come to the speaker's account of his preparations for murdering the old man that
we find his madness fully revealed. Even more convincingly than his earlier words
(for we might possibly think that someone who claims to hear things in heaven and
hell is a religious mystic), these preparations reveal him to be mad. What strikes us
is that they are so elaborate and meticulous. A significant detail is the exactness of
his schedule for spying: "every night just at midnight." The words with which he
describes his motions also convey the most extreme care (and I will indicate them
by italics): "how wisely I proceeded—with *what caution*," "I turned the latch of his
door and opened it—oh, so *gently!*" "how *cunningly* I thrust it [my head] in! I
moved it slowly—*very, very slowly*," "I undid the lantern *cautiously*—oh, *so
cautiously—cautiously*." Taking a whole hour to intrude his head into the room, he
asks, "Ha!—would a madman have been so wise as this?" But of course the word

> *Thesis sentence*

> *Textual evidence supports thesis*

Kim 2

wise is unconsciously ironic, for clearly it is not wisdom the speaker displays, but an absurd degree of care, an almost fiendish ingenuity. Such behavior, I understand, is typical of certain mental illnesses. All his careful preparations that he thinks prove him sane only convince us instead that he is mad.

Topic sentence on narrator's mad logic

Obviously his behavior is self-defeating. He wants to catch the "vulture eye" open, and yet he takes all these pains not to disturb the old man's sleep. If he behaved logically, he might go barging into the bedroom with his lantern ablaze, shouting at the top of his voice. And yet, if we can see things his way, there *is* a strange logic to his reasoning. He regards the eye as a creature in itself, quite apart from its possessor. "It was not," he says, "the old man who vexed me, but his Evil Eye." Apparently, to be inspired to do his deed, the madman needs to behold the eye—at least, this is my understanding of his remark, "I found the eye always closed; and so it was impossible to do the work." Poe's choice of the word *work*, by the way, is also revealing. Murder is made to seem a duty or a job; and anyone who so regards murder is either extremely cold-blooded, like a hired killer for a gangland assassination, or else deranged. Besides, the word suggests again the curious sense of detachment that the speaker feels toward the owner of the eye.

Conclusion pushes thesis further, making it more specific.

In still another of his assumptions, the speaker shows that he is madly logical, or operating on the logic of a dream. There seems a dreamlike relationship between his dark lantern "all closed, closed, so that no light shone out," and the sleeping victim. When the madman opens his lantern so that it emits a single ray, he is hoping that the eye in the old man's head will be open too, letting out its corresponding gleam. The latch that he turns so gently, too, seems like the eye, whose lid needs to be opened in order for the murderer to go ahead. It is as though the speaker is *trying* to get the eyelid to lift. By taking such great pains and by going through all this nightly ritual, he is practicing some kind of magic, whose rules are laid down not by our logic, but by the logic of dreams.

Kim 3

Work Cited

Poe, Edgar Allan. "The Tell-Tale Heart." *Literature: An Introduction to Fiction,*
Poetry, Drama, and Writing. Ed. X. J. Kennedy and Dana Gioia. 11th ed.
New York: Longman, 2010. 36–40. Print.

An unusually well-written essay, "By Lantern Light" cost its author two or three careful revisions. Rather than attempting to say something about *everything* in the passage from Poe, she selects only the details that strike her as most meaningful. In her very first sentence, she briefly shows us how the passage functions in the context of Poe's story: how it clinches our suspicions that the narrator is mad. Notice too that the student who wrote the essay doesn't inch through the passage sentence by sentence, but freely takes up its details in an order that seems appropriate to her argument.

Analysis

Examining a single component of a story can afford us a better understanding of the entire work. This is perhaps why in most literature classes students are asked to write at least one **analysis** (from the Greek: "breaking up"), an essay that breaks a story or novel into its elements and, usually, studies one part closely. One likely topic for an analysis might be "The Character of James Baldwin's Sonny," in which the writer would concentrate on showing us Sonny's highly individual features and traits of personality. Other topics for an analysis might be "Irony in Ha Jin's 'Saboteur,'" or "Setting in Kate Chopin's 'The Storm,'" or "The Unidentified Narrator in 'A Rose for Emily.'"

To be sure, no element of a story dwells in isolation from the story's other elements. In "The Tell-Tale Heart," the madness of the leading character apparently makes it necessary to tell the story from a special point of view and probably helps determine the author's choice of theme, setting, symbolism, tone, style, and ironies. But it would be mind-boggling to try to study all those elements simultaneously. For this reason, when we write an analysis, we generally study just one element, though we may suggest—probably at the start of the essay—its relation to the whole story. Here are two points to keep in mind when writing an analysis:

- **Decide upon a thesis, and include only relevant insights.** As tempting as it might be to include your every idea, stick to those that will help to prove your point.
- **Support your contentions with specific references to the story you are analyzing.** Quotations can be particularly convincing.

The following paper is an example of a solid, brief analysis. Written by a student, it focuses on just one element of "The Tell-Tale Heart"—the story's point of view.

Frederick 1

Mike Frederick

Professor Stone

English 110

18 January 2009

The Hearer of the Tell-Tale Heart

States author and work

Although there are many things we do not know about the narrator of Edgar Allan Poe's story "The Tell-Tale Heart"—is he a son? a servant? a companion?—there is one thing we are sure of from the start. He is mad. In the opening paragraph, Poe makes the narrator's condition unmistakable, not only from his excited and worked-up speech (full of dashes and exclamation points), but also from his wild claims. He says it is merely some disease which has sharpened his senses that has made people call him crazy. Who but a madman, however, would say, "I heard all things in the heaven and in the earth," and brag how his ear is a kind of radio, listening in on hell? The narrator's tenuous

Thesis statement

hold on reality and his wild shifts in mood indicate that he is insane and, therefore, that his point of view is untrustworthy.

Topic sentence— how point of view determines emphasis

Because the participating narrator is telling his story in the first person, some details in the story stand out more than others. When the narrator goes on to tell how he watches the old man sleeping, he rivets his attention on the old man's "vulture eye." When a ray from his lantern finds the Evil Eye open, he says, "I could see nothing else of the old man's face or person" (par. 9). Actually, the reader can see almost nothing else about the old man anywhere in the rest of the story. All we are told is that the old man treated the younger man well, and we gather that the old man was rich, because his house is full of treasures. We do not have a clear idea of what the old man looks like, though, nor do we know how he talks, for we are not given any of his words. Our knowledge of him is mainly confined to his eye and its effect on the narrator. This confinement gives that symbolic eye a lot of importance in the story. The narrator tells us all we know and directs our attention to parts of it.

Raises question, then explores answer

This point of view raises an interesting question. Since we are dependent on the narrator for all our information, how do we know the whole story isn't just a nightmare in his demented mind? We have really no way to be sure it isn't, as far as I can see. I assume, however, that there really is a dark shuttered house and an old man and real policemen who start snooping around when screams are heard in the neighborhood, because it is a more memorable story if

Frederick 2

it is a crazy man's view of reality than if it is all just a terrible dream. But we can't take stock in the madman's interpretation of what happens. Poe keeps putting distances between what the narrator says and what we are apparently supposed to think. For instance: the narrator has boasted that he is calm and clear in the head, but as soon as he starts trying to explain why he killed the old man, we gather that he is confused, to say the least. "I think it was his eye!" the narrator exclaims, as if not quite sure (par. 2). As he goes on to explain how he conducted the murder, we realize that he is a man with a fixed idea working with a patience that is certainly mad, almost diabolical.

Topic sentence on how narrator's madness is revealed

Some readers might wonder if "The Tell-Tale Heart" is a story of the supernatural. Is the heartbeat that the narrator hears a ghost come back to haunt him? Here, I think, the point of view is our best guide to what to believe. The simple explanation for the heartbeat is this: it is all in the madman's mind. Perhaps he feels such guilt that he starts hearing things. Another explanation is possible, one suggested by Daniel Hoffman, a critic who has discussed the story: the killer hears the sound of his *own* heart (227). Hoffman's explanation (which I don't like as well as mine) also is a natural one, and it fits the story as a whole. Back when the narrator first entered the old man's bedroom to kill him, the heartbeat sounded so loud to him that he was afraid the neighbors would hear it too. Evidently they didn't, and so Hoffman may be right in thinking that the sound was only that of his own heart pounding in his ears. Whichever explanation you take, it is a more down-to-earth and reasonable explanation than (as the narrator believes) that the heart is still alive, even though its owner has been cut to pieces. Then, too, the police keep chatting. If they heard the heartbeat, wouldn't they leap to their feet, draw their guns, and look all around the room? As the author keeps showing us in the rest of the story, the narrator's view of things is untrustworthy. You don't kill someone just because you dislike the look in his eye. You don't think that such a murder is funny. For all its Gothic atmosphere of the old dark house with a secret hidden inside, "The Tell-Tale Heart" is not a ghost story. We have only to see its point of view to know it is a study in abnormal psychology.

Raises question, then explores answer

Secondary source paraphrase

Restatement of thesis

Frederick 3

Works Cited

Hoffman, Daniel. *Poe Poe Poe Poe Poe Poe Poe*. New York: Anchor, 1973. Print.

Poe, Edgar Allan. "The Tell-Tale Heart." *Literature: An Introduction to Fiction,*
Poetry, Drama, and Writing. Ed. X. J. Kennedy and Dana Gioia. 11th ed.
New York: Longman, 2010. 36–40. Print.

The temptation in writing an analysis is to include all sorts of insights that the writer proudly wishes to display, even though they aren't related to the main idea. In the preceding essay, the student resists this temptation admirably. In fairly plump and ample paragraphs, he works out his ideas and supports his contentions with specific references to Poe's story. Although his paper is not brilliantly written and contains no insight so fresh as the suggestion (by the writer of the first paper) that the madman's lantern is like the old man's head, still, it is a good brief analysis. By sticking faithfully to his purpose and by confronting the problems he raises ("How do we know the whole story isn't just a nightmare?"), the writer persuades us that he understands not only the story's point of view but also the story in its entirety.

The Card Report

Another form of analysis, a **card report** breaks down a story into its various elements. Though card reports tend to include only as much information as can fit on both sides of a single 5- by 8-inch index card, they are at least as challenging to write as full-fledged essays. The author of a successful card report can dissect a story into its elements and describe them succinctly and accurately. A typical card report on "The Tell-Tale Heart" follows. In this assignment, the student was asked to include the following:

1. The story's title and the date of its original publication.
2. The author's name and dates of birth and death.
3. The name (if any) of the main character, along with a description of that character's dominant traits or features.
4. Similar information for other characters.
5. A short description of the setting.
6. The point of view from which the story is told.
7. A terse summary of the story's main events in chronological order.
8. A description of the general tone, or, in other words, the author's feelings toward the central character or the main event.
9. Some comments on the style in which the story is written. Brief illustrative quotations are helpful if space allows.
10. Whatever kinds of irony the story contains and what they contribute to the story.

11. The story's main theme, in a sentence.
12. Key symbols (if the story has any), with an educated guess at what each symbol suggests.
13. Finally, an evaluation of the story as a whole, concisely setting forth the student's opinion of it. (Some instructors consider this the most important part of the report, and most students find that, by the time they have so painstakingly separated the ingredients of the story, they have arrived at a definite opinion of its merits.)

As you might expect, fitting so much information on one card is like trying to engrave the Declaration of Independence on the head of a pin. The student who wrote this report had to spoil a few trial cards before he was able to complete the assignment. The card report is an extreme exercise in making every word count, a worthwhile discipline in almost any kind of writing. Some students enjoy the challenge, and most are surprised at how thoroughly they come to understand the story. A longer story, even a novel, may be analyzed in the same way, but insist on taking a second card if you are asked to analyze an especially hefty and complicated novel.

Front of Card

Carly Grace   English 101

<u>Story</u>: "The Tell-Tale Heart," 1850

<u>Author</u>: Edgar Allan Poe (1809-1849)

<u>Central character</u>: An unnamed younger man whom people call mad, who claims

that a nervous disease has greatly sharpened his sense perceptions. He is proud of his

own cleverness.

<u>Other characters</u>: The old man, whose leading feature is one pale blue, filmed

eye; said to be rich, kind, and lovable. Also three policemen, not individually

described.

<u>Setting</u>: A shuttered house full of wind, mice, and treasures; pitch dark even in

the afternoon.

<u>Narrator</u>: The madman himself.

<u>Events in summary</u>: (1) Dreading one vulture-like eye of the old man he shares

a house with, a madman determines to kill its owner. (2) Each night he spies on the

sleeping old man, but finding the eye shut, he stays his hand. (3) On the eighth

night, finding the eye open, he suffocates its owner beneath the mattress and

conceals the dismembered body under the floor of the bedchamber. (4) Entertaining

some inquiring police officers in the very room where the body lies hidden, the killer

again hears (or thinks he hears) the beat of the victim's heart. (5) Terrified,

convinced that the police also hear the heartbeat growing louder, the killer

confesses.

<u>Tone</u>: Horror at the events described, skepticism toward the narrator's claims to

be sane, detachment from his gaiety and laughter.

Back of Card

Style: Written as if told aloud by a deranged man eager to be believed, the story is punctuated by laughter, interjections ("Hearken!"), nervous halts, and fresh beginnings—indicated by dashes that grow more frequent as the story goes on and the narrator becomes more excited. Poe often relies on general adjectives ("mournful," "hideous," "hellish,") to convey atmosphere; also on exact details (the lantern that emits "a single dim ray, like the thread of a spider").

Irony: The whole story is ironic in its point of view. Presumably the author is not mad, nor does he share the madman's self-admiration. Many of the narrator's statements therefore seem verbal ironies: his account of taking an hour to move his head through the bedroom door.

Theme: Possibly "Murder will out," but I really don't find any theme either stated or clearly implied.

Symbols: The vulture eye, called an Evil Eye (in superstition, one that can implant a curse), perhaps suggesting too the all-seeing eye of God the Father, from whom no guilt can be concealed. The ghostly heartbeat, sound of the victim's coming back to be avenged (or the God who cannot be slain?). Death watches: beetles said to be death omens, whose ticking sound foreshadows the sound of the tell-tale heart *as a watch makes when enveloped in cotton.*

Evaluation: Despite the overwrought style (to me slightly comic-bookish), a powerful story, admirable for its conclusion and for its memorable portrait of a deranged killer. Poe knows how it is to be mad.

Comparison and Contrast

If you were to write on "The Humor of Alice Walker's 'Everyday Use' and John Updike's 'A & P,'" you would probably employ one or two methods. You might use **comparison**, placing the two stories side by side and pointing out their similarities, or **contrast**, pointing out their differences. Most of the time, in dealing with a pair of stories, you will find them similar in some ways and different in others, and you'll use both methods. Keep the following points in mind when writing a comparison-contrast paper:

- **Choose stories with something significant in common.** This will simplify your task, and also help ensure that your paper hangs together. Before you start writing, ask yourself if the two stories you've selected throw some light on each other. If the answer is no, rethink your story selection.

■ **Choose a focus.** Simply ticking off every similarity and difference between two stories would make for a slack and rambling essay. More compelling writing would result from better-focused topics such as "The Experience of Coming of Age in James Joyce's 'Araby' and William Faulkner's 'Barn Burning'" or "Mother-Daughter Relationships in Alice Walker's 'Everyday Use' and Tillie Olsen's 'I Stand Here Ironing.'"

■ **Don't feel you need to spend equal amounts of time on comparing and contrasting.** If your chosen stories are more similar than different, you naturally will spend more space on comparison, and vice versa.

■ **Don't devote the first half of your paper to one story and the second half to the other.** Such a paper wouldn't be a comparison or contrast so much as a pair of analyses yoked together. To reap the full benefits of the assignment, let the two stories mingle.

■ **Before you start writing, draw up a brief list of points you would like to touch on.** Then address each point, first in one story and then in the other. A sample outline follows for a paper on William Faulkner's "A Rose for Emily" and Katherine Mansfield's "Miss Brill." The essay's topic is "Adapting to Change: The Characters of Emily Grierson and Miss Brill."

> 1. Adapting to change (both women)
>   Miss Brill more successful
> 2. Portrait of women
>   Miss Emily—unflattering
>   Miss Brill—empathetic
> 3. Imagery
>   Miss Emily—morbid
>   Miss Brill—cheerful
> 4. Plot
>   Miss Emily
>   - loses sanity
>   - refuses to adapt
>   Miss Brill
>   - finds place in society
>   - adapts
> 5. Summary: Miss Brill is more successful

■ **Emphasize the points that interest you the most.** This strategy will help keep you from following your outline in a plodding fashion ("Well, now it's time to whip over to Miss Brill again . . .").

■ **If the assignment allows, consider applying comparison and contrast in an essay on a single story.** You might, for example, analyze the attitudes of the younger and older waiters in Hemingway's "A Clean, Well-Lighted Place." Or you might contrast Mrs. Turpin's smug view of herself with the young Mary Grace's merciless view of her in Flannery O'Connor's "Revelation."

The following student-written paper compares and contrasts the main characters in "A Rose for Emily" and "Miss Brill." Notice how the author focuses the discussion on a single aspect of each woman's personality—the ability to adapt to change and the passage of time. By looking through the lens of three different elements of the short story—diction, imagery, and plot—this clear and systematic essay convincingly argues its thesis.

Ortiz 1

Michelle Ortiz

Professor Gregg

English 200

25 May 2009

Successful Adaptation in

"A Rose for Emily" and "Miss Brill"

In William Faulkner's "A Rose for Emily" and Katherine Mansfield's "Miss Brill," the reader is given a glimpse into the lives of two old women living in different worlds but sharing many similar characteristics. Both Miss Emily and Miss Brill attempt to adapt to a changing environment as they grow older. Through the authors' use of language, imagery, and plot, it becomes clear to the reader that Miss Brill is more successful at adapting to the world around her and finding happiness.

> *Clear statement of thesis*

In "A Rose for Emily," Faulkner's use of language paints an unflattering picture of Miss Emily. His tone evokes pity and disgust rather than sympathy. The reader identifies with the narrator of the story and shares the townspeople's opinion that Miss Emily is somehow "perverse." In "Miss Brill," however, the reader can identify with the title character. Mansfield's attitude toward the young couple at the end makes the reader hate them for ruining the happiness that Miss Brill has found, however small it may be.

> *Textual evidence on language supports thesis.*

The imagery in "A Rose for Emily" keeps the reader from further identifying with Miss Emily by creating several morbid images of her. For example, there are several images of decay throughout the story. The house she lived in is falling apart and described as "filled with dust and shades . . . an eyesore among eyesores." Emily herself is described as being "bloated like a body long submerged in motionless water." Faulkner also uses words like "skeleton," "dank," "decay," and "cold" to reinforce these morbid, deathly images.

> *Imagery in Faulkner's story supports argument.*

Contrasting imagery in Mansfield's story supports argument.

In "Miss Brill," however, Mansfield uses more cheerful imagery. The music and the lively action in the park make Miss Brill feel alive inside. She notices the other old people that are in the park are "still as statues," "odd," and "silent." She says they "looked like they'd just come from dark little rooms or even—even cupboards." Her own room is later described as a "cupboard," but during the action of the story she does not include herself among those other old people. She still feels alive.

Characters contrasted with examples drawn from plots.

Through the plots of both stories the reader can also see that Miss Brill is more successful in adapting to her environment. Miss Emily loses her sanity and ends up committing a crime in order to control her environment. Throughout the story, she refuses to adapt to any of the changes going on in the town, such as the taxes or the mailboxes. Miss Brill is able to find her own special place in society where she can be happy and remain sane.

The final conclusion is stated and the thesis is restated.

In "A Rose for Emily" and "Miss Brill" the authors' use of language and the plots of the stories illustrate that Miss Brill is more successful in her story. Instead of hiding herself away she emerges from the "cupboard" to participate in life. She adapts to the world that is changing as she grows older, without losing her sanity or committing crimes, as Miss Emily does. The language of "Miss Brill" allows the reader to sympathize with the main character. The imagery in the story is lighter and less morbid than in "A Rose for Emily." The resulting portrait is of an aging woman who has found creative ways to adjust to her lonely life.

Response Paper

One popular form of writing assignment is the **response paper**, a short essay that expresses your personal reaction to a work of literature. Both instructors and students often find the response paper an ideal introductory writing assignment. It provides you with an opportunity to craft a focused essay about a literary work, but it does not usually require any outside research. What it does require is careful reading, clear thinking, and honest writing.

The purpose of a response paper is to convey your thoughts and feelings about an aspect of a particular literary work. It isn't a book report (summarizing the work's content) or a book review (evaluating the quality of a work). A response paper expresses what you experienced in reading and thinking about the assigned text. Your reaction should reflect your background, values, and attitudes in response to the work, not what the instructor thinks about it. You might even consider your response paper a conversation with the work you have just read. What questions does it seem to ask you? What reactions does it elicit? You might also regard your paper as a personal message to your instructor telling him or her what you really think about one of the reading assignments.

Of course, you can't say everything you thought and felt about your reading in a short paper. Focus on an important aspect (such as a main character, setting, or theme) and discuss your reaction to it. Don't gush or meander. Personal writing doesn't mean disorganized writing. Identify your main ideas and present your point of view in a clear and organized way. Once you get started you might surprise yourself by discovering that it's fun to explore your own responses. Stranger things have happened.

Here are some tips for writing a successful response paper of your own:

- **Make quick notes as you read or reread the work.** Don't worry about writing anything organized at this point. Just write a word or two in the margin noting your reactions as you read (e.g., "how unpleasant!" or "very interesting"). These little notes will jog your memory when you go back to write your paper.

- **Consider which aspect of the work affected you the most.** That aspect will probably be a good starting point for your response.

- **Be candid in your writing.** Remember that the literary work is only half of the subject matter of your paper. The other half is your reaction.

- **Try to understand and explain why you have reacted the way you did.** It's not enough just to state your responses. You also want to justify or explain them.

- **Refer to the text in your paper.** Demonstrate to the reader that your response is based on the text. Provide specific textual details and quotations wherever relevant.

The following paper is one student's response to Tim O'Brien's story "The Things They Carried" (page 595).

Martin 1

Ethan Martin

English 99

Professor Merrill

31 March 2009

Response to "The Things They Carried"

Reading Tim O'Brien's short story "The Things They Carried" became a very personal experience. It reminded me of my father, who is a Vietnam veteran, and the stories he used to tell me. Growing up, I regularly asked my dad to share stories from his past—especially about his service in the United States Marine Corps. He would rarely talk about his tour during the Vietnam War for more than a few minutes, and what he shared was usually the same: the monsoon rain could chill to the bone, the mosquitoes would never stop biting, and the M-16 rifles often jammed in a moment of crisis. He dug a new foxhole where he slept every night, he traded the cigarettes from his C-rations for food, and—since he was the radio man of his platoon—the combination of his backpack and radio was very heavy during the long, daily walks through rice paddies and jungles. For these reasons, "The Things They Carried" powerfully affected me.

While reading the story, I felt as if I was "humping" (597) through Vietnam with Lieutenant Jimmy Cross, Rat Kiley, Ted Lavender, and especially Mitchell Sanders—who carries the 26-pound radio and battery. Every day, we carry our backpacks to school. Inside are some objects that we need to use in class: books, paper, and pens. But most of us probably include "unnecessary" items that reveal something about who we are or what we value—photographs, perfume, or good-luck charms. O'Brien uses this device to tell his story. At times he lists the things that the soldiers literally carried, such as weapons, medicine, and flak jackets. These military items weigh between 30 and 70 pounds, depending on one's rank or function in the platoon. The narrator says, "They carried all they could bear, and then some, including a silent awe for the terrible power of the things they carried" (598).

Some of this "terrible power" comes from the sentimental objects the men keep. Although these are relatively light, they weigh down the hearts of the soldiers. Lt. Jimmy Cross carries 10-ounce letters and a pebble from Martha, a girl in his hometown who doesn't love him back. Rat Kiley carries comic books, and Norman Bowker carried a diary. I now own the small, water-logged Bible that my father carried through his tour in Vietnam, which was a gift from his mother. When I open its pages, I can almost hear his voice praying to survive the war.

The price of such survival is costly. O'Brien's platoon carries ghosts, memories, and "the land itself" (602). Their intangible burdens are heavier than what they carry in their backpacks. My father has always said that, while he was in Vietnam, an inexpressible feeling of death hung heavy in the air, which he could not escape. O'Brien notes that an emotional weight of fear and cowardice "could never be put down, it required perfect balance and perfect posture" (605), and I wonder if this may be part of what my father meant.

Both Tim O'Brien and my father were wounded by shrapnel, and now they both carry a Purple Heart. They carry the weight of survival. They carry memories that I will never know. "The Things They Carried" is not a war story about glory and honor. It is a portrait of the psychological damage that war can bring. It is a story about storytelling and how hard it can be to find the truth. And it is a beautiful account of what the human heart can endure.

Martin 3

Work Cited

O'Brien, Tim. "The Things They Carried." *Literature: An Introduction to Fiction, Poetry, Drama, and Writing.* Ed. X. J. Kennedy and Dana Gioia. 11th ed. New York: Longman, 2010. 595–607. Print.

TOPICS FOR WRITING

What kinds of topics are likely to result in papers that will reveal something about works of fiction? Here is a list of typical topics, suitable for papers of various lengths, offered in the hope of stimulating your own ideas. For additional ideas, see "More Topics for Writing" at the end of most chapters in this book.

TOPICS FOR WRITING BRIEF PAPERS (250–500 WORDS)

1. Explicate the opening paragraph or first few lines of a story. Show how the opening prepares the reader for what will follow. In an essay of this length, you will need to limit your discussion to the most important elements of the passage you explicate; there won't be room to deal with everything. Or, as thoroughly as the word count allows, explicate the final paragraph of a story. What does the ending imply about the fates of the story's characters, and about the story's take on its central theme?

2. Select a story that features a first-person narrator. Write a concise yet thorough analysis of how that character's point of view colors the story.

3. Following the directions on page 1926, write a card report on any short story in this book.

4. Consider a short story in which the central character has to make a decision or must take some decisive step that will alter the rest of his or her life. Faulkner's "Barn Burning" is one such story; another is Updike's "A & P." As concisely and as thoroughly as you can, explain the nature of the character's decision, the reasons for it, and its probable consequences (as suggested by what the author tells us).

5. Choose two stories that might be interesting to compare and contrast. Write a brief defense of your choice. How might these two stories illuminate each other?

6. Choose a key passage from a story you admire. As closely as the word count allows, explicate that passage and explain why it strikes you as an important moment in the story. Concentrate on the aspects of the passage that seem most essential.

7. Write a new ending to a story of your choice. Try to imitate the author's writing style. Add a paragraph explaining how this exercise illuminates the author's choices in the original.

8. Drawing on your own experience, make the case that a character in any short story behaves (or doesn't behave) as people do in real life. Your audience for this assignment is your classmates; tailor your tone and argument accordingly.

TOPICS FOR WRITING MORE EXTENDED PAPERS (600–1,000 WORDS)

1. Write an analysis of a short story, focusing on a single element, such as point of view, theme, symbolism, character, or the author's voice (tone, style, irony). For a sample paper in response to this assignment, see "The Hearer of the Tell-Tale Heart" (page 1924).
2. Compare and contrast two stories with protagonists who share an important personality trait. Make character the focus of your essay.
3. Write a thorough explication of a short passage (preferably not more than four sentences) in a story you admire. Pick a crucial moment in the plot, or a passage that reveals the story's theme. You might look to the paper "By Lantern Light" (page 1921) as a model.
4. Write an analysis of a story in which the protagonist experiences an epiphany or revelation of some sort. Describe the nature of this change of heart. How is the reader prepared for it? What are its repercussions in the character's life? Some possible story choices are Alice Walker's "Everyday Use," William Faulkner's "Barn Burning," Raymond Carver's "Cathedral," James Baldwin's "Sonny's Blues," and, not surprisingly, Flannery O'Connor's "Revelation."
5. Imagine you are given the task of teaching a story to your class. Write an explanation of how you would address this challenge.
6. Imagine a reluctant reader, one who would rather play video games than crack a book. Which story in this book would you recommend to him or her? Write an essay to that imagined reader, describing the story's merits.

TOPICS FOR WRITING LONG PAPERS (1,500 WORDS OR MORE)

1. Write an analysis of a longer work of fiction. Concentrate on a single element of the story, quoting as necessary to make your point.
2. Read three or four short stories by an author whose work you admire. Concentrating on a single element treated similarly in all of the stories, write an analysis of the author's work as exemplified by your chosen stories.
3. Adapt a short story in this book into a one-act play. This may prove harder than it sounds; be sure to choose a story in which most of the action takes place in the physical world and not in the protagonist's mind. Don't forget to include stage directions.
4. Describe the process of reading a story for the first time and gradually learning to understand and appreciate it. First, choose a story you haven't yet read. As you read it for the first time, take notes on aspects of the story you find difficult or puzzling. Read the story a second time. Now write about the experience. What uncertainties were resolved when you read the story the second time? What, if any, uncertainties remain? What has this experience taught you about reading fiction?
5. Choose two stories that treat a similar theme. Compare and contrast the stance each story takes toward that theme, marshalling quotations and specifics as necessary to back up your argument.
6. Browse through newspapers and magazines for a story with the elements of good fiction. Now rewrite the story *as* fiction. Then write a one-page accompanying essay explaining the challenges of the task. What did it teach you about the relative natures of journalism and fiction?

43 WRITING ABOUT A POEM

> *I love being a writer.*
> *What I can't stand is the paperwork.*
>
> —PETER DE VRIES

Many readers—even some enthusiastic ones—are wary of poems. "I don't know anything about poetry," some people say, if the subject arises. While poems aren't booby traps designed to trip up careless readers, it is true that poetry demands a special level of concentration. Poetry is language at its most intense and condensed, and in a good poem, every word counts. With practice, though, anyone can become a more confident reader—and critic—of poetry. Remember that the purpose of poetry isn't intimidation but wisdom and pleasure. Even writing a paper on poetry can occasion a certain enjoyment. Here are some tips.

- **Choose a poem that speaks to you.** Let pleasure be your guide in choosing the poem you write about. The act of writing is easier if your feelings are engaged. Write about something you dislike and don't understand, and your essay will be as dismal to read as it was for you to write. But write about something that interests you, and your essay will communicate that interest and enthusiasm.

- **Allow yourself time to get comfortable with your subject.** As most professors will tell you, when students try to fudge their way through a paper on a topic they don't fully understand, the lack of comfort shows, making for muddled, directionless prose. The more familiar you become with a poem, however, the easier and more pleasurable it will be to write about it. Expect to read the poem several times over before its meaning becomes clear. Better still, reread it over the course of several days.

READ ACTIVELY

A poem differs from most prose in that it should be read slowly, carefully, and attentively. Good poems yield more if read twice, and the best poems—after ten, twenty, or even thirty readings—keep on yielding. Here are some suggestions to enhance your reading of a poem you plan to write about.

■ **Read the poem aloud.** There is no better way to understand a poem than to effectively read it aloud. Read slowly, paying attention to punctuation cues. Listen for the audio effects.

■ **Read closely and painstakingly, annotating as you go.** Keep your mind (and your pencil) sharp and ready. The subtleties of language are essential to a poem. Pay attention to the connotations or suggestions of words, and to the rhythm of phrases and lines. Underline words and images that jump out at you. Use arrows to link phrases that seem connected. Highlight key passages or take notes in the margins as ideas or questions occur to you.

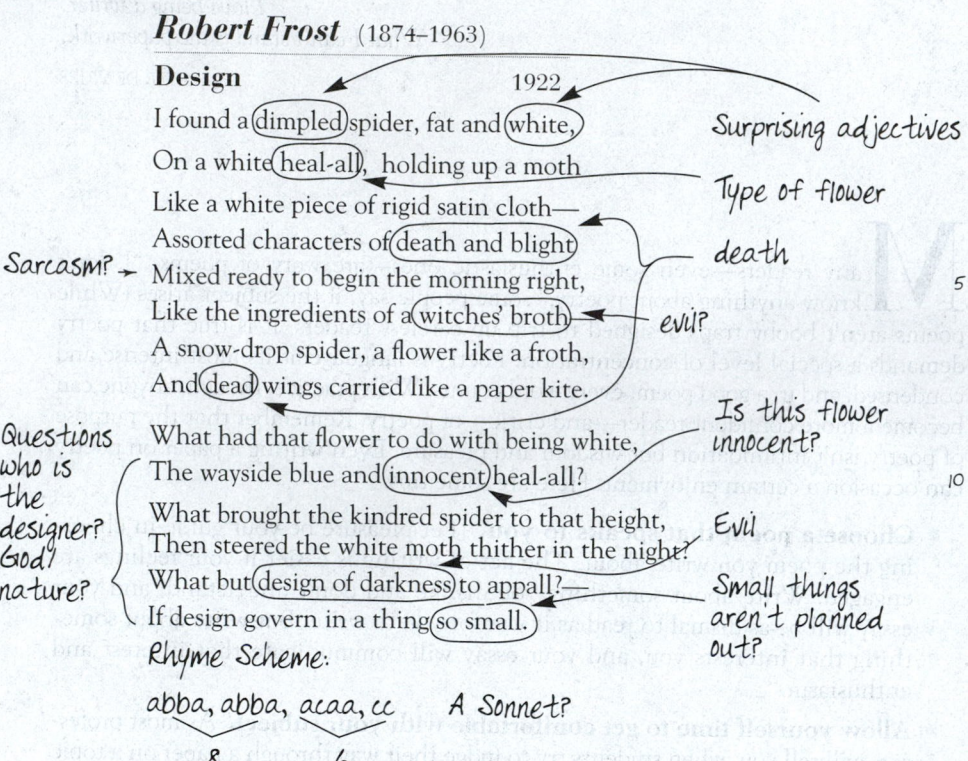

Robert Frost (1874–1963)

Design 1922

I found a (dimpled) spider, fat and (white,) — Surprising adjectives
On a white (heal-all,) holding up a moth — Type of flower
Like a white piece of rigid satin cloth—
Assorted characters of (death and blight) — death
Sarcasm? → Mixed ready to begin the morning right, 5
Like the ingredients of a (witches' broth) — evil?
A snow-drop spider, a flower like a froth,
And (dead) wings carried like a paper kite.

What had that flower to do with being white, — Is this flower innocent?
Questions who is the designer? God? nature? { The wayside blue and (innocent) heal-all? 10
What brought the kindred spider to that height, — Evil
Then steered the white moth thither in the night?
What but (design of darkness) to appall?— — Small things aren't planned out?
If design govern in a thing (so small.)

Rhyme Scheme:

abba, abba, acaa, cc   A Sonnet?

8   6

■ **Look up any unfamiliar words, allusions, or references.** Often the very words you may be tempted to skim over will provide the key to a poem's meaning. Thomas Hardy's "The Ruined Maid" will remain elusive to a reader unfamiliar with the archaic meaning of the word "ruin"—a woman's loss of virginity to a man other than her husband. Similarly, be sure to acquaint yourself with any references or allusions that appear in a poem. H. D.'s poem "Helen" will make sense only to readers who are familiar with the story of Helen of Troy.

THINK ABOUT THE POEM

Before you begin writing, take some time to collect your thoughts. The following steps can be useful in thinking about a poem.

- **Let your emotions guide you into the poem.** Do any images or phrases call up a strong emotional response? If so, try to puzzle out why those passages seem so emotionally loaded. In a word or two, describe the poem's tone.

- **Determine what's literally happening in the poem.** Separating literal language from figurative or symbolic language can be one of the trickiest—and most essential—tasks in poetic interpretation. Begin by working out the literal. Who is speaking the poem? To whom? Under what circumstances? What happens in the poem?

- **Ask what it all adds up to.** Once you've pinned down the literal action of the poem, it's time to take a leap into the figurative. What is the significance of the poem? Address symbolism, any figures of speech, and any language that means one thing literally but suggests something else. In "My Papa's Waltz," for example, Theodore Roethke tells a simple story of a father dancing his small son around a kitchen. The language of the poem suggests much more, however, implying that while the father is rough to the point of violence, the young boy hungers for his attention.

- **Consider the poem's shape on the page, and the way it sounds.** What patterns of sound do you notice? Are the lines long, short, or a mixture of both? How do these elements contribute to the poem's effect?

- **Pay attention to form.** If a poem makes use of rime or regular meter, ask yourself how those elements contribute to its meaning. If it is in a fixed form, such as a sonnet or villanelle, how do the demands of that form serve to set its tone? If the form calls for repetition—of sounds, words, or entire lines—how does that repetition underscore the poem's message? If, on the other hand, the poem is in free verse—without a consistent pattern of rime or regular meter—how does this choice affect the poem's feel?

- **Take note of line breaks.** If the poem is written in free verse, pay special attention to its line breaks. Poets break their lines with care, conscious that readers pause momentarily over the last word in any line, giving that word special emphasis. Notice whether the lines tend to be broken at the ends of whole phrases and sentences or in the middle of phrases. Then ask yourself what effect is created by the poet's choice of line breaks. How does that effect contribute to the poem's meaning?

PREWRITING: DISCOVER YOUR IDEAS

Now that you have thought the poem through, it's time to let your ideas crystallize on the page (or screen). One or more of the following prewriting exercises could help you collect your thoughts.

- **Brainstorm.** With the poem in front of you, jot down every single thing you can think of about it. Write quickly, without worrying about the value of your thoughts; you can sort that out later. Brainstorming works best if you set a time limit of ten or fifteen minutes and force yourself to keep working until the time is up, even if you feel as though you've said it all. A new idea might surprise you after you thought you were done. A list that results from brainstorming on "Design" might look something like this:

> white spider
> heal-all/flower
> dead moth like a kite
> white = innocence?
> death/blight
> begin the morning right=oddly cheerful
> irony
> witches' broth/scary
> white = strangeness
> heal-all usually blue
> flower doesn't heal all
> design = God or nature
> design of darkness = the devil?
> maybe no design (no God?)
> God doesn't govern small things

■ **Cluster.** If you are a visual thinker, you might find yourself drawn to clustering as a way to explore the relationship among your ideas. Begin by writing your subject at the center of a sheet of paper. Circle it. Then write ideas as they occur to you, drawing lines linking each new idea to ones that seem related. Here is an example of clustering on "Design."

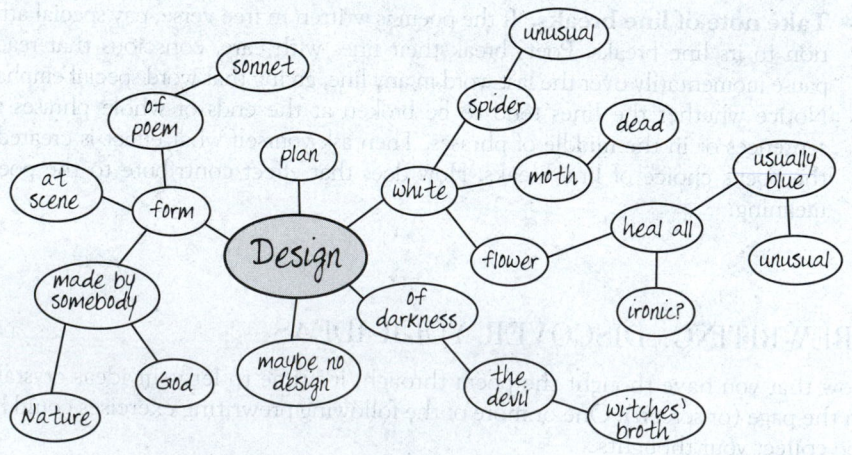

- **List.** Make a list of information that seems useful. Feel free to add notes that will help you to remember what you meant by each item. Headings can help you to organize related concepts. A list might look like this:

<u>Odd Coincidence</u>
white spider
white flower (not blue,
    innocent)
white moth (stiff, dead)
characters of death/blight
morning (hopeful) = ironic
witches' broth

<u>Questions</u>
Accidental or by design?
Whose design?
Nature or God?
Does God care?

<u>Form of Poem</u>
sonnet (strict, orderly)
form of universe =
    not so orderly?

- **Freewrite.** Another approach to generating ideas is to let your thoughts pour out onto the page. To freewrite, give yourself a time limit; fifteen or twenty minutes will work well. Then write, without stopping to think, for that whole time. Keep your hand moving. Don't worry about grammar or spelling or even logic; your task is to come up with fresh ideas that might evade you if you were writing more cautiously. Keep writing even (or especially) if you run out of ideas. New and surprising thoughts sometimes arrive when we least expect them. Here is a sample of freewriting on "Design."

> The scene seems strange. Spiders aren't usually white, and heal-alls are supposed to be blue. Moths are white, but this one is described as being like a rigid satin cloth or a paper kite. It's dead, which is why it is rigid, but the images seem to focus on its stiffness—its deadness—in a creepy way. The poet seems surprised at all this whiteness. Whiteness usually represents innocence, but here he says the flower would ordinarily be blue and innocent, so maybe it's not innocent now? I think he's saying this is a kind of deathly pageant; he calls the three things assorted characters though a flower can't be a character. The second part of the poem is all questions, no answers. What does he mean by "design of darkness"?
>
> Design seems to mean plan. It sounds like he's saying something sinister is going on. Like someone (God?) put the scene there for a purpose, maybe for him to notice. But then he seems to say no, God doesn't care about small things which maybe means he doesn't care about us either. I just noticed that this poem is (I think) a sonnet. It has rime and fourteen lines. It seems funny that a poem about there being no order to the universe is written in such a strict form.

- **Journal.** A journal of your reactions to the works you read can be an excellent place to look for raw material for more formal writing. If your instructor has assigned such a journal, page through to remind yourself of your first reactions to a poem you plan to write about.

■ **Outline.** To think through your argument before you begin to flesh it out, make an outline (a list of points arranged in a logical order). Not all writers work from outlines, but some find them indispensable. Here is a sample outline.

1. Italian sonnet (define)
    two parts
    octave draws picture
    sestet asks questions
2. Rime
    "ite" sound stresses whiteness
3. Sonnet form = order
    poem's subject = order
    irony/no order in universe
4. Design of poem is unpredictable
    looks orderly but isn't
5. Design of universe is unpredictable

WRITE A ROUGH DRAFT

When your prewriting work has given you a sense of direction, you will be ready to begin forming your thoughts and writing a first draft of your essay. Reread the section "Develop a Literary Argument" on page 1897 for help getting started.

■ **Review your purpose and audience.** Begin by referring back to the exact assignment you have been given. No matter how crystal clear your prose or intriguing your ideas, an essay that fails to respond to the assignment is likely to fall flat. As you begin your first draft, consider how best to focus your essay to fulfill the instructor's requirements. Whatever the assignment, you need to keep your purpose in mind as you write. You also need to consider your audience's needs, whether that audience is your professor, your fellow students, or some other hypothetical set of readers.

■ **Define your thesis.** To keep you focused on the task at hand, and to signal your intentions to your reader, you will need, first of all, to come up with a thesis. Like the rest of your first draft, that thesis sentence can be rough around the edges; you can refine it later in the process. For now, though, the thesis gives you something to work toward. You need to make a decisive statement that offers an insight that isn't entirely obvious about the work under discussion. In the final paper your task will be to convince readers that your thesis is sound. Here is a working thesis sentence for an analytical essay on Frost's poem "Design."

WORKING THESIS

The poem "Design" both is and isn't formal.

This rough thesis defines the essay's focus—the poem's form. But the statement is still very vague. A later, sharper version will clarify the idea, and show what the author means by the claim that the poem both is and isn't formal. The revision also will push this idea further by connecting the poem's form to its meaning.

> **REVISED THESIS**
>
> Although Frost's sonnet "Design" is a well-designed formal poem, the conclusions it presents are not predictable but both surprising and disturbing.

In its revised form, this thesis makes a stronger and more specific claim. Because the revision says something specific about how the poem works, it is more compelling than the vaguer original.

- **Supply evidence to prove your point.** Once you've settled on a working thesis, your next task is to decide what evidence will best prove your point. Be sure to quote from the poem to back up each point you make; there is no evidence more convincing than the poem itself.

- **Organize your argument.** You will need to make clear what each bit of evidence illustrates. Connect your argument back to the thesis as often as it takes to clarify your line of reasoning for the reader.

- **Concentrate on getting your ideas onto the page.** Later you will go back in and revise, making your prose clearer and more elegant. At that point, you can add information that seems to be missing, and discard passages that seem beside the point. For now, though, the goal is to spell out your argument while it is clear in your mind.

CHECKLIST: Writing a Rough Draft

- ☐ What is your assignment? Does the essay fulfill it?
- ☐ Who is your audience?
- ☐ What is your thesis?
- ☐ Is your thesis thought-provoking rather than obvious?
- ☐ Have you provided evidence to support your thesis?
- ☐ Does anything in your essay undercut your thesis?
- ☐ Have you quoted from the poem? Would more quotations strengthen your argument?
- ☐ Is your argument organized in a logical way?

REVISE YOUR DRAFT

- **Have a reader review your paper.** Once you have completed your rough draft, consider enlisting the aid of a reader, professional (a writing center tutor) or otherwise (a trusted friend). The author of the paragraph below used her instructor's comments to improve her paper's introduction.

DRAFT OF OPENING PARAGRAPH

Robert Frost's poem "Design" is an Italian sonnet, a form that divides its argument into two parts, an octave and a sestet. The octave, or first part of the poem, concentrates on telling the reader about a peculiar scene the poet has noticed: a white spider holding a dead moth on a white flower. The sestet, or second part of the poem, asks what the scene means. It doesn't really provide any answers.

Good start. I'm glad you're thinking about the poem's form. How does the form suit the content?

Does it hint at answers? Be more specific.

Add a little more. Is the scene significant? How so?

REVISED OPENING PARAGRAPH

For Robert Frost's poem "Design," the sonnet form has at least two advantages. As in most Italian sonnets, the poem's argument falls into two parts. In the octave Frost's persona draws a still life of a spider, a flower, and a moth; then in the sestet he contemplates the meaning of his still life. The sestet focuses on a universal: the possible existence of a vindictive deity who causes the spider to catch the moth and, no doubt, also causes—when viewed anthropomorphically—other suffering.

To see this essay in its entirety, turn to page 1951. (It's worth noting that while the thesis sentence often appears in an essay's first paragraph, this paper takes a different tack. The first paragraph introduces the essay's focus—the benefits of the sonnet form for this particular poem—then builds carefully toward its thesis, which appears in the last paragraph.)

■ **Make your argument more specific.** Use specifics instead of generalities in describing the poem. Writing imprecisely or vaguely, favoring the abstract over the concrete, is a common problem for student writers. When discussing ideas or principles, you can communicate more fully to your reader by supplying specific examples of those ideas or principles in action, as this student did when she reworked the ending of the paragraph above.

■ **Make your language fresh and accurate.** It is easy to fall into habitual expressions, especially to overuse a few convenient words. Mechanical language may tempt you to think of the poem in mechanical terms. Here, for instance is a plodding discussion of Frost's "Design":

DRAFT

The symbols Frost uses in "Design" are very successful. Frost makes the spider stand for Nature. He wants us to see nature as blind and cruel. He also employs good sounds. He uses a lot of *i*'s because he is trying to make you think of falling rain.

What's wrong with this "analysis"? The underscored words are worth questioning here. While understandable, the words *employs* and *uses* seem to lead the writer to see Frost only as a conscious tool-manipulator. To be sure, Frost in a sense "uses" symbols, but did he grab hold of them and lay them into his poem? For all we know, perhaps the symbols arrived quite unbidden and used the poet. To write a good poem, Frost maintained, a poet himself has to be surprised. (How, by the way, can we hope to know what a poet *wants* to do? And there isn't much point in saying that the poet is *trying* to do something. He has already done it, if he has written a good poem.) At least it is likely that Frost didn't plan to fulfill a certain quota of *i*-sounds. Writing his poem, not by following a blueprint but probably by bringing it slowly to the surface of his mind, Frost no doubt had enough to do without trying to engineer the reactions of his possible audience. Like all true symbols, Frost's spider doesn't *stand for* anything. The writer would be closer to the truth to say that the spider *suggests* or *reminds us* of nature or of certain forces in the natural world. (Symbols just hint; they don't indicate.)

After the student discussed the paper in a conference with her instructor, she rewrote her sentences:

REVISION

The symbols in Frost's "Design" are highly effective. The spider, for instance, suggests the blindness and cruelty of Nature. Frost's word-sounds, too, are part of the meaning of his poem, for the *i*'s remind the reader of falling rain.

Not every reader of "Design" will hear rain falling, but the student's revision probably comes closer to describing the experience of the poem most of us know.

■ **Be clear and precise.** Another very real pitfall of writing literary criticism is the temptation to write in official-sounding Critic Speak. Writers who aren't quite sure about what to say may try to compensate for this uncertainty with unnecessarily ornate sentences that don't say much of anything. Other times, they will begin a sentence and find themselves completely entangled in its structure, unable to make a perfectly sound idea clear to the reader. Should you feel yourself being tugged out to sea by an undertow of fancy language, here is a trick for getting back ashore: speak your ideas aloud, in the simplest terms possible, to a friend, or a tape recorder, or your mirror. When you've formulated your idea simply and clearly, write down your exact words. Most likely, your instructor will be grateful for the resulting clarity of expression.

CHECKLIST: Revising Your Draft

- ☐ Is your thesis clear and decisive?
- ☐ Does all your evidence advance your argument?
- ☐ Is information presented in the most logical order?
- ☐ Could your prose be clearer? More precise? More specific?
- ☐ Do transitional words and phrases signal movement from one idea to the next?

☐ Does your introduction draw the reader in? Does it prepare him or her for what follows?

☐ Does your conclusion tie up the essay's loose ends?

☐ Does each paragraph include a topic sentence?

☐ Does your title give a sense of the essay's subject?

COMMON APPROACHES TO WRITING ABOUT POETRY

Explication

In an **explication** (literally "an unfolding"), a writer explains an entire poem in detail, unraveling its complexities. An explication, however, should not be confused with a paraphrase, which puts the poem's literal meaning into plain prose. While an explication might include some paraphrasing, it does more than simply restate. It explains a poem, in great detail, showing how each part contributes to the whole. In writing an explication, keep the following tips in mind:

■ **Start with the poem's first line, and keep working straight through to the end.** As needed, though, you can take up points out of order.

■ **Read closely, addressing the poem's details.** You may choose to include allusions, the denotations or connotations of words, the possible meanings of symbols, the effects of certain sounds and rhythms and formal elements (rime schemes, for instance), the sense of any statements that contain irony, and other particulars.

■ **Show how each part of the poem contributes to the meaning of the whole.** Your explication should go beyond dissecting the pieces of a poem; it should also integrate them to cast light on the poem in its entirety.

Here is a successful student-authored explication of Frost's "Design." The assignment was to explain whatever in the poem seemed most essential, in not more than 750 words.

Jasper 1

Ted Jasper

Professor Koss

English 130

21 November 2009

An Unfolding of Robert Frost's "Design"

Interesting opening. Quotes author

Central question raised

"I always wanted to be very observing," Robert Frost once told an audience, after reading aloud his poem "Design." Then he added, "But I have always been afraid of my own observations" (qtd. in Cook 126–27). What could Frost have observed that could scare him? Let's examine the poem in question and see what we discover.

Jasper 2

Starting with the title, "Design," any reader of this poem will find it full of meaning. As the *Merriam-Webster Dictionary* defines *design,* the word can denote among other things a plan, purpose, or intention ("Design"). Some arguments for the existence of God (I remember from Sunday School) are based on the "argument from design": that because the world shows a systematic order, there must be a Designer who made it. But the word *design* can also mean "a deliberate undercover project or scheme" such as we attribute to a "designing person" ("Design"). As we shall see, Frost's poem incorporates all of these meanings. His poem raises the old philosophic question of whether there is a Designer, an evil Designer, or no Designer at all.

Like many other sonnets, "Design" is divided into two parts. The first eight lines draw a picture centering on the spider, who at first seems almost jolly. It is *dimpled* and *fat* like a baby, or Santa Claus. The spider stands on a wildflower whose name, *heal-all,* seems ironic: a heal-all is supposed to cure any disease, but this flower has no power to restore life to the dead moth. (Later, in line ten, we learn that the heal-all used to be blue. Presumably, it has died and become bleached-looking.) In the second line we discover, too, that the spider has hold of another creature, a dead moth. We then see the moth described with an odd simile in line three: "Like a white piece of rigid satin cloth." Suddenly, the moth becomes not a creature but a piece of fabric—lifeless and dead—and yet *satin* has connotations of beauty. Satin is a luxurious material used in rich formal clothing, such as coronation gowns and brides' dresses. Additionally, there is great accuracy in the word: the smooth and slightly plush surface of satin is like the powder-smooth surface of moths' wings. But this "cloth," rigid and white, could be the lining to Dracula's coffin.

In the fifth line an invisible hand enters. The characters are "mixed" like ingredients in an evil potion. Some force doing the mixing is behind the scene. The characters in themselves are innocent enough, but when brought together, their whiteness and look of *rigor mortis* are overwhelming. There is something diabolical in the spider's feast. The "morning right" echoes the word *rite,* a ritual—in this case apparently a Black Mass or a Witches' Sabbath. The simile in line seven ("a flower like a froth") is more ambiguous and harder to describe. Froth is white, foamy, and delicate—something found on a brook in the woods or on a beach after a wave recedes. However, in the natural world, froth also can be ugly: the foam on a polluted stream or a rabid dog's mouth. The dualism in nature—its beauty and its horror—is there in that one simile.

Defines key word. Sets up theme

Topic sentence on significance of title

Begins line-by-line unfolding of meaning

Discusses images

Explores language

Refers to sound

Jasper 3

Transition words

Quotes secondary source

Discusses theme

So far, the poem has portrayed a small, frozen scene, with the dimpled killer holding its victim as innocently as a boy holds a kite. Already, Frost has hinted that Nature may be, as Radcliffe Squires suggests, "Nothing but an ash-white plain without love or faith or hope, where ignorant appetites cross by chance" (87). Now, in the last six lines of the sonnet, Frost comes out and directly states his theme. What else could bring these deathly pale, stiff things together "but design of darkness to appall"? The question is clearly rhetorical; we are meant to answer, "Yes, there does seem to be an evil design at work here!" I take the next-to-last line to mean, "What except a design so dark and sinister that we're appalled by it?" "Appall," by the way, is the second pun in the poem: it sounds like *a pall* or shroud. (The

Defines key word

derivation of *appall*, according to *Merriam-Webster*, is ultimately from a Latin word meaning "to be pale"—an interesting word choice for a poem full of pale white images ["Appall"].) *Steered* carries the suggestion of a steering-wheel or rudder that some pilot had to control. Like the word *brought*, it implies that some invisible force charted the paths of spider, heal-all, and moth, so that they arrived together.

Answers question raised in introduction

Conclusion

Having suggested that the universe is in the hands of that sinister force (an indifferent God? Fate? the Devil?), Frost adds a note of doubt. The Bible tells us that "His eye is on the sparrow," but at the moment the poet doesn't seem sure. Maybe, he hints, when things in the universe drop below a certain size, they pass completely out of the Designer's notice. When creatures are this little, maybe God doesn't bother to govern them but just lets them run wild. And possibly the same mindless chance is all that governs human lives. And because this is even more senseless than having an angry God intent on punishing us, it is, Frost suggests, the worst suspicion of all.

Jasper 4

Works Cited

"Appall." *Merriam-Webster Online Dictionary*. Merriam-Webster, 2009. Web. 13
    November 2009.

Cook, Reginald. *Robert Frost: A Living Voice*. Amherst: U of Massachusetts
    P, 1974. Print.

"Design." *Merriam-Webster Online Dictionary*. Merriam-Webster, 2009. Web.
    11 November 2009.

Frost, Robert. "Design." *Collected Poems, Prose and Plays*. New York: Library
    of America, 1995. 275. Print.

Squires, Radcliffe. *The Major Themes of Robert Frost*. Ann Arbor: U of Michigan
    P, 1963. Print.

This excellent paper finds something worth unfolding in every line of Frost's poem, without seeming mechanical. Although the student proceeds sequentially through the poem from the title to the last line, he takes up some points out of order, when it serves his purpose. In paragraph two, for example, he looks ahead to the poem's ending and briefly states its main theme in order to relate it to the poem's title. In the third paragraph, he explicates the poem's later image of the heal-all, relating it to the first image. He also comments on the poem's form ("Like many other sonnets"), on its similes and puns, and on its denotations and connotations.

This paper also demonstrates good use of manuscript form, following the *MLA Handbook,* 7th ed. Brief references (in parentheses) tell us where the writer found Frost's remarks and give the page number for his quotation from the book by Radcliffe Squires. At the end of the paper, a list of works cited uses abbreviations that the *MLA Handbook* recommends.

A Critic's Explication of Frost's "Design"

It might seem that to work through a poem line by line is a mechanical task, and yet there can be genuine excitement in doing so. Randall Jarrell once wrote an explication of "Design" in which he managed to convey just such excitement. See if you can sense Jarrell's joy in writing about the poem.

> Frost's details are so diabolically good that it seems criminal to leave some unremarked; but notice how *dimpled, fat,* and *white* (all but one; all but one) come from our regular description of any baby; notice how the *heal-all,* because of its name, is the one flower in all the world picked to be the altar for this Devil's Mass; notice how *holding up* the moth brings something ritual and hieratic, a ghostly, ghastly formality, to this priest

and its sacrificial victim; notice how terrible to the fingers, how full of the stilling rigor of death, that *white piece of rigid satin cloth* is. And *assorted characters of death and blight* is, like so many things in this poem, sharply ambiguous: *a mixed bunch of actors* or *diverse representative signs*. The tone of the phrase *assorted characters of death and blight* is beautifully developed in the ironic Breakfast-Club-calisthenics, Radio-Kitchen heartiness of *mixed ready to begin the morning right* (which assures us, so unreassuringly, that this isn't any sort of Strindberg *Spook Sonata*, but hard fact), and concludes in the *ingredients* of the witches' broth, giving the soup a sort of cuddly shimmer that the cauldron in *Macbeth* never had; the *broth*, even, is brought to life—we realize that witches' broth *is* broth, to be supped with a long spoon.[1]

Evidently, Jarrell's cultural interests are broad: ranging from August Strindberg's ground-breaking modern play down to *The Breakfast Club* (a once-popular radio program that cheerfully exhorted its listeners to march around their tables). And yet breadth of knowledge, however much it deepens and enriches Jarrell's writing, isn't all that he brings to the reading of poetry. For him an explication isn't a dull plod, but a voyage of discovery. His prose—full of figures of speech (*diabolically good, cuddly shimmer*)—conveys the apparent delight he takes in showing off his findings. Such a joy, of course, can't be acquired deliberately. But it can grow, the more you read and study poetry.

Analysis

Like a news commentator's analysis of a crisis in the Middle East or a chemist's analysis of an unknown fluid, an **analysis** separates a poem into elements as a means to understanding that subject. Usually, the writer of an analysis focuses on one particular element: "Imagery of Light and Darkness in Frost's 'Design'" or "The Character of Satan in Milton's *Paradise Lost*." In this book, you probably already have encountered a few brief analyses: the discussion of connotations in John Masefield's "Cargoes" (pages 699–700), for instance, or the examination of symbols in T. S. Eliot's "The Boston Evening Transcript" (page 853). In fact, most of the discussions in this book are analyses. To write an analysis, remember two key points:

- ■ **Focus on a single, manageable element of a poem.** Some possible choices are tone, irony, literal meaning, imagery, figures of speech, sound, rhythm, theme, and symbolism.

- ■ **Show how this element of the poem contributes to the meaning of the whole.** While no element of a poem exists apart from all the others, by taking a closer look at one particular aspect of the poem, you can see the whole more clearly.

The paper that follows analyzes a particularly tricky subject—the formal and technical elements of Frost's "Design." Long analyses of metrical feet, rime schemes, and indentations can make for ponderous reading, but this paper proves that formal analysis can be interesting and can cast light on a poem in its entirety.

[1] *Poetry and the Age* (New York: Knopf, 1953), 42–43.

Lopez 1

Guadalupe Lopez
Professor Faber
English 210
16 April 2009

The Design of Robert Frost's "Design"

For Robert Frost's poem "Design," the sonnet form has at least two
advantages. As in most Italian sonnets, the poem's argument falls into two
parts. In the octave Frost's persona draws a still life of a spider, a flower, and a
moth; then in the sestet he contemplates the meaning of his still life. Although
the poem is perfectly formal in its shape, the ideas it presents are not
predictable, but are instead both surprising and disturbing. The sestet focuses
on a universal: the possible existence of a vindictive deity who causes the
spider to catch the moth and, no doubt, also causes—when viewed
anthropomorphically—other suffering.

Frost's persona weaves his own little web. The unwary audience is led
through the poem's argument from its opening "story" to a point at which
something must be made of the story's symbolic significance. Even the rhyme
scheme contributes to the poem's successful leading of the audience toward the
sestet's theological questioning. The word *white* ends the first line of the sestet,
and the same vowel sound is echoed in the lines that follow. All in all, half of
the sonnet's lines end in the "ite" sound, as if to render significant the
wh*ite*ness—the symbolic innocence—of nature's representation of a greater
truth.

A sonnet has a familiar design, and the poem's classical form points to
the thematic concern that there seems to be an order to the universe that
might be perceived by looking at even seemingly insignificant natural events.
The sonnet must follow certain conventions, and nature, though not as
readily apprehensible as a poetic form, is apparently governed by a set of
laws. There is a ready-made irony in Frost's choosing such an order-driven
form to meditate on whether or not there is any order in the universe.
However, whether or not his questioning sestet is actually approaching an
answer or, indeed, the answer, Frost has approached an order that seems to
echo a larger order in his using the sonnet form. An approach through poetic
form and substance is itself significant in Frost's own estimation, for Frost
argues that what a poet achieves in writing poetry is "a momentary stay against
confusion" (777).

Introduction gives overview of poem's form.

Thesis sentence

Topic sentence on how poem subtly makes its point

Topic sentence on how form relates to theme

Lopez 2

Although design clearly governs in this poem—in this "thing so small"—
the design is not entirely predictable. The poem does start out in the form of an
Italian sonnet, relying on only two rhyming sounds. However, unlike an Italian
sonnet, one of the octave's rhyming sounds—the "ite"—continues into the sestet.
And additionally, "Design" ends in a couplet, much in the manner of the
Shakespearean sonnet, which frequently offers, in the final couplet, a summing
up of the sonnet's argument. Perhaps not only nature's "story" of the spider,
the flower, and the moth but also Frost's poem itself echoes the larger universe.

Conclusion   It looks perfectly orderly until the details are given their due.

Lopez 3

Work Cited

Frost, Robert. "The Figure a Poem Makes." *Collected Poems, Prose and Plays*. New
    York: Library of America, 1995. 776–78. Print.

Comparison and Contrast

The process of **comparison** and **contrast** places two poems side by side and studies their
differences and similarities in order to shed light on both works. Writing an effective
comparison-contrast paper involves the following steps:

- **Pair two poems with much in common.** Comparing two poems with surface
  similarities—for example, Dorothy Parker's caustic "Résumé" and Ben Jonson's
  profoundly elegiac "On My First Son"—can be a futile endeavor. Though both
  poems are about death, the two seem hopelessly removed from each other in
  diction, tone, complexity, and scope. Instead, choose two poems with enough in
  common that their differences take on interesting weight.

- **Point to further, unsuspected resemblances.** Steer clear of the obvious
  ("'Design' and 'Wing-Spread' are both about bugs"). The interesting resemblances take some thought to discover.

- **Show noteworthy differences.** Avoid those your reader will see without any
  help.

- **Carefully consider your essay's organization.** While you may be tempted to
  discuss first one poem and then the other, this simple structure may weaken your

essay if it leads you to keep the two poems in total isolation from the other. After all, the point is to see what can be learned by comparison. There is nothing wrong in discussing all of poem A first, then discussing poem B—if in discussing B you keep referring back to A. Another strategy is to do a point-by-point comparison of the two poems all the way through your paper—dealing first, perhaps, with their themes, then with their central metaphors, and finally, with their respective merits.

A comparison-contrast essay is often a kind of analysis—a study of a theme common to two poems, perhaps, or of two poets' similar fondness for the myth of Eden. In some cases, though, a comparison can also involve evaluation—a judgment on the relative worth of two poems. Here, for example, is a poem by Abbie Huston Evans, followed by a paper that considers the merits of that poem and Frost's "Design." Through comparison and contrast, this student makes a case for his view of which poet deserves the brighter laurels.

Abbie Huston Evans (1881–1983)

Wing-Spread   1938

The midge spins out to safety
Through the spider's rope;
But the moth, less lucky,
Has to grope.

Mired in glue-like cable   5
See him foundered swing
By the gap he opened
With his wing,

Dusty web enlacing
All that blue and beryl.   10
In a netted universe
Wing-spread is peril.

Munjee 1

Tom Munjee

Professor Mickey

English 110

21 October 2009

"Wing-Spread" Does a Dip

    Abbie Huston Evans's "Wing-Spread" is an effective short poem, but it lacks the complexity and depth of Robert Frost's "Design." These two poems were published only two years apart, and both present a murderous spider and an unlucky moth, but Frost's treatment differs from Evans's approach in at least

Thesis sentence

Argument summary

two important ways. First, Frost uses poetic language more evocatively than Evans. Second, "Design" digs more deeply into the situation to uncover a more memorable theme.

Textual evidence—contrasts diction of 2 poems

If we compare the language of the two poems, we find "Design" is full of words and phrases rich with suggestions. The language of "Wing-Spread," by comparison, seems thinner. Frost's "dimpled spider, fat and white," for example, is certainly a more suggestive description. Actually, Evans does not describe her spider; she just says, "the spider's rope." (Evans does vividly show the spider and moth in action. In Frost's poem, they are already dead and petrified.) In "Design," the spider's dimples show that it is like a chubby little baby. This seems an odd way to look at a spider, but it is more original than Evans's conventional view (although I like her word *cable*, suggesting that the spider's web is a kind of high-tech food trap). Frost's word choice—his repetition of *white*—paints a more striking scene than Evans's slightly vague "All that blue and beryl." Except for her brief personification of the moth in the second stanza, Evans hardly uses any figures of speech, and even this one is not a clear personification—she simply gives the moth a sex by referring to it as "him." Frost's striking metaphors, similes, and even puns (*right*, *appall*) show him, as usual, to be a master of figures of speech. He calls the moth's wings "satin cloth" and "a paper kite"; Evans just refers in line 8 to a moth's wing. As far as the language of the two poems goes, we might as well compare a vase brimming with flowers and a single flower stuck in a vase. In fairness to Evans, I would say that her poem, while lacking complexity, still makes its point effectively. Her poem has powerful sounds: short lines with the riming words coming at us again and again.

Contrasts thematic approach

In theme, however, "Wing-Spread" seems much more narrow than "Design." The first time I read Evans's poem, all I felt was: Ho hum, the moth's wings were too wide and got stuck. The second time I read it, I realized that she was saying something with a universal application. This message comes out in line 11, in "a netted universe." That metaphorical phrase is the most interesting part of her poem. *Netted* makes me imagine the universe as being full of nets rigged by someone who is fishing for us. Maybe, like Frost, Evans sees an evil plan operating. She does not, though, investigate it. She says that the midge escapes because it is tiny. On the other hand, things with wide wing-spreads get stuck. Her theme as I read it is, "Be small and inconspicuous if you want to survive," or maybe, "Isn't it too bad that in this world the big beautiful types crack up and die, while the little puny punks keep sailing?" Now, this is a

Munjee 3

valuable idea. I have often thought that very same thing myself. But Frost's
closing note ("If design govern in a thing so small") is really devastating
because it raises a huge uncertainty. "Wing-Spread" leaves us with not
much besides a moth stuck in a web and a moral. In both language and
theme, "Design" climbs to a higher altitude.

*Conclusion
restates thesis*

Munjee 4

Works Cited

Evans, Abbie Huston. "Wing-Spread." *Literature: An Introduction to Fiction,
    Poetry, Drama, and Writing.* Ed. X. J. Kennedy and Dana Gioia. 11th ed.
    New York: Longman, 2010. 1953. Print.
Frost, Robert. "Design." *Collected Poems, Prose and Plays.* New York: Library of
    America, 1995. 275. Print.

HOW TO QUOTE A POEM

Quoted to illustrate some point, memorable lines can enliven your paper. Carefully
chosen quotations can serve to back up your thesis, or to alert your readers to a
phrase or passage they may have neglected. Quoting poetry accurately, however,
raises certain difficulties you don't face in quoting prose. Poets choose their line
breaks with deliberation, and part of a critic's job is to take those breaks into account.
Here are some guidelines for respecting a poet's line breaks and for making your essay
more polished in the bargain.

- **Quoting a few lines.** If you are quoting fewer than four lines of poetry, transform the passage into prose form, separating each line by a space, diagonal (/),
  and another space. The diagonal (/) indicates your respect for where the poet's
  lines begin and end. Two diagonals (//) signal a new stanza. Do not change the
  poet's capitalization or punctuation. Be sure to identify the line numbers you are
  quoting, as follows:

  > The color white preoccupies Frost. The spider is "fat and white, / On a
  > white heal-all" (1–2), and even the victim moth is pale, too.

■ **Quoting four or more lines.** If you are quoting four or more lines of verse, set them off from your text, and arrange them just as they occur on the page, white space and all. Be sure to identify the lines you are quoting. In general, follow these rules:

- Indent the quotation one inch, or ten spaces, from the left-hand margin.
- Double-space between the quoted lines.
- Type the poem exactly as it appears in the original. You do not need to use quotation marks.
- If you begin the quotation in the middle of a line of verse, position the starting word about where it occurs in the poem—not at the left-hand margin.
- If a line you are quoting runs too long to fit on one line, indent the return one-quarter inch, or three spaces.
- Cite the line numbers you are quoting in parentheses.

> At the end of the poem, the poet asks what deity or fate cursed this
> particular mutant flower
>   with being white,
> The wayside blue and innocent heal-all?
> What brought the kindred spider to that height,
> Then steered the white moth thither in the
>   night? (9–12)

■ **Omitting words.** If you omit words from the lines you quote, indicate the omission with an ellipsis (. . .), as in the following example:

> The color white preoccupies Frost in his description of the spider "fat
> and white, / On a white heal-all . . . / Like a white piece of rigid satin
> cloth" (1–3).

■ **Quoting only a brief phrase.** There's no need for an ellipsis if it is obvious that only a phrase is being quoted.

> The speaker says that he "found a dimpled spider," and he goes on to
> portray it as a kite-flying boy.

■ **Omitting full lines of verse.** If you leave out lines of verse, indicate the omission by spaced periods about the length of a line of the poem you are quoting.

> Maybe, she hints, when things in the universe drop below a certain size,
> they pass completely out of the Designer's notice:
>   The midge spins out to safety
>   Through the spider's rope;
>
>   . . . .
>   In a netted universe
>   Wing-spread is peril. (1–2, 11–12)

One last note: often a paper on a short poem will include the whole text of the poem at its beginning, with the lines numbered so that your reader can refer to it with ease. Ask your instructor whether he or she prefers the full text to be quoted this way.

TOPICS FOR WRITING BRIEF PAPERS (250–500 WORDS)

1. Write a concise *explication* of a short poem of your choice. Concentrate on those facets of the poem that you think most need explaining. (For a sample explication, see page 1946).

2. Write an *analysis* of a short poem, focusing on how a single key element shapes its meaning. (A sample analysis appears on page 1951.) Some possible topics are:

   - Tone in Edna St. Vincent Millay's "Recuerdo"
   - Rime and meter in Edgar Allan Poe's "A Dream Within a Dream"
   - Imagery in Wallace Stevens's "The Emperor of Ice Cream"
   - Kinds of irony in Thomas Hardy's "The Workbox"
   - Theme in W. H. Auden's "Musée des Beaux Arts"
   - Extended metaphor in Langston Hughes's "The Negro Speaks of Rivers" (Explain the one main comparison that the poem makes and show how the whole poem makes it. Other poems that would lend themselves to a paper on extended metaphor include: Emily Dickinson's "Because I could not stop for Death," Robert Frost's "The Silken Tent," Robert Lowell's "Skunk Hour," Adrienne Rich's "Aunt Jennifer's Tigers.")

   (To locate any of these poems, see the Index of Authors and Titles.)

3. Select a poem in which the main speaker is a character who for any reason interests you. You might consider, for instance, Robert Browning's "Soliloquy of the Spanish Cloister," T. S. Eliot's "The Love Song of J. Alfred Prufrock," or Rhina Espaillat's "Bilingual/ Bilingüe." Then write a brief profile of this character, drawing only on what the poem tells you (or reveals). What is the character's approximate age? Situation in life? Attitude toward self? Attitude toward others? General personality? Do you find this character admirable?

4. Choose a brief poem that you find difficult. Write an essay in which you begin by listing the points in the poem that strike you as most impenetrable. Next, reread the poem at least twice. In the essay's second half, describe how multiple readings changed your experience of the poem.

5. Although each of these poems tells a story, what happens in the poem isn't necessarily obvious: E. E. Cummings's "anyone lived in a pretty how town," T. S. Eliot's "The Love Song of J. Alfred Prufrock," Edwin Arlington Robinson's "Luke Havergal," James Wright's "A Blessing." Choose one of these poems, and in a paragraph sum up what you think happens in it. Then in a second paragraph, ask yourself: what, *besides* the element of story, did you consider in order to understand the poem?

6. Imagine a reader who categorically dislikes poetry. Choose a poem for that person to read, and, addressing your skeptical reader, explain the ways in which this particular poem rewards a careful reader.

TOPICS FOR WRITING MORE EXTENDED PAPERS (600–1,000 WORDS)

1. Perform a line-by-line explication of a brief poem of your choice. Imagine that your audience is unfamiliar with the poem and needs your assistance in interpreting it.
2. Explicate a passage from a longer poem. Choose a passage that is, in your opinion, central to the poem's meaning.
3. Compare and contrast any two poems that treat a similar theme. Let your comparison bring you to an evaluation of the poems. Which is the stronger, more satisfying one?
4. Write a comparison-contrast essay on any two or more poems by a single poet. Look for two poems that share a characteristic thematic concern. (This book contains multiple selections by Auden, Blake, Cummings, Dickinson, Donne, Eliot, Frost, Hardy, Hopkins, Hughes, Keats, Shakespeare, Stevens, Tennyson, Whitman, Williams, Wordsworth, Yeats, and many others.) Here are some possible topics:

   - Mortality in the work of John Keats
   - Nature in the poems of William Wordsworth
   - How Emily Dickinson's lyric poems resemble hymns
   - E. E. Cummings's approach to the free-verse line
   - Gerard Manley Hopkins's sonic effects

5. Evaluate by the method of comparison two versions of a poem, one an early draft and one a late draft, or perhaps two translations of the same poem from another language. For parallel versions to work on, see Chapter 27, "Translation."
6. If the previous topic appeals to you, consider this. In 1912, ten years before he published "Design," Robert Frost sent a correspondent this early version:

In White

A dented spider like a snow drop white
On a white Heal-all, holding up a moth
Like a white piece of lifeless satin cloth—
Saw ever curious eye so strange a sight?—
Portent in little, assorted death and blight
Like ingredients of a witches' broth?—
The beady spider, the flower like a froth,
And the moth carried like a paper kite.

What had that flower to do with being white,
The blue prunella every child's delight.
What brought the kindred spider to that height?
(Make we no thesis of the miller's plight.)
What but design of darkness and of night?
Design, design! Do I use the word aright?

Compare "In White" with "Design." In what respects is the finished poem superior?

7. Terry Ehret of Santa Rosa Junior College developed the following assignment:

> Compose your own answer to the question "What is poetry?" You may want to devise original metaphor(s) to define poetry and then develop your essay with examples and explanations. Select at least one poem from the anthology to illustrate your definition.

TOPICS FOR WRITING LONG PAPERS (1,500 WORDS OR MORE)

1. Review an entire poetry collection by a poet featured in this book. You will need to communicate to your reader a sense of the work's style and thematic preoccupations. Finally, make a value judgment about the work's quality.

2. Read five or six poems by a single author. Start with a poet featured in this book, and then find additional poems at the library or on the Internet. Write an analysis of a single element of that poet's work—for example, theme, imagery, diction, or form.

3. Write a line-by-line explication of a poem rich in matters to explain or of a longer poem that offers ample difficulty. While relatively short, John Donne's "A Valediction: Forbidding Mourning" and Gerard Manley Hopkins's "The Windhover" are poems that will take a good bit of time to explicate. Even a short, apparently simple poem such as Robert Frost's "Stopping by Woods on a Snowy Evening" can provide more than enough material to explicate thoughtfully in a longer paper.

4. Write an analysis of a certain theme (or other element) that you find in the work of two or more poets. It is probable that in your conclusion you will want to set the poets' works side by side, comparing or contrasting them, and perhaps making some evaluation. Here are some sample topics to consider:

   • Langston Hughes, Gwendolyn Brooks, and Dudley Randall as Prophets of Social Change
   • What It Is to Be a Woman: The Special Knowledge of Sylvia Plath, Anne Sexton, and Adrienne Rich
   • Popular Culture as Reflected in the Poetry of Wendy Cope, Michael B. Stillman, Gene Fehler, and Charles Martin
   • The Complex Relations Between Fathers and Children in the Poetry of Robert Hayden, Rhina Espaillat, Theodore Roethke, and A. E. Stallings.
   • Making Up New Words for New Meanings: Neologisms in Lewis Carroll and Kay Ryan

5. Apply the ideas in one of the critical excerpts in the "Writing Effectively" section found at the end of each chapter to a poem by the same author. Formulate a thesis about whether or not the prose excerpt sheds any light on the poetry. How do T. S. Eliot's thoughts on the music of poetry, or William Butler Yeats's observations on poetic symbolism, help you to better understand their poems? Quote as needed to back up your argument.

44

WRITING
ABOUT A PLAY

The play was a great success,
but the audience was a total failure.

—OSCAR WILDE

Writing about a play you've read is similar, in many ways, to writing about poetry or fiction. If your subject is a play you have actually seen performed, however, some differences will quickly become apparent. Although, like a story or a poem, a play in print is usually the work of a single author, a play on stage may be the joint effort of seventy or eighty people—actors, director, costumers, set designers, and technicians. Though a play on the page stays fixed and changeless, a play in performance changes in many details from season to season—and even from night to night.

Later in this chapter, you will find some advice on reviewing a performance of a play, as you might do for a class assignment or for publication in a campus newspaper. In a literature course, though, you will probably write about the plays you quietly read and behold only in the theater of your mind.

READ CRITICALLY

- **Read the whole play—not just the dialogue, but also everything in italics, including stage directions and descriptions of settings.** The meaning of a scene, or even of an entire play, may depend on the tone of voice in which an actor is supposed to deliver a significant line. At the end of *A Doll's House,* for example, we need to pay attention to *how* Helmer's last line is spoken—"*A hope flashes across his mind*"—if we are to understand that Nora ignores his last desperate hope for reconciliation when she slams the door emphatically. The meaning of a line may depend upon the actions described in the stage directions. If Nora did not leave the house or slam the door, but hesitated at Helmer's last line, the meaning of the play would be slightly different.

- **Highlight key passages and take notes as you read.** Later you will want to quote or refer to important moments in the play, and marking those moments will simplify your job.

Mrs. Peters (*to the other woman*): Oh, her fruit; it did freeze. (*To the County Attorney*) She worried about that when it turned so cold. She said the fire'd go out and her jars would break.

Sheriff: Well, can you beat the women! Held for murder and worryin' about her preserves.

Both men are insulting toward Mrs. Wright.

County Attorney: I guess before we're through she may have something more serious than preserves to worry about.

He thinks he's being kind.

Hale: Well, women are used to worrying over (trifles.)

Is housework really insignificant?

(*The two women move a little closer together.*)

The women side with each other.

County Attorney (*with the* (gallantry) *of a young politician*): And yet, for all their worries, what would we do without the ladies? ((*The women do not unbend.*)) *He goes to the sink, takes a dipperful of water from the pail and pouring it into a basin, washes his hands. Starts to wipe them on the roller towel, turns it for a cleaner place.*) Dirty towels! (*Kicks his foot against the pans under the sink.*) Not much of a housekeeper, would you say, ladies?

Courtesy toward women, but condescending

The two women aren't buying it.

Mrs. Hale ((stiffly)): There's a great deal of work to be done on a farm.

She holds back, but she's mad.

I don't like this guy!

Small, insignificant things or not?

Play's title. Significant word? The men miss the "clues"—too trifling.

■ **If your subject is a play in verse—such as those by Sophocles and Shakespeare—keep track of act, scene, and line numbers as you take notes.** This will help you to easily relocate any text you want to refer to or quote.

> Iago's hypocrisy is apparent in his speech defending his good name (3.3.108–74).

COMMON APPROACHES TO WRITING ABOUT DRAMA

The methods commonly used to write about fiction and poetry—for example, explication, analysis, or comparison and contrast—are all well suited to writing about drama. These methods are discussed in depth in the chapters "Writing About a

Story" and "Writing About a Poem." Here are a few suggestions for using these methods to write about plays in particular.

Explication

A whole play is too much to cover in an ordinary **explication**, a line-by-line unfolding of meaning in a literary work. In drama, explication is best suited to brief passages—a key soliloquy, for example, or a moment of dialogue that lays bare the play's theme. Closely examining a critical moment in a play can shed light on the play in its entirety. To be successful, an explication needs to concentrate on a brief passage, probably not much more than 20 lines long.

Analysis

A separation of a literary work into elements, **analysis** is a very useful method for writing about drama. To write an analysis, choose a single element in a play—for example, animal imagery in some speeches from *Othello,* or the theme of fragility in *The Glass Menagerie*. Plays certainly offer many choices of elements for analysis: characters, themes, tone, irony, imagery, figures of speech, and symbols, for example. Keep in mind, though, that not all plays contain the same elements you would find in poetry or fiction. Few plays have a narrator, and in most cases the point of view is that of the audience, which perceives the events not through a narrator's eyes but through its own. And while we might analyze a short story's all-pervading style, a play might contain as many styles as there are speaking characters. (Noteworthy exceptions do exist, though: you might argue that in Susan Glaspell's *Trifles,* both main characters speak the same language.) As for traditional poetic devices such as metaphors and metrical patterns, these may be found in plays such as *Othello,* but not in most contemporary plays, in which the dialogue tends to sound like ordinary conversation.

Comparison and Contrast

The method of **comparison** and **contrast** involves setting two plays side by side and pointing out their similarities and differences. Because plays are complicated entities, you need to choose a narrow focus, or you will find yourself overwhelmed. A profound topic—"The Self-Deception of Othello and Oedipus"—might do for a three-hundred-page dissertation, but an essay of a mere thousand words could never do it justice. A large but finite topic—say, attitudes toward marriage in *A Doll's House* and *Trifles*—would best suit a long term paper. To apply this method to a shorter term paper, you might compare and contrast a certain aspect of personality in two characters within the same play—for example, Willy's and Biff's illusions in *Death of a Salesman*.

Card Report

In place of an essay, some instructors like to assign a **card report**, a succinct but thorough method of analyzing the components of a play. For more information on this kind of assignment, see "The Card Report" on page 1926. Keep in mind, though, that when dealing with a play, you will find some elements that differ from those in a short story. Specifying the work's narrator may not be relevant to a play, for example. Also, for a full-length play, you may need to write on both sides of two 5- × 8-inch index cards instead of on one card, as you might for a short story. Still, in order to write a good card report, you have to be both brief and specific. Before you start, sort out your impressions of the play and try to decide which characters, scenes, and lines of dialogue are the most memorable and important. Reducing your scattered impressions to essentials, you will have to reexamine what you have read. When you finish, you will know the play much more thoroughly.

Here is an example: a card report on Susan Glaspell's one-act play *Trifles*. (For the play itself, see page 1111.) By including only the elements that seemed most important, the writer managed to analyze the brief play on the front and back of one card. Still, he managed to work in a few pertinent quotations to give a sense of the play's remarkable language. Although the report does not say everything about Glaspell's little masterpiece, an adequate criticism of the play could hardly be much briefer. For this report, the writer was assigned to include the following:

1. The playwright's name, nationality, and dates.
2. The title of the play and the date of its first performance.
3. The central character or characters, with a brief description that includes leading traits.
4. Other characters, also described.
5. The scene or scenes and, if the play does not take place in the present, the time of its action.
6. The dramatic question. This question is whatever the play leads us to ask ourselves: some conflict whose outcome we wonder about, some uncertainty whose resolution we look forward to. (For a more detailed discussion of dramatic questions, see page 1124.)
7. A brief summary of the play's principal events, in the order in which the playwright presents them. If you are reporting on a play longer than *Trifles*, you may find it simplest to sum up what happens in each act, perhaps in each scene.
8. The tone of the play, as best you can detect it. Try to describe the playwright's apparent feelings toward the characters or what happens to them.
9. The language spoken in the play. Try to describe it. Does any character speak with a choice of words or with figures of speech that strike you as unusual, distinctive, poetic—or maybe dull and drab? Does language indicate a character's background or place of birth? Brief quotations, in what space you have, will be valuable.
10. A one-sentence summary of the play's central theme. If you find none, say so. Plays often contain more than one theme. Which of them seems most clearly borne out by the main events?
11. Any symbols you notice and believe to be important. Try to state in a few words what each suggests.
12. A concise evaluation of the play. What did you think of it? (For more suggestions on being a drama critic, see Chapter 39, "Evaluating a Play.")

A card report on *Trifles* begins on the following page.

Front of Card

Ben Nelson   English 101

Susan Glaspell, American, 1876–1948   *Trifles*, 1916

<u>Central characters</u>: Mrs. Peters, the sheriff's nervous wife, dutiful but

independent, not "married to the law"—whose sorrows make her able to sympathize

with a woman accused of murder. Mrs. Hale, who knows the accused; more decisive.

<u>Other characters</u>: The County Attorney, self-important but short-sighted. The

Sheriff, a man of only middling intelligence, another sexist. Hale, a farmer, a cautious

man. Not seen on stage, two others are central: Minnie (Foster) Wright, the accused, a

music lover reduced to near despair by years of grim marriage and isolation; and John

Wright, the victim, known for his cruelty.

<u>Scene</u>: The kitchen of a gloomy farmhouse after the arrest of a wife on suspicion

of murder; little things left in disarray.

<u>Major dramatic question</u>: Why did Minnie Wright kill her husband? When this

question is answered, a new major dramatic question is raised: Will Mrs. Peters and Mrs.

Hale cover up incriminating evidence?

<u>Events</u>: In the exposition, Sheriff and C.A., investigating the death of Wright,

hear Hale tell how he found the body and a distracted Mrs. Wright. Then (1) C.A. starts

looking for a motive. (2) His jeering at Mrs. Wright (and all women) for their concern

with "trifles" causes Mrs. Peters and Mrs. Hale to rally to the woman's defense. (3) When

the two women find evidence that Mrs. Wright had panicked (a patch of wild sewing in a

quilt), Mrs. Hale destroys it.

[continued on back of card]

Back of Card

[*Events*, continued]

(4) Mrs. Peters finds more evidence: a wrecked birdcage. (5) The women find a canary with its neck wrung and realize that Minnie killed her husband in a similar way. (6) The women align themselves with Minnie when Mrs. Peters recalls her own sorrows, and Mrs. Hale decides her own failure to visit Minnie was "a crime." (7) The C.A. unwittingly provides Mrs. Peters with a means to smuggle out the canary. (8) The two women unite to seize the evidence.

Tone: Made clear in the women's dialogue: mingled horror and sadness at what has happened, compassion for a fellow woman, smoldering resentment toward men who crush women.

Language: The plain speech of farm people, with a dash of rural Midwestern slang (*red-up* for tidy; Hale's remark that the accused was "kind of done up"). Unschooled speech: Mrs. Hale says *ain't*—and yet her speech rises at moments to simple poetry: "She used to sing. He killed that too." Glaspell hints at the self-importance of the County Attorney by his heavy reliance on the first person.

Central theme: Women, in their supposed concern for trifles, see more deeply than men do.

Symbols: The broken birdcage and the dead canary, both suggesting the music and the joy that John Wright stifled in Minnie.

Evaluation: A powerful, successful, realistic play that conveys its theme with great economy—in its views, more than fifty years ahead of its time.

A Drama Review

Writing a play review, a brief critical account of an actual performance, involves going out on a limb and making an evaluation. It also can mean assessing various aspects of the production, including the acting, direction, sets, costumes, lighting, and possibly even the play itself. While reviews can be challenging to write, many students find them more stimulating—even more fun—than most writing assignments. There is no better way to understand—and appreciate—drama than by seeing live theater. Here are some tips for writing a review.

- **Clarify what you are evaluating.** Is it the play's script, or the performance? If the latter, are you concentrating on the performance in its entirety, or on certain elements, such as the acting or the direction? If the play is a classic one, the more urgent task for the reviewer will be not to evaluate the playwright's work but to comment on the success of the actors', director's, and production crew's particular interpretation of it. If the play is newer and less established, you may profitably evaluate the script itself.

- **If the play itself is your subject, be aware of the conventions within which the playwright is working.** For a list of considerations see "Judging a Play" on page 1678.

- **Don't simply sneer or gush; give reasons for your opinions.** Ground your praise or criticism of a production in specifics. Incidentally, harsh evaluations can tempt a reviewer to flashes of wit. One such celebrated flash is writer Eugene Field's observation of an actor in a production of *King Lear*, that "he played the king as though he were in constant fear that someone else was about to play the ace." The comment isn't merely nasty; it implies that Field had closely watched the actor's performance and had discerned what was wrong with it.

- **Early in the review, provide the basic facts.** Give the play's title and author, the theatrical company producing it, and the theater in which it is performed.

- **Give the names of actors in lead roles, and evaluate their performances.** How well cast do the leads seem? If an actor stands out—for good or ill—in a supporting role, he or she may deserve a mention as well.

- **Provide a brief plot summary.** Your reader may be unacquainted with the play, and will certainly want a general sense of what it is about. Out of general consideration to the reader, however, it is best not to reveal any plot surprises, unless the play is a classic one with an ending likely to be common knowledge.

- **If the play is unfamiliar, summarize its theme.** This exercise will not only help your reader understand your review but probably sharpen your analysis.

- **For a well-known play, evaluate the director's unique approach to familiar material.** Is the production exactly what you'd expect, or are there any fresh and apparently original innovations? If a production is unusual, does it achieve newness by violating the play? The director of one college production of *Othello* emphasized the play's being partly set in Venice by staging it in the campus swimming pool, with actors floating on barges and a homemade gondola—a fresh, but not entirely successful, innovation.

- **Comment on the director's work.** Can you discern the director's approach to the play? Do the actors hurry their lines or speak too slowly? Do they speak and gesture naturally, or in an awkward, stylized manner? Are these touches effective or distracting?

- **Pay attention to costumes, sets, and lighting, if they are noteworthy.** Though such matters may seem small, they have an effect on the play's overall tone.

- **Finally, to prepare yourself, read a few professional play reviews.** Reviews appear regularly in magazines such as the *New Yorker, Time,* the *New Criterion,* and *American Theatre,* and also on the entertainment pages of most metropolitan newspapers. Newspaper reviews can often be accessed online; for example, *New York Times* reviews may be found at <http://theater.nytimes.com.>

Here is a good, concise review of an amateur production of *Trifles,* as it might be written for a college newspaper or as a course assignment.

Trifles Scores Mixed Success in
Monday Players' Production

Women have come a long way since 1916. At least, that impression was conveyed yesterday when the Monday Players presented Susan Glaspell's classic one-act play *Trifles* in Alpaugh Theater.

Opening paragraph gives information on play and production

At first, in Glaspell's taut story of two subjugated farm women who figure out why a fellow farm woman strangled her husband, actors Lloyd Fox and Cal Federicci get to strut around. As a small-town sheriff and a county attorney, they lord it over the womenfolk, making sexist remarks about women in general. Fox and Federicci obviously enjoy themselves as the pompous types that Glaspell means them to be.

But of course it is the women with their keen eyes for small details who prove the superior detectives. In the demanding roles of the two Nebraska Miss Marples, Kathy Betts and Ruth Fine cope as best they can with what is asked of them. Fine is especially convincing. As Mrs. Hale, a friend of the wife accused of the murder, she projects a growing sense of independence. Visibly smarting under the verbal lashes of the menfolk, she seems to straighten her spine inch by inch as the play goes on.

Evaluates performances

Unluckily for Betts, director Alvin Klein seems determined to view Mrs. Peters as a comedian. Though Glaspell's stage directions call the woman "nervous," I doubt she is supposed to be quite so fidgety as Betts makes her. Betts vibrates like a tuning fork every time a new clue turns up, and when she is obliged to smell a dead canary bird (another clue), you would think she was whiffing a dead hippopotamus. Mrs. Peters, whose sad past includes a lost baby and a kitten some maniac chopped up

Analyzes direction

Further elaborates on stage direction

with a hatchet, is no figure of fun to my mind. Played for laughs, her character fails to grow visibly on stage, as Fine makes Mrs. Hale grow.

Klein, be it said in his favor, makes the quiet action proceed at a brisk pace. Feminists in the audience must have been a little embarrassed, though, by his having Betts and Fine deliver every speech defending women in an extra-loud voice. After all, Glaspell makes her points clearly enough just by showing us what she shows. Not everything is overstated, however. As a farmer who found the murder victim, Ron Valdez acts his part with quiet authority.

Overall evaluation

Despite flaws in its direction, this powerful play still spellbinds an audience. Anna Winterbright's set, seen last week as a background for *Dracula* and just slightly touched up, provides appropriate gloom.

HOW TO QUOTE A PLAY

The guidelines for quoting prose or poetry generally apply to quoting from a play. Plays present certain challenges of their own, however. When you quote an extended section of a play or dialogue that involves more than one character, use the following MLA format to set the passage off from the body of your paper:

- Indent one inch or ten spaces.
- Type the character's name in all capitals, followed by a period.
- If a speech runs for more than a single line, indent any additional lines one-quarter inch, or an additional three spaces.
- Provide a citation reference:

    If the play is written in prose, provide a page number.

    If the play is written in verse, provide the act, scene, and line numbers.

Here is an example of that format:

> The men never find a motive for the murder because, ironically, they consider all the real clues "trifles" that don't warrant their attention:
>
> > SHERIFF. Well, can you beat the women! Held for murder and
> >   worryin' about her preserves.
> > COUNTY ATTORNEY. I guess before we're through she may have
> >   something more serious than preserves to worry about.
> > HALE. Well, women are used to worrying over trifles. (1114)

When you are quoting a verse play, be careful to respect the line breaks. For citation references, you should provide the act, scene, and line numbers, so that your reader will be able to find the quotation in any edition of the play. A quotation from a verse play should look like this:

Even before her death, Othello will not confront Desdemona with his specific suspicions:

> OTHELLO. Think on thy sins.
>
> DESDEMONA.   They are loves I bear to you.
>
> OTHELLO. Ay, and for that thou diest.
>
> DESDEMONA. That death's unnatural that kills for loving. Alas,
>
> why gnaw you so your nether lip?
>
> Some bloody passion shakes your very frame.
>
> These are portents; but yet I hope, I hope,
>
> They do not point on me. (5.2.42–48)

TOPICS FOR WRITING BRIEF PAPERS (250–500 WORDS)

1. Analyze a key character from any of the plays in this book. Some choices might be Tom Wingfield in *The Glass Menagerie*, Torvald Helmer in *A Doll's House*, or Biff Loman in *Death of a Salesman*. What motivates that character? Point to specific moments in the play to make your case.

2. When the curtain comes down on the conclusion of some plays, the audience is left to decide exactly what finally happened. In a short informal essay, state your interpretation of the conclusion of one of these plays: *The Sound of a Voice, The Darker Face of the Earth, The Glass Menagerie*. Don't just give a plot summary; tell what you think the conclusion means.

3. Sum up the main suggestions you find in one of these meaningful objects (or actions): the handkerchief in *Othello*; the Christmas tree in *A Doll's House* (or Nora's doing a wild tarantella); Willy Loman's planting a garden in *Death of a Salesman*; Laura's collection of figurines in *The Glass Menagerie*.

4. Here is an exercise in being terse. Write a card report on a short, one-scene play (other than *Trifles*), and confine your remarks to both sides of one 5- × 8-inch card. (For further instructions see page 1963.) Possible subjects include *The Sound of a Voice, Tattoo, Soap Opera*.

5. Attend a play and write a review. In an assignment this brief, you will need to concentrate your remarks on either the performance or the script itself. Be sure to back up your opinions with specific observations.

TOPICS FOR WRITING MORE EXTENDED PAPERS (600–1,000 WORDS)

1. From a play you have enjoyed, choose a passage that strikes you as difficult, worth reading closely. Try to pick a passage not longer than about 20 lines. Explicate it—give it a close, sentence-by-sentence reading—and explain how this small part of the play relates to the whole. For instance, any of the following passages might be considered memorable (and essential to their plays):

   • Othello's soliloquy beginning "It is the cause, it is the cause, my soul" (*Othello*, 5.2.1–22).
   • Oedipus to Teiresias, speech beginning "Wealth, power, craft of statemanship!" (*Oedipus the King*, l.63–86).
   • Nora to Mrs. Linde, speech beginning "Yes, someday, maybe, in many years when I am not as pretty as I am now . . ." (*A Doll's House*, page 1567).

2. Analyze the complexities and contradictions to be found in a well-rounded character from a play of your choice. Some good subjects might be Hamlet, Othello, Nora Helmer (in *A Doll's House*), Willy Loman (in *Death of a Salesman*), or Tom Wingfield (in *The Glass Menagerie*).

3. Take just a single line or sentence from a play, one that stands out for some reason as greatly important. Perhaps it states a theme, reveals a character, or serves as a crisis (or turning point). Write an essay demonstrating its importance—how it functions, why it is necessary. Some possible lines include:

   • Iago to Roderigo: "I am not what I am" (*Othello*, 1.1.67).
   • Amanda to Tom: "You live in a dream; you manufacture illusions!" (*The Glass Menagerie*, Scene vii).
   • Charley to Biff: "A salesman is got to dream, boy. It comes with the territory" (*Death of a Salesman*, the closing Requiem).

4. Write an analysis essay in which you single out an element of a play for examination—character, plot, setting, theme, dramatic irony, tone, language, symbolism, conventions, or any other element. Try to relate this element to the play as a whole. Sample topics: "The Function of Teiresias in *Oedipus the King*," "Imagery of Poison in *Othello*," "Irony in *Antigonê*," "Williams's Use of Magic-Lantern Slides in *The Glass Menagerie*," "The Theme of Success in *Death of a Salesman*."

5. How would you stage an updated production of a play by Shakespeare, Sophocles, or Ibsen, transplanting it to our time? Choose a play, and describe the challenges and difficulties of this endeavor. How would you overcome them—or, if they cannot be overcome, why not?

6. Louis Phillips, of the School of Visual Arts in New York City, developed the following assignment. Read this statement from Woody Allen:

> Sports to me is like music. It's completely satisfying. There were times I would sit at a game with the old Knicks and think to myself in the fourth quarter, this is everything the theatre should be and isn't. There's an outcome that's unpredictable. The audience is not ahead of the dramatists. The drama is ahead of the audience.

What does Woody Allen mean by the notion of the audience being ahead of (or behind) the dramatist? Apply that notion to any play you have read. If Woody Allen truly feels that sports are more satisfying than drama, why does he continue to make movies?

TOPICS FOR WRITING LONG PAPERS (1,500 WORDS OR MORE)

1. Choose a play you have read and admire from this book, and read a second play by the same author. Compare and contrast the two plays with attention to a single element—a theme they have in common, or a particular kind of imagery, for example.
2. Compare and contrast the ways in which *The Glass Menagerie* and *Death of a Salesman* approach the theme of fantasy and wishful thinking.
3. Read *Othello* and view a movie version of the play. You might choose Oliver Parker's 1995 take on the play with Laurence Fishburne and Kenneth Branagh, or even *O* (2001), an updated version that takes a prep school as its setting and a basketball star as its protagonist. Review the movie. What does it manage to convey of the original? What gets lost in the translation?
4. Choosing any of the works in "Plays for Further Reading" or taking some other modern or contemporary play your instructor suggests, report any difficulties you encountered in reading and responding to it. Explicate any troublesome passages for the benefit of other readers.
5. Attend a play and write an in-depth review, taking into account many elements of the drama: acting, direction, staging, costumes, lighting, and—if the work is relatively new and not a classic—the play itself.
6. Have you ever taken part in a dramatic production, either as an actor or a member of the crew? What did the experience teach you about the nature of drama and about what makes a play effective?
7. Write a one-act play of your own, featuring a minor character from one of the plays you have read for class. Think about what motivates that character, and let the play's central conflict grow from his or her preoccupations.

45 WRITING A RESEARCH PAPER

A writer is a person for whom writing is more difficult than it is for other people.

—THOMAS MANN

Oh no! You have been assigned a research paper, and every time you even think about starting it, your spirits sink and your blood pressure rises. You really liked the story by Ernest Hemingway, but when you entered his name in the college library catalogue it listed 135 books about him. Time to switch authors, you decide. How about Emily Dickinson? She was fun to talk about in class, but when you Google her name, the computer states that there are over 8.4 million entries. What should you do? The paper is due in two weeks, not twenty years. Why would an otherwise very nice instructor put you through this mental trauma?

Why is it worthwhile to write a research paper? (Apart from the fact that you want a passing grade in the class, that is.) While you can learn much by exploring your own responses to a literary work, there is no substitute for entering into a conversation with others who have studied and thought about your topic. Literary criticism is that conversation. Your reading will expose you to the ideas of others who can shed light on a story, poem, or play. It will introduce you to the wide range of informed opinions that exist about literature, as about almost any subject. Sometimes, too, your research will uncover information about an author's life that leads you to new insights into a literary work. Undertaking a research paper gives you a chance to test your ideas against those of others, and in doing so to clarify your own opinions.

BROWSE THE RESEARCH

The most daunting aspect of the research paper may well be the mountains of information available on almost any literary subject. It can be hard to know where to begin. Sifting through books and articles is part of the research process. Unfortunately, the first material uncovered in the library or on the Internet is rarely the evidence you need to develop or support your thesis. Keep looking until you uncover helpful sources.

Another common pitfall in the process is the creeping feeling that your idea has already been examined a dozen times over. But take heart: like Odysseus, tie yourself to the mast so that when you hear the siren voices of published professors, you can listen without abandoning your own point of view. Your idea may have been treated, but not yet by you. Your particular take on a topic is bound to be different from some-one else's. After all, thousands of books have been written on Shakespeare's plays, but even so there are still new things to say.

CHOOSE A TOPIC

- **Find a topic that interests you.** A crucial first step in writing a research paper is coming up with a topic that interests you. Start with a topic that bores you, and the process will be a chore, and will yield dull results. But if you come up with an intriguing research question, seeking the answer will be a more engaging process. The paper that results will inevitably be stronger and more interesting.

- **Find a way to get started.** Browsing through books of literary criticism in the library, or glancing at online journal articles, can help to spark an idea or two. Prewriting techniques such as brainstorming, freewriting, listing, and clustering can also help you to generate ideas on a specific work of literature. If you take notes and jot down ideas as they occur to you, when you start the formal writing process you will discover you have already begun. For a closer discussion of preparing to write, see page 1893.

- **Keep your purpose and audience in mind.** Refer often to the assignment, and approach your essay accordingly. Think of your audience as well. Is it your professor, your classmates, or some other hypothetical reader? As you plan your essay, keep your audience's expectations and needs in mind.

- **Develop a general thesis that you hope to support with research, and look for material that will help you demonstrate its plausibility.** Remember: the ideal research paper is based on your own observations and interpretations of a literary text.

BEGIN YOUR RESEARCH

Print Resources

Writing a research paper on literature calls for two kinds of sources: primary sources, or the literary works that are your subject, and secondary sources, or the books, articles, and Web resources that discuss your primary sources. When you are hunting down sec-ondary sources, the best place to begin is your campus library. Plan to spend some time thumbing through scholarly books and journals, looking for passages that you find par-ticularly interesting or that pertain to your topic. Begin your search with the online catalog to get a sense of where you might find the books and journals you need.

To choose from the many books available on your library's shelves and through interlibrary loan, you might turn to book reviews for a sense of which volumes would best suit your purpose. *Book Review Digest* contains the full texts of many book reviews, and excerpts of others. The *Digest* may be found in printed form in the reference section of your campus library, which may also provide access to the online version. Whether you are using the online or print version, you will need the author's name, title, and date of first publication of any book for which you hope to find a review.

Scholarly journals are another excellent resource for articles on your topic. Indexes to magazines and journals may be found in your library's reference section. You may also find an index to print periodicals on your library's Web site.

Online Databases

Most college libraries subscribe to specialized online or CD-ROM database services covering all academic subjects—treasure troves of reliable sources. If you find yourself unsure how to use your library's database system, ask the reference librarian to help you get started. The following databases are particularly useful for literary research:

▪ The MLA *International Bibliography*, the Modern Language Association's database, is an excellent way to search for books and full-text articles on literary topics.

▪ *JSTOR*, a not-for-profit organization, indexes articles or abstracts from an archive of journals on language, literature, and African American studies.

▪ *Literature Resource Center* (Thomson Gale) provides biographies, bibliographies, and critical analyses of more than 120,000 authors and their work. This information is culled from journal articles and reference works.

▪ *Literature Online (LION)* provides a vast searchable database of critical articles and reference works as well as full texts of more than 300,000 works of prose, poetry, and drama.

▪ *Project MUSE*, a collaboration between publishers and libraries, offers access to more than 400 journals in the humanities, arts, and social sciences.

▪ EBSCO, a multisubject resource, covers literature and the humanities, as well as the social sciences, medical sciences, linguistics, and other fields.

Your library may provide access to some or all of these databases, or it may offer other useful ones. Many college library home pages provide students with access to subscription databases, which means that if you really can't bear to leave your comfy desk at home, you can still pay a virtual visit.

Reliable Web Sources

While online databases are a handy and reliable source for high-quality information, you may find yourself looking to supplement journal articles with information and quotations from the Internet. If so, proceed with care. While the journal articles in online databases have been reviewed for quality by specialists and librarians, Web sites may be written and published by anybody for any purpose, with no oversight. Even the online reference site *Wikipedia*, for example, is an amalgamation of voluntary contributors, and is rife with small factual errors and contributor biases. Carefully analyze the materials you gather online or you may find yourself tangled in the spidery threads of a dubious Web site. To garner the best sources possible, take these steps:

▪ **Learn to use Internet search engines effectively.** If you enter general terms such as the author's name and story title into an Internet search engine, you may well find yourself bombarded with thousands of hits. For a more efficient approach to navigating the Internet, try using an "advanced" search option, entering keywords to get results that contain those words (LITERARY CRITICISM A DOLL'S HOUSE or SYMBOLISM THE LOTTERY).

▪ **Begin your search at a reliable Web site.** Helpful as an advanced search may be, it won't separate valuable sources from useless ones. To weed out sloppy and inaccurate sites, begin your search with one of the following excellent guides through cyberspace:

- *Library of Congress.* Fortunately, you don't have to trek to Washington to visit this venerable institution's annotated collection of Web sites in the Humanities and Social Sciences Division. For your purpose—writing a literary research paper—access the Subject Index <http://www.loc.gov/rr/main/alcove9>, click on "Literatures in English" and then on "Literary Criticism." This will take you to a list of metapages and Web sites with collections of reliable critical and biographical materials on authors and their works. (A metapage provides links to other Web sites.)
- *Internet Public Library.* Created and maintained by the University of Michigan School of Information and Library Studies, this site <http://www.ipl.org> lets you search for literary criticism by author, work, country of origin, or literary period.
- *Library Spot.* Visit <http://www.libraryspot.com> for a portal to over 5,000 libraries around the world, and to periodicals, online texts, reference works, and links to metapages and Web sites on any topic including literary criticism. This carefully maintained site is published by Start Spot Mediaworks, Inc., in the Northwestern University/Evanston Research Park in Evanston, Illinois.
- *Voice of the Shuttle.* Research links in over 25 categories in the humanities and social sciences, including online texts, libraries, academic Web sites, and metapages may be found at this site. Located at <http://vos.ucsb.edu> it was developed and is maintained by Dr. Alan Liu in the English Department of the University of California.

CHECKLIST: Finding Reliable Sources

- ☐ Begin at your campus library. Ask the reference librarian for advice.
- ☐ Check the library catalog for books and journals on your topic.
- ☐ Look into the online databases subscribed to by your library.
- ☐ Locate reputable Web sites by starting at a reputable Web site designed for that purpose.

Visual Images

The Web is an excellent source of visual images. If a picture, chart, or graph will enhance your argument, you may find the perfect one via an image search on *Google, Ditto,* or other search engines. The Library of Congress offers a wealth of images documenting American political, social, and cultural history—including portraits, letters, and original manuscripts—at <http://memory.loc.gov>. Remember, though, that not all images are available for use by the general public. Check for a copyright notice to see if its originator allows that image to be reproduced. If so, you may include the photograph, provided you credit your source as you would if you were quoting text.

One note on images: use them carefully. Choose visuals that provide supporting evidence for the point you are trying to make or enhance your reader's understanding of the work. Label your images with captions. Your goal should be to make your argument more convincing. In the example below, a reproduction of Brueghel's painting helps to advance the author's argument and provide insight into Auden's poem.

Lombardo 4

Fig. 1. *Landscape with the Fall of Icarus* by Pieter Brueghel the Elder (c. 1558, Musées royaux des Beaux-Arts de Belgique, Brussels).

W. H. Auden's poem "Musée des Beaux Arts" refers to a specific painting to prove its point that the most honest depictions of death take into account the way life simply goes on even after the most tragic of events. In line 14, Auden turns specifically to Pieter Brueghel the Elder's masterwork *The Fall of Icarus* (see Fig. 1), pointing to the painting's understated depiction of tragedy. In this painting, the death of Icarus does not take place on center stage. A plowman and his horse take up the painting's foreground, while the leg of Icarus falling into the sea takes up a tiny portion of the painting's lower-right corner. A viewer who fails to take the painting's title into account might not even notice Icarus at all.

CHECKLIST: Using Visual Images

- ☐ Use images as evidence to support your argument.
- ☐ Use images to enhance communication and understanding.
- ☐ Refer to the images in your text.
- ☐ Label image as "Fig. 1" and provide title or caption.
- ☐ Check copyrights.
- ☐ Include source in works-cited list.

EVALUATE YOUR SOURCES

Print Resources

It's an old saying, but a useful one: don't believe everything you read. The fact that a book or article is printed and published doesn't necessarily mean it is accurate or unbiased. Be discriminating about printed resources.

Begin your search in a place that has taken some of the work out of quality control—your school library. Books and articles you find there are regarded by librarians as having some obvious merit. If your search takes you beyond the library, though, you will need to be discerning when choosing print resources. As you weigh the value of printed matter, take the following into account:

- **Look closely at information provided about the author.** Is he or she known for expertise in the field? What are the author's academic or association credentials? Is there any reason to believe that the author is biased in any way? For example, a biography of an author written by that author's child might not be as unbiased as one written by a scholar with no personal connections.

- **Determine the publisher's reliability.** Books or articles published by an advocacy group might be expected to take a particular—possibly biased—slant on an issue. Be aware also that some books are published by vanity presses, companies that are paid by an author to publish his or her books. As a result, vanity press-published books generally aren't subject to the same rigorous quality control as those put out by more reputable publishing houses.

- **Always check for a publication date.** If a document lists an edition number, check to see whether you are using the latest edition of the material.

- **For periodicals, decide whether a publication is an academic journal or a popular magazine.** What type of reputation does it have? Obviously, you do not want to use a magazine that periodically reports on Elvis sightings and alien births. And even articles on writers in magazines such as *Time* and *People* are likely to be too brief and superficial for purposes of serious research. Instead, choose scholarly journals designed to enhance the study of literature.

Web Resources

As handy and informative as the Internet is, it sometimes serves up some pretty iffy information. A Web site, after all, can be created by anyone with a computer and access to the Internet—no matter how poorly qualified that person might be. Be discerning when it comes to the Internet. Here are some tips on choosing your sources wisely:

- **Check a site's authorship or sponsorship.** Is the site's creator or sponsor known to you or reputable by association? Look closely at information provided about the author. Is he or she known for expertise in the field? What are the author's academic or association credentials? Is the Web entry unsigned and anonymous? If the Web site is sponsored by an organization, is it a reputable one? While government or university-sponsored sites may be considered reliable, think carefully about possible biases in sites sponsored by advocacy or special interest groups.

  A word of warning: individual student pages posted on university sites have not necessarily been reviewed by that university and are not reliable sources of information. Also, postings on the popular encyclopedia Web site

Wikipedia are not subject to a scholarly review process and have been noted to contain a number of inaccuracies. It's safer to use a published encyclopedia.

■ **Look at the site's date of publication.** When was it last updated? In some cases you may want to base your essay on the most current information or theories, so you will want to steer toward the most recently published material.

■ **Is this an online version of a print publication?** If so, what type of reputation does it have?

■ **Make your own assessment of the site.** Does the content seem consistent with demonstrated scholarship? Does it appear balanced in its point of view?

■ **Consult experts.** Cornell University has two good documents with guidance for analyzing sources, posted at <http://www.library.cornell.edu/services/guides. html>. The titles are "Critically Analyzing Information Sources" and "Distinguishing Scholarly from Non-Scholarly Periodicals." The UCLA College Library also provides useful information: "Thinking Critically About World Wide Web Resources" (<http://www2.library.ucla.edu/libraries>).

CHECKLIST: Evaluating Your Sources

Print

☐ Who wrote it? What are the author's credentials?
☐ Is he or she an expert in the field?
☐ Does he or she appear to be unbiased toward the subject matter?
☐ Is the publisher reputable? Is it an advocacy group or a vanity press?
☐ When was it published? Do later editions exist? If so, would a later edition be more useful?

Web

☐ Who wrote it? What are the author's credentials?
☐ Is he or she an expert in the field?
☐ Who sponsors the Web site? Is the sponsor reputable?
☐ When was the Web site published? When was it last updated?
☐ Is the Web site an online journal or magazine? Is it scholarly or popular?
☐ Does content seem consistent with demonstrated scholarship?
☐ Can you detect obvious bias?

ORGANIZE YOUR RESEARCH

■ **Get your thoughts down on notecards or the equivalent on your laptop.** Once you have amassed your secondary sources, it will be time to begin reading in earnest. As you do so, be sure to take notes on any passages that pertain to your topic. A convenient way to organize your many thoughts is to write them down on index cards, which are easy to shuffle and rearrange. You'll need 3- × 5-inch cards for brief notes and titles and 5- × 8-inch cards for more in-depth notes. Confine your jottings to one side of the card; notes on the back can easily be overlooked. Write a single fact or opinion on each card. This will make it easier for you to shuffle the deck and reenvision the order in which you deliver information to your reader.

■ **Keep careful track of the sources of quotations and paraphrases.** As you take notes, make it crystal clear which thoughts and phrases are yours and which derive from others. (Remember, *quotation* means using the exact words of your source and placing the entire passage in quotation marks and citing the author. *Paraphrase* means expressing the ideas of your source in your own words, again citing the author.) Bear in mind the cautionary tale of well-known historian Doris Kearns Goodwin. She was charged with plagiarizing sections of two of her famous books when her words were found to be jarringly similar to those published in other books. Because she had not clearly indicated on her notecards which ideas and passages were hers and which came from other sources, Goodwin was forced to admit to plagiarism. Her enormous reputation suffered from these charges, but you can learn from her mistakes and save your own reputation—and your grades.

■ **Keep track of the sources of ideas and concepts.** When an idea is inspired by or directly taken from someone else's writing, be sure to jot down the source on that same card or your computer file. Your deck of cards or computer list will function as a working bibliography, which later will help you put together a works-cited list. To save yourself work, keep a separate list of the sources you're using. Then, as you make the note, you need write only the material's author or title and page reference on the card in order to identify your source. It's also useful to classify the note in a way that will help you to organize your material, making it easy, for example, to separate cards that deal with a story's theme from cards that deal with point of view or symbolism.

■ **Make notes of your own thoughts and reactions to your research.** When a critical article sparks your own original idea, be sure to capture that thought in your notes and mark it as your own. As you plan your paper, these notes may form the outline for your arguments.

Some useful note cards taken on the critical essay on page 2030 about Joyce Carol Oates's short story "Where Are You Going, Where Have You Been?" might look something like this:

Direct quotation from critic

THEME

Schulz and Rockwood, p. 2030

"There is a terrible irony here, for although the story is full of fairy tales, Connie, its protagonist, is not. Connie represents an entire generation of young people who have grown up—or tried to—without the help of those bedtime stories which not only entertain the child, but also enable him vicariously to experience and work through problems which he will encounter in adolescence."

Paraphrase of critic

THEME

Schulz and Rockwood, p. 2030

Ironic that while story steeped in fairy tales, Connie is not. Connie stands for her whole generation that grew up without fairy tales.

Missed benefits of fairy tales for child: working through life's problems.

Critic's idea

THEME

Schulz and Rockwood, p. 2030

Many fairy tales underlie "Where Are You Going ?" e.g.
  Snow White
  Cinderella
  Sleeping Beauty
  Little Red Riding Hood

Your own idea

THEME or CHARACTER?

My Idea

Is Arnold the big bad wolf?
  Can I find clues in story?

■ **Make photocopies or printouts to simplify the process and ensure accuracy.** Scholars once had to spend long hours copying out prose passages by hand. Luckily, for a small investment you can simply photocopy your sources to ensure accuracy in quoting and citing your sources. In fact, some instructors will require you to hand in photocopies of your original sources with the final paper, along with printouts of articles downloaded from an Internet database. Even if this is not the case, photocopying your sources and holding onto your printouts can help you to reproduce quotations accurately in your essay—and accuracy is crucial.

REFINE YOUR THESIS

As you read secondary sources and take notes, you should begin to refine your essay's thesis. This, in turn, will help you to winnow your stacks of source material down to the secondary sources that will best help you to make your point. Even your revised thesis doesn't have to be etched in stone. It should simply give you a sense of direction as you start to plan your essay.

- **Be willing to fine-tune your thesis or even rework it completely.** Your research may reveal that you have misinterpreted an idea, or that others have already argued your thesis. Of course, it is annoying to find that you may be wrong about something, or that someone else has taken off with what you thought was your original argument, but don't let these discoveries put you off. If you run across arguments similar to your own, use them to refine your thoughts. (These sources also may well be useful to bolster your own thesis.)

- **Let your initial idea be the jumping-off point to other, better ideas.** Say, for example, that you plan to write about the peculiar physical description of Arnold Friend in Joyce Carol Oates's story "Where Are You Going, Where Have You Been?" You may have noticed he has trouble standing in his shoes, and you want to explore that odd detail. If you research this character, you may find Arnold Friend likened to the devil (whose cloven hooves might give him similar problems with standard-issue cowboy boots), or to the wolf in "Little Red Riding Hood" (also a character who would have a hard time managing human clothes). At that point, you may think, "Okay, my idea is shot. Everyone has written about this aspect of the Oates character." Well, just use your new knowledge to sharpen your focus. Can you think of other stories that deal with potentially supernatural, possibly even evil, characters? What about Nathaniel Hawthorne's "Young Goodman Brown"? Or Flannery O'Connor's "A Good Man Is Hard to Find"? How might you compare Arnold Friend with Hawthorne's devil or O'Connor's Misfit?

ORGANIZE YOUR PAPER

With your thesis in mind and your notes spread before you, draw up an outline—a rough map of how best to argue your thesis and present your material. Determine what main points you need to make, and look for quotations that support those points. Even if you generally prefer to navigate the paper-writing process without a map, you will find that an outline makes the research-paper writing process considerably smoother. When organizing information from many different sources, it pays to plan ahead.

WRITE AND REVISE

As with any other kind of essay, a research paper rarely, if ever, reaches its full potential in a single draft. Leave yourself time to rewrite. The knowledge that your first draft isn't your final one can free you up to take chances and to jot down your ideas as quickly as they occur to you. If your phrasing is less than elegant, it hardly matters in a first draft; the main point is to work out your ideas on paper. Rough out the paper, working as quickly as you can. Later you can rearrange paragraphs and smooth out any rough patches.

Once you've got the first draft down, it's an excellent idea to run it by a friend, a writing center tutor, or even your instructor. A writer can't know how clear or persuasive his or her argument is without a trusted reader to give feedback.

When you finally do revise, be open to making both large and small changes. Sometimes revising means adding needed paragraphs, or even refining the thesis a bit further. Be willing to start from scratch if you need to, but even as you take the whole picture into account, remember that details are important too. Before you hand in that final draft, be sure to proofread for small errors that could detract from the finished product.

MAINTAIN ACADEMIC INTEGRITY

Papers for Sale Are Papers that "F"ail

Do not be seduced by the apparent ease of cheating by computer. Your Internet searches may turn up several sites that offer term papers to download (just as you can find pornography, political propaganda, and questionable get-rich-quick schemes!). Most of these sites charge money for what they offer, but a few do not, happy to strike a blow against the "oppressive" insistence of English teachers that students learn to think and write.

Plagiarized term papers are an old game: the fraternity file and the "research assistance" service have been around far longer than the computer. It may seem easy enough to download a paper, put your name at the head of it, and turn it in for an easy grade. As any writing instructor can tell you, though, such papers usually stick out like a sore thumb. The style will be wrong, the work will not be consistent with other work by the same student in any number of ways, and the teacher will sometimes even have seen the same phony paper before. The ease with which electronic texts are reproduced makes this last possibility increasingly likely.

The odds of being caught and facing the unpleasant consequences are reasonably high. It is far better to take the grade you have earned for your own effort, no matter how mediocre, than to try to pass off someone else's work as your own. Even if, somehow, your instructor does not recognize your submission as a plagiarized paper, you have diminished your character through dishonesty and lost an opportunity to learn something on your own.

A Warning Against Internet Plagiarism

Plagiarism detection services are a professor's newest ally in the battle against academic dishonesty. Questionable research papers can be sent to these services (such as Turnitin.com and EVE2), which perform complex searches of the Internet and of a growing database of purchased term papers. The research paper will be returned to the professor with plagiarized sections annotated and the sources documented. The end result may be a failing grade on the essay, possibly a failing grade for the course, and, depending on the policies of your university, the very real possibility of expulsion.

ACKNOWLEDGE ALL SOURCES

The brand of straight-out dishonesty described above is one type of plagiarism. There is, however, another, subtler kind: when students incorporate somebody else's words *or* ideas into their papers without giving proper credit. To avoid this second—sometimes quite accidental—variety of plagiarism, familiarize yourself with the conventions for acknowledging sources. First and foremost, remember to give credit to any writer who supplies you with ideas, information, or specific words and phrases.

Quotations

- **Acknowledge your source when you quote a writer's words or phrases.** When you use someone else's words or phrases, you should reproduce his or her exact words in quotation marks, and be sure to properly credit the source.

> Already, Frost has hinted that Nature may be, as Radcliffe Squires
>
> suggests, "Nothing but an ash-white plain without love or faith or hope,
>
> where ignorant appetites cross by chance" (87).

- **If you quote more than four lines, set your quotation off from the body of the paper.** Start a new line; indent one inch (or ten spaces), and type the quotation, double-spaced. (You do not need to use quotation marks, as the format already tells the reader the passage is a quotation.)

> Samuel Maio made an astute observation about the nature of Weldon Kees's
>
> distinctive tone:
>
> > Kees has therefore combined a personal subject matter with an
> >
> > impersonal voice—that is, one that is consistent in its tone
> >
> > evenly recording the speaker's thoughts without showing any
> >
> > emotional intensity which might lie behind those thoughts. (136)

Citing Ideas

- **Acknowledge your source when you mention a critic's ideas.** Even if you are not quoting exact words or phrases, be sure to acknowledge the source of any original ideas or concepts you have used.

> Another explanation is suggested by Daniel Hoffman, a critic who has
>
> discussed the story: the killer hears the sound of his *own* heart (227).

- **Acknowledge your source when you paraphrase a writer's words.** To paraphrase a critic, you should do more than just rearrange his or her words: you should translate them into your own original sentences—again, always being sure to credit the original source. As an example, suppose you wish to refer to an insight of Randall Jarrell, who commented as follows on the images of spider, flower, and moth in Robert Frost's poem "Design":

RANDALL JARRELL'S ORIGINAL TEXT

Notice how the *heal-all*, because of its name, is the one flower in all the world picked to be the altar for this Devil's Mass; notice how *holding up* the moth brings something ritual and hieratic, a ghostly, ghastly formality, to this priest and its sacrificial victim.[1]

---

[1]*Poetry and the Age* (New York: Knopf, 1953) 42.

It would be too close to the original to write, without quotation marks, these sentences:

PLAGIARISTIC REWORDING

Frost picks the *heal-all* as the one flower in all the world to be the altar for this Devil's Mass. There is a ghostly, ghastly formality to the spider *holding up* the moth, like a priest holding a sacrificial victim.

This rewording, although not exactly in Jarrell's language, manages to steal his memorable phrases without giving him credit. Nor is it sufficient just to include Jarrell's essay in the works-cited list at the end of your paper. If you do, you are still a crook; you merely point to the scene of the crime. Instead, think through Jarrell's words to the point he is making, so that it can be restated in your own original way. If you want to keep any of his striking phrases (and why not?), put them exactly as he wrote them in quotations marks:

APPROPRIATE PARAPHRASE, ACKNOWLEDGES SOURCE

As Randall Jarrell points out, Frost portrays the spider as a kind of priest in a Mass, or Black Mass, elevating the moth like an object for sacrifice, with "a ghostly, ghastly formality" (42).

Note also that this improved passage gives Jarrell the credit not just for his words but for his insight into the poem. Both the idea and the words in which it was originally expressed are the properties of their originator. Finally, notice the page reference that follows the quotation (this system of documenting your sources is detailed in the next section).

DOCUMENT SOURCES USING MLA STYLE

You must document everything you take from another source. When you quote from other writers, when you borrow their information, when you summarize or paraphrase their ideas, make sure you give them proper credit. Identify the writer by name and cite the book, magazine, newspaper, pamphlet, Web site, or other source you have used.

The conventions that govern the proper way to document sources are available in the *MLA Handbook for Writers of Research Papers,* 7th ed. (New York: MLA, 2009). The following brief list of pointers is not meant to take the place of the *MLA Handbook* itself, but to give you a quick sense of the rules for documentation.

List of Sources

Keep a working list of your research sources—all the references from which you might quote, summarize, paraphrase, or take information. When your paper is in finished form, it will end with a neat copy of the works you actually used (once called a "Bibliography," now entitled "Works Cited").

Parenthetical References

In the body of your paper, every time you refer to a source, you need only to provide information to help a reader locate it in your works-cited list. You can usually give just the author's name and a page citation in parentheses. For example, if you are writing a paper on Weldon Kees's sonnet "For My Daughter" and want to include an observation you found on page 136 of Samuel Maio's book *Creating Another Self*, write:

> One critic has observed that the distinctive tone of "For My Daughter"
> depends on Kees's combination of personal subject matter with an
> impersonal voice (Maio 136).

If you mention the author's name in your sentence, you need give only the page number in your reference:

> As Samuel Maio has observed, Kees creates a distinctive tone in this sonnet
> by combining a personal subject with an impersonal voice (136).

If you have two books or magazine articles by Samuel Maio in your works-cited list, how will the reader tell them apart? In your text, refer to the title of each book or article by condensing it into a word or two. Condensed book titles are italicized, and condensed article titles are still placed within quotation marks.

> One critic has observed that the distinctive tone of "For My Daughter"
> depends on Kees's combination of personal subject matter with an
> impersonal voice (Maio, *Creating* 136).

Works-Cited List

Provide a full citation for each source on your works-cited page.   At the end of your paper, in your list of works cited, your reader will find a full description of your source—in the above examples, a critical book:

> Maio, Samuel. *Creating Another Self: Voices in Modern American Personal*
> *Poetry.* 2nd ed. Kirksville, MO: Thomas Jefferson UP, 2005. Print.

Put your works-cited list in proper form.   The *MLA Handbook* provides detailed instructions for citing a myriad of different types of sources, from books to online databases. Here is a partial checklist of the *Handbook*'s recommendations for presenting your works-cited list.

1. Start a new page for the works-cited list, and continue the page numbering from the body of your paper.
2. Center the title, "Works Cited," one inch from the top of the page.
3. Double-space between all lines (including after title and between entries).
4. Type each entry beginning at the left-hand margin. If an entry runs longer than a single line, indent the following lines one-half inch (or five full spaces) from the left-hand margin.
5. Alphabetize each entry according to the author's last name.
6. Include three sections in each entry: author, title, publication or access information. (You will, however, give slightly different information for a book, journal article, online source, or other reference.)

Citing Print Sources in MLA Style

For a book citation

    a. **Author's full name** as it appears on the title page, last name first, followed by a period.

    b. **Book's full title** (and subtitle, if it has one, separated by a colon) followed by a period. Remember to italicize the title. Also provide edition and volume information, if applicable, followed by a period.

    c. **Publication information:** City of publication followed by a colon; name of publisher followed by a comma; year of publication followed by a period; and publication medium—*Print*—followed by a period.

        (1) **Make your citation of the city of publication brief, but clear.** If the title page lists more than one city, cite only the first. For U.S. cities, you need not provide the state unless the name of the city alone may be confusing or is unfamiliar. For cities outside the United States, add a country abbreviation if the city is unfamiliar. For Canadian cities, use the province abbreviation. (Examples: Rome, GA; Leeds, Eng.; Victoria, BC)

        (2) **Shorten the publisher's name.** Eliminate articles (*A, An, The*), business abbreviations (*Co., Corp., Inc., Ltd.*), and descriptive words (*Books, House, Press, Publishers*). The exception is a university press, for which you should use the letters *U* (for University) and *P* (for Press). Use only the first listed *surname* of the publisher.

Publisher's Name	Proper Citation
Harvard University Press	Harvard UP
University of Chicago Press	U of Chicago P
Farrar, Straus and Giroux, Inc.	Farrar
Alfred A. Knopf, Inc.	Knopf

    d. **Optional additional information:** Any additional information that may be helpful for your reader can be provided at the end of a citation. For example, if the book is part of an established series or part of a multivolume set, put the name of the series or the complete work here.

The final citation for a book should read:

> Author's Last name, First name. *Book Title*. Ed. or vol. Publication city: Publisher, Year. Print.

For a journal or periodical article citation

    a. **Author's name,** last name first, followed by a period.

    b. **Title of article** followed by a period, all within quotation marks.

    c. **Journal publication information:** journal title (italicized); volume number followed by period, issue number; year of publication in parentheses followed by a colon; inclusive page numbers of the entire article followed by a period; and publication medium—*Print*—followed by a period.

or

> **Periodical publication information:** periodical title (italicized); day month year followed by a colon; page numbers of article (for continuous articles use inclusive pages, such as 31–33; for newspapers use starting page, such as C1+) followed by a period; and publication medium—*Print*—followed by a period.

The final citation for a journal article should read:

> Author's Last name, First name. "Article Title." *Journal* Volume.Issue
>
> (Year): Pages. Print.

The final citation for a periodical article should read:

> Author's Last name, First name. "Article Title." *Periodical* Day Month Year:
>
> Pages. Print.

Citing Web Sources in MLA Style

Like print sources, Internet sources should be documented with care. Before you begin your Internet search, be aware of the types of information you will want for your works-cited list. You can then record the information as you go. Keep track of the following information:

- Author's name
- Title of document
- Full information about publication in print form, when available
- Title of scholarly project, database, periodical, or professional or personal site
- Editor's name of project or database
- Date of electronic publication or last update
- Institution or organization sponsoring the Web site
- Date *you* accessed the source
- Web site address or URL

Although many Web sites provide much of this information at the beginning or ending of an article or at the bottom of the home page, you will find that it is not always available. Also note that as Web pages and even sites may sometimes disappear or change, you are well-advised to print out important pages for future reference.

For a Web resource citation

> a. **Author or editor's name,** last name first, followed by a period.
> b. **Title of work,** within quotation marks or italicized as appropriate, followed by a period.
> c. **Title of Web site,** in italics, followed by a period.
> d. **Sponsor or publisher of Web site** followed by a comma. If not available, use *N.p.*
> e. **Publication date** followed by a period. If data is not available, use *n.d.*
> f. **Publication medium—*Web*—**followed by a period.

g. **Date *you* accessed information:** day month year that you viewed document online.

h. **Optional URL:** if there is some reason your reader may not be able to access your Web page with the information provided, you may include the full URL, enclosed in angle brackets <>.

The final citation for a Web source should read:

> Author's Last name, First name. "Document Title." *Web site*. Web site
> Sponsor, Publication date. Web. Access Day Month Year.

For a print journal accessed on the Web

a. **Provide information for standard print citation**

   (1) **Author's name,** last name first, followed by a period.
   (2) **Title of work,** within quotation marks or italicized as appropriate, followed by a period.
   (3) **Print publication information:** journal title in italics; volume and issue number; year; page references, as available. If no pages are available, use *n. pag.*

b. **Provide Web access information**

   (1) **Title of Web site or database,** italicized.
   (2) **Publication medium—*Web*—**followed by period.
   (3) **Date *you* accessed information:** day month year that you viewed document online.

The final citation for a scholarly journal article obtained on the Web should read:

> Author's Last name, First name. "Article Title." *Journal* Volume.Issue (Year):
> Pages. *Web site or Online Database*. Web. Access Day Month Year.

Sample List of Works Cited

For a paper on Weldon Kees's "For My Daughter," a student's works-cited list might look as follows:

Works Cited

Grosholz, Emily. "The Poetry of Memory." *Weldon Kees: A Critical Introduction*. Ed. Jim Elledge. Metuchen, NJ: Scarecrow, 1985. 46–47. Print.

Kees, Weldon. *The Collected Poems of Weldon Kees*. Ed. Donald Justice. Lincoln: U of Nebraska P, 1975. Print.

Lane, Anthony. "The Disappearing Poet: What Ever Happened to Weldon Kees?" *New Yorker*. CondéNet, 4 July 2005. Web. 22 Aug. 2009.

Maio, Samuel. *Creating Another Self: Voice in Modern American Personal Poetry*. 2nd ed. Kirksville, MO: Thomas Jefferson UP, 2005. Print.

Nelson, Raymond. "The Fitful Life of Weldon Kees." *American Literary History* 1 (1989): 816–52. Print.

Reidel, James. *Vanished Act: The Life and Art of Weldon Kees*. Lincoln: U of Nebraska P, 2003. Print.

---, ed. *Weldon Kees*. Nebraska Center for Writers, Creighton U, n.d. Web. 26 Aug. 2009.

Ross, William T. *Weldon Kees*. Boston: Twayne, 1985. Print. Twayne's US Authors Ser. 484.

"Weldon Kees." *Poetry Out Loud*. National Endowment for the Arts and the Poetry Foundation, n.d. Web. 20 Sept. 2009.

See the Reference Guide for Citations at the end of this chapter for additional examples of the types of citations that you are likely to need for your essays, or check the seventh edition of the *MLA Handbook*.

As you put together your works-cited list, keep in mind that the little things—page numbers, quotation marks—count. Documentation may seem tedious, but it has an important purpose: it's for the reader of your paper who wants to pursue a topic you have researched. Luckily, you don't have to know the rules by heart. You can refer as necessary to the *MLA Handbook* or to the examples in this book.

Endnotes and Footnotes

Citations and quotations in the text of your essay should be brief and snappy, lest they bog down your prose. You may, however, wish to provide your reader with passages of less important (yet possibly valuable) information, or make qualifying statements ("On the other hand, not every expert agrees. John Binks finds poets are often a little magazine's only cash customers, while Molly MacGuire maintains that . . ."). To insert such information without awkwardly interrupting your paper, put it into an **endnote** (placed at the end of a paper) or a **footnote** (placed at the bottom of the page). Footnotes and endnotes are now used mainly for such asides, but they are also a time-honored way to document sources.

Adding footnotes

When an aside seems appropriate, insert a number in the text of your essay to send your reader to the corresponding note. Use the "Insert Footnote" option in your word processing program, or create a superscript number from the font menu. This will lift the number slightly above the level of your prose, so that it stands out.

> as many observers have claimed.[2]

Once you insert the number of your footnote into the text, your word processing program will cleverly take care of the formatting and placement of the footnote, automatically sending it to the bottom of the page.

> 2. On the other hand, not every expert agrees. John Binks, to name only one such observer, finds that poets are often a little magazine's only cash customers . . .

Citing sources with footnotes and endnotes

For a brief essay with only one or two citations, some professors prefer notes as simpler and more elegant than a very short works-cited list. Always check with your instructor on the preferred style. An endnote referencing a book looks like this:

1. Elizabeth Frank, *Louise Bogan: A Portrait* (New York: Knopf, 1985) 108–09.

If you later cite another passage in Frank's book, you need not repeat all its information. Just write:

2. Frank 192.

If your paper refers to two sources by Elizabeth Frank, give the full title of each in the first note citing it. Then, if you cite it again, use a shortened form of its title:

4. Frank, *Bogan* 192.

An endnote identifying a magazine article looks like this:

2. Louise Horton, "Who Reads Small Literary Magazines and What Good Do They Do?" *Texas Review* 9.1 (1984): 108–09.

If your professor prefers that you use endnotes to document sources, start a new page at the end of the body of your essay, titled "Notes."

Notes

1. Louise Horton, "Who Reads Small Literary Magazines and What Good Do They Do?" *Texas Review* 9.1 (1984): 108–10.

2. Elizabeth Frank, *Louise Bogan: A Portrait* (New York: Knopf, 1985): 108–25.

3. Frank 111.

SAMPLE STUDENT RESEARCH PAPER—PAGE 334

Professor Michael Cass of Mercer University asked his class to select the fiction writer on their reading list whose work had seemed most impressive and write a research paper defending that author's claim to literary greatness. See page 334 to read the research essay Stephanie Crowe wrote to fulfill the assignment.

CONCLUDING THOUGHTS

A well-crafted research essay is a wondrous thing—as delightful, in its own way, as a well-crafted poem or short story or play. Good essays prompt thought and add to knowledge. Writing a research paper sharpens your own mind and exposes you to the honed insights of other thinkers. Think of anything you write as a piece that could be published for the benefit of other people interested in your topic. After all, such a goal is not as far-fetched as it seems: this textbook, for example, features a number of papers written by students. Why shouldn't yours number among them? Aim high.

REFERENCE GUIDE FOR CITATIONS

Here is a comprehensive summary of the types of citations you are likely to need for most student papers. The format follows the current MLA standards for works-cited lists.

Print Publications
Books

No Author Listed

The Chicago Manual of Style, 15th ed. Chicago: U of Chicago P, 2003. Print.

One Author

Middlebrook, Diane Wood. *Anne Sexton: A Biography*. Boston: Houghton, 1991.
   Print.

Two or Three Authors

Jarman, Mark, and Robert McDowell. *The Reaper: Essays*. Brownsville, OR: Story
   Line, 1996. Print.

Four or More Authors

Phillips, Rodney, et al. *The Hand of the Poet*. New York: Rizzoli, 1997. Print.

or

Phillips, Rodney, Susan Benesch, Kenneth Benson, and Barbara Bergeron. *The Hand
   of the Poet*. New York: Rizzoli, 1997. Print.

Two Books by Same Author

Bawer, Bruce. *The Aspect of Eternity*. St. Paul: Graywolf, 1993. Print.

---. *Diminishing Fictions: Essays on the Modern American Novel and Its Critics*. St.
   Paul: Graywolf, 1988. Print.

Corporate Author

Poets and Writers. *A Writer's Guide to Copyright*. New York: Poets and Writers, 1979.
   Print.

Author and Editor

Shakespeare, William. *The Sonnets*. Ed. G. Blakemore Evans. Cambridge, Eng.: Cambridge UP, 1996. Print.

One Editor

Monteiro, George, ed. Conversations with Elizabeth Bishop. Jackson: UP of Mississippi, 1996. Print.

Two Editors

Craig, David, and Janet McCann, eds. *Odd Angles of Heaven: Contemporary Poetry by People of Faith*. Wheaton, IL: Shaw, 1994. Print.

Translation

Dante Alighieri. *Inferno: A New Verse Translation*. Trans. Michael Palma. New York: Norton, 2002. Print.

Introduction, Preface, Foreword, or Afterword

Thwaite, Anthony, Preface. *Contemporary Poets*. Ed. Thomas Riggs. 6th ed. New York: St. James, 1996. vii–viii. Print.

Lapham, Lewis. Introduction. *Understanding Media: The Extensions of Man*. By Marshall McLuhan. Cambridge: MIT P, 1994. vi–x. Print.

Work in an Anthology

Rodriguez, Richard. "Aria: A Memoir of a Bilingual Childhood." *The Best American Essays of the Century*. Ed. Robert Atwan and Joyce Carol Oates. Boston: Houghton, 2001. 447–66. Print. Best American Ser.

Translation in an Anthology

Neruda, Pablo. "We Are Many." Trans. Alastair Reid. *Literature: An Introduction to Fiction, Poetry, Drama, and Writing*. Ed. X. J. Kennedy and Dana Gioia. 11th ed. New York: Longman, 2010. 922. Print.

Multivolume Work

Wellek, René. *A History of Modern Criticism, 1750–1950*. 8 vols. New Haven: Yale UP, 1955–92. Print.

One Volume of a Multivolume Work

Wellek, René. *A History of Modern Criticism, 1750–1950*. Vol. 7. New Haven: Yale UP, 1991. Print.

Book in a Series

Ross, William T. *Weldon Kees*. Boston: Twayne, 1985. Print. Twayne's US Authors Ser. 484.

Republished Book

Ellison, Ralph. *Invisible Man*. 1952. New York: Vintage, 1995. Print.

Revised or Subsequent Editions

Janouch, Gustav. *Conversations with Kafka*. Trans. Goronwy Rees. Rev. ed. New York: New Directions, 1971. Print.

Reference Books

Signed Article in Reference Book

Cavoto, Janice E. "Harper Lee's *To Kill a Mockingbird*." *The Oxford Encyclopedia of American Literature*. Ed. Jay Parini. Vol. 2. New York: Oxford UP, 2004. 418–21. Print.

Unsigned Encyclopedia Article—Standard Reference Book

"James Dickey." *The New Encyclopaedia Britannica: Micropaedia*. 15th ed. 1987. Print.

Dictionary Entry

"Design." *Merriam-Webster's Collegiate Dictionary*. 11th ed. 2003. Print.

Periodicals

Journal

Salter, Mary Jo. "The Heart Is Slow to Learn." *New Criterion* 10.8 (1992): 23–29. Print.

Signed Magazine Article

Gioia, Dana. "Studying with Miss Bishop." *New Yorker* 5 Sept. 1986: 90–101. Print.

Unsigned Magazine Article

"The Real Test." *New Republic* 5 Feb. 2001: 7. Print.

Newspaper Article

Lyall, Sarah. "In Poetry, Ted Hughes Breaks His Silence on Sylvia Plath." *New York Times* 19 Jan. 1998, natl. ed.: A1+. Print.

Signed Book Review

Fugard, Lisa. "Divided We Love." Rev. of *Unaccustomed Earth,* by Jhumpa Lahiri. *Los Angeles Times* 30 Mar. 2008: R1. Print.

Unsigned, Untitled Book Review

Rev. of *Otherwise: New and Selected Poems,* by Jane Kenyon. *Virginia Quarterly Review* 72 (1996): 136. Print.

Web Publications

Web Site

Liu, Alan, ed. Home Page. *Voice of the Shuttle.* Dept. of English, U of California, Santa Barbara, n.d. Web. 17 Oct. 2008.

Document on a Web Site

"A Hughes Timeline." *PBS Online.* Public Broadcasting Service, 2001. Web. 20 Sept. 2008.

"Wallace Stevens." *Poets.org.* Academy of American Poets, n.d. Web. 20 Sept. 2009.

Online Reference Database

"Brooks, Gwendolyn." *Encyclopaedia Britannica Online.* Encyclopaedia Britannica, 2007. Web. 15 Feb. 2007.

Entire Online Book, Previously Appeared in Print

Jewett, Sarah Orne. *The Country of the Pointed Firs*. Boston: Houghton, 1910.
Bartleby.com. Web. 10 Oct. 2009.

Article in Online Newspaper

Atwood, Margaret. "The Writer: A New Canadian Life-Form." *New York Times*. New
York Times, 18 May 1997. Web. 20 Aug. 2008.

Article in Online Magazine

Garner, Dwight. "Jamaica Kincaid: The Salon Interview." *Salon*. Salon Media Group,
13 Jan. 1996. Web. 15 Feb. 2006.

Article in Online Scholarly Journal

Carter, Sarah. "From the Ridiculous to the Sublime: Ovidian and Neoplatonic
Registers in *A Midsummer Night's Dream*." *Early Modern Literary Studies* 12.1
(2006): 1–31. Web. 18 Jan. 2009.

Article from a Scholarly Journal, Part of an Archival Online Database

Finch, Annie, "My Father Dickinson: On Poetic Influence." *Emily Dickinson Journal*
17.2 (2008): 24–38. *Project Muse*. Web. 18 Jan. 2009.

Article Accessed via a Library Subscription Service

Seitler, Dana. "Unnatural Selection: Mothers, Eugenic Feminism, and Charlotte
Perkins Gilman's Regeneration Narratives." *American Quarterly* 55.1 (2003):
61–87. *ProQuest*. Web. 7 July 2008.

Painting or Photograph Accessed Online

Bruegel, Pieter, *Landscape with the Fall of Icarus*. 1558. Musées royaux des Beaux-
Arts de Belgique, Brussels. *ibiblio.org*. Center for the Public Domain and
UNC-CH. Web. 21 Nov. 2008.

CD-ROM Reference Works

CD-ROM Publication

"Appall." *The Oxford English Dictionary*. 2nd ed. Oxford: Oxford UP, 1992. CD-ROM.

Periodically Published Information, Collected on CD-ROM

Kakutani, Michiko. "Slogging Surreally in the Vietnamese Jungle." Rev. of *The Things They Carried*, by Tim O'Brien. *New York Times* 6 Mar. 1990: C6. CD-ROM. *New York Times Ondisc*. UMI-ProQuest. Oct. 1993.

Miscellaneous Sources

Compact Disc (CD)

Shakespeare, William. *The Complete Arkangel Shakespeare: 38 Fully-Dramatized Plays*. Narr. Eileen Atkins and John Gielgud. Read by Imogen Stubbs, Joseph Fiennes, et al. Audio Partners, 2003. CD.

Audiocassette

Roethke, Theodore. *Theodore Roethke Reads His Poetry*. Caedmon, 1972. Audiocassette.

Videocassette

Henry V. By William Shakespeare. Dir. Laurence Olivier. Perf. Laurence Olivier. Two Cities Films. 1944. Paramount, 1988. Videocassette.

DVD

Hamlet. By William Shakespeare. Perf. Laurence Olivier, Eileen Herlie, and Basil Sydney. Two Cities Films. 1948. Criterion, 2000. DVD.

Film

Hamlet. By William Shakespeare. Dir. Franco Zeffirelli. Perf. Mel Gibson, Glenn Close, Helena Bonham Carter, Alan Bates, and Paul Scofield. Warner, 1991. Film.

Television or Radio Program

Moby Dick. By Herman Melville. Dir. Franc Roddam. Perf. Patrick Stewart and Gregory Peck. 2 episodes. USA Network. 16–17 Mar. 1998. Television.

46 WRITING AS DISCOVERY: KEEPING A JOURNAL

I have all my life regretted
that I did not keep a regular journal.

—SIR WALTER SCOTT

The novelist E. M. Forster once remarked, "How do I know what I think until I see what I say?" Few writers know precisely what they are going to say before they begin. Writing isn't simply a way to communicate ideas; it is also a way to formulate them, to try out new thoughts and hash them through. It is also a wonderful way to explore ideas that may eventually grow into longer pieces of formal writing.

THE REWARDS OF KEEPING A JOURNAL

Many instructors ask students to respond to reading in a journal—a day-to-day account of what they read and how they react to it. One great advantage of a journal is that it allows you to express your thoughts and feelings immediately, in your own words, before they grow cold. You can set down all your miscellaneous reactions to the reading, whether or not they fit into a paper topic. (If you have to write a paper later on, your journal just might suggest topics galore.) Journals are a useful place for collecting impressions, working through your ideas, and trying out false starts until you find the one that leads you someplace interesting for both you and your reader.

Journals can be useful study tools, too. If your course includes a midterm or final examination, you may well find that rereading your journal will help you to remember details of the works you read earlier in the term.

While some instructors give directives for journal entries, assigning essay questions or particular topics to address, others will give a more open-ended assignment, asking only that students respond in a way that shows they are interacting with the material. Either way, to get the most out of the experience, you might consider a few tips:

- **Capture your first reaction.** Read with pen in hand, jotting down anything you wish to remember. Write about anything that catches your attention or defies your interpretation. Does a line of dialogue surprise you? Make a note of it. Does a particular sentence seem significant? Comment on it. Does something in the story not make sense? Record your bewilderment. Better still, try to push past

1997

it into understanding. If you're at first puzzled by a character's motivation or by a line of poetry that resists interpretation, try to work through your puzzlement. A snippet from a journal entry on Denise Levertov's poem "Ancient Stairway" (see page 830) might be as unprocessed as this:

> What does this poem mean? I'm on the first line, and I'm already confused. What does she mean by the line "Footsteps like water hollow?" How can water be hollow? Oh, wait . . . maybe hollow really goes with the line after it . . . so the footsteps hollow the "broad curves of stone" which I guess means the steps. But why didn't she break the lines to make the poem easier to read, I wonder. Why not break the line after water instead of hollow? But I like how the next line is just two words "ascending, descending." I guess this means the stairs go both ways like all stairs.

Writing as you read can help you to begin to get a handle on difficult passages. It can also focus your mind. If your thoughts tend to meander away from the pages before you, or if you find yourself tempted to skim instead of paying close attention, writing in your journal can keep you involved and alert.

▪ **Just get it down.** In keeping a journal, you are writing primarily for yourself. You aren't obliged to polish your prose. It isn't necessary to develop your ideas. Just jot them down. Your aim is to store information without delay, to record your observations and impressions. Although your instructor may read your journal, he or she is unlikely to be looking there for fully processed ideas; those will come in more formal pieces of writing. Your teacher will most likely be reading your journal to ascertain that you are thinking your way through the work and the issues it raises. To be safe, though, ask your professor how formal or informal the journal needs to be.

▪ **Get personal.** Your journal is a place in which to sound off and express gut reactions. Don't just copy your class notes into it. Don't simply record plot details: first X happened, then Y happened, then Z. Instead, note your own emotional responses to a piece of literature, and consider what about the work is causing you to react. Your first reactions can provide a jumping-off point for further exploration.

▪ **Keep writing after you've said it all.** You may think you've said everything you have to say after you've written for five minutes or covered half a page. Keep writing, working quickly, without agonizing over where your words are taking you. Sometimes when we write beyond the point where we'd rather stop, we surprise ourselves with new ideas and insights. This is why many instructors will assign a certain length to journal entries or ask students to write for a particular amount of time.

▪ **Read closely.** It can be tempting to paint your journal entries with a broad brush, writing about a poem's central theme or a story's plot. Don't forget the value of reading closely. Examine a paragraph, or a sentence, or even a particularly significant word. Like our DNA, which encodes genetic information about our whole selves, sometimes a small part of a poem, story, or play can reveal much about the work as a whole.

▪ **Stick with the text.** A moment in a story might remind you of something in your own past. Connie's encounter with Arnold Friend in "Where Are You

Going, Where Have You Been?," for example, may cause you to hearken back to your own brush with a creepy character. It might be tempting to leave the story behind and write about your own experience, but doing so won't teach you much about the story. You will learn more by giving the literary work itself your full attention.

- **Try out risky ideas.** A journal is no place to play it safe. Try for new insights—go out on a limb. You can try on new ideas and discard the ones that don't fit. By taking some risks, you may come up with a more provocative thesis than you otherwise would have, one that eventually will lead you to write a more dynamic term paper.

- **Follow your interests.** If you aren't given a specific topic to treat in your journal, attack the aspects of a literary work that most intrigue you. This will make your journaling more interesting—both for you and for your reader. If you should find yourself stumped, you can always turn to any of the "Topics for Writing" that appear at the end of the chapter in which your subject appears. These can provide a good starting point for a journal entry.

- **Write often.** Journals are useful only if you keep them up to date. Jot down your insights while you still have a story, poem, or play freshly in mind. Fall weeks behind, and you will have to grind out a journal from scratch, the night before it is due, and the whole project will decay into meaningless drudgery. Instead, if you faithfully do a little reading and writing every day or so, you will find yourself keeping track of the life of your mind. You will have a lively record not only of the literature you have read, but also of your personal involvement with it.

SAMPLE JOURNAL ENTRY

The following journal entry was written by Virginia Andros, a student at Saint Joseph's University in Philadelphia. Her subject was the opening of T. S. Eliot's "The Love Song of J. Alfred Prufrock," which can be found on page 995. She wrote these entries in longhand, in a notebook. (Some instructors will accept journals composed on and printed out from a computer; if unsure, have your professor clarify his or her preference.)

"Prufrock" Reflections

This poem begins with six lines written in a language I don't speak, Spanish, maybe, or Italian. I'm going to ignore those lines for now—they don't seem to be part of the poem itself. For now I'll worry about the actual poem. I like the first line: "Let us go then, you and I" because it feels like an invitation—like the lines are being spoken directly to me. I can picture the speaker stretching out his hand for me. The next lines are strange, though: "When the evening is spread out against the sky / Like a patient etherized upon a table." The part about the sky is beautiful, but the image that follows it is creepy. Already I'm wondering what kind of trip this is going to be, and if I should trust my guide.

So where are we going? We're traveling "through certain half-deserted streets" to get to "one-night cheap hotels / And sawdust restaurants with oyster-shells." What's a sawdust restaurant? Maybe the food tastes like sawdust? Or maybe the place is messy, with sawdust on the floor. It's interesting that the poem mentions "oyster shells" and not the oysters themselves. It's like we're concentrating on the garbage left over after the meal is done. The phrase "muttering retreats" is odd too . . . again, it sounds pretty negative. What's muttering? A crowd of people in the hotel lobby or the restaurant? They're not laughing or having pleasant conversation. The word "muttering" even sounds nasty . . . as though the people are complaining under their breath about the bad décor and lousy service.

Here's the next two lines. "Streets that follow like a tedious argument / Of insidious intent." How can streets be like a tedious argument? Confusion! But I picture cramped streets, in the center of a city. Maybe one leads to the next, which leads to the next, and the next . . . the way in a tedious argument one line of reasoning leads you to the next and pretty soon you've forgotten what you were arguing about in the first place, because you're bickering about something else entirely. I had to look up "insidious": it means slowly destructive. Is it the streets that have insidious intent, or the argument? I think maybe it's the argument . . . but maybe the streets do too in some way. The streets are slowly destructive? To whom? Okay, my head's starting to hurt. Maybe the streets are destructive to me, the person the speaker is speaking to.

Now the speaker talks to me (or at least to someone) directly again: "Oh, do not ask, 'What is it?' / Let us go and make our visit." I like these lines! I notice that they rhyme, so now I'm looking back to see if the other lines I've already read do too. Some do, but I hadn't noticed. Anyway, these lines make me wonder, who is the speaker? Is it J. Alfred Prufrock? And how is this a love poem? Maybe the "you" in the poem is a girlfriend? If so, this isn't much of a date.

New stanza: "In the room the women come and go / Talking of Michelangelo." Maybe we're in a museum?

Here comes more description of a sad, dirty city. The fog is "yellow" and there's chimney soot. If I'm right, and the speaker is taking his girlfriend around the city, he's sort of a loser. Why isn't he taking her someplace beautiful . . . to a nice restaurant, or out dancing? Why is he making her walk down a dirty street? Why is this poem so unromantic? If I were the girlfriend, there wouldn't be a second date.

This journal entry examines its subject closely, using key words and phrases to begin to get at the poem's meaning. Its author freely admits her confusion over certain challenging lines, but isn't content to rest on first impressions. By puzzling her way line by line through part of the poem, she begins to get at issues central to the entire poem: its speaker, its tone, its form, and its literal meaning. Doing your thinking on the page can be a crucial step in the writing—and reading—process. Even if keeping a journal isn't one of your course assignments, you might profitably apply these techniques to taking notes as you read through a poem, short story, or play. When it comes time to write a more formal paper, you're likely to be glad you've been actively thinking the material through all along.

47

WRITING AN
ESSAY EXAM

The test of literature is, I suppose,
whether we ourselves live more intensely for the reading of it.

—ELIZABETH DREW

Why might an instructor choose to give an essay examination? It may sometimes seem like sheer sadism, but there are good reasons for using essays to test your knowledge of a subject. Longer, more involved answers can reveal not just how well you have memorized course material but also how thoroughly you have processed it. An essay exam allows you to demonstrate that you can think critically about the literature you have read and the issues your reading has raised. It lets you show how well you can marshal evidence to support your assertions. It also gives you a chance to draw connections between the literary works you have read and the main themes of the course.

Whether your exam is take-home or in-class, open-book or closed, the following strategies will help you to show off what you know:

- **Be prepared.** Before you take the exam, review the readings. If you have been highlighting and annotating all semester, you will find yourself well rewarded for that extra bit of effort. A glance at highlighted portions of text can help refresh your memory about passages in a text that struck you as particularly important; your marginalia can help you to recall why that was the case.

- **Review your notes.** It is also a good idea to review any notes you have taken for the course. If you kept a reading journal, go back and reread it. (You will be surprised how many specific memories rereading your journal will trigger.) Even if you are permitted to use your books during the exam, reacquainting yourself with the material beforehand can help you better recall what it is you are looking for in those open books.

  As you review, be sure to think about the big picture. How do the literary works you have read relate to each other? If you have been reading theory and criticism, how might it apply to the course's content? If you have been given historical background about the period in which a work was written, how does the work embody its author's time? Sometimes it might help just to write down a few of the central ideas the course has explored on a separate sheet of paper—to summarize a few of the major insights the course has offered.

■ **Think it through.** Once you have been given the exam, be sure to read it all the way through before you begin writing. Figure out how much time you can afford to spend per section. Pay attention to how many points each question is worth; you may well want to budget your time accordingly. Leave yourself time to proofread your responses and add any missing information.

When you are ready to start, you might find it helpful first to attack questions about which you feel more confident. Go ahead, but save enough time to tackle the tougher ones as well.

■ **Read the questions carefully.** To ensure that you are answering the actual questions you have been asked, pay special attention to words in the directions that seem important. Verbs such as "analyze," "summarize," "explicate," "compare," "contrast," "evaluate," "interpret," and "explain" give clues to what your focus should be. Highlight or underline these action words so that you can more readily keep them in mind as you write. Understanding what you are being asked to do is crucial. Failing to follow directions might lose you precious points, no matter how brilliantly you write on your subject.

Careful reading and highlighting can also help you remember to address all parts of any given question. Don't get so caught up in answering one part of a question that you neglect the other parts.

■ **Understand your purpose.** Whenever you write, it pays to consider your audience and your purpose. Inevitably, the audience for an essay exam response will be your instructor. It's likely that he or she will be looking to see whether you have understood the material on which you are being tested. As you consider the questions you are about to answer, think back to concepts stressed by the instructor during in-class discussions. Try to touch on these concepts as you write, as long as you can do so without losing your focus. Also, since your instructor is familiar with the literary work under discussion, there's no need to relate the whole story in your exam response. Unless you are specifically asked to summarize, don't give any more plot details than are needed to accomplish the assigned task.

For clues about what your purpose should be, pay attention to those action words you have highlighted in the directions. Here are some common ones:

Analyze	Consider how a single element of the text contributes to its full meaning or effect.
Compare	Explore how two or more things resemble each other.
Contrast	Explore how two or more things differ from each other.
Evaluate	Examine a work with the purpose of determining its quality or importance.
Explain	Clarify a concept.
Explicate	Explain a brief work or a passage from a longer work in detail to show how its parts contribute to the work as a whole.
Interpret	Express a literary work's meaning in your own words.
Paraphrase	Restate a passage in your own words.
Prove	Provide evidence of the truth of a claim, drawing on information from the literary work under study.
Relate	Show a connection between two or more items.
Summarize	Give a shortened version of a literary work, touching on key points.

▪ **Plan before you write. Start with a clear thesis that accurately addresses the exam question.** A critical step in writing a good essay exam is creating a thesis sentence that succinctly expresses your main point. Using the exam question to provide direction for your thesis, come up with a statement that is both decisive and specific.

For example, if you have been asked to describe the grandmother's transformation in Flannery O'Connor's "A Good Man Is Hard to Find," your thesis should say something specific about *how* or *why* she gains insight in her last moments of life. The first thesis below does not address the assignment—it describes the grandmother, not the grandmother's transformation. It is accurate but incomplete since it does not lead anywhere useful.

IRRELEVANT THESIS
The grandmother in "A Good Man Is Hard to Find" is self-centered and silly.

The rough thesis that follows sticks with the merely obvious.

ROUGH THESIS
The grandmother in "A Good Man Is Hard to Find" is a silly, self-centered woman who undergoes a transformation at the end of the story.

The revised thesis makes a more decisive statement, providing specifics about what happens at the story's climax.

REVISED THESIS
In "A Good Man Is Hard to Find," the grandmother is transformed from a silly, self-centered woman into a wiser, more caring one.

A final revision goes further, venturing to say not only what happens in the story but why it happens. It provides a good road map for writing an essay exam.

FINAL THESIS
In "A Good Man Is Hard to Find," the grandmother is transformed by her proximity to death from a silly, self-centered woman into a wiser, more caring one.

▪ **Create a rough outline.** Though an essay question might seem like an occasion for off-the-cuff writing, it's a good idea to sketch a rough outline before you plunge in. As you write, follow the outline point by point. An outline for an essay response based on the final thesis above might look something like this:

1. Grandmother transformed by closeness to death
2. Starts out silly
   Lives in the past
   Gets directions wrong

3. Becomes wiser
    Sees her mistakes
    Sees her connection to the Misfit
4. Starts out self-centered
    Smuggles cat on trip
    Makes family drive out of way
5. Becomes caring
    Reaches out to Misfit
    Sees him as her own child
6. Nearness to death
    Hears her son get shot
    Misfit's quotation

- **Make it shapely.** Like a more formal piece of writing, your answer will need an introduction that establishes the point you will be making. It also should include a conclusion that summarizes your argument (preferably without too much bald-faced restatement) and reinforces your thesis. The paragraphs in between should be used to flesh out your argument.

- **Give evidence.** Back up your thesis, and any assertion you make along the way, with proof from the story, poem, or play you are discussing. Direct quotations generally make the most convincing evidence, but if you are working from memory, you can do the job with references to the text. To make your argument more convincing and establish how familiar you are with the material, be as specific as you can manage.

- **Keep your focus.** As you write, refer frequently to your outline. Be sure to keep your argument on track. Don't ramble or repeat yourself to fill up space; to do so will give the impression that you are uncertain about your response or the material.

- **Make smooth transitions.** Use transitional words and phrases to connect each new idea to the one that precedes it. These handy tools can signal your intentions. If your argument is changing directions, you might signal as much with words and phrases such as "in contrast," "on the other hand," "however," "yet," or "conversely." If you are continuing along the same track you've been traveling, try "in addition," "similarly," "furthermore," or "moreover." To indicate cause and effect, you might use "because," "therefore," "as a result," or "consequently." If you make it easy for your reader to follow your train of thought, the end result is likely to be a grateful reader.

- **Pay attention to detail.** Be sure to proofread your essay before handing it in. Nothing undermines a writer's authority faster than spelling mistakes and grammatical errors. Even illegible handwriting can try a reader's patience—never a good idea when a grade is involved.

CHECKLIST: Taking an Essay Exam

Exam Preparation

☐ Skim the literary works that will be on the exam.

☐ Reread all your notes and, if you have kept one, your reader's journal.

☐ Consider how the literary works on the exam relate to each other.

☐ Consider possible relationships between the literary works and any literary criticism, theory, or historical background you have been given in the course.

Taking the Exam

☐ When you are given the exam, quickly read it all the way through.

☐ Calculate how much time you can spend per question.

☐ Read each essay question carefully, underlining key words. Take note of multipart questions.

☐ Understand your purpose before you begin.

☐ Write a thesis sentence that accurately answers the exam question.

☐ Sketch an outline for the essay response.

☐ Include an introductory paragraph and a conclusion.

☐ Back up each point you make with evidence from the text.

☐ Don't give plot summaries unless asked to.

☐ Use transitional phrases to link paragraphs and ideas.

☐ Proofread your exam before handing it in.

PRACTICE ESSAY EXAM

The purpose of an essay exam is to test your ability to read and to effectively discuss a literary work in writing. A well-constructed exam response reveals both how well you read and interpret a work and how capably you organize and present your argument. An exam essay will not be as carefully prepared or polished as a paper you write and revise at home, but it still needs to be clear, intelligent, well-structured, and accurately based on the assigned text.

If you have never done an essay exam before, it will help to try your hand at a practice test. Here is a celebrated story by Toni Cade Bambara, along with a typical essay exam question. If you invest 45 minutes in writing a response to this sample question, you will find your actual essay exam far less intimidating.

Practice Essay Exam Question

Write a short essay on the main theme of Toni Cade Bambara's "The Lesson." In your interpretation, discuss the theme in relation to the story's narrator, main characters, setting, tone, style, and title. Demonstrate how each of these elements contributes to the effective communication of the theme. Provide specific examples to support your analysis.

Toni Cade Bambara

The Lesson   1972

Toni Cade Bambara (1939–1995), author, teacher, and civil rights activist, was born Miltona Cade in New York, and legally added her new last name in 1970. She grew up in Harlem and in the troubled Bedford-Stuyvesant section of Brooklyn. After taking her master's degree at City College, she worked for the New York State Welfare Department as a case investigator. Later she set out to learn dance and filmmaking; she studied commedia dell'arte in Florence and mime in Paris. After her fiction began to make her well known, she accepted invitations to teach at Duke, Stephens, Emory, Spelman College, and Rutgers University. Bambara's works of fiction are Gorilla, My Love *(1972), which contains the story "The Lesson,"* The Sea Birds Are Still Alive *(1977),* The Salt Eaters*

Toni Cade Bambara

(1980), and Those Bones Are Not My Child *(edited by Toni Morrison and posthumously published in 1999). She conducted workshops on writing and community organization at museums, prisons, libraries, colleges, and community centers, as well as recreation programs for psychiatric patients at New York City's Metropolitan Hospital. As a storyteller, Bambara devoted herself to correcting stereotypes of African Americans. She also wrote screenplays and edited two anthologies of African American literature,* The Black Woman *(1970) and* Tales and Stories for Black Folks *(1971). She died of cancer in 1995.*

Back in the days when everyone was old and stupid or young and foolish and me and Sugar were the only ones just right, this lady moved on our block with nappy hair and proper speech and no makeup. And quite naturally we laughed at her, laughed the way we did at the junk man who went about his business like he was some big-time president and his sorry-ass horse his secretary. And we kinda hated her too, hated the way we did the winos who cluttered up our parks and pissed on our handball walls and stank up our hallways and stairs so you couldn't halfway play hide-and-seek without a goddamn gas mask. Miss Moore was her name. The only woman on the block with no first name. And she was black as hell, cept for her feet, which were fish-white and spooky. And she was always planning these boring-ass things for us to do, us being my cousin, mostly, who lived on the block cause we all moved North the same time and to the same apartment then spread out gradual to breathe. And our parents would yank our heads into some kinda shape and crisp up our clothes so we'd be presentable for travel with Miss Moore, who always looked like she was going to church, though she never did. Which is just one of the things the grownups talked about when they talked behind her back like a dog. But when she came calling with some sachet she'd sewed up or some gingerbread she'd made or some book, why then they'd all be too embarrassed to turn her down and we'd get handed over all spruced up. She'd been to college and said it was only right that she should take responsibility for the young ones' education, and she not even related by marriage or blood. So they'd go for it. Specially Aunt Gretchen. She was the main gofer in the family. You got some ole dumb shit foolishness you want somebody to go for, you send for Aunt Gretchen. She been screwed into the go-along for so long, it's a blood-deep natural thing with her. Which is how she got saddled with me and Sugar and Junior in the first place while our mothers were in a la-de-da apartment up the block having a good ole time.

So this one day Miss Moore rounds us all up at the mailbox and it's puredee° hot and she's knockin herself out about arithmetic. And school suppose to let up in summer I heard, but she don't never let up. And the starch in my pinafore scratching the shit outta me and I'm really hating this nappy-head bitch and her goddamn college degree. I'd much rather go to the pool or to the show where it's cool. So me and Sugar leaning on the mailbox being surly, which is a Miss Moore word. And Flyboy checking out what everybody brought for lunch. And Fat Butt already wasting his peanut-butter-and-jelly sandwich like the pig he is. And Junebug punchin on Q.T.'s arm for potato chips. And Rosie Giraffe shifting from one hip to the other waiting for somebody to step on her foot or ask her if she from Georgia so she can kick ass, preferably Mercedes'. And Miss Moore asking us do we know what money is, like we a bunch of retards. I mean real money, she say, like it's only poker chips or Monopoly papers we lay on the grocer. So right away I'm tired of this and say so. And would much rather snatch Sugar and go to the Sunset and terrorize the West Indian kids and take their hair ribbons and their money too. And Miss Moore files that remark away for next week's lesson on brotherhood, I can tell. And finally I say we oughta get to the subway cause it's cooler and besides we might meet some cute boys. Sugar done swiped her mama's lipstick, so we ready.

So we heading down the street and she's boring us silly about what things cost and what our parents make and how much goes for rent and how money ain't divided

°*puredee*: pretty.

up right in this country. And then she gets to the part about we all poor and live in the slums, which I don't feature. And I'm ready to speak on that, but she steps out in the street and hails two cabs just like that. Then she hustles half the crew in with her and hands me a five-dollar bill and tells me to calculate 10 percent tip for the driver. And we're off. Me and Sugar and Junebug and Flyboy hangin out the window and hollering to everybody, putting lipstick on each other cause Flyboy a faggot anyway, and making farts with our sweaty armpits. But I'm mostly trying to figure how to spend this money. But they all fascinated with the meter ticking and Junebug starts laying bets as to how much it'll read when Flyboy can't hold his breath no more. Then Sugar lays bets as to how much it'll be when we get there. So I'm stuck. Don't nobody want to go for my plan, which is to jump out at the next light and run off to the first bar-b-que we can find. Then the driver tells us to get the hell out cause we there already. And the meter reads eighty-five cents. And I'm stalling to figure out the tip and Sugar say give him a dime. And I decide he don't need it bad as I do, so later for him. But then he tries to take off with Junebug foot still in the door so we talk about his mama something ferocious. Then we check out that we on Fifth Avenue and everybody dressed up in stockings. One lady in a fur coat, hot as it is. White folks crazy.

"This is the place," Miss Moore say, presenting it to us in the voice she uses at the museum. "Let's look in the windows before we go in."

"Can we steal?" Sugar asks very serious like she's getting the ground rules squared   5
away before she plays. "I beg your pardon," say Miss Moore, and we fall out. So she leads us around the windows of the toy store and me and Sugar screamin, "This is mine, that's mine, I gotta have that, that was made for me, I was born for that," till Big Butt drowns us out.

"Hey, I'm going to buy that there."

"That there? You don't even know what it is, stupid."

"I do so," he say punchin on Rosie Giraffe. "It's a microscope."

"Whatcha gonna do with a microscope, fool?"

"Look at things."   10

"Like what, Ronald?" ask Miss Moore. And Big Butt ain't got the first notion. So here go Miss Moore gabbing about the thousands of bacteria in a drop of water and the somethinorother in a speck of blood and the million and one living things in the air around us is invisible to the naked eye. And what she say that for? Junebug go to town on that "naked" and we rolling. Then Miss Moore ask what it cost. So we all jam into the window smudgin it up and the price tag say $300. So then she ask how long'd take for Big Butt and Junebug to save up their allowances. "Too long," I say. "Yeh," adds Sugar, "outgrown it by that time." And Miss Moore say no, you never outgrow learning instruments. "Why, even medical students and interns and," blah, blah, blah. And we ready to choke Big Butt for bringing it up in the first damn place.

"This here costs four hundred eighty dollars," say Rosie Giraffe. So we pile up all over her to see what she pointin out. My eyes tell me it's a chunk of glass cracked with something heavy, and different-color inks dripped into the splits, then the whole thing put into a oven or something. But for $480 it don't make sense.

"That's a paperweight made of semi-precious stones fused together under tremendous pressure," she explains slowly, with her hands doing the mining and all the factory work.

"So what's a paperweight?" asks Rosie Giraffe.

"To weigh paper with, dumbbell," say Flyboy, the wise man from the East.   15

"Not exactly," say Miss Moore, which is what she say when you warm or way off too. "It's to weigh paper down so it won't scatter and make your desk untidy." So right away me and Sugar curtsy to each other and then to Mercedes who is more the tidy type.

"We don't keep paper on top of the desk in my class," say Junebug, figuring Miss Moore crazy or lyin one.

"At home, then," she say. "Don't you have a calendar and a pencil case and a blotter and a letter-opener on your desk at home where you do your homework?" And she know damn well what our homes look like cause she nosys around in them every chance she gets.

"I don't even have a desk," say Junebug. "Do we?"

"No. And I don't get no homework neither," say Big Butt.   20

"And I don't even have a home," say Flyboy like he do at school to keep the white folks off his back and sorry for him. Send this poor kid to camp posters, is his specialty.

"I do," says Mercedes. "I have a box of stationery on my desk and a picture of my cat. My godmother bought the stationery and the desk. There's a big rose on each sheet and the envelopes smell like roses."

"Who wants to know about your smelly-ass stationery," say Rosie Giraffe fore I can get my two cents in.

"It's important to have a work area all your own so that . . ."

"Will you look at this sailboat, please," say Flyboy, cuttin her off and pointin to   25
the thing like it was his. So once again we tumble all over each other to gaze at this magnificent thing in the toy store which is just big enough to maybe sail two kittens across the pond if you strap them to the posts tight. We all start reciting the price tag like we in assembly. "Handcrafted sailboat of fiberglass at one thousand one hundred ninety-five dollars."

"Unbelievable," I hear myself say and am really stunned. I read it again for myself just in case the group recitation put me in a trance. Same thing. For some reason this pisses me off. We look at Miss Moore and she lookin at us, waiting for I dunno what.

"Who'd pay all that when you can buy a sailboat set for a quarter at Pop's, a tube of glue for a dime, and a ball of string for eight cents? It must have a motor and a whole lot else besides," I say. "My sailboat cost me about fifty cents."

"But will it take water?" say Mercedes with her smart ass.

"Took mine to Alley Pond Park once," say Flyboy. "String broke. Lost it. Pity."

"Sailed mine in Central Park and it keeled over and sank. Had to ask my father   30
for another dollar."

"And you got the strap," laugh Big Butt. "The jerk didn't even have a string on it. My old man wailed on his behind."

Little Q.T. was staring hard at the sailboat and you could see he wanted it bad. But he too little and somebody'd just take it from him. So what the hell. "This boat for kids, Miss Moore?"

"Parents silly to buy something like that just to get all broke up," say Rosie Giraffe.

"That much money it should last forever," I figure.

"My father'd buy it for me if I wanted it."

"Your father, my ass," say Rosie Giraffe getting a chance to finally push Mercedes.   35

"Must be rich people shop here," say Q.T.

"You are a very bright boy," say Flyboy. "What was your first clue?" And he rap him on the head with the back of his knuckles, since Q.T. the only one he could get away with. Though Q.T. liable to come up behind you years later and get his licks in when you half expect it.

"What I want to know is," I says to Miss Moore though I never talk to her, I wouldn't give the bitch that satisfaction, "is how much a real boat costs? I figure a thousand'd get you a yacht any day."

"Why don't you check that out," she says, "and report back to the group?" Which 40 really pains my ass. If you gonna mess up a perfectly good swim day least you could do is have some answers. "Let's go in," she say like she got something up her sleeve. Only she don't lead the way. So me and Sugar turn the corner to where the entrance is, but when we get there I kinda hang back. Not that I'm scared, what's there to be afraid of, just a toy store. But I feel funny, shame. But what I got to be shamed about? Got as much right to go in as anybody. But somehow I can't seem to get hold of the door, so I step away for Sugar to lead. But she hangs back too. And I look at her and she looks at me and this is ridiculous. I mean, damn, I have never ever been shy about doing nothing or going nowhere. But then Mercedes steps up and then Rosie Giraffe and Big Butt crowd in behind and shove, and next thing we all stuffed into the doorway with only Mercedes squeezing past us, smoothing out her jumper and walking right down the aisle. Then the rest of us tumble in like a glued-together jigsaw done all wrong. And people lookin at us. And it's like the time me and Sugar crashed into the Catholic church on a dare. But once we got in there and everything so hushed and holy and the candles and the bowin and the handkerchiefs on all the drooping heads, I just couldn't go through with the plan. Which was for me to run up to the altar and do a tap dance while Sugar played the nose flute and messed around in the holy water. And Sugar kept givin me the elbow. Then later teased me so bad I tied her up in the shower and turned it on and locked her in. And she'd be there till this day if Aunt Gretchen hadn't finally figured I was lyin about the boarder takin a shower.

Same thing in the store. We all walkin on tiptoe and hardly touchin the games and puzzles and things. And I watched Miss Moore who is steady watchin us like she waitin for a sign. Like Mama Drewery watches the sky and sniffs the air and takes note of just how much slant is in the bird formation. Then me and Sugar bump smack into each other, so busy gazing at the toys, 'specially the sailboat. But we don't laugh and go into our fat-lady bump-stomach routine. We just stare at that price tag. Then Sugar run a finger over the whole boat. And I'm jealous and want to hit her. Maybe not her, but I sure want to punch somebody in the mouth.

"Whatcha bring us here for, Miss Moore?"

"You sound angry, Sylvia. Are you mad about something?" Givin me one of them grins like she tellin a grown-up joke that never turns out to be funny. And she's lookin very closely at me like maybe she plannin to do my portrait from memory. I'm mad, but I won't give her that satisfaction. So I slouch around the store bein very bored and say, "Let's go."

Me and Sugar at the back of the train watchin the tracks whizzin by large then small then gettin gobbled up in the dark. I'm thinking about this tricky toy I saw in the store. A clown that somersaults on a bar then does chin-ups just cause you yank lightly at his leg. Cost $35. I could see me askin my mother for a $35 birthday clown. "You wanna who that costs what?" she'd say, cocking her head to the side to get a better view of the hole in my head. Thirty-five dollars could buy new bunk beds for Junior and Gretchen's boy. Thirty-five dollars and the whole household could go visit Granddaddy Nelson in the country. Thirty-five dollars would pay for the rent and the piano bill too. Who are these people that spend that much for performing clowns and $1000 for toy sailboats? What kinda work they do and how they live and how come we ain't in on it? Where we are is who we are, Miss Moore always pointin out. But it don't necessarily have to be that way, she always adds then waits for somebody to say that poor people have to wake up and demand their share of the pie and don't none of us know what kind of pie she talking about in the first damn place. But she ain't so smart cause I still got her four dollars from the taxi and she sure ain't gettin it. Messin up my day with this shit. Sugar nudges me in my pocket and winks.

Miss Moore lines us up in front of the mailbox where we started from, seem like years ago, and I got a headache for thinkin so hard. And we lean all over each other so we can hold up under the draggy-ass lecture she always finishes us off with at the end before we thank her for borin us to tears. But she just looks at us like she readin tea leaves. Finally she say, "Well, what did you think of F.A.O. Schwarz?" 45

Rosie Giraffe mumbles, "White folks crazy."

"I'd like to go there again when I get my birthday money," says Mercedes, and we shove her out the pack so she has to lean on the mailbox by herself.

"I'd like a shower. Tiring day," say Flyboy.

Then Sugar surprises me by sayin, "You know, Miss Moore, I don't think all of us here put together eat in a year what that sailboat costs." And Miss Moore lights up like somebody goosed her. "And?" she say, urging Sugar on. Only I'm standin on her foot so she don't continue.

"Imagine for a minute what kind of society it is in which some people can spend on a toy what it would cost to feed a family of six or seven. What do you think?" 50

"I think," say Sugar pushing me off her feet like she never done before, cause I whip her ass in a minute, "that this is not much of a democracy if you ask me. Equal chance to pursue happiness means an equal crack at the dough, don't it?" Miss Moore is besides herself and I am disgusted with Sugar's treachery. So I stand on her foot one more time to see if she'll shove me. She shuts up, and Miss Moore looks at me, sorrowfully I'm thinkin. And somethin weird is goin on, I can feel it in my chest.

"Anybody else learn anything today?" lookin dead at me. I walk away and Sugar has to run to catch up and don't even seem to notice when I shrug her arm off my shoulder.

"Well, we got four dollars anyway," she says.

"Uh hunh."

"We could go to Hascombs and get half a chocolate layer and then go to the Sunset and still have plenty money for potato chips and ice-cream sodas." 55

"Uh hunh."

"Race you to Hascombs," she say.

We start down the block and she gets ahead which is O.K. by me cause I'm going to the West End and then over to the Drive to think this day through. She can run if she want to and even run faster. But ain't nobody gonna beat me at nuthin.

48 CRITICAL APPROACHES TO LITERATURE

Literary criticism should arise out of a debt of love.

—GEORGE STEINER

Literary criticism is not an abstract, intellectual exercise; it is a natural human response to literature. If a friend informs you she is reading a book you have just finished, it would be odd indeed if you did not begin swapping opinions. Literary criticism is nothing more than discourse—spoken or written—about literature. A student who sits quietly in a morning English class, intimidated by the notion of literary criticism, will spend an hour that evening talking animatedly about the meaning of rock lyrics or comparing the relative merits of the *Star Wars* trilogies. It is inevitable that people will ponder, discuss, and analyze the works of art that interest them.

The informal criticism of friends talking about literature tends to be casual, unorganized, and subjective. Since Aristotle, however, philosophers, scholars, and writers have tried to create more precise and disciplined ways of discussing literature. Literary critics have borrowed concepts from other disciplines, such as philosophy, history, linguistics, psychology, and anthropology, to analyze imaginative literature more perceptively. Some critics have found it useful to work in the abstract area of **literary theory**, criticism that tries to formulate general principles rather than discuss specific texts. Mass media critics, such as newspaper reviewers, usually spend their time evaluating works—telling us which books are worth reading, which plays not to bother seeing. But most serious literary criticism is not primarily evaluative; it assumes we know that *Othello* or *The Metamorphosis* is worth reading. Instead, such criticism is analytic; it tries to help us better understand a literary work.

In the following pages you will find overviews of ten critical approaches to literature. While these ten methods do not exhaust the total possibilities of literary criticism, they represent the most widely used contemporary approaches. Although presented separately, the approaches are not necessarily mutually exclusive; many critics mix methods to suit their needs and interests. For example, a historical critic may use formalist techniques to analyze a poem; a biographical critic will frequently use psychological theories to analyze an author. The summaries try neither to provide a history of each approach nor to present the latest trends in each school. Their purpose is to give you a practical introduction to each critical method and then provide representative examples of it. If one of these critical methods interests you, why not try to write a class paper using the approach?

FORMALIST CRITICISM

Formalist criticism regards literature as a unique form of human knowledge that needs to be examined on its own terms. "The natural and sensible starting point for work in literary scholarship," René Wellek and Austin Warren wrote in their influential *Theory of Literature*, "is the interpretation and analysis of the works of literature themselves." To a formalist, a poem or story is not primarily a social, historical, or biographical document; it is a literary work that can be understood only by reference to its intrinsic literary features—that is, those elements found in the text itself. To analyze a poem or story, therefore, the formalist critic focuses on the words of the text rather than facts about the author's life or the historical milieu in which the text was written. The critic pays special attention to the formal features of the text—the style, structure, imagery, tone, and genre. These features, however, are usually not examined in isolation, because formalist critics believe that what gives a literary text its special status as art is how all its elements work together to create the reader's total experience. As Robert Penn Warren commented, "Poetry does not inhere in any particular element but depends upon the set of relationships, the structure, which we call the poem."

A key method that formalists use to explore the intense relationships within a poem is **close reading**, a careful step-by-step analysis and explication of a text. The purpose of close reading is to understand how various elements in a literary text work together to shape its effects on the reader. Since formalists believe that the various stylistic and thematic elements of a literary work influence each other, these critics insist that form and content cannot be meaningfully separated. The complete interdependence of form and content is what makes a text literary. When we extract a work's theme or paraphrase its meaning, we destroy the aesthetic experience of the work.

When Robert Langbaum examines Robert Browning's "My Last Duchess," he uses several techniques of formalist criticism. First, he places the poem in relation to its literary form, the dramatic monologue. Second, he discusses the dramatic structure of the poem—why the duke tells his story, whom he addresses, and the physical circumstances in which he speaks. Third, Langbaum analyzes how the duke tells his story—his tone, his manner, even the order in which he makes his disclosures. Langbaum neither introduces facts about Browning's life into his analysis, nor relates the poem to the historical period or social conditions that produced it. He focuses on the text itself to explain how it produces a complex effect on the reader.

Cleanth Brooks (1906–1994)

The Formalist Critic   1951

Here are some articles of faith I could subscribe to:

> *That literary criticism is a description and an evaluation of its object.*
>
> *That the primary concern of criticism is with the problem of unity—the kind of whole which the literary work forms or fails to form, and the relation of the various parts to each other in building up this whole.*
>
> *That the formal relations in a work of literature may include, but certainly exceed, those of logic.*

That in a successful work, form and content cannot be separated.

That form is meaning.

That literature is ultimately metaphorical and symbolic.

That the general and the universal are not seized upon by abstraction, but got at through the concrete and the particular.

That literature is not a surrogate for religion.

That, as Allen Tate says, "specific moral problems" are the subject matter of literature, but that the purpose of literature is not to point a moral.

That the principles of criticism define the area relevant to literary criticism; they do not constitute a method for carrying out the criticism.

• • •

The formalist critic knows as well as anyone that poems and plays and novels are written by men—that they do not somehow happen—and that they are written as expressions of particular personalities and are written from all sorts of motives—for money, from a desire to express oneself, for the sake of a cause, etc. Moreover, the formalist critic knows as well as anyone that literary works are merely potential until they are read—that is, that they are recreated in the minds of actual readers, who vary enormously in their capabilities, their interests, their prejudices, their ideas. But the formalist critic is concerned primarily with the work itself. Speculation on the mental processes of the author takes the critic away from the work into biography and psychology. There is no reason, of course, why he should not turn away into biography and psychology. Such explorations are very much worth making. But they should not be confused with an account of the work. Such studies describe the process of composition, not the structure of the thing composed, and they may be performed quite as validly for the poor work as for the good one. They may be validly performed for any kind of expression—non-literary as well as literary.

From "The Formalist Critic"

Michael Clark (b. 1946)

Light and Darkness in "Sonny's Blues"   1985

"Sonny's Blues" by James Baldwin is a sensitive story about the reconciliation of two brothers, but it is much more than that. It is, in addition, an examination of the importance of the black heritage and of the central importance of music in that heritage. Finally, the story probes the central role that art must play in human exis-tence. To examine all of these facets of human existence is a rather formidable undertaking in a short story, even in a longish short story such as this one. Baldwin not only undertakes this task, but he does it superbly. One of the central ways that Baldwin fuses all of these complex elements is by using a metaphor of childhood, which is supported by ancillary images of light and darkness. He does the job so well that the story is a *tour de force*, a penetrating study of American culture.

• • •

Sonny's quest is best described by himself when he writes to the narrator: "I feel like a man who's been trying to climb up out of some deep, real deep and funky hole and just saw the sun up there, outside. I got to get outside." Sonny is a person who finds his life a living hell, but he knows enough to strive for the "light." As it is chronicled in this story, his quest is for regaining something from the past—from his own childhood and from the pasts of all who have come before him. The means for doing this is his music, which is consistently portrayed in terms of light imagery. When Sonny has a discussion with the narrator about the future, the narrator describes Sonny's face as a mixture of concern and hope: "[T]he worry, the thoughtfulness, played on it still, the way shadows play on a face which is staring into the fire." This fire image is reinforced shortly afterward when the narrator describes Sonny's aspirations once more in terms of light: "[I]t was as though he were all wrapped up in some cloud, some fire, some vision all his own." To the narrator and to Isabel's family, the music that Sonny plays is simply "weird and disordered," but to Sonny, the music is seen in starkly positive terms: his failure to master the music will mean "death," while success will mean "life."

The light and dark imagery culminates in the final scene, where the narrator, apparently for the first time, listens to Sonny play the piano. The location is a Greenwich Village club. Appropriately enough, the narrator is seated "in a dark corner." In contrast, the stage is dominated by light, which Baldwin reiterates with a succession of images: "light . . . circle of light . . . light . . . flame . . . light." Although Sonny has a false start, he gradually settles into his playing and ends the first set with some intensity: "Everything had been burned out of [Sonny's face], and at the same time, things usually hidden were being burned in, by the fire and fury of the battle which was occurring in him up there."

The culmination of the set occurs when Creole, the leader of the players, begins to play "Am I Blue?" At this point, "something began to happen." Apparently, the narrator at this time realizes that this music *is* important. The music is central to the experience of the black experience, and it is described in terms of light imagery:

> Creole began to tell us what the blues were all about. They were not about anything very new. He and his boys up there were keeping it new, at the risk of ruin, destruction, madness, and death, in order to find new ways to make us listen. For, while the tale of how we suffer, and how we are delighted, and how we may triumph is never new, it always must be heard. There isn't any other tale to tell, it's the only light we've got in all this darkness.

From "James Baldwin's 'Sonny's Blues': Childhood, Light, and Art"

Robert Langbaum (b. 1924)

On Robert Browning's "My Last Duchess" 1957

When we have said all the objective things about Browning's "My Last Duchess," we will not have arrived at the meaning until we point out what can only be substantiated by an appeal to effect—that moral judgment does not figure importantly in our response to the duke, that we even identify ourselves with him. But how is such an effect produced in a poem about a cruel Italian duke of the Renaissance who out of unreasonable jealousy has had his last duchess put to death, and is now about to contract a second marriage for the sake of dowry? Certainly, no summary or paraphrase would indicate that condemnation is not our principal response. The difference must be laid to form, to that extra quantity which makes the difference in artistic discourse between content and meaning.

The objective fact that the poem is made up entirely of the duke's utterance has of course much to do with the final meaning, and it is important to say that the poem is in form a monologue. But much more remains to be said about the way in which the content is laid out, before we can come near accounting for the whole meaning. It is important that the duke tells the story of his kind and generous last duchess to, of all people, the envoy from his prospective duchess. It is important that he tells his story while showing off to the envoy the artistic merits of a portrait of the last duchess. It is above all important that the duke carries off his outrageous indiscretion, proceeding triumphantly in the end downstairs to conclude arrangements for the dowry. All this is important not only as content but also as form, because it establishes a relation between the duke on the one hand, and the portrait and the envoy on the other, which determines the reader's relation to the duke and therefore to the poem—which determines, in other words, the poem's meaning.

The utter outrageousness of the duke's behavior makes condemnation the least interesting response, certainly not the response that can account for the poem's success. What interests us more than the duke's wickedness is his immense attractiveness. His conviction of matchless superiority, his intelligence and bland amorality, his poise, his taste for art, his manners—high-handed aristocratic manners that break the ordinary rules and assert the duke's superiority when he is being most solicitous of the envoy, waiving their difference of rank ("Nay, we'll go / Together down, sir"); these qualities overwhelm the envoy, causing him apparently to suspend judgment of the duke, for he raises no demur. The reader is no less overwhelmed. We suspend moral judgment because we prefer to participate in the duke's power and freedom, in his hard core of character fiercely loyal to itself. Moral judgment is in fact important as the thing to be suspended, as a measure of the price we pay for the privilege of appreciating to the full this extraordinary man.

It is because the duke determines the arrangement and relative subordination of the parts that the poem means what it does. The duchess's goodness shines through the duke's utterance; he makes no attempt to conceal it, so preoccupied is he with his own standard of judgment and so oblivious of the world's. Thus the duchess's case is subordinated to the duke's, the novelty and complexity of which engages our attention. We are busy trying to understand the man who can combine the connoisseur's pride in the lady's beauty with a pride that caused him to murder the lady rather than tell her in what way she displeased him, for in that

> would be some stooping; and I choose
> Never to stoop.
>
> (lines 42–43)

The duke's paradoxical nature is fully revealed when, having boasted how at his command the duchess's life was extinguished, he turns back to the portrait to admire of all things its life-likeness:

> There she stands
> As if alive.
>
> (lines 46–47)

This occurs ten lines from the end, and we might suppose we have by now taken the duke's measure. But the next ten lines produce a series of shocks that outstrip each time our understanding of the duke, and keep us panting after revelation with no opportunity to consolidate our impression of him for moral judgment. For it is at this point that we learn to whom he has been talking; and he goes on to talk about dowry, even allowing himself to murmur the hypocritical assurance that the new bride's self and not the dowry is of course his object. It seems to me that one side of the duke's nature is here stretched as far as it will go; the dazzling figure threatens to decline into paltriness admitting moral judgment, when Browning retrieves it with two brilliant strokes. First, there is the lordly waiving of rank's privilege as the duke and the envoy are about to proceed downstairs, and then there is the perfect all-revealing gesture of the last two and a half lines when the duke stops to show off yet another object in his collection:

> Notice Neptune, though,
> Taming a sea-horse, thought a rarity,
> Which Claus of Innsbruck cast in bronze for me!

(lines 54–56)

The lines bring all the parts of the poem into final combination, with just the relative values that constitute the poem's meaning. The nobleman does not hurry on his way to business, the connoisseur cannot resist showing off yet another precious object, the possessive egotist counts up his possessions even as he moves toward the acquirement of a new possession, a well-dowered bride; and most important, the last duchess is seen in final perspective. She takes her place as one of a line of objects in an art collection; her sad story becomes the *cicerone's* anecdote° lending piquancy to the portrait. The duke has taken from her what he wants, her beauty, and thrown the life away; and we watch with awe as he proceeds to take what he wants from the envoy and by implication from the new duchess. He carries all before him by sheer force of will so undeflected by ordinary compunctions as even, I think, to call into question—the question rushes into place behind the startling illumination of the last lines, and lingers as the poem's haunting afternote—the duke's sanity.

From The Poetry of Experience

BIOGRAPHICAL CRITICISM

Biographical criticism begins with the simple but central insight that literature is written by actual people and that understanding an author's life can help readers more thoroughly comprehend the work. Anyone who reads the biography of a writer quickly sees how much an author's experience shapes—both directly and indirectly—what he or she creates. Reading that biography will also change (and usually deepen) our response to the work. Sometimes even knowing a single important fact illuminates our reading of a poem or story. Learning, for example, that poet Josephine Miles was confined to a wheelchair or that Weldon Kees committed suicide at forty-one will certainly make us pay attention to certain aspects of their poems we might otherwise have missed or considered unimportant. A formalist critic might complain that we would also have noticed those things through careful textual analysis, but biographical information provides the practical assistance of underscoring subtle but important meanings in the poems. Though many literary theorists have assailed biographical criticism on philosophical grounds, the biographical approach to literature has never disappeared because of its obvious practical advantage in illuminating literary texts.

---

cicerone's anecdote: the Duke's tale. (In Italian, a *cicerone* is one who conducts guided tours for sightseers.)

It may be helpful here to make a distinction between biography and biographical criticism. **Biography** is, strictly speaking, a branch of history; it provides a written account of a person's life. To establish and interpret the facts of a poet's life, for instance, a biographer would use all the available information—not just personal documents such as letters and diaries but also the poems—for the possible light they might shed on the subject's life. A biographical *critic*, however, is not concerned with re-creating the record of an author's life. Biographical criticism focuses on explicating the literary work by using the insight provided by knowledge of the author's life. Quite often, biographical critics, such as Brett C. Millier in her discussion of Elizabeth Bishop's "One Art," will examine the drafts of a poem or story to see both how the work came into being and how it might have been changed from its autobiographical origins.

A reader, however, must use biographical interpretations cautiously. Writers are notorious for revising the facts of their own lives; they often delete embarrassments and invent accomplishments while changing the details of real episodes to improve their literary impact. John Cheever, for example, frequently told reporters about his sunny, privileged youth; after the author's death, his biographer Scott Donaldson discovered a childhood scarred by a distant mother; a failed, alcoholic father; and nagging economic uncertainty. Likewise, Cheever's outwardly successful adulthood was plagued by alcoholism, sexual promiscuity, and family tension. The unsettling facts of Cheever's life significantly changed the way critics read his stories. The danger in the case of a famous writer (Sylvia Plath and F. Scott Fitzgerald are two modern examples) is that the life story can overwhelm and eventually distort the work. A shrewd biographical critic always remembers to base an interpretation on what is in the text itself; biographical data should amplify the meaning of the text, not drown it out with irrelevant material.

Virginia Llewellyn Smith

Chekhov's Attitude to Romantic Love   1973

It has been shown that the theme of love being destroyed by a cruel fate did not always have for Chekhov the appeal of the tragic: that it could also serve him as a good framework on which to build farce. Nor could one claim that the theme of illicit passion found its source in Chekhov's own imagination, let alone experience: Tolstoy's *Anna Karenina*° had been published in the later 1870s, before any of Chekhov's work. Nonetheless the coincidence of plot and emotion found in "About Love" and "The Lady with the Dog," together with the fact that the theme occupied Chekhov chiefly in the 1890s, has given rise to some speculation as to whether in fact Chekhov's own love-life during those years suffered as one critic puts it from the interference of a *force majeure*.° Since in this period Chekhov's private life is no longer a closed book (although many pages are indecipherable) the search for the romantic heroine becomes more complex. It becomes feasible to try to connect with her image certain women whose relations with Chekhov are at least partially illuminated and illuminating. Of Chekhov's female friends three in particular must now claim our attention.

Anna Karenina: Leo Tolstoy's novel (1875–1877) dealt explicitly with an adulterous affair.   *force majeure:* French for an "irresistible force."

No other single work of Chekhov's fiction constitutes a more meaningful comment on Chekhov's attitude to women and to love than does "The Lady with the Dog." So many threads of Chekhov's thought and experience appear to have been woven together into this succinct story that it may be regarded as something in the nature of a summary of the entire topic.

Gurov, the hero of the story, may at first appear no more closely identifiable with Chekhov himself than are many other sympathetic male characters in Chekhov's fiction: he has a post in a bank and is a married man with three children. It is because he has this wife and family that his love-affair with Anna Sergeevna leads him into an *impasse*. And the affair itself, involving Gurov's desperate trip to Anna's home town, has no obvious feature in common with anything we know of Chekhov's amorous liaisons.

And yet Chekhov's own attitudes and experience have clearly shaped Gurov's character and fate. The reader is told that Gurov "was not yet forty": Chekhov was thirty-nine when he wrote "The Lady with the Dog." Gurov "was married young" (*ego zhenili rano*): there is a faint implication in the phrase that an element of coercion played some part in his taking this step—a step which Chekhov, when he was young, managed to avoid. As in general with early marriages in Chekhov's fiction, Gurov's has not proved a success. His wife seems "much older than he" and imagines herself to be an intellectual: familiar danger-signals. She is summed-up in three words: "stiff, pompous, dignified" (*pryamaya, vazhnaya, solidnaya*) which epitomize a type of woman (and man) that Chekhov heartily disliked.

• • •

Gurov has had, however, liaisons that were, for him, enjoyable—and these we note, were brief: as was Chekhov's liaison with Yavorskaya and indeed, so far as we know, all the sexual relationships that he had before he met Olga Knipper.

"Frequent experience and indeed bitter experience had long since taught [Gurov] that every liaison which to begin with makes such a pleasant change . . . inevitably evolves into a real and extremely complex problem, and the situation eventually becomes a burden." That his friendships with, for instance, Lika and Avilova should evolve into a situation of this kind seems to have been exactly what Chekhov himself feared: he backed out of these friendships as soon as there appeared to be a danger of close involvement.

Gurov cannot do without the company of women, and yet he describes them as an "inferior breed": his experience of intimacy with women is limited to casual affairs and an unsatisfactory marriage. Chekhov also enjoyed the company of women and had many female friends and admirers: but he failed, or was unwilling, to involve himself deeply or lastingly with them. That in his work he should suggest that women are an inferior breed can be to some extent explained by the limited knowledge of women his self-contained attitude brought him—and perhaps, to some extent, by a sense of guilt concerning his inability to feel involved.

Gurov's behaviour to Anna Sergeevna at the beginning of their love-affair is characterized by an absence of emotional involvement, just such as appears in Chekhov's attitude towards certain women. There is a scene in "The Lady with the Dog" where, after they have been to bed together, Gurov eats a watermelon while Anna Sergeevna weeps over her corruption. It is not difficult to imagine Chekhov doing something similarly prosaic—weeding his garden, perhaps—while Lika poured out her emotional troubles to him.

Gurov's egocentricity is dispelled, however, by the potent influence of love, because Anna Sergeevna turns out to be the ideal type of woman: pitiable, defenseless, childlike, capable of offering Gurov an unquestioning love. Love is seen to operate as a force for good: under its influence Gurov feels revulsion for the philistinism of his normal life and associates.

• • •

Chekhov wrote "The Lady with the Dog" in Yalta in the autumn of 1899, not long after he and Olga were there together (although they were not, as yet, lovers) and had made the trip back to Moscow together. In the Kokkoz valley, it will be remembered, they apparently agreed to marry: and so by then, we may presume, Chekhov knew what it was to love.

From Anton Chekhov and the Lady with the Dog

Brett C. Millier   (b. 1958)

On Elizabeth Bishop's "One Art"   1993

Elizabeth Bishop left seventeen drafts of the poem "One Art" among her papers. In the first draft, she lists all the things she's lost in her life—keys, pens, glasses, cities— and then she writes "One might think this would have prepared me / for losing one average-sized not exceptionally / beautiful or dazzlingly intelligent person . . . / But it doesn't seem to have at all. . . ." By the seventeenth draft, nearly every word has been transformed, but most importantly, Bishop discovered along the way that there might be a way to master this loss.

One way to read Bishop's modulation between the first and last drafts from "the loss of you is impossible to master" to something like "I am still the master of losing even though losing you looks like a disaster" is that in the writing of such a disciplined, demanding poem as this villanelle ("[*Write* it!]") lies the potential mastery of the loss. Working through each of her losses—from the bold, painful catalog of the first draft to the finely-honed and privately meaningful final version—is the way to overcome them or, if not to overcome them, then to see the way in which she might possibly master herself in the face of loss. It is all, perhaps "one art"—writing elegy, mastering loss, mastering grief, self-mastery. Bishop had a precocious familiarity with loss. Her father died before her first birthday, and four years later her mother disappeared into a sanitarium, never to be seen by her daughter again. The losses in the poem are real: time in the form of the "hour badly spent" and, more tellingly for the orphaned Bishop, "my mother's watch": the lost houses, in Key West, Petrópolis, and Ouro Prêto, Brazil. The city of Rio de Janeiro and the whole South American continent (where she had lived for nearly two decades) were lost to her with the suicide of her Brazilian companion. And currently, in the fall of 1975, she seemed to have lost her dearest friend and lover, who was trying to end their relationship. But each version of the poem distanced the pain a little more, depersonalized it, moved it away from the tawdry self-pity and "confession" that Bishop disliked in so many of her contemporaries.

Bishop's friends remained for a long time protective of her personal reputation, and unwilling to have her grouped among lesbian poets or even among the other great poets of her generation—Robert Lowell, John Berryman, Theodore Roethke—as they seemed to self-destruct before their readers' eyes. Bishop herself taught them this reticence by keeping her private life to herself, and by investing what "confession" there was in her poems deeply in objects and places, thus deflecting biographical inquiry. In the development of this poem, discretion is both a poetic method and a part of a process of self-understanding, the seeing of a pattern in her own life.

Adapted by the author from Elizabeth Bishop: Life and the Memory of It

Emily Toth (b. 1944)

The Source for Alcée Laballière in "The Storm"   1990

In January 1898, right after Kate Chopin had finished writing her controversial novel *The Awakening*, about one woman's quest for love (and sexual fulfillment) outside of marriage, a St. Louis newspaper asked her to answer the question, "Is Love Divine?"

Chopin's response was telling. She wrote, "I am inclined to think that love springs from animal instinct, and therefore is, in a measure, divine. One can never resolve to love this man, this woman or child, and then carry out the resolution unless one feels irresistibly drawn by an indefinable current of magnetism."

In that case, it was no doubt magnetism that led Kate Chopin to the handsome, wealthy Creole planter Albert Sampité (pronounced "Al-bear Sam-pi-TAY") after the death of her husband Oscar. This may also be why Kate Chopin's widowhood stories emphasize hope, not bereavement; spring, not winter; possibility, not loss. After Oscar died, Kate—who had grown up in a house full of widows who managed their own lives and their own money—decided to run Oscar's businesses herself.

She became an accomplished entrepreneur, a brisk businesswoman during the day who nevertheless kept the dark night as her own, with its prospects for silence and mystery and sin. Men flocked to aid the handsome widow in 1883, but when villagers gossiped generations later about who was "sweet on Kate," one name kept recurring. It was no secret to anyone—including his wife—that Albert Sampité was pursuing Kate Chopin. An examination of Chopin's stories show that the male characters who kindle desire and who devote themselves to sexual pleasure are named Alcée, an abbreviated form of Albert Sampité. Al. S——é and Alcée are both pronounced "Al-say."

It was not unseemly, or even odd, for Monsieur Sampite (his family dropped the accent mark, though they continued to use French pronunciation) to meet with Madame Chopin at the point where their lands intersected. When merchandise arrived for Kate's store, by boat from New Orleans, she had to go down to the landing to get her goods. It was not uncommon for a local planter like Albert Sampite to be at the landing at the same time. Somehow, too, Albert Sampite became involved in Kate Chopin's money matters. Papers that he saved show that Albert was apparently helping Kate to collect money owed her—and he also valued her financial records enough to keep them with his own personal papers.

There were still other ways in which a willing couple could make connections. And in a sudden storm, it was not impossible for two people to take refuge alone together in a house—a sensual scenario Kate Chopin sketched out, years later, in her most explicit short story, "The Storm."

Kate and Albert were discreet about their romance, by the standards of a century later. If anyone wrote down dates and places and eyewitness descriptions, none of those survive—although Cloutierville residents would certainly have been able to recognize him in her writings. But an affair in the 1880s was not simply a matter of physical consummation. Much less than that could be called "making love": flirting, significant glances, stolen kisses, secret silences.

Kate Chopin, in her diary eleven years after the first spring of her widowhood, suggested that more than flirting had gone on in her life: "I had loved—lovers who were not divine," she wrote, and "And then, there are so many ways of saying good night!" And even in her published writings, Kate left proof that her relationship with

Albert Sampite was much more than a casual friendship. It shaped what she wrote about women and men, and love and lust and forbidden desires.

Adapted from Kate Chopin

HISTORICAL CRITICISM

Historical criticism seeks to understand a literary work by investigating the social, cultural, and intellectual context that produced it—a context that necessarily includes the artist's biography and milieu. Historical critics are less concerned with explaining a work's literary significance for today's readers than with helping us understand the work by recreating, as nearly as possible, the exact meaning and impact it had for its original audience. A historical reading of a literary work begins by exploring the possible ways in which the meaning of the text has changed over time. An analysis of William Blake's poem "London," for instance, carefully examines how certain words had different connotations for the poem's original readers than they do today. It also explores the probable associations an eighteenth-century English reader would have made with certain images and characters, like the poem's persona, the chimney sweep—a type of exploited child laborer who, fortunately, no longer exists in our society.

No one doubts the value of historical criticism in reading ancient literature. There have been so many social, cultural, and linguistic changes that some older texts are incomprehensible without scholarly assistance. But historical criticism can even help one better understand modern texts. To return to Weldon Kees's "For My Daughter," for example, one learns a great deal by considering two rudimentary historical facts—the year in which the poem was first published (1940) and the nationality of its author (American)—and then asking how this information has shaped the meaning of the poem. In 1940 war had already broken out in Europe, and most Americans realized that their country, still recovering from the Depression, would soon be drawn into it. For a young man like Kees, the future seemed bleak, uncertain, and personally dangerous. Even this simple historical analysis helps explain at least part of the bitter pessimism of Kees's poem, though a psychological critic would rightly insist that Kees's dark personality also played a crucial role. In writing a paper on a poem, you might explore how the time and place of its creation affect its meaning. For a splendid example of how to recreate the historical context of a poem's genesis, read the following account by Hugh Kenner of Ezra Pound's imagistic "In a Station of the Metro."

Hugh Kenner (1923–2003)

Imagism   1971

For it was English post-Symbolist verse that Pound's Imagism set out to reform, by deleting its self-indulgences, intensifying its virtues, and elevating the glimpse into the vision. The most famous of all Imagist poems commenced, like any poem by Arthur Symons,° with an accidental glimpse. Ezra Pound, on a visit to Paris in

---

Arthur Symons: Symons (1865–1945) was a British poet who helped introduce French symbolist verse into English. His own verse was often florid and impressionistic.

1911, got out of the Metro at La Concorde, and "saw suddenly a beautiful face, and then another and another, and then a beautiful child's face, and then another beautiful woman, and I tried all that day to find words for what they had meant to me, and I could not find any words that seemed to me worthy, or as lovely as that sudden emotion."

The oft-told story is worth one more retelling. This was just such an experience as Arthur Symons cultivated, bright unexpected glimpses in a dark setting, instantly to melt into the crowd's kaleidoscope. And a poem would not have given Symons any trouble. But Pound by 1911 was already unwilling to write a Symons poem.

He tells us that he first satisfied his mind when he hit on a wholly abstract vision of colors, splotches on darkness like some canvas of Kandinsky's (whose work he had not then seen). This is a most important fact. Satisfaction lay not in preserving the vision, but in devising with mental effort an abstract equivalent for it, reduced, intensified. He next wrote a 30-line poem and destroyed it; after six months he wrote a shorter poem, also destroyed; and after another year, with, as he tells us, the Japanese *hokku* in mind, he arrived at a poem which needs every one of its 20 words, including the six words of its title:

In a Station of the Metro

The apparition of these faces in the crowd;
Petals on a wet, black bough.

We need the title so that we can savor that vegetal contrast with the world of machines: this is not any crowd, moreover, but a crowd seen underground, as Odysseus and Orpheus and Koré saw crowds in Hades. And carrying forward the suggestion of wraiths, the word "apparition" detaches these faces from all the crowded faces, and presides over the image that conveys the quality of their separation:

Petals on a wet, black bough.

Flowers, underground; flowers, out of the sun; flowers seen as if against a natural gleam, the bough's wetness gleaming on its darkness, in this place where wheels turn and nothing grows. The mind is touched, it may be, with a memory of Persephone, as we read of her in the 106th Canto,

Dis' bride, Queen over Phlegethon,
girls faint as mist about her.

—the faces of those girls likewise "apparitions."

What is achieved, though it works by way of the visible, is no picture of the thing glimpsed, in the manner of

The light of our cigarettes
Went and came in the gloom.

It is a simile with "like" suppressed: Pound called it an equation, meaning not a redundancy, *a* equals *a*, but a generalization of unexpected exactness. The statements of analytic geometry, he said, "are 'lords' over fact. They are the thrones and dominations that rule over form and recurrence. And in like manner are great works of art lords over fact, over race-long recurrent moods, and over tomorrow." So this tiny poem, drawing on Gauguin and on Japan, on ghosts and on Persephone, on the Underworld and on the Underground, the Metro of Mallarmé's capital and a phrase that names a station of the Metro as it might a station of the Cross, concentrates far more than it need ever specify, and indicates the means of delivering post-Symbolist poetry from its pictorialist impasse. "An 'Image' is that which presents an intellectual and emotional complex in an instant of time": that is the elusive Doctrine of the Image. And, just 20 months later, "The image . . . is a radiant node or cluster; it is what I can, and must perforce, call a VORTEX, from which, and through which, and into which, ideas are constantly rushing." And: "An *image* . . . is real because we know it directly."

From *The Pound Era*

Joseph Moldenhauer (b. 1934)

"To His Coy Mistress" and the Renaissance Tradition   1968

Obedient to the neoclassical aesthetic which ruled his age, Andrew Marvell strove for excellence within established forms rather than trying to devise unique forms of his own. Like Herrick, Ben Jonson, and Campion, like Milton and the Shakespeare of the sonnets, Marvell was derivative. He held imitation to be no vice; he chose a proven type and exploited it with a professionalism rarely surpassed even in a century and a land as amply provided with verse craftsmen as his. Under a discipline so willingly assumed, Marvell's imagination flourished, producing superb and enduring examples of the verse types he attempted.

• • •

When he undertook to write a *carpe diem* lyric in "To His Coy Mistress," Marvell was working once more within a stylized form, one of the favorite types in the Renaissance lyric catalogue. Again he endowed the familiar model with his own special sensibility, composing what for many readers is the most vital English instance of the *carpe diem* poem. We can return to it often, with undiminished enthusiasm—drawn not by symbolic intricacy, though it contains two or three extraordinary conceits, nor by philosophical depth, though it lends an unusual seriousness to its theme—but drawn rather by its immediacy and concreteness, its sheer dynamism of statement within a controlled structure.

The *carpe diem* poem, whose label comes from a line of Horace and whose archetype for Renaissance poets was a lyric by Catullus, addresses the conflict of beauty and sensual desire on the one hand and the destructive force of time on the other. Its theme is the fleeting nature of life's joys; its counsel, overt or implied, is Horace's "seize the present," or, in the language of Herrick's "To the Virgins,"

> Gather ye rose-buds while ye may,
>   Old Time is still a flying.

It takes rise from that most pervasive and aesthetically viable of all Renaissance preoccupations, man's thralldom to time, the limitations of mortality upon his senses, his pleasures, his aspirations, his intellectual and creative capacities. Over the exuberance of Elizabethan and seventeenth-century poetry the pall of death continually hovers, and the lyrics of the age would supply a handbook of strategies for the circumvention of decay. The birth of an heir, the preservative balm of memory, the refuge of Christian resignation or Platonic ecstasy—these are some solutions which the poets offer. Another is the artist's ability to immortalize this world's values by means of his verse. Shakespeare's nineteenth and fifty-fifth sonnets, for example, employ this stratagem for the frustration of "Devouring Time," as does Michael Drayton's "How Many Paltry, Foolish, Painted Things." In such poems the speaker's praise of the merits of the beloved is coupled with a celebration of his own poetic gift, through which he can eternize those merits as a "pattern" for future men and women.

The *carpe diem* lyric proposes a more direct and immediate, if also more temporary, solution to the overwhelming problem. Whether subdued or gamesome in tone, it appeals to the young and beautiful to make time their own for a while, to indulge in the "harmless folly" of sensual enjoyment. Ordinarily, as in "To His Coy Mistress" and Herrick's "Corinna's Going A-Maying," the poem imitates an express invitation to love, a suitor's immodest proposal to his lady. Such works are both sharply dramatic and vitally rhetorical; to analyze their style and structure is, in effect, to analyze a persuasive appeal.

From "The Voices of Seduction in 'To His Coy Mistress'"

Kathryn Lee Seidel

The Economics of Zora Neale Hurston's "Sweat"   1991

"Sweat" functions at one level as a documentary of the economic situation of Eatonville in the early decades of the twentieth century. Hurston uses a naturalistic narrator to comment on the roles of Delia and Sykes Jones as workers as well as marriage partners, but ultimately the story veers away from naturalistic fiction and becomes a modernist rumination on Delia as an artist figure. The story's coherence of theme and structure makes it one of Hurston's most powerful pieces of fiction.

Preserved not only as a place but as an idea of a place, Eatonville, Florida, retains the atmosphere of which Hurston wrote. As putatively the oldest town in the United States incorporated by blacks, Eatonville possesses understandable pride in its unique history. When Hurston writes of Eatonville in "How It Feels To Be Colored Me," she implies that her childhood place was idyllic because "it is exclusively a colored town," one in which the young Zora was happily unaware of the restrictions that race conferred elsewhere. However, this gloss of nostalgia can be read simultaneously with "Sweat," published only two years earlier . . . [where] Hurston reveals the somber and multifaced variations of life in Eatonville in the first part of this century.

Economically Eatonville in "Sweat" exists as a twin, a double with its neighbor, the town of Winter Park. Far from being identical, the twin towns are configured like Siamese twins, joined as they are by economic necessity. Winter Park is an all-white, wealthy town that caters to rich northerners from New England who journey south each fall to "winter" in Florida—"snowbirds," as the natives call them. Winter Park then as now boasts brick streets, huge oaks, landscaped lakes, and large, spacious houses. To clean these houses, tend these gardens, cook the meals, and watch the children of Winter Park, residents of Eatonville made a daily exodus across the railroad tracks on which Amtrak now runs to work as domestics. . . . What is unique about Eatonville and Winter Park is that they are not one town divided in two but two towns. Eatonville's self-governance, its pride in its historic traditions, and its social mores were thus able to develop far more autonomously than those in the many towns . . . where the black community had to struggle to develop a sense of independent identity.

In "Sweat" we see the results of this economic situation. On Saturdays the men of the town congregate on the porch of the general store chewing sugarcane and discussing the lamentable marriage of Delia and Sykes Jones. Although these men may be employed during the week, Sykes is not. Some working people mentioned besides Joe Clarke, the store owner, are the woman who runs a rooming house where Bertha, Sykes's mistress, stays, the minister of the church Delia attends, and the people who organize dances that Sykes frequents. Work as farm laborers on land owned by whites is probably available, but it pays very little and is seasonal. Jacqueline Jones points out that in 1900, not long before the time of the story, 50 to 70 percent of adult black women were employed full time as compared to only 20 percent of men.[1] A black man might be unemployed 50 percent of the time. One reason that unemployed men congregated at the local general store was not merely out of idleness, as whites alleged, nor out of a desire to create oral narratives, as we Hurston critics would like to imagine, but there they could be "visible to potential employers," as Jones asserts.

There is not enough work for the men as it is, but the townspeople discuss Sykes's particular aversion to what work is available. Old man Anderson reports that Sykes was always "ovahbearin' . . . but since dat white w'oman from up north done teached 'im how to run a automobile, he done got too beggety to live—an' we oughter kill 'im." The identity of this woman and her exact role in Sykes's life is not referred to again, but if she was a Winter Park woman, then perhaps Sykes worked for a time as a driver for residents there. All the more ironic, then, his comment to Delia in which he berates her for doing white people's laundry: "ah done tole you time and again to keep them white folks' clothes outa this house." The comment suggests that Sykes does not work out of protest against the economic system of Eatonville in which blacks are dependent on whites for their livelihood. Has he chosen to be unemployed to resist the system? Within the story, this reading is fragile at best. The townspeople point out that Sykes has used and abused Delia; he has "squeezed" her dry, like a piece of sugarcane. They report that she was in her youth a pert, lively, and pretty girl, but that marriage to a man like Sykes has worn her out.

In fact, Delia's work is their only source of income. In the early days of their marriage Sykes was employed, but he "took his wages to Orlando," the large city about ten miles from Eatonville, where he spent every penny. At some point Sykes stopped working and began to rely entirely on Delia for income. As she says, "Mah tub of suds is filled yo' belly with vittles more times than yo' hands is filled it. Mah sweat is done paid for this house." Delia's sense of ownership is that of the traditional work ethic; if one works hard, one can buy a house and support a family. That Delia is the breadwinner, however, is a role reversal but not ostensibly a liberation; her sweat has brought her some meager material rewards but has enraged her husband.

Although she may at one time have considered stopping work so that Sykes might be impelled to "feel like man again" and become a worker once more, at the time of the story that possibility is long past. Sykes wants her to stop working so she can be dainty, not sweaty, fat, not thin. Moreover, he wants to oust her from the house so that he and his girlfriend can live there. . . . Sykes's brutality is a chosen compensation because he does not participate in the work of the community. He

[1]Jacqueline Jones, *Labor of Love, Labor of Sorrow: Black Women, Work, and the Family from Slavery to the Present* (New York: Basic Books, 1985) 113.

chooses instead to become the town's womanizer and bully who spends his earnings when he has them; he lives for the moment and for himself.

. . . With her house she possesses not only a piece of property, but she also gains the right to declare herself as a person, not a piece of property. Because Sykes has not shared in the labor that results in the purchase of this property, he remains in a dependent state. He is rebellious against Delia who he feels controls him by denying him the house he feels ought to be his; his only reason for this assertion is that he is a man and Delia is his wife.

Thus, the economics of slavery in "Sweat" becomes a meditation on marriage as an institution that perpetuates the possession of women for profit. Indeed, Sykes is the slaveholder here; he does not work, he is sustained by the harsh physical labor of a black woman, he relies on the work of another person to obtain his own pleasure (in this case buying presents for his mistress Bertha). He regards Delia's property and her body as his possessions to be disposed of as he pleases. Sykes's brutal beatings of Delia and his insulting remarks about her appearance are the tools with which he perpetuates her subordination to him for the sixteen years of their marriage.

From "The Artist in the Kitchen: The Economics of Creativity in Hurston's 'Sweat'"

PSYCHOLOGICAL CRITICISM

Modern psychology has had an immense effect on both literature and literary criticism. The psychoanalytic theories of the Austrian neurologist Sigmund Freud changed our notions of human behavior by exploring new or controversial areas such as wish fulfillment, sexuality, the unconscious, and repression. Perhaps Freud's greatest contribution to literary study was his elaborate demonstration of how much human mental process was unconscious. He analyzed language, often in the form of jokes and conversational slips of the tongue (now often called "Freudian slips"), to show how it reflected the speaker's unconscious fears and desires. He also examined symbols, not only in art and literature but also in dreams, to study how the unconscious mind expressed itself in coded form to avoid the censorship of the conscious mind. His theory of human cognition asserted that much of what we apparently forget is actually stored deep in the unconscious mind, including painful traumatic memories from childhood that have been repressed.

Freud admitted that he himself had learned a great deal about psychology from studying literature. Sophocles, Shakespeare, Goethe, and Dostoyevsky were as important to the development of his ideas as were his clinical studies. Some of Freud's most influential writing was, in a broad sense, literary criticism, such as his psychoanalytic examination of Sophocles' Oedipus in *The Interpretation of Dreams* (1900). In analyzing Sophocles' tragedy *Oedipus the King,* Freud paid the classical Greek dramatist the considerable compliment that the playwright had such profound insight into human nature that his characters display the depth and complexity of real people. In focusing on literature, Freud and his disciples such as Carl Jung, Ernest Jones, Marie Bonaparte, and Bruno Bettelheim endorsed the belief that great literature truthfully reflects life.

Psychological criticism is a diverse category, but it often employs three approaches. First, it investigates the creative process of the arts: what is the nature of literary genius, and how does it relate to normal mental functions? Such analysis may also focus on literature's effects on the reader. How does a particular work register its impact on the reader's mental and sensory faculties? The second approach involves the psychological study of a particular artist. Most modern literary biographers employ psychology to understand their subject's motivations and behavior. One book, Diane Middlebrook's controversial *Anne Sexton: A Biography* (1991), actually used tapes of the poet's sessions with her psychiatrist as material for the study. The third common approach is the analysis of fictional characters. Freud's study of Oedipus is the prototype for this approach, which tries to bring modern insights about human behavior into the study of how fictional people act. While psychological criticism carefully examines the surface of the literary work, it customarily speculates on what lies underneath the text—the unspoken or perhaps even unspeakable memories, motives, and fears that covertly shape the work, especially in fictional characterizations.

Sigmund Freud (1856–1939)

The Nature of Dreams   1933

Let us go back once more to the latent dream-thoughts. Their dominating element is the repressed impulse, which has obtained some kind of expression, toned down and disguised though it may be, by associating itself with stimuli which happen to be there and by tacking itself on the residue of the day before. Just like any other impulse this one presses forward toward satisfaction in action, but the path to motor discharge is closed to it on account of the physiological characteristics of the state of sleep, and so it is forced to travel in the retrograde direction to perception, and content itself with an hallucinatory satisfaction. The latent dream-thoughts are therefore turned into a collection of sensory images and visual scenes. As they are travelling in this direction something happens to them which seems to us new and bewildering. All the verbal apparatus by means of which the more subtle thought-relations are expressed, the conjunctions and prepositions, the variations of declension and conjugation, are lacking, because the means of portraying them are absent: just as in primitive, grammarless speech, only the raw material of thought can be expressed, and the abstract is merged again in the concrete from which it sprang. What is left over may very well seem to lack coherence. It is as much the result of the archaic regression in the mental apparatus as of the demands of the censorship that so much use is made of the representation of certain objects and processes by means of symbols which have become strange to conscious thought. But of more far-reaching import are the other alterations to which the elements comprising the dream-thoughts are subjected. Such of them as have any point of contact are *condensed* into new unities. When the thoughts are translated into pictures those forms are indubitably preferred which allow of this kind of telescoping, or condensation; it is as though a force were at work which subjected the material to a process of pressure or squeezing together. As a result of condensation one element in a manifest dream may correspond to a number of elements of the dream-thoughts; but conversely one of the elements from among the dream-thoughts may be represented by a number of pictures in the dream.

From *New Introductory Lectures on Psychoanalysis*

Gretchen Schulz (b. 1943)
and R. J. R. Rockwood

Fairy Tale Motifs in "Where Are You Going, Where Have You Been?"   1980

In her fiction both short and long Miss Oates makes frequent use of fairy tale material. Again and again she presents characters and situations which parallel corresponding motifs from the world of folk fantasy. And never is this more true than in the present story ["Where Are You Going, Where Have You Been?"]—never in all the novels and collections of short stories which she has written at last count. Woven into the complex texture of "Where Are You Going, Where Have You Been?" are motifs from such tales as "The Spirit in the Bottle," "Snow White," "Cinderella," "Sleeping Beauty," "Rapunzel," "Little Red Riding Hood," and "The Three Little Pigs." *The Pied Piper of Hamelin*, which ends tragically and so according to [Bruno] Bettelheim does not qualify as a proper fairy tale, serves as the "frame device" that contains all the other tales.

There is a terrible irony here, for although the story is full of fairy tales, Connie, its protagonist, is not. Connie represents an entire generation of young people who have grown up—or tried to—without the help of those bedtime stories which not only entertain the child, but also enable him vicariously to experience and work through problems which he will encounter in adolescence. The only "stories" Connie knows are those of the sexually provocative but superficial lyrics of the popular songs she loves or of the equally insubstantial movies she attends. Such songs and movies provide either no models of behavior for her to imitate, or dangerously inappropriate ones. Connie has thus been led to believe that life and, in particular, love will be "sweet, gentle, the way it was in the movies and promised in songs." She has no idea that life actually can be just as grim as in folk fairy tales. The society that is depicted in "Where Are You Going, Where Have You Been?" has failed to make available to children like Connie maps of the unconscious such as fairy tales provide, because it has failed to recognize that in the unconscious past and future coalesce, and that, psychologically, where the child is going is where he has already been. Since Connie has been left—in the words of yet another of the popular songs—to "wander through that wonderland alone"—it is small wonder, considering her lack of spiritual preparation, that Connie's journey there soon becomes a terrifying schizophrenic separation from reality, with prognosis for recovery extremely poor.

• • •

Bettelheim points out that a fairy tale like "Spirit in the Bottle" deals with two problems that confront the child as he struggles to establish a sense of identity: parental belittlement, and integration of a divided personality. In Connie's case, her mother's belittling remarks that "Connie couldn't do a thing, her mind was all filled with trashy daydreams," certainly have contributed to Connie's two-sidedness, with her one personality "for home" and another for "anywhere that was not home," a division also apparent in the relationship between Connie and the "girl friend" who accompanies her to the bottle-shaped restaurant—the two are so poorly differentiated as to suggest a mere *doubling* of Connie, rather than two separate individuals. While such personality division may at first glance seem pathological, it is not, according to Bettelheim, necessarily abnormal, since the "manner in which the child can bring some order into his world view is by dividing everything into opposites," and that "in the late-oedipal and post-oedipal ages, this splitting extends to the child himself."

• • •

To be assured of safe passage through what Bettelheim terms "that thorniest of thickets, the oedipal period," a child like Connie would need to have absorbed the wisdom of the other fairy tales to which Miss Oates alludes, tales such as "Snow White," "Cinderella," "Rapunzel," and "Little Red Riding Hood." By their applicability to Connie's situation, these tales reveal that at its deepest level Connie's most compelling psychological problem is *unresolved oedipal conflict, aggravated by sibling rivalry.*

Suggestive of "Snow White" is Connie's "habit of craning her neck to glance into mirrors, or checking other people's faces to make sure her own was all right" (as though other people's faces were mirrors, too); and we are told also that her mother, "who noticed everything and knew everything"—as though with the wicked queen's magic power—"hadn't much reason any longer to look at her own face," and so was jealous of her daughter's beauty and "always after Connie." Arnold Friend's sunglasses also mirror everything, which means that, in this instance, he personifies the Magic Mirror and, of course, he finds Connie the fairest one of all. In his words, "Seen you that night and thought, that's the one, yes sir, I never needed to look anymore." Though he thus serves as Prince, there is a hint of the dwarf motif in Arnold's short stature and obvious phallicism; and most particularly is this true of his friend, Ellie Oscar, a case of arrested development, whose face is that of a "forty-year-old baby." Connie's "Someday My Prince Will Come" daydreams, plus the many references to how dazed and sleepy she always is, especially the day Arnold comes for her, when she "lay languidly about the airless little room" and "breathed in and breathed out with each gentle rise and fall of her chest"—these too, suggest "Snow White" and, for that matter, "Sleeping Beauty," whose heroine in the Brothers Grimm is, like Connie, fifteen.

The oedipal implications of "Snow White" are evident in the fact that, as Bettelheim points out, the queen's Magic Mirror speaks not with the mother's but the daughter's voice, revealing the jealous child's own sense of inferiority and frustration projected onto her mother. The father's romantic feelings for the daughter are never at issue in such a fairy tale and he is generally depicted as weak, ineffectual, and oblivious to the struggle that issues between mother and daughter—exactly as in Miss Oates's story.

> From "In Fairyland Without a Map: Connie's Exploration Inward
> in Joyce Carol Oates's 'Where Are You Going, Where Have You Been?'"

Harold Bloom (b. 1930)

Poetic Influence

1975

Let me reduce my argument to the hopelessly simplistic; poems, I am saying, are neither about "subjects" nor about "themselves." They are necessarily about *other poems;* a poem is a response to a poem, as a poet is a response to a poet, or a person to his parent. Trying to write a poem takes the poet back to the origins of what a poem *first was* for him, and so takes the poet back beyond the pleasure principle to the decisive initial encounter and response that began him. We do not think of W. C. Williams as a Keatsian poet, yet he *began and ended as one,* and his late celebration of his Greeny Flower is another response to Keats's odes. *Only a poet challenges a poet as poet,* and so only a poet makes a poet. To the poet-in-a-poet, a poem is always *the other man,* the precursor, and so a poem is always a person, always the father of one's Second Birth. To live, the poet must *misinterpret* the father, by the crucial act of misprision, which is the rewriting of the father.

But who, what is the poetic father? The voice of the other, of the *daimon,* is always speaking in one; the voice that cannot die because already it has survived death—*the dead poet lives in one.* In the last phase of strong poets, they attempt to join the undying *by living in the dead poets* who are already alive in them. This late Return of the Dead recalls us, as readers, to a recognition of the original motive for the catastrophe of poetic incarnation. Vico, who identified the origins of poetry with the impulse towards divination (to foretell, but also to become a god by foretelling), implicitly understood (as did Emerson, and Wordsworth) that a poem is written to escape dying. Literally, poems are refusals of mortality. Every poem therefore has two makers: the precursor, and the ephebe's rejected mortality.

A poet, I argue in consequence, is not so much a man speaking to men as a man rebelling against being spoken to by a dead man (the precursor) outrageously more alive than himself.

From A Map of Misreading

MYTHOLOGICAL CRITICISM

Mythological critics look for the recurrent universal patterns underlying most literary works. **Mythological criticism** is an interdisciplinary approach that combines the insights of anthropology, psychology, history, and comparative religion. If psychological criticism examines the artist as an individual, mythological criticism explores the artist's common humanity by tracing how the individual imagination uses symbols and situations—consciously or unconsciously—in ways that transcend its own historical milieu and resemble the mythology of other cultures or epochs.

A central concept in mythological criticism is the **archetype**, a symbol, character, situation, or image that evokes a deep universal response. The idea of the archetype came into literary criticism from the Swiss psychologist Carl Jung, a lifetime student of myth and religion. Jung believed that all individuals share a "collective unconscious," a set of primal memories common to the human race, existing below each person's conscious mind. Archetypal images (which often relate to experiencing primordial phenomena like the sun, moon, fire, night, and blood), Jung believed, trigger the collective unconscious. We do not need to accept the literal truth of the collective unconscious, however, to endorse the archetype as a helpful critical concept. Northrop Frye defined the archetype in considerably less occult terms as "a symbol, usually an image, which recurs often enough in literature to be recognizable as an element of one's literary experience as a whole."

Identifying archetypal symbols and situations in literary works, mythological critics almost inevitably link the individual text under discussion to a broader context of works that share an underlying pattern. In discussing Shakespeare's *Hamlet,* for instance, a mythological critic might relate Shakespeare's Danish prince to other mythic sons avenging the deaths of their fathers, like Orestes from Greek myth or Sigmund of Norse legend; or, in discussing *Othello,* relate the sinister figure of Iago to the devil in traditional Christian belief. Critic Joseph Campbell took such comparisons even further; his compendious study *The Hero with a Thousand Faces* demonstrates how similar mythic characters appear in virtually every culture on every continent.

Carl Jung (1875–1961)

The Collective Unconscious and Archetypes   1931

Translated by R. F. C. Hull

A more or less superficial layer of the unconscious is undoubtedly personal. I call it the *personal unconscious*. But this personal unconscious rests upon a deeper layer, which does not derive from personal experience and is not a personal acquisition but is inborn. This deeper layer I call the *collective unconscious*. I have chosen the term "collective" because this part of the unconscious is not individual but universal; in contrast to the personal psyche, it has contents and modes of behavior that are more or less the same everywhere and in all individuals. It is, in other words, identical in all men and thus constitutes a common psyche substrate of a suprapersonal nature which is present in every one of us.

Psychic existence can be recognized only by the presence of contents that are *capable of consciousness*. We can therefore speak of an unconscious only in so far as we are able to demonstrate its contents. The contents of the personal unconscious are chiefly the *feeling-toned complexes*, as they are called; they constitute the personal and private side of psychic life. The contents of the collective unconscious, on the other hand, are known as *archetypes*. . . .

For our purposes this term is apposite and helpful, because it tells us that so far as the collective unconscious contents are concerned we are dealing with archaic or—I would say—primordial types, that is, with universal images that have existed since the remotest times. The term "representations collectives," used by Lévy-Bruhl to denote the symbolic figures in the primitive view of the world, could easily be applied to unconscious contents as well, since it means practically the same thing. Primitive tribal lore is concerned with archetypes that have been modified in a special way. They are no longer contents of the unconscious, but have already been changed into conscious formulae taught according to tradition, generally in the form of esoteric teaching. This last is a typical means of expression for the transmission of collective contents originally derived from the unconscious.

Another well-known expression of the archetypes is myth and fairy tale. But here too we are dealing with forms that have received a specific stamp and have been handed down through long periods of time. The term "archetype" thus applies only indirectly to the "representations collectives," since it designates only those psychic contents which have not yet been submitted to conscious elaboration and are therefore an immediate datum of psychic experience. In this sense there is a considerable difference between the archetype and the historical formula that has evolved. Especially on the higher levels of esoteric teaching the archetypes appear in a form that reveals quite unmistakably the critical and evaluating influence of conscious elaboration. Their immediate manifestation, as we encounter it in dreams and visions, is much more individual, less understandable, and more naïve than in myths, for example. The archetype is essentially an unconscious content that is altered by becoming conscious and by being perceived, and it takes its color from the individual consciousness in which it happens to appear.

From *The Collected Works of C. G. Jung*

Northrop Frye (1912–1991)

Mythic Archetypes   1957

We begin our study of archetypes, then, with a world of myth, an abstract or purely literary world of fictional and thematic design, unaffected by canons of plausible adaptation to familiar experience. In terms of narrative, myth is the imitation of actions near or at the conceivable limits of desire. The gods enjoy beautiful women, fight one another with prodigious strength, comfort and assist man, or else watch his miseries from the height of their immortal freedom. The fact that myth operates at the top level of human desire does not mean that it necessarily presents its world as attained or attainable by human beings. . . .

Realism, or the art of verisimilitude, evokes the response "How like that is to what we know!" When what is written is *like* what is known, we have an art of extended or implied simile. And as realism is an art of implicit simile, myth is an art of implicit metaphorical identity. The word "sun-god," with a hyphen used instead of a predicate, is a pure ideogram, in Pound's terminology, or literal metaphor, in ours. In myth we see the structural principles of literature isolated; in realism we see the *same* structural principles (not similar ones) fitting into a context of plausibility. (Similarly in music, a piece by Purcell and a piece by Benjamin Britten may not be in the least *like* each other, but if they are both in D major their tonality will be the same.) The presence of a mythical structure in realistic fiction, however, poses certain technical problems for making it plausible, and the devices used in solving these problems may be given the general name of *displacement*.

Myth, then, is one extreme of literary design; naturalism is the other, and in between lies the whole area of romance, using that term to mean, not the historical mode of the first essay, but the tendency, noted later in the same essay, to displace myth in a human direction and yet, in contrast to "realism," to conventionalize content in an idealized direction. The central principle of displacement is that what can be metaphorically identified in a myth can only be linked in romance by some form of simile: analogy, significant association, incidental accompanying imagery, and the like. In a myth we can have a sun-god or a tree-god; in a romance we may have a person who is significantly associated with the sun or trees.

From Anatomy of Criticism

Edmond Volpe (b. 1922)

Myth in Faulkner's "Barn Burning"   1964

"Barn Burning" however is not really concerned with class conflict. The story is centered upon Sarty's emotional dilemma. His conflict would not have been altered in any way if the person whose barn Ab burns had been a simple poor farmer, rather than an aristocratic plantation owner. The child's tension, in fact, begins to surface during the hearing in which a simple farmer accuses Ab of burning his barn. The moral antagonists mirrored in Sarty's conflict are not sharecropper and aristocrat. They are the father, Ab Snopes, versus the rest of mankind. Major De Spain is not developed as a character; his house is important to Sarty because it represents a totally new and totally different social and moral entity. Within the context of the society Faulkner is dealing with, the gap between the rich aristocrat and the poor sharecropper provides a viable metaphor for dramatizing the crisis Sarty is under-going. Ab Snopes is by no means a social crusader. The De Spain manor is Sarty's first contact with a rich man's house, though he can recall, in the short span of his life, at least a dozen times the family had to move because Ab burned barns. Ab does not discriminate between rich and poor. For him there are only two categories: blood kin and "they," into which he lumps all the rest of mankind. Ab's division relates to Sarty's crisis and only by defining precisely the nature of the conflict the boy is undergoing can we determine the moral significance Faulkner sees in it. The clue to Sarty's conflict rests in its resolution.

• • •

The boy's anxiety is created by his awakening sense of his own individuality. Torn between strong emotional attachment to the parent and his growing need to assert his own identity, Sarty's crisis is psychological and his battle is being waged far below the level of his intellectual and moral awareness.

Faulkner makes this clear in the opening scene with imagery that might be described as synesthesia. The real smell of cheese is linked with the smell of the hermetic meat in the tin cans with the scarlet devils on the label that his "intestines believed he smelled coming in intermittent gusts momentary and brief between the other constant one, the smell and sense just a little of fear because mostly of despair and grief, the old fierce pull of blood." The smells below the level of the olfactory sense link the devil image and the blood image to identify the anxiety the father creates in the child's psyche. Tension is created by the blood demanding identification with his father against "*our enemy* he thought in that despair; *ourn! mine and hisn both! He's my father!*" Sarty's conflict is played out in terms of identification, not in moral terms. He does not think of his father as bad, his father's enemies as good.

Ab unjustly accuses Sarty of intending to betray him at the hearing, but he correctly recognizes that his son is moving out of childhood, developing a mind and will of his own and is no longer blindly loyal. In instructing the boy that everyone is the enemy and his loyalty belongs to his blood, Ab's phrasing is revealing: "'Don't you know all they wanted was a chance to get at me because they knew I had them beat?'" Ab does not use the plural "us." It is "I" and "they." Blood loyalty means total identification with Ab, and in the ensuing scenes, Snopes attempts to make his son an extension of himself by taking him to the De Spain house, rise up before dawn to be with him when he returns the rug, accompany him to the hearing against De Spain and finally make him an accomplice in the burning of De Spain's barn.

The moral import of Ab's insistence on blood loyalty is fully developed by the satanic imagery Faulkner introduces in the scene at the mansion. As they go up the drive, Sarty follows his father, seeing the stiff black form against the white plantation house. Traditionally the devil casts no shadow, and Ab's figure appears to the child as having "that impervious quality of something cut ruthlessly from tin, depthless, as though sidewise to the sun it would cast no shadow." The cloven hoof of the devil is suggested by Ab's limp upon which the boy's eyes are fixed as the foot unwaveringly comes down into the manure. Sarty's increasing tension resounds in the magnified echo of the limping foot on the porch boards, "a sound out of all proportion to the displacement of the body it bore, as though it had attained to a sort of vicious and ravening minimum not to be dwarfed by anything." At first Sarty thought the house was impervious to his father, but his burgeoning fear of the threat the father poses is reflected in his vision of Ab becoming magnified and monstrous as the black arm reaches up the white door and Sarty sees "the lifted hand like a curled claw."

The satanic images are projected out of the son's nightmarish vision of his father, but they are reinforced by the comments of the adult narrator. Sarty believes Snopes fought bravely in the Civil War, but Ab, we are told, wore no uniform, gave his fealty to no cause, admitted the authority of no man. He went to war for booty. Ab's ego is so great it creates a centripetal force into which everything must flow or be destroyed. The will-less, abject creature who is his wife symbolizes the power of his will. What Ab had done to his wife, he sets out to do to the emerging will of his son. Ab cannot tolerate any entity that challenges the dominance of his will. By allowing his hog to forage in the farmer's corn and by dirtying and ruining De Spain's rug, he deliberately creates a conflict that requires the assertion of primacy. Fire, the element of the devil, is the weapon for the preservation of his dominance. Ab's rage is not fired by social injustice. It is fired by a pride, like Lucifer's, so absolute it can accept no order beyond its own. In the satanic myth, Lucifer asserts his will against the divine order and is cast out of heaven. The angels who fall with Lucifer become extensions of his will. In the same way, Ab is an outcast and pariah among men. He accepts no order that is not of his blood.

From "'Barn Burning': A Definition of Evil"

SOCIOLOGICAL CRITICISM

Sociological criticism examines literature in the cultural, economic, and political context in which it is written or received. "Art is not created in a vacuum," critic Wilbur Scott observed, "it is the work not simply of a person, but of an author fixed in time and space, answering a community of which he is an important, because articulate part." Sociological criticism explores the relationships between the artist and society. Sometimes it looks at the sociological status of the author to evaluate how the profession of the writer in a particular milieu affected what was written. Sociological criticism also analyzes the social content of literary works—what cultural, economic, or political values a particular text implicitly or explicitly promotes. Finally, sociological criticism examines the role the audience has in shaping literature. A sociological view of Shakespeare, for example, might look at the economic position of Elizabethan playwrights and actors; it might also study the political ideas expressed in the plays or discuss how the nature of an Elizabethan theatrical audience (which was usually all male unless the play was produced at court) helped determine the subject, tone, and language of the plays.

An influential type of sociological criticism has been Marxist criticism, which focuses on the economic and political elements of art. Marxist criticism, as in the work of the Hungarian philosopher Georg Lukacs, often explores the ideological content of literature. Whereas a formalist critic would maintain that form and content are inextricably blended, Lukacs believed that content determines form and that, therefore, all art is political. Even if a work of art ignores political issues, it makes a political statement, Marxist critics believe, because it endorses the economic and political status quo. Consequently, Marxist criticism is frequently evaluative and judges some literary work better than others on an ideological basis; this tendency can lead to reductive judgment, as when Soviet critics rated Jack London a novelist superior to William Faulkner, Ernest Hemingway, Edith Wharton, and Henry James, because he illustrated the principles of class struggle more clearly. London was America's first major working-class writer. To examine the political ideas and observations found in his fiction can be illuminating, but to fault other authors for lacking his instincts and ideas is not necessarily helpful in understanding their particular qualities. There is always a danger in sociological criticism—Marxist or otherwise—of imposing the critic's personal politics on the work in question and then evaluating it according to how closely it endorses that ideology. As an analytical tool, however, Marxist criticism and sociological methods can illuminate political and economic dimensions of literature that other approaches overlook.

Georg Lukacs (1885–1971)

Content Determines Form 1962

What determines the style of a given work of art? How does the intention determine the form? (We are concerned here, of course, with the intention realized in the work; it need not coincide with the writer's conscious intention.) The distinctions that concern us are not those between stylistic "techniques" in the formalistic sense. It is the view of the world, the ideology or *Weltanschauung*° underlying a writer's work, that counts. And it is the writer's attempt to reproduce this view of the world which constitutes his "intention" and is the formative principle underlying the style of a given piece of writing. Looked at in this way, style ceases to be a formalistic category. Rather, it is rooted in content; it is the specific form of a specific content.

Content determines form. But there is no content of which Man himself is not the focal point. However various the *données*° of literature (a particular experience, a didactic purpose), the basic question is, and will remain: what is Man?

Here is a point of division: if we put the question in abstract, philosophical terms, leaving aside all formal considerations, we arrive—for the realist school—at the traditional Aristotelian dictum (which was also reached by other than purely aesthetic considerations): Man is *zoon politikon*,° a social animal. The Aristotelian dictum is applicable to all great realistic literature. Achilles and Werther, Oedipus and Tom Jones, Antigone and Anna Karenina: their individual existence—their *Sein an sich*,° in the Hegelian terminology; their "ontological being," as a more fashionable terminology has it—cannot be distinguished from their social and historical environment. Their human significance, their specific individuality cannot be separated from the context in which they were created.

From *Realism in Our Time*

Daniel P. Watkins (b. 1952)

Money and Labor in "The Rocking-Horse Winner" 1987

It is a commonplace that D. H. Lawrence's "The Rocking-Horse Winner" is a story about the devastating effect that money can have on a family, and, further, that Lawrence's specific objections in the story are not to money abstractly conceived but

---

Weltanschauung: German for "world view," an outlook on life.   *données* French for "given"; it means the materials a writer uses to create his or her work or the subject or purpose of a literary work. *zoon politikon*: Greek for "political animal."   *Sein an sich*: the German philosopher G. W. F. Hegel's term for "pure existence."

to money as it is understood and valued by capitalist culture. This is one of Lawrence's most savage and compact critiques of what he elsewhere calls "the god-damn bourgeoisie" and of individuals who, despite their natural or potential goodness, "swallow the culture bait" and hence become victims to the world they (wrongly) believe holds the key to human happiness.

• • •

The class nature of labor under capital is presented symbolically in the story in terms of the adult and non-adult worlds. That is, social reality is controlled by parents whose primary concern is to bring in money sufficient to "the social position which they (have) to keep up." While they have a small income, and while "The father went in to town to some office," they never are really seen to work actively and productively. Rather, they set a tone of need in their world that generates intense and pervasive anxiety, which then is passed down to their children, who interiorize the values and attitudes of the adult world and set about (as best they can) to satisfy the demands of that world. Even when money is produced, however, the demands of the adult world are never fully met, but, quite the reverse, intensify further, so that more labor is necessary. In this context, work is not a means of meeting basic human needs, but rather only a way of producing greater sums of money, and thus it is clearly socially unproductive. Seen from this perspective, it is not important that the parents are not capitalists in the crudest sense (that is, they are not drawn as investors of money); what is important is that they both set the tone (economic scarcity) and determine the values (consumerism) of the world they inhabit, and in addition expropriate the wealth that others produce for their own private consumption.

Young Paul exemplifies vividly the sort of work that arises under capital. Simply put, he is a laborer for his mother, to whom he gives all of his money, only to find that the more he gives the more she needs. It is true, of course, that as a handicapper he invests money, betting on a profitable return on his investment, and that in this sense he is a sort of capitalist; indeed, it is his betting that is the literal sign of the economic relations controlling the world of the story. But at the same time his character is made to carry a much larger symbolic significance, for what he is investing, in real terms, is himself, selling his skills to generate wealth that he is not free to possess, but that is necessary to the maintenance of existing social relations. As his mother touches the money he earns, she uses it not to satisfy family needs—it has little or no *use* value—but to extend her social position and social power, and the process of extension of course is never-ending, requiring ever greater sums of money: "There were certain new furnishings, and Paul had a tutor. He was *really* going to Eton, his father's school, in the following autumn. There were flowers in the winter, and a blossoming of the luxury Paul's mother had been used to. And yet the voices in the house, behind the sprays of mimosa and almond-blossom, and from under the piles of iridescent cushions, simply trilled and screamed in a sort of ecstasy: 'There *must* be more money!'" This passage clearly focuses the priority of money over commodity and the relentlessness with which the power associated with money controls even the most personal dimension of life.

The work itself that Paul performs cannot, under such conditions, be personally satisfying, and this is shown powerfully by the sort of work he does. The rocking horse is a brilliant symbol of non-productive labor, for even while it moves it remains stationary: even while Paul is magically (humanly) creative, producing untold wealth for his mother, he does not advance in the least, and in fact becomes increasingly isolated and fearful that even the abilities he now possesses will be taken from him. The labor, which drives him to "a sort of madness," that consumes him to an ever greater degree, leaves him nothing for himself, driving him down a terrible path to emotional and then physical distress. He is never satisfied with what he produces because it in no way relieves the pressure that his world places on him, and thus his anxiety and alienation grow to the point of destroying any sense of real personal worth and removing him literally from all meaningful social exchange, as when he takes his rocking horse to his bedroom and rides alone late into the night trying to find the key to wealth.

From "Labor and Religion in D. H. Lawrence's
'The Rocking-Horse Winner'"

Alfred Kazin (1915–1998)

Walt Whitman and Abraham Lincoln 1984

In Lincoln's lifetime Whitman was the only major writer to describe him with love. Whitman identified Lincoln with himself in the worshipful fashion that became standard after Lincoln's death. That Lincoln was a class issue says a good deal about the prejudices of American society in the East. A leading New Yorker, George Templeton Strong, noted in his diary that while he never disavowed the "lank and hard featured man," Lincoln was "despised and rejected by a third of the community, and only tolerated by the other two-thirds." Whitman the professional man of the people had complicated reasons for loving Lincoln. The uneasiness about him among America's elite was based on the fear that this unknown, untried man, elected without administrative experience (and without a majority) might not be up to his "fearful task."

• • •

Whitman related himself to the popular passion released by war and gave himself to this passion as a political cause. He understood popular opinion in a way that Emerson, Thoreau, and Hawthorne did not attempt to understand it. Emerson said, like any conventional New England clergyman, that the war was holy. He could not speak for the masses who bore the brunt of the war. Whitman was able to get so much out of the war, to create a lasting image of it, because he knew what people were feeling. He was not above the battle like Thoreau and Hawthorne, not suspicious of the majority like his fellow New Yorker Herman Melville, who in "The House-top," the most personal poem in *Battle-Pieces*, denounced the "ship-rats" who had taken over the city in the anti-draft riots of 1863.

Despite Whitman's elusiveness—he made a career out of longings it would have ended that career to fulfill—he genuinely felt at home with soldiers and other "ordinary" people who were inarticulate by the standards of men "from the schools," He was always present, if far from available, presenting the picture of a nobly accessible and social creature. He certainly got on better with omnibus drivers, workingmen, and now "simple" soldiers (especially when they were wounded and open to his ministrations) than he did with "scribblers." By the time Whitman went down after Fredericksburg to look for brother George, the war was becoming a revolution of sorts and Whitman's old radical politics were becoming "the nation." This made him adore Lincoln as the symbol of the nation's unity. An essential quality of Whitman's Civil

War "memoranda" is Whitman's libidinous urge to associate himself with the great, growing, ever more powerful federal cause. Whitman's characteristic lifelong urge to join, to combine, to see life as movement, unity, totality, became during the Civil War an actively loving association with the broad masses of the people and *their* war. In his cult of the Civil War, Whitman allies himself with a heroic and creative energy which sees itself spreading out from the people and their representative men, Lincoln and Whitman.

Hawthorne's and Thoreau's horror of America as the Big State did not reflect Whitman's image of the Union. His passion for the "cause" reflected his intense faith in democracy at a juncture when the United States at war represented the revolutionary principle to Marx, the young Ibsen, Mill, Browning, Tolstoy. Whitman's deepest feeling was that his own rise from the city streets, his future as a poet of democracy, was tied up with the Northern armies.

From *An American Procession*

GENDER CRITICISM

Gender criticism examines how sexual identity influences the creation and reception of literary works. Gender studies began with the feminist movement and was influenced by such works as Simone de Beauvoir's *The Second Sex* (1949) and Kate Millett's *Sexual Politics* (1970) as well as sociology, psychology, and anthropology. Feminist critics believe that culture has been so completely dominated by men that literature is full of unexamined "male-produced" assumptions. They see their criticism correcting this imbalance by analyzing and combating patriarchal attitudes. Feminist criticism has explored how an author's gender influences—consciously or unconsciously—his or her writing. While a formalist critic such as Allen Tate emphasized the universality of Emily Dickinson's poetry by demonstrating how powerfully the language, imagery, and mythmaking of her poems combine to affect a generalized reader, Sandra M. Gilbert, a leading feminist critic, has identified attitudes and assumptions in Dickinson's poetry that she believes are essentially female. Another important theme in feminist criticism is analyzing how sexual identity influences the reader of a text. If Tate's hypothetical reader was deliberately sexless, Gilbert's reader sees a text through the eyes of his or her sex. Finally, feminist critics carefully examine how the images of men and women in imaginative literature reflect or reject the social forces that have historically kept the sexes from achieving total equality.

Recently, gender criticism has expanded beyond its original feminist perspective. In the last twenty years or so, critics in the field of gay and lesbian studies—some of whom describe their discipline as "queer theory"—have explored the impact of different sexual orientations on literary creation and reception. Seeking to establish a canon of classic gay and lesbian authors, these critics argue that sexual orientation is so central a component of human personality (especially when it necessarily puts one at odds with established social and moral norms) that to ignore it in connection with such writers amounts to a fundamental misreading and misunderstanding of their work. A men's movement has also emerged in response to feminism, seeking not to reject feminism but to rediscover masculine identity in an authentic, contemporary way. Led by poet Robert Bly, the men's movement has paid special attention to interpreting poetry and fables as myths of psychic growth and sexual identity.

Sandra M. Gilbert (b. 1936)
and Susan Gubar (b. 1944)

The Freedom of Emily Dickinson   1985

[Emily Dickinson] defined herself as a *woman* writer, reading the works of female pre-cursors with special care, attending to the implications of novels like Charlotte Brontë's *Jane Eyre*, Emily Brontë's *Wuthering Heights*, and George Eliot's *Middlemarch* with the same absorbed delight that characterized her devotion to Elizabeth Barrett Browning's *Aurora Leigh*. Finally, then, the key to her enigmatic identity as a "supposed person" who was called the "Myth of Amherst" may rest, not in investigations of her questionable romance, but in studies of her unquestionably serious reading as well as in analyses of her disquietingly powerful writing. Elliptically phrased, intensely compressed, her poems are more linguistically innovative than any other nineteenth-century verses, with the possible exception of some works by Walt Whitman and Gerard Manley Hopkins, her two most radical male contemporaries. Throughout her largely secret but always brilliant career, moreover, she confronted precisely the questions about the individual and society, time and death, flesh and spirit, that major precursors from Milton to Keats had faced. Dreaming of "Amplitude and Awe," she recorded sometimes vengeful, sometimes mystical visions of social and personal transformation in poems as inventively phrased and imaginatively constructed as any in the English language.

Clearly such accomplishments required not only extraordinary talent but also some measure of freedom. Yet because she was the unmarried daughter of conservative New Englanders, Dickinson was obliged to take on many household tasks; as a nineteenth-century New England wife, she would have had the same number of obligations, if not more. Some of these she performed with pleasure; in 1856, for instance, she was judge of a bread-baking contest, and in 1857 she won a prize in that contest. But as Higginson's "scholar," as a voracious reader and an ambitious writer, Dickinson had to win herself time for "Amplitude and Awe," and it is increasingly clear that she did so through a strategic withdrawal from her ordinary world. A story related by her niece Martha Dickinson Bianchi reveals that the poet herself knew from the first what both the price and the prize might be: on one occasion, said Mrs. Bianchi, Dickinson took her up to the room in which she regularly sequestered herself, and, mimicking locking herself in, "thumb and forefinger closed on an imaginary key," said "with a quick turn of her wrist, 'It's just a turn—and freedom, Matty!'"

In the freedom of her solitary, but not lonely, room, Dickinson may have become what her Amherst neighbors saw as a bewildering "myth." Yet there, too, she created myths of her own. Reading the Brontës and Barrett Browning, studying Transcendentalism and the Bible, she contrived a theology which is powerfully expressed in many of her poems. That it was at its most hopeful a female-centered theology is revealed in verses like those she wrote about the women artists she admired, as well as in more general works like her gravely pantheistic address to the "Sweet Mountains" who "tell me no lie," with its definition of the hills around Amherst as "strong Madonnas" and its description of the writer herself as "The Wayward Nun – beneath the Hill – / Whose service is to You – ." As Dickinson's admirer and descendant Adrienne Rich has accurately observed, this passionate poet consistently chose to confront her society—to "have it out"—"on her own premises."

From introduction to Emily Dickinson,
The Norton Anthology of Literature by Women

Nina Pelikan Straus

Transformations in *The Metamorphosis*   1989

Traditionally, critics of *Metamorphosis* have underplayed the fact that the story is about not only Gregor's but also his family's and, especially, Grete's metamorphosis. Yet it is mainly Grete, woman, daughter, sister, on whom the social and psychoanalytic resonances of the text depend. It is she who will ironically "blossom" as her brother deteriorates; it is she whose mirror reflects women's present situations as we attempt to critique patriarchal dominance in order to create new lives that avoid the replication of invalidation. . . .

If Grete is a symbol of anything, it is the irony of self-liberation in relation to the indeterminacy of gender roles. Grete's role as a woman unfolds as Gregor's life as a man collapses. It is no accident that this gender scrolling takes place in the literature of a writer who had curious experiences in his life with women—experiences of his own weakness and of women's strengths. Traditionally, the text has been read not as revealing brother-sister or gender-based relationships, however, but as revealing a father-son conflict or Oedipus complex.

• • •

The word "shame" is central to both Grete and Gregor's experiences. It is a shame that Gregor cannot get out of bed, that he cannot get up to go to work, that his voice fails him, that he cannot open the door of his room with his insect pincers, that he must be fed, that he stinks and must hide his body that is a shame to others. Shame comes from seeing oneself through another's eyes, from Gregor's seeing himself through Grete's eyes, and from the reader's seeing Grete through the narrator's eyes. The text graphically mirrors how we see each other in various shameful (and comic) conditions. Through Gregor's condition, ultimately shameful because he is reduced to the dependency of an ugly baby, Kafka imagines what it is like to be dependent on the care of women. And Kafka is impressed with women's efforts to keep their households and bodies clean and alive. This impression is enlarged with every detail that humiliates and weakens Gregor while simultaneously empowering Grete, who cares for Gregor, ironically, at his own—and perhaps at Kafka's—expense.

The change or metamorphosis is in this sense a literary experiment that plays with problems the story's title barely suggests. For Kafka there can be no change without an exchange, no flourishing of Grete without Gregor's withering; nor can the meaning of transformation entail a final closure that prevents further transformations. The metamorphosis occurs both in the first sentence of the text—"When Gregor Samsa awoke one morning from unsettling dreams, he found himself changed in his bed into a monstrous vermin"—and in the last paragraph of the story, which describes Grete's transformation into a woman "blossoming" and "stretching" toward the family's "new dreams" once Gregor has been transformed into garbage. Grete's final transformation, rendered in concrete bodily terms, is foreshadowed in Gregor's initial transformation from human into vermin. This deliberately reflective textual pattern implies that only when the distorting mirrors of the sexist fun house are dismantled can the sons of the patriarchs recognize themselves as dehumanized and dehumanizing. Only when Grete blooms into an eligible young woman, ripe for the job and marriage markets, can we recognize that her empowerment is also an ironic reification. She has been transformed at another's expense, and she will carry within her the marketplace value that has ultimately destroyed Gregor.

From "Transforming Franz Kafka's *Metamorphosis*"

Richard R. Bozorth (b. 1965)

"Tell Me the Truth About Love" 2001

The 1994 film *Four Weddings and a Funeral* has probably done more to popularize Auden than any other recent event. It is also an instructive moment in his reception, for where the academy has often praised his work for its universality, the film invokes him as a gay sage: before reciting "Funeral Blues" at his lover's funeral, the character Matthew prefaces it by calling Auden "another splendid bugger" like the late Gareth.

This scene makes visible a number of significant occlusions in Auden's love poetry, including those he himself instigated. This lyric first appeared in Auden and Isherwood's play *The Ascent of F6* (1936), recited to "A Blues" at the death of James Ransom, the protagonist's brother.[2] The version used in the film dates from 1938 and gained the title "Funeral Blues" in *Another Time* (1940). Included there as one of "Four Cabaret Songs for Miss Hedli Anderson," it is presented as an exercise in light verse. As Mendelson notes, its dedication to Benjamin Britten's favorite soprano was a form of disguise Auden used only for love poems with masculine pronouns.[3] By putting the text in the voice of a gay male character, *Four Weddings and a Funeral* outs the poem, much as Matthew uses it to affirm before the mourners the romantic nature of his relationship with Gareth. Auden's words become a poignant utterance about the public unspeakability of gay love:

> Let aeroplanes circle moaning overhead
> Scribbling on the sky the message He Is Dead,
> Put crêpe bows round the white necks of the public doves,
> Let the traffic policemen wear black cotton gloves.[4]

In cinematic context, such extravagance is not just an effect of the conventions of light verse, or an expression of anguish that the world goes blithely on—a feeling hardly limited, of course, to gay mourners. For these campy pleas for public ritual point up a gap between gay romantic loss and official forms of lament.

To read "Funeral Blues" as expressing a universal sense of the unfairness of death is to be so taken by Auden's facility with romantic commonplace as to be deaf to its sexual-political implications. For its part, *Four Weddings and a Funeral* risks another illusion in recovering Auden as a master of gay pathos. Perhaps his most touching line came with the 1938 revision: "I thought that love would last forever; I was wrong." Auden was evidently responding not to death but to the end of the affair that had generated most of his love poetry since 1932.[5] But while it is almost irresistible to see the poem as voicing utter desolation at a breakup, impermanence had always haunted Auden's love poems. "Certainty" and "fidelity," in his famous words, are delusions of lovers "in their ordinary swoon."[6] From this angle, "Funeral Blues" might sound contrived or even cruel, since it mourned someone still living. But the poem might also be read as a confession that grief can be a self-indulgent performance,

[2] W. H. Auden and Christopher Isherwood, *Plays and Other Dramatic Writings by W. H. Auden, 1928–1938*, ed. Edward Mendelson (Princeton: Princeton UP, 1988) 350–51.
[3] Edward Mendelson, *Later Auden* (New York: Farrar, 1999) 32.
[4] W. H. Auden, *The English Auden: Poems, Prose and Dramatic Writings* (London: Faber, 1977) 163.
[5] Mendelson, *Later Auden* 32.
[6] Auden, *English Auden* 207.

as manipulative of oneself as it is of others. Rather than obscuring the personal, Auden's title invites moral reflection: grieving can indeed be "Funeral Blues"—a way of acting out romantic pathos.

Both universalizing and "gay-positive" readings of "Funeral Blues" find it confirming what we—however "we" may be defined—already feel: we sentimentally construe the mourning voice as echoing our own desires. To read the poem instead as Auden's private response to the end of a homosexual love affair is to see its expression of grief as a means for reflection on love. We have seen how Auden used "parable" to articulate the social value of poetry as an antiuniversalizing form, and this chapter extends my concern with his poetic theory. My largest claim is that Auden came to treat poetry itself as a kind of lovers' discourse: a site of intimate relation between poet and reader in all their particularities. Poetry would be an erotic "game of knowledge," as Auden writes in the 1948 essay "Squares and Oblongs": "a bringing to consciousness . . . of emotions and their hidden relationships."[7]

From *Auden's Games of Knowledge: Poetry and the Meanings of Homosexuality*

READER-RESPONSE CRITICISM

Reader-response criticism attempts to describe what happens in the reader's mind while interpreting a text. If traditional criticism assumes that imaginative writing is a creative act, reader-response theory recognizes that reading is also a creative process. Reader-response critics believe that no text provides self-contained meaning; literary texts do not exist independently of readers' interpretations. A text, according to this critical school, is not finished until it is read and interpreted. As Oscar Wilde remarked in the preface to his novel *The Picture of Dorian Gray* (1891), "It is the spectator, and not life, that art really mirrors." The practical problem then arises, however, that no two individuals necessarily read a text in exactly the same way. Rather than declare one interpretation correct and the other mistaken, reader-response criticism recognizes the inevitable plurality of readings. Instead of trying to ignore or reconcile the contradictions inherent in this situation, it explores them.

The easiest way to explain reader-response criticism is to relate it to the common experience of rereading a favorite book after many years. Rereading a novel as an adult, for example, that "changed your life" as an adolescent, is often a shocking experience. The book may seem substantially different. The character you remembered liking most now seems less admirable, and another character you disliked now seems more sympathetic. Has the book changed? Very unlikely, but *you* certainly have in the intervening years. Reader-response criticism explores how different individuals (or classes of individuals) see the same text differently. It emphasizes how religious, cultural, and social values affect readings; it also overlaps with gender criticism in exploring how men and women read the same text with different assumptions.

While reader-response criticism rejects the notion that there can be a single correct reading for a literary text, it doesn't consider all readings permissible. Each text creates limits to its possible interpretations. As Stanley Fish admits in the following critical selection, we cannot arbitrarily place an Eskimo in William Faulkner's story "A Rose for Emily" (though Professor Fish does ingeniously imagine a hypothetical situation where this bizarre interpretation might actually be possible).

[7]W. H. Auden, "Squares and Oblongs," *Poets at Work*, ed. Charles D. Abbot (New York: Harcourt, 1948) 173.

Stanley Fish (b. 1938)

An Eskimo "A Rose for Emily"   1980

The fact that it remains easy to think of a reading that most of us would dismiss out of hand does not mean that the text excludes it but that there is as yet no elaborated interpretive procedure for producing that text. . . . Norman Holland's analysis of Faulkner's "A Rose for Emily" is a case in point. Holland is arguing for a kind of psychoanalytic pluralism. The text, he declares, is "at most a matrix of psychological possibilities for its readers," but, he insists, "only some possibilities . . . truly fit the matrix": "One would not say, for example, that a reader of . . . 'A Rose for Emily' who thought the 'tableau' [of Emily and her father in the doorway] described an Eskimo was really responding to the story at all—only pursuing some mysterious inner exploration."

Holland is making two arguments: first, that anyone who proposes an Eskimo reading of "A Rose for Emily" will not find a hearing in the literary community. And that, I think, is right. ("We are right to rule out at least some readings.") His second argument is that the unacceptability of the Eskimo reading is a function of the text, of what he calls its "sharable promptuary," the public "store of structured language" that sets limits to the interpretations the words can accommodate. And that, I think, is wrong. The Eskimo reading is unacceptable because there is at present no interpretive strategy for producing it, no way of "looking" or reading (and remember, all acts of looking or reading are "ways") that would result in the emergence of obviously Eskimo meanings. This does not mean, however, that no such strategy could ever come into play, and it is not difficult to imagine the circumstances under which it would establish itself. One such circumstance would be the discovery of a letter in which Faulkner confides that he has always believed himself to be an Eskimo changeling. (The example is absurd only if one forgets Yeats's *Vision* or Blake's Swedenborgianism° or James Miller's recent elaboration of a homosexual reading of *The Waste Land*.) Immediately the workers in the Faulkner industry would begin to reinterpret the canon in the light of this newly revealed "belief" and the work of reinterpretation would involve the elaboration of a symbolic or allusive system (not unlike mythological or typological criticism) whose application would immediately transform the text into one informed everywhere by Eskimo meanings. It might seem that I am admitting that there is a text to be transformed, but the object of transformation would be the text (or texts) given by whatever interpretive strategies the Eskimo strategy was in the process of dislodging or expanding. The result would be that whereas we now have a Freudian "A Rose for Emily," a mythological "A Rose for Emily," a Christological "A Rose for Emily," a regional "A Rose for Emily," a sociological "A Rose for Emily," a linguistic "A Rose for Emily," we would in addition have an Eskimo "A Rose for Emily," existing in some relation of compatibility or incompatibility with the others.

Again the point is that while there are always mechanisms for ruling out readings, their source is not the text but the presently recognized interpretive strategies for producing the text. It follows, then, that no reading, however outlandish it might appear, is inherently an impossible one.

From Is There a Text in This Class?

Yeats's Vision *or Blake's Swedenborgianism:* Irish poet William Butler Yeats and Swedish mystical writer Emanuel Swedenborg both claimed to have received revelations from the spirit world; some of Swedenborg's ideas are embodied in the long poems of William Blake.

Robert Scholes   (b. 1929)

"How Do We Make a Poem?"   1982

Let us begin with one of the shortest poetic texts in the English language, "Elegy" by
W. S. Merwin:

> Who would I show it to

One line, one sentence, unpunctuated, but proclaimed an interrogative by its grammar and syntax—what makes it a poem? Certainly without its title it would not be a
poem; but neither would the title alone constitute a poetic text. Nor do the two
together simply make a poem by themselves. Given the title and the text, the *reader*
is encouraged to make a poem. He is not forced to do so, but there is not much else
he can do with this material, and certainly nothing else so rewarding. (I will use the
masculine pronoun here to refer to the reader, not because all readers are male but
because I am, and my hypothetical reader is not a pure construct but an idealized version of myself.)

How do we make a poem out of this text? There are only two things to work on,
the title and the question posed by the single, colloquial line. The line is not simply
colloquial, it is prosaic; with no words of more than one syllable, concluded by a
preposition, it is within the utterance range of every speaker of English. It is, in a
sense, completely intelligible. But in another sense it is opaque, mysterious. Its three
pronouns—who, I, it—pose problems of reference. Its conditional verb phrase—would
. . . show to—poses a problem of situation. The context that would supply the information required to make that simple sentence meaningful as well as intelligible is not
there. It must be supplied by the reader.

To make a poem of this text the reader must not only know English, he must
know a poetic code as well: the code of the funeral elegy, as practiced in English from
the Renaissance to the present time. The "words on the page" do not constitute a
poetic "work," complete and self-sufficient, but a "text," a sketch or outline that must
be completed by the active participation of a reader equipped with the right sort of
information. In this case part of that information consists of an acquaintance with
the elegiac tradition: its procedures, assumptions, devices, and values. One needs to
know works like Milton's "Lycidas," Shelley's "Adonais," Tennyson's *In Memoriam*,
Whitman's "When Lilacs Last in the Dooryard Bloom'd," Thomas's "Refusal to
Mourn the Death, by Fire, of a Child in London," and so on, in order to "read" this
simple poem properly. In fact, it could be argued that the more elegies one can bring
to bear on a reading of this one, the better, richer poem this one becomes. I would go
even further, suggesting that a knowledge of the critical tradition—of Dr. Johnson's
objections to "Lycidas," for instance, or Wordsworth's critique of poetic diction—
will also enhance one's reading of this poem. For the poem is, of course, an anti-
elegy, a refusal not simply to mourn, but to write a sonorous, eloquent, mournful, but
finally acquiescent, accepting—in a word, "elegiac"—poem at all.

Reading the poem involves, then, a special knowledge of its tradition. It also
involves a special interpretive skill. The forms of the short, written poem as they
have developed in English over the past few centuries can be usefully seen as compressed, truncated, or fragmented imitations of other verbal forms, especially the
play, story, public oration, and personal essay. The reasons for this are too complicated for consideration here, but the fact will be apparent to all who reflect upon the
matter. Our short poems are almost always elliptical versions of what can easily be

conceived of as dramatic, narrative, oratorical, or meditative texts. Often, they are combinations of these and other modes of address. To take an obvious example, the dramatic monologue in the hands of Robert Browning is like a speech from a play (though usually more elongated than most such speeches). But to "read" such a monologue we must imagine the setting, the situation, the context, and so on. The dramatic monologue is "like" a play but gives us less information of certain sorts than a play would, requiring us to provide that information by decoding the clues in the monologue itself in the light of our understanding of the generic model. Most short poems work this way. They require both special knowledge and special skills to be "read."

To understand "Elegy" we must construct a situation out of the clues provided. The "it" in "Who would I show it to" is of course the elegy itself. The "I" is the potential writer of the elegy. The "Who" is the audience for the poem. But the verb phrase "would . . . show to" indicates a condition contrary to fact. Who would I show it to *if* I were to write it? This implies in turn that for the potential elegiac poet there is one person whose appreciation means more than that of all the rest of the potential audience for the poem he might write, and it further implies that the death of this particular person is the one imagined in the poem. If this person were dead, the poet suggests, so would his inspiration be dead. With no one to write for, no poem would be forthcoming. This poem is not only a "refusal to mourn," like that of Dylan Thomas, it is a refusal to elegize. The whole elegiac tradition, like its cousin the funeral oration, turns finally away from mourning toward acceptance, revival, renewal, a return to the concerns of life, symbolized by the very writing of the poem. Life goes on; there *is* an audience; and the mourned person will live through accomplishments, influence, descendants, and also (not least) in the elegiac poem itself. Merwin rejects all that. *If* I wrote an elegy for X, the person for whom I have always written, X would not be alive to read it; therefore, there is no reason to write an elegy for the one person in my life who most deserves one; therefore, there is no reason to write any elegy, anymore, ever. Finally, and of course, this poem called "Elegy" is not an elegy.

From *Semiotics and Interpretation*

Michael J. Colacurcio (b. 1936)

The End of Young Goodman Brown   1995

Having begun by assuming that all visible sanctity was real sanctity and by presuming his own final perseverance in faith, having next despaired of *all* virtue, he [Goodman Brown] ends by doubting the existence of any unblighted goodness but his own. There is simply no other way to account for the way Goodman Brown spends the rest of his life. Evidently he clings to the precious knowledge that he, at least, resisted the wicked one's final invitation to diabolical communion; accordingly, the lurid satisfactions of Satan's anti-covenant are not available to him. But neither are the sweet delights of the Communion of the Saints. He knows he resisted the "last, last crime" of witchcraft, but his deepest suspicion seems to be that Faith did not resist. Or if that seems too strong a formulation for tender-minded readers, he cannot make his faith in Faith prevail. Without such a prevailing faith, he is left outside the bounds of all communion: his own unbartered soul is the only certain locus of goodness in a world otherwise altogether blasted.

It would be easy enough to praise Young Goodman Brown for his recovery from the blasphemous nihilism of his mid-forest rage against the universe; for his refusal to translate his cosmic paranoia into an Ahabian plan of counterattack. Or, from another point of view, it would even be possible to suggest that if the Devil's proffered community of evil is the only community possible, perhaps he should have accepted membership instead of protecting the insular sacredness of his own separate and too precious soul. Perhaps salvation is not worth having—perhaps it is meaningless—in a universe where depravity has undone so many. But both of these moral prescriptions miss Hawthorne's principal emphasis, which, as I read the tale, is on the problem of faith and evidence; on that peculiar kind of "doubt" (in epistemological essence, really a kind of negative faith) which follows from a discrediting of evidences formerly trusted. Brown is damned to stony moral isolation because his "evidential" Puritan biases have led him all unprepared into a terrifying betrayal of Faith. He believes the Devil's spectral suggestions not merely because he is naive, though he is that; and not merely because he is incapable of the sort of evidential subtlety by which John Cotton instructed the very first members of those newly purified New England churches in the art of separating sheep and goats, or by which the Mathers sermonized the court of Oyer and Terminer on the occult art of the distinguishing of spirits. Brown believes the Devil because, at one level, the projected guilt of a man in bad faith *is* specter evidence and because, even more fundamentally, absolute moral quality is related to outward appearance as a real person is to his specter.

In short, Hawthorne suggests, one had better not raise such ultimate questions at all: to do so is to risk the appearance-and-reality question in its most pernicious, even "paranoic" form. At best one would be accepting the deceptive appearances of sanctity, as Goodman Brown evidently continued to be accepted at the communion table of a community which never suspected his presumption, despair, blasphemy, and his near approach to witchcraft. . . . And at worst, if one is already in bad faith, his penetrating glimpses into the "reality" behind the appearances will be no more than spectral projections of his own guilty wishes. . . . The truly naive will simply accept the smiling light of daytime, church-day appearances; the already compromised will "see" in others (as irrevocable commitment) what already pre-exists in themselves (as fantasy, wish, desire, or momentary intention). The only alternative would seem to be the acceptance of some ultimate and fundamental equality in a common moral struggle; a healthy skepticism about all moral appearances, firmly wedded to the faith that, whatever men may fantasize, or however they may fall, they generally love the good and hate the evil.

From *The Province of Piety: Moral History in Hawthorne's Early Tales*

DECONSTRUCTIONIST CRITICISM

Deconstructionist criticism rejects the traditional assumption that language can accurately represent reality. Language, according to deconstructionists, is a fundamentally unstable medium; consequently, literary texts, which are made up of words, have no fixed, single meaning. Deconstructionists insist, according to critic Paul de Man, on "the impossibility of making the actual expression coincide with what has to be expressed, of making the actual signs coincide with what is signified." Since they believe that literature cannot definitively express its subject matter, deconstructionists tend to shift their attention away from *what* is being said to *how* language is being used in a text.

Paradoxically, deconstructionist criticism often resembles formalist criticism; both methods usually involve close reading. But while a formalist usually tries to demonstrate how the diverse elements of a text cohere into meaning, the deconstructionist approach attempts to show how the text "deconstructs," that is, how it can be broken down—by a skeptical critic—into mutually irreconcilable positions. A biographical or historical critic might seek to establish the author's intention as a means to interpreting a literary work, but deconstructionists reject the notion that the critic should endorse the myth of authorial control over language. Deconstructionist critics like Roland Barthes and Michel Foucault have therefore called for "the death of the author," that is, the rejection of the assumption that the author, no matter how ingenious, can fully control the meaning of a text. They have also announced the death of literature as a special category of writing. In their view, poems and novels are merely words on a page that deserve no privileged status as art; all texts are created equal—equally untrustworthy, that is.

Deconstructionists focus on how language is used to achieve power. Since they believe, in the words of critic David Lehman, that "there are no truths, only rival interpretations," deconstructionists try to understand how some "interpretations" come to be regarded as truth. A major goal of deconstruction is to demonstrate how those supposed truths are at best provisional and at worst contradictory.

Deconstruction, as you may have inferred, calls for intellectual subtlety and skill. If you pursue your literary studies beyond the introductory stage, you will want to become more familiar with its assumptions. Deconstruction may strike you as a negative, even destructive, critical approach, and yet its best practitioners are adept at exposing the inadequacy of much conventional criticism. By patient analysis, they can sometimes open up the most familiar text and find unexpected significance.

Roland Barthes (1915–1980)

The Death of the Author   1968

Translated by Stephen Heath

Succeeding the Author, the scriptor no longer bears within him passions, humours, feelings, impressions, but rather this immense dictionary from which he draws a writing that can know no halt: life never does more than imitate the book, and the book itself is only a tissue of signs, an imitation that is lost, infinitely deferred.

Once the Author is removed, the claim to decipher a text becomes quite futile. To give a text an Author is to impose a limit on that text, to furnish it with a final signified, to close the writing. Such a conception suits criticism very well, the latter then allotting itself the important task of discovering the Author (or its hypostases: society, history, psyché, liberty) beneath the work: when the Author has been found, the text is "explained"—victory to the critic. Hence there is no surprise in the fact that, historically, the reign of the Author has also been that of the Critic, nor again in the fact that criticism (be it new) is today undermined along with the Author. In the multiplicity of writing, everything is to be *disentangled*, nothing *deciphered*; the structure can be followed, "run" (like the thread of a stocking) at every point and at every level, but there is nothing beneath: the space of writing is to be ranged over, not pierced; writing ceaselessly posits meaning ceaselessly to evaporate it, carrying out a systematic exemption of meaning. In precisely this way literature (it would be better from now on to say *writing*), by refusing to assign a "secret," an ultimate meaning, to the text (and to the world as text), liberates what may be called an anti-theological activity, an activity that is truly revolutionary since to refuse to fix meaning is, in the end, to refuse God and his hypostases—reason, science, law.

From "The Death of the Author"

Barbara Johnson (b. 1947)

Rigorous Unreliability   1987

As a critique of a certain Western conception of the nature of signification, deconstruction focuses on the functioning of claim-making and claim-subverting structures within texts. A deconstructive reading is an attempt to show how the conspicuously foregrounded statements in a text are systematically related to discordant signifying elements that the text has thrown into its shadows or margins, an attempt both to recover what is lost and to analyze what happens when a text is read solely in function of intentionality, meaningfulness, and representativity. Deconstruction thus confers a new kind of readability on those elements in a text that readers have traditionally been trained to disregard, overcome, explain away, or edit out— contradictions, obscurities, ambiguities, incoherences, discontinuities, ellipses, interruptions, repetitions, and plays of the signifier. In this sense it involves a reversal of values, a revaluation of the signifying function of everything that, in a signified-based theory of meaning, would constitute "noise." Derrida° has chosen to speak of the values involved in this reversal in terms of "speech" and "writing," in which "speech" stands for the privilege accorded to meaning as immediacy, unity, identity, truth, and presence, while "writing" stands for the devalued functions of distance, difference, dissimulation, and deferment.

This transvaluation has a number of consequences for the appreciation of literature. By shifting the attention from intentional meaning to writing as such, deconstruction has enabled readers to become sensitive to a number of recurrent literary topoi° in a new way.

• • •

In addition, by seeing interpretation itself as a fiction-making activity, deconstruction has both reversed and displaced the narrative categories of "showing" and "telling," mimesis and diegesis.° Instead of according moments of textual self-interpretation an authoritative metalinguistic status, deconstruction considers anything the text says about itself to be another fiction, an allegory of the reading process. Hence, the privilege traditionally granted to showing over telling is reversed: "telling" becomes a more sophisticated form of "showing," in which what is "shown" is the breakdown of the show/tell distinction. Far from doing the reader's work for her, the text's self-commentary only gives the reader more to do. Indeed, it is the way in which a text subverts the possibility of any authoritative reading by inscribing the reader's strategies into its own structures that often, for de Man, ends up being constitutive of literature as such.

Deconstructors, therefore, tend to privilege texts that are self-reflexive in interestingly and rigorously unreliable ways. Since self-reflexive texts often explicitly posit themselves as belated or revolutionary with respect to a tradition on which they comment, deconstruction can both reinstate the self-consciously outmoded or overwritten (such as Melville's *Pierre*°) and canonize the experimental or avant-garde. But because deconstruction has focused on the ways in which the Western white

---

Derrida: Jacques Derrida (1930–2004), French philosopher active in the development of deconstructionism.   *topoi:* the plural of the Greek *topos,* for "place"; it means a commonly used literary device.   *diegesis:* the main events of a story, the basic plot, as distinct from the narration. *Pierre: Pierre, or the Ambiguities* (1852), a complex novel by Herman Melville, was a failure during the author's lifetime; it was not widely read until the mid-twentieth century.

male philosophico-literary tradition subverts itself *from within*, it has often tended to remain within the confines of the established literary and philosophical canon. . . . If it has questioned the boundary lines of literature, it has done so not with respect to the noncanonical but with respect to the line between literature and philosophy or between literature and criticism. It is as a rethinking of those distinctions that deconstruction most radically displaces certain traditional evaluative assumptions.

From A World of Difference

Geoffrey Hartman (b. 1929)

On Wordsworth's "A Slumber Did My Spirit Seal"   1987

Take Wordsworth's well-known lyric of eight lines, one of the "Lucy" poems, which has been explicated so many times without its meaning being fully determined:

> A slumber did my spirit seal;
>   I had no human fears—
> She seemed a thing that could not feel
>   The touch of earthly years.
>
> No motion has she now, no force;
>   She neither hears nor sees;
> Rolled round in earth's diurnal course,
>   With rocks, and stones, and trees.

It does not matter whether you interpret the second stanza (especially its last line) as tending toward affirmation, or resignation, or a grief verging on bitterness. The tonal assignment of one rather than another possible meaning, to repeat Susanne Langer° on musical form, is curiously open or beside the point. Yet the lyric does not quite support Langer's general position, that "Articulation is its life, but not assertion," because the poem is composed of a series of short and definitive statements, very like assertions. You could still claim that the poem's life is not in the assertions but somewhere else: but where then? What would articulation mean in that case? Articulation is not anti-assertive here; indeed the sense of closure is so strong that it thematizes itself in the very first line.

　　Nevertheless, is not the harmony or aesthetic effect of the poem greater than this local conciseness; is not the sense of closure broader and deeper than our admiration for a perfect technical construct? The poem is surely something else than a fine box, a well-wrought coffin.

　　That it is a kind of epitaph is relevant, of course. We recognize, even if genre is not insisted on, that Wordsworth's style is laconic, even lapidary. There may be a mimetic or formal motive related to the ideal of epitaphic poetry. But the motive may also be, in a precise way, meta-epitaphic. The poem, first of all, marks the closure of a life that has never opened up: Lucy is likened in other poems to a hidden flower or the evening star. Setting overshadows rising, and her mode of existence is inherently inward, westering. I will suppose then, that Wordsworth was at some level giving expression to the traditional epitaphic wish: Let the earth rest lightly on the deceased. If so, his conversion of this epitaphic formula is so complete that to trace

---

Susanne Langer: Langer (1895–1985) was an American philosopher who discussed the relationship between aesthetics and artistic form.

the process of conversion might seem gratuitous. The formula, a trite if deeply grounded figure of speech, has been catalyzed out of existence. Here it is formula itself, or better, the adjusted words of the mourner that lie lightly on the girl and everyone who is a mourner.

I come back, then, to the "aesthetic" sense of a burden lifted, rather than denied. A heavy element is made lighter. One may still feel that the term "elation" is inappropriate in this context; yet elation is, as a mood, the very subject of the first stanza. For the mood described is love or desire when it *eternizes* the loved person, when it makes her a star-like being that "could not feel / The touch of earthly years." This *naive* elation, this spontaneous movement of the spirit upward, is reversed in the downturn or catastrophe of the second stanza. Yet this stanza does not close out the illusion; it preserves it within the elegiac form. The illusion is elated, in our use of the word: *aufgehoben°* seems the proper term. For the girl is still, and all the more, what she seemed to be: beyond touch, like a star, if the earth in its daily motion is a planetary and erring rather than a fixed star, and if all on this star of earth must partake of its sublunar, mortal, temporal nature.

• • •

To sum up: In Wordsworth's lyric the specific gravity of words is weighed in the balance of each stanza; and this balance is as much a judgment on speech in the context of our mortality as it is a meaningful response to the individual death. At the limit of the medium of words, and close to silence, what has been purged is not concreteness, or the empirical sphere of the emotions—shock, disillusion, trauma, recognition, grief, atonement—what has been purged is a series of flashy schematisms and false or partial mediations: artificial plot, inflated consolatory rhetoric, the coercive absolutes of logic or faith.

From "Elation in Hegel and Wordsworth"

CULTURAL STUDIES

Unlike the other critical approaches discussed in this chapter, cultural criticism (or **cultural studies**) does not offer a single way of analyzing literature. No central methodology is associated with cultural studies. Nor is cultural criticism solely, or even mainly, concerned with literary texts in the conventional sense. Instead, the term *cultural studies* refers to a relatively recent interdisciplinary field of academic inquiry. This field borrows methodologies from other approaches to analyze a wide range of cultural products and practices.

To understand cultural studies, it helps to know a bit about its origins. In the English-speaking world, the field was first defined at the Centre for Contemporary Cultural Studies of Birmingham University in Britain. Founded in 1964, this graduate program tried to expand the range of literary study beyond traditional approaches to canonic literature in order to explore a broader spectrum of historical, cultural, and political issues. The most influential teacher at the Birmingham Centre was Raymond Williams (1921–1983), a Welsh socialist with wide intellectual interests. Williams argued that scholars should not study culture as a canon of great works by individual artists but rather examine it as an evolutionary process that involves the

---

aufgehoben: German for "taken up" or "lifted up," but this term can also mean "canceled" or "nullified." Hartman uses the term for its double meaning.

entire society. "We cannot separate literature and art," Williams said, "from other kinds of social practice." The cultural critic, therefore, does not study fixed aesthetic objects so much as dynamic social processes. The critic's challenge is to identify and understand the complex forms and effects of the process of culture.

A Marxist intellectual, Williams called his approach cultural materialism (a reference to the Marxist doctrine of dialectical materialism), but later scholars soon discarded that name for two broader and more neutral terms, cultural criticism and cultural studies. From the start, this interdisciplinary field relied heavily on literary theory, especially Marxist and feminist criticism. It also employed the documentary techniques of historical criticism combined with political analysis focused on issues of social class, race, and gender. (This approach flourished in the United States, where it is called New Historicism.) Cultural studies is also deeply antiformalist, since the field concerns itself with investigating the complex relationships among history, politics, and literature. Cultural studies rejects the notion that literature exists in an aesthetic realm separate from ethical and political categories.

A chief goal of cultural studies is to understand the nature of social power as reflected in "texts." For example, if the object of analysis were a sonnet by Shakespeare, the cultural studies adherent might investigate the moral, psychological, and political assumptions reflected in the poem and then deconstruct them to see what individuals, social classes, or gender might benefit from having those assumptions perceived as true. The relevant mission of cultural studies is to identify both the overt and covert values reflected in a cultural practice. The cultural studies critic also tries to trace out and understand the structures of meaning that hold those assumptions in place and give them the appearance of objective representation. Any analytical technique that helps illuminate these issues is employed.

In theory, a cultural studies critic might employ any methodology. In practice, however, he or she will most often borrow concepts from deconstruction, Marxist analysis, gender criticism, race theory, and psychology. Each of these earlier methodologies provides particular analytical tools that cultural critics find useful. What cultural studies borrows from deconstructionism is its emphasis on uncovering conflict, dissent, and contradiction in the works under analysis. Whereas traditional critical approaches often sought to demonstrate the unity of a literary work, cultural studies often seeks to portray social, political, and psychological conflicts that the work masks. What cultural studies borrows from Marxist analysis is an attention to the ongoing struggle between social classes, each seeking economic (and therefore political) advantage. Cultural studies often asks questions about what social class created a work of art and what class (or classes) served as its audience. Among the many things that cultural studies borrowed from gender criticism and race theory is a concern with social inequality between the sexes and races. It seeks to investigate how these inequities have been reflected in the texts of a historical period or a society. Cultural studies is, above all, a political enterprise that views literary analysis as a means of furthering social justice.

Since cultural studies does not adhere to any single methodology (or even a consistent set of methodologies), it is impossible to characterize the field briefly, because there are exceptions to every generalization offered. What one sees most clearly are characteristic tendencies, especially the commitment to examining issues of class, race, and gender. There is also the insistence on expanding the focus of critical inquiry beyond traditional high literary culture. British cultural studies guru Anthony Easthope can, for example, analyze with equal aplomb Gerard Manley

Hopkins's "The Windhover," Edgar Rice Burroughs' *Tarzan of the Apes*, a Benson and Hedges cigarette advertisement, and Sean Connery's eyebrows. Cultural studies is infamous—even among its practitioners—for its habitual use of literary jargon. It is also notorious for its complex intellectual analysis of mundane materials, such as Easthope's analysis of a cigarette ad, which may be interesting in its own right but remote from most readers' literary experience. Some scholars, such as Camille Paglia, however, use the principles of cultural studies to provide new social, political, and historical insights into canonic texts such as William Blake's "The Chimney Sweeper." Omnivorous, iconoclastic, and relentlessly analytic, cultural criticism has become a major presence in contemporary literary studies.

Vincent B. Leitch (b. 1944)

Poststructuralist Cultural Critique   1992

Whereas a major goal of New Criticism and much other modern formalistic criticism is aesthetic evaluation of freestanding texts, a primary objective of cultural criticism is cultural critique, which entails investigation and assessment of ruling and oppositional beliefs, categories, practices, and representations, inquiring into the causes, constitutions, and consequences as well as the modes of circulation and consumption of linguistic, social, economic, political, historical, ethical, religious, legal, scientific, philosophical, educational, familial, and aesthetic discourses and institutions. In rendering a judgment on an aesthetic artifact, a New Critic privileges such key things as textual coherence and unity, intricacy and complexity, ambiguity and irony, tension and balance, economy and autonomy, literariness and spatial form. In mounting a critique of a cultural "text," an advocate of poststructuralist cultural criticism evaluates such things as degrees of exclusion and inclusion, of complicity and resistance, of domination and letting-be, of abstraction and situatedness, of violence and tolerance, of monologue and polylogue, of quietism and activism, of sameness and otherness, of oppression and emancipation, of centralization and decentralization. Just as the aforementioned system of evaluative criteria underlies the exegetical and judgmental labor of New Criticism, so too does the above named set of commitments undergird the work of poststructuralist cultural critique.

Given its commitments, poststructuralist cultural criticism is, as I have suggested, suspicious of literary formalism. Specifically, the trouble with New Criticism is its inclination to advocate a combination of quietism and asceticism, connoisseurship and exclusiveness, aestheticism and apoliticism. . . . The monotonous practical effect of New Critical reading is to illustrate the subservience of each textual element to a higher, overarching, economical poetic structure without remainders. What should be evident here is that the project of poststructuralist cultural criticism possesses a set of commitments and criteria that enable it to engage in the enterprise of cultural critique. It should also be evident that the cultural ethicopolitics of this enterprise is best characterized, using current terminology, as "liberal" or "leftist," meaning congruent with certain socialist, anarchist, and libertarian ideals, none of which, incidentally, are necessarily Marxian. Such congruence, derived from extrapolating a generalized stance for poststructuralism, constitutes neither a party platform nor an observable course of practical action; avowed tendencies often account for little in the unfolding of practical engagements.

From *Cultural Criticism, Literary Theory, Poststructuralism*

Mark Bauerlein (b. 1959)

What Is Cultural Studies?   1997

Traditionally, disciplines naturally fell into acknowledged subdivisions, for example, as literary criticism broke up into formalist literary criticism, philological criticism, narratological analysis, and other methodologically distinguished pursuits, all of which remained comfortably within the category "literary criticism." But cultural studies eschews such institutional disjunctions and will not let any straitening adjective precede the "cultural studies" heading. There is no distinct formalist cultural studies or historicist cultural studies, but only cultural studies. (Feminist cultural studies may be one exception.) Cultural studies is a field that will not be parceled out to the available disciplines. It spans culture at large, not this or that institutionally separated element of culture. To guarantee this transcendence of disciplinary institutions, cultural studies must select a name for itself that has no specificity, that has too great an extension to mark off any expedient boundaries for itself. "Cultural studies" serves well because, apart from distinguishing between "physical science" and "cultural analysis," the term provides no indication of where any other boundaries lie.

This is exactly the point. To blur disciplinary boundaries and frustrate the intellectual investments that go along with them is a fundamental motive for cultural studies practice, one that justifies the vagueness of the titular term. This explains why the related label "cultural criticism," so much in vogue in 1988, has declined. The term "criticism" has a narrower extension than does "studies," ruling out some empirical forms of inquiry (like field work) that "studies" admits. "Studies" preserves a methodological openness that "criticism" closes. Since such closures have suspect political intentions behind them, cultural studies maintains its institutional purity by disdaining disciplinary identity and methodological uniformity.

• • •

A single approach will miss too much, will overlook important aspects of culture not perceptible to that particular angle of vision. A multitude of approaches will pick up an insight here and a piece of knowledge there and more of culture will enter into the inquiry. A diversity of methods will match the diversity of culture, thereby sheltering the true nature of culture from the reductive appropriations of formal disciplines.

But how do cultural critics bring all these methods together into a coherent inquiry? Are there any established rules of incorporating "important insights and knowledge" coming out of different methods into a coherent scholarly project of cultural studies? How might a scholar use both phonemic analysis and deconstruction in a single inquiry when deconstructionist arguments call into question the basic premises of phonetics? What scholar has the competence to handle materials from so many disciplines in a rigorous and knowing manner? Does cultural criticism as a "studies" practice offer any transdisciplinary evaluative standards to apply to individual pieces of cultural criticism? If not, if there are no clear methodological procedures or evaluative principles in cultural studies, it is hard to see how one might popularize it, teach it, make it into a recognized scholarly activity. In practical terms, one does not know how to communicate it to others or show students how to do it when it assumes so many different methodological forms. How does one create an academic department out of an outspokenly antidisciplinary practice? What criteria can faculty members jointly invoke when they are trying to make curricular and personnel decisions?

Once again, this is precisely the point. One reason for the generality of the term is to render such institutional questions unanswerable. Cultural studies practice mingles methods from a variety of fields, jumps from one cultural subject matter to another, simultaneously proclaims superiority to other institutionalized inquiries (on a correspondence to culture basis) and renounces its own institutionalization—gestures that strategically forestall disciplinary standards being applied to it. By studying culture in heterogenous ways, by clumping texts, events, persons, objects, and ideologies into a cultural whole (which, cultural critics say, is reality) and bringing a melange of logical argument, speculative propositions, empirical data, and political outlooks to bear upon it, cultural critics invent a new kind of investigation immune to methodological attack.

From Literary Criticism: An Autopsy

Camille Paglia (b. 1947)

A Reading of William Blake's "The Chimney Sweeper" 2005

Romantic writers glorified childhood as a state of innocence. Blake's "The Chimney Sweeper," written in the same year as the French Revolution, combines the Romantic cult of the child with the new radical politics, which can both be traced to social thinker Jean-Jacques Rousseau. It is the boy sweep, rather than Blake, who speaks: he acts as the poet's dramatic persona or mask. There is no anger in his tale. On the contrary, the sweep's gentle acceptance of his miserable life makes his exploitation seem all the more atrocious. Blake shifts responsibility for protest onto us.

The poem begins as autobiography, a favorite Romantic genre. Having lost his mother, his natural protector, the small child was "sold" into slavery by his father (1–2). That is, he was apprenticed to a chimney-sweeping firm whose young teams would probably have worked simply for food, lodging, and clothing—basics that the boy's widowed working-class father might well have been unable to provide for his family. Children, soberly garbed in practical black, were used for chimney sweeping because they could wriggle into narrow, cramped spaces. The health risks of this filthy job were many—deformation of a boy's growing skeleton as well as long-term toxic effects from coal dust, now known to be carcinogenic. Chronic throat and lung problems as well as skin irritation must have been common. (Among the specimens floating in formaldehyde at Philadelphia's Mütter Museum, a nineteenth-century medical collection, is a chimney sweep's foot deformed by a bulbous tumor on the instep.)

Blake's sweep was so young when indentured into service that, he admits, he still lisped (2–3). The hawking of products and services by itinerant street vendors was once a lively, raucous feature of urban life. "Sweep, sweep, sweep!" cried the wandering crews seeking a day's employment. But this tiny boy couldn't even form the word: "Weep weep weep weep!" is how it came out—inadvertently sending a damning message to the oblivious world. It's really the thundering indictment of Blake as poet-prophet: Weep, you callous society that enslaves and murders its young; weep for yourself and your defenseless victims.

"So your chimneys I sweep and in soot I sleep": this singsong, matter-of-fact line implicates the reader in the poem's crimes—a confrontational device ordinarily associated with ironically self-conscious writers like Baudelaire (4). The boy may be peacefully resigned to the horror of his everyday reality, but we, locked in our own routines and distanced by genteel book reading, are forced to face our collective indifference. The boy represents the invisible army of manual laborers, charwomen, and janitors who do our dirty work. Scrubbing the infernal warren of brick and stone tunnels, he absorbs soot (symbolizing social sin) into his own skin and clothes, while we stay neat and clean.

The anonymous sweep—made faceless by his role—chatters cheerfully away about his friend "little Tom Dacre," whom he has taken under his wing (5). In this moral vacuum, where parents and caretakers are absent or negligent, the children must nurture each other. When the newcomer's curly hair was shaved off (to keep it from catching fire from live coals), he cried at his disfigurement, experienced as loss of self. Head shaving is a familiar initiatory practice in military and religious settings to reduce individuality and enforce group norms. To soothe little Tom, the solicitous sweep resorts to consolation of pitiful illogic: "when your head's bare / You know that the soot cannot spoil your white hair" (7–8). That's like saying, "Good thing you lost your leg—now you'll never stub your toe!" Tom's white (that is, blond) "lamb's back" hair represents the innocence of the Christlike sacrificial lamb: children, according to Blake, have become scapegoats for society's amorality and greed (6). Their white hair seems unnatural, as if the boys have been vaulted forward to old age without enjoying the freedoms and satisfactions of virile adulthood. For modern readers, the bald children's caged sameness is disturbingly reminiscent of that of emaciated survivors of Nazi concentration camps, where liberation was met with blank stoicism.

Amazingly, the sweep's desperate reassurance works: Tom goes "quiet," and for the next three stanzas, the whole center of the text, we enter his dreams (9–20). The poem seems to crack open in an ecstatic allegory of rebirth: the children of industrial London escape by the "thousands" from a living death, the locked "coffins of black" that are their soot-stained bodies as well as the chimneys where they spend their days (11–12). Alas, Tom's vision of paradise is nothing more than a simple, playful childhood—the birthright that was robbed from them. The poem overflows with the boys' repressed energy and vitality, as "leaping, laughing, they run" across the "green plain" of nature, then plunge into the purifying "river." Bathed "white," they "shine" with their own inner light, bright as the "sun" (15–18).

But something goes terribly wrong. The "Angel" with the "bright key" who was their liberator inexplicably turns oppressor (13, 19). As the sweeps "rise upon clouds" toward heaven and "sport in the wind" like prankish cherubs casting off their burdens (the "bags" of brushes and collected soot), an officiously moralistic voice cuts into the dream and terminates it: "And the Angel told Tom, if he'd be a good boy, / He'd have God for his father, and never want joy" (17–20). That Tom wakes right up suggests that the voice actually belongs to the boss or overseer, briskly rousing his charges before dawn. The angel's homily, heavy with conventional piety, stops the children's fun and free motion dead: If you'll be good boys—that is, do what we say—you'll win God's approval and find your reward in heaven. (In British English, to "never want joy" means never to *lack it*.) But God is another false father in this poem.

The trusting, optimistic children grab their bags and brushes and get right to work in the "cold" and "dark" (21–23). They want to do right, and their spirit is unquenched. But they've been brainwashed into pliability by manipulative maxims such as the one recited by our first sweep in the ominous last line: "So if all do their duty they need not fear harm" (24). This bromide is an outrageous lie. If the children were to rebel, to run away to the green paradise lying just outside the city, they would be safe. Their naive goodwill leads straight to their ruin—a short, limited life of sickliness and toil. The final stanza's off rhymes ("dark"/"work," "warm"/"harm") subtly unbalance us and make us sense the fractures in the sweep's world. The poem shows him betrayed by an ascending row of duplicitous male authority figures—his father, the profiteering boss, the turncoat angel, and God himself, who tacitly endorses or tolerates an unjust social system. As Tom's dream suggests, the only deliverance for the sweep and his friends will be death.

From *Break, Blow, Burn*

▶ TERMS FOR *review*

Formalist criticism ▶ A school of criticism that focuses on the *form* of a literary work. A key method that formalists use is close reading, a step-by-step analysis of the elements in a text.

Biographical criticism ▶ The practice of analyzing a literary work by using knowledge of the author's life to gain insight. Although the work is understood as an independent creation, the *biography* of the author provides the practical assistance of underscoring subtle but important meanings.

Historical criticism ▶ The practice of analyzing a literary work by investigating the social, cultural, and intellectual context that produced it, including the author's biography and milieu.

Psychological criticism ▶ The application of the analytical tools of psychology and psychoanalysis to authors and/or fictional characters in order to understand the underlying motivations and meanings of a literary work.

Mythological criticism ▶ The practice of analyzing a literary work by looking for recurrent universal patterns. It explores the ways in which an individual imagination uses myths and symbols shared by different cultures and epochs.

Sociological criticism ▶ The practice of analyzing a literary work by examining the cultural, economic, and political context in which it was written or received. It primarily explores the relationship between the artist and society.

Gender criticism ▶ The examination of the ways in which sexual identity influences the creation, interpretation, and evaluation of literary works. Feminism, gay culture, and the men's movement all play key roles in gender criticism.

Reader-response criticism ▶ The practice of analyzing a literary work by describing what happens in the reader's mind while interpreting the text, on the assumption that no literary text exists independently of readers' interpretations and that there is no single fixed interpretation of any literary work.

Deconstructionist criticism ▶ A school of criticism that rejects the traditional assumption that language can accurately represent reality. Deconstructionists believe that literary texts can have no single meaning; therefore, they concentrate their attention on *how* language is being used in a text, rather than what is being said.

Cultural studies ▶ A contemporary interdisciplinary field of academic study that focuses on understanding the social power encoded in "texts"—which may include any analyzable phenomenon from a traditional poem to an advertising image or actor's face.

GLOSSARY
OF LITERARY TERMS

Abstract diction *See* **Diction**.

Accent An emphasis or stress placed on a syllable in speech. Clear pronunciation of polysyllabic words almost always depends on correct placement of their accents (e.g., *de*-sert and de-*sert* are two different words and parts of speech, depending on their accent). Accent or speech stress is the basis of most meters in English. (*See also* **Accentual meter, Meter**.)

Accentual meter A meter that uses a consistent number of strong speech stresses per line. The number of unstressed syllables may vary, as long as the accented syllables do not. Much popular poetry, such as rap and nursery rhymes, is written in accentual meter.

Acrostic A poem in which the initial letters of each line, when read downward, spell out a hidden word or words (often the name of a beloved person). Acrostics date back as far as the Hebrew Bible and classical Greek poetry.

Allegory A narrative in verse or prose in which the literal events (persons, places, and things) consistently point to a parallel sequence of symbolic ideas. This narrative strategy is often used to dramatize abstract ideas, historical events, religious systems, or political issues. An allegory has two levels of meaning: a literal level that tells a surface story and a symbolic level in which the abstract ideas unfold. The names of allegorical characters often hint at their symbolic roles. For example, in Nathaniel Hawthorne's "Young Goodman Brown," Faith is not only the name of the protagonist's wife but also a symbol of the protagonist's religious faith.

Alliteration The repetition of two or more consonant sounds in successive words in a line of verse or prose. Alliteration can be used at the beginning of words ("cool cats"—**initial alliteration**) or internally on stressed syllables ("In kitchen cups concupiscent curds"—which combines initial and **internal alliteration**). Alliteration was a central feature of Anglo-Saxon poetry and is still used by contemporary writers.

All-knowing narrator *See* **Omniscient narrator**.

Allusion A brief (and sometimes indirect) reference in a text to a person, place, or thing—fictitious or actual. An allusion may appear in a literary work as an initial quotation, a passing mention of a name, or as a phrase borrowed from another writer—often carrying the meanings and implications of the original. Allusions imply a common set of knowledge between reader and writer and operate as a literary shorthand to enrich the meaning of a text.

Analysis The examination of a piece of literature as a means of understanding its subject or structure. An effective analysis often clarifies a work by focusing on a single element such as tone, irony, symbolism, imagery, or rhythm in a way that enhances the reader's understanding of the whole. *Analysis* comes from the Greek word meaning to "undo," to "loosen."

Anapest A metrical foot in verse in which two unstressed syllables are followed by a stressed syllable, as in "on a *boat*" or "in a *slump*." (*See also* **Meter**.)

Anecdote A short narrative usually consisting of a single incident or episode. Often humorous, anecdotes can be real or fictional. When they appear within a larger narrative as a brief story told by one character to another, the author usually employs them to reveal something significant to the larger narrative.

Antagonist The most significant character or force that opposes the protagonist in a narrative or drama. The antagonist may be another character, society itself, a force of nature, or even—in modern literature—conflicting impulses within the protagonist.

Anticlimax An unsatisfying and trivial turn of events in a literary work that occurs in place of a genuine climax. An anticlimax often involves a surprising shift in tone from the lofty or serious into the petty or ridiculous. The term is often used negatively to denote a feeble moment in a plot in which an author fails to create an intended effect. Anticlimax, however, can also be a strong dramatic device when a writer uses it for humorous or ironic effect.

Antihero A protagonist who is lacking in one or more of the conventional qualities attributed to a hero. Instead of being dignified, brave, idealistic, or purposeful, for instance, the antihero may be buffoonish, cowardly, self-interested, or weak. The antihero is often considered an essentially modern form of characterization, a satiric or frankly realistic commentary on traditional portrayals of idealized heroes or heroines. Modern examples range from Kafka's many protagonists to Beckett's tramps in *Waiting for Godot*.

Antithesis Words, phrases, clauses, or sentences set in deliberate contrast to one another. Antithesis balances opposing ideas, tones, or structures, usually to heighten the effect of a statement.

Apostrophe A direct address to someone or something. In poetry an apostrophe often addresses something not ordinarily spoken to (e.g., "O mountain!"). In an apostrophe, a speaker may address an inanimate object, a dead or absent person, an abstract thing, or a spirit. Apostrophe is often used to provide a speaker with means to articulate thoughts aloud.

Apprenticeship novel *See* **Bildungsroman**.

Archetype A recurring symbol, character, landscape, or event found in myth and literature across different cultures and eras. The idea of the archetype came into literary criticism from the Swiss psychologist Carl Jung who believed that all individuals share a "collective unconscious," a set of primal memories common to the human race that exists in our subconscious. An example of an archetypal character is the devil who may appear in pure mythic form (as in John Milton's *Paradise Lost*) but occurs more often in a disguised form like Fagin in Charles Dickens's *Oliver Twist* or Abner Snopes in William Faulkner's "Barn Burning."

Arena theater A modern, nontraditional performance space in which the audience surrounds the stage on four sides. The stage can be circular, square, rectangular, or ellipsoidal. In contrast to the **picture-frame stage**, with its privileged single point of view from the center of the orchestra seats, arena staging favors no one portion of the audience.

Aside In drama a few words or short passage spoken in an undertone or to the audience. By convention, other characters onstage are deaf to the aside.

Assonance The repetition of two or more vowel sounds in successive words, which creates a kind of rhyme. Like alliteration, the assonance may occur initially ("*all the awful auguries*") or internally ("white lilacs"). Assonance may be used to focus attention on key words or concepts. Assonance also helps make a phrase or line more memorable.

Atmosphere The dominant mood or feeling that pervades all or part of a literary work. Atmosphere is the total effect conveyed by the author's use of language, images, and physical setting. Atmosphere is often used to foreshadow the ultimate climax in a narrative.

Auditory imagery A word or sequence of words that refers to the sense of hearing. (*See also* **Imagery**.)

Augustan age This term has two related meanings. First, it originally referred to the greatest period of Roman literature under the Emperor Augustus (27 B.C.–14 A.D.) in which Virgil, Horace, and Ovid wrote. Second, it refers to the early eighteenth century in English literature, a neoclassical period dominated by Alexander Pope, Thomas Gray, and Jonathan Swift. English Augustan poetry was characteristically formal in both structure and diction.

Authorial intrusion *See* **Editorial point of view**.

Ballad Traditionally, a song that tells a story. The ballad was originally an oral verse form—sung or recited and transmitted from performer to performer without being written down. Ballads are characteristically compressed, dramatic, and objective in their narrative style. There are many variations to the ballad form, most consisting of quatrains (made up of lines of three or four metrical feet) in a simple rhyme scheme. (*See also* **Ballad stanza**.)

Ballad stanza The most common pattern of ballad makers consists of four lines rhymed *abcb*, in which the first and third lines have four metrical feet and the second and fourth lines have three feet (4, 3, 4, 3).

Bathos In poetry, an unintentional lapse from the sublime to the ridiculous or trivial. Bathos differs from anticlimax, in that the latter is a deliberate effect, often for the purpose of humor or contrast, whereas bathos occurs through failure.

Bildungsroman German for "novel of growth and development." Sometimes called an **apprenticeship novel**, this genre depicts a youth who struggles toward maturity, forming a worldview or philosophy of life. Dickens's *David Copperfield* and Joyce's *Portrait of the Artist as a Young Man* are classic examples of the genre.

Biographical criticism The practice of analyzing a literary work by using knowledge of the author's life to gain insight.

Biography A factual account of a person's life, examining all available information or texts relevant to the subject.

Blank verse The most common and well-known meter of unrhymed poetry in English. Blank verse contains five iambic feet per line and is never rhymed. (*Blank* means "unrhymed.") Many literary works have been written in blank verse, including Tennyson's "Ulysses" and Frost's "Mending Wall." Shakespeare's plays are written primarily in blank verse. (*See also* **Iambic pentameter**.)

Blues A type of folk music originally developed by African Americans in the South, often about some pain or loss. Blues lyrics traditionally consist of three-line stanzas in which the first two identical lines are followed by a third concluding, rhyming line. The influence of the blues is fundamental in virtually all styles of contemporary pop—jazz, rap, rock, gospel, country, and rhythm and blues.

Box set The illusion of scenic realism for interior rooms was achieved in the early nineteenth century with the development of the box set, consisting of three walls that joined in two corners and a ceiling that tilted as if seen in perspective. The "fourth wall," invisible, ran parallel to the proscenium arch. By the middle of the nineteenth century, the addition of realistic props and furnishings made it possible for actors to behave onstage as if they inhabited private space, oblivious to the presence of an audience, even turning their backs to the audience if the dramatic situation required it.

Broadside ballads Poems printed on a single sheet of paper, often set to traditional tunes. Most broadside ballads, which originated in the late sixteenth century, were an early form of verse journalism, cheap to print, and widely circulated. Often they were humorous or pathetic accounts of sensational news events.

Burlesque Incongruous imitation of either the style or subject matter of a serious genre, humorous due to the disparity between the treatment and the subject. On the nineteenth-century English stage, the burlesque was a broad caricature, parody, travesty, or take-off of popular plays, opera, or current events. Gilbert and Sullivan's Victorian operettas, for example, burlesqued grand opera.

Cacophony A harsh, discordant sound often mirroring the meaning of the context in which it is used. For example, "Grate on the scrannel pipes of wretched straw" (Milton's "Lycidas"). The opposite of cacophony is **euphony**.

Caesura, cesura A pause within a line of verse. Traditionally, caesuras appear near the middle of a line, but their placement may be varied to create expressive rhythmic effects. A caesura will usually occur at a mark of punctuation, but there can be a caesura even if no punctuation is present.

Carpe diem Latin for "seize the day." Originally said in Horace's famous "Odes I (11)," this phrase has been applied to characterize much lyric poetry concerned with human mortality and the passing of time.

Central intelligence The character through whose sensibility and mind a story is told. Henry James developed this term to describe a narrator—not the author—whose perceptions shape the way a story is presented. (*See also* **Narrator**.)

Character An imagined figure inhabiting a narrative or drama. By convention, the reader or spectator endows the fictional character with moral, dispositional, and emotional qualities expressed in what the character says—the dialogue—and by what he or she does—the action. What a character says and does in any particular situation is motivated by his or her desires, temperament, and moral nature. (*See also* **Dynamic character** and **Flat character**.)

Character development The process in which a character is introduced, advanced, and possibly transformed in a story. This development can prove to be either static (the character's personality is unchanging throughout the narrative) or dynamic (the character's personality undergoes some meaningful change during the course of the narrative). (*See also* **Dynamic character**.)

Characterization The techniques a writer uses to create, reveal, or develop the characters in a narrative. (*See also* **Character**.)

Child ballads American scholar Francis J. Child compiled a collection of over three hundred authentic ballads in his book *The English and Scottish Popular Ballads* (1882–1898). He demonstrated that these ballads were the creations of oral folk culture. These works have come to be called Child ballads.

Clerihew A comic verse form named for its inventor, Edmund Clerihew Bentley. A clerihew begins with the name of a person and consists of two metrically awkward, rhymed couplets. Humorous and often insulting, clerihews serve as ridiculous biographies, usually of famous people.

Climax The moment of greatest intensity in a story, which almost inevitably occurs toward the end of the work. The climax often takes the form of a decisive confrontation between the protagonist and antagonist. In a conventional story, the climax is followed by the **resolution** or **dénouement** in which the effects and results of the climactic action are presented. (*See also* **Falling action, Rising action.**)

Closed couplet Two rhymed lines that contain an independent and complete thought or statement. The closed couplet usually pauses lightly at the end of the first line; the second is more heavily end-stopped, or "closed." When such couplets are written in rhymed iambic pentameter, they are called **heroic couplets**. (*See also* **Couplet.**)

Closed dénouement One of two types of conventional dénouement or resolution in a narrative. In closed dénouement, the author ties everything up at the end of the story so that little is left unresolved. (*See also* **Open dénouement.**)

Closed form A generic term that describes poetry written in some preexisting pattern of meter, rhyme, line, or stanza. A closed form produces a prescribed structure as in the triolet, with a set rhyme scheme and line length. Closed forms include the sonnet, sestina, villanelle, ballade, and rondeau.

Close reading A method of analysis involving careful step-by-step explication of a poem in order to understand how various elements work together. Close reading is a common practice of formalist critics in the study of a text.

Closet drama A play or dramatic poem designed to be read aloud rather than performed. Many post-Renaissance verse dramas like Milton's *Samson Agonistes* (1671) or Byron's *Manfred* (1817) are examples of closet drama.

Colloquial English The casual or informal but correct language of ordinary native speakers, which may include contractions, slang, and shifts in grammar, vocabulary, and diction. Wordsworth helped introduce colloquialism into English poetry, challenging the past constraints of highly formal language in verse and calling for the poet to become "a man speaking to men." Conversational in tone, *colloquial* is derived from the Latin *colloquium*, "speaking together." (*See also* **Diction, Levels of diction.**)

Comedy A literary work aimed at amusing an audience. Comedy is one of the basic modes of storytelling and can be adapted to most literary forms—from poetry to film. In traditional comic plotting, the action often involves the adventures of young lovers, who face obstacles and complications that threaten disaster but are overturned at the last moment to produce a happy ending. Comic situations or comic characters can provide humor in tragicomedy and even in tragedies (the gravediggers in *Hamlet*).

Comedy of manners A realistic form of comic drama that flourished with seventeenth-century playwrights such as Molière and English Restoration dramatists. It deals with the social relations and sexual intrigues of sophisticated, intelligent, upper-class men and women, whose verbal fencing and witty repartee produce the principal comic effects. Stereotyped characters from contemporary life, such as would-be wits, jealous husbands, conniving rivals, country bumpkins, and foppish dandies, reveal by their deviations from the norm the decorum and conventional behaviors expected in polite society. William Congreve's *The Way of the World* (1700) is considered the finest example of Restoration comedy of manners. Modern examples include G. B. Shaw (*Arms and the Man*), Noel Coward (*Private Lives*), or Tom Stoppard (*Arcadia*).

Comic relief The appearance of a comic situation, character, or clownish humor in the midst of a serious action that introduces a sharp contrast in mood. The drunken porter in *Macbeth*, who imagines himself the doorkeeper of Hell, not only provides comic relief but intensifies the horror of Macbeth's murder of King Duncan.

Coming-of-age story *See* **Initiation story.**

Commedia dell'arte A form of comic drama developed by guilds of professional Italian actors in the mid-sixteenth century. Playing stock characters, masked *commedia* players improvised dialogue around a given scenario (a brief outline marking entrances of characters and the main course of action). In a typical play a pair of young lovers (played without masks), aided by a clever servant (Harlequin), outwit older masked characters.

Common meter A highly regular form of ballad meter with two sets of rhymes—*abab*. "Amazing Grace" and many other hymns are in common meter. (*See also* **Ballad stanza**.)

Comparison In the analysis or criticism of literature, one may place two works side-by-side to point out their similarities. The product of this, a comparison, may be more meaningful when paired with its counterpart, a **contrast**.

Complication The introduction of a significant development in the central conflict in a drama or narrative between characters (or between a character and his or her situation). Traditionally, a complication begins the rising action of a story's plot. Dramatic conflict (motivation versus obstacle) during the complication is the force that drives a literary work from action to action. Complications may be *external* or *internal* or a combination of the two. A fateful blow such as an illness or an accident that affects a character is a typical example of an *external* complication—a problem the characters cannot turn away from. An *internal* complication, in contrast, might not be immediately apparent, such as the result of some important aspect of a character's values or personality.

Conceit A poetic device using elaborate comparisons, such as equating a loved one with the graces and beauties of the world. Most notably used by the Italian poet Petrarch in praise of his beloved Laura, *conceit* comes from the Italian *concetto*, "concept" or "idea."

Conclusion In plotting, the logical end or outcome of a unified plot, shortly following the climax. Also called **resolution** or **dénouement** ("the untying of the knot"), as in resolving or untying the knots created by plot complications during the rising action. The action or intrigue ends in success or failure for the protagonist, the mystery is solved, or misunderstandings are dispelled. Sometimes a conclusion is ambiguous; at the climax of the story the characters are changed, but the conclusion suggests different possibilities for what that change is or means.

Concrete diction *See* **Diction**.

Concrete poetry A visual poetry composed exclusively for the page in which a picture or image is made of printed letters and words. Concrete poetry attempts to blur the line between language and visual art. Concrete poetry was especially popular as an experimental movement in the 1960s.

Confessional poetry A poetic genre emerging in the 1950s and 1960s primarily concerned with autobiography and the unexpurgated exposure of the poet's personal life. Notable practitioners included Robert Lowell, W. D. Snodgrass, and Anne Sexton.

Conflict In Greek, **agon**, or contest. The central struggle between two or more forces in a story. Conflict generally occurs when some person or thing prevents the protagonist from achieving his or her intended goal. Opposition can arise from another character, external events, preexisting situations, fate, or even some aspect of the main character's own personality. Conflict is the basic material out of which most plots are made. (*See also* **Antagonist, Character, Complication, Rising action**.)

Connotation An association or additional meaning that a word, image, or phrase may carry, apart from its literal denotation or dictionary definition. A word picks up connotations from all the uses to which it has been put in the past. For example, an owl in literature is not merely the literal bird. It also carries the many associations (connotations, that is) attached to it.

Consonance Also called **Slant rhyme**. A kind of rhyme in which the linked words share similar consonant sounds but different vowel sounds, as in *reason* and *raisin*, *mink* and *monk*. Sometimes only the final consonant sound is identical, as in *fame* and *room*, *crack* and *truck*. Used mostly by modern poets, consonance often registers more subtly than exact rhyme, lending itself to special poetic effects.

Contrast A contrast of two works of literature is developed by placing them side-by-side to point out their differences. This method of analysis works well with its opposite, a **comparison**, which focuses on likenesses.

Convention Any established feature or technique in literature that is commonly understood by both authors and readers. A convention is something generally agreed on to be appropriate for its customary uses, such as the sonnet form for a love poem or the opening "Once upon a time" for a fairy tale.

Conventional symbols Literary symbols that have a conventional or customary effect on most readers. We would respond similarly to a black cat crossing our path or a young bride in a white dress. These are conventional symbols because they carry recognizable connotations and suggestions.

Cosmic irony Also called **irony of fate**, it is the irony that exists between a character's aspiration and the treatment he or she receives at the hands of fate. Oedipus's ill-destined relationship with his parents is an example of cosmic irony.

Cothurni High thick-soled boots worn by Greek and Roman tragic actors in late classical times to make them appear taller than ordinary men. (Earlier, in the fifth-century classical Athenian theater, actors wore soft shoes or boots or went barefoot.)

Couplet A two-line stanza in poetry, usually rhymed, which tends to have lines of equal length. Shakespeare's sonnets were famous for ending with a summarizing, rhymed couplet: "Give my love fame faster than Time wastes life; / So thou prevent'st his scythe and crookèd knife." (*See also* **Closed couplet**.)

Cowboy poetry A contemporary genre of folk poetry written by people with firsthand experience in the life of horse, trail, and ranch. Plainspoken and often humorous, cowboy poetry is usually composed in rhymed ballad stanzas and meant to be recited aloud.

Crisis The point in a drama when the crucial action, decision, or realization must be made, marking the turning point or reversal of the protagonist's fortunes. From the Greek word *krisis*, meaning "decision." For example, Hamlet's decision to refrain from killing Claudius while the guilty king is praying is a crisis that leads directly to his accidental murder of Polonius, pointing forward to the catastrophe of Act V. Typically, the crisis inaugurates the falling action (after Hamlet's murder of Polonius, Claudius controls the events) until the catastrophe (or conclusion), which is decided by the death of the hero, King Claudius, Queen Gertrude, and Laertes. In *Oedipus*, the crisis occurs as the hero presses forward to the horrible truth, to realize he is an incestuous parricide and to take responsibility by blinding himself.

Cultural studies A contemporary interdisciplinary field of academic study that focuses on understanding the social power encoded in "texts." Cultural studies defines "texts" more broadly than literary works; they include any analyzable phenomenon from a traditional poem to an advertising image or an actor's face. Cultural studies has no central critical methodology but uses whatever intellectual tools are appropriate to the analysis at hand.

Dactyl A metrical foot of verse in which one stressed syllable is followed by two unstressed syllables (*bat*-ter-y or *par*-a-mour). The dactylic meter is less common to

English than it was to classical Greek and Latin verse. Longfellow's *Evangeline* is the most famous English-language long dactylic poem.

Deconstructionist criticism A school of criticism that rejects the traditional assumption that language can accurately represent reality. Deconstructionists believe that literary texts can have no single meaning; therefore, they concentrate their attentions on *how* language is being used in a text, rather than on *what* is being said.

Decorum Propriety or appropriateness. In poetry, decorum usually refers to a level of diction that is proper to use in a certain occasion. Decorum can also apply to characters, setting, and the harmony that exists between the elements in a poem. For example, aged nuns speaking inner-city jive might violate decorum.

Denotation The literal, dictionary meaning of a word. (*See also* **Connotation**.)

Dénouement The resolution or conclusion of a literary work as plot complications are unraveled after the climax. In French, *dénouement* means "unknotting" or "untying." (*See also* **Closed dénouement**, **Conclusion**, **Open dénouement**.)

Deus ex machina Latin for "a god from a machine." The phrase refers to the Greek playwrights' frequent use of a god, mechanically lowered to the stage from the skene roof, to resolve human conflict with judgments and commands. Conventionally, the phrase now refers to any forced or improbable device in plot resolution.

Dialect A particular variety of language spoken by an identifiable regional group or social class of persons. Dialects are often used in literature in an attempt to present a character more realistically and to express significant differences in class or background.

Dialogue The direct representation of the conversation between two or more characters. (*See also* **Monologue**.)

Diction Word choice or vocabulary. Diction refers to the class of words that an author decides is appropriate to use in a particular work. Literary history is the story of diction being challenged, upheld, and reinvented. **Concrete diction** involves a highly specific word choice in the naming of something or someone. **Abstract diction** contains words that express more general ideas or concepts. More concrete diction would offer *boxer puppy* rather than *young canine*, *Lake Ontario* rather than *body of fresh water*. Concrete words refer to what we can immediately perceive with our senses. (*See also* **Levels of diction**.)

Didactic fiction A narrative that intends to teach a specific moral lesson or provide a model for proper behavior. This term is now often used pejoratively to describe a story in which the events seem manipulated in order to convey an uplifting idea, but much classic fiction has been written in the didactic mode—Aesop's *Fables*, John Bunyan's *The Pilgrim's Progress*, and Harriet Beecher Stowe's *Uncle Tom's Cabin*.

Didactic poetry Kind of poetry intended to teach the reader a moral lesson or impart a body of knowledge. Poetry that aims for education over art.

Dimeter A verse meter consisting of two metrical feet, or two primary stresses, per line.

Doggerel Verse full of irregularities often due to the poet's incompetence. Doggerel is crude verse that brims with cliché, obvious rhyme, and inept rhythm.

Double plot Also called **subplot**. Familiar in Elizabethan drama, a second story or plotline that is complete and interesting in its own right, often doubling or inverting the main plot. By analogy or counterpoint, a skillful subplot broadens perspective on the main plot to enhance rather than dilute its effect. In Shakespeare's *Othello*, for instance, Iago's duping of Rodrigo reflects the main plot of Iago's treachery to Othello.

Drama Derived from the Greek *dran*, "to do," *drama* means "action" or "deed." Drama is the form of literary composition designed for performance in the theater, in which actors take the roles of the characters, perform the indicated action, and speak the written dialogue. In the *Poetics*, Aristotle described tragedy or dramatic enactment as the most fully evolved form of the impulse to imitate or make works of art.

Dramatic irony A special kind of suspenseful expectation, when the audience or reader understands the implication and meaning of a situation onstage and foresees the oncoming disaster (in tragedy) or triumph (in comedy) but the character does not. The irony forms between the contrasting levels of knowledge of the character and the audience. Dramatic irony is pervasive throughout Sophocles' *Oedipus*, for example, because we know from the beginning what Oedipus does not. We watch with dread and fascination the spectacle of a morally good man, committed to the salvation of his city, unwittingly preparing undeserved suffering for himself.

Dramatic monologue A poem written as a speech made by a character at some decisive moment. The speaker is usually addressing a silent listener as in T. S. Eliot's "The Love Song of J. Alfred Prufrock" or Robert Browning's "My Last Duchess."

Dramatic poetry Any verse written for the stage, as in the plays of classical Greece, the Renaissance (Shakespeare), and neoclassical periods (Molière, Racine). Also a kind of poetry that presents the voice of an imaginary character (or characters) speaking directly, without any additional narration by the author. In poetry, the term usually refers to the dramatic monologue, a lyric poem written as a speech made by a character at some decisive moment, such as Lord, Alfred Tennyson's "Ulysses." (*See also* **Dramatic monologue**.)

Dramatic point of view A point of view in which the narrator merely reports dialogue and action with minimal interpretation or access to the characters' minds. The dramatic point of view, as the name implies, uses prose fiction to approximate the method of plays (where readers are provided only with set descriptions, stage directions, and dialogue, and thus must supply motivations based solely on this external evidence).

Dramatic question The primary unresolved issue in a drama as it unfolds. The dramatic question is the result of artful plotting, raising suspense and expectation in a play's action as it moves toward its outcome. Will the Prince in *Hamlet*, for example, achieve what he has been instructed to do and what he intends to do?

Dramatic situation The basic conflict that initiates a work or establishes a scene. It usually describes both a protagonist's motivation and the forces that oppose its realization. (*See also* **Antagonist, Character, Complication, Plot, Rising action**.)

Dumb show In Renaissance theater, a mimed dramatic performance whose purpose is to prepare the audience for the main action of the play to follow. Jacobean playwrights like John Webster used it to show violent events that occur some distance from the play's locale. The most famous Renaissance example is the dumb show preceding the presentation of "The Murder of Gonzago" in *Hamlet*.

Dynamic character A character who, during the course of the narrative, grows or changes in some significant way. (*See also* **Character development**.)

Echo verse A poetic form in which the final syllables of the lines are repeated back as a reply or commentary, often using puns. Echo verse dates back to late classical Greek poetry.

Editing The act of rereading a draft in order to correct mistakes, cut excess words, and make improvements.

Editorial omniscience When an omniscient narrator goes beyond reporting the thoughts of his or her characters to make a critical judgment or commentary, making explicit the narrator's own thoughts or philosophies.

Editorial point of view Also called **Authorial intrusion**. The effect that occurs when a third-person narrator adds his or her own comments (which presumably represent the ideas and opinions of the author) into the narrative.

Elegy A lament or a sadly meditative poem, often written on the occasion of a death or other solemn theme. An elegy is usually a sustained poem in a formal style.

Endnote An additional piece of information that the author includes in a note at the end of a paper. Endnotes usually contain information that the author feels is important to convey but not appropriate to fit into the main body of text. (*See also* **Footnote**.)

End rhyme Rhyme that occurs at the ends of lines, rather than within them (as internal rhyme does). End rhyme is the most common kind of rhyme in English-language poetry.

End-stopped line A line of verse that ends in a full pause, usually indicated by a mark of punctuation.

English sonnet Also called **Shakespearean sonnet**. The English sonnet has a rhyme scheme organized into three quatrains with a final couplet: *abab cdcd efef gg*. The poem may turn, that is, shift in mood or tone, between any of the quatrains (although it usually occurs on the ninth line). (*See also* **Sonnet**.)

Envoy A short, often summarizing stanza that appears at the end of certain poetic forms (most notably the sestina, chant royal, and the French ballade). The envoy contains the poet's parting words. The word comes from the French *envoi*, meaning "sending forth."

Epic A long narrative poem usually composed in an elevated style tracing the adventures of a legendary or mythic hero. Epics are usually written in a consistent form and meter throughout. Famous epics include Homer's *Iliad* and *Odyssey*, Virgil's *Aeneid*, and Milton's *Paradise Lost*.

Epigram A very short poem, often comic, usually ending with some sharp turn of wit or meaning.

Epigraph A brief quotation preceding a story or other literary work. An epigraph usually suggests the subject, theme, or atmosphere the story will explore.

Epiphany A moment of insight, discovery, or revelation by which a character's life is greatly altered. An epiphany generally occurs near the end of a story. The term, which means "showing forth" in Greek, was first used in Christian theology to signify the manifestation of God's presence in the world. This theological idea was first borrowed by James Joyce to refer to a heightened moment of secular revelation.

Episode An incident in a large narrative that has unity in itself. An episode may bear close relation to the central narrative, but it can also be a digression.

Episodic plot, episodic structure A form of plotting where the individual scenes and events are presented chronologically without any profound sense of cause-and-effect relationship. In an episodic narrative the placement of many scenes could be changed without greatly altering the overall effect of the work.

Epistolary novel Novel in which the story is told by way of letters written by one or more of the characters. This form often lends an authenticity to the story, a sense that the author may have discovered these letters; but in fact they are a product of the author's invention.

Euphony The harmonious effect when the sounds of the words connect with the meaning in a way pleasing to the ear and mind. An example is found in Tennyson's lines, "The moan of doves in immemorial elms, / And murmuring of innumerable bees." The opposite of euphony is **cacophony**.

Exact rhyme A full rhyme in which the sounds following the initial letters of the words are identical in sound, as in *follow* and *hollow*, *go* and *slow*, *disband* and *this hand*.

Explication Literally, an "unfolding." In an explication an entire poem is explained in detail, addressing every element and unraveling any complexities as a means of analysis.

Exposition The opening portion of a narrative or drama. In the exposition, the scene is set, the protagonist is introduced, and the author discloses any other background information necessary to allow the reader to understand and relate to the events that are to follow.

Expressionism A dramatic style developed between 1910 and 1924 in Germany in reaction against realism's focus on surface details and external reality. To draw an audience into a dreamlike subjective realm, expressionistic artistic styles used episodic plots, distorted lines, exaggerated shapes, abnormally intense coloring, mechanical physical movement, and telegraphic speech (the broken syntax of a disordered psyche). Staging the contents of the unconscious, expressionist plays ranged from utopian visions of a fallen, materialistic world redeemed by the spirituality of "new men" to pessimistic nightmare visions of universal catastrophe.

Eye rhyme Rhyme in which the spelling of the words appears alike, but the pronunciations differ, as in *laughter* and *daughter*, *idea* and *flea*.

Fable A brief, often humorous narrative told to illustrate a moral. The characters in fables are traditionally animals whose personality traits symbolize human traits. Particular animals have conventionally come to represent specific human qualities or values. For example, the ant represents industry, the fox craftiness, and the lion nobility. A fable often concludes by summarizing its moral message in abstract terms. For example, Aesop's fable "The North Wind and the Sun" concludes with the moral "Persuasion is better than force." (*See also* **Allegory**.)

Fairy tale A traditional form of short narrative folklore, originally transmitted orally, that features supernatural characters such as witches, giants, fairies, or animals with human personality traits. Fairy tales often feature a hero or heroine who seems destined to achieve some desirable fate—such as marrying a prince or princess, becoming wealthy, or destroying an enemy.

Falling action The events in a narrative that follow the climax and bring the story to its conclusion, or dénouement.

Falling meter Trochaic and dactylic meters are called falling meters because their first syllable is accented, followed by one or more unaccented syllables. A foot of falling meter falls in its level of stress, as in the words *co*-medy or *aw*-ful.

Fantasy A narrative that depicts events, characters, or places that could not exist in the real world. Fantasy has limited interest in portraying experience realistically. Instead, it freely pursues the possibilities of the imagination. Fantasy usually includes elements of magic or the supernatural. Sometimes it is used to illustrate a moral message as in fables. Fantasy is a type of romance that emphasizes wish fulfillment (or nightmare fulfillment) instead of verisimilitude.

Farce A type of comedy featuring exaggerated character types in ludicrous and improbable situations, provoking belly laughs with sexual mix-ups, crude verbal jokes, pratfalls, and knockabout horseplay (like the comic violence of the Punch and Judy show).

Feminine rhyme A rhyme of two or more syllables with a stress on a syllable other than the last, as in *tur*-tle and *fer*-tile. (*See also* **Masculine rhyme**, **Rhyme**.)

Feminist criticism *See* **Gender criticism**.

Fiction From the Latin ficio, "act of fashioning, a shaping, a making." Fiction refers to any literary work that—although it might contain factual information—is not bound by factual accuracy, but creates a narrative shaped or made up by the author's imagination. Drama and poetry (especially narrative poetry) can be considered works of fiction, but the term now usually refers more specifically to prose stories and novels. Historical and other factual writing also requires shaping and making, but it is distinct from fiction because it is not free to invent people, places, and events; forays from documented fact must identify themselves as conjecture or hypothesis. Nonfiction, as the name suggests, is a category conventionally separate from fiction. Certainly an essay or work of literary journalism is "a made thing," and writers of nonfiction routinely employ the techniques used by fiction writers (moving forward and backward in time, reporting the inner thoughts of characters, etc.), but works of nonfiction must be not only true but factual. The truth of a work of fiction depends not on facts, but on how convincingly the writer creates the world of the story.

Figure of speech An expression or comparison that relies not on its literal meaning, but rather on its connotations and suggestions. For example, "He's dumber than dirt" is not literally true; it is a figure of speech. Major figures of speech include **metaphor, metonymy, simile,** and **synecdoche.**

First-person narrator A story in which the narrator is a participant in the action. Such a narrator refers to himself or herself as "I" and may be a major or minor character in the story. His or her attitude and understanding of characters and events shapes the reader's perception of the story being told.

Fixed form A traditional verse form requiring certain predetermined elements of structure, for example, a stanza pattern, set meter, or predetermined line length. A fixed form like the sonnet, for instance, must have no more or less than fourteen lines, rhymed according to certain conventional patterns. (*See also* **Closed form.**)

Flashback A scene relived in a character's memory. Flashbacks can be related by the narrator in a summary or they can be experienced by the characters themselves. Flashbacks allow the author to include events that occurred before the opening of the story, which may show the reader something significant that happened in the character's past or give an indication of what kind of person the character used to be.

Flat character A term coined by English novelist E. M. Forster to describe a character with only one outstanding trait. Flat characters are rarely the central characters in a narrative and are often based on **stock characters.** Flat characters stay the same throughout a story. (*See also* **Dynamic character.**)

Flexible theater Also called **black box** or **experimental theater space.** A modern, nontraditional performance space in which actor-audience relationships can be flexibly configured, with movable seating platforms. Usually seating anywhere from 100 to 250 spectators, black box theaters can accommodate staging in the round, thrust staging, tennis court staging, and even temporary proscenium arch (fourth wall) staging.

Folk ballads Anonymous narrative songs, usually in ballad meter, that were originally transmitted orally. Although most well-known ballads have been transcribed and published in order to protect them from being lost, they were originally created for oral performance, often resulting in many versions of a single ballad.

Folk epic Also called **Traditional epic.** A long narrative poem that traces the adventures of a tribe or nation's popular heroes. Some examples of epics are the *Iliad* and the *Odyssey* (Greek), *The Song of Roland* (French), and *The Cid* (Spanish). A folk epic originates in an oral tradition as opposed to a literary epic, which is written by an individual author consciously emulating earlier epic poetry.

Folklore The body of traditional wisdom and customs—including songs, stories, myths, and proverbs—of a people as collected and continued through oral tradition.

Folktale A short narrative drawn from folklore that has been passed down through an oral tradition. (*See also* **Fairy tale**, **Legend**.)

Foot The unit of measurement in metrical poetry. Different meters are identified by the pattern and order of stressed and unstressed syllables in their foot, usually containing two or three syllables, with one syllable accented.

Footnote An additional piece of information that the author includes at the bottom of a page, usually noted by a small reference number in the main text. A footnote might supply the reader with brief facts about a related historical figure or event, the definition of a foreign word or phrase, or any other relevant information that may help in understanding the text. (*See also* **Endnote**.)

Foreshadowing In plot construction, the technique of arranging events and information in such a way that later events are prepared for, or shadowed, beforehand. The author may introduce specific words, images, or actions in order to suggest significant later events. The effective use of foreshadowing by an author may prevent a story's outcome from seeming haphazard or contrived.

Form The means by which a literary work conveys its meaning. Traditionally, form refers to the way in which an artist expresses meaning rather than the content of that meaning, but it is now commonplace to note that form and content are inextricably related. Form, therefore, is more than the external framework of a literary work. It includes the totality of ways in which it unfolds and coheres as a structure of meaning and expression.

Formal English The heightened, impersonal language of educated persons, usually only written, although possibly spoken on dignified occasions. (*See also* **Levels of diction**.)

Formalist criticism A school of criticism which argues that literature may only be discussed on its own terms; that is, without outside influences or information. A key method that formalists use is close reading, a step-by-step analysis of the elements in a text.

Found poetry Poetry constructed by arranging bits of "found" prose. A found poem is a literary work made up of nonliterary language arranged for expressive effect.

Free verse From the French *vers libre*. Free verse describes poetry that organizes its lines without meter. It may be rhymed (as in some poems by H. D.), but it usually is not. There is no one means of organizing free verse, and different authors have used irreconcilable systems. What unites the two approaches is a freedom from metrical regularity. (*See also* **Open form**.)

Gender criticism Gender criticism examines how sexual identity influences the creation, interpretation, and evaluation of literary works. This critical approach began with feminist criticism in the 1960s and 1970s which stated that literary study had been so dominated by men that it contained many unexamined "male-produced" assumptions. Feminist criticism sought to address this imbalance in two ways: first in insisting that sexless interpretation was impossible, and second by articulating responses to the texts that were explicitly male or female. More recently, gender criticism has focused on gay and lesbian literary identity as interpretive strategies.

General English The ordinary speech of educated native speakers. Most literate speech and writing is general English. Its diction is more educated than **colloquial English**, yet not as elevated as **formal English**. (*See also* **Levels of diction**.)

Genre A conventional combination of literary form and subject matter, usually aimed at creating certain effects. A genre implies a preexisting understanding between the artist and the reader about the purpose and rules of the work. A horror story, for example, combines the form of the short story with certain conventional subjects, style, and theme with the expectation of frightening the reader. Major short story genres include science fiction, gothic, horror, and detective tales.

Gothic fiction A genre that creates terror and suspense, usually set in an isolated castle, mansion, or monastery populated by mysterious or threatening individuals. The Gothic form, invented by Horace Walpole in *The Castle of Otranto* (1764), has flourished in one form or another ever since. The term *Gothic* is also applied to medieval architecture, and Gothic fiction almost inevitably exploits claustrophobic interior architecture in its plotting—often featuring dungeons, crypts, torture chambers, locked rooms, and secret passageways. In the nineteenth century, writers such as Nathaniel Hawthorne, Edgar Allan Poe, and Charlotte Perkins Gilman brought the genre into the mainstream of American fiction.

Haiku A Japanese verse form that has three unrhymed lines of five, seven, and five syllables. Traditional haiku is often serious and spiritual in tone, relying mostly on imagery, and usually set in one of the four seasons.

Hamartia Greek for "error." An offense committed in ignorance of some material fact (without deliberate criminal intent) and therefore free of blameworthiness. A big mistake unintentionally made as a result of an intellectual error (not vice or criminal wickedness) by a morally good person, usually involving the identity of a blood relation. The *hamartia* of Oedipus, quite simply, is based on his ignorance of his true parentage; inadvertently and unwittingly, then, he commits the *hamartia* of patricide and incest. (*See also* **Recognition**.)

Heptameter A verse meter consisting of seven metrical feet, or seven primary stresses, per line.

Hero The central character in a narrative. The term is derived from the Greek epic tradition, in which *heroes* were the leading warriors among the princes. By extension, *hero* and *heroine* have come to mean the principal male and female figures in a narrative or dramatic literary work, although many today call protagonists of either sex *heroes*. When a critic terms the protagonist a *hero*, the choice of words often implies a positive moral assessment of the character. (*See also* **Antihero**.)

Heroic couplet *See* **Closed couplet**.

Hexameter A verse meter consisting of six metrical feet, or six primary stresses, per line.

High comedy A comic genre evoking so-called intellectual or thoughtful laughter from an audience that remains emotionally detached from the play's depiction of the folly, pretense, and incongruity of human behavior. The French playwright Molière and the English dramatists of the Restoration period developed a special form of high comedy in the **comedy of manners**, focused on the social relations and amorous intrigues of sophisticated upper-class men and women, conducted through witty repartee and verbal combat.

Historical criticism The practice of analyzing a literary work by investigating the social, cultural, and intellectual context that produced it—a context that necessarily includes the artist's biography and milieu. Historical critics strive to recreate the exact meaning and impact a work had on its original audience.

Historical fiction A type of fiction in which the narrative is set in another time or place. In historical fiction, the author usually attempts to recreate a faithful picture of daily life during the period. For example, Robert Graves's *I, Claudius* depicts the lives of the ancient Roman ruling class in the early Imperial age. Historical fiction sometimes introduces well-known figures from the past. More often it places imaginary characters in a carefully reconstructed version of a particular historical era.

Hubris Overweening pride, outrageous behavior, or the insolence that leads to ruin, *hubris* was in the Greek moral vocabulary the antithesis of moderation or rectitude. Creon, in Sophocles' *Antigonê*, is a good example of a character brought down by his *hubris*.

Hyperbole *See* **Overstatement**.

Iamb A metrical foot in verse in which an unaccented syllable is followed by an accented one, as in "ca-*ress*" or "a *cat*" (◡ ′). The iambic measure is the most common meter used in English poetry.

Iambic meter A verse meter consisting of a specific recurring number of iambic feet per line. (*See also* **Iamb**, **Iambic pentameter**.)

Iambic pentameter The most common meter in English verse—five iambic feet per line. Many fixed forms, such as the sonnet and heroic couplets, are written in iambic pentameter. Unrhymed iambic pentameter is called **blank verse**.

Image A word or series of words that refers to any sensory experience (usually sight, although also sound, smell, touch, or taste). An image is a direct or literal recreation of physical experience and adds immediacy to literary language.

Imagery The collective set of images in a poem or other literary work.

Impartial omniscience Refers to an omniscient narrator who, although he or she presents the thoughts and actions of the characters, does not judge them or comment on them. (Contrasts with **Editorial omniscience**.)

Implied metaphor A metaphor that uses neither connectives nor the verb *to be*. If we say, "John crowed over his victory," we imply metaphorically that John is a rooster but do not say so specifically. (*See also* **Metaphor**.)

Impressionism In fiction, a style of writing that emphasizes external events less than the impression those events make on the narrator or protagonist. Impressionist short stories, like Katherine Mansfield's "Miss Brill," usually center the narrative on the chief characters' mental lives rather than the reality around them.

Incremental refrain A refrain whose words change slightly with each recurrence. (*See also* **Refrain**.)

Initial alliteration *See* **Alliteration**.

Initiation story Also called **Coming-of-age story**. A narrative in which the main character, usually a child or adolescent, undergoes an important experience or rite of passage—often a difficult or disillusioning one—that prepares him or her for adulthood. James Joyce's "Araby" is a classic example of an initiation story.

In medias res A Latin phrase meaning "in the midst of things" that refers to a narrative device of beginning a story midway in the events it depicts (usually at an exciting or significant moment) before explaining the context or preceding actions. Epic poems such as Virgil's *Aeneid* or John Milton's *Paradise Lost* commonly begin *in medias res*, but the technique is also found in modern fiction.

Innocent narrator Also called **naive narrator**. A character who fails to understand all the implications of the story he or she tells. Of course, virtually any narrator has some degree of innocence or naiveté, but the innocent narrator—often a child or childlike adult—is used by an author trying to generate irony, sympathy, or pity by creating a gap between what the narrator knows and what the reader knows. Mark Twain's Huckleberry Finn—despite his mischievous nature—is an example of an innocent narrator.

Interior monologue An extended presentation of a character's thoughts in a narrative. Usually written in the present tense and printed without quotation marks, an interior monologue reads as if the character were speaking aloud to himself or herself, for the reader to overhear. A famous example of interior monologue comes at the end of *Ulysses* when Joyce gives us the rambling memories and reflections of Molly Bloom.

Internal alliteration *See* **Alliteration**.

Internal refrain A refrain that appears within a stanza, generally in a position that stays fixed throughout a poem. (*See also* **Refrain**.)

Internal rhyme Rhyme that occurs within a line of poetry, as opposed to **end rhyme**. Read aloud, these Wallace Stevens lines are rich in internal rhyme: "Chieftain Iffu-can of Azcan in caftan / Of tan with henna hackles, halt!" (from "Bantams in Pine-Woods").

Ironic point of view The perspective of a character or narrator whose voice or position is rich in ironic contradictions. (*See also* **Irony**.)

Irony A literary device in which a discrepancy of meaning is masked beneath the surface of the language. Irony is present when a writer says one thing but means something quite the opposite. There are many kinds of irony, but the two major varieties are **verbal irony** (in which the discrepancy is contained in words) and **situational irony** (in which the discrepancy exists when something is about to happen to a character or characters who expect the opposite outcome). (*See also* **Cosmic irony, Irony of fate, Sarcasm, Verbal irony**.)

Irony of fate A type of situational irony that can be used for either tragic or comic purposes. Irony of fate is the discrepancy between actions and their results, between what characters deserve and what they get, between appearance and reality. In Sophocles' tragedy, for instance, Oedipus unwittingly fulfills the prophecy even as he takes the actions a morally good man would take to avoid it. (*See also* **Cosmic irony**.)

Italian sonnet Also called **Petrarchan sonnet**, a sonnet with the following rhyme pattern for the first eight lines (the **octave**): *abba, abba*; the final six lines (the **sestet**) may follow any pattern of rhymes, as long as it does not end in a couplet. The poem traditionally turns, or shifts in mood or tone, after the octave. (*See also* **Sonnet**.)

Katharsis, **catharsis** Often translated as purgation or purification, the term is drawn from the last element of Aristotle's definition of tragedy, relating to the final cause or purpose of tragic art. Catharsis generally refers to the feeling of emotional release or calm the spectator feels at the end of tragedy. In Aristotle *katharsis* is the final effect of the playwright's skillful use of plotting, character, and poetry to elicit pity and fear from the audience. Through *katharsis*, drama taught the audience compassion for the vulnerabilities of others and schooled it in justice and other civic virtues.

Legend A traditional narrative handed down through popular oral tradition to illustrate and celebrate a remarkable character, an important event, or to explain the unexplainable. Legends, unlike other folktales, claim to be true and usually take place in real locations, often with genuine historical figures.

Levels of diction In English, there are conventionally four basic levels of formality in word choice, or four levels of diction. From the least formal to the most elevated they are **vulgate, colloquial English, general English**, and **formal English**. (*See also* **Diction**.)

Limerick A short and usually comic verse form of five anapestic lines usually rhyming *aabba*. The first, second, and fifth lines traditionally have three stressed syllables each; the third and fourth have two stresses each (3, 3, 2, 2, 3).

Limited omniscience Also called third-person limited point of view. A type of point of view in which the narrator sees into the minds of some but not all of the characters. Most typically, limited omniscience sees through the eyes of one major or minor character. In limited omniscience, the author can compromise between the immediacy of first-person narration and the mobility of third person.

Literary ballad Ballad not meant for singing, written for literate readers by sophisticated poets rather than arising from the anonymous oral tradition. (*See also* **Ballad**.)

Literary epic A crafted imitation of the oral folk epic written by an author living in a society where writing has been invented. Examples of the literary epic are *The Aeneid* by Virgil and *The Divine Comedy* by Dante Alighieri. (*See also* **Folk epic**.)

Literary genre *See* **Genre**.

Literary theory Literary criticism that tries to formulate general principles rather than discuss specific texts. Theory operates at a high level of abstraction and often focuses on understanding basic issues of language, communication, art, interpretation, culture, and ideological content.

Local color The use of specific regional material—unique customs, dress, habits, and speech patterns of ordinary people—to create atmosphere or realism in a literary work.

Locale The location where a story takes place.

Low comedy A comic style arousing laughter through jokes, slapstick humor, sight gags, and boisterous clowning. Unlike **high comedy**, it has little intellectual appeal. (*See also* **Comedy**.)

Lyric A short poem expressing the thoughts and feelings of a single speaker. Often written in the first person, lyric poetry traditionally has a songlike immediacy and emotional force.

Madrigal A short secular song for three or more voices arranged in counterpoint. The madrigal is often about love or pastoral themes. It originated in Italy in the fourteenth century and enjoyed great success during the Elizabethan Age.

Magic realism Also called **magical realism**. A type of contemporary narrative in which the magical and the mundane are mixed in an overall context of realistic storytelling. The term was coined by Cuban novelist Alejo Carpentier in 1949 to describe the matter-of-fact combination of the fantastic and everyday in Latin American fiction. Magic realism has become the standard name for an international trend in contemporary fiction such as Gabriel García Márquez's *One Hundred Years of Solitude*.

Masculine rhyme Either a rhyme of one syllable words (as in *fox* and *socks*) or—in polysyllabic words—a rhyme on the stressed final syllables: con-*trive* and sur-*vive*. (*See also* **Feminine rhyme**.)

Masks In Latin, *personae*. In classical Greek theater, full facial masks made of leather, linen, or light wood, with headdress, allowed male actors to embody the conventionalized characters (or *dramatis personae*) of the tragic and comic stage. Later, in the seventeenth and eighteenth centuries, stock characters of the *commedia dell' arte* wore characteristic half masks made of leather. (*See also* **Persona**.)

Melodrama Originally a stage play featuring background music and sometimes songs to underscore the emotional mood of each scene. Melodramas were notoriously weak in characterization and motivation but famously strong on action, suspense, and passion. Melodramatic characters were stereotyped villains, heroes, and young lovers. When the term *melodrama* is applied to fiction, it is almost inevitably a negative criticism implying that the author has sacrificed psychological depth and credibility for emotional excitement and adventurous plotting.

Metafiction Fiction that consciously explores its own nature as a literary creation. The Greek word *meta* means "upon"; metafiction consequently is a mode of narrative that does not try to create the illusion of verisimilitude but delights in its own fictional nature, often by speculating on the story it is telling. The term is usually associated with late-twentieth-century writers like John Barth, Italo Calvino, and Jorge Luis Borges.

Metaphor A statement that one thing *is* something else, which, in a literal sense, it is not. By asserting that a thing is something else, a metaphor creates a close association between the two entities and usually underscores some important similarity between them. An example of metaphor is "Richard is a pig."

Meter A recurrent, regular, rhythmic pattern in verse. When stresses recur at fixed intervals, the result is meter. Traditionally, meter has been the basic organizational device of world poetry. There are many existing meters, each identified by the different patterns of recurring sounds. In English most common meters involve the arrangement of stressed and unstressed syllables.

Metonymy Figure of speech in which the name of a thing is substituted for that of another closely associated with it. For instance, in saying "The White House decided," one could mean that the president decided.

Microcosm The small world as created by a poem, play, or story that reflects the tensions of the larger world beyond. In some sense, most successful literary works offer a microcosm that illuminates the greater world around it.

Mime Either a play or sketch without words, or the performer. (*See also* **Pantomime**.)

Minimalist fiction Contemporary fiction written in a deliberately flat, unemotional tone and an appropriately unadorned style. Minimalist fiction often relies more on dramatic action, scene, and dialogue than complex narration or authorial summary. Examples of minimalist fiction can be found in the short stories of Raymond Carver and Bobbie Ann Mason.

Mixed metaphor A metaphor that trips over another metaphor—usually unconsciously—already in the statement. Mixed metaphors are the result of combining two or more incompatible metaphors resulting in ridiculousness or nonsense. For example, "Mary was such a tower of strength that she breezed her way through all the work" ("towers" do not "breeze").

Monologue An extended speech by a single character. The term originated in drama, where it describes a solo speech that has listeners (as opposed to a **soliloquy**, where the character speaks only to himself or herself). A short story or even a novel can be written in monologue form if it is an unbroken speech by one character to another silent character or characters.

Monometer A verse meter consisting of one metrical foot, or one primary stress, per line.

Monosyllabic Foot A foot, or unit of meter, that contains only one syllable.

Moral A paraphrasable message or lesson implied or directly stated in a literary work. Commonly, a moral is stated at the end of a fable.

Motif An element that recurs significantly throughout a narrative. A motif can be an image, idea, theme, situation, or action (and was first commonly used as a musical term for a recurring melody or melodic fragment). A motif can also refer to an element that recurs across many literary works like a beautiful lady in medieval romances who turns out to be an evil fairy or three questions that are asked a protagonist to test his or her wisdom.

Motivation What a character in a story or drama wants. The reasons an author provides for a character's actions. Motivation can be either *explicit* (in which reasons are specifically stated in a story) or *implicit* (in which the reasons are only hinted at or partially revealed).

Myth A traditional narrative of anonymous authorship that arises out of a culture's oral tradition. The characters in traditional myths are usually gods or heroic figures. Myths characteristically explain the origins of things—gods, people, places, plants, animals, and natural events—usually from a cosmic view. A culture's values and belief systems are traditionally passed from generation to generation in myth. In literature, myth may also refer to boldly imagined narratives that embody primal truths about life. Myth is usually differentiated from legend, which has a specific historical base.

Mythological criticism The practice of analyzing a literary work by looking for recurrent universal patterns. Mythological criticism explores the artist's common humanity by tracing how the individual imagination uses myths and symbols that are shared by different cultures and epochs.

Naive narrator *See* **Innocent narrator**.

Narrative poem A poem that tells a story. Narrative is one of the four traditional modes of poetry, along with lyric, dramatic, and didactic. **Ballads** and **epics** are two common forms of narrative poetry.

Narrator A voice or character that provides the reader with information and insight about the characters and incidents in a narrative. A narrator's perspective and personality can greatly affect how a story is told. (*See also* **Omniscient narrator**, **Point of view**.)

Naturalism A type of fiction or drama in which the characters are presented as products or victims of environment and heredity. Naturalism, considered an extreme form of realism, customarily depicts the social, psychological, and economic milieu of the primary characters. Naturalism was first formally developed by French novelist Émile Zola in the 1870s. In promoting naturalism as a theory of animal behavior, Zola urged the modeling of naturalist literature and drama on the scientific case study. The writer, like the scientist, was to record objective reality with detachment; events onstage should be reproduced with sufficient exactness to demonstrate the strict laws of material causality. Important American Naturalists include Jack London, Theodore Dreiser, and Stephen Crane. (*See also* **Realism**.)

Neoclassical period *See* **Augustan age**.

New Formalism A term for a recent literary movement (begun around 1980) in which young poets began using rhyme, meter, and narrative again. New Formalists attempt to write poetry that appeals to an audience beyond academia. Timothy Steele, Gjertrud Schnackenberg, R. S. Gwynn, David Mason, and Marilyn Nelson are poets commonly associated with the movement.

New naturalism A term describing some American plays of the 1970s and 1980s, frankly showing the internal and external forces that shape the lives of unhappy, alienated, dehumanized, and often impoverished characters. Examples include the plays of Sam Shepard, August Wilson, and David Mamet.

Nonfiction novel A genre in which actual events are presented as a novel-length story, using the techniques of fiction (flashback, interior monologues, etc.). Truman Capote's *In Cold Blood* (1966), which depicts a multiple murder and subsequent trial in Kansas, is a classic example of this modern genre.

Nonparticipant narrator A narrator who does not appear in the story as a character but is capable of revealing the thoughts and motives of one or more characters. A nonparticipant narrator is also capable of moving from place to place in order to describe action and report dialogue. (*See also* **Omniscient narrator**.)

Nouvelle The French term for the short prose tale (called **novella** by Italian Renaissance writers) that usually depicted in relatively realistic terms illicit love, ingenious trickery, and sensational adventure, often with an underlying moral. Marguerite de Navarre's *Heptameron* is a classic collection of *nouvelle*.

Novel An extended work of fictional prose narrative. The term *novel* usually implies a book-length narrative (as compared to more compact forms of prose fiction such as the short story). Because of its extended length, a novel usually has more characters, more varied scenes, and a broader coverage of time than a short story.

Novella In modern terms, a prose narrative longer than a short story but shorter than a novel (approximately 30,000 to 50,000 words). Unlike a short story, a novella is long enough to be published independently as a brief book. Classic modern novellas include Franz Kafka's *The Metamorphosis*, Joseph Conrad's *Heart of Darkness*, and Thomas Mann's *Death in Venice*. During the Renaissance, however, the term *novella* originally referred to short prose narratives such as those found in Giovanni Boccaccio's *Decameron*.

Objective point of view *See* **Dramatic point of view**.

Observer A type of first-person narrator who is relatively detached from or plays only a minor role in the events described.

Octameter A verse meter consisting of eight metrical feet, or eight primary stresses, per line.

Octave A stanza of eight lines. *Octave* is a term usually used when speaking of sonnets to indicate the first eight-line section of the poem, as distinct from the *sestet* (the final six lines). Some poets also use octaves as separate stanzas as in W. B. Yeats's "Sailing to Byzantium," which employs the *ottava rima* ("eighth rhyme") stanza—*abababcc*.

Off rhyme *See* **Slant rhyme**.

O. Henry ending *See* **Trick ending**.

Omniscient narrator Also called **all-knowing narrator**. A narrator who has the ability to move freely through the consciousness of any character. The omniscient narrator also has complete knowledge of all of the external events in a story. (*See also* **Nonparticipant narrator**.)

Onomatopoeia A literary device that attempts to represent a thing or action by the word that imitates the sound associated with it (e.g., *crash, bang, pitter-patter*).

Open dénouement One of the two conventional types of dénouement or resolution. In open dénouement, the author ends a narrative with a few loose ends, or unresolved matters, on which the reader is left to speculate. (*See also* **Closed dénouement**.)

Open form Verse that has no set formal scheme—no meter, rhyme, or even set stanzaic pattern. Open form is always in free verse. (*See also* **Free verse**.)

Oral tradition The tradition within a culture that transmits narratives by word of mouth from one generation to another. Fables, folktales, ballads, and songs are examples of some types of narratives found originally in an oral tradition.

Orchestra In classical Greek theater architecture, "the place for dancing," a circular, level performance space at the base of a horseshoe-shaped amphitheater, where twelve, then later (in Sophocles' plays) fifteen, young, masked, male chorus members sang and danced the odes interspersed between dramatic episodes making up the classical Greek play. Today the orchestra refers to the ground floor seats in a theater or concert hall.

Overstatement Also called **hyperbole**. Exaggeration used to emphasize a point.

Pantomime Acting on the stage without speech, using only posture, gesture, bodily movement, and exaggerated facial expressions to mimic a character's actions and express feelings. Originally, in ancient Rome, a pantomime was a performer who played all the parts single-handedly. (*See also* **Mime**.)

Parable A brief, usually allegorical narrative that teaches a moral. The parables found in Christian literature, such as "The Parable of the Prodigal Son" (Luke 15:11–32), are classic examples of the form. In parables, unlike fables (where the moral is explicitly stated within the narrative), the moral themes are implicit and can often be interpreted in several ways. Modern parables can be found in the works of Franz Kafka and Jorge Luis Borges.

Paradox A statement that at first strikes one as self-contradictory, but that on reflection reveals some deeper sense. Paradox is often achieved by a play on words.

Parallelism An arrangement of words, phrases, clauses, or sentences side-by-side in a similar grammatical or structural way. Parallelism organizes ideas in a way that demonstrates their coordination to the reader.

Paraphrase The restatement in one's own words of what we understand a literary work to say. A paraphrase is similar to a summary, although not as brief or simple.

Parody A mocking imitation of a literary work or individual author's style, usually for comic effect. A parody typically exaggerates distinctive features of the original for humorous purposes.

Participant narrator A narrator that participates as a character within a story. (*See also* **First-person narrator**.)

Pentameter A verse meter consisting of five metrical feet, or five primary stresses, per line. In English, the most common form of pentameter is iambic.

Peripeteia Anglicized as *peripety*, Greek for "sudden change." Reversal of fortune. In a play's plotting, a sudden change of circumstance affecting the protagonist, often also including a reversal of intent on the protagonist's part. The play's peripety occurs usually when a certain result is expected and instead its opposite effect is produced. For example, at the beginning of *Oedipus*, the protagonist expects to discover the identity of the murderer of Laius. However, after the Corinthian messenger informs Oedipus that he was adopted, the hero's intent changes to encompass the search for his true parentage. A comedy's peripety restores a character to good fortune, when a moment in which the worst can happen is suddenly turned into happy circumstance.

Persona Latin for "mask." A fictitious character created by an author to be the speaker of a poem, story, or novel. A persona is always the narrator of the work and not merely a character in it.

Personification A figure of speech in which a thing, an animal, or an abstract term is endowed with human characteristics. Personification allows an author to dramatize the nonhuman world in tangibly human terms.

Petrarchan sonnet *See* **Italian sonnet**.

Picaresque A type of narrative, usually a novel, that presents the life of a likable scoundrel who is at odds with respectable society. The narrator of a picaresque was originally a *picaro* (Spanish for "rascal" or "rogue") who recounts his adventures tricking the rich and gullible. This type of narrative rarely has a tight plot, and the episodes or adventures follow in a loose chronological order.

Picture-frame stage Developed in sixteenth-century Italian playhouses, the picture-frame stage held the action within a proscenium arch, a gateway standing "in front of the scenery" (as the word *proscenium* indicates). The proscenium framed painted scene panels (receding into the middle distance) designed to give the illusion of three-dimensional perspective. Only one seat in the auditorium, reserved for the theater's royal patron or sponsor, enjoyed the complete perspectivist illusion. The raised and framed stage separated actors from the audience and the world of the play from the real world of the auditorium. Picture-frame stages became the norm throughout Europe and England up into the twentieth century.

Play *See* **Drama**.

Play review A critical account of a performance, providing the basic facts of the production, a brief plot summary, and an evaluation (with adequate rationale) of the chief elements of performance, including the acting, the direction, scene and light design, and the script, especially if the play is new or unfamiliar.

Plot The particular arrangement of actions, events, and situations that unfold in a narrative. A plot is not merely the general story of a narrative but the author's artistic pattern made from the parts of the narrative, including the exposition, complications, climax, and dénouement. How an author chooses to construct the plot determines the way the reader experiences the story. Manipulating a plot, therefore, can be the author's most important expressive device when writing a story. More than just a story made up of episodes or a bare synopsis of the temporal order of events, the plotting is the particular embodiment of an action that allows the audience to see the causal relationship between the parts of the action. (*See also* **Climax**, **Falling action**, **Rising action**.)

Poetic diction Strictly speaking, *poetic diction* means any language deemed suitable for verse, but the term generally refers to elevated language intended for poetry rather than common use. Poetic diction often refers to the ornate language used in literary periods such as the Augustan age, when authors employed a highly specialized vocabulary for their verse. (*See also* **Diction**.)

Point of view The perspective from which a story is told. There are many types of point of view, including first-person narrator (a story in which the narrator is a participant in the action) and third-person narrator (a type of narration in which the narrator is a nonparticipant).

Portmanteau word An artificial word that combines parts of other words to express some combination of their qualities. Sometimes portmanteau words prove so useful that they become part of the standard language. For example, *smog* from *smoke* and *fog*; or *brunch* from *breakfast* and *lunch*.

Print culture A culture that depends primarily on the printed word—in books, magazines, and newspapers—to distribute and preserve information. In recent decades the electronic media have taken over much of this role from print.

Projective verse Charles Olson's theory that poets compose by listening to their own breathing and using it as a rhythmic guide rather than poetic meter or form. (*See also* **Open form**.)

Proscenium arch Separating the auditorium from the raised stage and the world of the play, the architectural picture frame or gateway "standing in front of the scenery" (as the word *proscenium* indicates) in traditional European theaters from the sixteenth century on.

Prose poem Poetic language printed in prose paragraphs, but displaying the careful attention to sound, imagery, and figurative language characteristic of poetry.

Prosody The study of metrical structures in poetry. (*See also* **Scansion**.)

Protagonist The central character in a literary work. The protagonist usually initiates the main action of the story, often in conflict with the antagonist. (*See also* **Antagonist**.)

Psalms Sacred songs, usually referring to the 150 Hebrew poems collected in the Old Testament.

Psychological criticism The practice of analyzing a literary work through investigating three major areas: the nature of literary genius, the psychological study of a particular artist, and the analysis of fictional characters. This methodology uses the analytical tools of psychology and psychoanalysis to understand the underlying motivations and meanings of a literary work.

Pulp fiction A type of formulaic and quickly written fiction originally produced for cheap mass circulation magazines. The term *pulp* refers to the inexpensive wood-pulp paper developed in the mid-nineteenth century on which these magazines were printed. Most pulp fiction journals printed only melodramatic genre work—westerns, science fiction, romance, horror, adventure tales, or crime stories.

Pun A play on words in which one word is substituted for another similar or identical sound, but of very different meaning.

Purgation See **Katharsis**.

Quantitative meter A meter constructed on the principle of vowel length. Such quantities are difficult to hear in English, so this meter remains slightly foreign to our language. Classical Greek and Latin poetry were written in quantitative meters.

Quatrain A stanza consisting of four lines. Quatrains are the most common stanzas used in English-language poetry.

Rap A popular style of music that emerged in the 1980s in which lyrics are spoken or chanted over a steady beat, usually sampled or prerecorded. Rap lyrics are almost always rhymed and very rhythmic—syncopating a heavy metrical beat in a manner similar to jazz. Originally an African American form, rap is now international. In that way, rap can be seen as a form of popular poetry.

Reader-response criticism The practice of analyzing a literary work by describing what happens in the reader's mind while interpreting the text. Reader-response critics believe that no literary text exists independently of readers' interpretations and that there is no single fixed interpretation of any literary work.

Realism An attempt to reproduce faithfully the surface appearance of life, especially that of ordinary people in everyday situations. As a literary term, *realism* has two meanings—one general, the other historical. In a general sense, realism refers to the representation of characters, events, and settings in ways that the spectator will consider plausible, based on consistency and likeness to type. This sort of realism does not necessarily depend on elaborate factual description or documentation but more on the author's ability to draft plots and characters within a conventional framework of social, economic, and psychological reality. In a historical sense, Realism (usually capitalized) refers to a movement in nineteenth-century European literature and theater that rejected the idealism, elitism, and romanticism of earlier verse dramas and prose fiction in an attempt to represent life truthfully. Realist literature customarily focused on the middle class (and occasionally the working class) rather than the aristocracy, and it used social and economic detail to create an accurate account of human behavior. Realism began in France with Honoré de Balzac, Gustave Flaubert, and Guy de Maupassant and then moved internationally. Other major Realists include Leo Tolstoy, Henry James, Anton Chekhov, and Edith Wharton.

Recognition In tragic plotting, the moment of recognition occurs when ignorance gives way to knowledge, illusion to disillusion. In Aristotle's *Poetics*, this is usually a recognition of blood ties or kinship between the persons involved in grave actions involving suffering. According to Aristotle, the ideal moment of recognition coincides with *peripeteia* or reversal of fortune. The classic example occurs in *Oedipus* when Oedipus discovers that he had unwittingly killed his own father when defending himself at the crossroads and later married his own mother when assuming the Theban throne. (*See also* **Hamartia**, **Katharsis**, **Peripeteia**.)

Refrain A word, phrase, line, or stanza repeated at intervals in a song or poem. The repeated chorus of a song is a refrain.

Regionalism The literary representation of a specific locale that consciously uses the particulars of geography, custom, history, folklore, or speech. In regional narratives, the locale plays a crucial role in the presentation and progression of a story that could not be moved to another setting without artistic loss. Usually, regional narratives take place at some distance from the literary capital of a culture, often in small towns or rural areas. Examples of American regionalism can be found in the writing of Willa Cather, Kate Chopin, William Faulkner, and Eudora Welty.

Resolution The final part of a narrative, the concluding action or actions that follow the climax. (*See also* **Conclusion**, **Dénouement**.)

Restoration period In England, the period following the restoration of Charles II to the throne in 1660, extending to 1700. King Charles reopened the theaters that had been closed by the Puritans as sinful institutions. The Restoration period reintroduced a strong secular and urbane element back into English literature.

Retrospect *See* **Flashback**.

Reversal *See* **Peripeteia**.

Rhyme, **Rime** Two or more words that contain an identical or similar vowel sound, usually accented, with following consonant sounds (if any) identical as well: *queue* and *stew*, *prairie schooner* and *piano tuner*. (*See also* **Consonance**, **Exact rhyme**.)

Rhyme scheme, **Rime scheme** Any recurrent pattern of rhyme within an individual poem or fixed form. A rhyme scheme is usually described by using small letters to represent each end rhyme—*a* for the first rhyme, *b* for the second, and so on. The rhyme scheme of a stanza of **common meter** or hymn meter, for example, would be notated as *abab*.

Rhythm The pattern of stresses and pauses in a poem. A fixed and recurring rhythm in a poem is called **meter**.

Rising action That part of the play or narrative, including the exposition, in which events start moving toward a climax. In the rising action the protagonist usually faces the complications of the plot to reach his or her goal. In *Hamlet*, the rising action develops the conflict between Hamlet and Claudius, with Hamlet succeeding in controlling the course of events. Because the mainspring of the play's first half is the mystery of Claudius's guilt, the rising action reaches a climax when Hamlet proves the king's guilt by the device of the play within a play (3.2—the "mousetrap" scene), when Hamlet as heroic avenger has positive proof of Claudius's guilt.

Rising meter A meter whose movement rises from an unstressed syllable (or syllables) to a stressed syllable (for-*get*, De-*troit*). Iambic and anapestic are examples of rising meter.

Romance In general terms, romance is a narrative mode that employs exotic adventure and idealized emotion rather than realistic depiction of character and action. In the romantic mode—out of which most popular genre fictions develop—people, actions, and events are depicted more as we wish them to be (heroes are very brave, villains are very bad) rather than the complex ways they usually are. Medieval romances (in both prose and verse) presented chivalric tales of kings, knights, and aristocratic ladies. Modern romances, emerging in the nineteenth century, were represented by adventure novels like Sir Walter Scott's *Ivanhoe* or Nathaniel Hawthorne's *The House of the Seven Gables*, which embodied the symbolic quests and idealized characters of earlier, chivalric tales in slightly more realistic terms, a tradition carried on in contemporary popular works like the *Star Wars* and James Bond films.

Romantic comedy A form of comic drama in which the plot focuses on one or more pairs of young lovers who overcome difficulties to achieve a happy ending (usually marriage). Shakespeare's *A Midsummer Night's Dream* is a classic example of the genre.

Rondel A thirteen-line English verse form consisting of three rhymed stanzas with a refrain.

Round character A term coined by English novelist E. M. Forster to describe a complex character who is presented in depth and detail in a narrative. Round characters are those who change significantly during the course of a narrative. Most often, round characters are the central characters in a narrative. (*See also* **Flat character**.)

Run-on line A line of verse that does not end in punctuation, but carries on grammatically to the next line. Such lines are read aloud with only a slight pause at the end. A run-on line is also called *enjambment*.

Sarcasm A conspicuously bitter form of irony in which the ironic statement is designed to hurt or mock its target. (*See also* **Irony**.)

Satiric comedy A genre using derisive humor to ridicule human weakness and folly or attack political injustices and incompetence. Satiric comedy often focuses on ridiculing characters or killjoys, who resist the festive mood of comedy. Such characters, called humors, are often characterized by one dominant personality trait or ruling obsession.

Satiric poetry Poetry that blends criticism with humor to convey a message. Satire characteristically uses irony to make its points. Usually, its tone is one of detached amusement, withering contempt, and implied superiority.

Satyr play A type of Greek comic play that was performed after the tragedies at the City Dionysia, the principal civic and religious festival of Athens. The playwrights winning the right to perform their works in the festival wrote three tragedies and one satyr play to form the traditional tetralogy, or group of four. The structure of a satyr play was similar to tragedy's. Its subject matter, treated in burlesque, was drawn from myth or the epic cycles. Its chorus was composed of satyrs (half human and half horse or goat) under the leadership of Silenus, the adoptive father of Dionysius. Rascals and revelers, satyrs represented wild versions of humanity, opposing the values of civilized men. Euripides' *Cyclops* is the only complete surviving example of the genre.

Scansion A practice used to describe rhythmic patterns in a poem by separating the metrical feet, counting the syllables, marking the accents, and indicating the pauses. Scansion can be very useful in analyzing the sound of a poem and how it should be read aloud.

Scene In drama, the scene is a division of the action in an act of the play. There is no universal convention as to what constitutes a scene, and the practice differs by playwright and period. Usually, a scene represents a single dramatic action that builds to a climax (often ending in the entrance or exit of a major character). In this last sense of a vivid and unified action, the term can be applied to fiction.

Selective omniscience The point of view that sees the events of a narrative through the eyes of a single character. The selectively omniscient narrator is usually a nonparticipant narrator.

Sentimentality A usually pejorative description of the quality of a literary work that tries to convey great emotion but fails to give the reader sufficient grounds for sharing it.

Sestet A poem or stanza of six lines. *Sestet* is a term usually used when speaking of sonnets, to indicate the final six-line section of the poem, as distinct from the octave (the first eight lines). (*See also* **Sonnet.**)

Sestina A complex verse form ("song of sixes") in which six end words are repeated in a prescribed order through six stanzas. A sestina ends with an **envoy** of three lines in which all six words appear—for a total of thirty-nine lines. Originally used by French and Italian poets, the sestina has become a popular modern form in English.

Setting The time and place of a literary work. The setting may also include the climate and even the social, psychological, or spiritual state of the participants.

Shakespearean sonnet *See* **English sonnet**.

Short Story A prose narrative too brief to be published in a separate volume—as novellas and novels frequently are. The short story is usually a focused narrative that presents one or two main characters involved in a single compelling action.

Simile A comparison of two things, indicated by some connective, usually *like*, *as*, *than*, or a verb such as *resembles*. A simile usually compares two things that initially seem unlike but are shown to have a significant resemblance. "Cool as a cucumber" and "My love is like a red, red rose" are examples of similes.

Situational Irony *See* **Irony**.

Skene In classical Greek staging of the fifth century B.C., the temporary wooden stage building in which actors changed masks and costumes when changing roles. Its facade, with double center doors and possibly two side doors, served as the setting for action taking place before a palace, temple, cave, or other interior space.

Sketch A short, static, descriptive composition. Literary sketches can be either fiction or nonfiction. A sketch usually focuses on describing a person or place without providing a narrative.

Slack syllable An unstressed syllable in a line of verse.

Slant rhyme A rhyme in which the final consonant sounds are the same but the vowel sounds are different, as in letter and litter, bone and bean. Slant rhyme may also be called *near rhyme*, *off rhyme*, or *imperfect rhyme*. (*See also* **Consonance**.)

Slapstick comedy A kind of farce, featuring pratfalls, pie throwing, fisticuffs, and other violent action. It takes its name originally from the slapstick carried by the ***commedia dell'arte***'s main servant type, Harlequin.

Sociological criticism The practice of analyzing a literary work by examining the cultural, economic, and political context in which it was written or received. Sociological criticism primarily explores the relationship between the artist and society.

Soliloquy In drama, a speech by a character alone onstage in which he or she utters his or her thoughts aloud. The soliloquy is important in drama because it gives the audience insight into a character's inner life, private motivations, and uncertainties.

Sonnet From the Italian *sonnetto*: "little song." A traditional and widely used verse form, especially popular for love poetry. The sonnet is a fixed form of fourteen lines, traditionally written in iambic pentameter, usually made up of an **octave** (the first eight lines) and a concluding **sestet** (six lines). There are, however, several variations, most conspicuously the Shakespearean, or English sonnet, which consists of three quatrains and a concluding couplet. Most sonnets turn, or shift in tone or focus, after the first eight lines, although the placement may vary. (*See also* **English sonnet, Italian sonnet**.)

Spondee A metrical foot of verse containing two stressed syllables (′ ′) often substituted into a meter to create extra emphasis.

Stage business Nonverbal action that engages the attention of an audience. Expressing what cannot be said, stage business became a particularly important means of revealing the inner thoughts and feelings of a character in the development of Realism.

Stanza From the Italian, meaning "stopping-place" or "room." A recurring pattern of two or more lines of verse, poetry's equivalent to the paragraph in prose. The stanza is the basic organizational principle of most formal poetry.

Static character *See* **Flat character**.

Stock character A common or stereotypical character that occurs frequently in literature. Examples of stock characters are the mad scientist, the battle-scarred veteran, or the strong-but-silent cowboy. (*See also* **Archetype**.)

Stream of consciousness Not a specific technique, but a type of modern narration that uses various literary devices, especially interior monologue, in an attempt to duplicate the subjective and associative nature of human consciousness. Stream of consciousness often focuses on imagistic perception in order to capture the preverbal level of consciousness.

Stress An emphasis or accent placed on a syllable in speech. Clear pronunciation of polysyllabic words almost always depends on correct placement of their stress. (For instance, *de*-sert and de-*sert* are two different words and parts of speech, depending on their stress.) Stress is the basic principle of most English-language meter.

Style All the distinctive ways in which an author, genre, movement, or historical period uses language to create a literary work. An author's style depends on his or her characteristic use of diction, imagery, tone, syntax, and figurative language. Even sentence structure and punctuation can play a role in an author's style.

Subject The main topic of a poem, story, or play.

Subplot *See* **Double plot**.

Summary A brief condensation of the main idea or story of a literary work. A summary is similar to a paraphrase, but less detailed.

Surrealism A modernist movement in art and literature that tries to organize art according to the irrational dictates of the unconscious mind. Founded by the French poet André Breton, Surrealism sought to reach a higher plane of reality by abandoning logic for the seemingly absurd connections made in dreams and other unconscious mental activities.

Suspense Enjoyable anxiety created in the reader by the author's handling of plot. When the outcome of events is unclear, the author's suspension of resolution intensifies the reader's interest—particularly if the plot involves characters to whom the reader or audience is sympathetic. Suspense is also created when the fate of a character is clear to the audience, but not to the character. The suspense results from the audience's anticipation of how and when the character will meet his or her inevitable fate.

Syllabic verse A verse form in which the poet establishes a pattern of a certain number of syllables to a line. Syllabic verse is the most common meter in most Romance languages such as Italian, French, and Spanish; it is less common in English because it is difficult to hear syllable count. Syllabic verse was used by several Modernist poets, most conspicuously Marianne Moore.

Symbol A person, place, or thing in a narrative that suggests meanings beyond its literal sense. Symbol is related to allegory, but it works more complexly. In an allegory an object has a single additional significance. By contrast, a symbol usually contains multiple meanings and associations. In Herman Melville's *Moby-Dick*, for example, the great white whale does not have just a single significance but accrues powerful associations as the narrative progresses.

Symbolic act An action whose significance goes well beyond its literal meaning. In literature, symbolic acts usually involve some conscious or unconscious ritual element like rebirth, purification, forgiveness, vengeance, or initiation.

Symbolist movement An international literary movement that originated with nineteenth-century French poets such as Charles Baudelaire, Arthur Rimbaud, and Paul Verlaine. Symbolists aspired to make literature resemble music. They avoided direct statement and exposition for powerful evocation and suggestion. Symbolists also considered the poet as a seer who could look beyond the mundane aspects of the everyday world to capture visions of a higher reality.

Symbolists Members of the Symbolist movement.

Synecdoche The use of a significant part of a thing to stand for the whole of it or vice versa. To say *wheels* for *car* or *rhyme* for *poetry* are examples of synecdoche. (*See also* **Metonymy**.)

Synopsis A brief summary or outline of a story or dramatic work.

Tactile imagery A word or sequence of words that refers to the sense of touch. (*See also* **Imagery**.)

Tale A short narrative without a complex plot, the word originating from the Old English *talu*, or "speech." Tales are an ancient form of narrative found in folklore, and traditional tales often contain supernatural elements. A tale differs from a short story by its tendency toward less developed characters and linear plotting. British writer A. E. Coppard characterized the underlying difference by claiming that a story is something that is written and a tale is something that is told. The ambition of a tale is usually similar to that of a yarn: revelation of the marvelous rather than illumination of the everyday world.

Tall tale A humorous short narrative that provides a wildly exaggerated version of events. Originally an oral form, the tall tale assumes that its audience knows the narrator is distorting the events. The form is often associated with the American frontier.

Tercet A group of three lines of verse, usually all ending in the same rhyme. (*See also* *Terza rima*.)

Terminal refrain A refrain that appears at the end of each stanza in a song or poem. (*See also* **Refrain**.)

Terza rima A verse form made up of three-line stanzas that are connected by an overlapping rhyme scheme (*aba, bcb, cdc, ded*, etc.). Dante employs *terza rima* in *The Divine Comedy*.

Tetrameter A verse meter consisting of four metrical feet, or four primary stresses, per line.

Theater of the absurd Post World War II European genre depicting the grotesquely comic plight of human beings thrown by accident into an irrational and meaningless world. The critic Martin Esslin coined the term to characterize plays by writers such as Samuel Beckett, Jean Genet, and Eugene Ionesco. Samuel Beckett's *Waiting for Godot* (1955), considered to be the greatest example of the absurd, features in two nearly identical acts two tramps waiting almost without hope on a country road for an unidentified person, Godot. "Nothing happens, nobody comes, nobody goes, it's awful," one of them cries, perhaps echoing the unspoken thoughts of an audience confronted by a play that refuses to do anything.

Theme A generally recurring subject or idea conspicuously evident in a literary work. A short didactic work like a fable may have a single obvious theme, but longer works can contain multiple themes. Not all subjects in a work can be considered themes, only the central subject or subjects.

Thesis sentence A summing-up of the one main idea or argument that an essay or critical paper will embody.

Third-person narrator A type of narration in which the narrator is a nonparticipant. In a third-person narrative the characters are referred to as "he," "she," or "they." Third-person narrators are most commonly omniscient, but the level of their knowledge may vary from total omniscience (the narrator knows everything about the characters and their lives) to limited omniscience (the narrator is limited to the perceptions of a single character).

Tone The attitude toward a subject conveyed in a literary work. No single stylistic device creates tone; it is the net result of the various elements an author brings to creating the work's feeling and manner. Tone may be playful, sarcastic, ironic, sad, solemn, or any other possible attitude. A writer's tone plays an important role in establishing the reader's relationship to the characters or ideas presented in a literary work.

Total omniscience A type of point of view in which the narrator knows everything about all of the characters and events in a story. A narrator with total omniscience can also move freely from one character to another. Generally, a totally omniscient narrative is written in the third person.

Traditional epic *See* **Folk epic**.

Tragedy The representation of serious and important actions that lead to a disastrous end for the protagonist. The final purpose of tragedy in Aristotle's formulation is to evoke *katharsis* by means of events involving pity and fear. A unified tragic action, from beginning to end, brings a morally good but not perfect tragic hero from happiness to unhappiness because of a mistaken act, to which he or she is led by a *hamartia*, an error in judgment. Tragic heroes move us to pity because their misfortunes are greater than they deserve, because they are not evil, having committed the fateful deed or deeds unwittingly and involuntarily. They also move us to fear, because we recognize in ourselves similar possibilities of error. We share with the tragic hero a common world of mischance. (*See also* **Tragic flaw**.)

Tragic flaw A fatal weakness or moral flaw in the protagonist that brings him or her to a bad end, for example, Creon in *Antigonê* or Macbeth. Sometimes offered as an alternative translation of *hamartia*, in contrast to the idea that the tragic hero's catastrophe is caused by an error in judgment, the idea of a protagonist ruined by a tragic flaw makes more sense in relation to the Greek idea of *hubris*, commonly translated as "outrageous behavior," involving deliberate transgressions against moral or divine law.

Tragic irony A form of **dramatic irony** that ultimately arrives at some tragedy.

Tragicomedy A type of drama that combines elements of both tragedy and comedy. Usually, it creates potentially tragic situations that bring the protagonists to the brink of disaster but then ends happily. Tragicomedy can be traced as far back as the Renaissance (in plays likes Shakespeare's *Measure for Measure*), but it also refers to modern plays like Chekhov's *Cherry Orchard* and Beckett's *Waiting for Godot*.

Transferred epithet A figure of speech in which the poet attributes some characteristic of a thing to another thing closely associated with it. Transferred epithet is a kind of metonymy. It usually places an adjective next to a noun in which the connection is not strictly logical (Milton's phrase "blind mouths" or Hart Crane's "nimble blue plateaus") but has expressive power.

Trick ending A surprising climax that depends on a quick reversal of the situation from an unexpected source. The success of a trick ending is relative to the degree in which the reader is surprised but not left incredulous when it occurs. The American writer O. Henry popularized this type of ending.

Trimeter A verse meter consisting of three metrical feet, or three primary stresses, per line.

Triolet A short lyric form of eight rhymed lines borrowed from the French. The two opening lines are repeated according to a set pattern. Triolets are often playful, but dark lyric poems like Robert Bridge's "Triolet" demonstrate the form's flexibility.

Trochaic, trochee A metrical foot in which a stressed syllable is followed by an unstressed syllable (′ ◡) as in the words *sum*-mer and *chor*-us. The trochaic meter is often associated with songs, chants, and magic spells in English.

Troubadours The minstrels of the late Middle Ages. Originally, troubadours were lyric poets living in southern France and northern Italy who sang to aristocratic audiences mostly of chivalry and love.

Understatement An ironic figure of speech that deliberately describes something in a way that is less than the true case.

Unities The three formal qualities recommended by Italian Renaissance literary critics to unify a plot in order to give it a cohesive and complete integrity. Traditionally, good plots honored the three unities—of action, time, and place. The action in neoclassical drama, therefore, was patterned by cause and effect to occur within a 24-hour period. The setting took place in one unchanging locale. In the *Poetics*, Aristotle urged only the requirement of unity of plot, with events patterned in a cause-and-effect relationship from beginning through middle to the end of the single action imitated.

Unreliable narrator A narrator who—intentionally or unintentionally—relates events in a subjective or distorted manner. The author usually provides some indication early on in such stories that the narrator is not to be completely trusted.

Verbal irony A statement in which the speaker or writer says the opposite of what is really meant. For example, a friend might comment, "How graceful you are!" after you trip clumsily on a stair.

Verisimilitude The quality in a literary work of appearing true to life. In fiction, verisimilitude is usually achieved by careful use of realistic detail in description, characterization, and dialogue. (*See also* **Realism**.)

Verse From the Latin *versum*, "to turn." Verse has two major meanings. First, it refers to any single line of poetry. Second, it refers to any composition in lines of more or less regular rhythm—in contrast to prose.

Vers *libre* *See* **Free verse**.

Villanelle A fixed form developed by French courtly poets of the Middle Ages in imitation of Italian folk song. A villanelle consists of six rhymed stanzas in which two lines are repeated in a prescribed pattern.

Visual imagery A word or sequence of words that refers to the sense of sight or presents something one may see.

Vulgate From the Latin word *vulgus*, "mob" or "common people." The lowest level of formality in language, vulgate is the diction of the common people with no pretensions at refinement or elevation. The vulgate is not necessarily vulgar in the sense of containing foul or inappropriate language; it refers simply to unschooled, everyday language.

LITERARY CREDITS

Fiction

Chinua Achebe: "Dead Men's Path," copyright © 1972, 1973 by Chinua Achebe, from *Girls at War and Other Stories* by Chinua Achebe. Used by permission of Doubleday, a division of Random House, Inc.

Sherman Alexie: "This Is What It Means to Say Phoenix, Arizona" from *The Lone Ranger and Tonto Fistfight in Heaven* by Sherman Alexie. Copyright © 1993, 2005 by Sherman Alexie. Used by permission of Grove/Atlantic, Inc.

Elizabeth Ammons: "Biographical Echoes in 'The Yellow Wallpaper'" excerpted from *Conflicting Stories: American Women Writers at the Turn of The Century*, copyright © 1991. Reprinted by permission of Oxford University Press.

Inés Arredondo: "The Shunammite" by Inés Arredondo as translated by Alberto Manguel. © Alberto Manguel. Reprinted by permission of Guillermo Schavelzon & Asociados, Agencia Literaria.

Margaret Atwood: "Happy Endings" from *Good Bones and Simple Murders* by Margaret Atwood, copyright © 1983, 1992, 1994, by O.W. Toad Ltd. A Nan A. Talese Book. Used by permission of Doubleday, a division of Random House, Inc.

Houston A. Baker and Charlotte Pierce-Baker: Excerpt from "Patches: Quilts and Community in Alice Walker's 'Everyday Use'" by Houston A. Baker and Charlotte Pierce-Baker from *The Southern Review 21* (Summer 1985). Reprinted by permission of the authors.

James Baldwin: "Sonny's Blues" © 1957 by James Baldwin was originally published in *Partisan Review*. Copyright renewed. Collected in *Going to Meet the Man*, published by Vintage Books. Reprinted by arrangement with the James Baldwin Estate.

James Baldwin: From *Notes of a Native Son* by James Baldwin. Copyright © 1955, renewed 1983, by James Baldwin. Reprinted by permission of Beacon Press, Boston.

Jorge Luis Borges: "The Gospel According to Mark" from *Collected Fictions* by Jorge Luis Borges, translated by Andrew Hurley, copyright © 1998 by Maria Kodama; translation copyright © 1998 by Penguin Putnam Inc. Used by permission of Viking Penguin, a division of Penguin Group (USA) Inc.

T. Coraghessan Boyle: "Greasy Lake" from *Greasy Lake and Other Stories* by T. Coraghessan Boyle, © 1979, 1981, 1982, 1983, 1984, 1985 by T. Coraghessan Boyle. Used by permission of Viking Penguin, a division of Penguin Group (USA) Inc.

Nancy Bunge: From *Studies in Short Fiction Series-Nathaniel Hawthorne* © 1993 Gale, a part of Cengage Learning, Inc. Reproduced by permission. www.cengage.com/permissions.

Raymond Carver: "Cathedral" from *Cathedral* by Raymond Carver, copyright © 1981, 1982, 1983 by Raymond Carver. Used by permission of Alfred A. Knopf, a division of Random House, Inc.

Raymond Carver: Excerpts from "On Writing" from *Fires: Essays, Poems, Stories* by Raymond Carver. Copyright © 1983, 1984 by the Estate of Raymond Carver, reprinted with permission of The Wylie Agency LLC.

John Cheever: "The Swimmer" from *The Stories of John Cheever* by John Cheever, copyright © 1978 by John Cheever. Used by permission of Alfred A. Knopf, a division of Random House, Inc.

Anton Chekhov: "The Lady with the Pet Dog" translated by Avrahm Yarmolinsky, from *The Portable Chekhov* by Anton Chekhov, edited by Avrahm Yarmolinsky, copyright 1947, © 1968 by Viking Penguin, Inc., renewed © 1975 by Avrahm Yarmolinsky. Used by permission of Viking Penguin, a division of Penguin Group (USA) Inc.

Barbara Christian: Excerpt from the Introduction to *Everyday Use* by Alice Walker, edited by Barbara T. Christian, from *The Women Writers: Text and Context Series*. Copyright © 1994 by Rutgers, the State University. Reprinted by permission of Rutgers University Press.

Sandra Cisneros: "The House on Mango Street" from *The House on Mango Street*. Copyright © 1984 by Sandra Cisneros. Published by Vintage Books, a division of Random House, Inc., and in hardcover by Alfred A. Knopf in 1994. By permission of Susan Bergholz Literary Services, New York, NY and Lamy, NM. All rights reserved.

Louise S. Cowan: From "Passing by the Dragon" by Louise S. Cowan in "Revelation" by Flannery O'Connor, *The Trinity Forum Reading 40* (Summer 2005) (McLean, VA: The Trinity Forum, Inc., 2005). Used by permission.

Ralph Ellison: "Battle Royal," copyright 1948 by Ralph Ellison, from *Invisible Man* by Ralph Ellison. Used by permission of Random House, Inc.

William Faulkner: "A Rose for Emily," copyright 1930 and renewed 1958 by William Faulkner,

Poetry

Drama

Writing

PHOTO CREDITS

Fiction

1: © Jim McHugh Photography; 2: © Jim McHugh Photography; 3: Sara Krulwich/Redux Pictures; 8: From "The Tortoise and the Geese" by Maude Barrows Dutton. Illustrated by E. Boyd Smith. Yesterday's Classics, 2008; 11: Brown Brothers; 21: Bettmann/Corbis; 29: Bettmann/Corbis; 36: Bettmann/Corbis; 40: Hulton-Deutsch Collection/Corbis; 42: AP Photo; 73: Bettmann/Corbis; 79: © Jill Krementz, all rights reserved.; 86: Courtesy Alfred A. Knopf, Inc.; 90: Jean-Bernard Vernier/Corbis Sygma; 104: Scott, Foresman and Company; 110: Missouri Historical Society; 114: Bettmann/Corbis; 125: Nancy Crampton; 145: Nancy Crampton; 169: Bettmann/Corbis; 173: Jerry Bauer; 180: Bettmann/Corbis; 185: Courtesy the New York Public Library; 202: Jerry Bauer; 220: Nancy Crampton; 226: Scott, Foresman and Company; 234: Bettmann/Corbis; 242: Marian Wood; 253: AP Photo; 264: Bettmann/Corbis; 301: AP Photo; 344: Bettmann/Corbis; 348: AP Photo; 357: Familiar Segovia Camelo Archive; 365: Bernardo de Nlz/Corbis; 368: AP Photo; 407: Joe McTyre/The Atlanta Journal-Constitution; 411: Flannery O'Connor Collection, Ina Dillard Russell Library, Georgia College and State University; 412: © 2002 The Atlanta Journal-Constitution; 419: Courtesy Peabody Essex Museum (image# 14509); 432: Photofest, NYC; 436: The Granger Collection, NY; 450: Library of Congress; 455: Bettmann/Corbis; 464: Christie's Images; 471: AP Photo; 474: Christopher Felver/Corbis; 482: Corbis; 485: The Granger Collection, NY; 491: Nebraska Historical Society; 505: Bettmann/Corbis; 518: Courtesy Sandra Cisneros; 519: Nancy Crampton; 529: © Corbis; 538: Berenice Abbott/Commerce Graphics, Ltd, Inc.; 543: Sigrid Estrada; 545: Marion Ettlinger; 559: Bettmann/Corbis; 569: Jerry Bauer; 579: Andy Manis/AP Photo; 584: © Jill Krementz, all rights reserved.; 595: Jerry Bauer; 607: AP Photo; 613. Marion Ettlinger

Poetry

625: Christopher Felver/Corbis; 626: Steve Yeater/AP Photo; 627: Serena M. Agusto-Cox; 642: Ed Sousa/Stanford News Service; 668: The Imperial War Museum, London; 694: Brown Brothers; 707: Bettmann/Corbis; 724: David Lees/Corbis; 747: Brown Brothers; 751: David Lees/Corbis; 767: Bettmann/Corbis; 786: AP Photo; 805: Bettmann/Corbis; 827: John Psaropoulos; 835: Kunsthistorisches Museum, Vienna; 849: Bettmann/Corbis; 863: Culver Pictures; 881: Bettmann/Corbis; 902: Courtesy Rhina Espaillat; 916: Copyright Estate of Pamela Chandler/National Portrait Gallery, London; 920: Philadelphia Museum of Art, The Robert H. Lamborn Collection, 1903 (Acc# 1903–918); 921: RDA/Hulton Archives/Getty Images; 923: Bettmann/Corbis; 924: William Coupon/Getty Images; 926: © 2005 Banco de Mexico, Diego Rivera and Frida Kahlo Museum Trust, Av. Cinco de Mayo No.2, Col. Centro Del Cuauhtemoc 06059 Mexico D. F./photograph Bob Schalkwijk/Art Resource, NY.; 950: Scott, Foresman and Company; 957 left: Amherst College Archives and Special Collections; 957 right: Hulton Archive/Getty Images; 964: Courtesy Emily Dickinson Museum; 966: Warren/Picturehistory/Newscom; 974: Henri Cartier-Bresson/Magnum Photos; 982: Underwood & Underwood/Corbis; 984: Courtesy Aaron & Alta Sawyer Douglas Foundation, Private Collection.; 993: Houghton Library, Harvard University; 994: Bettman/Corbis; 1000: Newberry Library, Chicago; 1003: Houghton Library, Harvard University; 1006: Cover painting of T. S. Eliot by Wyndham Lewis, 1949. Courtesy the Master and Fellows, Magdalene College, Cambridge. From the book *Words Alone: The Poet T. S. Eliot* by Denis Donoghue, copyright © 2000 by Denis Donoghue. Reprinted with permission of Yale University Press.; 1016: Private Collection; 1020: Corbis; 1021: Bettmann/Corbis; 1023: Musées Royaux des Beaux-Arts de Belgique; 1025: Thomas Victor: 1026: Berg Collection of English and American Literature, New York Public Library; 1027: Private Collection; 1028: Bettmann/Corbis; 1034: Bettmann/Corbis; 1035: Library of Congress; 1036: Luigi Ciufetelli; 1037: Bettmann/Corbis; 1039: Christopher Felver/Corbis; 1043: Eric Schaal/Time Life Pictures/Getty Images; 1048: Courtesy of the National Portrait Gallery, London; 1051: Dorothy Alexander; 1052: Bettmann/Corbis; 1057: Ted Russell; 1060: By courtesy National Portrait Gallery, London; 1063: Fay Godwin/Network Photographers/Corbis Saba; 1064: Christopher Felver/Corbis; 1065: Courtesy the author; 1068: Brown Brothers; 1070: Photo by Doug Anderson; 1071: Gail & Bonnie Roub; 1072: Thomas Victor, Courtesy Poets.org/University of Pennsylvania; 1073: Dorothy Alexander;

1074: Bettmann/Corbis; 1078: Willie Williams; 1082 top: Photograph by Imogen Cunningham © 1978 The Imogen Cunningham Trust; 1082 bottom: Courtesy National Portrait Gallery, London; 1087: Reprinted from *School Figures* by Cathy Song © 1994 by permission of the University of Pittsburgh Press; 1089: Bettmann/Corbis; 1092: Jeff Towns/DBC; 1094: Bettmann/Corbis; 1095: Gabriel Harrison/Library of Congress; 1098: Courtesy of *New Directions;* 1099: Courtesy National Portrait Gallery, London; 1102: The Royal Photographic Society.

Drama

1105: Chris Goodne/Bloomberg News/Landov; 1106: Frank Franklin II/AP Photo; 1107: Damon Winter/Redux; 1119: Echo Theatre, Dallas, TX; 1126: AP Photo; 1136: Utah Shakespeare Festival; 1141: The Granger Collection, NY; 1146: © Mark Garvin; 1153: Courtesy Writers and Artists Agency; 1157: The Granger Collection, NY; 1159: R. C. Flickinger/*The Greek Theater and its Drama,* 1918; 1160: Bettmann/Corbis; 1163: Bettmann/Corbis; 1164: John Vickers Theatre Collection; 1203: Martha Swope; 1239: John Ross; 1242: Oli Scarff/Getty Images; 1243: Andrea Pistolesi/Getty Images; 1244: The National Portrait Gallery, London; 1245: Martha Swope; 1246 to 1346: © T. Charles Erickson; 1351: Bettmann/Corbis; 1352 to 1418: © T. Charles Erickson; 1443: Tate Gallery, London/Art Resource, NY; 1446 to 1461: © T. Charles Erickson; 1467: Photofest; 1468 to 1535: Utah Shakespeare Festival; 1546: National Portrait Gallery, London; 1560: The Harvard Theatre Collection, The Houghton Library; 1611: Bettmann/Corbis; 1613: Private Collection; 1658: Bettmann/Corbis; 1662: © Jim McHugh Photography; 1664 & 1668: Photo by Jay Thompson, Courtesy Center Theatre Group; 1670: Joe Kohen/Getty Images; 1680: © Michael Daniel; 1750: Tim Wright/Corbis; 1752: Photo by Richard Feldman for the American Repertory Theatre; 1765: Adam Rountree/Getty Images; 1772: Robbie Jack/Corbis; 1837: Bettmann/Corbis; 1840: Yale Repertory Theatre; 1887: Retna.

Writing

1889: The Berg Collection/New York Public Library; 1975: Musées Royaux des Beaux-Arts de Belgique; 2007: Random House, Inc.

INDEX OF MAJOR THEMES

If you prefer to study by theme or want to research possible subjects for an essay, here is a listing of stories, poems, and plays arranged into fourteen major themes.

Loneliness and Alienation

Love and Desire

Men and Women/Marriage

Woman's Identity

INDEX OF
FIRST LINES
OF POETRY

INDEX OF AUTHORS AND TITLES

Each page number immediately following a writer's name indicates a quotation from or reference to that writer. A number in **bold** refers you to the page on which you will find the author's biography.

INDEX OF LITERARY TERMS

Page numbers indicate discussion of terms in anthology. A page number in **bold** indicates entry in the **Glossary of Literary Terms.** n following a page number indicates entry in a note.